A Volcano Rekindled: The Renewed Eruption of Mount St. Helens, 2004–2006

Edited by David R. Sherrod, William E. Scott, and Peter H. Stauffer

Professional Paper 1750

U.S. Department of the Interior
U.S. Geological Survey

U.S. Department of the Interior
DIRK KEMPTHORNE, Secretary

U.S. Geological Survey
Mark D. Myers, Director

U.S. Geological Survey, Reston, Virginia: 2008

This report and any updates to it are available online at:
http://pubs.usgs.gov/pp/1750/

For product and ordering information:
World Wide Web: http://www.usgs.gov/pubprod
Telephone: 1-888-ASK-USGS (1-888-275-8747)

For more information on the USGS—the Federal source for science about the Earth,
its natural and living resources, natural hazards, and the environment:
World Wide Web: http://www.usgs.gov
Telephone: 1-888-ASK-USGS (1-888-275-8747)

Suggested citation:
Sherrod, D.R., Scott, W.E., and Stauffer, P.H., eds., 2008, A volcano rekindled; the renewed eruption of Mount St. Helens, 2004-2006: U.S. Geological Survey Professional Paper 1750, 856 p. and DVD-ROM.

Cataloging-in-publication data are on file with the Library of Congress (http://www.loc.gov/).

Produced in the Western Region, Menlo Park, California
Manuscript approved for publication, August 27, 2008
Text edited by Peter H. Stauffer, Tracey L. Suzuki,
James W. Hendley II, and George A. Havach
Layout by Judy Weathers and Susan Mayfield

Foreword

Late September and early October 2004 saw intense seismic unrest, rapid ground deformation, and explosions heralding the renewal of lava-dome growth in the crater of Mount St. Helens, Washington. Thus ended the relative calm of two decades since the renowned 1980–86 eruptions. Memories of the May 18, 1980, tragedy and its aftermath prompted a high level of concern among the public, public officials, and the media. Response to this unrest and eruption was led by scientists at the U.S. Geological Survey's (USGS) David A. Johnston Cascades Volcano Observatory (CVO). Established following the 1980 eruption, CVO was named for the spirited young USGS volcanologist who lost his life during the initial minutes of the May 18 cataclysm. USGS scientists worked in close cooperation with CVO's long-time partner in monitoring the volcanoes of Washington and Oregon, the Pacific Northwest Seismic Network at the University of Washington. This cooperation ensured that local land and emergency managers, public officials, key government agencies, media representatives, and the public received the information needed to protect life and property, as well as to appreciate the spectacle of an erupting volcano. USGS scientists from sister volcano observatories—Alaska, Hawaiian, Long Valley, and Yellowstone—and the broader USGS community contributed significantly to the effort. USGS scientists relied on lessons learned from responding to previous volcanic crises in the United States and abroad. Scientists from more than a dozen academic institutions undertook valuable scientific studies of the eruption. New instrumentation from the National Science Foundation-sponsored Plate Boundary Observatory aided in geodetic monitoring. The response was bolstered by vast improvements in monitoring technology, information management, and understanding of volcanic processes that were spawned by the 1980 eruption and other eruptions during the late 20th century.

The USGS is proud to have cooperated closely with the Gifford Pinchot National Forest, home of the Mount St. Helens National Volcanic Monument, the Washington State Emergency Management Division, county emergency-management agencies, the National Weather Service, the Federal Aviation Administration, and the Federal Emergency Management Agency in fulfilling its mandated role under the Disaster Relief Act of 1974 (P.L.93–288) "to provide technical assistance to State and local governments to ensure timely and effective disaster warning is provided." This multichaptered Professional Paper, released as the most recent period of the Mount St. Helens lava-dome building ends after nearly three and one-half years of continuous activity, adds to our understanding of how volcanic systems work, and how scientists must work together with a broad array of agencies and public officials to mitigate risk from volcanic activity.

Occurring more than a quarter century ago, the catastrophic 1980 eruption of Mount St. Helens may seem to some as just a historical footnote. This Professional Paper documenting both the volcano's recent activity and the need for coordinated warning and disaster response should serve the public well as a reminder of the challenges and consequences of living near an active volcano. Previous USGS Director Dallas Peck said it best: "The lessons of Mount St. Helens must not—and will not—be forgotten."

Mark D. Myers
Director,
U.S. Geological Survey

Anthony I. Qamar, 1943–2005

Research Assistant Professor, University of Washington
Co-Principal Investigator, Pacific Northwest Seismic Network
Washington State Seismologist, 1988–2005

Anthony "Tony" Qamar was a highly regarded, generous scientist whose career encompassed the Mount St. Helens eruptions of 1980–86 and 2004 (ongoing at this writing, June 2007). Tony and his colleague, Dan Johnson, were killed in a tragic auto accident October 4, 2005, while traveling to Washington's Olympic Peninsula to retrieve a GPS receiver.

Tony loved mountains, particularly volcanoes. Unbeknownst to many colleagues, Tony was an accomplished climber with major first ascents to his credit. He often combined his professional world with his love of the outdoors by accepting the task of repairing remote and inaccessible seismographs, such as those high on Mount Rainier and Glacier Peak. In 1980 he was one of the first scientists to appear at Mount St. Helens in response to precursory seismicity. Camping in the snow with a portable seismograph and thermal infrared imager, he witnessed and recorded many of the early phreatic eruptions.

In September 2004, Tony again became immersed in volcano seismology as Mount St. Helens reawakened. Moving from his regular office, he set up "camp" in a small, cramped room across from the seismology lab, where he was a resource for the staff and seismology students at the University of Washington's Department of Earth and Space Sciences and also for news media who used the lab during the early chaotic months of the eruption. He developed several automated computer codes (in FORTRAN) that enabled the staff of the Cascades Volcano Observatory and the Pacific Northwest Seismic Network to make sense of the overwhelming number of earthquakes and to track changes in real time. The paper on which he is first author in this volume (chap. 3) is based on these computational efforts and is, we hope, close to the paper he intended to write.

While fundamentally a seismologist interested in the stresses that trigger earthquakes, Tony let his curiosity drive his research in diverse directions. He published papers on the seismic structure of the Earth's inner core, seismic signals generated by meteors or the space shuttle, ice quakes from glaciers recorded by high-frequency seismographs, and the slowly straining tectonic plates as detected by GPS receivers.

Tony was an excellent classroom teacher and even better mentor. As a research collaborator he was generous with his time and ideas, interested more in working with others to achieve a better understanding of a scientific problem than in claiming his piece of the intellectual pie through first-author publications. Those around him were enriched by his presence, knowing he was a friend first and professor second. Students frequently approached him with questions, both technical and personal, and they always left with their answers in hand and their egos intact. The hole left by his passing is both wide and deep.

Tony Qamar poses near seismic equipment he helped to install on the flanks of Mount St. Helens in the summer of 2005

Contributors to This Professional Paper

Cascades Volcano Observatory

Beeler, Nick M.
Couchman, Marvin R.
Denlinger, Roger P.
Doukas, Michael P.
Driedger, Caroyn L.
Dzurisin, Daniel
Endo, Elliot T.
Gardner, Cynthia A.
Gerlach, Terrence M.
Gooding, Daniel J.
Iverson, Richard M.
Iwatsubo, Eugene Y.
Janda, Christine G.
Kingsbury, Cole G.
LaHusen, Richard G.
Lisowski, Michael
Lockhart, Andrew B.
Logan, Matthew
Lu, Zhong
Major, Jon J.
Mastin, Larry G.
McGee, Kenneth A.
Moran, Seth C.
Pallister, John S.
Roeloffs, Evelyn
Schilling, Steve P.
Scott, William E.
Sherrod, David R.
Spicer, Kurt R.
Swinford, Kelly J.
Thornber, Carl R.
Vallance, James W.
Walder, Joseph S.
Wolfe, Edward W.
U.S. Geological Survey
1300 SE Cardinal Court
Vancouver, WA 98683

Menlo Park

Bergfeld, Deborah
Calvert, Andrew T.
Clynne, Michael A.
Evans, William C.
Evarts, Russell C.
Fleck, Robert J.
Lanphere, Marvin A.
U.S. Geological Survey
345 Middlefield Road
Menlo Park, CA 94025

Denver

Brownfield, Isabelle K.
Lowers, Heather A.
Meeker, Gregory P.
Messerich, James A.
Thompson, Ren A.
U.S. Geological Survey
Denver Federal Center
Denver, CO 80225

Alaska Volcano Observatory

Neal, Christina A.
Schneider, David J.
Wessels, Rick L.
U.S. Geological Survey
4200 University Drive
Anchorage, AK 99508

Hawaiian Volcano Observatory

Poland, Michael P.
U.S. Geological Survey
PO Box 51
Hawaii National Park, HI 96718

University of Washington

Creager, Kenneth C.
Crosson, Robert S.
Donnelly, Carrie T.
Malone, Stephen D.
McChesney, Patrick J.
Norris, Robert D., USGS
Qamar, Anthony I. *
Steele, William P.
Thelen, Weston A.
Wright, Amy K.
Earth and Space Sciences
Box 351310
Seattle, WA 98195

U.S. Department of Agriculture, Forest Service

Frenzen, Peter M.
Knappenberger, Thomas H.
Lapcewich, Dennis
Matarrese, Michael T.
Gifford Pinchot National Forest
10600 N.E. 51st Circle
Vancouver, WA 98682

Brown University

Devine, Joseph D., III
Rutherford, Malcolm J.
Department of Geological Sciences
324 Brook Street
Providence, RI 02912

Iowa State University

Iverson, Neal R.
Moore, Peter L.
Department of Geological and Atmospheric Sciences
Ames, IA 50011

McGill University

Berlo, Kim
Earth & Planetary Sciences, McGill University
3450 University St.
Montreal, Quebec, Canada
H3A 2A7

Oregon State University

Kent, Adam J.R.
Department of Geosciences, OSU
Wilkinson Hall
Corvallis, OR 97331

Portland State University

Broderick, Cindy A.
Streck, Martin J.
Department of Geology, PSU
PO Box 751
Portland, OR 97207

Southern Methodist University

Quick, James E.
Office of Research and Graduate Studies
P.O. Box 750240
Dallas, TX 75275-0240

University of Bristol

Blundy, Jon
Department of Earth Sciences
Wills Memorial Building
Bristol BS8 1RJ, UK

* Deceased

University of California

Cooper, Kari M.
Geology Department, UC Davis
One Shields Avenue
Davis, CA 95616
Herriott, Trystan M.
Department of Earth Science, UC Santa Barbara
Webb Hall, Building 526
Santa Barbara, CA 93106

University of Cambridge

Edmonds, Marie
Downing Street
Cambridge CB2 3EQ, UK

University of Iowa

Reagan, Mark K.
Rowe, Michael C.
Wortel, Matthew
Department of Geoscience
121 Trowbridge Hall
Iowa City, IA 52242

University of Memphis

Horton, Stephen P.
Center for Earthquake Research and Information
3890 Central Ave
Memphis, TN 38152

University of Pittsburgh

Ramsey, Michael S.
Department of Geology & Planetary Science
200 SRCC Building
Pittsburgh, PA 15260

University of Oregon

Cashman, Katharine V.
Department of Geological Sciences, UO
1272 University of Oregon
Eugene, OR 97403

Western Washington University

Caplan-Auerbach, Jacqueline
Geology Department, WWU
516 High Street
Bellingham, WA 98225

Clark County

Needham, Deborah H.
Clark Regional Emergency Services Agency
710 W 13th St.
Vancouver, WA 98660

American Museum of Natural History

Mandeville, Charles W.
American Museum of Natural History
Central Park West at 79th Street
New York, NY 10024

Washington Military Department

Harper, Robert B.
Emergency Management Division
Building 20
Camp Murray, WA 98430

Contents

Chapters

Overview

Seismicity of the eruption

Geological observations of lava-dome growth

Geodesy and remote sensing

Models and mechanics of eruptive processes

Crisis management

Volcanic emissions

Petrologic and geochemical investigations of eruptive products

In pocket at back:

DVD-ROM containing the entire book, including digital appendixes to various chapters.

Overview

Basic facts of the 2004–2006, and continuing, eruption of Mount St. Helens, Washington

Early unrest	
Seismic swarm onset	September 23, 2004, 0200 hr Pacific daylight time (PDT)
First explosion	October 1, 2004, 1202 hr PDT
Lava extruded to surface	October 11, 2004 (not observed because of poor weather but deduced subsequently)
Explosions	
Number of explosions	6
Volcano explosivity index (VEI)	1–2 for early October 2004 vent-forming explosions
Largest VEI	2 (Oct. 5, 2004; Mar. 8, 2005)
Maximum known height of eruption clouds	11 km according to pilot reports 6 km minimum by Doppler radar (NEXRAD), March 8, 2005
Gases	
Sulfur dioxide, maximum	240 tons per day (Oct 27, 2004)
Carbon dioxide, maximum	2,415 tons per day (Oct 7, 2004)
Lava dome	
Composition	Dacite, 65% SiO_2
Phenocrysts	Plagioclase, amphibole, hypersthene
Total volume extruded	About 95×10^6 m^3 (as of September 11, 2007)
Maximum thickness of new dome	450 m
Highest altitude measured for new dome	2,368 m above sea level (spine 5, July 2005)
Volcano's summit (crater rim highest point)	2,540 m above sea level
Most notable rock avalanche	May 30, 2006, starting volume 50,000–100,000 m^3
Crater Glacier	
Volume before eruption	80×10^6 m^3
Volume after eruption	74×10^6 m^3
Maximum thickness of glacier	2004: about 150 m (datum is 1986 glacier surface) April 2005–July 2007: about 240 m, east arm, (deformed upper surface)
Monitoring sites within 10 km of volcano on September 22, 2004 (before onset)	
Seismometers	8
GPS receivers	1
Fixed transmitting cameras	1 (Gifford Pinchot National Forest)
Borehole tiltmeters	0
Number of monitoring sites installed within 10 km, September 2004–January 2008	
Seismometers (includes accelerometers)	20 (some destroyed or removed)
GPS receivers	20 (includes 14 installed by PBO *)
Fixed cameras	8
Tiltmeters	9 (includes 4 installed by PBO)
Borehole strainmeters	2 (installed by PBO)
Spiders	
Number deployed to crater for GPS or seismic monitoring	31
Number lost to natural causes	9

* Plate Boundary Observatory, a research component of EarthScope, which is sponsored by the National Science Foundation.

A Volcano Rekindled: The Renewed Eruption of Mount St. Helens, 2004–2006
Edited by David R. Sherrod, William E. Scott, and Peter H. Stauffer
U.S. Geological Survey Professional Paper 1750, 2008

Chapter 1

Overview of the 2004 to 2006, and Continuing, Eruption of Mount St. Helens, Washington

By William E. Scott[1], David R. Sherrod[1], and Cynthia A. Gardner[1]

Abstract

Rapid onset of unrest at Mount St. Helens on September 23, 2004, initiated an uninterrupted lava-dome-building eruption that continues to the time of writing this overview (spring 2006) for a volume of papers focused on this eruption. About three weeks of intense seismic unrest and localized surface uplift, punctuated by four brief explosions, constituted a vent-clearing phase, during which there was a frenzy of media attention and considerable uncertainty regarding the likely course of the eruption. The third week exhibited lessened seismicity and only minor venting of steam and ash, but rapid growth of the uplift, or welt, south of the 1980–86 lava dome proceeded as magma continued to push upward. Crystal-rich dacite (~65 weight percent SiO_2) lava first appeared at the surface on October 11, 2004, beginning the growth of a complex lava dome of uniform chemical composition accompanied by persistent but low levels of seismicity, rare explosions, low gas emissions, and frequent rockfalls. Petrologic studies suggest that the dome lava is chiefly of 1980s vintage, but with an admixed portion of new dacite. Alternatively, it may derive from a part of the magma chamber not tapped by 1980s eruptions. Regardless, detailed investigations of crystal chemistry, melt inclusions, and isotopes reveal a complex magmatic history.

Largely episodic extrusion between 1980 and 1986 produced a relatively symmetrical lava dome composed of stubby lobes. In contrast, continuous extrusion at mean rates of about 5 m^3/s in autumn 2004 to <1 m^3/s in early 2006 has produced an east-west ridge of three mounds with total volume about equal to that of the old dome. During much of late 2004 to summer 2005, a succession of spines, two recumbent and one steeply sloping and each mantled by striated gouge, grew to nearly 500 m in length in the southeastern sector of the 1980 crater and later disintegrated into two mounds. Since then, growth has been concentrated in the southwestern sector, producing a relatively symmetrical mound with steep gouge-covered slabs on its east flank. Throughout the eruption, the position of the extrusive vent has remained more or less fixed. Lack of geodetic evidence for either volume increase or pressure increase in the deep magmatic system since about 1990 and geodetic modeling that can account for only 20 to 30 percent of the 2004-to-present dome volume puzzles geodesists. Better constraints on parameters such as magma-chamber volume, crustal properties, and magma compressibility are needed to improve the models.

Development of the welt and the new dome bisected horseshoe-shaped Crater Glacier, which formerly wrapped around three sides of the 1980s dome, and fractured, compressed, and thickened the glacier's surviving east and west arms. Doubling of ice thickness resulted in increased flow rate and advance of termini, although rapid infiltration of water into the highly porous glacier bed prevented substantial basal sliding. Overall, dome growth and disintegration has removed surprisingly little ice.

The outcome of the ongoing eruption remains uncertain, but Mount St. Helens' varied eruptive history suggests multiple possibilities. One dynamical model and several petrologic investigations regard the current eruption as an extension of 1980s dome building that may persist continuously or episodically for years to come.

Introduction

A commonly asked question in the Pacific Northwest during the past 20 years, "When will Mount St. Helens erupt again?," was answered in late September to early October 2004, when a typical days-long swarm of small earthquakes escalated into intense unrest and eruption (Dzurisin and others, 2005). Many of the widely acknowledged principles of successful volcano-risk mitigation were reinforced:

[1] U.S. Geological Survey, 1300 SE Cardinal Court, Vancouver, WA 98683

- Understand a volcano's eruptive history and have an up-to-date hazard assessment.
- Have adequate monitoring systems installed and a good record of background behavior.
- Have a strong team of scientists and technicians on site, be able to draw on other experienced personnel, and have replacement monitoring equipment available.
- Have an interagency coordination or response plan in place and a working relationship with local emergency-response and land-management agencies.
- Have a well-coordinated joint information center to deliver updates to the media, public officials, and the public.

Fortunately, these conditions were largely met, owing to the volcano's memorable eruption in 1980 (Lipman and Mullineaux, 1981), to long-established monitoring systems operated by the U.S. Geological Survey (USGS) at its David A. Johnston Cascades Volcano Observatory (CVO) and the Pacific Northwest Seismic Network (PNSN) at the University of Washington, and to long-term cooperation in volcano-hazard and risk-mitigation issues by the Gifford Pinchot National Forest (GPNF; in which Mount St. Helens is located), Washington State Military Department–Emergency Management Division, and USGS–CVO. Nonetheless, scientific uncertainty, strong media interest and scrutiny, and the excitement of a volcanic crisis created an intense and, at times, chaotic scene.

As described in the contributions to this volume, more than 18 months of continuous activity has given scientists from the USGS and numerous academic institutions an opportunity to closely study an eruption that has progressed much differently from that of 1980–86. Rapid onset of unrest and eruption, apparently continuous extrusion of gas-poor, mostly crystallized lava into a glacier-filled crater, and month after month of monotonous seismicity, among numerous other observations and surprises, have led to new insights and models of eruptive processes. The eventual duration and outcome of the current eruption remain unknown, but scientists look forward to exploiting the rich research environment that Mount St. Helens continues to provide. Furthermore, the eruption has stimulated the seemingly insatiable interest of the public and media in volcanoes and reinvigorated visitation at the GPNF's Mount St. Helens National Volcanic Monument (herein, the Monument). The result is a more volcano-savvy citizenry in the Pacific Northwest, which is essential for maintaining awareness of potential volcano hazards posed by the other 12 Cascade volcanic centers in the U.S. and the three major Canadian volcanic centers in southern British Columbia.

This overview briefly summarizes the recent eruptive history of Mount St. Helens, including the 1980–86 eruption, the 1986–2004 period of quiescence punctuated by several notable periods of unrest and minor explosions, and the current eruption. Although not addressed in this overview, comparisons of the current eruption to historical dome-building eruptions at other volcanoes are provided in several papers in this volume (Schilling and others, chap. 8; Vallance and others, chap. 9; Cashman and others, chap. 19).

Previous Eruptive History

Mount St. Helens (fig. 1) has been by far the most frequently active volcano in the Cascade Range during the past few thousand years, producing eruptions of a wide variety of types and scales (Hoblitt and others, 1980; Crandell, 1987; Scott, 1989; Mullineaux, 1996; Clynne and others, this volume, chap. 28). Recent work shows that an eruptive center has existed in the Mount St. Helens area for at least 300,000 years. Early dacitic lava domes created a broad volcano surrounded by aprons of pyroclastic and volcaniclastic deposits. Only during the past few thousand years did the volcano grow into the high graceful cone of early 1980. Late Holocene cone building, which followed an apparent dormant period of about 7,000 years, began with several periods of lava-dome and plinian eruptions of dacite, not unlike earlier events in the volcano's history. However, starting about 2,500 years ago, substantial amounts of basalt and andesite began to erupt between dacitic eruptions. Such lava flows buried large parts of a central cluster of dacite domes and flanking fans and started cone building in earnest. Eruptions during the 17th and early 18th centuries raised the cone about 300 m, with emplacement of the summit dacitic lava dome, and added fans of debris on all flanks of the volcano. Eruptions during the early to middle 19th century did not alter the shape of the volcano greatly but provided an opportunity for early settlers to witness several small eruptions and to realize that Mount St. Helens is an active volcano.

1980–1986 Eruption

Although a detailed understanding of Mount St. Helens' eruptive history and a hazard-zonation map were available in spring 1980 (Crandell and Mullineaux, 1978), monitoring of the volcano was minimal (one telemetered seismometer on the west flank and one surveyed electronic-distance-measurement line on the east flank). With no recent eruptions having occurred, local officials and land managers had no experience with volcanic crises. The onset of seismicity in mid-March 1980, which accelerated greatly on March 25, and steam explosions starting on March 27 generated intense interest by public officials and the media. This interest required rapid creation of an emergency coordination center to bring together representatives of key agencies. GPNF's experience in fire operations helped greatly in organizing a response. Scientists learned numerous lessons, especially the need to speak with one voice and to quickly address rumors and conflicts (Miller and others, 1981). During April and early May 1980, a decrease in seismicity and frequency of steam explosions reduced public concern and intensified calls to open closed areas. However, the rapidly growing north-flank bulge, driven by intrusion of a cryptodome into the volcano, kept scientists wary.

Hopes that a distinctive change in seismicity or rapid acceleration of ground deformation would permit a short-term hazard forecast were dashed in minutes on May 18, when the north flank failed in a great debris avalanche (Glicken, 1998). This avalanche was the largest subaerial landslide on Earth in historical time. The resulting rapid decompression of the cryptodome generated explosions that produced a lateral blast, a rapidly moving pyroclastic density current that leveled ~600 km^2 of forest (Hoblitt, 2000) and killed most of the 57 victims of the eruption. The debris avalanche and blast were of a scale unknown in Mount St. Helens' history and proved milestones in the recognition of such events as an important hazard at composite volcanoes worldwide (Siebert, 1984). The hours-long eruption of pumice and ash that followed the blast was of expectable scale, although many affected communities in eastern Washing-

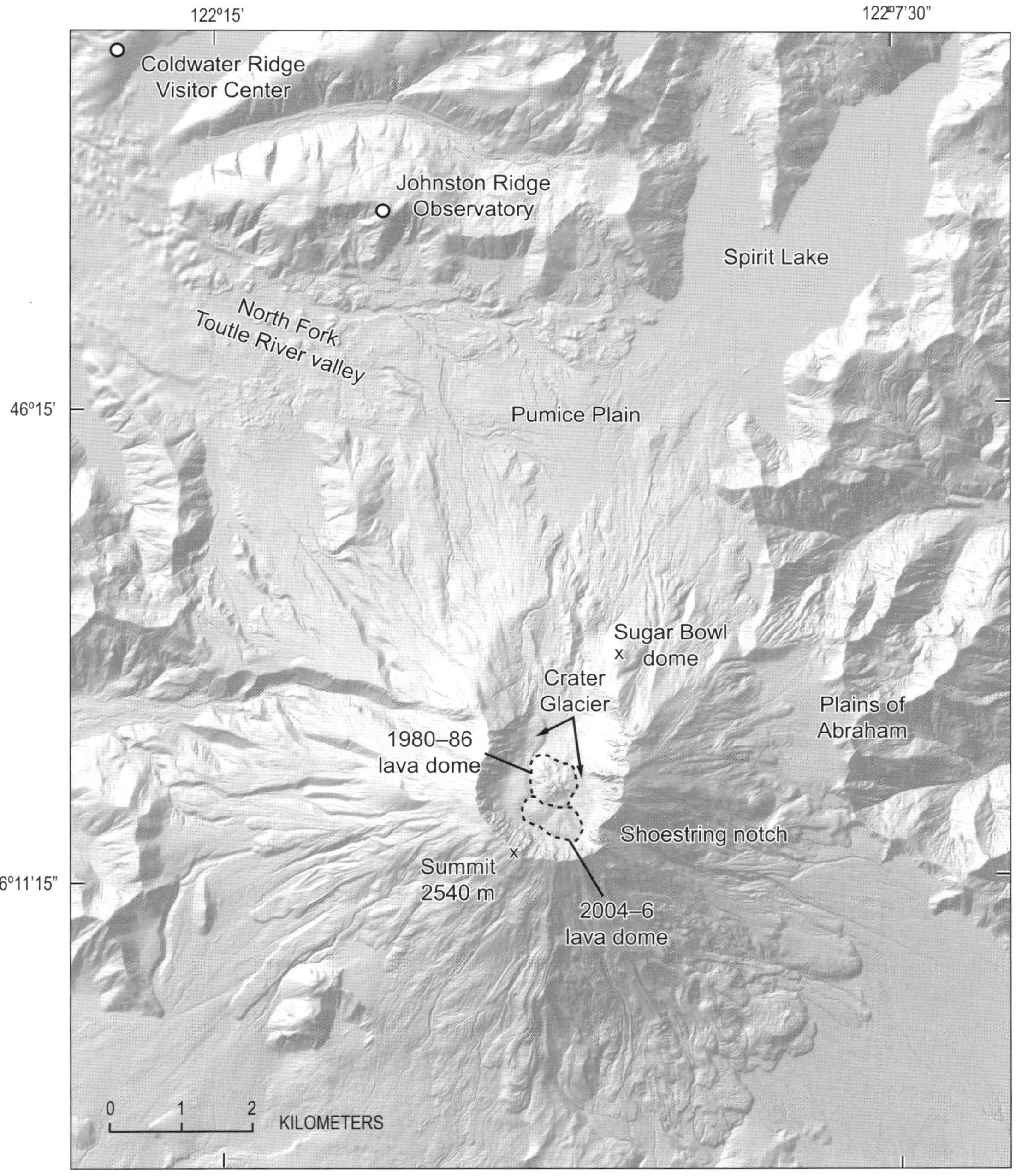

Figure 1. Shaded-relief index map of Mount St. Helens and adjacent areas, showing locations discussed in text. Base is chiefly from digital elevation model (DEM) of 2003 lidar survey (Schilling and others, chap. 8, this volume). Crater features are from DEM made from February 2006 aerial photographs, and northwest corner of map is from the National Elevation Dataset.

ton, northern Idaho, and western Montana were unaware of potential hazards and poorly prepared to respond to tephra fallout and resulting deposits on the order of millimeters to as much as 8 cm thick (Warrick and others, 1981).

Five smaller subplinian eruptions during summer 1980 were preceded by recognizable precursors, as were the 20 lava-dome-building eruptions that ended in October 1986 (Malone and others, 1981; Swanson and others, 1983). Dome-building eruptions were chiefly several-day episodes of extrusion of 1–6×10^6 m^3 of lava at average rates as high as 25 m^3/s. Three episodes lasted longer, including one of largely endogenous growth in 1982–83 that lasted 368 days and had an average eruption rate of 0.7 m^3/s. By October 1986, the lava dome stood about 270 m above the 1980 crater floor and had a total volume in the range of 77 to 91×10^6 m^3 (as estimated by Swanson and Holcomb, 1990, and Mills, 1992, respectively).

1986 to 2004

During 1980–86 dome building, seismicity was largely confined to shallow depth (<3 km) and related temporally to periods of extrusion. Starting in 1987, deeper earthquakes became more frequent. Stress-field modeling using focal mechanisms of deep earthquakes supported a hypothesis of pressurization of the magmatic system, which was thought to result from sealing of the shallow conduit (Moran, 1994). By late 1989, deep (3–10 km) seismicity was dominant and, over the next 22 months, 28 shallow, explosion-like seismic signals were recorded, at least 6 of which were accompanied by confirmed explosions that ejected blocks and produced ash clouds. Gas to drive these events was inferred to come from a deep magmatic source, likely from crystallization of magma in the conduit (Mastin, 1994).

Several other months-long periods of increased deep seismicity occurred after 1992; the most persistent and energetic was in summer 1998. A detectable efflux of CO_2 during this 1998 seismicity (Gerlach and others, this volume, chap. 26) suggested that magmatic intrusion was involved. Although scientists infer that some intrusion happened between 1987 and 2004 (Moran and others, this volume, chap. 2), geodetic surveys offer no support for a substantial increase in volume or pressure in the magmatic system after about 1990 (this volume: Dzurisin and others, chap. 14; Lisowski and others, chap. 15; Poland and Lu, chap. 18).

Throughout 1986–2004, winter snowfall and avalanche snow, alternating with summer rockfall debris from the crater walls, was accumulating in the moat between the 1980–86 lava dome and crater wall. By 1996 the mass was thick enough to initiate glacier flow and to form steep advancing snouts at a time when most of Earth's glaciers were shrinking (Schilling and others, 2004). As the volcano reawakened in 2004, the glacier, formally named Crater Glacier in 2006, formed a collar around three sides of the dome and was gaining mass yearly. South of the dome, the glacier's surface stood as much as 150 m above the 1986 crater floor.

During this time of relative quiescence, media attention to periods of increased seismicity and to anniversaries of the 1980 eruption, as well as other Mount St. Helens' issues, kept the volcano in the news and maintained awareness among the public that the volcano was active and could erupt again. Attention was periodically focused on the volcano as a result of policy discussions related to continuing high sediment production in the Toutle River basin (Major and others, 2000), to longevity and effectiveness of the sediment-retention structure built on the North Fork Toutle River, to the environmental impact of a proposed extension of State Route 504 across the Pumice Plain north of the crater, and to concerns regarding long-term funding issues at the Monument. Educational programs at the Monument and in local school districts also helped to maintain awareness of potential hazards.

Chronology of Events: 2004 to Early 2006

Beginning on September 23, 2004, three weeks of intense seismicity, punctuated by four brief explosions along with localized intense ground deformation, signaled a vent-clearing phase. During this phase there was great uncertainty as to how the unrest would progress and what style of eruption would likely result. The final week of vent clearing was characterized by lessened seismicity, but continued localized intense ground deformation. A phase of continuous lava-dome building, which is subdivided further by Vallance and others (this volume, chap. 9), began on October 11, 2004, and continues at the time of this writing (spring 2006). The highlights of each phase are summarized below, taken largely from contributions in this volume.

Vent Clearing—September 23 to October 5, 2004

A two-day swarm of tiny (mostly M_d<1), shallow volcano-tectonic earthquakes beginning early on September 23, 2004, resembled a swarm in November 2001 (Moran and others, this volume, chap. 2) and prompted release of an Information Statement by USGS–CVO and PNSN at 1800 PDT on September 23 (table 1, fig. 2). The statement discussed the swarm's similarity to previous ones and surmised that this swarm might reflect heavier-than-normal precipitation in the preceding four weeks. A rain gage at the mouth of the Mount St. Helens crater had recorded an abnormally wet last month of summer—more than 30 cm of rainfall. An update on the morning of September 24 noted the difference between the shallow seismicity of the past day and activity during summer 1998 that consisted of larger and deeper events and was considered evidence of deep magmatic intrusion. Both statements considered eruption unlikely without significant further precursors.

Beginning on the afternoon of Saturday, September 25, earthquakes increased in magnitude (M_d ≤2.8), and by the following morning a total of ten M_d >2.0 earthquakes had

Table 1. Systems used by U.S. Geological Survey–Cascades Volcano Observatory for event notification at Mount St. Helens during 2004–2006 eruption for hazards on the ground and for ash hazard to aircraft in flight.

[Terms in use when eruption began. On October 1, 2006, all U.S. Geological Survey volcano observatories adopted a new notification system for volcano hazards that uses some different terms and changes definitions of some levels. See http://volcanoes.usgs.gov/2006/warnschemes.html or http://pubs.usgs.gov/fs/2006/3139/fs2006-3139.pdf for details.]

Notification for Ground Hazard	
Information Statement	Describes short-lived events that may or may not be hazardous or gives commentary on status of volcano. May also be issued to provide commentary about notable events occurring within any staged alert level during volcanic unrest.
Staged alert levels	
1 Notice of Volcanic Unrest	First recognition of conditions that could lead to a hazardous event
2 Volcano Advisory	Hazardous volcanic event likely but not expected immediately, or ongoing eruption with localized hazards[1]
3 Volcano Alert	Hazardous volcanic event underway or expected within a few hours or days
Notification of Ash Hazards to Aircraft	
Aviation Color Code	
Green	Volcano is quiet; no eruption is anticipated
Yellow	Volcano is restless; eruption is possible but not known to be imminent
Orange	Small explosive eruption(s) either imminent or occurring; ash plume(s) not expected to reach 25,000 feet above sea level
Red	Major explosive eruption imminent or occurring; large ash plumes expected to reach at least 25,000 feet above sea level

[1] The second part of the definition was added during the current eruption.

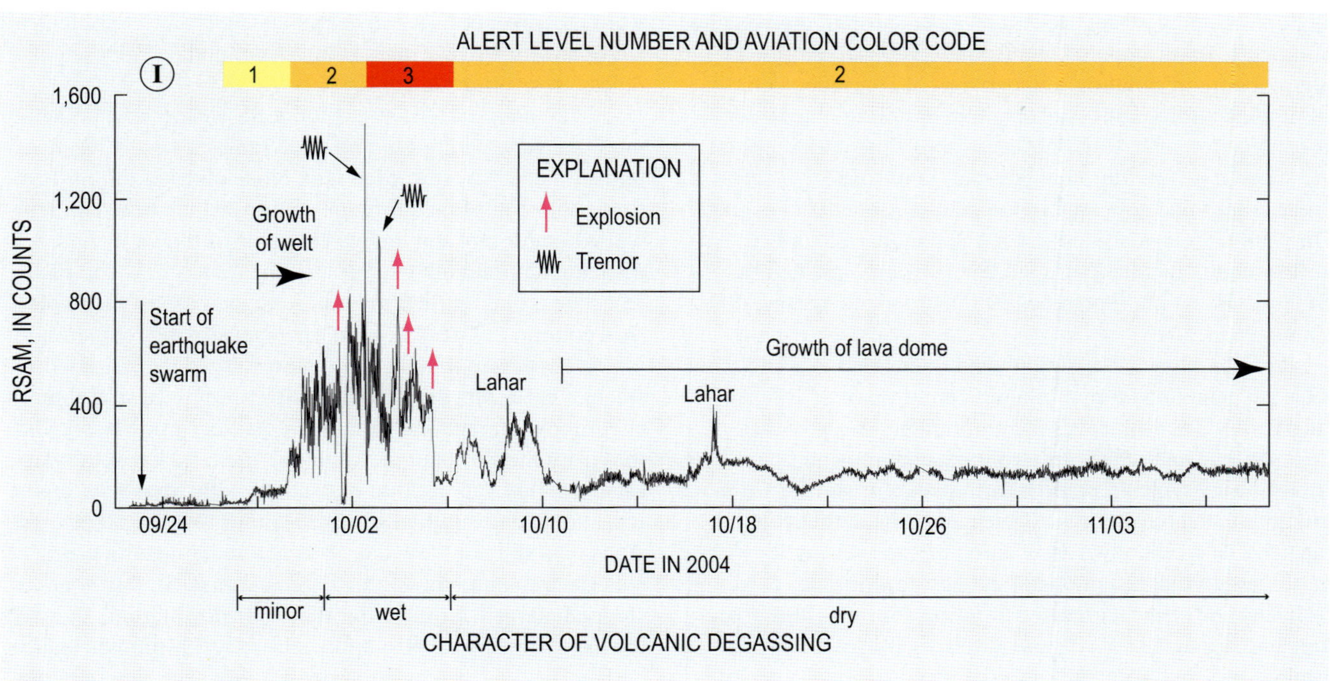

Figure 2. Real-time seismic amplitude measurement (RSAM) during first 6 weeks of unrest and eruption at Mount St. Helens served as proxy for rate of seismicity (modified from Moran and others, this volume, chap. 2). Times of explosions and periods of tremor are shown by symbols. Character of degassing from Dzurisin and others (2005). For meaning of numerals and colored bars indicating alert levels and aviation color codes, see table 1; I, release of first information statement.

been recorded—the most in a 24-hr period since lava-dome building ended in 1986. This increase in seismicity, along with the appearance of low-frequency and hybrid earthquakes, prompted reassessment of the probability of hazardous activity (Moran and others, this volume, chap. 2). At 1500 PDT on Sunday, September 26, after notifying the Washington State Emergency Management Division and GPNF, USGS–CVO and PNSN released a Notice of Volcanic Unrest (table 1; fig. 2), indicating that seismicity had surpassed background level and that the volcano was in a state that could evolve toward eruption. Greatest concern was for explosions such as those between 1989 and 1991 that could shower the crater and upper flanks with ballistic fragments and create ash clouds that could affect aircraft in flight and downwind communities.

The increase in alert level spurred several actions. The GPNF activated their Emergency Coordination Center and closed the south-flank climbers' trail and other trails near the crater (Frenzen and Matarrese, this volume, chap. 23). The number of daily media inquiries, chiefly to USGS–CVO, PNSN, and the Monument, rose rapidly, requiring a considerable effort to be directed toward interviews and briefings (Driedger and others, this volume, chap. 24). High rates of both seismicity and public interest in earthquake information compelled PNSN to develop new visualization tools for tracking seismicity and to establish independent Web sites for the public and for sharing information with USGS–CVO and other scientific partners (Qamar and others, this volume, chap. 3).

Field crews took advantage of uncommonly clear autumn weather to begin installation of additional seismometers and global positioning system (GPS) receivers around the volcano. Fortunately, Earthscope's Plate Boundary Observatory had been planning installation of a network of continuous GPS instruments at Mount St. Helens, and they were able to accelerate their program. Aerial observations of the crater at this time showed no obvious changes, but, in retrospect, a series of new cracks had appeared in the glacier immediately south of the 1980–86 lava dome between September 25 and 26. An uplifted area coincident with the cracks was confirmed by USGS observers on September 29 (Dzurisin and others, this volume, chap. 14).

By September 29 seismicity had intensified to about three events per minute with maximum magnitudes of M_d 2.4–2.8, rising RSAM (real-time seismic amplitude measurement) values (Moran and others, this volume, chap 2), and hours-long periods during which repetitive earthquakes of similar waveform dominated the records (Thelen and others, this volume, chap. 4). The well-known association of such seismicity with lava-dome-building eruptions of the past few decades at Mount St. Helens and elsewhere raised eruption concerns further and prompted issuance of a Volcano Advisory (table 1, fig. 2) midmorning on September 29. The aviation color code (see table 1) was raised to Orange because of increasing concern that explosions could send ash to altitudes where air traffic would be affected. The Volcano Advisory signified that processes were underway that could lead to hazardous eruptive events, but not imminently. Initial airborne missions to detect volcanic gases (carbon dioxide, sulfur dioxide, and hydrogen sulfide) found little, if any (Gerlach and others, this volume, chap. 26). Interpretation of the apparent lack of volcanic gas was tempered by the possibility that such gas had been scrubbed at the high water-to-gas mass ratios likely to be present at shallow levels beneath the nearly glacier-covered crater floor.

The alert-level rise to Advisory triggered the GPNF to activate a local Incident Management Team and to begin discussions with other agencies regarding a Joint Operation Center, which would be necessary if unrest continued to escalate or eruptions began (Frenzen and Matarrese, this volume, chap. 23). Intense media interest, directed chiefly toward USGS–CVO and the Monument, was beginning to adversely affect operations, so local and State emergency management agencies joined with USGS–CVO and the GPNF to begin organizing a Joint Information Center (Driedger and others, this volume, chap. 24).

Real-time seismic amplitude values increased again on the evening of September 29, reflecting an increase in maximum earthquake magnitudes (M_d 2.8–3.3) and rate of earthquakes of M_d>2 to about 1 per minute. The RSAM values fluctuated over the next 1.5 days. Flights during this time period again failed to detect significant amounts of volcanic gas. However, the uplifted and cracked area of the glacier south of the 1980–86 lava dome, along with a sliver of the dome, was continuing to fracture and rise several meters per day, creating what became known as the welt (Vallance and others, this volume, chap. 9; Dzurisin and others, this volume, chap. 14). Data from a GPS receiver on the west side of the 1980s lava dome showed northward movement of several centimeters per day, consistent with a shove from a rising mass south of the dome (LaHusen and others, this volume, chap. 16).

The inaugural flight at Mount St. Helens of a helicopter-mounted forward-looking infrared radiometer (FLIR) midday on October 1 was rewarded with close observation of the first explosion of the current eruption, which bored an ice-walled crater through the western part of the welt (figs. 3*A*, *B*; Schneider and others, this volume, chap. 17). The FLIR recorded a maximum temperature at the base of the explosion column of ~160°C, well below magmatic temperature, which suggested that the explosion was driven largely by steam. The explosion was also witnessed by several thousand cheering visitors at the Monument and became clearly visible from the Portland metropolitan area, 80 km southwest, as an ash and vapor cloud rose about 2 km above the crater rim and drifted southwestward. Neither this nor other explosions over the next few days had any recognizable precursors (Moran and others, this volume, chap. 6). Earthquakes stopped about 1 minute after the explosion started, and when the explosion signal also ended abruptly 19 minutes later, helicorders were quiet for about 3 hours. The rate of earthquakes rapidly increased again during the evening, and by late evening RSAM values exceeded those prior to the explosion, suggesting that the explosion had relieved elevated pressure in the conduit but that the system was repressurizing quickly (Moran and others, this volume, chap. 2).

For the next two days (October 2–3), seismicity remained at a high level of several thousand events per day, punctuated by earthquakes of M_d 3.5–3.9. Midday on October 2, a 50-minute episode of energetic, relatively broadband seismic tremor (Moran and others, this volume, chap. 2), coupled with hints of volcanic gas during the previous few days (Gerlach and others, this volume, chap. 26) and a continued high rate of growth of the welt, prompted USGS–CVO and PNSN to issue a Volcano Alert at 1400 PDT (table 1, fig. 2). Because of concern over an imminent and potentially hazardous event, the GPNF evacuated the Johnston Ridge Observatory (JRO), 8 km north of the crater, the Washington State Department of Transportation closed State Route 504 at the Coldwater Ridge Visitor Center, and land and air space was closed within 8 km (5 mi) of the crater (Frenzen and Matarrese, this volume, chap. 23). A key concern was that an explosive magmatic eruption could produce pyroclastic flows, swiftly melt large amounts of snow and ice surrounding the vent, and generate lahars that could sweep into the upper North Fork Toutle River valley. The increased possibility of ash clouds reaching high altitudes where they could affect air traffic warranted raising the aviation color code to Red.

Memories of the catastrophic events of May 18, 1980, preoccupied many media and citizens, so a major public-information effort was required to maintain a realistic hazard perspective (Driedger and others, this volume, chap. 24). An explanation that seemed to reduce anxiety was that the 1980 eruption had so eviscerated Mount St. Helens, creating a deep crater open to the north, that the volcano could no longer support a scenario of intrusion of a cryptodome, large flank failure, and catastrophic lateral blast. Consensus among scientists at USGS–CVO and PNSN was converging on two possible scenarios for volcanic activity over the coming weeks to months. These were transmitted to land and emergency managers. One focused on resumption of lava-dome growth accompanied by explosive events of volcanic explosivity index (VEI) 2–3. The other included the possibility of eruptions of VEI 4 to low 5, similar to the hours-long plinian eruption on the late morning and afternoon of May 18, 1980.

Interest on the part of the media and the public peaked during the first few days of October, resulting in high rates of inquiry and visits to Web sites (Driedger and others, this volume, chap. 24). A Joint Information Center opened on October 3, and a Joint Operations Center under unified command

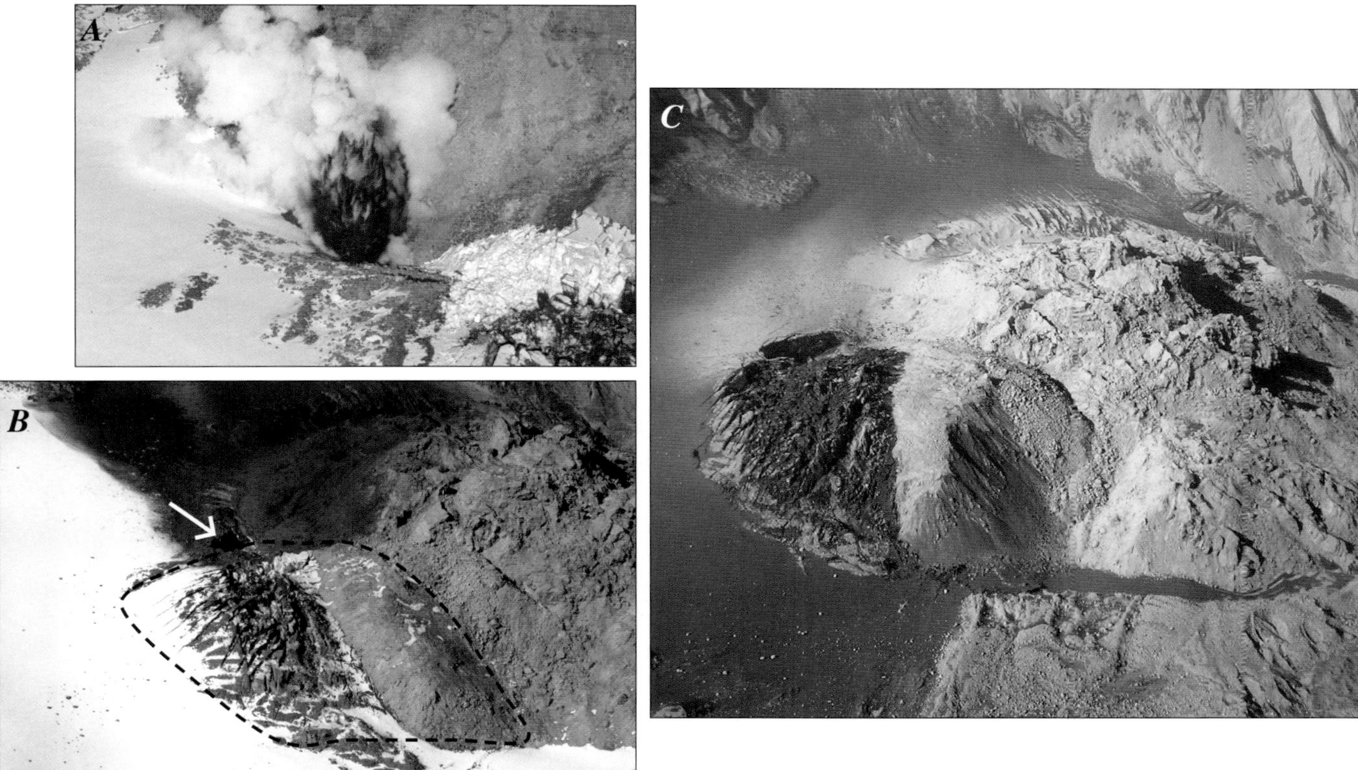

Figure 3. Crater features seen during first two weeks of the eruption of Mount St. Helens. *A*, Start of explosion of October 1, 2004, looking north across glacier toward 1980–86 lava dome. USGS photograph by J.S. Pallister. *B*, Looking west about 30 minutes after explosion of October 1, 2004, ended. USGS photograph by J.S. Pallister. Note tephra-covered snow and crater (white arrow) bored at west end of welt (dashed line), which is formed of uplifted glacier ice and southern part of 1980–86 lava dome. *C*, Noticeably larger welt on October 4, 2004, looking west. Some tephra of October 1 and 4 explosions is drying to light color. USGS photograph by S.F. Schilling.

was established the following day with representatives from key land-management and emergency-management agencies (Frenzen and Matarrese, this volume, chap. 23).

Additional explosions late on October 3 and midmorning on October 4 were followed by decreases and rebounds in seismicity much less dramatic than those on October 1; the last explosion on October 5 initiated a drop in RSAM that has never recovered (fig. 2; Moran and others, this volume, chap. 2). This last explosion, rating a VEI of 2, was the most vigorous, generating an ash plume that reached about 2 km above the crater rim. The plume drifted to the north-northeast, lightly dusting several communities and the eastern part of Mount Rainier National Park, about 100 km away.

The relatively low level of seismicity that followed the October 5 explosion, including multiplets of hybrid events with similar wave forms (Thelen and others, this volume, chap. 4), combined with moderate gas emissions (Gerlach and others, this volume, chap. 26) and continued growth of the welt (fig. 3*C*; Dzurisin and others, this volume, chap. 14), suggested that the eruption would probably progress to lava-dome extrusion. Under such conditions, the probability of hazardous events affecting areas beyond closures was small, except for ash clouds that could pose hazards to aircraft. Therefore, at 0915 PDT on October 6, USGS–CVO and PNSN lowered the alert level to Volcano Advisory, where it has remained since (table 1, fig. 2). Concurrently, the aviation color code was lowered to Orange. The GPNF reverted to a local Incident Management Team (Frenzen and Matarrese, this volume, chap. 23), and inquiries to the Joint Information Center began to decline, eventually leading to its being disbanded on October 13 (Driedger and others, this volume, chap. 24). USGS–CVO continued to update agencies through daily conference calls.

Vent Clearing—Waiting for Lava—October 5 to October 11, 2004

Several days of stormy weather beginning on October 6 drove visitors and media from the Monument, increased RSAM with storm noise, and generated a small lahar from the crater—a common occurrence with the onset of autumn rain. Brief views through the clouds showed that the welt continued to grow upward and outward, reaching more than 100 m above the former glacier surface. On October 10 a fixed camera on Sugar Bowl dome, at the northeast mouth of the crater, began transmitting images that tracked growth of part of the welt (Poland and others, this volume, chap. 11). Later analysis of digital elevation models (DEMs) showed that by October 11 the deformed area had a volume of about 10×10^6 m^3 (Schilling and others, this volume, chap. 8). FLIR measurements confirmed that by October 10 an area on the northwest part of the welt had reached temperatures >270°C, suggesting that the crater floor was being heated and pushed upward by rising magma (Schneider and others, this volume, chap. 17). An airborne survey on October 7 measured gas-emission rates of ~2,400 metric tons per day (t/d) CO_2, ~100 t/d SO_2, and ~10 t/d H_2S, which, although relatively modest for volcanoes such as Mount St. Helens, suggested that a dry pathway had been established and scrubbing of SO_2 reduced (Gerlach and others, this volume, chap. 26). The question on everyone's mind and asked repeatedly by the media was, "Has new lava appeared on the surface yet?"

Lava-Dome Growth—October 11, 2004, to Spring 2006

On October 11, a FLIR survey revealed a newly extruded fin-shaped rock spine (in retrospect designated spine 1) about 30 m high and 60 m long and having a maximum temperature of about 580°C (Schneider and others, this volume, chap. 17); this spine is considered to have been the initial appearance of new lava (fig. 4) and the start of growth of what we call the new lava dome (this volume: Schilling and others, chap. 8; Vallance and others, chap. 9; Herriott and others, chap. 10). The spine occupied the approximate location of the vent for early October explosions and stood >200 m above the crater floor. In the following days the spine grew, its base and cracks showed temperatures as high as 700°C, and additional areas of hot rock appeared to the south of spine 1 (designated spine 2; Vallance and others, this volume, chap. 9). The first samples of the new lava dome were dredged from spine 1 on October 20 using a weighted bucket on the end of a 30-m line slung from a helicopter. The samples looked like typical Mount St. Helens dacite (Pallister and others, this volume, chap. 30). During mid-October, RSAM fluctuated broadly, multiplets of hybrid earthquakes appeared and faded, and seismicity settled into a pattern of repetitive small (M_d <1) earthquakes, dubbed "drumbeats," occurring at a rate of one to two per minute, with larger events at longer intervals (Moran and others, this volume, chap. 2).

The potential for unpredictable explosions induced decisions to minimize the exposure of field crews; beginning in early October 2004, most new and replacement instruments in the crater were deployed by helicopter sling. Single-frequency GPS receivers and accelerometers (seismometers) mounted alone or together on tripods, dubbed "spiders," proved invaluable for maintaining close-in monitoring by telemetered seismic instruments (McChesney and others, this volume, chap. 7) and for allowing real-time geodetic measurements of rates and directions of movement of the welt and new dome, as well as movement of the glacier and deformation of the old lava dome (LaHusen and others, this volume, chap. 16; Dzurisin and others, this volume, chap. 14; Walder and others, this volume, chap. 13).

Growth of the new lava dome at Mount St. Helens has progressed steadily since mid-October 2004, apparently without pause (this volume: Schilling and others, chap. 8; Vallance and others, chap. 9; Herriott and others, chap 10; Poland and others, chap. 11; Major and others, chap. 12). In contrast, the old (1980–86) lava dome grew in episodic spurts on either side of a one-year period of continuous growth (Swanson and Holcomb, 1990). Rather than building a single dome-shaped structure similar to the old dome, the new dome grew initially as a series of recumbent, smoothly surfaced spines or "whalebacks" that extruded to lengths of almost 500 m. As is typical for such spines (Williams, 1932), their surfaces were striated and grooved and formed of powdery, crushed rock (gouge) and cataclasite that result from the solid extrusion grinding against the conduit walls during its last few hundred meters of ascent (Cashman and others, this volume, chap. 19; Moore and others, this volume, chap. 20). The gouge on early spines contained both dacite from the extrusion and more mafic constituents interpreted to have come from the conduit walls, but during most of the eruption, gouge has been formed entirely of dome dacite (Rowe and others, this volume, chap. 29; Pallister and others, this volume, chap. 30).

The dacite building the new dome is similar in chemical composition (~65 weight percent SiO_2) and mineralogy (plagioclase>hornblende≈hypersthene) to the dacite erupted on May 18, 1980, and is among the most silica-rich and incompatible-element-depleted magmas of the past 500 years at Mount St. Helens (Pallister and others, this volume, chap. 30). The dome lava contains 40–50 percent phenocrysts, and the groundmass is largely crystalline for most of its last 500 m of ascent (Cashman and others, this volume, chap. 19). In several contributions in this volume, petrologists and geochemists explore evidence for the origin of the lava and its recent history. Some of it is thought to represent residual magma from the 1980s, but several lines of evidence suggest that a component of a different dacite is mixed with the 1980s dacite—one newly arrived in the magma chamber or one from a part of the magma chamber that was not tapped in the 1980s (this volume: Pallister and others, chap. 30; Thornber and others, chap. 32; Blundy and others, chap. 33; Streck and others, chap. 34; Kent and others, chap. 35; Cooper and Donnelly, chap. 36; Reagan and others, chap. 37). Thin reaction rims on amphibole phenocrysts suggest storage for a prolonged period at depths of 4–5 km or deeper, followed by rapid ascent through the conduit (Rutherford and Devine, this volume, chap. 31).

Late Autumn 2004

The first of the whaleback-shaped spines (spine 3) started growing in late October 2004 from a spot just southeast of spine 1 and east of spine 2. A GPS spider riding on the spine moved at an average rate of about 10 m/d for 8 days (LaHusen

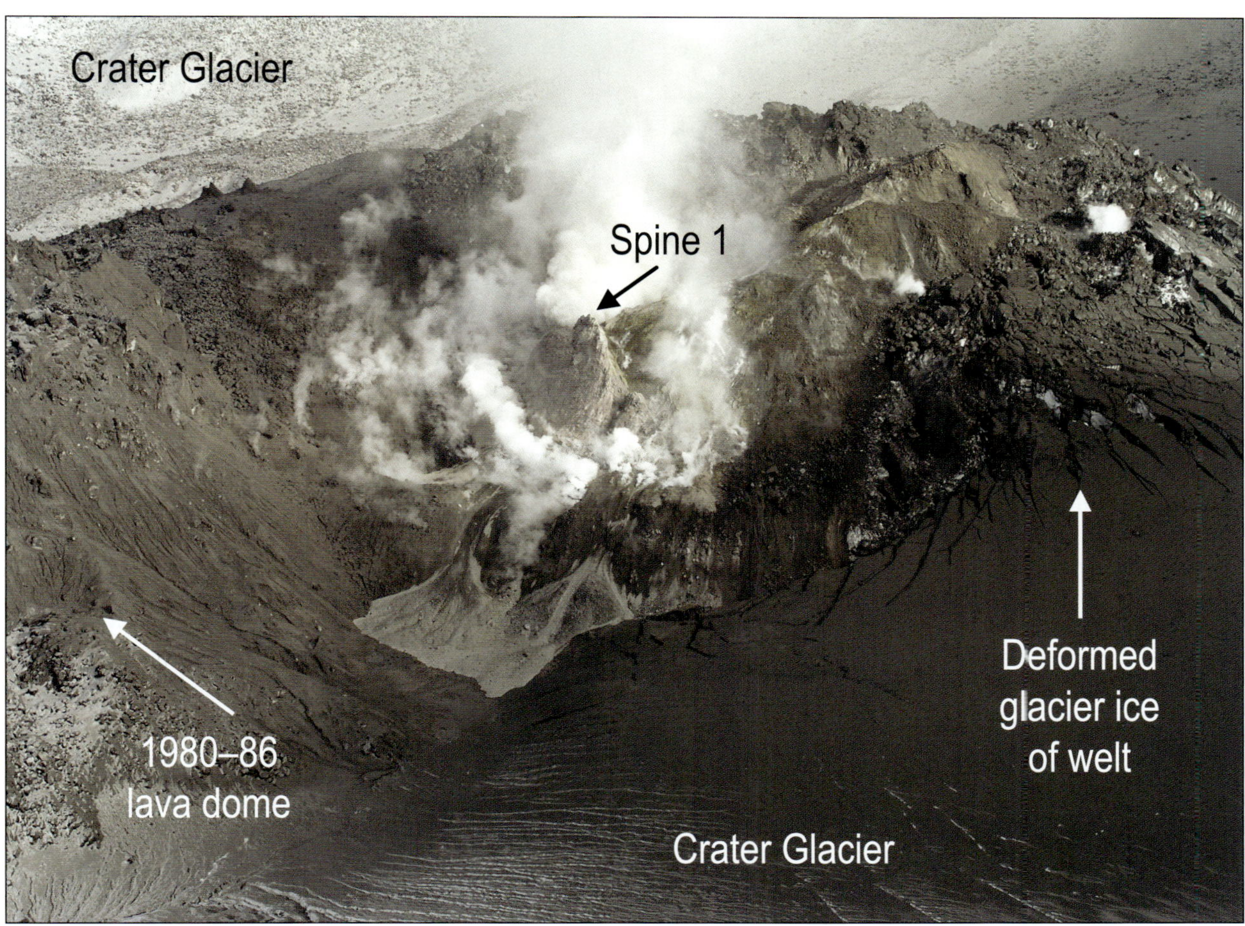

Figure 4. First view (toward southeast) of hot, new lava at surface in crater of Mount St. Helens, October 11, 2004. Spine 1 is composed of pinkish-gray dacite that is disintegrating and forming light-colored debris fans between welt, old dome, and west arm of glacier. USGS photograph by J.J. Major.

and others; this volume, chap. 16). By the end of November 2004, spine 3 was about 475 m long and had reached the base of the southeast crater wall; by mid-December, the total volume increase represented by the three spines of the new dome and welt, using the 1986 crater floor as a base datum, was about 30×10^6 m^3 (Schilling and others, this volume, chap. 8). Whether because of the increasing difficulty of extruding an ever-lengthening mass or because of stress imposed by impinging on the crater wall, longitudinal fractures appeared and widened and transverse fractures severed the spine from the vent in mid- to late December (fig. 5). The breakup of the spine was accompanied by sporadic earthquakes of M_d ~2.5–3.5, suggesting a causal relation (Moran and others, this volume, chap. 2). The remaining stump of spine 3 grew to form a new spine (spine 4) that pushed most of the old spine 3 aside to the east, except for a small amount that was stranded on the west side of spine 4 (Vallance and others, this volume, chap. 9; Herriott and others, this volume, chap. 10). As spine 3 was pushed eastward, it became increasingly fractured, and little of its original smooth, gouge-covered surface remained intact.

January to July 2005

Growth and disintegration of spines continued through the first 8 months of 2005. Spine 4 formed a prominent whaleback whose growth ended similarly to that of spine 3, whereas spine 5 grew at a steeper angle and its south end trended more southwesterly than did spines 3 and 4 (Vallance and others, this volume, chap. 9). Growth periods of spines 4 and 5 each lasted about 13 to 14 weeks. Extrusion rates during the growth of spines 4 and 5 were lower than during growth of spine 3 (Schilling and others, this volume, chap. 8), as were linear rates of motion measured by GPS spiders (LaHusen and others, this volume, chap. 16), by analysis of repeat photographs from the crater mouth (Major and others, this volume, chap. 12), and by tracking of points through sequential DEMs (Vallance and others, this volume, chap. 9). By midsummer 2005, the top of spine 5 reached the highest altitude attained by the new dome, 2,368 m. At that time the top stood only a few meters below the lowest point on the crater rim, Shoestring notch, and about 180 m below the present summit of Mount St. Helens; the dome then towered about 450 m above the 1986 crater floor. Spine 5 was a prominent feature in the view of the crater from JRO in midsummer 2005, with the crumbled remains of spine 4 and its large raft of intact gouge-covered surface lying off to the east (fig. 6*A*).

August 2005 to Spring 2006

A key change in the pattern of dome growth began in late July 2005, as towering spine 5 began to crumble rapidly. Rather than follow the previous pattern of a new spine growing southward and bulldozing the remains of older spines chiefly eastward, the growth of spine 6 progressed westward. The likeliest explanation is that spine 6 faced less resistance by plowing into the west arm of the glacier than by continuing to push into the previously extruded dome (Vallance and others, this volume, chap. 9). Although spine 6 had some areas displaying the smooth, gouge-covered surface typical of earlier whalebacks, it formed a more domical mass than had previous spines. Photogrammetric techniques estimated a rate of movement of several meters per day westward and upward (this volume: Major and others, chap. 12; Dzurizin and others, chap. 14). As spine 6 moved westward, the west side of spine 5, which was by then highly fractured, slumped westward into a widening sag forming between the two spines.

By mid-October 2005, a new spine was detected in FLIR imagery to be rising between spines 5 and 6 (Vallance and others, this volume, chap. 9). Spine 7 rode up the east side of spine 6, and both continued to move westward (fig.

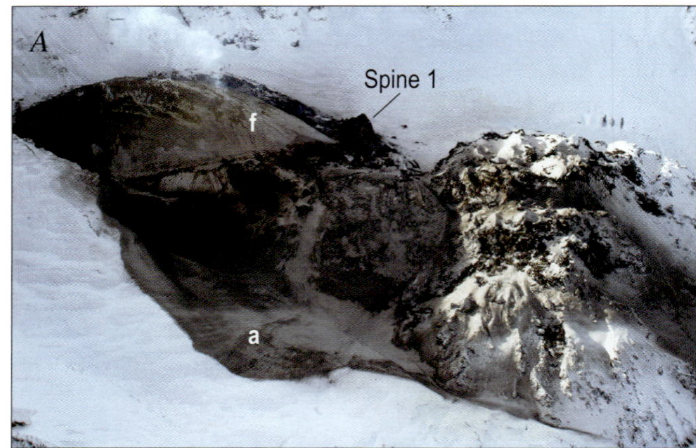

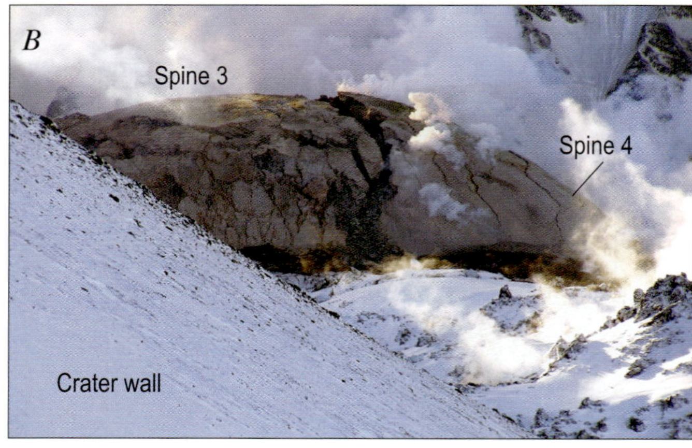

Figure 5. Views of spine 3. *A*, On December 16, 2004, spine was at its maximum extent just as fractures (f, right of the white vapor plume) were beginning to develop that would eventually sever the spine from the vent; view to west. Note thin deposit of ash formed by density current(s) of ash (a) originating as slough(s) of fine-grained gouge carapace. USGS photograph by W.E. Scott. *B*, One week later, fractures had expanded and severed spine 3 from vent; spine 4 was riding up on and pushing the disintegrating remains of spine 3 chiefly southeastward; view to southwest. USGS photograph by M.P. Poland.

6*B*). By spring 2006, much of spine 6 had been covered by spine 7 or by an apron of rockfall debris being shed westward from it. The combined mass of spines 6 and 7 continued to move west-northwestward and slightly downward at about 1 m/d during spring 2006 (LaHusen and others, this volume, chap. 16). Even though spines have formed and crumbled repeatedly throughout the eruption, the vent area (the area at which the extrusion breaches the ground surface) has remained in the same approximate position of the early October 2004 explosion pit and initial spine (this volume: Schilling and others, chap. 8; Vallance and others, chap. 9; Herriott and others, chap. 10).

Modest rates of gas emission during initial stages of dome growth in late 2004 diminished to lower rates throughout most of 2005 and early 2006. Typical daily average rates were a few hundred metric tons of CO_2 and a few tens of metric tons of SO_2 (Gerlach and others, this volume, chap. 26). In addition, during late August 2005, a survey from the crater rim using open-path Fourier-transform infrared spectroscopy yielded the first direct measurements of HCl in the plume at Mount St. Helens. The average daily emission rate of HCl was about 60 percent that of SO_2 (Edmonds and others, this volume, chap. 27). Intriguingly, studies of crater-floor and flank thermal and cold springs have shown no effect from the current eruption on either the content of dissolved magmatic volatiles or the temperatures of ground water (Bergfeld and others, this volume, chap. 25).

The future of dome growth at Mount St. Helens remains uncertain. By the end of 2005, the new dome had a total volume of about 73×10^6 m^3, nearly equaling the volume of the old lava dome in a time span about one-fifth as long (fig. 7). The rate of extrusion had declined from about 5 m^3/s in late 2004 to less than 1 m^3/s at the end of 2005. Overall, the rate of extrusion appeared to be either slowing exponentially or becoming relatively linear and fluctuating between <1 and 2 m^3/s (this volume: Schilling and others, chap. 8; Mastin and others, chap. 22). Will the eruption come slowly to a halt over the coming months or years, or will it stabilize at a steady long-term rate? Alternatively, will the rate of extrusion become variable and episodic—more reminiscent of dome growth during the 1980s? Textural similarity of current lava to that of the pre-1980 summit lava dome, which is known to have been emplaced over about 150 years during the 17th and 18th centuries, suggests that the current eruption may last for many more years (Pallister and others, 1992; Pallister and others, this volume, chap. 30). Finally, appreciating the varied eruptive history of Mount St. Helens

Figure 6. Views south to lava dome in Mount St. Helens' crater from fixed camera point at Johnston Ridge Observatory, 9 km to the north. Numerals denote spines of new lava dome. USGS photographs by E.T. Endo. *A*, June 24, 2005; actively extruding spine 5 is approaching its highest altitude. Note highly crevassed east (left) arm of Crater Glacier, which had been compressed by eastwardly migrating lava dome. *B*, December 5, 2005; spine 5 has disintegrated, and spines 6 and 7 are migrating westward (to right). Yellow dashed line marks profile of 1980s lava dome.

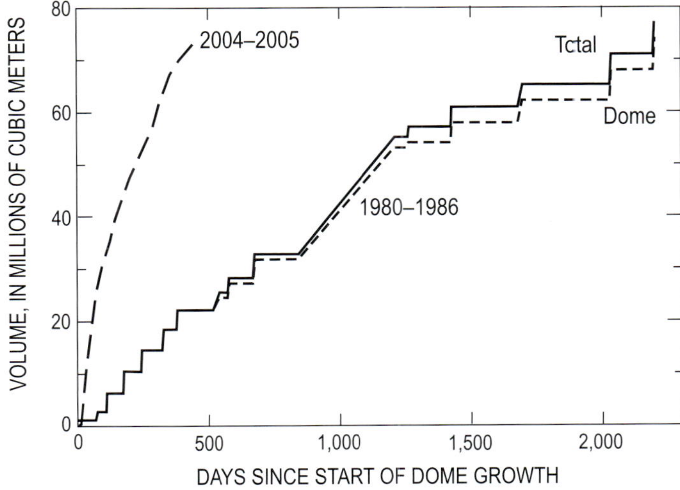

Figure 7. Comparison of cumulative extruded lava volumes for domes of 1980–86 (Swanson and Holcomb, 1990) and 2004–5 (Schilling and others, this volume, chap. 8) at Mount St. Helens. Total for 1980–86 includes tephra and rockfall debris from growing dome.

(Hoblitt and others, 1980), does the volcano have something entirely different in store?

Other Events Related to Dome Growth

Small Explosions Accompany Dome Growth

An explosion early on the stormy morning of January 16, 2005, was the first of two notable explosions during that year. There were no recognizable precursors to the explosion, but any subtle seismic precursors would probably have been lost in storm noise. Transmission from several crater instruments stopped for seconds-long intervals during the explosion's seismic signal, presumably as a result of ash in the air blocking radio signals (Moran and others, this volume, chap. 6). Reception from one near-vent seismometer stopped for several hours. Several other instruments on and close to the actively growing part of the lava dome were destroyed. Poor weather precluded field observations for several days, but a reconnaissance flight eventually revealed evidence of the explosion. Craters from ballistic blocks pockmarked the glacier surface, chiefly east of the new dome, for hundreds of meters. Ash covered the crater east and west of the new dome and formed a narrow deposit on the outer east flank of the volcano, consistent with strong westerly winds. About 5 mm of ash fell on the lower east flank; the extent of ashfall farther east is unknown because of a lack of snow-covered surface to preserve the ash and the heavy rainfall that accompanied and followed the explosion. Effects of the explosion were similar to those of the October 2004 events, but no visible vent crater was formed. A shallow trough along the northeast margin of spine 4 may have marked the vent. The similarity in texture and composition of the ash with previously collected samples of that spine's surficial gouge suggested that the explosion vented along the margin of the spine, entraining powdery gouge and blocks (Rowe and others, this volume, chap. 29).

The second explosion occurred under good viewing conditions late on the afternoon of March 8, 2005 (fig. 8*A*). Seismicity had increased slightly for several hours before the explosion and had initiated a close watch in the operations room at USGS–CVO, but it was not recognized as a precursor to an imminent explosion (Moran and others, this volume, chap. 6). The Sugar Bowl camera at the northeast mouth of the crater captured images of a dense ash cloud rising from near the new dome (Moran and others, this volume, chap. 6, fig. 10) and ballistic-impact craters in snow on the north flank of the old dome. Ballistic fragments destroyed one seismometer located between the old and new lava domes and one seismometer and two microphones located on the old lava

Figure 8. Explosion of March 8, 2005, at Mount St. Helens. *A*, Ash and vapor cloud as viewed toward north-northeast from Cascades Volcano Observatory, 70 km away. USGS photograph by M. Logan. *B*, View to southeast showing northwest base of 1980–86 lava dome and west arm of Crater Glacier pockmarked by craters (as large as 2 m across) formed by rain of ballistic fragments. USGS photograph by D. Dzurisin. *C*, Tephra deposit (a) on east-northeast flank of the volcano as seen from the Plains of Abraham. USGS photograph by D.R. Sherrod. Note the meager snowpack of the winter of 2004–5. *D*, Map showing extent of ballistic fragments and tephra fall from the explosion.

dome. A white vapor cloud billowed high above the crater rim and drifted east-northeastward. Pilots reported the top of the cloud reached an altitude of 11 km; the National Weather Service's NEXRAD detected it up to 6 km. The whiteness of the upper parts of the cloud suggested that it contained little ash. Application of a new one-dimensional steady-state model for wet volcanic plumes using that day's atmospheric conditions indicates that relatively high humidity may have boosted the plume height several additional kilometers (Mastin, 2007). The explosion continued vigorously for about 10 minutes and then waned over several tens of minutes. Investigations the following day revealed a field of ballistic craters (fig. 8*B*) extending about 1 km north-northwest of a poorly defined and vapor-shrouded possible vent area at the north end of the new lava dome. A narrow deposit of coarse ash and fine lapilli extended east-northeastward, discernible on snow for about 7 km from the vent (figs. 8*C*, 8*D*). This fallout deposit was about 20 mm thick on the crater rim and about 2 mm thick on the lower east flank of the volcano. Dustings of ash were reported in Ellensburg, Yakima, and Toppenish, Washington, as far as 150 km from Mount St. Helens. Lithic lapilli as large as 4 cm fell near the crater rim and fragments as large as 1 cm fell on the lower east flank.

Rockfalls and Rock Avalanches

Rockfalls and rock avalanches have both generated small pyroclastic density currents, with reaches of <1 km, and numerous ash clouds that rose above the crater rim. At most, such clouds only weakly dusted the outer flanks of the volcano and traveled only a short distance downwind. Signals of rockfalls and small rock avalanches were common on seismic records, and such events have been directly observed by scientists during hours-long occupations of sites on the old lava dome and crater rim, as well as during fortuitously timed flights (fig. 9). Many such events have also been recorded by fixed cameras (Poland and others, this volume, chap. 11). The largest avalanches observed have been on the order of tens of thousands of cubic meters, but most have been much smaller. Periods of rapid disintegration of spines and accompanying large earthquakes favored large avalanches and frequent rockfalls. The high degree of crystallinity and low gas content of the lava (this volume: Pallister and others, chap. 30; Gerlach and others, chap. 26; Edmonds and others, chap. 27) are probably responsible for the relatively small amount of ash generated by avalanches and rockfalls and the restricted distribution of deposits of

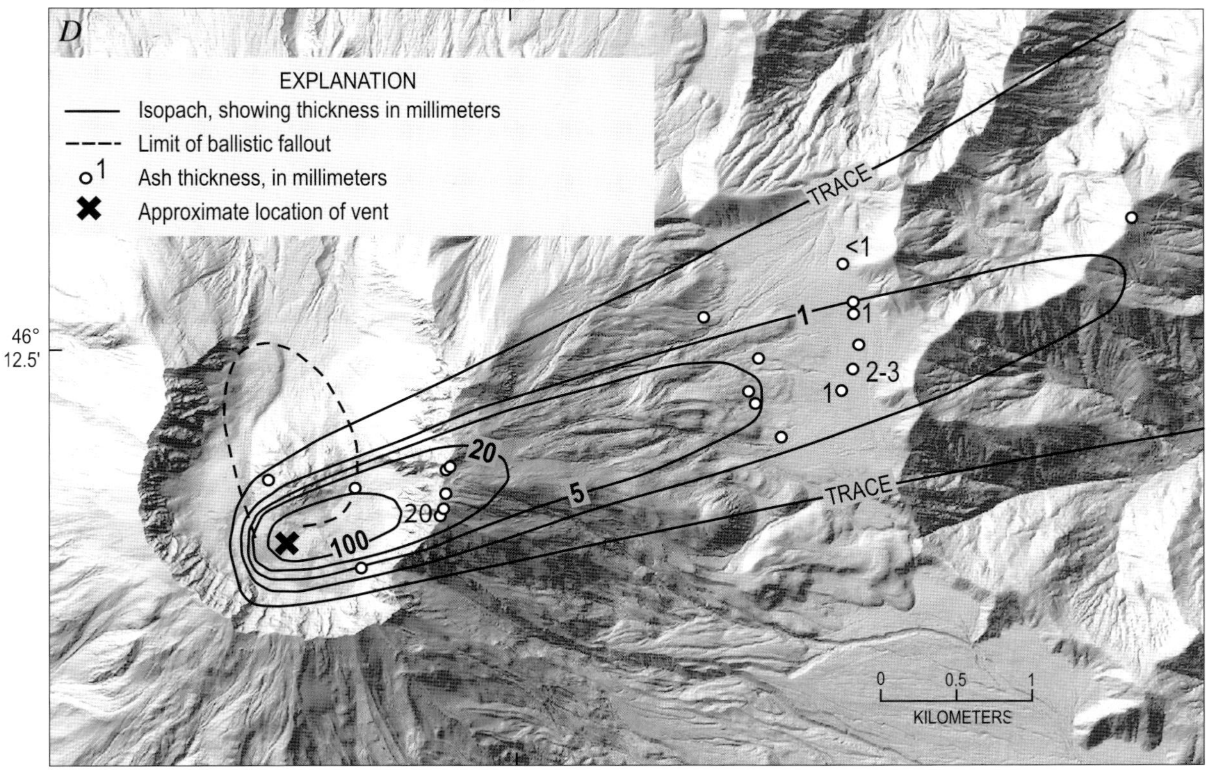

Figure 8—Continued.

resulting density currents. Sloughing of ashy gouge from the outer parts of whaleback-shaped spines, especially spine 3, has also created weak density currents of ash and accompanying ash clouds (fig. 5*A*).

Dome Growth Perturbs Glacier

Continued eastward movement of spines 3, 4, and 5 through late summer 2005 greatly compressed, thickened, and fractured the east arm of Crater Glacier (fig. 6*A*). Such conditions created an unprecedented glaciological experiment (Walder and others, this volume, chap. 13). The resulting doubling of thickness accelerated surface movement to more than 1 m/d, which, although high for such a small glacier, is less than would be expected from such a dramatic thickening. The explanation for lower-than-expected flow rate is that the bed of the glacier, which comprises talus and coarse pyroclastic debris, is so permeable that water pressure at the bed cannot rise sufficiently to induce rapid basal sliding (Walder and others, 2005). In response to this perturbation, the snout of the glacier's east arm thickened noticeably and advanced markedly during winter of 2005.

Beginning in late summer 2005, westward movement of spines 6 and 7 started compressing the west arm of Crater Glacier (fig. 10). As a result, a similar thickening and accelerated flow rate began to occur on the west arm (Walder and others, this volume, chap. 13).

A remarkable aspect of the interaction of the growing lava dome and glacier is the apparent lack of significant glacier melting (Walder and others, 2005; this volume, chap. 13). As the glacier grew in the crater between 1986 and 2004, USGS–CVO noted the potential for increasingly larger lahars if future explosive eruptions or lava-dome collapses generated pyroclastic flows. Such concerns dominated the hazard outlook for the first few weeks of unrest in 2004. Once lava-dome growth commenced, the lahar hazard assessment focused on the possibility of explosions from the dome swiftly melting snow in the crater, as had happened in 1982 and 1984 (Pierson, 1999), as well as on collapses from the new lava dome incorporating and melting snow and ice. Neither scenario has transpired to date (summer 2006). Explosions in January and March 2005 did not generate pyroclastic flows or surges of note and apparently melted little snow and ice. Rockfalls and rock avalanches from the dome have been of modest size, and neither they nor pyroclastic density currents derived from them have induced much melting (fig. 9*B*).

Figure 9. Rock avalanche from spine 5 and associated ash cloud and small pyroclastic density current of May 12, 2005; spine 5 and older spines designated by numerals. *A*, View from east crater rim of density current flowing northwestward and ash cloud rising and obscuring spine 5. USGS photograph by M. Logan. *B*, Aerial view from northwest following event, showing scar at rockfall source (arrow) and thin ash deposit (a) on snow. USGS photograph by D. Dzurisin.

New Insights from the Ongoing Eruption

Mount St. Helens' ongoing extrusion of gas-poor dacitic lava has presented an opportunity to develop and improve a variety of models. These models can illuminate controls on the volcano's eruptive behavior.

Scientists were tantalized by the persistent "drumbeat" earthquakes, at times amazingly periodic, that have accompanied nearly steady lava extrusion since early in the eruption (Moran and others, this volume, chap. 2). Were the drumbeats an indication of repetitive stick-slip motion along the margins of the extruding plug, producing the coating of striated fault gouge? Strength tests of gouge samples support this hypothesis and also show evidence for rate-weakening friction (Moore and others, this volume, chap. 20). A dynamical model demonstrates that repetitive stick-slip events are an almost inevitable consequence of magma influx at a near-equilibrium rate occurring in conjunction with rate-weakening frictional slip along the margins of an extruding solid plug (Iverson and others, 2006; Iverson, this volume, chap. 21). Because such a condition was attained very early in this eruption, the model implies that the magma-plug system was probably close to equilibrium at the onset and perhaps needed only a small perturbation to be triggered into action. It remains unknown whether the trigger was related to a small increase in magmatic pressure, to pressure increase caused by accumulation of an excess-volatile phase at the top of the magma chamber (Kent and others, 2007; Rowe and others, this volume, chap. 29), or to a shallow process such as weakening of the conduit cap rock through fracturing induced by late summer rain and glacier melt (Iverson, this volume, chap. 21). In any case, from the perspective of the model, the current eruption is a continuation of 1980s dome building, in which conditions of the magma-plug system differ little between eruptive and noneruptive periods.

Geodetic modeling of GPS data, primarily the long-term record from the receiver at Johnston Ridge Observatory, 9 km from the new lava dome, suggests that the source responsible for deformation is an ellipsoidal body that extends from about 5 km to 10–20 km deep, but that the volume lost from the source is only 20 to 30 percent of the erupted volume of lava (Lisowski and others, this volume, chap. 15). A model that incorporates geodetic and dome-growth data explores possible reasons for this apparent inconsistency, which include ongoing partial recharge, magma compressibility controlled by gas content, and size of the Mount St. Helens magma chamber (Mastin and others, this volume, chap. 22).

Summary

The contributions that follow in this volume represent the work of more than 100 scientists, emergency managers, and information specialists from numerous academic institutions, the USGS, the Gifford Pinchot National Forest, and State and local government. Together they provide a broad perspective of the ongoing eruption of Mount St. Helens and highlight the following events, findings, and lessons learned.

Figure 10. View of Mount St. Helens crater looking east-northeastward taken April 4, 2006. Spines 4 to 7 are identified by numerals; a steeply east-dipping gouge-covered slab of spine 7 (high point) is riding up over earlier parts of spine 7 and spine 6 and pushing them toward viewer's left. At time of photograph, a GPS spider riding to left of numeral 7 was moving about 1 m/d west-northwestward (to left) and slightly downward. Movement of spines 6 and 7 westward was compressing and fracturing west arm of Crater Glacier, but greater-than-normal snowfall during winter of 2005–6 was filling in crevasses and burying much of older part of new lava dome. Shoestring notch, lowest point on the east crater rim, lies just above spine 4. USGS photograph by J.W. Vallance.

The key requirements for successful volcano-crisis response were in place at Mount St. Helens when unrest began on September 23, 2004. These included geophysical monitoring systems, detailed knowledge of the volcano's eruptive history and hazards, a well-trained and highly experienced scientific staff, many public officials and citizens knowledgeable about volcano hazards, and years of close coordination among scientists, land managers, and emergency managers in planning for possible eruptions.

Once volcanic unrest began, intense interest from both media and the public required rapid establishment of a joint information center staffed by scientists and representatives of land-management, emergency-management, and other relevant State and local agencies. The center coordinated dissemination of clear, consistent messages and expanded and shrank as demand dictated.

The 2004-to-present eruption progressed rapidly from unrest to long-term lava extrusion. Between September 23 and October 11, 2004, intense seismic unrest and localized surface deformation, punctuated by four short-lived explosions, constituted a vent-clearing phase. During the final week of this phase, lessened seismicity, minor venting of steam and ash, and rapid localized surface deformation signaled that magma was continuing to push upward through crater-floor debris and glacier ice. Between October 11, 2004, and the present (spring 2006), persistent low levels of small, regular drumbeat earthquakes and sporadic larger seismic events, rare explosions, low gas emissions, and frequent rockfalls accompanied continuous lava-dome extrusion.

Ongoing continuous lava-dome growth has contrasted markedly with the largely episodic growth of the 1980s dome and has resulted in a strikingly different-looking dome. A succession of spines, some recumbent, smoothly gouge-coated, and nearly 500 m long, has built a dome about equal to the volume of the 1980s dome in about one-quarter of the time required to build that earlier dome. Rather than a single mound, the new dome currently comprises three main rock masses arrayed east-west across the crater between the 1980s dome and south crater wall. The vent for extruding lava has remained relatively fixed, and successive spines have been able to push older masses aside across the glacier-covered crater floor.

A dynamical model demonstrates that repetitive stick-slip events, such as drumbeat earthquakes might represent, are an almost inevitable consequence of magma influx at a near-equilibrium rate occurring in conjunction with rate weakening frictional slip along the margins of an extruding solid plug. Because such a condition was attained very early in the eruption, the model implies that the magma-plug system was close to equilibrium at the onset and perhaps needed only a small perturbation to be triggered into action. From this perspective, the current eruption is a continuation of 1980s dome building wherein conditions of the magma-plug system differ little between eruptive and noneruptive periods.

Crystal-rich dacite with a bulk chemical composition similar to that erupted explosively on May 18, 1980, has been building the new lava dome. Some of this is thought to be residual dacite from the 1980s, but a new component is likely admixed. The lava of the current eruption has texture similar to that of the pre-1980 summit dome, which was emplaced over about 150 years. This suggests that the current eruption may last for many more years.

The outcome of the ongoing eruption is uncertain. During the past few thousand years, Mount St. Helens has at times sustained dome growth for more than a century, as during construction of the pre-1980 summit dome; has alternated between explosive and effusive eruptions of dacite; and has also quickly switched from eruptions of dacite to eruptions of lava flows of more mafic composition.

Lava-dome extrusion in a glacier-covered crater has created an unprecedented glaciological experiment. The lava dome bisected the formerly horseshoe-shaped Crater Glacier into two arms that have been successively squeezed against the crater wall and thickened as lava spines bulldozed them outward. The arms were approximately doubled in thickness over a period of months. Flow rates increased, and both termini are advancing vigorously. However, rapid dewatering of glacier beds through the highly permeable crater-floor material has discouraged basal sliding, and most glacier movement consists of internal flow. In addition, extrusion of the lava dome through the glacier has resulted in amazingly little melting.

Localized surface deformation and dome growth, potential hazards to scientists and instruments in proximal areas, and a relatively slow but persistent pace of lava extrusion required development and adaptation of monitoring systems to study the eruption. Low-cost, portable alternatives to traditional GPS and seismic installations, dubbed "spiders," allowed helicopter deployment and retrieval of telemetered instruments in areas on and near the growing lava dome and highly crevassed glacier. Ingenuity combined with the skill of pilots ensured collection of a suite of lava samples from helicopter-borne dredges. Fixed cameras that telemetered images permitted visual observations and repeat images, from which rates of movement could be estimated. DEMs made from a succession of vertical aerial photographs tracked volumetric rates of lava-dome growth and provided detailed bases for a variety of investigations. Throughout the eruption, helicopter-mounted FLIR surveys, a relatively new technique for USGS scientists, provided key information regarding extrusion temperature, vent location, and dome structure.

Update of Recent Activity

Since preparation of this overview and the accompanying volume of reports in 2006, lava-dome growth continued at a slowing rate through 2007 and paused in late January 2008, after more than 39 months of continuous growth. This pause has been characterized by a very low level of seismicity, cessation of ground-tilt events that were discernible on shallow-borehole tiltmeters installed in late 2005 and summer 2006, and barely detectable efflux of sulfur dioxide. Analysis of repeat photographs from fixed cameras shows no evidence of extrusion, but rather only movement indicative of gravitational settling of spine 7, which is confirmed by a GPS spider atop the spine. As a result of these observations, USGS–CVO reduced the alert level to Volcano Advisory/Aviation Color Code Yellow on February 21, 2008, to signify that volcanic activity has decreased significantly but continues to be closely monitored for possible renewed increase. (As noted in table 1, the unified notification system adopted by all USGS volcano observatories in 2006 uses some new terms and redefines others from the system in use in 2004. Advisory/Yellow under the new system is roughly equivalent to Notice of Volcanic Unrest/Yellow in the old system).

From 2006 to early 2008, spine 7 continued to broaden. By July 2007, the new lava dome was slightly more than 1 km long (axis west-southwest to east-southeast) and about 0.6 km wide. Extruded volume had reached about 93×10^6 m^3, and average extrusion rate had dropped from about 0.5 m^3/s during 2006 to 0.1–0.2 m^3/s (S.P. Schilling, oral commun., 2007). Seismicity gradually diminished through 2006–7 and remained shallow (S.C. Moran, oral commun., 2007), the craterward motion of GPS instruments slowed greatly and probably ceased by mid-2007 (M. Lisowski, oral commun., 2007), gas emissions have remained at low levels (K.A. McGee, oral commun. 2007), and the composition of the erupting dacite remains unchanged from that reported in the first 2004 samples (Thornber and others, 2008b). No explosions have been detected since March 2005. Rockfalls and rock avalanches have continued, but the lack of high, steep fins and crags since autumn 2006 has kept their volume small. The arms of Crater Glacier continue to advance, the west arm most rapidly. As of February 2008, the snouts of the arms had touched, thereby enveloping the 1980–86 lava dome. Whether this pause in extrusion in early 2008 signals the end of dome growth or signals the start of a period of episodic lava extrusion, as happened in the 1980s, will become evident during the coming months to years.

References Cited

Bergfeld, D., Evans, W.C., McGee, K.A., and Spicer, K.R., 2008, Pre- and post-eruptive investigations of gas and water samples from Mount St. Helens, Washington, 2002 to 2005, chap. 25 *of* Sherrod, D.R., Scott, W.E., and Stauffer, P.H., eds., A volcano rekindled; the renewed eruption of Mount St. Helens, 2004–2006: U.S. Geological Survey Professional Paper 1750 (this volume).

Blundy, J., Cashman, K.V., and Berlo, K., 2008, Evolving magma storage conditions beneath Mount St. Helens inferred from chemical variations in melt inclusions from the 1980–1986 and current (2004–2006) eruptions, chap. 33 *of* Sherrod, D.R., Scott, W.E., and Stauffer, P.H., eds., A volcano rekindled; the renewed eruption of Mount St. Helens, 2004–2006: U.S. Geological Survey Professional Paper 1750 (this volume).

Cashman, K.V., Thornber, C.R., and Pallister, J.S., 2008, From dome to dust; shallow crystallization and fragmentation of conduit magma during the 2004–2006 dome extrusion of Mount St. Helens, Washington, chap. 19 *of* Sherrod, D.R., Scott, W.E., and Stauffer, P.H., eds., A volcano rekindled; the renewed eruption of Mount St. Helens, 2004–2006: U.S. Geological Survey Professional Paper 1750 (this volume).

Clynne, M.A., Calvert, A.T., Wolfe, E.W., Evarts, R.C., Fleck, R.J., and Lanphere, M.A., 2008, The Pleistocene eruptive history of Mount St. Helens, Washington, from 300,000 to 12,800 years before present, chap. 28 *of* Sherrod, D.R., Scott, W.E., and Stauffer, P.H., eds., A volcano rekindled; the renewed eruption of Mount St. Helens, 2004–2006: U.S. Geological Survey Professional Paper 1750 (this volume).

Cooper, K.M., and Donnelly, C.T., 2008, 238U-230Th-226Ra disequilibria in dacite and plagioclase from the 2004–2005 eruption of Mount St. Helens, chap. 36 *of* Sherrod, D.R., Scott, W.E., and Stauffer, P.H., eds., A volcano rekindled; the renewed eruption of Mount St. Helens, 2004–2006: U.S. Geological Survey Professional Paper 1750 (this volume).

Crandell, D.R., 1987, Deposits of pre-1980 pyroclastic flows and lahars from Mount St. Helens volcano, Washington: U.S. Geological Survey Professional Paper 1444, 91 p.

Crandell, D.R., and Mullineaux, D.R., 1978, Potential hazards from future eruptions of Mount St. Helens volcano, Washington: U.S. Geological Survey Bulletin 1383–C, 26 p.

Driedger, C.L., Neal, C.A., Knappenberger, T.H., Needham, D.H., Harper, R.B., and Steele, W.P., 2008, Hazard information management during the autumn 2004 reawakening of Mount St. Helens volcano, Washington, chap. 24 *of* Sherrod, D.R., Scott, W.E., and Stauffer, P.H., eds., A volcano rekindled; the renewed eruption of Mount St. Helens, 2004–2006: U.S. Geological Survey Professional Paper 1750 (this volume).

Dzurisin, D., Vallance, J.W., Gerlach, T.M., Moran, S.C., and Malone, S.D., 2005, Mount St. Helens reawakens: Eos (American Geophysical Union Transactions), v. 86, no. 3, p. 25, 29.

Dzurisin, D., Lisowski, M., Poland, M.P., Sherrod, D.R., and LaHusen, R.G., 2008, Constraints and conundrums resulting from ground-deformation measurements made during the 2004–2005 dome-building eruption of Mount St. Helens, Washington, chap. 14 *of* Sherrod, D.R., Scott, W.E., and Stauffer, P.H., eds., A volcano rekindled; the renewed eruption of Mount St. Helens, 2004–2006: U.S. Geological Survey Professional Paper 1750 (this volume).

Edmonds, M., McGee, K.A., and Doukas, M.P., 2008, Chlorine degassing during the lava dome-building eruption of Mount St. Helens, 2004–2005, chap. 27 *of* Sherrod, D.R., Scott, W.E., and Stauffer, P.H., eds., A volcano rekindled; the renewed eruption of Mount St. Helens, 2004–2006: U.S. Geological Survey Professional Paper 1750 (this volume).

Frenzen, P.M., and Matarrese, M.T., 2008, Managing public and media response to a reawakening volcano; lessons from the 2004 eruptive activity of Mount St. Helens, chap. 23 *of* Sherrod, D.R., Scott, W.E., and Stauffer, P.H., eds., A volcano rekindled; the renewed eruption of Mount St. Helens, 2004–2006: U.S. Geological Survey Professional Paper 1750 (this volume).

Gerlach, T.M., McGee, K.A., and Doukas, M.P., 2008, Emission rates of CO_2, SO_2, and H_2S, scrubbing, and preeruption excess volatiles at Mount St. Helens, 2004–2005, chap. 26 *of* Sherrod, D.R., Scott, W.E., and Stauffer, P.H., eds., A volcano rekindled; the renewed eruption of Mount St. Helens, 2004–2006: U.S. Geological Survey Professional Paper 1750 (this volume).

Glicken, H., 1998, Rockslide-debris avalanche of May 18, 1980, Mount St. Helens volcano, Washington: Bulletin of the Geological Survey of Japan, v. 49, nos. 2–3, p. 55–106, with 10 plates.

Herriott, T.M., Sherrod, D.R., Pallister, J.S., and Vallance, J.W., 2008, Photogeologic maps of the 2004–2005 Mount St. Helens eruption, chap. 10 *of* Sherrod, D.R., Scott, W.E., and Stauffer, P.H., eds., A volcano rekindled; the renewed eruption of Mount St. Helens, 2004–2006: U.S. Geological Survey Professional Paper 1750 (this volume).

Hoblitt, R.P., 2000, Was the 18 May 1980 lateral blast at Mt. St. Helens the product of two explosions?: Philosophical Transactions of the Royal Society of London, Series A, v. 358, no. 1770, p. 1639–1661.

Hoblitt, R.P., Crandell, D.R., and Mullineaux, D.R., 1980, Mount St. Helens eruptive behavior during the past 1,500 yr: Geology, v. 8, p. 555–559.

Iverson, R.M., 2008, Dynamics of seismogenic volcanic extrusion resisted by a solid surface plug, Mount St. Helens, 2004–2005, chap. 21 *of* Sherrod, D.R., Scott, W.E., and Stauffer, P.H., eds., A volcano rekindled; the renewed eruption of Mount St. Helens, 2004–2006: U.S. Geological Survey Professional Paper 1750 (this volume).

Iverson, R.M., Dzurisin, D., Gardner, C.A., Gerlach, T.M., LaHusen, R.G., Lisowski, M., Major, J.J., Malone, S.D., Messerich, J.A., Moran, S.C., Pallister, J.S., Qamar, A., Schilling, S.P., and Vallance, J.W., 2006, Dynamics of seismogenic volcanic extrusion at Mount St. Helens in 2004–05: Nature, v. 444, no. 7118, p. 439–443, doi:10.1038/nature05322.

Kent, A.J.R., Blundy, J., Cashman, K.V., Cooper, K.M., Donnelly, C., Pallister, J.S., Reagan, M., Rowe, M.C., and Thornber, C.R., 2007, Vapor transfer prior to the October 2004 eruption of Mount St. Helens, Washington: Geology, v. 35, no. 3, p. 231–234, doi: 10.1130/G22809A.1.

Kent, A.J.R., Rowe, M.C., Thornber, C.R., and Pallister, J.S., 2008, Trace element and Pb isotope composition of plagioclase from dome samples from the 2004–2005 eruption of Mount St Helens, Washington, chap. 35 *of* Sherrod, D.R., Scott, W.E., and Stauffer, P.H., eds., A volcano rekindled; the renewed eruption of Mount St. Helens, 2004–2006: U.S. Geological Survey Professional Paper 1750 (this volume).

LaHusen, R.G., Swinford, K.J., Logan, M., and Lisowski, M., 2008, Instrumentation in remote and dangerous settings; examples using data from GPS “spider” deployments during the 2004–2005 eruption of Mount St. Helens, Washington, chap. 16 *of* Sherrod, D.R., Scott, W.E., and Stauffer, P.H., eds., A volcano rekindled; the renewed eruption of Mount St. Helens, 2004–2006: U.S. Geological Survey Professional Paper 1750 (this volume).

Lipman, P.W., and Mullineaux, D.R., eds., 1981, The 1980 eruptions of Mount St. Helens, Washington: U.S. Geological Survey Professional Paper 1250, 844 p.

Lisowski, M., Dzurisin, D., Denlinger, R.P., and Iwatsubo, E.Y., 2008, Analysis of GPS-measured deformation associated with the 2004–2006 dome-building eruption of Mount St. Helens, Washington, chap. 15 *of* Sherrod, D.R., Scott, W.E., and Stauffer, P.H., eds., A volcano rekindled; the renewed eruption of Mount St. Helens, 2004–2006: U.S. Geological Survey Professional Paper 1750 (this volume).

Major, J.J., Pierson, T.C., Dinehart, R.L., and Costa, J.E., 2000, Sediment yield following severe volcanic disturbance—a two-decade perspective from Mount St. Helens: Geology. v. 28, p. 819–822.

Major, J.J., Kingsbury, C.G., Poland, M.P., and LaHusen, R.G., 2008, Extrusion rate of the Mount St. Helens lava dome estimated from terrestrial imagery, November 2004–December 2005, chap. 12 *of* Sherrod, D.R., Scott, W.E., and Stauffer, P.H., eds., A volcano rekindled; the renewed eruption of Mount St. Helens, 2004–2006: U.S. Geological Survey Professional Paper 1750 (this volume).

Malone, S.D., Endo, E.T., Weaver, C.S., and Ramey, J.W., 1981, Seismic monitoring for eruption prediction, *in* Lipman, P.W., and Mullineaux, D.R., eds., The 1980 eruptions of Mount St. Helens, Washington: U.S. Geological Survey Professional Paper 1250, p. 803–813.

Mastin, L.G., 1994, Explosive tephra emissions at Mount St. Helens, 1989–1991; the violent escape of magmatic gas following storms?: Geological Society of America Bulletin, v. 106, no. 2, p. 175–185.

Mastin, L.G., 2007, A user-friendly one-dimensional model for wet volcanic plumes: Geochemistry, Geophysics, Geosystems, v. 8, Q03014, doi:1029/2006GC001455.

Mastin, L.G., Roeloffs, E., Beeler, N.M., and Quick, J.E., 2008, Constraints on the size, overpressure, and volatile content of the Mount St. Helens magma system from geodetic and dome-growth measurements during the 2004–2006+ eruption, chap. 22 *of* Sherrod, D.R., Scott, W.E., and Stauffer, P.H., eds., A volcano rekindled; the renewed eruption of Mount St. Helens, 2004–2006: U.S. Geological Survey Professional Paper 1750 (this volume).

McChesney, P.J., Couchman, M.R., Moran, S.C., Lockhart, A.B., Swinford, K.J., and LaHusen, R.G., 2008, Seismic-monitoring changes and the remote deployment of seismic stations (seismic spider) at Mount St. Helens, 2004–2005, chap. 7 *of* Sherrod, D.R., Scott, W.E., and Stauffer, P.H., eds., A volcano rekindled; the renewed eruption of Mount St. Helens, 2004–2006: U.S. Geological Survey Professional Paper 1750 (this volume).

Miller, C.D., Mullineaux, D.R., and Crandell, D.R., 1981, Hazards assessments at Mount St. Helens, in Lipman, P.W., and Mullineaux, D.R., eds., The 1980 eruptions of Mount St. Helens, Washington: U.S. Geological Survey Professional Paper 1250, p. 789–801.

Mills, H.H., 1992, Post-eruption erosion and deposition in the 1980 crater of Mount St. Helens, Washington, determined from digital maps: Earth Surface Processes and Landforms, v. 17, no. 8, p. 739–754.

Moore, P.L., Iverson, N.R., and Iverson, R.M., 2008, Frictional properties of the Mount St. Helens gouge, chap. 20 *of* Sherrod, D.R., Scott, W.E., and Stauffer, P.H., eds., A volcano rekindled; the renewed eruption of Mount St. Helens, 2004–2006: U.S. Geological Survey Professional Paper 1750 (this volume).

Moran, S.C., 1994, Seismicity at Mount St. Helens, 1987–1992; evidence for repressurization of an active magmatic system: Journal of Geophysical Research, v. 99, no. B3, p. 4341–4354, doi:10.1029/93JB02993.

Moran, S.C., Malone, S.D., Qamar, A.I., Thelen, W.A., Wright, A.K., and Caplan-Auerbach, J., 2008a, Seismicity associated with renewed dome building at Mount St. Helens, 2004–2005, chap. 2 *of* Sherrod, D.R., Scott, W.E., and Stauffer, P.H., eds., A volcano rekindled; the renewed eruption of Mount St. Helens, 2004–2006: U.S. Geological Survey Professional Paper 1750 (this volume).

Moran, S.C., McChesney, P.J., and Lockhart, A.B., 2008b, Seismicity and infrasound associated with explosions at Mount St. Helens, 2004–2005, chap. 6 *of* Sherrod, D.R., Scott, W.E., and Stauffer, P.H., eds., A volcano rekindled; the renewed eruption of Mount St. Helens, 2004–2006: U.S. Geological Survey Professional Paper 1750 (this volume).

Mullineaux, D.R., 1996, Pre-1980 tephra-fall deposits erupted from Mount St. Helens, Washington: U.S. Geological Survey Professional Paper 1563, 99 p.

Pallister, J.S., Hoblitt, R.P., Crandell, D.R., and Mullineaux, D.R., 1992, Mount St. Helens a decade after the 1980 eruptions; magmatic models, chemical cycles, and a revised hazards assessment: Bulletin of Volcanology, v. 54, no. 2, p. 126–146, doi: 10.1007/BF00278003.

Pallister, J.S., Thornber, C.R., Cashman, K.V., Clynne, M.A., Lowers, H.A., Mandeville, C.W., Brownfield, I.K., and Meeker, G.P., 2008, Petrology of the 2004–2006 Mount St. Helens lava dome—implications for magmatic plumbing and eruption triggering, chap. 30 *of* Sherrod, D.R., Scott, W.E., and Stauffer, P.H., eds., A volcano rekindled; the renewed eruption of Mount St. Helens, 2004–2006: U.S. Geological Survey Professional Paper 1750 (this volume).

Pierson, T.C., ed., 1999, Hydrologic consequences of hot-rock/snowpack interactions at Mount St. Helens volcano, Washington, 1982–84: U.S. Geological Survey Professional Paper 1586, 117 p.

Poland, M.P., and Lu, Z., 2008, Radar interferometry observations of surface displacements during pre- and coeruptive periods at Mount St. Helens, Washington, 1992–2005, chap. 18 *of* Sherrod, D.R., Scott, W.E., and Stauffer, P.H., eds., A volcano rekindled; the renewed eruption of Mount St. Helens, 2004–2006: U.S. Geological Survey Professional Paper 1750 (this volume).

Poland, M.P., Dzurisin, D., LaHusen, R.G., Major, J.J., Lapcewich, D., Endo, E.T., Gooding, D.J., Schilling, S.P., and Janda, C.G., 2008, Remote camera observations of lava dome growth at Mount St. Helens, Washington, October 2004 to February 2006, chap. 11 *of* Sherrod, D.R., Scott, W.E., and Stauffer, P.H., eds., A volcano rekindled; the renewed eruption of Mount St. Helens, 2004–2006: U.S. Geological Survey Professional Paper 1750 (this volume).

Qamar, A.I., Malone, S.D., Moran, S.C., Steele, W.P., and Thelen, W.A., 2008, Near-real-time information products for Mount St. Helens—tracking the ongoing eruption, chap. 3 *of* Sherrod, D.R., Scott, W.E., and Stauffer, P.H., eds., A volcano rekindled; the renewed eruption of Mount St. Helens, 2004–2006: U.S. Geological Survey Professional Paper 1750 (this volume).

Reagan, M.K., Cooper, K.M., Pallister, J.S., Thornber, C.R., and Wortel, M., 2008, Timing of degassing and plagioclase growth in lavas erupted from Mount St. Helens, 2004–2005, from 210Po-210Pb-226Ra disequilibria, chap. 37 *of* Sherrod, D.R., Scott, W.E., and Stauffer, P.H., eds., A volcano rekindled; the renewed eruption of Mount St. Helens, 2004–2006: U.S. Geological Survey Professional Paper 1750 (this volume).

Rowe, M.C., Thornber, C.R., and Kent, A.J.R., 2008, Identification and evolution of the juvenile component in 2004–2005 Mount St. Helens ash, chap. 29 *of* Sherrod, D.R., Scott, W.E., and Stauffer, P.H., eds., A volcano rekindled; the renewed eruption of Mount St. Helens, 2004–2006: U.S. Geological Survey Professional Paper 1750 (this volume).

Rutherford, M.J., and Devine, J.D., III, 2008, Magmatic conditions and processes in the storage zone of the 2004–2006 Mount St. Helens dacite, chap. 31 *of* Sherrod, D.R., Scott, W.E., and Stauffer, P.H., eds., A volcano rekindled; the renewed eruption of Mount St. Helens, 2004–2006: U.S. Geological Survey Professional Paper 1750 (this volume).

Schilling, S.P., Carrara, P.E., Thompson, R.A., and Iwatsubo, E.Y., 2004, Posteruption glacier development within the crater of Mount St. Helens, Washington, USA: Quaternary Research, v. 61, no. 3, p. 325–329.

Schilling, S.P., Thompson, R.A., Messerich, J.A., and Iwatsubo, E.Y., 2008, Use of digital aerophotogrammetry to determine rates of lava dome growth, Mount St. Helens, Washington, 2004–2005, chap. 8 *of* Sherrod, D.R., Scott, W.E., and Stauffer, P.H., eds., A volcano rekindled; the renewed eruption of Mount St. Helens, 2004–2006: U.S. Geological Survey Professional Paper 1750 (this volume).

Schneider, D.J., Vallance, J.W., Wessels, R.L., Logan, M., and Ramsey, M.S., 2008, Use of thermal infrared imaging for monitoring renewed dome growth at Mount St. Helens, 2004, chap. 17 *of* Sherrod, D.R., Scott, W.E., and Stauffer, P.H., eds., A volcano rekindled; the renewed eruption of Mount St. Helens, 2004–2006: U.S. Geological Survey Professional Paper 1750 (this volume).

Scott, K.M., 1989, Magnitude and frequency of lahars and lahar-runout flows in the Toutle–Cowlitz River system: U.S. Geological Survey Professional Paper 1447–B, 33 p.

Siebert, L., 1984, Large volcanic debris avalanches; characteristics of source areas, deposits, and associated eruptions: Journal of Volcanology and Geothermal Research, v. 22, nos. 3–4, p. 163–197.

Streck, M.J., Broderick, C.A., Thornber, C.R., Clynne, M.A., and Pallister, J.S., 2008, Plagioclase populations and zoning in dacite of the 2004–2005 Mount St. Helens eruption; constraints for magma origin and dynamics, chap. 34 *of* Sherrod, D.R., Scott, W.E., and Stauffer, P.H., eds., A volcano rekindled; the renewed eruption of Mount St. Helens, 2004–2006: U.S. Geological Survey Professional Paper 1750 (this volume).

Swanson, D.A., Casadevall, T.J., Dzurisin, D., Malone, S.D., Newhall, C.G., and Weaver, C.S., 1983, Predicting eruptions at Mount St. Helens, June 1980 through December 1982: Science, v. 221, no. 4618, p. 1369–1376.

Swanson, D.A., and Holcomb, R.T., 1990, Regularities in growth of the Mount St. Helens dacite dome, 1980–1986, *in* Fink, J.H., ed., Lava flows and domes, emplacement mechanisms and hazard implications: Berlin, Springer-Verlag, International Association of Volcanology and Chemistry of the Earth's Interior, Proceedings in Volcanology 2, p. 3–24.

Thelen, W.A., Crosson, R.S., and Creager, K.C., 2008, Absolute and relative locations of earthquakes at Mount St. Helens, Washington, using continuous data; implications for magmatic processes, chap. 4 *of* Sherrod, D.R., Scott, W.E., and Stauffer, P.H., eds., A volcano rekindled; the renewed eruption of Mount St. Helens, 2004–2006: U.S. Geological Survey Professional Paper 1750 (this volume).

Thornber, C.R., Pallister, J.S., Lowers, H.A., Rowe, M.C., Mandeville, C.W., and Meeker, G.P., 2008a, Chemistry, mineralogy, and petrology of amphibole in Mount St. Helens 2004–2006 dacite, chap. 32 *of* Sherrod, D.R., Scott, W.E., and Stauffer, P.H., eds., A volcano rekindled; the renewed eruption of Mount St. Helens, 2004–2006: U.S. Geological Survey Professional Paper 1750 (this volume).

Thornber, C.R., Pallister, J.S., Rowe, M.C., McConnell, S., Herriott, T.M., Eckberg, A., Stokes, W.C., Johnson Cornelius, D., Conrey, R.M., Hannah, T., Taggart, J.E., Jr., Adams, M., Lamothe, P.J., Budahn, J.R., and Knaack, C.M., 2008b, Catalog of Mount St. Helens 2004–2007 dome samples with major- and trace-element chemistry: U.S. Geological Survey Open-File Report 2008–1130, 9 p., with digital database.

Vallance, J.W., Schneider, D.J., and Schilling, S.P., 2008, Growth of the 2004–2006 lava-dome complex at Mount St. Helens, Washington, chap. 9 *of* Sherrod, D.R., Scott, W.E., and Stauffer, P.H., eds., A volcano rekindled; the renewed eruption of Mount St. Helens, 2004–2006: U.S. Geological Survey Professional Paper 1750 (this volume).

Walder, J.S., LaHusen, R.G., Vallance, J.W., and Schilling, S.P., 2005, Crater glaciers on active volcanoes; hydrological anomalies: Eos (American Geophysical Union Transactions), v. 86, no. 50, p. 521, 528.

Walder, J.S., Schilling, S.P., Vallance, J.W., and LaHusen, R.G., 2008, Effects of lava-dome growth on the Crater Glacier of Mount St. Helens, Washington, chap. 13 *of* Sherrod, D.R., Scott, W.E., and Stauffer, P.H., eds., A volcano rekindled; the renewed eruption of Mount St. Helens, 2004–2006: U.S. Geological Survey Professional Paper 1750 (this volume).

Warrick, R.A., Anderson, J., Downing, T., Lyons, J., Ressler, J., Warrick, M., and Warrick, T., 1981, Four communities under ash after Mount St. Helens: University of Colorado, Institute of Behavioral Science, Program on Technology, Environment and Man Monograph 34, 143 p.

Williams, H., 1932, The history and character of volcanic domes: University of California, Bulletin of the Department of Geological Sciences, v. 21, p. 51–146.

USGS

Seismicity of the Eruption

Seismicity has long been the key monitoring tool for recognizing precursors to volcanic eruptions. The unrest at Mount St. Helens in 2004 was no different, beginning on September 23 as a seismic swarm that ultimately produced tens of thousands of earthquakes in the days before lava reached the surface on October 11. The sheer number of earthquakes forced adoption of new methods of processing and analyzing the data, as well as new techniques to ensure the rapid dissemination of seismic information over the Internet.

In this eruption, small earthquakes struck a cadence so regular that they became known as drumbeats—a phenomenon that persisted longer at Mount St. Helens than previously described elsewhere. Models to explain drumbeat earthquakes typically invoke stick-slip as the source mechanism. At Mount St. Helens, changes in drumbeat character were unrelated to variations in magma flux at the conduit; thus, drumbeat size and spacing are more likely a function of extrusion mechanics than of extrusion rate.

Also known from other eruptions and seen at Mount St. Helens were multiplets—families of earthquakes—so similar in their waveform that they must have originated from the same source in the shallow crust and traveled along similar paths to the seismometers. Their persistence indicated stationary sources that were stable over long periods of time.

Explosion detection capability was enhanced by the use of microphones to record infrasound. The infrasound signals were subtle, so multiple microphones were required at several sites within 1–2 km of the vent. The six explosions during this eruption lacked seismic precursors, although seismicity dropped after each in response to depressurization of the conduit. Seismic-amplitude values peaked an hour or two before at least one of the explosions, but such instances were too sporadic to serve as a predictive tool.

View west across 1980s dome and deformed glacial ice to explosion of October 1, 2004, the first eruptive event of renewed activity at Mount St. Helens. USGS photo by J.S. Pallister.

A Volcano Rekindled: The Renewed Eruption of Mount St. Helens, 2004–2006
Edited by David R. Sherrod, William E. Scott, and Peter H. Stauffer
U.S. Geological Survey Professional Paper 1750, 2008

Chapter 2

Seismicity Associated with Renewed Dome Building at Mount St. Helens, 2004–2005

By Seth C. Moran[1], Stephen D. Malone[2], Anthony I. Qamar[2*], Weston A. Thelen[2], Amy K. Wright[2], and Jacqueline Caplan-Auerbach[3]

Abstract

The reawakening of Mount St. Helens after 17 years and 11 months of slumber was heralded by a swarm of shallow (depth <2 km) volcano-tectonic earthquakes on September 23, 2004. After an initial decline on September 25, seismicity rapidly intensified; by September 29, M_d >2 earthquakes were occurring at a rate of ~1 per minute. A gradual transition from volcano-tectonic to hybrid and low-frequency events occurred along with this intensification, a characteristic of many precursory swarms at Mount St. Helens before dome-building eruptions in the 1980s. The first explosion occurred October 1, 2004, 8.5 days after the first earthquakes, and was followed by three other explosions over the next four days. Seismicity declined after each explosion and after two energetic noneruptive tremor episodes on October 2 and 3. Following the last explosion of this series, on October 5, seismicity declined significantly. Over the next ten days seismicity was dominated by several event families; by October 16, spacing between events had become so regular that we dubbed the earthquakes "drumbeats." Through the end of 2005 seismicity was dominated by these drumbeats, although occasional larger earthquakes (M_d 2.0–3.4) dominated seismic energy release. Over time there were significant variations in drumbeat size, spacing, and spectra that correlated with changes in the style of extrusion at the surface. Changes in drumbeat character did not correspond to variations in magma flux at the conduit, indicating that drumbeat size and spacing may be more a function of the mechanics of extrusion than of the extrusion rate.

[1] U.S. Geological Survey, 1300 SE Cardinal Court, Vancouver, WA 98683

[2] Pacific Northwest Seismic Network, Department of Earth and Space Sciences, University of Washington, Box 351310, Seattle, WA 98195

[3] Geology Department, Western Washington University, 516 High Street, Bellingham, WA 98225

* Deceased

Introduction

As of the writing of this paper (2006), more than 26 years of recorded seismic history have accumulated at Mount St. Helens since the Pacific Northwest Seismic Network's (PNSN) digital recording system began operation in March 1980. This 26-year period includes the precursory buildup to the May 18, 1980, eruption (Endo and others, 1981; Malone and others, 1981), post-May 18, 1980, seismicity associated with the 20 eruptions occurring between 1980 and 1986 (Malone, 1983; Malone and others, 1983; Swanson and others, 1985; Swanson and Holcomb, 1990), quiescence between 1987 and 2004 (Moran, 1994; Musumeci and others, 2002), and the onset of the eruption in 2004. This history is made all the richer by its being recorded on a relatively dense seismic network of short-period vertical-component seismometers in place since shortly after the first earthquakes began in late March of 1980 (fig. 1). Seismic data recorded by this network have been used in many studies, including (1) forecasting eruptions and detecting explosions (Endo and others, 1981; Malone and others, 1981; Malone and others, 1983; Swanson and others, 1983; Endo and others, 1990; Jonientz-Trisler and others, 1994); (2) eruption dynamics (Qamar and others, 1983; Weaver and others, 1983; Shemeta and Weaver, 1986); (3) modeling the Mount St. Helens magmatic system (Weaver and others, 1981; Scandone and Malone, 1985; Endo and others, 1990; Barker and Malone, 1991; Moran, 1994; Musumeci and others, 2002); (4) interpreting the structure of the magmatic system through tomography (Lees and Crosson, 1989; Lees, 1992; Moran and others, 1999), earthquake locations (Fehler, 1985; Weaver and others, 1987; Musumeci and others, 2002), and *b* values (Endo and others, 1981; Wiemer and McNutt, 1997); (5) determining the source process responsible for various type of seismic signals recorded at Mount St. Helens (Fehler and Chouet, 1982; Malone, 1983; Fehler, 1985; Norris, 1994); (6) describing the stress field associated with the magmatic system (Barker and Malone, 1991; Moran, 1994;

Giampiccolo and others, 1999; Musumeci and others, 2002); and (7) defining repetitive events (or earthquake families), including the first published study of repetitive events in a volcanic setting (Frémont and Malone, 1987).

As a result of these and other studies, by 2004 we had a fairly good working model of the magmatic system beneath Mount St. Helens. We also had a very good understanding of the character of typical eruptive and noneruptive seismicity. These perspectives proved vital to our ability to correctly assess the significance of seismicity when Mount St. Helens reawakened in 2004.

The reawakening of Mount St. Helens was heralded by a swarm of shallow (depth <2 km) volcano-tectonic (VT) earthquakes beginning at roughly 0200 Pacific daylight time (PDT) on September 23, 2004. More than one million earthquakes were recorded by the end of 2005, with events occurring every 1 to 5 minutes. Of these, roughly 8,000 events were located by the PNSN through the end of 2005. Many will likely never be located, even with sophisticated crosscorrelation and relative relocation techniques (for example, Thelen and others, this volume, chap. 4), because many are small, occur in the coda of previous events, and (or) have nonimpulsive arrivals. With such a sizable dataset we are still very much in discovery mode, and it is likely that at least some of what we present in this paper will be superseded by subsequent research. Our principal purpose is to give an overview of our understanding of seismicity that occurred before and during the eruption in 2004–5, as well as to put the eruption's seismicity in the broader context of the 26 years of seismic history of Mount St. Helens.

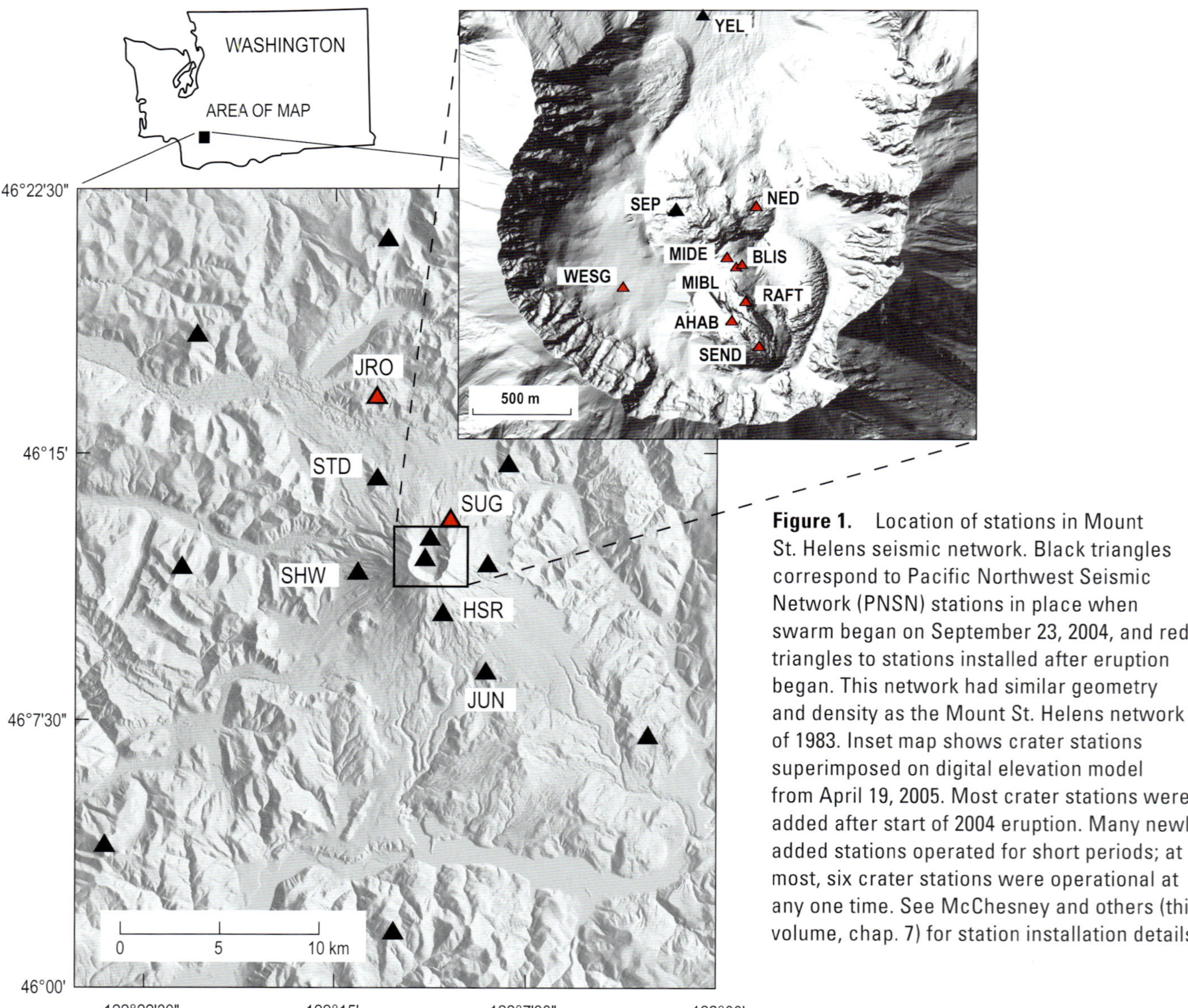

Figure 1. Location of stations in Mount St. Helens seismic network. Black triangles correspond to Pacific Northwest Seismic Network (PNSN) stations in place when swarm began on September 23, 2004, and red triangles to stations installed after eruption began. This network had similar geometry and density as the Mount St. Helens network of 1983. Inset map shows crater stations superimposed on digital elevation model from April 19, 2005. Most crater stations were added after start of 2004 eruption. Many newly added stations operated for short periods; at most, six crater stations were operational at any one time. See McChesney and others (this volume, chap. 7) for station installation details.

Seismicity During Quiescence, 1987–2004

Although short-term precursory seismicity began on September 23, 2004, in a longer term view the first precursory seismicity likely started as early as late 1987 (fig. 2), when the first of several years-long swarms of "deep" (>3 km) VT events began (Moran, 1994). The depth of these swarms contrasted sharply with the exclusively shallow (<3 km) precursory swarms associated with 19 of the 20 post-May 18, 1980, dome-building eruptions (Malone and others, 1983). In map view, the deeper events were concentrated to the north and south of the 1980–86 lava dome (Moran, 1994; Musumeci and others, 2002), in contrast to the east-west orientation of "deep" VT events that extended to 20 km immediately after the May 18, 1980, eruption (Weaver and others, 1981; Shemeta and Weaver, 1986; Barker and Malone, 1991; Moran, 1994). Fault-plane solutions for the post-May 18, 1980, "deep" events had tangentially oriented P axes with respect to the 1980 crater, in contrast to radially oriented P axes for post-1987 "deep" events (Barker and Malone, 1991; Moran, 1994; Musumeci and others, 2002). The changes in stress-field orientation and epicentral distribution are best explained by a pressure decrease in the magmatic plumbing system after 1980 and a pressure increase after 1986 (Barker and Malone, 1991; Moran, 1994; Musumeci and others, 2002). Moran (1994) argued that sizable swarms preceding the last two dome-building eruptions in 1986 were an indication of the formation of a plug in the conduit to the surface, a plug that subsequent batches of magma were unable to penetrate. The occurrence of six phreatic explosions in 1989–91 (Mastin, 1994) and detection of magmatic CO_2 in association with the last significant months-long swarm of deeper seismicity in 1998 (Gerlach and others, this volume, chap. 26) provide further evidence that intrusion of magma may have occurred between 1987 and 2004.

Most seismicity after 1998 was concentrated at depths ~2 km below the crater floor, although occasional deeper and shallower VT events also occurred (fig. 2). The 2-km-deep seismicity band could represent the development of a fracture system in the base of the plug inferred by Pallister and others (1992) and Moran (1994) to extend from the surface down to 2 km. The *b* values for earthquakes in this depth range increased marginally from 0.8–1.0 before 1992 to 1.0–1.4 after 1992 (fig. 3). The *b* values for events between 3 and 10 km showed no such change over the same time period, indicating that the shallow *b*-value change is not a result of a systematic bias in the PNSN catalog. The *b*-value increase, if real, could indicate an increase in the number of small fractures (Mogi, 1962) between 1991 and 1993 and is the type of change that would be expected in association with the

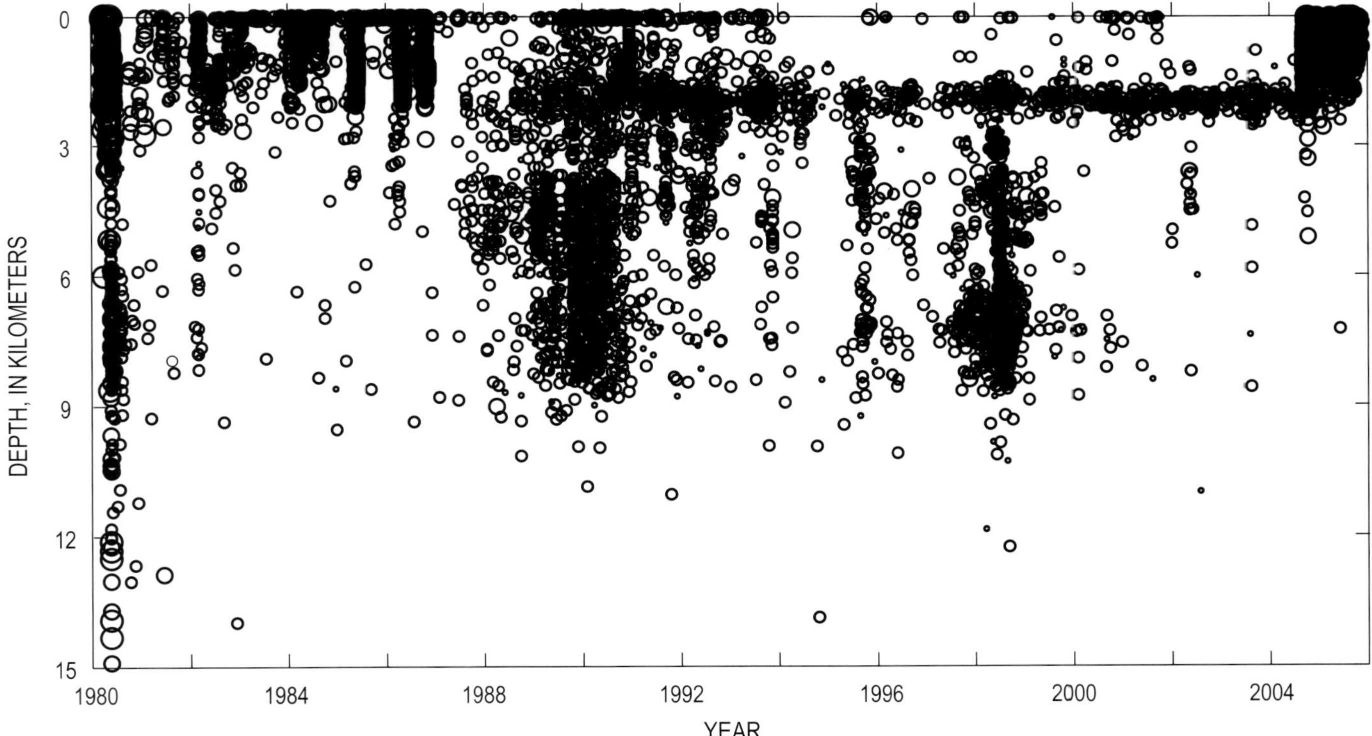

Figure 2. Time versus depth plot showing all earthquakes (circles) with well-constrained locations (gap <135°, nearest station <2 km, and arrival times on at least seven stations) occurring at Mount St. Helens between 1980 and 2005. Depths are relative to a datum corresponding to average altitude of stations in Mount St. Helens network, roughly 1.1 km above sea level. Horizontal-axis tick marks indicate start of a year, with gaps of 2 years between tick marks.

fracturing of the base of a plug (Vinciguerra and others, 2001). However, *b* values remained relatively constant in the subsequent 12 years leading up to the 2004 eruption (fig. 3), despite the evidence for a possible intrusion of magma in 1998.

The last significant earthquake swarm of the 1987–2004 quiescent period occurred on November 2–4, 2001. The swarm began relatively abruptly at around 1730 Pacific standard time (PST) on November 2 and consisted of many small (most with coda-duration magnitudes M_d <0.0, with the largest M_d 1.8) and shallow (<2 km) VT events occurring at a rate of 2–3 per minute. There were also a number of 10–30-minute-long spasmodic bursts of 8–10 VT events per minute. The Cascades Volcano Observatory (CVO) issued an Information Statement at 1800 PST on November 3, 2001, stating that a swarm was underway with no evidence that an eruption was imminent. Following the last spasmodic burst of VTs at 0400 PST on November 4, the number and size of earthquakes declined steadily, reaching background levels by November 5, 2001.

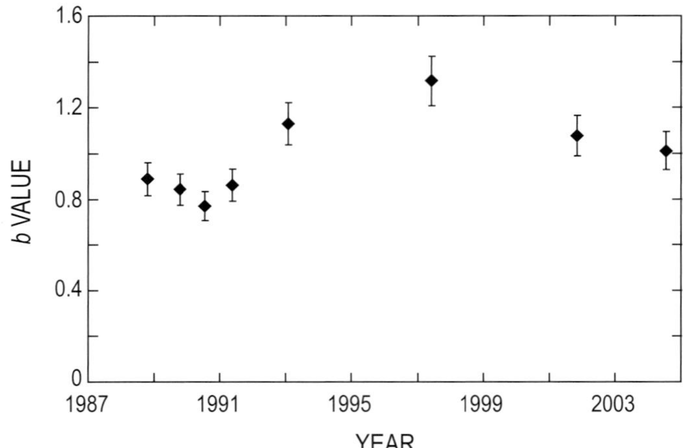

Figure 3. Plot of *b* values for shallow (depths <3 km) earthquakes occurring between 1987 and 09/23/2004, the last day for which the PNSN catalog is complete. Horizontal-axis tick marks indicate start of a year, with gaps of 2 years between tick marks. The *b* values are computed using maximum-likelihood method (Bender, 1983) and are determined for nonoverlapping groups of 150 events with M_d 0.4 (magnitude of completeness for entire interval) selected with same criteria used for earthquakes shown in figure 2.

September 23–October 5, 2004: Vent-Clearing Phase

September 23–September 25, 2004

The first short-term signs of unrest came in the form of a swarm of VT events starting at roughly 0200 PDT on September 23, 2004 (fig. 4), with the onset of unrest defined as the time when hourly event counts reached sustained levels above 1–2 events per hour. The number of earthquakes increased throughout September 23, peaked midday on September 24, and then declined to a minimum early on September 25, roughly 48 hours after the swarm began. By September 24, earthquakes had become so numerous that the PNSN began locating only a subset of them, and real-time seismic amplitude measurement (or RSAM; Endo and Murray, 1991), "webicorder," and spectrogram plots became the principal tools for tracking seismicity (Qamar and others, this volume, chap. 3). All located events were shallow (<2 km) and small, with the largest a M_d 2.2 and most having magnitudes <1.0. The *b* values for catalog locations were ~1, consistent with *b* values before 2004 (fig. 3). Fault-plane solutions from the PNSN catalog show a variety of failure mechanisms and stress-field orientations, with no clear dominant fracture pattern (appendix 1). To this point, seismicity closely resembled the swarm of November 2–4, 2001. This similarity governed initial interpretations by the PNSN and CVO. Although somewhat more energetic than the 2001 swarm, we judged that this swarm was within the bounds of noneruptive seismicity seen during the previous 18 years at Mount St. Helens. An information statement was released on September 24, stating that a seismic swarm was occurring at Mount St. Helens, with no indications that an eruption was imminent (Dzurisin and others, 2005; Scott and others, this volume, chap. 1).

September 25–October 1, 2004

Seismicity departed from the 2001 script midday on September 25, 2004. Instead of continuing to decline, the earthquake rate stabilized and then began to increase (fig. 5). Lower-frequency events, including hybrid and low-frequency (LF) events (previously identified as type "m" and "l" events at Mount St. Helens in the 1980s by Malone, 1983, and Malone and others, 1983) also began occurring alongside the VT events (fig. 6). We elected to refer to these as low-frequency, or "LF," events rather than the commonly used long-period, or "LP," event label, because the definition of an LP event includes a specific source mechanism (that is, the vibration of fluid- or gas-filled cracks; Lahr and others, 1994; Chouet, 1996). Experience with low-frequency events at Mount St. Helens in the 1980s indicated that other source mechanisms might be involved, and so we felt it best to use the purely descriptive "LF event" terminology without presuming a source mechanism. It should be noted that LF events commonly have extended codas at Mount St. Helens, resulting in overly large coda-duration magnitudes relative to amplitude-based magnitudes (Qamar and others, this volume, chap. 3).

The transition from VT to hybrid and LF events took place over several days, as illustrated by the earthquake spectral amplitude (or "ESAM") plot in figure 5 (see appendix 2 for details), with LF events becoming progressively more dominant through October 5. Similar transitions in earthquake types were seen in precursory swarms preceding many dome-building eruptions at Mount St. Helens in the 1980s (Malone,

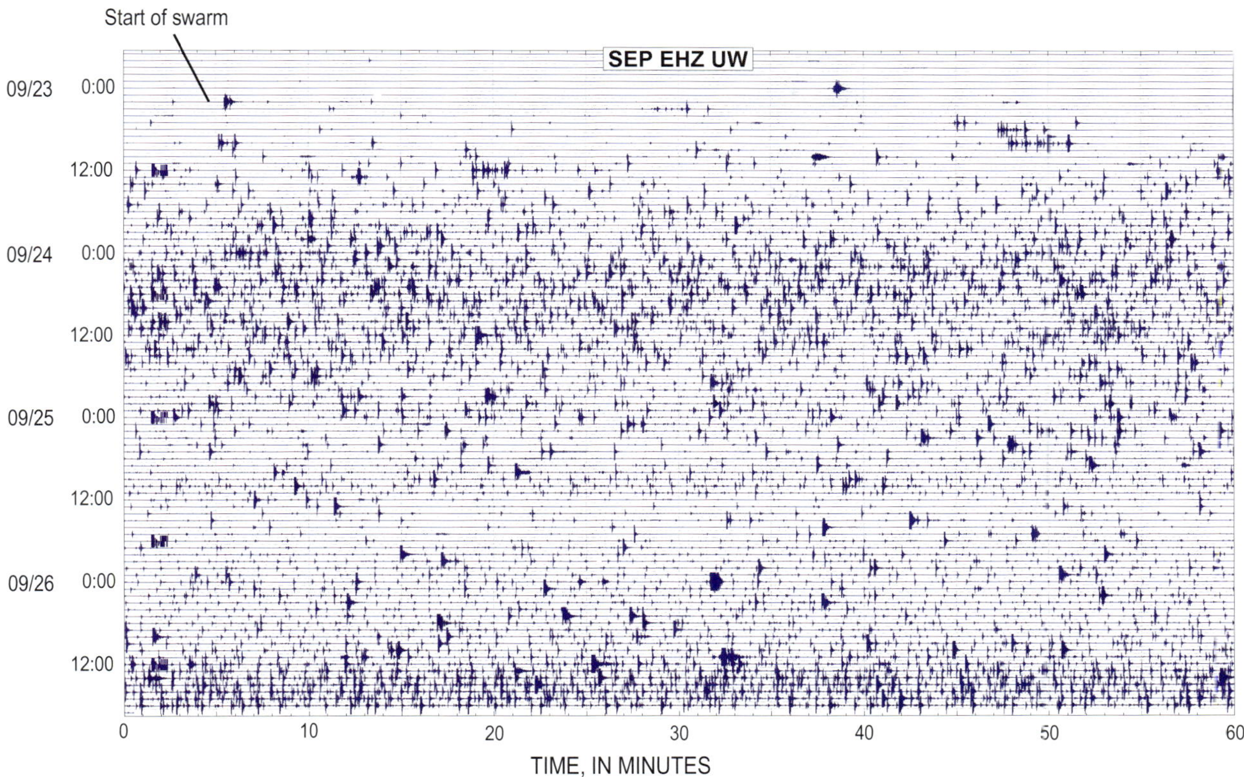

Figure 4. Seismic record from station SEP (~500 m north of the vent; see fig. 1) from 1900 PDT September 22 through 1900 PDT September 26, 2004, showing start of seismic swarm at 0200 PDT September 23 and buildup over next three days.

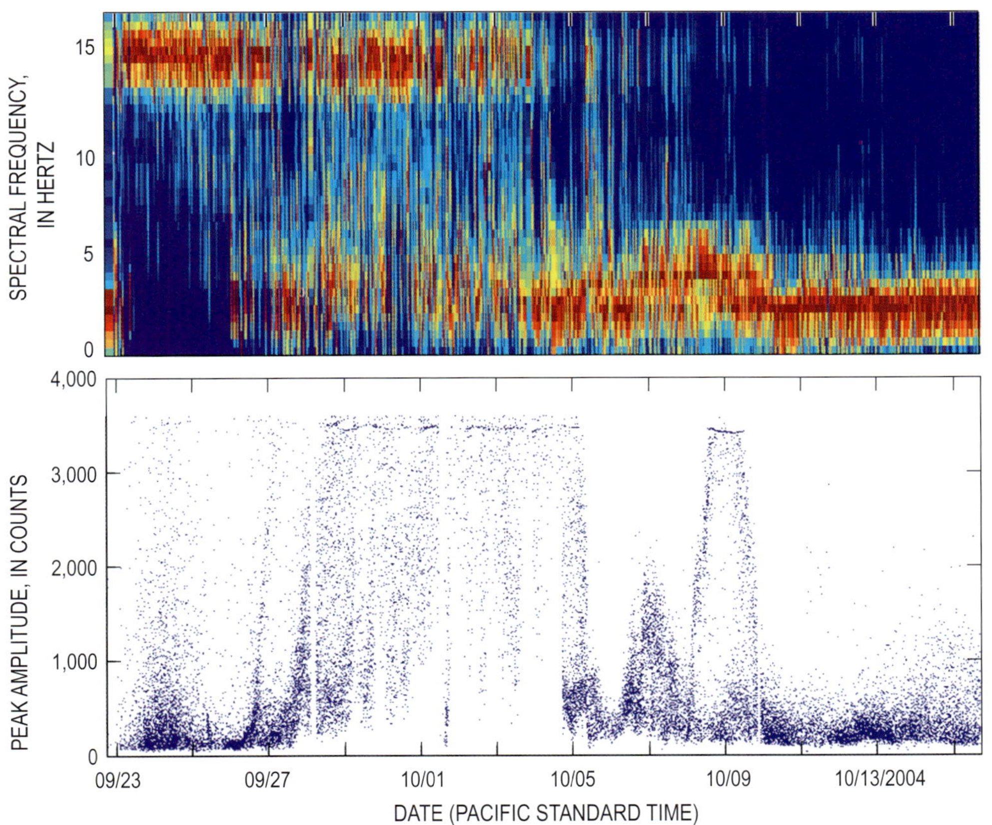

Figure 5. Plot of earthquake spectral amplitudes, or ESAM (top), and peak amplitudes (bottom) for detected events at station HSR (fig. 1) between September 23 and October 15, 2004 (see appendix 2 for event detection details). Horizontal-axis tick marks indicate start of a day, with gaps of 2 days between tick marks. Note that peak amplitudes clip at ~3,400 counts for station HSR.

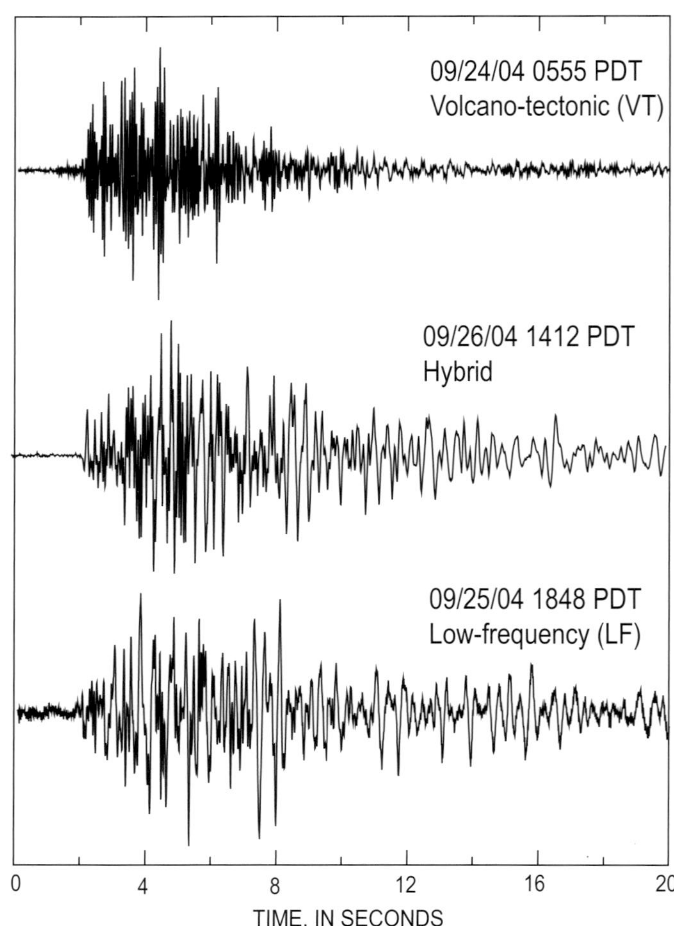

Figure 6. Waveforms for typical volcano-tectonic (VT), hybrid, and low-frequency (LF) events recorded at station HSR (fig. 1) during September 23–26, 2004.

1983; Malone and others, 1983), as well as in the first week of seismicity prior to the May 18, 1980, eruption (Malone and others, 1981; Endo and others, 1981). Those transitions were also gradual, taking place over periods of hours to days. The transitions before the 1980–86 dome-building eruptions were particularly noticeable several hours before eruptions commenced, and they therefore became one of the diagnostic tools that allowed for increasingly precise predictions of eruption onset times (Malone and others, 1983; Swanson and others, 1983; Swanson and others, 1985). Such changes in event character were inferred by Malone and others (1983) to represent a shallowing of the deformation front (as suggested by slightly shallower depths for type "l" events) and to be caused either by the fracturing of different rock types or by a change in source mechanism. In this context, the appearance of lower-frequency events on September 25, 2004, increased the likelihood in our minds that the seismic swarm would ultimately lead to an eruption.

By the morning of September 26 the earthquake rate had further intensified. By midday, maximum event sizes had also started increasing (fig. 5). The increase in event rate and event size and the change in event character caused CVO to issue a Notice of Volcanic Unrest (or Alert Level 1) in the afternoon of September 26. Earthquake locations showed no obvious temporal changes between September 25 and 26, in large part because station density within the crater and the velocity model were insufficient to locate shallow earthquakes in a geologically complex medium with a precision of less than several hundred meters. Between September 25 and 27, however, P-wave arrival-time differences increased between station SEP (fig. 1), located on the 1980–86 lava dome essentially on top of most earthquakes, and other stations located within 4 km of the vent (fig. 7). Daily average arrival-time differences between stations SEP and YEL increased the most (0.13 s), with differences at other stations increasing by 0.07–0.1 s. Arrival-time differences between station pairs not including SEP did not change significantly. We reexamined P-arrival picks and found no evidence that the changes in arrival-time differences were a result of analyst bias (multiple PNSN analysts were involved in picking earthquakes; Qamar and others, this volume, chap. 3) or decreased P-arrival impulsiveness at distant stations (which could result in late picks). The observed pattern is best explained by either a decrease in seismic velocity near station SEP or a decrease in earthquake depths below SEP. Although injection of magma and associated fracturing of country rock could result in lower velocities, shallowing of hypocenters is the simplest explanation for the increase in P-wave arrival-time differences. This shallowing is in part supported by the appearance on September 26 of cracks in the crater glacier (Dzurisin and others, 2005; Scott and others, this volume, chap. 1; Walder and others, this volume, chap. 13).

At roughly 1600 PDT on September 26, a series of earthquakes with similar waveforms (an earthquake "family" or multiplet; for example, see Frémont and Malone, 1987) began, at first mixed with other events with different waveforms (Thelen and others, this volume, chap. 4). By early morning of September 27, seismicity was dominated by this family, with magnitudes increasing through midday and reaching a maximum of M_d 1.9 by late afternoon. This was the first clear instance of repetitive earthquakes, something that was seen frequently before dome-building eruptions at Mount St. Helens in the 1980s (Frémont and Malone, 1987) and has also been observed during other dome-building eruptions, including Usu volcano[4] in Japan (Okada and others, 1981), Augustine Volcano (Power, 1988) and Redoubt Volcano (Power and others, 1994) in Alaska, Guagua Pichincha in Ecuador (Villagómez, 2000), Soufrière Hills volcano in Montserrat (Rowe and others, 2004), and Galeras Volcano in Columbia (R. White, oral commun., 2006). Preliminary fault-plane solutions for the larger events in this family have reverse-faulting

[4] Capitalization of "Volcano" indicates adoption of the word as part of the formal geographic name by the host country, as listed in the Geographic Names Information System, a database maintained by the U.S. Board on Geographic Names. Noncapitalized "volcano" is applied informally—eds.

mechanisms, in contrast to the mix of mechanisms generated during September 23–25 (appendix 1). By 1500 on September 27, the family had become less dominant, but similar events continued through September 28.

The event rate increased relatively rapidly, to 1 event per minute, around 1700 PDT on September 27, as smaller events began occurring between the larger earthquakes (fig. 8). The size of the larger earthquakes also increased, with maximum magnitudes reaching M_d 2.0–2.4 by midday on September 28. Most fault-plane solutions were dip-slip with a steeply dipping fault plane, in contrast to the reverse-faulting mechanisms dominant during the previous 24 hours (appendix 1). At this point, clipping of near-field (<4 km) stations occurred frequently. As a result, smaller events were frequently overwhelmed by the codas of the larger events, making it difficult to distinguish many individual events. It also became increasingly difficult to manually pick earthquakes and determine accurate coda magnitudes, because the coda from one event would be obscured by the onset of the next event. At this point, RSAM became the principal tool for monitoring seismicity (fig. 9), along with helicorder records from stations increasingly distant from Mount St. Helens.

Earthquakes further intensified between 0500 and 0800 on September 29 (fig. 8), when event rates increased to ~3 earthquakes per minute and maximum magnitudes rose to M_d 2.4–2.8, causing CVO to issue a Volcano Advisory (or Alert Level 2) at 1040 PST (Dzurisin and others, 2005). A second

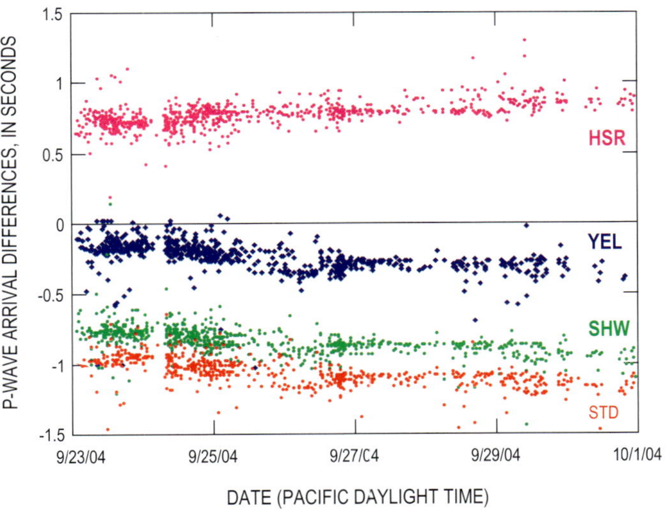

Figure 7. Plot of P-wave arrival-time differences between station SEP (located on the 1980–86 lava dome) and four other stations including HSR (magenta), YEL (dark blue), SHW (green), and STD (red), between September 23 and October 1, 2004. (see fig. 1 for station location). P-wave arrival-time differences were computed only for high-quality picks, with an estimated picking error of ≤0.05 s. Note that the absolute value of differences increases on all station pairs between September 25 and September 27. This increase was not apparent on other non-SEP station pairs and is consistent with shallowing of hypocenters.

rise in RSAM levels occurred 12 hours later, between 1700 and 2100 (fig. 9), when maximum magnitudes increased to M_d 2.8–3.3, with M_d >2 events occurring at a rate of ~1 per minute by the evening of September 29. Most fault-plane solutions for these events had normal-faulting mechanisms, although there were also occasional events with many, or all, down first-motions, consistent with reverse faulting (appendix 1). One side effect of the high rate of larger earthquakes was that they began to dominate seismic recordings at other Cascade volcano seismic networks (in particular at Mount Adams, Mount Hood, Mount Rainier, and Three Sisters), as well as at regional seismic stations in Washington and Oregon, resulting in a temporary reduction in PNSN sensitivity to smaller events in a broad area around Mount St. Helens.

Following the second intensification on September 29, the rate of larger earthquakes declined somewhat, resulting in a decline in RSAM values, which reached a relative minimum at roughly 0500 on September 30 (fig. 9). The rate of larger earthquakes increased and decreased two more times on September 30, with RSAM values always between the minimum and maximum levels achieved on September 29. The increases did not correspond with any known changes in the crater, although temporal resolution of visual observations and measurements from other geophysical instrumentation were insufficient to detect changes on an hourly scale. Fault-plane solutions from the PNSN catalog switched from dominantly normal-faulting to reverse-faulting solutions for a short time between 2300 September 30 and 0500 October 1 (appendix 1); then, three hours later at 0800, RSAM levels again increased as a result of an increase in event rate (figs. 8, 9). RSAM values peaked at 1100 at levels similar to previous maxima. The first phreatic explosion occurred an hour later at 1202 PDT, 8.5 days after the first precursory seismicity on September 23. This interval was one day longer than the 7-day interval between the first earthquakes and first phreatic explosion in March of 1980 (Endo and others, 1981; Malone and others, 1981). This similarity could indicate that a characteristic time interval exists between initiation of precursory activity and initial explosive activity at Mount St. Helens. If this is the case, then the time interval presumably is governed by the structure of the shallow conduit system and surrounding country rock, as well as the composition of the intruding magma.

Aside from the RSAM increase, there were no obvious precursors to the October 1 explosion. The explosion began aseismically, with no obvious changes in seismicity associated with the start of the explosion (Moran and others, this volume, chap. 6). Timing constraints for the explosion are excellent, because a CVO crew was flying around the vent when the explosion began (Schneider and others, this volume, chap. 17). The most obvious change in seismicity occurred at 1203, 1 minute after the explosion began, when earthquakes suddenly stopped (figs. 8, 9). This cessation was so dramatic that it caused one CVO crew working at seismic station STD (fig. 1) to look up at the crater when the sound of the earthquakes, heard through a scanner tuned to the frequency of a nearby seismic station, suddenly stopped. A relatively broadband

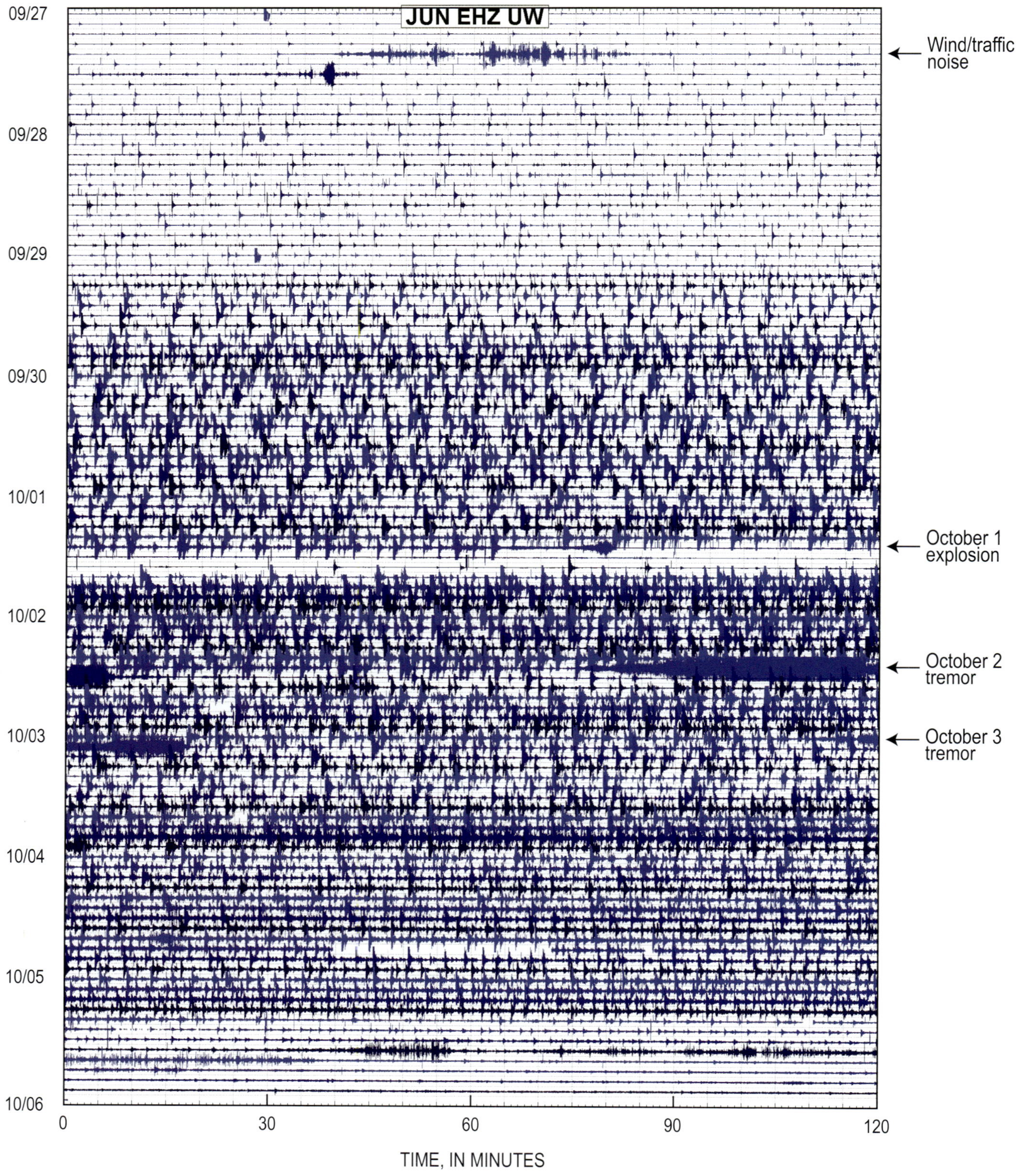

Figure 8. Seismic record from station JUN (6.5 km southeast of vent; fig. 1) from September 27 through October 5, 2004, showing seismicity trends during the vent-clearing phase.

(0.5–3 Hz) tremor signal accompanied the explosion after the last earthquake at 1203 (fig. 8), with tremor amplitudes roughly doubling between 1216 and 1221. At 1221 the tremor and the explosion stopped abruptly.

The October 1 explosion destroyed seismic station SEP, the closest station to the earthquakes (fig. 1). The loss of this station decreased the quality of PNSN catalog locations, with average hypocentral errors for well-constrained earthquakes (P waves on at least 7 stations, azimuthal gap <135°, nearest station within 3 km) increasing from 0.2 km in the 24 hours before October 1 to 0.34 km in the 24 hours after the explosion. This impact illustrates the importance of having seismic stations close to the source. Indeed, the loss of SEP was one of the primary motivations for the development of a seismic sensor package that could be remotely deployed at locations too hazardous for crews to work on the ground (McChesney and others, this volume, chap. 7).

October 1–October 5, 2004

Seismicity levels dropped precipitously following the 1202–1221 explosive event, with the first small earthquake not occurring until roughly 3 hours later at 1515. This drop indicated that seismicity was occurring in response to elevated pressure in the conduit system, pressure that was temporarily reduced by the October 1 explosion. Hybrid earthquakes slowly increased in number and size and then rapidly increased between 1700 and 2000 on October 1, with RSAM levels eventually exceeding those of September 29–October 1. As with previous intensifications, RSAM levels flattened and then gradually declined on October 2 (fig. 9). At roughly 1217 PDT on October 2, earthquakes were replaced abruptly by relatively broadband seismic tremor with dominant frequencies in the 0.5–3-Hz range (fig. 10). Tremor rapidly intensified over a period of 20 minutes, to peak reduced-displacement values of 28–43 cm^2, and was energetic enough to be recorded on seismic stations more than 240 km away. The energetic tremor, in combination with the October 1 explosion and continuing energetic earthquake activity, caused CVO to issue a Volcano Alert, the highest alert level. No explosions or other obvious surficial events (such as increased steaming or small ash emissions) were observed in association with the tremor. Tremor amplitudes began decreasing shortly after the alert level change, and, by 1315, tremor had virtually disappeared. As with the October 1 explosion, earthquake rates and sizes decreased significantly after tremor ceased, although the drop was not as abrupt or as long-lived (figs. 8, 9, 10). Earthquake rates and sizes began increasing again around 1400, and by 1900 RSAM values had returned to levels just below those before the October 2 tremor episode (fig. 9). A smaller tremor episode (reduced displacement 10–20 cm^2, peak frequencies 0.5–2.5 Hz) occurred between 0250–0315 PDT on October

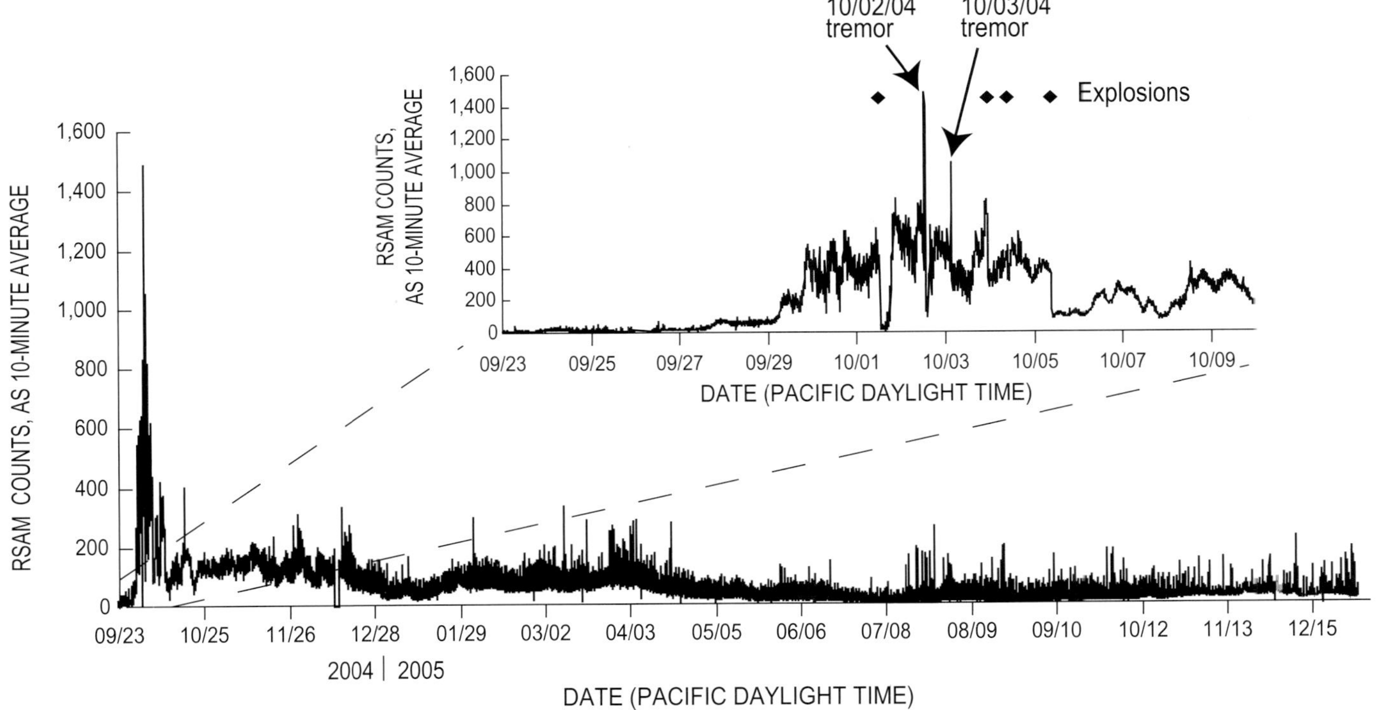

Figure 9. Plot of 10-minute real-time seismic amplitude measurement (RSAM) values from station SHW (3 km west of vent; fig. 1) between September 23, 2004, and December 31, 2005. Inset shows SHW RSAM between September 23 and October 10, timing of four phreatic explosions, and occurrence of two tremor episodes associated with a vent-clearing phase. Horizontal-axis tick marks in inset indicate start of a day, with gaps of 2 days between each tick mark.

3 (fig. 8), and, as with the October 2 episode, no eruptive plume was detected (M. Guffanti, written commun., 2004). In contrast to the October 2 episode, earthquakes continued to occur during the October 3 tremor episode. Although earthquake rates and RSAM levels dropped after the episode and remained low for the next 12 hours, the decrease was not as great as those that followed the October 1 explosion and the October 2 tremor.

Around 1500 PDT on October 3, earthquake rates again began increasing, with RSAM levels peaking at 1650 (fig. 9). After a brief drop, earthquake rates increased again, with seismicity dominated by many small-amplitude events. By 2100, earthquakes were occurring so close together in time that they became difficult to distinguish, forming a spasmodic tremorlike signal (fig. 8). Continuous, small-amplitude tremor was likely also occurring, although this signal can only be seen in the short gaps between individual earthquakes. Earthquake rates and the tremorlike signal decreased substantially around 2305, following a small steam-and-ash explosion at 2240 reported by U.S. Forest Service observers at the Coldwater Ridge Visitor Center, and RSAM dropped to levels similar to those from early in the day on October 3 (fig. 9). Following this small explosion, the number of larger (M_d >2) earthquakes decreased, with many smaller hybrid earthquakes occurring in the gaps between larger events (fig. 8). Earthquake rates and RSAM levels gradually increased again until another steam-and-ash explosion at 0943 PDT on October 4, and, as before, earthquake rates and RSAM levels briefly dropped following the explosion (figs. 8, 9). Shortly afterward, RSAM levels increased again, peaked at 1700 on October 4, and then gradually declined to a relative low at 2330. As with roughly two-thirds of the previous RSAM increases, the peak and subsequent decline were not associated with explosions or other anomalous surface activity. RSAM levels increased once again beginning at 0000 PDT on October 5, reaching a peak at 0600 that was maintained until the final explosion of the vent-clearing stage began at 0903. Earthquake sizes and rates began declining ~15 minutes after the explosion began and continued to decline over the next hour as the explosion continued through 1015. After the explosion, RSAM levels were lower than at any time since September 29, with the exception of the lull following the October 1 explosion. Although RSAM levels increased and decreased several times over subsequent weeks, they never again reached levels achieved before the October 5 explosion (fig. 9).

Between September 29 and October 5, earthquakes were too large and occurring too close together in time for more than a fraction of all earthquakes to be detected and located by the PNSN. Using the average event rates given above, we estimate that ~30,000 earthquakes occurred over these seven days. The largest located event was a M_d 3.9 on October 1, and 9 events had $M_d \geq 3.5$ between October 1 and October 4. To estimate the total amount of seismic energy expended during the vent-clearing phase, we calibrated RSAM values at station FMW (91 km north of Mount St. Helens) using 20 of the largest earthquakes and then integrated RSAM values from FMW between September 23 and October 5. The result was a cumulative magnitude equivalent to a M_d 5.5 earthquake, an order of magnitude lower than the cumulative magnitude of M_d 6.5 estimated for the March 28–May 18, 1980, precursory seismicity.

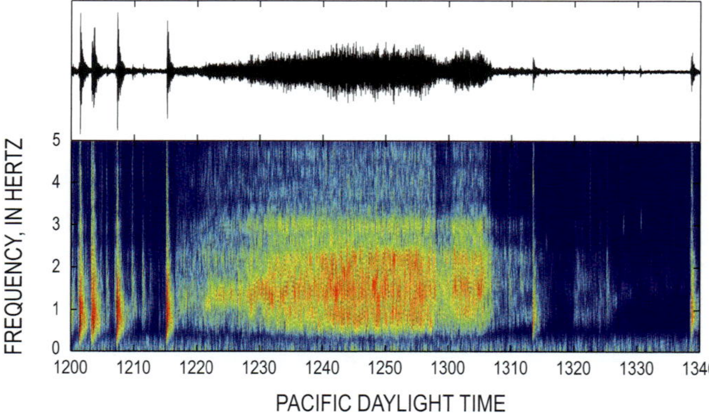

Figure 10. Tremor episode on October 2, 2004, as recorded on vertical component of broadband station JRO (8 km north of the vent; fig. 1). Time series (above) and spectrogram (below) for same time period. Note that discrete earthquakes stopped when tremor started at 1217 PDT and were significantly diminished after it ended at 1310.

October 5, 2004–December 31, 2005: Seismicity Accompanying Dome Building

The steep decline in seismicity following the October 5 explosion caused CVO to lower its alert level to Volcano Advisory (Alert Level 2), where it remained through the end of 2005. Although RSAM levels increased again between October 6–7 and October 8–9, 2004, as a result of increasing event sizes (largest were M_d 2.5–3.0), the increases were much more gradual and didn't reach September 29–October 5 levels (fig. 9). Because there had been a number of more rapid increases in seismicity between September 29 and October 5 that were not directly associated with eruptive activity, we did not change our alert status at the volcano during these more gradual intensifications. We noted during both those periods that earthquakes were dominated by a single event family, an attribute of Mount St. Helens seismicity that continues at the time of this writing (Moran and Malone, 2004; MacCarthy and Rowe, 2005; Thelen and others, this volume, chap. 4).

The October 8–9 earthquakes were a particularly spectacular example of an event family (fig. 11). Event magnitudes systematically increased over a ~12-hour period starting 0200 PDT, then stabilized at M_d 2.5–3.0 for almost 24 hours before systematically declining over a ~12-hour period back to M_d 1–1.5 (fig. 5). We generated hourly event stacks (fig.

11) to increase the signal-to-noise ratio of the P-wave arrivals and found that first motions were down at all stations, consistent with either very shallow reverse faulting or a deeper, nondouble-couple source (such as motion along a curved surface or an implosion). The appearance of event families, taken together with the overall decline in seismic levels, the change in event character to dominantly LF and hybrid events, the relatively low gas levels (Gerlach and others, this volume, chap. 26), and the observed deformation of the crater floor (Dzurisin and others, this volume, chap. 14), led CVO and the PNSN to believe that the most likely outcome was a new episode of lava dome building.

Seismicity declined significantly following the October 8–9 earthquake sequence. From October 10 to October 16, seismicity consisted of small (M_d <1) events occurring at a rate of 1–2 per minute, as well as slightly larger events with longer between-event intervals. At 0200 on October 16 the number of discrete M_d 1–1.5 events started decreasing, and between these events many tiny LF earthquakes appeared, spaced roughly 20 s apart (fig. 12). Event magnitudes of the tiny LF earthquakes steadily increased through October 17 before stabilizing at M_d ~0.5. When first observing these smaller events we noted a strong similarity to short-lived episodes of tiny, closely spaced LF events that were observed at Mount St. Helens in three separate instances associated with the 1983–84 continuous dome-building eruption (R. Norris, oral commun., 2006). On the basis of this similarity, we inferred that these LF events likely represented the extrusion of a new dome.

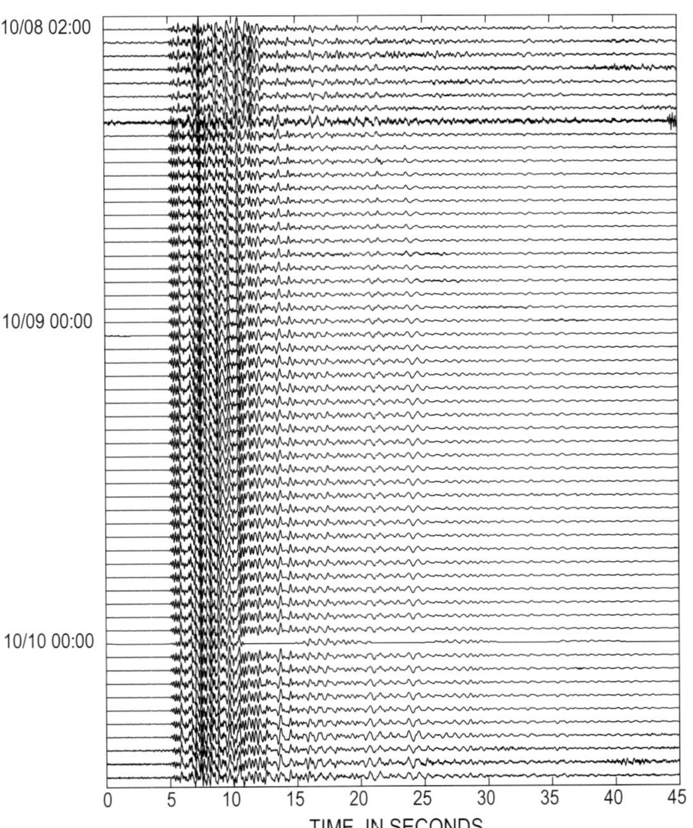

Figure 11. Plot of hourly stacks of events from earthquake family recorded on station HSR (2.5 km south of vent; fig. 1) between October 8 and October 10, 2004.

"Drumbeat" Earthquakes

The appearance of regularly spaced, small earthquakes on October 16, 2004, marked the beginning of the next seismic phase of the eruption, a phase that continues at the time of this writing. Seismicity in this phase was dominated by these events, which occurred at such remarkably constant intervals that we dubbed them "drumbeat" earthquakes. The drumbeats consisted of repetitive LF and hybrid earthquakes and were one of the hallmarks of the eruption in 2004–5. Indeed, we know of no instances at other volcanoes when drumbeatlike events have been observed over such a long period of time. The drumbeats accompanied the regular rate of extrusion of several dacite spines (in this volume: Schilling and others, chap. 8; Vallance and others, chap. 9; Herriott and others, chap. 10; Poland and others, chap. 11; Major and others, chap. 12). Many of the drumbeats had waveforms similar to other drumbeats (Thelen and others, this volume, chap. 4), a similarity that can be used to relatively relocate events within individual earthquake families with high precision, as was done in the 1980s at Mount St. Helens by Frémont and Malone (1987). Thelen and others (this volume, chap. 4) present a thorough analysis of a number of well-recorded families. Identifying and relocating all earthquake families occurring within the million-plus earthquakes of late 2004 and 2005 is a large task that will likely take years to complete, well beyond the scope of this paper.

Several investigators have proposed models that link drumbeats and extrusion rate (Harrington and Brodsky, 2006; Iverson and others, 2006; Iverson, this volume, chap. 21; Mastin and others, this volume, chap. 22), with most invoking stick slip as the source mechanism. Horton and others (this volume, chap. 5) note that spectral peaks from drumbeats recorded on broadband stations deployed in 2004–5 are suggestive of resonance within a structure such as a crack or conduit, with resonance initiated by a stick-slip event (Neuberg and others, 2006) or by a pressure transient in a crack (Chouet, 1996). Research into the drumbeat source mechanism is ongoing, and it is not our intent to present a thorough discussion of possible drumbeat source mechanisms. Instead we focus on describing general trends in drumbeat event spacing, size, and frequency content and how changes in these characteristics correlated with dome extrusion.

Event Spacing

Figure 13 shows that, to a first approximation, the time between drumbeats, or event spacing, changed little between October 16, 2004, and April 11, 2005, with daily averages ranging between 40 and 80 s. An important exception is that

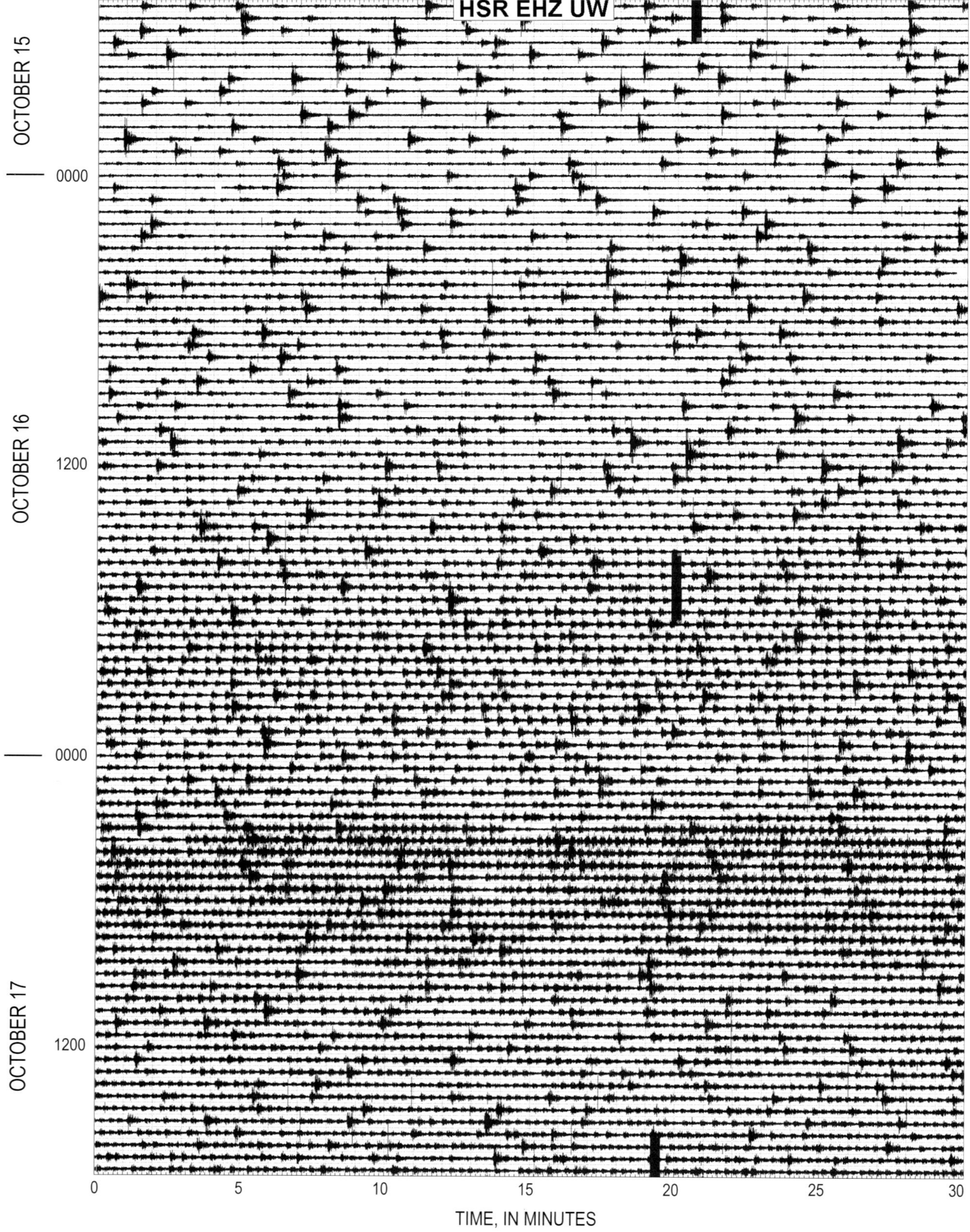

Figure 12. Seismic record from station HSR (2.5 km south of vent; fig. 1) from 1700 PDT on October 15 through 1800 PDT on October 17, 2004, showing onset of small, regularly spaced events ("drumbeats") occurring between larger events early on the morning of October 16. Drumbeat amplitudes increased gradually through the day.

between October 16 and November 12, 2004, events were occurring only ~20 s apart and were small enough that many went undetected by our detection algorithm (appendix 2). After November 12, event spacing increased to ~40 s, and visual inspections show that most events were detected. Between April 12 and July 8–10, 2005, the average event spacing gradually increased to more than 560 s, then briefly got shorter; on July 20 it became irregular, with spacing progressively increasing. In early August the events had become too small to be detected reliably by our algorithm on station HSR. Even on stations located within 1 km of the vent, earthquakes were occurring more as random earthquakes than drumbeats. By early October 2005, they had become so infrequent, emergent, and small that we began questioning whether the seismic events we were seeing were earthquakes or other surface sources, such as ice quakes and rockfalls. However, on October 9, 2005, earthquakes began to increase in size, and event spacing became remarkably regular again, with events occurring every ~70 s. Initially, event sizes were bimodal (fig. 13), with a population of larger-magnitude events (peak magnitude M_d ~2.5) occurring alongside a population of more frequent smaller events. The larger-magnitude events gradually decreased in size until by mid-November 2005 there was just a single dominant event size. Event spacing began increasing in mid-December and, by the end of December 2005, had again become irregular.

One important qualification to the drumbeat story is that many small earthquakes recorded on stations located inside the crater in 2004–5 were not drumbeats. This was particularly the case from May through July of 2005, when the spacing between drumbeats increased significantly (fig. 13). As drumbeats decreased in size and number starting in mid-June, there was a factor of 15 difference between numbers of detected events at station MIDE (located ~200 m from the vent) and station HSR (2.5 km from the vent) between May 20 and July 18, 2005 (fig. 14). Some of the events detected at MIDE were rockfalls, but most were earthquakes that were too small to be recorded on stations >0.5 km from the vent. The

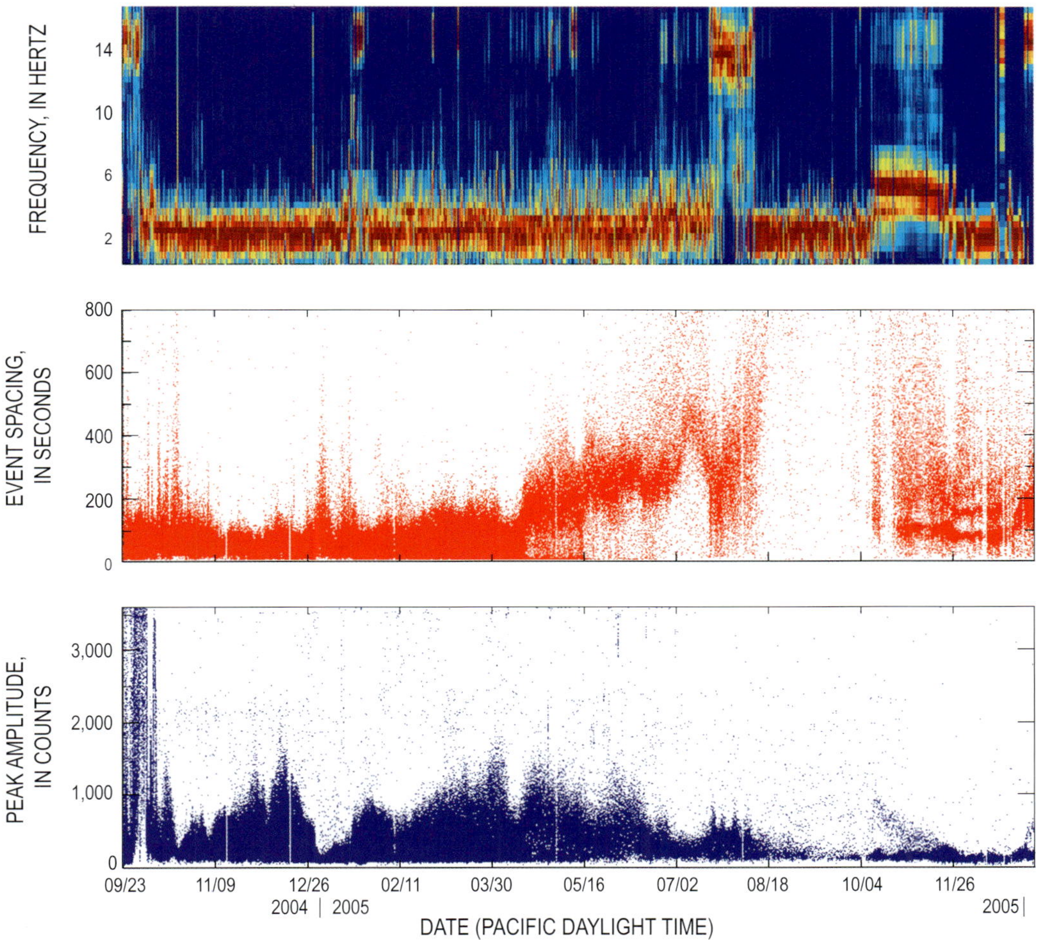

Figure 13. Plot showing ESAM (top), inter-event spacing (middle), and peak amplitudes (bottom) for detected events at station HSR (fig. 1) between September 23, 2004, and December 31, 2005 (see appendix 2 for event detection details). Roughly 370,000 events were detected during this time period, including occasional noise glitches and other false triggers.

events recorded on MIDE and other near-field stations lacked the regular spacing characteristic of drumbeats, and relative amplitudes and arrival-time patterns between MIDE and other near-field stations indicate that many were occurring within the extruded spines.

Event Size Distribution

There was a complex relation between drumbeat event spacing and event size. In general, increases in event spacing corresponded to increases in event size and vice versa (fig. 15). For example, on December 16, 2004, average drumbeat magnitudes were M_d ~1.5 and events were spaced ~90 s apart, whereas on December 23, 2004, average magnitudes had decreased to M_d ~0.5 and events were spaced ~40 s apart (although occasional M_d 1.0–1.5 events still occurred). If drumbeats are a result of stick-slip motion along a common fault plane and the steady extrusion rate corresponds to a constant slip rate (or stress accumulation rate) along the fault plane, then smaller drumbeats must be closer together if extrusion rate and seismic energy release are to remain constant. However, for seismic energy to have remained constant between December 16 and December 23, the event spacing would have had to decrease to ~3 s on December 23, a factor of 13 less than the observed ~40 s spacing. Thus there was a net reduction in seismic energy release between December 16 and December 23. Another drop in seismic energy release occurred in the evening of December 29, 2004, when drumbeat magnitudes dropped to M_d 0.0–0.5 while event spacing remained roughly constant (fig. 13).

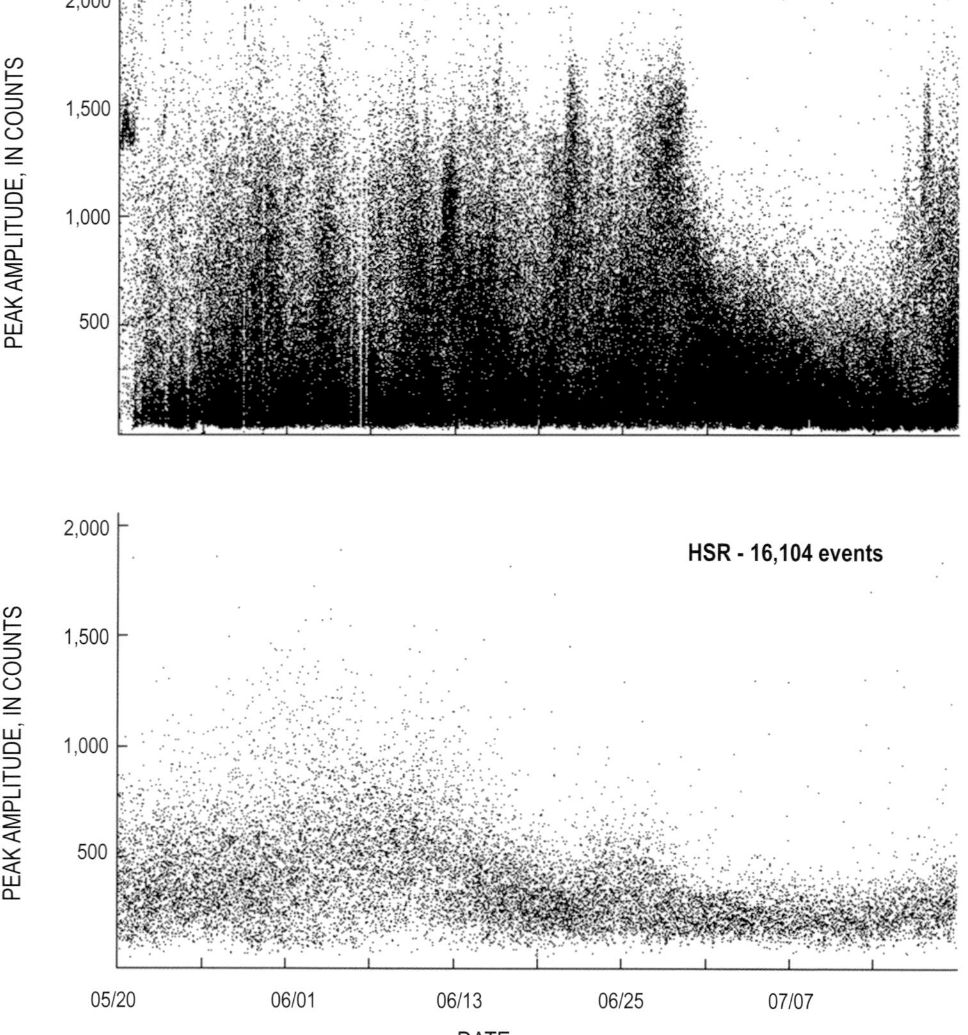

Figure 14. Detected events vs. time at stations MIDE (top) and HSR between May 20 and July 18, 2005. Note that the decline in events at HSR starting around June 13 is not seen at MIDE, evidence that many events detected on MIDE were occurring close to the station and were due to a process distinct from that responsible for the drumbeats.

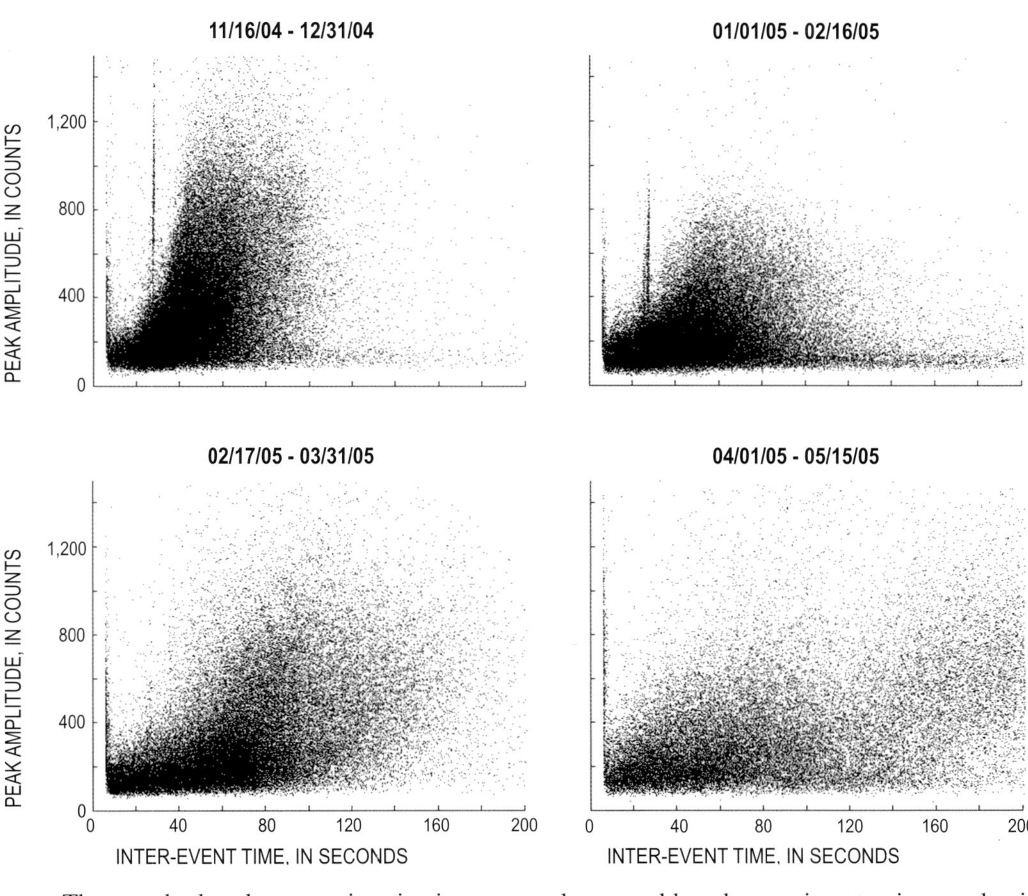

Figure 15. Plot of peak amplitudes vs. event spacing for detected events at HSR (fig. 1) for four time periods (all four plots have same vertical and horizontal scales). Although a general relation is seen between event size and inter-event time, particularly through mid-February (top two plots), the slope decreases over time, indicating that seismic energy release was declining as event spacing was increasing. Two linear features in the top two plots correspond to a sufficiently strong secondary phase arriving ~20 s after the P-wave at HSR to be occasionally detected as an event.

These and other decreases in seismic energy release could have been caused by decreases in extrusion rate, decreases in seismic coupling, or other changes in the mechanics of extrusion. Both December 2004 seismic energy drops (Dec. 23 and Dec. 29) occurred during the breakup of spine 3 and transition to spine 4 as the active locus of extrusion, a transition that began November 16 and continued through mid-January 2005 (Vallance and others, this volume, chap. 9). A mid-April 2005 drop in energy release, when event rates declined noticeably (fig. 13), coincided with the breakup of spine 4 and transition to spine 5, and another energy drop in mid-July coincided with the breakup of spine 5 and transition to spine 6 (Vallance and others, this volume, chap. 9). The correlation between transitions in extrusion style at the surface and changes in seismic energy release suggests that drumbeat seismicity was controlled to a certain extent by the mechanics of extrusion at the surface. Support for this interpretation comes from the observation that extrusion rates determined from digital elevation models (DEM) computed periodically throughout the eruption (Schilling and others, this volume, chap. 8) remained relatively constant despite fairly substantial changes in seismic energy release. In particular, the extrusion of spine 6 was associated with a significant drop in event rate and size from mid-August through early October of 2005, as described above. However, three DEMs spanning August–October 2005 show that the rate of extrusion remained roughly constant during the lull in seismicity. This lack of correspondence indicates that the rate and size of drumbeats may have been more a function of changes in extrusion mechanics than changes in magma flux through the conduit. Changes in extrusion mechanics that could have influenced earthquake occurrence include changes in the angle of extrusion (which would affect clamping forces), changes in the locus of extrusion, and (or) changes in the frictional properties along the conduit margin through rate hardening/softening or other processes.

A further complexity in the relation between event sizes and event spacing is that, although there clearly were extended periods of time when larger drumbeat events were followed by longer gaps, there also were many instances when larger events were followed by short gaps and smaller events followed by larger gaps. This complexity is not predicted by models that marry drumbeats with the regular extrusion rate (Iverson and others, 2006; Iverson, this volume, chap. 21; Mastin and others, this volume, chap. 22). If the drumbeats were a result of a stick-slip source, then this complexity indicates that drumbeats at times occurred at multiple locations within a complex network of shear zones, with individual faults having individual loading and unloading histories somewhat independent of those on other faults. It remains to be seen if individual drumbeat families (Thelen and others, this volume, chap. 4) show a more direct relation between event size and event spacing.

A final general characteristic of drumbeat magnitudes was their magnitude-frequency distribution over time. Most commonly, drumbeats occurred with a single dominant event size and, in general, did not follow a Gutenberg-Richter relation. This is consistent with the repetitive nature of the drumbeats and implies that source dimensions, as well as location, varied little between individual drumbeats. However, there were also time periods when event amplitudes appeared to follow a Gutenberg-Richter relation (fig. 13), in the sense that a greater number of small events occurred than large events. We note that there is no relation between event size and event spacing during many of these time periods, which also implies that multiple seismic sources were active at the same time.

P-Wave Spectra

With a thousand or more events occurring per day, it was difficult to notice changes in event character over time, although obvious variations from the norm, such as the sporadic occurrence of VT events, were noted, usually within hours. One means we used for tracking changes in drumbeat character was to plot event spectra over time (see appendix 2 for details). Earthquake spectral amplitude (ESAM) plots in figures 5 and 13 show that seismicity transitioned from hybrid events following the October 5 explosion to LF events by October 9 and was dominated by LF events (peak frequencies in the 2–3-Hz range) through early January 2005. Between January 8 and 25, hybrid events occurred along with LF events (fig. 16), with peak hybrid P-wave frequencies of 8–16 Hz on station HSR. Hybrids also occurred with LF events between mid-April and late May 2005 and were the dominant event type between July 20 and August 11, 2005 (fig. 16). In both cases, peak P-wave frequencies were in the 12–16-Hz range on station HSR. Hybrids again occurred alongside LF events between October 9 and November 18, with peak P-wave frequencies in the 4–6-Hz range and a weaker band between 14 and 16 Hz (fig. 13). These frequency changes are most notable on stations HSR and SHW, two stations located 2.5–3 km from the vent. Changes in event appearance are also apparent on station YEL, ~1 km from the vent (the closest station to have operated throughout the entire eruption), but peak frequencies for the hybrid events are 4–5 Hz, suggesting that the path to YEL attenuates much of the high-frequency energy apparent on flank stations.

The four instances of concentrated hybrid occurrence all coincide with transitions in spine extrusion, as well as with several changes in event amplitude and (or) event spacing described above. The best example of this was July–August 2005, when seismicity switched from dominantly LF to dominantly hybrid events. A time-lapse sequence of photos (fig. 17) from a remote camera located on the northeast edge of the crater (Poland and others, this volume, chap. 11; Major and others, this volume, chap. 12) shows that the hybrid events began as the south end of spine 5 stopped moving on July 20, resulting in differential motion within the spine. As time progressed, the resultant shear zone moved northward, until finally spine 6 split away from spine 5 and began moving westwards around August 9–10. Other major spine transitions occurred December 2004–January 2005, mid-April 2005, and early October 2005 (Vallance and others, this volume, chap. 9). Hybrid seismic events occurred to varying degrees during each of these transitions, a correlation that suggests a direct relation between hybrids and motion of the spines after extrusion from the vent. One speculative model is that the hybrids are a result of differential shearing occurring along the base of the spine during spine transitions, whereas the LF events, which do not have as clear a relation to changes in spine motion after extrusion, occur at shallow depths along the conduit margin.

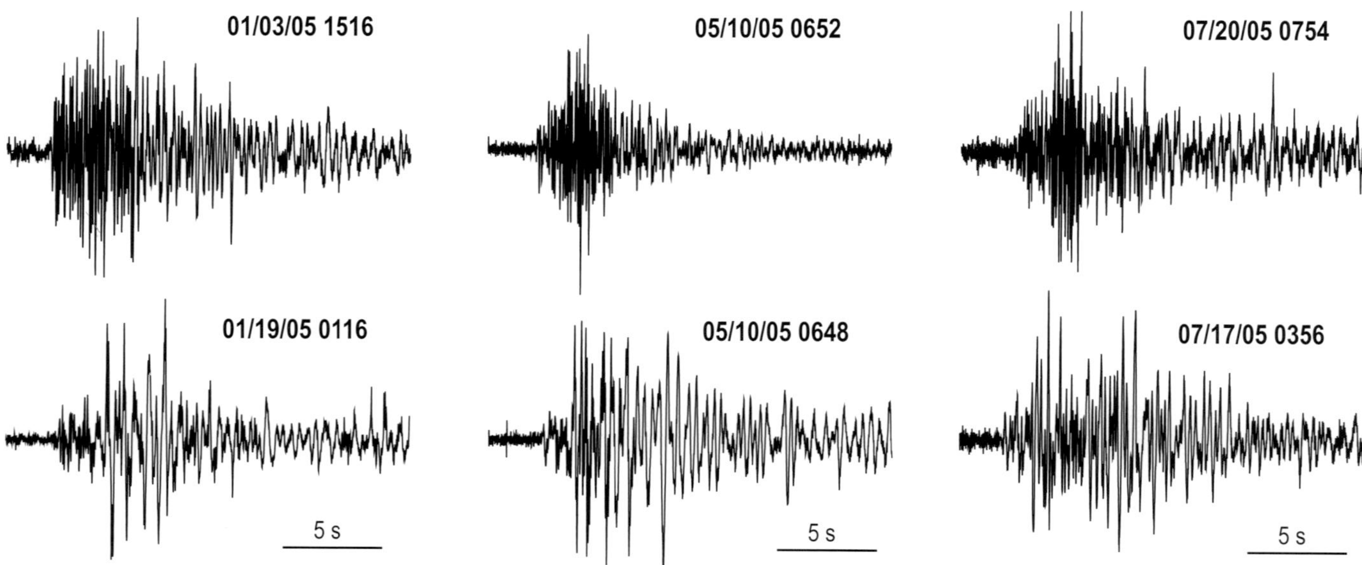

Figure 16. Examples of hybrid (top) and low-frequency drumbeats (bottom) as recorded at station HSR in January, May, and July 2005. Hybrid drumbeats were relatively rare and occurred in temporal clusters that are clearly visible on the ESAM plot in figure 13. Such clusters corresponded to transitional periods when one spine became inactive and a new spine began to grow.

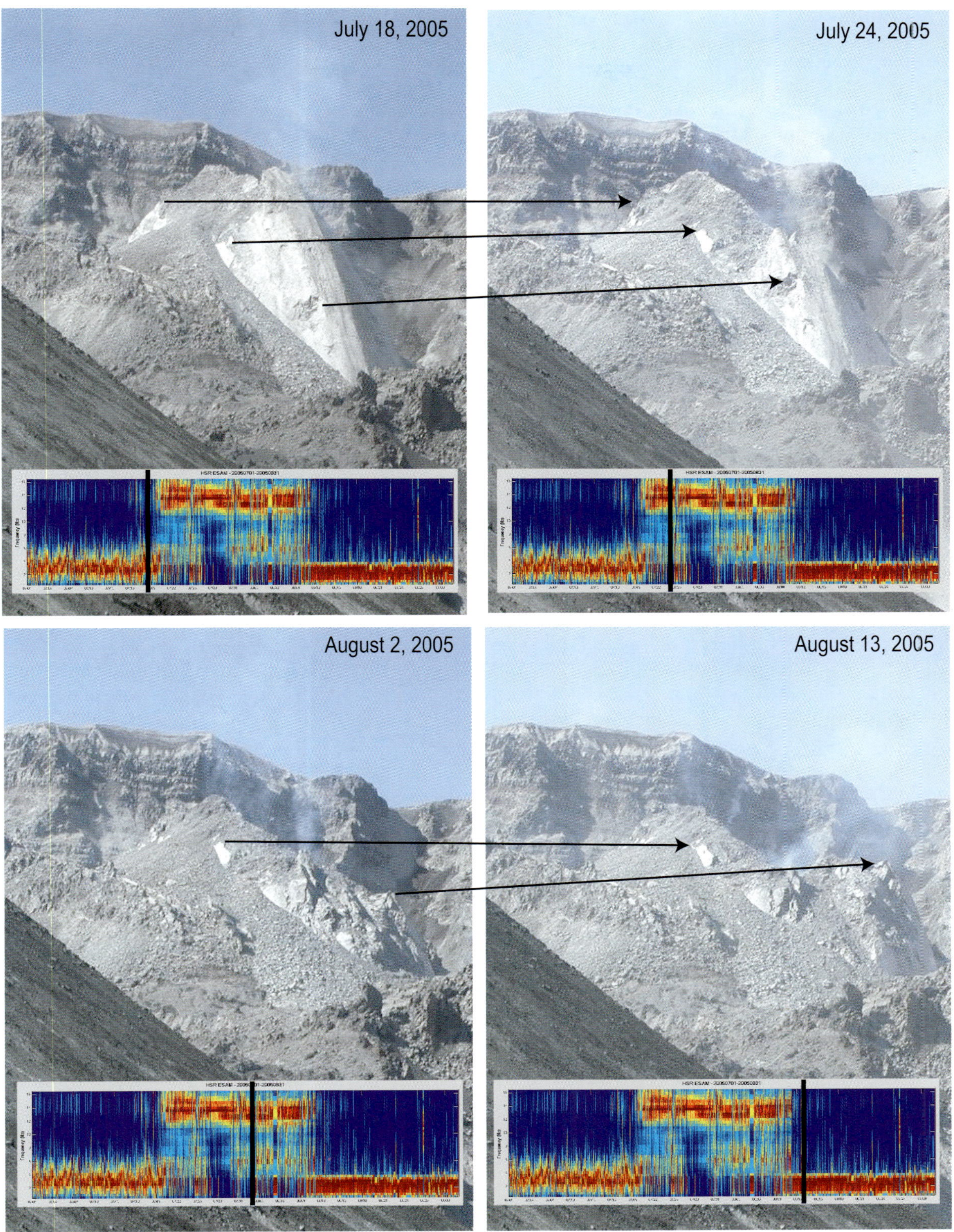

Figure 17. Four pictures taken from a camera station at SUG (fig. 1) showing transition from spine 5 to spine 6 that took place in late July–early August. Arrows indicate relative motion of common spots on spine 5. At bottom of each picture is an ESAM plot showing earthquake spectra between July 1 and August 31, 2005, with frequency ranging from 0 to 16 Hz (identical scale to figs. 5 and 13). Black vertical bar on each ESAM plot corresponds to date on which that picture was taken.

"Big" Earthquakes

Another intriguing aspect of seismicity after October 16, 2004, was the occasional occurrence of larger, or "big" (M_d >2.0, M_{max} = 3.4), shallow earthquakes. The first of these was a M_d 2.4 earthquake at 2048 PST on November 15, 2004, that was followed by 11 others over the next two weeks (fig. 18). These earthquakes were notable because they were much larger than the regular drumbeat events (fig. 19). They generated much interest among scientists and with the public, because they could be seen easily in the real-time digital helicorder plots displayed on the PNSN Web site (Qamar and others, this volume, chap. 3). Also, they often caused large rockfalls that, in turn, generated ash plumes, which frequently rose above the crater rim. The onset of the "big" events coincided with spine 3 encountering the south crater wall, as demonstrated by DEMs (Schilling and others, this volume, chap. 8). Spine 3 was likely in a state of uniaxial compression at this point, and the coincidence of its south-wall impingement and the occurrence of larger events suggests a causal relation.

The larger events cannot be distinguished from larger drumbeat events on the basis of PNSN catalog magnitudes alone, because drumbeats tend to have long codas that yield overly large M_d values relative to magnitudes determined using amplitudes. We therefore arbitrarily define larger events as those post-October 2004 events with amplitudes large enough to clip on station HSR. Through the end of 2005 there were more than 290 larger earthquakes with a cumulative magnitude of M_d 4.4. Most events occurred in one of four temporal clusters: November 15, 2004–January 14, 2005; January 25–March 9, 2005; March 22–April 22, 2005; and July 15–December 31, 2005 (fig. 18). The first and third clusters occurred in association with the breakup of spines 3 and 4, respectively, and the fourth occurred in association with the breakup of spines 5 and 6. In contrast, the second cluster occurred during steady extrusion of spine 4. The ends of the first and second clusters coincided with explosions on January 18, 2005, and March 8, 2005, respectively. The largest number of events in a single day was 11 on March 27, 2005, when several events occurred within an hour of their predecessors, and the largest daily moment release occurred April 4, 2005. Both peaks occurred during the transition in locus of active extrusion from spine 4 to spine 5.

Despite their size, the larger earthquakes are similar in several ways to the drumbeat events. Like the drumbeats, they are classified as either LF or hybrid events. Roughly 40 percent have impulsive arrivals on most stations, and, like the drumbeats, many of the events with impulsive arrivals have most or all down first motions (appendix 1). Many of the impulsive larger earthquakes have higher frequencies at the

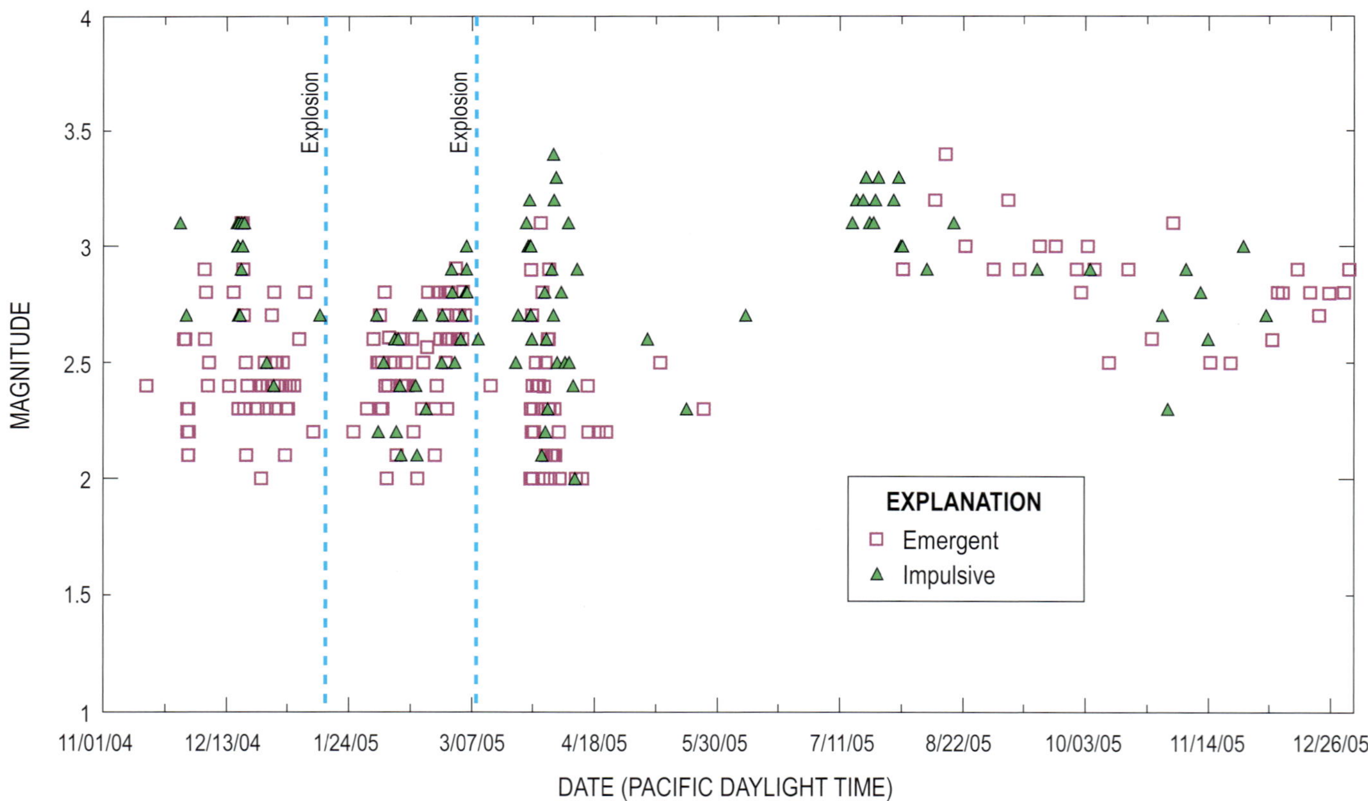

Figure 18. Plot showing occurrence of "big" earthquakes between November 1, 2004, and December 31, 2005. Green triangles correspond to impulsive events, hollow magenta squares to emergent events. Timing of two explosions on January 16 and March 8, 2005, are indicated by dashed blue lines.

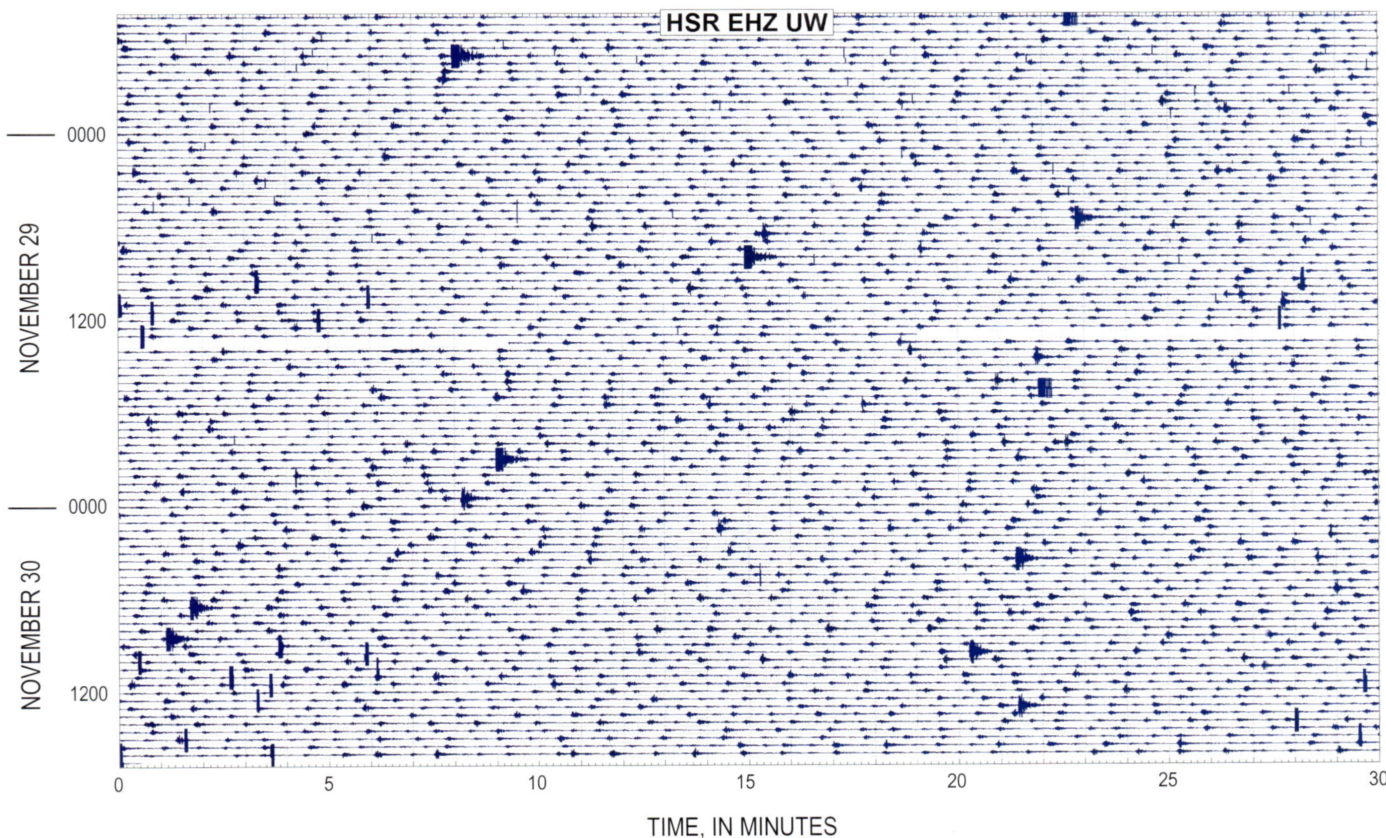

Figure 19. Seismic record from station HSR (see fig. 1) for 48 hours between 1700 PST on November 28 and 1700 PST on November 30, 2004, showing ten "big" earthquakes occurring along with regular drumbeats. Note that no change in drumbeat spacing or size occurs before or after the larger earthquakes, indicating that source processes are separate and distinct from one another.

start of the event and are classified as hybrid events, whereas the emergent events are dominantly LF events. Clipping of near-field sites makes event-family detection difficult, but on-scale recordings at broadband station JRO (~9 km from the vent; fig. 1) show that, although many of the larger events are dissimilar, there was at least one set of events occurring between December 2004 and April 2005 with similar waveforms (fig. 20). The similarity indicates not only that at least some of the larger earthquakes occurred in the same place with the same mechanism, but that the structure on which they occurred remained intact over a 4-month time span.

Spectra for drumbeats and the larger events are also similar. Figure 21 shows a set of waveforms and instrument-corrected spectra for a M_d 1.0 drumbeat and a M_d 3.0 "big" earthquake as recorded on stations plotted in order of distance from the earthquake. Spectra on all stations for both events have relatively flat curves for frequencies <1 Hz, a well-defined corner frequency at 1–2 Hz, and a ω^2 decrease in frequency content at higher frequencies, all characteristics of tectonic earthquake spectra (Brune, 1970). Horton and others (this volume, chap. 5) found similar characteristics for events recorded on their broadband network in 2004–5. Of particular note is the nearly identical corner frequency (F_c in fig. 21) of 1–2 Hz for all spectra, a frequency that is independent of distance and magnitude. One implication of this observation is that if the source is stick slip in nature, then the source duration is independent of source area. A source area independent of event size indicates that event magnitude is primarily a function of source displacement, rather than a combination of fault area and displacement as it is for tectonic earthquakes. This implies that the principal mechanical difference between drumbeats and "big" events is the amount of slip. If the earthquakes reflect stick-slip faulting within or at the periphery of the rising, rapidly solidifying magma plug (Iverson and others, 2006; Thelen and others, this volume, chap. 4; Iverson, this volume, chap. 21), then it is not surprising that the source area for these events is limited, because ruptures cannot propagate far outside of high-strain regions. The source duration of such a stick-slip event would then be a combination of the duration of motion of any part of the rupture surface and the area over which the rupture spreads, with the duration of this spreading being a function of the rupture velocity.

Locations for the impulsive larger events are more concentrated than drumbeat locations (fig. 22), although epicenters are still spread over an area 1 km by 1 km centered on the vent. Some of this scatter is likely due to changes in station

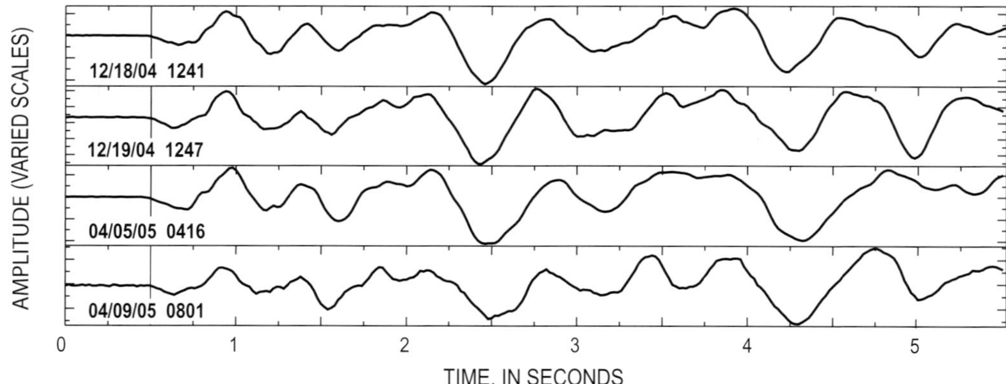

Figure 20. P-wave arrivals at broadband station JRO (fig. 1) for four "big" events occurring in December 2004 (upper two records) and April 2005 (lower two) with similar waveforms. Waveforms are scaled relative to the peak amplitude for each event. Although many "big" events do not have similar waveforms, the fact that some do indicates that these events on occasion occur at the same location with the same source mechanism. The 4-month time span between these four events also indicates that the structure on which these events occurred was not destroyed over that interval.

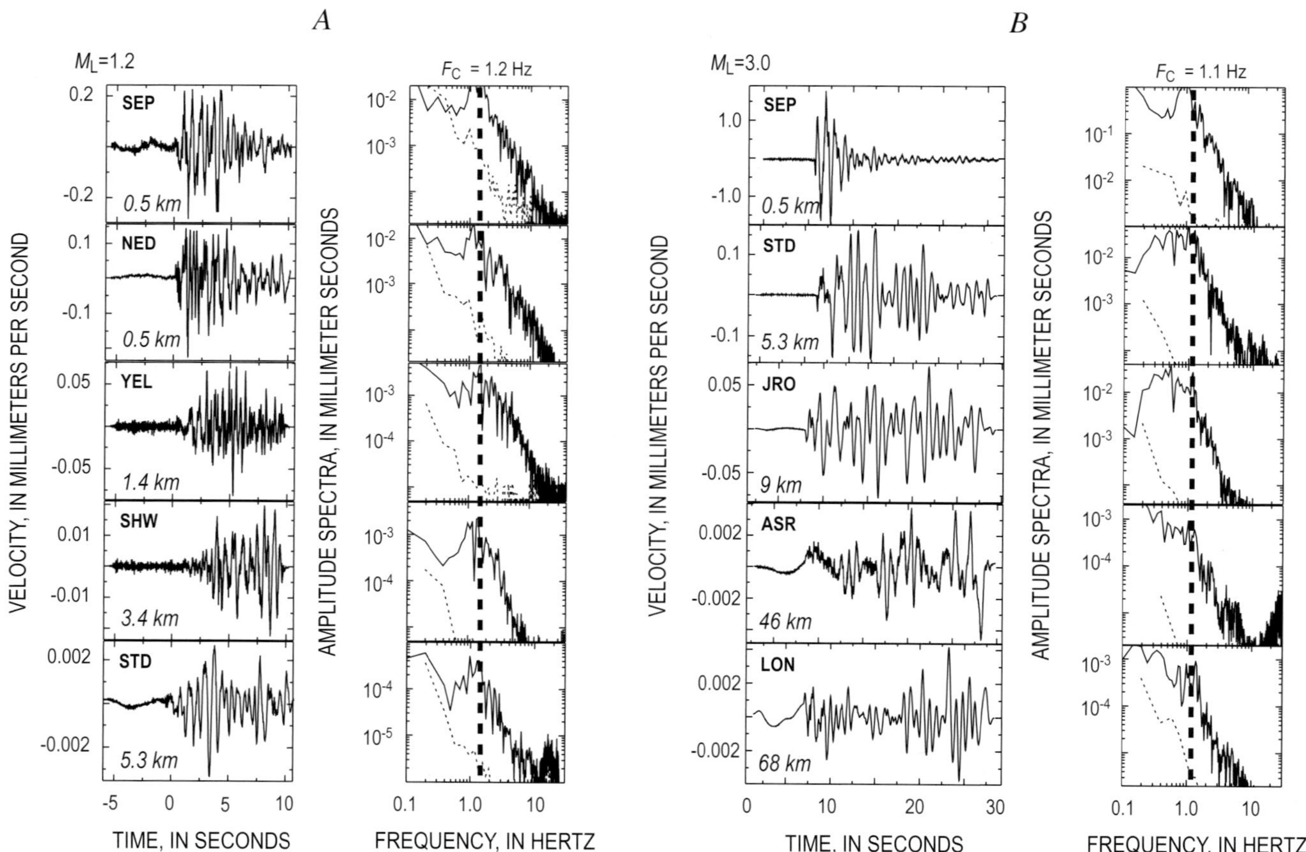

Figure 21. Instrument-corrected seismogram and frequency spectra for typical drumbeat (*A*) and "big" (*B*) seismic events. Stations are arranged in increasing distance from vent, with distance indicated for each station. All stations shown on location map (fig. 1) except ASR, located near Mount Adams, and LON, near Mount Rainier. Spectra are for 10.24-s windows starting with P-wave arrival. Thin dotted line below each spectral plot is noise estimate based on 10.24-s window taken before first arrival. Vertical thick dashed lines indicate corner frequencies (F_c) for each event. *A*, Drumbeat event, M_L 1.2, on August 20, 2005, at 1345 PDT. *B*, "Big" event, M_L 3.0, on March 26, 2005, at 1928 PST.

geometries and inaccuracies in the shallow velocity model (inaccuracies that, because of constantly changing velocity structure caused by the ongoing eruption, varied through time). Some scatter is also due to picking uncertainties, because arrival times, particularly on close-in stations, are difficult to pick to within ~0.1-s accuracy for all but the most impulsive events. However, some of the location scatter is real, the best evidence for which comes from differences in relative P-wave arrival times at stations placed close to the vent. As an example, figure 23 shows records on four crater stations from two events recorded ~9 hours apart on February 10 and 11, 2005. For the February 10 event, the P-wave arrived first at station BLIS (250 m east of the vent) and ~0.4 s later at AHAB (located 250 m southeast of the vent on top of spine 4); whereas for the February 11 event, the P wave arrived only 0.02 s later at AHAB. There was little change in relative P-wave arrivals at stations SEP and NED (~500 m north-northwest and ~500 m north-northeast of the vent, respectively). These patterns indicate that the February 11 event was located midway between AHAB and BLIS (350 m apart, including the altitude difference), whereas the February 10 event was located close to BLIS, a difference of as much as ~175 m (depending on P-wave velocities) between the two events. The 0.4-s difference in arrivals for the first event also implies remarkably low P-wave velocities (<1–2 km/s) at shallow depths, which is likely a result of AHAB and BLIS being placed on top of hot and highly fractured rock and crater-filling deposits (rockfall debris and ashfall deposits from the 1980 eruptions).

Hypotheses for the larger earthquake source include implosive-type mechanisms, fracturing of new rock (formation of new pathways to the surface), fracturing within spines before or after extrusion, and lurching of the active spine in a large-scale stick-slip event. Implosive mechanisms are consistent with all-down first-motion patterns observed for many of the impulsive events. However, none of these events occurred in association with explosions or significant degassing events. In addition, the extremely low levels of magmatic gases emanating from the vent (Gerlach and others, this volume, chap. 26) make it unlikely that sizable gas- or steam-filled cracks or pockets are able to accumulate below the surface and collapse to produce these events. We note, however, that Waite and others (2008) demonstrated that several events occurring in 2005 had a sig-

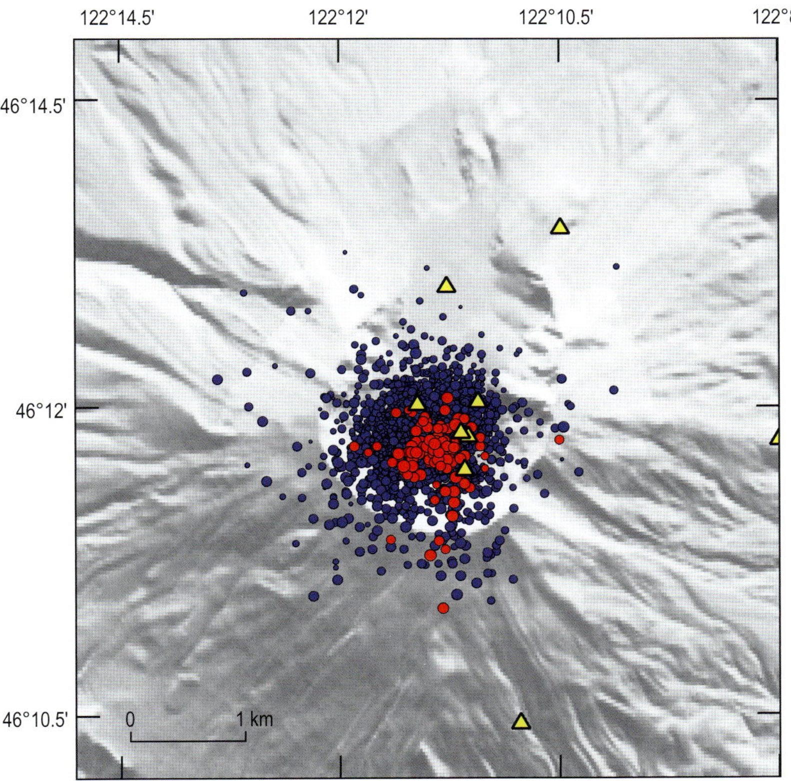

Figure 22. Map showing epicenters of drumbeat events (blue dots) and impulsive "big" events (red dots) occurring between November 1, 2004, and December 31, 2005. Dot sizes vary with magnitude. Drumbeat locations include events with P arrivals on at least seven stations, a nearest station within 2 km, and an azimuthal gap ≤135° (all impulsive "big" event locations meet these same criteria). Yellow triangles correspond to seismic station locations as of July 2005.

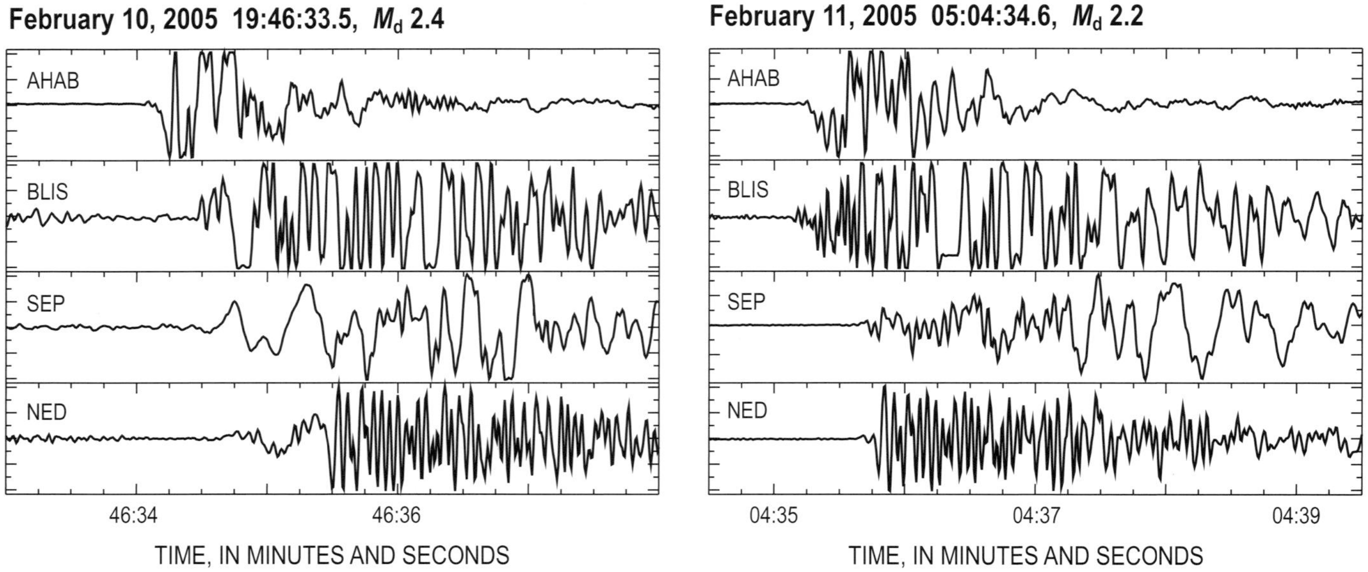

Figure 23. P-wave arrivals from two "big" earthquakes on four stations located within 0.5 km of vent (see fig. 1 for station locations). Note ~0.4-s difference in relative arrival times between stations AHAB and BLIS, indicating epicentral difference of more than one hundred meters for the two events.

nificant volumetric component, and they inferred that the source was a periodically collapsing, horizontal steam-filled crack.

Fracturing of new rock is also an unlikely process, as we would not expect to see repeating events or events with all-down first motions. Also, such a process would presumably not result in the emergent arrivals that we see at most stations in roughly half of the larger events. Fracturing within the spines is consistent with the observation that three of four large seismic-event clusters occur in association with the breakup of individual spines. However, events with all-down first motions are inconsistent with the observed failure mode in the spines, which occurred largely on shear, normal, and tensile fractures. Because the spines were, with one exception, higher than the seismometers, these failure modes would produce either a mixture of first motions or, in the case of normal faulting, dominantly up first motions. In addition, repetitive events spanning several months (and different spines) are incompatible with in-spine fracturing, because the fractures are destroyed in the spine breakup process.

Lurching of the active spine is our preferred hypothesis for the larger events. Lurches are consistent with shallow reverse faulting or upward thrusting of a piston that is indicated by the all-down first motions, as well as with long-lived event families. The fact that at least some events are located beneath the spine away from the vent indicates that they may have occurred along the interface between the base of the spine and the old crater floor. Because the 1980 crater floor is composed largely of ash and rockfall debris that fell from the crater walls in the years following the May 18, 1980, eruption, this interface likely is irregular and separates two poorly consolidated rock bodies. These lithologic and structural aspects could explain the emergent character of many larger seismic events and their low-frequency nature.

Volcano-Tectonic (VT) Earthquakes

Following the initial VT-rich days of the vent-clearing phase, VT events were a minor component of seismicity at Mount St. Helens. On a daily basis we scanned through seismic records in search of VT events, because we felt that VT events, especially those deeper than 2–3 km, might be an indicator either of a surge of new magma entering the system or adjustment of the magmatic system to magma withdrawal—and thus a potential harbinger of the eruption's end. VT events occurred as isolated events throughout the eruption and had small magnitudes (M_d <1), shallow (<2 km) depths, and epicenters similar to those for the drumbeats and larger events. The most notable occurrence of VT events was a swarm of more than 70 small (M_d <0.3) shallow earthquakes occurring between December 27, 2005, and January 4, 2006. The VT events in this swarm occurred independently of the low-frequency drumbeats, in some cases occurring just tens of seconds before or after a drumbeat (fig. 24). This swarm appears quite clearly in figure 13, as only the VT events were large enough to pass our amplitude threshold for the ESAM plot during this time period. Poor weather obscured the volcano from view during this interval, but tiltmeters located on the 1980–86 lava dome showed slight inflation while VT events were occurring, in contrast to deflation before and after (D. Sherrod and M. Lisowski, oral commun., 2006). Other periods of inflation, however, do not coincide with VT events, so we are uncertain whether this relation is coincidental. Given the lack of correspondence of VTs to any obvious changes in eruption dynamics or mechanics of extrusion, our best guess is that the VT events represent fracturing of more competent rock in the crater floor, such as basaltic andesite lava flows from the Castle Creek period (2,200–1,895 yr B.P.) that underlie much of the 1980 crater (Clynne and others, this volume, chap. 28).

Summary—Patterns and Trends in Mount St. Helens seismicity, 2004–2005

In several intriguing ways the precursory seismic sequence of September 23 to early October 2004 was similar to those before the May 18, 1980, eruption and the 20 eruptions that followed during 1980–86. The 8-day-long interval between the first earthquakes and the first phreatic explosion on October 1, 2004, is close to the 7-day interval seen in March of 1980 (Endo and others, 1981; Malone and others, 1981), suggesting a characteristic time interval for magma to reach the surface once it begins to move. In addition, the transition from VT events to hybrid and LF events starting September 25, 2004, was broadly similar to transitions in event type seen before many of the dome-building eruptions in the 1980s (Malone, 1983). The occurrence of the event families, starting with the first significant family on September 26, 2004, is also similar to occurrence of event families before and during 1983–86 dome-building eruptions (Frémont and Malone, 1987), as well as to those in association with many other dome-building eruptions (for example, Okada and others, 1981; Power, 1988; Power and others, 1994; Villagómez, 2000; Rowe and others, 2004). In retrospect, the combination of event-type transition and occurrence of event families on September 25, 2004, could have given us an early indication of the expected nature of eruptive activity at Mount St. Helens, although that knowledge would likely not have changed how CVO and the PNSN reacted to the developing seismic crisis.

A summary observation from the September 29–October 5 period is that, of the hours-long increases in seismic intensity, only 4 of 12 occurred before explosions (fig. 9). Furthermore, seismic energy levels had stabilized at least an hour before two of the four explosions (October 1 and October 5). Thus we find no statistical basis for using short-term increases in RSAM or other measures of seismic energy to make short-term forecasts of explosive activity.

The drumbeats and "big" earthquakes associated with the dome-building eruption represent a relatively new type of seismicity at Mount St. Helens that, with a few exceptions, was not a dominant characteristic of 1980–86 seismicity. Efforts

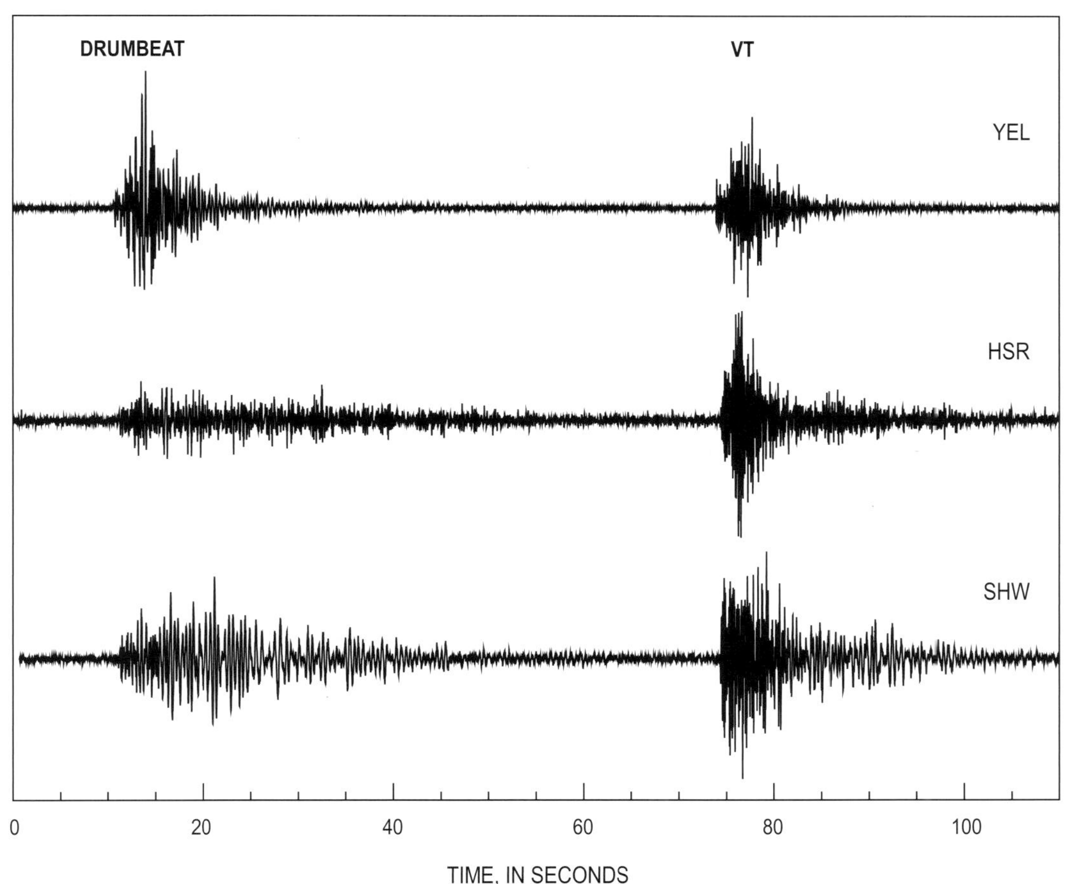

Figure 24. Seismograms from three stations for a drumbeat and a VT event occurring within 50 s of each other on December 29, 2005, at 1643 and 1644 PST, respectively. See figure 1 for station locations.

to characterize the nature of the drumbeat source are ongoing and likely will be the subject of research papers for years to come. Relatively new results with fascinating implications have already emerged from several field experiments run during 2004 and 2005, including the finding of infrasonic pulses associated with some drumbeats (Matoza and others, 2007) and the discovery of very long period (VLP) earthquakes in association with some of the larger drumbeats (Waite and others, 2008). These results provide evidence that processes operating at both deep (~500 m) and shallow (surface) levels are involved in the generation of drumbeats. The complexities in the relation between event spacing, event size, event spectra, and extrusion rate discussed in this paper, as well as in Thelen and others (this volume, chap. 4), further illustrate that the drumbeat source process is complex.

Finally, an important lesson that was reemphasized by the rapid escalation of seismicity during the first week of the eruption is that conditions can quickly become too dangerous to deploy additional seismometers after a volcano awakens. We were fortunate that the Mount St. Helens network installed in 1980–1983, particularly crater stations SEP (formerly REM) and YEL, was still in place and functional in 2004, because many of the events from the first two days were poorly recorded on stations outside of the crater. As the seismic crisis progressed, however, the limited dynamic range of the short-period analog stations was frequently exceeded at seismometers in the crater and on the flanks, resulting in lost information about seismic energy, spectral content, and event similarity. In addition, the absence of broadband three-component instruments in the crater meant that information was lost about the presence or absence of very low frequency signals and about source mechanisms for all types of events. As discussed by McChesney and others (this volume, chap. 7), seismicity intensified so rapidly during the first several days that we were unable to safely install such instruments in the crater. An important goal for seismic monitoring networks at any potentially active volcano should be to have seismometers, including broadband seismometers, installed at locations close to the presumed vent well before unrest begins.

Acknowledgments

The number of people involved in the seismic response to the renewed eruption in 2004–5 was huge, and it is impossible to give proper credit to all who helped us. Peggy Johnson, Josh Jones, Ruth Ludwin, Wendy McCausland, Karen Meagher, Guy Medema, Bob Norris, Bill Steele, George Thomas, and Tom Yelin all played critical roles in the PNSN/CVO seismic monitoring team, particularly with the immense tasks of data processing, production of Web graphics, around-the-clock monitoring of seismicity in the first several months of the eruption, and troubleshooting hardware problems brought on by the immense amount of seismic data and Web traffic. Marv Couchman, Rick LaHusen, Andy Lockhart, Jeff Marso, Pat McChesney, and Tim Plucinski all played critical roles in developing and installing new seismic and telemetry systems on and around the volcano, and we are extremely grateful to each of them for the many hours they devoted to improving real-time seismic monitoring at the volcano. Wendy McCausland calculated reduced displacement estimates for the October 2 and October 3 tremor episodes, and Bob Norris assisted with overnight shifts at CVO for more than a month, provided logistical support in the field, and was the first to recognize the similarity between 2004 drumbeats and "peppercorn" events seen in the 1980s.

We are grateful to Peter Cervelli for providing invaluable assistance in the drafting of all figures showing multiday seismic records and to Dave Ramsey for providing us with the station map showing crater station locations superimposed on the April 19, 2005, DEM in figure 1. We thank Jeff Johnson for his assistance with event-family identification during the first several weeks of the eruption and Helena Buurman for her assistance in processing and error-checking the results from our earthquake detection algorithm. We also thank Phil Dawson, John Power, Stephanie Prejean, and Randy White for their contributions to analysis and discussions of the significance of seismicity during the first critical weeks of renewed activity, for forming invaluable bridges to other researchers in the volcano seismology community when we were too busy to do so, and for providing greatly appreciated moral support during the first incredibly hectic weeks of the eruption. Finally, we are grateful to Charlotte Rowe and Randy White for thorough reviews that significantly improved this paper.

References Cited

Barker, S.E., and Malone, S.D., 1991, Magmatic system geometry at Mount St. Helens modeled from the stress field associated with posteruptive earthquakes: Journal of Geophysical Research, v. 96, no. B7, p. 11883–11894, doi:10.1029/91JB00430.

Bender, B., 1983, Maximum likelihood estimation of *b* values for magnitude grouped data: Bulletin of the Seismological Society of America, v. 73, p. 831–851.

Brune, J.N., 1970, Tectonic stress and the spectra of seismic shear waves from earthquakes: Journal of Geophysical Research, v. 75, no. 23, p. 4997–5009.

Chouet, B.A., 1996, Long-period volcano seismicity; its source and use in eruption forecasting: Nature, v. 380, p. 309–316.

Clynne, M.A., Calvert, A.T., Wolfe, E.W., Evarts, R.C., Fleck, R.J., and Lanphere, M.A., 2008, The Pleistocene eruptive history of Mount St. Helens, Washington, from 300,000 to 12,800 years before present, chap. 28 *of* Sherrod, D.R., Scott, W.E., and Stauffer, P.H., eds., A volcano rekindled;

the renewed eruption of Mount St. Helens, 2004–2006: U.S. Geological Survey Professional Paper 1750 (this volume).

Dzurisin, D., Vallance, J.W., Gerlach, T.M., Moran, S.C., and Malone, S.D., 2005, Mount St. Helens reawakens: Eos (American Geophysical Union Transactions), v. 86, no. 3, p. 25, 29.

Dzurisin, D., Lisowski, M., Poland, M.P., Sherrod, D.R., and LaHusen, R.G., 2008, Constraints and conundrums resulting from ground-deformation measurements made during the 2004–2005 dome-building eruption of Mount St. Helens, Washington, chap. 14 *of* Sherrod, D.R., Scott, W.E., and Stauffer, P.H., eds., A volcano rekindled; the renewed eruption of Mount St. Helens, 2004–2006: U.S. Geological Survey Professional Paper 1750 (this volume).

Endo, E.T., and Murray, T., 1991, Real-time seismic amplitude measurement (RSAM): a volcano monitoring and prediction tool: Bulletin of Volcanology, v. 53, no. 7, p. 533–545.

Endo, E.T., Dzurisin, D., and Swanson, D.A., 1990, Geophysical and observational constraints for ascent rates of dacitic magma at Mount St. Helens, *in* Ryan, M.P., ed., Magma transport and storage: New York, John Wiley, p. 317–334.

Endo, E.T., Malone, S.D., Noson, L.L., and Weaver, C.S., 1981, Locations, magnitudes, and statistics of the March 20–May 18 earthquake sequence, *in* Lipman, P.W., and Mullineaux, D.R., eds., The 1980 eruptions of Mount St. Helens, Washington: U.S. Geological Survey Professional Paper 1250, p. 93–107.

Fehler, M., 1985, Locations and spectral properties of earthquakes accompanying an eruption of Mount St. Helens: Journal of Geophysical Research, v. 90, p. 12729–12740.

Fehler, M., and Chouet, B.A., 1982, Operation of a digital seismic network on Mount St. Helens volcano and observations of long-period seismic events that originate under the volcano: Geophysical Research Letters, v. 9, no. 9, p. 1017–1020.

Frémont, M.J., and Malone, S.D., 1987, High precision relative locations of earthquakes at Mount St. Helens, Washington: Journal of Geophysical Research, v. 92, no. B10, p. 10223–10236.

Gerlach, T.M., McGee, K.A., and Doukas, M.P., 2008, Emission rates of CO_2, SO_2, and H_2S, scrubbing, and preeruption excess volatiles at Mount St. Helens, 2004–2005, chap. 26 *of* Sherrod, D.R., Scott, W.E., and Stauffer, P.H., eds., A volcano rekindled; the renewed eruption of Mount St. Helens, 2004–2006: U.S. Geological Survey Professional Paper 1750 (this volume).

Giampiccolo, E., Musumeci, C., Malone, S.D., Gresta, S., and Privitera, E., 1999, Seismicity and stress-tensor inversion in the central Washington Cascades mountains: Journal of Geophysical Research, v. 89, p. 811–821.

Harrington, R.M., and Brodsky, E.E., 2006, The Mount St. Helens hybrid earthquakes; stick-slip or resonating pipes [abs]: Eos (American Geophysical Union Transactions), v. 87, Fall Meeting Supplement, V52A-02.

Herriott, T.M., Sherrod, D.R., Pallister, J.S., and Vallance, J.W., 2008, Photogeologic maps of the 2004–2005 Mount St. Helens eruption, chap. 10 *of* Sherrod, D.R., Scott, W.E., and Stauffer, P.H., eds., A volcano rekindled; the renewed eruption of Mount St. Helens, 2004–2006: U.S. Geological Survey Professional Paper 1750 (this volume).

Horton, S.P., Norris, R.D., and Moran, S.C., 2008, Broadband characteristics of earthquakes recorded during a dome-building eruption at Mount St. Helens, Washington, between October 2004 and May 2005, chap. 5 *of* Sherrod, D.R., Scott, W.E., and Stauffer, P.H., eds., A volcano rekindled; the renewed eruption of Mount St. Helens, 2004–2006: U.S. Geological Survey Professional Paper 1750 (this volume).

Iverson, R.M., 2008, Dynamics of seismogenic volcanic extrusion resisted by a solid surface plug, Mount St. Helens, 2004–2005, chap. 21 *of* Sherrod, D.R., Scott, W.E., and Stauffer, P.H., eds., A volcano rekindled; the renewed eruption of Mount St. Helens, 2004–2006: U.S. Geological Survey Professional Paper 1750 (this volume).

Iverson, R.M., Dzurisin, D., Gardner, C.A., Gerlach, T.M., LaHusen, R.G., Lisowski, M., Major, J.J., Malone, S.D., Messerich, J.A., Moran, S.C., Pallister, J.S., Qamar, A.I., Schilling, S.P., and Vallance, J.W., 2006, Dynamics of seismogenic volcanic extrusion at Mount St. Helens in 2004–05: Nature, v. 444, no. 7118, p. 439–443, doi:10.1038/nature05322.

Jonientz-Trisler, C., Myers, B., and Power, J.A., 1994, Seismic identification of gas-and-ash explosions at Mount St. Helens—capabilities, limitations, and regional applications, *in* Casadevall, T.J., ed., Volcanic ash and aviation safety; proceedings of the First International Symposium on Volcanic Ash and Aviation Safety: U.S. Geological Survey Bulletin 2047, p. 351–356.

Lahr, J.C., Chouet, B.A., Stephens, C.D., Power, J.A., and Page, R.A., 1994, Earthquake classification, location, and error analysis in a volcanic environment; implications for the magmatic system of the 1989–1990 eruptions at Redoubt Volcano, Alaska: Journal of Volcanology and Geothermal Research, v. 62, nos. 1–4, p. 137–151, doi:10.1016/0377-0273(94)90031-0.

Lees, J.M., 1992, The magma system of Mount St. Helens: non-linear high-resolution P-wave tomography: Journal of Volcanology and Geothermal Research, v. 53, nos. 1–4, p. 103–116.

Lees, J.M., and Crosson, R.S., 1989, Tomographic inversion

for three-dimensional velocity structure at Mount St. Helens using earthquake data: Journal of Geophysical Research, v. 94, p. 5716–5728.

MacCarthy, J.K., and Rowe, C.A., 2005, Automatic scanning detection for characterization of dome-related seismic swarms at Mount St. Helens and their evolution through time [abs]: Eos (American Geophysical Union Transactions), v. 86, Fall Meeting Supplement, V53D-1591.

Major, J.J., Kingsbury, C.G., Poland, M.P., and LaHusen, R.G., 2008, Extrusion rate of the Mount St. Helens lava dome estimated from terrestrial imagery, November 2004–December 2005, chap. 12 *of* Sherrod, D.R., Scott, W.E., and Stauffer, P.H., eds., A volcano rekindled; the renewed eruption of Mount St. Helens, 2004–2006: U.S. Geological Survey Professional Paper 1750 (this volume).

Malone, S.D., 1983, Volcanic earthquakes; examples from Mount St. Helens, *in* Earthquakes—observations, theory and interpretation: Bologna, Italy, Società Italiana di Fisica, p. 436–455.

Malone, S.D., Endo, E.T., Weaver, C.S., and Ramey, J.W., 1981, Seismic monitoring for eruption prediction, *in* Lipman, P.W., and Mullineaux, D.R., eds., The 1980 eruptions of Mount St. Helens, Washington: U.S. Geological Survey Professional Paper 1250, p. 803–813.

Malone, S.D., Boyko, C., and Weaver, C.S., 1983, Seismic precursors to the Mount St. Helens eruptions in 1981 and 1982: Science, v. 221, p. 1376–1378.

Mastin, L.G., 1994, Explosive tephra emissions at Mount St. Helens, 1989–1991; the violent escape of magmatic gas following storms?: Geological Society of America Bulletin, v. 106, no. 2, p. 175–185.

Mastin, L.G., Roeloffs, E., Beeler, N.M., and Quick, J.E., 2008, Constraints on the size, overpressure, and volatile content of the Mount St. Helens magma system from geodetic and dome-growth measurements during the 2004–2006+ eruption, chap. 22 *of* Sherrod, D.R., Scott, W.E., and Stauffer, P.H., eds., A volcano rekindled; the renewed eruption of Mount St. Helens, 2004–2006: U.S. Geological Survey Professional Paper 1750 (this volume).

Matoza, R.S., Hedlin, M.A.H., and Garcés, M.A., 2007, An infrasound array study of Mount St. Helens: Journal of Volcanology and Geothermal Research, v. 160, p. 249–262, doi:10.1016/j.jvolgeores.2006.10.006.

McChesney, P.J., Couchman, M.R., Moran, S.C., Lockhart, A.B., Swinford, K.J., and LaHusen, R.G., 2008, Seismic-monitoring changes and the remote deployment of seismic stations (seismic spider) at Mount St. Helens, 2004–2005, chap. 7 *of* Sherrod, D.R., Scott, W.E., and Stauffer, P.H., eds., A volcano rekindled; the renewed eruption of Mount St. Helens, 2004–2006: U.S. Geological Survey Professional Paper 1750 (this volume).

Mogi, K., 1962, Magnitude-frequency relation for elastic shocks accompanying fractures of various materials and some related problems in earthquakes: Bulletin of the Earthquake Research Institute, v. 40, p. 831–853.

Moran, S.C., 1994, Seismicity at Mount St. Helens, 1987–1992; evidence for repressurization of an active magmatic system: Journal of Geophysical Research, v. 99, no. B3, p. 4341–4354, doi:10.1029/93JB02993.

Moran, S.C., and Malone, S.D., 2004, Seismicity associated with the first month of the 2004 eruption of Mount St. Helens [abs]: Eos (American Geophysical Union Transactions), v. 85, Fall Meeting Supplement, V31E-02.

Moran, S.C., Lees, J.M., and Malone, S.D., 1999, P-wave crustal velocity structure in the greater Mount Rainier area from local earthquake tomography: Journal of Geophysical Research, v. 104, p. 10775–10786.

Moran, S.C., McChesney, P.J., and Lockhart, A.B., 2008, Seismicity and infrasound associated with explosions at Mount St. Helens, 2004–2005, chap. 6 *of* Sherrod, D.R., Scott, W.E., and Stauffer, P.H., eds., A volcano rekindled; the renewed eruption of Mount St. Helens, 2004–2006: U.S. Geological Survey Professional Paper 1750 (this volume).

Musumeci, C., Gresta, S., and Malone, S.D., 2002, Magma system recharge of Mount St. Helens from precise relative hypocenter location of microearthquakes: Journal of Geophysical Research, v. 107, no. B10, 2264, p. ESE 16-1–ESE 16-9, doi:10.1029/2001JB000629.

Neuberg, J.W., Tuffen, H., Collier, L., Green, D., Powell, T., and Dingwell, D., 2006, The trigger mechanism of low-frequency earthquakes on Montserrat: Journal of Volcanology and Geothermal Research, v. 153, nos. 1–2, p. 37–50, doi:10.1016/j.jvolgeores.2005.08.00.

Norris, R.D., 1994, Seismicity of rockfalls and avalanches at three Cascade Range volcanoes; implications for seismic detection of hazardous mass movements: Bulletin of the Seismological Society of America, v. 84, p. 1925–1939.

Okada, H., Watanabe, H. Yamashita, H., and Yokoyama, I., 1981, Seismological significance of the 1977–1978 eruptions and the magma intrusion process of Usu Volcano, Hokkaido: Journal of Volcanology and Geothermal Research, v. 9, p. 311–334.

Pallister, J.S., Hoblitt, R.P., Crandell, D.R., and Mullineaux, D.R., 1992, Mount St. Helens a decade after the 1980 eruptions; magmatic models, chemical cycles, and a revised hazards assessment: Bulletin of Volcanology, v. 54, no. 2, p. 126–146, doi: 10.1007/BF00278003.

Poland, M.P., and Lu, Z., 2008, Radar interferometry observations of surface displacements during pre- and coeruptive periods at Mount St. Helens, Washington, 1992–2005, chap. 18 *of* Sherrod, D.R., Scott, W.E., and Stauffer, P.H., eds., A volcano rekindled; the renewed eruption of Mount St. Helens, 2004–2006: U.S. Geological Survey Professional Paper 1750 (this volume).

Power, J.A., 1988, Seismicity associated with the 1986 eruption of Augustine Volcano, Alaska: Fairbanks, University of Alaska, M.S. thesis, 142 p.

Power, J.A., Lahr, J.C., Page, R.A., Chouet, B.A., Stephens, C.D., Harlow, D.H., Murray, T.L., and Davies, J.N., 1994, Seismic evolution of the 1989–1990 eruption sequence of Redoubt Volcano, Alaska: Journal of Volcanology and Geothermal Research, v. 62, p. 69–94.

Qamar, A.I., St. Lawrence, W., Moore, J.N., and Kendrick, G., 1983, Seismic signals preceding the explosive eruption of Mount St. Helens, Washington, on 18 May 1980: Bulletin of the Seismological Society of America, v. 73, p. 1797–1813.

Qamar, A.I., Malone, S.D., Moran, S.C., Steele, W.P., and Thelen, W.A., 2008, Near-real-time information products for Mount St. Helens—tracking the ongoing eruption, chap. 3 *of* Sherrod, D.R., Scott, W.E., and Stauffer, P.H., eds., A volcano rekindled; the renewed eruption of Mount St. Helens, 2004–2006: U.S. Geological Survey Professional Paper 1750 (this volume).

Reasenberg, P.A., and Oppenheimer, D., 1985, FPFIT, FPPLOT, and FPPAGE: FORTRAN computer programs for calculating and plotting earthquake fault-plane solutions: U.S. Geological Survey Open-File Report 85–739, 109 p.

Rowe, C.A., Thurber, C.H., and White, R.A., 2004, Dome growth behavior at Soufriere Hills Volcano, Montserrat, revealed by relocation of volcanic event swarms, 1995–1996: Journal of Volcanology and Geothermal Research, v. 134, no. 3, p. 199–221.

Scandone, R., and Malone, S.D., 1985, Magma supply, magma discharge, and readjustment of the feeding system of Mount St. Helens during 1980: Journal of Volcanology and Geothermal Research, v. 23, nos. 3–4, p. 239–262, doi:10.1016/0377-0273(85)90036-8.

Schilling, S.P., Thompson, R.A., Messerich, J.A., and Iwatsubo, E.Y., 2008, Use of digital aerophotogrammetry to determine rates of lava dome growth, Mount St. Helens, Washington, 2004–2005, chap. 8 *of* Sherrod, D.R., Scott, W.E., and Stauffer, P.H., eds., A volcano rekindled; the renewed eruption of Mount St. Helens, 2004–2006: U.S. Geological Survey Professional Paper 1750 (this volume).

Schneider, D.J., Vallance, J.W., Wessels, R.L., Logan, M., and Ramsey, M.S., 2008, Use of thermal infrared imaging for monitoring renewed dome growth at Mount St. Helens, 2004, chap. 17 *of* Sherrod, D.R., Scott, W.E., and Stauffer, P.H., eds., A volcano rekindled; the renewed eruption of Mount St. Helens, 2004–2006: U.S. Geological Survey Professional Paper 1750 (this volume).

Scott, W.E., Sherrod, D.R., and Gardner, C.A., 2008, Overview of the 2004 to 2006, and continuing, eruption of Mount St. Helens, Washington, chap. 1 *of* Sherrod, D.R., Scott, W.E., and Stauffer, P.H., eds., A volcano rekindled; the renewed eruption of Mount St. Helens, 2004–2006: U.S. Geological Survey Professional Paper 1750 (this volume).

Shemeta, J., and Weaver, C.S., 1986, Seismicity accompanying the May 18, 1980, eruption of Mount St. Helens, Washington, *in* Keller, S.A.C., ed., Mount St. Helens, five years later: Cheney, Wash., Eastern Washington University Press, p. 44–58.

Swanson, D.A., and Holcomb, R.T., 1990, Regularities in growth of the Mount St. Helens dacite dome, 1980–1986, *in* Fink, J.H., ed., Lava flows and domes, emplacement mechanisms and hazard implications: Berlin, Springer-Verlag, International Association of Volcanology and Chemistry of the Earth's Interior, Proceedings in Volcanology 2, p. 3–24.

Swanson, D.A., Casadevall, T.J., Dzurisin, D., Malone, S.D., Newhall, C.G., and Weaver, C.S., 1983, Predicting eruptions at Mount St. Helens, June 1980 through December 1982: Science, v. 221, no. 4618, p. 1369–1376.

Swanson, D.A., Casadevall, T.J., Dzurisin, D., Malone, S.D., Holcomb, R.T., Newhall, C.G., and Weaver, C.S., 1985, Forecasts and predictions of eruptive activity at Mount St. Helens, USA; 1975–1984: Journal of Geodynamics, v. 3, p. 397–423.

Thelen, W.A., Crosson, R.S., and Creager, K.C., 2008, Absolute and relative locations of earthquakes at Mount St. Helens, Washington, using continuous data; implications for magmatic processes, chap. 4 *of* Sherrod, D.R., Scott, W.E., and Stauffer, P.H., eds., A volcano rekindled; the renewed eruption of Mount St. Helens, 2004–2006: U.S. Geological Survey Professional Paper 1750 (this volume).

Vallance, J.W., Schneider, D.J., and Schilling, S.P., 2008, Growth of the 2004–2006 lava-dome complex at Mount St. Helens, Washington, chap. 9 *of* Sherrod, D.R., Scott, W.E., and Stauffer, P.H., eds., A volcano rekindled; the renewed eruption of Mount St. Helens, 2004–2006: U.S. Geological Survey Professional Paper 1750 (this volume).

Villagómez, D., 2000, Sismícidad del volcán Guagua Pichincha 1998–1999: Quito, Ecuador, Escuela Politécnica Nacional, M.S. thesis.

Vinciguerra, S., Gresta, S., Barbano, M.S., and Distefano, G., 2001, The two behaviours of Mt. Etna Volcano before and after a large intrusive episode; evidences from *b* value and fractal dimension of seismicity: Geophysical Research Letters, v. 28, p. 2257–2260.

Waite, G.P., Chouet, B.A. and Dawson, P.B., 2008, Eruption dynamics at Mount St. Helens imaged from broadband seismic waveforms; interaction of the shallow magmatic and hydrothermal systems: Journal of Geophysical Research, v. 113, B02305, 22 p., doi:10.1029/2007JB005259.

Walder, J.S., Schilling, S.P., Vallance, J.W., and LaHusen, R.G., 2008, Effects of lava-dome growth on the Crater Glacier of Mount St. Helens, Washington, chap. 13 *of* Sherrod, D.R., Scott, W.E., and Stauffer, P.H., eds., A volcano rekindled; the renewed eruption of Mount St. Helens, 2004–2006: U.S. Geological Survey Professional Paper 1750 (this volume).

Weaver, C.S., Grant, W.G., Malone, S.D., and Endo, E.T., 1981, Post-May 18 seismicity; volcanic and tectonic implications, *in* Lipman, P.W., and Mullineaux, D.R., eds., The 1980 eruptions of Mount St. Helens, Washington: U.S. Geological Survey Professional Paper 1250, p. 109–121.

Weaver, C.S., Zollweg, J.E., and Malone, S.D., 1983, Deep earthquakes beneath Mount St. Helens; evidence for magmatic gas transport?: Science, v. 221, p. 1391–1394.

Weaver, C.S., Grant, W.C., and Shemeta, J.E., 1987, Local crustal extension at Mount St. Helens, Washington: Journal of Geophysical Research, v. 92, no. B10, p. 10170–10178.

Wiemer, S., and McNutt, S.R., 1997, Variations in the frequency-magnitude distribution with depth in two volcanic areas—Mount St. Helens, Washington, and Mt. Spurr, Alaska: Geophysical Research Letters, v. 24, p. 189–192.

Appendix 1. PNSN Fault-Plane Solutions, 09/23/04–12/31/05

This appendix comprises numerous plots showing first motions and preferred fault-plane solutions for well-constrained events (maximum azimuthal gap <135°, nearest station <1 km, and at least 10 picked phase arrivals) (fig. 25) in the PNSN catalog from September 24 to November 27, 2004, and for "big" events from November 27, 2004 to December 31, 2005 (fig. 26). We did not review fault-plane solutions from the PNSN catalog except those for the "big" events. Only those fault-plane solutions with at least 10 polarities are shown. Note that all fault-plane solutions times are in Coordinated Universal Time (UTC), in contrast to the local time convention used in the rest of this paper. All fault-plane solutions were determined using the FPFIT computer program (Reasenberg and Oppenheimer, 1985).

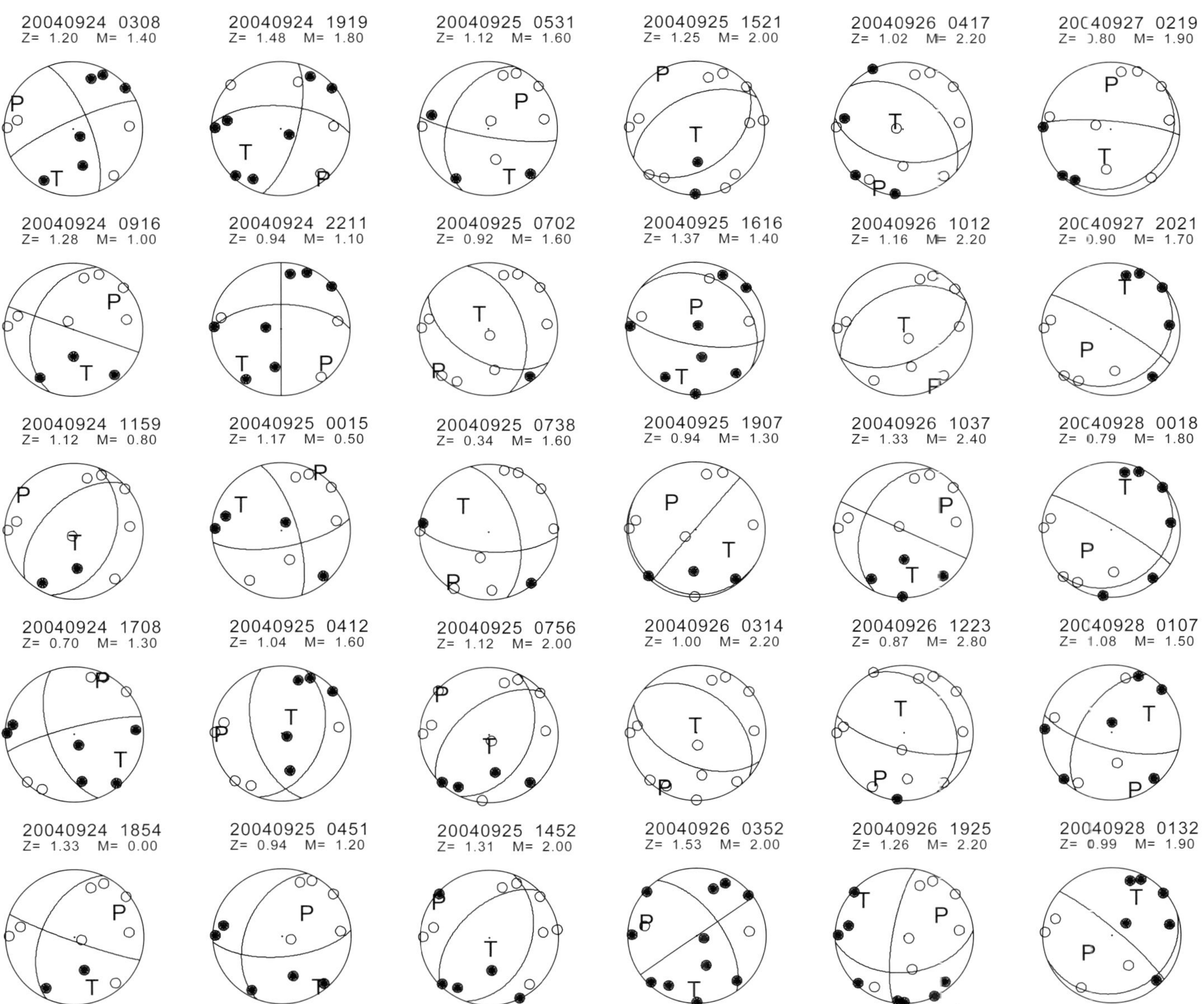

Figure 25. Fault-plane solutions for 161 earthquakes occurring at Mount St. Helens during the period from Sept. 24 to Oct. 11, 2004. P, compressional axis; T, tensional axis. Open circles correspond to dilatational (down) first motions, closed circles to compressional (up) first motions. Each solution is coded for date and time (UTC) in this format: YYYYMMDD hhmm. Z, depth, in kilometers; M, magnitude.

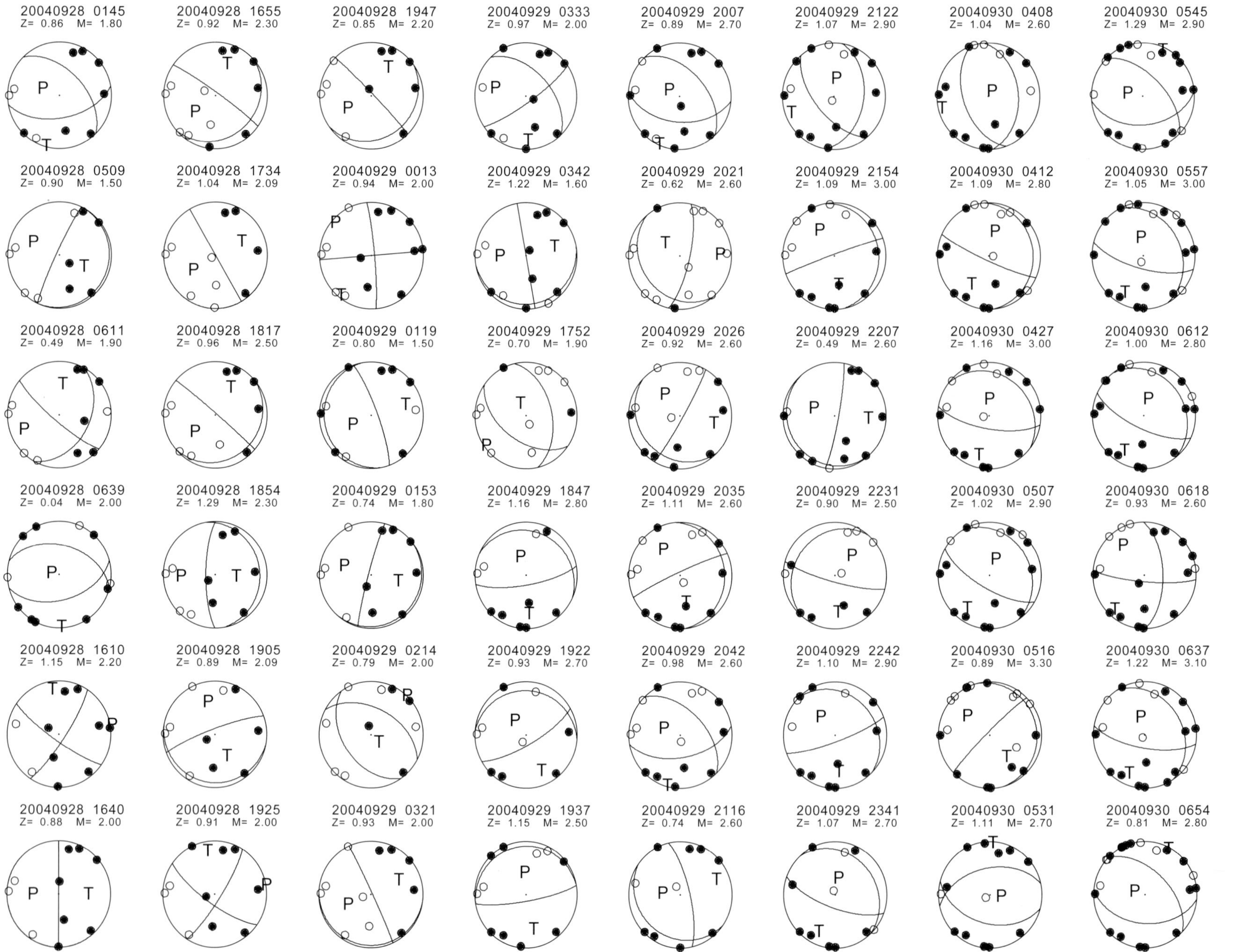

Figure 25—Continued.

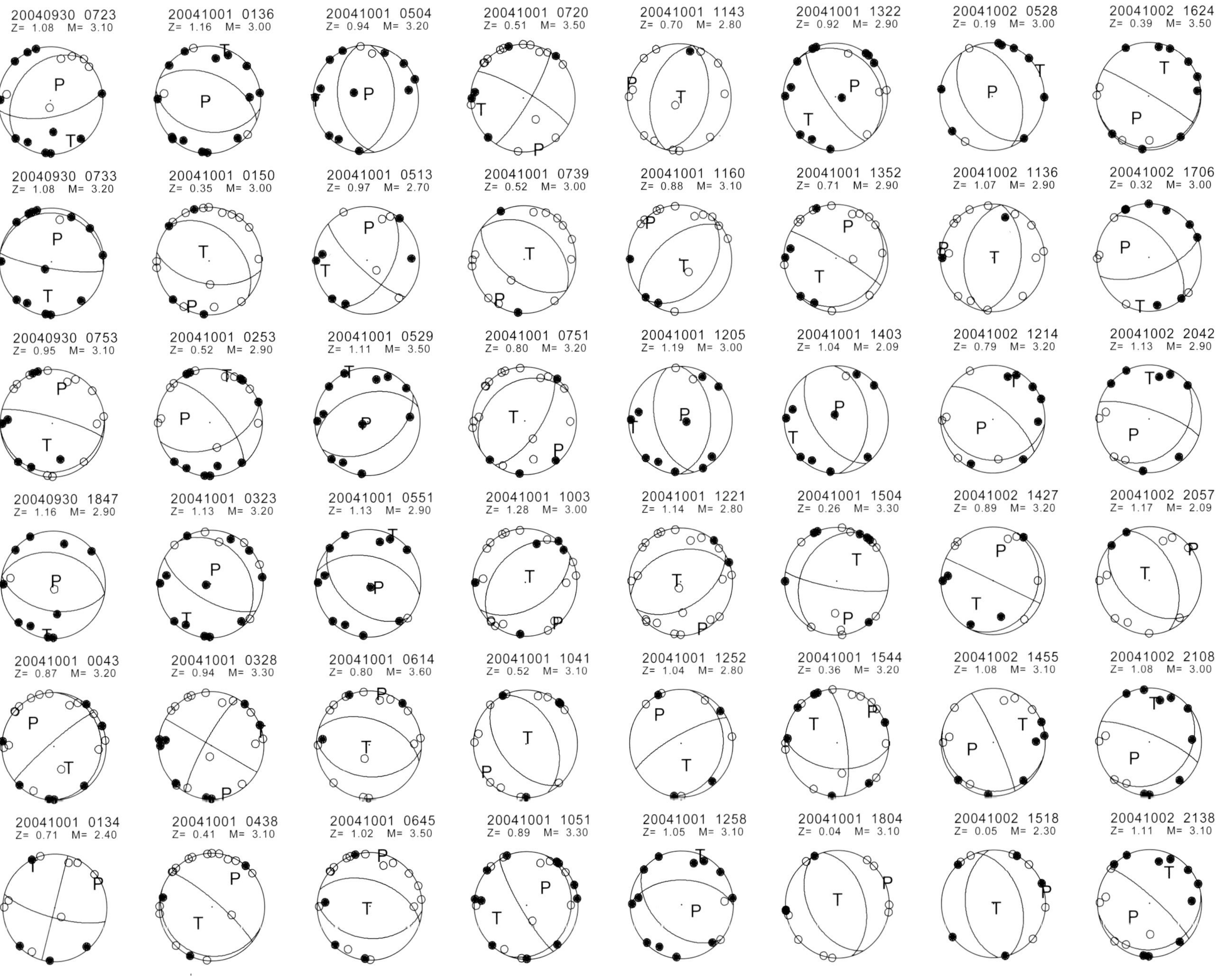

Figure 25—Continued.

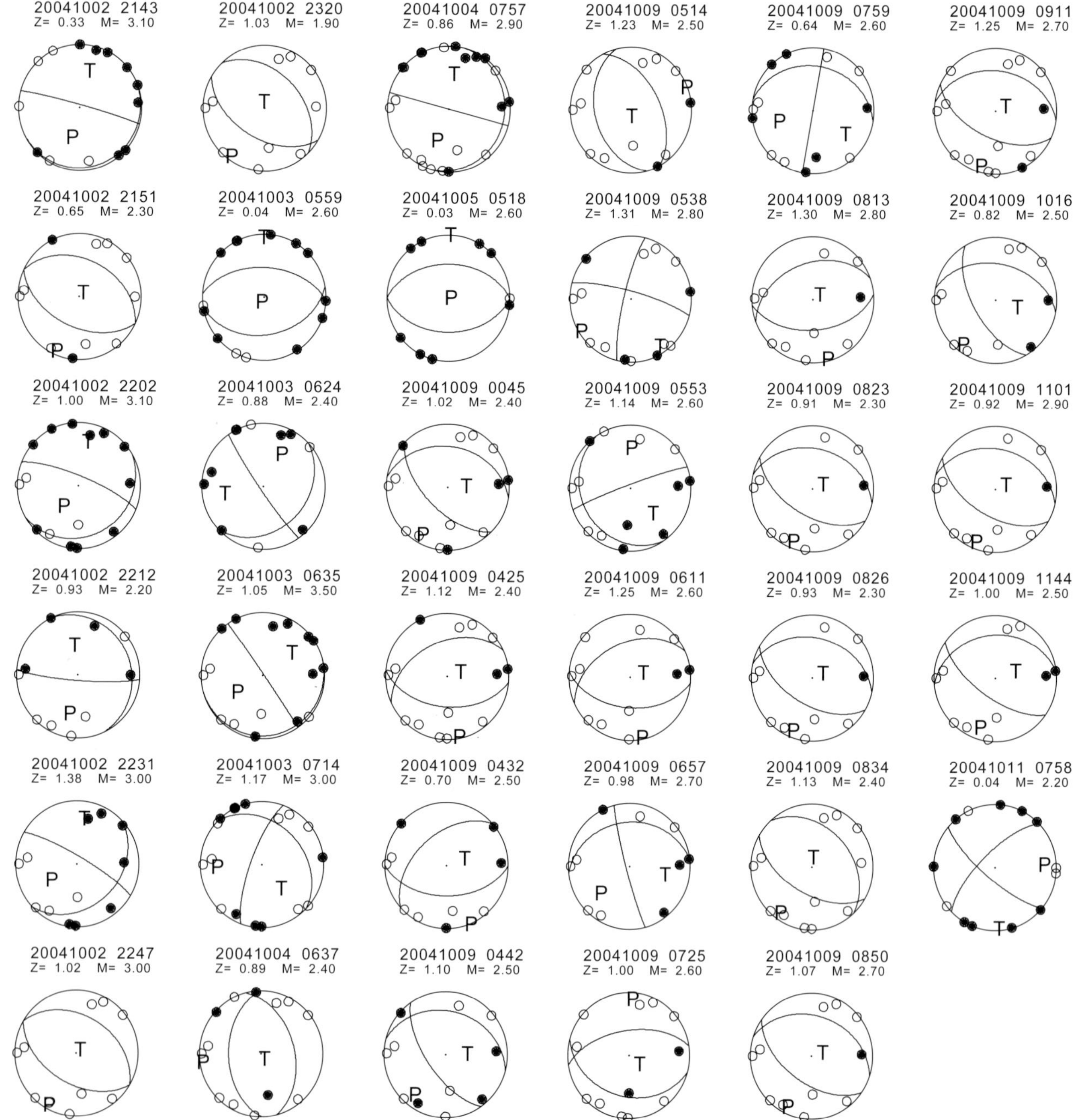

Figure 25—Continued.

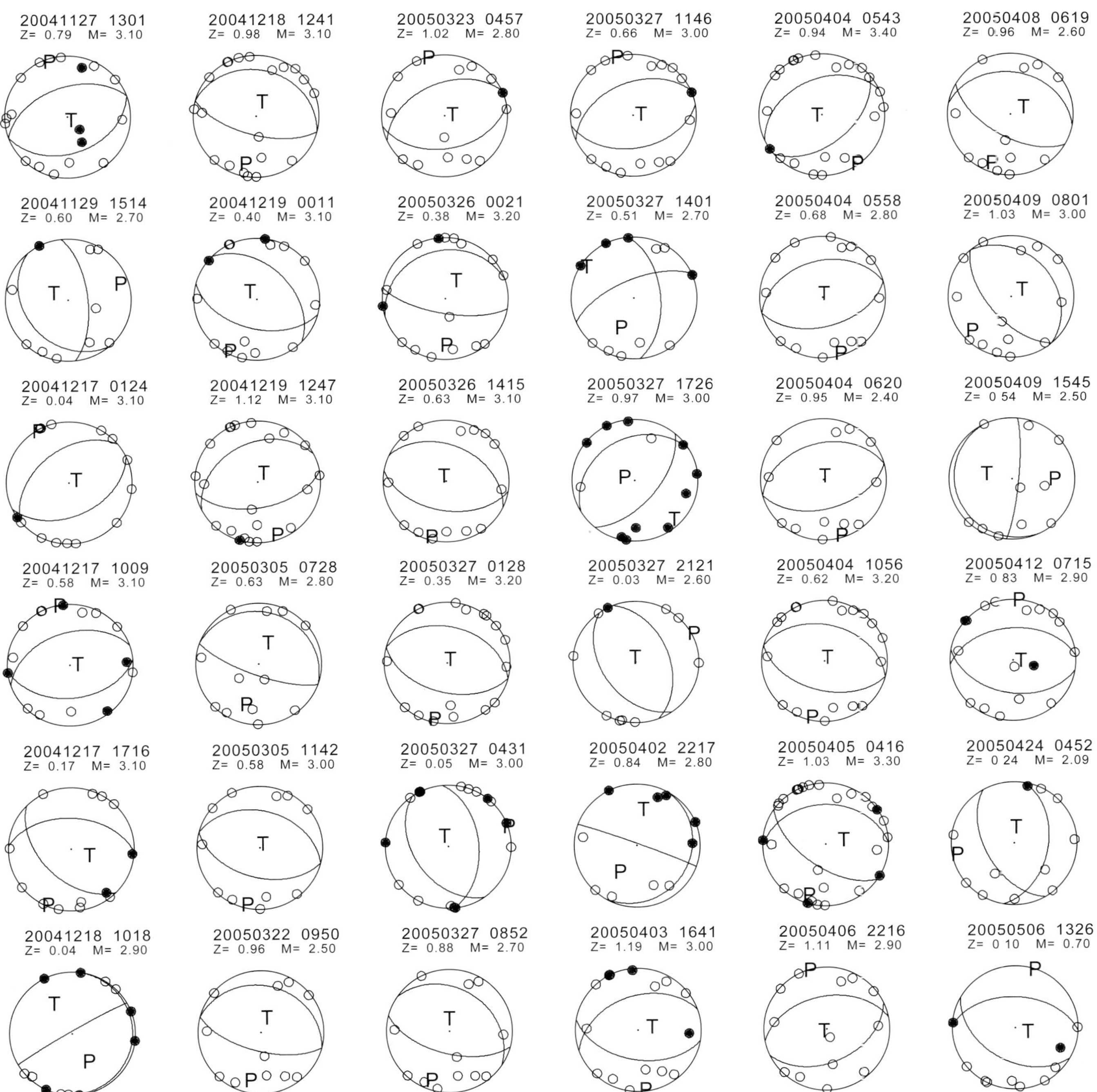

Figure 26. Fault-plane solutions for 55 earthquakes (M_d 0.7–3.4) occurring at Mount St. Helens during the period from Nov. 27, 2004, to Oct. 7, 2005. P, compressional axis; T, tensional axis. Open circles correspond to dilatational (down) first motions, closed circles to compressional (up) first motions. Each solution is coded for date and time (UTC) in this format: YYYYMMDD hhmm. Z, depth, in kilometers; M, magnitude.

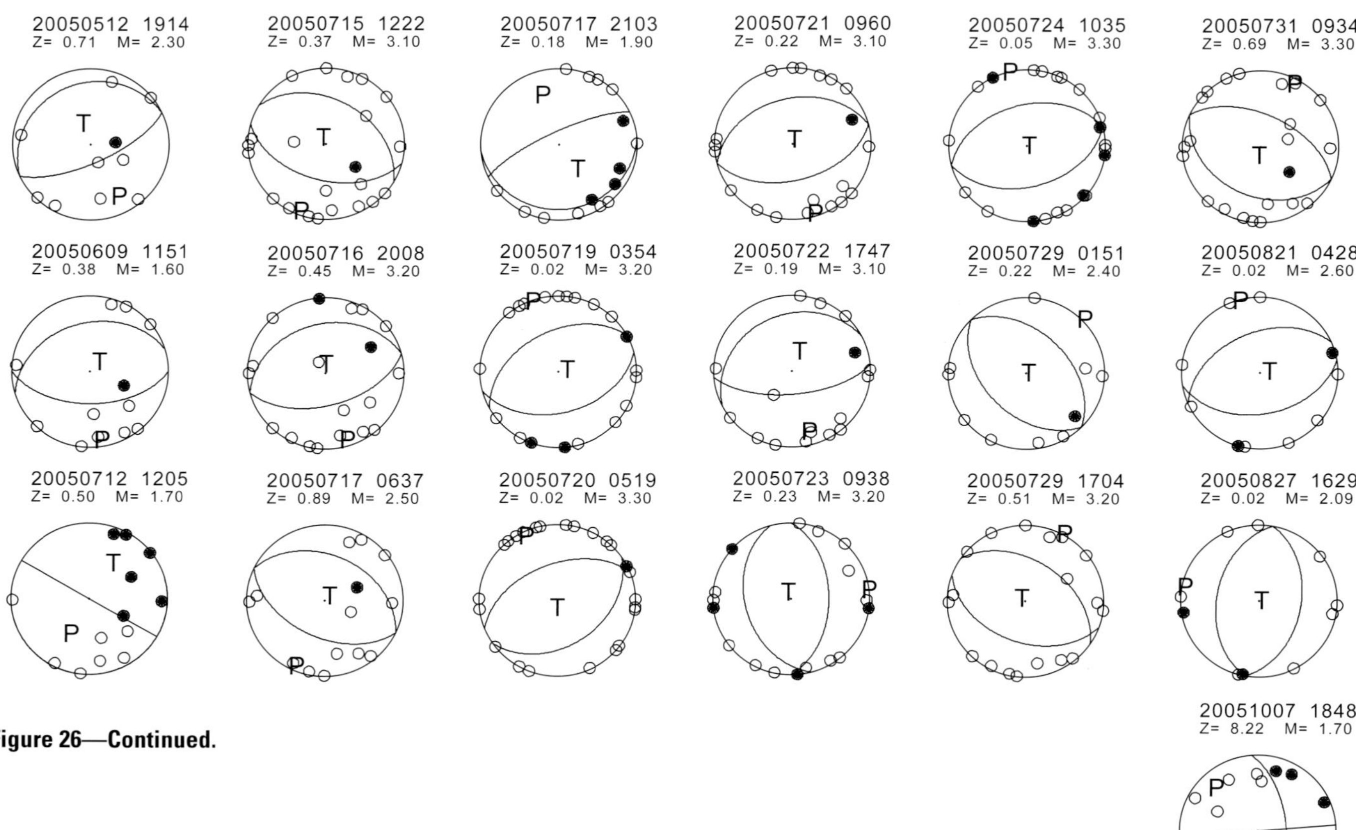

Figure 26—Continued.

Appendix 2. Automated Event Detection

Analyst-driven earthquake location quickly became infeasible as a means for tracking the course of the eruption because it was too slow (Qamar and others, this volume, chap. 3), so over subsequent months we developed methods for automatically detecting events and recording several event parameters of interest. Figures 5, 13, and 14 show results from one such method, a standard triggering algorithm that uses the ratio of average seismic amplitudes computed over short- and long-term time windows, as applied to station HSR (fig. 1). We chose HSR over other stations for three principal reasons: (1) it is a sensitive site that usually records even small earthquakes cleanly; (2) wind noise is usually insignificant; and (3) after a gain reduction on October 4, 2004, no changes were made to the site (McChesney and others, this volume, chap. 7). We used averaging windows of 1 s and 8 s for the short- and long-term averages and a triggering ratio of 2.3 that was determined to be optimal for HSR through trial and error. To avoid multiple triggers from the same event, we skipped forward 6 s after each trigger. We also devised station-specific algorithms for distinguishing between noise glitches (including telemetry and/or Internet dropouts, radio interference, and calibration pulses) and events, although some glitches still made it through our filters. To test the impact of such noise-induced event detections, we visually scanned through helicorder plots for selected time periods and removed glitches that had been recorded as events. Although the resulting plots were cleaner, the fundamental trends were unchanged; in essence, noise was overwhelmed by the shear number of earthquakes.

For each detected event we recorded the peak amplitude over the next 6 s (usually the S wave at HSR), the time gap between successive events, and the normalized power spectra for the first 256 samples following the P-wave arrival (or 2.56 s with the 100-Hz sample rate used by the PNSN and CVO for all short-period stations). We chose to look only at spectra for the first 2.56 s (256 samples) following the event trigger, as full-event spectra were dominated by surface-wave energy and were thus not useful in detecting subtle changes in source spectra, particularly between hybrid and LF events. We only show spectra for events with amplitudes greater than 300 counts (M_d ~1.0), because our algorithm commonly triggered on the S-wave for events smaller than this threshold. The resulting spectra plots, which we referred to as ESAM (Earthquake Spectral AMplitude) plots, proved to be more useful for assessing changes in earthquake source frequency than standard spectrograms of continuous seismic data, particularly because eruption-related seismicity was dominated by discrete seismic events.

A Volcano Rekindled: The Renewed Eruption of Mount St. Helens, 2004–2006
Edited by David R. Sherrod, William E. Scott, and Peter H. Stauffer
U.S. Geological Survey Professional Paper 1750, 2008

Chapter 3

Near-Real-Time Information Products for Mount St. Helens—Tracking the Ongoing Eruption

By Anthony I. Qamar[1*], Stephen D. Malone[1], Seth C. Moran[2], William P. Steele[1], and Weston A. Thelen[1]

Abstract

The rapid onset of energetic seismicity on September 23, 2004, at Mount St. Helens caused seismologists at the Pacific Northwest Seismic Network and the Cascades Volcano Observatory to quickly improve and develop techniques that summarized and displayed seismic parameters for use by scientists and the general public. Such techniques included webicorders (Web-based helicorder-like displays), graphs showing RSAM (real-time seismic amplitude measurements), RMS (root-mean-square) plots, spectrograms, location maps, automated seismic-event detectors, focal mechanism solutions, automated approximations of earthquake magnitudes, RSAM-based alarms, and time-depth plots for seismic events. Many of these visual-information products were made available publicly as Web pages generated and updated routinely. The graphs and maps included short written text that explained the concepts behind them, which increased their value to the nonseismologic community that was tracking the eruption. Laypeople could read online summaries of the scientific interpretations and, if they chose, review some of the basic data, thereby providing a better understanding of the data used by scientists to make interpretations about ongoing eruptive activity, as well as a better understanding of how scientists worked to monitor the volcano.

Introduction

The renewed activity of Mount St. Helens, which started in September 2004, caused the Pacific Northwest Seismic Network (PNSN) and the U.S. Geological Survey's Cascades Volcano Observatory (CVO) to rapidly adjust routine monitoring procedures and activities in order to accommodate additional data volume, data types, and real-time monitoring requirements. The speed with which the precursory earthquake swarm developed, the sheer number of earthquakes involved, and the need for rapid analysis and interpretation resulted in many changes being made to what had become routine processing procedures developed over the preceding years. The goal of providing accurate and timely interpretation of the evolving sequence was driven by the need of the emergency-response community to mitigate possible hazards and by intense public interest, as indicated by the horde of media that descended on any site where information might be available (Driedger and others, this volume, chap. 24). Through the precursory seismic swarm, the initial minor explosions, and the subsequent dome-building phase, seismic processing and display techniques were developed or expanded to help provide relevant information to the wide variety of users. This paper documents these techniques, focusing on why and how they were developed and what they contributed at the time to monitoring efforts.

Preexistence of Webicorders

Following the end of the previous eruption of Mount St. Helens in October 1986, seismicity at the volcano was monitored using standard seismic techniques, including earthquake locations and visual monitoring of continuous seismic records in the form of helicorders and webicorders. Data from 12 short-period, analog seismic stations were telemetered to the Pacific Northwest Seismic Network (PNSN) headquarters at the University of Washington (UW) for recording and analysis. A subset was also telemetered to the Cascades Volcano Observatory (CVO) for monitoring purposes.

The PNSN routinely processed events from Mount St. Helens through an event-triggered recording system as part

[1] Pacific Northwest Seismic Network, Department of Earth and Space Sciences, University of Washington, Box 351310, Seattle, WA 98195

[2] U.S. Geological Survey, 1300 SE Cardinal Court, Vancouver, WA 98683

* Deceased

of the routine catalog generation for the whole Pacific Northwest. These catalogs were originally only released in quarterly reports and distributed by surface mail. With the rapid evolution of the World-Wide Web, in the early 1990s the PNSN created a public Web site (www.pnsn.org) for online distribution of epicenter catalogs, maps, and other derived information products on earthquakes and volcanoes. As is common for many seismic networks, the PNSN also provided near-real-time Web images of selected seismograms, referred to as webicorder plots (fig. 1).

By 2004, webicorder plots were being produced for more than 60 of the approximately 250 PNSN seismic stations, including several Mount St. Helens stations. As soon as seismic unrest was recognized at Mount St. Helens (September 23, 2004), additional stations there were added to the volcano webicorder list at the expense of stations at other volcanoes; processing constraints limited the total number of webicorders that could be accommodated at any one time.

The webicorder plots were quickly discovered by many members of the public. By September 28, the number of hits on the PNSN departmental Web server was causing a substantial slowing of computer processing and increased Web-page delivery times. Because of the obvious public interest and the PNSN's mission to provide near-real-time information to the public, the PNSN requested assistance from the University of Washington Computers and Communications (CAC) group. Within 18 hours of our request the CAC had a high-capacity Web server connected directly to external high-volume routers to mirror our main pages. Within a few days this server was servicing requests at rates as high as 250,000 per hour, and the CAC group expanded the system to dual server machines with load-balancing routing. The first week's activity totaled more

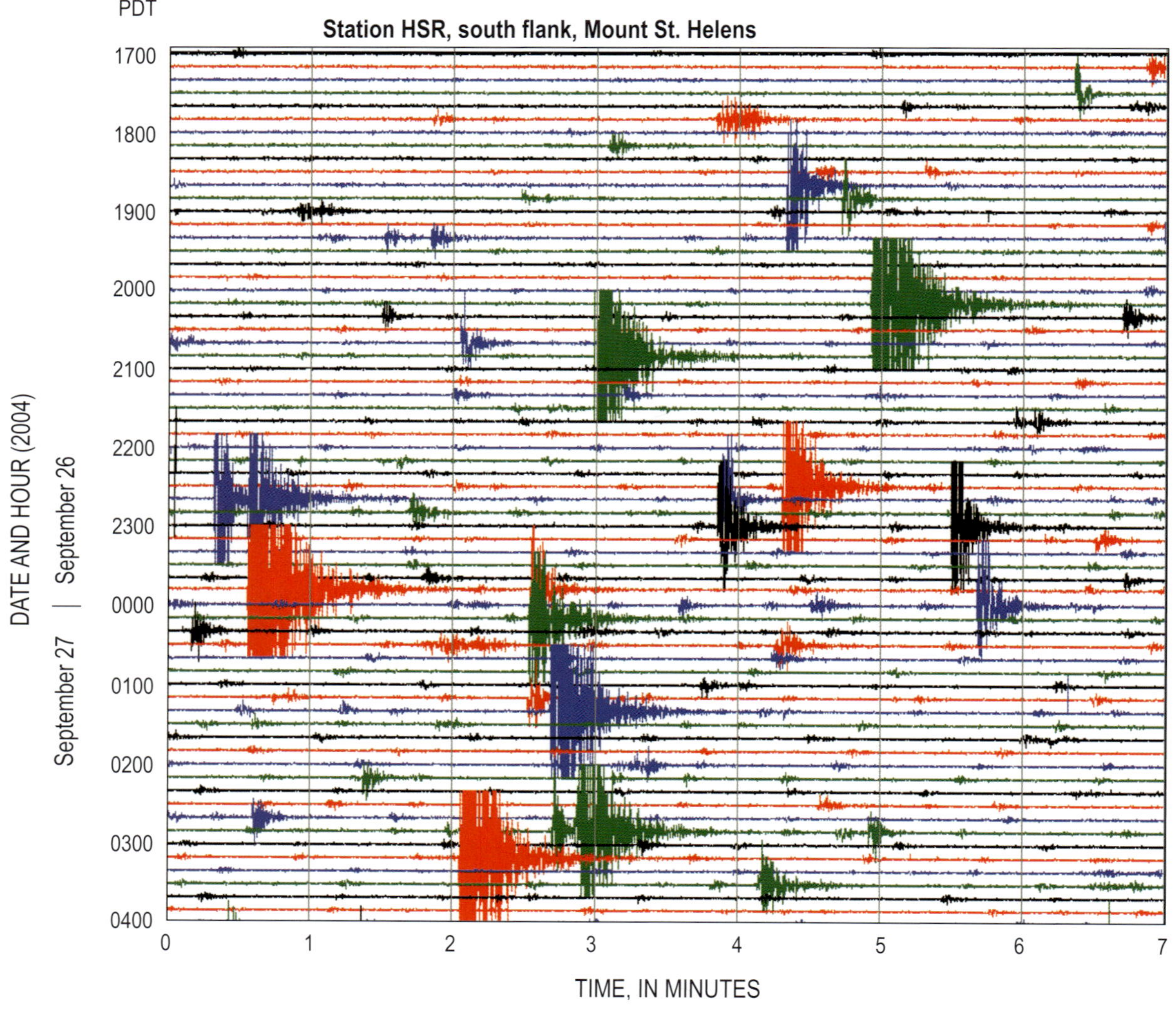

Figure 1. Part of a webicorder plot from station HSR on the south flank of Mount St. Helens from September 26 and 27, 2004. Time advances from left to right and top to bottom, as if reading a book. Each line begins a new 10-minute cycle (the last 3 minutes of each cycle are clipped off here), and gray vertical lines mark 1-minute intervals; color variations are merely to aid the eye in separating traces. Webicorder plots such as this one were updated in real time, available online before and during the 2004 restlessness and ensuing eruption, and were very popular with the public.

than 23 million hits, which translates to roughly 5 million complete pages of information served.

In addition to establishing a mirror site, the PNSN also established a semiprivate (nonlinked but otherwise open) Web server for use by the scientific staff at UW, CVO, and other institutions involved in monitoring the evolving crisis. A password-protected Web server at CVO hosted additional webicorders and other seismicity-related plots. The mix of public and private Web servers enabled us to satisfy the public's need for information while maintaining real-time data-sharing capabilities between CVO and the PNSN. Given the physical separation between the PNSN (located in Seattle, Wash.) and CVO (290 km south in Vancouver, Wash.), the capability for real-time data sharing was critical for effective telephone discussions between CVO and UW staff regarding the evolution of the unrest and eruption.

Real-Time Seismic Amplitude Measurements (RSAM)

Webicorders were valuable for seismologists to qualitatively gauge changes in event type, frequency, and size over the previous minutes to hours, but other tools were necessary to provide a quantitative basis for tracking seismicity changes through time. One such tool, which was quickly implemented at CVO (September 23), was the plotting of real-time seismic amplitude measurement (RSAM) values (Endo and Murray, 1991) (fig. 2). RSAM plots show the rectified amplitude of ground motion averaged over specified time intervals, commonly 10 minutes. Rather than focusing on individual events, RSAM provides a simplified but useful measure of the overall level of seismic activity. RSAM has become a widely used tool in volcano observatories around the world because it readily and quantitatively reflects changes in number and size of earthquakes, tremor, and background noise, each or all of which may be related to changes in volcanic activity. As a result of their previous widespread use, RSAM plots were generally well understood by all scientists at CVO and the PNSN.

The Earthworm seismic-data acquisition and processing system (Johnson and others, 1995; U.S. Geological Survey, 2006) is used both at CVO and at UW for the collection and analysis of seismic data. The "ew2rsam" module, a part of the Earthworm system, was used in the Mount St. Helens crisis to generate RSAM values in real time and plot them on multistation graphs at intervals ranging from several days to several months. Such multistation plots make it easier to determine whether seismic-amplitude changes result from local effects at each station (such as wind noise) or from volcanic processes. The RSAM plots were particularly important for recognizing trends when seismicity intensified on September 26, because webicorder plots for stations on or near the edifice became increasingly saturated and difficult to interpret (Moran and others, this volume, chap. 2).

Root-Mean-Square (RMS) Plots

The usefulness of the RSAM plots inspired the creation at the PNSN of root-mean-square (RMS) plots (fig. 2). Rather than just plotting the average of the rectified signal, these plots show the square root of the sum of squares of the signal averaged over fixed time intervals. Also, different plotting styles for the CVO RSAM and the PNSN RMS were used to emphasize different aspects of seismicity changes. Whereas the RSAM plots connect the points of each average with a line, the RMS plots just show individual averages over a fixed window length as isolated points. Such plots were routinely made for averaging windows of 1 minute and 10 minutes and posted

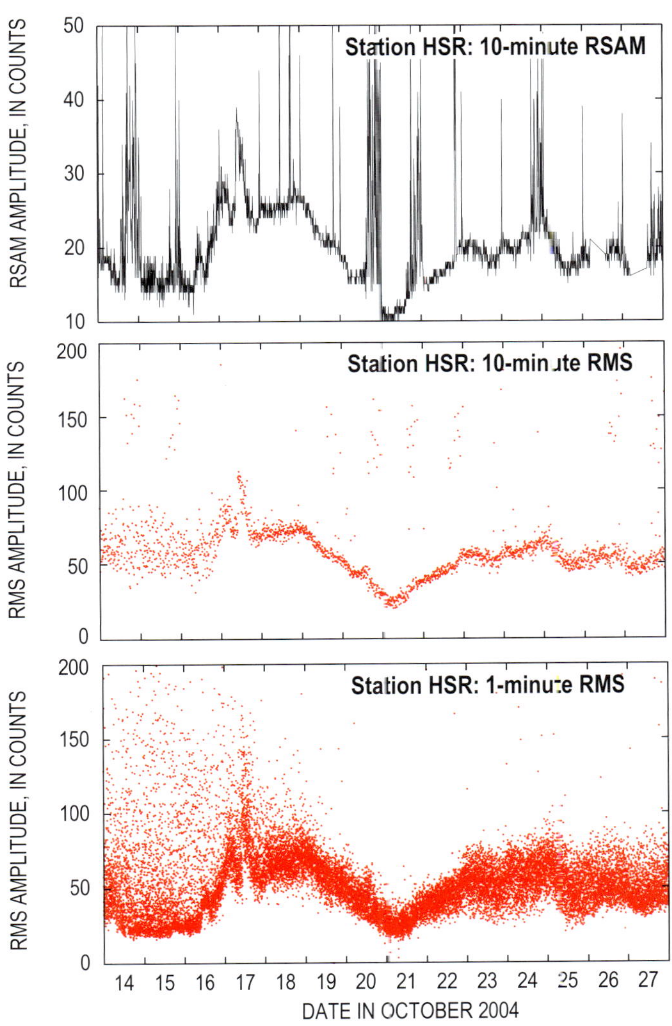

Figure 2. Real-time seismic amplitude measurement (RSAM, top) and root-mean-square (RMS, middle and bottom) plots for seismic signal levels from station HSR during mid- to late October 2004, early in the eruption. Besides the different algorithm to generate the points, plotting characteristics are also different to emphasize different aspects of the activity. Note how the 10-minute and 1-minute RMS plots differ in resolution for the variability of seismic activity.

in nearly real time on the PNSN public Web page. Although the RSAM and RMS plots generally show similar trends, the RMS plots can isolate changes caused by a few large events from cases in which there were an increased number of moderate-size events. From what we know, the inclusion of these plots on the PNSN public Web pages was the first time anywhere that reduced data, other than earthquake locations, were automatically released to the public in real time over the course of a volcanic eruption.

A modification of the RMS plotting routine was developed later in the eruption to show the largest and smallest RMS values determined over a specific time interval. For these plots, RMS values were computed every 5 s and only the largest and smallest during a 30-minute period were selected to plot. In effect these plots track the largest earthquakes and the lowest background level. The maximum-value RMS plots were used for tracking changes in maximum earthquake size over periods of days to weeks, whereas the minimum-value RMS plots were used for detecting elevated background levels that could have represented volcanic tremor (fig. 3).

Spectrograms

Spectrograms, sometimes called "Seismic Spectral Amplitude Measurements" (SSAM) (Rogers and Stephens, 1995) are plots of signal frequency versus time in which color or intensity is used to display the relative strength of a signal in a frequency band (fig. 4). Seismic spectrograms are generated by taking the Fourier spectrum of a fixed time window of signal (1 minute on 12-hour spectrograms at UW and 2.5 s on 10-minute spectrograms at CVO), smoothing the spectrum, and then plotting the amplitude as a color (warm for high amplitude, cool for low) on the vertical frequency axis.

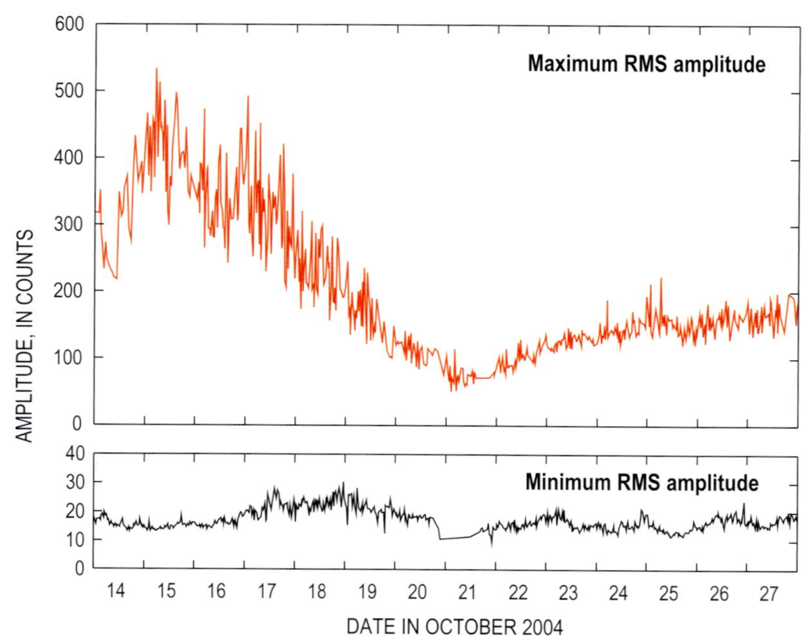

Figure 3. Maximum root-mean-square (RMS, top) and minimum RMS (bottom) plots for seismic-signal levels from station HSR during mid- to late October 2004, early in the eruption. Time period same as in figure 2. Minimum RMS shows background levels, which increased and diminished over roughly weekly intervals. Maximum RMS shows a substantial decrease in large earthquakes during this period.

Spectrograms for different sets of stations were being created at UW (12 hours per plot) and at CVO (10 minutes per plot) before September 23, 2004. The spectrograms added little to the interpretation of event types in the first few days of the seismic buildup. By September 26, however, they became useful for recognizing the decrease in higher frequencies as the earthquake sequence progressed from predominantly volcano-tectonic events, with their wide spectrum, through hybrids to dominantly low-frequency events, described by some as long-period (LP) events (Moran and others, this volume, chap. 2; Thelen and others, this volume, chap. 4). These changes of earthquake character were obvious on seismograms of individual events, but the spectrograms allowed us to track changes over time as well. Spectrograms also aided in distinguishing rockfalls, which have broad spectra and long durations, from small, emergent earthquakes. Spectrograms have continued to play an important role in the subsequent years of dome building, because they display variations in seismicity that correspond to different types of events.

Event Processing

At the PNSN, locations and magnitudes of earthquakes in the Pacific Northwest are routinely determined by manual review of waveforms selected by the Earthworm automatic event-triggering-and-recording system. This system uses a detector algorithm that determines a station "trigger" based on the ratio of short-term average over long-term average (STA/LTA) exceeding a specific threshold. Several station triggers must be active at roughly the same time from a subnetwork of nearby stations for the system to declare an event. This criterion helps to discriminate seismic events of real interest from noise bursts on individual stations. The triggering algorithm is tuned to be sensitive, so that very few events of interest are missed, at the cost of having many false triggers. Such a triggering system, in one form or another, has worked well since 1980, having detected for processing more than 100,000 earthquakes between 1980 and 2004.

With the onset of the Mount St. Helens seismic swarm in late September 2004, the routine processing procedures for the PNSN quickly were swamped with data. The automatic system triggered and recorded the early earthquakes with magnitudes as small as $M_d = -1.0$. Event triggering rates for the whole network went from an average of 2–5 events per hour (more than 50 percent noise triggers) before the swarm onset to 6–10 per hour by the end of the second day and to 25–40 per hour by the end of the third day. Soon thereafter the system was in an almost continuously triggered state. By the end of the second day, more than 250 events had been processed, and by the third day the analysis staff could not keep up with manually processing all triggered events. In addition to the burden of reviewing the triggered events, the volume of waveform data was filling available disk space, forcing us to move unprocessed data to tape and other media. Triage was necessary to ensure that at least a reasonable sampling of events were manually reviewed and that no trace data were lost. The task was twofold: first, we trained additional staff and students in the basic process and divided review tasks among them; then we experimented with different trigger parameters to achieve a representative, but not complete selection of events for manual processing.

After the first two months, with seismic activity continuing at a fairly high rate and the potential for a long-lasting eruption becoming evident, we changed the procedures in such a way that we could review the data for significant changes but process in detail only a selection of the larger or impulsive events. For this we started generating hour-long, sequential artificial trigger files of only Mount St. Helens stations, with a display order based on distance from the vent so that the waveforms could be easily scanned for events of interest and for changes in event or background signal characteristics. The trigger threshold for the automatic triggering system was raised for the Mount St. Helens subnet so that only larger events would generate a complete event trigger. This procedure sped up the routine analysis and provided a better way of detecting subtle changes in event types or characteristics, because an analyst could quickly scan through all of the data and easily see changes in both large and small events.

The hypocenter distribution determined by standard processing of well-recorded earthquakes changed very little over the course of the seismic restlessness and ensuing eruptive sequence. Hypocenter depths decreased during the first two weeks of restlessness from 2–3 km deep to less than 1 km. The scatter in epicenters is comparable to variation arising from picking errors. Some of the variation in locations can be attributed to changes in station configuration. Several times during the sequence, no station was located within 1.5 km of the source area because of station outages resulting from explosions, and thus depth control, in particular, was poor. Subsequent specialized analysis shows a much tighter clustering of hypocenters than that determined during the height of the sequence (Thelen and others, this volume, chap. 4).

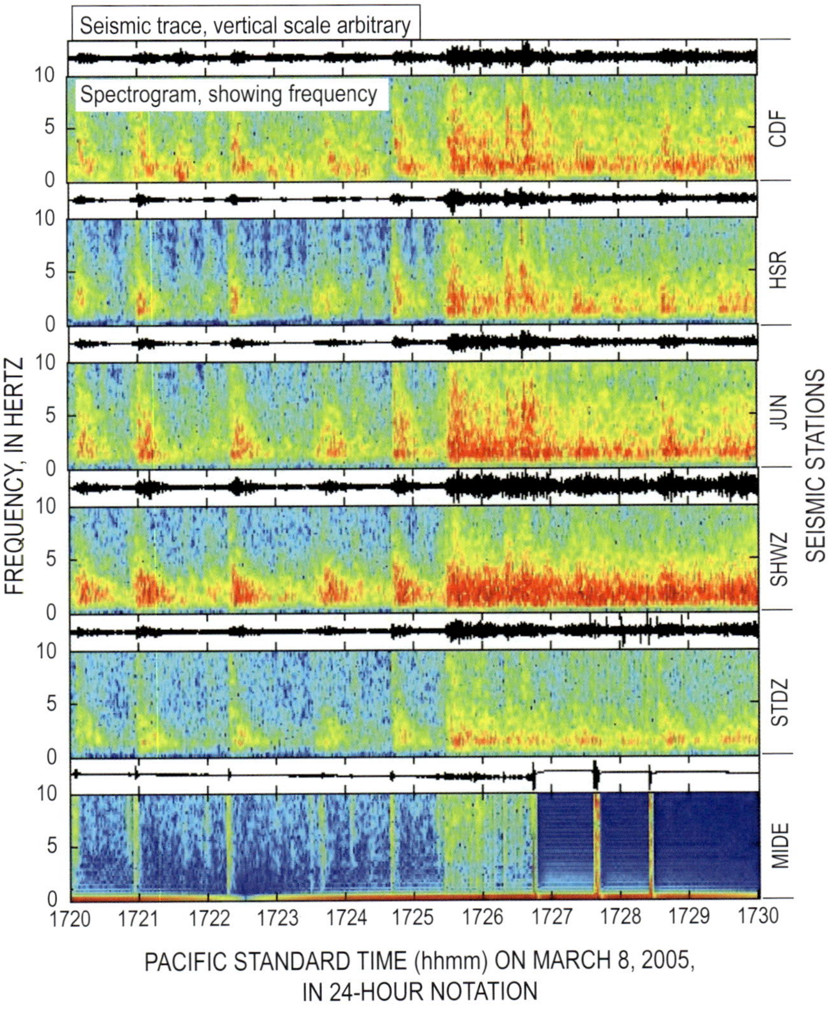

Figure 4. Sample spectrograms from six stations for a 10-minute period on March 8, 2005 (local date). Shown for each station are conventional seismogram (upper line trace) and corresponding spectrogram (color spectrum). Periodic earthquakes characterize the record until about 17:25:30 (1:25:30 UTC), when an explosion at the vent marks onset of sustained, low-frequency tremor. Station MIDE, lowermost of graphs, lost signal sporadically and then completely, owing to thick, airborne ash that interrupted radio transmission.

Automatic Trace Processing

Once it became apparent that the dominant seismic signals were from very regular earthquakes—so regular that they were named "drumbeat" earthquakes—we felt a need for tools to track the rate and type of individual earthquakes. A modification of an event-triggering algorithm was developed to detect characteristics of individual events. This algorithm was based on a ratio of short-term and long-term averages of RMS values computed at 5-s intervals for a key subset of close-in stations with good signal-to-noise ratios. The onset of an event was reliably detected, but determining the end of one event so that the algorithm would de-trigger and be ready for the next event required some tuning of parameters. Once an event was declared, several parameters, including its peak amplitude, average RMS value, and peak frequency, were determined from the original waveforms. The event was not located in the traditional sense, but an effective automatic event catalog was generated that included time, size, and general frequency content.

Focal Mechanisms

Focal mechanisms are traditionally difficult to obtain in volcanic areas because the emergent arrivals typical of low-frequency earthquakes and the high attenuation within the edifice result in low signal-to-noise ratios at more distant stations. Additionally, at Mount St. Helens, earthquakes located at shallow depth in the edifice are mostly small, contributing to poor signal-to-noise ratios. Shallow hypocenters mean that sampling the entire focal sphere, a requirement for a well-constrained focal mechanism, is difficult. Determination of focal mechanisms is therefore restricted to the relatively few large events for which good first motions are available on many stations. Typically focal mechanisms were generated at the PNSN during the event-location process by picking polarities (up or down) of the first motion. A modification of the program "FPFIT"(Reasenberg and Oppenheimer, 1985) was used to fit focal planes for a double-couple solution when there were 10 or more picked polarities. An unusual aspect of Mount St. Helens earthquakes is that a vast majority of first motions are dilatations. Many events have dilatations on all stations, giving the impression of an implosive or tensile source. However, because of poor sampling of the focal sphere, it is sometimes possible to fit a double-couple solution even to these cases. Figure 5 shows examples of four typical events with predominantly "all down" first motions. Of these four events only one clearly does not have a possible double couple solution.

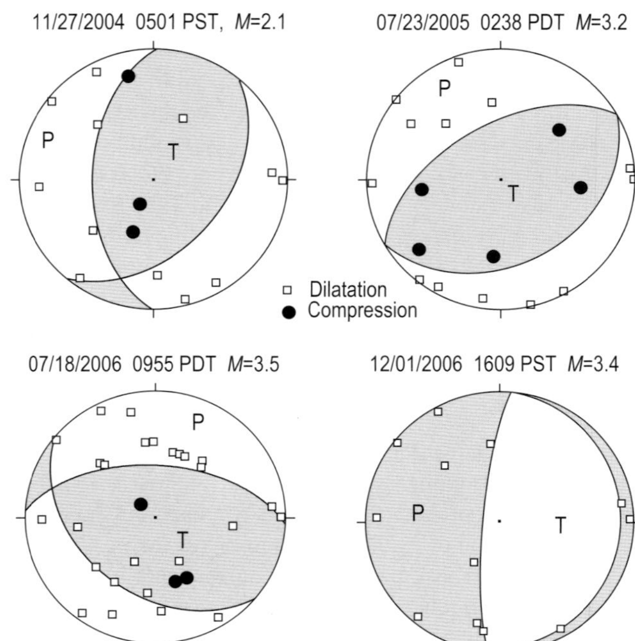

Figure 5. Examples of focal mechanisms determined from four of the many larger, well-recorded events. All such events are located within a few hundred meters of the vent. Note that while almost all polarities are dilatations, double-couple solutions can be fit in some cases. In other cases, such as the event of July 18, 2006, no double-couple solution is possible without many (five) inconsistent polarities.

Event Magnitudes

Routine earthquake processing by the PNSN uses coda duration to compute magnitudes (Crosson, 1972). For most tectonic earthquakes a consistent linear relation exists between the log of the coda duration and the local magnitude, M_L. However, this relation breaks down for earthquakes recorded on Cascade Range volcanoes. For shallow earthquakes in particular, the coda duration is much longer than expected for a given magnitude. Two calibrated broadband stations were installed near Mount St. Helens in October 2004, early in the eruption (McChesney and others, this volume, chap. 7). By deconvolving their known instrument responses and then convolving a Wood-Anderson response, equivalent maximum-trace amplitudes on standardized Wood-Anderson seismograms could be calculated. The resulting local magnitude (M_L) was determined for a suite of earthquakes over the magnitude range 0.5–3.4 (fig. 6). Coda durations for the larger events, mostly picked on stations distant from the volcano, gave duration magnitudes (M_d) comparable to the local magnitude (M_L). For smaller events, however, M_d is often grossly overestimated owing to the extended codas generated by the volcanic earthquakes recorded at stations on volcanic rocks.

Even though the coda duration magnitudes overestimate the true magnitude of the earthquake, coda magnitudes were still measured for located earthquakes to give a quantitative measure of the relative sizes of earthquakes at Mount St. Helens. Codas for the calculation of magnitude are measured only on stations off the edifice (beyond a 5-km radius) to minimize the effect of the extended codas.

Special Web Pages

For many years the PNSN Web site has maintained topical Web pages for all of the monitored Cascade Range volcanoes. Besides some general descriptive text for each volcano and links to the more extensive descriptions on CVO Web pages, these pages provide plots of epicenters, depth versus time, and energy release versus time at three different time scales. The plots have always been based on routine processing of earthquakes located at a volcano. During inter-eruption periods and for minor seismic swarms, these pages continue to be useful for seismologists and informative for the general public. As the current seismic sequence escalated, however, the plots often became outdated because the routine processing (and thus the catalog) was greatly delayed or incomplete. Thus the utility of these special pages to assist in the interpretation of changes was severely compromised. The automatic RSAM and RMS plots quickly became favored as the data product most used for tracking changes in the seismicity at Mount St. Helens. However, public interest in the special pages remained high, even though we frequently posted disclaimers concerning the accuracy and completeness of these plots.

By adopting the changes already described in this paper, earthquake processing again became routine enough that the special volcano-related pages for Mount St. Helens represented a near-real-time picture of seismicity, even though only a fraction of detected earthquakes were logged in the catalog of located events. For example, time-depth plots (fig. 7) of located events eventually made it obvious that the depths of earthquakes taking place beneath Mount St. Helens since the 1980s changed dramatically with the advent of the 2004 eruption. Earthquakes at depth of 2–3 km, with occasional deeper swarms, had been the norm at Mount St. Helens since the late 1980s. These events, particularly the deeper swarms, were interpreted as representing the repressurization of the magmatic system by recharge (Moran, 1994; Musumeci and others, 2002). With the advent of the 2004 (and ongoing) eruption, these deeper events ceased. This depth-pattern shift hints that if magma recharge is continuing during the eruption, it is not pressurizing the deeper system

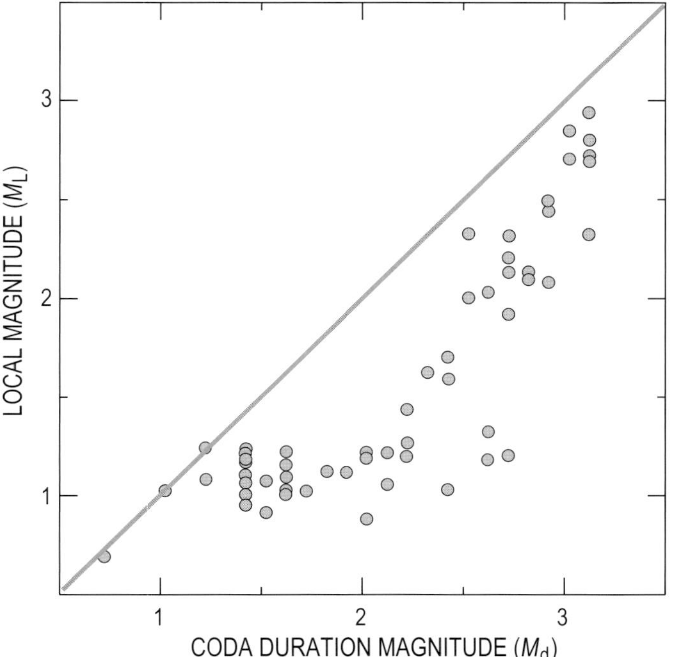

Figure 6. Coda duration magnitude versus local magnitude for a selection of Mount St. Helens earthquakes illustrates how use of coda duration magnitudes overestimates the local magnitudes for these earthquakes, particularly at lower magnitudes.

RSAM Alarms

In addition to magnitude-based earthquake alarms routinely used by the PNSN, several eruption-specific alarms were developed by CVO during the first 6 months of the eruption. RSAM alarms tuned to detect both large, discrete events ("event alarm") and smaller amplitude but longer duration events ("tremor alarm") were employed by CVO in mid-October 2004, shortly after the end of intense seismicity accompanying the vent-clearing phase. These alarms had previously been developed by the USGS Volcano Disaster Assistance Program as part of the "Glowworm" package of modules that operate as an add-on to the Earthworm acquisition system (Marso and others, 2003a). Before 2004, RSAM alarms had been used for more than a year to monitor the eruption of Anatahan volcano in the Commonwealth of the Northern Mariana Islands (Marso and others, 2003b).

The "event alarm" tracks RSAM values determined over a 2.56-s window (for 100-Hz data), with alarms issued if thresholds are exceeded at a prescribed number of stations for longer than 8 s. The "tremor alarm" uses RSAM values for 1-minute windows. When an alarm is issued, a separate module sends alerts via Short Message Service (SMS) to cell phones carried by on-call scientists. A potential weak link in this chain is the use of SMS, which requires that e-mail servers and SMS services be fully functional. Alerts were occasionally delayed by several minutes or even an hour before reaching individual phones. To partly address this limitation, SMS messages were sent to multiple cell phones (13 as of the summer of 2006) using multiple carriers. Nevertheless, these problems kept us from relying completely on SMS messaging, which we augmented by periodic data checks during off-hours.

Alert thresholds for the "event" and "tremor" alarms required refinement throughout the first 6 months of the eruption. Seismicity was so energetic initially that the alarms had to be desensitized to minimize the number of alerts. In mid-November 2004, larger earthquakes began occurring daily (Moran and others, this volume, chap. 2), and the "event alarm" was set so that thresholds were just barely exceeded by these events. Thresholds for the tremor alarm were much harder to determine, as we had no quantitative means for establishing thresholds. They initially were set at nominal values that were sufficiently high to prevent false triggers from wind and other noise sources. As a result, no alarms were issued for the January 16, 2005, explosion, which was accompanied by low-amplitude tremor that was barely detectable on stations outside the crater (Moran and others, this volume, chap. 6). Tremor alarm thresholds were reset on the basis of

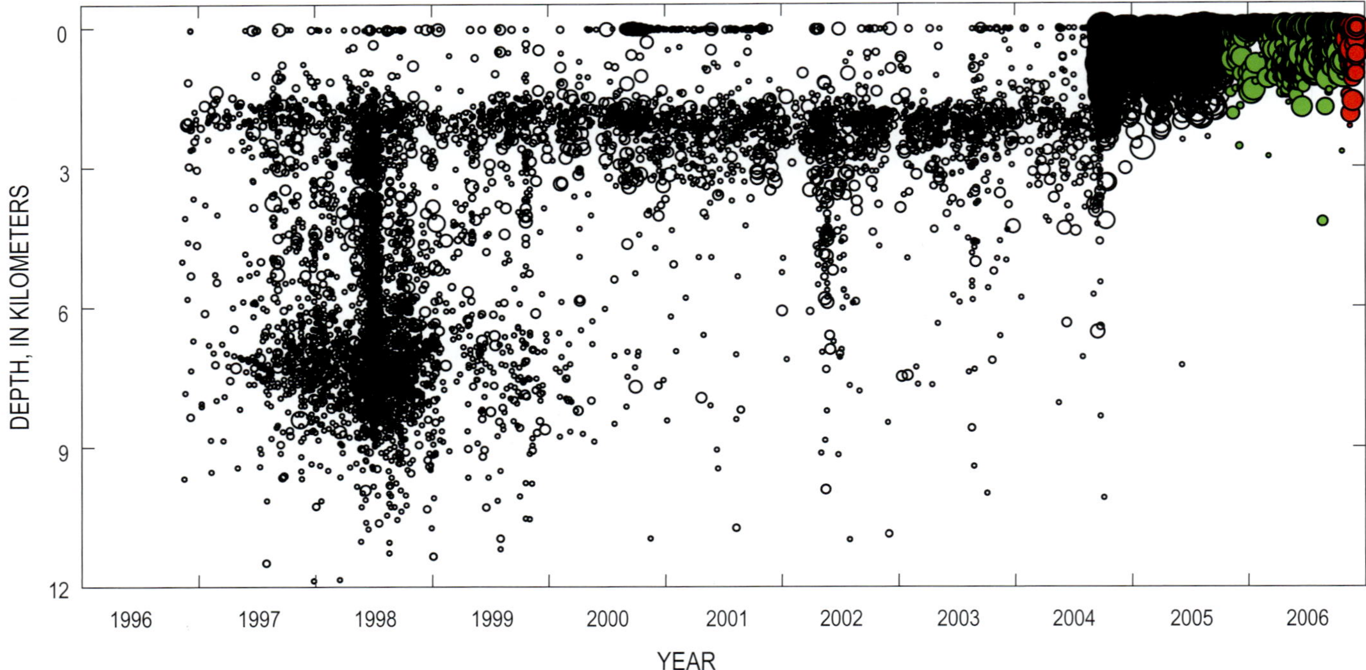

Figure 7. Time versus depth plot for a decade of seismicity at Mount St. Helens. Plot shows approximately 24,000 earthquakes located directly under the volcano (within 6-km radius of the new dome) between January 1997 and the end of 2006. Size of circles is proportional to event magnitude. Green circles, events in 2006; red circles, events in December 2006.

recordings of this explosion on stations located within the crater. However, the closest station became intermittent shortly after the January explosion and had stopped transmitting altogether by the time of the March 8, 2005, explosion. Seismicity associated with the March 8 explosion was more energetic (Moran and others, this volume, chap 6), but thresholds were not exceeded on enough stations to generate an alarm.

The failure of these alarms to generate alerts during explosions motivated us to develop a new alarm in the event of a loss of analog telemetry. Of the six explosions occurring during 2004–5, four, including the January 16 and March 8, 2005, explosions resulted in temporary or permanent loss of telemetry from at least one station. Traditional RSAM alarms have always used RSAM values from which the electronic bias or direct-current (DC) component has been removed, in large part to avoid false alarms resulting from common misalignment problems with analog telemetry circuitry that can impose a small DC offset on seismic data. However, the USGS J120 discriminator includes circuitry that detects the loss of the subcarrier and sets the discriminator output to a static 0.7-V DC level to distinguish loss of telemetry from a quiet seismic signal.

We created a new Earthworm module (based on the Earthworm ew2rsam module) that does not remove the DC component from RSAM values. Named FLOTSAM (not an acronym), this new alarm system sends alerts whenever values exceed a preset threshold at any station. The FLOTSAM system has sent out several alerts, some of which have been generated by loss of telemetry from crater stations destroyed during large rockfalls. Other alerts have resulted from stations that have stopped transmitting because of power outages at the site or weather-related disruptions of the radio signal.

The FLOTSAM alarm has become the alarm that the PNSN and CVO rely upon the most for detecting explosions, because no fine-tuning of amplitude and duration thresholds is required. All that is required is at least one seismometer placed close enough to the vent to have its radio signal disrupted by ash or by physical damage to the station. The event and tremor alarms are employed as well, with the event alarm proving to be a reliable detector of large earthquake-generated rockfalls, which sporadically produce ash clouds that reach from hundreds to several thousand meters above the crater rim.

Real-Time Traces for Remote Use

Early in the Mount St. Helens 2004 eruption, we became aware that researchers at other volcano observatories and academic institutions were interested in our seismic data. Besides the public Web pages, we provided access over the Internet to our real-time trace data wave-servers on a case-by-case basis. We also set up a direct export of selected data to the Alaska Volcano Observatory (AVO), where researchers were interested in following the seismic sequence in detail. At AVO and Stanford University the real-time data integration tool, VALVE (Cervelli and others, 2002), was used to track changes in seismic activity along with other parameters. The seismic-trace display program, SWARM (Alaska Volcano Observatory, 2006) was used at several different institutions to examine continuous seismic waveforms and their frequency content. In particular, researchers at the following institutions became near-real-time collaborators participating to some degree in the interpretation of specific aspects of Mount St. Helens seismicity:

- Alaska Volcano Observatory (Anchorage and Fairbanks)—event character, multiplet analysis
- U.S. Geological Survey (Menlo Park, Calif.)—event character, frequency shift
- University of California, Los Angeles—strong-motion portable monitoring, explosion analysis
- University of Memphis (Tennessee)—broadband portable monitoring
- Los Alamos National Laboratory (New Mexico)—multiplet analysis
- University of New Hampshire—multiplet analysis, acoustic signals.

Public Use and Response

The availability of relatively detailed information on the Web in nearly real time for this eruption of Mount St. Helens provided a new and powerful tool for public understanding. The availability of near-real-time original data (seismic traces) and analyzed products (RMS plots, maps, and time-depth plots) resulted in a change in the public perception of the eruption and their interaction with scientists. In previous eruption crises, the public has learned about the process primarily through the eyes of the news media, who may witness or photograph the physical events and talk with scientists about their interpretations. In this latest eruption of Mount St. Helens, the public could see for themselves on the Web many of the same data and products that the scientists were using. This availability improves the public understanding in two significant ways: Although the public still obtained the basic summary information from the news media, those wanting more or not trustful of the interpretations they were hearing could look at some of the data themselves.

The current eruption of Mount St. Helens is remarkable for the near absence of rumors and conspiracy theories purporting that critical information was being deliberately withheld from the public by scientists and emergency managers. The public also demonstrated the ability to digest a variety of sophisticated information products in order to follow the course of the eruption. Providing rich, open sources of eruption data enabled the public and media to monitor the ongoing eruption and may have encouraged them to seek further clarification from the scientific community when issues of interpretation arose. This public availability limited the kind of wild speculations that have sometimes occurred in the past.

Acknowledgments

The many staff and students associated with the Pacific Northwest Seismic Network (PNSN) and Cascades Volcano Observatory are too many to acknowledge individually but are greatly appreciated for their tireless help in the field and lab, often going much beyond what was expected to make the acquisition and processing of the huge amount of seismic data possible. Tom Murray, Peter Cervelli, Randy White, Jeff Johnson, Jackie Caplan-Auerbach, Chris Newhall, Giuliana Mele, Stephanie Prejean, and Steve Horton are thanked for their contributions to software, Web design, and general discussions relevant to our information products. David Sherrod and Jackie Caplan-Auerbach provided excellent reviews of our preliminary manuscript. The University of Washington's Office of Computing and Communications is acknowledged for their very rapid and effective Web server upgrades and extra telephone services. Partial support was provided by U.S. Geological Survey Cooperative Agreement 04HQAG005 for the operation of the PNSN.

References Cited

Alaska Volcano Observatory, 2006, Alaska Volcano Observatory software development page. SWARM version 1.2.3: U.S. Geological Survey online-only publication, including tutorial, manual, and software [http://www.avo.alaska.edu/Software/; last accessed Nov. 6, 2006].

Cervelli, D.P., Cervelli, P., Miklius, A., Krug, R., and Lisowski, M., 2002, VALVE; Volcano Analysis and Visualization Environment [abs.]: Eos (American Geophysical Union Transactions), v. 83, no. 47, Fall Meeting Supplement, U52A-07, p. F3.

Crosson, R.S., 1972, Small earthquakes, structure and tectonics of the Puget Sound region: Seismological Society of America Bulletin, v. 62, p. 1133–1171.

Driedger, C.L., Neal, C.A., Knappenberger, T.H., Needham, D.H., Harper, R.B., and Steele, W.P., 2008, Hazard information management during the autumn 2004 reawakening of Mount St. Helens volcano, Washington, chap. 24 *of* Sherrod, D.R., Scott, W.E., and Stauffer, P.H., eds., A volcano rekindled; the renewed eruption of Mount St. Helens, 2004–2006: U.S. Geological Survey Professional Paper 1750 (this volume).

Endo, E.T., and Murray, T., 1991, Real-time seismic amplitude measurement (RSAM); a volcano monitoring and prediction tool: Bulletin of Volcanology, v. 53, no. 7, p. 533–545.

Johnson C.E., Bittenbinder, A., Bogaert, B., Dietz, L., and Kohler, W., 1995, Earthworm—a flexible approach to seismic network processing: IRIS Newsletter, v. 14, no. 2, p. 1–4.

Marso, J.N., Murray, T.L., Lockhart, A.B., and Bryan, C.J., 2003a, Glowworm, an extended PC-based Earthworm system for volcano monitoring [abs], *in* Cities on Volcanoes 3: Hilo, Hawaii, International Association of Volcanology and Chemistry of the Earth's Interior (IAVCEI), Hilo, Hawaii, July 14–18, 2003, Abstract volume, p. 82.

Marso, J.N., Lockhart, A.B., White, R.A., Koyanagi, S.K., Trusdell, F.A., Camacho, J.T., and Chong, R., 2003b, The Anatahan volcano-monitoring system [abs.]: Eos (American Geophysical Union Transactions), v. 84, no. 46, Fall Meeting Supplement, V32B-1020.

McChesney, P.J., Couchman, M.R., Moran, S.C., Lockhart, A.B., Swinford, K.J., and LaHusen, R.G., 2008, Seismic-monitoring changes and the remote deployment of seismic stations (seismic spider) at Mount St. Helens, 2004–2005, chap. 7 *of* Sherrod, D.R., Scott, W.E., and Stauffer, P.H., eds., A volcano rekindled; the renewed eruption of Mount St. Helens, 2004–2006: U.S. Geological Survey Professional Paper 1750 (this volume).

Moran, S.C., 1994, Seismicity at Mount St. Helens, 1987–1992: Evidence for repressurization of an active magmatic system: Journal of Geophysical Research, v. 99, no. B3, p. 4341–4354, doi: 10.1029/93JB02993.

Moran, S.C., Malone, S.D., Qamar, A.I., Thelen, W.A., Wright, A.K., and Caplan-Auerbach, J., 2008a, Seismicity associated with renewed dome building at Mount St. Helens, 2004–2005, chap. 2 *of* Sherrod, D.R., Scott, W.E., and Stauffer, P.H., eds., A volcano rekindled; the renewed eruption of Mount St. Helens, 2004–2006: U.S. Geological Survey Professional Paper 1750 (this volume).

Moran, S.C., McChesney, P.J., and Lockhart, A.B., 2008b, Seismicity and infrasound associated with explosions at Mount St. Helens, 2004–2005, chap. 6 *of* Sherrod, D.R., Scott, W.E., and Stauffer, P.H., eds., A volcano rekindled; the renewed eruption of Mount St. Helens, 2004–2006: U.S. Geological Survey Professional Paper 1750 (this volume).

Musumeci, C., Gresta, S., and Malone, S.D., 2002, Magma system recharge of Mount St. Helens from precise relative hypocenter location of microearthquakes: Journal of Geophysical Research, v. 107, no. B10, 2264, p. ESE 16-1–ESE 16-9, doi:10.1029/2001JB000629.

Reasenberg, P.A., and Oppenheimer, D., 1985, FPFIT, FPPLOT, and FPPAGE: FORTRAN computer programs for calculating and plotting earthquake fault-plane solutions: U.S. Geological Survey Open-File Report 85–739, 109 p.

Rogers, J.A., and Stephens, C.D., 1995, SSAM: Real-time seismic spectral amplitude measurement on a PC and its application to volcano monitoring: Seismological Society of America Bulletin, v. 85, no. 2, p. 632–639.

Thelen, W.A., Crosson, R.S., and Creager, K.C., 2008, Absolute and relative locations of earthquakes at Mount St. Helens, Washington, using continuous data; implications for magmatic processes, chap. 4 *of* Sherrod, D.R., Scott, W.E., and Stauffer, P.H., eds., A volcano rekindled; the renewed eruption of Mount St. Helens, 2004–2006: U.S. Geological Survey Professional Paper 1750 (this volume).

U.S. Geological Survey, 2006, Earthworm documentation v. 7.0: U.S. Geological Survey online-only publication, including overview, release notes, and software [http://folkworm.ceri.memphis.edu/ew-doc/; last accessed Nov. 6, 2006].

A Volcano Rekindled: The Renewed Eruption of Mount St. Helens, 2004–2006
Edited by David R. Sherrod, William E. Scott, and Peter H. Stauffer
U.S. Geological Survey Professional Paper 1750, 2008

Chapter 4

Absolute and Relative Locations of Earthquakes at Mount St. Helens, Washington, Using Continuous Data: Implications for Magmatic Processes

By Weston A. Thelen[1], Robert S. Crosson[2], and Kenneth C. Creager[2]

Abstract

This study uses a combination of absolute and relative locations from earthquake multiplets to investigate the seismicity associated with the eruptive sequence at Mount St. Helens between September 23, 2004, and November 20, 2004. Multiplets, a prominent feature of seismicity during this time period, occurred as volcano-tectonic, hybrid, and low-frequency earthquakes spanning a large range of magnitudes and lifespans. Absolute locations were improved through the use of a new one-dimensional velocity model with excellent shallow constraints on P-wave velocities. We used jackknife tests to minimize possible biases in absolute and relative locations resulting from station outages and changing station configurations. In this paper, we show that earthquake hypocenters shallowed before the October 1 explosion along a north-dipping structure under the 1980–86 dome. Relative relocations of multiplets during the initial seismic unrest and ensuing eruption showed rather small source volumes before the October 1 explosion and larger tabular source volumes after October 5. All multiplets possess absolute locations very close to each other. However, the highly dissimilar waveforms displayed by each of the multiplets analyzed suggest that different sources and mechanisms were present within a very small source volume. We suggest that multiplets were related to pressurization of the conduit system that produced a stationary source that was highly stable over long time periods. On the basis of their response to explosions occurring in October 2004, earthquakes not associated with multiplets also appeared to be pressure dependent. The pressure source for these earthquakes appeared, however, to be different from the pressure source of the multiplets.

[1] Pacific Northwest Seismic Network, Department of Earth and Space Sciences, University of Washington, Box 351310, Seattle, WA 98195

[2] Department of Earth and Space Sciences, University of Washington, Box 351310, Seattle, WA 98195

Introduction

Because more than 1 million earthquakes occurred between the beginning of the latest eruption of Mount St. Helens in 2004 and the end of 2005 (Moran and others, this volume, chap. 2), there is a need to locate a representative set of earthquakes to search for first-order patterns and trends that may aid in future monitoring and research. Although locating most of the 1 million earthquakes would be possible and even somewhat practical with current methods and parallel computing, such a study is beyond the scope of this paper. Herein we concentrate on the seismicity leading up to the early October explosions and through about 1 month of dacitic dome building in order to characterize the seismicity associated with each eruptive phase.

One of the most striking features in this eruption's seismicity was the prominence of earthquake multiplets, or repetitious earthquakes. Earthquake multiplets are characteristically defined by their highly similar waveforms, often exceeding cross-correlation coefficients of 0.8 (Geller and Mueller, 1980; Frémont and Malone, 1987; fig. 1). This phenomenon is likely caused by earthquakes occurring very close to the same location with a similar source process (Geller and Mueller, 1980). Earthquake multiplets are a common occurrence in tectonic and volcanic areas worldwide, and many authors have exploited earthquake multiplets to determine highly precise relative relocations (for example, Poupinet and others, 1984; Fréchet, 1985; Frémont and Malone, 1987; Got and others, 1994; Waldhauser and Ellsworth, 2000). Every relative relocation method operates on the basic idea that closely spaced earthquakes recorded at a common station will have similar path and site effects. As long as the source region is homogeneous (or reasonably so) with respect to the dominant wavelength of the waveforms, the relative time lag between the earthquakes is a measure of the separation distance between the sources (Wolfe, 2002).

The classification and description of large suites of multiplets is also fairly common on volcanoes worldwide. Got and others (1994) relocated 250 earthquakes beneath Kīlauea, Hawai'i, to define a nearly horizontal plane of seismicity at 8-km depth. Stevens and Chouet (2001) analyzed long-period multiplets beneath Redoubt Volcano before its 1989 eruption and found smooth changes in amplitude and cross-correlation coefficient within multiplets. Rowe and others (2004) relocated approximately 17,000 similar earthquakes on Soufrière Hills volcano, Montserrat, by identifying multiplets through a hierarchical clustering algorithm and using those multiplets as stacks to refine phase picks. On Mount Pinatubo, Philippines, Battaglia and others (2004) used a similar approach to that of Got and others (1994) to relocate almost 11,000 events.

When locating similar earthquakes, a common approach is to use manually phase-picked events to seed stacks of similar events. Short windows of data are normally used, usually between 1.28 and 2.56 s after the P-wave arrival. Often such studies use triggered waveform data (records started by an amplitude trigger at the seismometer) instead of continuous waveform data, which are used here to identify multiplets. Past data sets are thus limited by what is triggered or located manually by the local seismic network and may be largely incomplete (Rowe and others, 2004).

Beginning in 1980, Mount St. Helens has been the most seismically active volcano in the Cascade Range. Increases in moment release in the shallow edifice are characteristically associated with explosive and effusive eruptions (Swanson and others, 1983). Earthquake multiplets at shallow depths were commonly observed at Mount St. Helens after 1982 and were used to obtain highly precise relative locations of earthquakes during the dome-building eruptions of September 10, 1984, and May–June 1985 (Frémont and Malone, 1987). Musumeci and others (2002) used similar events during the late 1990s to establish continuing magma recharge after 1992 into a storage zone at 5.5–10-km depth.

Since the beginning of the latest eruption in September 2004, less than 1 percent of the earthquakes detected have been routinely processed by the Pacific Northwest Seismic Network (PNSN) (Qamar and others, this volume, chap. 3), although care has been taken by PNSN analysts to extract a representative sampling of waveforms for the PNSN earthquake catalog. In this paper we (1) relocate the triggered earthquakes from the PNSN catalog to establish absolute locations, (2) identify and locate multiplets from the continuous seismic record, and (3) discuss the volcanological significance of our findings. We do not claim to classify every earthquake that has occurred during this period; instead, we present the absolute locations of the PNSN catalog data with a new velocity model and the characteristics of a representative set of multiplets that exhibit large populations and/or long lifespans. Especially of interest in this study are the relative locations and characters of the individual multiplets, how those characteristics change through time, and the relation of those characteristics to other phenomena. This information is important because we would like to assess the ability of multiplets to forecast eruptive activity or style.

This paper follows the time divisions used by Moran and others (this volume, chap. 2) to present the seismic evolution of the eruption. As it happens, station outages or station installations necessitated the use of additional time breaks to present consistent locations within a time period. Care has been taken across changes in network configurations to present a consistent and coherent picture of the seismicity.

Methods

Absolute Locations

Mount St. Helens has the densest seismic network of any volcano in the Pacific Northwest. Before the eruption in 2004, there were 13 permanent stations within 20 km of the volcano (fig. 2). Except for 11 days after the first phreatic explosion on October 1, a seismometer was positioned within 1 km of the new vent (McChesney and others, this volume, chap. 7), an arrangement that allowed an unusually accurate determination of absolute locations beneath the edifice compared to standard regional network locations. In this paper, we consider only earthquakes with eight picked P-wave arrival times, a maximum azimuthal gap of 135 degrees, and an arrival time pick within 3 km of the epicenter. The 3-km criterion is necessary for times when stations on the 1980s dome were saturated or destroyed. Additionally, we use a new velocity model (Thelen and others, 2006) to significantly reduce station corrections and improve locations (table 1, appendix 1). Absolute locations are determined with the program "SPONG," a PNSN adaptation of FASTHYPO (Herrmann, 1979).

Uncertainties in absolute event location are given by the program SPONG, which was benchmarked against Hypoinverse (Klein, 1989; S. Malone, oral commun., 2006). These include uncertainties in phase picks and in the earthquake-location inversion scheme itself. To evaluate the effect of changing station configurations, we performed jackknife tests (Efron and Gong, 1983) by systematically removing seismic stations. Generally, removing crater stations reduced depth constraint but did not change the distribution of epicenters significantly (appendix 2). The reduced resolution in depth often produced "airquakes," earthquakes with phase picks that resulted in depths above the velocity-model datum used in the solution. Airquakes were common in the existing PNSN earthquake catalog throughout the eruptive sequence at Mount St. Helens beginning in 2004. The uncertainties presented here do not include uncertainties in the velocity model, do not quantitatively account for changes in station configuration, and therefore are likely underestimates, especially in depth.

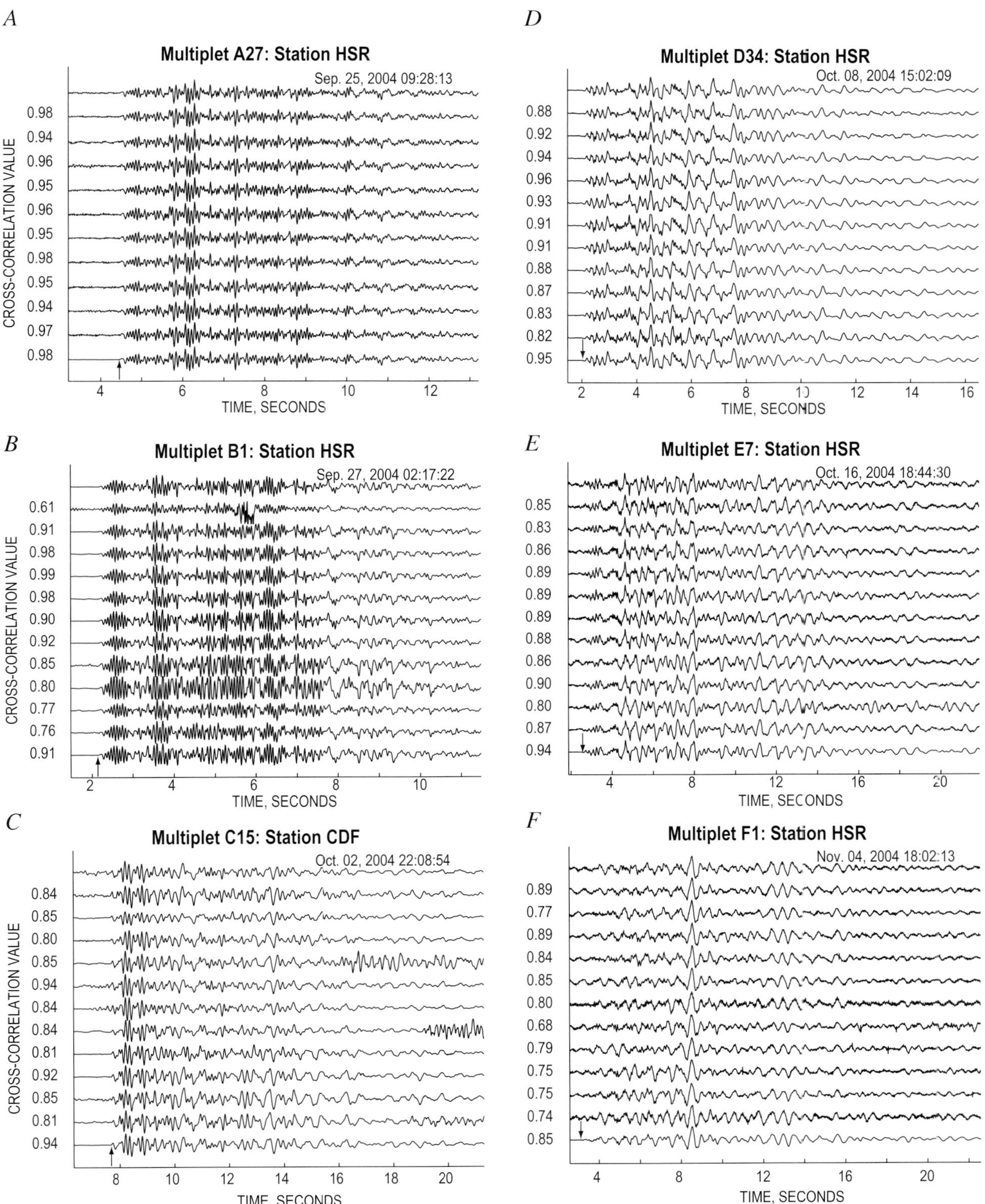

Figure 1. Example of waveforms from six multiplets analyzed in this study. Top trace in each is seed event for multiplet, and last trace is stack of all waveforms within multiplet at given station. Date and time on first trace are when seed event occurred. Arrow in bottom trace shows first arrival with polarity (up is compressional, down is dilatational). Station CDF has reversed polarity, so the first motion in *C* is actually down. Cross-correlation value of each trace with respect to seed event is shown on the y-axis. Waveforms are unfiltered and chosen at constant time intervals within the lifespan of their respective multiplets.

Classification of Multiplets

The PNSN catalog contains less than 1 percent of the total number of earthquakes, so entire groups of earthquakes have no representative in the catalog. As a result, we could not use the PNSN catalog as a starting point in searching for multiplets. Instead, our method for identifying multiplets started with a simple, highly sensitive threshold autopicker for which we selected a window of data around each trigger on the basis of the characteristic length of earthquakes in a given time period (10–20 s). Our autopicker typically missed the P-wave first arrival, so we included an empirically determined amount of time before the trigger (usually 1–3 s) in order to capture the entire event.

After the triggers were selected from the record, we cross-correlated, in the time domain, the first event to all other events at a particular station. Any event that was equal to or above the threshold cross-correlation coefficient (0.8) was considered part of that multiplet. The multiplet was then taken from the triggered events and stored. The next event that was not part of an existing multiplet was cross-correlated against all the remaining events and evaluated for events exceeding the cross-correlation coefficient cutoff. Any event that did not correlate with another event was considered an orphan and stored else-

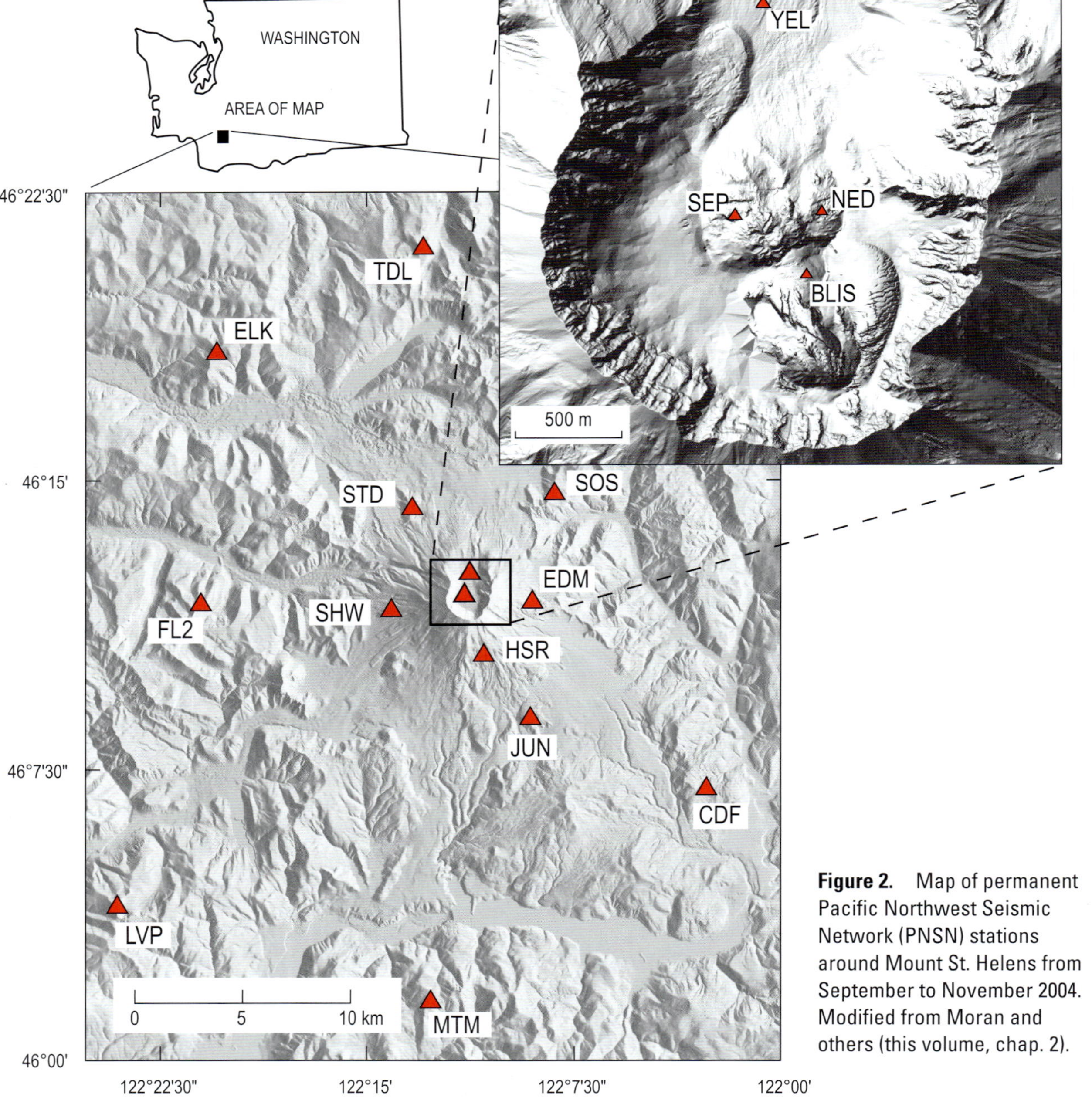

Figure 2. Map of permanent Pacific Northwest Seismic Network (PNSN) stations around Mount St. Helens from September to November 2004. Modified from Moran and others (this volume, chap. 2).

Table 1. Depth and velocity for P-wave model of Thelen and others (2006).

[Depth to top of layers defined by P-wave velocities; datum is altitude 2,200 m above sea level. Column 3 is the velocity model used for the relative locations, which assumes a Poisson solid in order to convert to S-wave velocity from the P-wave velocity of the one-dimensional model (appendix 1).]

Depth (km)	P-wave velocity (km/s)	S-wave velocity (km/s)
0	2.7	1.51
1.0	3.5	1.97
1.3	4.3	2.42
1.6	5.1	2.87
3.9	6.0	3.37
6.5	6.2	3.58
10.5	6.6	3.82
18.5	6.8	3.93
34.5	7.1	4.10
43.5	7.8	4.51

where. This process was repeated until all events were either classified into a multiplet or as an orphan. The multiplets were visually inspected to remove those with systematic noise such as calibration pulses and telemetry spikes, which can produce repeatable waveforms. Computer memory restrictions and the large number of triggers allowed us to process only about 10 days of data at a time. We therefore treated each time period individually and then combined the time periods by stacking multiplets from each time period and running the same analysis described above with event stacks instead of triggered data. This method served to combine time periods; however it also allowed for events with similar stacks to be combined even if individual events did not correlate at the initial threshold level. This technique of tracking multiplets has a disadvantage of using only one station to identify and classify multiplets, which makes it susceptible to near-site effects. However, Stephens and Chouet (2001) successfully used only one station to classify the multiplets before the 1989 eruption of Redoubt Volcano. We also visually checked other stations at the same distance range for the presence of the larger multiplets and ensured that near-site effects were not dominating the multiplet analysis.

Relative Location of Multiplets

After the identification of a multiplet, a representative event from that multiplet was chosen and cross-correlated against each hour of continuous data. Again, cross-correlation windows of 10–20 s were used, a choice based on the length of high signal-to-noise ratios throughout the waveform. Cross-correlation coefficients above a threshold were considered triggers. Three stations were required to have coincident triggers in order for the earthquake to be classified as a valid event. After the triggered events were compiled, all of the events were cross-correlated against each other at each station, and lags were noted at the maximum cross-correlation coefficient. Subsample estimates of lags were achieved in the time domain through polynomial interpolation of the cross-correlation coefficient peak. Lags were weighted by their normalized cross-correlation coefficient, and only lags with a cross-correlation above 0.8 were considered for earthquake locations. The lags for each event were then used to compute double-difference hypocenter locations with the hypoDD software (Waldhauser, 2001). For the initial location of the earthquakes within each multiplet, we stacked the multiplet and picked the first arrival of the stack at each station. Those picks were then applied to each earthquake in the stack on the basis of the lag derived from the cross-correlation. The picks were used to get absolute locations for each earthquake in the multiplet using the identical process as discussed above.

The use of long time windows meant that we were correlating dominantly S waves and Rayleigh waves. Most of the stations used in this study had a difference of 2 s or less between the P- and S-wave arrivals, meaning that at least 80 percent of the correlation window was composed of S waves and Rayleigh waves. Consequently, cross-correlating long time windows produced lags of phases that are traveling at S-wave velocities between the source and the receiver. We therefore elected to use an S-wave model for our relative locations. The S-wave model was obtained by assuming a Poisson's ratio for the crust and applying it to the P-wave model used in the absolute locations (table 1).

Errors in relative locations have several sources of uncertainty. One source is waveform alignment. Poorly aligned waveforms at a particular station may generate lineations in events toward that station (Battaglia and others, 2004). We minimized this source of uncertainty by using large time windows, which minimizes the occurrence of poorly aligned waveforms (Schaff and others, 2004). Another source of error in relative locations is uncertainty in the velocity model that the initial hypocenters start in (Michelini and Lomax, 2004). The path is canceled out by calculating the lag between two events, but the takeoff angle and azimuth are affected by the choice of an initial velocity model. In our analysis, we use a velocity model that is homogenous in the region of our cluster centroid. Changes in velocity, and therefore takeoff angle, only stretch or compress our cloud of hypocenters and do not affect the overall shape (appendix 3). Finally, artifacts in relative earthquake locations can be introduced through inhomogeneous phase lags on all stations in a solution. In other words, some stations will have a larger effect on the earthquake location than others, depending on the number of phase picks on that station. We tested this with the use of a jackknife test (Efron and Gong, 1983), a method in which one station is removed at a time and then all of the earthquakes within the multiplet are relocated, using the reduced station set (appendix 3). The change in location of each earthquake was tracked, and the maximum offset of all of the stations in the north, east, and vertical directions is presented as the uncertainty in relative location.

September 23–October 5, 2004: Vent-Clearing Phase

Absolute Locations, September 23, 0000 PDT, Through September 25, 1200 PDT

Relocating a subset of catalog PNSN events with the updated velocity model revealed a tight cluster of earthquakes with a radius of 250 m centered immediately southeast of station SEP (fig. 3*A*). The depth cross section showed a cluster of hypocenters that was elongate toward the future vent. The cluster spanned depths of approximately 400 to 1,100 m below the future vent. The average number of phases used in the earthquake location during this time period was 9.32, with a maximum of 52. The mean azimuthal gap in this subset of earthquake locations was 90 degrees. A total of 229 earthquakes were relocated with formal uncertainties averaging 132, 92 and 84 m in the north, east, and vertical directions, respectively. Reductions in estimated uncertainties for the north, east, and vertical directions were 20, 35, and 74 percent when compared to the routine network locations.

Multiplets, September 23, 0000 PDT, Through September 25, 1200 PDT

The buildup of multiplets occurred at an accelerating pace until approximately 0200 on September 24 (fig. 4). All multiplets were composed of volcano-tectonic (VT) events and, in most cases, many multiplets were occurring simultaneously. Here we distinguish VT earthquakes from hybrid and low-frequency earthquakes, as was done by Moran and others (this volume, chap. 2). Examples of frequency spectra of hybrid versus low-frequency earthquakes versus VT earthquakes, as defined in this paper, are shown in figure 5. The maximum number of multiplets with populations greater than 20 occurring concurrently was eight at 0200 PDT on September 24, coincident with the maximum of earthquake amplitudes on station JUN during this time period (fig. 4). After the maximum in earthquake amplitudes on September 24, seismic activity waned until September 26. None of the early multiplets recurred after seismic activity ramped up again on September 26, 2004.

The largest magnitude multiplet during this period, A27 (figs. 1, 6), was a group of 59 VT events that occurred over approximately 3 hours beginning at 1104 PDT on September 25. Picking the first arrivals of the stacked traces of A27 on each station and locating the multiplet with standard absolute-location techniques resulted in a location at the south end of the cluster of epicenters in figure 3*A*, at depths near the top of the cluster. The absolute location of the stack used only six phase picks, giving the location of the hypocentroid the largest uncertainty of any multiplet analyzed. Double-difference relocations of this swarm reveal a tight cluster, spanning less than 10 m in depth and about 5 m horizontally (fig. 6*A*). Orthogonal cross sections show mostly vertical orientations, which are an artifact of different stations' picks being used for different events. Uncertainty estimates are on the order of 3 m horizontally and 20 m vertically. In figure 6, the generally small average errors are masked by a few larger errors as great as 40 m. The cross-correlation values of the first event to subsequent events in the multiplet are nearly constant. Considering the location errors and constant cross-correlation values, we suggest that the earthquakes in this multiplet occurred at nearly the same location. The end of this multiplet coincided with the waning seismic activity of the swarm on September 25 (Moran and others, chap. 2, their figs. 4, 5).

Absolute Locations, September 25, 1200 PDT, Through October 1, 1200 PDT

Absolute locations of 313 PNSN catalog events during this time period showed a distinct shift up and to the south compared to those of the previous period (figs. 3*B*, 7). The decrease in earthquake depth was consistent with phase-pick differences identified by Moran and others (this volume, chap. 2; fig. 7) between September 25 and September 27. This cluster, too, was tightly spaced in depth (250 m radius) and in epicenter (300 m radius), with respect to other absolute locations. The hypocentroid shift compared to the swarm beginning September 23 was 133 m south, 69 m east, and 221 m up. The average number of stations used was 11, the average gap was 78 degrees, and the average distance from the epicenter to the closest station was 115 m. Uncertainties in event locations averaged 109 m north-south, 140 m east-west, and 119 m in depth.

Multiplets, September 25, 1200 PDT, Through October 1, 1659 PDT

Multiplets were present throughout this time period and occurred in two phases before the explosion on October 1 (fig. 4). The multiplets had lifespans of 1–2.5 days. Their first buildup started at approximately 1200 PDT on September 25, 2004. Accompanying an increase in the number and lifespan of the multiplets was an increase in the maximum amplitudes of the continuous data averaged over 1-minute intervals at station JUN (fig. 4). The second buildup started around midday on September 29 and continued until the explosion on October 1. The second phase is identified by the end of multiplets from the first phase of buildup and the occurrence of new multiplets. The transition coincided with a 250 percent increase in the maximum amplitude of signals recorded at station JUN (fig. 4). Thirteen multiplets that

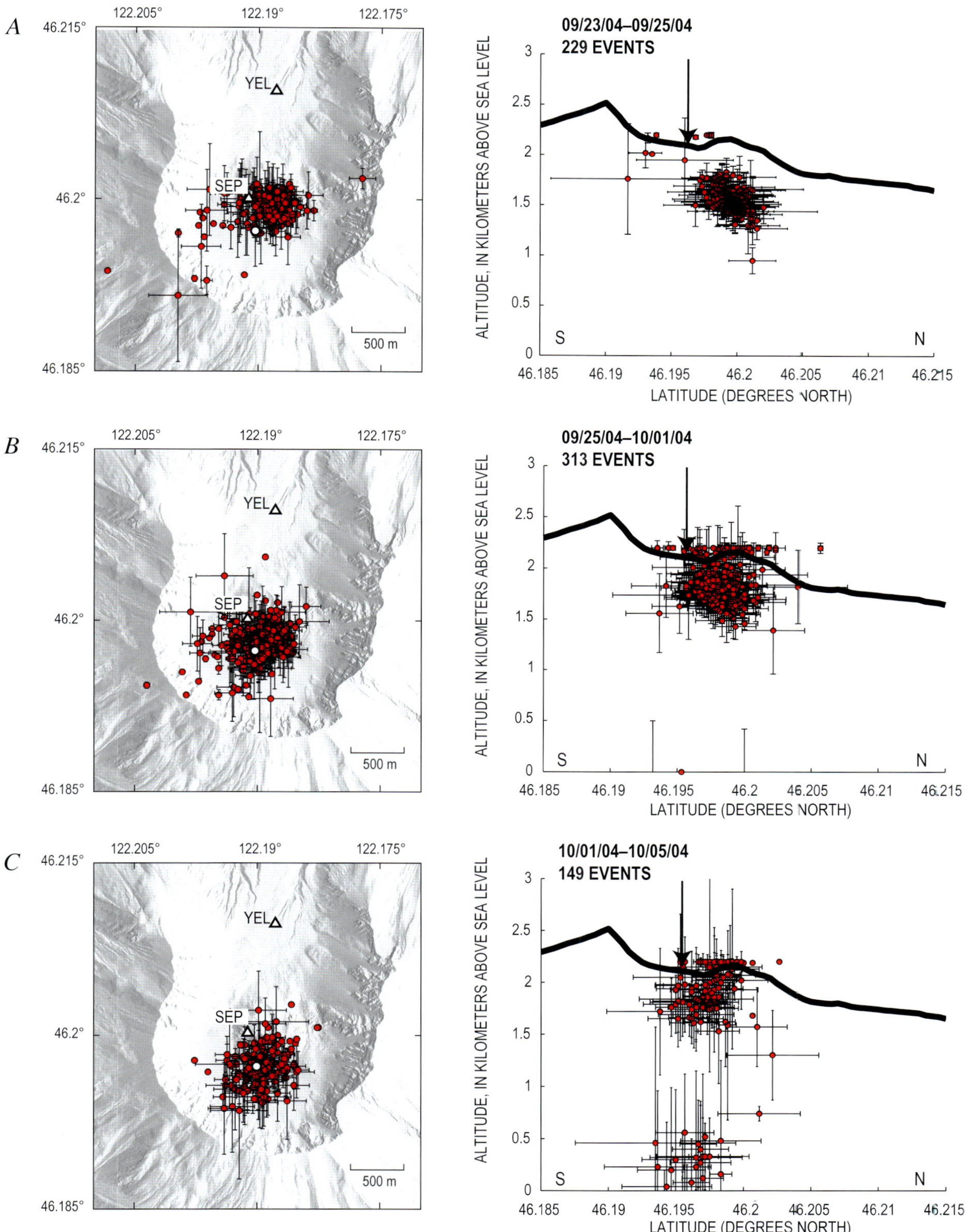

Figure 3. Absolute locations for Pacific Northwest Seismic Network (PNSN) catalog events for three time periods. Earthquakes plotted have eight or more phase picks, azimuthal gap of less than 135 degrees, and a phase pick at a station closer than 3 km from epicenter. Error bars are from SPONG location output. Permanent seismic stations shown on maps by black and white triangles. Cross sections show earthquake depth plots and topographic surface profile north-south through station SEP. White dot in map view and arrow in cross section show approximate location of vent.

were active before the October 1 explosion recurred after the explosion. Multiplets occurring after September 25 at 1200 PDT and through November 2004 were overwhelmingly hybrid and low-frequency earthquakes.

One multiplet, B1, started September 27 and continued for approximately 2.5 days (fig. 6*B*). The absolute location of the stacked traces formed a hypocentroid at 520-m depth, with an epicentroid centered in the cluster in figure 3*B*. The absolute location solution used 12 stations and had impulsive arrivals at all stations, making it one of the most reliable locations of the multiplets studied. The polarity of first arrivals was mixed and was consistent with reverse faulting on a north-striking, vertical or steeply dipping (85°–90°) fault. Relative locations of hypocenters are concentrated inside a sphere less than 15 m in diameter (fig. 6*B*). Location errors derived from jackknife techniques reveal uncertainties in the north, east, and vertical directions of 1.9 m, 1.3 m, and 1.3 m, respectively. The cross-correlation coefficient of the first event relative to each subsequent event decays with time, indicating a systematic temporal change in either the path between the earthquake and the receiver or a very small shift in location (Gret and others, 2005).

Absolute Locations, October 1, 1700 PDT, Through October 5, 1659 PDT

The absolute locations of 149 PNSN catalog events between the October 1 explosion and the end of October 5 apparently varied more widely in depth than those of the two previous time periods (fig. 3). However, with the destruction of station SEP during the October 1 explosion, the depths were less well constrained than in previous earthquake sets. In addition, emergent P-wave arrivals and overlapping codas made picks at the remaining crater station (YEL) and flank stations (HSR, EDM, SHW, and STD) sparse and imprecise, further affecting the depths. The effect of this can be seen as a cluster of seismicity that was falsely centered at 400-m

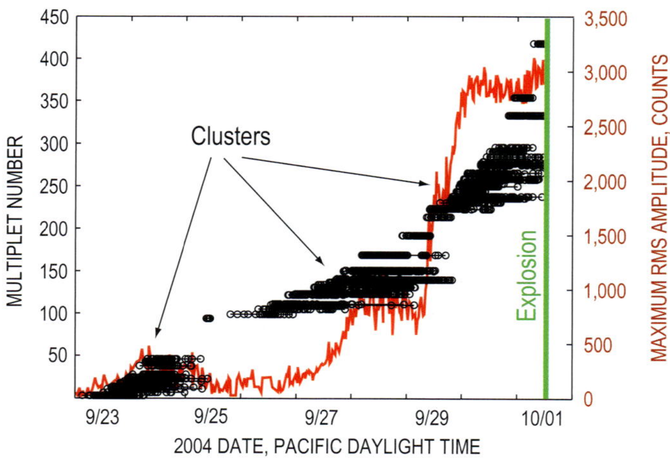

Figure 4. Timeline of multiplets from September 24, 2004, until explosion of October 1, 2004 (green line), detected on station HSR. Each earthquake is plotted as a circle, and multiplets are identified by a horizontal line through events that define multiplet. Only multiplets that have more than 20 events are plotted. Maximum root-mean-squared (RMS) amplitude averaged over 1 minute at station JUN shown in red.

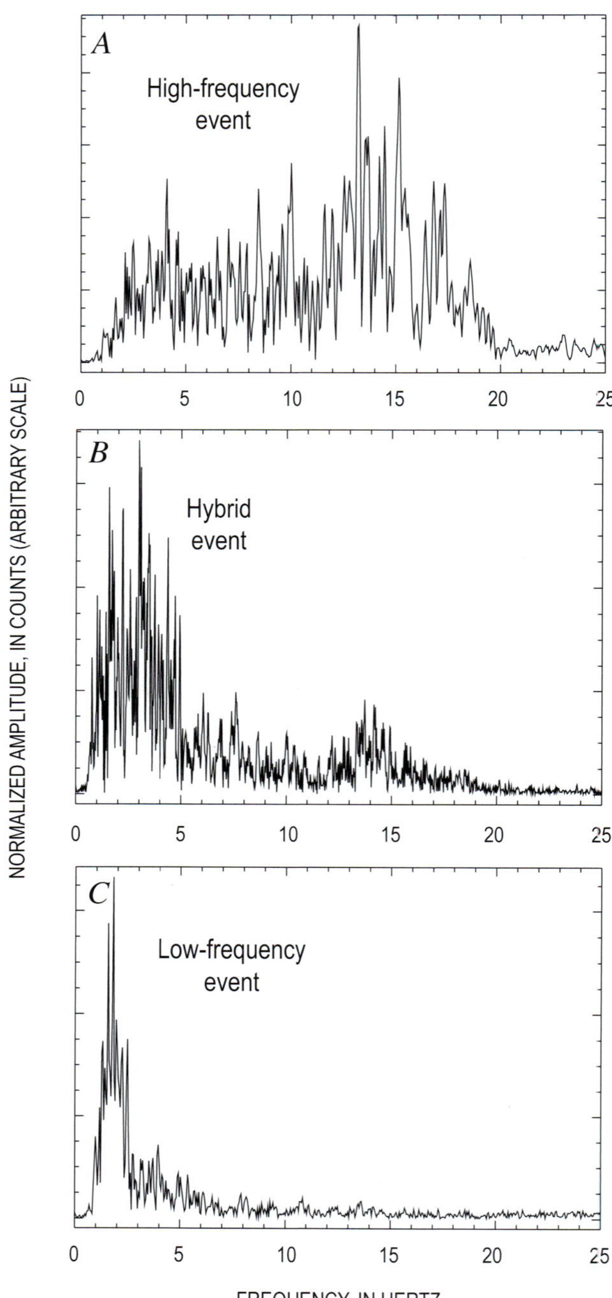

Figure 5. Examples of frequency spectra. High-frequency energy is seen between 12 and 20 Hz in high-frequency and hybrid events but not in low-frequency event. *A*, High-frequency event from September 25, 2004. *B*, Hybrid event from seed event of multiplet B1. *C*, Seed event of low-frequency multiplet F1 on station HSR.

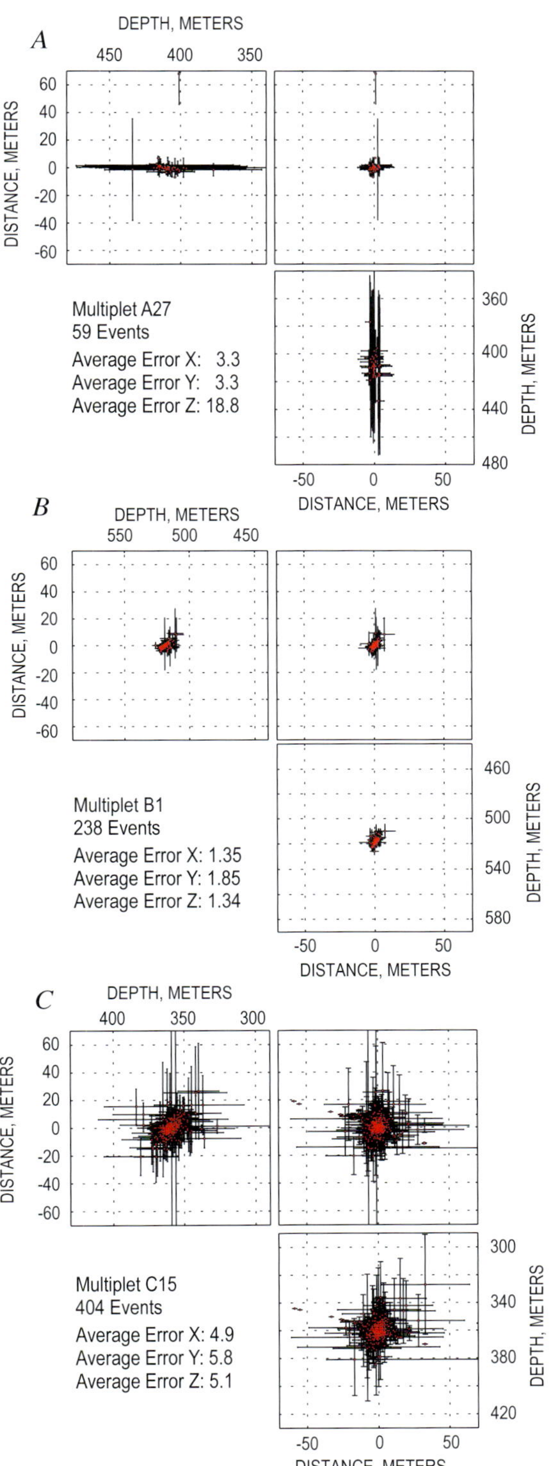

Figure 6. Relative relocations for three multiplets from the beginning of unrest through the period of phreatic explosions. For each, upper right square is map view (north at top), and left and bottom plots are cross sections. Plots are presented as cube with two sides folded out. Errors determined through jackknife techniques. Directions X, Y, and Z correspond to east, north, and vertical, respectively.

altitude owing to a lack of picks at station YEL (fig. 3*C*). Earthquake-location solutions used an average of 10 stations with an average gap of 81 degrees and an average delta of 1.52 km. Uncertainties in x, y, and z were 124, 146, and 244 m, respectively.

Multiplets, October 1, 1700 PDT, Through October 5, 1659 PDT

Several small-population multiplets were present during this time period (fig. 8). These multiplets consist of hybrid and low-frequency event families. There were three explosions and two episodes of tremor during this time period, in some cases concurrent with the start or stop of a multiplet. In most cases, however, multiplets during this time period continued largely unaffected by the occurrence of tremor or explosion.

One large low-frequency multiplet, C15, started 7 hours after the explosion on October 1. The absolute location of this multiplet using event stacks revealed a hypocentroid 100 m south and 160 m shallower than B1. Using a similar station configuration for both event stacks (no station SEP) shows approximately the same offset in location. Polarities from first arrivals of the multiplet stack were all dilatational, a characteristic for other earthquakes in this sequence, especially after October 1 (Moran and others, this volume, chap. 2; Qamar and others, this volume, chap. 3). This multiplet possessed highly stable amplitudes and cross-correlation coefficients in time. The relative relocations of 404 events from the C15 multiplet show a cluster of seismicity spanning approximately 20 m in diameter (fig. 6*C*). Some events of

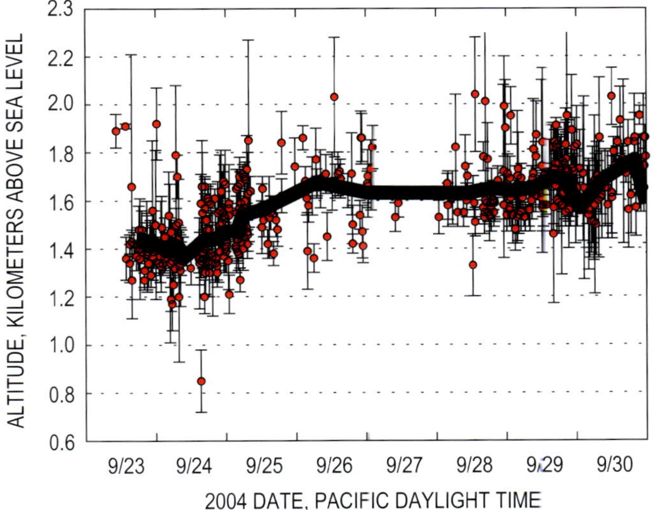

Figure 7. Earthquake altitude as function of time, September 23–30, 2004. Black line is running average altitude of 20 nearest earthquakes in time. The apparent gap in earthquakes between 9/26 and 9/28 is artificial, caused by a lack of earthquakes with location parameters that met our criteria and not by diminished seismicity.

the main cluster may have indicated a south-dipping structure; however, the overwhelming majority (75 percent) of the earthquake hypocenters were within the circular cluster. Using jackknife error techniques, we determined the locational uncertainties in north, east, and depth to be 5.8, 4.9, and 5.1 m, respectively.

October 5–November 20, 2004: Seismicity Associated with Dome Building

Absolute Locations, October 5, 0000 PDT, Through October 11, 1659 PDT

As with those between October 1 and October 5, earthquake arrivals at crater and flank stations were highly contaminated with earthquake codas from previous earthquakes and plagued with emergent signals. Thus, large uncertainties existed in the absolute locations, particularly in depth (fig. 9*A*). The spread of earthquake depth is suspect, owing to the absence of station SEP and the poor character of the first arrivals on station YEL. During this time period the absolute-location solutions of 227 events used an average of 10 stations, with an average gap of 89 degrees. The average distance to the nearest station was 1.15 km. Average uncertainties were 142 m in the north-south direction, 130 m in the east-west direction, and 226 m in depth.

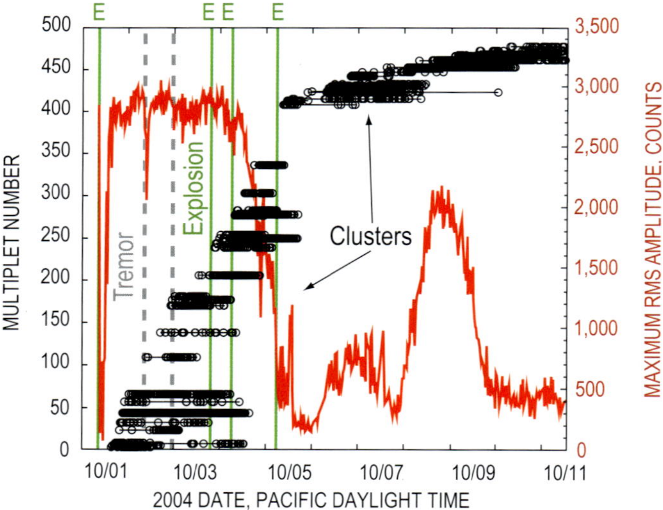

Figure 8. Timeline of multiplets from explosion of October 1 (leftmost green line) through October 11, 2004, detected on station ELK. Each earthquake is plotted as a circle, and multiplets are identified by a horizontal line through events that define multiplet. Only multiplets having more than 20 events are plotted. Maximum root-mean-squared (RMS) amplitude averaged over 1 minute at station JUN shown in red. Explosions, vertical green lines; tremor episodes, vertical gray lines.

Multiplets, October 5, 0000 PDT, Through October 11, 1659 PDT

Although four multiplets continued briefly through the explosion on October 5, a new temporal group of multiplets began about 1200 PDT on October 5. These multiplets generally had longer lifespans than previous multiplets, and fewer multiplets were occurring at the same time. Hybrids and low-frequency earthquakes dominated the seismic record. Multiplets during this time period did not obviously correspond to changes in the maximum amplitudes of signals recorded on station JUN.

The D34 hybrid multiplet discussed by Moran and others (this volume, chap. 2, their fig. 11) occurred during this time period. This multiplet consisted of 681 events starting October 8 at 0200 PDT. Absolute locations determined from the first arrivals of event stacks revealed a hypocentroid in the same location as multiplet C15. As was the case for C15, the polarities of the first arrivals were all dilatational. This multiplet methodically increased its amplitude before reaching a plateau and then decreased again to near the initial amplitude level (Moran and others, this volume, chap. 2). Magnitudes at the beginning were in the range M_d 1–1.5 and at the maximum were M_d 2.5–3.0. The cross-correlation coefficient of the first event to all others declined until the plateau in amplitude, and then remained constant for the rest of the sequence. Relative relocations of this cluster reveal a different pattern from that in previous multiplets. The hypocenter volume was tabular, striking to the southwest (fig. 10*A*). Uncertainties derived from jackknife tests showed errors of 2.7, 2.3, and 2.5 m, in the north-south, east-west, and vertical directions, respectively.

Absolute Locations, October 11, 1700 PDT, Through November 4, 1559 PST

During this period, low-frequency earthquakes dominated the seismic record. These earthquakes possessed emergent arrivals and thus had high uncertainties in absolute locations (fig. 9*B*). Earthquakes were extremely difficult to pick at stations outside the crater because of coda interference from previous events and poor arrivals. On October 12, station BLIS was installed on the saddle between the old and new domes (McChesney and others, this volume, chap. 7; fig. 2 for location). This station was used in less than half of the locations, however, owing to consistently emergent arrivals. Over the period of a month, only 130 earthquakes located by the PNSN met our selection criteria. For these earthquakes, an average of 10 stations were used for location solutions, with an average gap of 96 degrees and an average distance to the closest station of 431 m. Uncertainties in the north-south, east-west, and vertical directions were 142, 130, and 227 m, respectively.

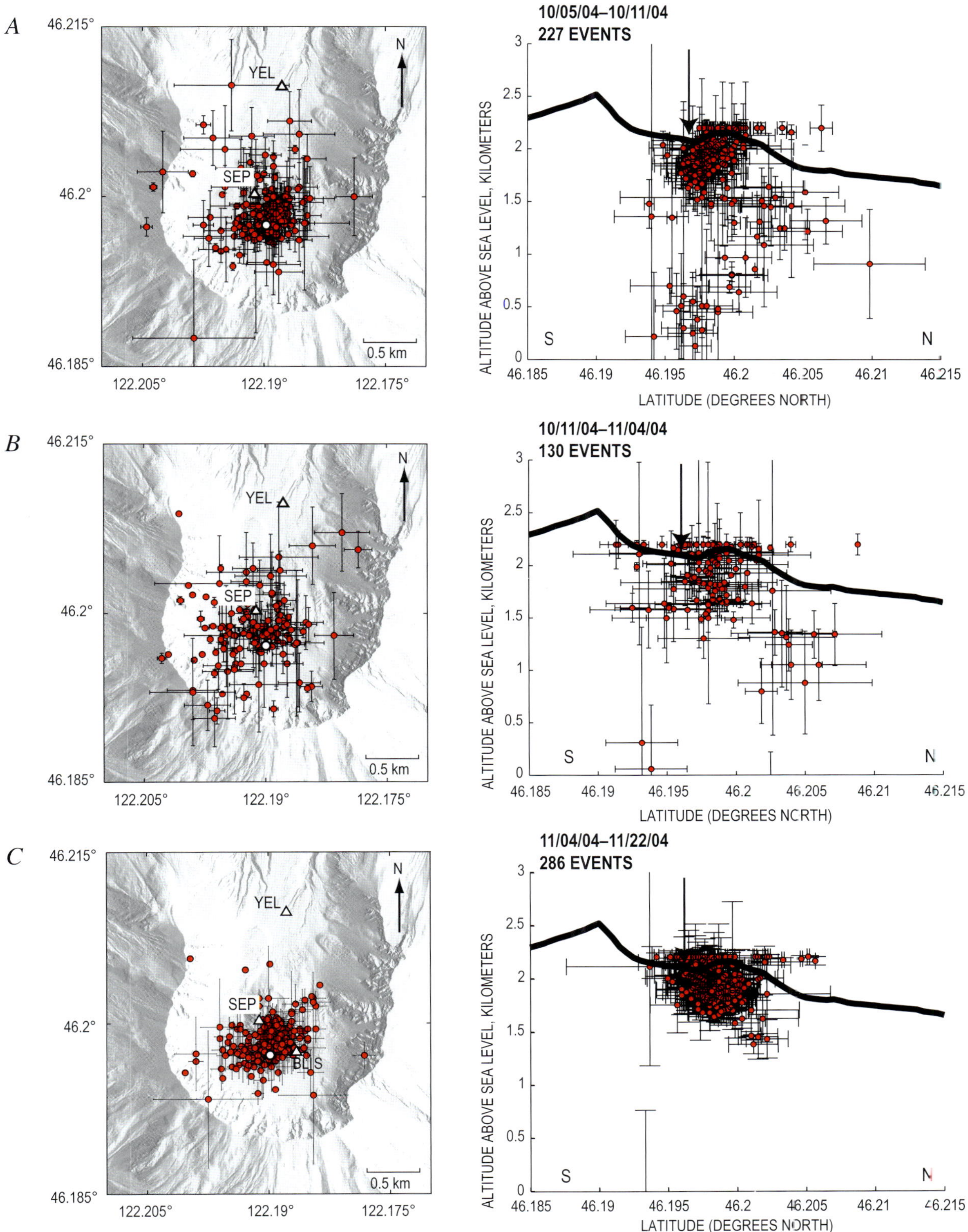

Figure 9. Absolute locations for Pacific Northwest Seismic Network (PNSN) catalog events for given time periods. Map views shown on left, cross sections on right. Permanent PNSN seismic stations shown with white triangles. Cross sections are north-south through station SEP, which was destroyed by explosion on October 1 and not reinstalled until November 5, 2004 (shown in top two plots only for reference). Earthquakes selected using same criteria as in figure 3. White dot (map view) and black arrow (cross section) show approximate location of vent.

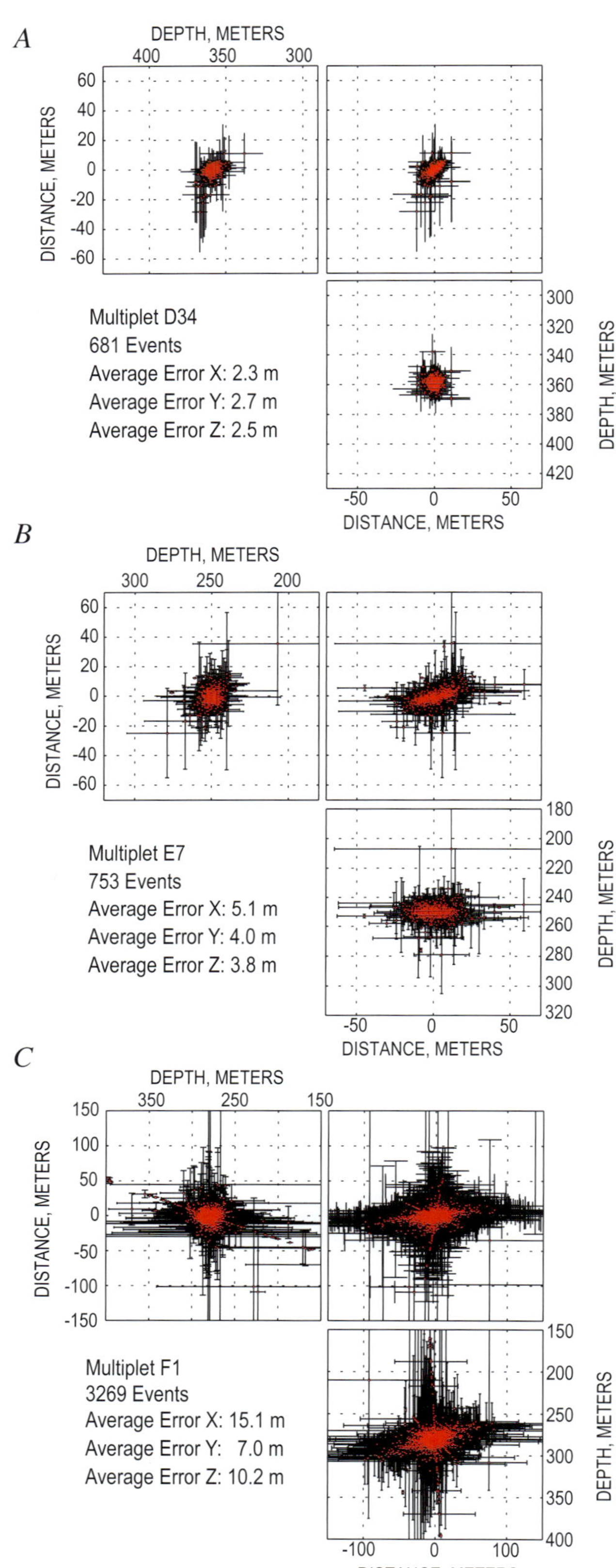

Figure 10. Relative relocations for three multiplets from early October to late November 2004. See figure 6 for explanation of views and errors.

Multiplets, October 11, 1700 PDT, Through November 4, 1559 PST

October 11, 2004, marked the first time new lava was seen at the surface (Vallance and others, this volume, chap. 9). Between then and November 4, three different spines were extruded, accompanied by comparatively low seismicity rates. Multiplets in the beginning of this time period had lifespans comparable to multiplets beginning after the October 5 explosion (figs. 8, 11), but multiplets with lifespans more than 1 month long began to occur later in the study period. In general, multiplets starting after October 22, 2004, had substantially longer lifespans than earlier multiplets. However, there was no obvious correlation between spine extrusion and the occurrence of multiplets during this time period.

One multiplet, E7, consisted of 753 events and started on October 16. Peak-to-peak amplitudes were stable and the cross-correlation coefficients of the first event compared to all others were nearly constant. The absolute hypocentroid from first-arrival picks of event stacks resulted in a location similar to that of multiplets C15 and D34. The polarities of first arrivals from event stacks all showed dilatation. The distribution of hypocenters was tabular, like that of D34, but had a more westerly strike (fig. 10*B*). The tabular distribution of epicenters had a long axis of approximately 40 m and a short axis of 10 m or less. The relative hypocenters spanned depths from 240 to 260 m. Uncertainties derived from jackknife analyses revealed average errors in location of 4.0, 5.1, and 3.8 m in the north-south, east-west, and vertical directions, respectively.

Absolute Locations, November 4, 1600 PST, Through November 22, 1559 PST

On November 5, station SEP was reinstalled (McChesney and others, this volume, chap. 7), increasing to three the number of stations within 2 km of the actively extruding spine. This addition proved important for locating earthquakes, as there were reliable picks from three close-in stations for almost all events. Absolute locations for 286 PNSN catalog events showed a 300-m-radius cluster with an epicentroid located only 160 m from the active vent (fig. 9*C*). The hypocentroid was located less than 400 m below the surface. The addition of the closest station, BLIS, on October 12, improved the sensitivity of the network to earthquakes, but comparing locations determined with and without BLIS is problematic. By ignoring station BLIS, we simulated the station configuration before October 1, 2004. The effect of taking out station BLIS was to make events slightly deeper on average, but the epicenters remained nearly unchanged. Details of these tests can be found in appendix 2. These tests suggest that the hypocentroid during this time period was at the same depth as the hypocentroid for the time period between September 25 and October 1, 2004, within error (figs. 3*B*, 6*C*). During the time period between November 4 and November 22, 2004, the earthquake-location solutions used an average of 10 stations, with an average gap of 96 degrees and an average distance from the epicenter to the nearest station of 45 m. Average uncertainties in the north-south, east-west, and vertical directions were 134, 107, and 122 m.

Multiplets, November 4, 1600 PST, Through November 22, 1559 PST

As was the case for the previous time period, multiplets during this time period possessed lengthy lifespans that included long periods of quiescence (fig. 11). As before, many multiplets were concurrent. One of the most prominent multiplets during this period, F1, consisted of 3,269 events that began on November 4 at approximately 1700 PST and lasted for more than 20 days. The absolute location derived from first-arrival picks of earthquake stacks resulted in a location south of all other multiplets analyzed in this study. The emergent first arrivals in the earthquake stacks produced large pick uncertainties. Resulting large uncertainties in the absolute locations as a result of the large pick uncertainties means that we cannot distinguish the absolute hypocentroid of F1 from those of other multiplet locations. Relative relocations of F1 formed a tabular volume similar in shape to multiplet E7 (Oct. 16 start) (fig. 10*B*). The epicentral distribution of multiplet F1 had a long axis of approximately 100 m and a short axis of 20 m. The cluster was confined to depths of 260 to 300 m. Average uncertainties derived from jackknife analyses in the north-south, east-west, and vertical directions were 7.0, 15.1, and 10.2 m, respectively.

Discussion

Absolute Locations

The high-frequency nature of the earthquakes between September 23 and September 25, 2004, suggests that the earthquakes during this time period were fracturing brittle rock. Although the uncertainties in latitude and longitude are on the same order of magnitude as the epicentral shift between September 23 and September 25, we believe the phase pick differences outlined by Moran and others (this volume, chap. 2) support the observed shift in epicentroid location. The upward and southward migration of

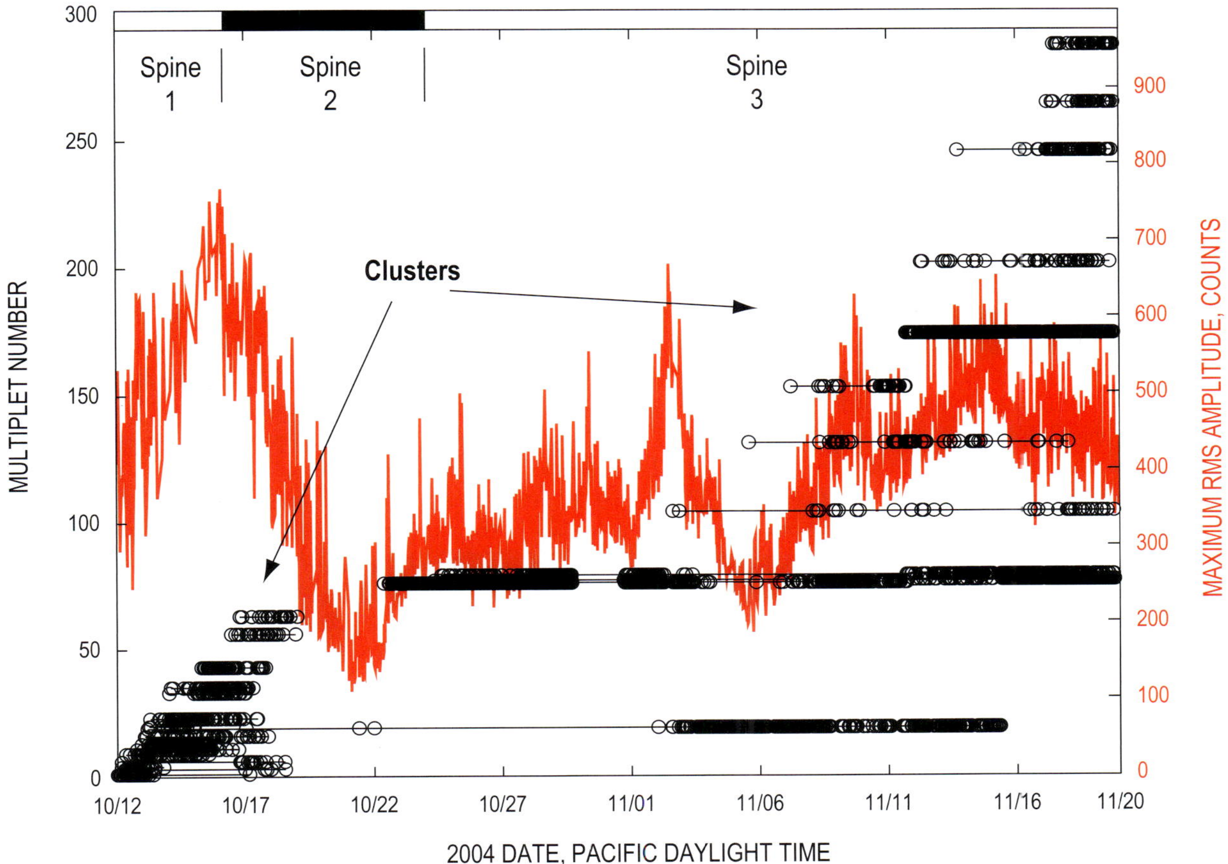

Figure 11. Timeline of multiplets detected on station ELK from October 12 through November 20, 2004. Each earthquake is plotted as a circle, and multiplets are identified by a horizontal line through events that define multiplet. Only multiplets that have more than 20 events are plotted. Maximum root-mean-squared (RMS) amplitude averaged over 1-minute intervals at station JUN shown in red. Date tickmarks are beginning of day, 0000 hr (midnight). Note change in amplitude scale compared to figures 4 and 8. Bar on top shows dome extrusion chronology (from Vallance and others, this volume, chap. 9).

absolute hypocenters between September 24 and September 26 and the shift to dominantly hybrid earthquakes suggest that the seismicity was occurring in response to a magmatic plug moving toward the surface (fig. 7). The shift occurred before any surface deformation near the 1980–86 dome (Dzurisin and others, this volume, chap. 14), although the continuous GPS at Johnston Ridge Observatory (JRO) did detect deflationary movement toward the volcano (Lisowski and others, this volume, chap. 15). An upward shift in hypocenters in the 1989 Ito-oki submarine eruption was explained as an upward propagating dike (Ukawa and Tsukahara, 1996). Their model showed that seismicity could occur above the crack tip in response to the dilatation of the crack below. Although this conclusion is plausible in hindsight at Mount St. Helens, the character and absolute locations of the earthquakes in the swarm between September 23 and September 25 alone probably would have not been enough to forecast an impending eruption.

After the first phreatic explosion on October 1, 2004, the loss of station SEP and consistently high seismic amplitudes on station YEL prevented the precise picking of events on crater stations. The absolute locations thus show greater scatter, have larger uncertainties, and are skewed in depth owing to the lessened station coverage. Jackknife tests performed by removing stations SEP and YEL from earthquake locations from September 25 to October 1 reveal depth patterns in seismicity similar to those seen for absolute earthquake locations calculated between October 1 and November 4. In essence, the precision in depth was poorer with the absence of stations SEP and YEL. This made relatively deep earthquakes deeper and shallow earthquakes become shallower (appendix 2). The locations were also more vertically aligned, similar to the absolute locations from October 1 through October 5 (fig. 3). The epicenter distribution in jackknife tests was nearly unchanged. We therefore suggest that the absolute locations for earthquakes from October 1 through October 5 were similar to those occurring before the first explosion. Similar tests indicate that locations for earthquakes after the October 5 explosion were similar to locations between September 25 and October 1 (appendix 2).

Absolute locations from November 5 to November 22 show that earthquake locations shifted slightly both up and south compared to pre-October 1 seismicity. The character of seismicity did not change significantly between October 16 and November 5, and we suggest that seismicity after the middle of October had similar absolute locations. The hypocentroid of absolute locations from November 5 to November 22 was ~290 m below the surface. Patterns in absolute locations between September 23 and November 22 indicate a conduit plunging 45°–60° northward at shallow depth beneath the old dome. The shape of the pattern is robust to changes in station layout (appendix 2); therefore we are confident the pattern is real.

Multiplets

A striking feature of seismicity during the early months of seismic unrest and eruption was the overwhelming presence of multiplets. Discrete multiplets occurred simultaneously throughout the study period; however, many can be further grouped into multiplet clusters. Here, we define a multiplet cluster as several multiplets that occurred simultaneously. Multiplet clusters often build slowly and end abruptly (figs. 4, 8, 11). On September 25, September 29, October 1, and October 5, the abrupt end of one cluster and the start of another was accompanied by changes in the amplitude of seismic signals recorded at station JUN (figs. 4, 8). No cluster recurred at any point during the study period, but in at least one case a multiplet within a previous cluster recurred after the cluster had ceased. The distinct clustering in time of multiplets may indicate that a particular source region was active during a cluster, with each multiplet having a different mechanism or occurring at a different location within the cluster source region. As each source region was altered or destroyed, a new cluster began from a new source region. Temporal clusters of multiplets were also observed at Soufrière Hills volcano, Montserrat, and were found to be related to the time derivative of the tilt (Green and Neuberg, 2006). Peaks in the real-time seismic amplitude measurement (RSAM), similar to the maximum amplitudes used here, were well correlated with peaks in the tilt at Soufrière Hills volcano; however, the relation between the RSAM and the occurrence of clusters of multiplets was not explicitly stated.

At Mount St. Helens, the absolute hypocentroid of each analyzed multiplet was similar when determined from stacks of each multiplet recorded at each station. All of the analyzed multiplets had locations within ~100 m of station BLIS at depths of 250 to 350 m (fig. 12). Further, the cross-correlation coefficients between each of the analyzed multiplets had values ranging between 0.17 and 0.50. This suggests that highly stable but distinct sources were present within a small source region at shallow depth beneath the 1980–86 dome. Similarly, the absolute location of multiplets that occurred at Soufrière Hills volcano in 1997 clustered tightly together, and Neuberg and others (2006) used this evidence to help argue for a pressure-dependent source for the occurrence of multiplets.

Multiplets also varied in lifespan. Generally, multiplets earlier in the study period had shorter lifespans than those occurring later. Lifespans of more than 1 month were observed for some multiplets during the dome-building phase of the eruption, suggesting a stable and stationary source region. Such long event families have only been reported at Shishaldin Volcano, Alaska (Petersen and others, 2006). However, very few studies have covered periods of time longer than days to weeks with continuous data. Amplitudes of events within individual multiplets were highly variable. However, changes typically varied smoothly with time. The magnitudes of events in large-population multiplets also ranged widely, from M_d –0.2 to M_d 3.0.

A steady decline in the cross-correlation coefficient between the first and subsequent events is observed in many multiplets. An example of this phenomenon is multiplet B1 (fig. 13). This change in cross-correlation coefficient could result from a shift in location or a change in the path between an earthquake and the recording station. Gret and others (2005) exploited the sensitivity of the coda to changes in path to distinguish changes in location from changes in path at Mount Erebus, Antarctica. They compared the cross-correlation values of event families using windows in different parts of the earthquake waveform. A similar analysis of multiplets here reveals similar patterns in correlation coefficients of the first event to each subsequent event, regardless of the time window used (fig. 13). We therefore interpret the change in cross-correlation values with time to result from small changes in location that are within the uncertainty of our relative locations.

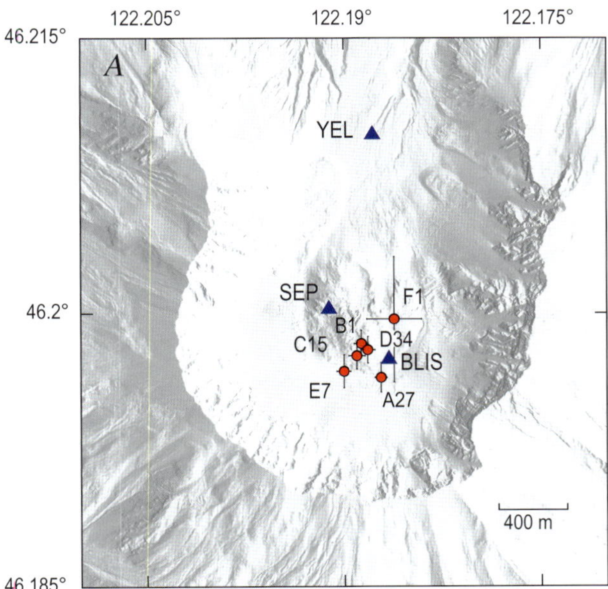

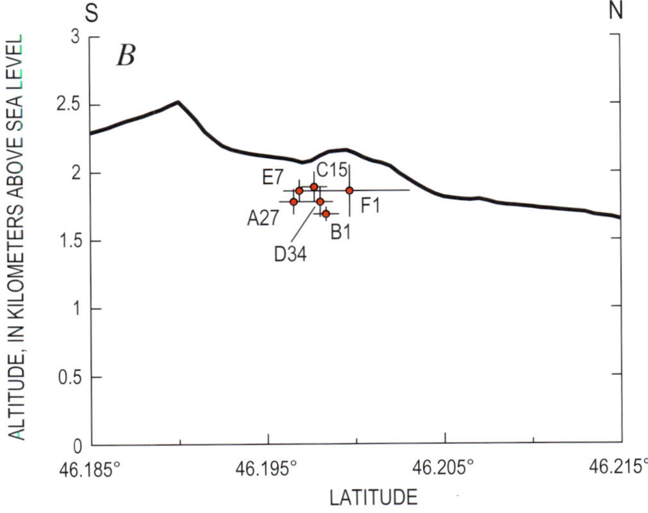

Figure 12. Absolute locations, obtained using first-arrival picks of event stacks, for multiplets depicted in figures 6 and 10. *A*, Map view. Blue triangles, permanent Pacific Northwest Seismic Network (PNSN) seismic stations as of November 4, 2004. *B*, Locations projected on north-south cross section through station SEP.

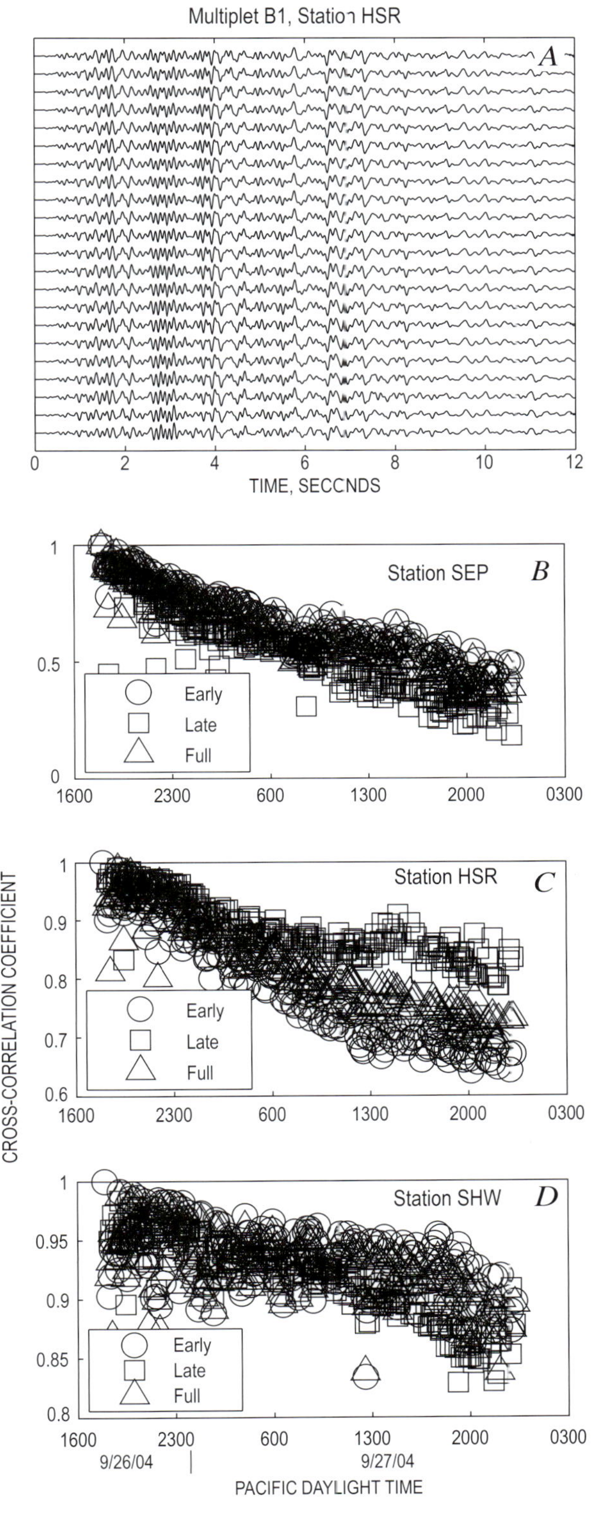

Figure 13. Cross-correlation analysis of first 220 events from multiplet B1. *A*, Waveforms filtered between 1 and 10 Hz of every tenth earthquake recorded on station HSR. *B–D*, Cross-correlation values as a function of time at stations SEP, HSR, and SHW, respectively. Three parts of waveform are used in each plot: first 4 s (early), next 4 s (late), and entire waveform (full).

Only the explosion on October 1 and, to a lesser extent, the explosion on October 5 significantly affected the occurrence of multiplets. After the October 1 explosion, all earthquakes, including multiplets, stopped for more than 3 hours (Moran and others, this volume, chap. 2). Several multiplets then restarted, and new multiplets began as the level of seismicity increased. This process repeated itself during periods of tremor and explosions occurring between October 1 and October 5; some multiplets already present continued and, in many cases, new multiplets began. The reactivation of multiplets and general seismicity after the October 1 explosion suggests that the phenomenon leading to the generation of multiplets during the time period around October 1 may be pressure dependent (Moran and others, this volume, chap. 2). The relation between the October 5 explosion and the occurrence of multiplets is less clear, because four multiplets continued through the explosion and another multiplet cluster started shortly after.

Relative locations of multiplets during the period we studied define a changing source volume. Between September 23 and October 5, hypocenters of multiplets defined a small equidimensional space, but after October 5 they defined larger, more tabular bodies striking west-southwest. In all cases except multiplet F1, depths spanned 20 m or less. The strike of the tabular bodies in E7 and F1 was also approximately perpendicular to the strike of spine 3, which extruded from October 24 to December 20, 2004 (Vallance and others, this volume, chap. 9). Such a progression is interesting in the context of volcanic activity. Moran and others (this volume, chap. 2) suggest that seismicity between September 23 and October 5 was associated with clearing of the conduit to allow subsequent lava extrusion. Smaller, more equidimensional source volumes early in the study period have relatively smaller surface area for gas escape. If the gas could not escape efficiently, excess overpressure may have caused fragmentation to occur in the conduit, resulting in the explosions seen between October 1 and October 5. After October 5, seismic amplitudes decreased, the lifespan of multiplets and source volumes increased, and extrusion of lava at the surface soon began. The tabular shape and orientation of the relative locations after October 1 are suggestive of a dike. Presumably, the larger source volume (and larger surface area) defined by the relative locations facilitated greater gas loss at shallow levels in the conduit, thereby contributing to steady degassing and suppression of explosions.

The cause for earthquakes at the restricted depths indicated by the absolute and relative locations is enigmatic. Seismogenic stresses around a plug of magma are dependent on the diameter, velocity, and viscosity of the plug (Webb and Dingwell, 1990; Goto, 1999). Indeed, it has been shown that stick-slip motion along the edges of an extruding plug can generate earthquakes that match the rates and sizes of observed drumbeat earthquakes at Mount St. Helens (Iverson, this volume, chap. 21). We might expect seismogenic zones at constrictions in the conduit (where the local magma flux increases), and we believe that this may be a reasonable source of seismogenic stress. We might also expect earthquakes in an area where the overburden pressure is low enough to allow solidification of the magma and force the viscosity across some threshold value. The viscosity is dependent mostly on pressure and, to a lesser extent, on temperature (Blundy and others, 2006). Viscosity can vary over many orders of magnitude, making it a difficult parameter to model in a context useful for interpreting the location of earthquakes (Goto, 1999). The lithostatic pressure, however, increased only slightly in the time period we describe. A decrease in the occurrence of earthquakes and multiplets after the October 1 explosion also suggests that the seismicity was dependent on pressure. We would therefore expect earthquake locations to remain fixed or to shallow slightly during the study period if the earthquakes were dependent on the lithostatic pressure, and the viscosity and velocity of the plug were fixed. The absolute depths of the multiplets were consistent with this observation and were also coincident with the depth of microlite crystallization of the rising magma (Cashman and others, this volume, chap. 19; Pallister and others, this volume, chap. 30). The depth of microlite crystallization is also thought to be a pressure-dependent phenomenon.

Not all earthquakes during the study period occurred as part of a multiplet. Indeed, the absolute locations show that earthquake hypocenters were spread across a wide range of depths, exceeding the depth range of the multiplets. The seismic energy declined after each explosion (Moran and others, this volume, chap. 6, their fig. 3), but for many of the explosions the multiplets persisted (fig. 8). This indicates that the earthquakes not associated with the multiplets declined in size and or number and therefore may also have been pressure dependent. Because the behavior of those earthquakes associated with multiplets and of those not associated with multiplets differs, we suggest that the cause of each phenomenon is distinct. In the case of the multiplets, the source is highly stable and nondestructive for long periods of time. In the case of earthquakes not associated with a multiplet, the source is nonrepeatable over short time scales.

Conclusions

Absolute and relative locations allowed us to characterize the possible source of earthquakes associated with renewed activity at Mount St. Helens beginning in September 2004. Absolute locations were improved with the use of a new velocity model. During periods of good depth constraint, absolute locations were found to be less than 1 km deep. A shallowing of earthquakes occurred between September 24 and 26, supported by changes in the difference of first-arrival picks at close-in stations (Moran and others, this volume, chap. 2). Absolute earthquake locations revealed a north-dipping structure which likely coincides with the shallow conduit that was formed during the initial vent-clearing phase.

Multiplets were prominent during the first months of the eruption. They included volcano-tectonic, hybrid, and low-frequency events with a wide range of magnitudes. Multiplets varied in lifespan, but those of the vent-clearing phase had much shorter lifespans than multiplets occurring during dome extrusion. Multiplets also occurred in temporal clusters that were usually associated with large changes in the maximum RMS seismic-signal amplitude. Absolute locations derived from earthquake stacks show that the individual multiplets likely originated in nearly the same area. Relative locations showed source volumes with diameters on the order of 25 m before October 5 and larger, tabular source volumes oriented to the west-southwest thereafter, a change concurrent with the transition from vent clearing to dome building. In some cases, the cross-correlation coefficients of the first event compared to all subsequent events showed a steady decline, suggesting movement of the source location at a level within our uncertainty. The properties and locations of multiplets suggest that their occurrence was based on changes in pressure.

Acknowledgments

We wish to thank the staff at the Pacific Northwest Seismic Network for their meticulous work in collecting and archiving data and generating a consistent catalog throughout the volcanic sequence—notably Steve Malone, Tony Qamar, Amy Wright, Tom Yelin, Guy Medema, Karen Meagher, Bill Steele, Bob Norris, and Ruth Ludwin. We also wish to thank our reviewers, Seth Moran and Clifford Thurber, for insightful comments that significantly improved the final version of the manuscript, and Dave Ramsey for the map in figure 2.

References Cited

Aster, R.C., Borchers, B., and Thurber, C.H., 2005, Parameter estimation and inverse problems: Amsterdam, Elsevier Academic Press, 301 p.

Battaglia, J., Thurber, C.H., Got, J.-L., Rowe, C.A., and White, R.A., 2004, Precise relocation of earthquakes following the 15 June 1991 eruption of Mount Pinatubo (Philippines): Journal of Geophysical Research, v. 109, p. B07302, doi:10.1029/2003JB002959.

Blundy, J., Cashman, K., and Humphreys, M., 2006, Magma heating by decompression-driven crystallization beneath andesite volcanoes: Nature, v. 443, no. 7107, p. 76–80, doi:10.1038/nature05100.

Cashman, K.V., Thornber, C.R., and Pallister, J.S., 2008, From dome to dust; shallow crystallization and fragmentation of conduit magma during the 2004–2006 dome extrusion of Mount St. Helens, Washington, chap. 19 *of* Sherrod, D.R., Scott, W.E., and Stauffer, P.H., eds., A volcano rekindled; the renewed eruption of Mount St. Helens, 2004–2006: U.S. Geological Survey Professional Paper 1750 (this volume).

Dzurisin, D., Lisowski, M., Poland, M.P., Sherrod, D R., and LaHusen, R.G., 2008, Constraints and conundrums resulting from ground-deformation measurements made during the 2004–2005 dome-building eruption of Mount St. Helens, Washington, chap. 14 *of* Sherrod, D.R., Scott, W.E., and Stauffer, P.H., eds., A volcano rekindled; the renewed eruption of Mount St. Helens, 2004–2006: U.S. Geological Survey Professional Paper 1750 (this volume).

Efron, B., and Gong G., 1983, A leisurely look at the bootstrap, the jackknife and cross-validation: American Statistician, v. 37, no. 1, p. 36–48.

Fréchet, J., 1985, Sismogenèse et doublets sismiques: Grenoble, France, Université Scientifique et Médicale de Grenoble, M.S. thesis, 206 p.

Frémont, M.J., and Malone, S.D., 1987, High precision relative locations of earthquakes at Mount St. Helens, Washington: Journal of Geophysical Research, v. 92, no B10, p. 10223–10236.

Geller, R.J., and Mueller, C.S., 1980, Four similar earthquakes in central California: Geophysical Research Letters, v. 7, p. 821–824.

Got, J.-L., Fréchet J., and Klein, F.W., 1994, Deep fault plane geometry inferred from multiplet relative relocation beneath the south flank of Kilauea Journal of Geophysical Research, v. 99, no. B8, p. 15375–15386.

Goto, A., 1999, A new model for volcanic earthquake at Unzen volcano; melt rupture model: Geophysical Research Letters, v. 26, no. 16, p. 2541–2544.

Green, D.N., and Neuberg, J., 2006, Waveform classification of volcanic low-frequency earthquake swarms and its implication at Soufrière Hills Volcano, Montserrat: Journal of Volcanology and Geothermal Research, v. 153, nos. 1–2, p. 51–63, doi: 10.1016/j.jvolgeores.2005.08.003.

Gret, A., Snieder, R., Aster, R.C., and Kyle, P.R., 2005, Monitoring rapid temporal change in a volcano with coda wave interferometry: Geophysical Research Letters, v. 32, L06304, doi: 10.1029/2004GL0211143.

Herrmann, R.B., 1979, FASTHYPO—a hypocenter location program: Earthquake Notes, v. 50, no. 2, p. 25–37.

Iverson, R.M., 2008, Dynamics of seismogenic volcanic extrusion resisted by a solid surface plug, Mount St. Helens, 2004–2005, chap. 21 *of* Sherrod, D.R., Scott, W.E., and Stauffer, P.H., eds., A volcano rekindled; the renewed eruption of Mount St. Helens, 2004–2006: U.S. Geological Survey Professional Paper 1750 (this volume).

Klein, F.W., 1989, HYPOINVERSE, a program for VAX computers to solve for earthquake locations and magnitudes: U.S. Geological Survey Open-File Report 89–314, 59 p.

Lahr, J.C., Chouet, B.A., Stephens, C.D., Power, J.A., and Page, R.A., 1994, Earthquake classification, location, and error analysis in a volcanic environment; implications for the magmatic system of the 1989–1990 eruptions at Redoubt Volcano, Alaska: Journal of Volcanology and Geothermal Research, v. 62, nos. 1–4, p. 137–151, doi:10.1016/0377-0273(94)90031-0.

Lees, J.M., and Crosson, R.S., 1989, Tomographic inversion for three-dimensional velocity structure at Mount St. Helens using earthquake data: Journal of Geophysical Research, v. 94, no. B5, p. 5716–5728.

Lisowski, M., Dzurisin, D., Denlinger, R.P., and Iwatsubo, E.Y., 2008, Analysis of GPS-measured deformation associated with the 2004–2006 dome-building eruption of Mount St. Helens, Washington, chap. 15 *of* Sherrod, D.R., Scott, W.E., and Stauffer, P.H., eds., A volcano rekindled; the renewed eruption of Mount St. Helens, 2004–2006: U.S. Geological Survey Professional Paper 1750 (this volume).

Malone, S.D., and Pavlis, G.L., 1983, Velocity structure and relocation of earthquakes at Mount St. Helens [abs.]: Eos (American Geophysical Union Transactions), v. 64, p. 895.

McChesney, P.J., Couchman, M.R., Moran, S.C., Lockhart, A.B., Swinford, K.J., and LaHusen, R.G., 2008, Seismic-monitoring changes and the remote deployment of seismic stations (seismic spider) at Mount St. Helens, 2004–2005, chap. 7 *of* Sherrod, D.R., Scott, W.E., and Stauffer, P.H., eds., A volcano rekindled; the renewed eruption of Mount St. Helens, 2004–2006: U.S. Geological Survey Professional Paper 1750 (this volume).

Michelini, A., and Lomax, A., 2004, The effect of velocity structure errors on double-difference earthquake location: Geophysical Research Letters, v. 31, L09602, doi:10.1029/2004GL019682.

Moran, S.C., Malone, S.D., Qamar, A.I., Thelen, W.A., Wright, A.K., and Caplan-Auerbach, J., 2008a, Seismicity associated with renewed dome building at Mount St. Helens, 2004–2005, chap. 2 *of* Sherrod, D.R., Scott, W.E., and Stauffer, P.H., eds., A volcano rekindled; the renewed eruption of Mount St. Helens, 2004–2006: U.S. Geological Survey Professional Paper 1750 (this volume).

Moran, S.C., McChesney, P.J., and Lockhart, A.B., 2008b, Seismicity and infrasound associated with explosions at Mount St. Helens, 2004–2005, chap. 6 *of* Sherrod, D.R., Scott, W.E., and Stauffer, P.H., eds., A volcano rekindled; the renewed eruption of Mount St. Helens, 2004–2006: U.S. Geological Survey Professional Paper 1750 (this volume).

Musumeci, C., Gresta, S., and Malone, S.D., 2002, Magma system recharge of Mount St. Helens from precise relative hypocenter location of microearthquakes: Journal of Geophysical Research, v. 107, no. B10, 2264, p. ESE 16-1–16-9, doi:10.1029/2001JB000629.

Neuberg, J.W., Tuffen, H., Collier, L., Green, D., Powell, T., and Dingwell, D., 2006, The trigger mechanism of low-frequency earthquakes on Montserrat: Journal of Volcanology and Geothermal Research, v. 153, nos. 1–2, p. 37–50, doi:10.1016/j.jvolgeores.2005.08.008.

Pallister, J.S., Thornber, C.R., Cashman, K.V., Clynne, M.A., Lowers, H.A., Mandeville, C.W., Brownfield, I.K., and Meeker, G.P., 2008, Petrology of the 2004–2006 Mount St. Helens lava dome—implications for magmatic plumbing and eruption triggering, chap. 30 *of* Sherrod, D.R., Scott, W.E., and Stauffer, P.H., eds., A volcano rekindled; the renewed eruption of Mount St. Helens, 2004–2006: U.S. Geological Survey Professional Paper 1750 (this volume).

Pearson, C.F., and Kienle, J., 1978, A seismic refraction study of Augustine volcano, Alaska [abs.]: Eos (American Geophysical Union Transactions), v. 59, no. 4, p. 311.

Petersen, T., Caplan-Auerbach, J., and McNutt, S.R., 2006, Sustained long-period seismicity at Shishaldin Volcano, Alaska: Journal of Volcanology and Geothermal Research, v. 151, p. 365–381.

Poupinet, G., Ellsworth, W.L., and Fréchet, J., 1984, Monitoring velocity variations in the crust using earthquake doublets; an application to the Calaveras Fault, California: Journal of Geophysical Research, v. 89, p. 5719–5731.

Pujol, J., 2000, Joint event location–the JHD technique and applications to data from local seismic networks, *in* Thurber, C.H., and Rabinowitz, N., eds., Advances in seismic event location: Dordrecht, Kluwer Academic Publishers, p. 163–204.

Qamar, A.I., Malone, S.D., Moran, S.C., Steele, W.P., and Thelen, W.A., 2008, Near-real-time information products for Mount St. Helens—tracking the ongoing eruption, chap. 3 *of* Sherrod, D.R., Scott, W.E., and Stauffer, P.H., eds., A volcano rekindled; the renewed eruption of Mount St. Helens, 2004–2006: U.S. Geological Survey Professional Paper 1750 (this volume).

Reeder, J.W., and Lahr, J.C., 1987, Seismological aspects of the 1976 eruption of Augustine Volcano, Alaska: U.S. Geological Survey Bulletin 1768, 32 p.

Rowe, C.A., Thurber, C.H., and White, R.A., 2004, Dome growth behavior at Soufriere Hills Volcano, Montserrat, revealed by relocation of volcanic event swarms, 1995–1996: Journal of Volcanology and Geothermal Research, v. 134, no. 3, p. 199–221.

Schaff, D.P., Bokelmann, G.H.R., Ellsworth, W.L., Zanzerkia, E., Waldhauser, F., and Beroza, G.C., 2004, Optimizing correlation techniques for improved earthquake location: Bulletin of the Seismological Society of America, v. 94, no. 2, p. 705–721.

Stephens, C.D., and Chouet, B.A., 2001, Evolution of the December 14, 1989 precursory long-period event swarm at Redoubt Volcano, Alaska: Journal of Volcanology and Geothermal Research, v. 109, p. 133–148.

Swanson, D.A., Casadevall, T.J., Dzurisin, D., Malone, S.D., Newhall, C.G., and Weaver, C.S., 1983, Predicting eruptions at Mount St. Helens, June 1980 through December 1982: Science, v. 221, no. 4618, p. 1369–1376.

Thelen, W.A., Malone, S.D., Qamar, A.I., and Pullammanappallil, S., 2006, Improvements to absolute locations from an updated velocity model at Mount St. Helens, Washington [abs.]: Seismological Research Letters, v. 77, no. 2, p. 238.

Ukawa, M., and Tsukahara, H., 1996, Earthquake swarms and dike intrusions off the east coast of Izu Peninsula, central Japan: Tectonophysics, v. 253, p. 285–303.

Vallance, J.W., Schneider, D.J., and Schilling, S.P., 2008, Growth of the 2004–2006 lava-dome complex at Mount St. Helens, Washington, chap. 9 *of* Sherrod, D.R., Scott, W.E., and Stauffer, P.H., eds., A volcano rekindled; the renewed eruption of Mount St. Helens, 2004–2006: U.S. Geological Survey Professional Paper 1750 (this volume).

Waite, G.P., and Moran, S.C., 2006, Crustal P-wave speed structure under Mount St. Helens from local earthquake tomography [abs.]: Eos (American Geophysical Union Transactions), v. 87, no. 52, Fall Meeting supplement, Abstract V11B-0578.

Waldhauser, F., 2001, HypoDD—a program to compute double-difference hypocenter locations (hypoDD version 1.0): United States Geologic Survey Open-File Report 01–113, 25 p.

Waldhauser, F., and Ellsworth, W.L., 2000, A double-difference earthquake location algorithm; method and application to the northern Hayward Fault, California: Bulletin of the Seismological Society of America, v. 90, p. 1353–1368.

Webb, S.L., and Dingwell, D.B., 1990, Non-Newtonian rheology of igneous melts at high stress and strain rates: experimental results for rhyolite, andesite, basalt, and nephelinite: Journal of Geophysical Research, v. 95, p. 15695–15701.

Williams, D.L., Abrams, G., Finn, C., Dzurisin, D., Johnson, D.J., and Denlinger, R., 1987, Evidence from gravity data for an intrusive complex beneath Mount St. Helens: Journal of Geophysical Research, v. 92, no. B10, p. 10207–10222.

Wolfe, C.J., 2002, On the mathematics of using difference operators to relocate earthquakes: Bulletin of the Seismological Society of America, v. 92, p. 2879–2892.

Appendix 1. Velocity Model

A velocity model serves an integral role in earthquake locations. Although many regions have three-dimensional velocity models available, computing power and speed requirements often mean that one-dimensional velocity models are used for routine locations. At Mount St. Helens, large static station corrections and earthquakes with locations above the velocity model datum (airquakes) were common during the beginning of the 2004 unrest and eruption, which demonstrated the need for a more accurate velocity model in the shallow part of the volcano. The velocity model used for routine locations by the Pacific Northwest Seismic Network (PNSN) was determined using nearby quarry blasts (Malone and Pavlis, 1983). That velocity model is regionally accurate, judging from the small station corrections on stations beyond the edifice of Mount St. Helens. The data used for the velocity model, however, had poor ray coverage through the shallow part of the edifice (<2 km). The result is a constant P-wave velocity of 4.6 km/s in the upper 2.2 km of the velocity model, far too fast for the pyroclastic deposits, thin lava flows, and fractured dacite lava domes found throughout the crater walls of the volcano. Exceedingly fast velocities resulted in large station corrections on edifice and crater stations used for routine processing (table 2). Three-dimensional P-wave velocity models exist for Mount St. Helens (Lees, 1989; Waite and Moran, 2006), but they also suffer from a lack of ray coverage and coarse resolution at the depths we are studying. Here we describe the method we used to develop a shallow (<2 km) one-dimensional P-wave velocity model to supplement the existing one-dimensional model (in use by the PNSN) for the Mount St. Helens area.

Table 2. Station corrections calculated for each velocity model with permanent Pacific Northwest Seismic Network (PNSN) stations used in routine earthquake locations between 2004 and 2006.

[See McChesney and others (this volume, chap. 7) for locations of seismic stations not shown in figure 2. Data shown here for each station are time residuals, in seconds, that result from the inadequacy of a one-dimensional model to represent the three-dimensional Earth. In theory, station residuals converge to zero as the computed velocity model converges toward the actual velocity structure between earthquake and station.]

PNSN Station	Existing PNSN Model[1] (s)	New Velocity Model[1] (s)	New Velocity Model[2] (s)
SEND	-0.087	0.000	-0.023
RAFT	-0.187	-0.083	0.063
MIBL	-0.218	-0.096	0.000
WESG	-0.179	-0.091	0.099
MIDE	-0.212	-0.190	0.000
SEP	-0.151	-0.102	0.071
BLIS	-0.393	-0.366	-0.170
NED	-0.050	0.000	0.131
SUG	0.200	0.000	0.064
YEL	0.024	0.000	0.078
EDM	0.179	0.059	0.033
HSR	0.192	0.070	0.088
SHW	0.108	0.042	-0.032
STD	0.070	0.057	0.000
SOS	0.017	0.039	0.000
JUN	-0.029	0.025	-0.034
FL2	-0.029	0.054	0.000
CDF	-0.043	0.134	0.062
ELK	-0.226	-0.177	-0.227
TDL	-0.163	-0.158	-0.223
LVP	-0.078	0.000	-0.060

[1]Datum is 1,700 m above sea level.

[2]Datum is 2,200 m above sea level.

Methods

In the summer of 2005, we deployed, at 100-m intervals, 39 RT-125 seismic recorders with alternating 4.5-Hz geophones and 1-Hz vertical seismometers (Thelen and others, 2006). The instruments were deployed for three days. The array began approximately 1 km north of the 2004–5 vent and extended northward 4 km onto the Pumice Plain (fig. 14).

We used an Occam's inversion scheme with second-order Tikhonov regularization to invert first-arrival data for a velocity model (Aster and others, 2005). The Occam's inversion scheme seeks a solution to $G(m) = d$ subject to the following constraints:

$$min \left\| Lm \right\|_2$$

$$\text{and} \left\| G(m) - d \right\|_2 \leq \delta ,$$

where $G(m)$ is a function of the model parameters that calculates the data, d, from the model. In this formulation, L is the roughening matrix (which is equal to the finite-difference approximation of the second derivative), and δ is the discrepancy parameter, $\sigma\sqrt{n}$, where n is the number of degrees of freedom and σ is the uncertainty of the time picks. Occam's inversion relies on an iteratively applied local linearization given by Taylor's theorem,

$$G(m^k + \Delta m) \approx G(m^k) + J(m^k)\Delta m \quad ,$$

where m^k is a trial model and $J(m^k)$ is the Jacobian. Using a damped least-squares approach, the constraints above, combined with the Taylor approximation, give

$$\min \left\| G(m^k) + J(m^k)\Delta m - d \right\|_2^2 + \alpha^2 \left\| L(m^k + \Delta m) \right\|_2^2 \quad ,$$

where the parameter α is adjusted after each iteration so that the solution will not exceed the allowable misfit. The inversion is terminated when $\delta^2 = \chi^2$, where

$$\chi^2 = \sum_{i=1}^{m} \frac{(d_i - (Gm_{L_2})_i)^2}{\sigma_i^2} .$$

Our "active sources" were earthquakes associated with dome building at Mount St. Helens. Twenty $M_d > 1.0$ earthquakes occurred within the crater from the surface to depths of 1 km while our instruments were recording. Of these, we chose the best earthquake (August 20, 2005, 21:28:37 PDT; $M_d = 2.6$) on the basis of its clarity of impulsive arrivals across the transect and the number of PNSN catalog picks used to routinely locate the earthquake. The epicenter of the earthquake is well constrained, owing to the excellent azimuthal coverage of seismometers around Mount St. Helens. The existing one-dimensional velocity model described above, however, allows for a tradeoff between the depth and the origin time within the upper 2.2 km of the velocity model. Thus, the depth is not as well constrained as the epicenter. With additional layers in the shallow part of the velocity model, this tradeoff is less important.

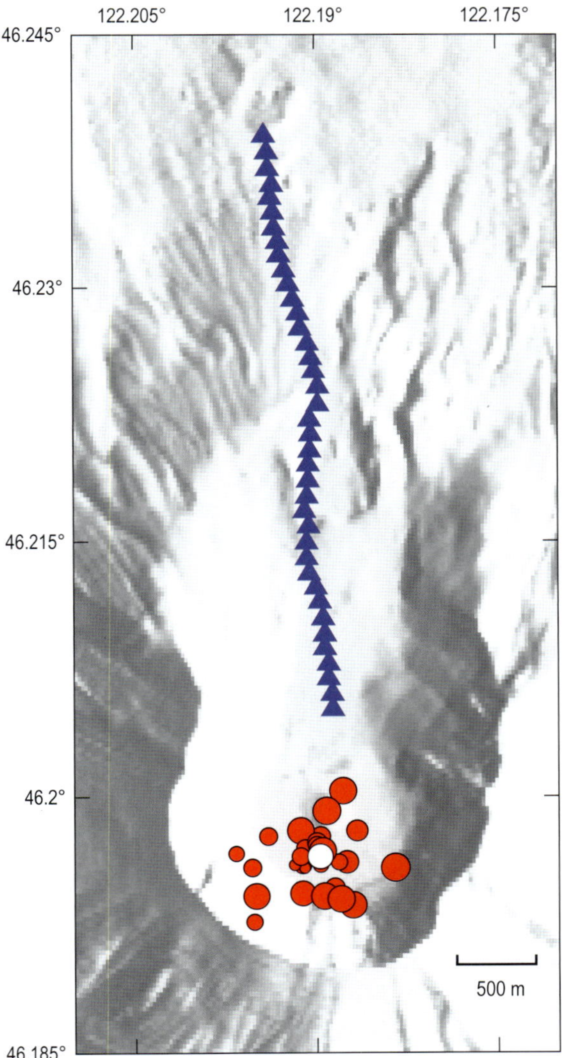

Figure 14. Instrument layout (blue triangles) with earthquake epicenters (red dots) used for P-wave inversion. Epicenter of primary earthquake used in inversion is shown by white dot.

Secondary arrivals were observed in the record section of the transect, but they were not easily picked across the array. We therefore used only the P-wave arrivals. Errors in picking first arrivals on the event used for the inversion were assumed to be constant and were estimated to be within five time samples (0.05 s) of the actual arrival. Our algorithm allows for the use of one earthquake at a time. We chose to use only one earthquake in our inversion for two reasons: (1) there was only one other earthquake (August 22, 2005, 03:32:45 PDT; $M_d = 1.4$) that possessed impulsive arrivals across the entire transect, and (2) that earthquake showed an identical pattern in first-arrival picks to the earthquake we used for the inversion. Using multiple earthquakes would not change or add to the information used in the inversion because the earthquakes that occurred during the deployment of the transect occurred in such a tight cluster. First arrivals from the other earthquakes that occurred during the deployment were picked only if they could be identified with a precision of better than 0.05 s. The time spread in picks at a given offset was used to define the standard deviation to ensure that the inversion did not overfit the data.

We used a one-dimensional travel-time calculator parameterized with constant velocity layers. The travel-time calculator allows for a three-dimensional geometry of stations and earthquake location. The setup of the inverse problem prescribes node depths and solves for the layer velocity between nodes. The node number and depths were based largely on constraints imparted by the program used for earthquake locations, SPONG. The first constraint is the use of a total of 10 layers in the velocity model. When combined with the existing PNSN velocity model, this only allowed for 4 layers. The second constraint is that different station altitudes can be used, but they must be included inside the top layer of the velocity model. Stations within 10 km of the crater, excluding the crater stations, span altitudes from 1,268 m to 1,700 m. We thus required a 500-m-thick top layer so that we could include the altitudes of these closest stations to the crater. Depths of the remaining three node-depths layers were found through a grid search with an increment of 100 m. The preferred model is the model that satisfies the condition above and has the smallest residual times ($t_{observed} - t_{calculated}$). Models with low-velocity inversions were poorly constrained using first-arrival data and thus were not considered.

The initial depth of the earthquake used in the inversion was 0.24 km (datum at 1,700 m above sea level). We iterated velocity-model solutions, each time updating the station corrections using a subset of PNSN catalog earthquakes with high-quality arrivals (see station correction discussion below) to get a new earthquake location and origin time. The new earthquake parameters were then used to update distance and time information of the transect, and the velocity model inversion was run again. Iterations stopped when the change in depth between iterations was less than the calculated uncertainty of the solution. The final depth of the earthquake was calculated to be 0.13 km. By alternately recalculating the location and the velocity model, we minimize errors in the location of the earthquake and in the velocity inversion results.

Location uncertainties in our nonlinear velocity inversion were calculated using the diagonal of the covariance, a method that is appropriate in linear inverse problems. We adapted this technique to our problem by linearizing the solution through a central difference and then calculating the error as if it were a linear problem. This approach is often used, though not strictly correct, and may underestimate the uncertainties in the model (Aster and others, 2005).

Station corrections are static time corrections used in earthquake hypocenter inversions using one-dimensional velocity models. Station corrections, which compensate for the one-dimensional modeling of a truly three-dimensional velocity structure, can be minimized by finding the closest one-dimensional approximation of the three-dimensional velocity structure under the volcano (Pujol, 2000). We do not minimize the station corrections here; however, we do use decreases in station corrections as a proxy for the quality of our velocity model.

Station corrections were calculated using a subset of 29 PNSN catalog events that occurred between 2004 and 2006. These events were selected for their exceptionally sharp impulsive arrivals and were already in use for calibrating PNSN velocity models for Mount St. Helens (S. Malone, oral commun., 2006). The first arrivals of these events were picked on the PNSN stations only if the arrival was unambiguous to ±0.05 s. Locations were then calculated using the existing velocity model and station corrections. The new velocity model was then used with the existing, fixed location to calculate new residuals for each station for each event. The station residuals were then averaged across events to obtain the station correction. This approach is not without flaws. Earthquake locations using the old velocity model may have errors imparted by the velocity model itself, which would lead to a bias in the station corrections. Near-site effects may also introduce a bias in the station corrections. Despite these disadvantages, we find that comparing station corrections gives us the best measure of spatial quality between two velocity models.

Results

P-Wave Model

The final result of our P-wave velocity inversion is shown in figure 15. Disappointingly, our inversion did not constrain velocities deeper than 1.5-km depth. This is because of the lack of deep earthquakes during the deployment and the final length of the transect used. Our deepest velocity (5.12 km/s) agrees well with the shallowest velocity of the existing model that spans depths of 0 to 2.2 km. Inverting a subset of the 12 closest picks to the hypocenter resulted in shallow velocities as low as 2.4 km/s, instead of the 2.7 km/s that is calculated in the final model. Residuals of the model show trends imparted by the constant velocity layers used in the inversion. The 13 picks farthest from the hypocenter show apparent velocities that are abnormally high (7–8 km/s). In our inversion, we discarded points (seven in all) with the largest offsets until inverted velocities at depths of 1 to 1.5 km below the transect were reasonable with respect to the existing velocity model. Removing time picks from the most distant stations resulted in depth constraints that were not as deep as we had initially planned, but it was required in order to get reasonable results. The apparent high velocities in our time picks may be a result of three-dimensional variations in wave speed. An alternative explanation may be a large amount of scattering that is shifting the energy of the direct arrival later in the signal and masking the energy remaining in the actual first arrival buried in the noise. Three-dimensional effects are also seen near the 2.1-km offset (fig. 15*A*), where three picks are advanced with respect to surrounding picks.

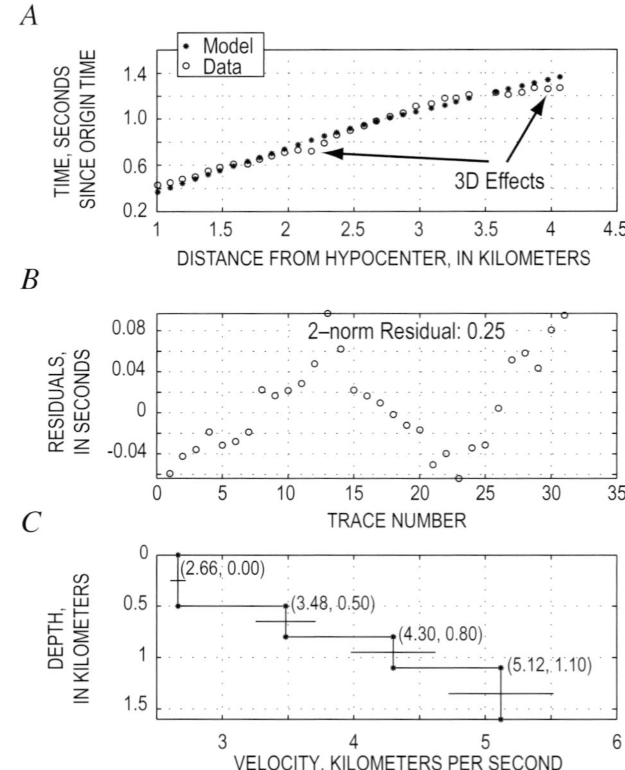

Figure 15. Results of final velocity inversion and grid search for P-wave model. *A*, Comparison of data (circles) and model (stars) for the final model. *B*, Plot of residuals. *C*, Velocity model plotted with 90-percent confidence intervals shown as horizontal lines.

Discussion

The results of our P-wave model show velocities of 2.4–2.7 km/s in the uppermost layer, approximately 1 km/s slower than found in the velocity model used at Mount St. Helens by Musumeci and others (2002). The discrepancy is due to different ray coverage within the crater. In our inversion, we had 39 instruments draping the crater floor and flank and recorded earthquakes less than 1 km deep. In the velocity model by Musumeci and others (2002), only three stations existed inside the crater and only earthquakes deeper than 2.5 km were recorded. The P waves used in our study thus better sampled the shallow structure of the volcano. Our shallowest velocities are similar to those measured at other volcanoes, including Augustine Volcano, Alaska (2.24–2.6 km/s; Pearson and Kienle, 1978), Redoubt Volcano, Alaska (2.9 km/s; Lahr and others, 1994), and Soufrière Hills, Montserrat (2.17 km/s; Rowe and others, 2004).

The new P-wave velocity model has relatively high velocities (4.3 km/s) at fairly shallow depths (0.8 km), considering the volcanic strata exposed within the crater. But such high velocities may be warranted, inasmuch as an intrusive suite at approximately 1-km depth has been interpreted from gravity data (Williams and others, 1987). Velocities of approximately 5.1 km/s have also been used in layered velocity models at Augustine Volcano at 0.9-km depth (Reeder and Lahr, 1987) and at Redoubt Volcano at 0.6-km depth (Lahr and others, 1994). Furthermore, the new P-wave model shows decreases in calculated station corrections at all stations on the volcano, suggesting that the new model is a closer approximation of the three-dimensional velocity structure under the edifice than the existing PNSN model (table 2).

By concatenating the existing S4 velocity model from the PNSN onto the bottom of the inverted velocity model, we are able to calculate improvements to station corrections resulting from the new model (table 2). The altitudes of our transect ranged between 1,100 m and 1,800 m above sea level. At best, our data only constrain the seismic velocities up to the maximum altitude of our transect. For consistency with the existing PNSN velocity model, we set our initial datum to 1,700 m. To allow for earthquake locations inside the new dome, we also considered a model identical to the final inverted velocity model, except with a datum at 2,200 m (datum-adjusted). The layer above the initial datum (1,700 m) has a constant velocity equal to the uppermost layer (2.66 km/s), and the layer depths are adjusted according to the new datum. Adjusting the datum to 2,200 m above sea level, the altitude of the highest seismic station, led to reduced station corrections. In particular, the station corrections on the dome are greatly reduced with respect to other velocity models we considered (table 2). The datum-adjusted model is preferred because it allows for earthquake locations within the new dome and results in lower station corrections for stations on the edifice and inside the crater. Admittedly, no dome material was present at 2,200-m altitude early in the study period, but in order to present the most consistent set of locations for the entire study period, a consistent velocity model should be used throughout the study period.

Appendix 2. Effect of Changing Station Configurations

We simulated the results of changing station configurations within the crater using PNSN catalog events from November 4 through November 20, 2004. During this time period, stations BLIS, YEL, and SEP were operational (McChesney and others, this volume, chap. 7), allowing an opportunity to understand the effect of particular stations on the geometry of the absolute locations. Absolute locations from September 23 until October 1 all lie along a north-dipping structure that descends beneath the 1980–86 dome. When good station coverage and impulsive arrivals were both present starting around November 4, 2004, a similar north-dipping structure emerged (fig. 16*A*). This north-dipping structure was found to be fairly robust analytically, persisting even when the two closest stations were excluded (figs. 16*B*, *C*). Only when station YEL is also excluded is there a breakdown in the shape of the cluster.

Generally, as we removed the close stations, the hypocentroid of the cluster moved deeper and the range of depths grew larger. For example, the original locations had a hypocentroidal depth of ~290 m. Upon removing station BLIS from calculation, the hypocentroid deepened to ~350 m. When both SEP and BLIS were removed, the hypocentroid was more than 400 m deep.

Appendix 3. Jackknife Tests

We show here the results of jackknife tests on the multiplet E7. The original relative locations show a tabular body with a surface projection spanning nearly 50 m. In depth the locations are restricted to a range of only about 20 m, outlining a cigar-shaped source region (figs. 10*E*, 17*A*). Multiplets D34 and F1 also show similar tabular bodies, so we are compelled to show the results of our jackknife tests to prove that the locations are not an artifact of station geometry or poor waveform alignment. In figure 17, we show the results of removing, one at a time, each of the four stations with the most observations. In almost all cases there is no change in the geometry of the source region. An exception is the source geometry when station YEL is removed (fig. 17*C*). In this test, the orientation of the source region is more southwest than in the original locations, and the relative hypocenters, viewed to the east, are elongate north-south.

We also tested the effect of a P-wave velocity model on the relative locations (fig. 17*F*). As mentioned previously, the velocity model that we chose lacks layer boundaries near the cluster centroid, so a change to higher velocities simply spreads the hypocenters out over a larger area without gross change in geometry.

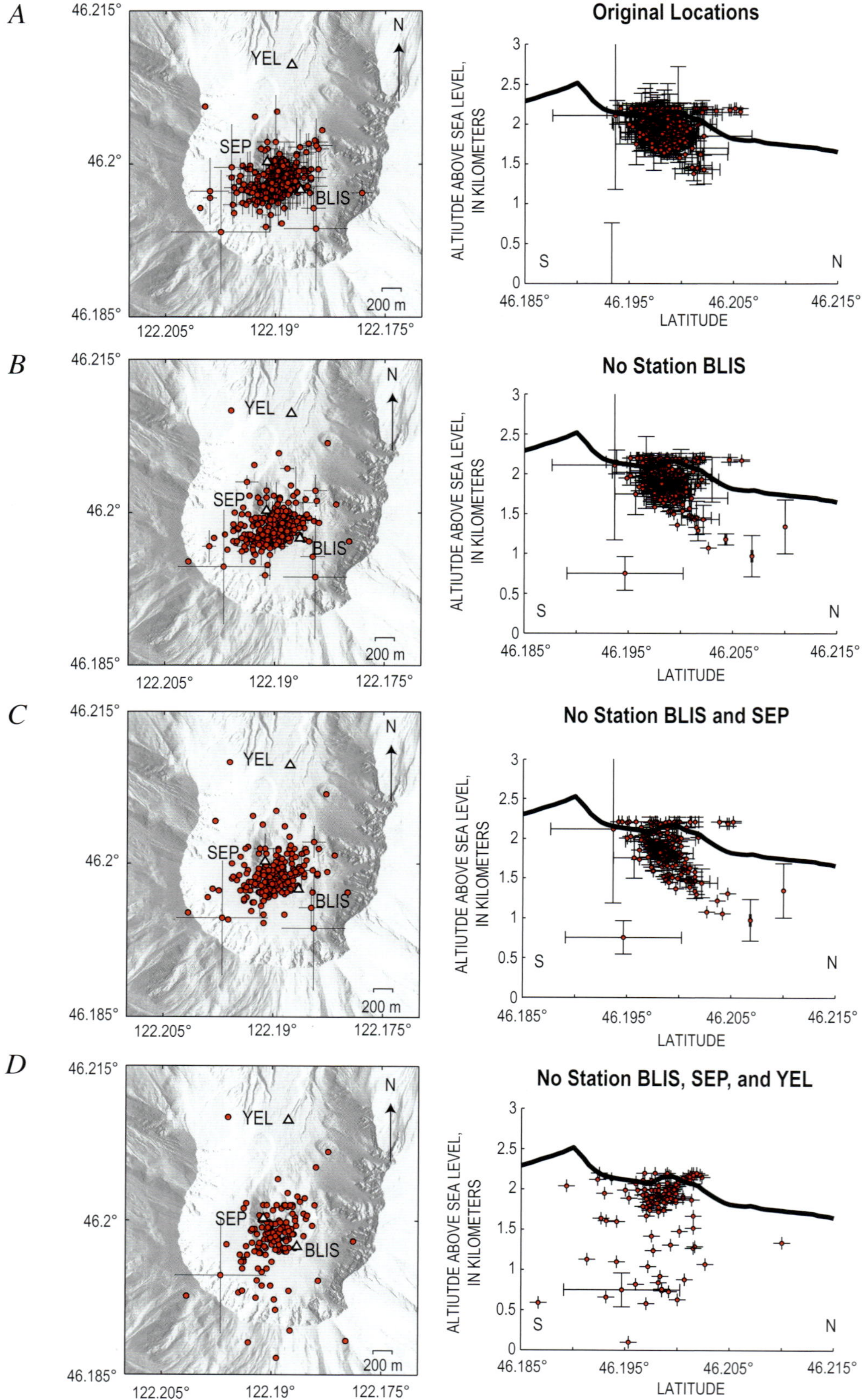

Figure 16. (*A–D*) Results of simulations of different station configurations using Pacific Northwest Seismic Network (PNSN) catalog earthquakes from November 4, 2004, to November 20, 2004.

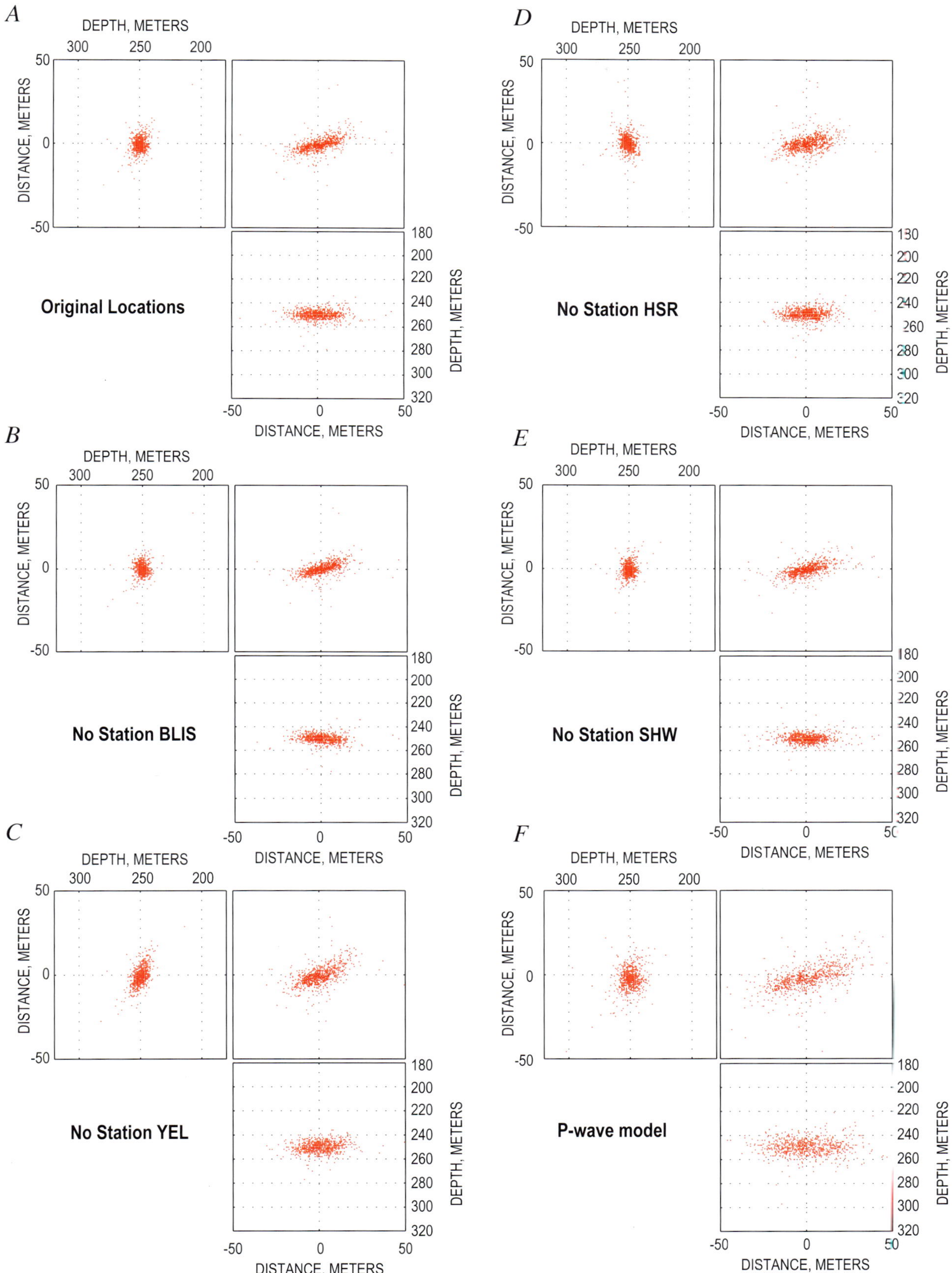

Figure 17. (*A–E*) Results of jackknife tests on multiplet E7. *F*, Results of the use of a P-wave model in the relative locations of multiplet E7.

A Volcano Rekindled: The Renewed Eruption of Mount St. Helens, 2004–2006
Edited by David R. Sherrod, William E. Scott, and Peter H. Stauffer
U.S. Geological Survey Professional Paper 1750, 2008

Chapter 5

Broadband Characteristics of Earthquakes Recorded During a Dome-Building Eruption at Mount St. Helens, Washington, Between October 2004 and May 2005

By Stephen P. Horton[1], Robert D. Norris[2], and Seth C. Moran[3]

Abstract

From October 2004 to May 2005, the Center for Earthquake Research and Information of the University of Memphis operated two to six broadband seismometers within 5 to 20 km of Mount St. Helens to help monitor recent seismic and volcanic activity. Approximately 57,000 earthquakes identified during the 7-month deployment had a normal magnitude distribution with a mean magnitude of 1.78 and a standard deviation of 0.24 magnitude units. Both the mode and range of earthquake magnitude and the rate of activity varied during the deployment. We examined the time domain and spectral characteristics of two classes of events seen during dome building. These include volcano-tectonic earthquakes and lower-frequency events. Lower-frequency events are further classified into hybrid earthquakes, low-frequency earthquakes, and long-duration volcanic tremor. Hybrid and low-frequency earthquakes showed a continuum of characteristics that varied systematically with time. A progressive loss of high-frequency seismic energy occurred in earthquakes as magma approached and eventually reached the surface. The spectral shape of large and small earthquakes occurring within days of each other did not vary with magnitude. Volcanic tremor events and lower-frequency earthquakes displayed consistent spectral peaks, although higher frequencies were more favorably excited during tremor than earthquakes.

[1] Center for Earthquake Research and Information, University of Memphis, 3890 Central Avenue, Memphis, TN 38155

[2] U.S. Geological Survey, at Pacific Northwest Seismic Network, Department of Earth and Space Sciences, University of Washington, Box 351310, Seattle, WA 98195

[3] U.S. Geological Survey, 1300 SE Cardinal Court, Vancouver, WA 98683

Introduction

Two classes of earthquakes are commonly observed at volcanoes around the world. One class, termed volcano-tectonic (VT) earthquakes by Latter (1981), consists of high-frequency events with sharp, well-defined body-wave phases. Volcano-tectonic events are produced by shear failure in solid rock; their broadband seismic waveforms are indistinguishable from normal tectonic earthquakes (Chouet, 1996). The second class of earthquakes observed at volcanoes consists of lower-frequency events that are thought to originate from a boundary between a fluid, such as magma or gas, and the solid surrounding rock (see, for example, Neuberg and others, 2006).

In this study we follow the convention of Moran and others (this volume, chap. 2), dividing lower-frequency earthquakes into two groups, hybrid and low-frequency (LF) earthquakes. Low-frequency events have a weak high-frequency onset followed by a harmonic waveform with one to several dominant frequencies in the range of 0.5–5 Hz (Chouet, 1996). In LF events, the P wave is often emergent, and the S wave is often obscured. Hybrid events blend the characteristics of both the VT and LF events (Lahr and others, 1994). The onset of the hybrid earthquake shows more pronounced high-frequency energy than the LF event, whereas the coda of both types is dominated by a high-amplitude, low-frequency waveform (Chouet, 1996). First-motion polarities are often mixed for both VT and hybrid events, whereas LF events generally display the same polarity at all stations (Lahr and others, 1994).

A network of eight broadband seismometers was installed at Mount St. Helens in October 2004 (fig. 1) to record seismic activity associated with the dome-building eruption that began with seismic unrest on September 23. The Cascades Volcano Observatory (CVO) installed two broadband seismometers northwest of the Mount St. Helens crater in October 2004. The Center for Earthquake Research and Information (CERI) at the University of Memphis installed six temporary stations at complementary azimuths around the volcano to provide better coverage of the eruption at about the same time. The CERI stations were removed in May 2005, and a separate temporary broadband network, installed by the U.S. Geological Survey in May 2005, was operated until October 2005. This analysis covers only the time period of the first temporary deployment.

Moran and others (this volume, chap. 2) separated the seismic activity associated with the dome-building eruption at Mount St. Helens into two temporal phases. The first was the vent-clearing phase that began with a swarm of shallow VT earthquakes on September 23 and ended with an explosion on October 5. A gradual transition from the VT events to lower-frequency earthquakes occurred between September 25 and October 1. This transition from VT to lower-frequency earthquakes was not recorded with broadband seismometers, because the first broadband seismometer was installed by CVO at Johnston Ridge Observatory (JRO; fig. 1) on October 1, 2004, about 1600 PDT. After October 5, seismicity was dominated by lower-frequency earthquakes. Tens of thousands of lower-frequency earthquakes were recorded by the broadband network between then and May 2005, with just one high-frequency (VT) earthquake. A few episodes of volcanic tremor were also observed, mostly before the CERI component of the broadband network became operational (Moran and others, this volume, chap. 2).

Lower-frequency earthquakes at Mount St. Helens were observed in association with eruptions in the 1980s (see, for example, Endo and others, 1981; Malone, 1983; and Malone and others, 1983). Those events were recorded using short-period, vertical-component seismometers. Since the mid-1990s, broadband seismometers have been used to record earthquakes and volcanic tremor on numerous volcanoes around the world, but the broadband recordings discussed here were the first at Mount St. Helens.

Because hybrid and LF earthquakes form the bulk of the signals recorded during the CERI broadband deployment, our analysis focuses on those events. We examine aspects of the seismicity that can be addressed by continuous, broadband, and unclipped recordings of the earthquakes. Following a brief description of the temporary broadband seismic network at Mount St. Helens, we discuss our search of the dataset for very

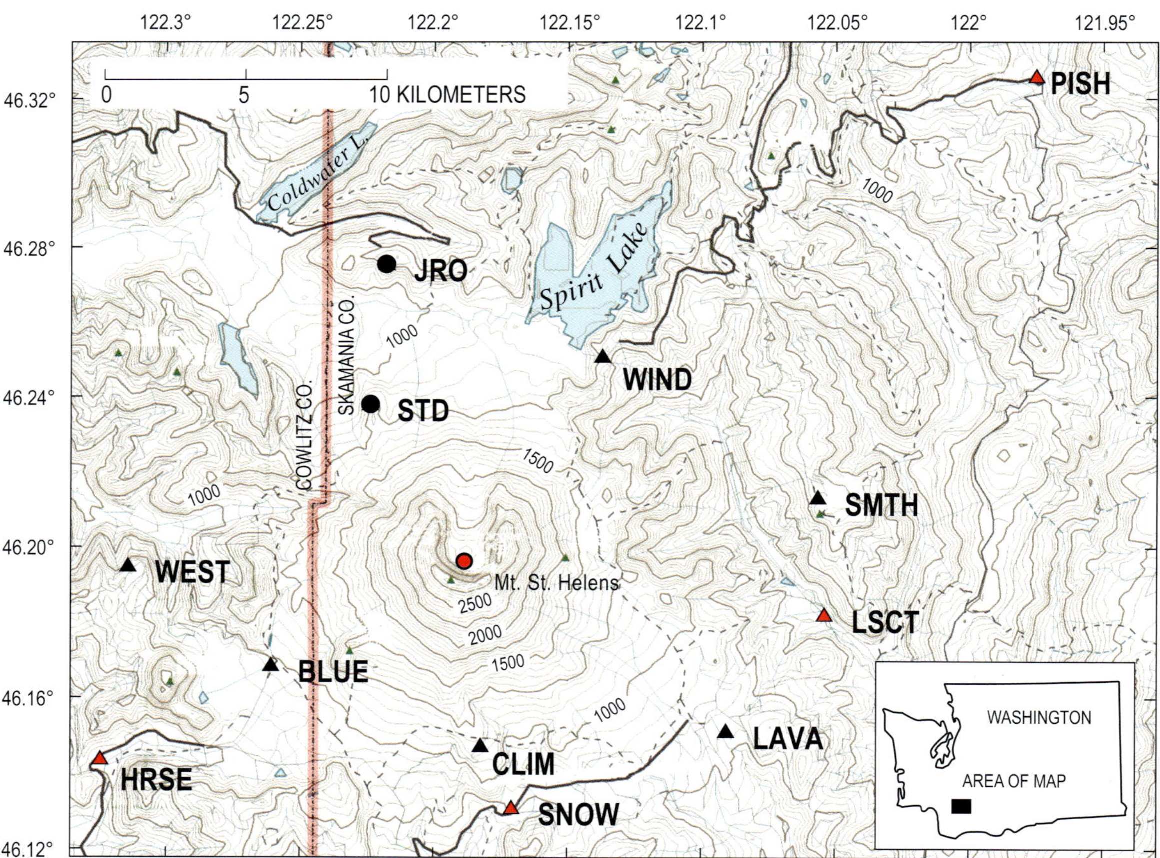

Figure 1. Broadband seismic stations at Mount St. Helens used in this study (from table 1). Black circles indicate location of CVO broadband seismometers. Black triangles indicate initial locations of CERI broadband seismometers. Red triangles show four CERI instruments redeployed to lower altitudes in early December 2004 to allow servicing throughout winter. Red circle indicates centroid of seismic activity. Roads shown in black; dashed lines are trails. Contours in meters, contour interval 50 m.

long period (VLP) pulses as described by Almendros and others (2002). We examine the variation in the rate and the magnitude distribution of the events identified by our trigger algorithm. We then look at the differences and similarities between hybrid and LF earthquakes and test a numerical measure of event character. Finally some issues are discussed related to wave propagation that make it difficult to determine focal mechanisms for these events through waveform modeling.

Broadband Network

Broadband seismic monitoring at Mount St. Helens began with CVO's installation of a Guralp CMG-6TD at JRO on October 1, 2004, approximately 1 week after the onset of increased seismic activity at the volcano (fig. 1). CVO installed a second instrument at Studebaker Ridge (STD) on October 5. Telemetry for both sites was established in late October, providing real-time broadband monitoring of Mount St. Helens seismicity (McChesney and others, this volume, chap. 7). On October 3, CERI, in cooperation with CVO and the Pacific Northwest Seismic Network (PNSN), began deploying broadband instruments with onsite recording capability. Station locations were chosen to provide the optimum azimuthal coverage, encircling the vent at the closest possible distance to Mount St. Helens. Budget, safety, and logistical considerations limited us to road-accessible sites. We deployed six Guralp CMG-6TD broadband seismometers within about 5 to 10 km of the seismic activity by October 5 (fig. 1). Four strong-motion instruments (Kinemetrics Altus K2 Recorder) were also deployed, although earthquakes in the sequence did not trigger the latter instruments.

A typical broadband station had a Guralp CMG-6TD sensor buried in a hole about 18 inches deep. Timing was provided by a GPS antenna. Power was provided by 12-V batteries recharged by a 30-W solar panel on a 1.2-m-tall stand. The broadband seismometers recorded three channels continuously at 50 samples per second and had a flat response to ground velocity between 0.033 and 25 Hz. Data were stored onsite using 2 GB of internal flash memory. With reasonable data compression, and a few sunny days for solar-power recharge, a service interval of 6 to 8 weeks was adequate to ensure no loss of data. In late October we started removing several temporary stations located in remote settings to avoid having them snowed under for the winter (table 1). By early November only two of the temporary stations, BLUE and LAVA, remained. Fortunately, these stations were southwest and southeast of the volcanic crater, so they, along with the two CVO stations, still provided reasonable azimuthal coverage. At the beginning of December, we moved stations to sites where the anticipated snow depth would not exceed 2.4 m. Three of these sites were winter recreational Sno-Parks maintained by the U.S. Forest Service, with plowed road access during normal snow years. The fourth site, LSCT, was sufficiently low in altitude to be accessible year-round.

Very Long Period Seismicity, October-November 2004

One of the principal reasons for our rapid deployment of broadband seismometers was to record any very long period (VLP) seismicity associated with the eruption that would otherwise have been missed by the PNSN short-period stations. We looked for evidence of VLP signals as described by Almendros and others (2002) in the period range 5–30 s. A moving root-mean-squared (RMS) average applied to bandpass-filtered seismograms was helpful in identifying trends and potential pulses. We checked peaks and trends observed in the moving average by visual inspection of the time series. For example, a moving RMS average was computed from seismograms recorded from October 5 through October 8 (fig. 2*A*). The two large peaks observed at station WIND in figure 2*A* at about 1600 (PDT) on October 6 and 0200 on October 8 can be correlated with spikes at other stations in the network. The first peak was produced by surface waves following a shallow M_w 6.2 earthquake that occurred in Indonesia at 1531 (PDT) on October 6. The second large peak was produced by body and surface waves following a shallow M_w 6.8 earthquake that occurred in the Solomon Islands at 0127 on October 8.

Two broad increases in RMS levels occurred between October 7 and 9. These trends were too broad to be teleseismic arrivals or VLP pulses but could have been caused by very long duration resonance of the volcano's magmatic-hydrologic system. We computed the RMS average at station LON, approximately 68 km north of Mount St. Helens and found that the broad trend increases observed at WIND, only 7.15 km from the vent, were matched by concurrent increases at LON, which suggests the source of the increase may be regional. Seismic waves that emanated from a local source below the Mount St. Helens crater should have attenuated with distance. To investigate amplitude as a function of distance from the crater, we plotted seismograms from October 7 to 9 arranged by the station distance from the crater (fig. 2*B*). The peak amplitudes and general character of the waveforms were similar at all stations, including LON. Because attenuation was not evident, we concluded that the broad energy increases did not result from a local source below the Mount St. Helens crater, but rather from a regional source. The increased long-period energy is best explained as seismic noise (microseisms) generated by a low-pressure weather system that approached the Pacific Northwest coast on October 7 and remained in the coastal area during the following 3 days. Microseisms, a nearly harmonic modulated waveform with periods around 6 s, have long been associated with storms over water, including normal low-pressure systems. Longuet-Higgins (1950) showed that the interaction of water waves with similar periods and different directions generates pressure waves that efficiently couple with the solid earth to produce seismic surface waves. These surface waves can propagate with gradual loss of energy over broad areas of the continent.

Table 1. Broadband station locations and dates of operation.

[Stations JRO and STD operated by Cascades Volcanic Observatory; others installed by Center for Earthquake Research and Information as part of this report. Datum is WGS84. Altitude is orthometric, interpolated from topographic maps after plotting locations. Distance is measured from centroid of seismic activity, the surface trace of which approximates the position of the vent.]

Station	Latitude (N)	Longitude (W)	Altitude (m)	Distance from vent (km)	Dates of operation
JRO	46.2751	122.2178	1,290	8.98	10/01/04–08/10/06
STD	46.2376	122.2240	1,250	5.28	10/25/04–present [1]
WIND	46.2504	122.1372	1,230	7.15	10/03/04–10/31/04
LAVA	46.1509	122.0908	850	9.13	10/03/04–12/02/04
BLUE	46.1682	122.2608	980	6.41	10/03/04–12/02/04
WEST	46.1946	122.3143	1,120	9.66	10/04/04–11/01/04
CLIM	46.1470	122.1825	1,140	5.58	10/04/04–11/01/04
SMTH	46.2128	122.0566	1,090	10.34	10/05/04–10/27/04
LSCT	46.1818	122.0540	500	10.52	12/03/04–05/07/05
SNOW	46.1306	122.1708	810	7.51	12/04/04–05/07/05
HRSE	46.1434	122.3244	620	12.02	12/05/04–05/06/05
PISH	46.3256	121.9754	860	21.77	12/07/04–05/08/05

[1] As of March 17, 2008.

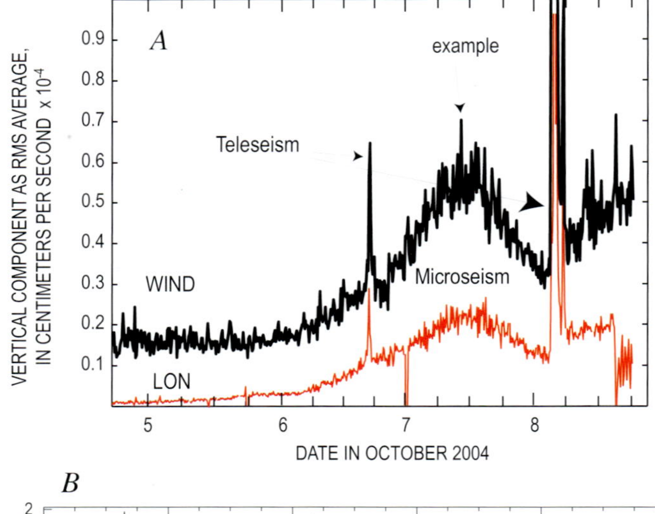

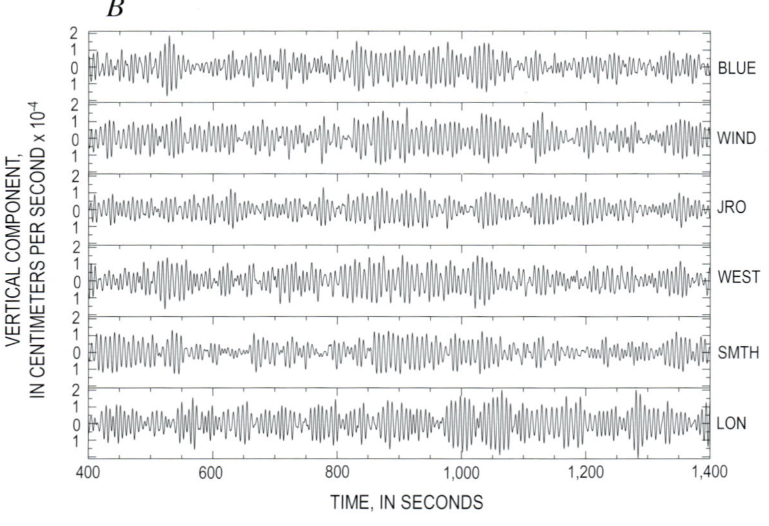

Figure 2. Ground motion recorded at Mount St. Helens, October 5–8, 2004. *A*, Moving RMS average (over consecutive 600-s window) of filtered (5–30 s) vertical component data at station WIND (black) and Pacific Northwest Seismic Network broadband station LON (red). Data from LON plotted in counts but scaled for visual comparison with velocity data from WIND. Date on x axis marks start of each day, PDT. Concurrent large sharp peaks at both stations are teleseismic arrivals. Broad increase that peaks about midday October 7 was most likely due to weather system impinging on region. Arrow labeled "example" shows approximate time displayed in bottom figure. *B*, Vertical component seismograms, all scaled to same absolute amplitude, for ~16-minute interval of intense low-frequency energy as recorded at six stations (listed at right edge).

Visual inspections of all moving RMS average peaks occurring in October and November 2004 revealed no VLP signals that originated below the Mount St. Helens crater. The absence of observed VLP signals could have been due in part to the distance of our stations from the source. Rapid decay of signal amplitude with distance is considered characteristic of VLP signals (Almendros and Chouet, 2003). VLP signals have been observed at other volcanoes at distances of less than 5 km (for example, Almendros and others, 2002; Aster and others, 2003). The closest broadband stations recording during the first deployment were STD and CLIM, about 5.28 km and 5.58 km respectively from the centroid of seismicity (fig. 1). Thus we cannot definitively rule out the occurrence of VLP signals at Mount St. Helens during this time period.

October 2004–May 2005 Seismicity Recorded by the Broadband Network

Event Magnitudes and Rates

Thousands of earthquakes were recorded during the 7-month broadband network deployment at Mount St. Helens. Because our data were not recorded in trigger mode, we developed a trigger algorithm based on the ratio of short-term (0.2 s) and long-term (320 s) averages to isolate individual events from the continuous records. We first applied a 0.5–3-Hz bandpass filter to the data and then used a short-term to long-term trigger ratio of 6 to identify 57,635 events. We assigned a magnitude for each event on the basis of the peak velocity (*pv*) measured on the vertical component at each CERI station. The body-wave arrivals of both hybrid and LF events were of smaller amplitude than the low-frequency waveforms that followed, so we assumed *pv* to be a surface-wave amplitude. We therefore adjusted the measured *pv* by the square root of the distance from the centroid of seismicity to the station (table 1) to account for geometrical spreading. The centroid location, 46.1964°N and 122.18882°W, was calculated from the PNSN catalog for events with $M_d \geq 2.5$ during this time period. The magnitude was given by $M_S = \log_{10}(pv) + 5.78$, where the distance-adjusted *pv* was averaged over all CERI stations and the constant (5.78) was calculated so that the largest event had M_S 3.4, equal to the PNSN duration-magnitude estimate for that event. Our magnitude estimates were reasonably consistent with PNSN magnitudes for events above M_d 2.6.

Figure 3*A* shows the distribution of event magnitudes selected by our trigger algorithm for the entire period of the network deployment. These have a normal distribution, with mean magnitude (M_S) of 1.78 and a standard deviation of 0.24 magnitude units. When comparing event triggers to the continuous seismograms, we observed that small earthquakes occurring in the coda of larger events were not likely to be selected by our trigger algorithm. Therefore, the distribution of smaller earthquakes in the sequence is probably not well characterized. The distribution of larger events, however, is probably well characterized. The distribution of earthquake size and the rate of activity varied with time, with larger earthquakes occurring irregularly throughout the sequence. To help discern patterns, we divided the entire dataset into 24-hour segments, calculated the magnitude distribution of each time interval as in figure 3*A*, and contoured the resulting magnitude distributions over time (fig. 3*B*). Most of the events with $M_S \geq 3$ occurred before October 5 and were associated with the closing days of the vent-clearing phase (Moran and others, this volume, chap. 2). The rate of seismic activity was quite high at that time, and the distribution of earthquake sizes was bimodal, with peaks around M_S 2.5 and M_S 2 and a range slightly greater than 2 magnitude units.

After October 5 the rate of seismic activity slowed drastically and the modal event size decreased to M_S 1.7 (fig. 3*B*). The minimum event size also increased to about M_S 1.5 from a minimum M_S of ~1.0 during the more active vent-clearing

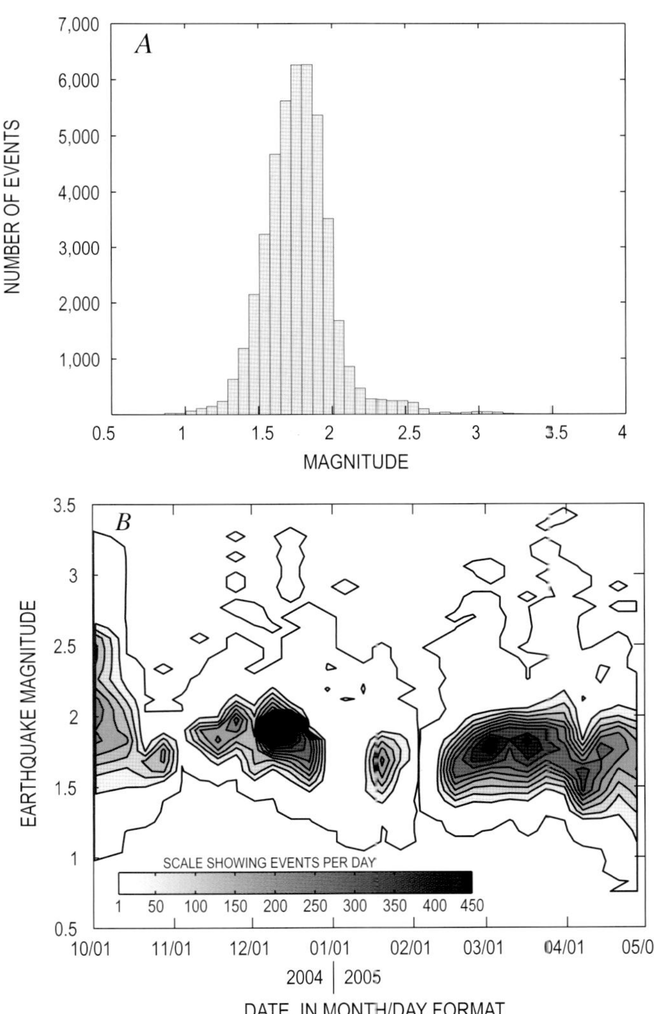

Figure 3. Event-magnitude occurrence for the more than 57,000 earthquakes identified during this deployment. Magnitudes are binned in 0.072-magnitude intervals. *A*, Histogram showing magnitude distribution. *B*, Time-series plot showing magnitude distribution. Contour interval is 50 events per day.

period. Because the trigger algorithm should have been more sensitive to small events when the rate of larger events was low, this increase of minimum event size during a period of reduced seismic activity suggests that the observed distribution for small events was not entirely due to lack of detection. Instead, small events were simply not plentiful during some time intervals.

Both the range and mode of earthquake size and the rate of seismic activity increased through the latter part of November 2004. These increases coincided with the approach and collision of spine 3 with the south crater wall (Schilling and others, this volume, chap. 8; Vallance and others, this volume, chap. 9). The seismic activity continued at a high rate through the middle of December, when 10 events with $M_S \geq 3.0$ occurred between December 17 and 19. Subsequently, both the rate of seismic activity and the modal size of events began to decrease. This trend continued through the middle of January, as spine 3 was disintegrating and being shoved aside by spine 4, and a large explosion occurred on January 16, 2005 (Moran and others, this volume, chap. 6). The seismicity rate increased through the latter part of January 2005. The small number of events between January 29 and February 6 was artificial, reflecting a loss of network data during that time interval. The seismicity rate remained high in March and April, when 14 $M_S \geq 3.0$ events occurred. It appears that the sporadic occurrence of events of $M_S \geq 3.0$ coincided with intervals of high seismicity rates.

Characteristics of Lower-Frequency Earthquakes at Mount St. Helens

Since the mid-1990s, broadband seismometers have been used to record earthquakes and tremor on numerous volcanoes around the world. Because our data were the first broadband recordings at Mount St. Helens, we looked with special care at the broadband character of the events recorded on our network. We recorded one high-frequency tectonic earthquake, two episodes of volcanic tremor, and thousands of lower-frequency earthquakes during the deployment. In this section we describe the characteristics of the lower-frequency events and compare our observations to the reported features of earthquakes observed at other volcanoes.

The first step was to compare a lower-frequency event to the high-frequency tectonic earthquake, because these form the two main types of earthquakes recorded at volcanoes (see, for example, Latter, 1981). We did not record volcano-tectonic events associated with the vent-clearing phase, because the broadband seismometers were only installed at the close of that phase. However, a small local tectonic event was recorded on November 22, 2004, at 0853 PST. Figure 4 shows seismograms and their associated spectra for that tectonic earthquake and an example LF earthquake, M_S 3.3, recorded on November 27, 2004, at 0601 PST. The tectonic event was not located by PNSN. However, a local hypocenter is required by the short S-P arrival-time differences at stations LAVA (1.5 s) and BLUE (2 s). We consider the event to be tectonic because it had sharp and well-defined P and S phases followed by a short high-frequency coda. Peak energy for this event was between 5 and 12 Hz, with very low spectral levels at frequencies less than 5 Hz. By contrast, the LF event had a low-amplitude onset, with frequencies as high as about 10 Hz, followed by a strong, long-duration, and lower-frequency waveform. The spectrum had significant energy between 0.3 and 5 Hz, with multiple spectral peaks suggestive of harmonic motion as observed for lower-frequency earthquakes at other volcanoes (for example, Chouet, 1996; Neuberg and others, 2006).

Next we compare the hybrid and LF earthquakes that form the two types of lower-frequency earthquakes recorded during the first year of renewed eruption at Mount St. Helens (Moran and others, this volume, chap. 2). For example, figure 5*A* shows the broadband seismograms for a M_S 3.13 hybrid earthquake recorded on October 3, 2004, at 1812 (PDT) and a M_S 3.2 LF earthquake recorded on November 28, 2004, at 1807 (PST). Figure 5*B* shows the same seismograms after 7-Hz highpass filters were applied, and figure 5*C* shows the Fourier displacement spectra for both events. The broadband waveforms of both events are dominated by the lower-

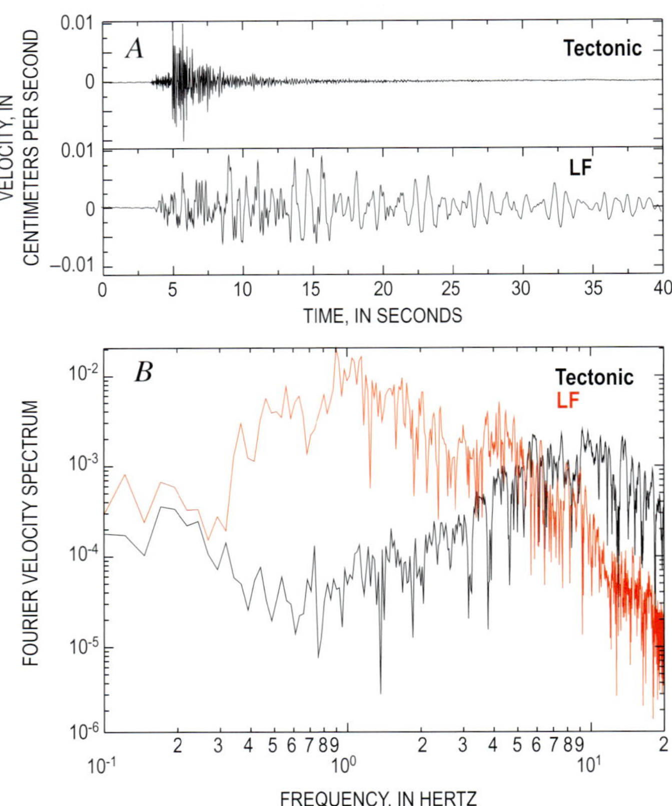

Figure 4. Seismograms and spectral characteristics for tectonic earthquake recorded November 22, 2004, and a low-frequency earthquake recorded November 27, 2004. *A*, Comparison of seismograms from station LAVA, plotted at same absolute scale. *B*, Fourier velocity spectra of associated seismograms. Tectonic earthquake is black trace; low-frequency event is red trace.

frequency (from 0.3 to about 5 Hz), nondispersive waves that give rise to the name of this class of earthquake. At frequencies between 0.3 and 2.0 Hz, the spectral amplitudes of the LF event slightly exceed those of the hybrid event (consistent with the slightly larger magnitude estimate), whereas at frequencies above 3.0 Hz, the spectral amplitudes of the hybrid event exceed the LF spectral amplitudes. This difference in high-frequency energy is also apparent in the time series, where the hybrid earthquake has a much more pronounced high-frequency onset (fig. 5*A*).

This difference in high-frequency energy is the primary difference between hybrid and LF earthquakes. It may result from a difference in the earthquake source process or a difference in the rock along the path from source to receiver that affects wave propagation (an increase in attenuation related to a reduction in source depth, for example). To investigate these possibilities, we filtered the lower-frequency energy from the signal. The filtered records (fig. 5*B*) show that both events actually have a high-frequency onset, although the amplitude is about five times larger for the hybrid event. Further, the high-frequency component of both events is similar in form and of comparable duration, extending well into the low-frequency waveform. This similarity in form and duration indicates that attenuation near the earthquake sources and along the paths to the receiver did not differ significantly. Rather, more high-frequency energy was generated at the source for the hybrid than for the LF earthquake. This is consistent with a larger component of shear faulting during the hybrid earthquake.

We explored the similarity in spectra between small and larger events in figure 6, where the velocity spectrum of the M_S 3.1 hybrid event (October 3, 2004) was compared to a randomly chosen M_S 1.7 event that occurred on October 11, 2004. The spectrum of the M_S 1.7 event was multiplied by a factor of 20 in order to compare the shape of the spectra of both events. The spectrum of the smaller event disappears into the background noise and is undetectable above 10 Hz and below 0.5 Hz. Between 0.5 and 10 Hz, the spectra of the large and small events were quite similar in shape and amplitude. The similarity in spectral shape suggests that both the source and path were similar for the two events. For tectonic earthquakes, the peak in the velocity spectrum would be expected to shift to lower frequencies as rupture zone size increased for larger earthquakes (Brune, 1970). The consistency in the frequency range of the peak of spectral energy for different-size earthquakes favors models such as that of Chouet (1996), in which a pressure transient resonates in a crack of constant dimension (a few centimeters in width), or that of Neuberg and others (2006), in which brittle failure of magma provides seismic energy that resonates in a conduit section of constant dimension (~30 m wide and several hundred meters long). In both cases the amplitude of the resonance would be determined by the strength of the pressure transient or size of the brittle failure, whereas the shape of the spectrum would be constrained by the size and properties of the resonator.

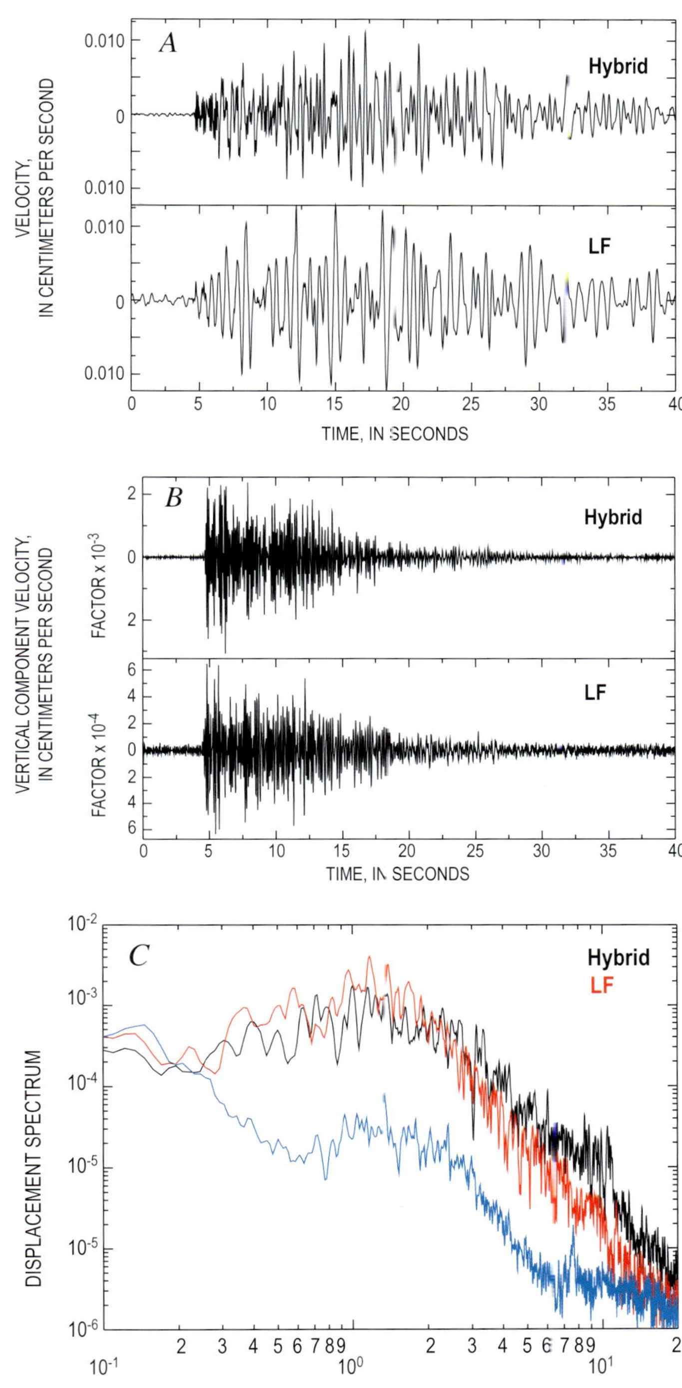

Figure 5. Comparison of seismic data from station BLUE for hybrid and low-frequency (LF) earthquakes. *A*, Vertical-component seismograms, plotted at same absolute scale. *B*, Corresponding 7-Hz highpass-filtered seismograms; note different scales. Decay of the waveforms is remarkably similar. *C*, Fourier displacement spectra of the original hybrid (black) and LF (red) seismograms. Spectrum of a 60-s interval from a "quiet" period on November 1, 2004, shows representative background noise level (blue). (This interval chosen because time intervals just before the two earthquakes contain the coda of other earthquakes.)

Resonance in a crack or conduit of constant dimensions produces amplitude spectra with strong peaks resulting from the summation of waves propagating between the boundaries of the structure. The specific frequencies of resonance are determined by the dimensions of the structure and the properties of the material within the conduit or crack. Identifying the frequencies of resonance would therefore place useful constraints on the volcanic process. Any given station can have a variety of peaks derived from its own particular source-receiver path and local site conditions, but the resonance peaks associated with a symmetric conduit or crack should be common to spectra observed at all stations independent of azimuth and distance. By comparing spectra at all stations, it should simply be a matter of identifying the common peaks.

A feature of the seismicity associated with this eruption of Mount St. Helens was the prominence of earthquake multiplets having highly similar waveforms (Thelen and others, this volume, chap. 4). Figure 7 shows the Fourier velocity spectra at six stations for a multiplet of 29 lower-frequency events ($2.1 \leq M_S \leq 2.2$) that occurred on October 16, 2004. The velocity spectra were normalized and overlaid for each station so that peaks that are consistent from event to event tend to stand out. Each station exhibits several consistent peaks in the range 0.4–2 Hz, but no peak appears consistently at all stations to indicate a specific frequency of source resonance. This lack of identifiable frequencies of source resonance is inconsistent with the resonance of a structure with simple geometry such as the rectangular crack of the Chouet (1996) model and the rectangular conduit of the Neuberg and others (2000) model. It suggests instead that wave propagation dominated the response at a given station and that source harmonics played a minor role. Alternatively, one can appeal to the excitation of a more complex, perhaps asymmetric, structure, where the harmonic response observed at a given station depends upon its location relative to the orientation of the source structure.

Fehler (1983) analyzed short-period records of tremor at Mount St. Helens that accompanied eruptions on August 7 and October 16–18, 1980. He found that the spectra of lower-frequency earthquakes were very similar to volcanic tremor, and he suggested that tremor was composed of many lower-frequency events inseparable in time. Neuberg and others (2000) observed that many episodes of volcanic tremor at Soufrière Hills volcano in Montserrat, West Indies, followed swarms of lower-frequency earthquakes in which the rate of earthquake occurrence continually increased until they merged into tremor. Figure 8*A* shows a seismogram with lower-frequency earthquakes followed by 58 minutes of volcanic tremor at Mount St. Helens on October 2, 2004. In this case, the lower-frequency earthquakes appeared to be distinct events occurring before and again after the volcanic tremor. There is no evidence to suggest that individual earthquakes merged to generate the volcanic tremor. Figure 8*B* shows the normalized velocity spectrum of one lower-frequency event and a 60-s window from the volcanic tremor. Neither spectrum displayed harmonic peaks at whole-number multiples of fundamental

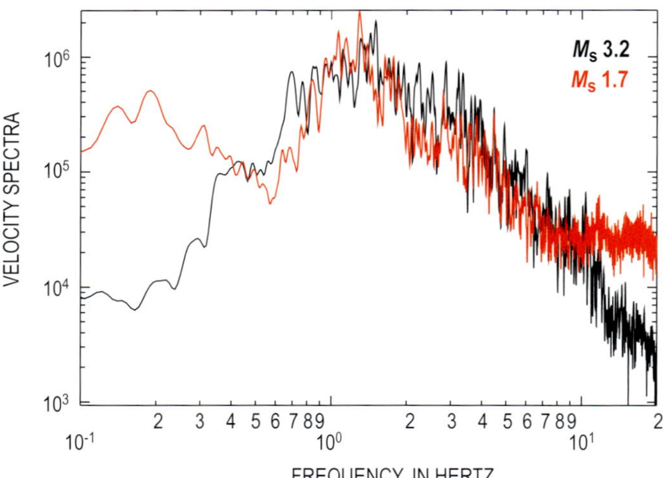

Figure 6. Spectral shapes of large and small events. Vertical-component Fourier velocity spectra recorded at station BLUE are shown for a M_S 3.2 hybrid event (black) and a randomly chosen M_S 1.7 event (red) occurring close together in time. Spectra of the small event (scaled up by a factor of 20) and large event are similar in shape between 0.5 and 10 Hz.

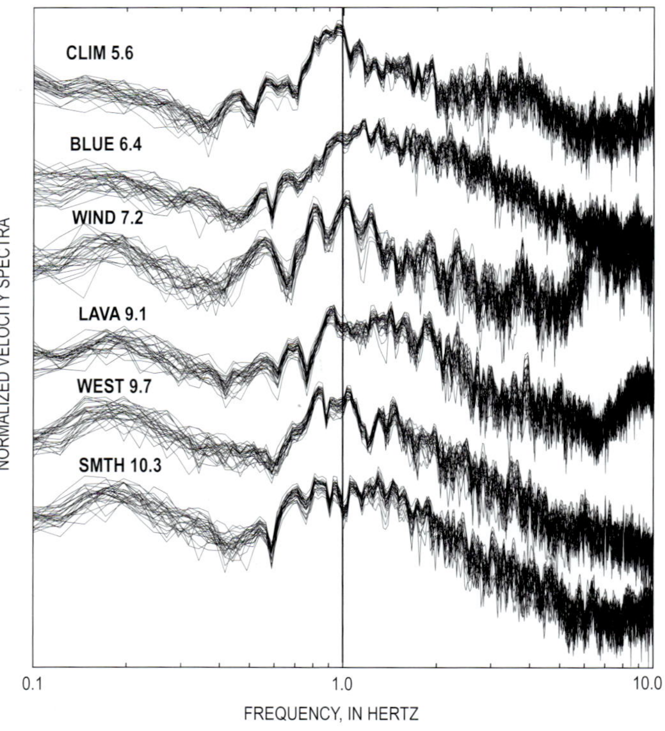

Figure 7. Comparison of spectra from six stations to identify source peaks. Fourier velocity spectra are plotted for a multiplet of 29 lower-frequency events ($2.1 \leq M_S \leq 2.2$) that occurred October 16, 2004. Velocity spectra are normalized and overlaid for each station so that peaks consistent from event to event become prominent. The distance to vent (see table 1) is to right of each station name.

frequencies. Both spectra had distinct peaks in common (for example, 0.8 and 1.1 Hz), consistent with Fehler's (1983) observations. However, the lower-frequency earthquake spectrum had a prominent peak at 0.6 Hz that was not observed in the spectrum of the volcanic tremor. This lower-frequency peak would be consistent with resonance of a structure having a larger dimension or with favorable excitation of the longer dimension of the same structure.

The progression from primarily volcano-tectonic events at the beginning of the 2004 eruption to combined hybrid and low-frequency (LF) events, then to dominantly LF events, reported by Moran and others (this volume, chap. 2), suggests a progressive loss of high-frequency seismic energy as magma moved toward and eventually onto the surface. Malone and collaborators have pointed out that gradual changes in event character were observed in many precursory swarms preceding dome-building eruptions at Mount St. Helens in the 1980s (Malone, 1983; Malone and others, 1983). During the 1980–86 dome-building eruptions, this transition became a diagnostic tool to predict eruption onset time (Malone and others, 1983; Swanson and others, 1983; Swanson and others, 1985). The high-frequency spectral difference between hybrid and LF events observed in figure 5*C* suggests that the slope of the high-frequency falloff could provide a measure to track the loss of high-frequency energy through time. To investigate this, the power spectra of an example hybrid and example LF event are compared in figure 9. Lines were fit by least squares to the high-frequency spectral amplitudes in the range 1–10 Hz. The slope of each line quantifies the rate of spectral amplitude decay with frequency or the high-frequency falloff of the velocity spectrum. The slope of the fitted line was −2.6 for the hybrid event and −4.9 for the LF event, indicating that this slope is a useful measure to quantify the high-frequency earthquake character.

We computed the high-frequency falloff for all events between October 4 and December 1, 2004 (CERI network station locations changed after December 1). Figure 10*A* shows earthquake magnitude versus time. Those events with magnitude in the range 1.5–2.0 are plotted in black, and other magnitudes are plotted in red. Because the high-frequency falloff could have a magnitude bias, the high-frequency falloff is plotted versus time (fig. 10*B*) with this same color convention. The slope of the high-frequency falloff ranged from approximately −1.75 to −5, defining a continuum between the ideal hybrid and LF events such as observed at Montserrat by Neuberg and others (2000). In early October, the slope values ranged from about −1.75 to −3.5, regardless of magnitude. The range was somewhat narrower for events with magnitude 1.5–2.0. Over time the slope values

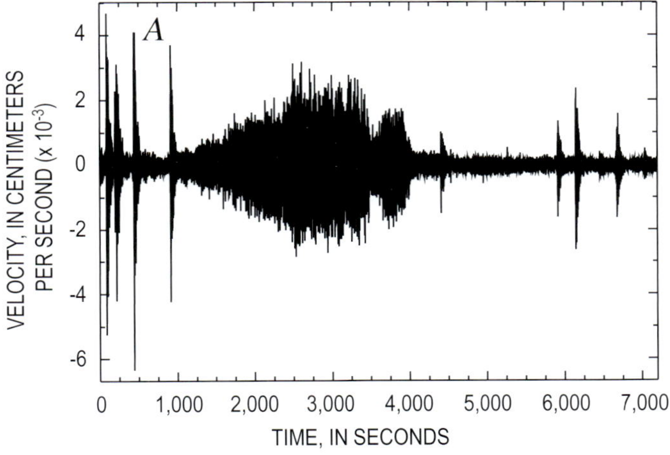

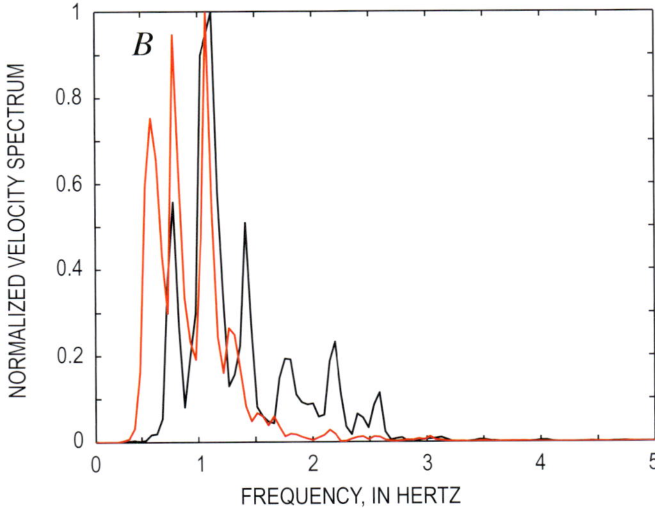

Figure 8. Seismic data showing 2-hour sequence of tremor recorded October 2, 2004, at JRO broadband station. *A*, Seismogram showing north component. Record of tremor is punctuated by impulsive earthquakes of lower-frequency type. *B*, Normalized velocity spectra for a lower-frequency earthquake (red) and the volcanic tremor (black) of October 2.

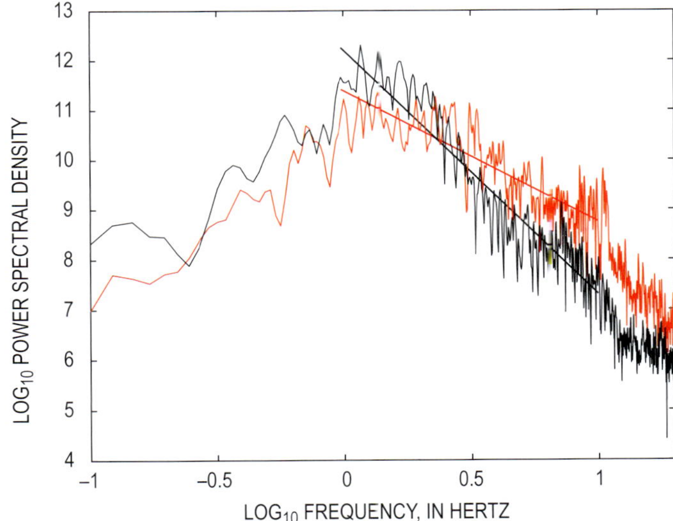

Figure 9. Power spectra of the vertical velocity components of a hybrid event (red) and a low-frequency event (black). Lines are least-squares fit to spectral amplitudes between ´ and 10 Hz; slopes are −2.6 for hybrid event and −4.9 for the LF event.

decreased to between about −3 and −4 at the end of October. The slope values continued at this level or decreased slightly until the end of November. If we arbitrarily declared a slope of −3.0 as the dividing line between hybrid and LF, then this figure would suggest about a 4:1 ratio of hybrid to LF events occurred between October 4 and October 5, decreasing smoothly to a 1:1 ratio by October 10, and decreasing to a 1:4 ratio by October 17. Other than a small increase around October 20, the slope continued to decrease so that by October 24, around 95 percent of the events were low frequency.

The gradual decrease in the slope of the high-frequency falloff over time reflects a progressive loss of high-frequency seismic energy. The loss of high-frequency seismic energy coincides with magma approaching and reaching the surface on October 11 (Scott and others, this volume, chap. 1). This lessening of high-frequency energy could be related to a decrease in earthquake source depth, with near-surface heterogeneity and anelasticity serving to filter out the higher-frequency parts of the seismograms. Alternatively, it may be related to a decrease in the static stress drop accompanying frictional slip as the magma plug, which initially needed to force its way through overlying rock, met with less resistance after the path to the surface was cleared.

Waveform Modeling

The record section in figure 11*A* shows bandpass-filtered (0.1–1 Hz) seismograms for a *M*s 2.9 LF earthquake that occurred on March 1, 2005, at 0928 PST. For this event, the acceleration record at station SEP in the crater was available. The SEP record was substantially clipped, but the filtered record should still illustrate the general character of ground acceleration in this passband. This earthquake was assigned a depth of 0.4 km by the PNSN. The seismograms all exhibited a low-amplitude onset followed by a long-duration, low-frequency waveform even at the closest station (SEP) recording acceleration. Signal duration increased with distance, from 15–20 s at less than 1 km epicentral distance from the source to ~50 s at 20 km distance. The first onset of larger-amplitude arrivals propagated at roughly 2 km/s. To investigate particle motion we chose a 6-s window having

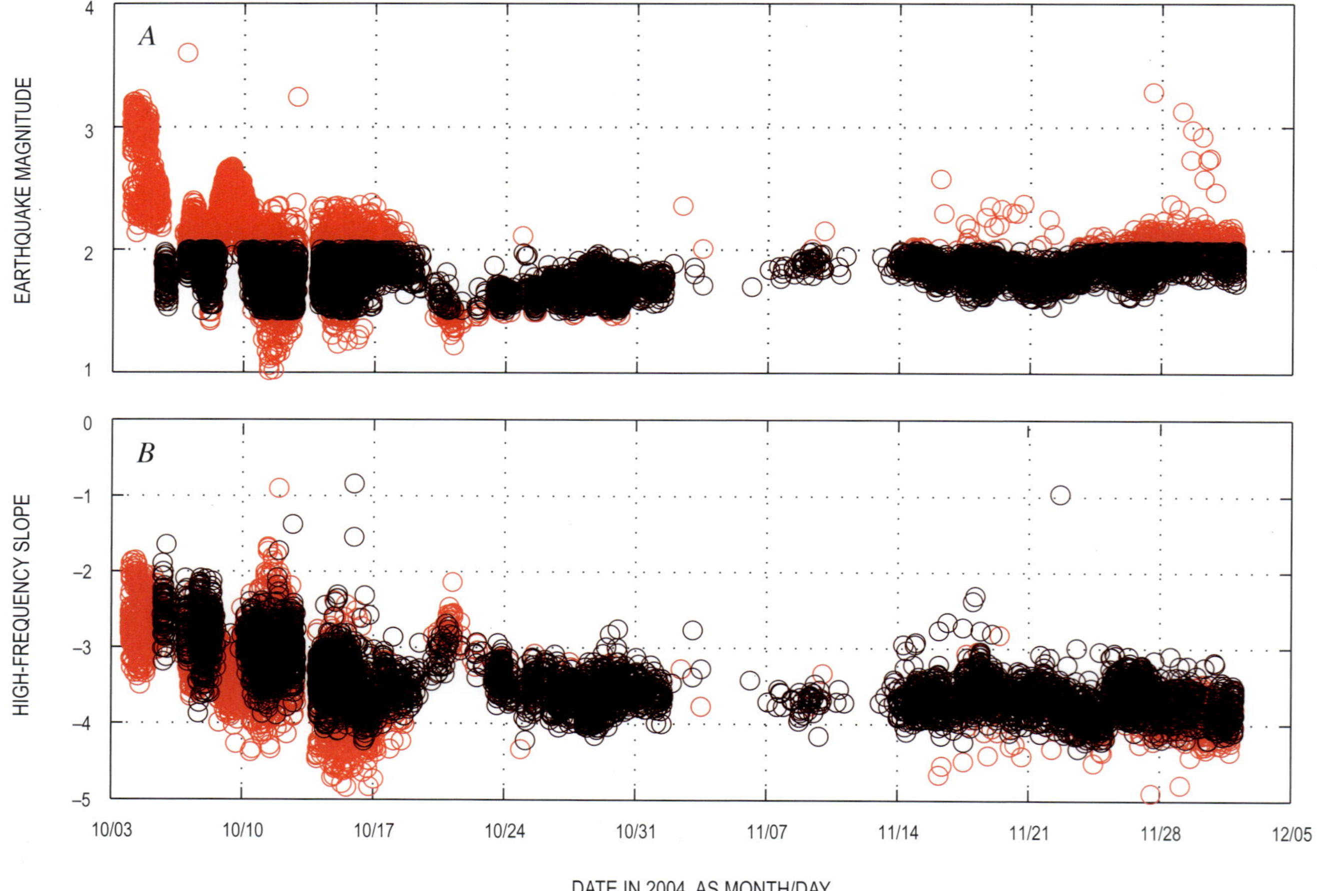

Figure 10. Time series showing seismic data from station BLUE. *A*, Magnitude versus time. Black circles show events in the range $1.5 \leq M_s \leq 2.0$; red circles are all other events. *B*, Plot of high-frequency slope versus time. Symbol color is determined by magnitude as in *A* (black circles, $1.5 \leq M_s \leq 2.0$).

a group velocity of 2 km/s for each station. At station PISH the particle motion in the vertical-radial plane was retrograde elliptical motion, characteristic of Rayleigh waves. However, the transverse component also had significant energy in this window, indicative either of Love waves or of multipathing. For the closer stations, the particle motion in the vertical-radial plane was more complex, suggesting interaction of body and surface waves in this window.

We used a reflection matrix method (Randall and others, 1995) to compute synthetic seismograms for a one-dimensional (1D) velocity model. The velocity model (table 2) was modified from the P-wave velocity model of Lees and Crosson (1989). The S-wave velocity in each layer was calculated from the P-wave velocity using a ratio of 1.7, based on the work of Sudo and Kong (2001), who found an average V_P / V_S ratio of 1.704 fit observed P- and S-wave travel times at all stations for a large number of well-recorded earthquakes at Aso volcano, Kyushu, Japan. A low-velocity surface layer with Swave velocity of 2 km/s was required to have the synthetic surface waves propagate at a velocity near 2 km/s. Moderate *Q* values were assumed (see table 2). We assumed an implosive source with −1 on the diagonal elements of the moment tensor and 0 on the off-diagonal elements. The synthetics were convolved with a triangular source pulse of 1-s duration and then lowpass filtered at 1 Hz.

The synthetic waveforms in figure 11*B* did a reasonable job of predicting the character of the initial arrivals and the beginning of the surface wave train. The synthetic P wave had a down first motion and was emergent at all azimuths. The synthetics do not have the long duration of the observed surface waves but rather a slightly dispersed surface wave traveling at approximately 2 km/s. We also tested other reasonable permutations of the layer velocities within a vertically stratified velocity model without producing the low-frequency coda. From this exercise we concluded that the low-frequency coda observed in figure 11*A* was not produced by a slow surface layer in a 1D velocity model. Scattering of low-frequency surface waves by the extreme local topography of the volcano would be a likely source of some of the coda. The resonance of a source structure (for example, Chouet, 1996, or Neuberg and others, 2006) could also contribute. Examination of surface-wave propagation in a 3D velocity model was beyond the scope of the current study. Unfortunately, we concluded that our simple 1D velocity model was inadequate for modeling waveforms for the purpose of determining the source time function and focal mechanism for these events, because the coda would map into the source.

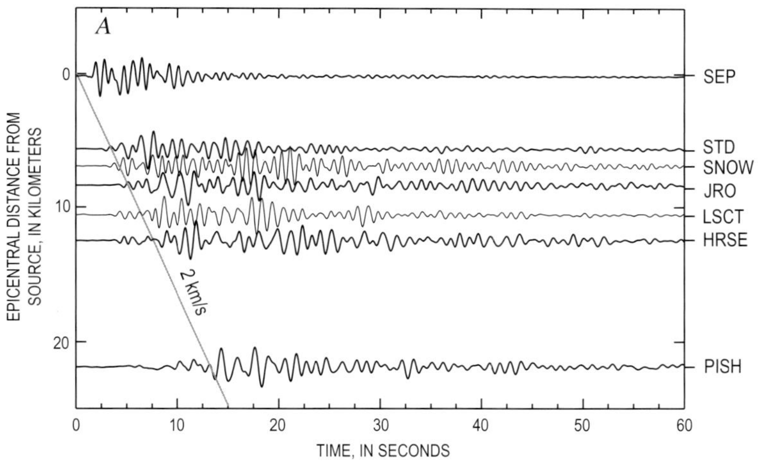

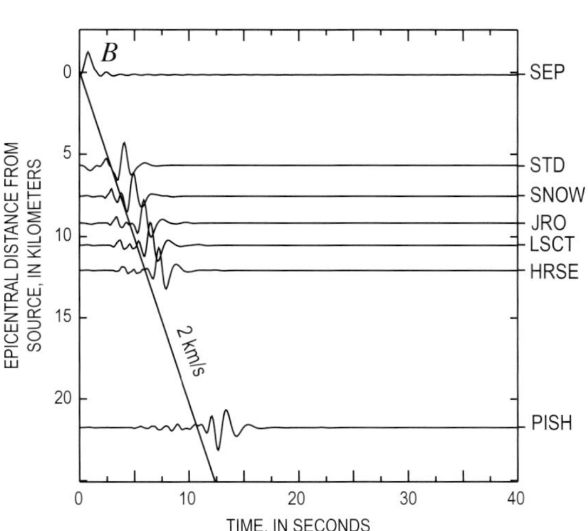

Figure 11. Seismic data for earthquake on March 1, 2005. Stations are identified at right. *A*, Time series for record section from vertical component. Vertical traces have been bandpass filtered between 0.1 and 1 Hz. First onset of the surface wave propagates at roughly 2 km/s. *B*, Synthetic record section assuming a one-dimensional velocity model (table 2) with a moderately slow surface layer (see text). Bandpass-filtered traces between 0.1 and 1 Hz are shown for an implosive, triangular source pulse. The surface wave propagates at roughly 2 km/s.

Table 2. Velocity structure of Mount St. Helens used in this study.

[For a material cycled in stress, Q is the inverse ratio of the energy lost each cycle to the peak strain energy. Q_P and Q_S specify the anelasticity of a material to P- and S-wave motion, respectively.]

Layer	Depth to top of layer (km)	S-wave velocity (km/s)	P-wave velocity (km/s)	Density (g/cm^3)	Q_S	Q_P
1	0	2.0	3.4	2.1	100	200
2	2	3.18	5.4	2.2	100	200
3	4	3.75	6.38	2.2	100	200
4	9	3.88	6.59	2.3	100	200
5	16	3.96	6.73	2.8	250	500
6	20	4.04	6.86	2.8	250	500
7	25	4.09	6.95	2.8	250	500
8	32	4.06	6.90	2.8	250	500
9	41	4.59	7.85	3.3	300	600

Summary

A network of broadband seismometers was rapidly deployed at Mount St. Helens when it became restless in September 2004 and maintained through the winter of 2004–5 without a significant loss of data. A principal reason for deploying broadband seismometers was to record any very long period (VLP) seismicity (5–30 s) associated with the eruption that would otherwise have been missed by the PNSN short-period stations. We found no evidence of VLP pulses at our stations in the first 2 months of recording. Our closest stations were more than 5 km distant from the centroid of seismic activity, and these pulses may attenuate too quickly to be observed at that distance.

More than 57,000 earthquakes were recorded during the 7-month deployment. They had a normal magnitude distribution, with a mean magnitude of 1.78 and a standard deviation of 0.24 magnitude units. Both the mode and range of earthquake size and the rate of activity varied during the 7-month period. Some cases of this variation can be associated with spine growth and breakup. In general, larger earthquakes tended to occur when the earthquake rate was high.

The dataset consisted largely of hybrid and low frequency (LF) earthquakes. These lower-frequency events typically had a low amplitude onset with frequencies up to about 10 or 20 Hz, followed by a strong, long-duration, and lower-frequency waveform. The shape of the Fourier spectrum at the low-frequency end was similar for both types of events, having significant energy between 0.3 and 5 Hz with multiple spectral peaks. Hybrid events exhibited more energetic high-frequency onsets than LF events, but the rate of high-frequency decay with time was similar for both types. The difference in high-frequency energy was more likely related to the source than to attenuation near the source or along the path, inasmuch as the high-frequency decay rate was the same for both events.

The spectra of large and small events that occurred close in time were quite similar in shape between 0.5 and 10 Hz. The similarity in spectral shape suggested that both the source and path were similar for the larger and smaller events. As opposed to the ideal tectonic earthquake spectra, in which the peak in the velocity spectrum changes to lower frequency as rupture zone area increases for larger earthquakes, the frequency range of the peak of spectral energy remained constant for different-size, lower-frequency earthquakes. This relative constancy is consistent with a resonating source, whereby the shape of the spectrum is constrained by the size and properties of the resonator. However, a search of spectra of the same events observed at multiple stations revealed no specific frequencies of source resonance, and so the spectra may reflect a complex, perhaps asymmetric, resonating structure.

The spectra of a lower-frequency earthquake and an episode of volcanic tremor had distinct peaks in common. However, the lower-frequency earthquake spectrum had a prominent peak at 0.6 Hz that was not observed in the spectrum of the volcanic tremor, and higher frequencies were more favorably excited during the tremor. This lower-frequency peak would be consistent with resonance of a larger structure during the earthquake or a change in the source such that excitation of the longer dimension of the same structure was favorable.

The high-frequency spectral difference between hybrid and LF events was quantified using the slope of the high-frequency falloff. The slope computed for several thousand lower-frequency earthquakes between October 4 and December 1, 2004, defined a continuum between the ideal hybrid and ideal LF events. The slope started relatively high on October 4 and transitioned smoothly to lower values until around October 14. The gradual decrease in the slope of the high-frequency falloff over time reflected a progressive loss of high-frequency seismic energy as magma approached and eventually reached the surface.

The first onset of the surface-wave train produced by low-frequency earthquakes propagated at roughly 2 km/s. This propagation velocity favors an areally extensive surface layer with an average S-wave velocity of about 2 km/s. A window of the vertical and radial components for a 2 km/s group velocity has retrograde elliptical particle motion when observed at 20 km distance. Signal duration ranges from 15 to 50 s. A one-dimensional velocity model was unsuitable for waveform modeling to determine the source time function and focal mechanism of the lower-frequency earthquakes.

Acknowledgments

Deployment and maintenance of the seismic network was facilitated by numerous individuals at the U.S. Forest Service, the Cascades Volcano Observatory, and the Pacific Northwest Seismic Network of the University of Washington. Federal Express shipped our equipment to Portland, Oregon, without cost. We are grateful to Thomas Brackman, Chris Watson, and Gary Patterson of the Center for Earthquake Research and Information (CERI) at the University of Memphis for taking time to assist in the field. We obtained seismic data for stations LON, JRO, and STD from the Incorporated Research Institutions for Seismology Data Management Center. Greg Waite and Charles Langston provided thoughtful and helpful reviews of this paper. This is CERI contribution 511.

References Cited

Almendros, J., and Chouet, B., 2003, Performance of the radial semblance method for the location of very long period volcanic signals: Seismological Society of America Bulletin, v. 93, p. 1890–1903.

Almendros, J., Chouet, B., Dawson, P., and Bond, T., 2002, Identifying elements of the plumbing system beneath Kilauea Volcano, Hawaii, from the source locations of very-long-period signals: Geophysical Journal International, v. 148, p. 303–312.

Aster, R., Mah, S., Kyle, P., McIntosh, W., Dunbar, N., Johnson, J., Ruiz, M., and McNamara, S., 2003, Very long period oscillations of Mount Erebus Volcano: Journal of Geophysical Research, v. 108, no. B11, 2522, doi:10.1029/2002JB002101.

Brune, J.N., 1970, Tectonic stress and the spectra of seismic shear waves from earthquakes: Journal of Geophysical Research, v. 75, no. 23, p. 4997–5009.

Chouet, B.A., 1996, Long-period volcano seismicity; its source and use in eruption forecasting: Nature, v. 380, p. 309–316.

Endo, E.T., Malone, S.D., Noson, L.L., and Weaver, C.S., 1981, Locations, magnitudes, and statistics of the March 20–May 18 earthquake sequence, *in* Lipman, P.W., and Mullineaux, D.R., eds., The 1980 eruptions of Mount St. Helens, Washington: U.S. Geological Survey Professional Paper 1250, p. 93–107.

Fehler, M., 1983, Observations of volcanic tremor at Mount St. Helens Volcano: Journal of Geophysical Research: v. 88, p. 3476–3484.

Lahr, J.C., Chouet, B.A., Stephens, C.D., Power, J.A., and Page, R.A., 1994, Earthquake classification, location, and tremor analysis in a volcanic environment; implications for the magmatic system of the 1989–1990 eruptions at Redoubt Volcano, Alaska: Journal of Volcanology and Geothermal Research, v. 62, nos. 1–4, p. 137–151, doi:10.1016/0377-0273(94)90031-0.

Latter, J.H., 1981, Volcanic earthquakes, and their relationship to eruptions at Ruapehu and Ngauruhoe volcanoes: Journal of Volcanology and Geothermal Research, v. 9, p. 293–309.

Lees, J.M., and Crosson, R.S., 1989, Tomographic inversion for three-dimensional velocity structure at Mount St. Helens using earthquake data: Journal of Geophysical Research, v. 94, no. B5, p. 5716–5728.

Longuet-Higgins, M.S., 1950, A theory of the origin of microseisms: Philosophical Transactions of the Royal Society of London, series A, v. 243, p. 1–35.

Malone, S.D., 1983, Volcanic earthquakes; examples from Mount St. Helens, *in* Earthquakes; observations, theory and interpretation: Bologna, Italy, Società Italiana di Fisica, p. 436–455.

Malone, S.D., Boyko, C., and Weaver, C.S., 1983, Seismic precursors to the Mount St. Helens eruptions in 1981 and 1982: Science, v. 221, p. 1376–1378.

McChesney, P.J., Couchman, M.R., Moran, S.C., Lockhart, A.B., Swinford, K.J., and LaHusen, R.G., 2008, Seismic-monitoring changes and the remote deployment of seismic stations (seismic spider) at Mount St. Helens, 2004–2005, chap. 7 *of* Sherrod, D.R., Scott, W.E., and Stauffer, P.H., eds., A volcano rekindled; the renewed eruption of Mount St. Helens, 2004–2006: U.S. Geological Survey Professional Paper 1750 (this volume).

Moran, S.C., Malone, S.D., Qamar, A.I., Thelen, W.A., Wright, A.K., and Caplan-Auerbach, J., 2008a, Seismicity associated with renewed dome building at Mount St. Helens, 2004–2005, chap. 2 *of* Sherrod, D.R., Scott, W.E., and Stauffer, P.H., eds., A volcano rekindled; the renewed eruption of Mount St. Helens, 2004–2006: U.S. Geological Survey Professional Paper 1750 (this volume).

Moran, S.C., McChesney, P.J., and Lockhart, A.B., 2008b, Seismicity and infrasound associated with explosions at Mount St. Helens, 2004–2005, chap. 6 *of* Sherrod, D.R., Scott, W.E., and Stauffer, P.H., eds., A volcano rekindled; the renewed eruption of Mount St. Helens, 2004–2006: U.S. Geological Survey Professional Paper 1750 (this volume).

Neuberg, J., Luckett, R., Baptie, B., and Olsen, K., 2000, Models of tremor and low-frequency earthquake swarms on Montserrat: Journal of Volcanology and Geothermal Research, v. 101, p. 83–104.

Neuberg, J.W., Tuffen, H., Collier, L., Green, D., Powell, T., and Dingwell, D., 2006, The trigger mechanism of low-frequency earthquakes on Montserrat: Journal of Volcanology and Geothermal Research, v. 153, nos. 1–2, p. 37–50, doi:10.1016/j.jvolgeores.2005.08.008.

Randall, G.R., Ammon, C.J., and Owens, T.J., 1995, Moment-tensor estimation using regional seismograms from a Tibetan Plateau portable network deployment: Geophysical Research Letters, v. 22, p. 1665–1668.

Schilling, S.P., Thompson, R.A., Messerich, J.A., and Iwatsubo, E.Y., 2008, Use of digital aerophotogrammetry to determine rates of lava dome growth, Mount St. Helens, Washington, 2004–2005, chap. 8 *of* Sherrod, D.R., Scott, W.E., and Stauffer, P.H., eds., A volcano rekindled; the renewed eruption of Mount St. Helens, 2004–2006: U.S. Geological Survey Professional Paper 1750 (this volume).

Scott, W.E., Sherrod, D.R., and Gardner, C.A., 2008, Overview of 2004 to 2006, and continuing, eruption of Mount St. Helens, Washington, chap. 1 *of* Sherrod, D.R., Scott, W.E., and Stauffer, P.H., eds., A volcano rekindled; the renewed eruption of Mount St. Helens, 2004–2006: U.S. Geological Survey Professional Paper 1750 (this volume).

Sudo, Y., and Kong, L.S.L., 2001, Three-dimensional seismic velocity structure beneath Aso Volcano, Kyushu, Japan: Bulletin of Volcanology, v. 63, p. 326–344.

Swanson, D.A., Casadevall, T.J., Dzurisin, D., Malone, S.D., Newhall, C.G., and Weaver, C.S., 1983, Predicting eruptions at Mount St. Helens, June 1980 through December 1982: Science, v. 221, no. 4618, p. 1369–1376.

Swanson, D.A., Casadevall, T.J., Dzurisin, D., Malone, S.D., Holcomb, R.T., Newhall, C.G., and Weaver, C.S., 1985, Forecasts and predictions of eruptive activity at Mount St. Helens, USA: 1975–1984: Journal of Geodynamics, v. 3, p. 397–423.

Thelen, W.A., Crosson, R.S., and Creager, K.C., 2008, Absolute and relative locations of earthquakes at Mount St. Helens, Washington, using continuous data; implications for magmatic processes, chap. 4 *of* Sherrod, D.R., Scott, W.E., and Stauffer, P.H., eds., A volcano rekindled; the renewed eruption of Mount St. Helens, 2004–2006: U.S. Geological Survey Professional Paper 1750 (this volume).

Vallance, J.W., Schneider, D.J., and Schilling, S.P., 2008, Growth of the 2004–2006 lava-dome complex at Mount St. Helens, Washington, chap. 9 *of* Sherrod, D.R., Scott, W.E., and Stauffer, P.H., eds., A volcano rekindled; the renewed eruption of Mount St. Helens, 2004–2006: U.S. Geological Survey Professional Paper 1750 (this volume).

A Volcano Rekindled: The Renewed Eruption of Mount St. Helens, 2004–2006
Edited by David R. Sherrod, William E. Scott, and Peter H. Stauffer
U.S. Geological Survey Professional Paper 1750, 2008

Chapter 6

Seismicity and Infrasound Associated with Explosions at Mount St. Helens, 2004–2005

By Seth C. Moran[1], Patrick J. McChesney[2], and Andrew B. Lockhart[1]

Abstract

Six explosions occurred during 2004–5 in association with renewed eruptive activity at Mount St. Helens, Washington. Of four explosions in October 2004, none had precursory seismicity and two had explosion-related seismic tremor that marked the end of the explosion. However, seismicity levels dropped following each of the October explosions, providing the primary instrumental means for explosion detection during the initial vent-clearing phase. In contrast, explosions on January 16 and March 8, 2005, produced noticeable seismicity in the form of explosion-related tremor, infrasonic signals, and, in the case of the March 8 explosion, an increase in event size ~2 hours before the explosion. In both 2005 cases seismic tremor appeared before any infrasonic signals and was best recorded on stations located within the crater. These explosions demonstrated that reliable explosion detection at volcanoes like Mount St. Helens requires seismic stations within 1–2 km of the vent and stations with multiple acoustic sensors.

Introduction

On September 23, 2004, a swarm of volcano-tectonic earthquakes heralded the reawakening of Mount St. Helens after 18 years of quiescence (Moran and others, this volume, chap. 2). On October 1 the first small explosion occurred, with three others following over the next four days (table 1). Several of these happened during daylight hours and were broadcast on live television across the United States, perhaps creating an impression that Mount St. Helens was building towards a larger explosive eruption. Instead, these explosions were followed by the steady-state extrusion of a new dome in the southern part of the 1980 crater. The relatively steady-state extrusion was punctuated by just two explosions, one on January 16, 2005, and the other on March 8, 2005 (table 1). All six explosions were phreatic, with no evidence, such as fresh pumice, of any significant magmatic component (Scott and others, this volume, chap. 1; Rowe and others, this volume, chap. 29). Overall, the eruption in 2004–5 featured very little explosive activity, a result of the gas-poor nature of the erupted magma (Gerlach and others, this volume, chap. 26).

We use the term "explosion" in this paper to refer to an impulsive, sudden yet sustained emission of volcanic gas and pyroclasts. Rapid detection of ash-producing explosions is of paramount importance because of the demonstrated dangers posed to aircraft by airborne ash particles (for example, Neal and others, 1997). Despite the paucity of explosions, seismic and acoustic recordings of the six explosions at Mount St. Helens have yielded several important insights into the utility and placement of seismic and acoustic sensors for improved explosion-detection capabilities, as well as insights into the nature of minor explosive activity during dome-building eruptions. In this paper we present a chronology of observations and recordings of explosions from 2004–5, focusing on our ability to detect the onset and termination of each explosion and on insights gained from seismic and acoustic data into the evolution of individual explosions.

Explosions During the Vent-Clearing Phase, October 1–October 5, 2004

Explosion 1: October 1, 1202 PDT

The first explosion occurred without warning at 1202 PDT on October 1 (fig. 1*A*, table 1), 8.5 days after the start of seismic unrest (Moran and others, this volume, chap. 2). The explosion was well documented, as it took place on a

[1] U.S. Geological Survey, 1300 SE Cardinal Court, Vancouver, WA 98683

[2] Pacific Northwest Seismic Network, Department of Earth and Space Sciences, University of Washington, Box 351310, Seattle, WA 98195

Table 1. Summary of eruption parameters and seismic and acoustic observations of the six explosions occurring at Mount St. Helens, Washington, during 2004–5.

[PDT, Pacific daylight (saving) time; PST, Pacific standard time.]

Explosion number, date, and time	Duration (minutes)	Seismicity before, during, and after	Infrasound detected?	Plume height (approximate, m above vent)	Eruption phase
Explosion 1: 10/01/04, 1202 PDT	19	No precursors; earthquakes stopped following onset; tremor associated with end of explosion; almost no earthquakes for several hours afterwards	N/A (no sensors)	2,400	Vent clearing
Explosion 2: 10/03/04, 2240 PDT	~25	No precursors; earthquake rates decreased after onset (drop not as pronounced as explosion 1); tremor associated with end of explosion; seismicity low following explosion	Possible, but could also be coseismic shaking	400	Vent clearing
Explosion 3: 10/04/04, 0943 PDT	~32	No precursors; earthquake rates gradually declined after onset (drop not as pronounced as explosion 2); no tremor associated with end of explosion	No	1,500	Vent clearing
Explosion 4: 10/05/04, 0905 PDT	70	No precursors; gradual but significant decline in earthquake rate and size after onset; no tremor associated with end of explosion	No	2,400	Vent clearing
Explosion 5: 01/16/05, 0312 PST	~33	No precursors; tremor occurred during entire event; no change in earthquake rate observed after explosion	Yes	Unknown	Dome building
Explosion 6: 03/08/05, 1725 PST	~20	Earthquake magnitudes increased ~2 hours before onset; tremor associated with entire event; short-lived increase in earthquake rate after explosion, rate returned to normal within 1–2 hours	Yes	9,000	Dome building

clear day with a U.S. Geological Survey (USGS) crew flying over the crater at the start of the explosion (Schneider and others, this volume, chap. 17), and many television cameras were transmitting images live from a site near Johnston Ridge Observatory (JRO) (fig. 2) to a nationwide audience (Driedger and others, this volume, chap. 24). Infrared recordings of the base of the eruption column showed peak temperatures around 160°C, consistent with visual observations that the explosion was phreatic (Schneider and others, this volume, chap. 17). Eruption cloud tops reached ~4,500 m above sea level (asl), or 2,400 m above the vent.

As described by Moran and others (this volume, chap. 2), seismicity had intensified in a series of steps through the first several days of the crisis that began on September 23, 2004 (fig. 3). By September 29, earthquakes of magnitude 2 and greater were occurring at a rate of ~1 per minute. Although seismicity intensified gradually between 0800 and 1100 PDT on October 1, several more-rapid intensifications had occurred in the previous two days, and so this intensification was not recognized as a short-term warning sign. Because preexplosion seismicity was so intense, it was difficult to see any obvious seismicity associated with the explosion in the first several minutes after 1202 PDT (fig. 1*A*). The most obvious seismic signal was the sudden cessation of earthquakes ~1 minute after the explosion began. After the earthquakes stopped, explosion-related tremor (defined here as seismic tremor accompanying an explosion) with frequencies of 1–3 Hz and a peak reduced displacement, or D_R (Aki and Koyanagi, 1981), of ~6 cm^2 could clearly be seen on many nearby stations (fig. 1*A*; see fig. 2 for station locations). Tremor began increasing in amplitude at 1216, then abruptly stopped at 1221, when the explosion also stopped. Weak tremor occurred again starting at 1240, but earthquakes did not occur again until ~3 hours later (Moran and others, this volume, chap. 2).

If the earthquakes had not ceased when the explosion started and the explosion had not occurred during daylight hours in clear conditions, it is possible that staff at the Cascades Volcano Observatory (CVO) and the Pacific Northwest Seismic Network (PNSN) might not have realized that an explosion had occurred. The intense earthquake activity at the time was continuously saturating nearby seismic stations, all of which had short-period vertical-component seismometers, and the explosion-related tremor would have been almost impossible to distinguish had the earthquakes not ceased. In an attempt to improve our explosion detection capability, 1-Hz infrasound-sensitive acoustic sensors (see appendix 1) were

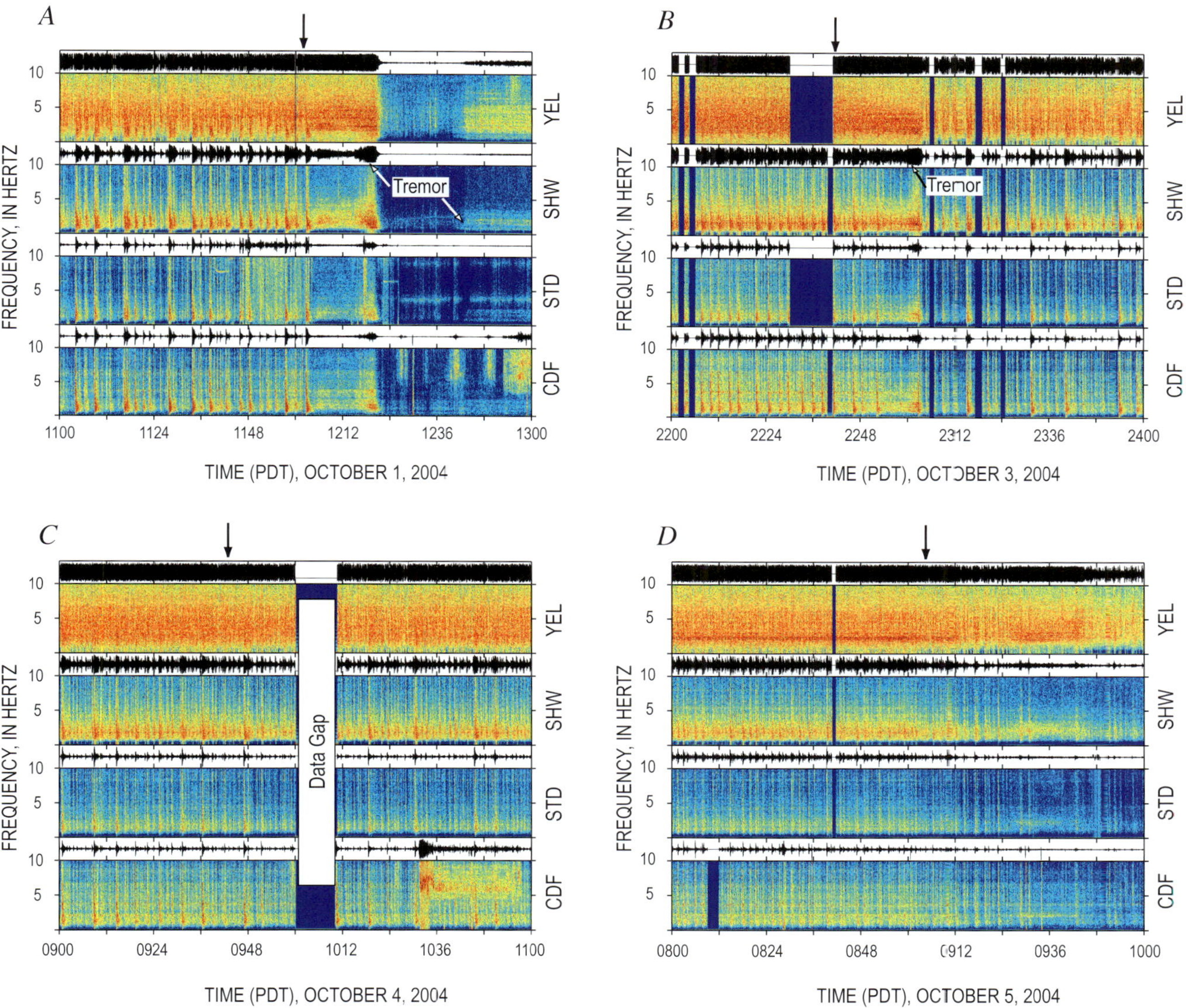

Figure 1. Multistation 2-hour-long spectrograms for explosions 1–4 at Mount St. Helens, Washington, October 2004. Time series (top) and frequency spectrogram (bottom) are shown for each of four seismic stations (see fig. 2 for station locations). Stations are shown in order of distance from vent, with closest station at top of the plot. Each time series is normalized to the maximum amplitude in each 2-hour window. Frequency spectrograms show spectral amplitudes for frequencies ranging from 0 to 10 Hz using a rainbow color palette, with dark blue corresponding to low spectral amplitudes (< 30 dB) and red to high amplitudes (>100 dB). Explosion onset time indicated by an arrow at top of each spectrogram. *A*, October 1, 2004, 1100–1300 PDT (explosion at 1202). *B*, October 3, 2004, 2200–2400 PDT (explosion at ~2240). *C*, October 4, 2004, 0900–1100 PDT (explosion at 0943). *D*, October 5, 2004, 0800–1000 PDT (explosion at 0905).

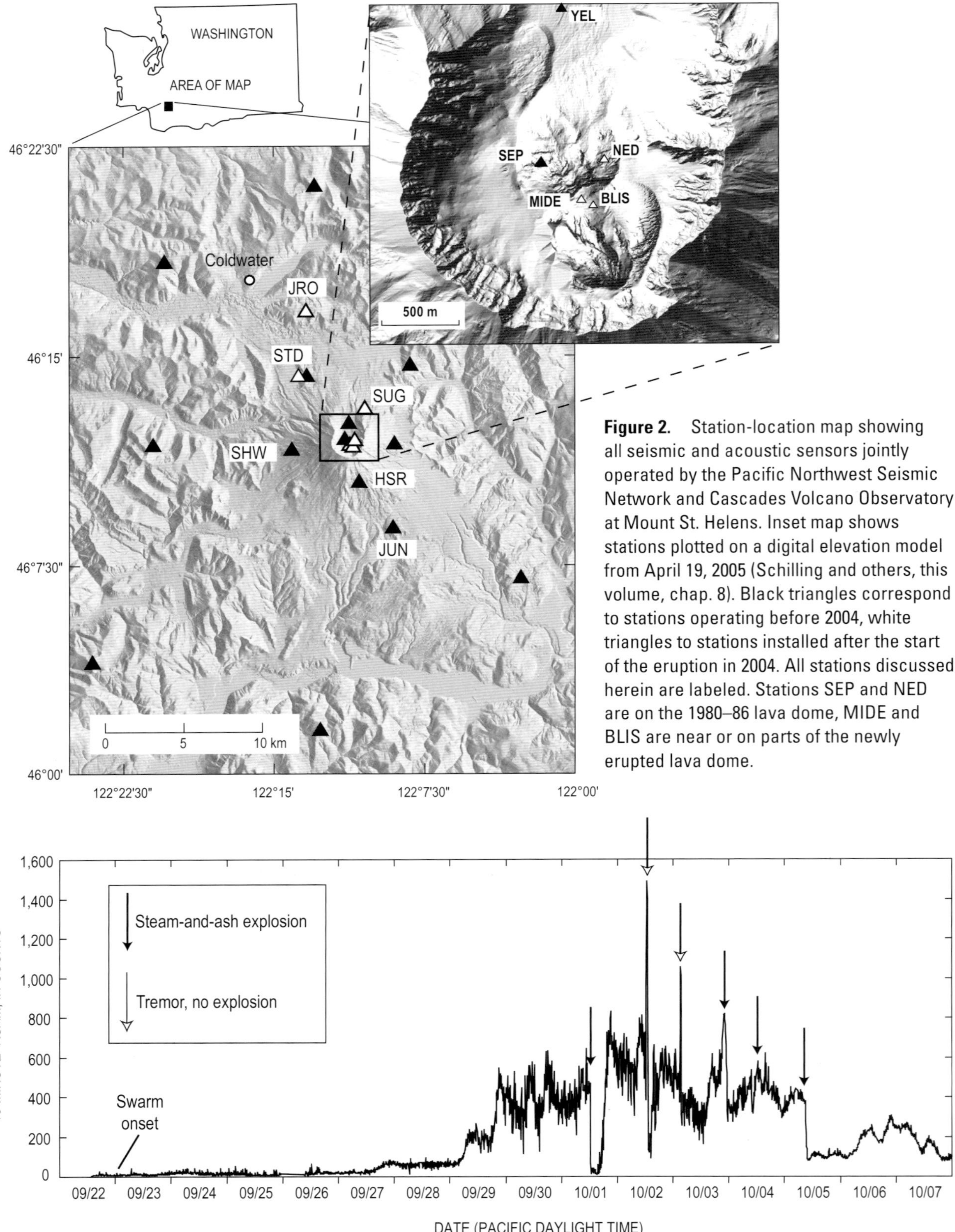

Figure 2. Station-location map showing all seismic and acoustic sensors jointly operated by the Pacific Northwest Seismic Network and Cascades Volcano Observatory at Mount St. Helens. Inset map shows stations plotted on a digital elevation model from April 19, 2005 (Schilling and others, this volume, chap. 8). Black triangles correspond to stations operating before 2004, white triangles to stations installed after the start of the eruption in 2004. All stations discussed herein are labeled. Stations SEP and NED are on the 1980–86 lava dome, MIDE and BLIS are near or on parts of the newly erupted lava dome.

Figure 3. Plot of 10-minute RSAM values (Endo and Murray, 1991) for station SHW (see fig. 2) from September 22 to October 8, 2004. Black arrows indicate timing of individual explosions; white arrows, timing of two tremor episodes that did not correspond to any explosions (the only two such cases during entire eruption; Moran and others, this volume, chap. 2).

installed at the Studebaker Ridge station (STD) on October 2 and at Sugar Bowl (SUG) on October 3 (McChesney and others, this volume, chap. 7; see fig. 2 for station locations).

Explosion 2: October 3, ~2240 PDT

The second explosion occurred at ~2240 PDT on October 3 (fig. 1*B*). Although this explosion occurred at night, the weather was clear and U.S. Forest Service observers stationed 13 km north-northwest of the crater at the Coldwater Ridge Visitor Center reported seeing an ash cloud that barely reached the crater rim (~2,500 m asl, or 400 m above the vent) starting at ~2240 PDT (M. Guffanti, written commun., 2004). Earthquake rates and real-time seismic amplitude measurement (RSAM; Endo and Murray, 1991) levels had increased several hours before the explosion (fig. 3), and by 2100 PDT events were occurring so close together that they were difficult to distinguish, forming a spasmodic, tremorlike signal (Moran and others, this volume, chap. 2). Because there had been much more energetic tremor earlier on October 2 and October 3 with no associated explosions, the spasmodic tremor was not regarded as a short-term warning sign. As with the October 1 explosion, earthquake rates dropped significantly at ~2305 PDT following a ~3-minute-long tremor episode (peak D_R ~3 cm^2) that presumably marked the end of the explosion (fig. 1*B*). A weak, continuous acoustic signal appeared on the newly deployed microphone at STD. However, with just that single sensor, we cannot distinguish between mechanical shaking of the microphone by passing seismic waves and explosion-related infrasound. The STD microphone did record many small (~0.5 Pa) infrasonic pulses associated with M >2 earthquakes, indicating that it was sufficiently close to record weak infrasonic signals from the crater.

Explosion 3: October 4, 0943 PDT

Earthquake rates gradually increased on the morning of October 4 until the third explosion occurred at 0943 PDT (maximum plume height ~3,650 m asl, or about 1,500 m above the vent), lasting until 1015 (fig. 1*C*). The explosion was recorded by a U.S. Forest Service Web camera at the JRO and was also noted by many observers. Earthquake rates decreased following the explosion (fig. 3), although not as markedly as either of the decreases following the previous two explosions. In contrast to the October 3 explosion, no obvious signal was apparent on the acoustic sensors and no explosion-related tremor was recorded on the nearby seismic stations (fig. 1*C*). The decline in seismicity was gradual and, unlike that accompanying the October 1 explosion, did not correspond in any direct way to the onset or termination of the explosion. Given the lack of obvious associated seismic signals, it is likely that the explosion would not have been detected had it occurred during bad weather.

Dzurisin and others (2005) show in their figure 1 a second steam-and-ash explosion on October 4 at ~1400 PDT. This was based on a report of anomalous steaming in the crater at that time (M. Guffanti, written commun., 2004), a report that coincided with a small drop in RSAM values. However, subsequent review of images from the JRO Web camera (taken every five minutes; Poland and others, this volume, chap. 11) showed no obvious steam or ash plume at that time, in contrast to the 0943 explosion. Given the absence of visible ash, we consider the 1400 event, if there was an event at all, to be at most a small steam explosion that is not comparable to the confirmed explosions, and we do not consider it further in this paper.

Explosion 4: October 5, 0905 PDT

The fourth and final explosion of the vent-clearing phase occurred at 0905 PDT on October 5 and lasted until 1015 (fig. 1*D*). This was the most vigorous and long-lasting explosion of the sequence, with the ash plume reaching ~4,500 m asl (2,400 m above the vent) and depositing trace amounts of ash ~100 km from the volcano (Scott and others, this volume, chap. 1). Before the explosion, RSAM levels had increased over a 6-hour period, reaching a peak level at 0600 that was maintained until the explosion (fig. 3). Earthquake sizes and rates began declining ~15 minutes after the explosion began (fig. 1*D*), with RSAM levels falling below post-September 29 levels by the end of the explosion (fig. 3). As with the October 4 explosion, no obvious explosion-related signals were apparent either on seismic or acoustic sensors (fig. 1*D*). However, the decline in seismicity was significant enough that an explosion could have been inferred if weather conditions had prohibited observation of the explosion. A delayed indicator of the explosion was the loss of the radio signal from station YEL from 1045 to 1238 following the explosion as a result of attenuation of its radio signal by the ash cloud.

Discussion

Because there was no attempt to maintain a full-time official observer near the volcano, there is a remote possibility that other small explosions occurred between October 1 and 5 that were not detected. We feel confident that no undetected explosions occurred during daylight hours, as clear weather provided excellent viewing conditions for the mass of people and media watching the volcano from various vantage points (Driedger and others, this volume, chap. 24). During nighttime hours clear viewing conditions still existed, aided by moonlight from an almost-full moon, and, as a result, members of the public and U.S. Forest Service staff were able to see one nighttime explosion (October 3). Nevertheless, we cannot rule out the possibility that other explosions occurred at night when the volcano was not watched.

Short-term declines in seismic energy following all four explosions were perhaps the most reliable indicator that an explosion had occurred. Seismicity declines following the explosions on October 1, 3, and 5 were particularly significant (fig. 3). However, similarly significant declines followed tremor episodes on October 2 and 3, which were not associated with explosions (Moran and others, this volume, chap. 2). In addition, smaller declines similar to that following the October 4 explosion (including several on October 4) did not correspond to known explosions. Thus short-term declines in seismic energy were not, by themselves, a reliable indicator that an explosion had occurred.

Explosions During the Dome-Building Phase

Several days after the October 5, 2004, explosion, a lava spine emerged from the vent (Vallance and others, this volume, chap. 9). The rest of 2004 was dominated by lava dome construction accompanied by low gas levels (Gerlach and others, this volume, chap. 26) and regularly spaced earthquakes (Moran and others, this volume, chap. 2). During October, November, and December of 2004 we installed several seismic stations within 500 m of the vent (fig. 2) and disabled the microphone at STD, because we needed the radio telemetry channel for data from another station (McChesney and others, this volume, chap. 7). One of the new stations on the 1980–86 lava dome (SEP) had a 2-Hz three-component velocity sensor and two 1-Hz acoustic sensors spaced ~15 m apart in a north-south alignment (appendix 1), roughly radial to the vent. With two microphones we hoped to be able to use relative arrival times of signals between the two sensors to distinguish between wind gusts (which would not necessarily produce similar waveforms, but any similar waveforms would have separations of as much as several seconds between the two sensors), coseismic signals due to shaking of the microphones by passing seismic waves (which would vary depending on the coupling of each microphone to the ground), and infrasonic signals (which would produce very similar waveforms with no more than ~0.05 s difference between the two sensors).

Explosion 5: January 16, 2005, ~0312 PST

The dome-building eruption was punctuated by a relatively short-lived explosion at ~03:12:50 PST on January 16, 2005. The explosion occurred at night during poor weather and was not visually observed. It was instead signaled by the sudden onset of a continuous broadband (1–10 Hz) tremor signal (fig. 4) accompanied by several larger-than-average low-frequency (dominant frequency <5 Hz) seismic events. The explosion-related tremor was relatively small (peak D_R of ~0.5 cm^2) and did not show up well on stations outside the crater (fig. 4). As a result, preestablished amplitude-based thresholds for generating automated alarms were not exceeded (Qamar and others, this volume, chap. 3) and the explosion was not detected by CVO and PNSN staff until more than an hour later during a routine scan of seismic records.

The explosion signal initially was most obvious on station BLIS (fig. 5), located ~250 m east of the vent (fig. 2). The estimated start time for the explosion is based on the onset of tremor at BLIS. Tremor did not become obvious on other stations, including two stations located ~500 m from the vent, until it increased in amplitude starting at ~0318 (figs. 4, 5). As BLIS was close to the actively growing spine 4, the tremor signal could conceivably have been caused by rockfalls coming off the spine. Rockfalls at Mount St. Helens commonly produce spindle-shaped signals 1–2 minutes long that often only appear on nearby stations. The tremor signal on BLIS was continuous between 0312 and 0318, however, indicating that the signal was the result of a longer duration process. We speculate that this signal could have been caused by relatively weak jetting before the more significant explosion that presumably occurred in association with the increase in tremor amplitudes starting at 0318.

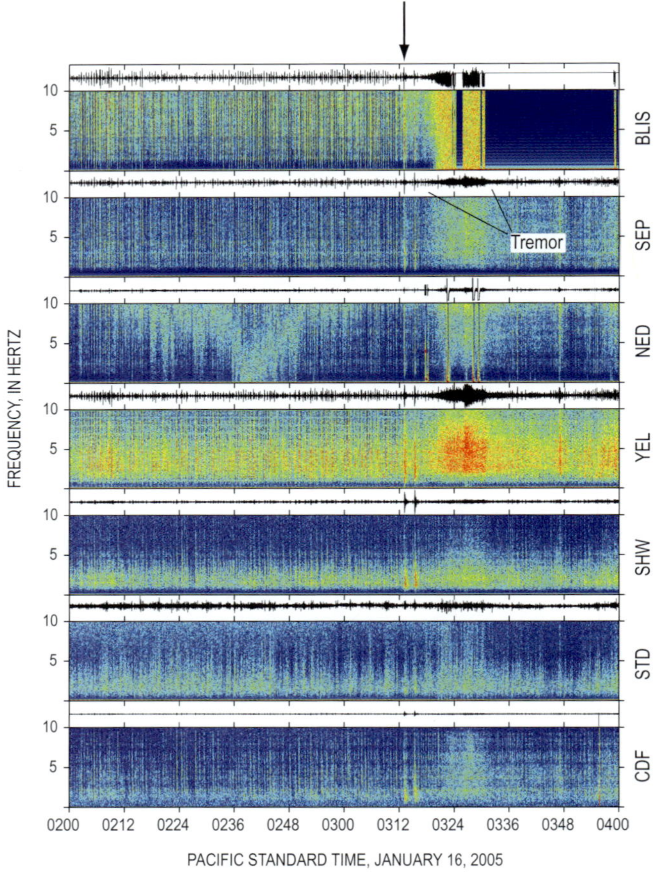

Figure 4. Multistation 2-hour-long spectrogram from 0200 to 0400 PST on January 16, 2005. See figure 2 for station locations and caption to figure 1 for description of spectrograms. Black-tipped arrow indicates estimated start time of explosion at 0312 PST; duration of tremor as seen on station SEP is indicated. Note that stations BLIS and NED had accelerometer sensors, SEP had a 2-Hz velocity sensor, and all other stations had 1-Hz velocity sensors. For more details on configuration of seismic stations, see McChesney and others (this volume, chap. 7).

Tremor rapidly intensified between 0318 and 0320. At ~0320 an emergent continuous signal became apparent on the SEP and SUG microphones (fig. 5). Given that these signals appeared in association with the seismic tremor, it is possible that some, if not most, of this signal reflects mechanical shaking of the microphones by seismic waves. We have no means of assessing this at the SUG site because it had just a single microphone and no collocated seismometer, but the near-simultaneous onset of acoustic signals at SEP and SUG suggest that at least a component of the SUG signal was due to shaking of the microphone housing. At 03:20:30, however, the two acoustic sensors at SEP began recording small-amplitude individual phases within the acoustic signals that were coherent between the two microphones and consistent with a source located at the vent. No correlative signals were apparent on the SUG acoustic sensor ~5 s later (the traveltime difference between SEP and SUG for acoustic waves traveling at 340 m/s). However, this is not surprising, given the fact that SUG is located on a ridgetop that was being buffeted by high winds from an oncoming storm system at the time. We infer that the coherent signals on the two acoustic sensors at SEP reflect the onset of explosion-related infrasound. Although the microphone recordings were still mostly incoherent at the onset of the continuous acoustic signal (fig. 5), individual phases in the signal became progressively more coherent with time. By ~0326, most of the signal was coherent and thus likely due to explosion-related infrasound (as opposed to explosion-related air currents or mechanical shaking of the sensors). The continuous acoustic signal peaked at ~0327 with maximum peak-to-peak amplitudes of 2–4 Pa (see appendix 1 for discussion of microphone calibration uncertainties) and faded to background levels by ~0331. The timing, size, duration, and character of the SEP infrasonic signals are consistent with an emergent infrasonic signal starting at 03:21:22 recorded on a microbarometer array located 13 km northwest of

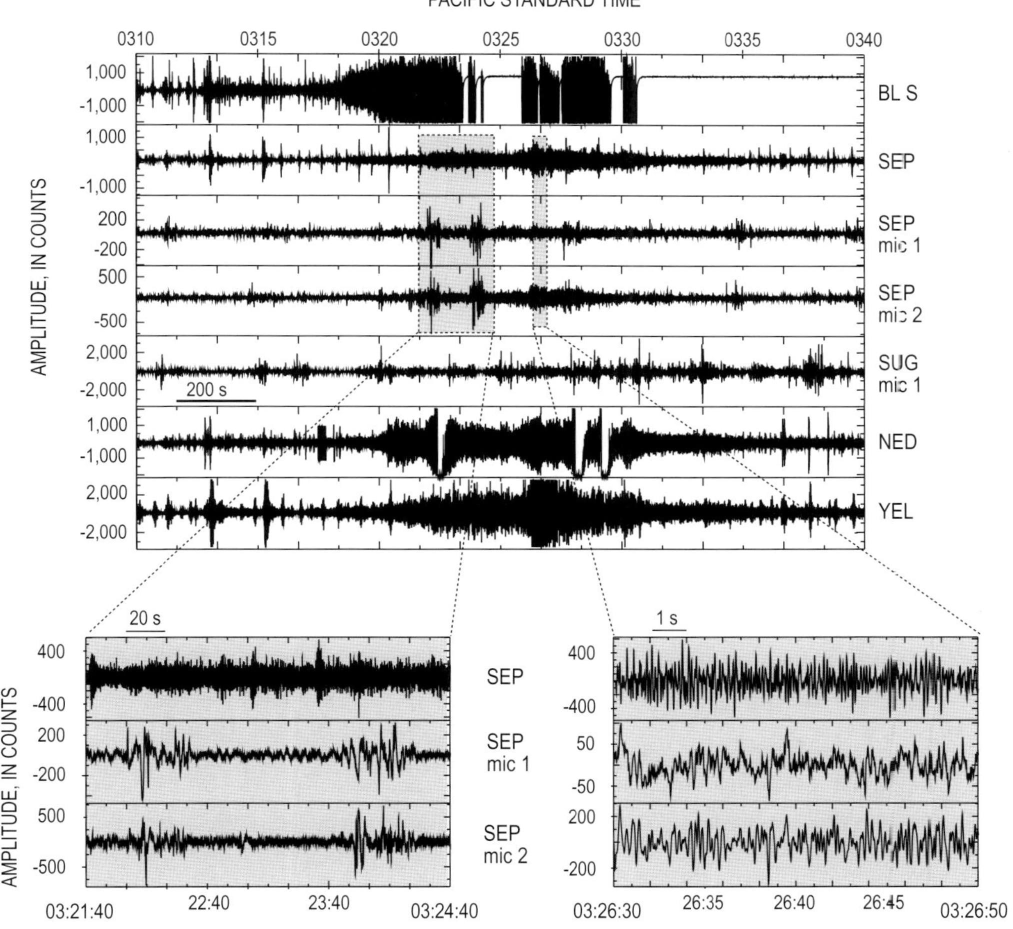

Figure 5. Multistation 30-minute plot showing unfiltered time-series data from 0310 to 0340 PST on January 16, 2005. See figure 2 for station locations. Insets at bottom of plot show 3 minutes (left) and 20 s (right) of data from vertical component of SEP seismometer (top) and two acoustic sensors (microphone 1, middle, and microphone 2, bottom), bandpass filtered with corner frequencies of 0.1 and 15 Hz. Left inset shows two events, recorded by acoustic sensors at ~03:22:00 and ~03:23:50, that we infer to be wind gusts associated with the explosion. Right inset shows mostly coherent signals between the two microphones, indicating that signals are mostly infrasonic energy produced by the explosion.

the vent near the U.S. Forest Service's Coldwater Ridge Visitor Center (Matoza and others, 2007).

Superimposed on the continuous infrasonic signal at SEP were several larger ~1 Hz pulses at 03:20:00, 03:22:05, and 03:23:50 (fig. 5). Although these pulses were broadly coherent between the two microphones, in detail the waveforms have significant variability. In addition, the time separation between relative peaks (as much as 2 s) is too large for an infrasonic signal, given the 15-m spacing of the microphones. The variability and large time differences between these pulses on the two microphones indicate that they were not traveling at sound velocities (~340 m/s) and are thus not infrasound. Other such signals were recorded in the hours before and after the explosion on both the SEP and SUG acoustic sensors, as well as at other times during stormy weather. Because a storm system was moving into the area at the time of the explosion, these pulses are likely wind gusts unrelated to the explosion. The 03:22:05 and 03:23:50 pulses, however, had larger-than-average amplitudes and broadly similar waveforms (fig. 5). On the basis of the admittedly subtle contrasts to other wind gust-related signals, we speculate that these pulses may have been caused by air flow from the explosion that swept across the SEP site at speeds of ~20 m/s.

Evidence that ash was moving across the 1980–86 lava dome shortly after the tremor-amplitude increase at 0318 comes from a several-second-long loss (or "dropout") of the radio signal from NED at 03:22:20 (fig. 5; see fig. 2 for site location). The radio signal from NED was known to be very strong. At the radio receiver for NED we measured a 30 dB fade margin—a quality determined by adding impedance at the receiver until it stops receiving the radio signal from the transmitter. The NED signal had never before been lost, even during stormy weather. The most likely explanation for the NED dropout is that the radio signal was temporarily blocked by ash. Radio telemetry was lost ~60 s later at BLIS, which had a much weaker radio signal (~10 dB fade margin at the receive site) and commonly dropped out during winter storms. Signals from both stations returned in time to record the peak of the tremor signal at 0327 (fig. 5). Shortly after this peak there were two more short-lived radio dropouts at 0328 and 0329 from station NED, followed by a dropout of several hours at station BLIS. The long duration of the BLIS dropout is consistent with a diffuse ash cloud lingering in the vent area following the explosion. Given that no dropouts occurred at SEP and that the first NED dropout occurred before the first BLIS dropout (despite BLIS being located much closer to the vent), we infer that ash was initially blown northeastwards across the dome towards NED.

Explosion-related seismic tremor gradually subsided after 0327, eventually fading to background levels at ~0345 PST on the crater stations. The tremor signal lasted for roughly 32 minutes, similar to the duration of the October 1, 2004, explosion. Subsequent geological reconnaissance on January 19 (3 days later but the first day of clear weather after the explosion) confirmed that an explosion had occurred (Scott and others, this volume, chap. 1), with the primary axis of ash deposition extending east-northeast from the vent toward both NED and BLIS (fig. 2). A field of impact craters as large as 1 m in diameter extended several hundred meters eastwards from the vent towards and beyond BLIS. Station BLIS survived in large part because it was mostly buried in snow. The distribution and thickness of deposits were similar in scope and size to those from the October 1, 2004, explosion (Scott and others, this volume, chap. 1), and it is reasonable to assume that the plume reached heights similar to the October 1 plume (~3,500–4,500 m asl).

In contrast to the October 1 explosion, nearby seismic stations were not saturated by large earthquakes before the January 16 explosion; as a result, the explosion-related tremor could clearly be seen on stations within the crater. Seismic signals from the explosion showed up poorly on stations outside the crater, however (fig. 4). If there had been no seismic stations inside the crater at the time of the explosion, it is conceivable that CVO and PNSN staff would not have known that an explosion had occurred until the next observation flight in the crater. This highlights the importance of having stations close to the vent for accurate and timely detection of explosions. In particular, the loss of telemetry on several crater stations, coupled with the tremor signal, made it clear that an ash-producing explosion had occurred.

As described above, the explosion produced infrasound that was recorded at SEP and at the Coldwater microbarometer array (Matoza and others, 2007). Had there been no crater stations, the Coldwater array might have provided the only definitive instrumental evidence that an explosion had occurred. The infrasonic signal was relatively subtle at both sites, however, and required multiple collocated acoustic sensors to distinguish between explosion-related infrasonic signals, wind noise, coseismic shaking of the acoustic sensors, and other acoustic noise sources. The subtlety of the infrasonic signals illustrates the important role that arrays of acoustic sensors can play in detecting explosions at volcanoes. Given the relatively small infrasonic signals, this explosion may represent an example of the type of ash-rich explosion that elsewhere has been found to be relatively inefficient at producing infrasound (Woulff and McGetchin, 1976; Johnson and Aster, 2005).

Explosion 6: March 8, 2005, 1725 PST

The dome-building eruption was not at all disturbed by the January 16 explosion, with earthquakes and steady-state lava-dome extrusion continuing unabated for the next seven weeks. The steady-state lava-dome extrusion was again punctuated by an explosion at ~17:25:20 PST on March 8, 2005. This was the largest of the six 2004–5 explosions; it was also the best documented and recorded of the six, as it occurred in the early evening of a cloudless day and as a result could be seen from the Portland, Oregon, metropolitan area, 85 km to the south. Tremor associated with the explosion was visible on all stations within 15 km (fig. 6), and CVO personnel who had seen the signal on seismic displays began contacting Federal, airline, and emergency officials within a minute of the start of the explosion. Explosion-related tremor appeared simultaneously at stations inside and outside the crater and achieved maximum amplitudes (peak D_R ~1 cm^2) within the first minute, indicating that the explosion rapidly reached maximum intensity, in contrast to the January 16 explosion. Visual observations confirmed the rapid intensification, with the resultant ash plume reaching heights of about 11,000 m (9,000 m above the vent) within 5 minutes (Scott and others, this volume, chap. 1). Explosion-related tremor began declining after ~8 minutes and became indistinct from normal seismic background levels within 20 minutes. All three stations within 500 m of the vent were destroyed by the explosion (fig. 7).

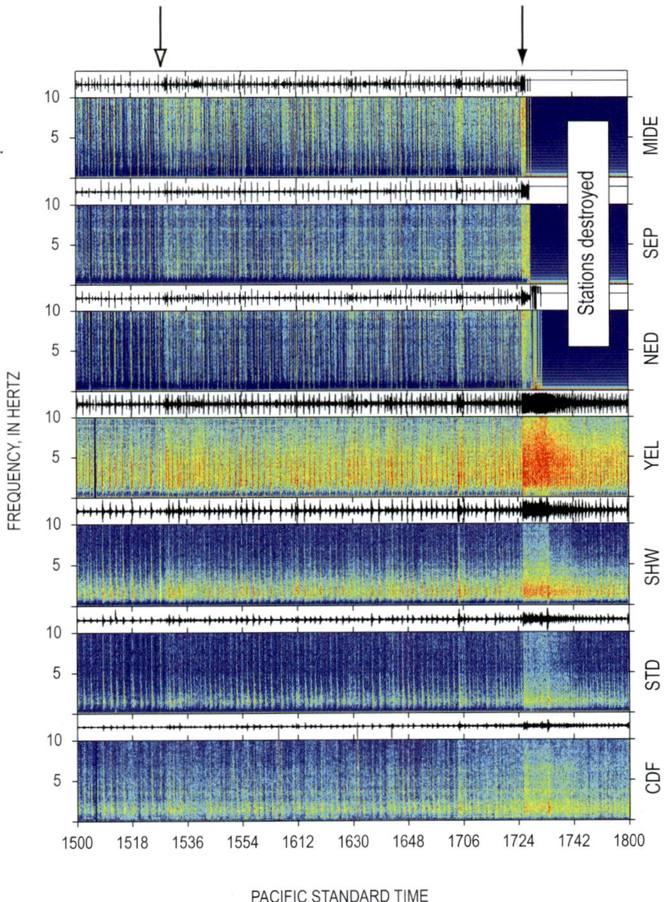

Figure 6. Multistation 3-hour-long spectrogram from March 8, 2005, between 1500 and 1800 PST. See figure 2 for station locations and caption to figure 1 for description of spectrograms. White-tipped arrow indicates start of an increase in number of larger events ~2 hour before the March 8 explosion; black-tipped arrow indicates start of explosion at 1725 PST. Note that stations MIDE and NED had accelerometer sensors, SEP had a 2-Hz velocity sensor, and all other stations had 1-Hz velocity sensors. For more details on configuration of seismic stations, see McChesney and others (this volume, chap. 7).

RSAM Increase

Roughly 2 hours before the March 8 explosion, RSAM levels began increasing at stations as far as 6 km from the vent (fig. 8). Although the increase was relatively small, particularly in comparison to increases seen in the first week of the eruption (Moran and others, this volume, chap. 2), the synchronous rise in RSAM at stations within and outside of the crater was unusual enough for CVO and PNSN staff to take notice roughly an hour before the explosion. This increase was one of the factors that contributed to the timely detection of the explosion, and it may be a relatively rare example of a short-term seismic precursor to an explosion. The RSAM increase was caused by an increase in the percentage of larger (M_d >1.5) earthquakes (fig. 9). Events in this magnitude range had been occurring at a rate of one every 3–4 minutes before the explosion. Starting at ~1529 the rate of larger events increased to one every 1–2 minutes, with the rate increasing through to the start of the explosion. No other attributes of the seismicity, including the total number of earthquakes per unit time (fig. 9), event frequency, event type, event location, and degree of similarity of waveforms between events, changed at this time.

Similar increases in event size occurred over short time intervals during the first week of seismic unrest in 2004. The fact that seismic energy levels dropped following the four explosions (particularly the October 1 and October 5, 2004, explosions) and two noneruptive tremor episodes indicates that the preexplosion elevated seismicity was a result of increased pressures in the shallow (<1 km) conduit system (Moran and others, this volume, chap. 2). We infer that the increase in seismic energy ~2 hours before the March 8 explosion similarly reflected an increase in pressure within the conduit. Given that an explosion occurred 2 hours after this increase, it is reasonable to assume that a pocket of steam and/or magmatic gas had accumulated within the conduit or along its margins at shallow depths shortly before the explosion, and that the gas pocket locally increased pressures. Given that there were no other significant changes in earthquakes before the explosion, we infer that the pressure increase merely perturbed the regular seismogenic process. Certainly, the increase in event size could reflect an increased pressurization in gas- or fluid-filled cracks (for example, Chouet, 1996). However, other factors, such as the ~1-m-thick layer of fault gouge found on most spines (Pallister and others, 2005; Cashman and others, this volume, chap. 19; Moore and others, this volume, chap. 20); the geologic evidence found for shearing within the extruded lava domes (Pallister and others, 2006); the low gas content (Gerlach and others, this volume, chap. 26); and the correlation of changes in earthquake character with changes in extrusive style at the surface (Moran and others, this volume, chap. 2), all combine to suggest that the regular earthquakes may have been a result of stick-slip motion (Iverson and others, 2006). If the earthquakes were the result of a stick-slip process, the pressure increase could have caused a seismic energy increase through (1) an increase in pressure at the base of the plug (Iverson and others, 2006); (2) a localized increase in applied shear stress along the conduit margins; (3) a change in fault properties in the seismogenic region; or (4) some combination of these factors. Because there are no constraints on the rate of motion of the active spine or the location of the gas pocket in the hours before the explosion, there is no basis for favoring or discarding any of these explanations. Nevertheless, the increase in RSAM values shortly before the March 8 explosion represents a relatively rare instance of a seismic precursor to a volcanic explosion and provides an example of a signal that could enable future short-term forecasts of explosive events during eruptions similar to the dome-building eruption at Mount St. Helens during 2004–5.

Acoustic Recordings

In contrast to the January 16 explosion, the March 8 explosion produced significant infrasonic signals that were well recorded on the two SEP microphones (the SUG microphone had stopped working before the March 8 explosion) as well as on the Coldwater infrasound array (Matoza and others, 2007). No infrasonic signals were recorded, however, until a discrete low-frequency (1–2 Hz) pulse at 17:26:20, ~60 s after the explosion signal first appeared on seismic stations (fig. 7). We note that the delay between seismic and infrasonic signals is similar to seismicity and infrasonic observations reported by Johnson and others (2003) in association with explosions at Guagua Pichnicha volcano, Ecuador, in 1998–99. These first infrasonic pulses were low frequency (1–2 Hz) and appeared on the SEP acoustic sensors ~2 s after a seismic event was recorded on the SEP seismometer (fig. 7), consistent with the time lapse expected between seismic and acoustic waves for a source ~500 m away. Matoza and others (2007) report seeing similar infrasonic signals at their Coldwater array starting at 17:26:55, 35 s after they appeared on the SEP acoustic sensors (35 s is the expected time difference, given the 12.5-km separation between the two sites). Several similar pulses occurred over the next 20 s, followed by much larger infrasonic signals

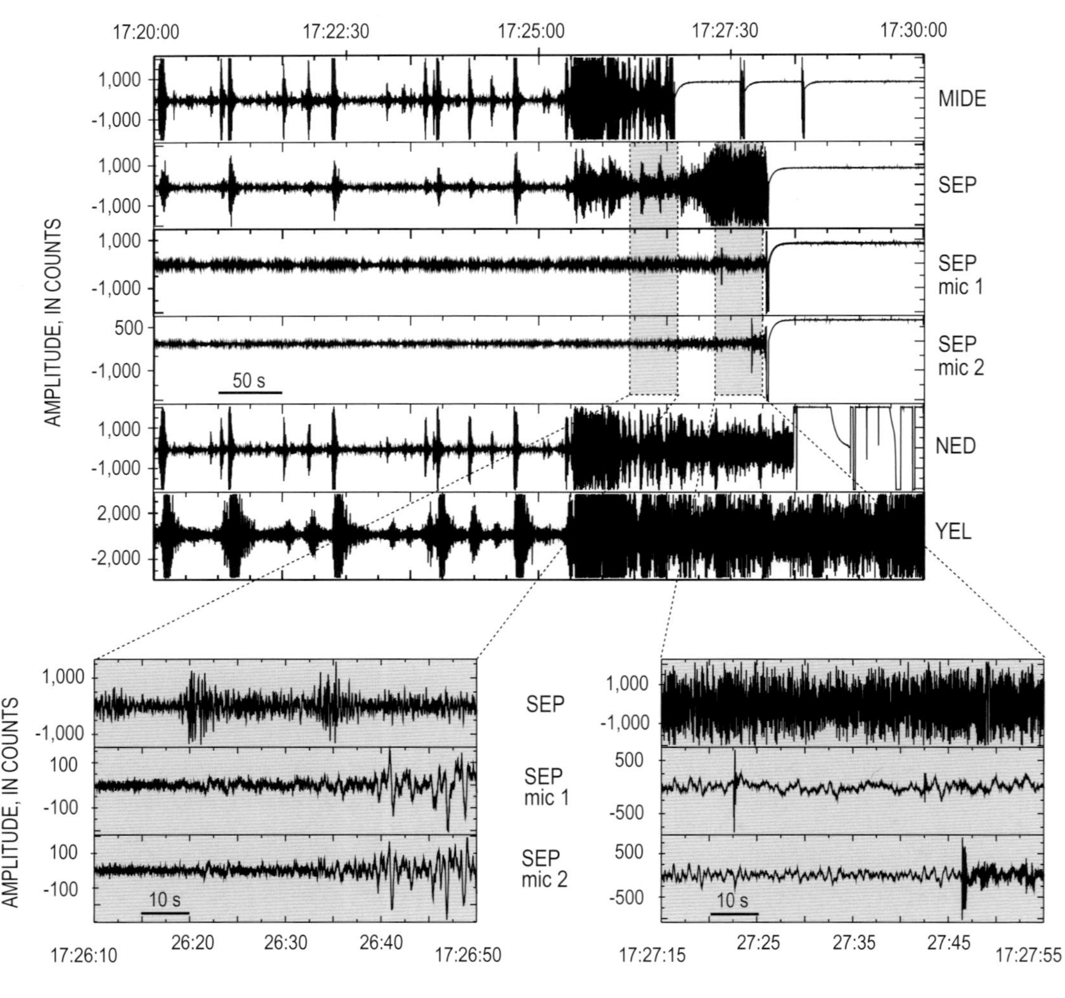

Figure 7. Multistation 10-minute plot showing time-series data from 1720 to 1730 PST on March 8, 2005. See figure 2 for station locations. Insets at bottom of plot show two 40-s windows of unfiltered data from the vertical component of the SEP seismometer (top) and two acoustic sensors (microphone 1, middle, and microphone 2, bottom). The left inset shows the onset of infrasonic signals at ~17:26:20, with amplitudes increasing significantly at ~17:26:40. Right inset shows several sharp spikes on acoustic sensors, which we infer to be caused by ballistic fragments landing close to each sensor. Conversion factor for counts to Pascals is nominally 44.5 counts/Pa for microphones at SEP (see appendix 1).

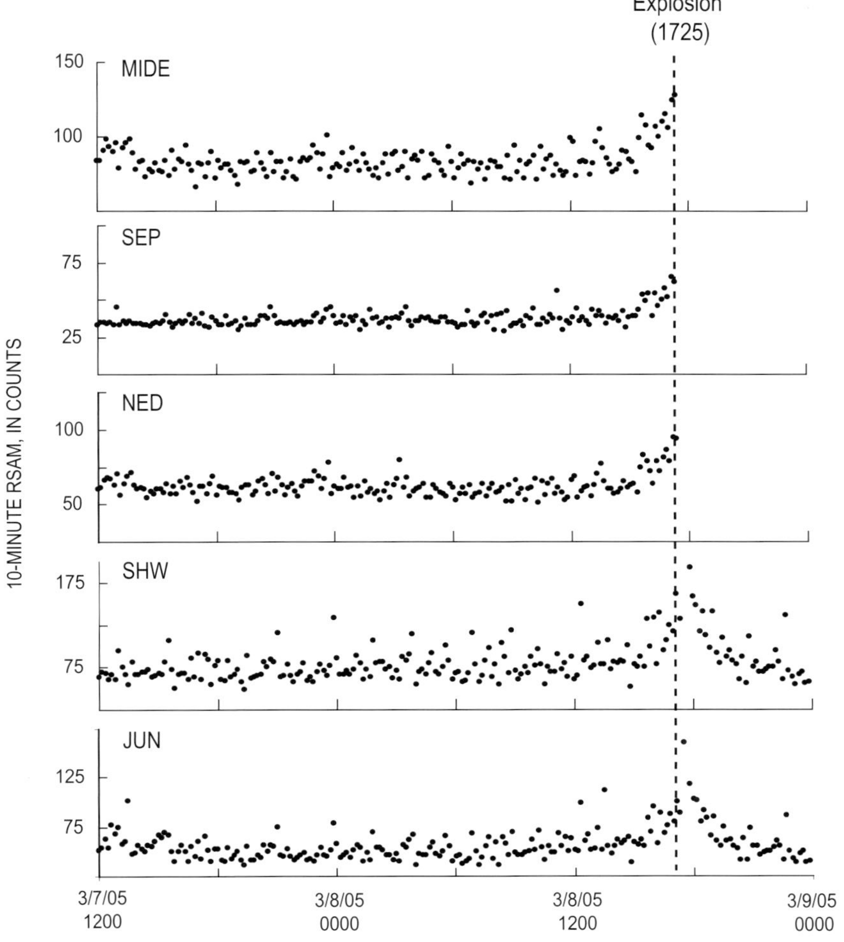

Figure 8. Plot of 10-minute RSAM values (Endo and Murray, 1991) on five stations over 36-hour time window extending from March 7 to March 9, 2005. Stations are ordered by distance from vent, nearest (MIDE, 0.25 km) to farthest (JUN, ~6.5 km). Vertical dashed line indicates start time for March 8 explosion.

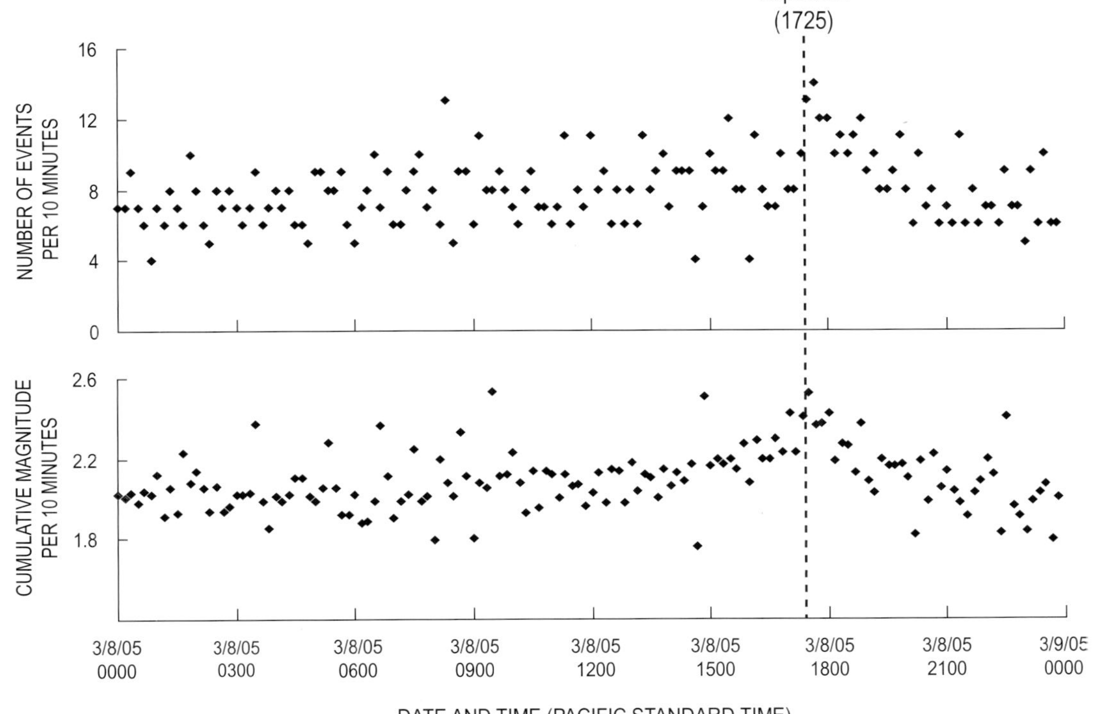

Figure 9. Plot showing number of events detected every 10 minutes at station HSR (top) and 10-minute cumulative event magnitude (bottom). Event detection is done using a standard STA/LTA trigger algorithm; for details see Moran and others (this volume, chap. 2). Event magnitudes determined using peak amplitudes at station HSR and a local magnitude relation calibrated to match the Pacific Northwest Seismic Network's coda-duration magnitude scale. Note that magnitudes began increasing slightly after 1500 PST, whereas number of events stayed constant until after explosion.

starting at 17:26:40. These larger signals were highly correlative between the two SEP acoustic sensors and did not correspond to seismic events on the SEP seismometer (fig. 7). Thus over the space of ~80 s the first phase of the explosion transitioned from producing mostly seismic signals in the first 60 s to producing both acoustic and seismic signals, and finally, 20 s later, to producing mostly acoustic signals.

Such variability in the production of acoustic and seismic energy during explosions has been documented at other volcanoes (Mori and others, 1989; Garcés and others, 1998; Johnson and others, 2003; Johnson and others, 2005; Johnson and Aster, 2005). Johnston and Aster (2005) demonstrated that this variability can be attributed to a variety of factors, including plume density, with dense plumes resulting in reduced acceleration of the atmosphere and reduced infrasonic amplitudes; magma/wall rock impedance contrast, with low impedances resulting in reduced seismic amplitudes; viscous flow in the conduit, with long and narrow conduits acting to reduce seismic and enhance infrasonic amplitudes; and source dimension, with large source regions yielding reduced infrasonic amplitudes. For the March 8 explosion, we favor an ash-rich plume as the primary reason for the apparent absence of acoustic signals in the first 60 s. Given that no open vent existed before the explosion, the initial explosion must have contained substantial amounts of ash and fractured rock mixed with steam and/or magmatic gas during the initial vent clearing. Evidence for this comes from a picture taken at 17:27:42 from a remote camera located 2.5 km northeast of the vent at SUG (fig. 10, lower photo; see fig. 2 for site location). That photograph shows a dark ash-rich cloud to the left (south) of the vent, a convecting lighter-colored plume to the right (north) that is relatively close to the SEP site, and impact craters (white patches) in snowfields on the northern side of the 1980–86 lava dome. The extent of the dark ash cloud, which enveloped most of the southern half of the crater just 140 s after the initial explosion signal (fig. 10), suggests that the initial plume contained a substantial amount of ash. The appearance of acoustic signals after 60 s could correspond to reduced ash content in the plume (and more efficient acoustic energy production) following vent clearing, with the subsequent increase in acoustic-to-seismic energy ratios over the next 20 s corresponding to progressively reduced amounts of ash entrained in the plume.

At 17:27:00 a high-frequency (>5 Hz) tremor signal that rapidly increased in amplitude appeared on the SEP seismometer (fig. 6), clipping the seismometer after 20 s. This increase was also registered at other stations within 15 km, although relative amplitude increases were much smaller, indicating that the source was close to the SEP seismometer and was likely shallow. There was no associated change in the nature or amplitude of the infrasonic signals recorded on the SEP microphones. We infer that this signal represents the generation of a second and perhaps more vigorous ash-rich plume. Although the explosion chronology is poorly detailed, photographs taken from Camas, Washington, (75 km south of Mount St. Helens), show a second plume starting to rise above the crater rim at 1727; by 1729 it had risen to the first plume's altitude at 1727 (fig. 11). The appearance of this second plume matches well with the timing of the onset of the more energetic tremor.

Further evidence for a second, more vigorous explosive phase comes from ballistic impacts. Most evidence comes from events that occurred after the tremor increase at 1727. At 17:27:22 the first of several sharp high-frequency signals appeared on the SEP microphones (fig. 7). Most of these signals appeared only on a single microphone, indicating that the source was small and very close to the sensors. We infer these to be caused by small ballistic fragments landing near individual microphones. This inference is supported by the appearance of impact craters in snow fields on the 1980–86 dome in a photo from the Sugar Bowl camera taken at 17:27:40 (fig. 10), indicating that ballistic fragments were falling at the time of the high-frequency spikes. Furthermore, the downward first-motion of the spikes (fig. 7) is inconsistent with an explosive source. We speculate that the downward first-motions might have been related to a pressure drop associated with nearby ballistic impacts. At 17:27:46, 12 s before SEP was destroyed, a low-amplitude, high-frequency signal appeared superimposed on the lower frequency infrasonic signals on both SEP microphones. On the basis of the high frequency content and small amplitude, we infer that this signal was caused by a rain of many small ballistic fragments across the SEP site. Finally, SEP and NED were both destroyed by hot ballistic fragments at 17:27:58 and 17:28:18, respectively, as indicated by multiple sharp punctures in enclosures, melted nylon ropes, and melted circuit-board solder found in equipment that was later retrieved from each site. The evidence for the bulk of ballistic impacts occurring after the tremor increase at 1727, coupled with the photographic evidence for a second plume starting at 1727, leads us to conclude that the 1727 tremor increase heralded the onset of the second and most energetic phase of the March 8 explosion.

Discussion

The explosions of 2004–5 at Mount St. Helens, although few in number and small in size, yielded a number of important insights regarding the use of acoustic and seismic instruments for reliable explosion detection, in particular for small explosions. One such insight comes from the observation that the most reliable seismic indicator for each of the four explosions occurring during the vent-clearing phase of October 1–5, 2004, was the seismicity decline following each explosion (table 1). None of the explosions had an obvious seismic precursor, and no seismic signals were recorded that heralded the start of any of the October 1–5 explosions. The lack of such obvious seismic signals may in part have been due to the intense seismicity associated with the vent-clearing phase, which would have obscured any moderate-amplitude seismic signals associated with the explosions. Despite the fact that seismicity declines followed each explosion, however,

Figure 10. Photographs of the crater of Mount St. Helens taken by a remote camera installed by the Cascades Volcano Observatory at SUG (2 km northeast of vent; see fig. 2) 10 s before (top) and ~140 s after (bottom) the start of the March 8 explosion at 17:25:20 PST. Times for each photo are accurate to nearest second, because time stamps were based on a clock periodically synchronized to Internet time server. View is to south; the south crater rim is in background and the northeast crater wall in foreground. The new lava dome is mostly shrouded by steam in upper image and completely obscured by ash clouds in lower image. The 1980–86 lava dome is in the center of each image (station NED is located on northeast side of that dome). Small white circles in the snow, visible in center of lower image, formed as impact craters from ballistic fragments that fell on all sides of the 1980–86 lava dome during explosion. (Pink diagonal lines in upper right corner of lower image result from damage to the camera in previous months when sun at low zenith shone directly into lens.)

seismicity declines also occurred during this phase that did not correspond to explosions. Clearly, real-time explosion detection cannot be based on seismic instruments alone.

Another insight comes from the fact that there were no obvious acoustic signals associated with the October 3–5 explosions that occurred after two single-sensor acoustic sites were established. The lack of acoustic signals in part indicates that the explosions were not large. However, because each site had only a single acoustic sensor, it is impossible to use methods such as those employed by Matoza and others (2007) on arrays of collocated acoustic sensors to significantly reduce noise levels. As illustrated by the subsequent explosion signals recorded at SEP in 2005, multiple acoustic sensors make it much easier to distinguish between explosion-related infrasonic signals and noninfrasonic noise sources such as wind and coseismic shaking of the microphone from passing seismic waves, especially if the explosion-related signals are weak.

Figure 11. Views of March 8, 2005, ash cloud at 1727 and 1729 PST as seen from Camas, Washington, 75 km south of Mount St. Helens. Time for each photo is precise to nearest minute (resolution of internal clock in camera used to take these photos). Two plumes are seen clearly in lower photograph, with second plume likely corresponding to intensification in tremor seen on SEP and other seismic stations starting at 17:27:00 (see fig. 7). Given that second plume can also be seen in the 1727 photo, we estimate that the photo was taken several tens of seconds after 17:27:00. Photographs by Elisa Wells, used with permission.

The intense seismicity during the first two weeks at Mount St. Helens highlighted an additional underappreciated attribute of acoustic sensors; because they are isolated from the ground, acoustic sensors are not nearly as susceptible as seismometers to saturation by energetic seismicity and thus may record explosion-related infrasound when seismic waves from frequent large earthquakes mask any explosion-related seismicity. Although acoustic sensors deployed 3–5 km from the vent did not record obvious infrasound associated with the October 3–5 explosions, at the same time the acoustic sensors were not overwhelmed by ground waves from the continuous large earthquakes and thus were more capable of detecting explosion-related signals than the seismic network. Because vigorous precursory seismicity can happen at any volcano, acoustic sensors with real-time telemetry, in particular arrays of sensors such as those deployed at SEP and Coldwater (Matoza and others, 2007), should be installed as soon as possible after the onset of volcanic unrest to improve explosion-detection capabilities. The destruction of SEP by the March 8 explosion (and the resultant loss of acoustic information about the evolution of the explosion) also demonstrates the value in placing some acoustic arrays at safe distances, despite the greater complexity of path effects, the higher signal attenuation, and the increased time delay in explosion detection inherent in recording explosion-related signals at more distant sites.

The January 16 and March 8, 2005, explosions also demonstrated the importance of having seismic stations within 1–2 km of a vent for reliable explosion detection. Explosion-related tremor from the January 16 explosion first appeared only on a station located ~250 m from the vent and only became apparent (albeit marginally) on stations outside the crater ~8 minutes later, when infrasonic signals also became apparent on acoustic sensors. Without seismic stations operating within 1–2 km of the vent, the explosion might have gone unnoticed until later field work by CVO staff. The March 8 explosion was also recorded first by the seismic network, with infrasound signals appearing ~60 s after the start of the explosion. Given the aviation sector's stated need to be alerted within 5 minutes of the start of an eruption (Ewert and others, 2005), such delays are potentially problematic. Seismic signals were large enough to be seen on stations within 15 km of the vent, but the explosion-related tremor was most clearly recorded on crater stations. An additional benefit of having stations in the crater came from the loss of telemetry experienced at one or more crater stations during the October 1, October 5, January 16, and March 8 explosions. These dropouts provided independent confirmation that ash was in the air, and for this reason the loss of telemetry from individual stations has since become a key element in the automated alarm system employed by CVO and PNSN (Qamar and others, this volume, chap. 3). Thus, installation of real-time seismic stations within 1–2 km of a volcanic vent is vital for improving explosion-detection capabilities at erupting volcanoes.

Acknowledgments

We are indebted to Marvin Couchman for his contributions in assembling, testing, and deploying the acoustic sensors at BLIS and SEP. We also wish to acknowledge Jeff Johnson for his advice on deploying multiple acoustic sensors at SEP; Robin Matoza and Michael Hedlin for generously sharing data and interpretations of acoustic signals recorded at their Coldwater infrasonic site; Mike Poland for having the foresight to install the Sugar Bowl camera in October 2004; Rick LaHusen, for maintaining the camera and associated telemetry system in the months after Mike's move to the Hawaiian Volcano Observatory; and Elisa Wells (wife of S. Moran) for having the presence of mind to start taking photos of the March 8, 2005, explosion cloud and for allowing us to publish them. Finally, we gratefully acknowledge Jackie Caplan-Auerbach and Jeff Johnson for their thoughtful and helpful reviews of this paper.

References Cited

Aki, K., and Koyanagi, R.Y., 1981, Deep volcanic tremor and magma ascent mechanism under Kilauea, Hawaii: Journal of Geophysical Research, v. 86, p. 7095–7110.

Cashman, K.V., Thornber, C.R., and Pallister, J.S., 2008, From dome to dust; shallow crystallization and fragmentation of conduit magma during the 2004–2006 dome extrusion of Mount St. Helens, Washington, chap. 19 *of* Sherrod, D.R., Scott, W.E., and Stauffer, P.H., eds., A volcano rekindled; the renewed eruption of Mount St. Helens, 2004–2006: U.S. Geological Survey Professional Paper 1750 (this volume).

Chouet, B.A., 1996, Long-period volcano seismicity; its source and use in eruption forecasting: Nature, v. 380, p. 309–316.

Driedger, C.L., Neal, C.A., Knappenberger, T.H., Needham, D.H., Harper, R.B., and Steele, W.P., 2008, Hazard information management during the autumn 2004 reawakening of Mount St. Helens volcano, Washington, chap. 24 *of* Sherrod, D.R., Scott, W.E., and Stauffer, P.H., eds., A volcano rekindled; the renewed eruption of Mount St. Helens, 2004–2006: U.S. Geological Survey Professional Paper 1750 (this volume).

Dzurisin, D., Vallance, J.W., Gerlach, T.M., Moran, S.C., and Malone, S.D., 2005, Mount St. Helens reawakens: Eos (American Geophysical Union Transactions), v. 86, no. 3, p. 25, 29.

Endo, E.T., and Murray, T., 1991, Real-time seismic amplitude measurement (RSAM); a volcano monitoring and prediction tool: Bulletin of Volcanology, v. 53, no. 7, p. 533–545.

Ewert, J.W., Guffanti, M., and Murray, T.L., 2005, An assessment of volcanic threat and monitoring capabilities in the United States; framework for a National Volcano Early Warning System: U.S. Geological Survey Open-File Report 2005–1164, 62 p.

Garcés, M.A., Hagerty, M.T., and Schwartz, S.Y., 1998, Magma acoustics and time-varying melt properties at Arenal Volcano, Costa Rica: Geophysical Research Letters, v. 25, p. 2293–2296.

Gerlach, T.M., McGee, K.A., and Doukas, M.P., 2008, Emission rates of CO_2, SO_2, and H_2S, scrubbing, and preeruption excess volatiles at Mount St. Helens, 2004–2005, chap. 26 *of* Sherrod, D.R., Scott, W.E., and Stauffer, P.H., eds., A volcano rekindled; the renewed eruption of Mount St. Helens, 2004–2006: U.S. Geological Survey Professional Paper 1750 (this volume).

Iverson, R.M., Dzurisin, D., Gardner, C.A., Gerlach, T.M., LaHusen, R.G., Lisowski, M., Major, J.J., Malone, S.D., Messerich, J.A., Moran, S.C., Pallister, J.S., Qamar, A.I., Schilling, S.P., and Vallance, J.W., 2006, Dynamics of seismogenic volcanic extrusion at Mount St. Helens in 2004–05: Nature, v. 444, no. 7118, p. 439–443, doi:10.1038/nature05322.

Johnson, J.B., and Aster, R.C., 2005, Relative partitioning of acoustic and seismic energy during Strombolian eruptions: Journal of Volcanology and Geothermal Research, v. 148, p. 334–354.

Johnson, J.B., Aster, R.C., Ruiz, M.C., Malone, S.D., McChesney, P.J., Lees, J.M., and Kyle, P.R., 2003, Interpretation and utility of infrasonic records from erupting volcanoes: Journal of Volcanology and Geothermal Research, v. 121, p. 15–63.

Johnson, J.B., Ruiz, M.C., Lees, J.M., and Ramon, P., 2005, Poor scaling between elastic energy release and eruption intensity at Tungurahua Volcano, Ecuador: Geophysical Research Letters, v. 32, L15304, 5 p., doi:10.1029/2005GL022847.

Matoza, R.S., Hedlin, M.A.H., and Garcés, M.A., 2007, An infrasound array study of Mount St. Helens: Journal of Volcanology and Geothermal Research, v. 160, p. 249–262, doi:10.1016/j.jvolgeores.2006.10.006.

McChesney, P.J., 1999, McVCO handbook 1999: U.S. Geological Survey Open-File Report 99–361, 48 p. [http://wrgis.wr.usgs.gov/open-file/of99-361.]

McChesney, P.J., Couchman, M.R., Moran, S.C., Lockhart, A.B., Swinford, K.J., and LaHusen, R.G., 2008, Seismic-monitoring changes and the remote deployment of seismic stations (seismic spider) at Mount St. Helens, 2004–2005, chap. 7 *of* Sherrod, D.R., Scott, W.E., and Stauffer, P.H., eds., A volcano rekindled; the renewed eruption of Mount St. Helens, 2004–2006: U.S. Geological Survey Professional Paper 1750 (this volume).

Moore, P.L., Iverson, N.R., and Iverson, R.M., 2008, Frictional properties of the Mount St. Helens gouge, chap. 20 *of* Sherrod, D.R., Scott, W.E., and Stauffer, P.H., eds., A volcano rekindled; the renewed eruption of Mount St. Helens, 2004–2006: U.S. Geological Survey Professional Paper 1750 (this volume).

Mori, J., Patia, H., McKee, C., Itikarai, I., Lowenstein, P., De Saint Ours, P., and Talai, B., 1989, Seismicity associated with eruptive activity at Langila Volcano, Papua New Guinea: Journal of Volcanology and Geothermal Research, v. 38, p. 243–255.

Moran, S.C., Malone, S.D., Qamar, A.I., Thelen, W.A., Wright, A.K., and Caplan-Auerbach, J., 2008, Seismicity associated with renewed dome building at Mount St. Helens, 2004–2005, chap. 2 *of* Sherrod, D.R., Scott, W.E., and Stauffer, P.H., eds., A volcano rekindled; the renewed eruption of Mount St. Helens, 2004–2006: U.S. Geological Survey Professional Paper 1750 (this volume).

Neal, C.A., Casadevall, T.J., Miller, T.P., Hendley, J.W., II, and Stauffer, P.H., 1997, Volcanic ash—danger to aircraft in the North Pacific: U.S. Geological Survey Fact Sheet 030–97, 2 p.

Pallister, J.S., Reagan, M., and Cashman, K., 2005, A new eruptive cycle at Mount St. Helens?: Eos (American Geophysical Union Transactions), v. 87, no. 48, p. 499–500, doi:10.1029/2005EO480006.

Pallister, J.S., Hoblitt, R., Denlinger, R., Sherrod, D., Cashman, K., Thornber, C., and Moran, S., 2006, Structural geology of the Mount St. Helens fault-gouge-zone field relations along the volcanic conduit-wallrock interface [abs.]: Eos (American Geophysical Union Transactions), v. 87, no. 52, Fall Meeting supplement, Abstract V41A-1703.

Poland, M.P., Dzurisin, D., LaHusen, R.G., Major, J.J., Lapcewich, D., Endo, E.T., Gooding, D.J., Schilling, S.P., and Janda, C.G., 2008, Remote camera observations of lava dome growth at Mount St. Helens, Washington, October 2004 to February 2006, chap. 11 *of* Sherrod, D.R., Scott, W.E., and Stauffer, P.H., eds., A volcano rekindled; the renewed eruption of Mount St. Helens, 2004–2006: U.S. Geological Survey Professional Paper 1750 (this volume).

Qamar, A.I., Malone, S.D., Moran, S.C., Steele, W.P., and Thelen, W.A., 2008, Near-real-time information products for Mount St. Helens—tracking the ongoing eruption, chap. 3 *of* Sherrod, D.R., Scott, W.E., and Stauffer, P.H., eds., A volcano rekindled; the renewed eruption of Mount St. Helens, 2004–2006: U.S. Geological Survey Professional Paper 1750 (this volume).

Rowe, M.C., Thornber, C.R., and Kent, A.J.R., 2008, Identification and evolution of the juvenile component in 2004–2005 Mount St. Helens ash, chap. 29 *of* Sherrod, D.R., Scott, W.E., and Stauffer, P.H., eds., A volcano rekindled; the renewed eruption of Mount St. Helens, 2004–2006: U.S. Geological Survey Professional Paper 1750 (this volume).

Schilling, S.P., Thompson, R.A., Messerich, J.A., and Iwatsubo, E.Y., 2008, Use of digital aerophotogrammetry to determine rates of lava dome growth, Mount St. Helens, Washington, 2004–2005, chap. 8 *of* Sherrod, D.R., Scott, W.E., and Stauffer, P.H., eds., A volcano rekindled; the renewed eruption of Mount St. Helens, 2004–2006: U.S. Geological Survey Professional Paper 1750 (this volume).

Schneider, D.J., Vallance, J.W., Wessels, R.L., Logan, M., and Ramsey, M.S., 2008, Use of thermal infrared imaging for monitoring renewed dome growth at Mount St. Helens, 2004, chap. 17 *of* Sherrod, D.R., Scott, W.E., and Stauffer, P.H., eds., A volcano rekindled; the renewed eruption of Mount St. Helens, 2004–2006: U.S. Geological Survey Professional Paper 1750 (this volume).

Scott, W.E., Sherrod, D.R., and Gardner, C.A., 2008, Overview of the 2004 to 2006, and continuing, eruption of Mount St. Helens, Washington, chap. 1 *of* Sherrod, D.R., Scott, W.E., and Stauffer, P.H., eds., A volcano rekindled; the renewed eruption of Mount St. Helens, 2004–2006: U.S. Geological Survey Professional Paper 1750 (this volume).

Vallance, J.W., Schneider, D.J., and Schilling, S.P., 2008, Growth of the 2004–2006 lava-dome complex at Mount St. Helens, Washington, chap. 9 *of* Sherrod, D.R., Scott, W.E., and Stauffer, P.H., eds., A volcano rekindled; the renewed eruption of Mount St. Helens, 2004–2006: U.S. Geological Survey Professional Paper 1750 (this volume).

Woulff, G., and McGetchin, T.R., 1976, Acoustic noise from volcanoes; theory and experiment: Geophysical Journal of the Royal Astronomic Society, v. 45, p. 601–616.

Appendix 1. Acoustic Sensors Used at Mount St. Helens

The acoustic sensors installed by CVO and PNSN at Mount St. Helens were previously designed as additions to the McVCO voltage-controlled oscillator (McChesney, 1999) that is in wide use by the PNSN and the USGS in the Cascades and elsewhere. The sensor consists of either 9 or 18 electret microphones with a 1-Hz frequency response, the signals from all microphones being summed to reduce electronic noise. Including the responses of other components in the recording system (for example, radio, digitizers, system gain), each 9-element microphone has a nominal response of 22.7 counts/Pascal (44.5 counts/Pascal for an 18-element microphone). The acoustic sensors installed at stations SEP and SUG had 18-element microphones, and the STD sensor had a 9-element microphone. An important caveat to the acoustic response of these sensors is that individual sensors were not calibrated before installation. Given that the sensitivity of individual electret sensors varies by ±3 dB and that their sensitivity is known to decline with time after installation (depending on environmental conditions), we estimate that the true response could vary by 30 percent or more for each nine-element microphone. For this reason we only give a range of possible pressure values in this paper.

The circuit board with electret sensors is typically placed in a PVC plastic tube with end caps and a hose connection on one end. The PVC tubing reduces bellows-type motion caused by wind or ground shaking. A soaker hose of variable length is attached to the hose connection to further reduce wind noise. At SUG and STD the sensors were placed inside an enclosure with the soaker hose strung in a line away from the enclosure. At SEP the two sensors were placed on the ground ~15 m apart, with rocks piled around the PVC tube to prevent movement and the soaker hose coiled next to each sensor.

A Volcano Rekindled: The Renewed Eruption of Mount St. Helens, 2004–2006
Edited by David R. Sherrod, William E. Scott, and Peter H. Stauffer
U.S. Geological Survey Professional Paper 1750, 2008

Chapter 7

Seismic-Monitoring Changes and the Remote Deployment of Seismic Stations (Seismic Spider) at Mount St. Helens, 2004–2005

By Patrick J. McChesney[1], Marvin R. Couchman[2], Seth C. Moran[2], Andrew B. Lockhart[2], Kelly J. Swinford[2], and Richard G. LaHusen[2]

Abstract

The instruments in place at the start of volcanic unrest at Mount St. Helens in 2004 were inadequate to record the large earthquakes and monitor the explosions that occurred as the eruption developed. To remedy this, new instruments were deployed and the short-period seismic network was modified. A new method of establishing near-field seismic monitoring was developed, using remote deployment by helicopter. The remotely deployed seismic sensor was a piezoelectric accelerometer mounted on a surface-coupled platform. Remote deployment enabled placement of stations within 250 m of the active vent.

Introduction

The earthquake swarm that signaled the start of the eruption at Mount St. Helens on September 23, 2004 (Scott and others, this volume, chap. 1), was recorded by a dense network of short-period stations operated jointly by the Pacific Northwest Seismic Network (PNSN), based at the University of Washington, and the U.S. Geological Survey (USGS) Cascades Volcano Observatory (CVO). The network consisted of 13 stations within 20 km of the volcano; 6 of these were within 5 km (fig. 1). Many stations had been in place since the early 1980s. Although the established monitoring was sufficient to detect the onset of the unrest, it proved inadequate to record and monitor the intense seismicity of the developing 2004–2005 eruption.

This paper recounts the changes made to the Mount St. Helens seismic network during the first year of the eruption. These include changes to the existing short-period network, the first installations of telemetered broadband seismometers, the addition of infrasonic microphones, and the remote deployment of piezoelectric accelerometers. The method of remote deployment is new—it relies on an innovative instrument package, called a "spider," that was developed during the first month of the eruption (LaHusen and others, this volume, chap. 16). The package enabled us to safely deploy fully functional seismic stations, by helicopter, to sites within a few hundred meters of the active vent without setting a foot on the crater floor (fig. 2). Seismic spider development occurred during the response to volcanic unrest, and the following chronological sections complement the technical discussion by showing how the seismic spiders were used and how our field experiences drove the design process. Because the seismic spider uses both an uncommon sensor and unconventional deployment, we describe it at length in a subsequent section, "Technical Description of the Seismic Spiders."

Deployment Chronology

The deployment chronology is divided into two sections. During the initial response we modified the existing short-period network and made new installations using traditional methods. Later, our focus was seismic spider deployment. To provide an overview, a summary of changes to the seismic monitoring system through 2005 is given in table 1. The instrument parameters for the spider deployments are described in a later section. The infrasonic microphones are described elsewhere (Moran and others, this volume, chap. 6).

[1] Pacific Northwest Seismic Network, Department of Earth and Space Sciences, University of Washington, Box 351310, Seattle, WA 98195

[2] U.S. Geological Survey, 1300 SE Cardinal Court, Vancouver, WA 98683

Initial Response to Seismic Unrest

Because Mount St. Helens was regarded as adequately monitored (Moran, 2004; Ewert and others, 2005), there was little urgency to install new instruments during the first several days of the seismic swarm that began on September 23, 2004. However, after seismicity intensified on September 26, the existing network proved inadequate in four ways (Moran and others, this volume, chap. 2): (1) The short-period network lacked dynamic range and repeatedly clipped on larger events. (2) There were no three-component instruments. (3) The network lacked the ability to record low-frequency signals. (4) There were no infrasonic sensors to record explosive activity. Consequently, CVO and the PNSN began mobilizing to put new stations in the field. Our priorities were the installation of broadband three-component seismometers and deployment of infrasonic microphones to complement the dense short-period network.

At the same time, other cooperating groups were mobilizing to deploy broadband and strong-motion sensors with onsite recording around the volcano (Horton and others, this volume, chap. 5). However, to overcome the limited dynamic range and frequency response of the short-period network, we felt it essential to have real-time data from several broadband stations transmitted to CVO and PNSN. Because of the added complication of providing telemetry, it took several days to organize the deployment.

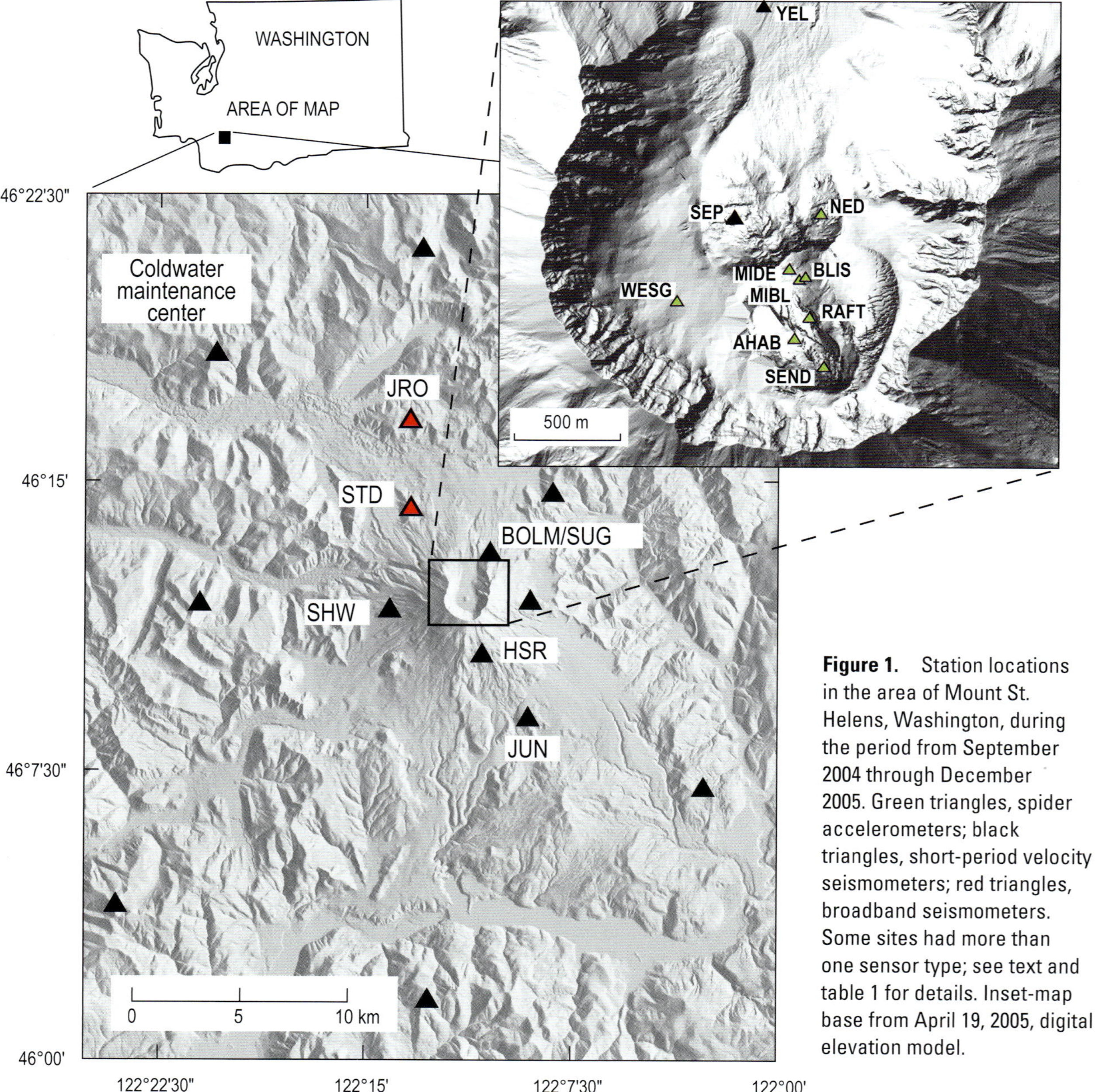

Figure 1. Station locations in the area of Mount St. Helens, Washington, during the period from September 2004 through December 2005. Green triangles, spider accelerometers; black triangles, short-period velocity seismometers; red triangles, broadband seismometers. Some sites had more than one sensor type; see text and table 1 for details. Inset-map base from April 19, 2005, digital elevation model.

On October 1, 2004, we made our first attempt to install a broadband seismometer and an infrasonic microphone at Studebaker Ridge, the site of an existing short-period station (STD; fig. 1). Work at the site, about 5 km from the vent, stopped when the first explosion of the eruption (at 1202 PDT) triggered a mandatory evacuation. As an alternative, we installed a broadband seismometer at the Johnston Ridge Observatory (JRO; fig. 1), 9 km north-northwest of the crater. Later, a broadband seismometer was successfully installed at Studebaker Ridge on October 5. Both seismometers were Guralp CMG-6TDs. These three-component instruments have a response of 30 s and were configured to measure each channel at 50 samples per second. Telemetry was not yet complete, so data were recorded initially in each instrument's 2-GB flash memory and collected later with a portable hard drive.

The interrupted installation of an infrasonic microphone at Studebaker Ridge (STDM) was completed on October 2, 2004, and another microphone (BOLM) was deployed at Sugar Bowl (fig. 1) on October 3 (Moran and others, this volume, chap. 6). The short-period seismic network was modified to provide telemetry for the microphone signals. Other changes to short-period stations were necessary in the first weeks of the eruption because signals were clipped for many earthquakes. To improve the dynamic range, a low-gain channel was added at several stations. Stations SHW and HSR were converted to dual gain on October 4 and JUN on October 7 (fig. 1). The sensitivity on the high-gain channel from HSR was also reduced, because signals from even relatively small earthquakes were severely clipped.

Figure 2. Overhead view of seismic spider deployed at station RAFT. Sensor platform (Marv lander) is at upper left. Instrument box on spider is 70 cm long. USGS photo by S.C. Moran, June 20, 2006.

Ideally the broadband instruments and microphones would have been located closer to the vent. Experience elsewhere has shown that very long period (VLP) earthquakes are best recorded on broadband instruments located within 4 km of the source region (B.A. Chouet, oral commun., 2004). By October 1, however, conditions inside the crater and on the crater rim were considered too dangerous for extended field work, so the instruments were installed more than 4 km from the source region. We will never know if VLP events occurred during the first several months of the eruption, a shortcoming that shows the importance of having at least one broadband instrument installed within 1–3 km of a potentially active vent before the beginning of unrest. None of the three explosions that occurred in the days after the October 1 event created an obvious signal on the microphones placed outside the crater (Moran and others, this volume, chap 6).

On October 20, an Earthworm data-processing node was established at the Gifford Pinchot National Forest's Coldwater Ridge maintenance facility, ~13 km northwest of the crater (fig. 1). This achievement marked a turning point in our response to the eruption by allowing Coldwater to function as a radio-telemetry terminus near the volcano. Links for the data from JRO and STD broadband seismometers were made to Coldwater with Freewave spread-spectrum digital radios (2.4 GHz). The presence of an Earthworm digitizer vastly expanded our analog channel capacity and allowed further seismic deployments to occur without long and difficult radio paths to CVO. Internet connectivity at Coldwater was through VSAT (very small aperture terminal) linked to a commercial communications network by microwave radio and satellite.

The explosion on October 1, 2004, destroyed the short-period seismic station at September lobe on the 1980–86 lava dome (SEP; fig. 1). Positioned ~500 m from the vent, SEP was the closest station to the earthquake sources. Losing this station greatly hampered earthquake location quality (Moran and others, this volume, chap. 2). The only remaining station within 3 km of the vent was the short-period station YEL (fig. 1) on the crater floor. However, the signal from YEL was clipped on many events until the gain was reduced by 12 dB during a quick visit on October 21.

Chronology of Seismic Spider Deployment

The need to reestablish near-field seismometers in the still-hazardous working conditions in the crater turned our attention to the development of a seismic station that could be deployed remotely. Available to us was the spider instrument package, originally developed for GPS deformation instruments and telemetry (LaHusen and others, this volume, chap. 16). We adapted this platform to carry an accelerometer (described in the next section) and an infrasonic microphone. The first seismic spider (BLIS, fig. 1) was deployed on October 12, 2004, at a location ~250 m east of the vent. The spider was

Table 1. Summary of changes to preeruption seismic network at Mount St. Helens, Washington, through 2005, including infrasonic microphones.

Station	Date	Change
SEP	10/1/04	Destroyed by explosion (L4-C seismometer)
JRO	10/1/04	Guralp CMG-6TD broadband installed
STDM	10/2/04	Nine-element infrasonic microphone installed
BOLM	10/3/04	Eighteen-element infrasonic microphone installed
SHW	10/4/04	Low gain added. High gain = 60 dB, low gain = 36.5 dB (L4-C seis.)
HSR	10/4/04	Dual gain. High gain = 28 dB, low gain = -1.32 dB (S-13 seis.)
STD	10/5/04	Guralp CMG-6TD broadband installed
JUN	10/7/04	Low gain added. High gain = 60 dB, Low gain = 36.5 dB (L4-C seis.)
STDM	10/12/04	Disconnected microphone telemetry for use at station BLIS
BLIS	10/12/04	Spider with accelerometer and 18-element infrasonic microphone
YEL	10/21/04	Gain reduced by 12 dB to 54 dB (L4-C seismometer)
SEP	11/4/04	Installed L22-3D and a pair of 18-element infrasonic microphones
NED	11/20/04	Spider with accelerometer
NED	12/20/04	Spider with accelerometer on separate platform (first Marv lander)
AHAB	2/8/05	Temporary spider deployment, accelerometer, and GPS
MIDE	2/16/05	Spider with accelerometer
SEP	3/8/05	Destroyed by explosion
NED	3/8/05	Destroyed by explosion
MIDE	3/8/05	Destroyed by explosion
SUG	3/9/05	L4-C seismometer at 42 dB added to station BOLM
SEP	3/14/05	Spider with accelerometer and two 18-element infrasonic microphones
YEL	3/15/05	Gain reduced by 6 dB to 48 dB
NED	4/6/05	Reinstalled spider with accelerometer
MIDE	4/6/05	Reinstalled spider with accelerometer, reinstalled again 04/14/05
SEND	6/30/05	Spider with accelerometer
WESG	7/12/05	Temporary spider deployment, accelerometer; removed 09/14/05
MIDE	7/19/05	Destroyed by rockfall
RAFT	7/28/05	Spider with accelerometer
MIBL	11/17/05	Spider with accelerometer

remarkably successful, despite noise spikes in the seismic signal caused by radio transmissions from the co-housed GPS system. These noise spikes were eliminated by remotely turning off the GPS instrument, which had been damaged during deployment.

Volcanic and seismic activity declined substantially after October 5, 2004 (Moran and others, this volume, chap. 2). After several weeks of reduced activity, we decided it was safe to work at SEP for a short time to replace the destroyed station with a three-component seismometer and a pair of infrasonic microphones. Usually such installations take hours, but by using the spider package we thought the visit would require less than one hour. On November 4, a spider was deployed in advance of the crew. Everything required for the station was preassembled and housed in the spider except the seismometer and microphones. It took only 45 minutes to install the Sercel L22-3D three-component seismometer and two infrasonic microphones. Even so, the helicopter was forced to depart hurriedly when an ash cloud advanced on the site, just as the crew was loading the ship to leave.

The success of the spider at BLIS led to another spider deployment at the northeast corner of the old dome (NED; fig. 1) on November 20, 2004. This site was selected because it improved the geometry of stations in the crater and included a patch of warm ground that was free of snow. Data became available on November 22, after an expansion of the analog telemetry channels at the Coldwater Earthworm node.

The first NED spider worked poorly. Unlike BLIS, the seismic signal from NED was often obscured by noise. At both stations the accelerometers were mounted in a leg of the spider platform. However, NED used a heavy radome antenna mounted on a mast, whereas BLIS had used a low-mass whip antenna. Wind or ground motion shook NED's antenna and sent vibrations through the spider to the sensor. We considered using whip antennas in the future, instead of radomes, but the heavier antenna had two advantages—increased signal strength and protection from icing. In addition, we could not be certain that the antenna was the only noise source. Consequently we decided to isolate the sensor from spider vibrations by mounting it in a separate platform, which we dubbed the "Marv lander" (see technical description in the next section). On December 23, 2004, a new spider equipped with a Marv lander was exchanged for the old one, solving the noise problem at NED.

On February 8, 2005, the spider AHAB was deployed atop the actively moving spine 4 (fig. 1). The location on the spine was chosen because it appeared stable and its slope of ~20° was not too steep for the spider. The objective of this short-term experiment was to record spine motion using GPS and to look for a correlation between "drumbeat" seismic events (Moran and others, this volume, chap. 2) and discrete movements of the spine. The spider housed an L-1 GPS receiver with an accelerometer and electronic thermometer mounted on a Marv lander. After 8 days of successful operation, AHAB was retrieved before the spine's process of growth and collapse could destroy it.

By the end of January 2005, following a period of intermittent operation, the BLIS spider stopped operating. We were unable to find the spider because it was buried in snow. Consequently, when AHAB was removed from spine 4, it was modified in the field to become a replacement for BLIS. The new location, MIDE, was a snowfree warm spot near the BLIS site (fig. 1). Station MIDE began operation on February 16, 2005.

A small but destructive explosion occurred on March 8, 2005 (Scott and others, this volume, chap 1; Moran and others, this volume, chap. 6). Ballistic fragments from the explosion destroyed MIDE, SEP, and NED. The MIDE equipment was never found. Scattered parts of SEP were barely visible under a blanket of ash. Although NED was recovered, little could be salvaged—even the apparently undamaged accelerometer no longer functioned. The loss of these three stations severely reduced our ability to record and locate earthquakes, and the loss of the close-in microphones at SEP eliminated our ability to detect small explosions.

The first step in restoring lost monitoring capacity was the installation of a short-period seismometer just north of the crater at SUG (fig. 1) on March 9. We chose this site because of its relative safety and the fact that the Sercel L4-C seismometer could be easily connected to the existing infrasonic microphone (BOLM) telemetry. A new seismic spider, including two 1-Hz microphones, was rapidly constructed and deployed at SEP on March 14. The crater station YEL was visited on March 15 and the gain lowered by another 6 dB because of continuing clipping problems.

The weather then took a turn for the worse, delaying replacement of spiders at MIDE and NED until April 6, 2005. The NED deployment went smoothly, but the MIDE spider toppled when released by the helicopter. We retrieved and inspected it and, finding no obvious problems, returned the spider to MIDE. However, it failed several days later and was retrieved again on April 10. Several of the power system's primary cell casings had melted, likely a result of internal damage caused by the spider's tumble on April 6. After replacing the cells, the spider was returned to MIDE on April 14.

With the arrival of summer, more sites were free of snow and available for seismic spider deployment. On June 30, 2005, in an effort to surround the source of the drumbeat earthquakes, a spider was placed at SEND, southeast of the former AHAB installation at the southeast end of spine 4, which by then was disintegrating (fig. 1). Another installation followed at WESG (western arm of the Crater Glacier) on July 12 (fig. 1). Unfortunately, the sensitivity of WESG was poor. We suspected bad ice-rock coupling or an electronic fault. Examination after the station was retrieved showed an intermittent problem with the accelerometer interface circuit. On July 19, MIDE was destroyed by a rock fall. On July 28, 2005, a replacement spider was deployed at RAFT, the only available patch of stable ground close to the vent (figs. 1, 2).

Finally, with the approach of winter we took several steps to improve the robustness of the crater spiders. WESG was removed on September 14, 2005, before it could be buried by snow. We also retrieved all spiders except RAFT to replace batteries and, if necessary, to add directional antennas. Subsequently, ice accumulation from an early winter storm damaged the coaxial cable for the radio transmitter at SEND. The SEND spider was retrieved and repaired on November 17. Because earthquakes had become much smaller, we relocated this spider to a new site, MIBL, closer to the vent (fig. 1). The MIBL site was warm and free of snow and near the previous MIDE and BLIS sites.

By the end of 2005, the CVO and PNSN real-time seismic network at Mount St. Helens consisted of 2 broadband seismometers, 13 conventional short-period instruments (3 with dual-gain channels), 4 seismic spiders, and 2 infrasonic microphones, all within 20 km of the volcano (table 1).

Technical Description of the Seismic Spiders

The loss of SEP during the explosion of October 1, 2004, forced us to improvise new techniques in order to restore seismic monitoring near the vent. Particularly for the first installations, we hurried to get something in the field, and each deployment was an experiment that led to changes in design. The evolving design complicates the description of the spider, because it is necessary to include the changes that were made. We trust that this section gives sufficient detail to satisfy both those who need to know the response parameters for a spider installation and those who are considering the design of remotely deployed seismic instruments.

Seismic Spider Overview

We designed the seismic spider for remote deployment close to an active volcanic vent where seismic signals were strong. Remote deployment ruled out the use of traditional seismic sensors, which require leveling by hand during installation. We knew of a sensor, used for measuring seismic activity of lava flowing through tubes in Hawai'i (R. Hoblitt, oral commun., 2004), that did not require leveling, could measure strong signals, and could survive the rigors of remote deployment. This sensor, a piezoelectric accelerometer, made the seismic spider possible.

Analog telemetry was used for a variety of reasons. Given strong signals, the contribution of some noise by the analog telemetry system did not detract much from the overall signal-to-noise ratio. The limited dynamic range of the telemetry system was overcome by using high- and low-gain channels. Analog telemetry allowed the use of lower frequency analog radios that, unlike digital spread-spectrum radios, do not require line-of-sight transmission paths and use much less power. The radios operated on the 406 to 420 MHz band, where antennas are fairly compact and their 100-mW transmissions can cover tens of kilometers. Several antennas were tried, but high-gain directional antennas were preferred because the radio path was often obstructed by terrain or snow. To prevent breakage from snow and ice loading, radome-protected antennas were favored.

Figure 3. Seismic spider slung by helicopter from staging area on March 14, 2005, for deployment at SEP. Included are two infrasonic microphones, one suspended immediately beneath the spider and another below it on the lander sensor platform (Marv lander), last item in the string. PNSN photo by P.J. McChesney, March 14, 2005.

Power was supplied by Air-Alkaline primary cells (Celair Corp.). Nine series-connected cells provided 12.6 V at 1,200 Ah. Total current drain was 110 mA, so 450 days of continuous operation were possible, but we planned for no more than a year because of capacity loss in cold weather.

The spider instrument package, developed early in this eruption to remotely deploy GPS instruments (LaHusen and others, this volume, chap. 16), provides an instrument compartment (~70×40×40 cm) optimized for helicopter transport and placement (fig. 3). We used the spider to house the power and telemetry systems and, initially, the sensor. Because of noise problems with the first two deployments, the sensor was moved to a separate platform, the Marv lander (described below).

Piezoelectric Accelerometer

Long used by industry for machine vibration measurement, piezoelectric accelerometers do not require leveling because they operate in any orientation. These devices convert dynamic forces to electrical energy through charge separation in a piezoelectric material. Acceleration (a) along the axis of the transducer acts on the seismic mass (M) to apply a force to the piezoelectric element. The force on the element produces a charge (q) such that $q = dMa$, where d is the piezoelectric constant. The stressed piezoelectric material acts as a capacitor (C), producing an open-circuit voltage (V) where $V = q/C$. Consequently the sensitivity of the accelerometer is V/g, where g is the unit of acceleration (Allocca and Stuart, 1984, p. 122).

Piezoelectric accelerometers respond to dynamic forces—to vibrations. The circuit model is a current generator in parallel with a capacitor, or its equivalent circuit, a voltage generator in series with a capacitor (Allocca and Stuart, 1984, p. 122–123). The model shows that there is an inherent low-frequency limit to a piezoelectric accelerometer. In addition, low-frequency vibrations produce weak acceleration signals, so piezoelectric accelerometers operating at low frequencies must use charge amplifiers to boost signal levels. The low-noise design of this amplifier is critical for low-frequency measurements because noise from the high input resistance of the charge amplifier increases with decreasing frequency (Schloss, 1993, p. 2). Consequently, poor signal-to-noise ratios at low frequency set the practical limit of piezoelectric response.

Sensor Parameters

We chose the Wilcoxon Model 731-207 Ultra Low Frequency Seismic Accelerometer for this application because of its relatively good low-frequency performance (see abbreviated specifications in table 2). There are other piezoelectric accelerometers with better low-frequency specifications than this model, but there is a tradeoff between increased low-frequency response and increased fragility. Because the sensors are subject to significant forces during deployment, the 250 *g* shock limit of the Model 731-207 was attractive. All units survived our handling and the helicopter deployment. However, one unit from NED, recovered after the explosion of March 8, 2005, was irreparably damaged, probably from ballistic impact.

The peak acceleration range of this model is more than sufficient for close-in monitoring. The low-gain telemetry channel was set for a maximum measurement of 0.1 *g*, a limit that was never exceeded despite recording M_L 3.4 earthquakes within 250 m of the source. The high sensitivity of the device permitted conservative seismic amplifier gain settings. Two telemetry channels were used for high- and low-gain recordings of the signal, with the low-gain channel set at 2.5 V/V. The high-gain channel was initially set at 83.17 V/V but was reduced to 41.75 V/V for later deployments. In the absence of noise, these gain settings achieve 16-bit dynamic range using two analog telemetry channels digitized at 12 bits each.

Response information for individual sensors is unavailable from the manufacturer. The nominal frequency response at 0.2 Hz is a worst-case limit. The design value for the low-frequency cutoff (−3 dB) is 0.1 Hz. This high-pass response has a pole at (−0.628319, 0) and a zero at (0, 0) set by charge amplifier components. Actual response is determined by component variation, and any particular unit may have a pole frequency from 0.1 to 0.15 Hz (Ron Denton, Application Engineer, Wilcoxon Research, written commun., 2006).

We attempted continuous electronic integration of the accelerometer output to produce a velocity response. Even though integration in the field was not satisfactory, it demonstrated the noise characteristics of the sensor. The data sheet for the Model 731-207 states that spectral noise, a 1-Hz bandwidth noise-density measurement at a particular frequency (Schloss, 1998, p. 1), increases as frequency decreases. At 2 Hz the noise density is 0.28 *g*/Hz. However, integration provides gain relative to the acceleration response; gain increases by a factor of two each time frequency is halved. In addition, below 2 Hz, sensor noise increases as $1/f$ (Ron Denton, Application Engineer, Wilcoxon Research, written commun., 2005). The combination of decreasing signal-to-noise ratio and increasing gain causes low-frequency noise to be prominent in the integrated response. Analog filtering of the low-frequency noise interfered with the integrator phase response. On the other hand, the acceleration response of the sensor has very good noise performance. Consequently the acceleration response was telemetered because we felt that digital postprocessing could do a better job if the velocity response was desired.

Piezoelectric Accelerometer Interfacing

The charge amplifier in the accelerometer can produce high-amplitude signals (5 V) and requires a power source. The voltage-controlled oscillators (VCOs) used to telemeter seismic signals are usually connected to passive seismometers that produce small-amplitude signals in the millivolt range. This mismatch required an interface circuit and VCO gain adjustments. We used McVCO, a microcontroller-based mimic of an analog VCO (McChesney, 1999). The interfacing problems are similar for other VCOs, but the details are best appreciated if the McVCO documentation is at hand.

Table 2. Abbreviated specifications for the Wilcoxon Model 731-207 piezoelectric accelerometer.

[Additional information online at www.wilcoxon.com.]

Accelerometer Specifications	
Sensitivity	10 V/*g*, ±10 %, 25°C
Acceleration Range	±0.5 *g*
Frequency Response	0.2–1300 Hz, −3 dB
Resonance Frequency	2,400 Hz
Temperature Response	−18% at 0°C, +8% at 80°C
Broadband Noise	2 μ*g*, 2.5 Hz to 25 kHz
Input Voltage Range	18–30 VDC, in series with a 2–10 mA current source diode
Shock Limit	250 *g*

The Model 731-207 accelerometer is a two-wire device. There is a ground connection and a combined signal and power connection. Power is provided through a current-source diode in series with a DC supply of 18–30 V. The signal rides on a 10-V bias. The most straightforward way to connect the accelerometer to the VCO is to raise the impedance of one VCO input and make a single-ended connection through a coupling capacitor. The nominal 24-V power required by the accelerometer can be generated from the 12-V telemetry power system with a voltage-doubler circuit.

This approach was used for the first deployments at BLIS and NED. The coupling capacitor at the VCO input produced a high-pass pole at 0.047 Hz, well below the nominal 0.2-Hz charge amplifier pole in the accelerometer. To achieve this low frequency, tantalum electrolytic capacitors were used. However, investigation of noise problems with the first NED deployment indicated that some sudden baseline shifts were due to the capacitor. The second deployment at NED used a polypropylene capacitor and higher input resistance to produce a pole at 0.04 Hz.

The polypropylene capacitor appeared to reduce some noise problems, but the design was still bothered by the spikes that occurred when GPS and seismic instruments cohabited the same spider. This and an interest in electronic integration of the accelerometer signal provoked the development of a different interface (fig. 4). The new interface used an input buffer to raise the impedance and a differential output stage that allowed connection directly to an unmodified VCO input. Rather than use a 24-V supply, the sensor ground was operated at −12 V, putting the output offset at −2 V and eliminating the need for a coupling capacitor at the sensor output. An optional integration stage was provided.

A high-pass pole (R4, C16) is included in the interface after the buffer stage. This was initially set to 0.017 Hz, making the charge amplifier pole dominant at low frequencies and reducing interaction with the optional integrator. This was later raised to 0.17 Hz when some low-frequency noise problems were seen in the accelerometer response. It has not been possible to duplicate this noise; it may have been unique, but for the sake of uniformity the pole continues to be set at 0.17 Hz. Table 3 lists deployment interface response characteristics and gains. Poles and zeros are from circuit simulation. All responses more than ten times the 30-Hz VCO low-pass filter are ignored.

This interface has been used for all our piezoelectric accelerometer deployments starting with the deployment of AHAB on February 8, 2005, and continuing through 2005, but it could be improved. Cohabitation with GPS still produces small glitches in the seismic signal when the GPS data transmission occurs. We expect that GPS noise could be reduced further by locating the interface on the sensor platform (fig. 3). This would change the connection in the long cable between the lander and the spider from a high impedance single-ended connection to a lower impedance differential connection. Better supply regulation might also help eliminate noise.

Gain Setting

The gain model for the dual-gain mode we used for all seismic spiders is shown in figure 5. Maximum acceleration of the Model 731-207 produces a maximum signal level of 5 V. This is greater than the input range of the McVCO, so the signal is reduced by half in all versions of the interface. The gain of two, created by the differential connection of the

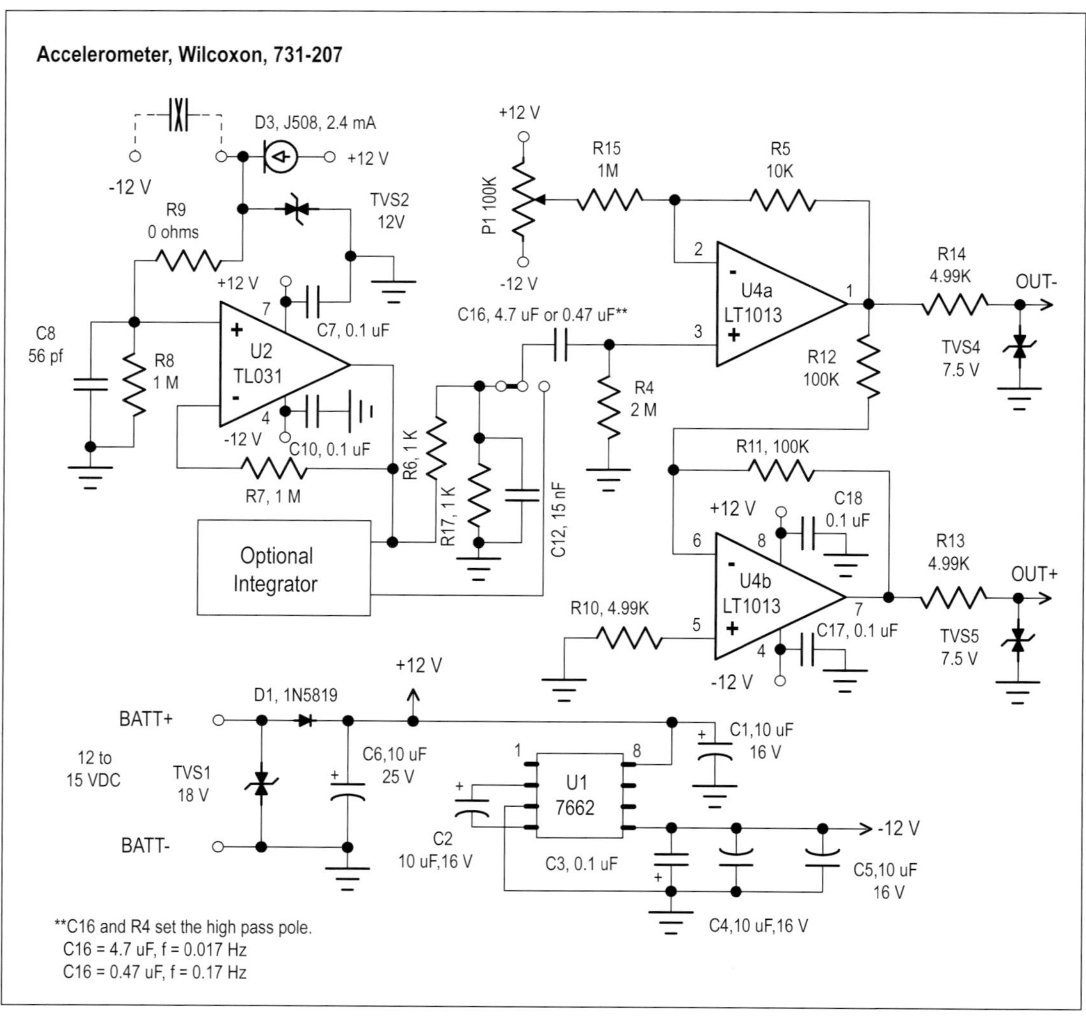

Figure 4. Piezoelectric accelerometer interface used from February 8, 2005, onward. Low-frequency response controlled by C16 and R4.

Table 3. Piezoelectric accelerometer channel gains and interface frequency responses.

[Different deployments to the same location are indicated by numerals in parentheses in station column. Last date for each station entry indicates modification or end of operation. nc, no change.]

Station	Date	High gain V/V	Low gain V/V	Interface response (poles), (zeros)
BLIS	10/12/04	83.17	2.5	(−0.294685, 0), (0, 0)
lost	01/31/05	--	--	--
NED(1)	11/20/04	83.17	2.5	(−0.294685, 0), (0, 0)
exchanged	12/20/04	--	--	--
NED(2)	12/20/04	83.17	2.5	(−0.249969, 0) (0, 0)
destroyed	03/08/05	--	--	--
AHAB	02/08/05	41.75	2.5	(−0.106357, 0), (0, 0)
removed	02/16/05	--	--	--
MIDE(1)	02/16/05	41.75	2.5	(−0.106357, 0), (0, 0)
destroyed	03/08/05	--	--	--
SEP	03/14/05	41.75	2.5	(−0.106357, 0), (0, 0)
modified	10/18/05	nc	nc	(1.06357, 0), (0, 0)
NED(3) modified	04/06/05	41.75	2.5	(−0.106357, 0), (0, 0)
	10/18/05	nc	nc	(−1.06357, 0), (0, 0)
MIDE(2)	04/06/05	41.75	2.5	(−0.106357, 0), (0, 0)
destroyed	07/19/05	--	--	--
SEND	06/30/05	41.75	2.5	(−1.06357, 0), (0, 0)
removed	11/17/05	--	--	--
WESG	07/12/05	41.75	2.5	(−1.06357, 0), (0, 0)
removed	09/14/05	--	--	--
RAFT	07/28/05	41.75	2.5	(−1.06357, 0), (0, 0)
MIBL	11/17/05	41.75	2.5	(−1.06357, 0), (0, 0)

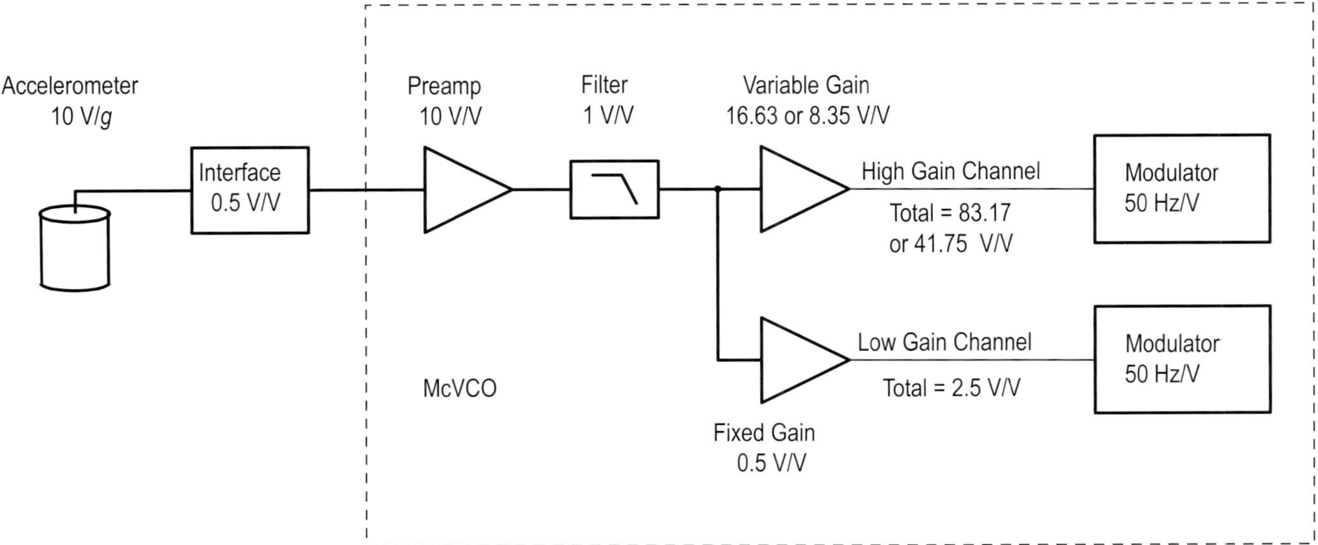

Figure 5. Dual-gain model of spider accelerometer. Additional gain and response terms result from demodulation and digitization. McVCO, microcontroller-based mimic of analog voltage-controlled oscillator.

later interfaces, is cancelled by the attenuation caused by the impedance match between interface and VCO, so the net gain of all interface stages is 0.5 V/V.

The input amplifier in the McVCO usually has a gain of 100 V/V. This was reduced to 10 V/V with jumpers on the input stage (McChesney, 1999, p. 31). After filtering (4th-order Butterworth, low-pass, 30-Hz filter) the signal splits into low- and high-gain channels. The low-gain channel is modified to have a gain of 0.5 V/V after the filter; consequently the total gain is 2.5 V/V from the interface input to the low-gain channel output. The maximum input signal swing of the channel's analog to digital converter is 2.5 V. A signal of 1 V from the sensor (0.1 *g*) produces a full-scale measurement on the low-gain channel.

The amplification of the high-gain channel after the filter stage depends on the gain switch setting and the microcontroller program version (McChesney, 1999, p. 15, p. 30–31). The high-gain channel after the filter stage was initially set for 16.63 V/V for a total gain of 83.17 V/V from the interface input to the high-gain channel output. As stated previously, this was reduced to 8.35 V/V for a total gain of 41.75 V/V for the deployments from AHAB onward (see table 3).

The McVCO modulator sensitivity is 50 Hz/V (McChesney, 1999, p. 30–31). The sensitivity of the discriminators used for demodulation was 0.02 V/Hz. The digitizer sensitivity was 819.2 counts/V. Where the total response to input excitation is the quotient of output counts divided by acceleration input, the scale factor for each channel voltage gain is shown in table 4.

Table 4. Scale factor for accelerometer channel gains.

Channel gain, V/V	Scale factor, counts/*g*
2.5	20,480
41.75	342,016
83.17	681,329

The "Marv Lander" Platform

We discovered a significant noise problem caused by spider vibrations during the first NED deployment. Later testing showed that soft tapping anywhere on the spider generated high levels of noise as long as the accelerometer was mounted on it. Our solution was to put the sensor on a separate platform, the "Marv lander," named for its developer, Marvin Couchman.

Previous experience with seismic installations at Mount St. Helens had shown that it was not always necessary to bury a seismometer to get good coupling and good noise performance. The installation at SEP before October 2004 was such an example. At the SEP site, warm temperatures a few centimeters below ground had caused rapid failures of several Sercel L4-C seismometers before a surface installation solved the problem. This approach was continued with the Sercel L22-3D installation at SEP on November 4, 2004. Other experiences with installations on rock, where digging was impossible, had also produced favorable results. In all these cases, isolation from surface noise was achieved by surrounding the seismometer with a rock pile, bags of sand, or concrete. We reasoned that a seismometer platform for remote deployment should provide significant mass around the sensor. Consequently the lander body is a 20-kg barbell weight (45 lb) with the piezoelectric sensor sealed with epoxy in the center hole (fig. 6).

The platform is coupled to the ground through three short legs formed by the eyebolts used to attach the rigging between it and the spider. Most of the spider sites had some ash cover, and, although we could not closely observe most of the platforms on the ground, we believe that the combination of tripod legs and weight helped root them in the ash and avoid tipping instability. The barbell weight also provided thermal mass, isolating the piezoelectric sensor from temperature changes rapid enough to produce an inband signal.

The lander rigging includes a 5-m length of 5-mm (3/16 in.) stainless steel cable attached to the spider's instrument box with a ring and thimble that protect the cable from wear during the helicopter flight (fig. 7). At the other end, a 10-mm (3/8 in.) rope harness attaches the lander to the cable. Soft rope is used to isolate the cable from the lander, eliminating cable vibrations as a source of seismic noise. Polypropylene rope was used for the first lander. When the instrument was retrieved after an explosion, one of the three leads was burned through, and hot rock was found embedded in the others. Subsequently, nylon rope was used because of its higher melting point and superior strength.

Separating the sensor from the spider body created some electrical problems. When the seismic spider is set down by the helicopter, the lander makes first contact with the ground. This can produce a strong static discharge between the lander

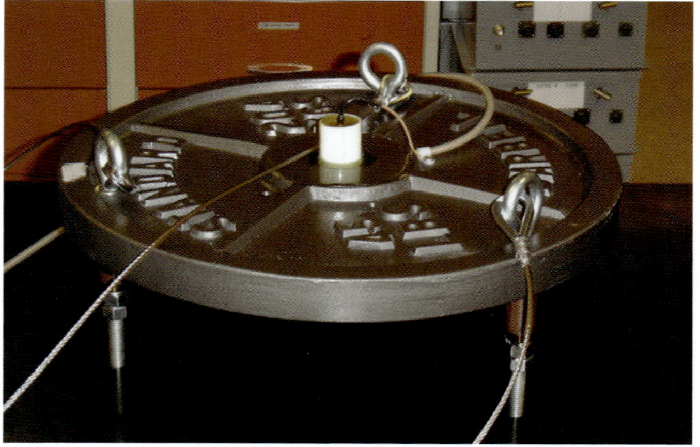

Figure 6. Marv lander under construction. Barbell weight stands on three legs formed by eyebolts that connect with rigging. Accelerometer is potted with epoxy inside the plastic pipe, which is cemented into center of the weight. USGS photo by M.R. Couchman, December 2, 2004.

Figure 7. Seismic spider laid out at staging area. Instrument box is approximately 70x40x40 cm. USGS photo by S.C. Moran, June 20, 2006.

and the spider that can damage the sensor and electronics. To provide a low-impedance discharge path, a grounding wire connects one of the lander's legs to the spider body. Discharge through the signal-cable shield is avoided by grounding it only at the spider end, and the sensor case is isolated from the lander body by potting it with epoxy inside a short length of PVC pipe (fig. 6). The signal cable is vulnerable to thermal and mechanical damage. Consequently, the two-pair shielded cable (Belden type 8723) is enclosed in thermal sleeving. Grounding wire and sensor cable are tied to the lander rigging.

The performance of an accelerometer mounted on the lander is illustrated in figure 8. The top trace is from the piezoelectric accelerometer installation at SEP shortly before it was replaced by a three-component velocity seismometer (Sercel L22-3D) on February 24, 2006. The bottom trace is from the L22 and shows an earthquake from February 26, 2006. The two earthquakes were chosen because signals from other stations indicated that they were very similar, having approximately the same magnitude, location, and source mechanism. The accelerometer data were integrated to produce a velocity response and then filtered (2 Hz, Butterworth high-pass filter) to remove long-period noise and produce an instrument response comparable to the L22. Despite the fact that the two sensor locations differed by ~15 m, their seismic traces share many similarities, particularly at the onsets. More to the point, the comparable signal-to-noise ratios show the effectiveness of the lander coupling.

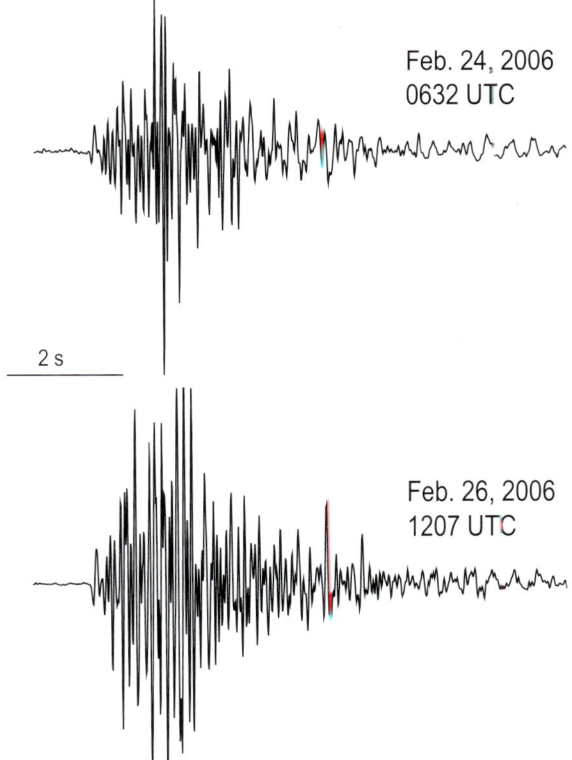

Figure 8. Comparison of numerically integrated response of piezoelectric accelerometer (top) and velocity seismometer (bottom) for similar earthquakes at station SEP. Accelerometer data were integrated to produce a velocity response and then filtered to remove long-period noise and produce an instrument response comparable to the velocity seismometer.

Summary

Even though Mount St. Helens was regarded as a well-monitored volcano, the September 2004 unrest exposed weaknesses in the seismic monitoring network. The explosion of October 1,

2004, removed our near-field monitoring capacity when station SEP was lost, reducing the quality of hypocenter determinations. One or more additional close-in stations would have increased the chance that near-field monitoring could survive a small explosion. Deployment of broadband seismometers before the start of volcanic unrest would have supplemented the short-period network by making up for its limited dynamic range and, if positioned within 4 km, could have detected any very long period events.

Once the eruption started, near-field sites quickly became too dangerous for fieldwork. However, with the seismic spider, we were able to improvise a solution that allowed us to establish close-in sites in comparative safety. The spider package not only enabled us to place a telemetered seismometer close to the vent but also to retrieve it for service or redeployment. This portability facilitated short-term studies such as AHAB on spine 4, and portability allowed us to adapt to changing field conditions during this prolonged eruption. A different choice of sensor and telemetry technology for remote deployment might have emerged from a less-hasty development process, but, given the advantage of strong signals in the near-field, both the sensor and analog telemetry were more than adequate for the task. We were particularly pleased with the performance of the Marv lander. It eliminated the spider platform noise and produced good coupling for the sensor. With the possible exception of the glacier site (WESG), there were no signal problems caused by poor sensor installation in 10 deployments.

Seismic spiders are not substitutes for well-established seismic stations because they lack the sensitivity to detect small earthquakes, unless they happen to be in the near field, or to detect the long-period earthquakes that may well mark the start of volcanic unrest. However, once unrest has begun, they can be used to supplement an existing network where additional near-field monitoring is desired. These portable, remotely deployed stations can be built in advance, allowing a very rapid response to events. The seismic spider is a new tool for monitoring erupting volcanoes, a tool that can be used in dangerous places with comparative safety.

Acknowledgments

The authors would like to thank Richard P. Hoblitt for suggesting the piezoelectric accelerometer used in the seismic spider and supplying them during the first deployments. His perceptive review of this paper greatly increased its coherence. Thomas L. Murray's review gave us a new perspective on the seismic spider design; this resulted in a more balanced paper and allowed us to avoid several shortcomings. Finally, we would like to thank Anthony Qamar for his initial calculation of the peak acceleration that a near-field sensor would measure and his many discussions of instrument response. Because of Tony, seismic spider data were "on scale" and calibrated.

References Cited

Allocca, J.A., and Stuart, A., 1984, Transducers—theory and applications: Reston, Va., Reston Publishing Company Inc., 497 p.

Ewert, J.W., Guffanti, M., and Murray, T.L., 2005, An assessment of volcanic threat and monitoring capabilities in the United States; framework for a National Volcano Early Warning System: U.S. Geological Survey Open-File Report 2005–1164, 62 p.

Horton, S.P., Norris, R.D., and Moran, S.C., 2008, Broadband characteristics of earthquakes recorded during a dome-building eruption at Mount St. Helens, Washington, between October 2004 and May 2005, chap. 5 *of* Sherrod, D.R., Scott, W.E., and Stauffer, P.H., eds., A volcano rekindled; the renewed eruption of Mount St. Helens, 2004–2006: U.S. Geological Survey Professional Paper 1750 (this volume).

LaHusen, R.G., Swinford, K.J., Logan, M., and Lisowski, M., 2008, Instrumentation in remote and dangerous settings; examples using data from GPS "spider" deployments during the 2004–2005 eruption of Mount St. Helens, Washington, chap. 16 *of* Sherrod, D.R., Scott, W.E., and Stauffer, P.H., eds., A volcano rekindled; the renewed eruption of Mount St. Helens, 2004–2006: U.S. Geological Survey Professional Paper 1750 (this volume).

McChesney, P.J., 1999, McVCO handbook 1999: U.S. Geological Survey Open-File Report 99–361, 48 p. [http://wrgis.wr.usgs.gov/open-file/of99-361/, last accessed Dec. 26, 2006].

Moran, S.C., 2004, Seismic monitoring at Cascade volcanic centers, 2004; status and recommendations: U.S. Geological Survey Scientific Investigations Report 2004–5211, 28 p.

Moran, S.C., Malone, S.D., Qamar, A.I., Thelen, W.A., Wright, A.K., and Caplan-Auerbach, J., 2008a, Seismicity associated with renewed dome building at Mount St. Helens, 2004–2005, chap. 2 *of* Sherrod, D.R., Scott, W.E., and Stauffer, P.H., eds., A volcano rekindled; the renewed eruption of Mount St. Helens, 2004–2006: U.S. Geological Survey Professional Paper 1750 (this volume).

Moran, S.C., McChesney, P.J., and Lockhart, A.B., 2008b, Seismicity and infrasound associated with explosions at Mount St. Helens, 2004–2005, chap. 6 *of* Sherrod, D.R., Scott, W.E., and Stauffer, P.H., eds., A volcano rekindled; the renewed eruption of Mount St. Helens, 2004–2006: U.S. Geological Survey Professional Paper 1750 (this volume).

Schloss, F., 1993, Accelerometer noise: Gaithersburg, Md., Wilcoxon Research, Inc., Sound and Vibration instrumentation reference issue, March 1993, 2 p. [http://www.wilcoxon.com/knowdesk/accelnoise.pdf, last accessed Dec. 26, 2006].

Schloss, F., 1998, Piezoelectric accelerometer specifications and specmanship: Gaithersburg, Md., Wilcoxon Research, Inc., Sound and Vibration, February 1998, 2 p. [http://www.wilcoxon.com/knowdesk/piezo_spec.pdf, last accessed Jan. 8, 2007].

Scott, W.E., Sherrod, D.R., and Gardner, C.A., 2008, Overview of 2004 to 2006, and continuing, eruption of Mount St. Helens, Washington, chap. 1 *of* Sherrod, D.R., Scott, W.E., and Stauffer, P.H., eds., A volcano rekindled; the renewed eruption of Mount St. Helens, 2004–2006: U.S. Geological Survey Professional Paper 1750 (this volume).

Geological Observations of Lava-Dome Growth

Seismic unrest at Mount St. Helens that started in September 2004 evolved into a dome-building eruption whose first new lava erupted 18 days later, on October 11. The dome grew as a series of spines within the existing 1980 crater. Each spine impinged upon the 1980–86 lava dome, on older parts of the new dome, and, in some cases, on the adjacent crater wall. Invariably, the stress of pushing caused the active spine to shear off, override previously extruded rock, and ultimately disintegrate. The numbered spines marked sequential growth episodes, whereas the vent itself never varied in location.

Crater Glacier, which was born in the deep shadows of the 1980 Mount St. Helens crater and grew in the years thereafter, was riven into two arms by the new dome, forced aside, doubled in thickness, and accelerated downslope. The glacier provided little resistance to the extruding lava. By being pushed away, the glacier was spared substantial melting—it lost only 10 percent of its volume despite years-long proximity to hot rock in its upslope reach.

On-the-ground field work within the crater was rarely undertaken in 2004–5, because of the persistent threat of small explosions. Consequently, most geologic monitoring was done through photography and periodic dredging of samples by helicopter. Some photographs were taken during helicopter overflights, others by fixed cameras (some of which transmitted images in near-real time), and overhead aerial photographs were taken from airplanes.

Through photogrammetry, the overhead aerial photographs provided digital elevation models of the new dome. From these digital data came the popular hillshade relief maps, deformation maps, and interpretive geologic maps and cross sections that illustrated the sequence of spine growth and decay. Successive digital elevation models also allowed the calculation of changing dome volumes and extrusion rates.

View east on October 12, 2004, to the first spine of the 2004 dome sequence soon after it breached the Crater Glacier and crater-floor debris. Spine is light-gray feature mostly encased in steam. USGS photo by J. C. Wynn.

A Volcano Rekindled: The Renewed Eruption of Mount St. Helens, 2004–2006
Edited by David R. Sherrod, William E. Scott, and Peter H. Stauffer
U.S. Geological Survey Professional Paper 1750, 2008

Chapter 8

Use of Digital Aerophotogrammetry to Determine Rates of Lava Dome Growth, Mount St. Helens, Washington, 2004–2005

By Steve P. Schilling[1], Ren A. Thompson[2], James A. Messerich[2], and Eugene Y. Iwatsubo[1]

Abstract

Beginning in October 2004, a new lava dome grew on the glacier-covered crater floor of Mount St. Helens, Washington, immediately south of the 1980s lava dome. Seventeen digital elevation models (DEMs) constructed from vertical aerial photographs have provided quantitative estimates of extruded lava volumes and total volume change. To extract volumetric changes and calculate volumetric extrusion rates (magma discharge rates), each DEM surface was compared to preeruption DEM reference surfaces from 1986 and 2003. Early in the 2004–5 eruption, DEMs documented deforming glacier ice and crater floor that formed a prominent "welt" having a volume of 10×10^6 m^3 and a growth rate of 8.9 m^3/s before dacite lava first appeared at the surface on October 11, 2004. Afterward, the rate was initially 5.9 m^3/s but slowed to 2.5 m^3/s by the beginning of January 2005. During 2005, the extrusion rate declined gradually to about 0.7 m^3/s. By December 15, 2005, the new dome complex was about 900 m long and 625 m wide and reached 190 m above the 2003 surface. More than 73×10^6 m^3 of dacite lava had extruded onto the crater floor.

Successful application of aerophotogrammetry was possible during the critical earliest parts of the eruption because we had baseline data and photogrammetric infrastructure in place before the eruption began. The vertical aerial photographs, including the DEMs and calculations derived from them, were one of the most widely used data sets collected during the 2004–5 eruption, as evidenced in numerous contributions to this volume. These data were used to construct photogeologic maps, deformation vector fields, and profiles of the evolving dome and glacier. Extruded volumes and rates proved to be critical parameters to constrain models and hypotheses of eruption dynamics and thus helped to assess volcano hazards.

Introduction

The volume of a growing lava dome and its extrusion rate are primary measurements that may be compared with other traditional volcano-monitoring data from ground deformation, gas geochemistry, and seismicity for the purpose of monitoring and studying erupting volcanoes. Such comparisons have been made for some recent dome-building eruptions, including Santiaguito, Guatemala (Harris and others, 2003); Unzen, Japan (Nakada and others, 1999); Redoubt, Alaska (Miller, 1994); and Soufrière Hills, Montserrat (Sparks and others, 1998). In addition to their value as a fundamental dataset, volumetric data are needed to explore such linkages as extrusion rate thresholds for transition to explosive activity and volume thresholds for initiation of large-scale dome collapse. In this paper, we describe a new application of traditional photogrammetric techniques to track the growth of the 2004–5 Mount St. Helens lava dome.

In October 2004, a new period of dome growth began at Mount St. Helens that changed the topography of the 1980 crater dramatically (fig. 1). Between October 2004 and December 2005, more than 73×10^6 m^3 of solid dacite lava extruded onto the crater floor immediately south of the lava dome that had formed in the 1980s. The new dome grew as a succession of large spines (Vallance and others, this volume, chap. 9). Dome growth intensely deformed and divided Crater Glacier, which had developed from a small debris-covered snowbank in 1985 into a glacier covering about 1 km^2 by 2001 (Schilling and others, 2004). We use the informal names "west

[1] U.S. Geological Survey, 1300 SE Cardinal Court, Vancouver, WA 98683

[2] U.S. Geological Survey, Box 25046, Denver Federal Center, Denver, CO 80225

Crater Glacier" and "east Crater Glacier" for the two ice bodies remaining within the crater. The growing dome compressed the east Crater Glacier against the east crater wall, resulting in spectacular thickening. Compression and thickening created crevasses and rapid advance of the terminus, about 185 m in two years, followed by similar effects on the west Crater Glacier (Walder and others, this volume, chap. 13).

The extruded volume and extrusion rate of lava associated with this protracted dome eruption are critical parameters used to constrain models of the magmatic system (Mastin and others, this volume, chap. 22) and eruption dynamics (Iverson, this volume, chap. 21), to determine how the magmatic system relates to surface measurements of magmatic gases (Gerlach and others, this volume, chap. 26) and seismicity (for example, to determine if extrusion rate correlates with size and rate of occurrence of volcano-related earthquakes; Moran and others, this volume, chap. 2), and to constrain calculations that address loading effects of the growing dome on surface deformation (Lisowski and others, this volume, chap. 15).

Photogrammetry based on vertical aerial photographs has been used previously to monitor, model, map, and measure surface change and deformation at volcanoes (Achilli and others, 1998; Baldi and others, 2000, 2005; Zlotnicki and others, 1990). A recent photogrammetric study of the Mount St. Helens crater (Schilling and others, 2004) tied a block of overlapping vertical aerial photographs to a network of global positioning system (GPS) stations on the volcano's flanks, dome, and crater floor (fig. 2*A*) resulting in a digital elevation model (DEM) of the volcanic edifice and entire crater configuration in October 2000.

The 2000 DEM has served as a baseline for comparison with past DEMs. Comparison of the 2000 surface with post-May 18, 1980, and 1990 DEMs, both derived from existing topographic contour maps, produced volume estimates of

Figure 1. Oblique photographs of Mount St. Helens crater from east rim; views to southwest. *A*, Preeruption crater on August 30, 2004, showing 1980s lava dome and Crater Glacier (mostly coated with rock debris). *B*, Crater on October 12, 2005, showing new lava dome dividing and deforming glacier. USGS photographs by S.P. Schilling.

glacier ice and talus accumulation, as well as crater-wall erosion (Thompson and Schilling, 2007). Near the beginning of the 2004–5 eruption, two other craterwide DEMs were constructed to estimate volume change. One was created from digital, photogrammetrically derived contours that depicted the crater in November 1986, and another was constructed from lidar data (Queija and others, 2005) obtained September 20–22, 2003, using the same network of GPS sites for ground control that was used for photogrammetric monitoring.

Throughout the 2004–5 eruption, we used analytical photogrammetry and a softcopy (that is, digital image) system to provide stereo imaging and accurate measurement of the rapidly changing crater morphology. Seventeen DEMs have been constructed from vertical aerial photographs (Messerich and others, 2008), collected approximately every three weeks, in order to quantify volumetric changes associated with dome growth and collapse as well as deformation of Crater Glacier (Walder and others, this volume, chap. 13). Each new DEM was compared to preeruption reference surfaces of the crater in 1986 and 2003 to extract volumetric changes. For viewing purposes, each DEM was also converted to a hillshade-relief map, in the form of digital raster images (tagged image file format) and corresponding georeferenced world files (ASCII format). These raster maps are found in appendix 1, which is available in the DVD that accompanies this volume and in online versions of this chapter.

Methods

Acquiring low-altitude aerial photographs in inclement weather over mountainous terrain presents logistical challenges, and taking them over an erupting composite volcano such as Mount St. Helens, where rapid turnaround of data is needed to evaluate hazards, adds urgency. These problems were simplified by taking advantage of photogrammetric infrastructure set up during previous work at the volcano (Schilling and others, 2004). When the 2004–5 eruption began, however, some established flight-planning procedures required modification, such as selection of new ground control sites and design of flight lines for appropriate photograph scale

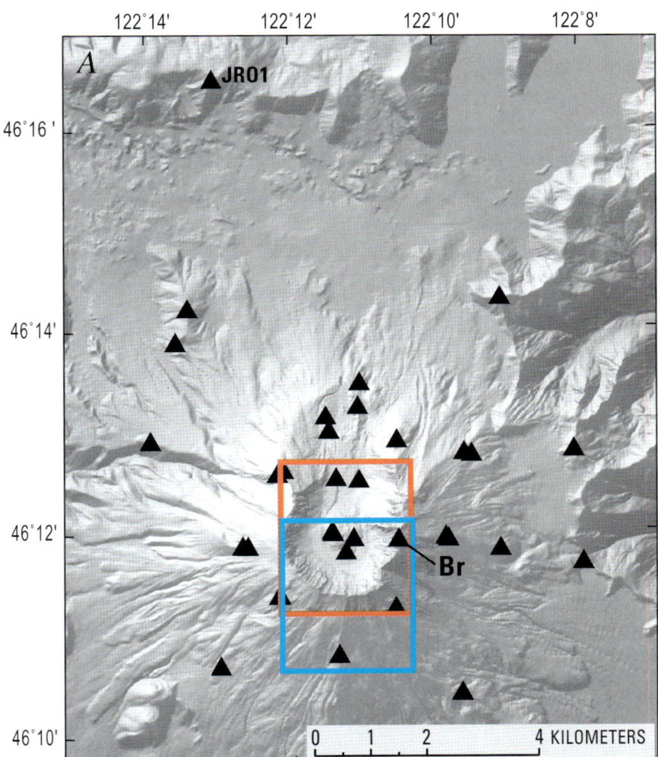

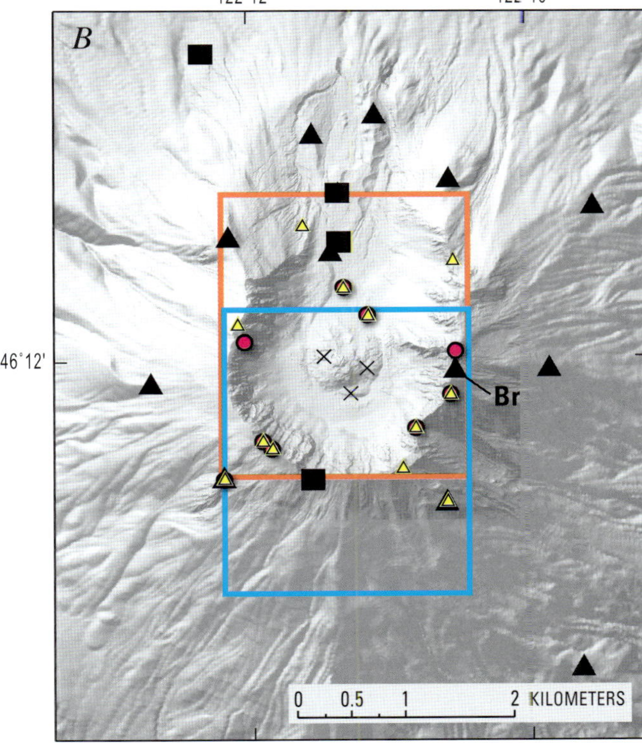

Figure 2. Shaded-relief maps of preeruption surface of Mount St. Helens (2003 DEM). Red and blue boxes show approximate areas covered by two overlapping, 1:12,000-scale vertical aerial photographs. *A*, Broad GPS ground control network (black triangles) used for aerotriangulation of block of photographs to extract coordinates for construction of 2000 DEM and to serve as control for 2003 lidar-based DEM. Br, Brutus control point on east rim. *B*, Ground control points for vertical aerial photographs obtained during 2004–5 eruption. Black X's, ground control points destroyed early in eruption. Red dots, photoidentified control points transferred from 2000 aerotriangulation for use early in eruption. Black squares, new, and black triangles, existing ground control points measured in summer 2005. Yellow triangles, photoidentified control points transferred from August 2005 aerotriangulation solution to serve as ground control for December 2005 aerotriangulation.

and overlap. Early in the eruption, having procedures already established meant that DEMs were constructed rapidly, at times within a few days of obtaining the aerial photographs.

Digital photogrammetry refers to photogrammetric systems that have been adapted from hardcopy (film) aerial photographs mounted on optical-mechanical stereo plotters to softcopy (scanned, digital) aerial photographs imported into a desktop computer workstation. Hardware for our softcopy system includes a fast central processing unit, abundant memory, two display screens (one for stereo images and one for control menus), polarizing spectacles for viewing onscreen images in stereo, and a customized mouse to control three-dimensional (3D) cursor movement. Socet Set software includes spatial resection and spatial intersection algorithms to calculate X, Y, and Z ground coordinates of features observed in stereo aerial photographs; it requires precise camera calibration parameters, carefully measured photograph coordinates, and accurate GPS ground control (Wolf and Dewitt, 2000; Thompson and Schilling, 2007). The softcopy system automates many standard photogrammetric tasks, such as inner and relative orientations of stereo models. However, the critical task of exterior orientation, which ties photographs to ground control, requires a skilled operator to maintain precision. Assuming minimal operator error, the accuracy of the final model solution is constrained by flight height, which determines scale, and by scanning resolution, which determines the minimum feature size that the operator can discern in the aerial photographs.

After considering many factors, such as safety and size of features to be measured, we selected a flying height of 3,900 m (12,800 ft), yielding a nominal photo scale of 1:12,000 with a 153.681-mm lens and 9×9-inch film format. Thus, 1 mm on the photograph at nominal scale represents 12 m on the ground. This nominal scale applies at about the altitude of the Crater Glacier surface immediately south of the 1980s lava dome, roughly midway through the range of relief within the Mount St. Helens crater—from about 2,540 m (8,330 ft) on the crater rim to about 1,815 m (5,955 ft) near the base of the 1980s dome. The variation in altitude corresponds to a variation in scale, often within a single photograph, from 1:8,964 at the rim to 1:13,726 at the base of the 1980s lava dome.

Each aerial photographic negative was scanned at 12 μm resolution, generating a graytone digital image roughly 350 megabytes in size. Owing to the scale variation within a photograph, each cell in the image may represent a different distance on the ground, from 0.108 to 0.165 m.

Global Positioning System (GPS) Control Network

Accurate ground control is equally as important as high-resolution scanning. About 30 GPS sites on the outer flanks, 1980s lava dome, and crater floor of Mount St. Helens (fig. 2*A*) form a network of ground control points for photogrammetric surveys. The sites were selected to accommodate the geometry needed for the exterior orientation (linking world and photograph coordinate systems) of blocks of overlapping photographs (multiple stereopairs along and between adjacent flight lines); each site was also accessible by helicopter. Most of the sites are part of a geodetic network established in 2000 (Dzurisin, 2003). Many are located near 3-m-high steel towers constructed after the 1980 eruption and used for electronic distance meter (EDM) surveys (Swanson and others, 1981). These towers or their shadows are relatively easy to find in the diapositive (film positives) rendering of aerial photographs used to help locate ground-control sites in the digital images. Using a helicopter and two crews, we were able to measure and place photo-targets at all of the stations in 1–2 days.

Measuring GPS locations in the field for ground control at Mount St. Helens is a straightforward task. We deploy a GPS receiver at each site, centering the antenna over a specific tower leg, piece of rebar, or benchmark. GPS receivers collect data at each site for about 1 hour. Before moving to the next site, three or four large plastic rectangular panels are placed radially about each GPS point to facilitate locating the control point in aerial photographs. The receiver data are downloaded and processed using Ashtech Office Suite for Survey ® (AOSS) software. The reference station for differential GPS processing is JRO1 (fig. 2*A*), which at the start of the eruption was the nearest continuous GPS station (approximately 9 km north of the crater). Altitudes from AOSS are converted to orthometric heights using the National Geodetic Survey (NGS) program GEOID03. The U.S. Army Corps of Engineer program CORPSCON is used to calculate X, Y, and Z coordinates using a horizontal datum of NAD83 and a vertical datum of NAVD88. The GPS data yield position accuracies of 2 to 3 cm in X and Y (horizontal) coordinates and 6 to 7 cm in the Z (vertical) coordinate.

Control points were remeasured annually from 2000 to 2004 before taking aerial photographs of the entire volcano. Repeated measurement improved and validated the positional accuracy of most sites. However, the landscape evolves quickly at Mount St. Helens, and site positions change, at times dramatically. For example, in 2002 the photo panels and rebar of the Brutus site on the east crater rim (fig. 2, station Br) were buried beneath about 20 cm of wind-blown pumice. The following year, the site toppled into the crater and had to be replaced.

New Ground Control Based on GPS Data and Photo-Identified Points

When the 2004–5 eruption began, four established flight lines used in previous studies to capture aerial photography of most of the volcano were abandoned in favor of a single, south-to-north flight line centered over the crater. A single flight line offered advantages of safety, simplicity, speed, and economy. However, it eliminated use of ground control points on the east and west outer flanks of the volcano and forced reliance on control points on the crater rim, floor, outer south flank, and 1980s lava dome. Unfortunately, explosions early in the eruption eliminated three critical ground control sites on the 1980s lava dome (fig. 2*B*). Several of the remaining control points were outside the stereo coverage of the single flight line.

Rather than increase the number of flight lines and incorporate the ground control on the volcano flanks in an aerotriangulated block or replace the ground control in the crater's potentially dangerous environment, we transferred control points from the stored orientation solution (aerotriangulation) of the 2000 block of aerial photographs. Photoidentifiable, measured points (fig. 2*B*), such as distinct boulders or topographic prominences, were carefully selected and passed from the aerotriangulated solution of 2000 models to the 2004 aerial photographs as ground control. These points or a subset of them provided control for successive sets of photographs obtained throughout the winter of 2004–5. The resulting ground-control accuracy was reduced from a few centimeters, based solely on GPS data, to a few decimeters using photogrammetrically transferred control points.

In July 2005 we remeasured and repaneled the network of existing ground-control points on the crater rim and flanks. In addition, we reestablished one of the points on the west side of the 1980s lava dome and added points on the crater floor north of the 1980s lava dome and a site on the south crater rim (fig. 2*B*).

Aerotriangulation

Aerotriangulation provided a means of transferring accurate control from earlier photogrammetric work at Mount St. Helens, rather than establishing new control in hazardous areas as the eruption progressed. Aerotriangulation refers to solving relative orientation equations for overlapping aerial photographs (stereo model), identifying common points (pass points) between adjacent models to form continuous strips or blocks of stereomodels, and solving simultaneous equations to adjust mathematically the strips or block of photographs to ground control. A series of nonlinear expressions with many unknowns are truncated by Taylor's theorem into a series of linear equations that are solved simultaneously by the method of least squares (Wolf and Dewitt, 2000). Our 2000 benchmark DEM was created from an aerotriangulation solution for a block of aerial photographs. The block comprised four adjacent, overlapping strips of photos; each strip was formed from seven or eight overlapping photographs. Point coordinates extracted from the 2000 stereomodels and aerotriangulation were used as control points for successive stereomodels and for aerotriangulation solutions during the early part of the 2004–5 eruption. The resulting root-mean-squared (RMS) residual error for the early aerotriangulation solutions was a few decimeters. New and remeasured GPS ground-control points in the aerial photographs taken in the summer and fall of 2005 resulted in an aerotriangulation RMS residual error of several millimeters to several centimeters. The average RMS error from all aerotriangulation solutions was 0.17 m in the X, Y, and Z coordinates. Extending that error over the area that has been affected by the eruption (about 1 km^2) gives rise to a volume of uncertainty of 1.7×10^5 m^3. This error is about 4 percent of the typical monthly extruded volume (4×10^6 m^3) estimated from comparison of the series of DEMs (Iverson and others, 2006, Supplementary Notes).

Digital Elevation Model (DEM) Construction

We used spatial resection calculations to derive an aerotriangulation solution and then used spatial triangulation algorithms to extract three-dimensional coordinates and construct a DEM that defines the crater surface. Two techniques were used for obtaining X, Y, and Z coordinates from the stereomodels.

The first method was a manual technique that relies on the skill of the operator. The operator examined one or more stereomodels and identified the area being deformed and the features to be measured. For each feature, the operator carefully placed a floating mark on the feature, stored the Z (elevation) coordinate, and triangulated and stored the X and Y (planimetric) coordinates. Points were collected individually or as a stream as the operator moved the floating mark along the terrain.

The second method was an automated technique in which Socet Set software used coplanarity equations to derive a plane intersecting three points: (1) an object in one image; (2) the same object in the overlapping area of a second, adjacent image; and (3) the triangulated position of the object on the ground. The software used the line formed where the plane intersected the two adjacent photographs to guide its search for matching cell patterns. When the X and Y coordinates of matching cell patterns were identified, the software calculated the corresponding Z coordinate. The operator defined an area and density of points for the automated calculations. The automated method did not work well in steep terrain but did work in the relatively flat-lying, glacier-covered parts of the crater, provided there was enough contrast (such as a dusting of ash) in the photographs to provide unique cell patterns. The automated technique identified, calculated, and stored X, Y, and Z coordinates for many locations relatively quickly. This technique was used sparingly, however, because it can be labor intensive. Automatically generated points must be checked by the operator, either individually or by generating contours of groups of collected points, to correct any errors.

Using these two techniques, individual points or streams of points marking breaks in slope (breaklines) were collected to better define topographic inflections, enabling intervening surfaces on the growing dome and deforming glacier to be represented by significantly fewer data points. The resulting three-dimensional surface is an array of triangular facets referred to as a triangulated irregular network (TIN), in which interpolated surfaces are triangles having measured points at each vertex. A TIN surface was checked for systematic errors or random operator error in a few seconds by generating digital contours for the surface. The operator easily located and repaired errors, such as points that caused contours to cross, and recalculated the TIN surface.

After error checking and visually determining that the TIN was an accurate representation of the three-dimensional surface depicted in the aerial photographs, the TIN data structure was stored and converted to a DEM. The DEM differs from the TIN in that the former is a regular array of square cells (or rasters), where each cell represents an area of the Earth's surface (X, Y) with a specific altitude value (Z). During this conversion process, the cell size or resolution did not dictate the accuracy of an altitude value. Rather, the resolution dictated how closely the DEM represents the TIN model. The accuracy of altitudes and horizontal positions was determined by the combined photogrammetric orientations, operator's skill, and in particular by the accuracy of the ground control.

Sources of error in the DEM construction included aerial camera calibration, film processing, flight parameters, ground control points, conversion of photos to digital form, stereomodel orientation (interior, relative, absolute), aerotriangulation, image-matching algorithms, operator bias, and random factors (Daniel and Tennant, 2001, p. 402–403). We estimated the uncertainty of any volume measurement to be a function of the area of the growing dome multiplied by the average RMS residual error (0.17 m). Thus, as the volume continued to increase, so did the estimated uncertainty of the volume calculation. However, the resulting uncertainty in volume-change calculations was about 4 percent—small compared to the ambiguity introduced by the unknown subsurface configuration of the lava dome (the lower part of the new dome masked by Crater Glacier).

Surface Depiction Using DEMs

The DEMs were imported into an ArcInfo Geographic Information System (GIS) for viewing and analysis after conversion to an ASCII text file in the softcopy system. This file, which was formatted for import to ArcInfo software, included a header containing the number of columns, number of rows, cell size, and X and Y coordinates of the lower left corner of the DEM, followed by a sequence in row-major order (top row first, bottom row last) of all the Z (elevation) values. The file was imported into the ArcInfo grid module as a high-resolution (2 m) grid (raster data structure).

Perhaps the most significant and primary use of any photogrammetrically constructed DEM is to examine the surface, either singly or in sequence with previous DEMs. Such a succession of DEMs for Mount St. Helens shows, qualitatively, the changing position, dimensions, and size of the growing dome and deforming glacier over time. The DEMs are difficult to examine or interpret directly. A hillshade algorithm was used to position an artificial "sun" at an arbitrary azimuth and altitude to render a gray-scale shaded-relief view of the changing dome and glacier. This rendition of the topography is free of potentially distracting details seen in the aerial photographs, such as steam, snow, or ash, and allows consistent and simplified viewing to study geomorphic change and compare cell alignment among DEMs.

The areal extent of the dome complex and deformed glacier increased throughout the 2004–5 eruption, forcing a corresponding increase in the extent of DEMs to document the change. To ensure proper alignment (registration) of the DEMs, they are cast within the same projection, same horizontal datum, and same vertical datum. We selected the Universal Transverse Mercator (UTM) projection's zone 10, which extends from 120° to 126° west longitude, the 1988 North American Vertical Datum (NAVD 88), and the 1983 North American horizontal datum (NAD 83). Previous DEMs derived from contours having a 1927 horizontal datum (NAD 27) were converted to NAD 83. In addition, a regional vertical correction of 1.25 m (Zilkoski and others, 1992) was applied to convert the 1929 vertical datum (NAGD 29) to NAVD 88. We confirmed this regional correction by calculating the difference between GPS control points stored in NAGD 29 and NAVD 88.

The extent of each DEM was varied in order to capture dome growth. Dome growth and the DEMs depicting the growth were bounded on the north by the relatively fixed 1980s lava dome and eventually bounded on the south by the south crater wall. The DEM edges on the east and west (as well as the south early in the eruption) were delineated visually to capture observed deformation, using the softcopy system. These results were confirmed by using GIS software to compare any current DEM to earlier DEMs. If we found that any of the DEMs had inadequate extent to represent the entire deformation field, the boundary could be extended using the scanned aerial photographs and aerotriangulation stored within the softcopy system.

Initially, the 2000 DEM was used as the baseline data set for all comparisons in order to keep the construction method consistent. However, the craterwide 2000 DEM had a cell size of 10 m, whereas DEMs constructed for the 2004–5 eruption had cell sizes of 2 m. The difference in cell size meant that each of the newer DEMs would have to be resampled to give a 10-m cell size. The error introduced by resampling outweighed the benefit of using consistent production methods; therefore, we later selected the craterwide 2003 DEM derived from lidar, and a 1986 DEM derived from contours, each having a 2-m cell size, for comparison with all subsequent DEMs.

Volume Calculation Methods

Although a single DEM surface offers a quick, synoptic portrayal of ongoing surface deformation, the comparison of successive DEM surfaces can yield estimates of erupted volume and average extrusion rate. We wrote software that uses GIS functions to subtract one DEM surface from another and generates a third, isoline surface showing net elevation change. The isoline surface stores the calculated difference between its two parent surfaces, retaining their 2-m cell size. In this manner, each cell of the isoline grid stores a positive, zero, or negative value resulting from the subtraction of the two corresponding parent cells. After the subtraction, the software sums values of all cells having a negative value (melting, erosion, or subsidence) and of all cells having a positive value (extrusion, deposition, or uplift) separately, and it also multiplies each total positive or total negative value by the area of a single cell (4 m^2). The software writes the resulting volumes to a text file and generates two additional grids, one showing the location of the positive and another showing the location of the negative results.

The potentially straightforward task of determining extruded volume from total-volume changes was complicated by the presence of Crater Glacier, in some places more than 150 m thick (greater than 200 m thick when including subglacial 1980–86 crater-floor deposits), which was displaced and severely disrupted as the eruption progressed. Two questions arose: (1) Does extrusion begin at the preexisting crater floor or at the glacier surface; and (2) how best to calculate erupted volume as a function of time? One approach (fig. 3*A*) is to difference each new DEM with the 2003 preeruption DEM and to use the total surface-volume change as a proxy for erupted volume. For example, 1 m^2 of glacier ice rising 2 m represents 2 m^3 of lava extruded beneath it or laterally displacing it. This approach has the advantage of accounting for all material that rose above the crater floor, some of which remains obscured by ice, and the method is simple and straightforward. Three disadvantages of this total volume-change technique are the unknown total amount of dilatation caused by ice deformation (though the largest crevasses are captured during DEM construction), volume gain by winter snow accumulation, and volume loss by melting.

Another approach (fig. 3*B*) is to assume that lava extends from the lava-ice contact at the surface vertically downward to the 1986 crater floor. This is a reasonable approach for three reasons: (1) field examples of ice-contact lava flows have steep sides that formed as they flowed against steep ice walls (Lescinsky and Fink, 2000); (2) where observed around the Mount St. Helens dome, ice-lava contacts are nearly vertical; and (3) this method is also simple and straightforward. One disadvantage is that this method ignores observed rising crater-floor material or glacier, especially early in the eruption, which probably deform in response to endogenous or subglacial lava emplacement.

Our solution was to use both approaches to track volume estimates. The first approach provided measurements of extruded rock independent of whether rock broke through the glacier surface. As the eruption proceeded, the dome grew larger and the impact of the glacier became proportionally smaller. The discrepancy between the two approaches therefore decreased over time.

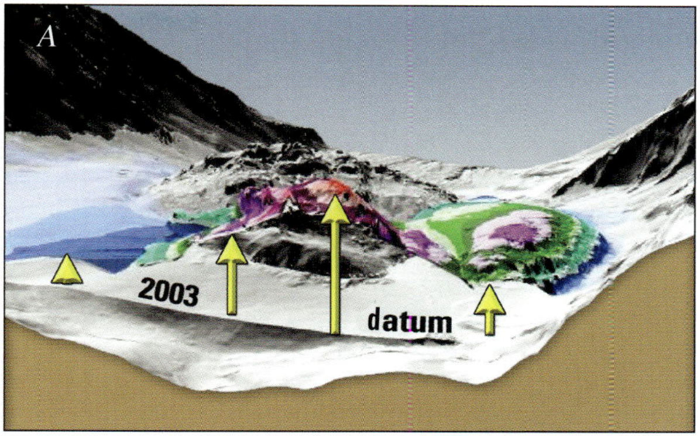

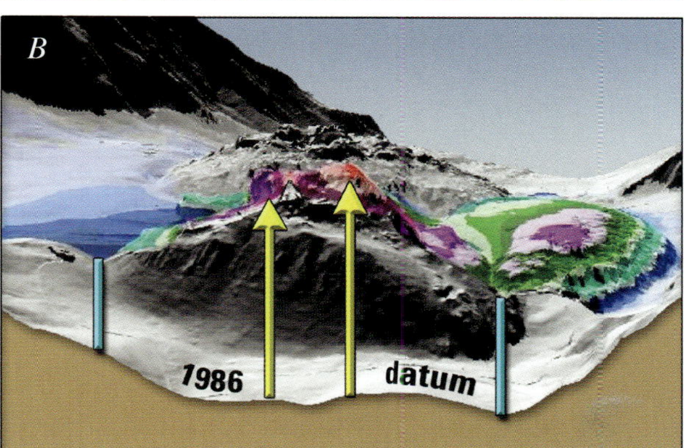

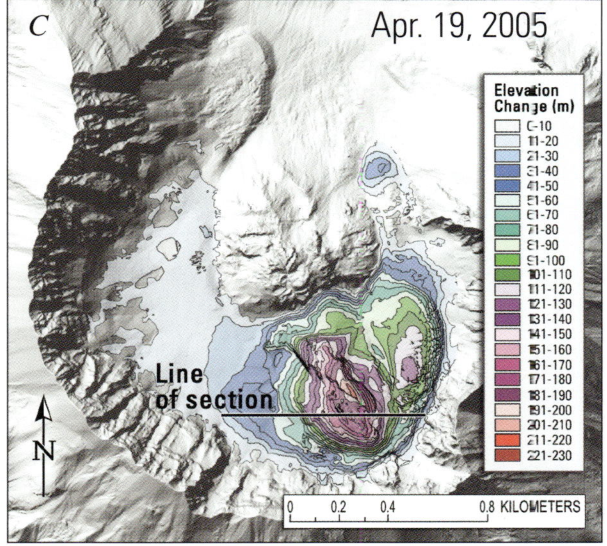

Figure 3. Diagrams (*A, B*) illustrating DEM differencing for volume-change calculations. Semitransparent oblique cutaway of surface defined by April 19, 2005, isolines (colored bands) draped on DEM showing 1986 ground topography and 2003 glacier surface. Yellow arrows, examples of local elevation changes. View to north-northwest. *A*, Total volume change. Note that differencing includes marginal areas, unlikely to be underlain by lava, that are composed of deformed glacier. *B*, Extruded-lava volume. Blue bars define inferred steep margins of extrusion. *C*, DEM and differencing surface of April 19, 2005. The DEM and differencing surface south of the line of section were removed to produce oblique views *A* and *B*.

Results

A sequence of 17 pairs of images derived from DEMs of October 4, 2004, through December 15, 2005, document lava dome growth and glacier deformation during the 2004–5 eruption (figs. 4, 6–8). For each pair, the left image is a shaded-relief map. Beginning with the October 13, 2004, map, a red line marks the approximate boundary of extruded lava on the surface that was extended vertically to the 1986 crater floor to calculate the extruded-lava volume. The right image is an isoline map draped over the shaded-relief image. Each 10-m interval of the isoline map is assigned a unique color to illustrate better the magnitude and location of elevation change relative to the 2003 crater surface. All isoline cells having an elevation difference equal to or greater than 10 m were summed to calculate total volume change. Some of the shaded-relief images, such as that for October 11, 2004 (fig. 4*E*), have triangular facets that portray areas where a

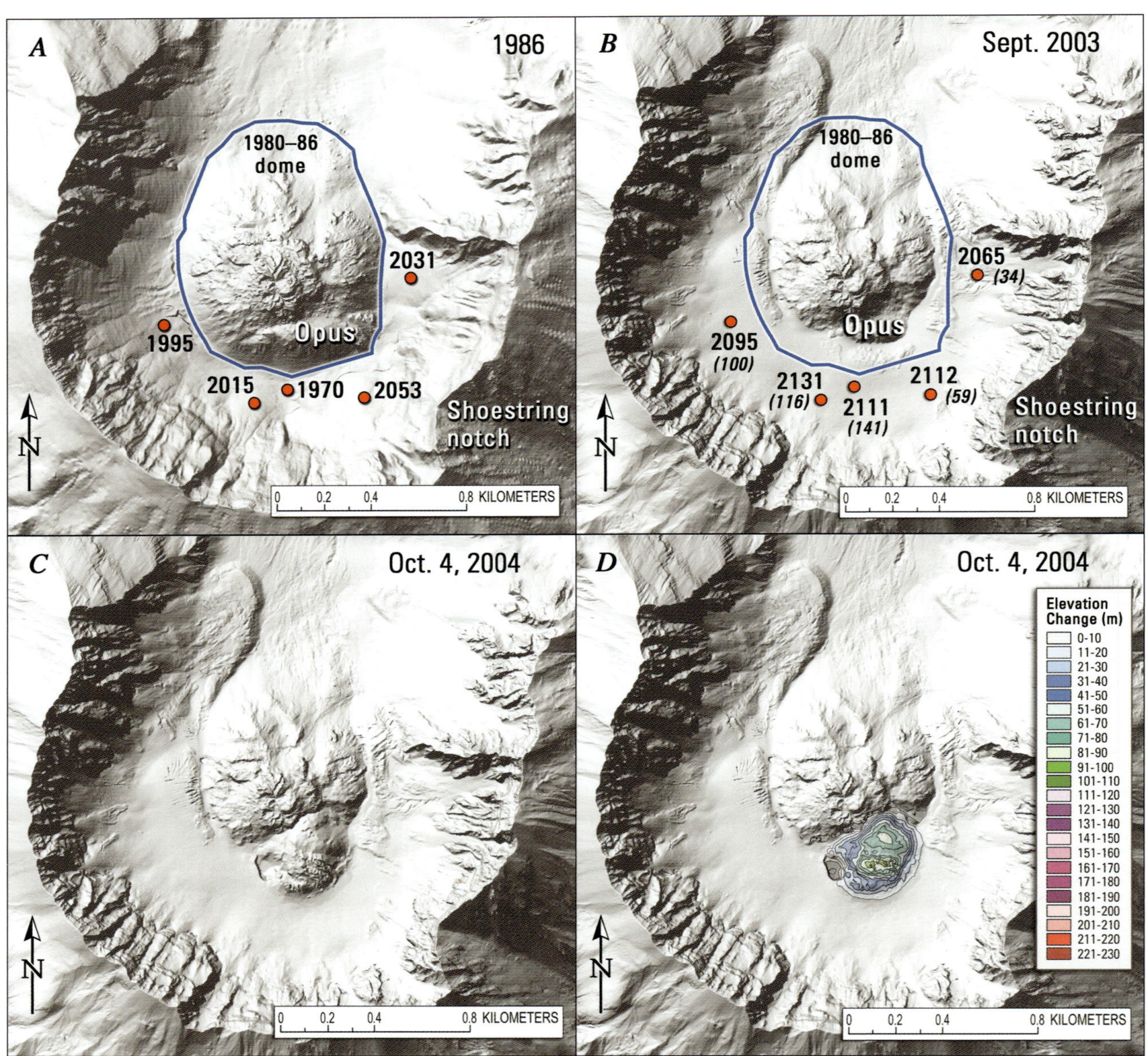

Figure 4. Shaded-relief images showing preeruption crater surface and growth of welt and initial lava extrusion (red outline in *G*). *A*, 1986 and *B*, 2003. Blue line, approximate boundary of 1980s lava dome. Red dots show altitude, in meters, of points on crater floor. Increases (in parentheses) caused by growth of Crater Glacier and deposits eroded from crater walls. Area labeled Opus is part of the 1980s lava dome involved in uplift in late September and early October 2004. *C–H*, sequence of three pairs of images from October 2004. Left image is shaded relief map; right image has 10-m isolines showing topographic changes relative to September 2003 (shown in *B*).

condensed steam plume in the aerial photographs prevented detailed coordinate collection.

Also shown for reference in figure 4 are shaded-relief images of the craterwide datum surfaces from 1986 (fig. 4*A*) and 2003 (fig. 4*B*). The shaded-relief map of the 1986 crater shows the configuration of crater walls, talus fans and other deposits on the crater floor, and the 1980s lava dome. The 2003 shaded-relief map also shows the newly formed glacier, which buries some margins of the 1980s lava dome. Spot altitudes show the magnitude of surface-elevation change from 1986 to 2003.

As the new lava dome grew, questions about the volume of the 1980s lava dome arose. We differenced DEMs to estimate a volume of 92×10^6 m^3 for the 1980s lava dome (Thompson and Schilling, 2007), which is larger than the 74×10^6 m^3 estimate of Swanson and Holcomb (1990) but is in agreement with volume calculations of Mills (1992). The difference in volume estimates may result from (1) differences in measurement methods, (2) exclusion by Swanson and Holcomb (1990) of crater-wall debris that was incorporated into the dome as it grew (Mills, 1992), and (3) different configurations for the base of the lava dome as a horizontal versus sloping surface.

The following discussion of the DEMs focuses on four time intervals and highlights key events related to dome building and deformation of Crater Glacier: (1) Growth of the so-called welt (Dzurisin and others, 2005), south of the 1980s lava dome, and its migration southward in late September and early October 2004 involved uplift of a part of the 1980s lava dome (area labeled Opus on figs. 4*A*, 4*B*),

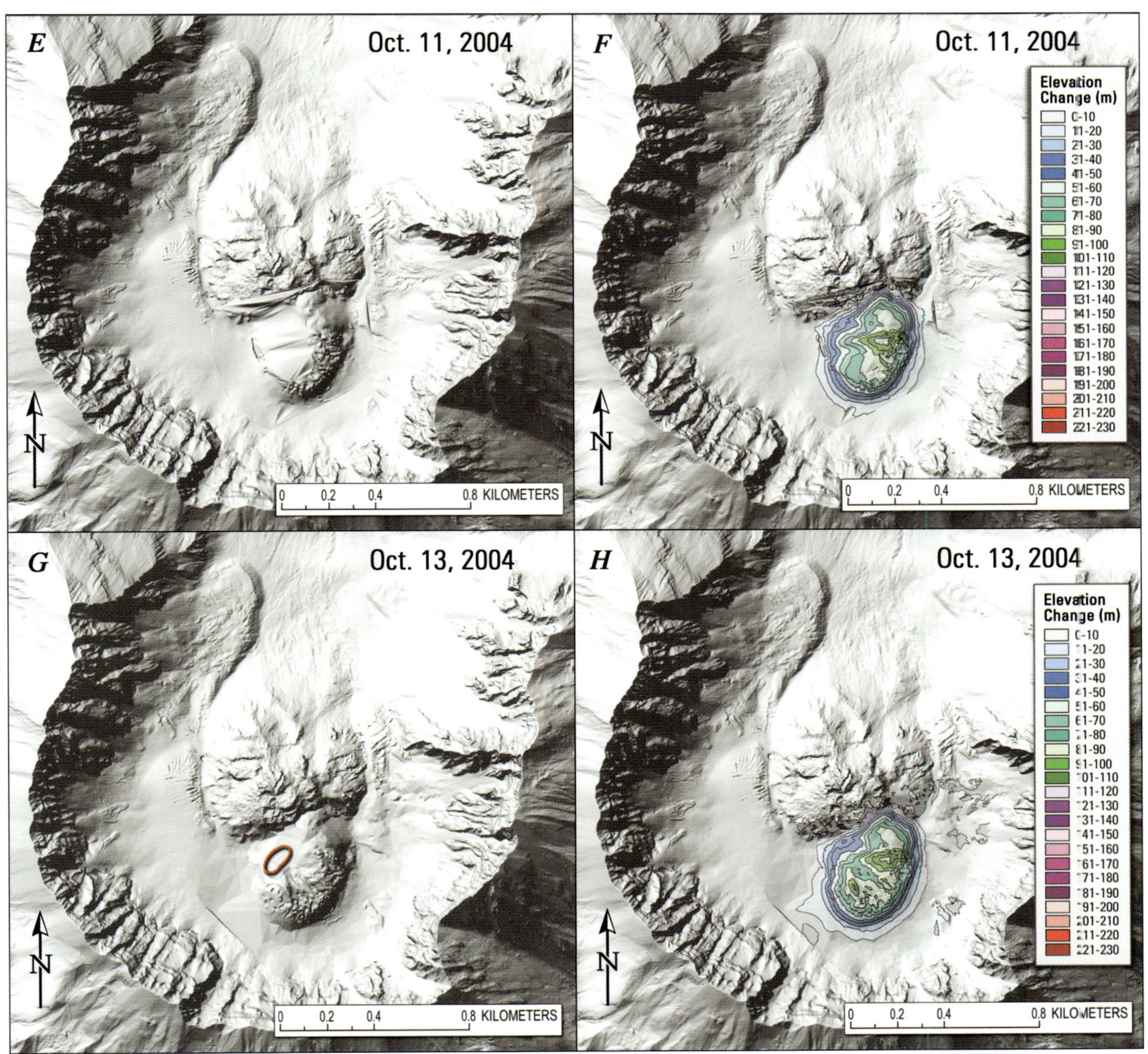

Figure 4—Continued.

crater-floor debris, and glacier ice. Initial lava spines 1 and 2 (see Vallance and others, this volume, chap. 9, for description of the lava-spine numbering scheme) rose through the northern part of the welt near the end of this interval. (2) From late October 2004 through mid-April 2005, extrusion, growth to the south and migration east, and breakup of curvilinear, smooth-surfaced spines 3 and 4, known as whalebacks, drove extraordinary deformation of the east Crater Glacier. The first evidence of lateral movement of the spines came from the DEMs. For example, the extrusion axis, a horizontal line oriented parallel to the direction of extrusion along the approximate center of a whaleback, initially moved southward, then shifted eastward from October 2004 through April 2005 (approximately 4° horizontal rotation of the whaleback axis towards the east occurred between November and December 2004 and about 6° between February and March 2005), as successive whalebacks emerged from the vent area, displacing older parts of the growing dome. (3) Between mid-April and late July 2005, smooth-surfaced spine 5 grew at a much steeper angle than had the previous whalebacks and began a trend toward west-directed movement. (4) In August 2005 spine 6 began to grow and migrate westward, followed by penetration of its eastern part by spine 7 in early October. Both spines moved west, which compressed and thickened west Crater Glacier. For a complete description of the geologic interpretation of dome growth, see Vallance and others (this volume, chap. 9). For a complete description of glacier deformation, refer to Walder and others (this volume, chap. 13).

October 4 Through October 13, 2004

Recognition of the welt (Dzurisin and others, this volume, chap. 14) a few days after seismic unrest began on September 23, 2004 (Moran and others, this volume, chap. 2), prompted efforts to obtain DEMs of the crater. The first group of images (figs. 4*C–H*) shows the remarkably rapid

Figure 5. Photographs of 2004–5 dome. *A*, View of crater after explosion of October 5, 2004. Welt formed of uplifted glacier, crater-floor debris, and southeast part of 1980s lava dome. Light-gray ash covers most of crater. View to west. *B*, Recumbent spine 3 on November 29, 2004, after impinging upon southeast crater wall. Its smooth carapace and leading wave of deformed glacier ice inspired the descriptive term, whaleback. View to southwest. *C*, Crater on February 22, 2005, showing spine 4 flanked by talus and, to left, remains of spine 3. Highly deformed east Crater Glacier prominent in left part of photograph. View to south. *D*, Close-up view about 5 m across of gouge-covered spine 4 extruding from vent, May 12, 2005. Striations parallel the direction of motion. Talus flanking spine is covered by dust from rockfalls and sloughing of gouge on right. View to south.
USGS photographs by S.P. Schilling (*A, C, D*) and S. Konfal (*B*).

Table 1. Total volume change, extruded lava volume, and rates of change during 2004–2005 eruption of Mount St. Helens.

[Extruded lava did not appear at the surface until October 11, 2004. Rates are calculated from the volume changes since the previous measurement.]

Date of photography	Total volume change (x 10^6 m^3)	Total volume change rate (m^3/s)	Extruded lava volume (x 10^6 m^3)	Lava extrusion rate (m^3/s)
10/4/2004	5 [1]	-- [1]	-- [2]	-- [2]
10/11/2004	10	8.9	-- [3]	-- [3]
10/13/2004	11	6.4	0.54 [4]	-- [4]
11/4/2004	20	4.6	12	5.9
11/29/2004	27	3.0	21	4.4
12/11/2004	30	3.4	26	4.1
1/3/2005	35	2.4	31	2.5
2/1/2005	40	1.9	35	1.8
2/21/2005	43	1.8	39	2.4
3/10/2005	45	1.5	42	1.8
4/19/2005	55	3.0	47	1.5
6/15/2005	59	0.8	54	1.4
7/14/2005	59	-0.2	57	1.3
8/10/2005	60	0.4	62	2.0
9/20/2005	62	0.7	67	1.6
10/24/2005	66	1.3	70	0.9
12/15/2005	75	1.9	73	0.7

[1] Volume is the welt, obtained by method of differencing from topographic surface of September 2003. Start date for growth of welt is imprecisely known, so no rate offered.

[2] Eruption has not begun; no extruded lava.

[3] Too steamy to confidently discern limits of new extrusion.

[4] Steamy; extruded lava volume is crude estimate, and no rate is offered.

changes that occurred in 10 days as the welt grew rapidly upward and southward, deforming parts of the 1980s lava dome, crater-floor material, and Crater Glacier (fig. 5*A*). By October 11 the welt had grown to about 425 m in width, 475 m in length, and 105 m in height (2,209 m altitude) above the 2003 glacier surface. (Length of welt and dome is measured along the approximate longest dimension of each shape, and width is measured along a line roughly perpendicular to the length.) The welt attained a volume of $10{\times}10^6$ m^3 (table 1) as lava spine 1 emerged on October 11 (Vallance and others, this volume, chap. 9; Pallister and others, this volume, chap. 30). Presumably the volume of the welt approximated the volume of lava emplaced onto the subglacial crater floor.

November 4, 2004, Through April 19, 2005

Nine image pairs (fig. 6*A–P*) show the sequential growth of lava spines 3 and 4, which shared a similar history in terms of form, growth, and demise. These two striated, gouge-covered, curvilinear, whaleback-shaped spines (figs. 5*B*, 5*C*, 5*D*) grew south-southeast from the vent. The southern ends were pushed eastward over time and broke apart after impinging upon the south crater wall. Both whalebacks were surrounded by talus aprons on the west, south, and east. Initially the disrupted glacier adjacent to the talus aprons formed a crevassed ridge that, in map view, looked like the bow wave of a ship (figs. 6*A*, 6*C*). West of the growing dome, the talus apron, gently flexed ice, and intervening depression formed a relatively stable configuration throughout this period.

The November 29, 2004, image (fig. 6*C*) shows that lava spine 3 had a wide center with tapering ends. It was about 145 m wide, 350 m long, and at its highest point 150 m above the 2003 surface (altitude 2,282 m). The December 11, 2004, image (fig. 6*E*) shows that a longitudinal fracture had formed and broken the whaleback into two parts. By January 3, 2005, prominent longitudinal and oblique transverse, northwest and north-northeast-striking fractures had broken spine 3 into many blocks, presumably as a result of the spine impinging on the south crater wall (Vallance and others, this volume, chap. 9). The resulting $31{\times}10^6$ m^3 dome was about 500 m long by 200 m wide and reached 184 m above the 2003 crater surface (altitude 2,293 m). East Crater Glacier was squeezed between the growing dome and the southeast crater wall (figs. 6*C*–*H*), becoming severely disrupted as it thickened more than 120 m into a conical form by December 11, 2004 (figs. 6*E*, 6*F*). The highest area of disrupted ice shifted about 100 m to the northeast by January 3, 2005 (figs. 6*G*, 6*H*). The west Crater Glacier experienced broad uplift of about 10 m near the 1980s lava dome and near the south crater wall (figs. 6*D*, 6*F*, 6*H*).

A second whaleback (spine 4) began forming in early January 2005 from the severed stump of spine 3. By February 1 it was 145 m wide, 320 m long, and 210 m above the 2003 surface (altitude 2,331 m) (elevation of corresponding point on 2003 surface varies slightly as location of high point of whalebacks changes) (figs. 6*I*, 6*J*). These dimensions are similar to those of spine 3 on November 29, 2004. Spine 4 grew south-southeastward to about 450 m in length, 150 m in width, and 210 m (altitude 2,343 m) above the 2003 surface on March 10, 2005 (figs. 6*M*, 6*N*). As with spine 3, longitudinal fractures cut the southwest edge of spine 4 (fig. 6*M*). In April 2005, longitudinal, northwest-striking fractures and oblique transverse, northeast-striking fractures broke spine 4 as it impinged on the south crater wall, forming rubble and several megablocks (fig. 6*O*).

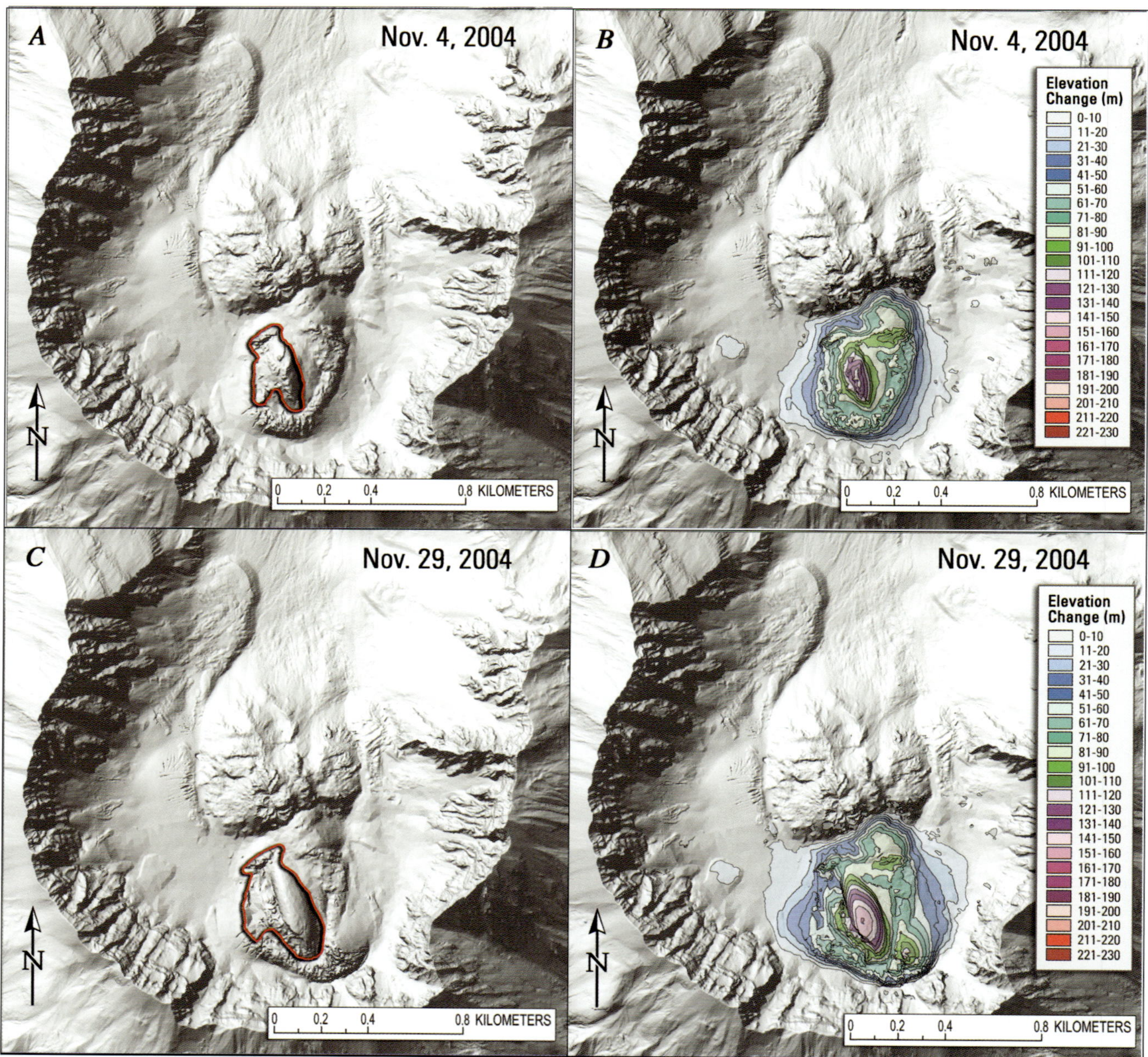

Figure 6. Sequence of eight pairs of shaded-relief images (*A*–*P*) showing growth of lava dome complex (red outline) and deformation of Crater Glacier from November 2004 to April 2005. Arrows (panel I) shows prominent, arcuate step on east Crater Glacier. For full explanation, see figure 3 and text.

The corresponding isoline maps for this time period show the response of the glacier to the growing dome (figs. 6*J*, 6*L*, 6*N*, 6*P*) as an increasing number of en echelon, east-trending, transverse crevasses cut east Crater Glacier. Apparent counterclockwise rotation and thickening of the glacier west of Shoestring notch to more than 110 m above its former surface in 2003 was in response to the dome-glacier margin moving eastward. In March 2005, a second small area of glacier ice had reached a similar height (fig. 6*N*) and, by April, an area about 100 by 50 m had attained a height of more than 120 m above the 2003 surface (fig. 6*P*). Between late February and April, new crevasses oblique and perpendicular to the existing crevasses cut the southern part of the glacier into blocks (fig. 6*O*). A prominent east-west, arcuate, steplike feature (figs. 6*I*–*P*; highlighted by arrows on fig. 6*I*) about 30 m high formed at the glacier surface east of the 1980s lava dome (see discussion in Walder and others, this volume, chap. 13). This ice step was cut by short radial crevasses. The broad thickening of west Crater Glacier continued primarily along the southwest edge of the 1980s lava dome. For example, the 20-m isoline lay about 130 m farther northwest in April than in February (figs. 6*J*, 6*P*).

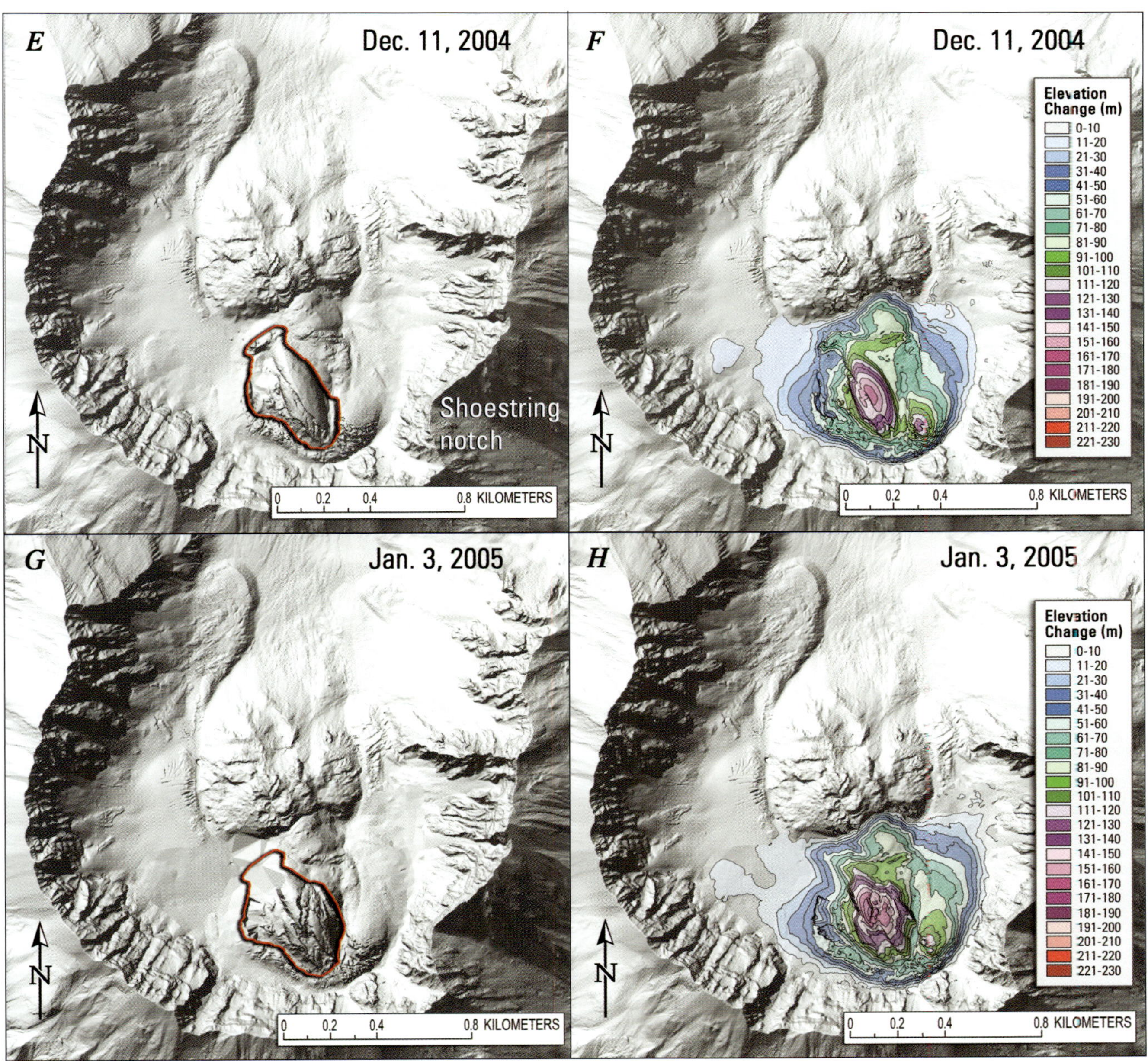

Figure 6—Continued.

June 15 Through August 10, 2005

The third group of image pairs (fig. 7*A–F*) shows that dome growth began to migrate west from its previous locus in the southeastern part of the crater. Though it is obscured in the June image (fig. 7*A*), the July image (fig. 7*C*) shows spine 5 was shorter (145 m in length), narrower (100 m across at the base), and higher (altitude 2,352 m, 250 m above the 2003 glacier surface) than the previous two spines, and it sloped steeply (about 60°) in all directions (see Vallance and others, this volume, chap. 9). Talus filled the substantial trough between west Crater Glacier and the dome that had existed for more than six months, eventually spilling onto the glacier surface. The slope angle of the talus on the northwest part of the new dome was about 32°. In July, spine 5 attained a height of 260 m (altitude 2,368 m) above the 2003 surface—the highest measured so far and within 2 m of the altitude of Shoestring notch, the lowest point on the crater rim. In August the dome was about 700 m in length and 600 m in width, with a volume of 62×10^6 m^3. Throughout the summer, crevasses continued to increase in number, disrupting the east Crater Glacier surface south of the prominent step, and they appeared in the elongate terminus of the glacier for the first time (fig.

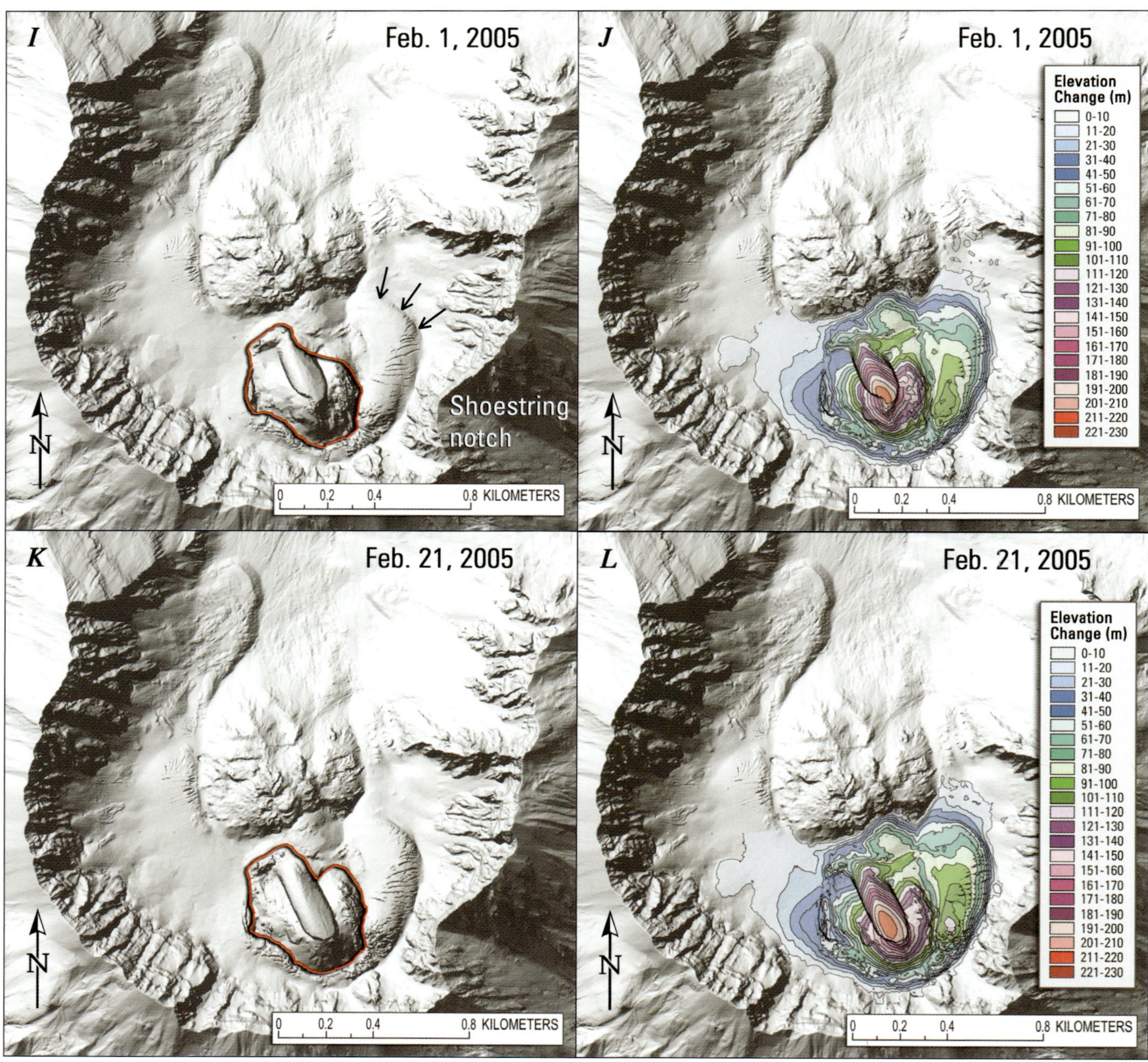

Figure 6—Continued.

7*A–F*). The effect of the northward advance of east Crater Glacier's terminus was to create an island of increased elevation shown by a series of closed isolines (for example, fig. 7*B*) (Walder and others, this volume, chap. 13). The isolines on west Crater Glacier indicate that thickening had slowed. However, subtracting the June 14 glacier surface from the July 15 glacier surface yields a negative change in volume (-1.5×10^6 m^3), likely a result of glacier melting. The west Crater Glacier-dome contact migrated about 60 m west between March and August, and radial and circumferential crevasses formed along the southeastern edge of the west glacier.

September 20 Through December 15, 2005

The fourth group of image pairs, (fig. 8*A–F*) shows that the locus of new dome growth migrated about 200 m west between August 10 and September 20, 2005. Part of spine 5 had decreased in elevation by about 75 m, forming a depression. Between September and December, spines 6 and 7 continued to grow westward, and the depression became a well-defined trough separating the newest growth from earlier spines. Spine 6 is difficult to distinguish within its flanking talus (fig. 8*A*), but it extruded on the northeast end of an elongate, arcuate ridge trending southwest along

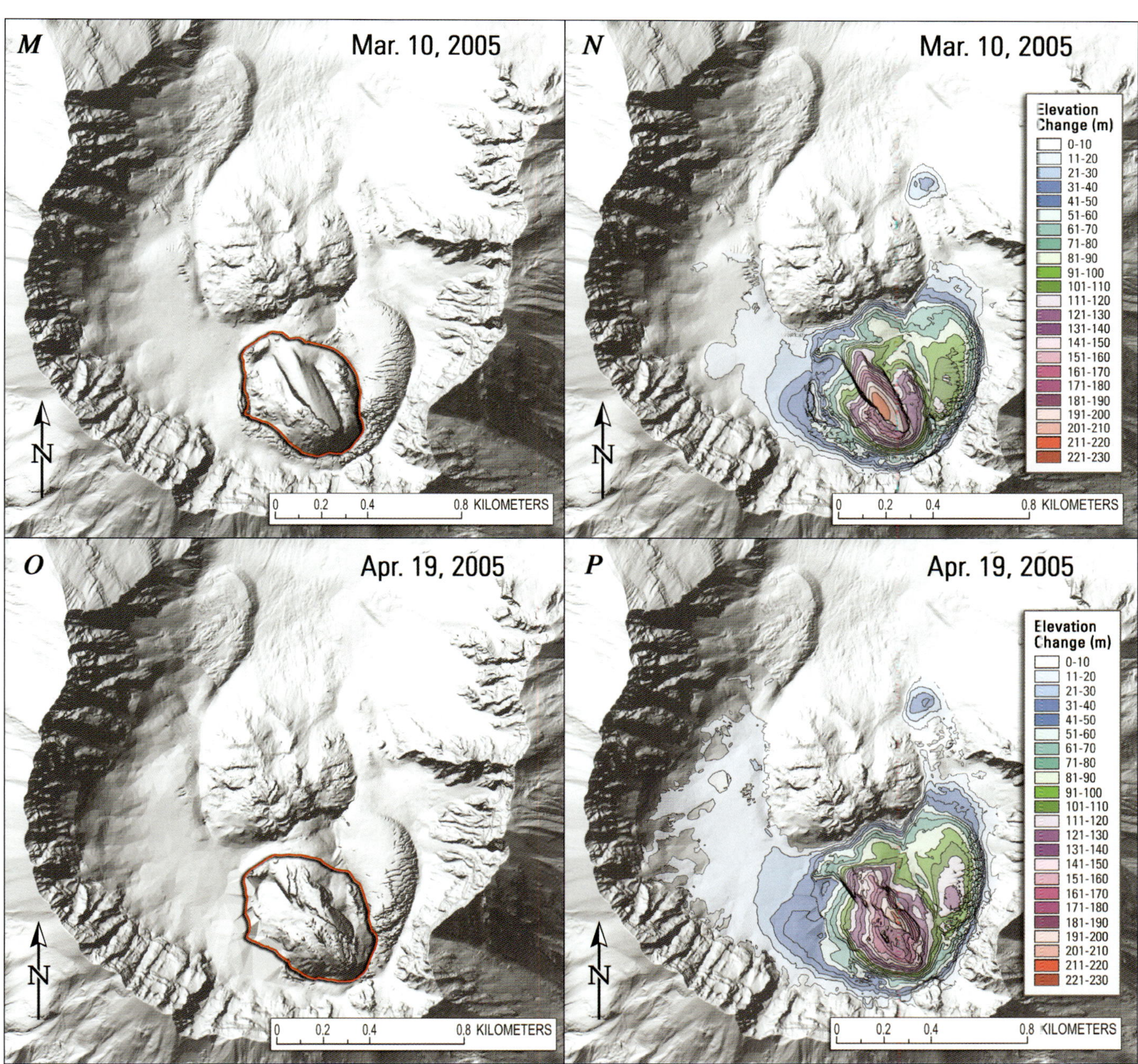

Figure 6—Continued.

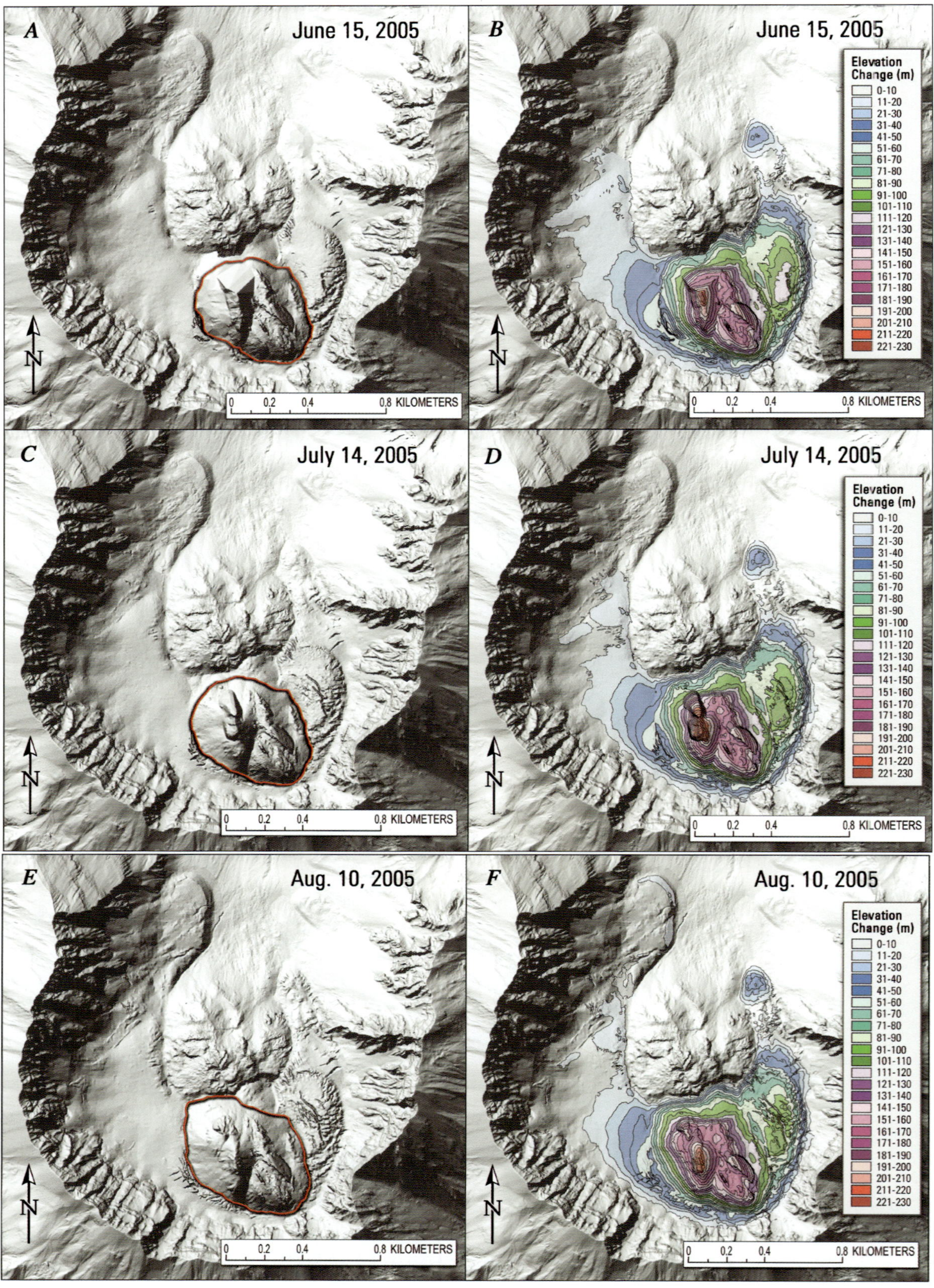

Figure 7. Sequence of three pairs of shaded-relief images (*A–F*) showing growth of lava dome complex (red outline) and deformation of Crater Glacier from June to August 2005. For full explanation, see figure 3 and text.

the top of the talus. In September, this newest part of the dome was about 420 m long, 285 m wide, and about 170 m (2,274 m altitude) above the 2003 glacier surface. By October, the highest point of spine 6 had migrated about 85 m west. Between October and December, spine 7 penetrated the eastern side of spine 6 and extruded upward and westward, bounded by a well-defined, nearly planar, gouge-covered surface striking approximately north-south. The nearly circular mass of talus and spines 6 and 7 was 430 m in length, 425 m in width, and about 180 m (altitude 2,280 m) above the 2003 surface. By December 2005, the entire dome complex was about 900 m long, 625 m wide, and 190 m (altitude 2,316 m) above the 2003 surface. Its volume, 73×10^6 m^3, was nearly equal to the 74×10^6 m^3 volume estimate of erupted lava for the 1980s lava dome (Swanson and Holcomb, 1990). East Crater Glacier was severely disrupted by both crevasses and summer ablation. The west glacier-dome contact migrated about 100 m west between September and December. Large crevasses formed on the west glacier, most likely in response to westward dome growth (Walder and others, this volume, chap. 13). Radial and circumferential crevasses increased in both size and number between September and December until the part of the glacier adjacent to the new dome took on the appearance of the disrupted east glacier. A prominent linear step, similar to the one on the east glacier, had migrated about 100 m north, and a broad area immediately south of the step had risen about 40 m.

Discussion

DEMs constructed from vertical aerial photographs provided an effective means to track and quantify dome growth and to calculate average magma-discharge rates of the 2004–5 lava dome at Mount St. Helens, as well as to gauge deformation of Crater Glacier. The DEMs met commonly identified needs in being (1) accurate—satisfying the appeal for precise, high-quality measurements at growing domes (Newhall and Melson, 1983); (2) safe—"acquired at low risk, and consequently * * * an important element in monitoring future activity of potentially explosive volcanoes" (Moore and Albee, 1981, p. 127); and (3) relatively inexpensive—acquisition costs of vertical aerial photographs and high-resolution scans are about 5 to 10 percent of those of other technologies such as lidar. Below we highlight suggestions for use of this technique at future eruptions, point out how DEMs and extruded-volume and extrusion-rate data were used in other studies, and draw a few brief comparisons between this and other dome-building eruptions.

Importance of Preparation and Suggestions for Improvements

Accurate measurements of the dome and glacier at Mount St. Helens were possible during even the critical earliest part of the 2004–5 eruption because we had baseline data and photogrammetric infrastructure in place before the eruption began. An earlier study of Crater Glacier (Schilling and others, 2004) had (1) identified an experienced photogrammetric contractor that ensured accuracy in camera calibration, film processing and scanning, and critical flight parameters such as altitude; (2) developed skills using aerotriangulation to orient blocks of photogrammetric stereomodels and to collect breaklines and points to create DEM surfaces with minimal operator bias and error; and (3) most importantly, established a network of ground control points on the flanks and crater floor of Mount St. Helens, validated by repeated measurements, with locational accuracy of a few centimeters. Hazards in the crater and uncertainty about the course of the eruption during late September and early October 2004 would have limited our ability to establish ground control. In retrospect, a greater number of control points in the crater area would have been useful, both to replace sites that were destroyed by explosions early in the eruption and to establish a set of points that could be remeasured to evaluate the accuracy of successive DEMs.

We spent days to weeks constructing each detailed DEM presented in this report, but, especially early in the eruption, a two-stage approach would have been advantageous to balance the need for rapid measurements for hazard-assessment purposes versus a greater level of detail for in-depth studies. Initial work would capture the minimal detail needed to obtain preliminary volume and extrusion-rate measurements. Later, as time allowed, we could add greater detail and improve accuracy.

Average Extrusion Rates

Plots of volume through time, whether comparing new crater-surface topography to the relatively uniform 2003 glacier surface (total volume change) or lava-dome volume as defined by the vertical projection of the dome outline to the 1986 crater floor (extruded volume), show that volume increased quickly early in the eruption and more slowly thereafter (fig. 9; table 1). Early in the eruption, measurements of total volume change document the deformation of glacier ice and existing crater floor to form a prominent welt (Dzurisin and others, 2005) having a volume of 10×10^6 m^3 and a growth rate of 8.9 m^3/s before lava first appeared at the surface on October 11, 2004. This volume estimate may be a minimum, because steam obscured some of the vent area. After the appearance of dacite lava at the surface, lava extrusion rates were initially 5.9 m^3/s, slowing to 2.5 m^3/s by the beginning of January 2005. After early 2005, the extrusion rate gradually declined to about 0.7 m^3/s, with a minor increase in rate during late summer 2005, and the total extruded volume gradually increased to 73×10^6 m^3 near the end of 2005.

For much of the eruption, the extruded-lava volume derived from the DEMs was the most appropriate measure of dome growth. However, especially early in the eruption, the unique situation of a lava dome erupting through a glacier required a second method, which included a measure of the total volume of surface deformation. This value was the sum of extruded volume and other surface volume change owing

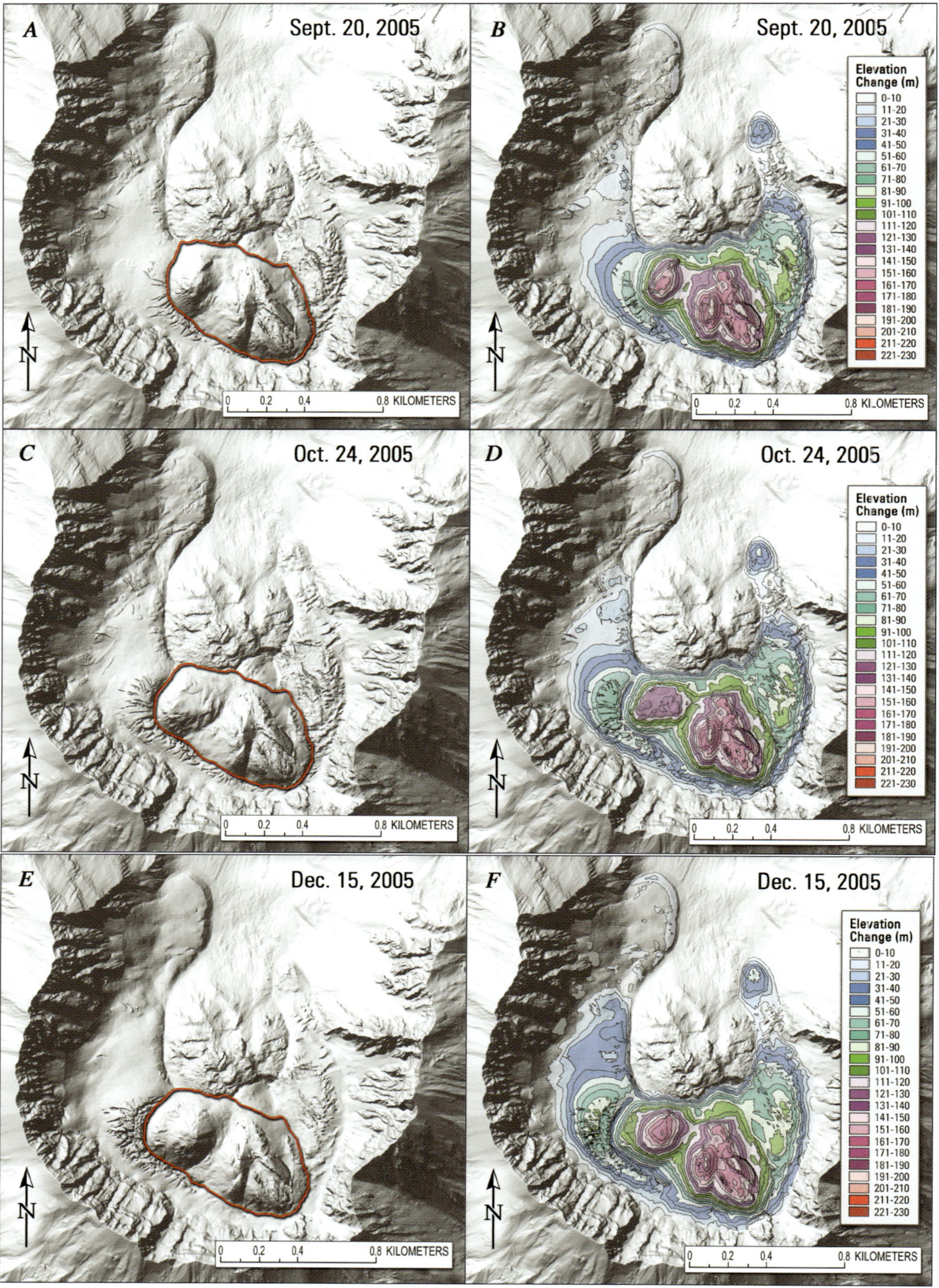

Figure 8. Sequence of three pairs of shaded-relief images (*A*–*F*) showing growth of lava dome complex (red outline) and deformation of Crater Glacier from September to December 2005. For full explanation, see figure 3 and text.

to deformation, snow and ice removal or accumulation, and addition of new talus from the crater walls. As the eruption continued, we used the extruded-lava volume to track dome growth and used the total volume change mainly to track changes in the glacier. Differences between the two rates resulted from factors unrelated to lava extrusion. For example, a prominent increase in the volume change rate in April 2005 (fig. 9*B*) coincided with including a larger part of west Crater Glacier in the April DEM, which resulted in adding more thickened glacier and seasonal snowfall to the total volume. A notable decrease of total volume change during a period of low extrusion rate during the summer of July 2005 likely reflects summer snowmelt and glacier ablation. The apparent slight increase in the extruded-lava rate in August 2005 is likely real.

Use of DEMs and Volume and Extrusion-Rate Data in Studies of the 2004–2005 Eruption

Vertical aerial photographs and the DEMs derived from them constitute one of the most widely used data sets collected during the 2004–5 eruption of Mount St. Helens. Scanned versions of the vertical aerial photographs provided a consistent base for interpretation and construction of photogeologic maps (Herriott and others, this volume, chap. 10). The DEMs provided numerical constraints to solve equations needed to estimate linear extrusion rates from a single remote camera (Major and others, this volume, chap. 12). Coupling the aerial photographic documentation with fields of deformation vectors and profiles of the dome derived from the DEMs yielded evidence to interpret the mechanics of dome growth (Vallance and others, this volume, chap. 9). Measurements and profiles from the DEMs helped to track the remarkable deformation of east and west Crater Glacier and showed that relatively little ice has been melted by dome growth (Walder and others, this volume, chap. 13).

Measurements of dome volume and extrusion rate were combined with other data sets such as seismology, gas geochemistry, and ground deformation to better understand eruptive processes. As the eruption continued, the extrusion rate remained relatively constant, even though the character of seismicity varied, suggesting that earthquakes were controlled more by changes in extrusion mechanics than by changes in extrusion rate (Moran and others, this volume, chap. 2). The

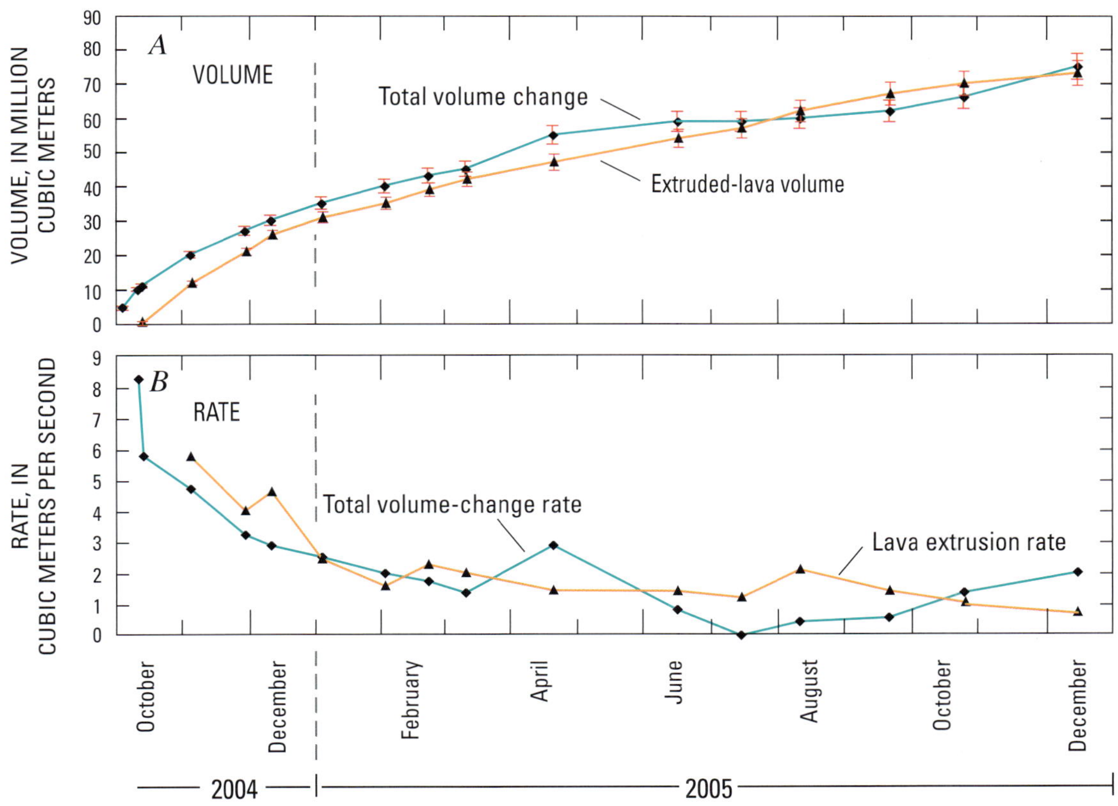

Figure 9. Time-series plots of dome growth at Mount St. Helens from start of eruption through December 2005. *A*, Total volume change (blue line) and extruded-lava volume (orange line) versus time. *B*, Total volume change rate (blue line) and volumetric extrusion rate (orange line) versus time. Early in eruption, all surface deformation likely resulted from extrusion or shallow intrusion of lava into glacier, and total volume change therefore would approximate lava extrusion rate.

nearly constant extrusion rate was also a key observation incorporated into a mechanistic model of extrusion driven by a nearly constant influx of magma from depth and resisted by a plug of solidified magma that slipped incrementally against the walls of the conduit (Iverson and others, 2006; Iverson, this volume, chap. 21). Models from GPS (Lisowski and others, this volume, chap. 15) and InSAR data (Poland and Lu, this volume, chap. 18) yield estimates of reservoir volume loss of 15–30×10^6 m^3, compared with a volume of 70–80×10^6 m^3 for the lava dome. This disparity most likely reflects a combination of expansion of magmatic volatiles and recharge (Mastin and others, this volume, chap. 22). However, erupted volumes and total volatile output for the 2004–5 eruption were used to estimate the volatile content of magma at 8.6-km depth. Gerlach and others (this volume, chap. 26) conclude that the magma was nearly depleted in excess volatiles, suggesting that new gas-rich magma has not been added into the reservoir during the months just before or during the eruption.

Volume measurements of the growing lava dome and derived extrusion rates help to place the 2004–5 eruption in context with those of other dome-building volcanoes (fig. 10) and within the growth history of Mount St. Helens since 1980. The average rate of growth of the current dome, about 2 m^3/s through the end of 2005, is an order of magnitude above the long-term (1980–present) eruption rate of Mount St. Helens (Iverson, this volume, chap. 21). However, when compared to other dome-growth episodes at Mount St. Helens and elsewhere the current growth rate is fairly typical (fig. 10).

Conclusions

Vertical aerial photographs, taken at time intervals ranging from successive days to every few weeks, and the digital elevation models (DEMs) constructed from them have been critical tools to document the remarkable growth history of the 2004–5 lava dome at Mount St. Helens, especially in providing estimates of volume and volumetric extrusion rate. Single DEMs provided length and width measurements of the dome and glacier; sequential DEMs recorded temporal and spatial changes. Moreover, measurements of volume and volumetric extrusion rate proved to be critical parameters. When combined with other primary data sets, they helped to form models and hypotheses that illuminated the mechanics and dynamics of the eruption, and thus helped to assess volcano hazards. The successful application of aerophotogrammetry to monitor this eruption was possible largely because baseline data and photogrammetric infrastructure were in place before the onset of activity. The aerial photos and DEMs obtained in this study are an enduring resource for addressing basic questions about the eruption, including many raised in other papers in this collection and, we suspect, others yet to be asked.

Acknowledgments

We thank Richard Iverson, Richard Herd, and Dan Dzurisin for their insightful and helpful reviews. Dan Dzuri-

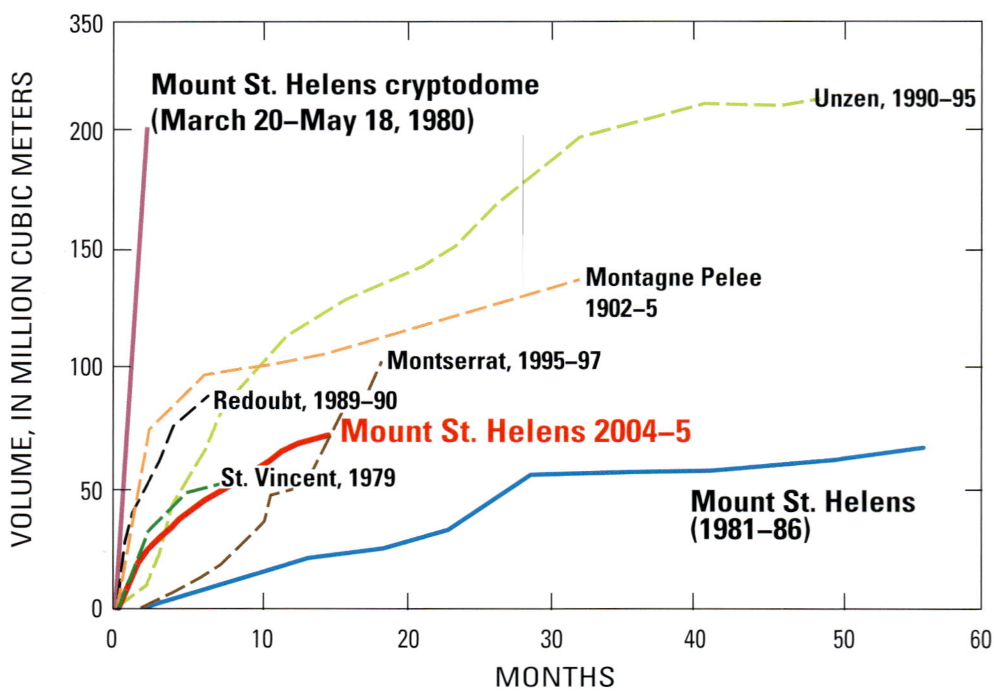

Figure 10. Mount St. Helens 2004–2005 growth rate curve compared with other historical lava domes (modified from Nakada and others, 1999; Tanguy, 2004).

sin also contributed insightful and helpful discussions. Bergman Photographic Services, including Larry and Bruce Bergman, Travis Marshall, Trevor Gray, Steve Tank, Kyla Dorsey, and John Hogl, have all contributed their expertise to ensure that we acquired excellent aerial photographs and scans. We are indebted to Jeff Linscott and the folks at JL Aviation for outstanding helicopter work, especially landing us gently in difficult places on the mountain for ground control work. Frank Trusdell, Mike Poland, Julie Griswold, Chris Harpel, Dave Ramsey, Joel Robinson, Stephanie Konfal, Angie Diefenbach, Sarah Thompson, and Susanne Ettinger helped with ground control work and offered insightful discussions. Last, but perhaps most important, we thank Bobbie Myers, who watched over us remotely, tracked our safety, and allowed us to focus on field tasks.

References Cited

Achilli, V., Baldi, P., Baratin, L., Bonini, C., Ercolani, E., Gandolfi, S., Anzidei, M., and Riguzzi, F., 1998, Digital photogrammetric survey on the island of Vulcano: Acta Vulcanologica, v. 10, no. 1, p. 1–5.

Baldi, P., Bonvalot, S., Briole, P., and Marsella, M., 2000, Digital photogrammetry and kinematic GPS applied to the monitoring of Vulcano Island, Aeolian arc, Italy: Geophysics Journal International, v. 142, no. 3, p. 801–811.

Baldi, P., Fabris, M., Marsella, M., and Monticelli, R., 2005, Monitoring the morphological evolution of the Sciara del Fuoco during the 2002–2003 Stromboli eruption using multi-temporal photogrammetry: ISPRS Journal of Photogrammetry and Remote Sensing, v. 59, no. 4, p. 199–211.

Daniel, C., and Tennant, K., 2001, DEM quality assessment, *in* Maune, D., ed., Digital elevation model technologies and applications; the DEM users manual: Town, Maryland, American Society of Photogrammetry and Remote Sensing, 539 p.

Dzurisin, D., 2003, A comprehensive approach to monitoring volcano deformation as a window on the eruption cycle: Reviews of Geophysics, v. 41, no. 1, 29 p., doi:10.1029/2001RG000107.

Dzurisin, D., Vallance, J.W., Gerlach, T.M., Moran, S.C., and Malone, S.D., 2005, Mount St. Helens reawakens: Eos (American Geophysical Union Transactions), v. 86, no. 3, p. 25, 29.

Dzurisin, D., Lisowski, M., Poland, M.P., Sherrod, D.R., and LaHusen, R.G., 2008, Constraints and conundrums resulting from ground-deformation measurements made during the 2004–2005 dome-building eruption of Mount St. Helens, Washington, chap. 14 *of* Sherrod, D.R., Scott, W.E., and Stauffer, P.H., eds., A volcano rekindled; the renewed eruption of Mount St. Helens, 2004–2006: U.S. Geological Survey Professional Paper 1750 (this volume).

Gerlach, T.M., McGee, K.A., and Doukas, M.P., 2008, Emission rates of CO_2, SO_2, and H_2S, scrubbing, and preeruption excess volatiles at Mount St. Helens, 2004–2005, chap. 26 *of* Sherrod, D.R., Scott, W.E., and Stauffer, P.H., eds., A volcano rekindled; the renewed eruption of Mount St. Helens, 2004–2006: U.S. Geological Survey Professional Paper 1750 (this volume).

Harris, A.J.L., Rose, W.I., and Flynn, L.P., 2003, Temporal trends in lava dome extrusion at Santiaguito 1922–2000: Bulletin of Volcanology, v. 65, p. 77–89.

Herriott, T.M., Sherrod, D.R., Pallister, J.S., and Vallance, J.W., 2008, Photogeologic maps of the 2004–2005 Mount St. Helens eruption, chap. 10 *of* Sherrod, D.R., Scott, W.E., and Stauffer, P.H., eds., A volcano rekindled; the renewed eruption of Mount St. Helens, 2004–2006: U.S. Geological Survey Professional Paper 1750 (this volume).

Iverson, R.M., 2008, Dynamics of seismogenic volcanic extrusion resisted by a solid surface plug, Mount St. Helens, 2004–2005, chap. 21 *of* Sherrod, D.R., Scott, W.E., and Stauffer, P.H., eds., A volcano rekindled; the renewed eruption of Mount St. Helens, 2004–2006: U.S. Geological Survey Professional Paper 1750 (this volume).

Iverson, R.M., Dzurisin, D., Gardner, C.A., Gerlach, T.M., LaHusen, R.G., Lisowski, M., Major, J.J., Malone, S.D., Messerich, J.A., Moran, S.C., Pallister, J.S., Qamar, A.I., Schilling, S.P., and Vallance, J.W., 2006, Dynamics of seismogenic volcanic extrusion at Mount St. Helens in 2004–2005: Nature, v. 444, no. 7118, p. 439–443, doi:10.1038/nature05322.

Lescinsky, D.T., and Fink, J.H., 2000, Lava and ice interaction at stratovolcanoes; use of characteristic features to determine past glacial extents and future volcanic hazards: Journal of Geophysical Research, v. 105, no. B10, p. 23711–23726.

Lisowski, M., Dzurisin, D., Denlinger, R.P., and Iwatsubo, E.Y., 2008, Analysis of GPS-measured deformation associated with the 2004–2006 dome-building eruption of Mount St. Helens, Washington, chap. 15 *of* Sherrod, D.R., Scott, W.E., and Stauffer, P.H., eds., A volcano rekindled; the renewed eruption of Mount St. Helens, 2004–2006: U.S. Geological Survey Professional Paper 1750 (this volume).

Major, J.J., Kingsbury, C.G., Poland, M.P., and LaHusen, R.G., 2008, Extrusion rate of the Mount St. Helens lava dome estimated from terrestrial imagery, November 2004–December 2005, chap. 12 *of* Sherrod, D.R., Scott, W.E., and Stauffer, P.H., eds., A volcano rekindled; the renewed eruption of Mount St. Helens, 2004–2006: U.S. Geological Survey Professional Paper 1750 (this volume).

Mastin, L.G., Roeloffs, E., Beeler, N.M., and Quick, J.E., 2008, Constraints on the size, overpressure, and volatile content of the Mount St. Helens magma system from geodetic and dome-growth measurements during the 2004–2006+ eruption, chap. 22 *of* Sherrod, D.R., Scott, W.E., and Stauffer, P.H., eds., A volcano rekindled; the renewed eruption of Mount St. Helens, 2004–2006: U.S. Geological Survey Professional Paper 1750 (this volume).

Messerich, J.A., Schilling, S.P., and Thompson, R.A., 2008, Digital elevation models of the pre-eruption 2000 crater and 2004–07 dome-building eruption at Mount St. Helens, Washington, U.S.A.: U.S. Geological Survey Open-File Report 2008–1169, 2 p., with digital database. [http://pubs.usgs.gov/of/2008/1169, last accessed July 15, 2008].

Miller, T.P., 1994, Dome growth and destruction during the 1989–1990 eruption of Redoubt Volcano: Journal of Volcanology and Geothermal Research, v. 62, nos. 1–4, p. 197–212.

Mills, H.H., 1992, Post-eruption erosion and deposition in the 1980 crater of Mount St. Helens, Washington, determined from digital maps: Earth Surface Processes and Landforms, v. 17, no. 8, p. 739–754.

Moore, J.G., and Albee, W.C., 1981, Topographic and structural changes, March–July 1980—photogrammetric data, *in* Lipman, P.W., and Mullineaux, D.R., eds,, The 1980 eruptions of Mount St. Helens, Washington: U.S. Geological Survey Professional Paper 1250, p. 123–134.

Moran, S.C., Malone, S.D., Qamar, A.I., Thelen, W.A., Wright, A.K., and Caplan-Auerbach, J., 2008, Seismicity associated with renewed dome building at Mount St. Helens, 2004–2005, chap. 2 *of* Sherrod, D.R., Scott, W.E., and Stauffer, P.H., eds., A volcano rekindled; the renewed eruption of Mount St. Helens, 2004–2006: U.S. Geological Survey Professional Paper 1750 (this volume).

Nakada, S., Shimizu, H., and Ohta, K., 1999, Overview of the 1990–1995 eruption at Unzen Volcano: Journal of Volcanology and Geothermal Research, v. 89, nos. 1–4, p. 1–22, doi:10.1016/S0377-0273(98)00118-8.

Newhall, C.G., and Melson, W.G., 1983, Explosive activity associated with the growth of volcanic domes: Journal of Volcanology and Geothermal Research, v. 17, p. 111–131.

Pallister, J.S., Thornber, C.R., Cashman, K.V., Clynne, M.A., Lowers, H.A., Mandeville, C.W., Brownfield, I.K., and Meeker, G.P., 2008, Petrology of the 2004–2006 Mount St. Helens lava dome—implications for magmatic plumbing and eruption triggering, chap. 30 *of* Sherrod, D.R., Scott, W.E., and Stauffer, P.H., eds., A volcano rekindled; the renewed eruption of Mount St. Helens, 2004–2006: U.S. Geological Survey Professional Paper 1750 (this volume).

Poland, M.P., and Lu, Z., 2008, Radar interferometry observations of surface displacements during pre- and coeruptive periods at Mount St. Helens, Washington, 1992–2005, chap. 18 *of* Sherrod, D.R., Scott, W.E., and Stauffer, P.H., eds., A volcano rekindled; the renewed eruption of Mount St. Helens, 2004–2006: U.S. Geological Survey Professional Paper 1750 (this volume).

Queija, V.R., Stoker, J.M., and Kosovich, J.J., 2005, Recent U.S. Geological Survey applications of Lidar: Photogrammetric Engineering and Remote Sensing, v. 71, no. 1, p. 5–9.

Schilling, S.P., Carrara, P.E., Thompson, R.A., and Iwatsubo, E.Y., 2004, Posteruption glacier development within the crater of Mount St. Helens, Washington, USA: Quaternary Research, v. 61, p. 325–329.

Sparks, R.S.J., Young, S.R., Barclay, J., Calder, E.S., Cole, P., Darroux, B., Davies, M.A., Druitt, T.H., Harford, C., Herd, R., James, M., Lejeune, A.M., Norton, G., Skerrit, G., Stasiuk, M.V., Stevens, N.S., Toothill, J., Wadge, G., and Watts, R., 1998, Magma production and growth of the lava dome of the Soufriere Hills Volcano, Montserrat, West Indies; November 1995 to December 1997: Geophysical Research Letters, v. 25, no. 18, p. 3421–3424.

Swanson, D.A., and Holcomb, R.T., 1990, Regularities in growth of the Mount St. Helens dacite dome, 1980–1986, *in* Fink, J.H., ed., Lava flows and domes, emplacement mechanisms and hazard implications: Berlin, Springer-Verlag, International Association of Volcanology and Chemistry of the Earth's Interior, Proceedings in Volcanology 2, p. 3–24.

Swanson, D.A., Lipman, P.W., Moore, J.G., Heliker, C.C., and Yamashita, K.M., 1981, Geodetic monitoring after the May 18 eruption, *in* Lipman, P.W., and Mullineaux, D.R., eds., The 1980 eruptions of Mount St. Helens, Washington: U.S. Geological Survey Professional Paper 1250, p. 157–168.

Tanguy, J.-C., 2004, Rapid dome growth at Montagne Pelée during the early stages of the 1902–1905 eruption; a reconstruction from Lacroix's data: Bulletin of Volcanology, v. 66, no. 7, p. 615–621, doi:10.1007/s00445-004-0344-z.

Thompson, R.A., and Schilling, S.P., 2007, Photogrammetry, *in* Dzurisin, D., ed., Volcano deformation—geodetic monitoring techniques: Berlin, Springer, Springer-Praxis Books in Geophysical Sciences, p. 195–221.

Vallance, J.W., Schneider, D.J., and Schilling, S.P., 2008, Growth of the 2004–2006 lava-dome complex at Mount St. Helens, Washington, chap. 9 *of* Sherrod, D.R., Scott, W.E., and Stauffer, P.H., eds., A volcano rekindled; the renewed eruption of Mount St. Helens, 2004–2006: U.S. Geological Survey Professional Paper 1750 (this volume).

Walder, J.S., Schilling, S.P., Vallance, J.W., and LaHusen, R.G., 2008, Effects of lava-dome growth on the Crater Glacier of Mount St. Helens, Washington, chap. 13 *of* Sherrod, D.R., Scott, W.E., and Stauffer, P.H., eds., A volcano rekindled; the renewed eruption of Mount St. Helens, 2004–2006: U.S. Geological Survey Professional Paper 1750 (this volume).

Wolf, P.R., and Dewitt, B.A., 2000, Elements of photogrammetry with applications in GIS (3d ed.): Boston, McGraw-Hill, 608 p.

Zilkoski, D.B., Richards, J.H., and Young, G.M., 1992, Special report—results of the general adjustment of the North American Vertical Datum of 1988: Surveying and Land Information Systems, v. 52, p. 133–149.

Zlotnicki, J., Ruegg, J.C., Bachelery, P., and Blum, P.A., 1990, Eruptive mechanism on Piton de la Fournaise volcano associated with the December 4, 1983, and January 18, 1984 eruptions from ground deformation monitoring and photogrammetric surveys: Journal of Volcanology and Geothermal Research, v. 40, no. 3, p. 197–217, doi:10.1016/0377-0273(90)90121-U.

Appendix 1. Hillslope Shaded-Relief Maps

[This appendix appears only in the digital versions of this work—in the DVD that accompanies the printed volume and as a separate file accompanying this chapter on the Web at: http://pubs.usgs.gov/pp/1750.]

The appendix contains 17 raster images in Tagged Image File Format (filename extension is "tif"), one for each of the hillshade relief maps used in figures 4, 6, 7, and 8. The filename contains the date (year-month-day) of the map. Corresponding ASCII world files (filename extension "tfw") for georeferencing the raster maps by GIS software are included, each using the Universal Transverse Mercator projection, zone 10, North American Datum 1983. A separate metadata file summarizes the pertinent details of image processing.

A Volcano Rekindled: The Renewed Eruption of Mount St. Helens, 2004–2006
Edited by David R. Sherrod, William E. Scott, and Peter H. Stauffer
U.S. Geological Survey Professional Paper 1750, 2008

Chapter 9

Growth of the 2004–2006 Lava-Dome Complex at Mount St. Helens, Washington

By James W. Vallance[1], David J. Schneider[2], and Steve P. Schilling[1]

Abstract

The eruption of Mount St. Helens from 2004 to 2006 has comprised extrusion of solid lava spines whose growth patterns were shaped by a large space south of the 1980–86 dome that was occupied by the unique combination of glacial ice, concealed subglacial slopes, the crater walls, and relics of previous spines. The eruption beginning September 2004 can be divided (as of April 2006) into five phases: (1) pre-dome deformation and phreatic activity, (2) initial extrusion of spines, (3) recumbent spine growth and repeated breakup, (4) southward extrusion across previous dome debris, and (5) normal faulting of the phase 4 dome to form a depression, a shift to westward extrusion and overthrusting of earlier phase 5 products. Overall, steady spine extrusion gradually slowed from 6 m^3/s in November 2004 to 0.6 m^3/s in February 2006.

Thermal camera data show that phase 1 activity included low-temperature thermal features, such as fumaroles, fractures, and ground warming related to rapid uplift, as well as deformation in the south moat of the crater. The relatively cold (<160°C) phreatic eruptions of early October heralded activity at a subglacial vent situated along the south-sloping margin of the 1980–86 dome. Thermal infrared imagery, documenting increased heat flow, presaged phase 2 extrusion of the October 11–15, 2004, lava spine. The thermal images of the extruding spine revealed a hot basal margin and highest temperatures of 600–730°C.

During phase 3, a recumbent whaleback-shaped spine with a low-temperature shroud of fault gouge and a hot, U-shaped basal margin extruded. This spine pushed southward along the bed of the glacier until it encountered the south wall of the 1980 crater, whereupon it broke up, decoupled, and regrew. Continued southward growth of the recumbent spine pushed cold deformed rock, hot dome rubble, and glacier ice eastward at a rate of 2 m/d. In April 2005, breakup of the whaleback and growth of a lava spine across previous dome rubble heralded phase 4 spine thrusting over previous spine remnants. During phase 4, the active spine pushed southward with an increasingly vertical component and increasing incidence of large rockfalls. In late July, the spine decoupled from its source, the vent reorganized, and a new spine began to grow westward at right angles to the previous growth direction, defining phase 5. Dome migration again plowed glacier ice out of the way at a rate of about 2 m/d, this time westward. In early October, the spine buckled near the vent and thrust over the previous one. A massive spine monolith had been constructed by December 2005, and growth of spines with increasingly steep slopes characterized activity through April 2006.

The chief near-surface controls on spine extrusion during 2004–6 have been vent location, relict topographic surfaces from the 1980s, and spine remnants emplaced previously during the present eruption. In contrast, glacier ice has had minimal influence on spine growth. Ice as thick as 150 m has prevented formation of marginal angle-of-repose talus fans but has not provided sufficient resistance to stop spine growth or slow it appreciably. Spines initially emerged along a relict south-facing slope as steep as 40° on the 1980s dome. The open space of the moat between that dome and the crater walls permitted initial southward migration of recumbent spines. An initial spine impinged on the opposing slopes of the crater and stopped; in contrast, recumbent whaleback spines of phase 3 impinged on opposing walls of the crater at oblique angles and rotated eastward before breaking up. Once spine remnants occupied all available open space to the south, spines thrust over previous remnants. Finally, with south and east portions of the moat filled, spine growth proceeded westward. Although Crater Glacier had only a small influence on the growing spines, spine growth affected the glacier dramatically, initially dividing it into two arms and then bulldozing it hundreds of meters, first east and then west, and heaping it more than 100 m higher than its original altitude.

[1] U.S. Geological Survey, 1300 SE Cardinal Court, Vancouver, WA 98683

[2] U.S. Geological Survey, Alaska Volcano Observatory, 4200 University Drive, Anchorage, AK 99508

Introduction

Continuous, steady extrusion of gas-poor, solidified dacitic magma through glacier ice has characterized the 2004–6 eruption of Mount St. Helens. Dome emplacement has been influenced by the geometry of the 1980 crater, an amphitheater ~2 km across, 500 m deep, and open to the north (fig. 1). In the exact middle of the amphitheater, the 1980–86 dome grew to a volume of about 77×10^6 m^3, attaining dimensions of 860 by 1,060 m in plan and reaching a height of 270 m above the flat-floored amphitheater (fig. 1*A*) (Swanson and Holcomb, 1990). By fall 2004, the north-facing aspect and steep walls, prolific annual snowfall, and frequent winter avalanches in the 1980 crater had given rise to a rapidly growing glacier, as thick as 150 m and with a volume of about 80×10^6 m^3, that wrapped the 1980s dome like a U (fig. 1*B*) (Schilling and others, 2004).

During initial volcanic unrest between September 23 and October 10, 2004, uplift and deformation along the southern part of the 1980s dome and glaciated areas to the south formed a welt more than 100 m high. Deformation of the 1980–86 dome, crater-floor debris, and glacier ice south of the 1980–86 dome has continued throughout the eruption. However, during subsequent dome growth, the locus of deformation has shifted southward, then alternately eastward and westward, as actively growing spines plowed old rocks, recently emplaced but inactive spines, and glacier ice out of their way (Dzurisin and others, 2005).

Following unrest that began on September 23, 2004, and culminated with phreatic eruptions 8–12 days later, intrusion and extrusion of solid magma has typified the eruption. The magma is unusually gas poor (Gerlach and others, this volume, chap. 26) and crystal rich (Pallister and others, this volume, chap. 30). Several meters of pulverized, variably sintered rock (Cashman and others, this volume, chap. 19) has commonly coated emergent lava spines, lending them a smooth appearance. Other spines have broken apart to become surrounded by hot talus fans.

Terminology used in this paper is as follows. A single lava dome was extruded at Mount St, Helens from 1980 to 1986 and a second from October 11, 2004, through the time of this writing. Because of their solid-state character, individual extrusions of the current dome-building eruption are termed "spines," not lobes. The term "recumbent" implies that the horizontal component of extrusion is greater than the vertical component. The term "whaleback" describes a form of smooth-surfaced recumbent spine. Several spines include upthrusted deformed rock of previous crumbled spines and older rock from the 1980–86 dome. Such spines are termed "compound" following Blake (1990) and distinguished from individual growing spines, which are typically monolithic rather than rubbly.

Spine morphologies of the current eruption are variants of Blake's (1990) upheaved plugs and peléean domes but do not include the more fluid, low lava domes and coulees. As of April 2006, the growing dome has included seven spines (figs. 2, 3) but no surface flowage features or extruded silicic lava flows. Spine shapes have included steeply inclined fins, broken blocky forms, and whalebacks (fig. 2). Four of the spines have grown recumbently, and five of them have pushed through thick glacial ice.

Thermal infrared imagery, petrography, and seismology all suggest that extrusion of these solid spines occurred at temperatures below the rock's solidus temperature. Rock samples that are porphyritic, microlite rich, and glass poor are consistent with subsolidus eruption (Pallister and others, this volume, chap. 30). Shallow seismic signals that locate within about 1 km of the surface and an absence of deeper signals (Moran and others, this volume, chap. 2; Thelen and others, this volume, chap. 4) suggest a possible viscous-to-solid transition of the magma at that depth. The hottest recorded temperatures of the extruding spines, culled from >10,000

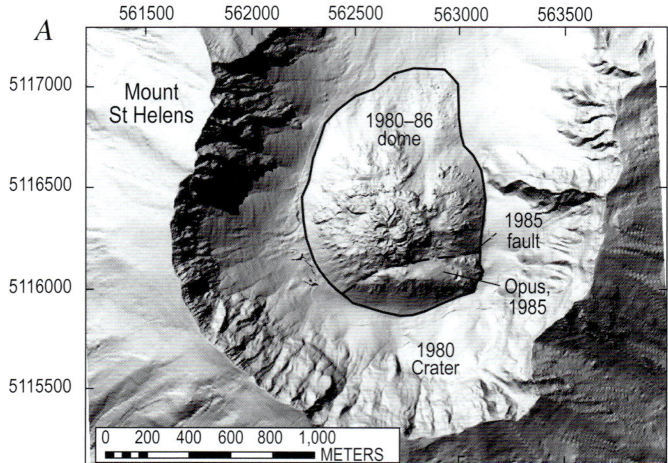

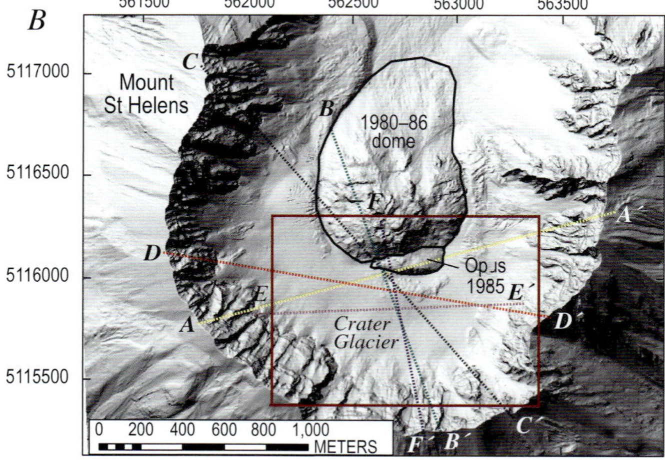

Figure 1. Digital elevation models (DEMs) of Mount St. Helens showing 1980 crater, 1980–86 dome, Opus, and Crater Glacier. Coordinate system is North American Datum 1927 Universal Transverse Mercator, zone 10N, in this and subsequent map figures. *A*, 1986 DEM. *B*, 2003 DEM. Solid rectangle locates DEMs in subsequent figures, and dashed lines locate cross sections illustrated in subsequent figures.

images collected during 37 missions, cluster where cracks and avalanches expose fresh interior surfaces and fall between 700°C and 730°C. These measurements provide a minimum limit for the temperature of extruded spines that is much lower than the solidus temperature of 920–960°C for the dacite of spines 1–7 (Pallister and others, this volume, chap. 30).

The purpose of this report is to document the characteristics of spine growth at Mount St. Helens, the dramatic near-field deformation that accompanied it, and the impact of dome growth on Crater Glacier. To achieve this we examined and analyzed oblique and vertical aerial photography, digital elevation models (DEMs), and thermal infrared imagery. In particular, we used DEMs and aerial photographs to document growth of spines and nearby deformation as a function of time. To illustrate how the dome has grown and how that growth has affected surrounding areas, we generated surface deformation maps and interpretive cross sections. As supporting evidence we considered results reported elsewhere in this volume, such as geologic mapping (Herriott and others, chap. 10), GPS instrumentation (LaHusen and others, chap. 16), and repeat photography from fixed sites (Major and others, chap. 12; Dzursin and others, chap. 14; Poland and others, chap. 11).

Deformation Within the Crater

Methods and Assumptions

During a period of about 18 months, repeated visual observations, oblique aerial photography, thermal infrared imagery, lidar, and high-resolution aerial photography delineated evolution of the 2004–6 dome at Mount St. Helens and deformation of nearby features in response to that growth. Frequent aerial reconnaissance allowed observations and oblique aerial photography as weather permitted. Cascades Volcano Observatory (CVO) staff collected such data almost daily in the period from September 27, 2004, until October 15, 2004. Thereafter, observations were less frequent, with repeat intervals increasing from a few days to as long as eight weeks.

Thermal Infrared Imagery

Thermal infrared (TIR) images allowed estimation of pixel-integrated temperatures for exposed dome-rock surfaces, fumaroles, and other features. More generally TIR surveys showed how surface areas were heated before the appearance of spines at the surface, allowed differentiation of individual spines, showed thermal structures within spines, and revealed how spines evolved and cooled once extruded (fig. 3). We conducted 37 TIR surveys of the deformed area and the growing dome between October 1, 2004, and April 30, 2006.

The instrument used, a FLIR Systems ThermaCAM™ PM595 infrared camera, mounted on a helicopter, is a microbolometer that measures brightness in the 7.5–13 µm waveband to detect temperatures in the range from –40°C to 1,500°C. It collects TIR images as frequently as once per second and can acquire both TIR and standard video (Schneider and others, this volume, chap. 17). Conversions to temperature depend on emissivity, atmospheric temperature, humidity, distance, viewing angle, steam, and gas (Ball and Pinkerton, 2006; Harris and others, 2005). We can independently measure atmospheric temperature, humidity, and distance well enough that resultant errors are about ±10°C; if emissivity is 0.96±0.1, additional errors would be ±5 percent (Schneider and others, this volume, chap. 17). We can only minimize errors owing to the other parameters by repeating measurements at multiple viewing angles and reporting temperature values for conditions with minimal gas and steam. Images from a TIR survey at a distance of about 1 km yield a horizontal field of view of about 210 m and a pixel resolution of about 1.5 m. Integration of brightness within individual pixels means that hottest reported temperatures could be averaged across areas less than 2 m^2 (Schneider and others, this volume, chap. 17).

Repeat Aerial Photographs, Lidar, and DEMs

A sequence of aerial photographs and lidar converted to DEMs provided vertical and planimetric control at intervals of 1 to 55 days during the 18-month study period. Lidar data from November 2003 (Queija and others, 2005) provided initial datum control, and DEMs generated from topographic maps provided control for the 1980 and 1986 surfaces (fig. 1). Three DEMs were derived from lidar surveys made early in the eruption between October 4 and November 20, 2004, (U.S. Geological Survey and National Aeronautics and Space Administration, unpub. data). In addition, Schilling and others (this volume, chap. 8) created 18 DEMs from vertical aerial photography taken between October 4, 2004, and February 9, 2006. The DEMs of October 4 and 13, 2004, (Schilling and others, this volume, chap. 8) provided a check of lidar DEMs collected October 4 and 14.

Identification and Tracking of Features

During the study period, we used aerial photographs and DEMs to identify and track primary and secondary features. Primary features could be located three dimensionally in two or more DEMs and included points at distinctive topographic crests or, less commonly, troughs and intersections of linear features. Examples of point features include distinctive spine formations (for example, fig. 2, point c), megablocks, stranded ice blocks, the toes of avalanches from the 1980 crater walls (fig. 2, points a and i), and seracs. Intersection features include crack networks on the growing dome (fig. 2, point h) and crevasses on Crater Glacier. In many cases, primary features formed of ice and snow persisted only from October 2004 through March 2005. Secondary features are those that we could track approximately in plan view but for which vertical control was difficult or impossible to obtain (fig. 2, features d, e, f, g). Secondary features included margins of actively

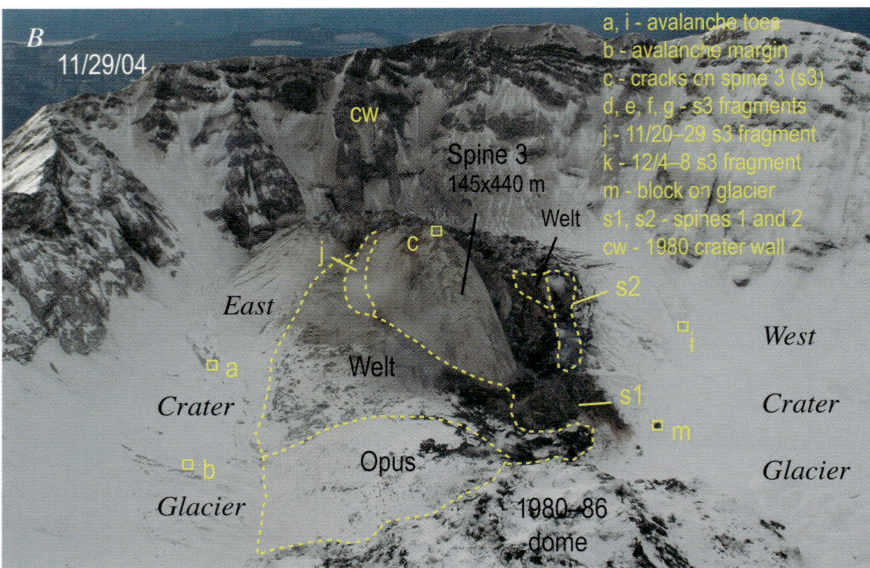

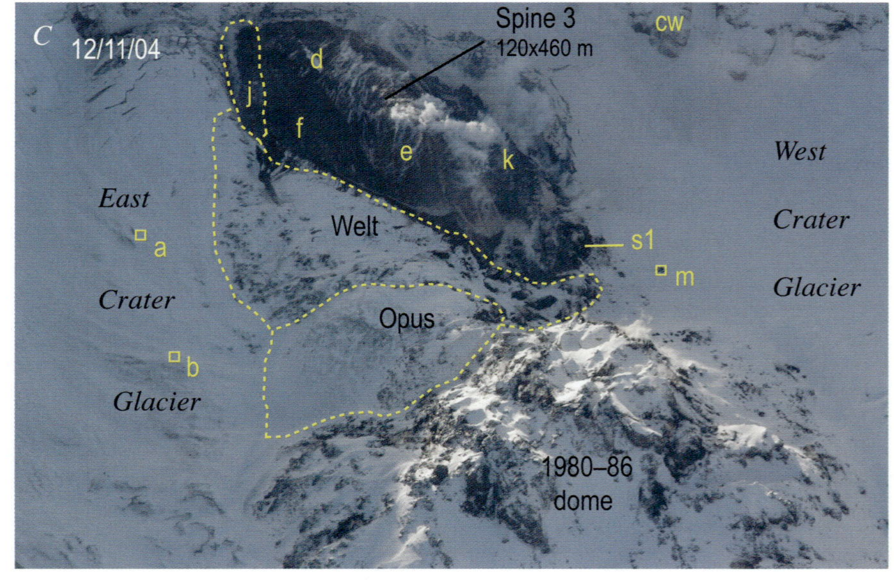

Figure 2. Photographs of Mount St. Helens crater and whaleback-form spines 3 and 4 taken looking south-southwest and illustrating primary and secondary features as they evolved during spine growth and deformation. Features denoted with squares are primary "point" features, and others are secondary features. *A*, November 20, 2004; USGS photo by J.N. Marso. *B*, November 29, 2004; USGS photo by M. Logan. *C*, December 11, 2004; USGS photo by J.S. Pallister. *D*, December 28, 2004; USGS photo by S. Konfal. *E*, January 3, 2005; USGS photo by M. Logan. *F*, January 14, 2005; USGS photo by M. Logan.

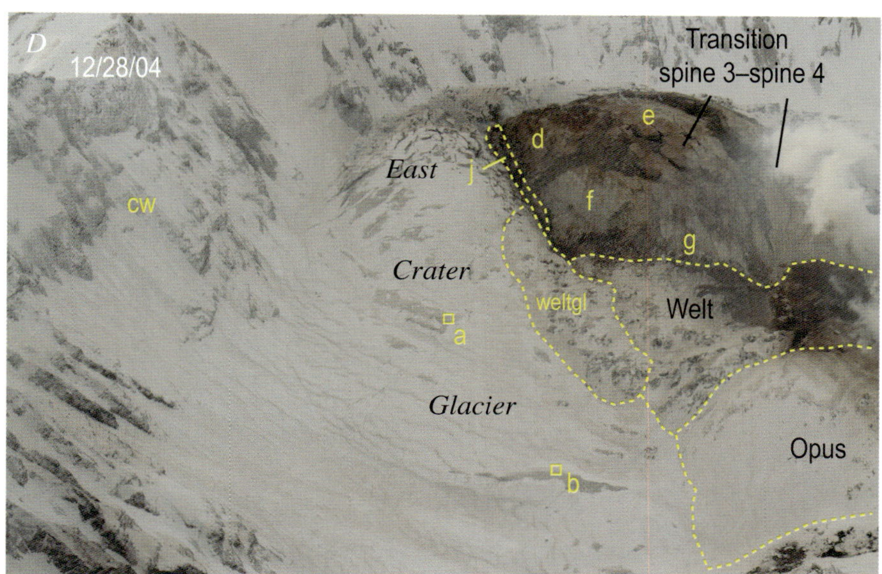

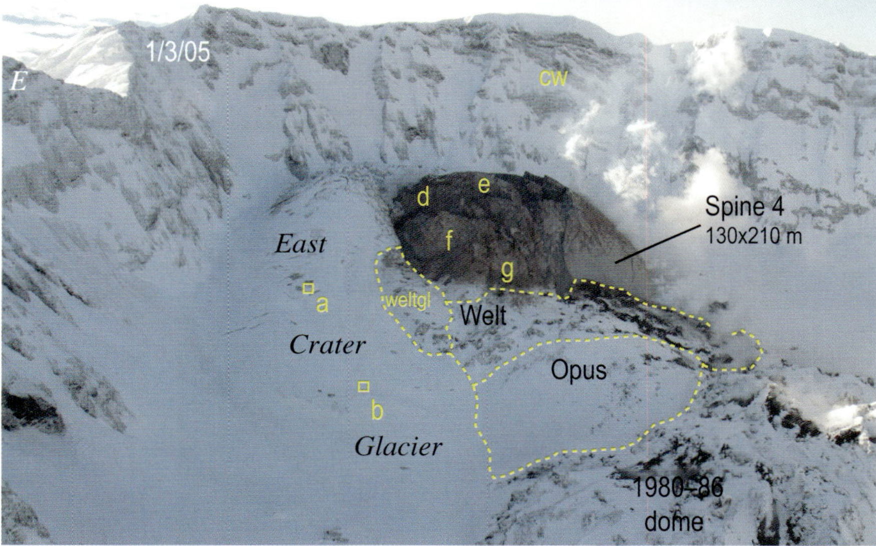

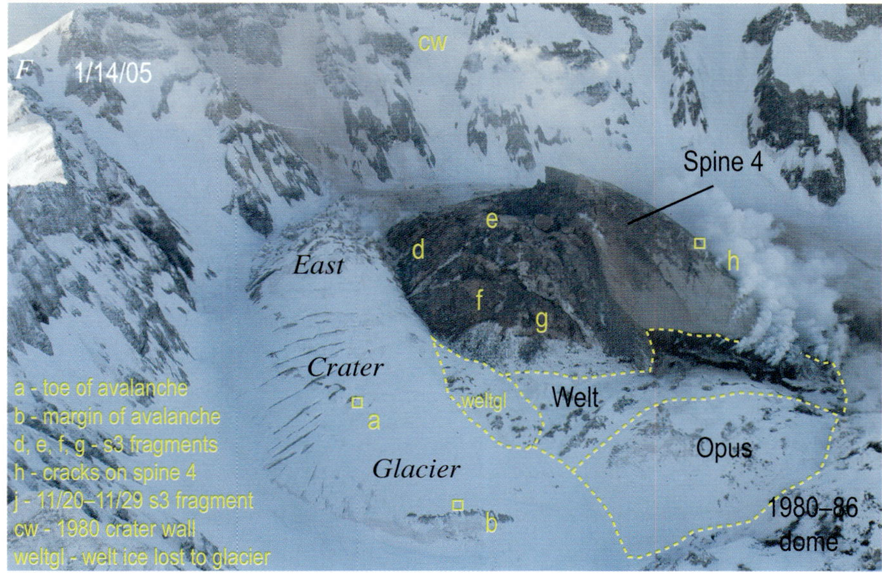

Figure 2—Continued.

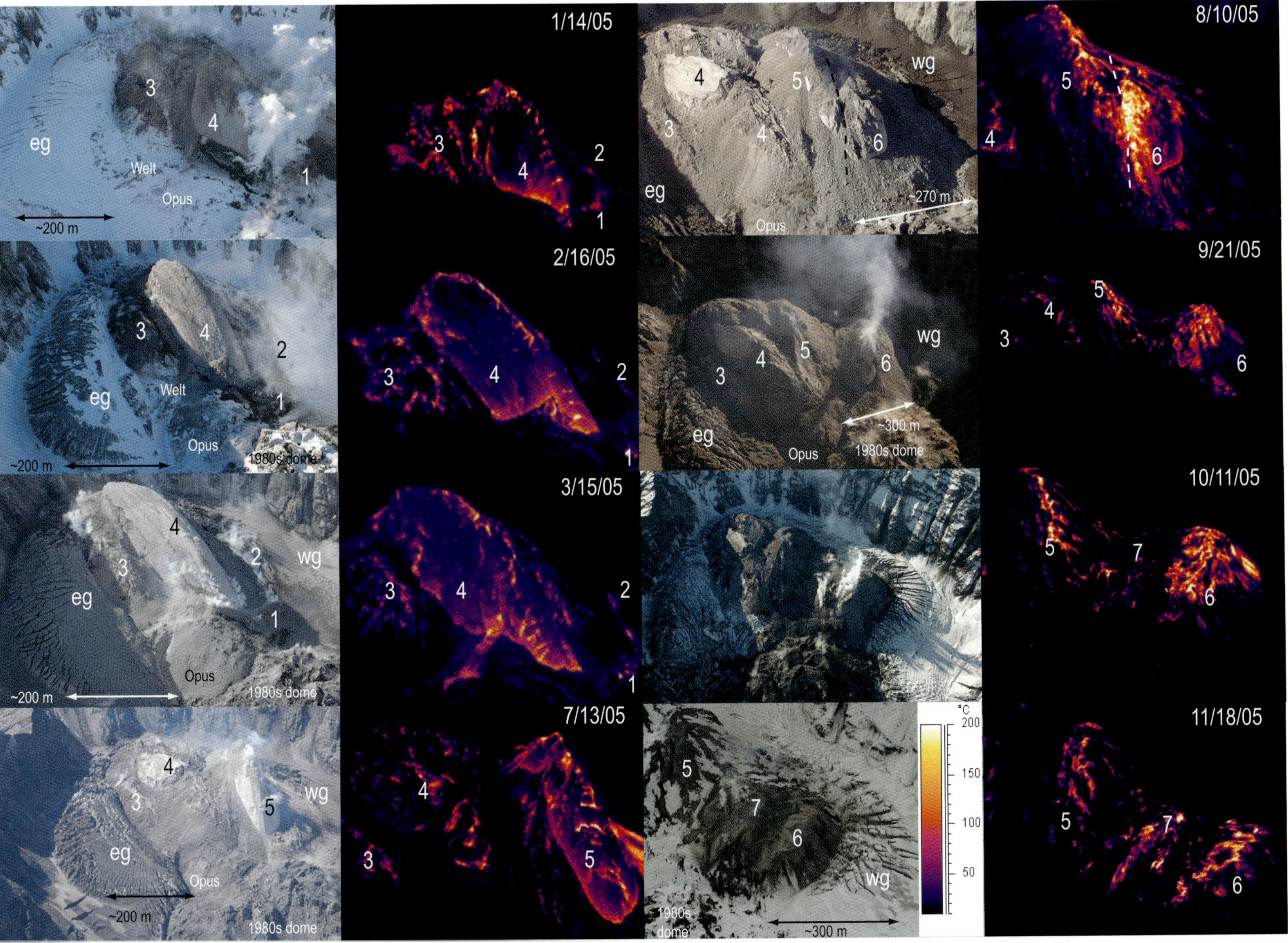

Figure 3. Photograph and thermal-infrared image pairs from Mount St. Helens, views from north-northeast (Jan. 14–Sep. 21, 2005), north (Oct. 11, 2005), and northwest (Nov. 18, 2005), illustrating evolution of the 2004–6 dome. Numbers designate spines 1–7; eg and wg designate east and west Crater Glacier. Dashed line in photograph of Aug. 10, 2005, is trace of fault developing between spines 5 and 6. USGS photos of Jan. 14, March 15, July 11, and Nov. 18, 2005, by J.W. Vallance; those of Feb. 16 and Sep. 21, 2005, by J.W. Ewert; those of Aug. 10 and Oct. 11, 2005, by C.A. Gardner and C. Fox-Lent. Thermal images of Feb. 16 and Sep. 21, 2005, by J.W. Vallance; the remainder by M. Logan.

growing spines, the contact of the 1980–86 dome with the new dome, the contacts of the glacier with the new dome and crater wall, and glacier snouts. Such secondary features provided useful constraints on deformation but could not be used to measure that deformation directly.

Sources of error in locating primary features included accuracy of DEMs, accuracy of repeating a location in a single DEM, identification and location of features in consecutive DEMs, deformation of features with time, melting or addition of snow to features, and misidentification of features in successive DEMs. Precision of DEMs is a few centimeters to about a decimeter (Schilling and others, this volume, chap. 8). On individual DEMs, distinctive features could be relocated to within ±2 m horizontally and ±1 m vertically.

Features were identified and relocated on successive DEMs with some certainty unless the features were obscured by snow, shadows, steam, or clouds or were so deformed during the interval between DEMs as to become difficult to recognize. Fresh snow and ablation may have affected relocation and ultimately even recognition of primary features, but some areas on or near the active dome were windswept or remained warm year-round; features in such areas were not subject to relocation errors related to melting or snowfall. Comparison of relative motion of groups of neighboring objects provided a check on correlations. We eliminated correlations that yielded results greatly at variance with those of neighboring objects.

Generally, error in locating primary features in successive DEMs is between ±2 m and ±5 m in the horizontal and vertical dimensions. Features subject to the most deformation—those on or near the actively growing dome—tend to be those with the greatest errors in relocation. Features away from the locus of deformation may have small absolute location errors but may not move far enough to register significant motion, given the magnitude of error in locating them.

Generation of Surface-Deformation Vectors

Primary features that can be located in two or more successive DEMs allow estimation of vector components from one time to another. This allows calculation of average rates of deformation (for example, points a, b, c, and h in fig. 2). As we know of no systematic source of error in locating primary features, errors should not tend to accumulate for features that can be located in three or more successive DEMs. Repeated locations of primary features indicated in figures by solid arrows thus allow generation of surface-deformation vectors within our stated error limits.

Successive locations of secondary features give a sense of magnitude and direction of deformation but do not yield true vectors. In such cases, the vertical component of deformation may be poorly known or unknown. Despite poor constraints on vertical position, plan-view locations of some secondary features are as accurate as those of primary features. Examples include features located in rectified aerial photographs for which no DEM exists and features that crumble as they move laterally yet still can be identified. Crumbling features are common on or near active spines. Relocations of such features can be accurate in plan; but vertical changes, if given, are minimum values. Relocations of secondary features such as the contact between the glacier and active dome give minimum constraints on deformation in both horizontal and vertical directions.

Vector Fields

Vector fields were derived from simultaneous tracking of numerous primary features on successive DEMs. Vector fields were used to delineate growth of active spines, deformation of inactive parts of the dome and its surroundings, and deformation of the glacier in locations where motion exceeded a threshold of about 4 m in the time between successive DEMs. Because DEMs were produced at intervals of 9–55 days and vertical and horizontal precision were ~5 m, detection limits for time-averaged deformation rates range from 0.6 to 0.09 m/d.

Comparison with GPS Data

During certain intervals, portable GPS receivers that provided nearly continuous measurement of deformation (LaHusen and others, this volume, chap. 16) were located near features tracked during this study using DEMs, thereby providing a check on our results. The GPS deformation measurements compared well with those of this study. For example, a GPS receiver placed on the spine during November 21–29, 2004, gave a vector almost identical in magnitude and direction (10.3 m/d, S. 19° E., up 6°) to that of a nearby feature 30 m east that we tracked November 20–29 (10.4 m/d, S. 21° E., up 8°).

Our deformation measurements have advantages and disadvantages compared with those derived from GPS receivers. The chief advantage of our approach is that we can track numerous features simultaneously and thus obtain a complete picture of dome growth and nearby deformation patterns. GPS sensors are advantageous in that their data streams can be sampled frequently and transmitted back to the observatory. Such real-time acquisition permits the use of GPS data in monitoring. In contrast, our measurements are values averaged over intervals between successive DEMs and have no application in real-time monitoring because of the additional time required to prepare DEMs.

Volume and Flux Calculations

All reported volumes assume the 1986 topographic surface as a datum and subtract it from DEMs of various dates over pertinent areas (hot-rock volumes given in Schilling and others, this volume, chap. 8). Because thick glacial ice overlay the 1986 debris fill of the moat by 2004, we chose the 1986 surface as a datum for volume calculations rather than the more recent ice-mantled surface of 2003–4. To facilitate calculations, we assumed that bounding surfaces between the datum and the areal extent of hot rock on any subsequent DEM were vertical. The assumption of vertical bounding surfaces dictates that calculated volumes are minimum values in cases where natural surfaces differ substantially from vertical. A steep, near-vertical contact between the extruding dome and glacier ice is probably a reasonable assumption for two reasons. First, visible upper parts of glacier contacts with hot rock were steep and nearly vertical. Second, relict ice-hot rock contacts exposed in other volcanic areas are commonly nearly vertical because the ice cools and buttresses the rock margin, preventing avalanches and rockfall that tend to form slopes more closely approaching the angle of repose.

Time-averaged volumetric extrusion rates for individual spines are derived by comparing volumes from one DEM to the next and dividing by the time between them. In many cases, volumetric rates are the same as the hot-rock extrusion rates of Schilling and others (this volume, chap. 8). Well-constrained growth intervals of certain spines allow more precise calculation of their volumetric extrusion rates.

Cross Sections

Cross sections were constructed from DEMs sampled at horizontal intervals of 10 m, are presented with no vertical exaggeration, and include both simple representations of successive surfaces and interpretive relations among units at depth. Our guiding philosophy in the construction of cross sections was not to extend geologic interpretation below levels for which we have no constraints. Therefore none is extended below our lowermost control surface, that of summer 1980.

Phases of Dome Growth at Mount St. Helens

Between the onset of unrest on September 23, 2004, and April 2006, the eruption developed in a manner that is divisible into five distinct phases, each with characteristic rate and pattern of eruption (table 1). An initial brief vent-clearing phase included seismic unrest, spectacular deformation features, and phreatic explosions developed in the moat between the 1980s dome and the 1980 crater walls. Initial spine extrusion began October 11, 2004. As extrusion continued, the locus of spine growth shifted, spines grew and stagnated, and new ones formed in their stead (table 1). As of April 2006, a total of seven discrete spines have erupted that we have grouped on the basis of similar growth patterns into four additional phases (table 1).

Phase 1, Precursory Vent Clearing, September 23–October 10, 2004: Phreatic Explosions and Deformation

The first indications of an impending eruption included a week of intensifying seismicity beginning September 23, 2004, deformation-induced surficial cracks in glacier ice south of the 1980–86 dome that began to appear by September 29 (Dzursin and others, this volume, chap. 14), and four phreatic explosions between October 1 and 5 (Moran and others, this volume, chap. 6). The phreatic explosions formed a vent at the west edge of deformed ice. Thermal IR images show that the explosions of early October had temperatures of no more than 160°C (Schneider and others, this volume, chap. 17). On the basis of these low temperatures, we infer that the explosions were phreatic rather than magmatic. However, the explosions did indicate interaction of hot rock with the shallow hydrothermal system, thus suggesting rise of magma to near the surface.

During early October, a zone of highly fractured ice developed and expanded southward as subsurface intrusion fractured and thrust the part of the 1980–86 dome called Opus, which had formed in 1985, and adjacent crater-floor debris upward to form a feature named "the welt" (fig. 4). This shallow intrusion of magma caused surface uplift in excess of 70 m (figs. 5, 6). Uplift was greatest along a north-south axis about 200 m east of the October vent (fig. 5) and diminished rapidly away from that axis.

The welt expanded southward, but motion of recognizable features through October 4 was upward and northward along a reverse fault with a strike of ~N. 80° E. and located between Opus and the remainder of the 1980–86 dome to the north (fig. 5). This faulting apparently reactivated a normal fault of 1985 that bounded the north margin of the Opus feature (fig. 1*A*). Surface deformation vectors south of the fault trace show motion of 25–30 m north and 50–70 m up. If deformation indicated motion along the fault, then its dip was ~60° south.

During October 4–14 the locus of deformation migrated south from Opus, and the sense of motion at the surface was radial, away from the most intense deformation. Motion on Opus was undetectable to barely detectable at ~5 m east and up (figs. 5, 6). On glacier surfaces, ballistic impact sites and distinctive avalanche toes near the periphery of the welt moved 5–15 m away from the welt (southwest to east) and up (fig. 5). The few traceable points on the eastern and central parts of the actively deforming welt moved 30–80 m eastward away from the axis of the welt (fig. 5).

The DEMs of October 13 and 14 recorded displacement in the range of 5–30 m along the surface of the expanding welt (fig. 5). Points along the deformation axis, which coincided with the axis of spine 3 when it later emerged in November, moved 15–30 m S. 10° E. along the axis and rose 6–8 m in one day. Nearby features to the east moved laterally 12–15 m S. 20° E. to S. 45° E., with little vertical motion. Features on fractured ice to the east also moved away from the growing welt, whereas those on Opus showed no detectable motion.

Phase 2, October 11–24, 2004: Spines 1 and 2

Initial Spine Growth

Spines 1 and 2 each extruded rapidly within a few days and thereafter remained inactive, though each was affected

Table 1. Timing, extrusion rates, character of dome growth, deformation within crater, and impact on glacier during each of five eruptive phases from September 2004 to April 2006, Mount St. Helens, Washington.

[Estimates of extrusion rates are derived from comparing DEMs from one date to the next (Schilling and others, this volume, chap. 8; and this chapter). Estimates of linear advance are obtained from tracking features in DEMs or aerial photographs (this chapter), from repeat photos from fixed positions (Major and others, this volume, chap. 12), and from portable GPS stations (LaHusen and others, this volume, chap. 16).]

Phase	Spine	Time period	Growth rate	Nature of eruptive activity	Deformation within 1980 crater	Effect on glacier
1—Precursory vent clearing	Pre-dome	Sept. 23 –Oct. 10, 2004	Not applicable	Vent clearing and phreatic explosions. Ascent of solid spine to surface.	Uplift of 1980–86 dome, and crater floor to north of 1980–86 dome to form welt. By Oct. 4, 2004, total volume of deformed area (welt) is ~5×10^6 m^3.	Disruption and uplift of Crater Glacier.
2—Initial spines	Spine 1	Oct. 11–15, 2004	2–3 m^3/s; 15–20 m/d	Near-vertical spine growth.	Continuing uplift of crater floor to south of 1980s dome; Volume of deformed welt increases, 5×10^6–11×10^6 m^3, Oct. 4–13, 2004.	Continuing uplift and disruption of glacier but no appreciable melting.
	Spine 2	Oct. 15–~Oct. 24, 2004	3 m^3/s; 25 m/d	Advance of spine 2 to the south; probable subterranean and subglacial intrusion of spine 3.	Locus of deformation shifts southward and eastward; formation of roof pendant over intruding spine.	
3—Recumbent growth of whaleback spines	Spine 3	Oct. 25–Dec. 18, 2004	4–6 m^3/s; 8–11 m/d	Recumbent growth of spine 3 toward south crater wall; spine 3 begins pushing against south crater wall ~Nov. 12, 2004.	Emerging spine displaces older rocks to east and south; roof pendant is transported to south end of spine 3; spine 2 subsides.	Growth of spine 3 divides Crater Glacier into east and west arms Spines 3 and 4 plow east Crater Glacier eastward and thereby thicken it as much as 100 m; crevasses form parallel to maximum principal-strain direction (~east–west) but no appreciable melting.
	Transition	Dec. 18, 2004–Jan. 3, 2005	No data	Spine 3 deflects off south crater wall, fractures, breaks up, and decouples from source.		
	Spine 4	Jan. 3–Apr. 9, 2005	1.5–2.5 m^3/s; 5–8 m/d	Continuing extrusion forms spine 4, which continues pushing to the south.	Southward growth of spine 4 tilts and pushes spine 3 to east; deformed 1980–86 debris migrates eastward; remnants of spines 1–3 to west are static	
4—Spine thrusts over previous spines	Transition	Apr. 10–19, 2005	No data	Spine 4 encounters south crater wall, fractures, and decouples from source.		East Crater Glacier deformation slows, then stops; glacier responds to thickening caused by previous deformation by accelerating downslope to north. West Crater Glacier is pushed west.
	Spine 5	Apr. 19-July 18, 2005	1–1.5 m^3/s; 3–6 m/d	Spine 5 thrusts over spine remnants west of spine 4. Smooth surface forms at north end of spine and gradually steepens. In June, spine fractures to the south and disintegrates.	Deformation to east is greatest near vent and diminishes south. This deformation slows and stops. Deformation to west is moderate and continual. Rockfall from spine 5 buries spine 2, then 1.	
		July 19–31, 2005		Spine 5 crumbles to feed rockfall avalanches and slumping events.		
5—Spines grow to west, then thrust over one another	Transition	Aug. 1–5, 2005	No data	Spine 5 fractures near its source and begins to slump.		West Crater Glacier thickens and cracks owing to westward migration of spines 6 and 7; cracks radiate westward along maximum principal-strain axes.
	Spine 6	Aug. 6– Oct. 9, 2005	1.5–2 m^3/s; 3–4 m/d	Sag depression grows owing to slumping of spine 5 and westward migration of spine 6; spine growth is chiefly recumbent and endogenous.	Deformation to west; east part of 2004–5 dome complex is stagnant.	
	Spine 7	Oct. 9, 2005 –Apr. 2006	0.5–1 m^3/s; 1–2 m/d	Endogenous growth followed by exogenous spine growth in depression.	Spine 7 pushes spine 6 to west and begins thrusting over elements both of itself and of spine 6.	

Figure 4. View of Mount St. Helens crater from north-northeast on October 10, 2004, illustrating welt, Opus, 1980–86 dome, crater wall, and Crater Glacier. USGS photo by R. Wessels.

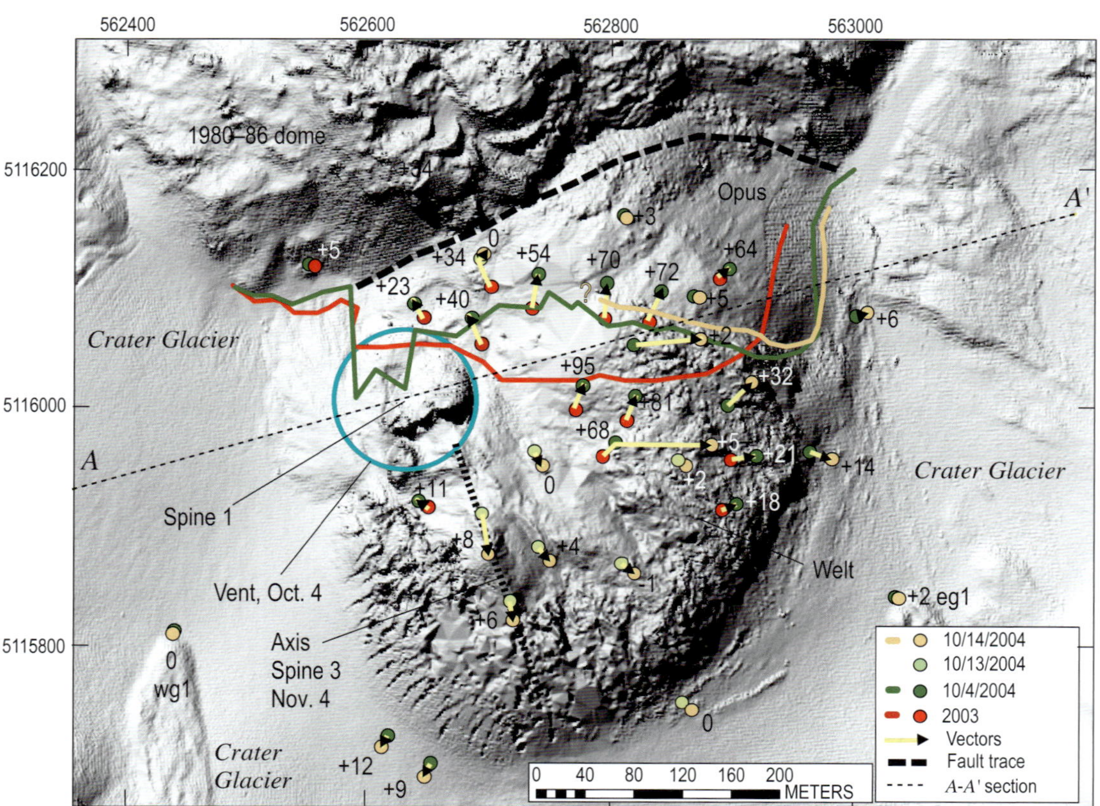

Figure 5. DEM of October 14, 2004, locating vent of October 4, 2004, and illustrating initial extrusion of spine 1 and locations of welt, Opus, 1980–86 dome, Crater Glacier, and cross section *A–A´* shown in figure 6. Dots indicate features tracked, and solid lines indicate changes in fractured ice margin for dates identified by color in key. Arrows show surface deformation vectors; numbers show vertical component of vectors in meters.

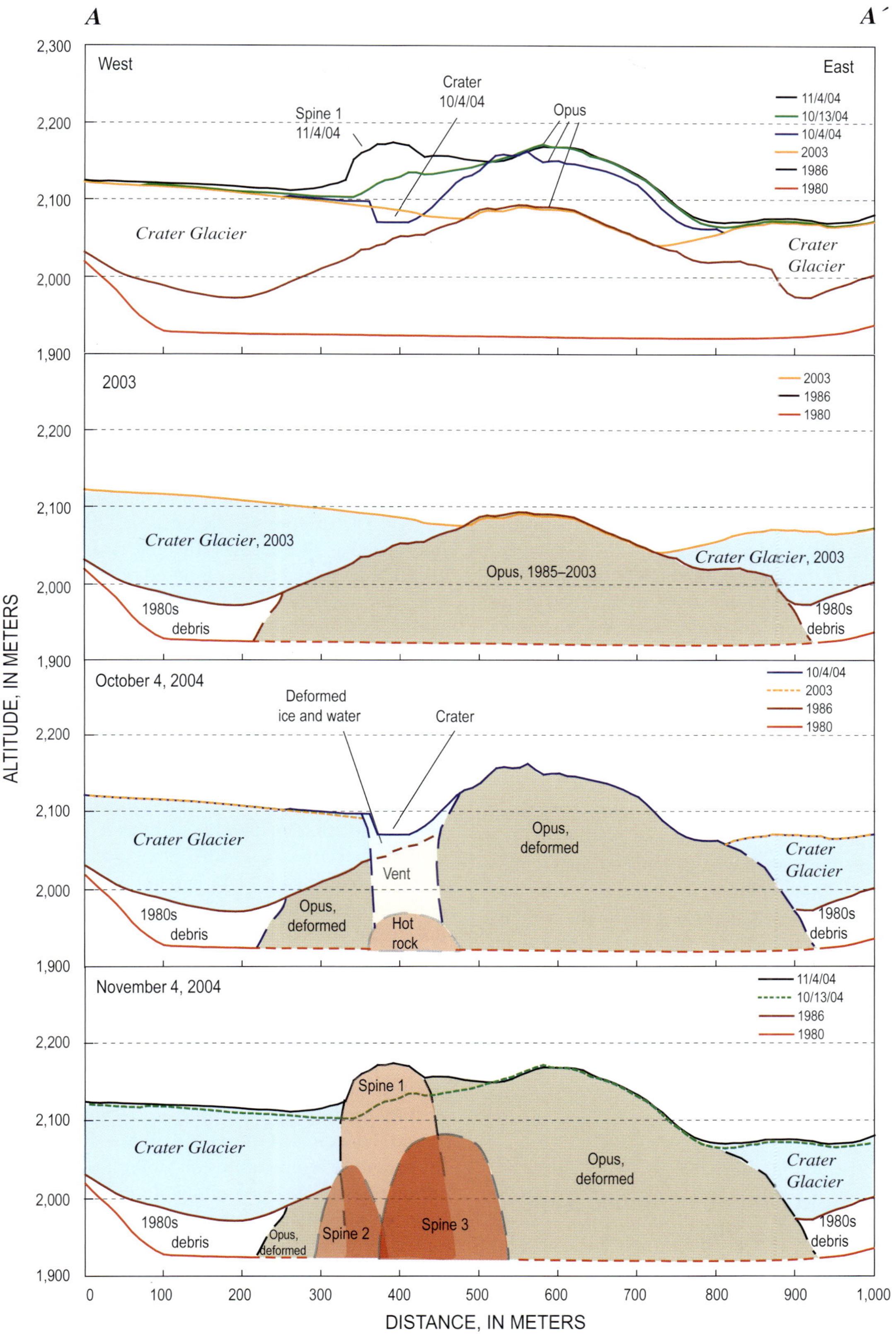

Figure 6. Cross section $A–A'$ (location shown in figure 5) illustrating extrusion of spine 1, intrusion of spines 2 and 3, and deformation of Opus and glacial ice. Top panel shows known profiles for the dates given, and other panels illustrate geologic interpretations on given dates.

subsequently by deformation and eventual burial. Warming at the surface of the welt to as much as 50°C on October 10, 2004, presaged the appearance of juvenile rock above ground on October 11 (Schneider and others, this volume, chap. 17). Spine 1 extruded from October 11 to 15. Owing to poor weather, the timing of spine 2 emplacement is less well constrained. Observations and study of oblique photographs showed that its growth began after October 15 and finished by October 24.

Spine 1 grew at a steep angle as a solid blocky slab from a south-facing slope on the west part of Opus. By October 14, it was 85×60 m, ~60 m high, dipping 50° northwest, and had volume of $\sim 0.6 \times 10^6$ m^3 (table 2, fig. 6). Using the outline of spine 1 on the DEM of November 4, we calculate that the total volume of spine 1 was then $\sim 0.9 \times 10^6$ m^3. Spine 1 extruded rapidly, 15–20 m/d and 2–3 m^3/s (table 2).

Although observations between October 15 and 24 were insufficient to delineate the nature of spine 2's growth directly, it emerged just south of spine 1 and appeared at the surface from north to south as though the deformed glacier ice from which it emerged had unzipped rapidly southward. It emanated from the October 4 vent (figs. 5, 7) and moved southward along subglacial slopes to form an elongate body oriented north–south at the surface (table 2). Its growth ceased when it encountered steep opposing slopes of the 1980 crater. Assuming vertical boundaries downward from the November 4 surface to the 1986 surface allows a volume calculation of about 2×10^6 m^3. The spine's estimated volume and interval of emplacement imply a time-averaged extrusion rate of ~3 m^3/s.

Deformation Accompanying Spine Growth

Between October 14 and November 4, the locus of maximum deformation propagated south along an axis oriented ~S. 20° W. Deformation diminished with distance normal to this axis. Opus and the 1980–86 dome were essentially static during this period (fig. 7). Severely deformed ice on the welt just east of its axis moved a few meters to the north; farther south, it moved as much as 60 m to the southeast and subsided (fig. 7). On glacier surfaces to the east, distinctive features moved 5–40 m eastward and rose 5–20 m. Farther north, glacial features moved a few meters northward. The few traceable points on ice west of the actively deforming welt rose a few meters, but only one feature nearest the northwest margin of the welt moved significantly westward, by ~10 m (fig. 7, point wg1).

Phase 3, Recumbent Growth of Spines 3 and 4: October 24, 2004–April 9, 2005

Growth of Whaleback Spine 3: October 24–December 18, 2004

During mid-October, spine 3 began intrusive growth and pushed into pre-2004 rock, deforming the welt, disrupting glacier ice, and forming a cryptodome beneath the welt (fig. 8). Evidence in support of intrusion included (1) deformation along an axis S. 19° E. that coincided with the axis of spine 3 when it later emerged (fig. 5), (2) upward and southward motion of pre-2004 rock along a trend similar to that of the whaleback when it emerged (figs. 5, 7), and (3) warming of rock at the surface near the axis of deformation (Schneider and others, this volume, chap. 17).

Spine 3 breached the deformed surface of the welt and advanced rapidly to the south-southeast between late October and mid-December to form a smooth-surfaced whaleback feature 300–460 m long and 120–145 m wide (tables 1, 2). Between October 24 and 27, spine 3 emerged from an area about 50 m southeast of spine 1, through older dome and crater-floor rock along the crest of the deforming welt (fig. 9). By early November, it was 320×125 m, with a long axis oriented S. 18° E. (fig. 7). As the spine pushed southward from mid-November through December, its long axis pivoted 9° eastward (to S. 27° E.) about its origin at the vent (table 2).

The surface of the whaleback had a cool and smooth, but striated, surface except on the west, where it was broken and blocky. The striations at the surface of the whaleback were interpreted as slickensides (fig. 10). Growth of the whaleback also lifted a partial roof composed of fractured 1980–86 dome rock and crater-floor debris and transported it southward during November 4–29 (fig. 10). Cashman and others (this volume, chap. 19) show that the smooth outer carapace of the whaleback comprised powdered, partially sintered 2004 dacite plus small amounts of 1980–86 dacite; they interpret this material as fault gouge formed through comminution as the solid spine rubbed and ground against older rock during its ascent in the conduit.

The stable crust of spine 3 insulated the hot rock within so that surface temperatures were low. Thermal images commonly showed a ~200°C zone around the base of the emerging spine (fig. 11*A*), and hot cracks showed rock temperatures as high as 730°C. The temperature of smooth, uncracked parts of the surface diminished exponentially with distance from the source at the base of the spine and approached ambient within 50 m (fig. 11*B*). Because the temperature also decreased exponentially with time (each 10 m from source represented about a day), the moving surface of the spine showed a classic Fourier's Law decline in temperature (Turcotte and Schubert, 1982). Such a temperature profile resembles those observed for blocky lavas at Santiaguito, Guatemala (Harris and others, 2002, 2004), though the lava core temperatures of Mount St. Helens spines differ from those of lavas at Santiaguito in likely being 100°C or more below solidus temperature.

Subtracting the spine 1 and 2 volumes from the total volume of hot rock emplaced by spines 1, 2, and 3 (Schilling and others, this volume, chap. 8) yields values for spine 3 volume and for its extrusion rate between late October 2004 and early January 2005 (table 2). Extrusion rate (flux through the 1986 surface) was ~5 m^3/s until November 4. Extrusion rates then declined from 4.4 to 2.5 m^3/s between late November and early January (table 2).

Table 2. Dimensions, orientation, volume, and growth rate of the welt and spines of Mount St. Helens, Washington, at various dates.

[Applicable interval for linear and volumetric growth rates and direction is from date of previous DEM to date of DEM given for row, unless specifically indicated.]

Phase	Date of DEM	Spine/ Welt	Dimensions (m)	Orientation of welt or spine	Linear growth rate, direction, period of interest, and GPS station name where applicable	Volume ($\times 10^6$ m^3)	Volumetric growth rate (m^3/s)
1—Precursory vent clearing	Oct. 4, 2004	Welt	370×370	Equant	~70 m/d, South, Sept. 29–Oct. 4	5 [a]	12 Sept. 29–Oct. 4
	Oct. 14, 2004	Welt	470×380	Long axis north-south	~10 m/d, South, Oct. 4–14	11 [a]	7
2—Initial spines	Oct. 14, 2004	Spine 1	85×60	Strikes S55W; dips 50° NW	15-20 m/d, S35E, Oct. 11–14	0.6	~2 Oct. 11–14
	Nov. 4, 2004	Spine 1	150×45	Strikes S58W; dips 80° NW		0.9	~3 Oct. 14–15
		Spine 2	240×50	Long axis, Due S	~25 m/d, South, Oct. 15–24	2	3 Oct. 15–24
3—Recumbent growth of whaleback spines	Nov. 4, 2004	Spine 3	320×125	Long axis S18E; dip at vent 30°	11.4 m/d, ~ S5W, Nov. 4–7	9	4.7 Oct. 13–Nov. 4
	Nov. 20, 2004	Spine 3	420×125	Long axis S19E	11 m/d, S22E, Nov. 4–20		
	Nov. 29, 2004	Spine 3	440×145	Long axis S23E	10.3 m/d, S19E, Nov. 21–29, ELEA [b] 10.5 m/d, S21E, Nov. 20–29	18	4.4 [a] Nov. 4–29
	Dec. 11, 2004	Spine 3	460×120	Long axis S27E	7–8 m/d, ~S20E [c]	23	4.1 [a]
	Jan. 3, 2005	Spine 4	210×130	Long axis S27E	4–7 m/d, ~S20E [c]	5.5	2.5 [a]
	Feb. 1, 2005	Spine 4	340×145	Long axis S28E	8.3 m/d, S19E, Jan. 15–16, CDAN [b]	10	1.8 [a]
	Feb. 21, 2005	Spine 4	400×150	Long axis S31E	5.8 m/d, S30E, Feb. 8–14, AHAD [b] 4.5 m/d, S32E, Feb. 1–21	14	2.4 [a]
	Mar. 10, 2005	Spine 4	440×140	Long axis S35E	3.9 m/d, S39E, Feb. 21–Mar. 10	17	1.8 [a]
	Apr. 19, 2005	Spine 4	490×140	Long axis S40E	2.6 m/d, S71E, Mar. 10–Apr. 19 Spine 4 decouples from vent during this interval.	21	1.5 [a]
4—Spine thrusts over previous spines	Apr. 19, 2005	Spine 5	100×90	Long axis S25E; dip at vent 40°	3.5–4.5 m/d, S10E [c]	1	1.5 [a]
	June 15, 2005	Spine 5	340×170	Long axis S9E	3–4 m/d, S along axis [c]	8	1.4 [a]
	July 14, 2005	Spine 5	285×105	Long axis; S5E; dip at vent 54°	2–3.5 m/d, S along axis [c]	11	1.3 [a]
	Aug. 10, 2005	Spine 5				15	
5—Spines grow to west then thrust over one another	Aug. 10, 2005	Spine 6	100×90	Long axis S43W	3–4 m/d, ~West [c]	1; compound spine 6 is ~12	2.0 [a]
	Sept. 20, 2005	Spine 6	350×280	Long axis S47W	3–4 m/d, ~West [c]	6; compound spine 6 is ~17	1.6 [a]
	Oct. 24, 2005	Spine 7	110×40	Long axis S44W	3–4 m/d, ~West [c]	New lava, spines 6+7, ~9	0.9 [a]
	Dec. 15, 2005	Spine 7	260×~250	Long axis S74W	~3 m/d, ~West [c]	New lava, spines 6+7, ~12	0.7 [a]
	Feb. 9, 2006	Spine 7	310×~300	Long axis S83W; dip at vent 50°	2.2 m/d, S80W, up 50°	New lava, spines 6+7, ~15	0.6

[a] Schilling and others (this volume, chap. 8).

[b] LaHusen and others (this volume, chap. 16).

[c] Major and others (this volume, chap. 12).

Growth of Spine 3: Onset of Recumbent Growth

Although the spine in early November 2004 appeared to grow more or less vertically from the axis of the welt, it in fact originated from a source beneath spine 1 and extended southward two to three times as fast as it pushed upward. Between November 4 and 7, identifiable features on the spine's surface moved ~32 m S. 5° W. (fig. 10). Vertical movement of the spine was poorly constrained but appeared to be ~12 m up. The south end of the spine extended almost 30 m S. 19° E., an orientation matching that of its long axis. A possible explanation for the contrast in surface-vector directions and overall spine extension is that, at this early stage of its growth, the spine rotated slightly westward while pushing south-southeast along its axis.

Deformation Adjacent to Spine 3 in Early November

Between November 4 and 7, areas to the east of spine 3 moved tens of meters parallel to the spine or were pushed in easterly directions, and areas to the west and north of spine 3 moved less than 10 m or remained static. Rock debris adjacent to the eastern margin of spine 3 moved parallel to the east margin by almost 30 m (fig. 10*A*). Rock debris farther east moved smaller distances. Motion of the rock debris had no detectable vertical component. Fractured and previously uplifted glacial ice less than 200 m east of the spine moved 10–15 m along trends ranging from southeast to east (fig. 10*A*). During November 4–7, a GPS unit west of the whaleback, CLF4, moved 8 m south-southwest and subsided 2 m

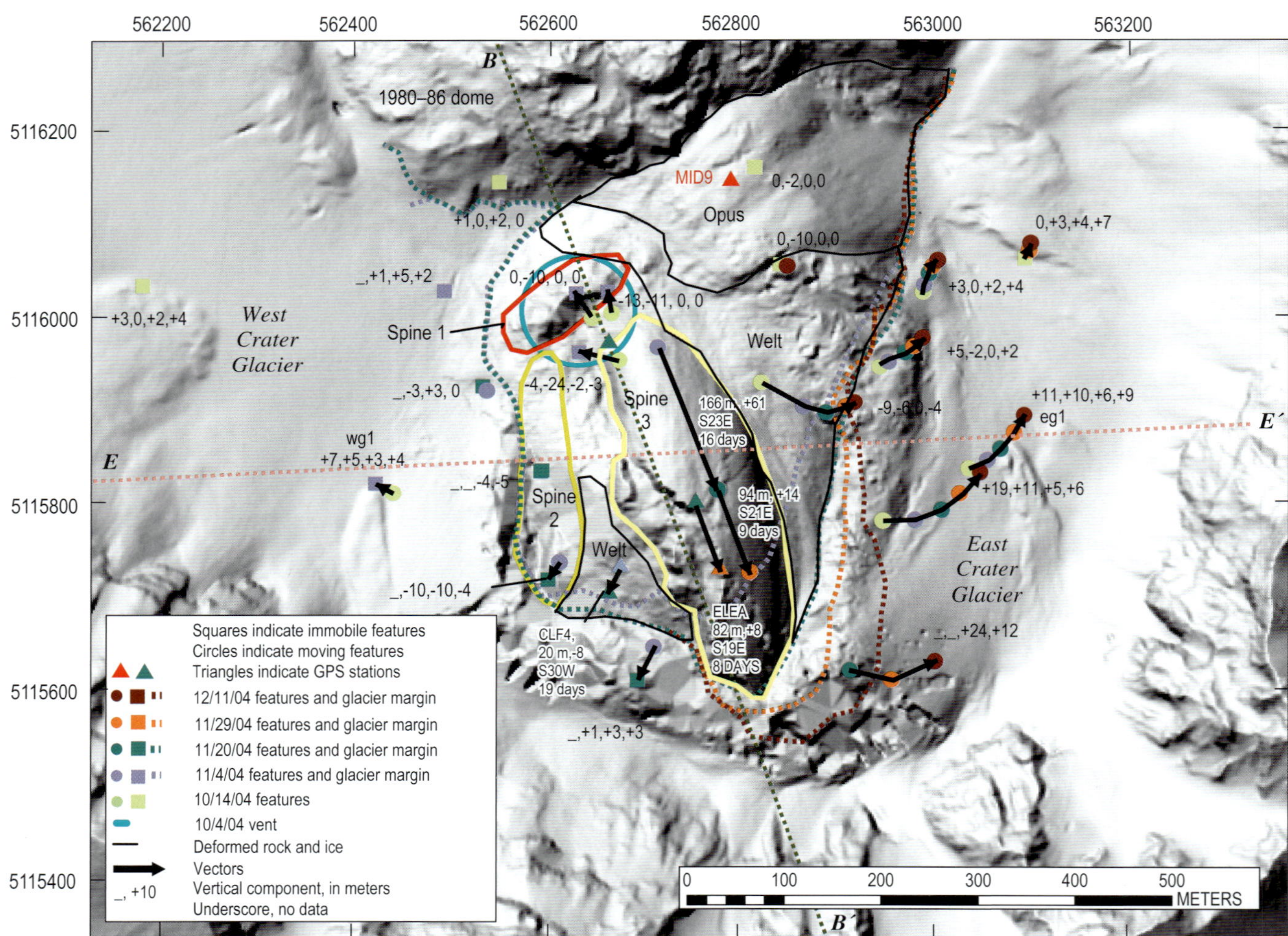

Figure 7. Deformation vectors for the period October 14–December 11, 2004, shown on DEM of November 20. Squares and dots indicate features tracked for dates identified by color in key. These colored symbols delimit deformation vectors of each of the four time intervals between relocation of features. For quantitative data (example: _, -3, +3, 0), numbers are vertical components of vectors, in meters, for each interval. Underscores indicate no data for that interval. Dotted lines indicate dome-glacier margins for dates indicated by color in key. Lines ***B–B´*** and ***E–E´*** are traces of cross sections shown in figures 8 and 14, respectively.

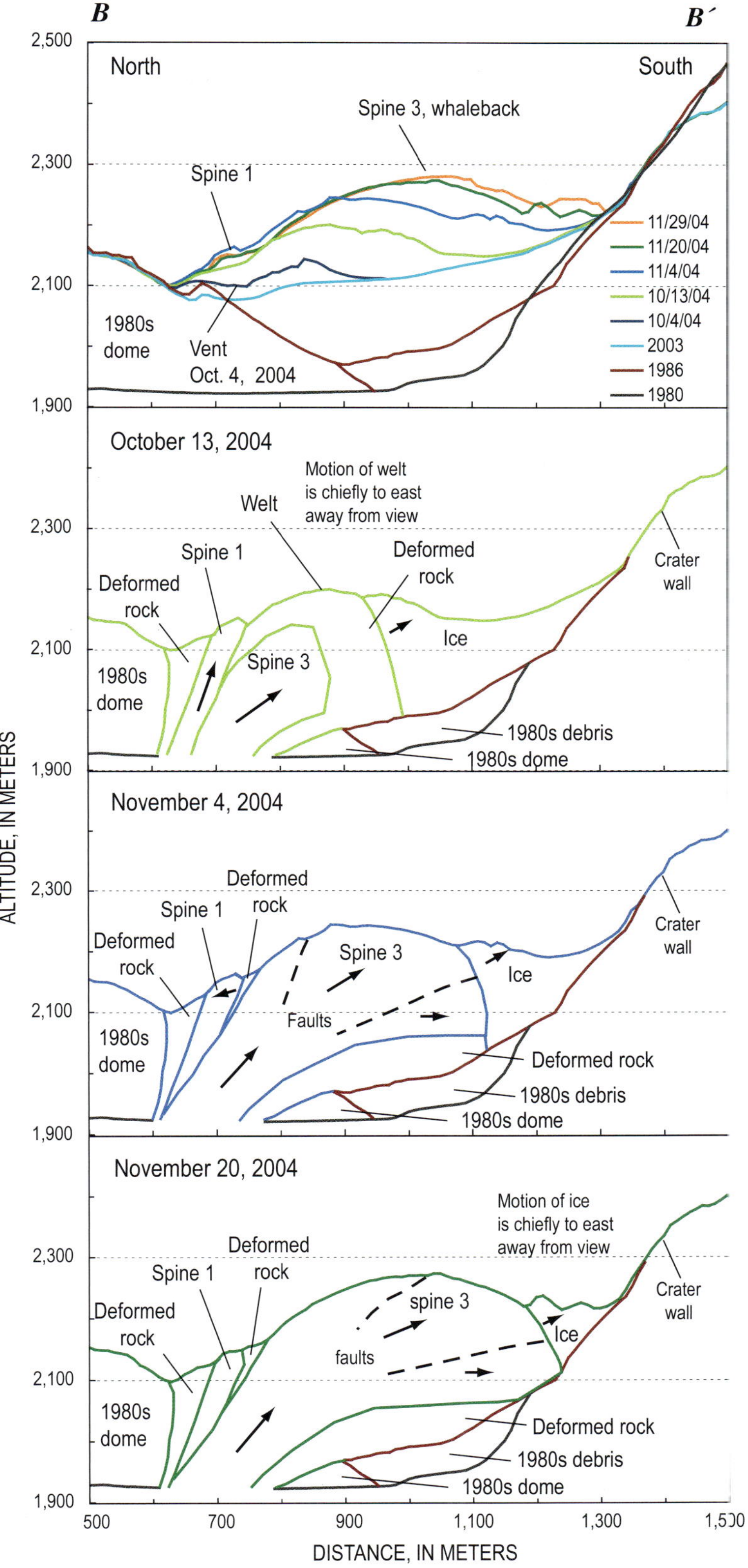

Figure 8. North-south cross section ***B–B′*** (location shown in figure 7) illustrating intrusion and recumbent growth of spine 3. Top panel shows known profiles for the dates given, and other panels illustrate geologic interpretations on given dates.

(LaHusen and others, this volume, chap. 16). Nearly static areas during this time included spines 1 and 2, Opus, and the west arm of Crater Glacier.

Striations and Relative Motion of Spine 3 in Early November

Growth of spine 3 and nearby deformation patterns explain otherwise enigmatic bidirectional striation patterns on the spine in early November 2004. On November 4, 7, and 10, striations plunging 31° N. 66° E. on the east face of spine 3 were superimposed on fainter striations plunging 20° N. 5° E. (fig. 10*B*). At the north end of the spine near the vent, only fainter N. 5° E. striations existed. A cursory analysis in early November suggested that the striations recorded a change in direction of spine growth, with the fresh striations indicating the most recent direction. However, our photogrammetric analysis indicates instead that welt debris adjacent to the whaleback was being dragged at a rate of almost 10 m/d along the base of the emerging spine along a ~S. 32° E. trend (fig. 10). This vector minus the true-growth vector yields a vector whose direction (N. 66° E.) matches the direction of the freshest east-flank striations (fig. 10*B*). Deformation patterns east of the spine thus suggest a simple explanation in which the fresh striations recorded a growth direction relative to debris being dragged southward, and the faint striations recorded the true growth direction of the spine.

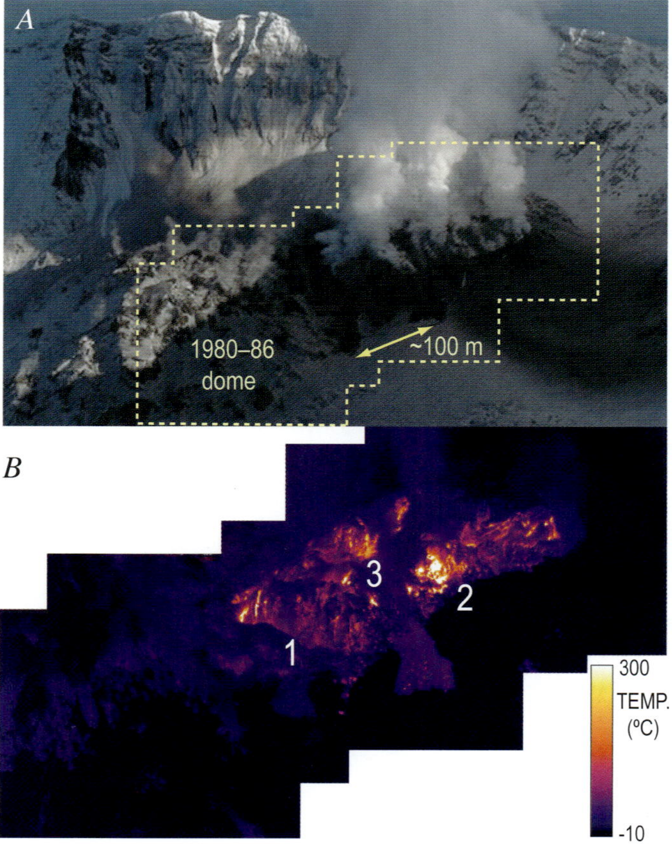

Figure 9. Mount St. Helens crater floor on October 27, 2004; view from northwest, illustrating spines 1–3. *A*, Photograph showing 1980–86 dome and ongoing extrusion, with fresh ash on Crater Glacier west of new dome. *B*, Mosaic of thermal-infrared images located in *A* from same date and time. Numbers indicate spines 1–3. Maximum temperature in field of view is 600°C (scale is set such that all temperatures greater than 300°C are white). Spine 3 has emerged since previous TIR survey on October 24. Thermal imagery shows hot debris fan and hot blocks on ice and firn near spine 1 and between spines 1 and 2. USGS photo by J.W. Vallance; thermal images by D.J. Schneider.

Continuing Recumbent Growth of Spine 3

Through November, spine 3 continued to advance to the south-southeast (S. 19° E. to S. 23° E.) at a linear rate of 10–11 m/d (fig. 7). Judging from the slope of the northern face, initial vertical components of motion were ~30°. As features on the spine moved to the south, their vertical motions gradually diminished to zero by ~300 m from the vent, and thereafter they began to subside (LaHusen and others, this volume, chap. 16; this study). The southerly (S. 5° W.) motion of features on the spine turned to south-southeast in mid-November (fig. 7). As the spine axis and growth direction converged, its whaleback form began to take on a smooth gouge-covered appearance on the east and west flanks.

Superposition of spine 3 outlines from November to December 2004 upon the 1986 surface suggests that the growing spine encountered opposing slopes of the 1980 crater wall in mid-November (fig. 8). The surface outline of the spine first overlapped the steep north-sloping crater wall at the bed of the glacier sometime between November 4 and 20 (fig. 12*A*). Northeastward acceleration of GPS spider MID9 north of spine 3 and south of the 1980–86 dome beginning November 12 probably corresponded to the time at which spine 3 began to push against the opposing slope of the 1980 crater beneath the glacier (fig. 13).

As spine 3 continued to impinge on steep, opposing subglacial slopes of the crater wall in late November and December, the spine axis began to rotate eastward (table 2, fig. 12*A*) and the spine began to break. Axis orientation changed 8° eastward from November 20 to December 11 (table 2). Between November 20 and 29, fracturing and separation of the first piece of spine 3 was apparent (figs. 2*A*, 2*B*), consistent with northeastward acceleration of GPS station MID9 during November 23–27 ("1st breakup" in fig. 13*A*). By November 29, this small spine fragment had completely separated, and by December 11, the rotating spine had pushed it into a steaming heap along its margin with east Crater Glacier (fig. 2*C*). A second, more substantial fragment separated and decoupled in early December. Northeastward acceleration and deceleration of MID9 suggests that the period of the fracture and decoupling of the resultant spine fragment spanned December 6–12 ("2nd breakup" in fig. 13*A*).

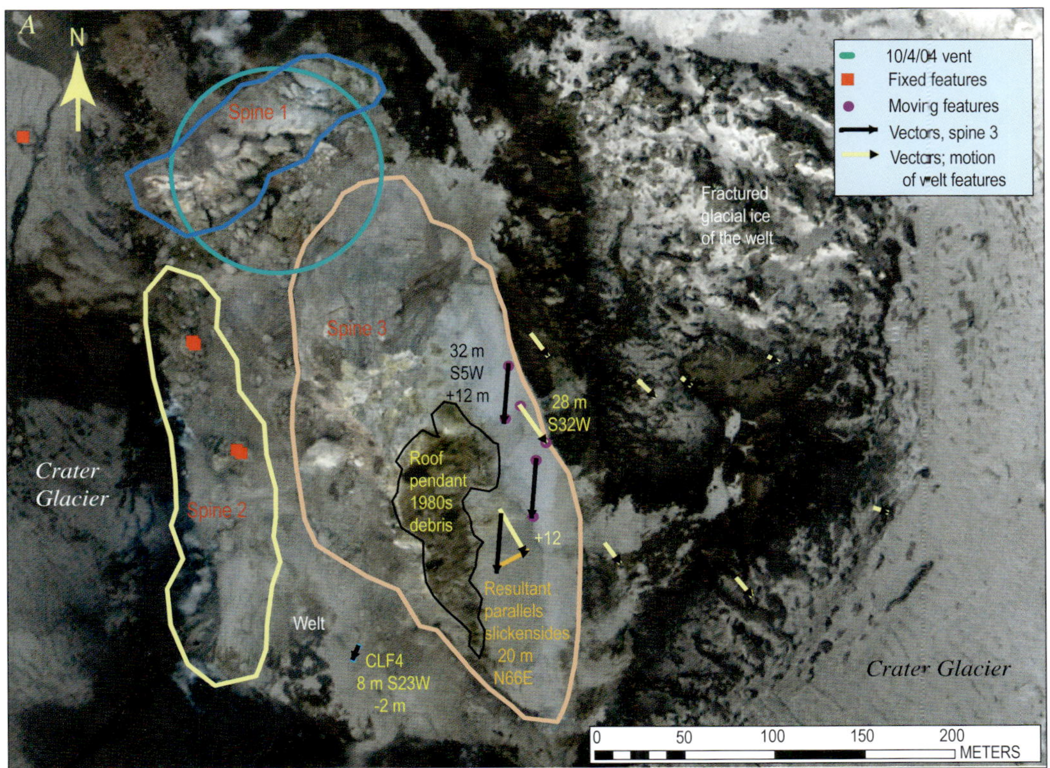

Figure 10. Mount St. Helens crater floor in early November 2004. *A*, Rectified vertical aerial photograph of dome taken November 7, 2004, with handheld camera from an airplane. The photograph was subsequently rectified using features on 1980–86 dome, Opus, and Crater Glacier for both November 4 and 7 so that its central part is tied to geographic coordinates of the November 4 DEM. The aerial photograph shows deformation vectors in plan view for November 4–7. *B*, Oblique photograph looking west at spine 3 on November 4, 2004, showing faint striations parallel to deformation vector, $\vec{V}_{black}$, and young pronounced striations parallel to vector $\vec{V}_{orange}$, where subscripts indicate vector colors in photograph. Debris adjacent to whaleback moves in the near-horizontal plane parallel to $\vec{V}_{yellow}$ such that $\vec{V}_{yellow} - \vec{V}_{black} = \vec{V}_{orange}$. USGS photos by J.S. Pallister.

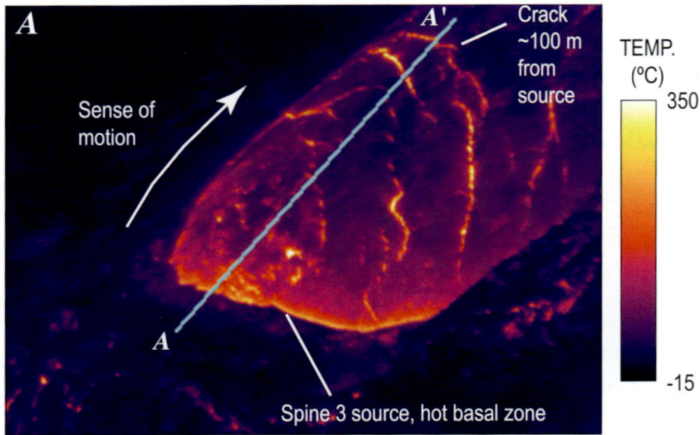

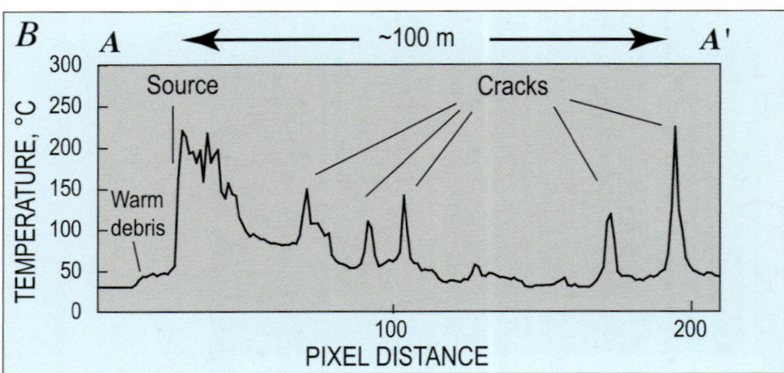

Figure 11. Thermal aspect of spine 3 surface on November 29, 2004. *A*, Thermal-infrared image from helicopter, view to southeast, by J.W. Vallance. *B*, Temperature profile from north to south.

There was no big north-south crack in a December 4 image (R.L. Helz, written commun., 2004). However, a December 8 image revealed a well-developed crack, confirming that during that interval a substantial part of the spine had begun to separate from its west flank along a longitudinal fracture oriented parallel to the spine's axis. December 11 photographs (fig. 2*C*), DEM (Schilling and others, this volume, chap. 8), and geologic map (Herriott and others, this volume, chap. 10) revealed that this fragment had largely decoupled and had begun to subside westward by that date. During November to mid-December numerous other small spine fragments separated from spine 3, mostly to the west. Generally, fragments separating to the west slowly subsided and stagnated, whereas the few separating to the east were bulldozed eastward.

Late October–Mid-December Deformation of Surrounding Areas during Spine 3 Growth

In response to recumbent dome growth from late October to mid-December, areas east of spine 3 rotated eastward about a pivot axis near Opus, showing horizontal displacements as great as 100 m. Areas west of spine 3 subsided or stagnated and moved less than 20 m (figs. 7, 14*A*). All areas east of spine 3 rotated eastward in such a fashion that displacement per unit time increased from north to south. Ice masses on the welt subsided and then migrated eastward across the boundary between stagnant ice and the Crater Glacier, whereupon they began to rise. During this interval all ice on the east Crater Glacier rose between 10 and 50 m, with largest vertical displacements occurring to the south and the smallest to the north (figs. 7, 14*A*). In effect, rotating dome and welt rock bulldozed the glacier eastward, compressing and lifting it such that its cross-sectional profile changed from concave to convex (figs. 2, 14*A*).

Spine 1 moved in response to the emerging spine 3, then stabilized as that new spine continued to grow. Spine 1 was displaced about 40 m north-northwest and tilted from a dip of 50° to 80° northwest between mid-October and early November (fig. 7). Comparison of the October 14 DEM with those of November (figs. 5, 7) shows the change in position of spine 1 with respect to the October 4 vent position. This displacement and rotation coincided with southward growth and emergence of spines 2 and 3. The displacement and rotation were to the northwest, directly away from the origin of spine 3's southward extrusion, and are likely to have been a response to spine 3 emergence rather than growth of spine 2.

Spine 2 and the area between spines 2 and 3 rotated slightly and subsided between October and December. In late October and early November, spine 2 moved as much as 20 m to the northwest at its south end but remained relatively stable to the north. In late October, the top of spine 2 was as much as 20 m higher than the adjacent glacier surface (fig. 9). As spine 3 grew, spine 2 subsided by 20–25 m (fig. 7). By late November, spine 2 had become a nondescript entity hidden below the level of west Crater Glacier, with talus and rockfall encroaching upon it from the more prominent spine 3 to the east (fig. 2*B*). The GPS spider CLF4, placed on the welt October 27, was perched between spines 2 and 3 as spine 3 emerged. The spider had moved ~44 m S. 24° W. and subsided 13 m by November 19, when it was buried by rockfall from spine 3 (LaHusen and others, this volume, chap. 16). As spine 3 advanced, it pushed parts of the dome south and west of it to the southwest, but, after its leading edge passed by and the spine began rotation in the opposite direction, subsidence of areas west of spine 3 began—possibly caused by removal of buttressing from the east.

West Crater Glacier, south and west of the spine complex, responded during a brief interval as spine 3 approached but otherwise remained relatively static from late October to mid-December (fig. 7). Dome growth after November 4 caused no detectable deflection of west Crater Glacier. A slow increase in altitude of the west glacier, caused in part by accumulation of snow, occurred as spine 3 grew. Areas of the glacier immediately south of the dome complex moved tens of meters as the whaleback approached (fig. 7), but then they stopped.

Breakup of Spine 3 and Formation of Spine 4: December 18, 2004–April 8, 2005

Spine 3 broke up and decoupled as spine 4 formed between mid-December 2004 and early January 2005. Photograph sequences showed fractures oriented diagonally across

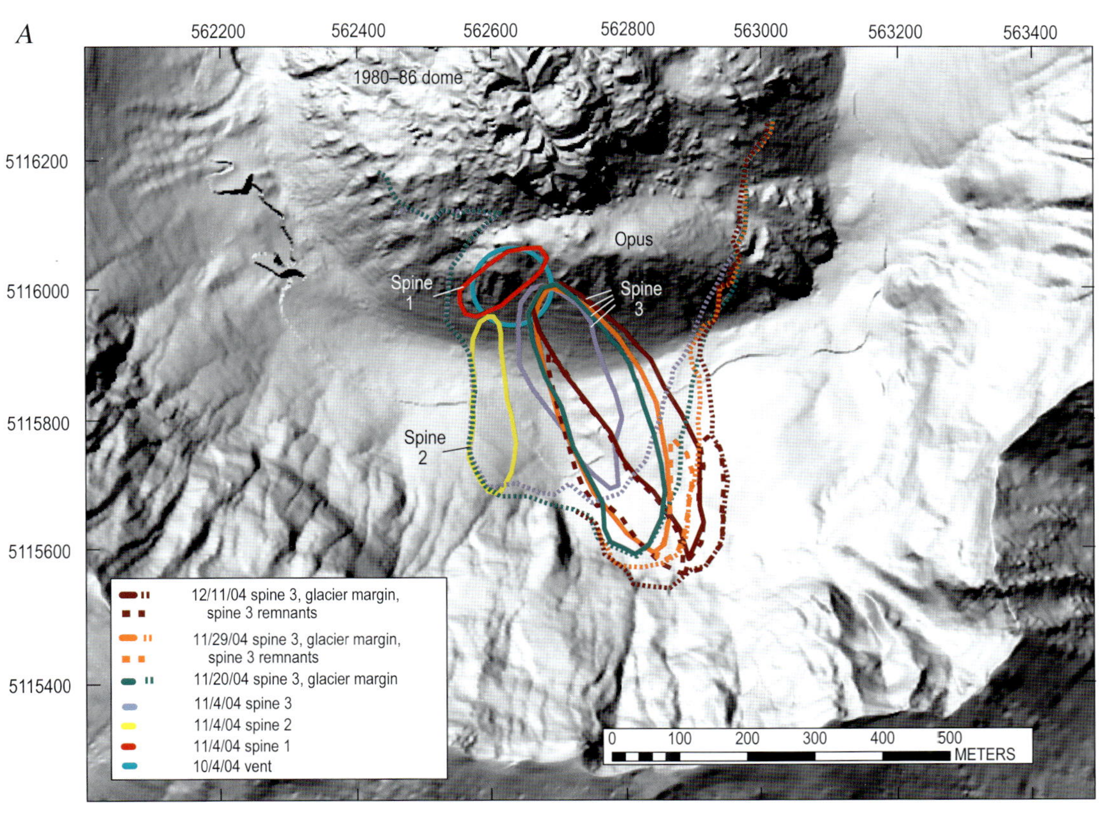

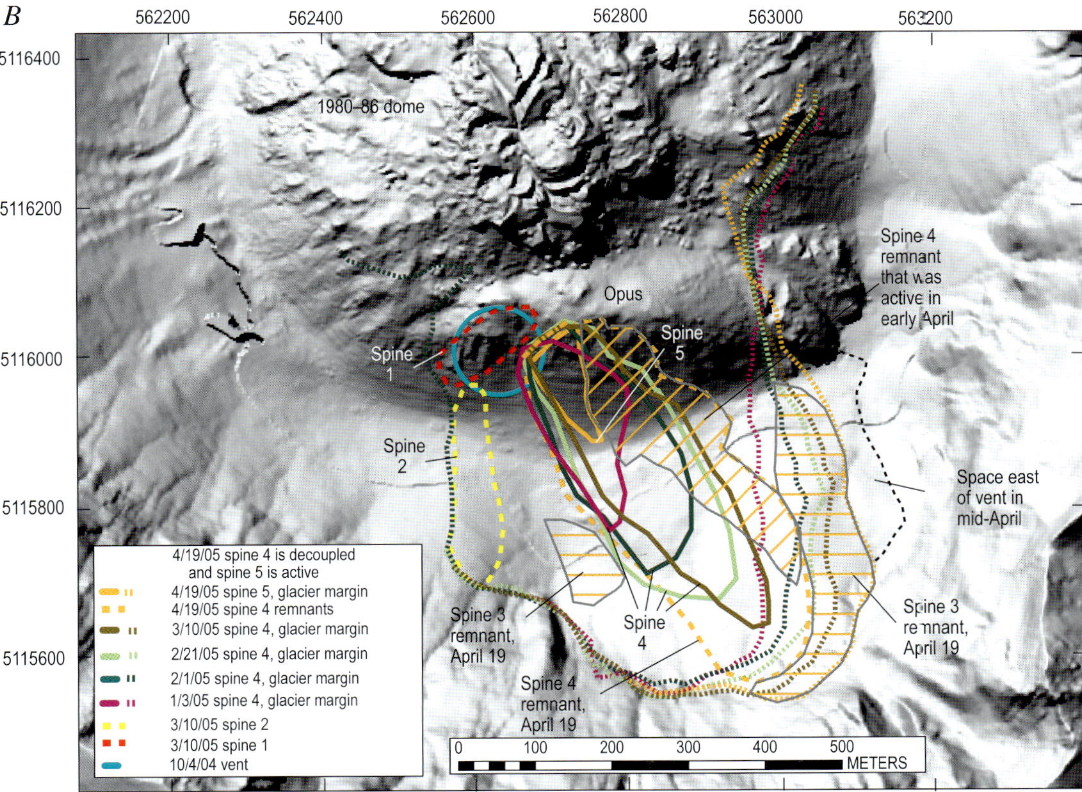

Figure 12. Outlines of active spines and dome-glacier margins at Mount St. Helens, Washington, superimposed on 1986 DEM. *A*, November 4–December 11, 2004. *B*, January 3–April 19, 2005.

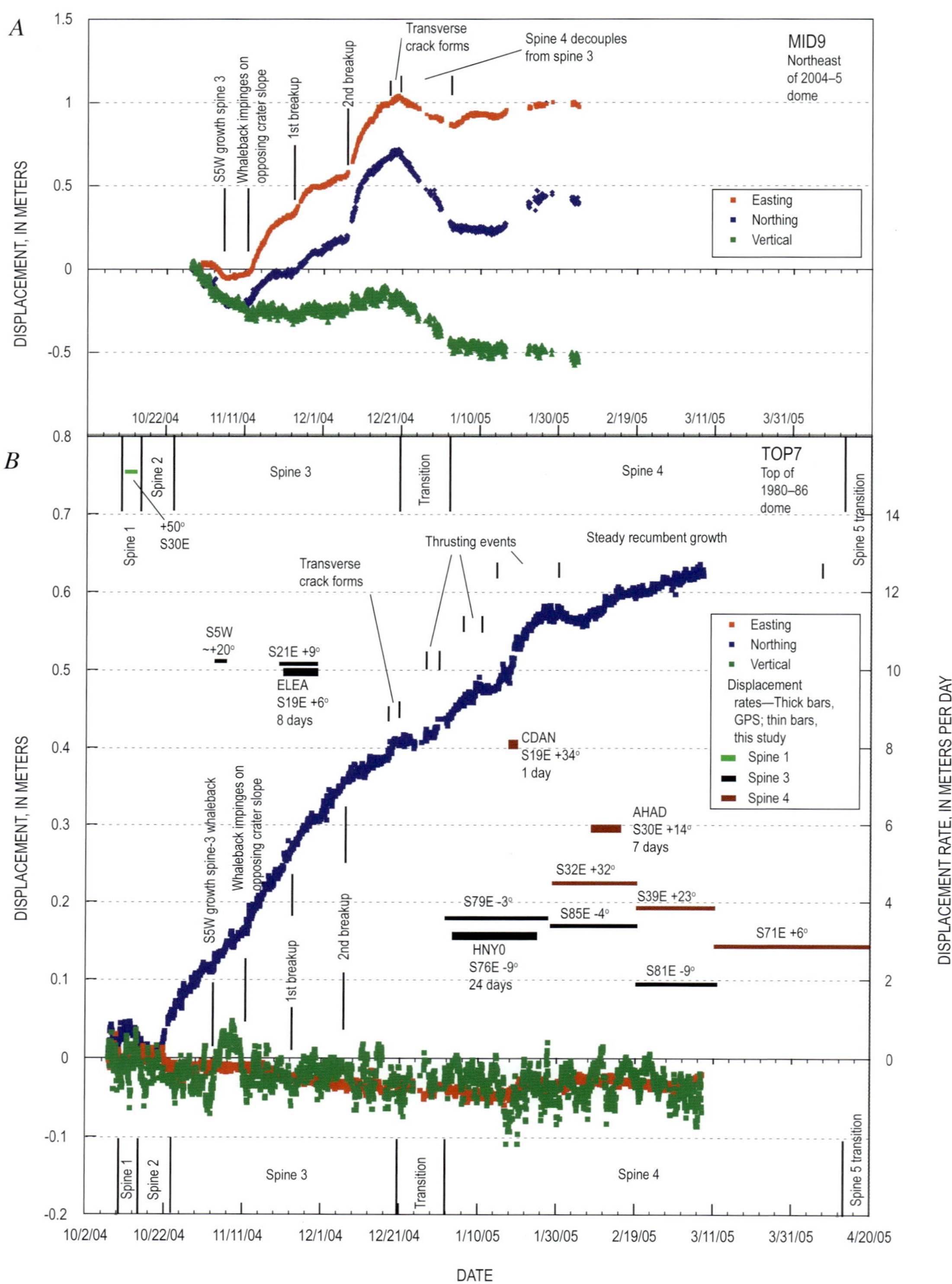

Figure 13. Plots of displacement versus time for GPS stations MID9 (*A*), located between 2004–5 and 1980–86 domes, and TOP7 (*B*), located at apex of 1980–86 dome, with intervals of spine growth and key events during spine growth, as well as linear extrusion rates of GPS receivers and features tracked in this study superimposed on GPS time series. Initial locations shown in figures 7 and 15. Because of their locations just northeast and north of spines 3 and 4, MID9 and TOP7 stations commonly accelerated opposite spine growth when spine met resistance to its growth and decelerated when that resistance was relieved. GPS data from LaHusen and others (this volume, chap. 16).

spine 3 that formed and became more prominent beginning about December 18 (Major and others, this volume, chap. 12). Station MID9 reversed its direction of motion from northeast to southwest on December 20 (LaHusen and others, this volume, chap. 16), an event correlated approximately to the formation of the transverse fractures (fig. 13). Southward thrusting of spine 4 over the slowing bulk of spine 3 had become evident by December 24–28 (figs. 2*D*, 2*E*; supplementary movie 2 in Iverson and others, 2006). A second fracture south of the first formed by January 3, 2005, and the decoupling of spine 4 from spine 3 could be considered complete by that time (fig. 2*E*). We infer that cessation of MID9's southwestward motion on January 3 corresponded to complete decoupling of spines 3 and 4.

Between January 3 and April 2005, spine 4 pushed south-southeast from a source located ~70 m east of spine 1. Spine 4 had whaleback morphology similar to that of spine 3 but underwent several cycles of thrusting over spine 3 before it established steady near-uniform growth. Photographs (figs. 2*E*, 2*F*) and time-lapse video (Iverson and others, 2006; Major and others, this volume, chap. 12, appendix 1) reveal thrusting events during January 6–12 and January 14–February 2. The TOP7 GPS spider accelerated northward during each of these events (fig. 13*B*). Time-lapse photography and GPS records for the period of February 2–April 9, 2005, suggest nearly uniform, steady southward growth and no further thrusting events.

By early January spine 4 had a crest oriented S. 27° E. and dimensions of 210×130 m (table 2, fig. 15). Spine 4 grew to ~440 m in length by early March before beginning to break up in April (fig. 16). As with spine 3 during November and December, the long axis of spine 4 began to pivot eastward about its origin at the vent. This rotation began once the spine started to impinge on slopes of the crater wall (figs. 12, 17); its long-axis orientation swung 12° eastward between mid-February and its breakup in mid-April (table 2, fig. 12*B*). This response suggests that the moving spine extended deep enough to be influenced by the slopes of the 1980 crater at depth, as modeled in cross sections (figs. 16, 17).

Linear extrusion rates of spine 4 diminished during January 3–April 10, as shown by analysis of photographs taken at hourly to daily intervals from fixed sites at the eastern crater mouth (Sugar Bowl) (Major and others, this volume, chap. 12), the motions of GPS spiders on the spine (LaHusen and others, this volume, chap. 16), and time-averaged results from this study (fig. 13, table 2). A GPS station, CDAN, moved 8 m/day along a path of S. 19° E. and 34° upward between January 15 and 16. A second station, AHAD, moved 5.9 m/d along a path of S. 30° E. and 14° upward between February 8 and 15 (fig. 13) (LaHusen and others, this volume, chap. 16). A rate and direction estimate using features on successive DEMs for the longer interval between February 1 and 21 was slower: 4.5 m/d along a path of S. 32° E.

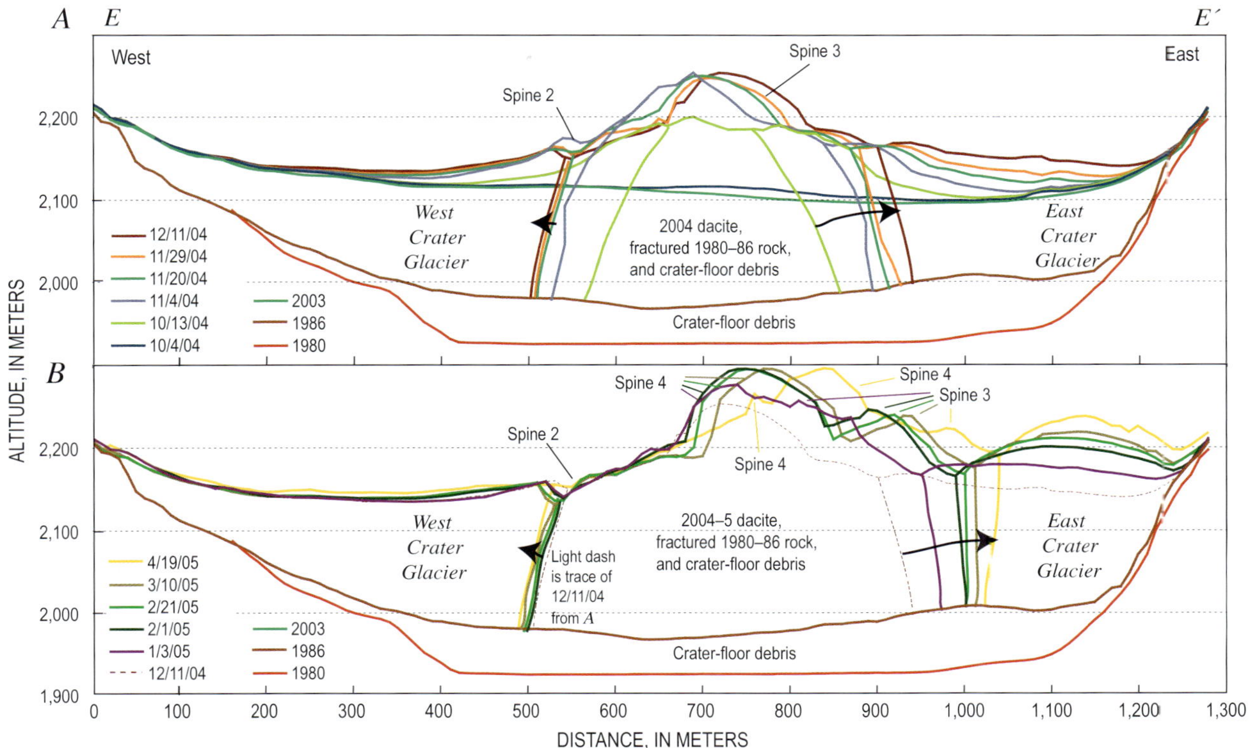

Figure 14. East-west cross section *E–E′* (location shown in figures 1 and 7) illustrating response of glacier to recumbent growth of spine 3. *A*, Profiles for October 13–December 11, 2004. *B*, Profiles for January 3–April 19, 2005.

and 32° upward (figs. 13, 15). This slower rate is about the same as spine 4 extrusion rates reported by Iverson and others (2006) and Major and others (this volume, chap. 12), who compared daily Sugar Bowl photographs. With time, extrusion rates diminished and directions became more easterly: 3.9 m/d along a path of S. 39° E. and 23° upward between February 21 and March 10. This decreased to 2.6 m/d along a path of S. 71° E. and 6° upward between March 10 and April 19. We estimated a time-averaged rate of advance for the period of January through mid-March by measuring advance of the leading edge of the whaleback in cross section (fig. 16). Between January 3 and March 10, the advance of ~300 m gave a rate between 4 and 5 m/d. Rates were as high as 8 m/d during some briefer intervals (table 2).

The initial volume of spine 4 on January 3, 2005, as it splintered from spine 3, was 5.5×10[6] m[3], and total volumes of hot rock reported for different times during the spine 4 extrusion (Schilling and others, this volume, chap. 8) allow calculation of spine 4 volumes and time-averaged, volumetric extrusion rates between January and April 2005 (table 2). Time-averaged extrusion rates for these intervals suggest a spurt in growth from February 1 to 21. The growth spurt occurred during the same interval in which spine 4 transitioned from intermittent thrusting to steady recumbent growth.

Deformation of Areas Surrounding Spine 4 Growth during January–April 2005

Spine 4 growth during January through April caused areas to the east to rotate eastward about a pivot near Opus. Displacements were as great as 200 m (fig. 15). In response to motion of the welt to the south of Opus, ice masses stranded

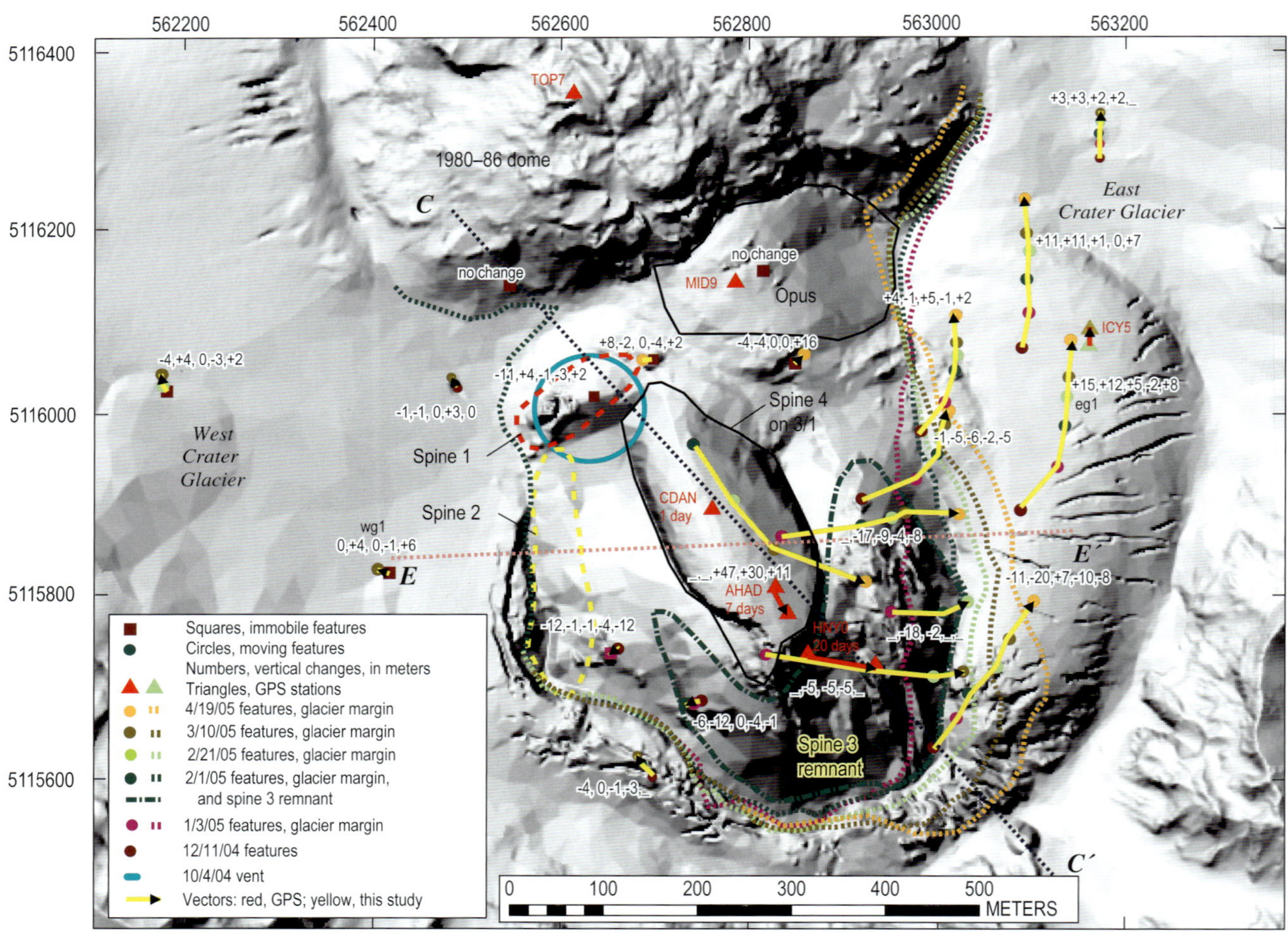

Figure 15. Deformation vectors for the period from January 3 to April 19, 2005, shown on DEM of February 1, 2005. Squares and dots indicate features tracked for dates identified by color in key. These colored symbols delimit deformation vectors of each of the five time intervals between relocation of features. Numbers are vertical components of vectors, in meters, for each interval. Underscores indicate no data for that interval. Dotted lines indicate dome-glacier margins for dates indicated by color in key. Dashed lines ***C–C′***, and ***E–E′*** are traces of cross sections shown in figures 16 and 17.

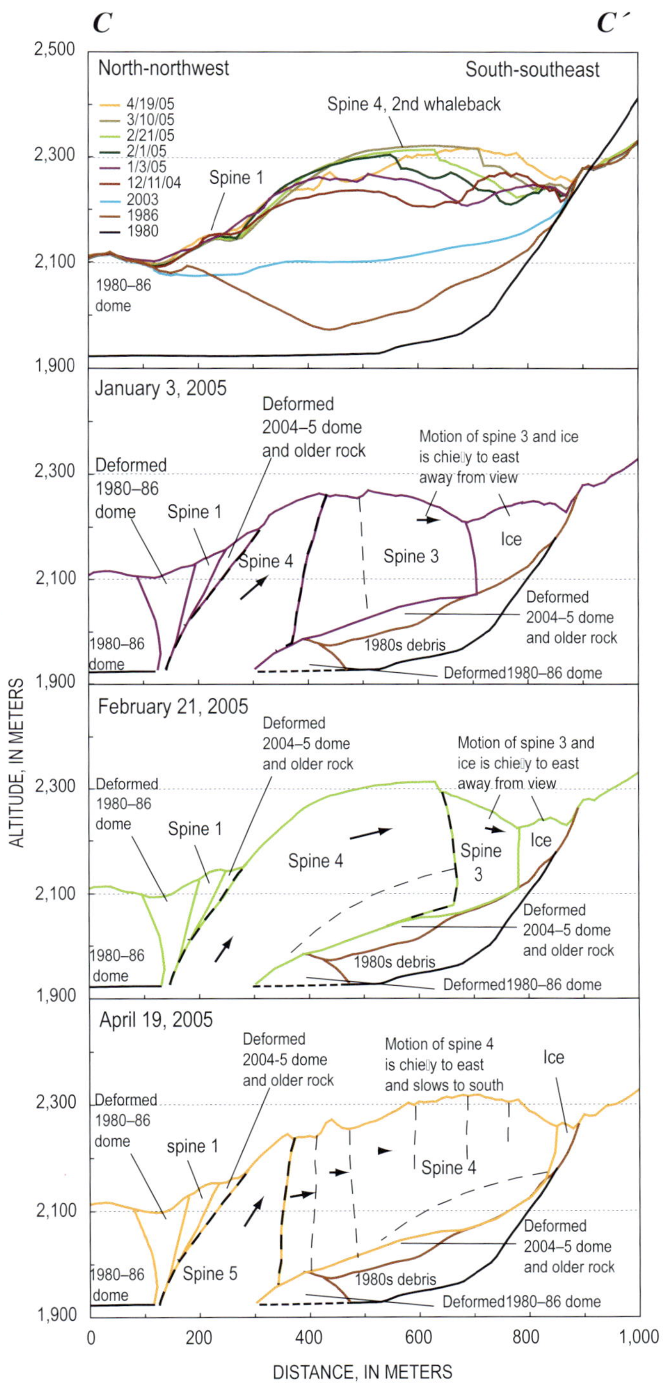

Figure 16. North-northwest to south-southeast cross section *C–C′* (location shown in figure 15) illustrating extrusion and recumbent growth of whaleback, spine 4. Top panel shows known profiles for dates given, and other panels illustrate geologic interpretations on given dates. Dashed lines indicate inferred faults.

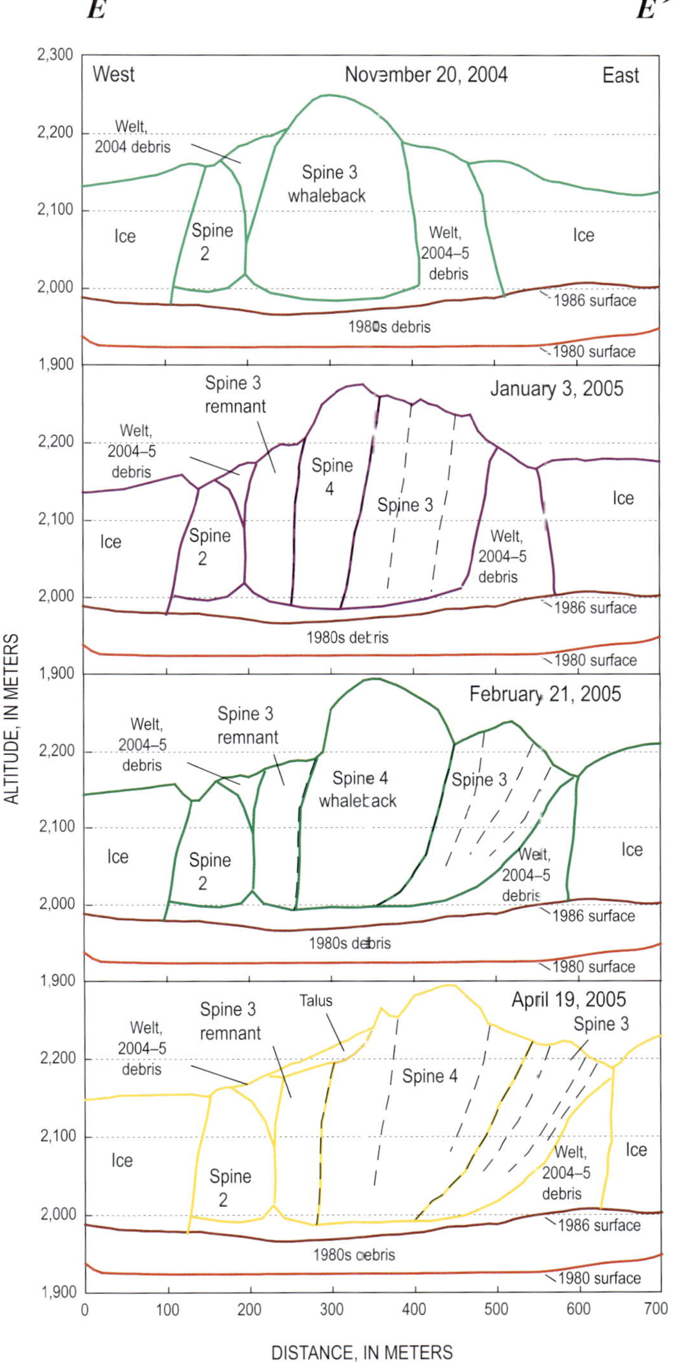

Figure 17. East-west cross section *E–E′* (location shown in figure 15) illustrating extrusion and recumbent growth of spines 3 and 4. Panels illustrate geologic interpretations on given dates. Dashed lines indicate inferred faults; heavy and light line weights indicate contacts between spines and within spines, respectively.

on the welt moved eastward until they crossed into the realm of the active east Crater Glacier, whereupon they flowed northward as part of the glacier. Recognizable remnants of the disintegrating spine 3 shifted eastward 100 m or more by February 1. Areas closest to spine 4 moved fastest. Between January 3 and February 1, an area on spine 3 south of spine 4 moved 107 m S. 79° E. at a rate of 3.7 m/d and subsided slightly (fig. 15). The GPS station HNY0, located ~40 m to the east, moved 3.2 m/d, S. 76° E., and also subsided (fig. 13) (LaHusen and others, this volume, chap. 16). Continuing deformation at nearby sites was S. 85° E., 3.6 m/d, and S. 81° E., 1.9 m/d, during February 1–March 10 (fig. 15).

Spine 4 bulldozed and tilted spine 3 eastward, rapidly fracturing it and causing it to disintegrate (figs. 2, 3, 17). By April 19, spine 3 had been reduced to a rubbly ridge adjacent to the east Crater Glacier, and its surface area had been reduced by a factor of five (Herriott and others, this volume, chap. 10). Overthrusting caused by eastward rotation of spine 4 as it deflected off the crater wall caused the reduction in area of spine 3 (fig. 17). Except for one small area, spine 3 remnants to the west were buried by spine 4 talus.

Areas on the 2004–5 dome west of spine 4 continued to subside but moved laterally no more than about 10 m. Spine 1 subsided in December but showed no significant motion thereafter. An area near the south end of spine 2 and another on a remnant of spine 3 west of spine 4 moved less than 10 m southwest between January and February and subsided 10–20 m. Thereafter, subsidence continued at a slower pace, and no further translation of these spine 2 and 3 fragments was detectable.

As the east Crater Glacier continued to be bulldozed eastward at rates as high as 1.5 m/d, it rose tens of meters and accelerated downstream. Between mid-December 2004 and mid-April 2005, the glacier profile bulged as much as 90 m and became markedly convex (fig. 14*B*). During this interval, individual surface features on east Crater Glacier rose as much as 50 m, with the largest vertical displacements in areas east and southeast of Opus. In contrast, farther upslope to the south, features lost tens of meters in altitude as they flowed north (fig. 15). Features with eastward components of displacement in the autumn of 2004 shifted to due north displacement during winter 2005 as the glacier accelerated away from the area of constriction between the rotating dome complex and the east crater wall. The glacier had thickened so much since the onset of the eruption (as much as 130 m) that its slope had increased dramatically, and it responded by flowing north to correct the imbalance.

The Crater Glacier west and north of the spine complex responded by moving a few meters northwest during late December to April, in places rising by a few meters. Although dome growth may have had a minor effect on west Crater Glacier (fig. 15) during the winter months of 2005, accumulation of snow and normal glacier flow downslope probably accounted for most of the observed change. Areas of the glacier immediately southwest of the 2004–5 dome complex moved about 30 m northwest in response to the approach of spine 4 (figs. 12, 15).

Phase 4, Extrusion of Spine 5 across Previous Spine Debris: April 10–July 31, 2005

Spine 4 broke up, decoupled, and changed direction in mid-April 2005. Continual pressure caused by spine 4 pushing against the opposing crater wall disrupted its steady southward propagation and caused it to break apart. Repeat photographs (Major and others, this volume, chap. 12) and time-lapse photography (Iverson and others, 2006) showed development of northeast- to southwest-striking fractures cutting spine 4 at this time. These fractures became progressively more prominent from April 10 to 19. Between April 19 and 24, as the fractures grew, spine 5 began to thrust over the top of spine 4 remnants. Like spine 4, the spine 5 source was ~50 m southeast of spine 1 (fig. 15).

Spine 5 had decoupled from spine 4 by April 19, though it continued to drag the southern parts of spine 4 southward until mid-May and to displace it to the east through June. Spine 5 displayed a smooth, gouge-covered surface near the vent. It became progressively steeper with time, the slope increasing from 40° on April 19 to 54° on July 14 (fig. 18). The spine tended to fracture and crumble as it grew higher, leading to a substantial breakup and decoupling of the southern section of the spine between mid-June and mid-July. During this interval spine growth began to resemble that of the Mont Pelée spine of 1903, with a steeply thrusting lithic core surrounded by an apron of debris at the angle of repose (Blake, 1990). The thrusting spine 5 acted as the driving force for a conveyer that transported at least half of the volume of the crumbling spine southward to form a ridge of disaggregated rock with a trend of S. 10° E. in mid-June and S. 5° E. in mid-July.

From April to August 2005, we were unable to use surface deformation vectors to make independent measurements of spine growth rate because of plumes that obscured key parts of the spine in aerial photos on two of four dates. A limiting, average, lineal growth rate of 4.3 m/d can be calculated from knowing that spine 5 was 100 m long on April 19 and 340 m long on June 15. Data from Major and others (this volume, chap. 12) suggest that extrusion rates of the smooth northern surface diminished from ~4 m/d in late June to ~2 m/d by early July. Time-averaged volume flux decreased slowly between April and July (table 2).

Deformation of Areas Surrounding Spine 5 from April to July 2005

Deformation of areas surrounding spine 5 showed that the spine was deep seated only near its source and was thrusting upward over previous parts of the dome complex to the south (fig. 19). Spine 4 remnants east of spine 5 rotated northeast or east, with the pivot point about 300 m southeast of the vent in an area of stagnant spine 4 rock (near point -7,-2,-3 in fig. 19). The areas of maximum displacement were in the north adjacent to the vent. Maximum displacement east of the vent on

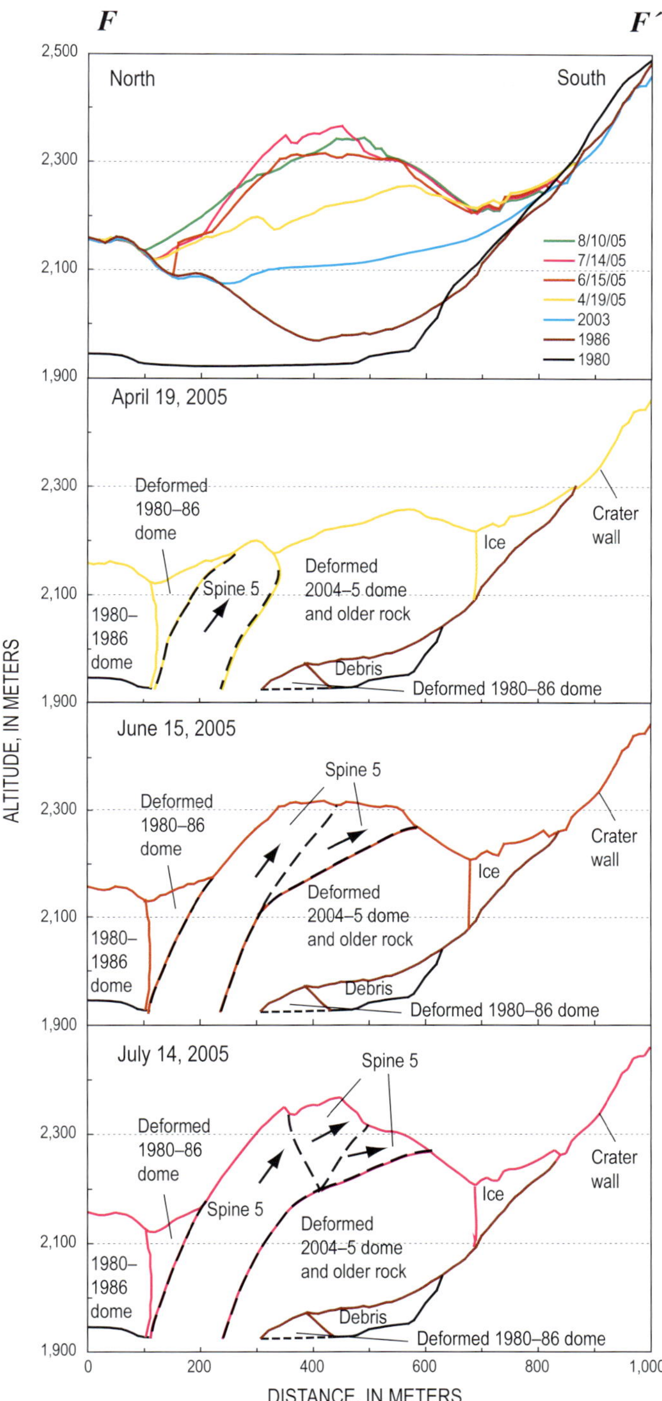

Figure 18. North-south cross section *F–F´* (location shown in figure 19) illustrating extrusion and thrusting growth of spine 5. Top panel shows known profiles for dates given, and other panels illustrate geologic interpretations on given dates. Southern part of spine 5 crumbled and broke up between June 15 and July 14, 2005.

spine 4 was 40–50 m, generally to the northeast. Most of the displacement occurred in April and May; very little occurred thereafter. A feature near GPS station SEV7 moved about 40 m to the northeast and subsided 16 m (point -7, -3, -6, fig. 19). All but 2 m of translation had occurred by June 15, but subsidence continued through August. The GPS station SEV7, located ~30 m west of this feature, was deployed on May 24. By June 15 it had moved only 7 m S. 70° E., implying that about 80 percent of the translation in this area had occurred between the time of the April 19 DEM and May 24. All remnants of spine 4, including those that did not translate significantly, subsided 10–20 m during spring and early summer of 2005. Farther east, spine 3 remnants also subsided between April and June but did not translate more than ~5 m.

Areas on the dome west and north of spine 5 moved northwestward 40–60 m (fig. 19). Spine 1 was pushed ~50 m northwest (point +10, fig. 19). An isolated remnant of spine 3 to the southwest of spine 5 (point -1, fig. 19) moved about 40 m westward before it was buried. Spine 2 was buried by encroaching spine 5 talus in June and then could not be tracked, but its contact with the west Crater Glacier receded as much as 100 m westward between April 19 and August 10 (fig. 19).

Nearby parts of the west Crater Glacier began to be pushed westward and were uplifted (fig. 19). Traceable features on the west glacier moved west as much as 80 m and rose as much as 20 m near the new dome's southwest margin, but areas farther to the north and west merely flowed downslope. Station WES6, a GPS receiver located on the west glacier ~200 m west of the dome, moved 10 m N. 51° W. and rose 0.8 m between July 14 and August 10. Meanwhile, the east Crater Glacier flowed passively to the north. East Crater Glacier fractured and became greatly crevassed as it descended rapidly to the north in response to the 100 m of excess thickness it had gained between November 2004 and April 2005. No further deformation of the east glacier occurred after mid-May, and its boundary with the dome became fairly stable (fig. 19).

Phase 5, Spines 6 and 7 Extrude Westward: August 1, 2005–April 2006 (Ongoing)

Normal Faulting and Westward Growth of Spine 6: August 1–October 9, 2005

Crumbling of spine 5 presaged reorganization of the vent and growth of spine 6 in late July and early August 2005. At least seven substantial rock avalanches and two slumping events between July 18 and 31 (table 3) reduced the smooth steep (54°) slabs of spine 5 of July 14 (fig. 3) to a rubbly ridge by August 10 (fig. 3). During this period, southward motion of segments of spine 5 slowed successively from south to north in such a way that, by the end of July, only the northernmost segment remained active.

During a transitional period August 1–5 (table 1), spine motion seen in time-lapse photography (Iverson and others, 2006) became localized to the vent area, where the sense of motion was nearly vertical, as the remainder of spine 5 began to slump slowly. A fracture system, somewhat concealed by rubble, developed along a S. 10° W. trend and divided the stagnating spine from the active extrusion as spine 6 developed and became the dominant feature, evident in images of August 10, 2005 (fig. 3).

From early to mid-August, spine 6 began moving westward, slowly at first but more rapidly. This westward motion of the extruding mass beginning on about August 6 marked the completion of the transition from spine 5 to spine 6 (table 1). Time-lapse photography of August 6–12 (Iverson and others, 2006) showed that spine 6 disintegrated continuously as it extended to the west.

The spine 6 mass comprised buried spines 1 and 2, a substantial part of spine 5 that had slumped to the west, debris shed from spines 3, 4, and 5, and welt rock caught between spines 1, 2, and 3 (fig. 20). This mass thus included massive lava, as well as deformed and disintegrating blocks and debris. On August 10, the extruded lava volume in spine 6 was ~1×10^6 m^3, but the total volume of the deformed mass was ~12×10^6 m^3 (table 2). A spurt in lava extrusion occurred during the transition from spine 5 to spine 6 and continued into September (table 2).

No specific feature on spine 6 could be tracked in DEMs and vertical aerial photos between August 10 and September 20. However, the trace of the active spine and the shift of the west glacier-spine margin constrain the magnitude of translation during this period (fig. 21). The most active part of the spine migrated ~140 m N. 75° W. during the 41 days at an average rate of 3.4 m/d. Overall the most active part of the spine subsided a net ~40 m, but this value ignores vertical growth—active disintegration removed tens of meters from the apex of spine 6. The center of most active extrusion moved westward away from the original (October 4, 2004) vent area

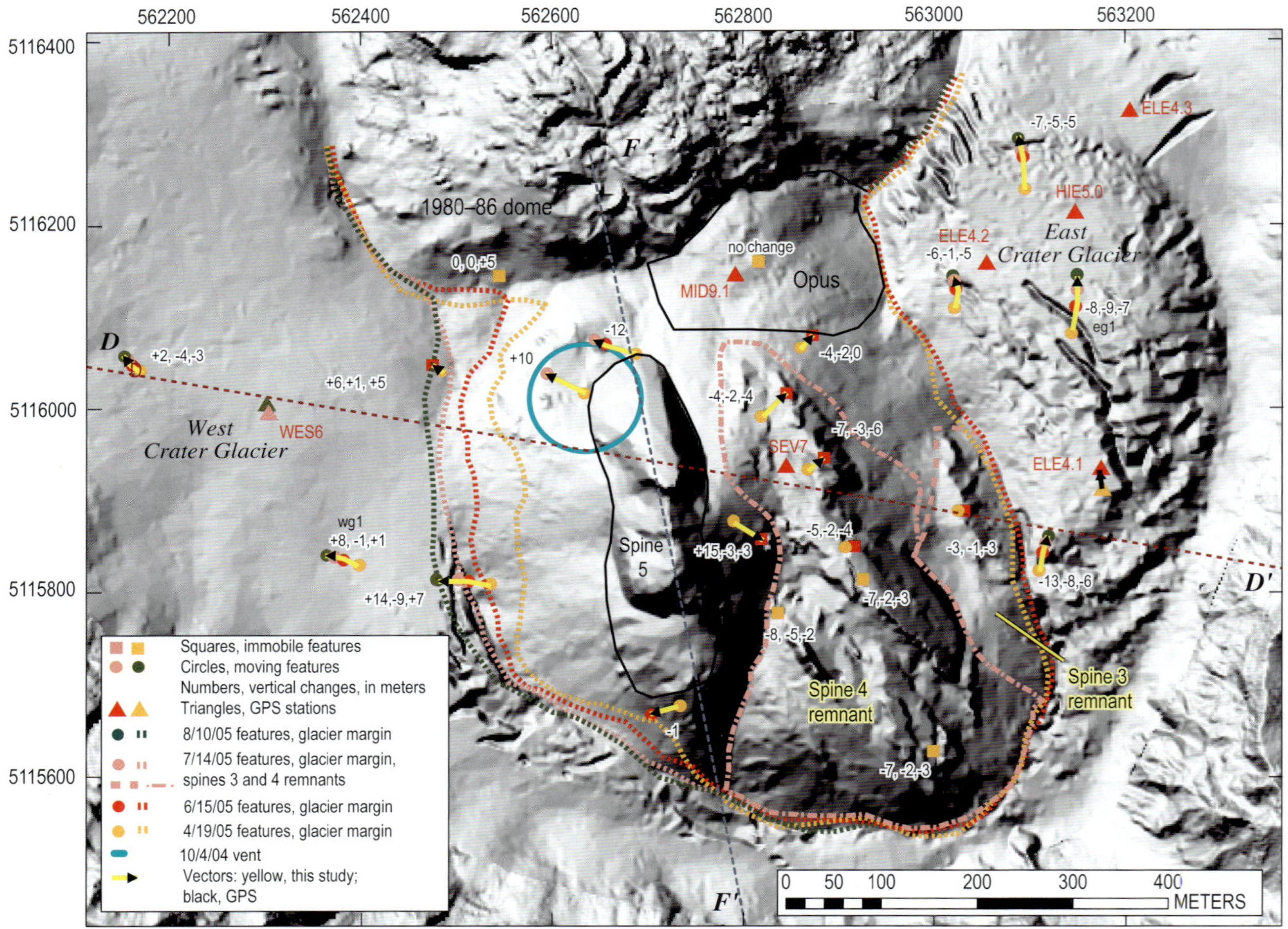

Figure 19. Deformation vectors for the period from April 19 to August 10, 2005, shown on DEM of July 14, 2005. Squares and dots indicate features tracked for dates identified by color in key. These colored symbols delimit deformation vectors of each of the three time intervals between relocation of features. Numbers are vertical components of vectors, in meters, for each interval. Underscores indicate no data for that interval. Dotted lines indicate dome-glacier margins for dates indicated by color in key. Line ***F–F′*** is trace of cross section shown in figure 18; line ***D–D′*** is trace of cross section shown in part in figure 22.

Table 3. Timing, style, and direction of mass-wasting events from spine 5 at Mount St. Helens, Washington, July 19–31, 2005.

[Timing and style of phenomena are inferred from time-lapse video (Iverson and others, 2006).]

Interval during which event occurred	Phenomenon	Direction
July 18–19	Avalanche	East
July 19–20	Avalanche	West
July 20–21	Avalanche	West from near apex of smooth slab
July 22–23	Avalanche	West
July 23–25	Slump	West
July 26–27	Avalanche	East
July 27–29	Slump	West from rubbly area of south part of spine
July 28–29	Avalanche	East
July 30–31	Avalanche	West

(fig. 21). Along an arc west to southwest of this new vent, the glacier-spine 6 contact receded 60–90 m westward at an average rate of 1.5–2.2 m/d (figs. 20–22).

Spine 5 Subsidence and Deformation of Surrounding Areas during August–September 2005

All parts of spine 5 translated westward and subsided as spine 6 moved away and removed its westward buttress (figs. 21, 22). Areas near spine 6 experienced maximum displacements of 40–60 m to the west and subsided by as much as 65 m. Areas close to the crest of spine 5 dropped by as much as 50 m while translating ~20 m westward. Such a pattern implies normal faulting along a northerly strike with westward dip as steep as 70°. The principal fault surface appears to coincide with a subsurface boundary sloping steeply to the west and demarcated by the contact between the subsurface remnants of spines 4 and 5 (fig. 22). This boundary could have formed a weak surface that was susceptible to subsequent subsidence. Features on spine 5 farther west of the fault trace translated more and subsided less than those near it, a pattern that implies rotational motion along a flattening fault (fig. 21). We infer that the fault is listric, dipping steeply westward along its near-surface trace and flattening as it extends deeper to the west (fig. 22).

The perspective provided by south-rim time-lapse photography (Poland and others, this volume, chap. 11) suggests that southwestern parts of spine 5 and southeastern parts of spine 6 subsided and migrated westward in tandem. Spine 5, near its eastern margin, subsided very little, apparently because the underlying spine 4–5 contact dipped gently compared to the steeper contact to the west. The most significant translation had occurred by September 20, but some areas continued to subside through October. Subsidence of spine 5, coupled with westward extension of spine 6, resulted in formation of a sag between spines 5 and 6 (figs. 21, 22).

To the east, Opus, spine 3, and spine 4 were relatively immobile, moving less than 4 m. In August and September, the GPS station SEV7, situated on spine 4 about 30 m to the east of spine 5, translated 2 m westward and subsided 3 m as the spine 5 buttress gave way. Motion on other parts of Opus, spine 3, and spine 4 was too small to be detectable (fig. 21).

While west Crater Glacier accelerated westward to northwestward and thickened, east Crater Glacier continued to flow passively northward (fig. 21). Between August 10 and October 24, traceable features on the west glacier moved west by 100–120 m and rose 20–35 m in response to the bulldozing caused by spine 6 advance (fig. 22). Ensuing crevasses radiated westward along the principal strain axis. Three GPS stations were located on west Crater Glacier for various time intervals (Walder and others, this volume, chap. 13). An example, WES6, originally about 150 m west of the dome, moved 50 m N. 51 W. and rose 13 m during August 10–September 14. In contrast, its motion in the 27 days before August 10 was only 10 m northwest and 1 m up. Advance of spine 6 pushed west Crater Glacier westward and heaped it as high as 30 m above its previous surface.

Westward Extrusion and Overthrusting of Spine 7: October 9, 2005–April 2006

Extrusion of spine 7 began in mid-October with subsurface spine intrusion centered east of spine 6 and near the trace of the October 4, 2004, vent. Subsurface intrusion gave way by November to spine extrusion, which continued through April 2006 (table 1, fig. 21*B*).

An increase in high-frequency earthquakes, beginning on October 9, 2005, marked the beginning of spine 7 growth (Moran and others, this volume, chap. 2). Fuming and heating of the surface area above the October 2004 vent observed in thermal images of October 11, 2005, revealed the first surface manifestation of the new intrusion (fig. 3). Time-lapse photographs from a camera on the south crater rim (Poland and others, this volume, chap. 11) showed general bulging of a rubbly area between spines 5 and 6 by October 13.

Uplift and westward motion that became increasingly evident between October 14 and 21 indicated extrusion of spine 7. From its origin in the depression between spines 5 and 6, spine 7 pushed upward and outward to the west, steepening on the east as it grew and overthrusting spine 6 to the west (fig. 20). By mid-November, a broken-up slabby spine had begun to emerge from the rubble-strewn slopes of the bulge. By mid-December, this slab of rock had become more coherent and prominent. As it continued to grow, the slab steepened eastward progressively, attaining a slope of 50° by April 2006. The extruding slab also pushed spine 6 and part of spine 7 across a sector extending from southwest

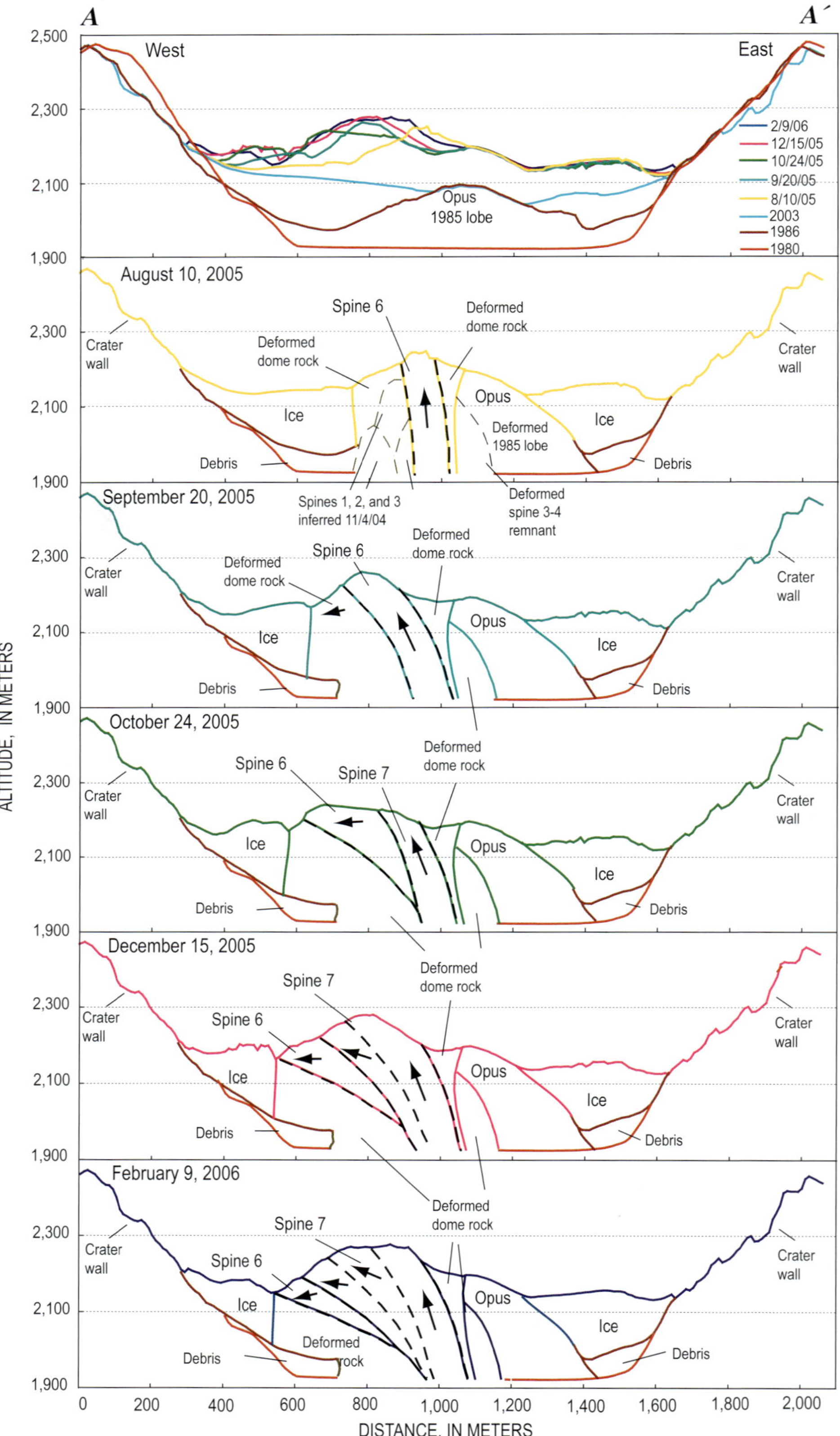

Figure 20. East-west cross section A–A' (location shown in figures 1 and 21) illustrating extrusion and thrusting of spines 6 and 7. Top panel shows known profiles for dates given, and the other panels illustrate geologic interpretations at labeled times. Dashed lines indicate thrust faults.

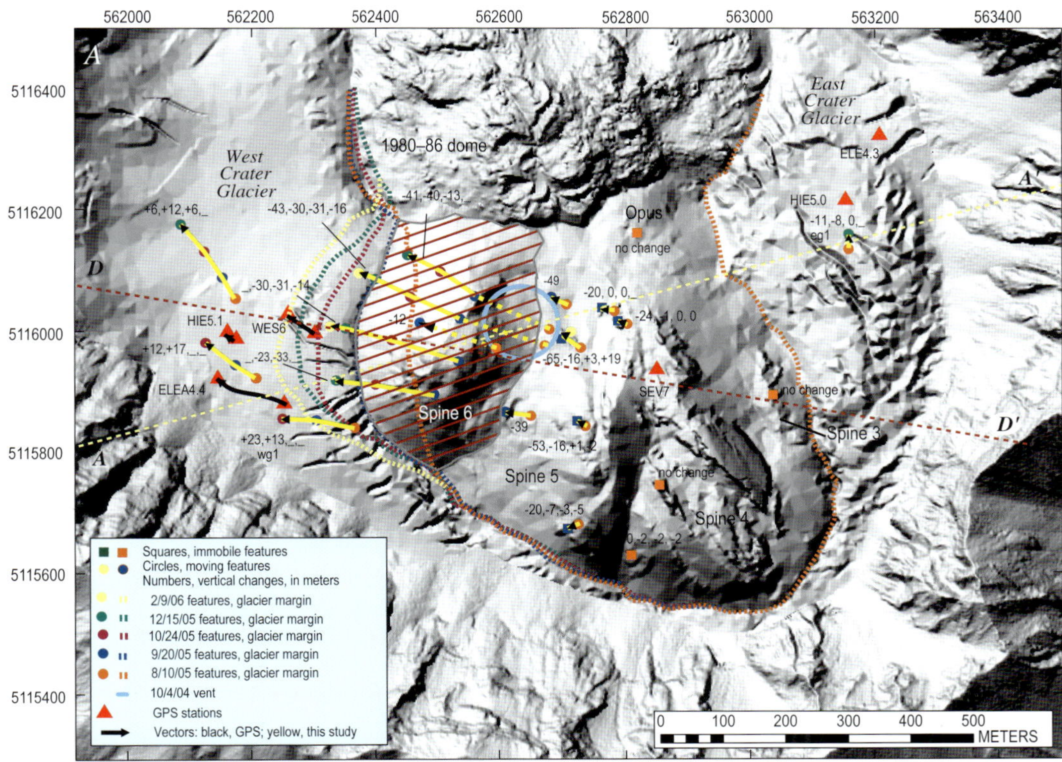

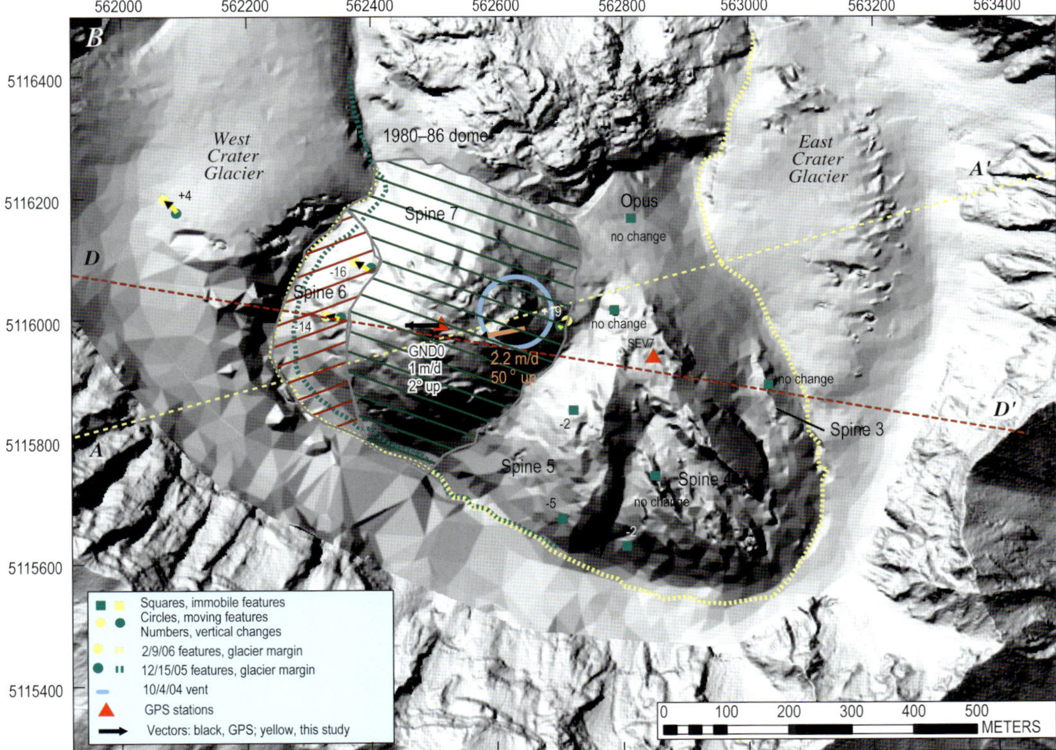

Figure 21. Deformation vectors for the period from August 10, 2005, to February 9, 2006, shown on DEMs. Squares and dots indicate features tracked for dates identified by color in key. These colored symbols delimit deformation vectors of each of the time intervals between relocation of features. Numbers are vertical components of vectors, in meters, for each interval; underscores indicate no data for interval. Red-lined pattern indicates spine 6; green-lined pattern indicates spine 7. Dotted lines indicate dome-glacier margins for dates indicated by color in key. Lines *A–A′* and *D–D′* are traces of cross sections shown in figures 20 and 22. *A*, September 20, 2005. *B*, February 9, 2006.

to northwest radially away from its source (fig. 21). Rock debris continually avalanching from the west face of spine 7 formed hot talus slopes on this side. As the spine grew through November, its rubbly western slope began to bury adjacent sections of spine 6.

Spine 7 formed a distinct entity between, and overlapping, spines 5 and spine 6. By October 24, the spine had been extruding for 10 days, and we estimate its volume as about a third of the total volume erupted since September 20, or ~1×10^6 m^3. Between October 24, 2005, and February 9, 2006, time-averaged magma flux gradually diminished (table 2).

As spine 7 moved westward and thrust over spine 6, it grew higher and steeper, and its solid eastern buttress became a progressively more prominent, finlike structure (figs. 23*A*, 23*B*). Cracks penetrated the gouge coat in distinctive patterns and moved upward and westward along with the fin (fig. 23*A*). From examination of photographs, spine 7 was ascending westward at an angle of 50° at a rate of ~2 m/d in early April (fig. 23*A*). At the same time, GPS station GND0, ~100 m west of the fin, was only moving 1 m/d horizontally westward (fig. 23*C*). This discrepancy in rate of deformation within spine 7, with steeper, faster displacement near source and slower subhorizontal displacement to the west, implies internal shearing (figs. 20, 23*D*).

Deformation during Spine 7 Extrusion: October 9, 2005–April 2006

All parts of spine 6 translated and subsided as spine 7 pushed it westward (figs. 21, 22). Features on spine 6 were subject to substantial but gradually diminishing deformation from October 9, 2005, to February 9, 2006, with maximum total displacement over this period in excess of 200 m to the west and subsidence as much as 80 m (table 4). Toward the end of this period, spine 7 moved about 1 m/d westward with no subsidence, while adjacent spine 6 moved at half that rate and subsided (table 4). Such a pattern implies shearing between spines 6 and 7 (figs. 20, 23*D*).

West Crater Glacier continued to move westward to northwestward (fig. 21). Between October and December, a single traceable feature on the west glacier moved northwest 60 m and rose 6 m in response to continuing spine impingement (fig. 21). Motion of GPS station ELE4.4, positioned farther south and closer to spine 7, slowed after October 24. It moved 1.6 m/d N. 68° W. and rose 19 m in the 34 days before October 24, whereas it moved 1.1 m/d N. 55° W. and rose 3 m in the 15 days after that date (LaHusen and others, this volume, chap. 16). Farther north, the glacier accelerated to the north in response

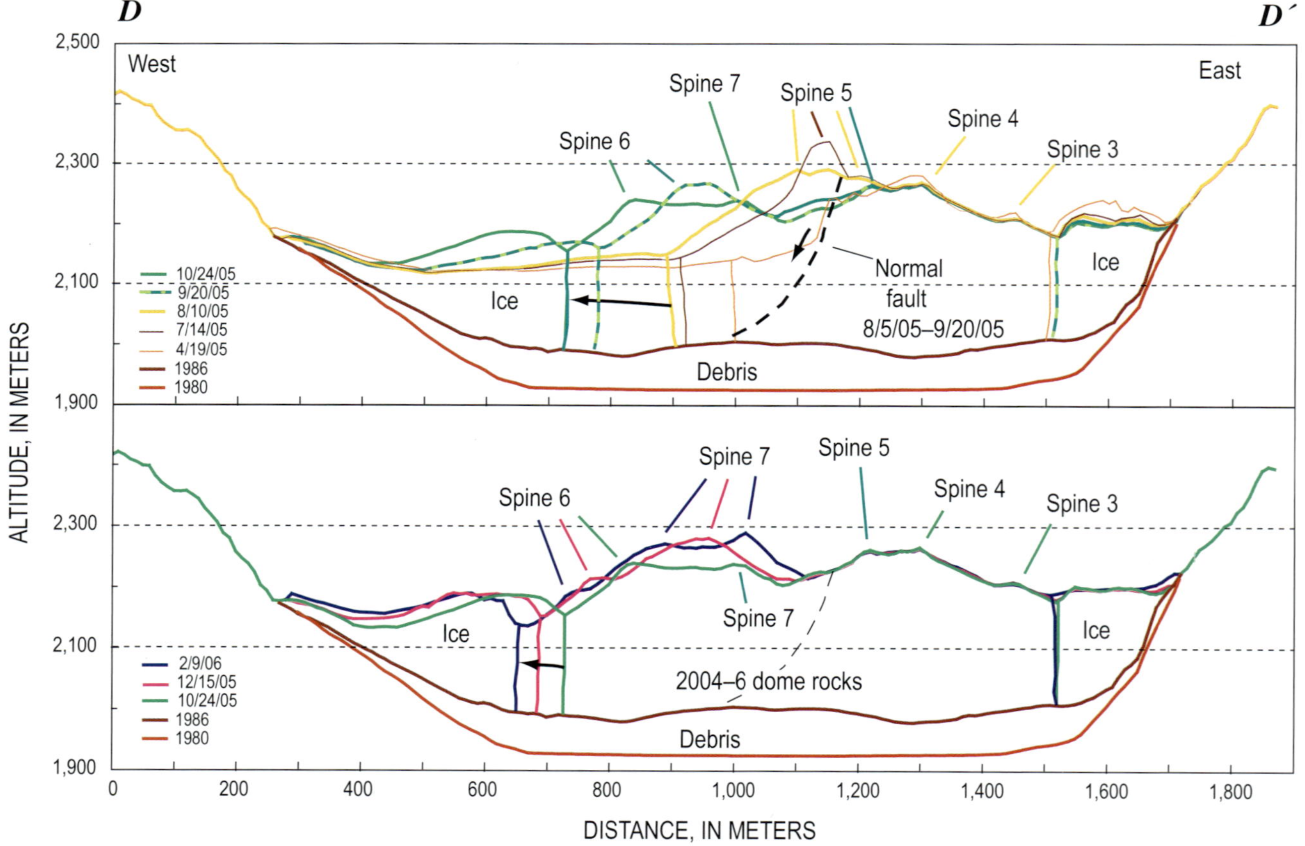

Figure 22. East-west cross section ***D–D´*** (location shown in figures 1 and 21) illustrating extrusion and thrusting of spines 6 and 7. Panels illustrate geologic interpretations at labeled times. Dashed line indicates inferred normal fault, which is located at steep west-dipping trace of spine 4 on April 19, 2005, surface.

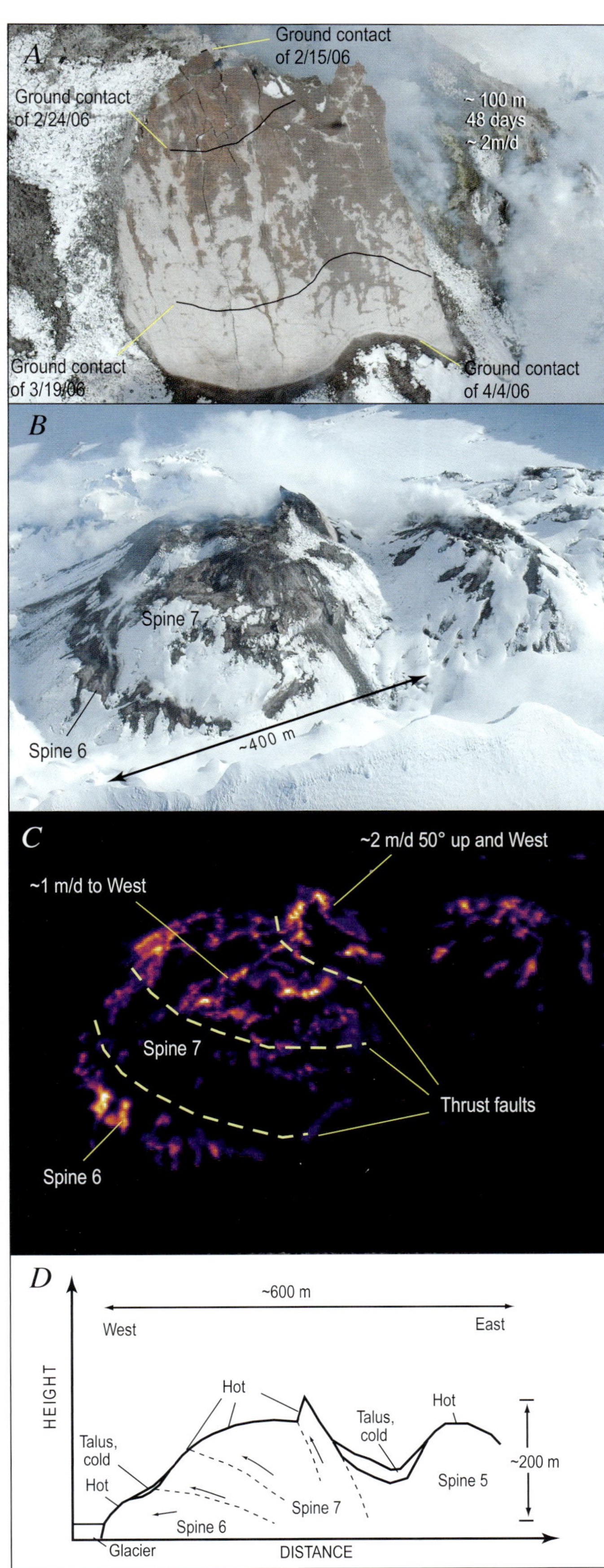

to the 30–40 m of excess elevation it had gained through uplift between August 2005 and February 2006 (fig. 21*A*).

Discussion

We consider here factors that influenced dome growth during the 2004–6 eruption. Potential near-surface controls on spine growth during the 2004–6 eruption include thick glacial ice, initial vent position and geometry, the 1986 topographic surface, and backpressure caused by spines pushing through and thrusting over debris from previous spines. We also consider the effects of dome growth on Crater Glacier. Lastly, we compare the 2004–6 Mount St. Helens dome-building eruption with well-documented historical examples at other volcanoes.

Effect of Glacier on Spine Growth

Glacier ice as thick as 150 m has apparently had little effect on the extrusion of the dome or on the growth of various spines, except to conceal substantial parts of them and to prevent shedding of disintegrating dome talus beneath the level of the glacier surface. As discussed in the introductory section, we infer that dome-glacier contacts have remained steep. Near-vertical contacts are consistent with ice-hot rock marginal boundaries observed at other locations. Examples include tuyas in British Columbia, Canada (Mathews, 1947), and ice-lava contacts at Mount Rainier (Lescinsky and Sisson, 1998). Glacial ice appeared not to impede spine growth significantly. Spines 2–4 grew recumbently to the south, pushing glacial ice aside as they progressed. Westward extension of spines 6 and 7 also pushed through thick glacial ice. The bed of the glacier was permeable enough that meltwater drained away without interacting with hot dome rock (Walder and others, this volume, chap. 13), except possibly during six brief phreatic explosions (Moran and others, this volume, chap. 6).

Vent Dimension and Location and Influence of 1980–86 Dome on Spine Growth

The depression from which the initial phreatic eruptions originated and from which the initial spine extruded was located at the west end of Opus and had an approximate

Figure 23. Photographs, thermal infrared image, and cross section of the Mount St. Helens crater on April 4, 2006. *A*, View looking west at 100-m fin showing previous ground-spine contacts. *B*, View looking northeast at spines 6 and 7. *C*, Thermal infrared image of view in *B*, looking northeast and showing thrust faults and relative motions. *D*, Schematic east-west cross section of growing spine 7, slowing spine 6, and stagnant spine 5. Orientation is roughly along line shown in *B* but extends east to spine 5. USGS photos by J.W. Vallance; thermal image by M. Logan.

Table 4. Timing, bearing, magnitude, and rate of deformation of one feature located on spine 6 at Mount St. Helens, Washington, between September 20, 2005, and February 9, 2006.

[Timing, direction, and magnitude of deformation are inferred from DEMs on given dates (Schilling and others, this volume, chap. 8).]

Interval	9/20/2005–10/24/2005	10/24/2005–12/15/2005	12/15/2005–2/9/2006
Days elapsed	34	52	56
Bearing	N80°W	N80°W	N85°W
Horizontal translation			
Displacement (m)	110	75	35
Rate (m/d)	3.2	1.4	0.6
Subsidence			
Displacement (m)	30	31	14
Rate (m/d)	0.9	0.6	0.3

diameter of 120 m (figs. 5, 12). Superimposing this vent location on the 1986 topographic surface (fig. 12) reveals that the initial vent was located on ice over the south-facing slope of the 1980–86 dome, in particular over the 1985 fault-formed ridge known as Opus. Just before the 2004 eruption, relief from the high point on Opus to the moat's floor beneath the glacier was ~130 m, and south-facing slopes were as steep as 40° under the trace of the vent (fig. 12).

The initial location of the 2004 vent, on steep south slopes of Opus, themselves buried beneath the glacier, clearly influenced the propensity of stiff spine extrusions to move southward. Several studies suggest that the magma ascending the conduit had largely solidified within a kilometer of the surface (Dzurisin and others, 2005; Iverson and others, 2006; and in this volume: Moran and others, chap. 2; Cashman and others, chap. 19; Pallister and others, chap. 30). We infer that, as the magma neared the surface in September 2004, the preexistent solid plug of 1980–86 dome rock deflected the rising mass southward so that, near the surface, it tilted southward.

We tracked successive extrusion points at the surface by centering circles on the center of each spine origin with appropriate diameters equal to spine width (fig. 24). As the extrusion transitioned from the initial spine formation of phase 2 to well-developed whaleback-style spines of phase 3, the surface trace of the vent moved south and east. These trends continued until spine 3 began its breakup in December 2004. During the spine 3–4 transition this sense of movement reversed. However, during growth of spine 4, the southward and eastward motion recommenced. With extrusion of spine 5 during phase 4, the vent gradually moved westward back toward its original location. This motion increased with phase 5 extrusion of spine 6. With the onset of spine 7 extrusion, the surface manifestation of the vent returned to and remained within 20 m of its original position. Between vent clearing of phase 1 and initial whaleback-style intrusion of phase 3, the surface trace of the vent rapidly rose 130 m because an increasingly thick pile of lava built beneath it. Elevation of the vent trace increased slowly through extrusion of spines 4 and 5 during phases 3 and 4, then diminished with extension of spine 6 as phase 5 commenced. Extrusion of spine 7 rebuilt the lava pile beneath the vent, so that by early 2006 its trace was 200 m higher than its altitude in October 2004, though it was back to its original position in plan view.

Superimposing the position of the original vent and the seven spines on the 1986 surface suggests that the vent or conduit need not have shifted substantially at the depth of the initial erup-

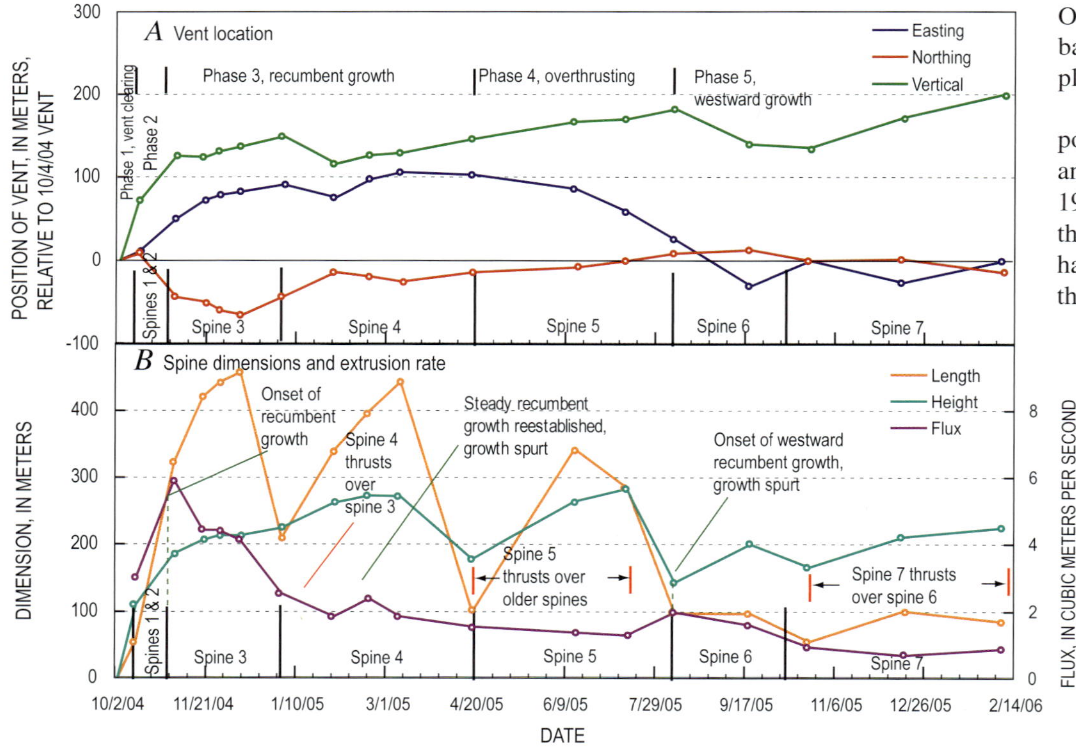

Figure 24. Plots of positions of vent, dimensions of spines, and extrusion flux versus time. *A*, Center of vent located in plan. *B*, Length of active spine, height of active spine, and lava discharge.

tion surface (figs. 12, 25). Geometry of the vent area permits origin of spines 1 through 4 from approximately the same initial vent location at the depth of the 1986 surface (fig. 12). Initially, extrusion of spines 1 and 2 covered the area directly above and to the south of the vent so that, as spine 3 began to grow upward and southward, previous spine and welt rubble diverted it eastward (fig. 12*A*). Additional dome rock and debris emplaced during spine 3 growth diverted spine 4 farther eastward. Eventually, so much dome rock had been pushed to the east that fragmented dome rock abutted the steep part of the east crater wall, and continuing spine extrusion could no longer push it aside. The subsequent spine (spine 5) therefore thrust instead over the older spines in a more southerly direction. When spine debris above the vent eventually built high enough, spine growth could extend westward across the rock debris of spines 1 and 2 (fig. 25). An inclined conduit did not simply increase in altitude; rather it shifted tens of meters southward, then south-southeastward, and finally southwestward as it evolved and grew higher (fig. 25). We suggest that vent geometry is such that spine extrusion throughout the eruption could have passed through approximately the same vent location at a depth near that of the 1986 surface and that migration of the vent's surface expression resulted from diversion by remnants of previous spines.

Influence of 1980–86 Surface on Spine Growth

Topography inherited from the 1980–86 eruption controlled growth patterns of the laterally propagating spines (figs. 12, 25). We superimposed the outlines of actively growing spines on topographic features concealed by glacier ice to assess their influence on growth patterns. Generally, we found that the 1986 topographic surface controlled recumbent

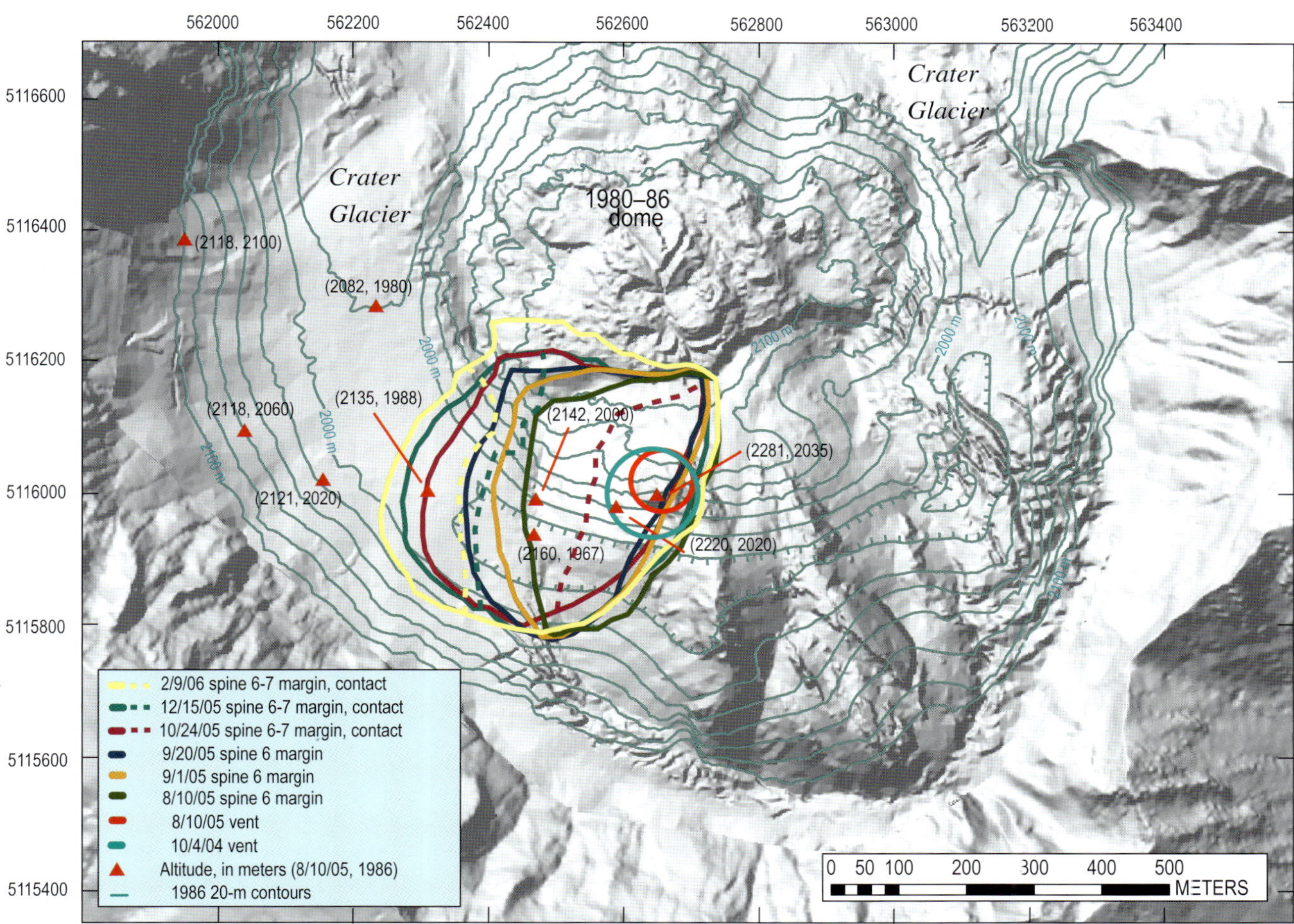

Figure 25. August 10, 2005, DEM showing outlines of spines 6 and 7 and their dome-glacier margins (solid lines) on dates indicated by colors in key. Dashed lines indicate contacts between spines 6 and 7 for appropriate dates indicated by colors in key. Select 20-m contours from 1986 DEM illustrate how composite spines 6 and 7 have migrated along a low topographic trough to west. Comparisons of altitudes on August 10, 2005, with those of 1986 are given for localities marked by red triangles.

growth directions, the rotation of spines, and how spines ultimately fragmented, but the ultimate barrier to continued lateral growth proved to be the walls of the 1980 crater modified by talus at their base and modified slightly by subsequent erosion.

After spine 1 grew, subsequent spines grew southward, in part because the crater floor sloped to the south. Spine 2 advanced due south until it encountered the steep opposing slopes of the south crater wall. Because spine 2 was then positioned directly south of the vent, the prominent whaleback of spine 3 that followed was forced slightly eastward as it advanced. Spine 3 extended across a broad basin to the south-southeast that was filled with glacial ice and welt debris. It then encountered the crater wall at an oblique angle (20°–30° from perpendicular) in mid-November 2004, and the influence of the wall deflected the snout of the spine eastward (fig. 12*A*). Once spine 4 had pushed remnants of its predecessor aside, it too progressed south-southeastward, encountered the 1980 crater wall at an oblique angle, and then rotated eastward (figs. 7, 15). A lack of such rotation before the spine arrived at buttressing slopes and fairly rapid rotation subsequently is strong evidence in support of the oblique-incidence hypothesis of rotation.

Both spines 3 and 4 began to fracture, crumble, and ultimately decouple from the source as a result of resistance to motion when they impinged on the crater wall. Spine 3 began to slow and break apart as it pushed against the crater walls in mid-November 2004. Two voluminous blocks and numerous smaller ones separated from the spine before it finally broke and fractured near its source on or about December 18, 2004. Thereafter, lava near the source slowly decoupled from remnants to the south to form spine 4. A similar sequence occurred when spine 4 itself met the wall, fractured at its root, and decoupled in April 2005 to form spine 5. In the April case, however, debris had filled the area east as far as the east crater wall, and thus spine 5 grew by southward thrusting across previous spine remnants.

Rotational motion of spines 3 and 4 in turn caused rotation of previously emplaced dome debris, welt debris, and glacier ice to the east. Southward spine propagation and oblique impingement on the crater wall apparently caused the rotation, and the less resistant expanse of glacial ice to the east permitted the rotation to proceed in that direction. By mid-April, when spine 4 and associated debris outboard of it had encountered steep slopes to the southeast as well as to the south, the counterclockwise rotation (map view) of phase 3 ceased (fig. 12*B*). Also at this time, the sense of rotation reversed from counterclockwise to clockwise, with a pivot 300 m south of the vent (fig. 19). The south end of spine 4 became fixed and the north end began to move east because the only available space east of the 2004–5 dome was located directly east of the vent (labeled "mid-April space east of vent" in fig. 12); no such space was available to the southeast.

Spine 5 thrust over remnants of spines 3 and 4 at steepening angles (fig. 18) until its perch atop those remnants became unstable. Failure along a north-south zone of weakness dipping steeply to the west allowed motion to resume along a 1986 topographic low, as spine 5 slumped together with westward growth of spine 6 (fig. 22). From April to August 2005, preexisting topography had little effect on spine growth because the active spine, 5, was shearing over previous spines rather than following old topographic surfaces. With extrusion of spine 6, westward spine migration pushed previous spine remnants and affiliated rubble westward into the topographic trough defined by the 1980–86 dome and the crater wall (fig. 25). This moat-like topography channeled growth of spine 6 such that it barely impinged on steeper slopes to the south and rode up on topographically high areas of the 1980–86 dome only near the vent, where some northward spreading and rockfall was underway. Similarly, as spine 7 thrust west into parts of spine 6, it pushed the earlier spine westward along the same topographic trough. As the volume of material to the west built, the rate of westward recession of the dome-glacier boundary slowed, and slabs of spine 7 extruded at steepening angles.

Extrinsic Control of Spine Growth Rate

An intrinsic exponential decline in overall extrusion rate (fig. 24) that probably derives from declining magma supply and pressurization is apparent during the course of the present eruption. Overprinted on this decline are several apparent increases in magma flux that may have been controlled extrinsically (spurts in fig. 24*B*). Time-averaged effusion rates commonly rise rapidly to a peak before falling slowly, resulting in an exponential decrease in eruption rate and declining growth (Harris and others, 2000). Such trends can be explained by the tapping of enclosed and pressurized magma chambers (Wadge, 1981; Harris and others, 2000). Extrinsic factors, such as changes in load, are thought to cause variation in effusion rates (Harris and others, 2003).

We hypothesized that increases or decreases in load near the surface might reduce or enhance extrusion rates, owing to increases and decreases in the mass displaced (fig. 24*B*). We plotted both relative height and length of active spines against time to test this idea. However, our results show no obvious correlation between spine length or height and extrusion rate (fig. 24*B*). A comparison between extrusion rate and style of extrusion suggests a possible correlation. Extrusion rate was greater when steady recumbent growth was established and smaller when active spines were thrusting upward at significant angles (fig. 24*B*). Steady lateral extrusion of spine 3 in late October and early November 2004 corresponded to an initial increase in discharge, and renewed steady extrusion of spine 4 in February 2005 corresponded to a slight increase in extrusion rate. A transition from thrusting to westward migration and slumping correlates to a third localized peak from late July to September 2005. Periods of resistance to movement caused by thrusting of spines at increasing angles over previous remnants also correlate with periods of diminished extrusion rate (fig. 24*B*). We suggest that such growth conditions may have acted to resist extrusion, suppressing the flux by backpressure. Slumping events and vent reorganization eased backpressure and thus enhanced flux.

Impact of Dome Growth on the Crater Glacier

Whereas the glacier had little affect on dome growth, spine growth did have a profound impact on the Crater Glacier—slicing it in two, pushing it hundreds of meters first one way then another, doubling it in thickness, but not melting it. As the response of Crater Glacier is the detailed subject of another contribution to this volume (Walder and others, chap. 13), we merely summarize the impact of spine growth on the glacier from the perspective of surface deformation vectors, which allowed us to track certain glacier features throughout nearly the entire course of the eruption. During October and November 2004, subsurface deformation owing to spine extrusion caused the glacier surface to take on first the appearance of a migrating wave of fractured ice and rock, then, with surfacing of spine 3 through that material, the appearance of bow waves of fractured snow and ice both west and east of the whaleback form. Once spine 3 divided the glacier in December 2004, it and its successor, spine 4, began slewing to the east, rotating about their tails and plowing the ice of the east glacier into a 100-m-high berm by January 2005. The berm then sluiced northward through the gap between the 1980–86 dome and the crater wall between April 2005 and February 2006 (fig. 26). Growth of spines 6 and 7, plus subsidence of dome remnants into west Crater Glacier, created a similar response between August and December 2005 whereby the glacier was first pushed up and westward (fig. 26) and then began to flow through the gap between the 1980–86 dome and crater wall. Despite its mistreatment, the glacier has lost no more than about 10 percent of its volume to contact melting as of February 2006 (Walder and others, this volume, chap. 13). Apparently, gouge-coated spines and shrouds of cold debris have effectively insulated glacier ice from hot spine interiors.

Comparison with Other Dome-Building Eruptions

Several factors set the 2004–6 dome-building eruption of Mount St. Helens apart from that of other well-documented historical domes such as those of Mount St. Helens 1980–86, Montserrat 1995–98, Santiaguito 1922–2006, and Unzen 1990–96. These include extrusion of solid spines, a propensity to form recumbent spines, interaction with glacier ice, and topographic setting. Mont Pelée in 1903 produced a spine that grew vertically but otherwise resembled whalebacks at Mount St. Helens. However, perhaps the historical dome-building eruption most similar to that of Mount St. Helens 2004–6 was the 1944–45 extrusion of the Showa-Shinzan dome at Usu volcano in Japan.

Mount St. Helens' 1980–86 dome extrusion differed from the present extrusion in extrusion rate, morphology, and process of emplacement. Excepting a one-year endogenous phase, extrusion of the 1980–86 dome occurred in discrete episodes, 16 of which were preceded by periods of accelerating endogenous growth, followed by extrusion of a viscous lobe, and terminated with periods of subsidence and lateral spreading (Swanson and Holcomb, 1990). In contrast, the present eruption has proceeded continuously with a general decline in discharge (fig. 24). Output of fresh dacite in the early phases of the present eruption occurred at a rate that is about one-half to one-third of rates measured during the 1980–86 episodes (Chadwick and others, 1988). The relentless growth during the 2004–6 eruption, however, has produced a total volume similar to that of the 1980–86 eruption in about one-fourth of the time.

Swanson and Holcomb (1990) document distinctive profiles for individual lobes emplaced during 1980–86, showing that lobes tended to adopt a characteristic slope (33°) and a characteristic height-to-diameter ratio (h/d) of about 0.32. The slope was approximately the angle of repose for coarse angular talus. In a more elaborate analysis, Iverson (1990) was able to model the characteristic slope in terms of a pressurized viscous magma enclosed by a brittle shell. Such a model is not applicable for spines of the present eruption because of the complicating influence of topographic barriers, glacial ice, and the subsolidus character of the magma, with the spines extruding in a near-solid state. Glacial ice within the crater has buttressed spines at slopes much greater than the angle of repose during the current eruption. Overall, the h/d ratio and slope for spines 3–7 ranged from 0.6 to 0.7 and from 50° to 60°, respectively. Those of initial spines were greater. Slopes higher than the angle of repose also reflect the massive and solid character of extruded spines. Such high h/d ratios are typical of upheaved domes and peléean spines (Blake, 1990).

Well-documented dome extrusion at Unzen, Japan, and Santiaguito, Guatemala, was continuous but varied in extru-

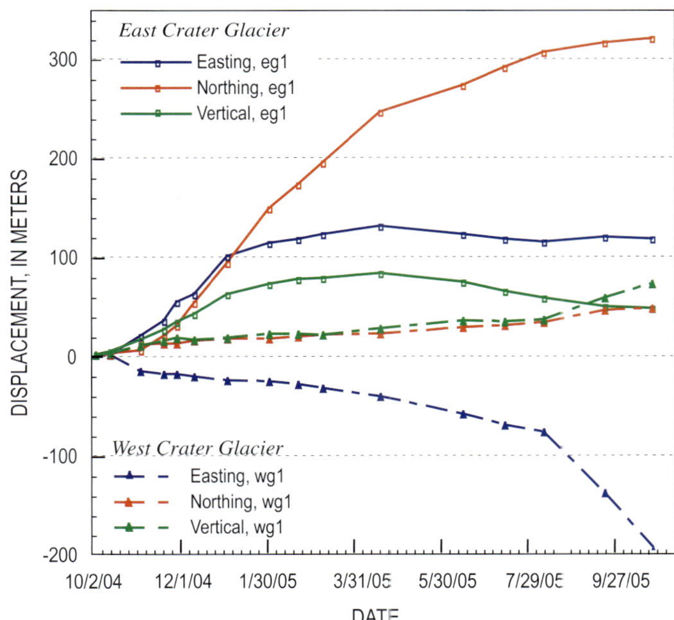

Figure 26. Displacement plots of a feature on east Crater Glacier (eg1 located at site a in fig. 2) and one on west Crater Glacier (wg1 located at site i in figs. 2*A*, 2*B*) versus time (both features are located at intervals in figs. 5, 7, 15, 19, 21).

sion rate and included both endogenous intrusion of viscous magma and extrusion of lava flows (Rose, 1980, 1987; Nakada and others, 1999; Harris and others, 2003). At Unzen, endogenous growth typified slow discharge, and exogenous growth typified more rapid discharge (Nakada and others, 1999). Over the course of the eruption, discharge slowed and endogenous growth increased proportionately (Nakada and others, 1999). Although Santiaguito has erupted continuously during 1922–2006, its growth has been episodic—waxing and waning over time scales of several years (Rose, 1987). In contrast to recent activity at Unzen, during Santiaguito's 84-year and ongoing eruption there has been a general tendency for the proportion of exogenous to endogenous growth to increase with time (Harris and others, 2003). Neither Unzen nor Santiaguito has shown the propensity to build solid-state spines at a low extrusion rate as observed during the current eruption at Mount St. Helens.

At Soufrière Hills volcano, Montserrat, Watts and others (2002) documented the morphology of lobes and spines, some of which superficially resemble those described here, and correlated them with extrusion rates. Watts and others (2002, their fig. 33) documented near-vertical spines, whaleback spines, and mega-spines that superficially resemble spines formed during the current eruption of Mount St. Helens, though similar forms here have had dimensions on a scale of hundreds of meters rather than tens of meters as observed at Soufrière Hills. With the exception of spine 1, the spines of the Mount St. Helens eruption have been larger and remained active longer than those at Soufrière Hills. Whaleback spines 3 and 4 grew during periods of months rather than days as at Montserrat, and spines 5 and 7 thrust over previous spines during periods of four months or more. The unusual, simultaneous slump and westward extrusion of spine 6 has no analogy to spine growth during any documented episode at Soufrière Hills volcano. More fluid morphologies, such as shear lobes and pancake lobes, did not occur during the Mount St. Helens 2004–6 eruption.

After its notorious eruption of 1902, Mont Pelée, Martinique, built a vertical spine that shares some characteristics with spines of the current Mount St. Helens eruption. That spine grew vertically to a height of more than 200 m in 1903 (Lacroix, 1904). Photographs (Lacroix, 1904) suggest that the spine was solid, had a gouge-coated and striated surface, and exposed a broken and massive surface on its opposite side. Like the Mount St. Helens spines, the Mont Pelée spine crumbled as it grew and eventually stagnated (Lacroix, 1904).

During its 1943–45 eruption, Showa-Shinzan dome of Mount Usu uplifted an area of as much as 1.5×1.5 km as much as 140 m (Mimatsu, 1995), generating a deformed zone reminiscent of the welt. Extrusion followed the deformation, as a jagged solid spine punched through the older roof rocks. As described by Mimatsu (1995), within nine days of initial unrest in December 1943, an area west of Mount Usu began to experience uplifting, folding, and faulting. Uplift to the west was initially strongest, after which its locus migrated in stages, eastward back toward the volcano. By June 1944, uplift ranged from 10 to 40 m. From June to November 1944, an additional 100 m of deformation accompanied 17 phreatic or phreatomagmatic explosions (Mimatsu, 1995). Finally, at the end of November 1944, the first lava spine pushed through the deformed and cratered uplifted area. Dacite spines continued to grow until August 1945. The spines commonly had a jagged appearance (Mimatsu, 1995), unlike those at Mount St. Helens. Like those at Mount St. Helens since 2004, the spines were completely solid on extrusion and showed no tendency to flow. The spines all rose more or less vertically, and none were described as having appreciable lateral components of motion (Mimatsu, 1995).

One spine at Mount Usu, Kobu-yama or Bump Mountain, did have a form more analogous to those of the present eruption of Mount St. Helens. Mimatsu (1995) describes it as having a shape like the bottom of a boat, with a coating of pulverized rock or dirt and grooves or scratches parallel to the direction of extrusion. The powdery surface is probably analogous to the gouge-coated surface of spines at Mount St. Helens. Mimatsu (1995) also described horizontal bands on Bump Mountain that were similar to the bands commonly observed on smooth surfaces of spines during 2004–6 at Mount St. Helens. The bands on Kobu-yama tended to form during periods of rain. Apparently, ash and debris that was constantly sloughing from the steep slopes of Kobu-yama stuck when the slopes were wetted. Furthermore, ash and debris accumulated at the base of the growing spine and stuck after heavy rains to form ledgelike bands that later rose as the spine extruded (Mimatsu, 1995). According to Mimatsu (1995), parts of these ledges were later shorn by falling debris.

Horizontal bands at Mount St. Helens are probably analogous, though not quite identical in origin, to those at Showa-Shinzan. Horizontal bands on spines at Mount St. Helens seem to have three forms, but all are plausibly related to moisture. The first, those most closely matching Mimatsu's (1995) description, are shelf-like accumulations of fine to coarse debris that stick to the smooth surfaces of spines at certain times, then rise with spine growth (fig. 27). At Mount St. Helens, these seem to correspond to stormy periods at the volcano. We suggest that, as at Showa-Shinzan, addition of water to mixtures of fine and coarse debris immediately adjacent to the hot base of the extruding spine creates a weak cement that subsequently dries against the hot spine. A variation on this process involves only the fine-grained ash at the base of the spine and requires relatively less moisture. These bands are much less prominent. Photographs show fine debris concentrated at the base of the spines (fig. 27). This material requires less water to form a cement and, hence less moisture is required to create horizontal bands of such fine ash. A third, most common but least prominent variety of band, appears to involve periodic darkening of the gouge-coated surface. No one has examined these closely enough to understand if there is an accumulation of material associated with them or if they are merely stains. We speculate that many of them are related to nightly dew. All of these bands are fragile and ephemeral.

Conclusions

Spine extrusion and associated near-vent deformation at Mount St. Helens during 2004–6 presented an opportunity to test and apply various methods to track, measure, and characterize the dynamics and morphologies of extrusion and nearby deformation during a dome-forming eruption. We summarize here our chief conclusions drawn from our data and the methodology that generated it.

Thermal infrared (TIR) surveys proved useful in differentiating events and structures that were cold from those that were hot. The TIR surveys showed that the explosions of October 1–5 were phreatic rather than magmatic. Imagery from TIR surveys also proved useful in identifying areas where spines were about to emerge. These were apparent as broad areas that warmed substantially in the days immediately prior to extrusion. Once spines began extruding, regular TIR surveys helped document their growth, character, and structures within them. Finally, TIR images helped monitoring crews identify places on

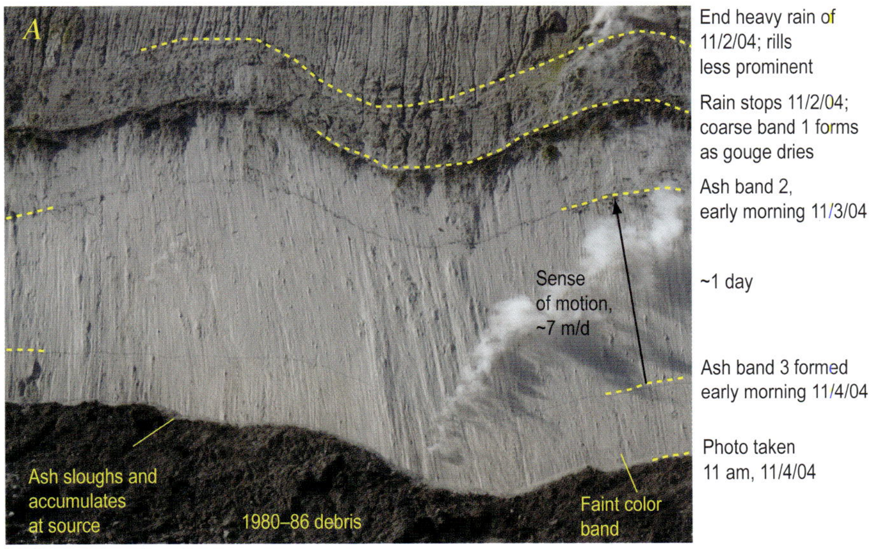

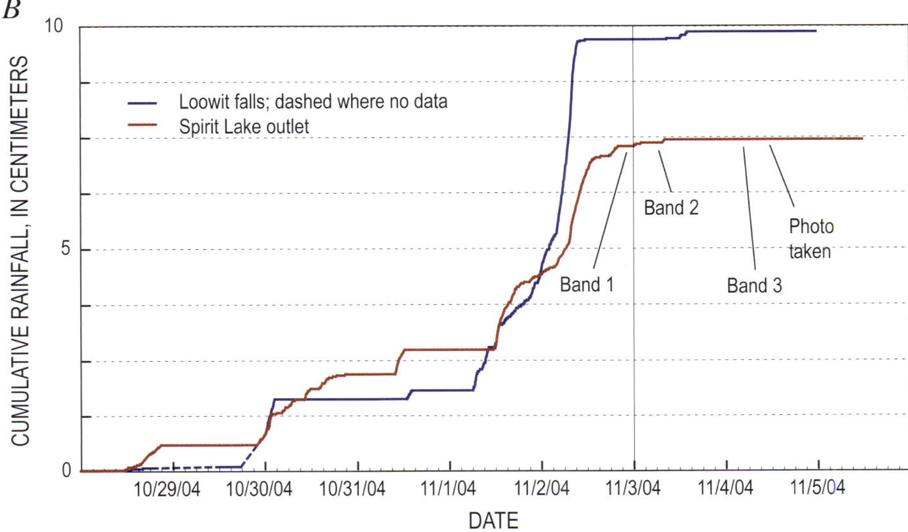

Figure 27. Photograph of emerging spine and plot of rainfall from October–November 2004. *A*, Close-up view of spine 3 east flank at 11 a.m. on November 4, 2004. Coarse band 1 consists of mixtures of ash and coarse lithic lapilli, more subtle bands 2 and 3 consist of ash, and very faint ones may be stains. Band formation is associated with increases in moisture. USGS photo by J.S. Pallister. *B*, Cumulative rainfall versus time from USGS gages at Loowit falls (crater mouth) and at Spirit Lake outlet and time of emergence of notable bands. Rainfall data courtesy of K. Spicer, USGS.

the dome cool enough to place GPS instruments and accelerometers (Schneider and others, this volume, chap. 17).

Data collected as part of this study along with others in this volume suggest solid-state extrusion throughout the current dome-building episode. TIR measurement of deep cracks and newly exposed surfaces give temperatures well below the solidus of the dacite magma being erupted. Morphology of the various spines exhibits no flowage features like lobes, coulees, or ramp structures. Indeed, yield strength has apparently been so high that the spines can stand at steep slopes until they crumble. New spines have typically formed as previous ones have undergone brittle failure and fracturing, then shearing off to form stagnant crumbling masses.

Tracking of features in successive sets of aerial photographs and DEMs has enabled the development of surface-deformation vector fields during 17 time intervals, which have varied in duration from 1 to 55 days. Each vector field gives a comprehensive spatial sense of deformation during that interval. Each also indicates the nature of advance or motion during the interval. Time-lapse photography and GPS instruments provided extra detail on much finer time scales for specific localities and localized fields of view, but the DEM tracking provided a valuable synoptic perspective.

Chief near-surface controls on spine extrusion during the 2004–6 eruption have been vent location, relict surfaces such as the 1980 crater structure and the 1980–86 dome, and spine remnants emplaced during previous phases of the present eruption—but not glacial ice. Ice as thick as 150 m has obscured eruptive processes, prevented formation of marginal angle-of-repose talus fans, and encouraged steep boundary slopes to the new dome complex through buttressing, but it has not significantly impeded spines pushing through it. Spines initially emerged at a location over the steep south-facing slope of the 1980–86 dome, which dictated their initial southward propagation. The glacier-filled space of the moat between the 1980 crater walls and the 1980–86 dome permitted southward propagation of spines 2 to 4 and funneled spines 6 and 7 westward. Spine 2 impinged on the opposing slope of the crater and stopped. In contrast, recumbent whaleback spines 3 and 4 impinged at oblique angles and rotated eastward before cracking up. Although the vent location at the 2004–6 surface shifted east and south more than 100 m before moving back to the west, its altitude increased ~200 m due to piling up of lava over the initial vent. The vent position relative to its initial trace at the 1986 surface need not have moved substantially. Once spine remnants occupied all available open space to the south, new spines thrust over previous remnants. Resistance to extrusion during intense periods of thrusting may have slowed extrusion rates because of backpressure effects during certain time intervals.

Although Crater Glacier had minimal influence on the growing spines, spine growth affected the glacier dramatically, initially dividing it into two arms and then bulldozing it hundreds of meters first east (east arm), then west (west arm), while heaping it more than 100 m higher than its original altitude.

The 2004–6 eruption has thus far differed from other well-documented historical eruptions in its solid-state character, its recumbent growth style, and its interaction with the glacier. On the basis of historical records, most domes grow endogenously; exogenously to produce thick units with a high aspect ratio and, sometimes, longer lava flows; or a combination of both (Blake, 1990). Peléean spines like those at Mont Pelée or Soufrière Hills are similar to those of the current eruption, but the 1943–45 eruption of Mount Usu provides the closest historical analogue. Perhaps the most similar of historically documented domes are those sometimes referred to as upheaved plugs (Blake, 1990). Such plugs appear to push up bodily like pistons and, when they reach the surface, have sufficient strength not to deform or spread outward but instead ascend vertically. Mimatsu (1995) beautifully documents the evolution of one such upheaval dome from 1943 to 1945 at Mount Usu in Japan. The intriguing variations in pluglike dome construction and evolution at Mount St. Helens since 2004, not previously well documented, have been recumbent growth and interaction with an unusual combination of topographic constraints and glacial ice.

Acknowledgments

We thank Andy Harris and Michelle Coombs for careful reviews of this manuscript. Andy's very detailed comments, in particular, greatly improved the paper. Cascades Volcano Observatory staff were generous with their time, their ideas, and their data.

References Cited

Ball, M., and Pinkerton, H., 2006, Factors affecting the accuracy of thermal imaging cameras in volcanology: Journal of Geophysical Research, v. 111, no. B11, B11203, doi.10.1029/2005Jb003829, 14 p.

Blake, S., 1990, Viscoplastic models of lava domes, *in* Fink, J.H., ed., Lava flows and domes, emplacement mechanisms and hazard implications: Berlin, Springer-Verlag, International Association of Volcanology and Chemistry of the Earth's Interior, Proceedings in Volcanology 2, p. 89–126.

Cashman, K.V., Thornber, C.R., and Pallister, J.S., 2008, From dome to dust; shallow crystallization and fragmentation of conduit magma during the 2004–2006 dome extrusion of Mount St. Helens, Washington, chap. 19 *of* Sherrod, D.R., Scott, W.E., and Stauffer, P.H., eds., A volcano rekindled; the renewed eruption of Mount St. Helens, 2004–2006: U.S. Geological Survey Professional Paper 1750 (this volume).

Chadwick, W.W., Archuleta, R.J., and Swanson, D.A., 1988, The mechanics of ground deformation precursory to dome-building extrusions at Mount St. Helens 1981–1982: Journal of Geophysical Research, v. 93, no. B5, p. 4351–4366, doi:10.1029/88JB01345.

Dzurisin, D., Vallance, J.W., Gerlach, T.M., Moran, S.C., and Malone, S.D., 2005, Mount St. Helens reawakens: Eos (American Geophysical Union Transactions), v. 86, no. 3, p. 25, 29.

Dzurisin, D., Lisowski, M., Poland, M.P., Sherrod, D.R., and LaHusen, R.G., 2008, Constraints and conundrums resulting from ground-deformation measurements made during the 2004–2005 dome-building eruption of Mount St. Helens, Washington, chap. 14 *of* Sherrod, D.R., Scott, W.E., and Stauffer, P.H., eds., A volcano rekindled; the renewed eruption of Mount St. Helens, 2004–2006: U.S. Geological Survey Professional Paper 1750 (this volume).

Gerlach, T.M., McGee, K.A., and Doukas, M.P., 2008, Emission rates of CO_2, SO_2, and H_2S, scrubbing, and preeruption excess volatiles at Mount St. Helens, 2004–2005, chap. 26 *of* Sherrod, D.R., Scott, W.E., and Stauffer, P.H., eds., A volcano rekindled; the renewed eruption of Mount St. Helens, 2004–2006: U.S. Geological Survey Professional Paper 1750 (this volume).

Harris, A.J.L., Murray, J.B., Aries, S.E., Davies, M.A., Flynn, L.P., Wooster, M.J., Wright, R., and Rothery, D.A., 2000, Effusion rate trends at Etna and Krafla and their implications for eruptive mechanisms: Journal of Volcanology and Geothermal Research, v. 102, p. 237–270.

Harris, A.J.L., Flynn, L.P., Matías, O., and Rose, W.I., 2002, The thermal stealth flows of Santiaguito dome, Guatemala: Implications for the cooling and emplacement of dacitic block-lava flows: Geological Society of America Bulletin, v. 114, no. 5, p. 533–546.

Harris, A.J.L., Rose, W.I., and Flynn, L.P., 2003, Temporal trends in lava dome extrusion at Santiaguito 1922–2000: Bulletin of Volcanology, v. 65, p. 77–89.

Harris, A.J.L., Flynn, L.P., Matías, O., Rose, W.I., and Cornejo, J., 2004, The evolution of an active lava flow field: an ETM+ perspective: Journal of Volcanology and Geothermal Research, v. 135, p. 147–168.

Harris, A.J.L., Dehn, J., Patrick, M.R., Calvari, S., Ripepe, M., and Lodato, L., 2005, Lava effusion rates from hand-held thermal infrared imagery; an example from the June 2003 effusive activity at Stromboli: Bulletin of Volcanology, v. 68, no. 2, p. 107–117.

Herriott, T.M., Sherrod, D.R., Pallister, J.S., and Vallance, J.W., 2008, Photogeologic maps of the 2004–2005 Mount St. Helens eruption, chap. 10 *of* Sherrod, D.R., Scott, W.E., and Stauffer, P.H., eds., A volcano rekindled; the renewed eruption of Mount St. Helens, 2004–2006: U.S. Geological Survey Professional Paper 1750 (this volume).

Iverson, R.M., 1990, Lava domes modeled as brittle shells that enclose pressurized magma, with application to Mount St. Helens, *in* Fink, J.H., ed., Lava flows and domes, emplacement mechanisms and hazard implications: Berlin, Springer-Verlag, International Association of Volcanology and Chemistry of the Earth's Interior, Proceedings in Volcanology 2, p. 47–69.

Iverson, R.M., Dzurisin, D., Gardner, C.A., Gerlach, T.M., LaHusen, R.G., Lisowski, M., Major, J.J., Malone, S.D., Messerich, J.A., Moran, S.C., Pallister, J.S., Qamar, A.I., Schilling, S.P., and Vallance, J.W., 2006, Dynamics of seismogenic volcanic extrusion at Mount St. Helens in 2004–05: Nature, v. 444, no. 7118, p. 439–443, doi:10.1038/nature05322, supplementary movie 2 at http://www.nature.com/nature/journal/v444/n7118/suppinfo/nature05322.html.

Lacroix, A., 1904, La Montagne Pelée et ses eruptions: Paris, Maison et Cie, 662 p.

LaHusen, R.G., Swinford, K.J., Logan, M., and Lisowski, M., 2008, Instrumentation in remote and dangerous settings; examples using data from GPS "spider" deployments during the 2004–2005 eruption of Mount St. Helens, Washington, chap. 16 *of* Sherrod, D.R., Scott, W.E., and Stauffer, P.H., eds., A volcano rekindled; the renewed eruption of Mount St. Helens, 2004–2006: U.S. Geological Survey Professional Paper 1750 (this volume).

Lescinsky, D.T., and Sisson, T.W., 1998, Ridge-forming, ice-bounded lava flows at Mount Rainier, Washington: Geology, v. 26, p. 943–946.

Major, J.J., Kingsbury, C.G., Poland, M.P., and LaHusen, R.G., 2008, Extrusion rate of the Mount St. Helens lava dome estimated from terrestrial imagery, November 2004–December 2005, chap. 12 *of* Sherrod, D.R., Scott, W.E., and Stauffer, P.H., eds., A volcano rekindled; the renewed eruption of Mount St. Helens, 2004–2006: U.S. Geological Survey Professional Paper 1750 (this volume).

Mathews, W.H., 1947, "Tuyas"; flat topped volcanoes in northern British Columbia: American Journal of Science, v. 245, p. 560–570.

Mimatsu, M., 1995, Showa-Shinzan diary, expanded reprint: Sapporo, Suda Seihan Co., 179 p.

Moran, S.C., Malone, S.D., Qamar, A.I., Thelen, W.A., Wright, A.K., and Caplan-Auerbach, J., 2008a, Seismicity associated with renewed dome building at Mount St. Helens, 2004–2005, chap. 2 *of* Sherrod, D.R., Scott, W.E., and Stauffer, P.H., eds., A volcano rekindled; the renewed eruption of Mount St. Helens, 2004–2006: U.S. Geological Survey Professional Paper 1750 (this volume).

Moran, S.C., McChesney, P.J., and Lockhart, A.B., 2008b, Seismicity and infrasound associated with explosions at Mount St. Helens, 2004–2005, chap. 6 *of* Sherrod, D.R.,

Scott, W.E., and Stauffer, P.H., eds., A volcano rekindled; the renewed eruption of Mount St. Helens, 2004–2006: U.S. Geological Survey Professional Paper 1750 (this volume).

Nakada, S., Shimizu, H., and Ohta, K., 1999, Overview of the 1990–1995 eruption at Unzen Volcano: Journal of Volcanology and Geothermal Research, v. 89, nos. 1–4, p. 1–22, doi:10.1016/S0377-0273(98)00118-8.

Pallister, J.S., Thornber, C.R., Cashman, K.V., Clynne, M.A., Lowers, H.A., Mandeville, C.W., Brownfield, I.K., and Meeker, G.P., 2008, Petrology of the 2004–2006 Mount St. Helens lava dome—implications for magmatic plumbing and eruption triggering, chap. 30 *of* Sherrod, D.R., Scott, W.E., and Stauffer, P.H., eds., A volcano rekindled; the renewed eruption of Mount St. Helens, 2004–2006: U.S. Geological Survey Professional Paper 1750 (this volume).

Poland, M.P., Dzurisin, D., LaHusen, R.G., Major, J.J., Lapcewich, D., Endo, E.T., Gooding, D.J., Schilling, S.P., and Janda, C.G., 2008, Remote camera observations of lava dome growth at Mount St. Helens, Washington, October 2004 to February 2006, chap. 11 *of* Sherrod, D.R., Scott, W.E., and Stauffer, P.H., eds., A volcano rekindled; the renewed eruption of Mount St. Helens, 2004–2006: U.S. Geological Survey Professional Paper 1750 (this volume).

Queija, V.R., Stoker, J.M., and Kosovich, J.J., 2005, Recent U.S. Geological Survey applications of Lidar: Photogrammetric Engineering and Remote Sensing, v. 71, no. 1, p. 5–9.

Rose, W.I., 1980, The geology of Santiaguito volcanic dome Guatemala: Hanover, N.H., Dartmouth College, Ph.D. dissertation, 253 p.

Rose, W.I., 1987, Volcanic activity at Santiaguito volcano, 1976–1984, *in* Fink, J.H., ed., The emplacement of silicic domes and lava flows: Geological Society of America Special Paper 212, p. 17–27.

Schilling, S.P., Carrara, P.E., Thompson, R.A., and Iwatsubo, E.Y., 2004, Posteruption glacier development within the crater of Mount St. Helens, Washington, USA: Quaternary Research, v. 61, no. 3, p. 325–329.

Schilling, S.P., Thompson, R.A., Messerich, J.A., and Iwatsubo, E.Y., 2008, Use of digital aerophotogrammetry to determine rates of lava dome growth, Mount St. Helens, Washington, 2004–2005, chap. 8 *of* Sherrod, D.R., Scott, W.E., and Stauffer, P.H., eds., A volcano rekindled; the renewed eruption of Mount St. Helens, 2004–2006: U.S. Geological Survey Professional Paper 1750 (this volume).

Schneider, D.J., Vallance, J.W., Wessels, R.L., Logan, M., and Ramsey, M.S., 2008, Use of thermal infrared imaging for monitoring renewed dome growth at Mount St. Helens, 2004, chap. 17 *of* Sherrod, D.R., Scott, W.E., and Stauffer, P.H., eds., A volcano rekindled; the renewed eruption of Mount St. Helens, 2004–2006: U.S. Geological Survey Professional Paper 1750 (this volume).

Swanson, D.A., and Holcomb, R.T., 1990, Regularities in growth of the Mount St. Helens dacite dome, 1980–1986, *in* Fink, J.H., ed., Lava flows and domes, emplacement mechanisms and hazard implications: Berlin, Springer-Verlag, International Association of Volcanology and Chemistry of the Earth's Interior, Proceedings in Volcanology 2, p. 3–24.

Thelen, W.A., Crosson, R.S., and Creager, K.C., 2008, Absolute and relative locations of earthquakes at Mount St. Helens, Washington, using continuous data; implications for magmatic processes, chap. 4 *of* Sherrod, D.R., Scott, W.E., and Stauffer, P.H., eds., A volcano rekindled; the renewed eruption of Mount St. Helens, 2004–2006: U.S. Geological Survey Professional Paper 1750 (this volume).

Turcotte, D.L., and Schubert, G., 1982, Geodynamics: New York, John Wiley, 450 p.

Wadge, G., 1981, The variation of magma discharge during basaltic eruptions: Journal of Volcanology and Geothermal Research, v. 11, p. 139–168.

Walder, J.S., Schilling, S.P., Vallance, J.W., and LaHusen, R.G., 2008, Effects of lava-dome growth on the Crater Glacier of Mount St. Helens, Washington, chap. 13 *of* Sherrod, D.R., Scott, W.E., and Stauffer, P.H., eds., A volcano rekindled; the renewed eruption of Mount St. Helens, 2004–2006: U.S. Geological Survey Professional Paper 1750 (this volume).

Watts, R.B., Herd, R.A., Sparks, R.S.J., and Young, S.R., 2002, Growth patterns and emplacement of the andesitic lava dome at Soufrière Hills Volcano, Montserrat, *in* Druitt, T.H., and Kokelaar, B.P., eds., The eruption of Soufrière Hills Volcano, Montserrat from 1995 to 1999: Geological Society of London Memoir 21, p. 115–152.

A Volcano Rekindled: The Renewed Eruption of Mount St. Helens, 2004–2006
Edited by David R. Sherrod, William E. Scott, and Peter H. Stauffer
U.S. Geological Survey Professional Paper 1750, 2008

Chapter 10

Photogeologic Maps of the 2004–2005 Mount St. Helens Eruption

By Trystan M. Herriott[1], David R. Sherrod[2], John S. Pallister[2], and James W. Vallance[2]

Abstract

The 2004–5 eruption of Mount St. Helens, still ongoing as of this writing (September 2006), has comprised chiefly lava dome extrusion that produced a series of solid, fault-gouge-mantled dacite spines. Vertical aerial photographs taken every 2 to 4 weeks, visual observations, and oblique photographs taken from aircraft and nearby observation points provide the basis for two types of photogeologic maps of the dome—photo-based maps and rectified maps. Eight map pairs, covering the period from October 1, 2004, through December 15, 2005, document the development of seven spines: an initial small, fin-shaped vertical spine; a north-south elongate wall of dacite; two large and elongate recumbent spines ("whalebacks"); a tall and elongate inclined spine; a smaller bulbous spine; and an initially endogenous spine extruded between remnants of preceding spines. All spines rose from the same general vent area near the southern margin of the 1980s lava dome. Maps also depict translation and rotation of active and abandoned spines, progressive deformation affecting Crater Glacier, and distribution of ash on the crater floor from phreatic and phreatomagmatic explosions. The maps help track key geologic and geographic features in the rapidly changing crater and help date dome, gouge, and ash samples that are no longer readily correlated to their original context because of deformation in a dynamic environment where spines extrude, deform, slough, and are overrun by newly erupted material.

Introduction

During its 2004–5 eruptive activity, Mount St. Helens extruded solid dacite lava onto the May 18, 1980, glacier-covered crater floor south of the 1980s lava dome. Beginning in October 2004, a series of seven spines extruded during the first 15 months of the eruption, following seismic unrest that began September 23, 2004. Two prominent whaleback-shaped spines (3 and 4) that erupted from late October 2004 to April 2005 followed two small spines (1 and 2) extruded in October 2004. From April through July 2005, tall, inclined spine 5 overrode remnants of previous spines to reach the dome's maximum altitude as of September 2006 (Schilling and others, this volume, chap. 8); this spine subsequently subsided and partially disintegrated. Finally, beginning in early August 2005, spines 6 and 7 extruded westward, a marked change from previous spines, which were shoved south along the crater floor. Remnant spines (those no longer actively extruding) were rapidly degraded and overrun by subsequent spines. Crater Glacier, which formed after the cataclysmic 1980 eruption (Schilling and others, 2004; Walder and others, this volume, chap. 13), was nearly bisected during the initial two months of the eruption and formed distinct east and west limbs that were substantially deformed in response to emplacement of the new lava dome.

Intensive monitoring of the eruption by the U.S. Geological Survey's Cascades Volcano Observatory (CVO) has been supplemented by photographic documentation of the dome's growth (this volume: Poland and others, chap. 11; Major and others, chap. 12; Dzurisin and others, chap. 14), including a series of 9×9-in. vertical aerial photographs. We present eight photogeologic maps traced from vertical aerial photographs of the Mount St. Helens crater that encompass 15 months of the eruption from October 1, 2004, through December 15, 2005. Each map is presented as both a photo-based and an accompanying rectified map without a photo base. The maps depict (1) the growth, stagnation, and subsequent burial or degradation of seven dacite spines (fig. 1); (2) the translation and rotation of geologic and geographic features throughout the evolution of the ongoing dome eruption; and (3) the progressive deformation of Crater Glacier as the growing dome displaced ice south of the 1980–86 dome. The photo-based maps also serve as a base for plotting locali-

[1] Department of Earth Science, Webb Hall, University of California, Santa Barbara, CA 93106; now at P.O. Box 750255, Fairbanks, AK 99775

[2] U.S. Geological Survey, 1300 SE Cardinal Court, Vancouver, WA 98683

ties of, and giving geologic and geographic context to, rock, gouge, and ash samples that were collected on the growing lava dome. Photographic documentation of sample context is crucial in a constantly changing setting in which a sample's original location loses significance, as when the base of a coherent spine sampled in January 2005 becomes a pile of transported and undifferentiated rubble by May 2005.

Methods

We compiled maps of the 2004–5 dacite dome eruption at Mount St. Helens on a sequence of ~1:12,000-scale vertical aerial photographs taken by Bergman Photographic Services on contract to CVO (Schilling and others, this volume, chap. 8). Photo pairs encompassing the crater rim, new lava dome, and the 1980–86 lava dome were selected and examined with a stereoscope. The crater rim and 1980s lava dome provided a reasonably stable frame of reference in the dynamic crater environment. On the photographs we mapped units that highlighted changes in dome growth and morphology, as well as changes in the 1980s dome, rock debris, and glacial ice surrounding the dome. Uncertainties of the map units result from working without the benefit of on-the-ground field mapping, which early in the eruption was deemed too hazardous owing to possible explosions or rockfalls and rock avalanches. Our intent is to provide a heightened visual record of the locations and characteristics of major features and deposits in the crater during the ongoing eruption.

Two types of photogeologic maps were prepared—photo-based and rectified. The latter lacks a base image in its final presentation. The visual content of the aerial photographs is immense, and unit boundaries are commonly vivid; however, the aerial photographs are not rectified, and therefore the photo-based maps are subject to scale variability and distortion within an individual image. Consequently, areas of, and distances between, map units on the photo-based maps are only comparable qualitatively. The rectified geologic maps allow quantitative comparison and complement the visually rich, nonrectified photo-based maps.

Although the two map series are based on the same photo pairs for any given date, variations exist within each map pair (photo-based and rectified). Dissimilarities result primarily from compiling the two types of maps at separate times but are compounded by employing different methods for assessing the contact locations (see below). Without doubt, the greater magnification and clarity possible with the plotter used to make the rectified maps resulted in a finer degree of detail, especially in differentiating gouge-covered surface, unroofed spine, and talus. Ultimately, small differences within map couplets persist. The two map series are not intended to be rigorously comparable but rather to be viewed and used for their individual strengths as discussed above.

Photo-Based Geologic Maps

We selected photographs on the basis of observable changes since previous photo coverage, visual clarity of crater

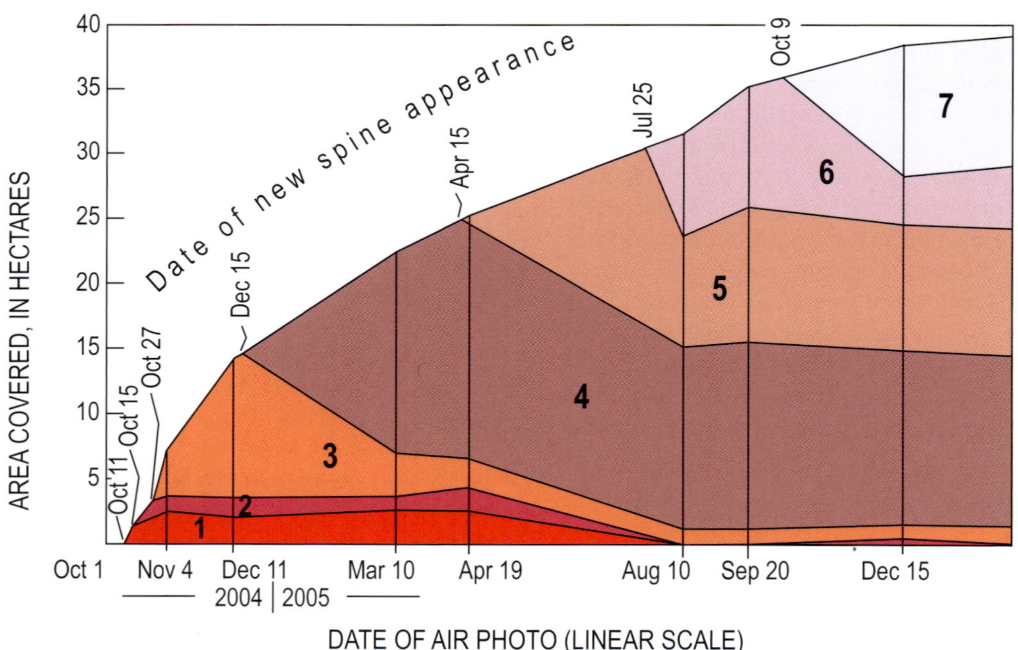

Figure 1. Area of Mount St. Helens' new dome and proportional coverage of individual spines through time. Areas measured from rectified photogeologic maps produced for dates of air photos shown. Date of new spine appearance from Vallance and others (this volume, chap. 9).

Table 1. Imagery used for photogeologic maps.

[Photo number (ex: 6-5) reported as flightline and frame number. Samples are whole-rock and gouge samples used for geochemical analyses described elsewhere in this volume. For brevity, sample numbers lack "SH" prefix (for example, complete sample No. is SH300). For stereographic pair, first listed is left-hand photo, southerly of pair; all flightlines oriented north-south. Column for georegistration points indicates number of points used in transformation to better rectify the photogrammetric geologic map.]

Date of photography	Figure No.	Photo used	Samples shown on photo map	Pair used for rectified map	Georegistration points
10/1/2004	2, 3A	6-5	No new dome	6-4, 6-5	19
11/4/2004	4, 3B	6-4	300, 301-1, 302-2, 304-1, 304-2	6-3, 6-4	15
12/11/2004	5, 3C	6-3	305	6-2, 6-3	19
3/10/2005	6, 3D	7-2	306, 307, 308, 309, 310, 311-1B, 312	7-2, 7-1	10
4/19/2005	7, 8A	6-4	313, 314, 315, 316	6-3, 6-4	19
8/10/2005	9, 8B	1-3	317, 318, 319, 320, 321, 322, 323	1-2, 1-3	22
9/20/2005	10, 8C	1-2		1-2, 1-3	15
12/15/2005	11, 8D	1-3	324	1-2, 1-3	25

features, and pertinence to appropriate geographic setting of sample localities. These selection criteria winnowed the aerial photograph series from 18 to 8 sets (table 1). Our procedure began by scanning (300 dpi) each of the chosen set of photographs. The scanned images were enlarged and framed to encompass a similar area at roughly similar scale. We then traced rock, ash, and glacier units using Adobe ® Illustrator 10 software. Although the photo-based maps are neither rectified nor georeferenced, we attempted to maintain the same field of view and azimuthal orientation (top to the north) of maps throughout the photo-based series.

We studied photo pairs stereoscopically and analyzed apparent three-dimensional surface morphology to identify photogeologic features and draw detailed map-unit contacts. Dashed lines on the maps indicate ambiguous contact locations. Thermal imagery and digital elevation models (DEMs) constructed from each set of photos (Schilling and others, this volume, chap. 8; Vallance and others, this volume, chap. 9) augmented the interpretation of geologic features and deposits viewed on the aerial photographs. We resolved additional crater details by referring to the extensive collection of oblique aerial photographs taken in the crater during field work by CVO scientists and by comparing aerial photographs with repeat images from time-lapse cameras at three fixed locations near the crater rim (this volume: Poland and others, chap. 11; Major and others, chap. 12; Dzurisin and others, chap. 14). These supplementary data elucidate areas within the crater that are obscured in the aerial photographs by condensed steam, shadows, or snow, or are difficult to interpret in plan view.

Rectified Geologic Maps

Conventional photogrammetric methods were used to rectify photogeologic maps. We mapped contacts while viewing paired vertical aerial photos stereoscopically on a Kern PG-2 optical-mechanical stereographic plotter. Our instrument at CVO lacks an electronic digitizer, so the resulting pencil-on-mylar maps were scanned and hand digitized using MapInfo ® Geographic Information System (GIS) software. Points of known geographic position, such as prominences on the crater rim and on the 1980s dome within the crater, served as pseudobenchmarks by which the maps were registered geographically. The crater-rim control points are prominent apices and craggy summits whose locations were derived from a lidar image with 2-m cells produced in November 2004. The 1980s-dome control points are rock spires recognizable on a 1988 high-resolution topographic map of the crater floor.

The PG-2 plotter produced rectified maps under most conditions; however, the photos encompass substantial altitude variation, more than 600 m, across short horizontal distances. Parallax-free models are therefore difficult to achieve, and a small amount of distortion may occur in the resulting maps. The problem is exacerbated by using the crater rim for geographic registration, whereas the area of geologic interest lies entirely on the crater floor, substantially lower in altitude. Moreover, snow cornices modify the crater rim in winter, with some forming prominent topographic apices recognizable in DEMs and aerial photos; these windblown snow and ice features can rebuild in slightly different geographic positions from photo to photo, a source of error for which we cannot systematically account. The crater rim itself retreats episodically by erosion, but no noticeable changes caused by this effect were observed in the 15 months that span our geologic maps.

To minimize distortion, the scanned pencil-on-mylar images were transformed by rubbersheeting methods. Specifically, the image was brought into its approximately correct position by a transformation matrix (general perspective projection transformation) and then by triangular irregular net adjustment (for fuller discussion of methodology, see Schilling and others, this volume, chap. 8). The transformations involved 15 to 25 registration points, except for the imagery of March 10, 2005, which used 10 points (table 1).

Ultimately, the resulting precision and probably the accuracy of the rectified maps is within plus or minus 12 m. This value is acceptable owing to the 1:12,000 scale of the aerial photographs and the standard convention that a geologic map should portray precision to at least 1 mm on the map. The precision was tested empirically by draping the resulting linework on existing DEMs. The crater rim was traced as part of each rectified map to provide a visual-empirical guide for comparison with the crater rim on the DEM. Rock spires on the 1980–86 dome provided intracrater tie points to further assess precision. The crater-rim test shows that all tracings lie within 5 m of each other. As a test of accuracy, the rock-spire test gives geographic coincidence generally within 1–5 m, with a few strays as far as 10 m. The resulting rectified maps are more than adequate, in both precision and accuracy, for the cataloging and archiving of geologic information.

Sample Localities

CVO staff collected (chiefly by helicopter dredge) and analyzed 26 samples of 2004–5 lava-dome dacite after the first dacite spine erupted in mid-October 2004 (Pallister and others, this volume, chap 30; Thornber and others, 2008). Sample localities (table 1) are plotted on the photo-based maps that depict relevant geologic and geographic features, providing approximate spatial and temporal context for the samples.

Description of Photogeologic Map Units

Map units described here include rock and debris from the 2004–5 dacite dome, phreatic or phreatomagmatic and rockfall-generated ash deposits, crater floor debris, 1980s lava dome, and deformed and undeformed glacial ice. Labels coupled with a plus sign (+) indicate where thin surficial deposits blanket other map units. The underlying map unit is listed first, followed by the symbol of the blanketing deposit. For example, unit label gd+a indicates deformed glacier overlain by a veneer of ash (see Dome Map Units, below).

We use lava dome, or simply dome, to describe the composite feature that comprises extrusive spines or lobes, endogenous growth, and talus. We mapped each spine as an individual unit of extrusive lava, typically massive, and analogous to a lobe or flow. Endogenous growth of some spines results in a rubbly surface. A whaleback is a smooth, striated spine, be it recumbent or vertical. The terms "new" and "old" dome are used informally to differentiate between the 2004–5 and 1980–86 lava domes, respectively.

The term Opus identifies an informally named part of the 1980s dome that was displaced southward during a 1985 eruption. The name originated from a benchmark used to track this movement and later was extended through casual usage to denote the entire elongate geographic ridge that resulted. Opus became important during the renewed eruption in 2004 because the conduit breached the surface near it, deforming both Opus and the adjacent Crater Glacier.

Crater Glacier deformed because of upwarping early in the eruption and then by lateral compression as extruded lava shoved the glacier aside. We demarcate deformed and undeformed glacial ice by tracing the abrupt topographic break in slope between them. This boundary was a deformation front within a compositionally coherent unit, unlike lithologic contacts, which are planar features separating discrete bodies of rocks or deposits.

2004–2005 Dacite Dome Map Units

Spines—Lava lobes, numbered 1–7 according to eruptive sequence of dacite lava extruded onto floor of Mount St. Helens crater during eruption ongoing since October 2004 (Vallance and others, this volume, chap. 9). Moderately porphyritic, with phenocrysts of plagioclase, amphibole, hypersthene, and Fe-Ti oxides. Includes three gross textural features—surface gouge; unroofed, ragged spine; and remnant spine—described below. Thus, map symbol may be a composite; for example, s4u indicates unroofed, ragged part of spine 4 after erosion has destroyed its smooth carapace. Spines defined as follows:

s7 Spine 7—Initially endogenous dacite spine; extruded between remnants of spines 5 and 6 beginning in October 2005. Longest-lived and latest in sequence as of September 2006

s6 Spine 6—Rubble-covered dacite spine; extruded during August and September 2005. Grew coincident with and adjacent to a graben, or sag, that developed west of spine 5

s5 Spine 5—Large south-trending dacite spine; extruded from late April through July 2005. Highest spine measured as of September 2006 (Schilling and others, this volume, chap. 8)

s4 Spine 4—Large, elongate, south-trending dacite whaleback; extruded from late December 2004 through late April 2005

s3 Spine 3—Large, elongate, south-trending dacite whaleback; extruded from late October through late December 2004. First occurrence of gouge-mantled spine with striated carapace, characteristic of all subsequent spines

s2 Spine 2—Elongate south-trending dacite spine; extruded in middle to late October 2004

s1 Spine 1—Small northeast-trending finlike dacite spine; initial effusive product; extruded in mid-October 2004

u Unroofed spine—Part of actively growing spine that no longer retains gouge-mantled carapace, which typically was shed through repeated rockfalls

r Spine remnants—Partially intact rubble of inactive spines. Moved constantly as growth of new spine wedged them away from vent

g Gouge—Cataclastic carapace 1–2 m thick that characterized surfaces of spines 3–7 where they first emerged from the vent. Commonly removed by fracturing and degradation

t Talus—2004–5 dacite dome talus resulting from rockfall from active and abandoned spines. May be darker in color than adjacent hot talus where wet or covered by damp ash

a Ash—Tephra, produced chiefly by phreatic or phreatomagmatic explosions and rockfalls. Shown separately on some maps are the following units:

a2 Ash from March 8, 2005, explosion—Primary magmatic and accidental lithic tephra generated during largest phreatomagmatic explosion of ongoing eruption. Resulted from near-vent fallout from plume of steam and ash that rose to about 11 km height

a1 Ash from October 1, 2004, explosion—Fine ash that blanketed northwest sector of Mount St. Helens crater

v Vent for October 1, 2004, explosion—Pit about 50 m in diameter that produced a short-lived steam-and-ash plume of phreatic or phreatomagmatic origin. Source of first explosive activity of ongoing eruption

b Ballistic craters—Depressions in glacier caused by bomb impacts during October 1, 2004, and March 8, 2005, explosions

Other Crater Map Units

rp Crater-floor roof pendant—Crater-floor debris that rested atop spine 3 upon its initial extrusion

gl Crater Glacier—Glacial ice and enclosed rock debris that accumulated subsequent to May 18, 1980, crater-forming eruption. Compression and thickening by crater-floor uplift and extrusion of new lava dome increased rate of flow northward around 1980s dome. Shown separately are the following:

gd Deformed Crater Glacier—Deformed, typically uplifted and crevassed glacial ice shoved aside as lava dome grew

gs Stranded glacial ice—Remnant of ice from east glacier left perched on flank of Opus by crater-floor uplift

la Lahar deposits—Remnants of small muddy debris flows and tiny pyroclastic flows generated by interaction of hot dacite dome rock and snow or glacial ice

cd Crater-floor debris and talus—Rubble uplifted by actively growing 2004–5 dacite dome

cw Crater wall—Strata forming crater walls and outer flanks of Mount St. Helens. Unit only appears on rectified maps

op Opus—Ridge created on south side of 1980s dome by a small graben that formed during October 1985 eruption

od 1980–86 lava dome—Older dome emplaced during a 6-year period following the May 18, 1980, crater-forming eruption

h Melt pit—Steeply walled pits at glacier/lava dome contact melted out by fumaroles. Unit only appears on rectified maps

***** 2004–5 sample location—Sample location, showing number (for example, 300; the SH prefix is not included in the map label); most samples collected by helicopter dredging tools. Shown only on photo-based maps

Discussion of Photogeologic Maps

Our discussion of the maps focuses on salient geologic, geographic, topographic, and glacial features generated during the first 15 months of the eruption. These include spine evolution, phreatic and phreatomagmatic explosions, uplifted crater-floor rocks, deformation of Opus, deformation of the Crater Glacier, and extensive rockfall-generated ash deposits. We do not discuss all features depicted in the images, as our goal is to provide a guide for visualizing the most notable changes on the crater floor between the dates of successive maps.

October 1, 2004

The October 1 phreatic explosion left its mark on the crater scene photographed that afternoon (fig. 2). Dark-gray ash (a1) mantles the western crater floor, having emanated from a prominent vent (v) in the Crater Glacier. Numerous craters on west Crater Glacier define a more restricted field of ballistic craters (a1b).

Adjacent to the vent on the east is highly fractured and uplifted glacial ice (gd), a welt approximately 52,000 m^2 in extent that grew rapidly as magma ascended toward the surface (fig. 3*A*). The base of the topographic rise to the welt, distinctive in stereo viewing but not readily apparent in the single base image of figure 2, defines the contact separating deformed from undeformed glacier. With time, some of the deformed ice seen in figure 2 became isolated from the main mass of Crater Glacier. The Opus ridge (op) is also deformed.

November 4, 2004

The November 4 image shows spine 3 (s3) and remnants of spines 1 (s1r) and spine 2 (s2r) of the new dome (fig. 4). The east-flank carapace of spine 3 is a well-preserved striated gouge surface (s3g). A distinctly whiter band marks the freshest gouge along the eastern base. Remnants of spines 1 and 2 are north and west, respectively, of spine 3.

At least one roof pendant (rp) of old dome and crater-floor debris is atop spine 3. In the photo, the pendant is seen as the darker area near the crest of the spine (fig. 4). Dark-gray

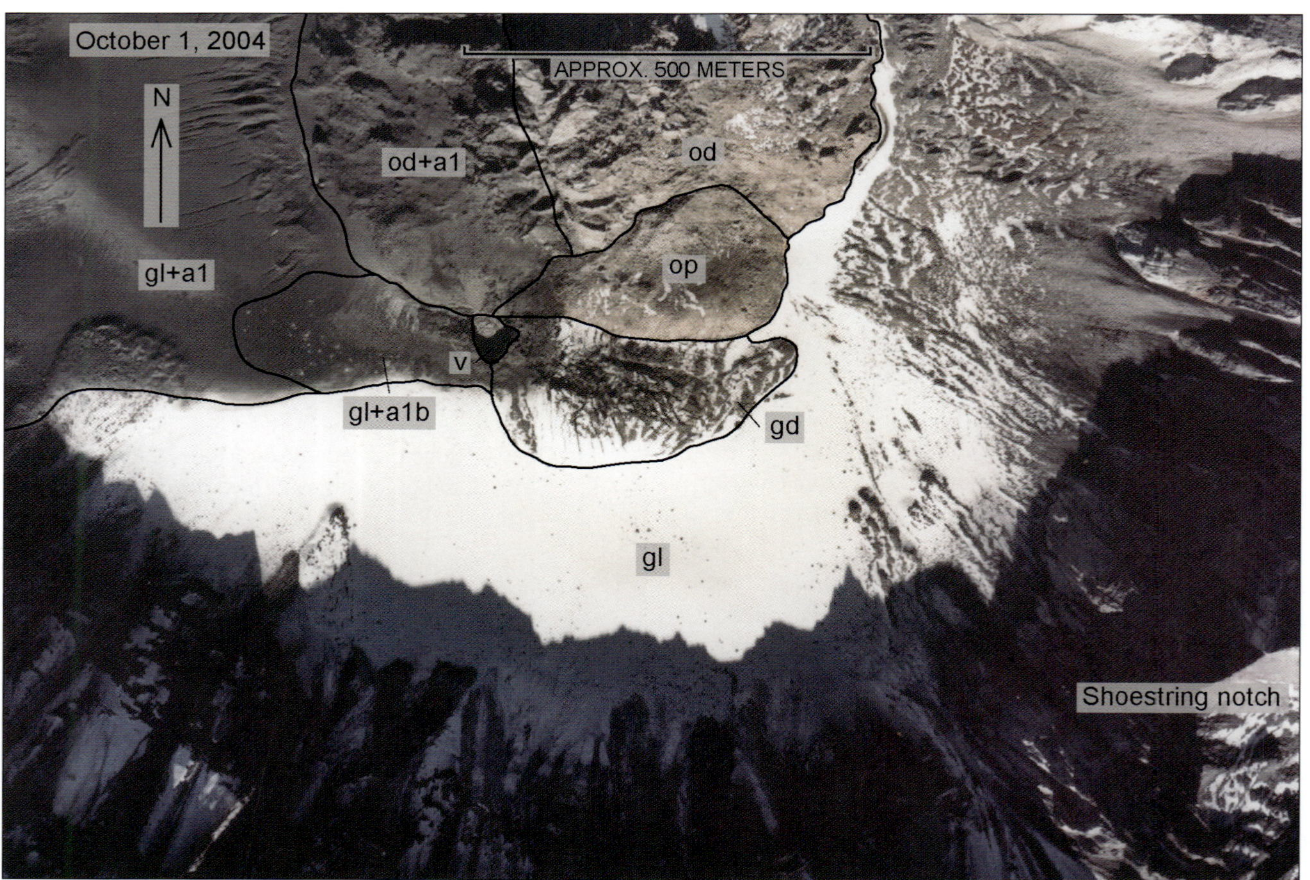

Figure 2. Photo-based geologic map of Mount St. Helens' new dome from aerial photo taken October 1, 2004. For explanation of unit symbols, see text. Shoestring notch is an informal geographic name for the topographic cleft that is the truncated head of the Shoestring Glacier, which was largely destroyed in the 1980 eruption of Mount St. Helens.

debris (cd) along the eastern periphery of spine 3 represents deformed fragments of the 1980–86 dome, first dragged southward 100–200 m on the roof of spine 3 and then eroded off (fig. 3*B*). Uplifted crater floor material lies east of the 1980s dome debris (fig. 3*B*).

East of the new dome is the highly deformed east limb of Crater Glacier (gd), crisscrossed by crevasses to form a serac field. The growing dome has nearly split the glacier, such that its east and west limbs have become geographically distinct. Nevertheless, the glacier remains contiguous around the south side of the new dome.

Deformation of Opus (op) is largely complete but is not easily discerned at the scale of this aerial image (fig. 4); stagnant and broken glacial ice mantles its south side. Increased heat flow on its western side has melted snow from an irregular area, but the exposed, darkened mass of jumbled rock is likely little different in form from the snow-covered nonthermal area of Opus.

Two or three small debris fans and more lobate, slurried deposits (la) originate from spine 1 remnants. Thinner lahar deposits extend along a narrow trace down the center of the cleft that separates the west flanks of the new and 1980s domes from the west limb of Crater Glacier (gl) (fig. 4).

December 11, 2004

Rain, melted snow, or condensed steam has left the snow-free areas very dark gray on this overcast day (fig. 5). Spine 3 has greatly lengthened, earning the name "whaleback." Its gouge-mantled surface (s3g), where wet, is dark grayish brown. The western slope of spine 3 has spalled to form talus (t), including some large house-size blocks. All the uplifted crater-floor debris seen along the west flank in previous images is now indistinguishable, likely buried by talus. Along the southeast side, steam and coarse blocks mark an elongate slab of spine 3 (s3u), detached, deformed, and wedged between spine 3 and the glacier (fig. 3*C*). Spine 1 and 2 remnants remain visible, although they are somewhat obscured by steam in this image (fig. 5).

Notable deformation continues on the east limb of Crater Glacier (gd), but only small changes occur along its west limb. The glacier remains intact along the south side of the new dome, but it has narrowed greatly to only about 60 m (fig. 3*C*). Glacial ice on parts of Opus has disappeared, causing an expansion of the area of Opus (compare figs. 3*B*, 3*C*).

March 10, 2005

Geomorphically prominent spine 4 has by this time supplanted spine 3, which underwent rapid fragmentation during early January 2005 (fig. 6). Spine 4 evolved as the northernmost part of spine 3 split along a vertical fracture and decoupled at its root from the rest of spine 3 to the south. As it grew southward, spine 4 isolated a small relic of spine 3 (s3ru) to the west as it bulldozed the remainder to the east (Vallance and others, this volume, chap. 9); these remnants emit steam where they abut glacial ice along the east margin. The stunning striated and gouge-mantled carapace of spine 4 (s4g), as well as the crevassed and thickened tongue of the deformed glacier (gd, east of spine 4; see below), take center stage in this photo. Remnants of spines 1 and 2 are increasingly ragged in appearance. Virtually no uplifted crater-floor debris remains adjacent to the new spines, as it has been buried by talus (t).

A large phreatomagmatic explosion on March 8 distributed ash (a2) across the north and east sectors of the crater, but large ballistic fragments fell chiefly north and northwest of the new dome. Opus and its shroud of snow and ice lie pinched between the new and 1980s domes. The stagnant ice on Opus (unit gs on fig. 3*D*) is now fully separated from the actively deforming glacier.

The east limb of Crater Glacier deformed dramatically through March and into April, producing the prominent, lobate deformation front visible near the southeast margin of the 1980–86 dome. The amplified glacial deformation slowed significantly in subsequent weeks.

April 19, 2005

Spine 5 (s5) at this time lies at the north end of the spine 4 whaleback remnants, with much of its gouge-covered surface (s4rg still intact (fig. 7). Extensive sloughing of spine 4 was first observed following a 2-week stormy period in late March 2005. Spine 4's southward growth and collision with the southern crater wall caused its breakup. Spine 3 (s3ru) is reduced to remnants flanking spine 4. Spine 1 and 2 remnants persist, although spine 2 (s2r) steams vigorously where shoved into the western limb of the glacier, so that little of it is visible in this photo (fig. 7).

Snowfall subsequent to the March 8 phreatomagmatic explosion buried the thin veneer of ash and ballistic fragments from that event. Distinctive ash (a) blanketing the east limb of the crater glacier on this image is a localized deposit that resulted from a large hot rockfall off the northeast face of spine 4 remnants (fig. 8*A*). Blocky rockfall material stopped abruptly at a topographic rise on the deformed east glacier; the rise is well pronounced in stereo viewing, but not readily apparent in figure 7. Ash elutriated and surged ahead for a short distance, forming the darkest of the deposit seen in the photo (gd+a, northern extent) (fig. 7). Even finer ash traveled south, presumably downwind, before being deposited (gd+a, southern extent).

August 10, 2005

Spine 6 (s6) separates from spine 5 at this time and edges westward (fig. 9), contrasting with previous spines that pushed along a south-southeastward trajectory. This new growth pattern focuses deformation of Crater Glacier in its west arm. The heretofore relentlessly moving terrain of spine 3, 4, and 5 remnants stagnates over the next few months (compare spatial relations in figs. 8*B*, 8*C*, 8*D*). Spine 3 remnants (s3ru) are vis-

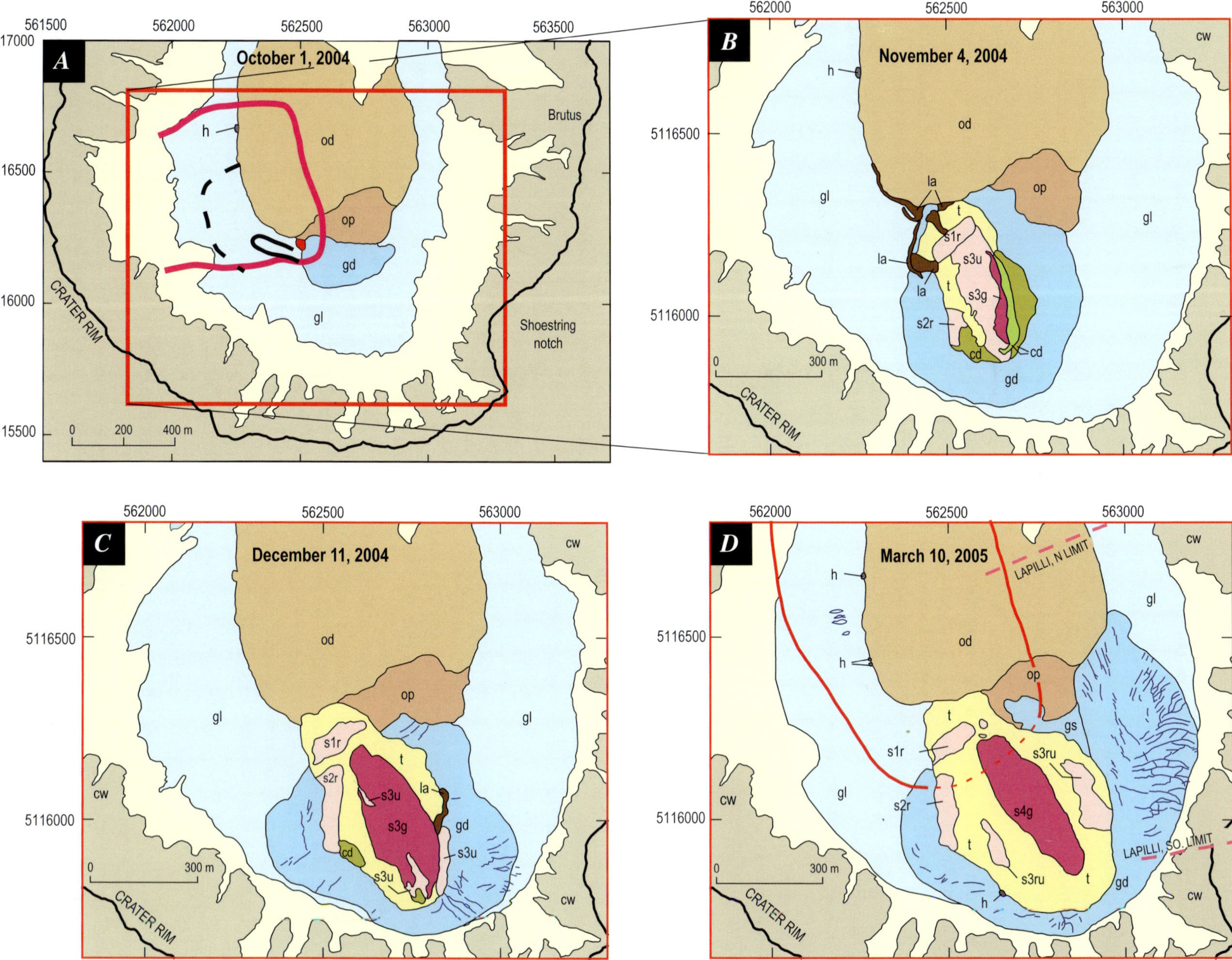

Figure 3. Rectified geologic maps of Mount St. Helens' new dome. *A*, October 1, 2004. *B*, November 4, 2004. *C*, December 11, 2004. *D*, March 10, 2005.

EXPLANATION

FEATURES ASSOCIATED WITH NEW DOME

s3u / s3g — Spine of 2004–2005 eruption (ongoing in December 2005)—Darker area mantled by gouge

t — Talus from flank of spine

la — Lahar deposits from area of new dome

cd — Crater-floor debris

Wedge of downdropped crater-floor debris

Vent for phreatomagmatic eruption of October 1, 2004

TEPHRA DEPOSITS ON MAP OF MARCH 10, 2005

Distribution of coarse ballistics—Dashed where lack of snow cover makes limit of cratering indistinct

Northern and southern limits of lapilli and ash

TEPHRA DEPOSITS ON MAP OF OCTOBER 1, 2004

Ash distribution

Ballistic fallout
- Inner, dense fall
- Outer limit of sparse fall

OTHER FEATURES IN CRATER

h — Melt pit at glacier margin

Talus from crater walls and 1980–86 dome

gl / gd — Glacial ice—Darker area deformed by dome growth

od / op — 1980–86 dome—Darker area is Opus ridge (op)

cw — Strata of crater walls and outer flanks

Notable crevasse on glacier—Resulting from dome emplacement. Only crevasses that developed after the previous map date are shown

Figure 3.—Continued.

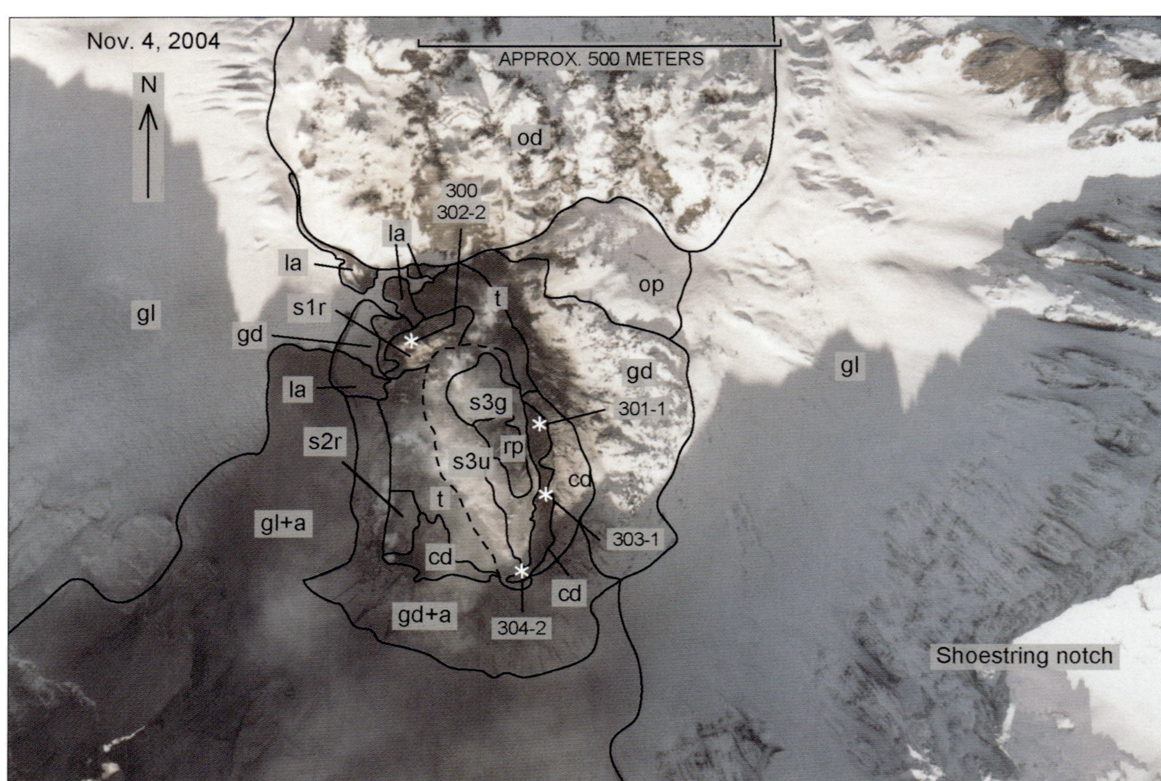

Figure 4. Photo-based geologic map of Mount St. Helens' new dome from aerial photo taken November 4, 2004. Stars mark sample localities; see table 1.

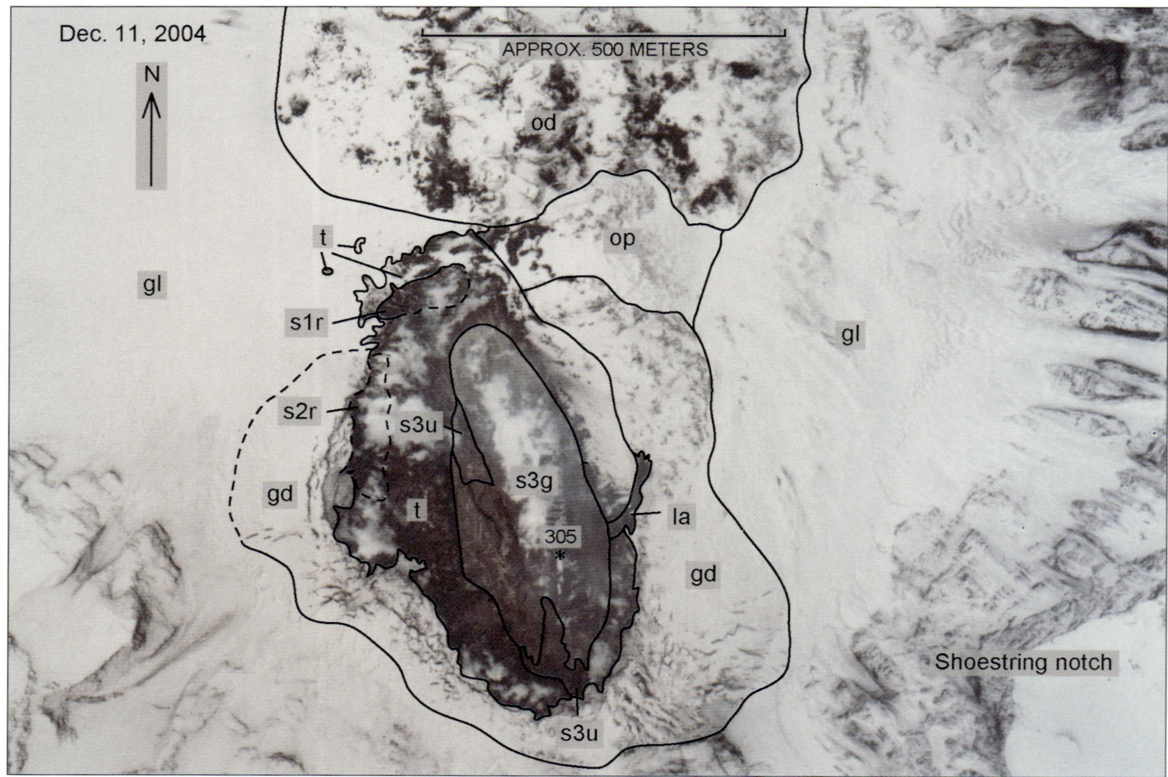

Figure 5. Photo-based geologic map of Mount St. Helens' new dome from aerial photo taken December 11, 2004. Star marks sample locality; see table 1.

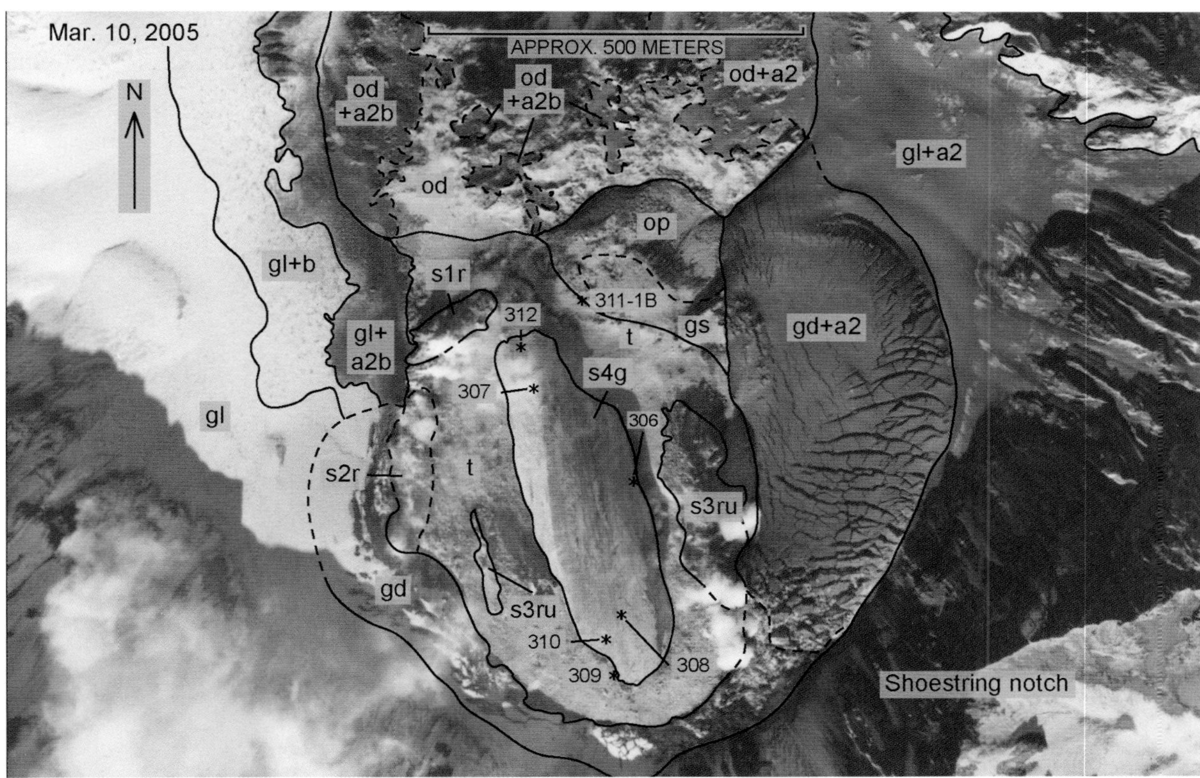

Figure 6. Photo-based geologic map of Mount St. Helens' new dome from aerial photo taken March 10, 2005. Stars mark sample localities; see table 1.

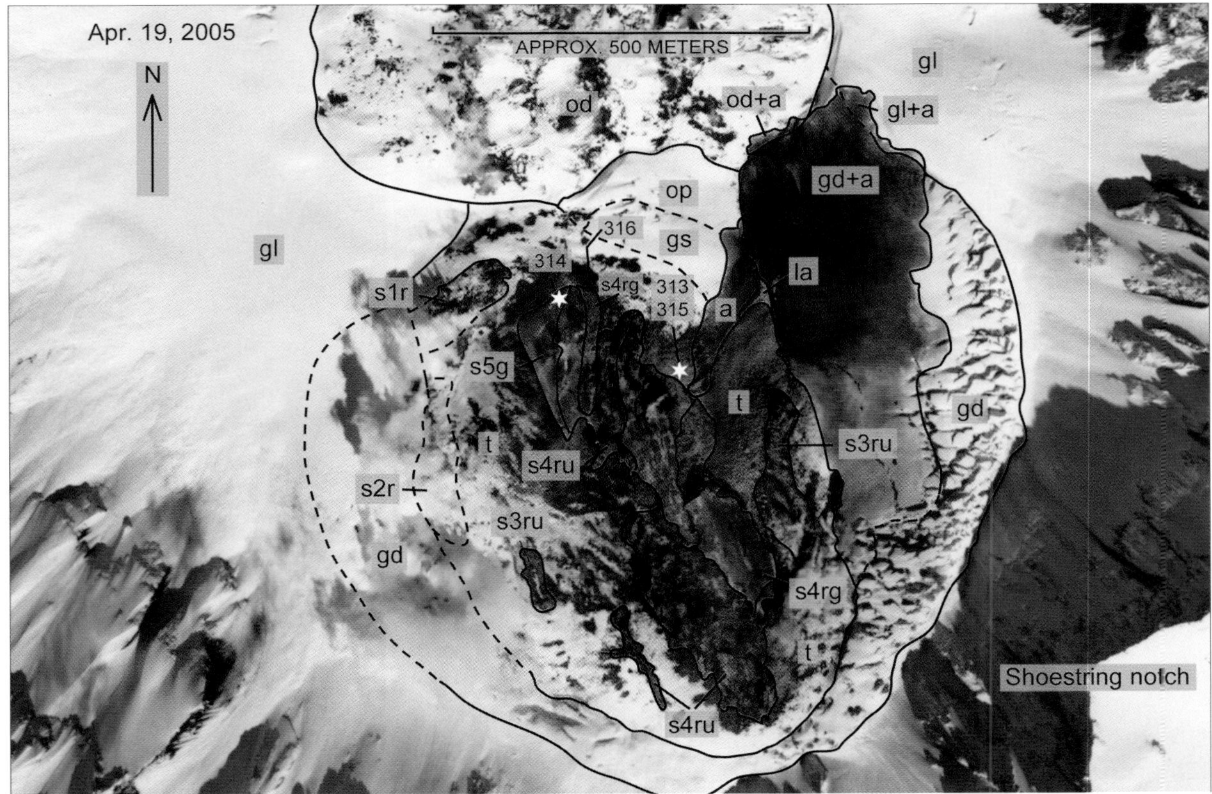

Figure 7. Photo-based geologic map of Mount St. Helens' new dome from aerial photo taken April 19, 2005. Stars mark sample localities; see table 1.

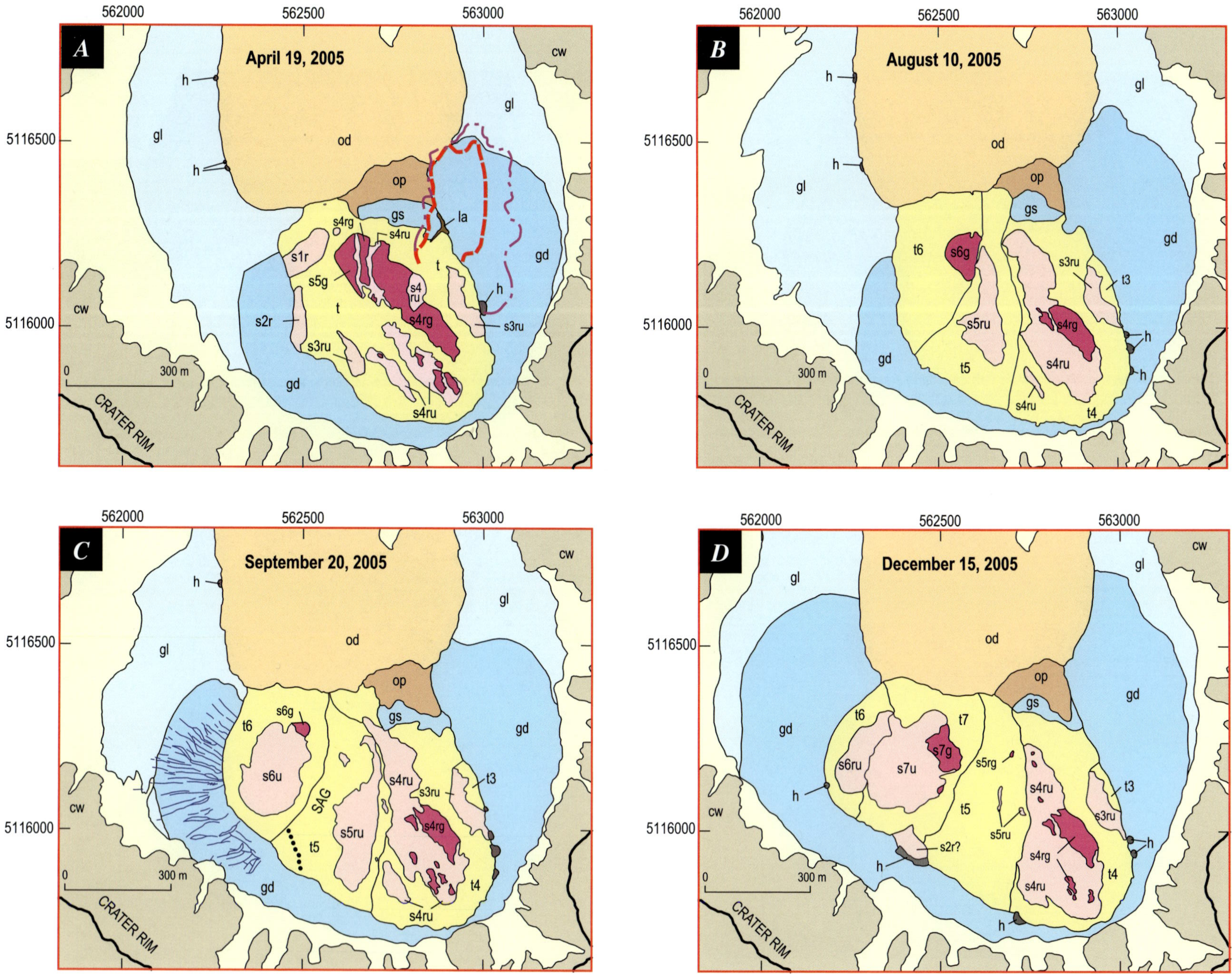

Figure 8. Rectified geologic maps of Mount St. Helens' new dome. *A*, April 19, 2005. *B*, August 10, 2005. *C*, September 20, 2005. *D*, December 15, 2005.

EXPLANATION

FEATURES ASSOCIATED WITH NEW DOME

Spine of 2004–2005 eruption (ongoing in December 2005)—Darker area mantled by gouge

Talus from flank of spine

Steaming lineament—On figure 8*C*. Likely marks incipient renewed exposure of spine 2 from beneath mantle of talus as seen on figure 8*D*

TEPHRA DEPOSITS ON MAP OF APRIL 19, 2005

Limit, density current of ashy sediment from rockfall

Outer limit of dilute ash from rockfall

OTHER FEATURES IN CRATER

Melt pit at glacier margin

Talus from crater walls and 1980–86 dome

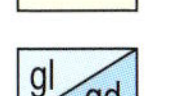

Glacial ice—Darker area deformed by dome growth

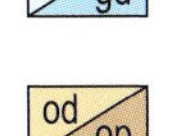

1980–86 dome—Darker area is Opus ridge (op)

Strata of crater walls and outer flanks

Notable crevasse on glacier—Resulting from dome emplacement. Only crevasses that developed after the previous map date are shown

Figure 8.—Continued.

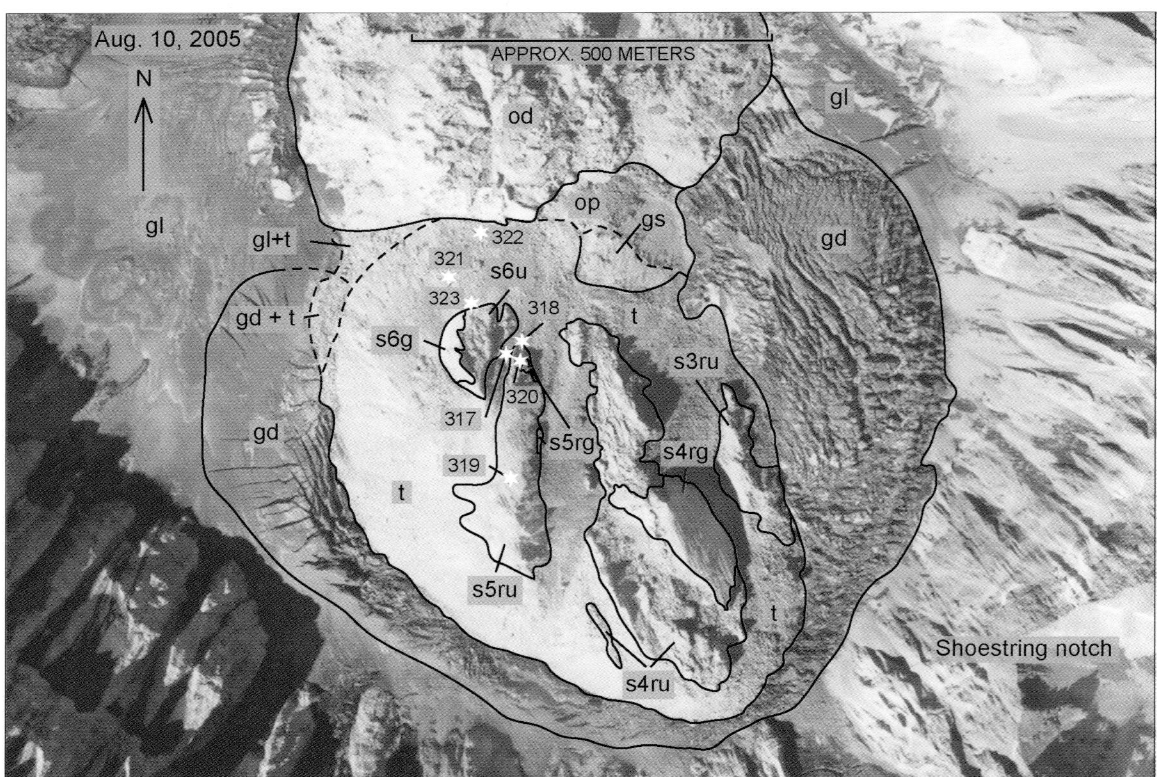

Figure 9. Photo-based geologic map of Mount St. Helens' new dome from aerial photo taken August 10, 2005. Stars mark sample localities; see table 1.

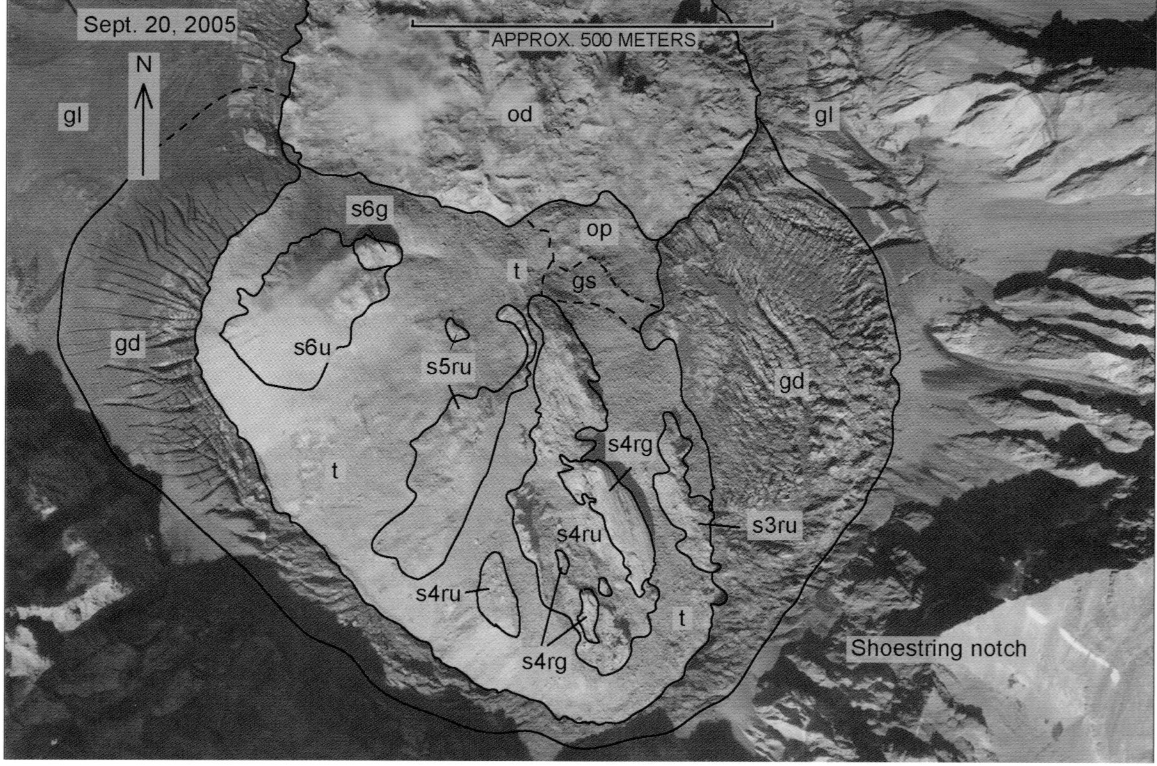

Figure 10. Photo-based geologic map of Mount St. Helens' new dome from aerial photo taken September 20, 2005.

ible only on the eastern periphery of the dome, whereas talus from spines 5 and 6 (t5, t6) now buries all remnants of spines 1, 2, and 3 to the west.

The washed-out appearance of the August 10 image (fig. 9) results from dust generated by summer rockfalls from both the new dome and the crater walls. Much of the light-dark color contrast in this photo arises from the water content of the dusted surface, which is darker where underlain by snow or ice.

September 20, 2005

Spine 6 (s6) continues to propagate westward (fig. 10). On its east side, rockfalls continue to incise the relatively small remaining parts of the gouge-mantled carapace (s6g). Abundant rockfalls from spine 5 have unroofed the core of that spine (s5ru), which now has a prominent axial crest. Spine 6's net westward motion is accompanied by subsidence between the actively growing part of the dome and the relatively stationary remnants of spines 3, 4, and 5 (fig. 8*C*).

Deformation in the west arm of Crater Glacier increases as spine 6 grows westward. Large new crevasses radiate outward from the contact with the expanding dome (fig. 8*C*). To the south, the band of glacial ice that bridges the east and west limbs of Crater Glacier has narrowed to about 6 m in width (fig. 8*C*).

December 15, 2005

In early October, spine 7 (s7) emerged from the sag that formed between spine 6 and remnants of spine 5 (fig. 11; Vallance and others, this volume, chap. 9). Spine 7 grew westward, pushing spine 6 remnants westward, overthrusting them, and burying them in talus. A small sliver of spine 6 (s6ru) still crops out along the margin of west Crater Glacier. Snow covers the largely cooled terrain of spines 3, 4, and 5, distinguishing it from the snow-free, hot, actively growing region of the dome. Spine 4 and 5 remnants are becoming more prominent as their cores are exhumed by rockfalls.

The deformation of Crater Glacier along its west arm is remarkable in this image (fig. 11). Deformation since August 2005 has created a jumbled serac field west of spine 6 remnants, and numerous crevasses underlie the snow-covered areas of the deformed west arm of the glacier.

Acknowledgments

We thank Christina Heliker and Steve Schilling for their insightful manuscript reviews, which led to greater clarity. Any remaining errors are the sole responsibility of the authors. The first author also thanks A.R. Wyss for his comments on an early version of the text.

Figure 11. Photo-based geologic map of Mount St. Helens' new dome from aerial photo taken December 15, 2005.

References Cited

Dzurisin, D., Lisowski, M., Poland, M.P., Sherrod, D.R., and LaHusen, R.G., 2008, Constraints and conundrums resulting from ground-deformation measurements made during the 2004–2005 dome-building eruption of Mount St. Helens, Washington, chap. 14 *of* Sherrod, D.R., Scott, W.E., and Stauffer, P.H., eds., A volcano rekindled; the renewed eruption of Mount St. Helens, 2004–2006: U.S. Geological Survey Professional Paper 1750 (this volume).

Major, J.J., Kingsbury, C.G., Poland, M.P., and LaHusen, R.G., 2008, Extrusion rate of the Mount St. Helens lava dome estimated from terrestrial imagery, November 2004–December 2005, chap. 12 *of* Sherrod, D.R., Scott, W.E., and Stauffer, P.H., eds., A volcano rekindled; the renewed eruption of Mount St. Helens, 2004–2006: U.S. Geological Survey Professional Paper 1750 (this volume).

Pallister, J.S., Thornber, C.R., Cashman, K.V., Clynne, M.A., Lowers, H.A., Mandeville, C.W., Brownfield, I.K., and Meeker, G.P., 2008, Petrology of the 2004–2006 Mount St. Helens lava dome—implications for magmatic plumbing and eruption triggering, chap. 30 *of* Sherrod, D.R., Scott, W.E., and Stauffer, P.H., eds., A volcano rekindled; the renewed eruption of Mount St. Helens, 2004–2006: U.S. Geological Survey Professional Paper 1750 (this volume).

Poland, M.P., Dzurisin, D., LaHusen, R.G., Major, J.J., Lapcewich, D., Endo, E.T., Gooding, D.J., Schilling, S.P., and Janda, C.G., 2008, Remote camera observations of lava dome growth at Mount St. Helens, Washington, October 2004 to February 2006, chap. 11 *of* Sherrod, D.R., Scott, W.E., and Stauffer, P.H., eds., A volcano rekindled; the renewed eruption of Mount St. Helens, 2004–2006: U.S. Geological Survey Professional Paper 1750 (this volume).

Schilling, S.P., Carrara, P.E., Thompson, R.A., and Iwatsubo, E.Y., 2004, Posteruption glacier development within the crater of Mount St. Helens, Washington, USA: Quaternary Research, v. 61, no. 3, p. 325–329.

Schilling, S.P., Thompson, R.A., Messerich, J.A., and Iwatsubo, E.Y., 2008, Use of digital aerophotogrammetry to determine rates of lava dome growth, Mount St. Helens, Washington, 2004–2005, chap. 8 *of* Sherrod, D.R., Scott, W.E., and Stauffer, P.H., eds., A volcano rekindled; the renewed eruption of Mount St. Helens, 2004–2006: U.S. Geological Survey Professional Paper 1750 (this volume).

Thornber, C.R., Pallister, J.S., Rowe, M.C., McConnell, S., Herriott, T.M., Eckberg, A., Stokes, W.C., Johnson Cornelius, D., Conrey, R.M., Hannah, T., Taggart, J.E., Jr., Adams, M., Lamothe, P.J., Budahn, J.R., and Knaack, C.M., 2008, Catalog of Mount St. Helens 2004–2007 dome samples with major- and trace-element chemistry: U.S. Geological Survey Open-File Report 2008–1130, 9 p., with digital database.

Vallance, J.W., Schneider, D.J., and Schilling, S.P., 2008, Growth of the 2004–2006 lava-dome complex at Mount St. Helens, Washington, chap. 9 *of* Sherrod, D.R., Scott, W.E., and Stauffer, P.H., eds., A volcano rekindled; the renewed eruption of Mount St. Helens, 2004–2006: U.S. Geological Survey Professional Paper 1750 (this volume).

Walder, J.S., Schilling, S.P., Vallance, J.W., and LaHusen, R.G., 2008, Effects of lava-dome growth on the Crater Glacier of Mount St. Helens, Washington, chap. 13 *of* Sherrod, D.R., Scott, W.E., and Stauffer, P.H., eds., A volcano rekindled; the renewed eruption of Mount St. Helens, 2004–2006: U.S. Geological Survey Professional Paper 1750 (this volume).

A Volcano Rekindled: The Renewed Eruption of Mount St. Helens, 2004–2006
Edited by David R. Sherrod, William E. Scott, and Peter H. Stauffer
U.S. Geological Survey Professional Paper 1750, 2008

Chapter 11

Remote Camera Observations of Lava Dome Growth at Mount St. Helens, Washington, October 2004 to February 2006

By Michael P. Poland[1], Daniel Dzurisin[2], Richard G. LaHusen[2], Jon J. Major[2], Dennis Lapcewich[3], Elliot T. Endo[2], Daniel J. Gooding[2], Steve P. Schilling[2], and Christine G. Janda[2]

Abstract

Images from a Web-based camera (Webcam) located 8 km north of Mount St. Helens and a network of remote, telemetered digital cameras were used to observe eruptive activity at the volcano between October 2004 and February 2006. The cameras offered the advantages of low cost, low power, flexibility in deployment, and high spatial and temporal resolution. Images obtained from the cameras provided important insights into several aspects of dome extrusion, including rockfalls, lava extrusion rates, and explosive activity. Images from the remote, telemetered digital cameras were assembled into time-lapse animations of dome extrusion that supported monitoring, research, and outreach efforts. The wide-ranging utility of remote camera imagery should motivate additional work, especially to develop the three-dimensional quantitative capabilities of terrestrial camera networks.

Introduction

During the 20th century, advances in technology have added an array of geophysical and geochemical instrumentation to the modern volcanologist's toolkit. The study of active volcanoes has relied increasingly upon datasets derived from such technology to infer the mechanics of volcanic processes, which often occur at depth. As detailed in this volume, many geophysical and geochemical techniques have been applied to improve understanding of eruptive activity at Mount St. Helens in 2004–6. Visual surveillance in volcanology, however, remains critical for providing "ground truth" necessary to confirm inferences drawn from geophysical and geochemical data.

Visual observations can be recorded by imaging systems on the ground or in an aircraft or spacecraft. For example, photogrammetric applications of aerial photography to volcanoes include quantification of large-scale deformation before the 1980 eruption of Mount St. Helens (Moore and Albee, 1981) and calculations of erupted volumes at Stromboli, Italy, in 2002–3 (Baldi and others, 2005) and at Mount St. Helens in 2004–6 (Schilling and others, this volume, chap. 8). Ground-based visual imagery is equally important for observing volcanic activity, having the advantages of low cost, frequent image acquisition, and flexibility in deployment. Starting in September 2004, we made extensive use of terrestrial cameras to investigate activity at Mount St. Helens using a continuously operating Webcam located 8 km north of the volcano and repeat photographs from a network of remote, telemetered digital cameras. The imagery was used to evaluate broad-scale eruptive activity in near real time, correlate geophysical signals with changes in eruptive activity, investigate dome extrusion processes, track the evolution of the eruption (including deformation of glacial ice) over time, and assess weather conditions for planning fieldwork.

We describe here the remote camera deployments and the activity recorded at Mount St. Helens during the period October 2004 to February 2006. Other types of camera deployments and applications at Mount St. Helens are described elsewhere in this volume. Results from high-rate, small field-of-view photography experiments designed to measure small-scale changes in dome extrusion are described by Dzurisin and others (this volume, chap. 14). Major and others (this volume, chap. 12) discuss quantitative dome-growth measurements

[1] U.S. Geological Survey, PO Box 51, Hawaii National Park, HI 96718

[2] U.S. Geological Survey, 1300 SE Cardinal Court, Vancouver, WA 98683

[3] U.S.D.A. Forest Service, Gifford Pinchot National Forest, 10600 NE 51st Circle, Vancouver, WA 98682

using images from a single remote camera in combination with a digital elevation model.

Previous Uses of Visual Observation Systems to Monitor Active Volcanoes

Volcanology is fundamentally an observational science, and repeat observations from fixed locations have proven critical to the documentation and interpretation of many volcanic processes. During dome extrusion in 1902–5 at La Montagne Pelée, Martinique, Lacroix (1908) collected photographs from fixed vantage points to record the development of the dome over the course of the extrusive phase of the eruption. In 1944–45, Mimatsu Masao, the postmaster of the Sobetsu Post Office in Japan, lacked camera equipment but documented the growth of the Showa-Shinzan dome at the base of Mount Usu in a detailed diary and with careful sketches. His unique surveying methods included a fixed observation point behind the post office, from where he viewed the growing dome by resting his chin on a level and by using a series of horizontally stretched cords as reference lines. His drawings of the uplift and dome growth from this vantage point were presented at the 1948 International Association of Volcanology conference in Oslo, Norway, and what came to be known as "Mimatsu diagrams" were praised as "the only existing records of the entire birth of a volcano" (Mimatsu, 1995).

One of the best known volcano photographic sequences was taken by Gary Rosenquist at Mount St. Helens during the landslide and lateral blast of May 18, 1980. The Rosenquist photos, and similar sequences taken from other locations around the volcano at the start of the eruption, were critical to understanding the development of the landslide and lateral blast (Voight, 1981; Voight and others, 1981; Moore and Rice, 1984), lahar initiation (Pierson, 1985), pyroclastic stratigraphy (Criswell, 1987), and the question of whether or not the blast was a product of one or two explosions (Hoblitt, 2000). Fixed-vantage-point cameras from more than 100 repeat terrestrial photography and time-lapse film stations were also a key tool for studying dome building at Mount St. Helens during 1980–86 (Topinka, 1992).

The development of digital cameras has facilitated the use of visual observation systems at volcanoes. At Kīlauea Volcano, Hawai'i, time-lapse digital cameras powered by solar panels and encased in weatherproof boxes now record details of volcanic events, including ground deformation, vent collapses, and surface breakouts of lava (Orr and Hoblitt, 2006). Repeat views from remote digital cameras have also been employed at Soufrière Hills volcano[4], Montserrat, where they provided important visual documentation of dome growth (Watts and others, 2002) and of the 2003 catastrophic dome collapse (Herd and others, 2005).

[4] Capitalization of "Volcano" indicates adoption of the word as part of the formal geographic name by the host country, as listed in the Geographic Names Information System, a database maintained by the U.S. Board on Geographic Names. Noncapitalized "volcano" is applied informally—eds.

Remote Camera Systems Used at Mount St. Helens

During October 2004 to February 2006, two types of remote camera systems were used for visually monitoring eruptive activity at Mount St. Helens—a Webcam and a network of remote, telemetered digital cameras. These systems are described below.

Webcam

A Webcam, herein referred to as the "VolcanoCam," was installed in 1996 at the U.S. Department of Agriculture–Forest Service's Johnston Ridge Observatory (JRO; fig. 1), 8 km north of Mount St. Helens (fig. 2*A*). At that time, the installation of the camera was more of an Internet novelty for the Gifford Pinchot National Forest (GPNF) and the Mount St. Helens National Volcanic Monument. The GPNF had just established one of the first Web sites within the Forest Service, and the addition of the VolcanoCam, they hoped, would provide a boost to forest recreation use by stimulating general interest in the area.

The VolcanoCam operated with minimal problems for 7 years until it suffered a mechanical failure in June 2003. Funding problems delayed replacement of the camera for more than a year. New equipment was finally procured and installed on September 23, 2004—coincidentally the day that seismic unrest began at Mount St. Helens. The new VolcanoCam was a color charge-coupled camera that provided a signal of 525 TV lines at 30 frames per second (terminology from the National Television System Committee standards). Still images were uploaded every five minutes to the Forest Service's national Web server. The clock on the camera was not synchronized to Internet time and was probably only accurate to within about 1 minute.

Access to the camera was initially limited to Forest Service and USGS staff, but the VolcanoCam was opened for public access on September 27, 2004, and immediately became a major attraction (http://www.fs.fed.us/gpnf/volcanocams/msh/, last accessed January 28, 2008). The number of hits on the VolcanoCam Web site became so large that the main Forest Service Web server crashed several times, and excessive bandwidth use threatened the main U.S. Department of Agriculture Web servers. A Web caching system alleviated the most serious bandwidth concerns. Fourth-quarter 2004 statistics for all Federal government Web sites later revealed that the Forest Service enjoyed the largest quarterly increase in customer satisfaction ever recorded for a Federal government Web site, due mainly to the worldwide popularity of the VolcanoCam.

Despite its relative simplicity, the VolcanoCam was a remarkably useful educational resource and volcano-monitoring tool. Many of the thousands of emails received by the Forest Service in late 2004 regarding the VolcanoCam were from teachers across the United States, offering their thanks for the opportunity to view volcanic activity in their classrooms. In addition, the VolcanoCam proved to be a valuable tool for volcanologists, enabling rapid assessment of volcanic activity and weather conditions from any location having Internet access. The camera also demonstrated limited infrared capabilities. Nighttime observations were important for detecting magma extrusion and rockfall events, and they garnered substantial interest from the general public. An independent Web site managed by Mr. Darryl Luscombe even made available daily movies from sequential "glow" images collected during the previous night (http://www.luscombe-carter.com/index.html, last accessed January 28, 2008).

Figure 1. Field setting for U.S. Department of Agriculture Forest Service VolcanoCam at Mount St. Helens, Washington. *A*, Camera position beneath eave of Johnston Ridge Observatory. USGS photo by J.P. Griswold, August 25, 2006. Inset shows camera. USGS photo by S.P. Schilling. *B*, Example of VolcanoCam view of the volcano acquired on September 24, 2004.

Remote, Telemetered Digital Cameras

In early October 2004, the value of having a visual monitoring station close to the volcano became obvious because the VolcanoCam's view of the locus of renewed activity was blocked by the 1980–86 lava dome. To meet this need, staff at the USGS Hawaiian Volcano Observatory constructed a remote, telemetered digital camera, based on models used at Soufrière Hills volcano, Montserrat (Herd and others, 2005), and sent it to the Cascades Volcano Observatory (CVO) for deployment at Mount St. Helens. The system included an Olympus C–3030 3.3-megapixel camera with a × 3 optical zoom lens. The camera was connected through a serial port to a 900-MHz radio mounted in a weatherproof box (fig. 3). The

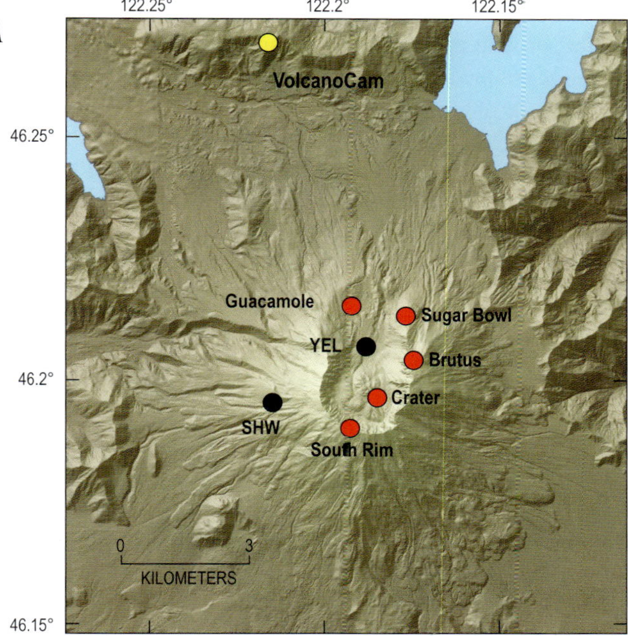

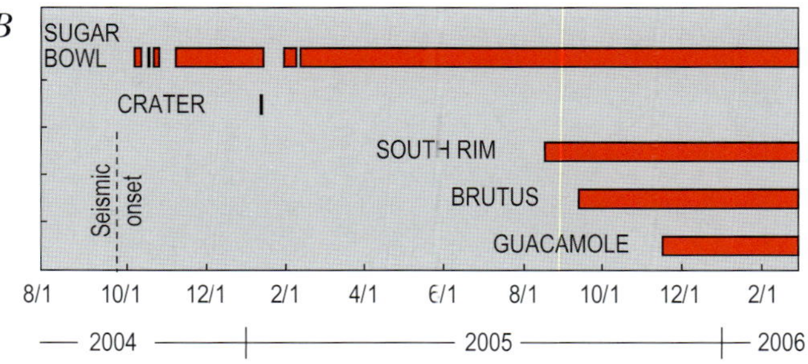

Figure 2. Remote, telemetered digital cameras used during monitoring of Mount St. Helens, Washington, 2004–6. *A*, Map showing locations of U.S. Geological Survey remote cameras (red dots) and U.S. Department of Agriculture Forest Service VolcanoCam (yellow dot). Black dots show locations of seismic stations that are referred to in figures 10 and 11. Hillshade-relief base map is from digital elevation model (DEM) of October 2005. *B*, Timeline with dates of operation (red bars) for remote, telemetered digital cameras through February 2006. Usable images were lacking on about half of all operating days, owing to inclement weather.

box was fastened to a tripod and pointed towards the deforming area in the southeast part of the crater (fig. 4). Power was supplied by a solar panel and batteries with enough capacity to ensure that the camera and radio would operate even during long periods of cloudy weather. Image resolution, zoom, and timing of acquisition were controlled from a computer located at the Forest Service's Coldwater Ridge Visitor Center, about 13 km northwest of the crater, using PhotoPC public domain software (http://www.lightner.net/lightner/bruce/photopc/ppc_use.html, last accessed January 28, 2008). Images were time stamped according to the camera time. The controlling computer could be reached via ftp from CVO through a satellite link, thereby providing access to imagery in near real time.

The remote camera was installed on October 10, 2004, on Sugar Bowl dome, immediately northeast of the breach in the 1980 crater wall and 2.3 km from the intensely deforming area, or welt (Dzurisin and others, this volume, chap. 14), in the southeast part of Mount St. Helens crater (fig. 2). The goals for the Sugar Bowl camera deployment were to (1) establish a visual record of volcanic activity, which could be used to test inferences drawn from geophysical, geological, and geochemical measurements, (2) monitor volcanic activity in near real time, and (3) provide a means of assessing general conditions in the volcano's crater to support field operations. Sugar Bowl offered a good view of the welt and subsequent dome growth (fig. 4*B*) from a point relatively safe from the mild explosive activity that characterized the early stages of the eruption.

A few problems resulted in a loss of imagery from the digital camera. Although high winds minimized snow accumulation, rime ice built up when temperatures were below freezing, obscuring the camera's view (fig. 5). The ice was removed manually during site visits, but it often persisted for weeks at a time when no field work was conducted. The system functioned well during the period October 2004 to February 2006, with only a few lapses in image acquisition (fig. 2*B*) caused by mechanical breakdowns and abrasion of the viewing window by blowing volcanic ash. When the camera was operating, cloudy or icy weather resulted in no usable imagery for approximately half of the total deployment time.

The Sugar Bowl camera became an important tool in monitoring, research, and public outreach efforts, and it motivated the deployment of four additional instruments (Crater, Brutus, South Rim, and Guacamole; fig. 2) by the end of 2005. These new systems used similar equipment and software as the Sugar Bowl camera (fig. 6*A*). The Crater camera was installed by a helicopter sling operation within a few hundred meters of the growing dome on January 14, 2005. A location close to the dome was selected to provide close-up images that might be used to test dome-growth models (fig 6*B*). This camera suffered a mechanical failure several hours after it was put into

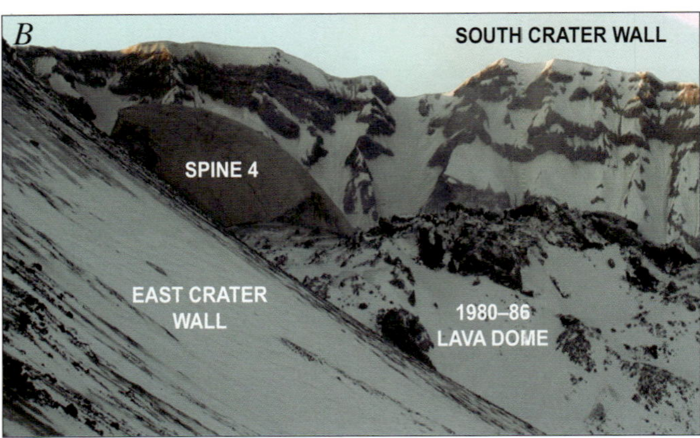

Figure 4. Setting and view for Sugar Bowl remote telemetered camera at Mount St. Helens, Washington. *A*, Field site atop Sugar Bowl dome, 2 km from active vent. Solar panel is out of view to the right. USGS photo by M.P. Poland, October 10, 2004. *B*, Example of camera view, acquired on February 10, 2005, showing spine 4.

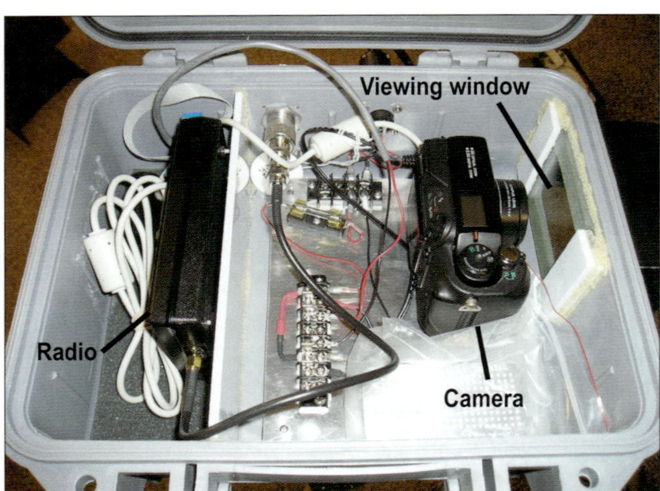

Figure 3. Interior of weatherproof box that contains camera and radio telemetry for Sugar Bowl remote, telemetered digital camera system. USGS photo by M.P. Poland, October 10, 2004.

place and was subsequently destroyed by a small explosion during the early morning of January 16, 2005. During the summer and fall of 2005, additional cameras were installed on the crater rim: Brutus (fig. 6*C*), 1.1 km east-northeast of the vent, and South Rim (fig. *6A, D*), 0.7 km southwest of the vent. As dome building focused in the southwestern part of the crater during late 2005, a camera was established on the floor of the breach in the 1980 crater: Guacamole (fig. 6*E*), 2.6 km north of the vent. Taken together, these camera systems provided a variety of different views of the growing lava dome.

Insights from Remote Camera Imagery

The remote cameras provided important, and sometimes unexpected, insights into volcanic activity at Mount St. Helens during 2004–2006. For example, the VolcanoCam confirmed that the extrusion of lava had begun in October 2004. Visual and infrared observations from a helicopter on October 11, 2004, noted a craggy, hot (maximum temperature of 580°C), rocky "fin," indicating that lava had reached the surface (Scott and others, this volume, chap. 1; Vallance and others, this volume, chap. 9). During the night of October 11 and the morning of October 12, the VolcanoCam showed signs of glow reflected off steam in the vicinity of the new spine, providing a valuable supplement to the earlier visual and infrared data and accessible to anyone with Internet access.

Both the VolcanoCam and the Sugar Bowl remote camera also had excellent views of explosive activity at Mount St. Helens. VolcanoCam photos posted to the Internet every five minutes provided useful, though approximate, constraints on the duration, magnitude, and timing of the early October 2004 explosions. Following that period, only two additional significant explosions occurred, on January 16 and March 8, 2005 (Scott and others, this volume, chap. 1; Moran and others, this volume, chap. 6). The January 16 explosion occurred shortly after 0300 Pacific standard time (PST, Greenwich mean time minus 8 hours) during a period of poor weather in the middle of the night and was not visible to either the VolcanoCam or Sugar Bowl systems. In contrast, the March 8 event took place at approximately 1725 PST during a time of clear weather (Scott and others, this volume, chap. 1; Moran and others, this volume, chap. 6). Analysis of Sugar Bowl imagery proved useful for the interpretation of seismic and acoustic data recorded during the event (Moran and others, this volume, chap. 6).

Figure 5. Rime-ice accumulation on Sugar Bowl telemetered digital camera at Mount St. Helens, Washington. Ice buildup was a common problem on camera systems during fall and winter months. USGS photo by S.P. Schilling, October 24, 2004.

Visual imagery from remote cameras was useful in the recognition and analysis of rockfall from the lava spines. Although background glow from the growing dome had been observed in VolcanoCam imagery starting on the night of October 11, 2004, brief, brighter flashes were noticed by Internet observers beginning on January 13, 2005 (such flashes probably occurred earlier than this date but were not observed because of either their low intensity or poor weather). These images prompted seismologists to review the overnight seismic records and led to the recognition that the flashes were associated with rockfall signals. A major VolcanoCam flash occurred at about 0303 PST on February 22, 2005, and was accompanied by a large seismic signal (fig. 7). Visual inspection by field crews on the following day recognized a new scar on the growing lava dome, confirming the occurrence of a large rockfall during the previous night.

Significant rockfall events during daylight hours were accompanied by bursts of ash that often drifted above the crater rim (Moran and others, this volume, chaps. 2 and 6). Combining imagery from the remote, telemetered digital cameras, which was available within minutes of acquisition, with real-time seismic data allowed for rapid recognition of the rockfall source. An example occurred on April 26, 2005, at approximately 1126 Pacific daylight time (PDT, Greenwich mean time minus 7 hours), when a part of spine 4 disintegrated, sending a small ash plume above the crater rim (fig. 8).

The volume of extruded lava at Mount St. Helens during 2004–2006 was calculated every 1–2 months by differencing digital elevation models (DEMs) derived from aerial photography or lidar data (Schilling and others, this volume, chap. 8). More frequent, but necessarily qualitative, estimates of the relative rate of lava extrusion could be made by examining time-lapse sequences acquired by the remote, telemetered digital cameras. For example, in December 2004, a marked decline in the release of seismic energy (Moran and others, this volume, chap. 2) suggested that the eruption was slowing. When a sequence of daily images from the Sugar Bowl remote camera was reviewed, however, it became clear that the overall rate of lava extrusion had not changed significantly across the lull in seismicity. The measurement of extrusion rates can be quantified by combining a DEM with the remote camera imagery, as demonstrated using data from the Sugar Bowl camera by Major and others (this volume, chap.

12). In an attempt to assess whether dome extrusion occurred smoothly or by a series of irregular surges correlative with seismicity, high-rate photography of a small field of view of patches on the growing lava dome was performed, but several factors limited the success of this experiment (Dzurisin and others, this volume, chap. 14).

Evolution of the Dome Complex Shown by Animations of Camera Imagery

Perhaps the most useful aspect of remote camera observations during 2004–6 at Mount St. Helens was the

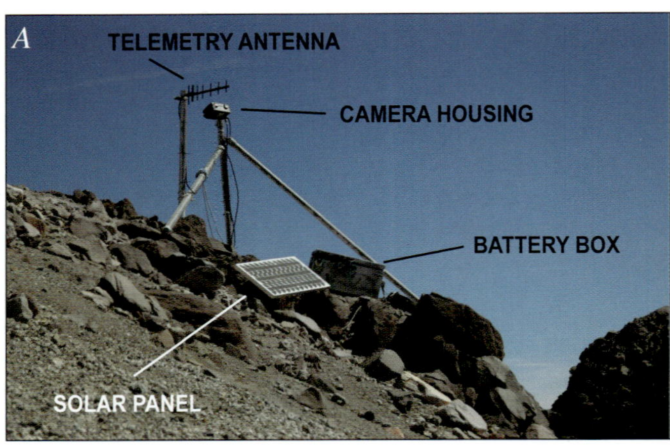

Figure 6. Other remote-camera setups and views at Mount St. Helens, Washington. Numbers on photos refer to spines as defined by Vallance and others (this volume, chap. 9). *A*, South Rim site, which also exemplifies equipment and installation style of Crater, Brutus, and Guacamole cameras. USGS photo by S.P. Schilling, August 19, 2005. *B*, Example of view from Crater camera, acquired January 15, 2005. *C*, Example of view from Brutus camera, acquired September 20, 2005. *D*, Example of view from South Rim camera, acquired August 19, 2005. *E*, Example of view from Guacamole camera, acquired February 24, 2006. Pink streak in middle of image is caused by sun damage to camera.

documentation of the lava dome complex's morphological evolution over time. During clear weather and rime ice-free conditions, and regardless of the presence of field personnel, the remote, telemetered cameras provided high-quality views of the volcano from common vantage points. Imagery was therefore directly comparable over time, and visualizing the changing morphology of the lava dome complex by animating images into time-lapse movies proved to be an important tool for monitoring and interpreting volcanic activity.

Time-lapse animations of images from the Sugar Bowl, Brutus, South Rim, and Guacamole remote camera are provided as supplementary digital data to this report (Major and others, this volume, chap. 12, appendix 1, found on the DVD accompanying the volume and on the Web version of the work). Below, we describe and interpret the time-lapse animations of dome growth at Mount St. Helens obtained from the remote, telemetered digital cameras during the period October 2004 to February 2006. This account relies heavily on the Sugar Bowl camera for observations during the first year of the eruption, when that was the only remote camera that had been deployed. The observations that follow are drawn solely from remote camera imagery and do not rely on other data. The account is not meant to supplant but rather to complement descriptions of dome growth derived from other types of observations and data that are contained elsewhere in this volume. The chronology of 2004–6 activity is reported in this volume by Scott and others (chap. 1), Schilling and others (chap. 8), Vallance and others (chap. 9), and Herriott and others (chap. 10). In addition, geophysical and geochemical time series from the eruption are summarized by Moran and others (chaps. 2 and 6), Lisowski and others, (chap. 15), LaHusen and others (chap. 16), Gerlach and others (chap. 26), and Pallister and others (chap. 30).

Between October 2004 and February 2006, dome growth at Mount St. Helens occurred through the extrusion of seven distinct spines (Scott and others, this volume, chap. 1; Vallance and others, this volume, chap. 9). Spines 1 and 2, formed in mid-October 2004, were the smallest of the extrusions, and they were active for the shortest periods of time. Owing to their location along the south margin of the 1980–86 lava dome, they were not visible to the Sugar Bowl camera or the VolcanoCam and were documented only by observations (including thermal imagery) from helicopter overflights. The growth of spines 3–7, however, was visible

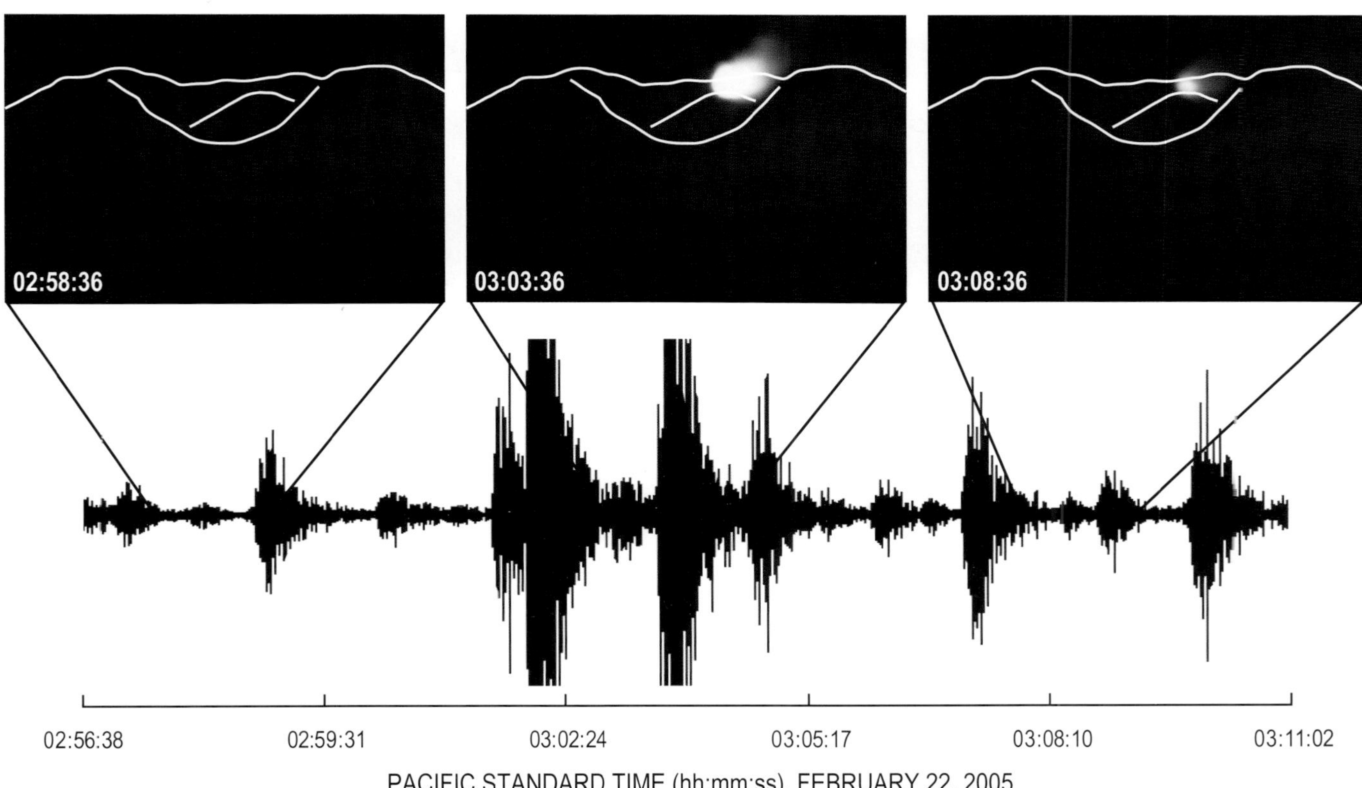

Figure 7. Use of nighttime images from the U.S. Department of Agriculture Forest Service VolcanoCam to track rockfalls at Mount St. Helens, Washington. Top, consecutive images from February 22, 2005 (PST), showing one of the largest rockfalls of that year. Bright patch is a reflection in steam clouds of incandescence created by the sudden exposure of hot material. Outline of Mount St. Helens and 1980–86 lava dome provided for context. VolcanoCam clock was not synchronized to Internet time, so it is probably only accurate to plus or minus 1 minute. Bottom, seismic record from station SHW (see fig. 2*A* for station location).

from the Sugar Bowl camera except for a brief interval during the growth of spine 6.

The Sugar Bowl camera was deployed after the welt had largely formed in the southeastern part of the crater. During the first week of image acquisition, the camera recorded growth of a small knob that protruded from the welt along the southeast margin of the 1980–86 lava dome. The knob disappeared during October 20–27, 2004, a period of inclement weather when no visual observations (either by remote camera or field personnel) were possible. Judging from oblique aerial photos, the bulge appeared to be crater-floor debris and ice that was pushed up and later collapsed during the initial stages of dome extrusion (J. Major, written commun., 2006).

Spine 3 first became apparent in Sugar Bowl camera imagery on October 29, 2004, when uplift of the welt accelerated rapidly. The spine continued to grow steadily towards the southeast until mid-December, when imagery from December 17 showed that cracks had formed along the north side of the extrusion. These cracks continued to develop throughout the remainder of the month, eventually leading to the formation of an independent spine of lava (spine 4). The breakup of spine 3 may have been caused when it impinged upon the

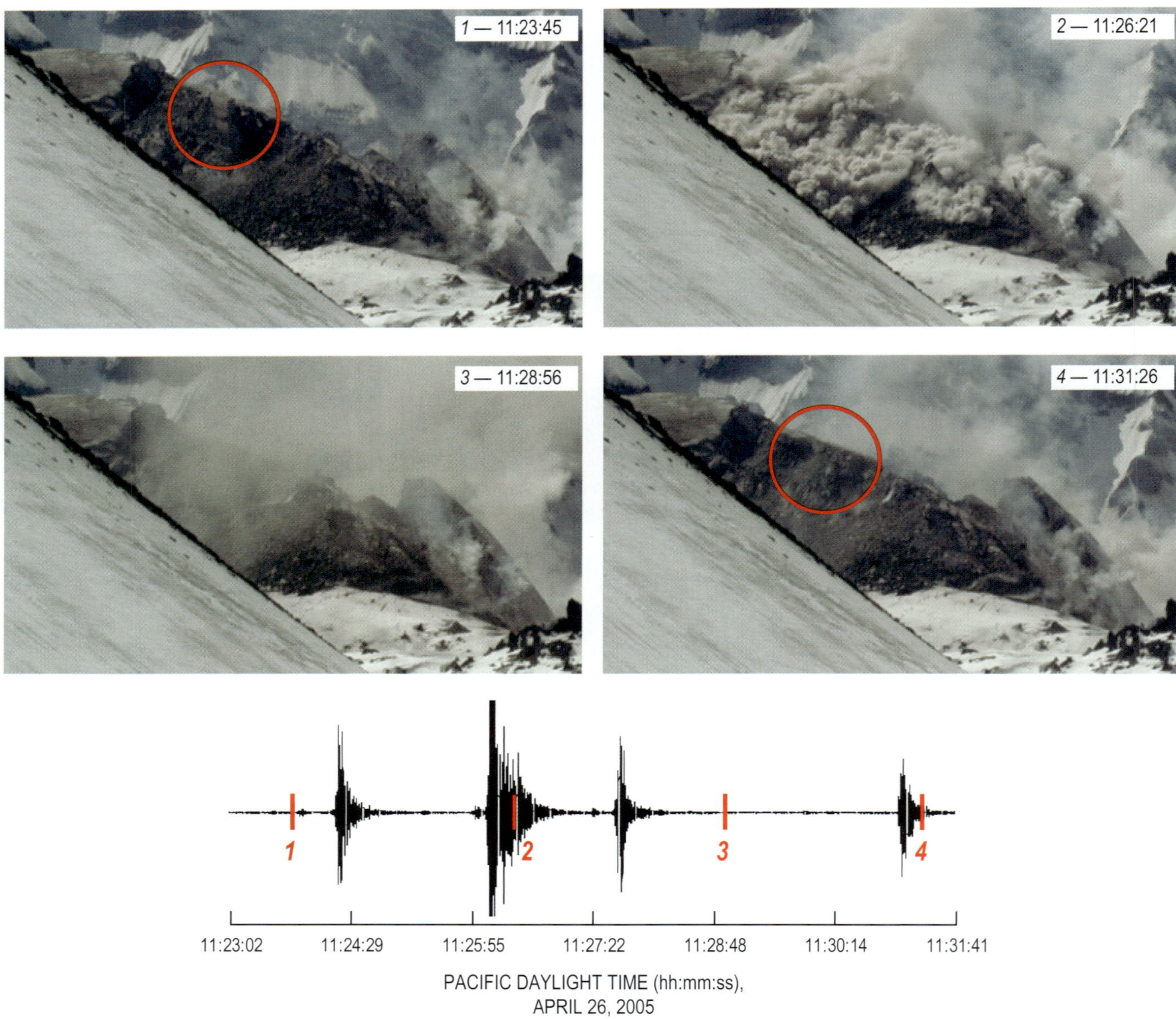

Figure 8. Seismic record from station YEL (bottom) and consecutive images from Sugar Bowl remote camera (top) for April 26, 2005 (PDT), showing major rockfall (source identified by red circle). See figure 2*A* for location of YEL.

southeastern crater wall (Vallance and others, this volume, chap. 9). The apparent extrusion velocity at the vent did not seem to change over this time period, judging from the photographic sequence from the Sugar Bowl camera and calculations of lineal extrusion rates (Major and others, this volume, chap. 12). If extrusion was constant, spine 3 was undergoing horizontal compression as lava continued to extrude from the vent, which probably caused it to fracture (Moran and others, this volume, chap. 2).

Spine 4, which was also characterized by dominantly southeastward motion, first rose to a higher altitude than spine 3, then began to override the latter in early January 2005. Sugar Bowl imagery suggests that the smooth surface of spine 4 began to fracture and disintegrate sometime between March 15 and April 13, 2005. A more definitive date is difficult to assign, because the view from Sugar Bowl was obscured by ice and clouds between those two dates, but field observations show that disintegration began about April 10 (Vallance and others, this volume, chap. 9). The increasingly fractured, but still coherent, spine continued to move to the southeast until April 24, 2005, by which time significant motion (that is, motion on the order of meters per day) had ceased and extrusive activity shifted from spine 4 to spine 5. Major and others (this volume, chap. 12) document this transition using quantitative lineal extrusion rates based on Sugar Bowl imagery.

The Sugar Bowl camera observed the initial formation of spine 5 between April 14 and 18, 2005, when upward motion and lineal extrusion rate (Major and others, this volume, chap. 12) of that spine became independent of spine 4. Spine 5 extruded at a steep angle (about 60°–70° from horizontal) from the vent and was subject to two cycles of construction and destruction during its life. Construction dominated until May 13, 2005, when a large part of the spine collapsed. Spine disintegration competed with extrusion to keep the spine at a relatively constant height from that time through June 4, 2005, when a second period dominated by construction began. By July 1, 2005, spine 5 had reached its highest altitude, although a period of more frequent collapses began around June 30, 2005. A few tens of meters of dome elevation were lost between July 1 and 3, 2005. Upward motion of spine 5 continued, but the highest altitude of the extrusion remained nearly constant between July 3 and 14, 2005, as collapses from the upper part of the spine compensated for the addition of new lava at its base. By July 15, 2005, destructive processes began to outpace spine construction, and the height of the spine decreased daily. Sugar Bowl imagery suggests that the second cycle of growth and destructive phases of spine 5 had mostly ceased by August 2, 2005.

The distinction between spines 5 and 6 is difficult to constrain, but Sugar Bowl images indicate that spine 6 was moving independently of spine 5 by August 1, 2005. Growth of spine 6 was mostly vertical until August 10, 2005, when it began to move to the west without increasing in height. Sugar Bowl imagery and lineal extrusion rates (Major and others, this volume, chap. 12) suggest an apparent acceleration in westward motion starting on about August 16, 2005, and the spine height began to decrease as large collapses destroyed its upper reaches. A consequence of the motion of spine 6 towards the west was the development of a depression between spine 6 and the mostly inactive spine 5. Continued extrusion to the west occurred throughout the remainder of August and September, with the spine's motion becoming almost completely horizontal. During this time period, the westernmost part of spine 5 gradually slumped into the growing depression, probably because it was left unsupported as spine 6 moved to the west (Vallance and others, this volume, chap. 9). Interestingly, unlike other spines, spine 6 apparently did not experience an extended period of collapse and destruction towards the end of its activity. This may have been a result of its relatively low height, compared to spines 3, 4, and 5.

Growth of spines 6 and 7 was well documented by the Brutus, South Rim, and Guacamole remote cameras, which were installed during late summer 2005. Sometime between September 28 and October 17, 2005 (a period of poor weather when few observations were possible), spine 6 gave way to spine 7, which grew out of the western side of the depression between spines 5 and 6. The direction of spine 7's motion was also toward the west but included a significant component of upward motion. As a result, spine 7 pushed and overrode spine 6, obscuring the distinction between the two extrusions. Although poor weather characterized much of late 2005 and early 2006, limited imagery indicates that spine 7 continued to grow into February 2006 with two cycles of alternating height increase (when the spine was gravitationally stable) and decrease (when the spine disintegrated gradually).

Time-lapse animation sequences from the remote, telemetered cameras reveal that spines 3 to 7 each experienced cycles of growth and destruction that lasted several months. The growth stages generally involved the extrusion of smooth-sided spines (with the exception of spine 6, which was mostly covered by rubble) with little accompanying large disintegration events. During destructive phases, spine extrusion continued, but abundant rockfall destroyed the smooth carapaces and resulted in highly fractured and blocky formations surrounded by talus. The onset of the destructive phase preceded the transition to a new spine in the cases of spines 3, 4, and 5. Spines 5 and 7 both experienced multiple constructive and destructive phases, perhaps related to their steeper extrusion angles. The "great spine" at La Montagne Pelée, Martinique, which was similar in appearance to the Mount St. Helens spines, also experienced multiple construction and destruction cycles during 1902–3, although the cycles appear to have been related to an unsteady, pulsing eruption rate (Jaupart and Allègre, 1991; Tanguy, 2004). At Mount St. Helens, lineal extrusion rates derived from Sugar Bowl imagery suggest that the eruption rate during the extrusion of spine 5 was nearly constant (Major and others, this volume, chap. 12); thus, alternating cycles of spine-height increase and erosion must have been controlled by other factors, for example, the strength of the dome carapace, thermal cooling, propagation of fractures, or gravitational stresses. Vallance and others (this volume, chap. 9) discuss the history and driving mechanisms of spine construction and destruction and the transitions between spines.

In addition to lava-dome processes and morphology, deformation of the Crater Glacier—which surrounded the 1980–86 lava dome on the east, west, and south before the onset of eruptive activity in 2004 (Schilling and others, 2004)—was recorded by several of the remote cameras. The Brutus camera's field of view included the contact between the western part of the dome complex and the west arm of the glacier. By the time the camera was installed in mid-September 2005, the west arm of Crater Glacier had already been extensively compressed, thickened, and fractured. The Brutus sequence of images showed continued thickening and cracking of glacial ice as spines 6 and 7 grew toward the west. A complementary perspective was provided by the Guacamole camera, which had a view of much of the glacier's west arm (including its terminus) and recorded glacier deformation from the time of its installation in mid-November 2005. Motion of the glacier's terminus occurred at an accelerated rate between January 23 and February 16, 2006, perhaps because of a downstream-moving bulge caused by compression of the glacier by spines 6 and 7 (Walder and others, this volume, chap. 13).

Strategies for Future Deployments of Remote Camera Systems

The bulk of the contributions from visual observation systems to monitoring efforts at Mount St. Helens in 2004–2006 are necessarily qualitative because of limitations in camera views and weather conditions. Images were generally used to support inferences drawn from geophysical and geological observations or to characterize transient events and long-term processes. As demonstrated by Major and others (this volume, chap. 12), however, quantitative measurements of surface change from single camera deployments are possible.

Future camera deployments at active volcanoes should take advantage of photogrammetric principles, which will allow for more detailed analyses of surface change. For example, oblique aerial photographs that include ground control points with known positions can be used to construct DEMs of the ground surface. The technique has been demonstrated in laboratory conditions (Cecchi and others, 2003), at small scales on active lava flows at Mount Etna (James and others, 2006), and at larger scales on an entire lava dome at Soufrière Hills volcano, Montserrat (Herd and others, 2005). Expanding the use of photogrammetry to terrestrial cameras can be accomplished by deploying a pair (or more) of remote, telemetered digital cameras with views that are separated by 30°–60° in azimuth from the target area and include several ground control points. A DEM of the areas viewed in common by a pair of cameras can then be constructed, and displacements, perhaps on the order of centimeters, may be calculated by differencing DEMs from different time periods. Although the principles involved in deriving such DEMs are not new, they have yet to be applied extensively using ground-based cameras. Terrestrial systems, although limited by weather conditions, offer the benefits of low cost, low power, flexibility, and high temporal and spatial measurement density. Dome-building eruptions characterized by steady topographic change over time, like the 2004–6 activity at Mount St. Helens, offer an excellent opportunity for developing terrestrial photogrammetric systems.

Conclusions

Remote camera systems have provided important information regarding volcanic activity at Mount St. Helens during 2004–6. A Webcam and a network of remote, telemetered digital cameras observed rockfalls, explosive activity, and the steady extrusion of lava on a nearly continuous basis, interrupted only by periods of inclement weather and infrequent mechanical failures. Time-lapse animations from the remote, telemetered digital cameras are outstanding records of lava dome emplacement that can be used to aid interpretations of volcanic activity and support education and outreach efforts.

Acknowledgments

The authors would like to thank the staff of the Hawaiian Volcano Observatory, particularly Rick Hoblitt (now at the USGS Cascades Volcano Observatory), Tim Orr, Richard Herd (now at the University of East Anglia in the United Kingdom), and Kevan Kamibayashi, for constructing and testing the first of the Mount St. Helens remote, telemetered cameras and sending the instrument to CVO for deployment at Sugar Bowl dome. Remote camera deployment was conducted with the assistance of Gene Iwatsubo, Stephanie Konfal, and Kirstie Simpson; Jon Major maintained the camera after it was installed and analyzed the imagery. Seismic data used in figures 7 and 8 were provided through the Incorporated Research Institutions for Seismology by the Pacific Northwest Seismic Network. Noise-filtered images from the VolcanoCam used to produce figure 7 were provided by Darryl Luscombe; David Ramsey generated the DEM that formed the backdrop for figure 2*A*. Jane Takahashi, Richard Herd, and Seth Moran provided valuable reviews.

References Cited

Baldi, P., Fabris, M., Marsella, M., and Monticelli, R., 2005, Monitoring the morphological evolution of the Sciara del Fuoco during the 2002–2003 Stromboli eruption using multi-temporal photogrammetry: ISPRS Journal of Photogrammetry and Remote Sensing, v. 59, no. 4, p. 199–211.

Cecchi, E., van Wyk de Vries, B., Lavest, J.M., Harris, A., and Davies, M., 2003, N-view reconstruction; a new method for morphological modeling and deformation measurement in volcanology: Journal of Volcanology and Geothermal Research, v. 123, nos. 1–2, p. 181–201.

Criswell, C.W., 1987, Chronology and pyroclastic stratigraphy of the May 18, 1980, eruption of Mount St. Helens, Washington: Journal of Geophysical Research, v. 92, no. B10, p. 10237–10266.

Dzurisin, D., Lisowski, M., Poland, M.P., Sherrod, D.R., and LaHusen, R.G., 2008, Constraints and conundrums resulting from ground-deformation measurements made during the 2004–2005 dome-building eruption of Mount St. Helens, Washington, chap. 14 *of* Sherrod, D.R., Scott, W.E., and Stauffer, P.H., eds., A volcano rekindled; the renewed eruption of Mount St. Helens, 2004–2006: U.S. Geological Survey Professional Paper 1750 (this volume).

Gerlach, T.M., McGee, K.A., and Doukas, M.P., 2008, Emission rates of CO_2, SO_2, and H_2S, scrubbing, and preeruption excess volatiles at Mount St. Helens, 2004–2005, chap. 26 *of* Sherrod, D.R., Scott, W.E., and Stauffer, P.H., eds., A volcano rekindled; the renewed eruption of Mount St. Helens, 2004–2006: U.S. Geological Survey Professional Paper 1750 (this volume).

Herd, R.A., Edmonds, M., and Bass, V.A., 2005, Catastrophic lava dome failure at Soufrière Hills Volcano, Montserrat, 12–13 July 2003: Journal of Volcanology and Geothermal Research, v. 148, nos. 3–4, p. 234–252, doi:10.1016/j.jvolgeores.2005.05.003.

Herriott, T.M., Sherrod, D.R., Pallister, J.S., and Vallance, J.W., 2008, Photogeologic maps of the 2004–2005 Mount St. Helens eruption, chap. 10 *of* Sherrod, D.R., Scott, W.E., and Stauffer, P.H., eds., A volcano rekindled; the renewed eruption of Mount St. Helens, 2004–2006: U.S. Geological Survey Professional Paper 1750 (this volume).

Hoblitt, R.P., 2000, Was the 18 May 1980 lateral blast at Mt. St. Helens the product of two explosions?: Philosophical Transactions of the Royal Society of London, Series A, v. 358, no. 1770, p. 1639–1661.

James, M.R., Robson, S., Pinkerton, H., and Ball, M., 2006, Oblique photogrammetry with visible and thermal images of active lava flows: Bulletin of Volcanology, v. 69, no. 1, p. 105–108.

Jaupart, C., and Allègre, C.J., 1991, Gas content, eruption rate, and instabilities of eruption regime in silicic volcanoes: Earth and Planetary Science Letters, v. 102, nos. 3–4, p. 413–429.

Lacroix, A., 1908, La Montagne Pelée apres ses eruptions: Paris, Académie des Sciences, 136 p.

LaHusen, R.G., Swinford, K.J., Logan, M., and Lisowski, M., 2008, Instrumentation in remote and dangerous settings; examples using data from GPS "spider" deployments during the 2004–2005 eruption of Mount St. Helens, Washington, chap. 16 *of* Sherrod, D.R., Scott, W.E., and Stauffer, P.H., eds., A volcano rekindled; the renewed eruption of Mount St. Helens, 2004–2006: U.S. Geological Survey Professional Paper 1750 (this volume).

Lisowski, M., Dzurisin, D., Denlinger, R.P., and Iwatsubo, E.Y., 2008, Analysis of GPS-measured deformation associated with the 2004–2006 dome-building eruption of Mount St. Helens, Washington, chap. 15 *of* Sherrod, D.R., Scott, W.E., and Stauffer, P.H., eds., A volcano rekindled; the renewed eruption of Mount St. Helens, 2004–2006: U.S. Geological Survey Professional Paper 1750 (this volume).

Major, J.J., Kingsbury, C.G., Poland, M.P., and LaHusen, R.G., 2008, Extrusion rate of the Mount St. Helens lava dome estimated from terrestrial imagery, November 2004–December 2005, chap. 12 *of* Sherrod, D.R., Scott, W.E., and Stauffer, P.H., eds., A volcano rekindled; the renewed eruption of Mount St. Helens, 2004–2006: U.S. Geological Survey Professional Paper 1750 (this volume).

Mimatsu, M., 1995, Showa-Shinzan diary; complete records of observation of the process of the birth of Showa-Shinzan, expanded reprint [Oshima, M., translator]: Sapporo, Suda Seihan Co., 179 p.

Moore, J.G., and Albee, W.C., 1981, Topographic and structural changes, March–July 1980—photogrammetric data, *in* Lipman, P.W., and Mullineaux, D.R., eds., The 1980 eruptions of Mount St. Helens, Washington: U.S. Geological Survey Professional Paper 1250, p. 123–141.

Moore, J.G., and Rice, C.R., 1984, Chronology and character of the May 18, 1980, explosive eruptions of Mount St. Helens, *in* Explosive volcanism; inception, evolution, and hazards: Washington D.C., National Academies Press, p. 133–142.

Moran, S.C., Malone, S.D., Qamar, A.I., Thelen, W.A., Wright, A.K., and Caplan-Auerbach, J., 2008a, Seismicity associated with renewed dome building at Mount St. Helens, 2004–2005, chap. 2 *of* Sherrod, D.R., Scott, W.E., and Stauffer, P.H., eds., A volcano rekindled; the renewed eruption of Mount St. Helens, 2004–2006: U.S. Geological Survey Professional Paper 1750 (this volume).

Moran, S.C., McChesney, P.J., and Lockhart, A.B., 2008b, Seismicity and infrasound associated with explosions at Mount St. Helens, 2004–2005, chap. 6 *of* Sherrod, D.R., Scott, W.E., and Stauffer, P.H., eds., A volcano rekindled; the renewed eruption of Mount St. Helens, 2004–2006: U.S. Geological Survey Professional Paper 1750 (this volume).

Orr, T., and Hoblitt, R.P., 2006, Monitoring Kilauea Volcano using non-telemetered time-lapse camera systems [abs.]: Eos (American Geophysical Union Transactions), v. 87, no. 52, Fall Meeting Supplement, Abstract G53A-0875.

Pallister, J.S., Thornber, C.R., Cashman, K.V., Clynne, M.A., Lowers, H.A., Mandeville, C.W., Brownfield, I.K., and Meeker, G.P., 2008, Petrology of the 2004–2006 Mount St. Helens lava dome—implications for magmatic plumbing and eruption triggering, chap. 30 *of* Sherrod, D.R., Scott, W.E., and Stauffer, P.H., eds., A volcano rekindled; the renewed eruption of Mount St. Helens, 2004–2006: U.S. Geological Survey Professional Paper 1750 (this volume).

Pierson, T.C., 1985, Initiation and flow behavior of the 1980 Pine Creek and Muddy River lahars, Mount St. Helens, Washington: Geological Society of America Bulletin, v. 96, no. 8, p. 1056–1069.

Schilling, S.P., Carrara, P.E., Thompson, R.A., and Iwatsubo, E.Y., 2004, Posteruption glacier development within the crater of Mount St. Helens, Washington, USA: Quaternary Research, v. 61, no. 3, p. 325–329.

Schilling, S.P., Thompson, R.A., Messerich, J.A., and Iwatsubo, E.Y., 2008, Use of digital aerophotogrammetry to determine rates of lava dome growth, Mount St. Helens, Washington, 2004–2005, chap. 8 *of* Sherrod, D.R., Scott, W.E., and Stauffer, P.H., eds., A volcano rekindled; the renewed eruption of Mount St. Helens, 2004–2006: U.S. Geological Survey Professional Paper 1750 (this volume).

Scott, W.E., Sherrod, D.R., and Gardner, C.A., 2008, Overview of the 2004 to 2006, and continuing, eruption of Mount St. Helens, Washington, chap. 1 *of* Sherrod, D.R., Scott, W.E., and Stauffer, P.H., eds., A volcano rekindled; the renewed eruption of Mount St. Helens, 2004–2006: U.S. Geological Survey Professional Paper 1750 (this volume).

Tanguy, J.-C., 2004, Rapid dome growth at Montagne Pelée during the early stages of the 1902–1905 eruption; a reconstruction from Lacroix's data: Bulletin of Volcanology, v. 66, no. 7, p. 615–621, doi:10.1007/s00445-004-0344-z.

Topinka, L., 1992, Basic photography at Mount St. Helens and other Cascade volcanoes, *in* Ewert, J. and Swanson, D., eds., Monitoring volcanoes; techniques and strategies used by the staff of the Cascades Volcano Observatory, 1980–90: U.S. Geological Survey Bulletin 1966, p. 195–217.

Vallance, J.W., Schneider, D.J., and Schilling, S.P., 2008, Growth of the 2004–2006 lava-dome complex at Mount St. Helens, Washington, chap. 9 *of* Sherrod, D.R., Scott, W.E., and Stauffer, P.H., eds., A volcano rekindled; the renewed eruption of Mount St. Helens, 2004–2006: U.S. Geological Survey Professional Paper 1750 (this volume).

Voight, B., 1981, Time scale for the first moments of the May 18 eruption, *in* Lipman, P.W., and Mullineaux, D.R., eds., The 1980 eruptions of Mount St. Helens, Washington: U.S. Geological Survey Professional Paper 1250, p. 69–86.

Voight, B., Glicken, H., Janda, R.J., and Douglass, P.M., 1981, Catastrophic rockslide avalanche of May 18, *in* Lipman, P.W., and Mullineaux, D.R., eds., The 1980 eruptions of Mount St. Helens, Washington: U.S. Geological Survey Professional Paper 1250, p. 347–377.

Walder, J.S., Schilling, S.P., Vallance, J.W., and LaHusen, R.G., 2008, Effects of lava-dome growth on the Crater Glacier of Mount St. Helens, Washington, chap. 13 *of* Sherrod, D.R., Scott, W.E., and Stauffer, P.H., eds., A volcano rekindled; the renewed eruption of Mount St. Helens, 2004–2006: U.S. Geological Survey Professional Paper 1750 (this volume).

Watts, R.B., Herd, R.A., Sparks, R.S.J., and Young, S.R., 2002, Growth patterns and emplacement of the andesitic lava dome at Soufrière Hills Volcano, Montserrat, *in* Druitt, T.H., and Kokelaar, B.P., eds., The eruption of Soufrière Hills Volcano, Montserrat, from 1995–1999: Geological Society of London Memoir 21, p. 115–152.

A Volcano Rekindled: The Renewed Eruption of Mount St. Helens, 2004–2006
Edited by David R. Sherrod, William E. Scott, and Peter H. Stauffer
U.S. Geological Survey Professional Paper 1750, 2008

Chapter 12

Extrusion Rate of the Mount St. Helens Lava Dome Estimated from Terrestrial Imagery, November 2004–December 2005

By Jon J. Major[1], Cole G. Kingsbury[1], Michael P. Poland[2], and Richard G. LaHusen[1]

Abstract

Oblique, terrestrial imagery from a single, fixed-position camera was used to estimate linear extrusion rates during sustained exogenous growth of the Mount St. Helens lava dome from November 2004 through December 2005. During that 14-month period, extrusion rates declined logarithmically from about 8–10 m/d to about 2 m/d. The overall ebbing of effusive output was punctuated, however, by episodes of fluctuating extrusion rates that varied on scales of days to weeks. The overall decline of effusive output and finer scale rate fluctuations correlated approximately with trends in seismicity and deformation. Those correlations portray an extrusion that underwent episodic, broad-scale stick-slip behavior superposed on the finer scale, smaller magnitude stick-slip behavior that has been hypothesized by other researchers to correlate with repetitive, nearly periodic shallow earthquakes.

Introduction

Aerial and terrestrial photography are effective ways of monitoring morphological changes that occur during volcanic eruptions (see, for example, Zlotnicki and others, 1990; Yamashina and others, 1999; Baldi and others, 2000, 2005; Honda and Nagai, 2002; Herd and others, 2005; Thompson and Schilling, 2007; Poland and others, this volume, chap. 11; Schilling and others, this volume, chap. 8). Some camera deployments and photography campaigns are aimed chiefly at monitoring volcanic activity qualitatively, whereas others endeavor to gather photographs sufficient to make quantitative (photogrammetric) measurements of static features or dynamic processes. For example, aerial photography has been used to estimate volumes of volcanic deposits and lava domes, to measure magnitudes of edifice deformation, to estimate volumetric loss during dome collapse, and to model development of volcano glaciers (for example, Moore and Albee, 1981; Jordan and Kieffer, 1981; Zlotnicki and others, 1990; Sparks and others, 1998; Schilling and others, 2004; Herd and others, 2005; Schilling and others, this volume, chap. 8). Similarly, ground-based photographs have been used to provide dynamic data of active processes, such as velocity estimates of large debris avalanches and lateral blasts (Voight, 1981), short-term (days) growth rates of lava domes (Yamashina and others, 1999), and motion of lava flows (James and others, 2006), and for geometric reconstructions of volcanic stratigraphy (Dungan and others, 2001). Commonly, stereoscopic imagery is used in such analyses, but apparent parallax caused by movement of an object in repeat photographs from a fixed position has also been exploited.

During the 2004–5 eruption of Mount St. Helens, oblique terrestrial imagery from remotely stationed cameras was one of the chief methods for monitoring the nature and pace of the eruption (Poland and others, this volume, chap. 11). Cameras were deployed principally to monitor the eruption visually without exposing scientists to unnecessary risk and to provide ancillary information on conditions in the crater (such as weather, the amount of steaming, or blowing ash) for purposes of planning field work. They were not deployed specifically for photogrammetric purposes.

Quantitative analysis of oblique terrestrial imagery commonly requires stereoscopic imagery or well-controlled nonstereoscopic imagery from multiple camera positions (Wolf and Dewitt, 2000). From October 2004 through December 2005 and beyond (Poland and others, this volume, chap. 11), however, we obtained repeat, ground-based imagery of the Mount St. Helens eruption from a single, fixed-position

[1] U.S. Geological Survey, 1300 SE Cardinal Court, Vancouver, WA 98683

[2] U.S. Geological Survey, PO Box 51, Hawaii National Park, HI 96718

camera located near the mouth of the volcano's crater. After August 2005, other ground-based cameras were located elsewhere around the volcano (Poland and others, this volume, chap. 11), but none of those provided stereoscopic imagery. In this paper, we employ a methodology for quantifying the linear extrusion rate of a growing silicic lava dome from the imagery obtained by the camera deployed near the crater mouth, summarize the results of spatial and temporal variations of dome growth and extrusion rates from November 2004 through December 2005, and compare our results with corresponding time series of seismic-energy release and local deformation measured by continuous Global Position System (GPS) receivers (Moran and others, this volume, chap. 2; LaHusen and others, this volume, chap. 16). Previously, average extrusion rates of silicic lava domes have been determined for discrete, short-lived eruptions or eruptive episodes (for example, Huppert and others, 1982; Swanson and others, 1987; Nakada and others, 1995; Sparks and others, 1998), although extrusion rates of a continuous, decadal-scale eruption have been measured by Rose (1987) and by Harris and others (2003). Demonstration of fine-scale temporal and spatial rate variation during a long-term, continuous extrusion is rare, however (for example, Sparks and others, 1998). Our data provide further insights on fine-scale behavior of sustained silicic dome growth, and they provide constraints for mathematical models that elucidate the physics of dome growth (for example, Barmin and others, 2002; Melnik and Sparks, 2005; Iverson and others, 2006; Iverson, this volume, chap. 21; Mastin and others, this volume, chap. 22).

The Sugar Bowl Camera

To photographically monitor dome growth at Mount St. Helens, we deployed a camera at the northeast end of the volcano's crater, on the Sugar Bowl lava dome, about 2.3 km from the locus of eruptive activity (fig. 1*A*). We used an Olympus 3030Z camera having a serial port (fig. 1*B*).

The camera utilizes a 1/1.8 inch solid-state sensor and has a nominal 6.5–19.5 mm focal length lens, equivalent to a 32–96 mm lens on a 35-mm camera. The camera was programmed to expose images at its maximum focal length and to record them at 1,280×960 pixels (~1.2-megapixel images). The relatively low-resolution setting was intended to permit rapid capture and transmission of images of explosions or other dynamic phenomena. Communications with the camera and transmission of images were enabled via radio through the serial port. Images were transmitted to a base-station computer located at the Mount St. Helens National Volcanic Monument's Coldwater Ridge Visitor Center, ~13 km down-valley (northwest) from the volcano. Once an image was transmitted, the camera acquired another image. The rate at which an image could be transmitted through the radio link governed the frequency of image acquisition, but in general images were acquired about every 3 minutes during daylight hours. Approximately once per hour the base-station computer transmitted an image to the Cascades Volcano Observatory. As needed, the computer could be queried to retrieve images more frequently. Periodically, all images were retrieved from the Coldwater Ridge Visitor Center.

The camera, deployed in a weatherproof housing (fig. 1*B*), began operating on October 10, 2004 (Poland and others, this volume, chap. 11). It was replaced by another camera and remounted on a fixed pipe in February 2006 and replaced again in May 2006. Owing to episodic cloud cover, ice rime, pitting of the window glass, and unit failures, usable imagery is discontinuous over the period of deployment. In this paper we focus on imagery obtained from November 2004 through December 2005, roughly the first year of the eruption that began in October 2004.

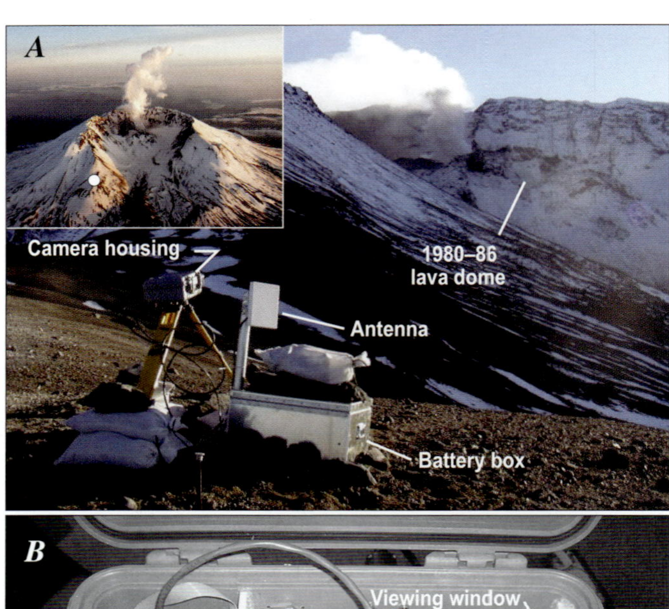

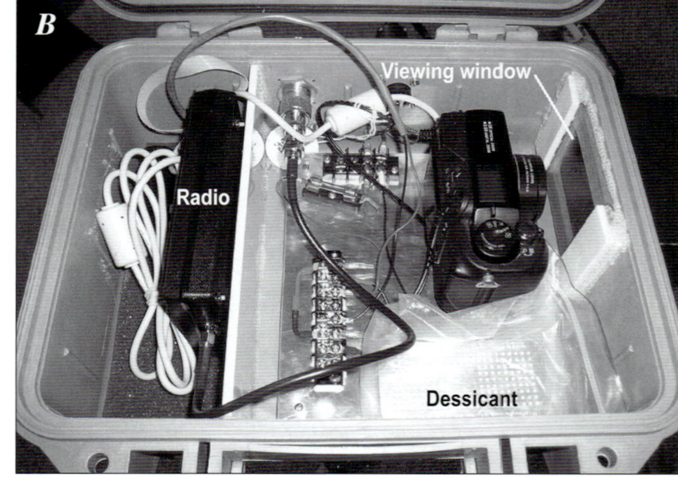

Figure 1. Photographs showing the camera system at Sugar Bowl lava dome. *A*, Deployed system at crater mouth. View is to southwest. Inset shows site location (white dot) on Sugar Bowl dome. Locus of eruptive activity is marked by emission of steam immediately to left rear of the partly snowclad 1980s lava dome. *B*, Camera and radio inside weatherproof housing.

Methodology

Theory of Terrestrial Image Analysis

The style of terrestrial imagery is defined on the basis of the orientation of the camera axis at the time of exposure. A horizontal terrestrial image is obtained when the camera axis is oriented horizontally at the time of exposure. If the camera is properly leveled before exposure, the x and z photographic axes are, respectively, oriented horizontally and vertically. Armed with precise information about camera and lens characteristics and an ability to pinpoint the optical center, or principal point, of a photograph, one can employ simple trigonometry to determine the horizontal and vertical angles between the camera axis and the rays to points in an object space (Wolf and Dewitt, 2000; fig. 2). If the camera is inclined from the horizontal, the resulting photograph is considered an oblique terrestrial image. In that case, computations of the angular differences between the camera axis, the rays to objects of interest, and a horizontal plane must account for the angle of inclination of the camera (Wolf and Dewitt, 2000).

The geometric relations among a camera's position, L, its focal length, f, the principal point of the photograph, o, the inclination angle of the camera axis, θ, and the horizontal and vertical angles to an image point are shown in figure 3. The horizontal angle, α_a, between the vertical plane containing image point a and the vertical plane containing the camera axis, Lo, is given by (Wolf and Dewitt, 2000):

$$\alpha_a = \tan^{-1}(x_a / f\sec\theta - z_a\sin\theta). \quad (1)$$

To conform to sign conventions, negative inclination angles refer to depression below, and positive inclination angles to elevation above, the horizontal (Wolf and Dewitt, 2000). In equation 1, correct algebraic signs must be applied to x_a, z_a, and θ. The vertical angle, β_a, to image point a is given by

$$\beta_a = \tan^{-1}(z_a\cos\theta / (f\sec\theta - z_a\sin\theta)\sec\alpha_a). \quad (2)$$

In equation 2, the algebraic sign of β is automatically obtained from the sign of the z_a coordinate (Wolf and Dewitt, 2000).

Although equations 1 and 2 allow determination of the horizontal and vertical angles to any image point relative to the camera axis, they represent an underdetermined system of equations with respect to quantifying horizontal or vertical distances unless some geodetic control can be established between the camera and an object of interest. Typically, control is provided by interior and exterior referenced orientations. Interior orientation includes camera

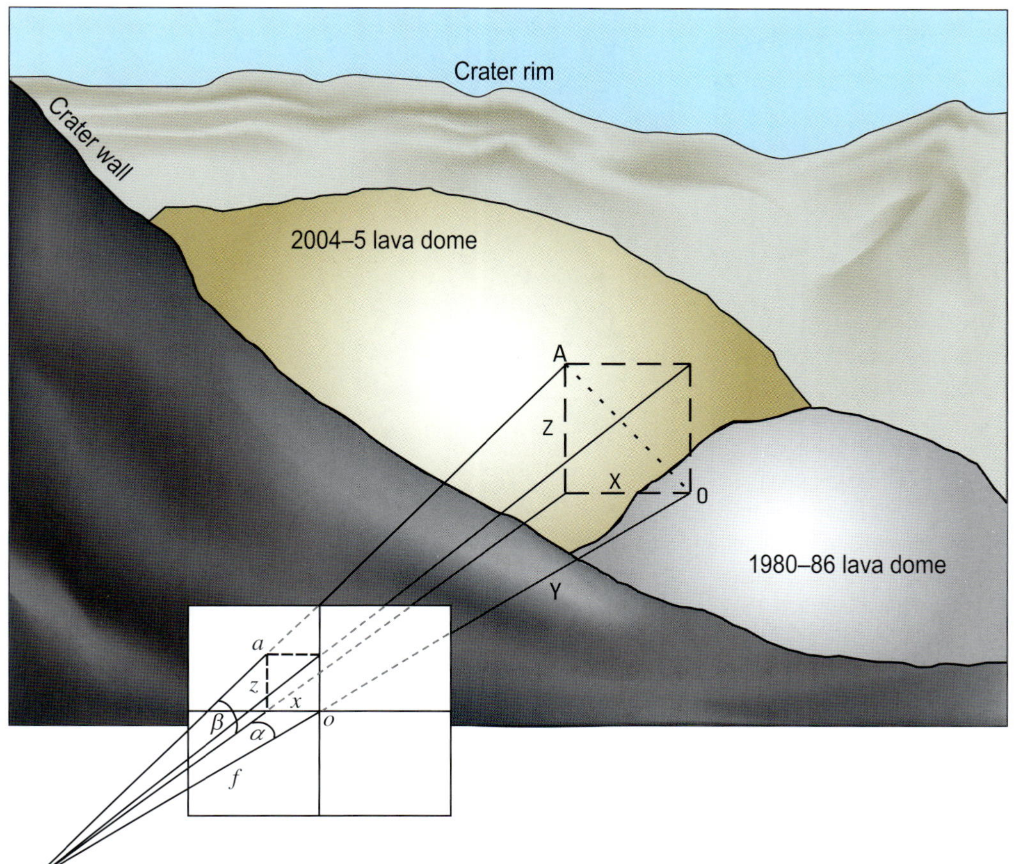

Figure 2. Diagram showing relations among optical rays from photographed objects and images projected in the focal plane for a horizontal terrestrial image. For clarity, positions of the focal plane and lens nodal point have been reversed. Focal length of the lens, f, and principal point of the image, o, are shown relative to L, the lens nodal point or position of the camera. Projections of object point, A, and the horizontal (X) and vertical (Z) distances of the object point relative to the camera axis are shown on the projected image as a, x, and z, respectively. Object distance, Y, horizontal angle, α, between the vertical plane containing the object point and the vertical plane containing the camera axis, and vertical angle, β, from a horizon line to the object point are also shown.

calibration parameters such as lens focal length, location of the image principal point, and corrections for lens distortion. Exterior orientation refers to the position and orientation of the camera with respect to a ground-based reference frame or with respect to the photographed object (Wolf and Dewitt, 2000; Molander, 2001). Orientation with respect to a ground-based reference frame is commonly accomplished by combining camera control (position and orientation) with object-space control (through established control points within the field of view).

In the absence of sound calibration parameters, one can approximate interior orientation of a digital camera from metadata contained in an image's exchangeable image format (EXIF) file and by assuming that the principal point is at the center of the image. At maximum focal length, zoom lenses commonly have minimal distortion, even on consumer-grade cameras. Such assumptions, of course, can introduce large errors to a photogrammetric analysis.

In the absence of independently established control points, one way to establish exterior orientation of a fixed camera is by measuring the orientation and position of the camera with respect to a photographed object. For the Sugar Bowl camera, we lack rigid calibration parameters. We do, however, have empirical calibration parameters from four similar cameras. In the absence of a solid camera calibration, we used averaged parameters obtained from the calibrations of those other cameras (table 1). We imposed exterior control on the imagery by measuring the camera orientation (direction of the camera axis and angle of inclination) and its location (using GPS), and we established its position relative to the proximal part of the actively growing dome by measuring coordinates and distances between the camera and the dome on sequential digital elevation models (DEMs) (Schilling and others, this volume, chap. 8; fig. 4). By fixing the distance between the camera and the near-vent area of the dome between sequential DEMs, knowing the camera orientation, and employing averaged lens characteristics, we solved all necessary trigonometric equations and roughly quantified magnitudes and rates of dome growth.

Resolving horizontal and vertical displacement rates within the focal plane of the image provided only apparent rates of extrusion, however. Quantifying more accurate linear

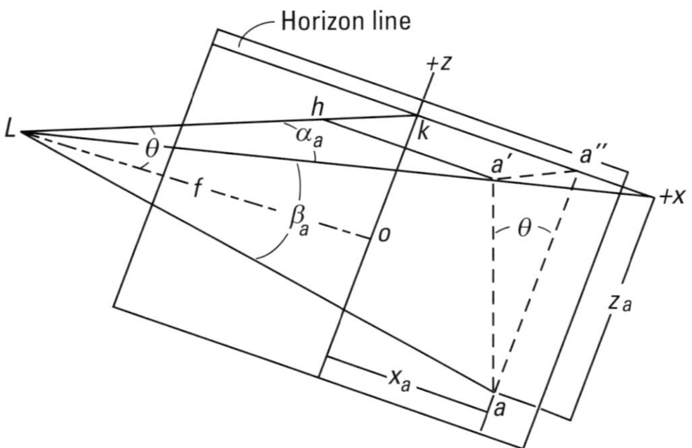

Figure 3. Diagram showing relations among optical rays from photographed objects and images projected in the focal plane of the camera for an oblique terrestrial image (slightly modified from Wolf and Dewitt, 2000; diagram copyright The McGraw-Hill Companies, Inc.). For clarity, the positions of the focal plane and lens nodal point have been reversed (see fig. 2). Focal length of the lens, *f*, principal point of the image, *o*, and angle of inclination of the camera axis, θ, are shown relative to *L*, the lens nodal point or position of the camera, and a horizontal line (*+x*). The projection of object point A (not shown) and its position relative to the photograph coordinate system (*+x*, *+z*) are shown on the projected image as *a*, x_a, and z_a, respectively. Line *Lk* is a horizontal line that intersects the photograph at point *k*. Line *aa′* is a vertical line, with *a′* located in a horizontal plane. Points *h* and *a″* represent geometric projections used in the derivation of equations 1 and 2. Angles α_a and β_a are the horizontal and vertical angles of the image point, *a*, relative to horizontal and vertical axes. See Wolf and Dewitt (2000) for detailed discussions of geometric relations and derivations of equations 1 and 2.

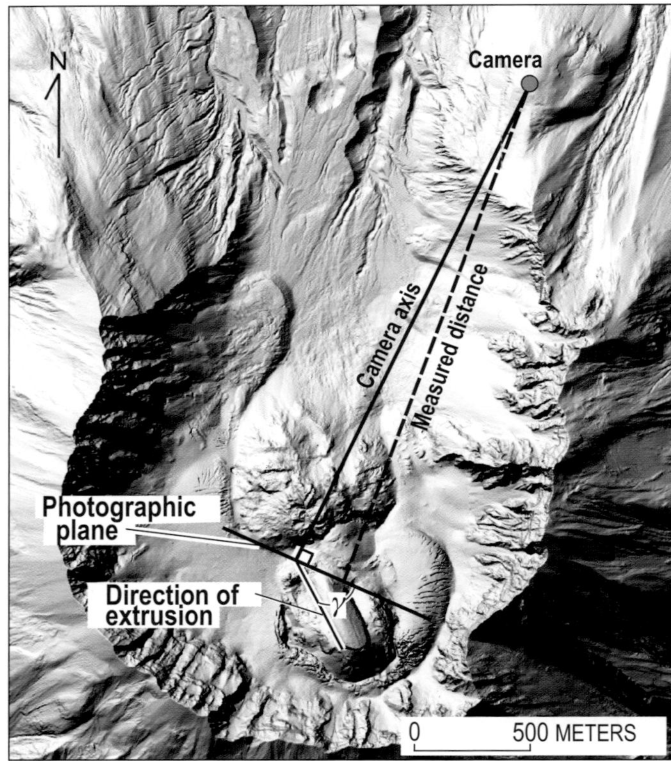

Figure 4. Digital elevation model of Mount St. Helens for February 21, 2005, showing positions of Sugar Bowl camera and 2004–5 lava dome, and relation between camera axis and obliquity of extrusion, γ. Measured distance is from camera to an identifiable feature on the dome. Trigonometric manipulation of this distance and the angular difference between that axis and the camera axis allowed computation of the distance along the camera axis.

Table 1. Camera characteristics and orientation parameters for the Sugar Bowl imagery, Mount St. Helens, Washington.

Parameter	Value
Camera characteristics	
Maximum sensor width [1]	7.76 mm
Maximum pixels at 1.2 megapixel setting	1,280 (1,280 × 960)
Field of view (at maximum focal length)	21°±1°
Resolvable pixel footprint at nominal distance to dome	~ 0.65 m
Lens characteristics	
Lens focal length (maximum) [1]	20.8 mm±1.2 mm
Lens distortion (radial) [1]	$\leq 10^{-4}$ mm
Camera orientation	
Inclination angle	7°±0.5°
Axis azimuth	207°±0.5°
Spatial measurements	
Camera location (UTM coordinates, zone 10, datum is WGS84)	5118137N, 563633E, ±10 m
Distance from camera to plane tangent to proximal dome	2,315 m ± 30 m
Obliquity of extrusion relative to focal plane	27°–53°±2°

[1] Values of these parameters represent averages obtained from empirical calibrations (using Photomodeler Pro 5) of four other Olympus C3030Z cameras.

extrusion rates of the dome required resolving trigonometric differences between the apparent direction of motion in the focal plane and the actual direction of motion. Again, by using sequential DEMs of the dome, we measured the angle of obliquity, γ, between the focal plane and the principal direction of dome growth (fig. 4). Analysis of a three-dimensional pyramid formed by the principal motion vectors (fig. 5) revealed that the angle, δ, between the vector of apparent motion in the focal plane (vector **c** in fig. 5) and the vector of actual motion (vector **V** in fig. 5) is related to the obliquity angle, γ, measured on the DEMs by

$$\delta = \tan^{-1}(R \tan\gamma)\,, \qquad (3)$$

where R is the ratio of the horizontal motion vector (vector **b** in fig. 5) to the resolved motion vector, **c**, in the focal plane (fig. 5). From that relation, simple trigonometric relations can be solved to estimate the extrusion rate in the direction of dome growth. Our methods and analysis are, of course, subject to many possible errors (discussed below) and are limited to extrusion rates that exceed about 1 to 1.5 m/d (displacements of about 2 to 3 pixels per day; table 1). Nevertheless, they represent useful procedures for extracting quantitative information from relatively low-resolution images from a fixed position obtained from an uncalibrated (and now damaged) camera.

Tracking Distinctive Features

To estimate extrusion rates, we followed movements of distinctive features on the lava dome between selected images. These features consisted of sharp edges, intersecting fractures, fracture tips, spots, or other stable, distinctive markers that could be readily identified and that persisted through multiple images, typically from a few days to about two weeks. To begin, an initial image (November 10, 2004) was imported into graphical design software and its apparent principal point (the center of the image) identified. Coordinates of features of interest on the dome were then computed relative to that apparent principal point (fig. 6). Subsequent images (separated by roughly 24 hours when possible) were then imported and manually coregistered with the preceding image, and the positions of displaced features of interest were updated. Coordinates of distinctive features on the dome in proximity to the vent area were entered into a spreadsheet, and equations 1 and 2 solved for the employed camera parameters (table 1) and measured distances between the camera and the dome (the distance was updated with each new DEM). The solutions, along with elapsed times between photographs, provided a time series of apparent horizontal and vertical displacement rates for selected proximal points on the actively growing dome. Typical rates of apparent horizontal and vertical displacement, and standard deviations of those rates, were estimated by averaging apparent displacement rates of 3 to 10 points per image. Apparent linear extrusion rates in the focal plane were determined by resolving the averaged horizontal and vertical displacement rates, and the standard deviation errors on those averaged rates were propagated to the resolved solution using standard methods (for example, Bevington and Robinson, 1992). An average extrusion rate in the direction of dome growth was determined by resolving the average apparent extrusion rate in the focal plane with respect to the angle of obliquity of extrusion.

Sources of Error

Several sources of error are inherent in a quantitative analysis of oblique imagery from the Sugar Bowl camera. A fixed source of error involves the quantification of lens characteristics, camera orientation, and spatial measurements (table 1) that affect the interior and exterior control imposed on the imagery. More random is the operator error incurred during image analysis.

Lens characteristics used in this analysis represent average values obtained from calibrations of four similar cameras. Variations of 1.2 mm about the assumed focal length (table 1) cause ±7 percent variation of the averaged apparent extrusion rates we report. Calibrated radial distortion in imagery was essentially negligible (table 1) and was thus ignored in our analyses. Repeated measurements of the inclination and azimuth of the camera housing during field visits minimized orientation error (table 1), although frequent misalignments among sequential photographs show that wind and transient snow and ice loads caused minor variations in orientation.

Spatial measurement errors revolve around accuracy of the camera location, inherent errors in the DEMs, measurement of the distance from the camera to the active extrusion, and measurement of the obliquity of the extrusion with respect to the camera axis. Replicable GPS measurements of the camera location and coordinate determinations in a GIS of selected locations on the active extrusion limit the error of the distance between the camera and the active extrusion to about ±30 m, or about 1-percent error on the measured distance (table 1). Inherent errors in the DEMs (Schilling and others, this volume, chap. 8) are small compared to other measurement errors and are thus ignored. For much of the period from November 2004 to August 2005, the dome grew along azimuths ranging from 150° to 170° (Schilling and others, this

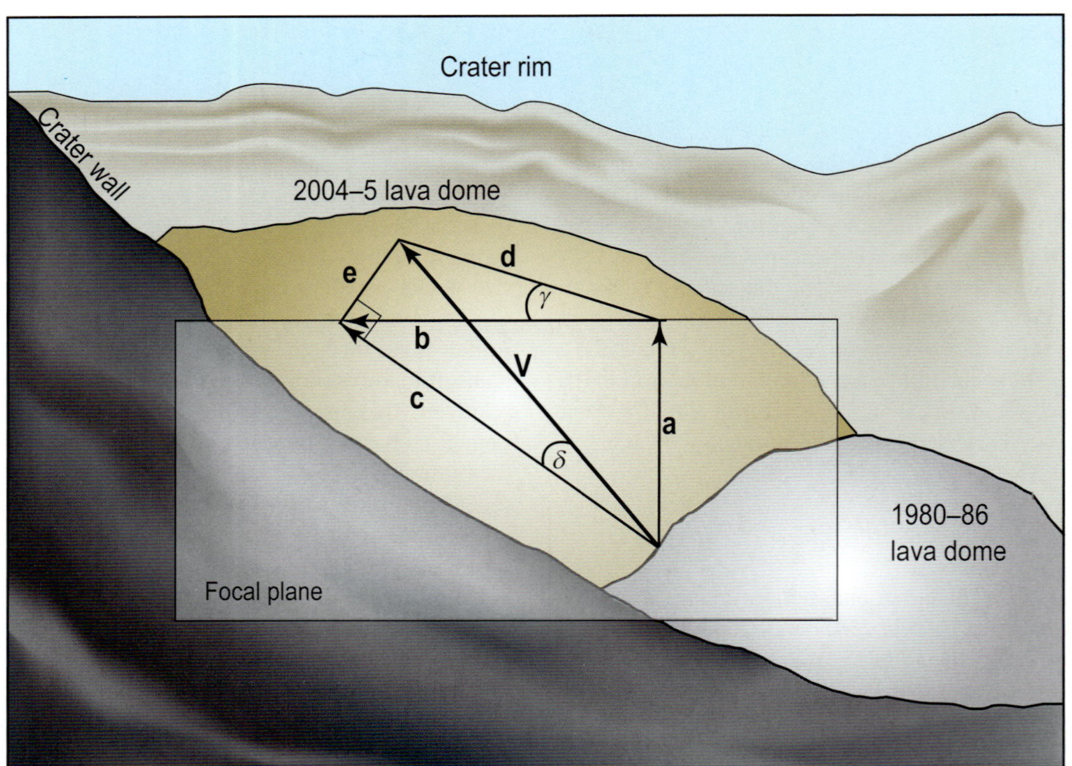

Figure 5. Diagram of a three-dimensional pyramid showing relations among the apparent vector of the average rate of motion, **c**, within a vertical plane perpendicular to the camera axis, the actual vector of extrusion, **V**, and the angle of obliquity of extrusion, γ. Triangle **abc** is oriented vertically and perpendicular to the camera axis, and triangle **ebd** is oriented orthogonally to triangle **abc** (that is, in the plane of the topographic digital elevation model). As a result, triangle **ecV** is a right triangle. Note that leg **e** is common to triangles **ecV** and **ebd**. Therefore, **e** = **b** tan γ = **c** tan δ. Solving this equality leads to tan δ = (**b**/**c**) tan γ, or $\delta = \tan^{-1}(R \tan \gamma)$, where R = **b**/**c**. Thus, by measuring the angle of obliquity of extrusion, γ, on a DEM, one can employ simple trigonometry to resolve the apparent average rate of motion in the focal plane to the estimated rate of extrusion in the direction of dome growth.

volume, chap. 8; Vallance and others, this volume, chap. 9), about 30°–50° oblique to the focal plane of the camera (which had an azimuth of 117°; table 1). From about mid-August through December 2005, motion was chiefly westward (~270° azimuth), about 25°–30° oblique to the focal plane of the camera. Repeated measurements of these obliquity angles within a GIS constrained these values to within a few degrees (table 1). Errors of ±2° about the measured obliquity angles cause ±2 percent variation in the reported averaged extrusion rates.

Aside from assumptions about lens characteristics and estimates of the distance from the camera to the dome, our most critical sources of error revolve around selection of the photographic principal point, the accuracy to which sequential photographs were coregistered, and the accuracy with which moving points were identified and tracked. For purposes of the analysis reported here, the principal point to which all measurements are referenced was selected simply as the center of the first base image, and all subsequent images were coregistered to that principal point. Owing to minor variations in fields of view resulting principally from winds and snow and ice loads on the housing, the principal point of the base image was not always the principal point of subsequent images. The distinctive dome features we followed were identified at the pixel level where possible, but the relatively low resolution of the images and the sometimes challenging lighting made pixel-level identification frequently difficult. Manual identification of displaced point positions could thus be in error by a few pixels. Overall, the greatest errors in the analysis were introduced through assumptions about lens focal length and through manual image registration and feature tracking.

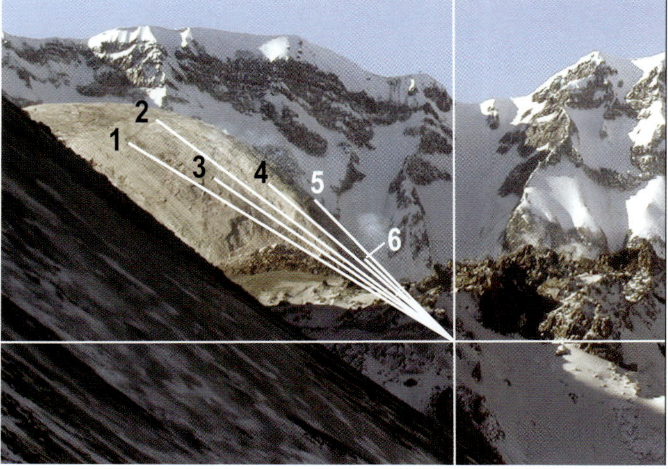

Figure 6. Example of photograph taken by the Sugar Bowl camera of the 2004–5 dome in the crater of Mount St. Helens, illustrating a distribution of points used to track motion. Because the image has been cropped, the principal point of the original photograph, which serves as the origin to which point coordinates (for example, 1 to 6) are referenced, is offset. In this image, the 2004–5 dome is about 130 m tall. Photograph taken on March 6, 2005, at 17:08:38 UTC.

Given the several sources of error that potentially affect our analysis, quantifying the cumulative error on our estimates of extrusion is a daunting task. Instead, we computed standard deviations of mean vertical and horizontal displacement rates in the focal plane from a collection of points on the proximal part of the active extrusion. Using standard practices (for example, Bevington and Robinson, 1992), we propagated the standard deviations of those mean values to the resolved extrusion rates in the focal plane and carried the propagated errors over to the resolved extrusion rates in the direction of dome growth to approximate a magnitude of error associated with our estimates of extrusion rate.

Results

Episodic growth and disintegration of several solidified lava spines characterized emplacement of the 2004–5 dome (Schilling and others, this volume, chap. 8; Vallance and others, this volume, chap. 9). Two minor spines, not visible from Sugar Bowl, breached the surface in October 2004. From late October 2004 until mid-April 2005, dome growth proceeded chiefly through emplacement and disintegration of two recumbent spines (spines 3 and 4) dubbed 'whalebacks' (Schilling and others, this volume, chap. 8; Vallance and others, this volume, chap. 9; fig. 7; supplemental movie in appendix 1). The character of growth changed following disintegration of spine 4 in mid-April 2005. More vertical, rather than recumbent, growth characterized spine 5 from mid-April until late July 2005 (fig. 7; supplemental movie). Following disintegration of spine 5 in late July 2005, vertical growth diminished and horizontal motion intensified as a new spine (spine 6) emerged and migrated rapidly westward. This phase of development persisted into October 2005, as a graben opened along the central part of the dome complex (see fig. 7 and supplemental movie) and growth of spine 6 became more endogenous. From mid-October through December 2005, the rapid westward migration of spine 6 slowed and vertical growth of another spine (spine 7) became notable (fig. 7; supplemental movie).

Rates of extrusion and associated motion of assorted segments of the 2004–5 lava dome varied in time and space, but for extended periods extrusion occurred at nearly steady rates. The average rate of vertical displacement varied between about 1 and 4 m/d, with a central tendency toward 2–3 m/d from November 2004 through June 2005 during growth of spines 3, 4, and 5 (fig. 8*A*). From about late June to mid-July 2005, the rate of vertical displacement of spine 5 slowed substantially, then increased from mid- to late July during a period of reinvigorated growth. Following a series of rockfalls in late July, vertical motion of spine 5 diminished, but another, though less vigorous, growth spurt occurred in early to mid-August as spine 6 emerged. In December 2005 the average vertical motion of spine 7 hovered around 1 m/d (fig. 8*A*). In contrast, the average rate of horizontal displacement (in the focal plane) during emplacement of recumbent spines 3 and

Figure 7. Time series of images from the Sugar Bowl camera illustrating growth, disintegration, and morphologic change of the new lava dome at Mount St. Helens between October 2004 and January 2006.

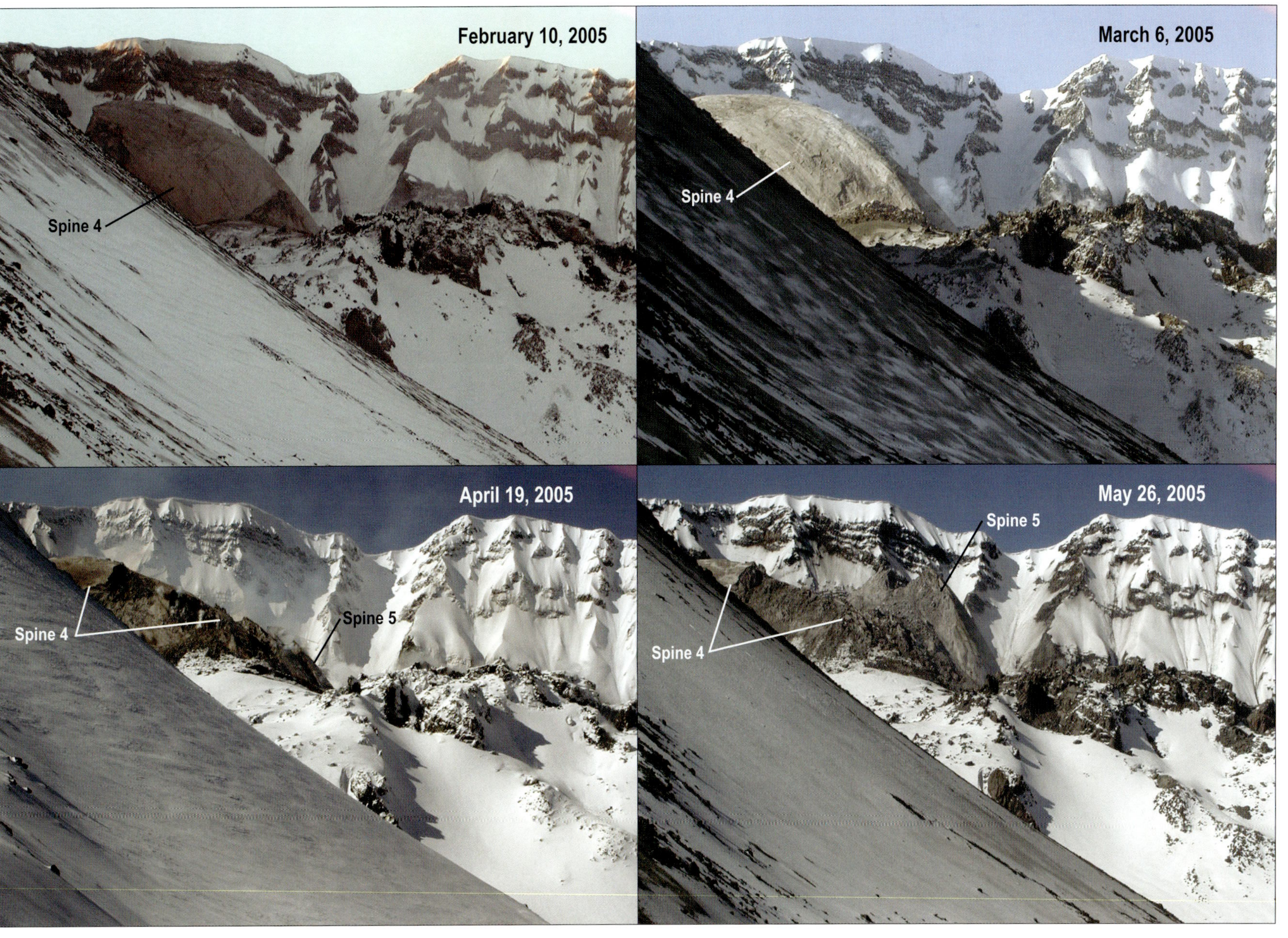

Figure 7.—Continued.

Figure 7.—Continued.

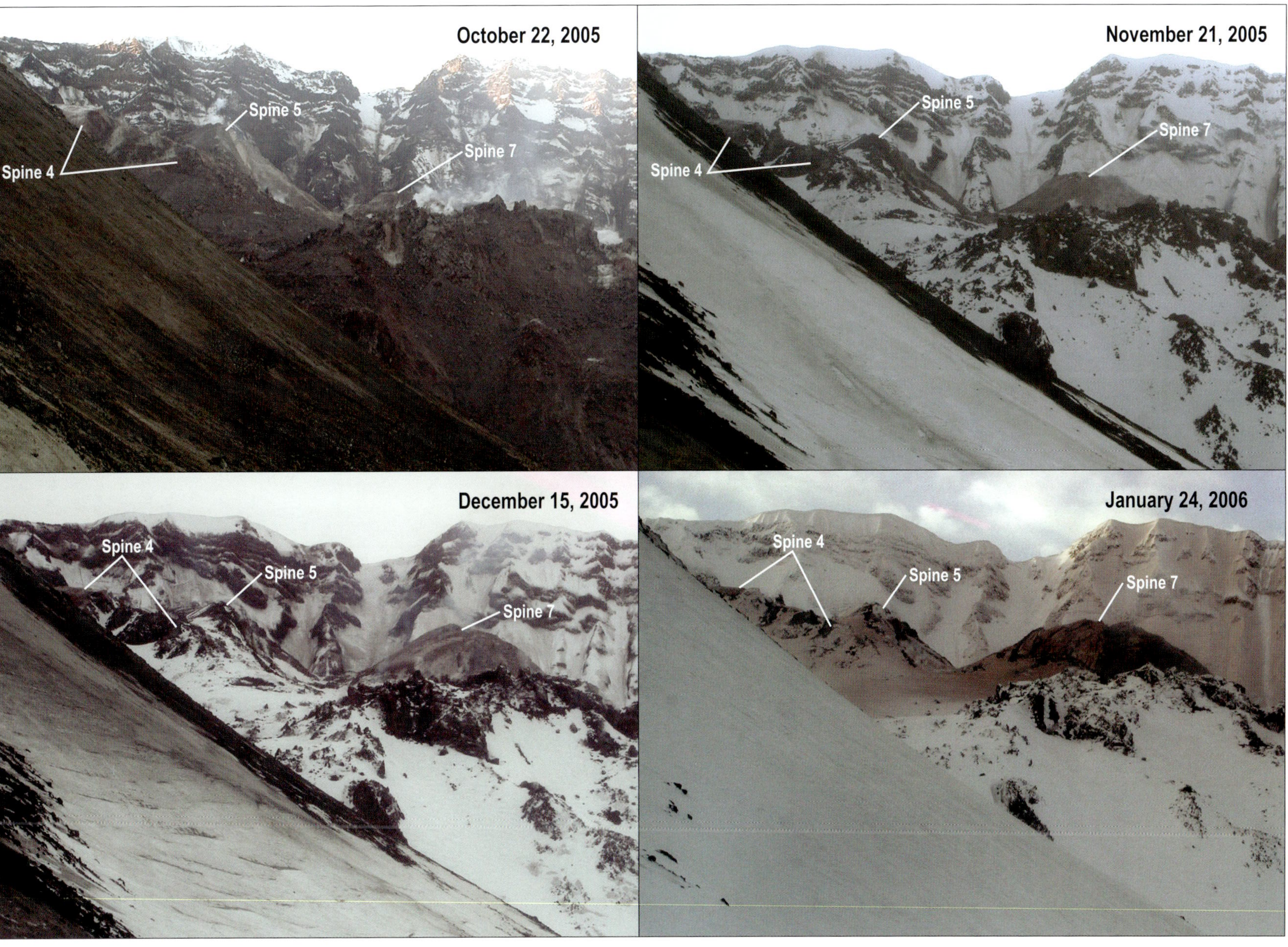

Figure 7.—Continued.

4 decreased progressively from about 5–7 m/d in November 2004 to about 3 m/d by mid-March 2005, then to fractions of a meter per day by late July 2005 after vertical growth of spine 5 became predominant (fig. 8*B*). Horizontal motion increased substantially in August (to >2 m/d) when growth of spine 6 migrated sharply westward; in December 2005, apparent horizontal motion of spine 7 hovered around 2 m/d.

Resolving the average horizontal and vertical displacement rates of the various spines into average rates of motion in the focal plane and then correcting those measurements for the angle of obliquity of extrusion shows that estimated extrusion rates declined logarithmically from November 2004 through December 2005 (fig. 8*C*). This decline is comparable to changes in magma discharge documented through analyses of DEMs (Schilling and others, this volume, chap. 8). However, several spurts of accelerated extrusion are superposed on the overall diminishing extrusion rate, and for several months lava extruded at a nearly steady rate (fig. 8*C*).

The estimated average linear extrusion rate was as great as 8–10 m/d in early November 2004 during emplacement of spine 3, hovered between 4 and 5 m/d from late December 2004 through mid-March 2005 during growth of spine 4, dropped to less than 2 m/d by mid-July 2005 during the waning stages of growth of spine 5, and then increased to about 4 m/d before spine 5 disintegrated in late July 2005. Following disintegration of spine 5, the extrusion rate again dropped to as low as 2 m/d before accelerating to about 4 m/d in August, when spine 6 emerged and migrated sharply westward. In December 2005, during growth of spine 7, the extrusion rate had again declined to about 2 m/d. GPS receivers deployed on spines 3 and 4 tracked extrusion rates in real time for limited periods (LaHusen and others, this volume, chap. 16). During the periods when usable imagery and GPS deployment coincided, estimates of extrusion rate compiled from imagery analyses are about 20–30 percent lower than the measured rates (fig. 8*C*). Given the assumptions in our analyses, our estimates of linear extrusion rate compare relatively favorably with measured rates.

Motion of the extruded lava varied spatially as well as temporally. Movement of the distal ends of recumbent spines 3 and 4 slowed as those spines enlarged, plowed over fragments of earlier spines, and impinged upon the crater wall. Differential rates of motion between distal and near-vent segments of those spines prompted development of thrust faults, large-scale fractures, and partial to complete disintegration in December 2004, January 2005, and April 2005 (fig. 7; supplemental movie; Schilling and others, this volume, chap. 8; Vallance and others, this volume, chap. 9). Such disintegration generated hot rockfalls and minor pyroclastic surges but did not trigger substantive pyroclastic flows similar to those produced by dome collapses elsewhere (for example, Ui and others, 1999; Herd and others, 2005). Following the disintegration of spine 4 (the largest of the recumbent spines) in mid-April 2005, the growth of spine 5 became focused along the western margin of the dome complex. During this phase of growth, active extrusion was effectively decoupled from the remnants of the earlier spines. From mid-April on, several remnants of spines 3 and 4 remained stable as spine 5 emerged (for example, note the stability of the intact block of spine 4 on the east margin of the dome complex between April and December 2005; fig. 7; supplemental movie). Local displacement of ground near the vent, however, showed that, on occasion, extruding solidified lava was well coupled to the immediately surrounding terrain (see supplemental movie).

Following the disintegration of spine 5 in July 2005, the dome became further segmented. As spine 6 emerged and migrated westward, the eastern segment of the dome complex remained stable, but the central segment slumped as its westward buttress was removed (fig. 7; supplemental movie). Such spatially differential motion and migration of the extruding solidified lava led to the segmented morphology of the 2004–5 dome (fig. 9), in contrast to the composite, but uniform morphology of the 1980s lava dome (see, for example, Swanson and others, 1987).

Extrusion rates estimated from the Sugar Bowl imagery are broadly correlated with overall trends in seismicity and deformation (fig. 10). From November 2004 until January 2005, the rapidly decreasing extrusion rate was synchronous with a general decline in seismic-energy release as indicated by real-time seismic amplitude measurements (RSAM) (Endo and Murray, 1991; Murray and Endo, 1992; Moran and others, this volume, chap. 2) (figs. 10*A*, *C*). The RSAM values are commonly invoked as a proxy highlighting overall seismic-energy release at volcanoes (for example, Power and others, 1994, 1995; Harlow and others, 1996; Mori and others, 1996; Voight and others, 1998). During phases of more or less steady extrusion from January to June 2005, minor increases in extrusion rate generally correlated with slight increases in RSAM. The extrusion-rate nadir and subsequent significant growth spurt in mid- to late July 2005 correspond with an equivalent nadir and subsequent minor increase in RSAM.

Correlations between trends in extrusion rate and geodetic measurements of deformation of a part of the 1980s lava dome are evident, but they are more subtle than are those with trends in seismicity (figs. 10*B*, *C*). We compare trends in extrusion rate with trends in the motion of station DOM1 located on the west side of the 1980s lava dome north-northwest of the vent of the 2004–5 eruption (Dzurisin and others, this volume, chap. 14; LaHusen and others, this volume, chap. 16). The overall logarithmic decay of the rate of lava extrusion is approximately mimicked by a corresponding logarithmic change in the northing component of motion of DOM1. Finer scale fluctuations in lava extrusion rate and motion of DOM1 are, however, typically out of phase, particularly after about the first 5 months of the eruption. For example, an increase in extrusion rate between late April and mid-June 2005 corresponds with southward movement of DOM1 (that is, a relaxation of the 1980s dome toward the 2004–5 vent). From late June through mid-July 2005, an ensuing period of declining extrusion rate corresponds with a period of increased northward movement of DOM1 (that is, movement of the 1980s dome away from the vent). An ensuing increase of extrusion

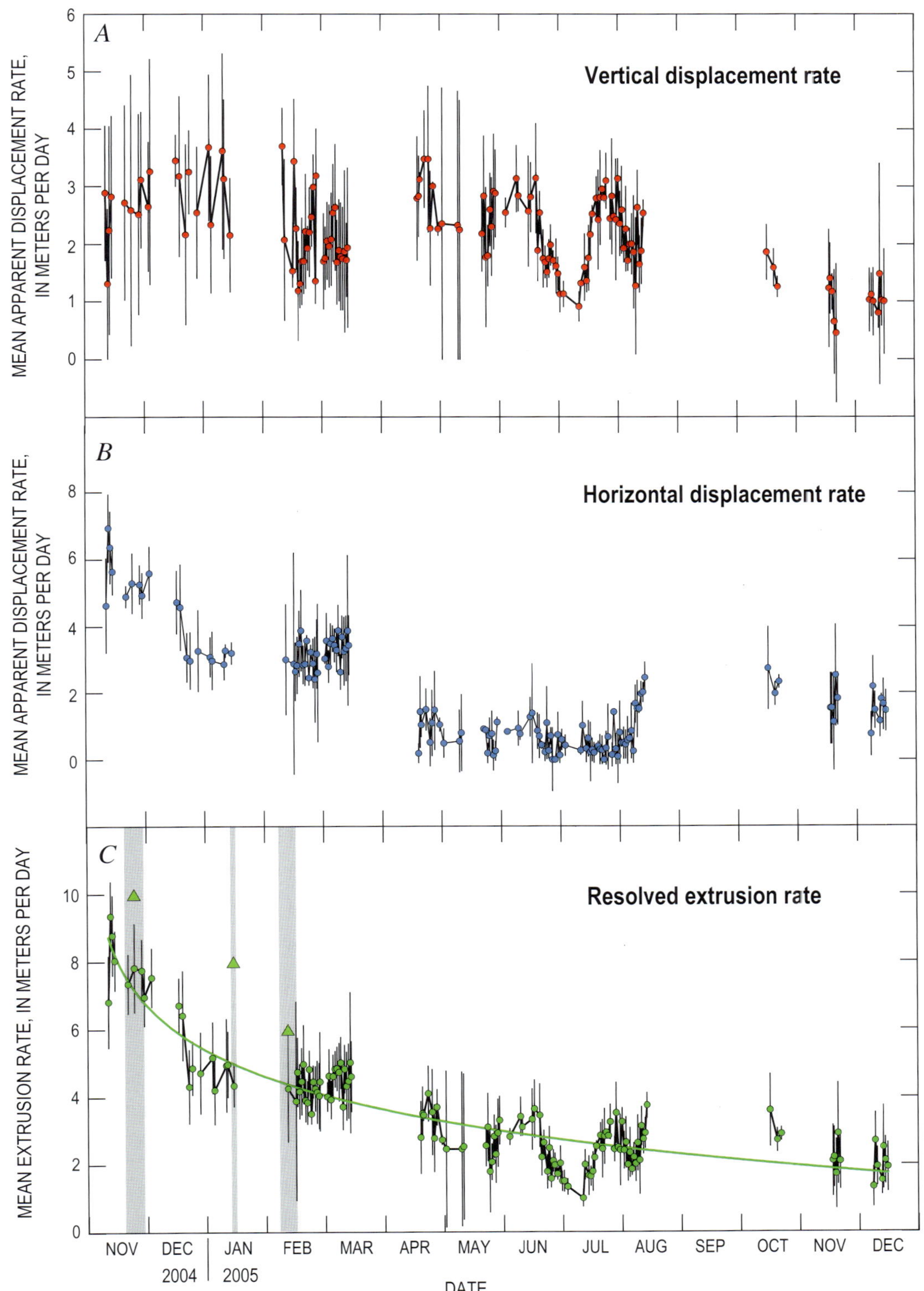

Figure 8. Time-series plot of displacement rates and extrusion rates of the 2004–5 lava dome at Mount St. Helens. Error bars represent ±1 standard deviation about the mean. *A*, Average rate of vertical displacement within the camera focal plane. *B*, Average rate of horizontal displacement within the camera focal plane. *C*, Estimated average extrusion rate of the 2004–5 lava dome in the direction of growth. The gray bands illustrate periods when GPS receivers were deployed on the lava dome, and the triangles represent the average rates of motion measured by GPS (LaHusen and others, this volume, chap. 16). A logarithmic decay curve is superposed on the data.

rate in late July again corresponds with southward movement of DOM1 (toward the vent), whereas the decrease of extrusion rate in early August corresponds with increased northward motion of DOM1 (again, away from the vent). The increase of extrusion rate documented in mid-August 2005 is not as well out of phase with the motion of DOM1 as are other periods of changing rates of extrusion, but it does correspond to a gradual change from northward motion (away from the vent) to southward motion (toward the vent). Only the northing component of motion of DOM1 appears to broadly correspond with variations in extrusion rate; there is little if any substantive correlation between extrusion rate and the easting or vertical components of motion of DOM1 (figs. 10*B*, *C*).

Discussion

Within the constraints of the interior and exterior control we imposed, the available oblique, terrestrial imagery from the Sugar Bowl camera provided a valuable means of estimating long-term linear extrusion rates over periods of weeks to months during the 2004–5 eruption of Mount St. Helens. The greatest sources of error revolved around our assumptions regarding the camera focal length and our ability to accurately coregister sequential images and follow features of interest through time. Pitting of the glass on the camera box, shadows, steam and clouds, weather-related loss of usable images, and physical changes to the dome during its growth and partial disintegration all contributed to the challenge of using the imagery. Although the locus of extrusion varied slightly during the period of analysis, errors in the imposed external control and measurements of the distance between the camera and the dome were relatively small compared to other sources of error. Indeed, the errors associated with the assumed focal length alone make the greatest difference in our comparisons of extracted versus measured extrusion rates.

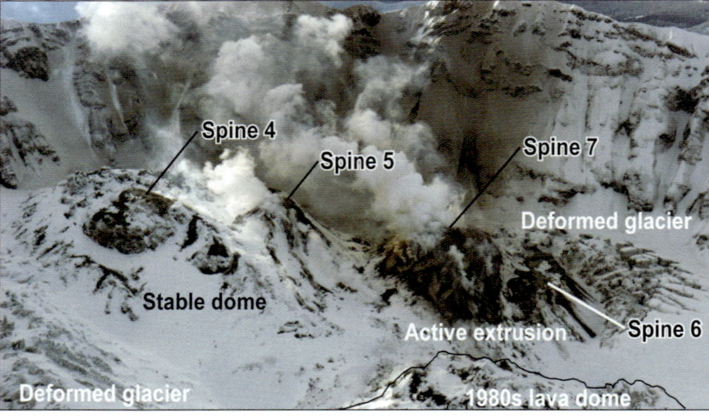

Figure 9. Oblique aerial photograph looking southwest into the crater of Mount St. Helens. Photograph illustrates the segmented morphology of the 2004–5 lava dome complex. Remnants of spines 4 and 5 are visible as discrete snowclad humps on the left and left-center of the image, and the locus of active growth, spine 7, is visible on the right side of the image. Fractured and deformed glacier ice is visible on the far left and far right sides of the image, and part of the snow-covered 1980s lava dome is visible in the bottom center of the image. USGS photograph by J.S. Pallister, December 6, 2005.

Our methodology for extracting quantitative information from the fixed-position imagery hinged upon an ability to impose external control. In the absence of a time series of DEMs, or even a single DEM, we would not have been able to solve the underdetermined system of equations posed by having imagery from only a single viewpoint. Traditional surveying could have provided the necessary measures of distance from the camera site to the dome, but the dangerous environment in the crater during the early phases of the eruption, the distance between the camera and the lava dome, the difficulty of precisely placing prisms even remotely, and the rapidly changing physical character of the dome inhibited such a strategy.

The ability to quantify the rate of extrusion, even crudely, greatly enhanced the value of the imagery. Rather than simply serving as a method to monitor the status of the eruption or the conditions in the crater, the imagery supplemented other geophysical monitoring equipment. For the most part, it provided the sole means of extracting long-term, semicontinuous quantitative information. Differencing of sequential DEMs provided long-term estimates of magma discharge (Schilling and others, this volume, chap. 8), but those DEMs were based on stereoscopic aerial photographs only acquired about once per month. Hence, DEM differencing could not provide information on the fine-scale fluctuations of extrusion rate apparent in the camera imagery. Thus, quantification of linear extrusion rate of the lava from the Sugar Bowl imagery provided information about the eruption that was unattainable by other means.

Deployment of remote cameras at Mount St. Helens clearly enhanced documentation and analysis of the eruption (Poland and others, this volume, chap. 11). The semicontinuous imagery obtained from the Sugar Bowl camera was particularly useful for analyzing long-term, relatively fine-scale (days to months) variations of the linear extrusion rate. It proved less useful for examining extrusion rate over periods of hours, given the low average rates of movement, the challenges of accurately following features of interest, and the resolution of the pixel footprint at the distances involved. Hence, the scale of the imagery had a direct bearing on the quality and utility of the information that could be extracted. Finer resolution at shorter time scales requires more narrowly focused, larger scale imagery, but obtaining such imagery can be extremely challenging (Dzurisin and others, this volume, chap. 14). Of course, measurements of linear extrusion rate do not necessarily correlate directly with measurements of volumetric extrusion rate (that is, magma discharge). Nevertheless, long-term estimates and documentation of fluctuations of this one-dimensional parameter are useful and shed insights

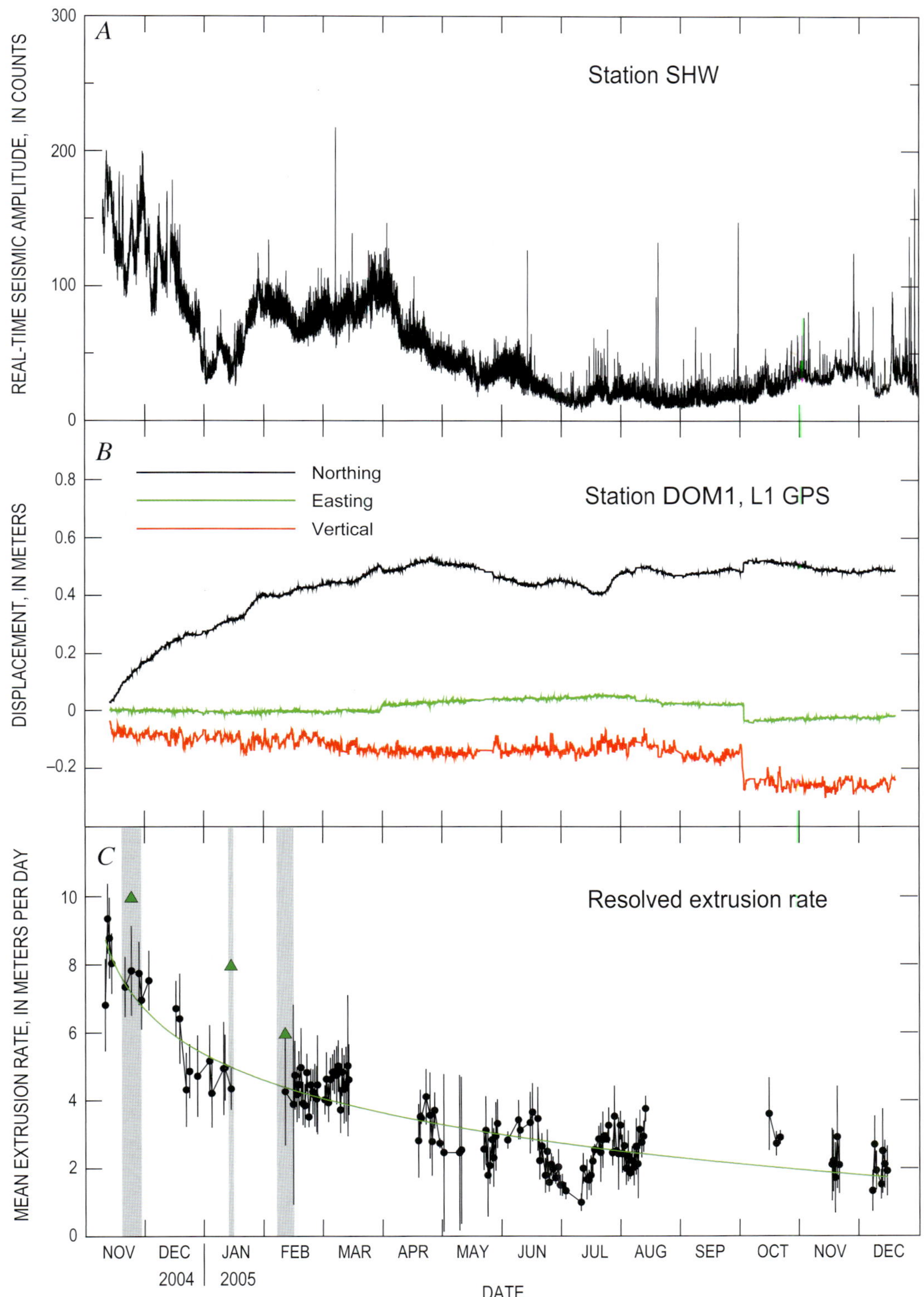

Figure 10. Time-series plots of RSAM, geodetic measurements, and extrusion rate at Mount St. Helens. *A*, Real-time seismic-amplitude measurements (RSAM) from station SHW located on the west flank of the volcano. Plot has been smoothed using a five-point moving average. *B*, GPS geodetic measurements at station DOM1 located on the western side of the 1980s lava dome. The data, obtained using the L1-band frequency, are referenced relative to a station located in the upper South Fork Toutle River valley (LaHusen and others, this volume, chap. 16). Plot has been smoothed using an 11-point moving median. *C*, Estimated average extrusion rate of the 2004–5 lava dome. See figure caption 8*C* for details.

into overall eruptive behavior, especially when trends in linear extrusion rate can be correlated with trends in other geophysical measurements.

The pulsating behavior of lava extrusion documented on time scales of days to weeks in our analysis has been observed on time scales of hours to years during emplacement of other silicic lava domes. At Soufrière Hills volcano, Montserrat, West Indies, Sparks and others (1998) noted that magma discharge pulsated on time scales of hours to months during a time when the overall discharge rate was increasing. In contrast, the pulsating behavior documented here occurred during an overall trend of declining magma discharge (Schilling and others, this volume, chap. 8). Fluctuating extrusion rates during an overall decline of magma discharge were also observed at Unzen volcano, Japan, from 1991 to 1995 (Nakada and others, 1999). Lava at Santiaguito dome, Guatemala, has extruded continuously since 1922, with 3–5-yr spurts of rapid discharge interspersed with 10–15-yr periods of slower discharge (Rose, 1987; Anderson and others, 1995; Harris and others, 2003). The Mount St. Helens 1980–86 lava dome grew through a series of 20 eruptive episodes between October 1980 and October 1986. However, each discrete extrusive episode was separated by pauses in eruptive activity that ranged from about one month to one year (Swanson and others, 1987), in contrast to the sustained, but fluctuating, extrusion that characterized the 2004–5 eruption. Sparks and others (1998) attribute pulsating extrusive behavior to a combination of deep and shallow volcanic processes. They speculate that discharge fluctuations on time scales of months to years are influenced chiefly by deep processes that control magmatic influx from the mantle and magma-chamber processes that affect magma ascent. In contrast, fluctuations on time scales of hours to weeks are attributed chiefly to pressure fluctuations caused by shallow-level processes, such as gas loss, crystallization kinetics, and mineral precipitation, which affect changes in magma properties and pressurization.

Correlations among seismicity, deformation, and extrusion rate during the 2004–5 Mount St. Helens eruption portray an extrusion that likely consisted of episodes of broad-scale stick-slip behavior. Relatively fine-scale correlations among periods of declining extrusion rate, relatively low seismicity, and northward movement of the 1980s lava dome (away from the eruptive vent) suggest episodes when the extruding solidified plug of lava was relatively well coupled to, and having difficulty evacuating, the conduit. Such a period of "stick" would be expected to result in lower seismicity, a low rate of extrusion, and increased deformation (that is, swelling) of the local terrain. In contrast, broad correlation among accelerated extrusion rate, slightly elevated seismicity, and southward movement of the 1980s lava dome (toward the eruptive vent) suggest episodes when the extruding solidified lava was relatively poorly coupled to, and slipping through, the conduit. Such periods of "slip" generated more or larger earthquakes as the lava dome lurched along (Moran and others, this volume, chap. 2) and allowed the local terrain deformed during the preceding period of stick to relax. Such episodes of broad-scale stick-slip movement complement a dynamic model of repetitive, fine-scale, stick-slip movement during sustained extrusion as proposed by Iverson and others (2006) and Iverson (this volume, chap. 21).

Long-term (months) and short-term (days) correlations between seismic intensity, deformation, and dome growth, such as documented here, have also been noted at other volcanoes. Broad correlations between seismic intensity and dome growth have been documented at Usu (Wano and Okada, 1980), Augustine (Power, 1988), Redoubt (Power and others, 1994), Unzen (Nakada and others, 1999), and Montserrat (Rowe and others, 2004), and short-term synchronicity and cyclicity between seismicity and deformation also have been observed (Voight and others, 1998). However, long-term, fine-scale correlations among fluctuations in extrusion rate, seismicity, and deformation generally have not been reported. Such correlations, as noted above, are clearly related to eruption mechanics. Indeed, Denlinger and Hoblitt (1999) have modeled short-term synchronicity and cyclicity in RSAM and deformation at Montserrat as a function of the interaction of volatile overpressure in magma and the overburden of an extruding lava dome, and Iverson (this volume, chap. 21) has hypothesized that the small, repetitive earthquakes that have occurred during the 2004–5 Mount St. Helens eruption, dubbed drumbeat earthquakes (Moran and others, this volume, chap. 2), reflect repetitive, small-magnitude (a few millimeters) stick-slip behavior of the extruding lava. Extraction of semicontinuous extrusion rates from long-term camera imagery, in conjunction with time-series of other geophysical data, clearly plays an important role in constraining dynamic eruption models and enabling forecasts of hazardous activity.

Conclusions

Imposition of interior and exterior controls on a semicontinuous series of oblique, terrestrial imagery from a fixed vantage point on the Sugar Bowl lava dome allowed quantification of fine-scale temporal behavior of the linear rate of lava extrusion during the 2004–5 eruption of Mount St. Helens. Analysis of the imagery showed that over a period of 14 months (November 2004–December 2005), the linear extrusion rate varied in both space and time. Overall, the extrusion rate declined approximately logarithmically from about 8–10 m/d in November 2004 to about 2 m/d by December 2005. However, the overall decline in the rate of extrusion was punctuated by fine-scale (days to weeks) fluctuations. The overall logarithmic decline of extrusion rate and the finer scale fluctuations correlated, approximately, with trends in seismicity and geodetic deformation. Those correlations portray an extrusion that underwent episodes of broad-scale stick-slip movement in addition to finer scale, smaller magnitude stick-slip episodes that others hypothesize to correlate with small, so-called drumbeat earthquakes. The ability to extract linear extrusion rates from the imagery from this fixed-position camera provided a significant, and sometimes the sole, means of semicontinuously quantifying eruption dynamics during much of the first year of eruption, and those data provide an important constraint for dynamic eruption models.

Acknowledgments

As noted in this chapter, the Sugar Bowl camera was not specifically deployed with the intention of extracting quantitative information. However, when viewing the images, especially after they have been compiled into a time-lapse movie, one cannot help but realize that they contain a plethora of information about the growth, and the rate of growth, of the new lava dome. The trick is to extract that information. We thank our colleagues at the Hawaiian Volcano Observatory for providing us with the original camera and communications software; Gene Iwatsubo, Kirstie Simpson, and Stephanie Konfal for helping install the camera; Seth Moran for providing us with RSAM data; Steve Schilling for stimulating discussions as we muddled along through our analyses; Matt Logan and Dan Gooding for compiling the imagery into the movie included in the supplemental movie of appendix 1; our many colleagues at CVO who asked pointed questions at staff meetings when we unveiled our analyses; and Ren Thompson and Ricky Herd for insightful, critical reviews that kept us from wandering beyond the limits of what we could reasonably do in our efforts to extract information from these photographs.

References Cited

Anderson, S.W., Fink, J.H., and Rose, W.I., 1995, Mount St. Helens and Santiaguito lava domes; the effect of short-term eruption rate on surface texture and degassing processes: Journal of Volcanology and Geothermal Research, v. 69, p. 105–116.

Baldi, P., Bonvalot, S., Briole, P., and Marsella, M., 2000, Digital photogrammetry and kinematic GPS applied to the monitoring of Vulcano Island, Aeolian arc, Italy: Geophysics Journal International, v. 142, no. 3, p. 801–811.

Baldi, P., Fabris, M., Marsella, M., and Monticelli, R., 2005, Monitoring the morphological evolution of the Sciara del Fuoco during the 2002–2003 Stromboli eruption using multi-temporal photogrammetry: ISPRS Journal of Photogrammetry and Remote Sensing, v. 59, no. 4, p. 199–211.

Barmin, A., Melnik, O., and Sparks, R.S.J., 2002, Periodic behavior in lava dome eruptions: Earth and Planetary Science Letters, v. 199, p. 173–184.

Bevington, P.R., and Robinson, D.K., 1992, Data reduction and error analysis for the physical sciences (2d ed.): Boston, McGraw-Hill, 328 p.

Denlinger, R.P., and Hoblitt, R.P., 1999, Cyclic eruptive behavior of silicic volcanoes: Geology, v. 27, p. 459–462.

Dungan, M.A., Wulff, A., and Thompson, R.A., 2001, Eruptive stratigraphy of the Tatara-San Pedro complex, 36°S, Southern Volcanic Zone, Chilean Andes; reconstruction method and implications for magma evolution at long-lived arc volcanic centers: Journal of Petrology, v. 42, p. 555–626.

Dzurisin, D., Lisowski, M., Poland, M.P., Sherrod, D.R., and LaHusen, R.G., 2008, Constraints and conundrums resulting from ground-deformation measurements made during the 2004–2005 dome-building eruption of Mount St. Helens, Washington, chap. 14 *of* Sherrod, D.R., Scott, W.E., and Stauffer, P.H., eds., A volcano rekindled; the renewed eruption of Mount St. Helens, 2004–2006: U.S. Geological Survey Professional Paper 1750 (this volume).

Endo, E.T., and Murray, T., 1991, Real-time seismic amplitude measurement (RSAM); a volcano monitoring and prediction tool: Bulletin of Volcanology, v. 53, no. 7, p. 533–545.

Harlow, D.H., Power, J.A., Laguerta, E.P., Ambubuyog, G., White, R.A., and Hoblitt, R.P., 1996, Precursory seismicity and forecasting of the June 15, 1991 eruption of Mount Pinatubo, *in* Newhall, C.G., and Punongbayan, R.S., eds., Fire and mud; eruptions and lahars of Mount Pinatubo, Philippines: Seattle, University of Washington Press, p. 285–305.

Harris, A.J.L., Rose, W.I., and Flynn, L.P., 2003, Temporal trends in lava dome extrusion at Santiaguito 1922–2000: Bulletin of Volcanology, v. 65, p. 77–89.

Herd, R.A., Edmonds, M., and Bass, V.A., 2005, Catastrophic lava dome failure at Soufriere Hills Volcano, Montserrat, 12–13 July 2003: Journal of Volcanology and Geothermal Research, v. 148, nos. 3–4, p. 234–252, doi:10.1016/j.jvolgeores.2005.05.003.

Honda, K., and Nagai, M., 2002, Real-time volcano activity mapping using ground-based digital imagery: ISPRS Journal of Photogrammetry and Remote Sensing, v. 57, p. 159–168.

Huppert, H.E., Shepherd, J.B., Sigurdsson, H., and Sparks, R.S.J., 1982, On lava dome growth, with application to the 1979 lava extrusion of the Soufrière of St. Vincent: Journal of Volcanology and Geothermal Research, v. 14, p. 199–222.

Iverson, R.M., 2008, Dynamics of seismogenic volcanic extrusion resisted by a solid surface plug, Mount St. Helens, 2004–2005, chap. 21 *of* Sherrod, D.R., Scott, W.E., and Stauffer, P.H., eds., A volcano rekindled; the renewed eruption of Mount St. Helens, 2004–2006: U.S. Geological Survey Professional Paper 1750 (this volume).

Iverson, R.M., Dzurisin, D., Gardner, C.A., Gerlach, T.M., LaHusen, R.G., Lisowski, M., Major, J.J., Malone, S.D., Messerich, J.A., Moran, S.C., Pallister, J.S., Qamar, A.I., Schilling, S.P., and Vallance, J.W., 2006, Dynamics of seismogenic volcanic extrusion at Mount St. Helens in 2004–05: Nature, v. 444, no. 7118, p. 439–443, doi:10.1038/nature05322.

James, M.R., Robson, S., Pinkerton, H., and Ball, M., 2006, Oblique photogrammetry with visible and thermal images of active lava flows: Bulletin of Volcanology, v. 69, no. 1, p. 105–108.

Jordan, R., and Kieffer, H.H., 1981, Topographic changes at Mount St. Helens—large-scale photogrammetry and digital terrain models, *in* Lipman, P.W., and Mullineaux, D.R., eds., The 1980 eruptions of Mount St. Helens, Washington: U.S. Geological Survey Professional Paper 1250, p. 135–141.

LaHusen, R.G., Swinford, K.J., Logan, M., and Lisowski, M., 2008, Instrumentation in remote and dangerous settings; examples using data from GPS "spider" deployments during the 2004–2005 eruption of Mount St. Helens, Washington, chap. 16 *of* Sherrod, D.R., Scott, W.E., and Stauffer, P.H., eds., A volcano rekindled; the renewed eruption of Mount St. Helens, 2004–2006: U.S. Geological Survey Professional Paper 1750 (this volume).

Mastin, L.G., Roeloffs, E., Beeler, N.M., and Quick, J.E., 2008, Constraints on the size, overpressure, and volatile content of the Mount St. Helens magma system from geodetic and dome-growth measurements during the 2004–2006+ eruption, chap. 22 *of* Sherrod, D.R., Scott, W.E., and Stauffer, P.H., eds., A volcano rekindled; the renewed eruption of Mount St. Helens, 2004–2006: U.S. Geological Survey Professional Paper 1750 (this volume).

Melnik, O., and Sparks, R.S.J., 2005, Controls on conduit magma flow dynamics during lava dome building eruptions: Journal of Geophysical Research, v. 110, no. B2, B02209, 21 p., doi:10.1029/2004JB003183.

Molander, C.W., 2001, Photogrammetry, *in* Maune, D.F., ed., Digital elevation model technologies and applications; the DEM users manual: The American Society for Photogrammetry and Remote Sensing, Bethesda, Maryland, p. 121–142.

Moore, J.G., and Albee, W.C., 1981, Topographic and structural changes, March–July 1980—photogrammetric data, *in* Lipman, P.W., and Mullineaux, D.R., eds., The 1980 eruptions of Mount St. Helens, Washington: U.S. Geological Survey Professional Paper 1250, p. 123–134.

Moran, S.C., Malone, S.D., Qamar, A.I., Thelen, W.A., Wright, A.K., and Caplan-Auerbach, J., 2008, Seismicity associated with renewed dome building at Mount St. Helens, 2004–2005, chap. 2 *of* Sherrod, D.R., Scott, W.E., and Stauffer, P.H., eds., A volcano rekindled; the renewed eruption of Mount St. Helens, 2004–2006: U.S. Geological Survey Professional Paper 1750 (this volume).

Mori, J., White, R.A., Harlow, D.H., Okubo, P., Power, J.A., Hoblitt, R.P., Laguerta, E.P., Lanuza, A., and Bautista, B.C., 1996, Volcanic earthquakes following the 1991 climactic eruption of Mount Pinatubo; strong seismicity during a waning eruption, *in* Newhall, C.G., and Punongbayan, R.S., eds., Fire and mud; eruptions and lahars of Mount Pinatubo, Philippines: Seattle, University of Washington Press, p. 339–350.

Murray, T., and Endo, E.T., 1992, A real-time seismic-amplitude measurement system (RSAM), *in* Ewert, J.A., and Swanson, D.A., eds., Monitoring volcanoes; techniques and strategies used by the staff of the Cascades Volcano Observatory, 1980–1990: U.S Geological Survey Bulletin 1966, p. 5–10.

Nakada, S., Miyake, Y., Sato, H., Oshima, O., and Fujinawa, A., 1995, Endogenous growth of dacite dome at Unzen volcano (Japan), 1993–1994: Geology, v. 23, no. 2, p. 157–160.

Nakada, S., Shimizu, H., and Ohta, K., 1999, Overview of the 1990–1995 eruption at Unzen Volcano: Journal of Volcanology and Geothermal Research, v. 89, p. 1–22.

Poland, M.P., Dzurisin, D., LaHusen, R.G., Major, J.J., Lapcewich, D., Endo, E.T., Gooding, D.J., Schilling, S.P., and Janda, C.G., 2008, Remote camera observations of lava dome growth at Mount St. Helens, Washington, October 2004 to February 2006, chap. 11 *of* Sherrod, D.R., Scott, W.E., and Stauffer, P.H., eds., A volcano rekindled; the renewed eruption of Mount St. Helens, 2004–2006: U.S. Geological Survey Professional Paper 1750 (this volume).

Power, J.A., 1988, Seismicity associated with the 1986 eruption of Augustine Volcano, Alaska: Fairbanks, University of Alaska, M.S. thesis, 142 p.

Power, J.A., Lahr, J.C., Page, R.A., Chouet, B.A., Stephens, C.D., Harlow, D.H., Murray, T.L., and Davies, J.N., 1994, Seismic evolution of the 1989–1990 eruption sequence of Redoubt Volcano, Alaska: Journal of Volcanology and Geothermal Research, v. 62, p. 69–94.

Power, J.A., Jolly, A.D., Page, R.A., and McNutt, S.R., 1995, Seismicity and forecasting of the 1992 eruptions of Crater Peak vent, Mount Spurr Volcano, Alaska; an overview, *in* Keith, T.C., ed., The 1992 eruptions of Crater Peak Vent, Mount Spurr Volcano, Alaska: U.S. Geological Survey Bulletin 2139, p. 149–159.

Rose, W.I., 1987, Volcanic activity at Santiaguito volcano, 1976–1984, *in* Fink, J.H., ed., The emplacement of silicic domes and lava flows: Geological Society of America Special Paper 212, p. 17–27.

Rowe, C.A., Thurber, C.H., and White, R.A., 2004, Dome growth behavior at Soufriere Hills Volcano, Montserrat, revealed by relocation of volcanic event swarms, 1995–1996: Journal of Volcanology and Geothermal Research, v. 134, no. 3, p. 199–221.

Schilling, S.P., Carrara, P.E., Thompson, R.A., and Iwatsubo, E.Y., 2004, Posteruption glacier development within the crater of Mount St. Helens, Washington, USA: Quaternary Research, v. 61, no. 3, p. 325–329.

Schilling, S.P., Thompson, R.A., Messerich, J.A., and Iwatsubo, E.Y., 2008, Use of digital aerophotogrammetry to determine rates of lava dome growth, Mount St. Helens, Washington, 2004–2005, chap. 8 *of* Sherrod, D.R., Scott, W.E., and Stauffer, P.H., eds., A volcano rekindled; the renewed eruption of Mount St. Helens, 2004–2006: U.S. Geological Survey Professional Paper 1750 (this volume).

Sparks, R.S.J., and 19 others, 1998, Magma production and growth of the lava dome of the Soufriere Hills Volcano, Montserrat, West Indies—November 1995 to December 1997: Geophysical Research Letters, v. 25, no. 18, p. 3421–3424.

Swanson, D.A., Dzurisin, D., Holcomb, R.T., Iwatsubo, E.Y., Chadwick, W.W., Jr., Casadevall, T.J., Ewert, J.W., and Heliker, C.C., 1987, Growth of the lava dome at Mount St. Helens, Washington (USA), 1981–1983, *in* Fink, J.H., ed., The emplacement of silicic domes and lava flows: Geological Society of America Special Paper 212, p. 1–16.

Thompson, R.A., and Schilling, S.P., 2007, Photogrammetry, *in* Dzurisin, D., ed., Volcano deformation—geodetic monitoring techniques: Berlin, Springer, Springer-Praxis Books in Geophysical Sciences, p. 195–221.

Ui, T., Matsuwo, N., Sumita, M., and Fujinawa, A., 1999, Generation of block and ash flows during the 1990–1995 eruption of Unzen volcano, Japan: Journal of Volcanology and Geothermal Research, v. 89, p. 123–137.

Vallance, J.W., Schneider, D.J., and Schilling, S.P., 2008, Growth of the 2004–2006 lava-dome complex at Mount St. Helens, Washington, chap. 9 *of* Sherrod, D.R., Scott, W.E., and Stauffer, P.H., eds., A volcano rekindled; the renewed eruption of Mount St. Helens, 2004–2006: U.S. Geological Survey Professional Paper 1750 (this volume).

Voight, B., 1981, Time scale for the first moments of the May 18 eruption, *in* Lipman, P.W., and Mullineaux, D.R., eds., The 1980 eruptions of Mount St. Helens, Washington: U.S. Geological Survey Professional Paper 1250, p. 69–86.

Voight, B., Hoblitt, R.P., Clarke, A.B., Lockhart, A.B., Miller, A.D., Lynch, L.L., and McMahon, J., 1998, Remarkable cyclic ground deformation monitored in real time on Montserrat, and its use in eruption forecasting: Geophysical Research Letters, v. 25, p. 3405–3408.

Wano, K., and Okada, H., 1980, Peculiar occurrence of Usu earthquake swarms associated with recent doming activity: Jishin, v. 33, p. 215–226.

Wolf, P.R., and Dewitt, B.A., 2000, Elements of photogrammetry with applications in GIS (3d ed.): Boston, McGraw-Hill, 608 p.

Yamashina, K., Matsushima, T., and Ohmi, S., 1999, Volcanic deformation at Unzen, Japan, visualized by a time-differential stereoscopy: Journal of Volcanology and Geothermal Research, v. 89, p. 73–80.

Zlotnicki, J., Ruegg, J.C., Bachelery, P., and Blum, P.A., 1990, Eruptive mechanism on Piton de la Fournaise volcano associated with the December 4, 1983, and January 18, 1984 eruptions from ground deformation monitoring and photogrammetric surveys: Journal of Volcanology and Geothermal Research, v. 40, no. 3, p. 197–217, doi:10.1016/0377-0273(90)90121-U.

Appendix 1. Time-Lapse Photography of Mount St. Helens, 2004–2006—Movie

[This appendix appears only in the digital versions of this work in the DVD-ROM that accompanies the printed volume and as a separate file accompanying this chapter on the Web at: http://pubs.usgs.gov/pp/1750.]

The appendix is a time-lapse movie showing dome growth at Mount St. Helens from November 10, 2004, to May 10, 2006. The movie, in mpeg-1 file format and titled "Sugarbowl to May10 2006_5000.mpg," is composed of 188 photographs taken by the Sugar Bowl remote camera. It was assembled by choosing the best image per day for times when weather was suitable for viewing the dome. File size is 23 Mb. Compiled by Matt Logan and Dan Gooding (USGS).

A Volcano Rekindled: The Renewed Eruption of Mount St. Helens, 2004–2006
Edited by David R. Sherrod, William E. Scott, and Peter H. Stauffer
U.S. Geological Survey Professional Paper 1750, 2008

Chapter 13

Effects of Lava-Dome Growth on the Crater Glacier of Mount St. Helens, Washington

By Joseph S. Walder[1], Steve P. Schilling[1], James W. Vallance[1], and Richard G. LaHusen[1]

Abstract

The process of lava-dome emplacement through a glacier was observed for the first time as the 2004–6 eruption of Mount St. Helens proceeded. The glacier that had grown in the crater since the cataclysmic 1980 eruption was split in two by the new lava dome. The two parts of the glacier were successively squeezed against the crater wall. Photography, photogrammetry, and geodetic measurements document glacier deformation of an extreme variety, with strain rates of extraordinary magnitude as compared to normal temperate alpine glaciers. Unlike such glaciers, the Mount St. Helens crater glacier shows no evidence of either speed-up at the beginning of the ablation season or diurnal speed fluctuations during the ablation season. Thus there is evidently no slip of the glacier over its bed. The most reasonable explanation for this anomaly is that meltwater penetrating the glacier is captured by a thick layer of coarse rubble at the bed and then enters the volcano's groundwater system rather than flowing through a drainage network along the bed. Mechanical consideration of the glacier-squeeze process also leads to an estimate for the driving pressure applied by the growing lava dome.

Introduction

Since October 2004, a silicic lava dome has been emplaced first through, and then alongside, glacier ice in the crater of Mount St. Helens. The dome has been emplaced in a near-solid state, not as liquid magma solidifying at the Earth's surface (Vallance and others, this volume, chap. 9). Heretofore, dome emplacement through a glacier was known only from a single published photograph (Simons and Mathewson, 1955, plate 6) showing a lava dome that had been emplaced through the caldera glacier of Great Sitkin Volcano, Alaska, sometime in 1945. Evidence bearing on lava-dome emplacement into ice has been presented by, for example, Gilbert and others (1996), who used geophysical methods to identify lava domes emplaced beneath the caldera glacier of Volcán Sollipulli, Chile, and by Tuffen and others (2001), who described a domelike rhyolite body that was evidently emplaced subglacially in Iceland and since exhumed. The 2004–6 eruption of Mount St. Helens has afforded the first-ever opportunity to actually document the process of lava-dome emplacement through a glacier.

The common picture of volcano-glacier interactions is one of rapid meltwater generation either as magma contacts the glacier bed—examples from Iceland have been especially well characterized, for example, the 1996 Gjálp eruption (Guðmundsson and others, 1997)—or as lava or pyroclasts are erupted onto the glacier surface (many examples are mentioned by Major and Newhall, 1989). At Mount St. Helens, however, glacier melt associated with dome emplacement has been minor, even as the glaciological consequences have been dramatic—Crater Glacier has been cut in half, and the resulting ice bodies have in succession been squeezed between the growing lava dome and the crater wall. In this paper we focus our attention on the glaciological consequences of the eruption. Condensed discussions of this material have been presented elsewhere by Walder and others (2005, 2007).

Field Setting: Crater Glacier Before October 2004

After the cataclysmic eruption of May 18, 1980, which beheaded, and in some cases completely destroyed, the glaciers that existed on the flanks of Mount St. Helens (Brugman and Meier, 1981), material from rock and snow avalanches began accumulating in the north-facing, amphitheaterlike crater (fig. 1). Mills (1992) used digitized topographic maps to

[1] U.S. Geological Survey, 1300 SE Cardinal Court, Vancouver, WA 98683

calculate the volumes of material eroded from the crater walls and accumulated on the crater floor. His results show that as of mid-1988, the thickness of accumulated material was 60 to 80 m across much of the crater floor south of the 1980–86 lava dome. The accumulated material as of mid-1988 was about 60 percent rock debris by volume and contained interstitial snow, but it was not flowing. The first reasonably clear evidence that a crater glacier had come into existence—the appearance of crevasses, which reflect flow—comes from photographs taken in September 1996 (Schilling and others, 2004). The glacier (now called Crater Glacier) at that time had a surface area of about 0.1 km^2; by September 2000, this area had increased to about 1 km^2. Proceeding similarly to Mills (1992) but using digital elevation models (DEMs), Schilling and others (2004) calculated that the material that had accumulated in the crater between May 18, 1980, and September 2000 had a thickness locally as great as 200 m and a volume of 1.2×10^8 m^3, of which about one-third comprised rock debris. If we interpret these figures in the context of Mills' discussion of what had accumulated on the crater floor as of 1988, it seems clear that the deepest part of the crater-floor fill consists primarily of rock-avalanche debris—a point to which we shall return—and would not be considered glacier ice by usual glaciological standards. The uppermost part of Crater Glacier, however, probably contains no more than 5 percent rock debris by volume, with such debris forming discrete, discontinuous layers that originate as rock-avalanche lobes (fig. 2), and glaciologists would call this material "dirty" firn and glacier ice.

To what extent is the material accumulated on the crater floor since 1980 a glacier? In framing an answer, we have to make explicit our reason for asking the question in the first place. Our focus here is not on morphology, but rather on the ice flow and deformation processes familiar to glaciologists, and how such processes affect the mechanical response of the crater-fill material to lava-dome emplacement. From this perspective, what one is tempted to call a glacier in a morphological sense is not the same as what is rheologically and mechanically glacier ice. Deformation of a material containing 60 percent rock debris by volume—Mills' (1992) estimate for the composition of the pre-1988 crater-floor fill—is surely dominated by rock-to-rock friction, not creep of any interstitial ice.

We choose to exclude from our mechanically defined glacier, as best we can, the deepest, rock-rich crater-floor fill. We do this by picking the glacier bed as the crater-floor surface

Figure 1. Oblique view of Mount St. Helens crater on October 5, 2000, looking south. Crater Glacier wraps around 1980–86 lava dome. East (left) arm of glacier is obscured by rock-avalanche debris; west (right) arm merges to the north of the lava dome with a rock-covered icy mass shed off the west crater wall. Crater width, as indicated by double-headed arrow, is about 2 km. USGS photograph by Bergman Photographic Services, Portland, Oreg.

Figure 2. Glacier features in crater of Mount St. Helens. *A*, Rock layers within uppermost part of Crater Glacier, as exposed on west side of new lava dome. Distance from glacier surface to prominent debris layer (arrow) is about 3 to 5 m. View to east. USGS photograph taken August 4, 2005, by W.P. Johnson. *B*, Surface of Crater Glacier on August 20, 2003, looking north along east side of 1980–86 lava dome. Rock-avalanche lobe in center of view extended from the crater wall nearly to the south side of the lava dome and had maximum thickness of about 1 m. USGS photograph by J.S. Walder.

defined by DEMs for October 12, 1986, and November 12, 1986. This is an approximate but defensible choice for several reasons: (1) The rate of accumulation of rock debris in the crater decreased markedly after 1986 (fig. 3). (2) 1986 marks the end of the previous dome-growth episode, so accumulation after 1986 occurred within a basin with reasonably stable boundaries. (3) As we argue in appendix 1, interstitial ice within the lowest, rock-rich crater-fill material has probably melted and not been replaced by ice intruding from above. With the 1986 surface thus defined as the glacier bed, we then differenced 2003 and 1986 DEMs to calculate the glacier thickness shortly before the start of the 2004 eruption (fig. 4). Using the Mills (1992) and Schilling and others (2004) figures for rock-debris accumulation, we estimate that Crater Glacier, so defined, has an average rock content of 15 percent by volume.

A note about names. The U.S. Board on Geographic Names on June 6, 2006, approved the name "Crater Glacier" for the feature that existed before the recent eruption. However, as is documented below, Crater Glacier has been split in two by dome growth, and it is both sensible and convenient to use the informal names "west Crater Glacier" and "east Crater Glacier" for the ice masses that exist in the crater as of the time of writing.

Changes in Crater Glacier Since October 2004

Methods

Hazards posed by Mount St. Helens' eruptions severely restricted field work in the crater, so we documented eruptive effects on Crater Glacier primarily by photography and photogrammetry. We managed to collect some glacier-motion data using single-frequency global positioning system (GPS) stations slung by helicopter onto the glacier surface in 2005 and 2006. The GPS stations (LaHusen and others, this volume, chap. 16) were available for glacier monitoring only intermittently, and on several occasions had to be moved, or else they would have toppled into crevasses. Station positions were determined from short-baseline differential fixed static solutions sampled at 10-second intervals over a 25-minute period every hour. Accuracy of individual solutions was approximately 20 mm in the horizontal and 50 mm in the vertical. A running-median filter was applied to solutions to remove spikes.

Morphological Changes

One of the first indirect signs of dome growth was the formation of a bulge in the south part of Crater Glacier during the last few days of September 2004 (fig. 5). An explosion on October 1, 2004, excavated a hole in the glacier (fig. 6). As the eruption proceeded, the southern part of Crater Glacier was eventually punctured by a rock spine surrounded by rubble (fig. 7), the latter perhaps comprising unconsolidated mate-

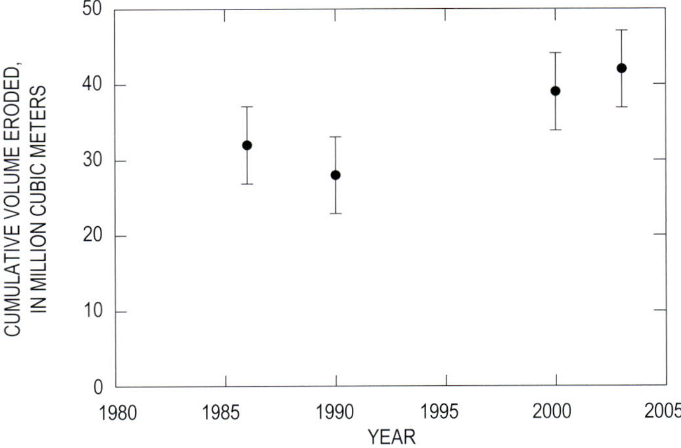

Figure 3. Cumulative volume eroded from walls of Mount St. Helens crater since the 1980 eruption, as determined by differencing digital elevation models for 1990, 2000, and 2003 with a DEM for 1980. Error bars ($\pm 1\sigma$) are shown. Despite uncertainties in the data, it is clear that erosion rate has fallen sharply since the mid-1980s.

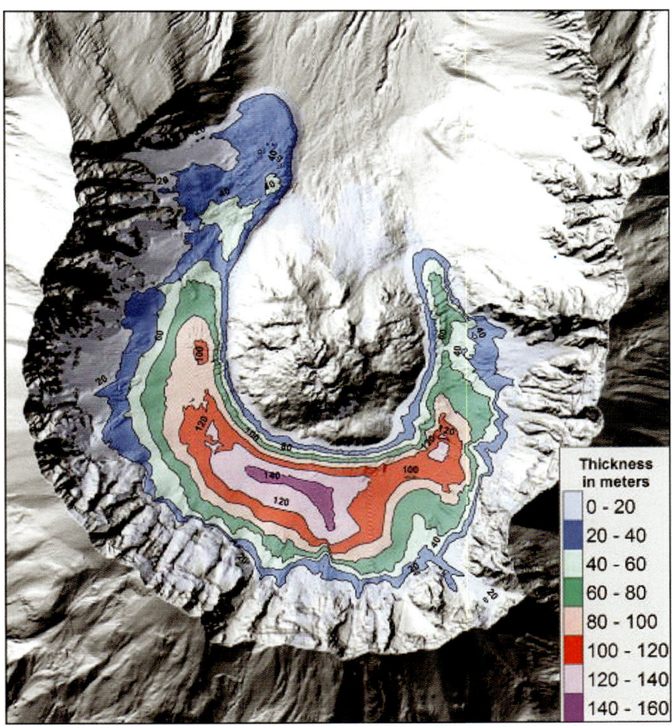

Figure 4. Map showing thickness of material accumulated on the crater floor of Mount St. Helens between October–November 1986 and September 2003. Background is a hillshade-relief map constructed from September 2003 digital elevation model. The 1980–86 lava dome is in center. As explained in text, the October–November 1986 surface is approximately the glacier bed, and the isopachs represent approximate glacier thickness.

rial that underlay the glacier. The lava dome as it exists as of October 4, 2006, is a complex of seven such spines extruded sequentially in the solid state from the same general vent area (fig. 8; Vallance and others, this volume, chap. 9). Spine 3, which began to be extruded in late October 2004, grew preferentially southward, developing a whaleback form and pushing aside firn and ice in a way reminiscent of the bow wave that precedes a ship through water (fig. 9). After spine 3 ran into the south crater wall in mid-November 2004, Crater Glacier was for all practical purposes split into two parts.

East Crater Glacier

Spine 3 spread to the east until late December 2004, then spalled greatly and was shouldered aside by spine 4—another "whaleback"—which grew until mid-April 2005. The east Crater Glacier (ECG) was effectively caught in a vise formed by the whaleback spines and the east crater wall. Owing to drought conditions that prevailed throughout most of the winter of 2004–5, there was practically no snow accumulation, and thus glacier-surface features showed very clearly. As eastward dome growth proceeded, the upwarped glacier apron on the east side of the dome (compare fig. 9) impinged against the east crater wall. However, the northernmost part of this ice apron was rotated until it formed a steplike feature trending nearly east to west (fig. 10). The ECG surface buckled, with east-west-trending crevasses forming parallel to the direction of dome spreading (fig. 11). Comparison of DEMs reveals that between mid-November 2004 and mid-April 2005, the dome/ECG contact migrated laterally by as much as 200 to 250 m and the glacier locally doubled in thickness (figs. 12, 13, 14). Expressed in terms of rates, the dome-ECG contact moved on average about 1 m/d and the glacier thickened at an astounding 0.6 m/d. By way of comparison, the average thickening rate for the "reservoir area" of a surging glacier, during the interval between surges, is perhaps 0.02 to 0.04 m/d (Raymond, 1987, p. 9123, fig. 1).

Since spine 4 quit growing in mid-April 2005, east Crater Glacier has thinned in its upper reach and thickened in its lower reach as normal flow processes redistribute ice mass downslope. Longitudinal crevasses became obvious by late April 2005; these crevasses probably reflect transverse spreading as the bowed-up surface—so evident during the squeezing episode—relaxed. As a result, the glacier surface became a field of seracs (fig. 15). The ECG terminus became steep (fig. 16) and advanced by about 150 m between April 19, 2005, and August 18, 2006.

Figure 5. Bulge in Crater Glacier next to south side of 1980–86 lava dome on September 30, 2004. Dark material on surface of fractured area is talus. Width of bulge is about 50 m. View to west. USGS photograph by D. Dzurisin.

Figure 6. Beginning of Mount St. Helens eruption through Crater Glacier on October 1, 2004. View to west. USGS photograph by J.S. Pallister.

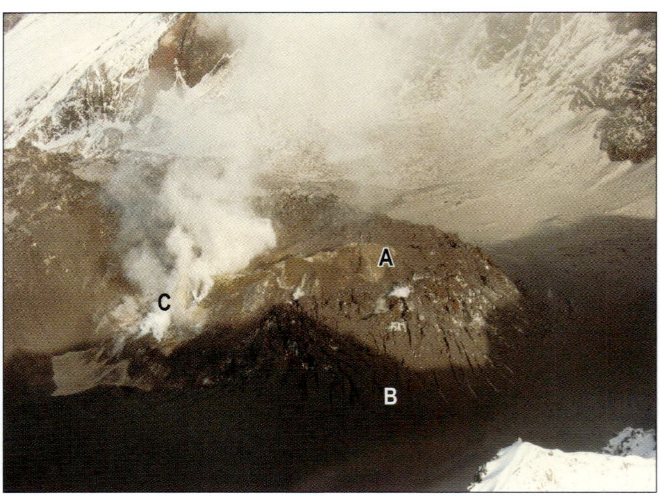

Figure 7. Upwarped, tephra-covered firn and ice around margins of new lava dome on October 11, 2004. View to northeast. A, Deformed rock at ambient temperature. B, Deformed firn and ice. C, Spine 1 (hot rock). USGS photograph by C.A. Neal.

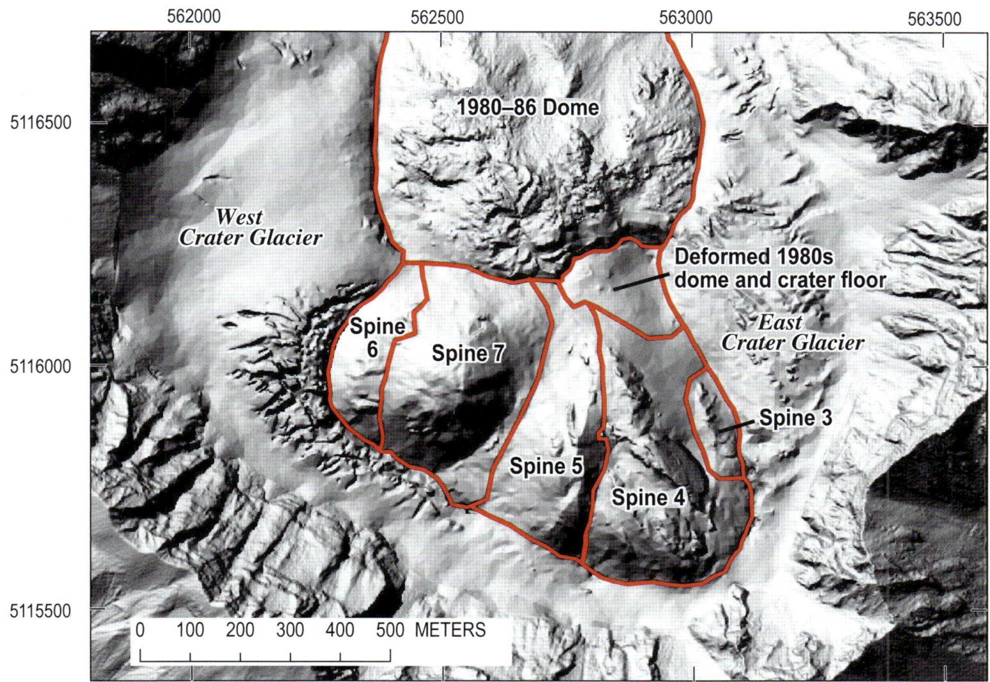

Figure 8. Map of the lava-dome spine complex in Mount St. Helens crater drawn on a hillshade-relief map from the October 24, 2005, DEM. Spines are numbered according to sequence of extrusion events, as discussed by Vallance and others (this volume, chap. 9). Coordinates referable to UTM zone 10, North American datum 1983.

Figure 9. Upwarped firn and ice around margin of new whaleback lava spine, November 20, 2004. View to east. USGS photograph by S.P. Schilling.

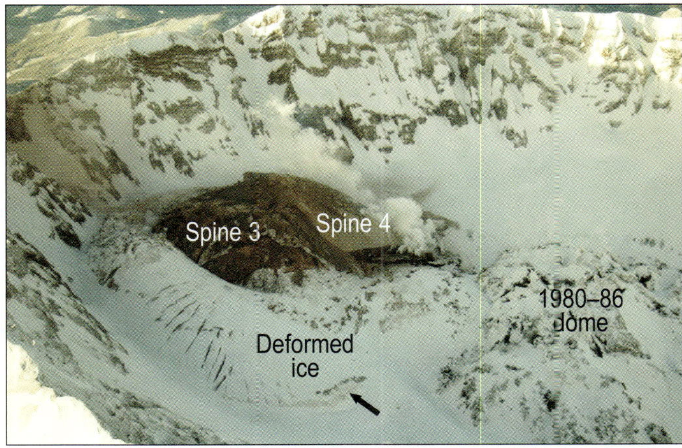

Figure 10. The new lava dome of Mount St. Helens (dominated by spines 3 and 4) and the by-then morphologically distinct east Crater Glacier (in foreground) on January 14, 2005. The bulge indicated by the arrow is not a kinematic wave but was instead formed when upwarped ice around the spine margins (see figs. 7, 8) was rotated as dome growth proceeded to east. View to southwest USGS photograph by J.W. Vallance.

Figure 11. Upwarped surface of east Crater Glacier on February 16, 2005. View to north. Crevasses are oriented roughly east-west, paralleling direction of squeeze by new lava dome (at left). 1980s dome in left-center distance. USGS photograph by J.S. Walder.

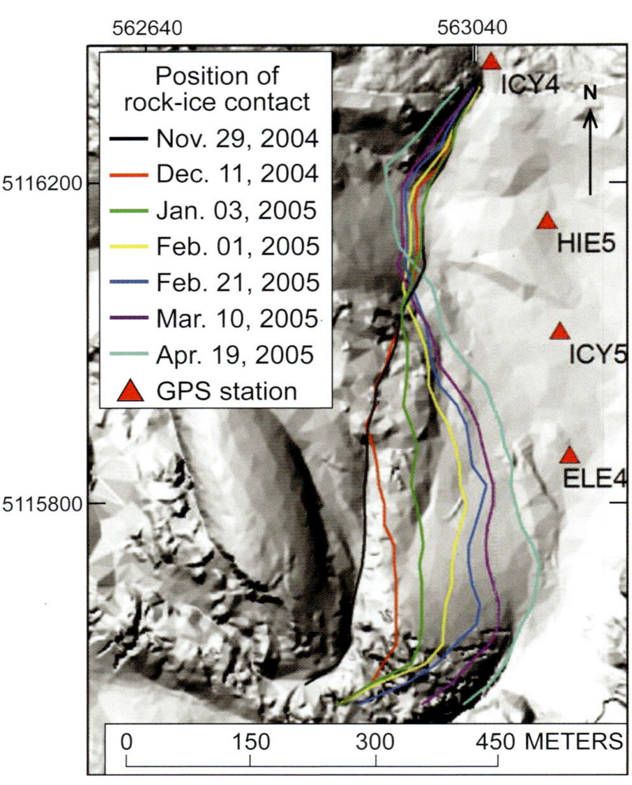

Figure 12. Migration of the contact between rock of the new lava dome and ice of east Crater Glacier during the period from November 29, 2004, to April 19, 2005. Contact position was determined from DEMs, with a probable error of about 5 m. Background image is hillshade-relief map for November 29, 2004. Coordinates are UTM zone 10 easting and northing, North American datum 1983. Eastward migration of rock-glacier contact for northing between about 5115500 and 5116000 reflects growth of new lava dome, which caused the glacier to thicken locally. The resulting enhanced ice flow to the north caused ice to encroach upon the margin of the old (1980–86) lava dome north of about northing 5116050. Also indicated are positions of four GPS stations deployed on the glacier at various times.

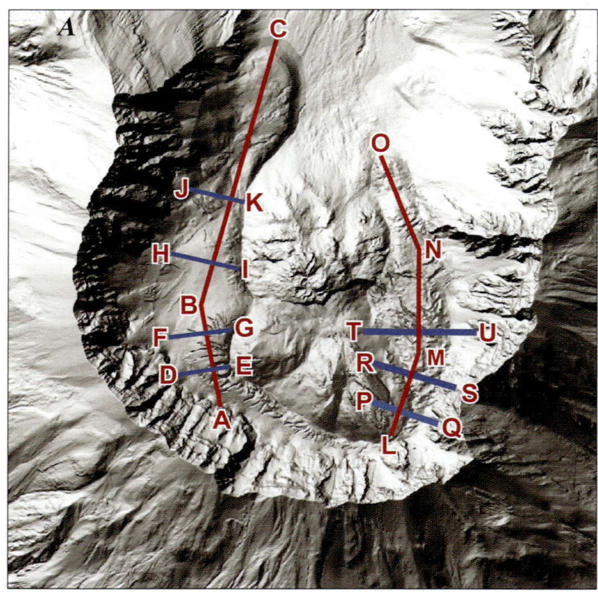

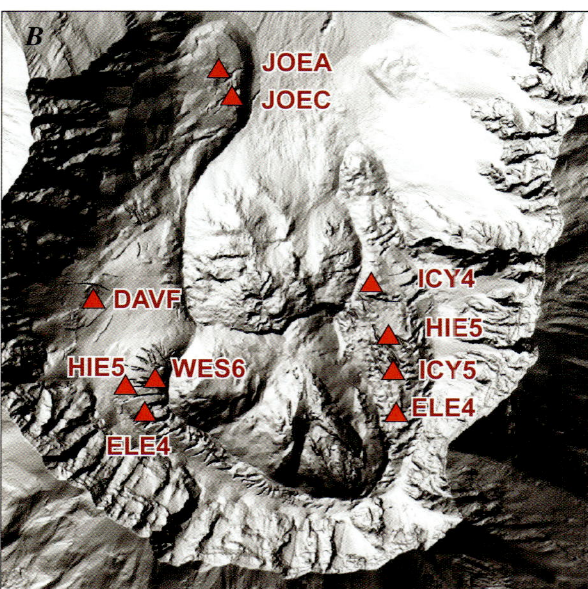

Figure 13. Hillshade-relief maps of Mount St. Helens crater constructed from photogrammetric analysis of aerial photographs dated October 24, 2005. *A*, Lines of section for which we calculated changes in glacier-surface altitude. *B*, Positions of GPS stations. Note that any individual station may not have been on the glacier on the date of the photographs. ELE4 appears twice because it was shifted from east Crater Glacier to west Crater Glacier during the course of the eruption.

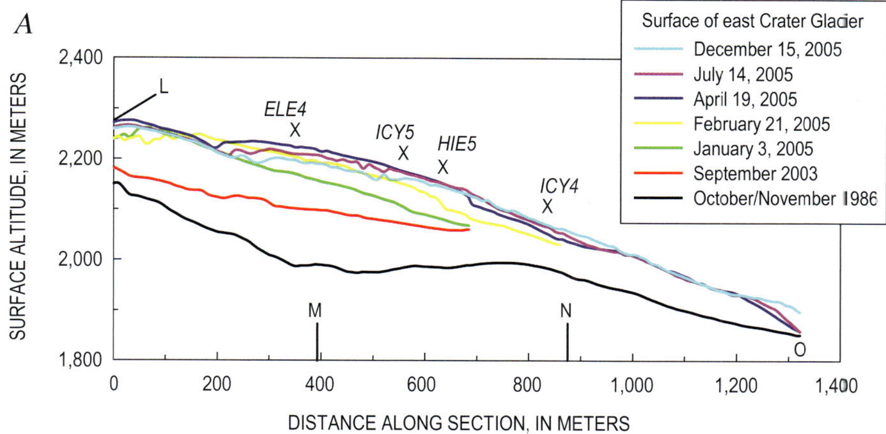

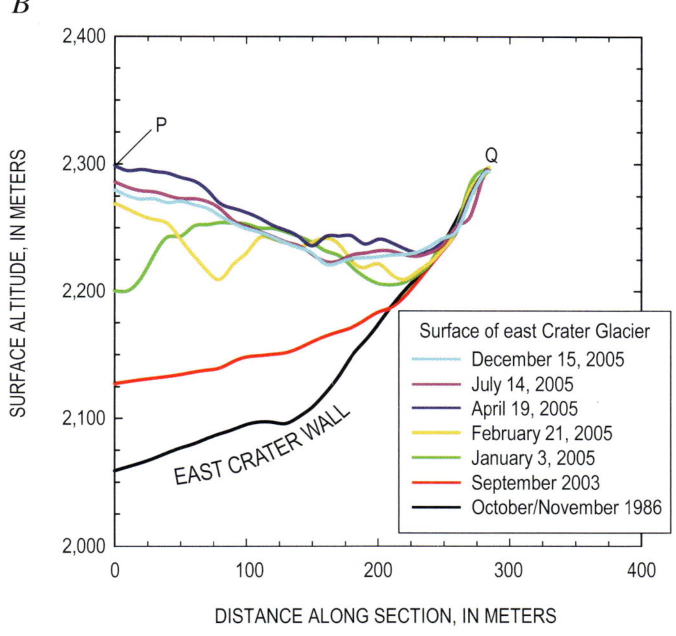

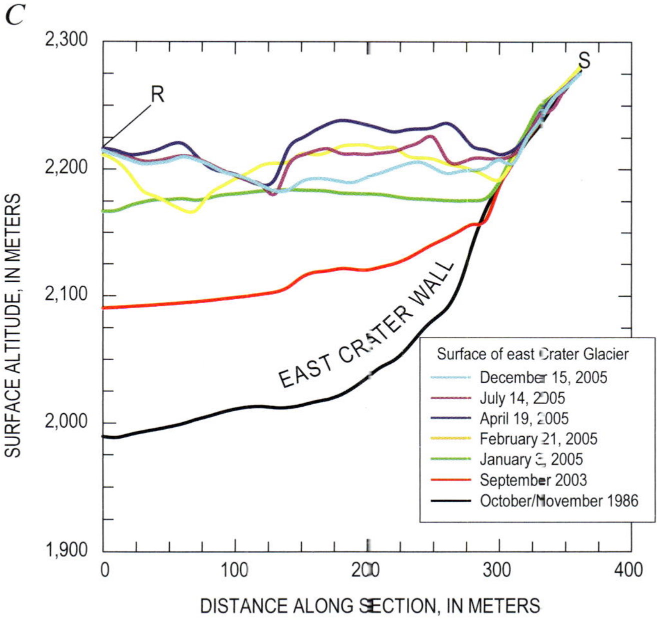

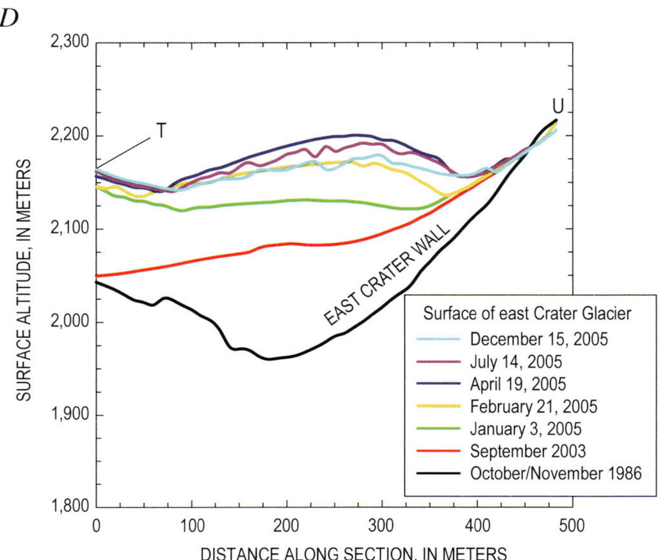

Figure 14. Cross sections showing changes in surface altitude of east Crater Glacier during the course of current eruption, based on sequential DEMs. Lines of section and GPS station locations shown in figure 13. (Note that GPS station ICY4 was adjacent to 1980–86 lava dome and thus north of the part of east Crater Glacier that was squeezed.) The 1986 profile represents the ground surface at the end of the 1980–86 dome-building episode and approximates the glacier bed. The 2003 profile should be within a few meters altitude of the glacier surface at beginning of current eruption. Not all DEM coverages extend to glacier terminus. *A*, Longitudinal section L–M–N–O approximately parallel to ice flow. *B*, Transverse section P–Q. *C*, Transverse section R–S. *D*, Transverse section T–U.

West Crater Glacier

Growth of spine 6 (Vallance and others, this volume, chap. 9) adjacent to west Crater Glacier (WCG) became noticeable in early August 2005. Surface bulging and crevassing of the glacier proceeded in much the same way as with ECG (fig. 17). Spine 6 quit growing, and spine 7 began growing and overriding spine 6, in early to mid-October 2005, but WCG continued to be squeezed owing to the push exerted by spine 7 on spine 6. Events unfolded much as with ECG: The dome-WCG contact migrated locally by >200 m (fig. 18), and the glacier locally doubled in thickness (fig. 19). A distinct bulge in the WCG surface began propagating downglacier (fig. 19*A*) and impinged upon the rather flat, mostly rock-covered terminus region, which arguably originated as a separate mass shed from the west crater wall (compare fig. 1). In summer 2006, it became clear that advance of the bulge was being accommodated by development of a shear zone within the flat terminus region (fig. 20).

Figure 15. Crevasses formed by lava-dome growth at Mount St. Helens. *A*, Longitudinal crevasses on east Crater Glacier cutting across transverse crevasses that had formed during eastward lava-dome growth (compare fig. 9), as seen on May 12, 2005. View to southwest. USGS photograph by M. Logan. *B*, Part of east Crater Glacier on July 26, 2005. View to south. Longitudinal crevasse growth by this date had effectively chopped the glacier surface into a field of seracs. USGS photograph by S.P. Schilling.

Change in Ice Volume During the Eruption

The change in glacier volume during the course of the eruption can be determined by comparing DEMs prepared for different dates. The method is discussed in appendix 2, and results are summarized in figure 21. The estimated volume decrease from the start of the eruption (October 2004) until October 2005—meaning (approximately) from the end of one ablation season to the end of the next ablation season—was $6.7\pm3.7\times10^6$ m^3, corresponding to an average rate of loss of 0.21 ± 0.12 m^3/s. The eruption has clearly not been marked by a process commonly associated with volcano-glacier interactions, namely, rapid meltwater generation (Major and Newhall, 1989). In retrospect, this is unsurprising—the eruption has been predominantly quiescent, not explosive, so scouring of the glacier surface by hot fragmental flows has been negligible; moreover, the spines have been extruded in a solid state, with surface temperature well below the solidus, and the glacier is well insulated from them by rubble (Schneider and others, this volume, chap. 17).

Ice Dynamics

Given the radical morphological changes to Crater Glacier during the eruption, described above, we should not be surprised if the glacier's dynamics were also significantly affected. Unfortunately, our complete lack of data on glacier-surface speed before the 2004 eruption complicates an assessment of how the eruption affected glacier dynamics. To try to infer a rough baseline for preeruption dynamics, we use mass-balance considerations to estimate the so-called balance velocity U_b, which is the cross-sectionally averaged speed that a glacier would have if it were in steady state (Paterson, 1994, p. 250):

$$U_b(x) = \frac{1}{W(x)\bar{H}(x)} \int_0^x \dot{b}(\xi) W(\xi)\, d\xi \ , \qquad (1)$$

where $W(x)$ is glacier width at distance x from the "headwall" or upstream end (in this case, the south crater wall), $\bar{H}(x)$ is average depth at a cross section, and $\dot{b}(x)$ is the local mass

Figure 16. Terminus (lower center) of east Crater Glacier on June 15, 2005. View to south. Compare to indistinct terminus as seen about 5 years earlier (fig. 1). Arrow indicates bulge similarly indicated in figure 10. The glacier is only about 100 to 150 m wide where it passes between crater wall and old lava dome (right center) USGS photograph by S.P. Schilling.

balance expressed as a thickness per unit time. Equation 1 is simply a mathematical statement of the steady-state assumption, namely, that the glacier is neither thickening nor thinning. We apply equation 1 to what would become (during the eruption) east Crater Glacier and estimate U_b near the terminus (at a position we denote by $x = L$) by taking $L \approx 1.2$ km, $\overline{H} \approx 60$ m (fig. 14*A*), and an average value $\dot{b} \approx 4$ m/yr (from a total ice accumulation of about 80×10^6 m^3 over an area of about 1 km^2

Figure 17. West Crater Glacier adjacent to westward-growing lava dome as seen on September 2, 2005. View to southeast. The crevasse pattern in the glacier is complicated and reflects shifting directions of dome growth, but those crevasses normal to the dome-glacier margin are the youngest.
USGS photograph by M. Logan.

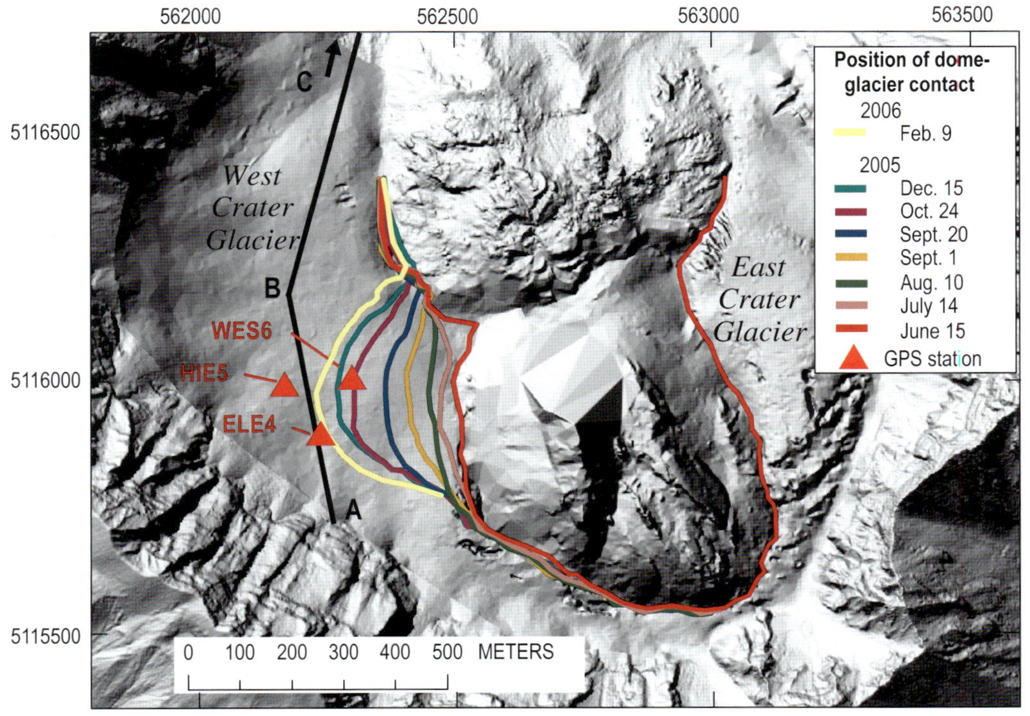

Figure 18. Migration of contact between the new lava dome and west Crater Glacier during the period June 15, 2005, to February 9, 2006. Contact position was determined from DEMs, with a probable error of about 5 m. Background image is hillshade-relief map for June 15, 2005. Coordinates are UTM zone 10 easting and northing, North American datum 1983. As the new dome grew, the glacier encroached upon margin of the old (1980–86) lava dome. Also shown are positions of three GPS stations that were deployed on the glacier at various times in 2005.

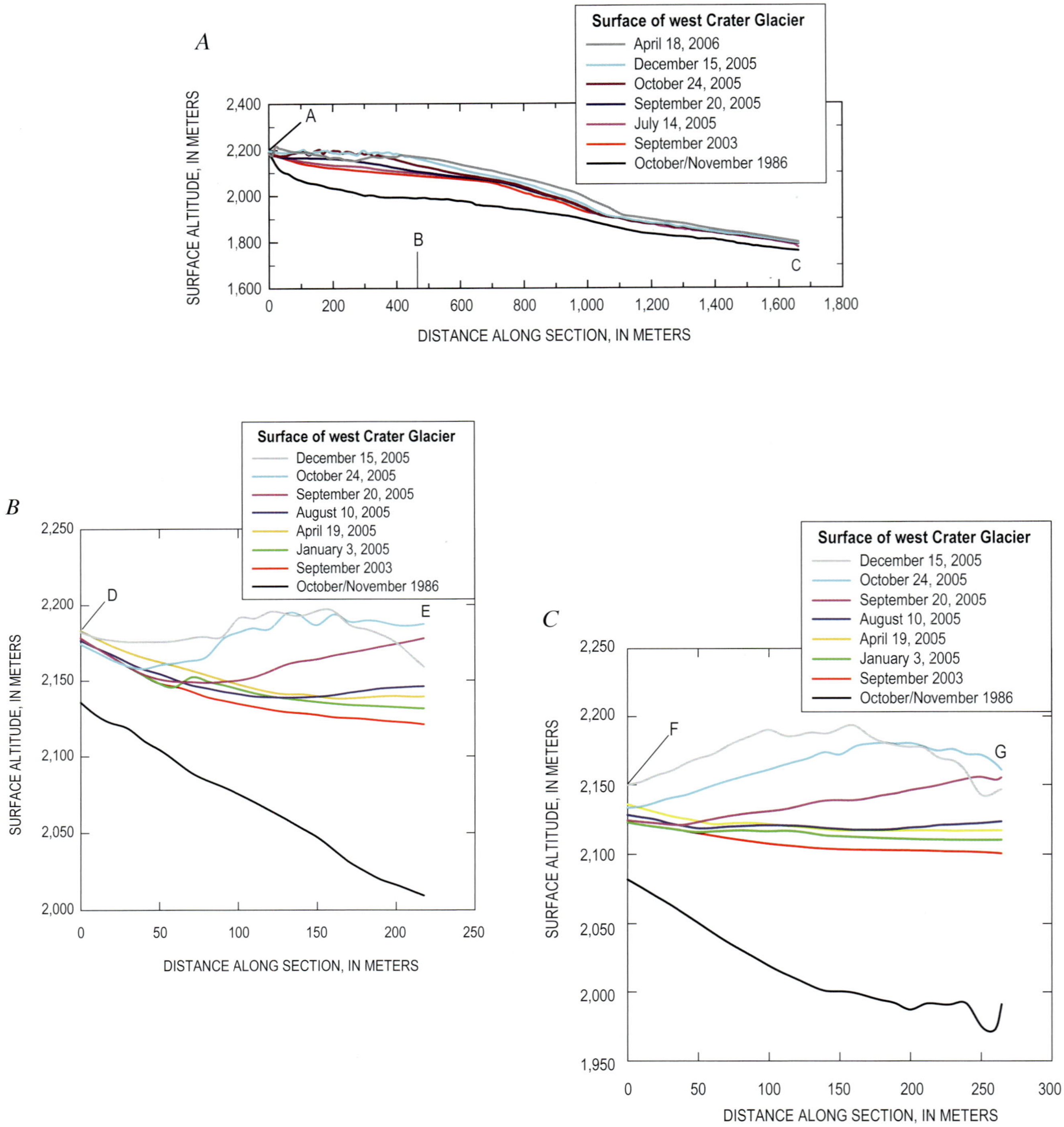

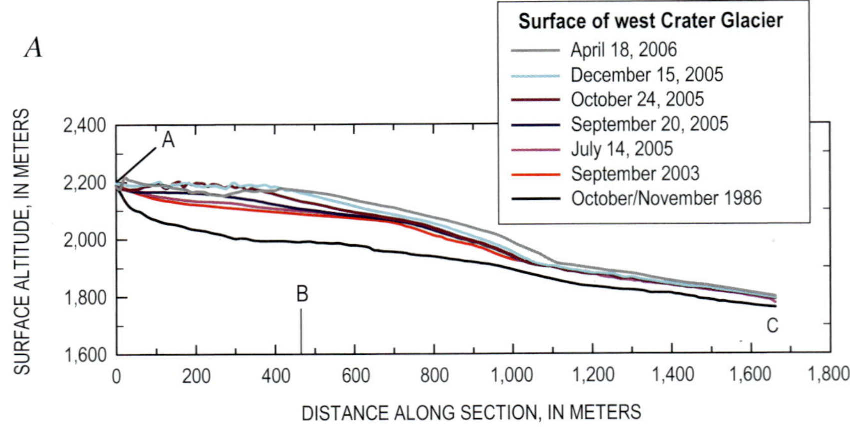

Figure 19. Change in surface altitude of west Crater Glacier during course of ongoing eruption, based on sequential DEMs. Lines of sections shown in figure 13. The 1986 profile represents the ground surface at end of the 1980–86 dome-building episode and is approximately the glacier bed. The 2003 profile should be within a few meters altitude of glacier surface at beginning of current eruption. *A*, Longitudinal section A–B–C, approximately following the thickest ice. The points labeled A, B, and C match those in figure 13*A*. *B*, Transverse section D–E. *C*, Transverse section F–G. *D*, Transverse section H–I. *E*, Transverse section J–K.

in 20 years), and by treating W as a constant. We find $U_b \approx 0.24$ m/d, which corresponds to a surface speed of about 0.29 m/d for ice with the flow-law exponent $n = 3$ (van der Veen, 1999, p. 103–106). We emphasize that this is at best a rough baseline for thinking about the preeruption surface speed, because the glacier was manifestly not in a steady state but rather growing.

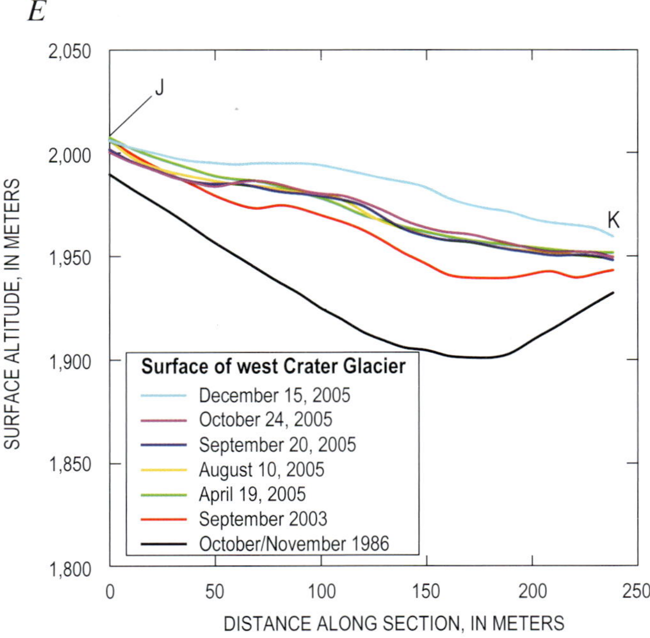

Figure 19—Continued.

East Crater Glacier

The GPS station positions during 2005 are shown in figure 13B; measured displacement rates are shown in figure 22. Interestingly, the balance velocity estimated above is comparable to the speed of station ICY4, which was downglacier of the

Figure 20. The glacier in Mount St. Helens crater as seen on September 12, 2006. View to south. As bulge on west Crater Glacier advanced and impinged on relatively flat terminus area, a shear zone delineated by echelon fractures developed (solid red curve). The shear zone at its northern end took on the character of a zone of compression, with crevasses parallel to direction of maximum compression (dotted red lines). Positions of GPS stations JOEA and JOEC are indicated. USGS photograph by W.E. Scott.

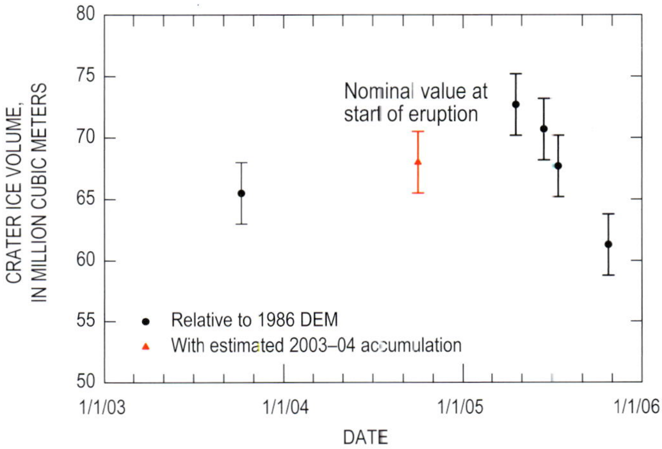

Figure 21. Total volume of glacier in Mount St. Helens crater as a function of time, with error bars (±1σ).

domain squeezed by the lava dome, on ice about 70 m thick and not far from the ECG terminus (fig. 10). In comparison, ICY5, about 300 m upglacier of ICY4, within the glacier reach being squeezed by dome growth (fig. 12) and on ice about 150 m thick, moved about 1.3 m/d, or about four times as fast as ICY4. This comparison presents a conundrum if deformation is only by simple shear and reflects a balance between gravitational driving stress and drag on the glacier bed and sides, in which case the difference in surface velocity between ICY4 and ICY5 should have been a factor of about $(150/70)^{n+1} \approx 21$ for a flow-law exponent $n = 3$ (van der Veen, 1999, p. 103–104). Moreover, owing to the nonlinear rheology of glacier ice (van der Veen, 1999, p. 13–15), the squeeze exerted on east Crater Glacier by the growing lava dome should have reduced the effective viscosity of the ice near ICY5 and made the difference in speed from ICY4 to ICY5 even greater. Resolution of the conundrum involves recognizing that gravitational driving stress is in fact resisted not only by drag but also by gradients in stress along the flow (van der Veen, 1999). A useful mechanical analogy is to think of east Crater Glacier, during the squeezing episode, as a tube of toothpaste with the cap removed. If the entire tube were squeezed uniformly, toothpaste would squirt out rapidly, but if squeezing is applied only to the part of the tube farthest from the opening, the toothpaste nearer the opening acts as a dam. Computational modeling by Price and Walder (2007) has confirmed the existence of a very strong longitudinal stress gradient.

Strain rates associated with ECG deformation can be estimated, in part, by considering the rate of eastward migration of the dome-glacier contact and the rate of glacier-surface uplift. Dividing the rate of eastward migration of the dome-glacier contact near ELE4 (fig. 12) by the glacier width (about 300 m), the average rate of contact migration for the period December 1, 2004, to January 3, 2005, corresponds to a squeeze strain rate of about –0.006/d; for the period January 3, 2005, to April 16, 2005, the squeeze strain rate was about –0.0036/d. Elongational strain rate in the downglacier direction cannot be estimated directly owing to the fact that there were never simultaneously two GPS units on the reach being squeezed. The strain rate associated with glacier thickening for the period January 3, 2005, to April 16, 2005, can be roughly estimated (see fig. 14*A*) at about $(0.6 \text{ m/d})/(100 \text{ m}) \approx 0.006/\text{d}$ near the centerline of east Crater Glacier.

To put the ECG strain-rate values in perspective, consider ice moving through a valley constriction at a rate of 100 m/y, with the valley narrowing by 25 percent over a length of 1 km—arguably a rather severe constriction. The lateral strain rate in this case would be –0.0001/d, or about 1–3 percent of the lateral strain rate associated with squeezing of the ECG. Thickening strain rate as large as that measured at ECG is known only from surge fronts (Kamb and others, 1985; Raymond and others, 1987), although in such cases the maximum compression is oriented along the normal ice-flow direction, whereas with ECG, maximum compression was transverse to the normal ice-flow direction.

West Crater Glacier

The GPS stations on west Crater Glacier during the summers of 2005 and 2006 (fig. 13*B*) recorded the response of the glacier to westward dome growth. We discuss results for 2005 and 2006 separately.

In 2005 (fig. 23), the peak in speed of ELE4 at about day 273 (September 30) occurred a few days before the appearance of spine 7 just east of spine 6 (fig. 8; Vallance and others, this volume, chap. 9). This peak in speed probably reflects a change in the stresses applied to WCG by the dome. During the 23-day period when the GPS records overlapped, all three stations on WCG accelerated rather smoothly (fig. 23*B*); differences in azimuth of motion reflect the local direction of dome growth. The displacement records for the overlap

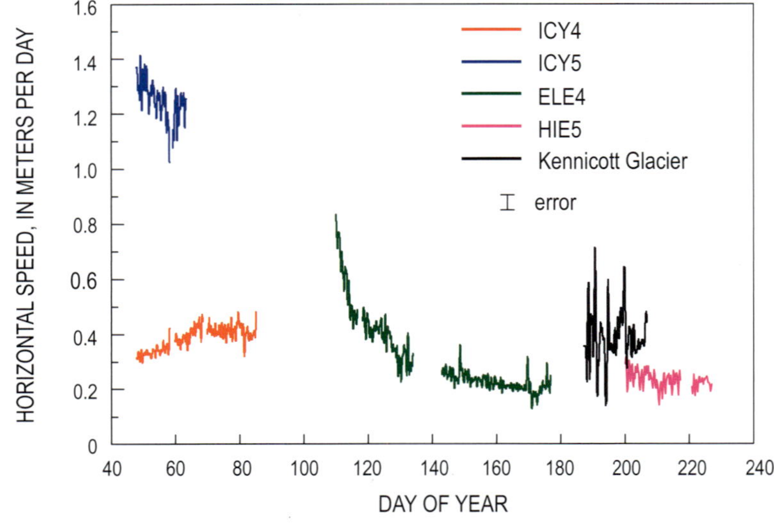

Figure 22 Horizontal speed of east Crater Glacier GPS stations. Locations of the stations shown in figure 12. Raw position data were filtered to remove spurious spikes and interpolated to 0.2-d intervals. Estimated error is 0.05 m/d. ICY4 and ICY5 were on glacier in mid- to late winter 2005 while the new lava dome was expanding eastward. ELE4 was fortuitously placed on glacier about the time that dome growth to east stopped, and it stayed on the glacier until early summer 2005. HIE5 was on the glacier in mid-summer 2005. Azimuth of motion for all stations was within 18° of north. Shown for comparison are surface-speed data (adapted from Anderson and others, 2005) for a target on Kennicott Glacier, a temperate valley glacier in Alaska, during the year 2000. The record for Kennicott Glacier shows large-amplitude, commonly diurnal fluctuations not seen at east Crater Glacier.

period were analyzed to determine direction and magnitude of the principal strain rates within the (approximately horizontal) plane determined by the three stations. Unsurprisingly, the direction of principal compression lined up closely with the trend of crevasses that formed during westward dome growth (fig. 17). Magnitudes of principal horizontal strain rates increased slowly over time, with their sum consistently negative at about −0.002/d. Making the plausible interpretation that surface uplift represents thickening of the glacier, vertical strain rate can be estimated as the average uplift rate divided by the glacier thickness, or about (0.25 m/d)/(120 m) = 0.002/d. The sum of the three principal strain rates was thus locally near zero, consistent with bulk incompressibility.

In 2006, we had motion data for three GPS stations located on WCG downglacier of the region being squeezed by the lava dome: DAVF, which operated for several months (during which time the station was relocated three times to prevent it from toppling into a crevasse), and JOEA and JOEC which operated for about six weeks during summer (fig. 24). Station DAVF was slightly upglacier of the cross section H–I (fig. 13*A*), on ice that thickened steadily as west Crater Glacier was squeezed (fig. 19*D*). Although the motion record for DAVF (fig. 24*A*) is complicated by the effect of crevasse growth and the need to move the instrument, there is again an absence of the diurnal speed variation we would expect if glacier sliding were occurring. The motion records for JOEA and JOEC (fig. 24*B*), located only about 150 m apart, nicely document deformation associated with the shear zone shown in figure 20. Station JOEA (east of the shear zone), on ice being shoved as the bulge in the WCG surface propagates downglacier and impinges upon the terminus region, moved nearly three times as fast as JOEC (west of the shear zone). The difference in azimuth of motion between JOEA and JOEC almost certainly reflects the opening of roughly north-south-striking crevasses (fig. 20).

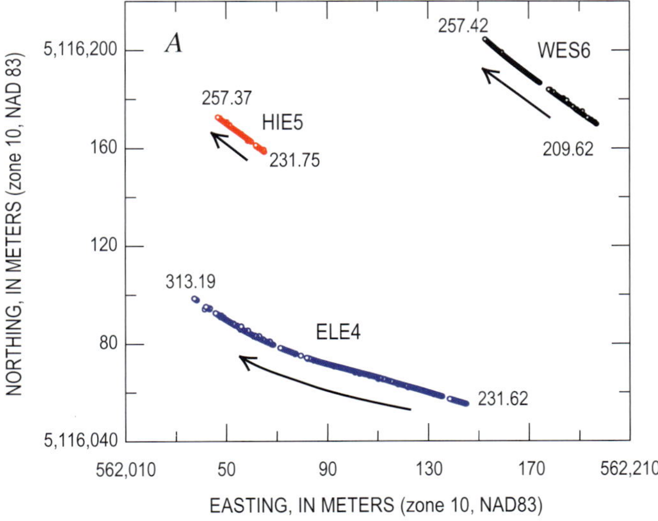

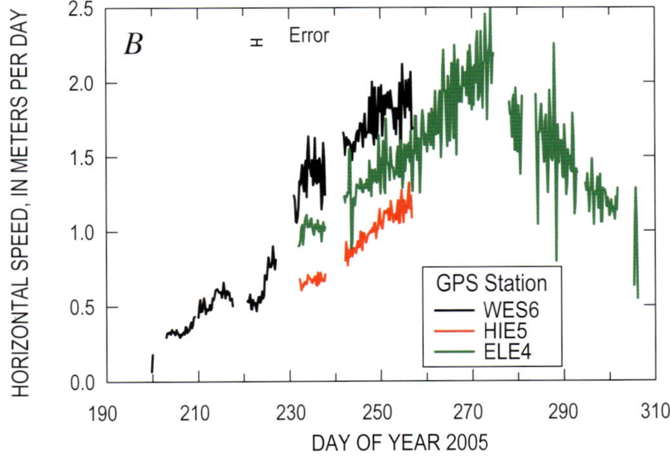

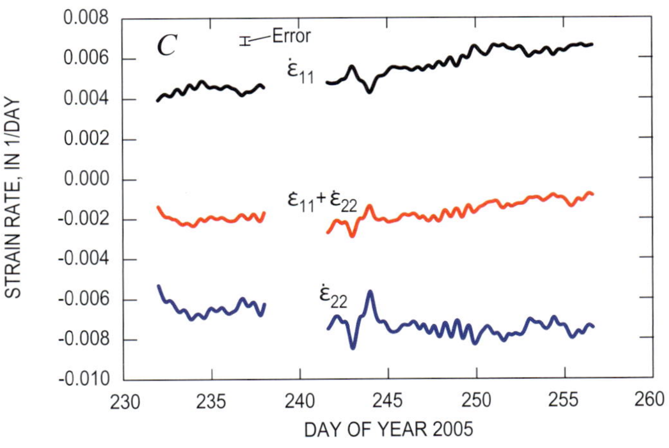

Inferences About Glacier and Volcano Hydrology

Temperate glaciers (those with ice at the melting point) move by a combination of internal creep and sliding of the ice over the bed (van der Veen, 1999). The creep component reflects the internal stress state of the glacier rather than conditions at the bed, whereas the sliding component reflects the boundary condition at the bed—in particular, how much friction there is against the bed. Measurements at many

Figure 23. GPS-derived motion data for west Crater Glacier in 2005. *A*, Displacement trajectories projected into horizontal plane, with day of year at beginning and end indicated. *B*, Horizontal speeds, calculated by filtering raw position data to remove spurious spikes, interpolating to 0.2-d intervals, and applying centered difference. Estimated error, shown by error bar, is 0.05 m/d. As with the east Crater Glacier record (fig. 22), diurnal speed fluctuations are not seen at west Crater Glacier. *C*, Principal strain rates in horizontal plane. Orientation of maximum extension ($\dot{\varepsilon}_{11}$) is N. 10° E.–S. 10° W.; orientation of maximum compression ($\dot{\varepsilon}_{22}$) is N. 80° W.–S. 80° E. For strictly incompressible ice, the sum $\dot{\varepsilon}_{11}+\dot{\varepsilon}_{22}$ would be zero.

glaciers have shown systematic differences between surface speed during the ablation (melt) season and during winter. For example, pulses of increased surface speed are commonly observed as the melt season begins (Anderson and others, 2004). More generally, surface speed in summer is higher than in winter, and large diurnal variations in surface speed are common (Fountain and Walder, 1998). As the creep component of glacier motion should be reasonably constant, variations in surface speed reflect variations in sliding speed, which is modulated by meltwater at the bed (see, for example, Harper and others, 2002). Our 2005 data for east Crater Glacier (fig. 22), however, show neither acceleration with the onset of the melt season nor a clear diurnal signal; data for west Crater Glacier from the summers of 2005 and 2006 (figs. 23, 24) similarly lack any diurnal signal. We propose as an explanation that there simply is no pressurized drainage system conveying water along the bed. Crater Glacier grew atop several tens of meters of rubble (mainly rock-avalanche debris) that had accumulated on the crater floor following the eruption of May 18, 1980 (Mills, 1992). As argued in appendix 1, much of this rubble is likely to be ice free because geothermal heat flow will have melted interstitial ice, and flow of the overlying ice downward into the rubble will have been slow. The volcanic edifice beneath this rubble is geologically complex, consisting of multiple lava flows, pyroclastic and lahar deposits, and other fragmental deposits (Crandell, 1987). Thus, water that reaches the glacier bed probably flows out of the crater through the rubble layer or downward into the volcano's groundwater system, rather than moving along the glacier bed. In support of this hypothesis, we note that there are no outlet streams at the glacier termini, although there are springs and seeps farther downslope. Discharge in Loowit Creek, which heads several hundred meters downstream of the WCG and ECG termini and drains the crater, is not measured regularly, owing to the impossibility of maintaining a permanent gaging station in the very unstable stream channel. However, such occasional discharge measurements as have been made (fig. 25) show no evidence for systematically elevated streamflow during the eruption.

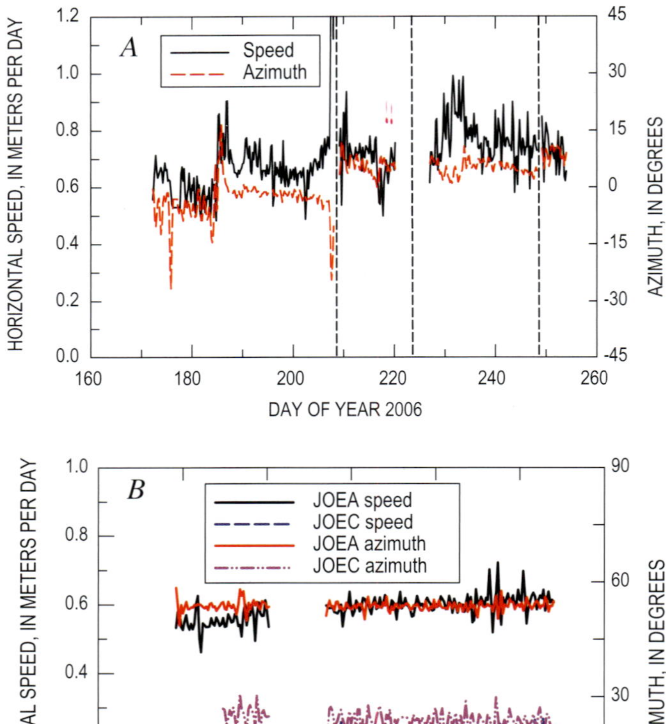

Figure 24. Motion data for GPS stations on the surface of west Crater Glacier in 2006. Estimated errors about 0.05 m/d for speed and 2 degrees for azimuth. See figure 13*B* for locations of the GPS stations. *A*, Horizontal speed and azimuth of GPS station DAVF. Dashed lines indicate breaks in data when instrument was moved to keep it from toppling into crevasses that formed during its stay. *B*, Horizontal speed and azimuth of GPS stations JOEA and JOEC.

Inferences from Glacier Dynamics Bearing on Lava-Dome Mechanics

We envisage outward push on Crater Glacier by the expanding Mount St. Helens dome as involving not glacier sliding, as usually considered by glaciologists, but low-angle thrust faulting. In our view, the glacier is being pushed over the underlying unconsolidated rock debris, with the décollement probably near the glacier bed (glacier bed being a rather ill-defined concept in the present case, as discussed earlier). Our conception of the process is sketched in figure 26. Glacier deformation

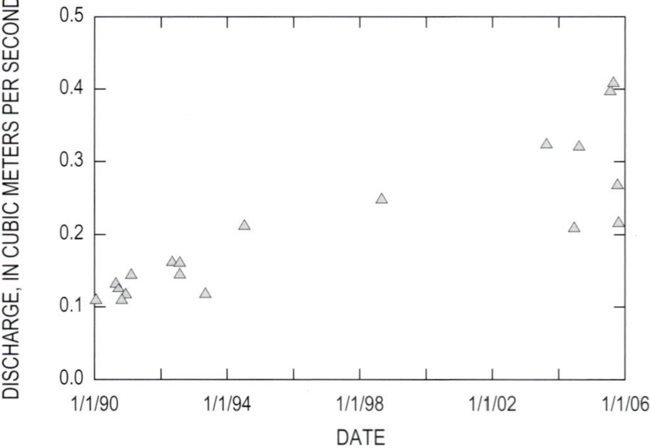

Figure 25. Discharge in Loowit Creek measured above Loowit Falls, from unpublished streamflow data collected by hydrologic surveillance staff at Cascades Volcano Observatory. Probable error in measurements is about 10 percent.

is for all intents and purposes quasistatic—accelerations can be ignored—so conservation of momentum reduces to a force balance. The force exerted by the lava dome will be balanced by the sum of resisting forces within the ice and at the glacier bed,

$$p \approx |\tau_{nn}| + (W/H)\tau_b, \tag{2}$$

where p is the pressure (force per unit area) exerted by the lava dome, τ_{nn} is the deviatoric stress within the ice normal to the dome-glacier contact, W is the width of the glacier (that is, the distance from the dome to the crater wall), H is a typical value of ice thickness, and τ_b is the magnitude of the shear stress opposing displacement of the glacier in a direction normal to the dome-ice margin (fig. 26). If motion on the décollement involves essentially Coulomb friction (that is, frictional resistance proportional to the normal load), then $\tau_b \approx \mu\rho_i gH$, where μ is the coefficient of friction, ρ_i is the density of ice, and g is acceleration due to gravity, and our estimate for p becomes

$$p \approx |\tau_{nn}| + \mu\rho_i gW. \tag{3}$$

We have taken the normal stress on the décollement to be equal to the ice-overburden pressure. Thus we are supposing that water pressure on the décollement is negligible, as is reasonable, because, as noted above, water at the glacier bed apparently flows downward into the volcano rather than in a pressurized drainage system along the bed.

We now estimate the magnitude of the two terms on the right-hand side of equation 3. The deviatoric stress within the ice normal to the dome-glacier contact, τ_{nn}, can be estimated if we take into account the rheological behavior of glacier ice as (see appendix 3):

$$\tau_{nn} = B|\dot{\varepsilon}_e|^{-2/3}\,\dot{\varepsilon}_{nn}, \tag{4}$$

where $\dot{\varepsilon}_{nn}$ is the strain rate normal to the dome-glacier contact and the so-called effective strain rate $\dot{\varepsilon}_e$ (equal to one-half the second invariant of the strain-rate tensor) is in this case given by

$$2\dot{\varepsilon}_e^{\,2} = \dot{\varepsilon}_{nn}^2 + \dot{\varepsilon}_{tt}^2 + \dot{\varepsilon}_{zz}^2, \tag{5}$$

where $\dot{\varepsilon}_{tt}$ is the strain rate tangential to the dome-glacier contact and $\dot{\varepsilon}_{zz}$ is the vertical strain rate. In writing equation 5, we assume that the directions normal and tangential to the dome-glacier contact are the directions of principal strain rates, an assumption that is supported by the available data. Using $B = 5.3\times10^7$ Pa·s$^{1/3}$ (Paterson, 1994; van der Veen, 1999) and the strain-rate calculations given above, we estimate $|\tau_{nn}| \approx$ 0.16–0.21 MPa. Taking $\mu \approx 0.5$ (consistent with there being considerable debris within the ice and thus much rock-to-rock friction at the décollement), $\rho_i = 900\,\text{kg/m}^3$ (corresponding to glacier ice, not snow or firn), g = 9.8 m/s^2, and $W \approx$ 250 m, the frictional term on the right-hand side of equation 3 has a magnitude of about 1.1 MPa. Frictional resistance on the décollement therefore dominates the force balance, with the estimated value of p being about 1.3 MPa. This estimate is admittedly rough, as we have not factored in the complicated geometry of the real system.

Summary and Outlook for the Future

The eruption of Mount St. Helens that began in fall 2004 has presented us with the first-ever opportunity to observe and document emplacement of a lava dome through glacier ice. The eruption has not caused any rapid melting of Crater Glacier, but the effects on the glacier have nonetheless been striking. Dome growth cut the glacier in two and then successively squeezed the two parts. Measurements using both specialized, helicopter-deployed GPS stations and photogrammetrically derived DEMs showed that the two glaciers underwent deformation of an extreme variety, with strain rates of extraordinary magnitude as compared to those in normal alpine temperate glaciers. Moreover, the GPS-derived motion records make clear that Crater Glacier is fundamentally unlike normal alpine glaciers, in that there is no evidence that it slides over its bed. The most reasonable explanation for this anomaly is that meltwater reaching the glacier bed enters the volcano's groundwater system rather than flowing toward the glacier terminus through a drainage network along the bed.

The part of east Crater Glacier that underwent thickening has been thinning since dome growth shifted to the west in April 2005, and normal ice flow has moved mass downstream. Terminus advance is likely to continue unless eruptive processes remove substantial glacier mass. West Crater Glacier is likely to evolve similarly in the short term, with terminus dynamics complicated by the formation of the shear zone shown in figure 20. The pattern of snow accumulation in the crater has been radically perturbed, with heat from the new lava dome locally preventing accumulation. Sufficiently prolonged dome growth could, of course, completely eliminate ice from the crater (and indeed completely eliminate the crater itself). Glaciers at Mount St. Helens come and go, modulated by the style and rhythm of eruptive behavior.

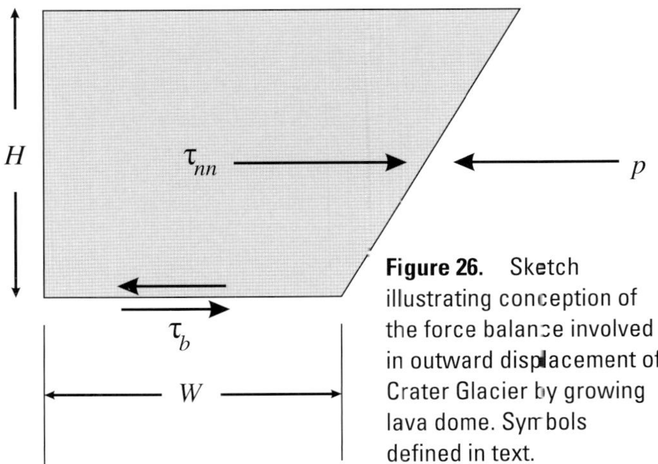

Figure 26. Sketch illustrating conception of the force balance involved in outward displacement of Crater Glacier by growing lava dome. Symbols defined in text.

Acknowledgments

R.M. Iverson and S.P. Anderson made helpful comments on an earlier version of this manuscript. DEMs were prepared by J. Messerich of the U.S. Geological Survey Photogrammetric Lab, Denver, Colorado, using aerial photographs taken by Bergman Photographic Services.

References Cited

Anderson, R.S., Anderson, S.P., MacGregor, K.R., Waddington, E.D., O'Neel, S., Riihimaki, C.A., and Loso, M.G., 2004, Strong feedbacks between hydrology and sliding of a small alpine glacier: Journal of Geophysical Research (Earth Surfaces), v. 109, F03005, 17 p., doi:10.1029/2004JF000120.

Anderson, R.S., Walder, J.S., Anderson, S.P., Trabant, D.C., and Fountain, A.G., 2005, The dynamic response of Kennicott Glacier to the Hidden Creek Lake outburst flood: Annals of Glaciology, v. 40, p. 237–242.

Brugman, M.M., and Meier, M.F., 1981, Response of glaciers to the eruptions of Mount St. Helens, *in* Lipman, P.W., and Mullineaux, D.R., eds., The 1980 eruptions of Mount St. Helens, Washington: U.S. Geological Survey Professional Paper 1250, p. 743–756.

Crandell, D.R., 1987, Deposits of pre-1980 pyroclastic flows and lahars from Mount St. Helens volcano, Washington: U.S. Geological Survey Professional Paper 1444, 91 p.

Fountain, A.G., and Walder, J.S., 1998, Water flow through temperate glaciers: Reviews of Geophysics, v. 36, no. 3, p. 299–328.

Gilbert, J.S., Stasiuk, M.V., Lane, S.J., Adam, C.R., Murphy, M.D., Sparks, R.S.J., and Naranjo, J.A., 1996, Non-explosive, constructional evolution of the ice-filled caldera at Volcán Sollipulli, Chile: Bulletin of Volcanology, v. 58, no. 1, p. 67–83.

Guðmundsson, M.T., Sigmundsson, F., and Björnsson, H., 1997, Ice–volcano interaction of the 1996 Gjálp subglacial eruption, Vatnajökull, Iceland: Nature, v. 389, no. 6654, p. 954–957.

Hallet, B., 1979, A theoretical model of glacial abrasion: Journal of Glaciology, v. 23, no. 89, p. 321–334.

Harper, J.T., Humphrey, N.F., and Greenwood, M.C., 2002, Basal conditions and glacier motion during the winter/spring transition, Worthington Glacier, Alaska, U.S.A.: Journal of Glaciology, v. 48, no. 160, p. 42–50.

Iverson, N.R., and Semmens, D., 1995. Intrusion of ice into porous media by regelation; a mechanism of sediment entrainment by glaciers: Journal of Geophysical Research, v. 100, no. B6, p. 10219–10230.

Kamb, B., Raymond, C.F., Harrison, W.D., Engelhardt, H., Echelmeyer, K.A., Humphrey, N., Brugman, M.M., and Pfeffer, T., 1985, Glacier surge mechanism; 1982–1983 surge of Variegated Glacier, Alaska: Science, v. 227, no. 4686, p. 469–479.

LaHusen, R.G., Swinford, K.J., Logan, M., and Lisowski, M., 2008, Instrumentation in remote and dangerous settings; examples using data from GPS "spider" deployments during the 2004–2005 eruption of Mount St. Helens, Washington, chap. 16 *of* Sherrod, D.R., Scott, W.E., and Stauffer, P.H., eds., A volcano rekindled; the renewed eruption of Mount St. Helens, 2004–2006: U.S. Geological Survey Professional Paper 1750 (this volume).

Major, J.J., and Newhall, C.G., 1989, Snow and ice perturbations during historical volcanic eruptions and the formation of lahars and floods: Bulletin of Volcanology, v. 52, no. 1, p. 1–27.

Mills, H.H., 1992, Post-eruption erosion and deposition in the 1980 crater of Mount St. Helens, Washington, determined from digital maps: Earth Surface Processes and Landforms, v.17, no. 8, p. 739–754.

Murav'ev, Ya.D., and Salamatin, A.N., 1990, Mass balance and thermal regime of a crater glacier at Ushkovskii Volcano: Volcanology and Seismology, v. 11, no. 3, p. 411–424.

Paterson, W.S.B., 1994, The physics of glaciers (3d ed.): Oxford, Pergamon, 480 p.

Philip, J.R., 1980, Thermal fields during regelation: Cold Regions Science and Technology, v. 3, nos. 2–3, p. 193–203.

Price, S.F., and Walder, J.S., 2007, Modeling the dynamic response of a crater glacier to lava-dome emplacement: Mount St. Helens, Washington, U.S.A.: Annals of Glaciology, v. 45, no. 1, p. 21–28, doi:10.3189/172756407782282525.

Raymond, C.F., 1987, How do glaciers surge?: Journal of Geophysical Research, v. 92, no. B9, p. 9121–9134.

Raymond, C., Johannesson, T., Pfeffer, T., and Sharp. M., 1987, Propagation of a glacier surge into stagnant ice: Journal of Geophysical Research, v. 92, no. B9, p. 9037–9049.

Salamatin, A.N., and Murav'ev, Ya.D., 1992, Some results of a study of the physical characteristics of the glacial stratum on the slopes of the Klyuchevskoy volcano: Volcanology and Seismology, v. 13, no. 2, p. 230–240.

Schilling, S.P., Carrara, P.E., Thompson, R.A., and Iwatsubo, E.Y., 2004, Posteruption glacier development within the crater of Mount St. Helens, Washington, USA: Quaternary

Research, v. 61, no. 3, p. 325–329.

Schilling, S.P., Thompson, R.A., Messerich, J.A., and Iwatsubo, E.Y., 2008, Use of digital aerophotogrammetry to determine rates of lava dome growth, Mount St. Helens, Washington, 2004–2005, chap. 8 *of* Sherrod, D.R., Scott, W.E., and Stauffer, P.H., eds., A volcano rekindled; the renewed eruption of Mount St. Helens, 2004–2006: U.S. Geological Survey Professional Paper 1750 (this volume).

Schneider, D.J., Vallance, J.W., Wessels, R.L., Logan, M., and Ramsey, M.S., 2008, Use of thermal infrared imaging for monitoring renewed dome growth at Mount St. Helens, 2004, chap. 17 *of* Sherrod, D.R., Scott, W.E., and Stauffer, P.H., eds., A volcano rekindled; the renewed eruption of Mount St. Helens, 2004–2006: U.S. Geological Survey Professional Paper 1750 (this volume).

Simons, F.S., and Mathewson, D.E., 1955, Geology of Great Sitkin Island, Alaska: U.S. Geological Survey Bulletin 1028–B, 43 p.

Tuffen, H., Gilbert, J., and McGarvie, D., 2001, Products of an effusive subglacial rhyolite eruption; Bláhnúkur, Torfajökull, Iceland: Bulletin of Volcanology, v. 63, nos. 2–3, p. 179–190.

Vallance, J.W., Schneider, D.J., and Schilling, S.P., 2008, Growth of the 2004–2006 lava-dome complex at Mount St. Helens, Washington, chap. 9 *of* Sherrod, D.R., Scott, W.E., and Stauffer, P.H., eds., A volcano rekindled; the renewed eruption of Mount St. Helens, 2004–2006: U.S. Geological Survey Professional Paper 1750 (this volume).

van der Veen, C.J., 1999, Fundamentals of glacier dynamics: Rotterdam, A.A. Balkema, 462 p.

Walder, J.S., LaHusen, R.G., Vallance, J.W., and Schilling, S.P., 2005, Crater glaciers on active volcanoes; hydrological anomalies: Eos (American Geophysical Union Transactions), v. 86, no. 50, p. 521, 528.

Walder, J.S., LaHusen, R.G., Vallance, J.W., and Schilling, S.P., 2007, Emplacement of a silicic lava dome through a crater glacier; Mount St Helens, 2004–06: Annals of Glaciology, v. 45, no. 1, p. 14–20, doi:10.3189/172756407782282426.

Appendix 1. Interstitial Ice in Crater-Floor Rock Debris

As shown by Mills (1992) and noted above, until about 1986, material accumulating on the Mount St. Helens crater floor consisted primarily of rock-avalanche material with interstitial snow. After 1986, the volumetric rate of snow accumulation exceeded the accumulation rate of rock debris. By the time the 2004 eruption began, the crater-fill material was locally as thick as 200 m, and it is hard to envisage that any interstitial snow within the lowermost fill would not have transformed to glacier ice (Paterson, 1994). However, there is reason to believe that some of the deepest fill may in fact be ice free, because interstitial ice within the rock framework will be melted by geothermal heat and not replaced by ice from above. If all heat flux from below causes melting, then the melt rate $\dot{m}$, expressed as thickness per unit time, will be given by the ratio of the geothermal heat flux, q_G, to the energy required to melt a unit volume of ice,

$$\dot{m} = \frac{q_G}{\phi \rho_i L}, \qquad (6)$$

where ϕ is porosity of the avalanche debris, ρ_i is the density of ice, and L is the heat of fusion. If one considers a glacier in a nonvolcanic setting, then taking $\phi = 0$, $L = 3.35 \quad 10^5$ J/kg, and $q_G = 0.05$ W/m^2, one finds $\dot{m} \approx 5$ mm/yr. In a volcanic setting, q_G could easily be one hundred times greater (Murav'ev and Salamatin, 1990; Salamatin and Murav'ev, 1992), and taking $\phi \approx 0.4$ for the crater-fill avalanche debris, one finds $\dot{m} \approx 1$ m/yr. Clearly melting can proceed rapidly, although we stress that these estimates for $\dot{m}$ are upper bounds, because ground water could carry away some of the geothermal heat flux.

The rate at which overlying glacier ice can flow into the avalanche debris is very low. The ice intrusion rate V is proportional to the gradient of ice pressure across the debris layer (Iverson and Semmens, 1995):

$$V = K_s P_g, \qquad (7)$$

where P_g is the gradient of ice pressure across the debris layer, and the proportionality constant K_s is analogous to hydraulic conductivity for ground-water flow. The constant K_s can be determined on theoretical grounds (Philip, 1980) in the case that the debris grain size is small enough that ice flow is dominantly by regelation, with plastic creep negligible; experimental results of Iverson and Semmens (1995) support Philip's theory. The crater-fill debris is coarse enough that plastic creep is necessary for the ice to flow through the pore space (Hallet, 1979), so the regelation-only value $K_S \approx 3 \times 10^{-15}$ m^2/Pa·s will give an overestimate of V. The ice pressure gradient P_g obviously depends upon the thickness of the ice-filled debris layer and the pressure of the overlying ice. For present purposes, suppose that the overburden pressure is 1 MPa (corresponding to an ice thickness of about 110 m) and the thickness of the ice-filled debris layer is 10 m. We then find from equation 7 that an upper-bound estimate of V is about 0.01 m/yr. A balance between $\dot{m}$ and V can exist only if the ice-filled debris layer is very thin—a few centimeters at most. We conclude that the ice within the deepest crater fill ought to, over time, melt out and not be replenished. It seems likely that the deepest crater fill will act as an aquifer conveying water along the crater floor toward the glacier terminus.

Appendix 2. Calculating Glacier Volume

The change in total glacier volume within the crater of Mount St. Helens, over the course of the eruption, was determined by GIS methods. Details of the method can be understood with reference to figure 27. The area covered by the glacier before the eruption was broken into three parts: part A1 includes the area within which dome rock was emplaced, and parts A2 and A3 are the east and west glacier arms that were not disrupted directly by dome growth. The glacier volumes in A2 and A3 were determined by differencing DEMs for various dates with the October–November 1986 DEM, the latter representing, as we argued in the main text, approximately the bed of the crater glacier.

As we are only trying to track the change in glacier volume with time, rather than total glacier volume, the exact choice of datum for the bed is not critical. (The ambiguity in determining the bed, upon which we commented in the main text, is thus not a problem.) The glacier volume in A1 is calculated as follows: Using the 1986 DEM as the datum, let the difference between the total volume above this surface at some date τ be denoted by V_τ, and the volume of extruded dome rock within A1 be given by V_d. (The calculation of V_d is described by Schilling and others, this volume, chap. 8.) The glacier volume within A1 is then $V_\tau - V_d$. This volume is added to the volumes in A2 and A3 to get the total glacier volume. The error in this total volume can be estimated as the total glacier surface area (1.0 km^2) times the root-mean-square error in the elevation-differencing procedure, which we take as 2.5 m. (This value follows from the 2.5 m error on the 1986 DEM, which was produced from a topographic map with contour interval of 5 m, and the 0.1 to 0.2 m error on later DEMs, which were produced directly from aerial photographs.

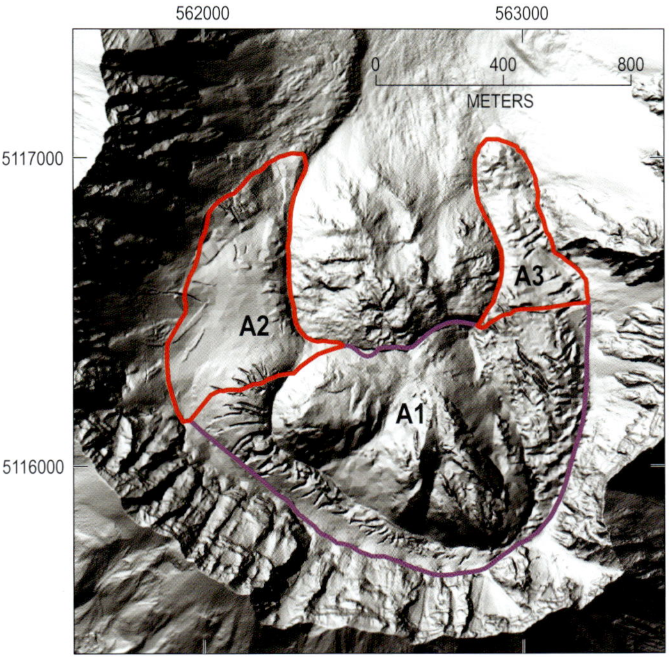

Figure 27. Separation of crater DEM coverages into three sections used in calculating total glacier volume as given in figure 21. Area A1 overlaps new lava dome, whereas areas A2 and A3 correspond to the downstream arms of west Crater Glacier and east Crater Glacier, respectively. Method of volume calculation is described in appendix 2. Background is hillshade-relief map based on DEM of October 24, 2005. Coodinates are UTM zone 10 easting and northing, North America datum 1983.

Appendix 3. Glacier Flow Dynamics

The flow law of ice is an empirical relation between stress and strain rate. For isotropic ice, the flow law is customarily written as the tensor relation (van der Veen, 1999)

$$\tau_{ij} = 2\eta\dot{\varepsilon}_{ij}, \qquad (8)$$

where τ_{ij} are deviatoric stresses, $\dot{\varepsilon}_{ij}$ are strain rates, and η is an effective viscosity that depends on the overall strain-rate field:

$$\eta = (B/2)\,\dot{\varepsilon}_e^{(1/n)-1}. \qquad (9)$$

B is a material property that depends on temperature, $n \approx 3$ for glacier ice (as compared to $n = 1$ for a Newtonian-viscous fluid like water), and $\dot{\varepsilon}_e$ is the effective strain rate, defined by the relation

$$2\dot{\varepsilon}_e^{\,2} = \dot{\varepsilon}_{xx}^2 + \dot{\varepsilon}_{yy}^2 + \dot{\varepsilon}_{zz}^2 + 2(\dot{\varepsilon}_{xy}^2 + \dot{\varepsilon}_{xz}^2 + \dot{\varepsilon}_{yz}^2). \qquad (10)$$

Here x, y, and z are arbitrary orthogonal coordinates. In the simple case of unidirectional slab flow—that is, flow driven by gravity and resisted by drag on the base (see, for example, van der Veen, 1999)—one could choose x as the downglacier coordinate, y as the cross-glacier coordinate, and z as normal to the glacier surface. The only nonzero strain-rate component would then be $\dot{\varepsilon}_{xz}$, in which case $\dot{\varepsilon}_e = |\dot{\varepsilon}_{xz}|$ and the flow law becomes a simple relation between shear stress and shear strain rate,

$$\tau_{xz} = B\,|\dot{\varepsilon}_{xz}|^{(1/n)-1}\,\dot{\varepsilon}_{xz}\,. \qquad (11)$$

We argued in the main text above that the crater glacier probably does not slide over its bed. The average strain rate $\dot{\varepsilon}_{xz}$ may therefore be estimated simply as the surface speed U divided by the glacier thickness H. Taking $U \approx 1$ m/d and $H \approx 150$ m in the part of east Crater Glacier experiencing lateral squeeze (see, for example, station ICY5 on fig. 14), the magnitude of the average strain rate $\dot{\varepsilon}_{xz}$ is then about 6.7×10^{-3}/d, comparable to the magnitude of the lateral strain rate $\dot{\varepsilon}_{yy}$ and vertical strain rate $\dot{\varepsilon}_{zz}$, which, as noted in the main text, averaged about 3×10^{-3}/d over the period of squeezing. The value $\dot{\varepsilon}_e$ is not well approximated by $|\dot{\varepsilon}_{xz}|$ in this case, and the nonzero (and in fact relatively large) values of $\dot{\varepsilon}_{yy}$ and $\dot{\varepsilon}_{zz}$ substantially reduce the effective viscosity (see equations 9 and 10).

In the slab-flow model, shear stress is simply proportional to depth and surface slope; that is, $\tau_{xz} = \rho_i g z \sin\theta$, where θ is surface slope and z increases downward from the glacier surface. One then finds that U depends upon flow ice thickness and slope according to the expression

$$U = \frac{2H}{n+1}\left(\frac{\rho_i g H \sin\theta}{B}\right)^n. \qquad (12)$$

With the usual value $n = 3$, the surface speed then varies as H^4.

Geodesy and Remote Sensing

The renewed eruption of Mount St. Helens provided many opportunities to bring modern geodetic tools—such as radar interferometry and GPS—to bear on monitoring what was, from 2004 to 2008, the only erupting volcano in the conterminous United States. The volume of lava extruded, about 0.1 km^3, proved small enough that geodetic signals associated with ground deformation were subtle and often difficult to interpret.

Surprises? The days and weeks leading to the seismic unrest of September 23, 2004, lacked demonstrable ground deformation. Presumably the volcano was already pressurized, its magma having moved into a position favorable for eruption as early as the late 1980s or early 1990s and awaiting only some incremental change that would initiate the final ascent. The amount of lava extruded between 2004 and 2006 was substantially greater than could be accounted for by reservoir withdrawal, according to models based on the GPS data. Instead, the discrepancy must be accounted for by some combination of magma recharge from greater depth and magma expansion by vesiculation in the shallow magma reservoir and its conduit.

It is this question of recharge by new magma—how much, from how deep, and of what composition?—that remains the inestimable puzzle, addressed partly by chapters in this section but raised again in sections describing modeling and mechanics, gas geochemistry, and petrology.

View southwest across spine 3 on November 29, 2004.
USGS photo by J.W. Vallance.

A Volcano Rekindled: The Renewed Eruption of Mount St. Helens, 2004–2006
Edited by David R. Sherrod, William E. Scott, and Peter H. Stauffer
U.S. Geological Survey Professional Paper 1750, 2008

Chapter 14

Constraints and Conundrums Resulting from Ground-Deformation Measurements Made During the 2004–2005 Dome-Building Eruption of Mount St. Helens, Washington

By Daniel Dzurisin[1], Michael Lisowski[1], Michael P. Poland[2], David R. Sherrod[1], and Richard G. LaHusen[1]

Abstract

A prolonged period of dome growth at Mount St. Helens starting in September–October 2004 provides an opportunity to study how the volcano deforms before, during, and after an eruption by using modern instruments and techniques, such as global positioning system (GPS) receivers and interferometric synthetic aperture radar (InSAR), together with more traditional ones, including tiltmeters, triangulation, photogrammetry, and time-lapse photography. No precursory ground deformation was detected by campaign GPS measurements made in 2000 and 2003, nor by a continuous GPS station (JRO1) operating ~9 km to the north-northwest of the vent area since May 1997. However, JRO1 abruptly began moving downward and southward, toward a source centered about 8 km beneath the volcano, concurrently with the start of a shallow earthquake swarm on September 23, 2004. The JRO1 velocity slowed from ~0.5 millimeters per day (mm/d) in late September–early October 2004 until spring 2005. Thereafter, it was essentially constant at ~0.04 mm/d through December 2005. In similar fashion, the growth rate of the welt on the south crater floor slowed from 8.9 m^3/s during October 4–11 to 6.4 m^3/s during October 11–13, 2004; this trend continued after emergence of the first lava spine on October 11. The volumetric extrusion rate decreased from 5.9 m^3/s during October 13–November 4, 2004, to 2.5 m^3/s during December 11, 2004–January 3, 2005, and for the remainder of 2005, it was in the range 2.0–0.7 m^3/s. Fifteen continuous GPS stations, installed soon after the eruption began, showed radially inward and downward ground motions through December 2005. Likewise, InSAR observations spanning the first year of the eruption indicate broad subsidence centered near the vent. Model-derived estimates of source-volume decrease from September 23, 2004, to October 31, 2006, are 16–24×10^6 m^3, substantially less than the volume erupted during the same period (87×10^6 m^3 through October 21, 2006). The discrepancy can be explained by a combination of magma expansion and recharge in the source region.

Lack of precursory deformation at JRO1 suggests that the conduit is poorly coupled to the rest of the edifice, so the rising magma column was able to push ahead older conduit material rather than intruding it. Constraints on conduit length and radius require that reservoir magma (as opposed to conduit-filling magma) reached the surface early during the eruption, probably soon after CO_2 emission rates peaked in early October 2004. If rapid emergence of spine 3 (the first whaleback-shaped extrusion) in late October 2004 marked the arrival of reservoir magma, then the volume of conduit material flushed from the system was about 20×10^6 m^3—the volume of surface deformation plus spines on November 4, 2004. The corresponding radius for a cylinder extending from the surface to depth d = 5 km is 35.7 m, or 28.2 m for d = 8 km. The average ascent rate through the conduit, assuming reservoir magma began its rise on September 23, 2004, was 120 m/d for d = 5 km, or 190 m/d for d = 8 km. Observed lineal extrusion rates were 2–10 m/d, so the conduit must widen considerably near the surface. Equating magma flux through the conduit to that at the surface, we obtain a vent radius of 125 m and an extrusion rate of 5.7 m^3/s—both values representative of the early part of the eruption.

Lack of precursory inflation suggests that the volcano was poised to erupt magma already stored in a crustal reservoir when JRO1 was installed in 1997. Trilateration and campaign GPS data indicate surface dilatation, presumably caused by reservoir expansion between 1982 and 1991, but no measurable deformation between 1991 and 2003. We conclude that all three of the traditionally reliable eruption

[1] U.S. Geological Survey, 1300 SE Cardinal Court, Vancouver, WA 98683

[2] U.S. Geological Survey, PO Box 51, Hawaii National Park, HI 96718

precursors (seismicity, ground deformation, and volcanic gas emission) failed to provide warning that an eruption was imminent until a few days before a visible welt appeared at the surface—a situation reminiscent of the 1980 north-flank bulge at Mount St. Helens.

Introduction

The deformational behavior of active basaltic shield volcanoes and large silicic magmatic systems (restless calderas) can be characterized in a general way by, respectively, (1) repeated inflation-deflation cycles in response to changes in crustal magma storage (for example, Kīlauea, Hawai'i, U.S.A., Dvorak and Okamura, 1987; Krafla, Iceland, Tryggvason, 1994), and (2) episodes of more gradual surface uplift or subsidence (bradyseisms) caused by magmatic inflation-deflation or hydrothermal system pressurization-depressurization (for example, Long Valley Caldera, Calif., U.S.A., Hill and others, 1985; Yellowstone caldera[3], Wyo., U.S.A., Dzurisin and others, 1999; Wicks and others, 2006; Phlegraean Fields caldera, Italy, Caputo, 1979). Deformation of stratovolcanoes of intermediate composition (andesite–dacite) is more varied and therefore more difficult to understand. Nonetheless, volcanoes of this type are numerous along the Pacific margin and, on short to intermediate time scales, they pose a greater threat to human populations than do basaltic shields or large silicic systems.

The reawakening of Mount St. Helens in 1980 following 123 years of quiescence provided a modern opportunity to study pre-, syn-, and post-eruptive deformation at an accessible and relatively well-studied stratovolcano. However, little was learned about any deep-seated deformation (source depth more than ~2 km) that might have occurred before the eruption because magma rose to shallow depth—as evidenced by the appearance of a bulge on the volcano's north flank by early April 1980 (fig. 1*A*)—before or soon after March 20, 1980, when a swarm of earthquakes caught volcanologists' attention and spurred the start of intensive monitoring (Lipman and others, 1981).

Renewed dome growth at Mount St. Helens starting in September–October 2004 (fig. 1*B*) provides a second opportunity to study how this volcano deforms before, during, and after an eruption—this time by using modern geodetic instruments and techniques, such as Global Positioning System (GPS) receivers (Lisowski and others, this volume, chap. 15; LaHusen and others, this volume, chap. 16) and interferometric synthetic aperture radar (InSAR, Poland and Lu, this volume, chap. 18), together with more traditional instruments and techniques, including tiltmeters, triangulation, photogrammetry, and time-lapse photography (Poland and others, this volume, chap. 11; Major and others, this volume, chap. 12). Deformation data from the first 15 months of the eruption (October 2004–December 2005) help to constrain (1) the depth and geometry of the magma plumbing system and (2) the time history of magma outflow and possible recharge to a crustal magma reservoir (Lisowski and others, this volume, chap. 15; Mastin and others, this volume, chap. 22). The 2004–5 deformation data, especially when considered together with other datasets, also raise several new questions.

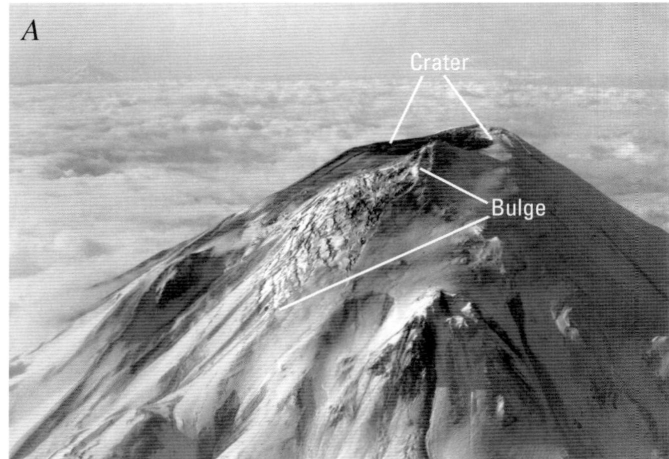

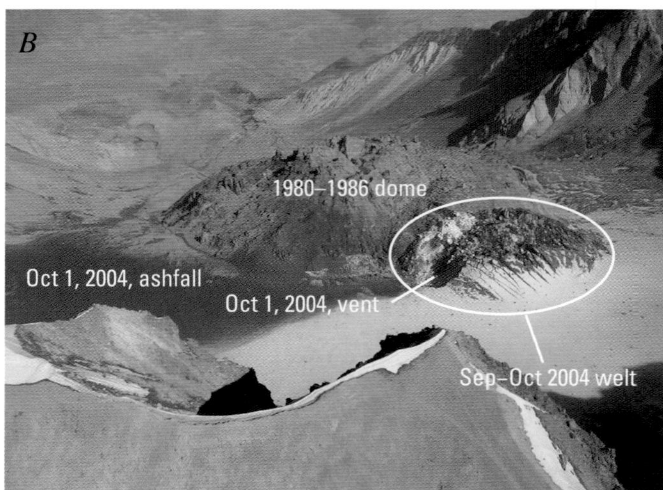

Figure 1. Examples of precursory surface deformation before eruptions at Mount St. Helens, Washington. *A*, Upper north flank on April 7, 1980. Series of phreatic eruptions that began on March 27, 1980, deposited ash and formed summit crater, which had grown to about 500 m west-east and 300 m north-south. Intensely cracked area below and north of crater shows distension of north flank. USGS photograph by R.B. Waitt. *B*, Crater floor as seen from above southwest crater rim on October 3, 2004. Vent for October 1 ash is visible at the west base of the welt of uplifted crater floor and glacial ice first recognized as deforming on September 27, 2004. USGS photograph by S. Konfal.

[3] Capitalization of "Caldera" or "Volcano" indicates adoption of the word as part of the formal geographic name by the host country, as listed in the Geographic Names Information System, a database maintained by the U.S. Board on Geographic Names. Noncapitalized "caldera" or "volcano" is applied informally—eds.

This paper draws freely on datasets and analyses presented elsewhere in this volume. Its main objectives are (1) to present an integrated overview of ground deformation observations, measurements, and results through December 2005 and (2) to explore some implications of these results, together with those from other disciplines, for the mechanism of the eruption and its future course.

Geodetic Techniques Used to Study the Eruption

This section summarizes the techniques used, successfully or unsuccessfully, to measure ground deformation during the 2004–5 eruption. The reader is referred to other papers in this volume for more thorough treatments of some of the techniques, results, and interpretations.

Regional Trilateration and Campaign-Style GPS Measurements

The Helens high-precision trilateration network was established in 1982 to track regional strain accumulation following the 1980 eruption at Mount St. Helens. Line lengths were measured with a Geodolite in 1982 and 1991 and with GPS in 2000. Lisowski and others (this volume, chap. 15) report that line lengths consistently increased by 1–3 cm between 1982 and 1991 but did not change significantly from 1991 to 2000. The line-length increases correspond to areal dilatation at a rate of 144±39 nanostrain/yr, which is an order of magnitude greater and distinctly different than the background tectonic strain. Lisowski and others (this volume, chap. 15) discount possible systematic error in the Geodolite surveys as the sole reason for the observed dilatation and invoke "... some other phenomenon, like recharge of the magma reservoir..." to account for the observations.

During summer 2000, the USGS Cascades Volcano Observatory (CVO) installed and made initial GPS observations at more than 40 benchmarks on and around Mount St. Helens (herein referred to as the large-aperture GPS network). The network is concentrated within 10 km of the volcano, but it extends more than 30 km and covers an area of more than 7,400 km^2 (fig. 2; Dzurisin, 2003). The first repeat survey was made in summer 2003. With effects of rigid-block rotation and regional strain removed, no significant strain was detected, with one exception: a station (DMSH) on the 1980–86 lava dome (fig. 2) moved down and east-northeastward, toward the center of the dome, at average rates of 9.0 cm/yr and 2.9 cm/yr, respectively (Lisowski and others, this volume, chap. 15).

The motion of DMSH is consistent with that seen at several nearby stations on the 1980–86 dome, which were observed each summer from 2000 to 2004 to provide geodetic control for vertical air photos and digital elevation models (Schilling and others, this volume, chap. 8). These stations generally moved down and toward the center of the dome at rates of a few centimeters per year, while stations on the crater floor moved very little (Lisowski and others, this volume, chap. 15). The motion of the stations is attributed to cooling and compaction of the uppermost conduit and dome. The latter consists mainly of stubby, highly deformed, dacite lava flows (lobes) and bouldery talus (Swanson and others, 1987). There is no evidence from the August 2004 control-point survey data of any change in trend that could be associated with the start of the current eruption.

The regional trilateration and campaign GPS data indicate that most of the surface deformation prior to the 2004–5 eruption took place in the decade following the 1980 eruption, and that little or no surface deformation occurred between 1991 and 2003. This is consistent with data from continuous GPS (CGPS) station JRO1, 8 km north-northwest of the volcano, which recorded no volcano-centric deformation from May 1997 to the beginning of seismic unrest on September 23, 2004 (see below). However, there is seismic evidence for pressurization of the magma reservoir and upward fluid intrusion starting in late 1987 and continuing at least until November 2001 (Moran, 1994; Moran and others, this volume, chap. 2). This apparent contradiction and other questions are addressed in the later Discussion section.

Continuous GPS (CGPS)

Johnston Ridge Observatory (JRO1)

Included in the large-aperture GPS network are 17 CGPS stations on or close to the volcano. The first station, JRO1, was installed in May 1997 at the Mount St. Helens National Volcanic Monument's Johnston Ridge Observatory. Lisowski and others (this volume, chap. 15) conclude that, within uncertainties, (1) the velocity of JRO1 was constant from May 1997 through mid-September 2004, and (2) JRO1 abruptly started moving south-southeast and down, toward a source beneath Mount St. Helens, on or about September 23, 2004. The anomalous motion was essentially concurrent (±1 day) with the start of a shallow earthquake swarm beneath the crater floor (Moran and others, this volume, chap. 2). Seismicity was accompanied by the growth of a large welt (fig. 1*B*), which was first visible in photographs taken on September 26. The first of several lava spines emerged from the welt on October 11, and extrusion of a dacite dome continued through the end of 2005 (Dzurisin and others, 2005; Vallance and others, this volume, chap. 9).

Fresh crevasses in glacier ice on the south crater floor, indicating intense deformation of the area that was to become the welt, were first recognized a few days after the start of shallow seismicity and anomalous motion at JRO1. New crevassing and uplift were confirmed by direct observation on September 29, 2004. In hindsight, they were recognized in photographs taken on September 26 by J.S. Pallister during a fixed-wing observation flight. Helicopter pilot Jeff Linscott (JL Aviation, Inc.) first noticed new cracks in the ice on September 28 while flying with members of the news media. He pointed out the cracks to us (D. Dzurisin and M.P. Poland) the next day, September 29. A photograph taken by a hiker from the south crater rim on September 25 shows no obvious disturbance in the area that became the welt; thus, the first surface cracks probably formed 2–3 days after the start of a shallow earthquake swarm at about 0200 PDT (0900 UTC) on September 23 and within 1 day of an uptick in seismicity on September 25 that culminated with the onset of the eruption.

On August 27, 2004, Linscott landed in the southern part of the crater with USGS–CVO staff; fresh cracks in glacier ice at their customary landing site forced them to use an alternate site nearby. Any significance of those cracks in terms of the impending eruption is undocumented. At the time, the cracks were attributed to summer snowmelt revealing crevasses in the advancing glacier. Similar features had been seen before and were visible at the time on the west arm of the glacier. Any relation to the recognized onset of volcanic unrest nearly a month later is speculative and not supported by the hiker's photograph taken on September 25.

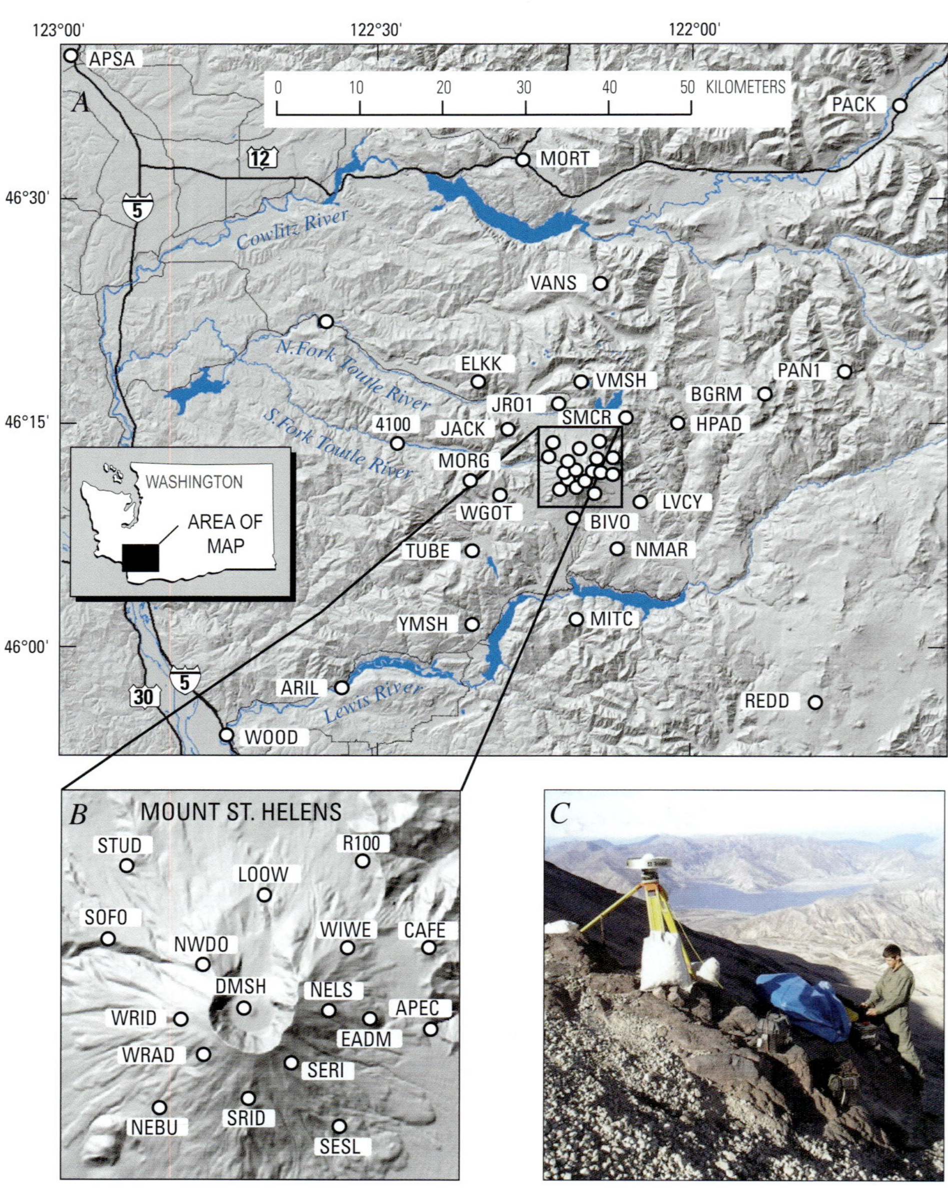

Figure 2. Large-aperture GPS network at Mount St. Helens, Washington. *A*, Location map showing 40 benchmarks observed during summers of 2000 and 2003. Base from shaded relief version of USGS digital elevation model. *B*, Benchmarks on or near the volcano. *C*, GPS receiver deployed at NELS (Nelson Ridge) on upper east flank of Mount St. Helens in October 2004.

Following a period of rapid motion toward a source beneath the volcano at a peak rate of ~0.5 mm/d in late September–early October 2004 (while the growth rate of the welt was as high as 8.9 m^3/s), the movement of JRO1 gradually slowed through December 2004. Meanwhile, the extrusion rate slowed from 5.9 m^3/s (October 13–November 4) to 2.5 m^3/s (December 11, 2004–January 3, 2005; Schilling and others, this volume, chap. 8). During May–December 2005, the velocity of JRO1 was essentially constant at ~0.04 mm/d toward the volcano. During the same interval, the rate of lava extrusion declined from 1.3 m^3/s (April 19–June 15) to 0.7 m^3/s (October 24–December 15), with somewhat higher rates during July 14–August 10 (2.0 m^3/s) and August 10–September 20 (1.6 m^3/s; Schilling and others, this volume, chap. 8).

Mount St. Helens CGPS Cluster

In response to the current eruption, CVO and the EarthScope Plate Boundary Observatory (PBO) installed 13 additional CGPS stations during October–November 2004. Most of the new stations are on the volcano, mounted 3–4 m high on steel tripods that served as EDM stations during the 1980s (fig. 3). Data from all 14 CGPS stations at Mount St. Helens are downloaded automatically to CVO and to the UNAVCO Boulder Facility Archive. The data are processed daily at the USGS Menlo Park facility to produce a 24-hour solution. Five additional stations, mounted on smaller tripods and without telemetry links, have operated intermittently since November 2004. Data from those stations are downloaded manually.

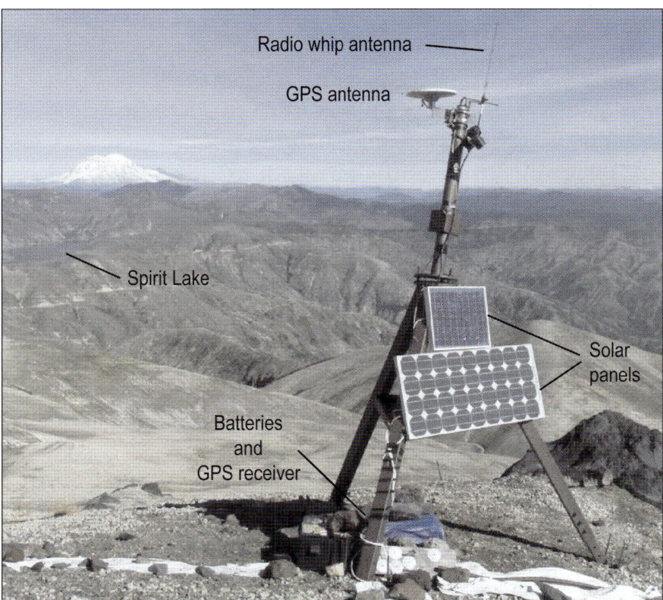

Figure 3. CGPS station WIWE (Windy West) on lower northeast flank of Mount St. Helens, Washington (fig. 2). Station is typical of several installed by CVO. View is to north-northeast. Mount Rainier is visible 77 km in distance.

Time-series plots of CGPS data show that the rate of motion toward the volcano peaked in late September or early October 2004, while the welt was growing rapidly but before the first lava emerged on October 11, 2004 (see figs. 10–13 in Lisowski and others, this volume, chap. 15). Both the far-field (beyond the crater floor) deformation rate and the extrusion rate declined progressively from mid-October through at least December 2004. Perhaps as early as January 2005, and surely by May 2005, the deformation rate and extrusion rate stabilized; both rates were relatively steady through December 2005.

Single-Frequency (L1-Only) GPS "Spiders"

It was clear from the early days of the eruption that extreme deformation of the south crater floor and glacier must attenuate rapidly with distance, because the 1980–86 dome and crater floor to the north remained essentially undisturbed, while the welt, just a few hundred meters to the south, grew to 500 m west-east, 600 m north-south, and 110–120 m high by October 11, 2004. LaHusen and others (this volume, chap. 16) report that a single-frequency CGPS station at SEP, on the 1980–86 dome less than 500 m north of the 2004–5 vent, moved anomalously about 20 cm north, 8 cm west, and 12 cm up during the 9-month period ending on September 27, 2004. This displacement was much less than we expected, given the large size and proximity of the welt. Likewise, all 13 of the CGPS stations that were installed on the volcano's flanks during October–November 2004 moved less than 2 cm during the ensuing 15 months. Therefore, it was necessary to install deformation sensors within a few hundred meters of the vent to monitor the course of the eruption. Conventional CGPS installations were not a reasonable option, because instrumentation in proximal areas had an expected lifetime of only days or weeks during the first few months of the eruption. Instead, we deployed and, in some cases, retrieved and redeployed a series of single-frequency (L1-only) CGPS stations aboard "spiders"—self-contained sensor platforms slung from a helicopter to otherwise inaccessible or hazardous sites (LaHusen and others, this volume, chap. 16). Here we summarize results of three GPS spider deployments to the growing dome, which provided reliable measurements of lineal extrusion rates for spines 3 and 4. See LaHusen and others (this volume, chap. 16) for discussion of additional deployments to the 2004–5 dome, 1980–86 dome, and Crater Glacier.

On November 20, 2004, GPS spider ELEA was set down astride spine 3, which was advancing south-southeastward across the crater floor. During the ensuing six days, before the instrument was destroyed in a rockfall, ELEA traveled 67 m southeast and 8 m up at an average rate of ~10 m/d and an average slope of 5.6° (LaHusen and others, this volume, chap. 16). The GPS spider CDAN was destroyed by a small explosive event starting at 0318 PST on January 16, 2005 (Scott and others, this volume, chap. 1), about 36 hours after it was deployed to spine 4. In the preceding 24 hours, CDAN moved 6.5 m south, 2.2 m east, and 4.7 m up, corresponding to an average velocity of 8.3 m/d at an average slope of 34.5°. The GPS spider AHAD was deployed to spine 4 on February 8, 2005. By the time it was retrieved on February 16, AHAD had moved 29 m south, 17 m east, and 9 m up, for an average velocity of 6.2 m/day at an average slope of 15.5° (LaHusen and others, this volume, chap. 16).

Velocities measured by ELEA, CDAN, and AHAD are not directly comparable for two reasons: (1) spines 3 and 4 differed in morphology (4 was, for the most part, steeper than 3), and (2) the three spiders occupied different positions with respect to the vent. Nonetheless, slowing of the extrusion velocity between late November 2004 and mid-February 2005, as indicated by the GPS spiders, is consistent with analysis of time-lapse images from the Sugar Bowl camera (Major and others, this volume, chap. 12) and with declining volumetric extrusion rates derived from analysis of digital elevation models (DEMs) for the same period (Schilling and others, this volume, chap. 8).

No additional GPS spiders were deployed to active parts of the growing dome from March to December 2005 because the surface was too steep, too rugged, or too hot. Meanwhile, spiders deployed to older parts of the 2004–5 dome, the 1980–86 dome, and Crater Glacier continued to provide data (LaHusen and others, this volume, chap. 16).

Interferometric Synthetic Aperture Radar (InSAR)

InSAR has been used successfully to study surface deformation at dozens of volcanoes worldwide (for example, Amelung and others, 2000; Zebker and others, 2000; Lu and others, 2007), but at Mount St. Helens three factors have limited its utility. First, EDM and GPS measurements show that any surface displacements that occurred at Mount St. Helens between InSAR's emergence in 1993 (Massonnet and others, 1993) and the start of the 2004–5 eruption were small compared to the resolution of InSAR (2.83 cm/fringe for C-band images; Lisowski and others, this volume, chap. 15). Second, persistent winter snow pack and frequent precipitation destroy coherence, except in small areas above the tree line in summer-to-summer interferograms. Third, the orbital repeat intervals for radar satellites ERS (35 days), RADARSAT (24 days), and ENVISAT (35 days) are too short to capture any slow, preeruption deformation and too long to capture rapid near-vent deformation while an eruption is underway. In the latter case, extreme deformation of the growing dome and displaced glacier make the in-crater part of all interferograms incoherent.

These difficulties with InSAR can be overcome to some extent by "stacking" (averaging) several interferograms for relatively short time periods (so coherence is maintained), which collectively span a period long enough for any deformation signal to emerge from the noise. Stacking works on the premise that a small deformation signal from a fixed source will accumulate with time, while random atmospheric noise sources will tend to cancel. Poland and Lu (this volume, chap. 18) stacked and analyzed hundreds of interferograms of Mount St. Helens acquired by ERS-1/2, ENVISAT, and RADARSAT satellites from 1992 to 2005. Stacks of preeruptive interferograms indicate no sign of volcanowide deformation, which is consistent with trilateration, campaign GPS, and CGPS data for the period from 1992 to 2005 (Lisowski and others, this volume, chap. 15). In contrast, the most reliable stack of coeruptive interferograms shows line-of-sight (LOS) increases (that is, surface subsidence) on the volcano's flanks at rates of 40–50 mm/yr, which is consistent with CGPS results for the coeruptive period.

Time-Lapse Oblique Photography

Several factors contributed to the widespread use of photography, both from aircraft and the ground, to record various aspects of the eruption including (1) growth, deformation, and geomorphic evolution of the lava dome, (2) perturbed motion and deformation of Crater Glacier, and (3) emergence of the lava column from the vent and resulting movement of spines across the crater floor. First, digital cameras are capable of producing high-quality images in near-real time (an advantage over film cameras) that can be shared among colleagues with ease. Second, the perceived level of risk to observers in the crater, especially during early phases of the eruption, was a factor that encouraged remote photo documentation. In hindsight, the 2004–5 eruption has been benign by comparison to most dacite dome eruptions; nonetheless, risks in proximal areas from rockfalls and small explosions were reduced by replacing human observers with cameras, especially for investigations that required repeated observations over long periods of time (for example, time-lapse images of dome growth). Third, it was recognized early in the 2004–5 eruption that cameras were providing a unique and valuable record of the measured pace, longevity, and character of events that transpired in the vent area. An unusual suite of circumstances—gas-poor, crystal-rich magma emerging from an inclined vent on a relatively flat crater floor beneath a newly formed glacier that is contained on three sides by steep crater walls—combined to create an unusual and visually captivating landscape. Over time scales ranging from minutes to months (from drumbeat earthquakes to gouge-covered, laterally mobile, whaleback-shaped spines), the eruption produced a variety of features that are suited to photo documentation and analysis. The following sections summarize two different approaches to time-lapse photo studies of the eruption. More detailed discussions of these and other camera applications can be found in Poland and others (this volume, chap. 11) and Major and others (this volume, chap. 12).

Synoptic Observations of Dome Growth and Glacier Deformation

Mount St. Helens lies 70 km north-northeast of CVO, within sight on a clear day but at a range suitable only for reconnaissance observations. The volcano's 1980 crater opens to the north, so the view of the current eruption site from CVO is blocked by the volcano's south flank. Continuous surveillance of the eruption by observers within sight of the vent was impractical for logistical reasons, so remote cameras were used instead to track the changing landscape in the crater. Time-lapse photography cannot be construed as deformation monitoring in a classical geodetic sense, but in the 2004–5 eruption, the disruption of the crater floor and glacier was so extreme that cameras became an effective tool for monitoring dramatic changes in the vent area. Elsewhere, CGPS stations and tiltmeters are better suited to measuring strains that are smaller by several orders of magnitude.

The first remote camera station was installed on October 10, 2004, at Sugar Bowl (altitude 1,859 m) on the east side of The Breach (open north end of 1980 crater), 2.3 km north-northeast of the vent. The Sugar Bowl camera recorded the changing morphology of the welt starting one day before emergence of spine 1 on October 11, 2004, followed by development, movement, and disintegration of three prominent whaleback spines (3, 4, and 5). The Sugar Bowl camera was poorly positioned for photographing the disintegration of spine 5 and westward migration of spine 6, which began in early August 2005, because the camera's view was blocked by the 1980–86 dome from August through early October 2005. But by mid-October 2005, spine 7 had grown into the field of view of the Sugar Bowl camera above the profile of the 1980–86 dome, where it remained through the end of 2005. Because the Sugar Bowl camera captured a large part of the dome growth that occurred from mid-October 2004 through December 2005, its images are well suited to systematic quantitative analysis. Major and others (this volume, chap. 12) used the Sugar Bowl images to estimate lineal extrusion rates as a function of time and to infer short-term (days to weeks) variations in the volumetric extrusion rate.

To complement the Sugar Bowl images, two additional camera stations were installed higher on the crater rim in August 2005. Brutus (BRUT) is located at 2,479 m altitude along the northeast rim, 1.1 km east-northeast of the vent. South Rim (SRIM) is located at 2,512 m altitude along the south-southwest crater rim, 0.7 km from the vent. BRUT sees most of the 2004–5 dome and Crater Glacier from the east-northeast; SRIM sees essentially the same area from a reciprocal vantage point.

Camera station Guacamole (GUAC), located at 1,634 m altitude on the floor of The Breach, 2.6 km north of the vent, was added in November 2005. Station GUAC provides a view of the western part of the 2004–5 dome, including spines 6 and 7, and of the deformed east and west arms of Crater Glacier. The lower altitude of GUAC, relative to the other cameras, allows for occasional glimpses under the clouds that obscure views from the higher cameras. See Poland and others (this volume, chap. 11) for additional description of the camera stations and telemetry system, including map locations, equipment used, method of storing and retrieving images, and capability for controlling camera parameters and shooting schedules.

Arguably the greatest value of the remote camera stations lies in the production of time-lapse "movies" (typically one image per day for several days, or all available three-minute images for a 24-hour period) that portray the changing morphology of the dome, deformation of Crater Glacier, rockfall sequences, and patterns of nighttime glow in an intuitive and easy-to-understand format. Several of these sequences are available on the DVD accompanying this volume and on the CVO Web site (http://vulcan.wr.usgs.gov/Volcanoes/MSH/Images/MSH04/repeat_views.html, last accessed January 14, 2008).

High-Resolution, Small Field-of-View Observations of Extrusion Site

In an attempt to capture any short-term (minutes to hours) variations in the lineal extrusion rate and to assess any correlation between these and "drumbeat" earthquakes, we deployed digital cameras with long focal-length lenses and time-lapse controllers at BRUT and on the September 1984 lobe (SEP) of the 1980–86 dome. Drumbeat earthquakes are repetitive, small earthquakes, many with waveforms similar to other drumbeats, that occurred at remarkably constant intervals during the 2004–5 eruption (Moran and others, this volume, chap. 2; Thelen and others, this volume, chap. 4). A correlation between drumbeats and lineal extrusion rate is suggested by a mathematical model that describes the extrusion process in terms of stick-slip motion of a rigid plug under the combined influences of magma pressure, gravity, and friction on the conduit wall (Iverson and others, 2006; Iverson, this volume, chap. 21). To avoid the need for longer-term power and protection from the elements, each of these camera deployments lasted for only a few hours. From BRUT, a Nikon ® CoolPix 990 camera coupled to a 12–36X spotting scope (fig. 4) produces a field of view at the vent (range ~1100 m) of approximately 60×90 m at 12X, or 20×30 m at 36X. From SEP (range ~400 m), the same camera coupled to a Questar ® 700 telephoto lens (3.5-inch diameter, f7.8) fitted with a 24-mm eyepiece (fig. 5) produces a 1.3×1.0 m field of view. Image size of the Nikon ® CoolPix 990 in "fine" resolution mode is 2048×1536 pixels (3.3 megapixels), so using it with the Questar ® 700 from SEP produces an image in which each pixel corresponds to ~0.6 mm on the ground.

Although the Nikon ® CoolPix 990–Questar ® 700 combination deployed at SEP is theoretically capable of millimeter-scale resolution at the vent, two factors combine to degrade the image quality in practice. First is the difficulty in establishing a sufficiently stable base for an imaging system with such high magnification—a problem with two parts. The first, coupling the camera system securely to the ground, can be overcome by mounting the camera and lens to a rigid plate or a short, heavy-duty tripod and by using sandbags to fix the plate or tripod firmly to the ground. The second part of the problem is ground motion associated with incessant drumbeat earthquakes and occasional larger shocks (M_{max} ~3.6).

On five occasions between September 2 and November 18, 2005, we tried frame intervals of 10 s or 30 s for periods of 1–6 hours at times when drumbeats were occurring every 2–3 minutes. Ground shaking is obvious in only a small fraction of the images, as would be expected from the framing interval, shutter speed (0.004–0.5 s), and average time between quakes. Each set of images reveals what appears to be relatively steady motion of the extrusion out of the vent, although any slight displacements of the camera system or underlying ground cannot be distinguished from apparent motion of the extrusion. We tried repeatedly to include in the images some part of the dome or crater wall that was relatively stable, but the camera's limited field of view and depth of field made this difficult and ultimately unproductive.

Figure 4. Temporary time-lapse photo station at Brutus (BRUT) on northeast crater rim, Mount St. Helens, Washington. Permanent camera station BRUT is ~100 m north (to the right) of this site.

Figure 5. Temporary time-lapse photo station at SEP on September 1984 lobe of 1980–86 dome, ~400 m north of the 2004–5 vent, Mount St. Helens, Washington. Sandbags at base of tripod are for added stability. Spirit Lake near center of photo. Mount Rainier on skyline.

A second factor that contributes to image degradation is heat shimmer caused by uneven refraction of light in unstable air along the camera's line of sight. Heat shimmer is exacerbated by numerous localized heat sources on the 1980–86 and 2004–5 domes and by extensive, hot talus deposits surrounding the active vent. The resulting image degradation can be mitigated to some extent by choosing the line of sight carefully, but this usually comes at the expense of the most desirable framing.

We have been unsuccessful in attempts to capture photographically any jerkiness in the extrusion process that might be associated with drumbeat or larger earthquakes. However, the high-resolution time-lapse images have been useful for another purpose. Because the images are at a known scale (determined empirically by photographing objects of known size with the same camera/lens combination at distances measured using a laser rangefinder), each set of images can be used to measure the average lineal extrusion velocity in the image plane. Motion of the extrusion can be discerned in images acquired only a few minutes apart.

The surface velocity of spine 6 was measured using high-resolution, time-lapse photography from SEP on three occasions from September 2, 2005, to October 18, 2005 (table 1, fig. 6). SEP was due north of the advancing front of spine 6 at the time, so the motion of features through the image frame can be used to measure west and up components of the velocity vector. The resultant velocity (west+up) is a reasonably good indicator of the lineal extrusion rate of spine 6, which was also advancing northward during this period owing to endogenous growth and spreading. The lineal extrusion rate determined in this way declined from 4.51 m/d on September 2 to 4.45 m/d on September 20 and to 2.51 m/d on October 18. Distances from the SEP camera station to the imaged part of spine 6 were measured with a laser rangefinder and are reported as the north component of velocity in table 1. The value for September 2 (>3.3 m/d) is a minimum value because there were no previous rangefinder measurements. The rate was greater than 3.3 m/d, the average value calculated from measurements made on September 2 and September 20, because the extrusion rate and growth rate of spine 6 generally slowed with time.

Figure 6 is based on a subset of 702 images acquired at SEP from 11:14:17 to 17:04:47 PDT (30-s interval) on September 20, 2005. Distance from the camera to the steep, gouge-covered north face of emerging spine 6, measured with a laser rangefinder, was 342±1 m. The camera's field of view included an aluminum target, 46×61 cm in size, for scale. The target was hung by steel cables from an anchor slung by helicopter to the top of the spine. For 58 of the sharpest images, the pixel coordinates of a distinctive feature on the target relative to a corner of the image were determined by inspection using a PC graphics program. A spreadsheet program was used to convert pixel coordinates to millimeters at the target, using the known image scale, to determine optimal linear fits to the data, to calculate departures from the best-fit line, and to plot the results as a function of time. Average velocity components (that is, slopes of the best-fit lines) are 3.89 m/d west and 2.17 m/d up. Departures from the best-fit lines are irregular and small, on the order of ±10 mm (fig. 6, middle). Therefore, the lineal extrusion rate during a 3.5-hr period on September 20, 2005, was constant within the uncertainty of the measurements. There is no evidence of stick-slip motion of the spine greater than about 10 mm associated with drumbeat earthquakes, which were occurring every 2–3 minutes, nor with two larger shallow quakes at 15:47:19 (M_d 2.9) and 16:05:26 (M_d 1.0) PDT.

Average velocities (west and up) determined from similar observations on September 2, 2005, and October 18, 2005, are 4.51 m/d and 2.51 m/d, respectively (table 1). No comparable measurements were possible from the Sugar Bowl camera on September 2 or September 20, but measurements on October 18, 22, and 24 are in the range 3–4 m/d. In all three cases in which these types of observations were made, the motion of the extruding spine was steady over time scales of a few hours; no evidence of short-term rate variations was seen in any of the photos. However, such variations likely are occurring in the conduit during earthquakes, and variations could also be occurring at the surface in millimeter-scale jerks too small to be resolved by this technique. During the first year of the eruption, drumbeat earthquakes occurred at rates of 0.3–3 per minute, while the lineal extrusion velocity was 1–10 m/d. If all of the motion were associated with drumbeat earthquakes, this would imply an average event size of 2.3 mm/drumbeat at the source. This value for average event size would be smaller if, as seems likely, extrusion is partly aseismic and seismic dislocations are attenuated between the earthquake source area and the surface.

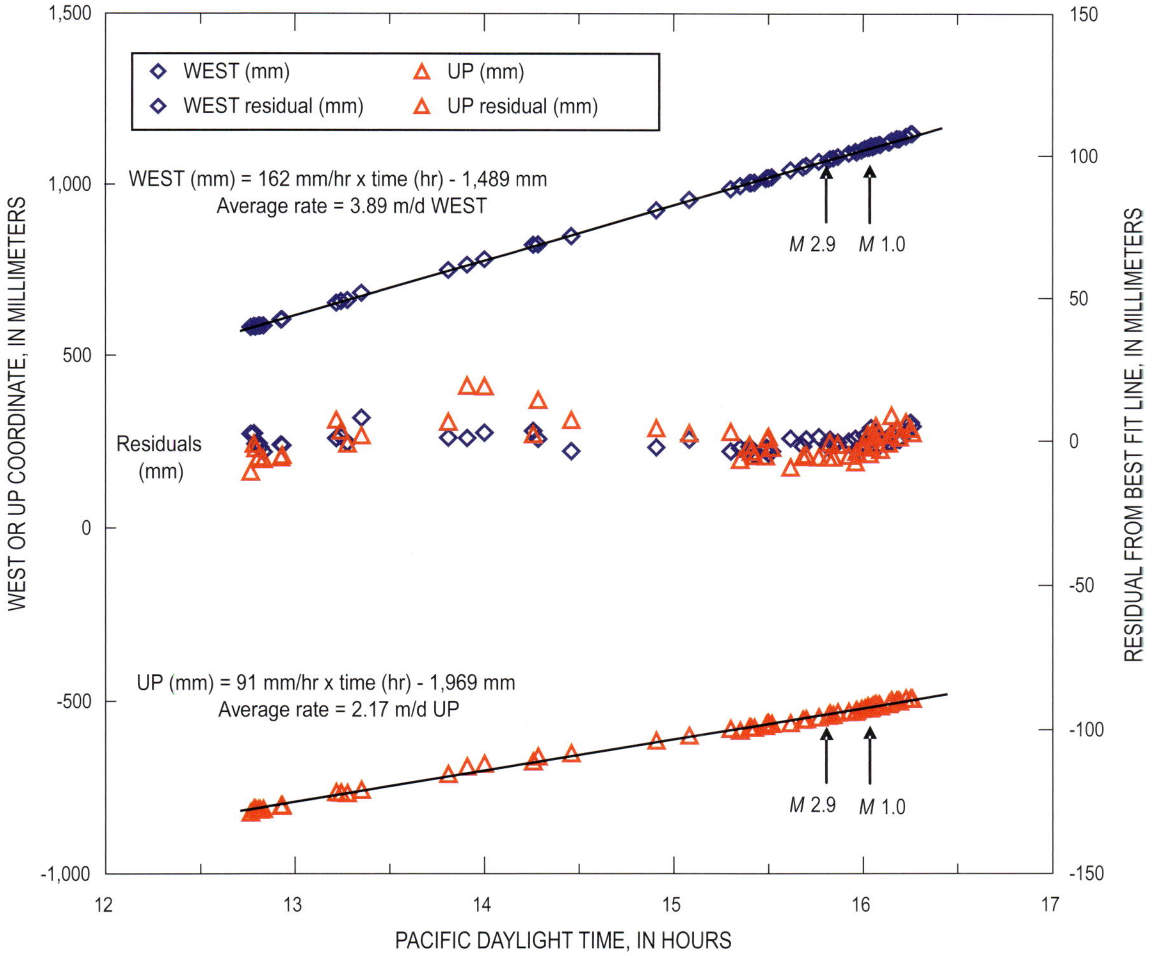

Figure 6. Lineal extrusion velocity of spine 6 for ~3.5-hour period on September 20, 2005, based on analysis of high magnification, small field-of-view, time-lapse (30 s interval) digital images from temporary camera station SEP, Mount St. Helens, Washington. Departures from best-fit lines for west and up components of motion are shown with corresponding symbols in middle ("Residuals").

Table 1. Velocities determined from high-magnification, small field-of-view, time-lapse images at station SEP, Mount St. Helens, Washington.

Date (2005)	West velocity (m/d)	Up velocity (m/d)	Extrusion velocity (west + up) (m/d)	North velocity (m/d)	Distance to target (m)
September 2	4.23	1.55	4.51	>3.3	402
September 20	3.89	2.17	4.45	3.3	342
October 18	2.41	0.69	2.51	1.3	306

Trilateration and Triangulation of Points on the Growing Dome

Classical trilateration and triangulation techniques were adapted with good results to measure changing displacement rates on the growing dome during 1980–86 which, together with changing patterns of seismicity, were used to predict the start of each dome-building episode from a few days to three weeks in advance (Swanson and others, 1983). Measurements were made by affixing prism reflectors to the dome and tracking their motion by using an EDM and theodolite from fixed points on the crater floor or, in some cases, from points on stable parts the dome itself. To increase the number of targets without continuously exposing a large number of reflectors to harsh conditions in the crater, some target points were marked with a survey pin so that a person on foot could accurately position a reflector at the point for a few minutes while a colleague made EDM and theodolite measurements. In this way, more than a dozen survey points distributed across the dome could be surveyed in a few hours.

We tried a similar approach to measure displacement rates on the 2004–5 dome, with lesser success. One difference from the 1980–86 dome is that continuous extrusion, frequent rockfalls, and the deeply crevassed glacier generally precluded foot travel on or around the 2004–5 dome. Instead, five targets, each consisting of a single prism reflector at the center of a painted wooden board attached to a barbell weight as a base, were slung from a helicopter to the 2004–5 dome and Crater Glacier. Three of the targets were set on spine 4, one to the east on rubble of spine 3, and one on the east arm of the glacier. None of the targets could be placed on active spine 5 because it was too steep and hot at the time. All of the targets were observed from BRUT (range ~1,100 m) using a Wild ® TC1000 total station tacheometer on April 21, May 3, and September 20, 2005. The tacheometer can produce surveys with angle measurements accurate to 3 arc seconds at range 1–2.5 km, depending on viewing conditions. Standard deviation of range measurements is 3 mm + 2 ppm, which corresponds to ±5 mm at 1 km range.

Four of the targets survived to the second survey, and three survived to the third survey. However, reflections were obtained from only two targets in the initial survey and from no targets in the second or third surveys, so we lack range measurements for the repeat surveys. The lack of reflections likely resulted from dust clinging to the prisms, etching of the glass by volcanic gases, and (or) changing alignment of the prisms with respect to the sight line as a result of earthquake shaking or slumping. The longest-surviving targets were near the top of spine 4, near the base of spine 3, and on the east arm of the glacier.

For the period May 3 to September 20, 2005, minimum average horizontal velocities of the three surviving targets declined to about one-fourth to one-third of the corresponding values for April 21 to May 3, 2005. For example, the average velocity of a target near the top of spine 4 declined from 0.28 m/d during the early period (April 21 to May 3) to 0.06 m/d during the latter period (May 3 to September 20). For the same periods, the target near the base of spine 3 slowed from 0.09 m/d to 0.02 m/d, and the eastside glacier target slowed from 0.49 m/d to 0.18 m/d. Steep, rugged, and hot terrain on the active dome precluded the use of GPS spiders during this period, so no data are available for comparison. Regardless, the observed slowing trend is consistent with what was happening in the crater at the time. When the first triangulation measurements were made on April 21, 2005, spine 5 was extruding southward, shoving the remnants of spines 3 and 4 southeastward and compressing the east arm of Crater Glacier, which resulted in thickening and increased rate of flow northward (Walder and others, this volume, chap. 13). Spine 6 emerged in early August 2005 and moved westward for the duration of the measurements. The movement of spine 6 eased the stress on spines 3 and 4 and on the glacier's east arm, which caused their velocities to slow.

Total-station surveys made by using helicopter-deployed targets are a feasible, albeit costly and manpower-intensive means to monitor surface displacements on a growing dome. This approach might be cost effective in some situations, but in our case the measurements were abandoned owing to the difficulty of maintaining targets on the dome and the cost of helicopter operations required for each survey. The long sight lines and consequent inability to obtain reflections from the prisms greatly weakened the value of the survey. Although the targets costs less than $200 each, their deployment and initial survey required about one hour of helicopter flight time (~$750/hr), as did each of two repeat surveys spaced 12 days and ~4.5 months apart, resulting in ~1 m accuracy at three surviving targets. For comparison, a GPS spider costs about $2,500, can be deployed to the dome in about one helicopter flight hour and later retrieved if desired. A spider provides three-dimensional positioning information every few minutes, with an accuracy of a few centimeters, without the need for field personnel, except for deployment and retrieval.

Borehole Tiltmeters

Two Pinnacle 5000 series borehole tiltmeters with tilt resolution of 5×10^{-9} radian (3×10^{-7} angular degree) were installed on the 1980–86 dome to record any transient (seconds to days) ground tilt that might accompany extrusion of the 2004–5 dome and consequent deformation of the crater floor and glacier. The installations were motivated in part by a dynamical model in which stick-slip motion of the plug produces repetitive, reversible strain in host rock near the conduit (Iverson and others, 2006; Iverson, this volume, chap. 21). If each drumbeat earthquake represents an upward "slip" of the plug, followed by a few minutes of increasing magma pressure while the plug remains "stuck," drumbeats should be associated with sudden inward tilt followed by gradual outward tilt between beats.

To test this hypothesis, the first tiltmeter was installed in a 2.3-m-deep hole bored into the September 1984 lobe of the 1980–86 dome (SEP), 480 m N. 16° W. of the 2004–5 vent, on August 5, 2005. A second tiltmeter (REM) was installed in a 1.8-m-deep hole on the northeast sector of the 1980–86 dome, 480 m N. 34° E. of the vent, on November 17, 2004. Both tiltmeters were modified by the manufacturer to enable one-second sampling. Data are telemetered to CVO by way of the U.S. Forest Service's Coldwater Ridge Visitor Center.

Analysis of the tiltmeter records is ongoing, and a complete discussion of results is beyond the scope of this paper. To date, we have seen no evidence of repetitive, reversible tilt events associated with drumbeat earthquakes. It is possible that tilts occur but are too small to be resolved by the tiltmeters, or that the tiltmeters are too far away from the source of the drumbeats. Fractured host rock surrounding the conduit wall or the rubbly interior of the 1980–86 dome might accommodate strains produced by stick-slip motion of the plug without transmitting them to the tiltmeter sites. Without further analysis, this null result should not be interpreted as negative evidence for the occurrence of stick-slip motion as predicted by the model.

Both tiltmeters have recorded tilt changes over time scales of a few minutes to weeks that are likely related to the extrusion process. The azimuths of tilt vectors for many of these events point either toward or away from the extrusion site within a few degrees. Consequently, the vectors from two tiltmeters tend to intersect close to the vent, indicating a shallow pressure source there. It seems plausible that some of the tilt signals are caused by relatively subtle changes in the shallow supply rate or extrusion rate, perhaps related to continual reorganization of the uppermost part of the conduit as the locus of surface activity shifts and the shape of the dome changes. Some of the larger earthquakes (M_d ~2) are associated with tilt events lasting several minutes, but most are not.

A tiltmeter and GPS spider (DOM1), located within 30 m of each other on the September 1984 lobe, responded to some of the same events. For example, the radial tilt component and DOM1 northings increased during September 1–23, 2005, by about 30 microradians and 12 cm, respectively. The instruments are nearly due north of the vent, and both measurements suggest inflation of the vent area. The simplest explanation is that increasing pressure beneath the vent caused the September 1984 lobe to tilt and move northward. At the time, spine 6 was extruding southwestward and migrating westward prior to the emergence of spine 7 in mid-October 2005. Northward tilting and displacement of the September 1984 lobe presaged the emergence of spine 7, possibly during a period of increased extrusion rate. Unfortunately, measurements of the lineal extrusion rate from Sugar Bowl were impossible in September 2005 because the camera's view of spine 6 was blocked by the 1980–86 dome (see earlier section titled Synoptic Observations of Dome Growth and Glacier Deformation).

Discussion

Although some of the techniques discussed above were more successful than others, all of them contributed to our evolving understanding of how Mount St. Helens deformed before and during eruptive activity in 2004–5. Rather than discussing the deformation results separately here, we also consider information from other disciplines (seismology, gas geochemistry, and petrology) and address a few broader issues. Our intent is to characterize current thinking about the eruption and to draw attention to some unresolved questions.

Where, and for how long, was the 2004–5 magma stored before the beginning of unrest on September 23, 2004? What is the nature of the magma reservoir and conduit system? How quickly did the 2004–5 magma rise to the surface? Why was there no inflation at JRO1 prior to September 23, 2004, given that the station clearly responded to deflation and shallow seismicity starting on that date? What are the implications for the future course of this eruption and for anticipating eruptions at similar volcanoes? None of these questions can be answered definitively from the geodetic data alone; however, when combined with other datasets, the geodetic data help to place useful constraints on Mount St. Helens' magma plumbing system and to highlight areas for additional research.

Source Models

The details of various source models fit to the geodetic data are discussed elsewhere in this volume, including Lisowski and others (chap. 15), Poland and Lu (chap. 18), and Mastin and others (chap. 22). Common elements of these source models are (1) depth in the range of 5–12 km (bottom possibly as deep as 20 km), and (2) volume loss through December 2005 in the range 15–30×10^6 m^3, compared to extruded volume of 73×10^6 m^3. Lisowski and others (this volume, chap. 15) modeled and removed the effects of plate motion, regional tectonics, and gravitational loading by the new dome before inverting CGPS data for a best-fit volcanic source model—a point prolate spheroid with its long axis vertical centered near 8 km depth, with a volume loss of 16–24×10^6 m^3 through October 31, 2006. Poland and Lu (this volume, chap. 18) modeled LOS changes from stacked co-eruptive interferograms by using a point source, which best fit the data with a depth of 12 km and a volume loss rate of 27×10^6 m^3/yr. They concluded that a more complicated model is not justified by the InSAR data alone, but they agreed with other authors in the volume that a vertically elongate source is probably more realistic and a better fit to the geodetic dataset as a whole. Mastin and others (this volume, chap. 22) used a vertical ellipsoidal source to fit surface displacements from CGPS data from November 8, 2004, to July 14, 2005. They concluded that the top of the source is 5±1 km deep, but the basal depth is poorly constrained—possibly 10–20 km. Their estimate of source-volume loss during that period is 11–15×10^6 m^3, increasing as the bottom of the source gets deeper. This corresponds to an average volume-loss rate of 16–22×10^6 m^3/yr, which we might double to account for the period of rapid motion at JRO1 from September 23, 2004, to November 8, 2004, which was not included in the model.

These geodetic models generally are consistent with the amount of CO_2 and other volcanic gases emitted during the eruption, which indicate that the erupting magma last equilibrated at 850°C and 130 MPa—conditions corresponding to a reservoir 5.2 km deep (Gerlach and others, this volume, chap. 26). Likewise, samples of the 2004–5 dome indicate that the pressure of last phenocryst growth corresponds to that near the apex of the magma reservoir at a depth of about 5 km (Pallister and others, this volume, chap. 30; Rutherford and Devine, this volume, chap. 31). Pallister and others (this volume, chap. 30) noted the possibility that the 2004–5 magma might be residual from the 1980–86 reservoir and went on to write: "Viewed in the context of seismic, deformation, and gas emission data, the petrologic and geochemical data can be explained by ascent of a geochemically distinct batch of magma into the apex of the [1980–86] reservoir during the period 1987–1997, followed by upward movement of magma into a new conduit, beginning in late September 2004."

In our opinion, the geodetic, gas-emission, and geochemical data from the 2004–5 eruption all point to involvement of magma that was stored in a vertically elongate reservoir centered near 8 km depth and extending upward to about 5 km. We believe this is the same reservoir that fed the plinian eruption of May 18, 1980, smaller explosive eruptions during the summer of 1980, and dome-building eruptions during 1980–86, as inferred by Scandone and Malone (1985) from seismic data (source centered at 9 km, extending from 7 km to 14 km) and Rutherford and others (1985) from the mineral phase assemblage found in May 18 pumice (7.2±1 km). It seems likely that the reservoir was replenished prior to (Moran, 1994; Moran and others, this volume, chap. 2) and possibly during the current eruption (Mastin and others, this volume, chap. 22; Pallister and others, this volume, chap. 30). Data from GPS and InSAR show that most of the surface deformation caused by pre-eruption reservoir inflation occurred prior to 1991, but there is seismic evidence for pressurization of the reservoir and upward fluid intrusion starting in 1987 and continuing at least until 2001. Apparently, reservoir replenishment and surface inflation occurred aseismically until shortly after the extended pause in dome building that began in 1986. Thereafter, increasing strain on rock hosting the reservoir and episodic intrusion of fluids induced microseismicity but no measurable surface deformation.

Implications for the Magma Plumbing System

On September 22, 2004, two things were clear: (1) seismicity at Mount St. Helens was at a low background level characteristic of long periods between sporadic earthquake swarms, and (2) JRO1 was moving northeastward relative to stable North America as part of a tectonic block undergoing clockwise rotation about a pole located either in south-central Oregon (Savage and others, 2000) or along the western part of the Oregon-Washington border where it intersects the Olympic-Wallowa lineament (McCaffrey and others, 2000). The emission rates of volcanic gases probably were low, as they had been each time they were measured after a temporary increase in CO_2 emission was noted during increased seismicity in spring–summer 1998. On four occasions from September 27 to October 2, 2004, measured emission rates of magmatic CO_2 and SO_2 were less than detection thresholds; the first notable increase did not occur until October 3, 2004 (Gerlach and others, this volume, chap. 26).

In hindsight, the September 22 calm belied a volcano poised to erupt. A swarm of small earthquakes, all within 2 km of the crater floor, began around 0200 PDT September 23. By midday on September 28, cracks large enough to be seen from a helicopter flying in the crater appeared in glacier ice on the south crater floor. Rapid uplift and intense seismicity continued for several days, and by October 7, a large welt growing on the south crater floor had approached the height of the 1980–86 dome (fig. 7). The first of several spines emerged from the welt on October 11, less than three weeks after the peaceful dawn of September 22.

Model-derived estimates of source-volume decrease during the first 15 months of the eruption are in the range 15–30×10^6 m^3, compared to an erupted volume of 73±4×10^6 m^3 through December 15, 2005. This suggests, but does not require, that the magma reservoir was partially recharged during the eruption. The lava extrusion rate declined from 5.9 m^3/s to 2.5 m^3/s during the 2.7 months from October 13, 2004, to January 3, 2005, but it varied only between 2.4 m^3/s and 0.7 m^3/s during the ensuing 14 months through the end of 2005 (Schilling and others, this volume, chap. 8). Meanwhile, the

JRO1 displacement rate slowed from a peak value of 0.5 mm/d in late September–early October 2004 to a steady 0.04 mm/d from May through December 2005. These trends suggest that the eruption might be approaching a steady-state condition in which the extrusion rate equals the recharge rate. If so, the situation could persist for years to decades, limited only by the volume of magma available for recharge.

Constraints and Conundrums

The geodetic data help to constrain the depth and geometry of the magma plumbing system and the time history of magma outflow and possible recharge to the reservoir. However, additional questions arise when the geodetic data are considered together with other datasets. For example, why did JRO1 immediately respond to the onset of shallow seismicity, presumably when magma began its ascent, but did not detect any precursory surface deformation during the preceding seven years? The most straightforward answer is that no such deformation occurred because the system was poised to erupt magma stored in the reservoir or conduit system since the 1980–86 eruption, long before JRO1 was installed in May 1997. This idea is consistent with data from trilateration surveys that show surface dilatation, presumably caused by magma accumulation beneath the volcano, between 1982 and 1991. It is also possible that the reservoir inflated during the series of earthquake swarms between 1987 and 2001 by an amount that was too small to cause measurable surface deformation. Mastin and others (this volume, chap. 22) make the point that magma compressibility could have significantly dampened any geodetic signal at Mount St. Helens. Perhaps reservoir magma is compressible enough and the host rock stiff enough that the amount of magma added to the reservoir since 1987 was accommodated without measurably deforming the surface.

How did material that resulted in rapid development of a welt on the south crater floor and subsequent extrusion of highly crystalline, gas-poor magma as gouge-covered spines (Cashman and others, this volume, chap. 19) move through or past the 1980–86 conduit system without substantially deforming more of the volcano and its surroundings? Station JRO1, 9 km north-northwest of the 2004–5 vent, recorded no anoma-

Figure 7. Welt growing on south crater floor, October 7, 2004, as seen from Brutus (BRUT) on northeast crater rim, Mount St. Helens, Washington. South (left) half of the welt is mantled by uplifted glacial ice and ash from small explosions on October 1 and October 5. The north (right) half comprises uplifted crater-floor material and part of the south flank of the 1980–86 dome. The latter was dubbed "Opus area" after 1980s-vintage EDM station Opus, which was located on south side of graben that formed during May 1985 dome-building episode (Swanson and others, 1987).

lous motion at millimeter scale before the eruption. A single-frequency GPS station at SEP on the 1980–86 dome, less than 500 m from the vent, moved anomalously about 20 cm north, 8 cm west, and 12 cm up during the 9-month period ending on September 27, 2004 (LaHusen and others, this volume, chap. 16)—seemingly not enough to accommodate the shallow intrusion of a meters-thick dacite magma body. One possibility is that the conduit is so poorly coupled to the rest of the volcano that the rising magma column was able to push ahead older conduit material, rather than intruding it. Otherwise, the conduit walls and surrounding host rock would have to be implausibly compliant to accommodate an intrusion without causing more widespread deformation.

If the former contents of the conduit were pushed ahead of reservoir magma, when did the latter first reach the surface? If rapid emergence of the first whaleback-shaped extrusion (spine 3) in late October 2004, following the more-labored extrusions of spines 1 and 2, marked the first arrival of reservoir magma, then the volume of conduit material flushed from the system was about 20×10^6 m^3—the volume of surface deformation plus spines on November 4, 2004. The corresponding radius r_c for a cylinder extending from the surface to depth $d = 5$ km is 35.7 m, or 28.2 m for $d = 8$ km. Using the volume of material extruded by November 4, 2004 (11.8×10^6 m^3), instead of the volume of surface deformation, we obtain $r_c = 27.4$ m for $d = 5$ km, or 21.7 m for $d = 8$ km. The average ascent rate through the conduit, v_c, assuming reservoir magma began its rise on September 23, 2004, is 120 m/d for $d = 5$ km, or 190 m/d for $d = 8$ km. If, instead, reservoir magma arrived at the surface as spine 1 on October 11, 2004, when the volume of the welt was 10.1×10^6 m^3, then $r_c = 25.4$ m for $d =$ 5 km, or 20.0 m for $d = 8$ km; and the average ascent rate was 280 m/d ($d = 5$ km), or 440 m/d ($d = 8$ km). Thus, for all plausible dimensions of the conduit system, reservoir magma must have reached the surface early in the eruption, probably about the time CO_2 emission rates peaked in October 2004 (Gerlach and others, this volume, chap. 26).

Calculated ascent rates in the conduit exceed observed lineal extrusion rates, $v_s = 2$–10 m/d, by more than an order of magnitude, so the conduit must widen considerably near the surface. Thornber and others (this volume, chap. 32) reach a similar conclusion (that is, a "wineglass shape" for the conduit) based on their interpretation of amphibole-rim thicknesses in post-November 2004 magma. Equating magma flux through the conduit to that at the surface for $d = 8$ km, $r_c =$ 28.2 m, $v_c = 190$ m/d, and $v_s = 10$ m/d, we obtain a vent radius, r_v, = 125 m and an extrusion rate of 5.7 m^3/s. Using $d = 5$ km, $r_c = 35.7$ m, $v_c = 120$ m/d, and $v_s = 10$ m/d produces essentially the same results, which are representative of the early part of the eruption. For comparison, Schilling and others (this volume, chap. 8) estimated the vent diameter to be 150–230 m east-west based on partial exposures of the basal perimeters of extruding spines. The north-south vent diameter is unconstrained owing to lack of adequate exposure.

Slowing of the JRO1 displacement rate suggests a corresponding reduction in the net rate at which magma is being withdrawn from the reservoir to a value that might be sustainable for the foreseeable future (0.5–1 m^3/s). If the lesser withdrawal rate is a result of recharge, the eruption could continue indefinitely. On the other hand, in the absence of sufficient recharge, the eruption will end when (1) the reservoir is depleted of eruptible magma, (2) the pressure difference between reservoir and surface falls below some threshold, or (3) friction in the upper part of the conduit chokes off magma flow (that is, stick-slip motion of the plug ceases—the plug stays stuck). In the latter case, increasing magma pressure beneath the plug could eventually result in an explosion; however, the low gas content of the 2004–5 magma makes an explosion less likely than it would be for gas-rich magma.

When gas-saturated magma rises, decreasing lithostatic pressure results in bubble formation. If some of the bubbles rise buoyantly through the magma and escape toward the surface, we might expect an eventual uptick in gas emission rates if, as we suspect, the Mount St. Helens magma reservoir has been recharged during the current eruption. The fact that no such increase was observed through the end of 2005 requires explanation. Emission rates of CO_2, SO_2, and H_2S were negligible during September 27–30, 2004, a period characterized by scrubbing or sealing-in of gases. Several days of wet degassing ensued, when scrubbing by the ground-water system dominated degassing. October 5–6, 2004, marked the beginning of a period of dry degassing when emission rates increased to 800–2,400 metric tons per day (t/d) CO_2, 40–250 t/d SO_2, and 0–10 t/d H_2S (Dzurisin and others, 2005). Throughout 2005, the emission rates of all three gases were near or below the low end of the October 2004 ranges (Gerlach and others, this volume, chap. 26).

It is possible that the 2004–5 eruption was triggered by a recharge event in September 2004 and that gases exsolved from the rising magma made their way to the surface by early October 2004, causing the observed uptick in emission rates; however, this seems unlikely for two reasons. First, the total amount of CO_2 emitted during the eruption is consistent with degassing the volume of magma that reached the surface, assuming the magma last equilibrated at about 5 km depth. In other words, there is no need to invoke recharge to account for the amount of CO_2 emitted. On the contrary, low CO_2 emission rates imply that the reservoir magma is "flat," that is, depleted of any significant exsolved-gas phase that might have accumulated in its upper part (Gerlach and others, this volume, chap. 26). Perhaps the catastrophic landslide and explosive eruptions of 1980 depleted a volatile-rich cap that formed since the end of the Goat Rocks eruptive period in 1857, and any exsolved gases that accumulated since then escaped before the current eruption began.

The second factor that weighs against a recharge event in September 2004 as the cause of increased CO_2 emission in early October is the short time interval involved. If, for example, recharge at 8 km depth beginning on September 23 was responsible for newly-exsolved CO_2 reaching the surface by October 1, the average ascent rate of the gas was ~1 km/d. This ascent rate is far greater than, for example, the bubble ascent rate of 1.7 m/hr inferred for the 1975 eruption of Mauna Loa volcano, Hawai'i (Ryan, 1995), even though bubble ascent rates in basalt are likely to be much greater than in dacite. It is possible that the existence of fracture permeability along the margins of the reservoir could allow this constraint to be bypassed. However, it is more straightforward and seems more likely that the source of CO_2 reaching the surface in early October 2004 was the same magma from the conduit or upper part of the reservoir that began extruding shortly thereafter. If so, any volatiles exsolved from magma entering the lower part of the reservoir since the eruption began have not yet fully traversed the length of the reservoir and conduit system. This implies an average rise rate less than about 10 km in 15 months, corresponding to 0.9 m/hr.

The foregoing paragraphs are not meant to imply that a reservoir recharge event could not have occurred during September and October 2004, but rather that such an event, if it did occur, might not have been the source of CO_2 that reached the surface in the next few days. The CO_2 that did reach the surface in early October 2004 could have come from magma previously stored in the conduit or reservoir. Furthermore, the lack of an uptick in CO_2 emission rates since peak values were measured in October 2004 suggests that the path for CO_2 from the base of the reservoir to the surface might be complex and time-consuming to the extent that the CO_2 signature of any recharge that occurred since the 2004–5 eruption began has yet to reach the surface.

Thus, all three of the traditionally reliable eruption precursors (seismicity, ground deformation, and volcanic gas emission) failed to provide warning that an eruption was imminent at Mount St. Helens until a few days before a visible welt appeared at the surface—both in September 2004 and March–April 1980 (the north-flank bulge). Sporadic earthquake swarms beneath the volcano from 1987 to 2003, at least one of which (1998) was accompanied by increased CO_2 emission, provided longer-term but nonspecific forewarning of the current eruption. Data from a single-frequency CGPS station on the 1980–86 dome might have provided several months warning that something anomalous was occurring, but the station was not operational during most of that period, and its data were not analyzed until after the eruption began. Crater-floor deformation might have been hidden beneath thick glacial ice for some time before the first surface cracks were noticed on September 28.

Implications for Volcano Monitoring

One obvious lesson from the 2004–5 eruption is the value of a dense network of CGPS stations operating long before the onset of unrest. The need for CGPS data from proximal stations was addressed at Mount St. Helens only after the 2004–5 eruption began. Most of the ground deformation that accompanied reservoir replenishment following the 1980–86 eruptions had ceased by 1991, before installation of the first CGPS station, JRO1, in 1997. Playing catch-up with a restless volcano is short sighted and dangerous. The best and safest time to install a comprehensive, integrated monitoring system is before unrest begins, when the need for such a system is less apparent.

There is much we do not understand about the 2004–5 eruption of Mount St. Helens, but the challenge does not end there. On January 11, 2006, Augustine Volcano in Cook Inlet, Alaska, began erupting for the first time since 1986. Augustine is a central dome and lava-flow complex surrounded by pyroclastic debris—not unlike Mount St. Helens in several respects. Both volcanoes are relatively young and frequently active. Mount St. Helens is notorious for its debris avalanche and eruption of May 18, 1980; Augustine has produced at least 11 debris avalanches in the past 2,000 years as a result of summit dome collapses (Waitt and Beget, 1996; Beget and Kienle, 1992). Mount St. Helens' eruptive products range from basalt through dacite (dominantly dacite). Augustine's products are dominantly andesite with small amounts of basaltic andesite and dacite. Before their current eruptions, both volcanoes last erupted in 1986, and both eruptions were dome-building events (Mount St. Helens, 1980–86; Augustine, March–September, 1986).

Given these similarities, we might expect that the precursors to Mount St. Helens' and Augustine's most recent eruptions were similar, too, and in several respects they were; however, there were some striking differences. On November 29, 2005, the Alaska Volcano Observatory (AVO) released the following statement (http://www.avo.alaska.edu/activity/avoreport.php?view=info&id=342&type=info&month=November&year=2005, last accessed January 14, 2008):

> Beginning in May 2005, there has been a slow increase in the number of earthquakes located under Augustine Volcano. The earthquakes are generally small (less than magnitude 1.0) and concentrate roughly 1 km below the volcano's summit. These earthquakes have slowly increased from 4–8 earthquakes/day to 20–35 earthquakes/day. Additionally, data from a 6-station Global Positioning System (GPS) network on Augustine Volcano indicate that a slow, steady inflation of the volcano started in mid-summer 2005 and continues at present. The GPS benchmark located nearest the summit has moved a total of 2.5 cm (1 inch). This motion is consistent with a source of inflation or pressure change centered under the volcano. This is the first such deformation detected at Augustine Volcano since measurements began just prior to the 1986 eruption.

Small explosions began on December 9, 2005, and there were reports of unusual "steaming" and sulfur smell downwind of the volcano, as well as a visible, condensed-steam plume extending at least 75 km from the volcano on December 12. The eruption began in earnest on January 11, 2006, characterized by magmatic explosions, pyroclastic flows and lahars, and extrusion of a new lava dome and flow that was first observed on January 16, 2006. Emission rates for SO_2 were about 1,000 t/d in early January and several thousand t/d during the first week of the eruption. Corresponding CO_2 emission rates were 2–3 times greater (Cervelli and others, 2006; Power and others, 2006).

The Augustine and Mount St. Helens eruptions were similar in the following respects:

1. No precursory inflation of a deep (>5 km) source was detected; modeling of GPS data indicates the preeruptive inflation source at Augustine was 1–2 km beneath the volcano's summit, at a depth of approximately sea level (Cervelli and others, 2006),

2. Deep deflation was associated with extrusion,

3. Phreatic explosions preceded the beginning of extrusion,

4. Energetic swarms of shallow earthquakes occurred in the days prior to the first explosion, and

5. Erupted products were predominantly effusive, with only minor tephra.

The eruptions differed in the following ways:

6. There were eight months of elevated seismicity at Augustine versus a few days of elevated seismicity at Mount St. Helens,

7. There were six months of precursory inflation at Augustine versus no precursory inflation at Mount St. Helens (but see below), and

8. There were several thousand tons per day of SO_2 and CO_2 recorded at Augustine versus 40–250 t/d SO_2 and 800–2,400 t/d CO_2 recorded at Mount St. Helens (Gerlach and others, this volume, chap. 26).

The differences in items 6 and 8 are supported by unambiguous seismic and gas emission-rate data, but the apparent lack of precursory inflation at Mount St. Helens (item 7) could be an artifact of inadequate geodetic monitoring. Station JRO1 might have been too distant (9 km) to detect inflation of a shallow source comparable to the one that inflated for months at Augustine. Even so, relatively deep sources at both volcanoes deflated during the eruptions but did not inflate in the years or months beforehand—a pattern unlikely to be sustainable over several eruption cycles. A possible explanation for this observation is that inflation of deep magma sources beneath arc volcanoes occurs mainly early in the eruption cycle, soon after an eruption ends, and slows as the next eruption approaches. This pattern has been observed in InSAR studies of Westdahl and Okmok volcanoes in the Aleutian arc by Lu and others (2003, 2005). Lu and his colleagues suggest that the magma supply rate is governed by the pressure gradient between a deep source and shallow reservoir. The pressure gradient and hence the flow rate are greatest immediately after eruptions. Pressurization of the reservoir decreases both the pressure gradient and flow rate, but eventually the reservoir ruptures, an eruption or intrusion occurs, and the cycle starts anew. This scenario is consistent with trilateration and campaign GPS results for Mount St. Helens that showed dilatation between 1982 and 1991, but no measurable deformation from 1991 to 2000 or from 2000 to 2003.

Given that the latest repose periods at Mount St. Helens and Augustine were similar, and that the magma erupted at Mount St. Helens is more viscous (greater SiO_2 content and crystallinity, lower temperature), why did Mount St. Helens erupt with less precursory seismicity and (perhaps) surface deformation? An important difference between the two eruptions is the higher gas-emission rates at Augustine. Gassy magma suggests a deep source, and the prolonged period of elevated seismicity and surface inflation at Augustine probably reflect the accumulation of rising magma in a shallow reservoir. In contrast, there are indications that gas-poor 2004–5 magma had already accumulated in a crustal reservoir long before the September 2004 earthquake swarm at Mount St. Helens. Inflation might have occurred anytime between 1982 and 1991, as suggested by trilateration and GPS results, episodically during repeated earthquake swarms between 1987 and 2001, or continuously and mostly aseismically.

Conjecture Regarding the Link Between 1980–1986 and 2004–2005 Eruptions

Continued low gas-emission rates at Mount St. Helens more than a year after the eruption began, and after extrusion of more than 73×10^6 m^3 of dacite, suggest that the eruption is being fed from a reservoir of mostly degassed magma. The most likely source is magma left over from the 1980s. The May 18, 1980, eruption was unusual in that it was triggered by a large landslide at 0832 PDT that unloaded the magmatic system suddenly and tapped gas-rich magma from a reservoir at 8 km depth. A devastating lateral blast and debris avalanche produced the most compelling images from the eruption, but an important change in the eruption's character did not occur until midday. Rowley and others (1981, p. 492, 489) reported: "At about noon, the eruption cloud lightened in color from medium gray to dirty white * * * (D.A. Swanson, oral commun., 1980)." and "Pyroclastic flows were first observed being emplaced at 1217 PDT (Pacific Daylight time) on May 18, nearly 4 hr after the start of the eruption, and successive pyroclastic flows continued to form intermittently for about 5 hr thereafter." It seems likely that the change in the eruption cloud at midday corresponded to the first arrival at the surface of gas-rich magma from a deeper source, presumably the 7-km-deep reservoir proposed by Rutherford and others (1985). This idea is consistent with the onset of vigorous harmonic tremor, indicative of magma movement, just before noon, and with its decline at about 1730 PDT (Malone and others, 1981).

If this scenario is correct, the hours-long delay between the initiation of the landslide and the first arrival of reservoir magma at the surface suggests that the latter might not have occurred without the former, that is, that the landslide interrupted a sequence of events that otherwise might not have tapped the reservoir on May 18. Without the landslide trigger, magma intruding the volcano to cause the famous north-flank bulge might have reached the surface in less spectacular fashion and might not have been followed by gas-rich magma from the reservoir. We speculate that catastrophic unloading of the magmatic system by the landslide decreased the reservoir-to-surface distance, thus increasing the pressure gradient abruptly. As a consequence of the greater pressure gradient, rapidly rising magma created and maintained an open conduit to the surface for 9 hours—enough time to release any separate gas phase that might have accumulated near the top of the reservoir. There would have been ample time, since the end of the previous eruption in 1857, for a volatile-rich cap to form by vesiculation and bubble-rise in the reservoir. Magma that rose into the lower-pressure environment of the reservoir prior to 1980 would have been temporarily oversaturated in volatiles. The "excess" volatiles would have exsolved to form bubbles that tend to aggregate and migrate toward the top of the reservoir. Given enough time and low enough permeability to the surface, a volatile-rich cap develops on the reservoir. The physics of this process is beyond the scope of this paper. We suggest only that the May 18, 1980, landslide might have initiated a cascade of events that resulted in, among the more obvious consequences, catastrophic loss of the gas-rich upper part of the reservoir. This set the stage for dome-building eruptions that followed in 1980–86 and 2004–5, which tapped reservoir magma that had been separated from its excess volatiles and only partly replenished during the interim.

The presence in the upper crust of magma remnant from the 1980s and earlier, which was devoid of its excess volatiles as a result of the May 18, 1980, eruption, might explain some aspects of the 2004–5 eruption. For example, the absence of precursory reservoir inflation is consistent with the idea that the magma erupted in 2004–5 was already present in the reservoir and conduit system when JRO1 was installed in 1997. Likewise, the short duration of precursory seismicity and the low gas emission rates throughout the 2004–5 eruption can be explained if the first few days of unrest involved the mobilization of magma that had been stored in the upper part of the conduit since the end of the 1980–86 eruption. This was soon followed by the rise of magma that arrived in the reservoir sometime before 1980, equilibrated to the pressure and temperature conditions in the reservoir, and lost its excess volatiles during the eruption on May 18, 1980. This explanation does not preclude partial recharge of the reservoir prior to or during the 2004–5 eruption. Mastin and others (this volume, chap. 22) conclude from their analysis of the geodetic data that "* * * erupted magma has been replaced in increasing proportions by recharge, but that the recharge rate remains somewhat less than the current effusion rate." Both the velocity of JRO1 and the effusion rate declined throughout 2006–7. During part or all of that period, the recharge rate might have been comparable to the effusion rate (L. Mastin, oral commun., 2008).

Although mostly speculative, we believe the following scenario is consistent with the current state of knowledge concerning the 1980–86 and 2004–5 eruptions. Both eruptions were fed from a reservoir centered near 8 km depth; magma erupted in the 1980s accumulated in the reservoir during an extended period, long enough for gas bubbles to rise and form a volatile-rich cap (Gerlach and McGee, 1994). The May 18, 1980, landslide and plinian eruption depressurized the reservoir catastrophically, releasing the volatile-rich cap and causing additional bubbles to form throughout the reservoir. Most of those bubbles managed to rise to the top of the reservoir at about 5 km depth and escape via the 1980 conduit system prior to the start of the 2004–5 eruption, leaving behind a large volume of gas-poor magma—at least several cubic kilometers according to Mastin and others (this volume, chap. 22). The 2004–5 eruption was preceded by and has been accompanied by reservoir recharge, which is continuing at a rate of ~1 m^3/s (early 2006). Any magmatic gas signature from recharge might be delayed and muted by the large vertical extent of the reservoir and relatively high viscosity of reservoir magma. Factors that will influence the future course of the eruption (for example, slowing and eventual cessation of dome growth, or a transition to either more explosive activity or effusion of more mafic magma) include (1) the recharge rate going forward, (2) bubble-rise rates in the reservoir–conduit system, and (3) the character of magma entering the base of the reservoir (that is, gas content and melt composition).

Volcanoes are complex natural systems. Effective hazards mitigation, even at well-monitored volcanoes such as Mount St. Helens, requires constant vigilance and better understanding of a wide variety of physical, chemical, and hydrologic processes that interact to produce eruptions. The events of late 2004 and 2005 at Mount St. Helens amazed and confounded us as they unfolded, and to some extent they still do. What were the perceived odds on September 22, 2004, that an enormous welt would rise on the crater floor in a matter of days, without producing far-field deformation, deep seismicity, or greatly increased gas emission? Or that the top of a dacite magma column would emerge from the welt in less than three weeks and extrude for more than a year as a series of gouge-covered spines, with older spines shunted aside as newer ones emerged? Or that during the eruption, Crater Glacier would be split in two and crumpled against the crater walls without producing even a trickle of water flow at the crater mouth? Clearly, there is much left to learn at this volcano before we can understand how, when, and why such amazing events occur, and to what extent they might be hazardous.

Acknowledgments

This is an overview and ideas paper, mostly devoid of its own data. The authors make no claim of originality or exclusivity. We accept responsibility for bad or half-baked ideas and credit any good ones to the eruption team at the USGS Cascades Volcano Observatory. We thank L.G. Mastin and P.F. Cervelli for helpful reviews.

References Cited

Amelung, F., Jónsson, S., Zebker, H., and Segall, P., 2000, Widespread uplift and 'trapdoor' faulting on Galápagos volcanoes observed with radar interferometry: Nature, v. 407, no. 6807, p. 993–996.

Beget, J.E., and Kienle, J., 1992, Cyclic formation of debris avalanches at Mount St. Augustine volcano: Nature, v. 356, no. 6371, p. 701–704.

Caputo, M., 1979, Two thousand years of geodetic and geophysical observations in the Phlegraean Fields near Naples: Geophysical Journal of the Royal Astronomical Society, v. 56, p. 319–328.

Cashman, K.V., Thornber, C.R., and Pallister, J.S., 2008, From dome to dust; shallow crystallization and fragmentation of conduit magma during the 2004–2006 dome extrusion of Mount St. Helens, Washington, chap. 19 *of* Sherrod, D.R., Scott, W.E., and Stauffer, P.H., eds., A volcano rekindled; the renewed eruption of Mount St. Helens, 2004–2006: U.S. Geological Survey Professional Paper 1750 (this volume).

Cervelli, P.F., Fournier, T., Freymueller, J., and Power, J.A., 2006, Ground deformation associated with the precursory unrest and early phases of the January 2006 eruption of Augustine Volcano, Alaska: Geophysical Research Letters, v. 33, L18304, doi: 10.1029/2006GL027219.

Dvorak, J.J., and Okamura, A.T., 1987, A hydraulic model to explain variations in summit tilt rate at Kilauea and Mauna Loa volcanoes, chap. 46 *of* Decker, R.W., Wright, T.L., and Stauffer, P.H., eds., Volcanism in Hawaii: U.S. Geological Survey Professional Paper 1350, v. 2, p. 1281–1296.

Dzurisin, D., 2003, A comprehensive approach to monitoring volcano deformation as a window on the eruption cycle: Reviews of Geophysics, v. 41, no. 1, p. 1.1–1.29, doi:10.1029/2001RG000107.

Dzurisin, D., Wicks, C., Jr., and Thatcher, W., 1999, Renewed uplift at the Yellowstone caldera measured by leveling surveys and satellite radar interferometry: Bulletin of Volcanology, v. 61, p. 349–355.

Dzurisin, D., Vallance, J.W., Gerlach, T.M., Moran, S.C., and Malone, S.D., 2005, Mount St. Helens reawakens: Eos (American Geophysical Union Transactions), v. 86, no. 3, p. 25, 29.

Gerlach, T.M., McGee, K.A., and Doukas, M.P., 2008, Emission rates of CO_2, SO_2, and H_2S, scrubbing, and preeruption excess volatiles at Mount St. Helens, 2004–2005, chap. 26 *of* Sherrod, D.R., Scott, W.E., and Stauffer, P.H., eds., A volcano rekindled; the renewed eruption of Mount St. Helens, 2004–2006: U.S. Geological Survey Professional Paper 1750 (this volume).

Herd, R.A., Edmonds, M., and Bass, V.A., 2005, Catastrophic lava dome failure at Soufrière Hills Volcano, Montserrat, 12–13 July 2003: Journal of Volcanology and Geothermal Research, v. 148, nos. 3–4, p. 234–252, doi:10.1016/j.jvolgeores.2005.05.003.

Hill, D.P., Bailey, R.A., and Ryall, A.S., 1985, Active tectonic and magmatic processes beneath Long Valley caldera, eastern California; an overview: Journal of Geophysical Research, v. 90, p. 11111–11120.

Iverson, R.M., 2008, Dynamics of seismogenic volcanic extrusion resisted by a solid surface plug, Mount St. Helens, 2004–2005, chap. 21 *of* Sherrod, D.R., Scott, W.E., and Stauffer, P.H., eds., A volcano rekindled; the renewed eruption of Mount St. Helens, 2004–2006: U.S. Geological Survey Professional Paper 1750 (this volume).

Iverson, R.M., Dzurisin, Daniel, Gardner, C.A., Gerlach, T.M., LaHusen, R.G., Lisowski, Michael, Major, J.J., Malone, S.D., Messerich, J.A., Moran, S.C., Pallister, J.S., Qamar, A.I., Schilling, S.P., and Vallance, J.W., 2006, Dynamics of seismogenic volcanic extrusion at Mount St. Helens in 2004–05: Nature, v. 444, no. 7118, p. 439–443, doi:10.1038/nature05322.

LaHusen, R.G., Swinford, K.J., Logan, M., and Lisowski, M., 2008, Instrumentation in remote and dangerous settings; examples using data from GPS "spider" deployments during the 2004–2005 eruption of Mount St. Helens, Washington, chap. 16 *of* Sherrod, D.R., Scott, W.E., and Stauffer, P.H., eds., A volcano rekindled; the renewed eruption of Mount St. Helens, 2004–2006: U.S. Geological Survey Professional Paper 1750 (this volume).

Lipman, P.W., Moore, J.G., and Swanson, D.A., 1981, Bulging of the north flank before the May 18 eruption—geodetic data, *in* Lipman, P.W., and Mullineaux, D.R., eds., The 1980 eruptions of Mount St. Helens, Washington: U.S. Geological Survey Professional Paper 1250, p. 143–155.

Lisowski, M., Dzurisin, D., Denlinger, R.P., and Iwatsubo, E.Y., 2008, Analysis of GPS-measured deformation associated with the 2004–2006 dome-building eruption of Mount St. Helens, Washington, chap. 15 *of* Sherrod, D.R., Scott, W.E., and Stauffer, P.H., eds., A volcano rekindled; the renewed eruption of Mount St. Helens, 2004–2006: U.S. Geological Survey Professional Paper 1750 (this volume).

Lu, Z., Masterlark, T., Dzurisin, D., Rykhus, R., and Wicks, C., Jr., 2003, Magma supply dynamics at Westdahl volcano, Alaska, modeled from satellite radar interferometry: Journal of Geophysical Research, v. 108, no. B7, 2354, 17 p., doi:10.1029/2002JB002311.

Lu, Z., Masterlark, T., and Dzurisin, D., 2005, Interferometric synthetic aperture radar (InSAR) Study of Okmok Volcano, Alaska, 1992–2003; magma supply dynamics and post-emplacement lava flow deformation: Journal of Geophysical Research, v. 110, no. B12, B02403, doi: 10.1029/2004JB003148, 18 p.

Lu, Z., Dzurisin, D., Wicks, C., Jr., Power, J., Kwoun, O., and Rykhus, R., 2007, Diverse deformation patterns of Aleutian volcanoes from satellite interferometric synthetic aperture radar (InSAR), *in* Eichelberger, J.C., Gordeev, E., Izbekov, P., Kasahara, M., and Lees, J.M., eds., Volcanism and tectonics of the Kamchatka Peninsula and adjacent arcs: American Geophysical Union Geophysical Monograph 172, p. 249–261.

Major, J.J., Kingsbury, C.G., Poland, M.P., and LaHusen, R.G., 2008, Extrusion rate of the Mount St. Helens lava dome estimated from terrestrial imagery, November 2004–December 2005, chap. 12 *of* Sherrod, D.R., Scott, W.E., and Stauffer, P.H., eds., A volcano rekindled; the renewed eruption of Mount St. Helens, 2004–2006: U.S. Geological Survey Professional Paper 1750 (this volume).

Malone, S.D., Endo, E.T., Weaver, C.S., and Ramey, J.W., 1981, Seismic monitoring for eruption prediction, *in* Lipman, P.W., and Mullineaux, D.R., eds., The 1980 eruptions of Mount St. Helens, Washington: U.S. Geological Survey Professional Paper 1250, p. 803–813.

Mastin, L.G., Roeloffs, E., Beeler, N.M., and Quick, J.E., 2008, Constraints on the size, overpressure, and volatile content of the Mount St. Helens magma system from geodetic and dome-growth measurements during the 2004–2006+ eruption, chap. 22 *of* Sherrod, D.R., Scott, W.E., and Stauffer, P.H., eds., A volcano rekindled; the renewed eruption of Mount St. Helens, 2004–2006: U.S. Geological Survey Professional Paper 1750 (this volume).

Massonnet, D., Rossi, M., Carmona, C., Adragna, F., Peltzer, G., Feigl, K., and Rabaute, T., 1993, The displacement field of the Landers earthquake mapped by radar interferometry: Nature, v. 364, p. 138–142.

McCaffrey, R., Long, M.D., Goldfinger, C., Zwick, P.C., Nabelek, J.L., Johnson, C.K., and Smith, C., 2000, Rotation and plate locking at the southern Cascadia subduction zone: Geophysical Research Letters, v. 27, no. 19, p. 3117–3120.

Moran, S.C., 1994, Seismicity at Mount St. Helens, 1987–1992: Evidence for repressurization of an active magmatic system: Journal of Geophysical Research, v. 99, p. 4341–4354.

Moran, S.C., Malone, S.D., Qamar, A.I., Thelen, W.A., Wright, A.K., and Caplan-Auerbach, J., 2008, Seismicity associated with renewed dome building at Mount St. Helens, 2004–2005, chap. 2 *of* Sherrod, D.R., Scott, W.E., and Stauffer, P.H., eds., A volcano rekindled; the renewed eruption of Mount St. Helens, 2004–2006: U.S. Geological Survey Professional Paper 1750 (this volume).

Pallister, J.S., Thornber, C.R., Cashman, K.V., Clynne, M.A., Lowers, H.A., Mandeville, C.W., Brownfield, I.K., and Meeker, G.P., 2008, Petrology of the 2004–2006 Mount St. Helens lava dome—implications for magmatic plumbing and eruption triggering, chap. 30 *of* Sherrod, D.R., Scott, W.E., and Stauffer, P.H., eds., A volcano rekindled; the renewed eruption of Mount St. Helens, 2004–2006: U.S. Geological Survey Professional Paper 1750 (this volume).

Poland, M.P., and Lu, Z., 2008, Radar interferometry observations of surface displacements during pre- and coeruptive periods at Mount St. Helens, Washington, 1992–2005, chap. 18 *of* Sherrod, D.R., Scott, W.E., and Stauffer, P.H., eds., A volcano rekindled; the renewed eruption of Mount St. Helens, 2004–2006: U.S. Geological Survey Professional Paper 1750 (this volume).

Poland, M.P., Dzurisin, D., LaHusen, R.G., Major, J.J., Lapcewich, D., Endo, E.T., Gooding, D.J., Schilling, S.P., and Janda, C.G., 2008, Remote camera observations of lava dome growth at Mount St. Helens, Washington, October 2004 to February 2006, chap. 11 *of* Sherrod, D.R., Scott, W.E., and Stauffer, P.H., eds., A volcano rekindled; the renewed eruption of Mount St. Helens, 2004–2006: U.S. Geological Survey Professional Paper 1750 (this volume).

Power, J.A., Nye, C.J., Coombs, M.L., Wessels, R.L., Cervelli, P.F., Dehn, J., Wallace, K.L., Freymueller, J.T., and Doukas, M.P., 2006, The reawakening of Alaska's Augustine Volcano [abs.]: Eos (American Geophysical Union Transactions), v. 87, no. 37, p. 373, doi:10.1029/2006EO370002.

Rowley, P.D., Kuntz, M.A., and MacLeod, N.S., 1981, Pyroclastic-flow deposits, *in* Lipman, P.W., and Mullineaux, D.R., eds., The 1980 eruptions of Mount St. Helens, Washington: U.S. Geological Survey Professional Paper 1250, p. 489–512.

Rutherford, M.J., and Devine, J.D., III, 2008, Magmatic conditions and processes in the storage zone of the 2004–2006 Mount St. Helens dacite, chap. 31 *of* Sherrod, D.R., Scott, W.E., and Stauffer, P.H., eds., A volcano rekindled; the renewed eruption of Mount St. Helens, 2004–2006: U.S. Geological Survey Professional Paper 1750 (this volume).

Rutherford, M.J., Sigurdsson, H., Carey, S., and Davis, A., 1985, The May 18, 1980, eruption of Mount St. Helens; 1. melt composition and experimental phase equilibria: Journal of Geophysical Research, v. 90, no. B4, p. 2929–2947.

Ryan, S.C., 1995, Quiescent outgassing of Mauna Loa volcano, 1958–1994, *in* Rhodes, J.M., and Lockwood, J.P., eds., Mauna Loa revealed; structure, composition, history, and hazards: Washington, D.C., American Geophysical Union Geophysical Monograph 92, p. 95–116.

Savage, J.C., Svarc, J.L., Prescott, W.H., and Murray, M.H., 2000, Deformation across the forearc of the Cascadia subduction zone at Cape Blanco, Oregon: Journal of Geophysical Research, v. 105, no. B2, p. 3095–3102.

Scandone, R., and Malone, S.D., 1985, Magma supply, magma discharge and readjustment of the feeding system of Mount St. Helens during 1980: Journal of Volcanology and Geothermal Research, v. 23, nos. 3–4, p. 239–262, doi:10.1016/0377-0273(85)90036-8.

Schilling, S.P., Thompson, R.A., Messerich, J.A., and Iwatsubo, E.Y., 2008, Use of digital aerophotogrammetry to determine rates of lava dome growth, Mount St. Helens, Washington, 2004–2005, chap. 8 *of* Sherrod, D.R., Scott, W.E., and Stauffer, P.H., eds., A volcano rekindled; the renewed eruption of Mount St. Helens, 2004–2006: U.S. Geological Survey Professional Paper 1750 (this volume).

Swanson, D.A., Lipman, P.W., Moore, J.G., Heliker, C.C., and Yamashita, K.M., 1981, Geodetic monitoring after the May 18 eruption, *in* Lipman, P.W., and Mullineaux, D.R., eds., The 1980 eruptions of Mount St. Helens, Washington: U.S. Geological Survey Professional Paper 1250, p. 157–168.

Swanson, D.A., Casadevall, T.J., Dzurisin, D., Malone, S.D., Newhall, C.G., and Weaver, C.S., 1983, Predicting eruptions at Mount St. Helens, June 1980 through December 1982: Science, v. 221, no. 4618, p. 1369–1376.

Swanson, D.A., Dzurisin, D., Holcomb, R.T., Iwatsubo, E.Y., Chadwick, W.W., Jr., Casadevall, T.J., Ewert, J.W., and Heliker, C.C., 1987, Growth of the lava dome at Mount St. Helens, Washington (USA), 1981–1983, *in* Fink, J.H., ed., Emplacement of silicic domes and lava flows: Geological Society of America Special Paper 212, p. 1–16.

Thelen, W.A., Crosson, R.S., and Creager, K.C., 2008, Absolute and relative locations of earthquakes at Mount St. Helens, Washington, using continuous data; implications for magmatic processes, chap. 4 *of* Sherrod, D.R., Scott, W.E., and Stauffer, P.H., eds., A volcano rekindled; the renewed eruption of Mount St. Helens, 2004–2006: U.S. Geological Survey Professional Paper 1750 (this volume).

Tryggvason, E., 1994, Surface deformation at the Krafla volcano, North Iceland, 1982–1992: Bulletin of Volcanology, v. 56, no. 2, p. 98–107.

Vallance, J.W., Schneider, D.J., and Schilling, S.P., 2008, Growth of the 2004–2006 lava-dome complex at Mount St. Helens, Washington, chap. 9 *of* Sherrod, D.R., Scott, W.E., and Stauffer, P.H., eds., A volcano rekindled; the renewed eruption of Mount St. Helens, 2004–2006: U.S. Geological Survey Professional Paper 1750 (this volume).

Waitt, R.B., and Beget, J.E., 1996, Provisional geologic map of Augustine Volcano, Alaska: U.S. Geological Survey Open-File Report 96–0516, 44 p., 1 plate, scale 1:25,000.

Walder, J.S., Schilling, S.P., Vallance, J.W., and LaHusen, R.G., 2008, Effects of lava-dome growth on the Crater Glacier of Mount St. Helens, Washington, chap. 13 *of* Sherrod, D.R., Scott, W.E., and Stauffer, P.H., eds., A volcano rekindled; the renewed eruption of Mount St. Helens, 2004–2006: U.S. Geological Survey Professional Paper 1750 (this volume).

Wicks, C.W., Thatcher, W., Dzurisin, D., and Svarc, J., 2006, Uplift, thermal unrest, and magma intrusion at Yellowstone caldera: Nature, v. 440, no. 7080, p. 72–75, doi:10.1038/nature04507.

Zebker, H.A., Amelung, F., and Jonsson, S., 2000, Remote sensing of volcano surface and internal processes using radar interferometry, *in* Mouginis-Mark, P.J., Crisp, J.A., and Fink, J.H., eds., Remote sensing of active volcanism: American Geophysical Union Geophysical Monograph 116, p. 179–205.

A Volcano Rekindled: The Renewed Eruption of Mount St. Helens, 2004–2006
Edited by David R. Sherrod, William E. Scott, and Peter H. Stauffer
U.S. Geological Survey Professional Paper 1750, 2008

Chapter 15

Analysis of GPS-Measured Deformation Associated with the 2004–2006 Dome-Building Eruption of Mount St. Helens, Washington

By Michael Lisowski[1], Daniel Dzurisin[1], Roger P. Denlinger[1], and Eugene Y. Iwatsubo[1]

Abstract

Detecting far-field deformation at Mount St. Helens since the crater-forming landslide and blast in 1980 has been difficult despite frequent volcanic activity and improved monitoring techniques. Between 1982 and 1991, the systematic extension of line lengths in a regional GPS trilateration network is consistent with recharge of a deep magma chamber during that interval. The rate of extension, however, averages only 3 mm/yr, and some of this apparent deformation may result from systematic scale error in the electronic distance measurements. Subsequent GPS surveys and data from a continuous GPS station, located 9 km north of Mount St. Helens and operating since 1997, show no significant volcanic deformation until the start of unrest on September 23, 2004. The current eruption has been accompanied by subtle but widespread inward and downward movement of GPS monitoring stations, exponentially decreasing with time and totaling as much as 30 mm. The observed deformation is consistent with the predictions of an elastic half-space model of a vertically elongate magma chamber with its center at a depth of around 7 to 8 km and with a total cavity-volume loss of about 16–24×10^6 m^3. The discrepancy between the estimated cavity-volume loss and the >83×10^6-m^3 volume of the erupted dome can be explained, for the most part, by exsolution of gas in the stored magma and by minor input of new magma during the eruption.

Introduction

The current episode of volcanic unrest at Mount St. Helens began suddenly with a shallow earthquake swarm on September 23, 2004. Geodetic monitoring of deformation in the months before and days after the start of unrest was limited to data from a single, continuous, dual-frequency GPS (CGPS) station, JRO1 (installed in 1997), having an antenna on the roof of Johnston Ridge Observatory (JRO) (fig. 1). Regional deformation in the years before the start of unrest was measured using campaign-style GPS surveys of a 43-station network during the summers of 2000 and 2003. Annual surveys of background deformation in the crater of Mount St. Helens began in 2000 at six GPS stations on and near the 1980s dome ("old dome") for the purpose of ground control (Schilling and others, this volume, chap. 8). A network of three single-frequency (L1) CGPS stations was installed in 2000 to monitor deformation on the September 1984 lobe of the 1980s dome, relative to two stations just outside of the crater (LaHusen and others, this volume, chap. 16). Only one of these L1 CGPS stations, SFOT (on the west flank), remained operational during most of 2004, and there is no GPS measurement of deformation in the crater until September 28, 2004. In the 1980s and 1990s, deformation of Mount St. Helens was measured by using (1) electronic distance meters (EDM) to track line-length changes, (2) theodolites to track angle changes, and (3) level arrays and electronic tiltmeters to monitor ground tilt (Dvorak and others, 1981; Lipman and others, 1981; Swanson and others, 1981; Ewert and Swanson, 1992).

The observed patterns and rates of deformation in volcanic areas are used to constrain possible sources and mechanisms of volcanic unrest. We did not detect a systematic pattern of deformation, other than secular tectonic motion, between the 2000 and 2003 campaign GPS surveys; nor were there anomalies in the JRO1 CGPS three-dimensional (3D), position-component time series before the start of unrest. By the time of the first phreatic explosion on October 1, 2004, the L1 CGPS network was restored to operational condition (the station on the September 1984

[1]U.S. Geological Survey, 1300 SE Cardinal Court, Vancouver, WA 98683

lobe of the dome was destroyed by ballistics on October 1) and several campaign GPS stations on the volcano's flanks were occupied. Within two weeks, additional CGPS stations were installed by the Cascades Volcano Observatory (CVO) and the Plate Boundary Observatory (PBO). Displacement of these stations during the eruption was small (a few centimeters maximum) and consistently inward toward Mount St. Helens and downward, the pattern of movement expected if a deep magma chamber were being depleted during the eruption. The deformation, however, is small given the volume of lava erupted at the surface. The pressure loss in the deep magma chamber that is feeding the eruption may be compensated by recharge and by exsolution of gas (Mastin and others, this volume, chap. 22).

We begin by discussing our methods of GPS data reduction and analysis, emphasizing the technique used to improve measurement precision by removing common-mode noise. We then use regional GPS surveys and CGPS data to calculate the pattern and rate of background tectonic deformation and to derive a simple tectonic model. Local deformation near Mount St. Helens is then calculated from EDM-measured, line-length data collected during the 1980s and 1990s and from GPS-measured position-change data collected between 2000 and 2003; these results are compared with the predictions indicated in the tectonic model. The time series of deformation at CGPS station JRO1 is examined carefully for anomalies in the years before the start of the current episode of volcanic unrest at Mount St. Helens. Finally, eruption-related deformation is calculated, and an elastic, half-space model of a deflating, spheroidal magma chamber is used to fit the observed deformation.

Figure 1. Radome-covered antenna for CGPS station JRO1, on the roof of the U.S.D.A. Forest Service's Johnston Ridge Observatory, 9 km north of Mount St. Helens, Washington. In the weeks before and days after September 23, 2004, when seismic unrest began, JRO1 was the only GPS station operating within 40 km of the volcano. USGS photo by E.Y. Iwatsubo.

GPS Data Collection and Analysis

Campaign GPS and Continuous Dual-Frequency GPS Networks

Regional and local deformation around Mount St. Helens is measured episodically with campaign GPS surveys and continuously with CGPS stations (fig. 2). The following is a simplified discussion of how GPS positions are determined. The basic principal is that a GPS position can be triangulated from distance measurements to several known locations. The GPS satellites transmit encoded timing signals (pseudoranges) at two carrier frequencies, L1 (1575.42 MHz) and L2 (1227.60 MHz). The orbits of the satellites are predictable, making them reference points from which the ground position can be triangulated. The distance is measured directly by using the travel time of the coded signal, but it is called a pseudorange because the satellite and ground clocks used to measure the travel time of the one-way satellite transmission are not synchronized. The most accurate measurement of distance is obtained from the relatively short-wavelength, continuous L1 and L2 carrier signals and from the so-called "ionospheric free" linear combination of L1 and L2 known as LC or L3. Generally, the LC observable is used to minimize scale error introduced by fluctuations in ionospheric activity. With the carrier signals, the range to the satellite is expressed as the sum of the observed carrier phase plus an ambiguous integer number of carrier wavelengths. Methods have been developed to determine or "fix" the phase ambiguities to their correct integer values, which removes them as an unknown in the solution and improves measurement precision.

The GPS data discussed here are acquired with geodetic-quality receivers that record pseudorange and carrier-phase data at least every 60 s, and most often at rates of 30, 15, or 10 s. During campaign GPS surveys, we collect data for a minimum of 6 hours (usually 24 hours) on multiple days.

Most of the campaign GPS stations around Mount St. Helens were surveyed initially in 2000, with the last complete survey of the network in 2003. Several stations were surveyed after the start of unrest on September 23, 2004, and again in 2005 and 2006. The center-punched, permanent tablets marking the campaign GPS stations generally are set in bedrock to provide a stable, long-term, ground-reference point. The only measure of deformation near Mount St. Helens at the start of unrest was provided by CGPS station JRO1. Other CGPS stations, operated by the Pacific Northwest Geodetic Array (PANGA) and the National Geodetic Survey's Continuous Operating Reference Stations (CORS), are found in the surrounding region and serve as stable local reference stations. Following the initial seismic swarm, a small number of the campaign GPS stations were reoccupied to measure deformation accumulated since 2003 and possible ongoing deformation during the early stages of the eruption.

By mid-October 2004 a new network of CGPS stations, installed by the USGS–CVO and the National Science Foundation's PBO, were tracking deformation associated with the eruption (table 1). Additional PBO and CVO CGPS stations were added in 2005 and 2006. In order to expedite obtaining site usage permits, and to keep the antennas above the winter snow pack, many of the new CGPS antennas were placed at the top of existing "winterized" 3- to 3.5-m-high steel towers that originally were installed in the fall of 1980 for EDM measurements (Swanson and others, 1981). Burial of the GPS antennas by snow has not been a problem, but ice buildup around the antenna and tower, particularly for stations high on the volcano's flank, has caused pseudodisplacements, two warped towers, and many communication and power failures.

GPS Data Processing: Minimally Constrained Daily Solution

We process GPS data with GIPSY/OASIS II software (Webb and Zumberge, 1995). Daily point-positioning solutions (Zumberge and others, 1997) use satellite orbit and clock

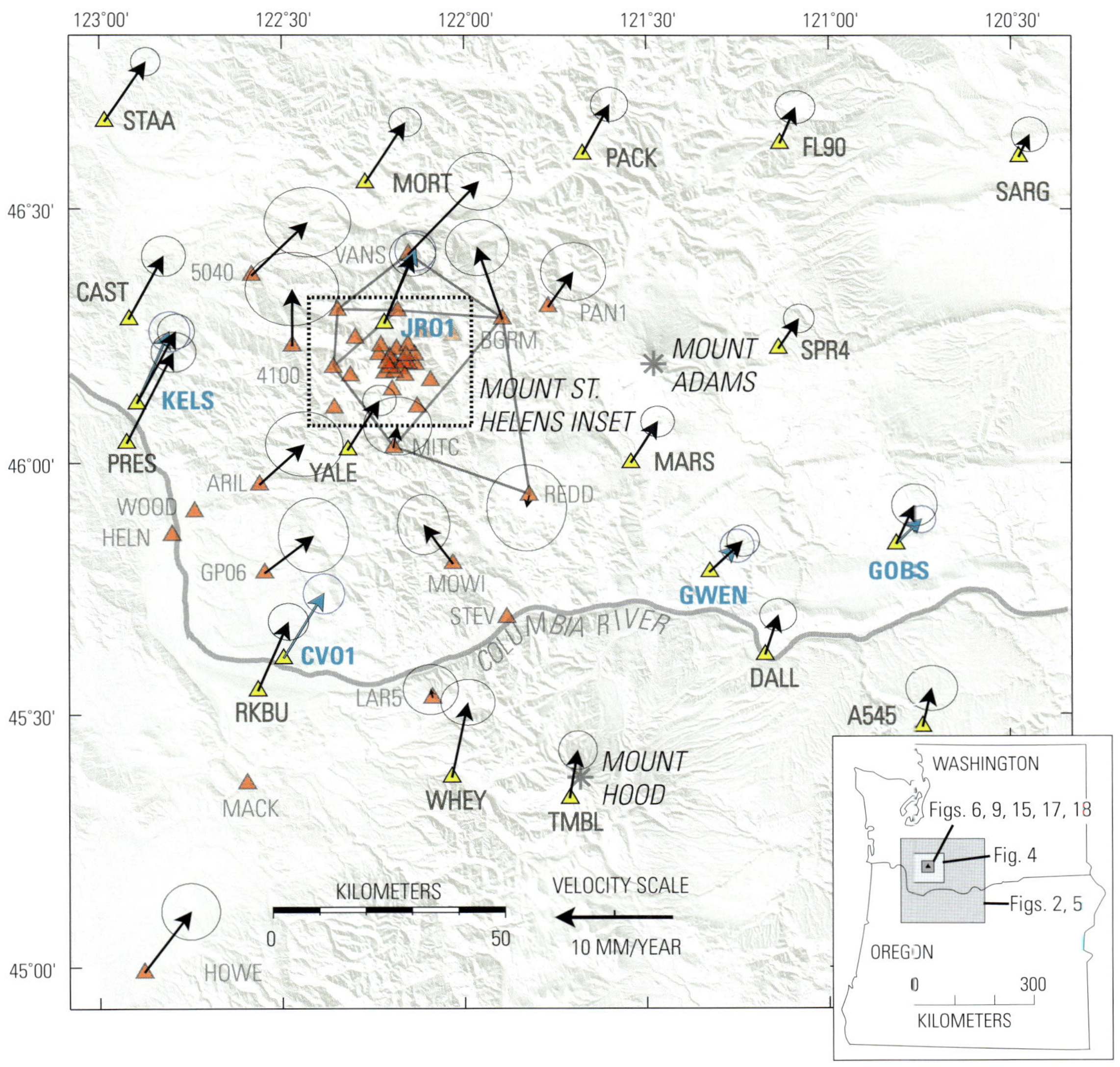

Figure 2. Map showing GPS stations in southwest Washington and northwest Oregon and their average horizontal-velocity vectors relative to stable North America (tipped with 95-percent-confidence error ellipses, vector scale at bottom) through September 2004. CGPS station names and velocity vectors are shown in blue. Black vectors at CGPS stations are calculated only from data coincident with campaign GPS surveys. Velocities at stations marked with yellow triangles are used to calculate background deformation for a tectonic model, which includes rigid-block motion and uniform-strain accumulation. The position of many stations was measured several times using campaign GPS, with some measurements made as early as 1992. However, the positions of most stations near Mount St. Helens (red triangles) were measured only in summers of 2000 and 2003. The Helens trilateration network, measured in 1982 and 1991, is shown here with faint solid lines between stations. The dashed box marks the local area around Mount St. Helens shown in figure 6.

Table 1. Regional and local continuously transmitting GPS (CGPS) stations near Mount St. Helens, Washington.

[Stations are listed in order of installation. PANGA, Pacific Northwest Geodetic Array; CVO, Cascades Volcano Observatory; PBO, Plate Boundary Observatory. See figure 2 for locations of most stations. Station names in bold type are within 20 km of Mount St. Helens.]

Station	Agency	Date operational	Monument type	Latitude (degrees)	Longitude (degrees)	Ellipsoidal elevation (m)
GOBS	PANGA	08/27/1997	Deep-drilled and braced	45.8388	-120.8147	621.49
KELS	PANGA	10/09/1997	Deep-drilled and braced	46.1182	-122.8961	-15.92
JRO1	CVO	05/23/1997	Roof mount	46.2751	-122.2176	1275.61
REDM	PANGA	07/24/1998	Shallow pier	44.2598	-121.1479	919.85
LIND	PANGA	07/28/1998	Roof mount	47.0003	-120.5390	471.93
LINH	PANGA	04/04/2002	Roof mount	47.0000	-120.5390	472.28
CVO1	CVO	01/04/2003	Roof mount	45.6109	-122.4961	66.67
P432	PBO	06/20/2004	Deep-drilled and braced	46.6228	-121.6832	318.88
P420	PBO	06/25/2004	Deep-drilled and braced	46.5886	-122.4961	74.11
P421	PBO	12/15/2004	Deep-drilled and braced	46.5318	-122.4292	220.60
TWRI	CVO	10/06/2004	EDM reflector tower	46.1979	-122.2119	2070.81
TWIW	CVO	10/11/2004	EDM reflector tower	46.2129	-122.1587	1630.55
P697	PBO	10/14/2004	EDM reflector tower	46.1876	-122.1766	2214.61
P693	PBO	10/14/2004	EDM reflector tower	46.2103	-122.2024	2113.00
P695	PBO	10/15/2004	EDM reflector tower	46.1990	-122.1642	2015.68
P696	PBO	10/15/2004	EDM reflector tower	46.1969	-122.1516	1600.03
TSTU	CVO	10/15/2004	EDM instrument tower	46.2369	-122.2241	1248.65
P687	PBO	10/16/2004	Shallow-drilled and braced	46.1096	-122.3546	391.10
TGAU	CVO	10/21/2004	EDM reflector tower	46.2192	-122.1923	1618.28
P698	PBO	11/04/2004	EDM reflector tower	46.1735	-122.1606	1479.39
P702	PBO	11/05/2004	Shallow-drilled and braced	46.3002	-122.3456	1305.70
P690	PBO	02/01/2005	EDM reflector tower	46.1800	-122.1899	2078.91
P699	PBO	02/02/2005	EDM reflector tower	46.1898	-122.2032	2274.11
P689	PBO	10/23/2005	Shallow-drilled and braced	46.1896	-122.3606	1359.46
THAR	CVO	06/28/2006	EDM instrument tower	46.2753	-122.1740	1430.55
P701	PBO	09/22/2006	Shallow-drilled and braced	46.1946	-122.1333	1247.79
P694	PBO	09/24/2006	Shallow-drilled and braced	46.2996	-122.1819	1726.03
P692	PBO	09/25/2006	Shallow-drilled and braced	46.2245	-122.1842	1492.23
P700	PBO	09/26/2006	Shallow-drilled and braced	46.1781	-122.2173	1522.03
P691	PBO	09/29/2006	Shallow-drilled and braced	46.2315	-122.2269	1183.26
P703	PBO	09/30/2006	Shallow-drilled and braced	46.1453	-122.1963	988.75
P705	PBO	09/30/2006	Shallow-drilled and braced	46.1730	-122.3106	1151.23

files obtained from the Jet Propulsion Laboratory (Pasadena, Calif.). The methods described by Blewitt (1989) are applied to the daily solutions of a network of stations, which improves measurement precision by estimating carrier-phase ambiguities within overlapping subsets of stations. The resulting minimally constrained network solution is in the reference frame of the satellite orbits (a nonfiducial reference frame—for example, Helfin and others, 1992). The GPS data processing to this point is standardized by using gp, a set of UNIX scripts and programs developed by Will Prescott and others at the USGS in Menlo Park, Calif. (see http://quake.wr.usgs.gov/research/deformation/gps/gpmanual/index.html).

Transformation of Minimally Constrained Solution to a Terrestrial Reference Frame

The next step in the GPS data-reduction process is experimental and has changed over time. The daily, minimally constrained, fixed-ambiguity network solution is merged with a point-position solution of a global network of CGPS stations (http://quake.wr.usgs.gov/research/deformation/gps/auto/*Track/*) that are in the stable interiors of the Earth's lithospheric plates; their positions and velocities are defined in the ITRF2000 terrestrial reference frame (Altimimi and others, 2002). No ambiguity resolution is attempted for the global network because of the large station separations. Station positions in the ITRF2000 frame station evolve following the no-net-rotation NNR-NUVEL-1A model of DeMets and others (1994). We are interested in deformation relative to the North American plate (NOAM), and for this purpose we created a nominal fixed-NOAM ITRF2000 reference frame using the Euler vector for NOAM given by Altimimi and others (2002, their table 6). We refer herein to this reference frame as "fixed-NOAMgp."

The combined (global and local), minimally constrained daily solution is transformed into ITRF2000 and to the fixed-NOAMgp terrestrial reference system by applying a seven-parameter Helmert transformation (x,y,z translations + rotations about the three axes + a scale change) that minimizes the misfit in the observed positions of the global reference stations with the positions predicted for that day. Misfit residuals from this adjustment are examined automatically to identify outliers, a reference station is removed from the solution if its residual exceeds five times the expected error, and the transformation process is iterated. Finally, the minimally constrained network solution and the combined ITRF and nominal fixed-NOAMgp solutions are archived, and Web-accessible plots of station time series and estimates of station velocities are updated.

GPS Networks Near Mount St. Helens

Campaign GPS and CGPS data from stations near Mount St. Helens are included in three regional groupings (networks): Cascadia includes most regional CGPS stations in the Pacific Northwest; Helens includes Mount St. Helens campaign GPS stations along with a subset of the regional CGPS stations that are processed only on the days campaign GPS data are collected; and HelensMonit includes CGPS stations around Mount St. Helens, a few regional GPS stations, and campaign GPS stations that provide bedrock local ties to the Mount St. Helens CGPS stations (for example, see http://quake.wr.usgs.gov/research/deformation/gps/auto/Helens/). These regional groupings are arbitrary and have resulted from the combination of a rapid increase in the number of stations over time and from the computational efficiency of processing data from networks having a smaller number of stations. New analysis techniques that detect and remove common-mode error in the station positions are most successful when all Mount St. Helens and related reference-station data are processed in a single group.

Local Terrestrial Reference Frames

The precision of regional GPS solutions can be improved by removing spatially correlated noise (Wdowinski and others, 1997). The transformation to a terrestrial reference frame is approximate, and it can be refined by using local stations (within a few hundred kilometers) with well-defined positions and velocities to estimate common-mode daily bias in the local solutions. Common-mode daily bias is estimated by either stacking the position component residuals (after removal of linear trends) of the local reference stations or by the equivalent procedure of estimating origin translations of the daily network solutions. We estimate the local network translations from a subset of CGPS reference stations included in the solutions.

We construct a local reference frame for the Mount St. Helens region to define the position of selected CGPS reference stations at any given time. The reference stations have long measurement histories, daily position measurements, and constant velocities. Starting with the daily combined, fixed-NOAMgp solutions, we remove all but the local reference stations and a subset of NOAM global stations. These solutions are merged to produce weekly averages of positions, outliers are identified and removed, and then the weekly averages for multiple years are adjusted to give an average position at a particular time and average station velocities (see Smith and others, 2004). We include the subset of ITRF2000 NOAM stations to keep the local reference frame aligned with our fixed-NOAMgp reference frame during the adjustment. Thereafter, most NOAM stations are removed from the final local reference frame because they are far from the region of interest.

The daily local solutions, which include several of the local reference stations, are then shifted into the local reference frame by applying a three-parameter Helmert transformation (3D translation), which minimizes the misfit between the observed positions of the local reference stations and those predicted by the local reference frame for that date. Occasionally, one or more of the local reference stations is poorly fit; it is removed from the regional solution and the transformation is iterated.

Removing the common-mode daily bias in the solutions can reduce the scatter in the station-component time series by a factor of 2 to 3 (Williams and others, 2004). Local-station seasonal wander, data offsets, and nonlinear deformation remain in the station-component time series after removing spatially correlated noise common to the reference stations. We use the QOCA (pronounced "coca") software (Quasi-Observation Combination Analysis) (Dong and others, 1998, 2002, 2006), designed and developed at NASA's Jet Propulsion Laboratory, for final analysis of the trends and noise in the GPS solutions. The QOCA software can be used to align the minimally constrained network solutions to any defined terrestrial reference frame, manipulate 3D station-position time series, and calculate spatial and temporal deformation.

Deformation in the Mount St. Helens Region Determined by Using GPS and Trilateration Survey Data

Tectonic interactions between the Pacific, Juan de Fuca, and North American plates displace and deform the ground in the Pacific Northwest (for example, Savage and others, 1991; Murray and Lisowski, 2000; McCaffrey and other, 2000; Savage and others, 2000; Miller and others, 2001; Svarc and others, 2002; Mazzotti and others, 2003). The widespread secular tectonic deformation can mask the more localized background and episodic deformation across the volcanic arc. For example, locking of the shallow interface between the Juan de Fuca and North American plates compresses the adjacent coastal region of the North American plate in the east-northeast direction of relative convergence between the plates. More enigmatic are the rigid-body movements of large continental regions (microplates) and possible strain accumulation or relative motion along their boundaries (for example, Wells and others, 1998; Wells and Simpson, 2001).

We use repeated GPS surveys and data from CGPS stations to derive a model for background tectonic deformation in the Mount St. Helens region. We then compare the modeled background rates of strain accumulation with that determined from line-length changes in an arc-crossing, regional trilateration network that was measured in 1982, 1991, and 2000. Finally, the tectonic model is used to adjust observed GPS station movements to determine the rate and pattern of volcanic deformation around Mount St. Helens since 2000.

Tectonic Rigid-Body Rotation and Strain Accumulation in the Mount St. Helens Region

The Helens GPS network includes several regional campaign stations with well-determined velocities, some occupied as early as 1992 (stations marked with yellow triangles in figs. 2 and 3). In addition, solutions for the Helens and Cascadia networks include several PANGA CGPS stations with well-determined velocities that are situated in the arc and back-arc regions (stations with blue names in figs. 2 and 3).

The GPS station velocities in the fixed-NOAMgp terrestrial reference frame reveal what appears to be a regional, clockwise, rigid-block rotation (figs. 2, 3). This microplate motion is roughly consistent with paleomagnetic studies that suggest widespread Cenozoic rotation in the Cascadia forearc (for example, Simpson and Cox, 1977; Magill and others, 1982; Wells and others, 1998) and is similar to widespread block rotation observed by using GPS to survey much of the Cascadia forearc, arc, and backarc region (McCaffrey and other, 2000; Savage and others, 2000; Svarc and other, 2002). In addition to the obvious block rotation, there may be a small amount of internal deformation (strain accumulation).

We use the method of Savage and others (2001, their appendix A) to simultaneously estimate an Euler vector for the rigid-body rotation and the rate of strain accumulation that best fits the observed regional-station velocities. Our best-fitting tectonic model was obtained by excluding the northern PANGA CGPS stations (CHWK, DRAO, SEDR, BREW) from the model. The resulting Euler vector, principal strain rates, and predicted station velocities are shown in figure 3 and summarized in table 2 (Helens GPS). An independent estimate of the rotation rate and strain was computed using QOCA, which gave similar results (table 2, Helens GPS QOCA). The computed Euler vector is roughly consistent with previous studies of GPS-measured deformation in Cascadia, which show a similar rate of clockwise block rotation (McCaffrey and other, 2000; Savage and others, 2000; Svarc and others, 2002). A small amount of uniaxial contraction (–18.0±1.9 nanostrain/yr, extension reckoned positive) accumulates in the ~N. 60° E. direction of relative convergence between the Juan de Fuca and North American plates. This rate of strain accumulation is equivalent to an average of 3.6 mm/yr of east-northeast-directed contraction across the 200-km-wide zone covered by the regional GPS stations and likely represents penetration of deformation from the locked subduction thrust into this region. The tectonic model does not define possible background vertical deformation, and we assume that there is none because regional studies of historical leveling data show little long-term elevation change across the Cascades (Verdonck, 2006).

Deformation in the 1980s and 1990s Within a Regional High-Precision Trilateration Network

The Helen trilateration network, which straddles the Cascade volcanic arc in southwestern Washington, was established to track regional strain accumulation following the 1980 crater-forming eruption of Mount St. Helens (fig. 4). Line lengths were measured in 1982 and 1991, and they were recovered with GPS in 2000 (EDM-measured line lengths can be downloaded from http://quake.wr.usgs.gov/research/deformation/gps/geodolite/index.html). The GPS-recovered line lengths were corrected for the –0.283 ppm systematic scale bias relative to Geodolite line lengths derived empirically by Savage and others (1996).

Table 2. EDM and GPS network strain and rotation rates.

[Strain rates within entire network assuming uniform strain accumulation. --, data not calculated.]

Network	Averaging interval	ε_1 (nano-strain/yr)	ε_2 (nano-strain /yr)	Azimuth ε_3 (degrees clockwise from north)	Rotation rate (nanoradian/yr)	Euler Pole latitude (degrees)	Euler Pole longitude (degrees)	Correlation latitude-longitude	Standard deviation unit weight
Helens EDM	1982.7–1991.7	82±28	62±27	44 ± 37	--	--	--	--	--
Helens EDM	1991.7–2000.7	11±29	–10±29	70 ± 35	--	--	--	--	--
Helens GPS	1992–2004	2.5±1.7	–18.0±1.9	63.8 ± 3.5	–15.4±1.2	44.476±0.141	–118.526±0.252	–0.804	1.0
Helens GPS (QOCA)	1992–2004	–0.8±2.7	–20.1±2.9	55.0 ± 6.0	–14.3±2.0	45.969±0.31	–117.876±0.540	–0.932	0.84

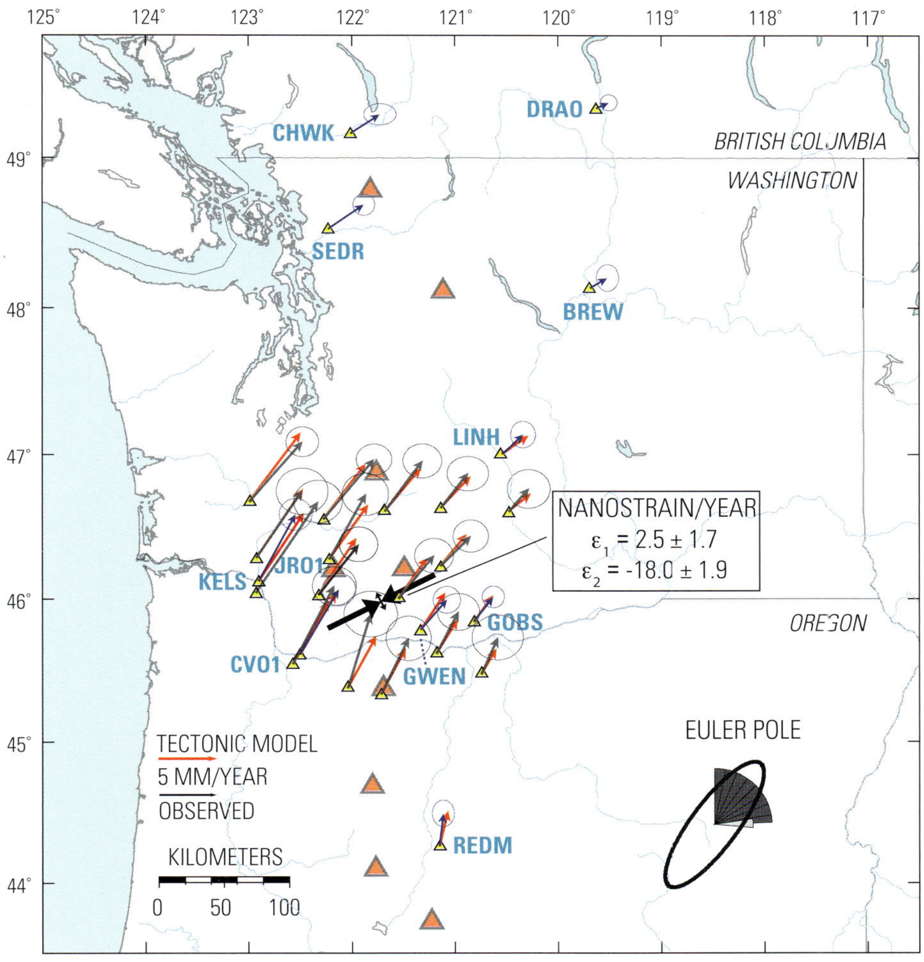

Figure 3. Map of GPS station velocities in Oregon, Washington, and British Columbia used to define the tectonic model of background rigid-block rotation and uniform strain accumulation. Observed station velocity vectors (black or blue arrows tipped with 95-percent-confidence error ellipses) are relative to stable North America. Velocity vectors predicted using the model are shown in red. Region for 95-percent confidence of the computed Euler pole is indicated by dark ellipse in eastern Oregon, rotation rate is indicated by dark wedges, and one-standard-deviation uncertainty in rotation rate is indicated by a light wedge. Large black arrows represent computed directions and rates of principal strains. The four most northerly CGPS stations (CHWK, DRAO, SEDR, BREW) are not included in the tectonic model calculation. Large orange triangles mark locations of major Cascade Range volcanoes.

Line lengths increased consistently by 1 to 3 cm between 1982 and 1991 but showed no significant change between 1991 and 2000. The uncertainty in a Helen line length measured with a Geodolite is between 4 and 8 mm, with the larger value for the longest lines in the network (see Savage and Prescott, 1973). By converting the observed line-length changes to extension rates and assuming that strain accumulates uniformly over the network, we can map variation in the extension rates as a function of line azimuth into surface tensor-strain-rate components. Between 1982 and 1991, areal dilatation ($\varepsilon_1 + \varepsilon_2$, where ε_1 and ε_2 are the principal strains and extension is reckoned positive) accumulated at a rate of 144±39 nanostrain/yr, which is equivalent to a ~3 mm/yr (~70 nanostrain/yr) average increase in the length across the ~40-km-aperture network in any direction. This rate of strain accumulation is distinctly different than the background areal dilatation rate (at −15±3 nanostrain/yr) estimated with the tectonic model (table 2 – note areal dilatation = $\varepsilon_1 + \varepsilon_2$). No significant strain accumulated between 1991 and 2000.

Surficial areal dilatation is expected to accompany recharge of a deep spheroidal magma reservoir. Areal dilatation is also a sensitive measure of possible systematic scale error in the individual EDM surveys because such error is proportional to distance measured and is independent of the direction of the line (Savage and others, 1986, p. 7471–7472). Systematic error in Geodolite line-length measurements is estimated to contribute about 0.14 ppm to the error in a line length, whereas a total systematic error of about 0.6 ppm between the two surveys is needed to reproduce the observed dilatation. The contribution of possible systematic error is included in the uncertainty in the rate of areal dilatation, and we conclude that the observed areal dilatation between 1982 and 1991 is too large for systematic error alone. Some other phenomenon, like recharge of the magma reservoir, contributes to this deformation.

Deformation in the Mount St. Helens GPS Network in the Years before September 23, 2004

The 43-station Helens campaign GPS network, surveyed in 2000 and 2003, extends for more than 50 km around Mount

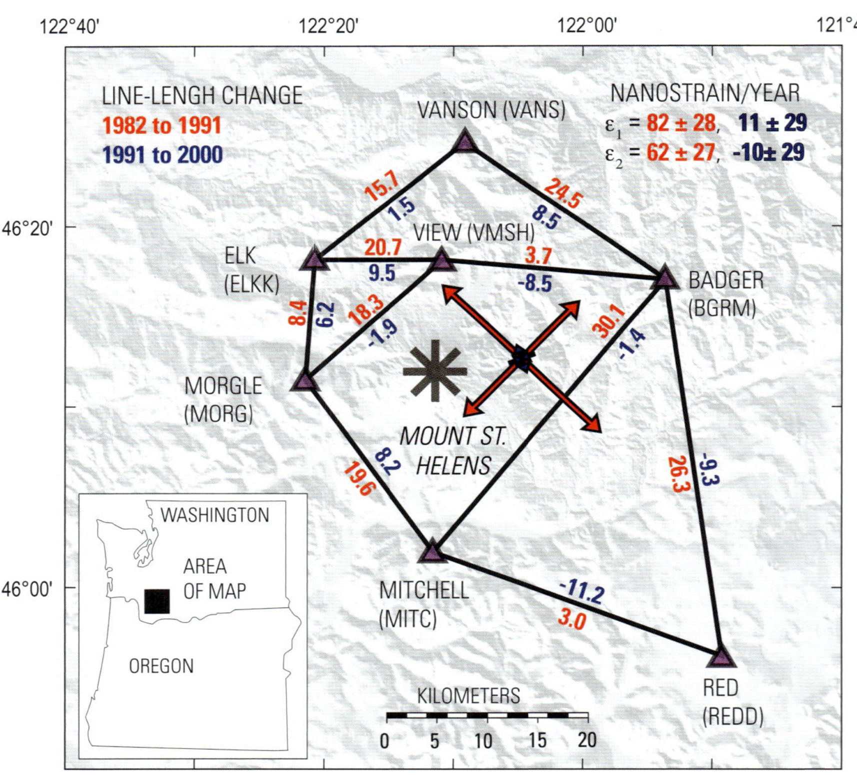

Figure 4. Map of the Helen trilateration network. Measured length changes and calculated uniform principal strain rates from 1982 to 1991 are shown in red. Corresponding values from 1991 to 2000 are shown in blue. EDM station names are given, with four-character GPS station name in parentheses. Line lengths in 2000 were measured with GPS. Directions and relative magnitudes of principal strain rates are shown with large arrows; their values are given in nanostrain per year.

St. Helens (stations marked with red triangles in fig. 2). Network coverage is increased in space and time by incorporating surveys of 13 nearby campaign GPS stations, some of which were measured as early as 1992, in the QOCA adjustment for average station velocities. Several PANGA CGPS stations, most in service since 1997 (table 1), are included in the solutions, and one of these, JRO1, is 9 km north of Mount St. Helens.

We use the predictions of the tectonic model given in table 2 (network Helens GPS) to remove regional secular deformation from the computed average GPS station velocities. We did not propagate uncertainty in the tectonic model into error in the corrected station velocities shown in figure 5 and listed in table 3. At the stations with well-defined velocities—those stations included in the tectonic-model calculation (stations marked with yellow triangles in fig. 5)—we see no significant motion. A few stations near Mount St. Helens have significant velocities, but their movements lack a consistent pattern, so we suspect they result from local instabilities or survey errors.

Examining the station velocities in the local network around Mount St. Helens (fig. 6), we observe no consistent pattern of deformation, but roughly half of the velocities exceed the 95-percent-confidence error ellipses. The highest velocity is found in the crater at station DMSH on the September 1984 lobe of the old dome, which moves to the east-northeast and down. This lobe is west of the old dome's center, and the observed motion is toward the center of the old dome, consistent with the motion expected as the old dome continues to cool and shrink. The westward velocity of stations MORG and WGOT, west of Mount St. Helens, is greater than 5 mm/yr, but other nearby stations show little or no significant motion. With surveys only in 2000 and 2003, it is difficult eliminate local instabilities or survey error, such as instrument setup, as a cause for the anomalous velocities. The daily measurements of position change at CGPS station JRO1 provide the strongest evidence for the lack of anomalous deformation in the years before September 2004. We examine the JRO1 data in the next section.

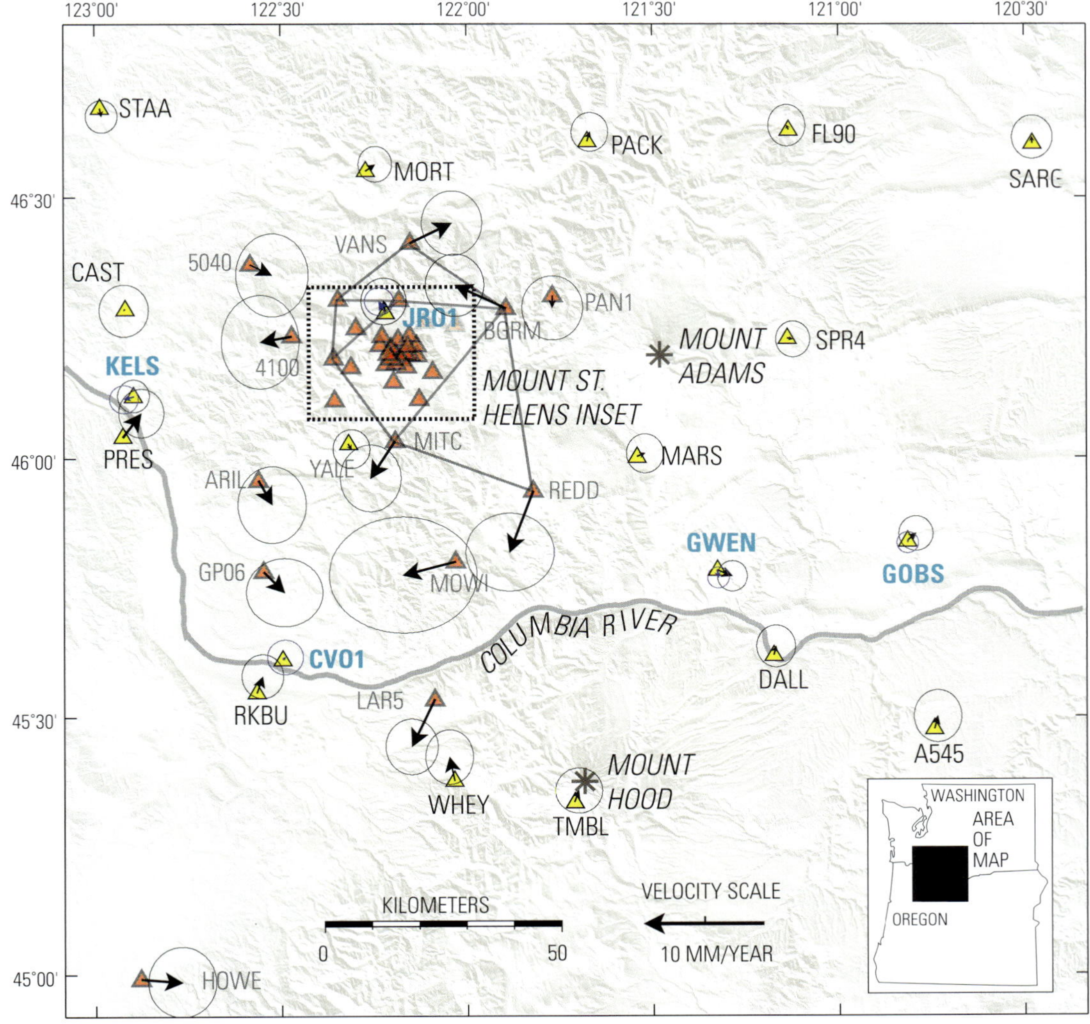

Figure 5. Map showing average GPS station horizontal-velocity vectors (tipped with 95-percent-confidence error ellipses, scale at bottom) for southwest Washington and northwest Oregon through September 2004, corrected for background motion predicted by a tectonic model. None of stations marked with yellow triangles, which were included in calculations for the tectonic model, have significant residual velocity. CGPS station names and velocity vectors are shown in blue. Most stations indicated with red triangles were surveyed only in the summers of 2000 and 2003.

Table 3. Adjusted Helens campaign GPS network average station velocities through September 23, 2004.

[Velocities are in nominal ITRF2000 fixed North American Plate terrestrial reference frame and are corrected for regional rigid-body rotation and strain.]

Station	Longitude (degrees)	Latitude (degrees)	East velocity ± 1σ error (mm/yr)	North velocity ± 1σ error (mm/yr)	E-N correlation	Up velocity ± 1σ error (mm/yr)
4100	-122.4706	46.2316	-2.65 ± 1.34	-0.50 ± 1.65	-0.04	-0.49 ± 6.64
5040	-122.5819	46.3695	1.86 ± 1.25	-0.95 ± 1.49	-0.06	13.87 ± 5.70
A545	-120.7435	45.4745	0.27 ± 0.82	1.08 ± 0.92	0.01	-1.76 ± 3.60
APEC	-122.1330	46.1950	-1.92 ± 1.06	4.00 ± 1.13	-0.01	-1.77 ± 4.93
ARIL	-122.5608	45.9561	1.16 ± 1.18	-2.10 ± 1.35	-0.05	4.29 ± 5.47
BGRM	-121.8943	46.2834	-4.32 ± 1.02	2.05 ± 1.12	0.00	0.14 ± 4.66
BIVO	-122.1962	46.1453	-2.37 ± 1.20	-4.60 ± 1.41	-0.03	11.24 ± 5.63
CAFE	-122.1349	46.2135	-2.56 ± 1.08	-0.39 ± 1.17	-0.03	0.36 ± 5.05
CANN	-123.9603	45.8617	4.29 ± 0.72	0.11 ± 0.77	-0.04	-0.94 ± 2.93
CAST	-122.9188	46.2833	-0.09 ± 0.85	-0.11 ± 0.92	-0.08	3.42 ± 3.30
CVO1	-122.4961	45.6109	-10.76 ± 6.44	1.92 ± 7.12	0.00	17.10 ± 29.68
DALL	-121.1752	45.6178	0.18 ± 0.67	0.76 ± 0.75	0.00	-3.40 ± 2.81
DMSH	-122.1910	46.2000	27.69 ± 1.04	9.39 ± 1.15	-0.01	-90.29 ± 4.86
DRAO	-119.6250	49.3226	-1.78 ± 0.43	1.46 ± 0.44	0.00	1.25 ± 1.39
EADM	-122.1521	46.1973	-1.18 ± 1.04	0.90 ± 1.12	-0.02	-3.54 ± 4.84
ELKK	-122.3452	46.3009	-0.65 ± 1.09	0.94 ± 1.18	-0.02	-0.24 ± 4.95
FL90	-121.1333	46.6288	-0.14 ± 0.64	0.36 ± 0.74	0.05	-6.53 ± 2.90
GOBS	-120.8147	45.8388	0.69 ± 0.59	0.61 ± 0.61	-0.02	0.33 ± 1.68
GP06	-122.5472	45.7810	1.76 ± 1.32	-1.80 ± 1.21	0.06	-5.07 ± 4.49
GWEN	-121.3276	45.7826	1.28 ± 0.52	-0.53 ± 0.54	-0.02	0.51 ± 1.58
HOWE	-122.8797	44.9900	3.50 ± 1.18	-0.29 ± 1.25	-0.07	-4.69 ± 4.57
HPAD	-122.0315	46.2520	-4.97 ± 1.03	1.09 ± 1.16	0.00	2.94 ± 4.70
JARD	-122.2973	46.2469	-1.89 ± 1.10	0.71 ± 1.19	-0.01	-28.35 ± 5.13
JRO1	-122.2176	46.2751	-0.16 ± 0.78	1.03 ± 0.83	-0.01	-2.93 ± 3.53
KELS	-122.8961	46.1182	-0.01 ± 0.55	0.02 ± 0.58	-0.02	-0.05 ± 1.64
LAR5	-122.0876	45.5327	-1.95 ± 0.90	-4.10 ± 0.98	-0.01	-1.77 ± 3.96
LOOW	-122.1843	46.2248	4.03 ± 1.05	0.77 ± 1.13	-0.01	1.29 ± 4.88
LVCY	-122.0912	46.1638	3.52 ± 3.69	2.02 ± 2.82	0.11	2.91 ± 8.44
MARS	-121.5419	46.0001	0.66 ± 0.64	0.28 ± 0.69	-0.02	1.29 ± 2.72
MITC	-122.1931	46.0309	-2.05 ± 1.05	-3.21 ± 1.18	-0.01	4.56 ± 4.73
MORG	-122.3572	46.1893	-7.42 ± 1.00	2.70 ± 1.11	-0.01	-0.66 ± 4.61
MORT	-122.2704	46.5506	0.80 ± 0.58	0.56 ± 0.64	-0.01	-1.76 ± 2.51
MOWI	-122.0308	45.7998	-4.45 ± 2.56	-1.17 ± 2.06	-0.12	-0.15 ± 6.61
NEBU	-122.2173	46.1782	-3.56 ± 1.08	2.41 ± 1.17	0.01	3.49 ± 5.02
NELR	-122.1649	46.1993	-1.33 ± 1.06	-1.07 ± 1.13	-0.03	1.99 ± 4.88
NESK	-123.9662	45.1343	5.07 ± 0.79	1.86 ± 0.83	-0.05	-1.51 ± 3.10
NMAR	-122.1280	46.1112	-1.23 ± 1.06	0.81 ± 1.20	0.03	5.58 ± 4.87

Table 3. Adjusted Helens campaign GPS network average station velocities through September 23, 2004. —Continued

[Velocities are in nominal ITRF2000 fixed North American Plate terrestrial reference frame and are corrected for regional rigid-body rotation and strain.]

Station	Longitude (degrees)	Latitude (degrees)	East velocity ± 1σ error (mm/yr)	North velocity ± 1σ error (mm/yr)	E-N correlation	Up velocity ± 1σ error (mm/yr)
NWDO	-122.2037	46.2096	2.72 ± 1.04	0.10 ± 1.13	-0.01	0.95 ± 4.79
PACK	-121.6752	46.6068	0.23 ± 0.64	0.80 ± 0.69	0.00	-5.60 ± 2.71
PAN1	-121.7685	46.3078	-0.02 ± 1.05	-1.04 ± 1.14	0.00	0.22 ± 4.84
PRES	-122.9245	46.0401	1.54 ± 0.78	2.06 ± 0.86	-0.04	-4.45 ± 3.23
R100	-122.1538	46.2322	1.16 ± 1.01	-1.01 ± 1.12	0.00	-0.64 ± 4.60
REDD	-121.8210	45.9349	-2.01 ± 1.53	-5.29 ± 1.38	-0.04	15.11 ± 5.71
RKBU	-122.5660	45.5467	0.49 ± 0.72	1.41 ± 0.78	-0.03	-5.58 ± 2.96
RS26	-123.4611	45.7968	3.37 ± 0.84	1.31 ± 0.94	-0.04	-2.90 ± 3.46
SARG	-120.4772	46.6024	-0.04 ± 0.71	0.53 ± 0.77	-0.01	-1.67 ± 2.83
SERI	-122.1765	46.1877	-2.81 ± 1.10	-4.41 ± 1.22	-0.05	-5.52 ± 5.07
SESL	-122.1615	46.1737	-1.37 ± 1.06	1.71 ± 1.14	-0.02	0.40 ± 4.94
SMCR	-122.1117	46.2586	-3.83 ± 0.96	2.37 ± 1.05	0.00	0.78 ± 4.33
SOFO	-122.2329	46.2153	0.83 ± 1.09	5.43 ± 1.18	-0.01	-1.88 ± 5.04
SPR4	-121.1371	46.2269	0.46 ± 0.59	-0.11 ± 0.63	-0.02	0.52 ± 2.47
SRID	-122.1899	46.1801	-1.65 ± 1.03	0.36 ± 1.12	-0.01	-5.21 ± 4.78
STAA	-122.9853	46.6708	0.15 ± 0.55	-0.72 ± 0.58	-0.03	1.60 ± 2.33
STUD	-122.2269	46.2314	2.99 ± 1.08	1.89 ± 1.18	0.00	-0.12 ± 5.03
TMBL	-121.7119	45.3340	0.35 ± 0.81	0.98 ± 0.80	-0.07	0.85 ± 3.22
TUBE	-122.3547	46.1095	2.22 ± 1.25	3.59 ± 1.41	-0.06	-2.24 ± 5.88
VANS	-122.1516	46.4101	3.54 ± 1.05	1.75 ± 1.16	0.01	0.47 ± 4.77
VMSH	-122.1820	46.2998	-1.54 ± 1.04	3.07 ± 1.12	-0.01	2.91 ± 4.81
WGOT	-122.3106	46.1730	-8.49 ± 0.88	0.80 ± 0.97	-0.01	-4.27 ± 3.94
WHEY	-122.0349	45.3762	-0.43 ± 0.83	2.02 ± 0.96	0.03	-4.67 ± 3.69
WIWE	-122.1587	46.2129	1.20 ± 1.05	-4.18 ± 1.13	0.00	2.21 ± 4.85
WRAD	-122.2035	46.1897	0.25 ± 1.07	7.46 ± 1.18	0.02	3.44 ± 5.00
WRID	-122.2107	46.1978	1.05 ± 1.05	-2.31 ± 1.13	0.00	0.23 ± 4.87
YALE	-122.3181	46.0262	0.26 ± 0.64	-0.47 ± 0.69	-0.07	1.18 ± 2.61

Time Series of Deformation from CGPS Data Collected at Johnston Ridge Observatory

A detailed history of deformation near Mount St. Helens since 1997 is found in the daily displacement components of CGPS station JRO1. The Cascadia network includes daily solutions in the fixed-NOAMgp reference frame and in a local reference frame that is defined by a subset of 11 CGPS stations in the network (table 4). QOCA's time-series analysis is used to simultaneously compute the component velocities, offsets, and repetitive seasonal displacements of JRO1. We do not include the anomalous data after September 23, 2004, in this analysis for background deformation. Outliers in the time series, found mainly in the winter when ice and snow accumulate around the GPS antenna, are defined as observations where the residual east or north displacement is larger than 5 mm, and the residual vertical displacement is larger than 15 mm. These residual outliers are about three times the weighted root-mean-square (WRMS) scatter observed in the JRO1 time-series analysis (table 4). Of the 2,267 daily observations, 130 (6 percent) were removed from the analysis because one or more of the components was identified as an outlier.

Small vertical offsets (~13 mm) in the time series were introduced on July 8, 1998, when a UNAVCO radome replaced the original Snow radome, and on July 16, 2002, when a SCIGN radome replaced the UNAVCO radome. The vertical offsets are calculated in QOCA by first setting assumed offset values based on estimates from a short span of data around the offset (we use 0.2 year), which is then given a weight of 0.25 times the offset; the final values are estimated simultaneously with other parameters. In our final analysis, only vertical offsets are estimated because initial analysis resulted in horizontal offsets that were small and insignificant. Nevertheless, the long-term trends could be biased slightly by error in the applied vertical offsets and possible small, horizontal offsets related to the antenna-radome changes.

The estimated JRO1 component velocities, offsets, and repetitive seasonal movements are removed to produce a resid-

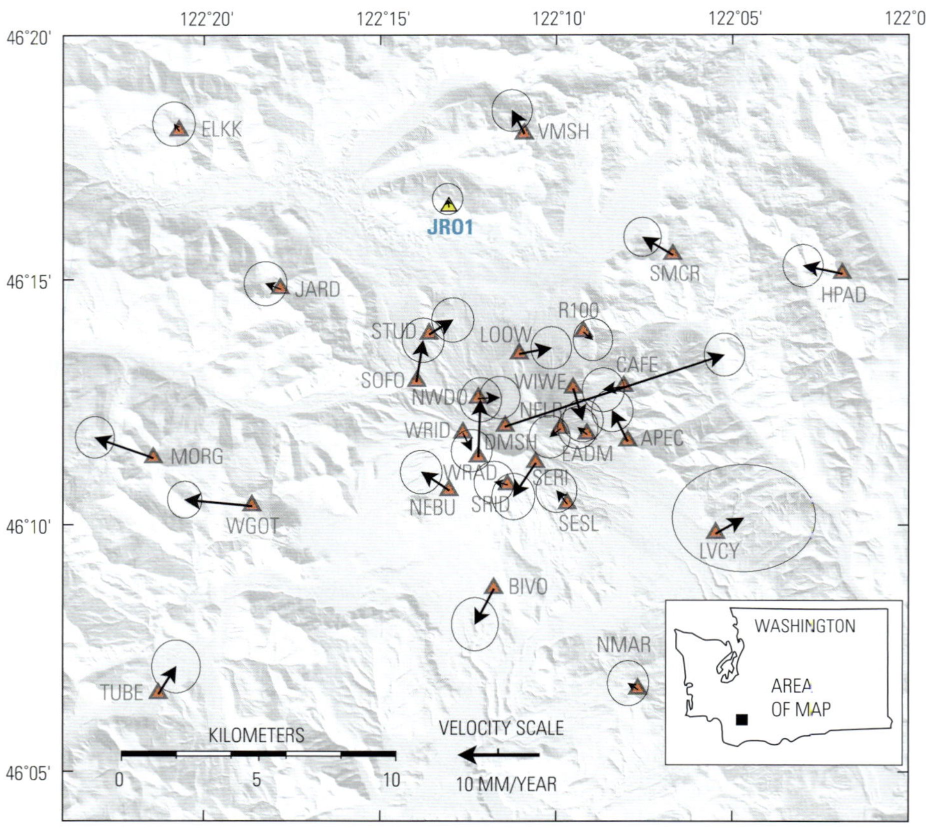

Figure 6. Map showing 2000–2003 corrected average GPS station horizontal-velocity vectors (tipped with 95-percent-confidence error ellipses, scale at bottom) for Mount St. Helens area. Although many stations show significant velocities, there is no systematic pattern that might suggest premonitory deformation before the start of the 2004 eruption. GPS station DMSH, on the 1980–86 lava dome, moved downward 87 mm/yr and east-northeastward 35 mm/yr, presumably as a result of cooling and compaction of the dome.

Table 4. Time-series analysis of Cascadia network local reference frame stations.

[WRMS is weighted root-mean-squared deviation (experimental standard deviation). Phases are relative to start of the calendar year. Data for station KELS are divided into two intervals to calculate velocities; other KELS data, equivalent between columns, are shown by dashes in second KELS column.]

Station	JRO1	KELS	KELS	BREW	CV01	GOBS	REDM
Start date (year month day)	19970523	19971010	20040923	19971010	20030104	19970827	19980725
End date (year month day)	20040922	20040922	20061013	20061013	20061013	20061013	20061013
Number of daily positions (post-1996)	2,137	2,977	--	1,669	1,308	3,149	2,889
Number of outliers	130	201	--	1	4	30	31
East WRMS (mm)	1.70	1.62	--	0.82	1.13	1.13	1.32
North WRMS (mm)	1.75	1.77	--	0.91	1.19	1.23	1.12
Up WRMS (mm)	5.01	4.62	--	3.23	3.50	3.36	3.25
East velocity (mm/yr)	2.76	3.07	6.14	1.33	3.26	1.52	0.16
North velocity (mm/yr)	5.82	5.84	5.03	0.75	5.63	2.09	2.80
Vertical velocity (mm/yr)	-1.99	-0.45	0.11	0.18	-1.54	-0.73	0.02
East annual amplitude (mm)	2.02	0.84	--	0.35	0.51	1.83	0.35
East annual phase (degrees)	52.35	37.32	--	239.69	288.89	139.06	351.70
North annual amplitude (mm)	1.96	0.98	--	0.10	0.06	1.30	0.62
North annual phase (degrees)	137.86	160.71	--	39.96	161.07	326.93	144.47
Vertical annual amplitude (mm)	1.70	1.10	--	0.35	1.66	0.49	0.97
Vertical annual phase (degrees)	25.41	354.79	--	284.29	356.08	277.76	50.14
East semiannual amplitude (mm)	0.34	0.34	--	0.06	0.12	0.25	0.20
East semiannual phase (degrees)	244.99	109.28	--	316.72	176.88	267.05	220.03
North semiannual amplitude (mm)	0.80	0.22	--	0.11	0.19	0.30	0.27
North semiannual phase (degrees)	263.56	236.34	--	199.17	87.40	85.48	330.50
Vertical semiannual amplitude (mm)	0.64	0.31	--	0.01	0.84	0.40	0.19
Vertical semiannual phase (degrees)	276.03	122.27	--	22.97	84.91	140.26	145.93

Station	LIND	LINH	GWEN	DRAO	CHWK	SEDR
Start date (year month day)	19980728	20020506	19970827	19970827	19981119	19971007
End date (year month day)	20061013	20061013	20061013	20061013	20061013	20061013
Number of daily positions (post 1996)	1,145	1,531	3,138	3,255	2,543	3,209
Number of outliers	13	16	72	12	11	7
East WRMS (mm)	1.3	1.11	1.55	1.00	1.10	1.14
North WRMS (mm)	1.19	1.15	1.50	1.16	1.42	1.33
Up WRMS (mm)	3.95	3.90	4.32	2.97	4.24	3.55
East velocity (mm/yr)	1.70	1.70	2.10	0.93	2.43	2.97
North velocity (mm/yr)	1.69	1.63	2.56	0.41	1.50	2.11
Vertical velocity (mm/yr)	-0.53	0.01	-0.85	1.61	0.25	-0.23
East annual amplitude (mm)	0.26	0.33	0.87	0.42	0.44	0.46
East annual phase (degrees)	90.92	75.29	278.58	73.03	322.58	305.77
North annual amplitude (mm)	0.81	0.48	0.39	0.24	0.37	0.23
North annual phase (degrees)	218.14	209.76	138.47	258.20	85.11	204.89
Vertical annual amplitude (mm)	0.47	1.64	1.69	0.71	0.47	0.09
Vertical annual phase (degrees)	83.08	25.46	229.45	98.87	160.64	279.40
East semiannual amplitude (mm)	0.11	0.37	0.15	0.12	0.02	0.28
East semiannual phase (degrees)	137.32	45.34	349.51	250.97	149.82	77.91
North semiannual amplitude (mm)	0.05	0.25	0.26	0.03	0.17	0.11
North semiannual phase (degrees)	306.59	269.95	232.06	278.87	168.30	30.14
Vertical semiannual amplitude (mm)	0.39	1.33	0.62	0.13	0.61	0.05
Vertical semiannual phase (degrees)	115.22	186.33	357.05	18.87	252.14	117.52

ual-component time series. The horizontal components are then rotated so that one component represents motion radial (N. 13.5° W.), and the other component represents tangential motion (N. 76.5° E.) to Mount St. Helens (fig. 7*A*). Previously identified outliers are included in these plots, but they will be outside the 5-mm (horizontal) and 15-mm (vertical) data-rejection criteria indicated by the yellow bands on figure 7.

Station JRO1 moved at the background rate (no slope in fig. 7*A*) until the start of unrest on September 23, 2004, when anomalous subsidence and movement toward Mount St. Helens began at the station. Intervals of low-level systematic noise remain in the residual-component time series, as do short periods of drift when winter snow and ice accumulate on the GPS antenna and distort its phase center.

The average velocity of station JRO1 derived from the time-series analysis is similar to the velocity estimated from the local reference-frame calculation, but it is 0.9 mm/yr faster in the north component and 0.5 mm/yr slower in the east component than the velocity predicted by the tectonic model. We later use the tectonic model to correct post-September 23, 2004, velocities at JRO1 and at other stations around Mount St. Helens having unknown secular velocities. The observed

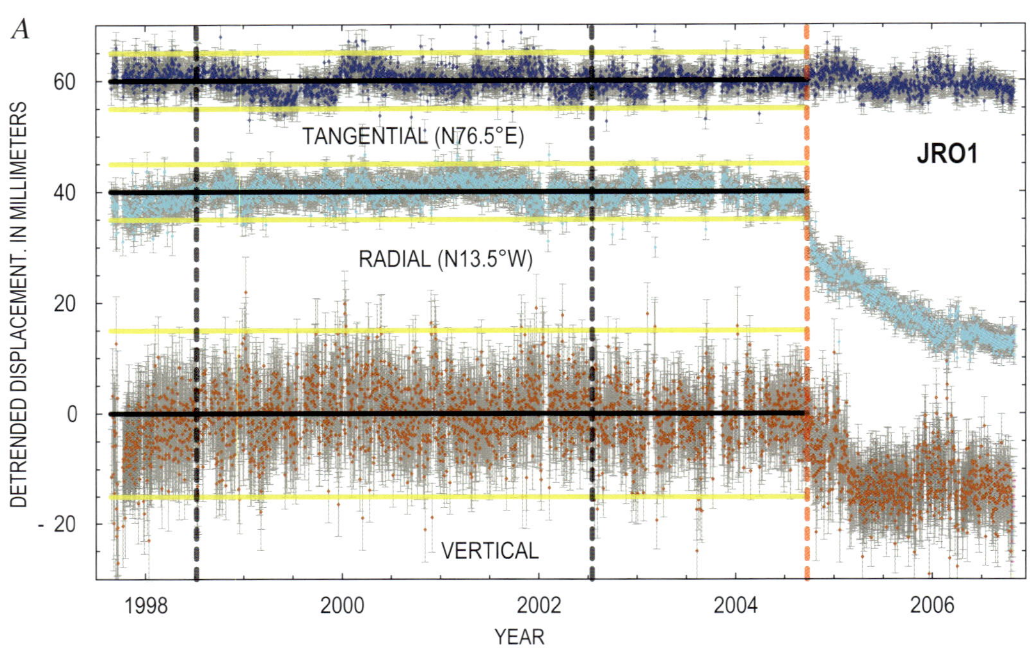

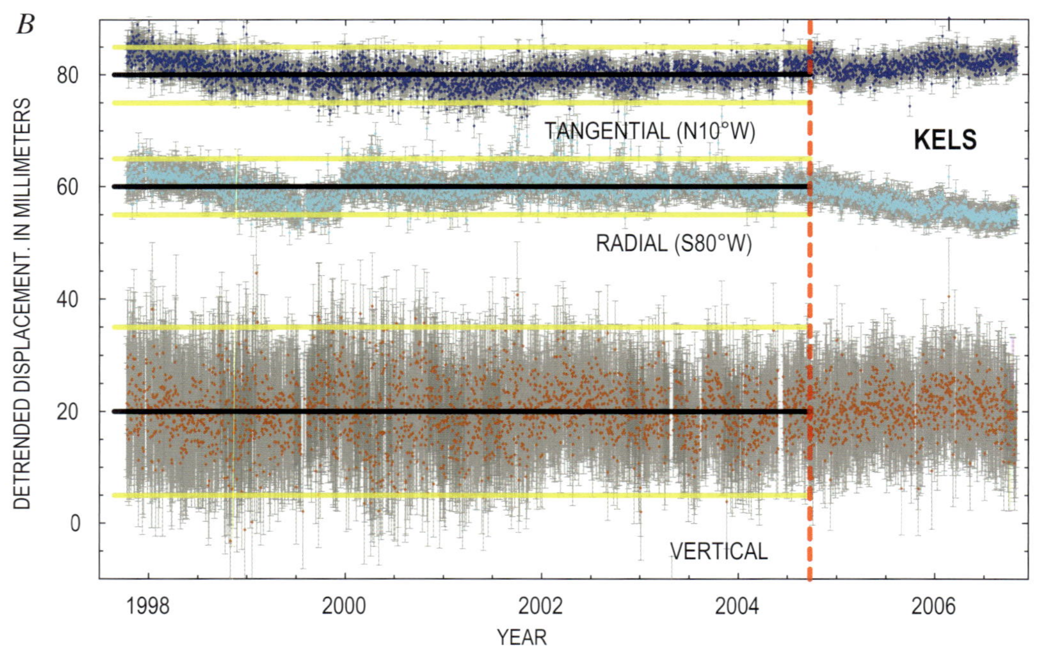

Figure 7. Stacked plots of detrended tangential, radial, and vertical daily average displacement of CGPS stations (*A*) JRO1, located 9 km north-northwest of Mount St. Helens, and (*B*) KELS, located 50 km west-southwest. Displacements are residuals from fitting a station velocity, mean value, cyclical annual and semiannual drift, and offsets from GPS antenna changes as determined by data collected through September 23, 2004. Vertical blue lines mark times that GPS antenna radomes were changed; vertical red line marks start of seismic unrest on September 23, 2004. Yellow horizontal lines are ±5 mm from pre-event tangential and radial mean values (outlier rejection limit) and ±15 mm from pre-event vertical mean value (outlier rejection limit). For station JRO1, one or more displacements were rejected for 130 of a total 2,267 days of data before September 23, 2004. For station KELS, one or more displacement components were rejected for 201 of 2,927 days of data.

discrepancy between the tectonic model and the observed motion at JRO1 is considered in the discussion of eruption-related deformation source models.

A small inward displacement of KELS, one of the PANGA CGPS stations used as a reference station in the local frame, also appears to have initiated at the start of volcanic unrest (fig. 7*B*). Station KELS is in Kelso, Wash., about 50 km west-southwest of Mount St. Helens, and the GPS antenna is mounted on a stable, deep-drilled, braced monument (Langbein and others, 1995) that is anchored at a depth of 10 m and isolated from the topsoil. The time-series analysis at KELS includes an additional term to resolve average velocities for the periods before and after September 23, 2004 (table 4). If deformation from the eruption of Mount St. Helens penetrated as far as station KELS, then it likely is the result of magma chamber pressure changes in a relatively deep (~10 km) source. We later examine data from several PBO CGPS stations located an equivalent distance to the north of Mount St. Helens to determine whether eruption-related deformation could be detected there.

GPS Station Displacements Early in the 2004–2006 Eruption

The only direct measure of deformation associated with the initiation of the eruption was made at JRO1, where slow, relatively steady motion toward Mount St. Helens was observed (fig. 8). The movement of station JRO1 was fastest in the two weeks after September 23, 2004, but even then it averaged only about 0.5 mm/day (inset, fig. 8). The inward movement continued at a nearly linear rate until a few days after the vigorous steam-and-ash explosion on October 5, 2004, when movement began to slow at a time-decaying rate. We later conclude that deformation has gradually slowed at other CGPS stations around Mount St. Helens.

The conduit that fed the eruptions in the 1980s is buried under the dome that developed in the years after the crater formed and that presumably was plugged with cooled magma. Was this plug pushed out at the start of the new dome-building eruption or was it bypassed? If a bypass formed, most likely it would appear as a dike that propagated to the

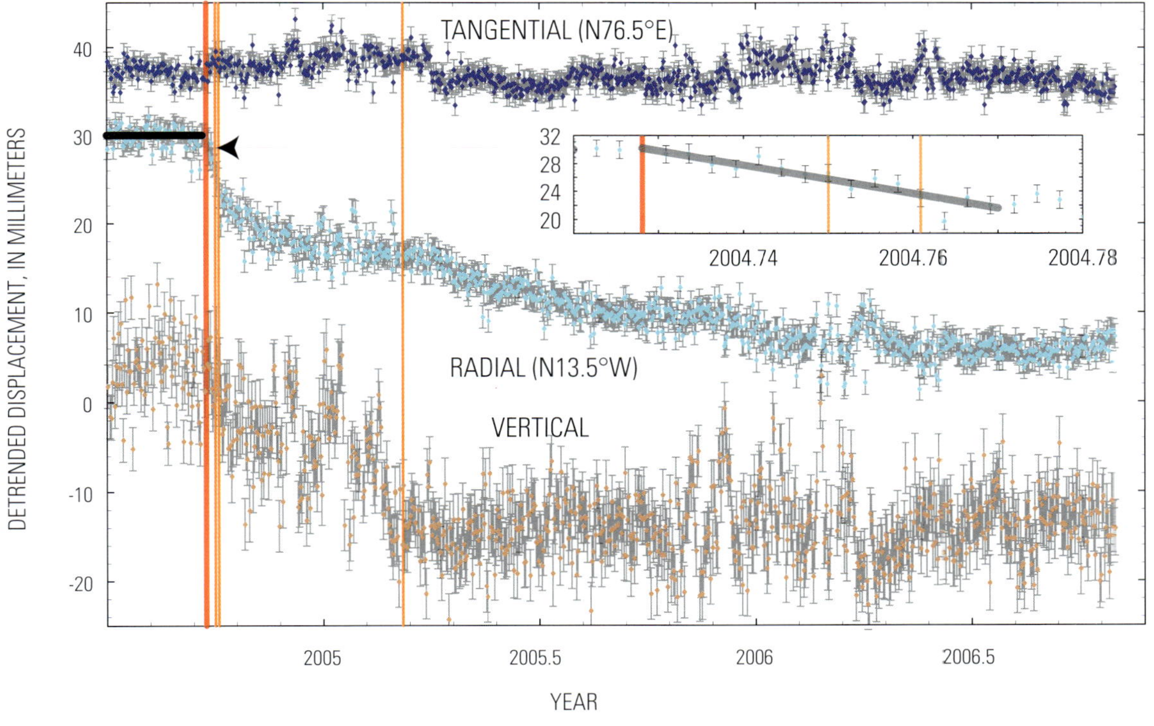

Figure 8. Stacked daily tangential (N. 76.5° E., top), radial (N. 13.5° W., middle), and vertical (bottom) displacements of CGPS station JRO1 from shortly before and during the 2004–2006 dome-building eruption of Mount St. Helens. Error bars are ±1 standard deviation. Bold horizontal black line represents projection of long-term trend in radial displacement, red vertical line marks start of unrest (seismic swarm beginning September 23, 2004), and orange vertical lines show start and end times of a series of phreatic explosions between October 1 and 5, 2004, and the time of last explosion on March 8, 2005. Vertical displacement appears to have ceased shortly after the March 8, 2005, explosion, whereas radial displacement has decayed more slowly. Inset shows a 23-day period at the start of unrest. Winter months show periods of anomalous displacements because of snow and ice accumulation on the GPS antenna radome.

surface, and we would expect associated deformation to be fairly widespread. The propagation of a shallow dike might not produce much deformation at station JRO1, located 9 km from the center of the crater, and we examine data from other stations closer to the newly formed vent for possible offsets at the start of the eruption.

An indirect measure of deformation associated with initial movement of magma to the surface is obtained at the subset of campaign GPS stations that were occupied within a week or two after the start of unrest. Displacement offset of these stations is estimated by projecting the observed 2000 to 2003 position-change trends to the start of unrest (September 23, 2004). We include data from an L1 CGPS station, DOM1, located on the September 1984 lobe of the old dome (see LaHusen and others, this volume, chap. 16). A power failure occurred at DOM1 in January 2004, and the station was not reactivated until September 27, 2004.

The large northward and upward offset at station DOM1 (in the same location as station DMSH) contrasts with the smaller and seemingly random pattern of offsets at surrounding stations (horizontal-displacement offset are shown in fig. 9, and component offsets are listed in table 5). Many of these offsets, though statistically significant on the basis of assumed error estimates, likely result from systematic error in the projected trends. Anomalous 2000 to 2003 velocities (fig. 6) were observed at many of the stations having relatively large event offsets (for example, stations WGOT, BIVO, and SERI, fig.9). These offsets are opposite of the anomalous trends, as might be expected if there were errors in the estimated station velocities. Event deformation appears to be limited to DOM1, which was about 300 m from the newly formed vent. The partially congealed magma plugging the conduit appears to have been pushed to the surface on the south side of the old dome, displacing the old dome slightly to the north and up. Most of the movement at station DOM1 had occurred by the time the station was reactivated (September 27, 2004). In its final days, the station continued moving north until it was destroyed by the first phreatic explosion on October 1, 2004 (LaHusen and others, this volume, chap. 16).

Displacement of GPS Stations During the 2004–2006 Eruption

The inward displacement of CGPS station JRO1 appears to start at about the same time as the first seismic swarm on

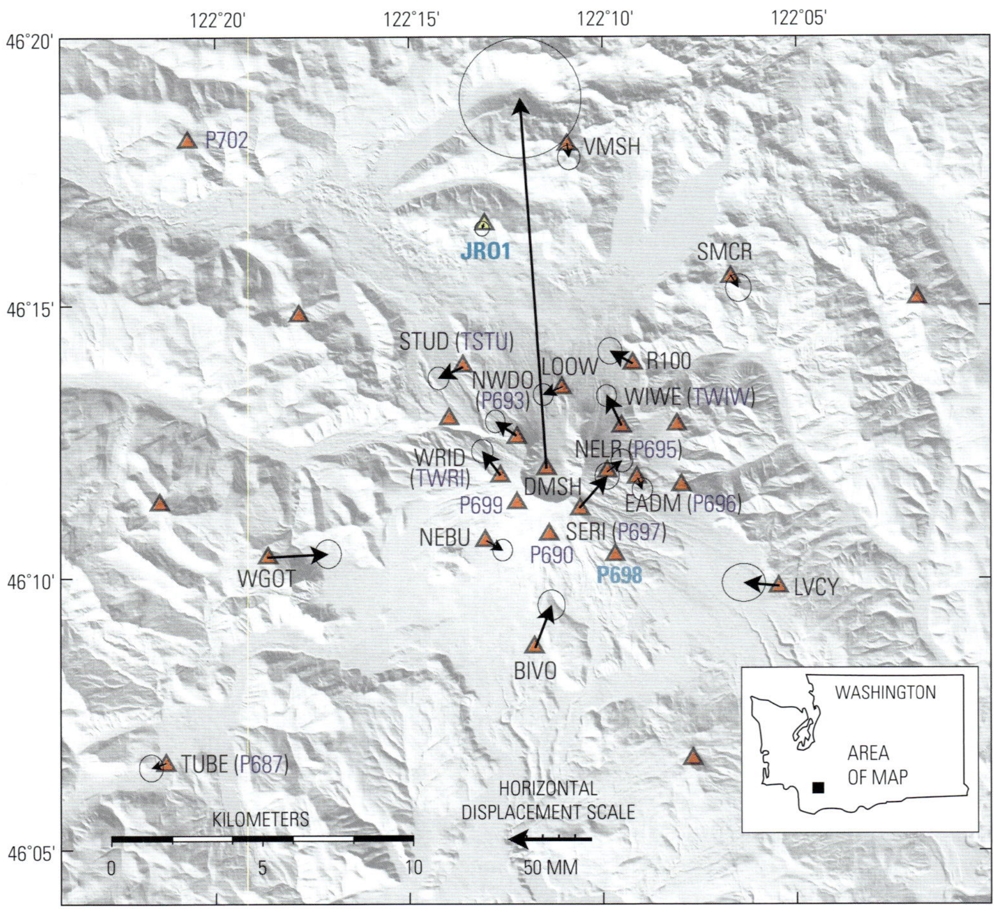

Figure 9. Map showing early event GPS station horizontal-displacement vectors (tipped with 95-percent-confidence error ellipses, vector scale on bottom) in the Mount St. Helens area. Displacements calculated by projecting station velocities to September 23, 2004, and estimating the offset between pre- and post-event positions. Many stations show significant movement, but there is no systematic pattern to suggest intrusion of a new dike to transport magma to the surface. Large displacement on the 1980–86 lava dome is that determined from measurements at DOM1 (same location as DMSH), an L1 CGPS station that was resurrected on September 27, 2004 (LaHusen and other, this volume, chap. 16).

Table 5. Estimated GPS station offsets at start of 2004 seismic unrest.

[Offsets are estimated by projecting 2000–2003 trends to September 23, 2004. Uncertainties are ±1 standard deviation.]

Station	Measurement date (2004)	Longitude (degrees)	Latitude (degrees)	East offset (mm)	North offset (mm)	East-North correlation	Vertical offset (mm)
JRO1	09/28	-122.218	46.275	-1 ± 1.8	-3 ± 1.9	0.004	6 ± 8.7
DOM1	09/28	-122.191	46.200	-16 ± 15.3	235 ± 15.7	0.014	90 ± 40.1
EADM	10/01-10/07	-122.152	46.197	3 ± 2.6	-7 ± 2.9	-0.007	-4 ± 12.2
LOOW	09/28-10/07	-122.184	46.225	-12 ± 2.5	-5 ± 2.8	0.012	-13 ± 11.8
NELR	09/29-10/07	-122.165	46.199	9 ± 2.7	7 ± 2.9	-0.038	3 ± 12.6
NEBU	09/28-10/07	-122.217	46.178	10 ± 2.5	-6 ± 2.8	0.043	-14 ± 12.0
NWDO	09/28-10/07	-122.204	46.210	-13 ± 2.5	9 ± 2.9	-0.002	-3 ± 12.0
SERI	09/30-10/05	-122.177	46.188	17 ± 3.0	20 ± 3.4	-0.070	24 ± 13.7
STUD	09/30-10/07	-122.227	46.231	-15 ± 2.6	-7 ± 2.9	0.016	0 ± 12.1
WIWE	09/29-10/07	-122.159	46.213	-9 ± 2.5	19 ± 2.8	0.021	-7 ± 11.8
WRID	10/01-10/05	-122.211	46.198	-11 ± 2.7	15 ± 3.0	0.024	2 ± 12.9
BIVO	11/03-11/09	-122.196	46.145	10 ± 3.4	27 ± 3.9	0.019	-41 ± 16.1
LVCY	11/04-11/09	-122.091	46.164	-22 ± 5.4	2 ± 4.6	0.057	-3 ± 17.1
R100	11/06 and 11/09	-122.154	46.232	-14 ± 3.0	8 ± 3.4	0.020	-3 ± 14.2
SMCR	11/06 and 11/09	-122.112	46.259	5 ± 3.2	-8 ± 3.6	0.010	-4 ± 14.7
TUBE	11/03-11/07	-122.355	46.110	-9 ± 3.0	-3 ± 3.4	-0.033	-13 ± 13.9
VMSH	11/04-11/09	-122.182	46.300	1 ± 2.8	-9 ± 3.2	0.009	-6 ± 13.3
WGOT	11/04 and 11/05	-122.311	46.173	37 ± 3.3	2 ± 3.7	0.014	-8 ± 15.1

September 23, 2004, and the displacement has continued at a decreasing rate throughout the eruption (fig. 8). The rate of subsidence, however, appears to have leveled off shortly after the March 8, 2005, explosion. Several short periods of anomalous vertical offsets in the winter of 2005, probably the result of snow and ice accumulation on the GPS antenna, make the subsidence appear jerky during the first few months of the eruption. The horizontal components of position change at JRO1 are affected less by winter anomalies, but outliers and short-term variations are apparent in the time series. At the measurement uncertainty of about ±1.7 mm in the horizontal components and ±5 mm in the vertical component of displacement (table 4), there is no apparent deformation anomaly in the months or days before the start of unrest.

The pattern and rate of deformation around Mount St. Helens during all but the first few weeks of the eruption are measured by a network of CGPS stations. Eleven new CGPS stations (seven from PBO and four from CVO) were installed by November 5, 2004 (see table 1 for installation dates and additional information). The PBO stations are part of a planned network of 20 CGPS stations (four with collocated borehole tiltmeters) and four strainmeter stations (each consisting of a borehole tensor strainmeter, a three-component seismometer, and a tiltmeter) in the NSF-funded PBO Mount St. Helens volcanic cluster. The data from new CGPS stations, along with data from JRO1, are processed by CVO as part of the HelensMonit network. Network solutions are transformed into fixed-NOAMgp, ITRF2000, and a local reference frame. The local reference frame for the HelensMonit network consists of five reference stations (GOBS, REDM, KELS, LINH, CVO1).

We use QOCA's time-series analysis to estimate and remove cyclical annual and semiannual seasonal noise from the daily CGPS solutions. We then remove secular tectonic motion predicted by the tectonic model and rotate the resulting cleaned, horizontal-component time series from the east and north geographic components into components that are radial and tangential to Mount St. Helens. At several stations, an eccentric offset correction (table 6) is used to transfer the positions measured at the campaign GPS station early in the eruption to the nearby CGPS station. Then, horizontal and vertical time-series data are stacked to compare position change over time (figs. 10, 11).

The CGPS stations near Mount St. Helens are divided into high- and low-altitude groups for the stacked-component time-series plots. The low-altitude stations have minor winter displacement anomalies, whereas stations at altitudes greater than 2,000 m experience frequent, and sometimes large, winter excursions. The locations of the CGPS stations are shown in figure 9.

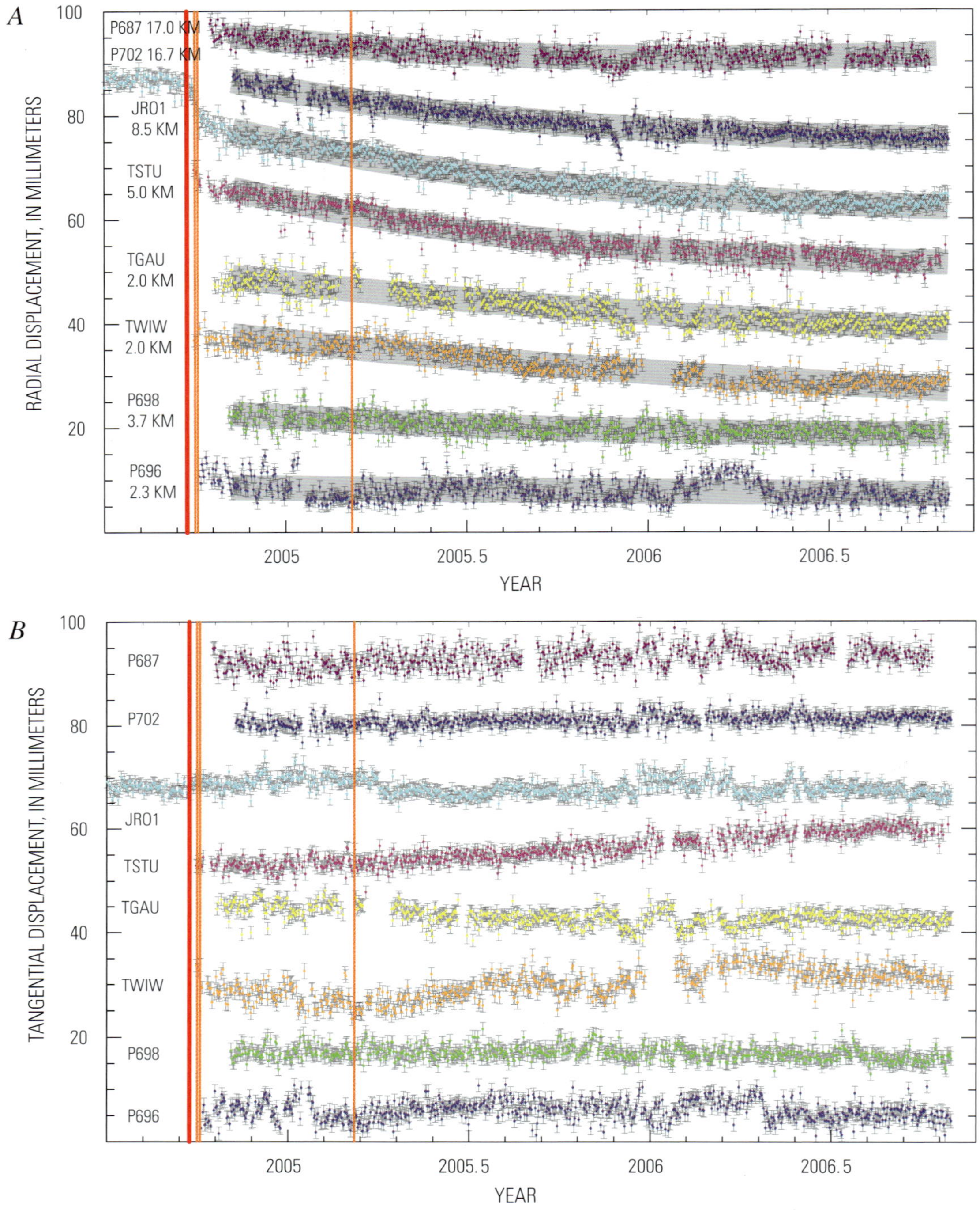

Figure 10. Plots of detrended and stacked time series of daily radial (*A*), tangential (*B*), and vertical (*C*) displacements at eight CGPS stations around Mount St. Helens at altitudes less than 2,000 m. Locations of stations shown in figure 9. Error bars are ±1 standard deviation, and gray bands in radial and vertical displacements are best-fitting rates of exponential decay. The red vertical line marks the start of unrest on September 23, 2004, and the orange vertical lines mark three phreatic explosions. A few of the earliest measurements at TSTU, TWIW, and P696 were made at a nearby campaign GPS station, and an eccentric correction was used to reduce positions to corresponding CGPS station. Tangential displacements at TSTU, TWIW, and TGAU are significantly different than zero. Station distances in *A* and *C* are computed relative to surface projection of modeled source (red cross in fig. 17*A*).

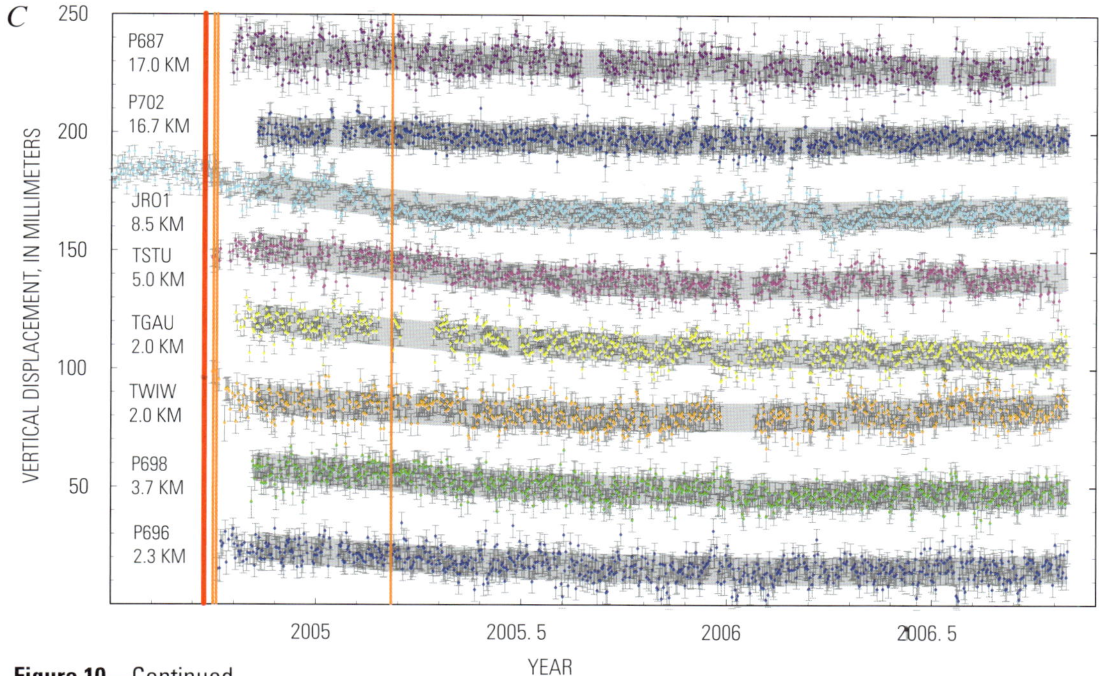

Figure 10—Continued.

The maximum radially inward movement of the low-altitude stations (fig. 10*A*) occurs at stations TSTU and JRO1, located at distances of 5 and 9 km from Mount St. Helens, respectively. Radial movement diminishes at stations located farther (P687, P702) and closer (TGAU, TWIW, P698, P696) to Mount St. Helens. The tangential component of motion is small, except at stations TSTU, TGAU, and TWIW (fig. 10*B*). Subsidence occurs at all stations and reaches its maximum at TSTU, but it diminishes at stations closest to and farthest from Mount St. Helens (fig. 10*C*).

During winter months, CGPS stations installed at altitudes above 2,000 m on Mount St. Helens (P695, P690, TWRI, P693, P697, P699) experience periods of temporary pseudo-displacements (fig. 11) from the accumulation of rime on the GPS antenna (fig. 12). At two high-altitude stations (P690 and P699) where the solar panels were mounted on the south side of the GPS antenna mast, asymmetrical ice loading permanently warped the towers.

The 2004–2005 winter displacements at station P697 were unusually large and constant (fig. 11). Initially we hypothesized that the apparent displacement of this station normal to the south crater wall resulted from the impact of the growing lava spine on that wall. With warming weather in the spring of 2005, the ice covering the GPS antenna melted, and the station returned to its initial position. The winter of 2004–2005 was unusually mild, and large, systematic pseudodisplacements were observed only at the highest stations (P699 and P697), and only the tower for station P699 was warped permanently by ice loading. During the more typical winter of 2005–2006, ice coated the GPS antennas at all high-altitude stations, and the towers at stations P699 and P690 were warped by ice loads on the attached solar panels.

Wintertime pseudodisplacements at the high-altitude CGPS stations complicate analysis of eruption-related deformation there. The application of suitable outlier-rejection criteria in the QOCA time-series analysis minimizes the need for hand-editing data outliers. The calculation of tower offsets at stations P699 (2005 and 2006) and P690 (2006), however, requires careful data editing, and even then the calculated horizontal offsets are poorly determined. The warping of the 3-m-high towers did not appear to cause significant vertical offset. A mechanical offset was introduced at station P699 in September 2006 during site maintenance when a UNAVCO field engineer removed the radome cover and reset the tilted GPS antenna. At the same time, the pole-mounted solar panels at P690 and P699 were removed and replaced with panels mounted on separate frames in an effort to prevent future load-induced offsets.

Time-Decaying Movement of GPS Stations During the 2004–2006 Eruption

The radial and vertical CGPS station displacements have been slowing over time, and the wide, gray bands shown in the stacked radial and vertical displacement plots are best-fitting curves of the form

$$y = ae^{-b(t-t_0)}, \qquad (1)$$

where a and b are constants, t is the observed time, and t_0 is the start time. In the data fit we use October 15, 2004, as the start time and include only data after that date. Our main inter-

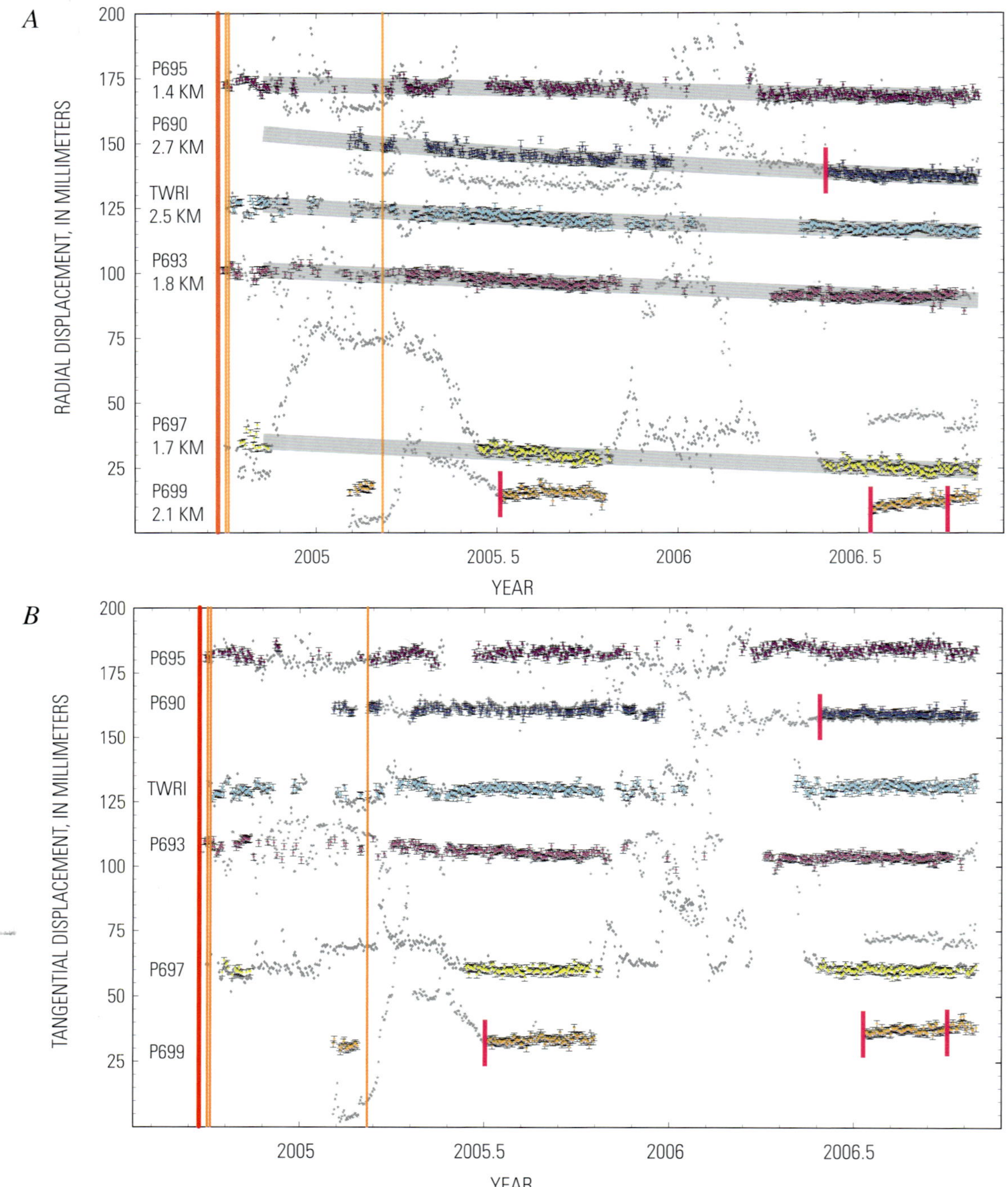

Figure 11. Plots of detrended and stacked time series of daily radial (*A*), tangential (*B*), and vertical (*C*) displacements at six CGPS stations around Mount St. Helens at altitudes greater than 2,000 m. Locations of stations shown in figure 9. Error bars are ±1 standard deviation, and gray bands in radial and vertical displacements are best-fitting rates of exponential decay. Gray dots are outliers (pseudodisplacements) that result from ice coating the GPS antennas, and they are not used in analysis. Short red vertical lines mark time used to calculate an offset for stations P690 and P699 to account for permanent warping of the tower from ice loading. The red vertical line marks the start of unrest on September 23, 2004, and the orange vertical lines mark three phreatic explosions. A few of earliest measurements at P695 and P693 were made at a nearby campaign GPS station, and an eccentric offset correction was used to reduce positions to corresponding CGPS station.

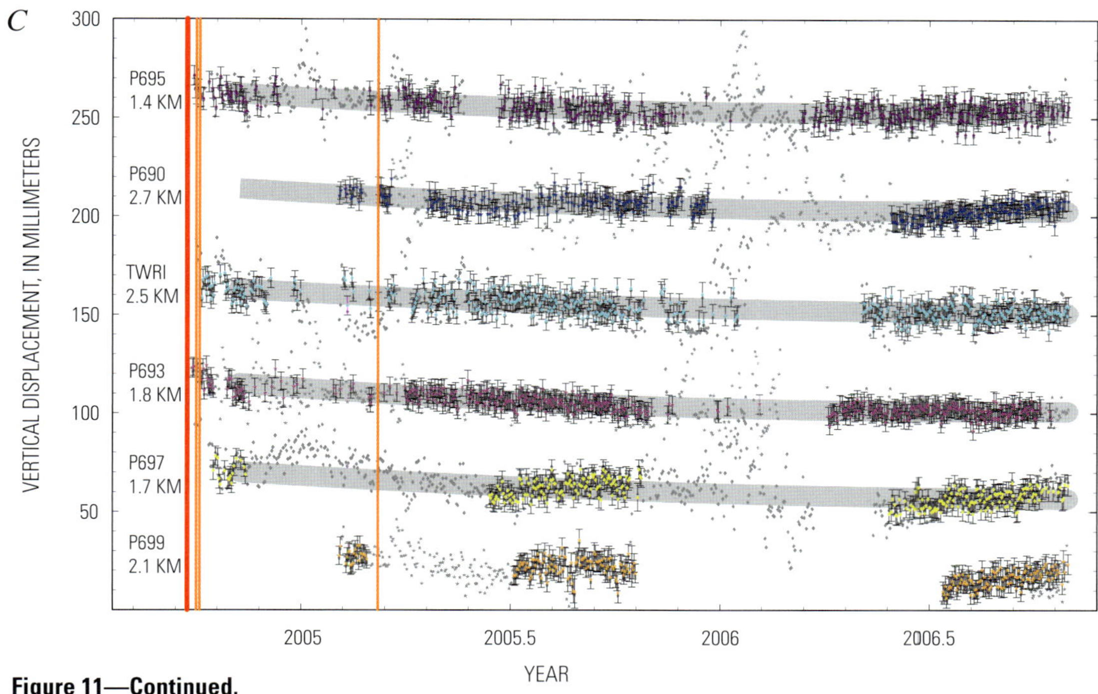

Figure 11—Continued.

Table 6. Surveyed offsets between bedrock campaign GPS stations and nearby tower or braced CGPS stations.

[Offsets may have been surveyed repeatedly and are given in Cartesian coordinates. CGPS, continuously transmitting GPS.]

Bedrock station	CGPS station	Measurement date	X offset (m)	Y offset (m)	Z offset (m)
WIWE	TWIW	2004/10/12	-4.2706	-0.2173	2.2044
WRID	TWRI	2005/08/11-08/18	-71.1883	71.0514	-10.0691
SERI	P697	2005/08/11-08/18	-11.1530	-2.2178	-0.8293
NWDO	P693	2004/10/15-10/19	121.0864	-5.9706	49.7039
STUD	TSTU	2004/10/15	394.1229	211.2114	465.2217
NELR	P695	2004/10/15	36.6088	-37.1623	-30.4480
TUBE	P687	2004/11/03-11/07	1.9623	1.2851	4.3265
SESL	P698	2005/07/13-07/22	50.0780	-53.8675	-15.3364
ELKK	P702	2004/11/05-11/07	-51.9197	-23.0480	-64.4552
EADM	P696	2004/10/15	10.7039	-46.8483	-36.9437
WRAD	P699	2005/08/19	18.1105	-12.8303	19.8468

est is in b, which gives the rate of time decay in the displacement components. We add a constant to the residual-component time-series data to make all residual components positive; thus intercept a is arbitrary. As discussed previously, the radially inward displacement of JRO1 between September 23 and approximately October 8 averaged 0.5 mm/day (inset, fig. 8). Equation 1 is one of several similar curves derived by Mastin and others (this volume, chap. 22) to fit the volume growth of the dome over time. Changes in the rate of dome growth might be expected to be matched by changes in the rate of volume or mass loss in the magma chamber feeding the eruption. We later test whether the observed deformation can be explained by depressurization of a magma chamber, but first we look for coherent patterns of deformation in the CGPS displacement time series.

Space-Time Correlated Deformation During the 2004–2006 Eruption

The CGPS station-component time series indicate small (total to several centimeters) radially inward and downward movements that appear to have slowed during the eruption. To determine whether these movements are correlated in time, as might be expected if they were in response to pressure loss in a magma reservoir, we apply principal component analysis (PCA; Preisendorfer, 1988). The PCA decomposes the collective station-displacement time series into a number of deformation modes, each of which consists of a common temporal response and a spatial scaling factor that varies between stations but remains constant over time at each station. This method of decomposing space-time data into the superposition of space- and time-separable modes is also called empirical orthogonal-function analysis (Menke, 1984) and eigenanalysis (Aubrey and Emery, 1983). Along with a similar method called Karhunen-Loeve expansion, Dong and others (2006) used PCA to identify and remove common-mode error in daily GPS station-coordinate time series. PCA also has been used to study interseismic deformation (for example, Savage, 1988, 1995).

A mathematical description of the method as applied in QOCA-based PCA analysis is given by Dong and others (2006). Summarizing their discussion, a data matrix X_{ij} is constructed such that each column (subscript i in equation 2) contains a single residual-displacement component (either east, north, or vertical) from a single station in the network. The rows of the matrix (subscript j) include displacement components from all network stations in each period of measurements (daily averages are used here). PCA allows one to represent X_{ij} by

$$X_{ij} = \sum_{k=1}^{N} A_{ik} C_k(t_j) \,, \qquad (2)$$

where the N products $A_{ik}C_k(t_j)$ are the individual modes, with A_{ik} as the spatially varying scale factor and $C_k(t_j)$ as the temporally varying time factor for each mode k. If the PCA-identified deformation modes are ordered by their contribution to the data variance, spatially correlated signals are contained in the first few modes, whereas the higher-order modes usually reflect more local effects.

We apply PCA to the cleaned, residual station-component time series from the 11 Mount St. Helens CGPS stations with the most complete time series (all stations except P690, P697, and P699), three PBO CGPS stations (P420, P421, and P432) located more than 40 km to the north, and the five distant CGPS reference stations (CVO1, KELS, LINH, GOBS, and REDM) included in the solutions. Outliers, predicted tectonic motion, and cyclical annual and semiannual noise are removed from the data. PCA requires observations at all included stations in each epoch. Therefore, Lagrangian interpolation is applied to fill small data gaps, and an iterative process that uses the predictions of the first three PCA modes is used to fill large data gaps (Dong and others, 2006). We examine deformation that occurred after October 15, 2004, when most of the new CGPS stations were operational.

The PCA can identify a single coherent mode of time-varying deformation. The first principal mode (mode 1) accounts for a large percentage (between 40 and 70 percent) of the data variance (fig. 13), particularly in the horizontal components, and only mode 1 temporal components (fig. 14*A*) vary systematically with time. The mode 2 (fig. 14*B*) and higher-order temporal components (not shown) have no long-term changes with time and likely represent random noise and systematic short-term fluctuations at one or more of the analyzed stations.

Mastin and others (this volume, chap. 22) derive logarithmic and exponential functions to fit the time decay in the

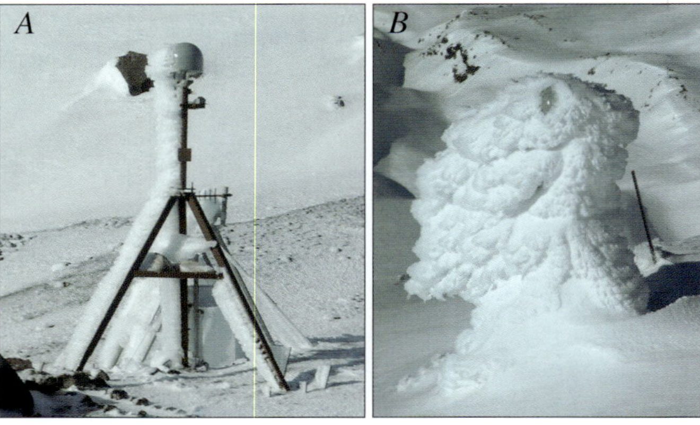

Figure 12. Examples of heavy winter rime on GPS station antennas and tower mounts at altitudes greater than 2,000 m. Locations of stations shown in figure 9. *A*, Station P697. Tower stands 3.5 m above ground, which has been blown free of snow. USGS photo by W.E. Scott. *B*, Station P699. Until September 2006, station P699 had a solar panel mounted on its GPS antenna mast, which exacerbated ice loading and resulted in permanent warping of the tower. USGS photo by M. Lisowski.

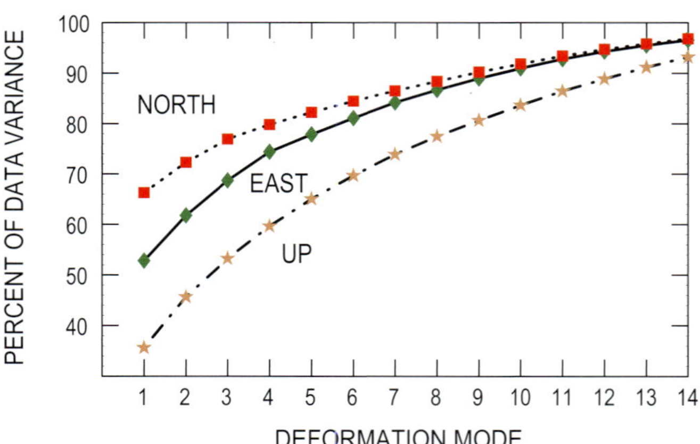

Figure 13. Cumulative percentage of data variance in 14 Mount St. Helens CGPS residual-component time series accounted for by the first 14 PCA deformation modes. North, east, and up spatial components are analyzed independently.

volumetric rate of dome growth and show that a logarithmic decay is expected if flow rate is controlled by frictional sliding of a near-surface plug (provided the coefficient of friction increases with displacement rate), whereas an exponential decay is expected if the effusion rate is a linear function of magma-chamber pressure. Ongoing, constant recharge adds a linear term to the equations of volumetric rate of dome growth.

The mode 1 deformation likely represents the loss of pressure in the magma chamber feeding the eruption, and the mode 1 temporal component can be fit with curves similar to those used by Mastin and others (this volume, chap. 22) to fit dome growth. The mode 1 east and north temporal components are best fit by an exponential decay (equation 1) and by exponential decay with a linear term (table 7). The relatively rapid decrease in the mode 1 vertical component is best fit by

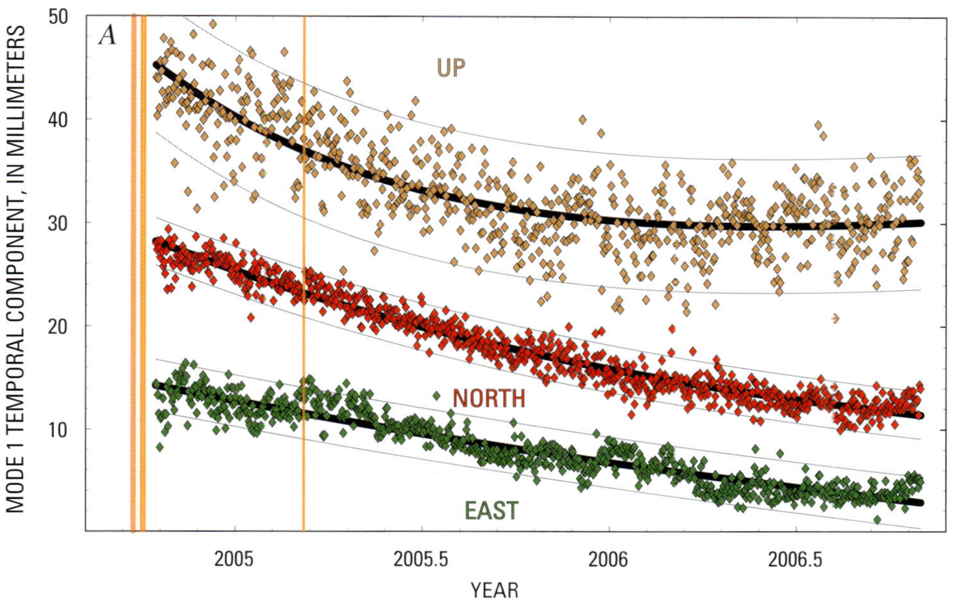

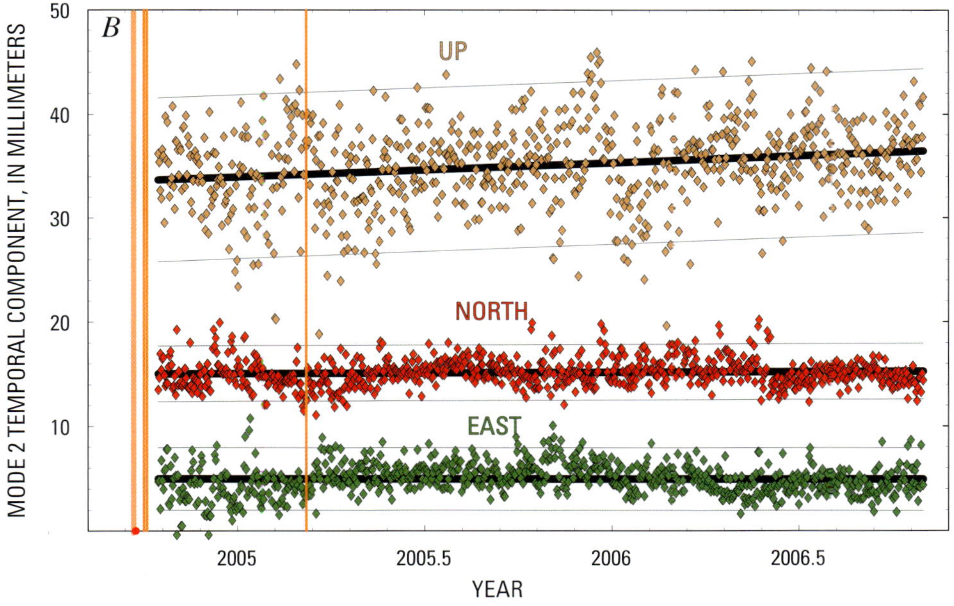

Figure 14. Temporal components from principal component analysis, in millimeters, from the combination of 14 Mount St. Helens CGPS stations and 5 CGPS reference-station residual-component time series. Dark lines are the fits to an exponential decay (equation 1) and light-gray lines are 95-percent-confidence limits of that fit. Vertical orange lines as in figures 10 and 11. *A*, Mode 1. *B*, Mode 2.

an exponential decay with a constant linear increase. The fit of the relatively noisy mode 1 temporal component without a linear term is only slightly worse. In all cases the inverted linear coefficient (*d*) and the exponential time coefficient (*b*) are highly correlated and, therefore, individually poorly determined. The best-fitting curves with the form of equation 1, along with their 95-percent-confidence limits, are shown in figure 14*A*.

So far we have examined only the PCA temporal components $C_k(t_j)$. Scaling the temporal components by the individual station response A_{ik} gives the corresponding station displacement. The scatter in the temporal components, when scaled, will result in scatter in the displacements. To calculate a station displacement for a specified time interval, we need to average or smooth the temporal components. The exponential fit supplies a smoothing that reproduces the data fairly well, and we use it to predict the temporal component and its uncertainty at any given time. The mode 1 horizontal and vertical displacements between October 15, 2004, and October 31, 2006, derived from the exponential fit, are shown in figure 15. Displacements are shown only for close-in stations, so that the map scale remains large enough to display details of deformation near Mount St. Helens, but all displacement values are listed in table 8.

Table 7. Exponential fits to PCA Mode 1 temporal components.

[Constant coefficients for $y=ae^{-b(t-t_0)} + d(t-t_0)$ with $t_0 = 2004.853$.]

Component	a (mm)	b (per yr)	d (mm/yr)	Variance (mm²)
East	22.057	0.366		1.764
East+linear	22.119	0.381	0.163	1.766
North	26.122	0.544		1.432
North+linear	26.077	0.536	-0.075	1.434
Up	24.333	0.471		15.713
Up+linear	29.207	1.171	4.492	13.112

Table 8. PCA Mode 1 station displacements from October 15, 2004, to October 31, 2006.

[Initial and final mode 1 temporal components are scaled by spatial eigenvalue for each station. Estimated 1 standard deviation uncertainty: east, 1.31 mm; north, 1.18 mm; up, 3.59 mm.]

CGPS station	Longitude (degrees)	Latitude (degrees)	East displacement (mm)	North displacement (mm)	Up displacement (mm)
JRO1	237.7824	46.2751	5.0	-14.8	-9.6
TGAU	237.8077	46.2192	4.2	-10.3	-15.3
TSTU	237.7759	46.2369	0.5	-17.2	-14.7
P687	237.6454	46.1096	4.3	-0.4	-8.8
P696	237.8484	46.1969	-0.9	-1.5	-10.3
P698	237.8394	46.1735	-2.7	1.2	-10.2
P702	237.6544	46.3002	6.1	-8.6	-5.5
KELS	237.1039	46.1182	3.7	-2.6	0.8
P693	237.7977	46.2103	8.1	-6.4	-9.3
P695	237.8358	46.1990	-3.2	-1.3	-9.2
TWIW	237.8413	46.2129	-11.5	-3.2	-9.3
P420	237.1337	46.5886	1.4	-3.9	-0.1
P421	237.5708	46.5319	2.4	-5.7	-5.0
P432	238.3168	46.6229	0.1	-3.7	-3.3
GOBS	239.1853	45.8388	-0.7	1.3	-0.8
LINH	239.4615	47.0003	0.3	-1.1	0.7
CVO1	237.5039	45.6109	0.1	-1.5	-1.4
REDM	238.8521	44.2598	0.3	-0.1	-0.7
TWRI	237.7881	46.1979	7.8	-4.5	-9.7

A few general features are apparent in the mode 1 displacements shown in figure 15. Maximum horizontal and vertical displacements are roughly equal, and subsidence is observed everywhere, with maximum values at distances greater than about 3 km and less than about 10 km. Horizontal displacements are toward Mount St. Helens, with maximum values at distances greater than about 5 km and less than about 20 km, and they are larger to the north of Mount St. Helens than to the south. Some of the apparent asymmetry in the deformation could result from the fact that there are more CGPS stations north of Mount St. Helens. Some other possible explanations for the asymmetry include error in the tectonic model that underestimates the background rate of northward motion, a source of deformation that is located to the south of the crater, a dipping source, and a laterally inhomogeneous crust.

The CGPS station displacements can be supplemented with data from a few campaign GPS stations to increase the areal coverage. This combination will be used to constrain possible sources of deformation. When we have a suitable model, we use the PCA mode 1 deformation to estimate the change in time.

Analytical Source Models

By using the PCA, a single mode of time-varying deformation was identified in the cleaned CGPS time series, which consists of an exponentially decaying downward and inward collapse toward Mount St. Helens. Such a collapse can result from pressure loss in the magma chamber feeding the eruption.

A simple model of an erupting volcano includes a magma chamber and a conduit to allow magma to escape to the surface (fig. 16). Magma chambers are idealized as fluid-pressurized, ellipsoidal cavities in an elastic half-space (Mogi, 1958; Davis and others, 1974; Davis, 1986; Yang and others, 1988; Fialko and others, 2001), and conduits are idealized as verti-

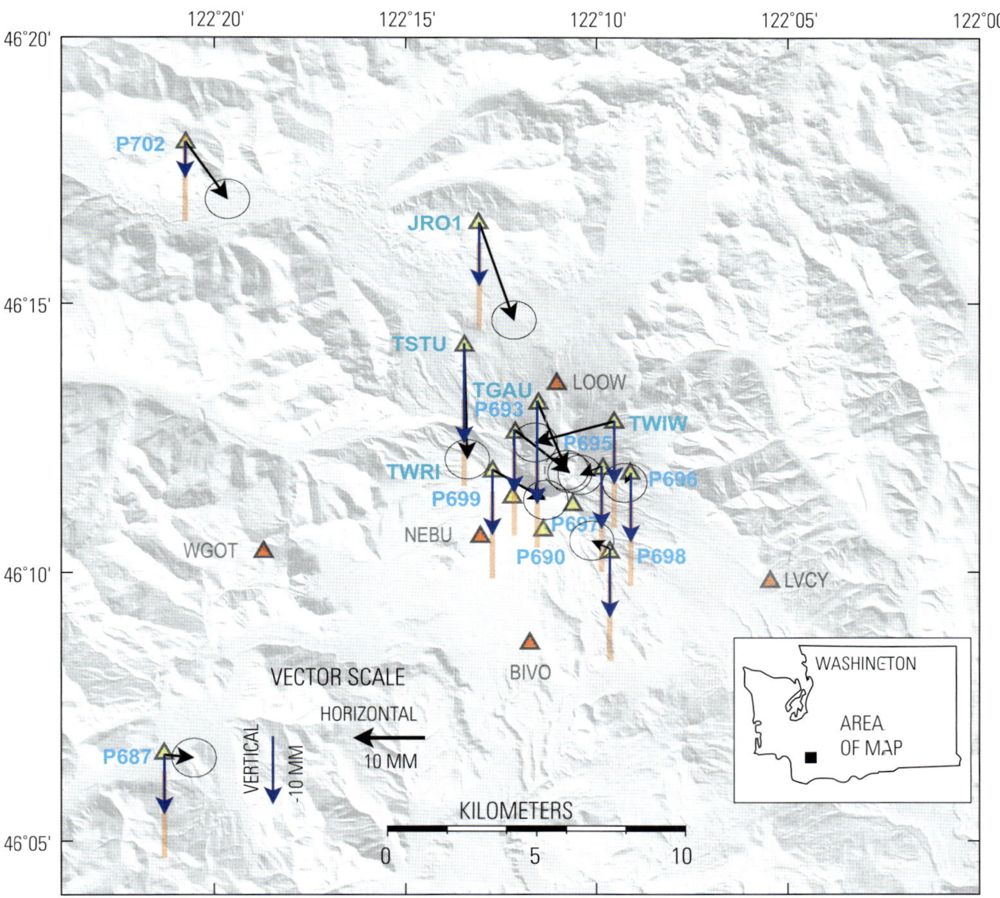

Figure 15. Map showing PCA mode 1 estimated horizontal (black arrows, tipped with 95-percent-confidence error ellipses) and vertical (blue arrows tipped with orange 95-percent-confidence error bars) displacements from October 15, 2004, to October 31, 2006, for the Mount St. Helens area. CGPS stations P699, P690, and P697 are not included in PCA analysis because of offsets and persistent winter excursions.

cal closed or open pipes (Bonaccorso and Davis, 1999). The eruption will continue until overpressure in the magma system drops below that of an equilibrated open magmatic system or until the conduit is blocked by congealing magma. As magma is withdrawn to feed an eruption, the pressure decrease in the magma system can be buffered by exsolution of gas (Mastin and others, this volume, chap. 22) and by input of new magma from depth.

Pressure change in a conduit with a radius of 10–50 m, typical for volcanoes (Bonaccorso and Davis, 1999), contributes little to the surface deformation, except near the vent; for the same reason, we can ignore deformation produced by shear tractions on the wall of the conduit exerted by magma flowing through the conduit. We assume that pressure change in the magma reservoir beneath the conduit is responsible for most of the observed deformation; therefore, we use the data to constrain the approximate limits of source depth, geometry, and the cavity volume change of a pressure source that represents the magma chamber. We limit our search to spheroidal pressure sources, which include spheres and prolate (elongate) and oblate (flattened) spheroids. We assume Poisson's ratio equals 0.25, and that the shear modulus equals 30 GPa in all the models. The pressure change that best reproduces the deformation is not estimated directly; rather, it is combined with the elastic parameters (shear modulus G, and Poisson's ratio ν) and the unknown source volume. Paradoxically, except for very shallow sources (where the chamber size is a large fraction of the depth), a large pressure change in a small source volume is indistinguishable from a small pressure change in a large source volume (McTigue, 1987). The ratio of pressure change to shear modulus must remain within the elastic limits of the surrounding rock.

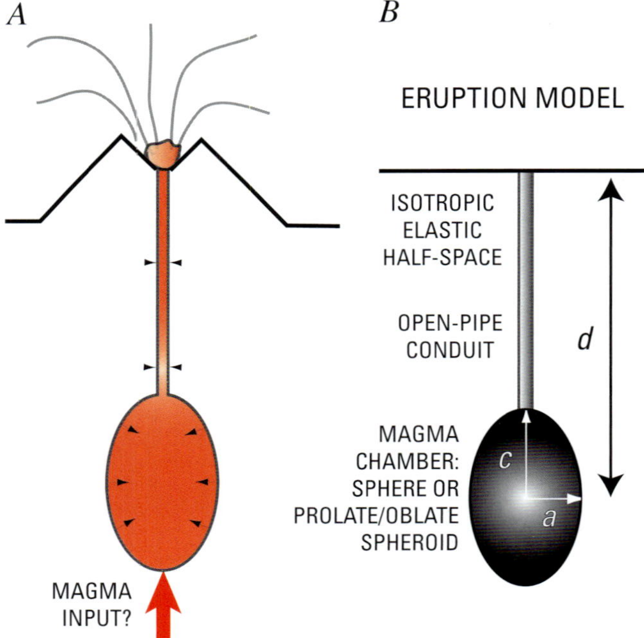

Figure 16. Schematic cross section of erupting volcano (*A*) and pressure sources (*B*) used to model surface deformation. Source depth, d, of magma chamber in half-space is relative to mean elevation of volcano.

Combined CGPS and Campaign GPS Data

Stations in the CGPS network are concentrated around the crater and to the north of Mount St. Helens. To improve spatial coverage of the deformation, we add data from campaign GPS surveys at five stations located at moderate distances from Mount St. Helens (red triangles in fig. 17). These stations were surveyed, at minimum, in late 2004 and again in 2005. We assume that deformation accumulates at a constant rate during the year after October 11, 2004, and obtain average station velocities for CGPS and campaign GPS stations (table 9). Our start and stop dates are arbitrary, but they include surveys of all the key campaign GPS stations. The mode 1 temporal components (fig. 14*A*) decay at approximately a linear rate during this year-long interval, except for the relatively noisy vertical component. The average horizontal (fig. 17) and vertical (fig. 18) station velocities for this one-year period are comparable in direction and relative magnitude to those derived from the PCA for a two-year period. Note that we include velocities for stations P690 and P697, which were excluded from the PCA analysis because of winter anomalies. The uncertainties in the station velocities are those from the QOCA time-series analysis supplemented in quadrature with a random-walk error of 1 mm/yr.

Elastic Half-Space Deformation Source Models

The nearly radial symmetry in the eruption-related deformation is consistent with a spheroidal-source geometry, and we first fit the data to a spherical-point (also called Mogi) pressure source by using a random-cost (Berg, 1993; Murray and others, 1996) search algorithm for the optimal location and depth of the source. Use of a point-source model is justified because the deformation is widespread, and, therefore, consistent with a source that is much deeper than its size (McTigue, 1987). The best-fitting spherical point-source depth (table 10) is deep (13 km), but, as indicated by the data misfit (reduced χ^2) of greater than 2, it is a poor choice when the maximum vertical and horizontal deformation are roughly equal (fig. 19*A*). A spherical source predicts a maximum horizontal deformation that is about 0.4 of the maximum vertical. Some of the misfit of the data to the model may be from the tectonic model used to correct the observed velocities. To account for such systematic error, we solve for a constant horizontal velocity in the data inversion. The point source with a systematic velocity shift fits the data slightly better, having a shallower source depth, and the center of deformation is shifted slightly to the northwest. The components of the translation (1.4 mm/yr west, 2.1 mm/yr north), however, are considerably larger than the misfit of the tectonic model to the pre-event velocity of JRO1 (0.5 mm/yr west, 0.9 mm/yr north).

A prolate spheroidal (cigar-shaped) pressure source predicts roughly equal maximum horizontal and vertical

Table 9. Adjusted Helens CGPS average station velocities from October 11, 2004, to October 11, 2005.

[Velocities are in nominal ITRF2000 fixed North American Plate terrestrial reference frame and are corrected for regional rigid-body rotation and strain.]

Station	Longitude (degrees)	Latitude (degrees)	East velocity ± 1 σ error (mm/yr)	North velocity ± 1 σ error (mm/yr)	Up velocity ± 1σ error (mm/yr)
JRO1	-122.2180	46.2750	5.42 ± 1.09	-10.50 ± 1.10	-13.19 ± 1.45
TSTU	-122.2240	46.2370	2.92 ± 1.09	-11.02 ± 1.10	-15.48 ± 1.46
TGAU	-122.1920	46.2190	3.78 ± 1.10	-5.32 ± 1.11	-12.58 ± 1.51
TWIW	-122.1590	46.2130	-5.53 ± 1.10	-2.24 ± 1.11	-8.49 ± 1.50
TWRI	-122.2120	46.1980	7.03 ± 1.13	-2.46 ± 1.14	-9.21 ± 1.64
P687	-122.3550	46.1100	4.56 ± 1.10	1.69 ± 1.11	-5.75 ± 1.54
P690	-122.1900	46.1800	0.56 ± 1.43	7.88 ± 1.48	-7.63 ± 2.71
P693	-122.2020	46.2100	7.41 ± 1.14	-2.59 ± 1.16	-8.98 ± 1.67
P695	-122.1640	46.1990	-2.08 ± 1.13	0.50 ± 1.14	-8.41 ± 1.66
P696	-122.1520	46.1970	-1.13 ± 1.10	0.32 ± 1.11	-9.11 ± 1.51
P697	-122.1770	46.1880	1.44 ± 1.33	0.58 ± 1.37	-3.30 ± 2.45
P698	-122.1610	46.1730	-1.72 ± 1.11	2.33 ± 1.12	-10.52 ± 1.56
P702	-122.3460	46.3000	5.44 ± 1.12	-7.10 ± 1.13	-3.45 ± 1.57
NEBU	-122.2170	46.1780	5.15 ± 1.77	0.65 ± 1.85	-14.71 ± 3.80
BIVO	-122.1960	46.1450	-1.43 ± 1.19	7.55 ± 1.21	-5.01 ± 1.88
LVCY	-122.0910	46.1640	-5.56 ± 2.16	3.25 ± 2.23	-11.54 ± 4.69
LOOW	-122.1840	46.2250	-0.35 ± 1.84	-7.65 ± 1.91	-10.02 ± 3.91
WGOT	-122.3110	46.1730	5.20 ± 2.40	1.90 ± 2.49	-15.80 ± 5.07
P420	-122.8660	46.5890	1.40 ± 1.08	-1.85 ± 1.09	0.94 ± 1.43
P421	-122.4290	46.5320	2.02 ± 1.17	-3.78 ± 1.19	-1.44 ± 1.79
P432	-121.6830	46.6230	-0.65 ± 1.09	-1.94 ± 1.10	-2.39 ± 1.44
KELS	-122.8960	46.1180	2.07 ± 1.08	-0.81 ± 1.09	-0.23 ± 1.38
GOBS	-120.8150	45.8390	0.86 ± 1.08	-1.55 ± 1.09	-1.10 ± 1.38
CVO1	-122.4960	45.6110	1.41 ± 1.08	0.04 ± 1.09	-0.65 ± 1.38
REDM	-121.1480	44.2600	-0.51 ± 1.08	-0.68 ± 1.09	0.65 ± 1.38
LINH	-120.5390	47.0000	-1.50 ± 1.08	-0.43 ± 1.09	2.26 ± 1.39

deformation. A point source of this type can be constructed by superimposing three collocated orthogonal point cracks (for example, Okada, 1985, 1992), with two of the cracks having equal amplitudes related to the aspect ratio w of the minor radii to the major radius of the spheroid by

$$M_0 = 1/(0.3 - 0.1w), \quad (3)$$

and the third crack having an amplitude

$$M_0 = 1/(0.4w - 0.2). \quad (4)$$

M_0 is the moment, which in this case is equivalent to volume change (the amount of opening times the area affected) multiplied by the shear modulus. If we substitute $w = 1$, then $M_0 = 5$ for the sum of all three cracks, and the source obtained is equivalent to a spherical point pressure source. Decreasing w elongates the spheroid.

A point prolate spheroidal pressure source with its long axis vertical fits the data better than do the spherical point-source models (table 10, fig. 19B). The best-fitting aspect ratio (0.66) and depth (7.9 km) is roughly consistent with other models of the Mount St. Helens magma chamber (Pallister and others, 1992). Only a slight improvement in the fit is obtained by adding a systematic horizontal velocity (0.2 mm/yr west, 1.4 mm/yr north), which shifts the center of the source to the southwest. The estimated velocity shift is similar to the misfit of the tectonic model to the pre-event velocity of JRO1.

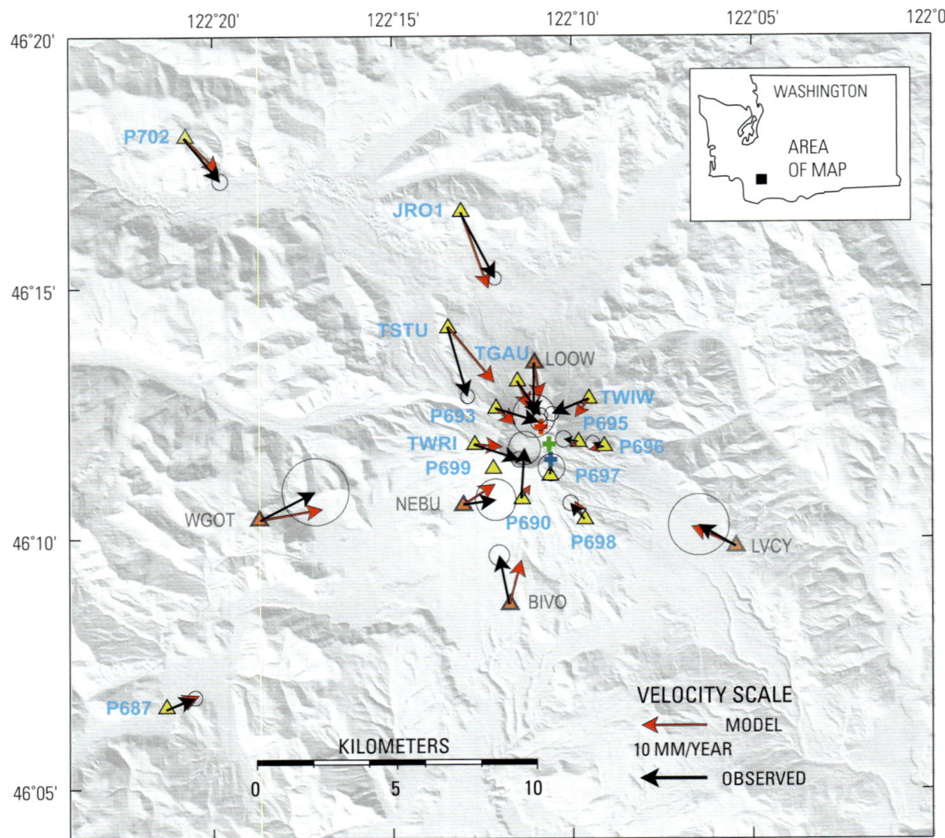

Figure 17. Map showing corrected average GPS station horizontal-velocity vectors (black arrows tipped with 95-percent-confidence error ellipses) and displacements predicted by best-fitting, tilted point prolate spheroid (red arrows, scale at bottom of figure) for the Mount St. Helens area from October 15, 2004, to October 15, 2005. See table 10 for model parameters. Surface projection of center of tilted point prolate spheroid marked by red cross, that of vertical prolate spheroid by blue cross, and that of spherical point pressure source by green cross.

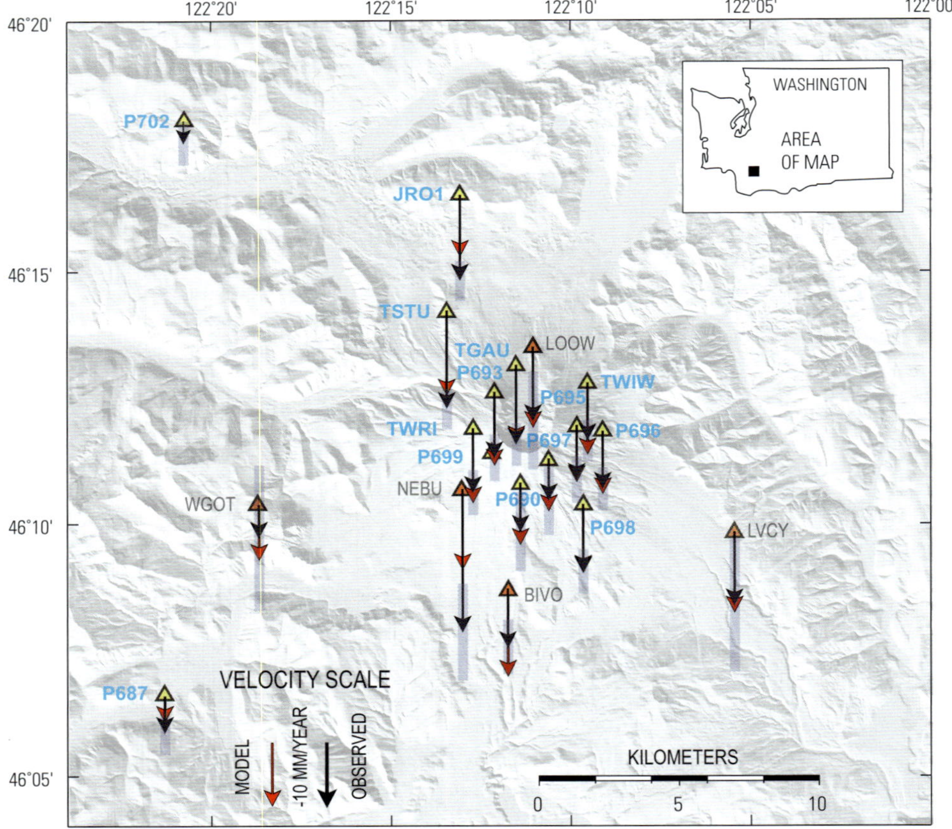

Figure 18. Map showing corrected average GPS station vertical-velocity vectors (black arrows tipped with light blue 95-percent-confidence error bar) and vertical displacements predicted by best-fitting, near-vertical, point-prolate spheroid (red arrows, scale at bottom) for Mount St. Helens area from October 15, 2004, to October 15, 2005. See table 10 for model parameters.

Another way for the model to account for asymmetry in the deformation is to allow the source to plunge at an angle less than 90° and to allow the azimuth of this axis to vary. If we do not allow for a systematic rate of translation, the parameter search returns a vertical optimal plunge. If we allow for a systematic velocity error, the best-fitting, plunging prolate source is nearly vertical (83°) with azimuth N. 37° W. (fig. 19*C*). The systematic velocity is again similar to the misfit of the tectonic model to the pre-event velocity of JRO1.

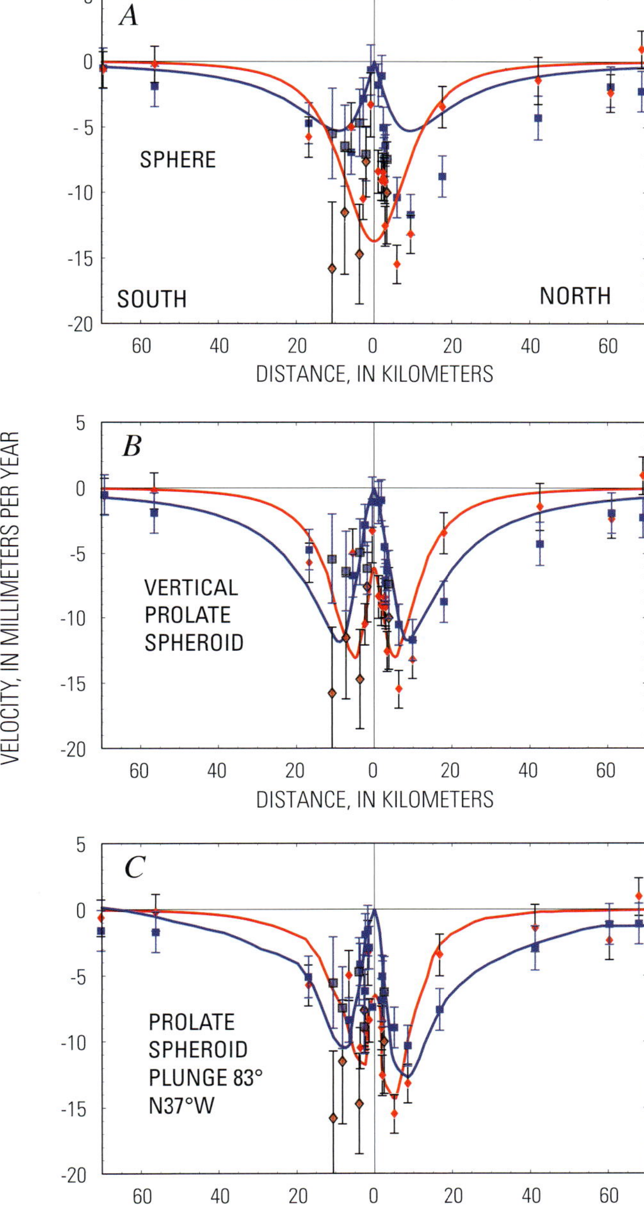

Figure 19. Observed radial (blue squares) and vertical (red diamonds) velocities for deformation of Mount St. Helens from October 15, 2004, to October 15, 2005, projected onto north-south profile and compared with predicted radial (solid blue curve) and vertical (red curve) velocities from best-fitting point sources. Error bars are ±1 standard deviation. Details of models given in table 9. *A*, spherical point pressure source; *B*, vertical point prolate spheroid; *C*, tilted or dipping point prolate spheroid with a small velocity correction.

To calculate the volume change consistent with the source strength, we assume that the spherical source has a radius of 1 km and the prolate spheroid has a minor radius of 1 km. Once the model geometry is fixed to the values obtained by the parameter search, the radius change (equivalent to strength of the source) is inverted directly. The equivalent source cavity-volume decrease for the one-year period covered by the data is in the range 8–12×10^6 m^3 in the various prolate spheroid models.

Only JRO1 recorded the relatively rapid deformation that occurred during the first two weeks of the eruption, and we use its motion as a proxy to estimate the total cavity-volume loss. The predicted 12.8 mm/yr of radially inward motion at JRO1 from the dipping prolate spheroid model with a systematic velocity correction is about half of the total movement of JRO1 from September 23, 2004, to October 31, 2006. A total cavity-volume loss of 16–24×10^6 m^3 is consistent with the JRO1 displacements, and it is a fraction of the >83×10^6 m^3 dome volume as of August 2006. Mastin and others (this volume, chap. 22) explain this discrepancy as a combination of exsolution of gas, which buffers pressure loss in the magma chamber, and recharge by new magma (recharge estimated to be only about one-tenth of the erupted volume). The recharge, if it is occurring, has thus far not increased the flux of volcanic gases (Gerlach and others, this volume, chap. 26).

Conclusions

Remarkably little far-field volcanic deformation has occurred around Mount St. Helens since shortly after the crater-forming collapse and eruption in 1980. Data collected in 1982 and 1991 for surveys of a regional high-precision trilateration network provide the clearest evidence for recharge of the volcano's magma system. During that interval, areal dilatation accumulated at an average rate of 144±39 nanostrain/yr, an order of magnitude greater than and opposite in sign to the estimated background rate of −15±3 nanostrain/yr. No significant deformation occurred in the same network between 1991 and 2000.

GPS surveys conducted since the 1990s reveal background deformation, which is used to define a tectonic model that includes a rigid-body clockwise rotation and a small amount of strain accumulation. The background strain accumulation within the network (in the absence of volcano deformation) is essentially a uniaxal contraction in the east-northeast direction, a possible effect of a locked Cascadia subduction-zone thrust fault. After removing this secular deformation, we find no coherent pattern of volcanic deformation around Mount St. Helens between 2000 and 2003. Furthermore, daily position measurements made at a CGPS

Table 10. Elastic half-space deformation source models.

[ΔEast and ΔNorth data show estimates for rigid-body translation rate that account for possible error in tectonic model. --, elements not part of solution; n.a., not applicable to long-axis trend because model is of vertical prolate geometry.]

Source description	Longitude (degrees)	Latitude (degrees)	Depth (km)	ΔRadius (m/yr)	ΔEast (m/yr)	ΔNorth (m/yr)	Aspect ratio	Long axis plunge (degrees)	Long axis (trend)	Model para-meters	Re-duced χ^2	ΔVolume (10^6 m^3/yr)
Spherical point pressure (Mogi)	-122.1765	46.1961	12.93	-0.7653	--	--	1.00 (fixed)	--	--	4	2.17	9.7
Spherical point pressure + translation rate	-122.1926	46.2119	10.39	-0.5028	-0.0014	0.0021	1.00 (fixed)	--	--	6	1.95	6.3
Vertical prolate spheroid	-122.1746	46.2133	7.99	-1.1485	--	--	0.66	90 (fixed)	n.a.	5	1.59	11.9
Vertical prolate spheroid + translation rate	-122.1758	46.2000	7.60	-0.9651	-0.0002	0.0014	0.673	--	n.a.	7	1.54	9.6
Tilted prolate spheroid	-122.1748	46.2133	7.94	-1.1356	--	--	0.660	90 (fixed)	n.a.	7	1.60	11.9
Tilted prolate spheroid + translation rate	-122.1811	46.2133	7.14	-0.7927	-0.0004	0.0013	0.676	82.4	N36°W	9	1.49	7.9

station 9 km north of Mount St. Helens show no anomalous deformation from 1997 until the start of seismic unrest on September 23, 2004.

The movement of magma to the surface at the start of unrest did not systematically displace GPS stations on the volcano's flanks, but it did displace station DOM1 on the September 1984 lobe of the old dome by more than 0.2 m to the north. The lack of systematic deformation around the crater suggests that solidified magma plugging the top of the conduit was pushed out, rather than being bypassed. Much of the movement of the L1 CGPS station DOM1 occurred by September 28, well before the first phreatic explosion, suggesting that the movement of magma began with the start of seismic unrest. At the same time, CGPS station JRO1 moved toward Mount St. Helens an average of about 0.5 mm/day from September 23 until a few days after the phreatic explosion on October 5, 2004, when its motion slowed and began to decay.

Analysis of eruption-related deformation data reveals a single space- and time-coherent mode of time-varying deformation, which has been decaying exponentially since the start of unrest. All GPS stations are moving toward Mount St. Helens and downward in a manner consistent with the predictions of an elastic half-space model that represents pressure loss in a vertically elongate magma chamber. The center of Mount St. Helens' magma chamber is estimated to be at a depth of 7 to 8 km, and the chamber's long axis, which is vertical or near vertical, is estimated to be approximately three times longer than its diameter. The actual dimensions of the magma chamber are poorly constrained by the deformation data. The source-cavity volume loss, which is proportional to the strength of the source, is about 16–24×10^6 m^3, about one-third of the erupted volume. This discrepancy can be accounted for mostly by buffering of pressure loss in the magma chamber through exsolution of gas and with a small amount of recharge (Mastin and others, this volume, chap. 22).

Acknowledgments

We thank the NSF-sponsored Plate Boundary Observatory for rapid installation of CGPS monitoring stations in October 2004 in response to renewed unrest at Mount St. Helens. In particular, we are grateful for the timely efforts of Katrin Hafner and other field engineers from UNAVCO, Inc., the contractor responsible for installing PBO stations.

We thank the CVO staff, temporary staff, and volunteers who helped with the field surveys and permanent CGPS station construction. We are grateful that Elliot Endo had the foresight to install a CGPS station at the Johnston Ridge Observatory. Richard LaHusen established telecommunications at the U.S. Forest Service's Coldwater Ridge maintenance shed in order to download CVO GPS data, and he provided L1 CGPS data. We used computer code from John Langbein of the USGS Earthquake Hazards Team to invert for best-fitting source-model parameters. The original code was developed by James C. Savage; Mark H. Murray added random-cost extensions and the Okada dislocation routines, and John Langbein added code for the ellipsoidal pressure sources. John Langbein and Larry Mastin provided constructive reviews of this paper.

References Cited

Aubrey, D.G., and Emery, K.O., 1983, Eigenanalysis of recent United States sea levels: Continental Shelf Research, v. 2, p. 21–33.

Altimimi, Z., Sillard, P., and Boucher, C., 2002, ITRF2000: A new release of the International Terrestrial Reference Frame for earth science applications: Journal of Geophysical Research, v. 107, no. B10, 2214, doi:10.1029/2001JB000561.

Berg, B., 1993, Locating global minima in optimization problems by a random-cost approach: Nature, v. 361, p. 708–710.

Blewitt, G., 1989, Carrier phase ambiguity resolution for the Global Positioning System applied to geodetic baselines up to 2000 km: Journal of Geophysical Research, v. 94, no. B8, p. 10187–10203.

Bonaccorso, A., and Davis, P.M., 1999, Models of ground deformation from vertical volcanic conduits with application to eruptions of Mount St. Helens and Mount Etna: Journal of Geophysical Research, v. 104, no. B5, p. 10531–10542.

Davis, P.M., 1986, Surface deformation due to inflation of an arbitrarily oriented triaxial ellipsoidal cavity in an elastic half-space, with reference to Kilauea volcano: Journal of Geophysical Research, v. 91, p. 7429–7438.

Davis, P.M., Hastie, L.M., and Stacey, F.D., 1974, Stresses within an active volcano, with particular reference to Kilauea: Tectonophysics, v. 22, p. 363–7438.

Demets, C., Gordon, R.G., Argus, D.F., and Stein, S., 1994, Effect of recent revisions of the geomagnetic reversal timescale on estimates of current plate motions: Geophysical Research Letters, v. 21, p. 2191–2194.

Dong, D., Herring, T.A., and King, R.W., 1998, Estimating regional deformation from a combination of space and terrestrial geodetic data: Journal of Geodesy, v. 72, p. 200–214.

Dong, D., Fang, P., Bock, Y., Cheng, M.K., and Miyazaki, S., 2002, Anatomy of apparent seasonal variations from GPS-derived site position time series: Journal of Geophysical Research, v. 107, no. B4, p. ETG 9-1–ETG 9-16.

Dong, D., Fang, P., Bock, Y., Webb, F., Prawirodirdjo, L., Kedar, S., and Jamason, P., 2006, Spatiotemporal filtering using principal component analysis and Karhunen-Loeve expansion approaches for regional GPS network analysis: Journal of Geophysical Research, v. 111, no. B03405, doi:10.1029/2005JB003806.

Dvorak, J., Okamura, A., Mortensen, C., and Johnston, M.J.S., 1981, Summary of electronic tilt studies at Mount St. Helens, *in* Lipman, P.W., and Mullineaux, D.R., eds., The 1980 eruptions of Mount St. Helens, Washington: U.S. Geological Survey Professional Paper 1250, p. 169–174.

Ewert, J.W., and Swanson, D.A., 1992, Monitoring volcanoes; techniques and strategies used by the staff of the Cascades Volcano Observatory, 1980–90: U.S. Geological Survey Bulletin 1966, 223 p.

Fialko, Y., Khazan, Y., and Simons, M., 2001, Deformation due to a pressurized horizontal circular crack in an elastic half-space, with applications to volcano geodesy: Geophysical Journal International, v. 146, p. 181–190.

Gerlach, T.M., McGee, K.A., and Doukas, M.P., 2008, Emission rates of CO_2, SO_2, and H_2S, scrubbing, and preeruption excess volatiles at Mount St. Helens, 2004–2005, chap. 26 *of* Sherrod, D.R., Scott, W.E., and Stauffer, P.H., eds., A volcano rekindled; the renewed eruption of Mount St. Helens, 2004–2006: U.S. Geological Survey Professional Paper 1750 (this volume).

Heflin, M., Bertiger, W., Blewitt, G., Freedman, A., Hurst, K., Licten, S., Lindqwister, U., Vigue, Y., Webb, F., Yunck, T., and Zumberge, J., 1992, Global geodesy using GPS without fiducial sites: Geophysical Research Letters, v. 19, no. 2, p. 131–134.

LaHusen, R.G., Swinford, K.J., Logan, M., and Lisowski, M., 2008, Instrumentation in remote and dangerous settings; examples using data from GPS "spider" deployments during the 2004–2005 eruption of Mount St. Helens, Washington, chap. 16 *of* Sherrod, D.R., Scott, W.E., and Stauffer, P.H., eds., A volcano rekindled; the renewed eruption of Mount St. Helens, 2004–2006: U.S. Geological Survey Professional Paper 1750 (this volume).

Langbein, J., Wyatt, F., Johnson, H., Hamann, D., and Zimmer, P., 1995, Improved stability of a deeply anchored geodetic monument for deformation monitoring: Geophysical Research Letters, v. 22, p. 3533–3536.

Lipman, P.W., Moore, J.G., and Swanson, D.A., 1981, Bulging of the north flank before the May 18 eruption—geodetic data, *in* Lipman, P.W., and Mullineaux, D.R., eds., The 1980 eruptions of Mount St. Helens, Washington: U.S. Geological Survey Professional Paper 1250, p. 143–155.

Magill, J., Wells, R.E., Simpson, R.W., and Cox, A.V., 1982, Post 12 m.y. rotations of southwestern Washington: Journal of Geophysical Research, v. 87, p. 3761–3776.

Mastin, L.G., Roeloffs, E., Beeler, N.M., and Quick, J.E., 2008, Constraints on the size, overpressure, and volatile content of the Mount St. Helens magma system from geodetic and dome-growth measurements during the 2004–2006+ eruption, chap. 22 *of* Sherrod, D.R., Scott, W.E., and Stauffer, P.H., eds., A volcano rekindled; the renewed eruption of Mount St. Helens, 2004–2006: U.S. Geological Survey Professional Paper 1750 (this volume).

Mazzotti, S., Dragert, H., Henton, J., Schmidt, M., Hyndman, R., James, T., Lu, Y., and Craymer, M., 2003, Current tectonics of northern Cascadia from a decade of GPS measurements: Journal of Geophysical Research, v. 108, no. B12, 2554, doi:10.1029/2003JB002653.

McCaffrey, R., Long, M.D., Goldfinger, C., Zwick, P.C., Nabelek, J.L., Johnson, C.K., and Smith, C., 2000, Rotation and plate locking at the southern Cascadia subduction zone: Geophysical Research Letters, v. 27, no. 19, p. 3117–3120.

McTigue, D.F., 1987, Elastic stress and deformation near a finite spherical magma body; resolution of the point source paradox: Journal of Geophysical Research, v. 92, no. B12, p. 12931–12940.

Menke, W., 1984, Geophysical data analysis; discrete inverse theory: New York, Elsevier, 260 p.

Miller, M.M., Johnson, D.J., Rubin, C.M., Dragert, H., Wang, K., Qamar, A., and Goldfinger, C., 2001, GPS determination of alongstrike variation in Cascadia margin kinematics; implications for relative plate motion, subduction zone coupling, and permanent deformation: Tectonics, v. 20, p. 161–176.

Mogi, K., 1958, Relations between the eruptions of various volcanoes and the deformations of the ground surfaces around them: Bulletin of the Earthquake Research Institute of University of Tokyo, v. 36, p. 99–134.

Murray, M., and Lisowski, M., 2000, Strain accumulation along the Cascadia subduction zone; Cape Mendocino to the Straits of Juan de Fuca: Geophysical Research Letters, v. 27, p. 3631–3634.

Murray, M.H., Marshall, G.A., Lisowski, M., and Stein, R.S., 1996, The 1992 M=7 Cape Mendocino, California, earthquake; coseismic deformation at the south end of the Cascadia megathrust: Journal of Geophysical Research, v. 101, no. B8, p. 17707–17725.

Okada, Y., 1985, Surface deformation due to shear and tensile faults in a half-space: Bulletin of the Seismological Society of America, v. 75, no. 4, p. 1135–1154.

Okada, Y., 1992, Internal deformation due to shear and tensile faults in a half-space: Bulletin of the Seismological Society of America, v. 82, no. 2, p. 1018–1040.

Pallister, J.S., Hoblitt, R.P., Crandell, D.R., and Mullineaux, D.R., 1992, Mount St. Helens a decade after the 1980 eruptions; magmatic models, chemical cycles, and a revised hazards assessment: Bulletin of Volcanology, v. 54, no. 2, p. 126–146, doi: 10.1007/BF00278003.

Preisendorfer, R.W., 1988, Principal component analysis in meteorology and oceanography, *in* Mobley, C.D., ed., Developments in Atmospheric Science 17: New York, Elsevier, 425 p.

Savage, J.C., 1988, Principal component analysis of geodetically measured deformation in Long Valley caldera, eastern California: Journal of Geophysical Research, v. 93, p. 1983–1987.

Savage, J.C., 1995, Principal component analysis of interseismic deformation in southern California: Journal of Geophysical Research, v. 100, p. 12691–12701.

Savage, J.C., and Prescott, W.H., 1973, Precision of Geodolite distance measurements for determining fault movements: Journal of Geophysical Research, v. 78, p. 6001–6008.

Savage, J.C., Prescott, W.H., and Gu, G., 1986, Strain accumulation in southern California, 1973–1984: Journal of Geophysical Research, v. 91, p. 7455–7473.

Savage, J.C., Lisowski, M., and Prescott, W.H., 1991, Strain accumulation in western Washington: Journal of Geophysical Research, v. 96, p. 14493–14507.

Savage, J.C., Lisowski, M., and Prescott, W.H., 1996, Observed discrepancy between Geodolite and GPS distance measurements: Journal of Geophysical Research, v. 101, p. 25547–25552.

Savage, J.C., Svarc, J.L., Prescott, W.H., and Murray, M.H., 2000, Deformation across the forearc of the Cascadia subduction zone at Cape Blanco, Oregon: Journal of Geophysical Research, v. 105, no. B2, p. 3095–3102.

Savage, J.C., Gan, W., and Svarc, J.L., 2001, Strain accumulation and rotation in the Eastern California Shear Zone: Journal of Geophysical Research, v. 106, no. B10, p. 21995–22007.

Schilling, S.P., Thompson, R.A., Messerich, J.A., and Iwatsubo, E.Y., 2008, Use of digital aerophotogrammetry to determine rates of lava dome growth, Mount St. Helens, Washington, 2004–2005, chap. 8 *of* Sherrod, D.R., Scott, W.E., and Stauffer, P.H., eds., A volcano rekindled; the renewed eruption of Mount St. Helens, 2004–2006: U.S. Geological Survey Professional Paper 1750 (this volume).

Simpson, R.W., and Cox, A.V., 1977, Paleomagnetic evidence for tectonic rotation of the Oregon Coast Range: Geology, v. 5, p. 585–598.

Smith, K.D., von Seggern, D., Blewitt, G., Preston, L., Anderson, J.G., Wernicke, B.P., and Davis, J.L., 2004, Evidence for deep magma injection beneath Lake Tahoe, Nevada–California: Science, v. 305, no. 5688, p. 1277–1280.

Svarc, J.L., Savage, J.C., Prescott, W.H., and Murray, M.H., 2002, Strain accumulation and rotation in western Oregon and southwestern Washington: Journal of Geophysical

Research, v. 107, no. B5, 2087, doi:10.1029/2000JB000033.

Swanson, D.A., Lipman, P.W., Moore, J.G., Heliker, C.C., and Yamashita, K.M., 1981, Geodetic monitoring after the May 18 eruption, *in* Lipman, P.W., and Mullineaux, D.R., eds., The 1980 eruptions of Mount St. Helens, Washington: U.S. Geological Survey Professional Paper 1250, p. 157–168.

Verdonck, D., 2006, Contemporary vertical crustal deformation in Cascadia: Tectonophysics, v. 417, nos. 3–4, p. 221–230.

Wdowinski, S., Bock, Y., Zhang, J., Fang, R., and Genrich, J.F., 1997, Southern California Permanent GPS Geodetic Array; spatial filtering of daily positions for estimating coseismic and postseismic displacements induced by the 1992 Landers earthquake: Journal of Geophysical Research, v. 102, no. B8, p. 18057–18070.

Webb, F.H., and Zumberge, J.F., 1995, An introduction to GIPSY/OASIS-II: Pasadena, Calif., Jet Propulsion Laboratory Publication No. JPL D-11088.

Wells, R.E., and Simpson, R.W., 2001, Northward migration of the Cascadia forearc in the northwestern U.S. and implications for the subduction deformation: Earth, Planets and Space, v. 53, p. 275–283.

Wells, R.E., Weaver, C.S., and Blakely, R.J., 1998, Fore-arc migration in Cascadia and its neotectonic significance: Geology, v. 26, no. 8, p. 759–762.

Williams, S.D., Bock, Y., Fang, P., Jamason, P., Nikolaidis, R.M., Prawirodirdjo, L., Miller, M., and Johnson, D.J., 2004, Error analysis of continuous GPS position time series: Journal of Geophysical Research, v. 109, no. B03412, doi:10.1029/2003JB00274.

Yang, X., Davis, P.M., and Dieterich, J.H., 1988, Deformation from inflation of a dipping finite prolate spheroid in an elastic half-space as a model for volcanic stressing: Journal of Geophysical Research, v. 93, no. B5, p. 4289–4257.

Zumberge, J.F., Heflin, M.B., Jefferson, D.C., Watkins, M.M., and Webb, F.H., 1997, Precise point positioning for the efficient and robust analysis of GPS data from large networks: Journal of Geophysical Research, v. 102, no. B3, p. 5005–5017.

A Volcano Rekindled: The Renewed Eruption of Mount St. Helens, 2004–2006
Edited by David R. Sherrod, William E. Scott, and Peter H. Stauffer
U.S. Geological Survey Professional Paper 1750, 2008

Chapter 16

Instrumentation in Remote and Dangerous Settings; Examples Using Data from GPS "Spider" Deployments During the 2004–2005 Eruption of Mount St. Helens, Washington

By Richard G. LaHusen[1], Kelly J. Swinford[1], Matthew Logan[1], and Michael Lisowski[1]

Abstract

Self-contained, single-frequency GPS instruments fitted on lightweight stations suitable for helicopter-sling payloads became a critical part of volcano monitoring during the September 2004 unrest and subsequent eruption of Mount St. Helens. Known as "spiders" because of their spindly frames, the stations were slung into the crater 29 times from September 2004 to December 2005 when conditions at the volcano were too dangerous for crews to install conventional equipment. Data were transmitted in near-real time to the Cascades Volcano Observatory in Vancouver, Washington. Each fully equipped unit cost about $2,500 in materials and, if not destroyed by natural events, was retrieved and redeployed as needed. The GPS spiders have been used to track the growth and decay of extruding dacite lava (meters per day), thickening and accelerated flow of Crater Glacier (meters per month), and movement of the 1980–86 dome from pressure and relaxation of the newly extruding lava dome (centimeters per day).

Introduction

Typically, volcano monitoring and associated eruption forecasting relies on several disciplines of volcanology, principally seismology, gas geochemistry, and geodesy (Dzurisin, 2006). No single tool or technique can adequately monitor or predict the range of volcanic behaviors—from aseismic deformation to relatively benign dome building to major explosive eruptions. Accordingly, volcanologists rely on an assortment of instruments and techniques to monitor volcanic unrest. Sensors and related instrumentation have been developed in attempts to accommodate the needs of each particular discipline. However, even when an instrument is available that is capable of making a desired measurement, use of the instrument may be limited by expense or by an inability to deploy it in dangerous or inaccessible sites close to volcanic vents. New techniques and instruments are notable to volcanologists when they are affordable and minimize exposure of personnel to hazards. This paper describes the rapid development and application of a self-contained instrument package that was used successfully to monitor deformation close to the vent during the renewed eruption of Mount St. Helens in 2004–2005.

Prior Near-Vent Geodesy at Mount St. Helens

Pioneering geodetic work done during the 1980–86 eruptions of Mount St. Helens demonstrated that some eruptions could be predicted by monitoring accelerating deformation on localized parts of the dome (fig. 1; Swanson and others, 1983; Dzurisin and others, 1983). The 1980s geodetic work demonstrated that substantial preeruptive dome deformation typically was limited to areas near the active vent. The geodetic-deformation measurements commonly required the repeated and prolonged presence of personnel working close to the vent to bury electronic tiltmeters or to measure distances between fixed monuments by using electronic distance meters. Fortunately, with the subsequent availability of commercial GPS instruments, it is now possible to make repeated high-precision geodetic measurements on the volcano without exposing personnel to prolonged periods of work in hazardous areas.

Prototype GPS Instrument

For 4 years prior to the September 2004 seismic unrest at Mount St. Helens, an automated L1 GPS system was intermittently operated as a prototype monitoring tool. The system was

[1] U.S. Geological Survey, 1300 SE Cardinal Court, Vancouver, WA 98683

being developed by the U.S. Geological Survey's Cascades Volcano Observatory (CVO) as an inexpensive, near-real-time, ground-deformation monitoring tool with design emphasis on low cost, power conservation, and telemetered data integrity (LaHusen and Reid, 2000). Station DOM1 was installed on the 1980–86 dome within the crater of Mount St. Helens, and stations SFT2 and POA3 were installed outside the crater about 4 km to the west and east of DOM1, respectively. Each station was powered by a 20-W solar panel and a rechargeable lead-acid battery. Within each was a USGS microcontroller controlled remotely from a desktop computer at CVO using a 100-km multi-hop 900-MHz radio link. The operational scheme conserves power at the remote stations by alternately powering the GPS receivers and radio-telemetry components. During data-acquisition cycles, a CMC Allstar model L1 GPS receiver coupled with a Micropulse model 1372 survey-grade GPS antenna is powered for 20 minutes while raw GPS data at 10-s epochs are logged to the microcontroller. At the end of each data-logging session, the GPS receiver is switched off to conserve power, and the radio is switched on to relay data packets to CVO. Each data-transmission session lasts several minutes and includes error

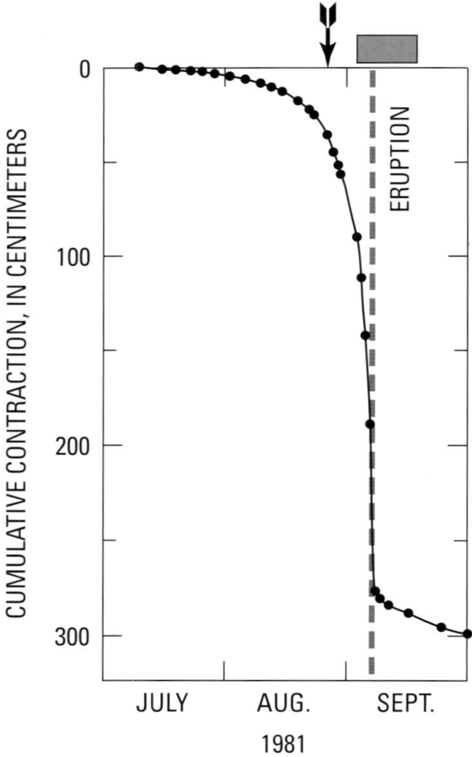

Figure 1. Movement of monument on lava dome in 1981 as determined by sequential EDM measurements, Mount St. Helens, Washington. Arrow indicates issuance of eruption prediction for time window shown by rectangular bar. Vertical dashed line shows time that dome eruption began (from Swanson and others, 1983).

checking and retransmission to achieve error-free blocks of raw GPS data. The operational duty cycle is adjustable to balance power conservation, frequency of measurement, and station longevity.

Fixed, static, double-differential solutions between stations were calculated automatically using USGS control and scheduling software that applied a commercial software module, Waypoint Precise DLL. An independent position solution was calculated for every 20-minute data-acquisition period. Although GPS data acquisition within the crater posed substantial challenges owing to obscured views of the sky, mantling by rime ice, and noise from multipath reflections, this monitoring scheme typically transferred data reliably and repeatedly. The accuracy of each single solution was 1 cm plus 1 ppm of the differential baseline length (4 km), or 1.4 cm for the horizontal components. Vertical accuracy was found to be about double the horizontal value. This noise, inherent to single-frequency GPS solutions, was reduced greatly by applying a moving median filter that allowed discrimination of more subtle motions of less than a centimeter over longer time periods. Between 2002 and February 2004, the system measured dome subsidence that possibly reflected contractive cooling of the dome interior. The subsidence was at an annual rate of about 8 cm/yr downward and 2 cm/yr eastward, toward the center of the dome (fig. 2). Batteries at DOM1 failed in February 2004 and were not replaced until September.

When the GPS system was reactivated on September 27, 2004, following initiation of seismicity at Mount St. Helens, station DOM1 was in a location significantly different from what would have been predicted based on the subsidence trend of the preceding years. It was about 20 cm north and 12 cm higher than the predicted location (fig. 2). These location changes occurred between February 2004 and September 27, 2004, but we cannot further constrain the rate and timing of this deformation. Automated measurements on September 27 showed that DOM1 was moving northward at 2 cm per day. This station and a companion seismometer, the only stations on the old dome, were destroyed 4 days later, on October 1, by ballistic fragments ejected during the first phreatic explosion of the 2004 eruption (fig. 3).

GPS Spider Deployments

Loss of the only GPS station in the crater presented a dilemma because near-vent deformation could no longer be monitored. The time-consuming task of reinstalling a solar-powered GPS station onsite was considered unsafe because of the risk of additional, unpredictable phreatic explosions. Other challenges for deformation monitoring in the crater included the likelihood of additional ashfall from explosions and the impending onset of winter snowfall.

As an alternative to installing a permanent, monumented station, we assembled three GPS stations electronically similar in design to the original DOM1. However, unlike DOM1, which

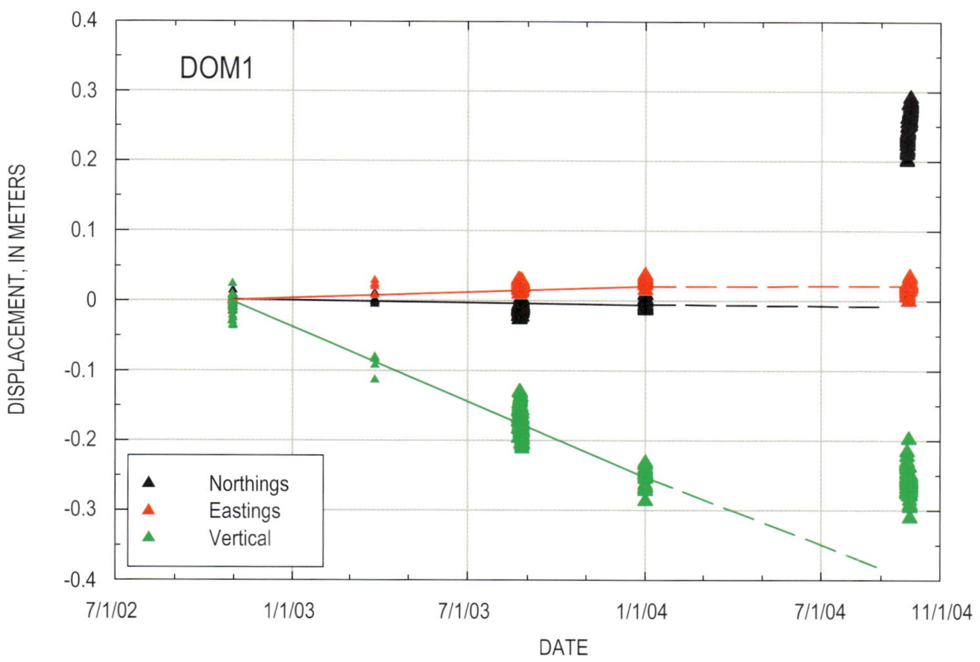

Figure 2. Time series of preeruptive deformation at GPS station DOM1, Mount St. Helens, Washington. Prior to February 2004, the 1980–86 dome was subsiding, possibly due to contraction of cooling interior. When DOM1 was reactivated on September 27, 2004, it was 20 cm north and 12 cm above its predicted location based on its previous trend (dashed lines).

Figure 3. Photographs showing station DOM1 GPS before and after its destruction by ballistic fragments from explosion at Mount St. Helens on October 1, 2004. *A*, Before explosion. Antenna mount (foreground behind boulder) and instrument shelter (black box), with helicopter hovering just beyond. USGS photo by R.G. LaHusen. *B*, After explosion, from slightly closer viewpoint. White jagged sheet of plywood is the only side of instrument box still erect. USGS photo by S.C. Moran, November 5, 2004.

was pieced together on site, these new stations were constructed as self-contained portable units. Each unit consisted of an aluminum case that housed a 1,200-Ah supply of nonrechargeable air-alkaline batteries and a weatherproof ABS plastic case enclosing the electronic components. A GPS antenna was attached to a 1.5-m-long steel pipe mast on one end of the aluminum case, and a similar mast on the other end supported a radio antenna. A rope sling with a swivel eye was bolted to the outer metal case for attachment to a helicopter sling-cable remote-release hook. Each of these three stations weighed approximately 70 kg, and parts for each unit cost about $2,500, making it practical to deploy several stations and constituting an acceptable loss if a station were destroyed. With this design, stations could be set in the crater near the source of the recent explosion, and personnel would be exposed only briefly to potential hazards. Initial results from these portable installations were promising, demonstrating that GPS stations could be installed quickly to provide repeatable results at centimeter accuracy in near-real time. One unit toppled shortly after deployment, so we redesigned the frame with three widely spaced legs for better stability on rocky, uneven terrain.

Spider Frame Design

Field tests of several frame prototypes helped to determine design requirements and constraints. These included the need for a frame that was: (1) strong and rigid for its weight, (2) corrosion resistant, (3) relatively inexpensive and simple to build, (4) capable of accommodating various onboard electronic instruments and antennas, (5) capable of being slung safely beneath a helicopter, (6) capable of deployment by helicopter sling cable onto uneven and rocky terrain, (7) stable when placed on uneven and rocky terrain, and (8) capable of being retrieved by grappling hook from a helicopter for redeployment to another site or transport to a safe location to replace batteries.

Using these design considerations, we constructed 18 frames at CVO (fig. 4). The frames were built of type 6061 stainless steel square tubing with 1.6-mm-thick walls and a 38×38-mm cross section. The tubing was cut with a horizontal band saw and welded using stainless steel welding wire.

The large leg span (1.4 m) of the three-legged frames and the low center of gravity of the welded aluminum battery and electronics box (0.34 m above ground surface) provided a stable platform for the onboard batteries and electronics. The GPS antenna was mounted to one of the three framing legs that extended higher than the other two, 1.7 m from the ground. A short leg served as a mount for a 1-m-long omnidirectional antenna for the data transceiver.

A pyramidal stainless steel tripod canopy of the same tubular material was welded to the legs, culminating 1.8 m above the ground where a lifting eye, cable, and swivel were attached. In addition to strengthening the frame, this canopy provided a centered attachment point for airborne transport and presented a large, open target for helicopter retrieval using a grappling hook. With the addition of the spindly-legged framework, these self-contained stations took on the appearance and nickname of "spiders."

The spider is stable when in flight beneath a helicopter, and the low center of gravity and wide leg span make the station resistant to tipping during deployment and retrieval, as well as resistant to toppling by high winds after deployment. Over the first 18 months of use, the stainless steel frames did not deteriorate in the harsh volcanic environment except for damage from direct ballistic impact. During 2004–5, we experimented with additional instruments on board some spiders including tiltmeters, cameras, gas sensors, and seismic accelerometers (McChesney and others, this volume, chap. 7).

Examples of GPS Spiders at Mount St. Helens, 2004–2005

GPS Spiders on the 1980–86 Dome

Remotely placed GPS spiders have occupied five sites on the 1980–86 dome. These sites were about 400–500 m from

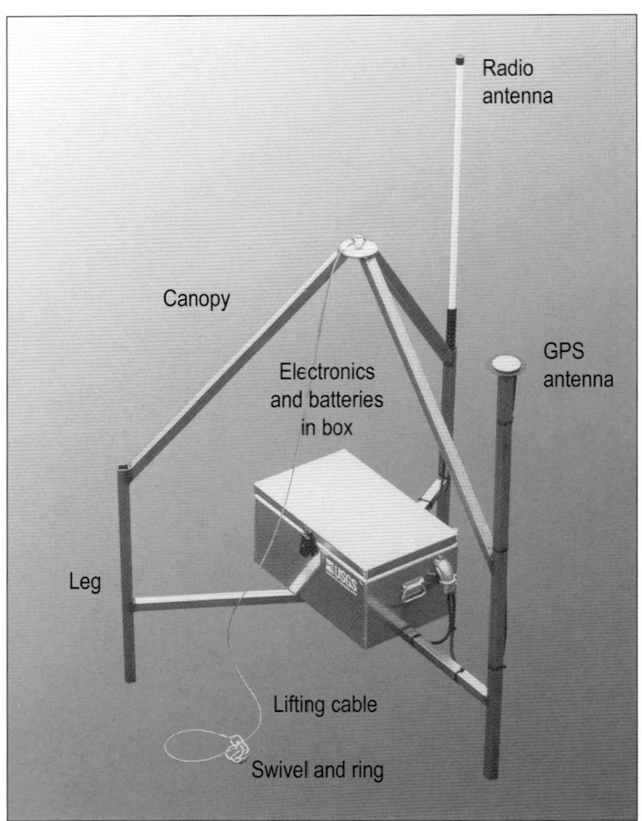

Figure 4. Photograph of GPS spider with stainless steel leg and canopy framework (leg span, 1.4 m) and aluminum box housing the unit's electronics and batteries. GPS antenna is located on extended leg in right foreground, and data radio antenna is attached to right rear leg. Stainless steel lifting cable with swivel and ring is attached to top of canopy. USGS photo by M. Logan.

Table 1. History of GPS spider deployments in the crater of Mount St. Helens, Washington, 2004–2005.

Station	Start date	End date	Displace-ment (m)	Fate
1980–86 dome				
DOM1.0 [1]	9/27/04	10/1/04	--	Explosion October 1, 2004
NDM5	10/3/04	1/2/05	0.15	Toppled, recovered
NRM6	10/4/04	11/20/04	--	Toppled, recovered
TOP7	10/4/04	3/8/05	--	Explosion March 8, 2005
DOM1.1	11/6/04	3/8/05	0.4	Explosion March 8, 2005
NEDB	11/20/04	3/8/05	0.16	Explosion March 8, 2005
DOM1.2	3/10/05	8/5/05	0.1	Moved
NEDB.1	4/6/05	3/2/06	0.1	Batteries expired
DOM1.3	8/5/05	12/25/05	0.05	Batteries expired
HIE5.2	9/21/05	12/31/05+	0.05	Continued operating into 2006
Middle zone				
MID9.0	10/27/04	2/3/05	1.4	Explosion damage Jan. 16, 2005
MIDE.0	2/11/05	3/8/05	0.22	Explosion March 8, 2005
MID9.1	4/6/05	6/29/05	2.3	Removed
MID9.2	11/17/05	12/16/05	0.17	Buried by talus
New dome				
CLF4	10/27/04	1/21/05	48	Rockfall
ELEA.0	11/20/04	11/27/04	67	Rockfall
HNY0	1/3/05	1/29/05	78	Rockfall
CDAN	1/15/05	1/16/05	8	Explosion Jan. 16, 2005
AHAD	2/8/05	2/16/05	41	Removed
ELE4.0	4/19/05	4/21/05	2	Moved
SEV7	5/24/05	3/24/06	10	Batteries expired
East Crater Glacier				
ICY4	2/16/05	4/8/05	22	Lost in crevasse
ICY5.0	2/16/05	3/8/05	28	Explosion March 8, 2005
ELE4.1	4/21/05	6/30/05	26	Moved
ELE4.2	6/30/05	7/28/05	6.7	Moved
HIE5.0	7/18/05	8/19/05	8.5	Moved
ELE4.3	7/28/05	8/19/05	7.8	Moved
West Crater Glacier				
WES6	7/14/05	9/14/05	70	Removed
ELE4.4	8/19/05	11/9/05	122	Batteries expired
HIE5.1	8/19/05	9/14/05	24	Moved

[1] Permanent monumented station; restarted Sept. 27, 2004.

the center of September 2004 deformation, ensuing phreatic explosions, and lava-spine extrusion. The history of emplacement and subsequent life is summarized in table 1; distribution and mapped progression is shown in figure 5.

The first three portable GPS stations were set on the north, east, and approximate center of the 1980–86 dome on October 3 and 4, 2004; station designations were NDM5, NRM6, and TOP7, respectively. Results from these installations showed that (1) motion of the three stations was similar, indicating the relative stability of the remotely deployed packages, and (2) the northward movement of the 1980–86 dome was continuing and was not restricted to the area of DOM1 on the west side of the dome. The 1980–86 dome lay north of the vent, so these spiders typically moved slightly northward. It appeared that the entire 1980–86 dome was moving to the north, away from the vent area, as if it were being shouldered aside in response to the growing mass beneath its south flank. Consequently, the northing component of the GPS solution best depicts the predominant motion. Magnitude of total motion during this period was less than 1 m (fig. 6). Rates were as much as 2 cm per day northward. Vertical displacement was typically within the noise of the analysis.

The 1980–86 dome appeared to behave as a semicoherent block so that, with few exceptions, spiders at different sites responded similarly (fig. 6). The rate of displacement varied with time. The limited evidence suggests that the rate of old-dome movement varied directly with the linear extrusion rate of the new dome, as shown by the coincidence of highest 1980–86 dome displacement rates with the greatest velocity for spiders riding on the extruding spine (fig. 6) We were

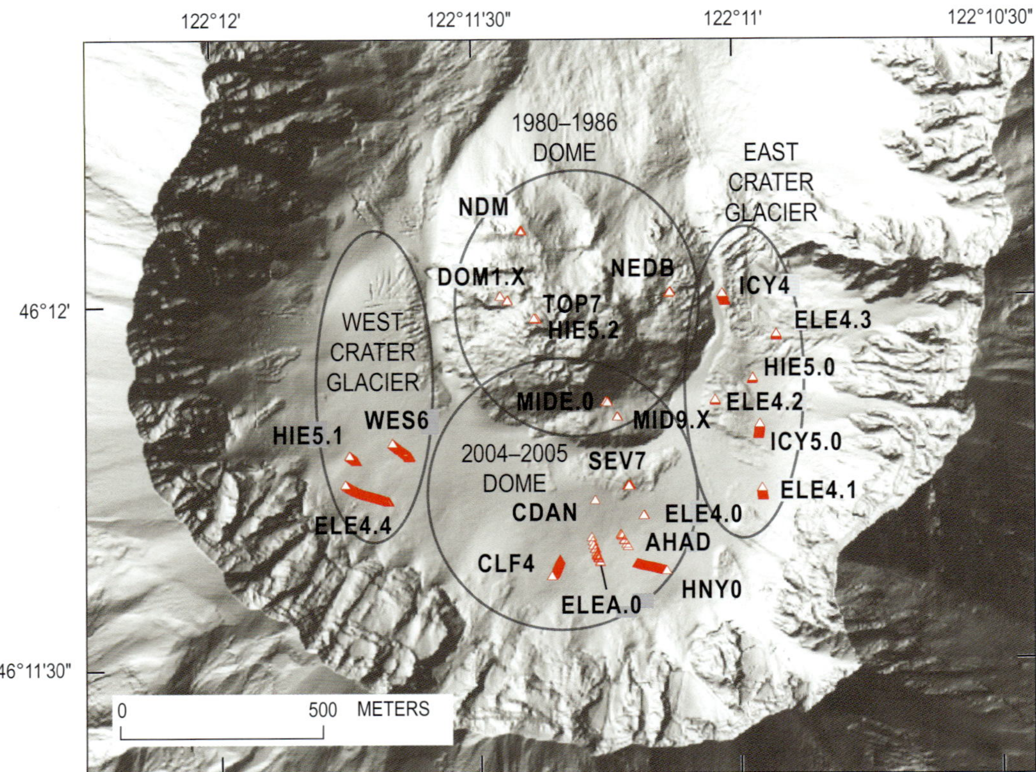

Figure 5. Shaded-relief digital elevation model (2003) showing GPS spider deployments (red triangles) in crater of Mount St. Helens, Washington. Tracks of triangles indicate total movement of stations (table 1).

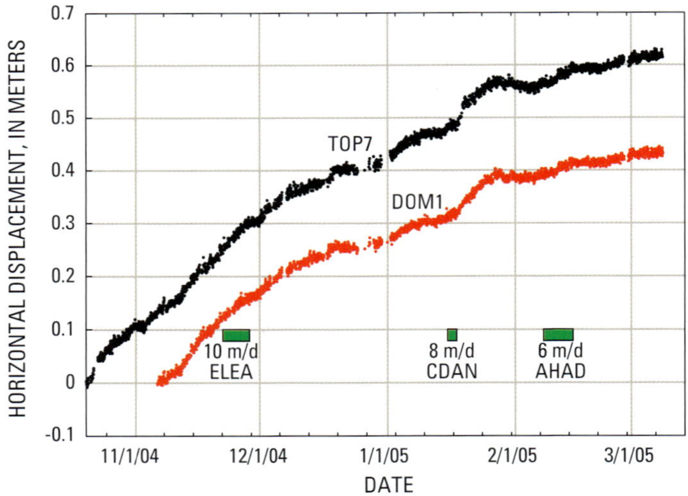

Figure 6. Graph showing movement of two GPS spiders on 1980–86 dome (DOM1, TOP7) and three GPS spiders on 2004–5 dome (ELEA, CDAN, and AHAD) during first 5 months of eruption. Location of stations shown in figure 5. The green boxes show duration of new-dome spiders, each labeled with elapsed horizontal velocity, which was nearly halved from November 2004 to March 2005. These three spiders had substantial displacements (as much as 67 m over a 7-day period for ELEA), which makes it difficult to portray their data in a manner comparable to the old-dome spiders TOP7 and DOM1.

unable to maintain a spider on the extruding spine long enough to demonstrate this relation more convincingly.

Intermittently, velocity of GPS spiders on the old dome increased as the rate of seismicity increased, as measured by real-time seismic amplitude measurements, or RSAM (Endo and Murray, 1991; Moran and others, this volume, chap. 2). One example of this correlation occurred on January 15, 2005, when TOP7 and other near-vent stations accelerated away from the vent as RSAM values started to increase (fig. 7). An explosion the following day destroyed several spiders (table 1).

GPS Spiders on the New Dome

Measurements of extrusive rates are the most effective way to monitor the progress of effusive eruptions. The best day-to-day proxy for extrusive rate at Mount St. Helens was the linear rate at which lava emerged from the vent; thus, we first targeted sites on and immediately adjacent to the actively extruding dome. Prior to new lava appearing at the surface on October 11, 2004, intense surface deformation created an uplift of part of the 1980–86 dome, deformed glacier ice, and crater-floor debris, or the "welt," through which the first lava spines emerged (Vallance and others, this volume, chap. 9). Sites on the welt had the advantage of longevity compared to placement directly on the active lava spines and were used first in October 2004. Although not directly on the extruding lava, these spiders were useful as proxies of eruption vigor because they were being actively pushed away from the vent. By late November 2004, we began placing spiders directly astride the actively extruding lava spine.

The first spider was set on the welt adjacent to the northeast side of the new dome on October 12, 2004, but its GPS antenna was damaged on deployment, rendering it geodetically useless. The spider also had seismic instrumentation on board that continued to function (McChesney and others, this volume, chap. 7). The next GPS spider, station CLF4, was installed on October 27, adjacent to the south flank of newly emergent spine 3, on uplifted crater-floor debris of the welt (fig. 5; table 1). Station CLF4 moved downward and to the south, traveling 10 m in the first three days as spine 3 plowed across the crater floor. Station CLF4 was pushed away from the growing spine as if riding the bow wave of a ship. It operated for 85 days, outliving the growth period of spine 3 and persisting into the first third of spine 4's life before succumbing to rockfall.

Some of the most interesting correlations between eruptive phenomena and movement of GPS spiders came from site MID9, which was on the saddle midway between the new and old domes (figs. 5, 8). On November 12, November 22, and December 8, 2004, MID9.0, the first of the MID9 spiders (table 1), accelerated away from the vent (fig. 9) coincident with increased RSAM counts. These velocity changes appeared as surge-pause-surge phases that lasted several days. The correlation with RSAM was masked for some other events that occurred in stormy weather, owing to heightened seismic noise that accompanied high wind.

On December 21, MID9.0 stalled and slowly reversed direction, heading back toward the vent and downward (figs. 9, 10). This change may have been in response to depressurization within the conduit and relaxation at the surface. Other crater GPS stations also slowed or stopped moving away from the vent. This event coincided with a change in seismicity, during which several large earthquakes had downward first motions as opposed to the typical pattern of upward first motions (S. Malone, written commun., 2004). But station MID9.0 continued its southward and down motion into 2005 while extrusion continued, so a more likely explanation for the ventward motion is that vent-adjacent bedrock was shifting in response to some other factor. Because this area between the

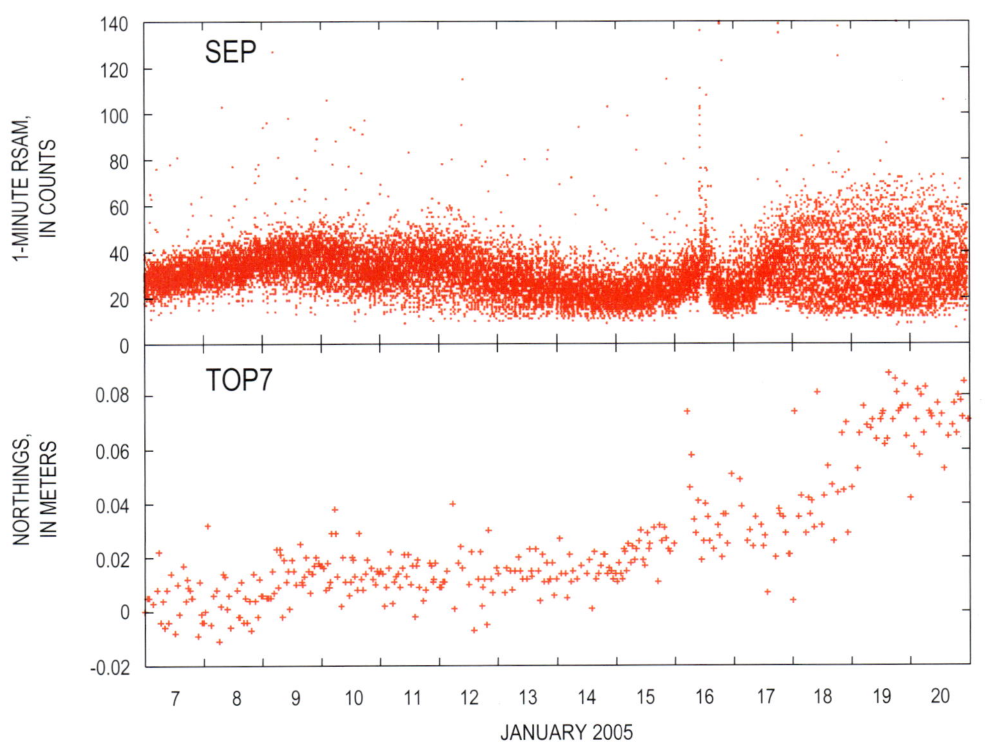

Figure 7. Graphs showing relation between increases in real-time seismic amplitude (RSAM) and northward motion of station TOP7 in mid-January 2005. Seismic station SEP is located 100 m northwest of TOP7, on the September lobe of the 1980–86 dome.

domes was so responsive to changes in eruption dynamics, we tried to keep a functioning GPS spider near the original MID9.0 location. Accordingly, after MID9.0 suffered antenna damage in an explosion on January 16, it was replaced by MIDE.0 followed by MID9.1 and MID9.2 (table 1).

On November 20, spider ELEA.0 was placed on the highest point of spine 3 (fig. 5). Its initial motion was an astonishing 10 m per day. Before it was destroyed by a rockfall 6 days later, ELEA.0 had moved 67 m south-southeastward and 8 m up.

The remarkable record of ELEA.0 reinforced our decision to keep a GPS spider on the actively growing spine of the new dome. A GPS spider, especially one carrying an accelerometer (seismometer), could add substantially to the amount of data available for evaluating steady-state extrusion models and for locating seismic sources more precisely. The task of slinging spiders onto hot lava spines proved more difficult than expected, owing to turbulence and decreased lift in heated air. Thermal surveys showed surface temperatures of spines away from the vent typically were less than 50°C, but cracks exposed interior lava as hot as 700°C (Vallance and others, chap. 9; Schneider and others, this volume, chap. 17) and created strong hot updrafts. A successful installation on January 3, 2005, deployed spider HNY0 (Happy New Year) on a large block near the south end of spine 4 (fig. 5). For more than 3 weeks, spider HNY0 moved 2–2.5 m/day east-southeastward, consistent with eastward spreading as the south end of the spine broke apart.

Figure 8. January 2005 photograph of station MID9 site (red box) between 1980–86 dome on the right and snow-free spine 4 on the left. Vent is marked by smooth emergent lava spine. Ground on which MID spiders were deployed was warm and was chosen to reduce burial by snow. USGS photo by D. Dzurisin, January 3, 2005.

Because spine 4's surface rose steeply from the vent, we built a spider with legs of differing length, cut appropriately to match the spine's 32° slope. This spider, CDAN, held fast in the soft fault gouge that mantled the spine (fig. 11). However, station CDAN was toppled and buried in talus during an explosion on the day after its installation, but not before it had moved about 8 m southward and upward (table 1).

Spiders were sited on the active spine sporadically into 2006 (table 1). Spines 5–7 grew more vertically than their recumbent predecessors and became increasingly mantled by talus, preventing us from finding sites suitable for setting a spider. Sites in talus were notably perilous, owing not only to instability of blocks on which spiders could be placed, but also to destruction by rockfalls from upslope debris. Summits of spines were free of risk from rockfall, but unlike the earlier recumbent spines that extended hundreds of meters from the vent—the site of greatest heat discharge—spines 5–7 grew more steeply, formed smooth surfaces for relatively short distances, and produced mostly rubble and large flanking talus aprons. Consequently, the summits of spines 5–7 were too hot and the air there too turbulent to safely deploy the instruments.

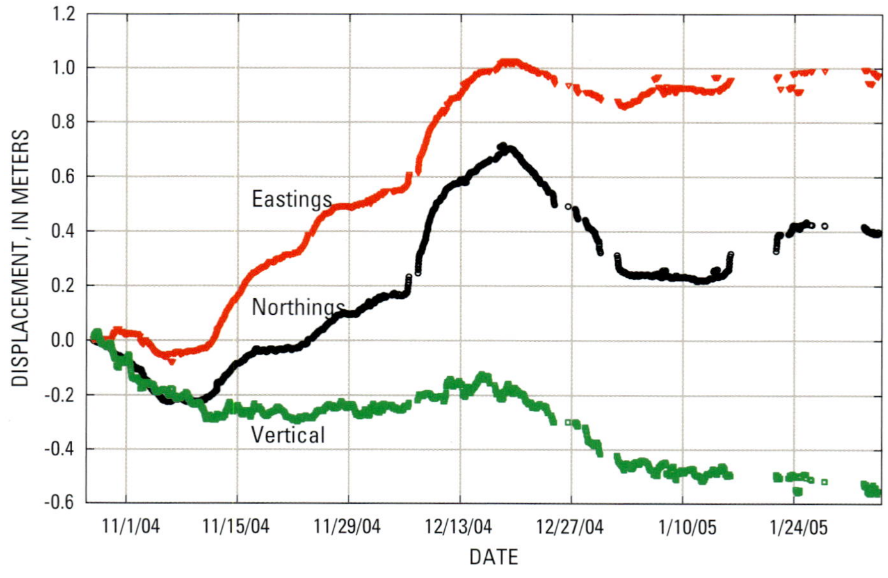

Figure 9. Graph of displacement of MID9.0 GPS spider, indicating accelerations, decelerations, and reversals as this near-vent station responded to subtle changes in eruption dynamics.

Spiders on Crater Glacier

Throughout the 2004–5 eruption, lava-dome growth through formerly horseshoe-shaped Crater Glacier has caused dramatic disruption and deformation (Walder and others, this volume, chap. 13). This remarkable process was documented with intermittent aerial photographs and creation of digital elevation models (Schilling and others, this volume, chap. 8), albeit with some difficulty owing to the lack of persistently identifiable features on the glacier surface. Those GPS spiders placed on the glacier provided a more continuous record of glacial deformation that allowed detailed examination of glacier compression, thickening, and increased rate of flow. Initially, growth of the welt and lava extrusions affected the southeastern part of the crater, cleaving Crater Glacier into east and west arms and compressing the east arm against the crater wall. Visual observations of this process indicated that the east arm was being greatly thickened. In response, the flow rate appeared to accelerate as a bulging lobe advanced northward toward the glacier's terminus east of the old lava dome. This deformation was accompanied by pervasive fracturing of the glacier with the formation of deep crevasses and, ultimately, extensive fields of seracs. In order to quantify these phenomena, several spiders were deployed temporarily on the glacier in nine locations between February and August 2005 (table 1).

Spiders ICY4 and ICY5.0 were installed on the east arm of Crater Glacier on February 16, 2005. Spider ICY5.0 was placed on the thickened and bulging part of the glacier, and ICY4 was placed on the relatively undisrupted part downslope of the bulge. Resultant velocity measurements from ICY4 showed the upper part of the glacier was moving 1.4 m/d and the lower undisturbed part was moving only 0.4 m/d. Of particular interest was the lack of diurnal velocity changes that typify temperate glaciers, indicating that Crater Glacier has a permeable bed that precludes basal slip resulting from meltwater accumulation (Walder and others, this volume, chap. 13). Additional spiders placed on the east and west arms confirmed these observations (table 1).

When dome growth shifted westward in midsummer 2005, the west arm of Crater Glacier started to show signs of bulging and crevassing, so in July and August 2005 a series of spider deployments was begun in order to collect data necessary to track changes. Stations WES6, ELE4.4 and HIE5.1 showed velocities of 1 m/d or more (fig. 12). Of particular interest was the stations' utility as an indirect confirmation of continuing lava extrusion because their instruments indicated continued upward motion as the advancing lava compressed the glacier against the crater wall. In times of limited visibility when remote cameras were ineffective, these spiders were our only means of confirming continuing dome growth. Their utility was limited by the occasional need to move them away from widening crevasses in the summer and by their inability to function under accumulation of several meters of snow during winter months.

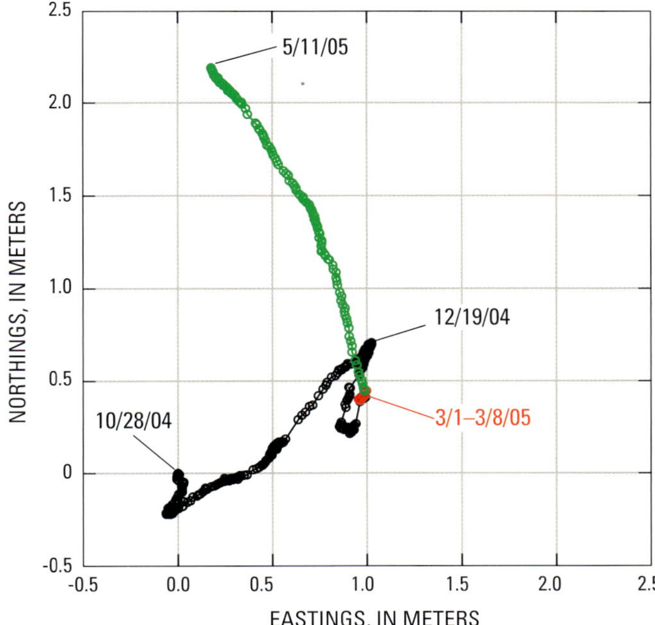

Figure 10. Schematic map showing horizontal path of three sequentially placed GPS spiders as they moved from the initial MID site. Site was alternately pushed away or relaxed toward the vent area during the course of deployment. Vent lay about 200 m southwest of MID. Change of symbol colors is solely to clarify the trace of displacement path.

Conclusions

During the 2004–5 eruption of Mount St. Helens, portable GPS stations, nicknamed spiders, installed by helicopter-sling operations proved to be an invaluable volcano-monitoring tool at sites in hazardous settings or where landing a helicopter was not possible. With real-time telemetry of data, spiders transmitted day and night. Cloudy weather that obscured camera images had no effect on the monitoring capability of GPS spiders. Although seismicity has become the most widely used real-time tool to detect explosive eruptions, real-time deformation monitoring may be equally or

Figure 11. Mid-January 2005 photograph of station CDAN GPS spider on extruding spine 4. Legs of differing lengths permitted level deployment on 32° slope. Legs are embedded several centimeters into soft gouge that mantles spine. USGS photo by J.S. Pallister, January 14, 2005.

more valuable to track dome-building eruptions. At present, nothing demonstrates ongoing extrusion of lava as directly as a GPS receiver riding on an active spine. Costing about $2,500 each in materials, spiders can be built relatively quickly and deployed in numbers needed to obtain data that provide a detailed record of near-vent deformation, lava extrusion, and effects on adjacent glaciers.

Acknowledgments

Our success with spiders stems in part from highly skilled helicopter pilots. In particular Jeff Linscott of JL Aviation and Morgan Kozloski of Hillsboro Aviation have carried greatest responsibility for installing and retrieving equipment. We gratefully acknowledge manuscript reviews by Tom Murray and Mark Reid.

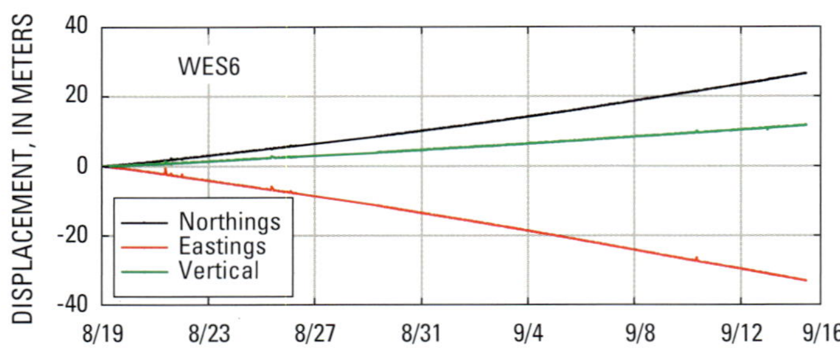

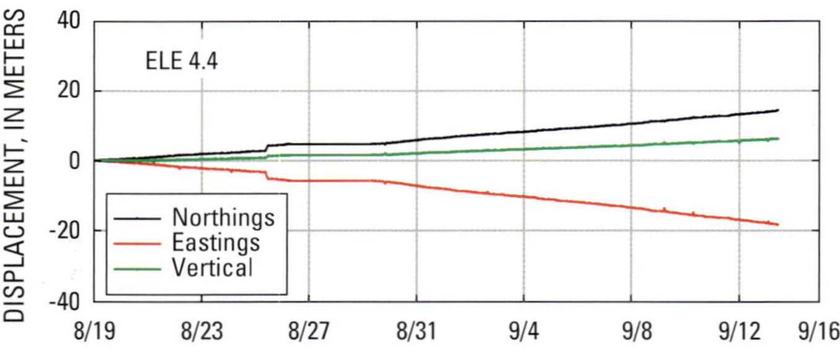

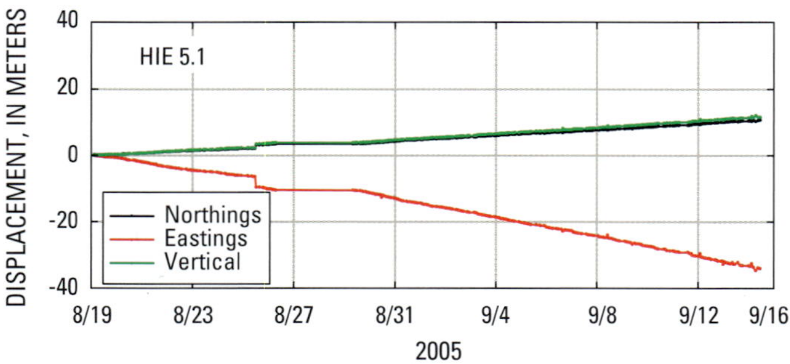

Figure 12. Plot of three GPS spiders on west arm of Crater Glacier during summer 2005, showing similar uplift and motion away from the advancing lava dome as the glacier was compressed against crater wall. Site locations shown in figure 5.

References Cited

Dzurisin, D., ed., 2006, Volcano deformation—geodetic monitoring techniques: Berlin, Springer, Springer-Praxis Books in Geophysical Sciences, 441 p.

Dzurisin, D., Westphal, J.A., and Johnson, D.J., 1983, Eruption prediction aided by electronic tiltmeter data at Mount St. Helens: Science, v. 221, no. 4618, p. 1381–1383.

Endo, E.T., and Murray, T., 1991, Real-time seismic amplitude measurement (RSAM); a volcano monitoring tool: Bulletin of Volcanology, v. 53, no. 7, p. 533–545.

LaHusen, R.G., and Reid, M.E., 2000, A versatile GPS system for monitoring deformation of active landslides and volcanoes [abs.]: Eos (American Geophysical Union Transactions), v. 81, no. 48, p. F320.

McChesney, P.J., Couchman, M.R., Moran, S.C., Lockhart, A.B., Swinford, K.J., and LaHusen, R.G., 2008, Seismic-monitoring changes and the remote deployment of seismic stations (seismic spider) at Mount St. Helens, 2004–2005, chap. 7 *of* Sherrod, D.R., Scott, W.E., and Stauffer, P.H., eds., A volcano rekindled; the renewed eruption of Mount St. Helens, 2004–2006: U.S. Geological Survey Professional Paper 1750 (this volume).

Moran, S.C., Malone, S.D., Qamar, A.I., Thelen, W.A., Wright, A.K., and Caplan-Auerbach, J., 2008, Seismicity associated with renewed dome building at Mount St. Helens, 2004–2005, chap. 2 *of* Sherrod, D.R., Scott, W.E., and Stauffer, P.H., eds., A volcano rekindled; the renewed eruption of Mount St. Helens, 2004–2006: U.S. Geological Survey Professional Paper 1750 (this volume).

Schilling, S.P., Thompson, R.A., Messerich, J.A., and Iwatsubo, E.Y., 2008, Use of digital aerophotogrammetry to determine rates of lava dome growth, Mount St. Helens, Washington, 2004–2005, chap. 8 *of* Sherrod, D.R., Scott, W.E., and Stauffer, P.H., eds., A volcano rekindled; the renewed eruption of Mount St. Helens, 2004–2006: U.S. Geological Survey Professional Paper 1750 (this volume).

Schneider, D.J., Vallance, J.W., Wessels, R.L., Logan, M., and Ramsey, M.S., 2008, Use of thermal infrared imaging for monitoring renewed dome growth at Mount St. Helens, 2004, chap. 17 *of* Sherrod, D.R., Scott, W.E., and Stauffer, P.H., eds., A volcano rekindled; the renewed eruption of Mount St. Helens, 2004–2006: U.S. Geological Survey Professional Paper 1750 (this volume).

Swanson, D.A., Casadevall, T.J., Dzurisin, D., Malone, S.D.,

Newhall, C.G., and Weaver, C.S., 1983, Predicting eruptions at Mount St. Helens, June 1980 through December 1982: Science, v. 221, no. 4618, p. 1369–1376.

Vallance, J.W., Schneider, D.J., and Schilling, S.P., 2008, Growth of the 2004–2006 lava-dome complex at Mount St. Helens, Washington, chap. 9 *of* Sherrod, D.R., Scott, W.E., and Stauffer, P.H., eds., A volcano rekindled; the renewed eruption of Mount St. Helens, 2004–2006: U.S. Geological Survey Professional Paper 1750 (this volume).

Walder, J.S., Schilling, S.P., Vallance, J.W., and LaHusen, R.G., 2008, Effects of lava-dome growth on the Crater Glacier of Mount St. Helens, Washington, chap. 13 *of* Sherrod, D.R., Scott, W.E., and Stauffer, P.H., eds., A volcano rekindled; the renewed eruption of Mount St. Helens, 2004–2006: U.S. Geological Survey Professional Paper 1750 (this volume).

Chapter 17

Use of Thermal Infrared Imaging for Monitoring Renewed Dome Growth at Mount St. Helens, 2004

By David J. Schneider[1], James W. Vallance[2], Rick L. Wessels[1], Matthew Logan[2], and Michael S. Ramsey[3]

Abstract

A helicopter-mounted thermal imaging radiometer documented the explosive vent-clearing and effusive phases of the eruption of Mount St. Helens in 2004. A gyrostabilized gimbal controlled by a crew member housed the radiometer and an optical video camera attached to the nose of the helicopter. Since October 1, 2004, the system has provided thermal and video observations of dome growth. Flights conducted as frequently as twice daily during the initial month of the eruption monitored rapid changes in the crater and 1980–86 lava dome. Thermal monitoring decreased to several times per week once dome extrusion began. The thermal imaging system provided unique observations, including timely recognition that the early explosive phase was phreatic, location of structures controlling thermal emissions and active faults, detection of increased heat flow prior to the extrusion of lava, and recognition of new lava extrusion. The first spines, 1 and 2, were hotter when they emerged (maximum temperature 700–730°C) than subsequent spines insulated by as much as several meters of fault gouge. Temperature of gouge-covered spines was about 200°C where they emerged from the vent, and it decreased rapidly with distance from the vent. The hottest parts of these spines were as high as 500–730°C in fractured and broken-up regions. Such temperature variation needs to be accounted for in the retrieval of eruption parameters using satellite-based techniques, as such features are smaller than pixels in satellite images.

[1] U.S. Geological Survey, 4200 University Drive, Anchorage, AK 99508

[2] U.S. Geological Survey, 1300 SE Cardinal Court, Vancouver, WA 98683

[3] Department of Geology and Planetary Science, University of Pittsburgh, 200 SRCC Building, Pittsburgh, PA 15260

Introduction

Detection and measurement of elevated temperature can play an important role in understanding the processes involved with active volcanic processes. As magma moves into a volcano, an increase in surface heat flow may occur that is manifested by various phenomena, such as increases in fumarole temperatures, opening of new fumaroles, development of hot faults and fractures, increases in hot spring and crater lake temperatures, and melting of snow and ice. Once an eruption begins there are numerous potential heat sources such as eruption columns, lava lakes, lava domes, lava flows, and pyroclastic-flow deposits. Analysis of thermal data can provide a means to detect unrest, observe phenomena not discernible at visible wavelengths, see through thin cloud cover and steam, and track changes in eruption style and eruption volume.

Thermal data are acquired at a variety of spatial and temporal resolutions: (1) low spatial resolution (kilometer scale) from high temporal resolution (multiple images per day) satellite sensors such as GOES, AVHRR, and MODIS (Dehn and others, 2002; Harris and others, 1997; Wright and others, 2002); (2) moderate spatial resolution (tens of meters) from low temporal resolution (weekly or greater) satellite sensors such as ASTER and Landsat TM/ETM+ (Flynn and others, 2001; Ramsey and Dehn, 2004; Vaughan and others, 2005); and (3) high spatial resolution (meter scale) from airborne or ground-based thermal imaging radiometers deployed on a tactical basis. This study focuses on an application of the latter—high-resolution thermal monitoring of eruptive activity at Mount St. Helens during October and November 2004.

The use of thermal imaging radiometers for monitoring volcanic activity has increased greatly over the past 5 years. A new generation of instruments that has entered the commercial marketplace utilizes detector arrays without external cooling (such as liquid nitrogen), thereby simplifying field logistics and increasing portability. These instruments provide calibrated temperature images and are useful in such applications as detecting heated fractures prior to lava eruption (Andronico and others, 2005) or flank collapse (Calvari and others, 2005), estimation of lava effusion rate (Harris and others, 2005a), and study of eruption dynamics (Harris and others, 2005b; Patrick and others, 2007).

The reawakening of Mount St. Helens in September 2004 began with a swarm of shallow earthquakes on September 23 (Moran and others, this volume, chap. 2) and progressed to deformation and cracking of glacier ice on the crater floor south of the 1980–86 dome to form the so-called welt, which was first observed on September 26 (Dzurisin and others, this volume, chap. 14). In response to this unrest, thermal-image monitoring began on October 1, 2004, to establish baseline thermal imagery and to examine the 1980–86 dome for signs of deformation. This paper reports results of the thermal surveys conducted during the first 2 months of activity during vent clearing and early stages of dome extrusion from October to December 2004. Thermal monitoring has continued throughout the eruption and has aided in the analysis of subsequent dome growth (Vallance and others, this volume, chap. 9).

Instrumentation and Methodology

The imaging system used in this study comprises a FLIR Systems ThermaCAM™ PM595 infrared camera and a Sony EVI-370 (visual-wavelength) video camera housed in a four-axis gyrostabilized gimbal that is mounted to the nose of a Bell-206 helicopter (fig. 1*A*). Although these types of thermal imaging cameras are generally referred to as FLIR, for Forward Looking Infrared, the gimbal can rotate in any direction. A crew member controls gimbal orientation and camera operation with a remote control (fig. 1*B*). The infrared camera utilizes a 320×240 microbolometer array that detects long-wave thermal radiation in the 7.5–13-µm atmospheric window and converts these values to brightness temperature. A 12°-wide telephoto lens provides a horizontal field of view of 210 m and a pixel resolution of 1.5 m at a distance of 1,000 m. Temperature is measured in three ranges: –40–200°C, 30–800°C, and 350–1,500°C. An internal flash memory card stores data from the infrared camera at 14-bit resolution and maximum frequency of 1 Hz. The visual video camera has a resolution of 720×480 pixels and a 12x auto-focus zoom lens. Analog video signals from the infrared and visual cameras are recorded simultaneously. These data are used to provide context and geographical reference for the individually calibrated thermal images.

The total radiant emittance measured by the infrared camera is

$$W_{tot} = \varepsilon\tau W_{obj} + (1 - \varepsilon)\,\tau W_{refl} + (1 - \tau)W_{atm}, \qquad (1)$$

where ε is the emissivity of the object (a measure of how much radiation is emitted from an object compared to a perfect blackbody emitter, see discussion), τ is the atmospheric transmission, W_{obj} is the emission from the object, W_{refl} is the reflected emission from ambient sources, and W_{atm} is the emission from the atmosphere. The camera system converts radiant emittance (as measured by camera detector voltage) to brightness temperature internally using factory-defined calibration coefficients. We use an average emissivity value of 0.96 based on laboratory measurements of a dacite reference (Vaughan and others, 2005). We use ThermaCAM™ Researcher software to calculate atmospheric transmissivity using measured values of the ambient air temperature, relative humidity, and atmospheric path length (from the object to the camera).

The telephoto capabilities of the infrared camera allowed for safe helicopter operations from outside the 1980 crater at a typical altitude of 3,000 m above sea level (600 m above the crater rim) and a horizontal distance of 1,000 m from the

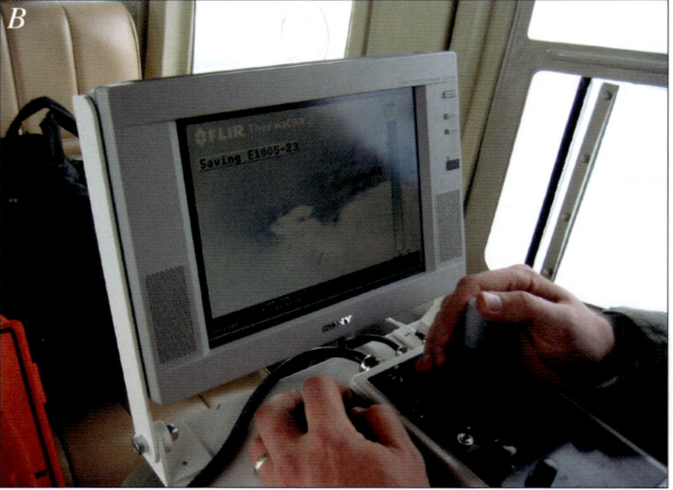

Figure 1. Forward Looking Infrared (FLIR) thermal and visual video imaging system used during airborne observations of Mount St. Helens, 2004–2007. *A*, FLIR instrument mounted on nose of Bell 206-L helicopter. Inset shows infrared (top) and visual video (bottom) lenses. *B*, Remote control panel used to display infrared and visual video streams, to control orientation of sensors using a joystick, and to capture data.

welt on the south crater floor. This was especially important for flights conducted during the first week of October 2004 when there was a high level of uncertainty regarding eruption prognosis and associated hazard. Infrared images, digital still photographs, and infrared and visual video were collected primarily at an oblique perspective, in many cases allowing for observation under steam and gas plumes that would have been impossible from a vertical viewing perspective. The thermal infrared and visual video collected using this system also provided striking graphical images for distribution to the media (Driedger and others, this volume, chap. 24).

In this study, thermal images are displayed in pseudocolor. Minimum and maximum temperature values (shown by a scale bar) are selected to provide optimal image enhancement. In some cases, the maximum temperature value reported in the text is higher than the maximum value shown by the scale bar.

Observations

Vent Clearing

We began thermal infrared monitoring on October 1, 2004, to develop baseline thermal images of the 1980–86 dome, to investigate the uplifted welt on the south crater floor, and to determine whether there was any thermal evidence for fracturing or faulting in the 1980–86 dome in response to ongoing uplift. Imaging began at 1156 PDT and showed several warm fumarolic regions with temperatures of 40°C to 65°C, primarily on the north flank of the dome, as well as the influence of solar heating on the south flank. The region of the dome and the south crater floor adjacent to the welt (an area of visible deformation and faulting) was near ambient temperature (0–15°C) except for a t-shaped thermal lineament (figs. 2*A*, 2*B*) at the west end of the graben that formed during dome extrusion in 1985 near the area of the dome informally known as Opus. This lineament had temperatures of 30°C to 38°C.

At approximately 1202 PDT an ash-rich explosion ruptured ice at the west end of the welt. This event began without recognizable precursory seismicity (Moran and others, this volume, chap. 6) and without any observable thermal change in images collected 15 seconds prior to onset. The eruption column comprised ballistic projectiles, jetting, ash-rich projections inclined northward, and a convecting steam-rich cloud (figs. 2*C*, 2*D*). The maximum temperature, 160°C, recorded from the base the column, indicated a phreatic rather than a magmatic mechanism. Infrared video shows that ballistic blocks were ejected primarily northward, where they destroyed seismic station SEP and GPS station DOM1 on the 1980–86 dome, located about 400 m north of the vent. Within 5 minutes of the eruption onset, a horizontally convecting ash-rich cloud developed and moved westward from the vent until it encountered the crater wall (figs. 2*E*, 2*F*). The steam-and-ash cloud ultimately reached an altitude of ~4,500 m above sea level. Ash emissions ended abruptly at 1220 PDT, and images collected several minutes later once the residual steam dispersed revealed a vent with a diameter of ~20 m in ice of the welt and a broad area of ash deposits on the west crater floor (fig. 2*G*). Vent temperatures were only slightly above freezing (2–6°C). Deposits adjacent to the vent had temperatures that ranged from 45°C to 50°C, and ballistic blocks with similar temperatures lay in small areas on the south and west flank of the 1980–86 dome (fig. 2*H*). The relatively low temperatures of the vent and deposits provide further evidence for a phreatic rather than magmatic eruption mechanism. A minor amount of snow and ice was melted, generating a small channelized flow that extended several hundred meters west from the vent.

Rapid deformation and uplift of the welt continued following the explosion, and thermal images tracked increasing temperatures of certain features (figs. 3, 4). Uplift of Opus (south of the 1985 graben) began to expose warmer interior rocks primarily on its eastern margin. Images of the Opus area collected on October 1, 2004 (figs. 3*A*, 3*B*), show several areas of elevated surface temperatures that ranged from 40°C to 50°C. Thermal images taken the following day showed that this area had been uplifted further and was the source of nearly constant warm rockfalls. By October 3, a broad region of oxidized rock from the interior of the dome was exposed (fig. 3*C*), and warm rockfalls and streaks of elevated temperature were more pronounced (fig. 3*D*). An elongate region of elevated temperature, detected at the north margin of the welt, trended east to west along the axis of the 1985 graben and intersected the October 1 vent (figs. 4*A*, 4*B*). Areas of enhanced heat flow along normal faults appeared in images as shorter lineaments perpendicular to the 1985 graben (fig. 4*B*).

Three additional phreatic explosions on October 3, 4, and 5 (Moran and others this volume, chap. 6) indicated the presence of a shallow heat source. These events reamed out a small basin on the west end of the welt, wherein water and ice collected (fig. 5*A*). On October 4, small ash-rich geysers (less than 50 m high) erupted through the lake, after which hot upwelling gas bubbles with temperatures as high as 200°C appeared (fig. 5*B*). The last phreatic explosion on October 5 produced a new vent north of the earlier one. Over the next several days, new fumaroles developed near these vent regions, with temperatures as high as 55°C observed on October 7.

On October 10, after 2 days of poor weather, thermal imagery detected a broad steaming area of ice- and snow-free rock at the west end of the welt (fig. 6*A*). Elevated temperatures that ranged from 30°C to 50°C characterized this broad area, and numerous hot point sources within it ranged from 100°C to more than 270°C (fig. 6*B*). This marked increase in temperature was the greatest yet observed and presented strong evidence that magma was nearing the surface.

Lava Extrusion Begins

Lava, first observed on October 11, extruded from the northern part of the zone of elevated temperatures shown in

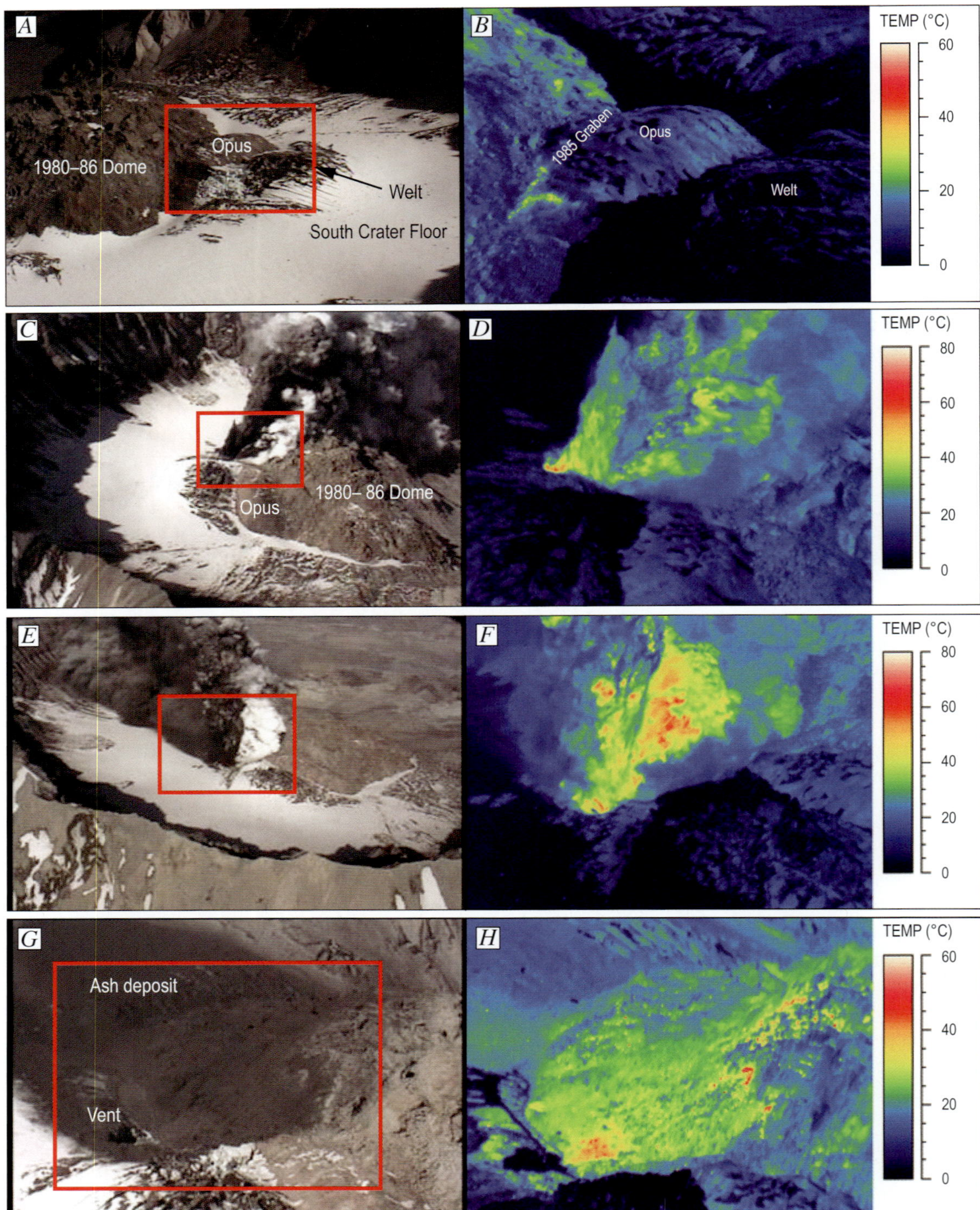

Figure 2. Comparisons between visual and infrared images of Mount St. Helens collected on October 1, 2004. Red rectangles in visual images show approximate boundaries of contemporaneous infrared images. *A*, Visual view from southwest of south crater floor and deforming welt collected at 11:56:30 PDT. *B*, Infrared image of area shown in *A*. *C*, Visual image from east showing phreatic eruption column collected at 12:05:50 PDT. *D*, Infrared image of area in *C*. *E*, Visual image from south showing phreatic eruption column collected at 12:07:07 PDT. *F*, Infrared image of area in *E*. *G*, Visual image from southeast showing vent region of phreatic explosion and associated ashfall deposits. *H*, Infrared image of area in *G*.

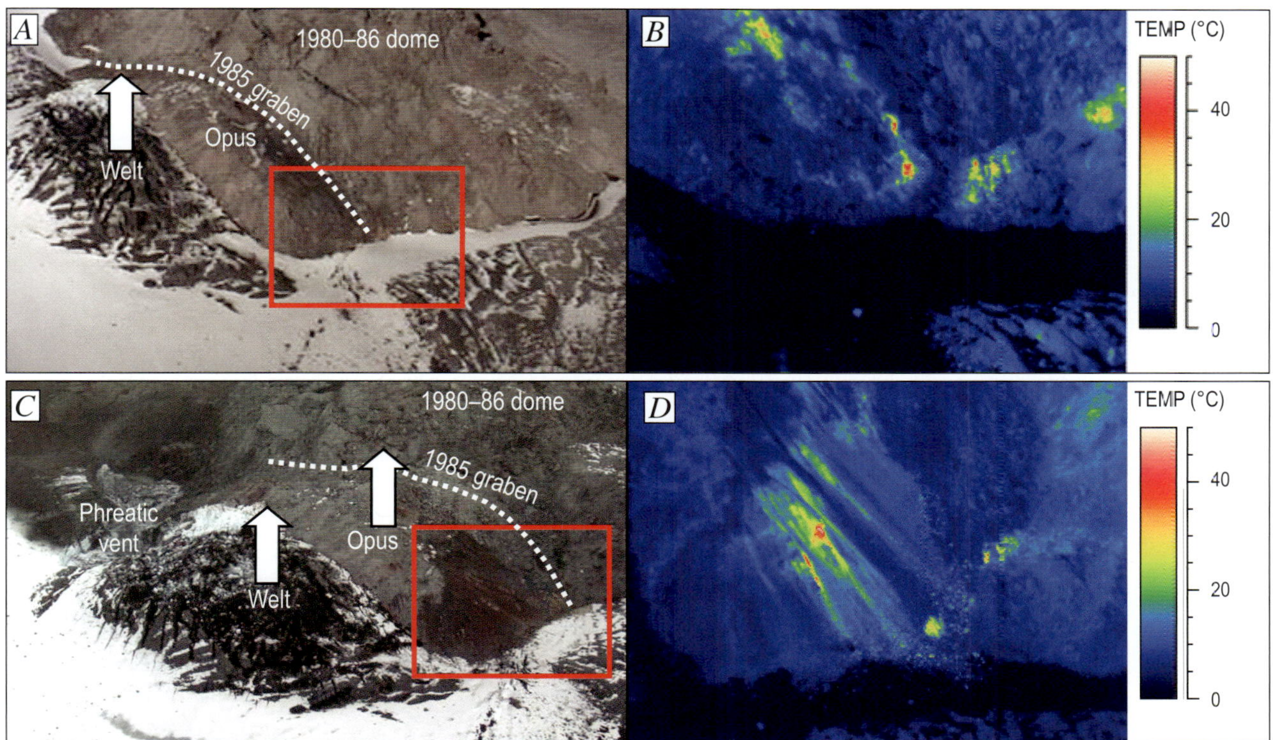

Figure 3. Comparisons between visual and infrared images of southeast part of 1980–86 dome and welt at Mount St. Helens. View from southeast. Red rectangles in visual images show approximate boundaries of contemporaneous infrared images. *A*, Visual image collected on October 1, 2004. *B*, Infrared image of area in *A*. *C*, Visual image collected on October 3, 2004. *D*, Infrared image of area in *C*.

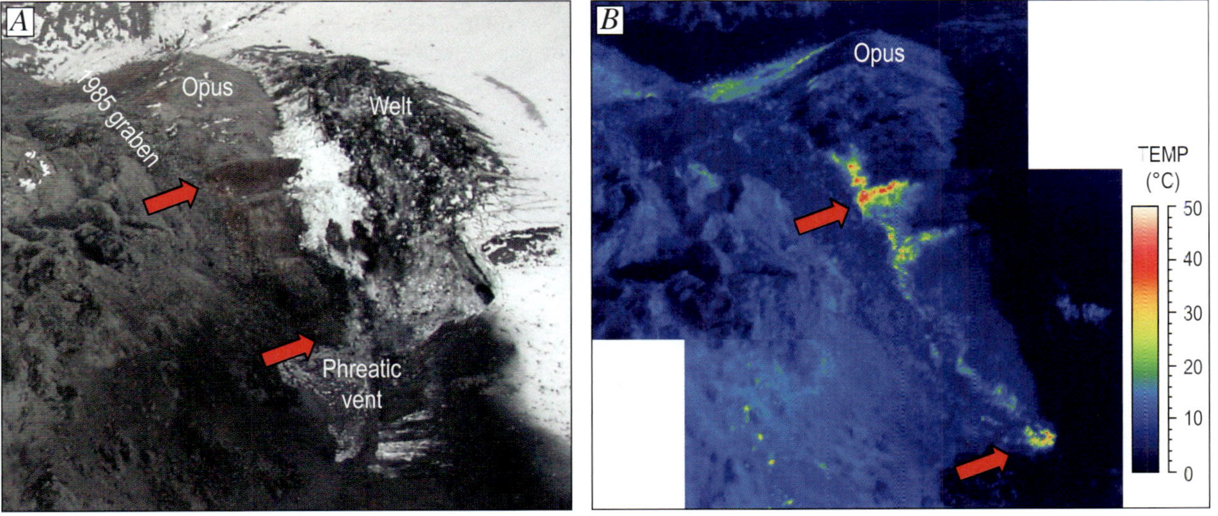

Figure 4. Comparison between visual and infrared images collected on October 3, 2004, of southern part of 1980–86 dome and welt at Mount St. Helens, showing thermal lineaments related to deformation. Red arrows indicate similar features between images. *A*, Visual image, view from the west. *B*, Contemporaneous infrared image.

figure 6. Following the usage of Cascades Volcano Observatory scientists, this and all subsequent lava extrusions are referred to as "spines," with a number assigned based on order of appearance. Spine 1 emerged as a fin-shaped slab approximately 80 m wide, 40 m high, and 10 m thick (fig. 7). Although the spine was partially obscured by steam during thermal observation (figs. 7*A*, 7*C*), temperatures as high as 580°C were measured at its base (figs. 7*B*, 7*D*). A small warm debris fan extended from spine 1, but there was little melting evident on adjacent snow and ice. Extrusion of spine 1 continued through at least October 14, with the hottest temperatures of the entire eruption sequence, 730°C, measured in cracks and fractures on that date.

Poor weather prevented thermal imaging flights from October 15 to 20, at which time extrusion of spine 2 had extended southward from spine 1 across the south crater floor. By October 24, spine 2 encountered the south crater wall (fig. 8). Spine 1 had cooled considerably since observation on October 14, with temperatures that ranged from 40°C to 60°C where it emerged from the ground, whereas the temperature of spine 2 ranged as high as 430°C within fractured and fragmented rock near the likely zone of extrusion (fig. 8*B*). Intense steaming, caused by high relative humidity on this day (~80 percent), attenuated measured temperatures. The surfaces of spines 1 and 2 were rough, fractured, and blocky. Hot rockfalls on their west sides caused minor melting of snow and ice. An overflight on October 27 detected temperatures as hot as 700°C where spine 2 emerged, as well as a broad warm area in the debris cover southeast of spine 1. Observations were hampered by thick steam, but retrospective analysis suggests that extrusion of spine 3 had begun by this time.

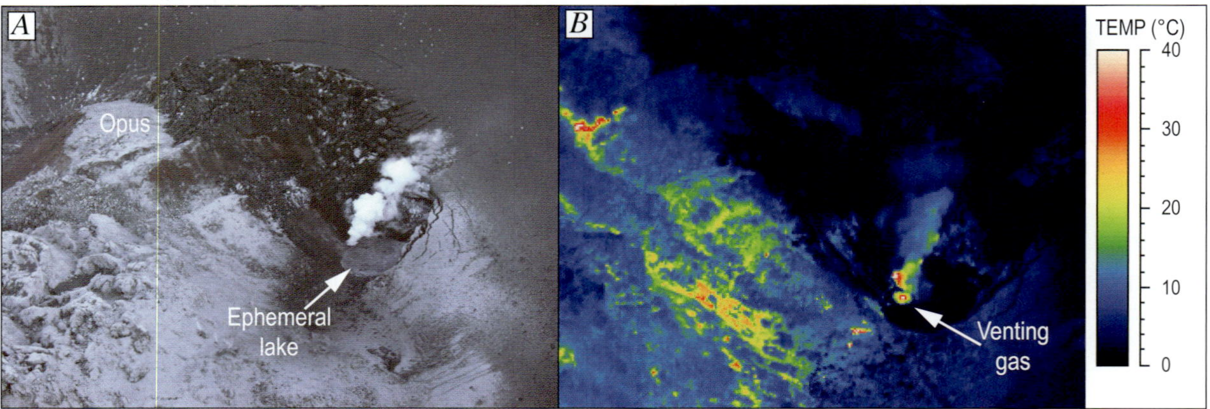

Figure 5. Comparison between visual and infrared images collected on October 4, 2004, of southern part of 1980–86 dome and phreatic vent on welt at Mount St. Helens, showing hot gas venting through ephemeral lake. *A*, Visual image, view from west. *B*, Contemporaneous infrared image.

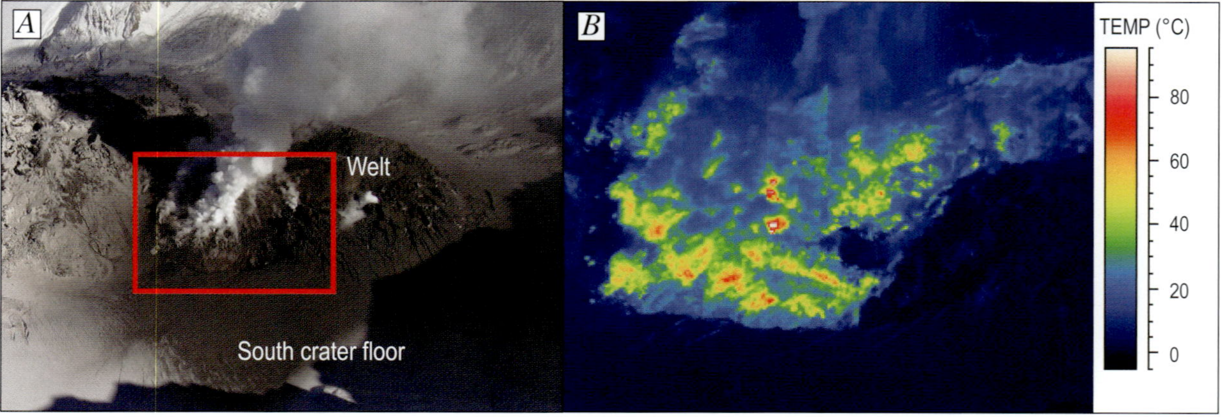

Figure 6. Comparison between visual and infrared images collected on October 10, 2004, of welt at Mount St. Helens, showing increased heat flow due to magma nearing surface. View from west. Red rectangle in visual image shows approximate boundary of contemporaneous infrared image. *A*, Visual image. *B*, Infrared image.

By November 4, spine 3 had grown considerably. Its surface was smooth with a few large cracks (fig. 9*A*), but its west and south sides were blocky and fractured. As much as several meters of fault gouge covering spine 3 formed as largely crystallized magma ascended the upper part of the conduit (Cashman and others, this volume, chap. 19). Its smooth surface and recumbent attitude gave spine 3 a whaleback-like morphology. The fault gouge served as an effective insulator so that surface temperatures where it emerged from the vent on its north end ranged from 150°C to 200°C and decreased exponentially to typical values of 25°C to 50°C within 50 to 75 m (fig. 9*B*). The hottest temperature observed in small regions of collapse and fractures was 625°C.

Spine 3 moved toward the south as it was extruded and encountered the south crater wall by November 12 (Vallance and others, this volume, chap. 9). By late November, continued southward compression against the crater wall resulted in crumbling of spine 3 at its south end (fig 10*A*). Large open fractures in the fault-gouge carapace observed in thermal images (fig. 10*B*) suggested tensional cracking caused by bending of the solid spine as the extrusion continued southward. A typical temperature profile during this time period is shown in figure 11 along a line parallel to direction of extrusion. Temperature at the vent was typically 200°C and decreased abruptly southward, but was as high as 700°C in fractures.

Thermal infrared images continue to be used as a monitoring tool to observe dome growth and have documented the thermal characteristics of recumbent (whaleback) extrusion from November 2004 to April 2005, vertical spine extrusion from April to July 2005, and composite spine growth (composed of massive rock and disintegrating rock debris) from July 2005 to present (April 2007) (Vallance and others, this volume, chap. 9).

Discussion

Sources of Temperature Measurement Error

Accurate measurement of temperature using a thermal radiometer depends on several factors including viewing angle, characteristics of the atmospheric path, absorption by volcanic gases (water and SO_2), and the emissivity of the

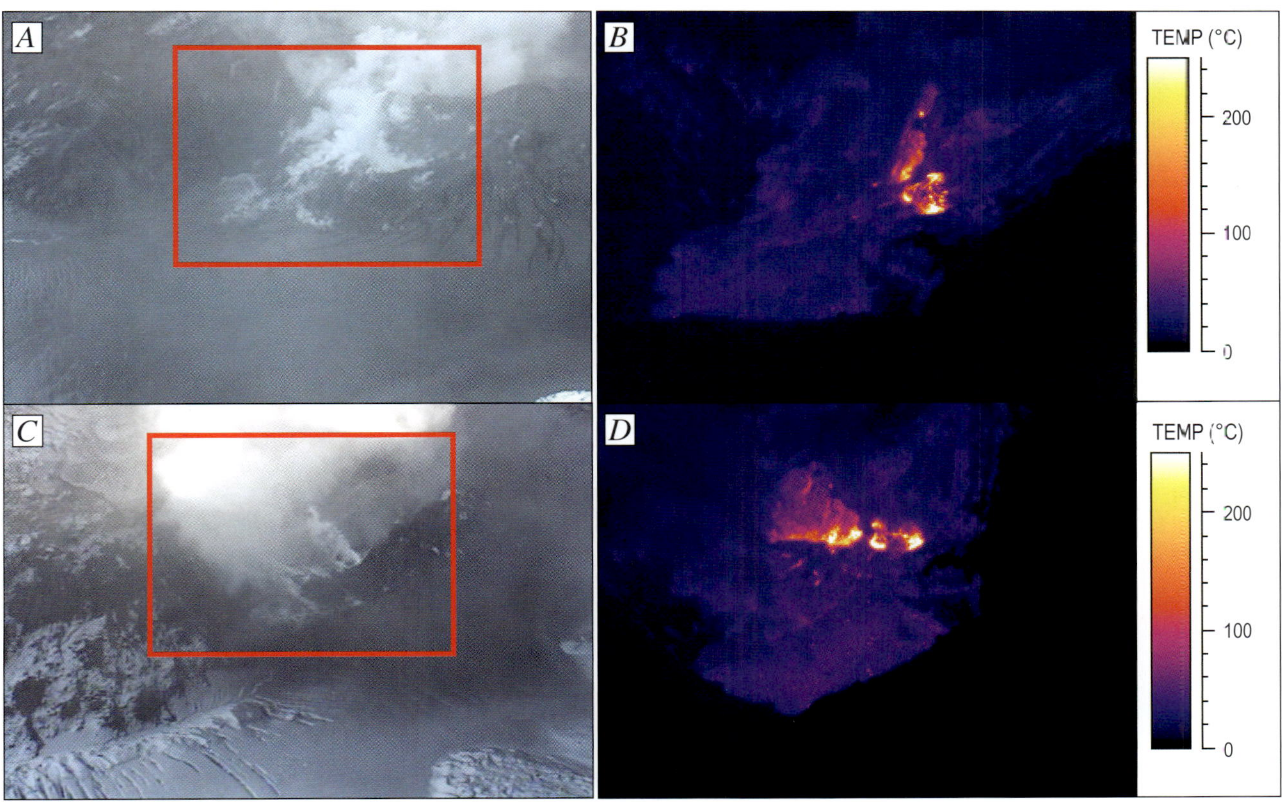

Figure 7. Comparison between visual and infrared images of Mount St. Helens collected on October 11, 2004, showing the first views of lava at the surface. Red rectangle in visual image shows approximate boundary of contemporaneous infrared image. *A*, Visual image, view from southwest. *B*, Infrared image, view from southwest. *C*, Visual image, view from northwest. *D*, Infrared image, view from northwest.

target (Ball and Pinkerton, 2006). The maximum temperature values reported herein are most strongly affected by viewing angle, because the source of heat typically was a fracture or fissure. In these cases, physical blockage of the source(s) of thermal emission occurred, and imaging of the target from multiple viewing angles was required to detect the maximum values. In other cases, opaque steam clouds completely obscured the source, making it impossible to measure the temperature accurately.

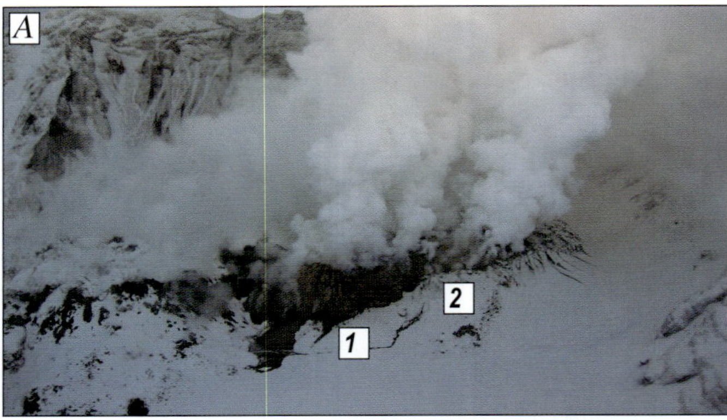

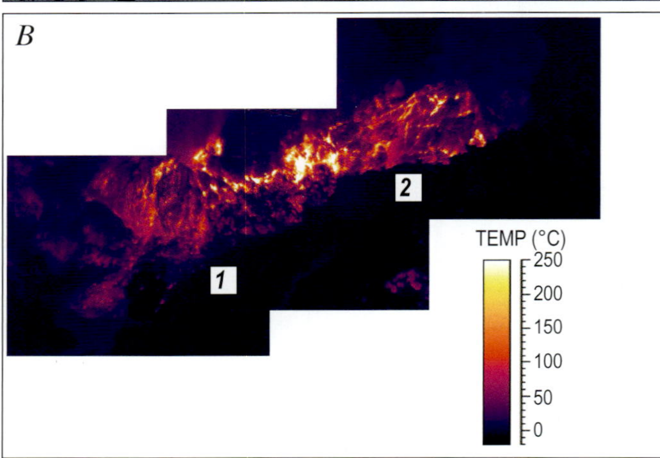

Figure 8. Comparison between visual and infrared images of Mount St. Helens collected on October 24, 2004, showing the development of spines 1 and 2 (as labeled). *A*, Visual image, view from the west. *B*, Composite infrared image.

Corrections for atmospheric-path absorption were made using ThermaCAM™ Researcher software and estimates of atmospheric temperature, relative humidity, and path length. For each mission, temperature and humidity values for Mount St. Helens were estimated using archived EDAS40 model sounding data provided by the NOAA Air Resources Laboratory (http//www.arl.noaa.gov/ready/amet.html). These values were used to compute the atmospheric transmission; the relation between these parameters is shown in figure 12 for a typical range of values. Uncertainty in estimating a representative relative humidity will contribute to a larger error in calculating transmission as the temperature of the atmosphere increases; the error will be compounded as the path length increases. Many of the thermal imaging missions were conducted at atmospheric temperatures near 0°C, the relative humidity values varied by a maximum of ±15 percent, and variation in path length was ±250 m. This results in a variation in atmospheric transmission of about ±2 percent. For an object with a temperature of 500°C, this results in a variation of ±10°C.

Although water is the dominant volcanic gas that absorbs infrared radiation, SO_2 has two strong absorption features (centered at wavelengths of 7.3 and 8.5 μm) within the spectral range of the thermal radiometer. Although techniques to quantify the systematic error in ground-based thermal infrared measurements caused by gas absorption are still being developed, it may be a significant issue in situations where gas concentrations are high (Sawyer and others, 2005). The SO_2 emission rates during the time period of this study were low, ranging from values at the lower detection limit of 1 metric ton per day (t/d) through October 4 and increasing to an average value of approximately 100 t/d thereafter (Gerlach and others, this volume, chap. 26). Thus, absorption of infrared emissions by SO_2 is likely to be a relatively small source of error.

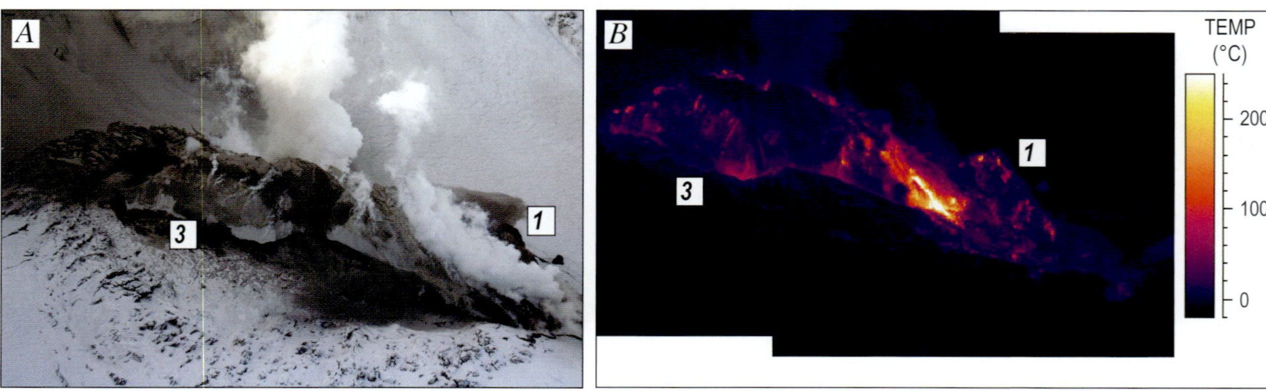

Figure 9. Comparison between visual and infrared images of Mount St. Helens collected on November 4, 2004, showing the development of spines 1 and 3 (as labeled). *A*, Visual image, view from the northeast. *B*, Composite infrared image.

Emissivity is a measure of how much energy is emitted from an object compared to a theoretical perfect emitter known as a blackbody. In nature, all materials emit less energy than a blackbody, because energy is absorbed by the vibration of molecular bonds. They are referred to as selective radiators wherein emissivity varies as a function of wavelength. Although the emissivity of silicate rocks has a characteristic decrease in emissivity at a wavelength range of 8 to 10 µm, an average value over the broader range of 7.5 to 13 µm is used where measuring temperatures with a broadband radiometer. Variations in emissivity can also occur for a given rock type as a result of vesicularity and particle size. In general, emissivity decreases as vesicularity decreases (Ramsey and Fink, 1999). The 2004 lava was largely degassed and dense (Pallister and others, this volume, chap. 30), suggesting that the actual emissivity may be lower than a laboratory reference. Furthermore, very fine grained silicates (<60 µm) exhibit a decrease in emissivity of the primary absorption band between 8 and 10 µm owing to the scattering of radiant energy (Ramsey and Christensen, 1998). It is possible that ash fallout and (or) the cover of the chalky fault-gouge carapace served to reduce the effective emissivity of the extruded lava (compared to the dacite reference value). The effect of an overestimated emissivity would be an increase in the temperatures above those reported herein. The result of a variation in emissivity was tested by changing the value by a factor of 0.1 within the ThermaCAM™ Researcher software, which resulted in a change in temperature on the order of 20°C for an area with a temperature of 450°C. Thus, variations in emissivity may account for changes on the order of 5 percent in the absolute temperature recorded.

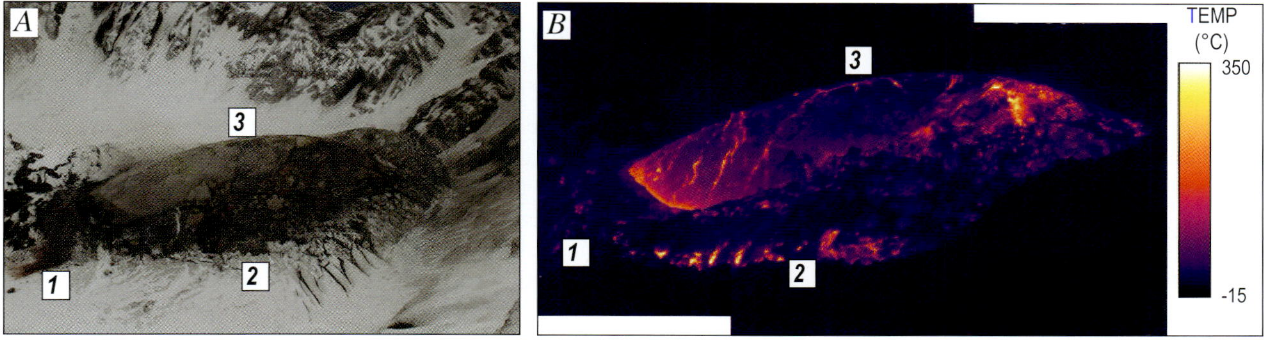

Figure 10. Comparison between visual and infrared images of Mount St. Helens collected on November 29, 2004, showing the development of spines 1 to 3. Spine 3 (as labeled) is actively being extruded and is crumbling as it encounters the south crater wall. *A*, Visual image, view from the west. *B*, Composite infrared image.

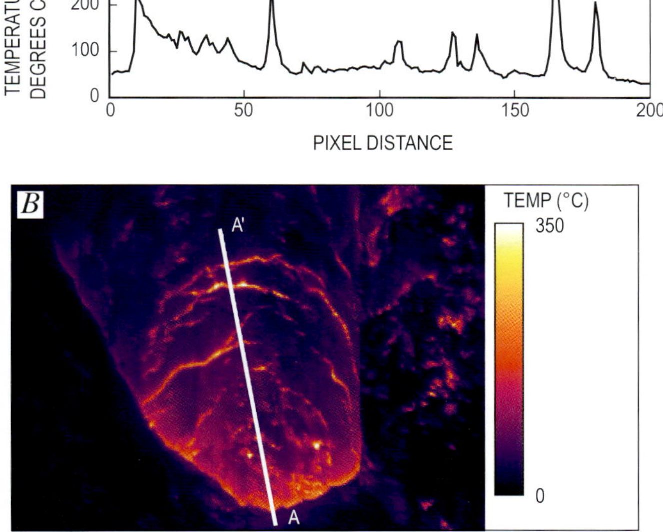

Figure 11. Temperature profile along north end of spine 3 at Mount St. Helens on November 29, 2004, showing typical temperatures observed during extrusion of whaleback spines. *A*, Temperature profile A–A', profile length approximately 125 m, north toward left. *B*, Infrared image of spine 3 viewed from the north showing the location of the north-south profile, A–A'.

Thermal Imaging as a Response Tool

The rapid pace of unrest associated with the reawakening of Mount St. Helens in September 2004 resulted in an intense monitoring response by the Cascades Volcano Observatory (CVO) and the broader U.S. Geological Survey Volcano Hazards Program (VHP). Although handheld thermal imaging cameras have been used successfully in eruption response by other volcano observatories worldwide (Kauahikaua and others, 2003; Andronico and others, 2005; Calvari and others, 2005; Harris and others, 2005a), the gimbal-mounted system used during this response was a relatively new tool for VHP scientists. It had been flown on several missions at the Alaska Volcano Observatory (AVO) to collect baseline thermal data and on one flight in response to unrest at Mount Spurr (Power, 2004). Thus, the gimbal-mounted instrument was largely untested for eruption response by the USGS when first flown at Mount St. Helens on October 1, 2004, arriving only 6 minutes prior to the initial phreatic explosion. The utility of the instrument was quickly recognized as it was determined rapidly that the initial explosion was of phreatic origin. This information was quickly radioed to the operations center at CVO and used to apprise land management and emergency response personnel. In addition, the thermal and visual video imagery was made available to the media and was broadcast widely. The ability to control the gimbal and shoot video in a wide range of orientations was extremely useful as the helicopter maneuvered in response to the eruption cloud, topographic barriers, and wind. The telephoto capabilities were also vital, allowing for observation at a safe distance beyond the crater rim.

In addition to documenting thermal features on the crater floor and dome, use of the instrument during the first 2 weeks of October provided opportunities to test thermal-observation strategies and to determine what kinds of useful information could be obtained. The stability of the 1980–86 dome in response to the deformation on the south crater floor was initially of great concern, as potential eruption scenarios were evaluated involving (1) large-scale collapse of the 1980s dome toward the northern open end of the 1980 crater and (2) potential hazards to the public who had come to view the volcano. Thus, an important early use of the system was to look for the thermal expression of faults or fractures on the northern flank of the dome. Observations made throughout the eruption have shown no significant change in thermal response of the 1980–86 dome and thus have eased concerns about its stability.

Structural Control of Heat Emissions

The south flank of the 1980–86 dome, which formed the northern part of the welt, showed several examples of structural control of heat emissions during a time of rapid uplift, faulting, and deformation (figs. 3, 4) along a graben formed during an episode of dome growth in 1985. Between flights on October 1 and 2, rapid uplift of tens of meters on the east end of the graben caused warm rockfalls from the newly exposed interior of the dome. Over the next several days, the thermal imaging system was able to record continued uplift in this region as expressed by displacement of thermal features and nearly continuous warm rockfalls. On the west end of the graben (fig. 4), the thermal expression of normal faulting was observed, suggesting that this area was not moving upward as rapidly as the east end. Although these features can be seen in visible images, the advantage of the thermal system was to highlight areas of interest during a time period of very rapid changes in surface topography. Similar phenomena (on a larger scale) were observed at Mount St. Helens in April and May 1980 during development of the bulge. For example, Kieffer and others (1981) documented increased heat flow from several faults, fractures, and brecciated zones using a variety of thermal imaging devices, and they reported

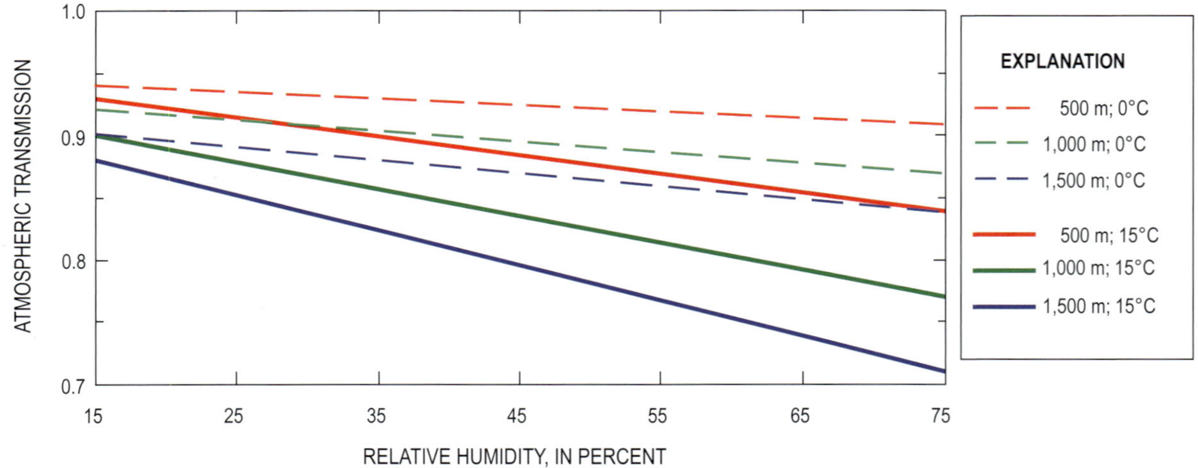

Figure 12. Atmospheric transmission as a function of relative humidity, atmospheric temperature, and path length.

temperature values in these regions of 15ºC to >25ºC above background, similar to those observed in October 2004. Structural control of heat emissions have also been noted at Mt. Etna in 2002 where hot fractures were observed several weeks prior to the eruption of a lava flow (Andronico and others, 2005), at Stromboli in 2002 where fractures were observed several hours prior to a major slope failure (Calvari and others, 2005), and at Augustine Volcano in 2006 where hot fractures and fissures were observed in the weeks preceding vulcanian explosions (D. Schneider, unpub. data). These studies suggest the broad utility of thermal imaging systems for detecting and monitoring deformation in the weeks and months prior to eruption.

The thermal measurements at Mount St. Helens documented an increase in heat flow on October 10 as magma neared the surface. On October 11, they provided unambiguous confirmation that lava (rather than uplifted crater floor) was being extruded. The imaging capabilities provided better viewing conditions at times when steam otherwise obscured observation (fig. 7) and allowed for an estimate of the volume of spine 1. The maximum temperature observed in fractures and regions of collapse during the eruption sequence was 730ºC, well below the solidus temperature of dacite. Although the thermal measurements may underestimate the maximum temperature as a result of thermal stratification due to radiative cooling, the observations are consistent with the petrologic (Pallister and others, this volume, chap. 30; Cashman and others, this volume, chap. 19) and seismic observations (Moran and others, this volume, chap. 2) that suggest a viscous to solid transition at a depth of approximately 1 km.

Comparisons to Satellite Methods

The detection limit of satellite-based measurements of thermal emissions is largely a matter of spatial resolution. With the exception of large thermal features (such as lava lakes, crater lakes, and pyroclastic-flow deposits), most sources of volcanogenic heat are subpixel in size when viewed with moderate-resolution sensors such as ASTER (90-m pixels) or coarse-resolution sensors such as AVHRR or MODIS (1-km pixels). Thus, the signal detected by the satellite is a pixel-integrated value of (at least) a hot and a cold (background) component. In order for a thermal anomaly to be detected, the proportion of hot material within a pixel, or the temperature of the hot component, needs to increase to the point where the integrated temperature exceeds a threshold (compared to neighboring pixels). So it follows that the smaller the spatial resolution of a sensor, the more sensitive it will be to detecting anomalous pixels.

Vaughan and Hook (2006) examined nighttime (to eliminate the solar reflected radiance) ASTER thermal infrared data for Mount St. Helens and reported that a single-pixel, weak (10°C) thermal feature was observed on the evening of October 1 approximately 11 hours after the first phreatic explosion. They noted that this value was within the range of typical ASTER-derived temperatures observed over the previous 5 years and would likely have not been viewed as significant without knowledge of the explosion. The next clear nighttime ASTER image was collected in February 2005 and showed an unambiguous maximum temperature of about 50°C. Although this instrument has been used successfully to monitor eruptive activity at many other volcanoes, the long period of time between successful, cloud-free nighttime images illustrates that significant eruptive activity can occur without being observed.

Manual analyses conducted by AVO of mid-infrared data from the AVHRR and MODIS sensors (1-km spatial resolution with multiple image collections per day) were not able to detect any unusual thermal (or volcanic ash) emissions during the precursory and vent-clearing phases of the eruption. The first weak thermal anomaly of 10°C (above background) was observed in data collected on the evening of October 11, shortly after the first observations of lava extrusion using the thermal imaging system (Alaska Volcano Observatory, unpub. data). It is unclear whether this level of activity would have been observed or reported without the knowledge of lava being extruded, as thermal anomalies of this magnitude can be masked by noise or other environmental factors. Thermal anomalies of 10°C to 20°C above background were reported by AVO throughout most of October during times of clear weather and increased to a one-pixel anomaly of 32°C above background in nighttime data on November 8 (Alaska Volcano Observatory, unpub. data). This observation corresponds most closely with the thermal image shown in figure 9 and occurred about 2 weeks after the start of the extrusion of spine 3. By comparison, MODVOLC, an automated global system designed to detect volcanic activity (with a rather high threshold to reduce false alarms) (Wright and others, 2004), did not trigger until December 18. By this time, spine 3 had encountered the south crater wall and started to disintegrate. Undoubtedly the detection of thermal activity by satellite techniques was greatly reduced by the insulating properties of the relatively cool fault-gouge carapace. Once the spines grew large and began to break apart, detection was more apparent. Still, lava extrusion was ongoing for a least a month before satellite methods utilizing 1-km-resolution data were able to unambiguously detect it.

Conclusions

The use of airborne thermal imaging to document eruptive activity at Mount St. Helens began in October 2004 to develop baseline thermal images of the 1980–86 dome and to investigate the rising welt on the south crater floor. Since that time, it has become a routine monitoring tool for tracking evolution of the lava dome (Vallance and others, this volume, chap. 9). Some of the unique information that has been derived from these data to date include (1) rapid identification of the phreatic nature of the early vent-clearing explosive phase; (2)

observation of the structural control of heat flow during times of large-scale deformation of the south flank of the 1980–86 dome, which was part of the welt; (3) observations of the venting of hot gas through an ephemeral crater lake and increased heat flow through the welt, indicative of a shallow magma source; (4) confirmation of new lava reaching the surface; (5) characterization of the change in surface temperature of the lava spines, from the initial, hotter spines 1 and 2 that were free of fault gouge, to the cooler gouge-covered whaleback spines (beginning with spine 3); (6) documentation that the relatively low maximum temperature of 730°C agreed with petrologic and seismic data suggesting a viscous-to-solid transition at shallow depth; and (7) identification of the source of active lava extrusion, dome collapse, and large variation in surface temperatures. Such temperature variation needs to be accounted for in the retrieval of eruption parameters using satellite-based techniques, because the thermal features are of subpixel size in satellite images.

Acknowledgments

We would like to thank Matthew Patrick and Cynthia Werner, who provided thoughtful and helpful reviews, and helicopter pilot Jeff Linscott of JL Aviation for his skillful, safe, and enthusiastic flying.

References Cited

Andronico, D., Branca, S., Calvari, S., Burton, M., Caltabiano, T., Corsaro, R.A., Del Carlo, P., Garfì, G., Lodato, L., Miraglia, L., Murè, F., Neri, M., Pecora, E., Pompilio, M., Salerno, G., and Spampinato, L., 2005, A multi-disciplinary study of the 2002–03 Etna eruption; insights into a complex plumbing system: Bulletin of Volcanology, v. 67, no. 4, p. 314–330, doi:10.1007/s00445-004-0372-8.

Ball, M., and Pinkerton, H., 2006, Factors affecting the accuracy of thermal imaging cameras in volcanology: Journal of Geophysical Research, v. 111, no. B11, B11203, 14 p., doi:10.1029/2005JB003829.

Calvari, S., Spampinato, L., Lodato, L., Harris, A.J.L., Patrick, M.R., Dehn, J., Burton, M.R., and Andronico, D., 2005, Chronology and complex volcanic processes during the 2002–2003 flank eruption at Stromboli volcano (Italy) reconstructed from direct observations and surveys with a handheld thermal camera: Journal of Geophysical Research, v. 110, no. B2, p. 1–23, doi:10.1029/2004JB003129.

Cashman, K.V., Thornber, C.R., and Pallister, J.S., 2008, From dome to dust; shallow crystallization and fragmentation of conduit magma during the 2004–2006 dome extrusion of Mount St. Helens, Washington, chap. 19 *of* Sherrod, D.R., Scott, W.E., and Stauffer, P.H., eds., A volcano rekindled; the renewed eruption of Mount St. Helens, 2004–2006: U.S. Geological Survey Professional Paper 1750 (this volume).

Dehn, J., Dean, K.G., Engle, K., and Izbekov, P., 2002, Thermal precursors in satellite images of the 1999 eruption of Shishaldin Volcano: Bulletin of Volcanology, v. 64, no. 8, p. 525–534, doi:10.1007/s00445-002-0227-0.

Driedger, C.L., Neal, C.A., Knappenberger, T.H., Needham, D.H., Harper, R.B., and Steele, W.P., 2008, Hazard information management during the autumn 2004 reawakening of Mount St. Helens volcano, Washington, chap. 24 *of* Sherrod, D.R., Scott, W.E., and Stauffer, P.H., eds., A volcano rekindled; the renewed eruption of Mount St. Helens, 2004–2006: U.S. Geological Survey Professional Paper 1750 (this volume).

Dzurisin, D., Lisowski, M., Poland, M.P., Sherrod, D.R., and LaHusen, R.G., 2008, Constraints and conundrums resulting from ground-deformation measurements made during the 2004–2005 dome-building eruption of Mount St. Helens, Washington, chap. 14 *of* Sherrod, D.R., Scott, W.E., and Stauffer, P.H., eds., A volcano rekindled; the renewed eruption of Mount St. Helens, 2004–2006: U.S. Geological Survey Professional Paper 1750 (this volume).

Flynn, L.P., Harris, A.J.L., and Wright, R., 2001, Improved identification of volcanic features using Landsat 7 ETM+: Remote Sensing of Environment, v. 78, nos. 1–2, p. 180–193.

Gerlach, T.M., McGee, K.A., and Doukas, M.P., 2008, Emission rates of CO_2, SO_2, and H_2S, scrubbing, and preeruption excess volatiles at Mount St. Helens, 2004–2005, chap. 26 *of* Sherrod, D.R., Scott, W.E., and Stauffer, P.H., eds., A volcano rekindled; the renewed eruption of Mount St. Helens, 2004–2006: U.S. Geological Survey Professional Paper 1750 (this volume).

Harris, A.J.L., Keszthelyi, L., Flynn, L.P., Mouginis-Mark, P.J., Thornber, C., Kauahikaua, J., Sherrod, D., Trusdell, F., Sawyer, M.W., and Flament, P., 1997, Chronology of the episode 54 eruption at Kilauea Volcano, Hawaii, from GOES-9 satellite data: Geophysical Research Letters, v. 24, no. 24, p. 3281–3284.

Harris, A., Dehn, J., Patrick, M., Calvari, S., Ripepe, M., and Lodato, L., 2005a, Lava effusion rates from hand-held thermal infrared imagery: an example from the June 2003 effusive activity at Stromboli: Bulletin of Volcanology, v. 68, no. 2, p. 107–117, doi:10.1007/s00445-005-0425-7.

Harris, A., Ripepe, M., Sahetapy-Engel, S., Marchetti, E., and Patrick, M., 2005b, Plume ascent velocities measured during explosive eruptions using thermal infrared thermometers [abs.]: Eos (American Geophysical Union Transactions), v. 86, no. 52, Fall Meeting Supplement, Abstract V24A-06.

Kauahikaua, J., Sherrod, D.R., Cashman, K.V., Heliker, C.,

Hon, K., Mattox, T.N., and Johnson, J.A., 2003, Hawaiian lava-flow dynamics during the Pu‘u ‘Ō‘ō-Kūpaianaha eruption; a tale of two decades, *in* Heliker, C., Swanson, D.A., and Takahashi, T.J., eds., The Pu‘u ‘Ō‘ō-Kūpaianaha eruption of Kīlauea Volcano, Hawai‘i; the first 20 years: U.S. Geological Survey Professional Paper 1676, p. 63–87.

Kiefer, H.H., Frank, D., and Friedman, J.D., 1981, Thermal infrared surveys at Mount St. Helens—observations prior to the eruption of May 18, *in* Lipman, P.W., and Mullineaux, D.R., eds., The 1980 eruptions of Mount St. Helens, Washington: U.S. Geological Survey Professional Paper 1250, p. 257–277.

Moran, S.C., Malone, S.D., Qamar, A.I., Thelen, W.A., Wright, A.K., and Caplan-Auerbach, J., 2008a, Seismicity associated with renewed dome building at Mount St. Helens, 2004–2005, chap. 2 *of* Sherrod, D.R., Scott, W.E., and Stauffer, P.H., eds., A volcano rekindled; the renewed eruption of Mount St. Helens, 2004–2006: U.S. Geological Survey Professional Paper 1750 (this volume).

Moran, S.C., McChesney, P.J., and Lockhart, A.B., 2008b, Seismicity and infrasound associated with explosions at Mount St. Helens, 2004–2005, chap. 6 *of* Sherrod, D.R., Scott, W.E., and Stauffer, P.H., eds., A volcano rekindled; the renewed eruption of Mount St. Helens, 2004–2006: U.S. Geological Survey Professional Paper 1750 (this volume).

Pallister, J.S., Thornber, C.R., Cashman, K.V., Clynne, M.A., Lowers, H.A., Mandeville, C.W., Brownfield, I.K., and Meeker, G.P., 2008, Petrology of the 2004–2006 Mount St. Helens lava dome—implications for magmatic plumbing and eruption triggering, chap. 30 *of* Sherrod, D.R., Scott, W.E., and Stauffer, P.H., eds., A volcano rekindled; the renewed eruption of Mount St. Helens, 2004–2006: U.S. Geological Survey Professional Paper 1750 (this volume).

Patrick M.R., Harris, A.J.L., Ripepe, M., Dehn, J., Rothery, D.A., and Calvari, S., 2007, Strombolian explosive styles and source conditions; insights from thermal (FLIR) video: Bulletin of Volcanology, v. 69, no. 7, p. 769–784, doi:10.1007/s00445-006-0107-0.

Power, J., 2004, Renewed unrest at Mount Spurr volcano, Alaska [abs.]: Eos (American Geophysical Union Transactions), v. 85, no. 43, p. 434.

Ramsey, M.S., and Christensen, P.R., 1998, Mineral abundance determination; Quantitative deconvolution of thermal emission spectra: Journal of Geophysical Research, v. 103, no. B1, p. 577–596.

Ramsey, M., and Dehn, J., 2004, Spaceborne observations of the 2000 Bezymianny, Kamchatka, eruption; the integration of high-resolution ASTER data into near real-time monitoring using AVHRR: Journal of Volcanology and Geothermal Research, v. 135, nos. 1–2, p. 127–146, doi:10.1016/j.jvolgeores.2003.12.014.

Ramsey, M.S., and Fink, J.H., 1999, Estimating silicic lava vesicularity with thermal remote sensing; a new technique for volcanic mapping and monitoring: Bulletin of Volcanology, v. 61, no. 1, p. 32–39.

Sawyer, G., Burton, M., and Oppenheimer, C., 2005, The effect of volcanic gases on quantitative temperature measurements using the FLIR thermal camera [abs.]: Eos (American Geophysical Union Transactions), v. 86, no. 52, Fall Meeting Supplement, Abstract V24A-08.

Vallance, J.W., Schneider, D.J., and Schilling, S.P., 2008, Growth of the 2004–2006 lava-dome complex at Mount St. Helens, Washington, chap. 9 *of* Sherrod, D.R., Scott, W.E., and Stauffer, P.H., eds., A volcano rekindled; the renewed eruption of Mount St. Helens, 2004–2006: U.S. Geological Survey Professional Paper 1750 (this volume).

Vaughan, R.G., and Hook, S.J., 2006, Using satellite data to characterize the temporal thermal behavior of an active volcano; Mount St. Helens, WA: Geophysical Research Letters, v. 33, L20303, doi:10.1029/2006GL027957.

Vaughan, R.G., Hook, S.J., Ramsey, M.S., Realmuto, V.J., and Schneider, D.J., 2005, Monitoring eruptive activity at Mount St. Helens with TIR image data: Geophysical Research Letters, v. 32, L19305, doi:10.1029/2005GL024112.

Wright, R., Flynn, L., Garbeil, H., Harris, A., and Pilger, E., 2002, Automated volcanic eruption detection using MODIS: Remote Sensing of Environment, v. 82, no. 1, p. 135–155.

Wright, R., Flynn, L.P., Garbeil, H., Harris, A.J.L., and Pilger, E., 2004, MODVOLC: Near-real-time thermal monitoring of global volcanism: Journal of Volcanology and Geothermal Research, v. 135, nos. 1–2, p. 29–49.

Chapter 18

Radar Interferometry Observations of Surface Displacements During Pre- and Coeruptive Periods at Mount St. Helens, Washington, 1992–2005

By Michael P. Poland[1] and Zhong Lu[2]

Abstract

We analyzed hundreds of interferograms of Mount St. Helens produced from radar images acquired by the ERS-1/2, ENVISAT, and RADARSAT satellites during the 1992–2004 preeruptive and 2004–2005 coeruptive periods for signs of deformation associated with magmatic activity at depth. Individual interferograms were often contaminated by atmospheric delay anomalies; therefore, we employed stacking to amplify any deformation patterns that might exist while minimizing random noise. Preeruptive interferograms show no signs of volcanowide deformation between 1992 and the onset of eruptive activity in 2004. Several patches of subsidence in the 1980 debris-avalanche deposit were identified, however, and are thought to be caused by viscoelastic relaxation of loosely consolidated substrate, consolidation of water-saturated sediment, or melting of buried ice. Coeruptive interferometric stacks are dominated by atmospheric noise, probably because individual interferograms span only short time intervals in 2004 and 2005. Nevertheless, we are confident that at least one of the seven coeruptive stacks we constructed is reliable at about the 1-cm level. This stack suggests deflation of Mount St. Helens driven by contraction of a source beneath the volcano.

Introduction

Continuous Global Positioning System (GPS) measurements at Mount St. Helens have provided unequivocal evidence of coeruptive deflation that started in 2004, coincident with the onset of seismicity in late September of that year (Lisowski and others, this volume, chap. 15). These data have been used to model an ellipsoidal source of volume loss between 6 and 12 km depth beneath the volcano (Lisowski and others, this volume, chap. 15; Mastin and others, this volume, chap. 22). In addition, GPS results from in and around the crater, including single-frequency instruments deployed on the growing lava dome, have recorded surface displacements associated with dome extrusion (LaHusen and others, this volume, chap. 16). Interferometric synthetic aperture radar (InSAR) data provide an excellent complement to these GPS data. Though lacking the high temporal resolution of continuous GPS or tiltmeter data, InSAR has the potential to provide much greater spatial resolution of deformation, which is useful both for identifying localized deformation sources and modeling complex source geometries. Further, radar images of Mount St. Helens are available from 1992 onward, making it possible to quantify surface displacements during the 1992–2004 preeruption period, when few other geodetic measurements were collected.

Although InSAR characterizations of surface deformation at shield volcanoes (for example, Amelung and others, 2000a) and calderas (for example, Hooper and others, 2004; Wicks and others, 1998; Wicks and others, 2006) have been quite successful, studies of stratovolcanoes have proven more challenging. This is largely due to the fact that most stratovolcanoes are steep sided and covered to varying degrees by vegetation, snow, and ice, leading to a loss of coherent interferometric signal on and around the volcano, especially for C-band radar wavelengths (Zebker and others, 2000; Lu and others, 2005b; Moran and others, 2006). The great height of many stratovolcanoes, relative to the surrounding terrain, can also create atmospheric conditions that introduce significant artifacts into InSAR results (Beaudecel and others, 2000; Wadge and others, 2006). The combined effects of these conditions prevented the use of coeruptive InSAR data for the analysis of deformation at numerous stratovolcanoes, includ-

[1] U.S. Geological Survey, PO Box 51, Hawaii National Park, HI 96718

[2] U.S. Geological Survey, 1300 SE Cardinal Court, Vancouver, WA 98683

ing Galeras, Colombia; Rincon de la Vieja, Costa Rica; Unzen, Japan; and Merapi, Indonesia (Zebker and others, 2000). Even when coeruptive data for a stratovolcano are coherent, there is no guarantee that deformation will be observed, as demonstrated by results from Fuego and Pacaya, Guatemala; Popocatepetl, Mexico; Sakurajima, Japan (Zebker and others, 2000); Irruputuncu (Zebker and others, 2000; Pritchard and Simons, 2004b) and Lascar (Pritchard and Simons, 2002; Pritchard and Simons, 2004a), Chile; and Shishaldin (Moran and others, 2006), Pavlof, Cleveland, and Korovin, Alaska (Lu and others, 2003b). Lu and others (2003b) and Moran and others (2006) suggested that, at least in the case of Shishaldin, the lack of observed line-of-sight displacements in coeruptive InSAR data may be caused by (1) posteruption motion that balanced preeruption displacements, resulting in no net deformation across the time spanned by the interferograms, (2) the occurrence of deformation in "blind zones" where InSAR data are not coherent, or (3) the lack of any significant deformation associated with the eruption. Pritchard and Simons (2004a; 2004b) suggest similar reasons for the lack of observed deformation in InSAR data from Cerro Irruputuncu and Volcán Lascar, two volcanoes in Chile, in addition to the possibility that the magma reservoir may be too deep to produce surface displacements detectable by InSAR.

Poor coherence at a volcano does not necessarily imply that surface displacements cannot be observed by InSAR. Cerro Hudson is a 10-km-diameter, ice-filled caldera in southern Chile. Despite a complete lack of coherence within and limited coherence outside the caldera, displacements were of sufficient magnitude (15-cm line-of-sight inflation over 3 years) to be detected and distinguished from atmospheric noise (Pritchard and Simons, 2004b). Although large displacements were not observed in individual coeruptive interferograms of Soufrière Hills volcano[1], Montserrat, Wadge and others (2006) identified deformation caused by a variety of processes once they stacked (averaged) multiple interferograms. At stratovolcanoes where coherence is excellent, InSAR studies have resulted in important discoveries of aseismic magma accumulation, including Peulik, Alaska (Lu and others, 2002b) and South Sister, Oregon (Dzurisin and others, 2006; Wicks and others, 2002). In addition, InSAR has been critical for characterizing deformation at many composite volcanoes that have experienced unrest or eruptions, including Westdahl (Lu and others, 2003a), Makushin (Lu and others, 2002a), Akutan (Lu and others, 2000; Lu and others, 2005b), Augustine (Masterlark and others, 2006), and Seguam (Masterlark and Lu, 2004), Alaska; Gada 'Ale, Ethiopia (Amelung and others, 2000b); and several volcanoes in the central and southern Andes (Pritchard and Simons, 2002; 2004a; 2004b). Clearly, the potential for advancing the understanding of pre- and coeruptive activity at Mount St. Helens through InSAR studies is substantial.

We completed an exhaustive analysis of InSAR data collected from Mount St. Helens between 1992 and 2005 from a variety of satellites, ground tracks, time spans, and satellite viewing geometries. Our goals were to (1) obtain high-spatial-resolution coeruptive surface displacement data of the known volcanowide deflation (Lisowski and others, this volume, chap. 15) for input into deformation source models, (2) identify any localized displacements that might not be detectable by GPS or other terrestrial measurements, and (3) identify any displacements precursory to the onset of eruptive activity in 2004. Coherence was poor and atmospheric artifacts were significant in most interferograms; nevertheless, we recognized localized displacements unrelated to volcanic activity and modeled coeruptive subsidence (although poor coherence prevented the use of complex model geometries). Preeruptive interferograms showed no evidence of precursory deformation; however, displacements localized within the crater cannot be ruled out, owing to poor coherence and atmospheric distortions.

Methodology

Traditional InSAR studies combine two radar images of the same area on the ground acquired at different times from nearly the same point in space to determine the deformation over the time spanned along the radar's line-of-sight (LOS). This procedure, unfortunately, does not produce satisfactory results at Mount St. Helens for three reasons: (1) atmospheric path delays, which often correlate with topography, can introduce artifacts that amount to several centimeters of apparent LOS displacement (fig. 1), (2) interferograms that include scenes acquired during nonsummer months are generally incoherent due to seasonal snow cover, and (3) coherence breaks down quickly over time, causing interferograms that span more than one or two years to be mostly incoherent. In fact, in interferograms spanning several months or more, coherence was generally maintained only on deposits that were emplaced during the explosive eruptions of 1980 (for example, May 18, May 25, June 12, July 22), especially north of the volcano and in the upper North Fork Toutle River. As a result, we relied on interferometric stacks to study deformation of Mount St. Helens.

Stacking is a procedure that adds the LOS displacements from multiple interferograms (which may or may not be overlapping in time) acquired along the same look angle. Dividing the summed displacements by the cumulative time spanned results in an average displacement rate (for example, Fialko and Simons, 2001; Peltzer and others, 2001). The technique decreases the magnitude of random noise (primarily atmospheric artifacts) by $N/u^{0.5}$, where N is the error in a single interferogram and u is the number of interferograms in the stack (Bevington and Robinson, 1992, p. 39–40). For

[1] Capitalization of "Volcano" indicates adoption of the word as part of the formal geographic name by the host country, as listed in the Geographic Names Information System, a database maintained by the U.S. Board on Geographic Names. Noncapitalized "volcano" is applied informally—eds.

example, if atmospheric variations typically result in an error of 10 mm/yr, a stack of 25 interferograms would reduce the noise level to about 2 mm/yr (assuming atmospheric path delay errors have similar magnitudes in all interferograms). In contrast, signals that persist over time—including steady deformation due to volcanic or tectonic activity—are emphasized because the signal is manifested in all interferograms in the stack. InSAR stacks have been able to distinguish displacement rates as low as a few millimeters per year (Wright and others, 2001, 2004) but are useful only when the strength and geometry of the deformation source do not vary significantly over time, meaning that nonlinear deformation rates or changes in source location or geometry are not easily recovered in interferometric stacks.

We do not expect changes in source geometry over time to bias the interferometric stacks. The geometry of the magmatic system of Mount St. Helens has been investigated using both petrologic (for example, Rutherford and others, 1985; Cashman, 1988; Cashman, 1992; Pallister and others, 1992) and seismic (Scandone and Malone, 1985; Barker and Malone, 1991; Lees, 1992; Moran, 1994; Musumeci and others, 2002) techniques and includes a reservoir at around 6–10 km depth connected to the surface by a near-vertical conduit. The conduit appears to have been sealed at a depth of about 2 km following the end of the 1980–86 eruptive period (Moran, 1994). Any pre- or coeruptive deformation associated with unrest beginning in 2004 will likely have a source within this system (especially at the levels around the 6–10-km-depth reservoir or 2-km-depth seal).

Similarly, deformation rates during both the pre- and coeruptive periods appear to be approximately linear, so time-variable displacements will not bias deformation rates derived by stacking. Electronic Distance Measurement (EDM) and campaign GPS measurements in the inter-eruptive period, from late 1986 through the first half of 2004, indicate that little deformation occurred, especially after 1991 (Lisowski and others, this volume, chap. 15). In addition, individual interferograms that span time periods before

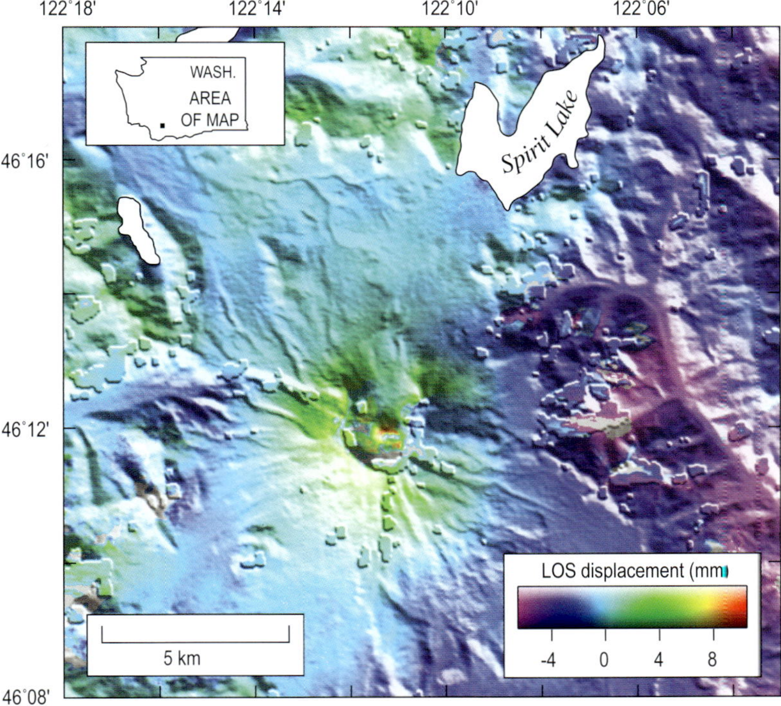

Figure 1. Interferogram of Mount St. Helens, Washington, formed from ERS-1 orbit 21415 (August 19, 1995) and ERS-2 orbit 2243 (September 24, 1995). Interferogram spans only 36 days during summer months, hence high level of coherence. Phase correlates strongly with topography, so Mount St. Helens shows apparent line-of-sight (LOS) lengthening, while lower valleys to east show LOS shortening. Such behavior is characteristic of strong atmospheric influence. Topographic irregularities caused by areas of no data in SRTM DEM.

the start of the unrest in September 2004 show no unambiguous signs of volcanowide deformation. If preeruptive surface displacements occurred, the motion must therefore have been small in magnitude but may have accumulated over time. Coeruptive displacements, measured by continuous GPS starting on September 23, 2004, are generally linear after the first few weeks of the activity (Lisowski and others, this volume, chap. 15) and suggest only minor temporal or spatial variations in the contraction of a source at depth beneath Mount St. Helens.

An unusually large InSAR data set, summarized in table 1, is available for Mount St. Helens, including multiple satellites with a variety of imaging geometries. For preeruptive time periods, we analyzed data from ERS-1, ERS-2, and ENVISAT. Usable data from the first two satellites span 1992–2001 and are available for four orbital tracks, whereas a sufficiently large archive of ENVISAT data is available from one track to allow an assessment of the surface displacement field in 2003–4. Our coeruptive InSAR data set includes five ENVISAT and two RADARSAT tracks. All possible interferograms from each independent track with perpendicular baselines of less than 300 m were created.

Topographic corrections to interferograms utilized the 30-m resolution Shuttle Radar Topography Mission (SRTM) digital elevation model (DEM), which was generated in 2000 (Farr and Kobrick, 2000). The older National Elevation Dataset (NED) 30-m DEM, created before 1986, contains fewer holes than the SRTM data, but its use resulted in deformation artifacts in interferograms in the area of Mount St. Helens crater. Significant topographic changes have occurred in the crater since the end of the 1980–86 eruptive period, most notably the growth of a glacier that had reached a maximum thickness of 200 m by the time eruptive activity resumed in 2004 (Schilling and others, 2004; Walder and others, this volume, chap. 13). The more recent SRTM DEM accounts for growth of the glacier and other changes since 1986 and does not introduce significant artifacts related to topographic change. Interferograms were smoothed using the filtering strategy of Goldstein and Werner (1998) and unwrapped following Chen and Zebker (2001).

From this collection of interferograms, we omitted all images that spanned less than 100 days (except for coeruptive ENVISAT mode 2, track 385, where the only interferograms with perpendicular baselines less than 300 m spanned 70 days or less), because images that span such short times have a low signal-to-noise ratio given the low displacement rates known from GPS (Lisowski and others, this volume, chap. 15). There is no upper limit on the time spanned, although interferograms that showed no or very limited coherence, including nearly all images that span more than two years, were omitted from the analysis. Stacks of each independent track were computed from this modified data set, and only pixels that are coherent in 60 percent of the input images are included in the final stack. Five preeruption and seven coeruption stacks were created, with 3 to 38 input interferograms each (table 1).

Preeruptive Stacks

Results

In preeruptive stacks (figs. 2–6), the range of displacements for each track is generally small, suggesting that the random atmospheric signal has been mostly removed. The lack of significant topography-correlated phase at Mount Adams (which we assume to be undeforming, based on the absence of other signs of unrest) in tracks that both cover and are coherent around both volcanoes (figs. 4, 5) further supports our assertion that atmospheric noise has been mostly suppressed by stacking.

None of the preeruption stacks show any signs of volcanowide deformation, suggesting that no significant surface displacements accumulated over the times spanned by the stacks. Unfortunately there are no InSAR results available between late 2001 and early 2003, so we cannot rule out deformation during this time period. No volcanowide displacements are apparent in the one stack that covers the early 2003 to September 2004 epoch (up to the start of the eruption), suggesting that no centimeter-level displacements on the flanks of the volcano occurred in the months immediately preceding the start of the eruption.

Despite this lack of signal, the five preeruption stacks do reveal at least three localized areas of surface displacement that are unrelated to the magmatic system of Mount St. Helens. All three regions are patches of subsidence located on the May 18, 1980, debris-avalanche deposit (fig. 2). The area with the highest subsidence rate, as much as 15 mm/yr (LOS), is directly north of the crater (site 1 in fig. 2), near the base of Johnston Ridge, and had been recognized previously in individual interferograms by Diefenbach and Poland (2003). A second, less distinct area located near the outlet of Coldwater Lake (site 2 in fig. 2) is subsiding at a rate of slightly less than 5 mm/yr (LOS). The third patch of subsidence, which is sinking at an LOS rate of approximately 6 mm/yr, is in the North Fork Toutle River valley, just southeast of Elk Rock and immediately upstream from a valley constriction (site 3 in fig. 2). The latter two patches had not been recognized previously.

The stacks presented in figures 2 through 6 give average deformation rates. To assess whether or not the subsidence rates of the three localized patches changed during 1992–2005, we used the individual unwrapped interferograms to reconstruct the temporal evolution of the deformation following the method of Berardino and others (2002). At Mount St. Helens, all five preeruption stacks suggest a constant subsidence rate of the area near the base of Johnston Ridge (fig. 7*A*). The four ERS-1/2 tracks are directly comparable in these time series, because they have similar look angles (table 1), and we assume that the deformation is dominated by vertical motion. In addition, the ENVISAT mode 2, track 156, time series confirms that the subsidence was continuing at least into 2004 at a similar rate. Subsidence near the mouth of Coldwater Lake (fig. 7*B*) and below Elk Rock (fig. 7*C*) may have decayed

Table 1. Characteristics of SAR data from Mount St. Helens, Washington, used in stacks and corresponding figures.

[Mode not shown for ERS-1/2 satellite data, which have only one mode. RADARSAT does not use track numbers. A, ascending; D, descending. Incidence angle is measured in degrees from vertical. Number of interferograms (igrams) indicates those used to construct the stack. Figure numbers correspond to this chapter.]

Satellite	Mode	Track	A or D	Incidence angle (deg)	Years spanned	Number of igrams	Figure No.
Preeruptive SAR data							
ERS-1/2	-	156	D	23.2	1992–2001	36	2
ERS-1/2	-	163	A	23.2	1993–2000	7	3
ERS-1/2	-	385	D	23.2	1992–2001	38	4
ERS-1/2	-	392	A	23.2	1995–2000	7	5
ENVISAT	IS 2	156	D	22.8	2003–2004	6	6
Coeruptive SAR data							
ENVISAT	IS 2	156	D	22.8	2004–2005	7	8
ENVISAT	IS 2	163	A	22.8	2004–2005	13	9
ENVISAT	IS 2	385	D	22.8	2004–2005	3[1]	10
ENVISAT	IS 2	392	A	22.8	2004–2005	6	11
ENVISAT	IS 6	20	A	40.9	2004–2005	13	12
RADARSAT	S 2	-	A	27.6	2004–2005	9	13
RADARSAT	S 5	-	A	39.1	2004–2005	6	14

[1] Note that all three input interferograms span 70 days or less.

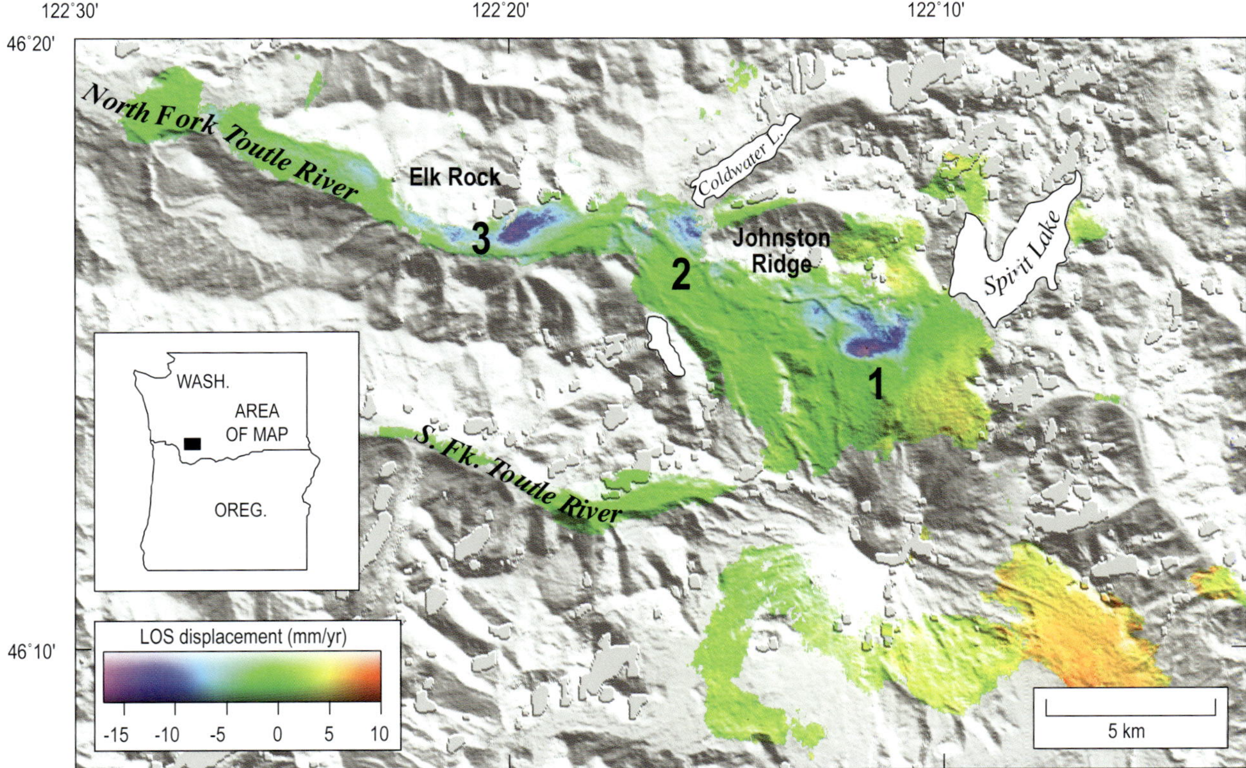

Figure 2. ERS-1/2, track 156, interferometric stack of Mount St. Helens, Washington, composed of 36 interferograms spanning preeruptive 1992–2001 period. Inset shows location of stack. Locations of major features referred to in the text are labeled. Image shows three areas of subsidence in debris-avalanche deposit—1 (Johnston Ridge), 2 (Coldwater), and 3 (Elk Rock).

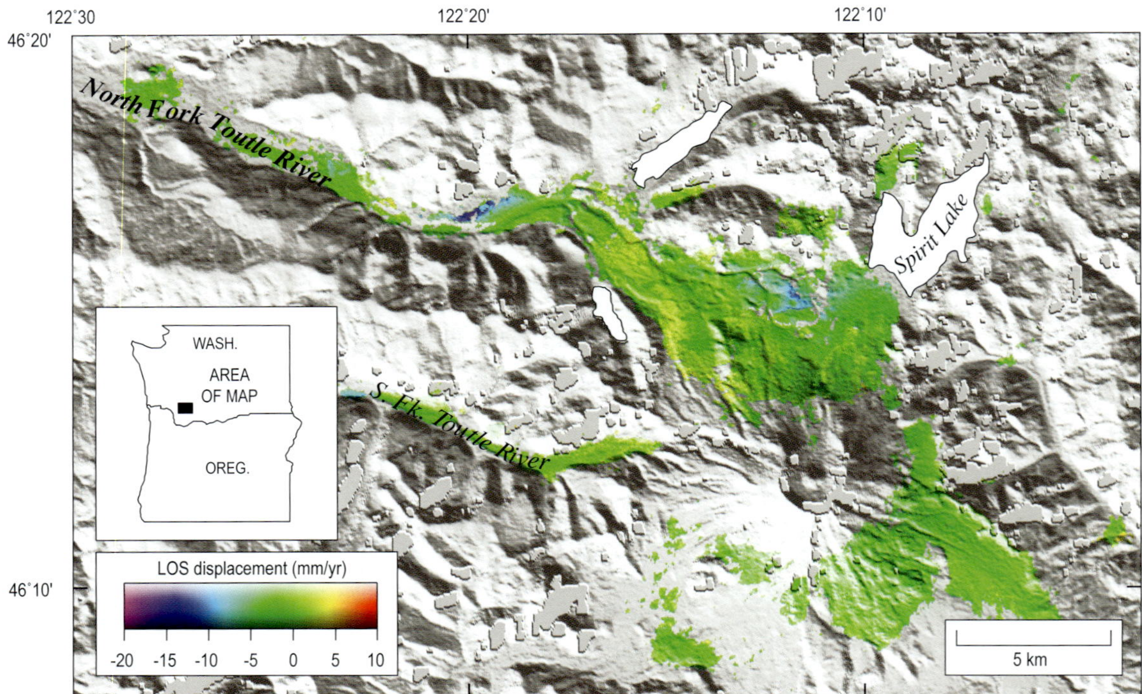

Figure 3. ERS-1/2, track 163, interferometric stack of Mount St. Helens, Washington, composed of seven interferograms spanning preeruptive 1993–2000 time period.

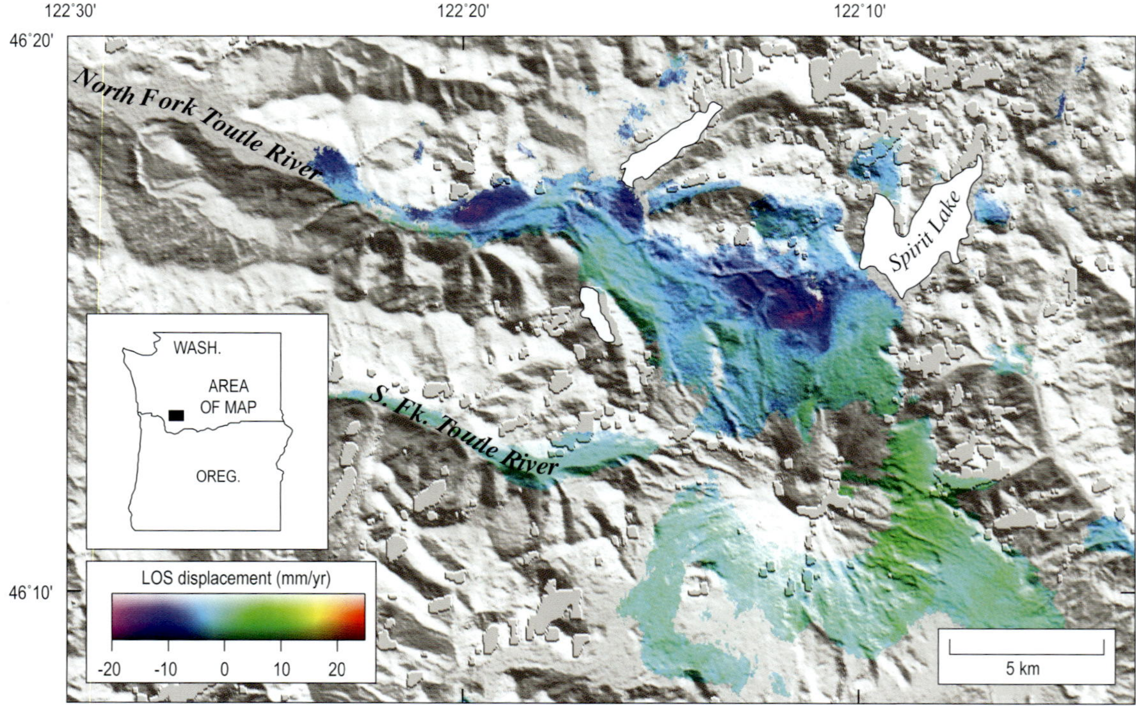

Figure 4. ERS-1/2, track 385, interferometric stack of Mount St. Helens, Washington, composed of 38 interferograms spanning preeruptive 1992–2001 time period.

slightly over the observation period, although the data are too noisy to be certain. Both regions, however, are apparent in coeruptive stacks that span 2004–5 (figs. 8–14), so neither area had ceased deforming by 2005.

Discussion

Lack of Preeruption Deformation

Dzurisin (2003) postulated that deep magma accumulation should precede volcanic unrest and eruption and might have gone undetected prior to the May 18, 1980, eruption of Mount St. Helens. He also suggested that InSAR is perhaps the best tool for detecting such deformation, as exemplified by discoveries of aseismic inflation at South Sister (Wicks and others, 2002) and Peulik (Lu and others, 2002b) volcanoes. Our results rule out surface displacements on the order of 1 cm or greater due to magma accumulation beneath Mount St. Helens between 1992 and late 2001 and between 2003 and the start of the 2004 eruption. It is unlikely that the period not covered by the InSAR stacks was the only time that displacements occurred; therefore, it is probable that no volcanowide

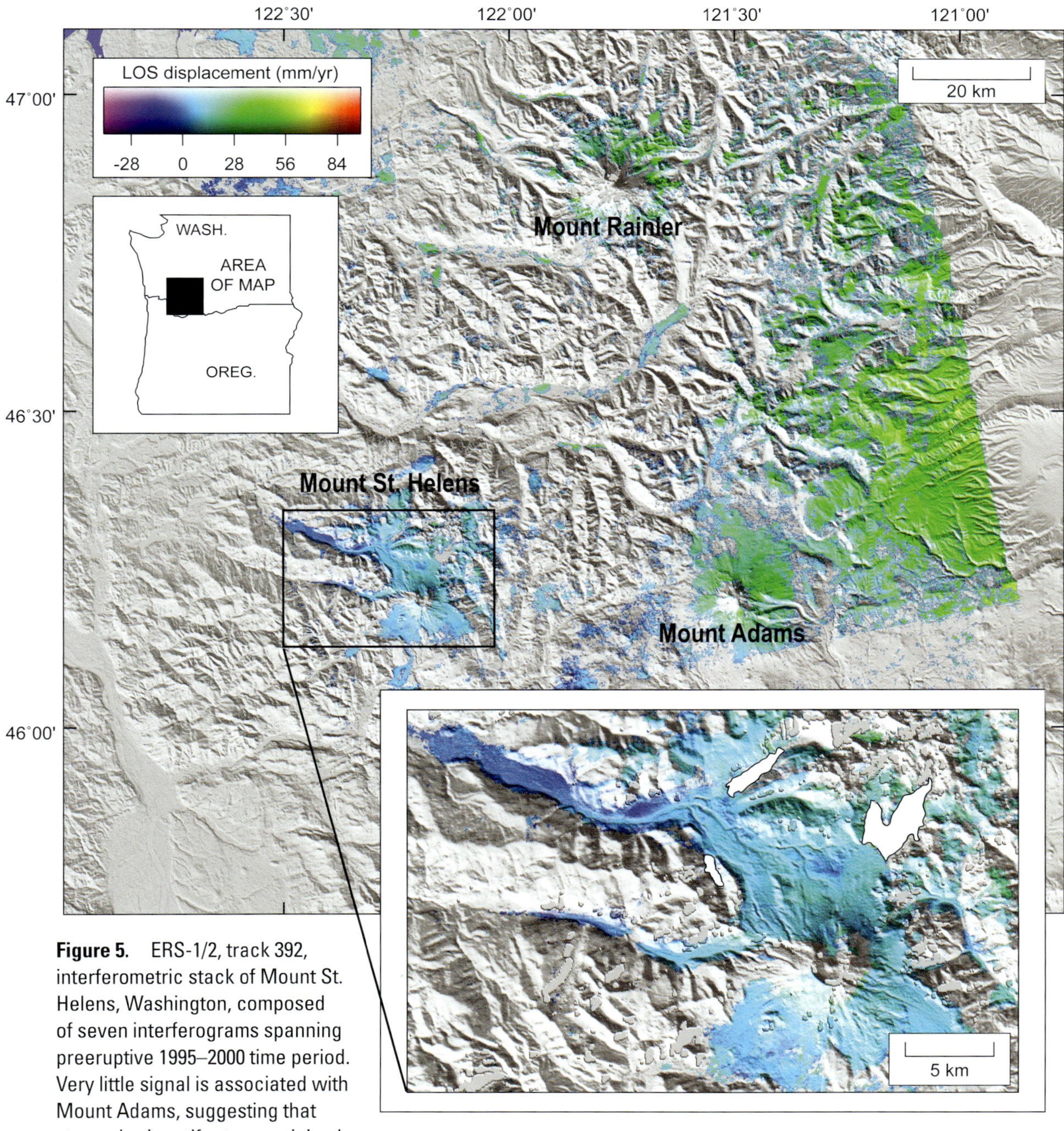

Figure 5. ERS-1/2, track 392, interferometric stack of Mount St. Helens, Washington, composed of seven interferograms spanning preeruptive 1995–2000 time period. Very little signal is associated with Mount Adams, suggesting that atmospheric artifacts are minimal.

displacements occurred during 1992–2004. How can this result be reconciled with Dzurisin's (2003) proposal?

Seismic and geodetic evidence from the late 1980s and early 1990s favor repressurization and possible resupply of the magma body located at about 6–10 km depth. Moran (1994) examined patterns of seismicity between 1987 and 1992 and concluded that the approximately 6- to 10-km-deep reservoir was being pressurized, probably by volatiles that exsolved during magma crystallization and were trapped beneath a seal in the shallow conduit. Seismicity, gas-emission events, and small explosions in 1989–91 may have been related to rupturing of this seal and escape of volatiles (Mastin, 1994). A seismic swarm in 1998 was accompanied by the emission of CO_2 (Gerlach and others, this volume, chap. 26), but whether this seismicity was related to magma migration or only the ascent of magmatic gases is unclear. Magma accumulation below 5.5 km depth is proposed by Musumeci and others (2002) to explain patterns of relocated seismicity. Lisowski and others (this volume, chap. 15) analyzed trilateration data collected in 1982 and 1991 and GPS data from 2000 and found evidence for areal dilatation between 1982 and 1991 that may indicate magma recharge. No significant changes were observed during the 1991–2000 time period. It is possible that magma was accumulating beneath Mount St. Helens only during the late 1980s and early 1990s and was manifested by deep seismicity, areal dilatation, and phreatic explosions (Mastin, 1994; Moran, 1994; Musumeci and others, 2002; Moran and others, this volume, chap. 2).

It seems that there is ample evidence for a pressure increase—either due to exsolution of volatiles, intrusion of new magma, or both—at ~6–10 km depth beneath Mount St. Helens in the years between the end of eruptive activity in 1986 and the start of the 2004 eruption. Changes in pressure or volume at this depth, if large enough, should result in displacements observable by InSAR because they would extend well outside the incoherent crater area without being overly broad or diffuse. The fact that no inflation was observed by InSAR during 1992–2004 (assuming that no deformation occurred during late 2001 to early 2003, when no InSAR data are available) suggests that either (1) the magnitude of volume increase (if magma accumulation occurred) or pressure increase (if only gas exsolution occurred) was insufficient to produce measurable surface displacements, (2) the increase in pressure or volume was accommodated by inelastic processes that did not deform the surface, or (3) the increase in pressure or volume occurred prior to 1992. Distinguishing among these mechanisms is not possible at present, although seismic and geodetic data (discussed above) that were collected after the end of the 1980–86 eruptive period and before InSAR results became available in 1992 favor option 3.

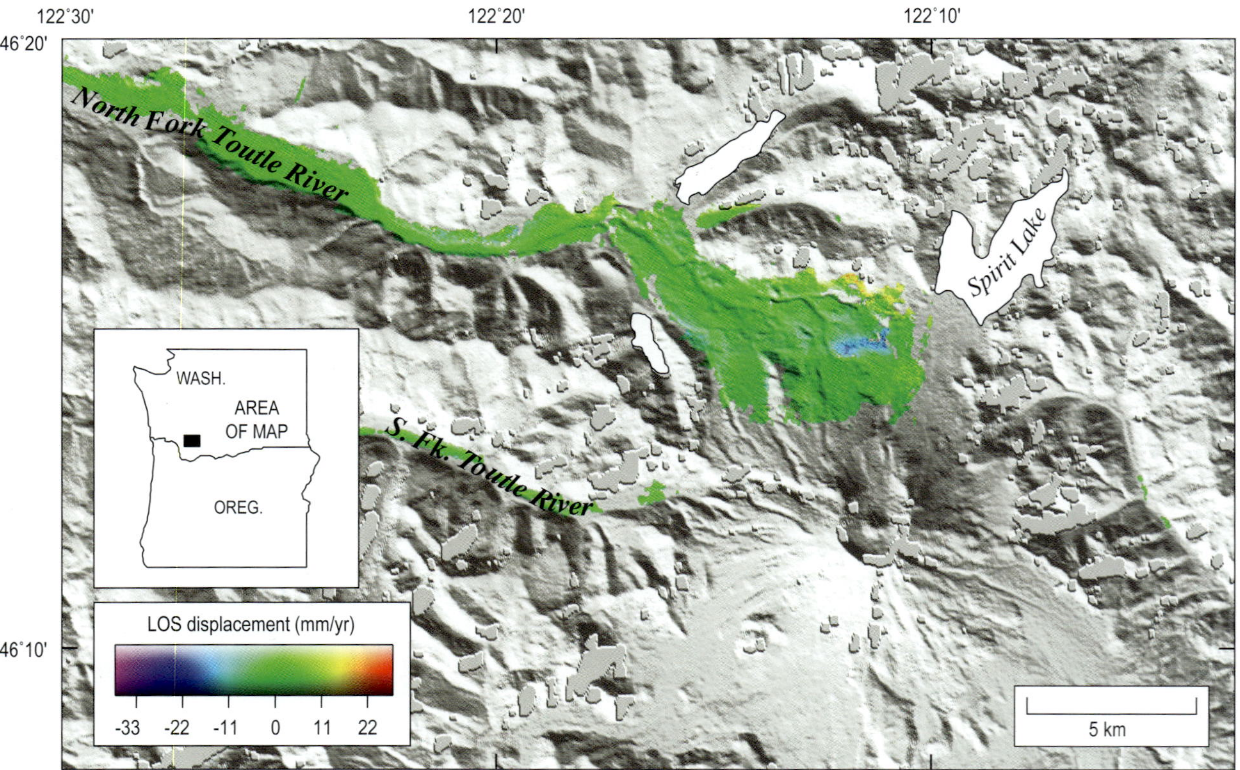

Figure 6. ENVISAT mode 2, track 156, interferometric stack of Mount St. Helens, Washington, composed of six interferograms spanning preeruptive 2003–2004 time period.

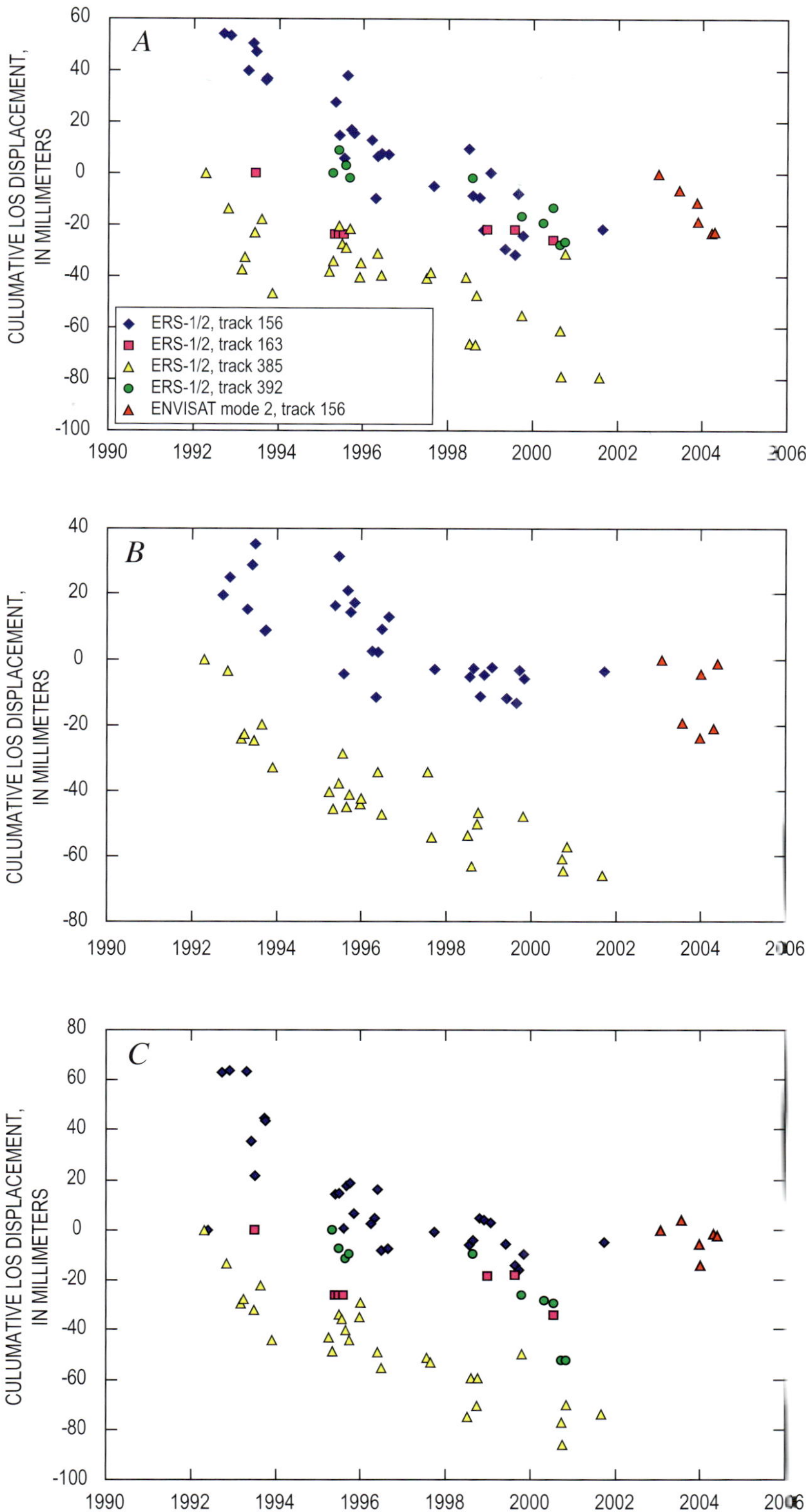

Figure 7. Time series showing line-of-sight (LOS) displacements of subsidence patches at (*A*) Johnston Ridge (site 1 in fig. 2), (*B*) Coldwater (site 2 in fig. 2), and (*C*) Elk Rock (site 3 in fig. 2). LOS displacements are relative to one another, so absolute value of Y axis is less important than changes in value over time. Note that more than 35 interferograms were used to generate time series for ERS tracks 156 and 385, whereas only 6–7 interferograms were used for ERS tracks 163 and 392, and ENVISAT track 156. Deformation rates determined from tracks with relatively few input interferograms could therefore be biased by atmospheric delay anomalies.

Subsidence Patches in the Debris-Avalanche Deposit

The origin of the localized subsidence patches on the debris-avalanche deposit is difficult to constrain and may be a result of several different processes. All three patches occur on the 1980 debris-avalanche deposit. Pyroclastic-flow deposits emplaced during explosive eruptions in 1980 bury the debris-avalanche unit at the base of Johnston Ridge near patch 1 but are not present at the other two patches (Rowley and others, 1981). The displacement patterns resemble poroelastic deformation caused by groundwater withdrawal (for example, Bawden and others, 2001), but there has been no deliberate removal of water from the debris-avalanche deposit. The subsidence has been occurring since at least 1992, and probably much longer, so subsidence mechanisms that occur on short time scales (days to months), including release of gas (Matthews and others, 2003), hydrocompaction due to rainfall (Hoblitt and others, 1985), and poroelastic deformation of the substrate (Lu and others, 2005a) cannot account for the longevity of the observed deformation and the lack of significant changes in subsidence rate over time (fig. 7). Instead, the deformation must be related to long-lived activity associated with the May 18, 1980, debris-avalanche deposit. Processes that have the potential to cause years-long subsidence of a loosely consolidated volcanic deposit like the Mount St. Helens debris-avalanche unit include cooling and contraction of an initially hot deposit (Masterlark and others, 2006), loading of a viscoelastic substrate (Briole and others, 1997; Stevens and others, 2001; Lu and others, 2005a; Masterlark and others, 2006), consolidation of a saturated or unusually dilated deposit (Major, 2000), and melting of buried ice (Branney and Gilbert, 1995; Everest and Bradwell, 2003).

The debris-avalanche deposit was emplaced onto a substrate of Tertiary volcanic rocks, with volcaniclastic sediments along river terraces of, and in, the upper part of the North Fork Toutle River valley and other drainages (Crandell, 1987; Evarts and others, 1987). The loosely consolidated debris-avalanche deposit has a volume of $2,500\times10^6$ m^3 and is composed mostly of cold dacite, andesite, and basalt, with probably less than 50×10^6 m^3 of the volume taken up by the hot (temperature greater than several hundred degrees Celsius) cryptodome that intruded the volcanic edifice in March–May 1980 (Voight and others, 1981; Glicken, 1996). The deposit reaches its maximum thickness, about 200 m, near the base of Johnston Ridge (but not at the exact location of the Johnston Ridge subsidence patch; Glicken, 1996). Glacial ice is thought to represent at least 100×10^6 m^3 of the volume of the unit (Brugman and Meier, 1981; Glicken, 1996). Much of this ice was buried by debris, and localized melting may have contributed to the formation of the North Fork Toutle River lahar on the afternoon of May 18, 1980 (Fairchild, 1987). Water derived from groundwater in the precollapse volcano and glacial ice incorporated into the debris avalanche amounted to approximately 250×10^6 m^3, about 12 percent of the total volume of the deposit (Glicken, 1996). A ground-water system developed in the unit following emplacement, as confirmed by numerous springs and seeps in the deposit, and seasonal changes in pond levels (J. Major, oral commun., 2006). Some parts of the debris-avalanche deposit were also saturated on emplacement, including two of the three patches of subsidence observed by InSAR (at the outlet of Coldwater Lake and below Elk Rock). The area below Elk Rock may have been the source of the May 18, 1980, North Fork Toutle River lahar (Fairchild, 1987; Glicken, 1996), and mud volcanoes caused by dewatering were observed near the outlet of Coldwater Lake in 1981 (J. Major, oral commun, 2006). In the weeks following May 18, 1980, Banks and Hoblitt (1996) measured the temperature of the deposit in shallow holes and found temperatures to be less than 100°C, with no increase in temperature below about 1.5 m. These data suggest that the maximum temperature of the deposit was no greater than boiling (Voight and others, 1981; Banks and Hoblitt, 1996), although temperatures probably varied widely depending on deposit composition (for example, shattered cryptodome versus cold volcanic edifice).

The initial emplacement temperature of the deposit would have to have been unreasonably high to cause subsidence due to cooling and contraction, as suggested by analogy with pyroclastic flows emplaced in 1986 at Augustine Volcano, Alaska. Masterlark and others (2006) used the known 3 cm/yr subsidence rate of Augustine's 1986 deposits (measured 13 years after the flows were emplaced) and the known maximum 126-m deposit thickness to model an initial temperature of 640°C. Decreasing the initial temperature to 500°C required a maximum pyroclastic-flow thickness of 336 m to produce the same subsidence rate. By analogy, the debris-avalanche deposit at Mount St. Helens would need to have an emplacement temperature of over 600°C to produce the subsidence observed by InSAR. Considering the small amount of hot cryptodome incorporated in the deposit and relatively low measured temperatures, it is unlikely that the temperature of significant volumes of the unit approached the required several hundred degrees.

Subsidence in response to a recently emplaced load occurs as the substrate relaxes viscoelastically beneath the load. The magnitude of the subsidence should be directly proportional to the size of the load and the thickness of the substrate (Briole and others, 1997). Subsidence patches on the Mount St. Helens debris-avalanche deposit, however, do not correlate with deposit thickness, although heterogeneity in pre-1980 surficial geology could still allow for subsidence due to loading. Loosely consolidated, relatively low-density sediment in and around the North Fork Toutle valley may be compacting under the load of the debris-avalanche deposit. Subsidence would occur only on parts of the debris-avalanche deposit that overlie accumulated sediment, explaining the patchiness of the subsidence and the fact that deformation occurs mostly where the unit lies near or above the buried channel and floodplains of the North Fork Toutle River. Testing this hypothesis is difficult without additional knowledge of the thickness and extent of sedimentary deposits prior to the catastrophic debris avalanche of May 18, 1980.

Consolidation of granular deposits is a function of water content and diffusivity; compaction and subsidence occur in saturated deposits as water is removed (Major, 2000). Localized subsidence undoubtedly resulted as water seeped from saturated parts of the debris-avalanche deposit, and dewatering persisted through 2005 on the basis of springs and seeps found throughout the unit (J. Major, oral commun., 2006). Depending on the diffusivity and saturated thickness of the deposit, gravitational consolidation resulting from dewatering and diffusion of fluid pressure in excess of hydrostatic pressure could last for years, causing subsidence for decades after the deposit was emplaced (Major, 2000).

Melting of buried ice as a long-term subsidence mechanism could only occur if ice within the debris-avalanche deposit melted slowly over decades. In cold deposits (for example, the terminal moraine of a retreating glacier), buried ice can persist for hundreds of years (Everest and Bradwell, 2003). Could ice have survived more than 25 years buried in the Mount St. Helens debris-avalanche deposit? The answer depends on the deposit temperature and whether ice survived as large blocks or pulverized grains. If the entire deposit were initially about boiling (Banks and Hoblitt, 1996), there is little chance that even large blocks of ice (25–50 m in diameter) could have survived more than a few months after May 18, 1980 (Fairchild, 1987). Some parts of the debris-avalanche deposit were probably at ambient temperature, however, because much of the collapsed edifice, including most of the first landslide block, was composed of the cold outer skin of the volcano (including glacial ice; Glicken, 1996). Evidence for long-term survival of buried ice at Mount St. Helens is suggested by the discovery of subsurface ice during excavations near Spirit Lake by the U.S. Army Corps of Engineers almost 2 years after the May 18, 1980, eruption (Glicken, 1996). Slow melting of buried ice would account for the patchiness of the subsidence, as well as the lack of correlation between debris avalanche thickness and subsidence magnitude. There is, unfortunately, no way to know whether or not buried ice is the source of subsidence of the Mount St. Helens debris-avalanche deposit, but it remains a viable mechanism.

All of the possible subsidence mechanisms are asymptotic processes, meaning that subsidence rates of the debris-avalanche deposit patches should decay over time. No significant rate changes are apparent from the InSAR time series (fig. 7), so the mechanism of subsidence for the debris-avalanche deposit patches must be a long-term process, with changes in the rate of deformation requiring decades to manifest. Based on the temperature and composition of the debris-avalanche deposit and substrate, the observed patches of subsidence may be caused by differential compaction of sedimentary substrate along the buried North Fork Toutle River, gravitational consolidation of locally saturated or unusually dilated areas of the debris-avalanche deposit, or melting of buried ice. Using current knowledge, the relative contributions of these mechanisms cannot be determined; thus all three processes are viable causes for localized areas of subsidence on the May 18, 1980, debris-avalanche deposit.

Coeruptive stacks

Results

Unlike the preeruptive stacks, coeruptive stacks are inconsistent and heavily affected by atmospheric artifacts (figs. 8 through 14). The seven coeruptive stacks show all possible deformation patterns—no surface displacements, volcanowide inflation, and volcanowide deflation. Deflation of Mount St. Helens is suggested by ENVISAT mode 2, track 163 (fig. 9), ENVISAT mode 6, track 20 (fig. 12), and RADARSAT mode 2 (fig. 13). No deformation is apparent in the ENVISAT mode 2, track 156 (fig. 8), ENVISAT mode 2, track 385 (fig. 10), and ENVISAT mode 2, track 392 (fig. 11) stacks. Inflation, at least in two quadrants of the volcano, is indicated in the RADARSAT mode 5 (fig. 14) stack. These contradictory results can be reconciled by examining the character of the subsidence patch located at the base of Johnston Ridge, which was probably active during the coeruptive time period based on its persistence during the preeruptive interval and lack of decay over time (fig. 7*A*). This feature is only apparent in ENVISAT mode 2, track 163 (fig. 9), ENVISAT mode 6, track 20 (fig. 12), and the two RADARSAT beam modes (figs. 13 and 14). Stacks that do not show the subsidence patches are not sensitive to displacement rates of 2–3 cm/yr, on the same order as the expected volcanowide deflation signal measured by GPS (Lisowski and others, this volume, chap. 15).

The three interferograms that show volcanowide subsidence (figs. 9, 12, 13) are the stacks produced from at least nine input interferograms (table 1). We suspect that the averaged range changes in figures 8, 10, 11, and 14 are biased by atmospheric delay anomalies due to the limited number of interferograms used in the stacks. These stacks should not be considered for further analysis. Atmospheric delay artifacts in the stacks may also be recognized by topography-correlated fringes at presumably undeforming mountains also covered by the scenes (Beaudecel and others, 2000). Unfortunately, no mountains other than Mount St. Helens are coherent within, or covered by, the ENVISAT mode 2, track 163 (fig. 9) and ENVISAT mode 6, track 20 (fig. 12) stacks, and their quality cannot be assessed independently. Mount Adams, 60 km east of Mount St. Helens, has no associated phase-correlated topography in the RADARSAT mode 2 stack (fig. 13) which, together with the debris-avalanche subsidence patches also visible in that image, suggests that the stack is sensitive to deformation on the order of 1 cm/yr. As a result, the stack that is most representative of the coeruptive deformation state of Mount St. Helens is RADARSAT mode 2 (fig. 13). This stack suggests

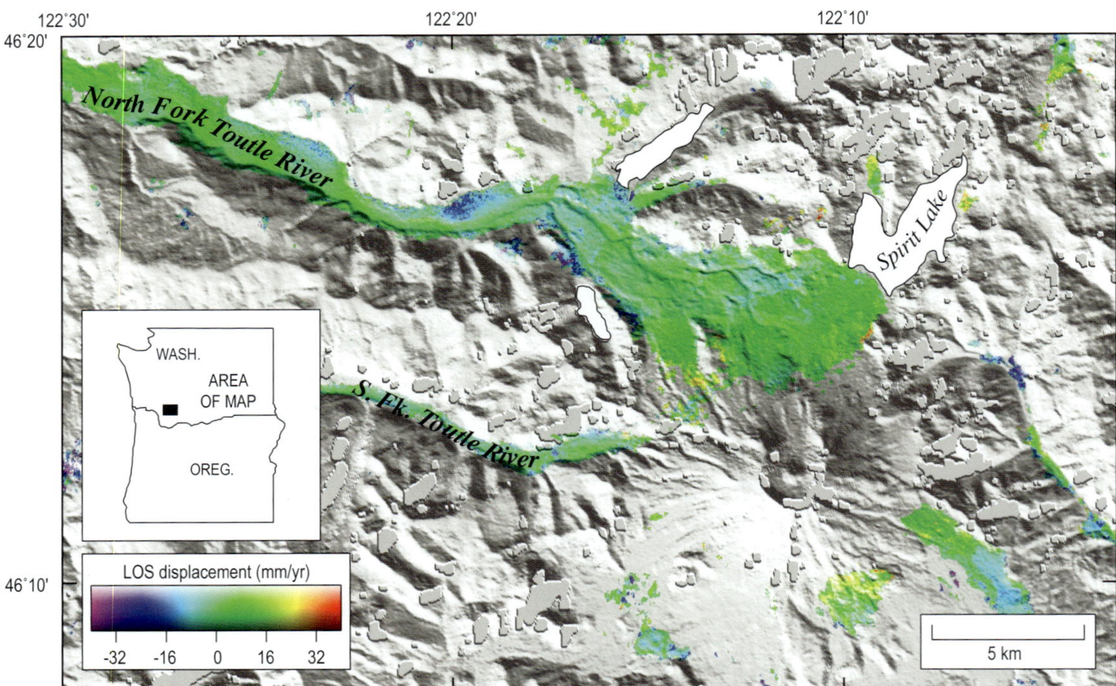

Figure 8. ENVISAT mode 2, track 156, interferometric stack of Mount St. Helens, Washington, composed of seven interferograms spanning coeruptive 2004–5 time period.

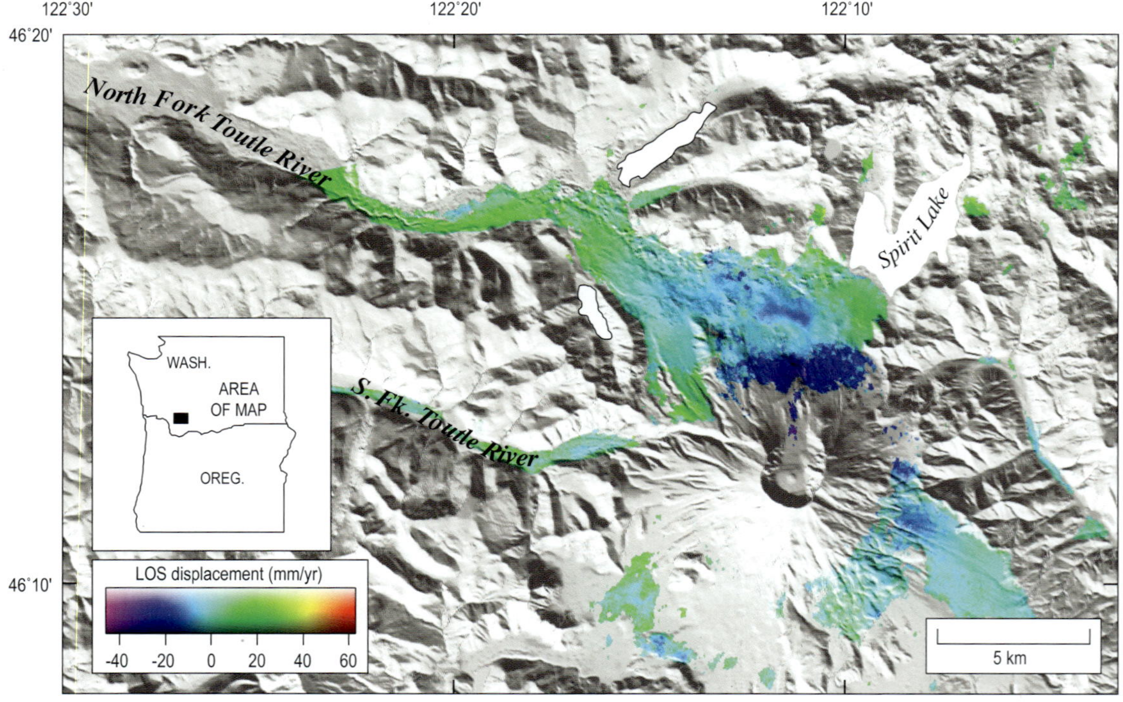

Figure 9. ENVISAT mode 2, track 163, interferometric stack of Mount St. Helens, Washington, composed of 13 interferograms spanning coeruptive 2004–5 time period.

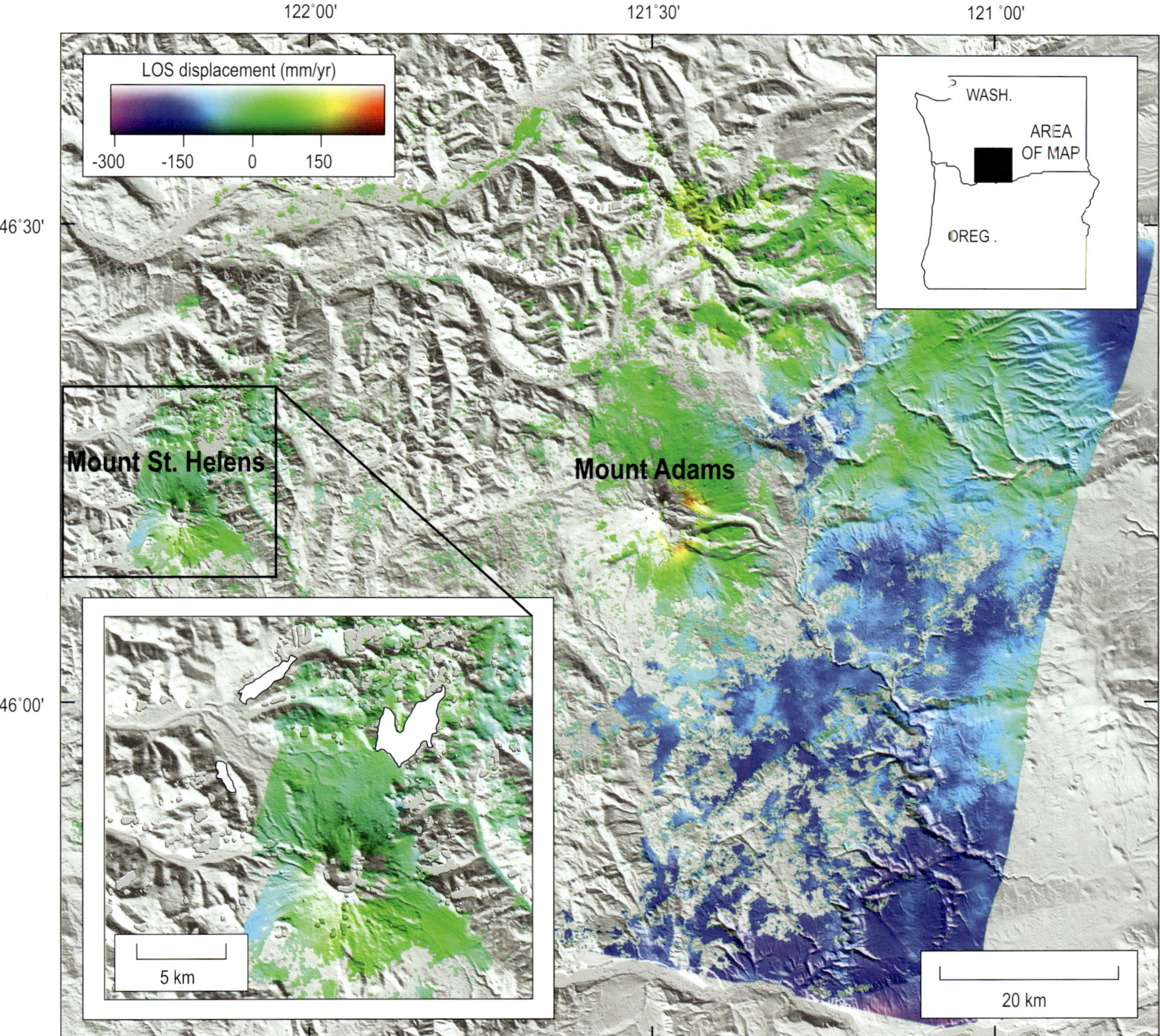

Figure 10. ENVISAT mode 2, track 385, interferometric stack of Mount St. Helens, Washington, composed of three interferograms spanning coeruptive 2004–5 time period. All three interferograms cover times of 70 days or fewer, so stacked phase has low signal-to-noise ratio and is characterized by phase that correlates with topography. This is especially apparent at Mount Adams.

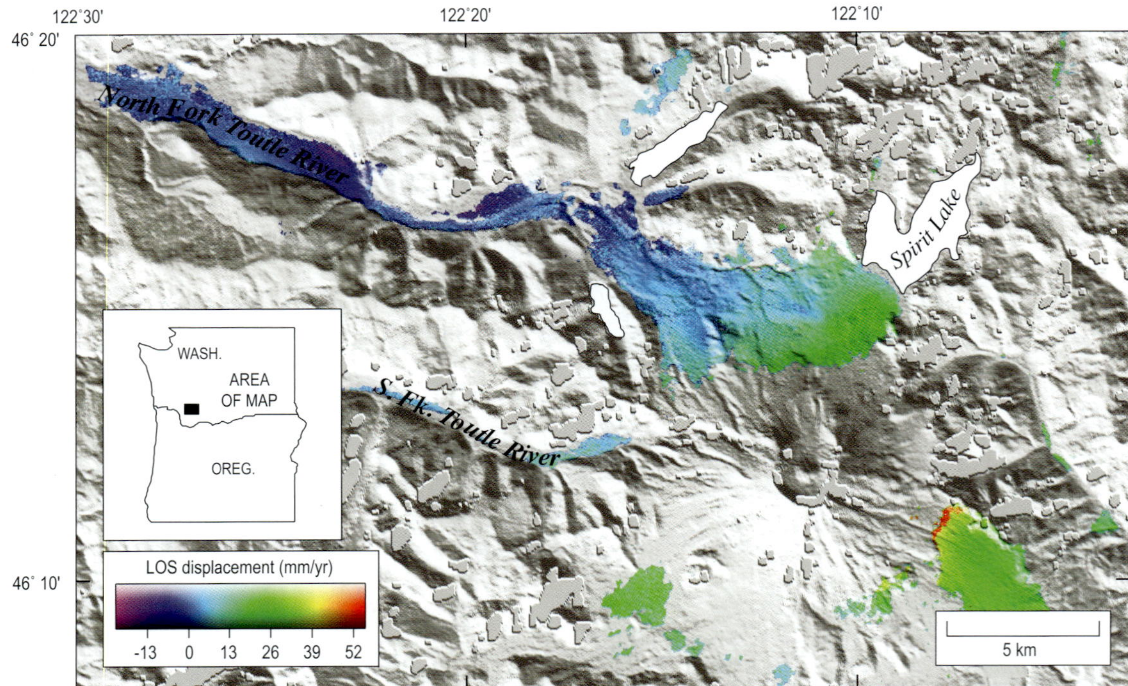

Figure 11. ENVISAT mode 2, track 392, interferometric stack of Mount St. Helens, Washington, composed of six interferograms spanning coeruptive 2004–5 time period.

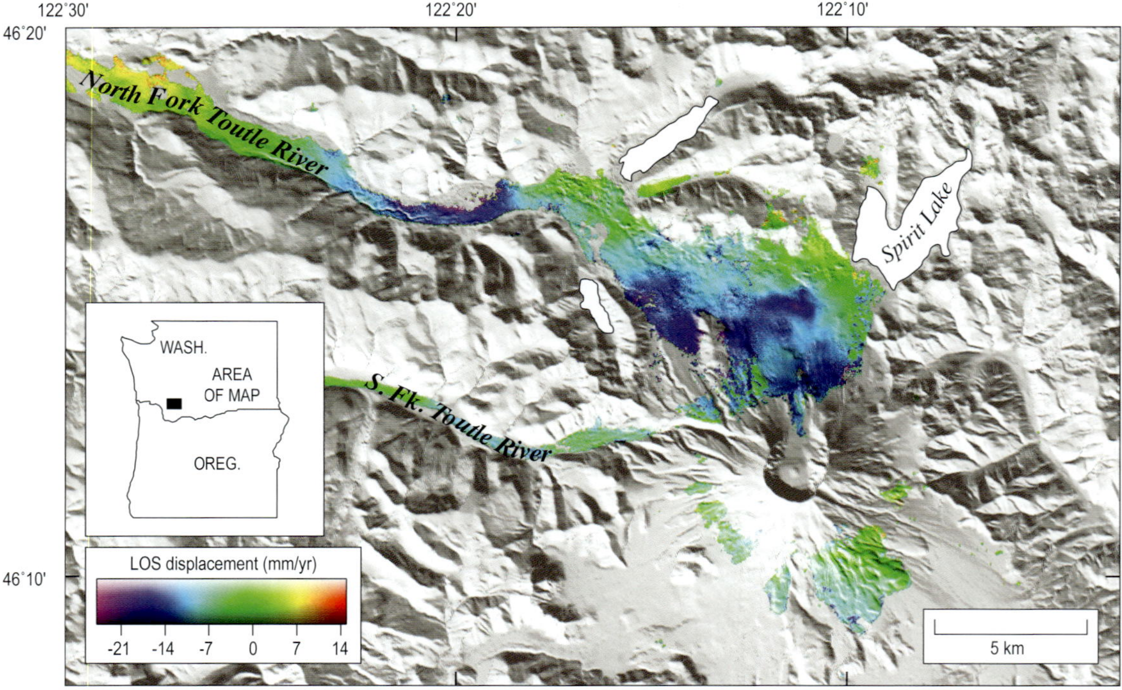

Figure 12. ENVISAT mode 6, track 20, interferometric stack of Mount St. Helens, Washington, composed of 13 interferograms spanning coeruptive 2004–5 time period.

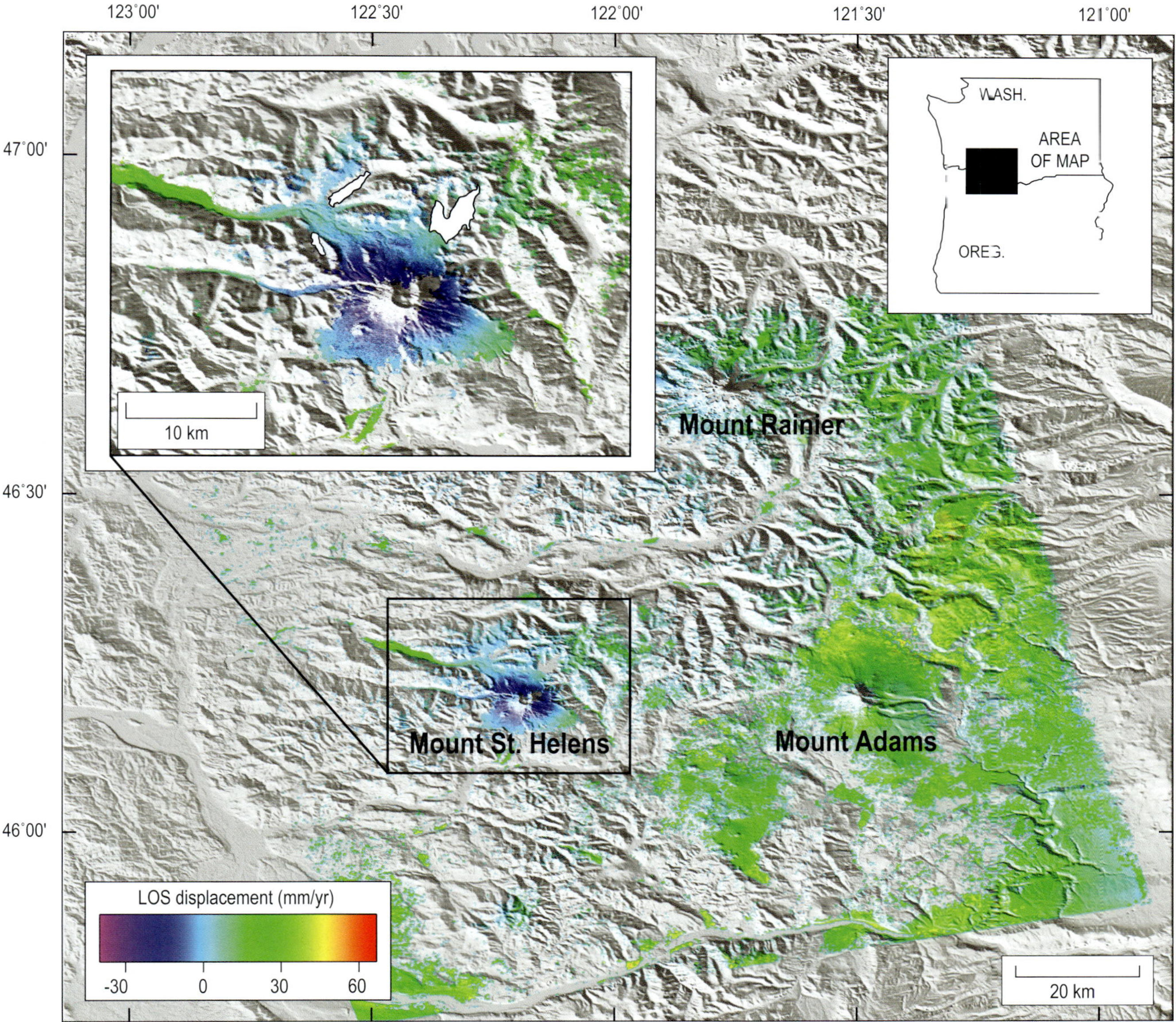

Figure 13. RADARSAT standard mode 2 ascending interferometric stack of Mount St. Helens, Washington, composed of nine interferograms spanning coeruptive 2004–5 time period. Stack clearly shows line-of-sight lengthening (subsidence) centered on Mount St. Helens which, as discussed in text, most likely reflects deformation of the ground surface. Atmospheric artifacts are probably minimized, as suggested by the lack of a significant signal associated with Mount Adams.

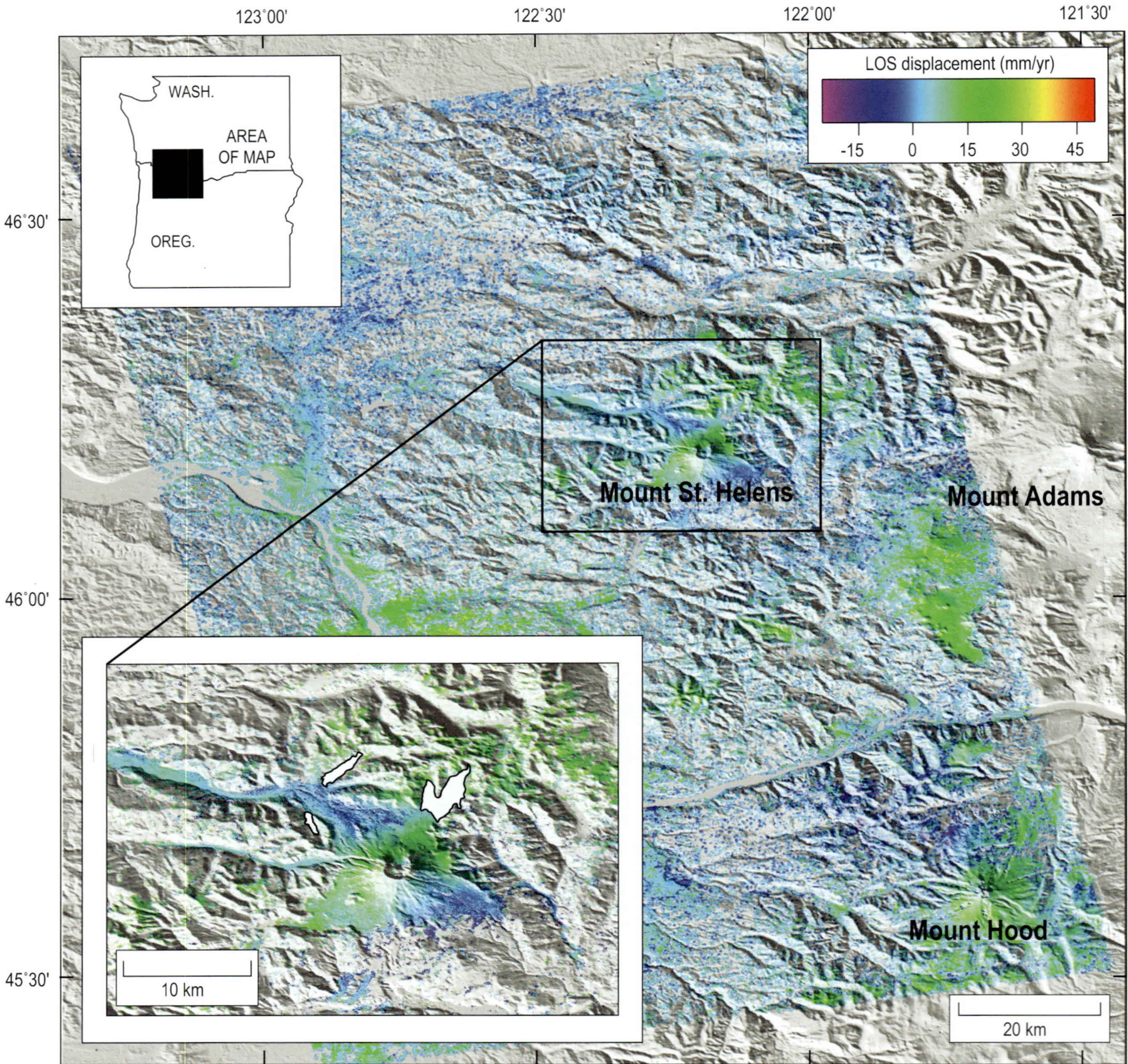

Figure 14. RADARSAT standard mode 5 ascending interferometric stack of Mount St. Helens, Washington, composed of six interferograms spanning coeruptive 2004–5 time period. Topography-correlated phase at Mount Hood suggests the presence of atmospheric artifacts in the stack.

LOS lengthening (subsidence) of at least 40–50 mm/yr centered on Mount St. Helens (the maximum is probably greater but not recoverable given the incoherence in the crater) and extends radially outwards beyond the flanks of the volcano.

Discussion

We modeled the RADARSAT mode 2 dataset (fig. 13) by inverting the LOS displacements for a buried point source of volume change (Mogi, 1958). Other types of sources (for example, an ellipsoid or circular crack) might yield a better fit to the data, but it is difficult to justify the use of more complicated source geometries in light of the limited coherence around Mount St. Helens, especially in the crater area where the deformation appears to reach a maximum. The best-fitting point source is located at a depth of 12 km directly beneath the crater of Mount St. Helens and has a volume loss of 27×10^6 m^3/yr (fig. 15). The depth compares favorably with a point source model based on GPS data (Lisowski and others, this volume, chap. 15), but it is deeper than more-complicated ellipsoidal source models (Lisowski and others, this volume, chap. 15; Mastin and others, this volume, chap. 22) and the 6–10-km-depth range for a proposed magma reservoir based on seismic data (Scandone and Malone, 1985; Barker and Malone, 1991; Moran, 1994; Musumeci and others, 2002). The greater InSAR-derived model depth is probably due to the lack of InSAR data in the crater area and the availability of only a single component of displacement from one interferometric stack.

We also modeled the data using a horizontal dislocation (Okada, 1985) constrained to uniform opening only, which approximates a sill. The best-fitting dislocation was located at a depth of 18 km, much deeper than the point source, but it had a similar volume change of about 30×10^6 m^3/yr. The difference in depths between the point source and dislocation models is unsurprising. A similar relation, for example, was found between point source and horizontal dislocation models of subsidence at Medicine Lake volcano, northern California (Dzurisin and others, 2002). The great variability in depths between the models is an indication of the strong dependence of model fits on model geometry (Delaney and McTigue, 1994). More data, especially from the crater region where displacement magnitudes are greatest, and varied look angles, which would provide additional components of displacement, are required to better constrain the geometry, volume change, and depth of the subsidence source, as well as model error estimates. Using only a single interferometric stack, results are unavoidably more ambiguous.

The modeled volume change is much smaller than the approximately 70×10^6 m^3 extruded over the first year of the eruption, as determined from analyses of digital elevation models (Schilling and others, this volume, chap. 8). Some of the difference may be explained by the fact that the stack averages the initially greater rates of subsidence and extrusion that occurred during the first few weeks of the eruption, but this is probably a minor effect. It is tempting to speculate that most of the discrepancy between modeled and extruded volumes is evidence for replenishment of the midcrustal magma reservoir by an even deeper source. Delaney and McTigue (1994), however, pointed out that the volume of injection should only equal the volume of eruption if the host rock is incompressible—clearly an unrealistic condition. They also demonstrated that modeled volume changes at depth are highly dependent on source geometry. In addition, our models assume a homogenous, isotropic, elastic rheology, which is almost certainly not the case beneath Mount St. Helens, where temperatures will be

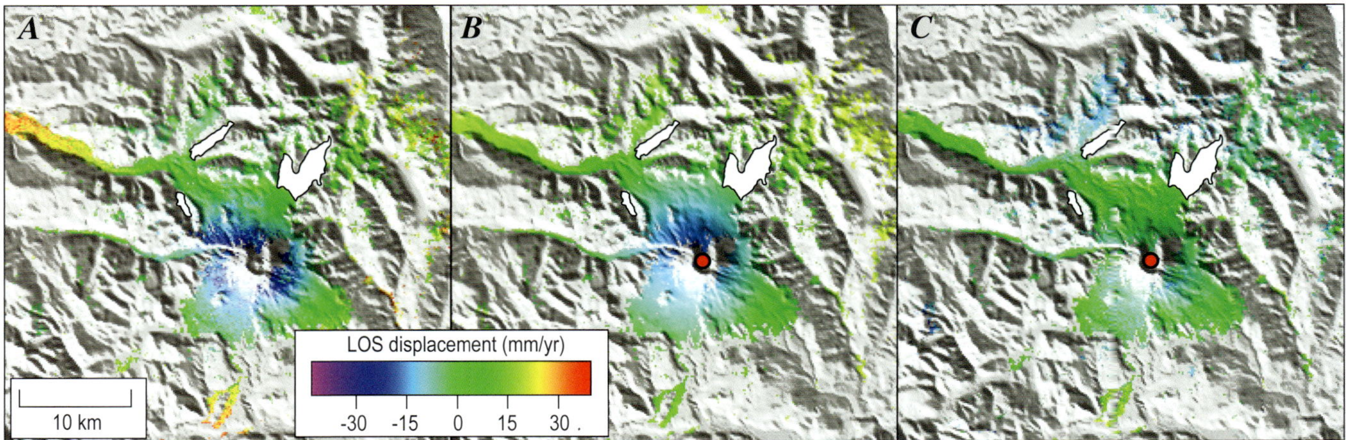

Figure 15. Observed (*A*), predicted (*B*), and residual (*C*) line-of-sight (LOS) displacements for RADARSAT standard mode 2 stack of Mount St. Helens, Washington (fig. 13), resulting from model that assumes point source of volume decrease (red circle) at depth of 12 km. LOS displacements scaled to maximize displacements around Mount St. Helens and differ from those in figure 13 for same interferogram.

elevated above the local geotherm due to the presence of the active magmatic system. Nonelastic rheologies can have a profound effect on the relation between surface deformation volume and source volume or pressure change (for example, Newman and others, 2001, 2006).

Nevertheless, it remains possible that the midcrustal magma reservoir was being replenished during the eruption, and that the discrepancy between modeled and extruded volumes was due to magma extrusion outpacing influx into the reservoir. Any surface inflation that might have resulted from recharge of the reservoir would have been masked by the greater deflation signal resulting from magma withdrawal and depressurization. Mastin and others (this volume, chap. 22) address this possibility in greater detail.

Conclusions

Interferograms from several independent tracks have been examined for signs of pre-and coeruptive deformation at Mount St. Helens. We can find no evidence for volcanowide displacements during time periods covered by stacks of radar interferograms (1992 to late 2001 and early 2003 until the onset of eruptive activity in September 2004). Seismic and geodetic evidence suggests repressurization, and possible resupply, of the 6- to 10-km-depth magma reservoir during the late 1980s and early 1990s, but this activity did not result in surface deformation detectable by InSAR during 1992–2004. We did find several small (1–2-km-diameter) patches of subsidence on the 1980 debris-avalanche deposit, one of which was recognized previously from individual interferograms of Mount St. Helens, and attribute this deformation to viscoelastic relaxation of loosely consolidated substrate under a load, differential consolidation of the deposit, or melting of ice buried within the deposit. Tracking the continued motion of these areas will serve as input for models of the post-depositional behavior of rapidly emplaced, unconsolidated deposits.

Coeruptive interferometric stacks are dominated by atmospheric noise, and only one of the seven stacks we assembled is demonstrably sensitive to deformation on the order of 1 cm or less. This stack indicates volcanowide deflation centered on the crater of Mount St. Helens and can be modeled by a point source of volume loss at a depth of 12 km beneath the edifice. This depth is at the lower boundary of a magma reservoir inferred from seismicity before 2004.

Both the pre- and coeruptive InSAR results have important implications for magma resupply, or lack thereof, before and during the 2004 eruption. Several papers in this volume address this question from differing perspectives and reach differing conclusions (for example, Moran and others, chap. 2; Dzurisin and others, chap. 14; Lisowski and others, chap. 15; Mastin and others, chap. 22; Gerlach and others, chap. 26; Pallister and others, chap. 30). Neither InSAR nor any other single data set can resolve the issue with certainty, but the weight of evidence seems to favor at least a minor amount of magma influx or pressurization of the midcrustal magma reservoir in the years before, and perhaps during, the eruption. The InSAR results, although not directly supportive of the idea, can be reconciled with it if the preeruption changes were small enough, accommodated by inelastic processes that did not measurably deform the surface, or occurred before 1992, and if the coeruption changes reflect a net deflation of the volcano due to extrusion outpacing recharge.

It is worth noting that, in general, the RADARSAT results are more coherent than those from ERS-1/2 and ENVISAT. A possible explanation for this discrepancy is that RADARSAT's H/H polarization provides better coherence in vegetated areas than V/V, which is the standard mode for ERS-1/2 and ENVISAT. Additional investigations into this possibility are warranted, as the result may suggest that one polarization mode is preferred over others for InSAR studies.

Our work has demonstrated the importance of including numerous interferograms in stacks. Coeruption stacks with less than nine input interferograms showed no signs of deflation that is known to be occurring from GPS. That our preeruption stacks span many more years and make use of many more interferograms than the coeruption stacks is the reason for the better signal-to-noise ratio in the preeruption stacks. The addition to the coeruptive stacks of InSAR data that extend through 2006 and beyond, assuming the eruption continues, will significantly reduce the magnitude of the atmospheric noise, allowing for more detailed analysis of surface deformation and associated source mechanisms.

Acknowledgments

Summer Miller provided invaluable assistance in preparing the ERS-1/2 and ENVISAT data sets for stacking. Paul Lundgren provided code for time series analysis, which Sarah Menassian modified for use with this project. Rick Hoblitt and Don Swanson offered much-needed guidance with respect to the emplacement of the Mount St. Helens debris avalanche, and discussions with Jon Major, Dick Iverson, and Joe Walder stimulated a closer look at the subsidence patches in the debris-avalanche deposit. Jon Major's advice concerning the behavior of saturated sedimentary deposits was especially valuable. Oh-Ig Kwoun assisted with processing RADARSAT data. We are indebted to Chuck Wicks, Daniel Dzurisin, and Seth Moran for thoughtful reviews and Jane Takahashi for thorough edits. Figures 1–6 and 8–15 were made using the Generic Mapping Tools (GMT) software (Wessel and Smith, 1998). ERS-1, ERS-2, and ENVISAT SAR data are copyrighted 1992–2005 by ESA and provided by Alaska Satellite Facility (ASF) and ESA Category-1 grants 2648 and 2765. RADARSAT-1 data are copyrighted by Canadian Space Agency and were provided by ASF. We thank the ASF for supporting RADARSAT-1 data acquisitions.

References Cited

Amelung, F., Jónsson, S., Zebker, H., and Segall, P., 2000a, Widespread uplift and 'trapdoor' faulting on Galápagos volcanoes observed with radar interferometry: Nature, v. 407, no. 6807. p. 993–996.

Amelung, F., Oppenheimer, C., Segall, P., and Zebker, H., 2000b, Ground deformation near Gada 'Ale Volcano, Afar, observed by radar interferometry: Geophysical Research Letters, v. 27, no. 19, p. 3093–3096.

Banks, N.G., and Hoblitt, R.P., 1996, Direct temperature studies of the Mount St. Helens deposits, 1980–1981: U.S. Geological Survey Professional Paper 1387, 76 p.

Barker, S.E., and Malone, S.D., 1991, Magmatic system geometry at Mount St. Helens modeled from the stress field associated with posteruptive earthquakes: Journal of Geophysical Research, v. 96, no. B7, p. 11883–11894.

Bawden, G.W., Thatcher, W., Stein, R.S., Hudnit, K.W., and Peltzer, G., 2001, Tectonic contraction across Los Angeles after removal of groundwater pumping effects: Nature, v. 412, no. 6849, p. 812–815.

Beaudecel, F., Briole, P., and Froger, J.-L., 2000, Volcano-wide fringes in ERS synthetic aperture radar interferograms of Etna (1992–1998); deformation or tropospheric effect?: Journal of Geophysical Research, v. 105, no. B7, p. 16391–16402.

Berardino, P., Fornaro, G., Lanari, R., and Sansosti, E., 2002, A new algorithm for surface deformation monitoring based on small baseline differential SAR interferograms: IEEE Transactions on Geoscience and Remote Sensing, v. 40, no. 11, p. 1–10.

Bevington, P.R., and Robinson, D.K., 1992, Data reduction and error analysis for the physical sciences (2d ed.): Boston, McGraw-Hill, 328 p.

Branney, M.J., and Gilbert, J.S., 1995, Ice-melt collapse pits and associated features in the 1991 lahar deposits of Volcán Hudson, Chile—criteria to distinguish eruption-induced glacier melt: Bulletin of Volcanology, v. 57, no. 5, p. 293–302.

Briole, P., Massonnet, D., and Delacourt, C., 1997, Post-eruptive deformation associated with the 1986–87 and 1989 lava flows of Etna detected by radar interferometry: Geophysical Research Letters, v. 24, no. 1, p. 37–40.

Brugman, M.M., and Meier, M.F., 1981, Response of glaciers to the eruptions of Mount St. Helens, *in* Lipman, P.W., and Mullineaux, D.R., eds., The 1980 eruptions of Mount St. Helens, Washington: U.S. Geological Survey Professional Paper 1250, p. 743–756.

Cashman, K.V., 1988, Crystallization of Mount St. Helens 1980–1986 dacite: a quantitative textural approach: Bulletin of Volcanology, v. 50, no. 3, p. 194–209.

Cashman, K.V., 1992, Groundmass crystallization of Mount St, Helens dacite, 1980–1986; a tool for interpreting shallow magmatic processes: Contributions to Mineralogy and Petrology, v. 109, no. 4, p. 431–449, doi:10.1007/BF00306547.

Chen, C.W., and Zebker, H.A., 2001, Two-dimensional phase unwrapping with use of statistical models for cost functions in nonlinear optimization: Journal of the Optical Society of America A, v. 18, no. 2, p. 338–351.

Crandell, D.R., 1987, Deposits of pre-1980 pyroclastic flows and lahars from Mount St. Helens volcano, Washington: U.S. Geological Survey Professional Paper 1444, 91 p.

Delaney, P.T., and McTigue, D.F., 1994, Volume of magma accumulation or withdrawal estimated from surface uplift or subsidence, with application to the 1960 collapse of Kilauea Volcano: Bulletin of Volcanology, v. 56, nos. 6–7, p. 417–424.

Diefenbach, A.K., and Poland, M.P., 2003, InSAR analysis of surface deformation at Mount St. Helens, Washington [abs.]: Geological Society of America Abstracts with Programs, v. 35, no. 6, p. 562.

Dzurisin, D., 2003, A comprehensive approach to monitoring volcano deformation as a window on the eruption cycle: Reviews of Geophysics, v. 41, no. 1, 29 p., doi:1010,1029/2001RG000107.

Dzurisin D., Poland, M.P., and Bürgmann, R., 2002, Steady subsidence of Medicine Lake volcano, northern California, revealed by repeated leveling surveys: Journal of Geophysical Research, v. 107, no. B12, doi:10.1029/2001JB000893.

Dzurisin, D., Lisowski, M., Wicks, C.W., Jr., Poland, M.P., and Endo, E.T., 2006, Geodetic observations and modeling of ongoing inflation at the Three Sisters volcanic center, central Oregon Cascade Range, USA: Journal of Volcanology and Geothermal Research, v. 150, nos. 1–3, p. 35–54.

Dzurisin, D., Lisowski, M., Poland, M P., Sherrod, D.R., and LaHusen, R.G., 2008, Constraints and conundrums resulting from ground-deformation measurements made during the 2004–2005 dome-building eruption of Mount St. Helens, Washington, chap. 14 *of* Sherrod, D.R., Scott, W.E., and Stauffer, P.H., eds., A volcano rekindled; the renewed eruption of Mount St. Helens, 2004–2006: U.S. Geological Survey Professional Paper 1750 (this volume).

Evarts, R.C., Ashley, R.P., and Smith, J.G., 1987, Geology of the Mount St. Helens area: Record of discontinuous volcanic and plutonic activity in the Cascade arc of southern Washington: Journal of Geophysical Research, v. 92, no. B10, p. 10155–10169.

Everest, J., and Bradwell, T., 2003, Buried glacier ice in southern Iceland and its wider significance: Geomorphology, v. 52, nos. 3–4, p. 347–358

Farr, T.G., and Kobrick, M., 2000, Shuttle Radar Topography Mission produces a wealth of data: Eos (American Geophysical Union Transactions), v. 81, no. 48, p. 583, 585.

Fairchild, L.H., 1987, The importance of lahar initiation processes, *in* Costa, J.E., and Wieczorek, G.F., eds., Debris flows/avalanches—processes, recognition, and mitigation: Geological Society of America Reviews in Engineering Geology 7, p. 51–61.

Fialko, Y., and Simons, M., 2001, Evidence for on-going inflation of the Socorro magma body, New Mexico, from Interferometric Synthetic Aperture Radar imaging: Geophysical Research Letters, v. 28, no. 18, p. 3549–3552.

Gerlach, T.M., McGee, K.A., and Doukas, M.P., 2008, Emission rates of CO_2, SO_2, and H_2S, scrubbing, and preeruption excess volatiles at Mount St. Helens, 2004–2005, chap. 26 *of* Sherrod, D.R., Scott, W.E., and Stauffer, P.H., eds., A volcano rekindled; the renewed eruption of Mount St. Helens, 2004–2006: U.S. Geological Survey Professional Paper 1750 (this volume).

Glicken, H., 1996, Rockslide-debris avalanche of May 18, 1980, Mount St. Helens volcano, Washington: U.S. Geological Survey Open-File Report 96–677, 90 p.

Goldstein, R.M., and Werner, C.L., 1998, Radar interferogram filtering for geophysical applications: Geophysical Research Letters, v. 25, no. 21, p. 4035–4038.

Hoblitt, R.P., Reynolds, R.L., and Larson, E.E., 1985, Suitability of nonwelded pyroclastic-flow deposits for studies of magnetic secular variation—a test based on deposits emplaced at Mount St. Helens, Washington, in 1980: Geology, v. 13, no. 4, p. 242–245.

Hooper, A., Zebker, H., Segall, P., and Kampes, B., 2004, A new method for measuring deformation on volcanoes and other natural terrains using InSAR persistent scatterers: Geophysical Research Letters, v. 31, no. 23, doi:10.1029/2004GL021737.

LaHusen, R.G., Swinford, K.J., Logan, M., and Lisowski, M., 2008, Instrumentation in remote and dangerous settings; examples using data from GPS "spider" deployments during the 2004–2005 eruption of Mount St. Helens, Washington, chap. 16 *of* Sherrod, D.R., Scott, W.E., and Stauffer, P.H., eds., A volcano rekindled; the renewed eruption of Mount St. Helens, 2004–2006: U.S. Geological Survey Professional Paper 1750 (this volume).

Lees, J.M., 1992, The magma system of Mount St. Helens; nonlinear high-resolution P-wave tomography: Journal of Volcanology and Geothermal Research, v. 53, nos. 1–4, p. 103–116.

Lisowski, M., Dzurisin, D., Endo, E.T., Iwatsubo, E.Y., and Poland, M.P., 2003, New results from a proposed PBO Cascade Volcano cluster III; post-eruptive deformation of Mount St. Helens, Washington, from EDM and GPS [abs.]: Geological Society of America Abstracts with Programs, v. 35, no. 6, p. 562.

Lisowski, M., Dzurisin, D., Denlinger, R.P., and Iwatsubo, E.Y., 2008, Analysis of GPS-measured deformation associated with the 2004–2006 dome-building eruption of Mount St. Helens, Washington, chap. 15 *of* Sherrod, D.R., Scott, W.E., and Stauffer, P.H., eds., A volcano rekindled; the renewed eruption of Mount St. Helens, 2004–2006: U.S. Geological Survey Professional Paper 1750 (this volume).

Lu, Z., Wicks, C.W., Jr., Power, J.A., and Dzurisin, D., 2000, Ground deformation associated with the March 1996 earthquake swarm at Akutan volcano, Alaska, revealed by satellite radar interferometry: Journal of Geophysical Research, v. 105, no. B9, p. 21483–21495.

Lu, Z., Power, J.A., McConnell, V.S., Wicks, C.W., Jr., and Dzurisin, D., 2002a, Preeruptive inflation and surface interferometric coherence characteristics revealed by satellite radar interferometry at Makushin Volcano, Alaska, 1993–2000: Journal of Geophysical Research, v. 107, no. B11, doi:10.1029/2001JB000970.

Lu, Z., Wicks, C.W., Jr., Dzurisin, D., Power, J.A., Moran, S.C., and Thatcher, W., 2002b, Magmatic inflation at a dormant stratovolcano; 1996–1998 activity at Mount Peulik volcano, Alaska, revealed by satellite radar interferometry: Journal of Geophysical Research, v. 107, no. B7, doi:10.1029/2001JB000471.

Lu, Z., Masterlark, T., Dzurisin, D., Rykhus, R., and Wicks, C.W., Jr., 2003a, Magma supply dynamics at Westdahl volcano, Alaska, modeled from satellite radar interferometry: Journal of Geophysical Research, v. 108, no. B7, 17 p., doi:10.1029/2002JB002311.

Lu, Z., Wicks, C.W., Jr., Dzurisin, D., Power, J., Thatcher, W., and Masterlark, T., 2003b, Interferometric Synthetic Aperture Radar studies of Alaska volcanoes: Earth Observation Magazine, v. 12, no. 3, p. 8–18.

Lu, Z., Masterlark, T., and Dzurisin, D., 2005a, Interferometric Synthetic Aperture Radar (InSAR) study of Okmok Volcano, Alaska, 1992–2003; magma supply dynamics and post-emplacement lava flow deformation: Journal of Geophysical Research, v. 110, no. B2, doi:10.01029/02004JB003148.

Lu, Z., Wicks, C.W., Jr., Kwoun, O.-I., Power, J.A., and Dzurisin, D., 2005b, Surface deformation associated with the March 1996 earthquake swarm at Akutan Island, Alaska, revealed by C-band ERS and L-band JERS radar interferometry: Canadian Journal of Remote Sensing, v. 31, no. 1, p. 7–20.

Lundgren, P., Casu, F., Manzo, M., Pepe, A., Berardino, P., Sansosti, E., and Lanari, R., 2004, Gravity and magma-induced spreading of Mount Etna Volcano revealed by satellite radar interferometry: Geophysical Research Letters, v. 31, no. 4, doi:10.01029/02003GL018736.

Major, J.J., 2000, Gravity-driven consolidation of granular slurries—implications for debris-flow deposition and deposit characteristics: Journal of Sedimentary Research, v. 70, no. 1, p. 64–83.

Masterlark, T., and Lu, Z., 2004, Transient volcano deformation sources imaged with interferometric synthetic aperture radar—application to Seguam Island, Alaska: Journal of Geophysical Research, v. 109, no. B1, doi:10.1029/2003JB002568.

Masterlark, T., Lu, Z., and Rykhus, R., 2006, Thickness distribution of a cooling pyroclastic flow deposit on Augustine Volcano, Alaska—optimization using InSAR, FEMs, and an adaptive mesh algorithm: Journal of Volcanology and Geothermal Research, v. 150, nos. 1–3, p. 186–201.

Mastin, L.G., 1994, Explosive tephra emissions at Mount St. Helens, 1989–1991; the violent escape of magmatic gas following storms?: Geological Society of America Bulletin, v. 106, no. 2, p. 175–185.

Mastin, L.G., Roeloffs, E., Beeler, N.M., and Quick, J.E., 2008, Constraints on the size, overpressure, and volatile content of the Mount St. Helens magma system from geodetic and dome-growth measurements during the 2004–2006+ eruption, chap. 22 *of* Sherrod, D.R., Scott, W.E., and Stauffer, P.H., eds., A volcano rekindled; the renewed eruption of Mount St. Helens, 2004–2006: U.S. Geological Survey Professional Paper 1750 (this volume).

Matthews, J.P., Kamata, H., Okuyama, S., Yusa, Y., and Shimizu, H., 2003, Surface height adjustments in pyroclastic-flow deposits observed at Unzen volcano by JERS-1 SAR interferometry: Journal of Volcanology and Geothermal Research, v. 125, nos. 3–4, p. 247–270.

Mogi, K., 1958, Relations between the eruptions of various volcanoes and the deformations of the ground surfaces around them: Bulletin of the Earthquake Research Institute, v. 36, no. 2, p. 99–134.

Moran, S.C., 1994, Seismicity at Mount St. Helens, 1987–1992: Evidence for repressurization of an active magmatic system: Journal of Geophysical Research, v. 99, no. B3, p. 4341–4354.

Moran, S.C., Kwoun, O.-I., Masterlark, T., and Lu, Z., 2006, On the absence of InSAR-detected volcano deformation spanning the 1995–1996 and 1999 eruptions of Shishaldin Volcano, Alaska: Journal of Volcanology and Geothermal Research, v. 150, nos. 1–3, p. 119–131.

Moran, S.C., Malone, S.D., Qamar, A.I., Thelen, W.A., Wright, A.K., and Caplan-Auerbach, J., 2008, Seismicity associated with renewed dome building at Mount St. Helens, 2004–2005, chap. 2 *of* Sherrod, D.R., Scott, W.E., and Stauffer, P.H., eds., A volcano rekindled; the renewed eruption of Mount St. Helens, 2004–2006: U.S. Geological Survey Professional Paper 1750 (this volume).

Musumeci, C., Gresta, S., and Malone, S.D., 2002, Magma system recharge of Mount St. Helens from precise relative hypocenter location of microearthquakes: Journal of Geophysical Research, v. 107, no. B10, 2264, p. ESE 16-1–ESE 16-9, doi:10.1029/2001JB000629.

Newman, A.V., Dixon, T.H., Ofoegbu, G.I., and Dixon, J.E., 2001, Geodetic and seismic constraints on recent activity at Long Valley Caldera, California; evidence for viscoelastic rheology: Journal of Volcanology and Geothermal Research, v. 105, no. 3, p. 183–206.

Newman, A.V., Dixon, T.H., and Gourmelen, N., 2006, A four-dimensional viscoelastic deformation model for Long Valley caldera, California, between 1995 and 2000: Journal of Volcanology and Geothermal Research, v. 150, nos. 1–3, p. 244–269.

Okada, Y., 1985, Surface deformation due to shear and tensile faults in a half-space: Bulletin of the Seismological Society of America, v. 75, no. 4, p. 1135–1154.

Pallister, J.S., Hoblitt, R.P., Crandell, D.R., and Mullineaux, D.R., 1992, Mount St. Helens a decade after the 1980 eruptions; magmatic models, chemical cycles, and a revised hazards assessment: Bulletin of Volcanology, v. 54, no. 2, p. 126–146, doi: 10.1007/BF00278003.

Pallister, J.S., Thornber, C.R., Cashman, K.V., Clynne, M.A., Lowers, H.A., Mandeville, C.W., Brownfield, I.K., and Meeker, G.P., 2008, Petrology of the 2004–2006 Mount St. Helens lava dome—implications for magmatic plumbing and eruption triggering, chap. 30 *of* Sherrod, D.R., Scott, W.E., and Stauffer, P.H., eds., A volcano rekindled; the renewed eruption of Mount St. Helens, 2004–2006: U.S. Geological Survey Professional Paper 1750 (this volume).

Peltzer, G., Crampé, F., Hensley, S., and Rosen, P., 2001, Transient strain accumulation and fault interaction in the Eastern California shear zone: Geology, v. 29, no. 11, p. 975–978.

Pritchard, M.E., and Simons, M., 2002, A satellite geodetic survey of large-scale deformation of volcanic centres in the central Andes: Nature, v. 418, no. 6894, p. 167–171.

Pritchard, M.E., and Simons, M., 2004a, An InSAR-based survey of volcanic deformation in the central Andes: Geochemistry, Geophysics, Geosystems, v. 5, no. 2, doi:02010.01029/02003GC000610.

Pritchard, M.E., and Simons, M., 2004b, An InSAR-based survey of volcanic deformation in the southern Andes: Geophysical Research Letters, v. 31, no. 15, doi:10.1029/2004GL020545.

Rowley, P.D., Kuntz, M.A., and MacLeod, N.S., 1981, Pyroclastic-flow deposits, *in* Lipman, P.W., and Mullineaux, D.R., eds., The 1980 eruptions of Mount St. Helens, Washington: U.S. Geological Survey Professional Paper 1250, p. 489–512.

Rutherford, M.J., Sigurdsson, H., Carey, S., and Davis, A., 1985, The May 18, 1980, eruption of Mount St. Helens—1. Melt composition and experimental phase equilibria: Journal of Geophysical Research, v. 90, no. B4, p. 2929–2947.

Scandone, R., and Malone, S.D., 1985, Magma supply, magma discharge and readjustment of the feeding system of Mount St. Helens during 1980: Journal of Volcanology and Geothermal Research, v. 23, nos. 3–4, p. 239–262, doi:10.1016/0377-0273(85)90036-8.

Schilling, S.P., Carrara, P.E., Thompson, R.A., and Iwatsubo, E.Y., 2004, Posteruption glacier development within the crater of Mount St. Helens, Washington, USA: Quaternary Research, v. 61, no. 3, p. 325–329.

Schilling, S.P., Thompson, R.A., Messerich, J.A., and Iwatsubo, E.Y., 2008, Use of digital aerophotogrammetry to determine rates of lava dome growth, Mount St. Helens, Washington, 2004–2005, chap. 8 *of* Sherrod, D.R., Scott, W.E., and Stauffer, P.H., eds., A volcano rekindled; the renewed eruption of Mount St. Helens, 2004–2006: U.S. Geological Survey Professional Paper 1750 (this volume).

Stevens, N.F., Wadge, G., Williams, C.A., Morley, J.G., Muller, J.-P., Murray, J.B., and Upton, M., 2001, Surface movements of emplaced lava flows measured by synthetic aperture radar interferometry: Journal of Geophysical Research, v. 106, no. B6, p. 11293–11313.

Voight, B., Glicken, H., Janda, R.J., and Douglass, P.M., 1981, Catastrophic rockslide avalanche of May 18, *in* Lipman, P.W., and Mullineaux, D.R., eds., The 1980 eruptions of Mount St. Helens, Washington: U.S. Geological Survey Professional Paper 1250, p. 347–377.

Wadge, G., Mattioli, G.S., and Herd, R.A., 2006, Ground deformation at Soufrière Hills Volcano, Montserrat during 1998–2000 measured by radar interferometry and GPS: Journal of Volcanology and Geothermal Research, v. 152, nos. 1–2, p. 157–173.

Walder, J.S., Schilling, S.P., Vallance, J.W., and LaHusen, R.G., 2008, Effects of lava-dome growth on the Crater Glacier of Mount St. Helens, Washington, chap. 13 *of* Sherrod, D.R., Scott, W.E., and Stauffer, P.H., eds., A volcano rekindled; the renewed eruption of Mount St. Helens, 2004–2006: U.S. Geological Survey Professional Paper 1750 (this volume).

Wessel, P., and Smith, W.H.F., 1998, New, improved version of Generic Mapping Tools released [abs.]: Eos (American Geophysical Union Transactions), v. 79, no. 47, p. 579.

Wicks, C.W., Jr., Thatcher, W., and Dzurisin, D., 1998, Migration of fluids beneath Yellowstone Caldera inferred from satellite radar interferometry: Science, v. 282, no. 5388, p. 458–462.

Wicks, C.W., Jr., Dzurisin, D., Ingebritsen, S., Thatcher, W., Lu, Z., and Iverson, J., 2002, Magmatic activity beneath the quiescent Three Sisters volcanic center, central Oregon Cascade Range, USA: Geophysical Research Letters, v. 29, no. 7, doi:10.1029/2001GL014205.

Wicks, C.W., Thatcher, W., Dzurisin, D., and Svarc, J., 2006, Uplift, thermal unrest, and magma intrusion at Yellowstone caldera: Nature, v. 440, no. 7080, p. 72–75, doi:10.1038/nature04507.

Wright, T., Parsons, B., and Fielding, E., 2001, Measurement of interseismic strain accumulation across the North Anatolian Fault by satellite radar interferometry: Geophysical Research Letters, v. 28, no. 10, p. 2117–2120.

Wright, T.J., Parsons, B., England, P.C., and Fielding, E.J., 2004, InSAR observations of low slip rates on the major faults of western Tibet: Science, v. 305, no. 5681, p. 236–239.

Zebker, H.A., Amelung, F., and Jonsson, S., 2000, Remote sensing of volcano surface and internal processes using radar interferometry, *in* Mouginis-Mark, P.J., Crisp, J.A., and Fink, J.H., eds., Remote sensing of active volcanism: Washington, D.C., American Geophysical Union Geophysical Monograph 116, p. 179–205.

Models and Mechanics of Eruptive Processes

Empirical data from seismology, geophysics, field geology, and petrology give us the precursory signals and ongoing history of the eruption. However, to understand how volcanoes work—and, consequently, to have a volcano-monitoring program with predictive value—requires deeper insight into an eruption's physical mechanisms. A "sticky piston" model of solid-state extrusion was suggested by the drumbeat aspect of the 2004–6 eruption's seismicity. Geologists made a renewed effort to catch the stick-slip process in action, using fixed-camera photography to monitor its visual manifestation and borehole tiltmeters to measure the associated inflation-deflation cycles expected in local ground deformation.

Laboratory testing of the gouge that encases the extruding dome indicates material properties suitable for the sticky-piston model to predict episodic, seismogenic slip, namely plug stiffness that exceeds that of the rising fluid magma and rate-weakening gouge friction at low slip rates. Textural evidence indicates that crystallization and solidification of the ascending magma preceded gouge formation. Comparison of groundmass textures from dome lavas and fault gouge suggests that brittle fracture was confined to the upper 1 km of the conduit. Textural similarity between gouge and the ash emitted by explosions from spine margins in January and March 2005 suggests that fragmentation preceded rather than accompanied these explosions.

Eruption rates and modeling of the magma reservoir allow reasonable fits to either exponential or logarithmic decay curves. For each of these, however, the history of reservoir decompression forms an imperfect match to the rapid, radially inward motion of the ground surface during the first month of the eruption, as deduced from displacement data from the continually transmitting GPS station located 9 km from the vent. That movement suggests that erupted magma was replaced by recharge, but that the recharge rate remained less than the eruption's characteristic effusion rate.

Spine 4 on February 22, 2005. View to east-southeast. Shoestring notch is low point on east crater rim. USGS photo by S.P. Schilling.

A Volcano Rekindled: The Renewed Eruption of Mount St. Helens, 2004–2006
Edited by David R. Sherrod, William E. Scott, and Peter H. Stauffer
U.S. Geological Survey Professional Paper 1750, 2008

Chapter 19

From Dome to Dust: Shallow Crystallization and Fragmentation of Conduit Magma During the 2004–2006 Dome Extrusion of Mount St. Helens, Washington

By Katharine V. Cashman[1], Carl R. Thornber[2], and John S. Pallister[2]

Abstract

An unusual feature of the 2004–6 eruptive activity of Mount St. Helens has been the continuous growth of successive spines that are mantled by thick fault gouge. Fault gouge formation requires, first, solidification of ascending magma within the conduit, then brittle fragmentation and cataclastic flow. We document these processes through field relations, hand samples, and thin-section textures. Field observations show that the gouge zone is typically 1–3 m thick and that it includes cataclasite and, locally, breccia in addition to unconsolidated (true) gouge. The gouge contains multiple slickenside sets oriented subparallel to each other and to the striation direction, as well as surface striations parallel to extrusion direction. Hand specimens show the cataclasite and gouge to be composed of a wide size range of broken dome and wall-rock fragments. This grain-size heterogeneity is even more pronounced in thin section, where individual samples contain fragments that span more than four orders of magnitude in size (from more than 10 to less than 10^{-3} mm).

Textures preserved within the gouge zone provide evidence of different processes operating in time and space. Most individual fragments are holocrystalline, suggesting that crystallization of the ascending magma preceded gouge formation. Cataclasite samples preserve a wide range of clast sizes; pronounced rounding of many clasts indicates extensive abrasion during transport. Within the gouge, crystals and lava fragments adjacent to finely comminuted shear zones (slickensides) are shattered into small, angular fragments that are either preserved in place, with little disruption, or incorporated into shear trains, creating a well-developed foliation. Together, evidence of initial grain shattering, followed by shear, grinding, and wear, suggests extensive transport distances (large strains). Textural transitions are often abrupt, indicating extreme shear localization during transport. Comparison of groundmass textures from dome lavas and fault gouge further suggests that brittle fracture was confined to the upper 400–500 m of the conduit. Observed magma extrusion (ascent) rates of ~7 m/d (8×10^{-5} m/s) permit several weeks for magma ascent from ~1,000 m (where groundmass crystallization becomes important) to ~500 m (where solidification nears completion). Brittle fracture, cataclastic flow, and shear localization (slickenside formation) probably dominated in the upper 500 m of the conduit.

Comparison of eruptive conditions during the 2004–6 activity at Mount St. Helens with those of other spine-forming eruptions suggests that magma ascent rates of about 10^{-4} m/s or less allow sufficient degassing and crystallization within the conduit to form large volcanic spines of intermediate composition (andesite to dacite). Solidification deep within the conduit, in turn, requires transport of the solid plug over long distances (hundreds of meters); resultant large strains are responsible for extensive brittle breakage and development of thick gouge zones. Moreover, similarities between gouge textures and those of ash emitted by explosions from spine margins indicate that fault gouge is the origin for the ash. As the comminution and generation of ash-sized particles was clearly a multistep process, this observation suggests that fragmentation preceded, rather than accompanied, these explosions.

Introduction

The 2004–6 eruption of Mount St. Helens has been characterized by steady lava effusion in the form of a succession of smooth-surfaced dacitic spines (Scott and others, this volume,

[1] Department of Geological Sciences, 1272 University of Oregon, Eugene, OR 97403

[2] U.S. Geological Survey, 1300 SE Cardinal Court, Vancouver, WA 98683

chap. 1) that are remarkable for the striated fault gouge that forms a carapace on each of the seven spines erupted between October 2004 and February 2006. This fault gouge is unusually well preserved and well sampled, thanks to helicopter dredging operations (see Pallister and others, this volume, chap. 30). Additional geophysical constraints on dome extrusion include photogrammetry (Schilling and others, this volume, chap. 8), thermal observations (Schneider and others, this volume, chap. 17), and seismic observations (Moran and others, this volume, chap. 2). Notable in these observations is the remarkable steadiness of both the extrusion and accompanying "drumbeat" earthquakes, all of which appear to originate at depths <1 km directly below the growing dome (Moran and others, this volume, chap. 2) and are interpreted to record steady stick-slip behavior of the ascending magma plug (Iverson and others, 2006; Iverson, this volume, chap. 21).

Individual outcrops document an abrupt transition from competent flow-banded dacite to a zone of breccia and cataclasite to finely comminuted and variably consolidated gouge. In this paper we use field, hand-specimen, and thin-section observations of these cataclastic dome facies to constrain some of the physical processes related to dome extrusion and gouge formation. Analysis of observations over this range in scale allows us to (1) describe progressive fragmentation of the solid dome rock to fine-grained fault gouge, (2) trace decompression/crystallization paths within the conduit, and (3) provide depth constraints on both solidification and onset of brittle deformation. We then link processes of fragmentation and gouge formation to relative rates of ascent (shear), degassing, and crystallization. This linkage is important both for recognizing conditions that may lead to changes in the emplacement conditions of the current dome at Mount St. Helens and for generalizing observations at Mount St. Helens to other recent effusive eruptions of intermediate composition magma. In addition, the spectacular preservation of fault textures allows us to extend analysis of tectonic gouge formation to volcanic environments and to compare brittle deformation processes in highly crystalline dacite with those of tuffisites in obsidian flows. Finally, the similarity of clasts preserved within the gouge to those found within ash from dome explosions (Rowe and others, this volume, chap. 29) allows us to speculate on the nature of explosions that have accompanied dome formation.

Background

As detailed descriptions of lava dome emplacement are provided in other papers in this volume (Scott and others, chap. 1; Schilling and others, chap. 8; Vallance and others, chap. 9), we briefly review only the elements of the dome's emplacement history that are directly relevant to the conditions of gouge formation. We then provide an overview of spine formation at other volcanoes, with a particular emphasis on both observations of spine emplacement and eruption conditions that produced these features. Finally, we discuss observational and experimental constraints on decompression-driven crystallization required to form spines.

2004–2006 Activity at Mount St. Helens

After about three weeks of precursory seismic unrest and phreatic explosions in late September and early October of 2004, a dacite lava spine emerged within the central crater of Mount St. Helens, to the south of the 1980–86 lava dome. Extrusion has been continuous since mid-October 2004, with emplacement and partial to complete disintegration of seven individual spines. Extrusion rates were highest, about 6 m^3/s, during the first month of the eruption, after which they dropped to 1–2 m^3/s. Linear rates of spine emergence from the vent have also been constant at 3–6 m/day ($3.5–7\times10^{-5}$ m/s), except during the early stages of extrusion when rates were about twice as fast. Extrusion has been accompanied by only two major explosions—one on January 16, 2005, and another on March 8, 2005. Ash produced by those explosions is described by Rowe and others (this volume, chap. 29).

Lava Dome Emplacement and Morphology

Howel Williams (1932) presented the first comprehensive description of volcanic dome emplacement. He used the term "dome" to describe viscous lava protrusions that could be subdivided into (1) "plug domes" (spines), (2) "endogenous domes" that grow by expansion from within and (3) "exogenous domes" built by surface effusion, usually from a central summit crater. He noted that effusion rate (Q) provided the strongest control on growth style, with the lowest effusion rate leading to plug dome (spine) formation. As a type example for plug-dome behavior he used the famous spine extruded from Mont Pelée, Martinique, in 1903. This massive spine reached a maximum height of >300 m, grew as rapidly as 25 meters in a day (2.9×10^{-4} m/s), and was disrupted continually by both collapse and explosions. The spine was described by Jaggar (1904) as " * * * a most extraordinary monolith, shaped like the dorsal fin of a shark, with a steep and almost overhanging escarpment on the east, while the western aspect of the spine was curved and smooth in profile. The field glass showed jagged surfaces on the steeper eastern side, and long smooth striated slopes on the western" (fig. 1). These smooth, striated slopes also preserved slickensides and breccias produced by differential movement of already solid lava. Lacroix (1904) noted both vertical striations parallel to the extrusion direction and horizontal ridges indicating "successive stages in its upheaval" (Williams, 1932).

Recent eruptions at Mount St. Helens, Washington; Unzen, Japan; and Soufrière Hills, Montserrat, confirm and extend these early concepts. Dome growth at Mount St. Helens from 1980 to 1986 had both exogenous and endogenous phases and erupted a total volume of 0.077 km^3 of dacite magma (62.5–63.5 weight percent SiO_2; Swanson and Holcomb 1990).

Exogenous growth of individual flow lobes was the dominant dome growth mechanism through 1981, with lobes emplaced at rates of 9–24 m^3/s during time periods of less than a week. Exogenous dome lobes were also emplaced from March 1984 until October 1986, although accompanying endogenous growth became increasingly important during this time period (Fink and others, 1990). Times of anomalous activity included (1) March 1982, when a protracted effusive event (24 days at an average rate of 1.6 m^3/s) was preceded by deep seismicity and a vulcanian explosion; (2) February 1983–February 1984, when effusion was continuous at a rate of 0.7 m^3/s (approximately equivalent to the long-term magma supply rate from October 1980 to October 1981) and dome growth was primarily endogenous; and (3) May 1985, when effusion lasted 17 days (at an average rate of 2.9 m^3/s). Only two spines were emplaced during the 1980–86 effusive activity, one in February 1983, during the period of continuous endogenous growth, and one in May 1985, at the end of a protracted (and largely endogenous) dome growth episode. Magma batches feeding individual exogenous dome lobes ascended at 0.1–1 m/s (Chadwick and others, 1988; Endo and others, 1990; Geschwind and Rutherford, 1995), corresponding to decompression rates of ~0.0025–0.025 MPa/s. Because effusion rates were 10–20 times lower during 1983, we infer that ascent rates during periods of continuous dome growth were correspondingly lower (at least by a factor of 2–5), with magma ascent rates for spine production even lower (probably <10^{-3} m/s).

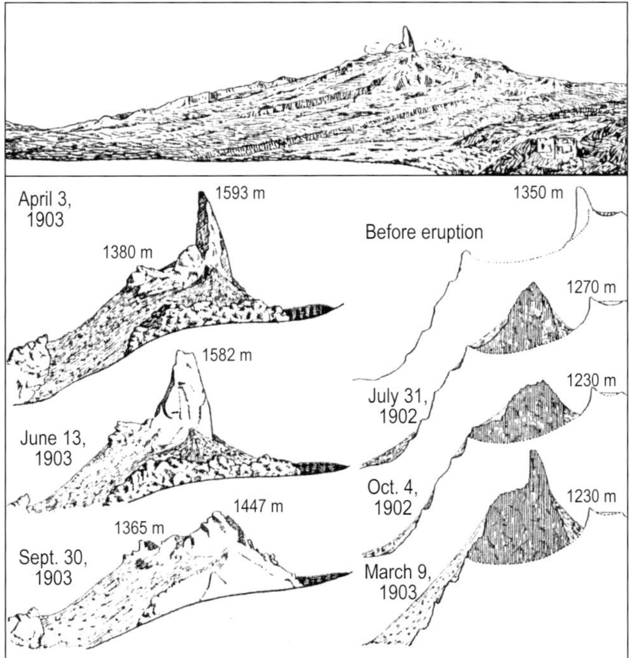

Figure 1. Sketches showing evolution of the great spine of Mont Pelée, Martinique, erupted in 1903. Note the difference between smooth, curved fault surface and rough, near-vertical face. From Williams (1932).

Links between eruption rate and dome morphology can be further constrained by examining two other eruptions of slightly different bulk composition. Unzen volcano, Japan, active from 1990 to 1995, constructed a 0.2-km^3 dome of dacitic composition (64.5–66 wt. percent SiO_2). Initial effusion (Q) at ~1 m^3/s produced a spine. Shortly thereafter a rapid increase in Q to ~5 m^3/s triggered a succession of pyroclastic flows accompanied by tremor spurts and two vulcanian eruptions (Nakada and Fujii, 1993; Nakada and others, 1995b, 1999; Nakada and Motomura, 1999). After this time the dome grew nearly continuously, with exogenous growth dominating during periods of higher effusion rates (>4 m^3/s) and endogenous growth dominant when effusion rates were low (<1 m^3/s). Magma ascent rates were estimated to be 13–40 m/d (1–5×10^{-4} m/s; Nakada and others, 1995b), more than an order of magnitude lower than during the time period of continuous magma ascent at Mount St. Helens in 1983. Effusion rates declined gradually until the end of the eruption, which was marked by the emergence of a spine from the endogenous dome (Nakada and others, 1995a).

Soufrière Hills volcano, Montserrat, intermittently active since 1995, has also shown a close correspondence between the rate of lava effusion and dome morphology. By 1999 the volcano had produced almost 0.3 km^3 of silicic andesite (57–61.5 wt. percent SiO_2), about two-thirds of which traveled as pumiceous and dense pyroclastic flows into valleys around the volcano. Low effusion rates (Q ~0.5–2 m^3/s) produced a range of spine and whaleback features, most of which grew in a matter of days. Moderate effusion rates (Q ~2–7 m^3/s) produced shear lobes that were active for days to weeks to months. High effusion rates (Q ~7–9 m^3/s) produced pancake-shaped lava lobes with flat tops and scoriaceous surfaces. Very high effusion rates (Q >9 m^3/s) resulted in vulcanian explosions (Watts and others, 2002). Of particular interest are features that bear close similarity to current activity at Mount St. Helens, specifically vertical spines and megaspines that characterized magma emplacement at low volumetric effusion rates (<2 m^3/s; Watts and others, 2002).

Together these case studies present a consistent story of spine growth under conditions of slow magma effusion (typically <1–2 m^3/s). Descriptions of both smooth and striated spine surfaces are common; Watts and others (2002) inferred that these characteristic curved surfaces were controlled by shear faults (for example, Donnadieu and Merle, 1998) in magma made highly viscous by late-stage decompression-driven crystallization. As noted above, spine morphology generally has been interpreted to reflect extrusion of a solid lava plug, which probably solidified more as a consequence of decompression-induced crystallization than of cooling on the way to the surface. However, there has been no detailed characterization of these bounding-fault surfaces or comparison of striated surfaces with tectonic fault textures, and no attempt has been made to use either fault-surface characteristics or crystallization textures to constrain the conditions of magma ascent and decompression that create these volcanic spine features.

The Importance of Decompression-Driven Crystallization

During the early part of the 20th century, there was great debate about the solidification mechanism that could generate the large Mont Pelée spine. Lacroix (1904) favored rapid cooling of lava on exit from the vent. Gilbert (1904) suggested that solidification of the spine might result from "escape of gases and formation of bubbles" rather than loss of heat by conduction. Gilbert's concept was extended by Shepherd and Merwin (1927), who argued that gas pressures required to support the spine (~10 MPa) resulted from crystallization; they went on to suggest that these high gas pressures also caused the explosive generation of nuées ardentes that accompanied spine extrusion. Williams (1932) extended the concept of crystallization-induced gas pressurization to explain late-stage explosions at several other domes, an association that Newhall and Melson (1983) find in most historical eruptions.

Dome growth during the 1980–86 eruption of Mount St. Helens provided the first quantitative documentation of decompression-driven crystallization in silicic magmas (Cashman, 1992). Decompression-driven crystallization has since been documented during effusive and intermittent explosive phases of numerous recent eruptions (for example, Nakada and others, 1995b; Wolf and Eichelberger, 1997; Gardner and others, 1998; Nakada and Motomura, 1999; Hammer and others, 1999, 2000; Cashman and Blundy, 2000; Martel and others, 2000; Sparks and others, 2000; Metrich and others, 2001; Blundy and Cashman, 2005; Cashman and McConnell, 2005) and is generally considered to be the dominant solidification mechanism in slowly ascending hydrous magma of intermediate composition. Petrographic observations show that plagioclase is the most abundant shallow-crystallizing phase, a consequence of the profound effect of dissolved H_2O on its stability. Quartz (or some other silica phase) joins the crystallizing assemblage when the quartz-feldspar cotectic is intersected, which typically occurs at low pressures, and rapidly increases the total crystal abundance. Both the number and mode of plagioclase crystals vary with decompression path (effective undercooling; ΔT_{eff}).

Decompression experiments on H_2O-saturated melts (Geschwind and Rutherford, 1995; Hammer and Rutherford, 2002; Martel and Schmidt, 2003; Couch and others, 2003) show that plagioclase number density, size, and morphology are controlled by the rate of decompression and the final pressure of equilibration. The extent of crystallization is dependent on both equilibration pressure and experiment duration (Hammer and Rutherford, 2002; fig. 2). Crystallinity increases as equilibration pressure decreases and with increasing time at a given pressure. At low pressure (≤25 MPa), extensive crystallization requires time scales of several weeks. Crystal nucleation rates also are highest at pressures between 25 and 10 MPa, although nucleation diminishes in importance at very low pressure (≤5 MPa) owing to the high viscosity of silicic melts with low H_2O (Hess and Dingwell, 1996). Extensive co-precipitation of quartz and feldspar appears to require equilibration at very low pressure (5–10 MPa).

An additional consequence of extensive late-stage decompression-driven crystallization is the release of latent heat. Evidence of late-stage heating in slowly erupted dome lavas includes both Ti-zoning of magnetite, which increases calculated Fe-Ti oxide temperatures, and reverse zoning of orthopyroxene (Devine and others, 2003; Pallister and others, 2005). These signs of heating have been interpreted as evidence of basaltic input at depth (for example, Devine and others, 2003). However, a recent study of samples erupted from Mount St. Helens in the early 1980s shows a strong correlation between late-stage heating and shallow crystallization, suggesting instead that this is a signature of shallow release of latent heat (Blundy and others, 2006). Because numerical models of conduit-flow dynamics show that even small changes in magma temperature have a large effect on magma discharge rate and eruptive behavior (Melnik and Sparks, 2005), localized crystallization-related heating may be an important component of shallow eruption dynamics.

In summary, the morphology of extruded spines—their asymmetric shape, smooth fault-bounded surfaces, and often imposing height—is controlled by effusion conditions. Formation of these spine features requires that magma ascent is sufficiently slow to allow near-complete volatile exsolution, degassing, and groundmass crystallization within the conduit. Outstanding questions include the relative timing of groundmass crystallization and fault formation, the potential role of latent heating in shear localization, the strain accommodated along these fault surfaces, the deformation mechanisms by which

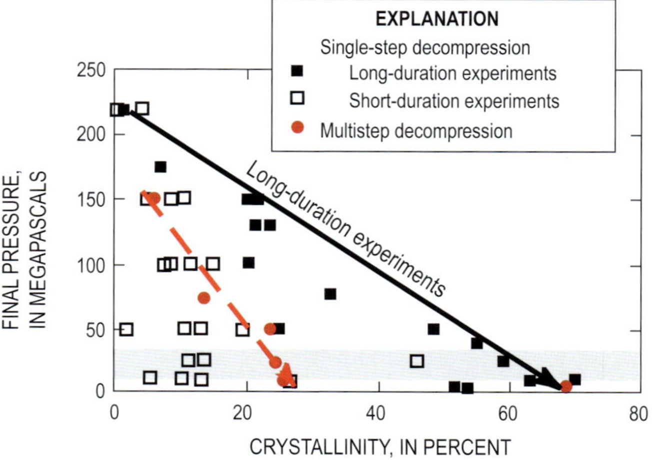

Figure 2. Relative effects of decompression time and equilibration pressure on crystallization of hydrous silicic melts. Single-step decompressions are followed by annealing at the final pressure; short-duration experiments, <30 hours; long-duration experiments, 168–931 hours. Multistep decompressions occur at constant rate of 1.2 MPa/hr. Data from Hammer and Rutherford (2002). Arrow shows equilibrium decompression-crystallization trend.

resulting fault gouge may affect plug extrusion, and the relation between observed seismic signals and spine emplacement.

Methods

Field observations and digital photography of the 2004–6 Mount St. Helens dome, made during two short ground-based sampling missions and numerous close-in helicopter flights, provide an outcrop-scale context for describing the character and origin of the gouge. Because of safety concerns, sampling of the dome and the dome carapace were accomplished primarily by helicopter dredging (Pallister and others, this volume, chap. 30). Although this remote technique did not allow detailed mapping of field relations, it did allow access to steep and unstable parts of the spines that could not have been reached on foot. The source areas for debris and talus samples are, in most cases, well constrained by field documentation. Moreover, both photographic and seismic records document the locations and timing of the specific rockfall events sampled. Finally, data collected during two days of field work in the summer of 2006 confirmed field relations inferred from remote techniques (Pallister and others, this volume, chap. 30). Distinct differences in sample lithology can be correlated with dome rock facies observed in the scree slopes on the dome flanks. A complete catalogue of sample information, including locations, brief descriptions, and bulk chemistry, is provided by Thornber and others (2008b).

All dome samples have been described and curated at the Cascades Volcano Observatory (Thornber and others, 2008b). Samples of unconsolidated fault gouge (SH303 and SH307) were processed in the Cascades Volcano Observatory Sediment Laboratory. Samples were dry sieved to 63 μm; size fractions <63 μm were analyzed using a Micrometrics Sedigraph III particle size analyzer. Additionally, both dome lava and fault gouge were characterized by petrographic analysis. Whole thin sections were scanned at high resolution for general textural characterization and quantitative analysis of plagioclase phenocryst and microphenocryst textures (that is, crystals >30 μm in diameter). Microscopic evaluation of sample textures was accomplished using a JSM-6300V scanning electron microscope at the University of Oregon. Thin sections were imaged in backscattered electron (BSE) mode using 10-kV accelerating voltage and 5-nA beam current. Both scanned and BSE digital images were processed and analyzed using Adobe Photoshop and ImageJ 1.34s (NIH Image for Mac OS X) software. Most techniques that were used are similar to those described elsewhere (for example, Cashman and McConnell, 2005); however, we also experimented with ways of analyzing the size distribution of clasts in the cataclasite for comparison with sieve data. Analysis of larger (>30 μm) dome fragments was performed on low magnification (20×) BSE images. Gray-scale thresholding of individual clasts provided binary images that could be easily processed to allow clast size analysis (fig. 3). All image-analysis data were then analyzed using Microsoft Excel.

Results

In this section we document processes related to spine extrusion. Because the observational record of spine extrusion is unique in the level of detail permitted by the sampling techniques, our primary goal is to provide comprehensive descriptions of textures produced as competent dacite lava is transformed into ultracataclastic fault gouge. We begin by reviewing details of field observations, followed by hand-specimen descriptions and thin-section observations. To describe the textural characteristics of fault rock samples, we follow Snoke and others (1998) in using the nomenclature conven-

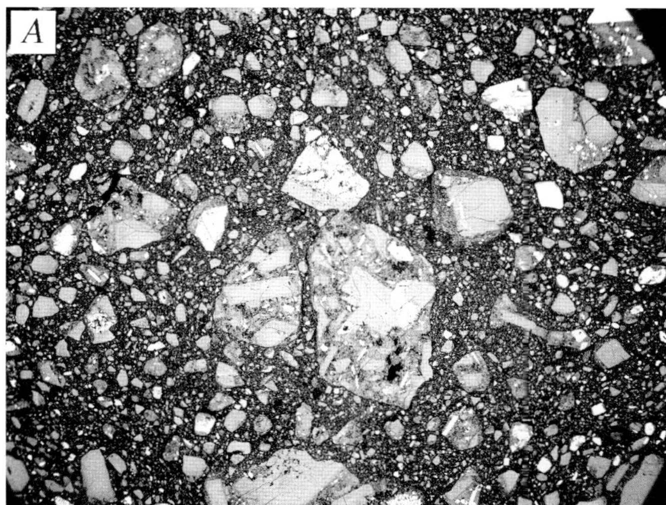

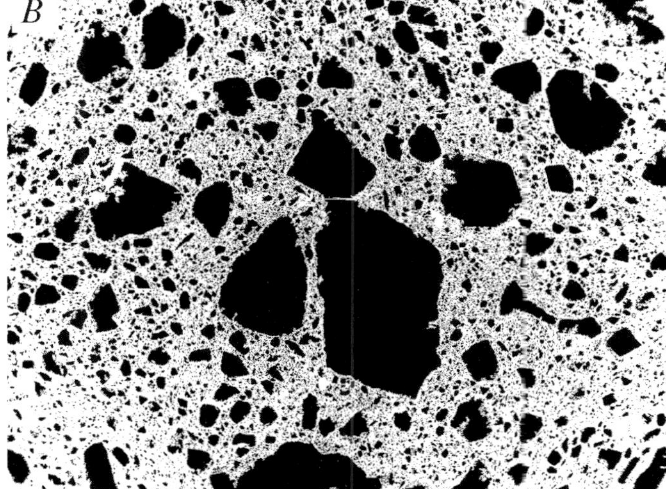

Figure 3. Examples from gouge sample SH326-2A illustrating the image-processing technique used to acquire grain-size data on cataclastic samples. Apparent circular concentration of very fine particles is an artifact of the image-acquisition technique; for this reason, only larger particles are used in final analysis. Images are 6.1 mm across. *A*, Backscattered electron image. *B*, Processed binary image.

tion of Sibson (1977), as modified by Scholz (1990), where "gouge" refers to noncohesive material with visible fragments constituting <30 percent (by volume) of the rock mass, in contrast to fault "breccia" that has >30 percent visible fragments. Although this naming convention would apply the term "cataclasite" to all cohesive brittle fault rocks, we distinguish cohesive breccia from cataclasite on the basis of apparent clast versus matrix support. Moreover, for simplicity we refer to the "gouge zone" when discussing the entire suite of cataclastic material that overlies massive dome dacite.

The View from the Field

The gouge carapace was first observed on November 7, 2004, on the surface of spine 3. At that time a large lava spine (300–400 m north-south by 50–150 m east-west) had been thrust to ~100 m above the surface of the already-uplifted glacier in the southeastern quadrant of the crater (figs. 4*A*, 4*B*). On the east face of the spine, a slope of gouge was exposed above a basal apron of wet, sandy debris containing angular lava blocks. The lower 10–20 m of the slope's exposed east face was composed of gouge that displayed prominent striations that plunged steeply east (parallel to the 45° slope of the spine) in exposures along the southeast face and more northerly along the northeast face. Along both faces a resistant surface layer was underlain by ≤1 m of white, powdery gouge (sample SH303) that was slightly warm to the touch (~30°C), dry, and friable. Sparse rock fragments within the gouge accumulated fine-grained material on their downslope sides, producing features akin to pressure shadows (Pabst, 1931) with a preserved sense of shear that was consistent with uplift of the spine core relative to marginal rocks (fig. 4*B*). Several curvilinear bands of discolored gouge and trails of embedded lithic fragments ("bathtub rings"; figs. 4*A*, 4*B*) paralleled the contact between the gouge and the debris apron at the base of the spine, recording earlier positions of this basal contact that shifted upward with growth. Disintegration of the south face of spine 3 (figs. 4*C*, 4*D*) allowed sampling of the (still hot) spine interior by helicopter dredging. The dominant rock type is dense hornblende-hypersthene-plagioclase-phyric dacite with a microcrystalline groundmass (SH304; Pallister and others, this volume, chap. 30).

The detailed descriptions of spine 3 provided above can be generalized to all other spines. A narrow band of mantling gouge typically forms an intact annulus at the vent margin (fig. 5*A*). Thermal data from a Forward-Looking Infrared Radiometer (FLIR) indicate temperatures of 100–200°C at this margin but show that the gouge surface cools to near ambient temperatures after about 10 m of uplift. A FLIR temperature maxima of 730°C (Schneider and others, this volume, chap. 17) indicates that temperatures remain high in the spine interior (within a few meters of the surface). Throughout the 2004–6 eruption, the thickness of the gouge zone has ranged from 1 to 3 m, always with surface striations oriented parallel to transport (fig. 5*B*). Most commonly, dense flow-banded dacite is abruptly overlain by 1–2 m of reddish cataclasite, which is overlain by poorly consolidated white to tan powdery gouge (fig. 5*C*). Occurring less frequently are examples of foliated gouge with parallel striations on the surface that form a penetrative shear foliation (fig. 5*D*). Samples of foliated gouge show multiple subparallel slickensides that indicate slight variations in slip direction at different depths. In some outcrops, a capping resistant (and striated) surface layer protects the unconsolidated gouge that, at times, posed challenges to sampling efforts. On one occasion, a 75-kg dredge was dragged along the surface of spine 4 without penetrating this surface layer. Bulk chemical analyses of gouge samples show that early gouge included a substantial fraction of older material from the conduit margin, whereas later gouge samples are mostly juvenile dacite (Rowe and others, this volume, chap. 29).

An unusual, well-exposed section of the lava-to-gouge boundary within a graben that formed in spine 4 was photographed in December 2005, more than a year after spine extrusion (fig. 6). Exposed cross sections of the gouge-lava contact showed both breccia and pink (altered) cataclasite separating massive flow-banded dacite from overlying powdery gouge. The abrupt contact between massive dacite and the overlying cataclasite indicates that this is an important mechanical boundary. The progression from breccia to gouge was well displayed, with blocks of intact dacite sheared from the underlying lava and progressively fragmented to produce breccia, cataclasite, and gouge. The sense of brittle shear derived from the inclination of shear surfaces within the breccia is consistent with upward transport from the vent. Photographic interpretations were confirmed by field observations made in the summer of 2006. The observations showed that the gouge formed over a vertical distance of 1–2 m by shear between the upward-thrusting dacite within the conduit and the conduit margins. Reidel shears within the cataclasite provide further evidence of brittle shear failure (Pallister and others, 2006).

Hand Samples

Rock samples collected from the talus of the growing 2004–6 Mount St. Helens dacite dome include both competent dacite (igneous rock) and a variety of fault rocks (cataclasite). Detailed descriptions of all samples can be found in Thornber and others (2008b). Here we briefly describe the varieties of pristine dome dacite before describing the range of fault rocks. Dacite samples vary in color from light gray to reddish or pink (a term used in deference to the first unequivocally juvenile samples of "hot pink" dacite SH304). The reddish alteration results from oxidation that is localized around hornblende, oxide, and hypersthene phenocrysts and does not noticeably affect the otherwise igneous fabric of the rocks.

In hand sample, the igneous facies of dome rocks may be broadly classified as (1) dense, light-gray (to pink) dacite, (2) flow-banded gray (to pink) dacite, or (3) vesicular dark-gray (to pink) dacite. Most samples also contain 1–5 volume percent of coarse-grained hornblende-gabbronorite xenoliths that are similar in abundance and character to those in 1980 to 1986 eruption products (Heliker, 1995). Lithic inclusions of dacite, andesite, and amphibolite are less abundant and typically of smaller size.

Dense light-gray dacite samples dominate the dome talus suite. Because these samples are both angular and dense (porosities <10 percent), and because several of these samples were dredged from collapsed faces of the spines, we infer that they are derived primarily from the dome interior. Flow fabric within the dome facies is not well developed and is indicated only by (1) alignment of acicular hornblende phenocrysts in some samples and (2) entrainment patterns of xenolithic fragments and vesicular pockets around them. Rare flow-banded dacite samples have distinctly light-colored or reddish bands (ranging from less than 10 to 20 mm in width) that are subparallel to foliation evident in dense, dacite host rock. Bands lack evidence of granular flow or other forms of brittle deformation and instead are characterized by high vesicularity relative to the host rock.

Vesicular dacite samples have 25–40 percent porosity and range in color from dark gray to red. In some vesicular samples, igneous flow is evidenced by fanned vesicle-distribution patterns and corresponding flow alignment of xenolith fragments and feldspar megacrysts. Proximity of the most

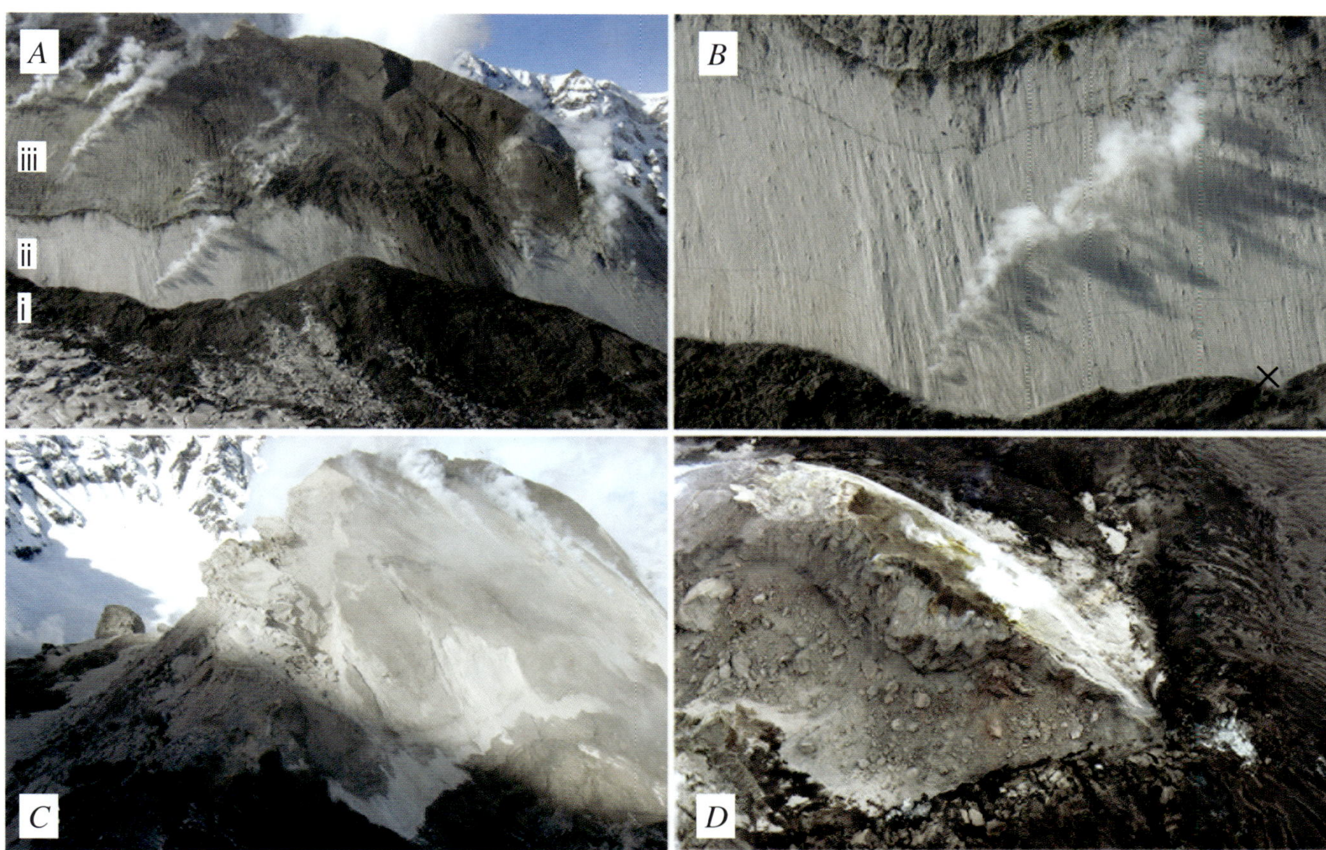

Figure 4. Spine 3 in early to mid-November 2004. USGS photographs by J.S. Pallister. *A*, West-looking view on November 4 showing, from the base upward: (i) an apron of sandy debris, snow, and glacial ice; (ii) 10–15-m-high wall of white slickenside-bearing gouge with "bathtub rings" that mark former contact levels between gouge surface and debris apron; (iii) dark tan (weathered) gouge or cataclasite with steeply dipping erosional furrows. Blocky outcrops (uppermost spine rough-weathering area near center-frame) are uplifted material from the debris apron. Steam is venting from fractures in gouge carapace. *B*, Close-up photograph on November 4 of gouge outcrop showing slickensides and "bathtub" rings that parallel contact between the gouge and the debris apron. Note shadows on the downslope sides of rock fragments within the gouge that suggest upward and westward movement of the spine relative to the debris fan. Sample SH303-1 was collected from the white powdery gouge at site marked by X, about 1 m above the debris apron 10 m north (right) of the prominent steam vent. *C*, Oblique aerial photograph on November 4 of the southeast collapsed terminus of spine 3 showing blocky outcrops of dense dacite of the spine interior. View to the north-northwest. *D*, Photograph on November 10 of the southwest face and south terminus of spine 3 with a dark (ash covered) "bulldozed" glacier on right. White gouge carapace is visible above the blocky interior of the collapsing southwest face; powdery gouge eroded from the carapace has been deposited on the debris apron on the east flank of the spine. View is to the northeast.

vesicular, glassy, and reddish dacite to the outer dome margins is inferred from in-place sampling (SH305-1; fig. 7) and is documented in the exposed cross sections of collapsed spines. Helium-pycnometer measurements of SH305-1 yield a He-accessible porosity of 30.4 percent, nearly identical to the 30.3 percent porosity determined from the measured bulk density of 1,829 kg/m^3 and measured solid density of 2,627 kg/m^3. The similarity of the connected and bulk porosity indicates that the pores are fully connected and, therefore, might allow permeable flow of gas upward along the margin of the conduit. Preliminary permeability measurements of the same samples yield permeabilities of 8–9×10^{-13} m^2, confirming the possible ease of gas flow through the more vesicular dome lavas.

Both abrupt and gradational changes from competent dacite to finely powdered gouge are found within the sample suite. Some fractured and foliated dacite samples reveal a subtle gradation between vesicular dacite and marginal granular gouge. For example, samples from 2–5 m below surface gouge collected in the SH309 dredge along the southern end of spine 4 are somewhat altered and show moderate crushing and compaction associated with postsolidification shearing. Cataclastic rocks are distinguished by visible frag-

Figure 5. Features of the new lava dome. USGS photos by J.S. Pallister. *A*, Oblique aerial photograph of crater and 2004–2005 lava dome taken from the northwest on June 29, 2005. Spine 3 is in a shadow on left; spine 4 is in the center (highly fractured and altered); and spine 5 is on the right, with white, striated gouge carapace on the north and west flanks, collapse scar on northwest face, and sharp, arcuate contact between hot, powdery gouge and talus marking the periphery of the vent. Crevassed and brown, ash-covered Crater Glacier surrounds the dome. The following three photos were taken on January 14, 2005. *B*, Striated surface of spine 4; direction of transport is from lower right to upper left. Orange box on instrument package at center of frame is 1 m long. *C*, Contacts between gouge (gray, weathered surface lacking distinct striations), underlying cataclastic breccia, and dense dacite exposed on the collapsed south face of spine 4. Note flow foliation in lower right of photograph and in some outcrops immediately below the gouge. Dacite lava is overlain abruptly by pink to yellow consolidated gouge, which in turn is mantled by powdery white to gray gouge. Preserved thickness of gouge zone above contact is 1–2 m, although original thickness was greater. *D*, Parallel striations on surface of spine 4; transport direction from lower right to upper left. Surface striations mark penetrative fabric that creates planar shear lamination of the cataclasite. Block of dacite collected from the interior of nearby spine 4 is flow foliated and displays a strong lineation of elongate amphiboles.

ments of dome lava suspended within a finer grained matrix (figs. 8*A*, 8*B*) and range from well consolidated to friable and from coarse to fine grained. Both the size and abundance of macroscopic lava fragments decrease toward the outer surface of fine-grained noncohesive gouge. Friable and foliated gouge from spine 4 (SH313-1) shows pronounced slickensides forming subparallel striations that permeate the loosely consolidated sample (fig. 8*C*). Powdery fault gouge is light in color and unconsolidated.

Samples in Thin Section

The petrography and petrology of dacite lava dome samples are described by Pallister and others (this volume, chap. 30) and will be reviewed only briefly here. The dacite lava has a uniform bulk composition (65 wt. percent SiO_2) and is highly crystalline, having 41–45 percent phenocrysts and microphenocrysts of plagioclase, hypersthene, amphiboles, and Fe-Ti oxides set in a microcrystalline matrix (fig. 9*A*). Iron-titanium oxide temperatures in early samples are 840–850°C; apparent temperatures increase in later samples in response to latent heat produced by extensive shallow crystallization (for example, Blundy and others, 2006).

Thin sections provide important insight into fine-scale cataclasis of competent dome lava. An unusual sample (SH324-4A) preserves an abrupt boundary between coherent dome lava and highly fragmented fault gouge. In thin section, the boundary between gouge and coherent lava is marked by thin, oxidized bands that are subparallel to the boundary (fig. 9*B*). Approximately parallel to these bands, more subtle variations in matrix density mark a throughgoing shear fabric within the boundary zone. More common are samples of cataclasite that are characterized by rounded fragments of dome lava within a finer grained matrix (SH326; fig. 9*C*). In thin section, dome fragments typically range in size from greater than 10 mm to less than 0.1 mm. The matrix comprises primarily shattered phenocrysts, although pieces of holocrystalline groundmass can also be identified. In friable, foliated gouge samples with obvious slickensides, the grain-size reduction vis-

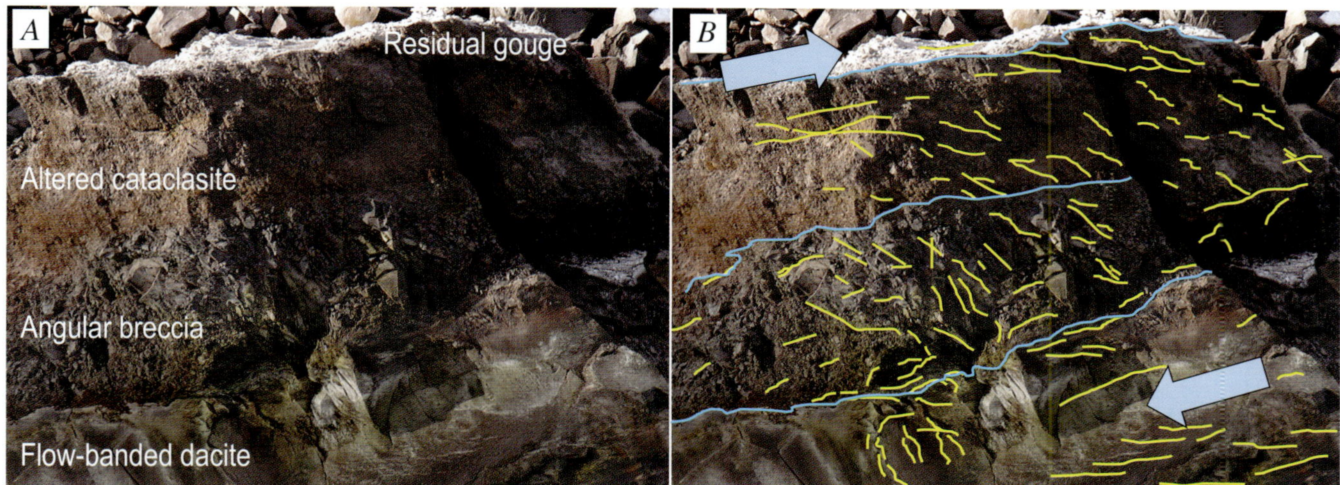

Figure 6. Dome-breccia relations. USGS photo by J.S. Pallister, December 15, 2005. *A*, Erosional remnant atop spine 4 preserves a breccia interval between massive to flow-banded dacite lava at base of outcrop and a thin surface layer of white powdery gouge. Brittle fractures (Reidel shears) are present in breccia and cataclasite. *B*, Trend lines indicate shear couple with basal dacite moving left (away from vent) relative to the upper (external) part of outcrop, consistent with shear between the dacite and the conduit wall during extrusion. Height of outcrop is approximately 3 m.

Figure 7. Outcrop and hand-specimen photographs of sample SH305, collected January 3, 2005, from spine 3.

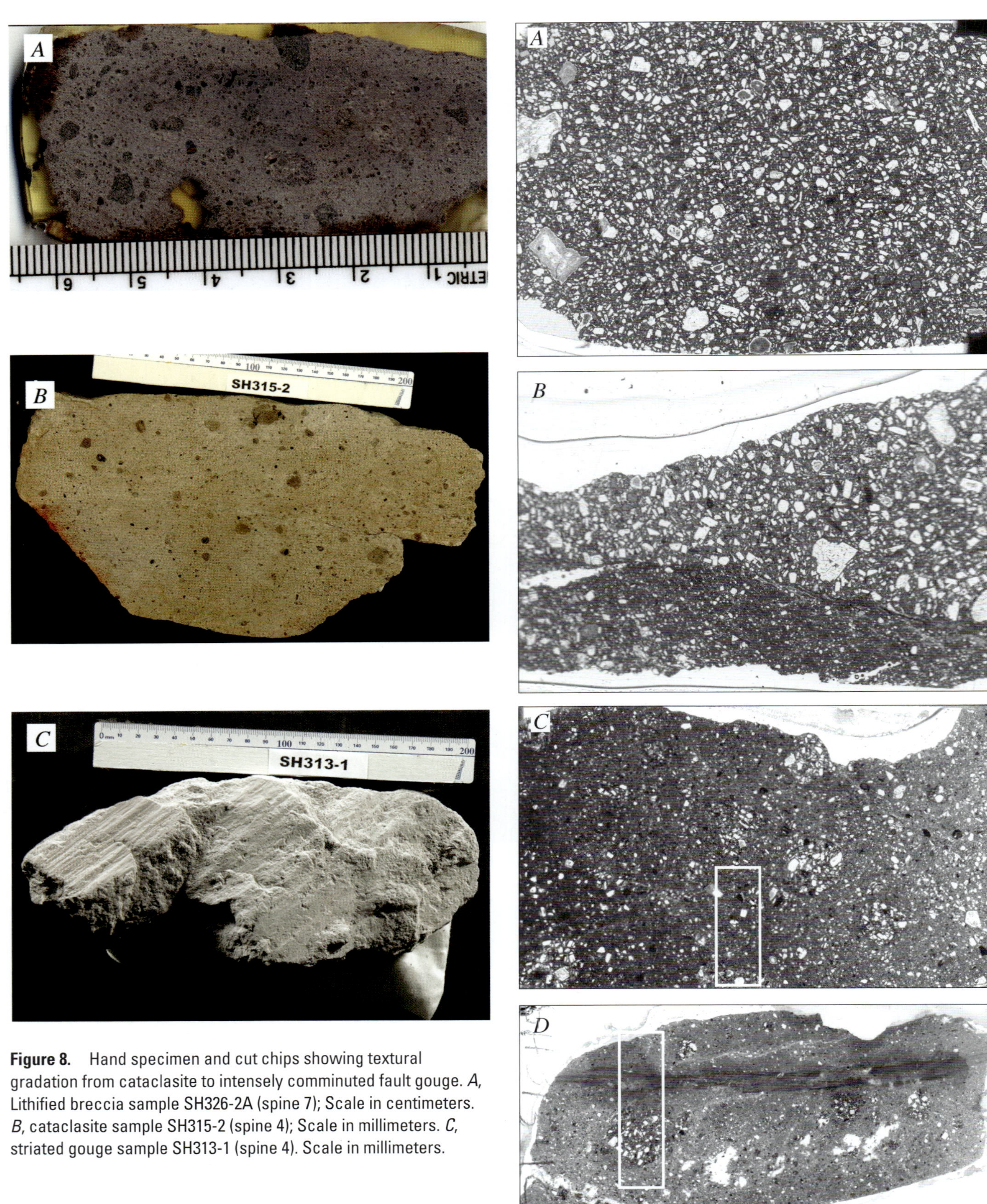

Figure 8. Hand specimen and cut chips showing textural gradation from cataclasite to intensely comminuted fault gouge. *A*, Lithified breccia sample SH326-2A (spine 7); Scale in centimeters. *B*, cataclasite sample SH315-2 (spine 4); Scale in millimeters. *C*, striated gouge sample SH313-1 (spine 4). Scale in millimeters.

ible in thin section is extreme (SH313-1; fig. 9*D*), with typical cataclasite (fig. 9*C*) cut by an extraordinarily fine-grained, foliated shear zone (an ultracataclasite, with grain size <1 μm). Other thin sections of the same gouge sample show anastomosing branches of foliated ultracataclasite that isolate areas of coarser cataclasite.

Backscattered Electron Imaging Observations

Field, hand-specimen, and thin-section observations of dome and gouge samples indicate that competent (and flow-banded) dome lava achieved threshold conditions for wholesale fragmentation, cataclastic flow, and strain localization to accommodate the large strains achieved during spine emplacement. Backscattered electron (BSE) imaging provides additional textural evidence for (1) the crystallization history of the dome magma that may have led to fragmentation, (2) fragmentation mechanisms, and (3) cataclastic flow.

Detailed characterization of phenocryst textures and composition is provided elsewhere in this volume (Pallister and others, chap. 30; Rutherford and Devine, chap. 31; Streck and others, chap. 34), so we limit our descriptions of phenocrysts to characteristics that may help to constrain shallow conduit processes. A striking feature of virtually all samples we have imaged is the presence of some plagioclase phenocrysts (>100 μm) with irregular margins on one or more growth faces that indicate rapid late-stage rim growth (fig. 10). In contrast, microphenocrysts (30–100 μm) typically are euhedral and prismatic. Phenocryst rim-growth irregularities range from a few to several tens of microns in width (fig. 10*A*) and include either multiple (fig. 10*B*) or single (fig. 10*C*) growth zones. In some samples, irregular growth protrusions partially entrap small pockets of groundmass glass that are substantially less crystalline and less vesicular than adjacent matrix (fig. 10*C*). The combined observations of rapid rim growth in both early-erupted (fast) and late-erupted (slow) dome lavas and clean glass preserved within the growth irregularities suggest that these features reflect relatively fast magma ascent (and overstepping of the plagioclase liquidus) at deeper levels in the conduit system. The prevalence of growth irregularities in large (and often outsized) phenocrysts further suggests that these crystals may have a unique decompression history.

Although the groundmass of all samples is highly crystalline, groundmass textures are variable. At one extreme are juvenile samples, collected by dredge in early November 2004 (SH304), that include several unusually glassy clasts. One such clast has only pyroxene and oxides as groundmass phases

◀ **Figure 9.** Full thin-section scans of samples showing transition from competent dome lava to highly comminuted fault gouge. Scale bar in *D* applies to all four panels. *A*, Sample SH316, from spine 5. *B*, Sample SH324-4A, from spine 7. *C*, Sample SH326-2A, from spine 7; box shows transect illustrated in figure 14*A*. *D*, Sample SH313-1C, from spine 4; box shows transect illustrated in figure 16*A*.

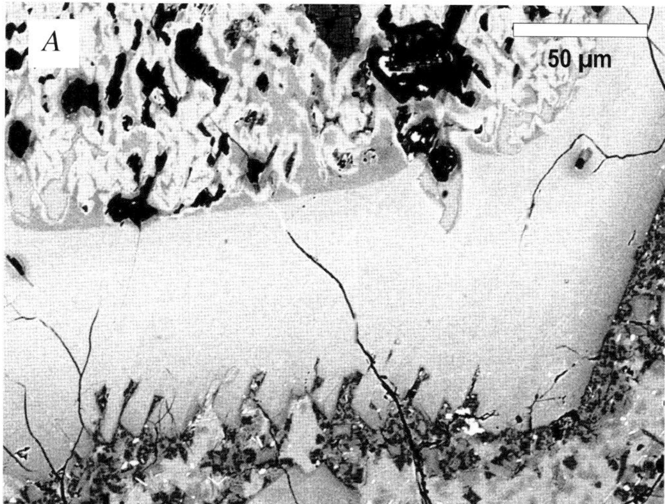

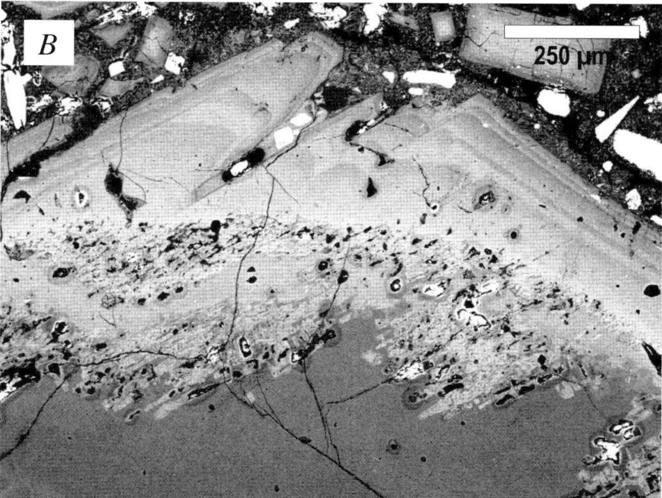

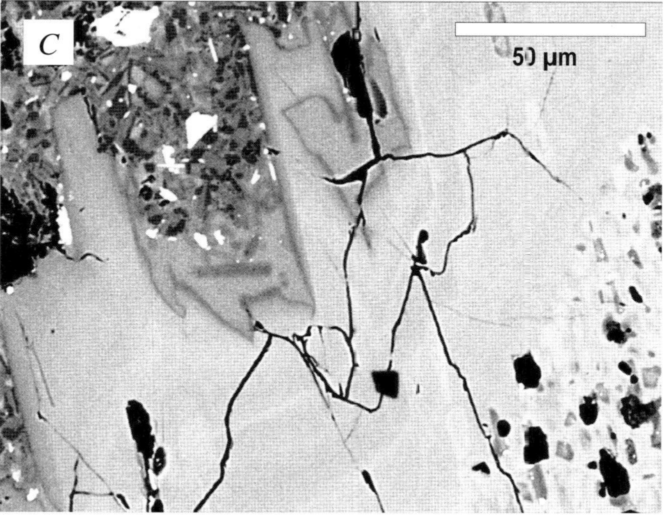

Figure 10. Plagioclase phenocryst textures indicative of rapid growth. *A*, Sample SH316. *B*, Sample SH315-2. *C*, Sample SH309-1.

and preserves ~ 2 weight percent H_2O in the groundmass glass (Pallister and others, this volume, chap. 30). Another sample (SH304-2G3; figs. 11*A*, 11*B*) has a groundmass composed primarily of feldspar microlites (<20 µm in length) with only minor pyroxene, oxides, and quartz. This sample is unusual in having abundant clean glass (~25 percent) and only minimal precipitation of silica phases. Many of the larger plagioclase microlites in this sample have swallowtail terminations that suggest rapid growth (for example, Hammer and Rutherford, 2002). High crystal number densities (~10^7/mm^3) preserved in this sample would suggest that most of the growth was both shallow (<25 MPa; see compilation in Cashman and McConnell, 2005) and rapid. These pressure estimates are roughly consistent with the ~30 MPa indicated by preserved H_2O contents of some other SH304 clasts, confirming that glassy SH304 samples appear to have been quenched at depths of ~1 km (for example, Pallister and others, this volume, chap. 30). More typical of early-erupted samples is SH305-1, from spine 3, emplaced in late November 2004 (for example, fig. 7). Sample SH305-1 is distinct from SH304-2G3 because it has less-numerous, but somewhat more-euhedral, plagioclase microlites in a groundmass mottled with 30–40-µm patches of cotectic feldspar and quartz crystallization, intergrowths that commonly nucleate along plagioclase phenocryst and microphenocryst boundaries and then grow into the melt (figs. 11*C*, 11*D*). Disequilibrium crystallization is a common feature of natural and experimental melts decompressed slowly to shallow levels (Hammer and Rutherford, 2002; Martel and Schmidt, 2003), the result of delayed quartz nucleation in these highly silicic melts (Cashman and Blundy, 2000; Blundy and Cashman, 2001). Quartz may have nucleated more easily along euhedral crystal margins if a thin, slightly SiO_2-enriched, boundary layer helped to overcome the activation energy required for quartz nucleation in the rhyolitic liquid.

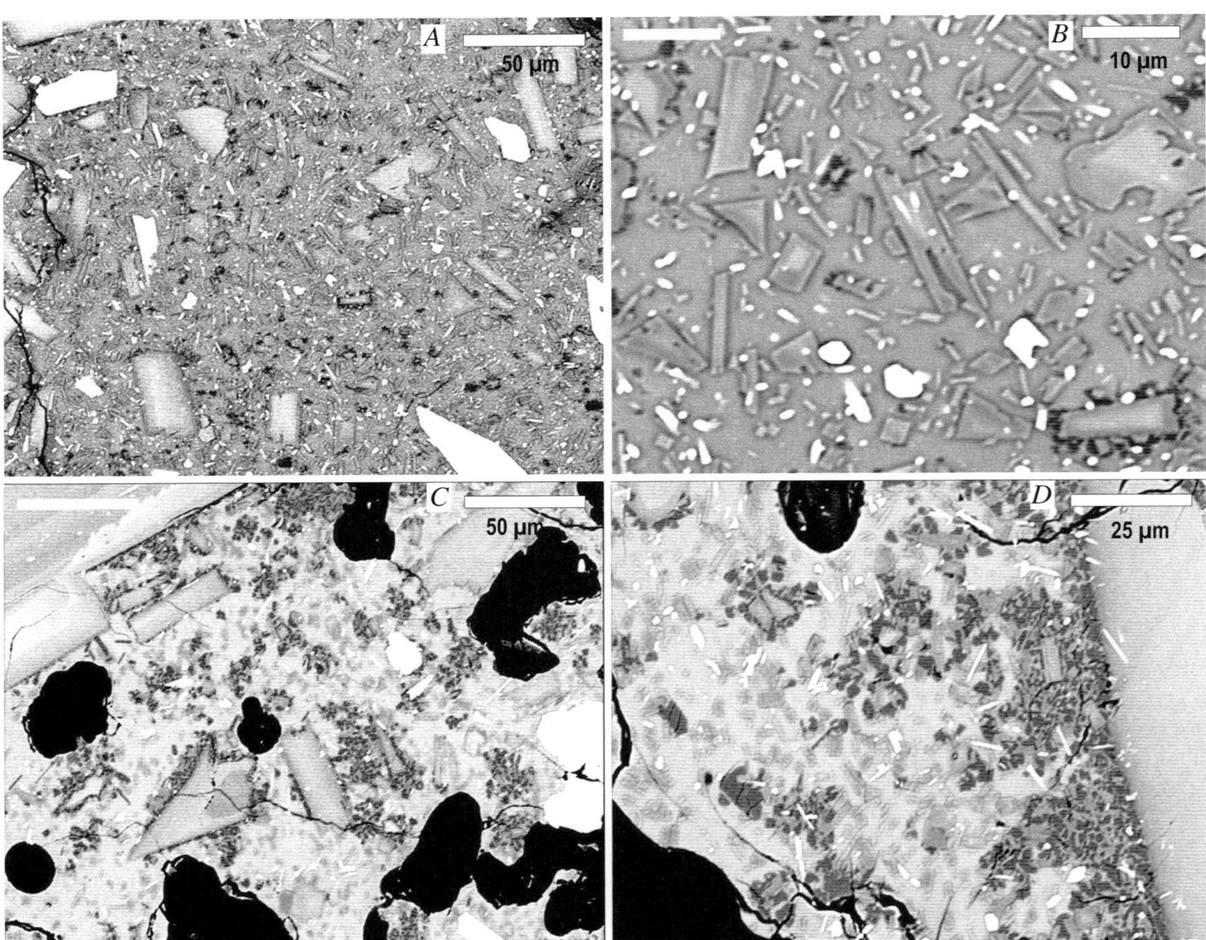

Figure 11. Backscattered electron images of groundmass textures from early-erupted samples (spine 3). *A*, Sample SH304-2G3 showing relatively high glass content and dominance of plagioclase microlites (medium- to light-gray crystals). *B*, Highly magnified view. *C*, Sample SH305-1 showing patchy development of cotectic quartz-feldspar intergrowths (blotchy dark-gray regions) with apparent nucleation on phenocryst margins. *D*, Highly magnified view.

By April 2005, the rate of dome extrusion had diminished and groundmass textures were correspondingly more crystalline. Dome dacite sample SH316 (from spine 5; fig. 9*A*) has a highly crystalline groundmass with abundant plagioclase crystals and patchy cotectic intergrowths of plagioclase and quartz (fig. 12*A*). Also apparent in the groundmass of SH316 are larger (~50 µm in length) acicular (platy in three dimensions) silica-phase crystals that appear to be a form of cristobalite (fig. 12*A*). Other samples, such as SH309, show abundant tridymite as a groundmass phase (figs. 12*B*, 12*C*), a feature that was also observed by Blundy and Cashman (2001) in some samples from the continuous growth phase of the 1983 Mount St. Helens dome. The long axes of tridymite crystals (fig. 12*B*) are aligned locally, recording late-stage deformation.

Backscattered electron imaging also provides a spectacular record of gouge development. As described above, dome dacite samples (fig. 13*A*) show little sign of deformation associated with magma ascent and extrusion, except for some samples with pronounced flow banding. Brittle breakage associated with flow is manifested first as throughgoing fractures, particularly along phenocryst boundaries (fig. 13*E*). Cataclasite sample SH326-2A shows more extensive evidence of crushing. Thin sections illustrate the textural heterogeneity of SH326-2A, with small (≤10 mm in diameter) dome lava clasts distributed randomly in a matrix of smaller clasts, individual crystals, and pulverized matrix (fig. 9*C*). Backscattered electron images show that the matrix itself contains a continuous range of fragment sizes, from intact lava clasts greater than 1 mm to tiny fragments smaller than 1 µm (fig. 14*A*), where

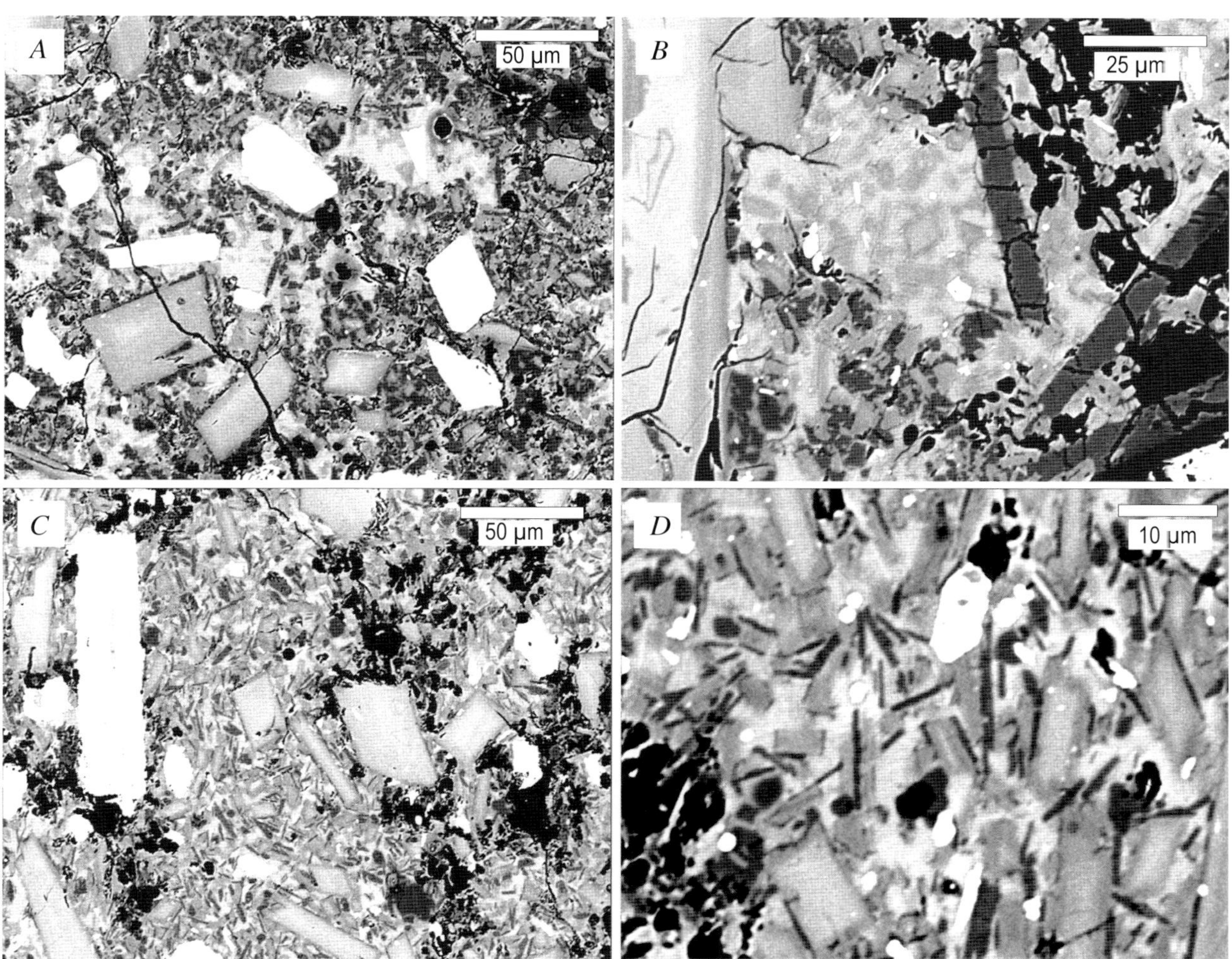

Figure 12. BSE images of groundmass textures from later-erupted samples. *A*, SH316 (spine 5) showing near-holocrystalline nature of groundmass. Dark-gray phase is quartz, medium-gray phase is plagioclase, light-gray phase is quenched glass, and white phases are mafic minerals. *B*, High-magnification view of SH316 groundmass showing high number density of plagioclase microlites in remnant, clean glass patches. *C*, SH309 (spine 4) showing unusual abundance of acicular aligned tridymite crystals in the groundmass. *D*, high magnification view of SH309 groundmass showing the intergrowths of plagioclase and tridymite (dark gray) and remnant patches of clean glass.

crude banding is suggested by regions of higher and lower fragment concentrations.

All samples of cataclasite and gouge show nearly complete groundmass crystallization; groundmass textures preserved within individual clasts are similar to the more crystalline parts of dome-lava groundmass. Larger fragments within the gouge typically are cored by plagioclase phenocrysts enclosed in holocrystalline (and microvesicular) groundmass (figs. 14*B*, 14*C*), although clasts composed entirely of microphenocrysts and microvesicular, holocrystalline groundmass are not uncommon. Commonly, the outer margin of clasts is distinctly rounded and is surrounded by very fine grained fragments, features that suggest extensive grinding, abrasion, and even rolling during transport.

Textural transitions from dome lava to gouge to ultracataclasite can be observed in more detail in samples SH324-4A (fig. 9*B*) and SH313-1 (fig. 9*D*). In SH324-4A (fig. 15), the pronounced boundary between dome lava and gouge seen in thin section marks an abrupt change from intact, holocrystalline, igneous groundmass to fragmented and disseminated matrix plus crystals and crystal fragments (fig. 15*A*). In detail, the boundary is composed of thin (~100 μm) slivers of intact holocrystalline groundmass separated by bands of loose crystal and groundmass fragments (fig. 15*B*). In figure 15*B*, the shear-zone margin shows a single plagioclase crystal in the process of being shattered, providing the source of the aligned crystal fragments seen in figure 15*D*. Patterns of fracture may provide a sense of shear, as in figure 15*C*, where conjugate fracture sets propagate through a dome lava fragment containing both crystals and holocrystalline groundmass.

A traverse across foliated gouge sample SH313-1 (figs. 8*C*, 9*D*) shows more spectacular grain-size variation (fig. 16*A*). Much of the thin section is similar to cataclasite sample SH326 (fig. 14), with intact clasts of dome lava suspended in a fine-grained matrix. However, as shown in BSE imagery, the narrow (≤1 mm) fault zone visible in thin section (fig. 9*D*) is composed of alternating bands (~100 μm wide) of fine-grained (tens of micrometers) and extremely fine grained (<1 μm) material (figs. 16*B*, 16*C*). By analogy with features observed in SH324-4A (fig. 15), we infer that banding develops by incorporation of shattered crystals (fig. 15*B*) and dome fragments

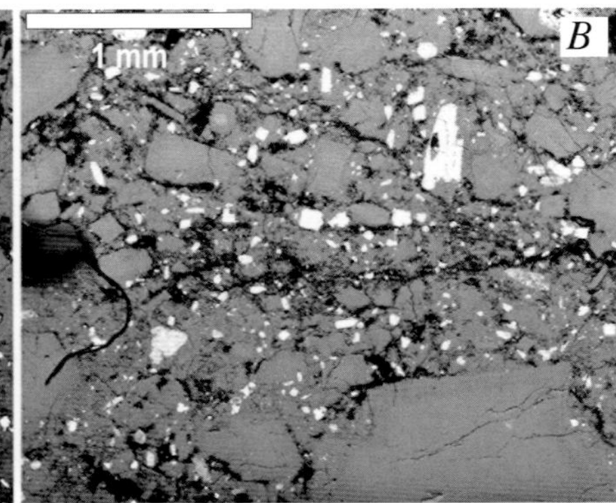

Figure 13. Low-magnification BSE images of two spine 4 samples. *A*, Competent dacite sample SH308-3A. *B*, partially fragmented sample SH309-1C. Note extensive fracturing (black areas indicate void space).

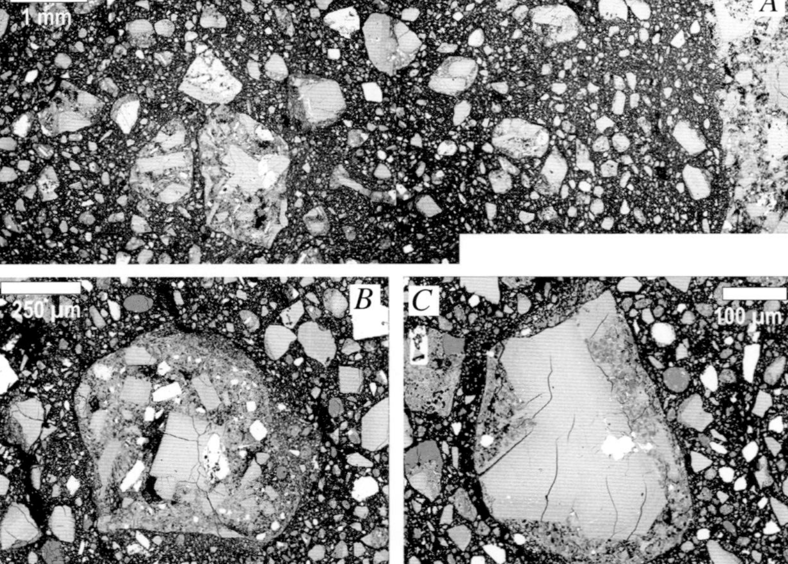

Figure 14. Backscattered electron images of fault gouge textures preserved in sample SH326-2A (spine 7; see fig. 9*C* for smaller-scale view). *A*, Composite transect illustrating textures characteristic of cataclasite samples. *B*, *C*, Typical gouge fragments composed of individual phenocrysts or broken dome matrix surrounded by holocrystalline matrix. Typically clasts are rounded and are surrounded by a halo of finely pulverized material.

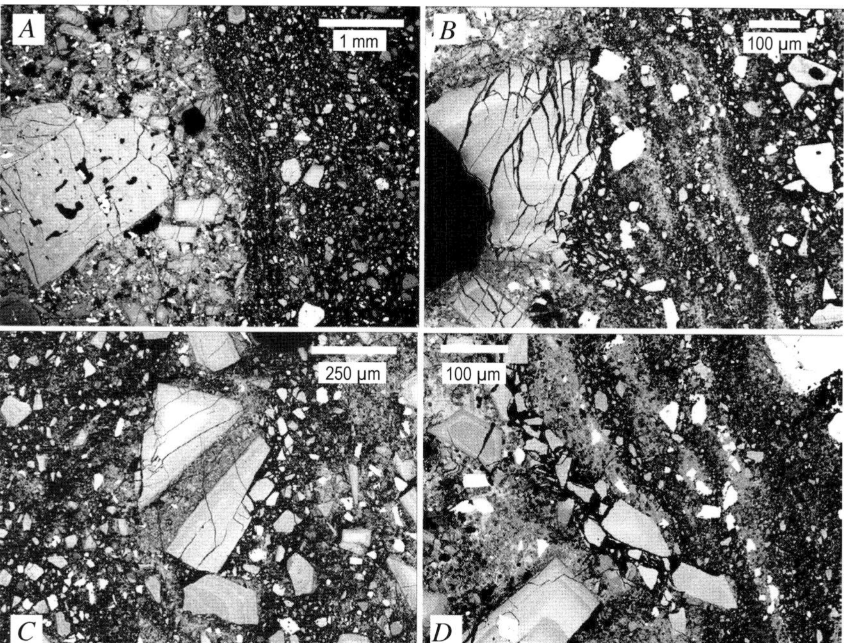

Figure 15. Backscattered electron images showing details of the lava-cataclasite boundary preserved in sample SH324-4A, from spine 7 (see fig. 9*B* for smaller-scale view of boundary). *A*, Low-magnification image across the boundary showing coherent dacite on left and cataclasite on right. *B*, Highly magnified view of boundary (from upper center of *A*) showing extensive fragmentation of a crystal next to the boundary and thin slivers of intact holocrystalline matrix parallel to the boundary. *C*, Lava fragment showing (Reidel?) fractures through plagioclase microphenocrysts and holocrystalline matrix within gouge. *D*, Broken slivers of holocrystalline matrix just below image of *B* that show lateral entrainment of broken crystal fragments into boundary zone.

(fig. 16*D*) into adjacent shear zones. Foliation orientations are both parallel and subparallel to the shear-zone orientation, consistent with macroscopic evidence for slight orientation variations among slickensides (fig. 8*C*). Moreover, in some locations along the shear zone, individual fragments of foliated gouge have been broken and rotated (figs. 16*C*, 16*D*). In other locations, the shear zone itself is anastomosing, forming an ultracataclastic zone that varies in width and complexity (fig. 16*E*). Here too, the orientation of individual foliated layers within the gouge is subparallel to the shear zone.

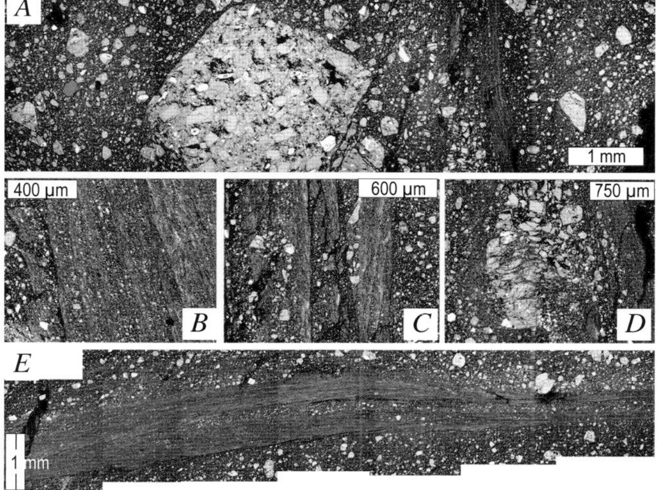

Figure 16. Backscattered electron images showing details of fault gouge sample SH313-1 from spine 4 (see fig. 9*D* for smaller-scale view). *A*, Transect across part of thin section SH313-1C showing a wide range of clast sizes in the gouge and extreme grain-size reduction within the "fault core," right of center. *B*, Detailed image of fine-scale foliated fault gouge showing slight offset in foliation orientation across the image. *C*, Breakage, disruption, and partial rotation of finely pulverized gouge. *D*, Shattered lava fragment adjacent to the fault core. *E*, Composite transect along the fault zone in thin section SH313-1A. Note fine-scale foliation oriented subparallel to the fault zone and anastomosing strands that isolate regions of less extensively pulverized gouge fragments.

Grain-Size Measurements

Sieve data for two powdery gouge samples—SH303-1 collected on November 4, 2004, from spine 3 and SH307-1 collected on February 22, 2005, from a collapsed part of spine 4—confirm the wide range in grain size of the gouge samples (fig. 17*A*). The two samples differ, however, in the extent of comminution. Sample SH307-1 has a bimodal size distribution with peaks at 10 and 350 µm; it has little material <1 µm in size and measurable clasts >5 mm. In contrast, the granulometric analysis for SH303-1 describes a rather broad peak with a poorly defined mode at about 32 µm, a substantial proportion of very fine grains, and no clasts >2.8 mm. This difference is best illustrated in a plot of cumulative volume, which shows the pronounced difference in volumetric contribution of very small particles (fig. 17*B*).

Grain size of fragments can also be estimated by analysis of BSE images. Although measurements of the number of clasts of a given size in area fraction are not directly comparable to measurements of the weight percent of a given sieve size, the image-analysis data provide another view of grain-size characteristics that can be compared directly with data from tectonic faults. Illustrative measurements on images from SH326-2A (figs. 3, 8*A*, 9*C*) show that the number-based data are dominated by the smallest size classes, which are difficult to measure accurately. When viewed as areal abundance, the data show a mode at 500 μm, similar to the volume-based (sieve) data for SH307-1 (fig. 18*A*). These data lack an equivalent peak at 8 μm because this was below our detection limit (~30 μm) for the imaging magnification used.

Quantifying the transition from intact dome lava to powdery gouge is more difficult. We experimented with measuring the reduction in size and abundance of plagioclase phenocrysts in thin section, a measurement that is easy to make using standard image-analysis techniques. The overall abundance of plagioclase, as measured in full thin-section scans (for example, fig. 9), decreases from a maximum of 32 percent in sample SH324-4A to 9.5 percent in consolidated gouge from the same sample (for example, fig. 9*B*; table 1). This range encompasses that of all other samples. Accompanying the decrease in crystal abundance is a decrease in average phenocryst size, which reflects breakage of large crystals to form numerous small crystal fragments. This breakage most severely affects the large phenocrysts, as shown by normalized cumulative plagioclase volume distributions (fig. 19). The median (50th percentile) plagioclase size decreases from about 300 μm in competent dome lava to about half of that in partially comminuted cataclasite sample 324-4A (fig. 19). More striking is the difference in maximum crystal size, which reaches several millimeters in the dome lava but only about 300 μm in SH324-4A cataclasite (table 1). If this analysis were extended to measurement of the finely laminated ultracataclasite zone of sample SH313-1 (fig. 16), the plagioclase size reduction would be even more extreme.

In summary, we have experimented with different ways of quantifying the observed fragmentation of competent dome rocks. Grain-size changes in fault gouge typi-

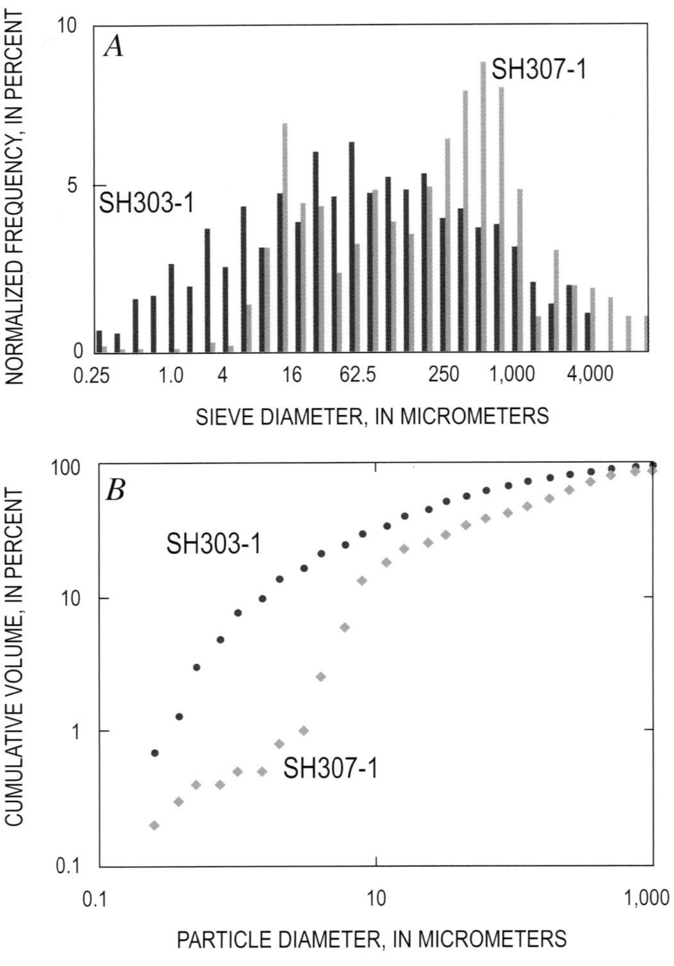

Figure 17. Sieve data for unconsolidated fault gouge samples SH303-1 (spine 3) and SH307-1 (spine 4). *A*, Histograms. *B*, Power-law plots. Note the difference in abundance of very fine particles (<10 μm) in the two samples and the absence of single power-law trend.

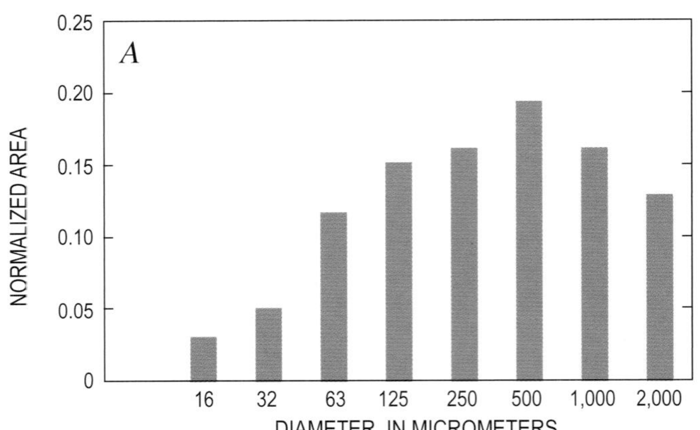

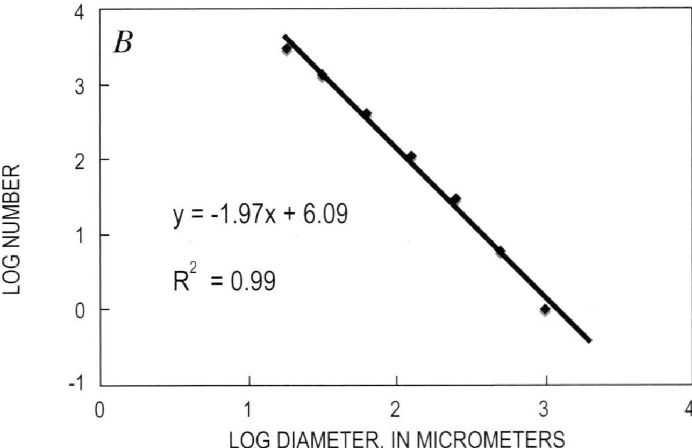

Figure 18. Grain-size data obtained by image analysis of BSE image of SH326-4A from spine 7. *A*, Histogram of data plotted by area (related to but not directly equivalent to volume-based sieve data). *B*, Power-law plot, with y-axis showing cumulative number of fragments greater than a given size. Data fit a power-law distribution over the size range 10–1,000 μm.

Table 1. Plagioclase phenocryst and microphenocryst data obtained from image analysis of whole thin-section scans.

[An example scan is shown in figure 9. Reported are the measured plagioclase area fraction, the total area measured, the total number of plagioclase crystals measured, the average plagioclase number per area, and the maximum and minimum plagioclase diameter. Where abrupt textural changes were preserved within a single thin section (for example, fig. 9*B*), different textural regimes were measured separately (denoted a and b).]

Sample No.	Plagioclase area fraction	Total area (mm^2)	Total number of crystals	Average crystal number	Maximum diameter (mm)	Minimum diameter (mm)
SH315	26.2	355	1,692	4.77	3.32	0.1
SH316(1)	27.9	222.5	2,441	10.97	1.19	0.03
SH316(2)	25.2	219.37	2,389	10.89	0.85	0.03
SH320-1C1(1)	11.7	185.54	2,404	12.96	1.01	0.02
SH320-1C1(2)	12.1	174.67	2,253	12.90	0.624	0.02
SH320-1A2	21.5	250.75	3,068	12.24	1.32	0.02
SH324-4A(1)-a	24	40.58	324	7.98	0.73	0.04
SH324-4A(2)-a	9.5	27.19	289	10.63	0.34	0.04
SH324-4A(1)-b	32	143.83	1,772	12.32	1.43	0.04
SH324-4A(2)-b	19.3	87.41	1,324	15.15	0.608	0.04
SH324-5(1)	25.8	198.9	3,496	17.58	0.91	0.02
SH324-5(2)	24.2	125.37	1,974	15.75	1.22	0.02
SH307-2A1	22.4	479.98	3,330	6.94	2.27	0.05

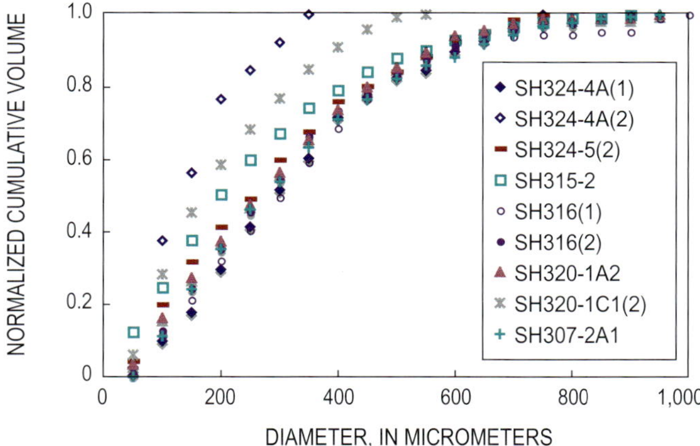

Figure 19. Plagioclase size distributions plotted as normalized cumulative volume for comparison with sieve data. Distributions determined by image analysis of full thin-section images, as shown in figure 9. Minimum size resolution approximately 30 µm (microphenocrysts and phenocrysts). Data show that plagioclase size distributions of undeformed dacite lava change progressively with increasing fragmentation toward smaller median and maximum crystal diameters. This change in size distribution is accompanied by a decrease in overall abundance of macroscopic plagioclase.

cally are measured by sieving, although this is possible only for unconsolidated samples. In cataclasite, clast size distributions may be analyzed using BSE images, although complete sample characterization would require combining multiple images at different magnifications. A simple characterization of progressive cataclasis of dome lava can be made using thin-section measurements of plagioclase phenocryst size and abundance. These data provide evidence of extensive fragmentation and grain-size reduction of dome lava during transport to the surface. Moreover, the common observations of abrupt textural transitions indicate extreme shear localization during transport. When combined with BSE evidence of initial grain shattering (figs. 15*B*, 16*D*) followed by shear, grinding, and wear (figs. 14*B*, 14*C*), these data suggest extensive transport distances (large strains) after initial breakage.

Discussion

The results presented above illustrate the range of processes that contributed to the transformation of dome lava to fault gouge and, in some cases, to ash emitted by small dome explosions (Rowe and others, this volume, chap. 29). In the following sections, we examine those processes in detail, paying particular attention to the role of degassing-induced crystallization and to conditions of fault formation. We generalize these observations by placing them first within the perspective provided by past activity (1980–1986) at Mount St. Helens and then within the context of other spine-forming eruptions.

The Role of Decompression Crystallization

All clasts within both cataclasite and fault gouge are nearly holocrystalline. Thus we infer that fragmentation of dome dacite occurred after most of the groundmass had crystallized. Extensive crystallization is most likely caused by decompression and degassing during the slow ascent of hydrous magma (reviewed above), although we cannot rule out the possibility of minor late-stage cooling along the conduit margin. Extensive crystallization, in turn, changes the rheology of the rising magma, particularly when coupled with changes in melt viscosity resulting from volatile exsolution (for example, Hess and Dingwell, 1996; Melnik and Sparks, 2002, 2005). At Mount St. Helens, these rheological changes transformed the deformation properties of the magma from plastic to brittle, fragmenting the rising magma plug and creating the resultant thick fault gouge. Constraining the depth at which this transformation initiates is important for accurate modeling of dome extrusion (Iverson and others, 2006), as well as for recognizing conditions that might lead to changes in the current eruptive activity.

Interpretation of the crystallization history of 2004–6 Mount St. Helens dacite is complicated by abundant evidence of nonequilibrium crystallization, including (1) rapid late-stage growth of rims on plagioclase phenocryst (fig. 10); (2) spatial heterogeneity of groundmass textures (both vesicles and crystals; fig. 11); (3) the presence of two or, sporadically, three silica phases (fig. 12); and (4) local temperature increases in the groundmass as the result of latent heat released by rapid groundmass crystallization (Blundy and others, this volume, chap. 33; Pallister and others, this volume, chap. 30). Here we briefly review the evidence for each before discussing the likely importance of each process to gouge formation.

Phenocryst textures that suggest rapid late-stage growth include swallowtail-like extensions from the corners of large crystals, irregular growth boundaries, and skeletal overgrowths that either partially or completely trap residual melt (fig. 10). These irregularities preserve glass within the growth protrusions, suggesting entrapment at moderately high pressures (that is, during early phases of groundmass crystallization), perhaps because microlite nucleation was inhibited by local increases in H_2O rejected from the rapidly growing crystal. Therefore it appears that this crystallization, while rapid, was not directly responsible for cataclasis and gouge formation, although it does reflect the overall importance of decompression-induced crystallization during this remarkably steady effusive activity.

More important for determining conditions of marginal fragmentation is the spatial inhomogeneity of groundmass textures found within the early dome lavas. Lavas are heterogeneous in both groundmass crystallinity and vesicularity. Heterogeneity in groundmass crystallinity is particularly evident in the concentration of cotectic quartz-plagioclase intergrowths along euhedral phenocryst margins (fig. 11). However, as most of the groundmass within the cataclasite and gouge samples is holocrystalline, it is unclear what effect, if any, the heterogeneities in groundmass crystallization may have had on brittle deformation of the dome dacite. Heterogeneous vesicle textures are more likely to affect the material properties of the lava when deformed. A feature of many of the holocrystalline clasts within the gouge is the presence of numerous tiny microvesicles that are probably a feature of second boiling during the last stages of crystallization. It is possible that variations in vesicle structure may play a role in clast breakage, although our observations suggest that this, also, does not dominate the failure behavior.

Most important for gouge formation seems to be near-complete solidification of the ascending magma. The depth of this solidification may be estimated using both groundmass phases and crystal textures. Three silica phases occur within the matrix of different gouge clasts: cristobalite, tridymite, and quartz. Cristobalite typically forms large crystals; similar crystals in cryptodome dacite from the 1980 eruption were interpreted by Hoblitt and Harmon (1993) to result from vapor-phase crystallization. Quartz can form discrete groundmass crystals, but it most commonly grows as fine-scale cotectic aggregates with plagioclase and anorthoclase. Tridymite forms discrete acicular grains (fig. 12) that are common in some samples, sparse in others, and completely absent in some dome lava. In their study of Mount St. Helens lava samples from 1980–1986, Blundy and Cashman (2001) found tridymite in a single lava sample erupted during the period of continuous slow effusion in 1983. They used experimental data to argue that equilibrium crystallization of tridymite in H_2O-saturated, anorthite-free melts requires a minimum pressure of 11 MPa and temperature of 885°C. Addition of anorthite to the melt will increase the temperature of the high quartz-tridymite boundary. Subsequently Cashman and McConnell (2005) found additional examples of tridymite-bearing dacite from pyroclasts stored temporarily at shallow levels prior to explosive eruptions of Mount St. Helens during the summer of 1980. When analyzed for volatile content using FTIR, one such glassy sample preserved ~0.6 weight percent H_2O, suggesting a minimum pressure of 5 MPa (A. Rust, oral commun., 2005). Thus it appears that the presence of tridymite requires shallow (<25 MPa) but not surface (>5–10 MPa) pressures (depths between 200 and 1,000 m for an average magma density of 2,500 kg/m^3). Patterns of silica-phase precipitation thus suggest (1) substantial delays in quartz nucleation to produce the observed high degree of spatial variability; (2) varying *P-T* paths during decompression, as illustrated by differences in the proportions of silica phases among samples; and (3) tridymite crystallization under a limited range of *P-T* conditions.

Experimental data (Hammer and Rutherford, 2002; Couch and others, 2003; Martel and Schmidt, 2003) further suggest that the common groundmass texture of holocrystalline quartz and feldspar intergrowths requires pressures >10 MPa (400 m) and crystallization time scales of weeks. If magma ascends at a constant rate from a storage region at >4 km (Rutherford and Devine, this volume, chap. 31), measured extrusion rates of ~7 m/d allow sufficient time for shallow crystallization (~3 months for ascent from 1,000 to 400 m). Pressures as low as 5 MPa were required to precipitate quartz-alkali feldspar intergrowths in decompression experiments on Pinatubo magma compositions (Hammer and Rutherford, 2002), whereas maximum rates of plagioclase nucleation typically require pressures between 25 and 5 MPa (Hammer and Rutherford, 2002; Couch and others, 2003; Martel and Schmidt, 2003). If gouge forms only after crystallization of the groundmass is nearly complete, these data suggest a shallow origin for the onset of brittle deformation (<400–500 m), consistent with the plug model of Iverson and others (2006). We note, however, that all of these estimates assume only minor cooling of magma during ascent, an assumption that appears reasonable given the high surface temperatures measured by FLIR (Schneider and others, this volume, chap. 17) and high Fe-Ti oxide temperatures from the dacite (Pallister and others, this volume, chap. 30).

Fault Gouge Formation

Extensive research on tectonic fault zones provides a framework for examining gouge formation during the extrusion of the 2004–6 Mount St. Helens spines. Tectonic fault zones commonly are characterized by narrow (millimeter to centimeter) slip planes composed of finely pulverized rock surrounded by broader cataclasite zones (typically meters in scale and locally foliated) mantled outward by a zone of less intensely deformed rock (for example, Chester and Logan, 1986, 1987; Chester and others, 1993; Schulz and Evans, 1998; Storti and others, 2003). These fault-zone characteristics are taken as evidence of strain-weakening behavior, with shear localization into narrow zones that act as the primary slip surfaces (for example, Ben-Zion and Sammis, 2003). Fault initiation in porous material commences with dispersed breakage, porosity reduction, and temporary strain hardening (for example, Mair and others, 2000; Cashman and Cashman, 2000). A change to strain-weakening behavior requires localization of shear through nucleation of interconnected slip surfaces (Biegel and others, 1989; Shipton and Cowie, 2003). Average particle size decreases with increasing strain (Marone and Scholz, 1989; Mair and others, 2000; Hadizadeh and Johnson, 2003) until that strain can be accommodated by rolling (Morgan and Boettcher, 1999), contact creep (Prasher, 1987), or development of new fault strands (if band formation results in local strain hardening; Mair and others, 2000).

In tectonic fault zones, gouge thickness shows a weak dependence on total displacement, a correlation that has been attributed to breakage of increasingly large asperities (Power and others, 1988). Sibson (1986) recognized three different types of natural fault gouge:

1. **Attrition breccia** resulting from wear. This gouge type is rare in tectonic faults, characterized by rolled clasts, and associated only with zones of significant fault slip.

2. **Distributed crush breccia** formed by destruction of local asperities. This gouge type is characterized by pervasive microfractures and jigsaw textures.

3. **Implosion breccia.** This gouge type has textures similar to those of distributed crush breccia.

Gouge within the cores of tectonic faults may contain ultrafine grains (micron to nanometer scale) whose origin has been variously attributed to quasi-static wear and attrition (Sammis and others, 1986; Chester and Chester, 1998), dynamic pulverization resulting from a single rupture event (Reches and Dewers, 2005; Wilson and others, 2005), and large strains (for example, Yund and others, 1990).

Our observations of textural characteristics of cataclasite and gouge samples from Mount St. Helens provide insight into fault gouge formation. Macroscopically, the structure of the fault zone along the conduit margin (for example, fig. 6) is similar to examples described in the fault literature, with an outer breccia that changes to cataclasite and, finally, into either fault gouge containing slickensides or areas of slip localization (figs. 8*C*, 16*A*) at the margin. Microscopically, localized extreme grain-size reduction along slickensides is consistent with experimental generation of ultrafine grains by large shear strains (Yund and others, 1990). Using the correlation for tectonic faults, a gouge thickness of 1–3 m suggests displacements of <1,000 m, in agreement with petrologic assessments of the depth of gouge formation presented above. Moreover, these values suggest total strains (displacement/thickness) less than or about 500. Assuming that all of the slip is concentrated along the conduit margin, observed slip rates of ~8×10^{-5} m/s are orders of magnitude higher than those of creeping faults and orders of magnitude lower than slip events on stick-slip faults. These slip velocities suggest strain rates (velocity/thickness) of 3–8×10^{-5}/s, intermediate to values typical for creeping and stick-slip tectonic faults.

The fault gouge itself appears to represent at least two of Sibson's (1986) types. Extensive grain fragmentation adjacent to the slickenside zones (figs. 15*B*, 16*D*) fits Sibson's description of distributed crush breccia, in that individual pieces of a grain have not been displaced from each other by shear. However, it is clear that these fragments are eventually distributed along the foliation bands by shear displacement after crushing (figs. 15*D*, 16*B*, 16*C*). In contrast, the common rounded fragments in cataclasite and gouge (figs. 14*B*, 14*C*) appear to be attrition breccia, with rounding that results from abrasion and wear during shear transport. The prevalence of these attrition features may reflect not only the large total displacements (shear strain) involved with dome emplacement but also the steadiness of movement. Whereas sporadic movement of tectonic faults allows healing or lithification of fault zones between slip events, steady movement of solidified magma along the conduit margin apparently prevents such healing. Instead, the observed gradual decrease in the percentage of larger clasts apparently allows them to be isolated from each other by the matrix, thus permitting individual clasts to roll and abrade. Continued brittle deformation of fragmented particles results in further grain-size reduction and shear localization along multiple slickensides.

An interesting discussion in the fault zone literature involves the mechanism by which fragmentation occurs. Patterns of grain-size reduction may be characterized by the fractal dimension D of particle grain size, where D relates cumulative particle frequency $N(S)$ (the number of particles less than S, usually measured per volume) to size (S):

$$N(S) \approx S^{-D}. \quad (1)$$

Thus D describes the relative proportion of small and large fragments; higher D values reflect samples where the grain-size distribution is dominated by smaller particles. Within this framework, the "pillar of strength" model (Allegre and others, 1982) predicts $D = 1.97$, the "plane of fragility" model (Turcotte, 1986) predicts $D = 2.84$, and the constrained comminution model (Sammis and others, 1986; Sammis and others, 1987; Sammis and Biegel, 1989; Turcotte, 1992) predicts $D = 2.6$. The latter model is based on sequential breakage of equal-size particles into a discrete (and relatively small) number of particles. Key to the constrained comminution model is that fragments of similar size are evenly distributed in space. Experimental studies of sheared quartz sand support a model of constrained comminution under conditions of high confining pressure (100 MPa) and particle size range of 10 μm to 1 mm (Biegel and others, 1989; Marone and Scholz, 1989). However, data from natural cataclastic samples are less easily interpreted (for example, Blenkinsop, 1991; An and Sammis, 1994; Storti and others, 2003; Cashman and others, 2007). In many fault zones, D values change from low in brecciated damage zones to high in intensely comminuted narrow shear zones (fig. 20). These high D values (high degrees of crushing) may result from slip-enhanced surface abrasion during shear transport, as suggested by Hooke and Iverson (1995) for glacially abraded sediment. High degrees of crushing also create the matrix support required to allow rolling and abrasion of remaining larger particles.

The fragmentation schematic shown in figure 20 provides a description of the process of gouge development at Mount St. Helens. Imaging data, which can be used to characterize the larger clast sizes in the cataclasite, yield fractal dimensions ~1.97 for particles from 10 to 1,000 μm in diameter (fig. 18*B*) when measured as number per area; this is equivalent to D ~ 2.97 on a volume basis. This high D value is identical to that measured by Chester and others (2005) in cataclasite and ultracataclasite of the Punchbowl Fault, a large-displacement fault in the San Andreas Fault system. Sieve data (fig. 17), however, show that grain size data are self similar (fractal) only within limited size ranges. As seen in other fault rocks, fits to straight-line segments suggest that D increases with decreasing grain size (for example, Blenkinsop, 1991; An and Sammis, 1994; Storti and others, 2003). High D values at very small grain sizes result from extensive comminution of individual clasts, as evidenced by the shattered large crystals and dome fragments that border the slickensides (figs. 15*B*, 16*D*). Thus we interpret the grain-size data to reflect (1) cataclasis and particulate flow over most of the observed gouge thickness and (2) strain localization and intense comminution within the slickensides, which are themselves distributed within the outer gouge zone.

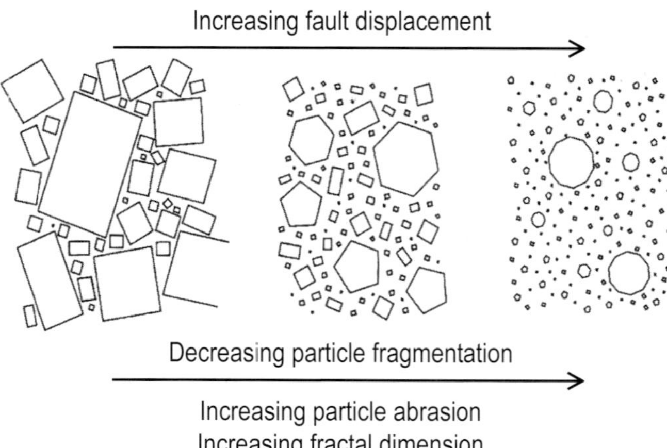

Figure 20. Diagram showing schematic change in size and shape of grains with increasing fault displacement. Although drawn for tectonic faults, this progression from coarse to fine grain sizes and angular to rounded shapes appears appropriate to fault behavior associated with spine emplacement at Mount St. Helens, Washington. Figure from Storti and others (2003).

The frictional properties of 2004–6 Mount St. Helens fault gouge have been investigated by Moore and others (this volume, chap. 20) at room temperature, shear rates of 1.5–5,000×10^{-6} m/s, and low normal stresses (5–195 kPa). They find rate-weakening behavior at shear rates <1×10^{-4} m/s and rate-strengthening behavior at >5×10^{-4} m/s, with stick-slip oscillations observed at the highest normal stress and lowest shear rates. However, although they observe shear localization into a narrow (1 mm) zone, they find no evidence of comminution or crushing of gouge, perhaps because the small cumulative strains and low normal stresses in the experiments were insufficient to produce the grain breakage observed in natural samples.

In summary, the unusually well developed fault gouge that has mantled all of the 2004–6 Mount St. Helens spines provides evidence of profound change in the rheological behavior of dome lava during ascent as a consequence of near-complete crystallization and subsequent brittle breakage and gouge formation. The effect of this extensive brittle deformation on dome extrusion is less clear. Iverson and others (2006) suggest that rate-weakening behavior is required to produce the stick-slip behavior suggested by the repetitive (drumbeat) earthquakes. Alternatively, Mastin and others (this volume, chap. 22) suggest a gouge zone that is, overall, rate strengthening but that fails in a patchwork fashion during extrusion. Field evidence for localized failure includes both observed Reidel shears in the cataclasite and in throughgoing ultracataclasite (slickenside) bands within the gouge.

Comparison with Other Dome Eruptions

The morphology and emplacement conditions of other recent domes and spines of intermediate composition are reviewed above. Here we use observations of the 2004–6 activity at Mount St. Helens to evaluate processes that may have affected extrusive behavior at other volcanoes.

Dome emplacement during the 1980–86 eruption of Mount St. Helens provides the most obvious comparison with current (2004–6) activity. Importantly, although the erupted composition in the 1980s was similar to that of the 2004–6 dacite and average effusion rates were comparable (or slightly lower), the 1980–86 magma had a higher temperature (880–900°C in the early 1980s compared with 840–850°C in 2004–6), and its extrusion was dominantly episodic rather than continuous. Spines were produced on only two occasions: (1) accompanying endogenous growth during continuous effusion in 1983 and (2) following a protracted, 17-day episode of (mostly endogenous) dome-lobe formation in May 1985. Backscattered electron images of a sample from the February 1983 spine look similar to early samples of the 2004 spine (compare fig. 21*A* with fig. 11*C*). In both samples the distribution of groundmass crystals is heterogeneous, as is the distribution of clean glass. In contrast, a marginal sample of the May 1985 spine is holocrystalline (fig. 21*B*), with the characteristic cotectic crystallization fabric seen in the more slowly extruded 2005–6 spine samples.

However, there are two differences between the spine sample from May 1985 and those of the current eruption. First, the extremely fine-scale "myrmekitic" textures occupying interstices between microlites in the May 1985 sample (and not observed in the 2004–6 spine samples) suggest that preeruptive crystallization occurred at shallow levels, most likely within the dome itself. Second, the boundary between the extruded spine and the dome lobe had a different character in 1985. In contrast to the thick gouge zones described above, the spine-dome lobe boundary in 1985 comprised a thin (~10 mm) cataclasite zone that, although showing some of the grain-size reduction characteristics of the recent gouge, was narrower and less

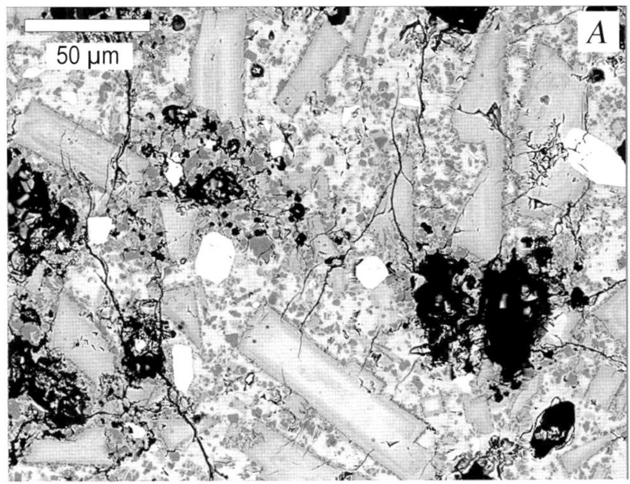

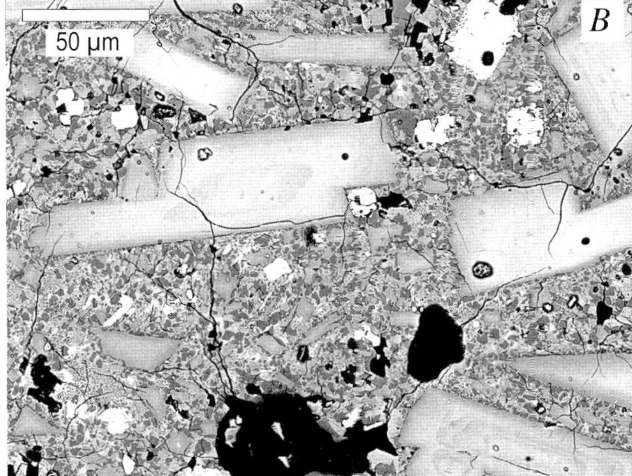

Figure 21. Backscattered electron images showing groundmass textures of 1980s lava spines of Mount St. Helens. Textures are similar to those observed in spines produced during current Mount St. Helens eruptive activity; for example, compare with figures 11*C*, 11*D*, 12*A*, or 12*B*. *A*, February 1983. *B*, May 1985.

comminuted (compare thin-section image of fig. 22 with those of fig. 9). These features suggest that the May 1985 dome was formed by late-stage solidification within the growing dome, with extrusion resulting in only small cumulative displacements (strain), consistent with its small size.

More similar are larger spines produced at Mont Pelée (1903), Unzen (1991–95), and Soufrière Hills (1995–present), which have macroscopic features similar to the 2004–6 spines at Mount St. Helens, including smooth curved forms and pronounced striations parallel to the extrusion direction (reviewed above). Descriptions in the literature suggest that gouge was present on the striated surface of the giant Mont Pelée spine (Jaggar, 1904); gouge and cataclasite also mantle some large dome fragments from Soufrière Hills, Montserrat. Conditions leading to spine formation also appear similar at all of these locations. Most important are estimated ascent rates of 1–3×10^{-4} m/s, rates that are sufficiently slow for the extensive crystallization necessary for both plug and fault gouge formation (see above). The comparison between the 1985 and current spines at Mount St. Helens further suggests that formation of large spines requires that magma solidify well within the conduit. This depth of solidification, in turn, means that solid dome rock must be transported large distances before exiting the vent, with resulting large strains responsible for the development of thick gouge zones.

From Dome to Dust

Brittle deformation is not unique to holocrystalline spines of intermediate composition. Numerous small-scale brittle deformation features have been described along shallow conduit margins and within basal shear zones of glassy obsidian domes, including anastomosing tuffisite veins and fractures, cataclasite zones, and trails of broken phenocrysts (for example, Stasiuk and others, 1996; Tuffen and Dingwell, 2005). Fracture and grain-size reduction in these systems have been explained by shear-strain rates at conduit margins exceeding experimentally determined critical rates for shear-induced fragmentation (for example, Dingwell and Webb, 1989) of high viscosity (10^{10}–10^{12} Pa s) melts at the low strain rates (10^{-3}–10^{-5}/s) anticipated for dome extrusion (Gonnermann and Manga, 2003; Tuffen and others, 2003).

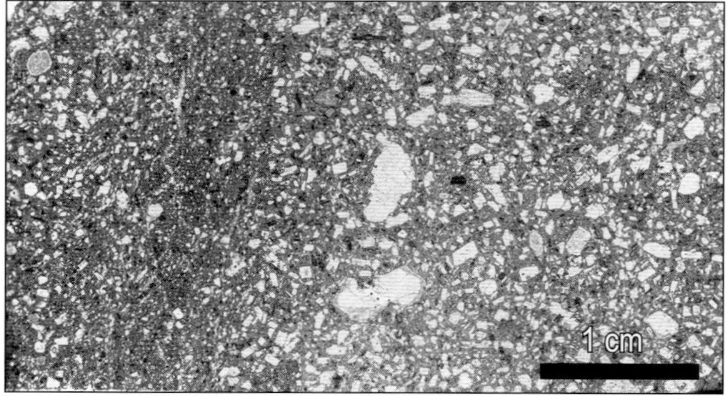

Figure 22. Full thin-section (4.5 cm x 2.5 cm) scan of sample collected across the margin of the May 1985 dome lobe (right) and spine (far left). The darker area of reduced phenocryst size toward the left side of the figure is a thin (<1 cm) cataclasite zone that marks the lava-spine boundary.

Deformation textures in obsidian domes, however, differ dramatically from those described here for the Mount St. Helens gouge zone. First, fracture networks in obsidian are limited to thin (<20 mm) fault and injection veins with limited to no displacement and thicker, irregular "injection voids" (≤80 mm in width; Tuffen and Dingwell, 2005). The largest fault complex observed by Tuffen and Dingwell (2005) is ~5 m in length, with a maximum offset of 0.13 m. Thus these features are substantially smaller than the zones of breccia, cataclasite, and gouge that line the shallow Mount St. Helens conduit, with the possible exception of basal breccia zones in some obsidian flows (Gonnermann and Manga, 2003). Moreover, both tuffisite veins and basal breccias show abundant evidence of annealing and ductile deformation (Gonnermann and Manga, 2003; Tuffen and others, 2003; Tuffen and Dingwell, 2005). In contrast, gouge zones at Mount St. Helens are dominated by brittle fracture and cataclastic flow, with no evidence of re-annealing between fracture events. Finally, fracture zones within obsidian domes appear to lack the distinct zones of breccia, cataclasite, and gouge seen at Mount St. Helens; instead, fragment sizes within the tuffisite veins are very small (much less than 1 mm), with no clasts of intermediate size.

What are the implications of these differences in fragmentation style? Annealing textures preserved within tuffisite veins and basal breccias of obsidian flows result from the strain-dependent rheology of viscous silicate melts; at the same temperature, the melt will flow at low strain rates but will fracture at higher strain rates. For this reason, a model of flow emplacement by repeated fracture and healing *of the same magma* has been suggested for obsidian (Tuffen and others, 2003; Tuffen and Dingwell, 2005). This model has been extended to explain repetitive seismic events accompanying andesitic dome growth at Soufrière Hills, Montserrat (for example, Neuberg and others, 2006). Our observations of fault gouge formation, however, would suggest caution in the direct application of deformation mechanisms in obsidian to the interpretation of seismicity associated with the emplacement of highly crystalline lava. Most importantly, we see no evidence of annealing within the gouge zone between fracture events. Instead, fault gouge forms by fracture and fragmentation of crystals and holocrystalline matrix into successively smaller fragments. For this reason, we suggest that the origin of the repetitive (drumbeat) earthquakes at Mount St. Helens most likely lies in progressive fragmentation of dome dacite rather than by process of repeated fracture and healing. Although definite assignment of individual slip features to specific earthquake characteristics is beyond the scope of this paper, we note that several types of slip zones are apparent at the outcrop to hand-specimen scale, from Reidel shears in the cataclasite (fig. 6) to slickensides in the gouge (fig. 8*C*). If individual drumbeat earthquakes represent slip events of ~5 mm (Iverson and others, 2006), then they may represent the composite effect of fracturing multiple smaller grains (as suggested by the dominance of fine (<10–20 μm) material within the cataclasite and gouge zone. Alternatively, perhaps only the initial fragmentation of larger dome fragments is seismogenic.

This leads to a final point—the role of fragmentation during dome explosions. A common assumption is that dome explosions result from sudden decompression of pressurized dome interiors and resultant brittle fragmentation (for example, Alidibirov and Dingwell, 1996). However, Rowe and others (this volume, chap. 29) demonstrate that ash released during the two substantial dome explosions associated with the current eruption (in January and March of 2005) bears a striking textural resemblance to the fault gouge described here. The implications of this observation are that the explosions themselves transported, but did not generate, much of the ash emitted during each event, an interpretation consistent with the source of the explosions at the junction of the spine and the conduit rather than from within the dome itself. We suspect that gouge formed along conduit margins may commonly supply ash to explosions that accompany spine growth (for example, Jaggar, 1904), a hypothesis that suggests that further studies of the physical properties of volcanic gouge (especially relations between deformation behavior and permeability) could improve our understanding of hazards related to the slow extrusion of lava spines.

Conclusions

We have documented field, hand-sample, and thin-section evidence for cataclasis and gouge formation along the margins of the smooth-surfaced spines extruded from Mount St. Helens from 2004 to present. These observations show brittle breakage and subsequent cataclastic flow to be important in the slow extrusion of intermediate-composition hydrous magma. Detailed textural observations document both crystallization accompanying magma ascent (decompression) and the sequential fragmentation of competent dome rock to produce fine-grained fault gouge. Taken together, these observations provide new constraints on interactions between rates of magma ascent, degassing, crystallization, and brittle fragmentation, interactions that control the dynamics of lava extrusion.

The groundmass of dacite lava samples is variably crystalline, with the extent of groundmass crystallinity apparently increasing with time (decreasing mass eruption rate). Most, if not all, of the crystallization is driven by decompression and degassing rather than cooling; Fe-Ti oxide temperatures suggest that the extensive crystallization may even help to heat the magma (for example, Blundy and others, 2006; Pallister and others, this volume, chap. 30). Within the gouge zone, dome fragments are holocrystalline, indicating solidification along conduit margins prior to brittle fragmentation. Detailed textural observations show that the transformation of competent dacite to fine powder occurred by sequential breakage of rock fragments to form zones of breccia, cataclasite, and gouge. Further concentration of slip along narrow slickenside planes produced thin (1 mm) zones of pulverized and foliated ultracataclasite. Both the extreme grain-size reduction along these slip zones and the shattering of individual grains observed adjacent to narrow slip surfaces are similar to textures observed in near-surface gouge produced by large tectonic faults (for example, Cashman and others, 2007) and suggest large strains. This inference is reasonable given a solidification depth of 400–500 m, above which deformation apparently is concentrated along the conduit margin (for example, Iverson and others, 2006). However, we see no evidence of subsequent annealing, as is commonly observed in tuffisite veins and obsidian flows (for example, Tuffen and others, 2003; Gonnermann and Manga, 2003), suggesting that earthquake-generating mechanisms based on repeated fracturing and healing do not apply to the extrusion of highly crystalline domes. Additionally, the two largest explosions at Mount St. Helens (in January and March of 2005) occurred at the contact between the spine and conduit wall and ejected ash that appears to have originated as fault gouge.

The physical characteristics of dome extrusion at Mount St. Helens from 2004–6 can be generalized to other recent examples of andesite and dacite extrusions. As surmised by Williams (1932), the complete decompression-driven solidification prior to magma extrusion necessary for spine formation requires magma ascent to be slow relative to the kinetics of crystallization and the dynamics of gas loss. Spine formation appears limited to magma ascent rates of <1–5×10^{-4} m/s, which allows several weeks for magma to transit from ~1,000 m (the point at which crystallinity increases dramatically as a function of decreasing pressure; Blundy and others, 2006) to ~400 m, where extensive cotectic crystallization of quartz and feldspar occurs. Comparison of marginal shear behavior of a small spine produced at Mount St. Helens in 1985 and the large spines produced from 2004 to 2006 also suggest a further point—that formation of large spines requires solidification to occur deep within the conduit, a condition that leads to extensive brittle deformation and gouge formation during transit to the surface.

Acknowledgments

The authors would like to acknowledge all CVO personnel who helped with field observations and sample collection, as well as a host of volunteers who helped to sort and catalogue the samples. We thank reviewers Rob Watts and Nick Beeler for their thoughtful comments on the first draft of the manuscript. Cashman acknowledges support from NSF EAR-0207362 and EAR-0510437.

References Cited

Alidibirov, M., and Dingwell, D.B., 1996, Magma fragmentation by rapid decompression: Nature, v. 380, no. 6570, p. 146–148, doi:10.1038/380146a0.

Allegre, C.J., LeMouel, J.L., and Provost, A., 1982, Scaling rules in rock fracture and possible implications for earthquake predictions: Nature, v. 297, p. 47–49.

An, L.J., and Sammis, C., 1994, Particle size distribution in cataclastic fault materials from Southern California; a 3-D study: Pure and Applied Geophysics, v. 143, p. 203–228.

Ben-Zion, Y., and Sammis, C., 2003, Characterization of fault zones: Pure and Applied Geophysics, v. 160, p. 677–715.

Biegel, R.L., Sammis, C.G., and Dieterich, J.H., 1989, The frictional properties of a simulated fault gouge having a fractal particle distribution: Journal of Structural Geology, v. 11, no. 7, p. 827–846.

Blenkinsop, T.G., 1991, Cataclasis and processes of particle size reduction: Pure and Applied Geophysics, v. 136, p. 59–86.

Blundy, J., and Cashman, K., 2001, Ascent-driven crystallisation of dacite magmas at Mount St. Helens, 1980–1986: Contributions to Mineralogy and Petrology, v. 140, no. 6, p. 631–650, doi:10.1007/s004100000219.

Blundy, J., and Cashman, K., 2005, Rapid decompression-driven crystallization recorded by melt inclusions from Mount St. Helens volcano: Geology, v. 33, no. 10, p. 793–796, doi:10.1130/G21668.1.

Blundy, J., Cashman, K., and Humphreys, M., 2006, Magma heating by decompression-driven crystallization beneath andesite volcanoes: Nature, v. 443, no. 7101, p. 76–80, doi:10.1038/nature05100.

Blundy, J., Cashman, K.V., and Berlo, K., 2008, Evolving magma storage conditions beneath Mount St. Helens inferred from chemical variations in melt inclusions from the 1980–1986 and current (2004–2006) eruptions, chap. 33 *of* Sherrod, D.R., Scott, W.E., and Stauffer, P.H., eds., A volcano rekindled; the renewed eruption of Mount St. Helens, 2004–2006: U.S. Geological Survey Professional Paper 1750 (this volume).

Cashman, K.V., 1992, Groundmass crystallization of Mount St. Helens dacite, 1980–1986; a tool for interpreting shallow magmatic processes: Contributions to Mineralogy and Petrology, v. 109, no. 4, p. 431–449, doi:10.1007/BF00306547.

Cashman, K.V., and Blundy, J., 2000, Degassing and crystallization of ascending andesite and dacite: Philosophical Transactions of the Royal Society of London, v. 358, p. 1487–1513.

Cashman, S.M., and Cashman, K.V., 2000, Cataclasis and deformation-band formation in unconsolidated marine terrace sand, Humboldt County, California: Geology, v. 28, p. 111–114.

Cashman, K.V., and McConnell, S.M., 2005, Multiple levels of magma storage during the 1980 summer eruptions of Mount St. Helens, WA: Bulletin of Volcanology, v. 68, no. 1, p. 57–75, doi:10.1007/s00445-005-0422-x.

Cashman, S.M., Baldwin, J.N., Cashman, K.V., Swanson, K., and Crawford, R., 2007, Microstructures developed by coseismic and aseismic faulting in unconsolidated near-surface sediments, San Andreas fault, California: Geology, v. 35, no. 7, p. 611–614, doi:10.1130/G23545A.1.

Chadwick, W.W., Archuleta, R.J., and Swanson, D.A., 1988, The mechanics of ground deformation precursory to dome-building extrusions at Mount St. Helens 1981–1982: Journal of Geophysical Research, v. 93, no. B5, p. 4351–4366, doi:10.1029/88JB01345.

Chester, F.M., and Logan, J.M., 1986, Implications for mechanical properties of brittle faults from observations of the Punchbowl fault zone, California: Pure and Applied Geophysics, v. 124, p. 79–106.

Chester, F.M., and Logan, J.M., 1987, Composite planar fabric of gouge from the Punchbowl fault, California: Journal of Structural Geology, v. 9, p. 621–634.

Chester, F.M., Evans, J.P., and Beigel, R.L., 1993, Internal structure and weakening mechanics of the San Andreas Fault: Journal of Geophysical Research, v. 98, p. 771–786.

Chester, J.S., Chester, F.M., and Kronenberg, A.K., 2005, Fracture surface energy of the Punchbowl fault, San Andreas system: Nature, v. 437, p. 133–136.

Couch, S., Sparks, R.S.J., and Carroll, M.R., 2003, The kinetics of degassing-induced crystallization at Soufrière Hills Volcano, Montserrat: Journal of Petrology, v. 44, p. 1477–1502.

Devine, J.D., Rutherford, M.J., Norton, G.E., and Young, S.R., 2003, Magma storage region processes inferred from geochemistry of Fe-Ti oxides in andesitic magma, Soufrière Hills volcano, Montserrat, W.I.: Journal of Petrology, v. 44, no. 8, p. 1375–1400, doi:10.1093/petrology/44.8.1375.

Dingwell, D.B., and Webb, S.L., 1989, Structural relaxation in silicate melts and non-Newtonian melt rheology in geological processes: Physics and Chemistry of Minerals, v. 16, p. 508–516.

Donnadieu, D., and Merle, O., 1998, Experiments on the indentation process during cryptodome intrusions; new insights into Mount St. Helens deformation: Geology, v. 26, p. 79–82.

Endo, E.T., Dzurisin, D., and Swanson, D.A., 1990, Geophysical and observational constraints for ascent rates of dacitic magma at Mount St. Helens, *in* Ryan, M.P., ed., Magma transport and storage: New York, John Wiley, p. 317–334.

Fink, J.H., Malin, M.C., and Anderson, S.W., 1990, Intrusive and extrusive growth of the Mount St Helens lava dome: Nature v. 348, p. 435–437.

Gardner, C.A., Cashman, K.V., and Neal, C.A., 1998, Tephra-fall deposits from the 1992 eruption of Crater Peak, Alaska; implications of clast textures for eruptive processes: Bulletin of Volcanology, v. 59, p. 537–555.

Geschwind, C.-H., and Rutherford, M.J., 1995, Crystallization of microlites during magma ascent; the fluid mechanics of 1980–1986 eruptions at Mount St. Helens: Bulletin of Volcanology, v. 57, no. 5, p. 356–370.

Gilbert, G.K., 1904, The mechanism of the Mont Pelée spine: Science, v. 19, p. 927–928.

Gonnermann, H.M., and Manga, M., 2003, Explosive volcanism may not be an inevitable consequence of magma fragmentation: Nature, v. 426, p. 432–435.

Hadizadeh, J., and Johnson, W.K., 2003, Estimating local strain due to comminution in experimental cataclastic textures: Journal of Structural Geology, v. 25, p. 1973–1979.

Hammer, J.E., and Rutherford, M.J., 2002, An experimental study of the kinetics of decompression-induced crystallization in silicic melt: Journal of Geophysical Research, v. 107, no. B1, p. ECV 8-1–8-24, doi:10.1029/2001JB000281.

Hammer, J.E., Cashman, K.V., Hoblitt, R., and Newman, S., 1999, Degassing and microlite crystallization during the pre-climactic events of the 1991 eruption of the Mt. Pinatubo, Philippines: Bulletin of Volcanology, v. 60, p. 355–380.

Hammer, J.E., Cashman, K.V., and Voight, B., 2000, Magmatic processes revealed by textural and compositional trends in Merapi dome lavas: Journal of Volcanology and Geothermal Research, v. 100, p. 165–192.

Heliker, C., 1995, Inclusions in the Mount St. Helens dacite erupted from 1980 through 1983: Journal of Volcanology and Geothermal Research, v. 66, nos. 1–3, p. 115–135, doi:10.1016/0377-0273(94)00074-Q.

Hess, K.-U., and Dingwell, D.B., 1996, Viscosities of hydrous leucogranitic melts; a non-Arrhenian model: American Mineralogist, v. 81, p. 1297–1300.

Hoblitt, R.P., and Harmon, R.S., 1993, Bimodal density distribution of cryptodome dacite from the 1980 eruption of Mount St. Helens, Washington: Bulletin of Volcanology, v. 55, no. 6, p. 421–437, 10.1007/BF00302002.

Hooke, R.L., and Iverson, N.R., 1995, Grain-size distribution in deforming subglacial tills; role of grain fracture: Geology, v. 23, p. 57–60.

Iverson, R.M., 2008, Dynamics of seismogenic volcanic extrusion resisted by a solid surface plug, Mount St. Helens, 2004–2005, chap. 21 *of* Sherrod, D.R., Scott, W.E., and Stauffer, P.H., eds., A volcano rekindled; the renewed eruption of Mount St. Helens, 2004–2006: U.S. Geological Survey Professional Paper 1750 (this volume).

Iverson, R.M., Dzurisin, D., Gardner, C.A., Gerlach, T.M., LaHusen, R.G., Lisowski, M., Major, J.J., Malone, S.D., Messerich, J.A., Moran, S.C., Pallister, J.S., Qamar, A.I., Schilling, S.P., and Vallance, J.W., 2006, Dynamics of seismogenic volcanic extrusion at Mount St. Helens in 2004–05: Nature, v. 444, no. 7118, p. 439–443, doi:10.1038/nature05322.

Jaggar, T.A., 1904, The initial stages of the spine on Pelée: American Journal of Science, v. 17, p. 34–40.

Lacroix, A., 1904, La Montagne Pelée et ses éruptions: Paris, Masson et Cie, 662 p.

Mair, K., Main, I., and Elphick, S., 2000, Sequential growth of deformation bands in the laboratory: Journal of Structural Geology, v. 22, p. 25–42.

Marone, C.J., and Scholz, C.H., 1989, Particle-size distribution and microstructures within simulated fault gouge: Journal of Structural Geology, v. 11, p. 799–814.

Martel, C., and Schmidt, B.C., 2003, Decompression experiments as an insight into ascent rates of silicic magmas: Contributions to Mineralogy and Petrology, v. 144, p. 397–415.

Martel, C., Bourdier, J.-L., Pichavant, M., and Traineau, H., 2000, Textures, water content and degassing of silicic andesites from recent plinian and dome-forming eruptions at Mont Pelée volcano (Martinique, Lesser Antilles arc): Journal of Volcanology and Geothermal Research, v. 96, p. 191–206.

Mastin, L.G., Roeloffs, E., Beeler, N.M., and Quick, J.E., 2008, Constraints on the size, overpressure, and volatile content of the Mount St. Helens magma system from geodetic and dome-growth measurements during the 2004–2006+ eruption, chap. 22 *of* Sherrod, D.R., Scott, W.E., and Stauffer, P.H., eds., A volcano rekindled; the renewed eruption of Mount St. Helens, 2004–2006: U.S. Geological Survey Professional Paper 1750 (this volume).

Melnik, O., and Sparks, R.S.J., 2002, Dynamics of magma ascent and lava extrusion at Soufrière Hills Volcano, Montserrat, *in* Druitt, T.H., and Kokelaar, B.P., eds., The eruption of Soufrière Hills Volcano, Montserrat, from 1995 to 1999: Geological Society of London Memoir 21, p. 153–171.

Melnik, O., and Sparks, R.S.J., 2005, Controls on conduit magma flow dynamics during lava dome building eruptions: Journal of Geophysical Research, v. 110, no. B2, B02209, 21 p, doi:10.1029/2004JB003183.

Metrich, N., Bertagnini, A., Landi, P., and Rosi, M., 2001, Crystallization driven by decompression and water loss at Stromboli Volcano (Aeolian Islands, Italy): Journal of Petrology, v. 42, p. 1471–1490.

Moore, P.L., Iverson, N.R., and Iverson, R.M., 2008, Frictional properties of the Mount St. Helens gouge, chap. 20 *of* Sherrod, D.R., Scott, W.E., and Stauffer, P.H., eds., A volcano rekindled; the renewed eruption of Mount St. Helens, 2004–2006: U.S. Geological Survey Professional Paper 1750 (this volume).

Moran, S.C., Malone, S.D., Qamar, A.I., Thelen, W.A., Wright, A.K., and Caplan-Auerbach, J., 2008, Seismicity associated with renewed dome building at Mount St. Helens, 2004–2005, chap. 2 *of* Sherrod, D.R., Scott, W.E., and Stauffer, P.H., eds., A volcano rekindled; the renewed eruption of Mount St. Helens, 2004–2006: U.S. Geological Survey Professional Paper 1750 (this volume).

Morgan, J.K., and Boettcher, M.S., 1999, Numerical simulations of granular shear zones using the distinct element method. 1. Shear zone kinematics and the micromechanics of localization: Journal of Geophysical Research, v. 104, p. 2703–2719.

Nakada, S., and Fujii, T., 1993, Preliminary report on the activity at Unzen Volcano (Japan), November 1990–November 1991; dacite lava domes and pyroclastic flows: Journal of Volcanology and Geothermal Research, v. 54, p. 319–333.

Nakada, S., and Motomura, Y., 1999, Petrology of the 1991–1995 eruption at Unzen—effusion pulsation and groundmass crystallization: Journal of Volcanology and Geothermal Research, v. 89, p. 173–196.

Nakada, S., Miyake, Y., Sato, H., Oshima, O., and Fujinawa, A., 1995a, Endogenous growth of dacite dome at Unzen volcano (Japan), 1993–1994: Geology, v. 23, no. 2, p. 157–160.

Nakada, S., Motomura, Y., and Shimizu, H., 1995b, Manner of magma ascent at Unzen Volcano (Japan): Geophysical Research Letters, v. 22, p. 567–570.

Neuberg, J.W., Tuffen, H., Collier, L., Green, D., Powell, T., and Dingwell, D., 2006, The trigger mechanism of low-frequency earthquakes on Montserrat: Journal of Volcanology and Geothermal Research, v. 153, nos. 1–2, p. 37–50, doi:10.1016/j.jvolgeores.2005.08.008.

Newhall, C.G., and Melson, W.G., 1983, Explosive activity associated with the growth of volcanic domes: Journal of Volcanology and Geothermal Research, v. 17, p. 111–131.

Pabst, A., 1931, Pressure-shadows and the measurement of the orientation of minerals in rocks: American Mineralogist, v. 16, p. 55–70.

Pallister, J.S., Reagan, M., and Cashman, K., 2005, A new eruptive cycle at Mount St. Helens?: Eos (American Geophysical Union Transactions), v. 86, no. 48, p. 499–500, doi:10.1029/2005EO480006.

Pallister, J.S., Thornber, C.R., Cashman, K.V., Clynne, M.A., Lowers, H.A., Mandeville, C.W., Brownfield, I.K., and Meeker, G.P., 2008, Petrology of the 2004–2006 Mount St. Helens lava dome—implications for magmatic plumbing and eruption triggering, chap. 30 *of* Sherrod, D.R., Scott, W.E., and Stauffer, P.H., eds., A volcano rekindled; the renewed eruption of Mount St. Helens, 2004–2006: U.S. Geological Survey Professional Paper 1750 (this volume).

Power, W.L., Tullis, T.E., and Weeks, J.D., 1988, Roughness and wear during brittle faulting: Journal of Geophysical Research, v. 93, no. B12, p. 15268–15278.

Prasher, C.L., 1987, Crushing and grinding process handbook: New York, John Wiley, 482 p.

Reches, Z., and Dewers, T.A., 2005, Gouge formation by dynamic pulverization during earthquake rupture: Earth and Planetary Science Letters, v. 235, p. 361–374.

Rowe, M.C., Thornber, C.R., and Kent, A.J.R., 2008, Identification and evolution of the juvenile component in 2004–2005 Mount St. Helens ash, chap. 29 *of* Sherrod, D.R., Scott, W.E., and Stauffer, P.H., eds., A volcano rekindled; the renewed eruption of Mount St. Helens, 2004–2006: U.S. Geological Survey Professional Paper 1750 (this volume).

Rutherford, M.J., and Devine, J.D., III, 2008, Magmatic conditions and processes in the storage zone of the 2004–2006 Mount St. Helens dacite, chap. 31 *of* Sherrod, D.R., Scott, W.E., and Stauffer, P.H., eds., A volcano rekindled; the renewed eruption of Mount St. Helens, 2004–2006: U.S. Geological Survey Professional Paper 1750 (this volume).

Sammis, C., and Biegel, R., 1989, Fractals, fault gouge and friction: Pure and Applied Geophysics, v. 131, p. 255–271.

Sammis, C., Osborne, R.H., Anderson, J.L., Banerdt, M., and White, P., 1986, Self-similar cataclasis in the formation of fault gouge: Pure and Applied Geophysics, v. 143, p. 54–77.

Sammis, C., King, G., and Biegel, R., 1987, The kinematics of gouge deformation: Pure and Applied Geophysics, v. 125, p. 777–812.

Schilling, S.P., Thompson, R.A., Messerich, J.A., and Iwatsubo, E.Y., 2008, Use of digital aerophotogrammetry to determine rates of lava dome growth, Mount St. Helens, Washington, 2004–2005, chap. 8 *of* Sherrod, D.R., Scott, W.E., and Stauffer, P.H., eds., A volcano rekindled; the renewed eruption of Mount St. Helens, 2004–2006: U.S. Geological Survey Professional Paper 1750 (this volume).

Schneider, D.J., Vallance, J.W., Wessels, R.L., Logan, M., and Ramsey, M.S., 2008, Use of thermal infrared imaging for monitoring renewed dome growth at Mount St. Helens, 2004, chap. 17 *of* Sherrod, D.R., Scott, W.E., and Stauffer, P.H., eds., A volcano rekindled; the renewed eruption of Mount St. Helens, 2004–2006: U.S. Geological Survey Professional Paper 1750 (this volume).

Scholz, C.H., 1990, The mechanics of earthquakes and faulting: New York, Cambridge University Press, 439 p.

Schulz, S.E., and Evans, J.P., 1998, Spatial variability in microscopic deformation and composition of the Punchbowl fault, southern California; implications for mechanism, fluid-rock interaction, and fault morphology: Tectonophysics, v. 295, p. 225–246.

Scott, W.E., Sherrod, D.R., and Gardner, C.A., 2008, Overview of the 2004 to 2006, and continuing, eruption of Mount St. Helens, Washington, chap. 1 *of* Sherrod, D.R., Scott, W.E., and Stauffer, P.H., eds., A volcano rekindled; the renewed eruption of Mount St. Helens, 2004–2006: U.S. Geological Survey Professional Paper 1750 (this volume).

Shepherd, E.S., and Merwin, H.E., 1927, Gases of the Mt. Pelée lavas of 1902: Journal of Geology, v. 35, p. 97–116.

Shipton, Z.K., and Cowie, P.A., 2003, A conceptual model for the origin of fault damage zone structures in high-porosity sandstone: Journal of Structural Geology, v. 25, p. 333–344.

Sibson, R.H., 1977, Fault rock and fault mechanisms: Journal of the Geological Society, London, v. 133, p. 191–213.

Sibson, R.H., 1986, Brecciation processes in fault zones; inferences from earthquake rupturing: Pure and Applied Geophysics, v. 124, p. 159–176.

Snoke, A.W., Tullis, J., and Todd, V.R., 1998, Fault-related rocks—a photographic atlas: Princeton, Princeton University Press, 617 p.

Sparks, R.S.J., Murphy, M.D., Lejeune, A.M., Watts, R.B., Barclay, J., and Young, S.R., 2000, Control on the emplacement of the andesite lava dome of the Soufrière Hills volcano, Montserrat by degassing-induced crystallization: Terra Nova, v. 12, no. 1, p. 14–20.

Stasiuk, M.V., Barclay, J., Carroll, M.R., Jaupart, C., Ratte, J.C., Sparks, R.S.J., and Tait, S.R., 1996, Degassing during magma ascent in the Mule Creek vent (USA): Bulletin of Volcanology, v. 58, p. 117–130.

Storti, F., Billi, A., and Salvini, F., 2003, Particle size distribution in natural carbonate fault rocks—insights for non-self-similar cataclasis: Earth and Planetary Science Letters, v. 206, p. 173–186.

Streck, M.J., Broderick, C.A., Thornber, C.R., Clynne, M.A., and Pallister, J.S., 2008, Plagioclase populations and zoning in dacite of the 2004–2005 Mount St. Helens eruption; constraints for magma origin and dynamics, chap. 34 *of* Sherrod, D.R., Scott, W.E., and Stauffer, P.H., eds., A volcano rekindled; the renewed eruption of Mount St. Helens, 2004–2006: U.S. Geological Survey Professional Paper 1750 (this volume).

Swanson, D.A., and Holcomb, R.T., 1990, Regularities in growth of the Mount St. Helens dacite dome, 1980–1986, *in* Fink, J.H., ed., Lava flows and domes, emplacement mechanisms and hazard implications: Berlin, Springer-Verlag, International Association of Volcanology and Chemistry of the Earth's Interior, Proceedings in Volcanology 2, p. 3–24.

Thornber, C.R., Pallister, J.S., Lowers, H.A., Rowe, M.C., Mandeville, C.W., and Meeker, G.P., 2008a, Chemistry, mineralogy, and petrology of amphibole in Mount St. Helens 2004–2006 dacite, chap. 32 *of* Sherrod, D.R., Scott, W.E., and Stauffer, P.H., eds., A volcano rekindled; the renewed eruption of Mount St. Helens, 2004–2006: U.S. Geological Survey Professional Paper 1750 (this volume).

Thornber, C.R., Pallister, J.S., Rowe, M.C., McConnell, S., Herriott, T.M., Eckberg, A., Stokes, W.C., Johnson Cornelius, D., Conrey, R.M., Hannah, T., Taggart, J.E., Jr., Adams, M., Lamothe, P.J., Budahn, J.R., and Knaack, C.M., 2008b, Catalog of Mount St. Helens 2004–2007 dome samples with major- and trace-element chemistry: U.S. Geological Survey Open-File Report 2008–1130, 9 p., with digital database.

Tuffen, H., and Dingwell, D., 2005, Fault textures in volcanic conduits—evidence for seismic trigger mechanisms during silicic eruptions: Bulletin of Volcanology, v. 67, p. 370–387.

Tuffen, H., Dingwell, D.B., and Pinkerton, H., 2003, Repeated fracture and healing of silicic magma generate flow banding and earthquakes?: Geology, v. 31, p. 1089–1092.

Turcotte, D.L., 1986, Fractals and fragmentation: Journal of Geophysical Research, v. 91, p. 1921–1926.

Turcotte, D.L., 1992, Fractals and chaos in geology and geophysics: Cambridge, Cambridge University Press, 221 p.

Vallance, J.W., Schneider, D.J., and Schilling, S.P., 2008, Growth of the 2004–2006 lava-dome complex at Mount St. Helens, Washington, chap. 9 *of* Sherrod, D.R., Scott, W.E., and Stauffer, P.H., eds., A volcano rekindled; the renewed eruption of Mount St. Helens, 2004–2006: U.S. Geological Survey Professional Paper 1750 (this volume).

Watts, R.B., Herd, R.A., Sparks, R.S.J., and Young, S.R., 2002, Growth patterns and emplacement of the andesitic lava dome at Soufrière Hills Volcano, Montserrat, *in* Druitt, T.H., and Kokelaar, B.P., eds., The eruption of Soufrière Hills Volcano, Montserrat from 1995 to 1999: Geological Society of London Memoir 21, p. 115–152.

Williams, H., 1932, The history and character of volcanic domes: University of California, Bulletin of the Department of Geological Sciences, v. 21, p. 51–146.

Wilson, B., Dewers, T., Reches, Z., and Brune, J., 2005, Particle size and energetics of gouge from earthquake rupture zones: Nature, v. 434, p. 749–752.

Wolf, K.J., and Eichelberger, J.C., 1997, Syneruptive mixing, degassing and crystallization at Redoubt Volcano, eruption of December 1989 to May, 1990: Journal of Volcanology and Geothermal Research, v. 75, p. 19–37.

Wong, T.-f., David, C., and Zhu, W., 1997, The transition from brittle faulting to cataclastic flow in porous sandstones—mechanical deformation: Journal of Geophysical Research, v. 102, no. B2, p. 3009–3025.

Yund, R.A., Blanpied, M.L., Tullis, T.E., and Weeks, J.D., 1990, Amorphous material in high strain experiment fault gouge: Journal of Geophysical Research, v. 95, p. 15589–15602.

A Volcano Rekindled: The Renewed Eruption of Mount St. Helens, 2004–2006
Edited by David R. Sherrod, William E. Scott, and Peter H. Stauffer
U.S. Geological Survey Professional Paper 1750, 2008

Chapter 20

Frictional Properties of the Mount St. Helens Gouge

By Peter L. Moore[1], Neal R. Iverson[1], and Richard M. Iverson[2]

Abstract

Frictional properties of gouge bounding the solid dacite plug that extruded at Mount St. Helens during 2004 and 2005 may have caused stick-slip upward motion of the plug and associated seismicity. Laboratory experiments were performed with a ring-shear device to test the dependence of the peak and steady-state frictional strength of the gouge on shearing rate and hold time. A remolded gouge specimen (~0.012 m^3) was sheared under constant normal stresses ranging from 5 to 200 kPa and at rates ranging from 10^{-6} to 10^{-3} m/s. The gouge exhibited rate-weakening behavior at rates lower than 1×10^{-4} m/s and rate-strengthening at rates above 5×10^{-4} m/s. Peak strengths occurred during the onset of shearing, when displacements were generally less than 0.5 mm. In slide-hold-slide tests, the peak strength of the gouge increased logarithmically as hold times increased from 3 s to almost 10^5 s.

Rate-weakening friction is a requirement for stick-slip behavior that is satisfied by the Mount St. Helens gouge. Indeed, regular stick-slip oscillations were observed in two experiments performed at the highest normal stress and lowest rates of shear. The conditions under which this stick-slip motion occurred indicate that the gouge also satisfies a second criterion for stick-slip behavior of materials exhibiting rate-and-state dependent friction—gouge stiffness exceeds that of the ascending magma that drives upward motion of the plug. The presence of highly compliant magma as a driving element may be crucial for generating stick-slip instabilities at the shallow earthquake focal depths observed during the eruption.

Introduction

Lava dome formation during the 2004–2005 eruption of Mount St. Helens was accompanied by abundant, nearly periodic, shallow-focus earthquakes. These "drumbeat" earthquakes had magnitudes <2, focal depths <1 km, and they typically recurred about every 1–2 minutes. This seismicity is thought to have resulted from incremental uplift of a solid dacite plug driven by magma ascent from below at rates of roughly 1–2 m^3/s (Iverson and others, 2006). Wear along the margin of the plug produced a layer of crushed rock, or gouge, of the same lithology as the extruding rock (fig. 1). Observed at the surface, this gouge formed a coating 0.1–1 m thick on freshly exposed faces of the lava dome. Moreover, these freshly exposed faces were conspicuously striated in directions mostly parallel to the direction of plug motion, indicating that gouge deformation probably accommodated much of the upward displacement of the plug mass. Interpretation of the source of drumbeat seismicity, therefore, requires knowledge of the frictional properties of this gouge.

Gouge is generated by the wear and cataclasis of rock during frictional shear and develops progressively with shear displacement (for example, Engelder, 1974). Although cataclasis may occur episodically in rapidly strained magma near its solidus (for example, Tuffen and Dingwell, 2005), granular gouge dredged from the margin of the new Mount St. Helens lava dome early in 2005 was cool, noncohesive, and bore evidence primarily of mechanical wear and comminution. Therefore, the frictional behavior of the gouge is likely similar to that of low-temperature gouge in shallow crustal faults. Consequently, frictional behavior observed in room-temperature laboratory experiments is relevant to interpreting dome extrusion processes during the 2004–2005 eruption of Mount St. Helens.

[1] Department of Geological and Atmospheric Sciences, Iowa State University, Ames, IA 50011

[2] U.S. Geological Survey, 1300 SE Cardinal Court, Vancouver, WA 98683

Theoretical Background

Rate- and State-Dependent Friction

Gouge behavior closely approximates that of a Coulomb material, such that its shear strength τ is described by $\tau = \mu\sigma'_n + c$, where σ'_n is the effective normal stress, c is cohesion and μ is the coefficient of friction. In most granular media at low temperatures, μ can be considered nearly constant, but laboratory experiments have routinely shown that μ is slightly sensitive to both shear rate and the history of deformation. These deviations from a constant coefficient of friction are small but of great interest because under the appropriate conditions they give rise to an instability that may be responsible for earthquakes. In fault mechanics literature, these shear-rate and deformation-history effects are termed "rate" and "state" dependencies, respectively (see Marone, 1998, for a review).

Stemming from the work of Dieterich (1979) and Ruina (1983), the most common expression of the rate- and state-dependence of friction is

$$\mu = \mu_0 + a\ln\left(\frac{V}{V_0}\right) + b\ln\left(\frac{\theta V_0}{D_c}\right) , \qquad (1)$$

where μ_0 is a reference coefficient of friction applicable at a reference shear displacement rate V_0, V is shear displacement rate (with dimensions of length/time), θ is a state variable (with dimensions of time), D_c is a characteristic slip distance over which friction adjusts to a steady state in response to a velocity change, and a and b are positive coefficients that are typically of order 10^{-3} to 10^{-2}. Individually, the parameters a and b describe the relative magnitude of the so-called "direct" and "evolution" effects, respectively. The direct effect is a near-instantaneous response of friction to a change in shear rate, whereas the evolution effect is a transient response that takes place over the characteristic length scale D_c. Note that in this paper, we use the term "shear rate" to denote shear displacement rates such as V. Where we wish to distinguish such rates from shear strain rates, which have dimensions of inverse time, we do so explicitly.

The state variable θ in equation 1 describes a time-dependent effect that can be viewed as the length of time that a set of grain contacts persists at a given velocity (Scholz, 2002). According to Dieterich (1979), the evolution of θ with time may be described by

$$\frac{d\theta}{dt} = 1 - \left(\frac{V\theta}{D_c}\right) . \qquad (2)$$

Although the characteristic slip distance can be determined from stress-displacement data from experiments with bare rock, it is difficult to determine in experiments with gouge because this displacement depends on the strain distribution in the gouge (Marone and Kilgore, 1993). In a steady state ($d\theta/dt = 0$), $\theta = D_c/V$ and equation 1 reduces to

$$\mu_{ss} = \mu_0 + (a - b)\ln\left(\frac{V}{V_0}\right) , \qquad (3)$$

where μ_{ss} is the steady-state friction coefficient. The sensitivity of steady-state frictional strength to shear rate, therefore, is given by the difference between the coefficients a and b for the direct and evolution effects:

$$a - b = \frac{\mu_{ss} - \mu_0}{\ln\left(V/V_0\right)} . \qquad (4)$$

If this difference is negative, the material weakens with increasing slip rate, and conversely, if $a - b$ is positive, the material strengthens with increasing slip rate (Scholz, 2002). The coefficients a and b are usually determined experimentally by conducting velocity-stepping triaxial or direct-shear experi-

Figure 1. Photograph of striated gouge near base of extruding spine at Mount St. Helens, July 28, 2005. Field of view approximately 20 m. USGS photo by S.P. Schilling.

ments in which shear rate is varied over a wide range during continuous shear.

Consistent with Dieterich's original reasoning (Dieterich, 1972, 1978, 1979), Beeler and others (1994) demonstrated that the parameter b can also be determined independently by measuring the variation in peak friction as a function of the time that shear is stopped ("hold time"), such that

$$b = \frac{d\mu_{peak}}{d\ln(t_{hold})} \quad . \tag{5}$$

Peak shear strength typically increases logarithmically with time as sliding surfaces are held in stationary contact. The mechanisms responsible for this aging effect are thought to be associated with compaction and growth of the area of solid-to-solid grain contact across the shear zone (Losert and others, 2000; Scholz, 2002).

Relation Between Gouge Frictional Behavior and Seismicity

If gouge becomes weaker as shear rate increases ($a - b < 0$), slip instability and stick-slip motion are possible, but according to the rate-and-state dependent friction model, rate weakening alone is not sufficient to induce stick-slip behavior (Rice and Ruina, 1983; Ruina, 1983). The stiffnesses of the gouge and the system that loads the gouge are also important. The decline from peak (static) frictional strength to steady-state (dynamic) strength of the gouge requires a finite displacement that exceeds but is proportional to the characteristic slip distance, D_c. If elastic strain in the materials loading the shear zone is relaxed over a displacement larger than D_c, the applied driving stress momentarily exceeds the resisting stress and slip accelerates until driving and resisting stresses become equal (fig. 2). As defined by Ruina (1983), the "critical stiffness" of the gouge, k_{crit}, is the ratio of shearing-resistance decline to characteristic slip distance upon a change in slip velocity, and k_{crit} has dimensions of stress per unit length. If the loading system requires a slip distance much greater than D_c to reduce the applied stress from the peak to steady-state strength, the loading system's stiffness is smaller than k_c and stick-slip behavior is possible (fig. 2).

According to the arguments summarized above, repetitive stick-slip motion along the subsurface margins of the extruding dacite plug at Mount St. Helens can occur if two conditions are met—(1) the gouge must exhibit rate-weakening behavior at the imposed loading rate, and (2) the most compliant component of the loading system (that is, the magma) must have a stiffness smaller than the critical stiffness of the gouge. The first requirement is readily evaluated with our laboratory experiments. The second requirement is more difficult to address, but our experiments and inferences about the magma-plug system at Mount St. Helens provide some constraints.

Experimental Methods

Gouge was obtained by dredging the surface of the newly extruded spine at Mount St. Helens by helicopter in February 2005. Ring-shear tests were performed at room temperature with dry, remolded specimens. Particles with diameters larger than one-tenth the smallest dimension of the specimen chamber (70 mm) were removed from the gouge, consistent with normal geotechnical testing procedure (Head, 1989). Shearing rates and normal stresses were varied among tests through the ranges permitted by the device (5×10^{-3} to 1.5×10^{-6} m/s and 5 to 195 kPa respectively). These experiments differed from velocity-stepping tests (for example, Blanpied and others, 1987; Biegel and others 1989; Marone and others, 1990) in that shear-rate changes were made only after first stopping shear.

The ring-shear device (detailed in Iverson and others, 1997) has been used to study the mechanical properties of a variety of granular geological materials (for example, Iverson and others, 1998; Iverson and others, 2000; Moore and Iverson, 2002; Scherer and others, 2004). Its large capacity permits inclusion of larger particles that are common in gouge, but the test specimen's large surface area limits the magnitude

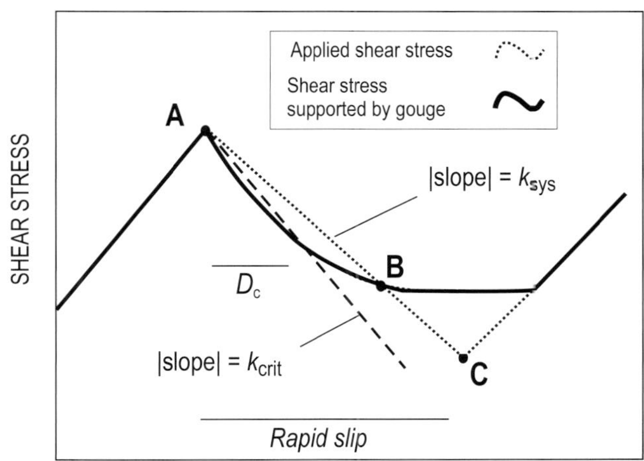

Figure 2. Stress applied by the loading system and shear stress supported by gouge during a stick-slip cycle. When slip commences at A, strength of the gouge initially declines more rapidly than the stress applied by the loading system, and acceleration occurs. When driving and resisting forces are equal again at B, slip begins to decelerate and stops at C. Slope of the decline in applied stress with displacement is the stiffness of the system (k_{sys}). When this stiffness is smaller than the critical stiffness of the gouge k_{crit} as defined by the shear stress decline and the gouge's characteristic slip distance D_c, the system is susceptible to stick-slip. D_c is the characteristic distance of exponential decay of gouge shearing resistance during rapid slip (after Scholz, 2002).

of the normal stress that can be applied. The ~70-mm-thick specimen rests in an annular chamber (annulus OD = 0.600 m, ID = 0.370 m) and is gripped at its base by a toothed platen (fig. 3). This platen is screwed to a base plate, and it and the lower walls bounding the specimen rotate. The toothed lid of the specimen chamber is prevented from rotating with the base by a pair of stationary, horizontally oriented load cells, causing the specimen to shear. The force exerted by the lid on these load cells is approximately the shear force supported by the specimen. Shear is focused in a lens-shaped zone that is 10–30 mm in thickness at the centerline of the specimen and is centered on the sliding interface between the upper and lower walls (fig. 3*B*) (for example, Hooyer and Iverson, 2000). A stress normal to the shearing direction is applied with a lever system that presses downward on the lid (fig. 3*A*). The lid is free to move vertically if the porosity of the specimen changes, and this vertical displacement is measured continuously with three equally spaced linear variable displacement transducers (LVDTs) that press on the perimeter of the lid.

Vertical and circumferential frictional forces between the gouge and the upper walls bounding the specimen are measured independently with a load cell and torque sensor, respectively, which are contained within a suspension called the "yoke" (fig. 3*A*). The yoke holds the upper walls stationary and is not coupled to the lid. The measured forces on the walls are used to correct both the normal stress applied to the shear zone, which is reduced by upward wall drag in a consolidating specimen, and the shear resistance on the lid, which is reduced due to circumferential drag between the specimen and walls. However, owing to extrusion of fine sediment along the interface between the upper and lower walls, a component of the measured circumferential wall force is due to friction between the upper and lower walls rather than between the upper wall and specimen. Thus, when applied normal stress is small, this friction represents an unknown fraction of the wall correction necessary to estimate the total resistance to shear. As a result, in experiments with the smallest applied normal stresses (5–23 kPa), uncertainty in the measured shear stresses and associated friction coefficients is large. Despite the uncertainty, these low-stress measurements are, nevertheless, included to qualitatively illustrate patterns that are available only from the low-stress tests.

Two variable-speed electric motors (1/17 and 1/2 hp) were used to turn the base and thereby shear the gouge specimen. Used in combination with either one or two gearboxes, these motors enabled two ranges of shear rate—1.5×10^{-6}–2.5×10^{-5} m/s and 5.0×10^{-4}–5.0×10^{-3} m/s. The higher-power motor coupled to a single gearbox allowed shearing at the higher range of rates, but this configuration could not deliver sufficient torque to shear the gouge under normal stresses greater than 23 kPa. When the smaller motor was used with both gearboxes normal stresses of as much as 200 kPa could be applied. At higher normal stresses this motor/gearbox configuration was not sufficient to turn the rotating base.

Two groups of experiments were conducted. In one group designed to investigate the rate dependence of gouge friction, shear was driven at a constant rate until shearing resistance became steady, usually after 1–10 mm of total centerline displacement. Shear was then stopped to adjust the motor speed and restarted under the same normal stress, but at a new rate, until shearing resistance again became steady. This process was repeated at multiple shearing rates, and whenever possible tests were repeated in sequences of increasing and decreasing shear rate. In a second group of experiments, periods of shear, which were terminated once shearing resistance became steady, were separated by intervals of hold (no shear) that ranged from 3 seconds to more than one day. In these experiments, shear rate and normal stress were held constant so that the effects of hold time on peak friction could be isolated.

A

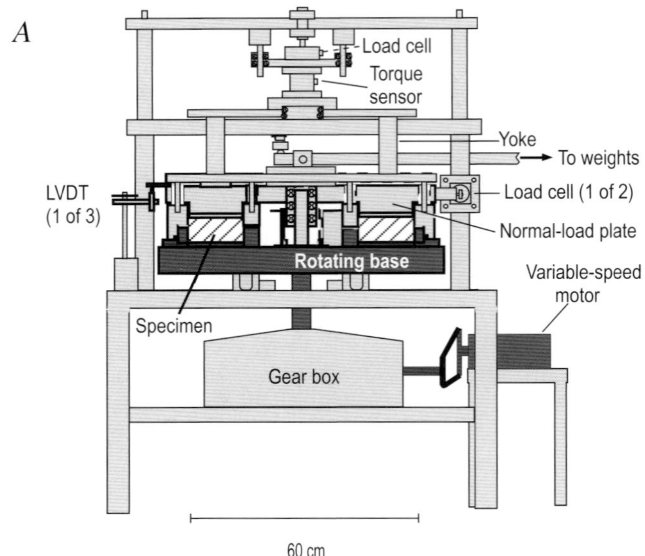

B

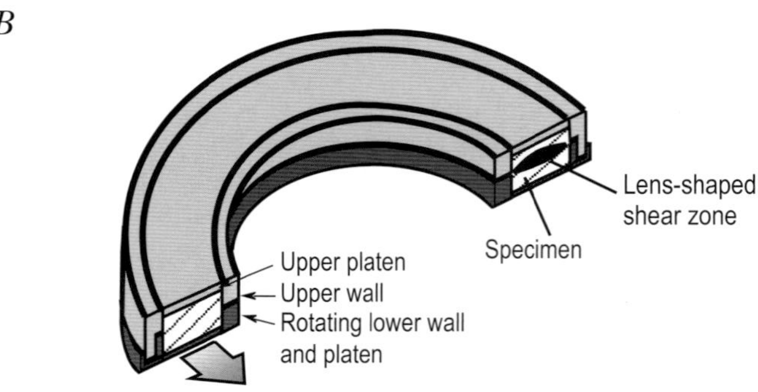

Figure 3. Ring-shear device. Gouge specimen is shown in crosshachure. *A*, Diagrammatic cross section. Dark-gray parts rotate when motor is on. A second gearbox between motor and large gearbox was used in the experiments conducted at low shear rates (1.5×10^{-6} – 2.5×10^{-5} m/s). LVDT, linear variable displacement transducers. *B*, Oblique sketch of the specimen chamber. Shearing in gouge typically is focused in a lens-shaped zone, shown in black, centered on interface between stationary upper wall and rotating lower wall.

After some of the experiments, the gouge was sieved to measure whether there had been a size reduction of the largest grains; no size reduction could be detected indicating that little comminution or crushing occurred in the experiments.

Results

Data obtained in two typical ring-shear experiments, conducted at different shear rates under an applied normal stress of 159 kPa, are shown in figure 4. Following initial stress peaks related to the "direct effect" of changing shear rate, shear stress became approximately steady after displacements of less than 10 mm. The key feature illustrated by these two data series is that the steady-state shear strength of the gouge was smaller at the faster shear rate. For rates smaller than 10^{-4} m/s, such rate weakening was always observed, except for experiments conducted at a normal stress of 23 kPa in which the shear-rate dependence was neutral or slightly positive, depending on how the data are regressed (fig. 5). In the two sets of experiments conducted at faster shearing rates and low normal stresses, rate strengthening was observed (fig. 5*B*). Unfortunately, because of the torque limitations of our motor/gearbox configurations, the shear rate at which the transition to rate strengthening occurs cannot be pinpointed, but it appears to be on the order of 10^{-4} m/s for the range of stresses considered. As described previously, measurements at the lowest applied normal stresses are uncertain, but the consistently larger apparent friction coefficient at normal stresses of 5 kPa may indicate that the gouge has some cohesion. (Cohesion of about 1 kPa would decrease the apparent friction coefficient at 5 kPa to about 0.4 or 0.5, comparable to values measured at higher normal stresses.) Alternatively, the larger friction coefficient at 5 kPa may reflect steepening of the Coulomb failure envelope that is commonly observed at low normal stresses in various laboratory tests on granular materials (Lambe and Whitman, 1969).

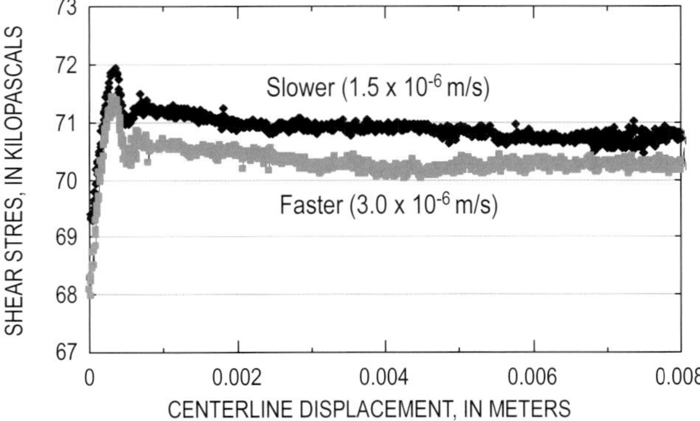

Figure 4. Stress-displacement data comparing two experiments conducted at normal stress of 159 kPa but at different shear rates. Prominent peaks in curves at ~0.5 mm of displacement are peak shear stresses, after which shear stress falls to steady-state value in both experiments.

Values of the rate-dependence parameter $a–b$ were estimated for each normal-stress level using equation 4 and a reference shear rate of 1.5×10^{-6} m/s, the smallest shear rate used in the experiments (table 1). Each value of $a–b$ was obtained from the slope of the linear regression of the steady-state friction coefficient against $\ln(V/V_0)$. Data from the "slow" (1.5×10^{-6} m/s to 2.5×10^{-5} m/s) and "fast" (5×10^{-4} m/s to 5×10^{-3} m/s) experiments were regressed separately. Values of $a–b$ at slow rates and high normal stresses (86–195 kPa) range from –0.0013 to –0.0103, indicating various degrees of rate weakening (fig. 5*A*).

In most of the ring-shear experiments, after a few millimeters of displacement, the shearing resistance of the gouge did not vary systematically, much as in the examples shown in figure 4. However, in the two experiments conducted at the largest normal stress and lowest shear rates, no steady shear stress developed. Instead, shear proceeded by regular stick-slip episodes (fig. 6). Major slip events were accompanied by abrupt consolidation, whereas dilation appeared to occur during "stick" intervals. Apparently the normal stresses and shear rates of these two experiments produced gouge stiffness and rate weakening that met both requirements for stick-slip behavior outlined previously.

In two sets of slide-hold-slide tests at a single shear rate and normal stress, peak strength increased logarithmically with hold time (fig. 7). Fitting these data to equation 5 indicates that $b = 0.0079$ (table 1). Hold time was also recorded during the variable-rate tests and, although these data have more scatter (perhaps due to a dependence of b on shear rate), they indicate a $b = 0.0075$. During hold periods compaction of the gouge was generally not observed, indicating either that growth of contact area between grains may not have been the key aging mechanism or that this effect was too subtle to be measured.

Discussion

Results of our ring-shear tests indicate that the Mount St. Helens gouge exhibits rate weakening at shear rates below about 10^{-4} m/s. At these rates, the magnitude of $a – b$ is comparable to typical published values for fault gouges, which vary from –0.001 to –0.01 (for example, Blanpied and others, 1987; Kilgore and others, 1993). Above 10^{-4} m/s and at the lowest normal stresses of these experiments, $a – b$ is positive, indicating that the gouge is rate strengthening. The apparent transition from negative to positive values of $a – b$ occurs at a shear rate similar to the same transition documented for other rock and gouge shear zones (for example, Shimamoto, 1986; Blanpied and others, 1987; Kilgore and others, 1993).

The transition shear rate in our experiments is only moderately larger than the rate of extrusion estimated for much of the 2004–2005 eruption (3×10^{-5} m/s to 7×10^{-5} m/s), but two observations indicate that gouge shear rates at Mount St. Helens may be well within the rate-weakening regime. Kilgore and others (1993) noted that the transition shear rate increases with increasing normal stress. Because normal stresses in our experiments were probably at least one order of magnitude smaller than those on the margins of the magma plug at depths of 100–500 m at Mount St. Helens (2–10 MPa), rate-weakening behavior at Mount St. Helens would likely be exhibited at higher shear rates than those of the experiments. Secondly, Marone and Kilgore (1993) showed that the characteristic slip distance D_c is more appropriately viewed as a characteristic shear strain (shear displacement divided by the shear-zone thickness) when considering shear within a gouge layer. In ring-shear experiments on the Mount St. Helens gouge in which we placed vertical columns of beads in the gouge to study the shear-strain distribution, more than 90 percent of the strain was distributed over a thickness of 10 mm. At Mount St. Helens, the shear-zone thickness is likely larger, given the ~1 m total thickness of the gouge layer and presence of particles too large to include in the ring-shear experiments. Thus, shear-strain rates in the ring-shear experiments were likely larger at a particular shear rate than those at Mount St. Helens, indicating that the gouge there would likely rate-weaken at higher shear rates than it did in the experiments. Thus, one of the conditions required for stick-slip ascent of the dacite plug—rate weakening of the gouge—appears to be met.

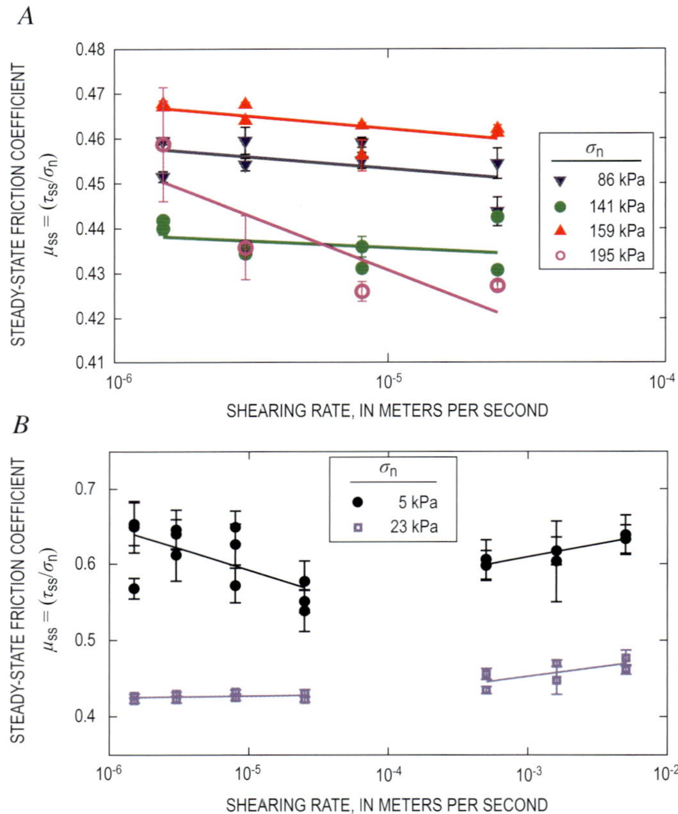

Figure 5. Steady-state friction coefficient as a function of shear rate. Each data point represents results of one experiment. Steady-state friction coefficient is shear stress supported by the gouge divided by corrected normal stress, both averaged over the part of experiment when time-averaged steady state had been attained (see fig. 4). Data are grouped by magnitude of applied normal stress. Error bars represent ±1 standard deviation of observed variability in friction coefficient during the period of the time-averaged steady state. *A*, High applied normal stresses. *B*, Low applied normal stresses.

Table 1. Rate-dependence parameters.

[Value *a–b* describes sign and magnitude of rate dependence of gouge friction. The *b* value alone describes magnitude of gouge strengthening as a function of hold time.]

Normal stress (kPa)	Shear-rate range (m/s)	*a–b*	*b*
Fast			
5	$5 \times 10^{-4} - 5 \times 10^{-3}$	0.0150	
23	$5 \times 10^{-4} - 5 \times 10^{-3}$	0.0105	
Slow			
5	$1.5 \times 10^{-6} - 2.5 \times 10^{-5}$	–0.0250	
23	$1.5 \times 10^{-6} - 2.5 \times 10^{-5}$	0.00099	
86	$1.5 \times 10^{-6} - 2.5 \times 10^{-5}$	–0.0022	
141	$1.5 \times 10^{-6} - 2.5 \times 10^{-5}$	–0.0013	
159	$1.5 \times 10^{-6} - 2.5 \times 10^{-5}$	–0.0024	0.0079
195	$1.5 \times 10^{-6} - 2.5 \times 10^{-5}$	–0.0103	

We now consider the second condition—that the stiffness of the loading system must be smaller than the critical stiffness defined by the evolution behavior of the gouge. Assessment of this condition requires independent estimates of both the in situ critical stiffness k_{crit} of the gouge and the stiffness k_{sys} of the magma that is driving extrusion.

The critical stiffness of the gouge was defined by Ruina (1983) as the post-peak reduction in shear stress divided by the characteristic slip distance over which this reduction occurs:

$$k_{crit} = \frac{-(a-b)\sigma_n'}{D_c}, \qquad \text{for } (a-b) < 0. \tag{6}$$

If a lithostatic stress state is assumed at the nucleation depth of the drumbeat earthquakes (~500 m) and pore-water pressure is neglected, such that the total normal stress equals the effective normal stress, then $\sigma_n' \sim 10$ MPa. A reasonable value of *a–b* indicated by our experimental results is –0.003. The characteristic slip distance D_c can be determined from the transition from steady slip to persistent stick-slip behavior that occurred in our experiments with high normal stresses. At this transition the experimental normal stress was 195 kPa (table 1), and k_{crit} equaled the stiffness of the test device. This stiffness is approximately 1.7×10^4 kPa/m (see appendix 1). (Here, again following Ruina (1983), we employ a stiffness having dimensions of stress per unit length (that is, mass/(time^2×length^2))). Substituting this value for k_{crit}, $a-b = -0.003$ and the experimental value of σ_n' (195 kPa) in equation 6 yields $D_c = 34$ µm, which is of the same order as typical laboratory values for gouge (for example, Marone and Kilgore, 1993). Assuming that $D_c = 34$ µm, $a-b = -0.003$, and $\sigma_n' = 10$ MPa are appropri-

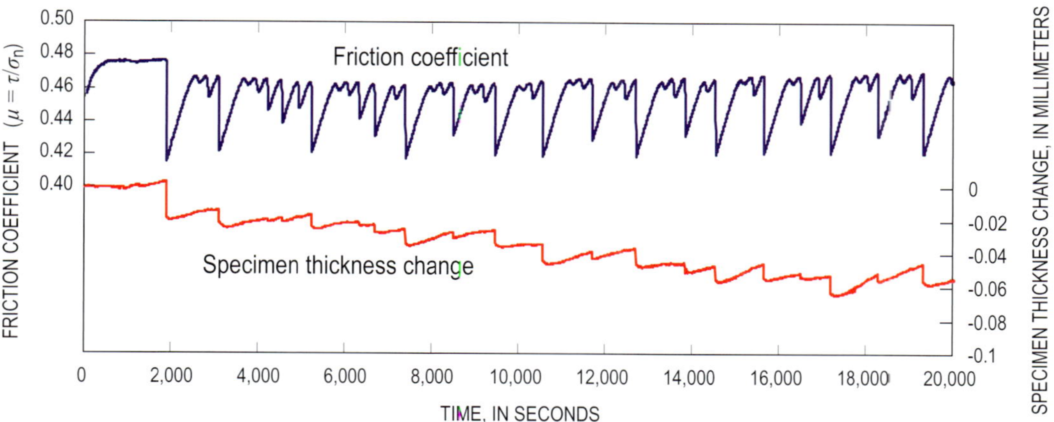

Figure 6. Part of one record of stick slip from experiments conducted at the two lowest shear rates (1.5×10^{-6} and 3.0×10^{-6} m/s) at 195 kPa normal stress. No direct measurement was made of displacement of the rotating base during these tests, so stick-slip displacement was inferred from shear-stress and specimen thickness records.

ate for the in situ gouge at Mount St. Helens, then equation 6 yields an in situ critical gouge stiffness of ~10^6 kPa/m.

To estimate the stiffness of the loading system, we assume that magma underlying the plug drives extrusion (fig. 8), and that the magma contains about 12 percent exsolved gas by volume (T. Gerlach, oral commun., 2005) and has a compressibility $\alpha = 10^{-4}$ per kPa (Iverson, this volume, chap. 21). The pertinent stiffness k is the magmatic "spring force" per unit area of plug-margin slip surface divided by the "spring displacement" associated with magma compression-relaxation cycles (compare with Ruina, 1983). To estimate this k, we approximate the magma body as a right circular column with height H = 8,000 m and cross sectional area $A=1/4(\pi d^2)$, where d is the mean column diameter, and we approximate the area of the slip surface on the margins of the plug as πdh, where h is the height of the plug in contact with the conduit walls. The spring force associated with magma compression is $(A/\alpha)(\delta/H)$, where δ is the characteristic displacement associated with magma compression or relaxation, and δ/H is the accompanying longitudinal strain of the magma column. Thus, the spring force per unit area of slip surface is $d\delta/(4\alpha hH)$, and dividing this expression by the displacement distance δ yields

$$k = d/(4\alpha hH). \quad (7)$$

If h is 500 m, and d is 50 m (these values are probably of the correct order of magnitude for the geometry at Mount St. Helens), then inserting these values and the α and H values noted above into equation 7 yields k ~10^{-1} kPa/m, seven orders of magnitude smaller than the critical gouge stiffness k_{crit} ~10^6 kPa/m. Therefore, even if the estimated values of magma compressibility or the geometrical parameters d, h, and H are greatly in error, the gouge is likely much stiffer than the magma column that drives upward movement of the plug. Thus, in addition to rate weakening of the gouge, the second requirement for stick-slip—that the critical stiffness of the gouge exceeds the stiffness of some part of the loading system—is likely satisfied.

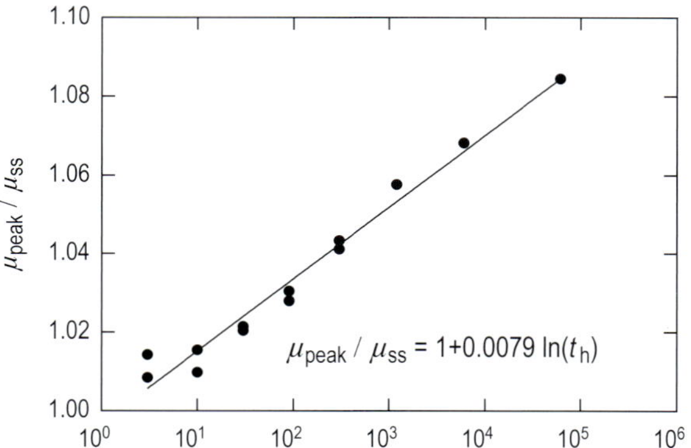

Figure 7. Normalized peak friction coefficient, μ_{peak}, as a function of logarithm of hold time. Standard error of b-value (slope of the regression) is 0.0004. All tests were at a normal stress of 159 kPa and shear rate of 2.5×10^{-5} m/s.

The finding that the magma-plug system can exhibit stick-slip behavior at shallow depths contrasts with the common observation that fault slip is aseismic within ~2 km of the surface (Scholz, 2002). The tendency for aseismic tectonic fault slip at shallow depths is commonly attributed either to rate strengthening in unconsolidated gouge or to the dependence of critical stiffness on normal stress, which is low near Earth's surface (Marone and Scholz, 1988; Scholz, 2002). Our results indicate that the Mount St. Helens gouge is rate weakening and the loading-system stiffness is exceptionally small owing to the presence of a large body of highly compressible magma. Therefore, stick-slip behavior should be possible at much smaller depths at Mount St. Helens than would be predicted for tectonically driven crustal faults.

Conclusions

Under normal stresses less than about 200 kPa, gouge sampled from the surface of the newly extruded Mount St. Helens dome in February 2005 exhibits frictional behavior that is described well by the rate- and state-dependent friction model. In our ring-shear device the gouge weakens with increasing steady shear rates up to about 10^{-4} m/s and strengthens at larger shear rates. This transition from weakening to strengthening occurs at an experimental shear rate only moderately larger than the observed time-averaged rate of extrusion at Mount St. Helens, but in situ the transition probably occurs at higher shear rates because in situ normal stresses in the gouge are probably significantly larger than those that could be applied experimentally. Also, the in situ stiffness of the gouge, as estimated using the conditions under which stick-slip occurred in the experiments, is roughly seven orders of magnitude greater than the stiffness of the most compliant component of the system driving uplift of the plug: the underlying magma. The rate weakening and high stiffness of the gouge relative to the magma are requirements for stick-slip behavior when rate-and-state dependent friction is present, so stick-slip behavior provides a viable hypothesis for the source of the observed shallow drumbeat earthquakes at Mount St. Helens. In addition, experiments showed that the peak strength of the gouge increased logarithmically with hold time, indicating that deformation history of the gouge could influence the character of stick-slip behavior and associated seismicity.

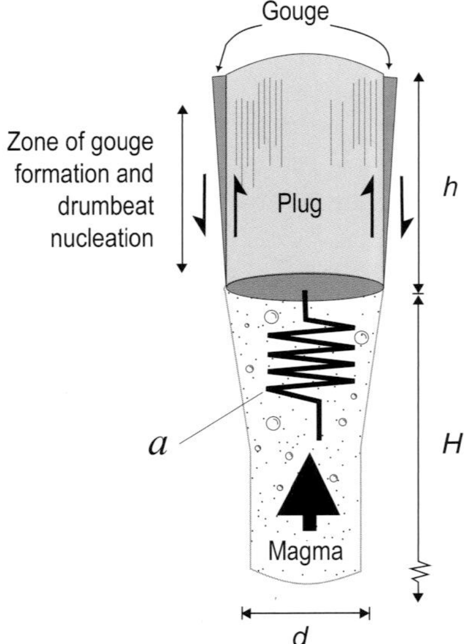

Figure 8. Schematic illustration of hypothesized magma-plug system at Mount St. Helens. Cool, rigid dacite plug is driven upward through upper conduit by ascending compressible magma. Gouge forms by frictional wear at interface between extruding plug and conduit. Because the gouge is stiffer than effective stiffness of the magma that is driving plug uplift, uplift occurs in stick-slip cycles, producing drumbeat earthquakes. Physical and geometrical variables (letters and symbols on figure) are discussed in text.

Acknowledgments

We thank John Pallister for collection of gouge samples from Mount St. Helens. Technical reviews by Nick Beeler and John Power and editorial suggestions by Jim Hendley significantly improved this paper.

References Cited

Beeler, N.M., Tullis, T.E., and Weeks, J.D., 1994, The roles of time and displacement in the evolution effect in rock friction: Geophysical Research Letters, v. 21, no. 18, p. 1987–1990.

Biegel, R.L., Sammis, C.G., and Dieterich, J.H., 1989, The frictional properties of a simulated gouge having a fractal particle distribution: Journal of Structural Geology, v. 11, no 7, p. 827–846.

Blanpied, M.L., Tullis, T.E., and Weeks, J.D., 1987, Frictional behavior of granite at low and high sliding velocities: Geophysical Research Letters, v. 15, no. 5, p. 554–557.

Dieterich, J.H., 1972, Time dependence of rock friction: Journal of Geophysical Research, v. 77, p. 3690–3697.

Dieterich, J.H., 1978, Time dependent friction and the mechanics of stick-slip: Pure and Applied Geophysics, v. 116, p. 790–806.

Dieterich, J.H., 1979, Modeling of rock friction 1—experimental results and constitutive equations: Journal of Geophysical Research, v. 84, no. B5, p. 2161–2168.

Engelder, J.T., 1974, Cataclasis and the generation of fault gouge: Geological Society of America Bulletin, v. 85, p. 1515–1522.

Head, K.H., 1989, Soil technician's handbook: New York, John Wiley, 83 p.

Hooyer, T.S., and Iverson, N.R., 2000, Clast-fabric development in a shearing granular material—implications for subglacial till and fault gouge: Geological Society of America Bulletin, v. 112, no. 5, p. 683–692.

Iverson, R.M., 2008, Dynamics of seismogenic volcanic extrusion resisted by a solid surface plug, Mount St. Helens, 2004–2005, chap. 21 *of* Sherrod, D.R., Scott, W.E., and Stauffer, P.H., eds., A volcano rekindled; the renewed eruption of Mount St. Helens, 2004–2006: U.S. Geological Survey Professional Paper 1750 (this volume).

Iverson, N.R., Baker, R.W., and Hooyer, T.S., 1997, A ring-shear device for the study of till deformation—tests on tills with contrasting clay contents: Quaternary Science Reviews, v. 16, no. 9, p. 1057–1066.

Iverson, N.R., Hooyer, T.S., and Baker, R.W., 1998, Ring-shear studies of till deformation—Coulomb-plastic behavior and distributed strain in glacier beds: Journal of Glaciology, v. 16, p. 1057–1066.

Iverson, R.M., Reid, M.E., Iverson, N.R., LaHusen, R.G., Logan, M., Mann, J.E., and Brien, D.L., 2000, Acute sensitivity of landslide rates to initial porosity: Science, v. 290, p. 513–516.

Iverson, R.M., Dzurisin, D., Gardner, C.A., Gerlach, T.M., LaHusen, R.G., Lisowski, M., Major, J.J., Malone, S.D., Messerich, J.A., Moran, S.C., Pallister, J.S., Qamar, A.I., Schilling, S.P., and Vallance, J.W., 2006, Dynamics of seismogenic volcanic extrusion at Mount St. Helens in 2004–05: Nature, v. 444, no. 7118, p. 439–443, doi:10.1038/nature05322.

Kilgore, B.D., Blanpied, M.L., and Dieterich, J.H., 1993, Velocity dependent friction of granite over a wide range of conditions: Geophysical Research Letters, v. 20, no. 10, p. 903–906.

Lambe, T.W., and Whitman, R.V., 1969, Soil Mechanics: New York, John Wiley, 553 p.

Losert, W., Géminard, J.-C., Nasuno, S., and Gollub, J.P., 2000, Mechanisms for slow strengthening in granular materials: Physical Review E, v. 61, no. 4, p. 4060–4068.

Marone, C., 1998, Laboratory-derived friction laws and their application to seismic faulting: Annual Reviews of Earth and Planetary Science, v. 26, p. 643–696.

Marone, C., and Kilgore, B., 1993, Scaling of the critical slip distance for seismic faulting with shear strain in fault zones: Nature, v. 362, p. 618–620.

Marone, C., and Scholz, C.H., 1988, The depth of seismic faulting and the upper transition from stable to unstable slip regimes: Geophysical Research Letters, v. 15, no. 6, p. 621–624.

Marone, C., Raleigh, C.B., and Scholz, C.H., 1990, Frictional behavior and constitutive modeling of simulated fault gouge: Journal of Geophysical Research, v. 95, no. B5, p. 7007–7025.

Moore, P.L., and Iverson, N.R., 2002, Slow episodic shear of granular materials regulated by dilatant strengthening: Geology, v. 30, p. 843–846.

Rice, J.R., and Ruina, A., 1983, Stability of steady frictional slipping: Journal of Applied Mechanics, v. 50, p. 343–349.

Ruina, A., 1983, Slip instability and state variable friction laws: Journal of Geophysical Research, v. 88, no. B12, p. 10359–10370.

Scherer, R.P., Sjunneskog, C.M., Iverson, N.R., and Hooyer, T.S., 2004, Assessing subglacial processes from diatom fragmentation patterns: Geology, v. 32, p. 557–560.

Scholz, C.H., 2002, Mechanics of earthquakes and faulting (2d ed.): New York, Cambridge University Press, 471 p.

Shimamoto, T., 1986, Transition between frictional slip and ductile flow for halite shear zones at room temperature: Science, v. 231, p. 711–714.

Tuffen, H., and Dingwell, D., 2005, Fault textures in volcanic conduits; evidence for seismic trigger mechanisms during silicic eruptions: Bulletin of Volcanology, v. 67, p. 370–387.

Appendix 1. Stiffness of the Ring-Shear Device

The stiffness of the ring-shear device can be estimated from stress-displacement transients that were common when shearing was initiated in experiments conducted at the highest normal stresses. Particularly after extended hold periods, the start of shear was characterized by sudden stress reductions that accompanied abrupt slip (fig. 9). Abrupt slip displacement was measured with a horizontally oriented LVDT that pressed on an armature extending from the rotating base of the device. This abrupt displacement of the rotating base occurred despite the constant speed of the motor driving the rotation of the base. These events reflect the release of elastic strain energy stored in the drive mechanism of the device, and therefore the ratio of abrupt stress reduction to abrupt slip describes the device stiffness, as applicable to the rate-and-state model of Ruina (1983)—1.7×10^4 kPa/m.

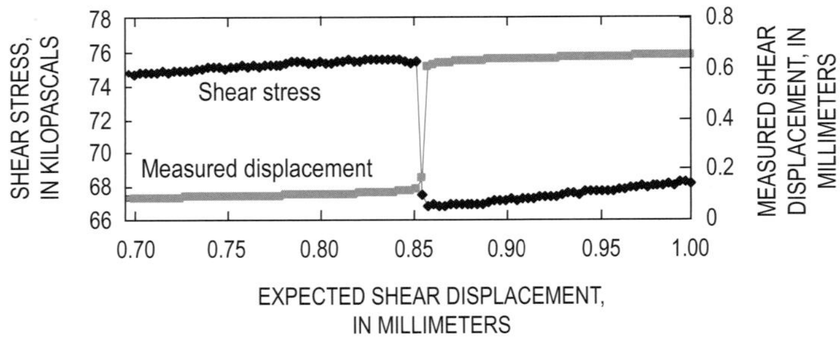

Figure 9. Shear stress and measured shear displacement during initial minutes of a ring-shear test conducted at a normal stress of 159 kPa. Data are plotted as a function of expected shear displacement calculated from rotation rate of motor that drives rotating base (fig. 3). Data begin when motor was actively driving rotation, but no displacement was measured at perimeter of the rotating base. During subsequent abrupt slip, there was a marked reduction in measured shear stress, well below steady-state strength of the gouge. This stress reduction and associated abrupt displacement are interpreted to reflect elastic compliance of the device.

Chapter 21

Dynamics of Seismogenic Volcanic Extrusion Resisted by a Solid Surface Plug, Mount St. Helens, 2004–2005

By Richard M. Iverson[1]

Abstract

The 2004–5 eruption of Mount St. Helens exhibited sustained, near-equilibrium behavior characterized by nearly steady extrusion of a solid dacite plug and nearly periodic occurrence of shallow earthquakes. Diverse data support the hypothesis that these earthquakes resulted from stick-slip motion along the margins of the plug as it was forced incrementally upward by ascending, solidifying, gas-poor magma. I formalize this hypothesis with a mathematical model derived by assuming that magma enters the base of the eruption conduit at a steady rate, invoking conservation of mass and momentum of the magma and plug, and postulating simple constitutive equations that describe magma and conduit compressibilities and friction along the plug margins. Reduction of the model equations reveals a strong mathematical analogy between the dynamics of the magma-plug system and those of a variably damped oscillator. Oscillations in extrusion velocity result from the interaction of plug inertia, a variable upward force due to magma pressure, and a downward force due to the plug weight. Damping of oscillations depends mostly on plug-boundary friction, and oscillations grow unstably if friction exhibits rate weakening similar to that observed in experiments. When growth of oscillations causes the extrusion rate to reach zero, however, gravity causes friction to reverse direction, and this reversal instigates a transition from unstable oscillations to self-regulating stick-slip cycles. The transition occurs irrespective of the details of rate-weakening behavior, and repetitive stick-slip cycles are, therefore, robust features of the system's dynamics. The presence of a highly compressible elastic driving element (that is, magma containing bubbles) appears crucial for enabling seismogenic slip events to occur repeatedly at the shallow earthquake focal depths (<1 km) observed during the 2004–5 eruption. Computations show that fluctuations in magma pressure accompanying such slip events are <3 kPa, indicating that deviations from mechanical equilibrium are slight and that coseismic force drops are <10^8 N. These results imply that the system's self-regulating behavior is not susceptible to dramatic change—provided that the rate of magma ascent remains similar to the rate of magma accretion at the base of the plug, that plug surface erosion more or less compensates for mass gain due to basal accretion, and that magma and rock properties do not change significantly. Even if disequilibrium initial conditions are imposed, the dynamics of the magma-plug system are strongly attracted to self-regulating stick-slip cycles, although this self-regulating behavior can be bypassed on the way to runaway behavior if the initial state is too far from equilibrium.

Introduction

The dome-building eruption of Mount St. Helens that began in October 2004 was remarkable in several respects. This paper describes formulation, analysis, and predictions of a mechanistic model that links three key aspects of the eruption. The first and perhaps most striking of these aspects was extrusion of solid rock that emerged from the crater floor as a sequence of spines with conspicuous fault gouge and striations on their freshly exposed bounding surfaces. Second, extrusion proceeded at a nearly constant long-term rate (~1–2 m^3/s) that was sustained from December 2004 through at least December 2005. Third, extrusion was accompanied by more than a million small earthquakes that occurred almost periodically at hypocentral locations <1 km beneath the extruding dome. These eruption characteristics motivate the hypothesis that extrusion was driven by a nearly constant influx of magma at depth and resisted by a plug of solidified magma that slipped incrementally and seismogenically against the wall rock forming the upper parts of the magma conduit. I refer to this hypothesis as SPASM, an acronym for Seismogenic Plug of Ascending, Solidifying Magma.

[1] U.S. Geological Survey, 1300 SE Cardinal Court, Vancouver, WA 98683

This paper formalizes the SPASM hypothesis mathematically and tests whether it is consistent quantitatively with behavior observed during the 2004–5 eruption of Mount St. Helens. The mechanistic framework of the SPASM model is simple, reflecting my belief that a relatively simple physical process (that is, one involving few special conditions and contingencies) is most likely responsible for producing persistent, repetitive, natural events—such as nearly periodic earthquakes. Although the SPASM model aims chiefly to explain the origin of these earthquakes, it can also provide insight into conditions under which the eruption style might significantly change, and the potential for such change has large implications for assessment of volcano hazards.

Below, following a brief overview of key features of the 2004–5 eruption of Mount St. Helens, I describe the conceptual basis of the SPASM model. I then present the mathematical formulation of the nonlinear SPASM equations and analytical results obtained from exact solutions of approximate (that is, linearized) versions of these equations. The analytical results demonstrate the plausibility of several broad classes of eruptive behavior, including both stable and unstable behavior. I then use numerical results obtained from approximate solutions of the exact, nonlinear model equations to clarify some consequences of instability. In particular, the numerical results show how stick-slip motion arises as a natural consequence of plug extrusion dynamics. In the final sections of the paper, I discuss implications of these findings for interpreting solid-state volcanic extrusion and accompanying seismicity.

Eruption Overview

Despite Mount St. Helens' famous explosive eruption in 1980, the dome-building activity that began in 2004 is consistent with the volcano's recent geologic history (Mullineaux and Crandell, 1981). Over the past ~4,000 years, Mount St. Helens has extruded rock at a mean rate of about 0.2 m^3/s while constructing a 26-km^3 modern edifice (defined here as the volume above 1,220 m altitude) composed primarily of andesite and dacite lava flows and domes and their detritus. From 1980 to 1986 a dacite dome grew episodically in the crater formed during the 1980 eruption, and its volume ultimately reached 7.4×10^7 m^3 (Swanson and Holcomb, 1990). From 1987 to 2004 Mount St. Helens did not erupt, although at least six phreatic explosions occurred from 1989 to 1991 (Mastin, 1994). Recurrent seismicity at depths of 2–8 km in the late 1980s and 1990s may have been associated with magma recharge but did not lead to eruptions (Moran, 1994).

Renewed eruptive activity began on October 1, 2004, when a small explosion formed a vent through the ~150-m-thick glacier that had grown in the southern part of Mount St. Helens' crater since 1986 (Schilling and others, 2004; Dzurisin and others, 2005; Walder and others, 2005). The explosion was preceded by about 7 days of increasingly intense seismicity at depths <1 km, but deeper seismicity (such as might be indicative of magma-chamber pressurization or depressurization) did not occur then and has not occurred subsequently (Moran and others, this volume, chap. 2). By October 11, explosions had largely ceased, seismic energy release had decreased to a rate about one-tenth that of the preceding two weeks, and extrusion of a solid dacite plug had begun (Dzurisin and others, 2005). By December 2004, extrusion rates had become nearly steady, and by December 15, 2005, the volume of the resulting new lava dome was ~7.3×10^7 m^3 (Schilling and others, this volume, chap. 8). This volume, added to that of the 1980–86 lava dome, implies that the mean extrusion rate at Mount St. Helens from 1980 to 2005 was about 0.2 m^3/s, similar to the mean rate for the past 4,000 years. Thus, the 2004–5 activity of Mount St. Helens was by no means unusual.

The remainder of this section focuses on the quasi-steady eruptive behavior observed at Mount St. Helens from December 2004 through December 2005, because understanding this behavior is the goal of SPASM. Other papers in this volume provide detailed descriptions of the findings briefly summarized below.

Extrusion Rates and Vent Size

After extrusion commenced, it appeared to occur continuously through December 2005, and it produced a sequence of monolithic dacite spines, with some reaching heights >100 m. The fourth of these spines had such a strikingly smooth, symmetrical, elongate form that it resembled a breaching whale and was accordingly dubbed the "whaleback" (fig. 1). Each spine emerged over a period of several weeks to several months and eventually disintegrated as a consequence of fracturing and avalanching of rock from its exposed surfaces. By late 2005, the sequence of spines had formed a composite dome with the appearance of a multicrested pile of rubble, and distinguishing individual spines would in retrospect have been difficult without knowledge of their emplacement history.

Despite the rather complicated details of spine emplacement, photogrammetric analysis showed that the rate of extrusion remained remarkably constant from about December 2004 to December 2005 (fig. 2) and typically ranged from about 1 to 2 m^3/s (Schilling and others, this volume, chap. 8). During the same period, the linear extrusion rate (that is, the speed of spine emergence from the ground) estimated from far-field, ground-based photography typically ranged from about 3×10^{-5} to 7×10^{-5} m/s (3–6 m/day) (Major and others, this volume, chap. 12), and these rates were largely consistent with high-precision data transmitted by short-lived GPS receivers placed intermittently on the extruding spines (LaHusen and others, this volume, chap. 16). Similar linear extrusion rates were inferred from short-duration, short-range photography, which detected centimeter-scale plug emergence over durations as brief as a few minutes (Dzurisin and others, this volume, chap. 14). Thus, all evidence indicates that extrusion rates were essentially constant over time scales longer than the duration of small earthquakes (about 10 s or less) but shorter than the multiyear duration of the eruption as a whole (>10^7 s).

According to the SPASM hypothesis, small, abrupt pulses in plug extrusion were responsible for generating small earthquakes. These pulses would have typically entailed upward plug displacements of ~5 mm (a value obtained by multiplying the typical 5×10^{-5} m/s linear extrusion rate by the typical 100-s interval between earthquakes), but abrupt movements this small were not resolvable by displacement measurements. Moreover, abrupt slip occurring at earthquake hypocentral depths may have been muted at shallower depths owing to inelastic deformation of weak near-surface materials. As a consequence, no direct measurements of coseismic pulses of plug extrusion were made during the eruption. Therefore, the SPASM model addresses the dynamics of stick-slip cycles with properties that have been inferred but not directly measured.

Inference also plays a role in estimating the size of the vent where extruding spines breached the crater floor, because the presence of fragmented glacier ice and accumulated talus, as well as previously extruded rock, partly obscured the vent margins. Moreover, different parts of the vent became visible as successive spines emerged and moved laterally as well as upward. From the standpoint of constraining the SPASM model, the most useful estimates of the effective cross-sectional area of the vent are obtained not from direct observations of spine geometry but from comparison of volumetric and linear extrusion rates measured over extended periods. Division of the typical volumetric rate of 1.5 m^3/s by the typical linear rate of 5×10^{-5} m/s yields an effective vent area of 30,000 m^2, which implies an effective vent diameter of ~200 m if the vent geometry is assumed to be circular. A vent of this size (but not necessarily circular) is assumed for all calculations I present in this paper.

Figure 1. Oblique aerial photograph of extruding "whaleback" spine 4 at Mount St. Helens, viewed from the northwest, on February 22, 2005. Horizontal length of the smooth whaleback is about 380 m. Arrow shows vent from which the spine emerged. USGS photo by S.P. Schilling.

Gouge Properties

Where fresh surfaces of newly extruded spines were exposed, they were coated with granulated, striated dacite interpreted to be fault gouge. The gouge presumably formed as a consequence of mechanical wear during localized shearing along the margins of the dacite plug as it moved upward relative to the adjacent conduit walls (compare Tuffen and Dingwell, 2005). Observations and dredge sampling from hovering helicopters indicated that the gouge thickness was typically about 1 m (J.S. Pallister, U.S. Geological Survey, oral commun., 2005). Striations on the gouge surface were abundant and generally aligned with the direction of extrusion (fig. 3).

Frictional properties of the gouge were measured using a large-scale ring-shear apparatus, in which a remolded, annular specimen (~0.012 m^3) was deformed in simple shear at various imposed rates (Moore and others, this volume, chap. 20). The measurements demonstrated that the gouge typically exhibited peak strength at displacements <0.5 mm, steady-state strength after about 3 mm of displacement, and reduction of steady-state strength with increasing shear rate (for example, fig. 4). At rates $\geq5\times10^{-4}$ m/s (about 43 m/day), this rate-weakening

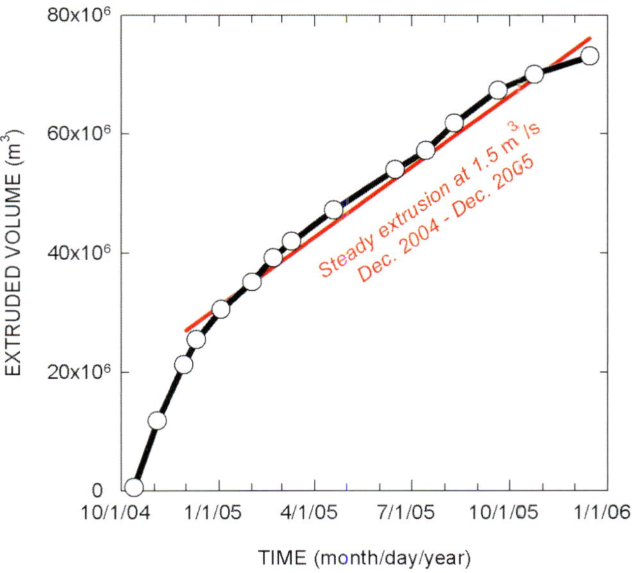

Figure 2. Measured volume of extruded dome rock at Mount St. Helens as a function of time (after Schilling and others, this volume, chap. 8). The red reference line shows growth of dome volume occurring with a constant extrusion rate of 1.5 m^3/s from December 2004 to December 2005.

behavior was supplanted by rate-strengthening behavior, but the relevance of this transition is questionable because the test equipment could shear the specimen at rates $\geq 5\times10^{-4}$ m/s only under very low confining stresses, ≤23 kPa (Moore and others, this volume, chap. 20).

Overall, the ring-shear tests of Moore and others (this volume, chap. 20) showed that frictional behavior of the Mount St. Helens gouge was largely consistent with that expected from models of rate- and state-dependent friction (for example, Dieterich, 1979; Ruina, 1983; Marone, 1998). Such models posit that frictional strength varies in proportion to the logarithms of the imposed shear rate and hold time (that is, the time a specimen is held in a static state between successive shear events). In rate-weakening materials, the combined effect of shear rate and hold time causes a reduction of frictional strength as steady shear rates increase. In tests of the Mount St. Helens fault gouge under confining stresses of 86–195 kPa, measured values of steady-state friction coefficients ranged from 0.42 to 0.47, and these values declined logarithmically as the imposed shear rate increased (Moore and others, this volume, chap. 20). Measured peak friction coefficients were 1–9 percent larger than steady-state friction coefficients, and peak values increased logarithmically with hold time. This hold-time effect is typical of rocks and densely packed granular materials (for example, Beeler and others, 1994; Losert and others, 2000).

Testing by Moore and others (this volume, chap. 20) also revealed that the effective in-place shear stiffness of the gouge was probably orders of magnitude larger than the effective stiffness of the magma body that loaded the gouge as it pushed the extruding plug upward. This contrast in stiffness, along with rate-weakening steady-state friction, provides a sufficient condition for stick-slip behavior in materials exhibiting rate- and state-dependent friction (Rice and Ruina, 1983; Ruina, 1983).

Figure 3. Photographs of striated, gouge-coated surfaces of extruding spines at Mount St. Helens. Arrows show direction of spine motion. *A*, Crest of spine 4 viewed from east on February 22, 2005. Hovering helicopter (circled) provides scale. *B*, Base of spine 5 viewed from north on July 28, 2005. Field of view is roughly 30 m wide. USGS photos by S.P. Schilling.

Drumbeat Earthquakes

An extraordinary feature of the 2004–5 eruption of Mount St. Helens was persistence of small ($M_d \leq 2$), shallow earthquakes that recurred so regularly they were dubbed "drumbeats" (Moran and others, this volume, chap. 2). The period between successive drumbeats shifted slowly with time but was commonly ~100 s (for example, fig. 5) and nearly always in the range 30–300 s. Seismograms showed

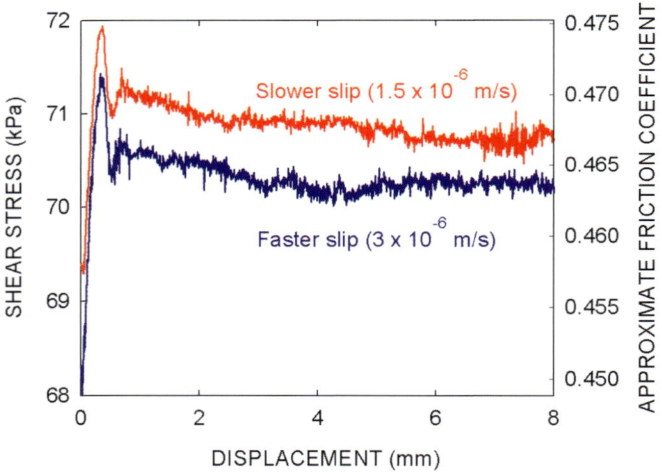

Figure 4. Example of data collected during ring-shear tests of gouge friction by Moore and others (this volume, chap. 20). Measured shear stress as a function of displacement is shown for two steady-state shear rates. Inferred friction coefficients (right-hand axis) represent shear stress divided by a nominally constant normal stress of 159 kPa, but normal stress fluctuated slightly (<1 percent) during the tests, such that friction coefficients are approximate (after Moore and others, this volume, chap. 20).

that drumbeat waveforms generally had impulsive, high-frequency onsets and low-frequency codas, similar to waveforms of other hybrid volcanic earthquakes (for example, Lahr and others, 1994; Neuberg, 2000). Over time scales of hours to weeks, drumbeats typically had consistent sizes and did not display a Gutenberg-Richter magnitude-frequency distribution typical of tectonic earthquakes (Moran and others, this volume, chap. 2). Precise location of drumbeat hypocenters was hindered by the geologic and topographic complexity of the Mount St. Helens crater and the low density of crater seismometers, but within resolution limits (~100 m), all drumbeats originated at depths <1 km directly around or beneath the growing dome. Accompanying the drumbeats at irregular intervals were smaller and larger earthquakes (as large as M_d 3.4) with differing seismic signatures, but these earthquakes had little lasting effect on the drumbeats.

The recurrence and character of drumbeat earthquakes implies the existence of a nondestructive seismic source, as has been inferred for other repetitive volcanic earthquakes (Lahr and others, 1994; Goto, 1999; Neuberg, 2000; Neuberg and others, 2006). The most outstanding attribute of the drumbeat earthquakes at Mount St. Helens, however, was their periodicity. This periodicity, together with the presence of striated fault gouge bounding the extruding plug, is the key motivation for the SPASM hypothesis.

Although the SPASM model aims to link plug extrusion and earthquake generation, it does not address resulting seismic radiation. Radiation of seismic waves could result from rapid propagation of rupture that spreads along the fault surface after nucleating in a strong "keystone" patch of fault gouge (see Scholz, 2002). Alternatively, the force drop accompanying frictional slip that occurs uniformly along the plug margins might be so abrupt as to radiate seismic energy (see Marone and Richardson, 2006), and this force drop is calculated by the SPASM model. In relating SPASM mechanics to seismic radiation, however, it must be borne

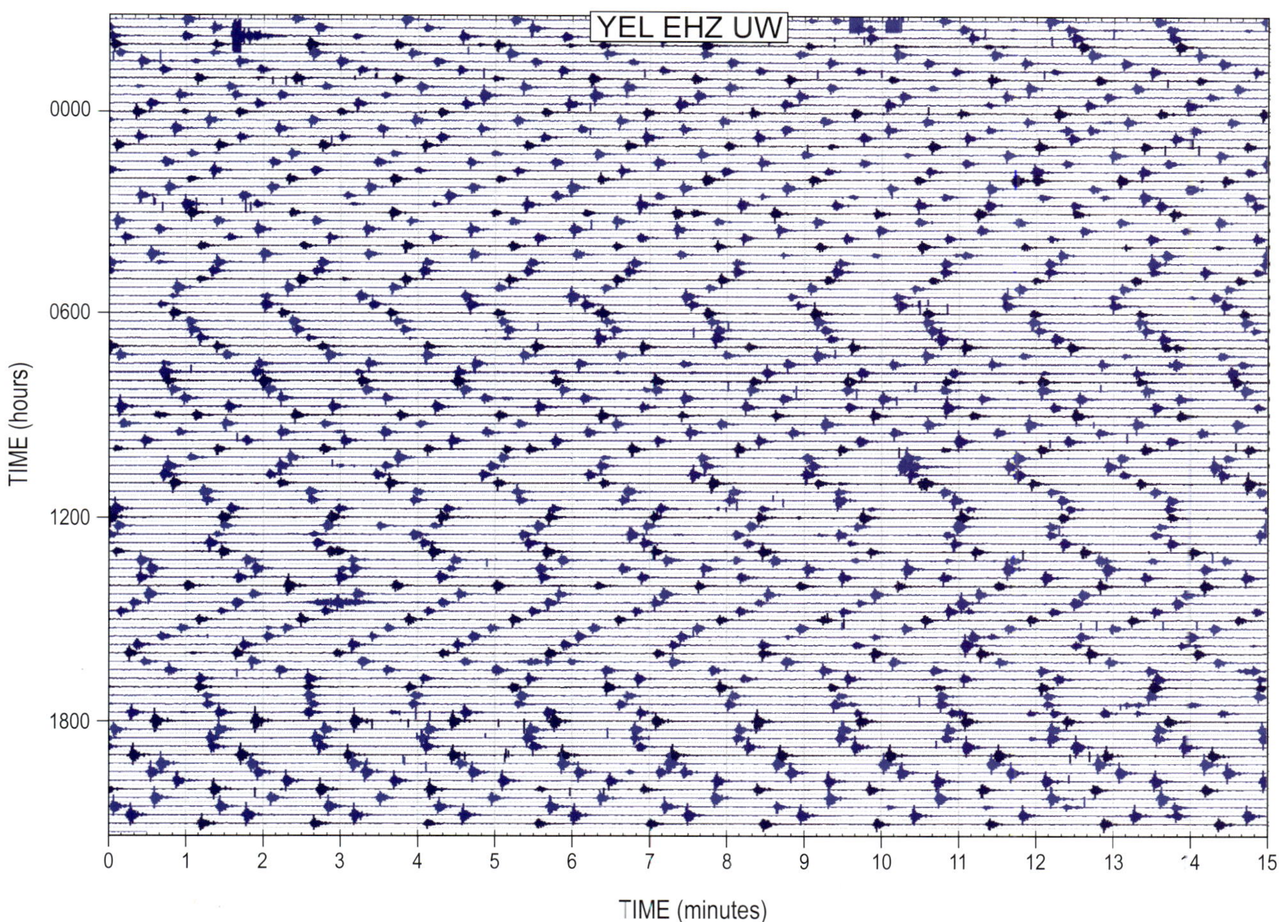

Figure 5. Example of 24-hour seismogram illustrating nearly periodic occurrence of "drumbeat" earthquakes at Mount St. Helens. Graph shows seismicity recorded at station YEL, located 1.5 km north of the 2004–5 vent. Time begins at 21:00 UTC on December 1, 2005, and scrolls from left to right and then top to bottom. Earthquake magnitudes were roughly 0.5–1 during this interval. Data courtesy of Pacific Northwest Seismic Network.

in mind that only a small fraction (<10 percent) of the work done during fault slip typically results in seismic radiation (McGarr, 1999). Generally, more work is done in overcoming friction, and the mechanics of the total work cycle is the primary focus of SPASM.

Magma Solidification and Compressibility

Although genesis of the magma that erupted in 2004–5 remains uncertain, petrologic data indicate that solidification occurred at depths <1 km. This inference derives from the fact that the composition of glass in the newly erupted dacite plots between the 0.1 and 50 MPa cotectics of the modified quartz-albite-orthoclase phase diagram for Mount St. Helens dacites (Blundy and Cashman, 2001) and from the presence of tridymite, which constrains the late stages of solidification to pressures of 10–20 MPa (equivalent to estimated lithostatic pressures at depths ~0.5–1 km) (Pallister and others, 2005, and this volume, chap. 30). These depths are consistent with the maximum hypocentral depths inferred for drumbeat earthquakes (Moran and others, this volume, chap. 2), and they imply that solid-state extrusion and earthquake generation were collocated.

The quantity and composition of volcanic gases emitted during the 2004–5 eruption demonstrate that the magma was gas poor in comparison to the 1980 Mount St. Helens magma but that the 2004–5 magma nonetheless contained sufficient exsolved gas to greatly influence its compressibility. At 8 km depth the gas volume fraction was probably <2 percent, but calculations using methods of Newman and Lowenstern (2002) indicate that the gas volume fraction grew during magma ascent and reached about 50 percent at ~1 km depth, where solidification began (Gerlach and others, this volume, chap. 26). The same calculations indicate that at depths between 8 and 1 km, the gas volume fraction averaged ~12 percent. Allowing for inevitable gas separation from rock during extrusion, these results are consistent with observed vesicle volume fractions of 11–34 percent in samples of the 2004–5 dacite (Gerlach and others, this volume, chap. 26). An exsolved gas volume fraction of 12 percent implies a magma compressibility ~10^{-7} Pa^{-1}, according to the model of Mastin and Ghiorso (2000). Although this value is, of course, inexact, its mechanical significance is clear: the magma was almost certainly much more compressible than solid rock, which generally has compressibilities <10^{-10} Pa^{-1} (Hatheway and Kiersch, 1989). As a consequence, magma compression almost certainly dominated elastic strain as pressure within the magma-conduit-plug system increased.

Geodetic Inferences About Magma Influx

Measured displacements of the volcano flanks and adjacent areas preceding and during the 2004–5 eruption imply that the volume of magma evacuated from depths <10 km was considerably less than the volume of extruded rock (Lisowski and others, this volume, chap. 15). No evidence of systematic preeruption surface displacement was found by global positioning system (GPS) surveys in 2000 and 2003 of a 40-station network centered on the volcano, nor by continuous operation of GPS station JRO1, located 9 km north of the eruption vent. Seismicity that heralded the eruption in late September 2004 was accompanied by only centimeter-scale downward and southward (that is, inward) surface displacements at JRO1 (Lisowski and others, this volume, chap. 15). The displacement pattern measured at all stations corresponds well with that predicted by an elastic half-space model that assumes pressure decrease within a vertically oriented, prolate spheroidal cavity with a mean depth of 8 km and volume loss ~2×10^7 m^3 during the period from October 1, 2004, to November 25, 2005 (Lisowski and others, this volume, chap. 15). This apparent volume loss is less than one-third the volume of rock extruded during the same period, and little of the apparent volume loss occurred after the onset of nearly steady extrusion in December 2004, implying that magma recharge from a deep (>10 km) source accompanied this phase of the eruption.

Conceptual Basis of Mathematical Model

The basic mechanical elements of the SPASM model are shown schematically in figure 6, and table 1 defines all mathematical symbols used in development and analysis of the model. The model assumes that magma flows into the base of a feeder conduit at a steady volumetric rate Q. The conduit is assumed to originate about 8 km beneath the Mount St. Helens crater, a depth inferred from hypocentral locations of pre-2004 earthquakes apparently associated with magma movement (Moran, 1994; Moran and others, this volume, chap. 2). Ascent of magma at the top of the conduit is resisted by force exerted by a near-surface plug of solidified magma, owing to its weight mg and boundary friction F. Seismic and petrologic data collected during the 2004–5 eruption imply that the plug extends to a depth <1 km, and as a baseline value I assume that it extends to a depth ~500 m. The plug mass m can change with time as a consequence of basal accretion of congealing magma at mass rate ρB, where ρ is the magma bulk density, and as a consequence of surface erosion by spalling and avalanching at mass rate $\rho_r E$, where ρ_r is the bulk density of the plug rock. The conduit volume can change with time as a result of motion of the base of the plug and changes in magma pressure that cause elastic deflection of the conduit walls. The magma pressure and density can change in response to the changing balance between the steady magma influx and changing conduit volume. The resulting mathematical model represents the simultaneous evolution of the upward plug velocity u, magma pressure against the base of the plug p, and conduit volume V, which are influenced by concurrent evolution of m and ρ.

Implicit in the SPASM model is a "top-down" perspective of eruption dynamics. The model focuses on observed surface and near-surface phenomena associated with eruptive behavior but does not consider phenomena associated with unobserved changes that might occur in a deep magma reservoir. Instead, in the SPASM model, variations in extrusion rate are postulated to arise naturally as a consequence of the dynamics of the solid plug responding to steady forcing. Unsteady forcing due to unsteady magma influx would complicate behavior exhibited by the SPASM model but would not change its fundamental character.

The SPASM model is one-dimensional and does not explicitly consider the effects of conduit and plug geometry. This simplification poses both an advantage and disadvantage. The advantage derives from the fact that predictions of the SPASM model are independent of geometrical effects and are, in a general sense, applicable to any geometry. The disadvantage is that SPASM yields no insight concerning the effects of geometrical complications such as variations in the shape of the magma conduit, vent, or growing lava dome.

Many previous eruption models have used a one-dimensional approach similar to the one used here, and some models have invoked stick-slip motion as a phenomenon responsible for cyclical eruptive behavior (for example, Denlinger and Hoblitt, 1999; Voight and others, 1999; Ozerov and others, 2003). The SPASM model, however, is the first to demonstrate how stick-slip behavior arises as a natural consequence of system dynamics. Indeed, a key feature of the SPASM model is that forces need not be balanced; therefore, the model can exhibit dynamical behavior not possible in eruption models that assume balanced forces (for example, Mastin and others, this volume, chap. 22).

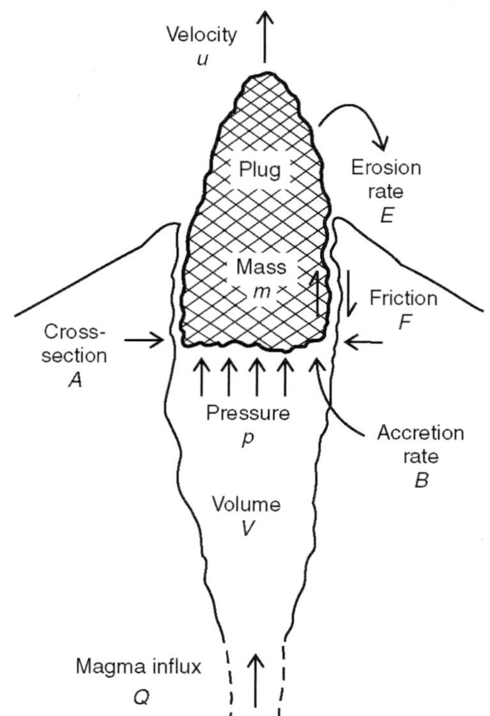

Figure 6. Schematic diagram illustrating the conceptual framework of the SPASM model.

Mathematical Formulation

The most fundamental equations used to derive the SPASM model express conservation of mass and linear momentum of the solid plug and conduit fluid. These conservation laws are supplemented by constitutive equations defining magma compressibility, conduit wall-rock compliance, and the frictional force acting where the plug contacts the conduit walls. In this section the conservation and constitutive equations are presented and reduced to a set of three simultaneous differential equations that describe behavior of the magma-conduit-plug system as a whole.

Conservation of Linear Momentum of Solid Plug

Changes in the upward momentum of the solid plug are described by Newton's second law of motion, expressed as

$$m\frac{du}{dt} + u\frac{dm}{dt} = pA - mg - F \ , \qquad (1)$$

where m is the plug mass, u is the vertical (upward) plug velocity, g is the magnitude of gravitational acceleration, and p is the magma pressure against the base of the plug, which has area A in horizontal projection. Upward motion of the plug is driven by the basal magma-pressure force pA and resisted by the plug weight mg and boundary friction force F. Implicit in equation 1 is the understanding that F would change sign (that is, friction would reverse its direction of action) if u were to change sign. A detailed specification of F is provided in the section on "Constitutive Equations," below.

Conservation of Mass of Solid Plug

Mass change of the solid plug depends on the rate of mass accretion at the base of the plug, ρB, and the rate of mass loss at the surface of plug due to erosion, $\rho_r E$, where B is the volumetric rate of magma conversion to solid rock and E is the volumetric erosion rate of the plug surface. Magma solidification may involve a change in mass density from ρ to ρ_r. Summing these effects yields the mass-conservation equation

$$\frac{dm}{dt} = \rho B - \rho_r E = \kappa, \qquad (2)$$

where κ is a convenient shorthand for $\rho B - \rho_r E$. For the sake of simplicity, κ is assumed constant, although this assumption is readily relaxed in numerical analyses if warranted. With constant κ, equation 2 yields the explicit solution

Table 1. Definitions of mathematical symbols.

Symbol	Dimensions	Definition
A	L^2	Horizontal cross-sectional area of base of plug
B	L^3/T	Volumetric rate of magma solidification at base of plug
C	M/T	Dimensional measure of rate dependence of plug friction force
c	none	Dimensionless measure of rate dependence of plug friction force
c_1, c_2	none	Arbitrary constants of integration
D	none	Dimensionless parameter summarizing effects of frictional damping
E	L^3/T	Volumetric rate of erosion of surface of plug
F	ML/T^2	Friction force on margins of plug
F_0	ML/T^2	Value of F at static limiting equilibrium
$F(u_0)$	ML/T^2	Value of F at the steady equilibrium extrusion rate u_0
F^*	none	F/F_0
G	none	Dimensionless parameter summarizing effects of gravity
g	L/T^2	Gravitational acceleration
H_{con}	L	Vertical height of magma-filled conduit
H_{plug}	L	Vertical height of extruding solid plug
K	none	Dimensionless parameter summarizing effects of plug mass change
m	M	Plug mass
m_0	M	Static or steady equilibrium value of m
p	M/LT^2	Magma pressure against base of plug
p_b	M/LT^2	Magma pressure at base of conduit
p_i	M/LT^2	Value of p at onset of a stick event
p_0	M/LT^2	Value of p at static limiting equilibrium
p_{ref}	M/LT^2	Reference value of p used in magma compression equation
Q	L^3/T	Volumetric rate of magma influx at base of conduit
R	none	Dimensionless parameter equal to $1-\rho/\rho_r$
R_0	none	Value of R when $\rho = \rho_0$
R^*	none	R/R_0
S	none	Dimensionless parameter summarizing rate dependent plug friction
$\hat{S}$	none	Dimensionless parameter summarizing static plug friction
T	T	Oscillation period
t	T	Time
t_0	T	Natural time scale of oscillations, defined in equation 25
t^*	none	t/t_0
u	L/T	Vertical extrusion velocity
u_0	L/T	Value of u at steady equilibrium
u_{ref}	L/T	Reference value of u used in friction equation
u'	L/T	$u-u_0$
u^*	none	u'/u_0
u_i^*	none	Initial value of u^*
V	L^3	Volume of magma-filled conduit
V_0	L^3	Static or steady equilibrium value of V
V'	L^3	$V-V_0$
V^*	none	V'/V_0

Table 1. Definitions of mathematical symbols.—Continued

Symbol	Dimensions	Definition
V_i	L^3	Value of V at onset of stick event
W	L^3/T	Parameter defined in equation 53
X	none	Dimensionless parameter defined in equation 44
Y	none	Dimensionless parameter defined in equation 44
Z	none	Dimensionless parameter defined in equation 44
α_1	LT^2/M	Elastic bulk compressibility of magma
α_2	LT^2/M	Elastic compliance of walls of magma-filled conduit
η	M/LT	Magma viscosity
κ	M/T	Rate of change of plug mass
λ	none	Parameter that relates plug weight to boundary normal stress
μ_0	none	Static friction coefficient
ν	none	Dimensionless parameter defined in equation 34
ρ	M/L^3	Bulk density of magma
ρ_0	M/L^3	Value of ρ at static limiting equilibrium
ρ_r	M/L^3	Bulk density of plug rock
ξ	none	Rescaled time variable defined in equation 34

$$m = \kappa t + m_0 \tag{3}$$

where m_0 is the initial value of m.

Conservation of Linear Momentum of Conduit Fluid

Newton's second law for upward motion of magma in the conduit takes a simple form if variations of magma properties and velocity with position are neglected:

$$\rho \frac{dQ}{dt} + Q\frac{d\rho}{dt} = A\left(\frac{p_b - p}{H_{con}} - \rho g - \frac{8\pi\eta}{A^2}Q\right). \tag{4}$$

Here Q is the vertical (upward) volumetric flux of magma, p_b is the magma pressure at the base of the conduit, and η is the magma viscosity. Equation 4 is the fluid-mechanical equivalent of equation 1 and is also equivalent to the Navier-Stokes equation for one-dimensional laminar flow, integrated over the conduit cross-sectional area A and height H_{con}. According to equation 4, upward motion of magma in the conduit is driven by the vertical pressure gradient $(p_b - p)/H_{con}$ and is resisted by the magma unit weight ρg and viscous drag, represented by the last term in the equation. The form of this drag term is inferred from an elementary analysis of Poiseuille flow in a cylindrical conduit, although alternative drag terms (appropriate for other conduit geometries or magma rheologies) could be used without difficulty.

A simplified momentum equation is obtained by assuming that the magma flux Q is independent of time and making the substitution $dQ/dt = 0$ in equation 4. Rearrangement of the resulting equation yields an explicit expression for Q,

$$Q = A\frac{\frac{p_b - p}{H_{con}} - \rho g}{\frac{d\rho}{dt} + \frac{8\pi\eta}{A}}. \tag{5}$$

Equation 5 shows that maintenance of constant Q in the presence of changing H_{con}, p, and ρ (all of which can occur in the context of the SPASM model) can imply that compensating changes occur in p_b and/or η. The model assumes that such compensating changes may indeed occur, but it does not evaluate such changes explicitly. A complete evaluation could be accomplished by using equation 4 together with a mass-conservation equation (see below) to model the dynamics of transient magma flow in the conduit (for example, Melnik and Sparks, 2002). However, such a model also requires specification of a basal boundary condition (for example, magma-chamber pressure) to drive magma inflow. Any such specification involves assumptions that are arbitrary, and the SPASM model minimizes use of arbitrary assumptions by specifying a constant basal magma influx Q.

Conservation of Mass of Conduit Fluid

The mass of the fluid magma in the conduit is ρV, where V is the conduit volume. Changes in ρV depend not only on changes in ρ and V but also on the influx of fluid mass at the base of the conduit ρQ and the loss of fluid mass at the top of the conduit ρB, which results from solidification at the base of the solid plug. These phenomena are summarized by the fluid mass-conservation equation

$$\rho\frac{dV}{dt}+V\frac{d\rho}{dt}=\rho(Q-B). \qquad (6)$$

Both Q and B are treated as constants.

Constitutive Equations

Although the conservation equations for Q and m reduce to the explicit forms shown above, the remaining two conservation equations (1 and 6) contain four dependent variables, u, p, V, and ρ and an as-yet-unspecified friction force F. Thus, three constitutive equations must be specified to attain mathematical closure.

Magma Compressibility

The first constitutive equation defines the compressibility of the fluid magma α_1 as

$$\alpha_1=\frac{1}{\rho}\frac{d\rho}{dp}, \qquad (7)$$

and integration of equation 7 yields $\rho=\rho_0\exp[\alpha_1(p-p_{ref})]$, where ρ_0 is the magma bulk density at a reference pressure p_{ref}. Combination of equation 7 with the chain rule $d\rho/dt=(d\rho/dp)(dp/dt)$ yields an equation that relates magma density change to pressure change:

$$\frac{d\rho}{dt}=\alpha_1\rho\frac{dp}{dt}. \qquad (8)$$

Below, this equation is used to replace density derivatives with pressure derivatives where advantageous.

Conduit Compliance

A second constitutive equation defines the bulk elastic compliance of the conduit walls α_2 as

$$\alpha_2=\frac{1}{V}\left[\frac{dV}{dp}\right]_0, \qquad (9)$$

where the subscript 0 denotes conduit volume change under a condition of zero plug velocity (u=0) and zero plug accretion (B=0). The utility of equation 9 is increased by embedding the equation in a definition of the total rate of conduit volume change that occurs when u and B are nonzero,

$$\frac{dV}{dt}=A\,u-\frac{\rho}{\rho_r}B+\left[\frac{dV}{dt}\right]_0. \qquad (10)$$

Here again, the subscript 0 denotes the rate of volume change that would exist if u=0 and B=0, whereas the terms Au and $(\rho/\rho_r)\,B$ describe conduit volume change due to upward plug motion and basal plug accretion, respectively. The factor ρ/ρ_r accounts for the influence of density change from ρ to ρ_r during magma solidification at the volumetric rate B.

To obtain a "systemic" constitutive equation for total conduit volume change, equation 9 is embedded in equation 10 by using the chain rule $[dV/dp]_0=[dV/dt]_0/(dp/dt)$, yielding

$$\frac{dV}{dt}=A\,u-\frac{\rho}{\rho_r}B+\alpha_2\frac{dp}{dt}V. \qquad (11)$$

The volume change described by equation 11 includes both an irreversible component and a reversible (elastic) component.

Plug Boundary Friction

The final constitutive equation defines the friction force F that acts where the plug contacts the conduit walls. This friction results from shearing of gouge, discussed briefly above in the section on "Gouge Properties" and in detail by Moore and others (this volume, chap. 20). Because friction might potentially exhibit diverse behaviors, and because this diversity has significant ramifications for extrusion dynamics, I represent F with a functional form that is consistent with the key findings of Moore and others (this volume, chap. 20) but that compromises between precision, generality, and simplicity:

$$F\;=\;\mathrm{sgn}(u)\,mg\lambda\,\mu_0\left[1+c\sinh^{-1}\left|\frac{u}{u_{ref}}\right|\right]. \qquad (12)$$

Here sgn(u) denotes the sign of u and stipulates that the frictional force always opposes motion; μ_0 is a static friction coefficient applicable when u=0; c is a parameter that describes the sign and magnitude of frictional rate dependence; and u_{ref} is a reference velocity that specifies the extent of nonlinearity of rate dependence (fig. 7). In the simplest case, with c=0, equation 12 specifies that the friction force has a constant value $F=F_0=\mathrm{sgn}(u)\,mg\lambda\mu_0$. If $c\neq 0$ and $u/u_{ref}<<1$, then equation 12 implies that friction depends almost linearly on slip rate ($F\approx\mathrm{sgn}(u)\,mg\lambda\mu_0[1+c\left|u/u_{ref}\right|]$), whereas for $u/u_{ref}>>1$, equation 12 implies that rate dependence of friction is essentially logarithmic ($F\approx\mathrm{sgn}(u)\,mg\lambda\mu_0[1+c\ln\left|2u/u_{ref}\right|]$) (see Abramowitz and Stegun, 1964, p. 87). This logarithmic dependence mimics behavior observed in the steady sliding experiments of Moore and others (this volume, chap. 20). The fact that nearly logarithmic behavior as well as other styles of frictional behavior may be represented by equation 12 is a significant advantage in analytical studies. Another advantage is that the equation implies that the maximum friction force is finite at u=0 (that is, $F = F_0 = = mg\lambda\mu_0$), whereas purely logarithmic friction rules imply that friction is infinite at u=0.

As specified by equation 12, the friction force F is proportional to the effective normal force on the sides of the plug, $mg\lambda$, where λ is a numerical factor that scales this normal force to the plug weight, mg. This definition implies that the maximum plausible value of λ is about 2 (assuming μ_0~0.5, as shown by the data of Moore and others, this volume, chap. 20), in which case sidewall friction suffices to support the entire plug weight. Realistic values of λ are likely to be considerably smaller than 2 and are dependent on the height of the plug in contact with the conduit walls and on the state of effective stress governing the normal traction on the plug margins. Although the effective stress state is unknown at Mount St. Helens, estimates of λ are constrained by the balance of forces implied by the right-hand side of equation 1 for the case of static limiting equilibrium: $F = F_0 = mg\lambda\mu_0 = pA - mg$. Algebraic rearrangement of this balance shows that λ must satisfy $\lambda = (1/\mu_0)[(pA/mg) - 1]$. Therefore, because the magma pressure p is unlikely to deviate much from lithostatic pressure (for if it did, it would cause hydraulic fracturing or conduit collapse), λ is largely determined by the plug geometry, which determines the plug mass m and basal area A, as well as the depth where p operates.

Although friction described by equation 12 represents both the peak-strength effect and shear-rate effect observed in the experiments by Moore and others (this volume, chap. 20), it includes no provision for the hold-time (or "state evolution") effect also observed in those experiments. In the context of equation 12, inclusion of such evolution would entail making μ_0 a time- or state-dependent quantity. This complication would introduce additional constitutive parameters, but it would add little to understanding the mechanism of regularly occurring drumbeat earthquakes at Mount St. Helens. Therefore, I have chosen to exclude state-evolution effects from the SPASM model.

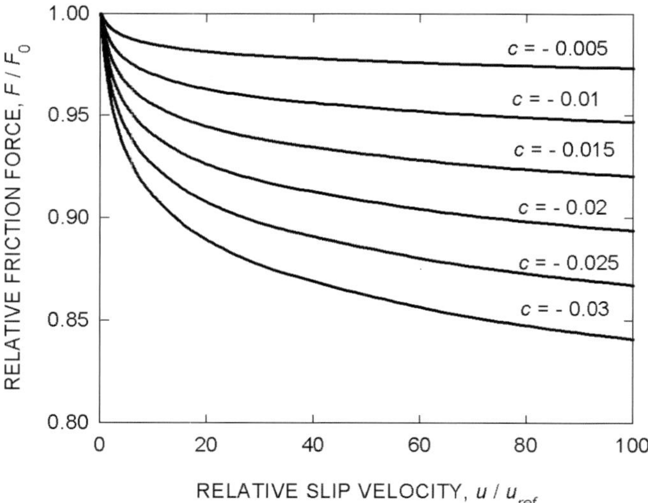

Figure 7. Graph of equation 12, illustrating nonlinear variation of relative friction force as a function of normalized slip rate u/u_{ref} and rate-dependence parameter c. Parameter F_0 is friction force at static, limiting equilibrium, $F_0 = m_0 g\lambda\mu_0$.

Friction represented by equation 12 does include a simple yet fundamental type of state dependence, however. The factor sgn(u) in equation 12 stipulates that the static (zero-velocity) friction force can jump from a positive value $mg\lambda\mu_0$ to a negative value $\geq -mg\lambda\mu_0$ if the extrusion velocity u changes from a positive value to a negative value. If u subsequently becomes positive again, then the friction force again becomes positive. Such jumps ensure that friction opposes motion, and they have great implications for the dynamical behavior of the extruding plug.

Reduced Governing Equations

The equations described above can be reduced to a compact system of three equations governing simultaneous evolution of the dependent variables u, V, and p. In this system the magma density ρ is eliminated as a dependent variable by using equation 8 to replace $d\rho/dt$ in equation 6 with dp/dt and then dividing all terms in the resulting equation by ρ, yielding

$$\frac{dV}{dt} + V\alpha_1 \frac{dp}{dt} = Q - B. \tag{13}$$

Equations 11 and 13 are then combined and rearranged algebraically to obtain explicit equations for dp/dt and dV/dt. These two equations accompany the equation of motion obtained by combining equations 2 and 12 with equation 1, thereby forming a system of three first-order differential equations,

$$\frac{du}{dt} = -g + \frac{1}{m_0 + \kappa t}\left[pA - \kappa u - F(u/u_{ref})\right], \tag{14}$$

$$\frac{dp}{dt} = \frac{-1/V}{\alpha_1 + \alpha_2}\left[Au + RB - Q\right], \text{ and} \tag{15}$$

$$\frac{dV}{dt} = \frac{\alpha_1}{\alpha_1 + \alpha_2}\left[Au + RB - Q\right] + Q - B, \tag{16}$$

where R is a nearly constant coefficient defined by

$$R = 1 - \frac{\rho}{\rho_r} = 1 - \frac{\rho_0}{\rho_r}\exp[\alpha_1(p - p_{ref})]. \tag{17}$$

The system of differential equations (14–16) contains four types of nonlinearities: one involving the quotient Au/V in equation 15, one involving the nonlinear dependence of R on p shown in equation 17, one involving the potential for jumps in F described in the section above on "Plug Boundary Friction," and one involving the dependence of F on $\sinh^{-1}|u/u_{ref}|$ shown in equation 12.

The Forced, Damped Oscillator Equation

The physical implications of the governing equations become clearer when equations 14 and 15 are combined to form a single, second-order equation. Differentiating equation 14 with respect to t, employing the chain rule $dF/dt = (dF/du)(du/dt)$, and substituting equation 15 into the resulting equation yields

$$(m_0 + \kappa t)\frac{d^2u}{dt^2} + \left(2\kappa + \frac{dF}{du}\right)\frac{du}{dt} + \left(\frac{A^2}{[\alpha_1 + \alpha_2]V}\right)u = -g\kappa + \frac{A(Q - RB)}{[\alpha_1 + \alpha_2]V}. \quad (18)$$

This equation has a form like that of equations governing behavior of forced, damped oscillators (Kreyszig, 1979, p. 82 ff.), and it implies that the extrusion velocity u has a natural tendency to oscillate about equilibrium. This tendency arises from the interplay of plug inertia, an upward "spring force" due to compression of the magma and conduit, and the downward force due to gravity. Oscillations of u are complicated by the presence of a time-dependent mass term $m_0 + \kappa t$, variable damping implicit in dF/du, and variable forcing due to the presence of R and V in the last term of equation 18, as well as by coupling of equation 18 to equations 16 and 17. Of course, equation 18 is strictly valid only insofar as F is a continuously differentiable function of u, and this restriction must be borne in mind when interpreting solutions of equation 18.

Linearized Dynamics: Analytical Results

Analytical solutions of equation 18 are important for guiding interpretation and numerical solution of the full equation set, 14–16, despite the fact that analytical solutions can be readily obtained only for various special cases. Analytical results also aid identification of diverse eruptive styles that are represented by the governing equations but are difficult to identify through numerical solutions alone.

Static, Steady-State, and Pseudosteady-State Solutions

The most basic special cases involve assumptions about the extrusion velocity u. A very simple special case with great physical importance assumes a condition of static limiting equilibrium, in which $u = 0$ and plug boundary friction just suffices to resist the upward force due to magma pressure. This case also assumes that the plug mass is constant (that is, $\kappa = 0$, $m = m_0$) and that the magma influx rate Q and basal accretion rate B are zero. These assumptions lead to the static equilibrium solution,

$$u = 0 \qquad p = p_0 = \frac{m_0 g + F_0}{A} \qquad V = V_0, \quad (19)$$

which satisfies equations 14–16 as well as 18. Here p_0 is the limiting equilibrium magma pressure at the base of the plug, F_0 is the friction force at static limiting equilibrium, $F_0 = m_0 g \lambda \mu_0$, and V_0 is an arbitrary but constant conduit volume.

An equally important special case assumes that the plug mass is constant ($\kappa = 0$, $m = m_0$) but that volumetric rate of basal plug accretion and volumetric rate of magma influx are finite and equal (B=Q). These conditions lead to an exact steady-state solution satisfying equations 14–16 as well as 18,

$$u = u_0 = \frac{Q - R_0 B}{A} \qquad p = \frac{m_0 g + F(u_0)}{A} \qquad V = V_0 \quad (20)$$

in which u_0 is the steady-state upward plug velocity, $F(u_0)$ is the steady-state friction force, $F(u_0) = m_0 g \lambda \mu_0 [1 + c \sinh^{-1}(u_0 / u_{ref})]$, and R_0 is a constant value of R that applies when $\rho = \rho_0$ (that is, $R_0 = 1 - (\rho_0 / \rho_r)$). The equation group 20 represents dynamic equilibrium of the steadily ascending magma-plug system, whereas transient states represent departures from this equilibrium. Below, analyses of these departures show that steady states can be stable in some circumstances and unstable in others.

In addition to the exact steady state described by equation group 20, pseudosteady states can exist in which the extrusion velocity u remains constant but the magma pressure p increases or decreases as the plug mass evolves according to $m = m_0 + \kappa t$. A pseudosteady-state solution that satisfies equations 14–16 and 18 is

$$u = \frac{Q - R_0 B}{A} - \frac{\kappa g(\alpha_1 + \alpha_2)V}{A^2} \qquad p = \frac{m_0 g + F(u)}{A} + \frac{\kappa(gt + u)}{A}$$

$$V = \frac{A(Q - B)}{\kappa g \alpha_1}. \quad (21)$$

Existence of this pseudosteady state requires that $B \neq Q$ and that R changes negligibly as p evolves. Despite these restrictions, the state described by equation group 21 has physical significance because it implies that essentially steady extrusion may occur in the presence of evolving plug mass and magma pressure, and it has mathematical significance because it provides a check on numerical results reported later in this paper. Additional pseudosteady states may, of course, exist if values of other parameters (for example, F_0, A, α_1, α_2) evolve, but such evolution is not addressed explicitly in this paper.

Linear Approximation of Transient States

Analysis of transient states is facilitated by linearization. As a first step, the dependent variables u and V in equation 18 are decomposed into sums of the steady-state values, defined in equation group 20, and transient deviations from steady state, denoted by primes:

$$u = u_0 + u'(t) \qquad V = V_0 + V'(t). \tag{22}$$

Substitution of equation group 22 into 18 and elimination of terms that sum to zero yields a simplified, but still nonlinear, version of equation 18 that describes the behavior of transient deviations. One linearization of this equation results from the assumption that magma density changes are small in comparison to the steady-state density, which enables R to be approximated by its steady-state value $R_0 = 1-(\rho_0/\rho_r)$. A second linearization involves the assumption that deviations in the magma-conduit volume are small in comparison to its steady-state volume (that is, $V'/V_0 << 1$). Then neglect of small terms involving V'/V_0 decouples equation 18 from 16 and removes the associated nonlinearity. These two linearizations generally have little effect on model predictions because they involve physical effects that are typically very subtle.

The most significant linearization involves approximation of dF/du in equation 18. If u remains positive, an exact, nonlinear expression for dF/du follows from the definition of F in equation 12 and can be written as (see Abramowitz and Stegun, 1964, p. 88)

$$\frac{dF}{du} = \frac{m_0 g \lambda \mu_0\, c}{u_{ref}} \left[1+\left(\frac{u}{u_{ref}}\right)^2\right]^{-1/2}. \tag{23a}$$

Substituting $u = u_0 + u'$ in equation 23a and simplifying the result algebraically yields an approximation of 23a that is valid if velocity deviations from steady state are sufficiently small that $u'/u_0 << 1$ and $u'/u_{ref} << 1$:

$$\frac{dF}{du} \approx \frac{m_0 g \lambda \mu_0\, c}{u_{ref}} \left[1+\left(\frac{u_0}{u_{ref}}\right)^2\right]^{-1/2} = C. \tag{23b}$$

Here C is a constant with the same sign as c but with dimensions of mass/time. If friction is rate independent, then C=0, whereas C>0 indicates rate-strengthening friction and C<0 indicates rate-weakening friction.

The linearized form of equation 18 results from making the substitutions shown in equations 21 and 23b and assuming $R = R_0$, $V'/V_0 << 1$, and $u'/u_0 << 1$, which yields

$$\left(1+\frac{\kappa t}{m_0}\right)\frac{d^2u'}{dt^2}+\left(\frac{2\kappa + C}{m_0}\right)\frac{du'}{dt}+\left(\frac{A^2}{m_0 V_0\left[\alpha_1+\alpha_2\right]}\right)u' = -\frac{g\kappa}{m_0}. \tag{24}$$

Except for the plug mass-growth factor $\kappa t/m_0$, all coefficients in equation 24 are constant, a property that facilitates analysis.

Natural Period of Oscillations

The form of equation 24 implies that if $\kappa = 0$ (that is, the plug mass is constant), then u' will oscillate freely with constant period $T = 2\pi t_0$, where t_0 is the natural time scale implied by the reciprocal of the coefficient that precedes u' in equation 24:

$$t_0 = \frac{[m_0 V_0(\alpha_1+\alpha_2)]^{1/2}}{A}. \tag{25}$$

This result is demonstrated more formally in the section on "Solution for Undamped Free Oscillations" below, but T and the time scale t_0 are introduced here as a basis for normalization of equation 24 and a first comparison of T and the typical interval between repetitive drumbeat earthquakes at Mount St. Helens. To facilitate this comparison, equation 25 is recast in a special form that is appropriate if the magma conduit and plug are approximated as right cylinders (not necessarily circular) with cross-sectional areas A and heights H_{con} and H_{plug}, respectively. In this case the oscillation period $T = 2\pi t_0$ can be expressed as

$$T = 2\pi[(\alpha_1+\alpha_2)\rho_r H_{con} H_{plug}]^{1/2}. \tag{26}$$

A graph of equation 26 for the values H_{con} = 8 km and ρ_r = 2,000 kg/m^3 is depicted in figure 8. The graph shows how the free oscillation period T varies as a function of the plug height H_{plug} and lumped compressibility $\alpha_1+\alpha_2$. For reasonable values of H_{plug} and $\alpha_1+\alpha_2$, the predicted T has values that range from about 10 s to several minutes. The similarity of these values to the observed recurrence period of drumbeat earthquakes during the 2004–5 eruption of Mount St. Helens helps support the hypothesis that the drumbeats were associated with oscillations of the extrusion rate u.

Normalized Oscillator Equation and Dimensionless Parameters

The quantity t_0 defined in equation 25 provides the appropriate time scale for normalization of equation 24, and this normalization leads to identification of the dimensionless parameters that control the linearized dynamics of the magma-plug system. Substitution of the normalized time $t^* = t/t_0$ and normalized velocity deviation $u^* = u'/u_0$ into equation 24 reduces the equation to

$$(1+Kt^*)\frac{d^2u^*}{dt^{*2}}+(2K+GS)\frac{du^*}{dt^*}+u^* = -KG, \tag{27}$$

in which K, S, and G are dimensionless parameters defined as

$$K = \frac{\kappa t_0}{m_0}, \tag{28}$$

$$S = \frac{Cu_0}{m_0 g}, \quad \text{and} \tag{29}$$

$$G = \frac{g t_0}{u_0}. \tag{30}$$

It is also useful to define a dimensionless damping factor D, which is half the coefficient in the second term of equation 27:

$$D = \frac{1}{2}(2K + GS) = \frac{t_0}{m_0}\left(\kappa + \frac{C}{2}\right). \quad (31)$$

If K=0, this damping factor plays a role like that of damping factors in textbook examples of linear oscillators, and D=1 constitutes critical damping (for example, Kreyszig, 1979, p. 82 ff.). This interpretation changes only subtly for cases with $K \neq 0$, as shown below.

A complete assessment of the magnitudes of the dimensionless parameters defined above is provided in the section on "Normalized Nonlinear Equations and Control Parameters" below, but for present purposes it suffices to note that typical magnitudes of K, G, and S imply that a satisfactory approximation of equation 27 commonly results from neglecting the plug growth term Kt^* as well as the effect of K on D. An even simpler but still relevant approximation is obtained by setting both K and S equal to 0 in equation 27. On the other hand, because solutions of equation 27 for nonzero values of these parameters imply diverse eruptive behaviors, which can differ qualitatively as well as quantitatively, I analyze the full spectrum of these behaviors before considering numerical solutions of the nonlinear system of equations 14–16.

Solution for Undamped Free Oscillations

For the case in which K=0 and S=0 (implying constant plug mass and constant plug-margin friction), equation 27 reduces to an elementary second–order equation describing undamped, free oscillations of the plug velocity. In this case the simplest nontrivial solution of equation 27 is

$$u^* = u_i^* \cos t^*, \quad (32)$$

which obeys the initial conditions $u^* = u_i^*$ and $du^* / dt^* = 0$. This solution demonstrates that the natural period of the plug's velocity oscillations is $T = 2\pi t_0$, as inferred in the section on "Natural Period of Free Oscillations" above. According to equation 32, sinusoidal oscillations with period T and amplitude u_i^* continue forever if an initial disturbance with magnitude u_i^* causes them to begin, provided that K=S=0.

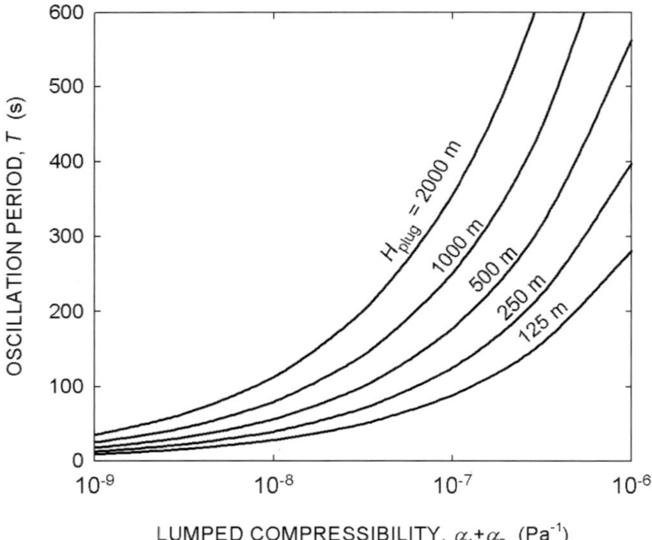

Figure 8. Graph of equation 26, illustrating predictions (from linearized theory) of variation of oscillation period T as a function of lumped compressibility $\alpha_1 + \alpha_2$ and plug height H_{plug}.

Solutions for Damped Free Oscillations—Stability of Quasi-Steady Extrusion

Another class of solutions of equation 27 exists if K=0 but $S \neq 0$. Physically, these conditions imply that the plug mass is constant $S \neq 0$ and that plug-margin friction depends linearly on the extrusion rate. In such cases the behavior of solutions depends on the value of D(= S/2) relative to the transition value D=0 and critical values $D=\pm$ 1, as summarized in table 2. In all cases the solutions imply stable eruptive behavior if D>0 (that is, if rate-strengthening friction exists), because u^* decays with time essentially like e^{-Dt^*}. On the other hand, if D<0 (that is, if rate-weakening friction exists), solutions containing the factor e^{-Dt^*} indicate unstable growth of u^*. The instability can be manifested as either runaway acceleration or oscillations that grow with time, as shown by the solutions listed in table 2.

The solutions listed in table 2 can also be used to infer whether the steady eruptive state represented by equation group 20 is physically accessible from an initial static state that exists before the onset of a volcanic eruption. For all cases with D>0, transient deviations in velocity (u^*) decay toward zero as time proceeds, implying that any transient state will eventually give way to a steady state. On the other hand, for cases in which D<0, dynamic steady states are inaccessible from an initial static state, because any transient motion grows without bound as time proceeds. Of course, this simple picture can change if $K \neq 0$ or if friction is nonlinear, as described in the section on "Nonlinear Dynamics: Numerical Results" below.

Solution for Damped, Forced Oscillations—Effects of Plug Growth on Extrusion Stability

The most complicated solutions of equation 27 apply to cases in which the plug mass changes with time such that $\kappa \neq 0$ and none of the parameters K, S, and G is zero. For such cases, solutions can be obtained by a multistep process that involves a simultaneous change of dependent and independent variables to transform equation 27 into Bessel's differential

Table 2. General solutions of equation 27 for cases with K=0 and D=$S/2$. All solutions contain arbitrary constants, c_1 and c_2, which are constrained by specifying initial conditions.

$\lvert D \rvert$	General solution of equation 27	Type of behavior
0	$u^* = c_1 \sin t^* + c_2 \cos t^*$	Undamped oscillations with constant amplitude
>0 but <1	$u^* = [c_1 \cos (t^* \sqrt{1-D^2}) + c_2 \sin (t^* \sqrt{1-D^2})]\ e^{-Dt^*}$	Underdamped oscillations; unstable growth if D<0
1	$u^* = (c_1 + c_2 t^*)\, e^{-Dt^*}$	Critically damped oscillation; unstable growth if D<0
>1	$u^* = c_1 e^{(-D+\sqrt{D^2-1})t^*} + c_2 e^{(-D-\sqrt{D^2-1})t^*}$	Overdamped, no oscillations; unstable growth if D<0

equation (appendix 1). Transformation of the well-known Bessel-equation solution back to the original variables u^* and t^* then yields the general solution

$$u^* = -KG + \frac{\xi^{\nu}}{4}\left[c_1 J_{\nu}(\xi) + c_2 Y_{\nu}(\xi)\right], \tag{33}$$

in which

$$\nu = \frac{K-2D}{K} \qquad \xi = 2\sqrt{\frac{1+Kt^*}{K^2}}. \tag{34}$$

Here c_1 and c_2 are arbitrary constants, and J_ν and Y_ν are Bessel functions of the first and second kind, of order ν (see Abramowitz and Stegun, 1964). Equation 33 describes diverse behaviors, partly analogous to those summarized in table 2. However, oscillations described by equation 33 have periods as well as amplitudes that evolve with time.

The relation between the solution for $K\neq0$ (equation 33) and the solutions for K=0 (table 2) has important physical implications. The relation is clarified by considering asymptotic approximations of J_ν and Y_ν that are valid for $\xi >> 1$. (The condition $\xi >> 1$ implies $t^* >> K - 1/K$, a criterion that is typically satisfied as time proceeds if K>0. If K<0, the criterion will not be satisfied as time proceeds, and equation 33 then implies that a singularity develops in which $u^* \to \infty$. Physically, this singularity represents a "catastrophe" in which the plug mass reaches zero, liquid magma reaches the surface, and the governing equations no longer apply.) For $\xi >> 1$ the Bessel function approximations are (Abramowitz and Stegun, 1964, p. 364)

$$J_\nu(\xi) \approx \sqrt{\frac{2}{\pi\,\xi}}\ \cos(\xi - \nu\pi/2 - \pi/4), \quad \text{and} \tag{35}$$

$$Y_\nu(\xi) \approx \sqrt{\frac{2}{\pi\,\xi}}\ \sin(\xi - \nu\pi/2 - \pi/4). \tag{36}$$

Substituting these approximations into equation 33 and collecting terms containing powers of ξ shows that, over time, u^* decays or grows according to

$$u^* \propto \left(\frac{1+Kt^*}{K^2}\right)^{1/4-D/K}. \tag{37}$$

The exponent $1/4 - D/K$ in equation 37 plays a physical role analogous to that of $-D$ in solutions with K=0 (table 2). The physical meaning of equation 37 becomes clearer if equations 29 and 31 are used to express the exponent in terms of physical parameters, yielding

$$u^* \propto \left(\frac{1+Kt^*}{K^2}\right)^{\frac{1}{2}\left(\frac{3}{2}+\frac{C}{\kappa}\right)}. \tag{38}$$

The exponent in equation 38 shows that oscillations in u^* will decay or grow depending on whether the criterion

$$\frac{C}{\kappa} > -\frac{3}{2} \tag{39}$$

is satisfied. Several classes of behavior are implied by this result and are summarized in table 3.

The chief physical implication of the results summarized in table 3 is that extrusion stability can depend on a tradeoff involving the rate dependence of the frictional resisting force and the rate of change of plug mass. Stable eruptive behavior can occur in the presence of rate-weakening friction (C<0) if the plug mass increases at a sufficient rate. This behavior contrasts with that of a system with constant plug mass, which necessarily exhibits unstable behavior if C<0 and, therefore, D<0 (table 2). Conversely, unstable behavior can occur in the presence of rate-strengthening friction (C>0) if the plug mass decreases at a sufficient rate.

Although further inferences can be drawn from the analytical results summarized by equations 38 and 39, for present purposes it

Table 3. Summary of behavior of equation 33, which is general solution of equation 27 for cases with changing plug mass ($K \neq 0, \kappa \neq 0$).

[Behavior for both rate-strengthening friction ($C > 0$) and rate-weakening friction ($C < 0$) is summarized.]

κ	C	Behavior of equation 33
$\kappa = -(2/3)C$	$C = -(3/2)\kappa$	Undamped, constant-amplitude oscillations
$\kappa > 0$	$C > 0$	Oscillations necessarily decay toward a steady state
$\kappa > 0$	$C < 0$	Oscillations grow if $\kappa < -(2/3)C$ and decay if $\kappa > -(2/3)C$
$\kappa < 0$	$C > 0$	Oscillations grow if $\kappa < -(2/3)C$ and decay if $\kappa > -(2/3)C$
$\kappa < 0$	$C < 0$	Behavior becomes singular

is more useful next to consider numerical solutions of the nonlinear equation set 14–16. Nonlinearities produce important effects that are not revealed by analytical results that strictly apply only when transient disturbances are small (that is, $u'/u_0 << 1$).

Nonlinear Dynamics: Numerical Results

Results of the linear theory point to several questions to be addressed through numerical solution of the nonlinear system of equations 14–16. Do the bounds of stable versus unstable eruptive behavior and character of oscillatory eruptive behavior change when nonlinearities exist? More specifically, can nonlinearities result in stick-slip instabilities like those inferred to produce drumbeat earthquakes at Mount St. Helens? What controls the magnitude and frequency of stick-slip events? Can such events occur repeatedly (that is, forever) until some attribute of the system changes? Can evolution of stick-slip periods and amplitudes yield inferences about evolution of system properties? Do complications such as plug mass change have significant effects? How sensitive are the system's dynamics to disequilibrium initial conditions? (Although the linear theory assumes that departures from equilibrium are always small, nature imposes no such constraint, and volcanic eruptions necessarily begin in disequilibrated states.)

Normalized Nonlinear Equations and Control Parameters

Guidance for investigating the behavior of numerical solutions comes from identification of dimensionless control parameters and their likely magnitudes. Behavior of the nonlinear equations is governed partly by the same dimensionless parameters that govern linearized behavior, but additional parameters also play a role. The additional control parameters are identified by normalizing the nonlinear system of first-order equations 14–16 through use of dimensionless variables defined as $u^* = u/u_0$, $p^* = p/p_0$, $V^* = V/V_0$, $t^* = t/t_0$.

Substituting these variables into equations 14–16 yields the normalized system

$$\frac{du^*}{dt^*} = -G + \frac{1}{1+Kt^*}\left[G(1+\hat{S})p^* - Ku^* - G\hat{S}F^*\right], \quad (40)$$

$$\frac{dp^*}{dt^*} = \frac{-1/V^*}{G(1+\hat{S})}\left[u^* - 1 + Z(R^* - 1)\right], \text{ and} \quad (41)$$

$$\frac{dV^*}{dt^*} = X\left[u^* - 1 + Z(R^* - 1)\right] + Y. \quad (42)$$

Here, G and K are dimensionless parameters defined exactly as in the linear model (that is, in equations 28 and 30). The dimensionless parameter $\hat{S}$ is related to S defined in the linear model (that is, in equation 29), but its definition is somewhat simpler because it involves F_0 rather than the derivative $C = dF/du$:

$$\hat{S} = \frac{F_0}{m_0 g} = \lambda \mu_0. \quad (43)$$

The dimensionless parameters X, Y, and Z have no analog in the linear model and are defined as

$$X = \frac{\alpha_1 m_0 u_0}{A t_0} \qquad Y = \frac{t_0(Q-B)}{V_0} \qquad Z = \frac{R_0 B}{u_0 A}. \quad (44)$$

The variables R^* and F^* in equations 40–42 are normalized versions of the density variable R defined in equation 17 and the friction force F defined in equation 12:

$$R^* = \frac{R}{R_0} = \frac{1 + (R_0 - 1)\exp\left[XG(1+\hat{S})(p^* - 1)\right]}{R_0}, \quad (45)$$

$$F^* = \frac{F}{F_0} = \mathrm{sgn}(u^*)\left(1 + c\sinh^{-1}[u^*(u_0/u_{ref})]\right). \quad (46)$$

In the nonlinear version of the SPASM model, equations 45 and 46 must be satisfied simultaneously with equations 40–42.

Plausible ranges of the values of the dimensionless parameters in equations 40–46 for the 2004–5 eruption of Mount St. Helens are listed in table 4. The tabulated values imply that some of the terms in equations 40–46 will have little influence on numerical results. For example, relevant values of the denominator $G(1+\hat{S})$ on the right-hand side of equation 41 are undoubtedly very much greater than 1, implying that p^* will remain close to its static equilibrium value $p^*=1$. This inference, together with the inference that $X<<1$ (table 4), implies that the argument of the exponential function in equation 45 will remain close to zero, despite the large probable value of $G(1+\hat{S})$. Therefore, $R^*=1$ is typically a good approximation of equation 45, and this approximation implies that the term $Z(R^*-1)$ in equations 41 and 42 will have only subtle effects. Similarly, the term Y in equation 42 will have subtle effects because $Y<<1$ (table 4). As a basis for prioritizing investigations, then, it is reasonable to assume initially that $Y=Z=0$.

With these simplifications in mind, equation 40 can be differentiated and combined with equation 41 to obtain a second-order equation, which can also be obtained through normalization of the original oscillator equation 18. For the case in which $R^*=1$ is a good approximation, the complete system of normalized nonlinear governing equations thereby reduces to

$$\left(1+Kt^*\right)\frac{d^2u^*}{dt^{*2}}+(2K+GS)\frac{du^*}{dt^*}+\frac{1}{V^*}u^*=\frac{1}{V^*}-K\,G, \quad \text{and} \tag{47}$$

$$\frac{dV^*}{dt}=X(u^*-1). \tag{48}$$

Note that S rather than $\hat{S}$ appears in equation 47, and that the entire set of dimensionless parameters has collapsed to K, G, X, and S in equations 47 and 48. Moreover, the values of K and X are typically much smaller than 1 (table 4), and the effects of terms containing K and X are therefore apt to be modest. On this basis, computational investigations aimed at illuminating the physics represented by the SPASM model can focus principally on the effects of G and S, secondarily on the effects of K, and lastly on the effects of X, Y, and Z.

The strategy of focusing primarily on effects of G and S reduces the need to explore a large, multidimensional parameter space numerically, and it parallels development of the linearized theory, in which D emerged as the key control parameter. Indeed, D defined in the linearized theory applies also to the nonlinear model, provided that D is viewed as a numerical index rather than a constant damping factor. For this purpose it is useful to define the index D as the value applicable when the slip rate equals the steady equilibrium rate ($u = u_0$):

$$D_{u=u_0}=\frac{1}{2}\,(2K+GS)= \tag{49}$$

$$\frac{1}{2}\left(\frac{2\kappa t_0}{m_0}+c\lambda\mu_0\frac{gt_0}{u_{ref}}\left[1+\left(\frac{u_0}{u_{ref}}\right)^2\right]^{-1/2}\right).$$

This equation is simply an algebraically expanded version of the definition given in equation 31, and I employ this definition of D to index numerical results.

It is also noteworthy that for cases in which $K=0$ and $u_0/u_{ref}>>1$, equation 49 reduces to the simplified form

$$D\approx\frac{1}{2}\left(c\lambda\mu_0\frac{gt_0}{u_0}\right), \tag{50}$$

which is commonly a satisfactory approximation. In the sparest distillation of the nonlinear SPASM model, then, numerical results can be expected to depend primarily on D as defined in equation 50, which in turn depends only on c, λ, and μ_0 if the equilibrium extrusion rate u_0 and oscillation time scale t_0 are fixed.

Computational Method

Numerical solutions were obtained by using a standard fourth-order Runge-Kutta method described by Press and others (1986). To implement the Runge-Kutta algorithm, a double-precision FORTRAN program was written and executed on a personal computer with a 2.26-GHz processor. Constant time steps were used to generate all solutions and were typically 0.0001 to 0.01 s. Although some exploratory computations required hours of CPU time, no computations reported in this paper required more than several minutes of CPU time when using this constant-time-step approach.

The accuracy of numerical solutions was checked against exact analytical solutions for simple linear cases with constant values of D and K (table 2 and equation 33). For nonlinear cases, some aspects of numerical solutions were checked analytically by exploiting the fact that the governing equations 14–16 yield nearly exact solutions for p and V for the special case in which $u = 0$. These solutions assume that $R=R_0$, and they have the form

$$V=V_i+Wt, \quad \text{and} \tag{51}$$

$$p=p_i+\frac{Q-R_0B}{(\alpha_1+\alpha_2)W}\ln\left[1+\frac{W}{V_i}t\right], \tag{52}$$

where

$$W=\frac{\alpha_1}{\alpha_1+\alpha_2}\left[R_0B-Q\right]+Q-B. \tag{53}$$

Here V_i and p_i are the values of V and p at the beginning of any "stick" episode with $u=0$. The duration of stick episodes, T_{stick}, may be calculated by solving equation 52 for t while setting p equal to the static limiting equilibrium pressure p_0 necessary to trigger any slip episode,

$$T_{stick}=\frac{V_i}{W}\left[\exp\left(\frac{(p_0-p_i)(\alpha_1+\alpha_2)W}{Q-R_0B}\right)-1\right]. \tag{54}$$

Table 4. Plausible values of SPASM model parameters applicable to the quasi-steady dome-building eruption of Mount St. Helens, 2004–2005.

[Derived dimensionless parameters determine model behavior and are formed from combinations of physical parameters.]

Parameter	Units	Value(s)	Comments on value(s)
Specified physical parameters			
A	m^2	30,000	Calculated using Q/u_0 and values tabulated here
B	m^3/s	0–10	Cannot differ greatly from Q
c	none	-0.01–0.01	Inferred from results of testing by Moore and others, (this volume, chap. 20)
C	kg/s	$\lvert C \rvert < 5\times10^{13}$	Calculated using equation 23 and values tabulated here
g	m/s^2	9.8	Typical value at Earth's surface
m_0	kg	5×10^{9}–7×10^{10}	Inferred from plug heights 100–1,000 m and A and ρ_r tabulated here
Q	m^3/s	1–2	Inferred from photogrammetric measurements of dome growth
R_0	none	-0.5–0.5	Calculated from typical values of ρ_0 and ρ_r tabulated here
t_0	s	0.4–150	Calculated from equation 25 and other values tabulated here
u_0	m/s	2×10^{-5}–7×10^{-5}	Inferred from measured linear extrusion rate
u_{ref}	m/s	7×10^{-8}–7×10^{-5}	Smaller than u_0 if friction rate-dependence is nonlinear
V_0	m^3	3×10^{6}–3×10^{8}	Inferred from 8 km conduit height and conduit radii 10–100 m
α_1	Pa^{-1}	10^{-8}–10^{-6}	Typical values for silicic magma with 1–50 vol percent bubble content
α_2	Pa^{-1}	$\leq 10^{-9}$	Typical values for fractured rock
κ	kg/s	$\lvert \kappa \rvert < 4{,}000$	Exceptions may occur during dome-collapse events
λ	none	0.1–1	Inferred from plug geometry and plausible effective stress states
μ_0	none	0.4–0.5	Inferred from results of testing by Moore and others, (this volume, chap. 20)
ρ_0	kg/m^3	1,200–2,400	Typical values for silicic magma with 1–50 vol percent bubble content
ρ_r	kg/m^3	1,600–2,400	Inferred from measurements on dome-rock specimens
Derived dimensionless parameters			
D	none	-10^{7}–10^{7}	Influence of D can be very significant
G	none	6×10^{4}–2×10^{7}	Influence of G is very significant
K	none	$\lvert K \rvert \leq 10^{-4}$	Influence of K is subtle except in event of abrupt dome collapse
S	none	-7–7	Influence of S is significant
$\hat{S}$	none	-0.5–0.5	Influence of $\hat{S}$ is significant if multiplied by G
X	none	4×10^{-4}–8×10^{-10}	Influence of X is subtle except perhaps where multiplied by G
Y	none	$\lvert Y \rvert \leq 10^{-4}$	Influence of Y is subtle
Z	none	$\lvert Z \rvert < 0.5$	Influence of Z may be significant, contingent on value of R^*

This equation is useful for checking computational results, and it also has a significant physical implication: the duration of stick episodes increases exponentially with $p_0 - p_i$. From this result it may be inferred that plug displacements during slip events also increase exponentially with $p_0 - p_i$, because the average extrusion velocity is fixed (as given by equation 20), and slip-event magnitude must therefore increase in proportion to stick duration. Although strict validity of equations 52 and 54 rests on the assumption that $R = R_0$, computations that do not employ this assumption show that, nonetheless, equations 52 and 54 generally provide good predictions.

Computational Results

Only a small number of computational solutions are presented here, but hundreds of additional solutions were computed and examined. Results chosen for presentation highlight a range of physical effects that appear particularly important for understanding the origin of drumbeat earthquakes at Mount St. Helens. To a lesser degree, results were also chosen to illustrate the spectrum of behaviors possible within the framework of the SPASM model.

Behavior with D Close to Zero

The most basic nonlinear features of solutions appear even when departures from linear behavior are slight. In particular, stick-slip cycles develop in any case in which D<0, provided that a jump in F is imposed at u=0. Figure 9 illustrates this behavior for a case in which $D=-0.01$, B=Q, and F depends linearly on u (that is, $F=\mathrm{sgn}(u)\,m_0 g\lambda\mu_0[1+c\left|u/u_{ref}\right|]$). The small value of D results from use of an unusually small value of λ, λ=0.01; physically, this value implies that frictional resistance and the damping it produces are small. The computation also used the initial conditions u=Q/A, $V=V_0$, and $p=p_0$, which imposed a slightly perturbed initial magma pressure (because the static equilibrium pressure p_0 slightly exceeds the steady equilibrium pressure) and used the parameter values K=0, Y=0, Z=0, X=5×10^{-6}, T=10 s, $\rho_0=\rho_r$= 2,000 kg/m^3, m_0=3.6×10^{10} kg, μ_0=0.5, c=–1.71×10^{-5}, and u_{ref}=0.1(Q/A)=6.66710^{-6} m/s. The fact that the value of u_{ref} is significantly smaller than that of the typical extrusion rate (Q/A) implies that effects of rate dependence in the friction rule are important.

Under the conditions described above, the computed extrusion behavior is initially identical to that predicted by the linear analytical theory, and u, p, and V each exhibit exponentially growing sinusoidal oscillations until u=0 occurs (at $t\approx$ 27 s in fig. 9). At that time F momentarily changes sign and thereby halts motion of the plug as it starts to descend. This event heralds the end of exponential oscillation growth and the onset of repetitive stick-slip cycles.

In both the sinusoidal and stick-slip cycles shown in figure 9, magma pressure oscillates ¼ cycle out of phase with slip velocity, and conduit volume oscillates ½ cycle out of phase with magma pressure. Although it may seem contradictory that conduit volume decreases as magma pressure increases, this out-of phase response results from conditions at the base of the extruding plug, where solidification and accretion occur continuously at the volumetric rate B, even as plug velocity diminishes to less than the steady-state value $u=Q/A$=6.667×10^{-5} m/s. Indeed, as a rough approximation, conduit volume declines whenever the plug extrusion rate is less than the basal accretion rate. The conduit volume also responds elastically to pressure changes, but this effect is typically overshadowed by volume changes associated with plug motion and basal accretion.

Key elements of the solution presented in figure 9 are recast in a phase-plane diagram in figure 10, which shows how pressure deviations from the static equilibrium pressure p_0 vary in concert with velocity deviations from the steady equilibrium velocity Q/A. As portrayed in the phase plane, the initial condition (u = Q/A, $p=p_0$, marked I.C. in fig. 10) is unstable. This instability leads to an outwardly diverging clockwise spiral representing simultaneous oscillations of u and p that grow with time. (Note that arrows in phase-plane diagrams throughout this paper point in the direction of advancing time.) When the spiral becomes large enough to encounter the condition u = 0, divergence ceases and the dynamics become locked in stick-slip limit cycles that repeat endlessly thereafter. If the initial condition is located elsewhere inside the stick-slip limit cycle of figure 10, behavior nonetheless diverges smoothly until locking in the same limit-cycle state. If friction exhibits rate-strengthening rather than

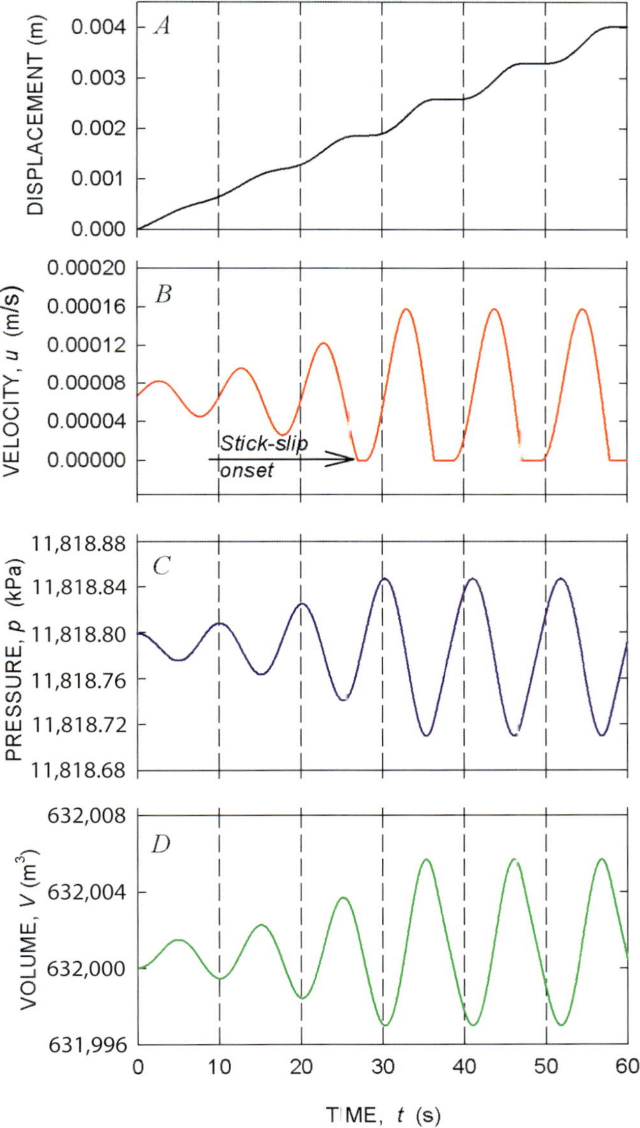

Figure 9. Start-up behavior of solution computed for D = –0.01 with linear rate weakening. Initial condition is $u=Q/A$, $p=p_0$, $V=V_0$. Oscillations of slip velocity (u), magma pressure (p) and conduit volume (V) are sinusoidal and match analytical predictions until u = 0 occurs and stick-slip behavior begins.

rate-weakening behavior (that is, $D>0$), then behavior converges smoothly to a steady fixed-point equilibrium instead. An analogous fixed-point equilibrium is exhibited by eruption models that assume forces are always balanced (for example, Mastin and others, this volume, chap. 22).

Modification of the behavior depicted in figures 9 and 10 by nonlinearity in the rate-weakening friction rule is illustrated in figures 11 and 12. Initial conditions and parameter values used to generate figures 11 and 12 were the same as those used to generate figures 9 and 10, but the nonlinear friction rule $F = \mathrm{sgn}(u)mg\lambda\mu_0[1 + c\sinh^{-1}|u/u_{ref}|]$ was employed. Comparison of figure 11 with figure 9 demonstrates that the most conspicuous effects of the nonlinearity are to delay the onset of stick-slip behavior and shorten the duration of individual stick events. These effects are unsurprising, because the nonlinearity represented by the $\sinh^{-1}$ function increasingly suppresses rate weakening as the slip rate increases.

Comparison of the phase-plane diagrams shown in figures 10 and 12 demonstrates that the dynamical effects of linear and nonlinear rate weakening also differ in other ways. In both figures 10 and 12 the feature of greatest interest is the outer loop representing stick-slip limit cycles. In the limit cycles shown in both figures, the maximum positive magma pressure deviates by a factor of only 4×10^{-6} from the static equilibrium pressure (~10^7 Pa), and the maximum slip velocity is only slightly more than double the equilibrium slip velocity. The maximum velocity is somewhat larger in the case with linear rate weakening (fig. 10), however, because linear rate weakening enables a larger dynamic overshoot of slip in response to increasing magma pressure. (Here, "dynamic overshoot" means that inertia carries the moving plug upward past an equilibrium point in which forces are balanced.) This larger overshoot produces a commensurately larger decline in magma pressure in response to slip, and the magma pressure deviation at the onset of stick-slip limit cycles is about three times larger in the case with linear rate weakening than with nonlinear weakening (~6×10^{-6} versus 2×10^{-6}). This difference in pressure deviation constitutes the single most important difference between the linear case (fig. 10) and the nonlinear case (fig. 12), because the duration of stick periods (T_{stick}) increases

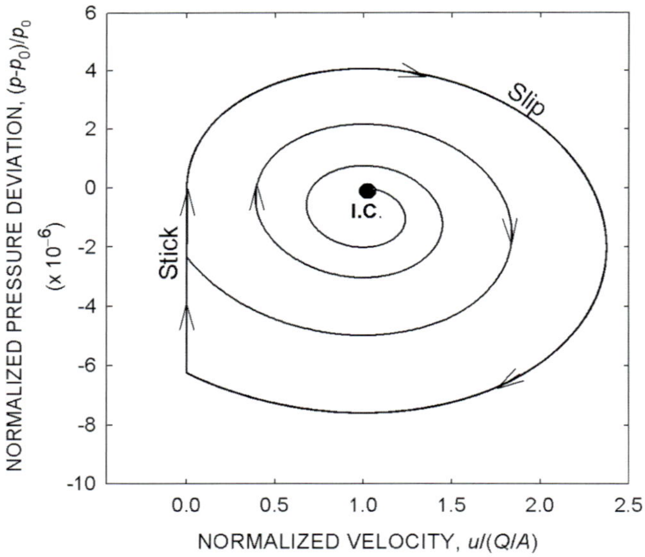

Figure 10. Phase-plane representation of simultaneous evolution of normalized slip velocity and normalized magma pressure computed for $D = -0.01$ with linear rate weakening. Initial condition (I.C.) is: $u = Q/A$, $p = p_0$, $V = V_0$. Arrows point in direction of advancing time.

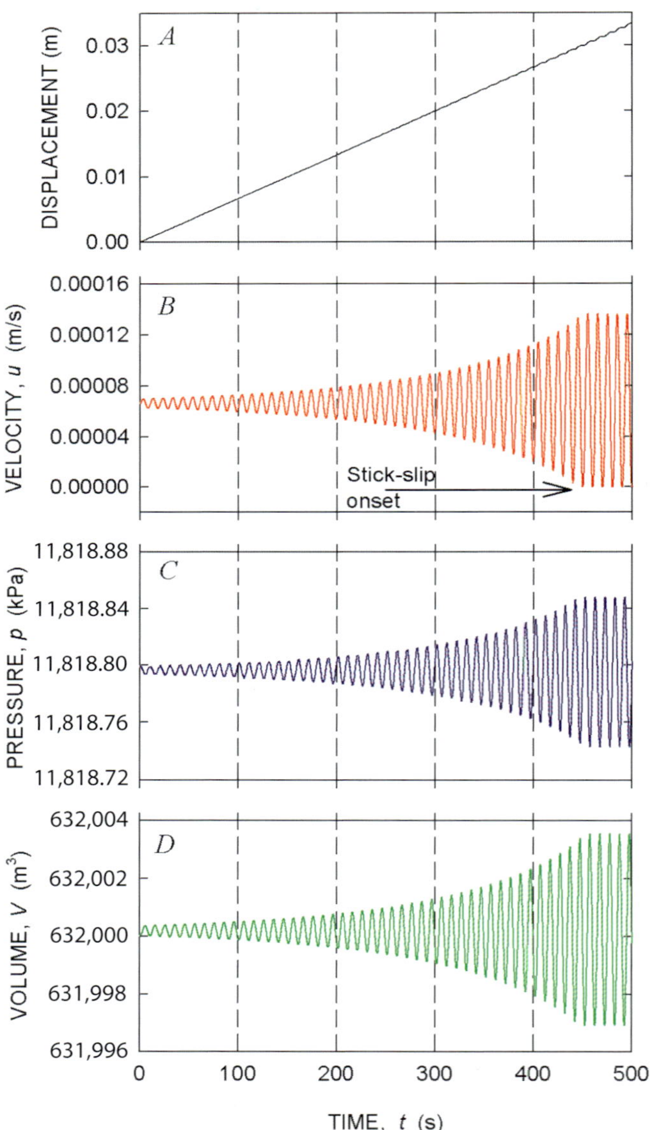

Figure 11. Start-up behavior of oscillatory solutions computed for $D = -0.01$ with nonlinear rate weakening. Initial condition is $u = Q/A$, $p = p_0$, $V = V_0$. Oscillations of slip velocity (u), magma pressure (p), and conduit volume (V) are sinusoidal until $u = 0$ occurs and stick-slip behavior begins.

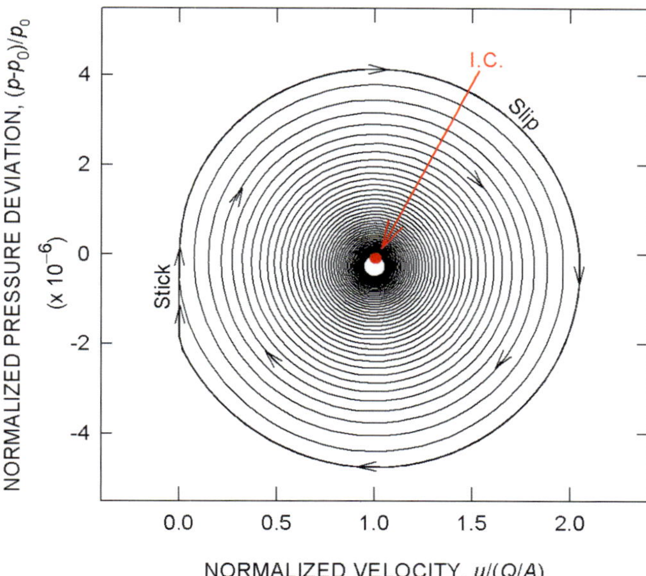

Figure 12. Phase-plane representation of simultaneous evolution of normalized slip velocity and normalized magma pressure computed for $D = -0.01$ with nonlinear rate weakening. Initial condition (I.C.) is $u = Q/A$, $p = p_0$, $V = V_0$. Arrows point in direction of advancing time.

exponentially with this pressure deviation, as indicated by equation 54. Therefore, nonlinearity in the friction rule has a significant effect on predictions of the periods and amplitudes of stick-slip oscillations, and the nonlinear rule was employed to generate all results presented subsequently in this paper.

Effects of the Damping Index *D*

Some of the most important findings of this study are summarized in figure 13, which illustrates computational results obtained by employing the nonlinear friction rule and various values of *D*. Computations that generated these results used the same parameter values used to generate figures 9–12, except that here $\lambda = 0.2$ was used and varying values of c were used to generate *D* values ranging from −0.2 to −4. (The value $\lambda = 0.2$ constitutes a "best-guess" value applicable to Mount St. Helens' plug geometry and state of effective stress, and c values ranging from 1.7×10^{-5} to 3.4×10^{-4} were used to simulate subtle rate weakening similar to that observed experimentally by Moore and others, this volume, chap. 20).

Displacement time series shown in figure 13*A* were computed for a family of stick-slip cycles with various values of *D*, and in figure 13*B* the same results are depicted as limit cycles in the velocity-pressure phase plane. Initial conditions used to generate figure 13 assumed a static, limiting equilibrium state (u=0, $p = p_0$, $V = V_0$) rather than the state with $u = u_0$ used to generate figures 9–12. Therefore, no divergent oscillations precede the development of stick-slip limit cycles.

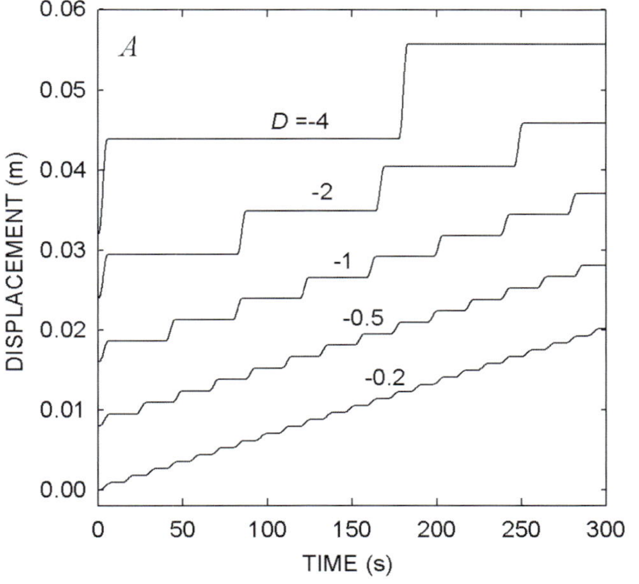

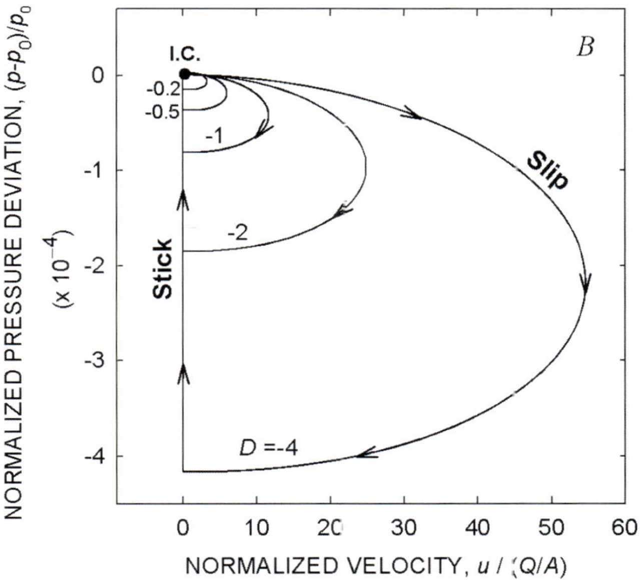

Figure 13. Stick-slip cycles computed for various values of parameter *D* with nonlinear rate weakening. All computations employed baseline parameter values Q=2 m^3/s, B=Q, $R_0 = 0$, K=0, Y=0, Z=0, X=5×10^{-6}, T=10 s, and employed m_0=3.6×10^{10} kg, λ=0.2, μ_0=0.5, and u_{ref}=0.1(Q/A)=6.667×10^{-6} m/s to determine *F*. Varying values of *c* were used to obtain varying values of *D*. *A*, Time series representation of stick-slip displacements. *B*, Phase-plane representation of velocity-pressure limit cycles. Arrows point in direction of advancing time.

The basic dynamics portrayed in figure 13*B* are simple. When basal magma influx produces pressure exceeding the static equilibrium value (p_0), it triggers slip at a rate that may slightly or greatly surpass the steady equilibrium rate (Q/A), depending on the value of *D*. When a combination of plug inertia and diminishing magma pressure no longer suffices to overcome the effects of gravity and friction, slip terminates and stick begins. Magma pressure then rebuilds until it triggers another slip event. Figure 13*A* shows that periods of stick-slip cycles with $D= -0.2$ differ little from the $T=10$ s period predicted by linear theory (that is, equation 25), but periods increase as *D* values range further from 0. For *D* values sufficiently far from 0, periods increase almost in direct proportion to the magnitude of *D*, and the amplitudes of slip events increase accordingly. Maximum slip speeds and associated pressure deviations during stick-slip cycles also increase in proportion to the magnitude of *D* (fig. 13*B*), bolstering the inference that *D* values encapsulate most of the important controls on system dynamics.

Stick-slip cycles computed with $D= -2$ closely resemble those thought to be responsible for generating drumbeat earthquakes at Mount St. Helens. With $D = -2$ individual slip events entail about 5 mm of displacement in about 5 s and maximum slip rates of ~1.7 mm/s. Attendant fluctuations in magma pressure are <0.02 percent of p_0 (fig. 13*B*), equivalent to only ~2.4 kPa or <0.2 m of static magma pressure head. This result implies that a remarkably delicate shift in the balance of forces distinguishes periods of slip from those with no slip. Multiplied by $A= 30{,}000$ m^2, the ~2.4 kPa pressure change also serves as a proxy for the force drop responsible for generating seismicity (~7×10^7 N).

Details of Baseline Case with $D=-2$

Deeper exploration of the dynamics computed with $D= -2$ provides further insight to physical phenomena that may be responsible for drumbeat seismicity at Mount St. Helens. Figure 14 illustrates details of repetitive earthquake cycles computed with $D=-2$. The histories of slip velocity, magma pressure, and conduit volume shown in figure 14 illustrate abrupt decreases in magma pressure and increases in conduit volume during slip events and also illustrate gradual changes of these quantities between slip events. As noted above, magma solidification at the base of the plug causes the volume of the fluid-filled conduit to decline between slip events, despite the fact that magma pressure rises.

Perhaps the most intriguing result illustrated in figure 14 involves the history of shear force along the plug margins. The shear force is large (~3.5×10^{10} N) because it must overcome the effects of both gravity and friction to move the massive plug upward, but the force drop during each slip event is comparatively small (~7×10^7 N) (fig. 14*E*). (This drop in shear force is closely related to the stress drop that occurs in conjunction with tectonic earthquakes, but force drop is, in fact, a more fundamental quantity. The force drop represents the product of the stress drop and the area of the slip surface—a product that appears directly in earthquake energy budgets (for example, Scholz, 2002, p. 184). Shear force might be concentrated in a relatively small patch of gouge bounding the extruding plug at Mount St. Helens, or it might be distributed evenly within the gouge; from the standpoint of force drop, this distinction makes no difference.) Standard estimation methods indicate that such a 7×10^7 N force drop, accompanied by 5 mm of slip (figs. 14*A*, *E*), implies about 2×10^5 J of seismic energy radiation (Scholz, 2002, p. 185), whereas the work done against friction during the slip events depicted in figure 14 is the total shear force times displacement, which yields an estimate of 2×10^8 J. These results are consistent with prior findings that only a small fraction of the work done during fault slip produces seismic radiation (McGarr, 1999).

The temporal pattern of the drop in shear force accompanying slip events also has significant implications. As slip accelerates, the shear force declines smoothly owing to the effects of rate-weakening friction (fig. 14*E*). Similarly, as slip decelerates, the force smoothly rises as friction gradually increases. When slip stops, however, the shear force drops abruptly because it suddenly returns to a static equilibrium value imposed by the plug weight and magma-pressure force, which has declined during slip. Before this reequilibration, the shear force is out of equilibrium with these static forces because rate-weakening friction allows slip to dynamically overshoot the equilibrium point. The net effect is that almost the full force drop (~7×10^7 N) occurs abruptly at the end of the slip cycle, and it thereby provides an impulse capable of radiating high-frequency seismic energy.

Sensitivity of Behavior to Variations of Parameters Within *D*

Values of *D* encapsulate the effects of most of the important parameters affecting stick-slip dynamics, but it is nevertheless necessary to examine whether variations in values of these individual parameters have significant effects. Results presented in figures 15 and 16 show that the behavior computed for $D= -2$ is quite insensitive to variations in c, λ, and u_0 / u_{ref}. For example, if values of c and λ range over orders of magnitude, while *D* is held constant, computed stick-slip limit cycles differ only slightly in a phase-plane diagram depicting coevolution of the normalized pressure deviation and normalized slip velocity (fig. 15*A*). Differences exist exclusively in the magnitude of normalized pressure deviations, reflecting the fact that smaller λ values imply that less magma pressure is needed to satisfy limiting equilibrium and trigger slip. Moreover, if the pressure deviations are "denormalized," as shown in figure 15*B*, such differences disappear entirely, and results for all values of c and λ collapse onto a single curve in the phase plane. This finding demonstrates that values of c and λ individually are unimportant in the system's dynamical behavior, provided that *D* is constant and the nonlinearity of the friction rule is unchanged.

Results shown in figure 16 illustrate the effects of changing the nonlinearity of the friction rule by allowing the value of u_0 / u_{ref} to range over four orders of magnitude while holding $D = -2$. To facilitate comparison with figure 13, figure 16 depicts results as both displacement time series and stick-slip limit cycles. These results show that reducing values of u_{ref} (that is, increasing values of u_0 / u_{ref}) produces stick-slip cycles with increased interevent periods, increased slip displacements, increased slip velocities, and increased deviations of magma pressure from its equilibrium value. However, effects of u_0 / u_{ref} ranging over four orders of magnitude (fig. 16) are similar to the effects of D ranging from about −2 to −4 (fig. 13), reinforcing the view that D values encapsulate most of the dynamical controls on system behavior. It is, however, unsurprising that effects of u_0 / u_{ref} are not captured entirely by values of D, as the effect of u_0 / u_{ref} is inherently nonlinear. For values of u_0 / u_{ref} smaller than 1, the periods of stick-slip oscillations lengthen, but this behavior is not pursued here because it has little relevance to plug extrusion at Mount St. Helens.

Effects of Plug Mass Change (Nonzero K)

Continuous changes in plug mass are represented by nonzero values of K (and of κ, its dimensional equivalent). If the condition $B=Q$ is assumed, nonzero values of K imply that the rate of mass loss due to surface erosion ($\rho_r E$) does not balance the rate of mass gain due to basal accretion (ρB), and the simplest example of such an imbalance occurs when the erosion rate is zero and the plug mass increases at the rate $\kappa = \rho B$. Figure 17 illustrates time-series behavior computed for this case (that is, κ=4,000 kg/s; K=1.78×10^{-7}) with D= −2 and $u_0 / u_{ref} = 10$. Comparison of figure 17 with figure 14

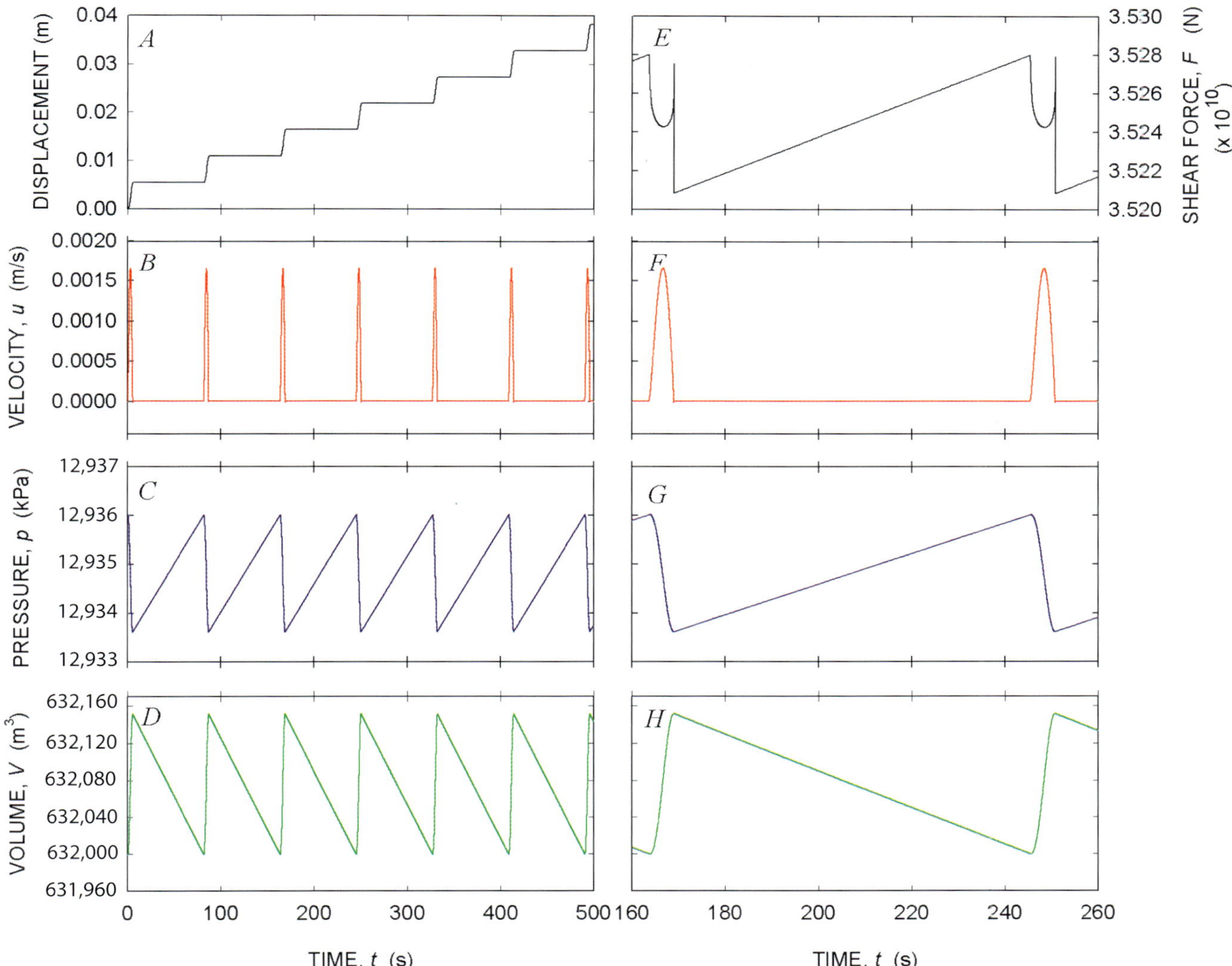

Figure 14. Time series depiction of concurrent changes in plug displacement, slip velocity, magma pressure, and conduit volume during earthquake cycles computed for baseline case with $D = -2$. Parameter values are same as those used to generate figure 13, and c = −1.71×10^{-4} is used to obtain $D = -2$. Panels *A–D* illustrate behavior during seven consecutive slip events, and panels *E–H* show details on an expanded time scale. Panel *E* is distinct from other panels because it shows force drops accompanying slip events.

shows that stick-slip cycles computed with K>0 have slightly larger periods and amplitudes than those computed with K=0, an unsurprising finding in view of analytical results indicating that positive K values will cause growth of oscillation periods (see equation 33). However, in contrast to analytical predictions, periods and amplitudes of stick-slip cycles computed with K>0 do not change with time.

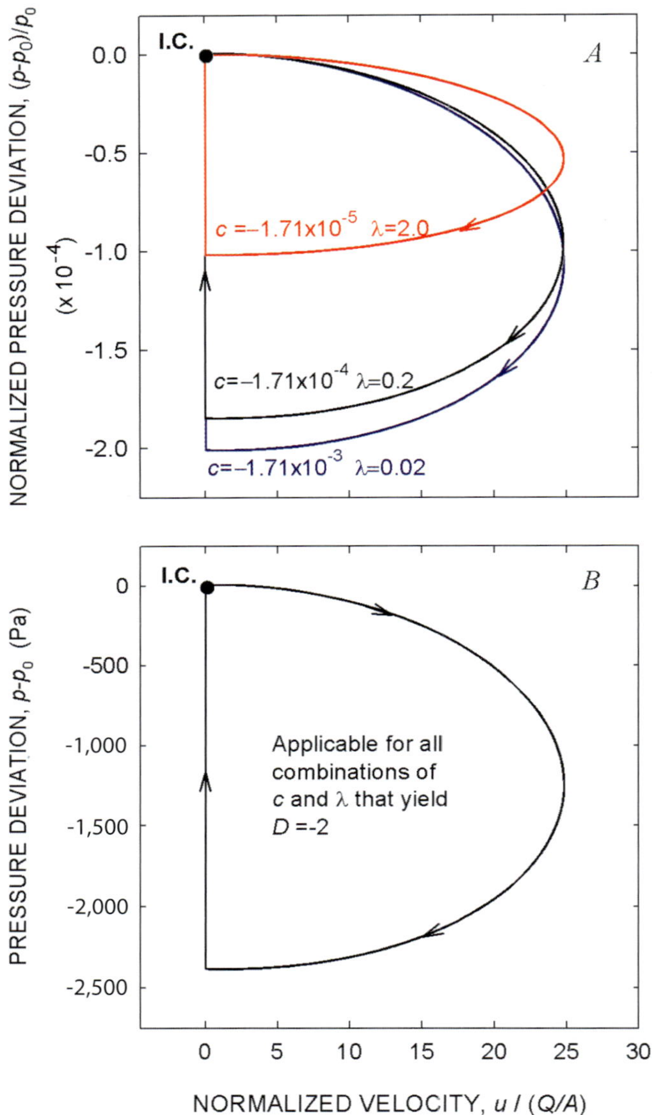

Figure 15. Sensitivity of stick-slip behavior with $D = -2$ to variations in parameters c and λ in the nonlinear rate-weakening friction rule. Other parameter values are same as those used to generate figure 14. Only phase-plane representations are shown, because time series are identical in all cases. Arrows point in direction of advancing time. *A*, Stick-slip cycles represented in terms of normalized pressure deviations. *B*, The same stick-slip cycles represented in terms of physical pressure deviations.

The linear analytical model yields spurious predictions of the effects of positive K values because it neglects explicit coupling between magma-pressure change and conduit-volume change, which is included in the nonlinear computational model. Figure 17 shows that magma pressure rises slightly in each successive stick-slip cycle, because increased pressure is required to drive uplift of the increasingly massive plug. This increasing pressure is accompanied by slightly decreasing conduit volume (fig. 17), because volume change due to compression of the highly compliant magma exceeds volume change due to conduit-wall deflection. Moreover, the percent decrease in conduit volume at the end of each stick-slip cycle is precisely the same as the percent increase in plug mass during the same cycle. Therefore, the effects of changes in conduit volume counterbalance the effects of changes in plug mass, such that the net effect of these changes on the oscillation period is zero. (As shown by equation 25, the time scale for the natural oscillation period, t_0, depends on the product of plug mass and conduit volume.) Numerical results show that the counterbalancing effect of mass changes and volume changes occurs for all positive K values—within reason. As suggested by analytical results, however, very large K or κ values (satisfying the criterion $\kappa > -(2/3)C$) might stabilize extrusion and diminish oscillations. Such large κ values are physically unreasonable, because C scales with the large quantity $m_0 g / u_{ref}$ (equation 23B), and mass accretion at a commensurately large rate is not plausible.

The magma pressure build-up depicted in figure 17 is further illustrated by its phase-plane representation in figure 18. As shown in the phase plane, each stick-slip limit cycle is like the preceding cycle, except that each successive slip event begins at a successively larger magma pressure. In this example, use of the maximum plausible rate of mass increase (that is, $\kappa = \rho B = 4{,}000$ kg/s) causes magma pressure to double after about 115,000 stick-slip cycles, or about 113 days. To within 1 percent, this result agrees with the pressure doubling time calculated by applying the analytical formula derived for pseudosteady-state extrusion (that is, equation 21) for the case in which $\kappa = 4{,}000$ kg/s. The chief implication of these results is that if the plug mass increases significantly, magma pressure can increase significantly without increasing the extrusion rate. Conversely, changes in extrusion rate need not be linked to changes in magma pressure if the plug mass changes.

Computational results obtained with K<0 differ in important ways from results obtained with K>0. Figure 19 depicts results computed using a negative K value with the same magnitude as the positive K value used to generate figures 17 and 18 (that is, $K = -1.78 \times 10^{-7}$), and this value implies that the mass erosion rate, $\rho_r E$, is twice the rate of basal mass accretion, ρB. Comparison of figures 17 and 19 shows that the negative K value produces changes in magma pressure and conduit volume with signs opposite to those for K>0 and also produces more frequent slip events (seven as opposed to six in 500 s). Slip events occur more frequently in the presence of diminishing plug mass, because less magma

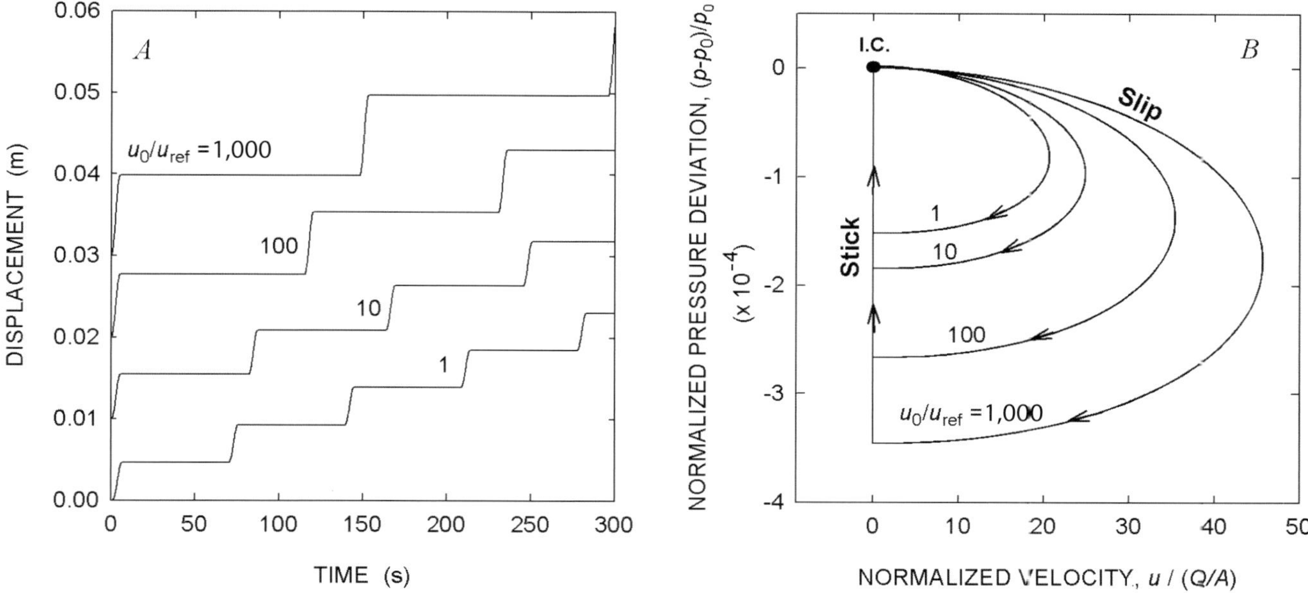

Figure 16. Sensitivity of stick-slip behavior with $D = -2$ to variations in u_0 / u_{ref} in the nonlinear rate-weakening friction rule. Other parameter values are the same as those used to generate figure 14. *A*, Time-series representation of stick-slip displacements. *B*, Phase-plane representation of velocity-pressure limit cycles corresponding to *A*. Arrows point in direction of advancing time.

pressure is necessary to trigger slip in each successive stick-slip cycle. Importantly, the increased frequency of slip events is accompanied by an increase in the mean extrusion rate (which occurs with a constant magma supply rate, Q=2 m^3/s), and this increase demonstrates the potential for runaway eruptive behavior. Moreover, decreasing plug mass eventually leads to a singularity in which fluid magma reaches the surface and the SPASM equations no longer apply (that is, the case with $C<0$ and $\kappa<0$ identified in table 3).

Runaway behavior is more evident in computational results obtained using negative K values with magnitudes much larger than the value -1.78×10^{-7} used to generate figure 19. Unlike large positive K values, large negative K values are physically plausible, because the plug mass can decrease rapidly if large-scale spalling or avalanching erodes the plug surface. Figure 20 depicts displacement time series computed with negative K values having magnitudes 100, 1,000, and 10,000 times greater than -1.78×10^{-7}. (The value -1.78×10^{-3} corresponds to mass loss at a rate of 4×10^7 kg/s or a volumetric rate of about 20,000 m^3/s—a rate high enough to remove the entire plug in less than one hour.) The key point illustrated by figure 20 is that, in the presence of significant mass loss, time-averaged displacement rates can be much larger than the steady equilibrium rate $u_0 = Q/A = 6.667\times10^{-5}$ m/s that prevails with K=0, and these high rates would likely lead to a change in eruptive style.

The unstable growth of extrusion rate that occurs with $K = -1.78\times10^{-3}$ is represented in the phase-plane diagram depicted in figure 21. The diagram shows that deviations from the equilibrium magma pressure and equilibrium slip rate are exceedingly large during each stick-slip cycle and that maximum slip rates increase during each successive slip cycle—while magma pressure successively declines. In such scenarios, then, extrusion occurs faster and faster until the plug is removed and liquid magma reaches the surface. The accompanying decline in magma pressure could also result in increased vesiculation and explosive potential, although this process is not represented by the SPASM model.

Effects of X

The dimensionless parameter X defined in equation 44 mediates the interaction between extrusion rate and conduit volume change, as shown by equations 42 and 43, and it also affects magma pressure change through its influence on R^* (that is, equation 45). The physical meaning of X can be clarified by writing its definition in a simplified, approximate form that is valid if $\alpha_1 >> \alpha_2$, which is almost certainly the case at Mount St. Helens:

$$X \approx u_0 \left(\frac{\alpha_1 m_0}{V_0} \right)^{1.2} . \quad (55)$$

This definition implies that, for systems in which u_0 and α_1 are constant, variations in X can be viewed as scaled variations in m_0 / V_0. Indeed, because values of m_0 / V_0 can be changed while holding t_0 and D constant, this strategy is used to assess the effects of variations in X computationally. The condition K=0 is also assumed in this assessment.

Computations in which X is increased or decreased by one order of magnitude from its baseline value (5×10^{-6}) show that stick-slip time series and phase-plane diagrams are identical for all values of X. However, figure 22 shows that some important details of the earthquake cycle change when X is increased by an order of magnitude (to 5×10^{-5}) by simultaneously increasing m_0 and decreasing V_0 by one order of magnitude each from their baseline values, while retaining D= −2. Comparison of figure 22 with figure 14 (the baseline case) shows that, although the timing and magnitude of slip events is unchanged when X is increased by one order of magnitude, the accompanying magma pressure, pressure change, shear force, and force drop are each increased by one order of magnitude, whereas the conduit volume change is reduced by somewhat less than an order of magnitude. These effects are all logical consequences of the increased plug mass and reduced conduit volume that are imposed by increasing the value of X.

The most important fact illustrated by figure 22 is that the predicted magma pressure at the base of the plug (~1.3×10^{8} Pa) is roughly an order of magnitude larger than the expected lithostatic pressure near the plug base (that is, at depths ~500 m). Such a large magma pressure is unrealistic, as it would probably cause hydraulic fracturing and a marked change in eruption style. This result implies that a value $X\approx5\times10^{-5}$ is too large to be realistic. Similarly, if X is reduced to 5×10^{-7} while holding t_0 and D constant, computed basal magma pressures are an order of magnitude smaller than the likely lithostatic pressure—a result that is also unrealistic. These findings imply that an X value similar to the baseline value (5×10^{-6}) is probably appropriate for Mount St. Helens. Therefore, the computed drop in shear force accompanying slip in the baseline case (fig. 14) is also probably appropriate.

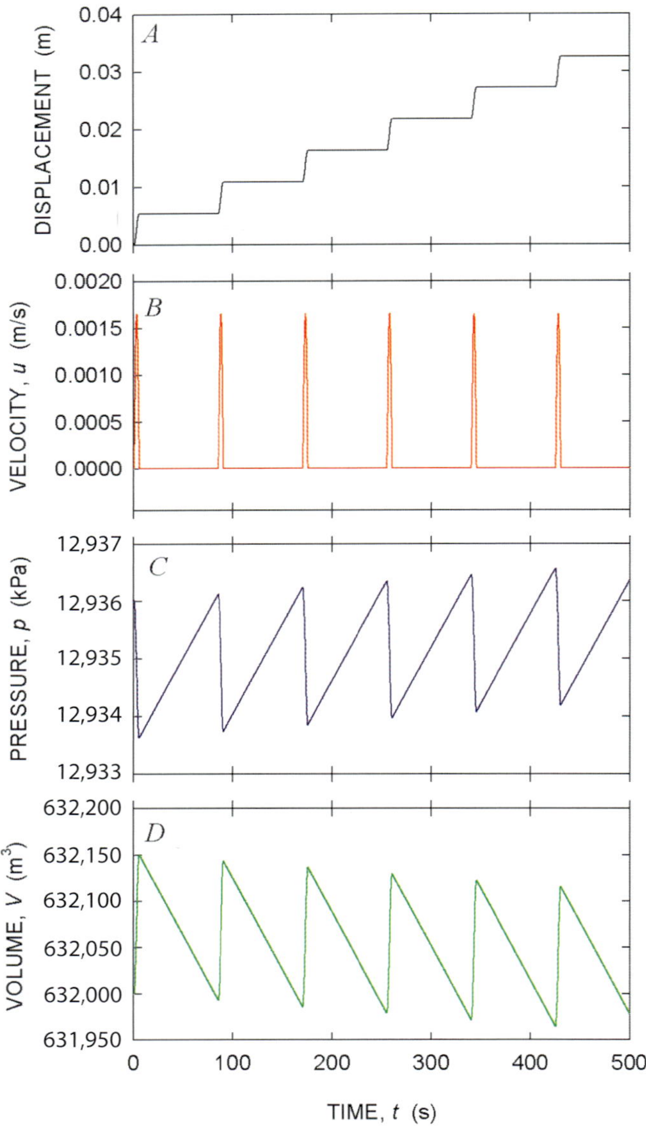

Figure 17. Time-series behavior of solutions computed with D= −2, u_0/u_{ref}=10, and increasing plug mass specified by K=1.78×10^{-7} (that is, κ =4,000 kg/s). Other parameter values are same as those used to generate figure 14.

Effects of Y

The dimensionless parameter Y defined in equation 44 represents the scaled difference between the magma-

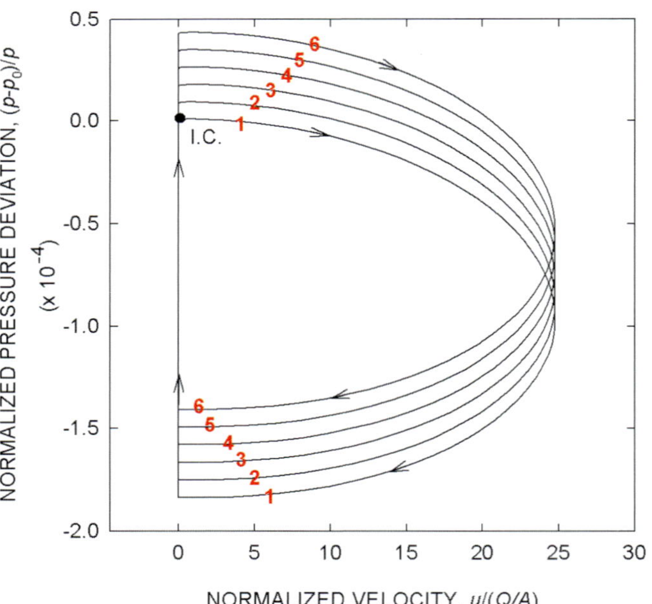

Figure 18. Phase-plane representation of solution depicted in figure 17. Numbers shown in red denote time sequence of successive limit cycles. Arrows point in direction of advancing time.

influx rate Q and magma-solidification rate B. All results presented thus far assume that $B=Q$, which is necessary for the magma-plug system to long remain close to equilibrium. Indeed, if $B \neq Q$ for a sustained period, a transition in eruptive behavior is inevitable. If $B>Q$, for example, the solidification front would propagate downward and the plug mass would increase unless mass loss due to surface erosion balances mass gain due to basal accretion. If such a balance were sustained, the plug would appear to sink progressively, even as extrusion continued, and friction on the plug margins would progressively increase. On the other hand, if $B<Q$, the solidification front would migrate

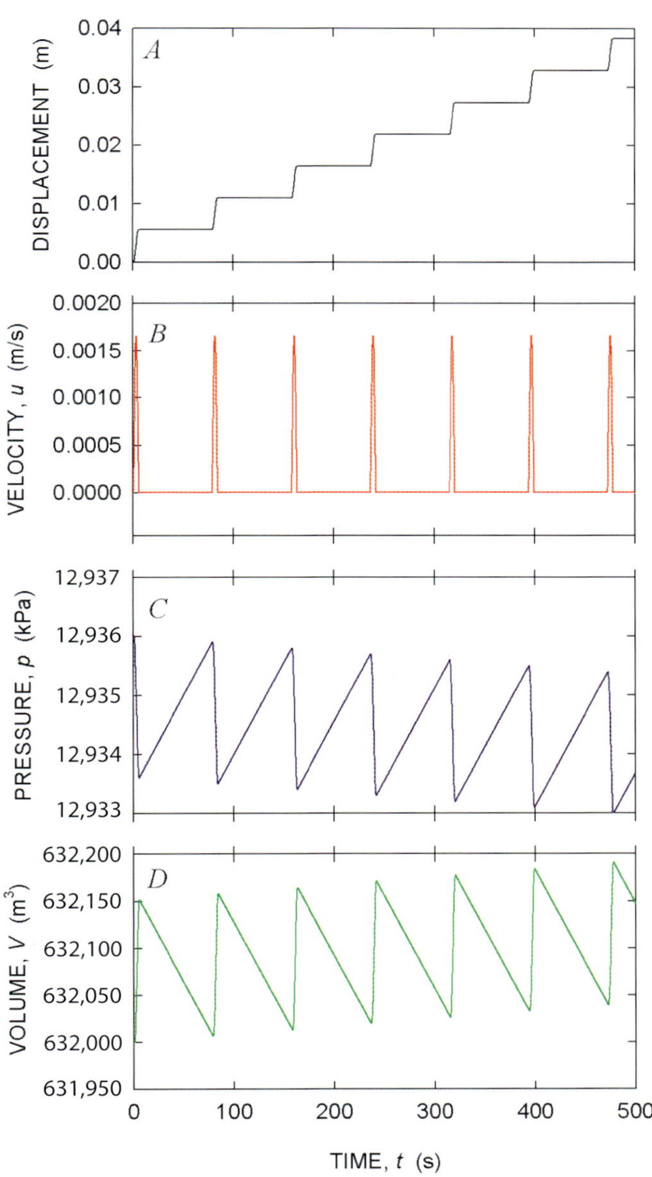

Figure 19. Time-series behavior of solutions computed with $D = -2$, $u_0/u_{ref} = 10$, and decreasing plug mass specified by $K = -1.78\times10^{-7}$ (that is, $\kappa = -4{,}000$ kg/s). Other parameter values are same as those used to generate figure 14.

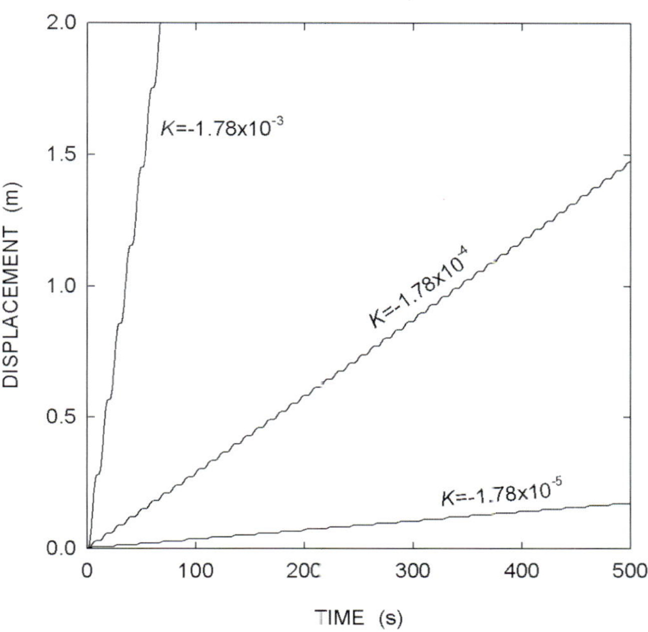

Figure 20. Comparison of displacement time series computed with $D = -2$, $u_0/u_{ref} = 10$, and differing rates of decreasing plug mass specified by differing values of K. Other parameter values are same as those used to generate figure 14.

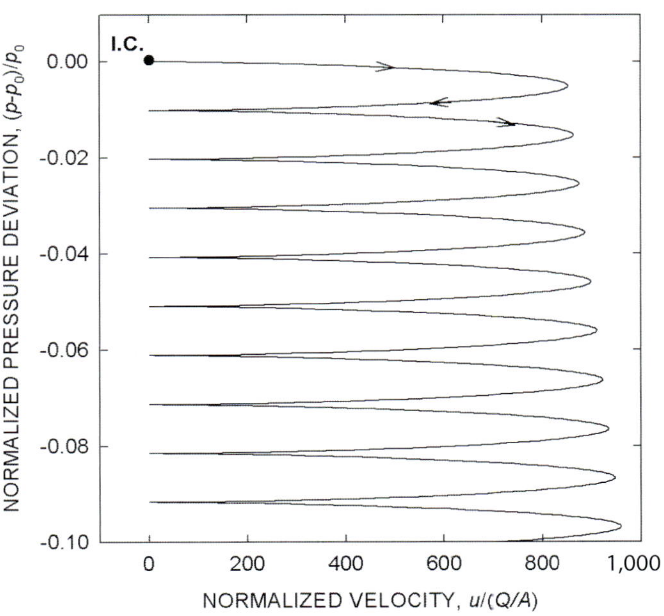

Figure 21. Phase-plane representation of stick-slip limit cycles occurring with $D = -2$, $u_0/u_{ref} = 10$, and rapid decrease in plug mass ($K = -1.78\times10^{-3}$; $\kappa = -4\times10$[illegible] kg/s). Other parameter values are same as those used to generate figure 14. Arrows point in direction of advancing time.

upward. In the extreme case of B=0, any changes in plug mass would result exclusively from surface erosion, and the plug would eventually be pushed out the ground as liquid magma reached the surface. This scenario represents singular behavior analogous to that occurring with a negative mass-change rate (K<0). Below, I focus only on short-time behavior for cases with $B>Q$ and B=0.

Behavior computed for a case with $B=2Q=4$ m^3/s and $K=1.78\times10^{-7}$ (that is, κ=4,000 kg/s) is shown in figure 23; this case is exactly like that illustrated in figure 17 except that, here, growth of plug mass occurs as a result of basal accretion in excess of Q. Thus, figure 23 depicts the response to growth of mass exclusively below the surface (with downward migration of the solidification front), whereas figure 17 depicts the response to growth exclusively above the surface (with no downward migration of the solidification front). The results shown in figures 23 and 17 are in most respects identical, except that the conduit volume decreases much more quickly in the case with basal accretion in excess of Q (fig. 23)—an obvious consequence of downward migration of the solidification front. Increasing pressurization of the conduit fluid accompanies this migration, and in the long run this combination of effects is unsustainable because magma pressure eventually would become large enough to fracture surrounding rock.

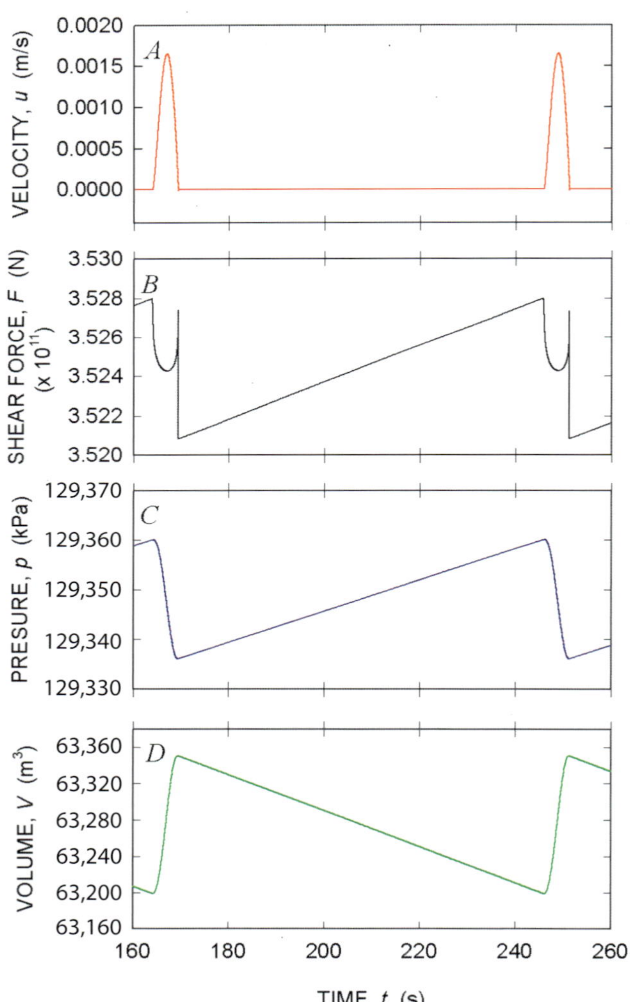

Figure 22. Details of an earthquake cycle computed with $D = -2$, $u_0/u_{ref}=10$, and $X = 5\times10^{-5}$ (one order of magnitude larger than the X value used to compute the baseline results shown in figure 14). Other parameter values are same as those used to generate figure 14.

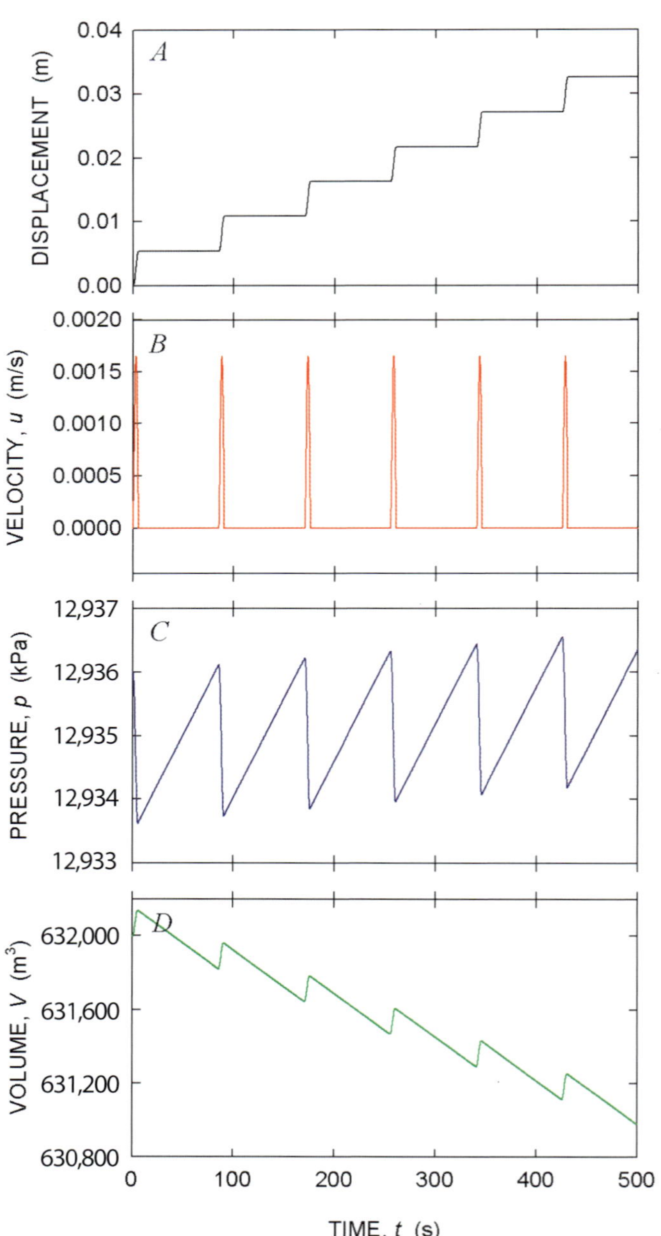

Figure 23. Time series behavior of solution computed with $D = -2$, $u_0/u_{ref}=10$, and excess basal accretion specified by $B = 2Q = 4$ m^3/s and $K = 1.78\times10^{-7}$ (that is, κ = 4,000 kg/s). Here $Y = -5\times10^{-6}$. Other parameter values are same as those used to generate figure 14.

The limiting case with small B (that is, B=0) exhibits behavior almost exactly like that computed for the baseline case with $B=Q$ and K=0. Indeed, with B=0, graphs of the behavior for early times are indistinguishable from those shown in figures 13 and 14, except that conduit volume increases with each successive stick-slip cycle (fig. 24). This increase is an obvious consequence of upward migration of the base of the plug, and although this migration affects plug dynamics negligibly in the short term, persistence of this migration eventually must lead to the singularity noted above (that is, magma reaching the surface).

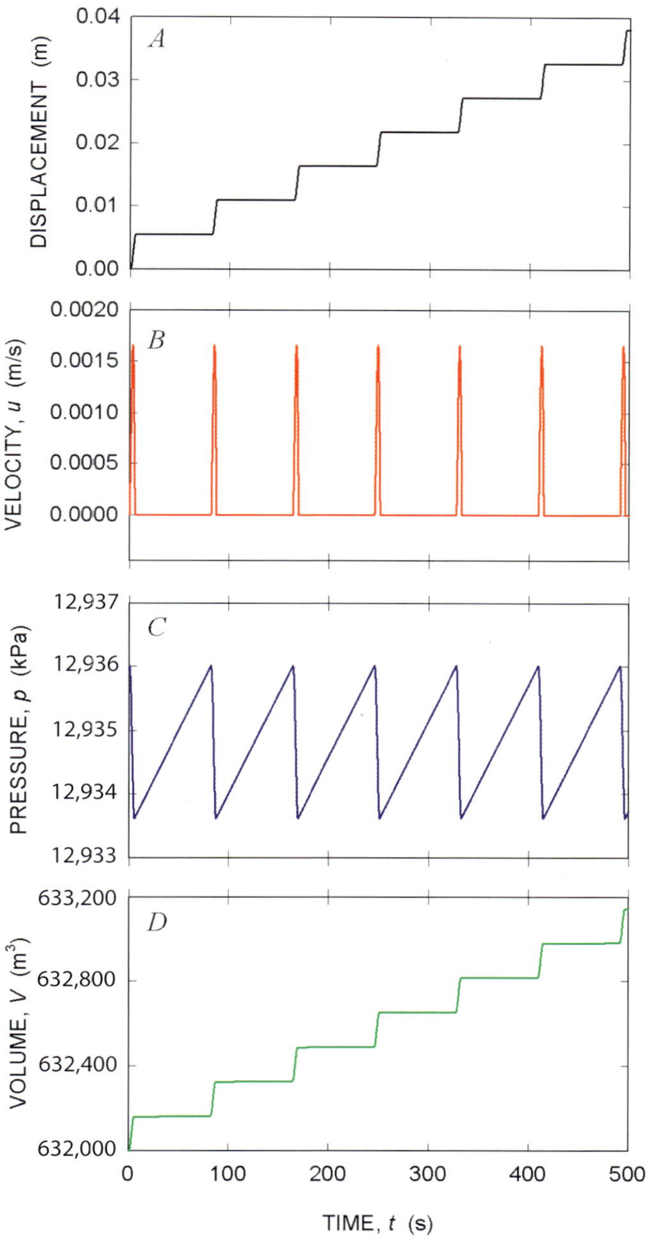

Figure 24. Time series behavior of solution computed with D = −2, u_0/u_{ref}=10, and zero basal accretion (B = 0). Here $Y = 5\times10^{-6}$. Other parameter values are same as those used to generate figure 14.

Effects of Z

The dimensionless parameter Z defined in equation 44 may be interpreted as a scaled version of the mass-density ratio difference, $R_0 = 1-(\rho_0/\rho_r)$, which plays its most important role in determining the mean (that is, time-averaged) extrusion rate, $u_0 = (Q - R_0 B)/A$ given by equation 19. The mean extrusion rate is affected by Z because R_0 determines the change in density that occurs as magma ascending at rate Q solidifies at rate B—such that an increase in density during solidification reduces the volumetric extrusion rate of the solid plug. Values of R_0 plausibly range from about −0.5 to 0.5, and for the case with $B=Q$, these values yield u_0 values ranging from 0.5(Q/A) to 1.5(Q/A). Moreover, with $B=Q$, the definition of Z also reduces to $Z = R_0/(1-R_0)$, so that Z depends exclusively on R_0. Examples of displacement time-series solutions computed for this case, with various values of Z, are shown in figure 25.

Interpretation of figure 25 is complicated by the fact that with A and B held constant, values of Z cannot be varied independently of values of D and X (because Z, X, and D all depend on u_0, which in turn depends on R_0). Therefore, the figure shows results of computations in which Z, X, and D vary simultaneously. Nevertheless, the effect of values of Z on the average extrusion rate is clearly evident in figure 25; large departures from the baseline value Z=0 yield similarly large departures from the average extrusion rate observed with Z=0 (that is, $u_0 = Q/A$). The period of stick-slip cycles remains nearly proportional to the magnitude of D (just as in the baseline case illustrated in fig. 13), despite variations in Z. Unlike

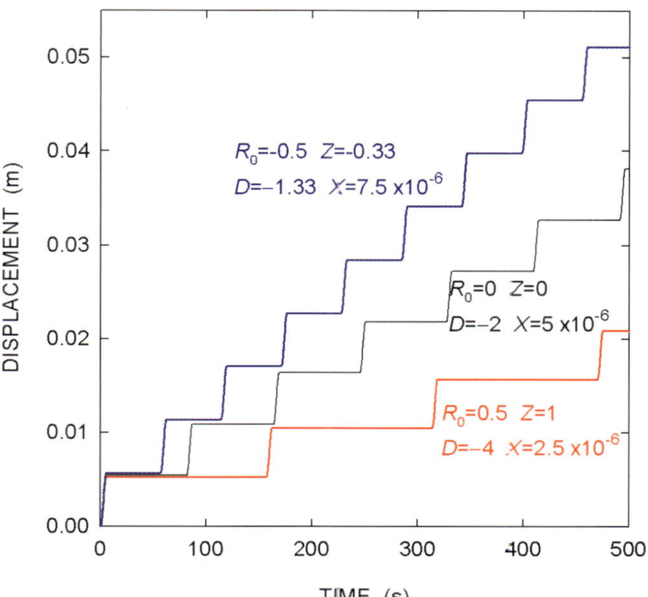

Figure 25. Displacement time series computed with varying values of R_0 and Z (with accompanying variation of D and X). Other parameter values are same as those used to generate figure 14.

the baseline case, however, the time series depicted in figure 25 each involve slip events with about the same magnitude of displacement (~5 mm). This behavior indicates that, while D largely controls the system's dynamics, the magnitude of slip events is additionally regulated by Z.

Effects of Initial Conditions

The preceding results were computed using initial conditions that assume a state of mechanical equilibrium, but volcanic eruptions presumably begin with an initial disequilibrium state, such as that due to magma pressure in excess of the static limiting equilibrium pressure ($p > p_0$). This section summarizes results of computations that used a disequilibrium initial condition of this type.

All computations with $p > p_0$ predict that an initial pulse of rapid motion occurs until plug momentum is depleted, magma pressure relaxes, and static equilibrium is restored, and this behavior occurs irrespective of the sign or value of D (figs. 26, 27). Pressure then rebuilds until it triggers a second stage of motion. For D<0 this stage consists of endlessly repetitive stick-slip limit cycles (closed loops in fig. 26) exactly like those produced with equilibrium initial conditions (for example, fig. 13), whereas for D>0 the second stage converges to a fixed-point equilibrium representing a state with dynamically balanced forces (fig. 27). It is noteworthy, however, that cases with rate-strengthening friction (D>0) and rate-weakening friction (D<0) exhibit similar initial pulses if the initial pressure disequilibrium is the same (for example, compare results for D=±0.2 in figs. 26*A* and 27).

A key point illustrated in figure 26 is that the maximum speed of the initial extrusion pulse and the magnitude of the associated pressure deviation increase almost linearly with increasing initial magma overpressure. Moreover, this trend is insensitive to the value of D, and linear extrapolation can therefore be used to infer the maximum extrusion speed (and pressure deviation) associated with any initial overpressure. With D= −2, for example, each increase of 0.005 percent in initial overpressure increases the maximum speed of the initial movement pulse u_{max} by about $u_{max}/(Q/A) = 14$ (fig. 26*B*).

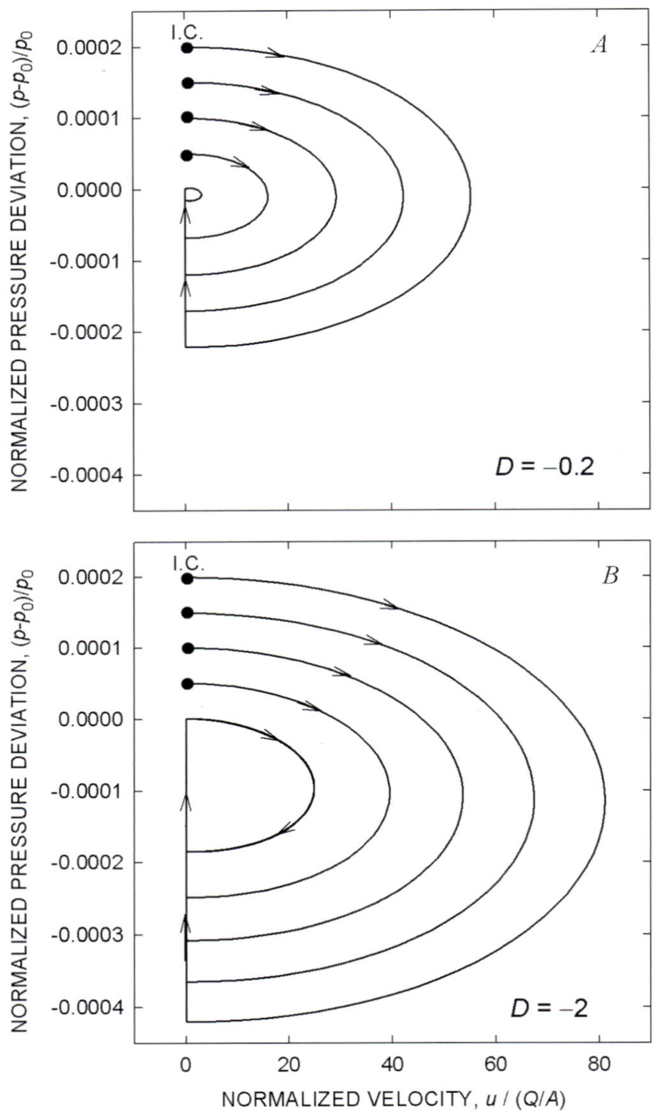

Figure 26. Phase-plane representation of behavior computed with four disequilibrium initial conditions (that is, initial excess magma pressures 0.005 percent, 0.01 percent, 0.015 percent, and 0.02 percent of p_0), for each of two negative values of D. Parameter values are same as those used to generate figure 14, except that $c = -1.71\times10^{-5}$ is used to obtain $D = -0.2$. Arrows point in direction of advancing time. *A*, $D = -0.2$. *B*, $D = -2$.

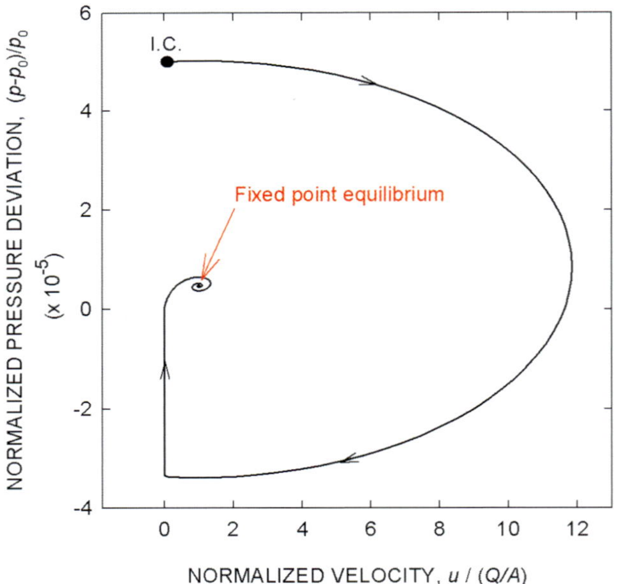

Figure 27. Phase-plane representation of extrusion behavior computed with an initial excess magma pressure (0.005 percent of p_0) and $D = 0.2$. Parameter values are same as those used to generate figure 14, except that $c = 1.71\times10^{-5}$ is used to obtain $D = 0.2$. Arrows point in direction of advancing time.

In conjunction with the baseline value $Q/A = 6.67\times10^{-5}$ m/s for Mount St. Helens, this result implies that a 0.005 percent magma overpressure (relative to the static limiting equilibrium pressure p_0) would produce a maximum extrusion velocity of about 3 mm/s, and that an overpressure of 5 percent would produce a maximum extrusion velocity of ~1 m/s.

Magnitudes of displacements that occur during the initial movement pulses shown in figures 26 and 27 can be estimated from the maximum pressure deviation $p_0 - p$, because the displacement during slip is proportional to the duration of the subsequent "stick time" (as shown by equation 54). By inference from equation 54, then, the displacement during the initial slip event increases like $e^{(\alpha_1+\alpha_2)(p_0-p_i)}$. On this basis, extrapolation from figure 26*B* shows that initial magma overpressures of even a few percent would lead to movement pulses of at least several meters, provided that $D=-2$.

Discussion

The SPASM model was developed to explain the relation between nearly steady solid-state extrusion and nearly periodic drumbeat earthquakes observed during the 2004–5 eruption of Mount St. Helens. Although this relation could result from a complicated interaction of numerous physical and chemical processes, the SPASM model aims for a parsimonious mechanical explanation that employs a minimum of postulates and variables. Some of the parsimony of the SPASM model derives from its central, simplifying assumption: that the volumetric flux of magma into the base of the eruption conduit (Q) is constant. This assumption is consistent with a top-down perspective of eruption dynamics, in which no time-dependent changes in a deep magmatic system are invoked to explain phenomena observed at Earth's surface.

From a mathematical standpoint, the assumption of constant Q enables the SPASM model to be reduced to a nonlinear system of three first-order ordinary differential equations. The relative simplicity of these equations facilitates both analytical and numerical studies of model properties. Indeed, the mathematical behavior of the SPASM model can be understood completely, and understanding of this simple model provides a steppingstone toward understanding behavior of Mount St. Helens during solid-state extrusion in 2004–5.

Analytical study of the SPASM model demonstrates that steady, solid-state extrusion is an equilibrium condition that can be satisfied exactly if the magma influx rate, Q, equals the rate of magma solidification at the base of an extruding plug, B, which in turn is balanced by erosion of the plug surface, E. In addition, pseudosteady states can exist in which the extrusion rate remains constant and changes in plug mass are accompanied by compensating changes in magma pressure. Such pseudosteady states cannot persist indefinitely, however, because changes in plug mass and magma pressure cannot continue without eventually causing a change in eruption style. Therefore, long-term steady-state extrusion at Mount St. Helens in 2004–5 probably involved a near-equilibrium state in which the plug mass effectively remained almost constant and $B \approx Q$ applied.

Analysis of the SPASM model shows that, even when a near-steady eruptive state persists, extrusion velocities have an inherent tendency to exhibit short-term oscillations about the long-term equilibrium rate. These oscillations are an inevitable consequence of the interaction of plug momentum, a variable upward force due to magma compression and pressure, and a downward force due to the plug weight. The oscillations are damped mostly by plug-boundary friction, and if friction exhibits rate-weakening behavior like that observed in experiments with fault gouge obtained from the surface of the Mount St. Helens plug, damping is negative and oscillation amplitudes grow unstably. Oscillation growth is necessarily arrested, however, because friction has the potential to reverse its direction of action when the plug extrusion velocity declines to zero. Growing oscillations are thereby transformed to repetitive stick-slip cycles, and these cycles continue indefinitely (that is, until a change in a parameter such as Q, B, or E occurs). According to the SPASM model, these repetitive stick-slip cycles are responsible for generating nearly periodic "drumbeat" earthquakes observed during solid-state extrusion at Mount St. Helens in 2004–5.

Properties of stick-slip cycles predicted by the SPASM model are controlled by a variety of factors, but both analytical and numerical results support the conclusion that the natural oscillation time scale t_0 and dimensionless damping D exert the most important controls. The oscillation time scale is fixed by conduit and plug properties that affect elastic strain in the system, whereas nonlinearly rate-dependent friction causes damping to vary as a function of the extrusion velocity u. Nevertheless, computational results show that most effects of variable damping are encapsulated by D evaluated at the steady equilibrium extrusion rate, $u=u_0$. These results show that the amplitudes and periods of stick-slip cycles increase almost in proportion to the magnitude of D, provided that t_0 remains constant.

Computations using diverse values of D show that $D=-2$ produces stick-slip cycles most similar to those inferred to generate drumbeat earthquakes at Mount St. Helens throughout much of the 2004–5 eruption, and the dynamics of these cycles are relatively insensitive to variations in values of the physical parameters that constitute D. With $D=-2$, computed interevent periods are about 80 s, the slip distance per event is about 5 mm, maximum slip speeds are about 2 mm/s, and reduction of magma pressure during slip is about 2.4 kPa. This reduction in magma pressure is strikingly small in comparison to the ambient, roughly lithostatic magma pressure (~1.3×10^4 kPa) inferred to exist at the base of the plug, about 500 m beneath the ground surface. The small size of magma-pressure fluctuations indicates that the system deviates little from mechanical equilibrium, even during slip events. Moreover, changes in basal magma pressure during slip events can be multiplied by the inferred basal area of the plug (~30,000 m^2) to provide a proxy for the force drop available to generate seismicity.

A more refined assessment of the force drop during slip events is provided by SPASM output that shows how the shear force due to plug-boundary friction (*F*) evolves during slip. With $D=-2$, the computed force drop is about 7×10^7 N, and much of the force drop occurs abruptly, despite the fact that slip events have durations of ~5 s. This nearly instantaneous force drop occurs just as the slip velocity, *u*, decreases from a finite value to zero, and its abruptness results from the interplay of three phenomena: (1) owing to rate-weakening friction during slip, the upward-moving plug gains momentum that causes it to overshoot an equilibrium state in which forces are dynamically balanced; (2) as the upward-moving plug decelerates, a potential for downward motion exists, because basal magma pressure has relaxed to a value smaller than its static equilibrium value; and (3) incipient downward motion of the plug is arrested immediately, however, because friction along the plug margin reverses direction so as to oppose motion. Friction adjusts just enough to stop motion and balance forces, of course, because friction can only oppose motion, not drive it. The abrupt adjustment of the friction force as plug motion ceases produces a sudden force drop that can radiate high-frequency seismic energy.

The mechanics that produce the stick-slip behavior and force drops predicted by the SPASM model are robust because they derive from basic physical principles, but the weakest link in the SPASM formulation involves the nature of friction and its rate dependence. Frictional properties of granulated solids such as fault gouge are poorly understood at a fundamental level, although some degree and type of rate weakening is generally observed in a variety of both idealized and geological granular media (for example, Nasuno and others, 1997; Marone, 1998). Rate-weakening behavior has also been measured in tests of fault gouge collected from the surface of the extruding plug at Mount St. Helens (Moore and others, this volume, chap. 20). In the context of the SPASM model, the most crucial point revealed by these tests is that some degree of rate-weakening occurs as slip velocities increase from zero to a steady equilibrium value u_0. This weakening suffices to generate stick-slip behavior, regardless of subtler nuances of friction. If rate-strengthening friction develops at higher slip rates, for example, it will help arrest slip events but not prevent them. Therefore, the occurrence of stick-slip cycles appears almost inevitable.

Occurrence of stick-slip cycles large enough and abrupt enough to generate drumbeat earthquakes is also contingent on elastic properties of the magma-plug-conduit system. At least one elastic element in the system must be soft enough to strain significantly in response to driving forces that are smaller than those required to shear the fault gouge irreversibly (compare Rice and Ruina, 1983). (The shallow depths of drumbeat earthquakes implies that these driving forces are probably smaller than those causing fault slip at hypocentral depths typical of nonvolcanic earthquakes (that is, >1 km), because confining stress and frictional resistance are relatively small at depths <1 km.) At Mount St. Helens, fluid magma underlying the extruding plug provides an exceptionally soft elastic element, because its estimated 12 percent (by volume) exsolved gas content makes it orders of magnitude more compressible than solid rock. In essence, then, the magma serves as a spongy spring that compresses significantly as it delivers the force to shear the plug-bounding gouge. Strain energy stored during magma compression is released in abrupt slip events that would be smaller and more frequent if the magma were stiffer. Therefore, the earthquake cycle described by the SPASM model differs from a typical tectonic earthquake cycle in two important ways: (1) in SPASM, strain energy is stored principally in a compressed fluid, not in a solid deformed in shear; repeated, nondestructive compression of "soft" fluid enables seismogenic plug slip to occur repeatedly at shallow depths; and (2) in SPASM, after slip has ceased, the plug is reloaded by forces due to gravity and magma influx. This reloading occurs very rapidly in comparison to reloading by tectonic strain accumulation, enabling drumbeat earthquakes to occur much more frequently than tectonic earthquakes.

Gradual evolution of the magnitude and periodicity of drumbeat earthquakes observed during the 2004–5 eruption of Mount St. Helens prompts questions about the cause. Can evolution of drumbeats be a harbinger of changes in eruption rate or style? The SPASM model provides insight to this issue, but it provides no unequivocal answers. According to the model, amplitudes and periods of slip events can change in response to changes in values of any of the parameters that constitute *D*, even when magma ascent and solidification rates are constant. Because *D* encompasses the effects of gouge frictional properties and the effective stress state, as well as the natural oscillation time scale t_0, evolution of any of a number of phenomena could be responsible for changing the character of drumbeats. Nonetheless, because field data can to some degree constrain changes in quantities such as plug mass or conduit volume, it is tempting to ascribe changes in drumbeats to unobserved changes in gouge properties or the state of effective stress. Computational results from SPASM indicate that rather subtle changes in these phenomena can alter drumbeat properties significantly. Indeed, it is easy to imagine that the source of drumbeats could migrate around the periphery of the extruding plug as scattered patches of particularly strong gouge form, fail, and reform. A model more elaborate than SPASM would be required to analyze the details of such behavior.

The SPASM model does provide a clear picture of potential changes in eruption style that can occur if conditions far from equilibrium develop. One type of disequilibrium develops if the rate of magma accretion at the base of the extruding plug differs significantly from the rate of plug extrusion. If the accretion rate is less than the extrusion rate, liquid magma eventually will reach the ground surface. Magma pressure will simultaneously decline, and this decline could enhance magma vesiculation and explosive potential. On the other hand, if the plug accretion rate exceeds the extrusion rate, the solidification front will propagate downward and magma pressure will increase, assuming that deep magma influx remains constant.

Increasing pressure could eventually trigger an exceptionally large slip event or fracture surrounding rock, causing a transition in eruption style—or it could suffice to stop magma influx, thereby halting the eruption.

Effects of magma pressure exceeding the static limiting equilibrium pressure can be treated as disequilibrium initial conditions in the SPASM model. If excess pressure exists but is insufficient to fracture rock, a rapid pulse of plug motion occurs until static equilibrium is restored. If magma pressure exceeds the equilibrium pressure by even a few percent, SPASM predicts that this pulse can involve velocities of meters per second and displacements of many meters. Such a pulse could even eject the plug from the volcanic vent and instigate the type of transition in eruption style described above.

The fact that no rapid pulses of extrusion or transitions in eruption style occurred during the 2004–5 eruption of Mount St. Helens implies that the magma-plug system never deviated much from equilibrium, even during the eruption onset. This behavior is, of course, very different from that during the cataclysmic eruption of Mount St. Helens on May 18, 1980. In that case explosive activity was caused by rapid depressurization of a shallow magma body triggered by a massive landslide. Without the landslide trigger, the 1980 eruptions of Mount St. Helens might have been relatively quiescent, much like the eruption of 2004–5.

Conclusion

The central conclusion of this study is that stick-slip oscillations are almost inevitable during an eruption in which steady ascent of compressible magma drives upward extrusion of a solidified plug with margins that exhibit rate-weakening friction. Whether such oscillations are large and abrupt enough to generate repetitive earthquakes like those observed at Mount St. Helens depends on a host of factors, nearly all of which are encompassed within two quantities derived in this paper: the natural oscillation time scale $t_0 = [m_0(\alpha_1 + \alpha_2)V_0]^{1/2} / A$ and the frictional damping index, which can be approximated as $D \approx (1/2)(c\lambda\mu_0 g t_0 / u_0)$. Large values of t_0 favor the occurrence of relatively large, infrequent slip events, because they imply that large elastic strains can be accommodated during magma compression. Large negative values of D have similar effects because they imply that effects of rate-weakening plug friction are significant, and rate weakening is responsible for "dynamic overshoot" during slip events. As a consequence, negative D values far from 0 cause the period between successive slip effects to exceed the period expected on the basis of t_0 alone.

Computations using $D = -2$ predict the occurrence of stick-slip cycles with interevent periods of ~80 s, slip displacements of ~5 mm, and force drops of ~7×10^7 N, and these properties appear consistent with those of events inferred to produce drumbeat earthquakes during the 2004–5 eruption of Mount St. Helens. Although individual modeled slip events last about 5 s, most of the accompanying force drop occurs in a fraction of a second, consistent with requirements for radiation of high-frequency seismic energy.

Persistence of nearly periodic drumbeat earthquakes also requires that slip events are driven by nearly steady forcing. At Mount St. Helens this forcing was provided by nearly steady ascent of magma. Magma solidification at the base of the extruding plug apparently occurred at a rate nearly equal to the rate of magma ascent, enabling the system to remain close to equilibrium. Indeed, model results show that a near-balance between ascent rate and solidification rate is essential for maintaining persistent drumbeats.

The presence of a near-surface body of compressible magma that serves as a driving element may be necessary to generate repetitive, seismogenic stick-slip events at the shallow focal depths (<1 km) observed during the 2004–5 eruption of Mount St. Helens. The strength of gouge at such shallow depths is relatively small (owing to relatively small normal stresses), and the gouge can therefore shear irreversibly before much elastic strain accumulates in a stiff adjacent body such as solid rock. Therefore, in the absence of a soft, near-surface magma body, stick-slip oscillations could still occur, but they would be reduced in size and period, perhaps to a degree that would make them aseismic. Moreover, near-surface fluid magma can undergo repeated elastic compression and decompression without accumulation of irreversible damage that would likely accompany similarly repetitive strain in solid rock.

Lack of large movement pulses during the 2004–5 eruption of Mount St. Helens reinforces the view that the magma-plug system remained close to equilibrium. Indeed, model results indicate that magma pressure exceeding the static equilibrium pressure by even a few percent was probably never present. An implication of this finding is that the dynamic equilibrium state exhibited during the eruption differs little from the static equilibrium state before the eruption onset. Therefore, the eruption trigger was likely very subtle, perhaps involving nothing more than weakening of the conduit cap rock by percolating water derived from late summer rains and glacier melt.

Acknowledgments

Virtually every member of the staffs of the Cascades Volcano Observatory and Pacific Northwest Seismic Network helped make this work possible through their contributions to monitoring the 2004–5 eruption of Mount St. Helens. I am indebted to all of them for their extraordinary efforts, and particularly to Seth Moran for fielding my many questions about volcano seismology. I am also indebted to Nico Gray of the Department of Mathematics, University of Manchester, U.K., who showed me how to obtain the analytical results summarized in equations 33–37 and appendix 1, and to Peter Moore and Neal Iverson, Department of Geological and Atmospheric Sciences, Iowa State University, who performed laboratory tests of the frictional properties of the Mount St. Helens gouge. Roger Denlinger and Joseph Walder provided insightful reviews that helped improve the manuscript.

References Cited

Abramowitz, M.K., and Stegun, I.A., eds., 1964, Handbook of mathematical functions with formulas, graphs, and mathematical tables: Washington, D.C., U.S. Government Printing Office, U.S. National Bureau of Standards Applied Mathematic Series 55, 1046 p.

Beeler, N.M., Tullis, T.E., and Weeks, J.D., 1994, The roles of time and displacement in the evolution effect in rock friction: Geophysical Research Letters, v. 21, no. 18, p. 1987–1990.

Blundy, J., and Cashman, K., 2001, Ascent-driven crystallisation of dacite magmas at Mount St. Helens, 1980–1986: Contributions to Mineralogy and Petrology, v.140, no. 6, p. 631–650, doi:10.1007/s004100000219.

Denlinger, R.P., and Hoblitt, R.P., 1999, Cyclic eruptive behavior of silicic volcanoes: Geology, v. 27, p. 459–462.

Dieterich. J.H., 1979, Modeling of rock friction 1; experimental results and constitutive equations: Journal of Geophysical Research, v. 84, no. B5, p. 2161–2168.

Dzurisin, D., Vallance, J.W., Gerlach, T.M., Moran, S.C., and Malone, S.D., 2005, Mount St. Helens reawakens: Eos (American Geophysical Union Transactions), v. 86, p. 25, 29.

Dzurisin, D., Lisowski, M., Poland, M.P., Sherrod, D.R., and LaHusen, R.G., 2008, Constraints and conundrums resulting from ground-deformation measurements made during the 2004–2005 dome-building eruption of Mount St. Helens, Washington, chap. 14 *of* Sherrod, D.R., Scott, W.E., and Stauffer, P.H., eds., A volcano rekindled; the renewed eruption of Mount St. Helens, 2004–2006: U.S. Geological Survey Professional Paper 1750 (this volume).

Gerlach, T.M., McGee, K.A., and Doukas, M.P., 2008, Emission rates of CO_2, SO_2, and H_2S, scrubbing, and preeruption excess volatiles at Mount St. Helens, 2004–2005, chap. 26 *of* Sherrod, D.R., Scott, W.E., and Stauffer, P.H., eds., A volcano rekindled; the renewed eruption of Mount St. Helens, 2004–2006: U.S. Geological Survey Professional Paper 1750 (this volume).

Goto, A., 1999, A new model for volcanic earthquake at Unzen volcano; melt rupture model: Geophysical Research Letters, v. 26, no. 16, 2541–2544.

Hatheway, A.W., and Kiersch, G.A., 1989, Engineering properties of rock, *in* Carmichael, R.S., ed., Practical handbook of the physical properties of rocks and minerals: Boca Raton, Florida, CRC Press, p. 673–715.

Kreyszig, E., 1979, Advanced engineering mathematics (4th ed.): New York, John Wiley, 939 p.

Lahr, J.C., Chouet, B.A., Stephens, C.D., Power, J.A., and Page, R.A., 1994, Earthquake classification, location, and error analysis in a volcanic environment; implications for the magmatic system of the 1989–1990 eruptions at Redoubt Volcano, Alaska: Journal of Volcanology and Geothermal Research, v. 62, nos. 1–4, p. 137–151, doi:10.1016/0377-0273(94)90031-0.

LaHusen, R.G., Swinford, K.J., Logan, M., and Lisowski, M., 2008, Instrumentation in remote and dangerous settings; examples using data from GPS “spider” deployments during the 2004–2005 eruption of Mount St. Helens, Washington, chap. 16 *of* Sherrod, D.R., Scott, W.E., and Stauffer, P.H., eds., A volcano rekindled; the renewed eruption of Mount St. Helens, 2004–2006: U.S. Geological Survey Professional Paper 1750 (this volume).

Lisowski, M., Dzurisin, D., Denlinger, R.P., and Iwatsubo, E.Y., 2008, Analysis of GPS-measured deformation associated with the 2004–2006 dome-building eruption of Mount St. Helens, Washington, chap. 15 *of* Sherrod, D.R., Scott, W.E., and Stauffer, P.H., eds., A volcano rekindled; the renewed eruption of Mount St. Helens, 2004–2006: U.S. Geological Survey Professional Paper 1750 (this volume).

Losert, W., Géminard, J.C., Nauson, S., and Gollub, J.P., 2000, Mechanisms for slow strengthening of granular materials: Physical Review E, v. 61, p. 4060–4068.

Major, J.J., Kingsbury, C.G., Poland, M.P., and LaHusen, R.G., 2008, Extrusion rate of the Mount St. Helens lava dome estimated from terrestrial imagery, November 2004–December 2005, chap. 12 *of* Sherrod, D.R., Scott, W.E., and Stauffer, P.H., eds., A volcano rekindled; the renewed eruption of Mount St. Helens, 2004–2006: U.S. Geological Survey Professional Paper 1750 (this volume).

Marone, C., 1998, Laboratory-derived friction laws and their application to seismic faulting: Annual Review of Earth and Planetary Sciences, v. 26, p. 643–696.

Marone, C., and Richardson, E., 2006, Do earthquakes rupture piece by piece or all together?: Science, v. 313, p.1748-1749.

Mastin, L.G., 1994, Explosive tephra emissions at Mount St. Helens, 1989–1991; the violent escape of magmatic gas following storms?: Geological Society of America Bulletin, v. 106, no. 2, p. 175–185.

Mastin, L.G., and Ghiorso, M.S., 2000, A numerical program for steady-state flow of magma-gas mixtures through vertical eruptive conduits: U.S. Geological Survey Open-File Report 00-209, 56 p.

Mastin, L.G., Roeloffs, E., Beeler, N.M., and Quick, J.E., 2008, Constraints on the size, overpressure, and volatile content of the Mount St. Helens magma system from geodetic and dome-growth measurements during the 2004–2006+ eruption, chap. 22 *of* Sherrod, D.R., Scott, W.E., and Stauffer, P.H., eds., A volcano rekindled; the renewed eruption of Mount St. Helens, 2004–2006: U.S. Geological Survey Professional Paper 1750 (this volume).

McGarr, A., 1999, On relating apparent stress to the stress causing earthquake slip: Journal of Geophysical Research, v. 104, no. B2, p. 3003–3011.

Melnik, O., and Sparks, R.S.J., 2002, Dynamics of magma ascent and lava extrusion at Soufrière Hills Volcano, Montserrat, *in* Druitt, T.H., and Kokelaar, B.P., eds., The eruption of Soufrière Hills Volcano, Montserrat, from 1995 to 1999: Geological Society of London Memoir 21, p. 153–171.

Moore, P.L., Iverson, N.R., and Iverson, R.M., 2008, Frictional properties of the Mount St. Helens gouge, chap. 20 *of* Sherrod, D.R., Scott, W.E., and Stauffer, P.H., eds., A volcano rekindled; the renewed eruption of Mount St. Helens, 2004–2006: U.S. Geological Survey Professional Paper 1750 (this volume).

Moran, S.C., 1994, Seismicity at Mount St. Helens, 1987–1992; evidence for repressurization of an active magmatic system: Journal of Geophysical Research, v. 99, no. B3, p. 4341–4354, doi:10.1029/93JB02993.

Moran, S.C., Malone, S.D., Qamar, A.I., Thelen, W.A., Wright, A.K., and Caplan-Auerbach, J., 2008, Seismicity associated with renewed dome building at Mount St. Helens, 2004–2005, chap. 2 *of* Sherrod, D.R., Scott, W.E., and Stauffer, P.H., eds., A volcano rekindled; the renewed eruption of Mount St. Helens, 2004–2006: U.S. Geological Survey Professional Paper 1750 (this volume).

Mullineaux, D.R., and Crandell, D.R., 1981, The eruptive history of Mount St. Helens, *in* Lipman, P.W., and Mullineaux, D.R., eds., The 1980 eruptions of Mount St. Helens, Washington: U.S. Geological Survey Professional Paper 1250, p. 3–15.

Nasuno, S., Kudrolli, A., and Gollub, J.P., 1997, Friction in granular layers; hysteresis and precursors: Physical Review Letters, v. 79, p. 949–952.

Neuberg, J.W., 2000, Characteristics and causes of shallow seismicity in andesite volcanoes: Philosophical Transactions Royal Society of London A, v. 358, p. 1533–1546.

Neuberg, J.W., Tuffen, H., Collier, L., Green, D., Powell, T., and Dingwell, D., 2006, The trigger mechanism of low-frequency earthquakes at Montserrat: Journal of Volcanology and Geothermal Research, v. 153, nos. 1–2, p. 37–50, doi:10.1016/j.jvolgeores.2005.08.008.

Newman, S., and Lowenstern, J.B., 2002, VolatileCalc—a silicate melt-H2O-CO2 solution model written in Visual Basic for excel®: Computers and Geosciences, v. 28, no. 5, p. 597–604, doi:10.1016/S0098-3004(01)00081-4.

Ozerov, A., Ispolatov, I., and Lees, J., 2003, Modeling Strombolian eruptions of Karymsky volcano, Kamchatka, Russia: Journal of Volcanology and Geothermal Research, v. 122, p. 265–280.

Pallister, J.S., Reagan, M., and Cashman, K., 2005, A new eruptive cycle at Mount St. Helens?: Eos (American Geophysical Union Transactions), v. 86, p. 499.

Pallister, J.S., Thornber, C.R., Cashman, K.V., Clynne, M.A., Lowers, H.A., Mandeville, C.W., Brownfield, I.K., and Meeker, G.P., 2008, Petrology of the 2004–2006 Mount St. Helens lava dome—implications for magmatic plumbing and eruption triggering, chap. 30 *of* Sherrod, D.R., Scott, W.E., and Stauffer, P.H., eds., A volcano rekindled; the renewed eruption of Mount St. Helens, 2004–2006: U.S. Geological Survey Professional Paper 1750 (this volume).

Press, W.H., Flannery, B.P., Teukolsky, S.A., and Vettering, W.T., 1986, Numerical recipes the art of scientific computing: Cambridge, Cambridge University Press, 818 p.

Rice, J.R., and Ruina, A., 1983, Stability of steady frictional slipping: Journal of Applied Mechanics, v. 50, p. 343–349.

Ruina, A., 1983, Slip instability and state variable friction laws: Journal of Geophysical Research, v. 88, no. B12, p. 10359–10370.

Schilling, S.P., Carrara, P.E., Thompson, R.A., and Iwatsubo, E.Y., 2004, Posteruption glacier development within the crater of Mount St. Helens, Washington, USA: Quaternary Research, v. 61, no. 3, p. 325–329.

Schilling, S.P., Thompson, R.A., Messerich, J.A., and Iwatsubo, E.Y., 2008, Use of digital aerophotogrammetry to determine rates of lava dome growth, Mount St. Helens, Washington, 2004–2005, chap. 8 *of* Sherrod, D R., Scott, W.E., and Stauffer, P.H., eds., A volcano rekindled; the renewed eruption of Mount St. Helens, 2004–2006: U.S. Geological Survey Professional Paper 1750 (this volume).

Scholz, C.H., 2002, The mechanics of earthquakes and faulting (2d ed.): Cambridge, Cambridge University Press, 471 p.

Swanson, D.A., and Holcomb, R.T., 1990, Regularities in growth of the Mount St. Helens dacite dome, 1980–1986, *in* Fink, J.H., ed., Lava flows and domes, emplacement mechanisms and hazard implications: Berlin, Springer-Verlag, International Association of Volcanology and Chemistry of the Earth's Interior, Proceedings in Volcanology 2, p. 3–24.

Tuffen, H., and Dingwell, D., 2005, Fault textures in volcanic conduits; evidence for seismic trigger mechanisms during silicic eruptions: Bulletin of Volcanology, v. 67, p. 370–387.

Voight, B., and 24 others, 1999, Magma flow instability and cyclic activity at Soufriere Hills Volcano, Montserrat, British West Indies: Science, v. 238, p. 1138–1142.

Walder, J.S., LaHusen, R.G., Vallance, J.W., and Schilling, S.P., 2005, Crater glaciers on active volcanoes; hydrological anomalies: Eos (American Geophysical Union Transactions), v. 86, p. 521, 528.

Appendix 1. Solution of Equation 27 by Transformation to Bessell's Equation

Conversion of the homogenous part of equation 27 into Bessel's equation is accomplished by using a simultaneous change of independent and dependent variables, given by

$$t^* = \frac{1}{K}\left[\left(\frac{Kz}{2}\right)^2 - 1\right] \qquad u^* = w\left(\frac{z}{2}\right)^{\frac{K-2D}{K}}. \tag{A1}$$

Substitution of equation group A1 into equation 27 converts it into Bessel's differential equation

$$z^2\frac{d^2w}{dz^2} + z\frac{dw}{dz} + (z^2 - v^2)\,w = 0, \tag{A2}$$

where

$$v = \frac{K-2D}{K}. \tag{A3}$$

The general solution of Bessel's equation is

$$w = c_1 J_v(z) + c_2 Y_v(z), \tag{A4}$$

where c_1 and c_2 are arbitrary constants and J_v and Y_v are Bessel functions of the first and second kind, of order v (Abramowitz and Stegun, 1964). Equation 33 is obtained by transforming equation A4 back to the original variables t^* and u^* and adding a particular solution of the inhomogeneous version of equation 27, $u^* = -KG$.

A Volcano Rekindled: The Renewed Eruption of Mount St. Helens, 2004–2006
Edited by David R. Sherrod, William E. Scott, and Peter H. Stauffer
U.S. Geological Survey Professional Paper 1750, 2008

Chapter 22

Constraints on the Size, Overpressure, and Volatile Content of the Mount St. Helens Magma System from Geodetic and Dome-Growth Measurements During the 2004–2006+ Eruption

By Larry G. Mastin[1], Evelyn Roeloffs[1], Nick M. Beeler[1], and James E. Quick[2]

Abstract

During the ongoing eruption at Mount St. Helens, Washington, lava has extruded continuously at a rate that decreased from ~7–9 m^3/s in October 2004 to 1–2 m^3/s by December 2005. The volume loss in the magma reservoir estimated from the geodetic data, $1.6–2.7\times10^7$ m^3, is only a few tens of percent of the 7.5×10^7 m^3 volume that had erupted by the end of 2005.

In this paper we use geodetic models to constrain the size and depth of the magma reservoir. We also ask whether the relations between extruded volume and geodetic deflation volume are consistent with drainage of a reservoir of compressible magma within a linearly elastic host rock. Finally, we compare the time histories of extrusion and geodetic deflation with idealized models of such a reservoir. Critical parameters include erupted volume V_e, dome density ρ_e, reservoir volume V_C, initial reservoir overpressure p_0^{ex}, pressure drop during the eruption Δp, reservoir compressibility $\kappa_C \equiv (1/V_C)(dV_C / dp)$, magma density ρ_M, and magma compressibility $\kappa_M \equiv (1/\rho_M)(d\rho_M/dp)$. Seismic velocity and reservoir geometry suggest $\kappa_C \approx 2\times10^{-11}$ Pa^{-1}, but mechanical considerations suggest $\kappa_C = 7–15\times10^{-11}$ Pa^{-1}.

The geodetic data are best fit with an ellipsoidal source whose top is 5±1 km deep and whose base is ~10–20+ km deep. In the absence of recharge, the decrease in magma-reservoir volume dV_C is theoretically related to the erupted volume V_e by $V_e/dV_C = (\rho_M/\rho_e)(1+\kappa_M/\kappa_C)$. For $\kappa_C = \sim7–15\times10^{-11}$ Pa^{-1} and $\rho_M \approx \rho_e$, estimates of V_e and dV_C suggest that $\kappa_M = 1.4–3.0\times10^{-10}$ Pa^{-1}, corresponding to a magmatic gas content in the reservoir of $v_g = 0$ to 1.8 percent by volume.

If we assume that effusion rate is linearly related to reservoir pressure and that the recharge rate into the reservoir is constant, the effusion rate should decrease exponentially with time to a value that equals the recharge rate. Best-fit curves of this form suggest recharge rates of 1.2–1.3 m^3/s over the first 500 days of the eruption. The best-fit constants include the product $V_C p_0^{ex} (\kappa_C + \kappa_M)$, making it possible to constrain reservoir volume using values of κ_C and κ_M constrained from ratios of erupted volume to geodetic deflation volume. If, on the other hand, we assume a logarithmic pressure-effusion rate relation and a constant recharge rate, the dome volume-time curve should follow a modified logarithmic relation, with the total erupted volume at a given time proportional to $V_C \Delta p (\kappa_C + \kappa_M)$. Using $\kappa_C = 7–15\times10^{-11}$ Pa^{-1}, results from log and exponential curves suggest a reservoir volume of at least several cubic kilometers if Δp or p_0^{ex} is less than ~30 MPa. Similar results are obtained from numerical calculations that consider temporal changes in (1) magma compressibility, (2) the weight of the lava dome suppressing effusion, and (3) recharge rate. These results are consistent with the notion that the reservoir volume is at least a few times larger than the largest Holocene eruption of Mount St. Helens (4 km^3 dense-rock-equivalent + volume for the 3.4-ka Yn eruption).

Both the exponential and logarithmic models predict a history of reservoir decompression that imperfectly matches displacement data at GPS station JRO1. Neither model, for example, predicts the rapid radially inward movement at JRO1 during the first month of the eruption. Such movement, followed by long-term linear deflation, suggests that erupted magma has been replaced in increasing proportions by recharge, but that the recharge rate remains somewhat less than the current (early 2006) effusion rate.

[1] U.S. Geological Survey, 1300 SE Cardinal Court, Vancouver, WA 98683

[2] U.S. Geological Survey, Reston, VA 20192; now at Southern Methodist University, Office of Research and Graduate Studies, P.O. Box 750240, Dallas, Texas 75275

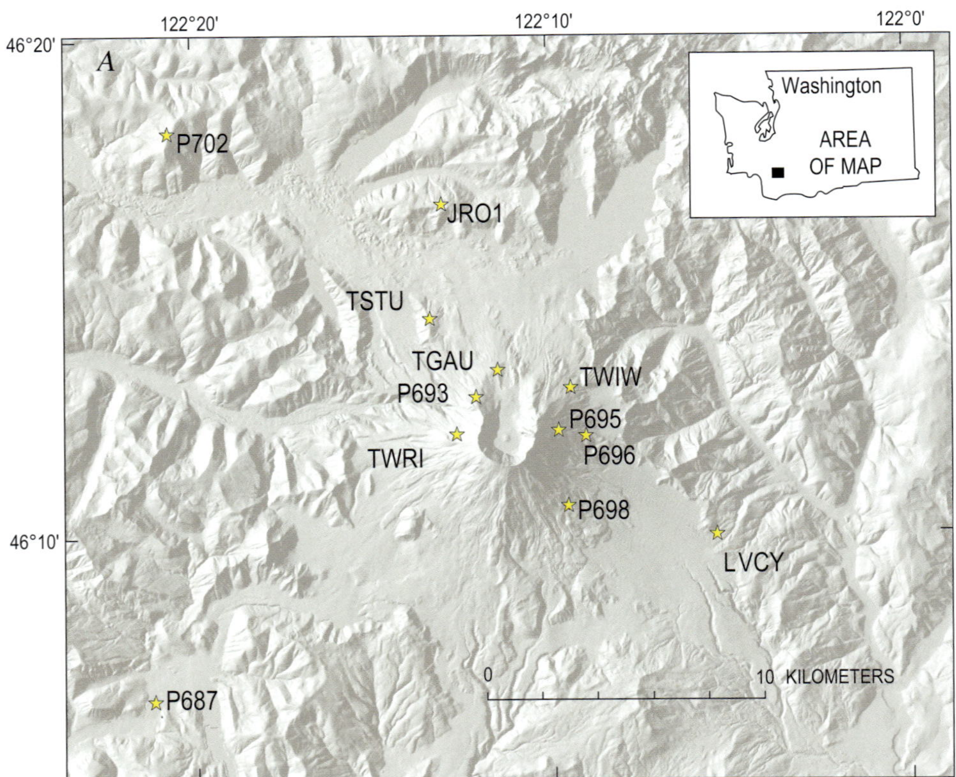

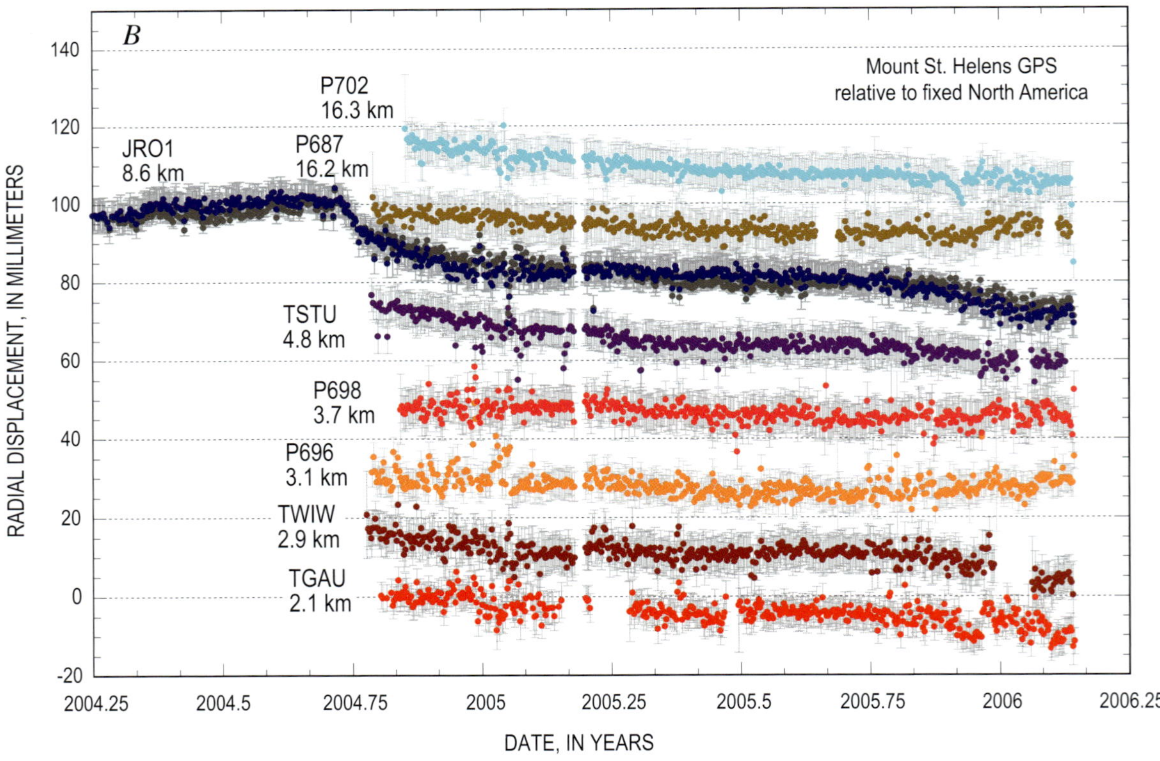

Figure 1. Geodetic stations and results. *A*, Map showing geodetic stations used to model the source of deflation at Mount St. Helens. *B*, Displacement radial to the Mount St. Helens crater versus time at geodetic stations. Outward radial displacements are positive. Error bars represent one standard deviation above and below the data point. Numbers beneath each station label indicate the map distance of each station from the crater center (46.2002° N, 122.1911° W).

Introduction

The current Mount St. Helens eruption extruded about 85 percent as much lava in 14 months (October 2004 to December 2005) as was extruded in 6 years to form the 1980–86 lava dome. At the time of writing (spring 2006), there is no obvious indication of waning growth; indeed, compared with other dome-building eruptions worldwide, the current eruption of Mount St. Helens only slightly exceeds the median duration (540 days) and volume (3.5×10^7 m^3) among historical dome-building eruptions (Newhall and Melson, 1983, and updates, C. Newhall, written commun., 2005). This eruption hardly approaches the duration (>50 years) of the dome building at Bezymianny Volcano, Kamchatka, whose growth followed a sector collapse and lateral blast in 1956 that resembled the 1980 Mount St. Helens sequence.

Dome-building eruptions, like eruptions of mafic lava flows, range in duration from days to decades and in volume from cubic meters to cubic kilometers. Eruption volume and duration are most strongly controlled by reservoir size, exsolved gas content, the amount of recharge into the magma system, and the composition and volatile content of recharging magma (Wadge, 1981; Newhall and Melson, 1983; Huppert and Woods, 2002; Woods and Huppert, 2003). In this study we use geodetic and growth-history data to constrain the volume, overpressure, history of recharge, and exsolved volatile content of the Mount St. Helens magma system.

Key Observations

Over several years prior to September 2004, campaign-style geodetic surveys and measurements at the only continuous global positioning system (CGPS) site at Mount St. Helens (JRO1, fig. 1*A*) showed no discernable inflation signal (Dzurisin and others, this volume, chap. 14; Lisowski and others, this volume, chap. 15). Deflation at JRO1 began with the onset of seismicity on September 23, 2004; uplift on the crater floor was first noticed on about September 26 (Dzurisin and others, this volume, chap. 14) and the first material at magmatic temperature on October 11. Eight new CGPS instruments installed between mid-October and early November 2004 (fig. 1*A*) have recorded more or less radially inward movement toward the crater (fig. 1), suggesting that the source of deflation (the magma reservoir) is roughly spherical or elliptical in shape rather than dike-shaped (Lisowski and others, this volume, chap. 15).

Throughout the eruption, lava has extruded as spines or lobes of more or less solid, nearly holocrystalline lava, their surfaces covered by unconsolidated fault gouge on the order of 1 m thick (fig. 2). The gouge thickness, considering relations between gouge thickness and displacement on tectonic faults (Robertson, 1983; Power and others, 1988), and petrologic information (Cashman and others, this volume, chap. 19) suggest that the faulting may extend from perhaps tens of meters to several hundred meters into the subsurface.

Figure 2. Photos of the growing lava dome of Mount St. Helens. *A*, View of spine 4 from the northwest on February 22, 2005. USGS photo by S.P. Schilling. *B*, Close-up of striated fault gouge covering the exterior of spine 3 as it emerged from the ground on November 11, 2004. Approximate location of that spine on February 22, 2005, shown by box *B* on panel *A*. USGS photo by J.S. Pallister. *C*, Close-up of fresh rockfall scar (~100 m long and 50 m high), revealing gouge thickness in cross section. Approximate location shown by box *C* on panel *A*. USGS photo taken February 22, 2005, by S.P. Schilling.

A series of digital elevation models (DEMs) based on 1:12,000-scale aerial photographs records the growth of the lava dome (Schilling and others, this volume, chap. 8). These DEMs show that in early October 2004 the rate of uplift of cold rock and glacial ice was on the order of 8–9 m^3/s, with nearly 1.1×10^7 m^3 uplifted by the time lava first became visible at the surface on October 11. Lava ("hot rock") extrusion rates were initially ~6–7 m^3/s in November 2004 but declined to less than 2 m^3/s in March 2005. Since March 2005 (about 150 days into the eruption) the extrusion rate has continued to decline gradually, such that the volume-time curve can be nearly fit with a straight line (fig. 3). Overall, the history of lava-dome volume versus time (fig. 3) has defined a remarkably regular monotonic, concave-downward curve that was noted in early 2005 and could be fit using simple exponential (fig. 3*C*) and logarithmic (fig. 3*A*) curves. In this study we endeavor to find the physical basis for these curve forms.

Geodetic Source Models

Using data from eight continuous GPS stations (fig. 1), we estimate the depth, location, and size of the source of deflation (the magma reservoir) by comparing inward displacements with those predicted for a vertical prolate ellipsoid embedded in a homogeneous, isotropic, linearly elastic half-space, using the equations of Bonaccorso and Davis (1999) (table 1). We evaluate the displacements during two time windows: (1) November 4, 2004, to February 5, 2005, and (2) February 5, 2005, to July 14, 2005. The start and end dates of these windows were chosen to coincide with DEM acquisition dates. We use only two time windows because data quality is insufficient to allow subdivision into shorter time windows. The second time window ends in summer 2005 because displacements since that time have been too small to be accurately modeled.

Measured displacements were adjusted for regional plate movement using the rates 3.461 mm/yr east, 5.91 mm/yr north, 1.46 mm/yr down; and for seasonal changes using sinusoidal adjustments having east, north, and z (vertical) amplitudes of 1.9149, 1.667, and 1.5289 mm and phase angles relative to January 1, 2004, of 51.86, 132.89, and 32.62 degrees, respectively (Lisowski and others, this volume, chap. 15). For the first time window, best-fit models place the top of the reservoir at 3–6 km below the mean altitude of the geodetic stations (which is ~1,300 m above sea level). In plan view the best-fit models lie 1.3–1.6 km east and 5–320 m south of the crater center (figs. 4, 5; table 1). Placing the top deeper than about 6 km tends to underestimate the radial displacement at stations proximal to the crater and overestimate both radial and vertical displacement components in the distal stations. The depth to the bottom of the reservoir is not well constrained but likely lies somewhere below 10 km (fig. 4*A*). Data from the second time period provide significantly poorer constraints (fig. 4*B*).

Geodetic Constraints on Reservoir Size and Pressure Drop

The amplitude of the geodetic signal scales with the product $R^2\Delta p/G$, where R is the horizontal radius of the ellipsoid, Δp is the pressure drop, and G is the host-rock shear modulus. Best-fit values of this product are listed in table 1. Using formulas for ellipsoid volume $V_C=(2/3)\pi R^2 h$ (where h is ellipsoid height) and elastic volume change of the ellipsoid $\Delta V_C=3V_C\Delta p/(4G)$ (McTigue, 1987; Tait and others, 1989; Tiampo and others, 2000), we find that $\Delta V_C=(\pi h/2)[R^2\Delta p/G]$. For the first time window, excluding sources at 4–7 km and 10–14 km depth that clearly do not fit the data, estimates of volume shrinkage of the magma body are $2.1–3.5\times10^6$ m^3. By comparison, the hot-rock volume (ΔV_e) erupted dur ing this time (Schilling and others, this volume, chap. 8; and fig. 3) was about 2.7×10^7 m^3—eight to twelve times the volume shrinkage of the reservoir. For the second time window, $\Delta V_C=$~$3–8\times10^6$ m^3 (poorly constrained), whereas the change in dome volume was $\Delta V_e=1.8\times10^7$ m^3. For the entire eruption through late 2005, Lisowski and others (this volume, chap. 15) and Poland and Lu (this volume, chap. 18)estimate ΔV_C ~$1.6–2.7\times10^7$ m^3 from geodetic and InSAR data, whereas hot-rock erupted volume by mid-December 2005 was about 7.3×10^7 m^3 (Schilling and others, this volume, chap. 8). Differences in density of the erupted versus unerupted magma (estimated later) are not great enough to account for these discrepancies.

The reservoir volume and pressure drop can be constrained if the shear modulus G can be estimated. On the basis of estimated seismic P-wave velocity $\upsilon_P=6.7\pm0.2$ km/s at 8–15 km depth (Musumeci and others, 2002, fig. 5), host-rock density $\rho_R=2{,}700\pm200$ kg/m^3 (Williams and others, 1987), an assumed Poisson's ratio ν of 0.25 ± 0.03, and the formula $G=\rho_R\upsilon_P^2(1-2\nu)/(2(1-\nu))$ (for example, Rubin, 1990), we obtain $G=40\pm4$ GPa. Using this value and $\Delta V_C=2.3\times10^7$ m^3 in the formula $\Delta V_C=3V_C\Delta p/(4G)$, we obtain $V_C\Delta p=1.2\times10^{18}$ $Pa{\cdot}m^3$. If we further assume that the pressure drop since the start of the eruption is less than a few tens of megapascals, the reservoir volume would have to exceed about 41 km^3—significantly larger than previously hypothesized at Mount St. Helens (>10 km^3 by Scandone and Malone, 1985; 5–7 km^3 by Barker and Malone, 1991). Several factors considered later and in appendix 1 suggest that a lower value of G, and hence smaller reservoir volume, is more appropriate.

An Idealized Magma Reservoir

We idealize the magma system (fig. 5) as an ellipsoidal magma body several kilometers deep within linearly elastic host rock, connected to the surface and to a source of recharge through relatively narrow conduits. The reservoir contains magma of density ρ_M and has a total mass $\rho_M V_C$. As long as the assumption of linear elastic host rock holds and the geometry of the reservoir does not change, the relation between

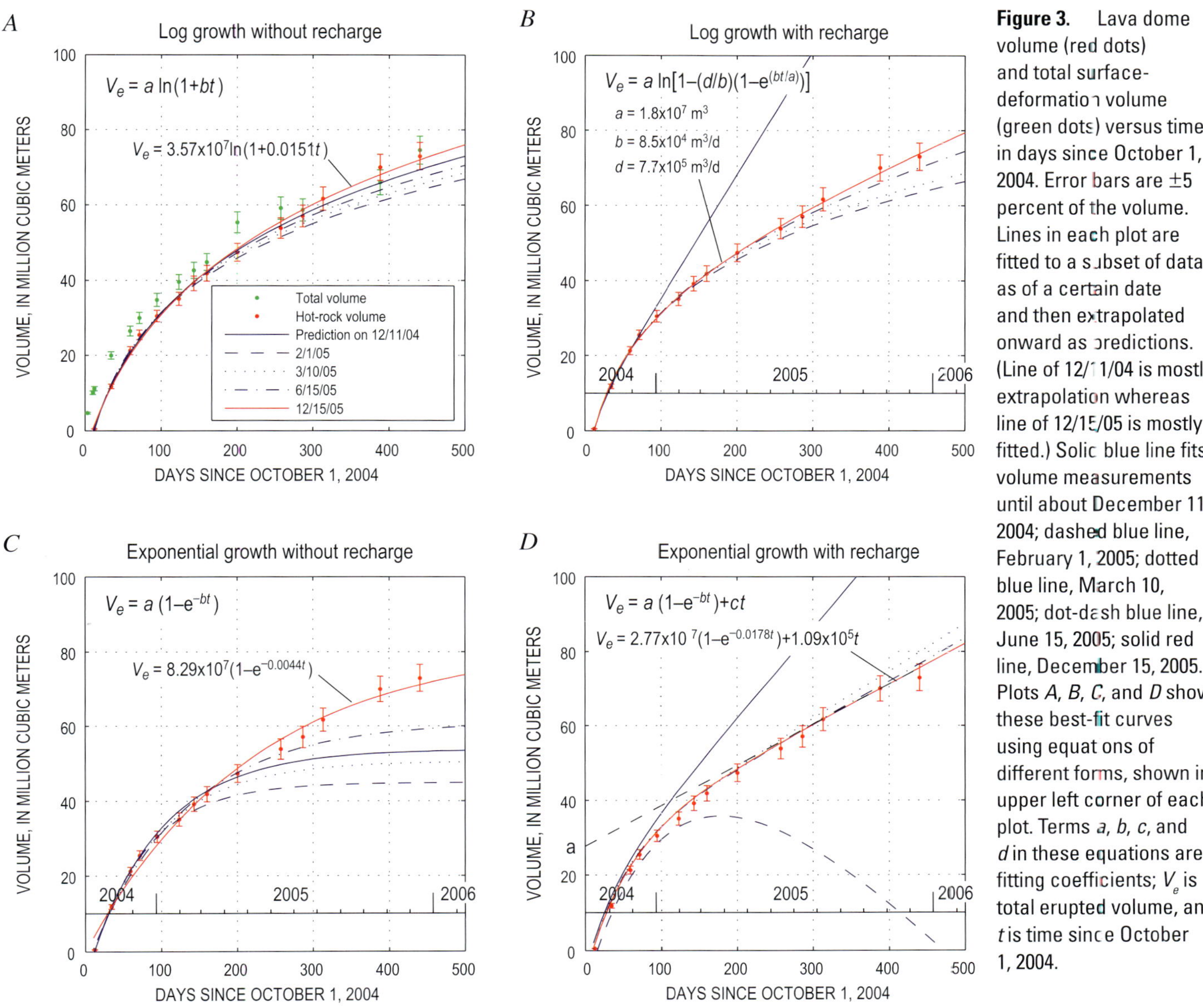

Figure 3. Lava dome volume (red dots) and total surface-deformation volume (green dots) versus time in days since October 1, 2004. Error bars are ±5 percent of the volume. Lines in each plot are fitted to a subset of data as of a certain date and then extrapolated onward as predictions. (Line of 12/11/04 is mostly extrapolation whereas line of 12/15/05 is mostly fitted.) Solid blue line fits volume measurements until about December 11, 2004; dashed blue line, February 1, 2005; dotted blue line, March 10, 2005; dot-dash blue line, June 15, 2005; solid red line, December 15, 2005. Plots *A*, *B*, *C*, and *D* show these best-fit curves using equations of different forms, shown in upper left corner of each plot. Terms *a*, *b*, *c*, and *d* in these equations are fitting coefficients; V_e is total erupted volume, and *t* is time since October 1, 2004.

Table 1. Parameters in geodetic source models plotted in figure 4.

[Parameters in plain type are specified by the user; those italicized are obtained by optimizing the fit between the model and the data.]

Model	Time period	Depth to top (m)	Depth to bottom (m)	Distance east of crater center (m)	Distance north of crater center (m)	Scale factor $\Delta pR^2/G$	$V_c\Delta p$ Pa•m^3 ×10^{17}	ΔV_c 10^6 m^3
1	11/4/04–2/5/05	*3,419*	20,000	*1,541*	*-68*	*-135*	-2.18	2.83
2	11/4/04–2/5/05	*3,654*	15,000	*1,511*	*-85*	*-155*	-1.72	3.69
3	11/4/04–2/5/05	*4,294*	10,000	*1,448*	*-100*	*-236*	-1.32	4.68
4	11/4/04–2/5/05	4,000	7,000	*1,492*	*-5*	*-286*	-0.84	1.80
5	11/4/04–2/5/05	6,000	10,000	*1,390*	*-321*	*-459*	-1.79	3.85
6	11/4/04–2/5/05	10,000	14,500	1,600	-500	*-885*	-3.89	8.34
7	2/5/05–7/14/05	3,500	15,500	1,400	-100	*-113*	-1.32	2.83
8	2/5/05–7/14/05	*7,191*	20,000	100	-3000	*-286*	-3.58	7.67

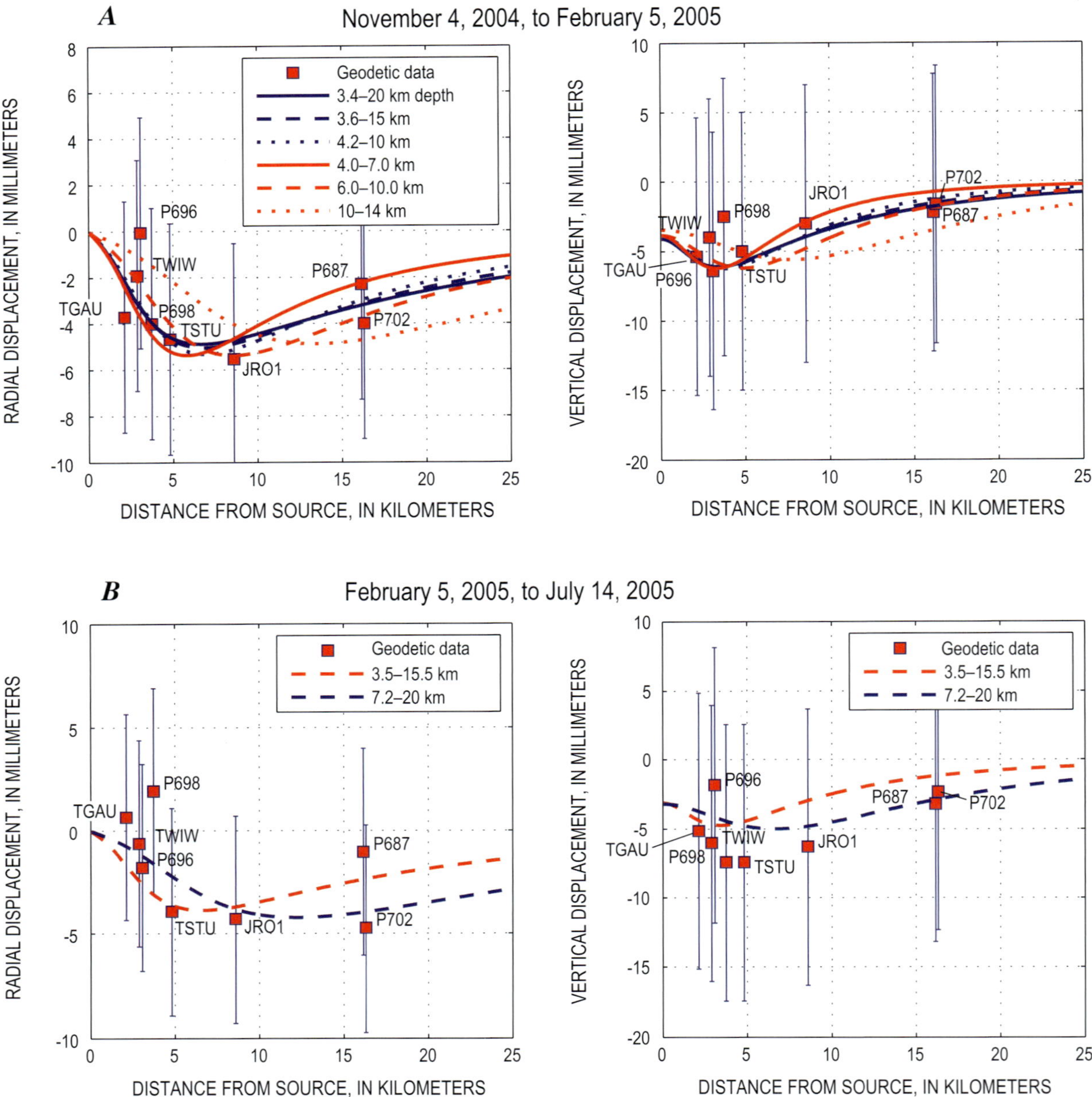

Figure 4 Measured and theoretical geodetic displacements for 252 days of eruption from November 4, 2004, to July 14, 2005. Data points, from continuous global positioning system (CGPS) receivers (fig 1*A*), show radial and vertical displacement; error bars are given as ±5 mm for radial displacement, ±10 mm for vertical displacement. Displacements are positive for outward radial and upward vertical directions. Lines represent theoretical displacements resulting from deflation of a vertical prolate ellipsoid in an elastic half-space. Depths in the explanation indicate, respectively, the depth to top and bottom of the ellipsoid below the mean altitude of the geodetic stations (1,300 m above sea level). *A*, Radial and vertical displacement between November 4, 2004, and February 5, 2005. *B*, Radial and vertical displacement between February 5 and July 14, 2005.

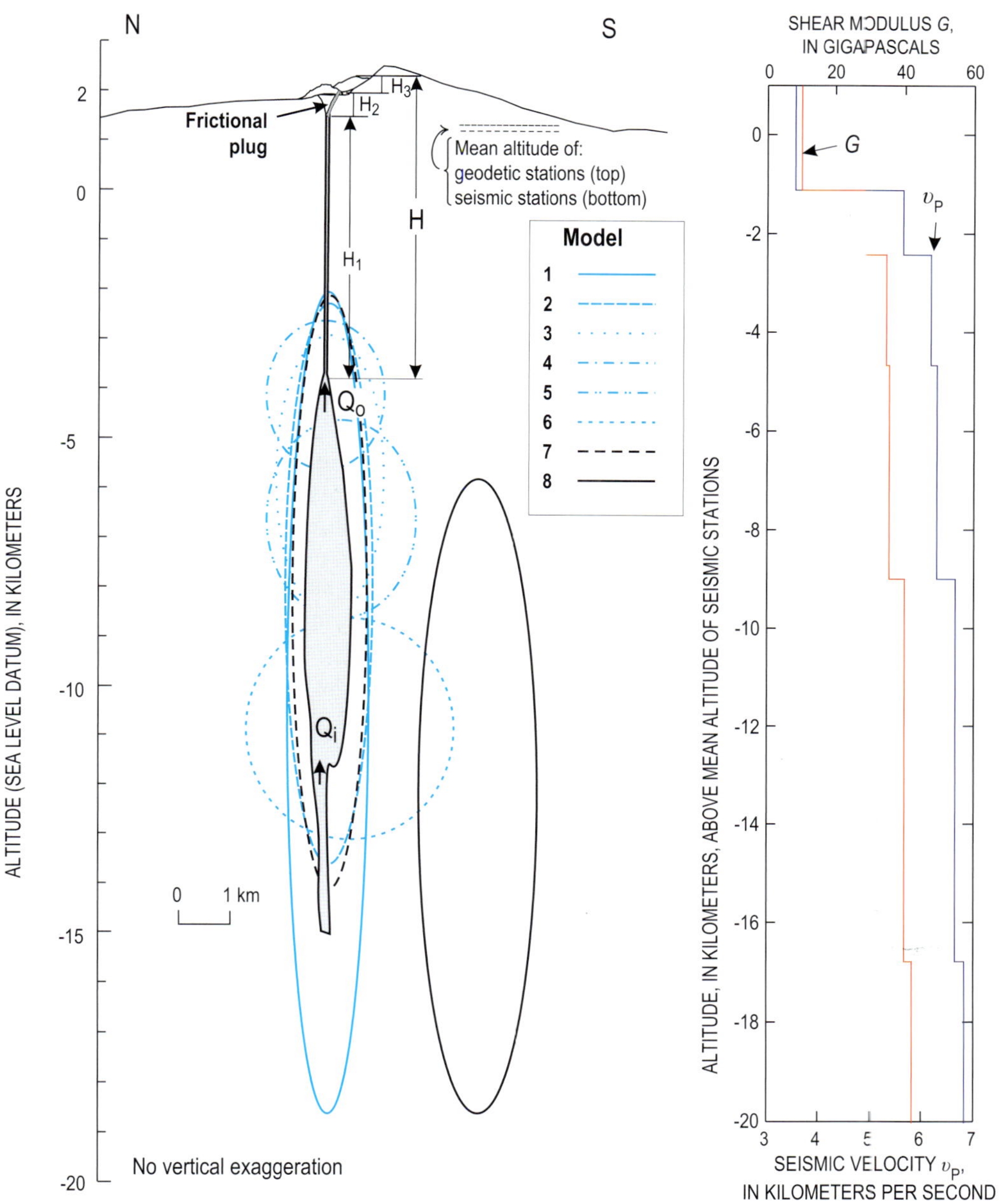

Figure 5. Left, Idealized north-south cross section through Mount St. Helens showing approximate location of the magma body (shaded), as judged from the geodetic modeling and some of the parameters used in this analysis. Blue and black dashed ellipses represent locations of geodetic models 1 through 8 listed in table 1; width of each ellipse represents its radius taken from value of $R^2\Delta p/G$ in table 1, using $\Delta p = 10$ MPa and $G = 35$ GPa. Right, Profile of seismic velocity (from Musumeci and others, 2002) and shear modulus G (estimated from seismic data and from density data of Williams and others, 1987). Shear modulus was estimated from the formula $G = \rho R v_P^2(1-2\nu)/(2(1-\nu))$, where Poisson's ratio, ν, is taken as 0.25 and ρ is taken as 2,150 kg/m^3 above the seismic datum and 2,700 kg/m^3 below it (Williams and others, 1987, fig. 8). Cross section and seismic profile have same vertical scales, but latter is set to datum of mean altitude of seismic stations.

reservoir pressure p and volume V_C is linear with a proportionality given by the reservoir compressibility κ_C:

$$\kappa_C \equiv \frac{1}{V_C}\frac{\partial V_C}{\partial p} \qquad (1)$$

For a sphere or prolate ellipsoid, $\kappa_C=3/(4G)$ (McTigue, 1987; Tiampo and others, 2000). We also assume that the magma has a finite compressibility (κ_M) given by:

$$\kappa_M \equiv \frac{1}{\rho_M}\frac{\partial \rho_M}{\partial p} \; . \qquad (2)$$

Finally, we assume that the change in reservoir mass (dM_C) equals the mass added by recharge ($dM_i=\rho_i dV_i$) minus the mass erupted ($dM_e \approx \rho_e dV_e$), where ρ_i, ρ_e, dV_i, and dV_e are the densities and volumes of injected and erupted magma, respectively. In mathematical terms,

$$\begin{aligned} d\left(\rho_M V_C\right) &= \rho_M dV_C + V_C d\,\rho_M \\ &= -\rho_e dV_e + \rho_i dV_i \end{aligned} \; . \qquad (3)$$

Adding terms for κ_C and κ_M into equation 3 and rearranging leads to:

$$dV_C = \frac{\rho_i dV_i - \rho_e dV_e}{\rho_M\left(1+\frac{\kappa_M}{\kappa_C}\right)} \; . \qquad (4)$$

In the absence of recharge we have:

$$\frac{dV_e}{dV_C} = -\frac{\rho_M}{\rho_e}\left(1+\frac{\kappa_M}{\kappa_C}\right) \; . \qquad (5)$$

Equation 5 carries the important implication that the erupted volume should not equal the volume shrinkage in the magma body except in the limiting case where the densities of erupted and unerupted magma are equal and the magma is incompressible ($\kappa_M \rightarrow 0$) (this was also pointed out by Johnson and others, 2000). If compressibility and density do not vary greatly with time during an eruption, equation 5 can be used to give the ratio of erupted volume V_e to the volume change of the magma reservoir ΔV_C. In spherical or ellipsoidal reservoirs, magma compressibility is generally thought to greatly exceed the reservoir compressibility (for example, Huppert and Woods, 2002); hence erupted volume should greatly exceed ΔV_C.

In the absence of recharge, what value of dV_e / dV_C might one expect at Mount St. Helens? The answer requires careful estimation of ρ_M, ρ_e, κ_M, and ρ_C, which we provide in the following several paragraphs.

The density of unerupted, volatile-saturated rhyolitic melt at ~200–250 MPa pressure is about 2,200 kg/m^3 (estimated using the method of Ghiorso and Sack in the program Conflow of Mastin, 2002). Combined with roughly 45 volume percent plagioclase crystals (Pallister and others, this volume, chap. 30) having a density of 2,600 kg/m^3, the bulk density of the magma ρ_M would be about 2,380 kg/m^3. Density measurements of most dome rock samples are about 2,300–2,500 kg/m^3 (K. Russell, written commun., 2006), although pores and voids could reduce the bulk density of the dome, ρ_e, by perhaps 10–20 percent below that of the dome rock. Within the uncertainties, we estimate the ratio ρ_M/ρ_e to be about 1.0 to 1.2. We use a reservoir compressibility of roughly 2×10^{-11} Pa^{-1} based on the formula $\kappa_C=3/(4G)$ for an ellipsoidal reservoir and the earlier estimate of G=40±4 GPa.

Magma Compressibility

Magma compressibility κ_M depends on gas volume fraction, solubility, crystallinity, and rate of loading. When changes in pressure are much more rapid than rates of gas exsolution (for example, the time scale of seismic-wave disturbances), the crystal, melt, and gas phases can be regarded as inert, and the bulk compressibility is simply the sum of the compressibilities of the crystal, melt, and gas phases (κ_x, κ_m, κ_g) multiplied by their respective volume fractions (v_x, v_m, v_g) (for example, Mastin, 2002):

$$\kappa_M = v_m\kappa_m + v_x\kappa_x + v_g\kappa_g \; . \qquad (6)$$

If, on the other hand, pressure changes occur over months or years, as in the current eruption, gas exsolution must be considered. Previous investigators (Tait and others, 1989; Huppert and Woods, 2002; Woods and Huppert, 2003) used a simple Henry's solubility law for H_2O and found an abrupt discontinuity in compressibility at the saturation pressure (~240 MPa in fig. 6*C*). Huppert and Woods (2002) and Woods and Huppert (2003) suggested that this discontinuity could have a dramatic, rejuvenating effect on the course of an effusive eruption once the magma reservoir reaches the saturation pressure.

The Mount St. Helens magma contains both H_2O and CO_2, and gas in such a two-component system should exsolve more gradually and over a wider range of pressures than it would if only H_2O were present. We estimate exsolved volatile content and magma compressibility using petrologic constraints from other studies. Phase equilibrium experiments (Rutherford and Devine, this volume, chap. 31) suggest that the currently erupting magma last equilibrated at a temperature of ~850°C, a pressure of ~120 MPa, and a source depth near 5 km. The crystallinity at this depth was 40 to 55 percent (Pallister and others, this volume, chap. 30). The center of deflation, however, is substantially deeper than 5 km, perhaps equal to that of the May 18, 1980, magma at around 8–9 km depth and 220 MPa pressure (Rutherford and Devine, 1988). Following Gerlach and others (this volume, chap. 26), we assume that present-day magma properties at the source resemble those in 1980, with a temperature of about 900°C, pressure of ~220 MPa, 30 percent crystals (Cashman and Taggart, 1983), and

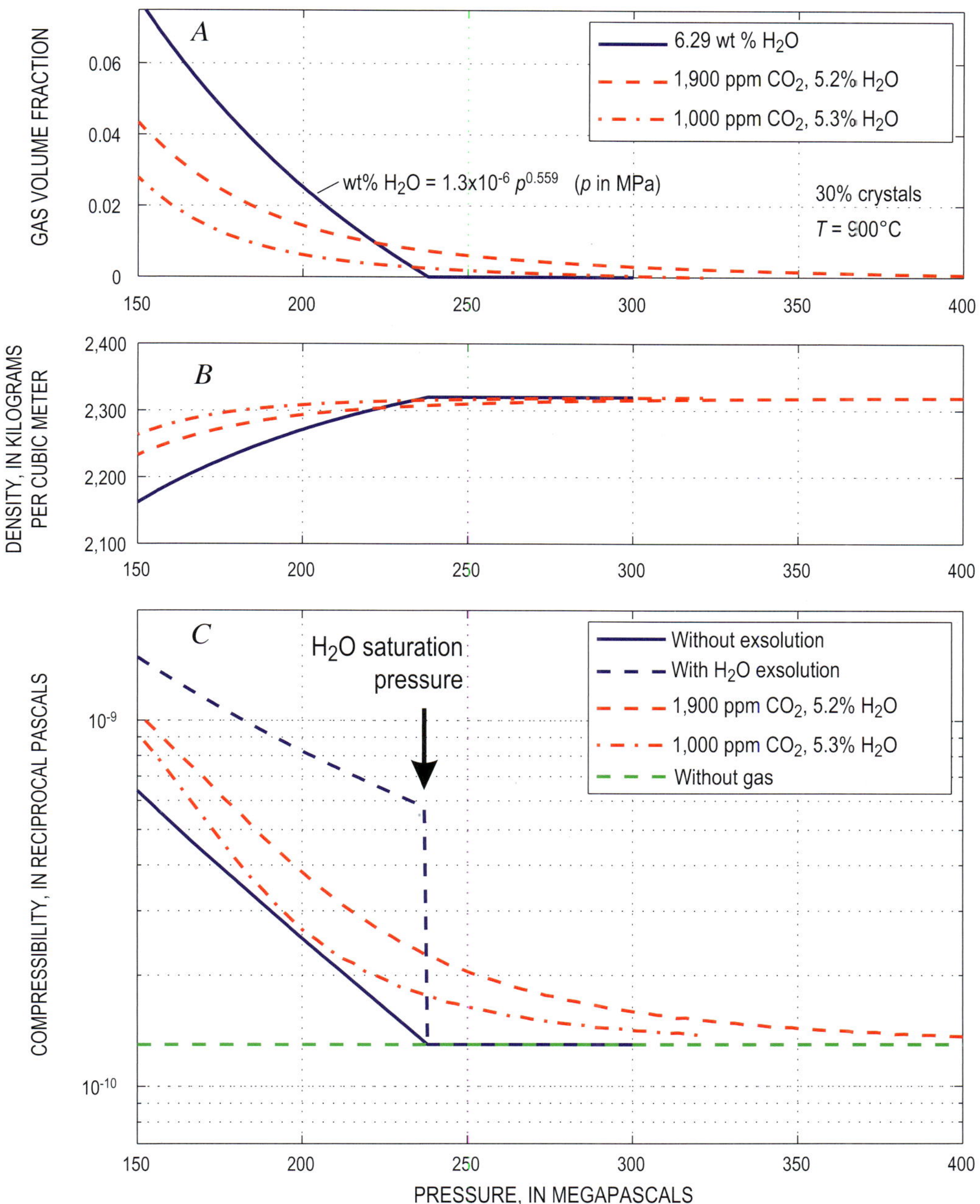

Figure 6. Characteristic features of magma having composition given in text, as function of pressure. Significance of the various lines is explained in text. *A*, Gas fraction by volume. *B*, Density. *C*, Compressibility.

a dissolved water concentration in the melt of about 5 weight percent (Blundy and Cashman, 2001).

Assuming that the CO_2 emitted into the atmosphere during this eruption originated from a mass of magma equal to that of the lava dome, Gerlach and others (this volume, chap. 26) estimate a preeruptive CO_2 concentration in the magma of about 1,100 ppm, or 1,900 ppm normalized to the melt alone (assuming 30 percent crystallinity). At 220 MPa pressure and 900°C temperature, with 5 weight percent dissolved H_2O, such a melt would contain roughly 350 ppm dissolved CO_2; the remaining CO_2 and H_2O would be exsolved in bubbles composing roughly 1.2 volume percent of the magma (Gerlach and others, this volume, chap. 26). The total water content normalized to the melt plus fluid phases would be about 5.2 weight percent.

Using the solubility code VolatileCalc 1.1 (Newman and Lowenstern, 2002), we calculate mass fractions of exsolved H_2O and CO_2 over pressures ranging from 150 to 400 MPa, and we combine these results with ideal gas relations to obtain the volume fraction of exsolved gas (fig. 6A). We assume a melt density ρ_m=2,200 kg/m^3 and crystal density ρ_x=2,600 kg/m^3; the melt density corresponds to a water-saturated melt of 1980 composition (sample SH-084 of Rutherford and others, 1985), calculated by the method of Ghiorso and Sack (1995) using the program Conflow (Mastin, 2002). From these volume fractions and phase densities we calculate the bulk density over the pressure range 150–400 MPa (fig. 6*B*) and then numerically calculate $(1/\rho_M)(\partial\rho_M/\partial p)$ to obtain κ_M (fig. 6*C*). We use a melt compressibility of 2.0×10^{-10} Pa^{-1}, estimated using the method of Ghiorso and Sack (1995) for water-saturated rhyolite at $p=220$ MPa, and a crystal compressibility of 2×10^{-11} Pa^{-1} obtained for albite at $T=900$°C and $p=220$ MPa from the program MELTS using the method of Elkins and Grove (1990).

Our calculations suggest that, over the pressure range of 150–400 MPa, the magma may have a bubble volume fraction of 0.0008 to 0.048 (fig. 6*A*). For comparison, we plot results for $CO_2=1{,}000$ ppm and $H_2O=5.3$ weight percent of the melt+fluid phases and also for a single-component (H_2O) volatile system using the Henry's law solubility illustrated in figure 6*A*, with the H_2O content (6.29 weight percent) set so that the volume fraction of gas at 220 MPa equals that of the two-component system. Both the two-component and the Henry's solubility laws show nearly an order-of-magnitude variation in compressibility over this pressure range, but the two-component systems show little or no discontinuity in κ_M at the saturation pressure. At $p=220$ MPa, the two-component system (1,900 ppm CO_2, 5.2 weight percent H_2O) gives $\kappa_M=2.8\times10^{-10}$ Pa^{-1}. We use this number as a starting point in our calculations. The relation between κ_M and volume fraction of gas for these two-component magma compositions is illustrated in figure 7.

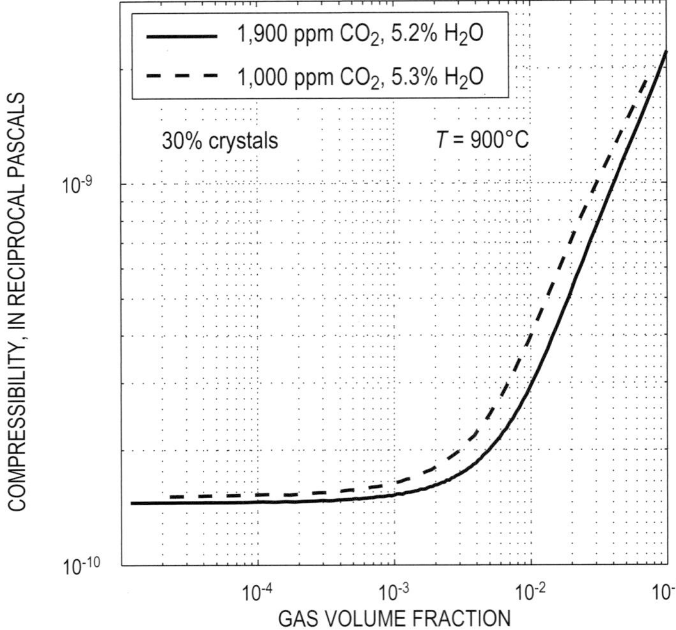

Figure 7. Compressibility versus volume fraction gas for a rhyolitic melt containing 30 percent crystals at 900°C temperature, using two different gas compositions.

Expected Ratio of Erupted Volume to Volume Change in the Reservoir

Using $\rho_M/\rho_e=1$, $\kappa_C=2\times10^{-11}$ Pa^{-1}, and $\kappa_M=2.8\times10^{-10}$ Pa^{-1} (~1.2 percent bubbles), then dV_e/dV_C predicted by equation 5 should be about 16, which is somewhat higher than the ranges of 7.7–12.8 and 2–6 calculated for the first and second time windows, respectively. A temporal increase in κ_M is suggested by the difference in apparent values of dV_e/dV_C between the first and second time windows, though uncertainties in these ratios are too great to make such an inference with confidence. For the overall eruption, the erupted volume by mid-December 2005, 7.3×10^7 m^3, was only about three times the reasonably well-constrained reservoir shrinkage dV_C of ~2.3×10^7 m^3 estimated by Lisowski and others (this volume, chap. 15). A ratio this low suggests a magma compressibility of ~4×10^{-11} Pa^{-1}, which is about one-fourth that of even a bubble-free magma of this crystallinity (fig. 7). If the magma reservoir is in fact bubble free, κ_C must be ~8×10^{-11} Pa^{-1} in order to have $dV_e/dV_C\approx3$; if it contains roughly 1 volume percent bubbles at the source depth, as inferred by Gerlach and others (this volume, chap. 26), κ_C must be ~1.4×10^{-10} Pa^{-1}. In either case, κ_M is only a few to several times greater than κ_C, which we take to indicate that the volume fraction of bubbles in the reservoir is zero or very small, consistent with the findings of Gerlach and others (this volume, chap. 26). If the reservoir was partially recharged during the eruption (a factor we consider later), a still lower ratio of κ_M/κ_C would be implied, suggesting still lower bubble content in the reservoir.

Idealized Models for History of Extrusion and Deflation

Previous studies (Wadge, 1981; Stasiuk and others, 1993; Huppert and Woods, 2002) point out that drainage of an elastic magma reservoir through a Newtonian conduit results in an exponentially decreasing extrusion rate. When combined with constant recharge rate into the magma system, the resulting curve has the form of an exponentially decreasing rate superimposed on a constant rate (fig. 3*D*). If these processes are responsible for determining the dome-growth curve at Mount St. Helens, then some information on the magma reservoir and conduit properties should be embedded in the coefficients to these equations. Information on the magma-reservoir volume and driving pressure are of particular importance.

We know that processes besides Newtonian flow and elastic relaxation may affect the growth history. The highly crystalline magma at Mount St. Helens, for example, probably has a non-Newtonian rheology. The extrusion of lava as a nearly solid plug bounded by frictional faults may also limit the growth rate. Different constitutive laws may predict different growth curves for the lava dome. Some curves fit to the hot-rock data (fig. 3) that have simple analytical forms are:

logarithmic (fig. 3*A*) $$V_e = a\ln\left(1+b\left(t-c\right)\right), \tag{7}$$

exponential (fig. 3*C*) $$V_e = a\left(1-\mathrm{e}^{-b(t-c)}\right), \tag{8}$$

modified log (fig. 3*B*) $$V_e = a\ln\left[1-\frac{d}{b}\left(1-e^{\frac{b(t-c)}{a}}\right)\right], \tag{9}$$

and exponential plus linear (fig. 3*D*)

$$V_e = a\left(1-e^{-b(t-c)}\right)+d\left(t-c\right). \tag{10}$$

The terms a, b, c, and d are fitting coefficients; their best-fit values are listed in table 2. (Parameter c, which represents the day of the eruption start, is used as a variable in these fits, even though its value is roughly known, making the number of truly unknown parameters equal to three.) Curve forms that fit the data best are equations 9 and 10, which, as shown later, assume a constant rate of recharge. The fitting errors are lower using these forms than using equations 7 and 8 (table 2). More importantly, however, curves of equations 9 and 10 have done a better job predicting future growth, as the best-fit coefficients for equations 9 and 10 have changed relatively little since early 2005 (table 2).

Exponential Growth Curve

Exponential curve forms of equations 8 and 10 are derived from two main assumptions. The first is that the magma-reservoir pressure p is linearly related to the mass of magma in the reservoir:

$$p = p_0 - \mathrm{C}\left(M_e - M_i\right), \tag{11}$$

where M_e is the mass that leaves the reservoir (assumed to equal the erupted mass), M_i is the mass that enters the reservoir as recharge, p_0 is initial reservoir pressure, and C is a constant that represents the change in pressure with reservoir mass, $\partial p/\partial M_C$. By substituting equations 2 and 1 into equation 3, and rearranging, we find that $\mathrm{C}=[(\kappa_C+\kappa_M)\rho_m V_C]^{-1}$.

The second assumption is that the mass effusion rate $\dot{M}_e$ is linearly related to magma reservoir pressure (p):

$$\dot{M}_e = \mathrm{A}p-\mathrm{B}, \tag{12}$$

where A and B are constants. This equation describes, among other possibilities, Newtonian (Poiseuille) flow (fig. 8*A*); Newtonian flow capped by a frictional plug (fig. 8*C*); flow of a solid mass through the conduit separated from the conduit walls by a Newtonian fluid (a "greased plug"; fig. 8*B*); and

Table 2. Fitting coefficients to curves in figure 3.

[Columns labeled $\Sigma(y_i-y)^2$ give the sum of the squares of errors between best-fit predictions and data.]

Date	Days since 10/1/04	Hot-rock volume $m^3\times10^6$	Rate m^3/s	Exponential best-fit parameters									Logarithmic best-fit parameters								
				With recharge					Without recharge				With recharge					Without recharge			
				a $m^3\times10^6$	b $s^{-1}\times10^{-7}$	c $s\times10^5$	d m^3/s	$\Sigma(y_i-y)^2$ $m^3\times10^{11}$	a $m^3\times10^6$	b $s^{-1}\times10^{-7}$	c $s\times10^5$	$\Sigma(y_i-y)^2$ $m^3\times10^{11}$	a $m^3\times10^6$	b m^3/s	c $s\times10^5$	d m^3/s	$\Sigma(y_i-y)^2$ $m^3\times10^{11}$	a $m^3\times10^6$	b $s^{-1}\times10^{-7}$	c $s\times10^5$	$\Sigma(y_i-y)^2$ $m^3\times10^{11}$
10/1/04	0	0																			
10/13/04	12	5.4																			
11/4/04	34	11.8	5.92																		
11/29/04	59	21.3	4.4																		
12/11/04	71	25.5	4.05	14.0	2.94	9.56	2.79	0.31	53.8	1.23	9.49	0.75	8.0	3.81	9.70	8.78	0.71	39.5	1.74	9.55	0.4
1/3/05	94	30.5	2.52	86.7	1.01	9.61	-1.98	1.76	46.7	1.49	9.66	2.27	29.7	1.47×10⁻⁷	9.71	7.55	2.42	29.5	2.58	9.75	4.8
2/1/05	123	35.1	1.84	94.3	0.96	9.59	-2.26	1.74	45.0	1.58	9.74	2.94	24.2	2.20×10⁻⁷	9.88	8.34	3.31	24.5	3.40	9.94	13.5
2/21/05	143	39.2	2.37	28.1	2.19	9.76	1.15	10.16	48.2	1.41	9.49	13.24	24.6	1.40×10⁻⁷	10.00	8.36	11.77	25.3	3.24	9.90	14.4
3/10/05	160	41.9	1.84	23.6	2.55	9.81	1.48	11.81	50.7	1.29	9.22	24.36	25.8	1.82×10⁻⁷	10.04	8.11	15.17	25.9	3.12	9.86	15.5
4/19/05	200	47.5	1.62	22.9	2.63	9.82	1.52	11.87	55.4	1.10	8.43	57.96	22.2	0.52	9.87	8.28	17.58	26.9	2.92	9.74	18.7
6/15/05	257	53.9	1.3	25.7	2.32	9.72	1.35	14.62	61.1	0.92	7.16	107.49	21.9	0.56	9.87	8.31	17.62	27.8	2.75	9.61	21.8
7/14/05	286	57.1	1.28	26.4	2.25	9.67	1.31	15.41	64.5	0.83	6.31	143.93	21.3	0.63	9.88	8.38	17.93	28.6	2.61	9.47	21.8
8/10/05	313	61.7	1.97	24.9	2.42	9.79	1.39	23.82	69.3	0.73	4.96	253.01	18.1	0.96	9.98	8.92	39.02	30.8	2.29	9.02	77.1
10/24/05	388	70.0	1.28	25.0	2.41	9.77	1.38	23.86	78.3	0.57	1.65	485.74	16.2	1.13	10.06	9.44	51.27	34.4	1.87	7.98	179.4
12/15/05	440	73.0	0.67	27.7	2.06	9.40	1.26	71.01	82.9	0.51	-0.16	551.65	18.0	0.98	9.96	8.89	61.32	35.7	1.75	7.54	195.1

greased-plug flow capped by a frictional plug (fig. 8*D*). We also assume that the linear relations in equations 11 and 12 do not change with time.

If one further assumes that the rate of mass recharge $(\dot{M}_i = Q_i)$ is constant, equations 11 and 12 can be combined and integrated (appendix 2) to give the erupted mass as a function of time. Noting that the erupted volume (V_e) is equal to M_e/ρ_e, we obtain:

$$V_e = \frac{1}{\rho_e}\frac{(\mathrm{A}p_0 - \mathrm{B}) - Q_i}{\mathrm{AC}}\left(1 - e^{-ACt}\right) + \frac{Q_i}{\rho_e}t\ . \qquad (13)$$

This equation has the same form as equation 10 with the following coefficients:

$$a = \frac{(\mathrm{A}p_0 - \mathrm{B}) - Q_i}{\rho_e \mathrm{AC}}\ , \qquad (14)$$

$$b = \mathrm{AC}\ \text{, and} \qquad (15)$$

$$d = \frac{Q_i}{\rho_e}\ . \qquad (16)$$

Differentiating equation 13 with respect to time, we find that this curve has an initial volumetric extrusion rate $\dot{V}_e^{t=0} = ab + d = (\mathrm{A}p_0 - \mathrm{B})/\rho_e$ but asymptotically approaches a linear trend having the slope $V_e^{t\to\infty} = d = Q_i/\rho_e$. Best-fit values of a, b, and d for the growth curve (table 2) suggest that $\dot{V}_e^{t=0} = \sim 7.0\ \mathrm{m^3/s}$ (605,000 $\mathrm{m^3}$/day) and $V_e^{t\to\infty} = \sim 1.26\ \mathrm{m^3/s}$ (109,000 $\mathrm{m^3}$/day). The latter value (the recharge rate) is several times greater than the long-term magma-supply rate of 0.2 $\mathrm{m^3/s}$ at Mount St. Helens, estimated by assuming that most of the volume of the edifice (~25 $\mathrm{km^3}$) was erupted in the past 4,000 years (Iverson and others, 2006). Finally, the volume constant a, roughly $2.8\times10^7\ \mathrm{m^3}$, is the y-intercept of the long-term growth line in fig. 3*D* (the black dashed line). The y-intercept represents the volume of magma that has erupted and has not been replaced in the reservoir by recharge. The remaining volume, more than $4.5\times10^7\ \mathrm{m^3}$, represents recharge.

The physical significance of terms in a and b can be further refined, depending on the type of flow in the conduit. For Poiseuille flow, the mass flow rate is (Mironer, 1979, p. 194):

$$\frac{dM_e}{dt} = \frac{\rho_e \pi R^4}{8\eta H}\left(p - \bar{\rho} g H\right), \qquad (17)$$

where H is the conduit length, η is the average viscosity, and $\bar{\rho}$ is the average magma density between the magma reservoir and the Earth's surface. This equation assumes that the pressure at the top of the conduit is negligible (an assumption we will evaluate later). For Poiseuille flow, the constants in equation 12 are $\mathrm{A} = \rho_e \pi R^4/(8\eta H)$ and $\mathrm{B} = \rho_e \pi R^4 \bar{\rho} g/(8\eta)$. Inserting these expressions into equation 13, we can recast a in the following form:

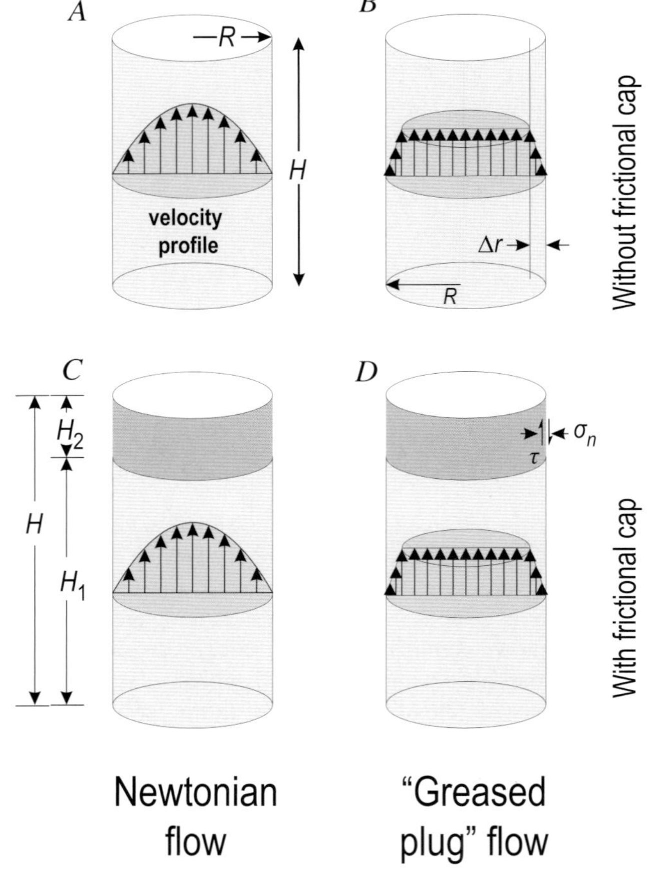

Figure 8. Types of conduit flow that are considered in deriving theoretical lava-dome growth curves. See text for full explanation.

$$a = \frac{\rho_M}{\rho_e}\left(\frac{\dot{V}_e^{t=0} - \dot{V}_e^{t\to\infty}}{\dot{V}_e^{t=0}}\right)\left(\kappa_C + \kappa_M\right)V_C\left(p_0 - \bar{\rho} g H\right). \quad (18)$$

Equation (18) can be generalized by noting that $(p_0 - \bar{\rho} g H)$ is the initial pressure at the base of the conduit in excess of that required to initiate upward flow. Denoting this term as p_0^{ex}, we can rewrite the equations as:

$$a = \frac{\rho_M}{\rho_e}\left(\frac{\dot{V}_e^{t=0} - \dot{V}_e^{t\to\infty}}{\dot{V}_e^{t=0}}\right)\left(\kappa_C + \kappa_M\right)V_C p_0^{ex}, \qquad (19)$$

$$b = AC = \frac{\rho_e}{\rho_M}\frac{\dot{V}_e^{t=0}}{\left(\kappa_C + \kappa_M\right)V_C p_0^{ex}}\ . \qquad (20)$$

It can be shown (appendix 3) that these equations also apply to greased-plug flow (fig. 8*B*) and to flow of either a Newtonian fluid or a greased plug capped by a frictional plug (figs. 8*C*, 8*D*; appendices 4, 5), so long as the plug's geometry and coefficient of friction do not change with time. If a frictional cap is present, p_0^{ex} represents the pressure in the magma reservoir in excess of both the pressure due to the weight of the overlying magma $(\bar{\rho}gH)$ and the pressure required to overcome frictional resistance of the plug.

Some important relations fall out of the equations above. In the absence of recharge, the final erupted volume is:

$$a = \frac{\rho_M}{\rho_e}(\kappa_C + \kappa_M)V_C p_0^{ex} . \quad (21)$$

Using $\kappa_C = 8\times10^{-11}$ Pa^{-1}, $\rho_M/\rho_e \approx 1$, $V_C = 10$ km^3, $p_0^{ex} = \sim30$ MPa, and $\kappa_M = 1.6\times10^{-10}$ Pa^{-1} appropriate for a bubble-free magma, the volume a is 7.2×10^7 m^3—roughly equal to the 7.3×10^7 m^3 that has erupted by the end of 2005. The time required for extrusion of 90 percent of this volume is about $3.5/b$, or ~416 days. Using a magma compressibility consistent with 1 percent bubbles ($\kappa_M = 2.8\times10^{-10}$ Pa^{-1}) and $\kappa_C = 1.4\times10^{-10}$ Pa^{-1} (to maintain $dV_e / dV_C \approx 3$ following equation 5), we obtain a theoretical extrusion volume $a = 1.26\times10^8$ m^3 and duration of 2.0 years. These results suggest that the eruption could continue beyond early 2006 without recharge, but only if the exsolved volatile fraction in the reservoir is significantly greater than ~1 percent or if the reservoir is significantly larger than ~10 km^3, or both.

For the case of recharge, taking $\dot{V}_e^{t\to\infty} = 1.26$ m^3/s and $a = 2.8\times10^7$ m^3 (table 2), the product $V_C p_0^{ex}(\kappa_M + \kappa_C)$ obtained from equation 19 is about 3.4×10^7 Pa·m^3. Constraining the reservoir volume and initial overpressure requires some additional constraint on magma compressibility, which is considered later.

Friction, Faulting, and the Growth Curve

A log-based formula having the form of equations 7 or 9 would be predicted if the growth of the lava dome were controlled by frictional resistance of a solid mass in the upper conduit, with the coefficient of friction increasing with the rate of slip.

Although the coefficient of friction is commonly taken as a constant with a value of ~0.6–1.0 (Byerlee, 1978), it actually varies slightly with sliding rate and with time between sliding events (for example, Scholz, 1998). When μ increases with displacement rate, acceleration is dampened out and stable sliding (or fault creep) results. When μ decreases with displacement rate, sliding can accelerate unstably, leading to earthquakes. In general, rate-strengthening friction is favored when the shear-zone temperature is near the brittle-ductile transition (Chester, 1994), when a thick gouge layer is present (Byerlee and Summers, 1976), and in near-surface conditions when normal stress on the fault plane is low (Marone and Scholz, 1988). These conditions all exist in the shallow conduit at Mount St. Helens.

On the other hand, experimental studies of the Mount St. Helens fault gouge at 25°C (Moore and others, this volume, chap. 20) suggest rate-weakening behavior when displacement rates are less than about 1×10^{-4} m/s and rate-strengthening behavior at rates above 5×10^{-4} m/s. Assuming a 100-m-diameter conduit near the surface, the range of observed volumetric extrusion rates (~1–7 m^3/s) translates into displacement rates of 1–9×10^{-4} m/s, crossing over the transition between these behavior types. We consider it likely that both rate-strengthening and rate-weakening sliding exist at shallow depth at any given time. Fault patches of rate-weakening gouge will slip abruptly to create small drumbeat earthquakes whereas other parts of the fault surface creep stably under rate-strengthening conditions. If rate-weakening behavior controls conduit flow, the appropriate friction coefficient to use in this model would be a value averaged over many stick-slip cycles. If that average doesn't change with time, the long-term growth curve will be exponential. But if rate-strengthening behavior controls conduit flow, we need to consider the stress-strain rate relations of rate-strengthening fault creep.

The Logarithmic Curve

When the coefficient of friction is rate-dependent, the shear stress that resists slip on a fault plane is commonly expressed as (for example, Scholz, 1998):

$$\tau = \tau_o + A_1\sigma_n \ln\frac{\dot{\delta}}{\dot{\delta}_o}. \quad (22)$$

Here σ_n is normal stress at the wall and A_1 is the rate dependence of fault strength. The constant τ_o is an arbitrary reference, the strength of the wall interface when the slip rate is $\dot{\delta}_o$.

In order to derive a growth curve, we assume that the frictional plug of mass M_p and length H_2 occupies a cylindrical conduit of radius R (fig. 8*C*). The frictional force along the plug margin is $2\pi RH_2\mu\bar{\sigma}_n$, where $\bar{\sigma}_n$ is the mean normal stress on the plug margin. The mass flow rate $\dot{M}_e$ is then related to $\dot{\delta}_o$ by $\dot{M}_e = \rho_e\pi R^2\dot{\delta}$, and pressure at the plug base (p) is related to mass flow rate as:

$$p = p_o + a\ln\frac{\dot{M}_e}{\dot{M}_o}, \quad (23)$$

where $a = 2A_1\bar{\sigma}_n H_2 / R$ and $p_0 = 2\tau_0 H_2 / R + Mg / \pi R^2$ are constants.

Rearranging this equation yields:

$$\dot{M}_e = e^{\dot{M}_0}\exp\left[\frac{(p - p_o)}{a}\right]. \quad (24)$$

Combining equation 24 with equation 11 (assuming recharge $M_i = 0$) and integrating leads to (appendix 6):

$$V_e = aD\ln\left(1 - \frac{t\dot{M}_0}{\rho_e Da}\right), \quad (25)$$

where $D = V_M(\kappa_C + \kappa_M)$ and V_M is the volume of the magma reservoir plus conduit. This equation has the same form as equation 7, with $a = \alpha V_M(\kappa_C + \kappa_M)$ and $b = \dot{V}_e^{t=0}/a$.

If recharge into the magma reservoir is included, the equation has the form (appendix 6):

$$V_e = \alpha D \ln\left[1 - \frac{\dot{M}_0}{Q_i}\left(1 - e^{\frac{Q_i t}{\rho_e \alpha D}}\right)\right]. \tag{26}$$

This equation has the form of equation 10, with a volume constant $a=\alpha D=1.47\times10^7$ m^3 (by regression through the most recent data set, table 2), a recharge rate $b=Q_i/\rho_e=1.0$ m^3/s, and an initial extrusion rate $d=\dot{M}_0/\rho_e=\dot{V}_e^{t=0}=8.9$ m^3/s (table 3). The recharge rate is about 30 percent less than the 1.26 m^3/s obtained from the exponential curve. By rearranging equation 23, substituting $\dot{M}_e=\rho_e\dot{V}_e$, $\dot{M}_0=\rho_e\dot{V}_e^{t=0}$, and $a=\alpha D=\alpha V_M(\kappa_C+\kappa_M)$, we can obtain a formula for the product of volume of the magma system and pressure drop from the beginning of the eruption until the time of the last data point used in this paper (December 15, 2005):

$$V_M\Delta p(\kappa_C + \kappa_M) = a\ln\left(\dot{V}_e^{t=0}/\dot{V}_e^{last}\right). \tag{27}$$

The parameters Δp and $\dot{V}_e^{last}$ are the pressure change at the base of the frictional plug and the extrusion rate at the end of this time period; the variable a is the numerical value of the fitting coefficient. From the first derivative of equation 9, $\dot{V}_e^{last}=1.20$ m^3/s as of December 15, 2005 (table 3), giving $V_M\Delta p(\kappa_C+\kappa_M)=3.0\times10^7$ m^3. It should be noted that this term contains slightly different parameters from $V_C p_0^{ex}(\kappa_C+\kappa_M)$ derived for the exponential curve: V_C represents reservoir volume, whereas V_M represents volume of the reservoir plus conduit below the frictional plug, and Δp represents pressure drop at the base of the plug, whereas p_0^{ex} gives the initial overpressure in the magma reservoir. Nevertheless, the values of these terms should be roughly comparable, and they are: $V_M\Delta p(\kappa_C+\kappa_M)=3.0\times10^7$ m^3 from the log fit (equation 9) versus $V_C p_0^{ex}(\kappa_C+\kappa_M)=3.4\times10^7$ m^3 from the exponential fit (equation 10). The fact that these values differ by only 10 to 15 percent suggests that inferences about magma-reservoir size and overpressure do not depend strongly on the assumptions regarding factors that control conduit flow.

Additional Constraints from the Geodetic Time Series

On the basis of their fit to the dome-growth data, neither the logarithmic (equation 9) nor the exponential (equation 10) model can be confidently eliminated. Each, however, predicts a history of reservoir deflation that can be compared with geodetic data. For the case of exponential dome growth, differentiating equation 13 with time under conditions of constant recharge and substituting in equations 4, 14, and 15 gives the following for reservoir deflation with time:

$$\Delta V_C = -\frac{\rho_e}{\rho_M}\frac{a\left(1-e^{-bt}\right)}{\left(1+\frac{\kappa_M}{\kappa_C}\right)}. \tag{28}$$

The reservoir deflates with the same time constant as the dome-growth curve, implying, for the best-fit value of b with recharge through December 15, 2005 (2.06×10^{-7} s^{-1}), that 90 percent of the geodetic deflation should have occurred after about 200 days, by mid-April 2005, and that by late summer 2005 the deflation should have essentially stopped. This is inconsistent with geodetic data, which show a nearly linear rate of inward displacement through at least the end of 2005. The log curve can theoretically provide a better match to the geodetic data, but the predictions at some point become physically unrealistic. For the case of zero recharge, for

Table 3. Calculations of $V_C p_0^{ex}(\kappa_M+\kappa_C)$ or $V_M\Delta p(\kappa_M+\kappa_C)$ obtained from exponential or logarithmic best-fit solutions.

Date	$V_C p_0^{ex}(\kappa_M+\kappa_C)$ exponential		Log with recharge			Log without recharge		
	With recharge m$^3\times10^6$	Without recharge m$^3\times10^6$	$\dot{V}_e^{t=0}$ m^3/s	$\dot{V}_e^{last}$ m^3/s	$V_M\Delta p(\kappa_M+\kappa_C)$ m$^3\times10^6$	$\dot{V}_e^{t=0}$ m^3/s	$\dot{V}_e^{last}$ m^3/s	$V_M\Delta p(\kappa_M+\kappa_C)$ m$^3\times10^6$
12/11/2004	24	54	8.3	3.94	5.9	6.9	3.4	28
1/3/2005	67	47	7.5	2.52	33	7.6	2.5	33
2/1/2005	71	45	8.3	1.82	37	8.3	1.8	37
2/21/2005	33	48	8.4	1.64	40	8.2	1.7	40
3/10/2005	29	51	8.1	1.54	43	8.1	1.5	43
4/19/2005	29	55	8.3	1.40	39	7.8	1.3	48
6/15/2005	31	61	8.3	1.20	42	7.6	1.1	54
7/14/2005	32	64	8.4	1.14	42	7.5	1.0	57
8/10/2005	31	69	8.9	1.23	36	7.1	1.0	61
10/24/2005	31	78	9.4	1.24	33	6.4	0.9	68
12/15/2005	34	83	8.9	1.11	38	6.2	0.8	72

example, combining equations 5 and 25 and substituting $a = \alpha V_C(\kappa_C + \kappa_M)$ and $b = \dot{V}_e^{t=0}/a$, the volume shrinkage of the magma system should follow the curve:

$$\Delta V_C = -\frac{\rho_e a \ln(1+bt)}{\rho_M\left(1+\frac{\kappa_M}{\kappa_C}\right)} . \tag{29}$$

In other words, the volume shrinkage of the magma reservoir with time should look like a negative mirror image of the dome growth curve, adjusted by the constant $\rho_e/(\rho_M(1+\kappa_M/\kappa_C))$. This curve leads to the physically unrealistic result that deflation continues indefinitely, even to negative reservoir volumes, at the same time that the lava dome keeps growing. This implication is an outcome of the logarithmic relation between stress and displacement rate (equation 22), which adequately fits experimental data on rate-dependent friction within the range of shear stresses applied during experiments but cannot be realistically extrapolated outside that range.

A More Realistic Model

We are therefore left with the result that neither the exponential curve nor the logarithmic curve can adequately fit both the lava-dome growth curve and the geodetic deflation history. What additional processes might account for the dome growth and deflation histories? Some possibilities include:

- *The effect of the dome's weight in suppressing further extrusion.*—Digital elevation models indicate that the dome rapidly grew to more than 200 m height in the first two months of the eruption, potentially adding several megapascals of increased pressure to the vent at the base of the dome. Our records on dome-height variations with time (fig. 9) can be used to constrain this effect.
- *Changes in magma compressibility with time.*—A decrease in reservoir pressure of 30 MPa can increase magma compressibility several tens of percent (fig. 6C), increasing the ability of the magma reservoir to maintain a long-term eruption with time.
- *A nonconstant rate of recharge.*—A more realistic model would have recharge into the reservoir increasing as reservoir pressure decreases.

These effects require a numerical solution to account for changing values with time. We solve the problem using differential equations described below.

To account for the relation between mass eruption rate and reservoir pressure, we assume again that the effusion rate is linearly related to the reservoir overpressure. For Poiseuille or greased-plug flow, the overpressure p^{ex} is simply $p - \bar{\rho} gH$. If a frictional cap is present, the overpressure is $p^{ex} = p - (\bar{\rho} gH + F)$, where F is the strength of the frictional cap (assumed constant). The growth of the lava dome changes the distance H from the reservoir to the free surface, and in order to account for this, we divide this term into two parts; $\bar{\rho} gH_0$, where H_0 is the distance from the top of the reservoir to the vent at the base of the lava dome, and $\rho_e gH_3$, where H_3 is the height of the lava dome. The relation between pressure and effusion rate is then:

$$\frac{dM_e}{dt} = \mathrm{A}_2\left[\frac{p - (\bar{\rho} gH_0 + \rho_e gH_3 + F)}{H_0 + H_3}\right] . \tag{30}$$

The constant A_2 has the value $\rho_e \pi R^4/(8\eta)$ for Poiseuille flow and $\rho_e \pi R^3 \Delta r/(8\eta)$ for greased-plug flow (appendix 4). This

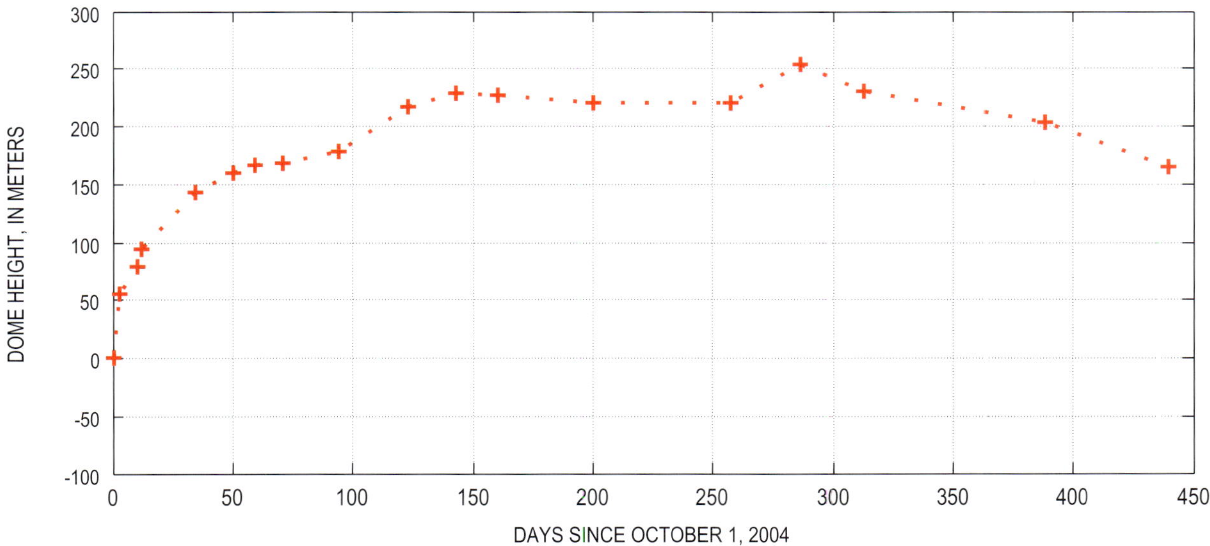

Figure 9. Maximum height of the Mount St. Helens lava dome above the 2003 crater floor (the Crater Glacier surface, approximately 2,115 m above sea level) during the course of the 2004–6 eruption.

equation can be simplified by noting that, at $t=0$, $p^{ex}=p_0^{ex}$ and $dM_e/dt=\dot{V}_e^{t=0}/\rho_e$:

$$\frac{dV_e}{dt}=\dot{V}_e^{t=0}\frac{p_0^{ex}+\Delta p-\rho_e g H_3}{p_0^{ex}} \quad . \qquad (31)$$

The initial extrusion rate $\dot{V}_e^{t=0}$, the dome height H_3, and the density ρ_e are constrained from measurements; the pressure change in the magma reservoir Δp is calculated by integration (below); and the initial overpressure p_0^{ex} is an adjustable parameter whose value is likely less than a few tens of megapascals.

The rate of pressure change in the reservoir is obtained by differentiating equation 11 with time and substituting $C=[(\kappa_C+\kappa_M)\rho_m V_C]^{-1}$:

$$\frac{dp}{dt}=\frac{\frac{dM_i}{dt}-\rho_e\frac{dV_e}{dt}}{\rho_M V_C(\kappa_C+\kappa_M)} \quad . \qquad (32)$$

In this calculation, the terms κ_C and ρ_e are considered known; dV_e/dt is obtained from equation 31, and the recharge rate dM_i/dt is calculated from a separate differential equation (below). The magma compressibility κ_M at the beginning of the eruption is an adjustable parameter; during the course of the eruption, it increases with decreasing pressure at a rate that equals the average slope of the curve of κ_M versus p in figure 6*C* (for CO_2=1,900 ppm, H_2O=5.2 weight percent). In each calculation, we use the magma density ρ_M shown in figure 6*B* at the given compressibility. Thus the magma density changes with pressure, though the changes are minor.

In accounting for recharge, we assume that the rate of input into the magma reservoir at the onset of the eruption was negligible but increased as reservoir pressure was depleted. The simplest such relation is linear, using an adjustable proportionality constant Q_{lt}:

$$\frac{dM_i}{dt}=-Q_{lt}\frac{\Delta p}{p_0^{ex}} \quad . \qquad (33)$$

The parameter Δp is the reservoir-pressure change since the start of the eruption (negative Δp implies a pressure decrease). Like Q_i in equation 13, Q_{lt} in equation 33 largely controls the long-term extrusion rate. The linear assumption implies laminar flow of magma into the reservoir from some deeper source whose pressure remains constant. A more realistic model would consider a finite source whose pressure decreased over time, but we have no constraints on the rate of pressure decrease and hence ignore it under the assumption that the deeper reservoir is much larger than the shallow one that feeds the eruption.

Equations 31, 32, and 33 can be simultaneously integrated to yield both a dome-growth curve and deflation history. The calculations involve four adjustable constants: V_C, p_0^{ex}, an initial value of κ_M, and Q_{lt}. Our solution takes κ_C to be a known quantity, although its value is known only approximately. The above estimates of $V_e/\Delta V_C$ suggest κ_C to be at least a few times greater than our initial estimate of 2×10^{-11} Pa^{-1}, but best-fit values of $V_C p_0^{ex}(\kappa_C+\kappa_M)$ in table 3 constrain $(\kappa_C+\kappa_M)$ to be less than about 5×10^{-10} Pa^{-1} for magma-reservoir volumes greater than about 5 km^3 and initial overpressures exceeding about 10 MPa. With these constraints, we run the model using two possible values of 7×10^{-11} and 1.5×10^{-10} Pa^{-1} for κ_C. In theory, the values of Q_{lt} and κ_M can be uniquely determined, as they are the only factors that significantly affect the long-term eruption rate and the ratio $V_e/\Delta V_C$, respectively. The values of V_C and p_0^{ex} are interdependent and nonunique, but ranges of possible combinations can be identified.

In order to compare the deflation history to geodetic measurements, we convert the history of pressure change Δp into a history of magma-chamber shrinkage ΔV_C, using $\Delta V_C=(V_C/\kappa_C)\Delta p$, and then convert ΔV_C into a theoretical displacement at JRO1 using one of the geodetic models in table 1 (fig. 4). For the first time period (fig. 4*A*), model 5 in table 1 (source depth 6–10 km) matches the JRO1 radial displacements best and predicts a radial displacement of 5.32 mm for a volume loss ΔV_C of 3.85×10^6 m^3, or 1.4×10^{-6} mm displacement per cubic meter volume loss.

Results

Numerical model results are compared with measurement histories of lava-dome volume and radial displacement at JRO1 in figures 10*A* and 10*B*, respectively. The solid black line in fig. 10*A* gives model results that match the hot-rock data for V_C=17 km^3, p_0^{ex}=17 MPa, and Q_{lt}/ρ_e = 1.7 m^3/s. The dashed black line gives analytical results using the exponential curve of equation 10 with $a=2.77\times10^7$ m^3, $b=2.06\times10^{-7}$ s^{-1} and d=1.26 m^3/s. These theoretical curves cannot be easily compared with the JRO1 data because deflation at JRO1 began around September 23, 2004, 20 days before the first lava appeared and three days before the first visible surface deformation (Dzurisin and others, this volume, chap. 14). The deflation between September 26 and October 11 was probably associated with extrusion of cold rock ahead of the rising magma. Deflation before September 26 may have been associated with intrusion at shallow depth or gas escape, neither of which can be easily quantified.

In order to simultaneously fit both curves, we add the volume of cold rock extruded before October 11 to the cumulative hot-rock volume (green data points, fig. 10*A*) and use September 27 as the start date (a date determined by a best-fit exponential curve through these new data). We also start with 3 mm of deflation at $t=0$, the approximate amount of deflation measured at JRO1 on September 27.

The blue dashed and solid lines in figure 10*A* represent best-fit analytical (using equation 10) and numerical curves through the modified dataset, respectively. Best-fit coefficients of the analytical curve give $a=3.61\times10^7$ m^3, $b=2.2\times10^{-7}$ s^{-1}, and d=1.28 m^3/s. Using $\kappa_C=7\times10^{-11}$ Pa^{-1}, $\kappa_M=1.2\times10^{-10}$ Pa^{-1} (adjusted to match the deflation curve) and equation 28 to calculate magma-reservoir deflation with time, the calculated displacements (dashed blue line, fig. 10*B*) roughly match the measurements during the first few months of the eruption and during the following summer (~250–400 days into the eruption), but they do not predict continued deflation that one would infer from a best-fit line through the JRO1 data after about 150 days.

A numerical solution (solid blue lines) provides a slightly better fit through the data using $V_C = 17$ km^3, $p_0^{ex} = 18$ MPa, $Q_{lt}/\rho_e = 1.7$ m^3/s, and κ_M ranging from an initial value of 1.85×10^{-10} Pa^{-1} to a final value of 1.98×10^{-10} Pa^{-1} (~0.40–0.48 percent bubbles). In this solution, the total volume of erupted magma that has not been replaced by recharge is about 3.9×10^7 m^3. This amount is 1.3×10^7 m^3 less than predicted by the analytical solution (fig. 10A). The lower total recharge implies more geodetic deflation; hence the numerical curve can be fit to the geodetic data using a slightly higher average κ_M than required by the analytical solution. Over the time window of the simulation, the magma-reservoir pressure drops by about 11 MPa, so that the excess pressure $(p - \bar{\rho} g H_1)$ by mid-December 2005 is about 7 MPa, three megapascals greater than the pressure $\rho_e g H_3$ at the vent, owing to the weight of the overlying dome (taking $\rho_e = 2300$ kg/m^3 and $H_3 = 167$ m on December 15, 2005).

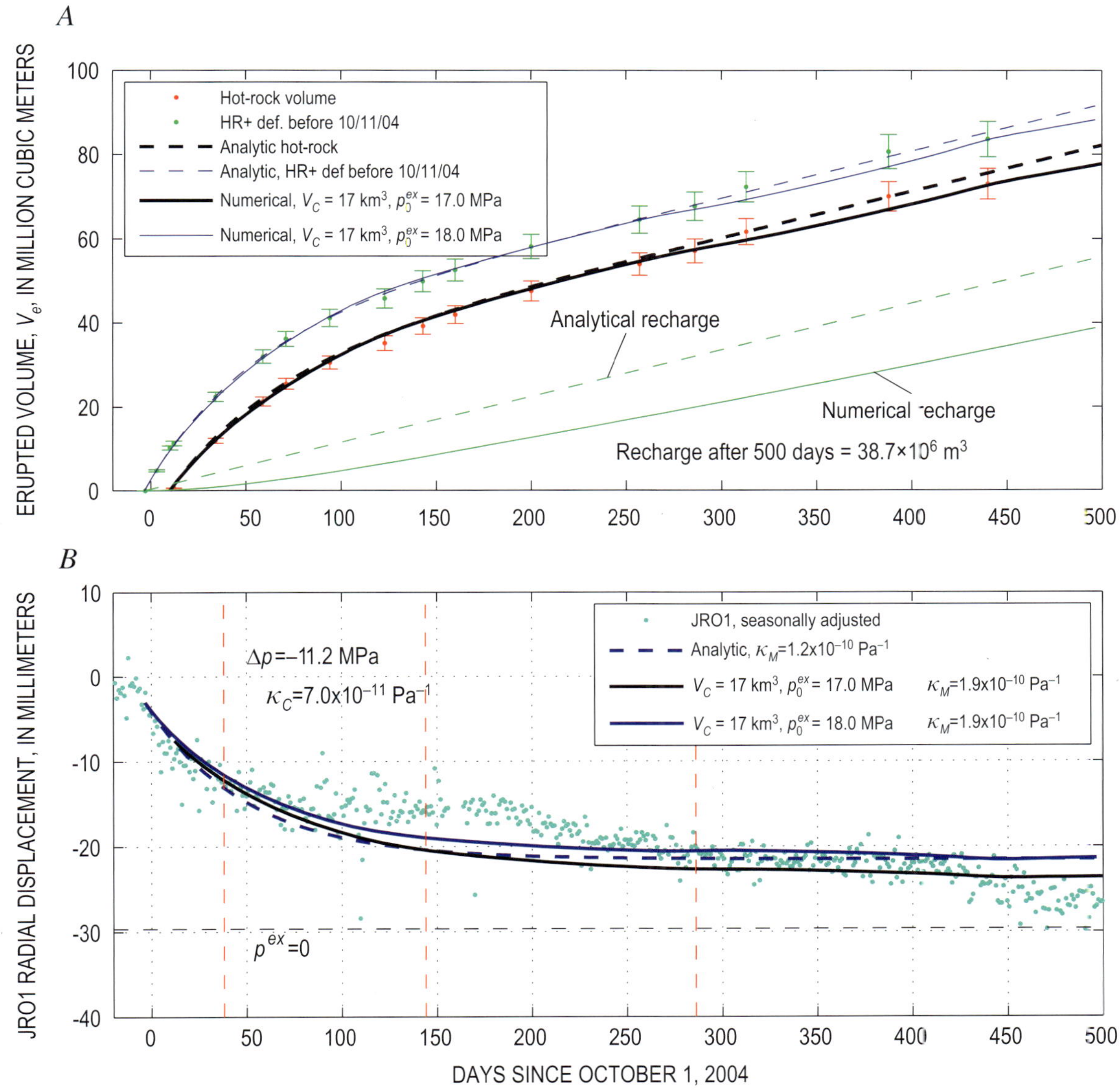

Figure 10. Comparison of theoretical and measured lava-dome volume and magma-reservoir deflation with time at Mount St. Helens. *A*, Erupted volume from digital elevation models. Phrase "HR+def before 10/11/04" refers to data points that represent hot-rock volume of the dome plus volume of uplifted cold crater-floor material that appears before the beginning of lava extrusion on October 11, 2004. Phrase "Analytic, HR+def before 10/11/04" refers to an analytical best-fit line through these data. Details are explained in text. *B*, Radial displacement measured at JRO1 continuous GPS station (fig 1*A*). Negative displacements are radially inward. Red vertical dashed lines in figure 10*B* refer to the start and end dates of time windows used in geodetic analysis (fig. 4 and table 1).

Other combinations of ΔV_C, p_0^{ex}, Q_{lt}, and κ_M that produce reasonable fits by numerical solution are listed in table 4. All combinations require Q_{lt}/ρ_e = 1.7±0.1 m³/s. Runs that use κ_C = 7×10⁻¹¹ Pa⁻¹ require average values of κ_M around 1.6–1.9×10⁻¹⁰ Pa⁻¹ (0.18–0.43 volume percent bubbles) and a magma-reservoir volume exceeding ~9 km³ for p_0^{ex}<~30 MPa. Runs that use κ_C = 15×10⁻¹¹ Pa⁻¹ require κ_M = 4.0–4.7×10⁻¹⁰ Pa⁻¹ (1.0–1.8 volume percent bubbles) and a magma-reservoir volume exceeding ~5 km³ for p_0^{ex} less than about 30 MPa. Using a still larger reservoir compressibility (κ_C = 3×10⁻¹⁰ Pa⁻¹), a magma reservoir larger than 2 km³ (for p_0^{ex} less than about 30 MPa) can still fit the curves using κ_M = 8.9–9.4×10⁻¹⁰ Pa⁻¹ (2.8–3.8 percent bubbles). The results that involve κ_C = 7 to 15×10⁻¹¹ Pa⁻¹ correspond to exsolved fluid contents in the source region that match most closely with gas emission data (Gerlach and others, this volume, chap. 26).

Table 4. Combinations of V_C, p_0^{ex}, Q_{lt}, and average value of κ_M that yield reasonable fits to the growth curve and geodetic data by numerical calculation; also given are the pressure drop Δp in the magma reservoir and the recharge volume calculated after 500 days of eruption.

κ_C Pa⁻¹×10⁻¹¹	V_C km³	p_0^{ex} MPa	avg κ_M Pa⁻¹×10⁻¹⁰	Q_{lt}/ρ_e m³/s	Δp MPa	Recharge m³×10⁶
7	6	41	1.6	1.7	-30.5	48.7
7	8	32	1.6	1.7	-23	46.7
7	10	27	1.8	1.7	-18.7	44.4
7	12	24	1.8	1.7	-16.3	42.9
7	14	21	1.9	1.7	-13.7	40.9
7	17	19	1.9	1.7	-12.0	39.0
7	20	16.5	1.9	1.7	-9.9	37.0
7	24	15	1.9	1.7	-8.6	34.9
7	27	14	1.9	1.7	-7.8	33.4
14	4	34	3.0	1.7	24.7	47.1
14	6	25	3.1	1.7	17.1	43.6
14	8	19	4.0	1.7	-12.0	39.2
14	10	16	4.1	1.7	-9.4	36.4
14	12	14.5	4.2	1.7	-8.2	34.2
14	14	13.3	4.2	1.7	-7.1	32.2
14	17	12	4.3	1.7	-6.0	29.6
14	20	11	4.7	1.7	-5.0	26.7
14	24	10.2	4.7	1.7	-4.3	24.3

The Quandary of Continued Deflation

Like the exponential function, the numerical solution predicts that deflation should have nearly ended several months after the eruption began, which does not agree with the geodetic data. Factors that might keep both the extrusion rate and the deflation rate more or less constant include (1) decreasing magma viscosity or friction coefficient with time; (2) increasing conduit diameter with time; and (or) (3) a nonlinear relation between extrusion rate and friction coefficient, similar to the logarithmic relation.

As of March 2006 there have been no obvious temporal changes in petrology or fault-gouge characteristics that might reflect changes in viscosity or friction coefficient (Pallister and others, this volume, chap. 30). Changes in conduit diameter cannot, however, be dismissed (our field observations are insufficient), nor can the possibility that conduit enlargement alone, in the absence of recharge, is responsible for sustained extrusion rates. Figure 11*B* shows a theoretical deflation curve calculated in the absence of recharge by solving equation 5 for reservoir volume loss dV_C using $(\rho_M/\rho_e)=1$, κ_M=3.3×10⁻¹⁰ Pa⁻¹ (adjusted to optimize fit), κ_C=7×10⁻¹¹ Pa⁻¹, and the erupted volume dV_e (= V_e) obtained from the best-fit curve, equation 10, through modified hot-rock data (fig. 11*A*). The theoretical curve matches the long-term linear trend quite well but underestimates the deflation in the first few months of the eruption. The rapid early deflation implies that the volume removed from the reservoir per unit erupted volume was initially high but then decreased with time, a characteristic that could be explained by either increasing recharge or by increasing magma compressibility with time. Starting with a slightly lower compressibility (3.2×10⁻¹⁰ Pa⁻¹) that increases to 4.1×10⁻¹⁰ Pa⁻¹ over the course of the eruption (fig. 11*B*, red dashed line) does not appear to reconcile the difference.

The pressure change Δp is related to the volume shrinkage dV_C by $\Delta p = dV_C/(V_C\kappa_C)$. For V_C = 15 km³, for example, the deflation in figure 11*B* represents a pressure drop of about 15–16 MPa, requiring an initial overpressure above this value to sustain the eruption for the observed time period. The conduit radius R that could give the instantaneous growth rate in figure 11*A* with the pressure in figure 11*B* can be calculated from equation 17 by substituting $p_0^{ex}+\Delta p-\rho_e gH_3$ for $(p-\rho gH)$, $\dot{V}_e^{t=0}$ for $(\pi R_0^4 p_0^{ex}/8\eta H)$, and $\rho_e\dot{V}_e$ for dM_e/dt:

$$R = R_0\left[\left(\frac{\dot{V}_e}{\dot{V}_e^{t=0}}\right)\left(\frac{p_0^{ex}}{p_0^{ex}+\Delta p-\rho_e gH_3}\right)\right]^{1/4}. \qquad (34)$$

Here, R_0 is the initial conduit radius. Calculating the change in R with time requires values of V_C and p_0^{ex} to be assumed in advance. For V_C = 15 km³ and p_0^{ex} = 30 MPa, the observed extrusion history can be produced by a roughly 15-percent decrease in conduit radius in the first few months of the eruption, followed by widening at a slow but accelerating rate (fig. 11*C*). As the overpressure approaches zero, the conduit radius must approach infinity to keep the extrusion rate constant (for example, the line for p_0^{ex} = 15 MPa in fig. 11*C*).

These results suggest that the changes in conduit radius required to maintain the observed eruption rate without recharge are less than a few tens of percent and thus probably too small to be easily detected by observed variations in lithic content of the lava or ratios in linear to volumetric extrusion rate. The changes shown in figure 11, however, involve a seemingly unrealistic shrinkage in radius early in the eruption, when effusion rates are high, followed by enlargement at an accelerating rate when effusion rates are low. We cannot dismiss conduit-radius changes in the absence of recharge, but we are inclined to consider them less likely than recharge-driven flow. Future developments may help distinguish these possibilities: If extrusion is sustained by conduit widening without recharge, geodetic deflation will continue and the eruption will eventually wane, then stop. If it is sustained by recharge, geodetic deflation will soon stabilize, but the eruption may continue for years and end gradually as the deeper magma source is depleted.

Finally, one explanation for continued deflation may lie in the results of the numerical models. Model runs using

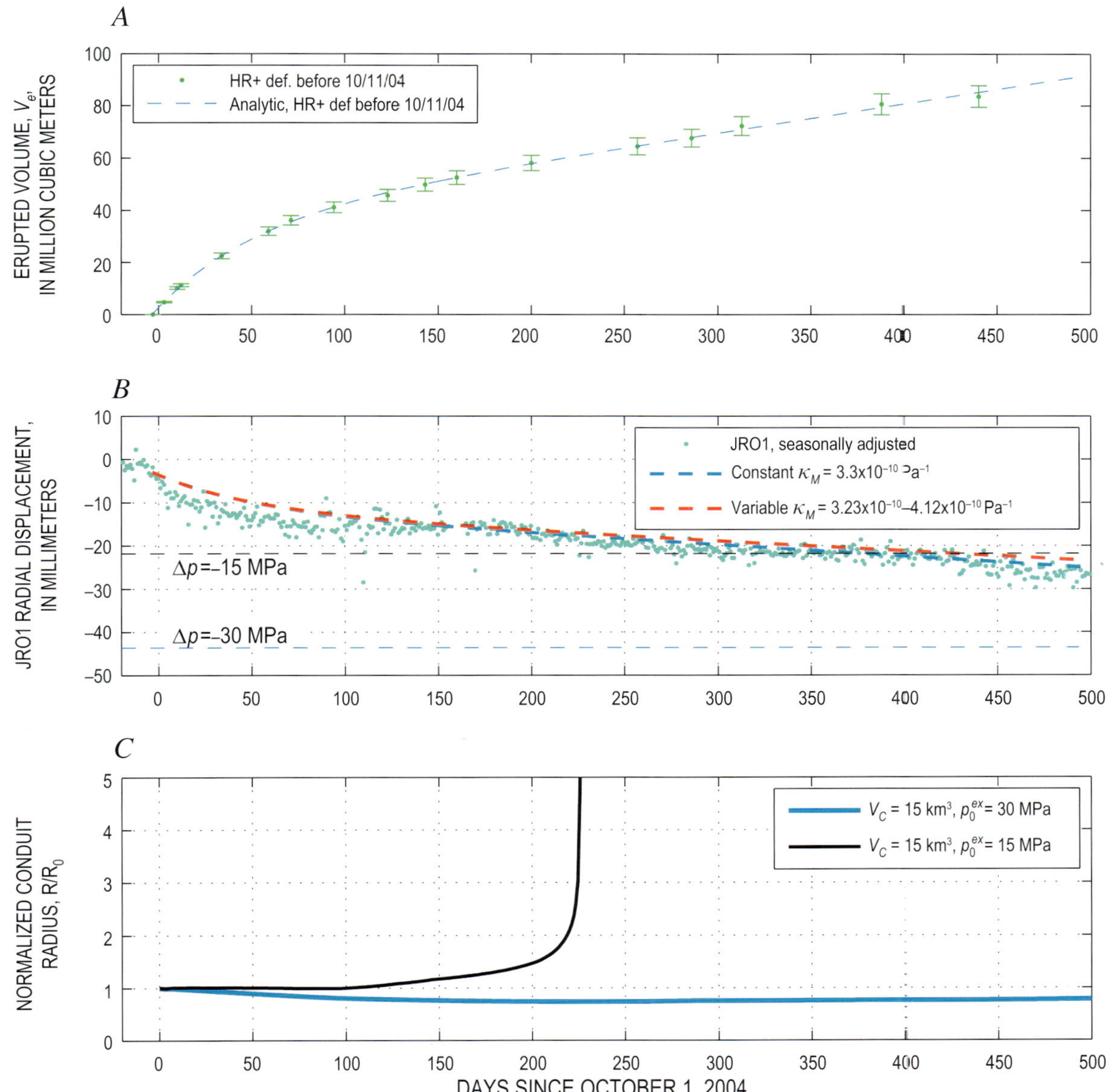

Figure 11. Modeled relation between extruded volume, magma pressure and overpressure, and conduit radius at Mount St. Helens. *A*, Erupted volume, V_e. Data points with error bars represent hot-rock volume of the lava dome plus volume of cold rock uplifted before October 11, 2004 (compare fig. 10*A*). Error bars are ±5 percent as in figures 2 and 10. *B*, Station JRO1 radial displacements (dots) compared with the displacements predicted at this point for deflation of a 15-km³ ellipsoidal magma body at 6–10 km depth with $\kappa_C = 7\times10^{-11}$ Pa^{-1} and (1) a constant $\kappa_M = 3.3\times10^{-10}$ (blue dashed line) or (2) κ_M increasing from 3.2×10^{-10} to 4.2×10^{-10} as pressure drops by 15 MPa (dashed red line). Negative displacements are radially inward. *C*, Conduit radius, *R*, required to maintain extrusion rate illustrated in figure 11*A*, normalized to the initial conduit radius, R_0. Magma pressure is inferred from deflation curve, assuming an initial overpressure of 30 MPa (blue line) or 15 MPa (black line). Method of calculating pressure change is explained in text.

a small magma body show a rapid deflation curve at JRO1 followed by stabilization as the recharge rate approaches the eruption rate. Runs that involve larger magma bodies show continued long-term deflation but cannot match the rapid deflation seen in the first several weeks of the eruption. The blue solid line in figure 10*B* represents an intermediate reservoir size that shows a little deflation still after 500 days of eruption but not enough to match the data. The steep deflation at short times and the long-term continued deflation at longer times may suggest that decompression initiated within a relatively small body of eruptible magma but expanded with time to a much larger volume that may include cooler or more crystalline, partially solidified material.

Discussion and Conclusions

Within the range of uncertainty, the above results are consistent with the view that the magma reservoir at Mount St. Helens is several to perhaps a few tens of cubic kilometers in size, that the pressure drop in the magma system is several to a few tens of megapascals, and that the reservoir contains less than a few volume percent exsolved gas at the source depth of 8–9 km. Numerous uncertainties prevent us from more accurate estimates of the size, overpressure, volatile content, and degree of recharge of the Mount St. Helens magma reservoir. The greatest limitation is the uncertainty in reservoir compressibility κ_C, which appears to be at least a few times greater over the period of this eruption than during the very brief time scale of seismic wave disturbance. Our conclusion that κ_C is only a few to several times less than magma compressibility contrasts with expectations (for example, Huppert and Woods, 2002) that κ_M would be much greater than κ_C in deep, equant, volatile-saturated magma bodies. The similarity between κ_M and κ_C during this eruption likely reflects both the lower rigidity of the Earth over long time scales and the low exsolved volatile content of the magma.

The observation that geodetic deflation volume dV_C is less than erupted volume V_e is an expected consequence of the finite compressibility of magma, and need not imply recharge. We expect dV_C to be less than V_e during nearly all eruptions. Conversely, in a reservoir that is intruded before an eruption, the injection volume V_i should be significantly greater than the resulting change in reservoir volume dV_C. Deep, stiff reservoirs containing volatile-rich magmas are likely to show the lowest ratios of dV_C/V_i, raising the question of whether preeruptive magma injection into a volatile-rich reservoir might fail to generate a detectable geodetic signal.

Finally, like Huppert and Woods (2002) and Woods and Huppert (2003), we find that the compressibility of magma, which is related to exsolved volatile content, has an overriding influence on the duration and final volume of effusive eruptions. Our study, however, advances those works by showing that, when exsolution of both H_2O and CO_2 is considered, there is little or no discontinuity in compressibility at the saturation pressure, and hence no dramatic change in eruptive style or the rate of decrease in eruptive activity when the saturation pressure is reached in a magma reservoir.

The idealizations in this paper are necessary for developing a simple model. In testing our assumptions, we acknowledge that many such idealizations are unrealistic. Our simple balloon-and-soda-straw cartoon of a magma reservoir may not even approximately resemble the complex of partially molten bodies that could make up the real magma system. Given this complexity, the question of whether the magma body is being recharged may be primarily a question of where one draws boundaries. We nevertheless hope that these simple models offer some insight.

Acknowledgments

Discussion of the form of the growth curve and its relation to physical processes was initiated by Terry Gerlach and Dan Dzurisin, to whom we owe many thanks. Mike Lisowski played a crucial role gathering deformation data used in this study and was offered coauthorship but politely declined. Dan Dzurisin and Peter Cervelli reviewed this manuscript and offered several improvements. Insights into various aspects of this study were provided by John Pallister, Carl Thornber, Richard Iverson, Shaul Hurwitz, Emily Brodsky, and Seth Moran.

References Cited

Barker, S.E., and Malone, S.D., 1991, Magmatic system geometry at Mount St. Helens modeled from the stress field associated with posteruptive earthquakes: Journal of Geophysical Research, v. 96, no. B7, p. 11883–11894, doi:10.1029/91JB00430.

Blackwell, D.D., Steele, J.L., Kelley, S.A., and Korosec, M.A., 1990, Heat flow in the State of Washington and thermal conditions in the Cascade Range: Journal of Geophysical Research, v. 95, no. B12, p. 19495–19516.

Blanpied, M.L., Marone, C.J., Lockner, D.A., Byerlee, J.D., and King, D.P., 1998, Quantitative measure of the variation in fault rheology due to fluid-rock interactions: Journal of Geophysical Research, v. 103, no. B5, p. 9691–9712.

Blundy, J., and Cashman, K., 2001, Ascent-driven crystallisation of dacite magmas at Mount St. Helens, 1980–1986: Contributions to Mineralogy and Petrology, v. 140, no. 6, p. 631–650, doi:10.1007/s004100000219.

Bonaccorso, A., and Davis, P.M., 1999, Models of ground deformation from vertical volcanic conduits with application to eruptions of Mount St. Helens and Mount Etna: Journal of Geophysical Research, v. 104, no. B5, p. 10531–10542.

Brace, W.F., and Kohlstedt, D.L., 1980, Limits on lithospheric stress imposed by laboratory experiments: Journal of Geophysical Research, v. 85, no. B11, p. 6248–6252.

Byerlee, J.D., 1978, Friction of rocks: Pure and Applied Geophysics, v. 116, p. 615–626.

Byerlee, J.D., and Summers, R., 1976, A note on the effect of fault gouge thickness on fault stability [abs.]: International Journal of Rock Mechanics and Mining Sciences and Geomechanics Abstracts, v. 13, p. 35–36.

Cashman, K.V., and Taggart, J.E., 1983, Petrologic monitoring of 1981 and 1982 eruptive products from Mount St. Helens: Science, v. 221, no. 4618, p. 1385–1387.

Cashman, K.V., Thornber, C.R., and Pallister, J.S., 2008, From dome to dust; shallow crystallization and fragmentation of conduit magma during the 2004–2006 dome extrusion of Mount St. Helens, Washington, chap. 19 *of* Sherrod, D.R., Scott, W.E., and Stauffer, P.H., eds., A volcano rekindled; the renewed eruption of Mount St. Helens, 2004–2006: U.S. Geological Survey Professional Paper 1750 (this volume).

Chester, F.M., 1994, Effects of temperature on friction; constitutive equations and experiments with quartz gouge: Journal of Geophysical Research, v. 99, no. B4, p. 7247–7261.

Clauser, C., and Huenges, E., 1995, Thermal conductivity of rocks and minerals, rock physics and phase relations, *in* A handbook of physical constants: Washington D.C., American Geophysical Union, p. 105–126.

Dieterich, J.H., 1979, Modeling of rock friction 1. Experimental results and constitutive equations: Journal of Geophysical Research, v. 84, no. B5, p. 2161–2168.

Dieterich, J.H., and Kilgore, B.D., 1996, Imaging surface contacts; power law contact distributions and contact stresses in quartz, calcite, glass and acrylic plastic: Tectonophysics, v. 256, p. 216–239.

Dzurisin, D., Lisowski, M., Poland, M.P., Sherrod, D.R., and LaHusen, R.G., 2008, Constraints and conundrums resulting from ground-deformation measurements made during the 2004–2005 dome-building eruption of Mount St. Helens, Washington, chap. 14 *of* Sherrod, D.R., Scott, W.E., and Stauffer, P.H., eds., A volcano rekindled; the renewed eruption of Mount St. Helens, 2004–2006: U.S. Geological Survey Professional Paper 1750 (this volume).

Elkins, L.T., and Grove, T.L., 1990, Ternary feldspar experiments and thermodynamic models: American Mineralogist, v. 75, p. 544–559.

Fournier, R.O., 1999, Hydrothermal processes related to movement of fluid from plastic into brittle rock in the magmatic-epithermal environment: Economic Geology, v. 94, no. 8, p. 1193–1211.

Gerlach, T.M., McGee, K.A., and Doukas, M.P., 2008, Emission rates of CO_2, SO_2, and H_2S, scrubbing, and preeruption excess volatiles at Mount St. Helens, 2004–2005, chap. 26 *of* Sherrod, D.R., Scott, W.E., and Stauffer, P.H., eds., A volcano rekindled; the renewed eruption of Mount St. Helens, 2004–2006: U.S. Geological Survey Professional Paper 1750 (this volume).

Ghiorso, M.S., and Sack, R.O., 1995, Chemical mass transfer in magmatic processes IV. A revised and internally consistent thermodynamic model for the interpolation and extrapolation of liquid-solid equilibria in magmatic systems at elevated temperatures and pressures: Contributions to Mineralogy and Petrology, v. 119, p. 197–212.

Heliker, C., 1995, Inclusions in the Mount St. Helens dacite erupted from 1980 through 1983: Journal of Volcanology and Geothermal Research, v. 66, nos. 1–3, p. 115–135, doi:10.1016/0377-0273(94)00074-Q.

Huppert, H.E., and Woods, A.W., 2002, The role of volatiles in magma chamber dynamics: Nature, v. 420, no. 6915, p. 493–495.

Iverson, R.M., Dzurisin, D., Gardner, C.A., Gerlach, T.M., LaHusen, R.G., Lisowski, M., Major, J.J., Malone, S.D., Messerich, J.A., Moran, S.C., Pallister, J.S., Qamar, A.I., Schilling, S.P., and Vallance, J.W., 2006, Dynamics of seismogenic volcanic extrusion at Mount St. Helens in 2004–05: Nature, v. 444, no. 7118, p. 439–443, doi:10.1038/nature05322.

Jaeger, J.C., and Cook, N.G.W., 1979, Fundamentals of rock mechanics (3d ed.): London, Chapman and Hall, 593 p.

Johnson, D.J., Sigmundsson, F., and Delaney, P.T., 2000, Comment on "Volume of magma accumulation or withdrawal estimated from surface uplift or subsidence, with application to the 1960 collapse of Kilauea volcano" by P.T. Delaney and D.F McTigue: Bulletin of Volcanology, v. 61, p. 491–493.

Linker, M.F., and Dieterich, J.H., 1992, Effects of variable normal stress on rock friction; observations and constitutive equations: Journal of Geophysical Research, v. 97, p. 4923–4940.

Lisowski, M., Dzurisin, D., Denlinger, R.P., and Iwatsubo, E.Y., 2008, Analysis of GPS-measured deformation associated with the 2004–2006 dome-building eruption of Mount St. Helens, Washington, chap. 15 *of* Sherrod, D.R., Scott, W.E., and Stauffer, P.H., eds., A volcano rekindled; the renewed eruption of Mount St. Helens, 2004–2006: U.S. Geological Survey Professional Paper 1750 (this volume).

Marone, C., and Scholz, C.H., 1988, The depth of seismic faulting and the upper transition from stable to unstable slip regimes: Geophysical Research Letters, v. 15, no. 6, p. 621–624.

Marone, C., Raleigh, C.B., and Scholz, C.H., 1990, Frictional behavior and constitutive modeling of simulated fault gouge: Journal of Geophysical Research, v. 95, no. B5, p. 7007–7025.

Marone, C.J., Scholz, C.H., and Bilham, R., 1991, On the mechanics of earthquake afterslip: Journal of Geophysical Research, v. 96, p. 8441–8452.

Mastin, L.G., 2002, Insights into volcanic conduit flow from an open-source numerical model: Geochemistry, Geophysics, Geosystems, v. 3, no. 7, 18p., doi:10.1029/2001GC000192.

McTigue, D.F., 1987, Elastic stress and deformation near a finite spherical magma body; resolution of the point source paradox: Journal of Geophysical Research, v. 92, no. B12, p. 12931–12940.

Mironer, A., 1979, Engineering fluid mechanics: New York, McGraw-Hill, 592 p.

Moore, P.L., Iverson, N.R., and Iverson, R.M., 2008, Frictional properties of the Mount St. Helens gouge, chap. 20 *of* Sherrod, D.R., Scott, W.E., and Stauffer, P.H., eds., A volcano rekindled; the renewed eruption of Mount St. Helens, 2004–2006: U.S. Geological Survey Professional Paper 1750 (this volume).

Musumeci, C., Gresta, S., and Malone, S.D., 2002, Magma system recharge of Mount St. Helens from precise relative hypocenter location of microearthquakes: Journal of Geophysical Research, v. 107, no. B10, 2264, p. ESE 16-1–ESE 16-9, doi:10.1029/2001JB000629.

Newhall, C.G., and Melson, W.G., 1983, Explosive activity associated with the growth of volcanic domes: Journal of Volcanology and Geothermal Research, v. 17, p. 111–131.

Newman, A.V., Dixon, T.H., Ofoegbu, G.I., and Dixon, J.E., 2001, Geodetic and seismic constraints on recent activity at Long Valley Caldera, California; evidence for viscoelastic rheology: Journal of Volcanology and Geothermal Research, v. 105, no. 3, p. 183–206.

Newman, A.V., Dixon, T.H., and Gourmelen, N., 2006, A four-dimensional viscoelastic deformation model for Long Valley Caldera, California, between 1995 and 2000: Journal of Volcanology and Geothermal Research, v. 150, nos. 1–3, p. doi:10.1016/j.jvolgeores.2005.1007.1017.

Newman, S., and Lowenstern, J.B., 2002, VolatileCalc; a silicate melt-H_2O-CO_2 solution model written in Visual Basic for Excel®: Computers and Geosciences, v. 28, no. 5, p. 597–604, doi:10.1016/S0098-3004(01)00081-4.

Pallister, J.S., Thornber, C.R., Cashman, K.V., Clynne, M.A., Lowers, H.A., Mandeville, C.W., Brownfield, I.K., and Meeker, G.P., 2008, Petrology of the 2004–2006 Mount St. Helens lava dome—implications for magmatic plumbing and eruption triggering, chap. 30 *of* Sherrod, D.R., Scott, W.E., and Stauffer, P.H., eds., A volcano rekindled; the renewed eruption of Mount St. Helens, 2004–2006: U.S. Geological Survey Professional Paper 1750 (this volume).

Poland, M.P., and Lu, Z., 2008, Radar interferometry observations of surface displacements during pre- and coeruptive periods at Mount St. Helens, Washington, 1992–2005: chap. 18 *of* Sherrod, D.R., Scott, W.E., and Stauffer, P.H., eds., A volcano rekindled; the renewed eruption of Mount St. Helens, 2004–2006: U.S. Geological Survey Professional Paper 1750 (this volume).

Pollard, D.D., and Fletcher, D.F., 2005, Fundamentals of structural geology: Cambridge, Cambridge University Press, 500 p.

Power, W.L., Tullis, T.E., and Weeks, J.D., 1988, Roughness and wear during brittle faulting: Journal of Geophysical Research, v. 93, no. B12, p. 15268–15278.

Reinen, L.A., Weeks, J.D., and Tullis, T.E., 1994, The frictional behavior of lizardite and antigorite serpentinites; experiments, constitutive models, and implications for natural faults: Pure and Applied Geophysics, v. 143, p. 317–358.

Robertson, E.C., 1983, Relationship of fault displacement to gouge and breccia thickness: Mining Engineering, v. 35, p. 1426–1432.

Rubin, A.M., 1990, A comparison of rift-zone tectonics in Iceland and Hawaii: Bulletin of Volcanology, v. 52, p. 302–319.

Ruina, A., 1983, Slip instability and state variable friction laws: Journal of Geophysical Research, v. 88, no. B12, p. 10359–10370.

Rutherford, M.J., and Devine, J.D., 1988, The May 18, 1980, eruption of Mount St. Helens; 3, Stability and chemistry of amphibole in the magma chamber: Journal of Geophysical Research, v. 93, no. B10, p. 11949–11959.

Rutherford, M.J., and Devine, J.D., III, 2008, Magmatic conditions and processes in the storage zone of the 2004–2006 Mount St. Helens dacite, chap. 31 *of* Sherrod, D.R., Scott, W.E., and Stauffer, P.H., eds., A volcano rekindled; the renewed eruption of Mount St. Helens, 2004–2006: U.S. Geological Survey Professional Paper 1750 (this volume).

Rutherford, M.J., Sigurdsson, H., Carey, S., and Davis, A., 1985, The May 18, 1980, eruption of Mount St. Helens; 1, Melt composition and experimental phase equilibria: Journal of Geophysical Research, v. 90, no. B4, p. 2929–2947.

Scandone, R., and Malone, S.D., 1985, Magma supply, magma discharge and readjustment of the feeding system of Mount St. Helens during 1980: Journal of Volcanology and Geothermal Research, v. 23, nos. 3–4, p. 239–262, doi:10.1016/0377-0273(85)90036-8.

Schaff, D.P., Beroza, G., and Shaw, B.E., 1999, Postseismic response of repeating aftershocks: Geophysical Research Letters, v. 25, p. 4559–4552.

Schilling, S.P., Thompson, R.A., Messerich, J.A., and Iwatsubo, E.Y., 2008, Use of digital aerophotogrammetry to determine rates of lava dome growth, Mount St. Helens, Washington, 2004–2005, chap. 8 *of* Sherrod, D.R., Scott,

W.E., and Stauffer, P.H., eds., A volcano rekindled; the renewed eruption of Mount St. Helens, 2004–2006: U.S. Geological Survey Professional Paper 1750 (this volume).

Scholz, C.H., 1998, Earthquakes and friction laws: Nature, v. 391, p. 37–42.

Stasiuk, M.V., Jaupart, C., and Sparks, R.S.J., 1993, On the variations of flow rate in non-explosive lava eruptions: Earth and Planetary Science Letters, v. 134, p. 505–516.

Tait, S., Jaupart, C., and Vergniolle, S., 1989, Pressure, gas content and eruption periodicity of a shallow, crystallising magma chamber: Earth and Planetary Science Letters, v. 92, p. 107–123.

Tiampo, K.F., Rundle, J.B., Fernandez, J., and Langbein, J.O., 2000, Spherical and ellipsoidal volcanic sources at Long Valley caldera, California, using a genetic algorithm inversion technique: Journal of Volcanology and Geothermal Research, v. 102, p. 189–206.

Turcotte, D.L., and Schubert, G., 2002, Geodynamics (2d ed.): Cambridge, Cambridge University Press, 456 p.

Wadge, G., 1981, The variation of magma discharge during basaltic eruptions: Journal of Volcanology and Geothermal Research, v. 11, p. 139–168.

Williams, D.L., Abrams, G., Finn, C., Dzurisin, D., Johnson, D.J., and Denlinger, R., 1987, Evidence from gravity data for an intrusive complex beneath Mount St Helens: Journal of Geophysical Research, v. 92, no. B10, p. 10207–10222.

Woods, A.W., and Huppert, H.E., 2003, On magma chamber evolution during slow effusive eruptions: Journal of Geophysical Research, v. 108, no. B8, 2403, p. doi:10.1029/2002JB002019.

Zoback, M.D., and Healy, J.H., 1984, Friction, faulting, and in situ stress: Annalen der Geophysik, v. 2, p. 689–698.

Appendix 1. Processes That Could Affect Reservoir Compressibility

The static shear modulus of large rock masses (kilometers in size) is generally known to be up to an order of magnitude less than that of laboratory-scale specimens (Pollard and Fletcher, 2005, p. 322). The reduction in shear modulus with increasing scale is generally attributed to the presence of fractures that can open or move (Rubin, 1990). In this paper we estimate host-rock shear modulus from the velocities of seismic waves whose wavelength is on the order of a kilometer and does not differ greatly from the dimensions of the rock mass under stress near the magma reservoir. On the other hand, seismic velocities are controlled by stress oscillations that act over a time scale of milliseconds, whereas eruption-associated stress changes evolve over a period of years. Over the longer time scale, subcritical crack growth, poroelasticity, and inelastic creep could deform rock and therefore reduce the shear modulus, G. Because the geodetic signal is measured at the surface, a low shear modulus at shallow depth could perhaps also affect the geodetic signal. These effects are considered below.

Crack growth and poroelasticity.—Crack growth may greatly reduce G at <1–2 km depth (Rubin, 1990), but at 6–12 km depth it is unclear whether cracks of any significant size exist. Near the hot reservoir, cracks are likely to anneal and seal off interstitial fluids (Fournier, 1999). Poroelastic effects theoretically have no effect on shear modulus, though they can decrease Poisson's ratio with time and change estimates of G if such estimates are based on the formula $G = \rho_R v_P^2(1-2\nu)/(2(1-\nu))$ (for example, Rubin, 1990). Poroelastic effects, however, change G by only a few tens of percent at most; at depths of 6–12 km, interstitial fluids are likely sparse and these effects even smaller.

Elastic inhomogeneity.—Figure 5 shows variations in G with depth estimated from the seismic-velocity profile and density data (explained in the figure caption). In the uppermost 1–2 km the estimated value of G may drop to about 11 GPa; however, at depths below 1–2 km the value of G remains above about 35 GPa. Because the surface displacements are affected by the elastic properties of all materials between the magma reservoir and the surface, the lower elastic moduli of near-surface materials must affect displacements to some degree, but the relation between reservoir stress drop and displacement should be primarily controlled by rock properties near the magma body. For this reason we consider that the effect of less stiff near-surface materials on G is likely to be less than about 20 percent.

High-temperature inelastic deformation near the magma body.—In long-lived magma systems, such as Long Valley in eastern California, viscoelastic creep may reduce by about two-thirds the pressure change required for a given volume change (Newman and others, 2001; Newman and others, 2006). However, the Mount St. Helens magma system is relatively young and surrounded by cooler rock that is gabbroic in composition (Heliker, 1995) and resistant to creep. Regional heat-flow studies suggest that the ambient temperature at 9–10 km depth in this region is about 350°C (Blackwell and others, 1990). If we assume the magma reservoir has existed at its present temperature for about 4,000 to 40,000 years, we can estimate the temperature profile around the magma reservoir by numerically integrating the following one-dimensional transient equation for conductive heat flow:

$$\frac{\partial T}{\partial t} = \frac{k_R}{\rho_R c_R r}\frac{\partial}{\partial r}\left(r\frac{\partial T}{\partial r}\right), \qquad (35)$$

where k_R and c_R are the thermal conductivity and specific heat, respectively, of the host rock, and r is the radial distance of a given point from the center of the magma body. Holding the temperature at the reservoir wall constant at 850°C and using $k_R = 2$ W/(m·K) (Clauser and Huenges, 1995) and $c_R = 1{,}300$ J/

(kg•K), we obtain the temperature profiles from a 1-km-radius magma body illustrated in figure 12*A*.

If decompression is rapid, the host rock will deform elastically, then relax with time as viscous creep reduces wall stress. The equations for the radial (σ_{rr}) and normal ($\sigma_{\theta\theta}$) stresses near a cylindrical body in an infinite linear elastic medium under plane-strain conditions are (Jaeger and Cook, 1979, p. 251):

$$\sigma_{rr} = \sigma_1\left(1-\frac{R^2}{r^2}\right)+p\left(\frac{R^2}{r^2}\right) , \quad (36)$$

$$\sigma_{\theta\theta} = \sigma_1\left(1+\frac{R^2}{r^2}\right)-p\left(\frac{R^2}{r^2}\right) , \quad (37)$$

where σ_1 is the far-field normal stress (assumed equal in all directions perpendicular to the cylinder axis), p is the internal pressure in the reservoir, and R is the cylinder radius. For $\sigma_1=240$ MPa and $p=210$ MPa, values of σ_{rr} and $\sigma_{\theta\theta}$ are plotted in figure 12*B*. Note that at the reservoir wall, the difference $\sigma_{\theta\theta}-\sigma_{rr}$ is equal to twice (σ_1-p).

The dominant form of stress relaxation is likely to be dislocation creep (Turcotte and Schubert, 2002), which involves a power-law dependence between normal strain rate ($\dot{\varepsilon}_{\theta\theta}$ or $\dot{\varepsilon}_{rr}$) and normal-stress difference ($\sigma_{\theta\theta}-\sigma_{rr}$) (Turcotte and Schubert, 2002, eq. 7-187):

$$\dot{\varepsilon}_{rr} = -\dot{\varepsilon}_{\theta\theta} = C_1\left(\sigma_{\theta\theta}-\sigma_{rr}\right)^n e^{-E_a/R_gT} , \quad (38)$$

where C_1, n, and E_a are fitting parameters, R_g is the gas constant, and T is temperature (in Kelvin). We use $C_1=520$ MPa^{-n}/s, $n=3$, and $E_a=356$ kJ/mol, which are appropriate for diabase (Turcotte and Schubert, 2002, table 7-4). The power-law dependence implies that viscosity is not constant at a given temperature; however, we can estimate a rough average viscosity from the relation:

$$\eta_{eff} \approx \frac{\left(\sigma_{\theta\theta}-\sigma_{rr}\right)}{\dot{\varepsilon}_{rr}} = \frac{e^{-E_a/RT}}{C_1\left(\sigma_{\theta\theta}-\sigma_{rr}\right)^{n-1}} . \quad (39)$$

Using this viscosity and Young's modulus $E = \rho\upsilon_P^2(1-2\nu)(1+\nu)/(1-\nu) = 1\times10^{11}$ Pa, (where $\nu=0.25$, $\upsilon_P=6.6$ km/s and $\rho=2{,}700$ kg/m^3), the viscous relaxation time τ_η is:

$$\tau_\eta = \frac{\eta_{eff}}{E} . \quad (40)$$

Rocks having $\eta_{eff}<\sim5\times10^{18}$ Pa·s will relax in less time than the 1.5-year duration of the eruption to date (early 2006). For a magma body that has existed for about 4,000–40,000 years, rocks within ~110–250 m of the reservoir wall will relax within this time period. If these rocks are considered part of the mechanical magma reservoir, its effective volume would be about 20 percent to 50 percent greater than the volume of magma alone. By comparison, no host rock was hot enough to relax during the 24-hour period following the Mount St. Helens eruptions of May and June 1980 (fig. 12*C*). Thus the aseismic body identified by Scandone and Malone (1985) could be as much as a few hundred meters smaller in diameter than the mechanical magma body that is deforming during the current eruption.

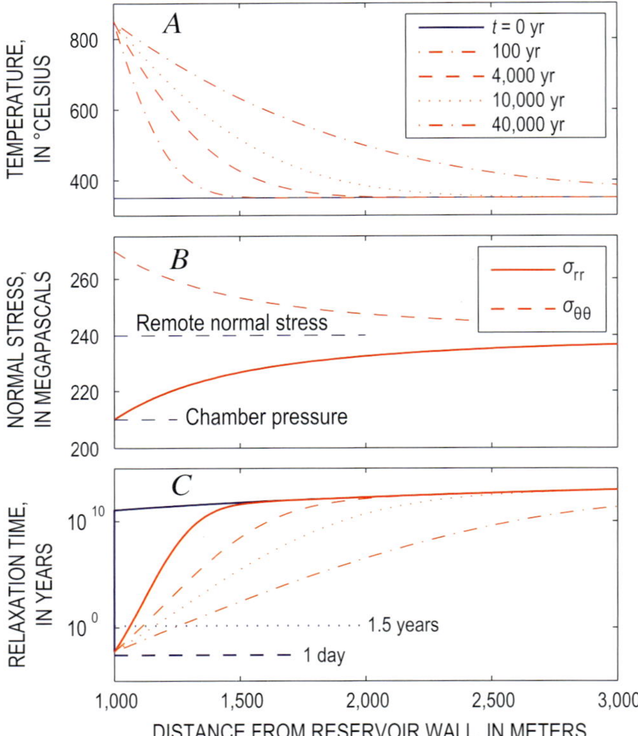

Figure 12. Response of a 1-km-radius magma body through time, as a function of distance from reservoir walls. *A*, Temperature over increasing time periods since emplacement of the magma body. Temperatures were calculated by integrating equation 35 with time. *B*, Circumferential ($\sigma_{\theta\theta}$) and radial (σ_{rr}) normal stresses versus radial distance from the reservoir wall, calculated assuming elastic deformation at short time periods following a rapid pressure change in the magma body. *C*, Viscous relaxation time versus distance for hot rock. The solid blue curve shows relaxation time versus distance assuming the host rock has a uniform temperature of 350°C. Red curves give relaxation time assuming the host-rock temperature varies with distance from the reservoir wall as illustrated by corresponding curves in panel *A*.

Appendix 2. Derivation of the Exponential Equation

Derivation of the exponential relation involves differentiating equation 11:

$$\frac{dp}{dt} = -C\left(\frac{dM_e}{dt}-Q_i\right) \quad (41)$$

and substituting equation 12 into this equation to give:

$$\frac{dp}{dt} = BC + CQ_i - ACp \ . \qquad (42)$$

Reversing the denominator in the left-hand term with the right-hand side of the equation and integrating gives:

$$-\frac{1}{AC}\ln\left(BC + CQ_i - ACp\right) + C_2 = t \ , \qquad (43)$$

where C_2 is the constant of integration. We find a value for C_2 by noting that, at $t=0$, $p=p_0$; hence

$$-\frac{1}{AC}\ln\left[\frac{BC + CQ_i - ACp}{BC + CQ_i - ACp_0}\right] =$$

$$-\frac{1}{AC}\ln\left[1 + \frac{AC\left(p_0 - p\right)}{BC + CQ_l - ACp_0}\right] = t \ . \qquad (44)$$

Further rearrangement leads to:

$$p = p_0 - \left(p_0 - \frac{B + Q_i}{A}\right)\left(1 - e^{-ACt}\right) . \qquad (45)$$

This equation can be substituted into equation 12 to give:

$$\begin{aligned}\frac{dM_e}{dt} &= Ap_0 + \left(B + Q_i - Ap_0\right)\left(1 - e^{-ACt}\right) - B \\ &= Q_i - \left(B + Q_i - Ap_0\right)e^{-ACt} \ ,\end{aligned} \qquad (46)$$

which can be integrated to give:

$$M_e = Qt + \frac{B + Q_i - Ap_0}{AC}e^{-ACt} + C_2 \ , \qquad (47)$$

where C_2 is a constant of integration, which can be evaluated by noting that, at $t=0$, $M_e=0$. After evaluating C_2, we get:

$$M_e = \frac{\left(Ap_0 - B\right) - Q_i}{AC}\left(1 - e^{-ACt}\right) + Q_i t \ . \qquad (48)$$

This equation can be expressed in eruptive volume (V_e) by dividing by lava density ρ_e:

$$V_e = \frac{1}{\rho_e}\frac{\left(Ap_0 - B\right) - Q_i}{AC}\left(1 - e^{-ACt}\right) + \frac{Q_i}{\rho_e}t \ . \qquad (49)$$

Appendix 3. The Exponential Equation for "Greased Plug" Flow

The assumption of Newtonian flow implies that the flow profile in the conduit is parabolic. Given the high crystal content of the magma, a more realistic scenario may be that the magma in the center of the conduit moves upward as a solid plug and that shear is concentrated along the conduit margins (fig. 8*B*). If the material in the shear acts in a Newtonian manner, a force balance leads to the following equation:

$$\pi R^2 p - \rho g \pi R^2 H - \frac{2H\eta}{\rho R \Delta r}\frac{dM_e}{dt} = 0 \ , \qquad (50)$$

where Δr is the thickness of the shear zone and ρ is the magma density in the conduit. The first term is the upward force at the base of the conduit, the second is the weight of the magma plug, and the third is the viscous force resisting upward flow. The equation can be rearranged as:

$$\frac{dM_e}{dt} = \frac{\rho \pi R^3 \Delta r}{2\eta H}\left(p - \rho g H\right) . \qquad (51)$$

In this case, the terms A and B in equation 12 have the value $A = \rho\pi R^3\Delta r/(8\eta H)$ and $B = \pi R^3\Delta r\rho^2 g/(8\eta)$. Substitution of these terms into equations 14 and 15 leads to expressions for a and b that are identical to equations 18 and 20; hence the constraints on the product $V_C(p_0 - \rho_m gH)$ are exactly the same for greased-plug flow as for Newtonian flow.

Appendix 4. Exponential Equation for Newtonian Flow Capped by a Frictional Plug with Constant Frictional Properties

The presence of fault gouge along the dome surface at Mount St. Helens suggests that, over some distance near the surface, magma moves upward as a solid plug with frictional sliding along its margins (fig. 8*D*). Assuming that flow below this plug is Newtonian, the equation for mass flux is:

$$\frac{dM_e}{dt} = \frac{\rho \pi R^4}{8\eta H_1}\left(\left(p - p_1\right) - \rho g H_1\right) , \qquad (52)$$

where H_l is the length of conduit over which flow is Newtonian and p_1 is the pressure at the base of the frictional plug (fig. 8*C*). That pressure is a function of both plug weight and friction. We assume that the shear stress along the plug margin must exceed the normal stress (σ_n) times a coefficient of friction (μ), which is assumed to be constant:

$$\tau \geq \mu\sigma_n \ . \qquad (53)$$

If the plug is cylindrical, vertical, of the same radius (R) as the conduit below, and of length H_2, the pressure (p_l) at the base of an upward-moving plug must exceed the sum of the plug weight and the frictional resistance:

$$p_1 \geq \rho g H_2 + \frac{2\mu\bar{\sigma}_n H_2}{R} \ . \qquad (54)$$

In this case, $\bar{\sigma}_n$ represents the mean normal stress on the conduit walls over the length of the plug. In solid rock, the horizontal normal stress could vary greatly even at shallow depth, depending on the state of gas pressure and on geometric factors. On the other hand, at Mount St. Helens, the crater floor is composed primarily of unconsolidated fallback from the 1980 eruptions. If we take this material to be cohesionless, faults of favorable orientation will form when the ratio of effective normal to shear stress on any potential fault plane exceeds that allowed by the coefficient of friction of the material (μ_h). Thus the ratio of most compressive (σ_1) to least compressive (σ_3) normal principal stress at any depth is limited to (Brace and Kohlstedt, 1980; Zoback and Healy, 1984):

$$\frac{\sigma_1 - p_p}{\sigma_3 - p_p} \le \left[\mu_h + \left(\mu_h^2 + 1\right)^{1/2}\right]^2 , \quad (55)$$

where p_p is the pore pressure in the host rock. For μ_h=0.6 and p_p ranging from 0 to σ_3, σ_1/σ_3 ranges from 1 to ~3. For this reason, we consider the normal stress on the conduit wall to be one-third to three times the vertical stress, and express the normal stress as the vertical stress times a constant γ of order 1. If the frictional plug extends from the surface to a depth H_2, the mean normal stress on the plug wall is $\overline{\sigma}_n=\gamma\overline{\rho}gH_2/2$. We also assume that $\mu \cong 0.5$; these simplifications allow us to rewrite equation 54 as:

$$p_1 \approx \rho g H_2 \left(1 + \gamma \frac{H_2}{R}\right) . \quad (56)$$

Inserting this value into equation 52 and noting that H_1+H_2=H, we have:

$$\frac{dV_e}{dt} = \frac{1}{\rho_e}\frac{\rho\pi R^4}{8\eta H_1}\left(p - \overline{\rho} g\left(H + \gamma\frac{H_2}{R}\right)\right) . \quad (57)$$

Hence A=$\rho_e\pi R^4/(8\eta H_1)$ and B=$\pi R^4 \rho_e{}^2 g(H+\gamma H_2/R)/(8\eta H_1)$. These terms lead to the following values of a and b:

$$a = \frac{(dV_e/dt)_{t=0} - (dV_e/dt)_{t\to\infty}}{\frac{\rho_M}{\rho_e}\left(\frac{dV_e}{dt}\right)_{t=0} \frac{K_M}{V_C\left(p_0 - \overline{\rho} g\left(H + \gamma\frac{H_2}{R}\right)\right)}}$$

$$\approx 0.8\frac{V_C\left(p_0 - \overline{\rho} g\left(H + \gamma\frac{H_2}{R}\right)\right)}{K_M} , \quad (58)$$

$$b = AC = \frac{\rho_e}{\rho_M}\left(\frac{dV_e}{dt}\right)_{t=0}\frac{K_M}{V_C\left(p_0 - \overline{\rho} g\left(H + \gamma\frac{H_2}{R}\right)\right)} . \quad (59)$$

Appendix 5. Exponential Equation for "Greased Plug" Flow Capped by a Frictional Plug with Constant Frictional Properties

As with the case above (appendix 4), this case involves modifying the greased plug equation to include a term for the pressure at the base of the frictional plug:

$$\frac{dM_e}{dt} = \frac{\rho\pi R^3 \Delta r}{2\eta H_1}\left((p - p_1) - \rho g H_1\right) . \quad (60)$$

Inserting the expression for p_1 in equation 56, we have:

$$\frac{dM_e}{dt} = \frac{\rho\pi R^3 \Delta r}{2\eta H_1}\left[p - \rho g\left(H + \gamma\frac{H_2}{R}\right)\right] . \quad (61)$$

Hence A=$\rho\pi R^3\Delta r/(2\eta H_1)$ and B=$\pi R^3\Delta r\rho^2 g(H+\gamma H_2/R)/(2\eta H_1)$.

Appendix 6. Derivation of Logarithmic Growth Curve

We envision a one-dimensional system consisting of a magma-filled reservoir and conduit system applying a pressure p to the base of an extruding solid rock plug of mass M_p and displacement rate $\dot{\delta}$ against gravity and frictional resistance to slip between the plug and the conduit wall. The rate of extrusion is controlled entirely by frictional resistance. That is, in this end-member model the magma below the plug has negligible viscosity.

Plug force balance.—Consider a "quasi-static" force balance for motion of a cylindrical plug (force resulting from acceleration is assumed to be negligible, $M\, d\dot{\delta}/dt \approx 0$). This quasi-static assumption is well justified by results of simulations in which inertia is considered; these "dynamic" simulations are not discussed in this appendix or elsewhere in this paper. The plug mass is assumed to be constant ($dM_p/dt \approx 0$), resulting from a balance between the rate of surface erosion of the plug and an equivalent subsurface accretion rate (for example, Iverson and others, 2006). The force balance per unit cross-sectional area in the conduit is:

$$p = \frac{M_p g}{\pi R^2} + \frac{2\tau H_2}{R} , \quad (62)$$

where p is the fluid pressure of the magma applied to the base of the plug, R is plug radius, H_2 is plug height, g is the acceleration due to gravity, and τ is the shear resistance of the interface between the plug and the conduit wall. Because the mass is assumed constant, R and H_2 are also constant.

Faults have a well-known second-order dependence of shear strength on slip rate $\dot{\delta}$ (Dieterich, 1979; Ruina, 1983) and related, somewhat complicated dependencies on accumulated slip and time of contact ("state" effects in rate and state friction) (for example, Linker and Dieterich, 1992). However, fault strength can be assumed to be purely slip-rate dependent when subject to sustained sliding if the ratio of asperity contact size to slip rate is small relative to the duration of sustained slip. Daily extrusion rates at Mount St. Helens from October 2004 to October 2005, converted to boundary slip rates, are in the range 70 to 7,000 μm/s, assuming that the plug has radius in the range of 25 to 75 m. Taking asperity contact size to be no more than 20 μm, as laboratory data on rock friction suggest (for example, Dieterich and Kilgore, 1996), its ratio to slip rate is 0.29 to 0.0029 seconds, meaning that time-dependent and slip-dependent changes and friction can be ignored for sustained slip durations longer than 0.5 to 1.0 seconds. Data on extruded volume are collected over intervals of a few weeks to a month. Therefore, we ignore complicated "state" effects on fault shear strength, and represent it by a simple slip-rate-dependent relation,

$$\tau = \tau_o + A_1 \sigma_n \ln \frac{\dot{\delta}}{\dot{\delta}_o} \ . \qquad (63)$$

Here σ_n is normal stress at the wall and A_1 is the rate dependence of fault strength. The constant τ_o is an arbitrary reference, the strength of the wall interface when the interface slip rate is $\dot{\delta}_o$.

For shear of thick fault-gouge layers (for example, Byerlee and Summers, 1976; Marone and others, 1990), for shear near the brittle-ductile transition (for example, Blanpied and others, 1998), and for near-surface faulting (Marone and Scholz, 1988), fault strength increases with slip rate (velocity strengthening, rate strengthening). Because all of these conditions are present at the plug wall at Mount St. Helens, we expect that fault slip is predominantly rate strengthening, and thus A_l in equation 63 is a small positive constant, typically between 0.001 and 0.03 (Marone and Scholz, 1988; Blanpied and others, 1998).

The volume of extruded material V_e is the product of the conduit cross-sectional area and the slip at the wall, and the extruded mass M_e is proportional to the extruded volume, so equation 63 is equivalently

$$\tau = \tau_o + A_1 \sigma_n \ln \frac{\dot{M}_e}{\dot{M}_o} \ , \qquad (64)$$

where notation for the mass rate of extrusion $dM_e/dt = \dot{M}_e$ is used. Combining equations 62 and 64 leads to a relation between magma pressure and the rate of plug extrusion

$$p = p_o + \alpha \ln \frac{\dot{M}_e}{\dot{M}_o} \ , \qquad (65)$$

where $\alpha = 2A_1\sigma_n H_2/R$ and $p_0 = 2\tau_0 H_2/R + Mg/\pi R^2$ are constants.

Magma mass balance.—During plug extrusion, the volume and driving pressure of the magma will change. To characterize these changes we consider, in turn, mass and volume balances for the magma. We define the magma mass $M_M = \rho_M V_M$ as the mass of magma in the magma reservoir and in the conduit below the frictional plug. The rate of change of mass can be expressed as

$$\frac{dM_M}{dt} = \rho_M \frac{dV_M}{dt} + V_M \frac{d\rho_M}{dt} \ , \qquad (66)$$

where ρ_M and V_M are magma density and volume, respectively. The mass change rate is also equivalent to the difference between the rate of mass input to the system Q_i and the rate out of the system Q_o, or

$$\frac{dM_M}{dt} = Q_i - Q_o \ . \qquad (67)$$

Because magma is not being extruded at the surface, Q_o represents the magma-volume loss due to magma freezing onto the plug (Iverson and others, 2006). Combining and rearranging so that fluid volume is the dependent variable yields

$$\frac{dV_M}{dt} = -\frac{V_M}{\rho_M}\frac{d\rho_M}{dt} + \frac{Q_i}{\rho_M} - \frac{Q_o}{\rho_M} \ . \qquad (68)$$

Reference to the magma density and its time derivative can be replaced by the pressure dependence through expanding the density derivative in equation 68:

$$\frac{d\rho_M}{dt} = \frac{\partial \rho_M}{\partial p}\frac{dp}{dt} \qquad (69)$$

and using the definition of the elastic compressibility of the magma $\kappa_M \equiv (1/\rho_M)(\partial\rho_M/\partial p)$. Making these substitutions into equation 68 leads to

$$\frac{dp}{dt} = -\frac{1}{V_M \kappa_M}\left(\frac{dV_M}{dt} + \frac{Q_o}{\rho_M} - \frac{Q_i}{\rho_M}\right) . \qquad (70)$$

Magma volume balance.—The volume of the magma system increases as the solid plug is extruded at a rate dV_e/dt, and decreases as magma freezes to the plug at the rate $-Q_o/\rho_M$. We also allow the walls of the magma system (reservoir and conduit) to respond elastically to changes in magma pressure using a representative reservoir and conduit compressibility κ_c so that the rate of elastic change of magma volume is $\kappa_c V_M \, dp/dt$. The combined rate of magma volume change is then

$$\frac{dV_M}{dt} = \frac{dV_e}{dt} - \frac{Q_o}{\rho_M} + \kappa_c V_M \frac{dp}{dt} \ . \qquad (71)$$

Combining equations 70 and 71 yields the relation between the mass rate of extrusion and the rate of change of the driving pressure

$$\frac{dp}{dt} = -\frac{\dot{M}_e/\rho_e - Q_i/\rho_M}{V_M(\kappa_C + \kappa_M)} \ , \qquad (72)$$

where the extruded mass is $M_e = V_e \rho_e$.

Solutions

Solutions for extrusion rate with time can be found by taking the time derivative of equation 65

$$\frac{dp}{dt} = \frac{\alpha}{\dot{M}_e}\frac{d\dot{M}_e}{dt} \qquad (73)$$

and equating to equation 71, resulting in the single differential equation

$$\frac{d\dot{M}_e}{dt} = -\frac{1}{\alpha V_M(\kappa_c + \kappa_M)}\left(\frac{\dot{M}_e^2}{\rho_e} - \frac{\dot{M}_e Q_i}{\rho_M}\right) . \qquad (74)$$

If the magma volume is large relative to the extruded volume, then V_M can be treated as a constant and equation 74 is separable. In the solution that follows we assume negligible density contrast between the magma and plug, $\rho_e = \rho_M$, as justified elsewhere in this paper.

No Recharge.—When Q_i=0 the extrusion rate is:

$$\dot{M}_e = \frac{Da\dot{M}_0}{t\dot{M}_0/\rho_e + aD} , \qquad (75)$$

where $\dot{M}_0$ is the extrusion rate at t=0, and $D = V_M(\kappa_C + \kappa_M)$. The cumulative mass of extruded material goes as

$$M_e = \rho_e a D \ln\left(1 + \frac{t\dot{M}_0}{\rho_e Da}\right) . \qquad (76)$$

This is the logarithmic form that well characterizes stress relaxation due to fault slip in some laboratory experiments (Reinen and others, 1994) and during earthquake afterslip (for example, Marone and others, 1991; Schaff and others, 1999).

With recharge.—If Q_i>0 the extrusion rate is

$$\dot{M}_e = \frac{Q_i}{1-\left(1-\frac{Q_i}{\dot{M}_0}\right)e^{\frac{-Q_i t}{\rho_e aD}}} . \qquad (77)$$

Note that equation 77 is for Q_i>0 and does not easily reduce to equation 75 for Q_i=0.

Cumulative extruded mass goes as

$$M_e = \rho_e aD\ln\left[1-\frac{\dot{M}_0}{Q_i}\left(1-e^{\frac{Q_i t}{\rho_e aD}}\right)\right] . \qquad (78)$$

This expression can be converted to erupted volume V_e by dividing by ρ_e.

USGS

Crisis Management

Mount St. Helens reawakened during the age of electronic media and an unprecedented public appetite for real-time information. The volcano's legacy of a large explosive eruption in the 1980s—still within the memory of many—added an element of interest and drama to the volcanic unrest of 2004. The effort to satisfy that interest and meet the information needs of both media and the public, while simultaneously providing prompt hazard information to Federal, State, and local government officials, forms a story of its own, told here in two chapters on crisis management.

The emergency-response discipline has, over the years, recognized the value of Joint Operations and Information Centers as useful management tools. These centers are implemented on a temporary basis in response to crisis situations—be it wildfire, severe weather, or volcano related—and are purposely terminated as a crisis winds down. Such centers operated for about two weeks early in the 2004 eruption to help coordinate interagency operations and maintain a consistent, centralized source of current information about volcanic activity, hazards, and area closures.

The case is made herein for the value of advance planning and teamwork during the actual crisis. Successes during the eruption that began in 2004 stem from the depth to which partner agencies with responsibilities for Mount St. Helens have built their collaborative networks during the past quarter century. State and county emergency response agencies, the Gifford Pinchot National Forest, and the U.S. Geological Survey have been working together in the business of volcano-hazard awareness and risk mitigation since the 1980s. The framework of cooperation and understanding among these groups has been longstanding, originated through rank-and-file employees and passed unbroken to successive managers.

View southwest on July 26, 2005, with spine 5 on the right and a partially distintegrated spine 4 in center. USGS photo by S.P. Schilling.

A Volcano Rekindled: The Renewed Eruption of Mount St. Helens, 2004–2006
Edited by David R. Sherrod, William E. Scott, and Peter H. Stauffer
U.S. Geological Survey Professional Paper 1750, 2008

Chapter 23

Managing Public and Media Response to a Reawakening Volcano: Lessons from the 2004 Eruptive Activity of Mount St. Helens

By Peter M. Frenzen[1] and Michael T. Matarrese[2]

Abstract

Volcanic eruptions and other infrequent, large-scale natural disturbances pose challenges and opportunities for public-land managers. In the days and weeks preceding an eruption, there can be considerable uncertainty surrounding the magnitude and areal extent of eruptive effects. At the same time, public and media interest in viewing developing events is high and concern for public safety on the part of local land managers and public safety officials is elevated. Land managers and collaborating Federal, State, and local officials must decide whether evacuations or restrictions to public access are necessary, the appropriate level of advance preparation, and how best to coordinate between overlapping jurisdictions. In the absence of a formal Federal or State emergency declaration, there is generally no identified source of supplemental funding for emergency-response preparation or managing extraordinary public and media response to developing events. In this chapter, we examine responses to escalating events that preceded the 2004 Mount St. Helens eruption and changes in public perception during the extended period of the largely nonexplosive, dome-building eruption that followed. Lessons learned include the importance of maintaining up-to-date emergency-response plans, cultivating close working relationships with collaborating agencies, and utilizing an organized response framework that incorporates clearly defined roles and responsibilities and effective communication strategies.

[1] Gifford Pinchot National Forest, Mount St. Helens National Volcanic Monument, 42218 NE Yale Bridge Rd, Amboy, WA 98601

[2] Gifford Pinchot National Forest, 10600 NE 51st Circle, Vancouver, WA 98682

Introduction

Mount St. Helens has undergone major changes in volcanic activity and land-management direction since 1979. Public perception has run the gamut from "tranquil, snow-covered mountain" to "notorious killer volcano" and, most recently, to "celebrated volcanic attraction and research laboratory." These transformations, together with the recent return to eruptive activity in 2004, provide useful insight into how infrequent events such as eruptions can influence people's perception of natural hazards. A person's perception of "normal volcanic behavior" changes as a function of degree of personal experience with a volcano and time since the last eruption. Managers need to be prepared to address a wide array of public perceptions and responses as they seek to provide for public access, education, and visitor safety in these dynamic landscapes. Our experience at Mount St. Helens suggests that, in the days and weeks leading up to a potentially explosive eruption, it is the management of people and their responses to perceived events that poses the greatest challenge.

Events Shape Human Responses

Since the 1980 eruption, management and education programs at Mount St. Helens have been developed largely in response to catastrophic eruptive events and the prevailing lens of public perception. Between 1980 and 1986, memory of the catastrophic eruption was intense, and agency efforts were largely centered on emergency response, restoration of damaged resources, and creation of the congressionally designated Mount St. Helens National Volcanic Monument (U.S. Department of Agriculture Forest Service, 1984). Response to volcanic activity was managed by an Emergency Coordination Center (ECC) at the Gifford Pinchot National Forest headquarters in Vancouver, Washington. After explosive eruptions ended in 1980, geologists focused their efforts on monitoring an intermittently growing lava dome and developing increasingly sophisticated methods of eruption forecasting. In the early 1990s, several years after the dome-building eruption ended, the general consensus among geologists and emergency managers was that eruptive activity that began in 1980 had run its course. The ECC was discontinued, and an emergency response plan was developed that formalized calldown procedures and the role of collaborating State and local authorities in the event of renewed activity (U.S. Department of Agriculture Forest Service, 1992). During the next decade, in the absence of volcanic activity, emphasis on volcano emergency planning was reduced and efforts focused on restoration of damaged roads and construction of visitor facilities in and around the Monument (U.S. Department of Agriculture Forest Service, 1984).

Following an 18-year period of quiet, the rapid acceleration of events leading up to the 2004 eruption surprised many geologists and emergency managers. Agency managers quickly shifted their focus from visitor education and protected-area stewardship to management of a fast-paced media event and renewal of multiagency working relationships and contingency closure zones around the volcano. Public reaction to renewed volcanic activity varied with people's memory of the catastrophic 1980 eruption and familiarity with volcanic processes. The level of concern of some residents and emergency responders was heightened by their memory of the largely unpredicted, devastating lateral blast and geologists' uncertainty expressed prior to the 1980 eruption about the expected degree of explosiveness and areal extent of the eruption.

Planning is Key to an Effective Response

Following the 1980 eruption, land managers implemented revised land-use allocations in the Monument, on the basis of existing hazards assessments and recent experience. Federal acquisition of private and leased lands effectively created an uninhabited 8-km (5-mi) buffer around the volcano. Facilities and roads were placed on ridges above the level of valleys draining the volcano outside of immediate hazard zones. Visitor Center roofs were designed to support the combined weight of projected ash fall and precipitation. This groundwork greatly reduced the potential hazard to life and property and simplified the situation faced by emergency managers in 2004. Federal ownership of adjacent lands also greatly facilitated the October 2, 2004, evacuation and identification of 5-, 8-, and 11-km radius (3, 5, and 7 mi) contingency closure zones around the volcano. Mount St. Helens offers a compelling example of the importance of incorporating volcanic-hazards mapping in land-use planning, road location, and facility design.

The rapid pace of public and media response to events leading up to the 2004 eruption provided a vivid reminder of the importance of an up-to-date emergency-response plan and clearly defined roles for collaborating local, State, and Federal responders (table 1). Within hours of the release of the initial U.S. Geological Survey (USGS) Information Statement on September 24, 2004, media flocked to the USGS Cascades Volcano Observatory (CVO). The Monument's visitor-center staff received hundreds of media phone calls, conducted numerous drop-in interviews, and saw increased visitation. Live media coverage of the eruption greatly accelerated the pace of events both for scientists monitoring the eruption and monument employees. Two days after the initial Information Statement, the USGS issued an Alert Level 1: Notice of Volcanic Unrest, the lowest of their three alert levels, triggering emergency calldown procedures and initiating a series of coordination meetings and consultations between Federal, State, and local officials. Prompt notification and consultation proved to be important, because in only nine days the volcano progressed from no activity (background levels of seismicity) to rapid deformation of the crater floor and steam and ash eruptions. The pace and intensity of media and public response and need for thoughtful coordination among Federal, State, and local partners proved to be a challenge for participating agencies. A key lesson learned during the 2004 eruption has been the importance of developing a shared understanding of interagency roles and responsibilities and of ensuring a timely flow of information at both the field and leadership levels.

Emergency Preparedness Requires a Long-Term Commitment

Before the onset of renewed volcanic activity in 2004, it was difficult for the Gifford Pinchot National Forest staff and multiagency partners engaged in the press of daily business to find time to update the emergency-response plan and calldown list. Fortunately, status of the emergency-response plan was monitored as one of the National Forest's internal performance measures, and an updated response plan was completed in 2003. Planning efforts were largely a paper exercise, however, and many years had passed since the participating agencies last engaged in a table-top response exercise or a field-implementation drill—the need for which has been an important lesson learned during the 2004 eruption. Since that time, participating local, State, and Federal agencies have engaged in a table-top exercise, and Monument employees have conducted periodic readiness reviews and field-implementation drills. The future challenge will be maintaining awareness of volcanic hazards and a long-term commitment to effective interagency response as memory of the 2004 eruption fades.

Use of the Incident Command System

Volcanic eruptions and other large-scale disturbances can potentially impact large areas, triggering emergency responses by numerous agencies from multiple, often overlapping jurisdictions. Coordination of the response to the 2004 eruption was greatly facilitated by activation of the Incident Command System (ICS; Federal Emergency Management Agency, 2004). ICS provided the framework for bringing together a regional, type-2 Incident Management Team (IMT–2) composed of Federal, State, and local emergency responders (fig. 1).

In 2004, following a USGS issuance of their highest alert level (Alert Level 3: Volcanic Alert), operations were directed through a Unified Command composed of a lead Incident Commander (IC) who shared command responsibility with a co-incident commander (Co-IC) from the Washington State Emergency Management Division (EMD) and a rotating Co-IC representing sheriffs from the four counties surrounding the volcano. Both the pace and efficiency of the response effort benefited from the resulting interagency coordination and unified voice.

The ICS is a highly organized, flexible structure that was developed for responding to fire and other emergency and nonemergency incidents on Federal lands. A major strength of ICS is the clear delegation of authority from the land-managing agency to the Incident Commander. The local Agency Administrator sets broad incident objectives and delegates management authority and responsibility for all aspects of the incident to the IC. This allows the IC to focus on a safe and effective response to the incident while the Agency Administrator focuses on day-to-day operations of the surrounding area. In cases where multiple jurisdictions are involved in response to a single incident, a Unified Command is established with command responsibility shared between two or more ICs, each representing his or her respective agency and Agency Administrator.

ICS offers the advantage of a uniform organizational structure composed of working groups that are universally recognized throughout the emergency-response community. This enables personnel trained in ICS functions to come together on a case-by-case basis and operate as an effective team. The size of an IMT is based on the size, complexity, or duration of the incident. On small (type 3) incidents, the IMT generally is staffed by personnel drawn from the local managing agency. As the incident grows in complexity—or if its duration exceeds local staffing capability—a larger, regional (type 2) IMT takes command. When size or complexity exceeds the capacity of a type-2 team, a national (type 1) IMT is brought in to manage the incident.

ICS is organized around five principal components or groups: Command, Planning, Operations, Logistics, and Finance (fig. 1). The Command component has primary authority and is responsible for setting overall objectives and priorities. Information and Safety are included in the Com-

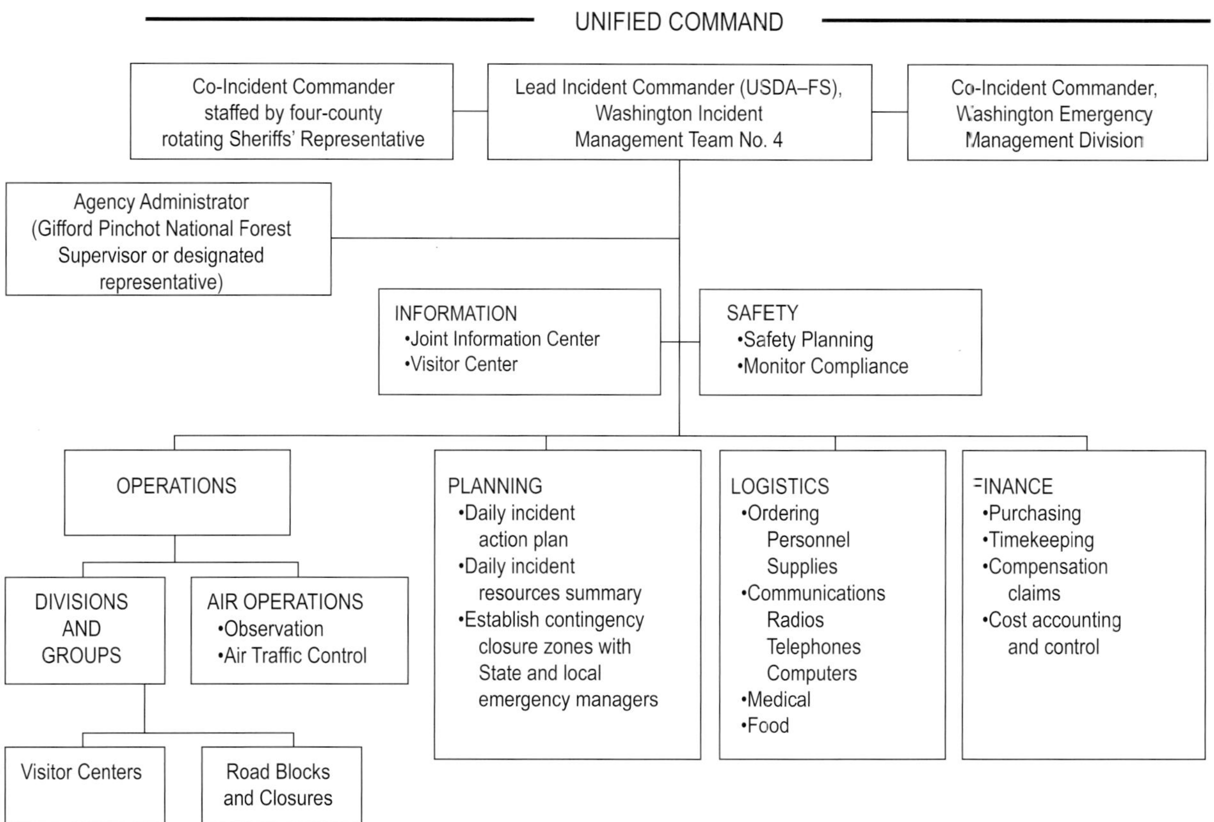

Figure 1. Organization chart for the short type-2 Incident Management Team that responded to the 2004 eruption of Mount St. Helens, Washington. USDA–FS, U.S. Department of Agriculture, Forest Service.

mand component because of their overall importance to ICS and the management of an incident. The Planning group develops action plans and collects and evaluates information about the status of the incident and available resources. The Operations group develops and conducts tactical operations to implement the plan; the Logistics group provides needed resources and support; and the Finance group provides cost accounting and procurement.

On October 3, 2004 (day 11 of the volcanic crisis), the Gifford Pinchot National Forest staff ordered a type-2 Incident Management Team known as a "short team" (fig. 1). Short teams are abbreviated versions of an IMT that provide an abbreviated command team and utilize local resources to fill in needed ICS functions. The National Forest staff utilized a Washington IMT that already included Gifford Pinchot employees and local collaborating agencies who were familiar with the volcano. The short team carried a full Command Staff composed of an Incident Commander, Deputy IC, Safety Officer, and Information Officer. Command was supported by a General Staff composed of Section Chiefs for Planning (responsible for contingency planning with collaborating agencies and preparation of daily action plans); Operations (responsible for managing area closures, patrols, and traffic management); Logistics (responsible for supporting field operations and the Joint Operations Center); Finance (responsible for managing business operations and cost containment); and Air Operations (responsible for a fixed-wing observation aircraft and managing air space around the volcano).

Factors Affecting Initial Response

The early phases of the 2004 eruption of Mount St. Helens did not fit any of the normal agency criteria for an incident response, which posed some interesting challenges for agency managers and field employees. Public interest was intense, but the eruption did not trigger resources for the logistical support and staffing normally associated with response to a forest fire or other large-scale event. At its public-interest peak, there were 24 satellite trucks at the volcano, media calls were arriving from around the world at

Figure 2. Television and print media gather at Castle Lake Viewpoint, Washington, on October 4, 2004. USGS photo by L.G. Mastin. Inset: Monument Scientist conducts twice-daily joint press conferences with U.S. Geological Survey scientists at the volcano. Inset photo by T.S. Warren, copyright © 2004, AP/WIDE WORLD PHOTOS.

Table 1. Initial management actions and lessons learned by local Ranger District personnel during days 1 through 5 of the 2004 eruption of Mount St. Helens, Washington.

[Volcanic events from this volume, Scott and others, chap. 1; Moran and others, chap. 2; Moran and others, chap.6. USGS, U.S. Geological Survey; CVO, Cascades Volcano Observatory; FS, U.S. Department of Agriculture Forest Service; M_d, earthquake coda magnitude.]

Day	Date	Volcanic events	Management challenges and responses	Lessons learned
1	Sept. 23	A swarm of small, shallow earthquakes begins at 0200 (depth less than 1 km, M_d less than 1) with 200 events recorded by 1700 PDT. The previous notable earthquake swarm occurred at 9 km depth in spring/summer, 1998.	Monument Scientist is notified by USGS–CVO, briefs other FS officials. CVO suggests earthquake swarm may be rock-fracturing from elevated ground water due to heavy rainfall.	On-staff science expertise helps transfer information from CVO to FS officials. Close working relationship with CVO staff proves invaluable for interpreting uncertain and rapidly changing events.
2	Sept. 24	CVO issues **Information Statement** describing earthquake swarm beneath 1980–86 lava dome and increased probability of small steam explosions in the crater. Number of seismic events peaks at midday and then starts to decline.	Monument posts information on Web site and at trailheads to notify climbers and hikers. Media flock to CVO, and visitor center (VC) staff responds to calls from media across the country. Staff familiarity with Mount St. Helens geology was an important ingredient in information transfer and effective response.	Monument response to fast-paced events was assisted by availability of employees well-trained in volcanic processes through past interpretive training by CVO staff. Managers of newly active volcanoes may need to bring in additional outside expertise for the short-term and (or) provide for needed employee training.
3	Sept. 25	Seismicity continues to decline through the afternoon and then begins to increase.	County sheriffs, emergency responders, and adjacent land managers all want to receive the latest information. FS and CVO initiate regular conference calls to brief collaborating State and local agencies.	The timely flow of information is a key element of an effective response. Since 2004, lead agencies have developed streamlined calldown procedures to facilitate the distribution of information and reduce duplication of effort.
4	Sept. 26	Shallow seismicity increases with 10 larger events (magnitude 2.0 to 2.8). **Alert Level 1: Notice of Volcano Unrest** is issued, the first such alert since October 1986. Character of some earthquakes suggests involvement of pressurized fluids (gas or steam) or perhaps magma. Increased possibility of small explosions, ashfalls above the crater rim, or small landslides and lahars.	Volcano is closed to climbing, and trails immediately north of the crater are closed. Satellite trucks, reporters, and volcano visitors continue to arrive, and a media center is established on a ridge west of VC. As number of media and visitors grows, logistics becomes increasingly challenging. By design, the FS Emergency Coordination Center (ECC) and Forest-Level Incident Management Team (IMT-3) are not activated until Alert Level 2.	Since 2004, the monument has developed local emergency-response procedures to support field operations during the early phases of a volcano-driven or public-interest-driven event. The plan recognizes the importance of maintaining strong working relationships between FS personnel and their local, State, and Federal counterparts. History of past collaboration with CVO and availability of CVO scientists for twice-daily briefings aids media response.
5	Sept. 27	Seismicity continues to increase slowly, although no events greater than magnitude 1.5 in last 24 hours. CVO crews report new crevasses in crater glacier south of 1980–86 lava dome. Gas flight does not detect magmatic gas.	FS officials review response plan and meet with collaborators to discuss interagency roles and responsibilities. The number of agencies and jurisdictions involved poses a challenge in the establishment of a Unified Command. Maintaining coordination and information flow is increasingly difficult as key personnel engage in interagency coordination and are assigned to VCs and other remote field sites.	2004 eruption demonstrated the need for maintaining up-to-date emergency-response plans that include clearly defined roles and lines of supervision for participating agencies. It is essential that co-incident commanders have a clear delegation of authority from the agencies that they represent. Periodic table-top exercises and response drills can help develop a shared vision of an effective multiagency response.

a rate of two per minute, and daily visits to the Monument's Web site exceeded 15 million (fig. 2).

By design, the Volcano Emergency Response Plan and Emergency Coordination Center (ECC) were not activated until CVO issued a Notice of Volcanic Unrest, three days after the earthquake swarm began. Activation of a local Incident Management Team (IMT–3) and associated logistical support was triggered when the Alert Level 2 (Volcano Advisory) was issued three days later (day 7). A major lesson learned in 2004 was the speed with which public and media response can outpace the actual progression of eruptive events. The task of responding to continuous, live media coverage and the many thousands of visitors who flocked to the volcano greatly exceeded the actual response needs generated by geologic events in what proved to be a remarkably quiet dome-building eruption (fig. 3). The Monument's response plan now includes provisions for augmented staffing and logistical support triggered by media and public response events irrespective of predetermined volcanic alert levels.

The use of predefined trigger points in emergency-response planning is useful because it focuses resources where and when they are most needed. In the case of the 2004 eruption, activation of ICS by the volcano alert system (Alert Level 1 on day 4 and Alert Level 2 on day 7; table 1) effectively compressed many critical response tasks into perhaps the busiest and most uncertain three-day period of the entire eruptive period. During

Figure 3. In the days following the evacuation of the Johnston Ridge Observatory, Washington, thousands of volcano watchers gather along State Route 504. USGS photo by M.P. Poland. Insets: Emergency managers were faced with a large "tailgate party" along the primary evacuation route northwest of the volcano. U.S. Forest Service photo by R.M. Petersen.

this three-day period, senior managers from the Gifford Pinchot National Forest and the Mount St. Helens National Volcanic Monument were engaged in coordination efforts involving multiple levels of the U.S. Department of Agriculture's Forest Service organization and those of collaborating local, State, and Federal agencies. Preparations were simultaneously underway to (1) establish a Joint Operations Center (JOC) managed under a multiagency Unified Command to respond to a potential large-scale eruption; (2) establish a Joint Information Center (JIC; Drieger and others, this volume, chap. 24) to handle steadily increasing national and international media coverage; and (3) activate a local Incident Management Team (IMT–3) to provide much-needed logistical support to field employees at the volcano. Local, State, and Federal managers were faced with considerable uncertainty as to the size of the potential eruption, the degree of hazard in adjacent areas, and the extent of a closure zone to implement around the volcano (fig. 4). In the absence of a State or Federal declared emergency, funding for associated personnel and response activities was also uncertain. To complicate matters further, these activities occurred at the end of the Federal fiscal year during a period of restricted purchasing and fiscal authority.

The combination of escalating earthquake activity and uncertainty about the anticipated eruption produced a heightened level of concern among emergency responders. Geologists at CVO did an excellent job of describing the most probable eruptive scenarios but were also careful to point out a broad range of less likely but potentially more destructive outcomes. Given the recent history and memory of the catastrophic eruption of May 18, 1980, geologists were careful to

Figure 4. Local, State, and Federal officials meet with Gifford Pinchot National Forest and U.S. Geological Survey officials on October 11, 2004, to discuss potential volcanic hazards and to define contingency closure zones. Photo courtesy of Pat Pringle.

frame potential eruptive scenarios within the context of how they differed from 1980. Geologists described the comparatively lower hazards associated with an open volcanic crater versus the magma-induced "bulge" that formed during the months preceding the 1980 eruption and failed so catastrophically. In the days preceding the Volcanic Alert and resulting October 2, 2004, evacuation of Johnston Ridge, there was considerable discussion about the presence or absence of gas-rich magma beneath the volcano. Geologists constructed probability trees in an effort to connect monitoring data with potential scenarios and to quantify the probability and magnitude of an explosive eruption.

The range of potential eruptive outcomes and potential for explosive activity formed the context within which local, State, and Federal agencies organized the emergency-response system. As live media coverage (fig. 2) fed a growing public interest and thousands of visitors gathered on Johnston Ridge, agency managers and geologists were actively discussing a potential pullback and the closure of an area 8 km (5 mi) radially around the volcano. Officials were concerned about potential human responses to a significant explosion or ashfall and the challenges posed by the evacuation of a large numbers of visitors on a single highway in steep, mountainous terrain. State and local officials who remembered the 1980 eruption were concerned about maintaining viable evacuation routes and providing an appropriate level of response in adjacent communities.

The steadily escalating tempo of earthquakes and rapid progression from Volcanic Advisory to Volcanic Alert (days 7 through 9; table 2) tested the emergency-response system. Implementation of the JOC and multiagency Unified Command was complicated by the fact that participating local, State, and Federal agencies each brought their own understanding of ICS, Unified Command, and its application to the process (table 2). Considerable effort was expended to work out the delegation of authority and lines of supervision associated with having a Unified Command composed of local, State, and Federal Co-Incident Commanders (lead IC from the IMT–2 for Federal; a representative of the Washington Emergency Management Division for State; and a rotating representative of the four county sheriffs for local jurisdictions). Communications and coordination were further challenged by the number of agencies, jurisdictions, and geographic locations involved in the response (CVO, JOC, GP National Forest headquarters, Monument visitor centers, and other remote sites).

The importance of instituting a Unified Command structure early in the process was a key lesson learned during the renewed eruptive activity of autumn 2004. Early activation allows collaborators time to familiarize their agencies with emerging issues, to make needed adjustments, and to implement needed agreements and delegations of authority. Early collaboration is important given the number of State and local agencies and jurisdictions involved in emergency response on National Forest and adjacent lands. Interagency response planning and periodic implementation drills can contribute to a shared understanding of roles, responsibilities, and supervisory structures and result in a more effective response.

Extended Eruptions Pose Challenges

During the fall of 2004, high levels of public and media interest were driven largely by the novelty of renewed eruptive activity and the opportunity to witness small steam and ash explosions. As the frequency of explosions diminished and winter weather increasingly obscured crater views, public interest evolved into fascination with the steaming volcano and amazement at the pace and longevity of the continuing eruption. Agency managers established closure boundaries and gate systems that restricted access to within 8 km (5 mi) of the volcano while providing access to adjacent areas for traditional forest activities (table 3). Since September 2004, the Monument has engaged in a sustained effort to manage evolving area closures, ensure adequate staffing during periods of increased visitation, and maintain a level of emergency preparedness among Monument employees. As geologists' confidence that any large-scale change in behavior will be detected by the monitoring network has increased, National Forest managers have reopened facilities and trails, restoring public access to most of the area surrounding the volcano.

The quiet, nonexplosive nature of the 2004 eruption provided a relatively safe opportunity for the public to watch volcanic processes firsthand and to increase their awareness of volcanic hazards in the Pacific Northwest. Since the fall of 2004, millions of people have learned about the ongoing eruption and monitoring through media coverage, Web sites, and personal experiences at the volcano. The continuing challenge for agency managers is to reaffirm the lessons learned during the 2004 eruption response and to periodically review and update interagency response plans and procedures. Given the intermittent nature of eruptive activity, we must adopt a long-term view and be prepared to act appropriately as volcanic events and associated public and media responses occur in the future.

Acknowledgments

The response to the 2004 eruption was truly a group effort. Our sincere thanks go to staff of the Gifford Pinchot National Forest; Mount St. Helens National Volcanic Monument; USGS Cascades Volcano Observatory; Washington Incident Management Team No. 4; Washington Emergency Management Division; Sheriff's Departments and supporting emergency responders from Clark, Cowlitz, Lewis, and Skamania Counties; Washington State Patrol; Washington Department of Transportation; Washington Department of Natural Resources; and the Federal Emergency Management Agency. Our response to worldwide media interest was greatly assisted by the availability of information officers from local, State, and Federal agencies whose voluntary assistance made the Joint Information Center possible. The manuscript benefited greatly from early reviews by Lynn Burditt and Tom Knappenberger and formal reviews by Drs. Shigeo Aramaki and Chris Newhall.

Table 2. Management actions and lessons learned following activation of the Emergency Coordination Center and type-3 Incident Management Team at the Gifford Pinchot National Forest Headquarters during days 7 through 11 of the 2004 eruption of Mount St. Helens, Washington.

[USGS, U.S. Geological Survey; CVO, Cascades Volcano Observatory; FS, U.S. Department of Agriculture Forest Service; M_d, earthquake coda magnitude. See table 1 for sources of volcanic events.]

Day	Date	Volcanic events	Management challenges and responses	Lessons learned
7	Sept. 29	Shallow seismicity accelerates overnight with four events per minute and increasing number of M_d 2–3 events. CVO issues **Alert Level 2: Volcano Advisory,** cautions that explosions, crater ballistics and ash clouds could occur at any time. GPS equipment detects northward movement of 1980–86 lava dome. No magmatic gas detected.	Emergency Coordination Center (ECC) and forest-level incident-management team (type 3) is activated, not all positions are filled. After 7 days, media-response capability at CVO and Visitor Centers begins to be strained. Federal and State officials discuss establishing a Joint Information Center to handle increasing demand for information and to allow CVO staff to focus on monitoring and eruption forecasting. Additional information officers arrive to help with media at Visitor Centers.	In 2004, public and media response to volcanic events was rapid and posed the biggest challenge to land managers. Current National Volcanic Monument response plans recognize the need for logistical support to field operations independent of volcano alert level. Plans include a trained cadre of local volcano-information officers to assist with phone calls and media inquiries at the Visitor Centers during the critical early phases of a volcanic or media-response event.
9	Oct. 1	CVO issues **Information Statement.** Seismicity continues at 1–2 events per minute, with largest up to M_d 3. Observations reveal uplift of Crater Glacier by several meters. At noon a small, 20-minute steam and ash explosion opens a vent in uplifted glacier. Elevated CO_2 detected on 1980–86 dome, and weak sulfurous odor but no SO_2 or H_2S.	Local, State, and Federal officials meet to discuss implementation of Unified Command and establishment of a Joint Operations Center. CVO and FS officials discuss potential hazards and trigger points for closure of the Johnston Ridge Observatory and viewpoints closest to the volcano. Visitor Center staff request additional help to handle expected crowds of volcano watchers for the coming weekend.	Maintaining timely flow of information to FS managers and field sites is the key to maintaining situational awareness and preparedness. Since 2004, CVO and FS have developed streamlined calldown procedures. As the eruption has continued, daily contacts have been replaced by weekly conference calls to keep Monument staff up-to-date on the latest monitoring information.
10	Oct. 2	Vigorous ~1-hour-long, low-frequency tremor occurs at 1215 PDT. Given that such tremors may indicate magma movement or pressurization, CVO issues **Alert Level 3: Volcano Alert**. Following the tremor, shallow seismicity continues at 1–2 per minute, with largest event M_d 3.	Visitor Center staff and State and local counterparts evacuate Johnston Ridge Observatory (JRO) and State Route 504. In less than an hour, 2,500 visitors and 14 satellite trucks are safely relocated. State highway, lands, and airspace within 8 km of volcano are closed. Some State and Federal officials express concern that evacuation of JRO exceeded the pace of official calldown procedures, but others view the 2004 evacuation of JRO as an example of front-line employees acting decisively to provide for public and employee safety.	The Monument emergency plan recognizes that field employees may need to act decisively in the interests of employee and visitor safety. Empowering field employees to implement clearly defined procedures can also be useful in the event that lines of communication fail. While empowerment of front-line employees is important, it is also critical to ensure that actions are well coordinated and communications are maintained across collaborating agencies and up and down the chain of command.
11	Oct. 3	25-minute low-frequency tremor occurs at 0250 PDT. Magnitude 3 earthquakes occur at a rate of one every 5 minutes. Large-scale uplift and fracturing of Crater Glacier continues.	Joint Information Center (JIC) is established at Gifford Pinchot National Forest Headquarters, providing relief for CVO staff and reducing media-call volume at Visitor Centers. CVO has difficulty reaching ECC after-hours contacts and finally reaches Visitor Center housing.	Afterhours calldown procedures have been amended to ensure that Visitor Centers are contacted directly by CVO. Maintaining vigilance in response to numerous seismic events and steam emissions over the long term is challenging.

Table 3. Management actions and lessons learned following activation of a short type-2 Incident Management Team from day 12 and onward in the 2004 eruption of Mount St. Helens, Washington.

[USGS, U.S. Geological Survey; CVO, Cascades Volcano Observatory; FS, U.S. Department of Agriculture Forest Service; M_d, earthquake coda magnitude. See table 1 for sources of volcanic events.]

Day	Date	Volcanic events	Management challenges and responses	Lessons learned
12	Oct. 4	22-minute-long steam and ash emission (3,700 m). Vent area is a bubbling lake. Visual observations assess tens of meters of uplift of Crater Glacier. Magma is at shallow level and could soon reach surface. Increased likelihood of larger steam and ash emissions. Gas flight detects CO_2 and low levels of H_2S.	FS brings in a regional Incident Management Team (IMT type 2) because Monument and Forest resources are becoming overextended. Unified Command coordinates the multiagency response effort. Providing resources to support IMT and field operations is challenging because a potential future eruption does not fit within the normal criteria for emergency-response funding or trigger an emergency declaration.	IMT-2 provides needed logistical support, organization, and supervision for increasingly complex multiagency effort. A key lesson learned is the importance of defining when Monument, National Forest, or regional-response officials are in charge. Since 2004, the Monument response plan clearly states that the Monument Manager is Incident Commander until the Forest Supervisor activates a Forest-level IMT.
13	Oct. 5	At 0905 PDT, a 70-minute-long steam and ash emission (4,500 m) deposits dusting of ash 60 miles to northeast. The ash plume is visible on Doppler weather radar. Seismicity drops and remains at low levels. Status remains at **Alert Level 3: Volcano Alert**.	Emergency response is directed by Incident Commander (IC) and two other co-ICs representing Washington State Emergency Management Division and four county sheriffs. Joint Operations Center is established. Resources include gate guards, traffic-control personnel at Visitor Centers, and fixed-wing observation aircraft.	IMT-2 provides welcome relief for Monument employees, many of whom have been on duty for more than 12 days. Current response plans recognize that Monument staff may need to be assisted by other Forest employees and resources during fast paced media events and prior to activation of a Forest or Regional IMT.
14	Oct. 6	Seismicity remains at reduced level. Probability of eruption that threatens life and property is decreased, so CVO steps back to **Alert Level 2: Volcano Advisory**. Rainfall overnight generates small debris flows in the crater. Low clouds and rain limit visibility and air operations.	IMT-2 and Forest representatives meet with local and State law enforcement and emergency managers to define closure zones; considerable discussion about the value of linking closure zones to specific alert levels. CVO and FS stress the importance of maintaining flexibility so closures can be adjusted according to current eruptive behavior and potential threats.	The Incident Command System (ICS) and Unified Command provide a useful structure for organizing a complex, multiagency response. However, in the absence of an emergency declaration or specific response funding, cost containment is a real concern. Response plans must ensure that key ICS functions are accounted for in a local response organization.
15 to 25	Oct. 7 to Oct.17	Shallow seismicity continues. After magma surfaces (day 19), seismicity gradually decreases. Small crater debris flows occur with rainfall. Status remains at **Alert Level 2: Volcano Advisory**.	Public and media interest declines as explosive activity subsides and weather obscures volcano. IMT-2 departs and operations are transitioned back to local IMT-3. As hazards diminish, closures are lifted and staffed temporary gates are replaced with unstaffed, permanent gates.	In absence of explosions, media and public interest in ongoing eruptive activity decreases. Outreach and information efforts are key to maintaining awareness of ongoing events and potential future hazards. Periodic press conferences and field visits aid outreach effort.
26 to 575	Oct.18, 2004 to June 2006	Continuous eruption and formation of spines. Extrusion rate and seismicity gradually decline. Periodic small steam and ash emissions with dome rockfall. Status remains at **Alert Level 2**.	Maintaining calldown procedures and response capability over months and years of continuous eruptive activity is a challenge. As comfort level with continuing nonexplosive eruption grows, additional areas around the volcano are reopened.	Confusion can occur when staff unfamiliar with volcanic processes and terminology relay technical information during calldowns. Need to ensure that contacts are knowledgeable about monitoring terminology and volcanic hazards.

References Cited

Driedger, C.L., Neal, C.A., Knappenberger, T.H., Needham, D.H., Harper, R.B., and Steele, W.P., 2008, Hazard information management during the autumn 2004 reawakening of Mount St. Helens volcano, Washington, chap. 24 *of* Sherrod, D.R., Scott, W.E., and Stauffer, P.H., eds., A volcano rekindled; the renewed eruption of Mount St. Helens, 2004–2006: U.S. Geological Survey Professional Paper 1750 (this volume).

Federal Emergency Management Agency, 2004, National Incident Management System: U.S. Department of Homeland Security, 139 p. [http://www.fema.gov/emergency/nims/nims_compliance.shtm; last accessed May 22, 2006].

Moran, S.C., Malone, S.D., Qamar, A.I., Thelen, W.A., Wright, A.K., and Caplan-Auerbach, J., 2008a, Seismicity associated with renewed dome building at Mount St. Helens, 2004–2005, chap. 2 *of* Sherrod, D.R., Scott, W.E., and Stauffer, P.H., eds., A volcano rekindled; the renewed eruption of Mount St. Helens, 2004–2006: U.S. Geological Survey Professional Paper 1750 (this volume).

Moran, S.C., McChesney, P.J., and Lockhart, A.B., 2008b, Seismicity and infrasound associated with explosions at Mount St. Helens, 2004–2005, chap. 6 *of* Sherrod, D.R., Scott, W.E., and Stauffer, P.H., eds., A volcano rekindled; the renewed eruption of Mount St. Helens, 2004–2006: U.S. Geological Survey Professional Paper 1750 (this volume).

Scott, W.E., Sherrod, D.R., and Gardner, C.A., 2008, Overview of the 2004 to 2006, and continuing, eruption of Mount St. Helens, Washington, chap. 1 *of* Sherrod, D.R., Scott, W.E., and Stauffer, P.H., eds., A volcano rekindled; the renewed eruption of Mount St. Helens, 2004–2006: U.S. Geological Survey Professional Paper 1750 (this volume).

U.S. Department of Agriculture Forest Service, 1984, Mount St. Helens National Volcanic Monument, Final Environmental Impact Statement, Comprehensive Management Plan: Vancouver, Wash., Gifford Pinchot National Forest, 450 p.

U.S. Department of Agriculture Forest Service, 1992, Mount St. Helens Contingency Plan: Vancouver, Wash., Gifford Pinchot National Forest, prepared in cooperation with the U.S. Geological Survey; Clark, Cowlitz, Skamania and Lewis County Sheriffs; Washington State Emergency Management Division; Federal Emergency Management Agency; U.S. Army Corps of Engineers; Pacific Power; and Portland General Electric, 48 p.

U.S. Department of Agriculture Forest Service, 2003, Mount St. Helens Volcanic Activity Response Plan: Vancouver, Wash., Gifford Pinchot National Forest, 30 p.

U.S. Department of Agriculture Forest Service, 2005, Mount St. Helens National Volcanic Monument, Initial Emergency Response Plan: Vancouver, Wash., Gifford Pinchot National Forest, Mount St. Helens National Volcanic Monument, 30 p.

A Volcano Rekindled: The Renewed Eruption of Mount St. Helens, 2004–2006
Edited by David R. Sherrod, William E. Scott, and Peter H. Stauffer
U.S. Geological Survey Professional Paper 1750, 2008

Chapter 24

Hazard Information Management During the Autumn 2004 Reawakening of Mount St. Helens Volcano, Washington

By Carolyn L. Driedger[1], Christina A. Neal[2], Tom H. Knappenberger[3], Deborah H. Needham[4], Robert B. Harper[5], and William P. Steele[6]

Abstract

The 2004 reawakening of Mount St. Helens quickly caught the attention of government agencies as well as the international news media and the public. Immediate concerns focused on a repeat of the catastrophic landslide and blast event of May 18, 1980, which remains a vivid memory for many individuals. Within several days of the onset of accelerating seismicity, media inquiries increased exponentially. Personnel at the U.S. Geological Survey, the Pacific Northwest Seismic Network, and the Gifford Pinchot National Forest soon handled hundreds of press inquiries and held several press briefings per day. About one week into the event, a Joint Information Center was established to help maintain a consistent hazard message and to provide a centralized information source about volcanic activity, hazards, area closures, and media briefings. Scientists, public-affairs specialists, and personnel from emergency-management, health, public-safety, and land-management agencies answered phones, helped in press briefings and interviews, and managed media access to colleagues working on science and safety issues. For scientists, in addition to managing the cycle of daily fieldwork, challenges included (1) balancing accurate interpretations of data under crisis conditions with the need to share information quickly, (2) articulating uncertainties for a variety of volcanic scenarios, (3) minimizing scientific jargon, and (4) frequently updating and effectively distributing talking points. Success of hazard information management during a volcanic crisis depends largely on scientists' clarity of communication and thorough preplanning among interagency partners. All parties must commit to after-action evaluation and improvement of communication plans, incorporating lessons learned during each event.

Introduction

In late September 2004, a sudden and rapidly accelerating increase in seismicity beneath Mount St. Helens heralded the onset of the first volcanic event of consequence in the contiguous 48 states since 1986 (Dzurisin and others, 2005). In addition to its volcanologic significance, the 2004 eruption captured the attention of the public worldwide, who, even after 24 years, vividly recalled the images and impacts of Mount St. Helens' catastrophic eruption on May 18, 1980. The 2004–2006 eruption was also the first in the contiguous 48 states since the establishment of widespread Internet use and development of the 24-hour international news cycle and its attendant around-the-clock demands. An Internet Web camera (VolcanoCam) installed and maintained by staff at the Gifford Pinchot National Forest (GPNF) gave unprecedented access to visual images of a Cascade Range eruption in near-real time. Real-time seismic information in the form of Internet-available seismograms maintained by the Pacific Northwest Seismic Network (PNSN) enabled the general public to monitor the volcano from home computers. At Mount St. Helens National Volcanic Monument (MSHNVM), scenic overlooks, such as the Johnston Ridge Observatory (JRO), provided an unprecedented view for thousands of visitors (fig. 1). All of these factors combined to create an enormous and urgent demand

[1] U.S. Geological Survey, 1300 SE Cardinal Court, Vancouver, WA 98683

[2] U.S. Geological Survey, 4200 University Drive, Anchorage, AK 99508

[3] USDA Forest Service, Gifford Pinchot National Forest, 10600 NE 51st Circle, Vancouver, WA 98682; now at USDA Forest Service Pacific Northwest Region Office, Box 3623, Portland, OR 97208.

[4] Clark Regional Emergency Services Agency, 710 W 13th St., Vancouver, WA 98660

[5] Washington Military Department, Emergency Management Division, Bldg. 20, Camp Murray, WA 98430

[6] University of Washington, Pacific Northwest Seismic Network, Box 351310, Seattle, WA 98195

for information and commentary regarding the volcano and its activity, hazards, likely outcomes, the daily activities of scientists, and any other available information about Mount St. Helens, one of the world's most famous volcanoes. This chapter describes some of the pre-event planning, the real-time development of strategies to respond to this demand, significant challenges, and lessons learned. Additional details regarding the first few weeks of unrest and eruption can be found in other contributions in this volume (Scott and others, chap. 1; Moran and others, chap. 2; Qamar and others, chap. 3; Moran and others, chap. 6).

Pre-Event Coordination and Planning

Since the mid-1990s, the U.S. Geological Survey (USGS) has produced a series of modern volcano-hazard assessments for each potentially active volcano in Washington and Oregon, including Mount St. Helens (Wolfe and Pierson, 1995). Each assessment was written in a format accessible to both technical and lay audiences and was distributed to public officials, educators, and public libraries in areas at risk.

Soon after this series of publications was completed, USGS staff began working with partner agencies in Washington and Oregon to develop hazard-response plans based on the assessments. These response plans define the roles of individual agencies and protocols for cooperation during volcanic unrest, such as the plan for Mount St. Helens (Gifford Pinchot National Forest, 2003). As of spring 2006, volcano-response plans now exist for Mounts Baker, Rainier, St. Helens, and Hood, and for Glacier Peak. Similar plans are in progress for Mount Adams and for the volcanoes of central Oregon.

Figure 1. Visitors at Mount St. Helens National Volcanic Monument's Johnston Ridge Observatory, Wash., view the October 1, 2004, explosion of steam and ash from vent approximately 9 km south, in crater. USGS photo by E.Y. Iwatsubo.

Ironically, the USGS was working with the GPNF and other agencies to update the Mount St. Helens plan when the 2004 volcanic unrest began.

In addition to collaborating on volcano response protocols, the USGS maintains active cooperation with its partners in hazard communication on the Federal, State, and local levels. This includes planning and practicing rapid initiation of a Joint Information Center (JIC), sharing expertise at news briefings, and assembling interagency-communication call-down lists. Since the 1980s unrest at Mount St. Helens, staff at the University of Washington's (UW) PNSN in Seattle have coordinated with the USGS in the development and release of Volcano Information Statements and Volcanic Alert Level changes. This close collaboration, refined over the years, enabled separate but well-synchronized media responses to the rapidly evolving unrest at Mount St. Helens that began on September 23, 2004.

Chronology of Events

The initial earthquake swarm on the morning of September 23, 2004, now commonly viewed as the onset of volcanic unrest, was noted in a Cascade Range update posted on the USGS-Cascades Volcano Observatory (CVO) Web site at 1800 PDT, but it brought little immediate inquiry from the media. The following morning CVO and PNSN released an Information Statement regarding the earthquake swarm, and veteran public viewers of seismograms on the PNSN Web site began to recognize the potential significance of the seismicity. This recognition culminated in approximately one dozen media inquires per day during the next few days at CVO. The PNSN, which provided information to Seattle television and radio stations and newspapers, was inundated by requests regarding the earthquakes. The growing public interest in the unrest resulted in a deluge of requests for information from members of the local press and other media providers. The PNSN published a press release on its Web site that described the onset of the earthquake swarm and provided links to seismicity pages on its own Web site and to Web sites of CVO, GPNF, and other sources. The PNSN Seismology Lab staff extended their operation to seven days per week, often working late into the night. As seismicity increased, the PNSN placed a disclaimer on its Web site, noting that postings for recent earthquakes were incomplete because staff could not keep up with processing these seismic events during regular working hours.

On September 26, the USGS issued an official Alert Level 1: Notice of Volcanic Unrest (unusual activity detected; Dzurisin and others, 2005), prompting inquiries to increase at both CVO and UW from about one dozen to more than 40 per day. Scientists at the USGS and PNSN consulted one another early each day about the increasing seismicity. After these conversations, USGS staff wrote formal talking points for use by information scientists, who were scientists recruited to speak to the media. On September 29, the USGS issued an Alert Level 2: Volcano Advisory (eruption likely but not imminent) and began to offer formal media briefings.

Staff at CVO and the USGS Office of Communications worked hard to address all inquiries in the face of increasing interest. Scientists identified the range of eruption potential. The ability to compile, synthesize, and understand the significance of the events was strained by mounting demands for information. The U.S. East Coast news cycle resulted in interviews at 0400 PDT, challenging USGS personnel as they struggled to maintain adequate 24-hour staffing. Only a few individuals rotating through the informal position of information scientist had the breadth of knowledge about all aspects of the volcanic unrest to answer all questions. Scientists found it challenging to interpret and distill the continuous stream of field data into timely public statements.

At the PNSN, television satellite trucks filled the parking lot, and staff and student volunteers struggled to keep up with phones and interview requests. In an attempt to make the monitoring and media response more sustainable, staff were ordered home after a 12-hour shift, and a number of key staff alternated on 12-hour shifts. By Monday, September 27, the PNSN Web site became completely congested, and system administrators were forced to configure high-capacity servers on the UW network backbone to serve the PNSN site.

During this time, USGS staff supplied information to the news media (many of whom kept satellite trucks present all day and night), critical operational partners, and other scientists, primarily by telephone and by the release of once- or twice-daily text updates by e-mail, faxes, and postings on the CVO Web site. Independently, colleagues at other USGS offices, the PNSN, the GPNF, and the Washington State Emergency Management Division (EMD) handled other inquiries. The communications landscape faced by USGS scientists is shown schematically in figure 2.

By September 28, five days into the event, USGS communications and technical staff were fielding 60 or more inquiries per day. It became apparent that media and public demands for information would soon exceed the capacity that could be managed effectively by any single agency. That notion, and the concern for the consistency and centralization of hazard messages, prompted the USGS to work with agency partners from the GPNF and the Washington EMD to plan and establish a JIC, described more completely later in this chapter. On September 29, GPNF officials and local emergency managers arriving at CVO to discuss the JIC encountered numerous media trucks in the parking lot and had to step over media cables that snaked through the CVO lobby, preventing the doors from closing at this normally secure government facility. It was clear that, in order for CVO staff to function, a JIC facility would need to be located away from CVO. The GPNF headquarters in Vancouver, only six miles distant, was chosen as a logical site.

During this time at the PNSN, UW Computing and Communications staff installed fiber-optic television circuits in the Seismology Lab to help meet the continually increasing demand for staff interviews, which now included national and international media providers. To help manage the more than 100 daily phone calls, a six-line phone bank was installed in the conference room adjacent to the lab. This facility was staffed by students and also was used for interviews with national and international media members.

As the rate and magnitude of earthquakes under Mount St. Helens continued to build, speculation about the nature of the coming eruption became the focus of many press reports. Daily teleconferences between PNSN and USGS–CVO scientists were crucial in formulating and sharing assessments of the volcano. Frequent consultation helped keep the public message from CVO and PNSN reasonably consistent.

On October 1, with JIC provisioning still in progress, a 20-minute-long steam and ash emission sent ash more than 3 km above the crater (Dzurisin and others, 2005; Moran and others, this volume, chap. 6). News of this event escalated inquiries to more than 80 per day at CVO. At PNSN, requests for information lessened slightly as attention shifted to CVO and the MSHNVM Castle Lake Viewpoint.

On October 2, intensified seismicity, including an hour-long period of energetic seismic tremor, prompted USGS–CVO to issue its highest warning level for the Cascade Range, an Alert Level 3: Volcano Alert, which means that a volcanic event threatening to life and property appears imminent or is underway. That afternoon millions of viewers worldwide watched a media briefing at CVO presented to U.S. Department of the Interior Secretary Gale Norton and a host of congressional dignitaries. Its political significance and public interest confirmed, Mount St. Helens unrest had become an incident of national and international prominence.

Late on the afternoon of October 2, the JIC opened its doors at GPNF headquarters. The media, at first reluctant to move from CVO, were eventually persuaded to relocate owing to the disciplined refusal of CVO staff to answer their inquiries onsite and by the ready availability of expertise at the new JIC. All information sources, including public-information officers (PIOs; a term that we use in a general sense to include a variety of professionals, other than volcanologists, who communicated with the media and public), scientists, staff at the USGS Office of Communications, and agency phone recordings, referred media to the JIC as the principal source of volcano information.

The JIC was fully activated from October 3 to October 13, spanning the buildup to and start of lava extrusion (Dzurisin and others, 2005). After October 13, media attention diminished sufficiently to allow JIC staff to return to normal agency facilities. Remaining calls were addressed at CVO by the outreach staff, information scientists, and USGS Office of Communications staff. The latest information, usually from the daily update, was made available on a 24-hour media line maintained and updated by the GPNF. Importantly, according to Incident Command principles for an evolving, ongoing situation, former JIC employees maintained contact so that in the event of later heightened activity, the information systems could be reestablished quickly. As of this writing in October

2006, no escalation of activity requiring JIC reactivation has occurred at Mount St. Helens.

Media interest in Mount St. Helens decreased owing to cessation of dramatic steam and ash explosions and the onset of cloudy weather, which blocked views of the volcano. Media managers were unwilling to pay for satellite trucks sitting idle and were less willing to report daily about lava dome-building events when interesting visual images were unavailable.

Development of Joint Operations Center and Joint Information Center

During the onset of volcanic unrest at Mount St. Helens, USGS and PNSN scientists and other public officials conducted their own hazard information dissemination according to each agency's protocols. As unrest escalated and the demand

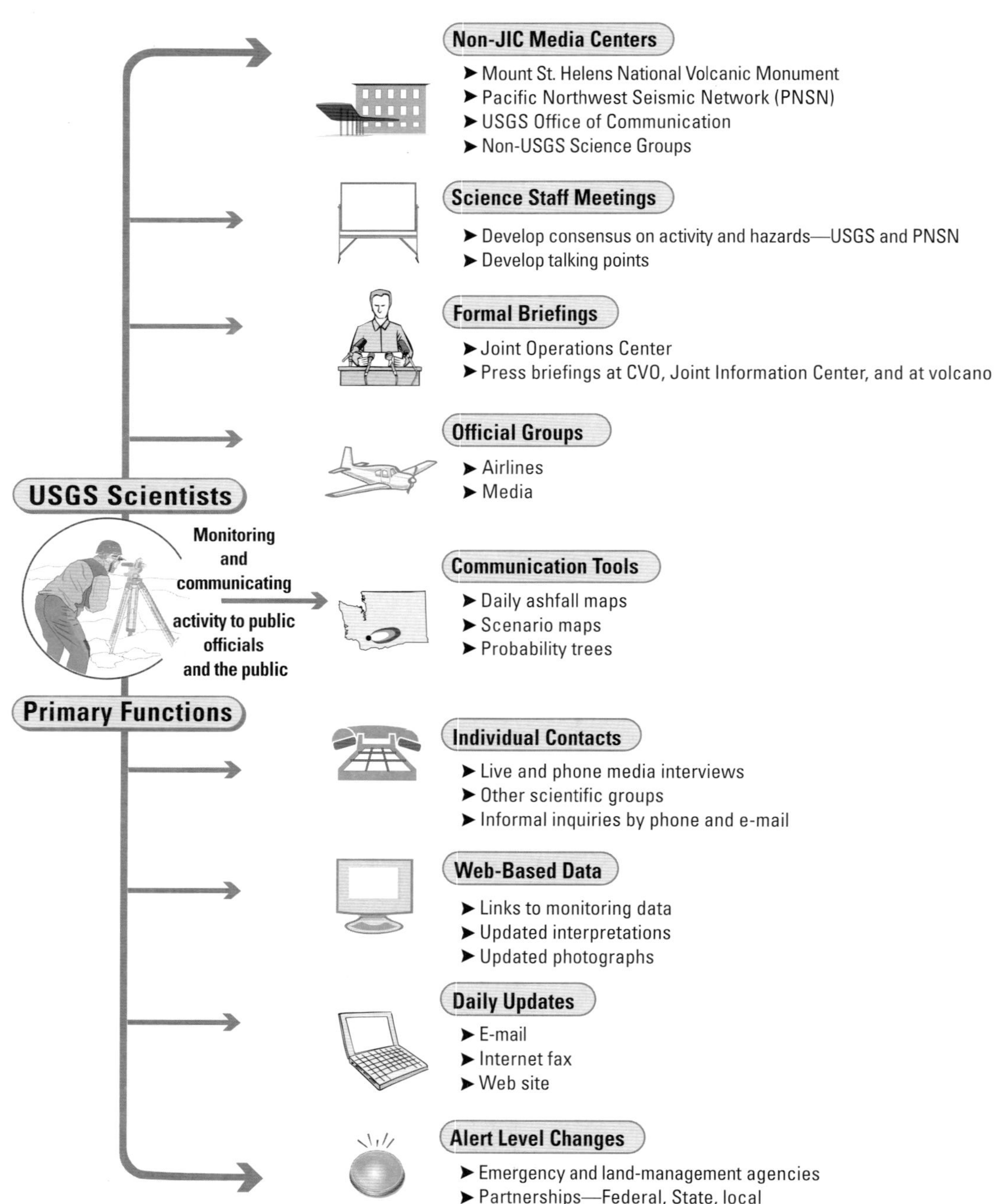

Figure 2. Graphic illustrating shared responsibilities of U.S. Geological Survey (USGS) scientists for communication with a broad range of individuals and agencies. CVO, Cascades Volcano Observatory.

for a more coordinated message grew, the agencies formally pooled their resources in a unified response that employed the precepts of the Incident Command System (ICS), a standard, on-scene, all-hazards incident management system already in use by emergency responders and codified nationally in 2004 as the National Incident Management System (NIMS; Federal Emergency Management Agency, 2004; Frenzen and Matarresse, this volume, chap. 23). Under this arrangement, agencies work together through designated members of a unified command (often the senior person from each agency) to establish a common strategy and a single Incident Action Plan (Federal Emergency Management Agency, 2004). In the case of the 2004 Mount St. Helens event, those stakeholder agencies created a Joint Operations Center (JOC; the term coined in present-day terms by NIMS is an "Incident Command Post"; Christine Jonientz-Trisler, oral commun., 2006). The JOC focused on operational aspects of the response (not scientific or research aspects) and took responsibility for the creation of the JIC.

This system of JOC and JIC (under NIMS terminology the JIC is called a "Joint Information System") is a well-known tool used in the ICS today. The JOC-JIC system enables interagency coordination, support for decision makers, flexibility based on changing circumstances, and, through the JIC, development and delivery of consistent messages. The system includes plans and protocols to provide information during incidents. A JIC (there can be several, although one is preferable) generally exists in a location where PIOs from involved organizations colocate to provide critical emergency information, crisis communications, and public-affairs functions. Although the public can receive information from many sources, a JIC allows the various organizations with responsibility during an incident to come together to ensure clear, timely, and consistent hazard messages.

The JIC can be viewed as a central hub for communication, a "one-stop shopping" facility where representatives from cooperating agencies can address inquiries with a single voice. A JIC can be assembled when communications needs exceed the capacity of individual agencies. The JIC provides interagency coordination and integration, development and delivery of coordinated messages, support for decision makers, and flexibility to meet demands based on changing circumstances. The use of a JIC reduces confusion, inaccuracies, and duplication of efforts and can help address rumor control. Each organization maintains its own authority and policies but still contributes to an overall unified message to the public (Federal Emergency Management Agency, 2004). A general call center and other office resources are shared, and technical representatives from specific agencies address inquiries germane to their agency's interest. The JIC is dynamic and can be resized to meet incident needs. To the detriment of the host agency, the JIC can displace normal agency operations for extended periods, such as the two weeks during 2004 that the headquarters conference room was unavailable to GPNF staff.

Physical Description, Responsibilities, and Operation of Joint Information Center

The Mount St. Helens JIC leadership (fig. 3) included the JIC Manager who reported to the Incident Commander at the JOC. The JIC Manager was responsible for functioning of the JIC and for maintaining records. Liaisons from Washington EMD, GPNF, and USGS were in constant contact with the JIC Manager or served in that role at some point during JIC operation. The Media Briefings Facilitator, Products Coordinator (news releases, for example), Call Center Supervisor, and PIOs at MSHNVM all reported to the JIC Manager, as did information scientists and other technical specialists. As needed, each agency in the command structure provided PIOs to coordinate their home agency's information (both internally and externally), act as spokespeople, and provide appropriate technical expertise. The PIOs also sent talking points to other information outlets, such as the PNSN, USGS staff in other cities, and to MSHNVM visitor facilities.

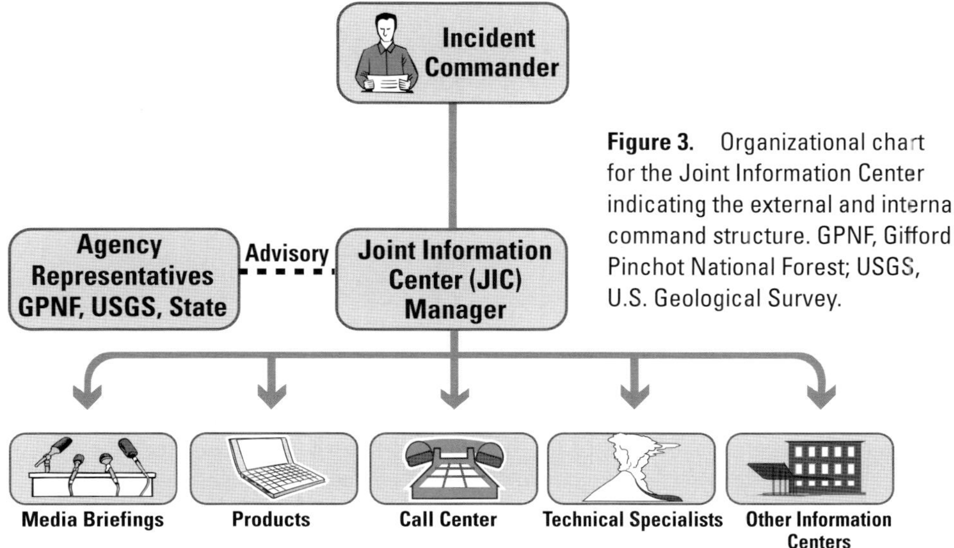

Figure 3. Organizational chart for the Joint Information Center indicating the external and internal command structure. GPNF, Gifford Pinchot National Forest; USGS, U.S. Geological Survey.

The JIC staff used a conference room at the GPNF headquarters (fig. 4). The room was dividable by heavy, soundproof curtains. During operation of the JIC, one-half of the room served as the Media Briefing Room, with areas reserved for television cameras, seating, and a podium. The other half of the conference room was arranged by function; one side housed the Call Center, and the other side housed the JIC Manager, technical experts, the news release production team, and the media briefings team.

The JIC Call Center consisted of a temporary six-line switchboard system that allowed call takers to simultaneously answer multiple incoming lines and to transfer media and public-affairs calls to the technical experts as needed. Call Center staff included employees of the GPNF and other national forests, USGS, Washington EMD, Oregon's Department of Geology and Mineral Industries, Washington's Department of Geology and Earth Resources, and many emergency-management and nontechnical public-affairs professionals from across the greater Portland-Vancouver metropolitan area. The Federal Emergency Management Agency (FEMA) also assisted with staffing and could have provided more formal assistance and resources had the incident escalated to an emergency or had an official Federal disaster declaration been issued. FEMA also pre-positioned management staff at the JOC and provided liaisons to the States of Washington and Oregon Emergency Operations Centers and a liaison to the USGS at CVO.

Call Center staff conveyed basic information about the current incident to media representatives, reading from daily talking points, updates compiled on a dry-erase whiteboard, and fact sheets compiled by the technical experts (fig. 5). This information satisfied many of the media callers. When an interview was requested and a technical expert was unavailable, the request was given to the Media Interview Coordinator. Detailed information (reporter name, media organization, publication or broadcast schedule or deadline, and nature of the questions) allowed the Media Interview Coordinator to prioritize pending requests and to assign USGS or other staff to the appropriate interview. This system was highly effective in meeting the vast majority of live interview requests. Technical experts, along with the JIC management from Washington

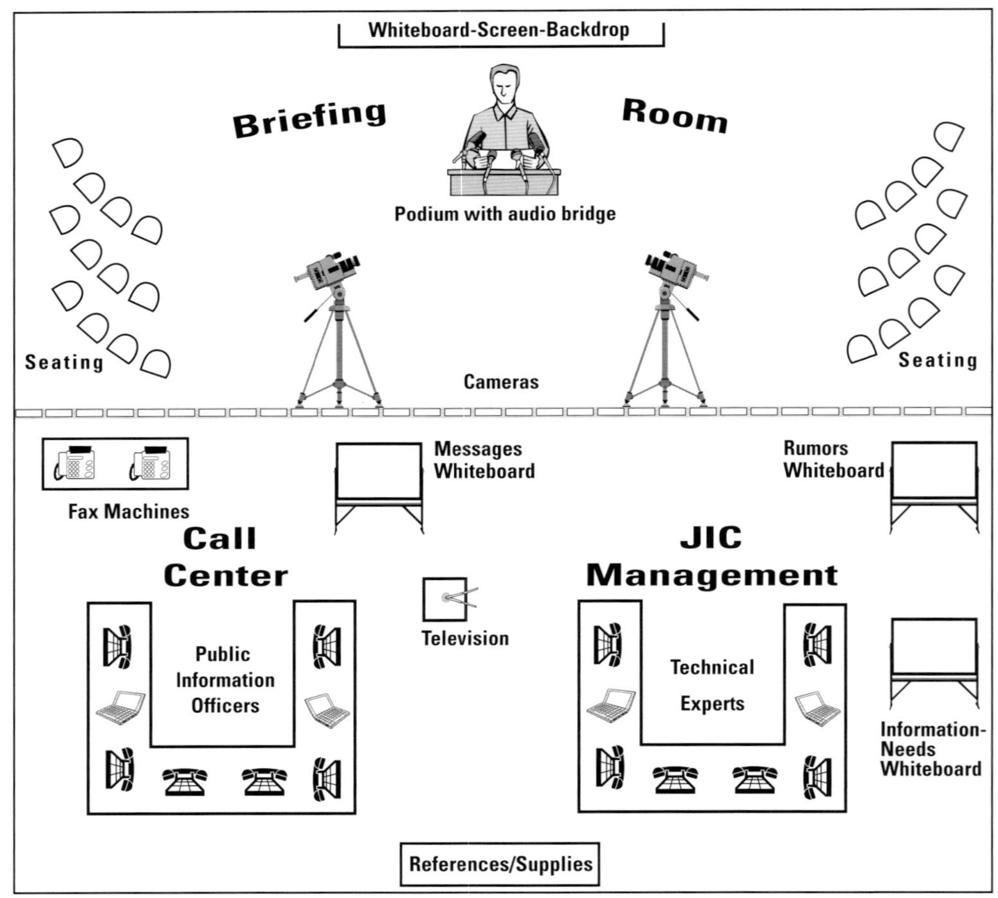

Figure 4. Layout of Joint Information Center (JIC), housed in conference room of Gifford Pinchot National Forest headquarters in Vancouver, Wash. The conference room was divided into three parts: a Media Briefing Room, a Call Center, and a section for JIC management and technical specialists.

EMD, the U.S. Department of the Interior Bureau of Land Management, and the GPNF and other national forests, posted new information prominently on the whiteboard so that it could be provided to media callers almost instantaneously. The Call Center's close proximity to scientists ensured that the nontechnical PIOs used the appropriate scientific descriptions.

Whereas CVO provided daily updates on volcanic activity and alert levels on its Web site, the JIC distributed news releases by e-mail or fax from information derived largely from CVO. Staffers combined rosters of media contacts from several agencies and amended them continuously in an effort to maximize distribution of information and to assure media that they would be informed of changes of volcano status. The JIC also established a recorded phone message line that summarized the current volcano conditions. This telephone number was widely advertised to the media, and the message was updated daily and provided in English and Spanish. The JIC also provided general volcano-hazards information that previously had been translated into eight languages.

News briefings at the JIC became an important regular source of authoritative information. The JIC initiated a rigorous, controlled protocol for briefing time, participation, and followup interviews with scientists or other officials. Briefings were conducted live on camera by designated scientists from USGS, often with equipment and graphics to illustrate content. Out-of-area media and radio station representatives called in during live briefings by way of a telephone audio link. The audio link enabled remote listeners to ask questions of presenters after the briefing. USGS Office of Communications staff often managed the media briefings. The JIC conducted two briefings on most days and a single briefing as demand decreased. During a period of several weeks, approximately 38 formal briefings were given at the JIC and at MSHNVM (see below).

Figure 5. Mount St. Helens Joint Information Center (JIC) housed at Gifford Pinchot National Forest headquarters, Vancouver, Wash. (USGS photos by C.L. Driedger, October 2004). *A*, Call Center, staffed by public-information officers from local agencies. *B*, JIC management and technical specialist center. *C*, Media Briefing Room.

Information Centers at Mount St. Helens

In addition to the JIC in Vancouver and the PNSN in Seattle, several other information centers provided updates in close coordination with the JIC. These included the interpretive facilities of MSHNVM, especially the Coldwater Ridge Visitor Center and nearby Castle Lake Viewpoint (fig. 6). At its peak, the Castle Lake Viewpoint hosted 24 television satellite trucks and accompanying media. Six GPNF PIOs and USGS information scientists staffed the viewpoint and held twice-daily news briefings. The multitude of media and public visitors at this remote viewpoint was substantial, and MSHNVM staff were soon overtaxed with the strain of conducting media interviews and providing crowd control for thousands of tourists who flocked to the monument. Media preferred to operate from Castle Lake Viewpoint because of its proximity to Mount St. Helens; however, scientists and the JOC preferred indoor briefings at the JIC in Vancouver, in close proximity to CVO.

Help in providing information also came from several colleges and universities with knowledgeable Earth science faculty, from State geological surveys in Washington and Oregon, and from other USGS offices throughout the nation. We have no satisfactory method to quantify the load of inquiries on these outlets.

Joint Information Center and Web Site Statistics

To document and evaluate the work of the JIC, staff tracked the number and type of inquiries (table 1) and maintained a master list of participants. During its 11-day operation, the JIC was staffed by 70 people from 30 different emergency-management, health, safety, and land-management agencies and the USGS, most of whom came from the Portland-Vancouver area. These individuals responded to more than 750 e-mail inquiries and more than 800 telephone inquiries from media staff in 12 countries.

Not surprisingly, the number of inquiries increased with a rise in real-time seismic amplitude measurements (RSAM) that reflected increased seismicity at the volcano (fig. 7). Inquiry frequency spiked when the alert level was raised, when volcanic tremor occurred, and when there were visible events, such as steam and ash explosions. USGS–CVO Web site statistics illustrate the same intense and event-driven demand for online information.

Table 1. Sources and numbers of inquiries to the Joint Information Center, Gifford Pinchot National Forest headquarters, Vancouver, Wash., from October 3 to October 13, 2004.

Sources of inquiries to the Joint Information Center	Number of inquiries
Television (local and affiliate)	278
Print (specific news publications)	228
Other (Associated Press wire service, public, and others)	163
Radio (local and affiliate stations)	137
Web-based news services	6

The PNSN Web site, where information about seismic activity related to volcanic unrest was available, received 31 million hits on the Web servers (equaling approximately 10 million pages viewed) between September 28 and October 5. Early during the event, in anticipation of this intense interest, UW staff separated the public Web site servers from computer servers that process scientific information, potentially saving both systems from failure.

As at PNSN, the record high number of hits on the CVO Web site prompted USGS system administrators to add servers and then to contract with temporary commercial service providers to accommodate the demand for online information. In September 2004, before onset of the erup-

Figure 6. Castle Lake Viewpoint, Mount St. Helens National Volcanic Monument, Wash., located approximately 15 km from Mount St. Helens, served as a nexus for media representatives during October 2004. Monument staff directed all media representatives to this viewpoint, dubbed "Satellite City," where media queries could be addressed efficiently by local staff and U.S. Geological Survey scientists. As many as 24 media trucks were on site at the height of media interest. USGS photo by L.G. Mastin, October 5, 2004.

tion, there were approximately 34,000 Web pages requested per day. During the steam and ash explosion on October 4, 2004, 1.43 million Web pages were requested—a 42-fold increase in daily CVO Web page requests. In the 2-week time period between September 24 and October 7, Web users requested 8.4 million pages, and 11.2 million pages were requested during October 2004. As of this writing in October 2006, the number of Web pages requested remains high. The volume of Web page requests has, on occasion, inexplicably risen tenfold, far exceeding October 2004 levels. CVO Web site access has yet to return to pre-October 2004 levels (Lyn Topinka, oral commun., 2006).

The majority of GPNF Web site hits were to the Mount St. Helens VolcanoCam Web page, which received an estimated 131 million hits (equaling approximately 18 million Web pages requested) between September 23 and October 31, 2004. The VolcanoCam's popularity resulted in a manyfold increase in Web page requests to the GPNF Web site.

Update Protocols at Cascades Volcano Observatory

USGS scientific and communications staff generated text updates on the status of the volcano each morning on the basis of consensus at daily scientific meetings. Although the JIC staff relied upon these daily updates, volcanic events sometimes rendered them obsolete. For example, during a scheduled news briefing at the JIC, scientist Willie Scott was inter-

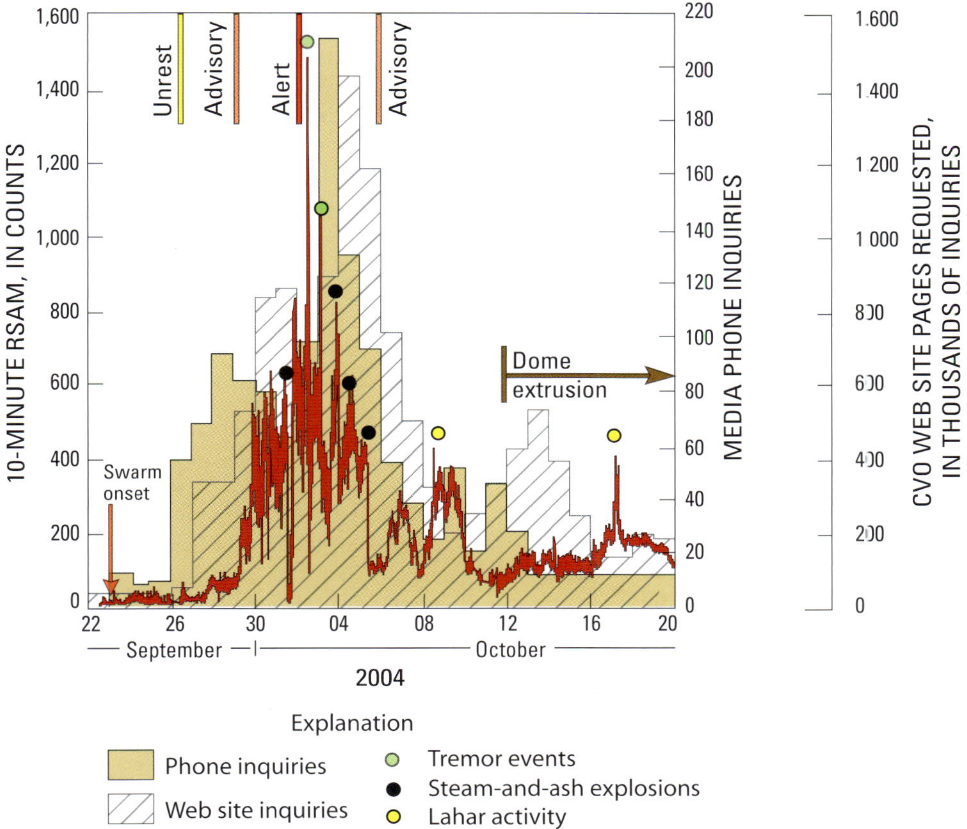

Figure 7. Relation between volcanic activity, alert levels, volume of media inquiries to the Cascades Volcano Observatory, and number of Web pages requested from the CVO Web site (Lyn Topinka, oral commun., 2005) during the first weeks of unrest at Mount St. Helens. Real-time seismic amplitude measurement (RSAM), in red, is a proxy for the level of seismicity at volcano. Media phone inquiries (daily counts, in tan) and public Web activity (hachured) generally increased with the rise in RSAM and spiked following changes of alert level and prominent volcanic events, such as steam and ash explosions.

rupted by a news reporter who announced that a steam and ash explosion was in progress. Scott was forced to abandon his prepared text and interpret the eruption as seen on a small monitor provided by one of the television stations.

Before the onset of the 2004 volcanic unrest at Mount St. Helens, CVO issued occasional written statements concerning volcanic activity and posted these to its Web site. Such statements were posted daily in the fall of 2004 and were supplemented by media advisories, information about news briefings, and notification of events released by fax and e-mail. In October 2004, CVO broadened daily update dissemination by e-mail to include media and aviation contacts; previously, e-mailed updates were sent primarily to government agencies. Broad update distribution has continued throughout 2006.

Hazard Information Management Through October 2006

Since cessation of the JIC on October 13, 2004, staff at CVO has replied to about 800 phone inquiries from the media, principally about the status of Mount St. Helens. As of October 2006, the combined number of media phone inquiries received by CVO and by the JIC during its 11 days of operation in 2004 exceeded 2,000. In addition to these general media inquiries, representatives of 41 documentary film projects contacted USGS–CVO for interviews, information, and graphics, mostly about the ongoing and 1980 eruptions at Mount St. Helens. Each year, the CVO staff has provided additional media briefings on the anniversary of the 2004 eruption and after significant explosive events. USGS staff assembled 10 rolls of video for use by media (b-rolls) between November 2004 and October 2006. As of this writing, the level of media interest is variable. The number of media inquiries rises with sightings of rockfall, with its subsequent suspension of dust and ash particles in the air, and with the onset of cold and clear weather, which initiates visible condensation plumes above the crater rim. CVO staff has taken the time to educate local media about these two phenomena. It is commonly accepted that this education has reduced the number of media inquiries considerably.

Challenges and Lessons Learned

The USGS and its partner agencies in emergency management faced a number of challenges in this episode of unrest at Mount St. Helens. Here, we present the most important challenges and lessons into four groupings: media and message management, JIC management, special needs of university cooperators, and organizational constraints. Many of these observations were compiled at an interagency after-action review of the eruption response, an important step in identifying lessons learned following any eruption crisis.

Media and Message Management

Pre-Event Planning for Communications with Media

A pre-event hazard communication and media management plan reduces the inevitable scramble to establish an effective information pipeline to the public and other constituencies (Peterson and Tilling, 1993; Newhall and Punongbayan, 1996). The plan should be written by agency representatives most likely to be in the "hot seat" during an event. Volcano observatories and cooperating scientific agencies need full-time scientists whose major roles are to manage media relations, community outreach, and education. These scientists should achieve a working understanding of emergency roles codified in NIMS, including their role in a JIC. The roles should address the following responsibilities:

1. Engage the media and educate them about hazards and agency roles in hazard response.
2. Prepare background information about a volcano and its hazards before a crisis begins and arrange for rapid development and dissemination of updated information, graphics, and maps required for briefings.
3. Maintain relations with media representatives so that they are prepared to reach broad audiences with agency messages. Media representatives should feel comfortable asking questions so that they can "get the story right."
4. Establish, exercise, and review phone, e-mail, fax, and other crisis-communication protocols.
5. Identify scientists who can dedicate their time to communication needs and offer media training for key staff.
6. Establish a system for obtaining photography and video footage for inclusion in media b-rolls.
7. Acquire official agency logos and apparel.
8. Consider a system for tracking media inquiries and workload.
9. Isolate public Web sites, by serving them from computer systems independent of the computers used for processing scientific data, to reduce the potential that increasing demand will crash either system.

Tools for First Moments Following an Event

After months or years of volcanic quiet, an eruption or onset of dramatic unrest can be a chaotic time with respect to media-communication protocols. Background fact sheets, FAQs, and other pre-event resources can help fill the immediate need for information. CVO developed a "Volcano Rapid Response Reference Page" that lists steps to be taken within the first few minutes of a visible volcanic event (fig. 8). The Reference Page can be customized for eruptions at any volcano.

Fighting Imaginations and Misperceptions

Agencies must devise a system to prepare, review, and update talking points that reinforce appropriate messages and terminology. A recurring challenge during the 2004 volcanic unrest concerned the widespread perception that any activity at Mount St. Helens was a prelude to another cataclysmic eruption resembling the event on May 18, 1980. Dispelling this image was a challenging exercise in wording and repetition. Once lodged in the public's mind, such misperceptions are hard to remove.

Disseminating Updates to Remote Information Centers

Maintaining contact, continuity, consistency, and completeness of message with remote information centers is both a technical and a human challenge. Communication and sharing

Volcano Rapid Response Reference Page

TASKS - *First* 10 MINUTES *of volcanic event*

1 - **Before Speaking To Media:** Visit operations room—obtain three known facts about situation for the development of talking points:

Talking Points

- ***What Is Happening?*** → (Example - At 1725 PDT a small explosive eruption began).
- ***What Is The Impact?*** → (Example - Ash from plume will fall east of volcano).
- ***What Are We Doing About It ?*** → (Example - USGS closely monitoring this event and advising local officials).

2 - **Update Talking Points:** Add some situation background.

3 - **Arrange Additional Help:** For liaison between operations room and outreach staff.

4 - **Recorded Message:** Place temporary messages on pertinent phone recorders, information lines, and Web sites.

5 - **Answer Inquiries:** Keep talking points visible while providing telephone interviews; maintain a record of inquiries.

6 - **Request Assistance From Other Offices/Agencies:** If it appears that a media event might overwhelm staff on hand.

ARRANGEMENTS - *During first* HOUR *of volcanic event*

1 - **News Briefing Arrangements:** Establish time and place; announce the briefing; arrange for audio bridge; choose speakers; develop messages to greater depth and information; assemble agenda; address needs for graphics.

2 - **Front Desk Duty:** Arrange for staffing in evenings and early mornings as necessary.

3 - **Joint Information Center Planning:** Initiate interagency arrangements as necessary.

4 - **Review Personal Needs For Outreach Staff:** Food, family schedules, for example.

5 - **Off-Hours Arrangements:** Advise duty scientists to check the front desk recorder for phone messages and respond to inquiries during nonwork hours. If inquiries require additional attention, contact outreach staff.

6 - **B-Roll:** Encourage scientific observers to take video that can be used for media b-roll; arrange for b-roll preparation and distribution.

7 - **Web Site Information:** Provide any necessary information about media briefings and b-roll to webmaster for b-roll preparation and distribution.

Contact Information for Outreach Staff:

Include contact information for additional help within office, within team and communication offices, and with partner agencies.

Figure 8. Volcano Rapid Response Reference Page illustrating how the Cascades Volcano Observatory addresses media inquiries during sudden volcanic events, such as steam-and-ash explosions and resultant plumes.

of talking points with PIOs and information scientists at Castle Lake Viewpoint were hampered by technological difficulties (fax and phone line service between information centers was intermittent) and the Viewpoint's physical distance from the JIC.

The Media's Need for Information, Now!

Agency representatives must be prepared to address nearly continuous information demands from the media for the 24-hour international news cycle. Scientists must create a steady stream of updated information to satisfy the appetite of media outlets and their constituencies. During the Mount St. Helens unrest, media photographers found it difficult to get close-range photographs because of temporary flight restrictions. At the request of the media, the 10 b-rolls released by the USGS provided close-up video coverage of the eruption, volcanologists working in the crater, and time-lapse and thermal-image video. Photographs taken by USGS observers were posted on the CVO Web site within a day of their being taken. There was a constant need for charts and illustrations for news briefings, especially for diagrams of volcano cross sections and schematics showing the relative sizes of the lava dome through time. Any media management plan should cover how these graphical products will be distributed efficiently.

Near-Simultaneous Observations by USGS Staff and Media

Scientists must often react to near-simultaneous observations by scientific staff and media. Today's media outlets have access to and budgets for fly-bys of the volcano by helicopters, which often are outfitted with modern infrared sensors and cameras similar to those used by scientists. At Mount St. Helens, there was pressure to interpret observations made by media representatives before the extended group of monitoring scientists had seen or analyzed the information.

Maintaining Appropriate Distance Between Media and Operational Staff

Maintaining appropriate distance between media representatives and operational staff is a primary reason for positioning the JIC away from science facilities. Prior to the 2004 volcanic unrest, many media members had developed links with scientists and contacted them at will. The creation of the information-scientist role freed operational scientists who had responsibilities for monitoring and analysis. The founding of the JIC and its media briefings allowed controlled access to scientists.

Consistent and Careful Use of Nomenclature

Another important concern in sharing information with the media and public is consistent use of terminology and nomenclature. In one particular case, USGS scientists unwittingly fed public concern through their casual use of geographical terms. Constant repetition of the "bulging crater floor…on the south side…of the old lava dome" gave rise to a mistaken notion that the south flank of the entire volcano was bulging in a manner similar to the north flank prior to the catastrophic May 18, 1980, event. Another source of terminology confusion concerned use of the word "eruption." For example, there were references to the events of early October 2004 as explosions, emissions, and eruptions. Although such distinctions appear trivial, and in many senses are purely semantic, to the reporting media representatives, these are important facts to get right.

The word "eruption" has a fairly specific image to many, and that includes visible lava, ash, and activity that is full of motion and potential danger. At this writing in October 2006, many people are unaware that Mount St. Helens continues to erupt. The same phenomenon occurred in Alaska during the 2005–6 eruption of Augustine Volcano. Once the volcano ceased ash-cloud production and began quietly producing lava flows, many people assumed the eruption had stopped altogether, despite the local volcano observatory's constant repetition of messages that the eruption continued.

Joint Information Center Management

Development and Concept

Agencies must recognize the value of a JIC and then plan for it. At Mount St. Helens there was a hesitancy to form a JIC, caused in part by immediate needs but in greater part by not understanding a JIC's value to all involved agencies. Volcano-response plans for each Cascade Range volcano refer to the use of a JIC, but, at the time of the 2004 event, no detailed plan existed for rapid development and staffing. It is important to understand the basics of the NIMS, each agency's role during a crisis, and how a JIC may help.

Adequate Space for Necessities

A JIC requires large and small rooms with secure entry points. The Mount St. Helens JIC lacked distinct and secure entry points that were out-of-view of JIC operations. Access to the Media Briefing Room required passage of media representatives through the inner workings of the JIC, which exposed sensitive information not intended for public release, such as private phone numbers. This required JIC workers temporarily to "sanitize" whiteboards of sensitive information. Such security issues can be addressed with good JIC design. The Mount St. Helens JIC suffered from a lack of small rooms for individual media interviews.

Staffing and Logistics

Agencies must plan for the details of assembling people and technological facilities rapidly during establishment and maintenance of a JIC. At the Mount St. Helens JIC, staff from the Clark Regional Emergency Services Agency took the initiative to locate call center personnel by announcing the need on an extensive PIO listserve in the Portland-Vancouver area. Many people responded to the call for help, but maintaining a refreshed staff of trained and knowledgeable call takers, technical specialists, and JIC managers was a constant challenge. Also of value was participation of volunteers from the City of Vancouver who could assist traveling media with requests for general local information. A JIC handbook of procedures and resources was extremely helpful for educating existing and newer personnel. Lines of authority were a subject of frequent discussion, with personnel adjusting to the roles placed upon them within the JIC. Security firewalls presented continuous technical roadblocks for communications, both within the JIC and to outside agencies. A general e-mail account could not be established, so staff had to use individual e-mail accounts for transmitting JIC business information.

Maintaining Consistent and Timely Messages

Agencies must consider that maintenance of a consistent, current message requires vigilance. At Mount St. Helens, volcanic events frequently eclipsed the Daily Update and necessitated hurried development of updated talking points, education of call takers and staff at other information outlets, and rumor control. An official JIC Daily Update required review by a representative of each agency. The duration of the production process often outlived the usefulness of the product. Early morning requests from East Coast media were most challenging because daily updates were not yet available. News briefings came too late for local morning news shows. There was demand for hourly updates, but no official process was available to provide this need. As a result of such media demands, the Alaska Volcano Observatory provided hourly status reports on its Web page during the height of the eruption of Augustine Volcano in early 2006. These were informal and nonreviewed snapshots of what was happening at the volcano, and they served to underscore that scientists were actively watching the volcano. Even remarking that nothing had changed in many hours apparently served to reassure Web users that the Observatory was aware of current conditions.

Special Needs of University Cooperators: Pacific Northwest Seismic Network

University cooperators must find the resources to protect monitoring capabilities while addressing media response. The greatest challenge faced by the PNSN was to find ways to satisfy the numerous requests for interviews while maintaining network operations and analyzing and interpreting data.

The PNSN PIO addressed media needs with support from student staff, who answered phones and organized requests for information and interviews. The PIO reviewed these requests and PNSN scientists monitoring the eruption were scheduled, when appropriate, to participate in interviews. The PNSN also received assistance from the UW Office of News and Information who assisted in scheduling interviews and disseminating press releases. At key moments, such as a change in alert level or following steam and ash explosions, reporters were pooled and the PNSN Director made a statement, answered questions for a few minutes, and then returned to work. National news outlets did not always get to talk to the scientist they requested, but all media requests were addressed. The PNSN concentrated their response onsite at the UW and turned down almost all requests for television-studio interviews. The PNSN also frequently referred many requests to the JIC, particularly those not directly related to seismicity.

Organizational Constraints

Staffing

The USGS volcano observatory system consists primarily of technical specialists with defined scientific roles and expertise to monitor volcanoes and assess hazards. For most staff, outreach and interaction with the media are ancillary duties; therefore, technical tasks may go unfinished when scientific staff are consumed by providing information. Even for observatories with professional communication and public-information specialists, a single eruption crisis can quickly overwhelm slim resources. To respond effectively and not diminish the technical efficacy of the observatory, it is key to call quickly for reinforcements from within and outside the USGS. It is helpful to have predetermined lists of staff available for temporary short-term duties to assist in this capacity. Crisis-related staffing should include information scientists, Web and illustration staff, and information technology support.

Cost

Establishing a JIC is not cost free. According to the GPNF, the total JIC operation costs for 11 days, including extra staffing by interpreters at MSHNVM, was approximately $88,400 in salaries and $7,500 in equipment and supplies. Most of the personnel who worked at the JIC either donated their time, or their agencies absorbed salary costs as a contribution to the regional response. For the Call Center, where 40 people rotated through various shifts to answer phones, the estimated cost of staff time alone totaled more than $17,000.

The State of Washington does not have a system to pay for JIC support without declarations of emergency or disaster, a situation common in other states. Once such a declaration exists, the State can request Federal resources from FEMA to support staff costs. Cultivating partnerships in advance, including the development of formal mutual-aid agreements, can help local offices deal with the staffing shortage during an information crisis. Although some agencies or jurisdictions were unable or unwilling to commit paid staff time to volunteer at the Mount St. Helens JIC, many others did donate personnel to the public-information effort. This volunteer opportunity provided PIOs with skill-building advantages, because it is rare to get the chance to work within a JIC.

Another expense of JIC operation is technological outfitting of the facility. The Mount St. Helens JIC at the GPNF headquarters already had phone lines and extensions available, so the cost of installing a switchboard and other phone lines was minimal. However, it was necessary to install fiber-optic cable to serve the needs of the media satellite trucks, and this involved some major contract work. By pre-identifying a facility with critical infrastructure in place and securing an agreement in advance for free or low-cost emergency use of that facility, technical costs can be minimized.

Media Training Needs

Scientists rarely, if ever, are trained to work with the media. For those who are likely to be directly involved in providing information to the media, many resources are available to provide an appropriate level of training, including classes in basic crisis communication available through local emergency-management offices.

Conclusions

Preeruption planning contributed significantly to the readiness of the USGS, PNSN, GPNF, and other key agencies to deliver timely and effective hazard information about the evolving eruption at Mount St. Helens, one of the world's most famous volcanoes. The success of the response speaks well of decisions by the USGS, a largely scientific agency, to enable communication planning to proceed on par with scientific response planning. Training of media representatives over the long term; practicing response plans; and ongoing communication among scientists, emergency managers, and community leaders about volcano hazards in the Pacific Northwest brings a cushion of support that bolstered effectiveness of the response. Despite this preparation, considerable flexibility, creativity, and rapid development of strategies to deal with unanticipated issues were essential. In particular, today's widespread use of the Internet and the around-the-clock news cycle required a fast, sustained pace of information delivery that frequently pushed the limits of staffing and internal communications. Establishing a JIC within the ICS structure contributed substantially to managing these expectations. The JIC also insulated the JOC and CVO and PNSN scientists from media attention, freeing managers and scientists to deal with critical aspects of the crisis.

To our knowledge, this was the first time that a fully developed JIC was used to address volcanic unrest. Earlier volcanic responses have tended toward multiple agencies providing information independently by specialists, such as at Ruapehu volcano, New Zealand (David Johnston, oral commun., 2005) and Volcán Santa Ana, El Salvador (John Ewert, oral commun., 2005). An exception was a single source at Pinatubo volcano, Philippines (Chris Newhall, oral commun., 2005). Our 2004 experience at Mount St. Helens confirms that volcano and seismic observatories benefit from the availability of a full-time scientist focusing on the needs of media relations, community outreach, and education.

Acknowledgments

We thank all those who contributed to successfully managing the hazard message during the 2004 unrest and eruption. We also acknowledge the critical feedback and constructive criticism from our partners in the media, at other agencies, and our own colleagues, all of whom helped improve our communication with the public. This manuscript was reviewed by Maggie Mangan and Chris Jonientz-Trisler.

References Cited

Dzurisin, D., Vallance, J.W., Gerlach, T.M., Moran, S.C., and Malone, S.D., 2005, Mount St. Helens reawakens: Eos (American Geophysical Union Transactions), v. 86, no. 3, p. 25, 29.

Federal Emergency Management Agency, 2004, National Incident Management System: U.S. Department of Homeland Security, 139 p. [http://www.fema.gov/emergency/nims/index.shtm, last accessed November 17, 2006].

Frenzen, P.M., and Mataresse, M.T., 2008, Managing public and media response to a reawakening volcano; lessons from the 2004 eruptive activity of Mount St. Helens, chap. 23 *of* Sherrod, D.R., Scott, W.E., and Stauffer, P.H., eds., A volcano rekindled; the renewed eruption of Mount St. Helens, 2004–2006: U.S. Geological Survey Professional Paper 1750 (this volume).

Gifford Pinchot National Forest, 2003, Mount St. Helens volcanic activity response plan update: Vancouver, Wash., Gifford Pinchot National Forest, 42 p.

Moran, S.C., Malone, S.D., Qamar, A.I., Thelen, W.A., Wright, A.K., and Caplan-Auerbach, J., 2008a, Seismicity associated with renewed dome building at Mount St. Helens, 2004–2005, chap. 2 *of* Sherrod, D.R., Scott, W.E., and Stauffer, P.H., eds., A volcano rekindled; the renewed eruption of Mount St. Helens, 2004–2006: U.S. Geological Survey Professional Paper 1750 (this volume).

Moran, S.C., McChesney, P.J., and Lockhart, A.B., 2008b, Seismicity and infrasound associated with explosions at Mount St. Helens, 2004–2005, chap. 6 *of* Sherrod, D.R., Scott, W.E., and Stauffer, P.H., eds., A volcano rekindled; the renewed eruption of Mount St. Helens, 2004–2006: U.S. Geological Survey Professional Paper 1750 (this volume).

Newhall, C.G., and Punongbayan, R.S., 1996. Successful volcanic-risk mitigation, *in* Scarpa, R., and Tilling, R.I., eds., Monitoring and mitigation of volcano hazards: Berlin, Springer-Verlag, p. 807–838.

Peterson, D.W., and Tilling, R.I., 1993, Interactions between scientists, civil authorities, and the public at hazardous volcanoes, *in* Kilburn, C.R.J., and Luongo, G., eds., Monitoring active lavas: London, UCL Press, p. 339–365.

Qamar, A.I., Malone, S.D., Moran, S.C., Steele, W.P., and Thelen, W.A., 2008, Near-real-time information products for Mount St. Helens—tracking the ongoing eruption, chap. 3 *of* Sherrod, D.R., Scott, W.E., and Stauffer, P.H., eds., A volcano rekindled; the renewed eruption of Mount St. Helens, 2004–2006: U.S. Geological Survey Professional Paper 1750 (this volume).

Scott, W.E., Sherrod, D.R., and Gardner, C.A., 2008, Overview of the 2004 to 2005, and continuing, eruption of Mount St. Helens, Washington, chap. 1 *of* Sherrod, D.R., Scott, W.E., and Stauffer, P.H., eds., A volcano rekindled; the renewed eruption of Mount St. Helens, 2004–2006: U.S. Geological Survey Professional Paper 1750 (this volume).

Wolfe, E.W., and Pierson, T.C., 1995, Volcanic-hazard zonation for Mount St. Helens, Washington: U.S. Geological Survey Open-File Report 95–497, 12 p.

MIDAC

Volcanic Emissions

Tracking the flow of gases from magma is perhaps the most vexing task of physical volcanology. To play upon a phrase, "gas waits for no man," because the gaseous species are volatile. Also, things get in the way, not the least of which are the volcanic edifice itself and ground water that permeates it.

The 2004–6 Mount St. Helens dacite was a "flat" magma—greatly depleted in excess (exsolved) volatiles compared to the May 18, 1980, dacite. If new magma entered the system as part of the 2004 eruption, it must have been gas poor, on the basis of modeling constrained by cumulative CO_2 emissions, cumulative dacite production, and measurement of dissolved H_2O and other volatile concentrations within the dacite glass.

This view, that the eruption was driven by degassed magma, is supported by chemical trends in hot springs and creek waters that drain the Mount St. Helens crater. Since 1994 these waters have shown decreasing SO_4 and Cl concentrations, most likely reflecting changing release rates of sulfur gases, HCl, and CO_2 from the magma and, to a varying degree, the efficiency of gas scrubbing by the water. Still unanswered is the question of what triggered the eruption of such gas-poor magma—was it influx of a small amount of hotter, gas-rich magma that was otherwise compositionally similar to the 1980s magma, infiltration of rainwater into the upper part of the conduit system, or some other mechanism?

The lessons from the 2004 eruption are clear: Scrubbing or simply having a magma already depleted in gases can mask the more typical signal of shallow magmatic sulfur-species degassing, so early monitoring of CO_2 should accompany early SO_2 monitoring. Indeed, the monitoring of CO_2, SO_2, and H_2S can track the drying out of a volcano and help distinguish the effects of gas scrubbing from the loss of permeability when pathways for gas are sealed by precipitates.

This eruption also provided an opportunity to further test new gas-emission monitoring tools. Results from open-path Fourier-transform infrared spectroscopy support the interpretation that closed-system degassing occurs as shallow as 1–2 km and that open-system degassing characterizes the shallowest part of the magmatic system.

View to south-southwest on September 19, 2005, as spine 6 grew westward away from disintegrating spines 4 and 5 (left of center) and compressed the highly crevassed west arm of Crater Glacier. Rocky terrain in lower right is 1980s dome. USGS photo by J.W. Ewert.

A Volcano Rekindled: The Renewed Eruption of Mount St. Helens, 2004–2006
Edited by David R. Sherrod, William E. Scott, and Peter H. Stauffer
U.S. Geological Survey Professional Paper 1750, 2008

Chapter 25

Pre- and Post-Eruptive Investigations of Gas and Water Samples from Mount St. Helens, Washington, 2002 to 2005

By Deborah Bergfeld[1], William C. Evans[1], Kenneth A. McGee[2], and Kurt R. Spicer[2]

Abstract

Samples of gas and water from thermal springs in Loowit and Step canyons and creeks that drain the crater at Mount St. Helens have been collected since October 2004 to monitor the flux of dissolved magmatic volatiles in the hydrologic system. The changing composition of the waters highlights a trend that began as early as 1994 and includes decreasing SO_4 and Cl concentrations and large increases in HCO_3. Geochemical models indicate that mineral sources and sinks are not the main controls on the changing water chemistry, and carbon and helium isotopes indicate that their sources in the gases and waters have remained unchanged during this time. The present-day molar ratios of C, S, and Cl in the springs approximate ratios measured in plume emissions in August 2005 and provide supporting evidence that changes in water chemistry most likely reflect changes in the release rates of sulfur gases, HCl, and CO_2 from the magma and a varying degree of efficiency of gas scrubbing by the overlying water. Results from coupled chemical analyses and discharge measurements on the creeks yield an estimate of the dissolved flux of magmatic HCl, SO_2, and CO_2 of around 5.2, 4.7, and 22 metric tons per day, respectively.

Introduction

Airborne gas measurements were a valuable tool in tracking magmatic emissions for Mount St. Helens during the 1980–86 eruptive sequence, but flights eventually were suspended as emission rates dropped to low levels. Between September 1988 and September 2004, attempts to measure the flux of magmatic volatiles at Mount St. Helens were restricted to analyses of gases and condensates from vents on the lava dome and thermal waters from springs in Loowit and Step canyons[3] in The Breach. Results from those analyses generally have shown a progressive decrease in magmatic volatile concentrations with time. Airborne gas-flux measurements over the crater at Mount St. Helens were resumed in September 2004 following the onset of seismic activity (Doukas and others, 2005). To date, those measurements have shown that plume CO_2 and SO_2 emission rates are much lower than emission rates during the 1980s eruptions (Gerlach and others, 2005, and this volume, chap. 26). Plume emission rates were one line of evidence that supported an early hypothesis that degassed magma was driving the current eruption.

To track the flux of dissolved magmatic volatiles in the hydrologic system during the current eruption, we established a surface-water sampling program on October 13, 2004. The first samples were collected on the Pumice Plain from two creeks that drain the crater. In mid-April 2005, as conditions nearer the crater stabilized, we expanded the monitoring network to include three locations in The Breach (fig. 1). These five sites were the main focus of our monitoring campaign during the first year after the 2004–5 eruption, but at times we also have collected samples from a warm spring on the west end of the Pumice Plain and from hot springs in Loowit and Step canyons in upper parts of The Breach. Thus far, our sample collection intervals have been irregular, but since October 2005 some continuous temperature and conductivity data have been collected by a probe installed near the top of Step creek.

In this report we present geochemical data from the monitoring sites; data from field campaigns in the crater and

[1] U.S. Geological Survey, 345 Middlefield Road, Menlo Park, CA 94025

[2] U.S. Geological Survey, 1300 SE Cardinal Court, Vancouver, WA 98683

[3] Many geographic features in the Mount St. Helens area are referred to informally by Earth scientists. Capitalization of "canyon," "creek," or "spring" indicates names formally adopted and listed in the Geographic Names Information System, a database maintained by the U.S. Board on Geographic Names. Noncapitalized names are applied informally—eds.

The Breach in 2002 and 2005, which focused on the chemistry of crater gases and hot spring waters; and data from a survey of regional cold springs. We also include data from previous investigations of the geochemistry of the hot springs at Mount St. Helens in order to evaluate long-term changes in gas sources or fluxes and, ultimately, to determine how magmatic processes at an active volcano are reflected in the hydrothermal system. We have adopted the names of the Loowit canyon hot springs that were used by Shevenell and Goff (1993) but have adhered to the policies of the U.S. Board on Geographic Names regarding capitalization of formal and informal names. Additional chemical data not discussed in the paper can be found in appendix 1, which appears only in the digital versions of this work (in the DVD that accompanies the printed volume and online at http://pubs.usgs.gov/pp/1750).

Background

After the May 1980 eruption of Mount St. Helens, gas samples were collected from cracks and fumaroles near the dome in the fall of 1980 (Evans and others, 1981; Gerlach and Casadevall, 1986). Due to dome growth and collapse and extrusions of new lava, the gas-sampling locations varied during the subsequent years. Before our work in 2002, the last

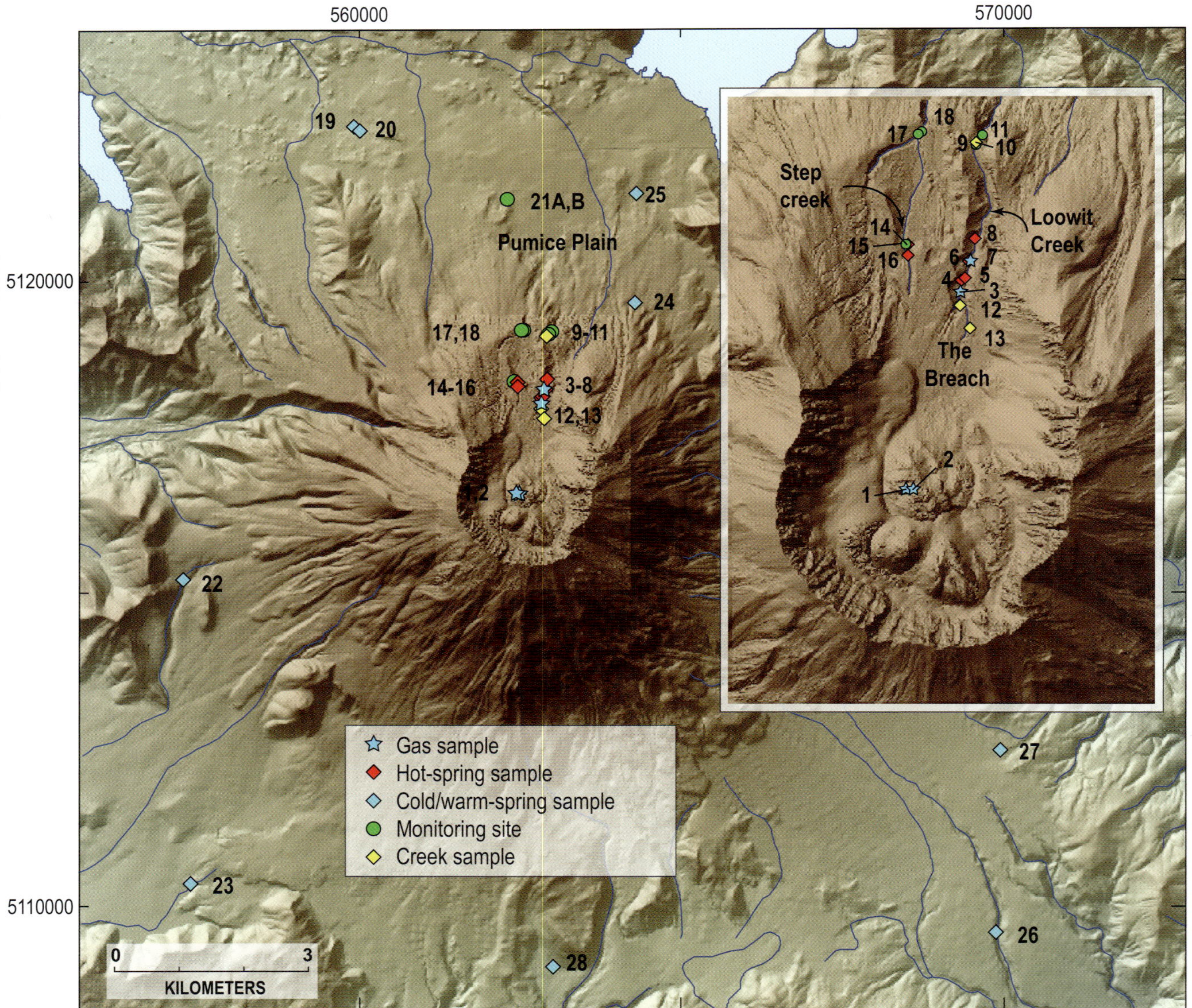

Figure 1. Maps showing sample locations for this study, 2002–2005, Mount St. Helens, Washington. Numbers for sample sites correspond to numbers listed in table 1. Inset shows crater and The Breach sample locations in more detail. Datum for geographic grid and UTM coordinates referenced to WGS84, zone 10.

gas sample from the crater was collected in June 1998 from an 86°C vent on the southwest side of the 1980–86 lava dome on a flow called the September 1984 lobe, herein referred to more briefly as "September lobe." The sampling site was formerly the hottest fumarole on the dome, but in 1998 it had cooled by 260–370°C relative to temperatures recorded in 1994–95 (Symonds and others, 2001).

Downcutting of avalanche deposits in The Breach of Mount St. Helens created Loowit and Step canyons, which drain to the north and represent the main discharge of surface water from the crater (fig. 1). Thermal springs were first observed discharging into Loowit Creek during the summer of 1983, and the first sample of spring water was collected in October 1983 (Thompson, 1990). Lower-temperature, low-discharge springs in Step canyon were discovered at a later date, and the first published analyses of the Step canyon springs are from 1988 (Shevenell and Goff, 1993). It has been estimated that more than 95 percent of the hot spring discharge from both canyons is provided by the springs in Loowit canyon (Shevenell and Goff, 1993). During the 1980s to mid-1990s, the hot springs in Loowit canyon were located in three areas along the length of the canyon. Each area contained clusters of hot springs of varying size and temperature. From south to north, the spring groups are called (1) Loowit source, (2) Loowit boulder basin, and (3) Loowit travertine. The name Loowit travertine is a misnomer that stems from the presence of gypsum-bearing precipitates on the rocks around the vent orifices (Shevenell and Goff, 1993). There are no names for the springs in Step canyon. The waters from both Loowit and Step canyons were sampled throughout the 1980s and 1990s, but because of the larger volume of thermal water, the Loowit canyon springs were sampled with the greatest frequency.

Post-2000 Field Campaigns

Gas and Water Samples from the Crater and The Breach

In August 2002 there were no fumaroles in the crater at Mount St. Helens, but diffuse steam was rising from several locations on the 1980–86 dome. We sampled gas at two locations from the strongest vents we could find on September lobe (fig. 1; table 1). Because of safety concerns we were unable to resample the sites in 2005. In August 2002 and July 2005 we also collected gases from bubbling hot springs in Loowit canyon. To our knowledge these are the first free-gas samples collected from springs in Loowit canyon.

Water samples were collected from the Loowit canyon hot springs in 2002 and 2005, and samples of the Step canyon springs were collected in July and October 2005. At springs with multiple orifices, our strategy was to choose the hottest spring for sample collection, and at times we also sampled water from a nearby spring. In 2002, the hottest vents at the Loowit boulder basin and Loowit travertine sites were along the west bank of Loowit Creek. The outflow from the southernmost spring, which we assume to be the Loowit source spring, was from a single vent on a bench above the canyon floor. The water cascaded down the west canyon wall into Loowit Creek. In July 2005 there was no visible outflow from the Loowit source spring; instead, a new large spring issued from the base of a small fan that abuts the west wall of the canyon. Additional cooler waters discharged from an upper part of the fan and small vents along the west bank of the creek.

The thermal waters in Step canyon occur in clusters and line the banks of the headwaters of Step creek. In 2005 there were no high-discharge vents, and all of the waters issued from areas composed of low-discharge seeps. Intermittent degassing was observed at both of the sites in July, but no gas was visible in October 2005.

Creeks and Regional Springs

The five sites that make up the monitoring network are along creeks that provide the major surface drainage from the crater at Mount St. Helens. The network includes two sites (LCBF and SCBF) on the Pumice Plain (fig. 1; table 1) and three sites (LCAF, EFSCAF, and WFSCAF) closer to the crater above the waterfalls on Loowit and Step creeks. The Pumice Plain sites are the most accessible and serve to monitor the surface drainage from locations just above the confluence of the two creeks. Of the higher-altitude sites, LCAF receives input from all of the hot springs in Loowit canyon and variable seasonal input of glacial meltwater; EFSCAF is on the east fork of Step creek, which is the fork that contains the Step canyon springs; and WFSCAF is a tributary to Step creek that drains the west wall of the crater. This channel (WFSCAF) carries seasonal runoff from the west arm of the Crater Glacier. We have not walked the length of this creek, but there are no obvious thermal waters that discharge to this drainage. In this report we also present water data from the probe locations (fig. 1; table 1) and three other locations on Loowit Creek, which were sampled in 2002 and 2005.

Several studies have used carbon and helium isotopes, together with water chemistry, to demonstrate that cold ground waters in volcanic regions can carry large amounts of dissolved magmatic carbon (Rose and Davisson, 1996; Chiodini and others, 2000; Evans and others, 2002). To investigate outflow of magmatic volatiles from the volcano to regional springs, we sampled eight mostly low-temperature springs in the area surrounding Mount St. Helens in July 2005. Kalama Spring, located southwest of Mount St. Helens, has the largest discharge of any spring in our sample set, followed by carbonate spring, a warm spring on the west end of the Pumice Plain (fig. 1; tables 1 and 2). Because the chemistry of carbonate spring has some similarities with the springs from The Breach, future discussion of this spring will be included with discussions of the hot springs. Of the seven other cold springs in this report, the most well-studied are Kalama, Willow, and Moss Springs, which have been sampled infrequently since

Table 1. Map number and location coordinates for samples collected during 2002–2005, Mount St. Helens, Washington.

[UTM coordinates and altitude are referenced to the WGS84 datum.]

Location	Map No.	Northing	Easting	Altitude (m)
Old dome Mount St. Helens				
September lobe, landing site	1	5116595	562436	2,122
September lobe, upper dome	2	5116600	562487	2,130
Springs in Loowit canyon				
2005 degassing spring	3	5118045	562819	1,664
Loowit source spring	4	5118136	562831	1,635
New spring on fan of Loowit canyon	5	5118157	562856	1,617
Loowit boulder basin spring	6	5118275	562882	1,604
Loowit boulder basin degassing spring	7	5118273	562891	1,604
Loowit travertine spring	8	5118442	562921	1,584
Springs in Step canyon				
Step canyon hottest spring	14	5118396	562453	1,644
Step canyon source spring	16	5118324	562453	1,645
Monitoring network sites				
Probe site, Loowit Creek above falls	9	5119128	562929	1,507
Loowit Creek above falls	11	5119198	562981	1,509
Probe site, east fork Step creek above falls	15	5118401	562446	1,617
West fork Step creek above falls	17	5119212	562519	1,512
East fork Step creek above falls	18	5119224	562546	1,512
Loowit Creek below falls	21A	5121306	562300	1,219
Step creek below falls	21B	5121306	562300	1,219
Other creek locations				
Lower Loowit Creek	10	5119150	562935	1,509
Upper Loowit Creek	12	5117947	562819	1,662
Upper Loowit Creek	13	5117784	562886	1,709
Pumice Plain spring				
Carbonate spring at gage	19	5122487	559926	935
Carbonate spring	20	5122421	560010	945
Regional cold springs				
Springs west of Cold Spring Creek	22	5115219	557268	1,132
Kalama Spring	23	5110368	557390	832
Spring on Loowit trail	24	5119654	564283	1,330
Willow spring	25	5121399	564292	1,125
Spring on Pine Creek	26	5109610	569886	731
Moss spring	27	5112493	569935	882
Spring west of Swift Creek	28	5109062	563021	756

the late 1980s. Four of the springs are unnamed and were identified on 24,000-scale quadrangle maps or were brought to our attention by Mike Clynne of the U.S. Geological Survey (USGS), who has mapped extensively in the area around Mount St. Helens. In the text that follows we refer to the regional springs by their associated map number (fig. 1; table 1). The eight springs we report on here are likely the largest on the margins of the volcano, although assuredly more cold springs are in the Mount St. Helens area.

Field and Laboratory Methods

Water and gas samples were collected for a suite of chemical analyses using standard field and laboratory techniques. At all sites the water temperature and conductivity were measured in the field using portable meters. Spring-water samples collected for bulk chemistry were preserved in the field by filtering them through a 0.45-µm filter into plastic bottles that were first rinsed with filtered water. Samples for cation analyses were preserved with high-purity nitric acid by dropwise addition to a pH < 2. Other nonfiltered (raw) spring-water samples were collected in glass bottles for alkalinity and δD and $\delta^{18}O$ analyses and in preevacuated glass bottles for $\delta^{13}C$ analysis of dissolved inorganic carbon (DIC), which consists of dissolved CO_2 + HCO_3 + CO_3. Depending on the sample size, waters collected for $\delta^{13}C$–DIC were acidified with 0.5 to 1.0 mL of high-purity hydrochloric acid to convert DIC to CO_2. Values for $\delta^{13}C$–DIC and ^{14}C–DIC were determined on purified CO_2 extracted from the water samples following methods described in Evans and others (2002).

Samples of creek waters from the monitoring sites typically were collected into prerinsed plastic bottles as raw waters. Filtering, sample preservation, and pH measurements were performed in the laboratory, at Menlo Park, Calif. Because samples from the monitoring sites were sometimes stored before they were received at the lab, we have not determined the bicarbonate concentrations of many of these water samples. A few samples of creek waters were collected for $\delta^{13}C$ analysis of DIC as described above. Creek discharge rate was measured using a pygmy meter. Visual estimates of discharge are identified in table 2.

Anion and cation concentrations in water samples were determined using ion chromatography and inductively coupled argon plasma spectrometry at USGS laboratories in Menlo Park, Calif. Isotope analyses were performed at USGS laboratories in Menlo Park, Calif., and Reston, Va., and at the Center for Accelerator Mass Spectrometry at Lawrence Livermore National Laboratory, Calif. Isotope analyses were performed using techniques outlined in Epstein and Mayeda (1953), Coplen (1973), Vogel and others (1987), and Coplen and others (1991).

Gas samples for bulk composition and $\delta^{13}C$–CO_2 analyses were collected into preevacuated glass bottles through a hollow titanium rod (from gas vents) or a funnel fitted with

Table 2. Spring and creek temperature and discharge measurements 2003–2005, Mount St. Helens, Washington.

[Letters following discharge rate indicate field method: EV, width and depth measured, velocity estimated; E, visual estimate; M, measured. Some locations coded to specify sites: ps, probe site; LCAF, Loowit Creek above falls; LCBF, Loowit Creek below falls; EFSCAF, east fork Step creek above falls; WFSCAF, west fork Step creek above falls; SCBF, Step creek below falls; CARB gs, carbonate spring gage site.]

Location	Date	Temp. (°C)	Discharge (L/s)	Method
Monitoring network sites				
LCAF	08/20/03	27.0	323	M
LCAF	06/17/04	24.4	208	M
LCAF	08/12/04	27.3	320	M
LCAF	04/21/05	27.5	170	E
LCAF	07/26/05	29.1	397	M
LCAF	08/26/05	30.1	408	M
LCAF	10/11/05	30.0	267	M
LCAF ps	10/25/05	25.9	215	M
LCBF	09/28/04	18.1	249	M
LCBF	10/13/04	16.3	306	M
LCBF	10/20/04	10.2	230	E
LCBF	12/02/04	8.4	110	E
LCBF	02/10/05	11.5	110	E
LCBF	04/21/05	16.9	187	M
LCBF	07/26/05	22.5	399	M
LCBF	08/26/05	19.8	279	M
EFSCAF	08/12/04	30.0	80	E
EFSCAF	04/21/05	19.5	60	E
EFSCAF	07/26/05	26.6	45	M
EFSCAF	08/26/05	24.1	40	EV
EFSCAF	10/11/05	17.6	19	M
EFSCAF ps	10/25/05	25.4	27	M
WFSCAF	08/12/04	10.5	120	E
WFSCAF	04/21/05	4.2	<30	E
WFSCAF	07/26/05	10.5	142	M
WFSCAF	08/26/05	16.4	30	EV
WFSCAF	10/11/05	7.5	10	E
SCBF	09/28/04	16.3	95	M
SCBF	10/13/04	14.5	112	M
SCBF	10/20/04	9.1	10	E
SCBF	11/05/04	9.7	10	E
SCBF	12/02/04	4.1	20	E
SCBF	02/10/05	5.6	10	E
SCBF	04/21/05	10.0	3	E
SCBF	07/26/05	21.2	110	M
SCBF	08/26/05	19.2	49	M
Pumice Plain spring				
CARB gs	10/25/05	15.7	354	M
Regional cold springs				
Spring 22	07/29/05	4.4	11	M
Spring 23	07/29/05	4.7	818	M
Spring 24	07/30/05	3.0	16	M
Spring 25	07/30/05	5.4	44	M
Spring 26	07/31/05	7.2	137	M
Spring 27	07/31/05	6.3	82	M
Spring 28	07/31/05	5.2	29	M

Tygon tubing (from bubbling springs). Prior to sampling, the entire collection system was purged of atmospheric gases. Gas samples were analyzed for bulk composition at the USGS in Menlo Park, Calif., using gas chromatography methods reported in Evans and others (1981). Carbon dioxide for stable isotope analysis was separated from the bulk gas sample using standard cryogenic techniques on a vacuum line (Evans and others, 2002). The spring gas samples for $^3He/^4He$ analysis were collected from the funnel and tubing apparatus into copper tubing that was then sealed at both ends with refrigeration clamps. The $^3He/^4He$ determination was run at Lawrence Berkeley National Laboratory in Berkeley, California, following methods outlined by Kennedy and van Soest (2006). Helium isotope ratios are reported as R/R_A values, which represent the $^3He/^4He$ ratio in the gas relative to the $^3He/^4He$ ratio in air. Values for $R/R_A > 1$ indicate that a percentage of the gas is derived from a mantle or magmatic source.

Results and Discussion

Chemistry of the Hot Springs, 1983 to 2005

The chemistry and temperature of the Loowit canyon hot springs changed rapidly after the springs appeared in 1983 (Thompson, 1990; Shevenell and Goff, 1993, 1995). The highest water temperature recorded was 92.6°C from the Loowit travertine spring group in 1986, and by then, concentrations of many of the dissolved constituents in the Loowit springs had peaked (Shevenell and Goff, 1993). The subsequent declining temperatures and variable chemistry were attributed to a rapidly cooling hydrothermal system that had formed just after the 1980 eruption. Several important conclusions were reached by Shevenell and Goff (1993, 1995, 2000) and Goff and McMurtry (2000), including (1) that the Loowit canyon hot springs discharged mixtures of recent meteoric water and about 10 percent magmatic water, (2) that the underground residence time of the mixed water was too short to allow water-rock equilibration or reliable geothermometry, and (3) that Cl, SO_4, and HCO_3 in the springs were mainly derived from magmatic volatiles.

More recent samples show that the chemistry of the hot springs at Mount St. Helens is still changing (F. Goff and the USGS, unpub. data, 1984–94), although water temperatures since 1990 appear to have stabilized (fig. 2). The early trend in anions from SO_4 toward Cl dominance stopped, and water samples from 1994, 2002, and 2005 show declines in both SO_4 and Cl relative to HCO_3 (table 3; fig. 3). The post-1989 data for the Step canyon springs follow a similar trend toward HCO_3-dominated water.

Overall, most elements in the Loowit springs show the effects of dilution by meteoric water over time (fig. 4). The plots in figure 4 may understate the dilution effects because of the increased focus on sampling the hottest springs in 2002 and 2005. Dilution effects also are seen in the δD and $\delta^{18}O$ composition of the waters from 2002 and 2005, which plot on or near the world meteoric water line (table 4; fig. 5). Previous $\delta^{18}O$ values of Loowit hot spring waters through 1994 were shifted by as much as 2 per mil to the right of the meteoric water line.

Simple dilution, however, does not fully explain all of the data. Concentrations of Na and SO_4 have decreased since 1984, whereas Cl and B concentrations remained high throughout the mid- to late 1980s and declined in later years (fig. 4). Concentrations of Mg increased in the 2002 and 2005 samples, and HCO_3 concentrations showed a large increase to concentrations higher than was recorded previously.

A clear response to the renewal of activity in 2004 has not yet been recognized in the hot springs. Just prior to the onset of seismicity in 2004, the discharge and water temperature at a spring in Loowit canyon appeared to be higher than normal (J.S. Pallister, USGS, oral commun., 2004), but no measurements were made. However, any possible temperature increase was short lived, as comparisons between the 2002 and 2005 samples from the hottest springs in Loowit canyon show little change in temperatures (table 3). Similarly, in July 2005 the temperature measured at the hottest spring in Step canyon was substantially higher than temperatures reported from 1994 (fig. 2), but three months later, in October, the temperature at the same location had declined 18°C, although the specific conductance had decreased only slightly. Because the flow from the Step canyon vents is low, this temperature decline is conceivably related to the change in surface air temperature and conductive cooling. The possible causes for rapid swings in temperature at the hot springs need further investigation, but at this point, it is difficult to attribute any temperature changes

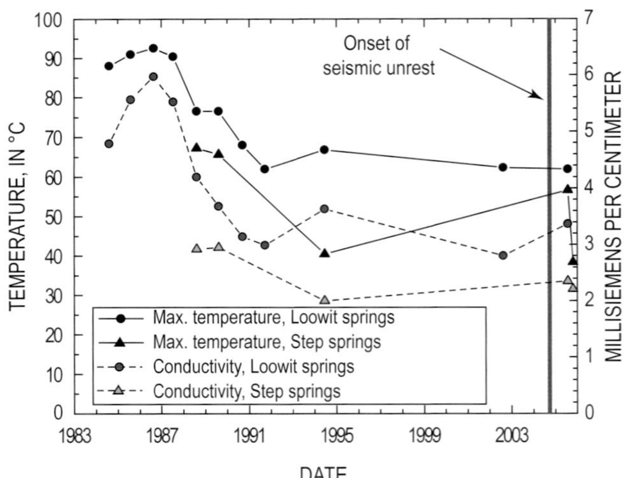

Figure 2. Change in maximum temperature and specific conductance of hot springs in The Breach of Mount St. Helens since 1984. Data from dates before 2002 are from Thompson (1990), Shevenell and Goff (1993), Goff and McMurtry (2000), and unpublished data from the U.S. Geological Survey.

Table 3. Water chemistry data from springs and creeks, 2002-2005, Mount St. Helens, Washington.

[Acidity (pH) and conductivity data in bold are from laboratory measurements, HCO_3 data in bold is determined on the basis of the measured amount of gas from the dissolved inorganic carbon extraction. Unless specified, all units are in parts per million. mS/cm, millisiemens per centimeter; --, no data. Additional chemical analyses are available in the digital appendix that accompanies electronic versions of this work.]

Sample No.	Date	Map No.	Temp. (°C)	pH	Cond (mS/cm)	B	Br	Ca	Cl	F	Fe	HCO_3	K	Li	Mg	Na	SiO_2	SO_4
Springs in Loowit canyon																		
MSH-02-01	08/16/02	4	58.9	6.4	2.6	4.9	0.56	55	310	2.3	3.5	727	44	0.74	24	474	186	330
MSH-02-02	08/17/02	6	61.0	6.3	2.7	5.7	0.61	62	330	2.2	4.0	769	46	0.82	28	497	196	360
MSH-02-03	08/17/02	7	62.3	6.3	2.8	5.9	0.61	68	340	2.2	3.9	844	46	0.83	28	515	197	360
MSH-02-04	08/18/02	8	57.6	6.5	2.8	5.6	0.59	68	350	2.6	2.3	779	45	0.75	31	508	184	360
MSH-05-02	07/26/05	3	59.1	--	2.6	6.0	0.44	67	281	2.5	4.0	--	47	0.94	36	511	196	400
MSH-05-03	07/26/05	3	57.0	**6.5**	3.0	5.9	0.44	66	280	2.6	4.2	761	46	0.90	35	495	191	399
MSH-05-04	07/26/05	5	61.9	**6.7**	3.4	6.7	0.48	69	291	2.4	4.3	807	48	1.01	37	521	205	395
MSH-05-05	07/26/05	5	60.5	--	2.7	6.5	0.48	72	288	2.4	3.3	--	48	1.00	38	512	201	392
Springs in Step canyon																		
MSH-05-07	07/26/05	14	56.6	**6.6**	2.4	5.7	0.32	67	217	1.3	4.7	752	30	0.95	49	375	190	235
MSH-05-06	07/26/05	16	45.1	**6.6**	1.9	4.3	0.24	73	171	1.2	7.7	706	22	0.74	50	271	162	171
MSH-05-22	10/25/05	14	38.4	**6.4**	2.2	5.7	0.36	66	241	1.9	17	--	21	0.84	57	316	166	249
Monitoring network sites																		
LCAF 042105	04/21/05	11	27.5	**8.5**	2.1	3.8	0.32	48	190	2.2	0.34	--	30	0.57	27	334	131	280
LCAF 063005	06/30/05	11	27.9	**8.6**	1.6	--	0.24	--	172	2.6	--	--	--	--	--	--	--	247
MSH-05-11	07/26/05	11	29.1	**8.8**	1.6	3.4	<0.003	54	172	2.2	1.1	487	27	0.52	24	287	123	247
LCAF 082605	08/26/05	11	30.1	**8.3**	1.6	2.9	0.28	32	169	2.3	0.29	--	24	0.46	20	248	105	236
LCAF 101105	10/11/05	11	30.0	**8.6**	1.9	--	0.32	--	197	2.3	--	--	--	--	--	--	--	273
MSH-05-24	10/25/05	9	25.9	**8.7**	1.8	3.5	0.32	55	193	2.5	0.85	**533**	28	0.54	24	304	130	268
LCBF 101304	10/13/04	21A	16.3	**8.5**	1.5	--	0.24	--	147	1.8	--	--	--	--	--	--	--	203
LCBF 102004	10/20/04	21A	10.2	**7.8**	1.6	2.9	0.30	15	151	2.2	<0.08	--	21	0.45	16	260	82	209
LCBF 120204	12/02/04	21A	8.4	**8.5**	1.8	--	0.24	--	167	2.0	--	--	--	--	--	--	--	234
LCBF 021005	02/10/05	21A	11.5	**8.6**	1.8	--	0.24	--	170	2.0	--	--	--	--	--	--	--	260
LCBF 042105	04/21/05	21A	16.9	**8.7**	1.9	3.7	0.32	31	180	2.1	0.48	--	28	0.56	24	312	121	270
LCBF 063005	06/30/05	21A	18.6	**8.7**	1.6	--	0.28	--	174	2.6	--	--	--	--	--	--	--	249
MSH-05-12	07/26/05	21A	22.5	8.9	1.6	3.5	0.26	45	167	2.2	0.47	--	27	0.53	24	291	123	244
LCBF 082605	08/26/05	21A	19.8	8.5	1.6	--	0.28	--	178	2.2	--	--	--	--	--	--	--	249
EFSCAF 042105	04/21/05	18	19.5	8.6	1.5	--	0.32	--	190	1.6	--	--	--	--	--	--	--	160
EFSCAF 063005	06/30/05	18	23.5	8.5	1.6	--	0.24	--	190	1.0	--	--	--	--	--		--	154
MSH 05 09	07/26/05	18	26.6	8.8	1.5	4.7	0.24	29	172	1.0	0.13	533	20	0.78	52	245	146	145
EFSCAF 082605	08/26/05	18	24.1	8.2	1.4	3.4	0.20	17	154	0.9	0.32	--	15	0.59	50	179	119	131
EFSCAF 101105	10/11/05	18	17.6	8.3	1.5	--	0.28	--	197	1.4	--	--	--	--	--	--	--	170

Table 3. Water chemistry data from springs and creeks, 2002-2005, Mount St. Helens, Washington.—Continued

[Acidity (pH) and conductivity data in bold are from laboratory measurements, HCO_3 data in bold is determined on the basis of the measured amount of gas from the dissolved inorganic carbon extraction. Unless specified, all units are in parts per million. mS/cm, millisiemens per centimeter; --, no data. Additional chemical analyses are available in the digital appendix that accompanies electronic versions of this work.]

Sample No.	Date	Map No.	Temp. (°C)	pH	Cond (mS/cm)	B	Br	Ca	Cl	F	Fe	HCO_3	K	Li	Mg	Na	SiO_2	SO_4
MSH-05-23	10/25/05	15	25.4	7.2	2.0	5.7	0.36	67	232	1.9	21	**787**	16	0.81	54	237	144	194
WFSCAF 042105	04/21/05	17	4.2	5.7	0.19	0.09	<0.003	12	47	2.2	0.0	--	0.90	0.01	6.0	6.5	19	6.5
WFSCAF 063005	06/30/05	17	6.6	5.7	0.09	--	0.01	--	20	3.2	--	--	--	--	--	--	--	2.5
MSH-05-10	07/26/05	17	10.5	5.8	0.06	0.03	<0.003	3.3	10	2.4	0.01	2.0	0.56	0.004	1.1	2.9	11	2.6
WFSCAF 082605	08/26/05	17	16.4	6.3	**0.05**	0.02	0.01	2.4	6	1.7	0.03	--	0.58	0.004	1.2	3.5	15	6.0
WFSCAF 101105	10/11/05	17	7.5	6.6	0.10	--	0.01	--	17	2.2	--	--	--	--	--	--	--	11
SCBF 101304	10/13/04	21B	14.5	8.5	0.79	--	0.100	--	84	0.9	--	--	--	--	--	--	--	84
SCBF 102004	10/20/04	21B	9.1	7.8	0.20	--	0.03	--	26	1.1	--	--	--	--	--	--	--	68
SCBF 120204	12/02/04	21B	4.1	8.5	1.0	2.6	0.14	31	94	1.3	0.10	--	8.6	0.39	24	135	65	118
SCBF 021005	02/10/05	21B	5.6	8.6	1.4	--	0.20	--	140	1.4	--	--	--	--	--	--	--	156
SCBF 063005	06/30/05	21B	14.5	7.9	0.34	--	0.06	--	48	3.0	--	--	--	--	--	--	--	28
MSH-05-13	07/26/05	21B	21.2	8.4	0.46	1.2	0.07	12	52	2.0	<0.04	--	5.6	0.20	13	69	44	44
SCBF 082605	08/26/05	21B	19.2	8.7	0.89	--	0.12	--	93	1.3	--	--	--	--	--	--	--	89
Other Loowit Creek locations																		
MSH-02-05	08/18/02	10	31.7	7.9	1.9	3.6	0.38	50	220	1.9	0.23	--	29	0.50	20	319	125	240
MSH-02-06	08/18/02	12	2.8	6.0	0.23	<0.02	0.004	23	1.3	1.4	0.62	92	3.4	0.03	6.3	12	39	39
MSH-05-01	07/26/05	13	7.7	**6.4**	0.08	0.04	0.010	7	16	2.3	0.02	4	0.54	0.005	2.0	3.3	17	2.0
Pumice Plain spring																		
CARB 081204	10/13/04	20	17.4	**7.8**	0.9	--	0.12	--	81	1.2	--	--	--	--	--	--	--	144
MSH-05-08	07/26/05	20	25.4	**7.3**	1.2	2.1	0.18	48	107	2.0	0.08	243	11	0.30	12	191	57	224
MSH-05-25	10/25/05	19	15.7	**7.4**	0.8	1.3	0.12	28	71	1.1	0.27	187	6.9	0.19	7.7	114	45	132
Regional cold springs																		
MSH-02-10	08/23/02	23	3.2	7.2	0.05	<0.02	0.003	3.5	1.0	0.1	0.01	25	0.73	0.004	1.2	4.6	22	1.9
MSH-05-15	07/29/05	22	4.4	5.7	0.04	0.004	<0.003	3.4	0.7	0.0	0.01	16	0.66	0.001	0.6	1.9	21	0.4
MSH-05-14	07/29/05	23	4.7	5.8	0.05	0.01	<0.003	3.6	1.1	0.1	0.01	28	0.74	0.006	1.2	4.9	24	1.9
MSH-05-17	07/30/05	24	3.0	8.2	0.08	0.01	<0.003	4.9	3.1	0.2	0.01	11	0.80	0.004	1.2	7.3	18	18
MSH-05-16	07/30/05	25	5.4	6.3	0.13	0.02	<0.003	13	1.4	0.2	<0.04	8	1.5	0.007	3.2	6.9	22	49
MSH-05-19	07/31/05	26	7.2	6.2	0.12	0.10	0.010	4.7	6.5	0.6	<0.04	54	1.8	0.048	2.6	18	43	8.5
MSH-05-18	07/31/05	27	6.3	6.5	0.09	0.08	<0.003	4.3	5.4	0.6	0.01	33	1.0	0.028	2.4	10	33	6.4
MSH-05-20	07/31/05	28	5.2	6.2	0.09	0.03	<0.003	7.0	2.1	0.2	<0.04	52	1.3	0.011	2.9	7.8	32	2.3

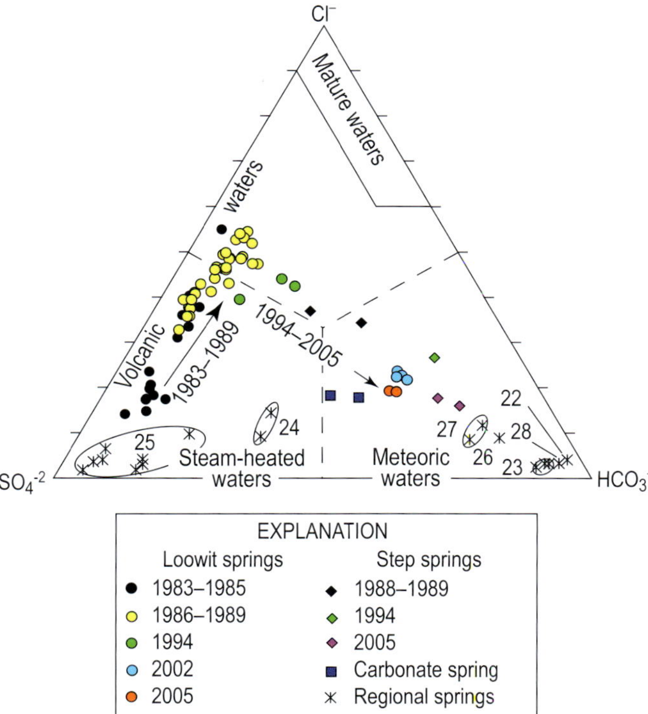

Figure 3. Ternary plot of anion proportion by mass for spring waters at or around Mount St. Helens, Washington (after Giggenbach, 1992). Arrows show change in major anions in Loowit springs since 1983 and Step springs since 1988. Data from dates before 2002 are from Thompson (1990), Shevenell and Goff (1993), Goff and McMurtry (2000), and unpublished data from the U.S. Geological Survey and Fraser Goff (University of New Mexico).

or the minor differences in the chemistry of the Loowit springs between 2002 and 2005 (table 3) to the current eruption.

Chemistry of the Regional Springs

All of the regional springs have temperatures <8°C and conductivities <150 µS/cm but can be divided into three groups based on variations in major anion concentrations (fig. 3; table 3). One group is defined by relatively high SO_4 concentrations, and the other groups are characterized as HCO_3-dominated waters but are subdivided on the basis of Cl concentrations.

The SO_4 waters consist of springs 24 and 25, which are north of Mount St. Helens on the eastern border of the Pumice Plain (fig. 1). Spring 25 has higher SO_4 concentrations than spring 24, and samples collected since 1988 show that anion compositions have been variable (fig. 3). In the late 1980s, SO_4-rich warm springs occurred in the cooling pyroclastic deposits of the Pumice Plain. Shevenell and Goff (1995) noted that these springs were not "steam-heated" waters, which are characteristically SO_4 rich, but instead probably were leaching SO_4 from $CaSO_4$ alteration minerals or from encrustations around the vents of short-lived fumaroles on the pyroclastic flows. Springs 24 and 25 are likely to be cold, dilute examples of this type of water.

The HCO_3-rich waters consist of springs 22, 23, and 28, which are solely HCO_3 waters, and springs 26 and 27, which have slightly elevated Cl in comparison with the other three springs (fig. 3; table 3). Springs 26 and 27 are southeast of Mount St. Helens and are of interest because (1) their anion chemistry lies along the dilution trend defined by the hot springs and (2) their ^{14}C values are greatly reduced relative to modern carbon (table 4), as discussed in more detail below. The elevated Cl in these springs may provide evidence for

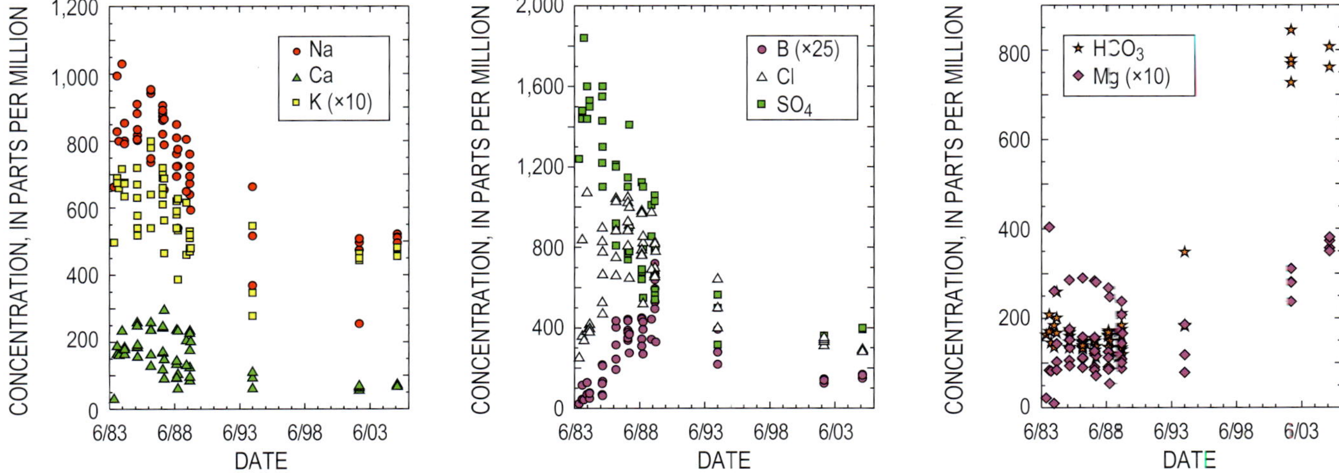

Figure 4. Chemistry of Loowit springs waters from 1983 to 2005, Mount St. Helens, Washington. Data from dates before 2002 are from Thompson (1990), Shevenell and Goff (1993), Goff and McMurtry (2000), and unpublished data (Fraser Goff, University of New Mexico).

some leakage of Loowit-type water through the southeastern wall of the crater.

Gas Transfer from Magma into Water

Gases released from magma can be variably dissolved into overlying cold water or released to a brine phase (Fournier, 1986) that can then mix with cold water. The resulting fluid is acidic, hot, and highly reactive with the surrounding rock. Mineral dissolution converts the acidic gas species H_2S, SO_2, HCl, and CO_2 into the anions SO_4, Cl, and HCO_3. The concentration of these anions in the spring waters can be related back to magmatic degassing only if the effects of variable gas solution and mineral dissolution/precipitation are constrained. Some constraints can be derived from the water chemistry.

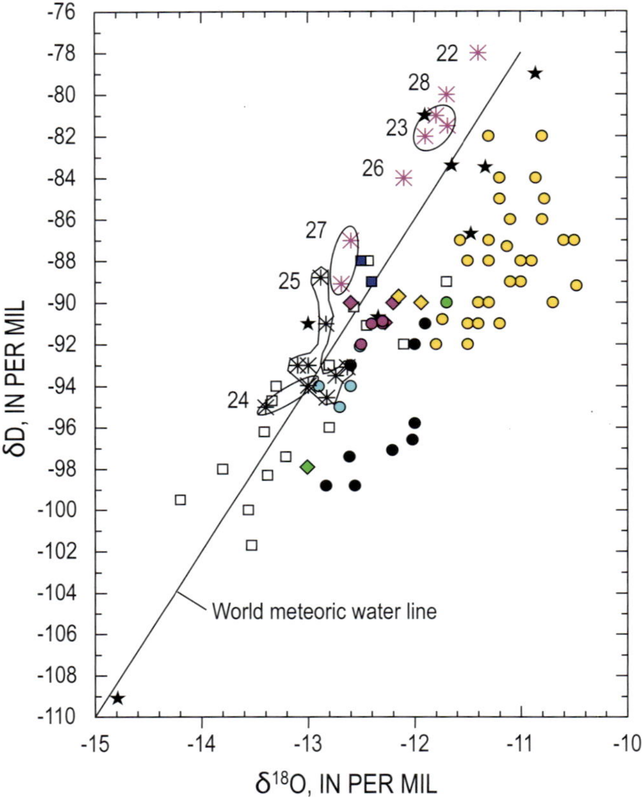

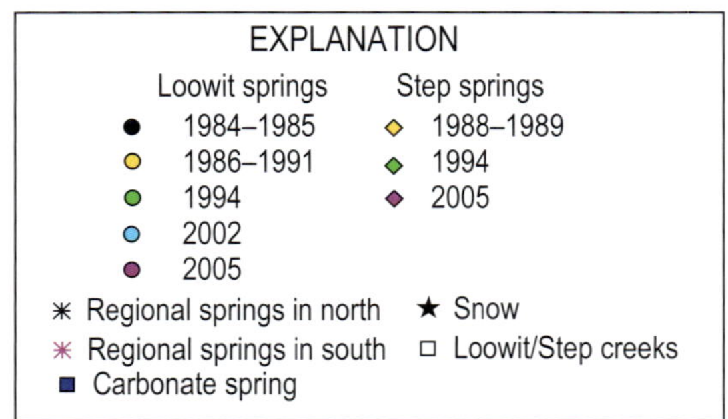

Figure 5. Stable-isotope composition of Loowit springs since 1980s, Mount St. Helens, Washington. Data from dates before 2002 are from Thompson (1990), Shevenell and Goff (1993, 1995), Goff and McMurtry (2000), and unpublished data from the U.S. Geological Survey.

Many metallic ions (such as Ca) are not transported in volatile form (Symonds and others, 1993), requiring that the major source of the cations in the springs be water-rock interaction. This process could ultimately remove SO_4 and HCO_3 from solution via precipitation. Attempts at geothermometry by Shevenell and Goff (1993; 1995) yielded maximum temperatures between 120°C and 175°C for the Loowit waters. For an assumed temperature of 150°C, calculations using SOLMNEQ88 (Kharaka and others, 1988) indicate saturation with anhydrite for waters collected in the 1980s but undersaturation for samples from 2002 and 2005. From the 1980s through 2005, Ca, Na, K, and SO_4 in the spring waters all show similar patterns of decline that are consistent with dilution (fig. 4), so there is no evidence that anhydrite was ever a significant control on SO_4 concentrations. Samples from all collection years are saturated with calcite at all temperatures above the discharge temperature. Calcite formation/dissolution may exert some influence on Ca and HCO_3. However, the large increase in HCO_3 after the 1980s cannot be attributed to calcite dissolution, which would also produce both higher Ca concentrations and higher pH values. Ca and pH have in fact dropped during this time (table 3).

Shevenell and Goff (2000) argued that halite formation in the magmatic fluid component was probably not a significant sink for Cl. Although Br and Cl concentrations in the springs have declined steadily over the years, it is noteworthy that for the past two decades the ratios of these two components have remained at a remarkably constant value around 0.002 (1984–2005, 44 samples, ± 0.001). The Step canyon springs and carbonate spring have lower concentrations of Br and Cl than the Loowit springs but fall along the same trend (fig. 6). The constant Cl/Br ratio shows that halite was never a major control on Cl in fluid sources to the hot springs.

In contrast, fumarole condensates have shown a large range in Cl/Br (fig. 6), possibly indicating that deposition of metal halides in the vent throats (Keith and others, 1981; Edmonds and others, this volume, chap. 27) can be a significant control on fumarolic Cl/Br ratios. The Cl/Br ratio in the springs, which lies within the range of the fumarolic condensates, may better represent the HCl/HBr ratio in gases released from magma. Additional Cl and Br could be leached from the volcanic rocks. Reported Br and Cl ratios in seven samples of andesite and dacite from the crater, The Breach, and Pumice Plain are variable, ranging between 0.002 and 0.01 (table 1 of Shevenell and Goff, 1993). However, the SO_4-rich nature of the transient hot springs in the Pumice Plain (Shevenell and Goff, 1995) indicates that rock leaching is not a major source of halides.

Overall, the data indicate that mineral sources and sinks for SO_4, Cl, and HCO_3 are not the main controls on the anions

Table 4. Isotope values determined for water samples collected during 2002–2005, Mount St. Helens, Washington.

[DIC, dissolved inorganic carbon; --, no data.]

Sample No.	Date	Map No.	Temperature (°C)	δD per mil	$\delta^{18}O$ per mil	$\delta^{13}C$-DIC per mil	^{14}C-DIC percent modern carbon
Springs in Loowit canyon							
MSH-02-01	08/16/02	4	58.9	-94	-12.9	-12.3	--
MSH-02-02	08/17/02	6	61.0	-95	-12.7	--	--
MSH-02-03	08/17/02	7	62.3	-94	-12.6	-12.2	--
MSH-02-04	08/18/02	8	57.6	-92	-12.5	-11.9	--
MSH-05-02	07/26/05	3	59.1	-91	-12.4	--	--
MSH-05-03	07/26/05	3	57.0	-92	-12.5	-12.1	--
MSH-05-04	07/26/05	5	61.9	-91	-12.3	-11.9	--
MSH-05-05	07/26/05	5	60.5	-91	-12.3	--	--
Springs in Step canyon							
MSH-05-06	07/26/05	16	45.1	-90	-12.6	-11.4	--
MSH-05-07	07/26/05	14	56.6	-91	-12.3	-10.9	--
MSH-05-22	10/25/05	14	38.4	-90	-12.2	--	--
Monitoring network sites							
MSH-05-23	10/25/05	15	25.4	-92	-12.1	-7.5	--
MSH-05-24	10/25/05	9	25.9	-89	-12.4	-8.1	--
Other Loowit Creek locations							
MSH-02-06	08/18/02	12	2.8	-98	-13.8	-11.2	--
MSH-05-01	07/26/05	13	7.7	-93	-12.8	--	--
Pumice Plain spring							
MSH-05-08	07/26/05	20	25.4	-89	-12.4	-11.5	5.5
MSH-05-25	10/25/05	19	15.7	-88	-12.5	--	--
Regional cold springs							
MSH-05-15	07/29/05	22	4.4	-78	-11.4	--	--
MSH-02-10	08/23/02	23	3.2	-82	-11.9	-14.2	93.8
MSH-05-14	07/29/05	23	4.7	-81	-11.8	-15.6	--
MSH-05-17	07/30/05	24	3.0	-95	-13.4	--	--
MSH-05-16	07/30/05	25	5.4	-93	-13.0	--	--
MSH-05-19	07/31/05	26	7.2	-84	-12.1	-16.5	50.0
MSH-05-18	07/31/05	27	6.3	-87	-12.6	-16.0	54.8
MSH-05-20	07/31/05	28	5.2	-80	-11.7	-15.9	53.1

in the hot springs. We conclude that the changing anion proportions shown in figure 3 reflect changes in the release rates of sulfur gases, HCl, and CO_2 from the magma and a varying degree of efficiency of gas scrubbing by the overlying water.

The 1983–89 trend in Loowit waters from SO_4 toward Cl (fig. 3) can be explained by the cessation in the supply of magma at the end of the 1980–86 dome-building eruptions. With declining output of sulfur gas from magma, less sulfur was available to be scrubbed into overlying meteoric water. The simultaneous increase in Cl can be attributed to crystallization of extruded and shallowly emplaced magma, with degassing of HCl or partitioning of Cl into an aqueous phase that then mixed with meteoric water. The ensuing trend toward HCO_3 dominance after 1989 (fig. 3) would logically be attributed to continuing declines in the supply of S and Cl as cooling and crystallization of the 1980–86 dome and shallow underlying magma progressed toward completion; CO_2, due to its low solubility even at high pressure, continued to exsolve from magma at greater depths. This scheme does not explain the large increase in HCO_3 concentrations in Loowit springs (fig. 4; table 3). Coupled with the drop in pH, the rise in HCO_3 concentrations between 1989 and 2002 represents an order-of-magnitude jump in DIC, an event of particular interest because it could indicate the ascent of fresh, CO_2-rich magma from depth beneath the chamber, leading up to the renewal of eruptive activity in 2004.

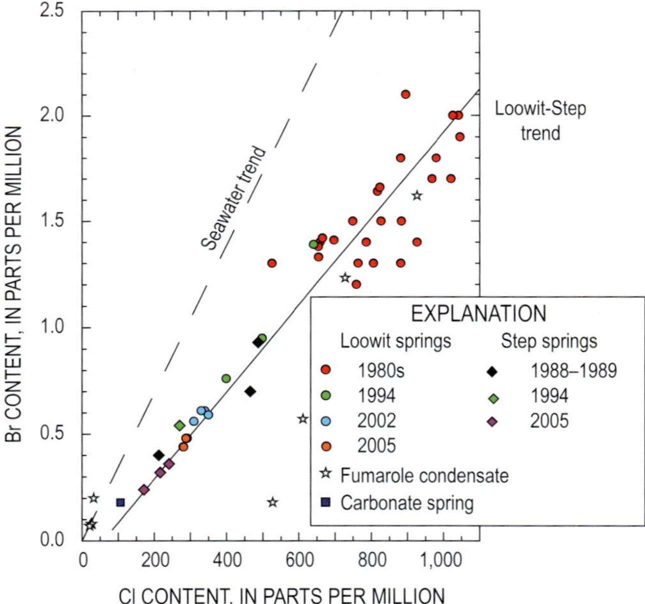

Figure 6. Trends in Br and Cl concentrations for 2002–2005 spring waters, compared with early data from springs and fumarole condensates from the 1980–86 dome at Mount St. Helens, Washington. One 1989 fumarole condensate sample that plots off the scale is not shown. Data from fumarole condensates and waters before 2002 are from Shevenell and Goff (1993, 2000), Goff and McMurtry (2000), and unpublished data (Fraser Goff, University of New Mexico).

However, the HCO_3 increase seems to have begun by 1994 (fig. 4), and carbon isotope data (discussed below) do not indicate CO_2 release from a new source of magma.

By 2002, the molar C:S:Cl ratio in Loowit waters had shifted from ~1:3:8 in the late 1980s to 10:1.4:3.6. This ratio is much closer to the 10:1.1:1.2 ratio measured in plume emissions by various techniques in 2005 (Gerlach and others, 2005; Edmonds and others, this volume, chap. 27). Our preferred explanation for the shift in the ratios is that for many years after dome emplacement in the 1980s, temperatures above boiling in the rocks of the 1980–86 dome prevented shallow waters from completely sealing off escape pathways for gas. Highly soluble HCl and SO_2 were effectively scrubbed by infiltrating water, but the CO_2 was still largely able to escape due to its much lower solubility. Once gas pathways were mostly blocked by liquid water, presumably after 1994, CO_2 scrubbing became efficient, and dissolved C:S:Cl ratios approached those of degassing magma. Note that the timeframe for these changes in chemistry is in fair agreement with the estimate that the 1980–86 dome would cool through its magnetization temperature in 18–36 years after emplacement (Dzurisin and others, 1990).

Carbon and Helium Isotope Evidence on Magmatic End Members

Gas from the Crater and The Breach

In spite of declining fumarole temperatures and the increasing amount of air in gases venting in the crater at Mount St. Helens, the carbon and helium isotopic compositions give evidence of a prolonged magmatic input. Gas collected in November 1980 from a >400°C fumarole near the dome provided the most representative $\delta^{13}C$–CO_2 value for the early magma at Mount St. Helens, −10.5 per mil (Evans and others, 1981; table 5). Over time the carbon isotope composition of CO_2 in fumarole gases shifted to lighter values (fig. 7*A*). The shift cannot be related to the increased air concentrations because the $\delta^{13}C$ value of atmospheric CO_2 is around −7 per mil (Faure, 1986). Since 1994 CO_2 concentrations in gases from the 1980–86 dome have declined, but $\delta^{13}C$–CO_2 values have stabilized (fig. 7). In June 1994, gas from a 560°C fumarole and other lower temperature fumaroles on the dome contained about 32 percent CO_2 and had $\delta^{13}C$ values between −11.7 and −12.0 per mil (Goff and McMurtry, 2000; F. Goff, unpub. data, 1994). In 1998, gas samples collected from an 86°C vent on September lobe contained 5 percent CO_2 with a $\delta^{13}C$ value of −11.9 per mil (Symonds and others, 2003; table 5), and gas samples collected from vents on September lobe in 2002 had less than 3 percent CO_2 with $\delta^{13}C$ values between −12.0 and −11.8 per mil (table 5).

Gas from the bubbling springs in 2002 and 2005 contained mostly CO_2 but also had considerable N_2 and Ar (table 5). The N_2/Ar ratio in the gas falls between the ratios for air and air-saturated meteoric water, but low O_2 values show that direct air contamination was not a factor. The R/R_A values for $^3He/^4He$ ratios in the gas were 5.5 and 5.8, respectively, similar to a 1989 hot spring water sample that had a value of 5.7 (Goff and McMurtry, 2000). The $\delta^{13}C$ value for the CO_2 in both years was −14.7 per mil, significantly lower than the isotopic composition of CO_2 in the vent gases. Analysis of the 2002 bubbling gas indicates that it is essentially ^{14}C dead, ruling out any significant biogenic CO_2 source (table 5; figs. 7*A*, 7*B*). An important consideration is that equilibrium fractionation processes call for lower $\delta^{13}C$ values in the gas-bubble CO_2, relative to the DIC, consisting of HCO_3 and dissolved CO_2.

Dissolved Inorganic Carbon in Spring Waters

The carbon isotope composition of DIC from the springs in Loowit and Step canyons and carbonate spring has a small range in values that is independent of water temperature (fig. 7*A*). The $\delta^{13}C$–DIC values in all these springs are similar to the $\delta^{13}C$ composition of fumarolic CO_2 from recent years but are lower than the 1980 fumarolic $\delta^{13}C$–CO_2 values. The $\delta^{13}C$–DIC data thus provide additional evidence for a change in the $\delta^{13}C$ of the CO_2 released from the underlying magma. This carbon isotope shift to lower values since 1980 is most easily attributed to fractional loss of ^{13}C-enriched CO_2 during degassing of the magma (Gerlach and Taylor, 1990) and is a strong argument against the involvement of fresh magma. A new pulse of gas-rich magma from great depth would likely cause a return toward heavier $\delta^{13}C$ values in gas vents and DIC, and a new pulse of basalt from mantle depths might bring an increase in $^3He/^4He$ ratios.

The regional springs have much lower HCO_3 concentrations than springs in the crater and The Breach and have lower $\delta^{13}C$–DIC values (tables 3, 4). The ^{14}C content of the DIC in springs 26, 27, and 28 contains about 50 percent modern carbon, and the ^{13}C–^{14}C isotope values fall on a mixing line between typical biogenic carbon and magmatic carbon in the dome vents and hot springs (fig. 7*B*). Springs 26, 27, and 28

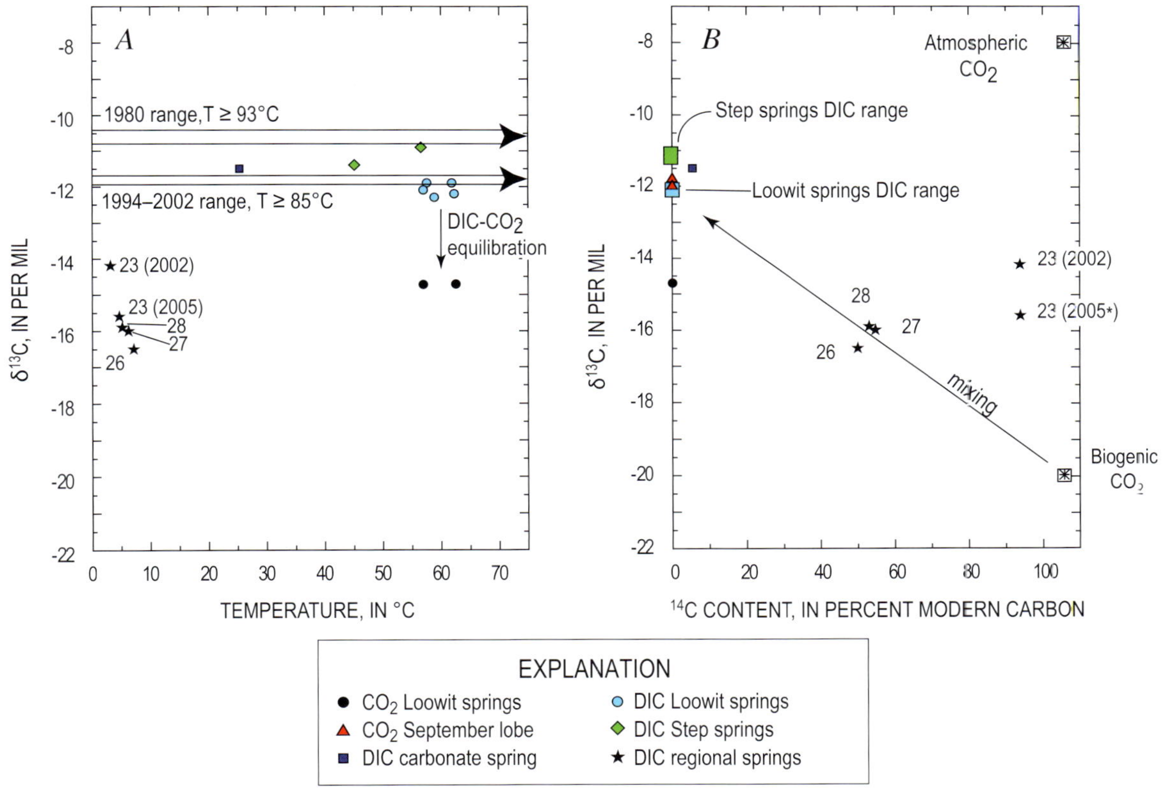

Figure 7. Water temperatures and carbon isotope compositions of dissolved inorganic carbon (DIC) and CO_2 from vents and springs at and around Mount St. Helens, Washington 1980–2005. *A*, $\delta^{13}C$–DIC values for hot and cold springs from this study compared to CO_2 gas collected from the 1980–86 dome. Horizontal arrows represent the range in $\delta^{13}C$–CO_2 values reported for 1980s dome gas samples from Evans (1981), Goff and McMurtry (2000), Symonds and others (2003), and this study. *B*, Comparison of $\delta^{13}C$–DIC and ^{14}C–DIC values for some regional cold springs with values of DIC and CO_2 from hot springs and atmospheric and biogenically derived CO_2. ^{14}C values for DIC in Loowit and Step springs and CO_2 from the September lobe are assumed to be zero. The 2005 analysis of sample 23, shown with asterisk, lacks a ^{14}C–DIC value, so it is arbitrarily assigned the 2002 analytical value, for purposes of plotting the $\delta^{13}C$ results.

Table 5. Chemical and isotopic results from gas analyses, 1980–2005, Mount St. Helens, Washington.

[Concentrations are reported as volume percent; --, no data; R/R_A, the $^3He/^4He$ ratio in the gas relative to the $^3He/^4He$ ratio in air.]

Sample No.	Date	Map No.	Temp. (°C)	He	H_2	Ar	O_2	N_2	CH_4	CO_2	C_2H_6	H_2S	CO	SO_2	N_2 / Ar	$\delta^{13}C$–CO_2 (‰)	$^3He/^4He$ $(R/R)_A$
Dome gas, 1980s dome																	
CQ244IB80 [1]	11/04/80	--	>400	<0.005	8.61	<0.02	0.03	1.6	<0.0002	86.6	<0.01	2.09	0.57	0.84	na	-10.5	--
981214 [2]	06/29/98	--	86	0.0005	0.0014	0.94	19.4	74.5	<0.0002	5.2	<0.0002	<0.0005	<0.001	--	79.1	-11.9	--
MSH-02-08 [3]	08/22/02	2	≥ 86	0.0005	0.0008	0.89	20.6	77.0	<0.0002	1.5	<0.0002	<0.0005	<0.001	--	86.2	-11.8	--
MSH-02-09 [3]	08/22/02	1	≥ 85	0.0006	0.0002	0.90	20.4	76.2	<0.0002	2.4	<0.0002	<0.0005	<0.001	--	84.4	-12.0	--
Hot spring gas, spring in Loowit canyon																	
MSH-02-03 [4]	08/17/02	7	62.3	0.0012	<0.0002	0.26	0.88	18.6	0.06	80.2	<0.0002	<0.0005	<0.001	--	72.4	-14.7	5.5
MSH-05-03	07/26/05	3	57.0	0.0019	0.0003	0.34	<0.0005	23.3	0.05	76.3	<0.0002	0.0026	<0.001	--	69.2	-14.7	5.8

[1] 1980 sample collected from crack near 1980 dome by W.C. Evans, from Evans and others (1981).

[2] 1998 sample collected from September lobe by R. Symonds; ^{13}C–CO_2 from Symonds and others (2003).

[3] Collected from September lobe.

[4] Value for ^{14}C–CO_2 equals 0.07 (percent modern carbon).

may contain some magmatic carbon, and the Cl concentrations in springs 26 and 27 support this idea. The DIC in spring 23 contains 94 percent modern carbon, and two samples from different years had variable $\delta^{13}C$ values that are higher than the other regional springs. The variation in the ^{13}C composition may indicate that some CO_2 degassing occurs from the water prior to its point of emergence. A small magmatic component in the spring is possible, but without additional study (for example, He isotopes), we cannot eliminate the possibility that the dead carbon in all four of these springs is derived from Tertiary-age hydrothermal carbonate in the volcanic rocks that underlie the edifice of Mount St. Helens (Evarts and others, 1987).

Total Discharges of Water, Heat, and Magmatic Volatiles

Creek-Water Discharge

During the course of this investigation, the measured surface discharge from Loowit Creek was about three to six times greater than the discharge from Step creek (table 2). Maximum seasonal discharge at the monitoring sites occurred in the midsummer to fall months. There are no historical data on discharge at Step creek, but measurements at LCAF show that flow rates have increased since 1989 (fig. 8; tables 2 and 6). The increase does not reflect variations in annual precipitation and more likely results from increased input of meltwater as Crater Glacier grew from a persistent snow bank in the shadow of the crater rim to an area of about 1 km^2 by September 2001 (Schilling and others, 2004).

Since October 2004, the emplacement of the new lava dome at Mount St. Helens resulted in extensive deformation of Crater Glacier and a concomitant decrease in the volume of glacial ice, without any large change in the surface flows of the creeks, indicating that some meltwater may exit the crater from leakage through the crater floor (Major and others, 2005; Walder and others, 2007; Walder and others, this volume, chap. 13). A complete hydrologic budget to address this idea has yet to be developed for Mount St. Helens and, until such time, our multiple measurements of stream flow and chemistry for Loowit and Step creeks (table 7) offer the most comprehensive picture of discharge and dissolved fluxes from the crater area.

Two major contributors to conductivity in the creek waters are Cl and SO_4 (fig. 9*A*). During the course of our investigation at both of the Loowit Creek monitoring sites, Cl/SO_4 ratios were essentially constant and mimicked ratios in Loowit springs in 2005 (fig. 9*B*). In contrast, Step creek waters show large variations in Cl to SO_4, which can be attributed directly to changes in the chemistry and discharge of water from WFSCAF. Combining the average flows of Loowit Creek and the east fork of Step creek yields a total thermal water discharge of 335 L/s with an average Cl concentration of 180 mg/L (table 7). The creek waters are composed primarily of meteoric water from melting ice and snow plus water from the

Table 6. Discharge measurements and meter information for Loowit Creek above the falls, 1985–98, Mount St. Helens, Washington.

Date	Discharge (L/s)	Meter type
08/15/85	161	Price AA meter
09/09/85	197	Price AA meter
08/09/88	195	Gurley meter
08/10/89	213	Gurley meter
09/14/89	220	Price AA meter
09/14/89	197	Price AA meter
10/16/89	116	Pygmy meter
01/17/90	109	Pygmy meter
08/24/90	132	Pygmy meter
09/20/90	126	Pygmy meter
10/23/90	109	Pygmy meter
12/07/90	117	Pygmy meter
02/08/91	144	Pygmy meter
05/01/92	161	Pygmy meter
07/28/92	160	Pygmy meter
07/28/92	144	Pygmy meter
05/05/93	118	Pygmy meter
07/07/94	212	Pygmy meter
09/01/98	248	Pygmy meter

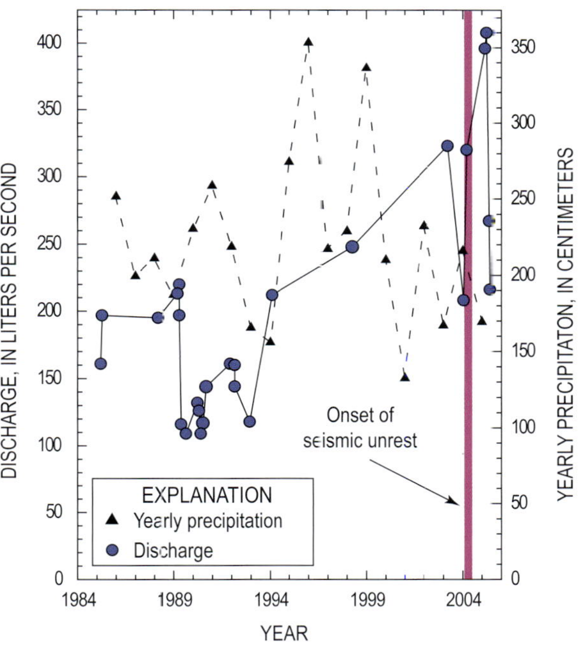

Figure 8. Discharge at site LCAF from 1985 to 2005 and yearly precipitation totals from the SNOTEL station at Spirit Lake, Mount St. Helens, Washington, from 1986 to 2005. Ticks on x axis correspond to month of June. Data from August 1988 and 1989 are from Shevenell (1990).

Table 7. Selected chemistry and discharge measurements for monitoring sites and some springs, 1988–2005, Mount St. Helens, Washington.

[CO_2 t/d, metric tons per day, calculated as CO_2 from measured HCO_3 flux; CO_2 mag., the corrected magmatic flux of CO_2 in metric tons per day based on measured spring pH values (see text); mS/cm, millisiemens per centimeter; ps, probe site; LCAF, Loowit Creek above falls; LCBF, Loowit Creek below falls; EFSCAF, east fork Step creek above falls; WFSCAF, west fork Step creek above falls; SCBF. Step creek below falls; CARB gs, carbonate spring gage site. Data from 1988 and 1989 are from Shevenell (1990). The ^{14}C data in bold were collected at a different time from the time the discharge was measured.]

Sample No.	Location	Date	Temp. (°C)	Conductivity (mS/cm)	Discharge (L/s)	^{14}C (% modern carbon)	HCO_3 (mg/L)	CO_2 (t/d)	CO_2 (mag. t/d)	Cl (mg/L)	SO_4 (mg/L)	Cl (t/d)	SO_4 (t/d)
Monitoring network sites													
MSH-05-11	LCAF	07/26/05	29.1	1.63	396		488	12.1	24	172	247	5.9	8.5
LCAF 082605	LCAF	08/26/05	30.1	1.61	408	--	--	--	--	169	236	5.9	8.3
LCAF 101105	LCAF	10/11/05	30.0	1.94	267	--	--	--	--	197	273	4.5	6.3
MSH-05-24	LCAF ps	10/25/05	25.9	1.83	215	--	533	7.1	14	193	268	3.6	5.0
LCBF 101304	LCBF	10/13/04	16.3	1.49	306	--	--	--	--	147	203	3.9	5.4
LCBF 042105	LCBF	04/21/05	16.9	1.87	187	--	--	--	--	180	270	2.9	4.4
MSH-05-12	LCBF	07/26/05	22.5	1.56	399	--	--	--	--	167	244	5.7	8.4
LCBF 082605	LCBF	08/26/05	19.8	1.63	279	--	--	--	--	178	249	4.3	6.0
Average flux									**19.0**			**4.6**	**6.5**
MSH-05-09	EFSCAF	07/26/05	26.6	1.45	45	--	535	1.5	3	172	145	0.7	0.6
EFSCAF 101105	EFSCAF	10/11/05	17.6	1.52	19	--	--	--	--	197	170	0.3	0.3
MSH-05-23	EFSCAF ps	10/25/05	25.4	1.96	27	--	787	1.3	2.6	232	194	0.5	0.5
Average flux									**2.8**			**0.5**	**0.4**
MSH-05-10	WFSCAF	07/26/05	10.5	0.06	142	--	12	0.1	0.1	10	3	0.1	0.03
SCBF 101304	SCBF	10/13/04	14.5	0.79	112	--	--	--	--	84	84	0.8	0.8
SCBF 082605	SCBF	08/26/05	19.2	0.89	49	--	--	--	--	93	89	0.4	0.4
MSH-05-13	SCBF	07/26/05	21.2	0.46	110	--	--	--	--	52	44	0.5	0.4
Average flux												**0.6**	**0.5**
Pumice Plain spring													
MSH-05-25	CARB gs	10/25/05	15.7	0.80	354	**5.5**	204	4.5	4.3	71	132	2.2	4.0
Regional cold springs													
MSH-05-14	#23	07/29/05	4.7	0.05	818	**93.8**	29	1.5	0.16	--	--	--	--
MSH-05-18 (nr)	#27	07/31/05	6.3	0.08	82	54.8	44	0.2	0.11	--	--	--	--
MSH-05-19	nr #26	07/31/05	7.2	0.12	137	50.0	94	0.8	0.42	--	--	--	--
MSH-05-20	#28	07/31/05	5.2	0.09	29	53.1	73	0.1	0.07	--	--	--	--
Loowit Creek above falls, 1988 and 1989													
SH-45	LCAF	08/09/88	41.0	3.36	195	--	87	1.1	1.1	600	567	10.1	9.6
SH-81	LCAF	08/10/89	41.6	3.02	213	--	88	1.2	1.2	549	507	10.1	9.3
Average flux									**1.1**			**10.1**	**9.4**

hot springs, and we can normalize the creek data to a source spring fluid with 280 mg/L by assuming that the meteoric water has no Cl (table 3). This calculation yields total water outputs of 215 L/s for the Loowit and Step springs. By using the density and enthalpy of water at 56°C, the heat output is ~50 MW. For perspective, a heat output of 50 MW would completely cool the 1980–86 dome in about 125 years.

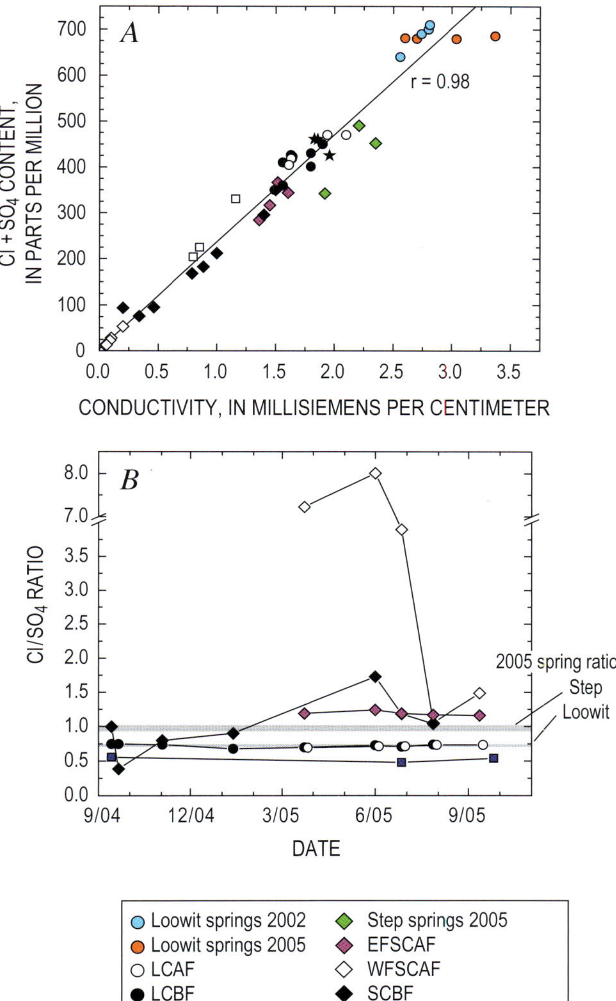

Figure 9. Cl and SO_4 concentrations for Loowit spring waters since 2002 and the creek-monitoring sites since October 2004, Mount St. Helens, Washington. *A*, Cl and SO_4 are major anions controlling conductivity in creek waters. *B*, Temporal plot showing Cl/SO_4 ratios at the monitoring sites. Loowit Creek sites show no change during the first year after the start of the 2004–5 eruption. Sites SCBF and WFSCAF show change in Cl and SO_4 ratios. Gray bars represent range in Cl and SO_4 for Loowit canyon and Step canyon springs in 2005. The LCAF site plot is shifted slightly so data can be shown.

Present-Day Flux of Magmatic Volatiles

Assuming that all of the dissolved carbon in the hot springs is derived from the underlying magma, we can couple the DIC concentration and the discharge to provide an estimate of the magmatic carbon flux. Table 7 shows six datasets for dates when a DIC sample was collected from a monitoring site concurrent with a discharge measurement. The largest flux measured was 12 metric tons per day (t/d), expressed as CO_2, from LCAF in July 2005. On the same day, another 1.5 t/d (as CO_2) discharged from EFSCAF. Measured pH values show that the DIC in Step and Loowit springs consists of approximately equal proportions of dissolved CO_2 and HCO_3, but nearly all of the dissolved CO_2 is outgassed upstream of the monitoring sites. The total output of magmatic carbon from the springs would, therefore, be double the amounts noted above. We did not gage carbonate spring in July 2005, but in October 2005 its magmatic CO_2 flux was 4.3 t/d. That value is adjusted for a small modern, nonmagmatic carbon contribution indicated by the ^{14}C value using mass balance, assuming the modern DIC component contains 105 percent modern carbon (James and others, 1999). Any potential flux of magmatic CO_2 from WFSCAF or the regional springs is less than 1 t/d.

We also estimated Cl and SO_4 fluxes for the creeks using the same methods. Apart from carbonate spring, which may have some nonmagmatic sources of Cl and SO_4, the data in table 7 show that the Loowit Creek sites are the main contributors of Cl and SO_4. Together, the Loowit and Step creeks yield average Cl and SO_4 fluxes of 5.2 t/d (expressed as HCl) and 4.7 t/d (expressed as SO_2) and, adjusting the DIC as discussed above, 22 t/d of CO_2. These data provide a first look at the flux of magmatic components dissolved in the waters at Mount St. Helens. For comparison, HCl and SO_2 fluxes in plume emissions on August 31, 2005, were 14 and 22 t/d, respectively (Edmonds and others, this volume, chap. 27), whereas CO_2 in the crater-plume emissions during the course of the 2004–6 eruption were in hundreds of tons per day (Doukas and others, 2005; Gerlach and others, this volume, chap. 26), and CO_2 emissions from the plume coming off Loowit springs were 27 t/d on June 9, 2005 (Gerlach and others, this volume, chap. 26).

Flux of Magmatic Volatiles 1988–1989

Estimates similar to those made for the 2004–5 data can be made for the flux of magmatic volatiles at LCAF in the late 1980s by using data from Shevenell (1990). Tables 2 and 7 show that the discharge at LCAF in August 1988 and 1989 was roughly 60 percent of the flow measured in the months of July and August 2003–5. In spite of lower discharges of creek water in the late 1980s, dissolved SO_4 and Cl fluxes were 1.4 and 2.2 times higher, respectively, than fluxes in 2004–5 (table 7). The dissolved magmatic CO_2 flux in 1988–89, however, was only 1.1 t/d, in comparison with 19 t/d from this study (table 7). Because the pH of the springs was about 7.2, we made no correction for outgassing of CO_2.

Conclusions

Data from springs and gas discharges in the crater are consistent with plume emission rates (Doukas and others, 2005; Gerlach and others, this volume, chap. 26) that indicate the current eruption is driven by degassed magma. From the early 1980s to 2002, gas vents on the 1980–86 dome grew weaker and more air-dominated, while magmatic Cl and SO_4 inputs to the Loowit springs declined, and the isotopic signal (D and ^{18}O) from magmatic water input disappeared. The large DIC increase in Loowit springs over time could indicate a pulse of new magma, but the $\delta^{13}C$ signatures of the DIC and of CO_2 gas are consistent with degassing of residual magma emplaced in the 1980s. No significant changes in Loowit springs occurred between 2002 and 2005. However, we note that the time for water to flow from the new dome to the spring vents could exceed one year, the time between the onset of unrest and the latest water sampling, so some caution must be applied to interpretations of the Loowit data. Carbon and helium isotope data for gas from the new dome might be more compelling but are unavailable.

Hot or mineralized springs occur on many volcanoes that lack summit plumes or obvious fumaroles and, in these cases, may provide the only opportunity to look for magmatic gases released at depth. The similarity in C:S:Cl ratios of recent Loowit springs samples and the 2005 plume emissions strongly supports the idea that spring geochemistry can accurately reflect magmatic degassing under favorable conditions. In this context, it is important to continue tracking the chemistry of the Mount St. Helens springs during the next few years in a search for responses to the current eruption.

Acknowledgments

We wish to thank several individuals who contributed to our research. Fraser Goff (Earth and Planetary Sciences Dept., Univ. of New Mexico) provided previously unpublished data from his work at Mount St. Helens. Helpful reviews were provided by Fraser Goff and Jon Major (USGS, Cascades Volcano Observatory). Peter Frenzen, the monument scientist at the Mount St. Helens National Volcanic Monument (USDA-Forest Service), provided logistical support and invaluable advice for several of our field campaigns. Student volunteers and interns Bryn Kimball (2002), Taryn López (2005), and Leif Rasmuson (2005) helped with sampling and stream gaging.

References Cited

Chiodini, G., Frondini, F., Cardellini, C., Parello, F., and Peruzzi, L., 2000, Rates of diffuse carbon dioxide Earth degassing estimated from carbon balance of regional aquifers—the case of central Apennine, Italy: Journal of Geophysical Research, v. 105, no. B4, p. 8423–8434.

Coplen, T.B., 1973, A double focusing, double collecting mass spectrometer for light stable isotope ratio analysis: International Journal of Mass Spectrometry and Ion Physics, v. 11, p. 37–40.

Coplen, T.B., Wildman, J.D., and Chen, J., 1991, Improvements in the gaseous hydrogen-water equilibration technique for hydrogen isotope-ratio analysis: Analytical Chemistry, v. 63, p. 910–912.

Doukas, M.P., McGee, K.A., and Gerlach, T.M., 2005, Airborne measurement of CO_2, SO_2, and H_2S emissions rates during the 2004–2005 eruption of Mount St. Helens [abs.]: Eos (American Geophysical Union Transactions), v. 86, no. 52, Fall Meet. Suppl., Abstract V53D-1590.

Dzurisin, D., Denlinger, R.P., and Rosenbaum, J.G., 1990, Cooling rate and thermal structure determined from progressive magnetization of the dacite dome at Mount St. Helens, Washington: Journal of Geophysical Research, v. 95, no. B3, p. 2763–2780.

Edmonds, M., McGee, K.A., and Doukas, M.P., 2008, Chlorine degassing during the lava dome-building eruption of Mount St. Helens, 2004–2005, chap. 27 *of* Sherrod, D.R., Scott, W.E., and Stauffer, P.H., eds., A volcano rekindled; the renewed eruption of Mount St. Helens, 2004–2006: U.S. Geological Survey Professional Paper 1750 (this volume).

Epstein, S., and Mayeda, T., 1953, Variation of ^{18}O content of waters from natural sources: Geochimica et Cosmochimica Acta, v. 4, no. 5, p. 213–224.

Evans, W.C., Banks, N.G., and White, L.D., 1981, Analyses of gas samples from the summit crater, *in* Lipman, P.W., and Mullineaux, D.R., eds., The 1980 eruptions of Mount St. Helens, Washington: U.S. Geological Survey Professional Paper 1250, p. 227–232.

Evans, W.C., Sorey, M.L., Cook, A.C., Kennedy, B.M., Shuster, D.L., Colvard, E.M., White, L.D., and Huebner, M.A., 2002, Tracing and quantifying magmatic carbon discharge in cold groundwaters—Lessons learned from Mammoth Mountain, USA: Journal of Volcanology and Geothermal Research, v. 114, p. 291–312.

Evarts, R.C., Ashley, R.P., and Smith, J.G., 1987, Geology of the Mount St. Helens area; record of discontinuous volcanic and plutonic activity in the Cascade arc of southern Washington: Journal of Geophysical Research, v. 92, no. B10, p. 10155–10169.

Faure, G., 1986, Principles of isotope geology: New York, John Wiley, 589 p.

Fournier, R.O., 1986, Conceptual models of brine evolution in magma-hydrothermal systems, chap. 55 *of* Decker, R.W., Wright, T.L., and Stauffer. P.H., eds., Volcanism in Hawaii: U.S. Geological Survey Professional Paper 1350, v. 2, p. 1487–1506.

Gerlach, T.M., and Casadevall, T.J., 1986, Fumarole emissions at Mount St. Helens volcano, June 1980 to October 1981; degassing of a magma-hydrothermal system: Journal of Volcanology and Geothermal Research, v. 28, nos. 1–2, p. 141–160, doi:10.1016/0377-0273(86)90009-0.

Gerlach, T.M., and Taylor, B.E., 1990, Carbon isotope constraints on degassing of carbon dioxide from Kilauea Volcano: Geochimica et Cosmochimica Acta, v. 54, no. 7, p. 2051–2058.

Gerlach, T.M., McGee, K.A., and Doukas, M.P., 2005, Emission rates, pre-eruption gas saturation and ascent degassing during the 2004–2005 eruption of Mount St. Helens [abs.]: Eos (American Geophysical Union Transactions), v. 86, no. 52, Fall Meet. Suppl., Abstract V52B-07.

Gerlach, T.M., McGee, K.A., and Doukas, M.P., 2008, Emission rates of CO_2, SO_2, and H_2S, scrubbing, and preeruption excess volatiles at Mount St. Helens, 2004–2005, chap. 26 *of* Sherrod, D.R., Scott, W.E., and Stauffer, P.H., eds., A volcano rekindled; the renewed eruption of Mount St. Helens, 2004–2006: U.S. Geological Survey Professional Paper 1750 (this volume).

Giggenbach, W.F., 1992, Chemical techniques in geothermal exploration, *in* D'Amore, F., ed., Applications of geochemistry in geothermal reservoir development: Rome, UNITAR/UNDP Guidebook, Center on Small Energy Resources, p. 119–144.

Goff, F., and McMurtry, G.M., 2000, Tritium and stable isotopes of magmatic waters: Journal of Volcanology and Geothermal Research, v. 97, p. 347–396.

James, E.R., Manga, M., and Rose, T.P., 1999, CO_2 degassing in the Oregon Cascades: Geology, v. 27, no. 9, p. 823–826.

Keith, T.E.C., Casadevall, T.J., and Johnston, D.A., 1981, Fumarole encrustations; occurrence, mineralogy and chemistry, *in* Lipman, P.W., and Mullineaux, D.R., eds., The 1980 eruptions of Mount St. Helens, Washington: U.S. Geological Survey Professional Paper 1250, p. 239–250.

Kennedy, B.M., and van Soest, M.C., 2006, A helium isotope perspective on the Dixie Valley, Nevada, hydrothermal system: Geothermics, v. 35, p. 26–43.

Kharaka, Y.K., Gunter, W.D., Aggarwal, P.K., Perkins, E.H., and DeBraal, J.D., 1988, SOLMINEQ.88—A computer program for geochemical modeling of water-rock interactions: U.S. Geological Survey Water Resources Investigation Report 88–4227, 420 p.

Major, J.J., Scott, W.E., Driedger, C., and Dzurisin, D., Mount St. Helens erupts again; activity from September 2004 through March 2005: U.S. Geological Survey Fact Sheet 2005–3036, 4 p.

Rose, T.P., and Davisson, M.L., 1996, Radiocarbon in hydrologic systems containing dissolved magmatic carbon dioxide: Science, v. 273, p. 1367–1370.

Schilling, S.P., Carrara, P.E., Thompson, R.A., and Iwatsubo, E.Y., 2004, Posteruption glacier development within the crater of Mount St. Helens, Washington, USA: Quaternary Research, v. 61, no. 3, p. 325–329.

Shevenell, L., 1990, Chemical and isotopic investigation of the new hydrothermal system at Mount St. Helens, Washington, USA: Reno, University of Nevada, Ph.D. dissertation, 282 p.

Shevenell, L., and Goff, F., 1993, Addition of magmatic volatiles into the hot spring waters of Loowit Canyon, Mount St. Helens, Washington, USA: Bulletin of Volcanology, v. 55, no. 7, p. 489–503, doi:10.1007/BF00304592.

Shevenell, L., and Goff, F., 1995, Evolution of hydrothermal waters at Mount St. Helens, Washington, USA: Journal of Volcanology and Geothermal Research, v. 69, p. 73–94.

Shevenell, L., and Goff, F., 2000, Temporal geochemical variations in volatile emissions from Mount St. Helens, USA, 1980–1994: Journal of Volcanology and Geothermal Research, v. 99, p. 123–138.

Symonds, R.B., and Reed, M.H., 1993, Calculation of multicomponent chemical equilibria in gas-solid-liquid systems; calculation methods, thermochemical data, and applications to studies of high-temperature volcanic gases with examples from Mount St. Helens: American Journal of Science, v. 293, no. 8, p. 758–864.

Symonds, R.B., Gerlach, T.M., and Reed, M.H., 2001, Magmatic gas scrubbing—implications for volcano monitoring: Journal of Volcanology and Geothermal Research, v. 108, nos. 1–4, p. 303–341, doi:10.1016/S0377-0273(00)00292-4.

Symonds, R.B., Poreda, R.J., Evans, W.C., Janik, C.J., and Ritchie, B.E., 2003, Mantle and crustal sources of carbon, nitrogen, and noble gases in Cascade-Range and Aleutian-Arc volcanic gases: U.S. Geological Survey Open-File Report 03–436, 26 p.

Thompson, M.J., 1990, Chemical data from thermal and nonthermal springs in Mount St. Helens National Monument, Washington: U.S. Geological Survey Open-File Report 90-0690–A, 16 p.

Vogel, J.S., Southon, J.R., and Nelson, D.E., 1987, Catalyst and binder effects in the use of filamentous graphite for AMS: Nuclear Instruments and Methods in Physics Research, v. B29, p. 50–56.

Walder, J.S., LaHusen, R.G., Vallance, J.W., and Schilling, S.P., 2007, Emplacement of a silicic lava dome through a crater glacier—Mount St Helens, 2004–06: Annals of Glaciology, v. 45, p. 14–20.

Walder, J.S., Schilling, S.P., Vallance, J.W., and LaHusen, R.G., 2008, Effects of lava-dome growth on the Crater Glacier of Mount St. Helens, Washington, chap. 13 *of* Sherrod, D.R., Scott, W.E., and Stauffer, P.H., eds., A volcano rekindled; the renewed eruption of Mount St. Helens, 2004–2006: U.S. Geological Survey Professional Paper 1750 (this volume).

Appendix 1. Trace-Element and Isotopic Data from Springs and Creeks in the Mount St. Helens Area, Washington, 2002–2005

[This appendix appears only in the digital versions of this work—in the DVD-ROM that accompanies the printed volume and as a separate file accompanying this chapter on the Web at: http://pubs.usgs.gov/pp/1750.]

This appendix is a spreadsheet of analytical data.

A Volcano Rekindled: The Renewed Eruption of Mount St. Helens, 2004–2006
Edited by David R. Sherrod, William E. Scott, and Peter H. Stauffer
U.S. Geological Survey Professional Paper 1750, 2008

Chapter 26

Emission Rates of CO_2, SO_2, and H_2S, Scrubbing, and Preeruption Excess Volatiles at Mount St. Helens, 2004–2005

By Terrence M. Gerlach[1], Kenneth A. McGee[1], and Michael P. Doukas[1]

Abstract

Airborne surveillance of gas emissions began at Mount St. Helens on September 27, 2004. Reconnaissance measurements—SO_2 column abundances and CO_2, SO_2, and H_2S concentrations—showed neither a gas plume downwind of the volcano nor gas sources within the crater. Subsequent measurements taken during the period of unrest before the eruption began on October 1 and for several days after October 1 showed only small point sources of gas within the crater. These sources defined a pattern of scrubbed degassing that evolved from near-zero emissions, to scattered CO_2-only sources, to growing sources of CO_2 with minor H_2S and SO_2, and finally to myriad sources of CO_2 with increasingly SO_2-dominant sulfur gases. Scrubbing strongly hydrolyzed SO_2 but also affected CO_2 and H_2S.

From October 7 on, a coherent plume spilled over the crater rim, yielding emission rates for CO_2 and SO_2, but not always for H_2S. Virtually all SO_2 and most CO_2 outgassed from the growing dome of new dacite; some CO_2 came from sources on the 1980–86 lava dome and in the Loowit springs area. The 2004–5 emission rates were notably low and variable. Emission rates for CO_2 peaked early (10/7/2004) at 2,415 metric tons per day (t/d), but the median rate was 655 t/d; only about 20 percent of the rates were greater than 1,000 t/d and about 45 percent were less than 500 t/d. Emission rates of SO_2 never exceeded 240 t/d, and the median rate was only 72 t/d; 70 percent of SO_2 emission rates were <100 t/d and about 40 percent were <50 t/d. Emission rates of H_2S were <10 t/d. Cumulative outputs through November 2005 were about 231,000 t CO_2 and 30,000 t SO_2.

The CO_2 and SO_2 emission rates are distinctly lower than those of the early 1980s, but they are similar to those of the 1980s lava-dome eruptions, possibly back as far as late 1981 or late 1980. However, the CO_2/SO_2 ratio of the 2004–5 emissions (11±1) is higher than that of the 1980s emissions (8) because of scrubbing during the early part of the eruption. The nonscrubbed CO_2/SO_2 of the 2004–5 gases is 9±1, similar to the1980s emissions.

Modeling constrained by cumulative CO_2 emissions, cumulative dacite production, and melt H_2O concentration confirms that the 2004–5 dacite is a "flat" magma—that is, a dacite magma greatly depleted in excess (exsolved) volatiles compared to May 18, 1980, dacite. The inferred excess-volatile content of the current dacite is only 1.2 volume percent (vol. percent), or 0.2 weight percent (wt. percent), compared to the 15 vol. percent (3 wt. percent) of the May 18 dacite at 900°C and 220 megapascals (MPa) (8.6 km depth). At the much lower pressure of 130 MPa prior to ascent from the shallowest part of the reservoir (5.2 km depth), the current dacite's inferred excess-volatile content is 1.2 wt. percent—significantly less than the 3 wt. percent of the May 18 dacite and on the low end of the 1–6-wt. percent range of deeper intermediate to silicic magmas commonly involved in explosive volcanism.

The modeling further indicates that before ascent from 5.2 km depth, the dacite's excess volatile phase was H_2O rich (X_{H_2O} = ~0.96, X_{CO_2} = ~0.04, mole fraction basis) with H_2S/SO_2 > 40, and its rhyolitic melt phase contained about 4.4 wt. percent H_2O and 37 parts per million (ppm) CO_2. After closed-system ascent to the depth range of groundmass crystallization (~0.5–1 km), X_{H_2O} is 0.98, H_2S/SO_2 is 4–7, and the melt contains 1.1–1.5 wt. percent H_2O and 1–3 ppm CO_2. Sulfur dioxide becomes dominant over H_2S at depths less than 0.2 km. Because of excess-volatile depletion, open-system degassing involves depths shallower than about 2.5 km, weak CO_2 and SO_2 emissions prone to the effects of scrubbing, and—in contrast to early 1980 degassing—no measurable effect on the equilibrium ($^{210}Pb/^{226}Ra$) values of the 2004–5 dacite.

The 2004–5 gas emissions are incompatible with "new" gas-rich magma introduced into the reservoir in the months

[1] U.S. Geological Survey, 1300 SE Cardinal Court, Vancouver, WA 98683

just before or since the onset of unrest and eruptive activity. However, the gas emissions are compatible with a flat magma—either leftover dacite from 1986 or dacite injected into the reservoir since 1986 as excess volatile-depleted magma, or as gas-rich magma subsequently mixed with larger amounts of leftover dacite or stripped of its excess volatiles by degassing prior to the current eruption.

Introduction

Airborne surveillance of gas emissions began on September 27, 2004, four days after a shallow earthquake swarm beneath the 1980–86 lava dome signaled Mount St. Helens' reawakening after 18 years (Scott and others, this volume, chap. 1; Moran and others, this volume, chap. 2). In this chapter we report the CO_2, SO_2, and H_2S gas emissions from the eruption's inception to the end of 2005, documenting their measurement, sources, and the magnitude and variability of the emission rates—presented in the context of gas-emission rates at Mount St. Helens in the 1980s and at several Cascade Range volcanoes since the late 1990s. The outstanding feature of the 2004–5 gas emissions is their persistently low emission rates. We attribute these low rates mainly to the extreme depletion of excess (that is, exsolved) volatiles in the current dacite compared to the May 18, 1980, dacite and secondarily to gas scrubbing. VolatileCalc modeling (Newman and Lowenstern, 2002) quantifies and confirms our hypothesis of excess-volatile depletion in the 2004–5 dacite. We exploit the modeling to reveal the amount and composition of excess-volatile fluid in the source dacite at depth, to track its evolution as the dacite ascends, and to quantify several related aspects of the degassing.

Background

Airborne Emission-Rate Measurements at Mount St. Helens in the 1980s

Airborne monitoring from a fixed-wing aircraft of SO_2 emission rates began at Mount St. Helens in May 1980 by making correlation spectrometer (COSPEC) measurements on the plume. More than 1,000 COSPEC flights followed during the next 8 years (McGee, 1992; McGee and Casadevall, 1994), most of which were made 1–2 km downwind of source vents during episodes of dome-building eruptions, endogenous dome growth, or intervening noneruptive periods. Casadevall and others (1981, 1983) describe the measurement technique and discuss the SO_2 emissions through 1982. McGee (1992) describes the structure, dynamics, and SO_2 cross sections of noneruptive plumes at Mount St. Helens that occurred from 1980 to 1988. McGee and Sutton (1994) discuss measurements made during four 1984–86 dome-building eruptions and compare results with various geophysical monitoring data. Early SO_2 emission rates frequently exceeded 1,000 metric tons per day (t/d), but rates declined to negligible levels by September 1988 when airborne COSPEC measurements ended, nearly 2 years after the last dome-building eruption of the 1980s (McGee and Casadevall, 1994). Airborne monitoring also included 119 measurements of CO_2 emission rates that ranged from >20,000 t/d in July 1980 to <1,000 t/d by the end of August 1981, when measurements were halted because concentrations of plume CO_2 had declined to levels indistinguishable from ambient atmospheric CO_2 by the analyzer employed at the time (Harris and others, 1981; McGee and Casadevall, 1994). McGee and Casadevall (1994) tabulate the 1980–1988 airborne emission-rate measurements and supplementary data, all of which can be downloaded from the USGS publications Web site, http://pubs.usgs.gov/of/1994/of94-212/ (last accessed March 14, 2008).

Airborne Emission-Rate Measurements in the Cascades Since the 1980s

We initiated a program of volcanic gas emission-rate measurements at Cascade Range volcanoes in the late 1990s after developing improved airborne monitoring techniques (described below). The program comprised airborne plume measurements at major volcanic centers, from Mount Baker in Washington to Lassen Peak in California, to establish baseline emission rates of CO_2, SO_2, and H_2S for identifying anomalous gas emissions at times of volcano unrest in the Cascade Range (table 1). Several volcanic centers—Glacier Peak, Mount Rainer, Mount Adams, Mount Jefferson, Medicine Lake caldera and Mount Shasta—produce no detectable emissions of the three gases; however, these airborne results do not rule out minor diffusive degassing and scattered spring and fumarole gas discharges derived from underlying magma. Other centers, such as Newberry caldera and South Sister, though lacking coherent plumes, do produce trace quantities of gas from small point sources that can be detected in airborne gas measurements. Besides Mount St. Helens, only three volcanoes in the Cascade Range produce coherent plumes with measurable gas output at the present time—Mount Baker, Mount Hood, and Lassen Peak. All of these volcanoes emit small amounts of gas: emission rates are <300 t/d for CO_2 and <10 t/d for H_2S; SO_2 is below detection.

Airborne Measurements at Mount St. Helens in 1998

In May 1998, background seismicity at Mount St. Helens increased markedly from the low levels recorded for the previous few years. Located directly below the lava dome, these small earthquakes clustered mainly in two distinct depth bands: 2–5 km and 7–9 km. Throughout June and the first half of July 1998, the seismicity continued to increase, with earthquake depths spanning the entire range from 2 to 9 km. The first of several airborne gas-surveillance flights recorded

Table 1. Gas measurements in the Cascade Range and nearby calderas after 1988.

[Platform indicates aircraft: FX, fixed-wing; Heli, helicopter. t/d, metric tons per day; –, no data; 0, measurement taken but gas was not detected; tr, trace.]

Volcano	Date	Platform	CO_2 (t/d)	SO_2 (t/d)	H_2S (t/d)
Mount Baker	07/08/1998	FX	273	0	–
	09/13/2000[1]	FX	187	0	5.5
	03/21/2001	FX	0	0	0
Glacier Peak	07/08/1998	FX	0	0	–
Mount Rainer	07/08/1998	FX	0	0	–
Mount Adams	08/03/1998	FX	0	0	–
	08/10/2005	FX	0	0	0
Mount St. Helens	06/22/1998	FX	1,900	0	–
	07/08/1998[2]	FX	tr	0	–
	07/08/1998[3]	FX	tr	0	–
	08/03/1998	FX	0	0	–
	09/14/1998	FX	0	0	–
Mount Hood	06/22/1998	FX	0	0	–
	08/03/1998	FX	0	0	–
	08/10/2005	FX	0	0	0
	09/15/2005	Heli	144	0	6.4
Mount Jefferson	08/11/1998	FX	0	0	–
Newberry caldera	09/19/2000	FX	tr	0	–
South Sister	04/25/2001	Heli	tr	0	–
	09/21/2001	Heli	0	0	–
Medicine Lake caldera	08/11/1998	FX	0	0	–
Mount Shasta	08/11/1998	FX	0	0	–
Lassen Peak	08/11/1998	FX	110	0	–
	09/19/2000	FX	20	0	2

[1]Data from McGee and others (2001).

[2]Morning flight.

[3]Afternoon flight.

a CO_2 emission rate of 1,900 t/d on June 22 (table 1). By July 8, morning and afternoon gas-measurement flights detected only trace CO_2 degassing, and by the end of July, seismicity returned to levels similar to those prior to May. Additional gas-surveillance flights on August 3 and September 14 failed to detect CO_2 degassing. All 1998 flights failed to detect SO_2; there were no H_2S measurements.

Instrumentation and Configuration of the Airborne Monitoring System

In this study, we used an airborne system developed during the past decade for measuring volcanic CO_2, SO_2, and H_2S emissions and intended primarily for application in the Cascade Range and the Aleutian arc. Sites of interest in these regions are remote, ground access is difficult, climates are wet, and thick snow pack and glaciers are present locally. Large volumes of recharge water foster hydrothermal systems and bodies of ground water and surficial water capable of scrubbing acidic magmatic volatiles (especially SO_2, HCl, HF) and masking magma degassing at depth during the early stages of unrest—hence the emphasis on an airborne system capable of measuring CO_2 and H_2S emissions (Doukas and Gerlach, 1995; Symonds and others, 2001).

The airborne system incorporates a LI-COR Model LI-6252 nondispersive infrared CO_2 analyzer and flow control unit to measure CO_2 concentrations. This instrument, with a fast 1-s response time and a high sensitivity to low concentrations of CO_2, is well suited for measuring small changes in CO_2 concentration. Its use for determining CO_2 in volcanic plumes is described in detail elsewhere (Gerlach and others, 1997; Gerlach and others, 1999). We used an Interscan Model 4170 H_2S analyzer to measure plume H_2S in the 0–1 ppm range. This instrument consists of an electrochemical voltametric sensor coupled to a 1-L/min sample-draw pump with H_2S concentration recorded from calibrated analog output. McGee and others (2001) describe the application of the Interscan analyzer to measuring H_2S in volcanic plumes. Similarly, an Interscan Model 4240 SO_2 analyzer with a 0–2 ppm range provides direct measurements of SO_2 in the plume. Assuming ambient air is largely devoid of H_2S and SO_2, our measurements indicate typical instrument noise values of 3–4 parts per billion (ppb)for these analyzers. Interscan analyzers show some cross sensitivity to other gases, so these gases are removed by appropriate chemical scrubbers installed on input lines. Because Interscan analyzers measure gas partial pressures, all calibrated output is corrected for the pressure and temperature at the altitude of measurement.

The airborne system is configured to employ two types of optical ultraviolet spectrometers for measuring SO_2 column abundances. For some of the early measurements in this study, we employed a Barringer correlation spectrometer (COSPEC V)—long the standard tool for monitoring volcanic SO_2 emission rates (Stoiber and Jepsen, 1973; Crafford, 1975; Malinconico, 1979; Stoiber and others, 1983). A data logger records the analog output of the instrument for later processing using USGS software. For the majority of the SO_2 flux measurements, we used a FLYSPEC built and configured as described in Horton and others (2006). This new, miniaturized, lightweight and low-power, ultraviolet correlation spectrometer incorporates an Ocean Optics USB2000 ultraviolet spectrometer with a fiber-optic collimating lens, a UV band-pass filter, and two SO_2 calibration cells. A subnotebook computer provides FLYSPEC power, control, and data collection through a USB port, and a small GPS receiver supplies location data for cosine corrections of traverses not perpendicular to the direction of plume travel.

The airborne instrument package also includes a type-K thermocouple, shielded from wind and direct sunlight, for measuring ambient air temperature and a chart recorder for in-flight logistical use. A pressure transducer mounted within the LI-COR analyzer provides measurements of ambient atmospheric pressure inside the unpressurized aircraft cabin. An onboard Rockwell GPS receiver continuously records the precise latitude, longitude, and altitude, so that the location of each measurement can be retrieved later for data processing. The data from all instruments except the FLYSPEC are recorded at 1-s frequency in a handheld PSC Falcon Model 310 portable data-collection terminal. Figure 1 illustrates schematically the configuration of all the instruments of the airborne system. Figure 2 displays instrument placement in both helicopter and fixed-wing aircraft and the external helicopter mounting of a FLYSPEC.

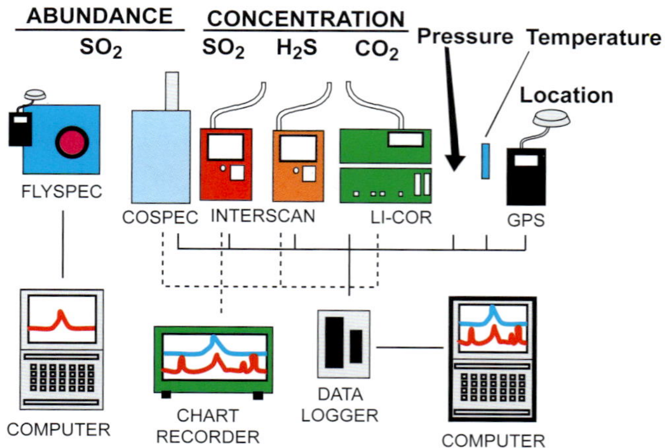

Figure 1. Airborne instrument package showing instruments used for measuring SO_2 column abundances (FLYSPEC and COSPEC); instruments for measuring CO_2, SO_2, and H_2S gas concentration (LI-COR and Interscan); sensors for measuring temperature, pressure, and location; and other components used during a typical airborne mission (computer, data logger, and chart recorder).

Figure 2. Gas-monitoring equipment installation for airborne surveillance, 2004–2005. *A*, FLYSPEC being attached to the strut of helicopter. The instrument's narrow field of view allows it to be mounted near the body of the aircraft without blocking the light. *B*, Typical mounting arrangement of instrumentation in helicopter. *C*, Instrumentation placed in a fixed-wing aircraft. Note COSPEC panel (right) protruding from behind copilot's seat. USGS photos by K.A. McGee (*A*, *C*) and M.P. Doukas (*B*).

Procedures and Methods

The gas measurements began on September 27, 2004. The five flights during the first week were primarily for reconnaissance purposes. At this stage of unrest, the volcano lacked a coherent gas plume but produced small fragmentary and ephemeral parcels of gas that—although detectable by the airborne system—were only useful for rough estimates of gas emission rates. Nevertheless, we were able to discover and follow the development of point sources of emerging gas emissions within the crater by mounting the direct-sampling instruments (LI-COR and Interscans) in a helicopter with an air intake tube attached to the lower left strut and making reconnaissance flights of the 1980–86 lava dome, the crater floor, and the crater walls (fig. 3).

After the first week of October 2004, a coherent plume developed and spilled over the crater rim, and accurate emission-rate determinations became feasible (fig. 4). We mounted and flew the direct-sampling instruments and the COSPEC V in a twin-engine aircraft configured for open-flow sampling of external air (Gerlach and others, 1997, 1999). The use of a twin-engine aircraft prevented contamination by combustion products from engine exhaust. Upward-looking COSPEC measurements taken while flying traverses beneath the plume perpendicular to the direction of plume transport provided SO_2 column abundances across an orthogonal section of the plume (fig. 5*A*). Flying traverses across the plume at different altitudes, each normal to its transport direction, allowed in-plume measurements and profiling of entire orthogonal sections of the plume by the direct-sampling instruments (LI-COR and Interscans) (fig. 5*B*). Figure 6 illustrates a series of airborne traverses across the plume, showing where the Interscan analyzer detected SO_2 in the orthogonal plume cross section. Later processing of these data into emission rates included corrections for curvature in the flight paths and for deviations from orthogonality. Contour maps of gas concentrations in the orthogonal plume cross section were produced using mapping software (Surfer v. 8).

By November 10, 2004, we made a transition to the use of a helicopter as the airborne platform for gas measurements, for these reasons: the availability of a helicopter for field work, the superior maneuverability of a helicopter for making plume measurements at the crater rim and within the crater, and the slower airspeed of the helicopter, which permits more measurements per meter across small plumes. Use of the helicopter also marked the transition to exclusive use of the FLYSPEC ultraviolet spectrometer for SO_2 emission-rate measurements. Although it is possible to utilize the COSPEC in a helicopter, "chopping" of light to the COSPEC telescope by the rotor blades creates interference in the signal output. This requires selection of longer time constants to dampen the interference, which negates the advantageous spatial resolution of the helicopter (Caltabiano and others, 1992; Galle and others, 2002; Elias and others, 2006). The FLYSPEC, however, is relatively immune to interference by the rotor blades, and no special filtering or processing of the data is required. The switch from COSPEC to FLYSPEC did not introduce inconsistencies into the SO_2 emission-rate dataset—side-by-side testing of these instruments shows they produce statistically equivalent results (Elias and others, 2006; Horton and others, 2006).

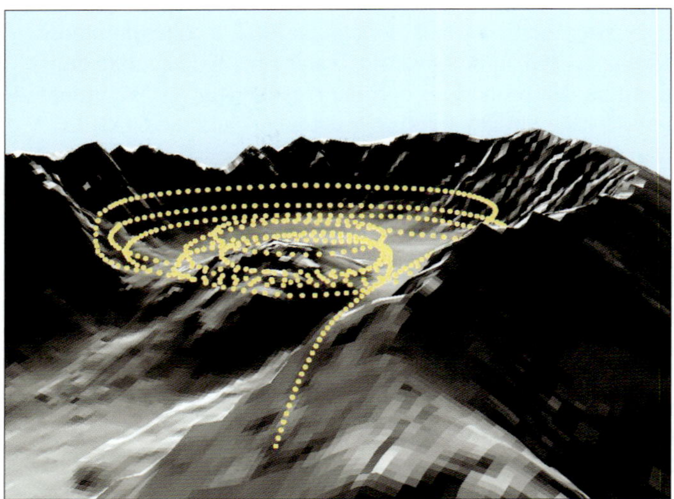

Figure 3. Shaded-relief elevation model of Mount St. Helens' crater indicating the flight path of a gas-measurement flight in October 2004. Early gas flights in fall 2004 before the emergence of a discrete plume, such as the flight illustrated here, were geared toward detecting point sources of CO_2, SO_2, and H_2S. View is to the southeast.

The relatively small field of view (2.5°) of the FLYSPEC allows it to be mounted on an external structural member close to the body of the helicopter and positioned to point vertically without loss of signal due to light obstruction (fig. 2*A*). We fed the USB signal and power cable through a side window of the helicopter to connect with the subnotebook computer. Prior to the plume measurements, we landed the helicopter at a calibration station high on the flank of Mount St. Helens and collected instrument spectra for the high and low calibration cells along with spectra for dark current and clear sky. Once the FLYSPEC was calibrated, we flew several traverses beneath the plume that were averaged to obtain the SO_2 column abundances of the plume. We reduced the data with the FluxCalc software program written by staff at the Hawai'i Institute of Geophysics and Planetology, University of Hawai'i at Mānoa. The program compares absorption values of as many as nine peak-and-trough combinations in each sample SO_2 spectrum to the two calibration cell spectra and then computes the column abundance of SO_2.

The standard method for determining emission rates from airborne in-plume measurements by the direct-sampling instruments is based on the volcanic gas concentrations measured in the cross section through the plume normal to wind direction, the average plume pressure and temperature in that section, and the wind speed (Harris and others, 1981; Gerlach and others, 1997). Gerlach and others (1999) adapted the method by using orbital traverses around a volcano and correcting the data from curved plume cross sections approximately normal to wind direction. McGee and others (2001) further adapted the method by using H_2S peaks as a guide for resolving the boundary between atmospheric-only CO_2 and atmospheric plus volcanic plume CO_2. In this study, we often used the location of SO_2 peaks recorded by the Interscan analyzer as markers to distinguish plume CO_2 from the atmospheric background CO_2 because H_2S was not always detected in the plume. Direct measurement of CO_2 and SO_2

Figure 4. Typical gas plumes from Mount St. Helens early in the 2004–2005 eruption. *A*, Plume observed on October 27, 2004. View is to southeast. *B*, Plume on November 4, 2004. View is to south. Crater diameter is about 2.1 km. USGS photos by M.P. Doukas (*A*) and K.A. McGee (*B*).

also allowed calculation of CO_2/SO_2 ratios at many locations in the plume.

Knowing the velocity of plume travel is essential in computing accurate gas-emission rates from either gas concentrations in a plume cross section or column-abundance measurements made beneath the plume. It is assumed that the speed of the plume as it moves downwind is the same as the ambient wind speed. We used the Doukas (2002) method of wind-speed measurement, in which a GPS receiver records the rate and direction of drift of the aircraft while flying neutral wind circles at the altitude of the plume. This information allows determination of wind speed and wind direction at the altitude of the plume with a windspeed uncertainty of <10 percent.

The equation of Gerlach and others (1997),

$$E_{CO_2} = 0.457329(ASP_{CO_2})/T, \quad (1)$$

calculates the CO_2 emission rate, E_{CO_2}, in t/d where A is the area of the plume cross section after corrections for curvature of orbital traverses (in m^2), S is the average plume speed (in m/s), P_{CO_2} is the average partial pressure of CO_2 in the plume (in pascals (Pa), calculated from the product of average barometric pressure in the plume and the average mole fraction concentration of CO_2 in the plume), and T is the average air temperature in the plume (in K). The constant (units: s t K Pa^{-1} m^{-3} d^{-1}) includes the kilogram molecular weight of CO_2 (0.04401 kg/mol), the universal gas constant (8.314510 Pa m^3 mol^{-1} K^{-1}), and the conversion factors 86,400 s/d and 10^3 kg/t. When calculating E_{H_2S}, P_{CO_2} is replaced by P_{H_2S}, and the con-

Figure 5. Schematic flight patterns for plume monitoring. *A*, Flight pattern for remote measurement of SO_2 column abundances in the plume. Flight traverses with the upward-looking FLYSPEC or COSPEC spectrometer are made beneath the plume perpendicular to its direction of travel. *B*, Instruments that measure concentration and require direct sampling of the plume, such as LI-COR and Interscan, are flown directly through the plume, perpendicular to its travel direction, in a series of top-to-bottom profiles forming a vertical plume cross section.

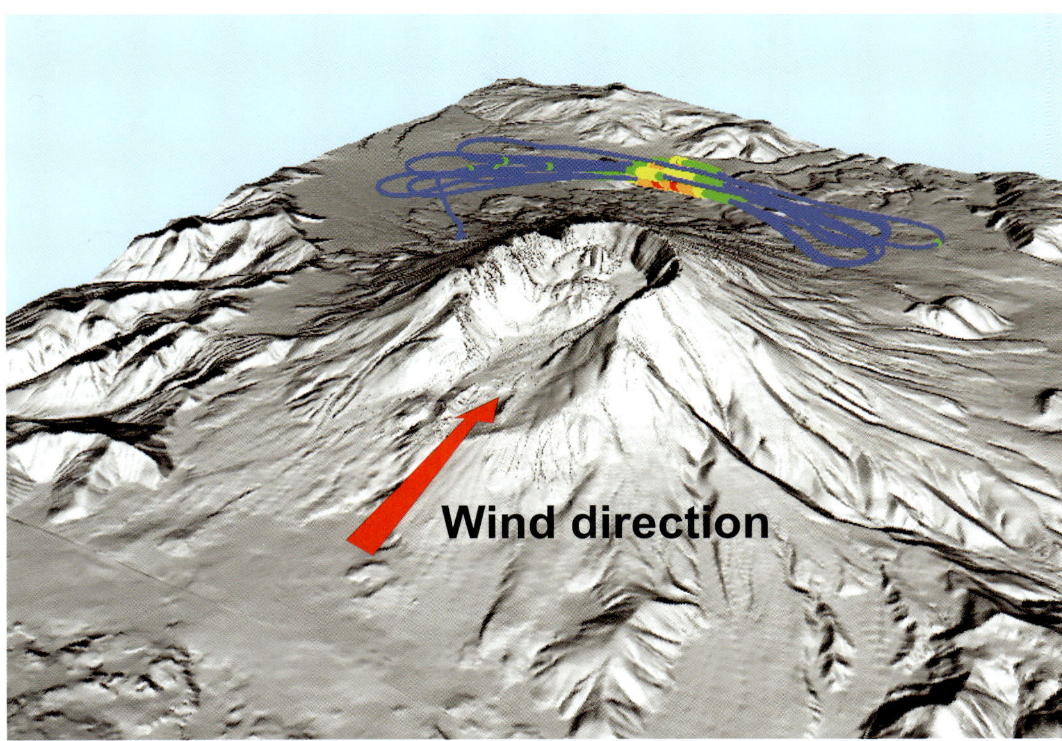

Figure 6. Illustration of a downwind airborne measurement of the plume from Mount St. Helens on July 13, 2005, plotted on shaded-relief elevation model. View is to the southeast. Blue line represents GPS tracks of several traverses through the plume, with hotter colors (yellow, orange, and red) representing locations where SO_2 was measured. Red arrow indicates wind direction; wind is from the north.

stant is 0.354141 (McGee and others, 2001); when calculating E_{SO_2}, P_{SO_2} and the constant 0.665665 are used.

Flight frequency varied because of a mix of factors, which included perceived flight safety, apparent necessity of the data for hazard assessments, rate of change of eruptive activity, and current and forecasted weather. Starting on September 27, 2004, we made 11 flights in the first 3 weeks, 1 to 2 flights per week during the next 5 weeks, and 1 or 2 flights per month thereafter throughout 2005, except during December 2005 when weather conditions did not permit access to the plume. Flight dates and aircraft platforms deployed (helicopter or fixed-wing) are recorded in table 2.

Description of Data and Statistical Tests

Gas emission-rate data, which form the backbone data of this report, tend to have skewed rather than symmetrical distributions. The skewed distributions are a reflection of two fundamental properties of gas emission-rate data: they can take on only positive values, and their standard deviations are typically large—commonly about as large or larger than their means. When distributions are skewed, means and standard deviations may no longer adequately describe population distributions, and interpreting these statistics in terms of a normal distribution can produce a misleading picture. It is preferable instead to report the median for skewed distributions (Glantz, 2005); we also report upper and lower percentile information as appropriate to give an indication of the dispersion of values in the sampled population.

If populations are skewed from normal distributions, parametric statistical tests may become unreliable, and nonparametric or distribution-free statistical tests should be used (Glantz, 2005). Therefore, we used statistical software (SigmaStat v. 3.1) to calculate the nonparametric Mann-Whitney rank-sum test (MWRST), instead of the parametric Student's *t* test, to test for significant differences in two groups of data. The MWRST can be used to evaluate significant difference in the medians of two groups, significant difference in the underlying population distributions of two groups, and significant difference between two groups caused by random sampling variations. We report the probability level (P) of MWRST results. Following the tradition of most physical-science research, the critical significance level for P is 5 percent ($P = 0.05$) in this report; that is, $P \leq 0.05$ indicates a significant difference. Several of the statistical calculations also included Kolmogorov-Smirnov normality testing (SigmaStat v. 3.1).

Results and Observations

Emission Rates, Cumulative Emissions, and CO_2/SO_2 Ratios

The measured CO_2, SO_2, and H_2S emission rates of the 2004–5 eruption spanned the period from September 27, 2004, to November 22, 2005 (fig. 7, table 2). Emission rates frequently were below detection limits before October 7, 2004 (fig. 7, table 2). Time series of the 24 CO_2 and 28 SO_2 emission rates measured from October 7, 2004, until the last 2005 measurement on November 22 were notably low and variable. Emission rates ranged from 2,415 t/d to 146 t/d for CO_2 and from 240 t/d to 14 t/d for SO_2; both CO_2 and SO_2 had low medians: 655 t/d for CO_2 and 72 t/d for SO_2. Less than 5 percent of the CO_2 emission rates were >2,000 t/d, about 80 percent were <1,000 t/d, more than 40 percent were <500 t/d, and about 25 percent were <250 t/d. Of the SO_2 emission rates, only 7 percent were >200 t/d, almost 70 percent were <100 t/d, and 40 percent were <50 t/d. At times, emission rates fell to <150 t/d for CO_2 and to <30 t/d for SO_2. Emission rates of H_2S were always low (<10 t/d). Multiple traverses under the plume gave comparable SO_2 emission rates, so the observed variation was not simply from puffing during times of measurement.[2]

Cumulative CO_2 and SO_2 emissions—calculated from the areas under emission-rate time-series plots—indicate total outputs of 231,150 t CO_2 and 29,700 t SO_2 from October 7, 2004, through November 22, 2005 (fig. 8; table 2). Weighted emission rates—calculated from cumulative emissions on measurement dates (fig. 8; table 2) divided by the number of days since October 7, 2004—are like multiday averages and thus smoother than measured emission rates. Although less variable, weighted emission rates also have low medians—830 t/d for CO_2 and 99 t/d for SO_2. However, these median rates are somewhat higher than the medians of measured values. Nevertheless, statistical tests confirm that no significant dif-

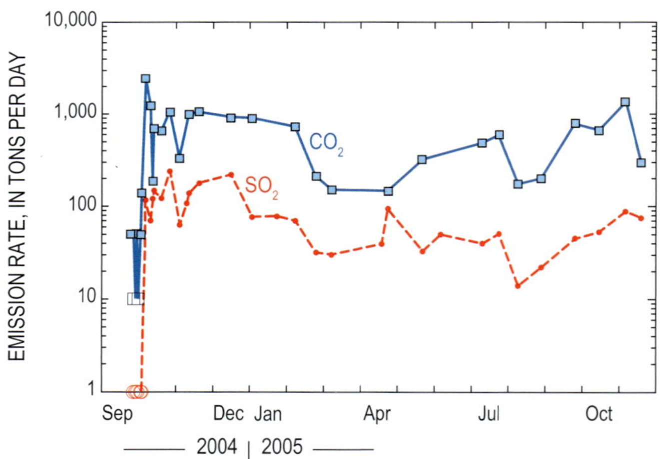

Figure 7. Time-series plots of CO_2 and SO_2 emission rates from September 27, 2004, to November 22, 2005 (table 2). The open symbols for some earlier measurements between September 27 and October 1, 2004, indicate estimated detection limit values of 10 t/d (CO_2) and 1 t/d (SO_2).

[2] Note added in proof: Low emission rates of 150–300 t/d CO_2, 5–35 t/d SO_2, and < 0.1 t/d H_2S persisted during 12 gas-monitoring flights from 2006 until the eruption paused in late January 2008.

Table 2. Emission rates and cumulative emissions for CO_2, SO_2, and H_2S during 2004–2005, Mount St. Helens, Washington.

[Emission rates are measured rates used in calculations of this study; significant figures were exaggerated to reduce roundoff errors. Cumulative emissions were determined as described in the text. Platform indicates aircraft: FX, fixed-wing; Heli, helicopter. t/d, metric tons per day; nd, not determined.]

Date	Plat-form	CO_2 (t/d)	SO_2 (t/d)	H_2S (t/d)	CO_2 (t)	SO_2 (t)
09/27/2004	Heli	50	1 [1]	0.1 [1]	nd	nd
09/29/2004	Heli	10 [1]	1 [1]	0.1 [1]	nd	nd
09/30/2004	Heli	50	1 [1]	0.1 [1]	nd	nd
10/01/2004	Heli	10 [1]	1 [1]	0.1 [1]	nd	nd
10/03/2004	Heli	50	1 [1]	0.1 [1]	nd	nd
10/04/2004	Heli	140	1 [1]	0.4	nd	nd
10/07/2004	FX	2,415	115	8	2,415	115
10/11/2004	FX	1,222	70	4	7,274	370
10/13/2004	FX	186	120	6	8,682	560
10/14/2004	FX	710	148	0.1 [1]	9,130	694
10/20/2004	FX	652	121	8	13,216	1,501
10/27/2004	Heli	1,060	240	8	19,208	2,764
11/04/2004	FX	332	63	0.1 [1]	24,776	3,976
11/10/2004	Heli	nd	107	6	nd	4,486
11/12/2004	Heli	981	138	nd	30,028	4,732
11/20/2004	Heli	1,053	177	6	38,164	5,993
12/17/2004	Heli	914	221	5	64,718	11,370
01/03/2005	Heli	887	76	0.1 [1]	80,027	13,393
01/24/2005	Heli	nd	78	11	nd	15,509
02/08/2005	Heli	718	70	0.3	108,917	16,619
02/25/2005	Heli	211	32	0.6	116,814	17,485
03/10/2005	Heli	149	30	0.3	119,154	17,888
04/21/2005	Heli	nd	40	0	nd	19,347
04/26/2005	Heli	146	94	0	126,086	19,681
05/25/2005	Heli	325	33	0	132,916	21,522
06/09/2005	Heli	nd	50	nd	nd	22,145
07/13/2005	Heli	485	40	nd	152,760	23,675
07/27/2005	Heli	594.3	51	0.1 [1]	160,316	24,312
08/12/2005	Heli	174	14	0.1 [1]	166,462	24,832
08/31/2005	Heli	198	22	0.1 [1]	169,996	25,174
09/28/2005	Heli	789	45	0.1 [1]	183,814	26,112
10/18/2005	Heli	658	53	0.3	198,284	27,092
11/09/2005	Heli	1,353	88	0.1 [1]	220,405	28,643
11/22/2005	Heli	300	75	0.1 [1]	231,150	29,702

[1]Estimated detection limits for CO_2, SO_2, and H_2S emission rates.

ference exists between the medians of measured and weighted CO_2 and SO_2 emission rates and the populations they sample (P >0.05).

The 24 contemporaneous CO_2 and SO_2 emission rates measured from October 7, 2004, to November 22, 2005, have a median molar CO_2/SO_2 ratio of ~12; about half of the CO_2/SO_2 ratios are between 7 and 18. The corresponding weighted emission rates have a median CO_2/SO_2 of ~10 and about half the CO_2/SO_2 ratios are between 9 and 11. Statistical tests confirm there is no significant difference between CO_2/SO_2 ratios calculated from measured and weighted emission rates (P >0.05). Total emissions for the entire period—231,150 t CO_2 and 29,700 t SO_2—indicate a CO_2/SO_2 of ~11. Thus, we employ a grand median CO_2/SO_2 ratio of 11±1 in this report.

Early Degassing

From the start of airborne gas measurements on September 27, 2004, throughout the period of unrest before the eruption began on October 1 and for almost a week thereafter, a volcanic plume was either absent or present as small fragmentary and ephemeral parcels of gas, yielding only rough gas-emission rates (table 2). Flights during this period served mainly as reconnaissance surveys for gas-emitting sources on the 1980–86 dome, the crater floor, and the crater walls (fig. 3) and led to the discovery and observation of point sources of gas emission that, over time, established a record of emergent degassing. The record began with SO_2 and H_2S concentrations at detection limits at all locations and CO_2 concentrations at ambient atmospheric levels at most locations (fig. 9), although sporadic CO_2 sources occurred with minor peaks <1.5 ppm above ambient levels. Similar results persisted through September 30. After the first steam-and-ash explosion at the start of the eruption on October 1, new CO_2 concentration peaks above ambient levels appeared—one new source on the northwest face of the 1980s dome produced an above-background peak of 36 ppm—but SO_2 and H_2S still remained largely at noise levels. There was some evidence, however, of the presence of H_2S—one minor peak was observed, and some observers in the air and on the ground downwind of the volcano reported the odor of H_2S.

The number of fumarole sources increased significantly by October 2, as did the number of above-ambient CO_2 concentration peaks—one reaching up to 16 ppm—while SO_2 and H_2S continued to be mostly absent, although field crews again reported H_2S odors (fig. 10). A further increase in the number of fumaroles and a broadening of CO_2 anomalies along with coincident low H_2S peaks (<0.02 ppm) appeared in the record on October 3. By October 4, CO_2 anomalies were as broad as a kilometer or more across, and SO_2 and H_2S formed coinci-

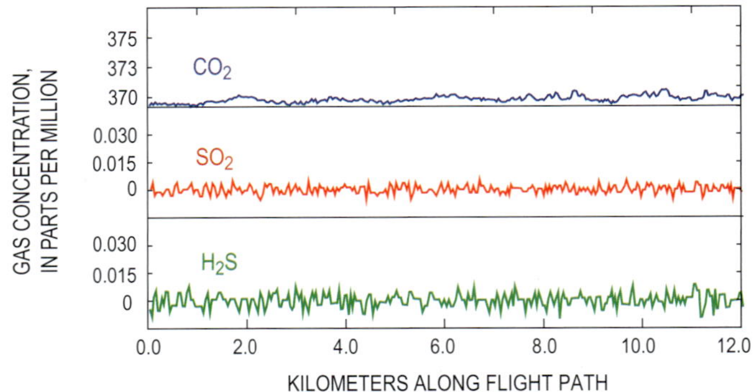

Figure 9. Concentrations of CO_2, SO_2, and H_2S measured along a helicopter flight path in Mount St. Helens crater on September 27, 2004. Concentrations of CO_2 are similar to ambient atmospheric levels; concentrations of SO_2 and H_2S are at sensor detection limits.

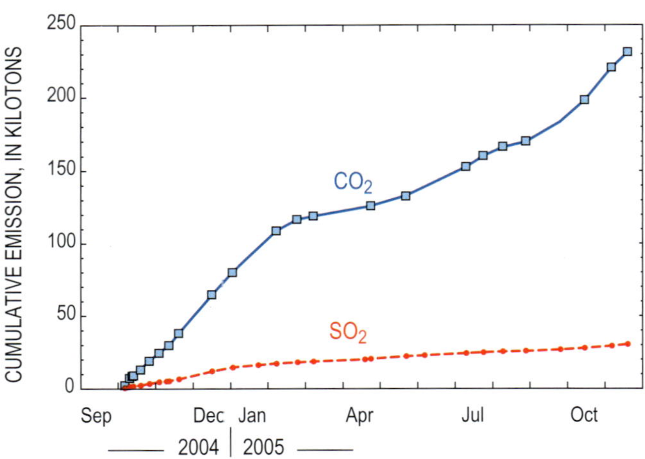

Figure 8. Time-series plots of cumulative CO_2 and SO_2 emissions from October 7, 2004, to November 22, 2005, when emission rates for both gases were above detection limits (fig. 7; table 2).

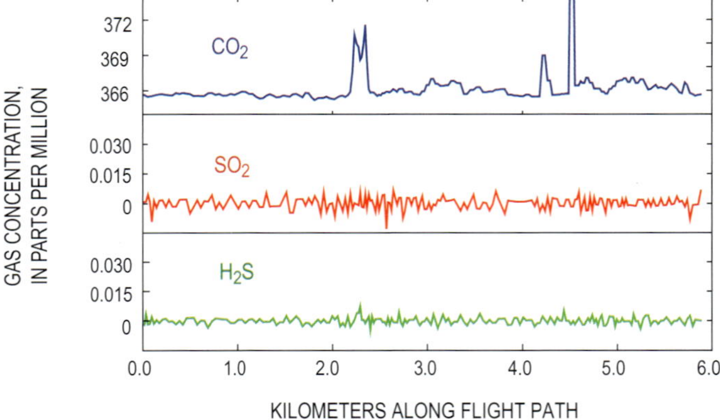

Figure 10. Concentrations of CO_2, SO_2, and H_2S measured along a helicopter flight path in Mount St. Helens crater on October 2, 2004. Concentrations of CO_2 show sporadic spikes above ambient atmospheric levels; concentrations of SO_2 and H_2S remain at sensor detection limits. The clipped CO_2 peak rises to 382 ppm.

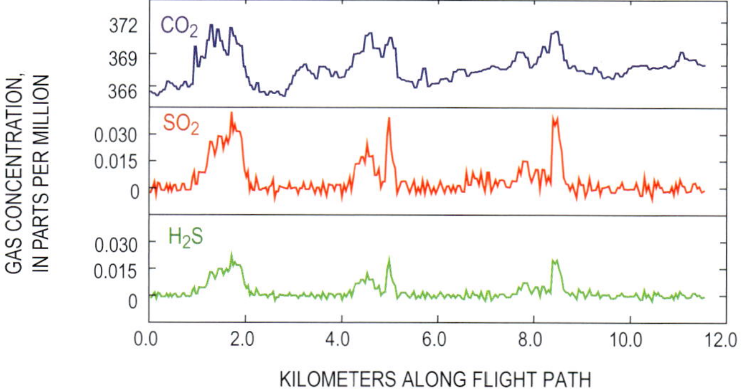

Figure 11. Concentrations of CO_2, SO_2, and H_2S measured along a helicopter flight path in Mount St. Helens crater on October 4, 2004. Concentrations of CO_2 show broad anomalies above ambient atmospheric levels; concentrations of SO_2 and H_2S show sharply coincident anomalies spiking above sensor detection limits. Note that SO_2 and H_2S anomalies have concentration levels of roughly similar magnitude.

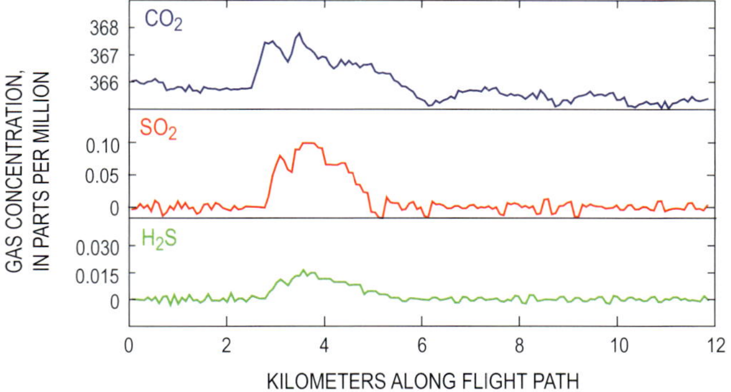

Figure 12. Concentrations of CO_2, SO_2, and H_2S measured along a helicopter flight path in Mount St. Helens crater on October 11, 2004. Concentrations of CO_2 show a broad anomaly above ambient atmospheric levels; concentrations of SO_2 and H_2S show coincident anomalies. Note that concentration levels of the SO_2 anomaly now are clearly greater than those of H_2S.

dent anomalies of roughly equivalent concentration levels (fig. 11). Wet degassing prevailed at this time as large gas bubbles were seen streaming through and ejecting from pools of water, which often contained chunks of floating ice that calved in from the adjacent melting glacier. By October 11, SO_2 clearly dominated H_2S as temperatures rose, pools of water dried up, and steaming increased greatly (fig. 12). Coherent plumes began to form regularly on or about October 7 and spilled over the crater rim (fig. 4), permitting acquisition of reliable emission rates by remote SO_2 column-abundance measurements and direct measurements of CO_2, SO_2, and H_2S gas concentrations (fig. 13).

Composite Degassing Sources

Mount St. Helens continued to produce buoyant plumes throughout the remainder of 2004 and all of 2005. In addition to the principal degassing site from the vent area on the north side of the new dome, several additional sites degassing both CO_2 and SO_2 were present at various locations on both old and new lobes of the growing new dome. By summer 2005, gas emissions were declining, and airborne gas measurements began to be conducted closer to the gas sources. These measurements provided more spatial resolution of gas concentrations within the proximal plume and revealed a minor source of the CO_2 within the plume coming from the 1980s dome. Since 2005, we have consistently detected CO_2 coming from the southwest side of the 1980s dome, just north of the vent area for the new dome. In addition, the older dome hosts a smaller CO_2 source on its east shoulder and several scattered point sources of CO_2. The spatial separation of new-dome and old-dome gas sources is best developed when winds are from the east or west. The degassing from the 1980s dome involves little or no SO_2. Nearly all of the SO_2 in the plume, and the majority of CO_2, originates from the hotter vents associated with the new dome. Under appropriate wind conditions, airborne traverses through the plume show CO_2 clearly degassing from both domes, whereas SO_2 is virtually absent from the

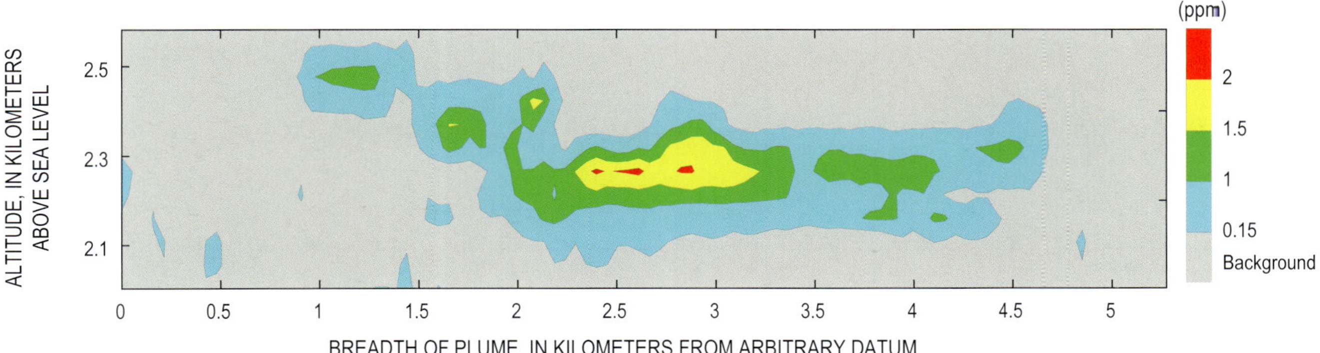

Figure 13. Concentrations of CO_2 in a vertical cross section of a coherent gas plume from Mount St. Helens on November 12, 2004, 1.7 km downwind of source. Bar on right shows scale for concentration of CO_2 above local atmospheric background. Plume cross section gives a CO_2 emission rate of 980 t/d.

1980s dome (fig. 14). Figure 14 shows CO_2 concentrations on a single plume traverse; most plume traverses show CO_2 concentrations are much higher over the new dome.

CO_2 Plume from Loowit Springs

During some of the airborne gas-measurement flights, a small CO_2 plume was observed that did not emanate from the new or the old dome. The source of this plume proved to be the Loowit springs area (Thompson, 1990), north of the 1980s dome and near the mouth of the crater, as determined by a series of low helicopter traverses on June 9, 2005, when winds from the north or northwest were favorable for distinguishing it. Orbital profiling around the upper part of the Loowit drainage defined the extent of the plume and quantified the CO_2 emission rate at 27 t/d (fig. 15), although the exact spring or springs involved could not be distinguished; neither SO_2 nor H_2S were detected. The spring discharge of magmatic CO_2 as inorganic carbon (aqueous CO_2 and HCO_3^- in about equal amounts) dissolved in Loowit waters and other thermal features draining the crater is ~22 t/d, which is similar to the emission rate of CO_2 gas around Loowit (Bergfeld and others, this volume, chap. 25). It is not known if the Loowit springs plume is a result of the current eruption or a longer-term feature.

Discussion

The key fact about the CO_2 and SO_2 emission rates is that they are generally low. This fact was evident early on and motivated our hypothesis that the CO_2 and SO_2 emissions of the 2004–5 eruption were derived from source dacite depleted in excess (that is, exsolved) volatiles at depth (Gerlach and others, 2005), herein termed "flat" magma. The corollary hypothesis—that gas emissions from flat dacite are expressly vulnerable to scrubbing, particularly during the unrest and early stages of the eruption—follows from the depletion in excess volatiles. The flat magma and gas scrubbing hypotheses underlie much of the discussion that follows.

Comparisons with 1980s Emission Rates

Comparisons of the 1980s and 2004–5 passive emission rates of SO_2 and CO_2 support the interpretation that the current eruption involves flat magma, possibly left over in the reservoir since the last lava-dome eruption in 1986. The 2004–5 SO_2 emission rates (fig. 7; table 2) are not significantly different from 1980s SO_2 emission rates during the period from October 18, 1980, to December 9, 1986 (fig. 16), according to the MWRST ($P \geq 0.05$). This time interval matches closely

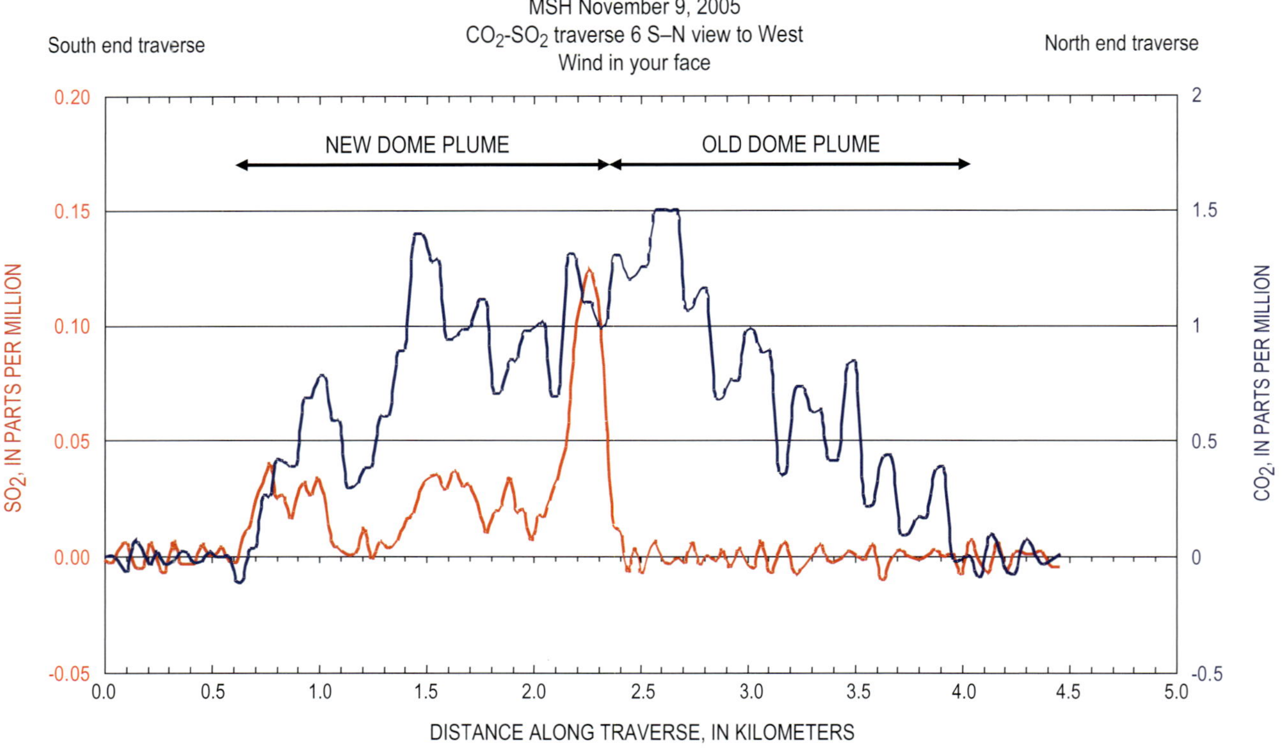

Figure 14. Airborne traverse of plume on November 9, 2005, showing above-background CO_2 concentration (blue) and SO_2 concentration (red). Wind direction from nearly due west allows comparison of plume data from the new dome complex with the older 1980–1986 dome. Traverse flown approximately 2.3 km downwind of central source area. The older dome is discharging CO_2 but little or no SO_2.

the period of 17 lava-dome eruptions and stable dome growth that produced the 1980s dome. October 18, 1980, is the date of the first SO_2 emission-rate measurement after the start of a lava-dome eruption on October 16, 1980—the first lava-dome eruption of the 1980s to produce a dome that survived. The last lava-dome eruption of the 1980s was on October 21, 1986, and the last significant SO_2 emission rate at the end of this eruption was 80 t/d on December 9, 1986. Of the 113 SO_2 emission-rate measurements made after this date, until measurements ceased on September 6, 1988, 95 percent were <25 t/d and 70 percent were <3 t/d—barely above detection limits. We did not include these data in the MWRST analysis in order to avoid confounding the emission rates associated with the 1980s lava-dome eruptions with emission rates of the protracted period of residual degassing at the end of the 1980s eruption cycle. The1980s dataset for the calculations started with the data from December 9, 1986, and was extended back in time by incrementally adding earlier SO_2 emission rates. Along this time line, the probability level decreased steadily from $P > 0.05$ and converged on the critical significance level ($P = 0.05$) when the October 18, 1980, data were added to the dataset. When still earlier 1980 data were included, P dropped abruptly below 0.05, indicating that the difference between the two groups of data became robustly significant. Thus, between October 18, 1980, and December 9, 1986, the two groups of data sample a similar population, and the differences between them—for example, median SO_2 emission rates of 72 t/d versus 100 t/d—can be explained by random sampling variations. However, we stress that the MWRST analysis operates only on the rates of the two groups of data without regard for the associated dates. This is important because if the dates are considered, it is evident that although the 10/18/1980–12/9/1986 SO_2 emission rates may share a common population with 2004–5 SO_2 emission rates, they are not randomly distributed in time, as indicated by the conspicuous skewing of their higher rates to earlier dates (fig. 16).

Plotting the SO_2 emission rates of the 1980s and 2004–5 together as time series on the same scale reveals that the emission rates of the 2004–5 eruption appear similar to those of the 1980s lava-dome eruptions back to at least late 1981 (fig. 16). MWRST comparisons back to late 1981 produce large P values indicating virtually no likelihood of a significant difference in the SO_2 emission rates of the 1980s and 2004–5 lava-dome eruptions; for example, comparisons back to October 1, 1981, give a P value of 0.7. Such differences as exist in the patterns of the two time-series plots are readily explained. The generally lower peak values of the 2004–5 eruption probably are related to the more-crystalline magma and steadier character of the present eruption; these properties act to curb extrusive surges that frequently caused SO_2 emission-rate peaks during the 1980s lava-dome eruptions. The 2004–5 emission rates appear blockier and less spiky on the graph, partly because of the steadier nature of the present eruption, but also because the steadier activity itself (along with tighter funding) led to less frequent monitoring flights—four to five times less frequent than in the 1980s. The fact that the current eruption has lasted considerably longer than the 1980s lava-dome eruptions also contributes to the blockier pattern of its SO_2 emission rates. The annualized 2004–5 SO_2 outputs also bear a noteworthy similarity to annual SO_2 outputs that occurred during the later years of the 1980s lava-dome eruptions. The 14-month, 30,000-t SO_2 output of the 2004–5 eruption (table 2) indicates an annualized output of 26,000 t, which is equivalent to the total Mount St. Helens SO_2 output for 1984 (Gerlach and McGee, 1994)—a year in which there were three lava-dome eruptions over a 6-month period. The 11-month output for 2005 of 18,000 t (computed from table 2 data) annualizes to an output of 19,600 t—comparable with the 1986 SO_2 output of 17,000 t (Gerlach and McGee, 1994). Thus, the MWRST analyses, the time-series patterns of SO_2 emission rates, and the annualized SO_2 outputs strongly suggest that the 2004–5 SO_2 emissions are similar to those of the 1980s lava-dome eruptions, possibly back as far as late 1981 or late 1980.

The CO_2 emission-rate measurements of the 1980s are restricted to the period between July 1980 and August 1981 (fig. 17; McGee and Casadevall, 1994); the measurements were terminated after August 1981 because the detection limit of the older measurement technique was reached. Applications of the MWRST to these data and the 2004–5 CO_2 emission-rate data (fig. 7, table 2), following the procedure described

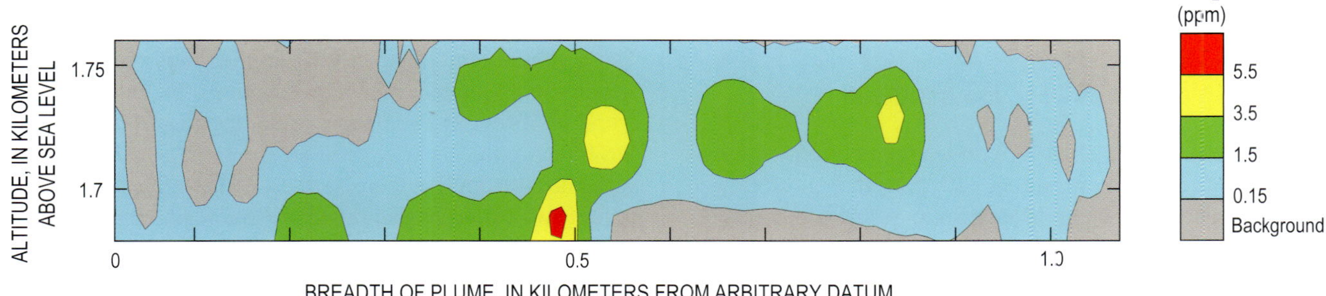

Figure 15. Vertical cross section of CO_2 gas plume 250 m downwind of Loowit springs area on June 9, 2005. The CO_2 emission rate computed from these data was 27 t/d. Scale bar on right shows CO_2 concentration above local atmospheric background.

above for comparing SO_2 emission rates, indicates that the 2004–5 data are significantly different from the July 1980–May 1981 data ($P \leq 0.05$). However, the 2004–5 data and the June–August 1981 data are not different and appear to be sampling the same population ($P > 0.05$). The similarity probably would have persisted beyond August 1981 had measurements been made by a more sensitive technique. Plotting the CO_2 emission rates of 1980–81 and 2004–5 together as time series on the same scale reinforces the MWRST analysis by revealing a pattern in which the latter CO_2 emission rates appear as an extension of the lower CO_2 emission rates of June–August 1981 (fig. 17). As in the case of the SO_2 emission rates, differences in magma physical properties and frequency of measurement account for the blockier, less spiky, and generally lower peak values of the 2004–5 CO_2 emission rates.

Thus, the time-series comparisons and MWRST results for CO_2 and SO_2 emission rates support a flat 2004–5 magma depleted in excess volatiles and producing generally low CO_2 and SO_2 emissions like those of the 1980s lava-dome eruptions. The flat magma is distinctly different from the gas-rich magma that produced the much higher CO_2 and SO_2 emissions earlier in 1980 (figs. 16, 17; Gerlach and McGee, 1994). The similarity to the gas emissions of the 1980s lava-dome eruptions suggests that the flat magma of the current eruption could involve leftover reservoir magma from 1986.

Comparison with 1980s CO_2/SO_2 Ratios

Contemporaneous measurements of CO_2 and SO_2 emission rates in the 1980s allow calculation of CO_2/SO_2 ratios on 117 days during a 418-day period from July 6, 1980, to August 28, 1981. The median CO_2/SO_2 ratio is 8, but there is considerable variation—25 percent of the ratios are ≤5 and 25 percent are ≥11. As noted earlier, measured and weighted CO_2 and SO_2 emission rates and total emissions of the current eruption imply a somewhat higher grand median CO_2/SO_2 ratio of 11±1. The MWRST indicates that the 117 1980–1981 CO_2/SO_2 ratios and the 24 2004–5 CO_2/SO_2 ratios—whether calculated from measured or weighted emission rates—are associated with significantly different populations ($P < 0.05$). Taking these results at face value would imply a real difference in CO_2/SO_2 ratios of the older and current gases, but we show below that the higher CO_2/SO_2 ratios of the current gases are caused by scrubbing.

Scrubbing in the 2004–2005 Eruption

Doukas and Gerlach (1995) drew attention to the unusually weak SO_2 emission rates that both preceded and followed eruptions at Crater Peak on Mount Spurr volcano, Alaska, in 1992 and noted the exceptionally strong and persistent H_2S odor in the Crater Peak plume during repose periods. They argued that liquid water present at or beneath the surface interacted with ascending magmatic gases, scrubbing SO_2 and other strongly acidic gases (HCl, HF) but impacting the weakly and moderately acidic gases (CO_2 and H_2S) less severely. The principal mechanisms for SO_2 scrubbing by liquid water are the hydrolysis reactions:

$$4SO_{2(g)} + 4H_2O_{(l)} = H_2S_{(g)} + 6H^+_{(aq)} + 3SO_4^{-2}{}_{(aq)}, \text{ and}$$

$$3SO_{2(g)} + 2H_2O_{(l)} = S_{(l,s)} + 4H^+_{(aq)} + 2SO_4^{-2}{}_{(aq)}.$$

These equilibria shift strongly to the right below 400°C, mainly converting SO_2 into dissolved sulfate as sulfuric acid. Some H_2S gas and native sulfur also are generated, which explained the intense H_2S odor at Crater Peak. Detailed thermochemical modeling (Symonds and others, 2001) confirms the significant scrubbing of magmatic SO_2, HCl, and HF by contact with surface, ground, and hydrothermal waters of volcanoes and indicates that scrubbing of CO_2 and H_2S also becomes significant at low gas-to-water ratios (<0.01, mass basis).

Carbon isotopes of dissolved inorganic carbon in hydrothermal, ground, spring, and stream waters reveal the scrubbing of magmatic CO_2 in the vicinity of several Cascade Range volcanoes: Lassen Peak, Mount Shasta, Crater Lake, Mount Bachelor, Broken Top, Three Sisters, Belknap Crater, and Mount Jefferson (Rose and Davisson, 1996; James and others, 1999; Evans and others, 2004). Scrubbing of potentially coexisting, more acidic magmatic gases (SO_2, H_2S, HCl, and HF) also probably occurs. Copious ground-water recharge in the High Cascades and subsequent downward and lateral flow (Ingebritsen and others, 1989, 1992, 1994) is probably chiefly responsible for the scrubbing and provides a basis for a conceptual model of scrubbing throughout much of the Cascade Range. Scrubbing processes may, therefore, be responsible for the currently absent to negligible emission rates of CO_2, SO_2, and H_2S at several Cascade Range volcanoes we have investigated with airborne measurements since the late 1990s (table 1). Although some of these volcanoes (for example, Mount Adams and Mount Jefferson) may simply be dormant, it is likely that much of the CO_2, SO_2, H_2S, HCl, and HF degassed from magmas at most of these volcanoes is captured by hydrothermal systems or ground water and is thus unavailable to form gas emissions at volcanic centers. Boiling of hydrothermal fluid containing captured magmatic gases may give rise to persistent degassing of CO_2 and H_2S (but not SO_2 because of hydrolysis to dissolved sulfate) at some volcanoes—Mount Baker and Lassen Peak being likely examples (table 1).

Symonds and others (2001) applied their thermochemical scrubbing models to several eruptions, including the 1980 eruption of Mount St. Helens, which they say illustrates SO_2 scrubbing in the early stage of an eruption. Low SO_2 emission rates—from less than 10 t/d to 48 t/d—during the period of phreatic eruptions and nonexplosive degassing that began on March 27, 1980, continued for 52 days up to the May 18 climactic explosion. Observations supporting early scrubbing of SO_2 include reports by COSPEC investigators of persistent H_2S odor in the crater at times when SO_2 emissions rarely exceeded 10 t/d (Stoiber and others, 1980). Emission rates of

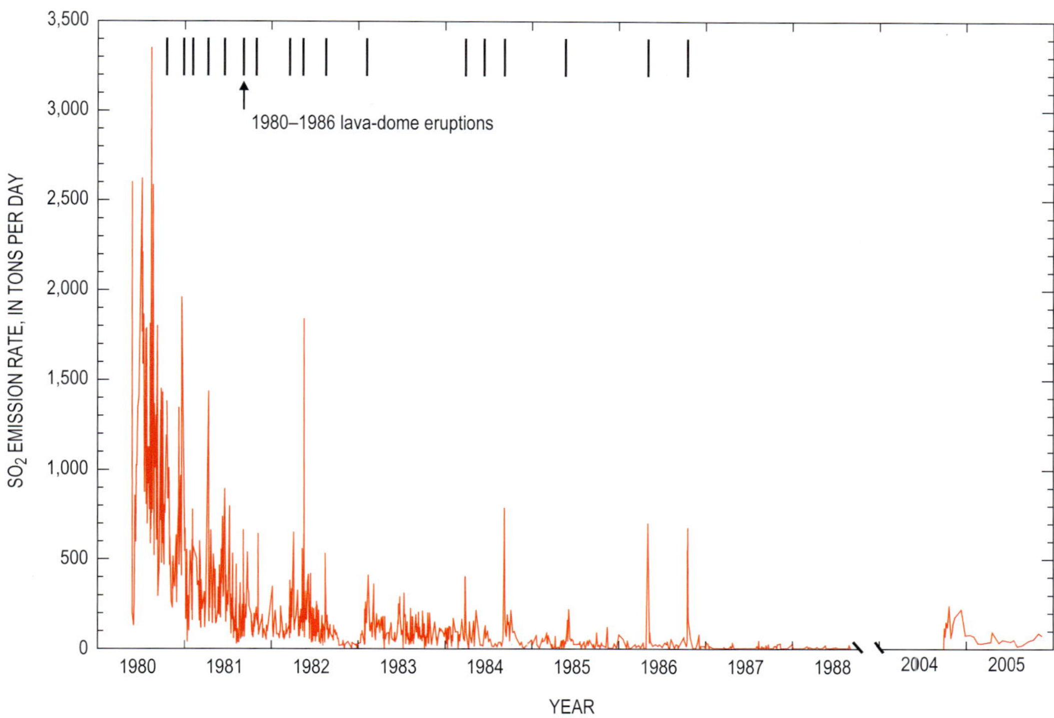

Figure 16. Time-series plots of all SO_2 emission rates measured during the 1980s (McGee and Casadevall, 1994) and during the 2004–2005 eruption. Scale break after last 1980s measurements in 1988 separates the two time series. Vertical lines indicate the starting dates of the 1980–1986 lava-dome eruptions. All 1980s and 2004–2005 time-series data are passive emission rates, except for the first 1980 data point—2,600 t/d measured in the May 25, 1980, explosive eruption. The May 18, 1980, explosive emission rate of 4,000,000 t/d is not included (Gerlach and McGee, 1994; Symonds and others, 2001).

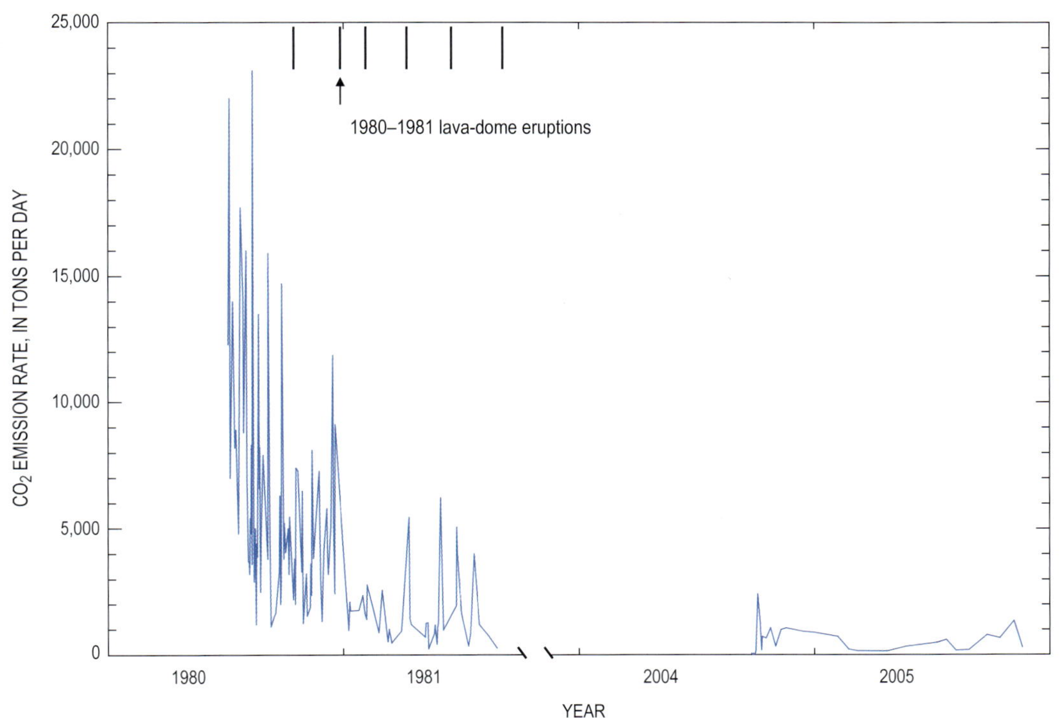

Figure 17. Time-series plots of all CO_2 emission rates measured during the 1980s (McGee and Casadevall, 1994) and during the 2004–2005 eruption. Scale break after the last measurements in 1981 separates the two time series. Vertical lines indicate starting dates of the 1980–1981 lava-dome eruptions. All 1980s and 2004–2005 time-series data are passive emission rates. The 1980 data begin with the 12,300 t/d CO_2 emission rate measured on July 6.

passively degassed SO_2 increased after the May 18 eruption and after the second explosion on May 25 but still remained relatively low (130–260 t/d). Twenty days later, on June 6, SO_2 emission rates jumped to 860 t/d and remained high (>600 t/d) until the end of October 1980 (fig. 16), finally attaining levels comparable to those of other erupting arc volcanoes and signaling the end of significant scrubbing. Note that the July 6, 1980, to August 28, 1981, CO_2/SO_2 ratios discussed above represent postscrubbing values.

Symonds and others (2001) also inferred that SO_2 scrubbing was active again during the period of seismic unrest at Mount St. Helens in the summer of 1998 when, as described above, an airborne survey on June 22 measured a CO_2 emission rate of 1,900 t/d (table 1), while concurrent COSPEC measurements failed to detect SO_2. These results are consistent with the degassing and scrubbing of SO_2 from an intrusion at a time when melting of snow from a permanent snowfield growing in the crater since 1986 (Anderson and others, 1998) helped create a wet edifice. Thus, an unknown amount of degassed CO_2 may also have been scrubbed at this time.

Scrubbing played a major role in the period of unrest and the early stages of the current eruption. We interpret the measurements during the September 27–30, 2004, period of insignificant gas emission with little or no detectable SO_2 or H_2S and with CO_2 largely at atmospheric levels (fig. 9) to be the result of fairly complete gas scrubbing at low gas-to-water mass ratios <0.01 (Symonds and others, 2001). Sealing of rock permeability in the old dome and the upper part of the 1980s conduit may also have played a role (Moran, 1994). It is likely, however, that scrubbing would soon have dominated sealing as a deterrent to gas emission. The concurrent shallow seismicity and deformation would tend to reestablish permeability. High seismicity was well established by September 26 and increased significantly on September 28 at shallow levels in and below the old lava dome (Moran and others, this volume, chap. 2). Radial fractures were visible in Crater Glacier adjacent to the old dome by September 26, and an area of deformation south of the dome was clearly evident on oblique photos on September 30 (Schilling and others, this volume, chap. 8). Furthermore, the 2004 unrest and eruption followed a period with an unusually large potential for groundwater recharge by surface water. No August–September interval since the cessation of dome-building eruptions in 1986 has had heavier rainfall than in 2004 (http://www.wcc.nrcs.usda.gov/snotel, last accessed March 15, 2008). The growth of Crater Glacier since 1986 provided increased storage of water available for release and ground-water recharge into late summer. Moreover, the earlier detection of sharp CO_2 concentration spikes on October 1 and 2, while SO_2 and H_2S remained at detection limits (fig. 10), strongly suggests scrubbing, rather than sealing, as the main cause restricting earlier gas emissions, since water does not scrub CO_2 as effectively as it scrubs SO_2 and H_2S. The subsequent appearance of wet degassing with large gas bubbles ejecting through pools of water obviously involved scrubbing. However, the subequal concentrations of SO_2 and H_2S at this time (fig. 11) reflected incomplete scrubbing of SO_2, which is likely because rapid transport in large bubbles restricted its interaction with water, thus allowing some of it to escape the pools. Wet degassing increasingly gave way to dry degassing, and SO_2 became the major sulfur gas (fig. 12). As temperatures rose and steaming increased, rock adjacent to the invading magma progressively dried out in the days before the initial emergence of a lava spine from the deforming area south of the 1980s dome on October 11. This date probably marks the end of significant scrubbing in the early stages of the eruption.

The composite degassing sources from the 1980s and 2004–5 domes bear the mark of gas scrubbing (fig. 14). Nearly all of the SO_2 in the plume comes from the hotter new dome. Degassing from the colder old dome involves minor CO_2 but little or no SO_2. We speculate that the source of gas at depth is the same for both domes but that the gas feeding the vents on the old dome is scrubbed of its SO_2 since water is more likely to be present within and beneath this colder dome. Edmonds and others (this volume, chap. 27) measured several gases, including SO_2 and HCl, in hot vent emissions on the new dome by remote Fourier-transform infrared spectroscopy from high on the east rim of Mount St. Helens. If our hypothesis is correct, both SO_2 and HCl—being strong acids—should be scrubbed in emissions from the old dome. Unfortunately, confirmation of concurrent scrubbing of both SO_2 and HCl at the old dome by similar measurements was not possible, owing to the absence of hot infrared sources.

The 24 CO_2/SO_2 ratios calculated from cumulative CO_2 and SO_2 emissions (fig. 8; table 2) show a striking pattern when plotted as a time series (fig. 18). The ratios decrease regularly and precipitously from October 7 until October 27, 2004, when they make a abrupt transition to nearly constant CO_2/SO_2 values of 9±1, close to the median value of 8 noted above for the 1980–81 CO_2/SO_2. They remain in this range (9±1) until September 28, 2005, after which subsequent 2005 values drift to CO_2/SO_2 values as high as 11.3.

We interpret the sharp decline in CO_2/SO_2 (fig. 18) to reflect the drying out of the shallow conduit and crater-floor rock adjacent to the invading dacite and the reduction of SO_2 scrubbing that dominated the early part of the 2004–5 eruption. However, cumulative emissions, although smoothing out short-term variations, can lag in their response to significant changes. In this case, measurements suggest early SO_2 scrubbing largely ceased on or about October 11, 2004, as discussed above, approximately two weeks before the October 27 date suggested by the cumulative emission data (fig. 18). After October 27, the CO_2/SO_2 ratio of cumulative emissions stabilized within the range of 9±1 for many months, grazing the median 1980–81 CO_2/SO_2 value of 8 (fig. 18). We interpret this range of values to represent the CO_2/SO_2 of nonscrubbed gas emissions of the current eruption, although it may be slightly high because of SO_2 scrubbing of gases from the old dome. The CO_2/SO_2 of the cumulative emissions rises above this range again after September 28, 2005 (fig. 18), presumably in response to renewed scrubbing. Because of the lag effect, the return to scrubbing may have started somewhat earlier. We have no data suggesting a specific cause of this return to scrubbing, but plausible factors may include the cracking and development of fracture permeability within the cooling and thickening carapace of the new dome and (or) seasonal changes affecting rainfall and groundwater recharge in the crater.

The CO_2/SO_2 time-series pattern in figure 18 illustrates the role of scrubbing in the early part of the current eruption and the close similarity of CO_2/SO_2 values in the nonscrubbed gas emissions of the 2004–5 eruption to those in the early 1980s. We contend, moreover, that scrubbing is the cause of the significant difference in CO_2/SO_2 indicated between the 1980–81 and 2004–5 gases by the MWRST analysis. The striking pattern of CO_2/SO_2 ratios (fig. 18) with their approach to the median 1980–81 CO_2/SO_2 ratio, hardly seems the result of chance, and it is consistent with flat magma remaining from 1986 that, although depleted in excess volatiles, still retains a similar CO_2/SO_2 ratio. However, the depletion of excess volatiles causes the emissions from the flat magma upon ascent and eruption to be generally weak and susceptible to scrubbing if water is present.

Fluid Content of the 2004–2005 Dacite at Depth

Recent studies indicate that the dacite erupted explosively at Mount St. Helens on May 18, 1980, had a fluid content (that is, excess volatiles) prior to ascent and eruption of ≥15 volume percent (vol. percent), which corresponds to ≥3 weight percent (wt. percent) (Wallace, 2001, 2003; P.J. Wallace, written commun., 2005). The May 18, 1980, dacite was decidedly not flat magma. We have tested the flat-magma hypothesis for the 2004–5 dacite by using the current CO_2 emission data to quantify the fluid content of the 2004–5 dacite at depth. If the flat-magma hypothesis is valid for the current dacite, its fluid content at depth should be significantly lower than that determined for the May 18, 1980, dacite.

Fluid Content of the 2004–2005 Dacite and the May 18, 1980, Dacite at 900°C and 220 MPa (8.6 km Depth)

The May 18, 1980, dacite last equilibrated prior to eruption at a temperature of 900°C and a pressure of 220 MPa (Rutherford, 1993), corresponding to 8.6 km depth (from crustal density model B-B' of Williams and others, 1987, used in this study to convert lithostatic pressures to depths beneath the crater). The rhyolitic melt of the May 18 dacite was relatively H_2O rich prior to eruption. Microprobe studies of melt inclusions give water-by-difference concentrations of 4.6±1 wt. percent (Rutherford, 1993), and recent ion-microprobe studies of melt inclusions in the May 18 white pumice show a clustering of H_2O concentrations around 5 wt. percent (Blundy and Cashman, 2005).

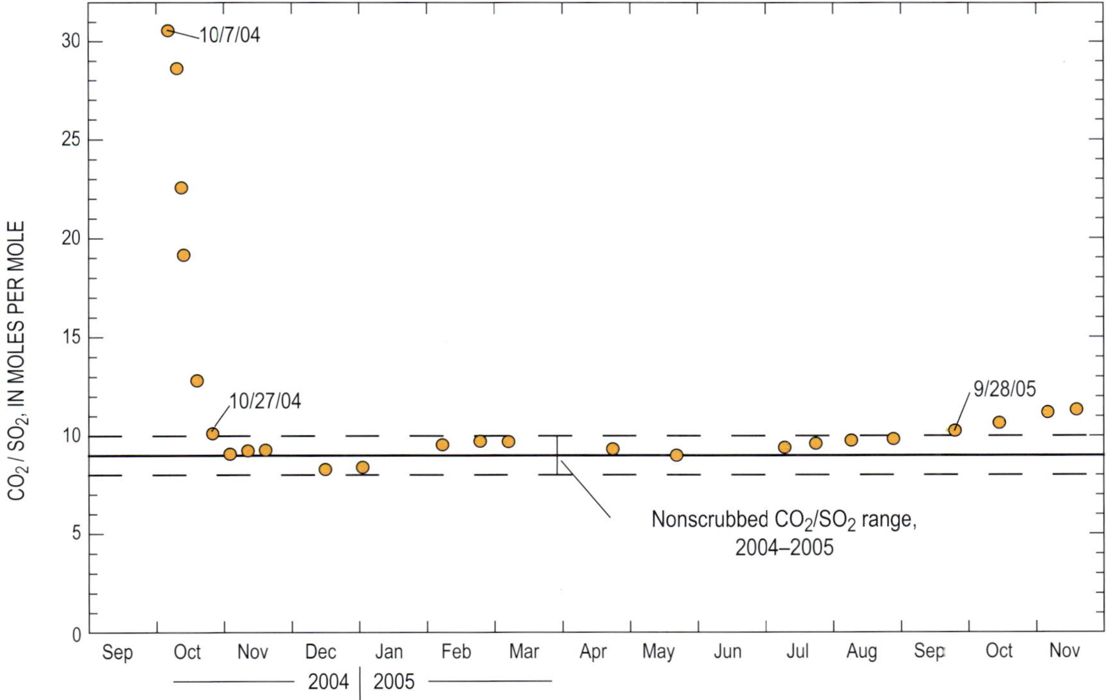

Figure 18. Time-series plot of molar CO_2/SO_2 ratios (dots) calculated from cumulative 2004–2005 emissions (fig. 8; table 2). Solid and dashed lines indicate nonscrubbed CO_2/SO_2 median and range of 9±1 for the 2004–5 gases. Lower dashed line also represents the median value (8) of the 1980–81 CO_2/SO_2 ratios as discussed in the text.

To maintain comparability with the May 18 dacite, we have used the constraints 900°C, 220 MPa, and a rhyolitic melt H_2O concentration of 5 wt. percent to estimate the fluid content of the 2004–5 dacite at 8.6 km depth. Several observations and experimental results support the use of these constraints. The current dacite contains phenocrysts of plagioclase, hypersthene, amphibole, and oxides—the same as the 1980–86 dacite, except for an absence of minor clinopyroxene (Pallister and others, this volume, chap. 30; Rutherford and Devine, this volume, chap. 31). The current dacite also is similar in bulk composition to the 1980–86 dacite, being only slightly more evolved (65 vs. 63 wt. percent SiO_2) and distinct in U-series isotopic ratios of plagioclases (Cooper and Donnelly, this volume, chap. 36) and in bulk-composition ratios of Ti and Cr to SiO_2 (Pallister and others, this volume, chap. 30)—differences that are most readily explained by addition of a minor fraction of new magma to the reservoir between 1986 and 2004 (Pallister and others, this volume, chap. 30). Melt inclusions provide no data on the H_2O concentration of preeruption melt in the current dacite (Pallister and others, this volume, chap. 30; Rutherford and Devine, this volume, chap. 31; Blundy and others, this volume, chap. 33). However, on the basis of phase equilibria experiments, Rutherford and Devine (this volume, chap. 31) propose that the new magma entered the storage reservoir as dacite with a melt concentration >4 wt. percent—implied by the amphiboles—and at a temperature of ~900°C—suggested by high-TiO_2 magnetite phenocrysts and the maximum anorthite content of cyclically zoned feldspar phenocrysts. These conditions are similar to those determined for the 1980 magma. To explain the cyclic zoning of the magma's phenocrysts, Rutherford and Devine invoke convective circulation of injected dacite, which would have involved exposure to pressures of 220 MPa at various times before rising to the shallower part of the reservoir, where they infer it last equilibrated at about 850°C and 120–140 MPa prior to final ascent and eruption.

We used VolatileCalc (Newman and H_2O Lowenstern, 2002) to model CO_2 solubility in hydrous rhyolitic melt at 900°C and 220 MPa to estimate the fluid content of the 2004–5 dacite for comparison with the May 18 dacite at 8.6 km depth. At these conditions, rhyolitic melt with 5 wt. percent H_2O would contain associated dissolved CO_2 at a concentration of ~350 ppm (fig. 19*A*). The mole fraction composition of the coexisting fluid would be ~0.76 for X_{H_2O} and ~0.24 for X_{CO_2} (fig. 19*B*), which is consistent with hydrothermal phase equilibria experiments on the current dacite that indicate X_{H_2O} would be ≥0.7 in the presence of a CO_2-bearing coexisting fluid (Rutherford and Devine, this volume, chap. 31). The fluid also would contain a small amount of sulfur, but since CO_2/SO_2 is ~9 in the nonscrubbed gas emissions—and CO_2/S would likely have been higher in the fluid at elevated pressure—we ignore sulfur in the present analysis.

We calculated the fluid content of the dacite at 8.6 km and the conditions delineated above for 14 dates in 2004–5 corresponding to the dates of digital elevation models (DEMs; Schilling and others, this volume, chap. 8). Table 3 lists values keyed to DEM dates for several parameters (defined in table 3 headnotes) used in the calculations. The last 2005 DEM date (12/15/2005) could not be used because weather conditions prevented measurement of CO_2 emission rates during December 2005, as noted above.

Table 3 contains values for two melt mass parameters: one for dacite like the 2004–5 dacite that contained 53.5 vol. percent melt prior to eruption (Pallister and others, this volume, chap. 30), which we discuss later, and the other for preeruption dacite with 70 vol. percent melt. The 70-vol. percent case for melt masses is based on the groundmass abundances of 65–80 vol. percent reported for the somewhat less evolved May 18, 1980, white pumice (Cashman and Taggert, 1983; Rutherford and others, 1985; Cashman, 1992) and a

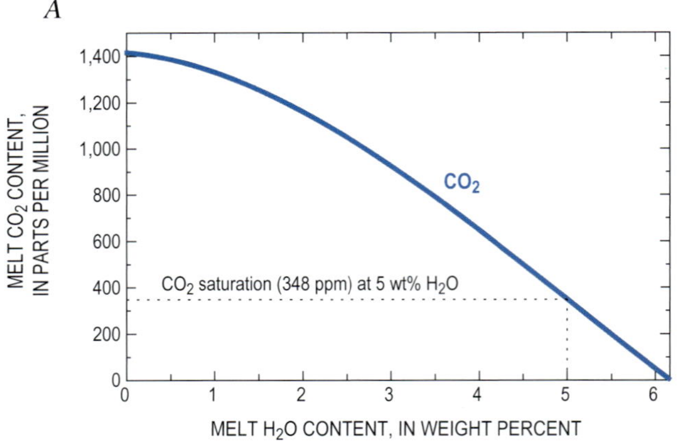

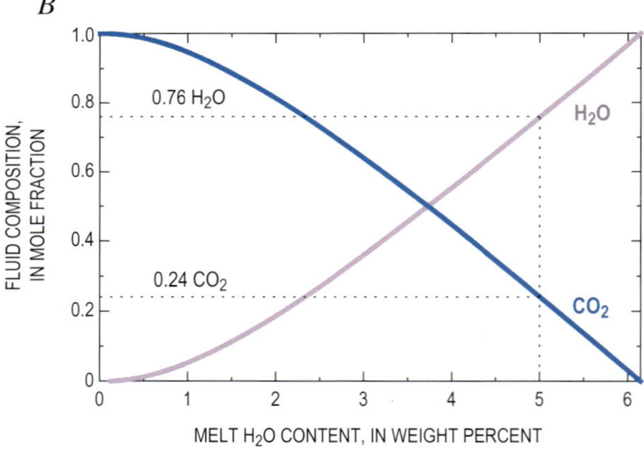

Figure 19. Concentration of CO_2 in hydrous rhyolitic melt and coexisting fluid composition at 220 MPa and 900°C (Newman and Lowenstern, 2002). *A*, Solubility of CO_2 (solid blue curve) in hydrous rhyolitic melts with a range of water concentrations. Dotted lines indicate a CO_2 saturation limit of 348 ppm for rhyolitic melt containing 5 wt. percent H_2O. Melt H_2O content is total H_2O—that is, OH and molecular H_2O. *B*, Mole fraction concentrations of H_2O and CO_2 (solid curves) in fluids coexisting with hydrous rhyolitic melts over a range of water concentrations. Dotted lines indicate fluid composition of 0.76 X_{H_2O} and 0.24 X_{CO_2} coexisting with rhyolitic melt containing 5 wt. percent water.

Table 3. Parameters for calculation of fluid content of the 2004–2005 dacite, Mount St. Helens, Washington.

[Digital elevation model (DEM) dates are the dates of DEMs of Schilling and others (this volume, chap. 8). Dacite volumes are estimated cumulative volumes of the newly extruded lava dome (Schilling and others, this volume, chap. 8). Dense rock equivalent (DRE) volumes are cumulative dacite volumes adjusted for an average porosity of 10 vol. percent (Cashman and others, this volume, chap. 19; Pallister and others, this volume, chap. 30; C. Thornber, written commun., 2006). Dacite masses are cumulative masses in metric tons (t) of dacite derived from the DRE volumes and the dacite DRE density of 2.62 g/cm^3 (K. Russell, written commun. 2006). Melt masses (t) are cumulative masses of melt estimated from DRE volumes and preeruption melt fractions of 53.5 vol. percent and 70 vol. percent, as described in the text. CO_2 masses (t) are cumulative masses of CO_2 output as of each DEM date, calculated from a curve fit to the cumulative CO_2 emissions (fig. 8). Significant figures were exaggerated to reduce roundoff errors.]

DEM date	Dacite volume (10^6 m^3)	DRE volume (10^6 m^3)	Dacite mass (10^6 t)	Melt mass for 53.5 vol. percent melt (10^6 t)	Melt mass for 70 vol. percent melt (10^6 t)	CO_2 mass (t)
11/04/2004	11.8	10.62	27.82	13.07	17.10	23,482
11/20/2004	18.4	16.56	43.39	20.38	26.66	39,380
11/29/2004	21.3	19.17	50.23	23.59	30.86	48,800
12/11/2004	25.5	22.95	60.13	28.24	36.95	61,162
01/03/2005	30.5	27.45	71.92	33.78	44.19	82,459
02/01/2005	35.1	31.59	82.77	38.87	50.86	102,639
02/21/2005	39.2	35.28	92.43	43.41	56.80	112,188
03/10/2005	41.9	37.71	98.80	46.40	60.71	118,092
04/19/2005	47.5	42.75	112.01	52.60	68.83	127,630
06/15/2005	53.9	48.51	127.10	59.69	78.10	141,901
07/14/2005	57.1	51.39	134.64	63.24	82.74	152,123
08/10/2005	61.7	55.53	145.49	68.33	89.40	163,184
09/20/2005	67.3	60.57	158.69	74.53	97.52	182,139
10/24/2005	70.0	63.00	165.06	77.52	101.43	202,885

melt density of 2.3 g/cm^3 reported for experimental investigations of rhyolite densities at elevated temperature and water pressure (Silver and others, 1990). The 70-vol. percent case maintains comparability with 1980 conditions of 900°C, 220 MPa, and rhyolitic melt containing 5 wt. percent dissolved H_2O at 8.6 km depth.

For each DEM date, the amount of dissolved CO_2 was calculated from the concentration of CO_2 in the melt (fig. 19*A*) and the mass of melt for the DEM date (table 3), as estimated from the 70-vol. percent melt fraction discussed above. In all cases, the amount of dissolved CO_2 was a minor fraction (<20 percent) of the cumulative (total) CO_2 output as of the DEM date (table 3), indicating that 2004–5 dacite containing 70 vol. percent rhyolitic melt with 5 wt. percent dissolved H_2O would indeed have been fluid saturated in the magma reservoir at 900°C and 220 MPa (8.6 km depth). We determined the amount of CO_2 in the fluid phase by subtracting the amount of CO_2 dissolved in the melt from the cumulative CO_2 emitted as of the DEM date (table 3). Having determined the amount of fluid CO_2, we calculated the amount of fluid H_2O from the H_2O-CO_2 fluid compositional relation (fig. 19*B*). We converted the amounts of fluid CO_2 and H_2O into a fluid volume by assuming ideal mixing and by using the modified Redlich-Kwong (MRK) equation of state (Holloway, 1977, 1981) to calculate molar volumes of CO_2 and H_2O at 900°C and 220 MPa. The volume of fluid and the DEM-based dacite volume (table 3), corrected to dense rock equivalent (DRE) basis (table 3), gave the fluid content as a volume percent of the dacite. The dacite masses (table 3) and the amounts of fluid CO_2 and H_2O also allowed expression of the fluid content as a weight percent of the dacite.

Figure 20 shows the fluid content of the dacite for the 14 DEM dates at 900°C and 220 MPa (8.6 km depth). The results, ranging from 0.82 to 1.32 vol. percent (0.15–0.24 wt. percent), indicate steady fluid content for the dacite at 8.6 km depth after a brief period of regularly increasing values involving the points for the first four DEM dates (November–December 2004). Steady fluid content begins with the January 3, 2005, DEM date and continues thereafter; it ranges from 1.16 to 1.32 vol. percent (0.21–0.24 wt. percent) and averages 1.23 vol. percent (0.22 wt. percent). These results are consistent with those of Mastin and others (this volume, chap. 22), who also inferred a low reservoir fluid content of <1.5 vol. percent from the relation between erupted-dacite volume and the volume shrinkage of the reservoir obtained from geodetic data (Lisowski and others, this volume, chap. 15).

It is noteworthy that the results are steady throughout 2005 despite the disparate datasets involved. Several factors may be at work during the brief period involving the four points of lower but steadily rising fluid content during November–December 2004 (fig. 20). These factors probably reflect the declining influence with time of CO_2 lost in scrubbing prior to November 2004 (or missed if airborne measurements were too infrequent) on the cumulative CO_2 output. Increasing the cumulative CO_2 outputs by 38 percent (11/4/2004) to 15 percent (12/11/2004) would bring the four points into the steady range of values. Alternatively, the lower fluid content may reflect a higher porosity of the earlier dacite—somewhere in the range 11–32 vol. percent (K. Russell, written commun., 2006)—compared to the eruption average of 10 vol. percent (table 3) used in the calculations, although there is presently no evidence that porosity declined in a steady way early in the eruption. A higher porosity decreases the DRE volume and mass of dacite in proportion to the cumulative amount of CO_2 and causes the volume percent fluid for the four 2004 DEM dates to increase—porosities of 35 vol. percent (11/4/2004) to 22 vol. percent (12/11/2004) would cause the fluid content of these dates to fall within the range of steady 2005 results. Involvement of shallower, more degassed magma early in the eruption might also account for the lower 2004 fluid content, but it is not obvious from the CO_2 emissions that the earlier magma was more degassed (figs. 7, 17). Lastly, the procedures used to estimate dacite volumes from DEMs may overestimate the smaller dacite volumes of the eruption-startup period, causing erroneously low calculated fluid content. Significant underestimation of early dacite volumes seems more likely, however, because of unaccounted for dacite residing in the conduit. Apparently, the volume of conduit dacite became a negligible fraction of the measurable dacite volume fairly early—sometime prior to the first DEM on 11/4/2004 (table 3).

The sensitivity of the modeling to the volume percent melt-fraction parameter is an important concern that is easily addressed. Recalculating the model for a melt fraction of 53.5 vol. percent (table 3), compared to the 70-vol. percent melt fraction used above, illustrates the low sensitivity of the results to a plausible range of values for the volume percent melt parameter. The resulting steady 2005 fluid content ranges from 1.23 to 1.39 vol. percent and averages 1.29 vol. percent—hardly different from the above results for 70 vol. percent melt.

Recently, Liu and others (2005) derived a new empirical model of CO_2 and H_2O solubility in fluid-saturated rhyolitic melt and recommended it over VolatileCalc (Newman and Lowenstern, 2002) for eruptive degassing and magma-chamber dynamics calculations because it gives better fits to experimental solubility data, especially at pressures above 200 MPa. At the conditions considered here, though, the two models agree closely on the dacite fluid content. For example, during the period of steady 2005 DEM dates, the model of Liu and others (2005) gives 1.17–1.33 vol. percent and a 1.24-vol. percent average versus 1.16–1.32 vol. percent and a 1.23-vol. percent average by VolatileCalc. The agreement becomes virtually exact in calculations at the lower pressures considered below. For these reasons, and because of VolatileCalc's user-friendly software, we have used it throughout this study.

We conclude that the average steady 2005 fluid content of 1.23 vol. percent (0.22 wt. percent; fig. 20) is the best estimate of the fluid content of the current dacite at a reservoir depth of 8.6 km, 900°C, and 220 MPa. This result and, indeed, all the results obtained above are significantly less than the ≥15-vol. percent (≥3 wt. percent) fluid determined for the May 18 dac-

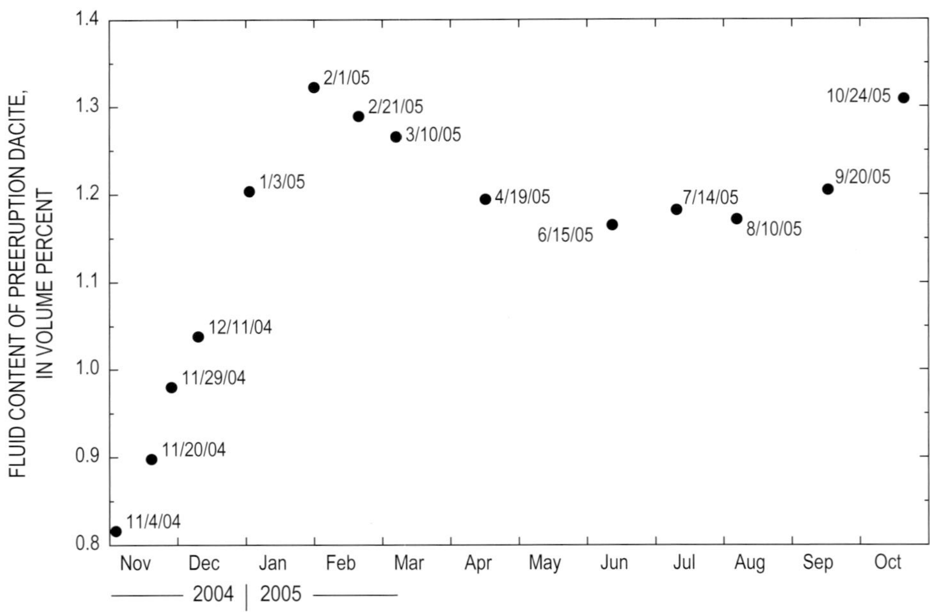

Figure 20. Fluid content of dacite at 900°C and 220 MPa (8.6 km) calculated as described in the text for 14 DEM dates in 2004–5.

ite; furthermore, they are much less than the 5–30-vol. percent (1–6 wt. percent) fluid indicated for several other explosive eruptions of silicic and intermediate magma (Wallace, 2001, 2003). The present analysis, therefore, indicates depletion of excess volatiles and thus confirms the flat-magma hypothesis for the dacite of the 2004–5 eruption.

Fluid Content of the 2004–2005 Dacite Prior to Ascent at 850°C and 130 MPa (5.2 km Depth)

As the dacite migrates to reservoir depths shallower than 8.6 km, its fluid content increases. Of particular interest is the fluid content where the dacite last equilibrated at about 850°C and 120–140 MPa in the presence of an H_2O-rich fluid ($X_{H_2O} \approx 1$) prior to ascent and eruption (Rutherford and Devine, this volume, chap. 31). The corresponding depth range of 4.8–5.6 km (Williams and others, 1987) places the preeruption dacite in the shallowest part of the ellipsoidal-cylindrical magma reservoir extending from 4.5–5 km to ≥12 km, as indicated by deformation data from the current eruption (Lisowski and others, this volume, chap. 15). The average volume percent groundmass of the 2004–5 dacite is 53.5 (Pallister and others, this volume, chap. 30; Rutherford and Devine, this volume, chap. 31). As such, it is a reasonable approximation of the rhyolitic melt fraction of the current dacite before its ascent and eruption from a shallow reservoir depth of 5.2 km (130 MPa)—the median of the 4.8–5.6-km depth range (120–140 MPa) where the dacite last equilibrated. This is the basis for the melt mass case corresponding to a melt fraction of 53.5 vol. percent in table 3. Accordingly, we have taken our results for all DEM dates obtained above (fig. 20) for dacite containing 70 vol. percent melt at 900°C, 220 MPa, and 8.6 km depth and repartitioned CO_2 and H_2O from melt to fluid to obtain a dacite with 53.5 vol. percent melt. To bring this dacite to the last equilibrium conditions within the shallow reservoir at 5.2 km (assuming a closed system), we used VolatileCalc to find the dissolved melt H_2O and CO_2 concentrations at 850°C and 130 MPa (fig. 21*A*) that—after further adjusting of H_2O and CO_2 partitioning between fluid and the 53.5-vol. percent melt phase—gave a fluid composition consistent with the X_{H_2O} and X_{CO_2} predicted by the model (fig. 21*B*). This iterative process consistently gave a melt H_2O concentration of ~4.4 wt. percent and an associated melt CO_2 concentration of ~37 ppm (fig. 21*A*) for each DEM date. The coexisting fluid composition is X_{H_2O}= ~0.96 and X_{CO_2} = ~0.04 (fig. 21*B*), consistent with experimental results of Rutherford and Devine (this volume, chap. 31) that indicate the X_{H_2O} of coexisting fluid would be close to 1.0 in the shallower part of the reservoir. These results also constrain the bulk dacite concentrations of CO_2 and H_2O—that is, fluid plus melt amounts of CO_2 and H_2O as mass fractions of the dacite—at average values of 1,167 ppm and 3.1 wt. percent, respectively, for the ten 2005 DEM dates. The corresponding average bulk dacite S concentration calculated from the cumulative SO_2 emissions (fig. 8; table 2) is 90 ppm for the 10 DEM dates.

The fluid content results for all the DEM dates range from 10.11 to 10.85 vol. percent (fig. 22); again, there is a tight grouping of steady fluid content for the ten 2005 DEM dates—10.63 to 10.85 vol. percent with an average 10.72 vol. percent. The large increase in the average volume percent fluid content from 1.23 to 10.72 vol. percent in going from 8.6 km to 5.2 km depth reflects the crystallization of melt (from 70 vol. percent melt to 53.5 vol. percent melt) and the decreased solubility of H_2O and CO_2 in rhyolite melt at lower pressure; it also includes the effect of fluid expansion as the pressure drops from 220 MPa to 130 MPa. The fluid expansion factor confounds comparisons of fluid content of magmas from different depths. This confusion is avoided by using mass units, which do

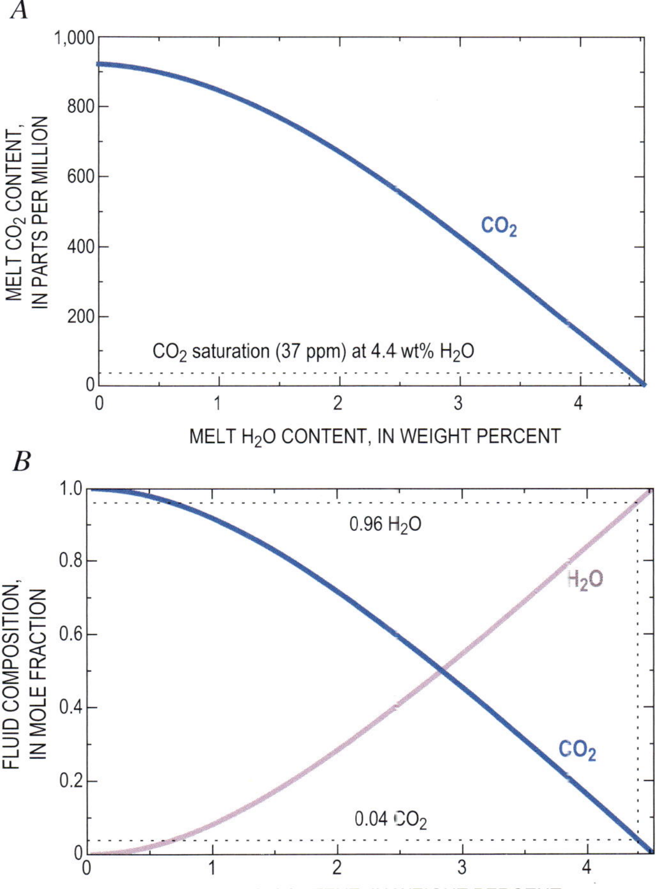

Figure 21. Concentration of CO_2 in hydrous rhyolitic melt and coexisting fluid composition at 130 MPa and 850°C (Newman and Lowenstern, 2002). *A*, Solubility of CO_2 (solid blue curve) in hydrous rhyolite melt with a range of water concentrations. Dotted lines indicate a CO_2 saturation limit of 37 ppm for rhyolitic melt containing 4.4 wt. percent H_2O. Melt H_2O content is total H_2O—that is, OH and molecular H_2O. *B*, Mole fraction concentrations of H_2O and CO_2 (solid curves) in fluids coexisting with hydrous rhyolitic melts over a range of water concentrations. Dotted lines indicate fluid composition of 0.96 X_{H_2O} and 0.04 X_{CO_2} coexisting with rhyolitic melt containing 4.4 wt. percent water.

not reflect fluid expansion; in the present case, the steady fluid content at 5.2 km depth ranges from 1.22 to 1.25 wt. percent and averages 1.23 wt. percent. Despite the relatively shallow depth, these results are still significantly smaller than Wallace's ≥3 wt. percent fluid content for the May 18 dacite at 8.6 km depth and on the low end of his 1–6 wt. percent range for deeper intermediate to silicic magmas involved in explosive volcanism (Wallace, 2001, 2003). These results further confirm the flat-magma hypothesis for the 2004–5 dacite.

We have assumed closed-system degassing with respect to the excess-volatile fluid phase's mobility in magma at depth. The steady excess-volatile fluid content of ~1.23 wt. percent calculated for the dacite at 5.2 km throughout 2005 is consistent with this assumption. Equilibrium (^{210}Pb)/(^{226}Ra) values reported for dacite erupted in 2004–5 (Reagan and others, this volume, chap. 37) also support closed-system degassing. Unlike those of the 1980 lava and tephra (Berlo and others, 2004), (^{210}Pb)/(^{226}Ra) values of the 2004–5 dacite were not affected by continuous open flow of fluid carrying ^{222}Rn from depth in sufficient amount or for sufficient duration to disturb secular equilibrium and generate ^{210}Pb deficits or excesses (Reagan and others, this volume, chap. 37); in our view, this reflects the depletion of excess volatiles compared to 1980 dacite. However, to explain the Li enrichment unique to plagioclase phenocrysts of the October 2004 dacite, Kent and others (2007) propose preferential partitioning of Li from deep melt into aqueous fluid migrating to the uppermost part of the magma chamber at 4.5 km, about 1 year before eruption; they argue that at this depth, which corresponds to 110 MPa (Williams and others, 1987), the fluid unmixed into a low-density vapor and a Li-rich brine that fostered the enrichment of Li in what became the October 2004 dacite's plagioclase phenocrysts. We suggest that Li in the dacite magma is partitioned preferentially into the accompanying excess-volatile fluid and that the Li-enriched plagioclase phenocrysts resulted when that fluid unmixed a Li-rich brine as the dacite ascended from 5.2 km to 4.5 km, where the magma stalled for several months before final ascent to the surface at the start of the eruption.

Ascent Degassing

We carried out calculations like those described above for the current dacite to model its closed-system degassing at 850°C during ascent from shallow reservoir depths. The calculations began at 5.2 km (130 MPa) and terminated at 0.47–0.95 km (10–20 MPa) where melt of the 1980s lava-dome eruptions crystallized extensively to groundmass (Blundy and Cashman, 2001). Figure 23 shows the fluid content, fluid composition, and melt H_2O and CO_2 concentrations of the dacite with ascent depth. We evaluated these variables for all DEM dates at each pressure of calculation and then correlated results to appropriate depths (Williams and others, 1987). The curves of figure 23 employ the average values of the ten 2005 DEM dates, which agreed within 5 percent.

Figure 23*A* shows the fluid content of the 2004–5 dacite during ascent; the fluid content of current dacite at 8.6 km and that of the May 18, 1980, dacite (Wallace, 2003) are included for comparison. The fluid content of the ascending 2004–5 dacite ranges from 10.7 vol. percent at the last equili-

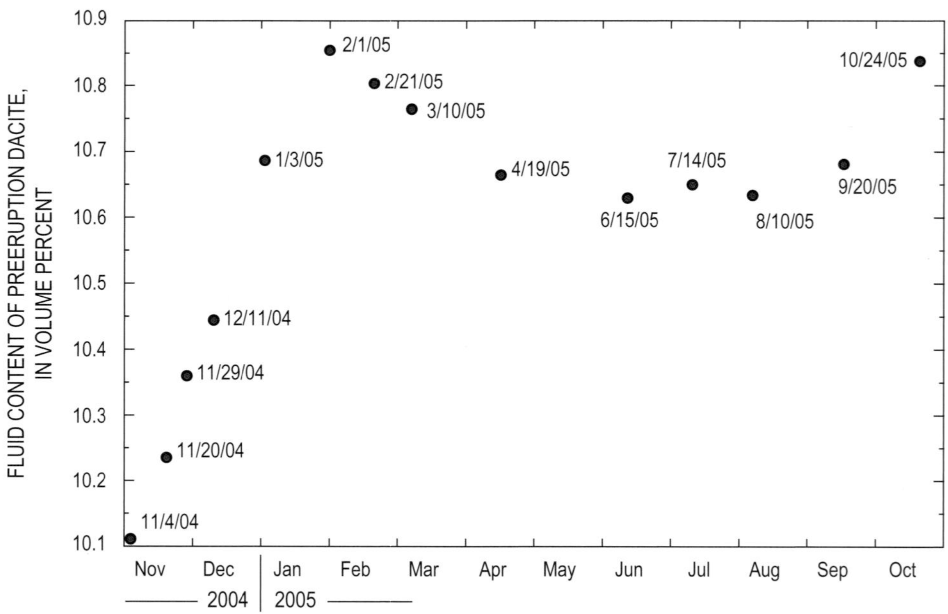

Figure 22. Fluid content of dacite at 850°C and 130 MPa (5.2 km) calculated as described in the text for 14 DEM dates in 2004–5.

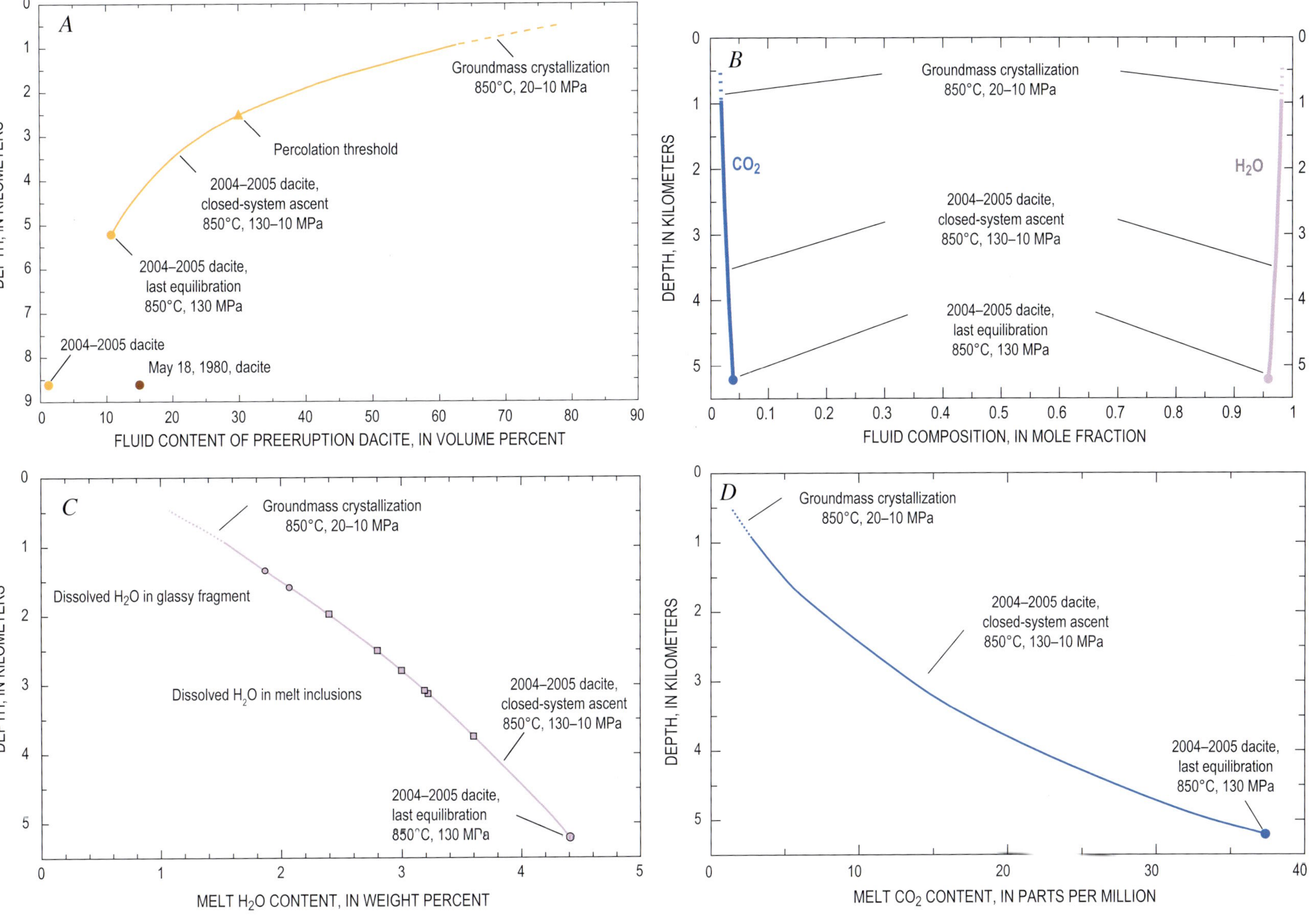

Figure 23. Closed-system ascent of 2004–2005 dacite from 5.2-km depth of last equilibration at 850°C and 130 MPa before eruption (Rutherford and Devine, this volume, chap. 31) to 0.47–0.95-km depth range of groundmass crystallization at 10–20 MPa (Blundy and Cashman, 2001). *A*, Fluid content (exolved fluid phase) of 2004–2005 dacite during ascent, and fluid content of 2004–2005 dacite and May 18, 1980, dacite (Wallace, 2003) at 8.6 km as discussed in the text. *B*, H_2O-CO_2 fluid composition of 2004–2005 dacite during ascent. *C*, Dissolved H_2O in melt of 2004–2005 dacite during ascent; dissolved H_2O in six melt inclusions (filled squares) with highest observed H_2O concentrations (Pallister and others, this volume, chap. 30; Blundy and others, this volume, chap. 33); and dissolved H_2O in a rare glassy fragment (filled circles) of October 2004 dacite sample SH304 (Pallister and others, 2005). *D*, Dissolved melt CO_2 concentration of 2004–2005 dacite during ascent.

bration depth to 60–80 vol. percent at depths of groundmass crystallization. The corresponding fluid composition of 2004–5 dacite during ascent (fig. 23*B*) is H_2O rich with X_{H_2O} always >0.96 and reaching 0.98 at the stage of groundmass crystallization. Extrapolating the compositional trends to near-surface conditions indicates that H_2O forms about 99 percent (molar basis) of the magmatic gases emitted to the atmosphere, whereas the monitored gases CO_2 and SO_2 account for only about 1 percent of the emitted magmatic gases. The implied magmatic $H_2O/(CO_2+SO_2)$ of ~99 is consistent with the value of 113 measured by open-path Fourier-transform infrared spectroscopy (Edmonds and others, this volume, chap. 27) on gas emissions from the new dome on August 31, 2005, considering that dome gases are likely to contain a meteoric component in addition to the magmatic component of water. Our CO_2 and SO_2 emission-rate data thus allow calculation of expected magmatic H_2O emission rates during 2004–5; the expected magmatic H_2O emission rates range from ~7 kt/d to ~100 kt/d with an estimated median of ~30 kt/d. We estimate cumulative H_2O production through 2005 at ~10 Mt from the cumulative production of CO_2 and SO_2.

The concentration of H_2O—that is, total OH and molecular H_2O—dissolved in the melt of the 2004–5 dacite ranges during ascent from the 4.4 wt. percent of last equilibration in the reservoir at 5.2 km to about 1.1–1.5 wt. percent at the conditions of groundmass crystallization (fig. 23*C*). The ascent curve for H_2O dissolved in melt indicates last equilibration depths of about 1.3–1.6 km for two measurements of H_2O concentration by Fourier-transform infrared spectrometry on a rare glassy fragment found in the October 2004 dacite sample SH304 (Pallister and others, 2005). Melt inclusions in the current dacite contain 0.0–3.6 wt. percent H_2O (Pallister and others, this volume, chap. 30; Blundy and others, this volume, chap. 33). The six highest melt-inclusion H_2O concentrations range from 2.4 to 3.6 wt. percent, corresponding to depths of only 2.0–3.7 km on the ascent curve for H_2O (fig. 23*C*). These results corroborate petrologic findings indicating that the melt inclusions provide no data on the volatile content of preeruption melt, apparently because slow ascent and eruption caused rupturing and (or) crystallization of virtually all melt inclusions, as suggested by their frequent mafic-mineral hosts, high crystallinity (≥70 percent), and variable SiO_2 concentrations (in this volume: Pallister and others, chap. 30; Rutherford and Devine, chap. 31; Blundy and others, chap. 33). Alternative explanations of the low melt-inclusion H_2O concentrations—for example, that they formed during ascent from 5.2 km, or that the source magma at 5.2 km depth was relatively dry (<4 wt. percent H_2O, which would imply X_{H_2O} <0.84)—are implausible in view of petrologic evidence. The concentration of CO_2 dissolved in the melt during ascent ranges from 37 ppm at the last equilibration in the reservoir at 5.2 km to about 1.3–2.9 ppm at the conditions of groundmass crystallization (fig. 23*D*).

The percolation threshold of 30 vol. percent indicated at ~2.5 km (fig. 23*A*) is a first-order approximation of the depth beyond which further ascent causes interconnected bubbles to increasingly dominate in overall degassing, ultimately transitioning to open-system degassing (Mueller and others, 2005). Melt concentrations of H_2O and CO_2 at the percolation threshold are about 2.8 wt. percent and 10 ppm, respectively, and the associated fluid composition is H_2O rich (X_{H_2O} = 0.975). The transition to open-system degassing during ascent at some depth shallower than ~2.5 km is an important step in the mobilization and flow of the H_2O-rich volcanic gases. Measured H_2O/HCl ratios of gas emissions on August 31, 2005, are consistent with a transition to open-system degassing at depths of ~1 km and prevailing to the surface (Edmonds and others, this volume, chap. 27). Open flow of H_2O-rich volcanic gases during ascent and dome emplacement purged shallow dacite of other volatile elements, including the entrainment of 210Po (Reagan and others, this volume, chap. 37) and the loss of Li from melt and the margins of plagioclase phenocrysts in the October 2004 dacite (Kent and others, 2007).

Fluid H_2S/SO_2 During Ascent

The gas-emission data show that SO_2 is the main sulfur species emitted to the atmosphere during the 2004–5 eruption. However, SO_2 may not be the dominant sulfur gas species at depth, where increased pressure can strongly affect sulfur speciation. Gerlach and Casadevall (1986) proposed from thermodynamic calculations constrained by fumarole gas compositions that H_2S was the dominant sulfur gas in the 1980s dacite at depth, whereas SO_2 dominated at pressures less than 4 MPa (depths less than 0.2 km). They cited reports of high H_2S/SO_2 in Mount St. Helens plumes from explosive eruptions of 1980–1981 in which 35–100 percent of the sulfur was present as H_2S (Hobbs and others, 1982) and suggested that rapid release of gas from depth prevented full equilibration to low pressure and allowed high H_2S/SO_2 to persist. They further suggested that rapid unloading during explosive eruptions of magma with oxygen fugacity as much as 1 order of magnitude above the Ni-NiO (NNO) buffer could burden the atmosphere with significant H_2S, as well as SO_2, and that SO_2 might increase as the H_2S oxidized, because the lifetime of H_2S in the atmosphere is only ~1 day (Graedel, 1977). Subsequent examination of TOMS satellite measurements made once a day on stratospheric volcanic clouds showed higher SO_2 masses for the May 18, 1980, cloud from Mount St. Helens on the second day than on the first day after eruption (Bluth and others, 1995).

We have taken a different approach to that of Gerlach and Casadevall (1986) and used the reaction

$$SO_2 + H_2O = H_2S + 1.5\ O_2$$

to estimate the H_2S/SO_2 ratio of the fluid phase during ascent of the current dacite from its last equilibration depth to the surface. For this reaction, the molar H_2S/SO_2 ratio is given by

$$H_2S/SO_2 = (pX_{H_2O}/Kf_{O_2}^{1.5})(\gamma_{H_2O}\gamma_{SO_2}/\gamma_{H_2S}), \quad (2)$$

where p is the total pressure in bars (1,300 bars to 1 bar), X_{H_2O} is the mole fraction of H_2O in the fluid (0.96 to 0.99, fig. 23*C*), K is the reaction equilibrium constant of $10^{20.03}$ at 850°C (HSC Chemistry for Windows v. 5.1), f_{O_2} is the current dacite's oxygen fugacity of $10^{-12.29}$ bar at 850°C (Pallister and others, this volume, chap. 30), and γ_i terms are dimensionless fugacity coefficients correcting for the nonideality of H_2O, SO_2, and H_2S. Fugacity coefficients from the MRK equation of state (Holloway, 1977, 1981), the corresponding state equation of Shi and Saxena (1992), and the ideal gas assumption ($\gamma_i = 1$) give H_2S/SO_2 results that agree within 10 percent, consistent with the relatively low-pressure, high-temperature conditions. The results confirm that H_2S is the dominant sulfur gas at depths >0.2 km (fig. 24), as in the 1980s (Gerlach and Casadevall, 1986); the H_2S/SO_2 ratio is >40 at the last equilibration depth in the shallow reservoir (5.2 km) and 3.3–6.5 in the depth range of groundmass crystallization (0.47 to 0.95 km). Compared to the explosive eruptions of the early 1980s, the slow ascent of magma from depth in the present eruption favors a closer approach to equilibrium with more complete conversion of H_2S to SO_2—consistent with the generally low H_2S emissions of the current eruption. Nevertheless, field crews often reported strong intermittent H_2S odor, especially after the early steam-and-ash events, and H_2S odor was reported by an airborne observer downwind of the volcano during and immediately after the first explosion of the eruption on October 1, 2004. These reports may be the result of rapid release of H_2S from depth. However, we cannot rule out an alternative H_2S origin by scrubbing and hydrolysis of SO_2, as discussed above, for the early days of the eruption in 2004.

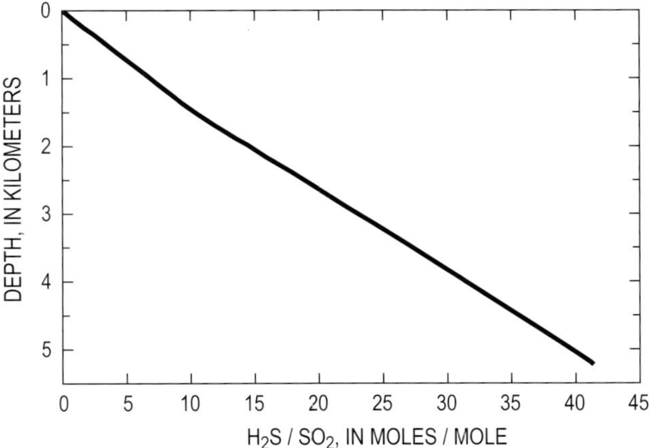

Figure 24. Calculated fluid H_2S/SO_2 of 2004–2005 dacite at 850°C ascending from the 5.2-km depth (130 MPa) of last equilibration in the shallow reservoir to the surface (0.1 MPa), as described in the text.

Excess Sulfur

The existence of an excess sulfur problem, although clear in the 1980s cycle of volcanism at Mount St. Helens (Gerlach and McGee, 1994), is problematic in the 2004–5 eruption. Assuming that the cumulative SO_2 emissions (table 2; fig. 8) for the DEM dates derived entirely from the melt fraction of the dacite prior to ascent implies a melt S concentration of 192 ppm at 5.2 km depth. The rupturing and high crystallinity of virtually all melt inclusions and the below-detection-limit sulfur concentrations of most melt inclusions and matrix glasses (Pallister and others, this volume, chap. 30), however, prevent the use of glass measurements to constrain the preeruption melt sulfur concentration of the current dacite prior to ascent from 5.2 km, thus precluding comparisons with the 192-ppm figure. Whether or not the preeruption melt sulfur concentration at 5.2 km depth accounts for the 2004–5 SO_2 emissions is therefore presently irresolvable, as is the question of excess sulfur for the 2004–5 eruption. The alternative source of the SO_2 emissions—that is, the fluid fraction of the dacite at 5.2 km—thus remains viable; this option would require a mole-fraction S concentration in the fluid (X_S) of only 0.004 prior to ascent (recall that the fluid X_{H_2O} and X_{CO_2} at 5.2 km are about 0.96 and 0.04, respectively). Moreover, experimental studies (Keppler, 1999) on haplogranitic melt at 850°C, 200 MPa, and f_{O_2} of 0.5 log units above the Ni-NiO buffer (NNO + 0.5)—close to the current dacite's f_{O_2} of NNO + ~1 (Pallister and others, this volume, chap. 30)—give fluid/melt partition coefficients for S of 47±4. These results strongly favor excess sulfur in the fluid fraction of the dacite at 5.2 km as the main source of the SO_2 emissions.

Concluding Remarks

The gas emissions of the 2004–5 eruption of Mount St. Helens provide no compelling evidence that gas-rich "new" magma was introduced into the reservoir during the months just prior to or since the onset of activity in September 2004, although additions of gas-poor new magma cannot be ruled out. The gas emissions are instead indicative of a flat source magma markedly depleted in excess volatiles compared to the May 18, 1980, dacite and the intermediate and silicic magmas commonly involved in explosive volcanism. However, the flat dacite of this eruption contains rhyolitic melt with appreciable dissolved water (4.4 wt. percent) despite its depletion in excess volatiles. It remains unclear whether flat dacite of this sort can give rise to large and violent explosive eruptions. The flat dacite has not done so in the present case, but this fact begs the question of how dependent explosive volcanism involving intermediate and silicic magma is on the magnitude of the excess-volatile load.

The 2004–5 gas emissions are plausibly compatible with 1980–86 dome-building magma left over in the reservoir and (or) with gas-poor new magma that entered the reservoir since 1986. Petrologic evidence favors the introduction of new magma (Pallister and others, this volume, chap. 30), but why is this new magma so gas poor compared to the May 18, 1980, magma? Perhaps the new magma was initially depleted in excess volatiles, or it may have mixed with a large amount of leftover 1980–86 magma already greatly depleted in exsolved volatiles. Alternatively, the new magma may simply have lost most of its excess-volatile load by fluid escape while stored at shallow reservoir depths long before the events of September 2004. The degassing of CO_2 measured on June 22, 1998, may represent the product of such fluid escape during a short period of seismicity accompanying recharge of the shallow reservoir. Although this is the strongest evidence of post-1986 fluid escaping and reaching the surface, we cannot rule out the possibility that fluid escaped from the shallow reservoir at other times since 1986 and was captured by hydrothermal fluid at depth or scrubbed by surficial water (Shevenell and Goff, 1993); the large increase of HCO_3^- in the waters of thermal springs at Loowit and Step canyons since 1994 (Bergfeld and others, this volume, chap. 25) may be the result of these processes.

The small load of excess volatiles in the 2004–5 dacite was an important factor in making it possible for scrubbing to shut down and strongly reduce gas emissions to the atmosphere in the period of unrest and the early stage of the eruption. The 2004–5 eruption affirms several implications of scrubbing for assessment of volcano hazards by volcanic gas monitoring: scrubbing can mask shallow magmatic degassing and thus severely restrict gas-emission monitoring as a volcano hazards assessment tool; scrubbing and its masking effects are most effective in the early stages of unrest; no great solace should be taken from low SO_2 emission rates during periods of unrest; early monitoring of CO_2 should accompany early SO_2 monitoring; the monitoring of CO_2, SO_2, and H_2S can track the drying out of a volcano and help distinguish the effects of gas scrubbing and permeability sealing on emissions; and emissions of CO_2 and H_2S in the early stages of unrest, when SO_2 and emissions are absent or trivial, should not be regarded as merely the degassing of hydrothermal fluid, as they can reflect significant shallow magmatic degassing combined with the effects of scrubbing.

Acknowledgments

We are indebted to the following, all of whom made valuable contributions to this paper by sharing ideas, observations and data: Roger Denlinger, Dan Dzurisin, Marie Edmonds, Mike Lisowski, Larry Mastin, John Pallister, Kelly Russell, Steve Schilling, Carl Thornber, and Paul Wallace. Our special thanks to Jeff Sutton for help with instrumentation and early monitoring flights, and to Larry Mastin and John Pallister for technical reviews. Finally, we acknowledge the support of the U.S. Geological Survey Volcano Hazards Program.

References Cited

Anderson, C.H., Jr., Behrens, C.J., Floyd, G.A., and Vining, M.R., 1998, Crater firn of Mount St. Helens, Washington: Journal of Cave Karst Studies, v. 60, p. 44–50.

Bergfeld, D., Evans, W.C., McGee, K.A., and Spicer, K.R., 2008, Pre- and post-eruptive investigations of gas and water samples from Mount St. Helens, Washington, 2002 to 2005, chap. 25 *of* Sherrod, D.R., Scott, W.E., and Stauffer, P.H., eds., A volcano rekindled; the renewed eruption of Mount St. Helens, 2004–2006: U.S. Geological Survey Professional Paper 1750 (this volume).

Berlo, K., Blundy, J., Turner, S., Cashman, K., Hawkesworth, C., and Black, S., 2004, Geochemical precursors to volcanic activity at Mount St. Helens, USA: Science, v. 306, p. 1167–1169.

Blundy, J., and Cashman, K., 2001, Ascent-driven crystallisation of dacite magmas at Mount St. Helens, 1980–1986: Contributions to Mineralogy and Petrology, v. 140, no. 6, p. 631–650, doi:10.1007/s004100000219.

Blundy, J., and Cashman, K., 2005, Rapid decompression-driven crystallization recorded by melt inclusions from Mount St. Helens volcano: Geology, v. 33, no. 10, p. 793–796, doi:10.1130/G21668.1.

Blundy, J., Cashman, K.V., and Berlo, K., 2008, Evolving magma storage conditions beneath Mount St. Helens inferred from chemical variations in melt inclusions from the 1980–1986 and current (2004–2006) eruptions, chap. 33 *of* Sherrod, D.R., Scott, W.E., and Stauffer, P.H., eds., A volcano rekindled; the renewed eruption of Mount St. Helens, 2004–2006: U.S. Geological Survey Professional Paper 1750 (this volume).

Bluth, G.J.S., Scott, C.J., Sprod, I.E., Schnetzler, C.C., Krueger, A.J., and Walter, L.S., 1995, Explosive emissions of sulfur dioxide from the 1992 Crater Peak eruptions, Mount Spurr volcano, Alaska, *in* Keith, T., ed., The 1992 eruptions of Crater Peak vent, Mount Spurr volcano, Alaska: U.S. Geological Survey Bulletin 2139, p. 37–45.

Caltabiano, T., Guiduzzi, G., Leuzzi, S., and Romano, R., 1992, Helicopter borne COSPEC SO_2 flux measurement: Acta Vulcanologica, v. 2, p. 95–98.

Casadevall, T.J., Johnston, D.A., Harris, D.M., Rose, W.I., Malinconico, L.L., Stoiber, R.E., Bornhorst, T.J., Williams, S.N., Woodruff, L., and Thompson, J.M., 1981, SO_2 emission rates at Mount St. Helens from March 29 through December, 1980, *in* Lipman, P.W., and Mullineaux, D.L., eds., The 1980 eruptions of Mount St. Helens, Washington: U.S. Geological Survey Professional Paper 1250, p. 193–200.

Casadevall, T.J., Johnston, D.A., Rose, W.I., Gerlach, T.M., Ewert, J., Wunderman, R., and Symonds, R., 1983, Gas emissions and the eruptions of Mount St. Helens through 1982: Science, v. 221, p. 1383–1385.

Cashman, K.V., 1992, Groundmass crystallization of Mount St. Helens dacite, 1980–1986—a tool for interpreting shallow magmatic processes: Contributions to Mineralogy and Petrology, v. 109, no. 4, p. 431–449, doi:10.1007/BF00306547.

Cashman, K.V., and Taggert, J.E., 1983, Petrologic monitoring of 1981 and 1982 eruptive products from Mount St. Helens: Science, v. 221, no. 4618, p. 1385–1387.

Cashman, K.V., Thornber, C.R., and Pallister, J.S., 2008, From dome to dust; shallow crystallization and fragmentation of conduit magma during the 2004–2006 dome extrusion of Mount St. Helens, Washington, chap. 19 *of* Sherrod, D.R., Scott, W.E., and Stauffer, P.H., eds., A volcano rekindled; the renewed eruption of Mount St. Helens, 2004–2006: U.S. Geological Survey Professional Paper 1750 (this volume).

Cooper, K.M., and Donnelly, C.T., 2008, ^{238}U-^{230}Th-^{226}Ra disequilibria in dacite and plagioclase from the 2004–2005 eruption of Mount St. Helens, chap. 36 *of* Sherrod, D.R., Scott, W.E., and Stauffer, P.H., eds., A volcano rekindled; the renewed eruption of Mount St. Helens, 2004–2006: U.S. Geological Survey Professional Paper 1750 (this volume).

Crafford, T.C., 1975, SO_2 emission of the 1974 eruption of Volcán Fuego, Guatemala: Bulletin Volcanologique, v. 39, p. 536–556.

Doukas, M.P., 2002, A new method for GPS-based wind speed determinations during airborne volcanic plume measurements: U.S. Geological Survey Open-File Report 02–395, 13 p.

Doukas, M.P., and Gerlach, T.M., 1995, Sulfur dioxide scrubbing during the 1992 eruption of Crater Peak, Mount Spurr, Alaska, *in* Keith, T., ed., The 1992 eruptions of Crater Peak vent, Mount Spurr volcano, Alaska: U.S. Geological Survey Bulletin 2139, p. 47–57.

Edmonds, M., McGee, K.A., and Doukas, M.P., 2008, Chlorine degassing during the lava dome-building eruption of Mount St. Helens, 2004–2005, chap. 27 *of* Sherrod, D.R., Scott, W.E., and Stauffer, P.H., eds., A volcano rekindled; the renewed eruption of Mount St. Helens, 2004–2006: U.S. Geological Survey Professional Paper 1750 (this volume).

Elias, T., Sutton, A.J., Oppenheimer, C., Horton, K.A., Garbeil, H., Tsanev, V., McGonigle, A.J.S., and Williams-Jones, G., 2006, Comparison of COSPEC and two miniature ultraviolet spectrometer systems for SO_2 measurements using scattered sunlight: Bulletin of Volcanology, v. 68, p. 313–322.

Evans, W.C., van Soest, M.C., Mariner, R.H., Hurwitz, S., Wicks, C.W., Jr., and Schmidt, M.E., 2004, Magmatic intrusion west of Three Sisters, central Oregon, USA: The perspective from spring geochemistry: Geology, v. 32, no. 1, p. 69–72.

Galle, B., Oppenheimer, C., Geyer, A., McGonigle, A.J.S., Edmonds, M., and Horrocks, L., 2002, A miniaturized ultraviolet spectrometer for remote sensing of SO_2 fluxes—a new tool for volcano surveillance: Journal of Volcanology and Geothermal Research, v. 119, p. 241–254.

Gerlach, T.M., and Casadevall, T.J., 1986, Fumarole emissions at Mount St. Helens volcano, June 1980 to October 1981—degassing of a magma-hydrothermal system: Journal of Volcanology and Geothermal Research, v. 28, nos. 1–2, p. 141–160, doi:10.1016/0377-0273(86)90009-0.

Gerlach, T.M., and McGee, K.A., 1994, Total sulfur dioxide emissions and pre-eruption vapor-saturated magma at Mount St. Helens, 1980–88: Geophysical Research Letters, v. 21, no. 25, p. 2833–2836, doi:10.1029/94GL02761.

Gerlach, T.M., Delgado, H., McGee, K.A., Doukas, M.P., Venegas, J.J., and Cardenas, L., 1997, Application of the LI-COR CO_2 analyzer to volcanic plumes—a case study, Volcán Popocateptl, Mexico, June 7 and 10, 1995: Journal of Geophysical Research, v. 102, p. 8005–8019.

Gerlach, T.M., Doukas, M.P., McGee, K.A., and Kessler, R., 1999, Airborne detection of diffuse carbon dioxide at Mammoth Mountain, California: Geophysical Research Letters, v. 26, 3661–3664.

Gerlach, T.M., McGee, K.A., and Doukas, M.P., 2005, Emission rates, pre-eruption gas saturation and ascent degassing during the 2004–2005 eruption of Mount St. Helens [abs.]: Eos (American Geophysical Union Transactions), v. 86, no. 52, Fall Meet. Suppl., Abstract V52B–07.

Glantz, S.A., 2005, Primer of biostatistics (5th ed.): New York, McGraw-Hill, 489 p.

Graedel, T.E., 1977, The homogeneous chemistry of atmospheric sulfur: Reviews of Geophysics and Space Physics, v. 15, p. 421–428.

Harris, D.M., Sato, M., Casadevall, T.J., Rose, W.I., and Bornhorst, T.J., 1981, Emission rates of CO_2 from plume measurements, *in* Lipman, P.W., and Mullineaux, D.L., eds., The 1980 eruptions of Mount St. Helens, Washington: U.S. Geological Survey Professional Paper 1250, p. 201–207.

Hobbs, P.V., Tuell, J.P., Hegg, D.A., Radke, L.F., and Eltgroth, M.W., 1982, Particles and gases in the emissions from the 1980–1981 volcanic eruptions of Mount St. Helens: Journal of Geophysical Research, v. 87, no. C12, p. 11062–11086.

Holloway, J.R., 1977, Fugacity and activity of molecular species in supercritical fluids, *in* Fraser, D., ed., Thermodynamics in Geology: Boston, D. Reidel, p. 161–181.

Holloway, J.R., 1981, Volatile interactions in magmas, *in* Newton, R.C., Navrotsky, A., and Wood, B.J., eds., Thermodynamics of Minerals and Melts: New York, Springer-Verlag, p. 273–293.

Horton, K.A., Williams-Jones, G., Garbeil, H., Elias, T., Sutton, A.J., Mouginis-Mark, P., Porter, J.N., and Clegg, S., 2006, Real-time measurement of volcanic SO_2 emissions: validation of a new UV correlation spectrometer (FLY-SPEC): Bulletin of Volcanology, v. 68, p. 323–327.

Ingebritsen, S.E., Sherrod, D.R., and Mariner, R.H., 1989, Heat flow and hydrothermal circulation in the Cascade Range, north-central Oregon: Science, v. 243, p. 1458–1462.

Ingebritsen, S.E., Sherrod, D.R., and Mariner, R.H., 1992, Rate and patterns of groundwater flow in the Cascade Range volcanic arc, and the effect on subsurface temperatures: Journal of Geophysical Research, v. 97, no. B4, p. 4599–4627.

Ingebritsen, S.E., Mariner, R.H., and Sherrod, D.R., 1994, Hydrothermal systems of the Cascade Range, north-central Oregon: U.S. Geological Survey Professional Paper 1044L, 86 p.

James, E.R., Manga, M., and Rose, T.P., 1999, CO_2 degassing in the Oregon Cascades: Geology, v. 27, no. 9, p. 823–826.

Kent, A.J.R., Blundy, J., Cashman, K.V., Cooper, K.M., Donnelly, C., Pallister, J.S., Reagan, M., Rowe, M.C., and Thornber, C.R., 2007, Vapor transfer prior to the October 2004 eruption of Mount St. Helens, Washington: Geology, v. 35, no. 3, p. 231–234, doi:10.1130/G22809A.1.

Keppler, H., 1999, Experimental evidence for the source of excess sulfur in explosive volcanic eruptions: Science, v. 284, p. 1652–1654.

Lisowski, M., Dzurisin, D., Denlinger, R.P., and Iwatsubo, E.Y., 2008, Analysis of GPS-measured deformation associated with the 2004–2006 dome-building eruption of Mount St. Helens, Washington, chap. 15 *of* Sherrod, D.R., Scott, W.E., and Stauffer, P.H., eds., A volcano rekindled; the renewed eruption of Mount St. Helens, 2004–2006: U.S. Geological Survey Professional Paper 1750 (this volume).

Liu, Y., Zhang, Y., and Behrens, H., 2005, Solubility of H_2O in rhyolite melts at low pressures and a new empirical model for mixed H_2O-CO_2 solubility in rhyolitic melts: Journal of Volcanology and Geothermal Research, v. 143, p. 219–235.

Malinconico, L.L., 1979, Fluctuations in SO_2 emission during recent eruptions of Etna: Nature, v. 278, p. 43–45.

Mastin, L.G., Roeloffs, E., Beeler, N.M., and Quick, J.E., 2008, Constraints on the size, overpressure, and volatile content of the Mount St. Helens magma system from geodetic and dome-growth measurements during the 2004–2006+ eruption, chap. 22 *of* Sherrod, D.R., Scott, W.E., and Stauffer, P.H., eds., A volcano rekindled; the renewed eruption of Mount St. Helens, 2004–2006: U.S. Geological Survey Professional Paper 1750 (this volume).

McGee, K.A., 1992, The structure, dynamics, and chemical composition of noneruptive plumes from Mount St. Helens, 1980–88: Journal of Volcanology and Geothermal Research, v. 51, p. 269–282.

McGee, K.A., and Casadevall, T.J., 1994, A compilation of sulfur dioxide and carbon dioxide emission-rate data from Mount St. Helens during 1980–88: U.S. Geological Survey Open-File Report 94–212, 24 p.

McGee, K.A., and Sutton, A.J., 1994, Eruptive activity at Mount St. Helens, Washington, USA, 1984–1988—a gas geochemistry perspective: Bulletin of Volcanology, v. 56, nos. 6–7, p. 435–446.

McGee, K.A., Doukas, M.P., and Gerlach, T.M., 2001, Quiescent hydrogen sulfide and carbon dioxide degassing from Mount Baker, Washington: Geophysical Research Letters, v. 28, p. 4479–4483.

Moran, S.C., 1994, Seismicity at Mount St. Helens, 1987–1992—evidence for repressurization of an active magmatic system: Journal of Geophysical Research, v. 99, no. B3, p. 4341–4354, doi:10.1029/93JB02993.

Moran, S.C., Malone, S.D., Qamar, A.I., Thelen, W.A., Wright, A.K., and Caplan-Auerbach, J., 2008, Seismicity associated with renewed dome building at Mount St. Helens, 2004–2005, chap. 2 *of* Sherrod, D.R., Scott, W.E., and Stauffer, P.H., eds., A volcano rekindled; the renewed eruption of Mount St. Helens, 2004–2006: U.S. Geological Survey Professional Paper 1750 (this volume).

Mueller, S., Melnik, O., Spieler, O., Scheu, B., and Dingwell, D.B., 2005, Permeability and degassing of dome lavas undergoing rapid decompression—an experimental determination: Bulletin of Volcanology, v. 67, no. 6, p. 526–538.

Newman, S., and Lowenstern, J.A., 2002, VolatileCalc—a silicate melt-H_2O-CO_2 solution model written in Visual Basic for excel®: Computers and Geosciences, v. 28, no. 5, p. 597–604, doi:10.1016/S0098-3004(01)00081-4.

Pallister, J.S., Reagan, M., and Cashman, K., 2005, A new eruptive cycle at Mount St. Helens?: Eos (American Geophysical Union Transactions), v. 86, no. 48, p. 499–500, doi:10.1029/2005EO480006.

Pallister, J.S., Thornber, C.R., Cashman, K.V., Clynne, M.A., Lowers, H.A., Mandeville, C.W., Brownfield, I.K., and Meeker, G.P., 2008, Petrology of the 2004–2006 Mount St. Helens lava dome—implications for magmatic plumbing and eruption triggering, chap. 30 *of* Sherrod, D.R., Scott, W.E., and Stauffer, P.H., eds., A volcano rekindled; the renewed eruption of Mount St. Helens, 2004–2006: U.S. Geological Survey Professional Paper 1750 (this volume).

Reagan, M.K., Cooper, K.M., Pallister, J.S., Thornber, C.R., and Wortel, M., 2008, Timing of degassing and plagioclase growth in lavas erupted from Mount St. Helens, 2004–2005, from ^{210}Po-^{210}Pb-^{226}Ra disequilibria, chap. 37 *of* Sherrod, D.R., Scott, W.E., and Stauffer, P.H., eds., A volcano rekindled; the renewed eruption of Mount St. Helens, 2004–2006: U.S. Geological Survey Professional Paper 1750 (this volume).

Rose, T.P., and Davisson, M.L., 1996, Radiocarbon in hydrologic systems containing dissolved magmatic carbon dioxide: Science, v. 273, p. 1367–1370.

Rutherford, M.J., 1993, Experimental petrology applied to volcanic processes: Eos (American Geophysical Union Transactions), v. 74, no. 5, p. 49 and 55.

Rutherford, M.J., and Devine, J.D., III, 2008, Magmatic conditions and processes in the storage zone of the 2004–2006 Mount St. Helens dacite, chap. 31 *of* Sherrod, D.R., Scott, W.E., and Stauffer, P.H., eds., A volcano rekindled; the renewed eruption of Mount St. Helens, 2004–2006: U.S. Geological Survey Professional Paper 1750 (this volume).

Rutherford, M.J., Sigurdsson, H., Carey, S., and Davis, A., 1985, The May 18, 1980, eruption of Mount St. Helens, 1. Melt composition and experimental phase equilibria: Journal of Geophysical Research, v. 90, no. B4, p. 2929–2947.

Schilling, S.P., Thompson, R.A., Messerich, J.A., and Iwatsubo, E.Y., 2008, Use of digital aerophotogrammetry to determine rates of lava dome growth, Mount St. Helens, Washington, 2004–2005, chap. 8 *of* Sherrod, D.R., Scott, W.E., and Stauffer, P.H., eds., A volcano rekindled; the renewed eruption of Mount St. Helens, 2004–2006: U.S. Geological Survey Professional Paper 1750 (this volume).

Scott, W.E., Sherrod, D.R., and Gardner, C.A., 2008, Overview of 2004 to 2006, and continuing, eruption of Mount St. Helens, Washington, chap. 1 *of* Sherrod, D.R., Scott, W.E., and Stauffer, P.H., eds., A volcano rekindled; the renewed eruption of Mount St. Helens, 2004–2006: U.S. Geological Survey Professional Paper 1750 (this volume).

Shevenell, L., and Goff, F., 1993, Addition of magmatic volatiles into the hot spring waters of Loowit Canyon, Mount St. Helens, Washington, USA: Bulletin of Volcanology, v. 55, no. 7, p. 489–503, doi:10.1007/BF00304592.

Shi, P., and Saxena, S.K., 1992, Thermodynamic modeling of the C-H-O-S fluid system: American Mineralogist, v. 77, p. 1038–1049.

Silver, L.A., Ihinger, P.D., and Stolper, E., 1990, The influence of bulk composition on the speciation of water in silicate glasses: Contributions to Mineralogy and Petrology, v. 104, p. 142–162.

Stoiber, R.E., and Jepsen, A., 1973, Sulfur dioxide contribution to the atmosphere by volcanoes: Science, v. 182, p. 577–578.

Stoiber, R.E., Williams, S.N., and Malinconico, L.L., 1980, Mount St. Helens, Washington, 1980, volcanic eruption—magmatic gas component during the first 16 days: Science, v. 208, p. 1258–1259.

Stoiber, R.E., Malinconico, L.L., and Williams, S.N., 1983, Use of the correlation spectrometer at volcanoes, *in* Tazieff, H., and Sabroux, J.C., eds., Forecasting volcanic events: Amsterdam, Elsevier, p. 425–444.

Symonds, R.B., Gerlach, T.M., and Reed, M.H., 2001, Magmatic gas scrubbing—implications for volcanic monitoring: Journal of Volcanology and Geothermal Research, v. 108, nos. 1–4, p. 303–341, doi:10.1016/S0377-0273(00)00292-4.

Thompson, J.M., 1990, Chemical data from thermal and nonthermal springs in Mount St. Helens National Monument, Washington: U.S. Geological Survey Open-File Report 90–690A, 16 p.

Wallace, P.J., 2001, Volcanic SO_2 emissions and the abundance and distribution of exsolved gas in magma bodies: Journal of Volcanology and Geothermal Research, v. 108, nos. 1–4, p. 85–106, doi:10.1016/S0377-0273(00)00279-1.

Wallace, P.J., 2003, From mantle to atmosphere—magma degassing, explosive eruptions, and volcanic volatile budgets, *in* De Vivo, B., and Bodnar, R.J., eds., Melt inclusions in volcanic systems—methods, applications and problems: Amsterdam, Elsevier, p. 105–128.

Williams, D.L., Abrams, G., Finn, C., Dzurisin, D., Johnson, D.J., and Denlinger, R., 1987, Evidence from gravity data for an intrusive complex beneath Mount St. Helens: Journal of Geophysical Research, v. 92, no. B10, p. 10207–10222.

A Volcano Rekindled: The Renewed Eruption of Mount St. Helens, 2004–2006
Edited by David R. Sherrod, William E. Scott, and Peter H. Stauffer
U.S. Geological Survey Professional Paper 1750, 2008

Chapter 27

Chlorine Degassing During the Lava Dome-Building Eruption of Mount St. Helens, 2004–2005

By Marie Edmonds[1], Kenneth A. McGee[2], and Michael P. Doukas[2]

Abstract

Remote measurements of volcanic gases from the Mount St. Helens lava dome were carried out using Open-Path Fourier-Transform Infrared spectroscopy on August 31, 2005. Measurements were performed at a site ~1 km from the lava dome, which was used as a source of IR radiation. On average, during the period of measurement, the volcanic gas contained 99 mol percent H_2O, 0.78 percent CO_2, 0.095 percent HCl, 0.085 percent SO_2, 0.027 percent HF, 4.8×10^{-4} percent CO, and 2.5×10^{-4} percent COS close to the active vent. The fluxes of these species, constrained by synchronous measurements of SO_2 flux, were 7,200 t/d H_2O, 140 t/d CO_2, 22 t/d SO_2, 14 t/d HCl, 2.0 t/d HF, 54 kg/d CO, and 59 kg/d COS, ±20 percent. Observations of H_2O/Cl in the vapor and melt are compared to models of closed- and open-system degassing and to models where a closed system dominates to depths as shallow as ~1 km, and gases are then allowed to escape through a permeable bubble network. Although several features are consistent with this model—for example, (1) H_2O/Cl in the gases emitted from stagnant parts of the lava dome, (2) the concentration of Cl in the matrix glass of erupted dacite, and (3) the glass H_2O/Cl—the gases emitted from the active part of the lava dome have much higher H_2O/Cl than expected. These higher H_2O/Cl levels result from a combination of two factors (1) the addition of substantial amounts of ground water or glacier-derived H_2O to the gases at shallow depths, such that only ~10 mol percent of the measured H_2O is magmatic, and (or) (2) some Cl present as alkali chloride (NaCl and KCl) in the gas phase. The mean molar Cl/S is similar to gases measured at other silicic subduction-zone volcanoes during effusive activity; this may be due to the influence of Cl in the vapor on S solubility in the melt, which produces a solubility maximum for S at vapor Cl/S ~1.

[1]U.S. Geological Survey, P.O. Box 51, Hawaii National Park, HI 96718; now at University of Cambridge, Downing Street, Cambridge, CB2 3EQ, U.K.

[2] U.S. Geological Survey, 1300 SE Cardinal Court, Vancouver, WA 98683

Introduction

Volcanic gases comprise water (H_2O), carbon dioxide (CO_2), sulfur dioxide (SO_2), hydrogen sulfide (H_2S), hydrogen chloride (HCl), and, to a lesser extent, hydrogen fluoride (HF), carbon monoxide (CO), and a host of trace species (for example, Symonds and others, 1994). Volatiles (mainly H_2O and CO_2) exsolve from magma during decompression, generating vesicularity and buoyancy relative to the surrounding rocks, thereby driving eruptions. The rate and style of degassing controls the rheological development of magma and governs eruptive style (for example, Sparks and others, 2000). Preeruptive dissolved H_2O, CO_2, S, and Cl contents in silicic magmas typically range from 1 to 6 weight percent and 0–400, 30–200 and 900–3,000 ppm, respectively, after having undergone ~60–70 percent vapor-saturated fractional crystallization at 2–5 kb in the crust to evolve from mafic magma compositions (Wallace, 2005).

Chlorine is a significant volatile component of magmas associated with subduction zones and is derived from devolatilization of the subducting lithospheric slab (Manning, 2004). Recent analysis of volatile fluxes at subduction zones indicates that the flux of subducted Cl in the form of seawater and sediments approximately balances the output from arc volcanism (~4–7×10^{12} g/yr), consistent with the low abundance of Cl in mantle plume-derived basalt tapping the deep mantle (Wallace, 2005). Along with other volatiles, Cl dissolves in the partial melt and, thereafter, behaves as an incompatible element during crystallization, although small amounts may be taken up by amphibole phases. Cl is finally removed from the melt by partitioning into a vapor phase during magma ascent through the crust. A high partition coefficient (vapor/melt) for Cl was first recognized by Kilinc and Burnham (1972). The release of Cl with H_2O and other volatiles from magma is important for the transport and concentration of ore metals, such as gold, copper, and iron, which may eventually form mineral deposits in large magmatic systems (Lowenstern and others, 1991). The acidic nature of HCl-containing gases may leach and alter volcanic rocks and contribute to instability in volcanic edifices (Le Friant and others, 2002).

Hydrogen chloride is the dominant chloride species in volcanic gases (Webster and Holloway, 1988); significant amounts of NaCl and KCl have also been detected (Le Guern and others, 1975). Gaseous HCl enters the atmosphere during volcanic eruptions; tropospheric emissions can cause local acid rain, and stratospheric injection of HCl gas can lead to degradation of the ozone layer (Tabazedeh and Turco, 1993). The rate of emission of HCl from volcanoes, compared to that of SO_2, has been linked to eruptive processes and has applications for volcano monitoring. Stoiber and Rose (1974) noted that gas Cl/S tends to increase throughout an eruptive episode, owing to the lower solubility of S. At Augustine Volcano, Symonds and others (1990) noted that older volcanic deposits exsolved gas with higher Cl/S than the main eruptive vents, suggesting that Cl continues to degas from melt after emplacement at the surface. At Soufrière Hills volcano[3], Montserrat, S-rich basaltic magma is supplied to the base of a porphyritic, Cl-rich andesite body. Volcanic gases with high levels of Cl/S are emitted during eruptive periods and gases with low levels of Cl/S are emitted during noneruptive periods. These emissions are caused by the degassing of negligible Cl but extensive S from the basalt to a vapor phase at 5–7 km; and the degassing of Cl but negligible S from the andesite during eruption (Edmonds and others, 2002).

During the current eruption of Mount St. Helens (ongoing in August 2006), CO_2, SO_2, and H_2S emission rates have been measured regularly and are well constrained (Gerlach and others, this volume, chap. 26); H_2O, HCl, and other minor species had not been quantified until this study. HCl is an important constituent of volcanic gases, yet fewer measurements of HCl than of SO_2 are carried out during volcanic eruptions. This paper presents new data on the composition of the volcanic gas plume emitted from the lava dome at Mount St. Helens in August 2005. Remote spectroscopic measurements of the volcanic plume made by using Open-Path Fourier-Transform Infrared spectroscopy (OP–FTIR) yield the relative proportions of magmatic H_2O, CO_2, HCl, SO_2, HF, CO, and COS of the gas phase. Synchronous measurements of SO_2 emission rates are used to calculate emission rates for the other six species.

The emission of Cl in the form of HCl gas is the focus of the analysis. In order to interpret the rate and mechanism of HCl emission from volcanoes, an understanding of how magmatic vapor evolves chemically with changes in pressure, temperature, and melt composition is necessary; this is reasonably constrained for H_2O, CO_2, and H_2O-CO_2 melt-vapor systems at shallow to intermediate pressures (for example, for basaltic melts, Dixon and others, 1995) but less well understood for systems containing S and Cl. The measured molar H_2O/Cl of the gases is compared to models describing different degassing regimes in order to evaluate the evolution of the vapor phase with magma ascent. The gas composition is compared to the compositions of volcanic gases at other silicic volcanoes and to observations made during 1980–86 at Mount St. Helens. The Cl/S molar ratio is evaluated with reference to the solubility of S and Cl in silicic melts.

Method

Open-path Fourier-transform infrared spectroscopy (OP–FTIR) is a spectroscopic technique that utilizes the absorptivity of specific gas molecules in order to quantify them accurately (fig. 1*A*). A spectrometer acquires infrared (IR) radiation from a source that has passed through volcanic gas. Di-atomic and monatomic compounds (for example, H_2, He) do not have an IR signature and, thus, cannot be measured by this technique. Absorption due to the gases is isolated and calibrated. OP–FTIR has been used successfully at several volcanoes, including Unzen, Japan (Mori and others, 1993); Vulcano, Italy (Francis and others, 1995); Etna, Italy (Burton and others, 2003); Soufrière Hills, Montserrat (Edmonds and others, 2002); and Kīlauea, USA (Edmonds and others, 2005). The OP–FTIR technique has advantages over direct methods of sampling, the most important of which is the remote aspect of the measurements and, hence, the higher level of safety, because it is not necessary to approach the fumaroles or vents closely. This technique is particularly useful for measuring gases at lava dome-building volcanoes, where explosions can occur with little warning; measurements can be collected throughout eruptive and noneruptive periods. For example, during the 1980–86 Mount St. Helens eruption, gas sampling was possible only from peripheral fumaroles, and when the lava dome was particularly active, no gas samples were collected at all (Gerlach and Casadevall, 1986). OP–FTIR also allows rapid measurements; several hundred spectra may be collected every hour, each containing information about the amount of various major and minor gas species in the pathlength.

The OP–FTIR data presented in this paper were collected on August 31, 2005, using the 2004–5 Mount St. Helens lava dome as a source of IR radiation (fig. 1). A digital elevation model formulated from photographs taken on September 1, 2005, (S.P. Schilling, written commun., 2008) is shown in figure 2. The massive parts of the dome were broken whaleback-shaped spines, each surrounded by a thick layer of blocky talus material. The measurements were taken in three sets; pathlengths ranged from 1,040 to 1,150 m (fig. 2). Temperatures on the surface of the lava dome were highly variable,

[3]Capitalization of "Volcano" indicates adoption of the word as part of the formal geographic name by the host country, as listed in the Geographic Names Information System, a database maintained by the U.S. Board on Geographic Names. Noncapitalized "volcano" is applied informally—eds.

ranging from ~10°C to >200°C (fig. 3). For the OP–FTIR measurements, cracks in the spine surfaces were used as IR sources and had temperatures as high as 600°C (Schneider and others, this volume, chap. 17). Volcanic gas rose from the lava dome (fig. 1*B*) and passed through the spectrometer's field of view.

A MIDAC IR spectrometer with a resolution of 0.5 cm^{-1} was mounted onto a 20-inch Newtonian telescope on a heavy-weight tripod (fig. 1*A*). The spectrometer design incorporates a Michelson interferometer, laser optics, CaF_2 optical windows, and an InSb Stirling-cycle cooled detector with a range of 5,000–1,800 cm^{-1}. The field of view of the instrument is 2–3 m at 800 m. A laptop computer and PCMCIA interface enable real-time data acquisition and processing, using Autoquant4 software (MIDAC Corp.). Analysis is based on a linear model of the sample absorbance known as Beer's Law, which can be written as:

$$A_i = \sum_{j=1}^{M} a_{ij} L C_j \qquad i = 1, 2 \ldots N, \tag{1}$$

where M is the number of compounds assumed to absorb in the spectral region analyzed; A_i is the observed sample absorbance at the ith frequency, C_j is the (unknown) concentration of the jth component of the mixture, L is the absorption pathlength used in recording the sample spectrum and a_{ij} is the absorptivity of the jth compound at the ith IR frequency. A_i, the absorbance spectrum, is obtained from the measured spectrum by normalizing the measured spectrum, S_i, by a background spectrum B, which is free of, or contains less, absorption due to volcanic gases:

$$A_i = -\log\left({S_i}/{B} \right). \tag{2}$$

The absorbance spectra, therefore, contain information pertaining only to the volcanic gas phase; all other background gases are canceled out by this procedure. The absorbance spectra, A_i, are baseline corrected (in each fitting region) before analysis, using a second-order polynomial, and they also are corrected for their temperature and pressure relative to the reference spectra. A calibration set of spectra of pure components at known concentrations are used to calculate the absorptivities a_{ij}.

The uncertainty in the measurements is calculated from the residual spectrum, which should have a mean of zero in the fitted region and is proportional to the square root of the sum of the squares of the residual:

$$\sigma^2 = \sum_i R_i^2 \Big/ (n-1), \tag{3}$$

where σ^2 is the error variance, R is the residual spectrum, and n is the number of observations. The standard error of the estimated concentration, ε, is equal to:

$$\varepsilon = \sigma C \Big/ \sqrt{\sum_i A_i^2}. \tag{4}$$

This technique allows the evaluation of precise concentration-pathlengths (*LCj* from equation 1) for each species, which have units of parts per million meters (ppm·m). The ratios of the concentration-pathlengths for different species in the plume typically are accurate to within a few percent, given appropriate analysis. The absolute values, however, are a minimum because the background spectrum, B, is not a clear-

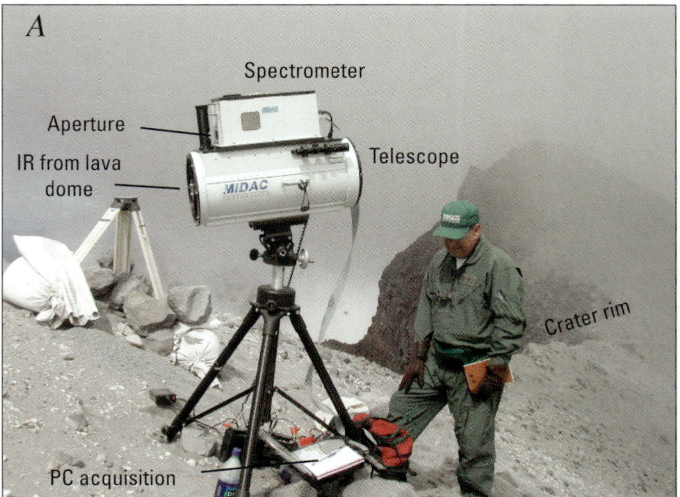

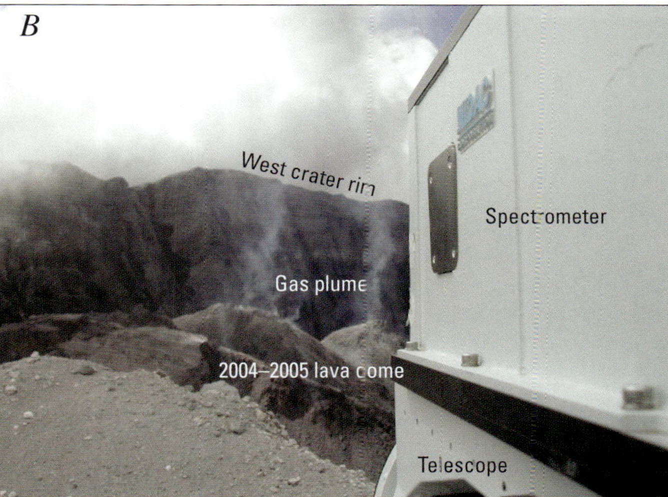

Figure 1. Fourier-transform infrared (FTIR) spectrometer in field settings. *A*, At FTIR measurement site (Brutus), on east crater rim of Mount St. Helens. *B*, Collecting radiation from hot cracks in the dacitic lava dome of Mount St. Helens, 2005. Volcanic gas is passing into the path in front of the infrared source.

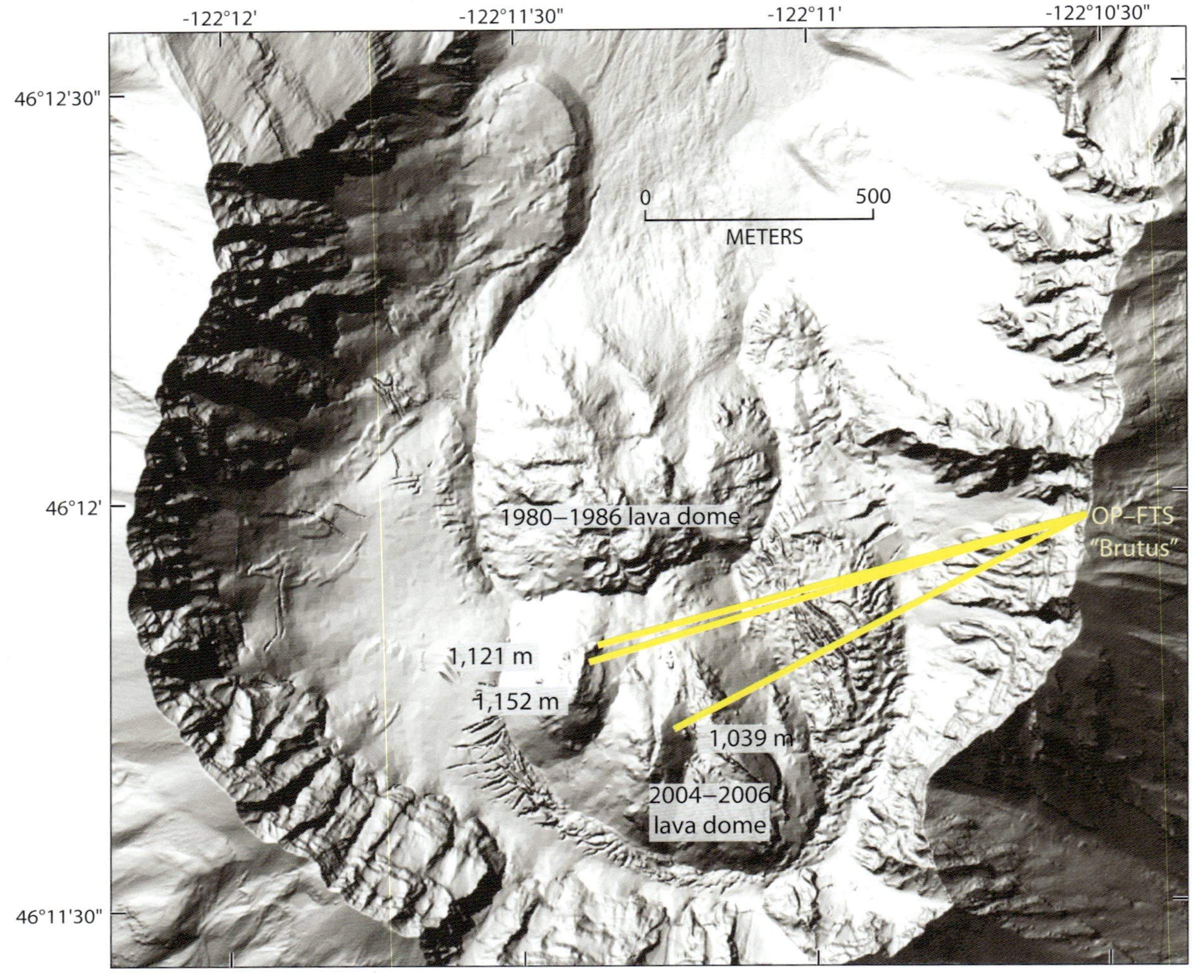

Figure 2. Shaded-relief digital elevation model of September 1, 2005, showing three paths used for OP–FTIR measurements in this study (courtesy of S.P. Schilling, USGS). Lengths of paths are labeled. Datum and projection are NAD83, UTM zone 10.

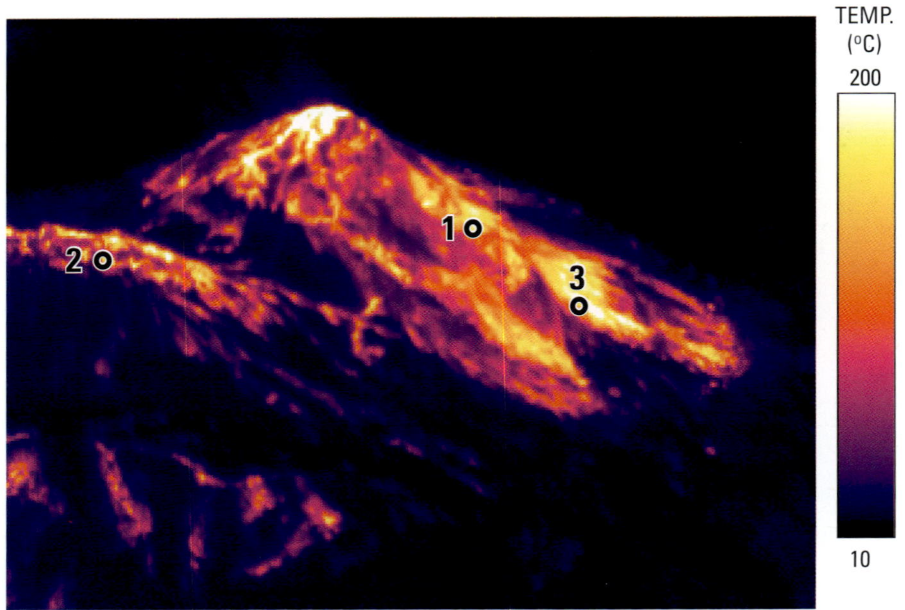

Figure 3. Thermal image, taken by forward-looking infrared radiometer (FLIR), showing lava dome from a helicopter near OP–FTIR measurement site (Brutus) on September 2, 2005 (courtesy of M. Logan, USGS). Numbers mark the parts of the lava dome used as infrared sources for measurement sets 1 to 3. Temperature scale on right.

Table 1. Summary of wavenumber windows used in analysis, detection limits, and mean errors for volcanic gas species detected by OP–FTIR in this study, Mount St. Helens, Washington, 2005.

Species	Wavenumber window (cm^{-1})	Detection limit (ppm·m)	Mean error (%)
H_2O	2134.80–2140.51	4,000	13.2
CO_2	2264.26–2273.20	2,000	15.3
HCl	2744.18–2848.38	3	7.6
SO_2	2447.36–2532.96	15	17.4
HF	4062.31–4089.16	20	14.1
CO	2089.29–2199.87	0.8	8.2
COS	2093.60–2020.87	0.7	7.6

sky spectrum for these measurements; rather, it is the spectrum containing the fewest molecules of volcanic gas in the series of measured spectra, S_i. A background spectrum under the exact conditions of the measurements containing no volcanic gas often is impossible to obtain in practice in this mode. Spectra were acquired once per second, and eight spectra were averaged, a procedure which typically took about 8 s.

In this study, retrievals for seven major volcanic gas species were carried out: H_2O, CO_2, HCl, SO_2, HF, CO, and COS. Retrievals for HCl and CO are relatively low in error, owing to their strong and fast absorption features; COS is detectable owing to its high absorptivity. Measured SO_2 exceeds detection limits, but the errors are larger owing to its weak absorption signature (at around 2,500 cm^{-1}). H_2O has a moderately high error owing to its high and variable background concentration derived from nonmagmatic, highly variable local sources, such as evaporating ground water, ice, and meteoric water. At these long pathlengths, background CO_2 is around 280,000 ppm·m, and, in order to be detected, volcanic CO_2 must be present at levels >5 percent above background levels. The errors and detection limits on the measurements are shown in table 1.

The results of the measurements take the form of molar ratios and gas compositions. The molar ratios are calculated by plotting the abundance (in concentration-pathlength units) of one gas species against another. The gas species will plot in a straight line if they are derived from a common origin (the volcanic vent) and a gas of constant composition is being emitted. All background gases, including random amounts of nonvolcanic H_2O, are eliminated from the results, owing to the normalization by background spectra. Any mixing of the volcanic gas with ambient air should, therefore, not affect the results unless chemical reactions are taking place, or unless there is significant heterogeneity in the atmospheric air composition in the pathlength (which is significant here for H_2O). The mean slope of the plots of gas abundances is equal to the molar ratio between the two species. Changes in the concentration-pathlength of a species with time are controlled by source effects (variations in the emission rate of gases), combined with fluctuating wind speeds and directions, which blow the plume gases out of the pathlength. Pairs of species concentration-pathlengths are used to calculate molar ratios, thereby eliminating these source and wind effects, as they will affect all gases similarly.

Emission rates for SO_2 were measured by absorption spectroscopy with a miniature spectrometer manufactured by Ocean Optics and an instrumental housing (incorporating calibration cells; FLYSPEC) and software developed by Horton and others (2006). Horizontal traverses were made beneath the plume, approximately 1.5 km downwind of the lava dome. Integrated concentration-pathlength across the plume width was multiplied by the plume speed (measured by using methodology developed by Doukas, 2002) to generate SO_2 emission rates. Three measurements of SO_2 emission rates were carried out, and errors are less than 10 percent.

Results

The spectra measured on August 31, 2005, record seven volcanic gas species: H_2O, CO_2, HCl, SO_2, HF, CO, and COS, in typical order of abundance for the three sets of measurements (fig. 2). The first set of measurements contained 109 spectra. The IR source for the measurements was part of spine 6, and the pathlength was 1,150 m (figs. 2, 3). These spectra recorded absorptions due to H_2O, HCl, CO, and COS gases; CO_2, SO_2, and HF were below detection, possibly due to a relatively low source temperature and (or) the long pathlength, both of which tend to decrease the signal-to-noise ratio. Figure 4 shows the characteristic absorption signature due to HCl gas in the measured spectra compared to a reference spectrum, the concentration-pathlength of H_2O and HCl, and the concentration-pathlengths of CO and COS with time for this set of measurements. Table 2 shows a summary of the data (labeled set 1) and includes mean and maximum concentrations measured for each species and the mean H_2O/Cl ratio. The relatively low abundances of all the detected gases (HCl, as much as 147 ppm·m, and H_2O, as much as 21,000 ppm·m) suggest that the abundances of CO_2 and SO_2 were probably below detection for this set of measurements. The mean H_2O/Cl molar ratio was 120 (table 2).

The second set of measurements were taken using a shorter pathlength of 1,040 m and a remnant of spine 5 as an IR source (figs. 2, 3). Figure 5 shows that HCl, HF, CO, and COS are detectable during the entire time period, whereas H_2O, CO_2, and SO_2 are detectable in only some of the spectra. Nondetection in some parts of the time series might be due to a weakening of the IR source or a decrease in gas-column abundance. The abundance of HCl ranged from 0 to 624 ppm·m over the pathlength, whereas SO_2 reached 251 ppm·m (table 2, set 2). Carbon monoxide reached a maximum concentration-pathlength of 15 ppm·m, and COS reached 2.6 ppm·m. The mean Cl/S ratio was 2.1, and H_2O/Cl was 85 (table 2).

The third set of measurements was taken using an IR source on spine 6, with a pathlength of 1,120 m (figs. 2, 3). This set of measurements imaged gases emitted from the

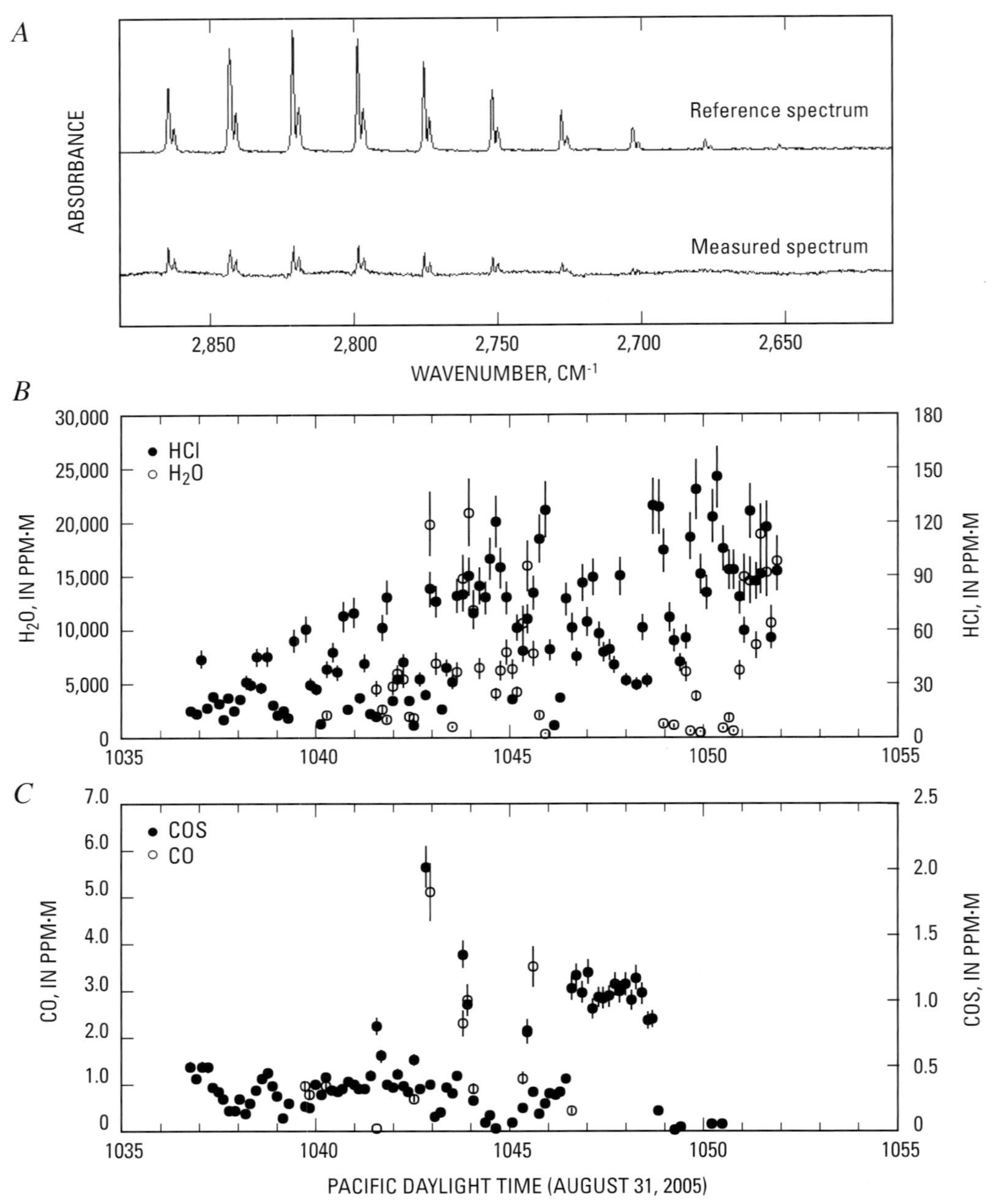

Figure 4. Data for measurement set 1, Mount St. Helens, Washington, 2005. *A*, Measured absorbance spectrum and reference spectrum for HCl gas for spectra collected along path 1. *B*, HCl and H_2O concentration pathlengths. *C*, CO and COS concentration pathlengths with time for measurement set 1.

Table 2. Summary of OP–FTIR measurements (sets 1, 2, and 3), Mount St. Helens, Washington, 2005.

[*N* is number of spectra in each set. Maximum $(LC)_{max}$ and mean $(LC)_{mean}$ are concentration pathlengths (in ppm·m) for the seven gas species detected; bd, below detection. Mean molar ratios are given with estimates of errors. Dashes show ratios not calculated where sulfur data are lacking.]

Set	HCl	SO_2	CO	CO_2	COS	H_2O	HF	Cl/S	Cl/F	H_2O/Cl	SO_2/COS	CO/CO_2
1 *N*=109												
$(LC)_{max}$	147	bd	5.1	bd	2.0	21,000	bd					
$(LC)_{mean}$	57.0	bd	1.7	bd	0.47	7,000	bd	--	--	120±25	--	--
2 *N*=479												
$(LC)_{max}$	624	251	15	10,300	2.6	51,000	310					
$(LC)_{mean}$	279	145	5.0	5,870	1.2	28,900	74	2.1±0.4	8.8±2.0	85±15	120±15	0.00086±0.0002
3 Active vent *N*=97												
$(LC)_{max}$	261	155	1.3	4,400	0.84	310,000	86					
$(LC)_{mean}$	110	121	0.42	1,300	0.35	64,000	40	1.1±0.3	3.5±2.0	1040±200	350±60	0.00032±0.00006

area closest to the active vent at the base of the most recently erupted spine. H_2O, CO_2, HCl, SO_2, HF, CO, and COS were detected in the absorption spectra (fig. 6 and table 2). The abundances of the gases were generally less than for measurement set 2; HCl concentration pathlengths reached 261 ppm·m, and SO_2 reached 155 ppm·m (table 2, set 3). The mean molar H_2O/Cl was 1,040 and Cl/S was 1.1. The molar ratios can be used to formulate a gas composition (table 3, column A). The gas was composed mainly of H_2O (99 mol percent), with 0.78 mol percent CO_2, 0.095 mol percent HCl, 0.085 mol percent SO_2, and minor amounts of HF, CO, and COS. For comparison, a gas sample collected in September 1981 (Gerlach and Casadevall, 1986) is shown in column D. Columns B and E show the same gas compositions recalculated to H_2O-free compositions, and columns C and F show them recalculated to H_2O- and CO_2-free compositions. The gas composition measured in 2005 is similar to that measured in 1981, albeit with less CO and more COS.

The ultraviolet spectrometer traverses carried out at 1400 PDT on August 31, 2005, yielded a mean SO_2 flux of 22 t/d. By converting the molar gas composition into the mass composition (table 4) for measurement set 3, the SO_2 emission rate (bold, table 4) can be used to calculate emission rates for the six other species. On August 31, 2005, H_2O was emitted at rates of about 83 kg/s (7,200 t/d), CO_2 at 1.6 kg/s (140 t/d), HCl at 0.16 kg/s (14 t/d), and HF at 0.024 kg/s (2.0 t/d). CO and COS were emitted at rates of 0.63 and 0.69 g/s, respectively; these fluxes are associated with errors of ~±20 percent. CO_2 emission rates were measured independently by using LICOR and were found to be 198 t/d (Gerlach and others, this volume, chap. 26). The excess can be attributed to a small amount of CO_2 degassing from the 1980–86 lava dome (Gerlach and others, this volume, chap. 26), which was not captured by the OP–FTIR measurements.

Discussion

Partitioning of Cl into Aqueous Vapor

Experimental work on Cl behavior in silicic magmas demonstrates the strong affinity that Cl has for a H_2O-rich vapor phase (Kilinc and Burnham, 1972; Webster and Holloway, 1988). The fluid-melt partition coefficient increases with decreasing temperature and with increasing dissolved melt Cl content; and decreases with decreasing pressure (Shinohara and others, 1989), although the latter is not well constrained. The partition coefficient is high for subaluminous melts and decreases with increasing aluminous or peralkaline character (Webster, 1992). Increasing the Cl molality of the vapor phase to high levels causes the formation of an immiscible Cl-rich liquid, as observed in the H_2O-NaCl system (Shinohara and others, 1989). Signorelli and Carroll (2002) determined Cl solubility limits of 4,800–6,800 ppm for the hydrous rhyolite melt of recent Soufrière Hills volcano eruptions, which has a (Na+K)/Al ~0.6. These concentrations are much higher than those observed in melt-inclusion glasses (Edmonds and others,

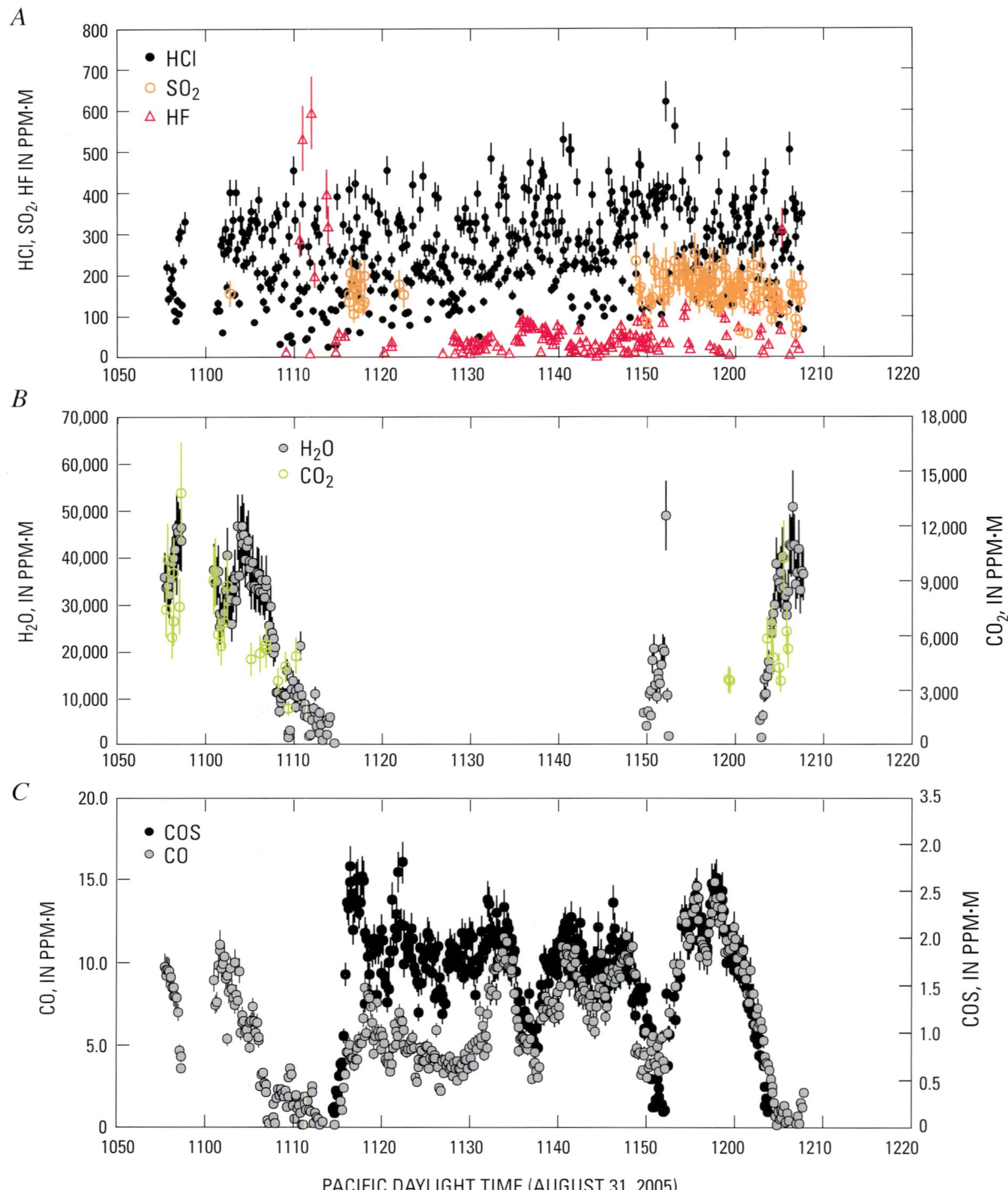

Figure 5. Data for measurement set 2, Mount St. Helens, Washington, 2005, as concentration pathlengths with time. *A*, HCl, HF, and SO_2. *B*, H_2O and CO_2. *C*, CO and COS.

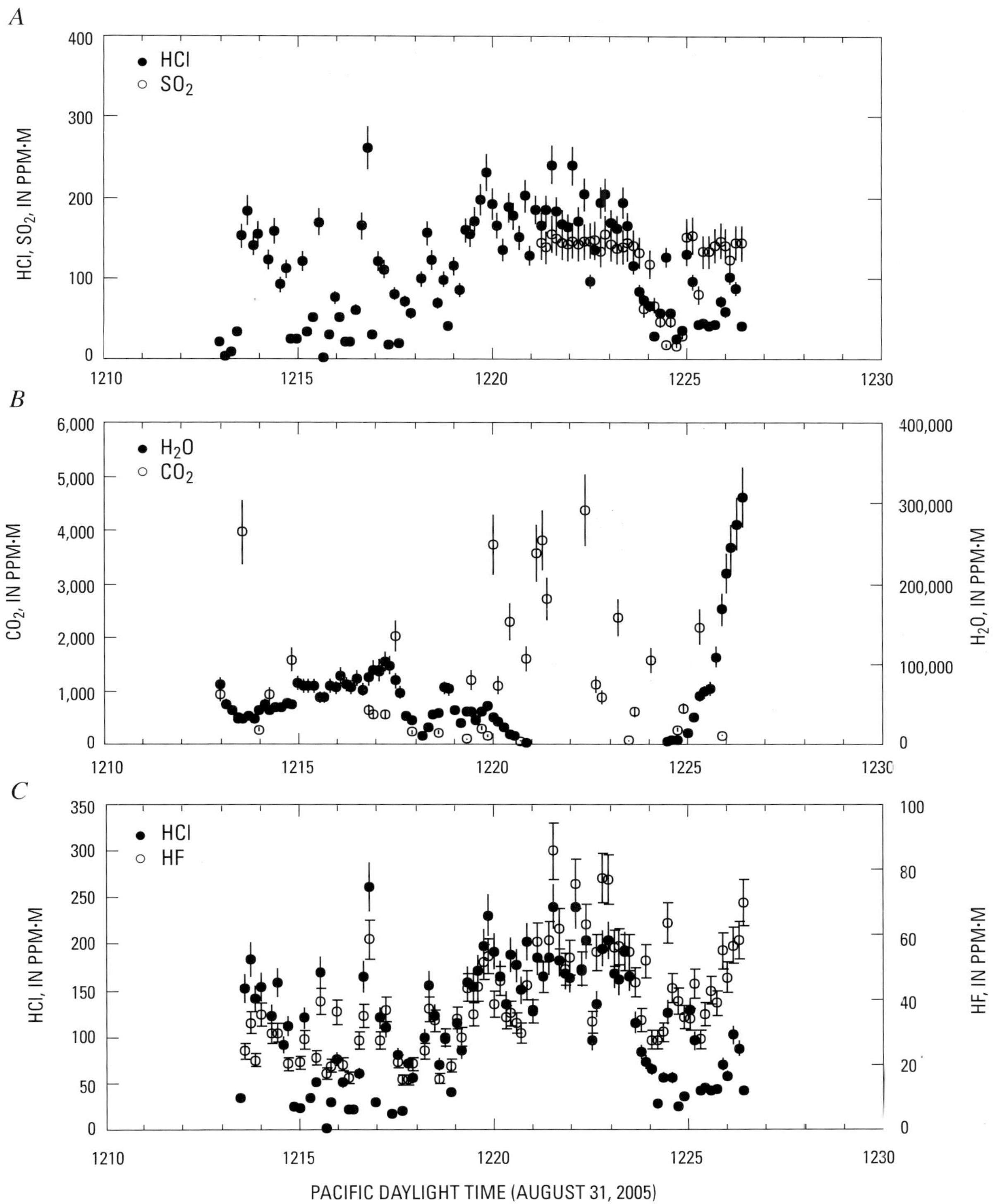

Figure 6. Data for measurement set 3, Mount St. Helens, Washington, 2005, as concentration pathlengths with time. *A*, HCl and SO_2. *B*, H_2O and CO_2. *C*, HCl and HF.

Table 3. Gas compositions at Mount St. Helens, 1981 and 2005.

[Compositions (in molar percent) derived from this study (column A) are compared with a representative gas composition derived from sampling of gases by using caustic soda in May 1981 (column D; Gerlach and Casadevall, 1986). Columns B and E show the gas compositions recalculated to H_2O-free compositions. Columns C and F show the gas compositions recalculated to H_2O- and CO_2-free compositions.]

	This study (set 3)			September 17, 1981		
	A	B	C	D	E	F
H_2O	99			99		
CO_2	0.78	79		0.89	83	
HCl	0.095	9.7	46	0.076	7.2	43
SO_2	0.085	8.6	41	0.067	6.3	38
HF	0.027	2.8	13	0.030	2.8	17
CO	0.00048	0.049	0.23	0.0023	0.22	1.3
COS	0.00025	0.025	0.12	1.8×10^{-5}	0.0017	0.010

Table 4. Gas composition derived from this study (from measurement set 3), Mount St. Helens, Washington, 2005, in molar percent and mass percent.

[Flux of each species is calculated using the flux of SO_2 gas measured with ultraviolet spectrometers (22 t/d; in bold). Fluxes expressed both in kg/s and in t/d.]

Species	Molar %	Mass %	Flux (kg/s)	Flux (t/d)
H_2O	99	98	83	7,200
CO_2	0.78	1.9	1.6	140
HCl	0.095	0.19	0.16	14
SO_2	0.085	0.30	0.25	**22**
HF	0.027	0.028	0.024	2.0
CO	0.00048	0.00073	0.00063	0.054
COS	0.00025	0.00080	0.00069	0.059

2002) and suggest that the aqueous vapor phase was relatively Cl poor. In the case of Mount St. Helens, melt-inclusion data for the erupted products of 1980–86 indicate that the maximum Cl content of the preeruptive melt was around 1,000 ppm (Rutherford and others, 1985), which is within the range of Cl concentrations in melt inclusions from the 2004–5 eruption of Mount St. Helens (Pallister and others, this volume, chap. 30) and is much lower than the solubility for Cl in a melt with (Na+K)/Al ~1 at 850–900°C and 200 MPa (around 2,000–2,500 ppm; Metrich and Rutherford, 1992). If the 2004–5 Mount St. Helens melt had an initial H_2O content of ~4.6 weight percent, similar to that obtained from melt-inclusion analysis for the 1980s erupted products (Rutherford and others, 1985), and if P_{total} is equal to P_{H_2O}, then the melt was in equilibrium with a H_2O-rich vapor at a depth of around 6 km (assuming lithostatic pressure with depth). The preeruption dissolved Cl content of the melt at about 6 km is assumed to be close to 1,000 ppm, on the basis of the maximum Cl concentration measured in melt inclusions (Pallister and others, this volume, chap. 30), which is within range of typical silicic arc magmas (Wallace, 2005).

The H_2O/HCl molar ratio of the vapor varies during melt ascent and eruption and is controlled by water solubility and degassing, partitioning of Cl into the vapor, the degassing regime (whether open- or closed-system degassing or some combination of the two is in operation), and microlite crystallization on ascent (which will tend to increase the concentration of volatiles in the melt and promote further degassing). These factors can be incorporated into models describing the evolution of the vapor phase on ascent and compared with the observations presented here. This analysis assumes there is no breakdown of hydrous phases (for example, amphibole), which would tend to increase the bulk H_2O of the system on magma ascent.

Closed-system degassing occurs when volatiles exsolve and remain in contact and in equilibrium with the host melt. The vesicularity of the melt is related to the amount of volatiles exsolved and the total pressure. Closed-system degassing can occur (1) during rapid ascent of magma from depth, resulting in fragmentation when the overpressure inside the expanding bubbles exceeds the strength of the magma, (2) in static magma bodies as a result of second boiling, and (3) during slow ascent of magma at depths of greater than a few kilometers, where gas fractions will typically be too low for fragmentation to occur. The partitioning of Cl between melt and aqueous vapor can be used to describe closed-system degassing:

$$\left(X^0_{H_2O} - X_{H_2O}\right) = \left(X^0_{Cl}/X_{Cl} - 1\right) \Big/ D_{Cl}^{fluid-melt}, \qquad (5)$$

where $X^0_{H_2O}$ and X^0_{Cl} are the original H_2O and Cl mass fractions, X_{H_2O} and X_{Cl} are the melt H_2O and Cl mass fractions, and $D_{Cl}^{fluid-melt}$ is the vapor-melt coefficient for Cl (assumed here to be constant). X_{H_2O} varies with pressure according to its solubility, which is calculated using VolatileCalc for a rhyolite melt at 920°C and with a $X^0_{H_2O}$ of 4.6 weight percent (Newman and Lowenstern, 2002).

Open-system degassing involves increments of vapor being removed from the host melt after exsolution. For volatiles that partition strongly into a vapor phase, this style of degassing results in efficient removal of the species from the melt. This style of degassing may occur (1) along conduit sidewalls, where exsolved volatiles can escape by migrating upward or through the conduit walls, or (2) during shallow, slow ascent of magma, when sufficient porosity develops to allow permeability and vapor escape through a three-dimensional bubble network (for example, Blower, 2001); significant gas loss through bubble ascent would be suppressed by the high viscosity of the magma and crystals. Open-system degassing can be modeled using a Rayleigh fractionation equation (for example, Villemant and Boudon, 1999):

$$X_{Cl} = X^0_{Cl} f^{\alpha}, \qquad (6)$$

$$\text{where } \alpha = \left(D_{Cl}^{fluid-melt} - 1\right), \qquad (7)$$

$$\text{and } f = 1 - \left[\left(X^0_{H_2O} - X_{H_2O}\right) \Big/ X^0_{H_2O}\right], \qquad (8)$$

where f is the fraction of water remaining in the melt. X_{Cl} is calculated for 5-MPa increments in pressure and converted to depth (km) assuming lithostatic pressures and a mean crustal density of 2,500 kg/m^3.

In order to account for microlite crystallization on ascent, which decreases the melt volume and causes increased exsolution of water, a factor q was introduced to the equation for the open-system degassing case, whereby

$$q = q^0 - q^0\left(\left(X^0_{H_2O} - X_{H_2O}\right) \Big/ X^0_{H_2O}\right), \qquad (9)$$

where q^0 is the initial melt fraction (taken to be 0.6). The expression for f, the fraction of H_2O remaining in the melt, is modified thus:

$$f = 1 - \left[\left(X^0_{H_2O} - X_{H_2O}\right) \Big/ X^0_{H_2O}\right] - \left[\left(\frac{q_n}{q_{n-1}}\right) X_{H_2O} - X_{H_2O}\right], \qquad (10)$$

where q_n is the melt fraction for the previous step and q_{n-1} is the melt fraction for the current step and $q_{n-1} < q_n$. This has the effect of decreasing f to a slightly greater degree at each step to account for the effects of microphenocryst and microlite crystallization.

Figure 7 shows the results for closed- and open-system degassing for three partition coefficients (*D*). These results show the large dependence of the vapor composition at the surface on degassing regime. The plots show the depletion of Cl in the melt, the ratio of dissolved H_2O/Cl, and the H_2O/Cl ratio in the vapor phase, with depth. Three measured parameters are marked on the plots to compare to the model data: (1) the mass fraction of dissolved Cl, (2) the H_2O/Cl in the matrix glass of the erupted products (for microcrystalline and flow-banded dacite; from Pallister and others, this volume, chap. 30; summarized in table 5), and (3) the mass ratio H_2O/Cl in the volcanic gases (converted from molar ratios given in table 2). The H_2O/Cl in gases from measurement sets 1 and 2 range from 35 to 70 and are labeled stagnant dome (SD), and those from measurement set 3 range from 430 to 630 and are labeled active dome (AD).

The mass fraction of Cl in the melt, dissolved melt H_2O/Cl, and vapor H_2O/Cl from the stagnant dome are consistent with closed-system degassing, with a large partition coefficient (*D*~50) for Cl, from depths of ~ 6 km. The active dome gases are richer in H_2O and are closer to the modeled H_2O/Cl for an open-system degassing regime. Open-system degassing from depth would deplete the melt almost entirely of Cl, however, which is not the case (figs. 7*A*, *B*); open-system degassing from depth is therefore inconsistent with observation. Closed-system degassing from depth with constant *D* is consistent with observation but unrealistic on two counts: (1) closed-system degassing could not physically lead to lava dome building, owing to the inevitably large gas fractions that would result at shallow depths, and (2) a constant partition coefficient for Cl is improbable, based on the experiments of Shinohara and others (1989), which suggests that *D* is strongly dependent on both dissolved melt Cl and on pressure.

Recent studies of degassing during the lava dome building of Soufrière Hills volcano, Montserrat, have shown that the degassing of H_2O in the upper conduit leads to cooling, crystallization, and an increase in viscosity of the magma (for example, Sparks and others, 2000). The development of permeability during degassing in the top ~1 km of the conduit leads to gas loss and effusive eruption. In order to investigate whether this mechanism is consistent with the proportions of H_2O and Cl in the melt and in volcanic gases at Mount St. Helens, the model is adjusted by using equation 5 in order to incorporate the effects of closed-system degassing at depths greater than 1 km with the same mean fluid-melt partition coefficients for Cl (3, 10, and 50), followed by open-system degassing along the top 1 km of the conduit (fig. 8), using equations 6–10 with fluid-melt partition coefficients of 1, 2, and 3 ($X^0_{H_2O}$ and X^0_{Cl} are set equal to the final X_{H_2O} and X_{Cl} given by the closed-system degassing model at 1-km depth; fig. 8). A partition coefficient of 1 represents the case whereby no further degassing of Cl occurs. The plots in figures 7 and 8 are, therefore, identical up to 1-km depth; at shallower depths, the effects of open-system degassing are shown in figure 8. Observations of the melt and gases are marked on figure 8 to compare to the models. The mass fraction of Cl remaining dissolved in the melt, the melt H_2O/Cl, and the H_2O/Cl for gases emitted from the stagnant part of the lava dome are consistent with deep, closed-system degassing (*D*~10), followed by open-system degassing with *D*~2–3 (fig. 8). A decrease in *D* to <5 was noted by Shinohara and others (1989) for lithostatic pressures corresponding to depths less than 2 km.

Table 5. Mean concentrations of Cl and H_2O in erupted matrix glasses of microcrystalline (from 5 measurements) and flow-banded (from 12 measurements) dacite, Mount St. Helens, Washington, 2004–2005.

[From Pallister and others, this volume, chap. 30.]

Matrix glass	Cl (ppm)	H_2O (wt%)	H_2O/Cl
Microcrystalline dacite			
Mean concentration	278	1.40	41
1σ deviation	53	0.98	24
Flow-banded dacite			
Mean concentration	853	2.40	28
1σ deviation	47	0.29	4.5

The H_2O/Cl of gases emitted from the active part of the lava dome, however, are not consistent with any of the theoretical models formulated here. This may be due to one or all of three factors: (1) a cessation of Cl degassing in the top 1 km of the conduit, (2) addition of substantial amounts of meteoric, ground-water, and glacier-derived H_2O to the gases at shallow

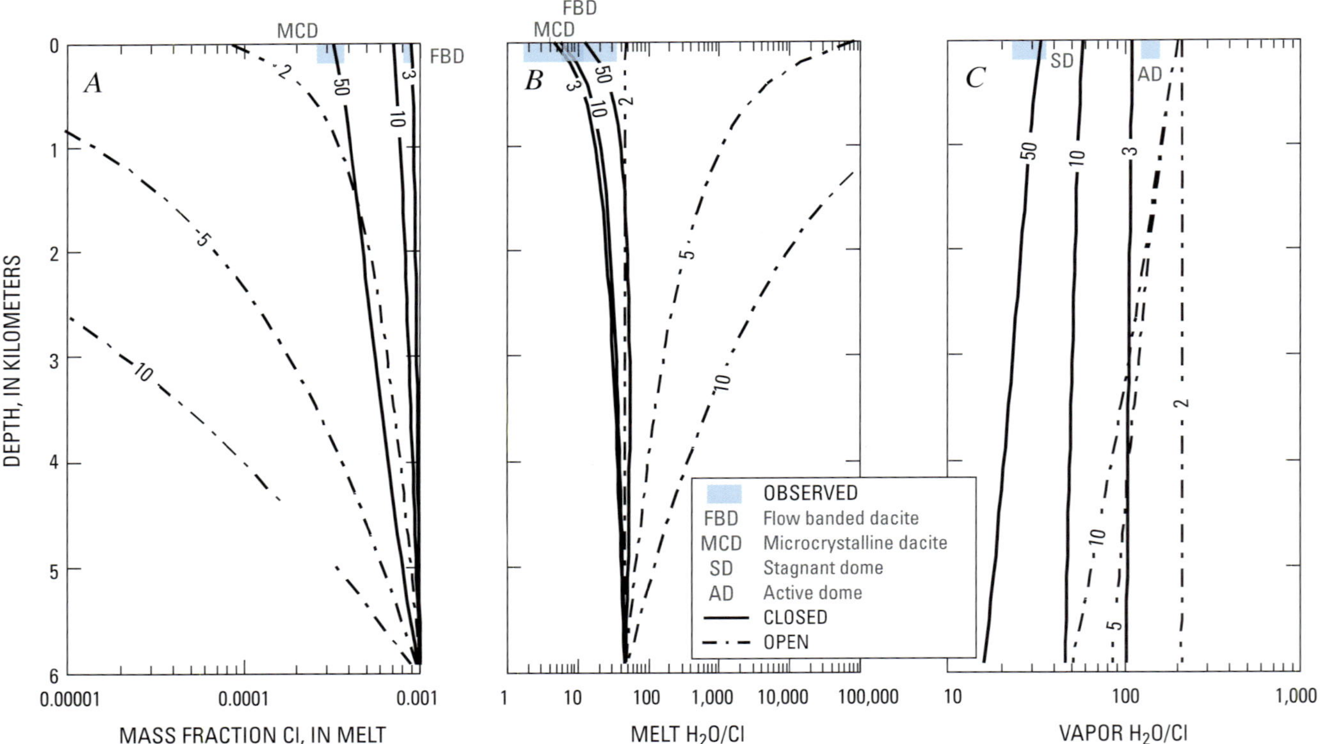

Figure 7. Effect on evolution of gases with depth for various models of degassing regime. Solid lines indicate closed-system degassing models and are labeled with the fluid-melt partition coefficient, D. Dot-dash lines indicate open-system degassing models and are labeled with the fluid-melt partition coefficient. Blue boxes indicate observed melt Cl, melt H_2O/Cl, and vapor H_2O/Cl. *A*, Fraction of Cl in melt. *B*, Dissolved melt H_2O/Cl. *C*, vapor H_2O/Cl.

depths, or (3) some Cl present as alkali chloride (NaCl and KCl) in the gas phase, as observed by Le Guern and Shinohara (1985) and studied experimentally by Shinohara and others (1989). The proportions of dissolved H_2O and Cl remaining in the erupted glasses suggests that there is no cessation of Cl degassing in the top 1 km of the conduit (fig. 8; compare observations to solid line presenting D=1), so this factor is discounted. Shevenell and Goff (1999) used oxygen- and hydrogen-isotope data from hot springs to show that only 30–70 mol percent of the H_2O in the fumaroles around the lava dome in 1981–86 was magmatic. In this case, the discrepancy between models and observations requires that only ~10 mol percent of the measured H_2O be magmatic. Modification of the gas composition is shown in table 3, column A; using this factor yields 91 mol percent H_2O and 7 mol percent CO_2, which might be more representative of the magmatic gas composition. The presence of alkali chlorides in the gas phase is consistent with the presence of chloride encrustations on the lava dome (possibly halite and (or) sylvite) observed during 2004–5 (C.R. Thornber, oral comm. 2005). Yellow encrustations on the September 1980 lava dome were noncrystalline and composed of Al, Cl, Fe, Ca, S, and H_2O. A sublimate film near fumaroles <250°C produced a yellow-brown stain on crack walls, which had a high Cl content (Keith and others, 1981).

Comparison and Significance of Molar Cl/S

The behavior of S in silicic melts differs significantly from both Cl and H_2O. The partitioning of sulfur into a vapor phase is controlled by several factors, the most significant being the fugacities of oxygen and sulfur in the vapor phase and melt composition (Carroll and Webster, 1994). The solubility of sulfur is much lower than that of Cl for a given set of magmatic conditions. Table 6 shows molar Cl/S measured using a variety of techniques during eruptions at a range of dacitic and andesitic subduction-zone volcanoes, including the 1980–86 Mount St. Helens lava-dome eruption. The molar ratio measured during this study is similar (within error) to ratios measured at most other volcanoes and to ratios measured during the 1980–86 Mount St. Helens eruption, with the notable exception of Soufrière Hills volcano, which shows considerably higher Cl/S during lava dome-building activity. A molar Cl/S of ~1 appears to be a dominant feature of most reported gas compositions measured during eruptions in subduction-zone settings.

Botcharnikov and others (2004) reported solubility data for melts coexisting with mixed H_2O-Cl-S gases to illustrate the effect of multiple volatile components on their solubility. The total Cl content of the melt-vapor system can affect the

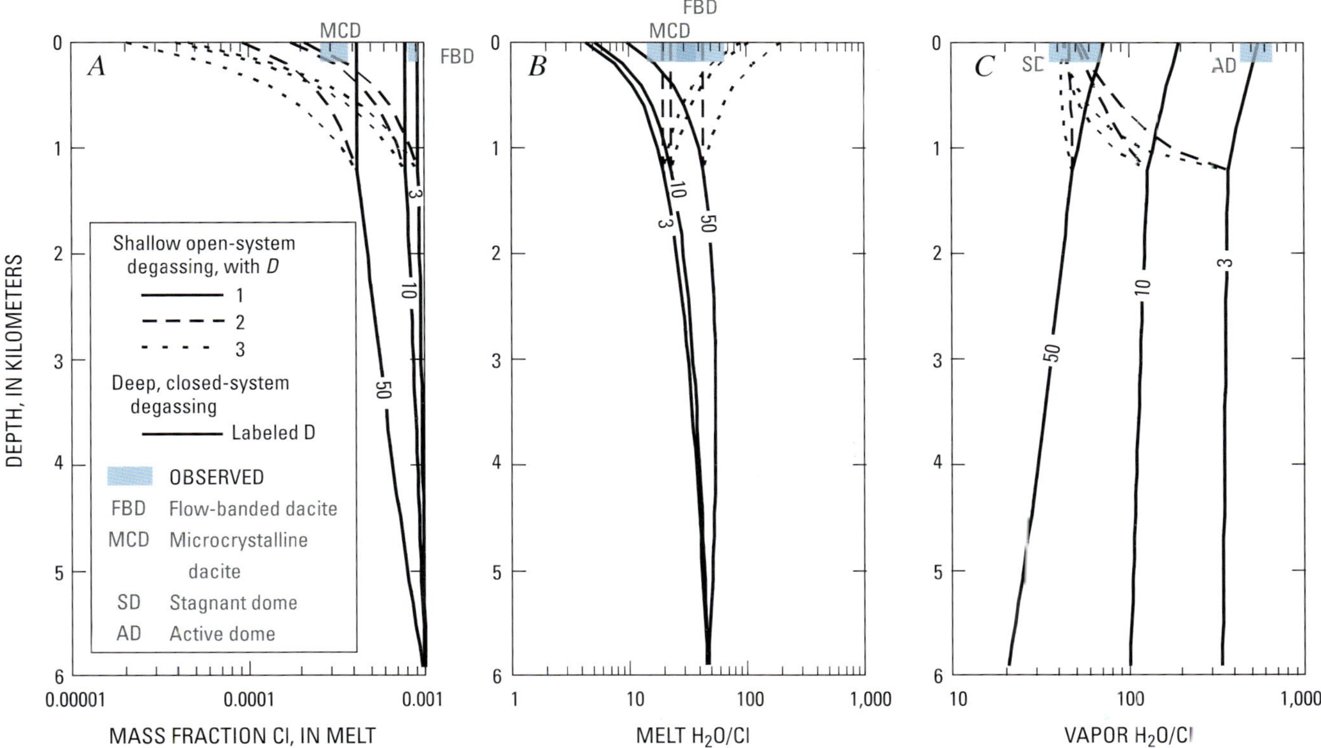

Figure 8. Effect of closed, then open-system (in the upper 1 km of the conduit) degassing on the composition of volcanic gases at the surface. The evolution of (*A*) the fraction of Cl in the melt, (*B*) dissolved melt H_2O/Cl, and (*C*) vapor H_2O/Cl with depth (km) for various models of degassing regime are shown. Closed-system degassing regimes are indicated by solid lines up to 1 km depth, labeled with values of D. Above 1 km depth, open-system degassing regimes are shown as dashed-dotted lines for three different values of D (see key). Observed melt Cl, melt H_2O/Cl, and vapor H_2O/Cl are shown as blue boxes.

Table 6. Molar Cl/S ratios in volcanic gases measured at other silicic subduction-zone volcanoes and at Mount St. Helens, Washington, 2005.

[Errors are estimated as ranging from 5 to 10 percent. OP–FTIR, open-path Fourier-transform IR spectroscopy; EBS, evacuated bottle sampling.]

Volcano	Type	Method	Cl/S
Usu-san, Japan[1]	Basaltic andesite	OP–FTIR	0.8
Mount St. Helens, USA[2]	Dacite	EBS	1.2
Mount St. Helens, USA[3]	Dacite	OP–FTIR	1.1
Augustine Volcano, USA[4]	Dacite	EBS	1.0
Unzen-dake, Japan[5]	Dacite	OP–FTIR	0.9
Soufrière Hills, Montserrat[6]	Andesite	OP–FTIR	2.0

[1]Mori and others, 1997.

[2]Gerlach and Casadevall, 1986.

[3]This study.

[4]Symonds and others, 1990.

[5]Mori and others, 1993.

[6]Edmonds and others, 2002.

solubility of S (Botcharnikov and others, 2004). The addition of 1 weight percent Cl increased S solubility by two times at 850°C and 200 MPa for a dacite-composition melt, with all other conditions constant. For a given H_2O vapor concentration, over a range of total S content and solubility, a maximum S solubility occurred corresponding to a vapor Cl/S of ~1. A vapor Cl/S of ~1 may, therefore, be a direct consequence of the presence of moderate amounts of Cl in the melt, which is typical for arc magmas; vapor Cl/S might further be buffered by the addition or depletion of small amounts of Cl to the system. The maximum in S solubility might be explained by two main factors (Botcharnikov and others, 2004): (1) S is dissolved as sulphate (SO_4^{2-}) in hydrous melts, where oxygen fugacity is relatively high, and as sulfide (S^{2-}) at low oxygen fugacities (Carroll and Webster, 1994); the transition occurs at oxygen fugacities close to NNO. The addition of Cl to an S-bearing system might shift the redox conditions to slightly more oxidized conditions. The other possibility is (2) that S-Cl-bearing complexes may form in the melt, which would increase the solubilities of both components.

The Abundance of Minor Gaseous Components (HF, CO, COS)

The solubility of fluorine (F) in silicic melts is generally much higher than that of Cl and, hence, does not degas to the same extent (Carroll and Webster, 1994). The vapor-melt partition coefficient for F is usually less than unity (Webster, 1990). Table 2 shows that the molar ratio of Cl/F in the volcanic gases is around 3.5. A similar molar Cl/F has been reported at a number of other silicic volcanoes in subduction-zone settings (Symonds and others, 1994) and compares well with the abundance of HF emitted from fumaroles at Mount St. Helens in September 1981 (table 3; Gerlach and Casadevall, 1986).

The mean CO/CO_2 ratio of the gases of around 3.2×10^{-4} (table 2) implies that the gases equilibrated at a temperature of about 570°C, on the basis of the relation:

$$\log\left(CO/CO_2\right) = 1.76 - 4417/T, \qquad (11)$$

where T is the temperature in Kelvin (Mori and Notsu, 1997). Collection temperatures derived from similar relations in gases sampled in 1981 ranged from 620°C to 762°C (Gerlach and Casadevall, 1986).

COS has been detected previously in volcanic plumes (for example, Le Guern and others, 1975), although measurements are few. Rasmussen and others (1982) reported abundances of 5 ppm by volume in the Mount St Helens gas plume of May 18, 1980, and suggested that injection of COS contributes to the stratospheric S burden during large silicic eruptions. Gerlach and Casadevall (1986) report molar SO_2/COS of 2,000 to 4,750 for gas samples collected at Mount St Helens from May to September 1981 from radial fumaroles around the lava dome. The mean molar ratios obtained August 31, 2005, using OP–FTIR are much lower than they were in the earlier samples, 350 (table 2, set 3) and 120 (set 2). Mori and Notsu (1997) reported SO_2 / COS of 400 for gases emitted from a fumarole at Aso, Japan, at a temperature of ~740°C.

Conclusions

Several conclusions can be drawn from the results and interpretation presented here:

- The fluxes of magmatic volatiles from Mount St. Helens on August 31, 2005, were 7,200 t/d H_2O, 140 t/d CO_2, 14 t/d HCl, 22 t/d SO_2, 2.0 t/d HF, 54 kg/d CO, and 59 kg/d COS.
- The H_2O/Cl ratio in the gases emitted from stagnant parts of the Mount St Helens lava dome, and the amount of Cl and the H_2O/Cl in the erupted glasses in the melt, are all consistent with a model of closed-system degassing up to ~ 1-km depth (with a fluid-melt partition coefficient, *D*, for Cl of ~10), followed by open-system degassing to the surface (with a *D* of ~2–3). This is similar to models proposed for lava dome-building eruptions elsewhere, where much of the gas loss occurs in the upper 1 km of the conduit, causing cooling, crystallization, and an increase in magma viscosity.
- The gases emitted from the active part of the Mount St Helens lava dome have an H_2O/Cl that is about one order of magnitude higher than that predicted for closed- or open-system degassing or the two-stage model above. This is explained by as much as 90 mol percent of the measured H_2O vapor being nonmagmatic (ground- or glacier-derived) and by some of the Cl being present as alkali chlorides in the gas phase (NaCl and KCl).
- Molar Cl/S in the gases measured in August 2005 is similar to that measured during 1980–86 at Mount St. Helens and at silicic subduction-zone volcanoes elsewhere during similar styles of eruption. This similarity may be caused by a maximum in S solubility when vapor Cl/S ~1, which is valid for the typical range in initial S and Cl (100–300 and 1,000–3,000 ppm, respectively) at silicic subduction-zone volcanoes.
- The gas analyses presented here confirm that remote spectroscopic techniques are capable of measuring the composition of high-temperature gases remotely and safely during lava dome building at silicic volcanoes, provided the measurements can be made using a pathlength ≤1 km with sufficient gas molecules in the path to enable detection. There is scope for automated measurements with more compact instruments that consume less power, enabling the development of time series and further analysis of the degassing regime throughout an eruption.

Acknowledgments

This work was done with the support of the USGS Mendenhall Postdoctoral Fellowship Program and the Center for the Study of Active Volcanoes (CSAV) at the University of Hawai`i, Hilo. Michelle Coombs and Jacob Lowenstern provided detailed and thorough reviews, which improved the manuscript enormously.

References Cited

Blower, J.D., 2001, Factors controlling permeability-porosity relationships in magma: Bulletin of Volcanology, v. 63, no. 7, p. 497–504.

Botcharnikov, R.E., Behrens, H., Holtz, F., Koepke, J., and Sato, H., 2004, Sulfur and chlorine solubility in Mt. Unzen rhyodacitic melt at 850°C and 200 MPa: Chemical Geology, v. 213, no. 1–3, p. 207–225.

Burton, M.R., Allard, P., Mure, F., and Oppenheimer, C., 2003, FTIR remote sensing of fractional magma degassing at Mount Etna, Sicily: Geological Society Special Publication, v. 213, p. 281–293.

Carroll, M.R., and Webster, J.D., 1994, Solubilities of sulfur, noble gases, nitrogen, chlorine and fluorine in magmas: Reviews in Mineralogy, v. 30, p. 231–280.

Dixon, J.E., Stolper, E.M., and Holloway, J.R., 1995, An experimental study of water and carbon dioxide solubilities in mid-ocean ridge basaltic liquids; Part I, Calibration and solubility models: Journal of Petrology, v. 36, no. 6, p. 1607–1631.

Doukas, M.P., 2002, A new method for GPS-based wind speed determinations during airborne volcanic plume measurements: U.S. Geological Survey Open-File Report 02–395, 13 p.

Edmonds, M., Pyle, D.M., and Oppenheimer, C., 2002, *HCl* emissions at Soufrière Hills Volcano, Montserrat, West Indies, during a second phase of dome building, November 1999 to September 2000: Bulletin of Volcanology, v. 64, p. 21–30.

Edmonds, M., Gerlach, T.M., Herd, R.A., Sutton, A.J., and Elias, T., 2005, The composition of volcanic gas issuing from Pu‘u ‘Ō‘ō, Kīlauea Volcano, Hawai‘i, 2004–5 [abs.]: Eos (American Geophysical Union Transactions), v. 86, no. 52, San Francisco, December 5–9, 2005. Fall Meet. Suppl. Abstract, V13G–08.

Francis, P.W., Maciejewski, A., and Oppenheimer, C., 1995, SO_2/HCl ratios in the plumes from Mt. Etna and Vulcano determined by Fourier transform spectroscopy: Geophysical Research Letters, v. 22, p. 1717–1720.

Gerlach, T.M., and Casadevall, T.J., 1986, Evaluation of gas data from high-temperature fumaroles at Mount St. Helens, 1980–1982: Journal of Volcanology and Geothermal Research, v. 28, nos. 1–2, p. 107–140, doi:10.1016/0377-0273(86)90008-9.

Gerlach, T.M., McGee, K.A., and Doukas, M.P., 2008, Emission rates of CO_2, SO_2, and H_2S, scrubbing, and preeruption excess volatiles at Mount St. Helens, 2004–2005, chap. 26 *of* Sherrod, D.R., Scott, W.E., and Stauffer, P.H., eds., A volcano rekindled; the renewed eruption of Mount St. Helens, 2004–2006: U.S. Geological Survey Professional Paper 1750 (this volume).

Horton, K.A., William-Jones, G., Garbeil, H., Elias, T., Sutton, A.J., Mouginis-Mark, P., Porter, J.N., and Clegg, S., 2006, Real-time measurement of volcanic SO_2 emissions—validation of a new UV correlation spectrometer (FLYSPEC): Bulletin of Volcanology, v. 68, no. 4, p. 323–327, doi:10.1007/s00445-005-0014-9.

Keith, T.E.C., Casadevall, T.J., and Johnston, D.A., 1981, Fumarole encrustations—occurrence, mineralogy and chemistry, *in* Lipman, P.W., and Mullineaux, D.R., eds., The 1980 eruptions of Mount St. Helens, Washington: U.S. Geological Survey Professional Paper 1250, p. 239–250.

Kilinc, I.A., and Burnham, C.W., 1972, Partitioning of chloride between a silicate melt and coexisting aqueous phase from 2 to 8 kilobars: Economic Geology, v. 67, p. 231–235.

Le Friant, A., Boudon, G., Komorowski, J.-C., and Deplus, C., 2002. The island of Dominica, site for the generation of the most voluminous debris avalanches in the Lesser Antilles: Comptes Rendus Geoscience, v. 334, no. 4, p. 235–243, doi:10.1016/S1631-0713(02)01742-X.

Le Guern, F., and Shinohara, H., 1985, Etna 1983 composition of the magmatic gases [abs.]: International Association of Volcanology and Chemistry of the Earth's Interior, General Assembly 1985, Giardini-Naxos, Italy, abstract vol. no. QE272 I58 A2 1985.

Le Guern, F., Giggenbach, W., and Tazieff, H., 1975, Equilibres chemiques des gaz eruptifs du volcan Erta`Ale (Ethiopie): Comptes Rendus Hebdominaires des Seances de l'Aacademie des Sciences, Serie D: Sciences naturelles, v. 280, p. 2093–2095.

Lowenstern, J.B., Mahood, G.A., Rivers, M.L., and Sutton, S.R., 1991, Evidence for extreme partitioning of copper into a magmatic vapor phase: Science, v. 252, p. 1405–1409.

Manning, C., 2004. The chemistry of subduction-zone fluids: Earth and Planetary Science Letters, v. 223, p. 1–16.

Metrich, N., and Rutherford, M.J., 1992, Experimental study of chlorine behavior in hydrous silicic melts: Geochimica et Cosmochimica Acta, v. 56, p. 607–616.

Mori, T., and Notsu, K., 1997, Remote CO, COS, CO_2, SO_2, HCl detection and temperature estimation of volcanic gas: Geophysical Research Letters, v. 24, no. 16, p. 2047–2050.

Mori, T., Notsu, K., Tohjima, Y., and Wakita, H., 1993, Remote detection of HCl and SO_2 in volcanic gas from Unzen Volcano, Japan: Geophysical Research Letters, v. 20, no. 13, p. 1355–1358.

Newman, S., and Lowenstern, J.B., 2002, VolatileCalc—a silicate melt-H_2O-CO_2 solution model written in Visual Basic for excel®: Computers and Geosciences, v. 28, no. 5, p. 597–604, doi:10.1016/S0098-3004(01)00081-4.

Pallister, J.S., Thornber, C.R., Cashman, K.V., Clynne, M.A., Lowers, H.A., Mandeville, C.W., Brownfield, I.K., and Meeker, G.P., 2008, Petrology of the 2004–2006 Mount St. Helens lava dome—implications for magmatic plumbing and eruption triggering, chap. 30 *of* Sherrod, D.R., Scott, W.E., and Stauffer, P.H., eds., A volcano rekindled; the renewed eruption of Mount St. Helens, 2004–2006: U.S. Geological Survey Professional Paper 1750 (this volume).

Rasmussen, R.A., Khalil, M.A.K., Dalluge, R.W., Penkett, S.A., and Jones, B., 1982, Carbonyl sulfide and carbon disulfide from the eruptions of Mount St. Helens: Science, v. 215, p. 665–667.

Rutherford, M.J., Sigurdsson, H., Carey, S., and Davis, A., 1985, The May 18, 1980 eruption of Mount St. Helens—1. Melt composition and experimental phase equilibria: Journal of Geophysical Research, v. 90, no. B4, p. 2929–2947.

Shevenell, L., and Goff, F., 1999, Addition of magmatic volatiles into the hot spring waters of Loowit Canyon, Mount St. Helens, Washington, USA: Bulletin of Volcanology, v. 55, no. 7, p. 489–503, doi:10.1007/BF00304592.

Shinohara, H., Iiyama, J.T., and Matsuo, S., 1989, Partition of chlorine compounds between silicate melt and hydrothermal solutions—1. Partition of NaCl-KCl: Geochimica et Cosmochimica Acta, v. 53, p. 2617–2630.

Signorelli, S., and Carroll, M.R., 2002, Experimental constraints on the origin of chlorine emissions at the Soufriere Hills Volcano, Montserrat: Bulletin of Volcanology, v. 62, p. 431–440.

Sparks, R.S.J., Murphy, M.D., Lejeune, A.M., Watts, R.B., Barclay, J., and Young, S.R., 2000, Control on the emplacement of the andesite lava dome of the Soufrière Hills Volcano, Montserrat, by degassing-induced crystallization: Terra Nova, v. 12, no. 1, p. 14–20.

Stoiber, R.E., and Rose, W.I., 1974, Cl, F, and SO_2 in Central American volcanic gases: Bulletin Volcanologique, v. 37, no. 3, p. 454–460.

Symonds, R.B., Rose, W.I., Gerlach, T.M., Briggs, P.H., and Harmon, R.S., 1990, Evaluation of gases, condensates, and

SO_2 emissions from Augustine Volcano, Alaska—the degassing of a Cl-rich volcanic system: Bulletin of Volcanology: v. 52, p. 355–374.

Symonds, R.B., Rose, W.I., Bluth, G.J.S., and Gerlach, T.M., 1994, Volcanic-gas studies—methods, results and applications: Reviews in Mineralogy, v. 30, p. 1–66.

Tabazedeh, A., and Turco, R.P., 1993, Stratospheric chlorine injection by volcanic eruptions; HCl scavenging and implications for ozone: Science, v. 260, no. 5111, p. 1082–1086.

Villemant, B., and Boudon, G., 1999, H_2O and halogen (F, Cl, Br) behaviour during shallow magma degassing processes: Earth and Planetary Sciences, v. 168, p. 271–286.

Wallace, P.J., 2005, Volatiles in subduction-zone magmas—concentrations and fluxes based on melt inclusion and volcanic gas data: Journal of Volcanology and Geothermal Research, v. 140, nos. 1–4, p. 217–240, doi:10.1016/j.jvolgeores.2004.07.023.

Webster, J.D., 1990, Partitioning of F between H_2O and CO_2 fluids and topaz rhyolite melt—implications for mineralizing magmatic-hydrothermal fluids in F-rich granitic system: Contributions to Mineralogy and Petrology, v. 104, p. 424–438.

Webster, J.D., 1992, Water solubility and Cl partitioning in Cl-rich granitic system; effects of melt composition at 2 kbar and 800°C: Geochimica et Cosmochimica Acta, v. 56, p. 679–687.

Webster, J.D., and Holloway, J.R., 1988, Experimental constraints on the partitioning of Cl between topaz rhyolite melt and H_2O and H_2O+CO_2 fluids—new implications for granitic differentiation and ore deposition: Geochimica et Cosmochimica Acta, v. 52, p. 2091–2105.

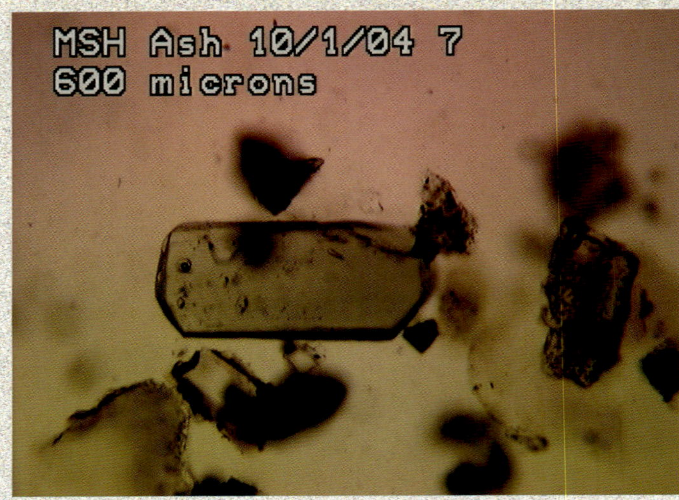
MSH Ash 10/1/04 7
600 microns

Petrological and Geochemical Investigations of Eruptive Products

Magma—erupt it passively to produce lava flows or domes; erupt it explosively and it is deposited as pyroclastic flows and tephra falls. Either way the products can be sampled and studied in great detail. Locked in the glass and minerals of lava flows and tephra is a complex, sometimes fragmentary record of a magma's temperature and pressure during ascent and eruption. Advances in analytical technology now allow the probing of single grains for their short-lived radioactive nuclides. The ratios of these isotopes vary at known rates, so that an absolute sense of time can be imposed on the petrologic processes. Thus texture, mineralogy, and chemistry provide wide-ranging insight into the conditions of magma formation, transport, storage, and eruption.

Is the 2004–6 lava the gas-depleted residuum of the 1980s eruption? Petrochemical details and short-lived isotopes suggest that it is—that the newly erupted dacite is mostly or entirely derived from the same reservoir as the 1980s magma.

Is new magma necessary to account for the compositional changes seen? That answer is less clear. Some component of hotter dacitic magma (possibly injected during earthquake swarms in the 1990s?) could have influenced the overall magma composition and shifted the abundance of certain indicator elements. Growth patterns and isotopic values tell us that a substantial proportion of the plagioclase phenocrysts grew at about the time of the 1980s eruption. The iron-titanium oxide geothermometer indicates magmatic temperatures of about 850°C; higher temperatures, above 1,000°C in some cases, may be explained by recharge of hotter magma at depth (which left no telltale geochemical, mineralogical, or petrographic signature) or by latent heat released during the rapid and shallow groundmass crystallization. The geochemical fingerprints of the 2004–6 magma are too fuzzy to identify a single scenario for the eruption, but they point toward a timeline that began more than a decade before magma reached the surface in October 2004.

An unusual perspective, this oblique view west as taken from the International Space Station on October 28, 2008. Much of the rugged terrain in the amphitheater is the new dome, but the 1980s dome can be recognized. The Breach drains north to Spirit Lake, seen at right of center. NASA photo by the Expeditiion 18 crew. (http://earthobservatory.nasa.gov/IOTD/view.php?id=36298)

A Volcano Rekindled: The Renewed Eruption of Mount St. Helens, 2004–2006
Edited by David R. Sherrod, William E. Scott, and Peter H. Stauffer
U.S. Geological Survey Professional Paper 1750, 2008

Chapter 28

The Pleistocene Eruptive History of Mount St. Helens, Washington, from 300,000 to 12,800 Years Before Present

By Michael A. Clynne[1], Andrew T. Calvert[1], Edward W. Wolfe[2], Russell C. Evarts[1], Robert J. Fleck[1], and Marvin A. Lanphere[1]

Abstract

We report the results of recent geologic mapping and radiometric dating that add considerable detail to our understanding of the eruptive history of Mount St. Helens before its latest, or Spirit Lake, stage. New data and reevaluation of earlier work indicate at least two eruptive periods during the earliest, or Ape Canyon, stage, possibly separated by a long hiatus: one about 300–250 ka and a second about 160–35 ka. Volcanism during this stage included eruption of biotite- and quartz-bearing dacite domes and pyroclastic flows in the area west of and beneath the present-day edifice, accompanied by the deposition of set C tephras. Ape Canyon-stage rocks are compositionally similar to younger Mount St. Helens dacite.

The Cougar stage, about 28–18 ka, was probably the most active eruptive stage in Mount St. Helens' history before the Spirit Lake stage. During the Cougar stage, a debris avalanche buried the area south of the present-day edifice, and voluminous pyroclastic flows, dacite domes, tephra, and a large-volume pyroxene andesite lava flow were erupted. Two tephra sets, M and K, were deposited midway through this stage.

Swift Creek-stage deposits were emplaced in two phases, beginning about 16 ka and ending about 12.8 ka. During the first phase, set S tephras and three large fans and at least one smaller fan of dacitic fragmental material were deposited on the northwest, west, south, and southeast flanks of Mount St. Helens. The fans are dominated by lithic pyroclastic-flow deposits associated with dome building but include both primary and reworked material from pumiceous pyroclastic flows and lahars. One Swift Creek-age dome on the west flank of the volcano has been located, and others must have been nearby. During the second phase, set J tephras were deposited, but no pyroclastic flows or domes are known to be associated with the andesitic set J tephras.

Preliminary petrographic analysis of these older rocks suggests that the volcano's magmatic system was simpler during the Ape Canyon stage than during subsequent stages and that the magmatic system has evolved from relatively simple to more complex as the volcano matured. Compositional cycles as envisioned by C.A. Hopson and W.G. Melson for the Spirit Lake stage probably did not occur during the Ape Canyon stage but developed later during the Cougar and Swift Creek stages.

Introduction

The general eruptive history of Mount St. Helens was established through the work of U.S. Geological Survey (USGS) scientists D.R. Mullineaux and D.R. Crandell. Although the edifice was constructed primarily by eruptions of lava domes and flows, the volcano's fallout tephra record is extensive; and away from the mountain and its fragmental apron, pumice and ash locally bury the older landscape, commonly to a depth of 3 m or more. Detailed study of these tephra deposits over a period of 30 years (see Mullineaux, 1996, and references therein) has established a general geochronologic framework for understanding the volcano's eruptive history. Four periods of intermittent volcanism, called stages, are recognized (fig. 1) on the basis of observed time-stratigraphic groups, or "sets," of similar-age tephras, separated by weathered intervals. Tephra set C is the dominant tephra of the earliest, or Ape Canyon, stage; tephra sets M and K mark the Cougar stage, tephra sets S and J mark the Swift Creek stage, and tephra sets Y, P, B, and W (and several less extensive ash layers) were deposited during the latest, or Spirit Lake, stage. An extensive apron of fragmental deposits surrounds the volcano and fills valleys draining the mountain

[1] U.S. Geological Survey, 345 Middlefield Road, Menlo Park, CA 94025

[2] U.S. Geological Survey, 1300 SE Cardinal Court, Vancouver, WA 98683

(fig. 2). Study of these deposits, which include sequences of pyroclastic flows, lahars, and debris avalanches, placed them into the general geochronologic framework (see Crandell, 1987, and references therein).

Age control on the eruptive history of Mount St. Helens was established by radiometric (^{14}C) dating of organic material in or directly beneath tephra, pyroclastic, and lahar deposits (Crandell and others, 1981; Crandell, 1987; Mullineaux, 1996); however, most dating focused on the youngest and best-preserved part of the volcano. Verhoogen (1937) published a crude geologic map, and Hopson (2008) a more detailed geologic map, of the edifice, both of which focus on the youngest part (Spirit Lake stage) of the volcano and provide little information on the older rocks.

New geologic mapping and radiometric dating allow us to refine and extend the general geochronologic framework—especially in the older part of the record that predates construction of the modern volcanic edifice. Here we report new radiometric (primarily $^{40}Ar/^{39}Ar$) ages of Ape Canyon- and Cougar-stage lavas and pyroclastic deposits and describe the older rocks erupted from Mount St. Helens and preserved in its debris apron and in river valleys draining the volcano. We integrate the tephrochronology of Mullineaux (1996) and the age information on lahars and pyroclastic flows reported by Crandell (1987) into a stratigraphy of the fragmental apron of the volcano. Although we modify the age ranges and intervals between eruptive stages at Mount St. Helens, we retain Mullineaux and Crandell's terminology. The single major modification to their scheme is that we assign volcanism substantially earlier than about 40 ka and not recognized by them to their Ape Canyon stage, which thus lasted from about 300 to about 35 ka. In all, ranges of the four stages are Ape Canyon, 300–35 ka; Cougar, 28–18 ka; Swift Creek, 16–12.8 ka; and Spirit Lake, 3.9–0 ka, as summarized in figure 1.

The eruptive products of Mount St. Helens are dominated by varied hypersthene-hornblende dacite but include olivine basalt, olivine and pyroxene andesite, and quartz- and biotite-bearing dacite. Since the 1980 eruption, a tremendous volume of geochemical data has been generated. Most analyses are of Spirit Lake-stage rocks, obtained to determine the general chemistry of the youngest part of the volcano; some analyses were applied to determining the origin of Mount St. Helens magmas, but most analyses were not carefully correlated with stratigraphy. Unlike their well-studied younger counterparts, the products of the earlier eruptive stages are inadequately characterized. Here we combine major-element geochemical data from the literature with data generated by USGS laboratories and correlate them with the petrography of the rocks to characterize the Ape Canyon, Cougar, and Swift Creek stages of Mount St. Helens.

Stage and age	Period and age	Tephra set
Spirit Lake stage, 3.9–0 ka	Modern period, 1980–present	**1980**
	Goat Rocks period, 1800–1857 C.E.	**layer T**
	Kalama period, 1479–1750 C.E.	**set X** **set W**
	Sugar Bowl period, 1,200–1,150 yr B.P.	**layer D**
	Castle Creek period, 2,200–1,895 yr B.P.	**set B**
	Pine Creek period, 3,000–2,500 yr B.P.	**set P**
	Smith Creek period, 3,900–3,300 yr B.P.	**set Y**
Dormant interval, 12.8–3.9 ka		
Swift Creek stage, 16–12.8 ka		**set J** **set S**
Dormant interval, 18–16 ka		
Cougar stage, 28–18 ka		**set K** **set M**
Dormant interval, 35–28 ka		
Ape Canyon stage, 300–35 ka		**set C**

Figure 1. Mount St. Helens eruptive history.

Analytical Techniques

K-Ar and $^{40}Ar/^{39}Ar$ Geochronology

Using $^{40}Ar/^{39}Ar$ incremental-heating techniques, we analyzed whole rock, groundmass, or plagioclase phenocrysts from 17 lava samples (see fig. 3 for locations). For whole rock experiments, samples were crushed, ultrasonicated, and sized to narrow ranges (typically 500–1,000 µm). For groundmass separates, samples were crushed, ultrasonicated, and sized to narrow ranges (typically 250–350 µm), depending on the distance between phenocrysts. Dense, clean groundmass was concentrated by using a Frantz magnetic separator and careful handpicking under a binocular microscope. For plagioclase separates, samples were crushed and sieved to narrow size ranges, depending on the sizes of inclusion-free plagioclase (typically 300–400 µm), and purified by using magnetic and density techniques, dilute HF etching, and handpicking. Samples were irradiated in six different packages between March 2000 and May 2005, all with identical technique. For irradiation, samples weighing 150–250 mg were packaged in Cu foil and placed in cylindrical quartz vials, together with 27.87-Ma Taylor Creek sanidine fluence monitors and K-glass and fluorite to measure interfering K and Ca isotopes; quartz vials were wrapped in 0.5-mm-thick Cd foil to shield samples

Figure 2. Mount St. Helens area, southwestern Washington, before the 1980 eruption. Dashed outline denotes approximate limit of Mount St. Helens debris apron. Fragmental deposits derived from Mount St. Helens extend farther down all major drainages heading on volcano. Swift Reservoir fills the Lewis River valley between Swift Creek and Pine Creek, and Yale Lake fills valley west of Rain Creek. Base is pre-1980 topographic quadrangle map (U.S. Geological Survey, 1919) in North American datum (later renamed North American Datum 1927), enhanced by D.W. Ramsey to create hillslope shading as if illuminated from northwest.

from thermal neutrons during irradiation. Samples were irradiated for 2 hours in the central thimble of the TRIGA reactor at the USGS laboratory in Denver, Colo. (Dalrymple and others, 1981); reactor vessel was rotated continuously during irradiation to avoid lateral neutron-flux gradients. The reactor constants determined for these irradiations were indistinguishable from those in other recent irradiations, and a weighted mean of constants obtained over the past 5 years yields $^{40}Ar/^{39}Ar_K$ = 0.000±0.0004, $^{39}Ar/^{37}Ar_{Ca}$ = 0.000706±0.000051, and $^{36}Ar/^{37}Ar_{Ca}$ = 0.000281±0.000009. Sanidine TCR-2 from the Taylor Creek Rhyolite (Duffield and Dalrymple, 1990) is a secondary standard calibrated against the primary intralaboratory standard, SB-3, which has an age of 162.9±0.9 Ma (Lanphere and Dalrymple, 2000). Fluence monitors were analyzed using a continuous laser system and a MAP 216 mass spectrometer, as described by Dalrymple (1989). Argon was extracted from groundmass and plagioclase separates using a Mo crucible in a custom resistance furnace modified from the design of Staudacher and others (1978) attached to the aforementioned mass spectrometer. Heating temperatures were monitored with an optical-fiber thermometer and controlled with an Accufiber model 10 controller. Gas was purified continuously during extraction using two SAES ST-172 getters operated at 2.5 and 4 A.

Mass-spectrometric discrimination and system blanks are important factors in the precision and accuracy of the $^{40}Ar/^{39}Ar$ age determinations of Pleistocene lavas because of low radiogenic yields. Discrimination was monitored by analyzing splits of atmospheric Ar from a reservoir attached to the extraction line. Typical system blanks, including mass-spectrometer backgrounds, were 1.5×10^{-18} mol of m/z 36, 9×10^{-17} mol of m/z 37, 3×10^{-18} mol of m/z 39, and 1.5×10^{-16} mol of m/z 40, where m/z is the mass/charge ratio.

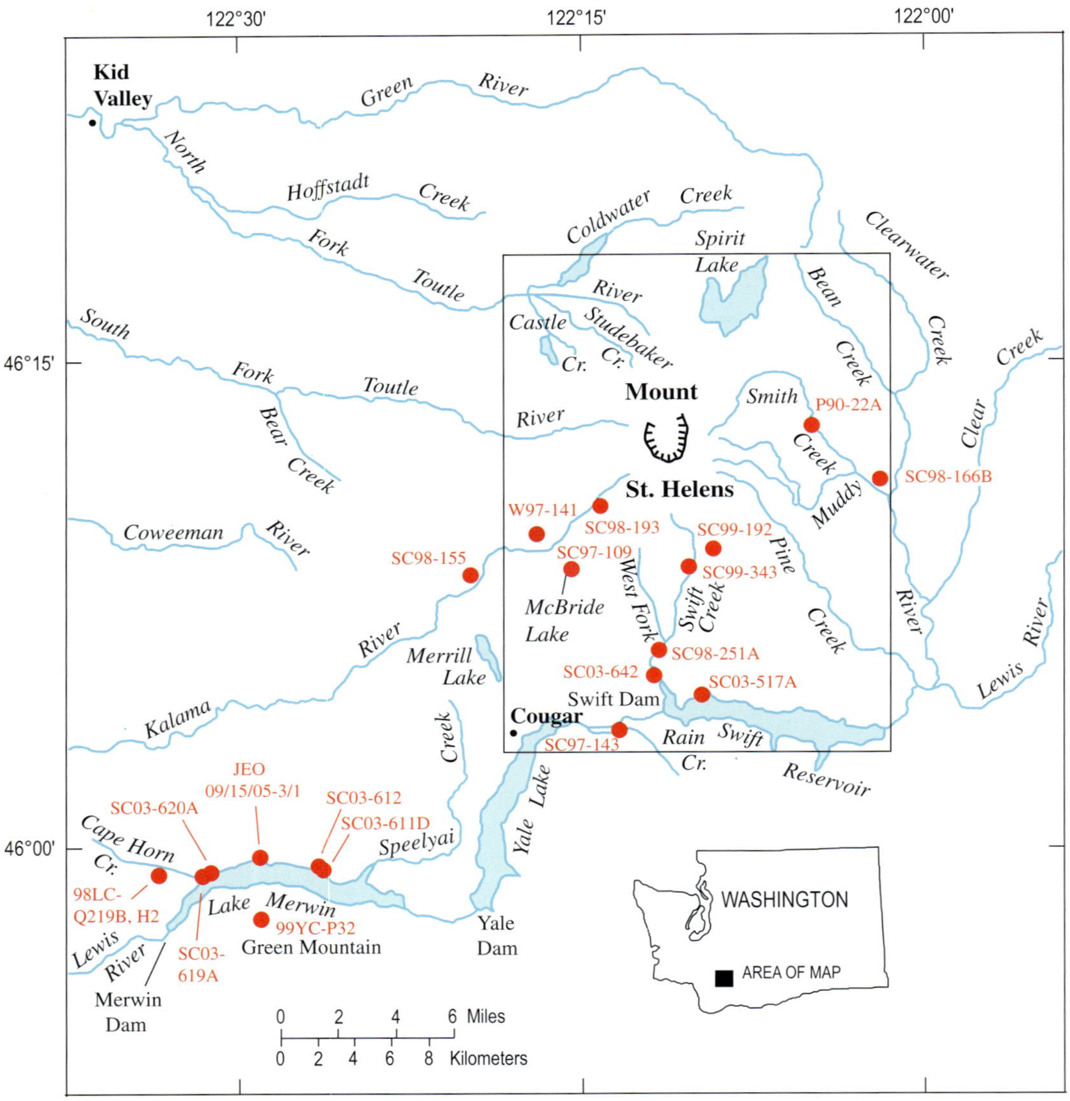

Figure 3. Sketch map of Mount St. Helens area, showing locations of newly dated samples reported in this chapter. Rectangle, area of figure 2.

Commonly accepted criteria (McDougall and Harrison, 1999) for a meaningful incremental-heating age are (1) a well-defined plateau (horizontal age spectrum with no significant slope) comprising more than 50 percent of ^{39}Ar released, (2) a well-defined isochron for plateau gas fractions, (3) concordant plateau and isochron ages, and (4) an ^{40}Ar/^{36}Ar isochron intercept not significantly different from 295.5. Because several of the samples violate one or more of these criteria, for those samples we favor the isochron age or report a plateau comprising less than 50 percent of ^{39}Ar released.

For isochron plots, data are not corrected by using an atmospheric ratio. Reported isochron ages include plateau steps on well-behaved samples or a data subset that includes the most steps yielding a reasonable goodness of fit. We commonly exclude the highest and lowest temperature steps because they are most strongly affected by ^{39}Ar recoil. We show normal isochron plots for these low-radiogenic-yield rocks because the data are easier to visualize. Isochron ages with a high probability-of-fit regression (a low mean square of weighted deviates, [MSWD ~1]; York, 1969) and an ^{40}Ar/^{36}Ar intercept not within the error of the present-day air ratio are interpreted to contain nonatmospheric initial Ar. For these samples, we interpret the isochron age as most meaningful. Isochron ages with an MSWD value greater than the critical value defined by Mahon (1996) are here reported with errors expanded by $\sqrt{\mathrm{MSWD}}$ (Ludwig, 1999); errors are reported at the 1σ level.

The K-Ar ages for samples SC97-141 and SC97-143 were determined in Menlo Park, Calif., using techniques delineated in Hildreth and Lanphere (1994).

Radiocarbon Dating

The samples with a laboratory number prefixed by "WW" were prepared at the USGS laboratory in Reston, Va., by John McGeehin and analyzed at the Center for Accelerator Mass Spectrometry of Lawrence Livermore National Laboratory in Livermore, Calif. The samples were pretreated with an acid-alkali-acid leaching process to remove contaminant C in the form of inorganic carbonates and organic soil acids before conversion to CO_2 and reduction with H_2 to pure C in the form of graphite over an Fe catalyst. Additional details of sample processing and analysis were reported by McGeehin and others (2001) and Roberts and others (1997), respectively.

All ^{14}C ages were calculated using the Libby 5,568-year half-life with $\delta^{13}C = -25$ and given in years before present (B.P.), defined as 1950 C.E. Errors as stated include one standard deviation (1σ) of counting statistics and an additional uncertainty attributable to isotope fractionation and sample processing. Radiocarbon ages of 0–22,000 yr B.P. were calibrated to calendar years by using the INTCAL04 terrestrial age calibration (Reimer and others, 2004); older ^{14}C ages were calibrated by using the method of Cutler and others (2004).

Geochemistry

Analytical methods for USGS major-element analyses by wavelength-dispersive X-ray spectroscopy were routine, as described by Taggart and others (1987). All analyses were recalculated to 100 percent anhydrous, with the Fe_2O_3/FeO ratio set to 0.2 of the total Fe analyzed as Fe_2O_3. Analyses from the literature were recalculated by using the same scheme. A few analyses, however, lack either P_2O_5 or MnO content, and so those two components were estimated on the basis of analyses of similar rocks. John Pallister, Cynthia Gardner, and Rick Hoblitt provided additional USGS analyses.

Results

K-Ar and ^{40}Ar/^{39}Ar Analyses

The results of K-Ar and ^{40}Ar/^{39}Ar analyses of Mount St. Helens rocks are summarized in table 1, and the data for incremental-heating experiments are listed in appendix 1. Plateau and isochron ages are plotted in figure 4. The dated samples are briefly described below, from youngest to oldest in the same order as in table 1. Sample locations (fig 3) are referable to North American Datum 1927 (NAD 27).

Sample SC98-155.—Dacite of Kalama Dome (Evarts and Ashley, 1990a), a small dome of porphyritic hornblende dacite with sparse resorbed biotite overlying till of Hayden Creek age in the Kalama River valley (lat 46°07.79' N., long 122°19.76' W.). Generally, only a single population of plagioclase is present, although a few phenocrysts are resorbed and all display oscillatory zoning with thick sodic rims. The groundmass is fresh and contains abundant microlites in clear glass. The whole-rock sample yielded all-negative apparent ages but has a well-constrained 16.3±12.9-ka isochron age comprising 94 percent of ^{39}Ar released, with an ^{40}Ar/^{36}Ar intercept of 289.2±0.9 and MSWD = 1.4. Higher-temperature steps contained little K-derived ^{39}Ar and had older apparent ages (see chemical analysis in table 5).

Sample SC99-343.—Andesite of Swift Creek, a thick andesite lava flow of porphyritic hornblende-augite-hypersthene andesite to dacite overlying Cougar-stage pyroclastic flows on the south flank of the volcano (lat 46°08.60' N., long 122°10.27' W.). Several populations of plagioclase phenocrysts are present, and most hornblende is converted to an aggregate of plagioclase, pyroxene, and Fe-Ti oxide. The groundmass is turbid, with tiny crystals set in cryptofelsite. The whole-rock sample yielded an excellent plateau age of 17.8±2.7 ka and an equivalent isochron age. The andesite of Swift Creek, named not for the stage but for its location along Swift Creek, was emplaced late in Cougar time.

Sample SC03-611D.—A clast of coarsely porphyritic hornblende dacite with sparse quartz from a Cougar-stage lahar deposit along the north shore of Lake Merwin in the Amboy quadrangle (lat 45°58.91' N., long 122°26.35'

Table 1. Summary of $^{40}Ar/^{39}Ar$ and K-Ar ages.

[See text for discussion of preferred ages, shown in bold. Maximum ages in italics. K-Ar ages calculated by using 1976 International Union of Geological Sciences constants (Steiger and Jäger, 1977): $\lambda_\beta = 4.962\times10^{-10}$/yr, $\lambda_\varepsilon = 0.581\times10^{-10}$/yr, $^{40}K/K_{total} = 1.167\times10^{-4}$ mol/mol. Errors are estimates of analytical precision at the 68-percent confidence level.]

$^{40}Ar/^{39}Ar$ data			Plateau age			Isochron age			
Sample	Material	Total-gas age (ka)	%^{39}Ar (steps)	Age (ka)	Error (1σ)	Age (ka)	Error (1σ)	MSWD	$^{40}Ar/^{36}Ar_i$
SC98-155	Whole rock	-95.1±8.6	72 (9 of 27)	-51.2	7.3	**16.3**	**12.9**	1.4	289.2±0.9
SC99-343	Whole rock	-52.4±8.7	79 (7 of 14)	**17.8**	**2.7**	18.7	4.5	0.94	294.1±1.4
SC03-611D	Groundmass	15.2±3.0	37 (4 of 14)*	21.7	1.8	**21.2**	**2.9**	1.8	298.7±2.3
SC03-612	Plagioclase	363.8±7.3	37 (3 of 9)	***24***	***11***	84.5	13.6	2.7	288.4±1.6
SC98-192	Whole rock	29.1±2.2	80 (6 of 14)	**27.9**	**1.7**	28.5	4.0	0.80	295.5±3.0
SC97-109	Groundmass	7.8±6.2	88 (6 of 12)	**34.9**	**4.6**	39.5	5.4	0.41	290.0±0.8
SC03-619A	Whole rock	34.1±1.1	97 (12 of 14)	**39.8**	**1.0**	40.0	2.4	1.6	295.0±2.2
P90-22A	Plagioclase	302.7±8.4	36 (2 of 8)	***54***	***10***				
SC03-620A	Plagioclase	754.1±8.5	36 (3 of 9)	***74***	***11***	79.8	29.9	1.8	293.2±5.1
SC98-251A	Whole rock	-361.9±12.4	83 (10 of 18)	*-184*	*10*	91.5	24.2	1.3	281.5±1.1
SC98-193	Groundmass	-42±18	20 (2 of 9)	112	24	147	37	0.65	289.7±1.8
SC98-193	Plagioclase	369.2±35.9	69 (5 of 9)	**107.4**	**39.2**	134	169	0.52	294.1±8.3
SC97-143	Plagioclase	695±31	42 (2 of 8)	113.8	40.8	-71.4	145.4	0.61	322.6±16.0
SC03-642	Plagioclase	530.4±8.8	52 (3 of 10)	**160**	**8.8**	166.6	46.0	2.9	288.8±4.1
99YC-P32	Plagioclase	519±122	77 (7 of 13)	**247**	**12**	155	55	1.3	318±15
98LC-Q219H2	Plagioclase	366±17	62 (3 of 9)	**263**	**19**				
98LC-Q219B	Plagioclase	404±28	85 (7 of 9)	**269**	**13**	276	19	0.81	292.2±4.1

K-Ar data				K_2O			Argon	
Sample	Material	K-Ar age (ka)	Weight (g)	wt %	No.	S.D.	$^{40}Ar_{rad}$ (mol/g)	$^{40}Ar_{rad}$ %
SC97-143	Whole rock	**109±24**	25.421	1.456	2	0.005	2.277×10^{-13}	1.8
W97-141	Whole rock	**296±7**	26.198	1.856	2	0.011	7.891×10^{-13}	25.4

* Weighted mean age, because the plateau does not comprise the required 50 percent of ^{39}Ar released.

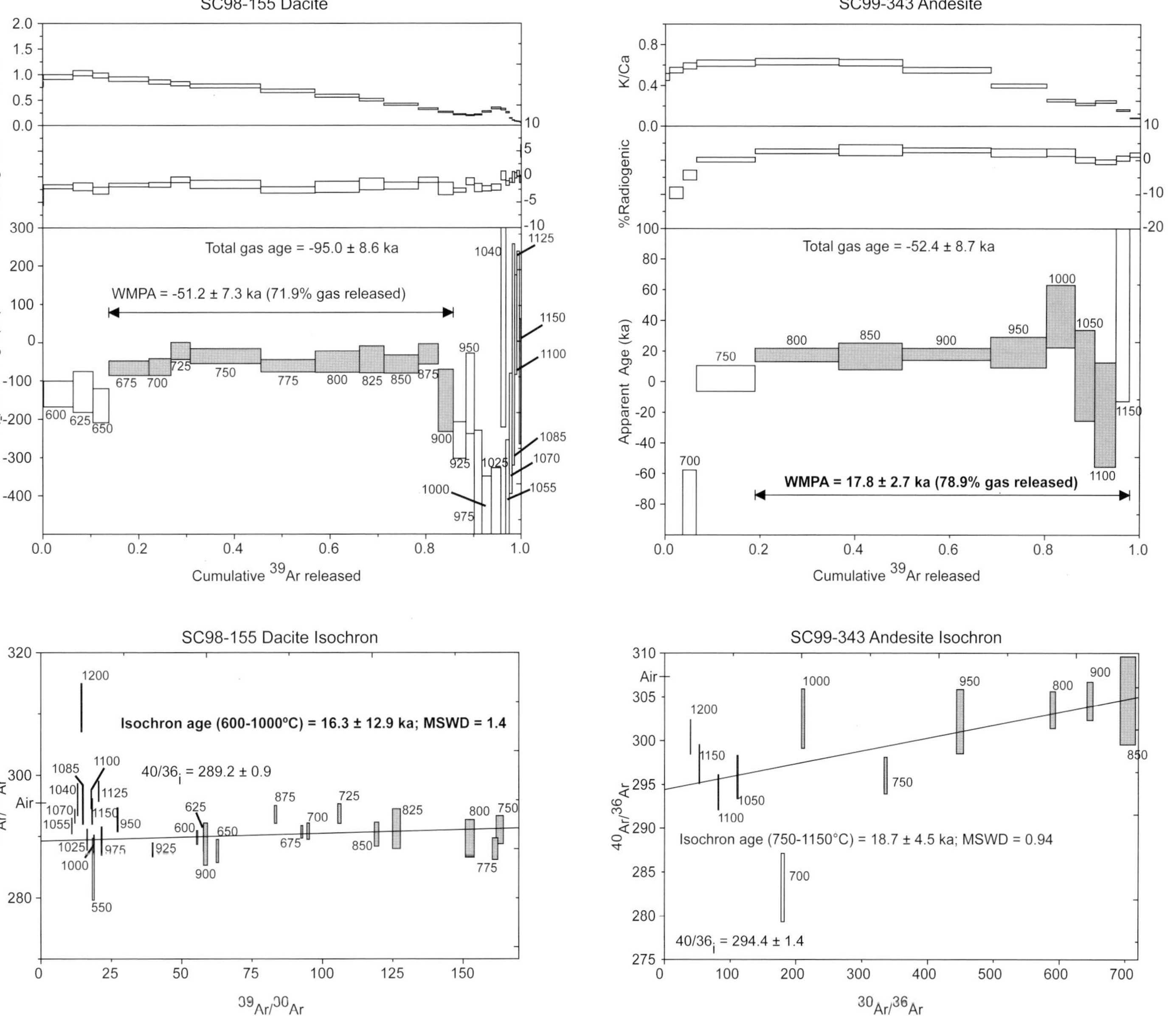

Figure 4. Argon plateau and isochron diagrams for dated samples from Mount St. Helens deposits (see fig. 3 for locations).

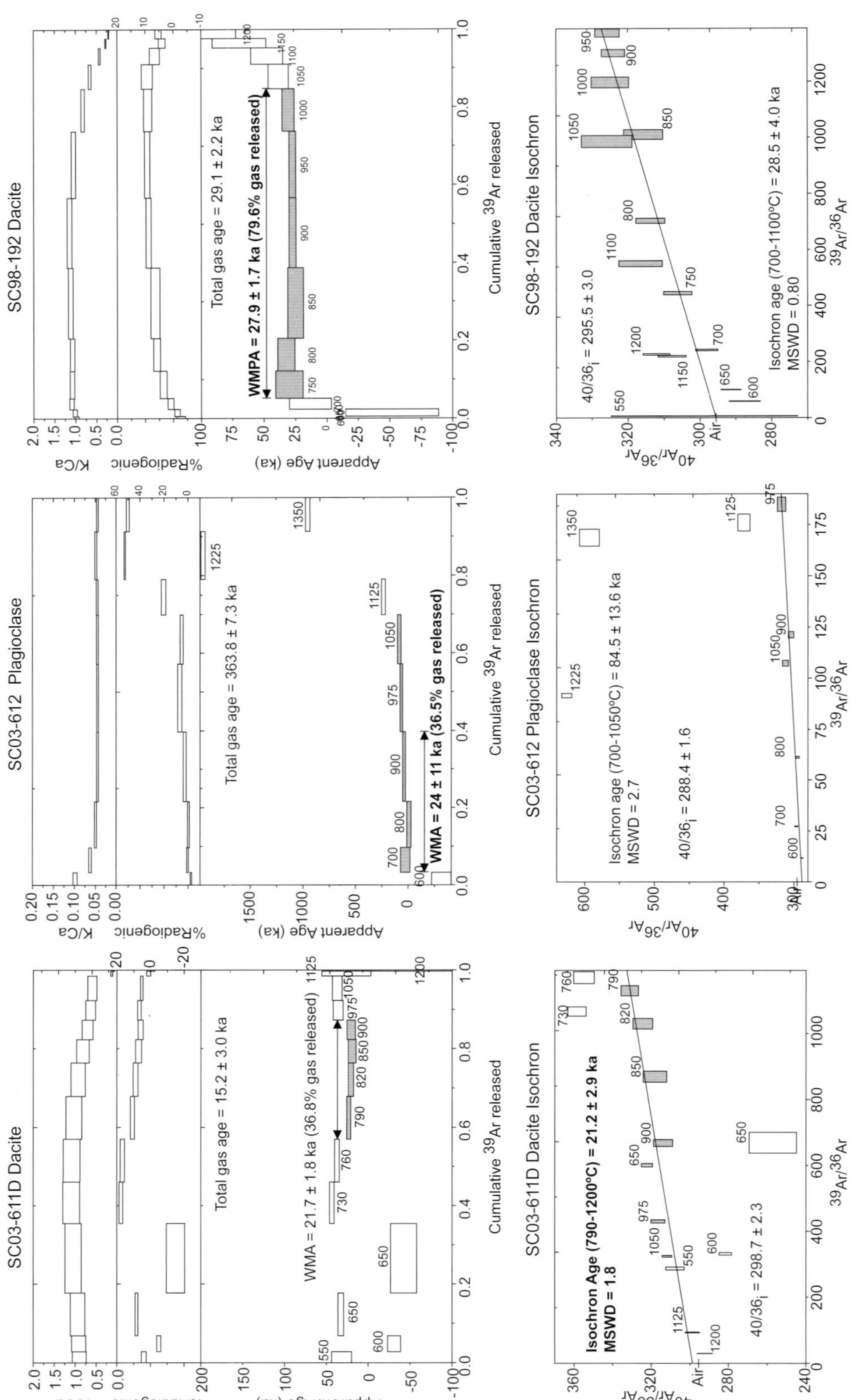

Figure 4.—Continued.

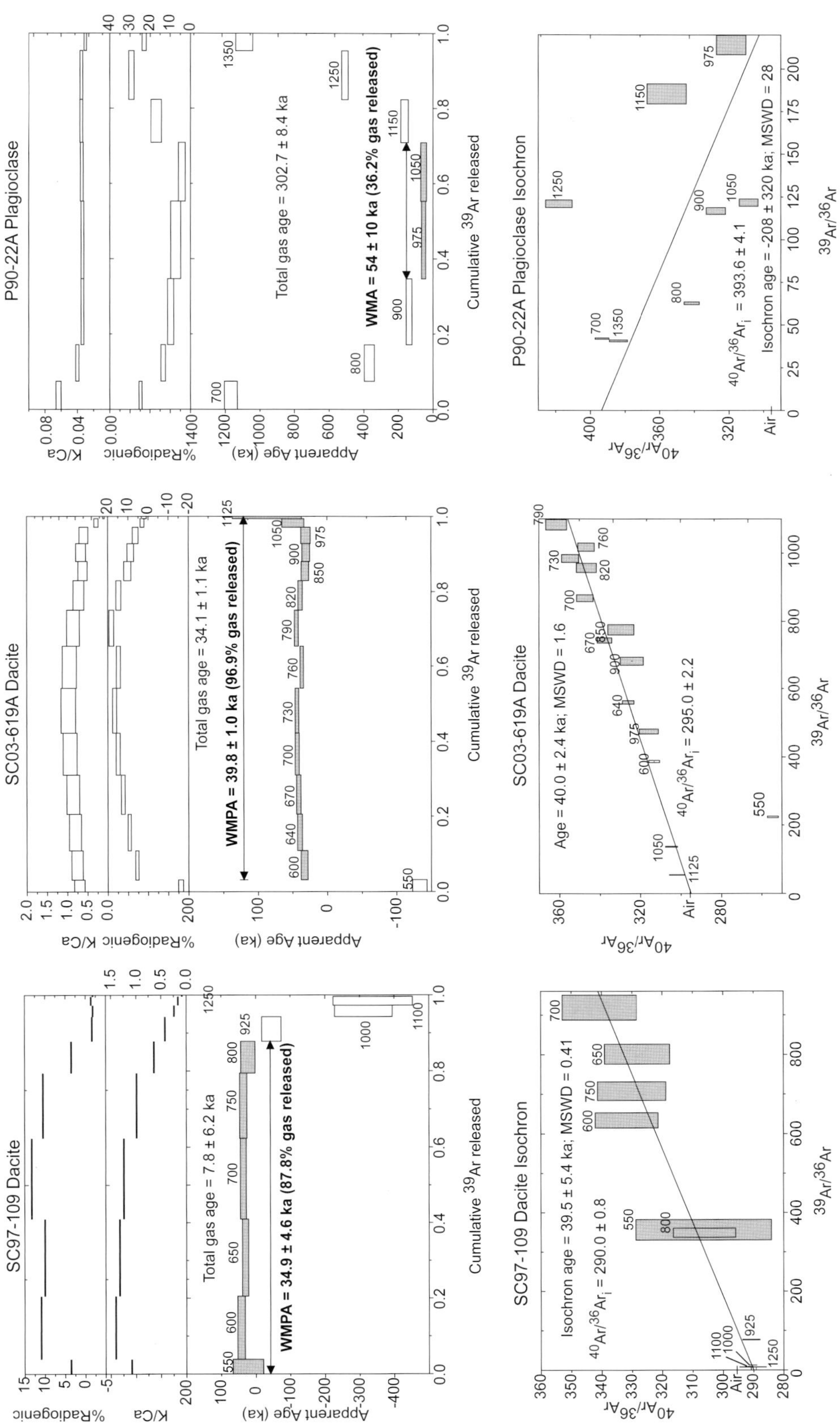

Figure 4.—Continued.

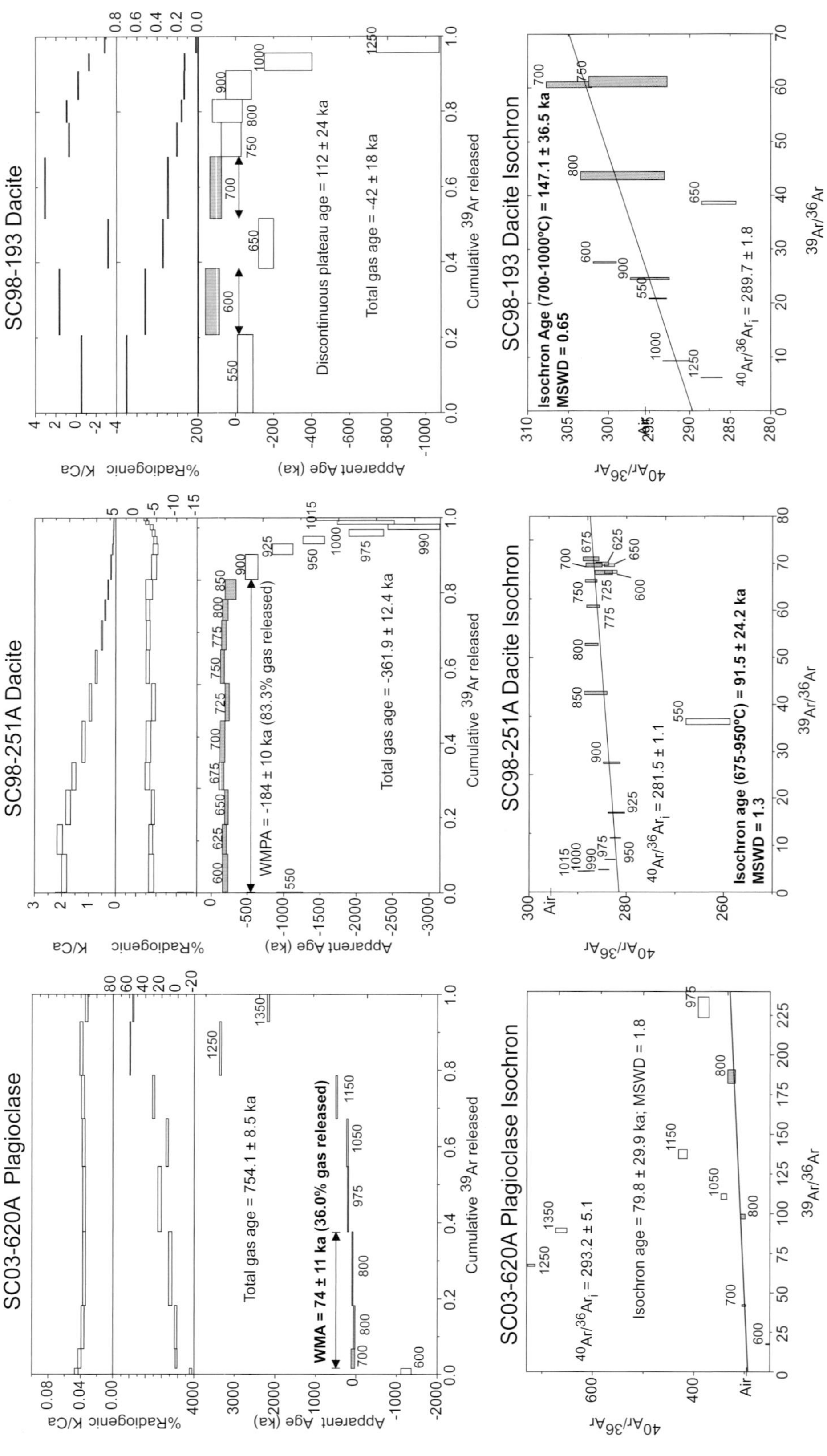

Figure 4.—Continued.

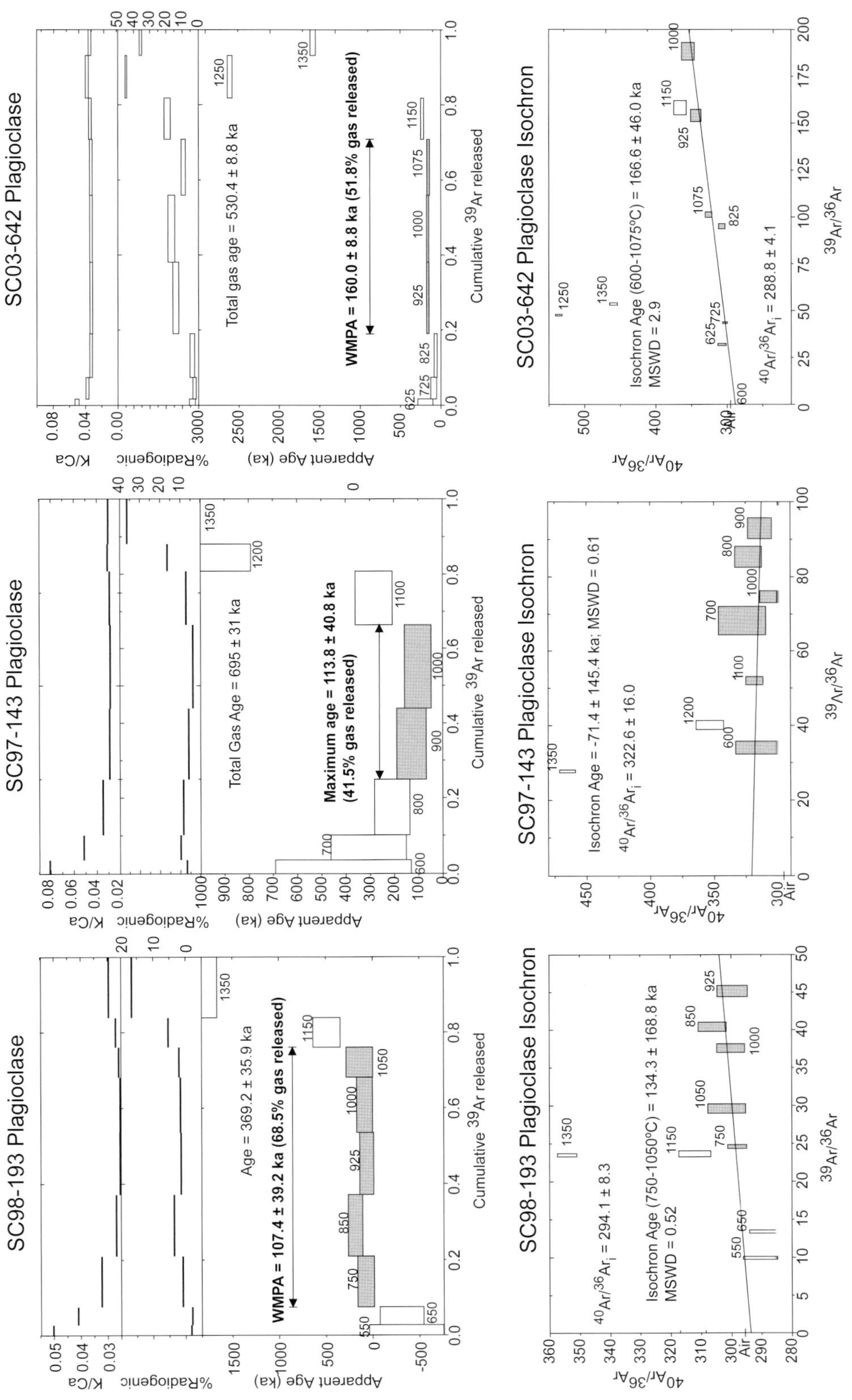

Figure 4.—Continued.

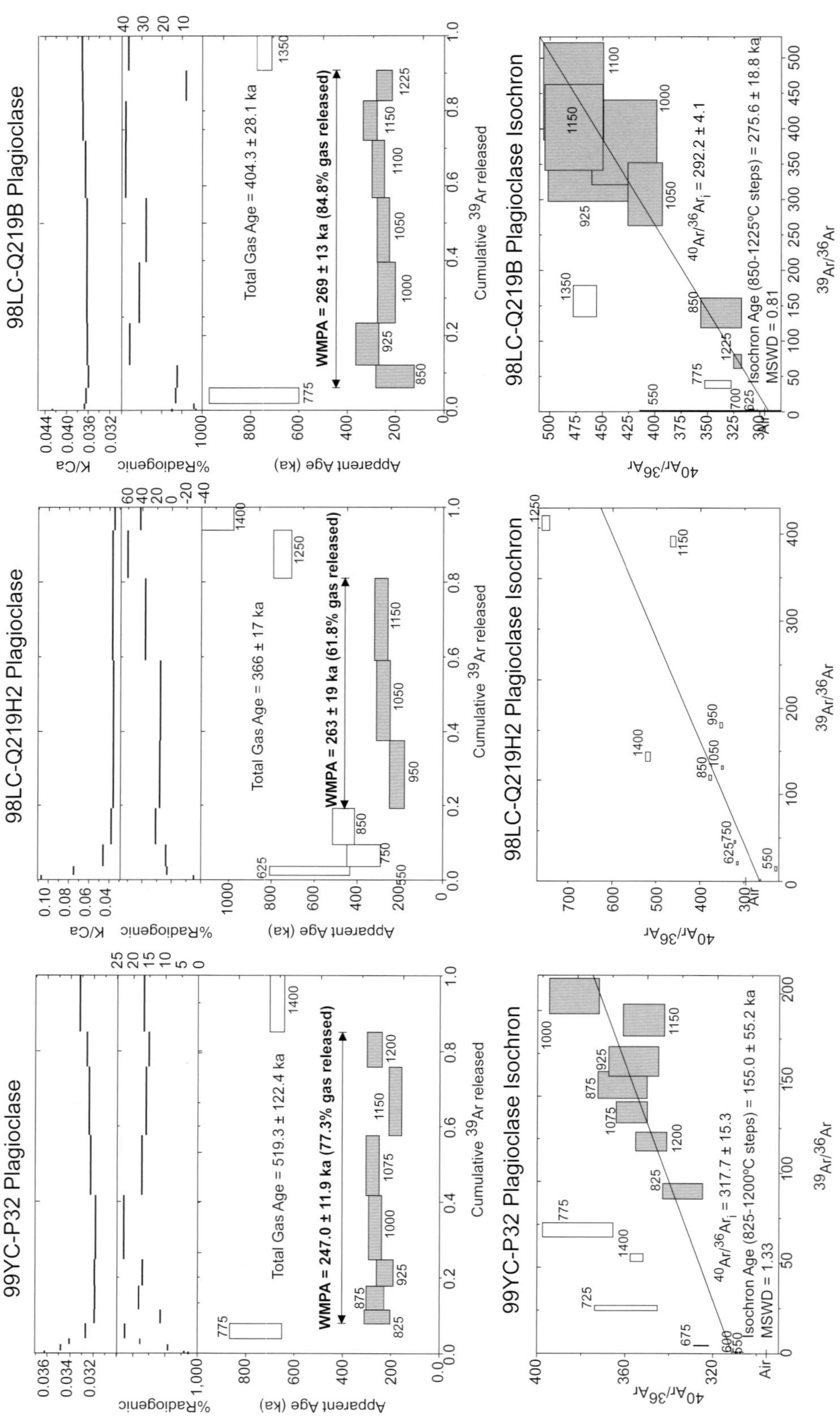

Figure 4.—Continued.

W.). The lahar deposit contains debris-avalanche dacite and, probably, andesite of Swift Creek, and so it must have been emplaced late in Cougar time. The amphibole is mostly converted to an aggregate of pyroxene, oxide, and plagioclase and originally may have been cummingtonite. Plagioclase displays various zoning patterns, but resorbed phenocrysts are relatively uncommon. The groundmass is mostly devitrified to a relatively coarse-grained intergrowth of plagioclase and quartz. The groundmass sample yielded a disturbed age spectrum containing only four concordant steps, with a weighted-mean age of 21.7±1.8 ka. A 21.2±2.9-ka isochron age comprising 43 percent of the ^{39}Ar released is indistinguishable from the weighted-mean age and has a higher-than-atmospheric intercept and a good fit. We interpret the isochron age as the most reliable (see chemical analysis in table 5).

Sample SC03-612.—A clast of porphyritic hornblende dacite with sparse quartz from a Cougar-stage lahar deposit along the north shore of Lake Merwin in the Amboy quadrangle (lat 45°58.93' N., long 122°26.45'W.). The lahar deposit contains debris-avalanche dacite and, probably, andesite of Swift Creek and is of late Cougar age. Plagioclase displays various zoning patterns, but resorbed phenocrysts are relatively uncommon. The groundmass is fresh and consists of crystallite-poor glass. A plagioclase separate from this rock yielded a climbing age spectrum from 27 ka to nearly 2 Ma. We interpret the weighted-mean age of three concordant low-temperature steps (24±11 ka) as a maximum age for the rock.

Sample SC98-192.—Dacite of June Lake, a thick, weakly welded lithic pyroclastic-flow deposit exposed at June Lake (lat 46°09.14' N., long 122°09.65' W.) on the south flank of the volcano. The deposit overlies mid-Tertiary arc volcanic rocks and is overlain by Cougar- and Swift Creek-stage pyroclastic-flow deposits. The rock is a porphyritic hypersthene-hornblende dacite. Most amphibole is converted to an anhydrous assemblage of pyroxene, plagioclase, and Fe-Ti oxides and may have originally been cummingtonite. The groundmass contains abundant tiny microlites and is nearly completely devitrified to cryptocrystalline material. The whole-rock sample yielded an excellent 27.9±1.7-ka plateau age and an equivalent isochron age.

Sample SC97-109.—Dacite of McBride Lake, a coarsely porphyritic hornblende dacite with sparse quartz from a Cougar-stage debris-avalanche or lahar deposit (loc. 55 of Crandell, 1987) near McBride Lake, on the southwest flank of the volcano (lat 46°08.49' N., long 122°15.45' W.). The rock is a common component of the lahar and reworked lahar deposits along the north shore of Lake Merwin (fig. 3). Plagioclase displays various zoning patterns, and a small proportion of phenocrysts have resorbed zones. The groundmass is cryptocrystalline and fresh. The groundmass sample yielded an excellent 34.9±4.6-ka plateau age comprising 88 percent of ^{39}Ar released. The highest-temperature steps have very low $^{40}Ar/^{36}Ar$ ratios, forcing the $^{40}Ar/^{36}Ar$ intercept to be low and the isochron age to be slightly older. We interpret the plateau age as the most reliable (see chemical analysis in table 4).

Sample SC03-619A.—Coarsely porphyritic hornblende dacite with sparse quartz from an Ape Canyon-stage lahar deposit that overlies Hayden Creek Drift and is exposed just above high water along the north shore of Lake Merwin in the Ariel quadrangle (lat 45°59.07' N., long 122°31.55' W.). The rock is a common component of Ape Canyon-stage lahar deposits in the Lewis River valley (fig. 2). The amphibole is mostly converted to an aggregate of pyroxene, Fe-Ti oxide, and plagioclase. Plagioclase displays various zoning patterns, and a small proportion of the phenocrysts have resorbed zones. The groundmass is mostly devitrified to a relatively coarse grained intergrowth of plagioclase and quartz. The groundmass sample yielded an excellent plateau age of 39.8±1.0 ka and an equivalent isochron age (see chemical analysis in table 4).

Sample P90-22A.—Porphyritic quartz-biotite-hornblende dacite clast from a pumiceous pyroclastic-flow deposit overlying Hayden Creek Drift. John Pallister collected this sample from locality 16 of Crandell (1987, probably unit P1, his fig. 7) in Smith Creek valley (lat 46°12.35' N., long 122°05.05' W.). At this locality, the pyroclastic-flow deposits are interbedded with set C tephras, and the abundance of hornblende and paucity of cummingtonite suggest that these pyroclastic-flow deposits may be equivalent to tephra layer Cy. Crandell and others (1981) reported an age older than 46.4 ka cal yr B.P. for this deposit. The rock is pumiceous and consists of plagioclase, abundant hornblende, biotite, quartz, and sparse cummingtonite in a glassy groundmass with very sparse microlites. Plagioclase displays various zoning patterns but phenocrysts are generally fresh and lack sieve textures. A plagioclase separate from this rock yielded a U-shaped age spectrum; no good fit to the isochron data is evident. We interpret the weighted mean of the youngest apparent ages (54±10 ka) as a maximum age for the rock.

Sample SC03-620A.—Coarsely porphyritic quartz-biotite-hornblende dacite from a lahar deposit exposed along the north shore of Lake Merwin in the Ariel quadrangle (lat 45°59.16' N., long 122°31.22' W.). The rock is a common component of Ape Canyon-stage lahar and derivative sedimentary deposits in the Lewis River from Yale Dam to Woodland, 32 km west. Smaller hornblende phenocrysts are converted to an aggregate of pyroxene, Fe-Ti oxide, and plagioclase, and larger ones have opacite rims. Plagioclase displays various zoning patterns, but resorbed phenocrysts are relatively uncommon. The groundmass is fresh and composed of crystallite-rich glass. A plagioclase separate from this rock yielded a climbing age spectrum from 72 ka to older than 3 Ma. We interpret the weighted-mean age of three concordant low-temperature steps (74±11 ka) as a maximum age for the rock.

Sample SC98-251A.—Light-colored, porphyritic hornblende-hypersthene dacite pumice from the two-pumice pyroclastic-flow deposit exposed in the cliffs west of Swift Creek (lat 46°05.87' N., long 122°11.95' W.). Most amphibole is converted to an anhydrous assemblage of pyroxene, plagioclase, and Fe-Ti oxide. Plagioclase is the most abundant phenocryst phase and displays several textures but is generally fresh and unresorbed. The groundmass consists of fresh glass choked with abundant tiny crystallites. The whole-rock sample yielded negative ages. An isochron comprising intermediate steps of the incremental-heating experiment yielded a good fit at 91.5±24.2 ka; however, we interpret the 24,380-yr age for laboratory No. W-2540 (table 2) as more reliable.

Sample SC98-193.—Andesite of Butte Camp, a porphyritic hypersthene-hornblende andesite from a glaciated lava dome at Butte Camp, collected from talus in an unnamed creek on the northwest side of the dome (lat 46°10.5' N., long 122°14.3' W.). The rock consists of porphyritic hypersthene-hornblende dacite without quartz and biotite. This rock is a component of Hayden Creek-age glacial deposits and Ape Canyon-age lahars in the Lewis River and North Fork of the Toutle River (fig. 3). Resorbed phenocrysts of plagioclase and hornblende are sparse; some phenocrysts are probably derived from disaggregation of cumulate-textured inclusions. The groundmass glass is clear and fresh but crowded with microlites. Age experiments on plagioclase and groundmass separates were attempted for this rock. Plagioclase yielded a good plateau age of 107.4±39.2 ka comprising 69 percent of ^{39}Ar released; isochron age is concordant but has a large error because of low radiogenic yields. The groundmass experiment was disturbed but yielded a 147.1±36.5-ka isochron, within the error of the plagioclase result. We interpret the plateau age as the most reliable (see chemical analysis in table 4).

Sample SC97-143.—Unnamed hypersthene-hornblende dacite from a Cougar-stage lahar deposit (lat 46°03.78' N., long 122°13.48' W.) along (Forest Service) Road 90, approximately 1 km west of Crandell's (1987) locality 45. The rock consists of coarsely porphyritic hypersthene-hornblende dacite with sparse quartz. This rock is a minor component of Cougar- and Ape Canyon-age lahar deposits in the Lewis River from Swift Dam to Woodland, 46 km west-southwest. Amphibole phenocrysts are fresh but have thin opacite rims; plagioclase phenocrysts are fresh and are present mostly in a single population. The groundmass consists of microlite-choked clear glass. A plagioclase separate yielded a U-shaped age spectrum; no good fit to the isochron data is evident. We interpret the weighted mean of the youngest apparent ages (113.8±40.8 ka) as a maximum age for the rock. This age is equivalent to a 109±24-ka K-Ar age obtained in a pilot study, which we interpret as the most reliable (see chemical analysis in table 4).

Sample SC03-642.—Unnamed porphyritic hypersthene-hornblende dacite from a megablock in the Cougar-stage debris-avalanche deposit exposed in Swift Creek (lat 46°05.25' N., long 122°12.40' W.). The rock consists of porphyritic hypersthene-hornblende dacite with no quartz or biotite. This rock is a minor component of the Cougar-stage debris-avalanche deposit (see "Discussion" section). Plagioclase displays various zoning patterns, including a few phenocrysts with resorption zones. The groundmass is fresh and consists of crystallite-choked glass. A plagioclase separate from this rock yielded a climbing age spectrum. Three intermediate incremental-heating steps yielded a plateau age of 160±8.8 ka, and an isochron age comprising the first 71 percent of ^{39}Ar released yielded a similar age of 167±46 ka. We interpret the plateau age as the most reliable (see chemical analysis in table 4).

Sample W97-141.—Dacite of Goat Mountain (Evarts and Ashley, 1990b), a coarsely porphyritic hornblende-biotite dacite with abundant quartz from the southeast flank of Goat Mountain (lat 46°08.85' N., long 122°16.96' W.). The rock is a common component of Hayden Creek-age glacial deposits and Ape Canyon-age lahars in the Lewis River from Yale Dam 32 km west to Woodland and in the Kalama River west of (Forest Service) Road 81 (fig. 3). Our K-Ar age of 296±7 ka (table 1) is significantly younger than the discordant K-Ar ages on hornblende (3.18±0.3 Ma) and biotite (1.06±0.6 and 0.76±0.6 Ma) reported by Engels and others (1976).

Sample 99YC-P32.—Bed of set C tephra beneath Amboy Drift (equivalent to Hayden Creek Drift) on the crest of Green Mountain, about 33 km southwest of the volcano in the Amboy quadrangle (lat 45°57.84' N., long 122°29.04' W.). The bed, which is about 2 m thick, is composed of coarse ash and scattered lapilli of weathered dacitic glass containing crystals of plagioclase, quartz, biotite, green hornblende, and cummingtonite, contains charred woodchips, and overlies a soil developed on Tertiary bedrock. Plagioclase yielded a plateau age of 247±12 ka comprising 78 percent of ^{39}Ar released. Isochron results suggest a high ^{40}Ar/^{36}Ar intercept but within the error of air. We interpret the plateau age as the most reliable.

Sample 98LC-Q219H2.—Block of slightly vesicular, coarsely and densely porphyritic dacite from a debris-flow(?) bed in the sequence of ice-contact deposits at Cape Horn Creek in the Ariel quadrangle (lat 45°59.16' N., long 122°33.48' W.). Phenocrysts of plagioclase, quartz, biotite, green hornblende, and cummingtonite occur in a groundmass of hydrated glass. Plagioclase exhibits complex zoning and some resorption but is fresh and free of inclusions. Some hornblende grains are zoned to cummingtonite rims. Plagioclase yielded a three-step plateau age of 263±19 ka comprising 62 percent of ^{39}Ar released but no usable isochron age.

Sample 98LC-Q219B.—Pumice-lapilli bed in a 9-m-thick sequence of ice-contact deposits exposed in a roadcut on the south valley wall of Cape Horn Creek, about 37 km southwest of the volcano in the Ariel quadrangle (lat 45°59.16' N., long 122°33.48' W.). The deposits consist almost entirely of Mount St. Helens-derived dacite debris and overlie Amboy Drift (Hayden Creek Drift). The sample, from a 0.5-m-thick bed of slightly reworked pumice lapilli, consists of phenocrysts of plagioclase, quartz, biotite, green-brown hornblende, and cummingtonite within a matrix of totally weathered glass. Plagioclase yielded an excellent plateau age of 269±13 ka comprising 85 percent of ^{39}Ar released and a comparable isochron age of 276±19 ka.

Radiocarbon Ages

Absolute time control for Crandell and Mullineaux's stratigraphy of the Ape Canyon and Cougar stages was based

Table 2. Radiocarbon and calibrated ages of Ape Canyon- and Cougar-stage deposits.

[All values in years ± 1σ. Samples with laboratory numbers prefixed by "WW" were prepared at the U.S. Geological Survey laboratory in Reston, Va., and analyzed by John McGeehin at Lawrence Livermore National Laboratory in Livermore, Calif. by accelerator mass spectrometry. These samples were pretreated with standard acid-alkali-acid wash, and ages were calculated with a ^{14}C half-life of 5,568 yr and $\delta^{13}C = -25$ (see text for sample descriptions and locations). Samples with laboratory numbers prefixed by "W" are from Crandell and others (1981) and were not pretreated (see Crandell and others, 1981, for sample descriptions and locations). Sample MS-5 is from Major and Scott (1988), and sample Scott BC from Scott (1989). Samples younger than 22 ka were calibrated by using the curve of Reimer and others (2004); samples older than 22 ka were calibrated by using the curve of Cutler and others (2004). Calibrated ages are reported as calendar years before 1950 C.E. Calibration curve of Cutler and others (2004) does not give uncertainties, which are rounded upward from the uncalibrated age.]

Laboratory No.	Sample No.	Radiometric age (^{14}C yr B.P.)	Calibrated age
	Cougar-stage deposits		
W-2413	—	18,560±180	22,170 (+190/−240)
W-4531	—	19,160±250	22,620 (+520/−210
WW-4543	SC03-517A	19,670±60	23,590 (+120/−150)
—	Scott BC	19,700±550	23,650 (+485/−965)
W-2540	—	20,350±350	24,380 (+510/−480)
—	MS-5	22,720±1,400	28,850 ±1,400
	Ape Canyon-stage deposits		
WW-3481	SC98-166B	42,950±560	47,430±600
WW-5561	JEO 09/15/05-3/1	44,960±930	49,540±1,000

on several uncalibrated ages of samples that were not pretreated before analysis (Crandell and others, 1981). Radiocarbon samples, when not pretreated to reduce contamination by modern organic material, commonly yield inconsistent or minimum ages. Furthermore, the calibrated ages, especially those in the range 20–50 ka, are 2–6 ka older than the uncalibrated ages. These factors lead to differences between the ages reported here and those reported by Crandell and others (1981), Crandell (1987), and Mullineaux (1996).

Brief descriptions of three new samples from the Ape Canyon and Cougar stages and two samples from the report by Crandell and others (1981) are given below and listed in table 2. Sample locations, which are referable to NAD 27, are shown in figure 3.

Sample WW-4543 (SC03-517A).—Charcoal from a Cougar-stage hypersthene-hornblende dacite pyroclastic-flow deposit ("Cougar-stage white pumice") exposed at lake level on the north shore of Swift Reservoir (figs. 2, 3), overlying set K tephra (lat 46°04.22' N., long 122°09.67' W.), in the Mount Mitchell quadrangle. The sample is stratigraphically equivalent to laboratory No. W-2413 (table 2, Crandell and others, 1981) from nearby locality 46 of Crandell (1987) and approximately stratigraphically equivalent to laboratory No. W-4531 (table 2; Crandell and others, 1981) on a hypersthene-hornblende dacite pyroclastic-flow deposit at locality 36 of Crandell (1987) in Pine Creek (figs. 2, 3).

Sample Scott BC.—Wood from sediment interbedded with Cougar-stage lahar deposits in the South Fork of the Toutle River (fig. 1) about 0.5 km upstream from the confluence with Bear Creek (approx. lat 46°14.0' N., long 122°12.65' W.) in the Elk Mountain quadrangle. The sample was described by Scott (1989, p. B32) as from the Bear Creek section but was unnumbered.

Sample W-2540.—Charcoal from a pumiceous pyroclastic-flow deposit ("two-pumice pyroclastic flow") exposed near Rain Creek, west of the Swift Reservoir (loc. 46 of Crandell, 1987), and underlying sets M and K tephras (approx. lat 46°03.25' N., long 122°12.9' W.) in the Mount Mitchell quadrangle.

Sample MS-5.—Charcoal from alluvial sediment below a lahar deposit (Major and Scott, 1988) at the intersection of Washington Highway 503 and Baker Road, near Speelyai Bay, Lake Merwin (lat 45°59.78' N., long 122°23.95' W.) in the Amboy quadrangle. The deposit contains Cougar-stage dacite but lacks debris-avalanche dacite, and so the deposit is Cougar age but predates the Cougar-stage debris-avalanche deposit (see next section).

Sample WW-3481 (SC98-166B).—Charcoal from unit 2, measured section C-2, upper zone of layer Cb, in the Muddy

River quarry (lat 46°11.06' N., long 122°03.09' W.) at the confluence of the Muddy River and Smith Creek (Mullineaux, 1996, p. 21) in the Smith Creek Butte quadrangle. The sample is equivalent to laboratory No. W-2661, the age of which is 37,600±1,300 ^{14}C yr B.P. (Crandell and others, 1981).

Sample WW-5561 (JEO 09/15/05-3/1).—Charcoal collected from a sandy lahar deposit along the north shore of Lake Merwin near Woodland Park (lat 45°59.48' N., long 122°29.11' W.) in the Amboy quadrangle. The clast population of the deposit is dominated by quartz-biotite dacite pumice, possibly equivalent to layer Cw (Vogel, 2005). Age courtesy of Jim O'Connor (U.S. Geological Survey).

Other Ages

Crandell and others (1981) reported 17 uncalibrated ages for the Swift Creek stage. Although these ages span a substantial period, some are internally inconsistent, and many are inconsistent with the ages reported by other workers from places where set S tephras are preserved. Here we present the most consistent raw ages and calibrated equivalents for the Swift Creek stage from Crandell and others (1981) and other literature (table 3).

Discussion

Ape Canyon Stage

Before the Ape Canyon stage, the Mount St. Helens area was an eroded terrain of moderate relief carved into mid-Tertiary (32–23 Ma) arc volcanic rocks (Evarts and others, 1987). The Cascade Range in southern Washington was repeatedly glaciated during the middle and late Pleistocene, and glaciers extended from the vicinity of the volcano westward to as low as about 30-m altitude in the Lewis River valley as recently as 60 ka (Grigg and Whitlock, 2002; Evarts, 2004b). Thus, the early record of Mount St. Helens volcanism is poorly preserved and incomplete. A few set C tephras and lava domes are locally preserved, but the most extensive record of early volcanism in the area is preserved as clasts in the Cougar-stage debris-avalanche deposit (see discussion below) and in glacial deposits and lahars in the lower Lewis River valley (Evarts, 2004a, b, 2005) and the valleys of the North and South Forks of the Toutle River (Scott, 1989; Evarts, 2001). Clasts of similar rock types in many younger Mount St. Helens pyroclastic deposits indicate that these older rocks also underlie the present-day edifice. New and existing radiometric ages of rocks and deposits emplaced during the Ape Canyon stage are plotted in figure 5.

Domes in the Goat Mountain and Butte Camp Area

Recent geologic mapping has established the extent of lava domes and remnants of lava domes that project above younger deposits in the area between Goat Mountain and the dome at Butte Camp (fig. 2), and additional rock types have been recognized in the Cougar-stage debris-avalanche deposit (see discussion below). The quartz-biotite dacite of Goat Mountain contains 68–69 weight percent SiO_2 and yielded a K-Ar age of 296±7 ka (sample W97-141, table 1). The hypersthene-hornblende andesite of Butte Camp contains 62–63 percent SiO_2 and yielded an $^{40}Ar/^{39}Ar$ plateau age of 107.4±39.2 ka (sample SC98-193, table 1). A small remnant of another dome east of Butte Camp is a quartz-biotite dacite containing 68 percent SiO_2. All these rocks occur in younger glacial deposits and lahars in the Toutle, Kalama, and Lewis River valleys. Similar rock types have been recognized as lithic clasts in Spirit Lake-stage pyroclastic deposits (for example, the Sugar Bowl blast deposit).

Debris-Avalanche Dacite and Rocks Preserved in the Cougar-Stage Debris-Avalanche Deposit

A substantial part of the Ape Canyon-stage edifice was removed by the Cougar-stage debris avalanche (see discussion below). A quartz-biotite dacite, called debris-avalanche dacite, which occurs as a few dome remnants and composes about 90 percent of the debris-avalanche deposit, is lithologically similar to other Ape Canyon-stage quartz-biotite dacites but is hydrothermally altered. Preliminary ion microprobe U-Th dating of zircons in debris-avalanche clasts indicates an age of about 71±9 ka for the dacite (J.S. Pallister, written commun., 2004). The debris-avalanche dacite and dome remnants vary little in composition and contain 64–65 percent SiO_2.

A few other dacite types constitute the remaining 10 percent of the Cougar-stage debris-avalanche deposit. A hornblende dacite containing 64 percent SiO_2 yielded an $^{40}Ar/^{39}Ar$ plateau age of 160±8.8 ka (sample SC03-642, table 1). A sample of the dacite of McBride Lake from the deposit at McBride Lake (sample SC97-109, fig. 3; loc. 44 of Crandell, 1987) yielded an age of 34.9±4.6 ka (table 1), one of the youngest ages from Ape Canyon-stage deposits.

Deposits Associated with Hayden Creek Drift in the Lewis River Valley

Near Mount St. Helens, the oldest preserved volcanic deposits overlie till that Crandell (1987) correlated with the Hayden Creek Drift of the Mount Rainier region (Crandell and Miller, 1974) on the basis of similar weathering characteristics. Crandell concluded that activity at the Mount St. Helens volcanic center entirely postdated this glaciation, which he inferred was age equivalent to marine isotope stage 4 (~60–75 ka)—too young, as we show below.

Equivalent deposits in the lower Lewis River valley mapped as Amboy Drift by Mundorff (1964) and Evarts (2004a, b, 2005), contain clasts of quartz- and biotite-bearing dacite compositionally indistinguishable from Ape Canyon-stage rocks, recording the occurrence of preglacial or syn-

Table 3. Radiocarbon and calibrated ages of Swift Creek-stage deposits.

[All values in years ± 1σ. Calibrated ages are reported as calendar years before 1950 C.E. All samples were pretreated except those with a laboratory number prefixed by "W." Most of those are from Crandell and others (1981) except samples W-5719 and W-5724, which are from Mullineaux (1996), and sample W-2983, which is from Hyde (1975) (see Crandell and others, 1981, for sample descriptions and locations). Samples Porter 1 and Porter 2 are from S.C. Porter and T.W. Swanson (written commun., 2006); sample Porter 3 is from Porter and others (1983); sample USGS-684 is from Waitt (1985); sample USGS-2780 is from Carrara and Trimble (1992); sample QL-1436 is from Davis and others (1982); sample WSU-2714 is from Baker and Bunker (1985); and sample Clague 1 is from Clague and others (2003). All samples were calibrated by using the curve of Reimer and others (2004).]

Laboratory No.	Description	Radiometric age (^{14}C yr B.P.)	Calibrated age
W-3548	Wood below layer Jg, South Fork of the Toutle River	10,710±150	12,790 (+80/−180)
W-5724	Peat below layer Jg, Fargher Lake	10,980±250	12,900 (+300/−150)
USGS-2780	Peat directly above and below layer Jyn	12,020±60	13,855 (+90/−50)
W-5719	Peat below layer Jy(?), Fargher Lake	11,580±250	13,400 (+300/−200)
W-2832	Base set J, east of Lahar	11,700±90	13,570 (+90/−130)
W-2441	Base set J, Smith Creek	11,880±110	13,750 (+120/−140)
W-2655	Pre-set J lahar, Muddy River, Cedar Flats fan	11,800±90	13,730 (+160/−250)
W-2866	Post set S, pre-set J lithic pyroclastic-flow deposit, Smith Creek, Cedar Flats fan	11,900±190	13,775 (+200/−225)
W-2870	Post set S, pre-set J lithic pyroclastic-flow deposit, Smith Creek, Cedar Flats fan	11,550±230	13,400 (+250/−200)
W-2868	Post set S, pre-set J lithic pyroclastic-flow deposit, Smith Creek, Cedar Flats fan	12,110±110	13,970 (+100/−140)
W-3145	Pre-set J lahar, South Fork of the Toutle River, Crescent Ridge fan	12,270±90	14,130 (+190/−140)
W-3133	Peat above set S, Tower Peak quadrangle	12,120±100	13,990 (+100/−140)
Porter 1	Sediment above set S, Skykomish Valley, Wash.	13,460±70	15,970 (+110/−180)
Porter 2	Sediment above set S, Skykomish Valley, Wash.	13,560±70	16,110 (+240/−160)
Porter 3	Peat above set S, Ohop Valley, Wash.	13,600±70*	16,150 (+230/−170)
QL-1436	Peat above set S, Davis Lake, Wash.	13,800±210	16,425 (+335/−320)
W-2983	Pyroclastic-flow deposit between layers Sg and So, mouth of Swift Creek	13,130±350	15,525 (+540/−470)
W-3141	Pumiceous pyroclastic-flow deposit, early set S, Forest Road 90 at Swift Creek	12,910±160	15,225 (+270/−210)
Clague 1	Estimated layer Sg age, Mono-Fish Lake paleomagnetic record	13,350±100*	15,850 (+200/−230)
WSU-2714	Shells below layer Sg, Mabton, Wash.	13,325±185	15,800 (+300/−300)
USGS-684	Shells below layer Sg, Touchet, Wash.	14,060±450	16,750 (+800/−600)

* Uncertainty not given and arbitrarily assumed to be 70 or 100 yr, respectively.

glacial eruptions at the Mount St. Helens volcanic center. Furthermore, small remnants of alluvial and possible debris-flow deposits composed mostly of Mount St. Helens-derived quartz-biotite±cummingtonite dacite are interbedded with drift at scattered sites in the Lewis River valley (Evarts and others, 2003; Evarts, 2004a, b, 2005). The largest such deposit, in the valley of Cape Horn Creek (fig. 3) about 37 km southwest of the modern volcano, is composed of well-bedded silt, sand, pumiceous pebble gravel, and probable debris-flow beds that contain prismatically jointed dacite clasts as large as 35 cm across. These beds, as thick as 9 m, consist almost entirely of quartz-biotite dacite debris and overlie till that contains sparse clasts of similar lithology. Several quartz-biotite dacite clasts from the Cape Horn Creek locality contain 65–67 percent SiO_2. The paucity of Tertiary rock fragments indicates that these beds are not typical fluvial sedimentary deposits of the Lewis River system, and their position—nearly 460 m above the valley floor—is much too high for them to be an erosional remnant of a valleywide fill. The sedimentary deposits are interpreted as freshly erupted dacitic debris that was transported across the surface of a glacier that occupied the Lewis River valley at that time and that accumulated in a small lake at the glacier margin. Plagioclase separated from a pumice-lapilli bed in the Cape Horn Creek section yielded an $^{40}Ar/^{39}Ar$ plateau age of 263±19 ka (sample 98LC-Q219H2, table 1), and plagioclase separated from a lithic dacite block in a debris-flow(?) bed yielded an analytically similar plateau age of 269±13 ka (sample 98LC-Q219B, table 1). Although both these ages are somewhat younger than the conventional K-Ar age of 296±7 ka for the dacite of Goat Mountain, they all indicate that the earliest activity at the Mount St. Helens volcanic center was considerably earlier than inferred by Crandell (1987) and Mullineaux (1996), and that the Hayden Creek or Amboy Drift is, at least partly, considerably older than inferred by Crandell and represents a glacial advance during marine isotope stage 8 (~300–250 ka).

Lahar Deposits in the Lewis River Valley

The most diverse known record of Ape Canyon-stage volcanism is preserved in lahar and related sedimentary deposits of post-Hayden Creek Drift age in the Lewis River valley. The occurrence of various similar rock types suggests the presence of several lava domes in the vicinity of the volcano and Goat Mountain before construction of the present-day edifice. Rocks from these domes are preserved in till and lahar deposits around Speelyai Bay, along the shores of Lake Merwin (fig. 3; Evarts, 2004a, b), and as far as 15 km farther downstream near Woodland (Evarts, 2005; Vogel, 2005). The lahar and lahar-runout deposits are dominated by Ape Canyon-stage dacite and contain little Tertiary bedrock material. Most of these deposits consist of dense dacite lava clasts that are well rounded, suggesting that they originated as stream alluvium derived from near the volcano and were incorporated into and transported by lahars. Typically, a few rock types dominate each lahar deposit, but several of the deposits are monolithologic, for example, the deposit exposed near the Speelyai Bay boat ramp (loc. E of Major and Scott, 1988) composed of dacite of McBride Lake. The dacite of McBride Lake from the deposit near McBride Lake (loc. 44 of Crandell, 1987) yielded a plateau age of 34.9±4.6 ka (sample SC97-109, table 1). Three other clasts of common, quartz-bearing hornblende dacite containing 65–66 percent SiO_2 collected from Ape Canyon- and Cougar-stage lahar deposits in the Lewis River valley yielded a plateau age of

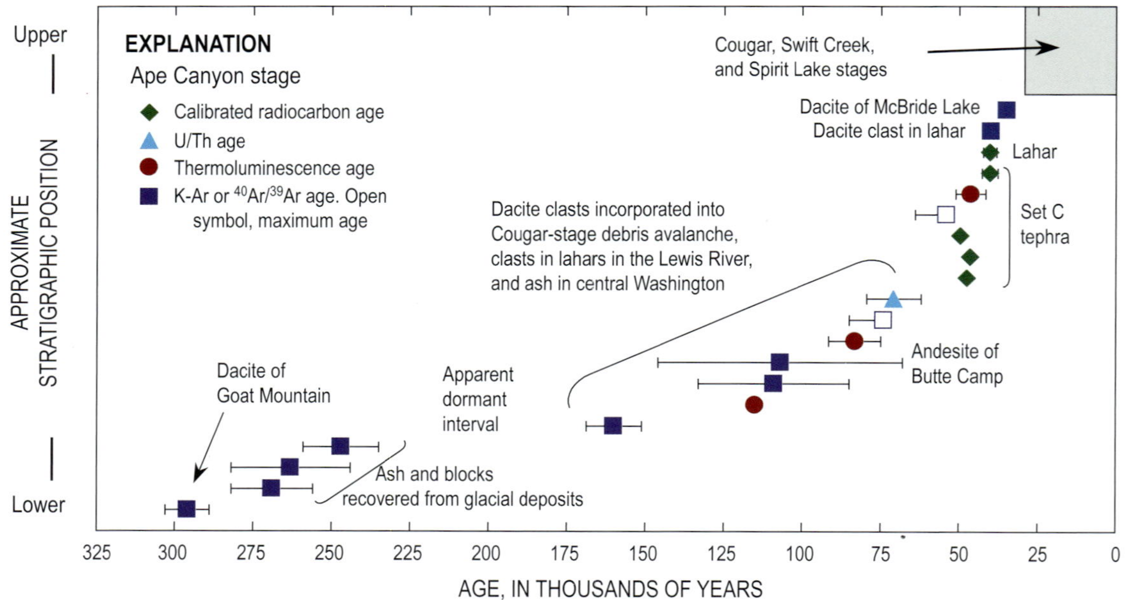

Figure 5. Dated samples for the Ape Canyon stage of Mount St. Helens' eruptive history, showing ages and analytical (1σ) errors. Samples without error bars have uncertainties smaller than symbol, except for oldest thermoluminescence age, which lacks an estimated error. Open symbols, maximum ages. Arranged in approximate stratigraphic order; direct stratigraphic relations do not exist or are unknown for some samples and deposits. See tables 1 and 2 and text for data and references. Radiocarbon ages in calibrated years before 1950 C.E. The Ape Canyon stage lasted from nearly 300 to about 35 ka, with a long hiatus from about 250 to about 160 ka. A second, smaller hiatus may have occurred from about 70 to about 50 ka; however, additional, as-yet-undated samples from glacial and lahar deposits in the Lewis River may partly or completely fill these gaps. Cougar, Swift Creek, and Spirit Lake stages of Mount St. Helens eruptive history fit into the small box at the upper right.

39.8±1.0 ka (sample SC03-619A, table 1), a K-Ar age of 109±24 ka (sample SC97-143, table 1), and a maximum age of 74±11 ka (sample SC03-620A, table 1). Some deposits that consist almost exclusively of well-rounded quartz-biotite dacite pumice clasts within a sandy matrix are interpreted as reworked set C tephra emplaced as lahars or reworked from lahar deposits, as discussed below.

Terraces of laharic gravel and dacite-bearing alluvium occupy several levels along the shore of Lake Merwin (fig. 3). These deposits, as high as 40 m above the pre-reservoir river level, demonstrate that during the Ape Canyon and Cougar stages and after the Hayden Creek-age glacier had retreated, the lower Lewis River valley (fig. 2) contained an extensive fill of volcaniclastic debris from Mount St. Helens. Alternatively, these deposits may represent remnants of lahars and till deposited along the margins of the valley at times when it was filled with glacial ice. The rock types in similar deposits in the North Fork of the Toutle River and lower Cowlitz River valleys (Evarts, 2001) are poorly studied.

Set C Tephra

The oldest deposits from Mount St. Helens recognized by Crandell and others (1981) are set C tephras, with age about 40 ka. A new calibrated age of 47,430±600 yr B.P. (laboratory No. WW-3481, table 2) for tephra layer Cb in the Muddy River quarry is from the same locality as laboratory No. W-2661 (uncalibrated age 37,600±1,300 yr B.P.) of Crandell and others. Charcoal from a monolithologic and probably syneruptive pumiceous sandy lahar on the north shore of Lake Merwin (fig. 3, loc. H of Major and Scott, 1988) yielded a calibrated age of 49,540±1,000 yr B.P. (laboratory No. WW-5561, table 2). Near the volcano, set C deposits that overlie Hayden Creek till are all younger than about 50 ka because any older tephras have been removed or obliterated by glaciation.

Deposits of quartz- and biotite-bearing tephra mineralogically equivalent to set C of Crandell (1987) and Mullineaux (1996) are widespread southwest of the volcano, where they are locally more than 2 m thick (Mundorff, 1964; Evarts and Ashley, 1990a, b; Evarts, 2004a, b, 2005). These deposits, which generally overlie Hayden Creek or Amboy Drift, were assumed to be coeval with the proximal C tephra and are no older than about 50 ka. However, at a few sites in the Lewis River valley (fig. 2), fallout beds of set C tephra underlie till (Evarts, 2005). Plagioclase from a tephra bed beneath till on Green Mountain, about 33 km southwest of Mount St. Helens (fig. 3; Evarts, 2005), yielded an $^{40}Ar/^{39}Ar$ plateau age of 247±12 ka (sample 99YC-P32, table 1), confirming that much-older set C tephras are preserved locally. Furthermore, two other tephras in central Washington that are correlated chemically with Mount St. Helens yielded thermoluminescence ages of 83.2±8.3 and about 115 ka (Busacca and others, 1992; Berger and Busacca, 1995). A thermoluminescence age of 46±5 ka for tephra layer Cy (Berger and Busacca, 1995) agrees closely with the calibrated ages for the adjacent layer Cb and the reworked set C pumice emplaced as lahars, as discussed above.

Set C tephras and related pyroclastic-flow deposits consist of coarsely porphyritic quartz-biotite-cummingtonite-hornblende dacite, mineralogically similar to dense quartz-biotite dacite of the Ape Canyon stage. Fresh set C pumice is rare because most deposits are deeply weathered. Two samples of set C tephra and pumice from pyroclastic-flow deposits at locality 16 of Crandell (1987) have compositions consistent with Ape Canyon-stage dacite. They contain 65–68 percent SiO_2, but most analyses have a loss on ignition of more than 5 percent and plot off the trends defined by dense dacites for most components, suggesting that their compositions have been affected by hydration and alkali and silica loss (fig. 6).

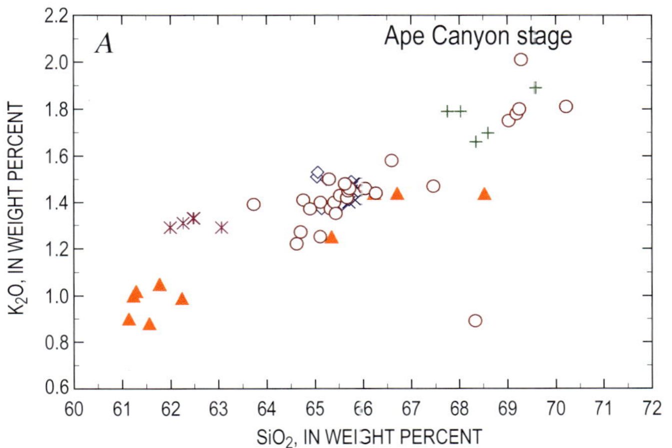

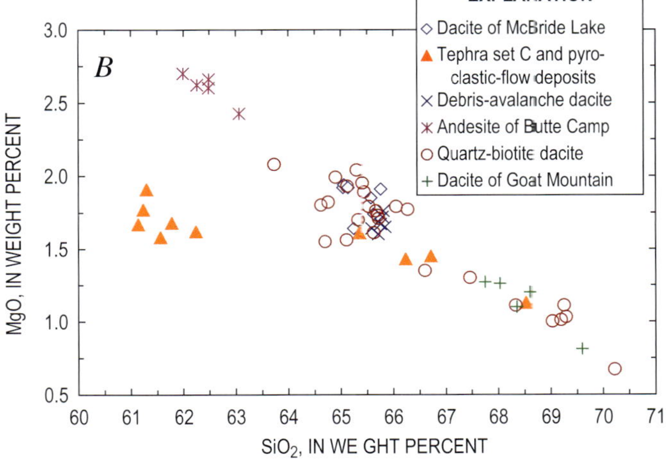

Figure 6. Silica-variation diagrams for Ape Canyon-stage rocks from the Mount St. Helens area (see figs. 2, 3). Samples are mostly U.S. Geological Survey analyses but include some analyses compiled from published reports (Crandell, 1987; Smith and Leeman, 1987; Mullineaux, 1996). *A*, K_2O versus SiO_2. *B*, MgO versus SiO_2.

Ape Canyon-Stage Petrography and Chemistry

Most Ape Canyon-stage rocks consist of coarsely porphyritic hornblende dacite characterized by the presence of quartz and, commonly, biotite. Phenocrysts typically constitute 30 to 40 volume percent of the rock. Plagioclase dominates the phenocryst assemblage and is commonly 0.5 to 1 cm across; complex zoning patterns are present, but resorption textures are sparse. Rounded and embayed quartz is generally present and locally abundant; in a few rocks, quartz is euhedral. Biotite is sparsely present in about half of Ape Canyon-stage dacites, and abundant in a few. Biotite phenocrysts are generally small but can be as large as 5 mm across—for example, in the dacite of Goat Mountain. Small phenocrysts of hypersthene are typically present, especially in rocks lacking biotite, but are generally sparse. Hornblende, commonly 0.5 to 1 cm long, is present in most Ape Canyon-stage dacites. Cummingtonite is sparsely present in a few samples. Complex zoning patterns in hornblende are sparse. Coarse-grained cumulate-textured inclusions and small quench-textured andesitic inclusions are rare in Ape Canyon-stage dacites (except in the andesite of Butte Camp).

Representative analyses of samples of Ape Canyon-stage rocks are listed in table 4, and a larger dataset is plotted in figure 6. The samples range in SiO_2 content from about 62 to 70 weight percent and, despite mineralogic differences, are compositionally similar to dacite from the other volcanic stages at Mount St. Helens (fig. 7). About half of the samples of Ape Canyon stage-rocks contain about 64–66 percent SiO_2, similar to the dacite from later volcanic stages, especially the Cougar and Swift Creek stages. Their contents of all other oxides are also similar to those of younger rocks, including high Na_2O, which distinguishes Mount St. Helens from other Cascade volcanoes. A few Ape Canyon-stage dacites have higher SiO_2 contents, as much as 68–69 percent. Andesite is the primary composition of the andesite of Butte Camp, and some weathered set C tephras may be andesitic. In summary, although little is known in detail about Ape Canyon-stage rocks, they are clearly related to younger Mount St. Helens dacites and are derived from the Mount St. Helens magmatic system.

Summary of Ape Canyon-Stage Volcanism

Radiometric dating of Ape Canyon-stage deposits indicates at least two periods of volcanism at Mount St. Helens during Ape Canyon time—one about 300–250 ka and another about 160–35 ka—possibly separated by a long hiatus. Alternatively, the evidence for eruptive events between 250 and 160 ka has been buried by younger volcanic deposits or simply not yet recognized. The earlier period is represented by the dacite dome of Goat Mountain (fig. 2), just west of the volcano, and by tephra and sediment associated with glacial till in the Lewis River valley and elsewhere (fig. 2). The later period is represented by megablocks in the Cougar-age debris-avalanche deposit, dacite clasts in lahar deposits in the river valleys draining the mountain, the andesite of Butte Camp and a few nearby eroded remnants of unnamed lava domes, set C tephra near the volcano, and older tephra in central Washington. A second, shorter hiatus may have occurred during the later period between about 70 and 50 ka. Some eruptions occurred while the Lewis River valley was occupied by ice.

An extensive hydrothermal system existed at Mount St. Helens late in Ape Canyon time. Most of the debris-avalanche dacite in the Cougar-stage debris-avalanche deposit and some

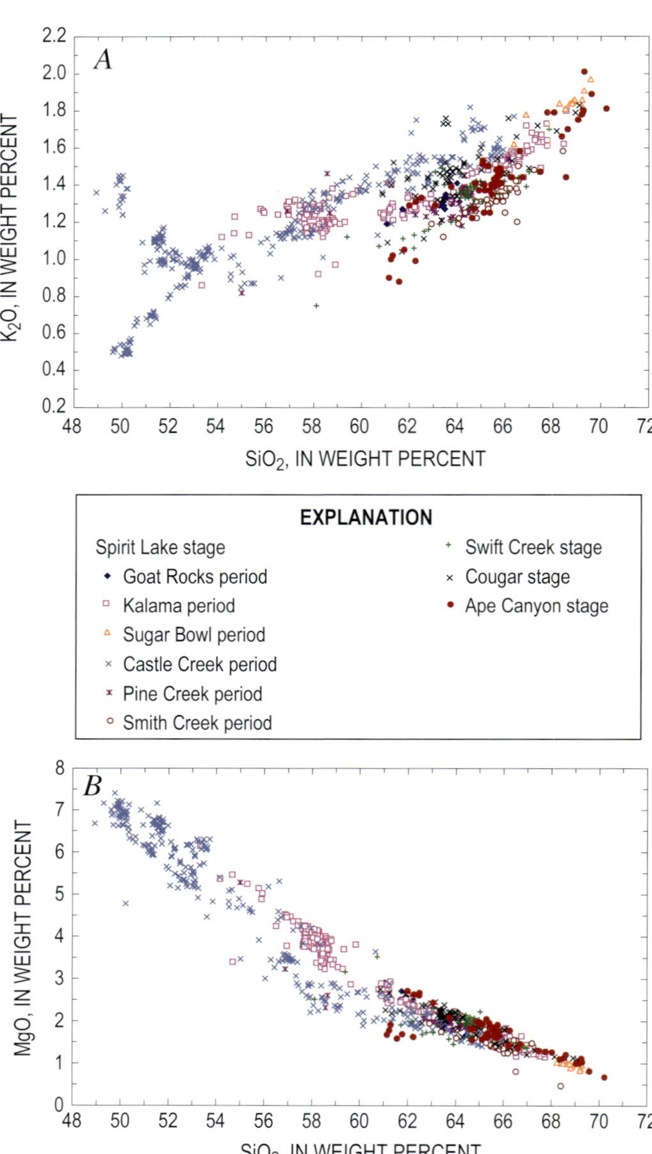

Figure 7. Silica-variation diagrams for 700 Mount St. Helens rocks plotted by eruptive stage or, for Spirit Lake-stage rocks, by eruptive period. Not shown are 1980–86 or 2004–6 rock compositions. Samples are mostly U.S. Geological Survey analyses but include some analyses compiled from published reports (Halliday and others, 1983; Crandell, 1987; Smith and Leeman, 1987, 1993; Gardner and others, 1995; Mullineaux, 1996; Hausback, 2000). *A*, K_2O versus SiO_2. *B*, MgO versus SiO_2.

Table 4. Composition of representative Ape Canyon-stage rocks.

[All samples analyzed at the U.S. Geological Survey laboratory in Denver, Colo.; analysts, David Siems and Joseph E. Taggart, Jr. All values in weight percent, recalculated to 100 weight percent on an anhydrous basis, with Fe_2O_3 = 0.2 total Fe, analyzed as Fe_2O_3. LOI, loss on ignition (in percent). Samples are coded to stratigraphic units as follows: abc, andesite of Butte Camp; dad, debris avalanche dacite; gm, dacite of Goat Mountain; hbd, quartz-bearing hornblende dacite; mcb, dacite of McBride Lake; qbp, quartz-biotite dacite; qbp*, lithic clast in the Sugar Bowl blast deposit.]

Sample --------	**SC98-193**	**SC03-642**	**SC03-619C**	**SC02-539A**	**SC97-143**	**SC03-603A**	**SC03-619A**
Unit-------------	**abc**	**hbd**	**qbp**	**qbp**	**hbd**	**qbp***	**hbd**
Latitude N -----	**46°10.5′**	**46°05.25′**	**45°59.07′**	**45°59.19′**	**46°03.78′**	**46°14.05′**	**45°59.07′**
Longitude W --	**122°14.3′**	**122°12.40′**	**122°31.55′**	**122°33.49′**	**122°13.48′**	**122°09.08′**	**122°31.55′**
			Major-element analyses, weight percent				
SiO_2	62.00	63.74	64.63	65.12	65.13	65.31	65.34
Al_2O_3	17.74	17.67	18.07	18.78	17.11	16.91	17.60
Fe_2O_3	1.08	0.93	0.89	0.82	0.94	0.93	0.82
FeO	3.90	3.33	3.22	2.93	3.38	3.35	2.96
MgO	2.70	2.08	1.80	1.56	1.93	2.04	1.70
CaO	5.68	5.38	4.74	4.18	4.64	4.56	4.75
Na_2O	4.53	4.48	4.53	4.62	4.48	4.48	4.62
K_2O	1.29	1.39	1.22	1.25	1.40	1.50	1.37
TiO_2	0.80	0.69	0.61	0.56	0.66	0.55	0.59
P_2O_5	0.20	0.22	0.23	0.11	0.26	0.21	0.18
MnO	0.08	0.07	0.07	0.07	0.08	0.07	0.07
LOI	0.02	1.02	1.93	3.04	0.84	0.14	0.20
FeO*/MgO	1.80	2.02	2.24	2.35	2.19	2.06	2.18

Sample --------	**SC03-620A**	**SC97-109**	**SC02-484**	**SC02-539B**	**P90-22A**	**W97-141**	**SC03-620B**
Unit-------------	**qbp**	**mcb**	**dad**	**qbp**	**C pf**	**gm**	**qbp**
Latitude N -----	**45°59.16′**	**46°08.49′**	**46°04.03′**	**45°59.19′**	**46°12.36′**	**46°08.85′**	**45°59.16′**
Longitude W--	**122°31.70′**	**122°15.45′**	**122°11.85′**	**122°33.49′**	**122°05.04′**	**122°16.96′**	**122°31.70′**
			Major-element analyses, weight percent				
SiO_2	65.54	65.77	65.82	66.61	67.42	67.76	70.23
Al_2O_3	17.24	16.91	17.12	18.20	16.73	16.78	17.00
Fe_2O_3	0.86	0.93	0.86	0.85	0.78	0.66	0.49
FeO	3.09	3.34	3.11	3.05	2.80	2.39	1.75
MgO	1.79	1.91	1.76	1.35	1.40	1.27	0.67
CaO	4.62	4.44	4.55	3.54	4.03	3.92	2.73
Na_2O	4.56	4.32	4.43	4.01	4.52	4.63	4.81
K_2O	1.43	1.49	1.48	1.58	1.57	1.79	1.81
TiO_2	0.59	0.65	0.60	0.60	0.53	0.48	0.34
P_2O_5	0.20	0.17	0.20	0.12	0.17	0.25	0.13
MnO	0.07	0.08	0.07	0.08	0.06	0.07	0.04
LOI	0.12	0.29	2.19	2.94	2.32	0.29	1.15
FeO*/MgO	2.15	2.19	2.21	2.81	2.49	2.36	3.26

remnants of similar rocks in the area between Goat Mountain and Butte Camp (fig. 2) are propylitically altered. Calcite is abundant and pyrite sparse within the matrix; mafic minerals are altered and replaced by chlorite and, rarely, epidote; and the groundmass of these rocks is thoroughly recrystallized, indicating alteration by hot water. Although the timing of this alteration is unclear, the debris-avalanche dacite is about 70 ka in age, and the absence of older altered rocks suggests that the hydrothermal system was active in the interval after about 70 ka and before about 30 ka.

The long period of intermittent volcanism during the Ape Canyon stage produced a cluster of dacite domes at an altitude as high as about 1,800 m slightly west of and at the present site of Mount St. Helens. In tephra sections, the interval between sets C and M (Cougar stage) is occupied by ash deposits, as thick as 1 m, that contain at least three weathering profiles (Mullineaux, 1996). Thus, the nature and duration of the hiatus between the Ape Canyon and Cougar stages is poorly constrained, but no lava flows or domes related to Mount St. Helens have ages corresponding to the period 35–28 ka.

Cougar Stage

The Cougar stage, between about 28 and 18 ka, was probably the most active stage in the volcano's history before its most recent, or Spirit Lake, stage. During the Cougar stage, voluminous pyroclastic flows, dacite domes, tephra, and a large-volume pyroxene andesite lava flow accompanied a debris avalanche. A few events have recently been recognized that preceded previous reconstructions of the Cougar stage. In combination with calibrated radiocarbon ages, these events reveal that the Cougar stage began somewhat before the 21–18 ka range proposed by Crandell (1987) and Mullineaux (1996). Cougar-stage stratigraphy is summarized in figure 8, and the ages of Cougar-stage rocks and deposits are listed in tables 1 and 2. These new ages and those presented in the subsection below entitled "Swift Creek stage" suggest that the Cougar and Swift Creek stages may have been separated by only a short hiatus; nevertheless, herein we retain the terminology of Crandell (1987) and Mullineaux (1996). The eruptions and deposits related to tephra sets M and K are designated "Cougar stage," whereas those related to tephra sets S and J are designated "Swift Creek stage."

Early Domes and Lahar Deposits

Early in the Cougar stage, an unknown number of hornblende dacite domes were erupted under the area covered by the present-day volcano (fig. 2). Though buried by younger volcanic deposits, these domes are represented by blocks in

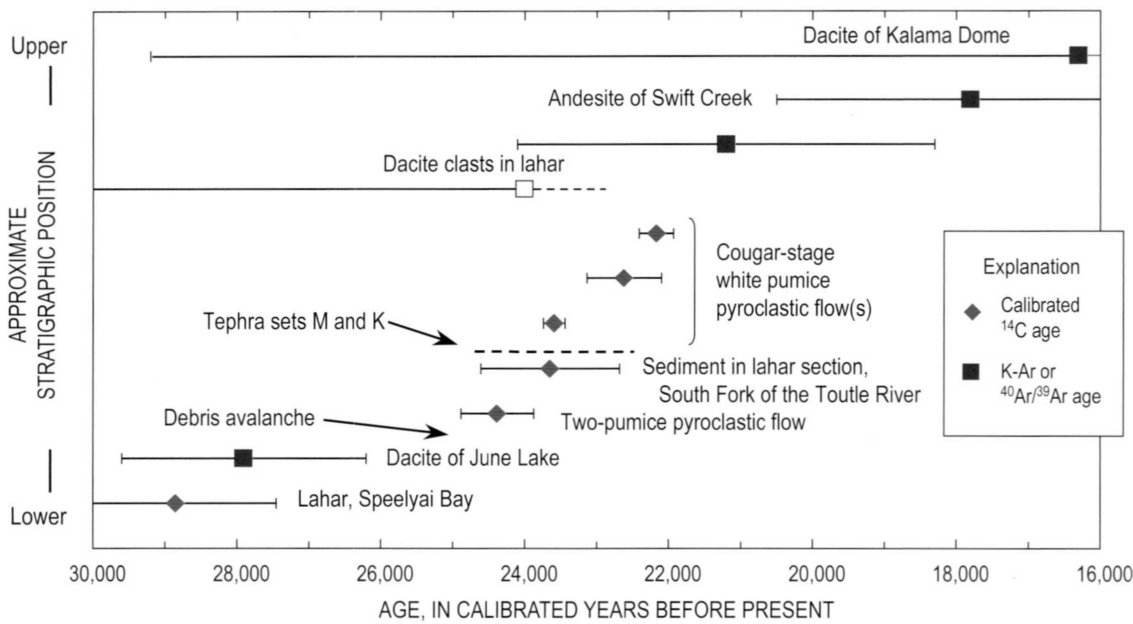

Figure 8. Dated samples for the Cougar stage of Mount St. Helens' eruptive history, showing ages and analytical (1σ) errors. Open symbols, maximum ages. Arranged in approximate stratigraphic order; direct stratigraphic relations do not exist or are unknown for some of these samples and deposits. Radiocarbon ages in calibrated years before 1950 C.E. The Cougar stage lasted from about 28 ka to about 18 ka. See tables 1 and 2 and text for data and references. Stratigraphic position of dacite clasts in Cougar-stage lahar is shown at approximate position of parent domes, which may be related to dome building that accompanied Cougar-stage white pumice eruptions. Lahar containing dacite clasts also contains andesite of Swift Creek and slightly postdates it. Same symbols and error bars as in figure 5.

lithic pyroclastic-flow deposits, blocks in the Cougar-stage debris-avalanche deposit, and clasts in Fraser-age glacial till and lahar deposits in the Lewis River valley. Lahar deposits containing various hypersthene-hornblende dacite clasts occur in the area around the east end of Swift Reservoir and in the lower Lewis River valley overlying Ape Canyon-stage lahar deposits. Some of these lahars probably traversed the Pine Creek drainage from a source in the vicinity of the present-day volcano. Lahar deposits and their reworked equivalents that lack debris-avalanche dacite are extensive in the Lewis River valley from Swift Dam to the east end of Lake Merwin and probably predate the Cougar-stage debris-avalanche deposit (see below). Charcoal in sediment from beneath a lahar deposit near Speelyai Bay yielded a calibrated age of 28,850±1,400 yr B.P. (sample MS-5, table 2) that is interpreted as a maximum age for the deposit (Major and Scott, 1988). A dacite clast from a similar nearby lahar deposit yielded an $^{40}Ar/^{39}Ar$ isochron age of 21.2±2.9 ka (sample SC03-611D, table 1). Lahar deposits of similar age and lithology also occur in the South Fork of the Toutle River and Cowlitz River drainages (fig. 3; Crandell, 1987; Scott, 1989; Evarts and Ashley, 1990b). Wood from sediment interbedded with these lahar deposits yielded a radiocarbon age of 23,650 (+485/−965) cal yr B.P. (sample Scott BC, table 2; Scott, 1989).

A small dome of hypersthene-hornblende dacite containing 63.5 percent SiO_2 in the Kalama River valley 13 km southwest of Mount St. Helens (figs. 1, 2) was informally designated the "dacite of Kalama Dome" by Evarts and Ashley (1990a). The rock yielded an $^{40}Ar/^{39}Ar$ isochron age of 16.3±12.9 ka (sample SC98-155, table 1), but the large uncertainty of the age and absence of stratigraphic context for this dome prevents interpreting its relation to other Cougar-stage events. The dacite of Kalama Dome probably was erupted during the Cougar stage, but a Swift Creek age is also possible. A small exposure of a cummingtonite-hypersthene-hornblende dacite lithic pyroclastic-flow deposit, called the dacite of June Lake, underlies Swift Creek-stage deposits near June Lake. The rock, which contains nearly 69 percent SiO_2, yielded an $^{40}Ar/^{39}Ar$ plateau age of 27.9±1.7 ka (sample SC98-192, table 1), indicating deposition during the Cougar stage. Fragments of this rock type also occur as lithic clasts in the two-pumice pyroclastic-flow deposit (see below). Early Cougar-stage rocks in the Cougar-stage debris-avalanche and lahar deposits near the east end of Swift Reservoir consist mostly of porphyritic hypersthene-hornblende dacite containing 64–65 percent SiO_2 that was emplaced as domes and lithic pyroclastic flows.

Cougar-Stage Debris-Avalanche Deposit and Two-Pumice Pyroclastic-Flow Deposit

The most devastating Cougar-stage event was a debris avalanche composed primarily of Ape Canyon-stage rocks. First noted by Mullineaux and Crandell (1981) and described briefly by Newhall (1982), the debris avalanche emplaced a 200- to 300-m-thick sheet of mostly hydrothermally altered debris in the drainage of ancestral Swift Creek as far south as the Lewis River (fig. 2). Crandell suggested that this debris avalanche originated in the area between Butte Camp and Goat Mountain. The approximately 17-km runout of the debris avalanche, however, suggests an origin from an altitude of about 2,000 to 2,200 m, estimated by using the length/distance relation of Siebert (1984). Together with remnants of the debris-avalanche deposit that are buried under younger deposits in the Cedar Flats area, the evidence suggests a source in the area of the present-day edifice. The volume of the Cougar-stage debris-avalanche deposit was at least 1 km^3, probably nearly 2 km^3, similar in volume to the 1980 debris avalanche. The Cougar-stage debris avalanche blocked the Lewis River at the present site of Swift Creek, and incision of the temporary dam generated flood-breakout lahars downstream in the Lewis River valley as far as the Columbia River and filled the lower Lewis River valley with lahar deposits to depths of at least 75 m. Filling of Yale Lake and Lake Merwin flooded many exposures of these lahar deposits, but they crop out sporadically along the shores of both reservoirs (Evarts, 2004a, b) and are well exposed in the vicinity of the community of Cougar. These lahar deposits are interpreted to be of Cougar age because they contain abundant clasts of debris-avalanche dacite and pumice from the overlying two-pumice pyroclastic-flow deposit. Lahar deposits and material eroded from the Cougar-stage debris-avalanche deposit also filled the east end of the valley now covered by Swift Reservoir to a depth of about 75 m.

Emplacement of the Cougar-age debris-avalanche deposit was followed immediately by a large dacitic pyroclastic eruption that produced the two-pumice pyroclastic-flow deposit, charcoal from which has a calibrated age of 24,380 (+510/–480) yr B.P. (laboratory No. W-2540, table 2). The contact between these two deposits displays no evidence of erosion or soil formation; thus, onset of the eruption that produced the two-pumice pyroclastic flow probably initiated the Cougar-stage debris avalanche, which in the Swift Creek drainage is buried under as much as 100 m of pumice and ash.

The two-pumice pyroclastic-flow deposit consists of many individual flow units and has a volume of at least 1 km^3. These flow units contain pumice of two distinct lithologic and compositional types: light-colored pumice of hypersthene-hornblende dacite containing 66–68 percent SiO_2, and homogeneous light- to dark-brown pumice of augite-hypersthene-hornblende dacite containing 63.5–64.5 percent SiO_2 (fig. 9; table 5). Blocks of banded pumice of both compositions are rare. The two-pumice pyroclastic-flow deposit can be recognized by abundant blocks of pumice, several meters across, as far as 12 km from the volcano. Dense, prismatically jointed blocks of dacite near the top of the two-pumice pyroclastic-flow deposit demonstrate that late in the eruption, dacite domes grew in the vent. Small amounts of the two-pumice pyroclastic-flow deposit or its reworked equivalent also occur in the Cedar Flats area and in some lahar deposits in the lower Lewis River and in the South Fork of the Toutle River west of Sheep Camp (fig. 3;

loc. 71 of Crandell, 1987). The distribution of the two-pumice pyroclastic-flow deposit is similar to that of the underlying Cougar-stage debris-avalanche deposit, suggesting that the vent was in the area of the present-day edifice.

Tephra Sets M and K and Cougar-Stage White Pumice

Sets M and K tephra were erupted in quick succession after the two-pumice pyroclastic flow and were followed by a second large-volume dacitic pyroclastic eruption that produced the herein-named Cougar-stage white pumice. Early-emplaced set M tephras consist of cummingtonite-hornblende dacite and are overlain by hypersthene-hornblende-cummingtonite dacite tephra, also in set M (Mullineaux, 1996). The composition of set M tephra is poorly known, because only a few analyses of weathered pumice that yielded andesitic compositions are available. Set K tephra consists of hypersthene-hornblende dacite (Mullineaux, 1996), and a single analyzed sample contains 67 percent SiO_2.

Extensive pyroclastic-flow deposits of the Cougar-stage white pumice overlie sets M and K tephras and the two-pumice pyroclastic-flow deposit on the south flank of Mount St. Helens from the Lewis River cliffs eastward to Marble Mountain (fig. 2). Smaller exposures occur in the Smith and Pine Creek drainages. Three calibrated ages for the Cougar-stage white pumice (samples W-2413, W-4531, WW-4543, table 2) range from 22.2 to 23.6 ka. The Cougar-stage white pumice consists of porphyritic hypersthene-hornblende dacite, with subtle variations in phenocryst content and abundance. Six analyses fall into two groups: one containing about 63 percent SiO_2 and a second containing about 65 percent SiO_2. The variations in lithology, composition, and age suggest that the Cougar-stage white pumice may represent more than one eruption, although no stratigraphic breaks within the unit have been observed.

Andesite of Swift Creek

The Cougar stage culminated with emplacement of the andesite of Swift Creek, a lava flow on the south flank of Mount St. Helens (fig. 2). The vent for the lava flow was near an altitude of about 1,830 m, probably at or near the summit of the volcano at that time. The andesite of Swift Creek consists of porphyritic hornblende-augite-hypersthene andesite to dacite containing 61–63.5 percent SiO_2 with a complex phenocryst assemblage. About 0.75 km^3 in volume, this lava flow was probably the largest in the history of Mount St. Helens. Its varying composition and multiple populations of plagioclase and mafic phenocrysts indicate a magma-mixing origin.

The andesite of Swift Creek, as thick as 200 m, flowed nearly 6 km down Swift Creek, where it presently forms the divide between the West Fork and main stem of Swift Creek. In contrast to the interpretation by Crandell (1987), the lava flow appears to overlie the two-pumice pyroclastic-flow deposit and probably overlies the Cougar-stage white pumice. Our radiometric dating of this lava flow indicates an $^{40}Ar/^{39}Ar$ plateau age of 17.8±2.7 ka (sample SC99-343, table 1). Fraser-age till (for example, locs. 39, 40, 47, and 49 of Crandell, 1987) contains abundant clasts derived from the andesite of Swift Creek and so must at least partly postdate its emplacement.

Petrography of Cougar-Stage Rocks

Most Cougar-stage rocks are less coarsely porphyritic than Ape Canyon-stage rocks. Crystal content commonly approaches 50 volume percent, although the crystals in Cougar-stage rocks are generally smaller. Cougar-stage rocks are dominated by plagioclase, with hornblende and hypersthene as the major mafic phenocryst phases. Cummingtonite and augite are present in a few units, especially set M tephra, but quartz and biotite are generally absent, even in high-silica dacite. Plagioclase phenocryst populations vary, but plagioclase in most Cougar-stage dacite displays complex zoning

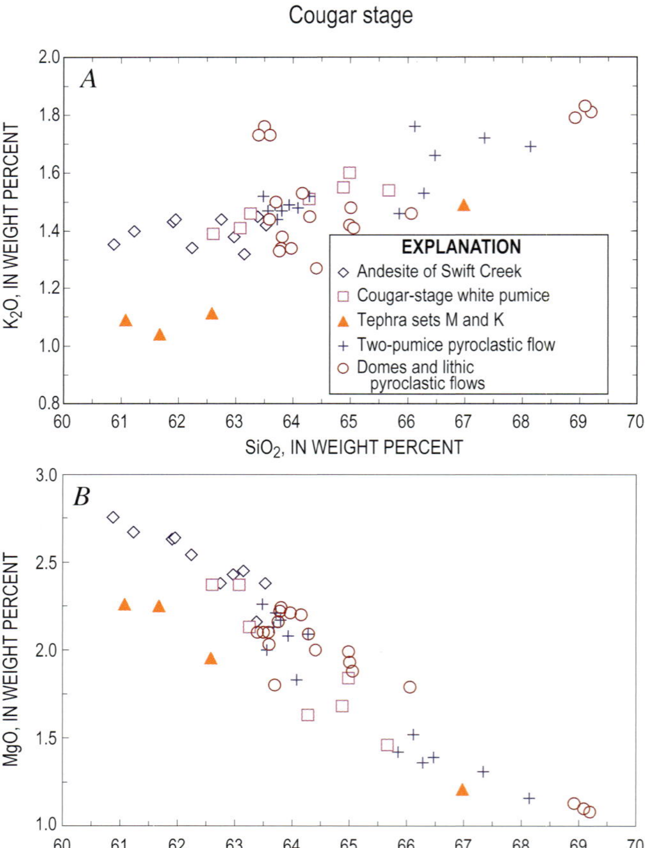

Figure 9. Silica-variation diagrams for Cougar-stage rocks from the Mount St. Helens area (figs. 2, 3). Samples are mostly U.S. Geological Survey analyses but include some analyses compiled from published reports (Crandell, 1987; Smith and Leeman, 1987, 1993; Evarts and Ashley, 1990a, b; Mullineaux, 1996). *A*, K_2O versus SiO_2. *B*, MgO versus SiO_2.

Table 5. Composition of representative Cougar-stage rocks.

[All samples analyzed at the U.S. Geological Survey laboratory in Denver, Colo.; analysts, David Siems and Joseph E. Taggart, Jr. All values in weight percent, recalculated to 100 weight percent on an anhydrous basis, with Fe_2O_3 = 0.2 total Fe, analyzed as Fe_2O_3. LOI, loss on ignition (in percent). Samples are coded to stratigraphic units as follows: asw, andesite of Swift Creek; djl, dacite of June Lake; dk, dacite of Kalama Dome; hbd, hornblende dacite clasts in debris-avalanche and lahar deposits at the east end of Swift Reservoir and in lahar deposits in the lower Lewis River valley; two-pum dk or two-pum lt, dark or light-colored pumice in two-pumice pyroclastic flow; white, Cougar-stage white pumice.]

Sample -------	**SC97-114**	**SC97-141**	**SC98-251A**	**SC98-250**	**SC01-440**	**SC02-487**	**SC98-155**
Unit------------	**asw**	**two-pum dk**	**two-pum dk**	**two-pum lt**	**white**	**white**	**dk**
Latitude N ----	**46°07.24′**	**46°04.19′**	**46°05.87′**	**46°05.16′**	**46°03.25′**	**46°06.62′**	**46°07.79′**
Longitude W--	**122°12.17′**	**122°11.84′**	**122°11.95′**	**122°12.25′**	**122°12.88′**	**122°10.69′**	**122°19.76′**
			Major-element analyses, weight percent				
SiO_2	61.23	63.72	64.28	66.12	64.88	63.26	63.50
Al_2O_3	17.66	17.29	17.24	17.16	17.56	17.87	17.55
Fe_2O_3	1.15	1.05	1.00	0.83	0.96	1.04	0.97
FeO	4.13	3.80	3.61	2.97	3.44	3.75	3.51
MgO	2.67	2.21	2.09	1.52	1.68	2.13	2.10
CaO	5.97	4.80	4.70	4.18	4.23	4.82	4.90
Na_2O	4.50	4.47	4.50	4.57	4.67	4.53	4.63
K_2O	1.40	1.44	1.52	1.76	1.55	1.46	1.76
TiO_2	0.84	0.77	0.72	0.58	0.63	0.76	0.73
P_2O_5	0.36	0.35	0.26	0.24	0.33	0.31	0.27
MnO	0.09	0.09	0.08	0.07	0.07	0.08	0.08
LOI	0.08	0.96	1.17	0.95	2.29	1.85	0.06
FeO*/MgO	1.93	2.14	2.17	2.44	2.56	2.20	2.09
Sample -------	**SC98-192**	**SC03-611D**	**SC03-580**	**SC03-581**	**SC04-696**	**SC04-700C**	**SC03-612**
Unit------------	**djl**	**hbd**	**hbd**	**hbd**	**hbd**	**hbd**	**hbd**
Latitude N ----	**46°09.14′**	**45°58.91′**	**46°06.29′**	**46°06.30′**	**46°02.43′**	**46°02.66′**	**45°58.93′**
Longitude W--	**122°09.65′**	**122°26.35′**	**122°00.40′**	**122°00.39′**	**122°04.53′**	**122°05.55′**	**122°26.45′**
			Major-element analyses, weight percent				
SiO_2	68.92	66.06	65.01	65.06	63.70	64.41	69.24
Al_2O_3	16.46	17.05	17.32	17.20	18.11	17.54	16.34
Fe_2O_3	0.62	0.86	0.88	0.89	1.01	0.92	0.60
FeO	2.23	3.09	3.16	3.21	3.64	3.32	2.18
MgO	1.13	1.79	1.93	1.88	1.80	2.00	1.08
CaO	3.51	4.37	4.87	4.78	4.62	5.04	3.43
Na_2O	4.72	4.45	4.46	4.66	4.50	4.58	4.68
K_2O	1.79	1.46	1.48	1.41	1.50	1.27	1.80
TiO_2	0.44	0.60	0.63	0.62	0.71	0.64	0.43
P_2O_5	0.14	0.19	0.18	0.21	0.32	0.21	0.17
MnO	0.06	0.07	0.07	0.08	0.08	0.08	0.05
LOI	0.09	0.46	1.28	0.04	2.58	0.01	1.30
FeO*/MgO	2.47	2.16	2.05	2.14	2.53	2.08	2.51

patterns; the zoning in larger crystals preserves an extended history of repeated crystallization and resorption, whereas smaller crystals are generally weakly zoned. Hornblende phenocrysts can be complexly zoned and commonly have thick to thin breakdown rims—features typical of those observed in younger Mount St. Helens dacites (Rutherford and Hill, 1993; Rutherford and Devine, this volume, chap. 31; Thornber and others, this volume, chap. 32).

Coarse-grained inclusions with cumulate or plutonic textures are present in Cougar-stage rocks but generally are smaller and less conspicuous than in Swift Creek- or Spirit Lake-stage rocks. Inclusions with quenched textures have been observed only in the dacite of June Lake and the two-pumice pyroclastic-flow deposit. Features indicating strong disequilibrium are generally absent in Cougar-stage dacite; however, Mullineaux (1996) reported the presence of olivine in separates of tephra layer Mo that suggests a basaltic component in the magmatic system at that time. Despite the petrographic differences, Cougar-stage rocks are compositionally similar to Ape Canyon-stage dacite (figs. 6, 9) and to younger Swift Creek- and Spirit Lake-stage dacites (fig. 7). The petrography and chemistry of Cougar-stage rocks indicate production from various magma batches of similar composition that were fractionated under similar conditions. Andesitic composition, shown by some set M tephras and the andesite of Swift Creek, suggest the presence of a more mafic component during the Cougar stage than earlier in Mount St. Helens' history. The magmatic system of the Spirit Lake stage probably first evolved during the Cougar stage.

Summary of Cougar Stage Volcanism

The earliest known Cougar-stage eruptive events were lahars in the South Fork of the Toutle River, Pine Creek, and the Lewis River (fig. 2) and lithic pyroclastic flows on the south flank of Mount St. Helens, which are about 28 ka in age. These deposits probably originated from lava domes erupted in the area of the present-day edifice. Many Ape Canyon-stage deposits in that area were removed and redeposited in ancestral Swift and Pine Creeks by the Cougar-stage debris avalanche, which was followed immediately by the two-pumice pyroclastic flow (about 24.4 ka) and then by sets M and K tephras and the Cougar-stage white pumice (about 23.6–22.2 ka). The debris flow and pyroclastic eruptions formed a thick sequence of fragmental deposits on the south flank of the volcano that blocked the Lewis River at Swift Creek. Subsequent failure of this blockage generated flood-breakout lahars that traversed the lower Lewis River. Emplacement of the andesite of Swift Creek about 18 ka divided the south flank into the West Fork of Swift Creek and the Swift Creek drainages.

At the end of the Cougar stage, Mount St. Helens consisted of a cluster of dacite domes at the site of the present-day edifice. No eruptions of the volcano are known between about 18 and about 16 ka, corresponding to the demise of the Cougar stage and the onset of the Swift Creek stage. The hiatus is probably shorter than that envisioned by Crandell (1987) and Mullineaux (1996), because additional eruptions, unrecognized by them, occurred between the Cougar-stage white pumice and the basal set S tephra of the Swift Creek stage.

Swift Creek Stage

During the Swift Creek stage, the widespread sets S and J tephras were erupted, and three extensive fans of fragmental debris were emplaced on the southeast, south, west, and northwest flanks of Mount St. Helens from dacite domes. Crandell (1987) speculated that these fans were emplaced by disruption of a single dome approximately in the center of the present-day edifice. However, though broadly lithologically similar, the dacitic clasts that occur within the Swift Creek, Crescent Ridge, and Cedar Flats fans are lithologically distinct and must each have had separate sources.

Swift Creek Fan

The Swift Creek fan covers much of the south flank of Mount St. Helens in the drainage of the West Fork of Swift Creek (fig. 2), where it overlies Cougar-stage deposits and Fraser-age till. This fan includes some of the deposits described by Hyde (1975) as the Swift Creek assemblage. The lower part of the fan, which predates late set S tephra (Crandell, 1987), consists of pumiceous and lithic pyroclastic-flow deposits of cummingtonite-bearing hypersthene-hornblende dacite containing about 67 percent SiO_2. The upper part of the fan, which postdates set S tephra, consists of lithic pyroclastic-flow deposits of hypersthene-hornblende dacite containing 64–65 percent SiO_2. The total thickness of the fan is about 30 m. Lahar deposits dominated by clasts of Swift Creek age cap the fan. Similar deposits in the small canyon just south of the old Timberline Campground at 1,340 m altitude on the northeast flank of the volcano are correlated with the Swift Creek fan. The site of the dome(s) that erupted the Swift Creek fan is poorly known, but it must have been in the vicinity of the present-day edifice. Hausback (2000) suggested that the Loowit and Archybacter domes, which are exposed in the walls of the 1980 eruption crater, are of Swift Creek age. If so, their petrography and lithology are most similar to Swift Creek fan rocks. The Swift Creek fan is smaller in volume than the Crescent Ridge or Cedar Flats fan. A lahar deposit exposed below Merwin Dam on the Lewis River (fig. 3) is probably related to the Swift Creek fan, and some lahar deposits in the vicinity of Cougar may be of Swift Creek age (Crandell, 1987).

Crescent Ridge Dome and Crescent Ridge Fan

The Crescent Ridge fan is a wedge of fragmental material that stretches from the Studebaker Creek area southward to Butte Camp on the northwest and west flanks of Mount St. Helens (fig. 2). This fan is at least 200 m thick, approximately centered below the Crescent Ridge dome, and consists dominantly of lithic pyroclastic-flow deposits. Pumiceous pyroclastic-flow deposits are also common in the lower part of the fan. Lahar deposits from the Crescent Ridge fan are preserved locally in the South Fork of the Toutle River (for example, loc. 72 of Crandell, 1987; Evarts and Ashley, 1990b) and in the Toutle River north of Silver Lake (Evarts, 2001).

Rocks of the Crescent Ridge fan are well exposed in the headwaters of the South Fork of the Toutle River (loc. 76 of Crandell, 1987) and in Studebaker Creek (fig. 2). The rocks fall into two lithologic groups: an early, primarily pumiceous group of cummingtonite-hornblende dacite (sparse small hypersthene) and a later, dominantly lithic group of augite-hypersthene-hornblende dacite (abundant hypersthene and sparse augite). Lithology varies somewhat in each group, especially in the abundances of different size ranges of plagioclase, but the textural characteristics of plagioclase are similar. The abundance of relatively large plagioclase crystals derived from gabbroic inclusions also varies. Both groups contain 64–65 percent SiO_2, although a few samples contain less. The composition and phenocryst mineralogy of the Crescent Ridge dome are similar to those of the lower, pumiceous part of the fan.

Most, and possibly all, of the Crescent Ridge fan probably postdates set S tephra (Crandell, 1987). No set S tephras have been observed within the fan, and layer Jg tephra overlies the fan. Preliminary paleomagnetic data (D.E. Champion, written commun., 2005) suggest that the early and late parts of the fan differ in age, possibly by decades or centuries. The distribution and mineralogy of the Crescent Ridge pyroclastic-fan deposits suggest that they originated partly from the currently exposed part of the Crescent Ridge dome, as well as from a now-buried uphill extension of the Crescent Ridge dome or from nearby domes no longer exposed. On the west flank of Mount St. Helens, drainage radial to the Crescent Ridge dome incised the Crescent Ridge pyroclastic fan; some of that drainage is still active, but part was later buried by voluminous pyroclastic-fan deposits of Spirit Lake (Kalama) age.

Cedar Flats Fan

The Cedar Flats fan completely filled the valley of Pine Creek and spilled into the Lewis River valley in the vicinity of Cedar Flats (fig. 2) during the period between the eruption of sets S and J tephra. This fan is at least 100 m thick in Pine Creek and 50 to 100 m thick in the Cedar Flats area. Remnants of lahar and lithic pyroclastic-flow deposits in the Smith Creek and Ape Canyon drainages indicate that a small component of the Cedar Flats fan originated on the east flank of Mount St. Helens and traveled down the Muddy River. The fan is dominated by lahar deposits but also contains lithic pyroclastic-flow deposits of dense hypersthene-hornblende dacite similar to set S tephra that were produced by hot collapses of growing domes which must have been situated near the present-day edifice. The Cedar Flats fan filled the Lewis River valley to a depth of at least 50 m in the area around the west end of Swift Reservoir and flowed an unknown distance down the Lewis River. Most clasts in the fan contain 64–65 percent SiO_2.

Age of Swift Creek-Stage Volcanism

The age of set S tephras (specifically the late set S layers Sg and So) is disputed. Radiocarbon ages (fig. 10; table 3) cited by Mullineaux (1996) seem to establish the onset of set S volcanism at about 15.5 ka, on the basis of the age of a pyroclastic flow interbedded in the set. However, additional radiocarbon ages from localities where layers Sg and So are interbedded with Missoula Flood deposits in eastern Washington and Vashon Drift in the Puget Lowland are as old as 16.5 ka (Davis and others, 1982; Porter and others, 1983; Baker and Bunker, 1985; Waitt, 1985; S.C. Porter and T.W. Swanson, written commun., 2006). These radiocarbon ages were determined on shells, peat, or sediment, and the results are neither internally nor stratigraphically consistent. Furthermore, in at least one sample, it is unclear which set S layer was being dated. The samples from set S pyroclastic flows were not pretreated, and so their ages may be slightly too young. Correlation using the Mono Lake-Fish Lake paleosecular-variation curve suggests an age for layers Sg and So of about 15.8 ka (Clague and others, 2003), depending on the assumptions used. Consideration of all these ages suggests the most reliable age for layers Sg and So is about 16 ka. The older set S tephras are probably no more than a few hundred years older, because they lack weathering zones (Mullineaux, 1996).

The precise ages of the Swift Creek-stage pyroclastic fans are unknown. Accumulation of the Swift Creek fan probably began around 16 ka and continued for an unknown period. The Crescent Ridge fan at least partly overlies set S tephras and is overlain by set J tephras. These fans may have accumulated quickly; a dated lahar deposit overlying the Crescent Ridge fan is younger than about 14 ka. The Cedar Flats fan postdates set S tephra and predates set J tephra; determinations on unpretreated samples from within the fan indicate an age of about 14 ka if the age for tephra layer Jyn is accurate. The apparent hiatus shown in figure 10 in the period of about 15–14 ka separates volcanism related to the older set, S, and the younger set, J, and is corroborated by the weak soil zone at the top of set S tephra (Mullineaux, 1996). However, nonexplosive volcanism probably continued during at least part of this period and formed the Crescent Ridge and Cedar Flats fans.

All three fans of Swift Creek stage are overlain by set J tephra. Calibrated ages are slightly contradictory, probably owing to a lack of pretreatment among the samples processed before 1990. The best single age may be that of Carrara and Trimble (1992) for layer Jyn in northeastern Washington. The sample was pretreated, and its calibrated age, 13,855 (+90/−50) yr B.P. (laboratory No. USGS-2780, table 3), suggests that set J tephra probably began accumulating at least as early as about 13.86 ka. Other ages suggest that the later set J tephras may be as young as about 12.8 ka. Additional geochronologic data are needed to refine the period represented by Swift Creek-stage volcanism.

Swift Creek Stage Petrography

Set S tephras consist of cummingtonite- and hornblende-bearing silicic andesite and dacite (fig. 11; table 6), and all but layer Sw also contain hypersthene (Mullineaux, 1986). Analyses indicate that layer So contains about 62–63 percent SiO_2 and layer Sg about 64 percent SiO_2. Varyingly porphyritic dacite, containing 63 to 67 percent SiO_2 and containing combinations of hornblende, hypersthene, and augite, were erupted from Mount St. Helens during the period equivalent to and shortly after set S tephras and deposited as the fans described above. Though similar macroscopically, the pyroclastic fans are distinguishable on the basis of their relative proportions of phenocrysts, textural characteristics of phenocryst minerals, and systematic differences in bulk chemistry. Plagioclase and hornblende display complex zoning patterns and evidence of reheating, resorption, and reaction.

Early set J tephras, layers Js and Jy, consist of hypersthene-hornblende silicic andesite containing 62–63 percent SiO_2; and later set J tephras, layers Jb and Jg, of hypersthene-hornblende andesite containing 58–61 percent SiO_2 (Mullineaux, 1996; Smith and Leeman, 1987). The youngest and most widespread set J tephra, layer Jg, also contains augite. No lava domes or flows are known to be associated with set J tephra; however, a dacite lava flow adjacent to, but clearly younger than, the Crescent Ridge dome may be similar in age to set J.

Some Swift Creek-stage dacite contains reacted cummingtonite or augite. Complexly sieve-textured plagioclase with thin overgrowth rims is common in tephra layer Jg, much more so than in any set S-related Swift Creek rocks described to date. Complexly zoned hornblende is also common. Coarse-grained inclusions with cumulate or plutonic textures are locally common in rocks of the Crescent Ridge and Cedar Flats fans but generally smaller and less conspicuous than in Spirit Lake-stage rocks. Inclusions exhibiting quench texture are absent in Swift Creek-stage rocks. Although no temperature data are available, the presence of cummingtonite in early Swift Creek-stage rocks suggests that the magmas may have evolved from relatively cool and wet to relatively hot and dry (Geschwind and Rutherford, 1992).

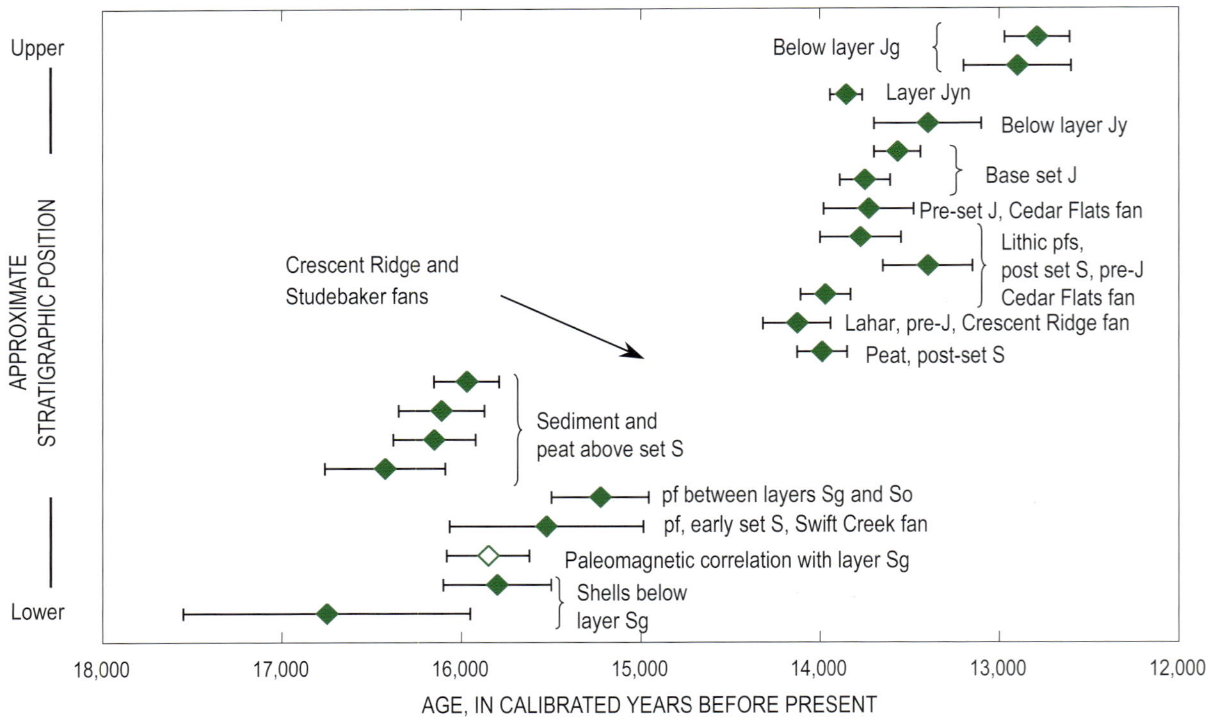

Figure 10. Dated samples for the Swift Creek stage of Mount St. Helens' eruptive history, showing ages and analytical (1σ) errors. Arranged in approximate stratigraphic order; direct stratigraphic relations do not exist or are unknown for some samples and deposits. Radiocarbon ages in calibrated years before 1950 C.E. The Swift Creek stage lasted from about 16 ka to possibly as late as about 12.8 ka. See table 3 and text for data and references. Same symbols and error bars as in figure 5, except open symbol, which represents estimated age for tephra layer Sg on the basis of correlation of radiocarbon ages with Fish Lake and Mono Lake paleomagnetic records.

Summary of Swift Creek-Stage Volcanism

Volcanism was intense during the relatively short Swift Creek stage, from about 16.0 to about 12.8 ka. Eruptions during this stage were dominated by the extrusion of dacite domes and the generation of lithic pyroclastic flows derived from them. Lithic pyroclastic-flow deposits were extensively reworked in the Pine Creek drainage, and two widespread tephra sets were erupted: set S before most of the dome building and set J after the dome building. The composition and lithology of Swift Creek-stage dacite vary little, but set J tephras are andesitic. At the end of the Swift Creek stage, Mount St. Helens consisted of a cluster of dacite domes with a summit altitude as high as about 2,100 m. Thick sequences of fragmental deposits filled the drainages of the mountain from Studebaker Creek south around to Pine Creek. Additional fans were probably emplaced on the north flank but, if so, have been buried by younger deposits. No eruptions are known between about 12.8 ka and the beginning of the Spirit Lake stage at about 3.9 ka (Crandell, 1987; Mullineaux, 1996).

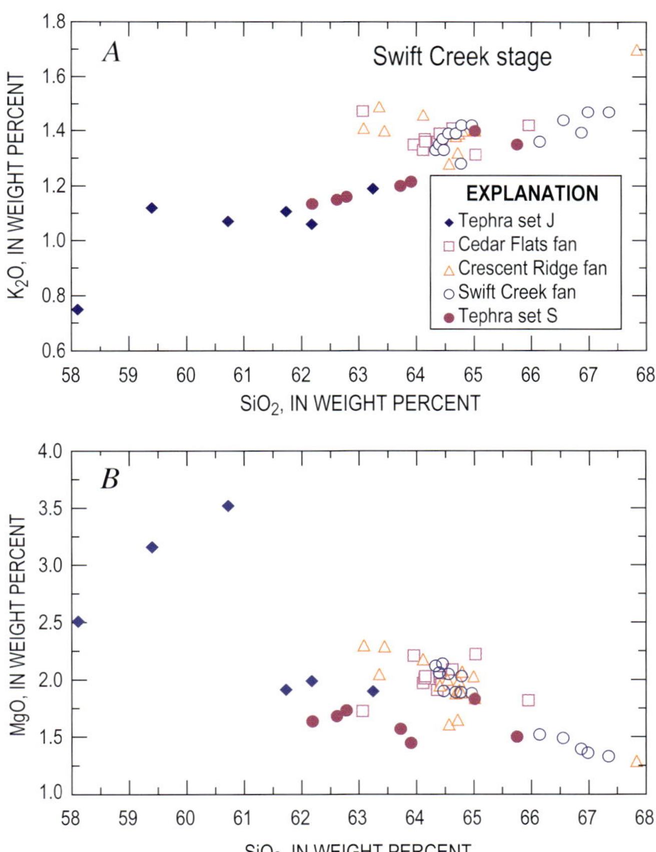

Figure 11. Silica-variation diagrams for Swift Creek-stage rocks from the Mount St. Helens area (figs. 2, 3). Samples are mostly U.S. Geological Survey analyses but include some analyses compiled from published reports (Halliday and others, 1983; Crandell, 1987; Smith and Leeman, 1987; Mullineaux, 1996; Hausback, 2000). *A*, K_2O versus SiO_2. *B*, MgO versus SiO_2.

Spirit Lake Stage

The Spirit Lake stage (3.9–0 ka), which includes the youngest and most complex part of the eruptive history of Mount St. Helens, has been described in several reports, particularly those by Hoblitt and others (1980) and Mullineaux and Crandell (1981), and so only a brief summary is given here. The excellent preservation of deposits, abundance of radiocarbon ages (Crandell and others, 1981; Hausback and Swanson, 1990), tree-ring chronology (Yamaguchi, 1983, 1985; Yamaguchi and Lawrence, 1993; Yamaguchi and Hoblitt, 1995; Yamaguchi and others, 1990) and paleomagnetic work (Hagstrum and others, 2002) have elucidated considerable detail for this period. Although volcanism was intermittent, with hiatuses of a few to about 600 years, at the scale of our knowledge of other stages the Spirit Lake stage appears continuous. The Spirit Lake stage is divided into seven eruptive periods (fig. 1): the Smith Creek (3.9–3.3 ka), Pine Creek (3–2.5 ka), Castle Creek (2.2–1.9 ka), Sugar Bowl (1,200–1,150 yr B.P.), Kalama (1479–1750 C.E.), Goat Rocks (1800–1857 C.E.), and Modern (1980–present) (data and terminology of Mullineaux, 1996; slightly modified by Clynne and others, 2004; Clynne and others, 2005). Volcanism during the Spirit Lake stage is dominated by dacite, as were earlier stages, but various compositions from basalt to high-silica dacite have also been erupted (fig. 7). Basalt and basaltic andesite dominated during the Castle Creek period, andesite was erupted during the Pine Creek and Kalama periods, and basaltic to andesitic magmatic inclusions sparsely occur in some dacites of the Pine Creek, Sugar Bowl, and Kalama periods.

The bulk of the pre-1980 edifice of Mount St. Helens above about 1,800-m altitude was constructed during the Spirit Lake stage. During the Smith Creek period, Mount St. Helens was highly explosive and erupted mostly tephra and pyroclastic flows, but at least one lava dome was also emplaced, and large lahars swept down the North Fork of the Toutle River to at least the Columbia River. During the Pine Creek period, Mount St. Helens erupted at least three dacite domes, and two large fans of lithic dacite were deposited by lithic pyroclastic flows and lahars, one in the Pine Creek and Swift Creek drainages and another in the Studebaker and Castle Creek drainages. During the late Pine Creek period, Mount St. Helens erupted andesite and basaltic andesite lava flows; then, after a short hiatus, volcanism resumed. During the Castle Creek period, Mount St. Helens erupted dacite, andesite, and basalt as tephra, pyroclastic flows, and lava domes and flows. During the Pine Creek and Castle Creek periods, Mount St. Helens gained much of its cone shape, and by their end, it had attained an altitude of about 2,450 m. During the Sugar Bowl period, three dacitic lava domes were emplaced, and a small lateral blast and tephra layer were erupted. The early Kalama period was initiated by two large tephra eruptions and followed by the growth of dacite lava domes and pumiceous and lithic pyroclastic flows; the middle Kalama period was dominated by eruption of andesite lava flows; and during the

Table 6. Composition of representative of Swift Creek-stage rocks.

[All samples analyzed at the U.S. Geological Survey laboratory in Denver, Colo.; analysts, David Siems and Joseph E. Taggart, Jr. All values in weight percent, recalculated to 100 weight percent on an anhydrous basis, with Fe_2O_3 = 0.2 total Fe, analyzed as Fe_2O_3. LOI, loss on ignition (in percent). Samples are coded to stratigraphic units as follows: cd, Crescent Ridge dome; cff, Cedar Flats fan; csf, Crescent Ridge fan; J, layer Jg pumice; S, set S pumice; swf, Swift Creek fan.]

Sample -------	**SC98-201**	**SC03-573**	**SC03-583**	**SC03-587A**	**W95-84**	**W94-32**
Unit------------	**Jg**	**cff**	**cff**	**cff**	**cd**	**csf**
Latitude N ----	**46°11.4′**	**46°04.53′**	**46°04.45′**	**46°09.92′**	**46°12.04′**	**46°11.47′**
Longitude W--	**122°14.1′**	**122°00.25′**	**122°00.07′**	**122°05.51′**	**122°12.73′**	**122°13.85′**
Major-element analyses, weight percent						
SiO_2	59.40	64.63	64.44	63.96	64.41	64.75
Al_2O_3	19.02	17.32	17.59	17.33	17.46	17.39
Fe_2O_3	1.26	0.90	0.91	0.97	0.95	0.91
FeO	4.54	3.23	3.27	3.50	3.40	3.29
MgO	3.16	2.09	1.96	2.21	1.95	1.91
CaO	5.94	4.98	4.91	5.13	4.97	4.78
Na_2O	4.29	4.54	4.64	4.55	4.58	4.65
K_2O	1.12	1.41	1.34	1.35	1.36	1.40
TiO_2	0.93	0.63	0.63	0.71	0.67	0.63
P_2O_5	0.25	0.19	0.22	0.22	0.18	0.20
MnO	0.10	0.07	0.08	0.08	0.08	0.08
LOI	2.73	0.20	0.01	0.15	0.09	0.14
FeO*/MgO	1.79	1.93	2.09	1.98	2.18	2.16
Sample -------	**W94-72B**	**W01-211**	**SC98-270A**	**SC98-266**	**SC98-269**	**SC03-587B**
Unit------------	**csf**	**swf**	**swf**	**swf**	**swf**	**S**
Latitude N ----	**46°12.81′**	**46°07.79′**	**46°05.64′**	**46°07.21′**	**46°07.23′**	**46°09.92′**
Longitude W--	**122°14.13′**	**122°12.02′**	**122°13.36′**	**122°12.08′**	**122°12.35′**	**122°05.51′**
Major-element analyses, weight percent						
SiO_2	65.02	64.46	64.69	64.97	66.99	65.76
Al_2O_3	17.41	17.48	17.65	17.37	17.14	18.12
Fe_2O_3	0.87	0.90	0.91	0.90	0.75	0.81
FeO	3.15	3.24	3.28	3.23	2.72	2.93
MgO	1.84	2.14	1.89	1.88	1.36	1.50
CaO	4.90	4.98	4.80	4.73	4.09	4.17
Na_2O	4.57	4.54	4.52	4.63	4.74	4.52
K_2O	1.40	1.37	1.39	1.42	1.47	1.35
TiO_2	0.60	0.63	0.64	0.62	0.50	0.57
P_2O_5	0.17	0.19	0.16	0.17	0.15	0.21
MnO	0.07	0.07	0.08	0.08	0.07	0.07
LOI	0.96	0.55	0.20	0.06	0.15	3.58
FeO*/MgO	2.14	1.89	2.17	2.14	2.49	2.44

late Kalama period, a large dome was emplaced at the summit of the volcano. Overall, during the Kalama period, lava flows and a summit dome added about 500 m height to the volcano and gave Mount St. Helens its pre-1980 form. During the Goat Rocks period, a tephra layer, lava flow, and a dome and small lithic pyroclastic fan were emplaced.

Implications of Older Rocks for the Mount St. Helens Magmatic System

Although only limited data are available to characterize the magmatic system of Mount St. Helens before the Spirit Lake stage, a few generalizations are possible. On the basis of the data discussed above, we infer that the general interpretations of Smith and Leeman (1987, 1993) that were derived primarily from their study of the Spirit Lake stage are generally applicable to the earlier stages. Dacite at Mount St. Helens probably originates by melting of mafic rocks in the lower crust (Smith and Leeman, 1987), and andesite is the result of mixing between dacite and basalt derived from the mantle (Smith and Leeman, 1993). The more detailed mixing model of Pallister and others (1992) for the Kalama period is probably applicable to other periods of the Spirit Lake stage. Disaggregation of the abundant coarse-grained inclusions in many Mount St. Helens dacites and andesites are a complicating factor for interpreting these rocks (Cooper and Reid, 2003).

Hopson and Melson (1990) recognized similarities in the composition of Mount St. Helens rocks that were repeated over time, and they introduced the concept of compositional cycles. They noted a tendency for eruptions early in a cycle to be highly explosive and the magma to contain cummingtonite and (or) quartz plus biotite. They inferred that the magma is relatively cool and water rich at the beginning of a cycle. As the cycle proceeds, the magma becomes hotter and less water rich, eruptions less explosive, and the mafic phenocrysts dominated by hornblende and hypersthene. The volcano tends to produce dacite that varies only slightly lithologically over a period of decades to centuries, probably indicating replenishment of the shallow magma chamber with hotter and dryer magma from deeper in the magmatic system. Cycles end with effusive eruptions of relatively mafic composition containing an anhydrous mineral assemblage of hypersthene, augite, and, sporadically, olivine. Hopson and Melson (1990) attributed the cycles to establishment of a compositional gradient in the magmatic system during repose of the volcano, eruption of part of the system, and reestablishment of the compositional gradient during the following repose.

Hopson and Melson's compositional-cycle concept, which was developed before any comprehensive understanding of the eruptive history of Mount St. Helens, fails to explain many details of this history. These details are probably better explained by the occasional interaction of a fundamentally dacitic magmatic system with basalt from the mantle. Nevertheless, evidence suggests that volatile enrichment of the shallow magmatic system from below plays a role in the evolution of Mount St. Helens magmas.

Compositional cycles as envisioned by Hopson and Melson (1990) for the Spirit Lake stage were probably absent during the Ape Canyon stage. The common presence of biotite and quartz during the Ape Canyon stage indicates that early Mount St. Helens magmas were generally cooler and wetter than those later in its eruptive history. Successive eruptive units vary considerably petrographically, and equilibrium phenocryst textures suggest probably much less interaction between magma batches, possibly because recharge and eruptions were more intermittent. The volume erupted per unit of time was smaller and the magmatic system less integrated during the Ape Canyon stage, especially before about 50 ka. However, the detailed stratigraphy of the Ape Canyon stage is poorly known, and the incomplete preservation of Ape Canyon-stage deposits makes recognition of compositional cycles difficult.

By the Cougar stage, the magmatic system was beginning to resemble that of the present day. At times during the Cougar stage, Mount St. Helen erupted cool and wet magmas containing cummingtonite, although most Cougar-stage rocks lack cummingtonite, biotite, or quartz, are less crystalline than most Ape Canyon-stage rocks, and probably represent hotter, less evolved magma. Although the magmatic system was still primarily dacitic, more interaction occurred between magma batches, and the volcano was probably more continually active than during the Ape Canyon stage. Sequences of pumiceous pyroclastic-flow deposits as thick and widespread as those emplaced in Cougar time have not been erupted since. The Cougar stage probably culminated with eruption of the voluminous andesite of Swift Creek, a mixed-magma lava flow.

The Swift Creek stage may be the first well-developed magmatic cycle at Mount St. Helens. The thin weathering zone between the Cougar and Swift Creek stages and the return to cummingtonite-bearing magma suggests a short hiatus between the stages. After an initial explosive phase, the Swift Creek stage was primarily a period of dacite dome building. During this period, the volcano erupted dacite with decreasing chemical variation and an increasingly anhydrous mafic phenocryst assemblage. Complex zoning of plagioclase and hornblende phenocrysts and evidence of disequilibrium conditions indicate that interaction between dacitic magma batches was extensive. These features suggest cryptic interaction of the Swift Creek dacitic magma with a hotter, probably more mafic magma as the Swift Creek stage progressed. The Swift Creek stage ended with the eruption of set J tephras, which are sparsely porphyritic and andesitic and contain resorbed phenocrysts, indicating interaction with hot or mafic magma.

During the earlier stages, the Mount St. Helens magmatic system erupted proportionately more dacite than during the Spirit Lake stage. The mafic component is subtler, possibly because it represents a smaller proportion of the total magmatic system. Alternatively, interaction with mafic magma may have occurred at a deeper level during the earlier stages than during the Spirit Lake stage. Much additional study of the petrology of rocks from the Ape Canyon, Cougar, and Swift Creek stages is needed to further evaluate the magmatic system during the early history of Mount St. Helens.

Summary

The stratigraphy and radiometric dating described herein provide more detail on the early history of Mount St. Helens than was previously available, and the petrographic and bulk-rock chemical data are useful for a preliminary evaluation of the long-term magmatic history of the volcano. Radiometric dating of rocks preserved in debris-avalanche, lahar, and glacial deposits demonstrates that Mount St. Helens has a much longer history than previously appreciated. Rocks as old as 300 ka are recognized and assigned to the Ape Canyon stage of Crandell (1987) and Mullineaux (1996). Many Ape Canyon-stage rocks are recognized by the presence of quartz and (or) biotite but are chemically similar to younger Mount St. Helens dacite.

During the Cougar and Swift Creek stages, the eruptive style of Mount St. Helens changed from intermittent dacitic activity of the Ape Canyon stage to the episodic and compositionally varying activity of the Spirit Lake stage. Significant eruptive events of the Cougar stage included dacite dome building, removal of part of the edifice by a debris avalanche, and emplacement of large-volume pyroclastic flows and an andesite lava flow. The Swift Creek stage was relatively short lived and dominated by the construction of dacite domes on the edifice and fans of fragmental material on the flanks of the volcano. Preliminary petrographic analysis of Cougar- and Swift Creek-stage rocks suggests that Cougar-stage rocks resemble Ape Canyon-stage rocks, whereas Swift Creek-stage rocks are more like those of the Spirit Lake stage. These characteristics indicate that the volcano's magmatic system has evolved from relatively simple to more complex as the volcano matured and that interaction between dacitic magma batches with more mafic magma increased from the Ape Canyon to Spirit Lake stages. Further work may allow us to subdivide the history of the Ape Canyon stage and will clarify the magma processes active during the Ape Canyon, Cougar, and Swift Creek stages.

Acknowledgments

We thank Jim O'Connor for discussions on deposits in the Lewis River and age of the Swift Creek stage. Chemical analyses of USGS samples were expertly performed by Dave Siems, Joe Taggart, and Tammy Hannah. John Pallister, Cynthia Gardner, and Rick Hoblitt graciously contributed chemical analyses of some Spirit Lake-stage samples to our compilation. John McGeehin performed the radiocarbon analyses reported for the samples in table 2 with a laboratory number prefixed by "WW." John Pallister provided preliminary data on the debris-avalanche dacite zircon age. Michelle Coombs, Duane Champion, and Scott Starratt provided technical reviews that improved the manuscript.

References Cited

Baker, V.R., and Bunker, R.C., 1985, Cataclysmic late Pleistocene flooding from glacial Lake Missoula; a review: Quaternary Science Reviews, v. 4, p. 1–44.

Berger, G.W., and Busacca, A.J., 1995, Thermoluminescence dating of late Pleistocene loess and tephra from eastern Washington and southern Oregon and implications for the eruptive history of Mount St. Helens: Journal of Geophysical Research, v. 100, p. 22361–22374.

Busacca, A.J., Nelstead, K.T., McDonald, E.V., and Purser, M.D., 1992, Correlation of distal tephra layers in loess in the channeled scablands and Palouse of Washington State: Quaternary Research, v. 37, p. 281–303.

Carrara, P.E., and Trimble, D.A., 1992, A Glacier Peak and Mount St. Helens J volcanic ash couplet and the timing of deglaciation in the Colville Valley area, Washington: Canadian Journal of Earth Sciences, v. 29, p. 2397–2405.

Clague, J.J., Barendregt, R., Enkin, R.J., and Foit, F.F., Jr., 2003, Paleomagnetic and tephra evidence for tens of Missoula floods in southern Washington: Geology, v. 31, p. 247–250.

Clynne, M.A., Champion, D.E., Wolfe, E.W., Gardner, C.A., and Pallister, J.S., 2004, Stratigraphy and paleomagnetism of the Pine Creek and Castle Creek eruptive episodes, Mount St. Helens, Washington [abs.]: Eos (American Geophysical Union Transactions), v. 85, no. 47, Fall Meeting Supplement Abstract V43E-1453.

Clynne, M.A., Ramsey, D.W., and Wolfe, E.W., 2005, The pre-1980 eruptive history of Mount St. Helens, Washington: U.S. Geological Survey Fact Sheet 2005–3045, 4 p.

Cooper, K.M., and Reid, M.R., 2003, Re-examination of crystal ages in recent Mount St. Helens lavas: implications for magma reservoir processes: Earth and Planetary Science Letters, v. 213, nos. 1–2, p. 149–167.

Crandell, D.R., 1987, Deposits of pre-1980 pyroclastic flows and lahars from Mount St. Helens Volcano, Washington: U.S. Geological Survey Professional Paper 1444, 91 p.

Crandell, D.R., and Miller, R.D., 1974, Quaternary stratigraphy and extent of glaciation in the Mount Rainier region, Washington: U.S. Geological Survey Professional Paper 847, 59 p.

Crandell, D.R., Mullineaux, D.R., Rubin, M., Spiker, E., and Kelley, M.L., 1981, Radiocarbon dates from volcanic deposits at Mount St. Helens, Washington: U.S. Geological Survey Open-File Report 81–844, 15 p.

Cutler, K.B., Gray, S.C., Burr, G.S., Edwards, R.L., Taylor, F.W., Cabioch, G., Beck, J.W., Cheng, H., and Moore, J., 2004, Radiocarbon calibration and comparison to 50 kyr B.P. with paired ^{14}C and ^{230}Th dating of corals from Vanuatu and Papua New Guinea: Radiocarbon, v. 46, p. 1127–1160.

Dalrymple, G.B., 1989, The GLM continuous laser system for $^{40}Ar/^{39}Ar$ dating; description and performance characteristics: U.S. Geological Survey Bulletin 1890, p. 89–96.

Dalrymple, G.B., Alexander, E.C., Jr., Lanphere, M.A., and Kraker, G.P., 1981, Irradiation of samples for $^{40}Ar/^{39}Ar$ dating using the Geological Survey TRIGA reactor: U.S. Geological Survey Professional Paper 1176, 55 p.

Davis, P.T., Barnosky, C.W., and Stuiver, M., 1982, A 20,000 year record of volcanic ashfalls, Davis Lake, southwestern Washington [abs.]: American Quaternary Association Annual Conference, 7th, Seattle, 1982, Program and Abstracts, June 28–30, p. 87.

Duffield, W.A., and Dalrymple, G.B., 1990. The Taylor Creek Rhyolite of New Mexico, a rapidly emplaced field of lava domes and flows: Bulletin of Volcanology, v. 52, p. 475–487.

Engels, J.C., Tabor, R.W., Miller, F.K., and Obradovich, J.D., 1976, Summary of K-Ar, Rb-Sr, U-Pb, Pb-α and fission track ages of rocks from Washington prior to 1975 (exclusive of Columbia Plateau basalts): U.S. Geological Survey Miscellaneous Field Studies Map MF–710, scale 1:1,000,000.

Evarts, R.C., 2001, Geologic map of the Silver Lake quadrangle, Cowlitz County, Washington: U.S. Geological Survey Miscellaneous Field Studies Map MF–2371, scale 1:24,000.

Evarts, R.C., 2004a, Geologic map of the Ariel quadrangle, Clark and Cowlitz Counties, Washington: U.S. Geological Survey Scientific Investigations Map 2826, 35 p., scale 1:24,000 [http://pubs.usgs.gov/sim/2004/2826].

Evarts, R.C., 2004b, Geologic map of the Woodland quadrangle, Clark and Cowlitz Counties, Washington: U.S. Geological Survey Scientific Investigations Map 2827, 38 p., scale 1:24,000 [http://pubs.usgs.gov/sim/2004/2827].

Evarts, R.C., 2005, Geologic map of the Amboy quadrangle, Clark and Cowlitz Counties, Washington: U.S. Geological Survey Scientific Investigations Map 2885, 25 p., scale 1:24,000 [http://pubs.usgs.gov/sim/2005/2885].

Evarts, R.C., and Ashley, R.P., 1990a, Preliminary geologic map of the Cougar quadrangle, Cowlitz County, Washington: U.S. Geological Survey Open-File Report 90–632, 47 p., scale 1:24,000.

Evarts, R.C., and Ashley, R.P., 1990b, Preliminary geologic map of the Goat Mountain quadrangle, Cowlitz and Clark Counties, Washington: U.S. Geological Survey Open-File Report 90–631, 40 p., scale 1:24,000.

Evarts, R.C., Ashley, R.P., and Smith, J.G., 1987, Geology of the Mount St. Helens area; record of discontinuous volcanic and plutonic activity in the Cascade Arc of southern Washington: Journal of Geophysical Research, v. 92, no. B10, p. 10155–10169.

Evarts, R.C., Clynne, M.A., Fleck, R.J., Lanphere, M.A., Calvert, A.T., and Sarna-Wojcicki, A.W., 2003, The antiquity of Mount St. Helens and the age of the Hayden Creek Drift [abs.]: Geological Society of America Annual Meeting Abstracts with Programs, v. 35, no. 6, p. 80.

Gardner, J.E., Carey, S., Rutherford, M.J., and Sigurdsson, H., 1995, Petrologic diversity in Mount St. Helens dacites during the last 4,000 years; implications for magma mixing: Contributions to Mineralogy and Petrology, v. 119, nos. 2–3, p. 224–238.

Geschwind, C.-H., and Rutherford, M.J., 1992, Cummingtonite and the evolution of the Mount St. Helens (Washington) magma system; an experimental study: Geology, v. 20, p. 1011–1014.

Grigg, L.D., and Whitlock, C., 2002, Patterns and causes of millennial-scale climate change in the Pacific Northwest during Marine Isotope stages 2 and 3: Quaternary Science Reviews, v. 21, p. 2067–2083.

Hagstrum, J.T., Hoblitt, R.P., Gardner, C.A., and Gray, T.E., 2002, Holocene geomagnetic secular variation recorded by volcanic deposits at Mount St. Helens, Washington: Bulletin of Volcanology, v. 63, p. 545–556.

Halliday, A.N., Fallick, A.E., Dickin, A.P., Mackenzie, A.B., Stephens, W.E., and Hildreth, W., 1983, The isotopic and chemical evolution of Mount St. Helens: Earth and Planetary Science Letters, v. 63, no. 2, p. 241–256, doi:10.1016/0012-821X(83)90040-7.

Hausback, B.P., 2000, Geologic map of the Sasquatch Steps area, north flank of Mount St. Helens, Washington: U.S. Geological Survey Map I–2463, scale 1:4,000.

Hausback, B.P., and Swanson, D.A., 1990, Record of prehistoric debris avalanches on the north flank of Mount St. Helens volcano, Washington: Geoscience Canada, v. 17, p. 142–145.

Hildreth, W., and Lanphere, M.A., 1994, Potassium-argon geochronology of a basalt-andesite-dacite arc system; the Mount Adams volcanic field, Cascade Range of southern Washington: Geological Society of America Bulletin, v. 106, p. 1413–1429.

Hoblitt, R.P., Crandell, D.R., and Mullineaux, D.R., 1980,

Mount St. Helens eruptive behavior during the past 1,500 yr: Geology, v. 8, p. 555–559.

Hopson, C.A., 2008, Geologic map of Mount St. Helens, Washington prior to the 1980 eruption: U.S. Geological Survey Open-File Report 02–468, scale 1:31,250.

Hopson, C.A., and Melson, W.G., 1990, Compositional trends and eruptive cycles at Mount St. Helens: Geoscience Canada, v. 17, p. 131–141.

Hyde, J.H., 1975, Upper Pleistocene pyroclastic flow deposits and lahars south of Mount St. Helens volcano: U.S. Geological Survey Bulletin 1383–B, 20 p.

Lanphere, M.A., and Dalrymple, G.B., 2000, First-principles calibration of ^{38}Ar tracers; implications for the ages of ^{40}Ar/^{39}Ar fluence standards: U.S. Geological Survey Professional Paper 1621, 10 p.

Ludwig, K.R., 1999, User's manual for Isoplot/Ex version 2, a geochronological toolkit for Microsoft Excel: Berkeley, Calif., Berkeley Geochronology Center Special Publication 1a, 47 p.

Mahon, K., 1996, The new "York" regression; application of an improved statistical method to geochemistry: International Geology Reviews, v. 38, p. 293–303.

Major, J.J., and Scott, K.M., 1988, Volcaniclastic sedimentation in the Lewis River Valley, Mount St. Helens, Washington—processes, extent, and hazards: U.S. Geological Survey Bulletin 1383–D, 38 p.

McDougall, I., and Harrison, T.M., 1999, Geochronology and thermochronology by the ^{40}Ar/^{39}Ar method (2d ed.): Oxford, U.K., Oxford University Press, 269 p.

McGeehin, J., Burr, G.S., Jull, A.J.T., Reines, D., Gosse, J., Davis, P.T., Muhs, D., and Southon, J.R., 2001, Stepped-combustion ^{14}C dating of sediment: A comparison with established techniques: Radiocarbon, v. 43-2A, no. 1, p. 255–262.

Mullineaux, D.R., 1986, Summary of pre-1980 tephra-fall deposits erupted from Mount St. Helens, Washington State, USA: Bulletin of Volcanology, v. 48, p. 17–26.

Mullineaux, D.R., 1996, Pre-1980 tephra fall deposits erupted from Mount St. Helens, Washington: U.S. Geological Survey Professional Paper 1563, 99 p.

Mullineaux, D.R., and Crandell, D.R., 1981, The eruptive history of Mount St. Helens, *in* Lipman, P.W., and Mullineaux, D.R., eds., The 1980 eruptions of Mount St. Helens, Washington: U.S. Geological Survey Professional Paper 1250, p. 3–15.

Mundorff, M.J., 1964, Geology and ground-water conditions of Clark County, Washington, with a description of a major alluvial aquifer along the Columbia River: U.S. Geological Survey Water-Supply Paper 1600, scale 1:48,000, 268 p.

Newhall, C.G., 1982, A prehistoric debris avalanche from Mount St. Helens [abs.]: Eos (American Geophysical Union Transactions), v. 63, p. 1141.

Pallister, J.S., Hoblitt, R.P., Crandell, D.R., and Mullineaux, D.R., 1992, Mount St. Helens a decade after the 1980 eruptions; magmatic models, chemical cycles, and a revised hazards assessment: Bulletin of Volcanology, v. 54, no. 2, p. 126–146, doi:10.1007/BF00278003.

Porter, S.C., Pierce, K.L., and Hamilton, T.D., 1983, Late Wisconsin mountain glaciation in the western United States, *in* Porter, S.C., ed., The late Pleistocene, v. 1 *of* Late-Quaternary environments of the United States: Minneapolis, University of Minnesota Press, p. 71–111.

Reimer, P.J., Baillie, M.G.L., Bard, E., Bayliss, A., Beck, J.W., Bertrand, C.J.H., Blackwell, P.G., Buck, C.E., Burr, G.S., Cutler, K.B., Damon, P.E., Edwards, R.L., Fairbanks, R.G., Friedrich, M., Guilderson, T.P., Hogg, A.G., Hughen, K.A., Kromer, B., McCormac, G., Manning, S., Ramsey, C.B., Reimer, R.W., Remmele, S., Southon, J.R., Stuiver, M., Talamo, S., Taylor, F.W., van der Plicht, J., and Weyhenmeyer, C.E., 2004, INTCAL04 terrestrial radiocarbon age calibration, 0–26 cal kyr B.P.: Radiocarbon, v. 46, p. 1029–1058.

Roberts, M.L., Bench, G.S., Brown, T.A., Caffee, M.W., Finkel, R.C., Freeman, S.P.H.T., Hainsworth, L.J., Kashgarian, M., McAninch, J.E., Proctor, I.D., Southon, J.R., and Vogel, J.S., 1997, The LLNL AMS Facility, *in* Jull, A.J.T., Beck, J.W., and Burr, G.S., eds., Proceedings of the Seventh International Conference on Accelerator Mass Spectrometry, Tucson, Ariz., USA, May 20–24, 1996: Amsterdam, North-Holland Press, p. 57–61.

Rutherford, M.J., and Devine, J.D., III, 2008, Magmatic conditions and processes in the storage zone of the 2004–2006 Mount St. Helens dacite, chap. 31 *of* Sherrod, D.R., Scott, W.E., and Stauffer, P.H., eds., A volcano rekindled; the renewed eruption of Mount St. Helens, 2004–2006: U.S. Geological Survey Professional Paper 1750 (this volume).

Rutherford, M.J., and Hill, P.M., 1993, Magma ascent rates from amphibole breakdown: an experimental study applied to the 1980–1986 Mount St. Helens eruptions: Journal of Geophysical Research, v. 98, no. B11, p. 19667–19685.

Scott, K.M., 1989, Magnitude and frequency of lahars and lahar-runout flows in the Toutle-Cowlitz River system: U.S. Geological Survey Professional Paper 1447–B, 33 p.

Siebert, L., 1984, Large volcanic debris avalanches; characteristics of source areas, deposits and associated eruptions: Journal of Volcanology and Geothermal Research, v. 22, nos. 3–4, p. 163–197.

Smith, D.R., and Leeman, W.P., 1987, Petrogenesis of Mount St. Helens dacitic magmas: Journal of Geophysical Research, v. 92, no. B10, p. 10313–10334.

Smith, D.R., and Leeman, W.P., 1993, The origin of Mount St. Helens andesites: Journal of Volcanology and Geothermal Research, v. 55, nos. 3–4, p. 271–303, doi:10.1016/0377-0273(93)90042-P.

Staudacher, T., Jessberger, E.K., Dorflinger, J., and Kiko, J., 1978, A refined ultrahigh-vacuum furnace for rare gas analysis: Journal of Physics E: Scientific Instruments, v. 11, p. 781–784.

Steiger, R.H., and Jäger, E., 1977, Subcommission on Geochronology; convention on the use of decay constants in geo- and cosmochronology: Earth and Planetary Science Letters, v. 36, p. 359–362.

Taggart, J.E., Jr., Lindsey, J.R., Scott, B.A., Vivet, D.V., Bartel, A.J., and Stewart, K.C., 1987, Analysis of geologic materials by wavelength-dispersive X-ray fluorescence spectrometry, chapt. E *of* Baedecker, P.A., ed., Methods for geochemical analysis: U.S. Geological Survey Bulletin 1770, p. E1–E19.

Thornber, C.R., Pallister, J.S., Lowers, H.A., Rowe, M.C., Mandeville, C.W., and Meeker, G.P., 2008, Chemistry, mineralogy, and petrology of amphibole in Mount St. Helens 2004–2006 dacite, chap. 32 *of* Sherrod, D.R., Scott, W.E., and Stauffer, P.H., eds., A volcano rekindled; the renewed eruption of Mount St. Helens, 2004–2006: U.S. Geological Survey Professional Paper 1750 (this volume).

U.S. Geological Survey, 1919, Mt. St. Helens quadrangle: U.S. Geological Survey topographic map series, scale 1:125,000 [reprinted 1943].

Verhoogen, J., 1937, Mount St. Helens, a recent Cascade volcano: University of California, Bulletin of the Department of Geological Sciences, v. 24, p. 263–302.

Vogel, M.S., 2005, Quaternary geology of the lower Lewis River valley, Washington; influence of volcanogenic sedimentation following Mount St. Helens eruptions: Pullman, Washington State University, M.S. thesis, 146 p.

Waitt, R.B., Jr., 1985, The case for periodic, colossal jökulhlaups from Pleistocene glacial Lake Missoula: Geological Society of America Bulletin, v. 96, p. 1271–1286.

Yamaguchi, D.K., 1983, New tree-ring dates for Recent eruptions of Mount St. Helens: Quaternary Research, v. 20, p. 246–250.

Yamaguchi, D.K., 1985, Tree-ring evidence for a two-year interval between recent prehistoric explosive eruptions of Mount St. Helens: Geology, v. 13, p. 554–557.

Yamaguchi, D.K., and Hoblitt, R.P., 1995, Tree-ring dating of pre-1980 volcanic flowage deposits at Mount St. Helens, Washington: Geological Society of America Bulletin, v. 107, p. 1077–1093.

Yamaguchi, D.K., and Lawrence, D.B., 1993, Tree-ring evidence for 1842–1843 eruptive activity at the Goat Rocks dome, Mount St. Helens, Washington: Bulletin of Volcanology, v. 55, p. 264–272.

Yamaguchi, D.K., Hoblitt, R.P., and Lawrence, D.B., 1990, A new tree-ring date for the "floating island" lava flow, Mount St. Helens, Washington: Bulletin of Volcanology, v. 52, p. 545–550.

York, D., 1969, Least squares fitting of a straight line with correlated errors: Earth and Planetary Science Letters, v. 5, p. 320–324.

Appendix 1. $^{40}Ar/^{39}Ar$ Analyses of Mount St. Helens Rocks

[This appendix appears only in the digital versions of this work—in the DVD-ROM that accompanies the printed volume and as a separate file accompanying this chapter on the Web at: http://pubs.usgs.gov/pp/1750.]

Complete incremental-heating, gas extraction, and radiometric age data from 17 experiments on 16 rock samples are tabulated in nine worksheets of a Microsoft Excel file.

Chapter 29

Identification and Evolution of the Juvenile Component in 2004–2005 Mount St. Helens Ash

By Michael C. Rowe[1], Carl R. Thornber[2], and Adam J.R. Kent[3]

Abstract

Petrologic studies of volcanic ash are commonly used to identify juvenile volcanic material and observe changes in the composition and style of volcanic eruptions. During the 2004–5 eruption of Mount St. Helens, recognition of the juvenile component in ash produced by early phreatic explosions was complicated by the presence of a substantial proportion of 1980–86 lava-dome fragments and glassy tephra, in addition to older volcanic fragments possibly derived from crater debris. In this report, we correlate groundmass textures and compositions of glass, mafic phases, and feldspar from 2004–5 ash in an attempt to identify juvenile material in early phreatic explosions and to distinguish among the various processes that generate and distribute ash. We conclude that clean glass in the ash is derived mostly from nonjuvenile sources and is not particularly useful for identifying the proportion of juvenile material in ash samples. High Li contents (>30 µg/g) in feldspars provide a useful tracer for juvenile material and suggest an increase in the proportion of the juvenile component between October 1 and October 4, 2004, before the emergence of hot dacite on the surface of the crater on October 11, 2004. The presence of Li-rich feldspar out of equilibrium (based on Li-plagioclase/melt partitioning) with groundmass and bulk dacite early in the eruption also suggests vapor enrichment in the initially erupted dacite. If an excess vapor phase was, indeed, present, it may have provided a catalyst to initiate the eruption. Textural and compositional comparisons between dome fault gouge and the ash produced by rockfalls, rock avalanches, and vent explosions indicate that the fault gouge is a likely source of ash particles for both types of events. Comparison of the ash from vent explosions and rockfalls suggests that the fault gouge and new dome were initially heterogeneous, containing a mixture of conduit and crater debris and juvenile material, but became increasingly homogeneous, dominated by juvenile material, by early January 2005.

Introduction

The phreatic explosion at Mount St. Helens, Wash., on October 1, 2004, was the first of four such events that occurred between October 1 and 5, 2004, preceding the emergence of hot dacitic lava on the crater floor on October 11, 2004. From October 5, 2004, through December 2005, two additional explosions and numerous rockfalls sent volcanic ash over the crater rim (Scott and others, this volume, chap. 1).

Petrologic characterization of volcanic ash provides a means to monitor volcanic activity and to assess precursory evidence of changes in eruptive behavior (Taddeucci and others, 2002). Volcanic monitoring by way of ash characterization is commonly conducted because ash may be collected easily at relatively low cost. Also, because the volcanic edifice is not always accessible, volcanic ash may provide the only petrologic evidence for changes in eruptive behavior.

Juvenile magmatic glass has been observed in the tephra produced before extrusion of lava flows and domes or before large magmatic eruptions (Watanabe and others, 1999; Cashman and Hoblitt, 2004). "Juvenile," as defined in this study, refers to ash and dome lava erupted hot, with textural and geochemical characteristics similar to the earliest dome material (sample SH304, collected Nov. 4, 2004) and later dome samples. (Dome samples dredged from the crater floor before sample SH304 was collected consist of a heterogeneous mixture of crater and conduit debris and minor juvenile material; Pallister and others, this volume, chap. 30). Monitor-

[1] Department of Geosciences, 104 Wilkinson Hall, Oregon State University, Corvallis, OR 97331; now at Department of Geoscience, 121 Trowbridge Hall, University of Iowa, Iowa City, IA 52242

[2] U.S. Geological Survey, 1300 SE Cardinal Court, Vancouver, WA 98683

[3] Department of Geosciences, 104 Wilkinson Hall, Oregon State University, Corvallis, OR 97331

ing of glass compositions in volcanic ash has also identified multiple magmatic components in eruptions and recorded compositional change over the course of a single eruption (for example, Pallister and others, 1992; Swanson and others, 1994, 1995; Schiavi and others, 2006).

At Mount St. Helens, previous eruptive products complicate the ash story, making petrologic monitoring of volcanic ash more difficult. Lava-dome growth from 1980 to 1986 generated a thick (~250 m) cap of dacitic lava over the preexisting conduit. In addition, crater-filling breccia and tephra from 1980 and earlier eruptions may underlie the 1980–86 lava dome for 500 m or more (Friedman and others, 1981). Ash produced by explosions is therefore likely to contain a substantial proportion of "older" Mount St. Helens material. Analysis and comparison of ash is further complicated by mechanical sorting during transport, requiring consideration of such variables as sample location relative to the vent and windspeed and wind direction (for example, Sparks and others, 1997; Houghton and others, 2000).

Petrologic studies of older Mount St. Helens tephra provide a basis for comparing the products of the 2004 eruption (ongoing at time of writing, early 2007). Glass analyses of 1980–82 tephra and dome samples demonstrated trends of increasing crystallinity and decreasing water content, with lower water content likely associated with progressively lower volume and less intense post-May 18 explosive eruptions (Sarna-Wojcicki and others, 1981a; Melson, 1983). Textural comparisons of the May 18, 1980, blast material with that from precursory eruptions indicate that juvenile material appeared as early as 2 months before the climactic eruption and that the juvenile component was reflected by ash particles with either glassy or microcrystalline matrices, characteristic of shallow crystallization (Cashman and Hoblitt, 2004). Cashman and Hoblitt's study is significant in that it identifies the need to consider partially crystalline material in addition to glassy fragments as potentially juvenile. Also, it provides a textural comparison for current eruptive products.

Several previous studies of trace elements, capable of transport within volatile phases, in tephras were undertaken to identify evidence for magmatic degassing associated with explosive events before and after May 18, 1980 (Thomas and others, 1982; Berlo and others, 2004). Whole-rock ^{210}Pb excess and Li enrichment (max ~23 µg/g) in plagioclase feldspar in the 1980 cryptodome, followed by significantly lower Li contents in feldspar within the May 18 fallout tephra and pyroclastic-flow deposits and subsequent eruptive events, led Berlo and others (2004) to propose that the anomalously high Li contents resulted from vapor transfer from a deeper magma source to shallow stored/stalled magma.

The goals of this study of 2004–5 Mount St. Helens ash were to (1) identify and track changes over time in the composition and proportion of juvenile eruptive material in explosive events associated with the reactivation of Mount St. Helens; and (2) combine textural and geochemical observations to distinguish between the processes and products of ash generation, including a comparison of ash from rockfalls and vent explosions. Accomplishing these goals required a detailed examination of the textures and geochemical characteristics of erupted ash samples in comparison with dome petrology and geochemistry, discussed elsewhere in this volume (Cashman and others, this volume, chap. 19; Pallister and others, this volume, chap. 30; Thornber and others, this volume, chap. 32; Kent and others, this volume, chap. 35).

Methods

Sample Collection

After the October 1, 2004, phreatic eruption of Mount St. Helens, 27 ash-collection stations were established around the perimeter of the volcano (fig. 1). Ash samples collected before the placement of stations were from relatively clean flat surfaces (fig. 2*A*). Collection stations were distributed radially along line-of-sight to the volcano, ranging in distance from 2.4 to 10 km from the vent (fig. 1). Each station consisted of a rebar-suspended double bucket (fig. 2*B*); the inner bucket, with drainage slits approximately a third up from its base, was suspended within the outer bucket to allow excess water to drain without significant loss of ash. Ash was collected at stations over periods ranging in length from less than 3 to more than 15 days until November 29, 2004 (fig. 3). Ultimately, ash collection at the established stations was a function of station accessibility, whereas the presence of ash depended on predominant wind directions during the period preceding

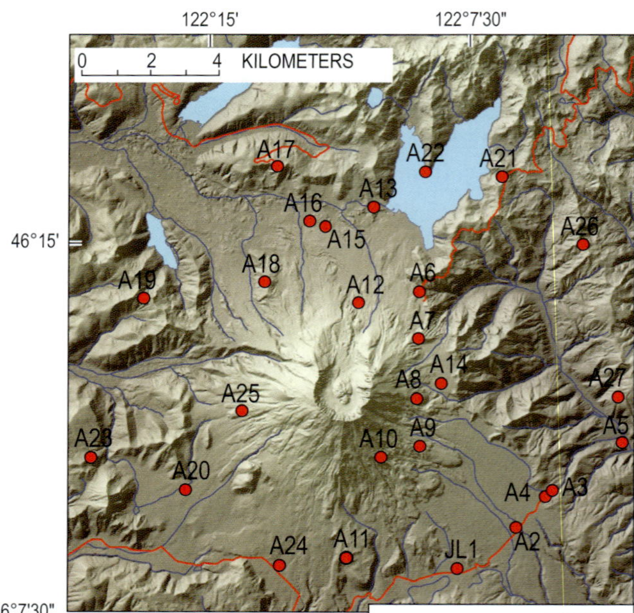

Figure 1. Mount St. Helens area, Washington, showing locations of ash-collection stations.

collection. After November 29, 2004, most ash samples were collected from discrete ash-producing events (either explosions or rockfalls and rock avalanches) on snow-covered (fig. 2*C*) or otherwise-clean surfaces. Snow-covered surfaces provided easy identification of new ash and allowed for tracking of deposited ash to its source (fig. 2*C*). Additional ash samples were collected in August 2005 from collection devices placed in the crater ("petrology spiders," fig. 2*D*), similar to those deployed for seismic and deformation monitoring (LaHusen and others, this volume, chap. 16).

A total of 15 samples collected between October 1, 2004, and March 9, 2005, were analyzed in this study (table 1), of which 12 are of ash spanning the period October 1, 2004, through March 9, 2005, two are of dome fault gouge (collected Nov. 4, 2004, and Feb. 22, 2005), and one is from a crater debris flow (collected Oct. 20, 2004) associated with collapse of the initial spine (table 1). (See Pallister and others this volume, chap. 30, for a detailed description of dome fault gouge and crater debris flow collection.)

Of the four early explosive events, only the three included in this study (12:02 p.m. Oct. 1, 9:43 a.m. Oct. 4, and 9:05 a.m. Oct. 5) produced downwind ash fallout between October 1 and October 5, 2004 (Major and others, 2005). Samples from the suite of Mount St. Helens 2004–5 ash deposits (Rowe and others, 2008) were selected for our purposes on the basis of emplacement date, wind directions, and volume of material collected.

Analytical Methods

Major-element compositions of groundmass glass, melt inclusions (where possible), feldspar, and mafic minerals (amphibole, clinopyroxene, and hypersthene) were measured

Figure 2. Examples of ash-collection sites. *A*, Clean, flat surfaces. *B*, At an ash collection station. Inset is a schematic drawing of the ash-collection buckets, showing drainage slits in upper bucket and drainage holes in base of lower bucket; bolts in lower bucket provide support and suspension of upper bucket. *C*, On snow-covered surfaces. *D*, In petrology spiders (see text for description). Inset is top view of petrology spider, with nylon netting for identification and collection of hot ballistic material on left and baffled compartments for ash and lithic fragments on right.

Table 1. Ash, gouge, and crater debris samples analyzed in this study.

[Eruption dates for crater debris and gouge samples estimated by J.S. Pallister. Further details of ash samples are available in Rowe and others (2008).]

Sample	Type	Date collected	Eruption date
MSH04E1DZ_1	ash	10/1/2004	10/1/2004
MSH04E2A03_A1	ash	10/4/2004	10/4/2004
MSH04E3RANDLE_2	ash	10/5/2004	10/5/2004
MSH04A20_10_11	ash	10/11/2004	10/5/04–10/11/04
MSH04A09_10_12	ash	10/12/2004	10/4/04–10/12/04
MSH04A20_10_16	ash	10/16/2004	10/11/04–10/16/04
MSH04A21_10_20	ash	10/20/2004	10/15/04–10/20/04
MSH04A04_11_2	ash	11/2/2004	10/16/04–11/2/04
MSH04MR_11_4	ash	11/4/2004	11/4/2004
MSH05JP_1_14A	ash	1/14/2005	1/13/2005
MSH05JV_1_19	ash	1/19/2005	1/16/2005
MSH05DRS_3_9_4	ash	3/9/2005	3/8/2005
SH303-1	gouge	11/4/2004	10/18/04
SH307-1	gouge	2/22/2005	2/12/05
SH300-1	crater debris[1]	10/20/2004	10/15/04

[1]Only fine material collected from the crater debris flow is included in this study; includes 2004 dacite as well as older crater-floor debris.

for all 12 ash samples by electron microprobe analysis. To reduce potential sampling biases, 25 to 50 feldspar phenocrysts, ~20 mafic phenocrysts, and 10 to 20 glass specimens were analyzed from each sample, approximately proportional to their relative abundances in ash samples, as estimated visually. Backscattered electron images were taken of all the ash and dome gouge samples to document the heterogeneity of ash particles within and between samples. Trace-element contents in feldspar from 14 samples were measured by laser-ablation inductively coupled plasma mass spectrometry (LA-ICP-MS). In addition, major- and trace-element contents in feldspar from the two dome fault-gouge samples (SH303-1 and SH307-1, table 1) and trace-element contents in feldspar from the crater debris sample (sample SH300-1, table 1) were determined.

Electron microprobe analyses were conducted on a Cameca SX–100 instrument at Oregon State University. Analyzed samples were not sieved, and phenocrysts and glasses of all sizes were analyzed to reduce the possible bias created by mechanical sorting during transport (Houghton and others, 2000). Wherever possible, electron microprobe analyses of phenocryst phases were made within 15 µm of the grain boundary. Electron microprobe analyses of glass were conducted according a procedure modified from that of Morgan and London (1996). Na and K were counted for 60 s, using a 2-nA beam current, a 15-keV accelerating voltage, and a 10-µm beam diameter. Al, Ca, Cl, Fe, Mg, Mn, P, S, Si, and Ti were analyzed by using a 30-nA beam current, a 15-keV accelerating voltage, and 10-µm beam diameter, with count times ranging from 10 to 50 s. The narrow beam diameter (~20 µm is optimal) was required by the small size of glassy fragments in the ash (Morgan and London, 1996). Feldspar (30 nA) and mafic phases (50 nA) were measured by using a 15-keV accelerating voltage and 5- and 1-µm beam diameters, respectively. A rhyolite glass standard (USNM 72854 VG–568), a feldspar standard (Labradorite USNM 115900), and a pyroxene standard (Kakanui augite USNM 122142) were analyzed before each analytical session. Glass standard statistics are presented in Rowe and others (2008).

Trace-element (Ba, Ce, Eu, La, Li, Nd, Pb, Pr, Sr, and Ti) contents in feldspar were determined by LA-ICP-MS analysis in the W.M. Keck Collaboratory for Plasma Spectrometry at Oregon State University, using a 193-nm ArF Excimer laser. Analyses were performed by using a stationary laser (70-µm spot size) to ablate a progressively deepening crater in the sample materials, requiring targeted feldspar phenocrysts to be larger than ~80 µm in diameter. Owing to the large spot size required and the fine grain size of the feldspar in the ash, analyses were made close to the center of inclusion-free grains. Each individual analysis represents 40 s of data acquisition during ablation, with background count rates measured for 30 s before ablation. A 4-Hz pulse frequency resulted in an ablation crater 15 to 20 µm deep. Trace-element abundances were calculated relative to the NIST 612 glass standard, which was analyzed under identical conditions throughout the analytical session. U.S. Geological Survey glass BCR-2G was also analyzed as a secondary standard. Counts were normalized to ^{29}Si, also measured during ablation, and contents were determined according to the method of Kent and others (this volume, chap. 35). Precision of trace-element analysis is presented by Kent and others (this volume, chap. 35). Li contents, most relevant to this study, have a precision of 7 to 8 percent (1σ), although for one session, involving measurement of samples SH300-1, MSH04A20_10_16, and MSH05DRS_3_9_4 (table 1), analytical uncertainties calculated from repeated analyses of standard BCR-2G may be as high as 25 percent (1σ). Overall, uncertainties are similar to those in the analyses by Berlo and others (2004) and Kent and others (this volume, chap. 35), who reported analytical uncertainties of ~10–15 percent.

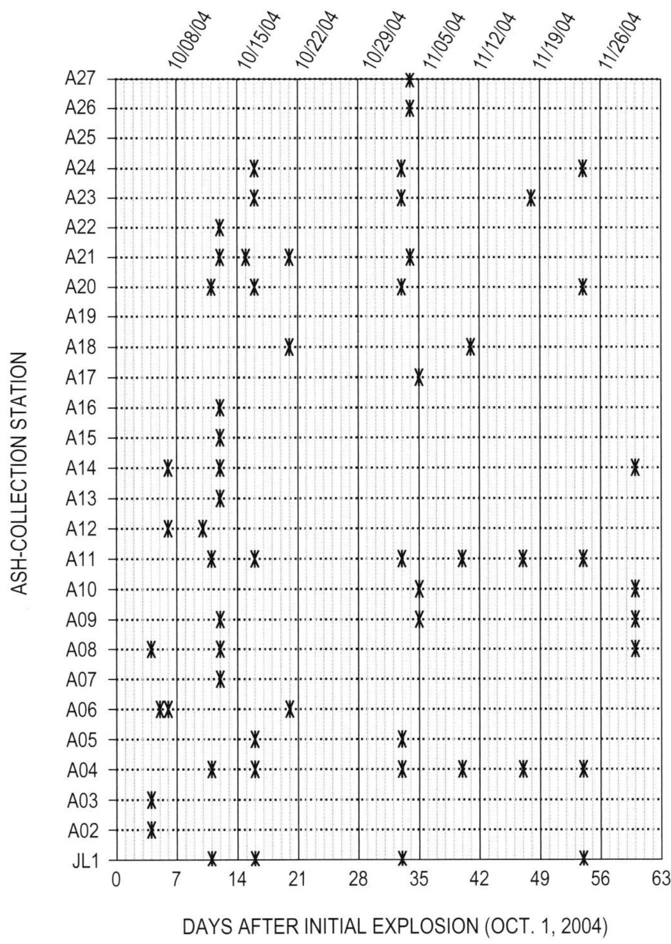

Figure 3. Collection dates for ash-collection stations (see fig. 1) from October 1 (day 0) through November 29 (day 60), 2004.

Results

Glass and Groundmass

The groundmass in ash samples is dominated by crystalline to microcrystalline textures, with groundmass crystallization resulting in the formation of crystalline silica and feldspar microlites (fig. 4). Matrix textures of the juvenile dacite are described elsewhere in this volume (Cashman and others, this volume, chap. 19; Pallister and others, this volume, chap. 30). Late crystallization of the groundmass significantly influenced glass analyses. Al_2O_3 and SiO_2 contents were used to screen glass analyses for microlite crystallization (fig. 4), resulting in 81 reliable analyses of glass, herein referred to as "clean glass." Most clean-glass analyses were obtained from pumice fragments and glass adhering to phenocrysts. Major-element contents in clean glass vary widely, likely owing to localized effects of melt crystallization and the inherent heterogeneity of the ash, especially in early explosions. SiO_2 contents in clean glass range from 52 to 79 weight percent but dominantly are from 72 to 78 percent (table 2). No temporal trend is apparent to suggest a systematic change in the melt composition over the course of 2004–5 sampling (fig. 5).

Mafic Minerals

Mafic minerals analyzed in the ash samples include hypersthene, amphibole, clinopyroxene, and olivine. Hypersthene, which is the dominant mafic mineral in the ash, varies widely in composition ($En_{47.1–73.7}$). Hypersthene in dome sample SH304-2 ($En_{53.3–65.8}$), as well as in older 1980s dome samples ($En_{44.3–69.8}$), similarly varies widely in composition (fig. 6). Amphibole compositions in the ash, new dome dacite, and the 1980–86 dome dacite are essentially identical, most easily observed in Al_2O_3 and FeO* contents. Al_2O_3 content ranges from ~7 to 14 weight percent in the ash and 1980–86 dome material and from ~6 to 15 weight percent in the 2004–6 dome dacite, although in all three samples Al_2O_3 contents cluster between 10 and 13 weight percent (fig. 7). Similarly, total Fe contents range from ~10 to 18 weight percent FeO* in the ash, 1980–86 dome, and 2004–6 dome (fig. 7; Rutherford and Devine, this volume, chap. 31; Thornber and others, this volume, chap. 32).

The thickness of the outermost disequilibrium-reaction rims on amphibole phenocrysts in the ash varies widely, with thick reaction rims (>15–20 µm) present on some grains. Disequilibrium-reaction rims on amphiboles from new dome dacite typically are ~5 µm thick, sporadically 6 to 10 µm thick, and rarely 50 to 100 µm thick, with larger rims commonly associated with amphibole xenocrysts (Thornber and others, this volume, chap. 32). Variations in thickness of amphibole disequilibrium-reaction rims decreased over the course of the eruption, with only rare thick rims in March 8, 2005, tephra. The presence of thick-rimmed amphibole grains is characteristic of 1980–86 magmas (Rutherford and Hill, 1993) but differs from the uni-

Table 2. Electron microprobe analyses of clean, juvenile glass.

[Juvenile glass as described in text is based on MgO and K_2O fields defined by glass and inclusion analyses of samples SH304 and SH305. Specific analysis from among a suite is listed in "Analysis" column. Total Fe reported as FeO. nd, not determined. Sample prefixes MSH04 and MSH05 have been removed; see table 1 for complete sample numbers.]

Sample	Analysis	SiO_2	TiO_2	Al_2O_3	FeO	MnO	MgO	CaO	Na_2O	K_2O	P_2O_5	SO_2	Cl	Total
E2A03_A1	2	73.30	0.47	14.72	1.19	0.05	0.22	1.40	4.37	2.75	0.09	0.01	0.14	98.71
E2A03_A1	7	74.00	0.27	15.91	0.89	0.00	0.06	2.09	4.28	2.83	0.07	0.00	0.04	100.44
A20_10_11	11	72.32	0.26	15.02	1.21	0.04	0.09	1.66	4.77	2.28	0.08	0.01	0.12	97.86
A20_10_16	2	76.81	0.24	13.79	1.42	0.02	0.16	0.52	2.92	4.52	0.04	0.00	0.09	100.53
A20_10_16	4	77.63	0.34	12.64	0.97	0.00	0.05	0.57	3.15	4.21	0.03	0.00	0.02	99.61
A21_10_20	14	74.75	0.34	14.24	0.53	0.00	0.02	1.24	3.97	3.41	0.07	0.01	0.01	98.59
A04_11_2	16	71.52	0.22	18.38	0.97	0.00	0.06	2.70	4.26	3.28	0.06	0.00	0.00	101.45
JP_1_14A	1	75.49	0.22	14.00	0.47	0.00	0.10	1.00	4.47	4.12	0.05	0.01	0.05	99.98
JP_1_14A	2	76.06	0.23	12.60	1.32	0.00	0.00	0.33	5.49	3.19	0.18	0.01	0.05	99.46
JP_1_14A	3	73.83	0.18	15.34	0.63	0.02	0.04	1.70	4.45	4.49	0.03	0.01	0.01	100.73
JP_1_14A	6	76.01	0.22	13.78	0.53	0.00	0.09	1.22	2.77	5.33	0.23	0.01	0.03	100.22
JP_1_14A	9	78.38	0.16	12.69	0.64	0.01	0.03	1.29	1.62	5.01	0.04	0.00	0.03	99.90
JV_1_19	4	74.14	0.26	16.05	1.44	0.05	0.07	1.50	5.54	3.03	0.09	0.00	0.02	102.19
JV_1_19	8	71.17	0.09	16.05	0.42	0.01	0.03	1.68	4.55	2.28	0.05	0.02	0.03	96.38
SH304-2 [1]	A9b hb1	75.2	0.19	13.5	0.87	0.00	0.01	0.88	2.32	5.09	0.01	nd	0.103	98.27
SH305-1 [1]	kc g-22	76.6	0.34	12.4	1.35	0.01	0.03	0.27	3.01	5.72	0.08	nd	0.110	99.92

[1]Representative analyses of dome samples SH304 and SH305 from Pallister and others (this volume, chap. 30).

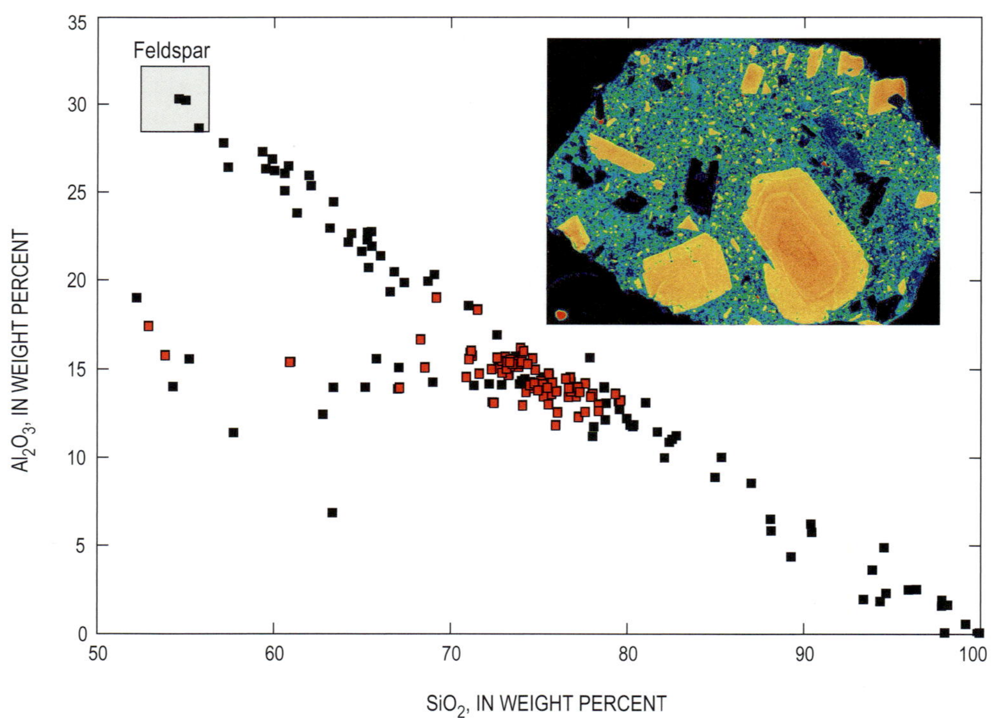

Figure 4. Silica-variation diagram showing Al_2O_3 versus SiO_2 contents in groundmass glass of ash fragments. Compositional range between feldspar and quartz end members is characteristic of highly crystalline groundmass. Red data points, clean glass (see text for explanation). Inset X-ray map (Al Kα) shows crystallization of feldspar (orange) and quartz (blue) in juvenile groundmass.

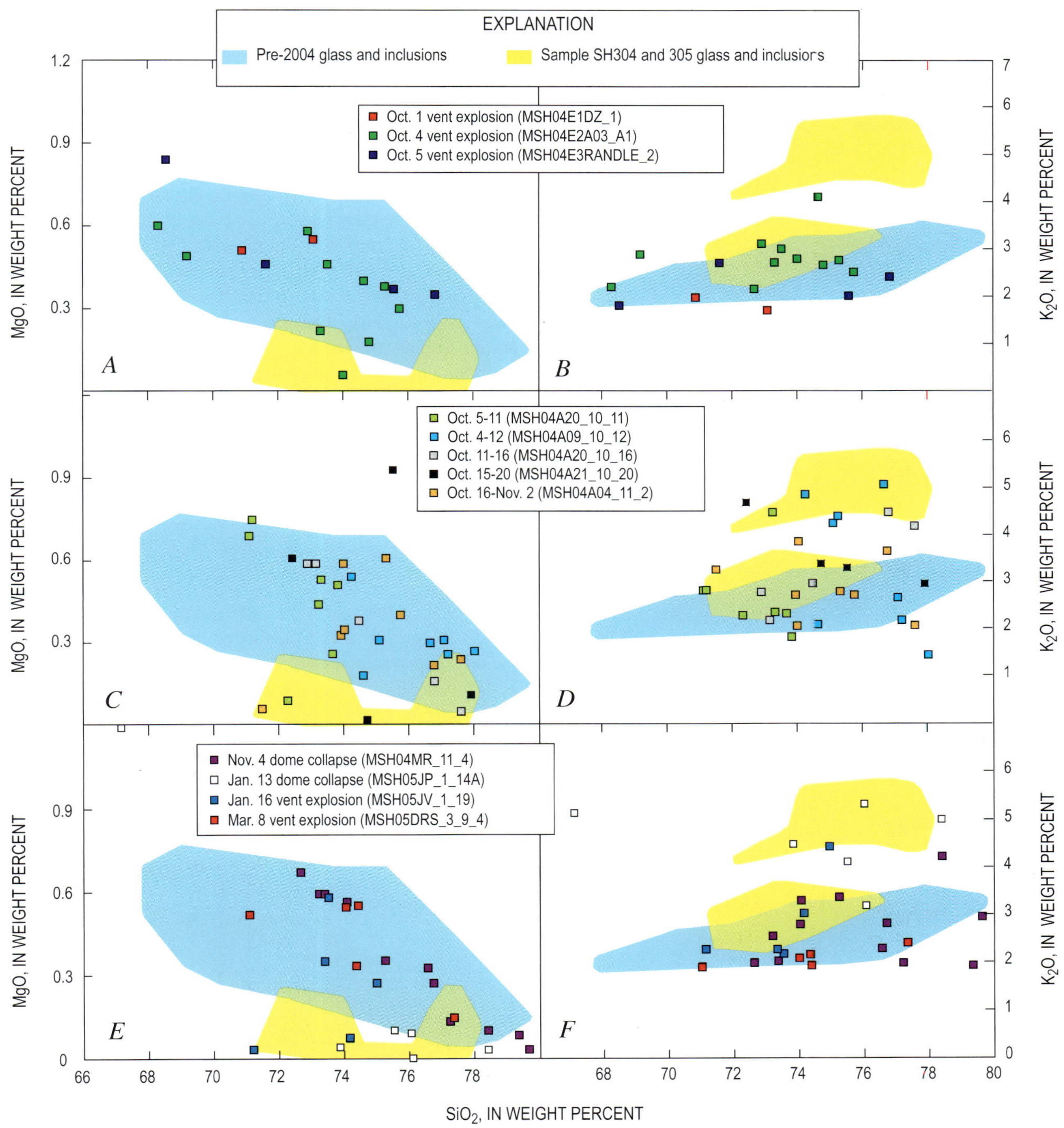

Figure 5. Silica-variation diagrams of MgO and K_2O versus SiO_2 contents in clean glass (see text for explanation) Blue field, pre-2004 tephra and dome glass compositions (Sarna-Wojcicki and others, 1981a; Melson, 1983); yellow field, glass and melt-inclusion compositions for dome samples SH304 and SH305 from current explosions (see Pallister and others, this volume, chap. 30). Plots are paired to show tephra from early vent explosions *(A, B)*, tephra from October 5 to November 2, 2005 *(C, D)*, and tephra from rockfalls and vent explosions from November 4, 2004, to March 8, 2005 *(E, F)*.

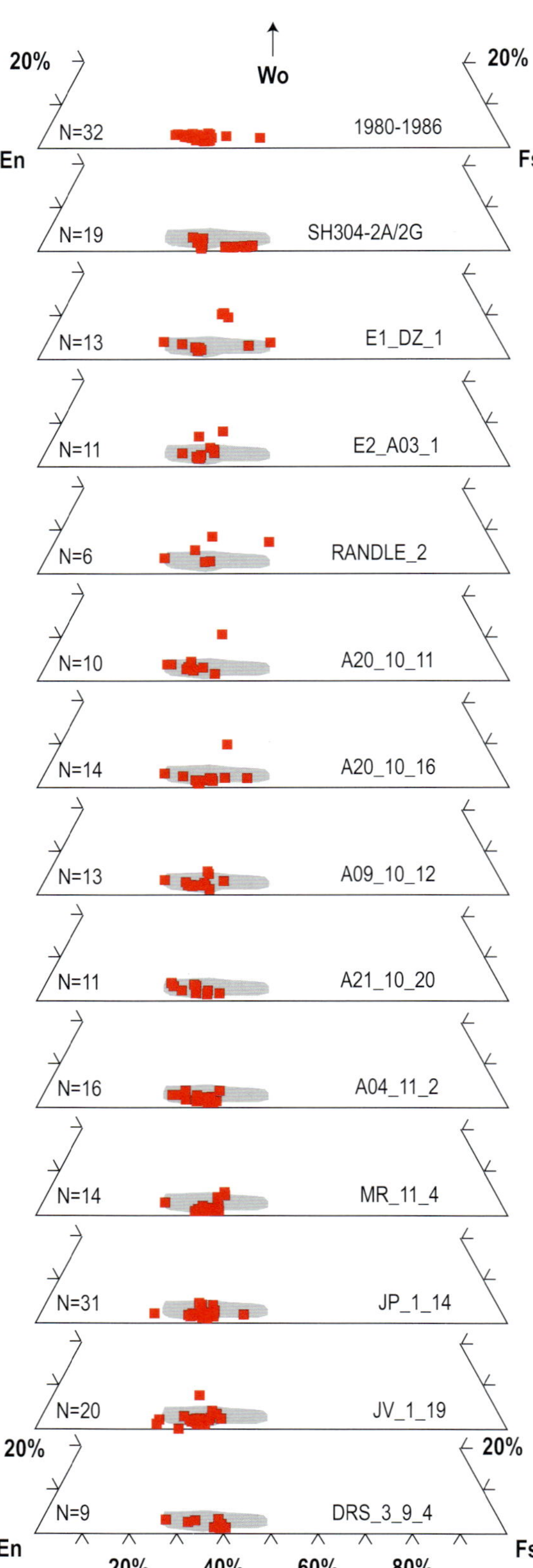

Figure 6. Compositions of hypersthene phenocrysts analyzed from 1980–86 Mount St. Helens, dome sample SH304-2A, and 2004–5 ash samples. Shaded field, range of 1980–86 hypersthene compositions from top panel.

formly thin (~5 µm thick) decompression rim around 2004–5 dacitic amphiboles, an observation suggesting that the early ash samples have older Mount St. Helens material mixed with juvenile ash particles.

In addition to the presence of thick reaction rims on amphibole phenocrysts in the ash, the identification of clinopyroxene and rare olivine phenocrysts in the early ash supports the interpretation that these samples were a heterogeneous mixture containing some proportion of older Mount St. Helens eruptive material. Discrete clinopyroxene phenocrysts are present in the early ash samples but rare in the new dome material, where they typically are associated with xenolith fragments. Clinopyroxene phenocrysts were not observed in the ash samples collected after October 20, 2004.

Owing to the compositional variation of hypersthene and amphibole phenocrysts in the ash samples and the complete compositional overlap between these phases in the new dome and 1980–86 dome, mafic-mineral phases are of limited value for identification of juvenile material and are not discussed further here. (See Rutherford and Devine, this volume, chap. 31, and Thornber and others this volume, chap. 32, for discussion of the textural and compositional variations of Mount St. Helens 2004–5 amphiboles.)

Feldspars

Feldspar phenocrysts in ash, gouge, and crater debris vary widely in composition. Feldspar phenocryst compositions in the ash range from An_{87} to An_{28}, overlapping samples from both the new dome (An_{53-33}) and 1980–85 dome (An_{51-34}). As with mafic-mineral phases, major-element contents in feldspar

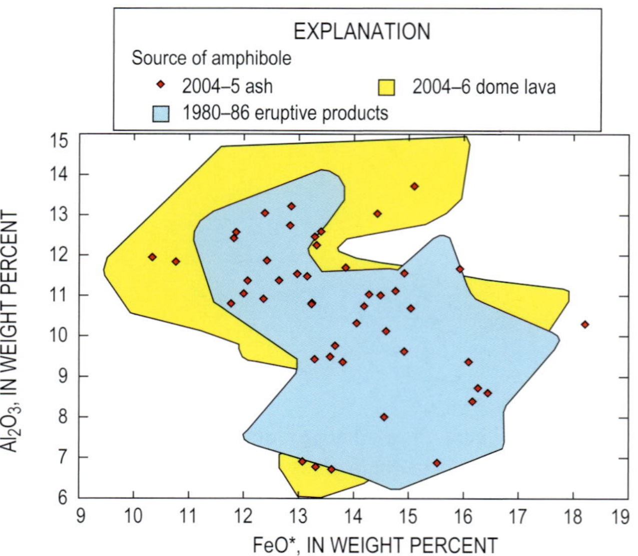

Figure 7. Al_2O_3 versus total Fe (FeO*) in amphiboles in ash samples. Blue field, amphibole in 1980–86 eruptive material; yellow field, amphibole in 2004–6 dome material.

in the ash and new dome samples are indistinguishable from older Mount St. Helens eruptive material (Rowe and others, 2005; Streck and others, this volume, chap. 34). A total of 266 LA-ICP-MS analyses were completed on 14 of the samples included in this study. Significant variations were noted in the contents of Ba (14.5–224 µg/g), Sr (532–1,603 µg/g), La (1.0–9.7 µg/g), Pb (0.3–7.0 µg/g), and Li (6.9–48.5 µg/g) (Rowe and others, 2008). La has a well-defined, and Pb a weakly defined, positive correlation with Ba, whereas Sr is negatively correlated with Ba (fig. 8). Correlations between trace elements (excluding Li) and anorthite content are believed to be due both to variations in feldspar/melt partition coefficients with anorthite content and to changes in melt composition as a result of fractionation of plagioclase, hornblende, hypersthene, and oxides during melt evolution (Kent and others, this volume, chap. 35).

Li in feldspar, in contrast to other trace elements, does not correlate with other major or trace elements. In addition, on the basis of feldspar/melt partitioning, the highest Li contents would require >>200 µg/g Li in the melt (Bindeman and others, 1998), significantly greater than that observed in the bulk dacite (21–28 µg/g; Kent and others, 2007; Thornber and others, 2008b). In ash samples collected after November 4, 2004, Li contents are more homogenous and consistently lower relative to earlier ash samples, with a maximum Li content of 30 µg/g (fig. 9). This decrease in Li content was also observed in dome samples collected after Mount St. Helens dome sample SH304, which was estimated to have been erupted on or about October 18, 2004 (Kent and others, 2007; Pallister and others, this volume, chap. 30; Kent and others, this volume, chap. 35).

Discussion

October 1–5, 2004, Ash Explosions

Identification of a Juvenile Component

Identification and quantification of the juvenile component in the products of early Mount St. Helens eruptive events can be used to evaluate the likely course of a reawakening volcano. By comparing glass compositions and feldspar trace-element contents in the ash with those of 1980–86 and 2004–5 dome materials, the proportion of juvenile material (if present), as previously defined, in the early erupted ash may be

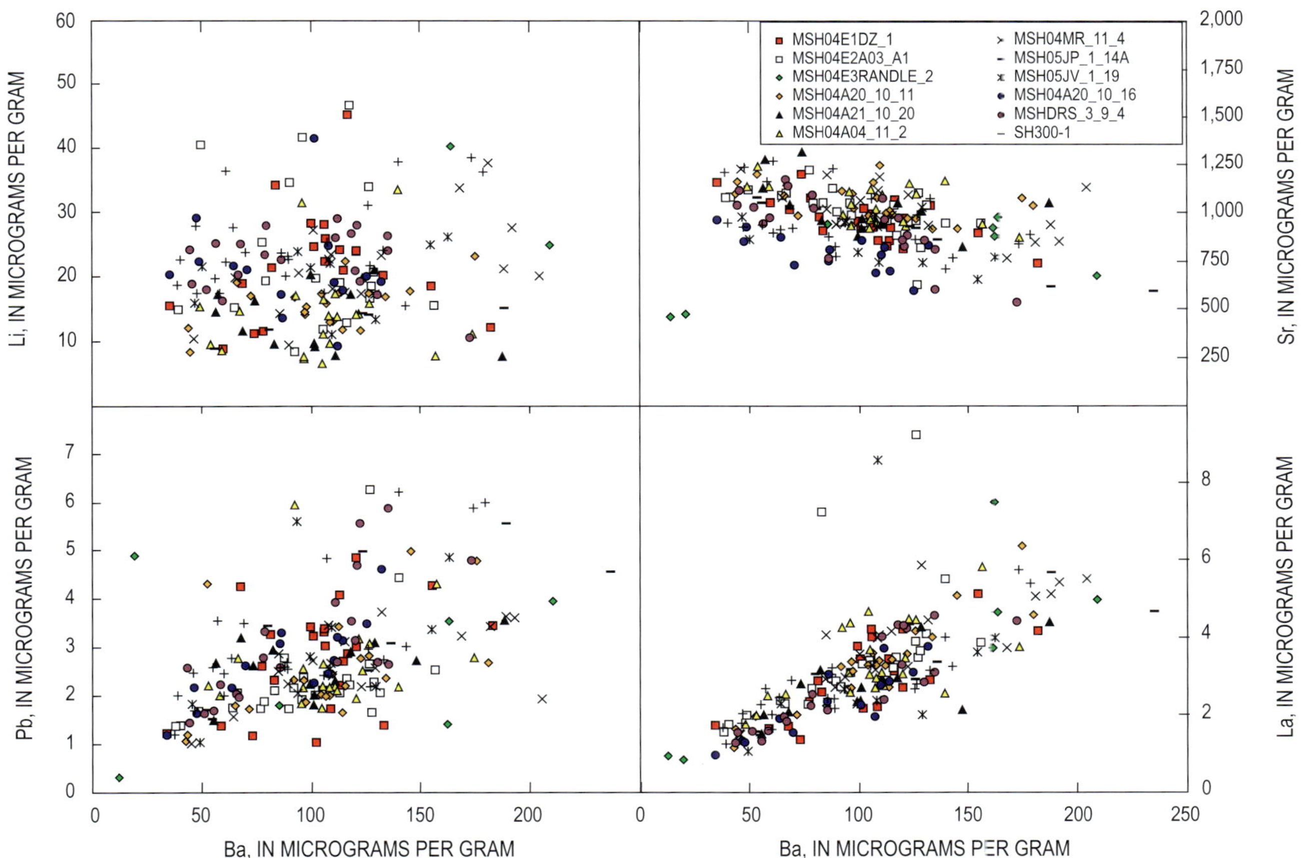

Figure 8. Selected trace-element contents in feldspar in ash samples.

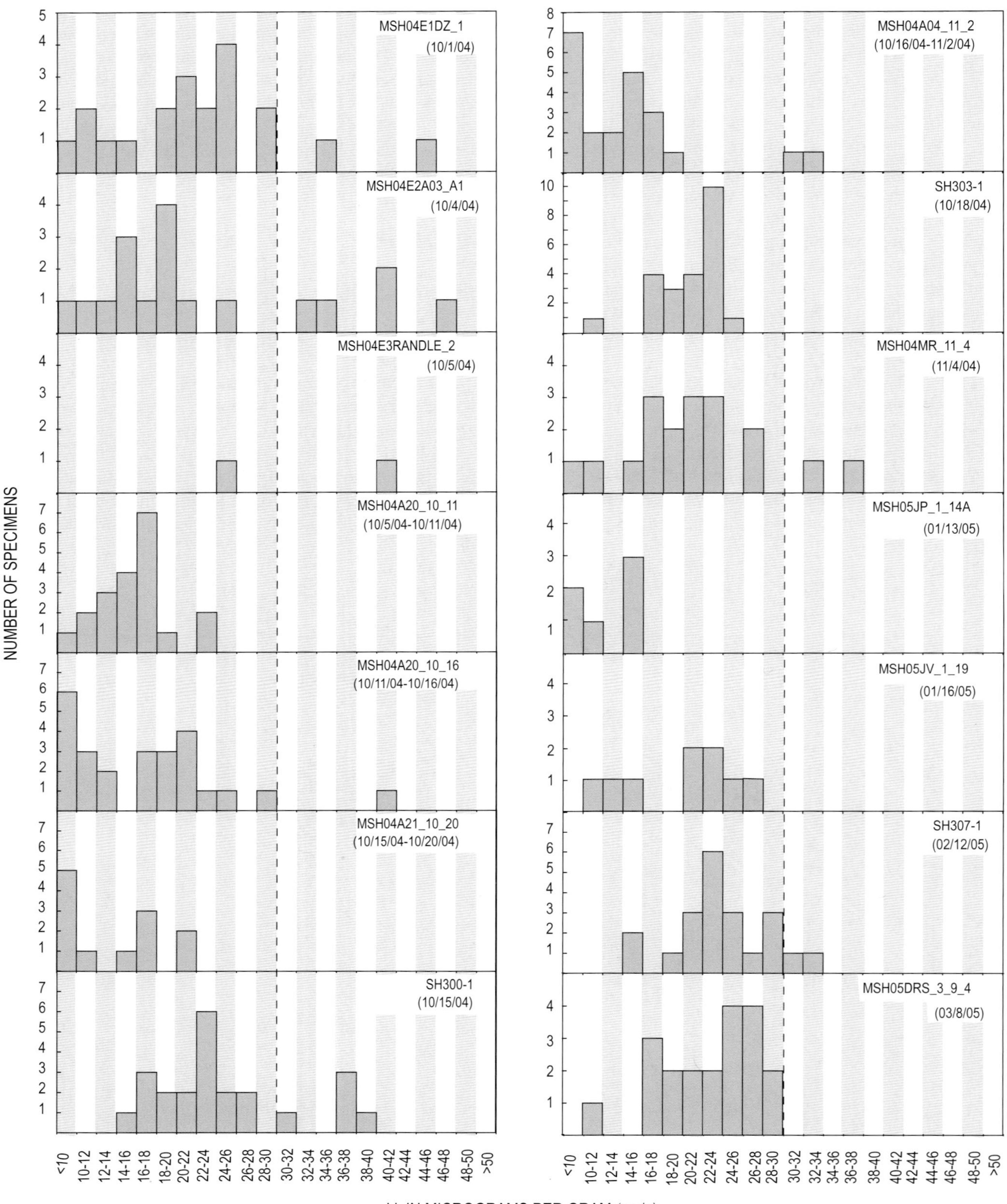

Figure 9. Histograms of Li contents in feldspar from each of 14 analyzed samples. Feldspar Li contents >30 µg/g (dashed line) in ash samples collected before November 4, 2004, coincide with Li contents in juvenile feldspar from dome sample SH304. Eruption dates of samples are given in parentheses.

calculable. Most major-element contents in glass overlap with those in eruptive products of 1980–82 (Sarna-Wojcicki and others, 1981a; Melson, 1983) and pre-1980 (Sarna-Wojcicki and others, 1981a). However, matrix glass and melt inclusions from 2004–5 Mount St. Helens samples SH304 and SH305 have distinctly lower MgO contents (<0.5 weight percent) and higher K_2O contents (max 5.5 weight percent) at comparable SiO_2 contents (fig. 5; table 2; Pallister and others, this volume, chap. 30). On the basis of variations in MgO and K_2O contents, glasses can be divided into what appear to be older glassy ash fragments and juvenile material. Judging from these criteria, none of the clean-glass analyses from the October 1 and 5, 2004, explosions are considered juvenile, although glasses with juvenile characteristics were observed in ash from the October 4, 2004, explosion (fig. 5). However, the high crystallinity of the groundmass, resulting in few clean-glass analyses, precludes definitive estimates of the proportion of juvenile glass observed in early eruptive material. In addition, all of the analyzed pumice fragments fall within the compositional fields defining older volcanic deposits (fig. 5).

Backscattered electron images provide a textural comparison between juvenile crystalline groundmass (fig. 10*B*) and a pumiceous glass fragment compositionally similar to older volcanic deposits (fig. 10*D*). Both textural and compositional comparisons between the various groundmass types are critical to avoiding a common misconception that glassy ash particles (for example, fig. 10*D*) are always representative of the juvenile component associated with an eruption, as previously attributed (for example, Sarna-Wojcicki and others, 1981b; Swanson and others, 1995; Watanabe and others, 1999).

Previous studies of 1980s tephra and dome samples indicate that the Li content in feldspar from 1980–85 lavas and tephras is as high as ~25 μg/g (fig. 11; Berlo and others, 2004; Kent and others, this volume, chap. 35). In contrast, the Li content in plagioclase from early 2004 dome sample SH304-2A (erupted approx. Oct. 18, 2004) ranges from 28 to 43 μg/g Li, distinctly higher than that in older Mount St. Helens feldspar (Kent and others, this volume, chap. 35). This difference provides a means to trace the contribution to ash samples collected between October 1 to October 5, 2004, from juvenile magma (figs. 9, 11). As previously discussed, after dome sample SH304-2A was collected, Li contents dropped to levels similar those in 1980–85 materials (<30 μg/g), thus limiting the usefulness of this approach to material produced only at the start of an eruption.

Measured Li contents in plagioclase in ash erupted from October 1, 2004, to March 9, 2005, form two populations. The Li contents of most plagioclase phenocrysts range from 10 to 25 μg/g and appear to be broadly normally distributed around a mean of 19 μg/g (fig. 9), whereas a smaller subset (~25 percent) of grains have distinctly higher Li contents (max 46 μg/g). On a cumulative-probability plot (fig. 11*B*), most plagioclase phenocrysts lie on a straight-line segment, with a mean of ~18 μg/g, consistent with a near-normal distribution; however, a distinct break in slope occurs at ~30 μg/g, suggesting that the higher Li contents may derive from a different population. If we divide the samples into two groups, using a Li content of 30 μg/g as a boundary, application of Student's *t* test (appropriate for comparing the means of small samples that may show some departure from a normal distribution; for example, Borradaile, 2003) suggests that these two sample

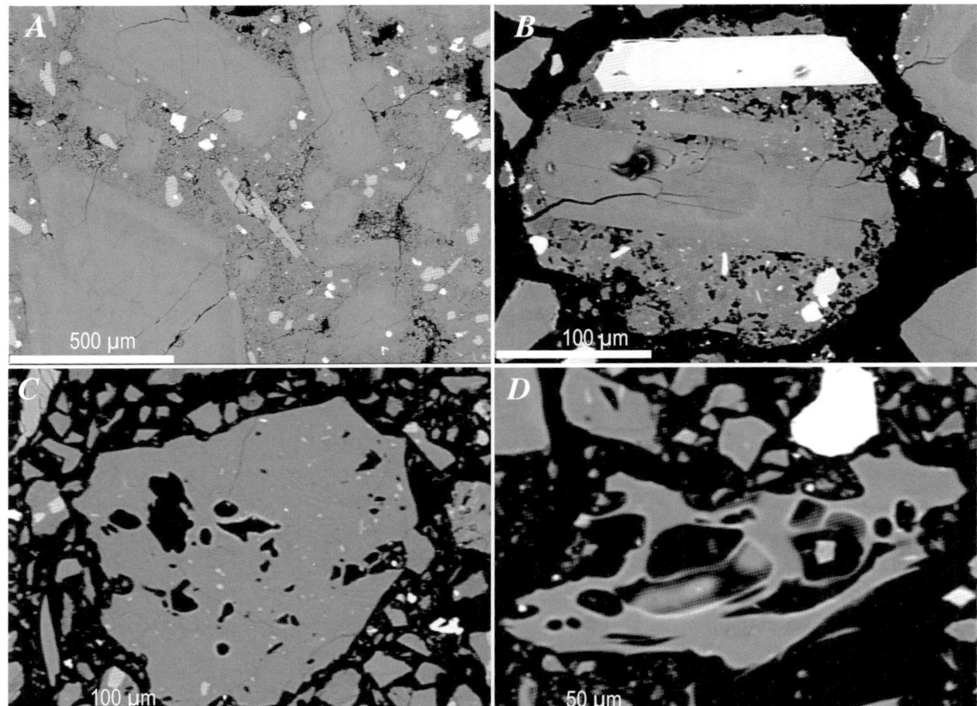

Figure 10. Backscattered electron images of dome rock, ash fragments, and pumice fragments. *A,* Groundmass from dome sample SH304. *B,* Ash fragment from sample MSH04MR_11_4 (feldspar Li content of 33.7 μg/g). *C,* Glassy fragment of ash with extensive plagioclase microlite crystallization from sample MSH04E2A03_A1. *D,* Pumice fragment from sample MSH04E2A03_A1.

groups are significantly different at the >99.9-percent confidence level. Furthermore, the >30-µg/g-Li sample group is indistinguishable from plagioclase from samples SH304-2A and SH304-2C, whereas the <30-µg/g-Li sample group is indistinguishable from plagioclase from the 1981–85 dome samples (table 3). From this we suggest that the plagioclase containing >30 µg/g Li in ash produced by explosions from October 1 to 5, 2004, was derived from Li-enriched juvenile magma similar to that sampled by dome samples SH304-2A and SH304-2C.

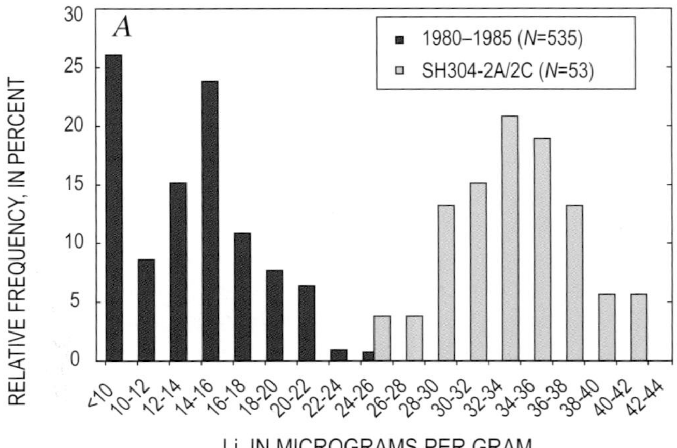

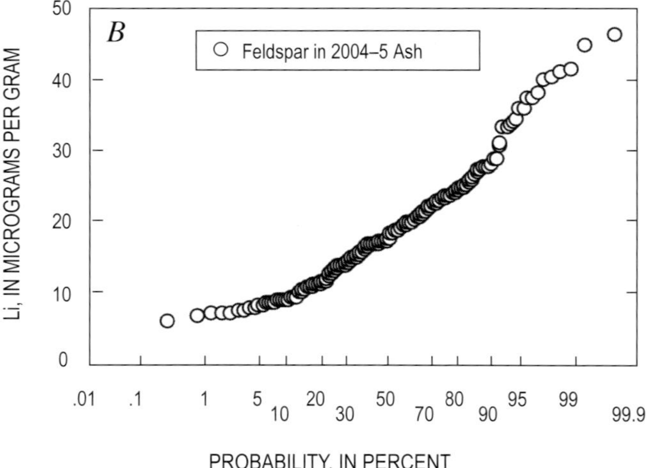

Figure 11. Li contents in feldspar in dome rocks. *A*, Histogram of Li contents in feldspar in 1980–85 dome rocks (black bars, *N*=535) and in sample SH304 (gray bars; *N*=53). Data for 1980–85 samples from Berlo and others (2004) and Kent and others (this volume, chap. 35); data for sample SH304 from Kent and others (this volume, chap. 35). *B*, Li content versus probability for 2004–5 feldspar in ash. In a single normally distributed population, this relation would plot as a straight line. Distinct change in slope at 30 µg/g Li content suggests that multiple populations of plagioclase grains are present in ash samples.

Li enrichment in feldspar, which is interpreted to result from transfer of a magmatic vapor phase, is expected to occur only within juvenile material, not in older conduit material or debris covering the conduit (Kent and others, 2007). This interpretation is supported by (1) the absence of anomalous Li contents in plagioclase in gabbroic inclusions; and (2) the high Li contents (max ~200 µg/g) in amphibole-hosted melt inclusions, consistent with concentrations required in the melt, as estimated from plagioclase/melt partitioning (Bindeman and others, 1998; Kent and others, 2007). On the basis of this evidence, 8 out of 39 (~20 percent) of the feldspars from the October 1 to 5, 2004, ash deposits are juvenile. Though not definitive, the proportion of juvenile material also increases from October 1 to October 4, 2004, suggesting a possible increased involvement of juvenile material in explosions. One explanation for this increase is upward movement of magma within the shallow conduit, consistent with the appearance of hot dacite on the surface of the crater floor on October 11, 2004.

A discrepancy is evident between estimates of the proportion of juvenile material in ash based on Li contents in feldspars versus the compositions of glass fragments. A possible cause for this discrepancy is that only a few clean-glass analyses were obtained as a result of quartz and feldspar microlite crystallization (figs. 4, 10). This same microcrystalline texture is also observed in dome samples, suggesting that the shallow magmatic crystallization observed in dome rocks occurred before fragmentation of the dacite. Because most of the juvenile groundmass had crystallized before eruption, clean-glass analyses ultimately underestimate the proportion of juvenile material in early ash samples.

Evidence for a Volatile Eruption Trigger

The high Li contents measured in early-erupted feldspar from the ash (max 48 µg/g) and dome samples (max 41 µg/g) may indicate an increase in volatile components at the initiation of the 2004 eruption. As previously discussed, the high Li content measured in feldspar would require a Li content in melt of ~200 µg/g, on the basis of plagioclase/melt partition coefficients (Bindeman and others, 1998), despite the lower Li contents (21–28 µg/g) measured in bulk dacite. As suggested by Berlo and others (2004), the Li-rich feldspar could be explained by enrichment of shallow-stored magma through upward movement of an alkali-enriched vapor from deeper within the magmatic system. Because the highest Li contents were measured only before collection of sample SH305-1 (estimated eruption date, Nov. 20, 2004), this difference suggests greater vapor enrichment during the early stages of the eruption. Kent and others (2007) estimate that vapor enrichment must have occurred within the year before the eruption (potentially within just a few days) before the eruption, because earlier enrichment would have resulted in diffusional equilibration of feldspar in gabbroic inclusions—which have lower Li contents than groundmass plagioclase. The decrease in feldspar Li contents over time observed in the dome dacite samples may indicate that the volatile-enriched magma

Table 3. Statistics of Li contents in feldspar in 2004–5 ash, new dome lava, and 1980–85 dome lava.

[2004 sample is SH304-2A, erupted about Oct. 18 and collected Nov. 4, 2004, showing data from Kent and others (this volume, chap. 35). Li contents in feldspar for 1980 materials from Berlo and others (2004). Data for 1981–85 from samples SH100, SH141, and SH187, analyzed at Oregon State University (Kent and others, this volume, chap. 35). Li contents in feldspars from ash produced during the 2004–5 eruption are divided into "Li-poor" (<30 μg/g) and "Li-rich" (>30 μg/g) groups on the basis of statistical analysis (fig. 11; see text for discussion).]

	Feldspar in dome rocks			Feldspar in 2004–5 ash	
	2004	**1981–85**	**1980**	**Li-poor**	**Li-rich**
Mean	33.4	17.1	13.1	17.6	37.5
Standard deviation (1σ)	3.8	4.3	4.6	5.8	4.5
Number of samples (N)	53	28	507	177	18

was only a shallow cap on a larger magma body (Kent and others, this volume, chap. 35).

A CO_2 output of 2,415 t/d, measured on October 7, 2004, followed by a steady decline in ensuing months also suggests a greater volume of gas early in the eruption, although the higher gas output could also result from higher extrusion rates early in the eruption (Gerlach and others, this volume, chap. 26). Together, both the high Li contents in feldspar and the highest CO_2 output measured on October 7, 2004, may indicate the presence of an excess volatile phase, partly resulting from volatile components transferred from a deeper magma, before the onset of the eruption. An increase in vapor pressure may have helped drive the explosions of October 2004. (For a more detailed discussion on the formation of the vapor phase, see Berlo and others, 2004, and Kent and others, this volume, chap. 35.)

Ash Generation

Airborne ash at Mount St. Helens is produced by both vent explosions and rockfalls or rock avalanches. Two general mechanisms are typically described for the generation of ash during vent explosions. In magmatic explosions, exsolution and expansion of gases in magma during its ascent leads to vesiculation and fragmentation of the magma (Heiken, 1972; Cashman and others, 2000). In contrast, phreatomagmatic eruptions result primarily from the rapid expansion, at Mount St. Helens, of meteoric water as it interacts with magma and (or) hot rock at depth (Morrissey and others, 2000).

Ash from Mount St. Helens' 2004–5 vent explosions is dispersed more widely than ash from rockfalls, with fallout reported as far as Ellensburg, Wash., after the March 8, 2005, vent explosion (Mastin and others, 2005; Scott and others, this volume, chap. 1). Rockfalls and rock avalanches in this eruption resulted from dome growth and oversteepening (Vallance and others, this volume, chap. 9). Rockfalls and rock avalanches, with elutriation of fine ash particles, occur much more frequently than vent explosions and are typically smaller, sending ash as high as 3,000 m into the air before it falls proximal to the edifice (Scott and others, this volume, chap. 1). In addition to vent explosions and rockfalls, small volumes of airborne ash may be distributed by elutriation during steaming of the dome or resuspended off crater walls by strong winds—relatively low energy mechanisms for ash transportation.

Mechanisms of ash generation and distribution of the 2004–5 Mount St. Helens eruption are not easily discernible by using criteria of grain shape, volume of glass, or textural and compositional heterogeneity of ash particles (see above descriptions). In this eruption, very little glassy material was present in the ash, and <5 percent of the clean-glass samples are considered juvenile. Juvenile groundmass observed in the dome and in the ash is mostly crystalline (quartz and feldspar), with localized vesiculation and devitrification (figs. 10*A*, 10*B*). Water-by-difference measurements of melt inclusions in phenocrysts from dome samples SH304 and SH305 support gas emission data which, for this eruption, indicate that juvenile magma had degassed extensively before eruption (Gerlach and others, this volume, chap. 26; Pallister and others, this volume, chap. 30). The degassed and crystallized nature of the magma may have reduced the role of expansion of magmatic volatile components in the generation of ash, during either vent explosions or rockfalls and rock avalanches. In addition, the abundance of lithic fragments and paucity of glass shards or pumice fragments suggest that vent explosions (Oct. 1, 4, and 5, 2004; Jan. 16, 2005; Mar. 8, 2005) are dominantly phreatic in origin and that crystallization of the rising magma had occurred before the explosive events.

By comparing geochemical analyses of feldspar and glass in conjunction with the backscattered electron imaging of ash derived from vent explosions and rockfalls or rock avalanches, we attempted to distinguish between possible causes and mechanisms for the dispersal of ash. Major-element compositions of matrix glass and glass inclusions from the January 13, 2005, rockfall ash correlate well with juvenile compositions determined from glass analyses of dome samples SH304 and SH305 (fig. 5). In contrast, less than half of the glass analyses from the January 16, 2005, vent explosion correlate with juvenile fields. This discrepancy demonstrates that the vent eruptions entrain more of the exotic fragments derived from crater debris in the vent area.

A distinct contrast is observed when comparing glass compositions from the rockfall events of November 4, 2004, and January 13, 2005. Whereas the ash from the November 4, 2004, event is dominated by older glass, the ash from the January 13, 2005, event is dominated by juvenile glass (fig. 5), suggesting that the part of the early dome (or uplift area) responsible for ash generation contained a significant amount of older material but by January 2005 was composed dominantly of juvenile dacitic material. This conclusion is also supported by field observations and pre-November 2004 dome samples (Pallister and others, this volume, chap. 30; Reagan and others, this volume, chap. 37).

Juvenile ash fragments from large rockfalls (Nov. 4, 2004, and Jan. 13, 2005) and vent explosions (Jan. 16, 2005, and Mar. 8, 2005) have nearly identical groundmass textures, as described above (fig. 12). Both processes produce strikingly similar grain shapes. Ash particles dominated by large phenocrysts commonly reflect the general shape of those phenocrysts and are more angular, whereas ash particles dominated by groundmass typically range in shape from subangular to round. In principle, particle shape in magmatic eruptions is controlled by the shape and abundance of vesicles, whereas glassy fragments in phreatomagmatic eruptions are commonly pyramidal or blocky (Heiken, 1972). In both magmatic and phreatomagmatic eruptions, however, relatively rapid cooling should result in the generation of glassy material. In contrast, in an experimental study of dacite fragmentation using Mount St. Helens 1980 gray dacite, similar to the cryptodome with low H_2O contents and composed of ~30 volume percent phenocrysts, the material produced brittle, angular fragments (Alidibirov and Dingwell, 1996). This material more closely resembles some of the particles observed in recent rockfalls and explosions, suggesting

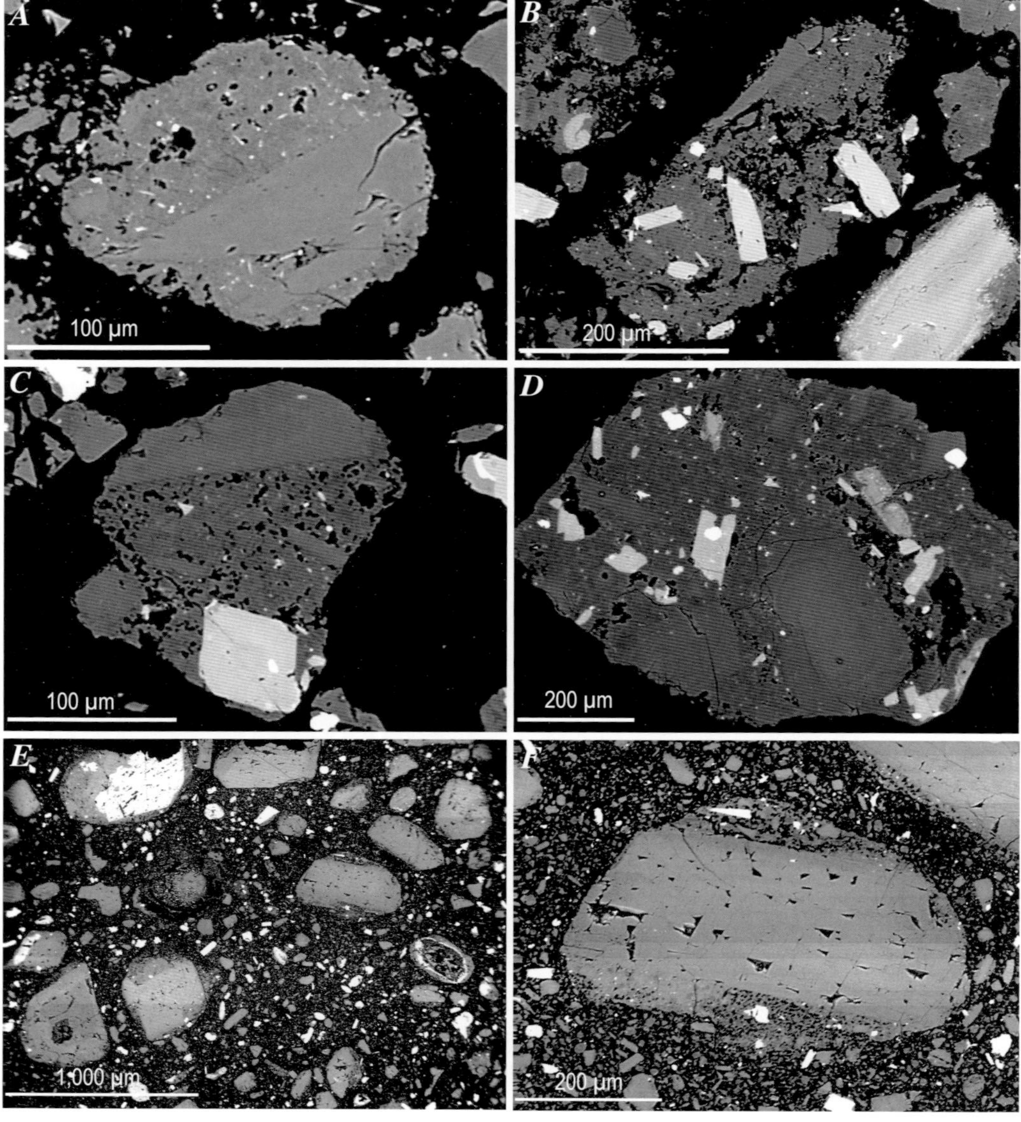

Figure 12. Backscattered electron images of characteristic ash particles from dome rockfalls *(A, B)*, vent explosions *(C, D)* and dome gouge *(E, F)*. *A*, Rounded ash fragment from sample MSH05JP_1_14A, from rockfall on January 13, 2005. *B*, More highly disaggregated ash particle from same sample as in figure 12*A*. *C*, Subrounded ash fragment with grain shape controlled by larger feldspar and hypersthene phenocrysts from sample MSH05JV_1_19, from explosion of January 16, 2005. *D*, Largely devitrified ash particle (see X-ray map in fig. 3) from explosion of March 8, 2005. *E*, Low-magnification image of disaggregated dome gouge from sample SH307-1. *F*, Enlargement of rounded clast in figure 12*E*, showing characteristic ash morphology.

that fragmentation may have occurred by brittle failure without frothing or vesiculation of the magma. Similarities in grain shape and texture of the juvenile matrix from different types of events suggest that the ash is generated by related processes.

The disaggregation of the outer 1 to 3 m of the dome (dome fault gouge; see Cashman and others, this volume, chap. 19, for a detailed description) provides an additional potential source for ash particles, independent of magmatic fragmentation. Gouge particles are dominantly subangular to rounded, similar to the particles observed in a large proportion of the ash (figs. 12*E*, 12*F*). Groundmass textures of dome gouge (sample SH303-1, table 1) extruded on October 18, 2004, are heterogeneous, suggesting that at that time the gouge contained a high percentage of exotic wallrock fragments.

The heterogeneity of the dome gouge may also explain the dominance of glass compositions representative of older eruptive events in the November 4, 2004, dome-collapse ash. In addition, Li contents in feldspar from the November 4, 2004, ash closely resemble those of the gouge, which are dominantly low (<30 µg/g) and do not correlate well with those of either dome samples SH304 or SH305 (figs. 9, 11; Kent and others, this volume, chap. 35). Recall that feldspars with Li contents below 30 µg/g are a statistically distinct group from the Li-rich population and correlate with older Mount St. Helens eruptive products (fig. 11). In contrast, the January 13, 2005, dome-collapse ash is significantly more homogenous, with glass compositions matching that of the growing dome (fig. 5). This homogeneity was also observed in the dome fault gouge (sample SH307-1, table 1) collected on February 22, 2005, with groundmass textures resembling those of the growing dome, and groundmass textures and grain shapes similar to those observed in the ash.

Textural and geochemical evidence presented here suggests that airborne ash in the 2004–6 eruption is largely generated from the dome fault gouge. Large dome-collapse events and explosions may also produce a significant component of material resulting from brittle failure of the dacite during expansion of volatile components, despite low volatile contents. These particles would have groundmass textures similar to dome gouge but would likely have angular to subangular grain shapes instead of the more rounded particles found within the gouge (Alidibirov and Dingwell, 1996; Cashman and others, this volume, chap. 19).

The particle size distributions of ash samples generated from both dome collapse and vent explosions overlap significantly, largely owing to the distance to the vent at which samples were collected; therefore, particle size is inconclusive for distinguishing source mechanism (fig. 13). Mean particle size varies but generally decreases with increasing distance from the vent. In addition, the mean particle size of ash from vent explosions is significantly greater than that from dome-collapse events, despite collection farther from the vent, illustrating the farther transport of coarse ash during more explosive events. The particle size distribution of dome gouge differs from that of ash deposited from either dome-collapse events or vent explosions (fig. 13). However, because variables resulting in mechanical sorting of the ash, including explosivity of the eruption, windspeed, height of the ash cloud, and distance to the vent, are not taken into account in this comparison, particle size distributions cannot be used to corroborate textural evidence which suggests that a large proportion of the ash is derived from the dome fault gouge.

Distal ash believed to remobilize during steaming or from strong winds is dissimilar to ash from the rockfalls and vent explosions. The ash collected between October 6 and November 2, 2004, contains abundant exotic particles and pumice fragments and substantially less of the highly crystalline groundmass characteristic of the juvenile dome material commonly erupted during discrete ash-producing events. Only a small proportion of clean juvenile glass is present in all of the ash samples collected during this interval, and no systematic variation is observed in the proportion of juvenile glass over time, despite the appearance of hot dacite on October 11, 2004. Similar results are observed for Li contents in feldspar during this period, with high Li contents in only ~4 percent (3 of 79) of analyzed feldspar, despite identifying ~22 percent (5 of 23) of juvenile feldspar in the fine material in the sample collected from the October 20, 2004, crater debris flow (sample SH300-1, table 1). Remobilization of ash particles from the crater walls by strong winds, and elutriation of fine ash particles from rising steam, appear to have (1) preferentially transported low-density material, such as pumice fragments; and (2) resulted in apparent dilution of the estimated proportion of juvenile material as a result of greater contamination from older volcanic rocks. Despite the continuous ash collection, therefore, sampling of discrete events appears to provide a more representative depiction of current eruptive conditions.

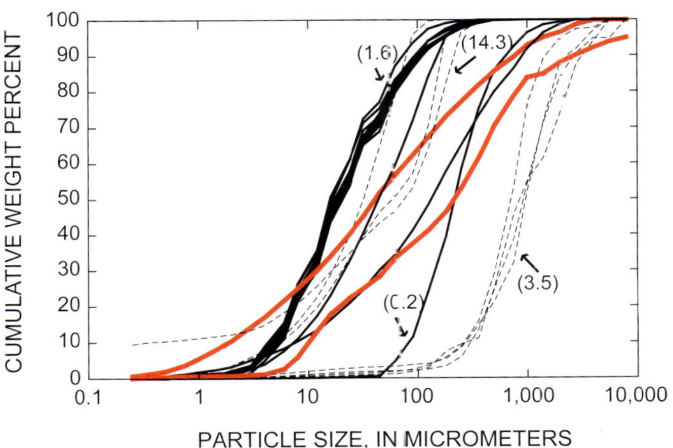

Figure 13. Particle size distribution for ash derived from rockfalls and rock avalanches (black solid lines, *N*=13), vent explosions (dashed lines, *N*=7), and dome gouge (red solid lines, *N*=2). Wide variation is partly attributable to varying distance from vent (numbers in parentheses are distance in kilometers to vent) and explosivity of eruption. Note that even at greater distance from vent, explosive deposits generally have a larger average particle size.

Conclusions

This textural and geochemical examination of 2004–5 Mount St. Helens ash provides several important observations and conclusions with regard to early eruptive events and processes of ash generation and transportation.

1. The Li content in feldspar from dome sample SH304 is >30 µg/g, significantly higher than in older Mount St. Helens eruptive material, allowing for the identification of juvenile plagioclase in the ash. Li contents may indicate an increase in the proportion of juvenile material from October 1 through 4, 2004. High Li contents in feldspar are useful as a tracer for juvenile material only during the beginning stages of the eruption—within 6 weeks after eruptive onset—because after about November 20, 2004 (estimated eruption date of sample SH305), Li contents in feldspar dropped to levels similar to that observed during the period 1980–86. The decrease in Li content also suggests that the volatile-enriched magma was only a shallow cap on a larger magma body.

2. The clean glass in ash samples is mostly older volcanic material. Juvenile groundmass is typically crystalline (quartz and feldspar), with localized devitrification and patchy, very fine vesiculation, contrary to the traditional assumption that clean glass is juvenile volcanic material. Estimates of the proportion of juvenile material based on glass analyses are significantly lower than those based on Li content in plagioclase.

3. Groundmass textures, grain shapes, and compositional similarities among ash from vent explosions, rockfalls, and dome fault gouge particles suggest that the gouge is a significant source of ash material. Despite differences in particle size, the grain shapes and textures of particles from rockfalls and vent explosions are relatively similar, suggesting that the ash is derived by a similar mechanism in both events. The heterogeneity observed in early ash samples correlates with observations that the early extruded dome material and fault gouge contained a significant proportion of older volcanic material. The increase in the homogeneity of ash over time is consistent with a similar trend in dome and fault gouge samples.

4. The presence of an excess volatile phase, as indicated by the high Li contents in feldspar, may indicate the presence of a greater proportion of vapor at the top of the conduit where shallow-stored magmas had stalled. This excess vapor may have been the catalyst for initiation of the 2004–6 eruption.

5. Continuous monitoring of ash samples during periods of relatively low eruptive activity may not provide a representative depiction of the current eruptive processes, owing to contamination from other debris. Therefore, collection and monitoring of discrete dome-collapse events and vent explosions provides the most accurate record of the current eruption.

Acknowledgments

We thank all of the Cascades Volcano Observatory staff and volunteers who assisted in the collection of Mount St. Helens ash, especially S. McConnell, T. Herriott, and A. Eckberg, who assisted with drying, sorting, and weighing of ash samples, and D. Gooding and D. Ramsey for assistance in the field and with the collection site mapping. Electron microprobe time at Oregon State University was provided by F. Tepley. LA-ICP-MS analyses were performed at the W.M. Keck Collaboratory for Plasma Spectrometry, Oregon State University. Detailed reviews by J. Larsen and R. Hoblitt greatly improved the manuscript. The Mount St. Helens petrology working group provided valuable discussion and feedback for this study. This research was supported in part by National Science Foundation grant EAR 0440382.

References Cited

Alidibirov, M., and Dingwell, D.B., 1996, Magma fragmentation by rapid decompression: Nature, v. 380, no. 6570, p. 146–148, doi:10.1038/380146a0.

Berlo, K., Blundy, J., Turner, S., Cashman, K., Hawkesworth, C., and Black, S., 2004, Geochemical precursors to volcanic activity at Mount St. Helens, USA: Science, v. 306, p. 1167–1169.

Bindeman, I.N., Davis, A.M., and Drake, M.J., 1998, Ion microprobe study of plagioclase-basalt partition experiments at natural concentration levels of trace elements: Geochimica et Cosmochimica Acta, v. 62, p. 1175–1193.

Borradaile, G., 2003, Statistics of Earth Science data; their distribution in time, space, and orientation: New York, Springer, 351 p.

Cashman, K.V., and Hoblitt, R.P., 2004, Magmatic precursors to the 18 May 1980 eruption of Mount St. Helens, USA: Geology, v. 32, no. 2, p. 141–144, doi:10.1130/G20078.1.

Cashman, K.V., Sturtevant, B., Papale, P., and Navon, O., 2000, Magmatic fragmentation, *in* Sigurdsson, H., ed., Encyclopedia of volcanoes: London, Academic Press, p. 421–430.

Cashman, K.V., Thornber, C.R., and Pallister, J.S., 2008, From dome to dust; shallow crystallization and fragmentation of conduit magma during the 2004–2006 dome extrusion of Mount St. Helens, Washington, chap. 19 *of* Sherrod, D.R., Scott, W.E., and Stauffer, P.H., eds., A volcano rekindled; the renewed eruption of Mount St. Helens, 2004–2006: U.S. Geological Survey Professional Paper 1750 (this volume).

Friedman, J.D., Olhoeft, G.R., Johnson, G.R., and Frank, D., 1981, Heat content and thermal energy of the June dacite dome in relation to total energy yield, May–October 1980, *in* Lipman, P.W., and Mullineaux, D.R., eds., The 1980 eruptions of Mount St. Helens, Washington: U.S. Geological Survey Professional Paper 1250, p. 557–567.

Gerlach, T.M., McGee, K.A., and Doukas, M.P., 2008, Emission rates of CO_2, SO_2, and H_2S, scrubbing, and preeruption excess volatiles at Mount St. Helens, 2004–2005, chap. 26 *of* Sherrod, D.R., Scott, W.E., and Stauffer, P.H., eds., A volcano rekindled; the renewed eruption of Mount St. Helens, 2004–2006: U.S. Geological Survey Professional Paper 1750 (this volume).

Heiken, G., 1972, Morphology and petrography of volcanic ashes: Geological Society of America Bulletin, v. 83, no. 7, p. 1961–1987.

Houghton, B.F., Wilson, C.J.N., Smith, R.T., and Gilbert, J.S., 2000, Phreatoplinian eruptions, *in* Sigurdsson, H., ed., Encyclopedia of volcanoes: London, Academic Press, p. 513–525.

Kent, A.J.R., Blundy, J., Cashman, K.V., Cooper, K.M., Donnelly, C., Pallister, J.S., Reagan, M., Rowe, M.C., and Thornber, C.R., 2007, Vapor transfer prior to the October 2004 eruption of Mount St. Helens, Washington: Geology, v. 35, no. 3, p. 231–234, doi:10.1130/G22809A.1.

Kent, A.J.R., Rowe, M.C., Thornber, C.R., and Pallister, J.S., 2008, Trace element and Pb isotope composition of plagioclase from dome samples from the 2004–2005 eruption of Mount St Helens, Washington, chap. 35 *of* Sherrod, D.R., Scott, W.E., and Stauffer, P.H., eds., A volcano rekindled; the renewed eruption of Mount St. Helens, 2004–2006: U.S. Geological Survey Professional Paper 1750 (this volume).

LaHusen, R.G., Swinford, K.J., Logan, M., and Lisowski, M., 2008, Instrumentation in remote and dangerous settings; examples using data from GPS "spider" deployments during the 2004–2005 eruption of Mount St. Helens, Washington, chap. 16 *of* Sherrod, D.R., Scott, W.E., and Stauffer, P.H., eds., A volcano rekindled; the renewed eruption of Mount St. Helens, 2004–2006: U.S. Geological Survey Professional Paper 1750 (this volume).

Major, J.J., Scott, W.E., Driedger, C., and Dzurisin, D., 2005, Mount St. Helens erupts again; activity from September 2004 through March 2005: U.S. Geological Survey Fact Sheet 2005–3036, 4 p.

Mastin, L.G., Sherrod, D.R., Vallance, J.W., Thornber, C.R., and Ewert, J.W., 2005, The roles of magmatic and external water in the March 8 tephra eruption at Mount St. Helens as assessed by a 1-D steady plume-height model [abs.]: Eos (American Geophysical Union Transactions), v. 86, no. 52, Fall Meeting Supplement, Abs. V53D-1597.

Melson, W.G., 1983, Monitoring the 1980–1982 eruptions of Mount St. Helens; compositions and abundances of glass: Science, v. 221, no. 4618, p. 1387–1391.

Morgan, G.B., IV, and London, D., 1996, Optimizing the electron microprobe analysis of hydrous alkali aluminosilicate glasses: American Mineralogist, v. 81, 1176–1185.

Morrissey, M., Zimanowski, B., Wohletz, K., and Buettner, R., 2000, Phreatomagmatic fragmentation, *in* Sigurdsson, H., ed., Encyclopedia of volcanoes: London, Academic Press, p. 431–445.

Pallister, J.S., Hoblitt, R.P., and Reyes, A.G, 1992, A basalt trigger for the 1991 eruptions of Pinatubo volcano?: Nature, v. 356, p. 426–428.

Pallister, J.S., Thornber, C.R., Cashman, K.V., Clynne, M.A., Lowers, H.A., Mandeville, C.W., Brownfield, I.K., and Meeker, G.P., 2008, Petrology of the 2004–2006 Mount St. Helens lava dome—implications for magmatic plumbing and eruption triggering, chap. 30 *of* Sherrod, D.R., Scott, W.E., and Stauffer, P.H., eds., A volcano rekindled; the renewed eruption of Mount St. Helens, 2004–2006: U.S. Geological Survey Professional Paper 1750 (this volume).

Reagan, M.K., Cooper, K.M., Pallister, J.S., Thornber, C.R., and Wortel, M., 2008, Timing of degassing and plagioclase growth in lavas erupted from Mount St. Helens, 2004–2005, from ^{210}Po-^{210}Pb-^{226}Ra disequilibria, chap. 37 *of* Sherrod, D.R., Scott, W.E., and Stauffer, P.H., eds., A volcano rekindled; the renewed eruption of Mount St. Helens, 2004–2006: U.S. Geological Survey Professional Paper 1750 (this volume).

Rowe, M.C., Thornber, C., and Kent, A.J.R., 2005, Petrology and geochemistry of Mount St. Helens ash before and during continuous dome extrusion [abs.]: Geochimica et Cosmochimica Acta, v. 69, no. 10, supp. 1, p. A272.

Rowe, M.C., Thornber, C.R., Gooding, D.J., and Pallister, J.S., 2008, Catalog of Mount St. Helens 2004–2005 tephra samples with major- and trace-element geochemistry: U.S. Geological Survey Open-File Report 2008–1131, 7 p, with digital database.

Rutherford, M.J., and Devine, J.D., III, 2008, Magmatic conditions and processes in the storage zone of the 2004–2006 Mount St. Helens dacite, chap. 31 *of* Sherrod, D.R., Scott, W.E., and Stauffer, P.H., eds., A volcano rekindled; the renewed eruption of Mount St. Helens, 2004–2006: U.S. Geological Survey Professional Paper 1750 (this volume).

Rutherford, M.J., and Hill, P.M., 1993, Magma ascent rates from amphibole breakdown; an experimental study applied to the 1980–1986 Mount St. Helens eruptions: Journal of Geophysical Research, v. 98, no B11, p. 19667–19685.

Sarna-Wojcicki, A.M., Meyer, C.E., Woodward, M.J., and Lamothe, P.J., 1981a, Composition of air-fall ash erupted on May 18, May 25, June 12, July 22, and August 7, *in* Lipman, P.W., and Mullineaux, D.R., eds., The 1980 eruptions of Mount St. Helens, Washington: U.S. Geological Survey Professional Paper 1250, p. 667–681.

Sarna-Wojcicki, A.M., Waitt, R.B., Jr., Woodward, M.J., Shipley, S., and Rivera, J., 1981b, Premagmatic ash erupted from March 27 through May 14, 1980—extent, mass, volume, and composition, *in* Lipman, P.W., and Mullineaux, D.R., eds., The 1980 eruptions of Mount St. Helens, Washington: U.S. Geological Survey Professional Paper 1250, p. 569–575.

Schiavi, F., Tiepolo, M., Pompilio, M., and Vannucci, R., 2006, Tracking magma dynamics by laser ablation (LA)-ICPMS trace element analysis of glass in volcanic ash: the 1995 activity of Mt. Etna: Geophysical Research Letters, v. 33, L05304, 4p., doi:10.1029/2005GL024789.

Scott, W.E., Sherrod, D.R., and Gardner, C.A., 2008, Overview of the 2004 to 2006, and continuing, eruption of Mount St. Helens, Washington, chap. 1 *of* Sherrod, D.R., Scott, W.E., and Stauffer, P.H., eds., A volcano rekindled; the renewed eruption of Mount St. Helens, 2004–2006: U.S. Geological Survey Professional Paper 1750 (this volume).

Sparks, R.S.J., Bursik, M.I., Carey, S.N., Gilbert, J.S., Glaze, L.S., Sigurdsson, H., and Woods, A.W., 1997, Volcanic plumes: New York, John Wiley, 574 p.

Streck, M.J., Broderick, C.A., Thornber, C.R., Clynne, M.A., and Pallister, J.S., 2008, Plagioclase populations and zoning in dacite of the 2004–2005 Mount St. Helens eruption; constraints for magma origin and dynamics, chap. 34 *of* Sherrod, D.R., Scott, W.E., and Stauffer, P.H., eds., A volcano rekindled; the renewed eruption of Mount St. Helens, 2004–2006: U.S. Geological Survey Professional Paper 1750 (this volume).

Swanson, S.E., Nye, C.J., Miller, T.P., and Avery, V.F., 1994, Geochemistry of the 1989–1990 eruption of Redoubt Volcano; part II, mineral and glass chemistry: Journal of Volcanology and Geothermal Research, v. 62, nos. 1–4, p. 453–468.

Swanson, S.E., Harbin, M.L., and Riehle, J.R., 1995, Use of volcanic glass from ash as a monitoring tool; an example from the 1992 eruptions of Crater Peak, Mount Spurr volcano, Alaska, *in* Keith, T.E.C., ed., The 1992 eruptions of Crater Peak vent, Mount Spurr volcano, Alaska: U.S. Geological Survey Bulletin 2139, p. 129–137.

Taddeucci, J., Pompilio, M., and Scarlato, P., 2002, Monitoring the explosive activity of the July–August 2001 eruption of Mt. Etna (Italy) by ash characterization: Geophysical Research Letters, v. 29, no. 8, 1230, 4 p., doi:10.1029/2001GL014372.

Thomas, E., Varekamp, J.C., and Busheck P.R., 1982, Zinc enrichment in the phreatic ashes of Mt. St. Helens, April 1980: Journal of Volcanology and Geothermal Research, v. 12, nos. 3–4, p. 339–350.

Thornber, C.R., Pallister, J.S., Lowers, H.A., Rowe, M.C., Mandeville, C.W., and Meeker, G.P., 2008a, Chemistry, mineralogy, and petrology of amphibole in Mount St. Helens 2004–2006 dacite, chap. 32 *of* Sherrod, D.R., Scott, W.E., and Stauffer, P.H., eds., A volcano rekindled; the renewed eruption of Mount St. Helens, 2004–2006: U.S. Geological Survey Professional Paper 1750 (this volume).

Thornber, C.R., Pallister, J.S., Rowe, M.C., McConnell, S., Herriott, T.M., Eckberg, A., Stokes, W.C., Johnson Cornelius, D., Conrey, R.M., Hannah, T., Taggart, J.E., Jr., Adams, M., Lamothe, P.J., Budahn, J.R., and Knaack, C.M., 2008b, Catalog of Mount St. Helens 2004–2007 dome samples with major- and trace-element chemistry: U.S. Geological Survey Open-File Report 2008–1130, 9 p., with digital database.

Vallance, J.W., Schneider, D.J., and Schilling, S.P., 2008, Growth of the 2004–2006 lava-dome complex at Mount St. Helens, Washington, chap. 9 *of* Sherrod, D.R., Scott, W.E., and Stauffer, P.H., eds., A volcano rekindled; the renewed eruption of Mount St. Helens, 2004–2006: U.S. Geological Survey Professional Paper 1750 (this volume).

Watanabe, K., Danhara, T., Watanabe, K., Terai, K., and Yamashita, T., 1999, Juvenile volcanic glass erupted before the appearance of the 1991 lava dome, Unzen volcano, Kyushu, Japan: Journal of Volcanology and Geothermal Research, v. 89, p. 113–121.

A Volcano Rekindled: The Renewed Eruption of Mount St. Helens, 2004–2006
Edited by David R. Sherrod, William E. Scott, and Peter H. Stauffer
U.S. Geological Survey Professional Paper 1750, 2008

Chapter 30

Petrology of the 2004–2006 Mount St. Helens Lava Dome—Implications for Magmatic Plumbing and Eruption Triggering

By John S. Pallister[1], Carl R. Thornber[1], Katharine V. Cashman[2], Michael A. Clynne[3], Heather A. Lowers[4], Charles W. Mandeville[5], Isabelle K. Brownfield[4], and Gregory P. Meeker[4]

Abstract

Eighteen years after dome-forming eruptions ended in 1986, and with little warning, Mount St. Helens began to erupt again in October 2004. During the ensuing two years, the volcano extruded more than 80×10^6 m^3 of gas-poor, crystal-rich dacite lava. The 2004–6 dacite is remarkably uniform in bulk-rock composition and, at 65 percent SiO_2, among the richest in silica and most depleted in incompatible elements of the magmas erupted at Mount St. Helens during the past 500 years. Since shortly after the first spine of lava appeared, samples have been collected using a steel box dredge ("Jaws") suspended 20–35 m below a helicopter and, occasionally, by hand sampling. As of the spring of 2006, 25 age-controlled samples have been collected from the seven spines of the new lava dome. Samples were obtained from both the interiors of spines and from their carapaces, which are composed of fault gouge and cataclasite 1–2 m thick. The dacite lava is crystal rich, with 40–50 percent phenocrysts. The groundmass is extensively crystallized to a cotectic assemblage of quartz, tridymite, and Na- and K-rich feldspar microlites, raising the total crystal content to more than 80 percent on a vesicle-free basis in all but the earliest erupted samples. Early samples and those collected from near the spine margin are more glassy and vesicular that those collected later and from the interior of the spines. Oxide thermobarometer determinations for the earliest erupted samples we collected cluster at temperatures of approximately 850°C and at an oxygen fugacity one log unit above the nickel-nickel oxide (NNO) buffer curve. In contrast, samples from relatively glass-poor samples erupted in late 2004 and early 2005 have zoned oxides with apparent temperatures that range to greater than 950°C. The higher temperatures in these microlite-rich rocks are attributed to latent heat evolved during extensive and rapid groundmass crystallization. Low volatile contents of matrix glasses and presence of tridymite and quartz in the high-silica rhyolite matrix glass indicate extensive shallow (<1 km) crystallization of the matrix, driven by degassing of water and solidifying the magma below the level of the vent. The mode of eruption of the dacite as a series of fault-gouge-mantled spines is explained by this process of extensive subvent degassing and solidification.

Although the dacite from this eruption is more silica rich than 1980–86 dome rocks, most major and trace element concentrations of the 1980–86 and 2004–6 magma batches are similar, and magmatic gas emissions have been low and have had similar ratios to those of the 1980s, raising the possibility that the magma might be residual from the 1980–86 reservoir. However, titanium and chromium are enriched slightly relative to the most recent 1980–86 and Goat Rocks (A.D. 1800–1857) eruptive cycles, and heavy rare-earth-element abundances are slightly depleted relative to those erupted during the past 500 years at Mount St. Helens. These data suggest either addition of new gas-poor dacite magma or tapping of a region of the preexisting reservoir that was not erupted previously.

A relatively low pressure of last phenocryst growth suggests that the magma was derived from near the apex of the Mount St. Helens magma reservoir at a depth of about

[1] U.S. Geological Survey, 1300 SE Cardinal Court, Vancouver, WA 98683

[2] Department of Geological Sciences, 1272 University of Oregon, Eugene, OR 97403

[3] U.S. Geological Survey, 345 Middlefield Rd, Menlo Park, CA 94025

[4] U.S. Geological Survey, Box 25046, Denver Federal Center, Denver, CO 80225

[5] American Museum of Natural History, Central Park West at 79th Street, New York, NY 10024

5 km. Viewed in the context of seismic, deformation, and gas-emission data, the petrologic and geochemical data can be explained by ascent of a geochemically distinct batch of magma into the apex of the reservoir during the period 1987–97, followed by upward movement of magma into a new conduit beginning in late September 2004.

The question of new versus residual magma has implications for the long-term eruptive behavior of Mount St. Helens, because arrival of a new batch of dacitic magma from the deep crust could herald the beginning of a new long-term cycle of eruptive activity. It is also important to our understanding of what triggered the eruption and its future course. Two hypotheses for triggering are considered: (1) top-down fracturing related to the shallow groundwater system and (2) an increase in reservoir pressure brought about by recent magmatic replenishment. With respect to the future course of the eruption, similarities between textures and character of eruption of the 2004–6 dome and the long-duration (greater than 100 years) pre-1980 summit dome, along with the low eruptive rate of the current eruption, suggest that the eruption could continue sluggishly or intermittently for years to come.

Introduction

End members of natural phenomena offer important constraints on processes, in part because they provide a means to understand boundary conditions. The ongoing eruption of Mount St. Helens is such an end member, as it represents a sustained low-rate dacite eruption at a potentially explosive volcano. A fortunate combination of conditions has allowed us to investigate fundamental questions about volcanic plumbing systems, triggers for eruptions, and controls on explosivity.

The dacite has largely solidified to crystalline rock beneath the surface, such that the first two years of the eruption have been characterized by nearly continuous extrusion of lava spines. Furthermore, because the spines have been extruded at an angle, the vent has been partially exposed through most of the eruption, allowing up-close access by helicopter to install instruments, document the character of the spines, and collect a series of lava and gouge samples through time. The sample collection, along with field observations and seismic, deformation, thermal, and gas monitoring, form the basis for this and other petrologic papers in this volume.

We have employed an unusual method of sampling borrowed from the oceanographic community. A dredge bucket suspended beneath a helicopter was used repeatedly to collect samples from the actively extruding spines over the course of the eruption. Samples have been distributed widely to petrologists and geochemists at a variety of institutions in the U.S. and overseas. Accordingly, petrologic studies of the 2004–6 eruption were undertaken through a team approach, which brought together more than 25 petrologists from a dozen institutions to contribute to the interpretation of the eruption (Pallister and others, 2005). We thank these scientists and acknowledge their contributions and those of our USGS colleagues, as through this community approach and synthesis of different types of data we have advanced our understanding.

This report deals primarily with the general petrology of the dacite lava and what it tells us about magmatic processes when viewed in the broader context of monitoring data and Mount St. Helens' history. We report results from field observations and petrographic studies using optical and scanning electron microscopy, microprobe analyses of glasses and Fe-Ti oxide minerals, Fourier-transform infrared (FTIR) spectroscopy, and a comparison of the whole-rock major- and trace-element compositions of 2004–6 samples with those of previous eruptive episodes at Mount St. Helens. Other petrologic reports in this volume focus on silicate mineral chemistry and zoning, isotopic data, phase equilibria, and the petrology and chemistry of ash samples, as well as detailed studies of the chemistry of the dacite and textures of the fault gouge that mantles the lava spines.

Field Geology and Sampling

A chronology of the 2004–6 eruption is given by Scott and others (this volume, chap. 1), and details of lava-dome growth are described and illustrated by Vallance and others (this volume, chap. 9) and summarized in digital elevation models and photogeologic maps (Schilling and others, this volume, chap. 8; Herriott and others, this volume, chap. 10). Here we provide only a brief outline of field relations used to establish eruption ages of samples and field observations that are important to interpretation of the petrology. The 2004–6 eruption sequence began with intense seismic unrest, uplift of crater floor, and deformation of glacial ice during late September 2004, which were followed by a series of phreatic explosions during the first week of October. Beginning October 11, 2004, spines of juvenile lava extruded in the deformed area, and these have continued to extrude virtually continuously ever since. On January 16, 2005, and March 8, 2005, the only sizable explosions since early October 2004 blanketed the crater floor with ash and ballistic fragments. For safety, a steel dredge (fig. 1), sling-loaded to a helicopter, and a few short-duration landings were used to collect rock and gouge samples from the spines. A total of 25 locations were sampled on 16 days during the period between October 2004 and February 2006, as shown in table 1 and in the photogeologic maps of Herriott and others (this volume, chap. 10).

There have been no pumiceous eruptions in this eruptive sequence, and, except for small flows formed during collapse of the initial spine in October–November 2004 (fig. 2), there have been no dome-collapse pyroclastic flows. Descriptions of ash samples collected from deposits of the few small explosive eruptions and many small rockfalls and rock avalanches are given in Rowe and others (this volume, chap. 29), and descriptions of the fault gouge, which mantles the dacite spines, are given in Cashman and others (this volume, chap. 19).

Figure 1. Photographs illustrating use and design of rock dredge. Dredge allowed collection from normally inaccessible locations, as shown in the main photos. *A*, Upper lip of spine 7, where fragments of consolidated gouge and lava from close to the gouge carapace were collected on February 15, 2006. USGS photo by J.S. Pallister *B*, View looking down at dredge from helicopter while sampling blocks of dacite from near gouge contact. As shown in the inset photos, the dredge is a plate-steel frame, 30 by 60 cm and 30 cm deep, beneath which hangs a removable heavy-gauge wire-screen basket for collecting rocks (lower inset). Upper edge of frame is serrated to better bite into rock or gouge, giving dredge its informal name, "Jaws." Basket can be replaced with steel box for sampling fine-grained material such as gouge (upper inset). Dredge is lifted from a steel ring attached to 1-m-long steel lift arm bolted to sides of frame to allow adjustment of bite angle. A steel leader cable 6 mm in diameter and 5 m long is attached to steel ring on lift arm. The ring allows side loads to be imparted on dredge to help dislodge it if it becomes wedged in rock face. Steel cable is attached to standard electrically released sling-load cable from helicopter. USGS photo by J.S. Pallister.

Table 1. Rock samples collected in the crater of Mount St. Helens from October 2004 to February 2006.

[All samples of new dome are multiple rock fragments collected by helicopter dredging except SH301 and SH325, collected by hand. Sample numbering sequence continues that adopted for Mount St. Helens reference collection from 1980–86. Sample numbers with hyphenated suffixes (for example, SH304-2G1) elsewhere in the report refer to individual fragments in these composite samples (Thornber and others, 2008b). Eruption dates are estimated by using collection locations and known lineal rate of extrusion to track samples back to vent, as described in text. Limiting dates specify time interval for emplacement, from known field relations.]

Sample No.	Spine	Collection date	Eruption date	Limiting dates
SH300	1	10/20/2004	10/15/2004	10/11/04–10/20/04
SH300[1]		10/20/2004	<1986[1]	
SH301[2]		10/27/2004	<1986[2]	
SH302	1 or 2	10/27/2004	10/14/2004	10/12/04–10/27/04
SH304	3	11/4/2004	10/18/2004	10/12/04–11/04/04
SH305	3	1/3/2005	11/20/2004	10/27/04–12/01/04
SH306	4	1/14/2005	12/15/2004	12/07/04–12/21/04
SH307	4	2/22/2005	2/12/2005	02/01/05–02/15/05
SH308	4	2/22/2005	1/21/2005	01/15/05–02/01/05
SH309	4	2/22/2005	1/13/2005	01/07/05–01/25/05
SH310	4	2/22/2005	1/16/2005	01/10/05–01/28/05
SH311	4	1/19/2005	1/16/2005	01/16/05–01/19/05
SH312	4	4/10/2005	3/8/2005	03/08/05–03/08/05
SH313	4	4/19/2005	4/1/2005	03/15/05–04/05/05
SH314	5	4/19/2005	4/17/2005	04/16/04–04/19/05
SH315	4	4/19/2005	4/1/2005	03/15/05–04/05/05
SH316	5	5/24/2005	4/15/2005	04/01/05–05/10/05
SH317	5	6/15/2005	5/1/2005	04/10/05–05/30/05
SH318	5	7/13/2005	7/7/2005	07/01/05–07/09/05
SH319	5	7/13/2005	5/15/2005	05/01/05–05/25/05
SH320	5	7/13/2005	7/1/2005	06/26/05–07/06/05
SH321	6	8/19/2005	8/10/2005	08/05/05–08/19/05
SH322	6	8/19/2005	8/15/2005	08/10/05–08/19/05
SH323	6	10/18/2005	9/10/2005	08/10/05–10/19/05
SH324	7	12/15/2005	12/5/2005	11/23/05–12/07/05
SH325	7	02/07/2006	12/20/2005	12/05/05–01/01/06
SH326	7	02/15/2006	1/10/2006	01/01/06–01/20/06

[1] Dredge sample SH300 contained 2004 dacite and rock fragments uplifted from crater floor (1980–86 dome or shallow conduit rock).

[2] Hand sample SH301 contained several dacite blocks pushed up from crater floor (1980–86 dome or shallow conduit rock).

On October 11, 2004, the first spine (spine 1) of new lava was extruded through uplifted glacier near the south flank of the 1980–86 lava dome, and we began collecting lava samples soon after. During the remainder of October, spine 2 emerged and extended to the south, while a new area of the glacier was uplifted east and then southeast of spine 1. Our initial samples were collected from spine 1 by helicopter dredging using a makeshift bucket dredge, followed by landings and hand sampling on October 27 and November 4. By October 27, protuberances of hot lava had breached the area of uplifted glacier in the southeastern part of the crater, and by November 4 an elongate wedge of new lava had emerged from the uplift, risen to a height of about 100 m (fig. 3), and been thrust laterally toward the south crater wall, plowing the glacier aside. Because of its elongate, recumbent form, this spine 3 became known as a "whaleback," a term used to describe similar recumbent spines during an early stage of the eruption at Soufrière Hills volcano, Montserrat (Watts and others, 2002). Initially, the whaleback had a smooth east face mantled by soft white fault gouge; this face dipped 40º–60º degrees east and was marked by down-plunge striations and darker colored "bathtub rings," the latter recording uplifted positions where the spine had previously been in contact with a debris apron at its base. During November and December 2004, global positioning system (GPS) data and fixed-camera observations recorded the whaleback moving southward in conveyorlike fashion, transporting new lava from a vent at its north end and shedding it as hot talus blocks to the south and west (Schilling and others, this volume, chap. 8; Vallance and others, this volume, chap. 9).

By mid-December 2004, oblique longitudinal fractures developed in spine 3. By early January 2005, spine 3 had broken into multiple fracture-bounded segments and spine 4 began to emerge from the vent. Spine 4 was also extruded to the southeast as a whaleback. It overrode rubble from spine 3 until it too reached the south crater wall and fragmented in mid to late April as spine 5 emerged from the vent. Spine 5 overrode the two earliest spines. It began to fragment into rubble in late July 2005. Smaller, rubbly spine 6 then emerged, but it was extruded to the southwest from the vent and extended farther west than previous spines. During the fall of 2005, a sag opened between spines 5 and 6 as spine 6 continued to extrude and thrust upward and to the southwest. Finally, during October 2005 and continuing into 2006, spine 7 emerged and was thrust steeply to the southwest; it overrode spine 6, and part of it collapsed to form a talus apron that extended onto the narrowing west arm of Crater Glacier, which was trapped between the westward-thrusting dome and the crater wall. The eruption of spine 7 has continued to the time of this writing (September 2006) and has been characterized by near-vertical spine growth and collapse, producing a large mass of dacite rubble in the western part of the crater.

Figure 2. Oblique aerial photograph (view to southeast) of small pyroclastic flow (with vapor clouds rising from it) produced by rockfall from spine 2 (shrouded in cloud) on October 27, 2004. Snowmelt from flow produced watery lahar in small channel on snow-covered glacier, forming small debris fan in basin at base of spine 1. USGS photo by J.S. Pallister.

The relatively low angle of extrusion through most of the eruption produced inclined spines that were extruded to the south (spines 2–5), such that the northern half of the vent margin was exposed at the surface. This margin consisted of an arcuate rim of hot gouge, convex on its north side. The southern margin of the vent has not been exposed. Extrapolation of the exposed rim as a circle yields a vent diameter of 100–200 m; however, variably exposed extensions of the gouge rim along the east and west margins of the spines (on occasions for several hundred meters) suggest an oval vent outline. This oval outline may be the result of the inclined intersection of a north-plunging cylindrical conduit with the crater floor, or it may indicate a true elongation of the vent.

Each of the spines displayed a carapace of white to tan fault gouge or cataclasite 1–2 m thick as it emerged from the vent (Cashman and others, this volume, chap. 19). The gouge zone is striated, with multiple layers of subparallel slickensides oriented parallel to the transport direction at the point of emergence from the vent. The orientation of the slickensides, combined with photographically or GPS-determined rates of linear spine transport, provide a means to "backtrack" sample localities to the vent and thereby establish eruption ages. The vent is assumed to be at the altitude of the crater floor below Crater Glacier. Using this method, approximate eruption dates have been estimated for each of the dome samples, along with age ranges, the latter reflecting uncertainty in rate of transport from the vent to the collection locality (table 1). One sample (SH312) is assigned a unique eruption age, coincident with the explosion of March 8, 2005, because it was melted into a nylon rope on a near-vent monitoring station (McChesney and others, this volume, chap. 7; LaHusen and others, this volume, chap. 16).

Laboratory Methods

Petrography and Microbeam Analysis

Polished thin sections of representative samples were prepared and examined using petrographic and scanning electron microscopes (SEM), electron microprobe, and imaging

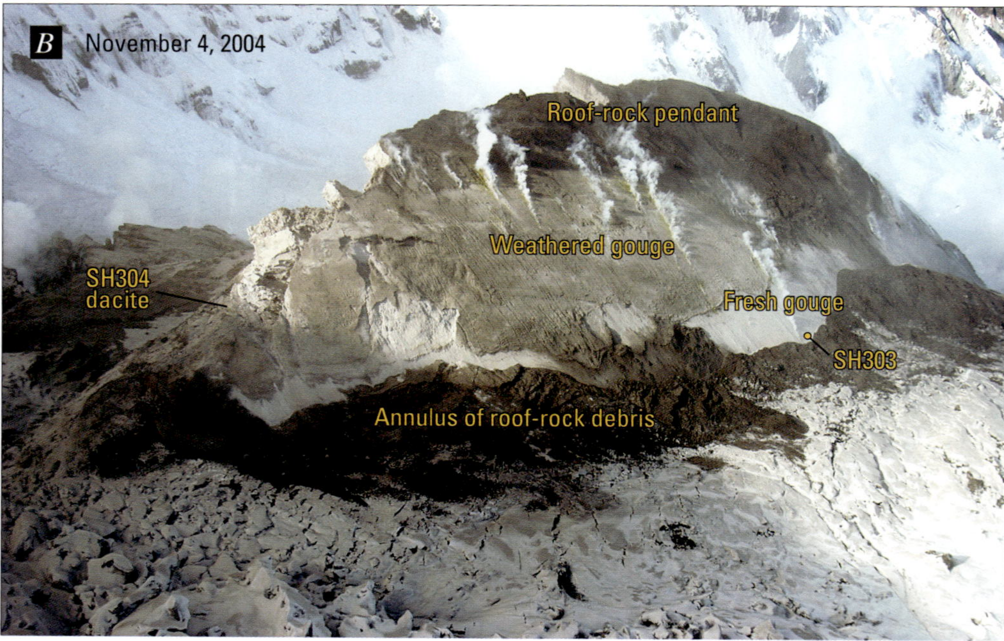

Figure 3. Sampling sites for new dome rocks early in eruption. *A*, View to west of lava exposed at crest of uplifted glacier in southeast crater on October 27, 2004; USGS photo by J.S. Pallister. Steam emanates from surface of spine 3, surrounded by dark (wet) debris from the crater floor and root of the 1980–86 dome that was brought to surface atop spine. Inset shows initial window through crater-floor debris, exposing gouge on spine 3 surface. Our sample SH301 was from roof rock collected near helicopter (circled). *B*, View to west of same area on November 4, 2004, showing fault-gouge mantled and striated east face of spine 3, now about 100 m above uplifted surface of the deformed glacier. USGS photo by J.S. Pallister. First dense dacite sample of the spine interior (SH304) was dredged from southeast end of spine 3 and was still hot when returned to a staging area 10 km distant. First gouge sample was collected during a short-duration landing at SH303. Note roof-rock pendant of crater-floor debris, which was transported upward as spine emerged from glacier and rose upward and obliquely to the southeast. See Cashman and others (this volume, chap. 19) for additional details of gouge carapace.

methods. Because of extensive, very fine grained groundmass crystallization, modal analyses were done using a combination of optical point counting, low- and high-magnification SEM image analysis of backscattered electron images, and multielement microprobe-stage raster maps. Thin-section raster map data were processed using image analysis software to give area percentages for a series of color bins, which were adjusted to differentiate phases in the sample and then combined through a series of additions, subtractions, and normalizations to yield approximate area percentages of the phases. Stage raster maps were made for large (1 cm^2) and small (2.56 mm^2) areas, the latter to yield a high-resolution image (2-μm pixel spacing), which was required to resolve microlites. For example, the color spectrum was adjusted so that red areas in the large-area aluminum (Al) map equal the area percentage of plagioclase phenocrysts (fig. 4). When added to percent of small green lath-shaped microlites in the high-resolution aluminum map, this gives the total feldspar abundance. Similarly, red to yellow areas of the two iron (Fe) maps (fig. 4) gives the percentage of oxides, which is subtracted from the percentage of nonblack areas in the high-resolution silicon (Si) map to determine percentage of void space. Yellow areas in the high-resolution Si map give the percentage of SiO_2 phases, which are present only in the groundmass. Glass abundance is obtained from the potassium (K) maps by subtracting the area percentage of K-rich phases (yellow, alkali feldspar) in the high-resolution map from the percentage of glass (blue) in the large-area, lower resolution map. Using these types of mapping and image analysis techniques, it has been possible to quantify the abundance and textures of crystals, glass, and vesicles at scales ranging from centimeters to microns (table 2).[6]

Matrix glass, glass inclusions, oxide minerals, and selected silicate minerals were analyzed using the electron microprobe, and the results are summarized in tables 3 and 4 and in appendix 1 (included in the digital version of this paper). Most microprobe analyses were conducted at 15-kV accelerating voltage and 20-nA beam current, using the JEOL 8900 microprobes at U.S. Geological Survey (USGS) laboratories in Denver, Colo., and Menlo Park, Calif. SEM analyses were conducted using a JEOL 5800LV SEM equipped with an energy-dispersive X-ray system (EDS) at the USGS microbeam laboratory in Denver. Natural and synthetic silicate standards were used and off-peak background corrections were applied to standards and unknowns; secondary silicate-mineral standards were used to verify and monitor the analytical routines. Glass standard NIST SRM 610 (Ihinger and others, 1994; Pearce and others, 1997) was used as a secondary standard for sulfur (S) and chlorine (Cl).

Beam spot sizes were varied according to the material being analyzed and the nature of the problem being examined. Point beams were used for oxides and to examine zoning profiles, larger spot sizes (to 40 μm) were used where possible to analyze glasses, and iterative counting techniques, similar to those pioneered by Nielson and Sigurdsson (1981), were used during all glass analyses to monitor and, where indicated, to correct for alkali and silica migration. To avoid loss related to electron beam damage, the elements sodium (Na), K, and Si were analyzed before other elements in glasses, and count rates were collected for these elements starting immediately when the beam was unblanked. Curves were individually fit to the count-rate data for each analysis, and the intercept at time zero was used in the data reduction routines. Long count times (>300 seconds on and off peak) were used for S and Cl analyses, yielding detection limits of 70–90 ppm for S and about 50 ppm for Cl. On the basis of long-term reproducibility of standard analyses, analytical reproducibility for microprobe analyses is estimated as 1–2 percent of the reported amounts for major elements, except for H_2O, which is calculated by the difference of complete major- and minor-element probe analyses from 100 percent and is subject to uncertainties of about 1 weight percent.

In addition, two sets of approximately 700–1,000 microprobe point analyses each were done in polygonal grids and averaged to characterize the bulk composition of two small quenched inclusions in two samples. A third set of gridded point analyses were done over a similar-size grid in the host dacite of one of the samples to test the method. To save time, mean atomic number background corrections and short (approximately 20 s) dwell times were used for these analyses, cutting analytical time to approximately 36 hours for each area. The resulting data for the dacite host were also used to calculate an analytical mode by binning analyses into mineral types, glass, and void space according to a series of compositional and stoichiometric rules (see tables 2 and 5).

IR Spectroscopic Analysis

Dissolved water and carbon dioxide in two unusual glassy samples, SH304-2G1 and SH304-2G2, were determined by Fourier-transform infrared (FTIR) spectroscopy in the Department of Earth and Planetary Sciences at the American Museum of Natural History, using a Nicolet 20SXB FTIR spectrometer attached to a Spectra Tech IR Plan microscope, according to methods described by Mandeville and others (2002). A total of 10 to 16 spots were measured in the most microlite-free (Fe-Ti oxides and orthopyroxene) regions of matrix glass in each sample, and IR results are reported in table 6. Because of the small thicknesses of films of glass in the matrix of typical microcrystalline dacite, it has only been possible to determine water contents by FTIR on the matrix glass in the one glass-rich sample (SH304-2G).

Bulk-Rock Analysis

Representative samples of the dacite lava were coarsely crushed in a hydraulic press and hand-picked for bulk-rock analyses. Splits of the crushed dacite were cleaned of xenolithic material, and the cleaned samples were submitted for analysis at USGS labs in Denver, Colo. Splits of many of the samples were also analyzed at Washington State University's Geoanalytical

[6] Tables 2 through 9 are grouped at the back of this chapter, after "References Cited."

Laboratory. Major-element analyses of whole-rock samples were obtained by X-ray fluorescence (XRF) methods (Taggart and others, 1987). Trace-element abundances for selected samples were determined by Induction Coupled Plasma–Mass Spectrometric (ICP–MS) and Instrumental Neutron Activation Analysis (INAA) methods (Baedecker and McKown, 1987). On the basis of replicate analyses of standards, analytical reproducibility of major-element abundances is estimated to be better than 0.4 percent of the reported values for SiO_2 and Al_2O_3. For other elements, reproducibility is better than ±2 percent of values in the range 1–10 wt. percent and better than ±6 percent for abundances less than 1 wt. percent. Coefficients of variation ($100 \times (\sigma / \bar{x})$, in percent) for INAA analyses, based on counting statistics, are given in table 8.

Modal Compositions and Textures of the Dacite Lava

Microcrystalline Dacite

The spines erupted from Mount St. Helens in 2004–6 are composed of remarkably crystal-rich hornblende-hypersthene dacite. For consistency with past usage at Mount St. Helens, the term hornblende is used informally herein for rock names. In fact, the amphiboles in the 2004–6 dacite range in composition from magnesiohornblende and tschermakite to magnesiohastingsite (Rutherford and Devine, this volume, chap. 31; Thornber and others, this volume, chap. 32), and therefore

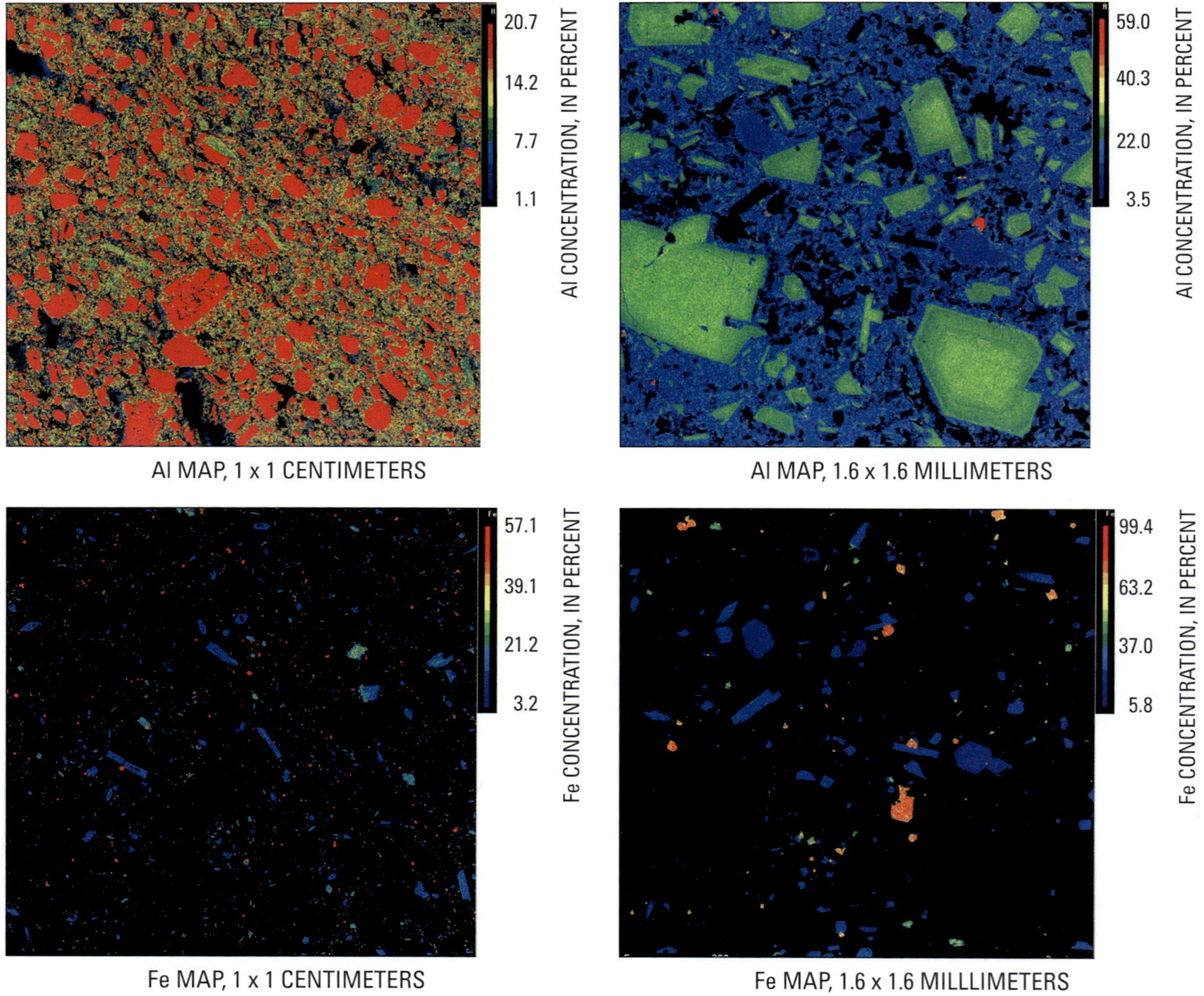

Figure 4. Electron microprobe-stage raster maps of sample SH305-1A illustrating the procedure for deriving abundance of phases from image analysis. Each map was produced by driving microprobe stage over areas approximately 1 cm^2 (left images) and then 2.6 mm^2 (right images; to differentiate matrix phases) while simultaneously recording X-ray peak intensities from five wavelength-dispersive spectrometers and from backscattered electron detector. The X-ray intensities are compared to standard intensities to derive approximate concentrations of major elements as oxides and are plotted according to stage position to produce images shown here. Note that each map has a unique color scale.

we use the more general term amphibole when referring to individual crystals. Microbeam mapping of three microcrystalline dacite samples (SH304-2A, SH305-1A, SH315-4) yields total crystal contents that range from 69 percent to 87 percent (phenocrysts+microlites) on a void-free basis. Phenocryst content of the microcrystalline dacite averages 46.0 percent (±4.3 percent), also on a void-free basis (table 2). The high total crystal content is a result of extensive groundmass crystallization, which produced fine-grained mosaics of microlites, residual glass, and vesicles. For consistency with previous work (Cashman, 1992) a cutoff of approximately 30 µm is used to distinguish microlites from phenocrysts in modes. The microlite-rich groundmass texture of the 2004–6 dacite is referred to as "microcrystalline" to distinguish it from the more typical hyalopilitic textures of the 1980s lavas.

Samples collected from spine 3 during the early stages of the eruption (table 1), when the eruption rate was high (that is, greater than 5 m^3/s; Schilling and others, this volume, chap. 8; LaHusen and others, this volume, chap. 16), and from the exterior margin of the spines are relatively glassy. For example, interior sample SH304-2A has, by microbeam map analysis, approximately 45 percent phenocrysts of plagioclase, amphibole, hypersthene, and Fe-Ti oxides set in a microcrystal-rich matrix that contains approximately 33 percent microlites and 22 percent glass on a vesicle-free basis (table 2). Exterior sample SH305-1A is also relatively vesicular (37 per-

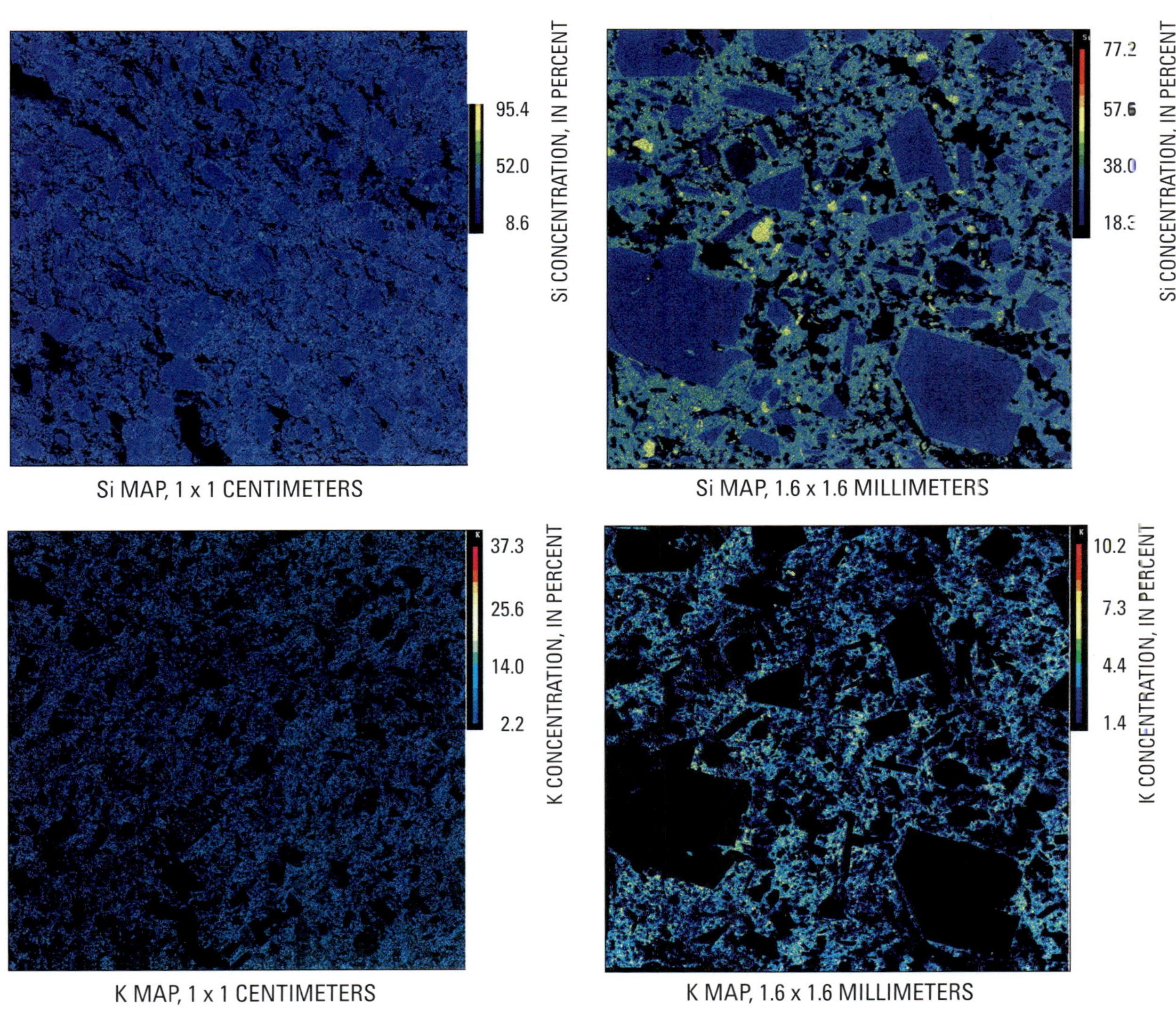

Figure 4.—Continued.

cent) and glassy (30 percent on a vesicle-free basis). However, samples erupted subsequently have less glass. For example, sample SH315-4 from spine 4 (erupted approximately April 1, 2005) has only about 13 percent glass (table 2), and samples collected later in 2005 and in 2006 have only trace amounts of glass. The presence of two populations of vesicles in the microcrystalline dacite, one with larger (100–500 μm long) irregular vesicles, and a second with small (1 μm) spherical vesicles implies continued degassing during microlite crystallization (figs. 5*A*, 5*B*).

A detailed look at SH305-1A shows several features that are characteristic of the 2004–6 dacite. First, plagioclase phenocrysts commonly have overgrowth rims that are partly irregular in form and appear to have grown rapidly (fig. 5*A*). Amphibole crystals are complexly zoned and have thin, fine-grained breakdown rims (fig. 5*C*) that average 5 μm in thickness (Thornber and others, this volume, chap. 32). The groundmass contains abundant plagioclase microphenocrysts and microlites in a glassy matrix (figs. 5*B*, 5*D*). The matrix of this sample shows the onset of very late stage cotectic precipitation of Na- and K-rich feldspar and quartz, which commonly nucleate at the margins of larger plagioclase crystals. Additionally, there is a minor component of tridymite (acicular dark-gray crystals in fig. 5*D*), as also reported by Blundy and Cashman (2001) for slowly cooled samples of the March 1983 Mount St. Helens dacite.

Later erupted samples preserve noticeably less glass in the matrix. For example, sample SH315-4 from spine 4 (erupted approximately April 1, 2005) has only about 13 percent glass (table 2; fig. 6*A*). The groundmass has some still-distinguishable plagioclase microlites, but these have been largely subsumed into a near-holocrystalline matrix (fig. 6*B*). Also common in this sample are fairly large, discrete crystals of quartz (fig. 6*B*). Sample SH316 from spine 5 shows similar features to samples from spines 3 and 4, with evidence of rapid rim growth on many plagioclase phenocrysts (figs. 6*C*) and small patches of preserved glass in a near-holocrystalline matrix (fig. 6*D*). Sample SH315 also contains broadly folded, vesicular, pink-colored veins a few millimeters to a few centimeters in cross section and extending for tens of centimeters across large blocks (fig. 7*A*). Scanning electron micrograph images from within one of the veins display an irregular network of matrix phases between the phenocrysts, formed by finely intergrown tridymite, quartz, Na- and K-rich feldspar, and void space (fig. 7*B*). Where larger cavities are transected by the plane of the thin section, the silica-feldspar intergrowth is seen to extend into the vesicle space (fig. 7*C*), exposing delicate networks of tridymite and feldspar (figs. 7*D*, 7*E*). Magnetite grains in the vein zones have undergone oxidation exsolution (fig. 7*F*). These features document a continuum of matrix crystallization, extending from a fluid-saturated magma into a vapor-dominated phase of crystallization.

Samples collected later in 2005 and in 2006 have only trace amounts of glass and show even more extensive groundmass and vapor-phase crystallization. An examination of SH321 and SH322 from spine 6 (samples erupted on approximately August 10 and August 15, 2005, respectively) reveals groundmasses composed entirely of microlites (figs. 8*A*–*D*) and consisting of graphic intergrowths of a "granite minimum" assemblage of sodic plagioclase (An_{20-30}), quartz, tridymite, and a more potassic feldspar (anorthoclase to sanidine). Quartz and the feldspars occur as subhedral crystals within the intergrowths. Tridymite occurs within the graphic intergrowths and protrudes into vesicle space (fig. 8*A*), attesting to crystallization from both melt and gas phases. Microprobe analyses of representative groundmass phases are given in table 3, and many are keyed to figure 8.

Cristobalite is a common groundmass phase in samples from each of the spines. It displays a characteristic microbotryoidal texture and commonly fills vesicles and interstices in the dacite, as well as within rare diktytaxitic quenched inclusions. The occurrence is indicative of late-stage vapor-phase crystallization, similar to that described for cristobalite in the 1980 Mount St. Helens cryptodome (Hoblitt and Harmon, 1993).

Glassy Dacite

The dredge haul from spine 3 on November 4, 2004 (SH304 sample series, Thornber and others, 2008b), contained principally blocks of still-hot, pink to gray, microcrystalline dacite. However, the haul also contained several small (2–5-cm diameter) dark glassy dacite fragments. Most of these have bulk compositions, phenocryst assemblages, Fe-Ti oxide temperatures, and textures that indicate they are derived from uplifted parts of the 1980–86 lava dome. However, one flow-banded glassy fragment (SH304-2G) has characteristics that suggest it may be juvenile (for example, overlapping Fe-Ti oxide temperature and similar bulk composition compared to the microcrystalline dacite). Sample SH304-2G is a hornblende-hypersthene dacite with 72 percent glass (fig. 9, table 2). The ratio of K_2O in the glass compared to that of the whole rock is indicative of a glass content of only 54 percent and suggests that the sample is enriched in glass and depleted in crystal components (table 2), such as would occur by flow segregation or filter-pressing, an effect that is consistent with the flow-banded character of the fragment (fig. 9*A*). Although there is some uncertainty in establishing that this sample is juvenile, it is investigated in more detail here as a possible analogue for the melt phase of the 2004 magma before the extensive groundmass crystallization. Unlike the amphibole phenocrysts in the microcrystalline dacite, which have reaction-rim thicknesses that cluster at about 5 μm (Rutherford and Devine, this volume, chap. 31; Thornber and others, this volume, chap. 32), the amphibole phenocrysts in SH304-2G lack reaction rims (fig. 9*B*), indicating more rapid ascent, as might be expected during the earliest phase of the eruption. The glass in this sample contains swarms of very small (less than 1 μm diameter) hypersthene microlites (figs. 9*C*, 9*D*), similar to those found in the outer zones of plagioclase phenocrysts in the 2004–6 dacite (Streck and others, this volume, chap. 34).

Inclusions

Inclusions in volcanic rocks provide glimpses of country rock surrounding magma reservoirs and conduits, plutonic equivalents or cumulates from host magmas, quenched blebs of other magmas, and potentially even partially melted source rocks for the magmas (Bacon, 1986; Costa and others, 2002; Jackson, 1968; Smith, 2000). Mount St. Helens dacites contain a rich suite of inclusions, consisting primarily of dioritic to gabbroic plutonic rocks, and the 2004–6 lava dome is no exception.

Plutonic and Metamorphic Inclusions

The 2004–6 dacite contains relatively abundant medium-grained gabbroic to dioritic inclusions as well as minor banded and granoblastic amphibolite inclusions. They are present in both dome lava and gouge samples; we estimate their abundance at 1–5 percent. Although not yet studied in detail, in hand sample the inclusions appear to be similar to the gabbroic and metamorphic inclusions that make up 3–5 percent of the 1980–86 lava dome (Heliker, 1995; Pallister and others, 1991). We previously thought that

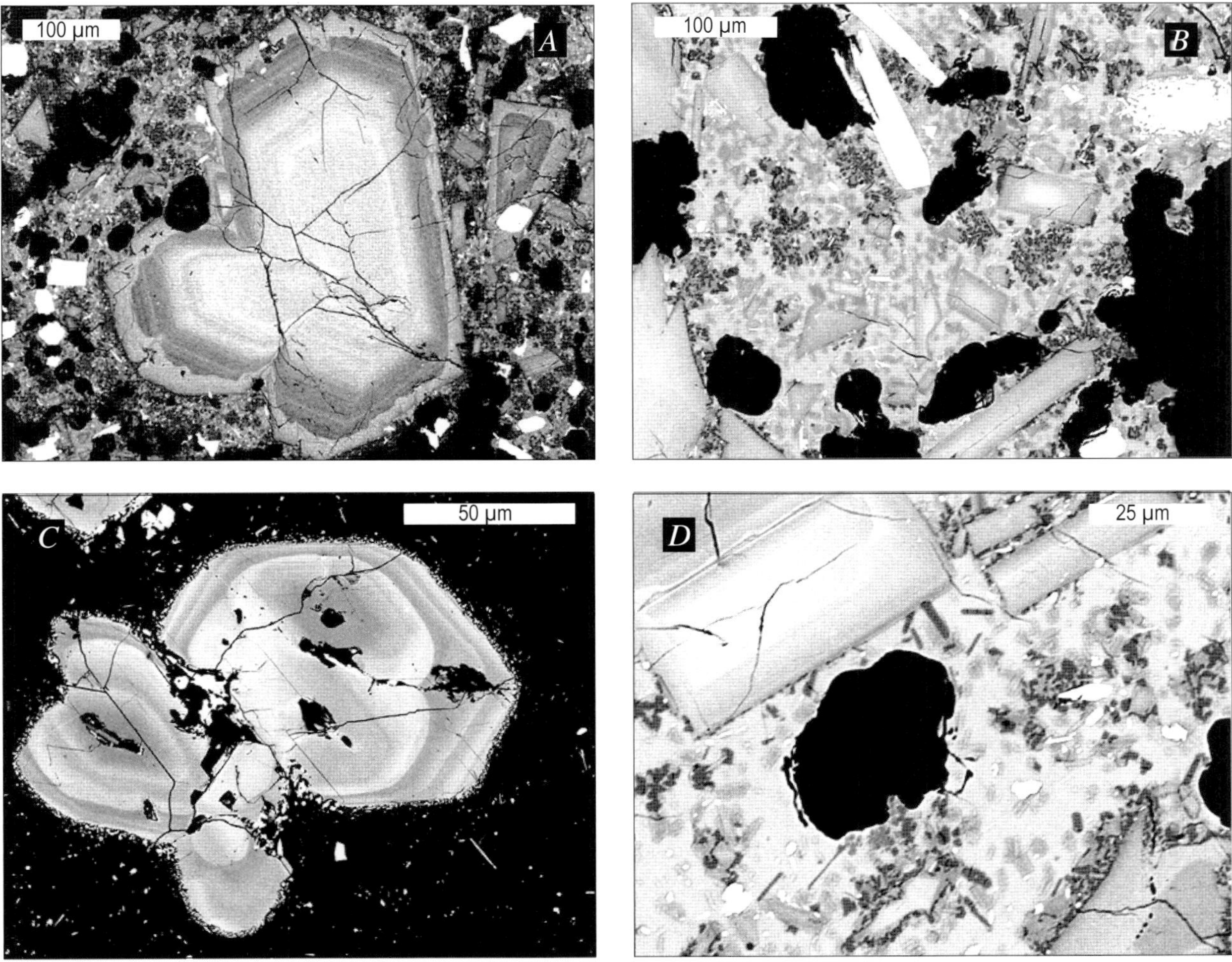

Figure 5. SEM backscattered electron images (*A, B, D*) and one optical image (*C*) of microcrystalline dacite sample SH305-1. This early 2004 sample (eruption date, November 20, 2004, table 1) has relatively glass-rich groundmass and shows early stages of shallow cotectic groundmass crystallization. Magnification varies; scale bars labeled on images. *A*, Plagioclase phenocryst. Note irregular, cuspate margins, indicative of rapid growth. *B*, Groundmass. Visible in *A* and *B* are two size populations of vesicles: large (irregular) and smaller (oval to spherical). *C*, Zoned amphibole with thin (5 µm) reaction rim. *D*, Small plates of tridymite (dark gray).

some of the gabbroic inclusions represented cumulates from the Mount St. Helens magma reservoir, but U-Pb ion-probe zircon ages of about 25 Ma for several samples (our unpublished ion microprobe data) suggest that many of these may instead be derived from a Miocene gabbroic to quartz diorite intrusive complex inferred from gravity data to underlie the volcano (Williams and others, 1987).

Dacite Inclusions

Some samples collected from the later spines of the 2004–6 eruption contain small (1–5 cm) inclusions of dacite with slightly different textures or degrees of alteration compared to the host dacite. Petrographic examination and electron microprobe analyses of one of these inclusions in sample SH321-1C show little difference in mineralogy or composition across the inclusion boundary. Another (SH316-1A) has a bulk composition distinct from the host dacite, with 63.4 percent SiO_2, and it likely represents a xenolith entrained in the conduit magma and derived from the root of the 1980–86 lava dome. We suspect that many such "dacite-in-dacite" inclusions are fragments of shallow conduit lava and wall rocks, incorporated as the conduit shifted slightly to feed subsequent spines. Consistent with this idea, an examination of inclusions in the gouge carapace and variations in bulk composition of the gouge (Cashman and others, this volume, chap. 19) indicate

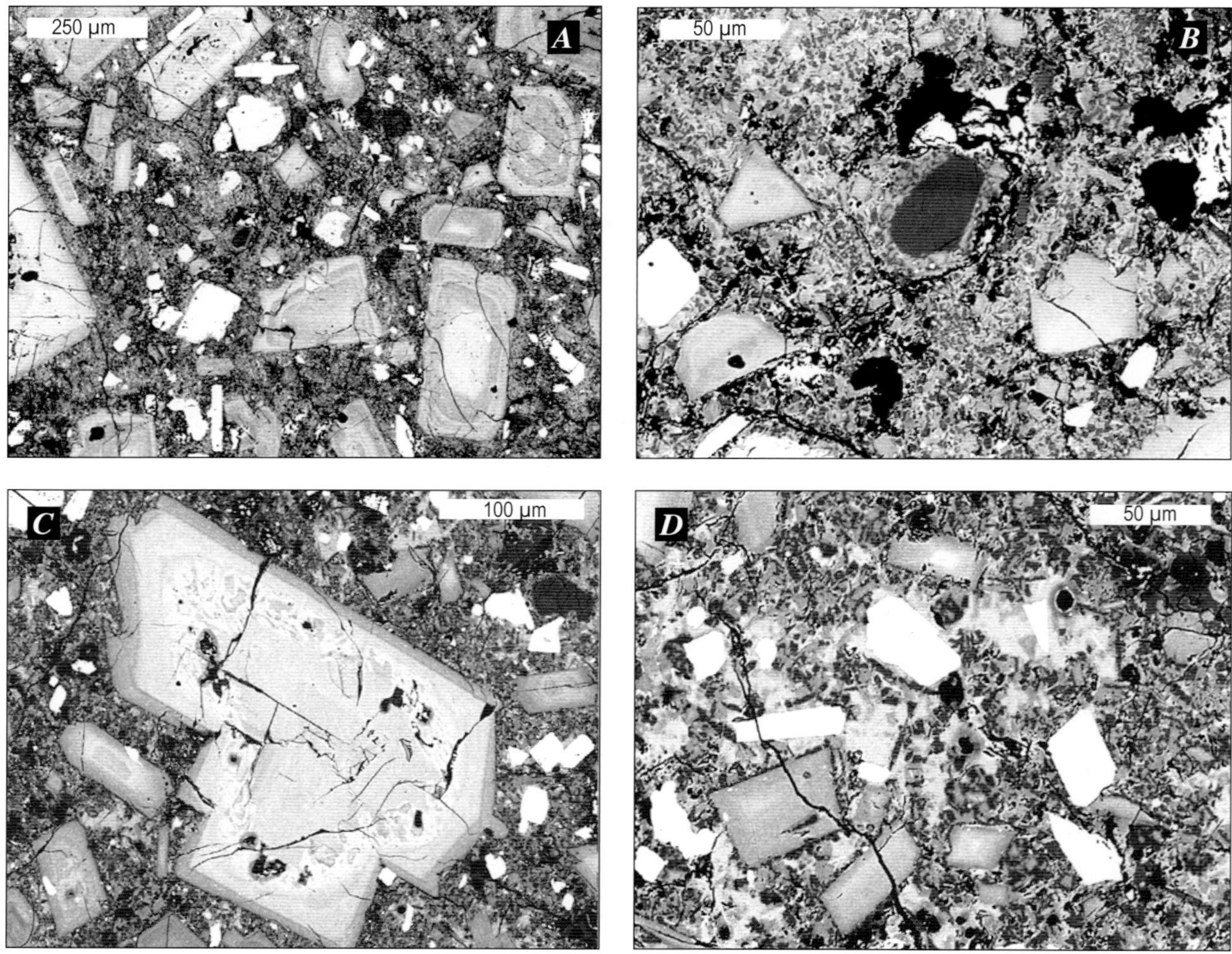

Figure 6. SEM backscattered electron images of microcrystalline dacite samples emplaced in April 2005. These samples have experienced rapid and extensive groundmass crystallization, producing a nearly holocrystalline groundmass. Magnification varies; scale bars labeled on images. *A* and *B*, sample SH315-4, erupted April 1, 2005. In *B* note dark-gray quartz grain (center) and micrographic intergrowth of feldspar and quartz forming the groundmass. *C* and *D*, Sample SH316, erupted April 15, 2005.

that the conduit margins incorporated a range of crater floor rocks as the gouge formed.

Quenched Magmatic Inclusions

Two small (<1-cm diameter) inclusions, composed of diktytaxitic networks of plagioclase and amphibole crystals and containing variable amounts of glass and void space, were found in samples SH315-4 (figs. 10*A*, 10*B*) and SH321-1C. As magma mixing has been involved in the evolution of magmas erupted at Mount St. Helens during the past 4,000 years (Pallister and others, 1992; Smith and Leeman, 1993) and has been implicated as a trigger for explosive eruptions (Pallister and others, 1996), we searched the 2004–6 rock collection for additional examples, and we examined these two inclusions in detail. Our search indicates that although dacite-in-dacite inclusions are relatively common, quenched inclusions are exceedingly rare in the suite of 2004–6 samples. In the approximately 500 kg of samples collected to date (Thornber and others, 2008b), we have found only the two small quenched inclusions, with a total mass less than 5 g.

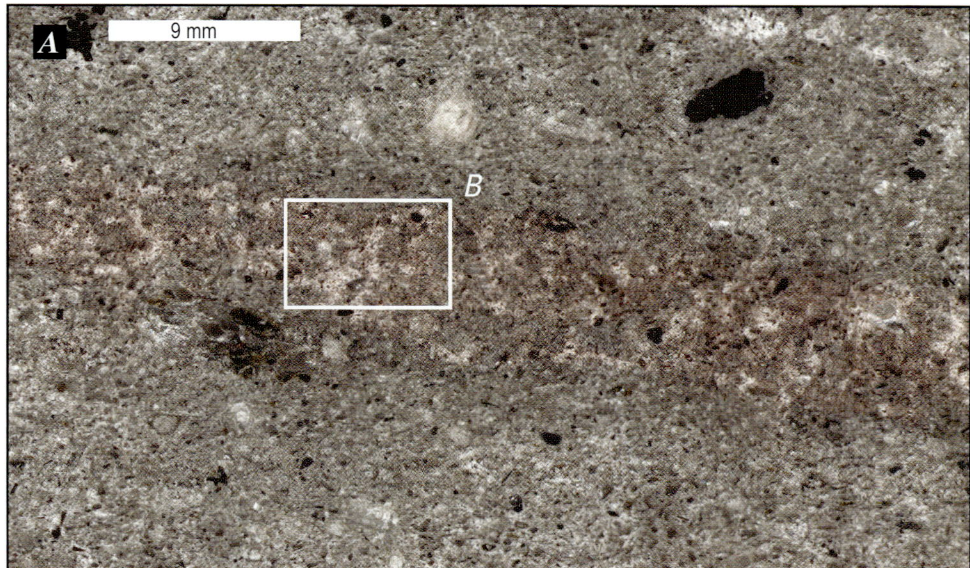

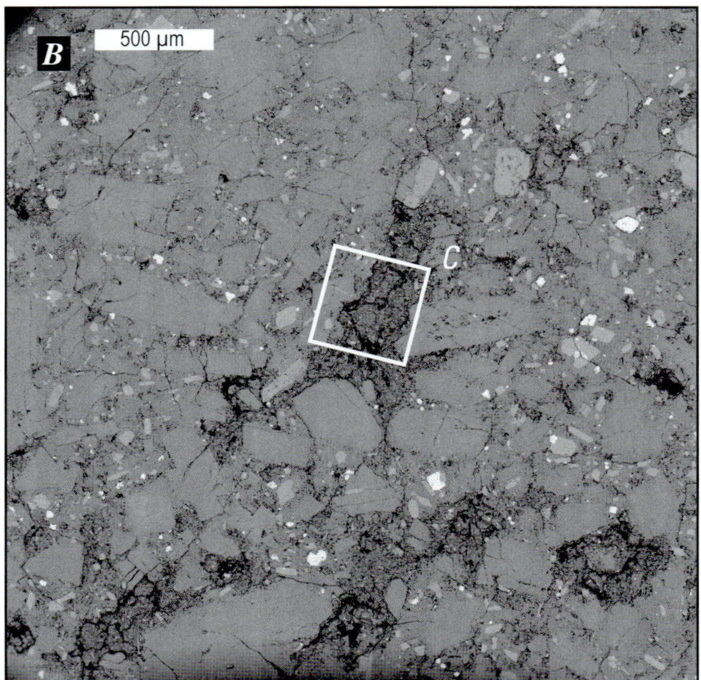

Figure 7. Photograph and SEM backscattered electron (BSE) images of microcrystalline dacite sample SH315-5. Sequence shows progressive increase in magnification, and locations are mapped on preceding images. *A*, Polished thin section, 4.5 cm in long dimension, showing pink-colored vesicular vein. *B* and *C*, BSE images showing network of fine-grained microlite-rich matrix between phenocrysts. *D* and *E*, BSE images showing phases identified by morphology and energy-dispersive spectrometric (EDS) analysis: Fsp = Na+K-rich feldspar; Mt = titanomagnetite; Opx = orthopyroxene (hypersthene). *F*, BSE image of titanomagnetite grains in the vein zone showing development of oxidation-exsolution lamellae.

A more-detailed examination of an inclusion in sample SH315-4 reveals elongate and hopper-shaped crystals of amphibole and plagioclase (figs. 10*C*, 10*D*), as would be produced by rapid growth during undercooling of a hotter and more mafic magma in the dacite host magma. The amphiboles are high in Al_2O_3 (to 14 percent) and they lack reaction rims, except at the margins of the inclusion, where they reacted with the host dacite during decompression to produce thin breakdown rims (Thornber and others, this volume, chap. 32). Plagioclase phenocrysts have normally zoned An_{60-40} cores bounded by cuspate dissolution zones, which are rimmed by much more sodic and potassic plagioclase (to An_{20}, Or_9). These rims extend into the rhyolitic groundmass glass (75–76 percent SiO_2) as angular and hopper-form crystals (figs. 10*D*, 10*E*). Cristobalite, with a characteristic microbotryoidal texture, is relatively abundant as a late vapor-phase product.

To determine the bulk compositions of the inclusions, we used a microprobe to analyze 736 and 960 points distributed over the polished surface of each of the two inclusions and 1,021 points over a similar area of the host dacite (fig. 10*A*;

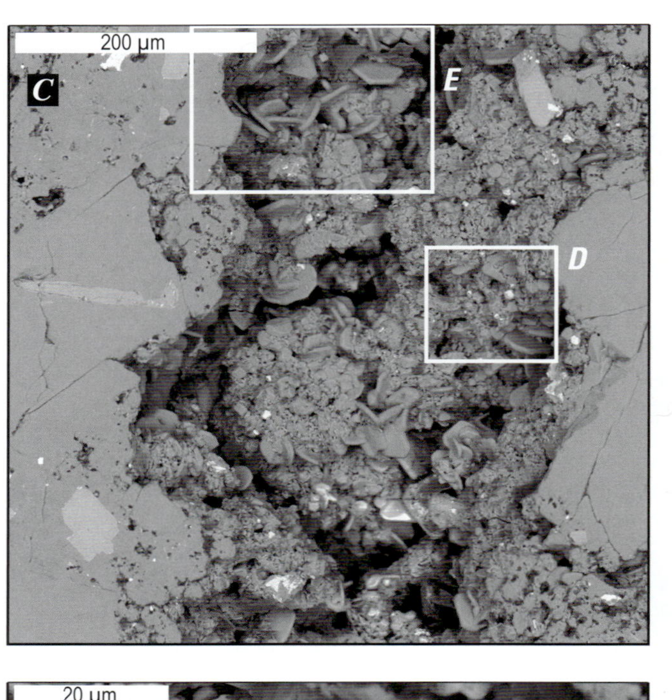

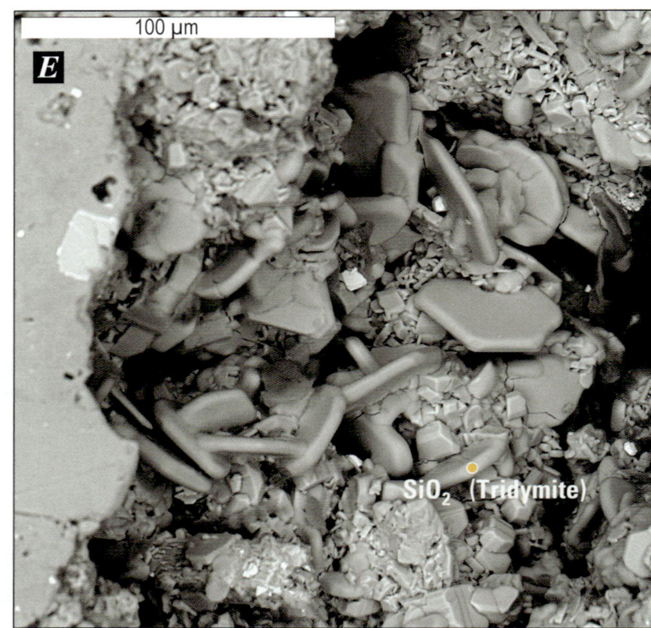

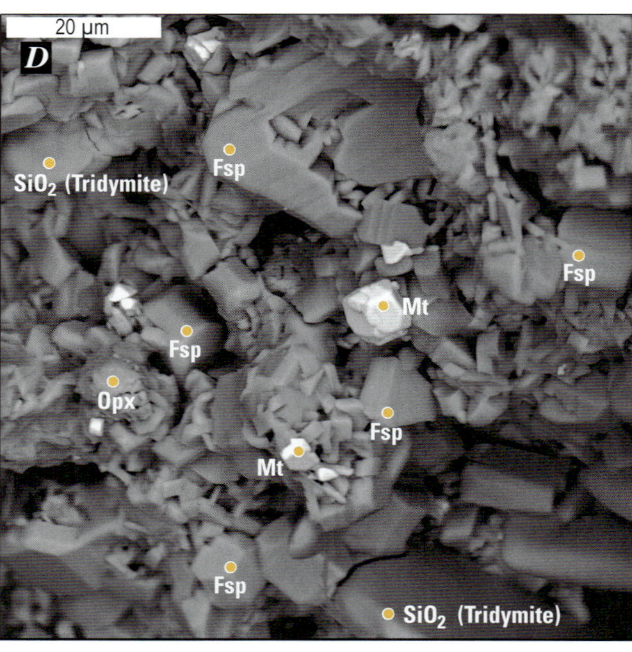

Figure 7.—Continued.

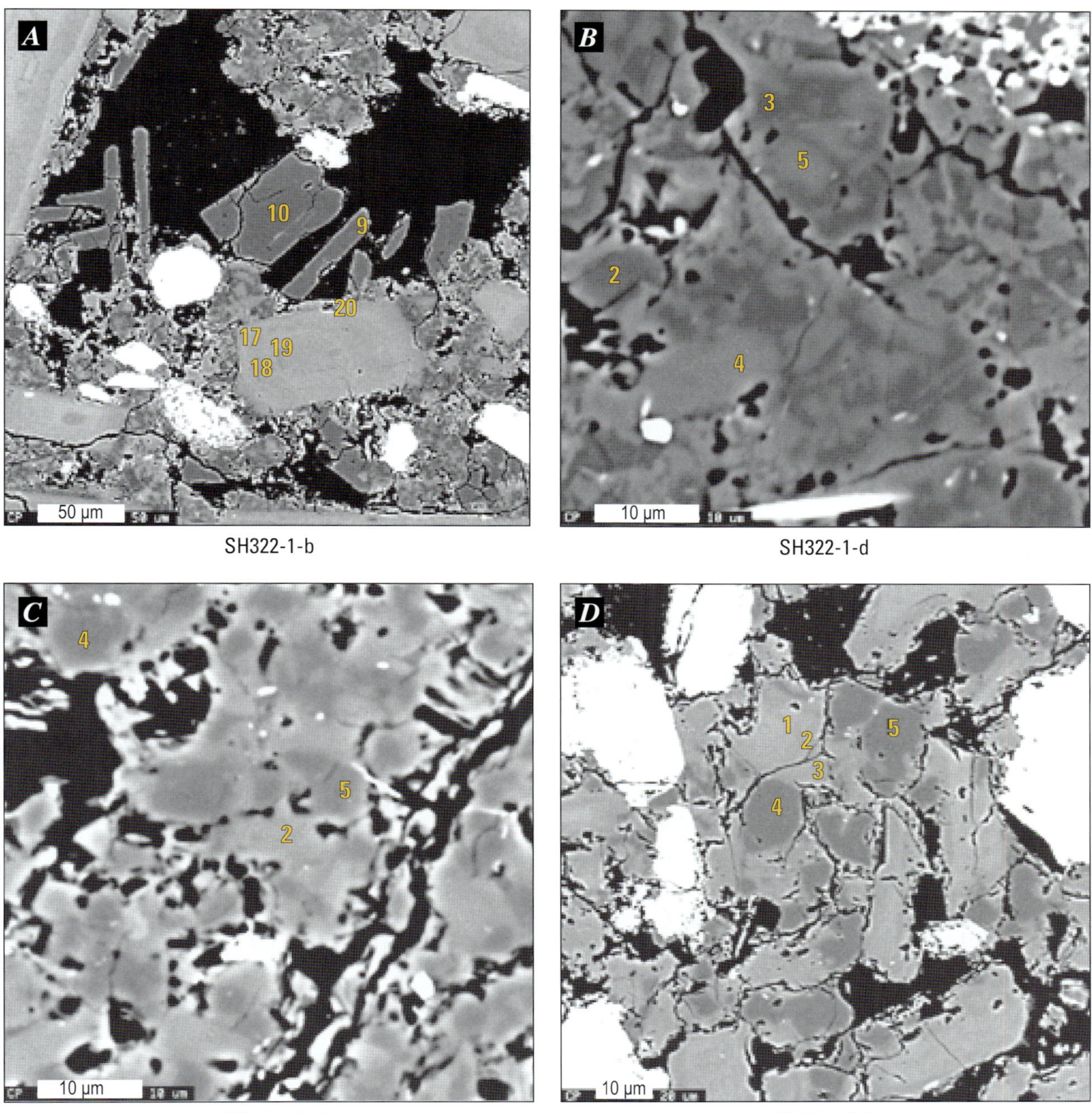

SH322-1-b

SH322-1-d

SH321-1C-7b

SH321-1C-7d

Figure 8. SEM backscattered electron images of microcrystalline dacite samples, documenting continued matrix crystallization. Microprobe analysis points keyed by number to table 3 (final suffix numbers in sample-number list of table 3 refer to locations shown here). *A* and *B*, Sample SH322-1. *C* and *D*, Sample SH321-1C. Minerals probed include tridymite with approximately 1 percent Al_2O_3 (*A*, 9–10; *B*, 2), quartz with less than 0.7 percent Al_2O_3 (*B*, 3; *C*, 4; *D*, 4–5), An_{19-39}/Or_{3-9} plagioclase microlites (*B*, 4; *C*, 2, *D*, 1–3) and An_{33-36}/Or_{1-4} plagioclase microphenocryst (*A*, 17–20), anorthoclase (*B*, 5), and cristobalite with more than 3 percent Al_2O_3 (*C*, 5).

table 5). Averages of these analyses reveal that the inclusion in sample SH315-4 is andesitic (60.0 percent SiO_2), consistent with the relatively high An content of plagioclase cores. It is regarded as a bleb of a more mafic magma that mingled with the dacite at some point in the past (see under "Discussion"). The second inclusion, in SH321-1C, has a bulk composition that overlaps with the host dacite, at 64.8 percent SiO_2 (table 5). However, this sample has a similar quench texture and phenocryst assemblage to the inclusion in SH315-4. It probably represents an entrained bleb of hotter dacite that quenched in the cooler host dacite. However, we cannot rule out the possibility that formerly it was a more mafic magma that quenched in the dacite and then accumulated late-stage rhyolite melt in its matrix through filter pressing (to account for its higher silica content). Quenched inclusions are often heterogeneous in composition because of the effects of postentrainment crystallization (Bacon, 1986). During crystallization of a more mafic inclusion in a cooler and more silicic melt, the melt reaches vapor saturation; it vesiculates, and pressure in the inclusion increases. This process may force residual melt

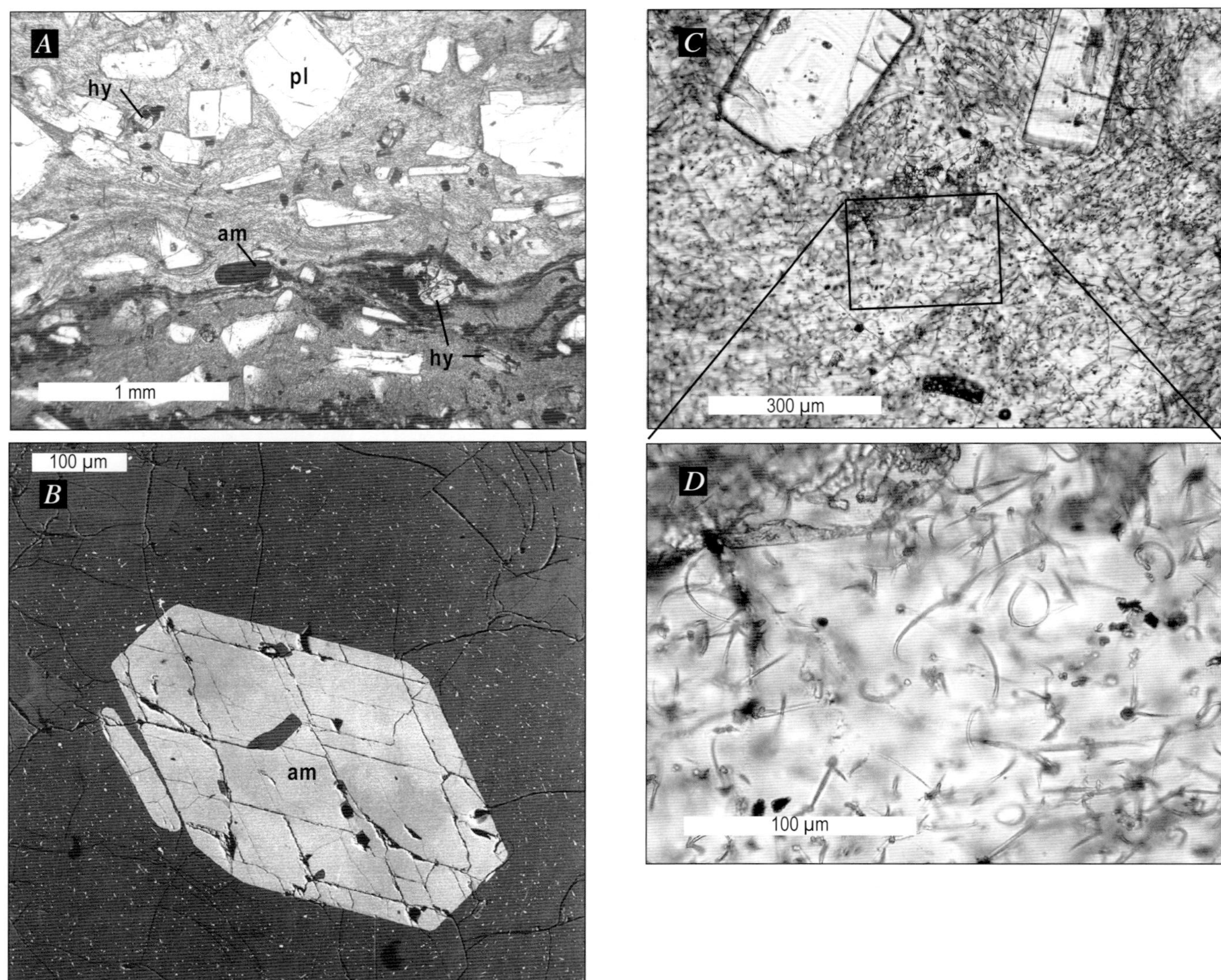

Figure 9. Photomicrographs (*A, C, D*) and SEM backscattered image (*B*) of glassy fragment SH304-2G1, collected on November 4, 2004. *A*, Phenocrysts of plagioclase (pl), hypersthene (hy), and amphibole (am) lie within a flow-foliated groundmass marked by dark bands bearing micron-size oxides. *B*, Microlites of hypersthene and oxides appear as bright specks in backscattered image, and subhedral to euhedral amphibole microphenocryst lacks reaction rims. *C* and enlargement *D*, Glass-rich matrix is peppered with submicron-size curvilinear hypersthene microlites and oxide grains.

toward the margins of the inclusion as the interior gains void space (vesicles). Thus, inclusions may autofractionate, some parts gaining high-silica residual melt and some parts losing residual melt.

Compositions of Matrix Phases and Oxides

Silicate Minerals

Matrix silicate minerals include hypersthene, plagioclase, anorthoclase, quartz, tridymite, and cristobalite. The compositions of phenocrysts in the dacite are the subject of other reports in this volume (Rutherford and Devine, chap. 31; Thornber and others, chap. 32; Streck and others, chap. 34; Kent and others, chap. 35). Here we focus only on the compositions of mineral grains in the microcrystalline groundmass of samples—grains that have textures indicative of late and shallow crystallization. These include microlites (grains <30 µm in diameter), matrix silica phases, and edge compositions of plagioclase phenocrysts. Compositions of these minerals are listed in table 3, and textures of the matrix phases are illustrated in figures 5 through 8. Cristobalite is a common minor phase in all but the most glassy dome rocks. The cristobalite grains have a distinctive botryoidal texture and multiple contraction fractures. They commonly occur at the margins of irregular void space, indicating deposition from a late-stage, silica-rich vapor phase. This occurrence is similar to that seen in the 1980 cryptodome (Hoblitt and Harmon, 1993). Bladed crystals of tridymite are present in low

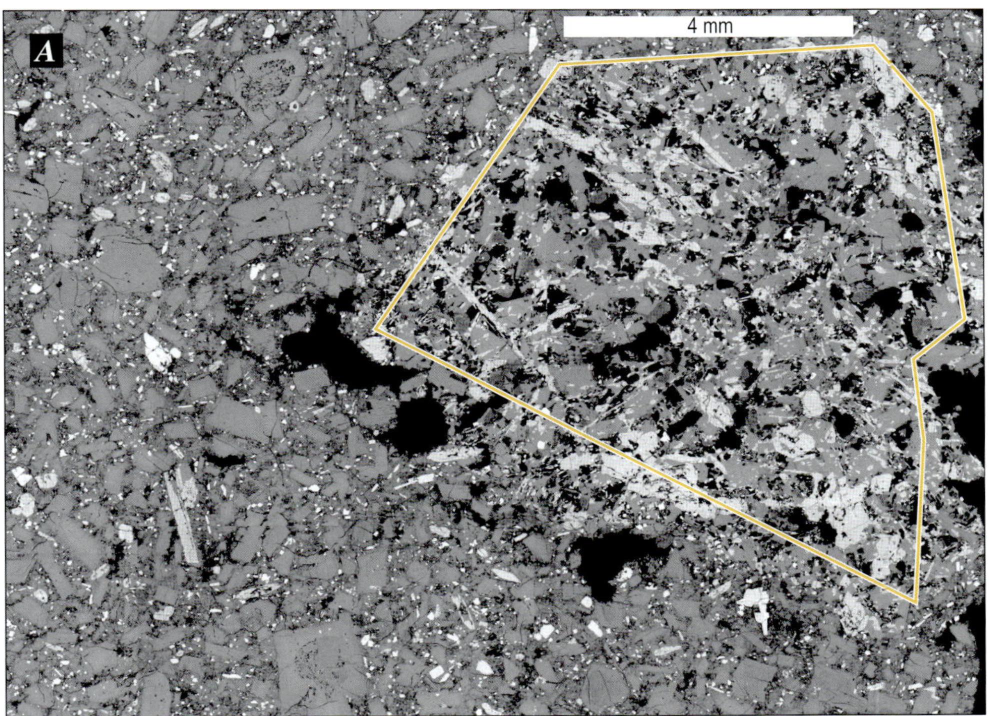

Figure 10. Backscattered electron SEM stage raster-map images of sample SH315-4. Abbreviations: am, amphibole; cr, cristobalite; pl, plagioclase; gl, glass; vo, void space. *A*, Composite of 24 smaller images, shows a mafic (60 percent SiO_2) quenched inclusion at upper right, with acicular amphiboles (light gray) and glassy vesicular groundmass. Irregular box encloses an area that was analyzed using a grid pattern to determine inclusion's bulk composition (table 5). *B*, Enlargement of part of inclusion, showing diktytaxitic texture (visible also in *A*) and void-filling cristobalite (cr) with microbotryoidal texture. *C, D,* and *E*, differing views and magnification showing cristobalite (in image *C*), elongate and hopper crystals of amphibole and plagioclase (*C,D,E*), brown high-silica rhyolite glass (*D, E*) and irregular dissolution and overgrowth textures in plagioclase (*E*). Numbers in images *D* and *E* refer to An content of plagioclase and percent SiO_2 in glass (the latter determined by broad-beam microprobe analysis).

abundance in most samples, although they are common in one of the samples, SH309-1. Quartz microlites occur as anhedral intergrowths with anorthoclase and sodic plagioclase, in some cases forming a patchy texture extending into small glass pools at the margins of plagioclase grains, which have experienced rapid edge growth. The compositions of plagioclase microlites and the final few microns of some phenocryst rims extend to An_{20}, well below the average rim composition of An_{35} measured in hundreds of zoning profiles (Rutherford and Devine, this volume, chap. 31; Streck and others, this volume, chap. 34) and thought to represent the late stages of plagioclase equilibration at depth. A second feldspar, which ranges from anorthoclase to sanidine in composition, with as much as 43 percent Or component (table 3), is also present in the matrix of some samples, where it is intergrown with sodic plagioclase and quartz, forming a "granite minimum" assemblage (Tuttle and Bowen, 1958).

Glasses

Microprobe analyses of matrix glass and glass inclusions reveal mostly dry, high-silica rhyolite compositions (table 4). Most of our analyses of matrix glasses come from early phases

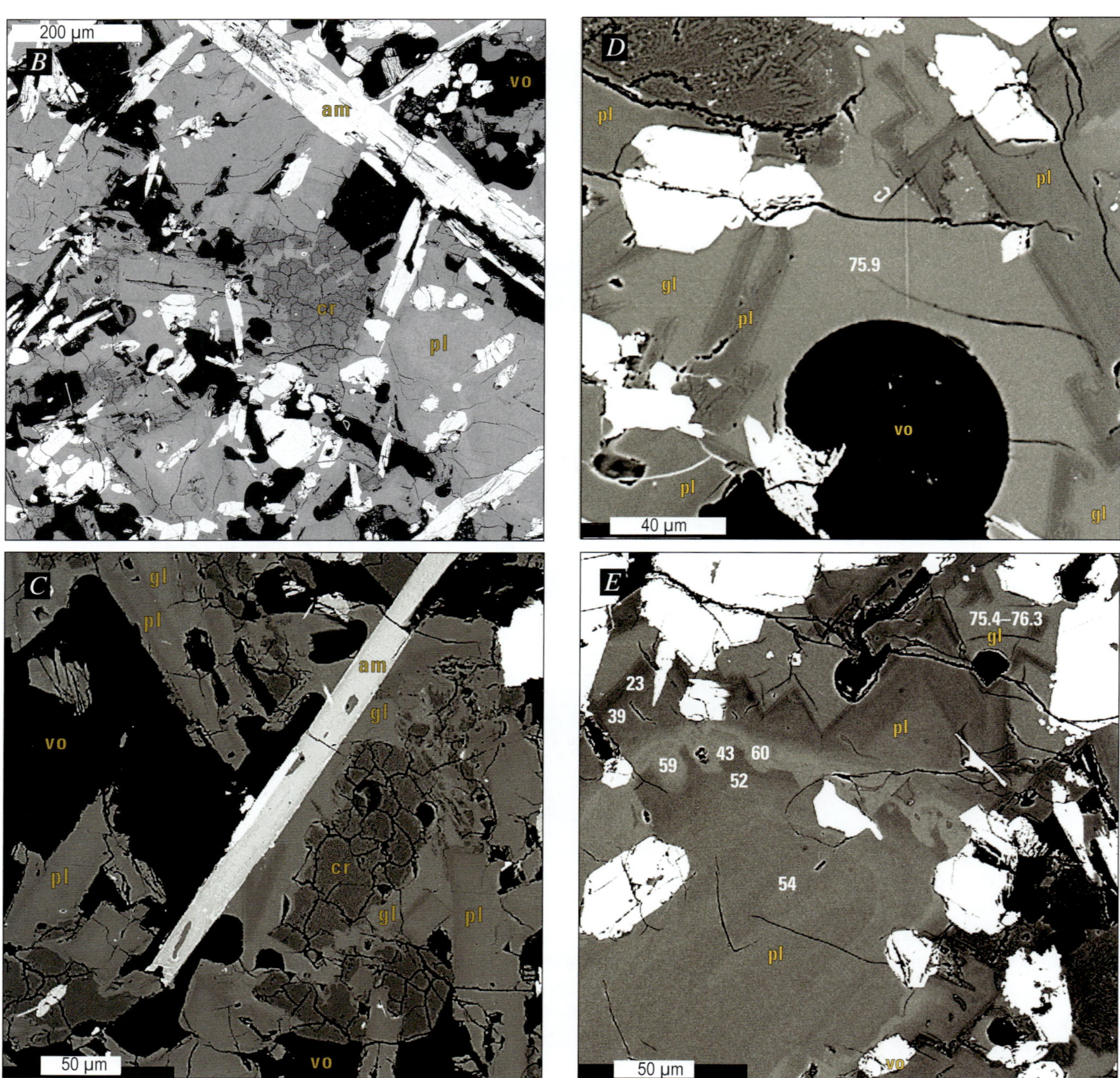

Figure10.—Continued.

of spine 3. In subsequent samples, matrix glass occurs only as thin films that are difficult or impossible to analyze with the electron microprobe without exciting nearby mineral grains. Available matrix-glass compositions are all rhyolitic, ranging from 73 to 78 percent SiO_2 and containing <0.5 to 2.2 wt. percent H_2O (fig. 11). Most glass inclusions also have low water-by-difference values. A single inclusion in amphibole from SH304 has about 3.6 percent H_2O (by difference); all others have <3 percent and many have <0.5 percent H_2O. Secondary ion mass spectrometric (SIMS) analyses of glass inclusions in samples SH305 and SH315 range from 0.03 to 0.20 wt. percent (Jon Blundy, written commun., 2005), confirming the dry character of the inclusions.

Two sections of the glassy fragment SH304-2G were analyzed using FTIR spectroscopy. These measurements of total dissolved water in the matrix glass of sample SH304-2G2, based on the intensity of the absorbance at 3,570 cm^{-1}, yielded 1.9±0.18 wt. percent H_2O (16 spots, table 6), with a range from 1.4 to 2.1 wt. percent, overlapping the microprobe water-by-difference value reported here for the same sample (fig. 11). Total water in matrix glass of SH304-2G1 is 1.7±0.14 wt. percent on the basis of summation of water dissolved as hydroxyl groups determined from the absorbance peak at 4,500 cm^{-1} and molecular water determined from the intensity of the absorbance peak at 1,630 cm^{-1}, in agreement with the value determined from the 3,570 cm^{-1} peak. Total dissolved

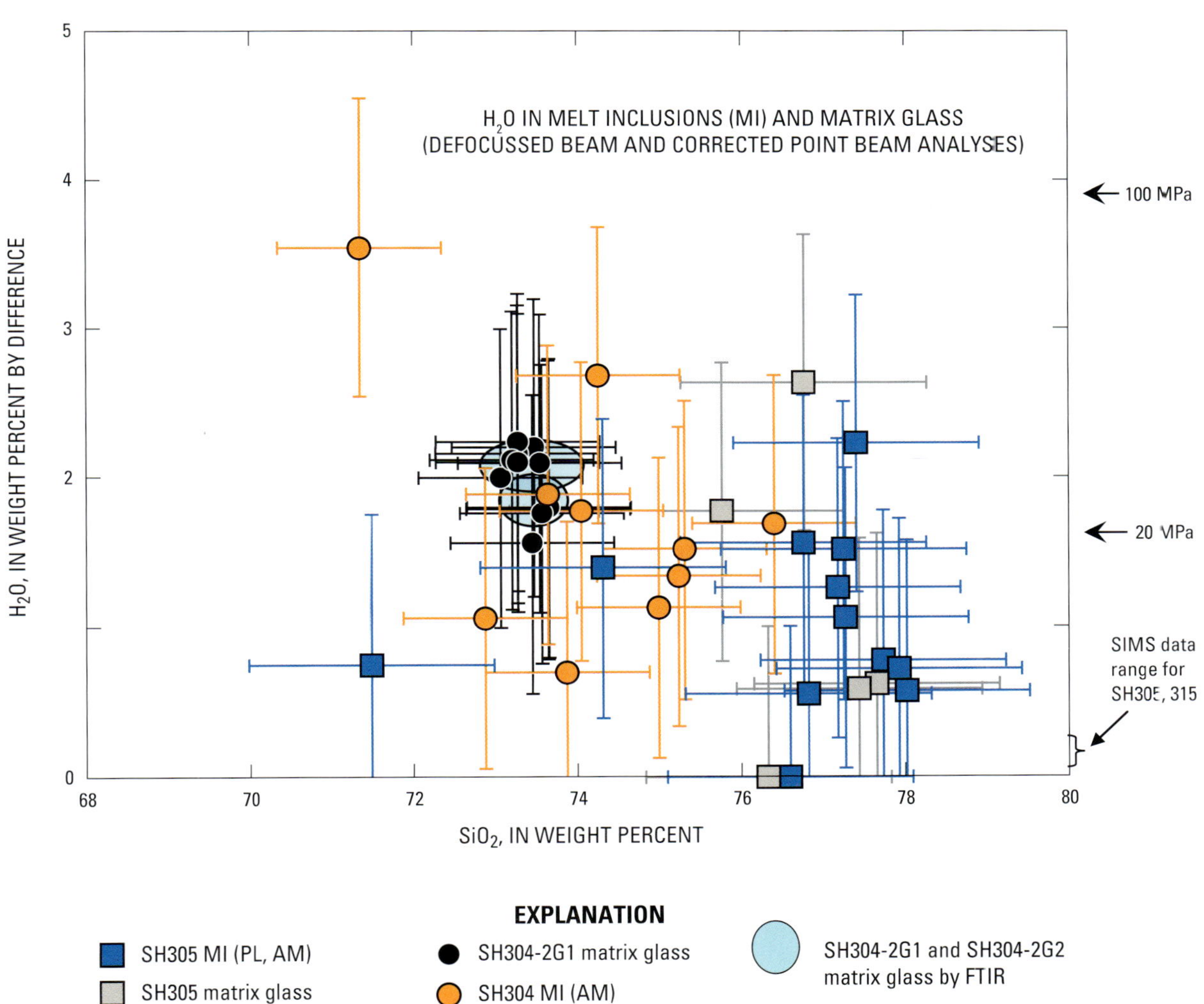

Figure 11. Abundance of H_2O in matrix glass and glass inclusions from spine 3, determined by differencing the totals of microprobe analyses from 100 percent and plotted against SiO_2. Abbreviations: PL, plagioclase; AM, amphibole; MI, melt inclusion. Circled fields represent average and standard deviation for Fourier-transform infrared (FTIR) analyses of matrix glass in SH304-2G1 and SH304-2G2, which overlap with microprobe analyses of same sample. Concentrations of water at saturation in silicate melts at 20 and 30 MPa (Moore and others, 1995) are shown for comparison, as is the range of secondary ion mass spectrometer (SIMS) data for matrix glass in samples erupted later (J. Blundy and K. Cashman, written commun., 2005).

water concentration in the matrix glass of sample SH304-2G2, estimated from the measured intensity of the absorbance peak at 3,570 cm^{-1}, is 2.3±0.15 wt. percent (10 spots, table 6) and ranging from 2.0 to 2.5 wt. percent. Total dissolved water in SH304-2G2 matrix glass, determined from summation of water dissolved as hydroxyl and molecular components, is 2.1±0.17 wt. percent, in agreement with the value from the 3,570 cm^{-1} peak (table 6).

In matrix glass from samples SH304-2G1 and SH304-2G2, the concentration of dissolved water present as molecular H_2O slightly exceeds that of water dissolved as hydroxyl groups (table 6). The observed water speciation in SH304-2G matrix glasses is in contrast to that observed in rapidly quenched (cooling by hundreds of degrees per minute) experimental glasses or in silicate melts at high temperature and pressure with similar total dissolved water concentrations (Dixon and others, 1995; Mandeville and others, 2002; Nowak and Behrens, 1995; Shen and Keppler, 1995; Silver and Stolper, 1989; Sowerby and Keppler, 1999). This most likely reflects species reequilibration during slower cooling and magma ascent. In none of the acquired spectra from SH-04-2G1 and SH304-2G2 matrix glass was a CO_2 absorbance peak above background observed. Dissolved CO_2 concentration is below our detection limit (<20 ppm).

Most matrix glasses and glass inclusions have sulfur abundances less than detection limits (70–86 ppm, table 4). However, four glass inclusions from dacite erupted in October 2004 have between about 80 and 130 ppm S, and one inclusion contains about 250 ppm S (table 4, fig. 12). Chlorine abundances in glass inclusions reach a high of 1,450 ppm; they average 829±309 ppm in microcrystalline sample SH305-1 and 1,155±142 ppm in microcrystalline sample SH304-2A9b. Chlorine abundance in matrix glasses averages 278±53 ppm in the high-silica rhyolite glass of the microcrystalline dacite; in contrast, it averages 852±47 ppm in low-silica rhyolite glasses from the flow-banded glassy

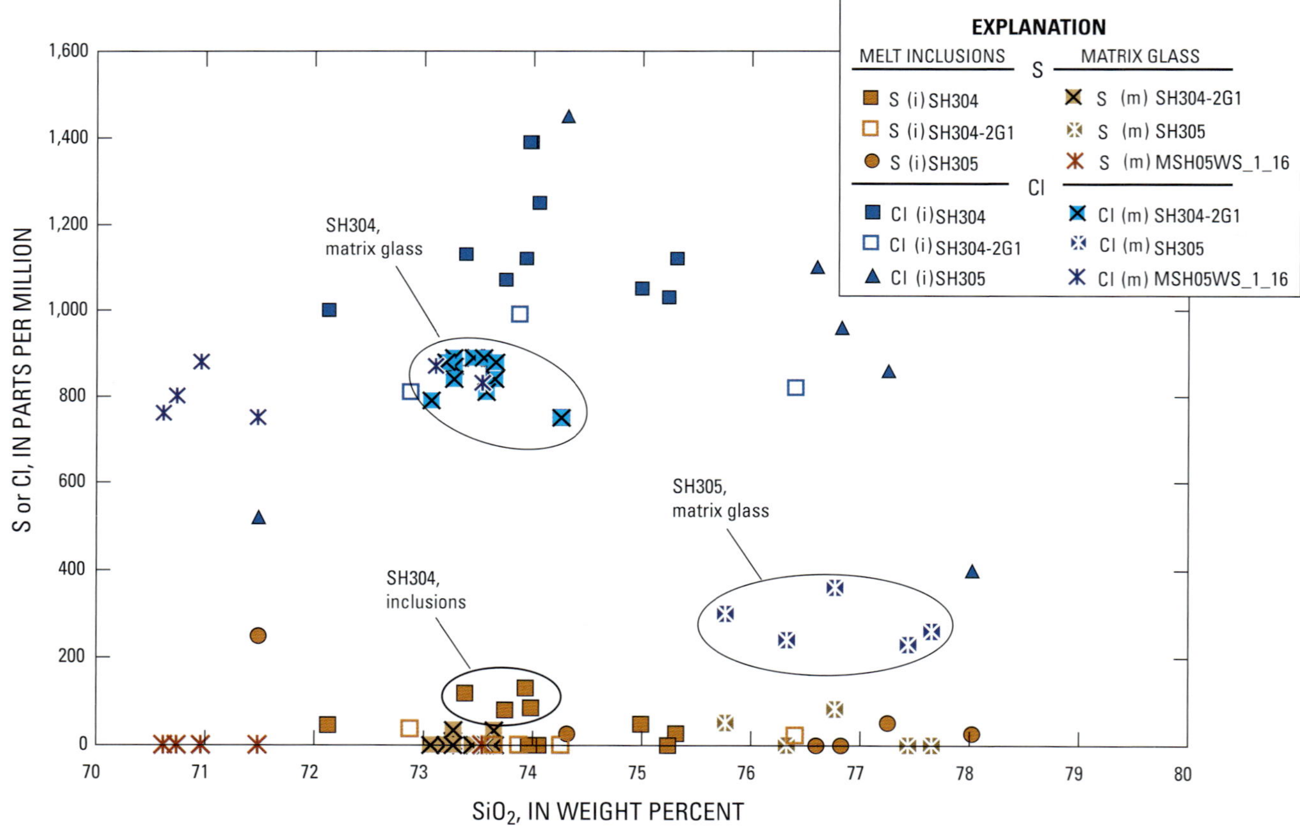

Figure 12. Abundance of sulfur (S) and chlorine (Cl) in matrix glass and glass inclusions from spine 3 plotted against SiO_2. Note low concentrations for S in matrix glass and most glass inclusions. Only glass inclusions in sample SH304 (eruption date, October 18, 2004), and one inclusion from SH305 have more than 200 ppm SO_2 (or >100 ppm S). Chlorine abundances in glasses show a wider range, with early matrix glass of the glassy fragment SH304-2G1 having more than 800 ppm Cl, whereas matrix glass in SH305, erupted later, is depleted, with less than 400 ppm Cl, consistent with more extensive degassing of microcrystalline SH305. The matrix glass with the lowest SiO_2 is in a fragment from tephra sample MSH05WS_1_16, collected from the January 16, 2005, explosion deposit.

sample SH304-1G and in glassy fragments from the January 16, 2005, tephra. As the high-silica rhyolite is a differentiation product of decompression-driven matrix crystallization, the lower Cl in these glasses is consistent with very shallow degassing of Cl during the latest stages of solidification, accompanied by development of fracture permeability in the conduit (Edmonds and others, this volume, chap. 27).

Oxides

Equilibrium temperatures and oxygen fugacities were calculated using a spreadsheet routine (Lepage, 2003), which yields results from multiple solution models for the Fe-Ti exchange thermometer and oxygen barometer (Andersen and Lindsay, 1988). Results calculated using the solution model of

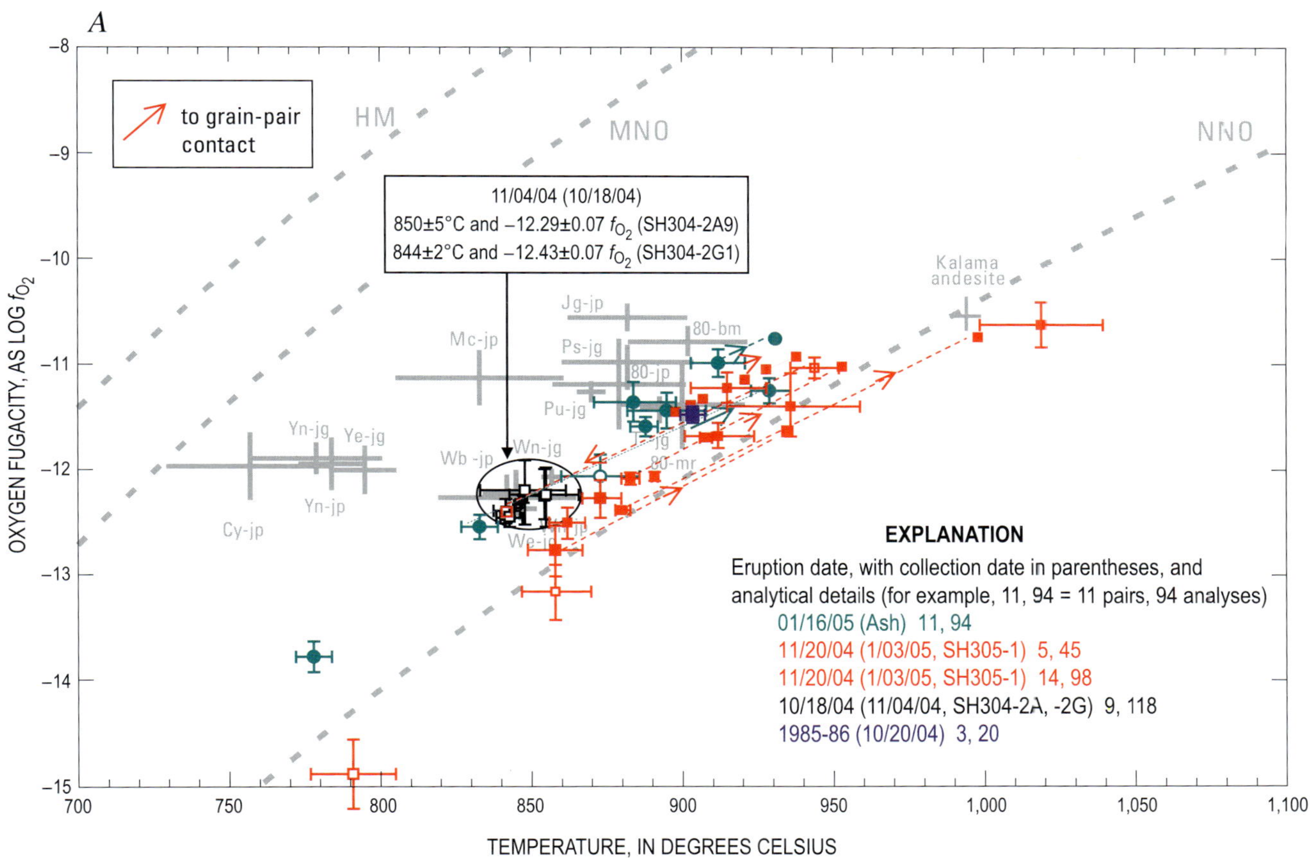

Figure 13. Results of Fe-Ti oxide thermobarometry for 2004–6 lava dome (*A, B*), plotted with respect to oxygen fugacity and temperature. Buffer curves for nickel-nickel oxide (NNO), manganese-manganese oxide (MNO) and hematite-magnetite (HM), and results for samples from earlier eruptive episodes at Mount St. Helens plotted for comparison. Samples color coded by eruption date. Number of grain pairs of the two solid-solution series ilmenite ($FeTiO_3$)–hematite (Fe_2O_3) and magnetite (Fe_3O_4)–ulvöspinel (Fe_2TiO_4) for each sample are indicated in the explanation. In cases in which temperatures and oxygen fugacities cluster, error bars represent ranges derived from the thermobarometer by using maximum and minimum values of standard deviations of Fe and Ti. In cases in which zoning was apparent from analytical profiles, backscattered-electron imagery, or stage mapping, temperatures and oxygen fugacities are plotted for each analyzed point in the zoned phase. Arrows show trends as contact between the two oxide grains is approached. Most zoned grains show increasing apparent temperature and oxygen fugacity toward grain contact, indicative of recent heating, although latest erupted samples analyzed (April 2005) show apparent cooling and reduction in oxygen fugacity. *A*, Data from samples erupted between October 18, 2004, and January 16, 2004, as well as data from 1980 and previous eruptions at Mount St. Helens. Two-letter symbols such as "Cy" refer to tephra units of Mullineaux (1996), suffixes refer to source of data as follows: -jg = Jim Gardner (Gardner and others, 1995a, 1995c), -mr = Malcolm Rutherford (Rutherford and others, 1985), -bm = Bill Melson (Melson and Hopson, 1981), -jp = John Pallister (unpublished). *B*, Data from samples erupted between January 21 and April 17, 2005. *C*, Average atomic Mg/Mn ratios for ilmenite-magnetite pairs used in generating thermobarometric results presented in *A* and *B*. Also shown are equilibrium line and error limits (2σ) for oxide pairs from volcanic rocks (Bacon and Hirschmann, 1988).

Stormer (1983) are most consistent with experimental calibrations and are given in table 9 and displayed in figure 13. Only analyses of touching Fe- and Ti-rich oxide pairs were used for thermobarometry, and individual analyses of oxide minerals in the dacite are given in appendix 1 (in the digital version of this chapter). Typically 5 to 25 analyses were made of each grain pair. For unzoned grains or for grain pairs that were too small to demonstrate zoning, the average compositions of each phase are plotted, along with error bars for temperatures and oxygen fugacities (f_{O_2}) (figs. 13*A*, 13*B*). The error bars were calculated from the maximum and minimum of the ±1 standard deviation ranges for Ti and Fe in each grain pair. As shown in figure 13*C*, all of the grain pairs used for thermobarometry in this study have Mg/Mn ratios within error limits of the equilibrium line of Bacon and Hirschmann (1988).

We have observed apparent zoning in both the titanomagnetite and ilmenite with respect to distance from the boundary between these two phases (fig. 14), although the abrupt

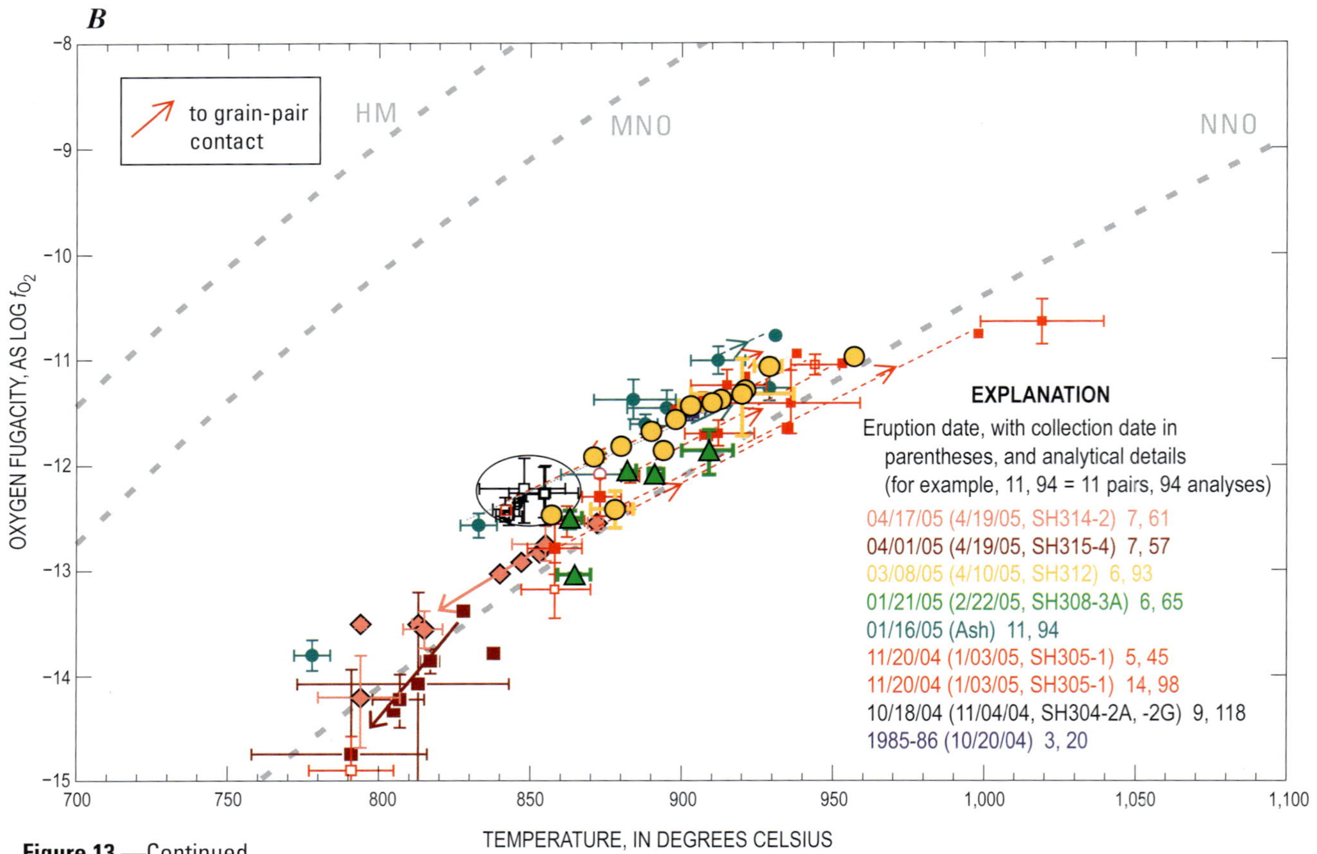

Figure 13.—Continued.

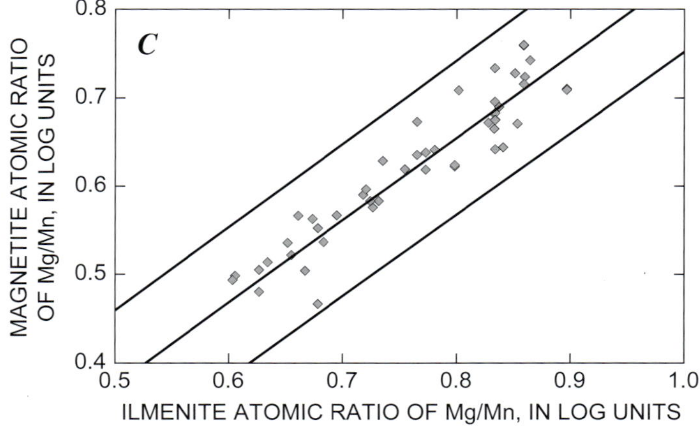

Figure 13.—Continued.

increase in Ti in the ilmenite near the boundary has been attributed to submicron-scale recrystallization of the ilmenite (Devine and others, 2003; Rutherford and Devine, this volume, chap. 31). For grain pairs in which zoning is apparent in one phase but not the other, we calculated multiple apparent temperatures and oxygen fugacities using each individual analysis of the zoned phase and the average composition of the unzoned phase. Temperatures for the first seven months of the eruption are plotted against eruption dates and permissive date ranges (from table 1) in figure 15.

The early sample of microcrystalline dacite (SH304-2A9; eruption date approximately October 18, 2004; table 1) yields a temperature of 850±5°C at an oxygen fugacity of $10^{-12.29 \pm 0.07}$ (table 9), which we take to be the conditions of last equilibration of the magma before ascent in 2004. Zoning in oxides erupted subsequently yield Fe-Ti oxide thermometer results that range to apparent temperatures of 950°C or more before plunging to less than 800°C in April 2005. Our samples that were erupted since April 2005, after the eruption rate slowed substantially, all contain titanomagnetite with oxidation lamellae of titanohematite, such that we have been unable to obtain meaningful thermometry results for the later part of the eruption.

Bulk-Rock Geochemistry

No significant variation in average major- and trace-element whole-rock compositions of the 2004–6 dome samples is apparent in the major-element data; standard deviations for more than 20 samples are close to the range of uncertainty expected for replicate analysis of standard rocks (table 7). The 2004–6 dacite has 64.93±0.09 percent SiO_2 and a relatively high Na_2O/K_2O ratio of 3.2, similar to other Mount St. Helens dacite. The lack of variation in SiO_2 with eruption date is evident in figure 16, which also shows SiO_2 abundances for gouge and dacite collected from the roof of spine 3 (SH300,

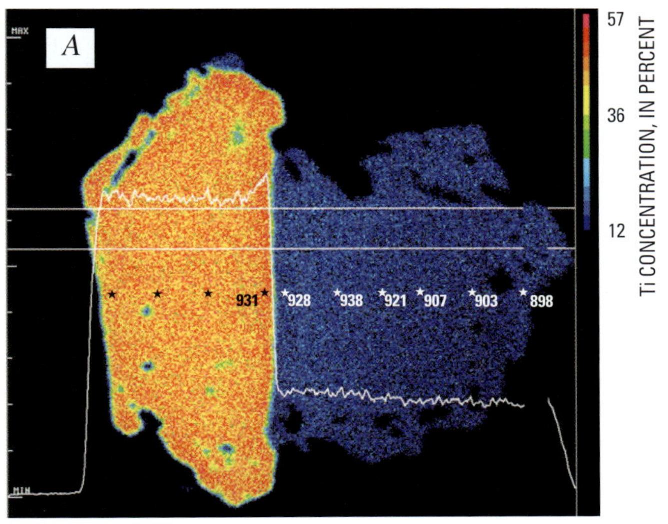

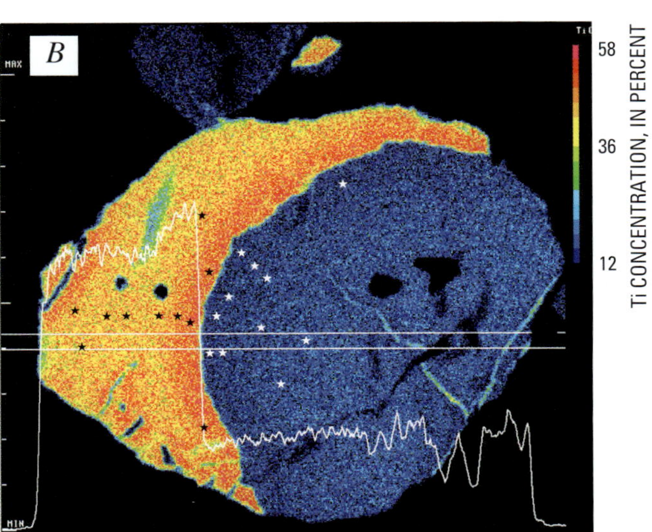

Figure 14. Electron microprobe stage maps showing abundance of TiO_2 in oxide grain pairs from samples SH305-1 (*A*) erupted approximately November 20, 2004, and MSH05JV_1_19 (*B*) from a dacite fragment in the ash deposit from the January 16, 2005, explosion. Maps are 100 X 100 µm in dimension. The SH305-1 grain pair (*A*) shows a relatively uniform or slightly decreasing TiO_2 trend across ilmenite grain (orange), with a steep increase in abundance within 10 µm of the contact with the adjacent titanomagnetite grain (blue) and a gradual increase in TiO_2 across the titanomagnetite grain toward the ilmenite grain. Apparent temperatures, calculated for individual analytical points in the titanomagnetite (as indicated by the asterisks and numbers in the figure) compared to the average composition of the ilmenite show a decrease from 928°C at the grain contact to 898°C at the rim. The apparent temperature for the two analytical points closest to the grain boundary yielded 931°C. The MSH05JV_1_19 grain pair (*B*) displays the same abrupt decrease in Ti in the ilmenite with distance from the titanomagnetite, but the opposite trend in the titanomagnetite, which shows a gradual decrease in TiO_2 abundance as the grain boundary is approached. The superimposed line graphs show the relative abundance of TiO_2 in the band outlined by the two horizontal lines in each image. The MSH05JV_1_19 grain pair (number 7 in table 9) shows a decrease from an average of 830°C for points within 10 microns of the grain boundary to 938°C for the average compositions of the two grain interiors.

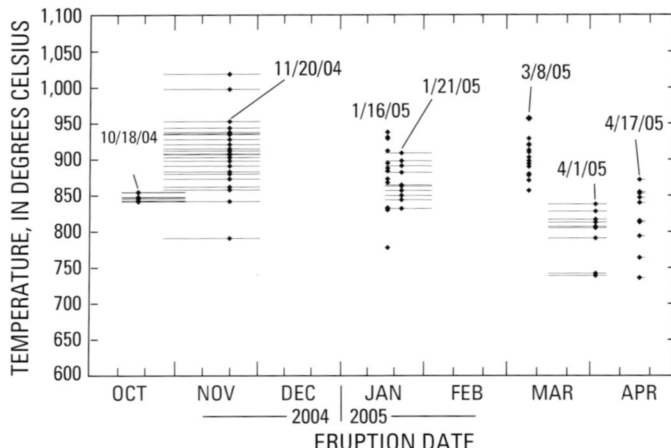

Figure 15. Fe-Ti oxide temperatures for 2004–5 Mount St. Helens dacite lava samples plotted against eruption dates; diamonds indicate best estimate of eruption dates. Bars show full range of permissible eruption dates (table 1). Wide range in apparent temperatures results from zoned oxide pairs (fig. 14).

SH301), when it first breached glacial ice in the southeastern crater on October 25, 2004. These roof-rock samples have distinctly lower SiO_2 and alkalis and higher MgO, CaO, and $FeTO_3$ (total iron expressed as Fe_2O_3), and their compositions overlap with those of lava erupted in 1985–86 (table 7, fig. 17), suggesting that they are crater-floor rocks uplifted by the 2004 dacite as it punched through the crater floor. Analyses of several small glassy fragments that were collected in dredge samples from early spines (spines 1 and 3) are also listed in table 7. These are higher in silica than samples from the 1980–86 dome and may represent fragments of dacite that were intruded early in the 2004 eruption.

Compositions of the 2004–6 samples lie along the high-SiO_2 projections of most major- and minor-element variation trends defined by the Goat Rocks and 1980–86 dome lavas (Pallister and others, 1992). However, they lie off the trend for TiO_2, which is present in higher abundance than would be expected from the 1980–86 trend (fig. 17). High-precision analyses of Cr by instrumental neutron activation analysis (INAA) are diagnostic of the presence of basaltic mixing components within Mount St. Helens andesites and dacites (Pallister and others, 1992). Chromium abundances in 2004–6 dome rocks are compared to those of Kalama (A.D. 1479–1750[7]), Goat Rocks (A.D. 1800–1857), and the 1980–86 eruptive periods in figure 18 (full INAA analyses and uncertainties are reported in Thornber and others, 2008b). As with TiO_2, the 2004–6 dacites have higher Cr abundances than would be expected from a continuation of the Goat Rocks and 1980–86 trends, as well as lower Cr at 65 percent SiO_2 than the dacites from the early Kalama eruptive period. Analyses were conducted at the same laboratory using the same procedures and standards to ensure reproducibility, and duplicate samples from 1985 and 1986 dome rocks were rerun to verify the differences.

A characteristic feature of Mount St. Helens dacites, including 2004–6 lava, is the lack of europium anomalies and a decrease in total rare-earth-element (REE) abundance with increasing SiO_2, thereby ruling out progressive crystal fractionation in their origins (table 8, fig. 19). The 2004–6 dacite is distinct in having the lowest heavy-REE abundances of any of the dacites we have analyzed from eruptive products of the past 500 years at Mount St. Helens.

Discussion

Petrology of the 2004–6 dacite at Mount St. Helens provides constraints on both shallow and deep magmatic processes and insights into the roles that degassing and crystallization play in controlling the explosivity of volcanic eruptions and how the past history of the volcano helps in forecasting the future course of the eruption. Accordingly, the discussion is presented in four parts: (1) shallow conduit processes, (2) deep reservoir processes, (3) implications for magmatic plumbing, explosivity, and eruption triggering, and (4) lessons from the past and implications for the future.

Shallow Conduit Processes

Field relations, petrography, volatile contents of glasses, and oxide thermobarometry help us understand the processes that were operative in the shallow conduit beneath the 2004–6 vent. Together with geophysical and gas geochemical monitoring data, they show that magma within the conduit solidified at shallow levels beneath the vent, producing a nearly solid seismogenic plug (Iverson and others, 2006) that has fed the series of spines that constitute the new lava dome.

Constraints from Field Geology

The 2004–6 eruption of Mount St. Helens represents a nonexplosive end member in the range of eruptive behavior of dacitic magmas. By the spring of 2006 the volume of the new dome exceeded 80×10^6 m^3 (Schilling and others, this volume, chap. 8), a volume similar to the 1980–86 lava dome ($74–77 \times 10^6$ m^3, Swanson and Holcomb, 1990). Eruption rates during 2004–6 have ranged from as high as 9 m^3/s in the initial phase to less than 1 m^3/s (Schilling and others, this volume, chap. 8). The style of eruption, with continued extrusion of solid dacite spines, contrasts with most of the 1980–86

[7]In this report we use an age range of A.D. 1479–1750 for the Kalama period, on the basis of a tree-kill date of A.D. 1722 for a summit-dome lahar in the Muddy River drainage and a bracketing youngest age of A.D. 1750 determined for trees that subsequently rooted on a late summit dome-derived hot lahar in upper Pine Creek (Yamaguchi and Hoblitt, 1995). The age of final summit dome eruptions in the Kalama eruptive period remains uncertain.

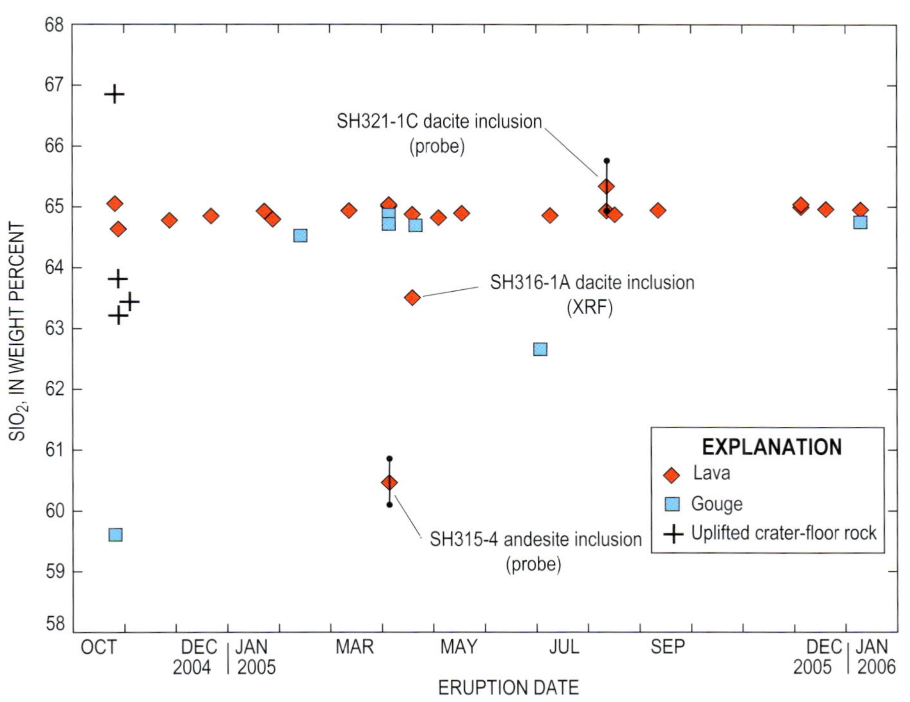

Figure 16. Content of SiO_2 in Mount St. Helens samples plotted against likely eruption date (table 1), except for SH300 and SH301, which are samples of crater-floor rocks and plotted against collection date. Note uniform abundance of SiO_2 (65 percent) in most dome and gouge samples. Exceptions include low abundances (<63 percent) in inclusion samples and in two gouge samples, and wide range in crater floor samples collected on October 20, 2004.

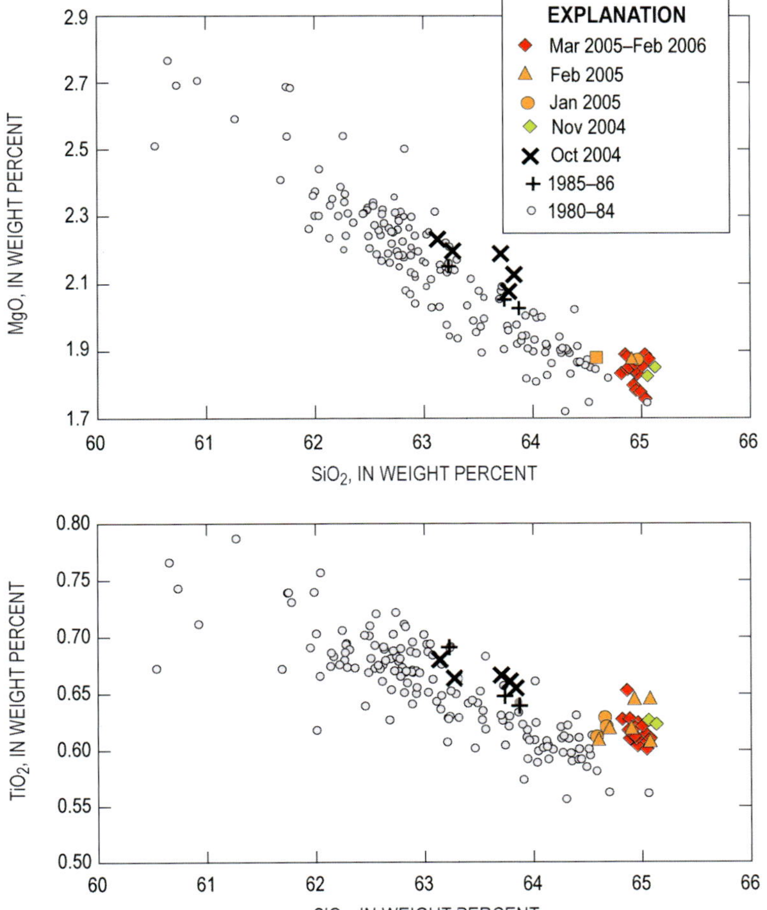

Figure 17. Variation diagrams of MgO and TiO_2 against silica, showing trends in juvenile eruptive products from 1980–86 eruptions at Mount St. Helens (Pallister and others, 1992) and 2004–6 eruptions. Note that 2004–6 samples lie at high-SiO_2 projection of the linear arrays, except for TiO_2, which is distinctly higher for given SiO_2 content in the 2004–6 lavas than in previous eruptive episodes.

dome-forming eruptions at Mount St. Helens, as well as with most other dome-forming eruptions worldwide. The development of gouge-mantled spines is unusual but not unique. Photographs of the Showa-Shinzan lava dome (extruded in a Japanese wheat field on the flank of Mount Usu in 1944–45) show spines with striations that look remarkably like those on the Mount St. Helens dome (Mimatsu, 1995). The 200-m-diameter cylindrical and striated spine of Mont Pelée, Martinique, is another example. The original Peléean spine rose at rates of 3–6 m per day and reached a height of 115 m above the crater floor by the time of the explosive eruptions on May 6–8, 1902 (Chrétien and Brousse, 1989; Smith and Roobol, 1990). A larger spine grew in 1903, rose to 300 m, and bore vertical striations and slickensides (Williams, 1932, quoting Lacroix, 1904). Similarly, the andesitic Soufrière Hills volcano, Montserrat, has produced multiple, gouge-covered and striated spines during some phases of dome construction (Watts and others, 2002). What is unusual about the 2004–6 Mount St. Helens eruption is continuous spine extrusion over such a long period, nearly continuous extrusion of relatively thick gouge and cataclasite at the spine margins, and the low level of explosivity that has accompanied spine growth and disintegration. Of known analogs, the gouge-covered spines of Showa-Shinzan are considered most similar to those at Mount St. Helens (Vallance and others, this volume, chap. 9).

The 2004–6 spine-forming mode of eruption also contrasts with eruptions that produced the 1980–86 lava dome at Mont St. Helens. The 17 eruptive episodes in the 1980s produced 20 short (200–400 m), thick (20 m) flows (lobes) and included periods of endogenous growth and small explosions (Swanson and others, 1987; Swanson and Holcomb, 1990). Lava flows produced through mid-February 1984 had scoriaceous carapaces, as opposed to the gouge carapaces on spines of the current eruption. Two small spines were extruded during these episodes (in late February–March 1983 and during May 1985), but these also lacked gouge carapaces. Also in contrast with the hotter dome lavas of the 1980s, the 2004–6 lava generally lacks augite phenocrysts and is much more crystal rich

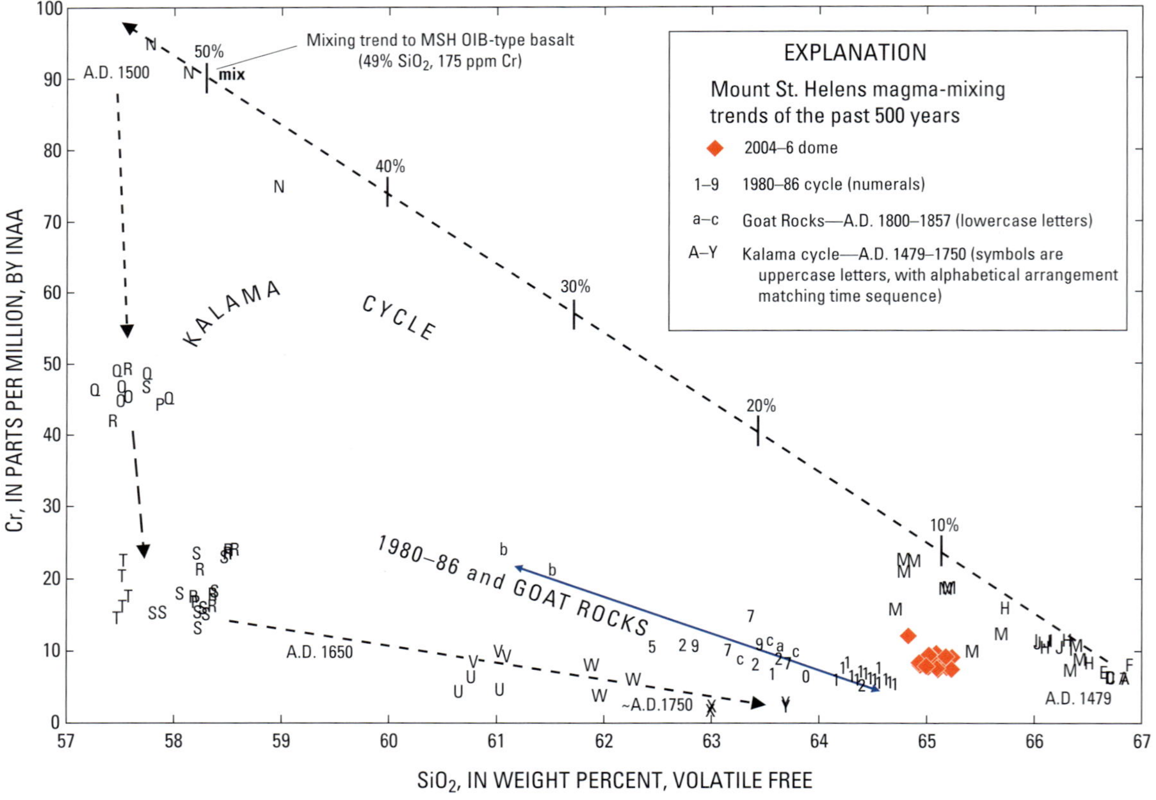

Figure 18. Variation diagram of Cr against SiO_2 for juvenile eruptive products from Mount St. Helens erupted during past 500 years (Pallister and others, 1992). Note that 2004–6 samples have higher Cr abundance than the projection of the Goat Rocks eruptive period and 1980–86 trend but lower abundance than the early phase of the Kalama eruptive period (A.D. 1479–1750). Analytical uncertainty for Cr is ±3 ppm at the 10-ppm level (by instrumental neutron activation analysis, INAA) and for SiO_2 (XRF data) is ±0.2 percent on the basis of counting statistics and replicate analyses. Magma mixing with basaltic magmas at Mount St. Helens is called on to explain the cyclic trends (Pallister and others, 1992). Letters and numbers refer to stratigraphic sequence, and percentages refer to proportions of a basaltic mixing end member as explained in Pallister and others (1992).

and glass poor compared to the more glass-rich augite-bearing hornblende-hypersthene dacite of the 1980s dome (Cashman, 1992; Geschwind and Rutherford, 1995; Melson, 1983). We suggest that a primary control on the low level of explosivity of the 2004–6 lava is the combined effect of lower gas abundance in the magma and a greater degree of shallow matrix crystallization, which produced virtually dry and rheologically solid dacite lava hundreds of meters beneath the vent.

The "megaspines" of the early (1995–98) eruptive phase of the Soufrière Hills volcano, Montserrat, also had striated surfaces and cataclastic textures, judging from observations by one of us (Cashman). Because their morphologies are correlated with eruption rate and character of seismicity (Watts and others, 2002), it is instructive to compare these with the Mount St. Helens examples. At Montserrat, vertical spines and whaleback structures dominated at rates of <1 m^3/s, and their emplacement was accompanied by periodic hybrid earthquake swarms. Megaspines were emplaced aseismically at 1–2 m^3/s. Broad shear-lobe spines were emplaced aseismically at 2–5 m^3/s, but their collapse was accompanied by intense hybrid swarms. Blocky shear-lobes were emplaced at 2–5 m^3/s, accompanied by repetitive hybrid swarms and tremor. Pancake lobes were emplaced at 7–9 m^3/s, also with repetitive hybrid swarms and tremor. Explosions at Montserrat occurred at eruption rates greater than 9 m^3/s and commonly followed large dome-collapse events.

The Mount St. Helens spines are similar to the vertical spines, whaleback structures, and megaspines of Montserrat. However, instead of being restricted to eruption rates of less than 2 m^3/s, these morphologies at Mount St. Helens have occurred over the full range of eruption rates, and collapse events have been small—rockfalls and sparse rock avalanches that have not triggered substantial pyroclastic flows. These differences are likely related to compositional differences (andesite at Soufrière Hills, dacite at Mount St. Helens), and to a much larger vent diameter of 100–200 m at Mount St. Helens, compared to about 30 m at Soufrière Hills. The larger vent diameter allows slower ascent rates and more extensive shallow crystallization for similar volumetric rates of extrusion.

Compared with activity at Soufrière Hills, Montserrat, collapse events at Mount St. Helens have been minor. Lim-

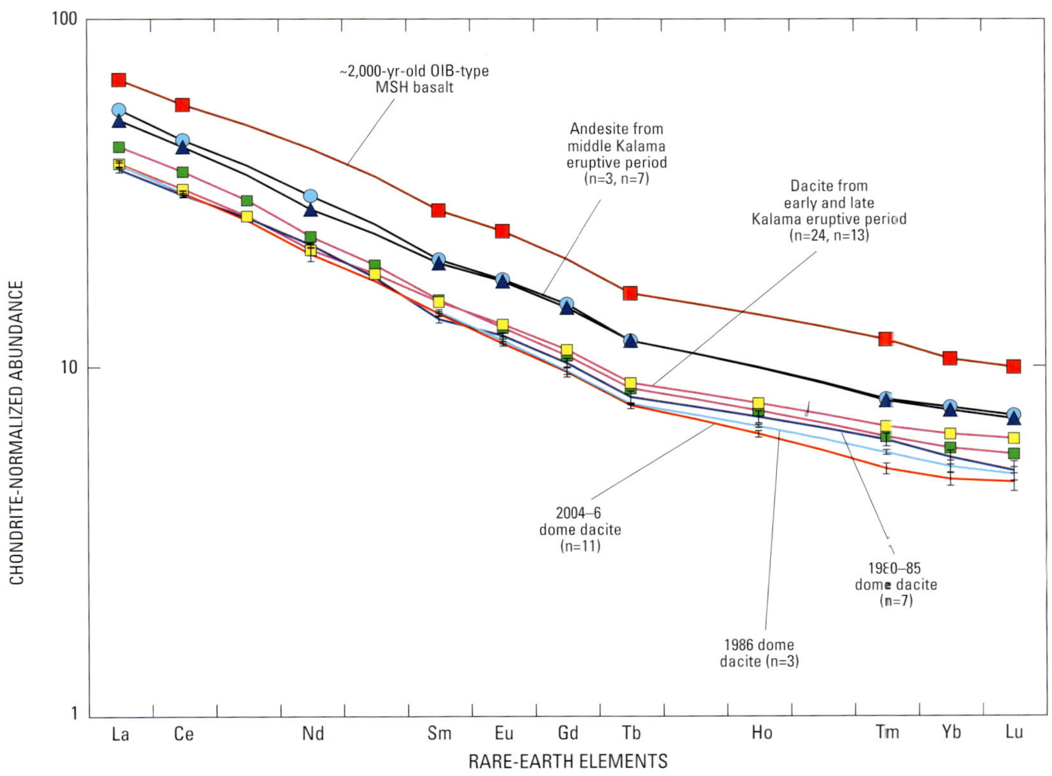

Figure 19. Chondrite-normalized rare-earth-element (REE) abundance patterns for juvenile eruptive products from Mount St. Helens erupted during the past 500 years. Note that the 2004–6 lavas have the lowest heavy-REE abundances. Error bars (±1σ) are given for analyses of 1980 and subsequent samples. Error bars (±1σ) for older, higher-REE abundance samples are smaller than the symbols and are not plotted.

ited disintegration of collapsing blocks during short runouts onto the low-relief crater floor at Mount St. Helens is likely due to a drier composition and the more solid (microlite-rich and glass-poor) character of the Mount St. Helens dacite lava compared to the more glass- and water-rich matrix glasses of the Montserrat andesite lava (Couch and others, 2003; Harford and others, 2003). Furthermore, greater topographic relief at Soufrière Hills has contributed to greater runout distances.

Constraints from Petrography and Major-Element Compositions of Matrix Glasses and Microlites

As shown in figures 4 through 8, the matrix of the 2004–6 dacite is remarkably rich in microlites, even compared to the dome lava of the 1980s (with the exception of spine samples from 1983 and 1985, which are also highly crystalline). We interpret these matrix textures to result from extensive depressurization-driven crystallization during ascent of the magma through the conduit, similar to the process envisioned for the 1980–86 dome (Blundy and Cashman, 2001; Cashman, 1988, 1992). In contrast to the episodes of the 1980s, we see no evidence for stagnation of magma at multiple levels of the conduit. Instead, an analysis of eruptive volumes and likely conduit dimensions (discussed below) and of consistency of amphibole reaction-rim thicknesses (Rutherford and Devine, this volume, chap. 31; Thornber and others, this volume, chap. 32) indicates that dacite lava of the current eruption is a product of continuous ascent of magma through a conduit that taps the top of the deeper reservoir at about 5-km depth. We see a continuum in the degree of matrix crystallization, from early 2004–early 2005 samples with variable fractions of matrix glass to late 2005–6 samples, which have only trace amounts of glass remaining. Such a pattern is consistent with more rapid ascent and eruption rates during the early phase of the eruption.

The crystallization of a granite-minimum microlite assemblage of tridymite or quartz, An_{20-30} plagioclase, and anorthoclase (table 4) is consistent with extensive groundmass crystallization. The high-silica rhyolite composition of residual glass is indicative of very shallow final crystallization. Following the arguments of Blundy and Cashman (2001), the presence of quartz and the projection of glass compositions onto the modified Qz-Ab-Or ternary diagram of Blundy and Cashman (2001) yield crystallization pressures for the most evolved matrix glasses between 50 MPa and 0.1 MPa (fig. 20). This result indicates crystallization at a depth considerably less than 2.2 km, on the basis of a density model (Williams and others, 1987, section B–B') in which the crustal column consists of 1.5 km with density of 2.15 g/cm^3 overlying an extensive diorite to gabbroic pluton with average crustal density of 2.7 g/cm^3. The presence of tridymite in some samples further restricts the pressure for matrix crystallization and solidification to the range 11–25 MPa (depth 0.5–1.0 km) at temperature 885–915°C (Blundy and Cashman, 2001), consistent with the shallow location of earthquakes that have accompanied the eruption (Thelen and others, this volume, chap. 4).

Constraints from SO_2, Cl, and H_2O Abundances in Glasses

The abundance of H_2O in glasses can also be used to constrain depths, owing to the variation in solubility of water in silicate melts with pressure (Moore and others, 1995, 1998). Matrix and inclusion glasses show a decline in water content from approximately 2.3 wt. percent H_2O at 73.5 percent SiO_2 to less than 0.1 percent at 77 percent SiO_2 (fig. 11). The upper end of this H_2O range is indicative of quenching at a pressure of about 30 MPa (depth of 1.4 km) followed by decompression-driven crystallization and quenching of residual melt, which continued to pressures of less than 10 MPa (depth about 0.5 km). Most of the glass inclusions analyzed so far have water and SO_2 contents that overlap with the matrix glasses, indicating that most of the inclusions have leaked (fig. 11).

Total dissolved water concentrations determined in the matrix glass of samples SH304-2G1 and SH304-2G2 were used to constrain the pressure and depth at which residual melt in this glassy sample solidified. Water solubility in the melt at 850°C was computed from electron microprobe determinations of the matrix-glass bulk composition and the 0–300-MPa water solubility model of Moore and others (1998). Given saturation, the total water concentration in matrix glass of

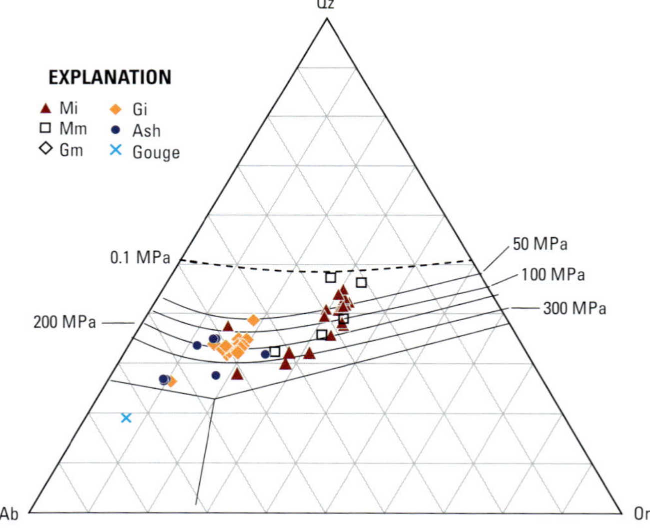

Figure 20. Projection of glass compositions from SH304 and SH305 Mount St. Helens samples onto modified quartz-albite-orthoclase haplogranite ternary diagram of Blundy and Cashman (2001). Cotectic lines and water-saturated minima and eutectics are plotted as function of pressure for comparison. Dashed line is approximate position of the 1-atmosphere cotectic. Solid symbols refer to melt inclusions, open symbols to matrix melt. Other labels as follows: Mi, melt inclusion in dacite lava; Mm, matrix melt in dacite lava; Gi, melt inclusion in dacite fragment in gouge; Gm, matrix glass in dacite fragment in gouge; Ash, melt inclusion within tephra fragment in ash; Gouge, matrix melt within dacite fragment in gouge.

sample SH304-2G2, which has the most microlite-free matrix glass and the greatest water content (2.3±0.15 wt. percent), indicates quench to glass from approximately 33 to 41 MPa, or approximately 1.5 to 2 km depth, on the basis of the density distribution in crustal section B–B' of Williams and others (1987). Assuming this unusual glassy sample represents a quenched equivalent of the microcrystalline 2004 dacite, these results would indicate incipient matrix crystallization at a depth of 1.5–2 km, although, as noted above, most of the groundmass crystallization and solidification is constrained by the microlite phase assemblage in the more typical microcrystalline dacite to depths of less than 1 km.

The abundance of sulfur in glass inclusions (table 4, fig. 12) is lower than that in glass inclusions from the 1980 Mount St. Helens dacite (Blundy and Cashman, 2005; Devine and others, 1984; Gardner and others, 1995a; Melson, 1983). This indicates that the magma was depleted in sulfur before eruption and is consistent with the hypothesis that the 2004–6 magma was residual from the reservoir of the 1980s. The highest sulfur contents (as well as highest Cl and H_2O) are found in the earliest erupted samples, coincident with the highest SO_2 and CO_2 emissions (Gerlach and others, this volume, chap. 26). This suggests more rapid ascent, less matrix crystallization, and less gas loss as the initial magma made its way relatively rapidly to the surface.

Abundance of Cl in matrix glass is lower than that in glass inclusions (table 4, fig. 12) and decreases with increasing SiO_2 and K_2O (indicators of increasing matrix crystallization), consistent with degassing accompanying decompression crystallization at shallow levels, as also seen at Soufrière Hills volcano (Edmonds and others, 2001; Harford and others, 2003). The abundance of Cl in glass inclusions and matrix melts can be used to calculate emission rates of Cl for the eruption. We use our average Cl abundance of 1,155±142 ppm in glass inclusions as representative of the dacite at magma reservoir depths (4–5 km) (Rutherford and Devine, this volume, chap. 31), 852±47 ppm for the magma at a depth of 1.4 km (as inferred from the water content of the glass in SH304-2G1), and 278±53 ppm for the residual Cl in the microcrystalline dacite lava (table 4). The average Cl value for glass inclusions (1,155±142 ppm) is based on inclusions in amphibole crystals (a Cl-bearing phase) from sample SH305-2A9b. Although exchange of Cl with the host crystal is a possibility, the average abundance is similar to the higher Cl abundances in plagioclase and hypersthene inclusions, which range widely from 400 to 1,450 ppm; the lower abundances likely result from leakage. The differences between the abundance in the glass inclusions and that in the matrix glasses, multiplied by the dacite density (approximately 2,400 kg/m^3) yields emissions of 400±249 metric tons per million cubic meters of dacite for the ascent interval from 5 to 1.4 km depth and 758±132 metric tons for the interval from 1.4 km to the surface. The total emission is 1,158±381 metric tons per million cubic meters of dacite extruded, or about 100×10^3 metric tons for the 85×10^6 m^3 extruded through August 2006.

On the basis of this analysis, we would predict Cl emissions of 100±33 and 700±231 metric tons per day for extrusion rates of 1 m^3/s and 7 m^3/s, respectively, exclusive of any contribution from a separate fluid phase. This value is greater than the rate of 12–25 metric tons per day measured on August 31, 2005, by open-path FTIR (Edmonds and others, this volume, chap. 27). The discrepancy may be due to (1) precipitation of chlorides in dome rocks (yellow efflorescence has been common near fumaroles and attributed to deposition of iron chlorides), (2) shallow scrubbing of Cl into groundwater (however, only 5.2 tons per day of dissolved Cl was measured in water from Loowit and Step springs at the crater mouth, and no spike in Cl abundance has yet been detected (Bergfeld and others, this volume, chap. 25)), or (3) a lower Cl abundance in the August 2005 dacite compared to that from late 2004, when our glass inclusion-bearing samples were erupted. We consider the last possibility most likely.

Constraints from Oxide Thermobarometry

Zoned oxides similar to those in the 2004–6 dacite are known to occur in volcanic rocks that have undergone recent heating due to magma mingling, and the time scales for preservation of zoning in oxide minerals have been determined experimentally to be on the order of a few days to a few months, depending on the size of the oxide grains and degree of heating (Devine and others, 2003; Gardner and others, 1995a; Nakamura, 1995; Pallister and others, 1996; Venezky and Rutherford, 1999). Although there is clear petrographic and geochemical evidence for magma mixing in older rocks from Mount St. Helens (Pallister and others, 1992; Smith and Leeman, 1993), there is little such evidence in the 2004–6 dacite, which is uniform in bulk-rock composition and has only extremely rare and small (less than 1-cm diameter) quenched mafic inclusions.

In several cases, the source of the heating to produce zoned oxides is evident, such as in the case of the June 7–12, 1991, andesites at Mount Pinatubo, which show clear petrographic and geochemical evidence of derivation by mingling of basalt with dacite in proportions of about 1:2 (Pallister and others, 1996). In other cases, the physical evidence of heating by a hotter and more mafic magma consists only of a small proportion of quenched mafic inclusions, such as in the andesite of Soufrière Hills volcano (Murphy and others, 2000). In the Soufrière Hills case, the zoned oxides indicate apparent heating of about 30°C, which led Devine and others (2003) to propose a model in which underplated basalt heated a boundary zone in an andesitic reservoir. The boundary layer was then mobilized and erupted, with only minor entrainment of the underlying basalt, as seen in ubiquitous blade-shaped laths of pargasite in the groundmass of all samples.

In their study of microlite formation in the Soufrière Hills andesite, Couch and others (2003) calculated that a temperature rise of as much as 45°C would be expected from latent heat evolved during the extensive (32 percent), shallow (less than 2 km), and relatively rapid (1–2 day) decompression-driven groundmass crystallization, given the measured extrusion rates and estimated conduit diameter (Melnik and Sparks, 2002). However, neither Couch and others (2003) nor Devine and others (2003) concluded that latent heating at shallow levels was responsible for the zoned oxides, because it was not possible to experimentally produce the zoning profiles of the Soufrière Hills titanomagnetites in short-duration (2 day) heating experiments without extensive amphibole breakdown, which was not seen in natural samples. However, longer-duration (2 week) heating experiments at magma reservoir pressure of 130 MPa (5–6 km depth) did reproduce the natural zoning profiles without amphibole breakdown.

The zoned oxides in the Mount St. Helens samples share some features with those from Soufrière Hills. First, the earliest samples from October 2004, when eruption rates were high (greater than 5 m^3/s) have oxide pairs that lack zonation. Second, the Mount St. Helens oxide pairs erupted during the winter of 2004–5 are zoned in a sense that indicates heating (fig. 14). As was also seen in a sample from the explosive eruption of September 29, 1997, at Soufrière Hills (Devine and others, 2003), the zoning in the winter 2004–5 oxides is best developed at the grain boundary between the titanomagnetite and ilmenite phases, with little zonation developed at melt-crystal boundaries. As is evident from the range of temperature-f_{O_2} trends for grain pairs in figure 13, the Mount St. Helens thermobarometric results are parallel to the common buffer curves, a characteristic of heating with melt present (Devine and others, 2003). The above features could be interpreted as indicating a similar process of heating by hot magma underplating. However, there is considerable variation in degree of zoning from grain pair to grain pair in the Mount St. Helens samples, even within the same thin section. These features indicate that heating was of relatively short duration and was variable at the scale of millimeters. That the zoning is best developed at the two-crystal grain boundaries indicates redistribution of Ti and Fe within the crystal structures of titanomagnetite and ilmenite, but with little, if any, redistribution between the oxide minerals and the adjacent groundmass glass.

We believe that these small-scale relations are best explained by latent heating during groundmass crystallization, as was also suggested for 1980–86 pumice and lava samples (Blundy and others, 2006). Variation of heating at the millimeter scale is most readily explained by inhomogeneity in rate and extent of groundmass crystallization and localized variability in transport of heat by vapor expansion, conduction, and access to the hydrothermal system at shallow conduit levels. The fact that zoning is developed with respect to distance from the titanomagnetite-magnetite phase boundary, and not at grain-melt boundaries, is probably a result of the rapidly changing composition and crystallinity of the adjacent groundmass, such that consistent zoning of Fe-Ti oxides by diffusive exchange with melt was not possible. In contrast to the situation at Soufrière Hills, where transport from 2 km to the surface is thought to have been too rapid for latent heating, by the beginning of 2005 the eruption rate at Mount St. Helens had slowed to less than 2.5 m^3/s (Schilling and others, this volume, chap. 8) and the conduit at shallow levels was of much larger diameter—100 to 200 m, as opposed to about 30 m for Soufrière Hills (Melnik and Sparks, 2002). Consequently, the ascent time through the shallow interval of groundmass crystallization was longer at Mount St. Helens. Using our estimate that most groundmass crystallization took place mainly in the uppermost 500 m, with a near-surface conduit diameter of 200 m and a volumetric ascent rate of 2.5 m^3/s, we derive an ascent rate of 7 m/d, which is consistent with the measured rates of linear extrusion of spines (Dzurisin and others, this volume, chap. 14; LaHusen and others, this volume, chap. 16), and an ascent time of about 2.5 months. Allowing the conduit to decrease in diameter with depth, such that it averages only 100 m in diameter over the uppermost 0.5–1 km, would yield an average rate of 28–56 m/d and an ascent time of 2.6–5.2 weeks. These ascent times are in the appropriate range for development and preservation of zoning in oxides (Devine and others, 2003).

We can estimate the maximum amount of latent heating that is theoretically possible from the amount of groundmass crystallization in the 2004–6 dacite using thermodynamic data, much as was done by Couch and others (2003) for the Soufrière Hills andesite. Latent heat is equal to the enthalpy of melting divided by the heat capacity at the temperature of interest. As the microlite population is dominated by plagioclase, we can use the range of enthalpies of melting of plagioclase, from 59,280 J/mol for albite to 81,000 J/mol for anorthite, to approximate the amount of latent heat available and the maximum temperature rise. At an initial temperature of about 850°C, the heat capacity of albite would be about 318 J/mol per K; and of anorthite, about 328 J/mol per K. Therefore, isenthalpic crystallization of 30–40 percent of the dacite would produce a temperature rise of about 30–45°C. A more complete analysis, by Mark Ghiorso using the thermodynamic modeling program pMELTS (Ghiorso and others, 2002) for decompressing a water-saturated 2004–6 dacite composition at 855°C and $f_{O_2} = 10^{-12}$ from 20 MPa to 0.1 MPa, estimates a temperature rise of 30°C and results in a magma with 0.5 g ilmenite, 2.5 g magnetite, 7.6 g orthopyroxene, 13 g quartz, 84 g of An_{31} plagioclase, and 12.3 g of 76.6 percent SiO_2 melt with 80 ppm H_2O (Mark Ghiorso, written commun., 2005)—a reasonable match to the natural assemblage. Loss of some of the heat would result in appearance of alkali feldspar in the assemblage, an increase in the abundance of quartz, and a decrease of the melt fraction remaining. Further discussion of the role of latent heating in decompression crystallization of volcanic rocks is available in Blundy and others (2006).

The maximum quantity of latent heat available from groundmass crystallization is less than the degree of apparent heating recorded by the zoned oxides in the dome rocks. We attribute this discrepancy to the fact that the zoned oxides can only give apparent temperatures. They indicate heating, but the extent of heating must be less than the maximum indicated by the zoning. If the diffusion rates were fast enough, the distribution of Ti and Fe in the grains would rehomogenize to a value intermediate between the minimum and maximum ranges seen in the zoned crystals and would also reequilibrate with the melt; consequently, the actual temperatures would be less than the maximum apparent temperatures in figure 13.

The analyses from samples collected later in 2005 and in 2006 offer additional insights into the process responsible for the oxide zoning (fig. 13*B*, table 9). Samples erupted during April 2005, when the extrusion rate was less than 2 m^3/s, show a wide range in apparent temperature and oxygen fugacity. Seven grain pairs in sample SH314-2 are unzoned or weakly zoned; three of these yield average temperatures of 794–814°C, two of 840–874°C, and two grain pairs yield a wide range of temperatures (726–821°C). The titanomagnetite of one grain pair appears to be reversely zoned (cooled), with lower Ti near the boundary with ilmenite, yielding an apparent temperature for the two core areas of about 872°C but decreasing to 840°C at the boundary.

Sample SH315-4 shows an even wider and cooler range in apparent temperatures, with reverse zoning of both titanomagnetite and ilmenite and apparent temperatures ranging from a low of 644°C to a high of 839°C. Sample SH315-4 is also distinct from most of the other samples with respect to a lower oxygen fugacity, extending below the NNO buffer curve at temperatures below 800°C. As previously noted, we have been unable to obtain meaningful oxide thermobarometry results for samples erupted after April 2005 owing to the presence of extensive oxidation lamellae.

The lower apparent oxidation state of April 2005 samples may be the result of extensive degassing driving precipitation of oxides and extraction of Fe^{+3} from the melt, thereby lowering f_{O_2}. In addition, as the liquid gains more SiO_2, the increased concentrations of Na_2O and K_2O in the melt would complex with Fe^{+3} and lower its activity, having the same effect of lowering the f_{O_2}. This explanation is consistent with a predicted decrease in oxidation accompanying extensive crystallization at less than 10 MPa pressure by pMELTS modeling (Mark Ghiorso, written commun., 2005).

The progression in time from (1) tightly clustered temperatures and oxygen fugacities for the early erupted samples to (2) zoned oxides indicative of heating to (3) wide-ranging apparent temperatures, reverse zoning, and low oxygen fugacities to (4) development of oxidation lamellae is coincident with a decrease in eruption rate from more than 5 m^3/s to less than 2 m^3/s and with a decrease in the abundance of glass from as much as 30 percent to less than 10 percent. Consequently, we attribute the changes in the oxides to result from latent heating due to groundmass crystallization, coupled with, and then dominated by, heterogeneous heat loss and vapor transport, and finally by oxidation at the shallowest levels of the conduit and vent.

To answer questions about the source of the explosions of January 16 and March 8, 2005 (Moran and others, this volume, chap. 6; Rowe and others, this volume, chap. 29), we analyzed oxide grain pairs in 11 small tephra fragments from the January 16, 2005, tephra deposit (table 9). All but two of these grain pairs are unzoned, and they each produce tightly clustered temperatures and oxygen fugacities ranging from 780°C at f_{O_2} of $10^{-13.8}$ to 930°C at f_{O_2} of $10^{-11.3}$. None of these overlap with the temperature and oxygen fugacity of the initial 2004 dacite samples; however, two of the grain-pairs have zoned titanomagnetite indicative of heating. With grain size about 100 μm, they are larger than the range of 20–40 μm that is typical of the 2004–6 dacite. From these data, we conclude that most of the dacite tephra fragments in the January 16 tephra are not juvenile, suggesting that this explosion emanated from the margins of the conduit and favoring a phreatic rather than magmatic explosion source. However, the story may be different for the March 8, 2005, explosion. The analyses of oxide grain pairs from that ash result in temperatures that average 852±22°C, indistinguishable from the initial 2004 dacite temperature of 850±5°C.

Shallow Conduit Processes—A Petrologic Synthesis

In figure 21 we summarize petrologic features that explain how and where the conduit magma solidified to become a plug. Viscous and relatively melt-rich dacite magma with approximately 55 percent melt ascended from depth, decompressed, lost volatiles, and began to undergo rapid groundmass crystallization at a depth of about 1 km. The earliest erupted dacite preserved equilibrium Fe-Ti oxide temperatures of about 850°C, which we assume is the temperature at the top of the source reservoir. With increasing crystallization and decreasing melt fractionation, plagioclase became more sodic (reaching An_{20-25} at final stages), and the crystallizing assemblage was joined by anorthoclase and quartz or tridymite (table 3) at depths of less than 0.5 km. Latent heat that was evolved during decompression-driven groundmass crystallization raised temperatures above 850°C until magma approached the surface. During the earliest stages of the eruption, when extrusion rates were high, the residual high-silica rhyolite matrix melt quenched through the glass transition, especially near the more rapidly cooling conduit margins, and locally preserved as much as 30 percent glass. However, within the spine interior and during later stages of the eruption when eruption rates were slower, groundmass crystallization continued virtually to completion, producing microcrystalline groundmasses with a granite-minimum composition, and latent heating produced zoned oxides. The petrologic constraints outlined here helped define the pressure and depth of solidification used in the quantitative dynamical model of Iverson and others (2006) and Iverson (this volume, chap. 21) for seismogenic stick-slip extrusion of the solid Mount St. Helens dacite plug.

Deep Reservoir Processes

Constraints from Petrography, Textures, and Fe-Ti Oxide Thermobarometry

Isotopic data elsewhere in this volume (Kent and others, chap. 35; Cooper and Donnelly, chap. 36; Reagan and others, chap. 37) indicate a complex history for the 2004–6 magma. For example, U-Th-series phenocryst model ages vary over time scales of decades to thousands of years, and some crystals have variable initial Sr isotopic ratios. The dacite contains amphiboles with widely varying Al and Fe content, which indicate derivation over wide ranges in temperature and depth—most readily explained by crystallization during convection of magma over a depth range of about 5 to more than 12 km within the source reservoir (Rutherford and Devine, this volume, chap. 31). In addition, normal and reverse zoning of plagioclase phenocrysts and entrainment of hypersthene microlites in the outer zones of plagioclase resulted from changes in temperature and pressure as magma cycled within a convecting reservoir (Streck and others, this volume, chap. 34). It seems clear that many of the phenocrysts were recycled from previous crystallization episodes and from crystal mush resident in the reservoir.

Modal data and textures described previously (table 2; figs. 4, 5), in combination with isotopic, phase-equilibria, and phenocryst relations described above, indicate multiple stages in the history of the dacite. The phenocryst assemblage of oxides, amphibole, hypersthene, and plagioclase grew slowly in the deep convecting reservoir. Our earliest samples of the 2004 dacite, erupted in October, provide our best constraints on temperature, oxygen fugacity, P_{H_2O}, and depth of magma at the roof of the deep reservoir (850 ±5°C, $f_{O_2} = 10^{-12.4 \pm 0.1}$, 130 MPa, and about 5 km depth, respectively; see also Rutherford and Devine (this volume, chap. 31)). The equilibration depth for 2004 is significantly shallower than the equilibration depth for May 18, 1980, dacite, which by the same method yields a depth of 8.6±1 km (220±30 MPa) (Rutherford, 1993). These differences suggest that the roof of the reservoir became shallower after the 1980 eruption, a relation also suggested by shallowing of storage areas inferred from water contents of melt inclusions in pumice from eruptions in the summer of 1980 (Cashman and McConnell, 2005). A greater abundance of phenocrysts and more sodic plagioclase rims in the 2004–6 dacite, along with shallower equilibration depths and more evolved bulk composition, is consistent with this eruption tapping a shallower and more phenocryst-rich part of the magma reservoir than was tapped in 1980–86 (Cashman, 1992; Cashman and Taggart, 1983; Geschwind and Rutherford, 1995; Rutherford and others, 1985).

Glass-rich dacite sample SH304-2G initially had all major phenocryst phases, namely plagioclase, hypersthene,

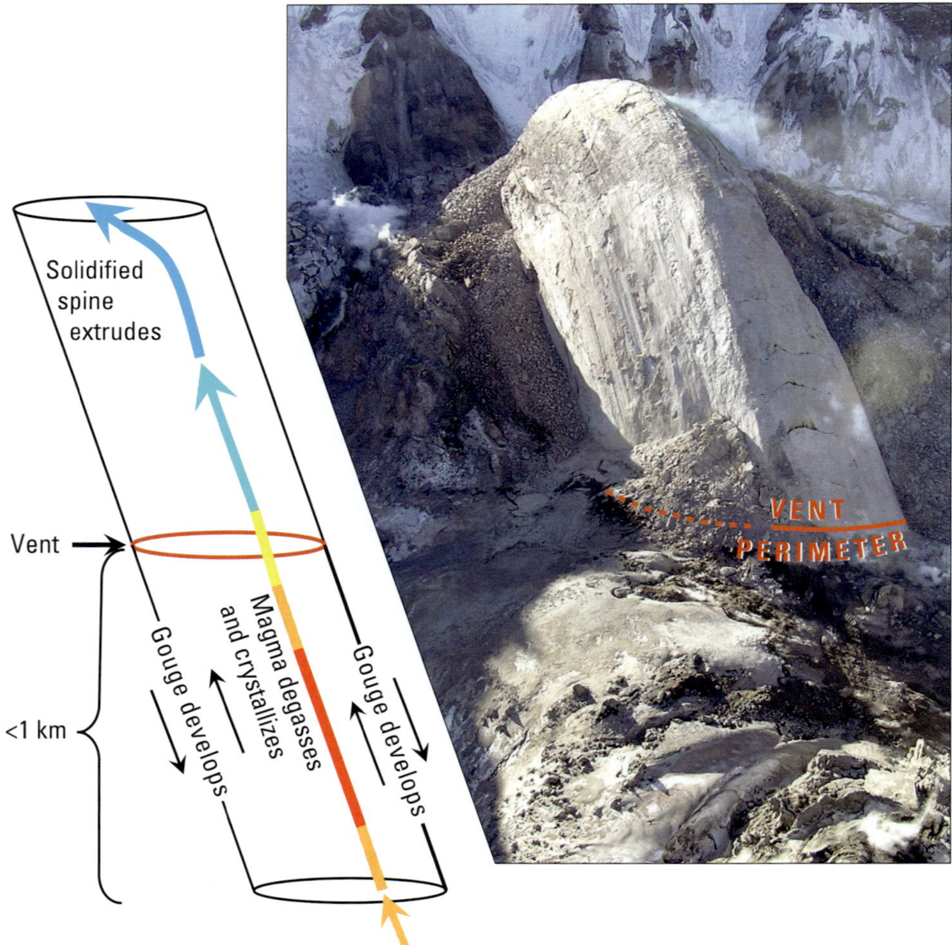

Figure 21. Diagram showing stages in development of a solid spine, drawn approximately to scale, using oblique aerial photograph of spine 4, February 22, 2005. View in photograph is to south-southwest from above east margin of 1980–86 lava dome; USGS photo by D. Dzurisin. South crater wall is visible in background. Spine is inclined and is being extruded parallel to slickenside striations, which are formed in meter-thick gouge carapace. Blocky talus flanks spine on east and west and was derived from areas where dome is disintegrating. Bracket on diagram indicates depth range of solidification, estimated to be less than 1 km. Colors of arrows diagrammatically represent intervals of decompression crystallization, latent heating, and subsequent cooling at the surface.

amphibole, and Fe-Ti oxides, coexisting with melt at 844±2°C and an oxygen fugacity of $10^{-12.43\pm0.07}$, overlapping with the temperature and oxygen fugacity of the microcrystalline dacite SH304-2A9 (table 9). The presence of tiny elongate hypersthene and oxides (less than 5 µm in diameter; fig. 9*D*) as the only microlite phases is therefore surprising. At pressures less than about 100 MPa, amphibole is unstable, and one would expect to see plagioclase on the liquidus and crystallizing in the groundmass. In contrast, at high temperatures, the Mount St. Helens dacite composition does have hypersthene first on the liquidus (Rutherford, 1993; Rutherford and Devine, this volume, chap. 31). Could the glassy sample SH304-2G represent magma that was heated during convection in the deep reservoir? Heating would preferentially melt the groundmass phases, such that subsequent cooling and rapid ascent would lead to nucleation of early hypersthene. However, late-stage heating is ruled out by tight clustering of Fe-Ti oxide thermobarometric data at low temperatures in SH304-2G (844±2°C for 65 analyses of six equilibrium grain pairs) and overlap of these oxide temperatures with those in the microcrystalline dacite, SH-04-2A9 (850±5°C). In addition, absence of resorbed margins on plagioclase and amphibole phenocrysts argues against an earlier stage of extensive heating. Consequently, we are left with the interpretation that the absence of plagioclase microlites is a kinetic effect and that SH304-2G is a fragment from the selvage of a vanguard dike that was emplaced to shallow levels and quenched during the earliest phase of the eruption in September 2004.

The presence of extremely rare mafic inclusions in two of the samples indicates mingling and quenching of andesite magma in the dacite at some time during its history. The lack of decompression rims on the high-Al amphiboles of the quenched inclusions, except where they were exposed to the dacite host magma, is consistent with quenching at depths where amphibole was stable (>100 MPa). The difference in bulk composition between inclusions in SH315-4 and SH321-1C, and their small sizes, suggests that these are fragments of larger inclusions, which may display a range in vesiculation and filter-pressing textures (Bacon, 1986). How long small fragments of quenched inclusions can be preserved in convecting, crystal-rich dacite magma is unknown. Their scarcity, coupled with the remarkably uniform composition of the 2004–6 dacite, suggest that they date from a past mingling event. As discussed later, geophysical and gas data suggest that no new magma was added to the reservoir between the summer of 1980 and late 1987 (Moran, 1994; Moran and others, this volume, chap. 2). However, it is possible that new magma was added during seismic swarms that took place during the period after 1987. Consequently, we suggest that these rare inclusions may have been entrained during a period of mingling with hotter and more mafic magma at depth preceding the 1980 eruption or during the repressurization of the reservoir recorded by seismicity between 1987 and 1998 (Moran, 1994).

Constraints from Bulk-Rock Geochemistry

Upper regions of magma reservoirs, by virtue of lower temperature and higher viscosity, may be bypassed during eruptions (Sparks and others, 1984), such that hot, lower viscosity plumes of magma from lower levels of a reservoir may intrude through overlying magma to be erupted first, only to be followed by higher viscosity magma entrained into the newly established conduit. Such a model was proposed to explain the cycle of initially decreasing and then increasing SiO_2 in 1980–86 dome lava at Mount St. Helens (Carey and others, 1990; Pallister and others, 1992). However, the difference in minor and trace-element compositions of the 2004–6 and 1980–86 dacites, including lower heavy rare-earth elements (HREE) (fig. 19) and higher Ti and Cr (figs. 17, 18), indicate that this magma was not derived by continued closed-system crystallization of 1980 dacite magma. Instead, we suggest that the 2004–6 magma was derived from a distinct batch of dacite, as explained below.

The rare-earth-element (REE) abundances in Mount St. Helens rocks are especially informative because they decrease in abundance with increasing SiO_2. Owing to their overall incompatibility in major phenocryst phases, the decrease in their abundance cannot be explained by major-phase crystal fractionation (Pallister and others, 1992; Smith and Leeman, 1987). The highest REE abundances in recent Mount St. Helens magmas are in mafic magmas (basalts and basaltic andesites) erupted during the Castle Creek eruptive period, about 2,000 years ago (fig. 19). This factor, as well as other geochemical and petrologic trends in Mount St. Helens magmas, are most readily explained by variable amounts of mixing between dacite magma (derived by partial melting of lower crustal metabasaltic rocks) and mafic magma enriched in high-field-strength elements (HFSE) and REE (Gardner and others, 1995b; Pallister and others, 1992; Smith and Leeman, 1987, 1993). The 2004–6 dacites have the lowest HREE abundances seen in any Mount St. Helens rocks erupted during the past 500 years. Consequently, they appear to be the least contaminated by mixing with REE- and HFSE-enriched basaltic magmas. Like other Mount St. Helens dacites, the 2004–6 samples have several characteristics that have been attributed to adakites (Defant, 1993; Drummond and Defant, 1990), such as high SiO_2, Al_2O_3, and Na_2O, low Y and Yb, and relatively high Sr (about 400 ppm), and they lack or have only small Eu anomalies. However, they are not as enriched in LREE as adakites (with La/Yb ratios of about 10, as opposed to ratios greater than 20 in the archetypical adakite). The same residual phases responsible for depletion of the HREE (garnet, amphibole, and pyroxene) are also expected at the base of the crust, a source we prefer, as it does not require transport of the dacite through a hot mantle wedge without modification (Dawes and others, 1994). Consequently, we do not consider the Mount St. Helens dacites as partial melts of slab eclogites but more likely as melts of lower crustal metabasaltic rocks that have undergone variable amounts of crystallization and geochemical modification in the shallow crustal reservoir beneath the volcano (Smith and Leeman, 1987).

Regardless of the ultimate source of the 2004–6 dacite, its distinct TiO_2, Cr, and HREE abundances suggest that either it is an entirely new batch of dacite magma from the deep crust or it is derived from a geochemically isolated region of a crustal reservoir. The question of new versus residual magma has implications for the long-term eruptive behavior of Mount St. Helens, because arrival of a new batch of dacitic magma from the deep crust could herald the beginning of a new long-term cycle of eruptive activity (Pallister and others, 2005). Despite the heterogeneity in phenocryst ages and zoning history, the erupted magma is remarkably homogeneous in bulk composition, indicating that this batch of magma is well mixed. Although we cannot rule out the possibility that a batch of dacite magma from the deep crust is involved in the current eruption, the low levels of gas emissions (Gerlach and others, this volume, chap. 26), U-series evidence for multiple ages of crystals (Cooper and others, this volume, chap. 36), and the wide range in crystallization depths of phenocrysts, indicative of convection (Rutherford and Devine, this volume, chap. 31), lead us to favor the hypothesis that the 2004–6 magma is derived from a geochemically distinct batch of magma that had accumulated recently at the apex of the crustal magma reservoir. This magma had been depleted in SO_2 and CO_2 during multiple cycles of reservoir convection, as explained in the section below on eruption triggering.

An Updated Reservoir and Conduit Model

In figure 22 we update a diagrammatic cross section of the Mount St. Helens magmatic system that was drawn on the basis of seismic, petrologic, and deformation data (Pallister and others, 1992; Scandone and Malone, 1985). The principal changes to the diagram that make it different from a 1980s interpretation are listed here.

1. The top of the reservoir is raised from a depth of about 6 km to about 5 km on the basis of the equilibration pressure of 130 MPa for the 2004–6 magma (Rutherford and Devine, this volume, chap. 31). Assuming that magma ascent was accompanied by an increase in pressure in the reservoir and not accomplished simply by collapse of the roof into the magma, this top-of-reservoir level is bracketed by seismic and deformation data to the time interval 1987–97, as described below.

2. The geometry of the conduit from 5 km to the surface is poorly constrained. It may consist of a complex of dikes and irregular intrusions that represent the conduit pathways of previous eruptions (suggested by textural and petrologic evidence that the 1980–86 dome lavas experienced a multistage decompression history; see Cashman, 1992). However, because of the distinct and uniform dacite composition, consistency of amphibole reaction-rim thicknesses, and continuous eruption, the 2004–6 eruption is thought to have established a new conduit pathway, at least partly distinct from that of the 1980–86 dome-forming eruptions. But how was a new conduit emplaced without large-scale inflation prior to the eruption? One possibility is that the new volume of dacite magma and spine that was emplaced at shallow levels between September 23 and October 11, 2004, was compensated by extrusion under the glacier of an equal volume of solidified rock from the 1980–86 conduit. Uplift of 12×10^6 m^3 was recorded during this period before the first spine emerged (Schilling and others, this volume, chap. 8). Such a model would help explain the presence "crater floor" samples that are geochemically similar to 1985 or 1986 dacite, bits of which were uplifted with the glacier and sampled on October 20 and 27, 2004 (table 1).

3. We reduce the model size of the reservoir to a magma volume of about 4 to 5 km^3, a compromise between the smaller volumes inferred from seismic data (Lees, 1992; Moran, 1994; Musumeci and others, 2002) and magma volumes of as much as 8 km^3, which are suggested by eruptive volumes of the largest historical eruptions at Mount St. Helens. The largest plinian eruptions of Mount St. Helens during the past 4,000 years had magmatic volumes of 4 km^3 (tephra layer Yn) and 2 km^3 (tephra layer Wn) (Carey and others, 1995). Reservoir volumes are likely at least twice this volume, based on the assumption that individual explosive (but noncaldera-forming) eruptions are unlikely to withdraw more than half of their shallow crustal reservoir volumes without extensive surface deformation or caldera collapse. The presence of a continuous magma reservoir within the seismically defined depth range between about 5 and greater than 12 km during the past 4,000 years is based on variation in depths of equilibration of magmas erupted during this time span, including changes in equilibration depths of as much as 6 km in less than 3 years (Gardner and others, 1995c). In addition, conductive cooling models suggest cooling times on the order of several thousand years for magma reservoirs of these depths and volumes (see Hawkesworth and others, 2000). That the magma reservoir is spatially continuous over its depth range and convecting, rather than discontinuous as in Lees' (1992) model, is consistent with the petrologic evidence of large-scale convection cited above and with new seismic tomographic modeling, which indicates a continuous reservoir over the interval between 6 and at least 10 km (Waite and Moran, 2006).

We follow Gardner and others (1995c) in interpreting the rapid change in equilibration depths for successive eruptions at Mount St. Helens to reflect tapping of different levels of the reservoir at different times. Such would appear to be the case for the source regions for the 2004–6 magma (130 MPa, about 5.2 km) compared to the 1980 magma (220 MPa, about 8.6 km) (Rutherford, 1993; Rutherford and Devine, this volume, chap. 31). An increase in seismicity at depths of 3 to 10 km,

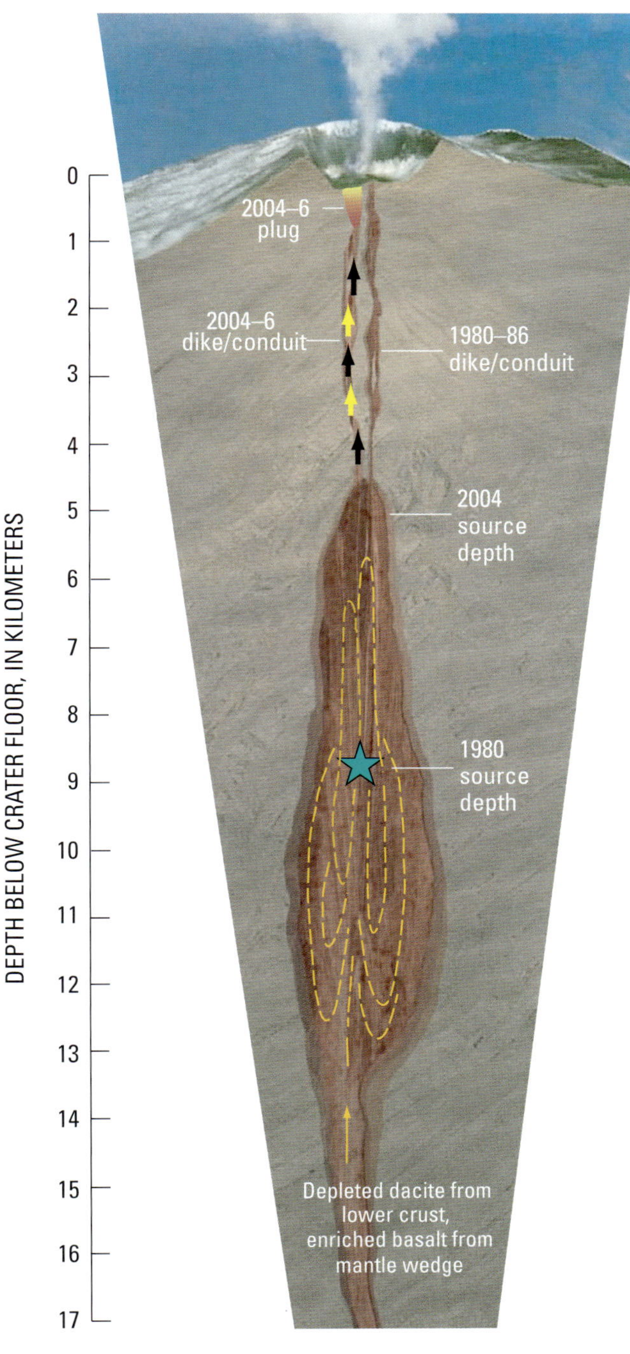

Figure 22. Schematic cross section of Mount St. Helens plumbing system, updated from Pallister and others (1992) to include constraints from current eruption. Yellow dashed lines are inferred convection paths in reservoir (Rutherford and Devine, this volume, chap. 31) and are overlain by a stagnant crystal-rich mush zone considered as the source for the 2004–6 eruption. Diagram used here is modified from an illustration published Nov. 28, 2005, by the New York Times News Service; copyright © 2005 The New York Times Company.

including an initial cluster at 4–6 km, and accompanying repressurization of the reservoir and conduit between 1987 and 1992 (Moran, 1994), may reflect foundering of the roof of the reservoir and migration of a batch of magma to the shallower equilibration depths. As noted above, we suggest that the 2004–6 dacite was derived from the apical region of the reservoir. It originated from a geochemically distinct batch of crystal-rich magma not tapped during the 1980–86 eruptions that rose into the apical region after 1986.

The deep levels of the reservoir probably occupy a tensional dikelike structure within the St. Helens seismic zone (Musumeci and others, 2002), and the 1980–86 conduit may well consist of multiple intrusions and dikes (Cashman, 1992). However, unlike the situation at other volcanic centers (see, for example, Eichelberger and Izbekov, 2000), we see little surface geologic evidence for extensive dacitic dikes at shallow levels outside of the immediate crater area or alignment of older satellitic domes.

Studies of the plutonic substrate of volcanic arcs offer additional insights. Composite arc plutons and stocks with volumes of 10 km^3 or more are common at paleodepths of 5–15 km, and arc batholiths, such as in the Sierra Nevada, are increasingly recognized to consist of multiple smaller magma bodies. However, many of these plutonic complexes developed over time spans measured in millions of years, not over a period of less than 300,000 years (Clynne and others, this volume, chap. 28; Crandell, 1987) in the tensional offset of a fault zone (Weaver and others, 1987). A better analogue for the Mount St. Helens plumbing system comes from a composite stratovolcano model based on ore deposits in the Andes (Sillitoe, 1973). Sillitoe's composite model is similar to figure 22 and consists of a complex composite stock of multiple feeder dikes and plugs of various ages overlying a shallow crustal pluton. We recognize that diagrams such as figure 22 are at best oversimplified cartoons compared to the complexity seen in eroded volcanic terranes, yet we believe they serve as useful constructs to evaluate volcano monitoring and petrologic data and to consider how magmas move through the crust.

Reservoir Pressurization and Eruption Triggering

One of the most important questions in volcanology and volcano-hazard mitigation is to understand what triggers eruptions. Before addressing this question for the 2004–6 Mount St. Helens eruption, however, we need to define what we mean by triggering. A pressurized reservoir-conduit system is a necessary condition for an eruption, but it is not a trigger, because pressure can be released slowly—for example, through passive degassing. A trigger requires a rapid increase in relative pressure of sufficient magnitude to fracture a new pathway to the surface (for a volcano with a solidified conduit or hydrothermal seal) or to raise the level of magma above the vent in an active magma-filled conduit. Accordingly, triggers can result by unloading from above or from a rapid increase in pressure or volume at depth. Candidates for triggers from above include edifice collapse (as in 1980 at Mount St. Helens) or more subtle changes affecting an already pressurized system (an example: increased rainfall, Mastin, 1994). Indeed, Iverson and others (2006) calculate that once the system is pressurized, changes in pressure that are equivalent to a magma head of less than one meter are sufficient to start and stop the stick-slip cycles that they model for the current Mount St. Helens eruption.

Rapid addition of new magma and fluids to a crustal reservoir can increase pressure and trigger an eruption from below. This was the case for the eruption of Pinatubo in 1991, in which new hydrous mafic magma from depth entered a crystal-rich dacite reservoir, vesiculated, mingled, and created a buoyant plume, which rose through the viscous and crystal-rich upper part of the reservoir, increased pressure in the hydrothermal system, fractured a new pathway to the surface, and triggered the eruption (Pallister and others, 1996). In the Pinatubo case, deep long-period seismicity recorded and tracked ascent of basalt from 35 or 40 km deep to the crustal reservoir at depths of less than 14 km before the eruption (White, 1996).

For the 2004 Mount St. Helens eruption, the long-term pattern of seismicity since the 1980 eruption indicates that the reservoir and conduit system began to repressurize in late 1987 after the cessation of 1980–86 dome eruptions (Moran, 1994; Musumeci and others, 2002). Pressurization led to repeated seismic swarms at depths of less than about 8 km, and rainfall-induced fracturing weakened hydrothermal seals and triggered small gas explosions in 1989–91 (Mastin, 1994). Only a few deep (>3 km) earthquakes were located in the months before the 2004 eruption, and there have been no deep earthquakes during the 2004–6 eruptive period; the hundreds of thousands of small hybrid earthquakes that accompanied spine extrusion have been shallow (Moran and others, this volume, chap. 2; Thelen and others, this volume, chap. 4). These relations indicate that the reservoir-conduit system was already pressurized before the eruption. The highest rate of seismic energy release took place during the September 30–October 5, 2004, time period of shallow volcano-tectonic earthquakes and explosions that preceded extrusion of the initial spine (Moran and others, this volume, chap. 2). Given the small amount of pressure required for the hypothesized stick-slip cycles of spine extrusion (Iverson and others, 2006; Iverson, this volume, chap. 21), this initial period of greater energy release in early October 2004 indicates that the trigger for the eruption involved a somewhat larger pressure differential, which was accompanied by upward migration and venting of overpressured hydrothermal fluids.

Pressurization of a magma reservoir may result either from addition of mass (replenishment) or by fluid exsolution and expansion (driven by cooling and/or decompression). Long-term magmatic replenishment and magma mixing is a characteristic of the past at Mount St. Helens (Pallister and others, 1992; Gardner and others, 1995a; Clynne and others, this volume, chap. 28). However, as previously noted, the paucity of mafic inclusions, homogeneity of the dacite composition, lack of deep seismicity, and the low levels of gas emissions argue against ongoing (2004–6) replenishment, as does a lack of volcanic deformation during the period from at least as early as late 1997 (when continuous GPS monitoring was established) to late September 2004 (Lisowski and others, this volume, chap. 15).

Deformation data for the current eruption are best fit by an ellipsoidal reservoir with a centroid depth of 7 to 8 km (Lisowski and others, this volume, chap. 15) and are consistent with both recent seismic tomography models (Waite and Moran, 2006) and with the petrologic constraints outlined above. However, the volume of erupted dacite falls short of the modeled volume decrease at depth, requiring either magmatic replenishment or expansion of the reservoir magma (Lisowski and others, this volume, chap. 15). Geochemical modeling of gas-emission data suggests about 1.2–1.4 volume percent separate fluid phase at 220 MPa (about 8.6 km depth), which would increase to about 9–10 volume percent at 130 MPa (5.2 km), near the apex of the magma reservoir (Gerlach and others, this volume, chap. 26). Modeling of magma and wall-rock physical properties (Mastin and others, this volume, chap. 22) to match the geodetically constrained rate of change in eruptive volume indicates only limited magma compressibility (low average volatile content of less than 2 volume percent) and a large magma reservoir (a few to as much as 10 km^3 at depths of 5 to >10 km), consistent with the recent seismic tomography (Waite and Moran, 2006). The modeling by Mastin and others of deformation data from the first 1.5 year (this volume, chap. 22) also favors ongoing magmatic replenishment at a rate of about 1–1.3 m^3/s. On balance, and given the uncertainties in the models, at this time it remains uncertain if the reservoir is being recharged, if the fluid phase in the reservoir is expanding, or both. Furthermore, if the reservoir is being recharged from below and erupted from the top, any significant additions of SO_2 and CO_2 gases have not yet made their way through the >10-km vertical extent of magma in the reservoir and conduit system to the surface.

A Petrologic Explanation

Magma in the upwelling limbs of convection cells exsolves volatiles because of their reduced solubility in the silicate melt on ascent to lower pressures. Therefore, without addition of new volatile-rich magma at depth, magma in a convecting reservoir will be progressively depleted by multiple convection cycles as volatiles in upwelling magma are lost to overlying stagnant magma and reservoir roof rocks. Any nonconvecting magmatic mush present at the roof of the reservoir would either be enriched or depleted in volatiles, depending on the ratio of volatile addition from upwelling magma to volatile loss through wall and roof rocks. During periods of frequent or continuous magmatic replenishment of the deep reservoir by hot and gas-rich magmas, enhanced convection would tend to enrich an upper mush zone in volatiles. During such periods, undercooling of newly introduced magmas at depth could also produce highly gas-rich plumes of buoyant mingled magma. Energetic plumes would be capable of penetrating and mobilizing previously gas-enriched mush in the reservoir roof to trigger large explosive eruptions. Evidence for such a process is seen in the eruptive products of Pinatubo volcano (Pallister and others, 1996) and is suggested by the presence of mingled pumices found in the basal set W tephra from the A.D. 1479 explosive eruption of Mount St. Helens, which initiated the Kalama eruptive period (Pallister and others, 1992). In contrast, in the absence of replenishment (or with diminished volumes of replenishment), continued convection would slowly deplete the reservoir in the lower-solubility volatiles, and the magmatic fluid phase would shift from relatively SO_2- and CO_2-rich to H_2O- and Cl-rich compositions.

This latter condition is what we propose for the current eruption of Mount St. Helens. Since 1980, the magma reservoir has seen minimal replenishment, such that convection has produced a batch of well-mixed, crystal-rich magma with 65 percent SiO_2 near the reservoir roof. A slow increase in pressure was brought about beginning in late 1987 by convection-driven exsolution of a water-rich volatile phase (which outpaced volatile losses through roof rocks). Magmatic pressure finally exceeded lithostatic load in late September 2004, and the eruption ensued. As conduit pressures during the 2004–6 eruption have not greatly exceeded lithostatic pressure and have been modulated by continuous crystallization of a shallow seismogenic plug (Iverson and others, 2006; Iverson, this volume, chap. 21), the eruption has been sustained at a low nonexplosive rate.

Lessons from the Past, Implications for the Future

Of dacites erupted at Mount St. Helens during the past 500 years, the 17th-18th century summit-dome dacite (63–64 percent SiO_2), which erupted at the end of the Kalama eruptive period and formed the pre-1980 summit of the volcano (Crandell, 1987; Mullineaux, 1996; Pallister and others, 1992), is most akin to the dacite from the current eruption. Pre-1980 summit-dome samples are characterized by extensive groundmass crystallization, resulting in a vesicle- and glass-poor microcrystalline groundmass. Although geochemically distinct from the 2004–6 dacite and texturally finer grained, the summit dome dacite has numerous similarities with it. Like the 2004–6 eruption, the summit-dome eruptions were relatively low in explosivity, producing only one pumiceous pyroclastic flow down the Toutle River drainage in early summit-dome time (R.P. Hoblitt, oral commun., 2006). The dominant deposits from the summit dome originated from small lithic pyroclastic flows and hot lahars, which were shed off the growing and collapsing lava dome, blanketed the upper slopes of the volcano, and fed multiple small lahars that spread out onto the flanks of the volcano. The nonpumiceous pink "z" ash (Mullineaux, 1996) is the only tephra layer associated with summit-dome eruptions. It occurs as a thin (typically less than 1 cm) ash deposit on all flanks of the volcano and was likely derived from small ash clouds produced during dome collapse events over an extended period of time. Also, like some of the 2004–6 dome rocks, lithic fragments in summit-dome deposits are characterized by red oxidation fractures and rinds.

The greater extent of summit-dome deposits is a consequence of prolonged emplacement over 100 years or more (Clynne and others, 2005; Hoblitt, 1989; Yamaguchi and Hoblitt, 1995), large volume, and its location high atop the steep-sided cone. We do not know if the summit dome was built as a series of spines, for such features are rarely preserved in the geologic record. However, the summit dome was clearly built at a low mean eruptive rate. It spalled and disintegrated in place, forming the rubbly pre-1980 summit, and it shed multiple lithic pyroclastic flows and lahars. It produced only relatively small and diffuse ash clouds, similar to those produced during the 2004–6 eruption. If the current eruption were to follow a similar path, it could produce continuous or intermittent dome-forming eruptions for decades. Although low eruption rates do not guarantee a long-duration episode, a global compilation of historical dome-forming eruptions indicates that only low-rate eruptions last for many years or decades (Chris Newhall, written commun., 2005).

Acknowledgments

The authors wish to acknowledge the several dozen petrologists and geochemists from a variety of academic and government institutions who joined us during the ongoing eruption to form an informal Mount St. Helens petrology working group (Pallister and others, 2005; Rowe and others, 2008b). The contributions of these scientists are well represented in this volume and contribute greatly to our understanding of the ongoing eruption. We thank our U.S. Geological Survey (USGS) colleagues from the Cascades Volcano Observatory (CVO) and other USGS offices and from the Pacific Northwest Seismic Network at the University of Washington for sharing of data and discussion of ideas and interpretations, which have made our work on this eruption scientifically stimulating and rewarding. We thank Bobbie Myers of CVO and Jeff Linscott of JL Aviation for their emphasis on safety as well as innovation during our helicopter missions at Mount St. Helens. And finally, we thank Charlie Bacon and Malcolm Rutherford for technical reviews of this manuscript.

References Cited

Andersen, D.J., and Lindsay, D.H., 1988, Internally consistent solution models for Fe-Mg-Mn-Ti oxides; Fe-Ti oxides: American Mineralogist, v. 73, nos. 7–8, p. 714–726.

Bacon, C.R., 1986, Magmatic inclusions in silicic and intermediate volcanic rocks: Journal of Geophysical Research, v. 91, no. B6, p. 6091–6112.

Bacon, C.R., and Hirschmann, M.M., 1988, Mg/Mn partitioning as a test for equilibrium between coexisting Fe-Ti oxides: American Mineralogist, v. 73, p. 57–61.

Baedecker, P.A., and McKown, D.M., 1987, Instrumental neutron activation analysis of geochemical samples, chapter H *of* Baedecker, P.A. ed., Methods for geochemical analysis: U.S. Geological Survey Bulletin 1770, p. H1–H14.

Bergfeld, D., Evans, W.C., McGee, K.A., and Spicer, K.R., 2008, Pre- and post-eruptive investigations of gas and water samples from Mount St. Helens, Washington, 2002 to 2005, chap. 25 *of* Sherrod, D.R., Scott, W.E., and Stauffer, P.H., eds., A volcano rekindled; the renewed eruption of Mount St. Helens, 2004–2006: U.S. Geological Survey Professional Paper 1750 (this volume).

Blundy, J., and Cashman, K., 2001, Ascent-driven crystallisation of dacite magmas at Mount St. Helens, 1980–86: Contributions to Mineralogy and Petrology, v. 140, no. 6, p. 631–650, doi:10.1007/s004100000219.

Blundy, J., and Cashman, K., 2005, Rapid decompression-driven crystallization recorded by melt inclusions from Mount St. Helens volcano: Geology, v. 33, no. 10, p. 793–796, doi:10.1130/G21668.1.

Blundy, J., Cashman, K., and Humphreys, M., 2006, Magma heating by decompression-driven crystallization beneath andesite volcanoes: Nature, v. 443, p. 76–80, doi:10.1038/nature05100.

Carey, S., Sigurdsson, H., Gardner, J.E., and Criswell, W., 1990, Variations in column height and magma discharge during the May 18, 1980 eruption of Mount St. Helens: Journal of Volcanology and Geothermal Research, v. 43, p. 99–112.

Carey, S., Gardner, J., and Sigurdsson, H., 1995, The intensity and magnitude of Holocene plinian eruptions of Mount St. Helens volcano: Journal of Volcanology and Geothermal Research, v. 66, p. 185–202.

Cashman, K.V., 1988, Crystallization of Mount St. Helens 1980–1986 dacite; a quantitative textural approach: Bulletin of Volcanology, v. 50, no. 3, p. 194–209.

Cashman, K.V., 1992, Groundmass crystallization of Mount St. Helens dacite, 1980–1986: a tool for interpreting shallow magmatic processes: Contributions to Mineralogy and Petrology, v. 109, no. 4, p. 431–449, doi:10.1007/BF00306547.

Cashman, K.V., and McConnell, S.M., 2005, Multiple levels of magma storage during the 1980 summer eruptions of Mount St. Helens, WA: Bulletin of Volcanology, v. 68, no. 1, p. 57–75, doi:10.1007/s00445-005-0422-x.

Cashman, K.V., and Taggart, J.E., 1983, Petrologic monitoring of 1981 and 1982 eruptive products from Mount St. Helens: Science, v. 221, p. 1385–1387.

Cashman, K.V., Thornber, C.R., and Pallister, J.S., 2008, From dome to dust; shallow crystallization and fragmentation of conduit magma during the 2004–2006 dome extrusion of Mount St. Helens, Washington, chap. 19 *of* Sherrod, D.R., Scott, W.E., and Stauffer, P.H., eds., A volcano rekindled; the renewed eruption of Mount St. Helens, 2004–2006: U.S. Geological Survey Professional Paper 1750 (this volume).

Chrétien, S., and Brousse, R., 1989, Events preceding the great eruption of 8 May, 1902 at Mount Pelee, Martinique: Journal of Volcanology and Geothermal Research, v. 38, p. 67–75.

Clynne, M.A., Ramsey, D.W., and Wolfe, E.W., 2005, The pre-1980 eruptive history of Mount St. Helens, Washington: U.S Geological Survey Fact Sheet 2005–3045, 4 p.

Clynne, M.A., Calvert, A.T., Wolfe, E.W., Evarts, R.C., Fleck, R.J., and Lanphere, M.A., 2008, The Pleistocene eruptive history of Mount St. Helens, Washington, from 300,000 to 12,800 years before present, chap. 28 *of* Sherrod, D.R., Scott, W.E., and Stauffer, P.H., eds., A volcano rekindled; the renewed eruption of Mount St. Helens, 2004–2006: U.S. Geological Survey Professional Paper 1750 (this volume).

Cooper, K.M., and Donnelly, C.T., 2008, ^{238}U-^{230}Th-^{226}Ra disequilibria in dacite and plagioclase from the 2004–2005 eruption of Mount St. Helens, chap. 36 *of* Sherrod, D.R., Scott, W.E., and Stauffer, P.H., eds., A volcano rekindled; the renewed eruption of Mount St. Helens, 2004–2006: U.S. Geological Survey Professional Paper 1750 (this volume).

Costa, F., Dungan, M.A., and Singer, B.S., 2002, Hornblende- and phlogopite-bearing gabbroic xenoliths from Volcán San Pedro (36°S), Chilean Andes; evidence for melt and fluid migration and reactions in subduction-related plutons: Journal of Petrology, v. 43, no. 2, p. 219–241.

Couch, S., Harford, C.L., Sparks, R.S.J., and Carroll, M.R., 2003, Experimental constraints on the conditions of formation of highly calcic plagioclase microlites at the Soufriere Hills Volcano, Montserrat: Journal of Petrology, v. 44, no. 8, p. 1455–1475.

Crandell, D.R., 1987, Deposits of pre-1980 pyroclastic flows and lahars from Mount St. Helens volcano, Washington: USGS Professional Paper 1444, 91 p.

Dawes, R.L., Green, N.L., Defant, M.J., and Drummond, M.S., 1994, Mount St. Helens; potential example of the partial melting of the subducted lithosphere in a volcanic arc—comments and reply: Geology, v. 22, p. 187–190.

Defant, M.J., 1993, Mount St. Helens; potential example of the partial melting of the subducted lithosphere in a volcanic arc: Geology, v. 21, p. 547–550.

Devine, J.D., Sigurdsson, H., Davis, A.N., and Self, S., 1984,

Estimates of sulfur and chlorine yield to the atmosphere from volcanic eruptions and potential climatic effects: Journal of Geophysical Research, v. 89, no. B7, p. 6309–6325.

Devine, J.D., Rutherford, M.J., Norton, G.E., and Young, S.R., 2003, Magma storage region processes inferred from geochemistry of Fe-Ti oxides in andesitic magma, Soufrière Hills Volcano, Montserrat, W.I.: Journal of Petrology, v. 44, no. 8, p. 1375–1400, doi:10.1093/petrology/44.8.1375.

Dixon, J.E., Stolper, E.M., and Holloway, J.R., 1995, An experimental study of water and carbon dioxide solubilities in mid-ocean ridge basaltic liquids. Part I, calibration and solubility models: Journal of Petrology, v. 36, no. 6, p. 1607–1631.

Drummond, M.S., and Defant, M.J., 1990, A model for trondhjemite-tonalite-dacite genesis and crustal growth via slab-melting; Archean to modern comparisons: Journal of Geophysical Research, v. 95, p. 21503–21521.

Dzurisin, D., Lisowski, M., Poland, M.P., Sherrod, D.R., and LaHusen, R.G., 2008, Constraints and conundrums resulting from ground-deformation measurements made during the 2004–2005 dome-building eruption of Mount St. Helens, Washington, chap. 14 *of* Sherrod, D.R., Scott, W.E., and Stauffer, P.H., eds., A volcano rekindled; the renewed eruption of Mount St. Helens, 2004–2006: U.S. Geological Survey Professional Paper 1750 (this volume).

Edmonds, M., Pyle, D., and Oppenheimer, C., 2001, A model for degassing at the Soufrière Hills Volcano, Montserrat, West Indies, based on geochemical data: Earth and Planetary Science Letters, v. 186, no. 2, p. 159–173.

Edmonds, M., McGee, K.A., and Doukas, M.P., 2008, Chlorine degassing during the lava dome-building eruption of Mount St. Helens, 2004–2005, chap. 27 *of* Sherrod, D.R., Scott, W.E., and Stauffer, P.H., eds., A volcano rekindled; the renewed eruption of Mount St. Helens, 2004–2006: U.S. Geological Survey Professional Paper 1750 (this volume).

Eichelberger, J.C., and Izbekov, P.E., 2000, Eruption of andesite triggered by dyke injection; contrasting cases at Karymsky Volcano, Kamchatka and Mt Katmai, Alaska: Philosophical Transactions of the Royal Society A. Mathematical, Physical and Engineering Sciences, v. 358, no. 1770, p. 1465–1485.

Gardner, J.E., Carey, S., Rutherford, M.J., and Sigurdsson, H., 1995a, Petrologic diversity in Mount St. Helens dacites during the last 4,000 years; implications for magma mixing: Contributions to Mineralogy and Petrology, v. 119, nos. 2–3, p. 224–238.

Gardner, J.E., Carey, S., Sigurdsson, H., and Rutherford, M.J., 1995b, Influence of magma composition on the eruptive activity of Mount St. Helens, Washington: Geology, v. 23, no. 6, p. 523–526.

Gardner, J.E., Rutherford, M., Carey, S., and Sigurdsson, H., 1995c, Experimental constraints on pre-eruptive water contents and changing magma storage prior to explosive eruptions of Mount St Helens volcano: Bulletin of Volcanology, v. 57, no. 1, p. 1–17.

Gerlach, T.M., McGee, K.A., and Doukas, M.P., 2008, Emission rates of CO_2, SO_2, and H_2S, scrubbing, and preeruption excess volatiles at Mount St. Helens, 2004–2005, chap. 26 *of* Sherrod, D.R., Scott, W.E., and Stauffer, P.H., eds., A volcano rekindled; the renewed eruption of Mount St. Helens, 2004–2006: U.S. Geological Survey Professional Paper 1750 (this volume).

Geschwind, C.-H., and Rutherford, M.J., 1995, Crystallization of microlites during magma ascent; the fluid mechanics of 1980–1986 eruptions at Mount St Helens: Bulletin of Volcanology, v. 57, no. 5, p. 356–370.

Ghiorso, M.S., Hirschmann, M.M., Reiners, P.W., and Kress, V.C., 2002, The pMELTS; A revision of MELTS for improved calculation of phase relations and major element partitioning related to partial melting of the mantle to 3 GPa: Geochemistry, Geophysics, Geosystems, v. 3, no. 5, 36 p., doi: 10.1029/2001GC000217.

Harford, C.L., Sparks, R.S.J., and Fallick, A.E., 2003, Degassing at the Soufrière Hills Volcano, Montserrat, recorded in matrix glass compositions: Journal of Petrology, v. 44, no. 8, p. 1503–1523.

Hawkesworth, C.J., Blake, S., Evans, P., Hughes, R., Macdonald, R., Thomas, L.E., Turner, S.P., and Zellmer, G., 2000, Time scales of crystal fractionation in magma chambers—integrating physical, isotopic and geochemical perspectives: Journal of Petrology, v. 41, no. 7, p. 991–1006.

Heliker, C., 1995, Inclusions in Mount St. Helens dacite erupted from 1980 through 1983: Journal of Volcanology and Geothermal Research, v. 66, nos. 1–4, p. 115–135, doi:10.1016/0377-0273(94)00074-Q.

Herriott, T.M., Sherrod, D.R., Pallister, J.S., and Vallance, J.W., 2008, Photogeologic maps of the 2004–2005 Mount St. Helens eruption, chap. 10 *of* Sherrod, D.R., Scott, W.E., and Stauffer, P.H., eds., A volcano rekindled; the renewed eruption of Mount St. Helens, 2004–2006: U.S. Geological Survey Professional Paper 1750 (this volume).

Hoblitt, R.P., 1989, The Kalama eruptive period, southwest and south flanks, *in* Chapin, C.E., and Zidek, J., eds., Field excursions to volcanic terranes in the western United States, v. 2, Cascades and Intermountain West: New Mexico Bureau of Mines and Mineral Resources Memoir 47, p. 65–69.

Hoblitt, R.P., and Harmon, R.S., 1993, Bimodal density distribution of cryptodome dacite from the 1980 eruption of Mount St. Helens, Washington: Bulletin of Volcanology, v.

55, no. 6, p. 421–437, doi:10.1007/BF00302002.

Ihinger, P.D., Hervig, R.L., and McMillan, P.F., 1994, Analytical methods for volatiles in glasses, *in* Carroll, M.R., and Holloway, J.R., eds., Volatiles in magmas: Reviews in Mineralogy and Geochemistry, v. 30, p. 67–121.

Iverson, R.M., 2008, Dynamics of seismogenic volcanic extrusion resisted by a solid surface plug, Mount St. Helens, 2004–2005, chap. 21 *of* Sherrod, D.R., Scott, W.E., and Stauffer, P.H., eds., A volcano rekindled; the renewed eruption of Mount St. Helens, 2004–2006: U.S. Geological Survey Professional Paper 1750 (this volume).

Iverson, R.M., Dzurisin, D., Gardner, C.A., Gerlach, T.M., LaHusen, R.G., Lisowski, M., Major, J.J., Malone, S.D., Messerich, J.A., Moran, S.C., Pallister, J.S., Qamar, A.I., Schilling, S.P., and Vallance, J.W., 2006, Dynamics of seismogenic volcanic extrusion at Mount St. Helens in 2004–05: Nature, v. 444, no. 7118, p. 439–443, doi:10.1038/nature05322.

Jackson, E.D., 1968, The character of the lower crust and upper mantle beneath the Hawaiian Islands: Proceedings of the 23rd International Geological Congress, v. 1, p. 131–150.

Kent, A.J.R., Rowe, M.C., Thornber, C.R., and Pallister, J.S., 2008, Trace element and Pb isotope composition of plagioclase from dome samples from the 2004–2005 eruption of Mount St Helens, Washington, chap. 35 *of* Sherrod, D.R., Scott, W.E., and Stauffer, P.H., eds., A volcano rekindled; the renewed eruption of Mount St. Helens, 2004–2006: U.S. Geological Survey Professional Paper 1750 (this volume).

Lacroix, A., 1904, La Montagne Pelée et ses éruptions: Paris, Masson et cie, 662 p.

LaHusen, R.G., Swinford, K.J., Logan, M., and Lisowski, M., 2008, Instrumentation in remote and dangerous settings; examples using data from GPS "spider" deployments during the 2004–2005 eruption of Mount St. Helens, Washington, chap. 16 *of* Sherrod, D.R., Scott, W.E., and Stauffer, P.H., eds., A volcano rekindled; the renewed eruption of Mount St. Helens, 2004–2006: U.S. Geological Survey Professional Paper 1750 (this volume).

Lees, J.M., 1992, The magma system of Mount St. Helens; non-linear high resolution P-wave tomography: Journal of Volcanology and Geothermal Research, v. 53, nos. 1–4, p. 103–116.

Lepage, L.D., 2003, ILMAT; an Excel worksheet for ilmenite-magnetite geothermometry and geobarometry: Computers and Geosciences, v. 29, p. 673–678.

Lisowski, M., Dzurisin, D., Denlinger, R.P., and Iwatsubo, E.Y., 2008, Analysis of GPS-measured deformation associated with the 2004–2006 dome-building eruption of Mount St. Helens, Washington, chap. 15 *of* Sherrod, D.R., Scott, W.E., and Stauffer, P.H., eds., A volcano rekindled; the renewed eruption of Mount St. Helens, 2004–2006: U.S. Geological Survey Professional Paper 1750 (this volume).

Mandeville, C.W., Webster, J.D., Rutherford, M.J., Taylor, B.E., Timbal, A., and Faure, K., 2002, Determination of molar absorptivities for infrared absorption bands of H_2O in andesitic glasses: American Mineralogist, v. 87, p. 813–821.

Mastin, L.G., 1994, Explosive tephra emissions at Mount St. Helens, 1989–1991; the violent escape of magmatic gas following storms?: Geological Society of America Bulletin, v. 106, no. 2, p. 175–185.

Mastin, L.G., Roeloffs, E., Beeler, N.M., and Quick, J.E., 2008, Constraints on the size, overpressure, and volatile content of the Mount St. Helens magma system from geodetic and dome-growth measurements during the 2004–2006+ eruption, chap. 22 *of* Sherrod, D.R., Scott, W.E., and Stauffer, P.H., eds., A volcano rekindled; the renewed eruption of Mount St. Helens, 2004–2006: U.S. Geological Survey Professional Paper 1750 (this volume).

McChesney, P.J., Couchman, M.R., Moran, S.C., Lockhart, A.B., Swinford, K.J., and LaHusen, R.G., 2008, Seismic-monitoring changes and the remote deployment of seismic stations (seismic spider) at Mount St. Helens, 2004–2005, chap. 7 *of* Sherrod, D.R., Scott, W.E., and Stauffer, P.H., eds., A volcano rekindled; the renewed eruption of Mount St. Helens, 2004–2006: U.S. Geological Survey Professional Paper 1750 (this volume).

Melnik, O., and Sparks, R.S.J., 2002, Dynamics of magma ascent and lava extrusion at Soufriere Hills Volcano, Montserrat, *in* Druitt, T.H., and Kokelaar, B.P., eds., The eruption of Soufriere Hills Volcano, Montserrat, from 1995 to 1999: Geological Society of London Memoir 21, p. 153–171.

Melson, W.G., 1983, Monitoring the 1980–1982 eruption of Mount St. Helens; compositions and abundances of glass: Science, v. 221, p. 1387–1391.

Melson, W.G., and Hopson, C.A., 1981, Preeruption temperatures and oxygen fugacities in the 1980 eruptive sequence, *in* Lipman, P.W., and Mullineaux, D.R., eds., The 1980 eruptions of Mount St. Helens, Washington: U.S. Geological Survey Professional Paper 1250, p. 641–648.

Mimatsu, M., 1995, Showa-Shinzan diary; complete records of observation of the process of the birth of Showa-Shinzan, expanded reprint [Oshima, M., translator]: Sapporo, Suda Seihan Co., 179 p.

Moore, G., Vennemann, T., and Carmichael, I.S.E., 1995, Solubility of water in magma to 2 kbar: Geology, v. 23, p. 1099–1102.

Moore, G., Vennemann, T., and Carmichael, I.S.E., 1998, An

empirical model for the solubility of H_2O in magmas to 3 kilobars: American Mineralogist, v. 83, nos. 1–2, p. 36–42.

Moran, S.C., 1994, Seismicity at Mount St. Helens, 1987–1992; evidence for repressurization of an active magmatic system: Journal of Geophysical Research, v. 90, no. B3, p. 4341–4354, doi:10.1029/93JB02993.

Moran, S.C., Malone, S.D., Qamar, A.I., Thelen, W.A., Wright, A.K., and Caplan-Auerbach, J., 2008a, Seismicity associated with renewed dome building at Mount St. Helens, 2004–2005, chap. 2 *of* Sherrod, D.R., Scott, W.E., and Stauffer, P.H., eds., A volcano rekindled; the renewed eruption of Mount St. Helens, 2004–2006: U.S. Geological Survey Professional Paper 1750 (this volume).

Moran, S.C., McChesney, P.J., and Lockhart, A.B., 2008b, Seismicity and infrasound associated with explosions at Mount St. Helens, 2004–2005, chap. 6 *of* Sherrod, D.R., Scott, W.E., and Stauffer, P.H., eds., A volcano rekindled; the renewed eruption of Mount St. Helens, 2004–2006: U.S. Geological Survey Professional Paper 1750 (this volume).

Mullineaux, D.R., 1996, Pre-1980 tephra-fall deposits erupted from Mount St. Helens, Washington: U.S. Geological Survey Professional Paper 1563, 99 p.

Murphy, M.D., Sparks, R.S.J., Barclay, J., Carroll, M.R., Lejeune, A.-M., Brewer, T.S., Macdonald, R., Black, S., and Young, S., 2000, The role of magma mixing in triggering the current eruption at the Soufriere Hills volcano, Montserrat, West Indies: Geophysical Research Letters, v. 25, no. 18, p. 3433–3436

Musumeci, C., Gresta, S., and Malone, S.D., 2002, Magma system recharge of Mount St. Helens from precise relative hypocenter location of microearthquakes: Journal of Geophysical Research, v. 107, no. B10, p. ESE16-1–ESE16-9, doi:10.1029/2001JB000629, 002002.

Nakamura, M., 1995, Continuous mixing of crystal mush and replenished magma in the ongoing Unzen eruption: Geology, v. 23, no. 9, p. 807–810.

Newman S., Stolper, E.M., and Epstein, S., 1986, Measurement of water in rhyolitic glasses; calibration of an infrared spectroscopic technique: American Mineralogist, v. 71, p. 1527–1541.

Nielson, C.H., and Sigurdsson, H., 1981, Quantitative methods for electron microprobe analysis of sodium in natural and synthetic glasses: American Mineralogist, v. 66, p. 547–552.

Nowak, M., and Behrens, H., 1995, The speciation of water in haplogranite melts determined by in situ near-infrared spectroscopy: Geochmica et Cosmochimica Acta, v. 59, p. 3445–3450.

Pallister, J.S., Heliker, C., and Hoblitt, R.P., 1991, Glimpses of the active pluton below Mount St. Helens [abs.]: Eos (American Geophysical Union Transactions), v. 72, no. 44, supplement, p. 576.

Pallister, J.S., Hoblitt, R.P., Crandell, D.R., and Mullineaux, D.R., 1992, Mount St. Helens a decade after the 1980 eruptions; magmatic models, chemical cycles, and a revised hazards assessment: Bulletin of Volcanology, v. 54, no. 2, p. 126–146, doi: 10.1007/BF00278003.

Pallister, J.S., Hoblitt, R.P., Meeker, G.P., Knight, R.J., and Siems, D.F., 1996, Magma mixing at Mount Pinatubo; petrographic and chemical evidence from the 1991 deposits, *in* Newhall, C.G., and Punongbayan, R., eds., Fire and mud; eruptions and lahars of Mount Pinatubo, Philippines: Seattle, University of Washington Press, p. 687–732.

Pallister, J.S., Reagan, M., and Cashman, K, 2005, A new eruptive cycle at Mount St. Helens?: Eos (American Geophysical Union Transactions), v. 86, no. 48, p. 499–500, doi:10.1029/2005EO480006.

Pallister, J.S., Hoblitt, R., Denlinger, R., Sherrod, D., Cashman, K., Thornber, C., and Moran, S., 2006, Structural geology of the Mount St. Helens fault-gouge zone—field relations along the volcanic conduit-wallrock interface [abs.]: Eos (American Geophysical Union Transactions), v. 87, no. 52, Fall Meeting supplement, Abstract V41A-1703.

Pearce, N.J.G., Perkins, W.T., Westgate, J.A., Gorton, M.P., Jackson, S.E., Neal, C.R., and Chenery, S.P., 1997, A compilation of new and published major and trace element data for NIST SRM 610 and NIST SRM 612 glass reference materials: Geostandards Newsletter, v. 21, p. 115–144.

Reagan, M.K., Cooper, K.M., Pallister, J.S., Thornber, C.R., and Wortel, M., 2008, Timing of degassing and plagioclase growth in lavas erupted from Mount St. Helens, 2004–2005, from ^{210}Po-^{210}Pb-^{226}Ra disequilibria, chap. 37 *of* Sherrod, D.R., Scott, W.E., and Stauffer, P.H., eds., A volcano rekindled; the renewed eruption of Mount St. Helens, 2004–2006: U.S. Geological Survey Professional Paper 1750 (this volume).

Rowe, M.C., Thornber, C.R., and Kent, A.J.R., 2008a, Identification and evolution of the juvenile component in 2004–2005 Mount St. Helens ash, chap. 29 *of* Sherrod, D.R., Scott, W.E., and Stauffer, P.H., eds., A volcano rekindled; the renewed eruption of Mount St. Helens, 2004–2006: U.S. Geological Survey Professional Paper 1750 (this volume).

Rowe, M.C., Thornber, C.R., Gooding, D.J., and Pallister, J.S., 2008b, Catalog of Mount St. Helens 2004–2005 tephra samples with major- and trace-element geochemistry: U.S. Geological Survey Open-File Report 2008–1131, 7 p, with digital database.

Rutherford, M.J., 1993, Experimental petrology applied to volcanic processes: Eos (American Geophysical Union Transactions), v. 74, no. 5, p. 49, 55.

Rutherford, M.J., and Devine, J.D., III, 2008, Magmatic conditions and processes in the storage zone of the 2004–2006 Mount St. Helens dacite, chap. 31 *of* Sherrod, D.R., Scott, W.E., and Stauffer, P.H., eds., A volcano rekindled; the renewed eruption of Mount St. Helens, 2004–2006: U.S. Geological Survey Professional Paper 1750 (this volume).

Rutherford, M.J., and Hill, P.M., 1993, Magma ascent rates from amphibole breakdown; an experimental study applied to the 1980–1986 Mount St. Helens eruptions: Journal of Geophysical Research, v. 98, no. B11, p. 19667–19685.

Rutherford, M.J., Sigurdsson, H., Carey, S., and Davis, A., 1985, The May 18, 1980, eruption of Mount St. Helens; 1, Melt composition and experimental phase equilibria: Journal of Geophysical Research, v. 90, no. B4, p. 2929–2947.

Scandone, R., and Malone, S.D., 1985, Magma supply, magma discharge, and readjustment of the feeding system of Mount St. Helens during 1980: Journal of Volcanology and Geothermal Research, v. 23, nos. 3–4, p. 239–262, doi:10.1016/0377-0273(85)90036-8.

Schilling, S.P., Thompson, R.A., Messerich, J.A., and Iwatsubo, E.Y., 2008, Use of digital aerophotogrammetry to determine rates of lava dome growth, Mount St. Helens, Washington, 2004–2005, chap. 8 *of* Sherrod, D.R., Scott, W.E., and Stauffer, P.H., eds., A volcano rekindled; the renewed eruption of Mount St. Helens, 2004–2006: U.S. Geological Survey Professional Paper 1750 (this volume).

Scott, W.E., Sherrod, D.R., and Gardner, C.A., 2008, Overview of 2004 to 2006, and continuing, eruption of Mount St. Helens, Washington, chap. 1 *of* Sherrod, D.R., Scott, W.E., and Stauffer, P.H., eds., A volcano rekindled; the renewed eruption of Mount St. Helens, 2004–2006: U.S. Geological Survey Professional Paper 1750 (this volume).

Shen, A., and Keppler, H., 1995, Infrared spectroscopy of hydrous silicate melts to 1000°C and 10 kbar; direct observations of H_2O speciation in a diamond anvil cell: American Mineralogist, v. 80, p. 1335–1338.

Sillitoe, R.H., 1973, The tops and bottoms of porphyry copper deposits: Economic Geology, v. 68, no. 6, p. 799–815.

Silver, L.A., and Stolper, E.M., 1989, Water in albitic glasses: Journal of Petrology, v. 30, p. 667–709.

Smith, A.L., and Roobol, M.J., 1990, Mt. Pelée, Martinique; a study of an active island arc volcano: Geological Society of America Memoir 175, 105 p.

Smith, D., 2000, Insights into the evolution of the uppermost continental mantle from xenolith localities on and near the Colorado Plateau and regional comparisons: Journal of Geophysical Research, v. 105, no. B7, p. 16769–16781.

Smith, D.R., and Leeman, W.P., 1987, Petrogenesis of Mount St. Helens dacitic magmas: Journal of Geophysical Research, v. 92, no. B10, p. 10313–10334.

Smith, D.R., and Leeman, W.P., 1993, The origin of Mount St. Helens andesites: Journal of Volcanology and Geothermal Research, v. 55, nos. 3–4, p. 271–303, doi:10.1016/0377-0273(93)90042-P.

Sowerby, J.R., and Keppler, H., 1999, Water speciation in rhyolitic melt determined by in-situ infrared spectroscopy: American Mineralogist, v. 84, p. 1843–1849.

Sparks, R.S.J., Huppert, H.E., Turner, J.S., Sakuyama, M., and O'Hara, M.J., 1984, The fluid dynamics of evolving magma chambers: Philosophical Transactions of the Royal Society of London, Series A, Mathematical and Physical Sciences, v. 310, no. 1514, p. 511–534.

Stormer, J.C., 1983, The effects of recalculation on estimates of temperature and oxygen fugacity from analyses of multicomponent iron-titanium oxides: American Mineralogist, v. 68, p. 586–594.

Streck, M.J., Broderick, C.A., Thornber, C.R., Clynne, M.A., and Pallister, J.S., 2008, Plagioclase populations and zoning in dacite of the 2004–2005 Mount St. Helens eruption; constraints for magma origin and dynamics, chap. 34 *of* Sherrod, D.R., Scott, W.E., and Stauffer, P.H., eds., A volcano rekindled; the renewed eruption of Mount St. Helens, 2004–2006: U.S. Geological Survey Professional Paper 1750 (this volume).

Sun, S.-s., and McDonough, W.F., 1989, Chemical and isotopic systematics of oceanic basalts; implications for mantle composition and processes, *in* Saunders, A.D., and Norry, M.J., eds., Magmatism in the ocean basins: Geological Society of London Special Publication 42, p. 313–345.

Swanson, D.A., and Holcomb, R.T., 1990, Regularities in growth of the Mount St. Helens dacite dome, 1980–1986, *in* Fink, J.H., ed., Lava flows and domes, emplacement mechanisms and hazard implications: Berlin, Springer-Verlag, International Association of Volcanology and Chemistry of the Earth's Interior, Proceedings in Volcanology 2, p. 3–24.

Swanson, D.A., Dzurisin, D., Holcomb, R.T., Iwatsubo, E.Y., Chadwick, W.W., Jr., Casadevall, T.J., Ewert, J.W., and Heliker, C.C., 1987, Growth of the lava dome at Mount St. Helens, Washington (USA), 1981–1983, *in* Fink, J.H., ed., The emplacement of silicic domes and lava flows: Boulder, Colo., Geological Society of America Special Paper 212, p. 1–16.

Taggart, J.E., Jr., Lindsay, J.R., Scott, B.A., Vivit, D.V., Bartel, A.J., and Stewart, K.C., 1987, Analysis of geologic materials by wavelength-dispersive X-ray fluorescence spectrometry, chapter E *of* Baedecker, P.A., ed., Methods for geochemical analysis: U.S Geological Survey Bulletin 1770, p. E1–E19.

Thelen, W.A., Crosson, R.S., and Creager, K.C., 2008, Absolute and relative locations of earthquakes at Mount St. Helens, Washington, using continuous data; implications for magmatic processes, chap. 4 *of* Sherrod, D.R., Scott, W.E., and Stauffer, P.H., eds., A volcano rekindled; the renewed eruption of Mount St. Helens, 2004–2006: U.S. Geological Survey Professional Paper 1750 (this volume).

Thornber, C.R., Pallister, J.S., Lowers, H.A., Rowe, M.C., Mandeville, C.W., and Meeker, G.P., 2008a, Chemistry, mineralogy, and petrology of amphibole in Mount St. Helens 2004–2006 dacite, chap. 32 *of* Sherrod, D.R., Scott, W.E., and Stauffer, P.H., eds., A volcano rekindled; the renewed eruption of Mount St. Helens, 2004–2006: U.S. Geological Survey Professional Paper 1750 (this volume).

Thornber, C.R., Pallister, J.S., Rowe, M.C., McConnell, S., Herriott, T.M., Eckberg, A., Stokes, W.C., Johnson Cornelius, D., Conrey, R.M., Hannah, T., Taggart, J.E., Jr., Adams, M., Lamothe, P.J., Budahn, J.R., and Knaack, C.M., 2008b, Catalog of Mount St. Helens 2004–2007 dome samples with major- and trace-element chemistry: U.S. Geological Survey Open-File Report 2008–1130, 9 p., with digital database.

Tuttle, O.F., and Bowen, N.L., 1958, Origin of granite in the light of experimental studies in the system $NaAlSi_3O_8$-$KAlSi_3O_8$-SiO_2-H_2O: Geological Society of America Memoir 74, 153 p.

Vallance, J.W., Schneider, D.J., and Schilling, S.P., 2008, Growth of the 2004–2006 lava-dome complex at Mount St. Helens, Washington, chap. 9 *of* Sherrod, D.R., Scott, W.E., and Stauffer, P.H., eds., A volcano rekindled; the renewed eruption of Mount St. Helens, 2004–2006: U.S. Geological Survey Professional Paper 1750 (this volume).

Venezky, D.Y., and Rutherford, M.J., 1999, Petrology and Fe-Ti oxide reequilibration of the 1991 Mount Unzen mixed magma: Journal of Volcanology and Geothermal Research, v. 89, no. 1, p. 213–230, doi:10.1016/S0377-0273(98)00133-4.

Waite, G.P., and Moran, S.C., 2006, Crustal P-wave speed structure under Mount St. Helens from local earthquake tomography [abs.]: Eos (American Geophysical Union Transactions), v. 87, no. 52, Fall Meeting supplement, Abstract V11B-0578.

Watts, R.B., Heard, R.A., Sparks, R.S.J., and Young, S.R., 2002, Growth patterns and emplacement of the andesitic lava dome at Soufrière Hills Volcano, Montserrat, *in* Druitt, T.H., and Kokelaar, B.P., eds., The eruption of Soufrière Hills Volcano, Montserrat, from 1995 to 1999: Geological Society of London Memoir 21, p. 115–152.

Weaver, C.S., Grant, W.C., and Shemeta, J.E., 1987, Local crustal extension at Mount St. Helens, Washington: Journal of Geophysical Research, v. 92, no. B10, p. 10170–10178.

White, R.A., 1996, Precursory deep long-period earthquakes at Mount Pinatubo; spatio-temporal link to basalt trigger, *in* Newhall, C.G., and Punongbayan, R.S., Fire and mud; eruptions and lahars of Mount Pinatubo, Philippines: Seattle, University of Washington Press, p. 307–328.

Williams, D.L., Abrams, G., Finn., C., Dzurisin, D., Johnson, D.J., and Denlinger, R., 1987, Evidence from gravity data for an intrusive complex beneath Mount St Helens: Journal of Geophysical Research, v. 92, no. B10, p. 10207–10222.

Williams, H., 1932, The history and character of volcanic domes: University of California Bulletin of the Department of Geological Science, v. 21, p. 51–146.

Yamaguchi, D.K., and Hoblitt, R.P., 1995, Tree-ring dating of pre-1980 volcanic flowage deposits at Mount St. Helens, Washington: Geological Society of America Bulletin, v. 107, p. 1077–1093.

Tables 2–9

Table 2. Modal data for samples from 2004–2006 Mount St. Helens lava dome. Further explanation of methods in "Laboratory Methods" section.

[Optical modes, as volume percent, are derived by counting 1,000 or 1,300 points at 100× magnification. Grains and voids smaller than 30 μm in maximum dimension are counted as matrix, consequently most silica phases, which occur mainly as late-stage microlites, were not detected (n.d.) by optical point counting. Some grains were large enough to detect and count, but as late-stage phases, they were not included in the total phenocryst counts. TS, thin section; DRE, dense-rock-equivalent abundances. DRE calculated by subtracting voids and renormalizing the optical modes and microbeam "ALL" modes. Dashes indicate absence of a value (for example, as in no void space in recalculated DRE columns). Hornblende, used informally for a range of amphibole compositions, forms large (1–3 mm) phenocrysts; consequently its abundance in individual sections may not be statistically representative.

Microbeam map analysis modes, as volume percent, derived from image analysis of 1-cm^2 microprobe-stage raster maps of X-ray intensities for Si, Al, Mg, Fe, K and backscattered electron intensity, combined with image analysis of SEM backscattered electron images of 100-μm^2 areas.

Columns labeled "All" tabulate complete modal analysis, including microlites (1–30 μm maximum diameter), obtained by microbeam imaging at scales of 1 cm^2 and 100 μm^2.

Probe DRE for phenocryst abundance calculated from 1,024 analyses of 1-μm spots distributed over a 1-cm^2 grid and binned (after excluding 262 analyses with totals >102 percent or <85 percent) according to mineral types and glass using the following compositional and stoichiometric rules:
Plagioclase if Si+Al = 3.85–4.15 (based on 8 oxygens) and K_2O <2 percent;
Anorthoclase if Si+Al = 3.85–4.15 (based on 8 oxygens) and K_2O >2 percent;
Hypersthene if MgO >17 percent;
Hornblende if MgO = 8–17 percent and Na_2O>1 percent;
Quartz if SiO_2>78 percent;
Silica phase (tridymite, cristobalite) if SiO_2 =72–78 percent;
Fe-Ti oxide if FeO+TiO_2 >30 percent and SiO_2 <10 percent.

Plagioclase category as part of microprobe analysis may include anorthoclase, except where counted separately in the analysis of SH315-4.

Microlite abundance calculated by subtracting total crystals determined by microbeam analysis from phenocryst abundance determined by microbeam (m) or optical (o) methods.

Values for glass by K_2O balance are weight percent and calculated on a volatile-free basis from the percentage of glass needed to give the K_2O determined by bulk chemical analysis. To convert to volume percent, multiply by 1.1]

	SH304-2A, spine 3 1,000 points counted				SH304-2G1, spine 3 1,000 points counted		SH305-1A, spine 3 1,300 points counted			SH315-4, spine 4 1,300 points counted	
Optical mode, percent	TS	DRE	TS	DRE	TS	DRE	TS	TS	DRE	TS	DRE
Plagioclase	30	31	31	32	22	22	27	27	30	39	39
Hypersthene	4	4	4	4	3	3	4	4	5	6	6
Hornblende	8	8	2	2	2	2	4	4	4	4	4
Oxides	2	2	2	2	1	1	2	2	2	2	2
Silica phases	n.d.	n.d.	n.d.	n.d.	n.d.	n.d.	0.2	0.2	0.2	n.d.	n.d.
Voids	2	--	2	--	0.4	--	9	9	--	1	--
Matrix	55	55	59	60	72	73	53	53	59	49	49
Sum	100	100	100	100	100	100	100	100	100	100	100
Phenocrysts	44	45	39	40	27	27	37	37	41	51	51

Table 2. Modal data for samples from 2004–2006 Mount St. Helens lava dome. Further explanation of methods in "Laboratory Methods" section.—Continued

	SH304-2A, spine 3 1,000 points counted				SH304-2G1, spine 3 1,000 points counted			SH305-1A, spine 3 1,300 points counted			SH315-4, spine 4 1,300 points counted
								SH-305-1A			Probe (DRE)
Microbeam map analysis, percent	TS	DRE	ALL	DRE	TS	All	DRE	TS	All	DRE	DRE
Plagioclase	32	35	47	64	22	22	22	32	33	52	48
Anorthoclase	n.d.	n.d.	n.d.	n.d.	n.d.	n.d.	n.d.	n.d.	n.d.	n.d.	15
Hypersthene	3	4	4	5	2	4	4	5	5	8	5
Hornblende	5	6	6	8	2	2	2	3	3	6	3
Oxides	1	1	1	1	0.3	0.4	0.4	1	1	2	1
Silica phases	n.d.	n.d.	n.d.	n.d.	n.d.	n.d.	n.d.	n.d.	1	2	16
Voids	8	--	25	--	1	1	--	36	37	--	--
Glass	n.d.	n.d.	17	22	73	71	72	18	19	30	13
Matrix	50	55	—	—	—	—	—	4	—	—	—
Sum	100	100	100	100	100	100	100	100	100	100	100
Phenocrysts	42	45	--	45	26	--	--	41	--	--	--
Total crystals	--	--	58	78	--	28	28	--	43	69	87
Microlites (m)	--	--	--	33	--	--	2	--	--	29	--
Microlites (o)	--	--	--	38	--	--	1	--	--	28	37
					Glass K_2O	Bulk K_2O	Percent glass	Glass K_2O	Bulk K_2O	Percent glass	
K_2O weight percent					3.38	1.83		5.09	1.41		
Glass by K_2O balance							54			28	

	SH319-1, spine 5 1,300 points counted		SH321-1A, spine 6 1,300 points counted		SH325-1A, spine 7 1,300 points counted		Average microcrystalline dacite		
Optical mode, percent	TS	DRE	TS	DRE	TS	DRE	TS	DRE	SD
Plagioclase	36.3	36.9	37.1	37.8	33.8	34.4	33.9	34.8	3.7
Hypersthene	5.2	5.3	6.3	6.4	2.5	2.6	4.7	4.8	1.4
Hornblende	5.5	5.6	3.5	3.6	2.6	2.7	4.6	4.7	2.0
Oxides	1.4	1.4	1.1	1.1	1.4	1.4	1.6	1.6	0.4
Silica phases	1.1	1.1	1.0	1.0	1.1	1.1	0.8	0.9	0.4
Voids	1.6	--	1.8	--	1.8	--	2.8	--	--
Matrix	48.8	49.6	49.2	50.1	56.8	57.8	51.9	53.5	4.4
Sum	100.0	100.0	100.0	100.0	100.0	100.0	100.3	100.3	0.1
Phenocrysts	48.5	49.3	49.0	48.9	41.4	41.1	45.6	46.0	4.3

Table 3. Electron-microprobe analyses of matrix minerals in 2004–2006 dacite.

[Oxides in weight percent. Anorthite (An), albite (Ab), and orthoclase (Or) components expressed as molecular percent. Cation totals based on recalculation of atomic proportions using eight oxygen anions. Detection limits are about 0.01 percent; values less than this amount are reported as 0.00 percent.]

Sample No.	SiO_2	Al_2O_3	FeO	MgO	CaO	Na_2O	K_2O	TiO_2	P_2O_5	MnO	BaO	Total	An	Ab	Or	Total
Anorthoclase and orthoclase microlites (less than 30 µm)																
SH322-1-d-7	68.3	18.3	0.47	0.00	0.40	5.73	6.70	0.06	0.02	0.01	0.13	100.1	2	55	43	4.91
SH322-1-d-5	65.3	21.5	0.37	0.02	2.95	7.54	2.50	0.04	0.03	0.00	0.04	100.2	15	70	15	4.95
Plagioclase microlites (less than 30 µm)																
SH322-1-d-4	60.9	24.0	0.36	0.00	5.05	7.58	1.48	0.03	0.01	0.00	0.07	99.5	25	67	9	5.00
SH321-1C-7d-3 (i)	62.3	23.0	0.52	0.00	3.77	8.00	1.42	0.05	0.01	0.00	0.10	99.2	19	73	8	4.99
SH321-1C-7b-2 (h)	60.8	24.5	0.48	0.00	5.43	7.53	1.11	0.04	0.00	0.01	0.04	99.9	27	67	6	4.99
SH321-1C-7c-7 (h)	59.9	25.0	0.47	0.00	6.14	7.42	0.93	0.01	0.00	0.00	0.03	99.8	30	65	5	5.01
SH321-1C-7d-2 (i)	60.3	24.3	0.51	0.02	5.32	7.62	0.82	0.01	0.01	0.01	0.07	99.0	26	69	5	5.00
SH321-1C-7d-1 (i)	57.0	26.6	0.58	0.00	8.14	6.66	0.45	0.03	0.00	0.01	0.02	99.5	39	58	3	5.02
Plagioclase microphenocryst (100 µm)																
SH322-1-b-17	58.6	26.2	0.43	0.01	7.46	6.94	0.58	0.00	0.01	0.01	0.03	100.3	36	61	3	5.01
SH322-1-b-18	59.5	25.8	0.35	0.01	6.76	7.45	0.40	0.02	0.02	0.00	0.05	100.3	33	65	2	5.01
SH322-1-b-19	58.5	26.0	0.31	0.00	7.36	7.23	0.23	0.03	0.00	0.00	0.06	99.7	36	63	1	5.01
SH322-1-b-20	59.8	25.5	0.49	0.00	6.83	7.35	0.67	0.01	0.00	0.01	0.07	100.7	33	64	4	5.01
Quartz microlites																
SH321-1C-7c-6 (h)	100.0	0.14	0.29	0.01	0.01	0.00	0.03	0.04	0.00	0.01	0.02	100.6				4.01
SH321-1C-7b-4 (h)	98.3	0.38	0.16	0.01	0.02	0.07	0.05	0.07	0.01	0.00	0.05	99.2				4.01
SH321-1C-7d-4 (i)	99.6	0.12	0.17	0.01	0.01	0.02	0.00	0.04	0.00	0.00	0.01	99.9				4.01
SH321-1C-7d-5 (i)	99.5	0.07	0.16	0.00	0.03	0.00	0.01	0.06	0.00	0.00	0.02	99.9				4.00
SH322-1-d-3	98.7	0.63	0.11	0.02	0.05	0.13	0.05	0.10	0.00	0.02	0.03	99.8				4.02
Tridymite microlites																
SH322-1-b-9	99.1	1.06	0.07	0.00	0.01	0.40	0.02	0.12	0.00	0.00	0.02	100.8				4.04
SH322-1-b-10	99.3	0.94	0.07	0.00	0.02	0.34	0.02	0.06	0.01	0.01	0.01	100.7				4.03
SH322-1-b-11	98.7	1.02	0.11	0.00	0.03	0.39	0.02	0.10	0.01	0.00	0.00	100.3				4.04
SH322-1-d-2	97.0	1.52	0.09	0.00	0.03	0.41	0.11	0.11	0.00	0.02	0.07	99.4				4.05
Cristobalite microlites																
SH312-1	93.9	4.27	0.35	0.00	0.15	0.71	0.68	0.15	0.00	0.01	0.04	100.3				4.13
SH321-1C-7b-5 (h)	93.3	3.57	0.25	0.03	0.36	1.27	0.39	0.08	0.01	0.02	0.00	99.3				4.15

Table 4. Electron-microprobe analyses of matrix glass and glass inclusions in 2004–2006 Mount St. Helens dacite and two quenched inclusions from the dacite.

[Oxide abundances in weight percent; Cl and S recalculated as ppm. Sample numbers follow standard format (for example, SH305-1) but have additional coding for specific thin section, spot number; may show additional feature, "core," to refer to melt inclusions in reacted core of plagioclase. Size indicates beam diameter, in microns. Phases coded as m, matrix; i, inclusion; p, plagioclase; h, hypersthene; a, amphibole; o, oxide. For inclusions, codes combined to show host mineral. Count rates were monitored for Na, K, and Si during each analysis, and these elements were corrected for migration as described in "Laboratory Methods" section. H_2O calculated by difference. Detection limit, D.L., for S ranges between 70 and 86 ppm and corresponds to the value at which one standard deviation is equivalent to 66 percent of the reported value. Lower values reported for S whenever a peak is detected above background, along with larger standard deviation. None detected, n.d., indicates no peak detected above background levels. Column headed "SD, S" shows standard deviation for S, in percent, based on counting statistics for individual analyses; dashes in this column are for analyses in which no S peak was detected. Dashes in other columns indicate insufficient data to calculate meaningful averages or standard deviations.]

Sample and Spot No.	Size	Phase	SiO_2	Al_2O_3	FeO	MgO	CaO	Na_2O	K_2O	TiO_2	P_2O_5	MnO	BaO	Cl	SO_3	Total	H_2O	Cl	S	D.L.	SD, S
Glass inclusions in microcrystalline dacite																					
SH305-1kc g-6 (core)	1	ip	77.7	11.2	1.02	0.22	0.34	2.82	5.33	0.33	0.05	0.01	0.08	0.081	n.d.	99.23	0.8	810	n.d.	70	--
SH305-1kc g-7 (core)	1	ip	77.3	10.7	1.52	0.26	0.38	2.66	5.32	0.54	0.05	0.00	0.07	0.120	n.d.	98.94	1.1	1,200	n.d.	73	--
SH305-1kc g-8 (core)	1	ip	76.8	11.2	1.28	0.18	0.31	2.56	5.36	0.55	0.09	0.02	0.07	0.084	n.d.	98.45	1.6	840	n.d.	76	--
SH305-1kc g-9 (core)	1	ip	77.2	11.1	1.19	0.18	0.37	2.59	5.40	0.49	0.07	0.01	0.08	0.064	n.d.	98.74	1.3	640	n.d.	70	--
SH305-1kc g-10 (core)	1	ip	77.9	11.1	1.25	0.18	0.33	2.60	5.24	0.46	0.05	0.03	0.09	0.057	n.d.	99.28	0.7	570	n.d.	74	--
SH305-1kc g-12 (core)	1	ip	77.4	10.8	0.96	0.04	0.23	2.68	5.16	0.35	0.07	0.00	0.05	0.060	n.d.	97.77	2.2	600	n.d.	73	--
SH305-1kc g-5	1	ip	77.3	11.0	1.14	0.26	0.37	2.61	5.37	0.27	0.04	0.01	0.07	0.086	0.013	98.49	1.5	860	52	66	75
SH305-1kc g-21	1	ip	78.0	11.6	1.21	0.11	0.38	2.49	5.01	0.45	0.10	0.01	0.04	0.040	0.007	99.43	0.6	400	26	70	150
SH305-1kc g-22	1	ih	76.6	12.4	1.35	0.03	0.27	3.01	5.72	0.34	0.08	0.01	0.05	0.110	n.d.	99.97	0.0	1,100	n.d.	75	--
SH305-1kc g-27	1	ih	71.5	16.8	1.61	1.42	0.99	4.09	2.37	0.17	0.09	0.05	0.06	0.052	0.062	99.27	0.7	520	250	71	18
SH305-1kc g-23	1	ih	76.8	12.1	1.12	0.01	0.24	3.02	5.63	0.31	0.05	0.02	0.06	0.096	n.d.	99.45	0.5	960	n.d.	75	--
SH305-1kc g-25	1	ia	74.3	13.3	0.98	0.08	0.38	3.14	5.50	0.64	0.07	0.00	0.07	0.145	0.007	98.61	1.4	1,450	26	70	154
Average			76.6	11.9	1.22	0.25	0.38	2.85	5.12	0.41	0.07	0.02	0.07	0.08	0.022	98.97	1.0	829	--	72	--
Standard deviation			1.9	1.7	0.20	0.38	0.20	0.44	0.88	0.14	0.02	0.01	0.01	0.03	0.027	0.59	0.6	309	--	--	--
SH304-2A9b hb1	1	ia	75.0	13.7	0.84	0.01	0.88	2.45	5.23	0.20	0.02	0.01	0.10	0.105	0.012	98.54	1.5	1,050	48	86	110
SH304-2A9b hb1	20	ia	75.3	13.6	0.86	0.01	0.85	2.03	4.98	0.23	0.06	0.04	0.11	0.112	0.007	98.16	1.8	1,120	27	86	216
SH304-2A9b hb1	20	ia	75.2	13.5	0.87	0.01	0.88	2.32	5.09	0.19	0.01	0.00	0.10	0.103	n.d.	98.37	1.6	1,030	n.d.	85	--
SH304-2A9b hb6	5	ia	74.1	12.9	0.81	0.01	0.63	3.44	5.55	0.22	0.03	0.03	0.10	0.125	n.d.	97.93	2.1	1,250	n.d.	85	--
SH304-2A9b lghb gl1	1	ia	74.0	14.2	0.91	0.12	0.80	3.69	5.02	0.17	0.05	0.02	0.10	0.139	0.022	99.25	0.7	1,390	86	84	63
SH304-2A9b lghb gl2	1	ia	74.0	14.1	0.93	0.11	0.77	3.96	5.17	0.21	0.07	0.03	0.08	0.139	n.d.	99.58	0.4	1,390	n.d.	85	--
SH304-2A9b lghb gl3	1	ia	72.1	15.7	1.00	0.24	1.40	4.38	4.20	0.17	0.16	0.02	0.06	0.100	0.012	99.54	0.5	1,000	48	85	106
SH304-2A9b lghb gl4	1	ia	73.4	15.6	0.84	0.19	1.35	4.21	3.42	0.19	0.08	0.04	0.08	0.113	0.030	99.55	0.4	1,130	118	84	45
SH304-2A9b lghb gl5	1	ia	73.9	15.7	0.83	0.20	1.25	4.12	3.36	0.12	0.10	0.05	0.12	0.112	0.032	99.93	0.1	1,120	129	83	41
SH304-2A9b lghb gl6-1	1	ia	73.7	15.7	0.82	0.18	1.33	4.24	3.38	0.16	0.12	0.05	0.08	0.107	0.020	99.92	0.1	1,070	81	85	69
Average			74.1	14.5	0.87	0.11	1.01	3.48	4.54	0.19	0.07	0.03	0.09	0.12	0.019	99.08	0.9	1,155	--	--	--
Standard deviation			1.0	1.1	0.06	0.09	0.29	0.89	0.87	0.03	0.05	0.02	0.02	0.01	0.010	0.75	0.8	142	--	--	--
Matrix glass in microcrystalline dacite																					
SH305-1kc g-1	1	m	77.7	13.3	0.63	0.02	0.69	2.20	4.47	0.27	0.06	0.02	0.06	0.026	n.d.	99.38	0.6	260	n.d.	75	--
SH305-1kc g-30	1	m	75.8	12.1	0.70	0.02	0.41	3.36	5.37	0.34	0.07	0.01	0.03	0.030	0.013	98.24	1.8	300	52	76	91
SH305-1kc g-33	1	m	76.8	11.8	0.68	0.02	0.19	2.21	5.24	0.33	0.08	0.00	0.04	0.036	0.021	97.41	2.6	360	83	74	56
SH305-1ag-1	1	m	76.3	14.2	0.64	0.03	0.92	4.00	4.74	0.27	0.07	0.01	0.04	0.024	n.d.	101.28	0.0	240	n.d.	75	--
SH305-1ag-35	1	m	77.4	11.9	0.83	0.03	0.23	2.97	5.63	0.31	0.05	0.01	0.03	0.023	n.d.	99.42	0.6	230	n.d.	75	--
Average			76.8	12.7	0.69	0.02	0.49	2.95	5.09	0.30	0.07	0.01	0.04	0.03	0.017	99.15	1.1	278	--	--	--
Standard deviation			0.8	1.0	0.08	0.01	0.31	0.77	0.48	0.03	0.01	0.01	0.01	0.01	0.006	1.46	1.0	53	--	--	--

Table 4. Electron-microprobe analyses of matrix glass and glass inclusions in 2004–2006 Mount St. Helens dacite and two quenched inclusions from the dacite.—Continued

[Oxide abundances in weight percent; Cl and S recalculated as ppm. Sample numbers follow standard format (for example, SH305-1) but have additional coding for specific thin section, spot number; may show additional feature, "core," to refer to melt inclusions in reacted core of plagioclase. Size indicates beam diameter, in microns. Phases coded as m, matrix; i, inclusion; p, plagioclase; h, hypersthene; a, amphibole; o, oxide. For inclusions, codes combined to show host mineral. Count rates were monitored for Na, K, and Si during each analysis, and these elements were corrected for migration as described in "Laboratory Methods" section. H_2O calculated by difference. Detection limit, D.L., for S ranges between 70 and 86 ppm and corresponds to the value at which one standard deviation is equivalent to 66 percent of the reported value. Lower values reported for S whenever a peak is detected above background, along with larger standard deviation. None detected, n.d., indicates no peak detected above background levels. Column headed "SD, S" shows standard deviation for S, in percent, based on counting statistics for individual analyses; dashes in this column are for analyses in which no S peak was detected. Dashes in other columns indicate insufficient data to calculate meaningful averages or standard deviations.]

Sample and Spot No.	Size	Phase	SiO2	Al2O3	FeO	MgO	CaO	Na_2O	K_2O	TiO_2	P_2O_5	MnO	BaO	Cl	SO_3	Total	H_2O	Cl	S	D.L.	SD, S
Matrix glass in glassy flow-banded dacite																					
SH304-2G1g1-m1	5	m	73.5	13.9	0.91	0.04	1.31	3.96	3.30	0.22	0.07	0.01	0.09	0.089	n.d.	97.40	2.6	890	n.d.	85	--
SH304-2G1g1-m2	5	m	73.1	13.9	1.17	0.17	1.40	4.26	3.38	0.16	0.06	0.01	0.04	0.079	n.d.	97.67	2.3	790	n.d.	85	--
SH304-2G1g1-m3	5	m	73.5	13.9	1.22	0.11	1.37	4.22	3.39	0.21	0.04	0.03	0.07	0.089	n.d.	98.08	1.9	890	n.d.	85	--
SH304-2G1g1-m4	20	m	73.5	13.8	0.98	0.10	1.06	4.19	3.50	0.19	0.02	0.02	0.07	0.089	n.d.	97.59	2.4	890	n.d.	85	--
SH304-2G1g1-m5	1	m	73.6	14.0	0.87	0.04	1.30	4.15	3.46	0.21	0.04	0.00	0.07	0.084	0.008	97.87	2.1	840	34	84	139
SH304-2G1g1-m6	1	m	73.3	13.9	1.02	0.10	1.28	4.05	3.45	0.17	0.05	0.04	0.09	0.089	n.d.	97.49	2.5	890	n.d.	85	--
SH304-2G1g1-m7	1	m	73.3	13.9	1.09	0.12	1.19	3.92	3.51	0.18	0.07	0.03	0.08	0.087	0.008	97.41	2.6	870	34	84	142
SH304-2G1g1-m8	1	m	73.2	14.0	0.96	0.08	1.18	4.09	3.55	0.21	0.07	0.03	0.09	0.088	n.d.	97.55	2.5	880	n.d.	85	--
SH304-2G1g1-m9	1	m	73.7	13.8	0.89	0.04	1.18	4.17	3.59	0.18	0.05	0.02	0.09	0.088	n.d.	97.81	2.2	880	n.d.	85	--
SH304-2G1g1-m10	1	m	73.3	14.0	0.79	0.04	1.19	4.23	3.62	0.22	0.03	0.01	0.06	0.084	n.d.	97.52	2.5	840	n.d.	85	--
SH304-2G1g1-m11	1	m	73.6	14.0	0.94	0.06	1.44	4.20	3.16	0.20	0.09	0.04	0.07	0.081	n.d.	97.89	2.1	810	n.d.	85	--
SH304-2G5g1	40	m	74.3	12.5	1.18	0.10	1.15	4.76	2.61	0.24	0.02	0.00	0.07	0.075	n.d.	96.98	3.0	750	n.d.	85	--
Average			73.5	13.8	1.00	0.08	1.25	4.18	3.38	0.20	0.05	0.02	0.07	0.09	0.008	97.61	2.4	852	--	--	--
Standard deviation			0.3	0.4	0.14	0.04	0.11	0.21	0.27	0.02	0.02	0.01	0.01	0.00	0.000	0.29	0.3	47	--	--	--
Glass inclusions in glassy flow-banded dacite																					
SH304-2G1g1-g1	1	io	73.9	14.0	1.33	0.10	1.43	4.34	3.11	0.48	0.07	0.00	0.09	0.099	n.d.	98.95	1.1	990	n.d.	85	--
SH304-2G1g3-1	1	ih	73.6	14.0	0.94	0.02	1.48	4.08	3.17	0.21	0.01	0.01	0.08	0.086	n.d.	97.74	2.3	860	n.d.	85	--
SH304-2Gg4-1	1	ih	76.4	12.2	0.85	0.07	1.00	3.88	3.29	0.03	0.06	0.05	0.08	0.082	0.005	97.96	2.0	820	19	86	232
SH304-2Gg6-1	1	ip	72.9	14.5	0.54	0.01	2.47	5.59	2.26	0.13	0.06	0.03	0.06	0.081	0.010	98.59	1.4	810	38	85	132
Average			74.2	13.7	0.92	0.05	1.60	4.47	2.96	0.21	0.05	0.02	0.08	0.09	0.007	98.31	1.7	870	--	--	--
Standard deviation			1.5	1.0	0.33	0.04	0.62	0.77	0.47	0.19	0.02	0.02	0.01	0.01	0.003	0.56	0.6	83	--	--	--
Glass inclusion in dacite fragment in gouge																					
11-4 gou gr7	1	ih	63.7	17.8	2.78	0.23	3.32	4.90	2.41	1.24	0.41	0.03	0.06	0.281	0.031	97.17	2.8	2,810	125	75	37
Matrix glass in fragments from tephra erupted January 16, 2005																					
WS_1_19 g1	20	m	70.6	14.7	2.10	0.52	2.21	4.89	2.17	0.38	0.11	0.07	0.08	0.076	n.d.	97.96	2.0	760	n.d.	75	--
WS_1_19 g2	20	m	70.7	14.7	2.11	0.54	2.25	4.90	2.19	0.37	0.07	0.05	0.07	0.080	n.d.	98.07	1.9	800	n.d.	75	--
WS_1_19 2-22	20	m	71.0	14.5	2.13	0.46	2.07	3.88	2.16	0.32	0.07	0.04	0.07	0.088	n.d.	96.73	3.3	880	n.d.	75	--
WS_1_19 2-23	20	m	71.5	14.8	1.99	0.48	2.24	4.97	2.09	0.33	0.08	0.04	0.04	0.075	n.d.	98.58	1.4	750	n.d.	75	--
WS_1_19 5-25	20	m	73.5	12.7	1.80	0.28	1.30	4.41	2.56	0.36	0.09	0.03	0.07	0.083	n.d.	97.26	2.7	830	n.d.	75	--
WS_1_19 5-26	20	m	73.1	12.8	1.84	0.26	1.30	4.43	2.46	0.41	0.08	0.03	0.06	0.087	n.d.	96.84	3.2	870	n.d.	75	--
Average			71.7	14.0	2.0	0.4	1.9	4.6	2.3	0.4	0.1	0.0	0.1	0.1	n.d.	97.6	2.4	815	--	--	--
Standard deviation			1.3	1.0	0.1	0.1	0.5	0.4	0.2	0.0	0.0	0.0	0.0	0.0	n.d.	0.7	0.7	55	--	--	--
Glass inclusions in fragments from tephra erupted January 16, 2005																					
WS_1_19 gi-43	1	io	73.8	14.9	1.01	0.02	0.30	4.71	4.00	0.61	0.05	0.03	0.07	0.389	0.012	99.87	0.1	3,890	47	72	97
WS_1_19 gi-44	1	io	74.3	15.1	0.94	0.02	0.58	5.84	3.14	0.55	0.12	0.01	0.07	0.369	n.d.	101.05	0.0	3,690	n.d.	75	--

Table 5. Major-element compositions of host dacite and small quenched inclusions from 2004–2006 Mount St. Helens dome lava.

[Oxides reported as weight percent. Compositions determined by automated electron-microprobe, sampling from 736 to 1,021 points distributed across gridded areas of polished sections and compared with bulk rock X-ray fluorescence (XRF) analyses of the dacite. Rejected were analyses with totals greater than 102 percent or less than 85 percent (resulting from, for example, beam overlap with void space in the microprobe mount). Comparison of normalized average composition of host by microprobe to that by XRF shows excellent agreement (within 1 percent) for SiO_2 and Na_2O, good agreement (within 7 percent of reported value) for Al_2O_3, CaO, and K_2O, and moderate (microprobe average is 30 percent low relative to XRF analysis MgO) to poor agreement (microprobe average is 47–72 percent low for TiO_2, FeO, and MnO). Poor agreement attributed to undersampling of small oxide grains in the microprobe analyses, many of which were likely rejected due to low totals. See "Laboratory Methods" section for additional information on methodology.]

Sample No.	SiO_2	Al_2O_3	$FeTO_3$	MgO	CaO	Na_2O	K_2O	TiO_2	MnO	Total
SH315-4 host [1]										
758 point average	62.11	17.54	2.82	1.36	4.83	4.30	1.25	0.34	0.04	94.57
Normalized to 100%	65.67	18.54	2.98	1.44	5.10	4.55	1.32	0.36	0.05	100.00
SH315-4 host by XRF	65.16	17.24	4.38	1.87	4.75	4.49	1.41	0.61	0.07	100.00
Correction factors[2]	0.99	0.93	1.47	1.30	0.93	0.99	1.07	1.72	1.53	1.00
SH315-4 inclusion [3]										
724 point average	58.95	16.47	5.95	4.06	6.40	3.54	1.19	0.87	0.06	97.50
Normalized to 100%	60.47	16.89	6.10	4.17	6.56	3.63	1.22	0.89	0.06	100.00
Corrected analysis	60.00	15.71	8.98	5.43	6.11	3.59	1.31	1.54	0.10	100.00
SH321-1C inclusion [4]										
523 point average	64.31	16.99	4.30	1.85	5.09	4.07	1.23	0.52	0.05	98.42
Normalized to 100%	65.34	17.27	4.37	1.88	5.17	4.14	1.25	0.53	0.05	100.00
Corrected analysis	64.84	16.06	6.43	2.45	4.81	4.09	1.34	0.92	0.07	100.00

[1] Rejected were 263 analyses from 1,021 total points analyzed.

[2] Correction factors are abundance ratios of microprobe to XRF data, used to correct microprobe analyses.

[3] Rejected were 236 analyses from 960 total points analyzed.

[4] Rejected were 213 analyses from 736 total points analyzed.

Table 6. Fourier-transform infrared (FTIR) spectrographic analyses of matrix glass in samples SH304-2G1 and SH304-2G2.

[Abs, absorbance at the indicated wavenumber (for example, 4,500 cm^{-1}). Absorbance at wavenumber 2,350 cm^{-1} was below detection level of 20 ppm as CO_2. Water and hydroxyl groups all reported in weight percent; H_2Ot, total dissolved water; H_2Om, molecular water; OH^-, dissolved water as hydroxyl groups. For data reduction purposes, standard values from Newman and others (1986) used for molar absorptivity, ε, for water in rhyolitic glass. They are ε_{3750} cm^{-1}=68; ε_{1630} cm^{-1}=55; ε_{5200} cm^{-1}=1.61; ε_{4500} cm^{-1}=1.73.]

Sample No.	Abs 4500 cm^{-1}	Abs 5200 cm^{-1}	Abs 3570 cm^{-1}	Abs 1630 cm^{-1}	Thickness cm	Density g/L	H_2Ot 3570 cm^{-1}	H_2Om 1630 cm^{-1}	H_2Om 5200 cm^{-1}	$OH^{=}$ 4500 cm^{-1}	H_2Ot[3] 4500 + 5200 cm^{-1}	H_2Ot 4500 + 1630 cm^{-1}
SH304-2G1-s1	0.0045	0.0069	0.520	0.248	0.00372	2317	1.598	0.942	0.896	0.544	1.439	1.486
SH304-2G1-s2	0.0057	0.0070	0.672	0.307	0.00372	2317	2.066	1.167	0.909	0.689	1.597	1.855
SH304-2G1-s3	0.0041	0.0075	0.469	0.230	0.00372	2317	1.442	0.874	0.974	0.495	1.469	1.369
SH304-2G1-s4	0.0062	0.0070	0.649	0.285	0.00372	2317	1.995	1.083	0.909	0.749	1.658	1.832
SH304-2G1-s5	0.0056	0.0066	0.639	0.289	0.00372	2317	1.964	1.098	0.857	0.677	1.533	1.775
SH304-2G1-s6	0.0070	0.0090	0.837	0.369	0.0053	2317	1.806	0.984	0.820	0.594	1.414	1.578
SH304-2G1-s7	0.0080	0.0100	0.879	0.406	0.0053	2317	1.896	1.083	0.911	0.678	1.590	1.761
SH304-2G1-s8	0.0077	0.0098	0.859	0.382	0.0053	2317	1.853	1.019	0.893	0.653	1.546	1.672
SH304-2G1-s9	0.0088	0.0100	1.020	0.436	0.0062	2317	1.881	0.994	0.779	0.638	1.417	1.632
SH304-2G1-s10	0.0090	0.0110	1.028	0.462	0.0062	2317	1.896	1.053	0.857	0.652	1.509	1.706
SH304-2G1-s11	0.0049	0.0079	0.662	0.292	0.00372	2317	2.035	1.110	1.026	0.592	1.618	1.702
SH304-2G1-s12	0.007	0.0066	0.778	0.347	0.005	2317	1.779	0.981	0.637	0.629	1.267	1.610
SH304-2G1-s13	0.005	0.0070	0.645	0.315	0.00372	2317	1.983	1.197	0.909	0.604	1.513	1.801
SH304-2G1-s14	0.0064	0.0067	0.544	0.256	0.00372	2317	1.672	0.973	0.870	0.773	1.643	1.746
SH304-2G1-s15	0.008	0.0110	0.876	0.396	0.0053	2317	1.890	1.056	1.002	0.678	1.681	1.735
SH304-2G1-s16	0.01	0.0130	1.148	0.516	0.0062	2317	2.117	1.177	1.013	0.725	1.737	1.901
Average							1.867	1.049	0.891	0.648	1.539	1.698
Standard deviation							0.178	0.090	0.096	0.072	0.121	0.139
SH304-2G2-s1	0.0097	0.0137	1.069	0.484	0.0052	2323	2.345	1.312	1.269	0.836	2.105	2.149
SH304-2G2-s2	0.0084	0.0127	1.053	0.488	0.0052	2323	2.309	1.323	1.176	0.724	1.901	2.047
SH304-2G2-s3	0.0145	0.0172	1.558	0.651	0.0078	2323	2.278	1.177	1.062	0.833	1.896	2.010
SH304-2G2-s4	0.0095	0.0155	1.149	0.514	0.0052	2323	2.520	1.394	1.436	0.819	2.255	2.213
SH304-2G2-s5	0.017	0.0160	1.685	0.767	0.0078	2323	2.464	1.387	0.988	0.977	1.965	2.364
SH304-2G2-s6	0.0129	0.0172	1.601	0.723	0.0078	2323	2.341	1.307	1.062	0.741	1.804	2.048
SH304-2G2-s7	0.0092	0.0110	0.988	0.445	0.0052	2323	2.167	1.207	1.019	0.793	1.812	2.000
SH304-2G2-s8	0.0142	0.0163	1.619	0.733	0.0078	2323	2.367	1.325	1.007	0.816	1.823	2.141
SH304-2G2-s9	0.0106	0.0165	1.357	0.612	0.0078	2323	1.984	1.106	1.019	0.609	1.628	1.716
SH304-2G2-s10	0.013	0.0162	1.549	0.716	0.0078	2323	2.265	1.294	1.000	0.747	1.748	2.041
Average							2.304	1.283	1.104	0.790	1.894	2.073
Standard deviation							0.150	0.092	0.147	0.095	0.180	0.168

Table 7. Major elements and Zr by X-ray fluorescence (XRF) and selected trace-element analyses by inductively coupled plasma mass spectrometry (ICP-MS) for bulk samples from 2004–2006 Mount St. Helens lava dome and sample of lava erupted in October 1986.

[Oxide abundances in wt. percent, elemental abundances in parts per million. Numbers in parentheses represent number of analyses in average (AVG) and standard deviation (SD). Complete analyses of all samples are given in Thornber and others (2008b), and additional geochemical data for bulk analyses of samples from past 500 years of eruptive activity at Mount St. Helens are summarized in Pallister and others (1992).]

	2004–6 dacite		Glassy fragments			Roof of spine 1		Roof of spine 3		1986
Spine No.	3–7		3	1	1	1		3		
Sample --			SH304-2G1	SH300-1A3A	SH300-1C2	SH300 (dense)		SH301		SH226
XRF	AVG (23)	SD (23)				AVG(3)	SD(3)	AVG(3)	SD(3)	
SiO_2	64.93	0.09	66.85	64.64	64.65	63.43	0.35	63.38	0.29	63.78
Al_2O_3	17.21	0.08	16.77	17.12	17.23	17.45	0.12	17.49	0.02	17.35
$FeTO_3$	4.40	0.05	3.87	4.65	4.43	4.93	0.03	4.97	0.13	4.89
MgO	1.85	0.05	1.24	2.01	1.85	2.17	0.05	2.16	0.08	2.02
CaO	4.73	0.03	3.99	4.86	4.77	5.30	0.09	5.26	0.08	5.04
Na_2O	4.61	0.08	4.64	4.50	4.73	4.56	0.05	4.55	0.04	4.60
K_2O	1.42	0.02	1.83	1.34	1.44	1.24	0.01	1.27	0.02	1.37
TiO_2	0.62	0.01	0.52	0.63	0.62	0.66	0.01	0.67	0.01	0.67
P_2O_5	0.15	0.02	0.21	0.17	0.21	0.19	0.00	0.17	0.01	0.18
MnO	0.07	0.00	0.07	0.07	0.07	0.08	0.00	0.08	0.00	0.08
Total	100.00	0.00	100.00	100.00	100.00	100.00	0.00	100.00	0.00	100.00
LOI	0.09	0.10	2.21	0.41	0.35	0.06	0.03	0.25	0.15	1.16
ICP-MS	AVG (23)	SD (23)								
Ba	340	18	335	335	373	290	2	312	3	333
Be	1.35	0.11	1.50	1.30	1.70	1.20	0.00	1.30	0.10	1.42
Cd	0.10	0.09	0.07	0.07	0.09	0.04	0.00	0.08	0.06	0.07
Ce	24.61	1.05	25.70	25.40	28.10	21.75	0.49	23.80	0.10	26.00
Co	11.50	0.73	13.40	12.60	7.70	12.90	0.42	13.57	0.45	13.10
Cr	8.91	1.14	24.10	11.40	13.80	12.40	1.56	12.00	2.15	14.00
Cs	1.56	0.10	1.50	1.50	2.10	0.66	0.18	1.37	0.15	1.49
Cu	33.30	3.16	30.80	41.00	25.80	38.20	5.94	37.60	2.19	23.80
Ga	19.50	0.81	20.00	19.40	20.00	17.70	0.14	19.00	0.00	19.90
La	12.69	0.43	13.00	12.50	14.30	11.20	0.14	11.83	0.06	13.00
Li	24.66	1.98	28.30	25.00	11.90	11.45	2.05	13.43	4.15	22.70
Mn	544	23	591	581	529	561	14	590	12	618
Mo	0.75	0.09	1.10	0.69	1.50	0.82	0.04	0.78	0.09	0.95
Nb	5.38	1.26	6.40	7.00	7.60	7.75	2.76	4.50	0.20	7.02
Ni	8.28	0.97	16.90	8.10	7.00	10.20	0.85	12.73	1.94	11.40
P	616	41	720	659	690	563	15	613	6	684
Pb	7.63	0.62	7.80	7.28	8.50	5.24	0.08	5.97	1.34	7.04
Rb	33.65	1.14	32.60	31.40	41.10	23.45	3.46	29.07	0.76	32.40
Sb	0.17	0.12	0.20	0.20	0.26	0.10	0.00	0.20	0.00	<0.02
Sc	9.38	0.64	9.90	10.80	6.00	10.25	0.35	10.50	0.50	10.50
Sr	471	11	462	462	447	457	10	473	9	489
Th	2.75	0.24	2.90	2.55	3.00	2.21	0.01	2.40	0.00	2.56
Tl	0.33	0.34	0.20	0.28	0.40	0.13	0.00	0.11	0.08	0.29
U	1.05	0.11	1.20	1.10	1.20	1.06	0.01	0.97	0.01	1.07
V	75.17	6.12	90.20	83.30	42.00	87.30	3.39	86.43	2.51	86.90
Y	11.79	0.73	12.90	11.70	13.20	12.40	0.00	13.37	0.25	13.30
Zn	60.35	3.40	68.70	66.40	64.00	66.70	6.93	70.10	1.61	65.20
ED-XRF										
Zr	119	19		136				119	1	149

Table 8. Trace-element analyses by instrumental neutron activation analysis of bulk samples from 2004–2006 Mount St. Helens lava dome and sample of lava erupted in October 1986.

[Elemental abundances in parts per million (ppm), except Au in parts per billion (ppb). Numbers in parentheses indicate number of analyses in average (AVG) and standard deviation (SD). Standard deviation for SH300-1A3A and SH226 are based on multiple counts for the same element. Dashes indicate insufficient data to calculate meaningful standard deviations. Normalization to chondrite abundance uses chondritic composition reported by Sun and McDonough (1989). Complete analyses of all samples are given in Thornber and others (2008b), and additional geochemical data for bulk analyses of samples from past 500 years of eruptive activity at Mount St. Helens are summarized in Pallister and others (1992).]

	2004–6 dacite Average		2004–6 dacite glassy fragment		Roof of spine 1		1986 dacite	
Spine No.-----	3–7		1		1			
Sample -------			SH300-1A3A		SH300 (dense)		SH226	
INAA (ppm)	AVG (5)	SD (5)		SD	AVG(3)	SD (3)		SD
Rb	35.38	1.22	33.80	1.39	27.60	1.73	33.20	0.80
Sr	463	42	472	19.82	475	18.23	485	14.07
Cs	1.65	0.05	1.51	0.04	0.70	0.13	1.53	0.04
Ba	350	6	357	7.85	284	1.15	329	4.94
Th	2.61	0.07	2.51	0.04	2.17	0.01	2.53	0.03
U	1.23	0.02	1.26	0.05	1.11	0.05	1.20	0.04
La	11.92	0.16	11.60	0.10	10.80	0.00	12.10	0.08
Ce	24.36	0.94	22.90	0.23	23.13	0.15	25.30	0.23
Nd	12.84	0.47	12.80	0.45	12.20	0.20	13.30	0.39
Sm	2.80	0.09	2.78	0.02	2.67	0.02	2.92	0.02
Eu	0.85	0.01	0.89	0.02	0.87	0.02	0.90	0.02
Gd	1.01	1.38	2.56	0.29	2.50	0.06		
Tb	0.35	0.02	0.34	0.01	0.37	0.01	0.39	0.01
Ho	0.41	0.02	0.43	0.08	0.46	0.01	0.47	0.06
Tm	0.06	0.09	0.16	0.02	0.18	0.00		
Yb	0.99	0.04	0.98	0.03	1.06	0.03	1.12	0.02
Lu	0.15	0.01	0.15	0.004	0.15	0.00	0.16	0.003
Zr	119	15	107	10	115	2.52	143	16.16
Hf	3.10	0.10	2.95	0.04	2.99	0.08	3.28	0.04
Ta	0.35	0.01	0.37	0.01	0.36	0.01	0.40	0.01
W	0.47	0.38	0.77	0.77	0.79	0.16	0.79	0.13
Sc	8.89	0.15	9.61	0.07	10.07	0.31	9.81	0.07
Cr	8.40	0.61	12.20	0.35	12.10	0.98	10.70	0.24
Co	11.44	0.13	12.70	0.11	13.63	0.55	12.40	0.12
Ni	9.96	4.52	8.48	1.26	16.67	0.86	14.60	1.59
Zn	55.08	1.68	58.30	1.69	67.97	1.10	57.90	1.22
As	0.94	0.11	1.07	1.07	0.56	0.08	1.28	0.08
Sb	0.17	0.01	0.19	0.01	0.12	0.02	0.18	0.01
Au, (ppb)	4.84	8.87	0.82	0.49	8.83	5.96	0.56	0.33
Chondrite-normalized REE abundances								
La	50.30	0.69	48.95	0.22	45.57	0.00	51.05	0.18
Ce	39.80	1.54	37.42	0.14	37.80	0.25	41.34	0.15
Pr								
Nd	27.49	1.00	27.41	0.26	26.12	0.43	28.48	0.24
Sm	18.27	0.57	18.17	0.02	17.45	0.13	19.08	0.03
Eu	14.58	0.20	15.38	0.04	14.94	0.39	15.50	0.04
Gd	4.91	6.72	12.46	0.18	12.18	0.27		
Tb	9.36	0.56	8.98	0.03	9.90	0.22	10.45	0.02
Dy								
Ho	7.25	0.27	7.60	0.11	8.15	0.15	8.32	0.09
Tm	2.49	3.42	6.27	0.05	7.15	0.08		
Yb	5.81	0.24	5.79	0.01	6.24	0.16	6.59	0.01
Lu	5.75	0.20	5.87	0.01	6.05	0.18	6.38	0.01

Table 9. Fe-Ti oxide thermobarometry results for 2004–2005 eruptive products.

[Temperatures and oxygen fugacities calculated using Fe-Ti exchange thermometer and oxygen barometer of Andersen and Lindsay (1988) and the solution model of Stormer (1983). Complete oxide analyses, by electron microprobe, are presented in digital appendix. Grain number indicates each of successive individual grains analyzed by electron microprobe; c indicates composite grain, typically with two or more magnetite crystals attached to single ilmenite. Grain pair size shows maximum dimension of combined grains. Zoning coded as follows: U, unzoned; Z (IL), zoned ilmenite; Z (MT), zoned titanomagnetite; Z (B), zoning in both oxide grains; (ZR), reversely zoned with lower Ti in magnetite near contact with ilmenite; (S) = slight zoning detected but inadequate to warrant separate calculations of temperature and oxygen fugacity (f_{O_2}); Ux = unzoned, but partially exsolved; broad beam analyses used. "?" = zoning not determined. Eruption dates and related uncertainty described in table 1.

Averages and standard deviation (std. dev.) calculated only for unzoned or weakly zoned grains. Dashes, insufficient data to determine standard deviation. For zoned grains, temperature (T) and oxygen fugacity (f_{O_2}) calculated for individual spot analyses of zoned phase vs. average composition of the unzoned phase, or for near-contact single ilmenite-magnetite pairs. Column for analyses/grain pairs refers to total number of analyses used in calculation, followed by number of grain pairs for samples with homogeneous distributions of oxide temperatures. Samples SH300 and SH304 yield results that are tightly clustered, reflecting primary magmatic equilibration conditions in the Mount St. Helens magma reservoir at depth. All other samples of the 2004–6 dacite have heterogeneous oxide mineral populations that show evidence of disequilibrium, attributed mainly to transient heating.]

Grain No.	Sample No. and eruption date	Grain pair size	Zoning	T, °C	Std. dev.	f_{O_2}	Std. dev.	Analyses/ grain pairs
SH300-1A3 (1980–86) [1]			U	904	4	-11.50	0.08	21/3
SH304-2A9 (10/18/04)			U	850	5	-12.29	0.07	65/4
SH304-2Gg1 (10/18/04)			U	844	2	-12.43	0.07	61/6
SH305-1 (11/20/04)								
1	Average (40 µm)		Z (MT)	883	3	-12.11	0.06	5
1	±3 µm from contact	40 µm	Z (MT)	953	--	-11.05	--	2
2	43 µm from IL	65 µm	Z (MT)	898	--	-11.48	--	2
2	32 µm from IL	65 µm	Z (MT)	903	--	-11.41	--	2
2	26 µm from IL	65 µm	Z (MT)	907	--	-11.35	--	2
2	18 µm from IL	65 µm	Z (MT)	921	--	-11.17	--	2
2	10 µm from IL	65 µm	Z (MT)	938	--	-10.95	--	2
2	4 µm from IL	65 µm	Z (MT)	928	--	-11.07	--	2
2	Average	65 µm	Z (MT)	915	13	-11.25	0.15	11
3	Average interior	20 µm	Z (MT)	880	3	-12.41	0.02	10
3c	±3 µm from contact	20 µm	Z (B)	998	--	-10.77	--	2
4c	weakly zoned	20 µm	S (MT)	912	12	-11.71	0.13	6
5	small grain pair	8 µm	Z (MT)	1019	83	-10.65	1.07	4
6	Average	40 µm	U	908	2	-11.72	0.03	6
7c	first MT grain (6 µm)	15 µm	U	858	9	-12.79	0.25	5
7c	second MT grain (4 µm)	15 µm	U	935	--	-11.66	--	4
8	Average	25 µm	U	891	1	-12.09	0.04	10
9	Average	25 µm	U	883	1	-12.03	0.01	9
10c	Average	40 µm	S (MT)	871	10	-12.50	0.19	10
11	Average	40 µm	U	857	1	-12.80	0.02	10
SH305-1 (kc) (11/20/04)								
1	Average	14 µm	S (MT)	873	7	-12.30	0.18	5
2	Average	12 µm	U	862	6	-12.53	0.15	6
SH305-2A (11/20/04)								
1	Average	30 µm	Z (MT)	936	23	-11.42	0.31	15
2	Average	40 µm	S (MT)	791	14	-14.91	0.33	8

Table 9. Fe-Ti oxide thermobarometry results for 2004–2005 eruptive products.—Continued

Grain No.	Sample No. and eruption date	Grain pair size	Zoning	T, °C	Std. dev.	f_{O_2}	Std. dev.	Analyses/ grain pairs
3	Average	30 µm	U	858	12	-13.19	0.27	11
4	<20 µm from IL	100 µm	Z (MT)	944	8	-11.06	0.10	9
4	Core of MT vs. IL	100 µm	"	842	--	-12.43	--	7
MSH05JV_1_19 (1/16/05 grains in ash) (1980–86) [1]								
1	Average	100 µm	Ux	884	14	-11.38	0.19	9
3	Average	100 µm	U	888	5	-11.61	0.09	8
4	Interior of grains	100 µm	S (MT)	912	9	-11.01	0.13	8
4	5 µm from IL	100 µm	S (MT)	931	--	-10.78	--	5
5	Average	130 µm	Ux	895	13	-11.46	0.17	6
6	Average	100 µm	U	778	6	-13.80	0.15	10
7	Average grain interiors	120 µm	Z(B)	938	8	-10.66	0.12	12
7	Average ±15 µm of contact	120 µm	"	830	13	-13.28	0.40	8
8	Average	120 µm	U	873	13	-12.09	0.20	18
9	Average	70 µm	U	833	6	-12.57	0.12	10
10	Average	35 µm	U	750	5	-14.73	0.22	9
MSH05WS_1_19 (1/16/05 grains in ash) (1980–86)								
9b	Average grain interiors	200 µm	Z(MT)	833	6	-12.57	0.12	7
9b	Average ±8 µm of contact	200 µm	"	929	6	-11.27	0.12	8
SH308-3A (02/22/05)								
1	Average	12 µm	U	865	6	-13.04	0.01	8
2	Average	20 µm	U	909	9	-11.86	0.23	9
3	Average	40 µm	S (MT)	891	2	-12.08	0.06	17
4	Average	25 µm	U	882	1	-12.05	0.01	11
5	Average	17 µm	U	863	6	-12.50	0.10	8
6	Average	40 µm	U	882	1	-12.05	0.01	13
7	Average	40 µm	U	863	6	-12.50	0.09	12
SH308-3A (CT) (02/22/05)								
1	Grain 3-4	40 µm	?	850	--	-13.40	--	2
2	Grain 7-8	30 µm	?	898	--	-12.01	--	2
3	Grain 9-10	30 µm	?	844	--	-13.26	--	2
4	Grain f2 1-2	40 µm	?	850	--	-13.40	--	2
5	Grain f2 3-4	30 µm	?	857	--	-12.49	--	2
	Average of above			860	22	-12.91	0.63	
SH309-1 (CT) (02/22/05)								
1	Grain 7-5	50 µm	?	958	--	-10.35	--	2
2	Grain 8-9	60 µm	?	990	--	-10.07	--	2
3-08-05 grains in ash (CT) (03/08/05)								
1	DRS4g1 1-2	15 µm	?	868	--	-12.86	--	2
2	DRS4g1 3-4	15 µm	?	887	--	-12.42	--	2
3	DRS4g1 5-6	30 µm	?	842	--	-13.75	--	2
4	DRS4g2 1-2	25 µm	?	846	--	-13.31	--	2
5	DRS4g2 3-4	40 µm	?	825	--	-13.85	--	2
6	DRS4g2 5-6	50 µm	?	828	--	-13.85	--	2

Table 9. Fe-Ti oxide thermobarometry results for 2004–2005 eruptive products.—Continued

Grain No.	Sample No. and eruption date	Grain pair size	Zoning	T, °C	Std. dev.	f_{O_2}	Std. dev.	Analyses/ grain pairs
7	DRS4f3g1-2	50 µm	?	871	--	-12.66	--	2
8	DRS4f51 1-2	25 µm	?	846	--	-13.51	--	2
	Average of above			852	22	-13.28	0.56	
SH312-1 (03/08/05)								
1	Average	40 µm	Z (MT)	894	2	-11.86	0.03	11
1	±5 µm from contact	40 µm	Z (MT)	957	--	-10.98	--	2
2	Average grain interiors	80 µm	Z (MT)	871	2	-11.92	0.04	13
2	5 µm from IL	80 µm	Z (MT)	898	--	-11.57	--	7
2	12 µm from IL	80 µm	Z (MT)	913	--	-11.38	--	7
2	18 µm from IL	80 µm	Z (MT)	910	--	-11.41	--	7
2	25 µm from IL	80 µm	Z (MT)	898	--	-11.57	--	7
2	32 µm from IL	80 µm	Z (MT)	890	--	-11.68	--	7
2	40 µm from IL	80 µm	Z (MT)	880	--	-11.82	--	7
3c	Average	40 µm	U	878	8	-12.42	0.17	20
4c	first MT grain (15 µm)	55 µm	U	929	5	-11.07	0.07	11
4c	second MT grain (10 µm)	55 µm	U	921	1	-11.29	0.04	6
5	SH312 gr5	30 µm	U	920	17	-11.33	0.33	4
8	SH312 gr5c	25 µm	U	857	2	-12.47	0.05	3
6	SH312 gr6	50 µm	U	903	4	-11.44	0.02	10
7	SH312 gr7	50 µm	U	895	3	-11.85	0.08	12
SH314-2 (04/17/05)								
1	Average	20 µm	U	794	14	-14.21	0.48	5
2	Average	50 µm	U	813	2	-13.51	0.01	8
3	Average grain interiors	50 µm	ZR(MT)	872	3	-12.55	0.07	11
3	SH314-2 gr3 ct	50 µm	ZR(MT)	840		-13.03		6
3	4 µm from IL	50 µm	ZR(MT)	847		-12.92		6
3	8 µm from IL	50 µm	ZR(MT)	853		-12.83		6
4	SH314-2 gr4 sm	25 µm	U	794	1	-13.51	0.03	5
5	Average	45 µm	U	855	11	-12.75	0.16	11
7	Average	40 µm	U	764	38	-15.23	1.34	8
8	Average grain interiors	30 µm	Z (MT)	736	1	-16.62	0.02	8
8	5 µm from IL	30 µm	Z (MT)	815	7	-13.56	0.18	5
SH315-2 (04/01/05)								
1	Average	300 µm	Z (IL)	739	24	-16.29	0.83	6
1	High Fe IL core vs. avg. MT	300 µm	Z (IL)	828		-13.39		4
2	Average grain interiors	60 µm	Z (MT)	838	1	-13.79	0.05	8
2	4 µm from IL	60 µm	Z (MT)	805	1	-14.34	0.07	9
3	Average	50 µm	S (IL)	807	9	-14.23	0.27	7
4	Average	25 µm	U	791	33	-14.75	1.14	6
5c	Average	30 µm	U	742	98	-16.40	3.81	9
6	Average	30 µm	U	817	3	-13.86	0.12	7
7	Average	35 µm	U	813	40	-14.08	1.22	7

[1] Crater floor debris dragged up by extruding spines but that probably originated by dome growth in the period 1980–86.

[2] Emitted as ash during explosion that disrupted crater-floor debris adjacent to spine 4.

Appendix 1. Oxide Analyses used in Thermobarometic Calculations

[This appendix appears only in the digital versions of this work—in the DVD-ROM that accompanies the printed volume and as a separate file accompanying this chapter on the Web at: http://pubs.usgs.gov/pp/1750.]

The database for oxide analyses described in this chapter is tabulated in a spreadsheet file.

A Volcano Rekindled: The Renewed Eruption of Mount St. Helens, 2004–2006
Edited by David R. Sherrod, William E. Scott, and Peter H. Stauffer
U.S. Geological Survey Professional Paper 1750, 2008

Chapter 31

Magmatic Conditions and Processes in the Storage Zone of the 2004–2006 Mount St. Helens Dacite

By Malcolm J. Rutherford[1] and Joseph D. Devine III[1]

Abstract

The 2004–6 eruption of Mount St. Helens produced dacite that contains 40–50 volume percent phenocrysts of plagioclase, amphibole, low-Ca pyroxene, magnetite, and ilmenite in a groundmass that is nearly totally crystallized. Phenocrysts of amphibole and pyroxene range from 3 to 5 mm long and are cyclically zoned, with one to three alternations of Fe- and Al-rich to Mg- and Si-rich layers showing little indication of phenocryst dissolution between zones. Similar-size plagioclase phenocrysts also contain several cyclic zones ranging between ~An_{68} and An_{45-35}. Textural evidence indicates that amphibole, pyroxene, and ilmenite began to crystallize before the most An-rich plagioclase. Magnetite and ilmenite phenocrysts are small (less than 100 μm), vary somewhat in composition from grain to grain, and are sporadically zoned. Magnetite-ilmenite pairs yield temperatures of equilibration ranging from 820°C to 890°C and f_{O_2} values of NNO +1 log unit. Magnetite compositions suggest that the 2004–6 magma was formed by mingling of magmas less than 5–8 weeks before eruption and that the magma last equilibrated within this temperature range. The amphibole phenocryst zoning involves approximately equal amounts of a pressure-sensitive Al-Tschermak molecular substitution and a temperature-sensitive edenite substitution in one cycle of growth. Hydrothermal experiments done on the natural dacite show that crystallization of the Fe- and Al-rich amphibole end member requires pressures of 200–300 MPa at temperatures of 900°C, conditions approaching the upper temperature limit of amphibole stability. The dacitic magma crystallizes the An_{68} plagioclase when the pressure drops to 200 MPa at 900°C. The magma must cool at this depth to produce a complete An_{68}–An_{40} plagioclase zone and a Mg-rich layer on the amphiboles before the magma is cycled back to a high pressure, when a new layer of Fe-rich amphibole is acquired. The amphibole crystallizing in the dacite experiments at less than 200 MPa is lower in aluminum than any compositions in the natural cyclically zoned phenocrysts. The outer rim on some 2004–6 amphibole phenocrysts appears to have formed in the 100–200 MPa range, as do some phenocrysts in the May 1980 dacite pumice. Plagioclase rims of An_{35} in the 2004–6 magmas indicate that phenocryst growth continued until the pressure decreased to 130 MPa and that ascent was slow until this depth. Magma then entered the conduit for a relatively rapid ascent to the surface as indicated by the very thin (less than 5 μm) decompression-induced rims on the amphibole phenocrysts.

Introduction

Mount St. Helens began to erupt in 2004 after 18 years of relatively shallow seismic activity and no eruptions, aside from a few gas explosions during 1989–91 (Mastin, 1994). The extrusion of a lava dome onto the 1980 crater floor during the 1980–86 time period marked the end of the eruption that began in 1980. However, seismic data collected during the past two decades (Moran, 1994; Moran and others, this volume, chap. 2) showed a continuous, moderate level of small-magnitude seismic activity directly beneath the volcano, particularly in the depth range of 3–12 km. In addition, there were significant increases in the level of seismic activity at 3–10-km depths in 1995, 1998, and 2002, suggesting the possibility that magma was ascending to a depth of 3 to 4 km beneath the crater floor at these times. In October 2004, following a brief period of steam-and-ash explosions, lava began erupting within the crater at the south margin of the 1980–86 lava dome, and a new lava dome has been building slowly from a steady eruption of dacite magma (Pallister and Thornber, 2005; Pallister and others, this volume, chap. 30).

[1] Geological Sciences Department, Brown University, 324 Brook Street, Providence, RI 02912

Samples of the new dome collected by the U.S. Geological Survey's Cascades Volcano Observatory (USGS–CVO) scientists in late October 2004 were very oxidized, reddish in color, and crystal rich; they are considered likely to be material left in the upper conduit from the 1986 eruption. Samples that were collected within 1–2 weeks of eruption in late November 2004 (SH304), in early January 2005 (SH305), and more recently are interpreted to be samples of new magma. Initially, it appeared that this new magma was simply remobilized 1980–86 magma, stored at some level, possibly at 3–4 km, as suggested by the seismic record. In support of this idea, the bulk compositions determined for the new lava (Pallister and others, this volume, chap. 30) show it to be only slightly more evolved than lava from the 1980–86 eruptions (65 rather than 63 weight percent SiO_2). However, some characteristics of the new lava samples pointed to a new magma source at depth, or at least reestablishment of the 1986 magma storage system at 7–12 km depth (Scandone and Malone, 1985). These characteristics included the presence of apparently stable amphibole phenocrysts, the presence of significant amounts of glass in many samples, and, most particularly, the identification of magnetite-ilmenite pairs yielding temperatures >900°C (Pallister and Thornber, 2005; Rutherford and Devine, 2005). If the erupting magma had been stored at pressures less than 100 MPa (~4 km below the summit; Geschwind and Rutherford, 1995) then amphibole phenocrysts would have developed a thick reaction rim according to earlier work (Rutherford and Hill, 1993). Amphiboles in the 2004–6 magma generally lack evidence of any significant breakdown except for a thin (less than 5 μm) rim that is attributed to reaction with melt during ascent in the conduit (Rutherford and Devine, 2005). The greater than 900°C temperatures from the 2004–6 oxides are higher than temperatures (860°C) recorded from samples of the 1986 Mount St. Helens eruption (Rutherford and Hill, 1993), suggesting that hotter magma was involved in the 2004–6 eruptions.

The observations and the initial analyses of the 2004–6 lava samples (Pallister and Thornber, 2005) give rise to a number of questions that we have attempted to answer in this paper: (1) Where did phenocrysts in these magmas last equilibrate with the surrounding melt before entering the conduit and undergoing transport to the surface? This question can be addressed by studying the rim compositions of the phenocryst phases in the natural samples and by doing experiments designed to reproduce the phenocryst rim-melt equilibrium at different possible preeruption conditions. (2) Can the cyclic compositional zoning observed in all of the silicate phenocryst phases (plagioclase, amphibole and orthopyroxene) of the 2004–6 magma (Rutherford and Devine, 2005) be explained by crystallization of a dacite magma at different conditions, and, if so, what are those conditions? We have studied the phenocryst zoning analytically and experimentally to determine the range of conditions experienced by the magma over its preeruption crystallization history, and herein we use the data to create a model of magma dynamics within this subvolcanic system. (3) Finally, what are the preeruption conditions for the 2004–6 magma, and how do they compare with those determined for the 1980–86 magma samples (Rutherford and others, 1985; Rutherford and Devine, 1988)? What are the possible reasons for any differences observed?

Analytical and Experimental Methods

Samples of the new 2004–6 Mount St. Helens dacite dome were supplied by members of the USGS–CVO staff shortly after it became possible to collect them. Polished thin sections were made for mineral-chemistry and textural investigations of the different samples, and crushed powders were made of some samples for use in hydrothermal experiments. The phases in the natural samples were analyzed using a CAMECA SX100 microprobe for the crystalline phases and a CAMECA Camebax microprobe for glasses. Analytical methods used are identical to those of Rutherford and Devine (2003). Amphibole cation proportions were calculated using the method of Holland and Blundy (1994). The method of Cosca and others (1991) was used to calculate amphibole stoichiometry on the basis of 13 cations (Si, Al, Fe, Mg, Mn, and Ti) and to estimate ferric iron contents.

Experiments were performed on sample SH305-1 (erupted in November 2004), which was crushed to form a mixture of matrix and small (less than 0.2 mm) phenocryst fragments. This crushed sample was used in hydrothermal melting experiments and to create a glass-rich starting material for use in crystallization experiments. Melting and crystallization experiments were done in adjacent sealed tubes. The objective was to reversibly create new phenocryst growth under controlled conditions of pressure, temperature, and oxygen fugacity (P, T, and f_{O_2}). All of the experiments were done with $P_{H_2O} = P_{total}$ using previously described methods. The textural data indicate that amphibole crystallized before plagioclase in the 2004–6 magma, and this requires that the melt contain at least 4 weight percent dissolved H_2O (Merzbacher and Eggler, 1984) at this early stage of crystallization. With additional crystallization (primarily plagioclase and orthopyroxene), the melt would have rapidly approached water saturation for total pressures less than 300 MPa. The possibility that the 2004–6 magma initially contained some dissolved CO_2 cannot be ruled out, however, and is considered in the discussion.

Petrology of the 2004–2006 Dacite

General Petrology

The 2004–6 Mount St. Helens dacite is macroscopically similar to the material erupted in 1980–86. It is a crystal-rich dacite (~45 volume percent phenocrysts on a bubble-free basis) with phenocrysts of plagioclase, orthopyroxene, amphibole, Ti-magnetite, and ilmenite in a groundmass that is nearly totally crystallized in most of the samples (fig. 1;

Pallister and Thornber, 2005; Rutherford and Devine, 2005). Phenocrysts range up to 6 mm across and sporadically show some preferred orientation owing to magma flow. The groundmass and phenocryst assemblages are the same, except that amphibole is lacking in the groundmass and, instead, there is Ca-rich pyroxene and minor cristobalite and quartz. The bulk compositions of the 2004–6 magma samples have been remarkably uniform at 65 weight percent SiO_2 throughout the eruption (Pallister and others, this volume, chap. 30). The erupting magma resembles the magma that erupted in 1980–86 in that it contains several volume percent (fragments and crystal clots) of "gabbroic" material that is rich in plagioclase, pyroxenes, and amphibole (Heliker, 1995). As in the earlier eruption, a few of the inclusions in the 2004–6 samples contain interstitial melt (glass) that appears to represent partial melting, but many inclusions do not contain a glass phase. The smallest inclusions are difficult to distinguish macroscopically from phenocryst clots, but their amphibole differs from the phenocrysts compositionally and generally is not chemically zoned. Additionally, Ca-rich pyroxene commonly is associated with amphibole in the inclusions (Rutherford and Devine, 2005).

Plagioclase

The plagioclase phenocrysts in the Mount St. Helens 2004–6 magma are euhedral, complexly zoned crystals (fig. 1) as large as 5 mm in diameter, although most are less than 3 mm. These phenocrysts have a complex core-to-rim cyclic zoning easily observable in backscattered electron (BSE) images (fig. 2). The composition of the outer plagioclase rim ranges from An_{60} to An_{35}, but the great majority of the rims are relatively albite rich (An_{30-35}). Core compositions of the plagioclase phenocrysts range up to An_{68}. Plots of composition versus distance (rim to rim) across typical phenocrysts in the 2004–6 lava are shown in figure 2, and the compositions of a typical core and rim are given in table 1. Most boundaries between compositional zones are parallel to growth faces, with relatively little evidence of resorption involved in the zoning reversals (fig. 2). However, some resorption did occur during the plagioclase growth history, and 5 to 10 volume percent of the phenocrysts, including both small and large crystals, have a strongly sieved core with a relatively thin rim of clear plagioclase. A similar population of sieve-cored plagioclase phenocrysts was also observed in 1980–86 lava (Rutherford and others, 1985). Another characteristic of the plagioclase phenocrysts in the new lava is the relatively common presence of included crystals of amphibole, orthopyroxene, and Ti-magnetite, in decreasing order of abundance, particularly in the outer half of the phenocryst.

Amphibole

Amphibole phenocrysts in the Mount St. Helens dacite are euhedral, mostly 1–3 mm long but infrequently up to 5 mm in length, and commonly exhibit an internal cyclic compositional zoning parallel to growth faces (fig. 3). Petrographic examination shows some variability in amphiboles from samples erupted at different times during the 2004–6 eruption, particularly different amounts of opacitization due to variable syneruptive oxidation (Garcia and Jacobson, 1979; Rutherford and Hill, 1993) or decompression-induced rim development. The outer margins of some amphiboles appear somewhat rounded and possibly eroded or abraded (fig. 3*C*); whereas evidence for rounding or dissolution at internal zone boundaries is inconclusive (fig. 3). Inclusions in amphiboles are relatively uncommon compared to plagioclase phenocrysts, but magnetite and sulfide inclusions do occur. Larger inclu-

Figure 1. Photomicrographs showing thin section of typical Mount St Helens dacite assemblage. Phenocryst phases are plagioclase (Plg), amphibole (Hb), low-Ca pyroxene (Opx), all with obvious cyclic zoning, and magnetite (Mt); ilmenite is other phenocryst, not shown. Groundmass is largely crystallized and slightly vesicular. *A*, Plane-polarized transmitted light. *B*, Backscattered electron image. M.I., melt inclusion.

Table 1. Compositions of representative natural plagioclase and orthopyroxene phenocrysts in dacite erupted at Mount St. Helens, Washington, 2004–2006.

[Chemical analyses determined by electron microprobe at Brown University, Providence, R.I.; J.D. Devine, analyst. Compositions in weight percent; all Fe as FeO in pyroxene and as Fe_2O_3 in plagioclase. Magnesium number, Mg# = (Mg×100)/(Mg+(Fe^{2+} in octahedral site)).]

Plagioclase phenocrysts						
Sample No.---	**SH304c**	**SH304r**	**SH305c**	**SH305r**	**SH323r**	**SH323c**
SiO_2	53.54	60.19	52.16	58.69	58.46	51.86
Al_2O_3	29.56	25.16	29.86	26.73	26.40	30.81
Fe_2O_3	0.30	0.24	0.59	0.33	0.32	0.63
CaO	12.21	6.71	13.44	8.04	7.91	13.54
Na_2O	4.33	6.85	3.31	6.33	6.46	3.37
K_2O	0.11	0.25	0.17	0.25	0.24	0.08
Total	100.05	99.40	99.53	100.37	99.79	100.29
An content	60	35	69	40	39	68
Orthopyroxene phenocrysts						
Sample No.---	**SH304 Px1**	**SH304 Px2**	**SH305 Px1**	**SH305 Px2**	**SH323 Opx 1**	**SH323 Opx 2**
SiO_2	52.60	52.56	52.17	53.45	52.14	53.09
TiO_2	0.22	0.13	0.17	0.12	0.21	0.29
Al_2O_3	1.56	0.54	0.44	0.56	1.37	1.74
FeO	21.07	23.50	23.28	20.47	22.60	16.97
MgO	22.30	20.80	20.85	23.65	20.40	25.23
CaO	1.16	1.15	1.21	0.86	1.20	0.99
MnO	0.70	0.69	0.63	0.71	0.69	0.41
Cr_2O_3	0.00	0.01	0.02	0.01	0.01	0.06
Total	99.61	99.38	98.77	99.83	98.62	99.78
Mg#	63	60	60	63.5	61	64

sions in amphibole are generally multicrystalline and appear to represent trapped melts that have crystallized in what appears to have been a hollow-cored crystal (figs. 1, 3*A–C*). The amphiboles that occur in gabbroic inclusions are commonly not in contact with glass, except on the inclusion margins. Amphibole crystals in these inclusions are also generally anhedral, do not show cyclic compositional zoning, and are low in Al_2O_3 (8–11 weight percent) compared to the phenocrysts. Some isolated crystals in the dacite magma have similar characteristics.

The cyclic internal zoning present in the majority of amphibole phenocrysts in the 2004–6 Mount St. Helens lava is present in even the smallest (~100 µm) phenocrysts and is observable optically, as well as in BSE images. This zoning tends to begin with a bright BSE zone in the center of a phenocryst, involves one or two cycles of alternating bright-dark zoning, and ends with a dark, low-FeO zone adjacent to the groundmass (fig. 3). A similar zoning occurs in the amphiboles from the 1986 lava dome (fig. 3*D*), although the outer rim in these samples is intermediate to Fe-rich rather than Mg-rich. The Mg# (Mg/(Mg+Fe^{2+})) and ^{VI}Al profiles across representative amphibole phenocrysts are shown in figure 3, and compositions at points across typical cycles of amphibole growth are given in table 2.

The cyclic compositional zoning in the Mount St. Helens amphiboles involves Fe-, Al-, Na-, and K-enriched bright zones (BSE images) that alternate with, and grade into, Mg- and Si-rich dark BSE zones (figs. 3, 4). The cation substitutions involved in this zoning are similar to those observed in phenocrysts from the 1995–2002 Soufrière Hills andesite erupted on Montserrat (Rutherford and Devine, 2003) and in Fish Canyon latite (Bachmann and Dungan, 2002), but they differ in one significant aspect. A pressure-sensitive Al-Tschermak substitution was not inferred for either the Soufrière Hills or the

Fish Canyon amphibole zoning. In contrast, phenocrysts in the 2004–6 Mount St. Helens lava are marked by compositional variations that are ~50 mol percent Al-Tschermak substitution (^{M}(Mg, Fe) + ^{T}Si = ^{M}Al + ^{T}Al; fig. 5*A*), with the remaining change in ^{T}Al attributed to the temperature-dependent edenite (^{T}Si + ^{A}vacancy = ^{T}Al + ^{A}(Na+K)) and Ti-Tschermak exchanges (2^{T}Si + ^{M}Mn = 2^{T}Al + ^{M}Ti), as shown in figures 5*B* and 5*C*. In going from the Fe-rich to the Mg-rich zones, the decrease in Fe appears to be completely balanced by the increase in Mg in the octahedral position (fig. 6), as was found to be the case in previous studies (Bachmann and Dungan, 2002; Rutherford and Devine, 2003). In other words, the increase in ^{VI}Al in the amphibole structure is accompanied by an increase in Fe^{2+} at the expense of Mg^{2+} in the octahedral site (fig. 3).

One potentially important aspect of the amphibole phenocryst zoning in the 2004–6 Mount St. Helens magma is illustrated by the zoning in sample SH323 (fig. 7). Most amphibole phenocrysts in this sample have, in contrast to 2004–6 magma erupted earlier, a relatively bright (Fe-rich) rim, but the Al_2O_3 content is low and the SiO_2 content (fig. 4) is relatively high in this layer. Analytical electron-microprobe traverses across such phenocrysts show that the fluorine (F) content increases significantly over a distance of 20–40 μm at the phenocryst margin as Si increases and Al decreases. The core of the amphibole phenocryst contains 960±200 ppm F; the very outer margin of the phenocryst contains as much as 7,700 ppm (fig. 7*C*; table 2). A similar increase in F and Si was noted where the rim-to-rim analytical profile passed close to a melt channel in the phenocryst. Another, possibly related, observation is that the amphiboles in the gabbroic inclusions also are low in octahedral as well as total Al and Si relative to the cyclically zoned phenocrysts, and they are somewhat enriched in F (2,500 ppm) relative to the cyclically zoned phenocrysts (average of 900 ppm F). The presence of a thin, decompression-induced reaction rim at the contact of these phenocrysts with the groundmass indicates that the fluorine enrichment occurs before the final magma ascent and decompression. One possible explanation of the fluorine zoning is that these crystals and crystal rims represent a partial recrystallization of amphiboles at conditions of low *P* and high activity of SiO_2 just outside the OH-bearing amphibole stability field. Similar overgrowths are observed on amphibole phenocrysts

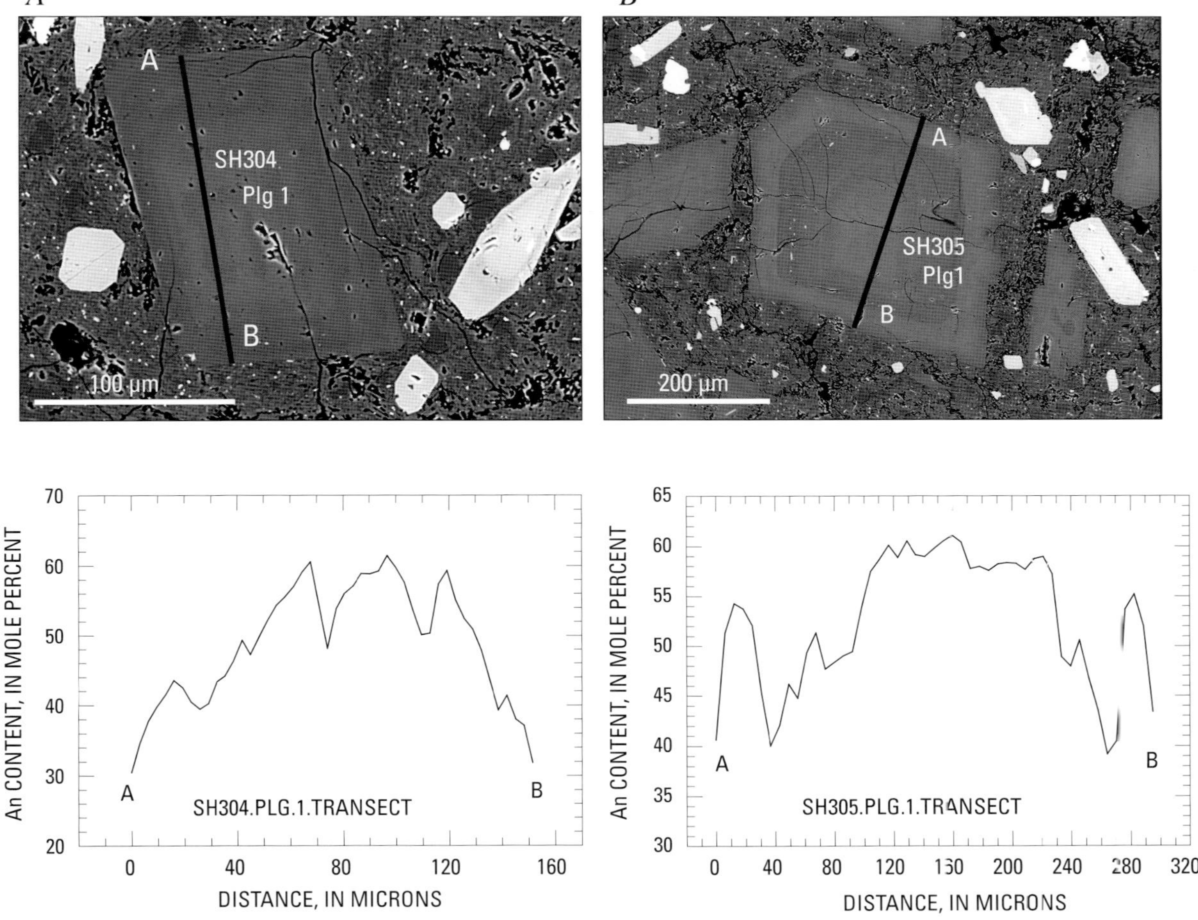

Figure 2. Backscattered electron images from thin section of Mount St. Helens lava, showing typical plagioclase phenocryst of 2004–6 lava. Images show cycles of light (Ca-rich) and dark (Na-rich) phenocryst growth; accompanying graphs depict An concentrations along the A–B profiles. *A*, Plagioclase in sample SH304. *B*, Plagioclase in sample SH305.

Table 2. Representative natural amphibole compositions in dacite erupted at Mount St. Helens, Washington, 2004–2006.

[Chemical analyses determined by electron microprobe at Brown University, Providence, R.I.; J.D. Devine, analyst. Compositions in weight percent; all Fe as FeO; n.d., not determined. Structure formula calculated after Holland and Blundy (1994). Magnesium number, Mg# = (Mg×100)/(Mg+(Fe^{2+} in Y site)).]

Sample No.---	SH304-1-2	SH304-1	SH304-1	SH305a	SH305b
Site------------	Hb7 rim	Hb7 interior	Hb7 core	Hb rim	Core
Character-----	Hi-Mg	Med.-Al	Hi-Al	Low-Al	Hi-Al
			Major-element analyses, weight percent		
SiO_2	44.80	42.86	40.97	43.51	40.40
TiO_2	1.95	2.41	2.56	2.72	2.40
Al_2O_3	11.40	13.09	14.30	11.97	14.86
FeO	12.30	12.90	15.31	11.99	16.05
MgO	15.43	13.92	11.82	14.97	10.54
CaO	11.29	10.67	10.74	11.58	11.39
Na_2O	1.98	2.37	2.39	2.39	2.26
K_2O	0.20	0.30	0.31	0.32	0.35
MnO	0.16	0.15	0.21	0.10	0.16
Cr_2O_3	0.02	0.01	0.01	0.00	0.00
Total	99.51	98.92	98.61	99.55	98.41
			Cation abundance in structure formula		
Si	6.305	6.128	5.942	6.170	5.923
^{IV}Al	1.695	1.872	2.058	1.830	2.077
Ti	0.206	0.259	0.279	0.290	0.265
^{VI}Al	0.196	0.333	0.386	0.171	0.490
Cr	0.007	0.001	0.008	0.000	0.000
Fe^{3+}	0.893	0.802	0.842	0.725	0.681
Fe^{2+}(Y)	0.468	0.639	0.938	0.649	1.261
Mg	3.237	2.966	2.555	3.164	2.303
Ca	1.702	1.634	1.669	1.760	1.809
Fe^{2+}(X)	0.087	0.101	0.077	0.047	0.026
Mn	0.019	0.018	0.026	0.012	0.020
Na	0.541	0.657	0.673	0.676	0.642
K	0.036	0.055	0.057	0.058	0.065
Mg#	87.37	82.27	73.14	82.98	64.62
$Fe^{3+}/\Sigma Fe$	0.617	0.520	0.453	0.510	0.346

erupted later in 2005 (SH324) and in 2006 (SH328), when the magma mass-eruption rate was also relatively low (Pallister and others, this volume, chap. 30).

Low-Ca Pyroxene (Orthopyroxene)

The orthopyroxene phenocrysts present in the 2004–6 magma are commonly cyclically zoned parallel to growth surfaces, similar to the zoning observed in amphibole. Examples where the zoning stands out as alternating light and dark bands are present in figures 1*B*, 3*A*, and 3*B*. Compositional profiles across a typical zoned phenocryst are shown in figure 8 for the pyroxene that is present in figure 1*B*. Like the amphibole, pyroxene phenocrysts can have as many as four cycles of light and dark zones rich in Fe and Mg, respectively, but many have only two. The smaller number of cycles visible in BSE and compositional profiles across orthopyroxene phenocrysts might be related to their smaller size, although some 100-μm-diameter crystals have as many as three light-dark growth cycles (fig. 3*A*). The trend from cycle to cycle is similar in both amphibole and orthopyroxene, in that the transition from dark, Mg-rich to bright, Fe-rich bands is sharp, whereas the bright to dark transition is gradational (figs. 1, 3). This similar-

Table 2. Representative natural amphibole compositions in dacite erupted at Mount St. Helens, Washington, 2004–2006.—Continued

[Chemical analyses determined by electron microprobe at Brown University, Providence, R.I.; J.D. Devine, analyst. Compositions in weight percent; all Fe as FeO; n.d., not determined. Structure formula calculated after Holland and Blundy (1994). Magnesium number, Mg# = (Mg×100)/(Mg+(Fe^{2+} in Y site)).]

Sample No.------ Site--------------- Character-------	SH308-1 #1 rim Low-Al	SH308-1 #3 core Med.-Al	SH323 Rim Low-Al	SH323 Near rim Med.-Al	SH323 27 core Hi-Al
Major-element analyses, weight percent					
SiO_2	43.89	41.53	43.88	41.15	42.08
TiO_2	2.43	2.27	2.56	2.88	2.22
Al_2O_3	11.38	13.31	10.25	13.88	14.11
FeO	12.48	14.97	14.69	14.65	14.79
MgO	15.15	12.12	13.69	12.23	12.65
CaO	10.71	11.02	11.07	11.40	10.74
Na_2O	2.32	2.25	2.46	2.96	2.83
K_2O	0.23	0.35	0.31	0.27	0.27
MnO	0.08	0.23	0.21	0.14	0.23
Cr_2O_3	0.06	0.01	0.01	0.00	0.00
F	n.d.	n.d.	0.77	0.102	0.096
Total	98.73	98.06	99.90	99.66	100.02
Cation abundance in structure formula					
Si	6.251	6.054	6.375	5.957	6.017
^{IV}Al	1.749	1.946	1.625	2.043	1.983
Ti	0.260	0.249	0.280	0.314	0.239
^{VI}Al	0.162	0.341	0.130	0.325	0.395
Cr	0.007	0.001	0.001	0.000	0.000
Fe^{3+}	0.827	0.807	0.716	0.584	0.777
Fe^{2+}(Y)	0.528	0.968	0.909	1.139	0.893
Mg	3.216	2.633	2.964	2.639	2.696
Ca	1.634	1.721	1.723	1.768	1.645
Fe^{2+}(X)	0.131	0.049	0.160	0.051	0.098
Mn	0.010	0.028	0.026	0.017	0.028
Na	0.641	0.636	0.693	0.831	0.785
K	0.042	0.065	0.057	0.050	0.049
Mg#	85.89	73.12	76.53	69.86	75.12
$Fe^{3+}/\Sigma Fe$	0.556	0.442	0.401	0.329	0.440

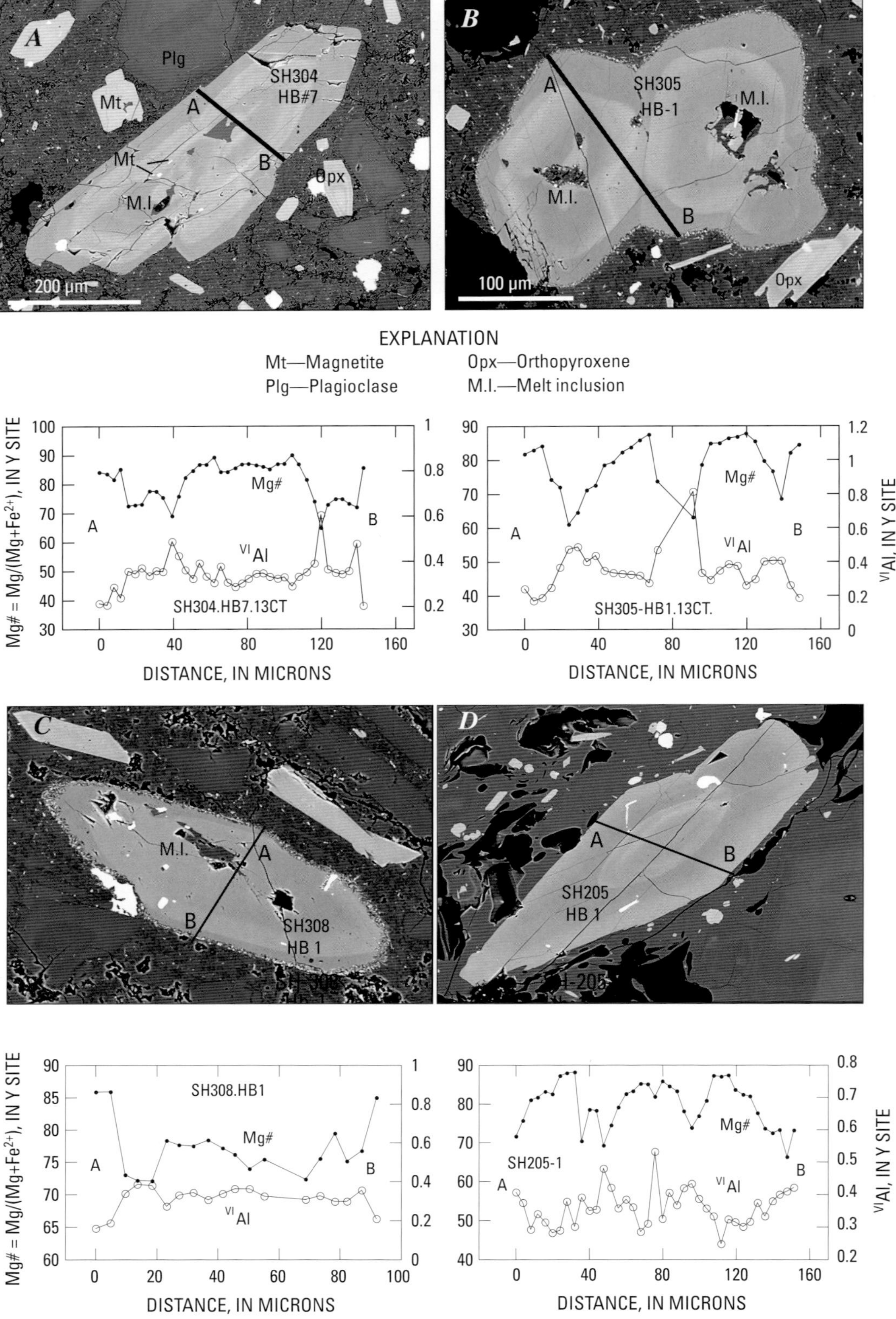

Figure 3. Backscattered electron images of typical amphibole and orthopyroxene phenocrysts; accompanying graphs show compositional profiles along lines A–B in each image. Note growth cycles of alternating Fe-rich (bright) and Mg-rich (dark) zoning. Compositional profiles show the Fe-rich zones are also rich in octahedral-coordinated Al (^{VI}Al). *A*, Sample SH304. *B*, Sample SH305. *C*, Sample SH308. *D*, Sample SH205 from 1986 dacite lava dome.

ity in compositional zoning implies that the two minerals were co-crystallizing as *P–T* conditions in the magma went through a series of cycles. As in the amphibole, the Al and Ti concentrations in orthopyroxene are slightly higher in the Fe-rich zones, but the correlation is not strong (fig. 8). The lack of a correlation of Fe with Al in pyroxene is probably due in part to the fact that the Al_2O_3 content is low (0.5–1.5 weight percent). Analyses of representative pyroxene phenocrysts are given in table 1.

Fe-Ti Oxides

Subhedral to rounded Fe-Ti oxide crystals (<150 µm rim to rim) are present in all samples studied. Titanomagnetite phenocrysts in dome lavas characterized by relatively rapid volumetric extrusion rates (6.5 m³/s; Pallister and others, this volume, chap. 30) are commonly homogeneous in composition from core to rim, although TiO_2 contents may vary

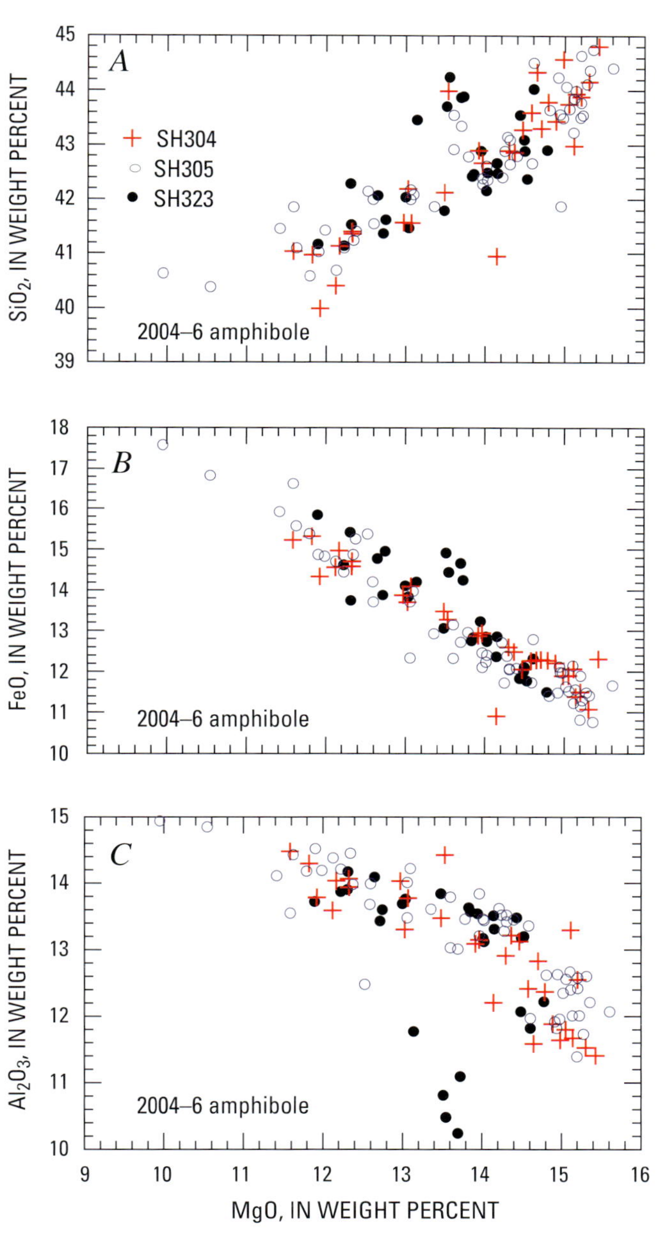

Figure 4. Chemical variation diagrams showing rim-to-rim compositional zoning in typical amphibole phenocrysts from three samples of the 2004–6 eruption. *A*, MgO vs. SiO_2. *B*, MgO vs. FeO. *C*, MgO vs. Al_2O_3. Crystal rims in SH323 (five points) with anomalously high SiO_2 (panel *A*) and low Al_2O_3 (panel *C*) are discussed elsewhere in the paper.

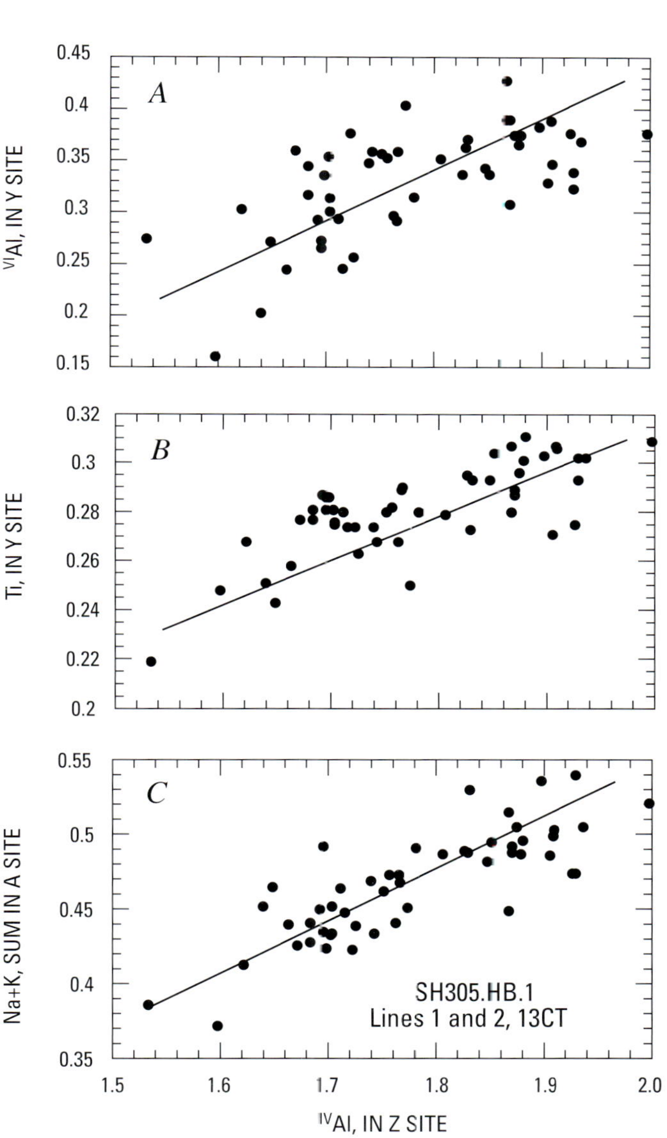

Figure 5. Plots showing position of chemical species in crystallographic sites versus tetrahedrally coordinated Al (^{IV}Al) in Z site for typical, cyclically zoned amphibole in lava samples from Mount St. Helens 2004–6 eruption. *A*, Octahedrally coordinated Al (^{VI}Al) in the Y site. *B*, Ti in the Y site. *C*, Sum of Na+K in the A site. Note that approximately equal amounts of the ^{IV}Al increase are balanced by increases in ^{VI}Al and the sum of Na and K.

substantially from grain to grain, even within the same hand sample (fig. 9). There is no apparent correlation between TiO_2 content and grain size (fig. 9). Lava samples characterized by relatively low volumetric extrusion rates have titanomagnetite crystals that contain lamellae of titanohematite that occur in trellis-like intergrowths with titanomagnetite that is higher in TiO_2 content than the presumed parent. Titanohematite grains in the groundmass of such oxidized samples impart a reddish color to the rocks.

Subhedral to anhedral ilmenite grains (typically less than 50 μm), though rare, are present in every sample. Many grains appear to be embayed to a greater or lesser extent. The TiO_2 contents of the ilmenite grains in rapidly extruded lavas are essentially bimodally distributed, with one group somewhat higher in TiO_2 (~44 weight percent) and lower in FeO* (~48 weight percent, all iron as FeO) than the other (TiO_2 ~42 weight percent; FeO* ~50 weight percent). Analyses of representative phenocrysts are included in table 3. Individual grains are essentially homogeneous in composition except for the outermost rim, which may be somewhat higher in TiO_2 than the cores. In some slowly extruded samples, near-surface oxidation processes have resulted in decomposition of the ilmenite and its replacement by veinlets of titanohematite, interspersed with rare small patches of a TiO_2 polymorph (greater than 83 weight percent TiO_2), likely rutile.

Rare ilmenite-titanomagnetite in-contact pairs are present in all samples examined. Concentration gradients for TiO_2 in titanomagnetite crystals in contact with ilmenite are commonly observed in these oxide pairs, with high TiO_2 adjacent to the ilmenite. Analyses of coexisting oxide pairs are given in table 3, together with the temperature and oxygen fugacity indicated by the coexisting compositions.

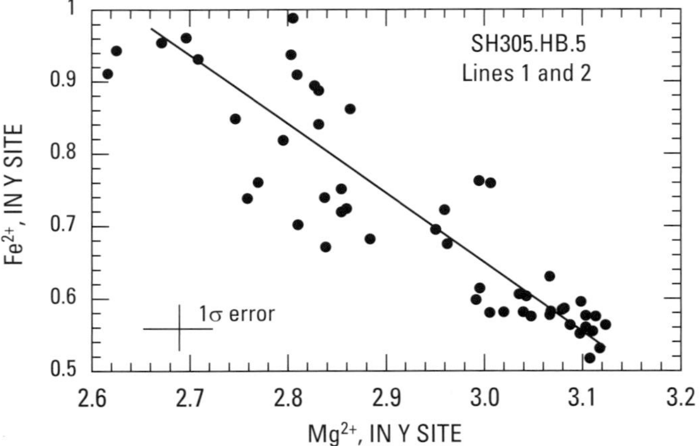

Figure 6. Plot of Mg^{2+} versus Fe^{2+} for the same amphibole phenocryst data plotted in figure 5, illustrating 1:1 correlation of Fe and Mg in the Y site of cyclically zoned 2004–2006 phenocrysts.

Preeruption Magma Conditions Inferred from the Phenocrysts

The compositions of the coexisting Fe-Ti oxides in the different samples of the 2004–6 Mount St. Helens dacite have been used to obtain estimates of temperature and f_{O_2} of the magma during the period of last magnetite-ilmenite equilibration. Methods of conversion are those described by Devine

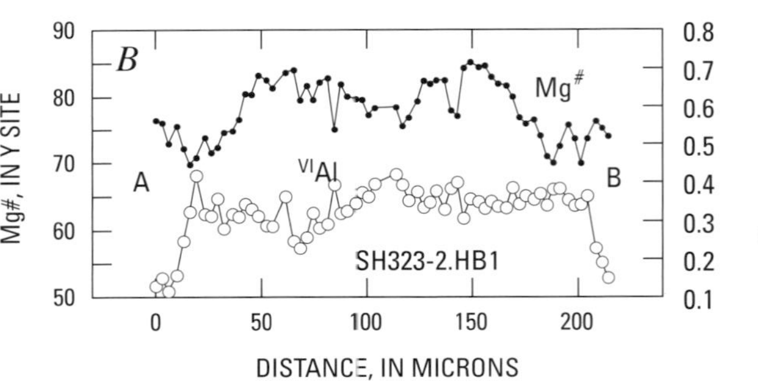

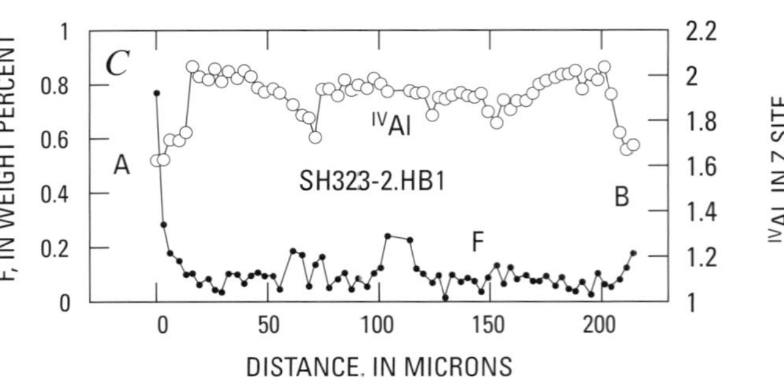

Figure 7. Typical amphibole phenocryst in sample SH323 erupted in September 2005 when the mass eruption rate had dropped to about 1 m^3/s (Pallister and others, this volume, chap. 30). *A*, Backscattered electron image showing compositional traverse as line A–B. *B*, *C*, Compositional traverses, showing presence of a rim less than 30 μm thick with low Al and Mg (panel *B*) and high F (panel *C*). Profile for SiO_2 across same phenocryst (fig. 4) shows the rim is also enriched in Si.

and others (2003) and utilize the algorithm of Andersen and Lindsley (1988) as amended by Andersen and others (1993). However, meaningful geothermometry based on analysis of ilmenite-titanomagnetite (two-oxide) pairs in these samples is hampered by the common presence of TiO_2 concentration gradients in the titanomagnetite grains, especially near the contact with ilmenite. Similar occurrences in the 1995–2003 Soufrière Hills volcano (Montserrat) andesite dome lavas were interpreted to be caused by replacement of the ilmenite grains by the in-contact encroaching titanomagnetite grain (Devine and others, 2003). The concentration gradients were interpreted as arising from submicron-scale mixtures of encroaching titanomagnetite upon islands of relict ilmenite. It was concluded in that case that temperature estimates based on analysis of the titanomagnetite crystal in the gradient zone (likely a two-phase mixture) were spurious. In some cases, two-oxide geothermometry calculations for the gradient zones yielded temperature estimates greater than 1,000°C, far above the experimentally determined upper stability limit (855°C) of the amphibole crystals observed to be stable in the natural magma (Rutherford and Devine, 2003). The two-oxide geothermometry calculations produced spurious results for zoned oxide pairs. Similar high-Ti magnetite zones adjacent to ilmenite in the Mount St. Helens 2004–6 magma are interpreted to give spurious temperature estimates for the same reasons.

In addition to using pairs of titanomagnetite and ilmenite (table 3), estimates of preeruptive magma temperatures also were attempted by analyzing the cores of large individual titanomagnetite and ilmenite grains in the 2004–6 lava samples. The titanomagnetite analyses in SH305 fall into three groups, with high, intermediate, and low TiO_2 contents (fig. 9). The range of TiO_2 contents observed in the titanomagnetite crystals might, in part, reflect incorporation of xenolithic material from the conduit walls. Temperature estimates based on the combined analytical transects range from 816°C to 889°C for sample SH305 and from 823°C to 884°C for sample SH315. A significant part of the variance in the estimates is due to the wide range of compositions observed in the respective phases. Temperature estimates based on analyses of titanomagnetite grains in the intermediate-TiO_2 group range from 823°C to 846°C when used in combination with the high-TiO_2 ilmenite the range of temperature estimates is 854–875°C when the low-TiO_2 ilmenite is used in the calculations. Oxygen fugacities generally are less than one log unit above the NNO synthetic buffer (range +0.6 to +1.2 log units) at the calculated temperatures in all cases.

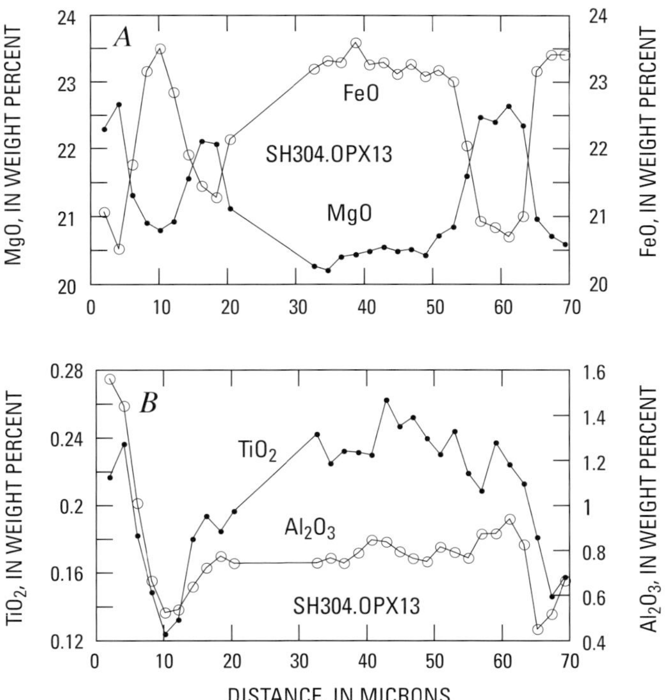

Figure 8. Compositional profiles (rim to rim) across typical zoned orthopyroxene in sample SH304 (phenocryst imaged in fig. 1*B*). Note tendency of Ti and Al to be correlated with Fe in the pyroxene growth cycles as they are in amphibole (figs. 5, 6). *A*, MgO and FeO. *B*, TiO_2 and Al_2O_3.

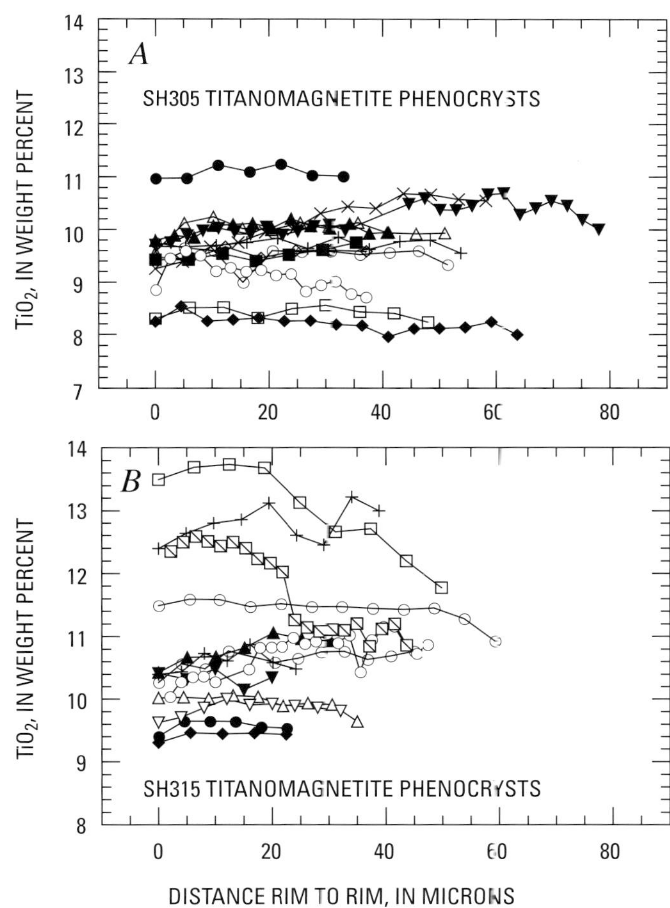

Figure 9. Composition (TiO_2) profiles across representative titanomagnetite phenocrysts in samples SH305 (*A*) and SH315 (*B*) from the 2004–6 eruption, showing range of relatively homogeneous crystals present.

Table 3. Chemical composition of ilmenite and titanomagnetite occurring as pairs, with calculated temperature and f_{O_2} of last equilibration geothermometry and oxygen geobarometry, Mount St. Helens, Washington, 2004–2006.

[Chemical analyses determined by electron microprobe at Brown University, Providence, R.I.; J.D. Devine, analyst. Compositions in weight percent; all Fe as FeO. Structural formula, temperature, and oxygen fugacity calculated after Devine and others (2003). Oxide phases abbreviated as follows: ILM, ilmenite; MT, magnetite.]

Sample No.----	SH304-1b2		SH305-1-8		SH305-1-8	
Date erupted--	10/18/04		11/20/04		11/20/04	
Relation--------	Oxide pair in plag		Oxide pair in proximity		Oxide pair, small grains	
Oxide	ILM	MT	ILM	MT	ILM	MT
FeO	51.39	82.85	49.94	80.67	50.34	74.88
TiO_2	42.98	8.54	44.02	11.13	44.36	12.73
Al_2O_3	0.21	2.33	0.17	1.79	0.21	1.74
Cr_2O_3	0.01	0.02	0.02	0.03	0	0.02
MgO	1.83	0.92	2.04	1.09	1.75	0.84
MnO	0.54	0.4	0.62	0.43	0.62	0.41
Total	96.96	95.06	96.82	95.15	97.29	90.63
Analyses	14	5	4	11	3	3
T°C	847		879		922	
$Log_{10} f_{O_2}$	−11.82		−11.10		−11.59	
ΔNNO	+1.16		+0.79		+0.50	
Sample No.----	**SH305-1-8**		**SH315-1a**		**SH315-1a**	
Date erupted---	**11/20/04**		**4/1/05**		**4/1/05**	
Relation--------	**Oxide pair in contact**		**Oxide pair in proximity**		**Oxide pair in proximity**	
Oxide	ILM	MT	ILM	MT	ILM	MT
FeO	51.90	78.65	49.24	82.63	51.27	82.29
TiO_2	41.75	13.77	45.07	9.57	43.22	7.86
Al_2O_3	0.22	1.48	0.14	1.47	0.16	2.80
Cr_2O_3	0.02	0.03	0.02	0.06	0.02	0.02
MgO	1.90	1.20	1.74	0.91	1.80	1.23
MnO	0.56	0.52	0.63	0.44	0.44	0.37
Total	96.35	95.65	96.84	95.09	96.91	94.57
Analyses	5	7	14	6	5	7
T°C	963		828		832	
$Log_{10} f_{O_2}$	−10.22		−12.57		−12.07	
ΔNNO	+0.70		+0.79		+1.21	

In spite of the difficulty of obtaining meaningful temperature estimates from in-contact Fe-Ti oxide pairs in the Mount St. Helens 2004–6 magma, the presence of the TiO_2 concentration gradients is evidence of a recent heating event (Nakamura, 1995; Venezky and Rutherford, 1999). However, the general lack of rim-to-core TiO_2 diffusion gradients in titanomagnetite phenocrysts suggests that heating of the crystals must have taken place some weeks before eruption, judging from experimental work on similar samples (Rutherford and Devine, 2003; Devine and others, 2003) and from diffusion data on Ti in magnetite (Venezky and Rutherford, 1999). It appears likely that the variability of TiO_2 contents in titanomagnetite is due in part to commingling of parcels of magma that experienced different *P–T* histories prior to eruption. This interpretation is consistent with observations of cyclic variations of amphibole and orthopyroxene chemistry described above.

Two other important intensive parameters that can occasionally be determined for a preeruption magma using phenocryst and melt compositions are the pressure (depth) and the P_{H_2O} (for example, Rutherford and others, 1985). The phenocryst assemblage in the 2004–6 magma suggests an intermediate depth (greater than 3.5–4 km) because the stability of amphibole in a melt requires that the water content of the melt be at least equal to H_2O saturation at 100 MPa (Merzbacher and Eggler, 1984). The compositions of coexisting amphibole and plagioclase can also potentially yield both pressure and temperature information (Holland and Blundy, 1994), but the complex compositional zoning in both these phases makes it difficult to determine what amphibole coexists with a given plagioclase. In an attempt to circumvent this problem, the margins of amphibole crystals included in plagioclase were analyzed along with the immediately adjacent plagioclase for the 2004–6 magma samples. The results showed a complete range of amphibole compositions in contact with a given plagioclase and, thus, no decipherable indication of pressure or temperature. Similarly, the analysis of glassy melt inclusions in phenocrysts have yielded important data on the volatile content of the preeruption melt for other eruptions (for example, Rutherford and others, 1985; Wallace, 2005), but the relatively slow ascent and eruption of the 2004–6 dacite appears to have caused cracking and/or crystallization of almost all melt inclusions in the new Mount St. Helens magma. Analyses of 2004–6 samples indicate dissolved water contents less than 3 weight percent (J. Blundy, oral commun., 2006), and CO_2 below FTIR detection limits (less than 40 ppm).

The observation that amphibole crystallized before plagioclase in the 2004–6 samples indicates that this dacite contained at least 4 weight percent dissolved H_2O when the crystallinity was very low (less than 4–8 volume percent), as discussed above. This means that when the phenocryst content of the dacite reached the preeruption 40–50 volume percent as the result of decompression and/or cooling, the dissolved H_2O in the remaining melt would have almost doubled. In fact, the residual melt probably would have reached H_2O saturation where the storage-region pressure was less than 300 MPa. These arguments assume that all magma entering the magma storage zone was similar in composition, including dissolved volatiles. The fact that the erupted dacite has been uniform in composition and contains no mafic melt-bearing enclaves (Pallister and others, this volume, chap. 30) suggests that this assumption is justified.

Experimental Phase Equilibrium Constraints

In order to determine the *P–T* conditions where the compositions of the phenocrysts observed in the 2004 Mount St. Helens magma are stable, hydrothermal experiments were performed on a crushed powder of SH305. Experiments were done using water-saturated conditions, a decision justified by arguments presented in the previous section. Most experiments were at a log f_{O_2} close to NNO+1 because of the f_{O_2} conditions determined from the Fe-Ti oxide phenocrysts, but higher and lower oxidation states also were investigated using solid-state buffers. Sample and buffer were contained in Ag or Ag-Pd tubes. Details of the experiments are given in table 4, and the results are plotted in figure 10. The main objective of these experiments was to determine the composition of the amphibole and plagioclase that is stable (grows in experimental charges previously equilibrated at somewhat higher or lower P_{H_2O} and *T*) at each point in the range of *P–T* conditions where amphibole is stable in the magma. Our interest in the amphibole stability in this dacite magma stems from the observation that the main amphibole population appears to have crystallized at a range of conditions within the amphibole stability field prior to the final magma ascent to the surface. The final magma ascent is represented by the 0- to 5-μm-thick reaction rims that occur at the amphibole-melt contact (Rutherford and Devine, 2005).

As expected, the general hydrothermal phase equilibria of the 2004–6 dacite are similar to those determined for the slightly less evolved 1980 lava (63 versus 65 weight percent SiO_2). The amphibole stability field at the f_{O_2} conditions (NNO +1.0±0.5) of the many reconnaissance experiments is essentially unchanged by the composition difference, with the breakdown at 200 MPa occurring at 910±8°C (fig. 10). Above 200 MPa, the reaction to form amphibole with decreasing temperature does not involve Ca-rich pyroxene, as it does at lower pressures. Orthopyroxene, plagioclase, magnetite, and ilmenite appear almost simultaneously on the liquidus (920±5°C at 200 MPa) of the 2004–6 dacite for H_2O-saturated conditions. Melt and phenocryst abundances were determined for representative experiments using the bulk-rock and melt compositions (table 5), along with phenocryst compositions from each experiment, in a mass-balance calculation (Wright and Doherty, 1971). Just within the amphibole stability field at 200 MPa (900°C), the magma contains 8 weight percent crystals (4 percent plagioclase, 2 percent each of orthopyroxene and amphibole, and less than 1 percent of magnetite and ilmenite). At 850°C and 200 MPa, the crystals make up 32 weight percent of the magma (M-27; table 4), and at 850°C and 100 MPa, they make up 52 weight percent of the magma.

The composition of the plagioclase that is stable at any set of *P–T* conditions is contoured in figure 10 primarily on the basis of long-duration crystallization experiments, but reversals also were achieved. New-growth plagioclase is readily identifiable morphologically in higher temperature experiments (900±25°C), and it was analyzed. Very long duration (15 to 30 days) crystallization experiments used a starting material created at 235 MPa to determine the stable plagioclase-composition contours at lower pressures, all at 850°C. Plagioclase compositions used to create the contours in figure 10 are recorded in table 4.

The compositions of the amphibole produced are plotted in figure 11 for the experiments where new growth could be identified optically and in BSE images (table 6). Plotted for comparison are the data from representative natural phenocrysts in sample SH305. Six experiments run at 850°C or 870°C and pressures of 100–230 MPa all have amphiboles with 9–10.5 weight percent Al_2O_3, well outside the range observed in the normal cyclically zoned natural amphiboles (11.5–15 weight percent). The range of MgO (and FeO) in these low-temperature amphiboles is partly a function of the differences in f_{O_2} in this group of experiments, as illustrated by the most oxidized experi-

Table 4. Hydrothermal experiments on Mount St. Helens 2004 dacite.

[Total of 48 runs, arranged in order of decreasing pressure, from 260 to 70 MPa. Temperature ranges from 940°C to 840°C. Starting material was powder derived from sample SH305 (dome lava erupted November 2004) for 20 runs (shown as 305pdr); whereas starting material for other runs was product of an intervening run, shown listed. Oxygen fugacity buffered within 2 log units of nickel-nickel oxide (NNO). Crystallization products, listed in order of decreasing abundance (except glass), are plagioclase, Plg; amphibole; A; orthopyroxene, Opx; Cpx, clinopyroxene; magnetite, Mt; ilmenite, Il; and glass, L. Product listed in square brackets indicates phase is breaking down, is not in contact with melt, and is considered unstable at conditions of experiment; number in brackets refers to rim thickness on amphibole. Weight percent crystals shown parenthetically for some runs, determined by mass balance methods. Anorthite content of plagioclase, specified for 60 percent of runs, ranges from An_{71} to An_{34}.]

Run No.	Starting material	Pressure (MPa)	Temperature (°C)	Buffer (Δ NNO)	Time (days)	Products	
M-45a	M-41	260	915	1	1.0	L	
M-63a	305pdr	260	850	-1	1.0	Plg, A, Opx, Mt, I, L	(25%)
M-63b	M-16	260	850	-1	1.0	An_{53}, A, Opx, Mt, I, L	(25%)
M-73	305pdr	250	895	0	1.5	Plg, A, Opx, Mt, I, L	
M-35	M-31	235	900	1	2	An_{68}, A, M, L	(3%)
M-20	305pdr	235	850	1	1.5	An_{50}, A, Opx, Mt, I, L	(32%)
M-49	M-17	225	860	1	5	An_{51}, Opx, A, Mt, L	
M-62	M-58+s	210	900	-1	2	An_{64}, Opx,A, Mt, L	
M-59a	M-56a	205	900	-2	1	An_{62}, A, Opx, Mt, L	
M-59b	M-19	205	900	-2	1	An_{62}, A, Opx, Mt, L	
M-60b	M-16	205	900	-2	1.5	Plg, A, Opx, Mt, L	
M-58	305pdr	200	930	1	1	L	
M-16	305pdr	200	922	1	2	Opx, Mt, [Plg], L	
M-24	305pdr	200	920	1	1.8	An_{71}, Opx, Mt, M, L	
M-19	M-17	200	915	1	0.5	Plg, Opx, M, L	(4%)
M-36	M-17	200	915	1	2	An_{70}, Opx, Mt, L	(2%)
M-41a	305pdr	200	910	1	2	An_{67}, Opx, A, Cpx, Mt, L	
M-41b	M-24	200	910	1	2	Plg, Opx, A, M, L	
M-50b	M-24	200	900	2	2	An_{62}, Opx, A, Mt, L	(8%)
M-51a	M-41a	200	900	-1	1	Plg, Opx, A, Mt, I, L	
M-51b	305pdr	200	900	-1	1	Plg, Opx, A, Mt, I, L	
M-56a	305pdr	200	900	-2	0.7	Plg, A, Opx, Mt, L	
M-25	M-24	200	885	1	2	An_{58}, A, Opx, Mt, I, L	
M-26	M-24	200	870	1	3	An_{52}, A, Opx, Mt, I, L	
M-66	305pdr	200	850	1	2	An_{42}, A, Opx, Mt, I, L	
M-27	M-24	200	850	1	6	An_{44}, A, Opx, Mt, I, L	
M-17	305pdr	200	840	1	4	Plg, A, Opx, Mt, I, L	
M-21	M-20	180	850	1	28	An_{40}, A, Opx, Mt, I, L	
M-48	M-34	150	905	1	2	Plg, A, Opx, Mt, I, L	
M-34	305pdr	150	880	1	2	An_{58}, A, Opx, Mt, I, L	
M-32	M-31	150	860	1	6	An_{42}, A, Opx, Mt, I, L	
M-28	M-24	150	860	1	6	Plg, A, Opx, Mt, I, L	
M-22	M-20	140	850	2	28	An_{37}, A, Opx, Mt, I, L	
M-54	305pdr	125	940	1	2	An_{70}, Opx, Mt, I, L	
M-44	M-39	125	930	1	3	An_{68}, Opx, Mt, I, L	
M-39	305pdr	125	920	1	1	An_{58}, A, Opx, Mt, I, L	
M-38	305pdr	125	910	1	2	An_{54}, Opx, Cpx, Mt, I, L	
M-31	305pdr	125	875	1	4	An_{44}, Opx, Cpx, [A], Mt, I, L	
M-46	M-30	125	864	1	6	An_{40}, A, Opx, Mt, I, L	
M-53	M-38	125	860	1	6	An_{39}, A, Opx, Mt, I, L	

Table 4. Hydrothermal experiments on Mount St. Helens 2004 dacite.—Continued

[Total of 48 runs, arranged in order of decreasing pressure, from 260 to 70 MPa. Temperature ranges from 940°C to 840°C. Starting material was powder derived from sample SH305 (dome lava erupted November 2004) for 20 runs (shown as 305pdr); whereas starting material for other runs was product of an intervening run, shown listed. Oxygen fugacity buffered within 2 log units of nickel-nickel oxide (NNO). Crystallization products, listed in order of decreasing abundance (except glass), are plagioclase, Plg; amphibole; A; orthopyroxene, Opx; Cpx, clinopyroxene; magnetite, Mt; ilmenite, Il; and glass, L. Product listed in square brackets indicates phase is breaking down, is not in contact with melt, and is considered unstable at conditions of experiment; number in brackets refers to rim thickness on amphibole. Weight percent crystals shown parenthetically for some runs, determined by mass balance methods. Anorthite content of plagioclase, specified for 60 percent of runs, ranges from An_{71} to An_{34}.]

Run No.	Starting material	Pressure (MPa)	Temperature (°C)	Buffer (Δ NNO)	Time (days)	Products	
M-54a	M-44	120	912	1	2.5	An_{56}, Opx, Cpx, Mt, I, L	
M-54b	M-38	120	912	1	2.5	Plg, Opx, Cpx, Mt, I, L	
M-52	305pdr	120	845	1	21	An_{56}, Opx, A, Mt, I, L	(51 %)
M-47	305pdr	115	890	1	3	Plg, Opx, Cpx, Mt, I, L	
M-30	305pdr	100	865	1	4	Plg, Opx, Cpx, Mt, I, [A, 8 m], L	
M-23	M-20	100	850	1	30	An_{34}, Opx, A, Mt, I, L	
M-12	305pdr	82	850	1	10	Plg, Opx, Cpx, Mt, I, [A, 10 m]	
M-11	M-20	70	850	1	6	Plg, Opx, Cpx, Mt, I, [A, 8 m]	

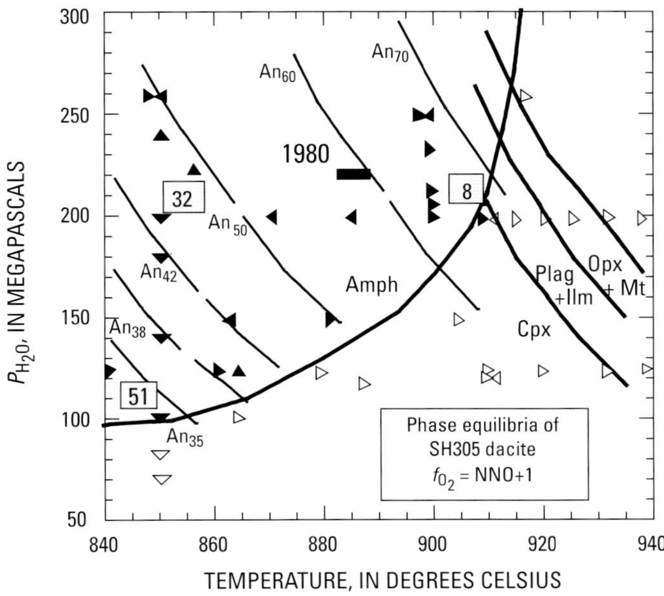

Figure 10. Pressure-temperature phase diagram determined for the Mount St. Helens 2004–6 dacite at water-saturated conditions and oxygen fugacity equal to NNO+1 log units. Symbols for individual experiments (table 4) point in the direction of approach to the final *P* and *T* plotted; solid symbols indicate amphibole is stable. Solid heavy lines mark upper stability limit for a given phenocryst phase: Cpx, Ca-pyroxene; Amph, amphibole; Plag, plagioclase; Opx, orthopyroxene; Mt, magnetite; Ilm, ilmenite. Medium-weight lines are contours labeled with plagioclase anorthite content (for example, An_{70}), on basis of data in table 4. Boxed numbers (8, 32, 51) indicate weight percent crystals present at *P–T* conditions occupied by box, as determined by a mass balance calculation (see text). Solid bar labeled 1980 shows estimated conditions in preeruption 1980 magma (Rutherford and others, 1985; Venezky and Rutherford, 1999).

Table 5. Bulk and experimental glass compositions, Mount St. Helens, Washington, 2004–2006.

[Chemical analyses determined by electron microprobe at Brown University, Providence, R.I.; J.D. Devine, analyst. Each analysis is an average; total number of analyses for each sample listed in row "Analyses." Compositions in weight percent; all Fe as FeO. Parenthetical numbers, standard deviation on average for the last places given. VBD, dissolved volatiles (H_2O) by difference. Column 1 (all glass), SH305 bulk composition.]

Sample ---	SH-305	M-62	M-59a	M-51a	M-27	M-17	M-23	M-34
T(°C) ------	1300	900	900	900	850	850	850	890
P(MPa)---	0.1	210	205	200	200	200	100	150
f_{O_2} (ΔNNO)	+1	−1	−2	−1	+1	+1	+1	+1
				Major-element analyses, weight percent				
SiO_2	64.80 (24)	62.48 (28)	62.48 (26)	61.59 (39)	65.30 (98)	67.69 (52)	72.83 (24)	67.95 (32)
TiO_2	0.64 (5)	0.60 (5)	0.54 (7)	0.52 (6)	0.32 (9)	0.25 (3)	0.25 (4)	0.34 (4)
Al_2O_3	17.23 (14)	15.85 (13)	15.94 (19)	16.06 (4)	14.46 (28)	13.91 (18)	12.38 (12)	13.68 (10)
FeO	4.35 (10)	3.24 (12)	3.22 (8)	3.15 (16)	2.10 (52)	2.11 (17)	1.42 (11)	2.40 (9)
MgO	1.91 (4)	1.26 (5)	1.24 (7)	1.45 (11)	0.68 (51)	0.46 (3)	0.21 (2)	0.53 (11)
CaO	4.68 (8)	3.93 (7)	3.93 (7)	4.28 (19)	1.96 (44)	2.13 (11)	1.20 (7)	2.27 (6)
Na_2O	4.58 (9)	4.84 (10)	4.84 (10)	4.64 (19)	5.60 (25)	4.77 (19)	4.60 (14)	4.66 (17)
K_2O	1.45 (7)	1.53 (6)	1.53 (6)	1.33 (11)	2.40 (14)	1.83 (9)	2.43 (11)	1.97 (4)
MnO	0.10 (3)	0.02 (3)	0.02 (3)	0.05 (2)	0.06 (5)	0.04 (3)	0.02 (4)	0.04 (3)
Total	99.74	93.75	93.68	93.07	92.89	93.19	95.34	93.84
Analyses	9	6	6	6	6	7	6	6
VBD	0	6.25	6.32	6.93	7.11	6.81	4.66	6.16

ment, M-22 (fig. 11*A*). The externally imposed f_{O_2} in the 900°C experiments ranges from 2 log units below to 2 log units above NNO, bracketing the f_{O_2} indicated by the Fe-Ti oxides (NNO +1) in the natural sample.

The variation in Al_2O_3 content (including Al_{total} and ^{VI}Al) of amphibole that crystallizes from the 2004–6 dacite (table 6) should be a function of temperature and pressure as discussed earlier in this paper, and the experimental data (fig. 11) show this to be the case. It is notable, however, that only experiments done at 200 MPa and higher pressures have compositions that plot in the zone defined by the cyclically zoned natural phenocrysts. Additionally, none of the experiments in the pressure range 200–250 MPa produced amphiboles comparable to the highest Al- and Fe-rich zones in the natural amphibole. Experiments at 200 MPa, 900°C, and a log f_{O_2} in the range NNO+2 to NNO-2 produce the low and intermediate Al_2O_3 compositions in the cyclically zoned natural phenocrysts. Experiments at 900°C and pressures of 235 MPa (NNO+1) and 250 MPa using the NNO buffer did not produce an amphibole with higher Al. Both the Al_2O_3 and ^{VI}Al composition data indicate that a pressure somewhat greater than 250 MPa is required to stabilize the highest Al- and Fe-rich amphibole end members of the natural phenocrysts.

Depth of the Preeruptive 2004–2006 Magma System

The question of preeruptive magma-storage depth is of considerable interest and importance for understanding the ongoing Mount St. Helens eruption and for predicting how the eruption is likely to progress. Is the magma erupting from the same storage zone determined for the 1980–86 eruptions (Scandone and Malone, 1985; Rutherford and others, 1985), or has the system changed? The seismic record over the decade before the new eruption suggests that magma may have moved to a relatively shallow depth (3–4 km) below the crater floor, particularly at one or two times during this period (Moran, 1994; Moran and others, this volume, chap. 2). Seismicity accompanying the 2004 eruption appears to have been largely in the region from 2 km to the surface, consistent with magma erupting from storage below this depth. Theoretically, the abundance and composition of phenocrysts, particularly the rim compositions, are dependent on the final P and T of phenocryst-melt equilibration in the erupting magma. We have attempted to use this knowledge and the phenocryst data from the natural sample and experiments to determine the depth of the magma storage upper boundary.

As described in the previous section, most of the amphibole-phenocryst growth in the 2004–6 dacite was at pressures of 200 MPa or higher and at temperatures greater than 850°C. The phenocryst abundance in the dacite at these high pressures is less than 32 volume percent at temperatures greater than 850°C (fig. 10). However, given that much of the magma erupted at 850°C with ~45 volume percent phenocrysts (Pallister and others, this volume, chap. 30), plagioclase phenocryst growth must have continued to a much lower pressure (fig. 10). Analytical data from experiments designed to achieve a good approach to plagioclase phenocryst rim-melt equilibrium as a function of pressure at 850°C are compared with rim-composition measurements in the natural samples (figure 12).

Table 6. Representative experimental amphibole compositions and structure formulas, Mount St. Helens, Washington, 2004–2006.

[Chemical analyses determined by electron microprobe at Brown University, Providence, R.I.; J.D. Devine, analyst. Compositions in weight percent; all Fe as FeO. Structure formula calculated after Holland and Blundy (1994). Magnesium number, Mg# = (Mg×100)/(Mg+(Fe^{2+} in Y site)).]

Sample No.---	**M-62**	**M-59b**	**M-59a**	**M-51a**	**M-49**
***P* (MPa)-------**	**210**	**205**	**205**	**200**	**225**
***T* (°C)----------**	**900**	**900**	**900**	**900**	**860**
f_{O_2} (ΔNNO)--	**-1**	**-2**	**-2**	**-1**	**1**
Major-element analyses, weight percent					
SiO_2	42.63	43.68	43.58	42.07	44.44
TiO_2	2.48	2.28	2.62	2.72	1.89
Al_2O_3	13.38	12.54	11.31	13.00	10.31
FeO	13.13	10.72	11.48	14.07	14.95
MgO	13.30	15.21	14.90	13.14	13.15
CaO	10.95	11.07	11.06	11.58	10.56
Na_2O	2.25	2.37	2.26	2.39	1.89
K_2O	0.27	0.33	0.26	0.32	0.26
MnO	0.19	0.11	0.21	0.10	0.26
Total	98.58	98.31	97.68	99.39	97.71
Cation abundance in structure formula					
Si	6.119	6.224	6.275	6.041	6.452
Al^{IV}	1.881	1.776	1.725	1.959	1.548
Ti	0.268	0.244	0.284	0.294	0.206
Al^{VI}	0.383	0.331	0.195	0.241	0.216
Fe^{3+}	0.728	0.654	0.701	0.745	0.823
Fe^{2+}(Y)	0.776	0.536	0.622	0.908	0.909
Mg	2.846	3.231	3.198	2.812	2.846
Ca	1.684	1.690	1.706	1.782	1.643
Fe^{2+}(X)	0.072	0.088	0.059	0.037	0.083
Na	0.627	0.609	0.631	0.665	0.532
Mg#	78.57	85.78	83.71	75.60	75.80
$Fe^{3+}/\Sigma Fe$	0.462	0.512	0.507	0.441	0.454

Sample No.---	**M-32**	**M-28**	**M-20**	**M-27**	**M-22**
***P* (MPa)-------**	**150**	**150**	**234**	**200**	**140**
***T* (°C)----------**	**200**	**860**	**850**	**850**	**850**
f_{O_2} (ΔNNO)--	**1**	**1**	**1**	**1**	**1**
Major-element analyses, weight percent					
SiO_2	44.72	45.19	45.59	42.92	46.04
TiO_2	2.46	1.73	1.68	2.14	1.49
Al_2O_3	9.29	10.26	9.48	11.49	8.58
FeO	14.58	13.12	14.21	15.80	11.60
MgO	13.07	14.04	13.71	12.19	15.48
CaO	11.14	11.28	11.32	10.97	11.36
Na_2O	1.97	1.98	1.79	2.23	1.94
K_2O	0.27	0.28	0.26	0.32	0.24
MnO	0.14	0.18	0.28	0.21	0.29
Total	97.64	98.06	98.32	98.27	97.02
Cation abundance in structure formula					
Si	6.540	6.515	6.575	6.264	6.659
Al^{IV}	1.460	1.485	1.425	1.736	1.341
Ti	0.271	0.188	0.182	0.235	0.162
Al^{VI}	0.141	0.259	0.187	0.240	0.121
Fe^{3+}	0.558	0.625	0.698	0.745	0.670
Fe^{2+}(Y)	1.182	0.911	0.986	1.129	0.709
Mg	2.849	3.017	2.947	2.652	3.337
Ca	1.745	1.77	1.749	1.715	1.761
Fe^{2+}(X)	0.043	0.046	0.030	0.055	0.024
Na	0.558	0.554	0.500	0.631	0.542
Mg#	70.68	76.81	74.93	70.14	82.47
$Fe^{3+}/\Sigma Fe0$	0.313	0.395	0.407	0.386	0.478

The results of the plagioclase-growth experiments indicate that if the 2004–6 magma was stored for more than 30 days at 180 MPa before experiencing a fairly rapid ascent to the surface, the rim compositions would be approximately An_{40}. The similarity of the 14- and 28-day experimental results suggest that much longer storage at this depth would not change the most albite-rich composition observed, as long as the temperature and P_{H_2O} remained unchanged. At 140 and 100 MPa, the plagioclase in equilibrium with the residual melt at 850ºC is An_{35} and An_{32}, respectively. Comparing these experimental plagioclase compositions to the most Na-rich rims on natural phenocrysts in SH304 and SH305 suggests that the phenocrysts in the 2004–6 magma were crystallizing at a pressure as low as 120–140 MPa before the final ascent. The natural phenocrysts with more Ca-rich rims (fig. 12) are interpreted to have experienced little or no growth in the decompression accompanying ascent to 120 MPa. This lack of new plagioclase growth is expected in an ascending magma when the phenocryst content is high, because the melt immediately adjacent to some phenocrysts is limited in volume by other phenocrysts that are close or touching. Additionally, because the ascent from the storage zone to the surface did not produce significant reaction rims on amphiboles, we conclude that measurable additions to the plagioclase phenocrysts are unlikely to be added during the final (100 to 0.1 MPa) ascent. We make this conclusion because H_2O loss from the melt in ascending magma is the main cause of both amphibole breakdown and plagioclase crystallization. The amphibole rims are less than 5 µm thick in these samples, indicating a relatively rapid magma ascent (Rutherford and Hill, 1993; Rutherford and Devine, 2003). Although nucleation and growth of plagioclase microlites occurs readily in such decompressions (Geschwind and Rutherford, 1995), the experimental data indicate that additions to associated phenocrysts would be minor and too thin to analyze by electron microprobe.

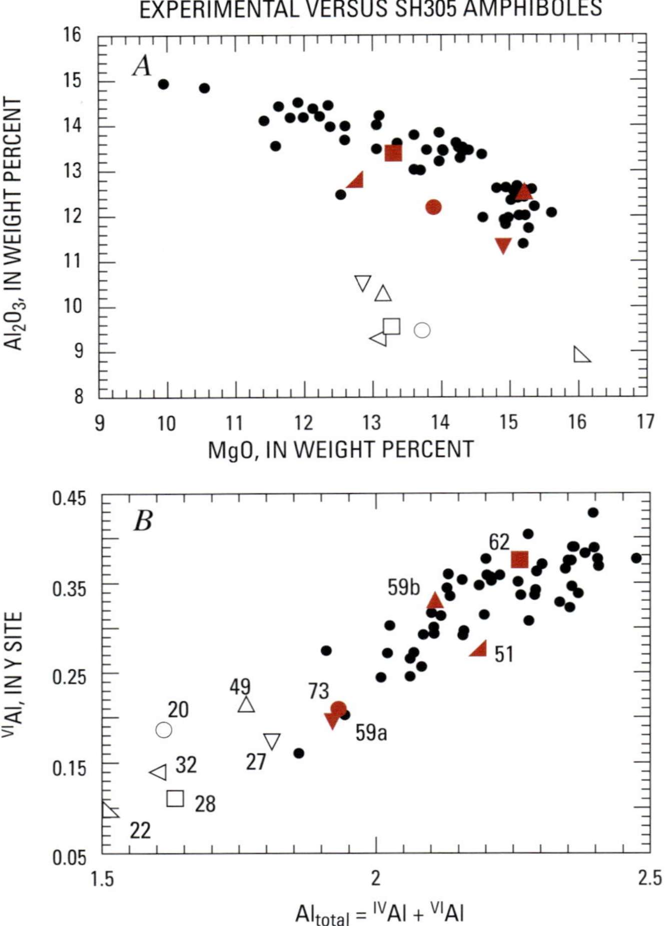

Figure 11. Compositions of amphiboles produced in hydrothermal experiments (table 4) compared with those of natural cyclically zoned phenocrysts in SH305, a representative phenocryst in 2004–6 magma. Black solid dots, natural amphiboles; open symbols, experimental results at temperatures from 840ºC to 870ºC and pressures less than 200 MPa. Solid red symbols represent experiments at 900ºC and pressures of 200–260 MPa. The f_{O_2} of the 900ºC experiments ranged from NNO-2 to NNO+2; others were all at NNO+1 log units. Numbered symbols indicate amphibole compositions (table 6) produced in experiments; numbers correspond to sample numbers in table 4. *A*, Al_2O_3 versus MgO. *B*, ^{VI}Al versus Al_{total}.

To summarize, the plagioclase rim compositional data indicate that the 2004–6 magma could have been stored at a pressure as low as 120 MPa, or a depth of 4–5 km below the crater floor for a relatively prolonged period before eruption. When these data are considered together with the depth range indicated by seismic data during the eruption (Moran and others, this volume, chap. 2), the 4–5-km depth appears to represent the top of the magma storage zone. However, it is also obvious that the preeruptive magma storage extended to much greater depths, and the Na-rich plagioclase phenocryst rims may have developed during the slow, final ascent process that began somewhere below 4 km.

The amphibole phenocryst compositions and their very thin decompression-induced reaction rims do not significantly constrain estimates of the preeruptive magma storage-zone depth, except to indicate that it was greater than 100 MPa (4–5 km) for magma at 850ºC. If the storage zone pressure had been less than 100 MPa, there would have been thick, coarse-grained reaction rims on all amphiboles. For example, 10-µm-thick rims were produced in experiments at 85 and 70 MPa on the 2004–6 dacite in as little as 7 days (experiments M-11 and M-12; table 4). However, as discussed in the following section, the crystallization of the cyclically zoned amphiboles must have occurred at pressures more than twice the 100 MPa estimated for the final pressure of phenocryst-melt equilibration. No attempt was made to use the Al-in-hornblende geobarometer to estimate the pressure because the phenocryst phase assemblage in the 2004–6 dacite is not silica saturated as required by the geobarometer calibration (Johnson and Rutherford, 1989). Using the geobarometer (Thornber and others, this volume, chap. 32) should give an upper-pressure limit, particularly for the early crystallization of the Al-rich amphiboles.

Origin of the Cyclically Zoned Phenocrysts: Preeruptive Magma History

A second objective of this project was to determine the origin and significance of the cyclic compositional zonation observed in 2004–6 magma phenocrysts. Is it possible to crystallize the cyclically zoned plagioclase, amphibole, and orthopyroxene phenocrysts by simply changing conditions in the dacite magma, or are injections of mafic magma required? For example, the presence of cyclically zoned phenocrysts in the silicic andesite magma erupted recently (1995–2002) at Soufrière Hills, Montserrat, was clearly the result of recrystallization following injections of a more mafic basaltic andesite (Rutherford and Devine, 2003). Vesicular blobs of the mafic magma were carried up in the erupting magma, and small, blade-shaped crystals of high-An plagioclase and pargasitic amphibole from the mafic magma are present in the andesite groundmass. However, there is no evidence of recent mafic magma injections into the 2004–6 dacite (Pallister and others, this volume, chap. 30). Thus, we have concentrated on determining how the 2004–6 phenocryst compositions could have been formed from dacite magma by trying to determine the range of pressure-temperature conditions where the various phenocryst compositions would crystallize.

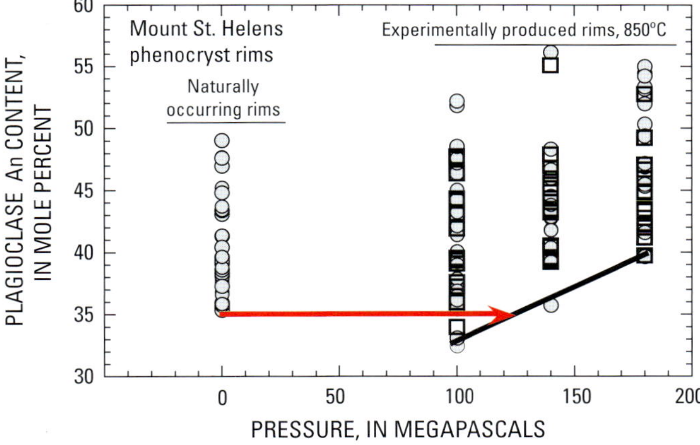

Figure 12. Comparison of plagioclase phenocryst-rim compositions in samples from 2004–2006 Mount St. Helens eruption (SH304 and SH305) with those produced in long-duration crystallization experiments at 850°C and pressures of 100 to 180 MPa (table 4). Squares, 15-day runs; circles, 30-day runs. Similarity between different run durations indicates experiments were sufficiently long to approach chemical equilibrium. Arrow indicates pressure (about 120 MPa) where these experiments produce new plagioclase that is compositionally equal to most Na-rich rims on the natural phenocrysts. More Ca-rich rims in natural plagioclase are interpreted as rims where there was limited late-stage growth.

Figure 13 is a model of the Mount St. Helens 2004–6 magma storage zone that uses the experimental data described above to explain the cyclic zoning of the natural amphibole, plagioclase, and orthopyroxene phenocrysts. Because there is no evidence, such as mafic enclaves, to indicate other magma compositions were mixed or mingled with the 2004–6 dacite, our model assumes a dacite magma input. The timing of this input is not known; it could have been associated with the beginning stages of the 2004–6 eruption, or it could have been associated with past (1986–98) peaks in deep seismic activity (Moran and others, this volume, chap. 2). Given that the preeruptive magmatic temperatures decreased from 1980 to 1986 (Rutherford and Hill, 1993), it seems unlikely that the hot 2004–6 magma was emplaced during the 1980–86 eruptions, although this possibility cannot be ruled out. The homogeneity of the 2004–6 dacite suggests that the magma composition entering the base of the storage zone is similar to the magma that has been erupting. Uranium-series dating of mineral separates from the 2004–6 magma indicate there is an old component present in the erupting magma (Cooper and others, this volume, chap. 36), but this may be explained by the xenolithic material, and it does not appear to affect our conclusions about magma entering the 2004–6 system.

If the incoming dacite magma had a high dissolved water content, as the phenocryst phase assemblage suggests, it would crystallize Fe- and Al-rich amphibole before or during its invasion of the storage zone at about 900°C (fig. 13). This temperature for the incoming magma is suggested by the high-TiO_2 magnetite phenocrysts in some of the samples (fig. 9), by the lack of plagioclase inclusions in amphibole phenocrysts that indicate that amphibole crystallized before plagioclase, and by the anorthite content (An_{68}) in the cores of cyclically zoned plagioclase phenocrysts. Small amounts of orthopyroxene, magnetite, and ilmenite crystallized along with the early amphibole as indicated by inclusions in amphibole and the experimental phase equilibria. The pressure on the magma as it enters the storage zone is interpreted to be ~300 MPa (12 km depth) on the basis of the experiments (fig. 11) that indicate such pressures are required to stabilize the high-Al zones in the amphibole phenocrysts. Importantly, An_{68} plagioclase is not stable above 200 MPa at 880–900°C, according to the water-saturated experiments (fig. 10), and would be lacking in the phenocryst-poor magma just after it entered the storage zone.

As the water-rich magma moved higher in the storage zone, the high-An (An_{68}) zones in plagioclase would begin to crystallize at 200 MPa and temperatures near 900°C. At this point (about 7–8 km depth), much of the magma must stagnate and cool in the storage zone in order to form the more Ab-rich zones in the plagioclase and the more Mg-rich zones in the amphiboles. The plagioclase phenocrysts require that the magma cools to 850°C in order to stabilize and grow the albite-rich layer (An_{45-50}) in the first growth cycle. We interpret this cooling as occurring in a lateral flow (fig. 13). If cooling did not occur, the original phenocrysts would tend to dissolve during convection to depth, and textures within phenocrysts indicate dissolution was not extensive. The second cycle of amphibole growth begins with an Fe- and Al-rich material that is stable only at pressures substantially greater than 200 MPa (fig. 11); the amphibole data require the convection system shown in figure 13. Sharp chemical transitions—those between Na-rich and Na-poor zones in plagioclase (200 MPa and 850°C) and those between Mg-rich and Fe-rich zones in amphibole—are consistent with the convection process, in that crystallization would not occur in the sinking magma.

The forces to drive the convection certainly are present. The melt-rich character, relatively high temperature, and high dissolved H_2O content would tend to make the incoming magma buoyant in the storage zone occupied by older, cooler, and more crystal-rich magma. During ascent from the 12-km depth, the buoyancy of this magma would decrease as a result of decompression-induced crystallization. Cooling, crystallization, and loss of released gas at the top of the convective cell would further reduce the buoyancy of the magma, apparently to the point where the combination of density and viscosity cause it to sink in the chamber. Using the data of Geschwind and Rutherford (1995) for the densities of the phases, the density of the magma would increase from 2,310 kg/m^3, as magma with 5 volume percent crystals (amphibole and orthopyroxene) enters the storage zone, to 2,450 kg/m^3 at 850°C where magma contains 30 volume percent phenocrysts (in the proportions plag:amph:opx:mt = 23:3:3:1 on a volume percent basis). This represents a 6-percent density increase of the crystal-rich magma relative to the incoming melt-rich magma, assuming gas released in the upwelling process is able to escape during the crystallization. Given that viscosity of the H_2O-rich melt will be relatively low, the viscosity of the phenocryst-poor magmas should facilitate the convection. Sharp increases in viscosity when the phenocryst content goes above 30 volume percent (Marsh, 1981) may indicate why the cycle ends and why there are only two zoning cycles, on average, in amphibole.

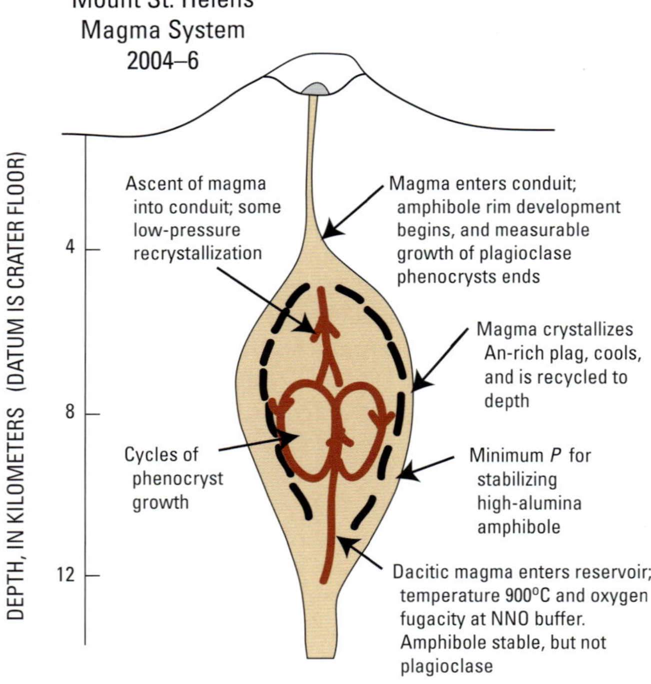

Figure 13. Simplified cross section showing model of the Mount St. Helens magma storage zone and transport system based on petrologic data for the 2004–6 samples discussed in this paper (see also Pallister and others, this volume, chap. 30) and the seismic depths associated with magma movement before and during the 2004 eruption (Moran and others, this volume, chap. 2). Depth scale is relative to the crater floor.

Following an average of two cycles of phenocryst growth and convective overturn, some fraction of the magma would separate and rise toward the conduit. Although there were additions to the plagioclase phenocrysts in this stage of magma ascent (fig. 12), there was almost no additional amphibole crystallization, because the interstitial H_2O-saturated melt at 200 MPa and 850°C has essentially no amphibole component, and there is no Ca-rich pyroxene in the H_2O-rich dacite. However, amphibole recrystallization to form Fe-rich, Al-poor amphibole rims, as observed in SH323 (fig. 7) may occur in magma that spent a somewhat longer-than-average time in the less-than-200-MPa pressure range during this ascent.

A variation of the above model involving an incoming magma that has a somewhat lower initial dissolved H_2O content cannot be ruled out. Rather than H_2O-saturated, the incoming magma could have a P_{H_2O} as low as 0.7 P_{total}, in which case the amphibole stability would not have been affected, but plagioclase phenocrysts would have been stabilized to a higher temperature at a given pressure. This is equivalent to proposing that the magma was saturated with a CO_2-bearing fluid when it entered the storage zone. As discussed above, however, the initial melt-rich magma must have contained at least 4 weight percent dissolved H_2O in order to stabilize amphibole, and this limits the CO_2 content of the coexisting fluid (Newman and Lowenstern, 2002) to ~600 ppm. The maximum temperature of the magma coming into the storage zone at 260–300 MPa is still required to be less than 910°C in order to stabilize the high-Al amphibole. However, in this case, the An_{68} plagioclase cores could have formed at pressures greater than 200 MPa, possibly as early as the amphibole. The absence of plagioclase inclusions in the amphibole cores suggests this variant of the storage zone model is unlikely.

Comparison of 2004–2006 and 1980–1986 Preeruption Magmas

Some additional data collected for the 1986 lava dome (sample SH205) and for the 1980 pumice (SH084) during the course of this study indicate that a set of convective processes similar to those described above was operating in the magma storage zone during the 1980–86 eruptions. Magma erupted in 1986 last equilibrated at 860±10ºC (Rutherford and Hill, 1993) and contained amphiboles with cyclic zoning generally indistinguishable from that in the 2004–6 magma. A plot of Al_2O_3 versus MgO for amphiboles (fig. 14) shows essentially total overlap between typical amphiboles from SH205 (1986) and SH323 (2005; table 2 and fig. 4). A cyclical set of phenocryst growth conditions similar to that outlined for the 2004–6 magmas (fig. 13) appears to be required for the 1986 dome-forming lava. The lack of decompression-induced rims on amphibole in the 1986 sample (fig. 3*D*) is one significant example of how the 1986 magma differs from that erupted in 2004–6. This observation seems to require an even more rapid ascent for the 1986 magma over the final 4–5 km. Outer rims on the 1986 amphibole that are higher in FeO, relative to those in the 2004–6 magma, might also be explained by a rapid ascent of magma from depth. This mineralogical evidence of amphibole crystallization over a pressure range suggests a process similar to one proposed recently (Blundy and Cashman, 2005; Cashman and McConnell, 2005) as operating in the Mount St. Helens magma system, on the basis of melt-inclusion data. The magma ascent history, however, appears to have been more complicated than can be determined from the melt inclusions.

Compositional zoning in representative amphibole phenocrysts from the May 18, 1980, white pumice is shown in figure 14. The Al_2O_3 versus MgO zoning within individual 1980 phenocrysts defines line segments that are parallel to the 2004–6 trend, but they range down to significantly lower Al_2O_3. The lower-Al_2O_3 phenocrysts are similar in composition to the Al-poor rims analyzed on amphiboles in SH323 (fig. 7) and other more recently erupted 2004–6 samples. In a previous section we suggested that the composition of the anomalous Al-poor rims on SH323 amphiboles are best explained by recrystallization at pressures of 100–200 MPa, possibly even just outside (below) the stability limit of OH-amphibole. This would help explain the fluorine enrichment of these rim compositions. These observations suggest that the convective process described in the model for the 2004–6 magma storage zone also was working in 1986 and 1980. However, at least some of the 1980 magma seems to have experienced a significant part of the amphibole crystallization at a pressure in the 150–200 MPa range at the 880ºC temperature (Rutherford and Devine, 1988; Venezky and Rutherford, 1999) of this system. The 1980 phenocrysts generally are higher in F (~1,200 ppm) than are the cores of 2004–6 samples (900 ppm) but are not as high as the 2004–6 rims (SH323), consistent with this lower-pressure origin.

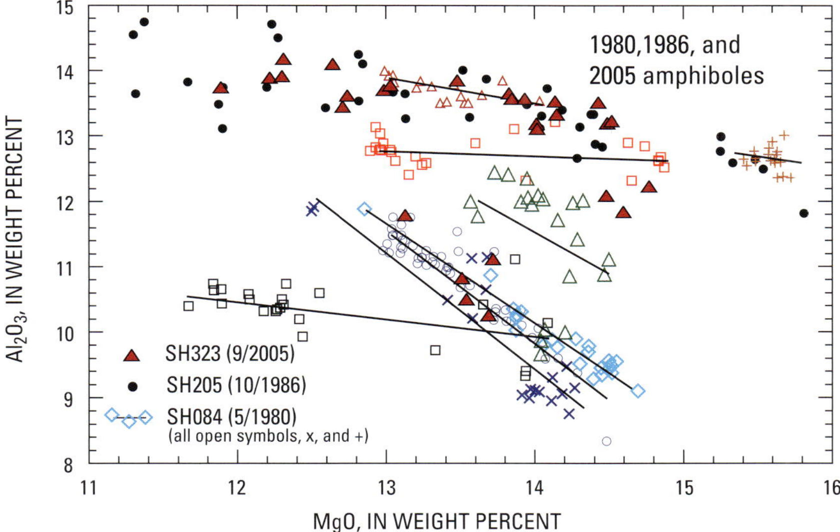

Figure 14. Compositions of eight amphibole phenocrysts (rim to rim transects) in the 1980 Mount St. Helens pumice (SH084) compared with similar amphibole transects for a typical sample of the 2004–6 lava dome (SH323) and 1986 dome (SH205). Lines are fit to the eight SH084 amphibole profiles. Zoning in the 1980 pumice phenocrysts is similar to that in the 2004–6 phenocrysts except that it occurs at lower Al_2O_3 in most crystals. Note that rims on SH323 amphiboles spread over the low-Al_2O_3 compositions found in the May 1980 samples, whereas the zoning profile in SH205 (1986 lava) is indistinguishable from 2004–6 samples such as SH304 and SH305 (fig. 4).

Conclusions

In summary, and in answer to the questions posed in the introduction to this paper, the following conclusions can be made: (1) The phenocryst assemblage that occurs in the 2004–6 Mount St. Helens dacite lava-dome samples can be attributed to crystallization from dacite magma; no mafic magma injection is required. (2) The compositions of the Fe-Ti oxides, magnetite and ilmenite, although somewhat variable, indicate that the temperature of equilibration was in the range of 820–890ºC and the f_{O_2} was NNO + 1 log unit. The existence of a range of TiO_2 in different, relatively homogenous titanomagnetite phenocrysts also suggests there was mingling of different batches of dacite with different thermal histories to create each batch of erupting magma. (3) Cyclic zoning observed in amphiboles in the 2004–6 magma consists of Al- and Fe-rich zones alternating with Mg- and Si-rich zones and can be explained as approximately equal amounts of two substitutions: a pressure-sensitive Al-Tschermak substitution and a temperature-controlled edenite substitution. Significantly, different amounts of the Al-Tschermak end member, in different zones of each amphibole phenocryst, require crystallization over a range of total pressure. Hydrothermal experiments on the dacite composition show that the Fe- and Al-rich end member of the amphibole zoning must have crystallized at pressures of ~300 MPa, whereas more Mg- and Si-rich amphibole zones crystallized in the 200-MPa range. (4) Cyclical zoning in natural plagioclase phenocrysts, ranging from An_{68} to An_{35}, also requires the magma to cycle through a range of crystallization conditions. The hydrothermal experiments indicate that An_{68} plagioclase would crystallize at ~200 MPa and 900ºC, well after the initial crystallization of amphibole in an ascending dacite magma. Cooling to ~850ºC is required to develop the first layer of Ab-rich plagioclase. (5) In order to explain the cyclic zoning in the phenocrysts, each batch of magma must have experienced convective overturn, going back to near the original high pressure at the lower temperature (850ºC), where it interacted with new incoming dacite magma, as illustrated in figure 13. (6) Rims on plagioclase phenocrysts, as sodic as An_{35}, indicate that plagioclase phenocryst growth continued in ascending magma until the pressure was ~130 MPa. This pressure is interpreted to represent the top of the magma storage zone at 4–5 km depth. (7) Compositional zoning in the 1980 and 1986 amphibole phenocrysts indicates that convective conditions also existed during phenocryst growth in that magma system.

Acknowledgments

We acknowledge the financial support of the National Science Foundation and field support from the Cascades Volcano Observatory staff for providing samples. We thank the members of the Mount St. Helens petrology working group for assistance and ideas and for providing access to manuscripts during their preparation. Finally, we acknowledge productive discussions with John Pallister and Carl Thornber and insightful reviews by Jon Blundy and Wes Hildreth.

References Cited

Andersen, D.J., and Lindsley, D.H., 1988, Internally consistent solution models for Fe-Mg-Mn-Ti oxides: Fe-Ti oxides: American Mineralogist, v. 73, nos. 7–8, p. 714–726.

Andersen, D.J., Lindsley, D.H., and Davidson, P.M., 1993, QUILF; a Pascal program to assess equilibria among Fe-Mg-Mn-Ti oxides, pyroxenes, olivine, and quartz: Computers and Geosciences, v. 19, p. 1333–1350.

Bachmann, O., and Dungan, M.A., 2002, Temperature-induced Al-zoning in hornblendes of the Fish Canyon magma, Colorado: American Mineralogist, v. 87, p. 1062–1076.

Blundy, J., and Cashman, K., 2005, Rapid decompression-driven crystallization recorded by melt inclusions from Mount St. Helens volcano: Geology, v. 33, no. 10, p. 793–796, doi:10.1130/G21668.1.

Cashman, K.V., and McConnell, S.M., 2005, Multiple levels of magma storage during the 1980 summer eruptions of Mount St. Helens, WA: Bulletin of Volcanology, v. 68, no. 1, p. 57–75, doi:10.1007/s00445-005-0422-x.

Cooper, K.M., and Donnelly, C.T., 2008, ^{238}U-^{230}Th-^{226}Ra disequilibria in dacite and plagioclase from the 2004–2005 eruption of Mount St. Helens, chap. 36 *of* Sherrod, D.R., Scott, W.E., and Stauffer, P.H., eds., A volcano rekindled; the renewed eruption of Mount St. Helens, 2004–2006: U.S. Geological Survey Professional Paper 1750 (this volume).

Cosca, M.A., Essene, E.J., and Bowman, J.R., 1991, Complete chemical analyses of metamorphic hornblendes; implications for normalizations, calculated H_2O activities, and thermobarometry: Contributions to Mineralogy and Petrology, v. 108, p. 472–484.

Devine, J.D., Rutherford, M.J., Norton, G.E., and Young, S.R., 2003, Magma storage region processes inferred from geochemistry of Fe-Ti oxides in andesitic magma, Soufrière Hills volcano, Montserrat, W.I.: Journal of Petrology, v. 44, no. 8, p. 1375–1400, doi:10.1093/petrology/44.8.1375.

Garcia, M.O., and Jacobson, S.S., 1979, Crystal clots, amphibole fraction, and the evolution of calc-alkaline magmas: Contributions to Mineralogy and Petrology, v. 69, p. 319–327.

Geschwind, C.-H., and Rutherford, M.J., 1995, Crystallization of microlites during magma ascent; the fluid mechanics of 1980–1986 eruptions at Mount St. Helens: Bulletin of Volcanology, v. 57, no. 5, p. 356–370.

Heliker, C., 1995, Inclusions in Mount St. Helens dacite erupted from 1980 through 1983: Journal of Volcanology and Geothermal Research, v. 66, nos. 1–4, p. 115–135, doi:10.1016/0377-0273(94)00074-Q.

Holland, T., and Blundy, J., 1994, Non-ideal interactions in calcic amphiboles and their bearing on amphibole-plagioclase thermometry: Contributions to Mineralogy and Petrology, v. 116, no. 4, p. 433–447, doi:10.1007/BF00310910.

Johnson, M.C., and Rutherford, M.J., 1989, Experimental calibration of the Al-in-hornblende geobarometer with application to the Long valley caldera (California) volcanic rocks: Geology, v. 17, p. 837–841.

Marsh, B.D., 1981, On the crystallinity, probability of occurrence, and rheology of lava and magma: Contributions to Mineralogy and Petrology, v. 78, p. 85–98.

Mastin, L.G., 1994, Explosive tephra emissions at Mount St. Helens, 1989–1991; the violent escape of magmatic gas following storms?: Geological Society of America Bulletin, v. 106, no. 2, p. 175–185.

Merzbacher, C., and Eggler, D.H., 1984, A magmatic geohygrometer; application to Mount St. Helens and other dacitic magmas: Geology, v. 12, p. 587–590.

Moran, S.C., 1994, Seismicity at Mount St. Helens, 1987–1992; evidence for repressurization of an active magmatic system: Journal of Geophysical Research, v. 90, no. B3, p. 4341–4354, doi:10.1029/93JB02993.

Moran, S.C., Malone, S.D., Qamar, A.I., Thelen, W.A., Wright, A.K., and Caplan-Auerbach, J., 2008, Seismicity associated with renewed dome building at Mount St. Helens, 2004–2005, chap. 2 *of* Sherrod, D.R., Scott, W.E., and Stauffer, P.H., eds., A volcano rekindled; the renewed eruption of Mount St. Helens, 2004–2006: U.S. Geological Survey Professional Paper 1750 (this volume).

Nakamura, M., 1995, Continuous mixing of crystal mush and replenished magma in the ongoing Unzen eruption: Geology, v. 23, p. 807–810.

Newman, S., and Lowenstern, J.B., 2002, Volatilecalc; a silicate melt-H_2O-CO_2 solution model written in Visual Basic for exel®: Computers and Geosciences, v. 28, no. 5, p. 597–604, doi:10.1016/S0098-3004(01)00081-4.

Pallister, J.S., and Thornber, C.R., 2005, Is the 2004–05 eruption of Mount St. Helens tapping new dacite from the deep crust? [abs.]: Eos (American Geophysical Union Transactions), v. 86, no. 52, Fall Meeting Supplement, Abstract V52B–05.

Pallister, J.S., Thornber, C.R., Cashman, K.V., Clynne, M.A., Lowers, H.A., Mandeville, C.W., Brownfield, I.K., and Meeker, G.P., 2008, Petrology of the 2004–2006 Mount St. Helens lava dome—implications for magmatic plumbing and eruption triggering, chap. 30 *of* Sherrod, D.R., Scott, W.E., and Stauffer, P.H., eds., A volcano rekindled; the renewed eruption of Mount St. Helens, 2004–2006: U.S. Geological Survey Professional Paper 1750 (this volume).

Rutherford, M.J., and Devine, J.D., 1988, The May 18, 1980, eruption of Mount St. Helens, III; stability and chemistry of amphibole in the magma chamber: Journal of Geophysical Research, v. 93, no. B10, p. 11949–11959.

Rutherford, M.J., and Devine, J.D., 2003, Magmatic conditions and magma ascent as indicated by hornblende phase equilibria and reactions in the 1995–2002 Soufrière Hills magma: Journal of Petrology, v. 44, p. 1433–1454.

Rutherford, M.J., and Devine, J.D., 2005, Crystallization of and conditions in the MSH 2004–05 dacite magma as indicated by phenocryst compositions and experiments [abs]: Eos (American Geophysical Union Transactions), v. 86, no. 52, Fall Meeting Supplement, Abstract V52B–05.

Rutherford, M.J., and Hill, P.M., 1993, Magma ascent rates from amphibole breakdown; an experimental study applied to the 1980–1986 Mount St. Helens eruptions: Journal of Geophysical Research, v. 98, no. B11, p. 19667–19685.

Rutherford, M.J., Sigurdsson, H., Carey, S., and Davis, A., 1985, The May 18, 1980, eruption of Mount St. Helens, 1; melt composition and experimental phase equilibria: Journal of Geophysical Research, v. 90, no. B4, p. 2929–2947.

Scandone, R., and Malone, S.D., 1985, Magma supply, magma discharge and readjustment of the feeding system of Mount St. Helens during 1980: Journal of Volcanology and Geothermal Research, v. 23, nos. 3–4, p. 239–262, doi:10.1016/0377-0273(85)90036-8.

Thornber, C.R., Pallister, J.S., Lowers, H.A., Rowe, M.C., Mandeville, C.W., and Meeker, G.P., 2008, Chemistry, mineralogy, and petrology of amphibole in Mount St. Helens 2004–2006 dacite, chap. 32 *of* Sherrod, D.R., Scott, W.E., and Stauffer, P.H., eds., A volcano rekindled; the renewed eruption of Mount St. Helens, 2004–2006: U.S. Geological Survey Professional Paper 1750 (this volume).

Venezky, D.Y., and Rutherford, M.J., 1999, Petrology and Fe-Ti oxide reequilibration of the 1991 Mount Unzen mixed magma: Journal of Volcanology and Geothermal Research, v. 89, p. 213–230, doi:10.1016/S0377-0273(98)00133-4.

Wallace, P.J., 2005, Volatiles in subduction zone magmas; concentrations and fluxes based on melt inclusion and volcanic gas data: Journal of Volcanology and Geothermal Research, v. 140, nos. 1–4, p. 217–240, doi:10.1016/j.jvolgeores.2004.07.023.

Wright, T.L., and Doherty, P.C., 1971, A linear programming and least squares method for solving petrologic mixing problems: Geological Society of America Bulletin, v. 81, p. 1995–2008.

A Volcano Rekindled: The Renewed Eruption of Mount St. Helens, 2004–2006
Edited by David R. Sherrod, William E. Scott, and Peter H. Stauffer
U.S. Geological Survey Professional Paper 1750, 2008

Chapter 32

Chemistry, Mineralogy, and Petrology of Amphibole in Mount St. Helens 2004–2006 Dacite

By Carl R. Thornber[1], John S. Pallister[1], Heather A. Lowers[2], Michael C. Rowe[3], Charles W. Mandeville[4], and Gregory P. Meeker[2]

Abstract

Textural, compositional, and mineralogical data are reported and interpreted for a large population of clinoamphibole phenocrysts in 22 samples from the seven successive dacite spines erupted at Mount St. Helens between October 2004 and January 2006. Despite the uniformity in bulk composition of magma erupted since 2004, there is striking textural and compositional diversity among amphibole phenocrysts and crystal fragments that have grown from, partly dissolved in, or been accidentally incorporated in the new dacite. This study demonstrates that magma erupted throughout the current dome-building episode is the end product of small-scale, thorough mixing of multiple generations of crystal-laden magma. The mixed amphibole population provides important clues to magma conditions within the dacite magma reservoir prior to ascent and, to some extent, the dynamics of mixing and ascent.

The predominant amphibole in new dome rock ranges from moderate- to high-alumina tschermakite and magnesiohastingsite compositions. As substantiated by major- and trace-element geochemistry and barometry calculations, this compositional range of crystals, along with plagioclase, orthopyroxene, and iron-titanium oxide, is likely to have precipitated from dacite magma over a range of pressures and temperatures consistent with experimentally determined phase relations (~900°C to ~800°C between 100 MPa and ~350–400 MPa or ~4-km and 13.5–15-km depth). Along with trace-element characteristics, textural and compositional data help to distinguish some low-alumina magnesiohornblende crystals as xenocrysts. The diverse range in composition of amphibole in all samples of 2004–6 dacite, and the complex zonation observed in many phenocrysts, suggests a well-mixed source magma with components that are subjected to repeated heating and (or) pressurization within this pressure-temperature window. Amphibole textural and compositional diversity suggest dynamic conditions in the upper-reservoir zone, which has been tapped steadily during ~2 years of continuous and monotonous eruption. This well-mixed crystal mush is likely to have been subjected to repeated injection of hotter magma into cooler crystal-laden magma while simultaneously assimilating earlier generations of dacitic roof material and surrounding gabbroic rock.

Decompression-related reaction rims around subhedral, rounded, resorbed, and fragmented amphibole phenocrysts, regardless of composition, indicate that this mixed-crystal assemblage was being broken, abraded, and dissolved in the magma as a result of mechanical mixing before and during early stages of ascent from conduit roots extending into a mushy cupola of the shallow reservoir. In the earliest lava samples (October 2004), amphiboles with <3-μm rims associated with a glassier matrix than later samples suggest a slightly faster ascent rate consistent with the relatively high eruptive flux of the earliest phases of dome extrusion. Reaction rim widths of ~5 μm on amphibole in all subsequently extruded lava result from a steady influx and upward transport of magma from 3.5–2.5-km to ~1-km depth at rates of ~600 to ~1,200 m/day, through a conduit less than 10 m in radius. Slower ascent rates inferred from volumetric-flux and matrix-crystallization parameters are explained by a widening of the conduit to greater than 60 m radius within 1 km of the surface.

[1] U.S. Geological Survey, 1300 SE Cardinal Court, Vancouver, WA 98683

[2] U.S. Geological Survey, Box 25046, Denver Federal Center, Denver, CO 80225

[3] Department of Geosciences, 104 Wilkinson Hall, Oregon State University, Corvallis, OR 97331; now at Department of Geoscience, 121 Trowbridge Hall, University of Iowa, Iowa City, IA 52242

[4] American Museum of Natural History, Central Park West at 79th Street, New York, NY 10024

Introduction

The cooled and degassed dacite magma that has been tapped continuously by the 2004–6 eruption at Mount St. Helens is a mixture of 45 percent phenocrysts and 55 percent dacite melt (Pallister and others, this volume, chap. 30, table 4). As shown by Pallister and others (this volume, chap. 30), the whole-rock composition of lava erupted from 2004 to 2006 is strikingly uniform (64.9±0.09 weight percent SiO_2), and the dense-rock-equivalent (DRE) volume proportion of plagioclase (30–40 percent), amphibole (4–8 percent), orthopyroxene (3–5 percent), and iron-titanium-oxide (1–2 percent) phenocrysts is consistent throughout the eruption. Similarity of bulk-rock and bulk-matrix compositions, as well as the experimental phase equilibria of Rutherford and Devine (this volume, chap. 31), suggest that the dominant phenocryst assemblage shares a dacite parentage. However, the isotopic, mineralogical, and textural diversity of phenocrysts leaves little doubt that the bulk compositional uniformity is the end result of repeated and thorough mixing of phenocryst-laden magma with preexisting crystalline material.

Petrologic models of magmatic processes for this eruption rely, in part, upon mineral-melt criteria that are clouded by a genetically mixed population of phenocrysts. The phenocrysts, including variably resorbed, reacted, and fragmented crystals, are discrete pieces of a complicated "dacite puzzle." Some crystal populations look alike but did not necessarily crystallize together at the same depth, temperature, magma composition, and time. Detailed studies of phenocryst morphology and chemistry provide petrologic context for establishing the genetic affinities of the crystals. This chapter provides detailed documentation of the potpourri of amphibole phenocrysts in the 2004–6 lava at Mount St. Helens.

All amphibole found in 1980–86 and 2004–6 Mount St. Helens dome lava is calcium-rich, monoclinic amphibole (clinoamphibole). In fresh gray pieces of plagioclase-rich dacite (fig. 1), amphibole phenocrysts are conspicuous as dark-brown to black, lustrous to semitranslucent flecks, chunks, and, locally, flow-aligned acicular blades.

The ubiquitous amphibole phase in 1980–86 and 2004–6 Mount St. Helens dome rock incorporates all of the major-element components of a water-saturated dacite melt and, thus, records changes in the pressure-temperature (*P-T*) paths and the compositional variations of host magmas at depths in excess of ~ 4 km, where amphibole is stable (~100 MPa, Rutherford and Devine, this volume, chap. 31). Clinoamphibole phenocrysts dissolve in magmas undergoing decompression and degassing during ascent. The nature and extent of amphibole breakdown reactions record the rates and paths of magma ascent from depth (Rutherford and Hill, 1993; Browne and Gardner, 2006; Buckley and others, 2006). In this study of newly erupted Mount St. Helens lava, we establish and correlate variations in texture, chemistry, and mineralogy among amphibole crystals, and we document and interpret the characteristics of amphibole reaction rims. Aluminum-in-amphibole thermobarometry is applied to infer the relative *P-T* conditions for the range of amphiboles likely to have crystallized from host dacite or similar magma. We aim to provide an

Figure 1. Photograph showing freshly broken surface of SH325-1A, a typical sample of Mount St. Helens 2004–6 dacite lava.

"amphibolic" perspective toward understanding the character and disposition of a well-mixed, cooled, and degassed magma beneath Mount St. Helens during its near-steady-state transport to the surface from 2004 to 2006.

Samples Used in this Study

This investigation is based on microbeam studies of 22 Mount St. Helens dacite samples erupted during the October 2004 to January 2006 interval of spine emergence and dome growth (table 1). Aside from the samples derived unequivocally from newly extruded material (including the March 8, 2005, ash-fall sample, MSH05DRS3/8-4), the suite described here includes two unusual glassy dacite fragments (SH300-1A3, SH304-2G) dredged from debris shed by the emergent dome in early October 2004. Because these two samples are of uncertain origin and are uniquely glassy, their data, along with data for lithic inclusions of nonjuvenile andesite and dacite found in lava samples SH315-4, SH325-1A, and SH321-1, are discussed separately. Petrologic attributes of several samples reported here are also reviewed elsewhere in this volume; for example, the petrology of the early glassy fragment (SH-04-2G) and the small, glassy andesite inclusion in SH315-4 are discussed by Pallister and others (this volume, chap. 30). An overview and complete catalog of samples collected during the 2004–6 eruption, including sampling methods, locations, brief descriptions, and chemistry, is presented for dome samples by Thornber and others (2008) and for tephra samples by Rowe and others (2008).

Three older dome samples from the Cascades Volcano Observatory (CVO) archive were also analyzed to assess differences between clinoamphibole chemistry from the current eruption suite and the 1980–86 dacite (table 1). Compositional data on amphiboles in two gabbro xenoliths from the 1986 dome rock (791-8a, 791-8b samples of Pallister and others, 1991) provide a basis for identifying xenolith-derived crystal fragments among the diverse population of amphiboles in the 2004–6 dacite.

Overview of Amphibole Data

Amphiboles in polished thin sections were selected for analysis without bias to size or morphology. Microbeam analyses and imagery used in this study were accomplished at three different laboratories (details of microbeam methods are in appendix 1). All amphibole analyses used in this investigation fit the mineralogical criteria established for calcic amphiboles by Leake and others (1997). The stoichiometric calculation used to assess cation site occupancy and proper nomenclature is discussed in a separate section below. Compositional data acquired include 458 major-element analyses of 399 individual crystals with 373 interior and 85 outer (20 μm) rim analyses. These data include 26 analyses of 17 crystals in lithic inclusions of andesite or dacite and 49 analyses of 28 crystals in glassy lithic samples. In addition, rare-earth elements were analyzed for 80 amphibole cores in nine samples spanning the 2004–6 eruption. No amphibole trace-element data are currently available for 1980–86 lava or xenolithic inclusions. All chemical analyses of 2004–6 amphibole phenocrysts compiled for this investigation are tabulated in appendix 2, which appears only in the digital versions of this work (in the DVD that accompanies the printed volume and online at http://pubs.usgs.gov/pp/1750). For purposes of the comparison with current eruptive products, major-element analyses of amphibole in 1980–86 Mount St. Helens dacite and in gabbroic xenoliths in the 1980–86 dome material also were compiled and are provided in appendix 2.

Maximum length and width measurements of 391 (98 percent) of the analyzed phenocrysts were made using scaled scanning electron microscope (SEM) images. Although providing a general assessment of amphibole crystal sizes and aspect ratios, this method does not consider variations resulting from crystal orientation within the plane of the thin section. Measurements of the average width of amphibole-breakdown rims resulting from decompression (Rutherford and Hill, 1993; Browne and Gardner, 2006) were made on 195 crystals having rims in contact with the 2004–6 dacite matrix. Care was taken to exclude any anomalous rim widths for crystals sectioned unevenly along their outer edges.

Amphibole Morphology and Reaction Textures

In typical new-dome material, amphibole grains range in size from phenocrysts <4 mm long to microphenocrysts ranging from 100 to 10 μm. An amphibole size distribution based upon approximate surface areas (length-by-width measurements) shows that nearly all of the smallest crystals observed ($<1\times10^3$ μm^2) are fragments with broken or irregular edges and that the amphibole population as a whole is more normally distributed about a range of $10–100\times10^3$ μm^2 (fig. 2). Distinctly resorbed edges are observed among broken and unbroken crystals. A 62-percent majority of the amphibole phenocryst population is equant to slightly acicular (0–10 percent acicularity) and 23 percent is distinctly acicular, with length/width ratios ranging from 2.5:1 to 5:1 (20–30 percent acicularity, fig. 3).

Morphologic variants of isolated amphibole grains in 2004–6 dacite-lava samples include (1) subhedral, equant to acicular crystals with well-defined faces and typically, but not always, multiple, compositionally distinct growth zones (fig. 4); (2) angular fragments, variably rounded or embayed and commonly broken along cleavage planes that intersect normal growth zones (fig. 5); (3) well-rounded and seemingly abraded grains lacking substantially embayed or cuspate grain boundaries (fig. 6); and (4) irregularly shaped, rounded and embayed crystals or crystal fragments, commonly with fine

Table 1. Summary of Mount St. Helens 2004–2006 samples used in this investigation.

Sample No.	Spine No.	Collection date	Eruption date[1]	Sample type	Rock type
SH100		9/8/1981	9/6/1981	Dome talus	Dacite
SH133		6/5/1985	2/1–3/31/1983	Dome rock	Dacite
SH187		6/6/1989	5/30/1985	Dome rock	Dacite
SH300-1A3	1	10/20/2004	10/15/2004	Crater debris, either 1985 or Oct 2004 (?)	Dense dark-gray glassy dacite fragment
SH300-1C	1	10/20/2004	10/15/2004	Crater debris, either 1985 or Oct 2004 (?)	Vesicular dark-gray dacite fragment
SH302-1A	1 or 2	10/27/2004	10/14/2004	Crater debris, either1985 or Oct 2004 (?)	Vesicular dark-gray dacite fragment
SH304-2A	3	11/4/2004	10/18/2004	Dome talus and debris	Vesicular “hot-pink” dacite
SH304-2G	3	11/4/2004	10/18/2004	Dome talus and debris	Dense dark-gray glassy dacite fragment
SH305-1	3	1/3/2005	11/20/2004	Spine margin	Vesicular gray dacite
SH306-A	4	1/14/2005	12/15/2004	Dome talus	Vesicular pink-gray dacite
SH308-3	4	2/22/2005	1/21/2005	Dome talus	Vesicular gray dacite
SH309-1C	4	2/22/2005	1/13/2005	Spine margin	Vesicular gray-pink dacite, fractured foliated
SH311-1B	4	1/19/2005	1/16/2005	Ballistic block, 1/16/2005 explosion	Vesicular gray dacite
MSH05DRS_3_9_4	4	3/9/2005	3/8/2005	Coarse fragments in tephra-fall deposit from 3/8/2005 explosion	Vesicular gray-pink dacite
SH312-1	4	4/10/2005	3/8/2005	Ballistic block, 3/8/2005 explosion	Vesicular gray dacite
SH314-1A1	5	4/19/2005	4/17/2005	Gouge fragment	Vesicular dacite fragment
SH315-3	4	4/19/2005	4/1/2005	Dome talus, 4/18/2005 collapse	Dense gray dacite
SH315-4	4	4/19/2005	4/1/2005	Dome talus, 4/18/2005 collapse	Dense gray dacite
SH317-4	5	6/15/2005	5/1/2005	Dome talus	Dense pink-gray dacite
SH319-1	5	7/13/2005	5/15/2005	Dome talus	Dense gray-pink dacite, foliated, “pink” margins
SH321-1	6	8/19/2005	8/10/2005	Dome talus, 8/19/2005 collapse	Dense gray-pink dacite, “pink” margins
SH323-2, -3	6	10/18/2005	9/10/2005	Dome talus, 8/19/2005 collapse	Dense gray dacite
SH324-1A	7	12/15/2005	12/5/2005	Spine margin	Vesicular gray-pink dacite
SH324-3	7	12/15/2005	12/5/2005	Spine margin	Dense gray dacite
SH325-1	7	2/7/2006	12/20/2005	Dome talus	Dense gray dacite

[1] Estimate of when sampled lava was extruded from vent, whose altitude is assumed to be that of the crated floor below Crater Glacier.

to coarse cuspate margins indicative of magmatic resorption (fig. 7). The patterns of compositional zoning apparent in SEM backscattered electron images of many crystals or fragments typically define subparallel growth bands. In numerous cases, regardless of grain morphology, zoning patterns have an irregular or patchy appearance. This characteristic has been attributed to late-stage igneous (near-solidus) diffusion (Hammarstrom and Zen, 1992) but could result from patchy dissolution and regrowth (M.J. Rutherford, written commun., 2006).

Many amphibole crystals or fragments in the new Mount St. Helens dacite have glass inclusions (fig. 4) or partially to wholly crystallized melt inclusions (glass±opx±plg±oxides; for example, fig. 5*B*), suggestive of variable cooling or reaction rates among a mixed phenocryst population. Amphibole phenocrysts of subhedral and resorbed morphology also are present in glomerophyric clusters, coupled during growth with various combinations of plagioclase, orthopyroxene, or oxide crystals (fig. 8). Although some of the more pristine-looking glomerophyric aggregates appear as though they grew in the dacite host, those cored by resorbed amphiboles may have resulted from prolonged amphibole-melt reaction, as discussed further below.

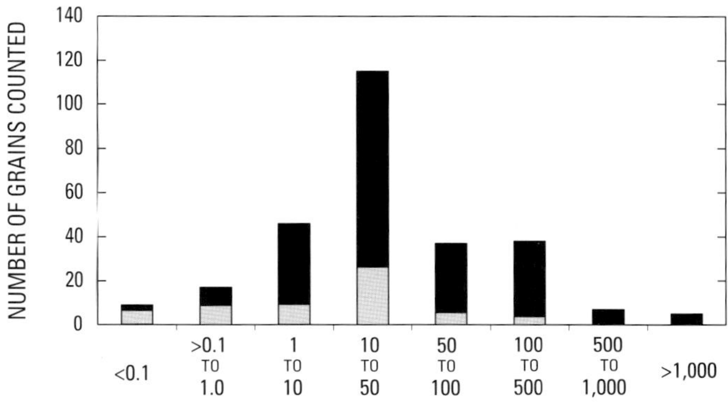

Figure 2. Histogram of size distribution of amphibole phenocrysts in Mount St. Helens 2004–6 dacite lava presented as approximate surface area. The size distribution of fragmented crystals, shown in gray, is compared to that of the overall population, shown in black.

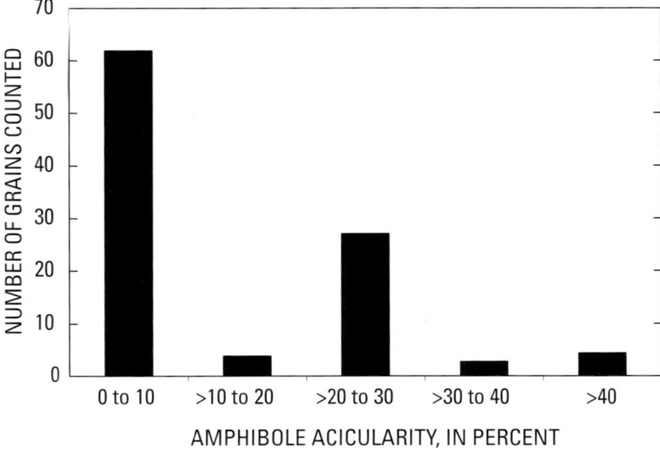

Figure 3. Histogram of acicularity of amphibole phenocrysts in Mount St. Helens 2004–6 dacite lava. Percent acicularity = [100 × length/(length + width)] – 50. (Equant crystals have zero-percent acicularity).

Because of similarities in texture and degree of reaction, there might be no definitive textural distinction between cognate and xenocrystic aggregates, such as those derived from gabbroic xenolith fragmentation. The latter could appear relatively pristine (unreacted or unresorbed) if exposed to the degassed host melt during xenolith fragmentation at near-solidus temperatures and shallow depths.

The edges of all amphibole crystals in contact with matrix in 2004–6 dacite lava are armored by an aureole of acicular microlites of plagioclase and orthopyroxene (±Fe-Ti oxide). As demonstrated by experiments, such rims result from reaction of clinoamphibole with dacite melt during decompression and degassing (Rutherford and Hill, 1993; Browne and Gardner, 2006). Rim widths are a function of the rate and path of ascent of the host magma during transport to the surface from a minimum P_{H_2O} of 100 MPa where amphibole is stable (>3.5–4 km depth at Mount St. Helens).

Essentially all of the amphibole crystals measured have decompression reaction rims between 3 and 8 μm thick; average reaction-rim width is 5±1 μm. Typical reaction rims pseudomorphically replace the outer edges of subhedral, rounded, or resorbed crystals and fragments (fig. 9). Exceptions to the normal reaction-rim thickness are observed in the earliest dome sample (SH304-2A, fig. 9*B*), which has <3-μm-thick rims, and the glassy lithic fragment (SH304-2G, fig. 9*A*), in which amphibole crystals lack reaction rims. Atypically thick rims (30–200 μm) are found among isolated amphibole crystals in 2004–6 dacite. These rims are defined by relatively coarse-grained plagioclase-orthopyroxene-oxide intergrowths that surround embayed (resorbed) amphibole grains (fig. 10).

An unusual but recurrent texture observed in SH314-1 and DRS_3_9_4 indicates amphibole reacting with the host melt to form second-generation amphibole + liquid (fig. 11). Such amphibole-to-amphibole reaction reflects exposure to a hotter or chemically incompatible melt under amphibole saturation conditions. As discussed further within the context of the compositions of these crystals, this amphibole-to-amphibole reaction is likely to occur at depths near the low-pressure limits of amphibole stability (100 MPa).

Amphibole phenocrysts in lithic inclusions (SH315-4inc, SH325-1Ainc, and SH321-1inc) have reaction-rim characteristics that differ from those of the host 2004–6 dacite. The SH315-4 glass-bearing inclusion has distinctly acicular amphibole intergrown with plagioclase and minor clinopyroxene, and it has an andesitic bulk composition (Pallister and others,

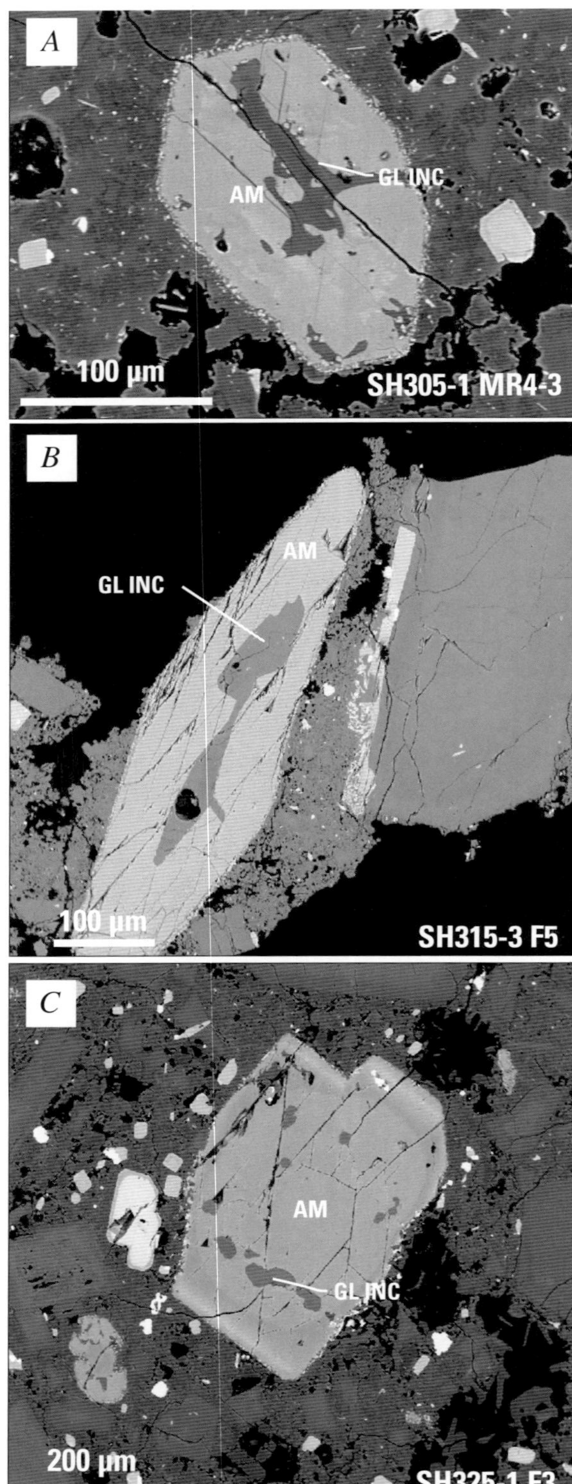

Figure 4. SEM backscattered electron images of analyzed subhedral amphibole grains (AM) in Mount St. Helens 2004–6 dacite lava. Glass inclusions (GL INC) indicated where confirmed by microbeam analysis. The sample and image numbers shown on the lower right side in each image correspond to analysis numbers in appendix 2. *A*, Sample SH305-1. *B*, Sample SH315-3. *C*, Sample SH325-1.

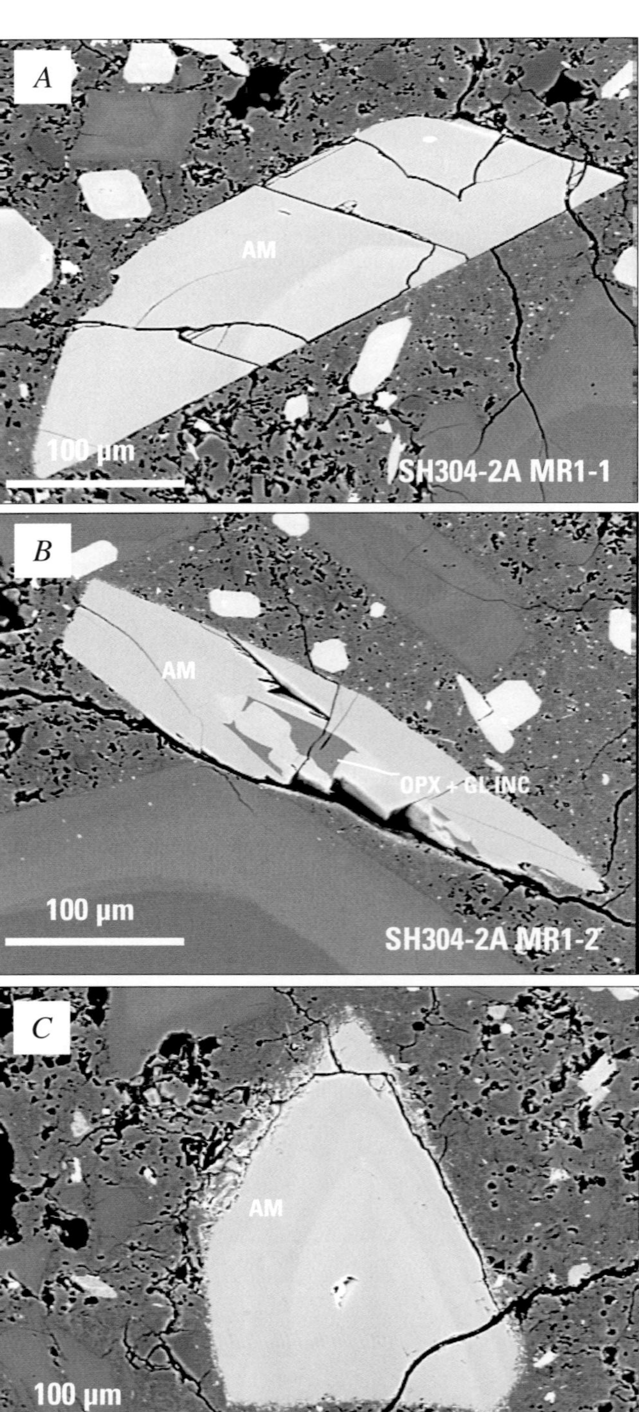

Figure 5. SEM backscattered electron images of analyzed broken amphibole grains (AM) in Mount St. Helens 2004–6 dacite lava. Orthopyroxene and glass inclusions (OPX + GL INC) are indicated where confirmed by microbeam analysis. The sample and image numbers shown on the lower right side in each image correspond to analysis numbers in appendix 2. *A*, Sample SH304-2A. *B*, Sample SH304-2A. *C*, Sample SH319-1.

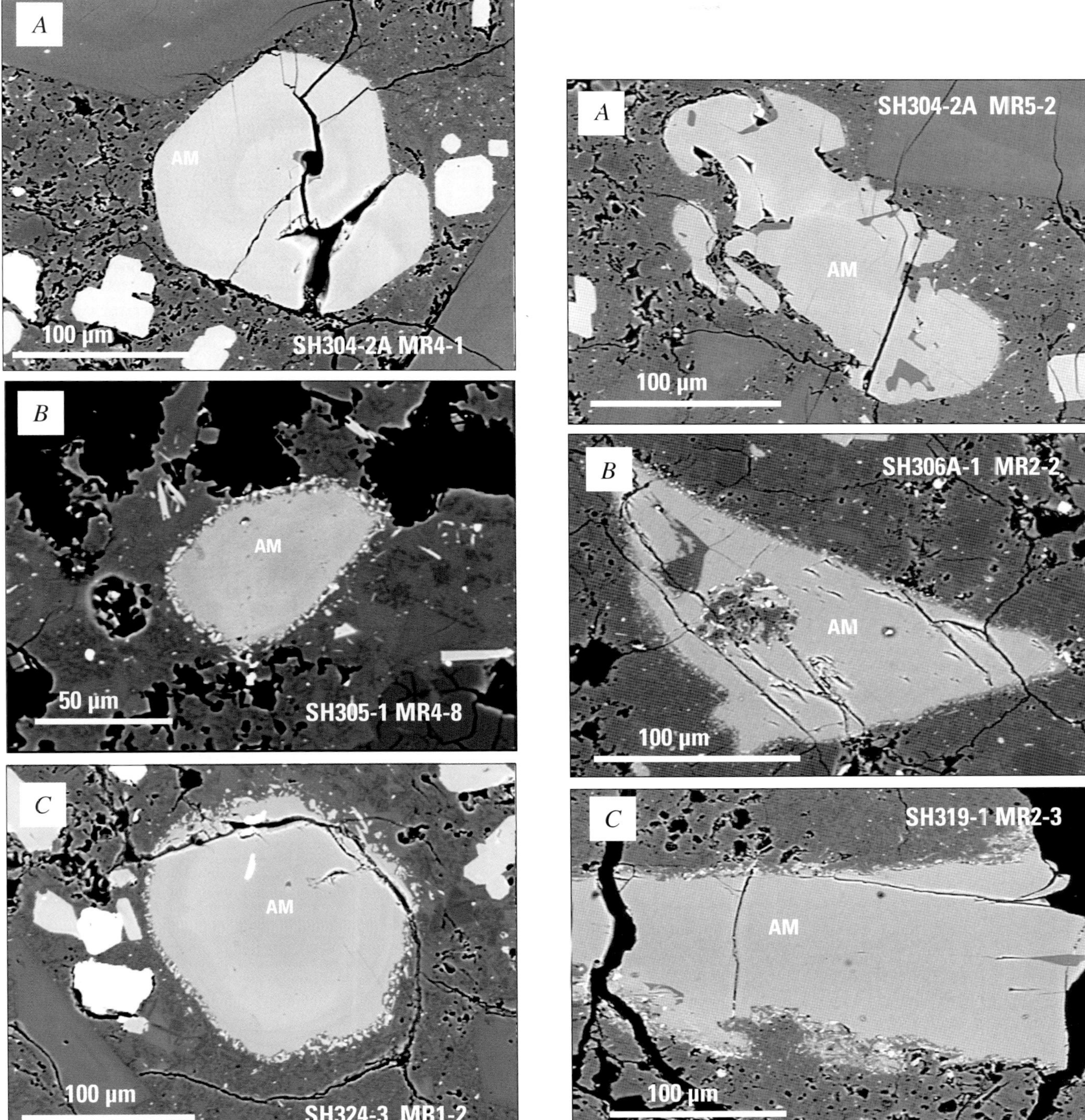

Figure 6. SEM backscattered electron images of analyzed rounded or abraded amphibole grains (AM) in Mount St. Helens 2004–6 dacite lava. The sample and image numbers shown on the lower right side in each image correspond to analysis numbers in appendix 2. *A*, Sample SH304-2A. *B*, Sample SH305-1. *C*, Sample SH324-3.

Figure 7. SEM backscattered electron images of resorbed amphibole crystals (AM) with embayed and cuspate margins in Mount St. Helens 2004–6 dacite lava. The sample and image numbers shown on the upper right side in each image correspond to analysis numbers in appendix 2. *A*, Sample SH304-2A. *B*, Sample SH306A-1. *C*, Sample SH319-1.

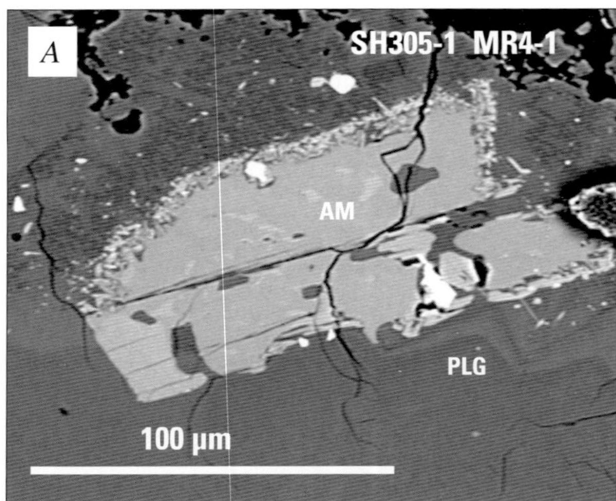

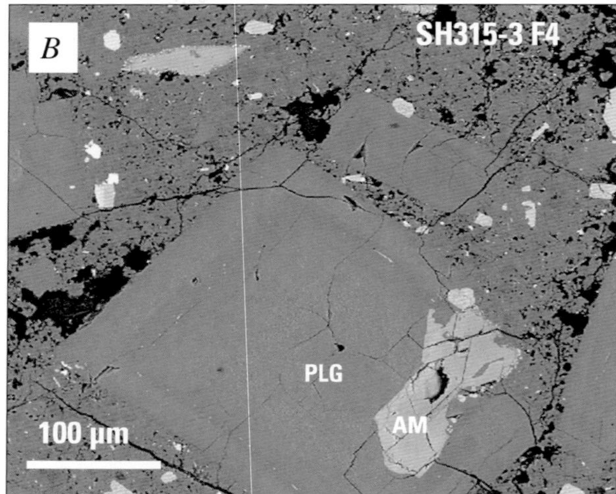

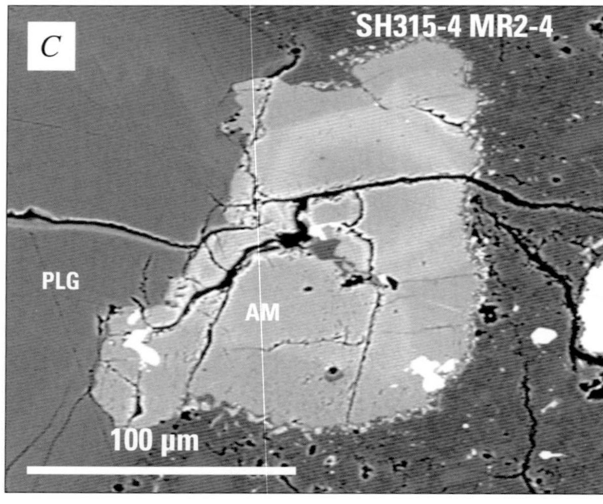

Figure 8. SEM backscattered electron images of amphibole grains (AM) intergrown with plagioclase (PLG) in Mount St. Helens 2004–6 dacite lava. The sample and image numbers shown on the upper right side in each image correspond to analysis numbers in appendix 2. *A*, Sample SH305-1. *B*, Sample SH315-3. *C*, Sample SH315-4.

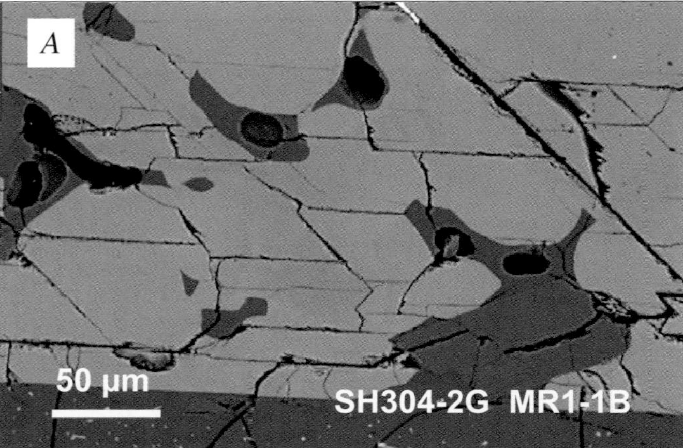

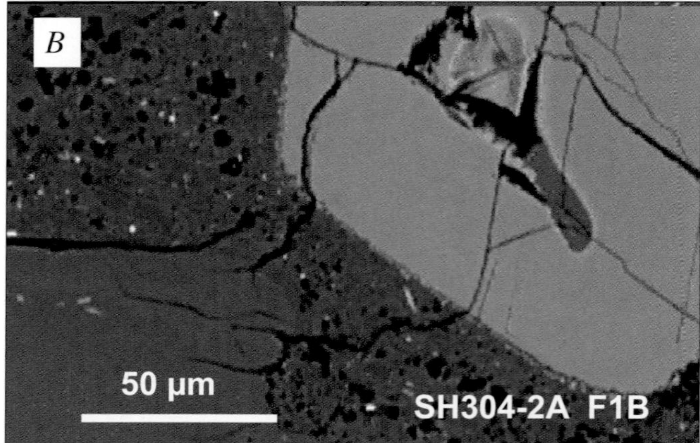

Figure 9. SEM backscattered electron images showing reaction rims around amphibole phenocrysts in Mount St. Helens 2004–6 dacite lava. The sample and image numbers shown on the lower right side in each image correspond to analysis numbers in appendix 2. *A*, No reaction rims present on amphiboles in glassy lithic fragment, SH304-2G. *B*, Rim widths are ~3 µm in October 2004 spine lava, SH304-2A. *C*, Typical 5-µm rims in all subsequent 2004–6 spine samples (SH305-1 shown here) are composed of an acicular microcrystalline intergrowth of plagioclase (dark colored), orthopyroxene (lighter colored), and Fe-Ti oxide (white).

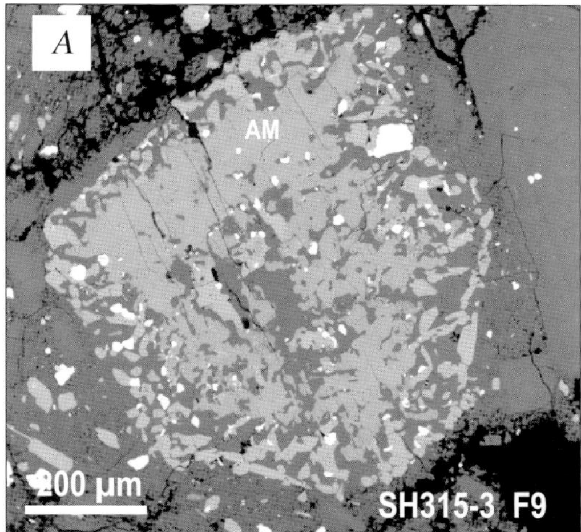

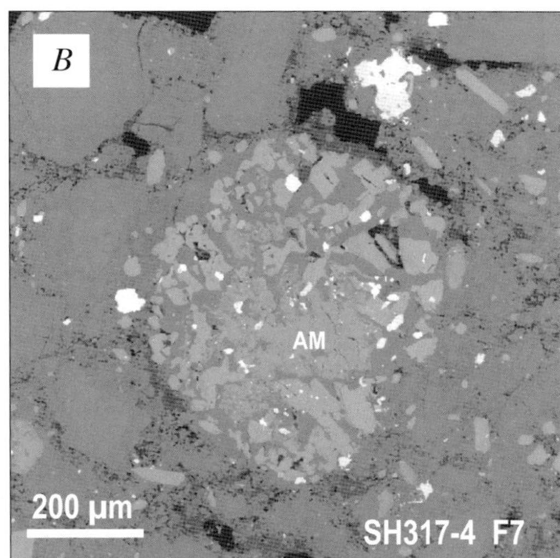

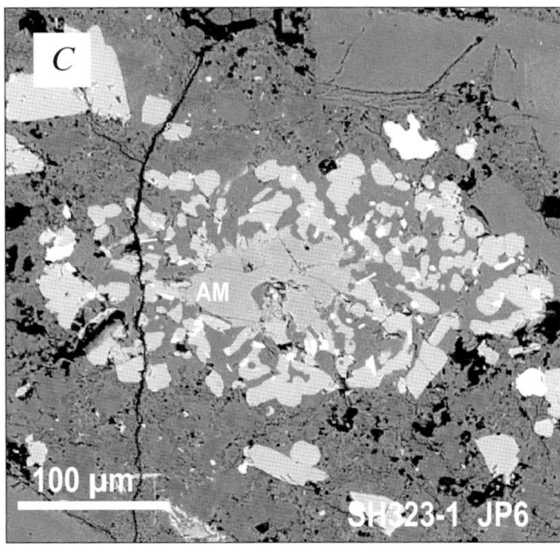

Figure 10. SEM backscattered electron images showing rare coarse-grained reaction rims (plagioclase + orthopyroxene + Fe-Ti oxide) around amphibole phenocryst remnants (AM) in Mount St. Helens 2004–6 dacite lava. The sample and image numbers shown on the lower right side in each image correspond to analysis numbers in appendix 2. *A*, Sample SH315-3. *B*, Sample SH317-4. *C*, Sample SH323-1.

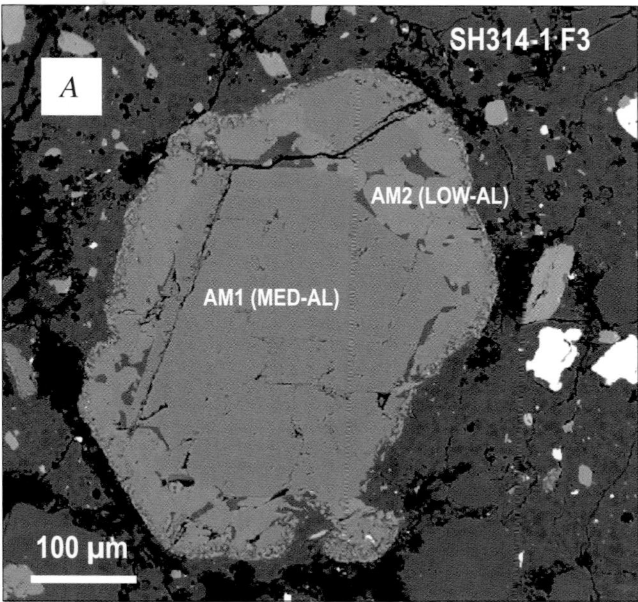

Figure 11. SEM backscattered electron images showing examples of amphibole-to-amphibole+melt reaction in Mount St. Helens 2004–6 dacite lava. The sample and image numbers shown on the upper right side in each image correspond to analysis numbers in table 2 and appendix 2. *A*, In sample SH314-1, amphibole with ~12.5 percent Al_2O_3 (AM1) is surrounded by aggregate of amphibole crystals (AM2) with ~7.2 percent Al_2O_3 and high fluorine (~0.18 percent) and glass (dark gray). *B*, In sample DRS_3_9_4, amphibole with ~12.2 percent Al_2O_3 (AM1) is surrounded by an aggregate of amphibole crystals (AM2) with ~6.9 percent Al_2O_3 and high fluorine (~0.25 percent) and glass (dark gray).

this volume, chap. 30). Reaction rims ~5-µm wide are found on the inclusion edge, where amphibole crystals are in contact with the dacite matrix, but no such rims occur along interior contacts between amphibole and glass. Inclusion SH325-1Ainc has a bulk texture similar to that of SH315-4inc, but the matrix lacks a significant glass component. Reaction rims are similarly restricted to grains in contact with the host dacite. These are the only andesite inclusions found among the well-scrutinized suite of 2004–6 dacite samples. They are small (<1.5 cm) and are likely accidental fragments derived from conduit walls. We do not consider them evidence of mafic-magma mixing.

Dacite inclusions such as SH321-1inc contain resorbed amphibole crystals with broad reaction rims similar to those found in the bimodal population in 1980–86 dacite (Rutherford and Hill, 1993; Cashman and McConnell, 2005). This inclusion also is distinguished from the 2004–6 host lava by the presence of clinopyroxene microphenocrysts in the matrix around amphibole, which is suggestive of isobaric heating of a cooler crystal-laden magma or of slow decompression of a newer hotter one (see Rutherford and Devine, this volume, chap. 31, fig. 10). It is theoretically possible that such fragments could have originated from eruption-related magmatic processes. However, like the andesite inclusions, these rounded fragments are more likely to be inconsequential xenoliths eroded from the shallow conduit walls.

We discern some fundamental characteristics of the 2004–6 dacite magma from the textures of its amphibole phenocrysts. The well-dispersed population of texturally diverse amphibole described above is a strong indication that the uniform composition of the dacite is inherited from a process of small-scale mingling and intermixing of crystal-laden magmas at depth. The consistent presence of variably zoned, broken, abraded, and resorbed amphibole crystals suggests that a number of temporally (and spatially) distinct crystallization environments are represented. Because similar 5-µm reaction rims are observed around all morphologic variants of amphibole, crystal fragmentation, abrasion, and resorption must have occurred at depth after assembly of the diverse crystal population and during initial stages of decompression with upward transport. Further discussion of amphibole-melt reaction textures and implications for dynamics of magma ascent is presented later in this chapter.

In the following sections, the chemistry and mineralogy of this textural medley of amphibole phenocrysts are reviewed to ascertain genetic distinctions and to gain insight into magmatic conditions associated with the 2004–6 eruption.

Amphibole Major-Element Chemistry

Amphibole phenocrysts analyzed to date in 2004–6 Mount St. Helens dacite (fig. 12; table 2; appendix 2) are all clinoamphibole with a calcium content of ~11.0 weight percent (11.0±0.3 percent CaO). Their silica and alumina contents span a continuous range that varies inversely between average end members with high silica and low alumina (47.5 percent SiO_2, 6.4 percent Al_2O_3) and low silica and high alumina (41.8 percent SiO_2, 15.0 percent Al_2O_3) (fig. 13*A*). The prevalent

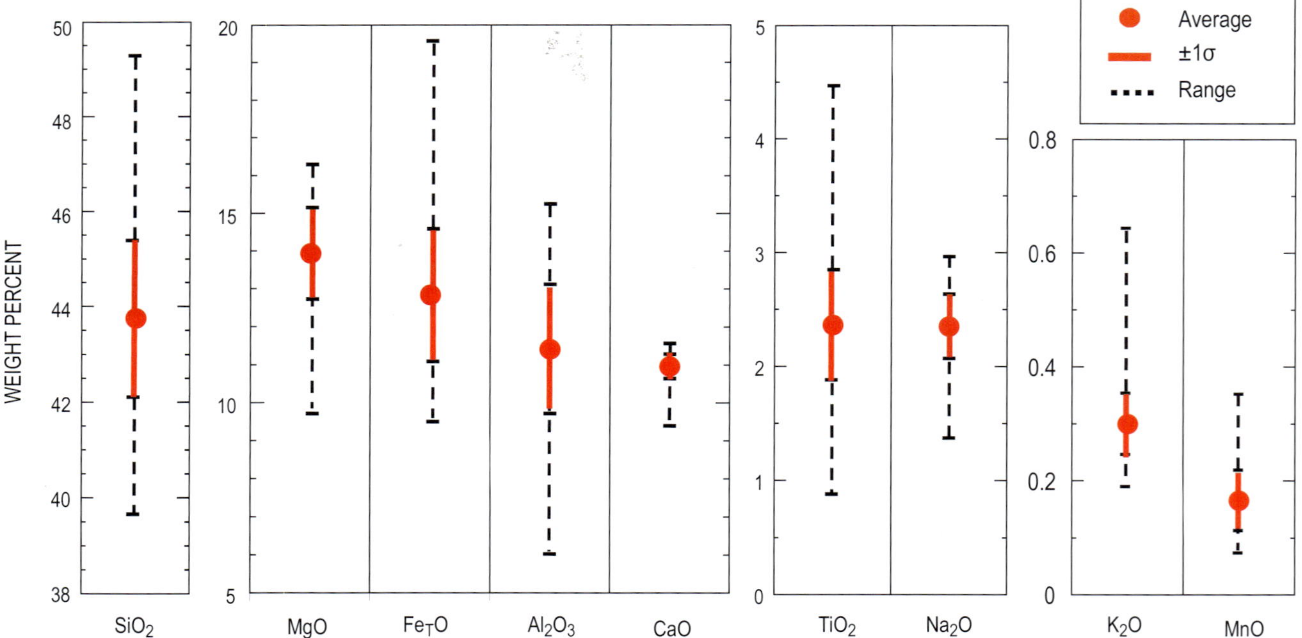

Figure 12. Average, range, and standard deviation of major elements analyzed in Mount St. Helens 2004–6 amphibole phenocrysts (excluding data from crystals in lithic inclusions and glassy lithic fragments). Fe_TO is all iron calculated as Fe^{2+}.

2004–6 amphibole compositional range, defined as ±1σ variation from the mean, is from 42.1 to 43.8 percent SiO_2 and 11.4 to 9.7 percent Al_2O_3.

Three compositional trends are evident within the silica/alumina range of amphibole crystals in dome dacite (and dome-derived ash) by the patterns of Mg and Fe variation with Al (figs. 13*B*, 13*C*). The low-alumina range (low-Al), from 6 to ~9 percent Al_2O_3, has a sympathetic increase in Fe_TO (all iron calculated as Fe^{2+}) averaging from 12 to 15.5 percent associated with decreasing MgO from 16 to 12 percent. Over the mid-alumina range (medium-Al), from ~9 to 12 percent Al_2O_3, average Fe_TO decreases to 12 percent and MgO increases to 12–16 percent. High-alumina (high-Al) amphibole ranges from ~12 to 15 percent Al_2O_3, with a corresponding average Fe_TO increase to 16 percent and a MgO decrease to ~11 percent.

Amphibole phenocrysts of high-Al, medium-Al, and low-Al compositions are present and distributed similarly in nearly all 2004–6 samples examined, as well as in 1980–86 dacite samples (fig. 14*A*). Our data reveal that amphibole in 2004–6 and 1980–86 dacites have the same range of major-element compositions. The low-Al amphiboles in old and new dacite overlap the phenocryst compositions in gabbroic xenoliths (fig. 14*A*). Amphibole crystals in the SH304-2G glassy lithic fragment are chiefly medium-Al in composition but display a low- to high-Al range similar to that of the 2004–6 population (fig. 14*B*). The high-Al amphibole compositions of lithic inclusions (SH315-4inc and SH325-1Ainc) are similar to those

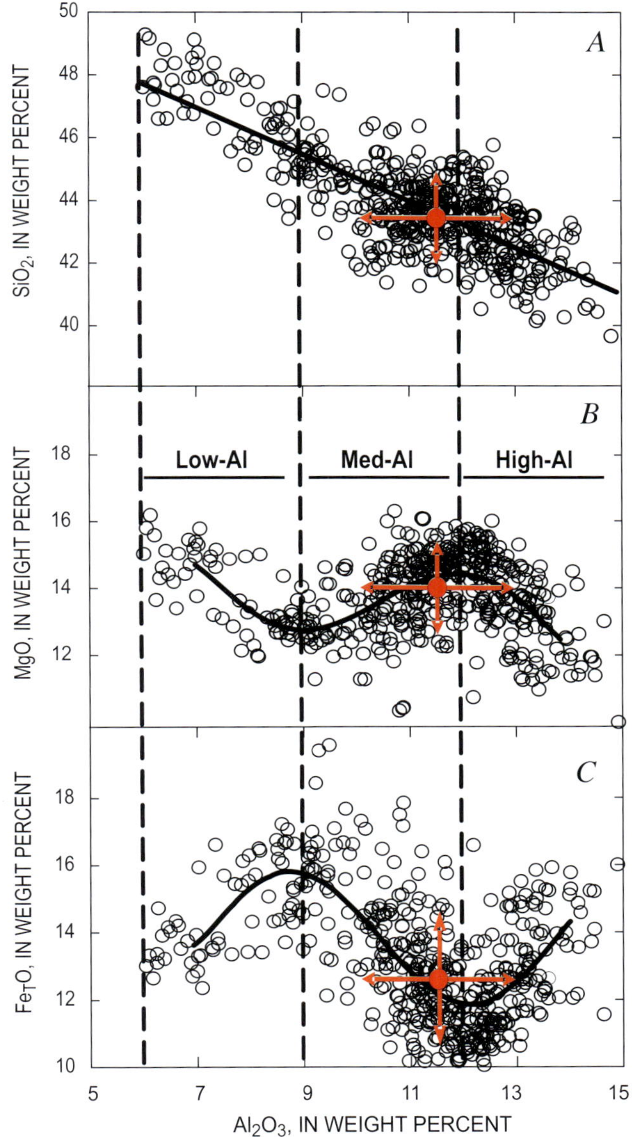

Figure 13. Alumina variation diagrams for Mount St. Helens 2004–6 amphibole phenocrysts (excluding data from crystals in lithic inclusions and glassy lithic fragments); average and 1σ standard deviation in red. Curves are high-order polynomial fits. *A*, Silica. *B*, Magnesia. *C*, Iron oxide (Fe_TO calculated as 100 percent ferrous iron). Reversals in Fe_TO and MgO with increasing Al_2O_3 define low-Al (6 to 9 percent), medium-Al (9 to 12 percent), and high-Al (>12 percent) compositions.

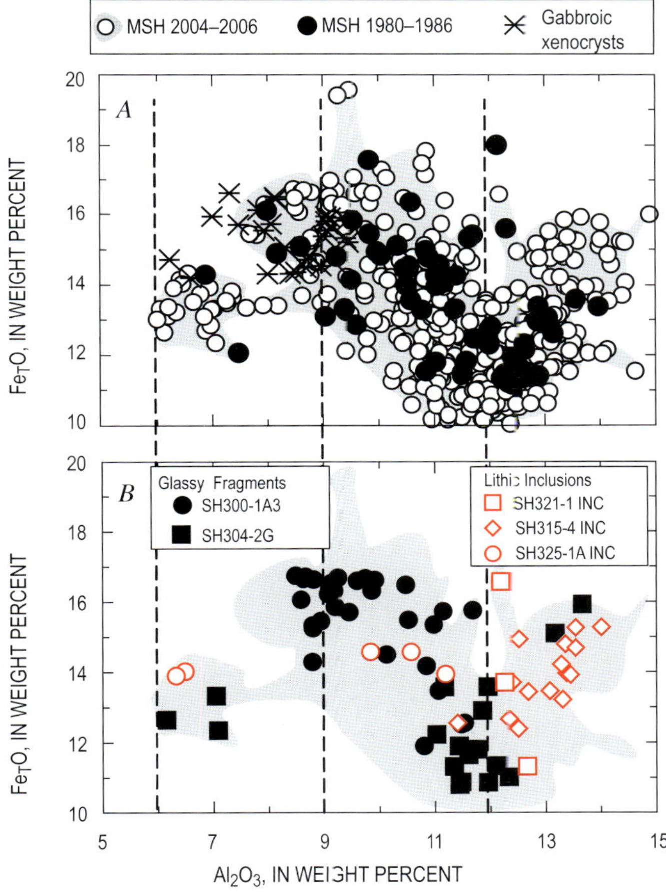

Figure 14. Iron oxide versus alumina in Mount St. Helens amphibole phenocrysts. *A*, 2004–6 amphibole phenocrysts (open circles and gray-shaded area) compared to those in 1980–86 Mount St. Helens dacite and gabbroic xenocrysts. *B*, Amphiboles in lithic inclusions and glassy lithic fragments; shaded area corresponds to field of 2004–6 amphibole phenocrysts shown in *A*.

Table 2. Selected electron microprobe analyses of amphibole phenocrysts in Mount St. Helens 2004–2006 dacite.

[Laboratories identified by first two letters in analysis number: AM, American Museum of Natural History; GS, U.S. Geological Survey, Denver; OS, Oregon State University. Relative position of analyzed spot: inZ, inner zone; outZ, outer zone. Nomenclature from Leake and others (1997): mghst, magnesiohastingsite; tscher, tschermakite; mghb, magnesiohornblende; eden, edenite; parg, pargasite. See appendix 2, table A2, for all analytical data.]

Sample No.--	SH304-2A			SH305-1			SH306-A		DRS_3_9_4		SH314-1		SH315-3			SH315-4		SH317-4	
Analysis No. ------------	OS-MR4-3	AM-G24C	AM-G24R	OS-MR3-2	OS-MR3-3	OS-MR3-4	OS-MR2-2	OS-MR2-5	GS-F3P13	GS-F3P9	GS-F3P1	GS-F3P5	GS-F16G1 P1	GS-F16G1 P2	GS-F16G1 P3	GS-F1G1 P1	GS-F1G1 P2	GS-F7G2 P2	GS-F1G2 P7
Position-------	core	core	rim	core	core	core	core	core	core	rim	core	rim	inZ	core	rim	core	rim	core	rim
SiO_2	48.4	42.0	44.0	43.1	42.9	46.9	42.6	47.8	43.1	47.9	42.6	47.1	43.7	44.0	45.1	42.2	43.3	40.5	42.3
TiO_2	1.54	2.53	2.39	2.37	2.24	2.09	1.97	1.46	2.21	1.46	2.37	1.48	1.46	1.61	0.88	2.38	2.11	3.06	2.35
Al_2O_3	7.4	12.8	12.5	14.2	14.0	8.6	13.1	7.9	12.2	6.9	12.4	6.9	9.4	8.5	8.0	12.1	11.2	14.4	13.2
FeO	13.7	11.3	10.7	14.6	12.0	13.7	14.8	13.4	10.8	12.7	10.9	13.1	16.3	16.2	16.3	10.4	9.9	13.7	13.1
MnO	0.3	0.1	0.1	0.12	0.13	0.16	0.20	0.28	0.12	0.23	0.12	0.24	0.35	0.29	0.35	0.11	0.11	0.17	0.12
MgO	15.2	14.7	15.5	11.6	14.5	14.4	12.0	15.0	14.8	14.7	14.9	15.5	12.4	12.7	13.3	15.3	16.1	11.9	13.3
CaO	11.0	11.2	11.4	10.4	10.3	11.3	11.2	10.6	10.8	10.8	11.5	11.2	10.4	10.4	9.8	11.1	11.1	11.3	10.7
Na_2O	1.5	2.4	2.4	2.4	2.6	1.8	2.1	1.7	2.5	1.5	2.8	1.8	1.8	2.1	1.6	2.9	2.8	2.6	2.6
K_2O	0.28	0.30	0.32	0.38	0.29	0.34	0.35	0.23	0.30	0.22	0.29	0.22	0.26	0.31	0.20	0.30	0.30	0.31	0.34
F	0.02	0.08	0.10	0.00	0.00	0.01	0.01	0.02	0.06	0.25	0.07	0.08	0.22	0.00	0.14	0.19	0.10	0.02	0.04
Cl	0.05	0.02	0.01	0.03	0.02	0.05	0.03	0.04	0.02	0.04	0.01	0.04	0.02	0.02	0.02	0.02	0.01	0.26	0.14
O = F,Cl	0.00	0.04	0.05	0.01	0.00	0.01	0.00	0.00	0.03	0.11	0.03	0.04	0.10	0.00	0.06	0.08	0.04	0.06	0.05
Total	99.19	97.37	99.38	99.19	99.11	99.33	98.36	98.39	96.94	96.63	97.99	97.60	96.20	96.16	95.56	96.98	97.03	98.28	98.25
T-Site Si^{+4}	6.869	6.074	6.209	6.176	6.088	6.690	6.189	6.830	6.242	6.969	6.149	6.862	6.490	6.587	6.717	6.144	6.271	5.929	6.119
T-Site $^{IV}Al^{+3}$	1.131	1.926	1.791	1.824	1.912	1.310	1.811	1.170	1.758	1.031	1.851	1.138	1.510	1.413	1.283	1.856	1.729	2.071	1.881
C-Site $^{VI}Al^{+3}$	0.105	0.250	0.284	0.576	0.437	0.141	0.432	0.165	0.331	0.153	0.258	0.041	0.128	0.089	0.114	0.213	0.186	0.412	0.376
C-Site Ti^{+4}	0.165	0.275	0.253	0.255	0.239	0.224	0.215	0.156	0.241	0.160	0.258	0.162	0.163	0.181	0.099	0.261	0.229	0.337	0.255
C-Site Fe^{+3}	0.620	0.772	0.660	0.643	0.704	0.585	0.673	0.667	0.642	0.571	0.591	0.370	0.963	0.621	0.896	0.626	0.615	0.536	0.681
C-Site Mg^{+2}	3.212	3.161	3.272	2.487	3.070	3.052	2.604	3.184	3.187	3.192	3.202	3.355	2.752	2.828	2.946	3.316	3.468	2.604	2.859
C-Site Fe^{+2}	0.901	0.527	0.522	1.036	0.546	0.999	1.077	0.826	0.599	0.925	0.691	1.072	0.995	1.281	0.946	0.584	0.502	1.108	0.827
B-Site Fe^{+2}	0.102	0.066	0.080	0.070	0.179	0.049	0.043	0.110	0.071	0.049	0.036	0.153	0.064	0.125	0.187	0.059	0.079	0.032	0.082
B-Site Mn^{+2}	0.033	0.011	0.010	0.015	0.015	0.019	0.025	0.034	0.014	0.028	0.015	0.029	0.044	0.037	0.044	0.013	0.014	0.022	0.015
B-Site Ca^{+2}	1.674	1.734	1.720	1.595	1.571	1.722	1.742	1.615	1.682	1.678	1.778	1.741	1.660	1.674	1.560	1.734	1.722	1.767	1.661
B-Site Na^{+}	0.192	0.189	0.191	0.319	0.235	0.209	0.190	0.242	0.233	0.245	0.171	0.076	0.232	0.164	0.209	0.195	0.185	0.179	0.243
A-Site Na^{+}	0.220	0.471	0.465	0.341	0.470	0.285	0.403	0.224	0.481	0.191	0.605	0.438	0.275	0.444	0.247	0.634	0.600	0.566	0.491
A-Site K^{+}	0.051	0.056	0.058	0.070	0.053	0.061	0.064	0.042	0.055	0.041	0.053	0.041	0.049	0.060	0.038	0.055	0.055	0.058	0.063
Total	15.27	15.53	15.52	15.41	15.52	15.35	15.47	15.27	15.54	15.23	15.66	15.48	15.32	15.50	15.28	15.69	15.65	15.62	15.55

Table 2. Selected electron microprobe analyses of amphibole phenocrysts in Mount St. Helens 2004–2006 dacite.—Continued

[Laboratories identified by first two letters in analysis number: AM, American Museum of Natural History; GS, U.S. Geological Survey, Denver; OS, Oregon State University. Relative position of analyzed spot: inZ, inner zone; outZ, outer zone. Nomenclature from Leake and others (1997): mghst, magnesiohastingsite; tscher, tschermakite; mghb, magnesiohornblende; eden, edenite; parg, pargasite. See appendix 2, table A2, for all analytical data.]

Sample No--	SH319-1			SH321-1			SH323-2		SH323-3				SH324-3				SH325-1		
Analysis No.-----------	OS-MR2-1	OS-MR2-3	OS-MR3-1	GS-F0P3	GS-F2P3	OS-MR1-3	OS-MR2-3	OS-MR3-2	GS-G1-2	GS-G1-7	GS-G1-6	GS-G1-8	GS-F0P3	GS-F0P8	OS-MR1-1	OS-MR1-2	GS-F1B-G1P3	GS-F1B-G1P4	GS-F1B-G1P5
Position-------	core	core	core	core	core	core	core	core	core	inZ	outZ	rim	core	core	core	core	core	inZ	rim
SiO_2	44.3	45.2	43.4	43.7	43.5	44.8	46.4	42.8	43.6	43.7	44.2	43.8	42.7	45.6	44.5	43.5	44.9	42.0	44.9
TiO_2	2.24	2.13	2.38	2.48	2.74	2.55	1.31	2.79	2.19	2.20	2.17	2.78	2.42	1.11	2.51	2.27	1.63	2.31	1.71
Al_2O_3	11.7	12.3	13.2	10.8	9.8	10.3	9.2	14.2	10.9	12.3	11.7	10.1	11.6	9.4	11.0	13.4	9.0	12.7	9.1
FeO	12.3	10.6	11.7	11.1	13.7	13.7	17.0	13.5	13.6	11.6	10.5	12.9	14.8	15.6	13.1	12.7	13.5	12.7	13.7
MnO	0.17	0.12	0.10	0.14	0.15	0.19	0.27	0.13	0.19	0.15	0.12	0.19	0.20	0.26	0.16	0.12	0.21	0.15	0.23
MgO	14.6	15.6	14.5	15.0	13.8	13.9	12.5	12.6	13.2	14.5	15.2	13.7	12.3	13.5	13.8	13.9	14.0	13.0	13.8
CaO	11.2	10.9	11.1	11.1	10.7	11.0	11.0	10.9	10.8	10.8	10.9	10.5	10.8	10.0	11.4	11.1	10.8	10.8	10.6
Na_2O	2.2	2.3	2.4	2.3	2.7	2.0	1.9	2.4	2.3	2.3	2.3	2.3	2.6	1.9	2.1	2.4	2.4	2.4	1.9
K_2O	0.29	0.29	0.32	0.25	0.29	0.31	0.24	0.36	0.25	0.30	0.28	0.30	0.29	0.23	0.31	0.34	0.24	0.28	0.23
F	0.00	0.00	0.00	0.02	0.03	0.00	0.00	0.01	0.69	0.16	0.10	0.19	0.02	0.04	0.01	0.00	0.04	0.01	0.03
Cl	0.02	0.01	0.02	0.18	1.55	0.04	0.02	0.02	0.02	0.01	0.01	0.02	0.11	0.16	0.02	0.02	0.17	0.11	0.19
O=F,Cl	0.00	0.00	0.00	0.05	0.35	0.01	0.00	0.00	0.29	0.07	0.04	0.08	0.03	0.05	0.00	0.00	0.05	0.03	0.06
Total	98.88	99.53	99.16	97.17	98.59	98.72	99.83	99.71	97.34	98.08	97.31	96.61	97.85	97.82	98.91	99.64	96.81	96.39	96.32
T-Site Si^{+4}	6.312	6.343	6.165	6.341	6.395	6.430	6.665	6.097	6.388	6.261	6.360	6.431	6.270	6.609	6.381	6.167	6.593	6.181	6.599
T-Site $^{IV}Al^{+3}$	1.688	1.657	1.835	1.659	1.605	1.570	1.335	1.903	1.612	1.739	1.640	1.569	1.730	1.391	1.619	1.833	1.407	1.819	1.401
C-Site $^{VI}Al^{+3}$	0.268	0.369	0.369	0.192	0.087	0.172	0.213	0.473	0.267	0.346	0.334	0.172	0.277	0.210	0.240	0.408	0.147	0.379	0.177
C-Site Ti^{+4}	0.240	0.225	0.254	0.270	0.303	0.276	0.142	0.298	0.242	0.238	0.234	0.307	0.267	0.120	0.271	0.242	0.180	0.256	0.189
C-Site Fe^{+3}	0.700	0.615	0.671	0.613	0.492	0.665	0.687	0.623	0.620	0.685	0.620	0.610	0.585	0.884	0.573	0.681	0.629	0.622	0.716
C-Site Mg^{+2}	3.092	3.273	3.074	3.233	3.017	2.968	2.666	2.681	2.877	3.108	3.251	2.990	2.682	2.917	2.958	2.929	3.073	2.857	3.016
C-Site Fe^{+2}	0.697	0.514	0.631	0.673	1.100	0.916	1.292	0.926	0.995	0.623	0.560	0.921	1.190	0.864	0.959	0.742	0.972	0.886	0.902
B-Site Fe^{+2}	0.063	0.117	0.081	0.060	0.091	0.068	0.060	0.064	0.055	0.083	0.077	0.052	0.043	0.148	0.045	0.082	0.056	0.061	0.072
B-Site Mn^{+2}	0.021	0.014	0.012	0.017	0.019	0.024	0.033	0.016	0.024	0.018	0.015	0.023	0.025	0.032	0.020	0.014	0.025	0.018	0.029
B-Site Ca^{+2}	1.709	1.645	1.689	1.724	1.692	1.686	1.691	1.667	1.690	1.665	1.676	1.657	1.700	1.559	1.746	1.679	1.695	1.706	1.673
B-Site Na^{+}	0.207	0.224	0.218	0.200	0.198	0.222	0.217	0.253	0.231	0.234	0.232	0.267	0.232	0.260	0.190	0.224	0.224	0.215	0.226
A-Site Na^{+}	0.391	0.391	0.446	0.449	0.563	0.343	0.324	0.399	0.425	0.413	0.399	0.384	0.513	0.270	0.399	0.424	0.450	0.469	0.315
A-Site K^{+}	0.053	0.053	0.059	0.047	0.054	0.057	0.045	0.066	0.047	0.054	0.051	0.056	0.053	0.042	0.056	0.062	0.045	0.052	0.043
Total	15.44	15.44	15.50	15.50	15.62	15.40	15.37	15.46	15.47	15.47	15.45	15.44	15.57	15.31	15.46	15.49	15.50	15.52	15.36
Name	tscher	tscher	mghst	tscher	mghst	tscher	mghb	tscher	tscher	tscher	tscher	tscher	mghst	mghb	tscher	tscher	mghb	mghst	mghb

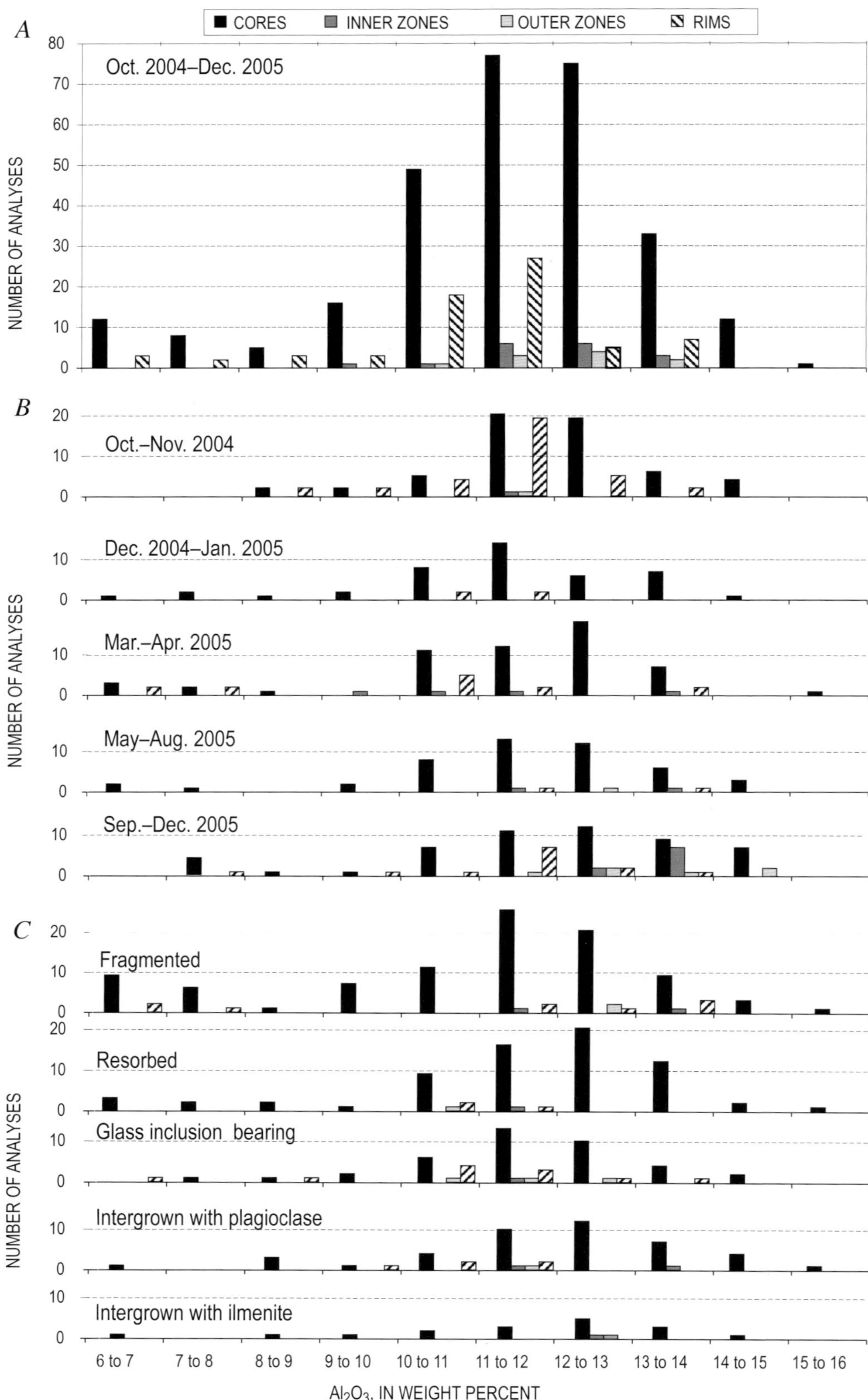

Figure 15. Histograms showing the frequency distribution of Al_2O_3 in cores, inner zones, outer zones, and rims of amphibole crystals in Mount St. Helens 2004–6 dacite lava (excluding crystals in glassy lithic fragments and lithic inclusions). *A,* For all 2004–6 amphiboles. *B,* For consecutive time intervals. *C,* For phenocrysts with specific textural attributes.

crystallized from andesite at high pressures (for example, Allen and Boettcher, 1978; Grove and others 2003). High-Al amphibole compositions, along with differences in reaction textures, are consistent with these inclusions originating from an andesite magma (Pallister and others, this volume, chap. 30), but there is no clear evidence in support of a comagmatic relation between the andesitic magma and the host dacite.

The one dacitic inclusion studied (SH321-1inc) has a range of amphibole chemistry similar to that of 1980–86 and 2004–6 lava. As inferred from the presence of clinopyroxene and the distinctly thick amphibole reaction rims (see reaction-rim discussion), this inclusion could be an accidental piece of shallow 1980s conduit material.

The frequency distribution of alumina concentrations in cores, inner zones, outer zones, and rims of amphiboles in the 2004–6 dacite indicate an approximately normal distribution about the mean value of 11.4±1.7 percent Al_2O_3 (fig. 15). A similar distribution is observed for a smaller population of 1980–86 amphiboles, but amphiboles in gabbroic xenoliths overlap the low end of the 2004–6 population (fig. 14*A*).

Correlations between alumina content and size of amphibole crystals reveal a normal distribution about the mean alumina content of ~11 percent and about a median size range within 10–100×10^3 μm^2 (fig. 2), suggestive of compositional and morphologic consistency of the mean population. In contrast, most of the crystal fragment population (gray bars in fig. 2) has low-Al compositions, supporting the likelihood of a xenocrystic origin. There is no clear correlation between alumina content and acicularity. Both equant and relatively acicular populations have nearly similar distributions about the alumina average.

The abundance of low- to high-Al amphiboles, just as the overall amphibole modal abundance and bulk-dacite composition, has not changed throughout the duration of the 2004–6 eruption (fig. 15). Furthermore, the same overall distribution of alumina contents is apparent among amphiboles of similar texture or mineral associations (fig. 15).

Multiple analyses from core to rim were obtained for numerous amphibole crystals. The compositional variation of amphibole rims within and among samples is similar to the broad range of core compositions and the amphibole population as a whole (fig. 16). Detailed analyses of amphiboles with multiple growth zones reveal some systematic tendencies within limited populations of crystals. For example, analyses of cores, inner zones, and outer zones of several SH323-3 amphiboles vary widely and are without obvious correlations of core-to-rim progressions between crystals, but the rims all trend toward an average 10.8±0.6 percent Al_2O_3 (fig. 16*A*). This convergence of rims toward the amphibole composition to last equilibrate with the host magma is within the 1σ uncertainty of the 11.4 percent average of Al_2O_3 in all 2004–6 amphiboles. Such is not the case for core-to-rim analyses of crystals in SH325-1A (fig. 16*B*), which are similar to the overall broad dispersion of rim data. The variable rim compositions must reflect changing conditions in the magma reservoir and during ascent from it.

Amphibole Rare-Earth-Element (REE) Chemistry

The REE concentrations in all 2004–6 dacite amphibole phenocrysts display middle rare-earth-element (MREE) enrichment patterns typical of igneous clinoamphiboles (fig. 17; appendix 2). Similar MREE-enriched patterns for different crystals in each sample are distinguished by varying degrees of overall REE enrichment, accompanied by progressive Eu depletion. Like other amphibole characteristics discussed above, there are no clear distinctions of REE patterns among samples over time or, in most cases, with textural attributes. However, a distinct trend of overall REE enrichment (typified by La) and Eu depletion (relative to Nd) with decreasing alumina content in medium- to low-Al amphibole crystals is clearly observed (fig. 18).

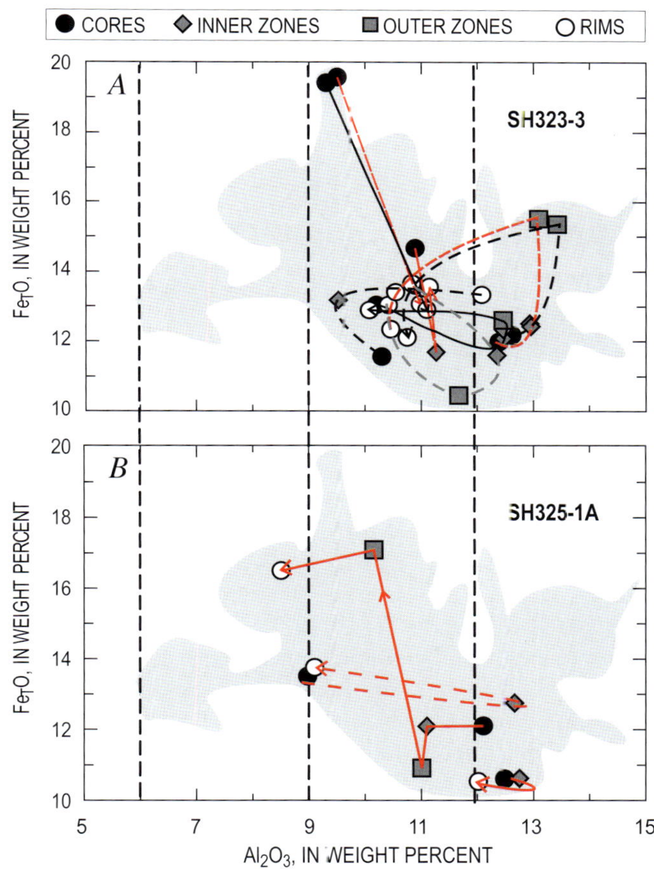

Figure 16. Iron oxide (Fe_TO) versus alumina within individual amphibole phenocrysts in Mount St. Helens 2004–6 dacite lava. Arrows connect core, inner-zone, outer-zone, and rim compositions. Shaded area is the field of 2004–6 amphibole phenocrysts from figure 14*A*. *A*, Interior compositions of amphiboles vary widely, but rim compositions converge toward an average of 10.8±0.6 percent Al_2O_3. *B*, Example of amphiboles that do not show consistent variations.

Concentration patterns for the REE-enriched and Eu-depleted (Eu/Nd<1) amphibole crystals suggest that some are not comagmatic (fig. 19). The three most extreme patterns (from samples SH304-2A, SH305-1, SH311-1B) are all low-Al amphiboles (7.4–8.9 percent Al_2O_3) with patchy zoning and variable resorption (for example, fig. 4*A*). They must be derived from a strongly Eu-depleted melt that has undergone significant Eu^{3+}-enriched plagioclase crystallization in an oxidizing environment. Such distinctive REE patterns suggest that these low-Al amphiboles are xenocrysts. New trace-element data for gabbroic xenoliths, in which amphibole is a late cumulus phase, would help to test this hypothesis.

There are no textural distinctions among the group of slightly LREE-enriched, low- to medium-Al amphiboles with Eu/Nd <1 (fig. 18*B*). The slight REE enrichment reflects a normal magmatic fractionation trend from one or more dacite magmas. Low-Al amphiboles with slight Eu depletion may have been derived from earlier generations of solidified dacite accumulated at the top of the Mount St. Helens magma reservoir or by shallow low-temperature crystallization within the host magma. For the medium- to high-Al amphiboles, the most prevalent of our 2004–6 samples, LREE concentrations are consistently low, and Eu is not depleted relative to Nd.

Amphibole Stoichiometry and Nomenclature

The amphibole nomenclature used here, as recommended by the International Mineralogical Association, is that of Leake and others (1997). Nomenclatorial guidelines are based upon occupancies of the A, B, C, and T sites within the amphibole mineral structural formula,

$$\mathbf{A}[Na{+}K]\ \mathbf{B}Ca_{2-x}\ [x{=}Mg, Fe^{2+}, Mn, Mg]\ \mathbf{C}^{M1,M2,M3}\ Mg_{5-y}\ [y{=}Fe^{2+}, Mn, {}^{VI}Al, Ti, Fe^{3+}]\ \mathbf{T}Si_{8-z}\ [z{=}{}^{IV}Al]\ O_{22}\ OH_{2-n}\ [n{=}F, Cl]).$$

Herein, the Leake and others (1997) nomenclature was applied to the amphibole stoichiometry determined using the Holland and Blundy (1994) method. This method was chosen because it allows for each amphibole to be normalized to the best stoichiometric constraint for ferric iron determination and gives the most reasonable amphibole formula for calculating pressure using the Anderson and Smith (1995) Al-in-hornblende barometer. Leake and others (1997) propose a method for calculating amphibole formula from electron microprobe analysis that is similar to that of Holland and Blundy (1994). Amphibole classification using the two methods typically results in the same name except for species that are sensitive to ferric iron determinations, such as pargasite and magnesiohastingsite.

The complete 2004–6 amphibole data set, plotted using the classification diagram of Leake and others (1997), is shown in figure 20. High-silica, low-Al amphiboles in dacite and gabbroic xenoliths are magnesiohornblende, but they also include some alkaline, edenite compositions. Medium- to high-Al ranges of the data set fall in tschermakite to magnesiohastingsite fields. The medium-Al group, consisting mostly of tschermakite, gives way to magnesiohastingsite with increasing alumina and alkali contents, extending toward rare pargasite compositions. Aside from mineral classification, the main purpose of calculating amphibole stoichiometry is to evaluate crystallographically controlled cationic variations that are sensitive to pressure and temperature.

As is widely documented in studies of clinoamphibole thermobarometry of igneous and metamorphic rocks, the extent of Tschermak's molecule substitution is a function of relative pressure and temperature of equilibration (Helz, 1982; Hammarstrom and Zen, 1986; Anderson and Smith, 1995; Bachmann and Dungan, 2002). At higher pressures and temperatures, the amount of Al in octahedral (C) sites (^{VI}Al) increases together with the amount in tetrahedral Al (^{IV}Al) sites. Most of this coupled alumina substitution occurs at the expense of divalent cations (for example, Mg^{2+} and Fe^{2+}) in the octahedral C-site and silica in tetrahedral sites in a pressure-sensitive Al-Tschermak exchange ($^{C}(Mg,Fe) + {}^{T}Si \leftrightarrow {}^{IV}Al + {}^{VI}Al$). At higher temperatures, increased concentrations of alkali cations (Na^+ and K^+) and Ti^{4+} are accommodated with additional ^{IV}Al in the amphibole lattice and form edenite (^{A}vacancy + $^{T}Si \leftrightarrow {}^{A}(Na{+}K) + {}^{IV}Al$) and Ti-Tschermak ($^{B}Mn{+}2^{T}Si \leftrightarrow {}^{C}Ti{+}2^{IV}Al$) substitutions. There is a broad, continuous range of pressure-sensitive Al-Tschermak component substitution exhibited by the complete array of amphibole compositions in 2004–6 Mount St. Helens dacite (fig. 21*A*). In addition, a broad range of temperature-sensitive Ti-Tschermak and edenite cationic exchanges also are apparent (figs. 21*B–D*).

The amphibole calculation optimizes ferric iron (Fe^{3+}) in the stoichiometric scheme and is a means of "ironing out" the secondary deviations in total iron and magnesium with alumina (figs. 13*B*, 13*C*). The exchange of Fe^{2+} and Mg^{2+} in the C site is consistently linear in high- and medium-Al amphiboles (fig. 22). At higher alumina contents and consistent with Al-Tschermak substitution, the absolute concentrations of Mg and Fe^{2+} are lower along lines of constant Mg number (Mg#, 100*(Mg/(Mg+ Fe^{2+}))). The Mg# variation in low-Al amphibole is more erratic. The Mg# increases with increasing proportion of Fe^{3+} (fig. 23*A*), suggesting that the Mg# trends are at least partly affected by differences in the oxidation state of host magmas. The variations of Ti and Mn with Mg# reveal distinctly different trends of low-Al magnesiohornblendes and the prevalent medium- to high-Al tschermakites and magnesiohastingsites (figs. 23*B*, 23*C*). Inverse trends of Ti versus Mg# (or Fe^{3+}) exhibited by the range of common amphibole compositions (±1σ population trend in fig. 23) are consistent with growth at variable temperature and f_{O_2} under buffered conditions, as suggested by temperature-f_{O_2} ranges calculated for Fe-Ti oxide pairs in 2004–6 dacite (Pallister and others, this volume, chap. 30, fig. 13).

Within the dataset there is no clear correlation between the Mg# and the relative partitioning of ^{VI}Al and ^{IV}Al (Al-

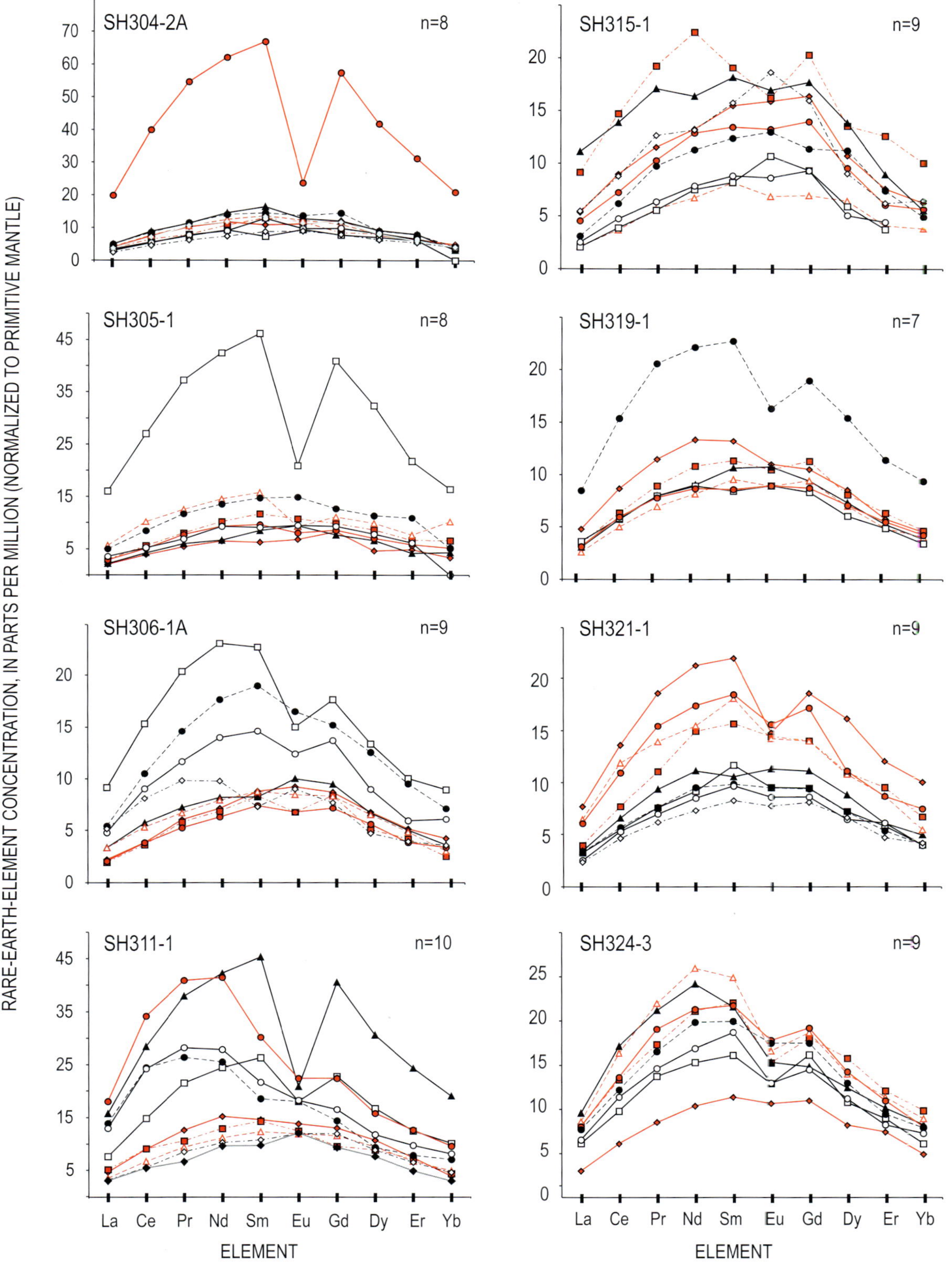

Figure 17. Rare-earth-element (REE) concentrations of amphibole phenocryst cores in eight consecutive Mount St. Helens 2004–6 dacite lava samples (normalized to "primitive mantle" of Sun and McDonough, 1989). Spidergrams show middle REE enrichment patterns that are typical of clinoamphibole and distinguished by varying degrees of REE enrichment and Eu depletion. Number of analyzed grains indicated (for example, n=8).

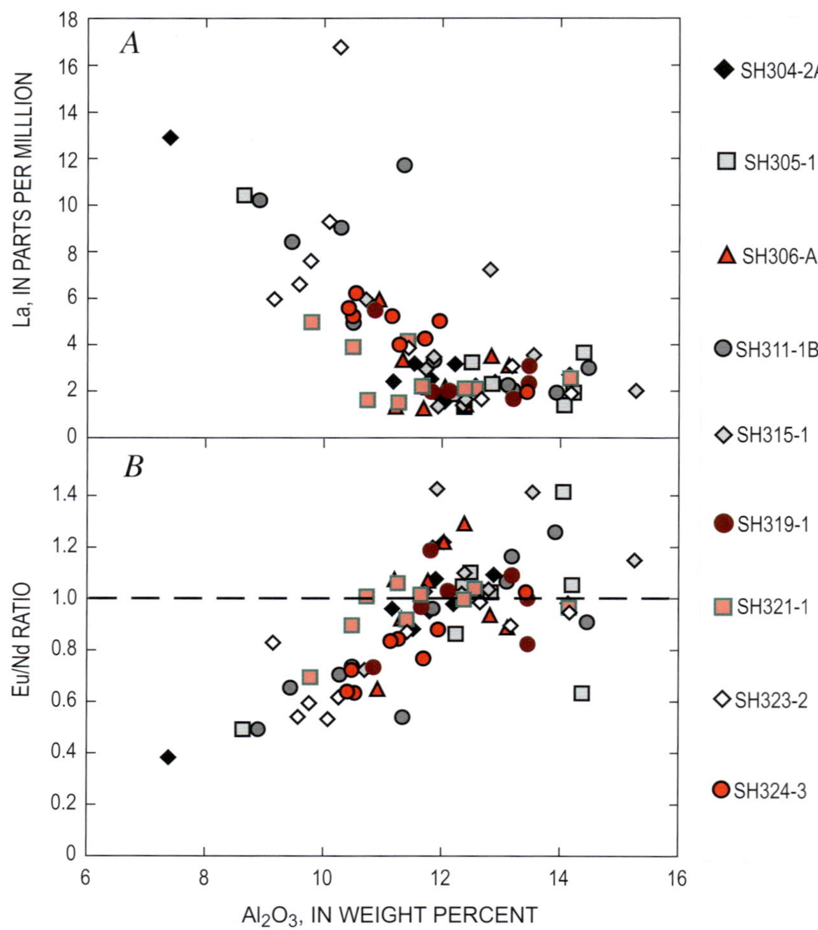

Figure 18. Rare-earth element (REE) versus alumina among amphibole phenocryst cores in consecutive Mount St. Helens 2004–6 dacite lava samples, showing trends reflective of overall REE enrichment and Eu depletion with decreasing alumina in medium- to low-Al amphiboles. *A*, La versus alumina. *B*, Eu/Nd versus alumina; Eu/Nd values <1 are Eu depleted.

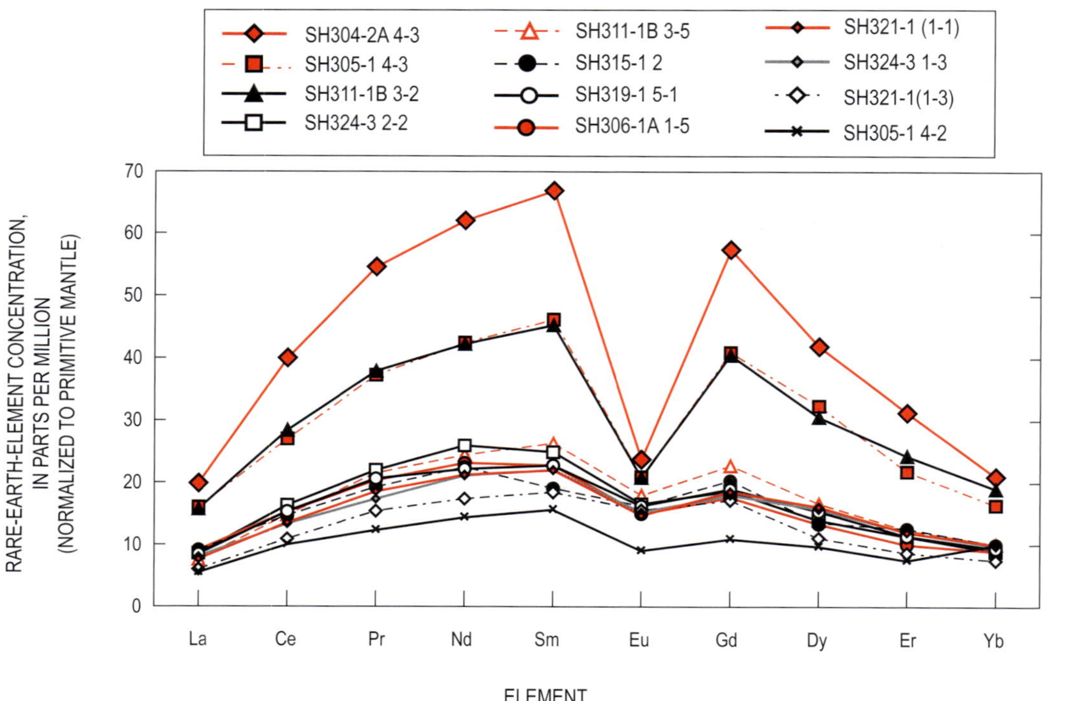

Figure 19. Rare-earth-element (REE) concentrations in Eu-depleted 2004–6 amphibole phenocrysts (normalized to "primitive mantle" of Sun and McDonough, 1989). Samples with the three most extreme REE patterns, likely xenocrysts, have low Al (7.4–8.9 percent Al_2O_3), patchy zoning, and resorbed edges.

Tschermak exchange; fig. 23*D*), indicating that Mg-Fe exchange is independent of relative pressure of crystallization. Also, no consistent differences are observed between core and rim Mg# and ^{VI}Al or ^{IV}Al. These observations and interpretations are in contrast to the inverse relation of Mg# and ^{IV}Al documented within individual 2004–6 amphibole crystals by Rutherford and Devine (this volume, chap. 31). The covariance of Mn, Ti, and Fe^{2+} in the medium- to high-Al amphibole suite likely reflects differences in the abundance and composition of coexisting Fe-Ti oxides in the crystallizing assemblage, which are affected by changes in temperature and the oxidation state over a range of pressures reflected by Al-Tschermak substitution.

Amphibole Thermobarometry

Rutherford and Devine (this volume, chap. 31) conducted phase-equilibria experiments on 2004 dacite that establish lower P_{H_2O} and upper T limits of amphibole+plagioclase+orthopyroxene+Fe-Ti-oxide saturation. Their results reproduce the observed phenocrysts of the dacite between pressures of 130 and 300 MPa (~5–12 km depth) at 850°C to 920°C, respectively (Rutherford and Devine, this volume, chap. 31, fig. 10). They observed increased Tschermak component of Mount St. Helens amphibole equilibrated at 200–300 MPa and 900°C in comparison with that at or below 200 MPa at ~860–850°C. These data suggest that the Tschermak and edenite substitutions, exhibited by the predominant 2004–6 tschermakite and magnesiohastingsite compositions, ought to constrain the relative P–T path of dacite magmas that have contributed to the phenocryst mix observed in new lava.

The Al-in-hornblende thermobarometer of Anderson and Smith (1995) is used here to estimate relative equilibration pressures over the ~850–900°C temperature range established by iron-titanium oxide thermometry and experimental petrology of new dacite lava (Pallister and others, this volume, chap. 30; Rutherford and Devine, this volume, chap. 31). As expressed by Anderson and Smith (1995, p. 554) and debated by others (for example, Blundy and Holland, 1990; Rutherford and Johnson, 1992; Hammarstrom and Zen, 1992), this algorithm may not yield accurate results at temperatures in excess of experimental calibration (800°C) and without all of the Tschermak-buffering phases in the barometric assemblage. We assume that most amphiboles in the 2004–6 dacite were crystallized from similar dacite magmas at temperature <920°C and that all were cosaturated with fluid, plagioclase, orthopyroxene, and oxide. The covariance of alumina and silica in these phases is not fixed for every amphibole that crystallizes, but the Tschermak molecular substitution should be constrained by this same five-phase assemblage throughout the pressure range in which the amphibole crystallized, thus providing a relative indication of crystallization pressures and temperatures.

Calculated pressures for amphiboles equilibrated under known P and T conditions help validate application of Al-in-hornblende thermobarometry to Mount St. Helens dacite (fig. 24). The Anderson and Smith (1995) algorithm is accurate for the 200- to 800-MPa range of experimental amphiboles at

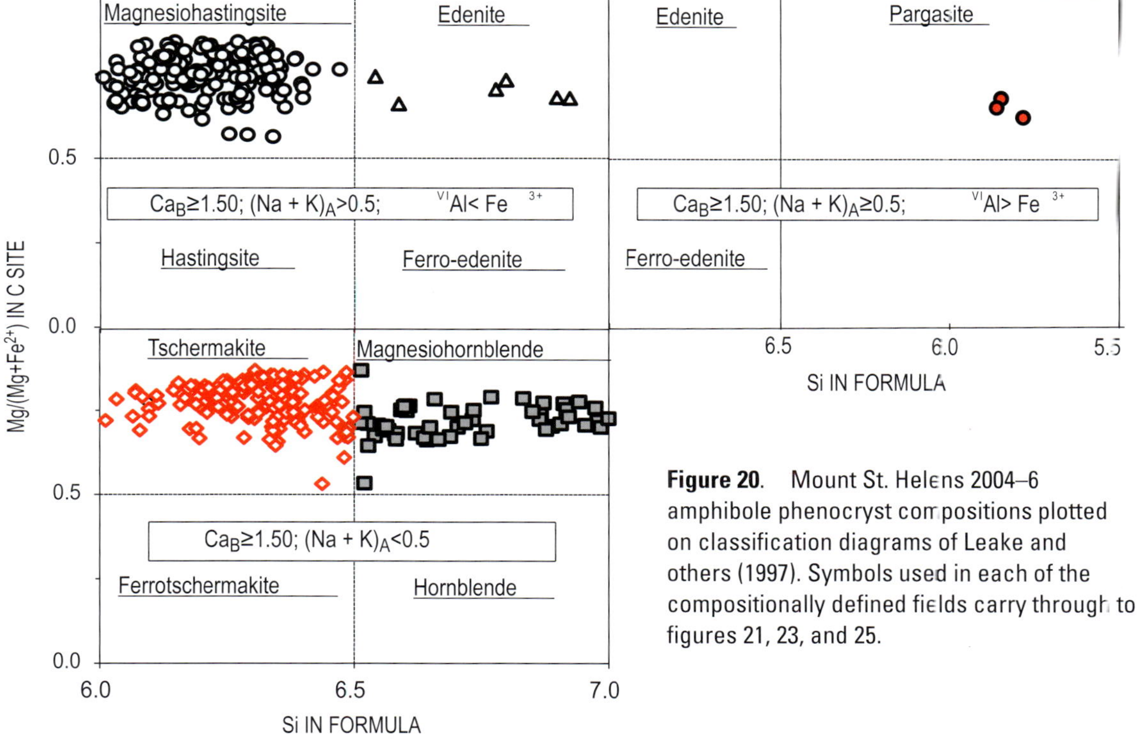

Figure 20. Mount St. Helens 2004–6 amphibole phenocryst compositions plotted on classification diagrams of Leake and others (1997). Symbols used in each of the compositionally defined fields carry through to figures 21, 23, and 25.

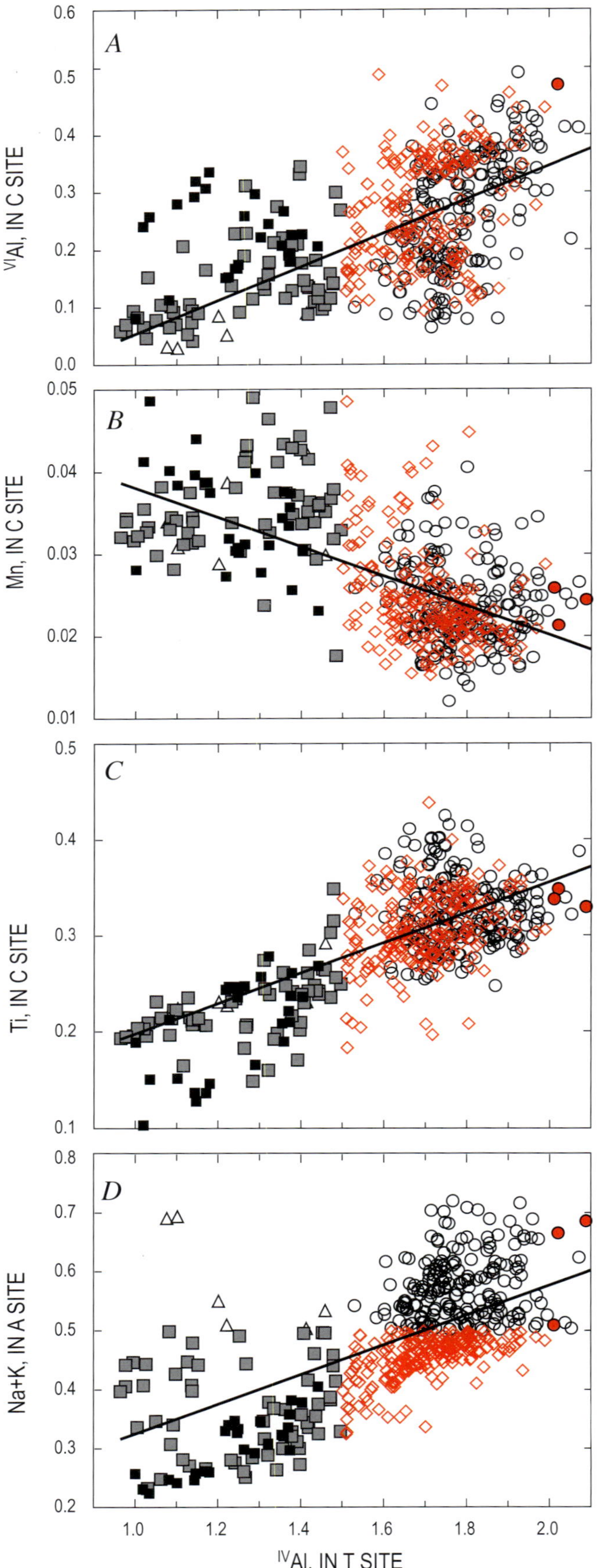

Figure 21. Site-specific cation concentrations versus tetrahedrally coordinated Al (^{IV}Al) in Mount St. Helens 2004–6 amphibole phenocrysts grouped according to amphibole type, with symbols as defined in figure 20. Magnesiohornblendes of 1986 gabbroic xenoliths, shown with black squares, are included for comparison. Lines shown represent best-fit linear regressions. *A*, Increasing octahedral alumina (^{VI}Al) concentrations roughly coincide with increasing tetrahedral alumina (^{IV}Al), reflecting a range of pressure-sensitive Al-Tschermak substitution. *B* and *C*, Antithetic variations of Mn and Ti with increasing ^{IV}Al demonstrate a continuous range of temperature-sensitive Ti-Tschermak substitution. *D*, Total alkali concentrations (Na+K in A site) increase with increasing ^{IV}Al in an edenite exchange, also indicative of increasing temperature of crystallization.

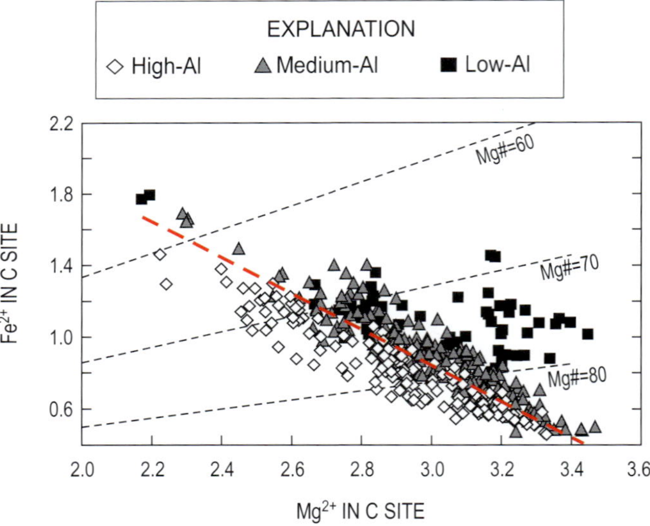

Figure 22. Fe^{2+} versus Mg^{2+} variation diagram for low-Al, medium-Al, and high-Al groups of Mount St. Helens 2004–6 amphiboles. At higher alumina contents, concentrations of Mg and Fe^{2+} (in C sites) are lower along lines of constant Mg# (=Mg/(Mg+Fe^{2+}), shown as dashed black lines. A well-balanced Fe-Mg C-site exchange is observed among medium-Al to high-Al amphiboles. The dashed red line shows best-fit linear regression of predominant 2004–6 amphibole population (defined as ±1σ from average composition).

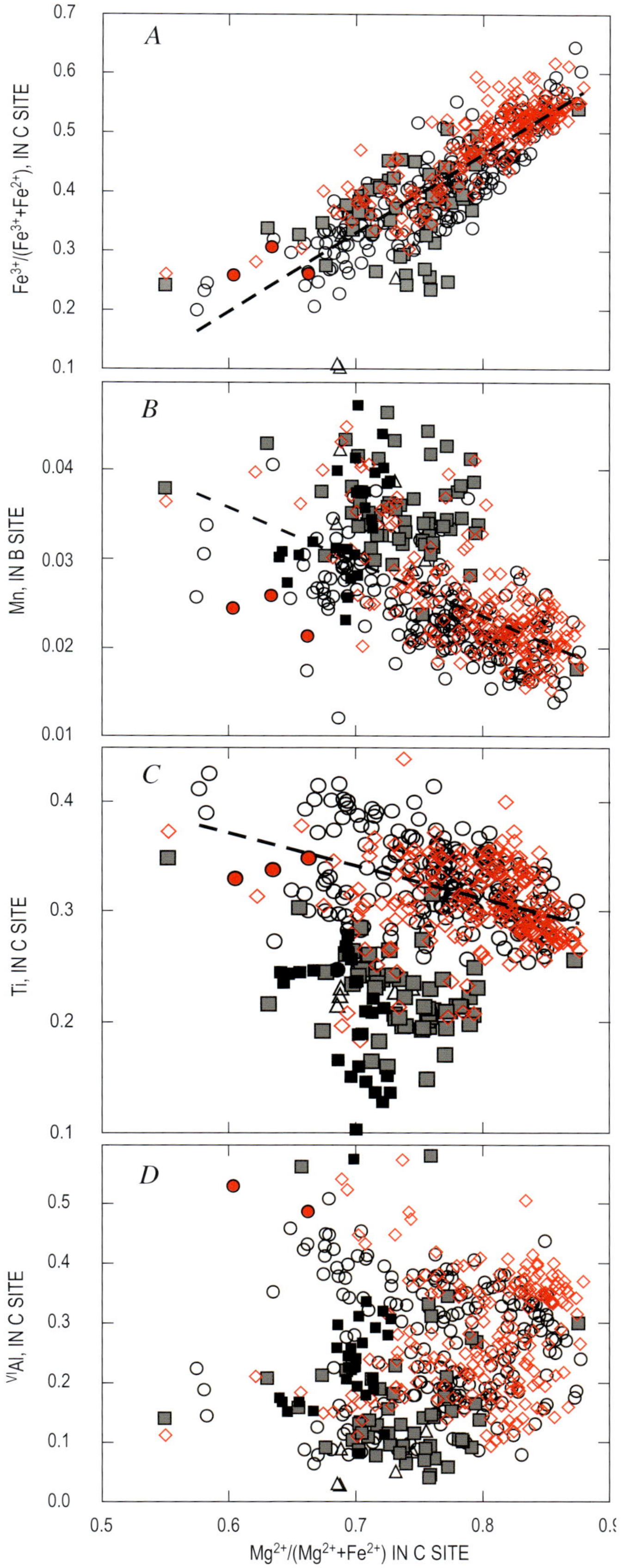

Figure 23. Site-specific cation concentrations versus Mg# in C site ($Mg^{2+}/(Mg^{2+}+Fe^{2+})$) in Mount St. Helens 2004–6 amphibole phenocrysts, grouped according to amphibole type, with symbols as defined in figure 20. Dashed lines represent best-fit linear regressions of predominant 2004–6 amphibole population (defined as ±1σ from average). Magnesiohornblendes in 1986 gabbroic xenoliths, shown as black squares, are presented for comparison. *A*, Mg# increases with increasing proportion of Fe^{3+} relative to total iron (Fe^{3+} + Fe^{2+}), suggesting that Mg# is largely affected by magmatic oxidation state. *B* and *C*, Covariance of Mn and Ti with Mg# in predominant amphibole population indicates Mg# varies independently of temperature-sensitive Ti-Tschermak exchange (figs. 21*B*, 21*C*). *D*, Octahedral alumina (^{VI}Al) concentrations show no systematic correlation with Mg#, indicating that Fe^{2+}-Mg exchange is independent of pressure-sensitive Al-Tschermak substitution.

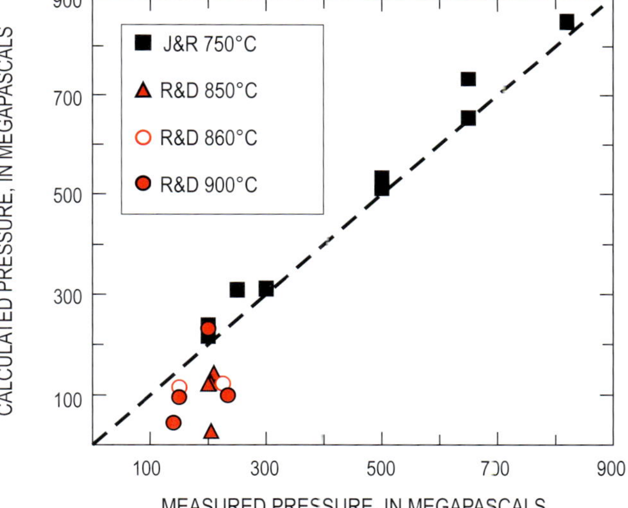

Figure 24. Plot of experimentally measured pressures versus pressures calculated by Al-in-hornblende barometer of Anderson and Smith (1995), using temperatures and amphibole compositions from experimental runs. J&R, Johnson and Rutherford (1989) experiments at 750°C on dacite from Fish Canyon Tuff (64.4 percent SiO_2) and Round Valley, Idaho (65.2 percent SiO_2), in which amphibole coexists with melt, fluid, quartz, biotite, plagioclase, sphene, and Fe-Ti oxides. R&D, Rutherford and Devine (this volume, chap. 31) experiments on 2004 Mount St. Helens dacite at 850°C, 860°C, and 900°C in which amphibole coexists with melt, fluid, plagioclase, orthopyroxene and Fe-Ti oxides.

740°C in three calc-alkaline magma compositions (64.4–65.2 percent SiO_2, Johnson and Rutherford, 1989) for which it was calibrated. In those experiments, the coexisting phase assemblage (melt, fluid, quartz, biotite, plagioclase, alkali-feldspar, sphene, and Fe-Ti oxides) provides a complete Tschermak-buffering capacity (Anderson and Smith, 1995). In experiments on 2004 Mount St. Helens dacite at pressures of 100–200 MPa and temperatures of 850–860°C and 900°C (Rutherford and Devine, this volume, chap. 31), amphibole coexists with a fluid+melt+plagiclase+orthopyroxene+oxide assemblage, similar to that of newly erupted lava. Overall, barometric calculations for amphibole equilibrated in the silica undersaturated dacite (analyses from table 6 of Rutherford and Devine, this volume, chap. 31) yield results consistent with the <200 MPa run conditions. Most of the estimates are low by more than 50 MPa, but there is closer agreement for the highest-Al amphiboles in runs at both 900°C and 850°C.

Barometric calculations for the predominant 2004–6 amphibole population (±1σ range, fig. 25) define a depth range for crystallization from 13.5 to ~4 km depth (350 MPa to 100 MPa) at temperatures between 850°C and 900°C. The overall average of phenocryst compositions yields barometry results of 220 MPa at 850°C. As restricted by the minimum pressure of amphibole stability (100 MPa), our calculations show that the bulk of amphibole crystallization occurred at temperatures less than ~875°C. At ~900°C, only high-Al amphiboles yield tenable calculated pressures, ranging from 100 to ~250 MPa, and perhaps to 300 MPa. Judging from the apparent error in applying Al-barometry to experimentally produced amphiboles at <200 MPa (fig. 24), it may be that actual equilibration pressures are higher by about 50–100 MPa. At 850°C this correction would increase the maximum depth range of average amphibole crystallization from ~8.5 km (220 MPa) to ~10.5 or perhaps to 12.5 km (270–320 MPa) and would increase the maximum depth range of the more aluminous tschermakite and magnesiohastingsite to >15 km (400 MPa).

The relative calculated pressures for the majority of amphibole compositions suggests two *P-T* scenarios for the 2004–6 magma and for prior generations of hostlike, precursory magma that are preserved in the crystal-laden mixture: (1) high-Al amphiboles formed at relatively low temperature and great depth (>15 km at <850°C), and the subsequent bulk of amphibole crystallization occurred during nearly isothermal ascent, or (2) crystallization during cooling between 900°C and 800°C at shallower depths within the magma reservoir (from 4 km to ~8 or possibly ~10 km), or a combination of (1) and (2). In either case, the range of calculated thermobarometric conditions reflected by tschermakite to magnesiohasting-

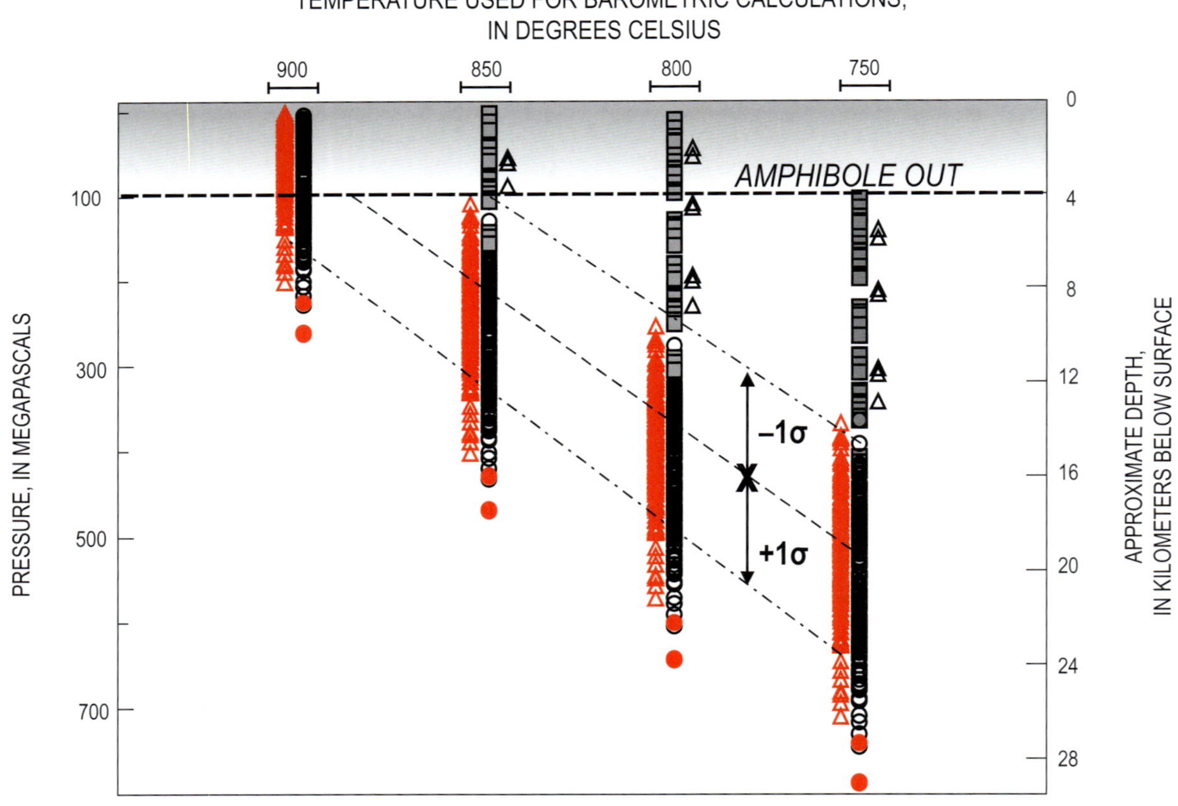

Figure 25. Plot showing results of Al-in-hornblende barometry applied to 2004–6 amphiboles at 750°C, 800°C, 850°C, and 900°C. Symbols correspond to amphibole types, as shown in figure 20. Inferred pressure (depth) versus temperature window for the average (X) and predominant amphibole population (±1σ range) is indicated.

site compositions in new lava reflects a well-mixed population of crystals formed in similar dacite magma over a likely depth range of 4–13.5 km, or possibly as deep as 15 km.

Our calculations suggest that low-Al magnesiohornblendes require low crystallization temperatures (750–850°C) to yield minimum pressures of amphibole stability (>100 MPa, fig. 25). Their presence in the mix suggests entrainment of near-solidus, and perhaps older, dacite mush (along with gabbroic material) in hotter 2004–6 magma. Those low-Al amphiboles that are not xenocrysts may have crystallized at low pressures and temperatures from host dacite melt. The highest Al-tschermakite, magnesiohastingsite, and pargasite could be derived from a mafic source (magma or wall rock) or could have crystallized from dacite under high *P-T* conditions above plagioclase saturation. In either case, magma crystallizing the end-member, high-Al amphiboles may not be close to quartz-saturation or to five-phase saturation conditions. In this case, barometry calculations would yield untenably low pressures over the temperature range of interest.

Amphibole Decompression Reactions, Magma Ascent Dynamics, and Conduit Geometry

The nature and extent of amphibole dissolution and reaction associated with variable decompression paths of dacite magma are documented in the recently published experimental study of Browne and Gardner (2006). Data from their series of isothermal decompression runs, performed on similar compositions and initially equilibrated under conditions analogous to those of the Mount St. Helens 2004–6 magma (840°C and 150 MPa), help to constrain paths of magma ascent. Reaction rims similar to the typical 5-μm rims on subhedral, resorbed, or fragmented amphibole crystals in the 2004–6 Mount St. Helens dacite were reproduced by isothermal decompression from 60 to <30 MPa (~2.5- to <1-km depth) over an interval of 3 to 4 days (compare textures in our fig. 7 with those in fig. 4 of Browne and Gardner, 2006). Such 5-μm rims must have formed by the time magma reached the uppermost conduit because amphibole ceases to react at depths less than ~0.6 km in a highly viscous, nearly solidified, and completely degassed host (Browne and Gardner, 2006).

Textures of resorbed amphibole crystals seen in the 2004–6 Mount St. Helens dacite (fig. 7) could be produced if the host magma stalled for ~2 days at ~3.5 to 2.5-km depth (90 to 60 MPa) during ascent (Browne and Gardner, 2006). Under such conditions, amphibole dissolves without forming pseudomorph reaction rims, which develop subsequent to resorption during further ascent. The disappearance of amphibole, as documented by resorption textures and decreased modal abundance in experimental products, is accompanied by nucleation and growth of orthopyroxene and plagioclase (±Fe-Ti oxide) microphenocrysts in the vicinity of dissolved amphibole. Such microphenocrysts are likely to have contributed to the microcrystalline matrix, which further develops during ascent (Blundy and Cashman, 2001; Cashman and others, this volume, chap. 19).

Amphiboles with <3-μm rims in early dome samples with a glassier matrix (figs. 9*A*, 9*B*; and Pallister and others, this volume, chap. 30) suggest faster ascent rates through the 60–30-MPa pressure range than later dacite, consistent with the relatively high eruptive flux during the earliest phases of dome extrusion (Schilling and others, this volume, chap. 8; Reagan and others, this volume, chap. 37).

The sporadic occurrence of wider reaction rims (30–200 μm) may be attributed to the haphazard entrainment of amphibole phenocrysts subjected to extensive reaction while occluded to walls of the lower conduit. Alternatively, some phenocrysts with wide reaction rims could be xenolithic fragments of 1980s dacite, which is known to have two reaction-rim populations (10–12 and 30 μm; Rutherford and Hill, 1993). Composite phenocrysts with resorbed and patchy cores surrounded by subhedral zoned overgrowths and amphibole-to-amphibole reactions probably reflect xenocryst assimilation at depth. It is evident from less commonly observed examples of resorbed medium-Al amphibole crystals with low-Al (and high fluorine) amphibole overgrowths (for example, in SH314-1 and DRS_3_9_4; fig. 11, table 2) that this style of amphibole dissolution and reaction has occurred in magma stored at depths near to and perhaps slightly above the limits of amphibole stability. Such cases would seem to reflect the disruption of a crystal mush by a hotter or chemically incompatible melt. Rutherford and Devine (this volume, chap. 31) suggest that fluorine has the effect of stabilizing amphibole at depths above that of H_2O-only amphibole saturation. Thus, it is possible that late-stage fluorine enrichment could promote the occurrence of such amphibole-to-amphibole–melt reactions in the lower conduit.

The persistent 5-μm amphibole rims in all post-November 2004 spine lava reflect steady influx and upward transport of magma through the lower conduit, possibly on the order of 2–4 days, from 3.5–2.5-km depths to as shallow as ~1 km. Thus, an amphibole-based rate of magma ascent for this depth interval is between ~600 and ~1,200 m/day. As constrained by a first-year erupted volume of about 70×10^6 m^3 (Schilling and others, this volume, chap. 8), such rates infer a conduit radius between 10 and 5 m. In contrast, ground deformation and eruptive flux infer a significantly larger average conduit radius of ~35 m (down to 5 km depth) (Dzurisin and others, this volume, chap. 14).

A similar discrepancy existed between conduit dimensions inferred from amphibole-rim and volumetric-flux modeling of the 1980s dome-building eruption (Cashman, 1992; Pallister and others, 1992). For the current eruption, both interpretations might be valid, but for different depth ranges. Taken together, these analyses suggest that the conduit may have a wineglass shape. At ~3.5–1-km depth, the conduit might be a narrow pipe (or short dike) that accommodates relatively rapid transit of dacite magma, as recorded by the thin amphibole reaction rims. Above ~1 km, where matrix crystallization of magma occurs (Cashman and others, this volume, chap. 19; Pallister and others this volume, chap. 30) and amphibole reactions cease, a cooling, solidifying, and sluggishly moving magma is accommodated by a wider conduit (>60 m radius). Such a wineglass shape for the conduit also might help explain (1) the apparent localization of deformation to the crater and to a deep region whose centroid lies at depth of ~8 km (Dzurisin and others, this volume, chap. 14; Lisowski and others, this volume, chap. 15) and (2) the lack of geophysical or petrologic evidence for magma storage between ~4–5-km and ~1-km depths.

The Amphibole Perspective: from Source to Surface

Our study of amphibole systematics shows the near-solid magma recently extruded from Mount St. Helens is a well-blended, crystal-rich dacite mush that originated from depths of at least ~4 km and ascended to within 1 km of the surface at rates in the range ~0.6–1.2 km/day. The compositional ranges of amphibole phenocrysts in the 2004–6 dacite reflect multiple generations of (primarily) dacite magma crystallization in different *P-T* environments. Amphibole morphology and texture reveal a dynamic magma-mixing regime in which a genetically disparate, amphibole phenocryst assemblage is variably dissolved, overgrown, broken, and abraded. The same ranges of amphibole compositions and textures are found in all thin sections of dome material. An obvious implication of the well-dispersed amphibole variability is that the monotonous bulk chemistry of new lava is the result of fine-scale (less than a cubic centimeter) blending of multiple, crystal-laden dacite magmas.

Petrologic constraints, including complex zoning in some amphibole phenocrysts, have spawned models in which this latest generation of Mount St. Helens lava evolved physically and chemically to its preeruptive condition by convective recycling of crystal-laden dacite magma through a contiguous *P-T* regime (such as that depicted in the simplified magma-reservoir diagrams of Pallister and others, this volume, chap. 30, fig. 22; Rutherford and Devine, this volume, chap. 31, fig. 13). Our thermobarometric calculations place amphibole crystallization in a *P-T* window between 100 and ~350–400 MPa (~4- and 13.5–15-km depth) and ~900°C and ~800°C. This interpretation of the *P-T* regime for eruption-related magmatism is within that constrained by experimentally determined phase relations (Rutherford and Devine, this volume, chap 31) and is consistent with the seismologically defined 4–12-km-deep magma source (Moran, 1994).

The broad *P-T* regime reflected in the variety of phenocrysts also could be an artifact of repeated injection of different crystal-laden, dacite magma batches under more restricted *P-T* conditions in the uppermost zone of the magma reservoir. Amphibole petrology and several other lines of evidence suggest that much of the blending of the 2004–6 dacite mush is achieved between ~8- and 4-km depth. The average amphibole in 2004–6 magma is interpreted to have crystallized at 850°C and 220 MPa (fig. 25). Coincidentally, those same source conditions were interpreted for the May 18, 1980, pumice (Rutherford and others, 1985). Considering that the range of amphibole compositions of 2004–6 dacite is comparable to that of amphibole in 1980–86 lava, we suggest a consistent staging area at and above ~8-km depth for both eruptions. Thermobarometric calculations indicate that cyclic variations within the range of the predominant 2004–6 amphibole compositions could result from heating and cooling within this upper part of a magma reservoir (fig. 25). Compositional zoning in the outer parts of plagioclase in the 2004–6 dacite are likewise consistent with injections of hotter, porphyritic dacite magma into crystal-laden dacite mush (Streck and others, this volume, chap. 34).

Isotopic studies of plagioclase in 2004–6 dacite (Cooper and Donnelly, this volume, chap. 36; Kent and others, this volume, chap. 35) suggest that the majority of phenocrysts are "zero-age" and cognate to the host dacite. Of the remaining phenocrysts, a small proportion are Tertiary xenocrysts, but 20–40 percent of analyzed plagioclase crystals are considered antecrysts, derived from prior generations of Mount St. Helens dacite (see Bacon and Lowenstern, 2005, for further discussion of the term, antecryst). Our data indicate that amphibole phenocrysts have a similarly diverse heritage. Although 2004–6 dacite antecrysts may be an inevitable product of long-term mixing, it is also likely that some of them, as well as xenocrysts, are assimilated from variably aged roof rocks and surrounding crustal materials by intrusive processes.

The disequilibrium reflected both in the textural variety of amphiboles and in the wide variation of their outermost rim compositions is a clear indication of a dynamic, preeruptive, magma-mixing environment for the 2004–6 dacite. Uniform reaction rims on all subhedral, rounded, resorbed, and fragmented amphibole phenocrysts of all compositional affinities indicate that this crystal assemblage was being broken, abraded, and dissolved in the magma immediately before and during early stages of ascent. An ascent path that accommodates these features involves differential flow rates through regions of the lowermost conduit and uppermost magma reservoir. In this scenario, supported by experimental observations of Browne and Gardner (2006), some magma must stagnate long enough at 90–60 MPa (~3.5–2.5-km depth) for amphiboles to be resorbed, but other magma does not. This situation seems plausible for a magma ascending through deep conduit roots that must extend into a mushy reservoir cupola. The crystal-laden magma is viscous enough to fragment and entrain additional amphibole phenocrysts during ascent through crystal mushes in the upper reservoir and lower conduit at ~5–3.5 km. Small reaction rims on the well-mixed amphibole assemblage result from rapid decompression of host-dacite magma during ascent through a small conduit (≤10-m radius) extending upward from ~3.5 km to within ~1 km of the crater floor. From ~1 km to the surface, the final preeruptive condition of amphibole is frozen in as the magma quenches into a nearly solid plug of porphyritic lava. During and after this magma-to-lava transition, a relatively sluggish plug ascent is accommodated by an enlarged (≥60-m radius) uppermost conduit, in which the fresh dacite lava is sheared and gouged during forceful expulsion as lava spines.

Acknowledgments

We thank Jeff Linscott of JL Aviation, whose adept piloting skills enabled heli-dredge collection of lava samples, and Bobbie Myers of the U.S. Geological Survey's Cascades Volcano Observatory (USGS–CVO), who helped to ensure the safety of our dome-sampling forays. Assistance with sample processing and archiving by Winston Stokes (USGS–CVO) and dedicated volunteers in the CVO Petrology Laboratory (Siobhan McConnell, Trystan Herriott, Taryn Lopez, and Alison Eckberg) is gratefully acknowledged. Isabelle Brownfield (USGS, Denver) provided many of the SEM images used in the course of this investigation. Thoughtful reviews of an early version of this chapter by Roz Helz (USGS, emeritus) and Mac Rutherford (Brown University) resulted in significant improvements.

References Cited

Allen, J.C., and Boettcher, A.L., 1978, Amphiboles in andesite and basalt, II—Stability as a function of P-T-f_{H_2O}-f_{O_2}: American Mineralogist, v. 63, nos. 11–12, p. 1074–1087.

Anderson, J.L., and Smith, D.R., 1995, The effects of temperature and f_{O_2} on the Al-in-hornblende barometer: American Mineralogist, v. 80, p. 549–599.

Bachmann, O., and Dungan, M.A., 2002, Temperature-induced Al-zoning in hornblendes of the Fish Canyon magma, Colorado: American Mineralogist, v. 87, p. 1062–1076.

Bacon, C.R., and Lowenstern, J.B., 2005, Late Pleistocene granodiorite source for recycled zircon and phenocrysts in rhyodacite lava at Crater Lake, Oregon: Earth and Planetary Science Letters, v. 233, p. 277–293.

Blundy, J., and Cashman, K., 2001, Ascent-driven crystallisation of dacite magmas at Mount St. Helens, 1980–1986: Contributions to Mineralogy and Petrology, v. 140, no. 6, p. 631–650, doi:10.1007/s004100000219.

Blundy, J.D., and Holland, T.J.B., 1990, Calcic amphibole equilibria and a new plagioclase-amphibole geothermometer: Contributions to Mineralogy and Petrology, v. 104, no. 2, p. 208–224, doi:10.1007/BF00306444.

Browne, B.L., and Gardner, J.E., 2006, The influence of magma ascent path on the texture, mineralogy, and formation of hornblende reaction rims Earth and Planetary Science Letters, v. 246, p. 161–176

Buckley, V.J.E., Sparks, R.S.J., and Wood, B.J., 2006, Hornblende dehydration reactions during magma ascent at Soufrière Hills Volcano, Montserrat: Contributions to Mineralogy and Petrology, v. 151, no. 2, p. 121–140, doi:10.1007/s00410-005-0060-5.

Cashman, K.V., 1992, Groundmass crystallization of Mount St, Helens dacite, 1980–1986—a tool for interpreting shallow magmatic processes: Contributions to Mineralogy and Petrology, v. 109, no. 4, p. 431–449, doi:10.1007/BF00306547.

Cashman, K.V., and McConnell, S.M., 2005, Multiple levels of magma storage during the 1980 summer eruptions of Mount St. Helens, WA: Bulletin of Volcanology, v. 68, no. 1, p. 57–75, doi:10.1007/s00445-005-0422-x.

Cashman, K.V., Thornber, C.R., and Pallister, J.S., 2008, From dome to dust; shallow crystallization and fragmentation of conduit magma during the 2004–2006 dome extrusion of Mount St. Helens, Washington, chap. 19 *of* Sherrod, D.R., Scott, W.E., and Stauffer, P.H., eds., A volcano rekindled; the renewed eruption of Mount St. Helens, 2004–2006: U.S. Geological Survey Professional Paper 1750 (this volume).

Cooper, K.M., and Donnelly, C.T., 2008, ^{238}U-^{230}Th-^{226}Ra disequilibria in dacite and plagioclase from the 2004–2005 eruption of Mount St. Helens, chap. 36 *of* Sherrod, D.R., Scott, W.E., and Stauffer, P.H., eds., A volcano rekindled; the renewed eruption of Mount St. Helens, 2004–2006: U.S. Geological Survey Professional Paper 1750 (this volume).

Dzurisin, D., Lisowski, M., Poland, M.P., Sherrod, D.R., and LaHusen, R.G., 2008, Constraints and conundrums posed by ground deformation measurements during the 2004–2006 dome-building eruption of Mount St. Helens, Washington, chap. 14 *of* Sherrod, D.R., Scott, W.E., and Stauffer, P.H., eds., A volcano rekindled; the renewed eruption of Mount St. Helens, 2004–2006: U.S. Geological Survey Professional Paper 1750 (this volume).

Grove, T.L., Elkins-Tanton, L.T., Parman, S.W., Chatterjee, N., Müntener, O., and Gaetani, G.A., 2003, Fractional crystallization and mantle melting controls on calc-alkaline differentiation trends: Contributions to Mineralogy and Petrology, v. 145, p. 515–533.

Hammarstrom, J.M, and Zen, E-an, 1986, Aluminum in hornblende; an empirical igneous geobarometer: American Mineralogist, v. 71, p. 1297–1313.

Hammarstrom, J.M., and Zen, E-an, 1992, Discussion of Blundy and Holland's (1990) "Calcic amphibole equilibria and a new amphibole-plagioclase geothermometer":

Contributions to Mineralogy and Petrology, v. 111, no. 2, p. 264–266, doi:10.1007/BF00348957.

Helz, R.T., 1982, Phase relations and compositions of amphiboles produced in studies of the melting behavior of rocks, *in* Veblen, D.R., and Ribbe, P.H., eds., Amphiboles—petrology and experimental phase relations: Reviews in Mineralogy, v. 9B, p. 279–346.

Holland, T., and Blundy, J., 1994, Non-ideal interactions in calcic amphiboles and their bearing on amphibole-plagioclase thermometry: Contributions to Mineralogy and Petrology, v. 116, no. 4, p. 433–447, doi:10.1007/BF00310910.

Jarosewich, E., Nelen, J.A., and Norberg, J.A., 1980, Reference samples for electron microprobe analyses: Geostandards Newsletter, v. 4, no. 1, p. 43–47.

Johnson, M.C., and Rutherford, M.J., 1989, Experimental calibration of the aluminum-in-hornblende geobarometer with application to Long Valley caldera (California) volcanic rocks: Geology, v. 17, p. 837–841.

Kent, A.J.R., Jacobsen, B., Peate, D.W., Waight, T.E., and Baker, J.A., 2004, Isotope dilution MC-ICP-MS rare earth element analysis of geochemical reference materials NIST SRM 610, NIST SRM 612, NIST SRM 614, BHVO-2G, BHVO-2, BCR-2G, JB-2, WS-1, W-2, AGV-1, AGV-2: Geostandards Newsletter, v. 28, p. 417–430.

Kent, A.J.R., Rowe, M.C., Thornber, C.R., and Pallister, J.S., 2008, Trace element and Pb isotope composition of plagioclase from dome samples from the 2004–2005 eruption of Mount St Helens, Washington, chap. 35 *of* Sherrod, D.R., Scott, W.E., and Stauffer, P.H., eds., A volcano rekindled; the renewed eruption of Mount St. Helens, 2004–2006: U.S. Geological Survey Professional Paper 1750 (this volume).

Leake, B.E., Woolley, A.R., Arps, C.E.S., Birch, W.D., Gilbert, M.C., Grice, J.D., Hawthorne, F.C., Kato, A., Kisch, H.J., Krivovichev, V.G., Linthout, K., Laird, J., Mandarino, J.A., Maresch, W.V., Nickel, E.H., Rock, N.M.S., Schumacher, J.C., Smith, D.C., Stephenson, N.C.N., Ungaretti, L., Whittaker, E.J.W., and Youzhi, G., 1997, Nomenclature of amphiboles—report of the subcommittee on amphiboles of the International Mineralogical Association, Commission on New Minerals and Mineral Names: American Mineralogist, v. 82, nos. 9–10, p. 1019–1037.

Lisowski, M., Dzurisin, D., Denlinger, R.P., and Iwatsubo, E.Y., 2008, GPS-measured deformation associated with the 2004–2006 dome-building eruption of Mount St. Helens, Washington, chap. 15 *of* Sherrod, D.R., Scott, W.E., and Stauffer, P.H., eds., A volcano rekindled; the renewed eruption of Mount St. Helens, 2004–2006: U.S. Geological Survey Professional Paper 1750 (this volume).

Moran, S.C., 1994, Seismicity at Mount St. Helens, 1987–1992; evidence for repressurization of an active magmatic system: Journal of Geophysical Research, v. 99, no. B3, p. 4341–4354, doi:10.1029/93JB02993.

Pallister, J.S., Heliker, C., and Hoblitt, R.P., 1991, Glimpses of the active pluton below Mount St. Helens [abs.]: Eos (American Geophysical Union Transactions), v. 72, no. 44, supplement, p. 576.

Pallister, J.S., Hoblitt, R.P., Crandell, D.R., and Mullineaux, D.R., 1992, Mount St. Helens a decade after the 1980 eruptions—magmatic models, chemical cycles, and a revised hazards assessment: Bulletin of Volcanology, v. 54, no. 2, p. 126–146, doi:10.1007/BF00278003.

Pallister, J.S., Thornber, C.R., Cashman, K.V., Clynne, M.A., Lowers, H.A., Mandeville, C.W., Brownfield, I.K., and Meeker, G.P., 2008, Petrology of the 2004–2006 Mount St. Helens lava dome—implications for magmatic plumbing and eruption triggering, chap. 30 *of* Sherrod, D.R., Scott, W.E., and Stauffer, P.H., eds., A volcano rekindled; the renewed eruption of Mount St. Helens, 2004–2006: U.S. Geological Survey Professional Paper 1750 (this volume).

Pearce, N.J.G., Perkins, W.T., Westgate, J.A., Gorton, M.P., Jackson, S.E., Neal, C.R., and Chenery, S.P., 1997, A compilation of new and published major and trace element data for NIST SRM 610 and NIST SRM 612 glass reference materials: Geostandards Newsletter, v. 21, p. 115–144.

Pichavant, M., Valencia, H.J., Boulmier, S., Briqueu, L., Joron, J., Juteau, M., Marin, L., Michard, A., Sheppard, S.M.F., Treuil, M., and Vernet, M., 1987, The Macusani glasses, SE Peru; evidence of chemical fractionation in peraluminous magmas, *in* Mysen, B.O., ed., Magmatic processes—physiochemical principles: Geochemical Society Special Publication No. 1, p. 359–373.

Reagan, M.K., Cooper, K.M., Pallister, J.S., Thornber, C.R., and Wortel, M., 2008, Timing of degassing and plagioclase growth in lavas erupted from Mount St. Helens, 2004–2005, from ^{210}Po-^{210}Pb-^{226}Ra disequilibria, chap. 37 *of* Sherrod, D.R., Scott, W.E., and Stauffer, P.H., eds., A volcano rekindled; the renewed eruption of Mount St. Helens, 2004–2006: U.S. Geological Survey Professional Paper 1750 (this volume).

Rowe, M.C., Thornber, C.R., Gooding, D.J., and Pallister, J.S., 2008, Catalog of Mount St. Helens 2004–2005 tephra samples with major- and trace-element geochemistry: U.S. Geological Survey Open-File Report 2008–1131, 7 p, with digital database.

Rutherford, M.J., and Devine, J.D., III, 2008, Magmatic conditions and processes in the storage zone of the 2004–2006 Mount St. Helens dacite, chap. 31 *of* Sherrod, D.R., Scott, W.E., and Stauffer, P.H., eds., A volcano rekindled; the renewed eruption of Mount St. Helens, 2004–2006: U.S. Geological Survey Professional Paper 1750 (this volume).

Rutherford, M.J., and Hill, P.M., 1993, Magma ascent rates from amphibole breakdown—an experimental study applied to the 1980–1986 Mount St. Helens eruptions: Journal of Geophysical Research, v. 98, no. B11, p. 19667–19685.

Rutherford, M.J., and Johnson, M.C., 1992, Comment on Blundy and Holland's (1990) "Calcic amphibole equilibria and a new amphibole-plagioclase geothermometer": Contributions to Mineralogy and Petrology, v. 111, no. 2, p. 266–268.

Rutherford, M.J., Sigurdsson, H., Carey, S., and Davis, A., 1985, The May 18, 1980, eruption of Mount St. Helens; 1. melt composition and experimental phase equilibria: Journal of Geophysical Research, v. 90, no. B4, p. 2929–2947.

Schilling, S.P., Thompson, R.A., Messerich, J.A., and Iwatsubo, E.Y., 2008, Use of digital aerophotogrammetry to determine rates of lava dome growth, Mount St. Helens, 2004–2005, chap. 8 *of* Sherrod, D.R., Scott, W.E., and Stauffer, P.H., eds., A volcano rekindled; the renewed eruption of Mount St. Helens, 2004–2006: U.S. Geological Survey Professional Paper 1750 (this volume).

Streck, M.J., Broderick, C.A., Thornber, C.R., Clynne, M.A., and Pallister, J.S., 2008, Plagioclase populations and zoning in dacite of the 2004–2005 Mount St. Helens eruption—constraints for magma origin and dynamics, chap. 34 *of* Sherrod, D.R., Scott, W.E., and Stauffer, P.H., eds., A volcano rekindled; the renewed eruption of Mount St. Helens, 2004–2006: U.S. Geological Survey Professional Paper 1750 (this volume).

Sun, S.-s., and McDonough, W.F., 1989, Chemical and isotopic systematics of oceanic basalts—implications for mantle composition and processes, *in* Saunders, A.D., and Norry, M.J., eds., Magmatism in the ocean basins: Geological Society of London Special Publications 42, p. 313–345.

Thornber, C.R., Pallister, J.S., Rowe, M.C., McConnell, S., Herriott, T.M., Eckberg, A., Stokes, W.C., Johnson Cornelius, D., Conrey, R.M., Hannah, T., Taggart, J.E., Jr., Adams, M., Lamothe, P.J., Budahn, J.R., and Knaack, C.M., 2008, Catalog of Mount St. Helens 2004–2007 dome samples with major- and trace-element chemistry: U.S. Geological Survey Open-File Report 2008–1130, 9 p., with digital database.

Appendix 1. Analytical Methods

Microbeam analyses and imagery used in this study were accomplished at three different laboratories. Most data were obtained using the USGS Denver JEOL 8900 electron microprobe and a JEOL 5800-LV scanning electron microscope (SEM). Nine samples were analyzed and imaged by M. Rowe at Oregon State University on a Cameca SX-100 electron microprobe. At both laboratories, amphibole grains were analyzed using 20-nA beam current and a 15 keV accelerating voltage. For all but the smallest of grains, which required a fully focused beam, a 10-µm beam diameter was used for crystal interiors and near-rim analyses. Count times for major elements varied between 30 and 10 s on peak (15 to 5 s background count times). For F and Cl, count times on peak were increased to 60 and 40 s, respectively. USNM natural silicate mineral standards were used for calibration. Kakanui hornblende (Jarosewich and others, 1980) was repeatedly analyzed to monitor accuracy and precision during and among runs.

Additional analyses of SH304-2A (early dacite) and SH304-2G (glassy lithic fragment) amphibole crystals were done by C. Mandeville at the American Museum of Natural History (AMNH) using a Cameca SX-100 electron microprobe utilizing a 15-keV accelerating voltage, 10-nA beam current for major elements, 15-µm beam diameter, 30 s count time on peak and 15 s on background. F, Cl, and Cr analyses of amphiboles by electron microprobe at AMNH were done during the same analytical session with 15-keV accelerating voltage, 40-nA beam current, and 140 s count time on peak and 70 s on background. Precision and accuracy of major-element analyses were checked by repeated analyses of Kakanui hornblende. Precision and accuracy of F, Cl, and Cr analyses at AMNH were monitored by repeated analyses of Macusani peraluminous rhyolite glass (1.3 percent F, 450 ppm Cl; Pichavant and others, 1987), NMNH 164905 chromium-augite (0.85 percent Cr; Jarosewich and others, 1980), and NIST SRM 610 glass (415±49.5 ppm Cr; Pearce and others, 1997).

All amphibole analyses used in this investigation fit the mineralogical criteria established for clinoamphiboles by Leake and others (1997). See text for discussion of the stoichiometric calculation used to assess cation site occupancy and proper nomenclature.

Trace-element concentrations of amphiboles were analyzed by laser ablation inductively coupled plasma mass spectrometry (LA ICP-MS) in the W.M. Keck Collaboratory for Plasma Spectrometry, Oregon State University, and collected from the same phenocryst areas that were analyzed and imaged by the Cameca SX-100 electron microprobe. Amphiboles were ablated with a NuWave 213 nm Nd:YAG laser using a 40-µm stationary spot and 20-Hz pulse rate. Ablation time and data acquisition for each analysis was 30 s, with 45 s of washout time before and after ablation. Measured counts were normalized to ^{43}Ca. Trace-element concentrations were then calculated relative to the BCR-2G glass standard. BHVO-2G glass standard was ablated under identical conditions as the amphiboles as a secondary standard. Precision, estimated by repeated analysis of BHVO-2G, is within 10 percent of reported values for all trace elements (Kent and others, 2004).

Appendix 2. Major- and Trace-Element Compositions of Amphibole Phenocrysts in Mount St. Helens 2004–2006 and 1980–1986 Dacite Lava

[This appendix appears only in the digital versions of this work—in the DVD-ROM that accompanies the printed volume and as a separate file accompanying this chapter on the Web at: http://pubs.usgs.gov/pp/1750.]

The Mount St. Helens amphibole phenocryst chemistry described in this chapter is tabulated in six worksheets of a Microsoft Excel file. The six worksheets are organized as follows:

Worksheet 1. Electron microprobe analyses of amphibole phenocrysts in Mount St. Helens 2004–6 dacite.
Worksheet 2. Electron microprobe analyses of amphibole phenocrysts in Mount St. Helens 2004 glassy lithic fragments.
Worksheet 3. Electron microprobe analyses of amphibole phenocrysts in Mount St. Helens 2004–6 lithic inclusions.
Worksheet 4. Electron microprobe analyses of amphibole phenocryst cores in Mount St. Helens 1986 gabbro xenoliths.
Worksheet 5. Electron microprobe analyses of amphibole phenocryst cores in Mount St. Helens 1980–86 dacite.
Worksheet 6. LA-ICPMS rare-earth-element analyses of amphibole phenocrysts in Mount St. Helens 2004–6 dacite.

Chapter 33

Evolving Magma Storage Conditions Beneath Mount St. Helens Inferred from Chemical Variations in Melt Inclusions from the 1980–1986 and Current (2004–2006) Eruptions

By Jon Blundy[1], Katharine V. Cashman[2], and Kim Berlo[3]

Abstract

Major element, trace element, and volatile concentrations in 187 glassy melt inclusions and 25 groundmass glasses from the 1980–86 eruption of Mount St. Helens are presented, together with 103 analyses of touching Fe-Ti oxide pairs from the same samples. These data are used to evaluate the temporal evolution of the magmatic plumbing system beneath the volcano during 1980–86 and so provide a framework in which to interpret analyses of melt inclusions from the current (2004–2006) eruption.

Major and trace element concentrations of all melt inclusions lie at the high-SiO_2 end of the data array defined by eruptive products of late Quaternary age from Mount St. Helens. For several major and trace elements, the glasses define a trend that is oblique to the whole-rock trend, indicating that different mineral assemblages were responsible for the two trends. The whole-rock trend can be ascribed to differentiation of hydrous basaltic parents in a deep-seated magma reservoir, probably at depths great enough to stabilize garnet. In contrast, the glass trends were generated by closed-system crystallization of the phenocryst and microlite mineral assemblages at low pressures.

The dissolved H_2O content of the melt inclusions from 1980–86, as measured by ion microprobe, ranges from 0 to 6.7 wt. percent, with the highest values obtained from the plinian phase of May 18, 1980. Water contents decrease with increasing SiO_2, consistent with decompression-driven crystallization. Preliminary data for dissolved CO_2 in melt inclusions from the May 18 plinian phase and from August 7, 1980, indicate that X_{H_2O} in the vapor phase was approximately constant at 0.80, irrespective of H_2O content, suggestive of closed-system degassing with a high bubble fraction or gas streaming through the subvolcanic system. Temperature and f_{O_2} estimates for touching Fe-Ti oxides show evidence for heating during crystallization owing to release of latent heat. Consequently, magmas with the highest microlite crystallinities record the highest temperatures. Magmas also become progressively reduced during ascent and degassing, probably as a result of redox equilibria between exsolving S-bearing gases and magmas. The lowest temperature oxides have $f_{O_2} \approx$ NNO, similar to high-temperature fumarole gases from the volcano. The temperature and f_{O_2} of the magma tapped by the plinian phase of May 18, 1980, are 870–875°C and NNO+0.8, respectively.

The dissolved volatile contents of the melt inclusions have been used to calculate sealing pressures; that is, the pressure at which chemical exchange between inclusion and matrix melt ceased. These are greatest for the May 18 plinian magma (120 to 320 MPa); lower pressures are recorded by samples of the preplinian cryptodome and by all post-May 18 magmas. Magma crystallinity, calculated from melt-inclusion Rb contents, is negatively correlated with sealing pressure, consistent with decompression crystallization. Elevated contents of Li in melt inclusions from the cryptodome and post-May 18 samples are consistent with transfer of Li in a magmatic vapor phase from deeper parts of the magma system to magma stored at shallower levels. The Li enrichment attains its maximum extent at ~150 MPa, which is ascribed to separation of a single vapor phase into H_2O-rich gas and dense Li-rich brine at the top of the magma column.

There are striking correlations between melt-inclusion chemistry and monitoring data for the 1980–86 eruption. Dissolved SO_2 contents of melt inclusions from any given event, multiplied by the mass of magma erupted during that event,

[1] Department of Earth Sciences, University of Bristol, Wills Memorial Building, Bristol BS8 1RJ, United Kingdom

[2] Department of Geological Sciences, 1272 University of Oregon, Eugene, OR 97403

[3] Department of Earth Sciences, Wills Memorial Building, Bristol BS8 1RJ, UK; now at Earth & Planetary Sciences, McGill University, 3450 University St., Montreal, Quebec, Canada H3A 2A7

correlate with the measured flux of SO_2 at the surface, suggesting that magma degassing and melt-inclusion sealing are closely related in time and space.

Textural and chemical evidence indicates that melt inclusions became effectively sealed (physically or kinetically) shortly before eruption. Thus by converting pressure to depth using a density model and edifice-loading algorithm for the volcano, changing depths of magma extraction with time can be tracked and compared to the seismic record. The plinian eruption of May 18, 1980, involved magma stored 5–11 km below sea level; this is inferred to be the subvolcanic magma chamber. The preceding eruptions, including the May 18, 1980, blast, involved magma withdrawal from the cryptodome and conduit down to 5 km below sea level. Subsequent 1980 eruptions tapped magma down to depths of ≤10 km below sea level. Tapping of magma stored deeper than 2 km below sea level stopped abruptly at the end of 1980, coincident with the onset of extensive shallow seismicity and a change from explosive to effusive eruption style from 1981 to 1986. Overall, the 1980–86 eruption is consistent with the evisceration of a thin, vertically extensive body of magma extending from 5 to at least 11 km below sea level and connected to the surface by a thin conduit. In the absence of sustained high magma-supply rates from depth, decompression crystallization of magma ascending through the system leads eventually to plugging of the conduit.

The current eruption of Mount St. Helens shares some similarities with the 1981–86 dome-building phase of the previous eruption, in that there is extensive shallow seismicity and extrusion of highly crystalline material in the form of a sequence of flows and spines. Melt inclusions from the current eruption have low H_2O contents, consistent with magma extraction from shallow depths. Highly enriched Li in melt inclusions suggests that vapor transport of Li is a characteristic feature of Mount St. Helens. Melt inclusions from the current eruption have subtly different trace-element chemistry from all but one of the 1980–86 melt inclusions, with steeper rare-earth-element (REE) patterns and low U, Th, and high-field-strength elements (HFSE), indicating addition of a new melt component to the magma system. It is anticipated that increasing involvement of the new melt component will be evident as the current eruption proceeds.

Introduction

Quenched melt inclusions in phenocrysts from volcanic rocks can provide information on preeruptive conditions within the subvolcanic magma body. Concentrations of H_2O and other volatile species can be used to infer preeruptive storage depths, whereas concentrations of major and trace elements can be used to elucidate the arrival of new magma batches and, in the case of highly incompatible elements, the crystallinity of the magma at the time of inclusion entrapment. Of particular value are plagioclase-hosted melt inclusions, because of their ubiquity in calc-alkaline magmatic rocks and because of their ability to record a wide range of magmatic conditions through partial reequilibration with the matrix melt during magma ascent and crystallization (Blundy and Cashman, 2005). By allying melt inclusion data to determinations of temperature and oxygen fugacity (f_{O_2}) from coexisting iron-titanium oxides, it is possible to provide a detailed image of evolving subvolcanic magmatic conditions, which can in turn be linked to monitoring data such as volatile flux and seismicity.

We have previously published data on H_2O and major elements in melt inclusions from the 1980–86 eruption of Mount St. Helens. Here we augment the published dataset with additional data, including previously unpublished trace-element data. The total dataset for the 1980–86 eruption now comprises 212 glasses, including 172 melt inclusions hosted in plagioclase, 8 in amphibole, 4 in orthopyroxene, 3 in clinopyroxene, and 25 groundmass glasses. Major elements, H_2O, and light trace elements (Li-Ti) have been determined for all of these glasses; heavy trace elements (Ti-U) have been determined for 74 of them. A preliminary study of dissolved CO_2 was carried out on two samples from the May 18 and August 7, 1980, eruptive episodes. In order to compare the conditions of magma storage during the 1980–86 eruption with those of the current (2004–2006) eruption, we have analyzed 11 melt inclusions in three samples from the current eruption for the same suite of elements. We also present new data on touching Fe-Ti oxide pairs for 14 samples spanning the entire 1980–86 eruption, for comparison with data from the new eruption (Pallister and others, this volume, chap. 30).

Materials and Methods

A full list and brief description of the 32 samples analyzed, together with their origin and any previous publications that describe them, are presented in table 1. Most of the samples were prepared as grain mounts of plagioclase and mafic minerals; in some cases thin sections were also used.

Melt inclusions are widespread in plagioclase phenocrysts from all samples studied. Most inclusions are glassy without evidence of daughter crystals. About 20 percent of all inclusions analyzed contain small vapor bubbles exposed at the surface of the thin section or grain mount. Thin rims or embayments of plagioclase around the walls of most plagioclase-hosted inclusions testify to some crystallization after the inclusion was first formed (Blundy and others, 2006). Melt inclusions are less common in mafic phenocrysts (amphibole, clinopyroxene, orthopyroxene). These inclusions typically lack clear evidence of host-crystal precipitation on their walls. Some of the 1980–86 samples with relatively low (or zero) microlite abundance also have matrix glass pools large enough for analysis. It was not possible to find any large matrix glass pools in samples from the current eruption.

After initially examining each sample for melt inclusions using a scanning electron microscope (SEM), a subset of the

Table 1. Inventory of samples studied.

[Samples prefixed SH (and May 25 sample) are from the Cascades Volcano Observatory collection except SH80D (collected by D. Pyle). Samples prefixed USNM are from Smithsonian Institution (see Melson, 1983). Samples prefixed KC are from collection of K. Cashman. Samples prefixed SHKB were collected by the authors in September 2003; UTM eastings and northings referable to zone 10, datum WGS84. Sample MSH006 was provided by S. Carey.]

Sample No.	Eruption date	Days since Mar. 17, 1980	Sample type (and location)
SH10	Apr. 12, 1980	27	Dense juvenile clast
USNM115379-34	May 18, 1980	62	Cryptodome gray dacite erupted during lateral blast
SH80D	May 18, 1980	62	Cryptodome gray dacite erupted during lateral blast. Collected from Pumice Plain
SHKB24	May 18, 1980	62	Blast deposit, nonvesicular margin of cryptodome (UTM 565536E, 5119874N)
C85-310	May 18, 1980	62	Pale gray (microlite-bearing) pumice erupted during early stage of plinian eruption
MSH006	May 18, 1980	62	Plinian pumice
KC518PFB	May 18, 1980	62	Microlite-free pumice, pyroclastic flow. Multiple sample splits (KCHB, KCPL, PLZ, MAY)
May25	May 25, 1980	69	Fallout pumice
KC612PF	June 12, 1980	87	Pumice from pyroclastic flow
KC722U	July 22, 1980	127	Pumice
KC807B	Aug. 7, 1980	143	Pumice from pyroclastic flow
SHKB23	Aug. 7, 1980	143	Denser pumice in the levee of October 1980 pyroclastic flow (UTM 562602E, 5117871N)
USNM115418-60	Oct. 16, 1980	213	Dome fragment
USNM115418-60-2	Oct. 16, 1980	213	Dome fragment
USNM115418-42	Oct. 16, 1980	213	Pumice
USNM115418-61	Oct. 16, 1980	213	Dome
USNM115427-1	Dec. 27, 1980	285	Pumice
USNM115427-4	Dec. 27, 1980	285	Dome
USNM115465	June 18, 1981	458	Dome
KC681	June 18, 1981	458	Dome
USNM115773-18	Mar. 19, 1982	732	Dome
USNM115773-3	Mar. 19, 1982	732	Pumice
SH127	May 14, 1982	788	Dome
SH131	Aug. 18, 1982	884	Dome
SH135	Feb. 7, 1983	1,057	Spine
SH156	June 17, 1984	1,553	Dome (collected in June, probably erupted March 1984)
SH201	May 24, 1985	1,894	Spine
SHKB20	May 8, 1986	2,243	Vesicular dome rock from top of dome (UTM 562619E, 5116559N)
SHKB21	Oct. 21, 1986	2,409	Light-colored sample from top of dome (UTM 562619E, 5116559N)
SH304-2A	Oct. 18, 2004	8,981	Spine
SH305-1	Nov. 20, 2004	9,014	Spine
SH315-4	Apr. 1, 2005	9,146	Spine

inclusions was selected for analysis of H_2O and trace elements by ion microprobe. The same inclusions were then analyzed by electron microprobe analysis (EMPA). The analyses were performed in this order because of the known damage that results from EMPA, especially for volatile elements (Humphreys and others, 2006). In choosing melt inclusions for analysis we used backscattered electron intensity to select melt inclusions with a range of compositions. Because backscatter intensity correlates strongly with dissolved H_2O, our analyses bracket the full range of observed H_2O in each sample.

Ion microprobe analyses were carried out on Au-coated polished mounts using a CAMECA IMS-4f instrument at the University of Edinburgh with a primary beam of O^- ions and detection of positive secondary ions. Typical operating conditions were 10 kV (nominal) primary beam and 2–6-nA current at the sample surface, corresponding to an 8–15-μm sputtered area. To prevent sample charging, a small raster (typically ≤10 μm diameter) was applied when analyzing ^{1}H and light trace elements (up to ^{47}Ti). Secondary ions were extracted at 4.5 kV with an offset of 75±20 V to reduce transmission of molecular ions. To minimize magnet hysteresis we analyzed isotopes in two separate batches. The first batch included the light element isotopes: ^{1}H, ^{7}Li, ^{9}Be, ^{11}B, ^{30}Si, ^{45}Sc, and ^{47}Ti. Interference on ^{45}Sc by $^{29}Si^{16}O$ was monitored using ^{42}Ca and ^{44}Ca and then subtracted by peak-stripping. The second batch of isotopes, measured on a subset of melt inclusions, included the heavier isotopes: ^{30}Si, ^{47}Ti, ^{85}Rb, ^{88}Sr, ^{89}Y, ^{90}Zr, ^{93}Nb, ^{133}Cs, ^{138}Ba, ^{139}La, ^{140}Ce, ^{141}Pr, ^{143}Nd, ^{149}Sm, ^{157}Gd, ^{159}Tb, ^{161}Dy, ^{165}Ho, ^{171}Yb, ^{178}Hf, ^{181}Ta, ^{232}Th, and ^{238}U. Background was monitored at mass 130.5 and found to be consistently <0.01 counts per second.

Interferences of light rare-earth-element (REE) oxide ions on heavy REE, Ta, and Hf were removed by peak-stripping using the oxide/ion ratios of Hinton (1990). The efficacy of the peak-stripping procedure was monitored by analyzing two isotopes of Gd (156 and 157) to check for consistency. The high Ba content of all glasses and the large interference of BaO on both Eu isotopes (BaO/Ba ≈ 0.05) means that Eu cannot be precisely determined. The largest oxide corrections are those involving Ce (CeO/Ce ≈ 0.21), which imparts an uncertainty of ±20 percent (relative) on peak-stripped Gd count rates. Count times varied from isotope to isotope, according to abundance in the glass, but were always sufficient to generate a minimum of 100 counts over the analysis period. For both batches of isotopes, ^{30}Si was used as an internal standard, and values were corrected for their SiO_2 content using the subsequent analysis of each inclusion by EMPA. Trace element calibration was carried out using NIST SRM610 multielement glass. Analyses of natural-glass secondary standards reveal that accuracy is within ±15 percent relative for all elements. This indicates that differences in ion yield between SRM610 and natural silica-rich glasses are small. There is evidence that some of these small ion yield differences are systematic, but we have not corrected for this effect, which would make only a small difference to the data presented.

Water was measured using ^{1}H and a working curve of $^{1}H/^{30}Si$ versus H_2O based on analysis of 5–12 hydrous andesite, dacite, and rhyolite glasses of known H_2O content (0.09–5.8 wt. percent). A working curve was generated on each day of analysis. There are small variations in ^{1}H ion yield between different sessions, but the working curves are consistently linear with correlation coefficients in excess of 0.99. We used $^{1}H/^{30}Si$ for calibration, rather than $^{1}H/^{30}Si \times SiO_2$, because of the systematic variation in ^{1}H ion yield with matrix SiO_2 content (Blundy and Cashman, 2005). Our working curves can be used for glasses ranging in composition from basalt to rhyolite, although all of the glasses analyzed in this study are rhyolitic. In a typical analysis of 15 cycles across the mass range, only the final 10 cycles were averaged owing to the presence of a small amount of signal instability at the onset of the analysis. This routine corresponds to a presputter period of a few minutes for ^{1}H analysis. No such effect is observed for other light isotopes, for which all 15 cycles were included in the averaging.

Electron microprobe analysis for major elements plus total S (expressed as equivalent SO_2), F, and Cl, was carried out on a CAMECA SX100 five-spectrometer WDS instrument, using a range of minerals, oxides, and metals for calibration. Operating conditions (2-nA beam current, 15-μm diameter spot) were those shown by Humphreys and others (2006) to minimize the loss of alkalis (especially Na) during analysis. This analytical protocol reproduces the measured H_2O content (as estimated from the analytical total) of hydrous glass standards to within 0.4 weight percent average absolute deviation. A few of the major element analyses, obtained early in the study, were analyzed on a JEOL-733 four-spectrometer instrument using slightly higher beam currents (Blundy and Cashman, 2005). These analyses did show some Na loss, as measured by ion microprobe analysis of ^{23}Na. For these analyses we have used the ion microprobe value of Na_2O in preference to the EMPA value.

After performing both ion microprobe analysis and EMPA, the data were screened for quality according to the following criteria: the analytical total, including H_2O, must lie between 98.5 and 100.5 percent; Ti contents measured by EMPA and ion microprobe (heavy and light element routine) for a single inclusion must be within 15 percent relative; and the ion microprobe spot, as examined by SEM, must not have any contact with the host mineral. Analyses that failed one or more of these tests were discarded. Representative analyses are presented in tables 2 and 3, and the full dataset of accepted analyses can be found in appendix 1 (included in the digital version of this paper).

Touching Fe-Ti oxide pairs were analyzed by EMPA in thin sections of selected 1980–86 samples using a Cameca SX100 with 20-nA beam current and a focused spot. We used only touching pairs because of the known rapid reequilibration of Fe-Ti oxides to changes in temperature and f_{O_2} (for example, Venezky and Rutherford, 1999). By selecting only oxides in direct contact it is possible to get the closest approximation to equilibrium compositions. This approach is used in preference to the conventional practice of averaging large numbers of separate ilmenite and magnetite analyses. We screened each magnetite-ilmenite pair for Mg-Mn exchange equilibrium using the method of Bacon and Hirschmann (1988) and then calculated T–f_{O_2} using the recalculation procedure of Spencer and Lindsley (1981) and the thermometer of Andersen and Lindsley (1988) (table 4; see digital appendix 2 for geochemical analyses of oxide minerals).

Major Element Systematics

Melt inclusions from the 1980–86 eruption are rhyolites with 68–79 percent SiO_2 (on an anhydrous basis). Matrix glasses span the same range. Melt inclusions from the current eruption extend the range in SiO_2 to 80 percent. As previously shown by Blundy and Cashman (2001), the high SiO_2 of the glasses requires crystallization at low pressures because of the increase in SiO_2 solubility with decreasing pressure. It is therefore likely that the major element variation in melt inclusions records crystallization of magma within the magma chamber and conduit.

In figure 1 we compare the major-element chemistry of melt inclusions and matrix glasses to whole-rock data from the

Table 2. Selected major-element and H_2O analyses, in weight percent, of subset of inclusion and groundmass glasses from Mount St. Helens.

[Entire dataset is in appendix 1; host of inclusion—P, plagioclase; A, amphibole; O, orthopyroxene; C, clinopyroxene; gm, groundmass; tube, tube connecting inclusion and groundmass. Analyses by electron microprobe except H_2O and some Na_2O (* follows analyzed point) by ion microprobe. Dashes, element not analyzed. sd, 1 standard deviation of H_2O measurement propagated through counting statistics and uncertainties on H_2O working curve. As described in text, p_{H_2O} is H_2O saturation pressure in MPa at 900°C from Newman and Lowenstern (2002).]

Sample No.	Analyzed point	Host	Na_2O	Al_2O_3	SiO_2	MgO	K_2O	CaO	TiO_2	FeO	MnO	P_2O_5	Cl	F	SO_2	H_2O	s.d.	Total	p_{H_2O}
1980–86 eruption																			
sh10	s4-1	P	4.07	11.27	75.12	0.83	2.74	0.66	0.52	3.16	0.04	0.12	0.13	0.10	0.00	0.99	0.04	99.72	8.8
USNM115379-34	11A*	O	5.86	14.65	71.15	0.35	2.45	2.21	0.29	2.27	0.26	--	--	--	--	1.83	0.02	101.31	28.2
USNM115379-34	2A*	P	6.18	13.63	69.48	0.54	2.25	1.80	0.23	2.00	0.13	0.31	--	--	--	3.76	0.05	100.31	101.3
USNM115379-34	3B	P	4.56	12.27	72.57	0.70	2.70	1.07	0.38	2.65	0.05	0.10	0.14	0.04	0.05	2.12	0.03	99.40	37.0
USNM115379-34	6A*	P	5.47	11.78	73.58	0.81	2.76	0.91	0.34	3.15	0.03	--	--	--	--	2.21	0.03	101.02	39.9
SH80D	2A	P	4.34	11.17	73.66	0.77	3.45	0.81	0.40	2.52	0.10	0.15	0.15	0.01	0.02	1.95	0.03	99.50	31.7
SH80D	8A	P	4.42	11.15	75.26	0.30	3.41	0.68	0.52	1.69	0.06	0.11	0.16	0.10	0.00	1.28	0.02	99.15	14.4
C85-310	pl3-3	P	4.30	11.41	75.49	0.53	2.61	0.70	0.38	2.32	0.03	0.03	0.16	0.03	0.01	1.91	0.09	99.87	30.5
MSH006	gm1*	gm	5.93	14.20	71.96	0.49	2.17	2.14	0.32	2.13	--	--	--	--	--	1.58	0.02	100.93	21.4
MSH006	9A*	P	5.75	13.74	65.91	0.71	2.15	2.27	0.33	2.03	--	0.76	--	--	--	5.92	0.10	99.57	208.1
MSH006	10A*	P	5.49	13.31	64.91	0.71	1.99	1.95	0.41	2.78	0.02	0.33	--	--	--	6.38	0.11	98.27	231.5
KC518PFB	518b-4-1	P	3.92	14.50	67.94	0.47	1.97	2.54	0.34	1.75	0.01	0.09	0.14	0.06	0.01	5.14	0.09	98.90	168.3
KC518PFB(KCHB)	7A	A	5.54	14.07	69.01	0.36	1.85	2.25	0.37	2.19	0.02	0.00	0.11	0.00	0.15	3.19	0.06	99.09	76.8
KC518PFB(KCHB)	11A*	A	5.65	15.03	65.81	0.37	2.44	2.35	0.51	2.13	0.00	--	--	--	--	4.92	0.21	99.20	156.9
KC518PFB(KCHB)	GM3*	gm	6.28	14.87	71.10	0.51	1.66	2.62	0.35	2.06	0.16	--	--	--	--	1.17	0.02	100.78	12.1
KC518PFB(KCPL)	13A*	P	5.76	12.71	69.58	0.26	2.10	1.59	--	1.01	0.00	0.18	--	--	--	4.79	0.09	97.99	150.6
KC518PFB(MAY)	6-2	P	4.89	17.04	63.99	0.35	1.58	4.15	0.24	1.49	0.00	0.30	0.10	0.07	0.00	6.40	0.89	100.60	232.7
KC518PFB(MAY)	02-1	P	4.40	13.88	65.35	0.48	2.01	2.00	0.38	2.17	0.05	0.10	0.14	0.00	0.02	6.70	0.21	97.67	248.0
KC518PFB(PLZ)	gm3*	gm	5.96	15.26	69.44	0.45	1.99	2.29	0.36	2.27	0.00	--	--	--	--	2.22	0.03	100.24	40.1
KC518PFB(PLZ)	33A2*	P	6.36	12.84	68.48	0.63	1.89	1.74	0.37	2.18	0.06	0.16	--	--	--	4.60	0.08	99.31	141.4
KC518PFB(PLZ)	plz-51-1	P	3.82	14.56	67.65	0.64	1.65	2.36	0.36	2.12	0.09	0.03	0.10	0.36	0.02	4.92	0.09	98.68	157.2
May25	PL6-1	P	4.82	13.16	69.97	0.48	2.23	1.52	0.38	2.11	0.02	0.05	0.14	0.12	0.01	4.95	0.45	99.93	158.5
KC612PF	14-2	P	5.57	12.61	70.58	0.51	2.45	1.27	0.35	2.37	0.00	0.27	0.14	0.05	0.00	3.92	0.10	100.08	109.0
KC612PF	14-GM	tube	5.17	11.90	73.07	0.53	2.54	1.08	0.56	2.19	0.06	0.22	0.12	0.02	0.02	2.48	0.06	99.94	49.1
KC722U	1-GM*	gm	4.62	12.04	77.02	0.20	2.85	0.90	0.45	1.58	--	--	--	--	--	0.25	0.01	99.90	0.6
KC722U	12-1	P	5.08	12.61	71.74	0.28	2.33	1.22	0.37	1.85	0.04	0.12	0.17	0.08	0.09	4.26	0.11	100.23	124.7
KC807B	807b-9-1	O	4.75	12.82	73.89	0.18	2.57	1.29	0.38	2.22	0.06	0.00	0.15	0.10	0.02	1.09	0.02	99.51	10.5
KC807B	807b-9-2	P	3.42	12.92	70.94	0.67	2.28	1.43	0.39	2.52	0.02	0.08	0.16	0.12	0.01	4.21	0.07	99.16	122.4
KC807B	15-1	P	5.04	12.98	72.13	0.55	2.26	1.42	0.37	2.15	0.00	0.07	0.12	0.10	0.05	3.95	0.14	101.20	110.4
KC807B	11-1	P	5.71	12.99	71.79	0.30	2.23	1.32	0.19	1.29	0.01	0.00	0.11	0.02	0.08	4.17	0.15	100.21	120.7
KC807B	17GM	tube	4.52	11.65	75.88	0.17	2.85	0.72	0.56	1.65	0.05	0.05	0.18	0.11	0.00	1.35	0.05	99.72	16.0
USNM115418-42	c1-gm	gm	4.56	11.03	77.69	0.11	2.90	0.53	0.36	1.59	0.19	0.11	0.21	0.00	0.01	0.93	0.02	100.22	7.8

Table 2. Selected major-element and H_2O analyses, in weight percent, of subset of inclusion and groundmass glasses from Mount St. Helens. —Continued

[Entire dataset is in appendix 1; host of inclusion—P, plagioclase; A, amphibole; O, orthopyroxene; C, clinopyroxene; gm, groundmass; tube, tube connecting inclusion and groundmass. Analyses by electron microprobe except H_2O and some Na_2O (* follows analyzed point) by ion microprobe. Dashes, element not analyzed. sd, 1 standard deviation of H_2O measurement propagated through counting statistics and uncertainties on H_2O working curve. As described in text, p_{H_2O} is H_2O saturation pressure in MPa at 900°C from Newman and Lowenstern (2002).]

Sample No.	Analyzed point	Host	Na_2O	Al_2O_3	SiO_2	MgO	K_2O	CaO	TiO_2	FeO	MnO	P_2O_5	Cl	F	SO_2	H_2O	s.d.	Total	p_{H_2O}
USNM115418-42	b5-1	P	5.17	12.27	72.99	0.52	2.32	1.13	0.31	1.81	0.02	0.01	0.13	0.12	0.01	2.73	0.08	99.52	58.6
USNM115418-60	16A	P	4.51	11.57	72.08	0.63	2.76	0.94	0.52	2.40	0.07	0.09	0.15	0.11	0.01	6.38	0.11	102.22	231.5
USNM115418-60	17C	P	4.41	10.27	71.52	0.67	2.50	0.85	0.40	3.45	0.10	0.08	0.14	0.09	0.37	2.51	0.04	97.36	50.3
USNM115418-60-2	pl1-1	A	4.23	14.11	72.86	0.21	3.07	1.17	0.31	2.10	0.02	0.09	0.28	0.04	0.00	1.81	0.07	100.30	27.7
USNM115427-1	a7-1	P	4.89	12.00	74.44	0.39	3.20	0.67	0.40	1.70	0.04	0.12	0.19	0.14	0.00	2.01	0.05	100.19	33.5
USNM115773-3	pl10-1	P	5.42	12.15	75.01	0.55	2.63	0.87	0.27	2.06	0.09	0.13	0.14	0.21	0.02	0.60	0.02	100.12	3.3
USNM115773-3	pl4-1	P	4.53	11.53	74.64	0.41	2.62	0.77	0.41	1.99	0.06	0.10	0.11	0.18	0.00	2.79	0.08	100.14	60.6
USNM115773-3	pl8-1	P	5.05	11.72	73.20	0.48	2.93	1.23	0.81	2.70	0.06	0.23	0.26	0.20	0.00	1.33	0.04	100.18	15.4
SH127	sh127-5-1	P	5.94	10.68	74.21	0.39	3.33	1.00	0.52	2.01	0.06	0.07	0.19	0.21	0.00	1.09	0.02	99.71	10.6
SH131	sh131-1-1	O	3.28	12.80	75.62	0.42	2.74	0.89	0.33	2.08	0.05	0.12	0.19	0.11	0.02	0.30	0.01	98.95	0.9
SH131	sh131-3-gm	gm	3.91	11.35	78.44	0.08	3.28	0.77	0.35	1.33	0.01	0.09	0.10	0.25	0.02	0.04	0.00	100.01	0.0
SH131	sh131-5-1	P	5.26	11.11	75.32	0.13	3.36	0.62	0.40	1.54	0.07	0.00	0.17	0.48	0.00	0.86	0.02	99.31	6.7
SH135	sh135-1-1	P	3.58	11.10	75.81	0.09	5.32	0.46	0.48	1.32	0.05	0.09	0.13	0.22	0.03	0.11	0.01	98.79	0.1
SH156	sh156-1-1	P	3.68	10.46	76.58	0.21	3.71	0.26	0.43	1.62	0.03	0.07	0.23	0.00	0.00	1.81	0.07	99.08	27.6
SH156	sh156-6-gm	gm	4.29	11.10	78.34	0.09	3.57	0.41	0.30	1.25	0.01	0.07	0.11	0.03	0.00	0.12	0.01	99.68	0.1
SH156	sh156-7-1	P	4.52	10.88	77.19	0.16	3.42	0.61	0.32	1.24	0.01	0.03	0.17	0.24	0.01	1.09	0.03	99.90	10.6
SH156	sh156-8-2	A	6.18	15.23	72.44	0.12	3.48	0.77	0.30	1.60	0.03	0.09	0.21	0.07	0.00	0.12	0.00	100.63	0.1
SHKB21	shkb21-2-1	C	4.71	11.02	75.61	0.08	5.12	0.40	0.33	1.40	0.04	0.10	0.24	0.11	0.00	0.17	0.00	99.31	0.3
Current eruption																			
SH304-2A	sh304-1-1	A	2.83	13.84	72.70	0.84	5.65	0.82	0.29	2.24	0.09	0.08	0.10	0.21	0.00	0.15	0.00	99.83	0.2
SH304-2A	sh304-2-1	O	6.63	19.05	69.70	0.27	0.68	3.65	0.09	0.89	0.01	0.09	0.03	0.00	0.01	0.06	0.01	101.15	0.0
SH304-2A	sh304-4-2	P	4.68	10.32	77.34	0.07	2.62	0.15	0.05	0.73	0.06	0.05	0.04	0.00	0.01	2.99	0.03	99.12	68.5
SH305-1	a1-1	A	5.27	13.56	72.08	0.08	6.04	0.06	0.44	1.78	0.16	0.07	0.19	0.00	0.04	0.18	0.01	99.96	0.3
SH305-1	a3-1	A	3.75	12.07	76.56	0.08	5.47	0.38	0.27	1.27	0.00	0.01	0.12	0.00	0.02	0.20	0.01	100.17	0.4
SH315-4	a11-1	O	2.73	12.46	76.48	0.46	4.64	0.15	0.22	2.27	0.15	0.05	0.08	0.33	0.00	0.03	0.00	100.05	0.0
SH315-4	d4-1	P	3.91	13.44	73.94	0.25	4.27	1.79	0.19	1.17	0.05	0.07	0.12	0.15	0.04	0.09	0.01	99.47	0.1

Table 3. Selected trace-element analyses, in parts per million, of subset of inclusion and groundmass glasses from Mount St. Helens.

[Entire dataset is in appendix 1; host of inclusion—P, plagioclase; A, amphibole; O, orthopyroxene; C, clinopyroxene; gm, groundmass; tube, tube connecting inclusion and groundmass. Analyses by ion microprobe. Dashes, element not analyzed.]

Sample	Analyzed point	Host	Li	B	Sc	Rb	Sr	Y	Zr	Nb	Cs	Ba	La	Ce	Pr	Nd	Sm	Gd	Dy	Ho	Yb	Hf	Th	U
1980–86 eruption																								
USNM115379-34	11A	O	57	--	2.0	44	200	7.3	183	6.2	2.1	383	13.6	27.4	3.2	14.4	3.0	--	--	--	--	7.8	3.3	1.8
USNM115379-34	3B	P	48	--	5.6	49	68	11.2	206	6.6	2.8	447	14.9	32.3	3.3	18.1	3.7	4.2	3.5	0.56	--	6.4	3.0	1.6
USNM115379-34	6A	P	47	--	6.5	51	61	11.9	226	9.5	2.6	460	16.2	34.5	3.9	17.3	3.4	3.7	3.1	0.59	1.8	8.8	3.9	1.6
SH80D	2A	P	33	--	7.1	69	57	11.6	224	6.9	--	361	15.0	28.7	3.7	--	--	--	--	--	--	--	2.8	1.5
SH80D	8A	P	32	--	7.5	58	38	12.0	234	8.3	--	378	15.7	33.0	4.0	--	--	--	--	--	--	--	3.1	1.3
MSH006	gm1	gm	34	--	5.4	40	180	9.5	179	6.6	1.8	360	13.3	26.8	3.5	12.6	2.6	2.0	2.6	0.46	1.2	5.6	3.1	1.5
MSH006	9A	P	32	--	3.8	36	212	7.6	154	5.4	1.5	317	11.9	22.9	2.9	12.1	2.4	2.1	2.1	0.34	1.0	4.5	2.4	1.1
MSH006	10A	P	38	--	4.0	34	192	6.9	136	5.2	--	276	11.3	21.8	2.2	--	--	--	--	--	--	--	2.1	1.1
KC518PFB(KCHB)	11A	A	32	--	3.2	47	267	7.0	320	28.8	1.8	439	20.3	35.8	3.7	12.6	3.4	2.1	1.9	0.41	--	10.3	5.1	2.2
KC518PFB(KCHB)	GM3	gm	35	--	4.5	36	224	8.5	180	5.8	1.5	341	12.4	26.3	3.2	13.4	2.7		--	--	--	5.6	2.5	1.0
KC518PFB(KCPL)	13A	P	32	--	1.9	45	190	2.9	87	4.3	3.0	421	11.6	20.7	2.1	8.6	1.5	1.1	--	--	--	4.0	3.7	1.5
KC518PFB(PLZ)	33A2	P	37	--	6.5	50	195	11.0	240	8.6	2.7	454	17.9	36.2	4.1	17.4	3.2	3.3	2.5	0.55	1.7	7.8	4.4	2.3
KC612PF	14-2	P	47	25	4.8	45	88	9.5	176	5.9	2.5	424	14.1	26.5	3.1	12.3	3.0	3.3	--	0.53	1.5	5.3	2.6	1.5
KC612PF	14-GM	tube	42	25	5.6	52	64	9.5	205	6.8	2.8	385	12.3	28.2	3.3	15.1	3.5	3.6	2.8	0.55	1.7	6.4	2.8	1.4
KC722U	1-GM	gm	37	31	6.3	49	150	12.0	233	8.5	2.6	452	15.1	33.6	4.0	16.8	3.2	4.2	3.5	0.70	2.0	8.5	3.7	1.8
KC722U	12-1	P	58	21	3.2	40	129	7.7	168	6.5	2.3	479	14.3	27.8	3.1	13.7	2.8	2.1	2.3	0.42	1.4	5.8	3.3	1.2
KC807B	807b-9-1	O	37	23	5.8	45	86	11.1	230	8.9	2.4	426	14.4	31.2	3.8	14.7	3.1	2.6	2.9	0.61	1.9	8.7	4.7	1.9
KC807B	807b-9-2	P	61	21	5.7	44	118	9.5	205	8.3	2.0	459	15.6	33.7	3.8	16.6	3.1	2.8	2.9	0.54	1.4	6.8	3.9	1.9
KC807B	15-1	P	98	25	5.7	50	117	8.5	191	6.9	3.3	425	13.4	27.1	3.3	13.0	2.5	2.7	2.9	--	1.8	6.9	3.3	2.1
KC807B	11-1	P	89	25	3.6	47	144	7.8	155	6.2	2.5	423	13.1	26.3	3.4	12.9	3.1	2.2	2.3	0.58	1.3	6.7	4.1	1.8
USNM115418-42	b5-1	P	60	23	5.6	40	89	8.8	186	5.8	2.3	385	13.3	26.7	3.0	12.2	2.3	3.5	2.3	0.42	1.08	4.9	2.7	1.4
USNM115427-1	a7-1	P	57	21	9.1	42	38	4.1	239	11.6	1.7	492	4.3	8.8	1.0	3.8	0.6	0.7	1.1	0.24	0.81	7.2	2.6	1.2
USNM115773-3	pl10-1	P	34	25	3.2	41	56	5.2	214	5.6	2.1	354	13.0	25.0	2.6	10.2	1.6	2.5	1.4	0.30	0.65	6.1	3.0	1.5
USNM115773-3	pl4-1	P	65	19	4.3	43	57	7.6	185	6.2	1.9	346	13.6	27.9	3.0	12.8	2.0	2.8	2.0	0.41	1.21	6.2	2.9	1.5
SH127	sh127-5-1	P	118	29	7.9	61	36	14.6	264	11.0	2.8	457	17.3	37.3	4.1	18.7	3.9	2.7	3.6	0.78	2.2	8.8	4.3	2.0
SH131	sh131-1-1	O	23	37	4.6	49	42	13.5	213	7.6	1.9	479	15.9	32.0	3.8	16.5	3.3	2.4	2.9	0.72	2.1	7.4	3.5	1.7
SH131	sh131-3-gm	gm	38	37	5.3	50	30	13.6	286	9.6	2.4	417	14.3	32.3	3.3	15.5	3.3	2.8	3.4	0.62	2.0	9.4	5.2	2.1
SH131	sh131-5-1	P	71	33	5.8	53	24	13.5	268	9.1	2.3	408	15.8	35.0	4.2	15.1	3.1	--	3.4	0.66	2.6	9.6	5.0	2.1
SH156	sh156-1-1	P	276	28	5.9	64	22	12.0	235	8.9	3.2	498	18.5	37.1	4.2	17.8	3.2	2.6	3.0	0.66	2.0	8.9	5.5	2.3
SH156	sh156-7-1	P	63	33	4.6	58	26	11.1	275	8.7	3.4	416	13.7	29.2	3.3	14.1	2.9	--	3.0	0.67	1.8	10.2	5.1	2.1
SHKB21	shkb21-2-1	C	122	44	3.0	66	15	14.4	379	8.3	3.2	260	18.1	38.8	4.6	18.7	3.4	2.9	3.6	0.79	1.9	13.0	6.5	2.6
Current eruption																								
SH304-2A	sh304-1-1	A	60	24	1.5	172	66	8.7	150	6.4	2.4	512	12.8	27.1	3.2	12.3	2.3	2.4	1.8	0.38	1.3	4.2	1.8	0.3
SH304-2A	sh304-4-2	P	169	28	3.0	53	156	4.6	42	4.9	3.2	370	9.6	19.6	2.2	8.7	1.9	2.0	1.2	0.21	0.5	1.7	1.9	0.6
SH305-1	a3-1	A	159	27	11.8	109	22	11.2	172	5.3	4.0	356	14.0	28.8	3.5	15.2	3.2	3.8	3.3	0.61	1.6	6.2	3.7	1.7
SH315-4	d4-1	P	28	34	3.4	187	7	7.0	148	5.6	4.2	116	12.1	26.4	2.8	12.1	2.1	--	1.5	--	0.6	6.1	3.3	1.4

Table 4. Calculated temperature and oxygen fugacity (f_{O_2}) for selected touching pairs of magnetite and ilmenite in Mount St. Helens samples from 1980–86 and current (2004–2006) eruptions.

[All data plotted in figure 12. Each oxide pair is identified in the column labeled "pair," for cross-referencing to appendix 2 (in digital versions of this work in CD and on Web), which contains the entire dataset and full oxide analyses. Texture: P, phenocryst; G, groundmass; I, inclusion in silicate phenocryst; E, exsolution lamellae and host.]

Sample	Texture	Pair	T, °C	log f_{O_2}
1980–86 eruption				
SH80D	P	SH80Dpr3	891	-11.79
C85-310	P	C85_310 pr3	942	-10.54
C85-310	I	C85_310 pr6 inc opx	870	-11.23
C85-310	G	C85_310 pr7tiny	904	-11.55
KC518PFB	P	518pfapr1	874	-11.51
KC518PFB	P	518pfapr4	899	-11.04
May-25	P	may25pair2	908	-10.94
May-25	P	may25pr1	958	-10.50
May-25	P	may25pr2	914	-11.44
May-25	P	may25pr8	869	-12.06
KC612PF	P	june12pr3	877	-11.71
KC612PF	P	june12p6	901	-11.29
KC722U	P	722upr4	895	-11.37
KC722U	P	722upr6	878	-11.80
SHKB23	I	SHKB23pr1 incPl	859	-12.32
SHKB23	G	SHKB23pr2late gm	872	-11.99
SHKB23	P	SHKB23pr3pheno	949	-10.93
KC681	P	681 pair 2	902	-11.61
KC681	P	681 pair 4	751	-14.65
KC681	P	681 pair 5	950	-10.73
SH131	G	SH131gm	862	-12.39
SH131	P	SH131pr8	883	-11.21
SH131	G	SH131pr9gm	911	-11.33
SH135	P	SH135_10pr6	479	-29.05
SH156	E	SH156pr3ex	871	-12.07
SH156	P	SH156pr4	864	-11.90
SH156	G	SH156pr8tiny	927	-10.63
SH156	G	SH156pr9tiny	864	-12.19
SH156	P	SH156pr11	899	-11.40
SH201	P	sh201pr2	833	-13.41
SH201	P	sh201pr3	857	-11.76
SHKB20	P	SHKB20pr6	848	-12.35
SHKB20	P	SHKB20pr6bpheno	893	-11.83
Current eruption				
SH315-4	P	a5pair7	850	-12.19
SH315-4	P	a5pair2rpt	868	-11.95
SH315-4	P	a5pair6gmsrpt	1,022	-9.96

1980–86 and current eruptions, as well as to data for magmas erupted at Mount St. Helens throughout late Quaternary time, taken from a compilation of 94 published analyses (Cashman and Taggart, 1983; Criswell, 1987; Fruchter and others, 1980; Gardner and others, 1995; Halliday and others, 1983; Hooper and others, 1980; Irving and others, 1980; Leeman and others, 1990; Melson, 1983; Pallister and others, 1992; Rutherford and Devine, 1988; Sarna-Wojcicki and others, 1981; Scheidegger and others, 1982; Smith and Leeman, 1987, 1993; Smithsonian Institution, 1980) and eight additional unpublished analyses. These data show a number of key systematics. Whole-rock compositions of 1980–86 magmas and those from the current eruption are silicic andesite or dacite with similar major-element compositions, which lie within the overall range for pre-1980 late Quaternary magmas from Mount St. Helens. In terms of both compatible (CaO, Al_2O_3, MgO, FeO, TiO_2) and incompatible (K_2O, Na_2O) oxides, the glasses all lie at and beyond the high SiO_2 end of the whole-rock data.

The relatively smooth chemical trends through the whole-rock data are consistent with derivation of the dacites by fractional crystallization or partial melting of basaltic rocks at depth (Smith and Leeman, 1987) or a combination of these processes. We cannot rule out mixing of magmas of different SiO_2 contents to generate some of the chemical diversity in the whole rocks, especially those with >62 percent SiO_2. However, marked inflections in the trends for some major and trace elements require a change in fractionating or residual mineralogy during differentiation. For example, the inflection in Al_2O_3 (fig. 1*A*) and TiO_2 (fig. 1*D*) at ~60 percent SiO_2 is interpreted as the arrival of plagioclase as a controlling phase, and the inflection in the FeO versus MgO plot at ~1.5 percent MgO (fig. 1*C*) marks the arrival of magnetite. The continuous linear drop in CaO with increasing SiO_2 (fig. 1*B*) is a result of the involvement of amphibole and clinopyroxene in addition to plagioclase, such that the bulk CaO content of the crystalline residue remains approximately constant.

The location of the glass analyses at the high-SiO_2 extrapolation of the whole-rock trends suggests that they represent the continued crystallization of magma to low pressures. The fact that the dacites in which the glasses are found have such limited compositional range, whereas the glasses themselves cover a wide compositional range, even within a single sample, indicates that low-pressure crystallization involved very little change in bulk composition. In other words, the glasses record a process of closed-system crystallization in which some crystals (for example, plagioclase) are overgrown by rims of different composition, whereas others (for example, mafic minerals, oxides) are able to partially or fully reequilibrate. There is no evidence for significant physical removal of crystals from the melt, because the compositional vectors defined by the glasses are oblique to those defined by their host rocks. This is consistent with the high viscosity of silicic melts, which would preclude efficient crystal separation on appropriate time scales.

The variation in K_2O with SiO_2 in glasses (fig. 1*E*) curves strongly upward at high SiO_2, consistent with the saturation of a silica phase (tridymite or quartz), as observed in the most evolved glasses of both the 1980–86 (Blundy and Cashman, 2001) and current eruptions (Pallister and others, this volume, chap. 30). The elevated K_2O of glasses from the current eruption distinguishes them from those of the 1980–86 eruption, although a single glass from the current eruption plots at anomalously low K_2O (0.67 percent). The overall trend suggests that most of the glasses of the current eruption reached

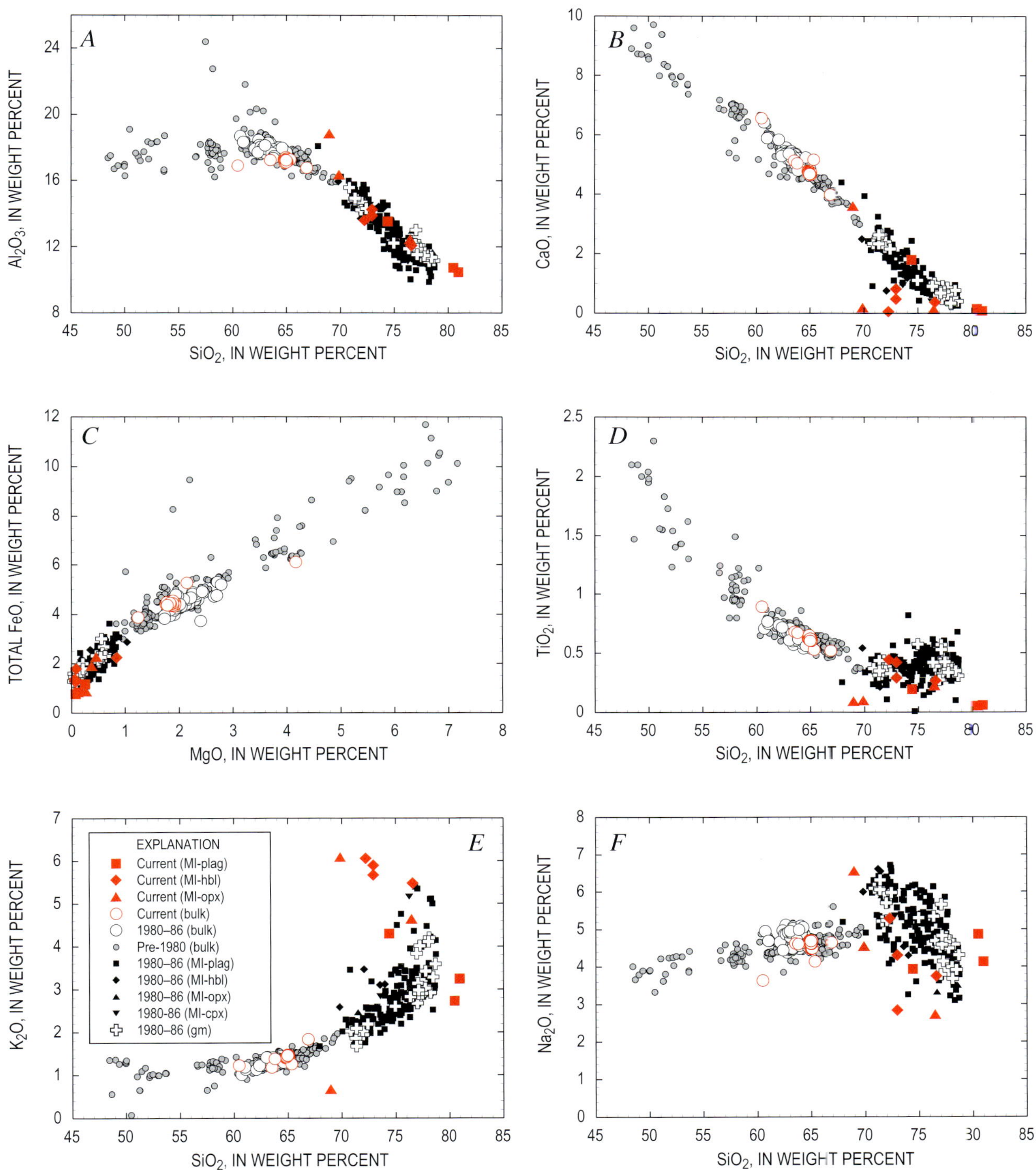

Figure 1. Major-element variation diagrams (normalized to 100 percent anhydrous) for Mount St. Helens whole rocks of late Quaternary age (sources given in text) and melt inclusion (MI) and groundmass (gm) glasses from 1980–86 and current (2004–2006) eruptions (data from table 2). All glass data by electron microprobe analysis. Explanation indicates host mineral for melt inclusions (MI): plag, plagioclase; hbl, hornblende; opx, orthopyroxene; cpx, clinopyroxene. *A*, Al_2O_3–SiO_2. *B*, CaO–SiO_2. *C*, FeO^{tot}–MgO. *D*, TiO_2–SiO_2. *E*, K_2O–SiO_2. *F*, Na_2O–SiO_2.

the silica-saturation surface at low pressure, whereas silica saturation was relatively rare in 1980–86 glasses. Silica saturation requires higher degrees of crystallization, cooler temperatures, or an initially more SiO_2-rich melt.

The Na_2O-SiO_2 variation (fig. 1*F*) is unusual in that it shows a marked inflection between the whole-rock data, which show increasing Na_2O with SiO_2, and the glasses, which show the opposite. This cannot be a result of analytical error, as the technique used for glass analyses effectively eliminates Na loss (Humphreys and others, 2006). The decrease in Na_2O with SiO_2 in the glasses cannot be generated by fractionation of an Na-rich crystal phase, because the most sodic phase in any of these rocks is groundmass plagioclase (An_{35}) with ~7 percent Na_2O. Instead, we suggest that Na is preferentially partitioned into the exsolving vapor phase during volatile-saturated crystallization, causing it to decrease in the melt. This is consistent with the elevated Na content of fumarole gases from the volcano (Symonds and Reed, 1993). The slight increase in Na_2O with SiO_2 in the whole-rock data suggests that, in contrast to the glasses, differentiation did not involve a free-vapor phase. The fact that the glass trend is markedly oblique to the whole-rock trend indicates that the onset of low-pressure crystallization and the onset of volatile saturation were almost coincident, as is typical of volatile-saturated decompression crystallization (Blundy and Cashman, 2001, 2005; Annen and others, 2006).

Trace Element Systematics

In figure 2 we compare the trace-element concentrations in glasses with the whole-rock data for magma erupted before 1980, from 1980 to 1986, and during the current eruption. The trace-element behavior can be divided into compatible elements (for example, Sr, fig. 2*A*), which decrease with increasing SiO_2; incompatible elements (Cs, Rb, Th, figs. 2*B*–*D*), which increase; and those elements that show inflections (Ba, Zr, Nb, Y, figs. 2*E*–*H*). The compatible behavior of Sr at ≥65 percent SiO_2 is consistent with plagioclase becoming the controlling phase. The curvature of the Sr-SiO_2 trend (fig. 2*A*) is reminiscent of the Al_2O_3-SiO_2 trend (fig. 1*A*) and testifies to an

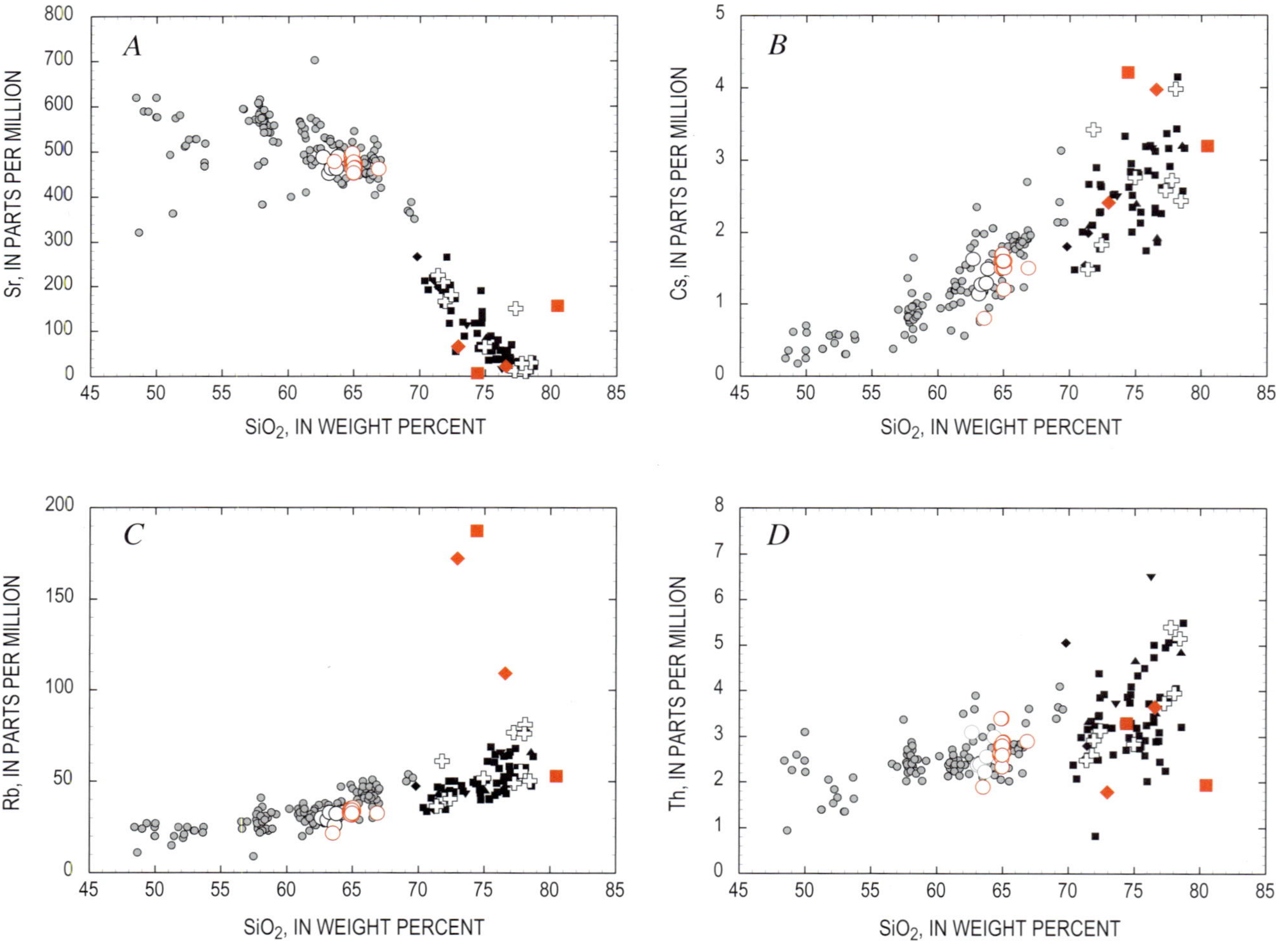

Figure 2. Trace element variation versus SiO_2 (normalized to 100-percent anhydrous) for Mount St. Helens whole rocks of late Quaternary age (sources as in fig. 1) and melt inclusion and groundmass glasses from 1980–86 and current (2004–2006) eruptions (data from tables 2 and 3). *A*, Strontium. *B*, Cesium. *C*, Rubidium. *D*, Thorium. *E*, Barium. *F*, Zirconium. *G*, Niobium. *H*, Yttrium. Symbols as in figure 1.

increasingly important role for plagioclase as differentiation proceeds. This is allied to the fact that the plagioclase-melt partition coefficient for Sr (D_{Sr}) increases as plagioclase An content decreases (Blundy and Wood, 1991).

The increase of Cs, Rb, and Th with increasing SiO_2 reflects their high incompatibility in all phenocryst phases at Mount St. Helens. Trends for Cs and Th, although showing greater scatter, are similar for the 1980–86 and current eruptions, showing a steady increase with increasing SiO_2 in both whole rocks and glasses. In contrast, the behavior of Rb at high SiO_2 is enigmatic. Three glasses for the current eruption are displaced to very high Rb, as previously noted for K_2O. It is hard to ascribe this to silica saturation alone, because there is no such displacement in Cs, Ba, or Th. Decoupling of Rb (and K) from other trace elements could be generated by involvement of a crystal phase with high partition coefficients for Rb and K, such as mica. However, as micas have $D_{Ba}>D_{Rb}$ (Icenhower and London, 1995), the effect should be greater for Ba than for Rb, which is the opposite of what is observed. We suggest instead that high initial Rb is a distinctive feature of a small number of melt inclusions from the current eruption.

The slight inflection in the Ba-SiO_2 trend (fig. 2*E*) at >74 percent SiO_2 is consistent with the increase in D_{Ba} for plagioclase with decreasing An content (Blundy and Wood, 1991). According to the model of Blundy and Wood, at 900°C Ba becomes compatible in plagioclase at An_{27}, a composition slightly more sodic than the most An-poor microlite observed at Mount St. Helens (An_{33}). However, as this is within the uncertainty of the Blundy and Wood model, we suggest that crystallization of sodic plagioclase microlites is the most likely cause of the inflection to lower Ba at high SiO_2. Early stages of fractionation involved Ca-rich plagioclase, and so Ba remained incompatible.

The inflections in the behavior of Zr, Nb, and Y (figs. 2*F–H*) cannot be attributed to microlite crystallization. These elements behave incompatibly during differentiation of the glasses (that is, concentrations increase with SiO_2, but compatibly (decrease with SiO_2) in the differentiation trend from

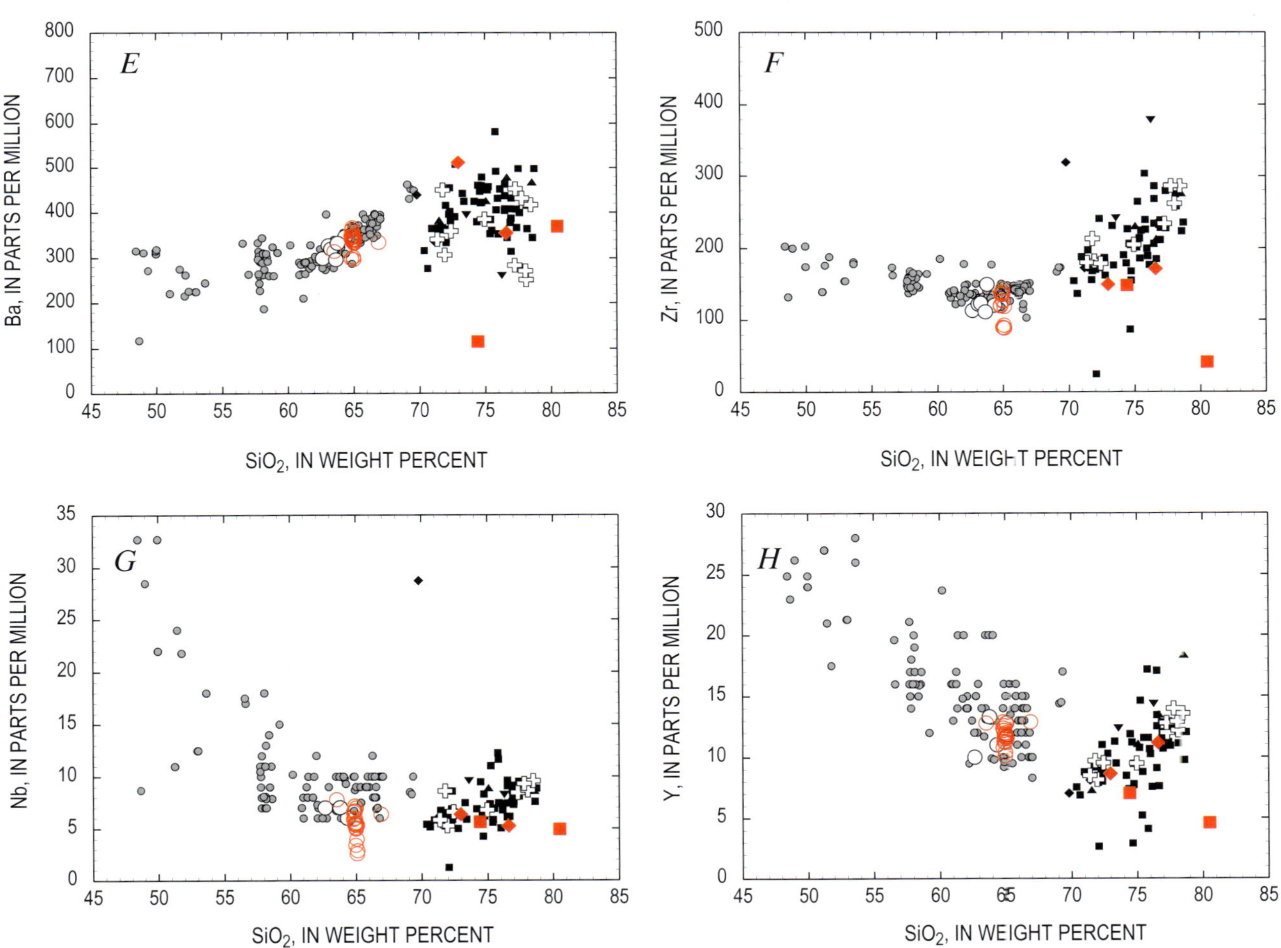

Figure 2.—Continued.

basalt to dacite. This behavior was previously noted by Smith and Leeman (1987), who attributed the low concentration of many incompatible trace elements in dacite to their generation by melting of basalt in the lower crust. During this process, garnet was stable in the residue and residual amphibole occurred at much higher modal proportion than it occurs as a phenocryst phase in the dacite. We agree with this interpretation in a general sense, although we note that crystallization of hydrous basalt, rather than melting of basalt, can also produce residues with garnet and modally abundant amphibole. Annen and others (2006) have argued on the basis of thermal models that deep crustal crystallization of hydrous basalt is the most effective method of producing andesite and dacite. We suggest that high-pressure crystallization accounts for the trends of decreasing Y, Zr, and Nb with increasing SiO_2 in the bulk rocks. Garnet and/or amphibole crystallization best explains the behavior of Y and possibly Zr, whereas crystallization of rutile or ilmenite can account for the behavior of Nb. We note that the Zr concentrations in all Mount St. Helens rocks are too low for zircon saturation at ≥850°C (Watson and Harrison, 1983), and it is unlikely that this mineral plays a role in controlling the behavior of Zr in the whole rocks. It is possible, however, that the three melt inclusions with Zr concentrations <100 ppm in figure 2*F* attained zircon saturation during cooling, although this would require a temperature ≤720°C (Watson and Harrison, 1983), which is below the H_2O-saturated haplogranite solidus at pressures ≤50 MPa (Johannes and Holtz, 1996).

Detailed quantitative modeling of the whole-rock and melt-inclusion differentiation trends is beyond the scope of this paper. However, we conclude that the whole-rock chemical variations seen in figures 1 and 2 are consistent with a high-pressure, vapor-undersaturated differentiation episode to generate the silicic andesite and dacite and that this is followed by low-pressure, vapor-saturated crystallization to generate the compositional variation in the glasses. Mixing of more and less differentiated magmas at depth (Annen and others, 2006) or entrainment of crystalline residues from depth may be responsible for some of the linearity observed in the whole-rock data, especially in rocks with >62 percent SiO_2. However, the overall whole-rock trend from basalt to dacite cannot be attributed to magma mixing alone.

For the 1980–86 eruption, melt inclusions hosted by plagioclase, amphibole, orthopyroxene, and clinopyroxene lie on the same overall trends (figs. 1, 2). In keeping with Rutherford and Devine (1988), we observe that amphibole-hosted inclusions are confined to the SiO_2-poor end of the array, but they do not show a consistent offset relative to plagioclase- or pyroxene-hosted inclusions. This observation indicates that the major and trace-element chemistry of a melt inclusion is not a product of simple closed-system postentrapment crystallization or dissolution of the host mineral. If it were, then elements that are compatible in only one host phase (for example, Sr in plagioclase) would show different behavior from one host mineral to another; but figure 2*A* indicates that this is not the case. Similarly, we see no consistent offset in MgO and FeO contents of those inclusions hosted in mafic minerals compared to those in plagioclase (fig. 1*C*; Blundy and Cashman, 2005).

Rare-Earth Elements (REE)

Rare-earth elements (except Eu) have been measured in melt inclusions and groundmass glasses from the 1980–86 eruption and from melt inclusions in three samples of the current eruption. Selected data are plotted on chondrite-normalized (Sun and McDonough, 1989) variation diagrams in figures 3*B*–*D*, together with whole-rock data (fig. 3*A*) from the literature and from Pallister and others (this volume, chap. 30). As noted by Pallister and others, bulk rock REE patterns of samples from both the current and 1980–86 eruptions are similar. The only difference is a lower overall content of heavy REE in the current eruption. Neither eruption produced rocks with any detectable Eu anomaly (fig. 3*A*), despite the abundance of plagioclase as a major crystallizing phase at low pressure. This is consistent with the suggestion above that much of the chemical variation in the basalt to dacite magmas at Mount St. Helens was generated in the lower crust (~30 km depth), where plagioclase was a minor phase (Berlo and others, 2007). Elevated f_{O_2} in these magmas would also serve to minimize any Eu anomaly due to the low Eu^{2+}/Eu^{3+} ratio. Plagioclase appears to have become a major crystallizing phase only above 62 percent SiO_2. We cannot rule out some plagioclase fractionation followed by plagioclase addition at a later stage to eliminate any Eu anomaly, although it would be surprising if this process precisely eliminated the Eu anomaly in all samples analyzed.

The melt inclusion and groundmass glasses have slightly elevated REE concentrations relative to the bulk rocks owing to crystallization. This crystallization demonstrably involved plagioclase, and we would expect the glasses to show negative Eu anomalies if this element could be measured by ion microprobe. Plagioclase has higher partition coefficients for the light REE relative to the heavy REE; hence the increase in heavy REE concentration with fractionation is greater than that of the light REE. This is clearly seen in the groundmass glasses (fig. 3*B*). A characteristic of almost all inclusion and groundmass glasses is a flattening out of the REE patterns between Sm and Yb, leading to a relatively low chondrite-normalized ratio (Sm/Yb_N) of ~2. This behavior is characteristic of silicic magmas that have equilibrated with amphibole, which has elevated, but near-constant, partition coefficients for Sm to Yb (Sisson, 1994). The Sm/Yb_N of most glasses and the whole rocks is broadly similar, suggesting that at least some of the amphibole fractionation occurred in the source region of the dacites, in accord with inferences from trace-element systematics. Melt inclusions in amphibole and orthopyroxene from the current eruption (fig. 3*C*) are broadly similar in REE chemistry to those of 1980–86, with $Sm/Yb_N \approx 2$.

Most plagioclase-hosted melt inclusions have similar REE patterns to melt inclusions in mafic phenocrysts and groundmass glasses, with $Sm/Yb_N \approx 2$ (fig. 3*D*). However, of the 172 plagioclase-hosted inclusions from 1980–86, we have identified two with anomalous patterns. The first (KCPL-12A), from the plinian phase of May 18, 1980, has similar overall light REE concentrations but a much higher Sm/Yb_N of 4. The second (427-1-A7-1), from December 27, 1980, has very low REE concentrations and a distinctive spoon-shaped pattern, strongly suggestive of amphibole fractionation from the melt inclusion after entrapment. The steep pattern from the May 18 sample cannot have been generated by any postentrapment process and appears to represent a chemically distinctive, but rare, batch of melt within the system, trapped in plagioclase before the melt could be fully homogenized with the rest of the melt in the system. Two plagioclase-hosted melt inclusions from SH304-2A, an early erupted sample from the current eruption (see Pallister and others, this volume, chap. 30), also show significantly steeper REE patterns (for example, SH304-4-2 on fig. 3*D*), similar to the plagioclase-hosted inclusion of May 18, 1980, described above. This similarity is borne out by other distinctive chemical features, including significantly lower U, Th, Y, TiO_2, Zr, and Hf and higher Sr for its SiO_2 concentration (table 3).

Given the limited number of melt inclusions analyzed from the current eruption compared to 1980–86, the fact that two plagioclase-hosted melt inclusions show anomalous chemistry suggests that this component was considerably more common in the current eruption than in 1980–86. The preservation of melt inclusions with distinctive chemistry suggests a magma system that is continually replenished with melts from depth. These melts can be trapped sufficiently rapidly that extensive chemical interaction with the dominant matrix melt cannot occur. Humphreys and others (2008) drew similar conclusions regarding "exotic" melt inclusions from Shiveluch Volcano, Kamchatka.

There are several chemical lines of evidence to support the involvement of a new type of magma in the current eruption. When other trace elements are plotted against Sm/Yb_N, three anomalous melt inclusions lie at the high Sm/Yb_N

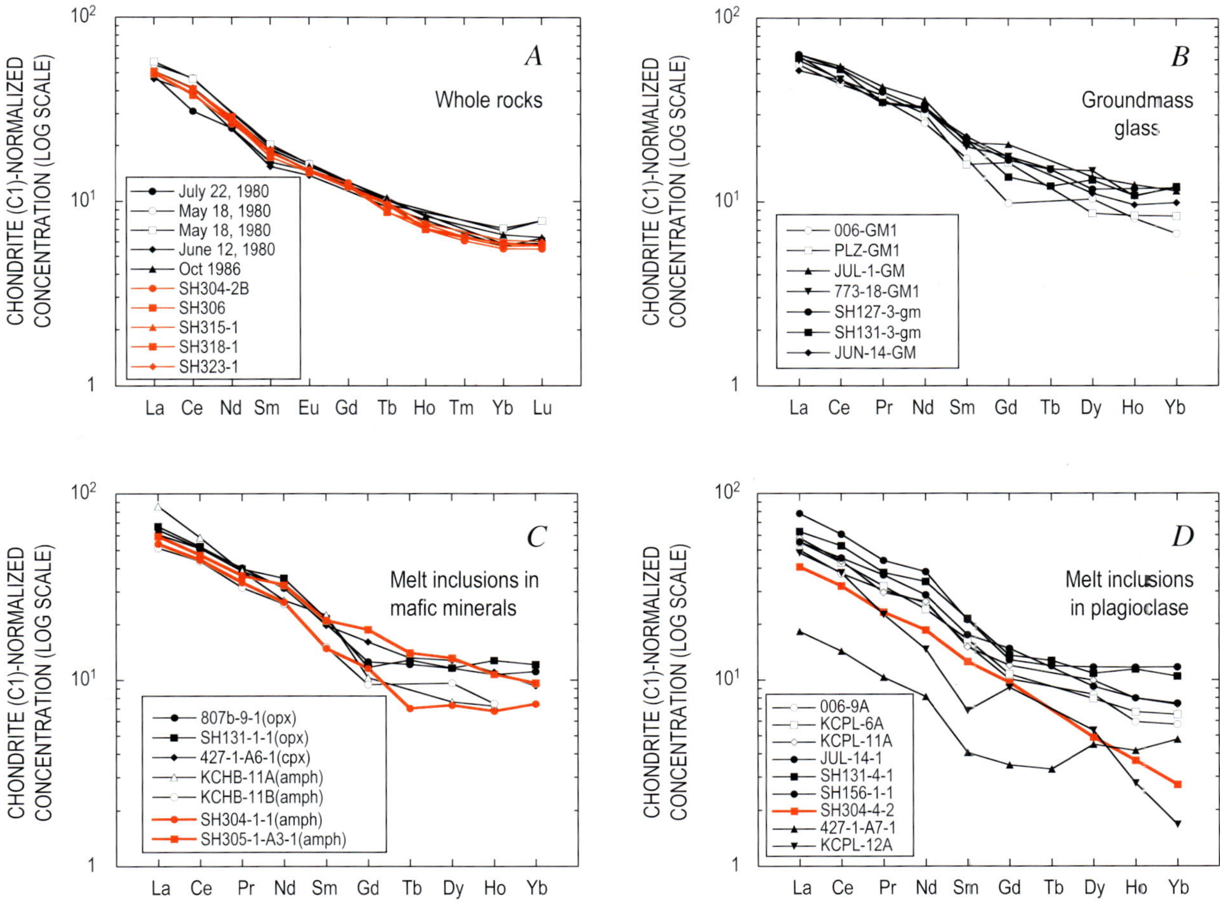

Figure 3. Chondrite-normalized REE patterns for selected glasses (data from table 3) and whole rocks from Mount St. Helens. Samples from current (2004–2006) eruption shown in red. *A*, Whole rocks (Halliday and others, 1983; Smith and Leeman, 1987; Pallister and others, this volume, chap. 30). *B*, Groundmass glasses. *C*, Melt inclusions in mafic minerals, identified in parentheses in legend. *D*, Melt inclusions in plagioclase. Low value for Sm in KCPL-12A is probably an analytical artifact. Note that horizontal axis differs slightly between panels *A* and *B–D*.

extreme of the trend defined by the majority of melt inclusions and whole rocks (fig. 4). The anomalous melts are defined by slightly lower U, Th, and high-field-strength elements (HFSE). Significantly, the whole-rock trace element chemistry of the samples from the current eruption is also displaced towards this high Sm/Yb_N component (fig. 4), consistent with its greater prevalence in the current eruption than in 1980–86 (Pallister and others, this volume, chap. 30). Conversely, the major-element chemistry of this component is not sufficiently different from that of other melt components in the system to significantly modify the major element chemistry of magmas from the current eruption. We suggest that input of melts with this chemistry into the magmatic system before the current eruption has played an important but subtle role in modifying its bulk trace-element chemistry. The only whole-rock analyses from Mount St. Helens that lie close to this postulated high Sm/Yb_N, low-HFSE component (fig. 4) are from the Ape Canyon eruptive stage (300–35 ka) and the Smith Creek eruptive period (3.3–3.9 ka) (Halliday and others, 1983; Clynne and others, this volume, chap. 28).

Water

Using a subset of the data presented here for the various 1980 eruptive phases, Blundy and Cashman (2005) showed that the variation in H_2O with SiO_2 is consistent with vapor-saturated crystallization in response to decompression. Those data, augmented by new data for May 18 and July 22, 1980, and June 18, 1981, are presented in figure 5*A*. The data describe a trend of decreasing H_2O with increasing SiO_2. The maximum H_2O content is 6.7 percent, in a plagioclase-hosted melt inclusion from the plinian phase of May 18, 1980; the minimum is at the ion microprobe detection limit (~0.04 weight percent). The lowest H_2O (and highest SiO_2) values occur in highly crystalline samples erupted during the preplin-

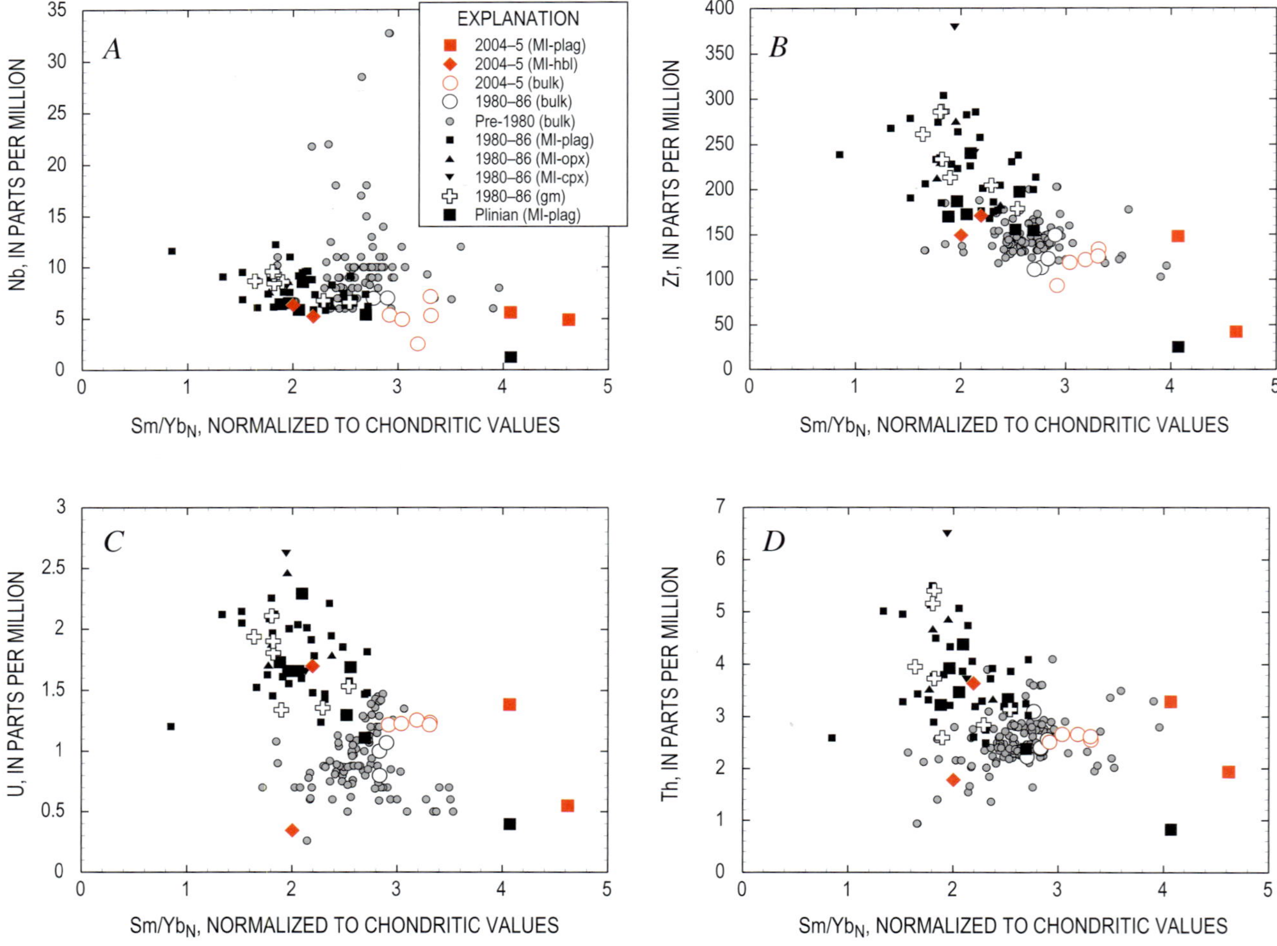

Figure 4. Variation in selected trace-element concentrations as function of chondrite-normalized Sm/Yb_N for Mount St. Helens whole rocks of late Quaternary age (sources as in fig. 1) and melt inclusion and groundmass glasses from 1980–86 and current (2004–2006) eruptions (data from table 3). *A*, Niobium. *B*, Zirconium. *C*, Uranium. *D*, Thorium.

ian phase (cryptodome) of May 18, 1980, and during the subsequent dome-forming eruptions. This variation in melt-inclusion composition can be attributed to rapid extraction of the plinian magma from relatively deep in the subvolcanic plumbing system, whereas the cryptodome and post-May 18 domes were derived from magma that either ascended more slowly from the same depths as the plinian magma or had stalled at shallower levels (lower pressure) before extrusion (Blundy and Cashman, 2005). All subplinian eruptions of 1980 contain melt inclusions that show some affinity with those of the May 18 plinian eruption in having elevated H_2O and low SiO_2.

Superimposed upon the trend of decreasing H_2O with increasing SiO_2 is a vertical trend of decreasing H_2O at nearly constant SiO_2 (shaded oval in fig. 5*A*). This trend is seen in some plagioclase-hosted melt inclusions from the plinian eruption of May 18 and the June 12 and October 16 domes (all 1980). The trend is also evident in many amphibole-hosted inclusions and a single orthopyroxene-hosted inclusion. The vertical trend terminates in the groundmass glasses of the plinian pumices, which contain 0.5 to 2.2 percent H_2O; the pumice analyses represent the H_2O content of the melt at or close to the point of fragmentation during eruption. As magma ascent during the plinian eruption was extremely rapid, there was insufficient time for full chemical exchange between phenocrysts and matrix; thus the groundmass glasses had sufficient time to lose H_2O syneruptively but not enough time to modify their SiO_2 (Blundy and Cashman, 2005). We consider that some plagioclase, amphibole, and orthopyroxene crystals fractured during ascent, allowing H_2O to escape without concomitant crystallization, such that they are displaced towards the groundmass glasses in figure 5*A*. This process primarily affected explosively erupted samples. In subsequent discussions we will refer, informally, to those inclusions lying within the shaded region of figure 5*A* as "ruptured inclusions."

Melt inclusions from the 1982–86 phase of the eruption (fig. 5*B*) lie at the low-H_2O, high-SiO_2 end of the 1980–81 trend. Only the March 19, 1982, sample contains melt inclusions with >2 percent H_2O. The 1982–86 phases of the eruption therefore appear to derive largely from slowly ascending magma stored preeruptively at shallow levels, with the possible exception of March 19, 1982, where there is seismic evidence for involvement of new deeper magma (Malone and others, 1983).

Melt inclusions from the current eruption (fig. 5*C*) show contrasting behavior to those of 1980–86. All but two of the

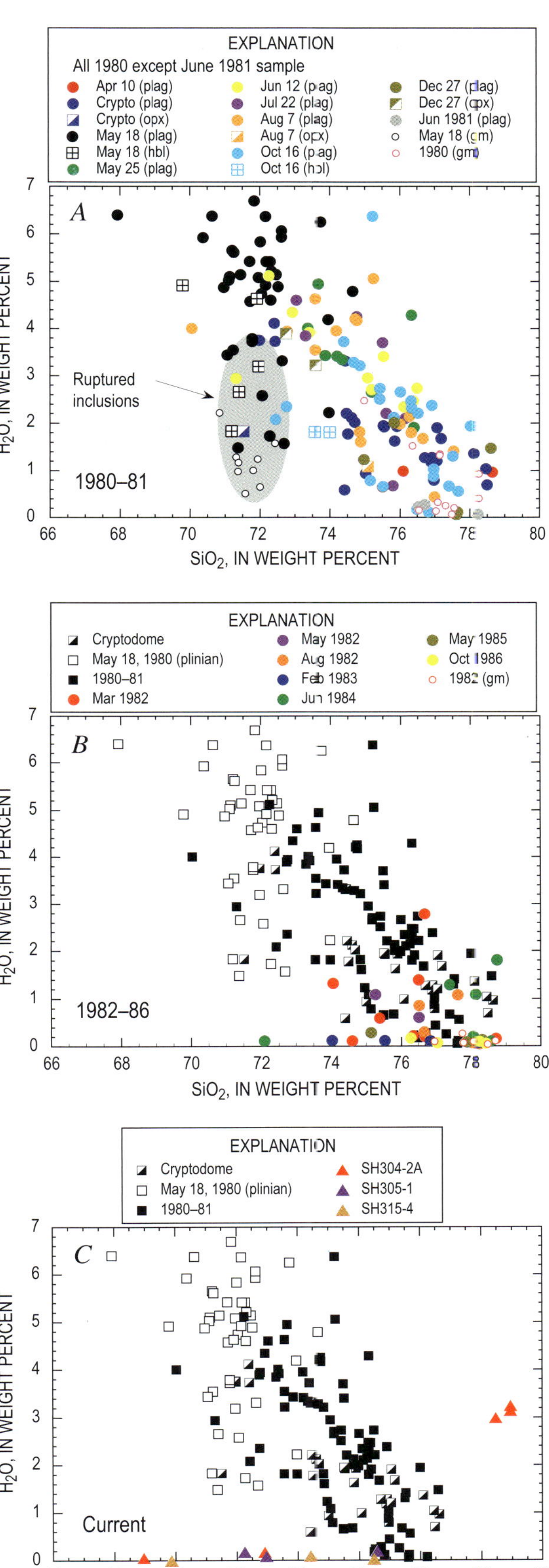

Figure 5. Variation in dissolved H_2O versus SiO_2 (normalized to 100 percent anhydrous) for melt inclusion and groundmass glasses, distinguished on basis of host mineral and eruption age. *A*, 1980–81. Gray oval denotes field of groundmass glasses and ruptured melt inclusions, thought to have lost H_2O syneruptively (Blundy and Cashman, 2005). *B*, 1982–86. *C*, Current eruption (2004–2006). The 1980–81 variation is reprised in panels *B* and *C* for comparative purposes.

inclusions have negligible H_2O contents, close to ion microprobe detection limits. The variable SiO_2 contents of these inclusions strongly suggest that they fall into the ruptured inclusion category. The striking exceptions are three inclusions from SH304-2A with elevated H_2O (~3 percent) and SiO_2 (~81 percent). These inclusions lie quite remote from the 1980–86 trend, suggesting that different processes have shaped their chemistry. The same inclusions have the anomalous REE patterns seen in figure 3*C*. We noted previously that there is evidence for significant silica-phase fractionation in glasses from the current eruption (for example, fig. 1*E*). The elevated H_2O content of the inclusions from SH304-2A suggests that they encountered the silica-saturation surface at higher pressures than those of the 1980–86 eruption. Higher pressure saturation with silica can occur if the magma is initially more silica rich, cooler, or both (Blundy and Cashman, 2001, fig. 2).

Partial Pressure of H_2O and Other Volatile Species

Changes in inclusion-sealing conditions can be conveniently expressed in terms of the partial pressure of H_2O (p_{H_2O}) (Blundy and Cashman, 2005). The p_{H_2O} can be calculated from the measured H_2O content and well-known solubility-pressure relations. We have used the software VolatileCalc of Newman and Lowenstern (2002) for rhyolitic melts at a nominal temperature of 900°C. Pressures calculated in this way are reported in table 2. The p_{H_2O} varies from 248 MPa (for the maximum H_2O content of 6.7 percent) to zero. The p_{H_2O} values calculated for pumice erupted during the May 18, 1980, plinian event are consistently higher than those of subsequent explosive and effusive eruptive episodes.

Partial pressure of H_2O does not equate directly to total pressure (P_{tot}) because of the presence of other volatiles, notably CO_2, halogens, and sulfur species. We can use the measured concentrations of F, Cl, and S (as SO_2) in glasses (table 2) to estimate partial pressures of other volatile species.

The chlorine content of glasses in the 1980–86 eruptive products ranges from 0.05 to 0.30 weight percent (fig. 6*A*) and shows a slight increase with decreasing p_{H_2O}. This variation is consistent with the known negative pressure dependence of Cl solubility in silicate melts (Metrich and Rutherford, 1992). Enrichment of melt in Cl at low pressure can result either from crystallization or from interaction between Cl-rich vapor liberated from magma at higher pressures and magma stored at lower pressure, or a combination of both processes. The higher values measured are close to the measured solubility of Cl in hydrous rhyolite melts in equilibrium with a NaCl-KCl-H_2O vapor (Shinohara and others, 1989). Metrich and Rutherford (1992) report slightly higher values, probably attributable to subtle differences in rhyolite starting composition. The fact that the measured solubilities lie at the upper end of the measured Cl contents strongly suggests that the 1980–86 Mount St. Helens melts were at or close to saturation with Cl-bearing vapor. However, this does not imply high p_{Cl_2} (or p_{HCl_2}) in the vapor phase. For example, the Cl-saturated 60–120-MPa experiments of Shinohara and others (1989) involve fluids with Cl molalities as low as 1, which equates to a mole fraction of Cl in an H_2O-rich vapor of less than 2 percent. Thus the contribution of p_{Cl_2} (or p_{HCl}) to P_{tot} is negligible. We note that at pressures of ≤120 MPa the experiments of Shinohara and others (1989) show evidence for exsolution of a dense brine phase from the vapor. Thus it is possible that the Mount St. Helens melt inclusions from 1980–86 trapped at p_{H_2O} <120 MPa were also brine saturated, which has implications for the chemical signature of fumarole gases released at the surface. Chlorine contents of two glasses from the current eruption plot at the lower end of the 1980–86 range (≤0.06 percent; fig. 6*A*).

The fluorine content of the glasses ranges from the EMPA detection limit of ~0.1 weight percent up to 0.5 weight percent (fig. 6*B*). No F was detected in the two melt inclusions from the current eruption with elevated H_2O contents. There is considerable scatter in the data, largely a consequence of low count rates for F at the analytical conditions. Overall, however, F contents are similar to Cl in any given melt inclusion and show a similar slight tendency for increase in F with decreasing p_{H_2O}. Fluorine contents are below the experimentally determined fluorite solubility of Dolejš and Baker (2006) and Price and others (1999).

Concentrations of SO_2 (fig. 6*C*) are typically less than 0.1 percent, with only two melt inclusions having significantly higher concentrations. Surprisingly, the highest SO_2 concentrations are observed at lower pressures, and mostly in post-May 18 samples. The highest values of SO_2 lie at p_{H_2O} of 50–150 MPa, suggesting that S may be concentrated in the upper reaches of the subvolcanic plumbing system. The solubility and speciation of S in silicate melts depend on pressure, temperature, f_{O_2}, f_{S_2}, and melt composition (see, for example, Carroll and Rutherford, 1985; Luhr, 1990; Clemente and others, 2004; Scaillet and Pichavant, 2005). For the May 18 plinian eruption of Mount St. Helens, Whitney (1984) calculated f_{H_2S} = 3.3 MPa and f_{SO_2} = 2.0 MPa, indicating that the contribution of sulfur species to the overall fluid pressure is small. Sulfur dioxide contents of melt inclusions from the current eruption are similar to the lower values from 1980–86.

Concentrations of CO_2 in melt inclusions were not measured routinely as part of this study. Even small amounts of dissolved CO_2 equate to significant partial pressures, however, because of its low solubility in rhyolitic melts. Thus knowing CO_2 concentrations is a prerequisite for converting p_{H_2O} to P_{tot} and thence to depth. Many of the characteristics of the 1980–86 eruption are consistent with volatile-saturated dacite magma (Rutherford and others, 1985), but the coexisting vapor need not be pure H_2O. Recently we have measured CO_2 concentrations in bubble-free melt inclusions from the May 18 plinian eruption and the August 7, 1980, eruption using ion microprobe analysis of ^{12}C calibrated against a working curve consisting of rhyolite and andesite glasses of known CO_2 content. The data and analytical method will be described in detail elsewhere. However, we note here that the analyzed melt inclusions do contain detectable CO_2. The most H_2O-rich

(6.1 percent H_2O) melt inclusion of those analyzed for CO_2, from May 18, contains 400 ppm CO_2. This equates to P_{tot} of 281 MPa, using the model of Newman and Lowenstern (2002) at 900°C, compared to 216 MPa if only the H_2O content is considered. Thus the presence of CO_2 contributes 65 MPa to the calculated P_{tot}. Samples with lower H_2O have lower CO_2. For example, at 4 percent H_2O, the maximum CO_2 content is 160 ppm, which equates to P_{tot} of 140 MPa, compared to 113 MPa for the CO_2-free case. The August 7, 1980, melt inclusions lie at the low H_2O extrapolation of the May 18 samples and extend down to 1.6 percent H_2O and 60 ppm CO_2, where the incorporation of CO_2 increases P_{tot} from 23 to 31 MPa. We do not yet have any CO_2 measurements for melt inclusions in samples of the current eruption.

These preliminary results confirm the conclusions of Rutherford and others (1985) and Rutherford and Devine (1988) that the fluid phase in equilibrium with the May 18, 1980, magma was a mixed H_2O-CO_2-SO_2-H_2S fluid. On the basis of experimental determination of phase relations and composition, they proposed a preeruptive equilibration pressure (P_{tot}) for the May 18 plinian magma of ~220 MPa with X_{H_2O} in the fluid of 0.67. Our most H_2O- and CO_2-rich melt-inclusion analysis from this eruption corresponds to P_{tot}=281 MPa and X_{H_2O}≈0.8. As pressure decreases, our preliminary data show that X_{H_2O} remains approximately constant, suggestive of nearly closed-system degassing with high bubble fractions (Newman and Lowenstern, 2002) or gas streaming through the magma system, buffering X_{H_2O} (Rust and others, 2004).

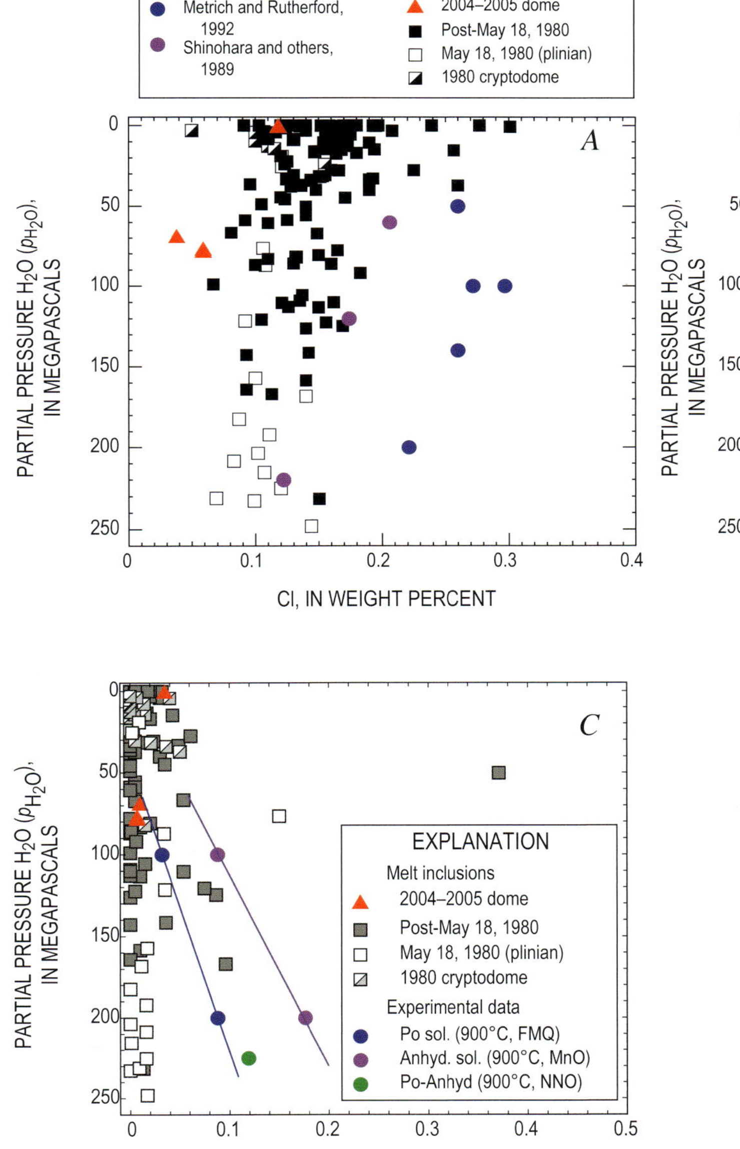

Figure 6. Concentration of volatile elements in melt inclusions as a function of p_{H_2O}, as calculated from H_2O contents using VolatileCalc (Newman and Lowenstern, 2002) at 900°C. Data are subdivided on basis of eruption age. Also plotted are experimental solubility data for comparison. *A*, Chlorine. Experimentally determined Cl solubility in system rhyolite-vapor±brine from Metrich and Rutherford (1992) at 830–850°C and Shinohara (1989) at 810°C. *B*, Fluorine. Experimentally determined fluorine solubility from Dolejš and Baker (2006) and Price and others (1999). *C*, Sulfur, expressed as SO_2. Experimentally determined pyrrhotite (Po) and anhydrite (Anhyd) solubility at FMQ, NNO, and MnO buffers (Luhr, 1990).

Without CO_2 data for all of the analyzed melt inclusions, it is impossible to calculate P_{tot} for each one. However, we can use the preliminary results for CO_2 to bracket the correction required to convert p_{H_2O} to P_{tot}. We will assume that $X_{H_2O} = 0.8$ for all melt inclusions and use the model of Newman and Lowenstern (2002) to derive a relation between p_{H_2O} (calculated CO_2 free) and P_{tot} (calculated at measured H_2O and $X_{H_2O} = 0.8$). This simple procedure gives the following empirical correction for the presence of CO_2:

$$P_{tot} = 1.287 \times p_{H_2O} . \qquad (1)$$

The maximum P_{tot} for any melt inclusion in table 2, calculated in this way, is 248×1.287 = 319 MPa. In the following discussion we will use both p_{H_2O} and P_{tot} (calculated from equation 1) as the ordinate axes for plotting.

Lithium

One of the most striking geochemical features of Mount St. Helens is the considerable variability in lithium (Li) content of melt inclusions and plagioclase phenocrysts (Berlo and others, 2004; Kent and others, 2007). For the 1980–86 eruption, Li in melt inclusions ranges from 20 to 100 ppm (Berlo and others, 2004). New data for the 1982–86 phase of that eruption extends the range to 270 ppm (table 3). There is a corresponding elevation of Li contents in plagioclase phenocrysts from the same samples that show elevated melt-inclusion Li (Berlo and others, 2004; Kent and others, 2007; Kent and others, this volume, chap. 35). For the 1980 samples (fig. 7*A*), Li reaches its maximum level at P_{tot}≈140 MPa. The high Li concentrations are confined to the cryptodome and post-May 18 eruptive phases. At lower P_{tot}, Li contents fall systematically to ~25 ppm, the same concentration observed in quenched matrix glasses from these samples. Melt inclusions from the plinian phase of May 18 have near-constant 30 ppm Li over a wide range of P_{tot}. Quenched matrix glasses from this phase of the eruption also have 25–30 ppm Li.

Berlo and others (2004) ascribed the behavior of Li in the post-May 18, 1980, to 1981 phases of the eruption to transfer of Li from deeper parts of the magma system to magma stored at shallower level. Enrichment of Li in cryptodome samples suggests that a similar pattern of Li transfer preceded the May 18 eruption. A vapor phase was considered the most likely transport agent. The fact that Li enrichment reaches a maximum at a value of P_{tot} that marks the upper limit of the range

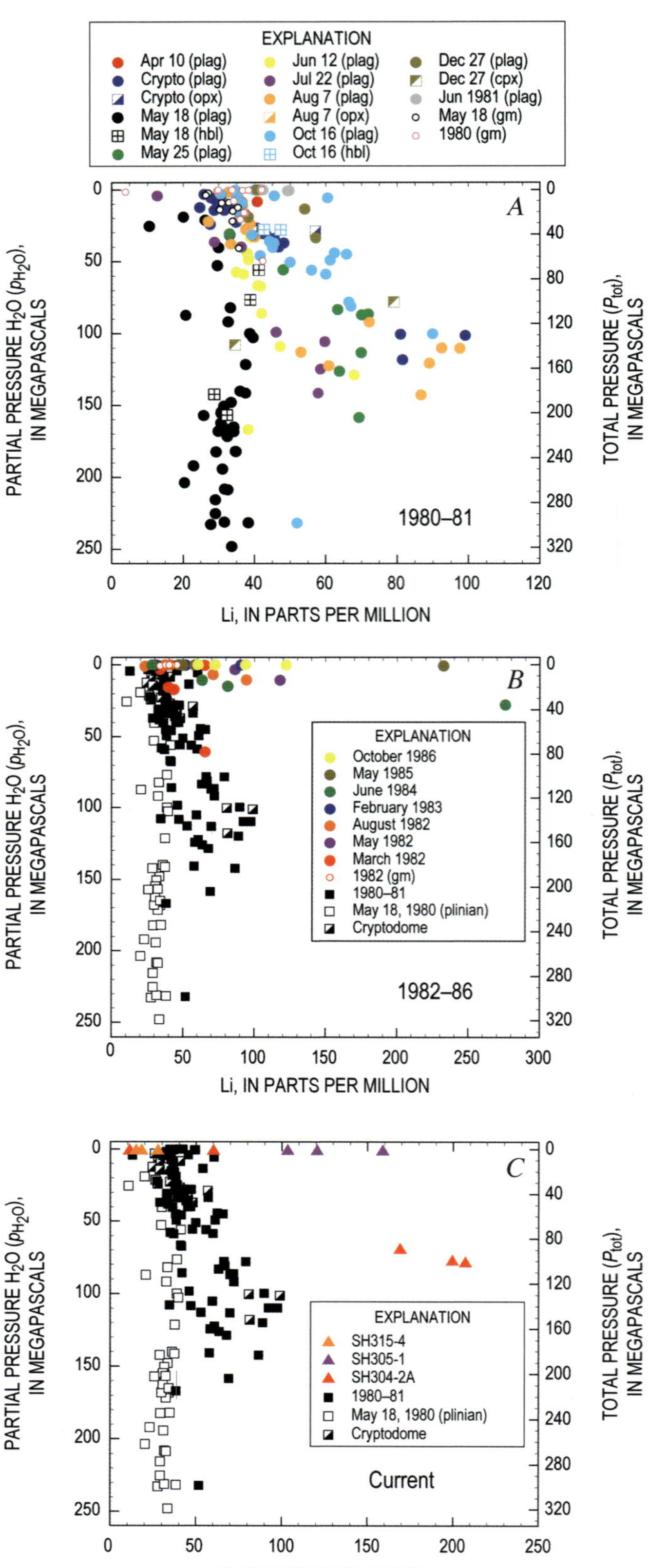

Figure 7. Lithium variation as a function of p_{H_2O} and P_{tot} in melt-inclusion and groundmass glasses. Values for P_{tot} calculated from p_{H_2O} using equation 1. *A*, 1980–81. *B*, 1982–88. *C*, Current (2004–2006) eruption. The 1980–81 variation is reprised in panels B and C for comparative purposes. Horizontal scale differs in each panel.

defined by melt inclusions from the May 18 plinian samples that have not suffered syneruptive H_2O loss (fig. 7*A*) suggests that Li enrichment takes place at the top of the main magma reservoir. May 18 melt inclusions with > 4 percent H_2O (and two melt inclusions from June 12 and October 16, 1980) lack significant Li enrichment. Berlo and others (2004) argued that the longer a magma batch is stored at low pressure ($P_{tot} \leq 150$ MPa) before eruption, the greater the extent of Li enrichment observed. As magma continues to ascend above the level of Li enrichment, further degassing occurs, stripping the highly vesicular groundmass melt of its elevated Li but preserving high Li in melt inclusions and plagioclase.

New data for the 1982–86 phase of eruption (fig. 7*B*) paint a slightly different picture. A single melt inclusion from the March 1982 eruption has elevated H_2O (p_{H_2O}=60 MPa) and a Li content of 60 ppm, similar to melt inclusions in samples produced by the explosive-effusive activity of 1980. All subsequent eruptions, however, show Li enrichment at significantly lower pressures; the maximum Li concentration (276 ppm) occurs at P_{tot}=40 MPa. These data suggest that the locus of maximum Li enrichment shifted to lower pressures after 1981. The greater extent of Li enrichment in these inclusions is consistent with a longer period of shallow magma storage between eruptions. Groundmass Li from these samples has much lower Li, about 35–40 ppm.

The current eruption also shows elevated Li, as high as 210 ppm (table 3; Kent and others, 2007). The high levels of Li enrichment in the current eruption probably reflect the long dormancy between 1986 and 2004. Most of the melt inclusions from the current eruption have experienced both syneruptive H_2O loss (fig. 5*C*) and extensive shallow crystallization, such that the p_{H_2O} recorded by the most Li-rich inclusions may be meaningless. However, three melt inclusions from SH304-2A have high Li and high H_2O (p_{H_2O}=80 MPa; fig. 7*C*). They therefore plot near the pressure level of maximum Li enrichment of the 1980 samples (p_{H_2O}=110). A corresponding elevation of Li in plagioclase is seen in the same samples (Kent and others, 2007). These observations suggest that the locus of Li enrichment for the current eruption may have shifted back to higher pressures, although the data are too sparse to determine whether this is the same depth as that during the 1980–81 eruptive phase.

Kent and others (2007) propose that the mechanism of Li enrichment at Mount St. Helens involves upwards streaming of volatiles derived from deeper parts of the subvolcanic system, combined with condensation of a magmatic brine and loss of a low-salinity vapor phase at shallow levels. Lithium will be concentrated in the brine relative to the vapor, thereby providing a means of enriching the shallow-stored magmas in Li. This interpretation is consistent with the observed variation in Cl, which increases in concentration with decreasing P_{tot} (fig. 6*A*). Fractional degassing alone could not produce this enrichment. Concentrations of Cl in melt inclusions from the 1980–86 eruption are consistent, within error, with the experimentally measured solubility of Cl in brine-saturated rhyolite at pressures below ~160 MPa (Shinohara and others, 1989). The discrete levels at which Li enrichment is observed at Mount St. Helens would then correspond not only to depths at which gas streaming was most intense (for example, at the top of the magma chamber), but also to depths at which phase separation occurs. The latter depth would be controlled by the NaCl content of the vapor (for example, Heinrich and others, 1999). The proposed mechanism is analogous to that often invoked for the origin of hydrothermal ore deposits (Shinohara, 1994; Heinrich and others, 1999; Webster, 2004).

Crystallinity

We can use trace-element data from the melt inclusions to investigate the proposal that Li enrichment is associated with crystal-rich magmas at the top of the main magma reservoir. Incompatible elements, such as Cs and Rb, show increases in concentration with SiO_2 (figs. 2*B*, 2*C*) that are most easily related to increases in crystallinity. As the 1980–86 eruption produced silicic andesite and dacite of near-constant bulk composition, it is possible to use the average bulk-rock trace element content to calculate the crystallinity of the magma at the time of trapping for each melt inclusion and then see how this varies with pressure (for example, Blundy and others, 2006). For this exercise we have used Rb, because more melt inclusions have been analyzed for this element than for Cs and because Rb has a lower bulk partition coefficient than K. The average whole-rock Rb content of all magmas analyzed for the 1980–86 eruption (n=5) is 31±3 ppm. We have used this value to calculate the crystallinity at the time of trapping for each melt inclusion assuming that bulk $D_{Rb} = 0$. The exact value of whole-rock Rb used is not crucial to these calculations. They provide a relative means of assessing crystallinity, provided that there are no significant secular variations in Rb from magma batch to magma batch. The typical 1σ uncertainty on each calculated crystallinity, based on propagation of the uncertainty in bulk Rb, is ±0.09.

Calculated crystallinities are plotted against pressure in figure 8*A* for the 1980–81 eruptive phases and in figure 8*B* for 1982–86. The data are scattered, indicating either that there were variations in the initial Rb content of the magma or that the magma did not follow a single decompression crystallization trajectory. This is not surprising given the likely complex geometry of the subvolcanic system, which will lead to spatial gradients in crystallinity that depend, for example, on the storage period and proximity of a particular plagioclase grain to conduit or chamber walls. Nonetheless, the 1980–81 melt inclusions show two crude trends of increasing crystallinity, shown by arrows in figure 8*A*. The first is recorded by the plagioclase-hosted melt inclusions from the plinian phase of May 18 and shows an overall increase from 0.10 at P_{tot} = 300 MPa to around 0.35 at 160 MPa. The latter value is in good agreement with the modal abundance of phenocrysts in samples of the microlite-free white pumice from May 18 (on a vesicle-free weight basis; Kuntz and others, 1981). This suggests that a significant proportion of the phenocrysts grew during decompression from $P_{tot} \geq 300$ to 160 MPa (Blundy and Cashman, 2005). Some plagioclase-hosted melt inclusions from the cryptodome and post-May 18 eruptions of 1980 plot at the lower pressure end of this trend at 130–210 MPa (fig. 8*A*).

The second trend is defined chiefly by microlite-rich cryptodome and post-May 18 samples and extends from a crystallinity of ~0.35 at $P_{tot} \approx 80$ MPa to 0.55 at the lowest pressures. This increase in crystallinity is consistent with the growth of microlites in these samples, augmented possibly by overgrowth rims on phenocrysts (Cashman, 1992). The highest crystallinities are recorded by microlite-rich cryptodome samples. Between the two trends of increasing crystallinity, from P_{tot} of ~180 to ~100 MPa, there is no marked change in crystallinity. Interestingly, this pressure interval brackets the P_{tot} at which the maximum Li enrichment occurs in the same samples (fig. 7*A*).

Melt inclusions from 1982–86 (fig. 8*B*) overlap the second trend described above ($P_{tot} \leq 40$ MPa), with broadly similar maximum crystallinities at low P_{tot}. The only exception is one melt inclusion from March 1982, which records P_{tot} (78 MPa) and crystallinity (0.30) similar to the lowest values from the May 18 plinian pumice. Interestingly, the March 19, 1982, eruption not only was preceded by deep earthquakes but also produced the only post-1980 explosive eruption (Malone and others, 1983; Weaver and others, 1983). These observations are consistent with recharge (and subsequent degassing) of the deeper parts of the system at that time (Weaver and others, 1983).

The crystallinity recorded by melt inclusions from the current eruption (fig. 8*C*) is less well constrained, owing both to paucity of data and the fact that all but one of the inclusions analyzed for heavy trace elements appear to have ruptured (fig. 5*C*). We have again used Rb for the crystallinity calculations, but with a slightly different bulk Rb content based on an average of dacites from the current eruption (33±3 ppm; Pallister and others, this volume, chap. 30). The one unruptured melt inclusion (from SH304-2A; fig. 8*C*) shows similar crystallinity and pressure ($p_{H_2O} \approx 70$ MPa) to melt inclusions from post-May 18, 1980, and March 1982 samples (fig. 8*B*). Evidence was presented above that melt inclusions of the current eruption encountered the silica-saturation surface at higher pressures than the 1980–86 magma. The fact that the crystallinity is comparable to those of 1980–86 inclusions, many of which lack evidence for silica saturation, suggests that the reason for higher pressure silica saturation in the current magmas is a result of their higher initial SiO_2 contents rather than cooling. Ruptured melt inclusions from the current eruption imply very high magma crystallinities (≥0.7) at the time of trapping, consistent with textural evidence (Cashman and others, this volume, chap. 19). The loss of H_2O from these inclusions, however, precludes any constraint on the pressure at which this high crystallinity was reached.

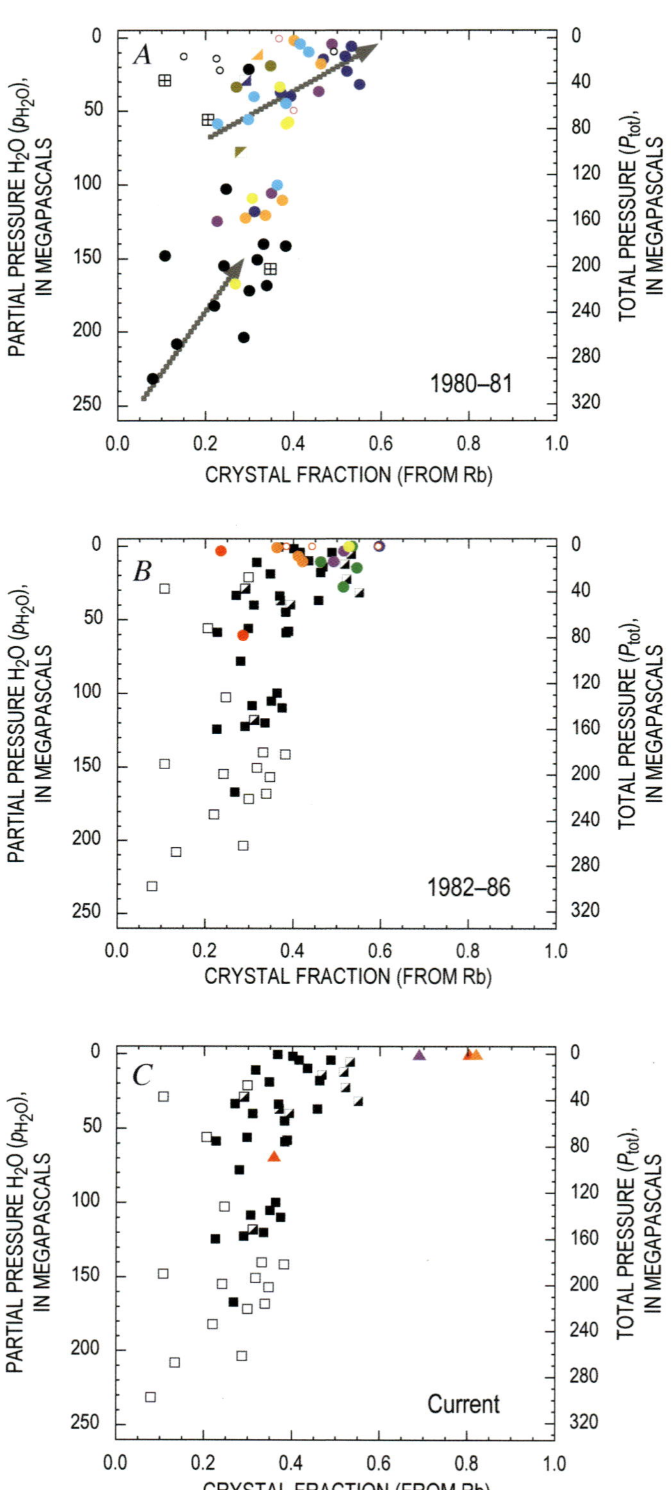

Figure 8. Crystallinity calculated from Rb concentration of melt-inclusion and groundmass glasses as a function of p_{H_2O} and P_{tot}. Symbols as in figure 7. *A*, 1980–81. Arrows denote the two episodes of crystallization described in text. *B*, 1982–86. *C*, Current eruption (2004–2006).

Oxide Thermobarometry

In order to assess the relative importance of decompression and cooling in driving crystallization at Mount St. Helens, we have analyzed touching pairs of oxides from the 1980–86 and current eruptions (table 4). A more comprehensive discussion of the oxide data from the current eruption is presented by Pallister and others (this volume, chap. 30).

The majority of phenocryst temperatures from 1980–86 span a range from 840 to 960°C; f_{O_2} ranges from 0 to 0.8 log units above the NNO buffer (fig. 9*A*). A single oxidized pair from August 1982, showing exsolution lamellae, lies at NNO+1.8. Four phenocryst pairs define lower temperatures: one pair each from June 1981 and the cryptodome, and two pairs from a spine sample erupted in 1985. These lower temperature oxides straddle the NNO buffer and overlap the range of f_{O_2} of high-temperature fumarole gases from Mount St. Helens (Gerlach and Casadevall, 1986; fig. 9*A*). Some oxides from August 1982 and June 1984 show exsolution textures typical of slow cooling, as often observed in plutonic rocks. In detail (fig. 9*B*), individual eruptions show discrete f_{O_2} variations, with a tendency for f_{O_2} to decrease (relative to NNO) progressively from the May 18 plinian eruption to subsequent subplinian and dome-forming eruptions. Thus, the highest f_{O_2} phenocrysts (at NNO+0.8) come from the microlite-free, H_2O-rich plinian phase of May 18, 1980, whereas subsequent eruptions of microlite-bearing, H_2O-poor magmas define subparallel trends but displaced to slightly lower f_{O_2} (fig. 9*B*). The most reduced samples lie at NNO and come from August 7, 1980, and June 1981. Microlite oxides from 1980–86 (fig. 9*C*) cover essentially the same spreads in temperature and f_{O_2} as the phenocrysts from post-May 18 plinian samples; that is, displaced to slightly lower f_{O_2} relative to NNO.

The reduced nature of groundmass oxides relative to phenocrysts (fig. 9*C*) and the progressive reduction of the phenocrysts as magmas become progressively less H_2O rich and more crystalline (fig. 9*B*) suggests that magma reduction occurs concomitantly with degassing and crystallization. This is consistent with the relatively reduced nature of the high-temperature fumarole gases (Gerlach and Casadevall, 1986) relative to the phenocryst oxides from the May 18 plinian phase (fig. 9*A*). The lower temperature (≤850°C) and f_{O_2} of oxide pairs from several samples appear to have equilibrated with the fumarole gases at very low pressures. Reduction of the magma during degassing suggests that equilibria between exsolved gases and magma are important in constraining the redox state of the melt. For the case of sulfur-free, H_2O- and Fe-bearing melt, Candela (1986) and Burgisser and Scaillet (2007) show that degassing results in oxidation of the melt. Our contrary observation that degas-

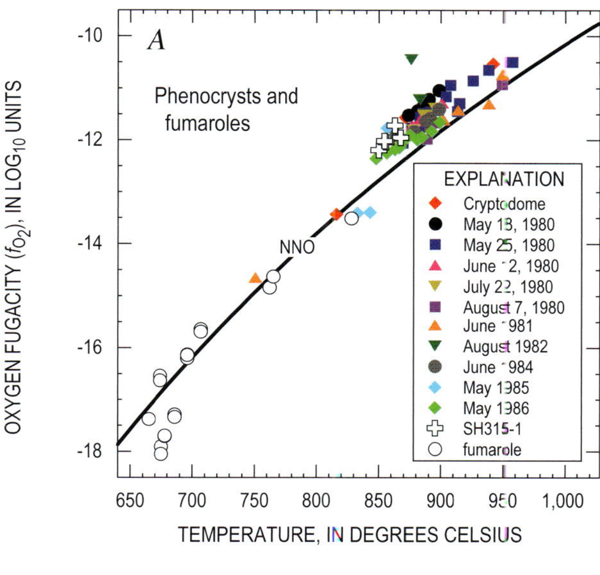

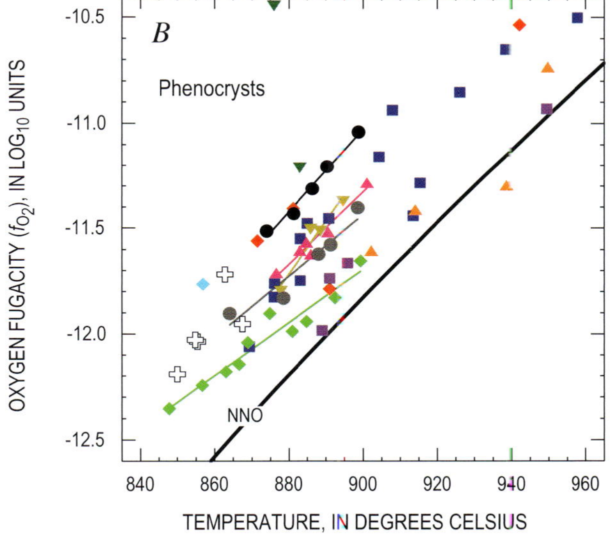

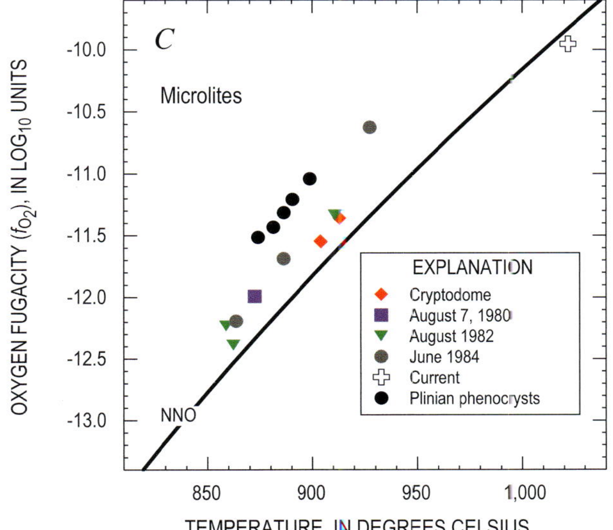

Figure 9. Temperature versus f_{O_2} variations for selected 1980–86 and current samples calculated from touching Fe-Ti oxide pairs. Data from table 4. *A*, Phenocrysts and fumarole gases (Gerlach and Casadevall, 1986). *B*, Detail of phenocrysts, showing temporal evolution of f_{O_2}; lines show linear fits to oxides from selected eruptions. Explanation same as in *A*. *C*, Groundmass microlites, with May 18, 1980, plinian-deposit oxides from panel *A* for comparison. Nickel-nickel oxide (NNO) buffer (at 200 MPa) shown for reference.

sing leads to reduction of the melt is consistent with the presence of reduced sulfur (S^{2-}) in the melt, and the degassing equilibrium (Whitney, 1984; Candela, 1986; Burgisser and Scaillet, 2007):

$6Fe_2O_3$(melt) + $3S^{2-}$(melt) = 12FeO(melt) + $3SO_2$(vap).

The magnitude of the observed reduction (≤0.7 log units in f_{O_2}) is consistent with the thermodynamic calculations of Burgisser and Scaillet (2007) for degassing and ascent of sulfur-rich, relatively oxidized (NNO+1) silicic magma.

The process of reduction can also account for the observed increase in melt sulfur contents at lower pressures (fig. 6*C*). For example, the experimental data of Clemente and others (2004) show that a modest decrease in f_{O_2} from NNO+1 to NNO increases sulfur solubility in rhyolite melt by a factor of three.

Following Blundy and others (2006), we consider the phenocryst temperature spread in figure 9*B* to reflect real temperature variations within the magma body. The preservation of the spread indicates that there was insufficient time for all oxides to fully equilibrate to changing temperatures before eruption. Possible causes of the spread include injection of new magma from depth into the system, loss of heat to wall rocks during magma storage, and latent heat release during decompression crystallization. Blundy and others (2006) argue that the latter process, which amounts to ~2.5°C for each 1 percent crystallized, dominates during isenthalpic magma ascent. This explains why microlite-bearing samples with the highest crystallinities tend to have the highest maximum temperatures. Interestingly, the highest temperatures, and largest range of temperatures, are found in a May 25, 1980, pumice sample (fig. 9*B*) that shows evidence of extensive, very shallow crystallization. Extensive crystallization, coupled with a short repose interval (one week), would limit the extent to which the shallow magma could thermally reequilibrate after the rapid crystallization pulse. The profound effect of late-stage heating indicates that the most reliable estimate of temperature in the deep magma body that fueled the May 18 plinian event lies at the low temperature end of the spread, that is, ~870°C, in good agreement with the estimate (880±10°C) of Venezky and Rutherford (1999) but somewhat lower than earlier estimates by Melson and Hopson (1981) and Rutherford and others (1985).

Temperature estimates from touching phenocrysts in a single sample (SH315-4) of the current eruption are displaced to slightly lower temperatures (850–870°C) relative to the main 1980–86 trend as observed by Pallister and others (this volume, chap. 30). A curious feature of SH315-4 is the unusually high temperature (1,020°C) recorded by a single touching microlite pair (fig. 9*C*). Pallister and others (this volume, chap. 30) also present sparse high Fe-Ti-oxide temperatures (≤1,019°C) from other samples of the current eruption. These data raise the possibility of some recharge of the magma system by hotter magma at depth. Alternatively, they could result from significant latent-heat release as ascending magmas undergo rapid and considerable crystallization (Pallister and others, this volume, chap. 30).

Temporal Variations

In this section we track temporal trends in several parameters at Mount St. Helens since March 17, 1980, the approximate date on which the first seismic activity was observed (Endo and others, 1990), in order to investigate evolving magma-storage conditions beneath the volcano. The most useful parameters to examine in time series are: (1) the volatile elements H_2O, SO_2, and Cl (fig. 10), which monitor changes in degassing; (2) the major elements K_2O, MgO, and TiO_2 (fig. 11), which monitor variations in crystallinity and the arrival of new, less-evolved magma batches; and (3) temperature and f_{O_2} (fig. 12), which monitor cooling (or heating) and redox conditions.

There is an overall drop in the maximum H_2O content of melt inclusions with time, from a maximum of nearly 7 percent during the plinian phase of May 18, 1980, to almost zero in 1986 (fig. 10*A*). Maximum H_2O content of groundmass glass decreases from 2.2 to 0 percent over the same period. In general, explosive eruptions are characterized by melt inclusions with high H_2O contents, whereas effusive eruptions are characterized by low-H_2O inclusions. This strongly suggests a relation between magma storage conditions and eruptive style. In detail, the decrease in maximum H_2O content with time is nonlinear and appears to describe a crude sawtooth cyclic pattern in which abrupt peaks in H_2O are followed by a steady fall. Although this may in part be an artifact of sample size, our attempts to analyze the most H_2O-rich melt inclusions from each sample using SEM screening, as described above, suggest that this variability is real. Peaks are observed on May 18, 1980 (plinian eruption), March 19, 1982, and June 17, 1984. It is unclear whether the single H_2O-rich melt inclusion from October 16, 1980, represents a peak or simply an inherited crystal from an earlier eruption. The three peaks delineate cycles in eruptive behavior. The first cycle started with the plinian eruption on May 18, after which a steady decrease in magma supply rate led to increasingly short explosive eruptions that finally changed to discrete effusive events (Scandone and Malone, 1985). The second cycle initiated with an explosive eruption on March 19, 1982, preceded and accompanied by deep earthquakes, after an unusually long repose interval of 5 months. This cycle then evolved to a year (February 1983–February 1984) of continuous slow magma effusion and endogenous dome growth. The third cycle began with renewal of discrete extrusive dome growth events in March 1984 (although the first sample we have of this cycle was collected in June 1984) and continued until the end of effusive activity in 1986. This cyclicity suggests that changes in eruptive activity in March 1982 and March 1984 may reflect new inputs of magma. There are too few melt-inclusion data from the current eruption to discern any trend.

Chlorine shows the opposite behavior with time to H_2O, with an overall increase in Cl from May 18, 1980, to 1986 (fig. 10*B*). This is consistent with the increase in solubility of Cl with decreasing p_{H_2O} (for example, fig. 6*A*). As is the case for H_2O, the change in Cl is nonlinear with time and appears to

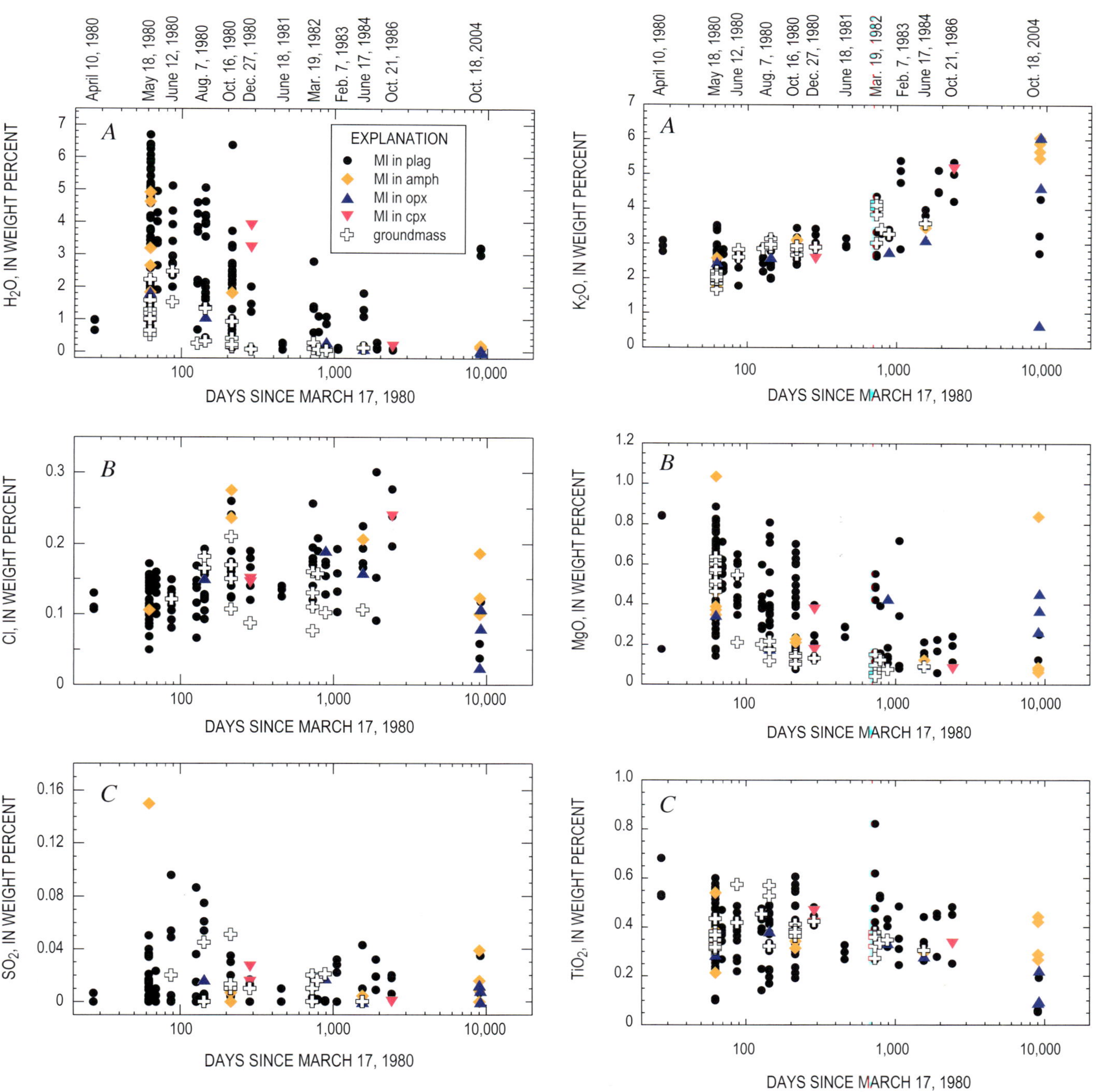

Figure 10. Temporal variation of volatile components in melt inclusion and groundmass glasses for 1980–86 and current (2004–2006) eruptions, plotted as a function of days since March 17, 1980 (log scale). Melt inclusions (MI) distinguished on basis of host mineral: plag, plagioclase; amph, amphibole; opx, orthopyroxene; cpx, clinopyroxene. Selected eruptive episodes are marked on the upper abscissa in panel *A* for reference. *A*, Water. *B*, Chlorine. *C*, Sulfur dioxide.

Figure 11. Temporal variation of major-element oxides (normalized to 100-percent anhydrous) in melt inclusion (MI) and groundmass glasses for the 1980–86 and current (2004–2006) eruptions, plotted as a function of days since March 17, 1980 (log scale). Symbols as in figure 10. *A*, K_2O. *B*, MgO. *C*, TiO_2. All elements analyzed by electron microprobe.

show distinct peaks (for example, October 1980) and troughs (for example, June 1981). The increase in Cl with time is particularly marked during the 1980 events, with the highest values reached in October. The temporal trend for Cl in groundmass glass broadly mirrors that of the melt inclusions. Chlorine contents of melt inclusions from the current eruption are variable but generally displaced to values lower than those of the 1980–86 eruption.

Total sulfur (expressed as SO_2) drops abruptly from May 18 through December 1980 to 1986, with consistently low values thereafter (fig. 10*C*), except for a slight elevation in March 1982. As with H_2O and Cl, the June 1981 melt inclusions are distinguished by low SO_2 contents. The highest value recorded (0.37 weight percent) comes from a melt inclusion in an October 16, 1980, sample (table 2; not plotted). This unusually high value, which greatly exceeds the known solubility of sulfur in rhyolite melts (Clemente and others, 2004), may result from sample contamination by tiny sulfide grains, although none were evident in backscattered electron images. Like H_2O, SO_2 exhibits a secondary peak in 1984 with the resumption of episodic dome-building eruptions. Groundmass glasses also show diminishing sulfur with time. The SO_2 contents of melt inclusions from the current eruption are comparable to those of post-1980 melt inclusions.

Another monitor, K_2O, which like Rb serves as a proxy for crystallinity (Cashman, 1992; Blundy and Cashman, 2005; Cashman and McConnell, 2005), shows a steady increase with time, from ≤2 percent on May 18, 1980, to ≥5 percent in February 1983 and October 1986 (fig. 11*A*). Minimum K_2O values increase during 1980–81, before decreasing slightly in March 1982 pumice. Minimum K_2O then increases again, with maximum values achieved in May 1985 (see also Cashman 1992; Geschwind and Rutherford, 1995). The maximum K_2O content during 1982–86 is highly variable, reaching a maximum in a February 7, 1983, sample from a highly crystalline lava spine. Overall these temporal trends are consistent with

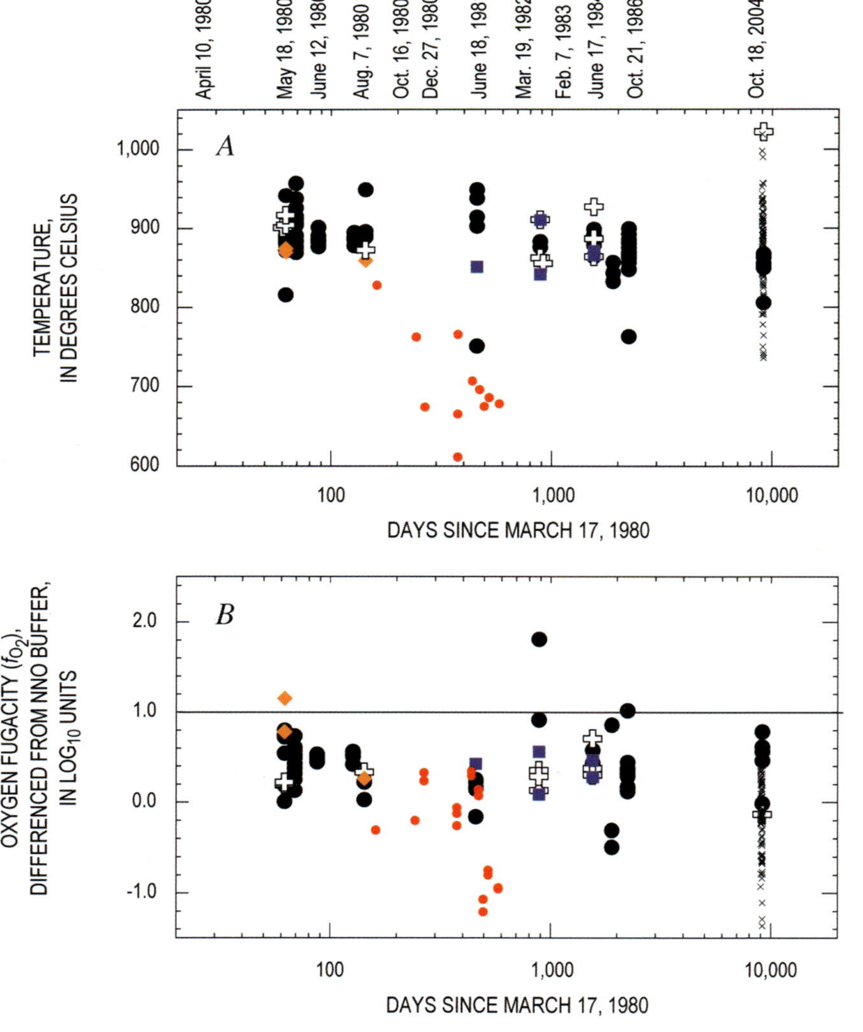

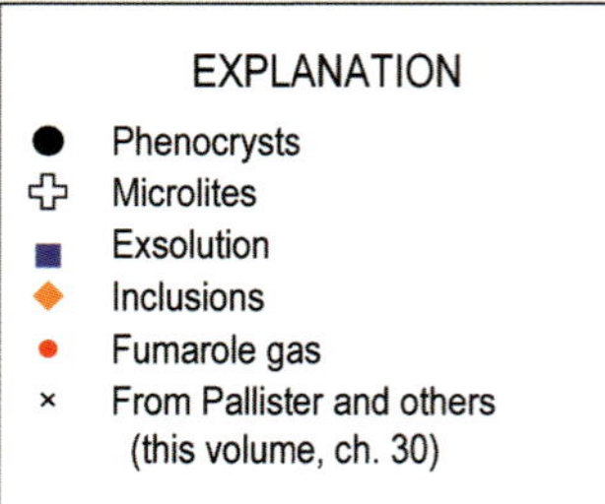

Figure 12. Temporal variation of (*A*) temperature and (*B*) $\log_{10} f_{O_2}$ (relative to NNO) in touching oxide pairs for 1980–86 and current eruptions, plotted as a function of days since March 17, 1980 (log scale). Fe-Ti oxide pairs are distinguished on a textural basis; "inclusions" denotes two oxides included in a single silicate phenocryst. Data from table 4. Small red dots denote temperature and f_{O_2} in high-temperature fumarole gases (Gerlach and Casadevall, 1986). Horizontal lines show best estimate of conditions in magma body erupted in plinian phase of May 18, 1980, based on touching phenocrysts. Also shown for comparison are current eruption data of Pallister and others (this volume, chap. 30).

increasing microlite crystallization with time in response to decreasing H_2O. Interestingly, the temporal trends for K_2O and H_2O (fig. 10*A*) are not closely correlated, a reflection of the varying rates of degassing and crystallization, also seen as scatter in the pressure-crystallinity plot (fig. 8). Groundmass glasses have similar K_2O contents to melt inclusions. The current eruption shows highly variable K_2O, spanning more than the total variation from 1980–86. A single melt inclusion in orthopyroxene from October 18, 2004, shows unusually low K_2O, whereas several melt inclusions preserve K_2O values that exceed anything seen in 1980–86. The wide variability in K_2O for the current eruption is consistent with extrusion of magma of highly variable crystallinity (Cashman and others, this volume, chap. 19), although we cannot rule out involvement of melts with initially very different K_2O contents.

The MgO contents of melt inclusions (fig. 11*B*) are inversely correlated with K_2O but show considerably greater variability for any one eruptive phase. From May 18, 1980, to June 1981, the maximum MgO content drops off sharply from <1 percent to ~0.25 percent, consistent with increasing amounts of microlite crystallization. There is then a marked increase in maximum MgO during the period March 1982 to February 1983, more evidence suggestive of the involvement of slightly less crystalline magma during this eruption. After 1983 the MgO content falls to low levels similar to the minimum MgO contents of the earlier effusive phases. Groundmass glasses lie consistently at the low end of the melt-inclusion data. As with K_2O, MgO in melt inclusions from the current eruption is extremely variable, spanning almost the entire range observed in 1980–86 (fig. 11*B*).

The behavior of TiO_2 (fig. 11*C*) differs from that of MgO. During 1980, minimum TiO_2 contents increase slightly with time. After 1980 the TiO_2 baseline remains almost constant through 1986, but the maximum TiO_2 peaks between 1982 and 1983. Groundmass glasses lie consistently at the low end of the melt-inclusion range. Melt inclusions from the current eruption are also variable in TiO_2 but generally displaced to lower levels than 1980–86.

Iron-titanium oxide temperatures (fig. 12*A*) show a span of values throughout the 1980–86 eruption, with a slight (~50°C) overall decrease in maximum temperature with time, suggestive of some secular cooling within the subvolcanic magma reservoir. Oxide inclusions in phenocrysts from the May 18, 1980, plinian eruption give temperatures of 875°C. Phenocryst and groundmass oxide pairs from subsequent eruptions in 1980 are displaced to higher temperatures, which Blundy and others (2006) attribute to the latent-heat release during crystallization of phenocryst rims and microlites. Several phenocryst oxide pairs from post-May 18 samples show significantly lower temperatures that decrease with time. This trend matches that of high-temperature fumarole gases from Mount St. Helens collected in 1980–81 (Gerlach and Casadevall, 1986; fig. 12*A*), suggesting that these low-temperature oxides equilibrated with fumarole gases as they streamed though the shallow magma-storage system. Over the same period f_{O_2} (relative to the NNO buffer; fig. 12*B*) shows fluctuations of ~1 log unit, decreasing during 1980, showing a marked increase in March 1982, and then decreasing again to 1986. For the 1980–81 period, the f_{O_2} values of the most reduced oxide pairs match those of the high-temperature fumarole gases (Gerlach and Casadevall, 1986; fig. 12*B*), also suggestive of equilibration of selected oxide pairs with vapors exsolved from underlying magma.

Iron-titanium oxide temperatures for the current eruption (fig. 12*A*) span a considerable range (730–1,020°C). The lowest temperatures are close to those of the coolest oxides recorded in 1986. The trend to temperatures ≥960°C may be caused by the addition of significantly hotter new magma or latent-heat release during crystallization (Pallister and others, this volume, chap. 30). In either case it is likely that the lowest oxide temperatures correspond to magmas held over from the end of the 1986 eruptive phase and that the heating event was sufficiently recent that no wholesale resetting of phenocryst oxide temperatures was possible. Oxygen fugacity estimates for the current eruption (fig. 12*B*) also cover almost the entire 1980–86 range. This may result from extensive redox reactions involving fumarole gases or from addition of more oxidized magmas into the system.

Relation Between Petrological and Monitoring Data

In principle there should be a relation between the subterranean magmatic record, as preserved in melt inclusions, and the monitoring record, in the form of seismic events, ground deformation, volatile flux, and so forth. A relation has already been demonstrated for Fe-Ti oxide temperature-f_{O_2} measurements and fumarole gases (fig. 12). In this section we will explore two further correlations, between the SO_2 content of melt inclusions and the SO_2 flux from the volcano, and between the pressures recorded by melt inclusions and the depths of subvolcanic earthquakes.

In figure 13*A* we compare the SO_2 content of melt inclusions with the measured SO_2 flux (McGee and Casadevall, 1994). Sulfur dioxide degasses both during and between eruptive events, with some of the highest fluxes unassociated with the appearance of magma at the surface. A striking correlation is apparent between the two datasets. The high SO_2 content of melt inclusions during May to August 1980 corresponds to high SO_2 fluxes over the same period. The melt-inclusion data show a slight decrease in SO_2 from October 1980 to June 1981, before increasing again slightly through March 1982 to June 1984. It is difficult to correlate this increase with the slight increase in SO_2 flux over this period because of the sparseness of data. The clear temporal correlation between SO_2 in melt inclusions and the SO_2 flux suggests that magma degassing and the sealing off of melt inclusions are closely associated in time. Indeed it is possible that gas loss (which drives the SO_2 flux) and sealing of melt inclusions (which traps SO_2) are related processes. Significantly, SO_2 degassing between eruptions produces spikes in SO_2 flux which are not matched in the melt-inclusion data.

For those eruptive phases in which the total erupted volume and duration are known, it is possible to calculate a mean SO_2 flux from the melt-inclusion data for comparison with the monitoring data. To perform the calculations we have taken the erupted volumes and eruption durations from Swanson and others (1987) and Swanson and Holcomb (1990), assumed a magmatic density of 2,500 kg/m^3, and used the maximum measured SO_2 in melt inclusions for each eruption (that is, assuming negligible SO_2 in the groundmass glass). The calculations for October 16, 1980, using the measured maximum of 0.37 weight percent, yielded anomalously high fluxes, confirming our suspicion that this is an anomalously high value and not representative of the eruption as a whole. We have therefore adopted the second highest value (0.04 percent) for this eruption. To calculate the average measured SO_2 flux for each eruptive phase, we have taken the data of McGee and Casadevall (1994) and averaged them over the duration of the phase. The standard deviation is also calculated. In figure 13*B* we plot the observed SO_2 flux versus calculated ("petrological") SO_2 flux. The agreement between the two estimates is striking and within the combined errors on both sets of measurements. This is in contrast to calculated petrological fluxes for major plinian eruptions (Wallace, 2001), which consistently underestimate the measured fluxes by factors of up to 10. This suggests that plinian eruptions are driven in part by gas derived from deeply stored volatile-rich magma that is not erupted (Wallace, 2001). This interpretation is consistent with the SO_2 flux between dome-forming eruptions: the good correlation between the calculated and observed eruptive fluxes during eruptions in figure 13*B* suggests that SO_2 expelled between eruptions derives from a deeper source rather than from the magma that subsequently appears at the surface. Certainly there is evidence that syneruptive degassing processes differ between large plinian eruptions and smaller dome-forming eruptions.

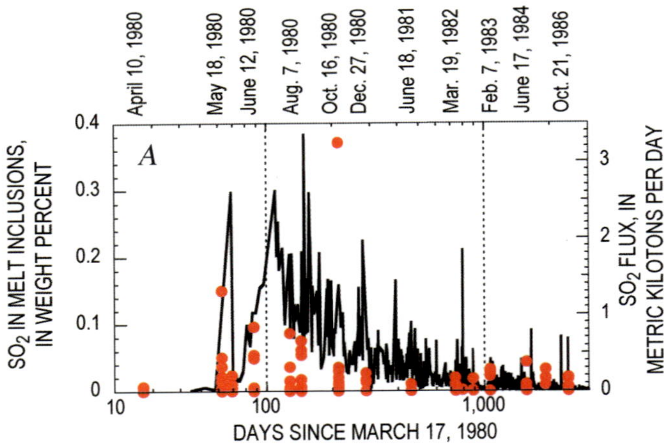

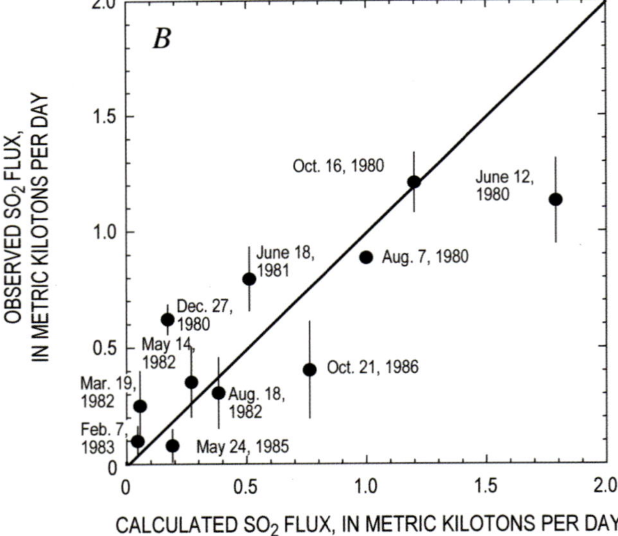

Figure 13. Comparison of dissolved SO_2 in melt inclusions and measured SO_2 flux (in metric kilotons per day) for post-May 18, 1980, episodes of 1980–86 eruption (McGee and Casadevall, 1994). *A*, Temporal evolution of melt inclusion SO_2 (left hand axis, red dots) and SO_2 flux (right hand axis, black line). Key eruptive events shown on top axis for clarity. *B*, Observed SO_2 flux versus calculated SO_2 flux, based on duration of each eruptive phase, erupted volume, and maximum SO_2 content in melt inclusions. Bars show 1 standard deviation error of observed flux. Error on calculated flux is ~10–20 percent relative. Full details of calculation procedure are given in text. Black line denotes a 1:1 correlation.

The relation between the pressures recorded by melt inclusions and the seismic record for 1980–86 is equally significant. For each plagioclase-hosted melt inclusion we have calculated p_{H_2O} and P_{tot}, using the methodology described above. We have not used melt inclusions hosted in mafic minerals, because of their tendency to lose H_2O syneruptively. In addition, we have filtered the dataset for plagioclase-hosted melt inclusions that appear to have ruptured (that is, they plot within the gray ellipse in fig. 5*A*). The resultant dataset is plotted in figure 14*A*. There is a clear decrease in maximum pressure with time; a small amount of the decrease in pressure immediately after May 18, 1980, results from decompression of the entire system following removal of the upper 400–1,000 m of the edifice during the sector collapse that preceded the lateral blast (Moore and Albee, 1981). In detail, we note that each eruption contains melt inclusions with a pressure range (for example, Cashman and McConnell, 2005), which diminishes with time. Magmas erupted during 1980 cover a wide range in P_{tot}, from 320 to 0 MPa. There is a clear distinction between melt inclusions in the blast dacite, which tapped magma from the cryptodome and conduit over a pressure range of 0–160 MPa, and the main plinian phase, which tapped magma with melt inclusions stored from 120 to 320 MPa. The minimum melt-inclusion pressure for the plinian magmas is slightly greater than the minimum pressure at which amphibole is stable at ~875°C, consistent with the lack of amphibole breakdown rims in these samples (Rutherford and Hill, 1993). Eruptions after October 1980 produced magma with melt inclusions that record P_{tot} <50 MPa, with the exception of a single melt inclusion from March 1982 at 80 MPa. All of these magmas contain amphibole with reaction rims (Rutherford and Hill, 1993). The clear impression from figure 14*A* is that the 1980 eruptions of Mount St. Helens sampled magma (as recorded by melt inclusions) stored over a wide pressure range, whereas the subsequent eruptions predominantly involved magma stored preeruptively at shallow levels. This change occurs abruptly between October 16 and December 27, 1980, and is accompanied by an abrupt change in eruptive activity from transitional explosive-effusive to predominantly effusive.

Earthquake depths for the period 1980–86 are available from the Pacific Northwest Seismic Network catalog. These data adopt as their datum the mean seismic station altitude at Mount St. Helens, which is ~1.1 km above sea level. In order to compare earthquake depths to P_{tot}, we require a relation between these two variables. We have integrated the depth-density model for rocks beneath the volcano from Williams and others (1987), coupled with the volcano edifice-loading algorithm of Pinel and Jaupart (2000), to calculate lithostatic pressure as a function of depth. For the period before and including May 18, 1980, we assume a conical edifice 2.95 km high standing 1.5 km above the surrounding landscape and having a basal radius of 3.2 km. The edifice density is taken as 2,170 kg/m^3 (as in Moran, 1994). The calculated pressures are then parameterized in terms of depth, *z*, (below sea level) using a polynomial:

$$z\ (\mathrm{km}) = 0.029654\ P_{tot} + 0.22704 P_{tot}^{0.5} - 2.95\ , \qquad (2a)$$

where P_{tot} is the calculated total pressure, in MPa, for each melt inclusion using the relation between P_{tot} and p_{H_2O} in equation 1.

Following the removal of the volcanic summit on May 18, 1980, there is a small pressure readjustment in the rocks beneath the volcano. We have modeled this change using a truncated conical edifice with its top 2.55 km above sea level and the method of Pinel and Jaupart (2005) to derive a second expression for calculating depths in samples erupted after May 18, 1980, as follows:

$$z\ (\mathrm{km}) = 0.03074\ P_{tot} + 0.18334 P_{tot}^{0.5} - 2.55\ . \qquad (2b)$$

Note that the pressure drop is small (≤6 MPa) and confined to the upper reaches of the subvolcanic system (above 500 m above sea level).

In applying equations 2a and 2b we are making a number of assumptions. First, we assume that the pressure in the magma reservoir is lithostatic, without significant magmatic overpressure through volatile buildup, for example, or significant regional deviatoric stresses. As magmatic overpressures are likely to be ≤20 MPa (Massol and Jaupart, 1999), we consider this effect to be small. Second, implicit in our use of equation 1 is the assumption that X_{H_2O} is approximately constant at 0.8 throughout the magma column and that the partial pressures of other volatile species (such as SO_2, H_2S, HCl, HF) are very low.

We have calculated *z* for all unruptured plagioclase-hosted melt inclusions, for comparison to the earthquake depths (fig. 14*B*), after subtracting 1.1 km from the latter to account for the mean station altitude. There is a striking overall consistency between the calculated ranges of

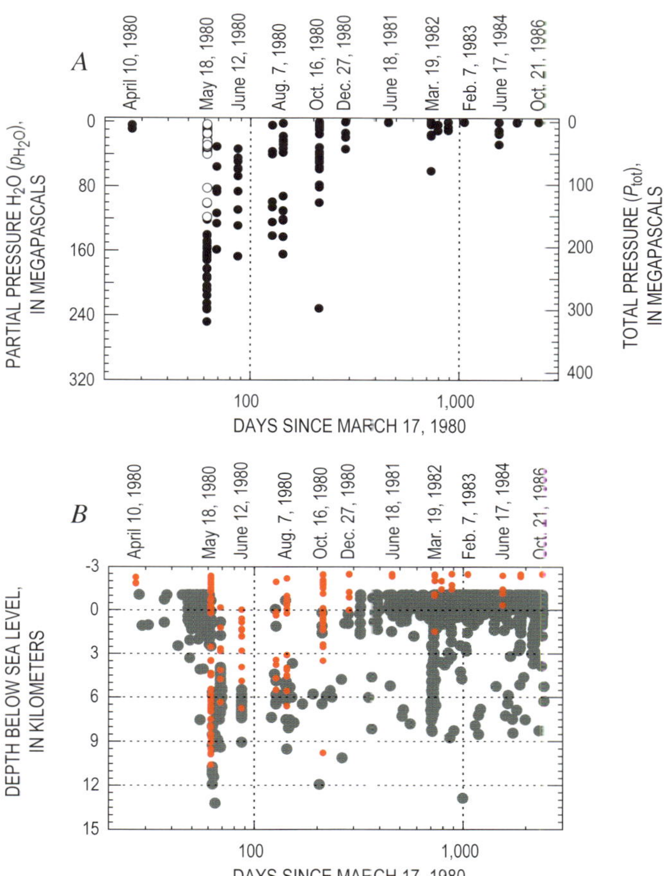

Figure 14. Evolution of melt-inclusion sealing pressures and depths with time for unruptured melt inclusions from 1980–86. *A*, Variation in p_{H_2O} and P_{tot} as calculated from H_2O contents and equation 1, respectively. May 18, 1980, cryptodome samples, erupted during blast phase and early plinian phase (Criswell, 1987) are shown as open circles; all other eruptions, including main plinian phase of May 18, 1980, shown as dots. *B*, Comparison of melt-inclusion sealing depths (red dots), as calculated from equation 2a for eruptions of May 18, 1980, and earlier and from equation 2b for subsequent eruptions, with earthquake hypocenters (gray dots) from Pacific Northwest Seismic Network catalog, corrected by 1.1 km to account for mean seismic-station altitude. Note development of a shallow seismic lid before May 18, 1980, and after December 27, 1980. Magmas erupted during the interval between these dates show consistently higher maximum extraction depths than those erupted before or after.

melt-inclusion depths and the range of earthquake depths associated with any given phase of the eruption. This agreement is particularly strong for May 18, 1980, for which the maximum melt inclusion and earthquake depth ranges agree to within 1–2 km. Here we note that the deep earthquakes followed the explosive eruption and have been interpreted to reflect collapse in response to magma withdrawal (Scandone and others, 2006). Following May 18, 1980, there is a dramatic dropoff in earthquake event frequency throughout 1980. Melt-inclusion depths over the same period extend down to ~10 km below sea level but are consistently shallower than those in the plinian deposit. Here again, deep seismic activity occurred in response to, rather than before, eruptive activity, an interpretation that is consistent with the observed correlation between earthquake and melt-inclusion depths. This pattern changed in March 1982, when deep earthquakes preceded the explosive eruption by about a week (Scandone and others, 2006). Here we see a mismatch between the earthquake depth and maximum recorded melt-inclusion depth that suggests that the week of intrusion was sufficient for degassing and equilibration at intermediate storage levels before eruption.

After 1980 there is an increase in the number of shallow earthquakes, reflecting a gradual closing of the conduit system that remained open through the summer of 1980 (Scandone and others, 2006). During this period no melt inclusions record depths greater than 1.5 km below sea level. Apparently the development of extensive shallow-level seismicity in December 1980 marks the formation of a barrier to the eruption and/or preservation of deeper melt inclusions. This may be a consequence of slower magma-ascent rates during this period, such that higher pressure melt inclusions are not preserved, or the preeruptive stalling of each magma batch at depths corresponding to the region of shallow seismicity. This scenario is consistent with effective sealing off of the subvolcanic system after December 27, 1980 (for example, Scandone and Malone, 1985). Shallow seismicity persisted throughout the noneruptive period of 1986–2004, gradually deepening with time and leading eventually to the formation of a distinct "seismic lid" at depths of ~1 km below sea level after 1992 (Moran and others, this volume, chap. 2). Seismic activity associated with the current eruption has been consistently shallow (within the seismic lid). Melt inclusions from the current activity tell the same story; most record very low pressures, whereas the most H_2O-rich originate approximately at the base of the pre-October 2004 seismic lid.

Discussion

The melt-inclusion data are consistent with a vapor-undersaturated silicic magma generated in the deep crust, ascending to the point of vapor saturation, and undergoing decompression crystallization (Blundy and Cashman, 2001, 2005; Annen and others, 2006). Melt inclusions from the 1980–86 samples record a vertical variation in crystallinity with pressure, such that the lowest pressure samples have the highest crystallinity and the lowest bulk magmatic H_2O content. The plinian phase of May 18, 1980, tapped the deeper, less crystalline part of the magma reservoir—from a relatively crystal-rich cap at P_{tot}=120 to a crystal-poor, deeper part at P_{tot}=320 MPa. The few plagioclase- and amphibole-hosted melt inclusions that record lower pressures lost H_2O syneruptively (fig. 5*A*). Preplinian and postplinian eruptions tapped magma stored at somewhat shallower levels, which had undergone further decompression crystallization. The deepest, most crystal poor of these magmas came from P_{tot} of 150–220 MPa during 1980, that is, overlapping the shallowest plinian magmas, and from much smaller P_{tot} during 1982–86. This picture of the subvolcanic magma system is consistent with seismic (Lees, 1992; Moran 1994), petrologic (Pallister and others, 1992; Rutherford and Hill, 1993), and geodetic (Mastin and others, this volume, chap. 22) data that suggest a thin, vertically extensive magma chamber less than 500 m in diameter at a depth of ~5 km below sea level, connected to the surface by a narrow conduit (≤40 m in radius) that may be only intermittently filled with magma (Scandone and others 2006). As magma ascends through this system, it loses H_2O and crystallizes, leading to a vertical gradient in H_2O content and crystallinity.

Within the magma chamber, crystallinity increases from ~10 to 30 weight percent. It is unclear whether 10-percent crystallinity represents the crystal content of the magma as it enters the deep system or whether the magma is essentially aphyric at that point. A possibility that we favor is that the 10 percent initial crystal load was entrained from the deep-seated magma generation zone, as proposed by Annen and others (2006). Alternatively, rapid crystallization of initially aphyric magma at the point of vapor saturation may have prevented the preservation of any melt inclusions with compositions matching the bulk Mount St. Helens magmas. Magma from the deeper reservoir periodically fills the shallow plumbing system, undergoing further crystallization en route. This crystallization involves both rim overgrowths on phenocrysts and microlite nucleation. Total crystallinity reaches a maximum of ~60 weight percent at the shallowest levels.

Between eruptions, magmatic gases streaming out of the deeper part of the system interact with the shallow-stored magma, enriching the magma in Li at the point of phase separation to a brine. The same process of intereruption gas streaming enriches shallow-stored magmas in Cl and F (figs. 6*A*, *B*) and ^{210}Pb (Berlo and others, 2006), enriches plagioclase phenocrysts in Li (Berlo and others, 2004), generates pulses in the SO_2 flux (fig. 13*A*), and may also buffer X_{H_2O} in the vapor phase. The observed ^{210}Pb excesses in the same magmas that show Li enrichments (Berlo and others, 2004, 2006) suggest a subvolcanic magma system wherein a large deep reservoir episodically supplies ^{222}Rn-bearing gas to a much smaller shallow reservoir.

The significance of melt-inclusion pressures (and corresponding depths) hinges on the mechanisms by which inclusions form, evolve, and become sealed. Melt inclusions trapped in plagioclase, amphibole, and pyroxenes show similar chemical characteristics (figs. 1, 2), indicating that the compositions of the melt inclusions are not controlled by host-inclusion exchange. There is, nonetheless, clear evidence that melt-inclusion compositions have been modified since they first became incorporated. The fact that melt inclusions and groundmass glasses have overlapping compositions for all nonvolatile components suggests that the dominant process of melt-inclusion modification is exchange with the groundmass melt, rather than exclusively by reaction with the host mineral. We suggest that exchange of components between inclusion and groundmass melts, via thin channels or capillaries connecting inclusion and matrix, persists for some time after the inclusion is first trapped (Anderson, 1991; Stewart and Pearce, 2004; Blundy and Cashman, 2005; Humphreys and others, 2008). Thus, melt-inclusion chemistry follows groundmass-liquid lines of descent, despite the absence of daughter minerals in the inclusion, up to the point that the inclusion becomes sealed off (occluded) from the matrix.

Occlusion may be a physical process, whereby a new overgrowth of plagioclase blocks the channel connecting inclusion and groundmass, or it may be a kinetic process, limited by the time available for chemical exchange. For a typical channel length of 100 μm (Blundy and others, 2006) and magma temperature of ~900°C, the diffusivity data of Baker (1991) indicate that diffusive exchange of Si (the slowest diffusing species) will occur on time scales of 7 to 46 hours for melt H_2O contents of 3 and 6 percent, respectively. Thus, even without physical occlusion, melt inclusions are unlikely to equilibrate chemically with the groundmass in the last day or so before eruption. Whether physically or kinetically occluded, there comes a point after which each melt inclusion undergoes no further chemical modification, except for syneruptive loss of H_2O and other volatiles from ruptured inclusions. We refer to this as the "melt-inclusion sealing point," which corresponds to a depth and time coordinate in the overall magma ascent trajectory. There may be a considerable time gap between the moment when the inclusion first exists as a physical entity within the crystal, the "melt-inclusion formation point," and the sealing point. During this time gap the melt-inclusion chemistry evolves in harmony with the groundmass melt.

There are several lines of evidence from this study to suggest that the melt-inclusion sealing point corresponds closely in time to the onset of the event in which the host crystal is erupted. For example, the correlation between SO_2 contents of melt inclusions and the SO_2 flux associated with a particular eruptive event (fig. 13*B*) suggests sealing off shortly before eruption. If the inclusion were sealed several weeks or more before the eruption, the petrological sulfur flux and the measured sulfur flux would be out of phase. The correspondence between inclusion-sealing pressures and eruptive style (fig. 14*A*) suggests that rapid upwards movement of the magma may be sufficient to seal off the inclusion. Thus, the explosive eruptions of 1980 preserve melt inclusions sealed over a wide pressure range, because there was insufficient time to allow the inclusions to modify their chemistry during the final stages of ascent. Conversely, after 1980, when eruptions were less vigorous and predominantly effusive, sealing depths are consistently shallow, reflecting accumulation of magma beneath the growing seismic lid between eruptions as well as slower ascent and more time to chemically exchange with the groundmass.

There is also evidence to suggest that the melt-inclusion sealing point corresponds closely in space to the region of the subvolcanic system where the host crystal was stored before eruption. The close temporal correspondence between sealing depths and earthquake depths (fig. 14*B*) suggests that there is a relation between magma withdrawal and earthquakes. During the period May 18 to December 27, 1980, sealing depths show a wide range, down to 11 km below sea level. During this time period, earthquakes occurring in response to evacuation of magma from the system cover the same depth range. At the same time, limited precursory seismic activity and high intereruptive gas fluxes show that the conduit system was relatively open (Scandone and others, 2006). After December 27, shallow earthquakes increase dramatically in abundance to form a seismic lid, and sealing depths become almost exclusively shallow. The only post-December 1980 melt inclusion with a sealing depth below sea level is found in the explosive event of March 19, 1982, which punctuated nearly 5 years of predominantly effusive activity. This event was preceded by a deep earthquake swarm, apparently testifying to renewed magma supply from depth and tapping of a small part of this magma during the eruption. The dominant control over the transition in eruptive behavior after December 1980 is likely to have been dwindling magma supply from depth (Scandone and Malone, 1985), such that the addition of new magma to the base of the system was unable to maintain a fully connected conduit or to keep pace with the effects of decompression crystallization. The current (2004–2006) eruption appears to be a continuation of this process, with magma ascent now sufficiently slow that a plug of largely crystallized magma is being extruded as a spine from depths at which there are abundant shallow earthquakes (Iverson and others, 2006).

We propose that, for any given eruptive event, the melt inclusion sealing depths are a good indication of both the depth range over which magma was stored preeruptively and the rate at which it was extracted. Before May 18, 1980, magma resided from just below the volcanic summit to at least 11 km below sea level. The maximum Li enrichment observed at ~5 km below sea level probably marks a constriction at the top of the magma column. All magma at shallower levels was probably stored in a plexus of dikes that formed the conduit or within the growing cryptodome. Magma stored at very shallow depths in the nascent cryptodome was erupted as early as April 10, 1980 (Cashman and Hoblitt, 2004). The lateral blast of May 18 eviscerated the cryptodome and magma residing in the conduit down to ~5 km below sea level (see, for example, Scandone and others, 2006). The May 18 plinian event erupted a large volume of magma stored within the subvolcanic chamber from 5 to 11 km below sea level. Residual magma left at shallow levels was probably the source of much of the May 25 eruption. The subvolcanic system was then efficiently recharged, leading once again to a system in which a relatively deep magmatic reservoir supplied gas to shallow stored magma, giving rise to Li (and ^{210}Pb) enrichments (Berlo and others, 2004, 2006). The post-May 18 transitional eruptions tapped magma stored at depths ≤10 km below sea level, probably as a result of evacuation of the vestigial conduit system developed after the plinian event (see also Cashman and McConnell, 2005). This was the last "deep" magma to be erupted from Mount St. Helens.

After December 27, 1980, all melt inclusions have sealing depths at or above sea level, a single exception being a melt inclusion from the March 19, 1982, explosive event. Coincident with the change in inclusion sealing depths, there is the development of extensive shallow seismicity and the change to dominantly effusive behavior. The depth at which maximum Li enrichment occurs is also displaced to sea level or shallower, indicating either a change in the composition of gas released from depth, such that the brine condensation pressure is reduced, or a change in magma storage depth. In either case it is clear that after October 1980 the subvolcanic magma system contained predominantly crystalline magma that was unable to sustain explosive activity. An earthquake swarm in March 1982 may testify to limited recharge of the deeper system (≤ 9 km below sea level) by new magma. However, very little of this deeper magma was erupted directly, most being stored instead at shallow level (<2 km below sea level) before eruption.

There are similarities between the post-December 1980 preeruptive magma-storage conditions and those of the current eruption, where once again exclusively shallow-stored magma (≤2 km below sea level) is extruded. However, continuous slow magma extrusion during the current eruption results in a conduit plugged by largely crystalline magma, leading to successively erupted holocrystalline spines lubricated along their margins by well-developed fault gouge (Iverson and others, 2006; Cashman and others, this volume, chap. 19; Iverson, this volume, chap. 21). We would expect activity to revert to a more explosive eruptive style only after the conduit has been completely cleared to liberate magma stored beneath. This would require a substantial increase in the magma supply rate from depth or destruction of the shallow volcanic plumbing system.

The decay of ^{222}Rn to ^{210}Pb and diffusion of Li in plagioclase provide important time constraints on the process of degassing and the storage and ascent of magma at shallow level. Berlo and others (2006) argue that the enrichment in ^{210}Pb occurs because significant decay of ^{222}Rn occurs during gas transport from depth. Given the 3.8-day half-life of ^{222}Rn, the ^{210}Pb enrichment constrains gas transport time to be at least of this order. The rapid diffusion of Li in plagioclase (Giletti and Shanahan, 1997) indicates that diffusive enrichment (and loss) of Li on the scale of millimeters (a typical plagioclase phenocryst diameter) occurs on time scales of hours to days at 900°C. Thus magma must be stored at shallow levels for at least hours to days in order to acquire the observed Li enrichment. The magma must then ascend on a time scale that is long enough to allow Li to diffuse out of the melt and into the vapor phase but too short to allow the Li to escape from the plagioclase phenocrysts. This behavior is consistent with repose periods of a week or more between those eruptive events showing Li-enriched plagioclase (Berlo and others, 2004), and with ascent times of several days or less for post-18 May eruptions of Mount St. Helens (Rutherford and Hill, 1993).

The current eruption also shows very high Li concentrations in melt inclusions and plagioclase (Kent and others, 2007). Although the data are insufficient to discern the depth of Li enrichment, it is clear that substantial time is required to generate such high Li levels via the gas-streaming mechanism. Certainly it appears that the process of enrichment is similar in the current eruption to that of 1980–86 and this represents a characteristic feature of magma ascent and degassing at Mount St. Helens.

A key question about the current eruption is whether, petrologically, it represents a continuation of the 1980–86 eruption, following a brief period of dormancy, or whether it heralds the arrival of new magma at depth. There are several lines of evidence presented elsewhere in this volume that support the involvement of some new magma, not present at the time of the 1980–86 eruption. First, there is seismic evidence for recharge of the deeper system as early as 1987–92 (Moran, 1994). Focal mechanisms for these events are consistent with repressurization of the system at depths of 5–9 km below sea level, in the depth range of the 1980–86 magma chamber. Additional deep (8–10 km below sea level) earthquake swarms occurred in 1996 and 1998–99, suggesting continued recharge (Musumeci and others, 2002). Second, whole-rock geochemical data (Pallister and others, this volume, chap. 30) reveal that, although the bulk chemistry of the currently erupting dacite is slightly more evolved than that of 1980–86, the concentrations of some compatible trace elements (Ni, Cr) are higher, suggestive of addition of a more mafic input into the system. Third, Fe-Ti oxide temperatures (Pallister and others, this volume, chap. 30) indicate the appearance of high-temperature (>1,000°C) pairs in the groundmass of some recent samples, in accord with data presented in this work. No such high temperatures were evident in 1980–86. This is suggestive of heating by a new hotter magma at depth, although we cannot rule out the effects of significant latent heat release in these highly crystalline magmas.

The melt-inclusion data presented here also support the arrival of new magma at depth. The trace-element compositions of two melt inclusions from the current eruption are in marked contrast to all but one of the melt inclusions analyzed from 1980–86 in their steep REE pattern and lower U, Th, Y, Zr, and Hf. In terms of major elements, there are subtle differences between the current and 1980–86 eruptions. Although the melt inclusions of the current eruption are still rhyolitic in composition, the range of MgO and K_2O contents in them almost equals the entire range seen in 1980–86, whereas TiO_2 and Cl contents are uniformly lower. The simplest interpretation of these data is mixing of a new and different magma into a reservoir filled with the unerupted residue of the 1980–86 eruption. At present the evidence for this mixing event is subtle, and it is inferred only through slight changes in trace-element chemistry consistent with small parcels of the new magma invading volumetrically dominant older magma stored at shallow levels. This interpretation is consistent with seismic evidence for such batches (for example, Scandone and others, 2006). Over time, the addition of increasing quantities of this melt component displaces slightly the bulk chemical composition of the currently erupting magma, as evinced by figure 4. The melt-inclusion data do not necessarily require input of a more mafic magma into the system, just a more silicic magma with elevated Ni and Cr contents, similar, for example, to the dacites erupted during the Kalama period (Pallister and others, 1992, and this volume, chap. 30). Continued monitoring of melt inclusions from the current eruption is required to track the progressive involvement of the new magma as the eruption taps progressively deeper levels of the subvolcanic reservoir.

Conclusions

Whole-rock chemical variations in magma erupted from or around Mount St. Helens during late Quaternary time testify to extensive chemical differentiation of basaltic magma beneath the volcano to produce silicic andesite and dacite, such as those erupted in 1980–86 and since 2004. Plagioclase involvement was minimal during the early stages of differentiation, probably because of elevated H_2O contents in the parental magmas (Berlo and others, 2007). The compatible behavior of Y, Zr, and Nb during whole-rock differentiation points to the involvement of garnet, amphibole, and ilmenite in modal proportions at odds with the observed phenocryst assemblages. This suggests that differentiation occurred at considerable depth below Mount St. Helens, probably at the base of the crust ($P_{tot} \geq 1$ GPa), where garnet becomes a stable crystallizing phase (see, for example, Müntener and others, 2001). The curvature of many whole-rock geochemical trends rules out magma mixing as the primary source of chemical variation at Mount St. Helens. However, limited amounts of mixing of different magmas in the source region, and entrainment of crystal residues from depth, may account for some of the linearity in rocks with >62 percent SiO_2, including those from the 1980–86 and current (2004–2006) eruptions.

Melt-inclusion and groundmass-glass compositions lie at the high-SiO_2 end of the whole-rock arrays. The chemical trends exhibited by the glasses commonly are oblique to those of the whole rocks, indicative of a marked change in crystallizing assemblage. We interpret the glass trends to result from low-pressure crystallization of a dacite magma that was generated in the lower crust and ascended to the point of volatile saturation, ~11 km below sea level. Low-pressure crystallization involved the plagioclase-rich phenocryst assemblage, rather than the high-pressure amphibole-rich assemblage, which controls the whole-rock chemistry. The wide variety of matrix and inclusion glass compositions within host dacites of restricted composition indicates that low-pressure crystallization involved negligible physical segregation of crystals and melts.

Melt inclusions and Fe-Ti oxide data from the 1980–86 eruption provide constraints on the evolving subvolcanic magma plumbing. The dissolved volatile contents of the melt inclusions have enabled us to determine the storage pressure of a magma batch just before its eruption. By converting pressure to depth, we have been able to track the changing magma-extraction depths with time. The plinian eruption of May 18, 1980, involved magma that last equilibrated 5–11 km below sea level. The preceding eruptions, including the May 18, 1980, blast deposit, tapped magma from just below the edifice to ~5 km below sea level. Subsequent episodes in 1980 tapped magma down to 10 km below sea level. The tapping of deeper magma stopped abruptly at the end of 1980, coincident with the onset of shallow preeruptive seismicity and the transition to purely effusive activity. All subsequent 1981–86 eruptive episodes tapped exclusively shallow-stored magma. We interpret the development of shallow seismicity to mark the effective closure of the conduit system by stalled, highly crystallized magma in response to diminished magma supply. Therefore, 1980 corresponds to a period during which the conduit formed on May 18 remained sufficiently open that magma could be tapped over a wide range of depths.

The current eruption of Mount St. Helens shares similarities with the 1981–86 phase of the previous eruption, in that magma appears to be fed from shallow levels, beneath a seismic lid. However, the continuous slow effusion that characterizes the current activity is different from the more rapid episodic effusion of most of the 1980s and produces highly crystalline conduit material in the form of a sequence of collapsing spines. Several subtle petrological and chemical lines of evidence indicate that the deep magma driving spine extrusion differs from that previously present at Mount St. Helens. Melt-inclusion data suggest that the new magma has lower concentrations of REE, U, Th, and HFSE; higher Ni and Cr; and a steeper REE pattern than melts from 1980–86. To date, very little of this magma has insinuated its way into the choked conduit system. With time, however, we anticipate that the proportion of new magma in erupted products will increase. A careful integration of petrologic, seismologic, and gas-monitoring data will help to mark the progressive rise of any new magma through the system and, possibly, its eventual appearance at the surface.

Acknowledgments

This work was funded through research fellowships from the Natural Environment Research Council (U.K.) and the Royal Society to Blundy, National Science Foundation grants EAR-0207362 and EAR-0510437 to Cashman, and a University of Bristol Ph.D. studentship to Berlo. We would like to thank J. Craven, S. Kaseman, and R. Hinton for support on the Edinburgh ion microprobe, S. Kearns for help on the Bristol electron microprobe, and informative discussions with M. Humphreys, O. Melnik, S. Sparks, J. Pallister, and

S. Moran. L. Mastin, R. Scandone, and S. Sparks provided thorough and helpful reviews. We are indebted to B. Chappell for painstaking compilation of the published whole-rock data from Mount St. Helens, S. Moran for providing seismic data, S. Carey for providing sample MSH006, D. Pyle for providing sample SH80D, and V. Pinel for providing details of the depth-pressure relation. This work is dedicated to the memory of Ben John (1935–2006).

References Cited

Andersen, D.J., and Lindsley, D.H., 1988, Internally consistent solution models for Fe-Mg-Mn-Ti oxides; Fe-Ti oxides: American Mineralogist, v. 73, nos. 7–8, p. 714–726.

Anderson, A.T., 1991, Hourglass inclusions; theory and application to the Bishop rhyolitic Tuff: American Mineralogist, v. 76, p. 530–547.

Annen, C., Blundy, J.D., and Sparks, R.S.J., 2006, The genesis of intermediate and silicic magmas in deep crustal hot zones: Journal of Petrology, v. 47, p. 505–539.

Bacon, C.R., and Hirschmann, M.M., 1988, Mg/Mn partitioning as a test for equilibrium between coexisting Fe-Ti oxides: American Mineralogist, v. 73, p. 57–61.

Baker, D.R., 1991, Interdiffusion of hydrous dacitic and rhyolitic melts and the efficacy of rhyolite contamination of dacitic enclaves: Contributions to Mineralogy and Petrology, v. 106, p. 462–473.

Berlo, K., Blundy. J., Turner, S., Cashman, K., Hawkesworth, C., and Black, S., 2004, Geochemical precursors to volcanic activity at Mount St. Helens, USA: Science, v. 306, p. 1167–1169.

Berlo, K., Turner, S., Blundy, J., Black, S., and Hawkesworth, C., 2006, Tracing pre-eruptive magma degassing using (^{210}Pb/^{226}Ra) disequilibria in volcanic deposits of the 1980–1986 eruptions of Mount St. Helens: Earth and Planetary Science Letters v. 249, nos. 3–4, p. 337–349, doi:10.1016/j.epsl.2006.07.018.

Berlo, K., Blundy, J., Turner, S., Hawkesworth, C., 2007, Textural and chemical variation in plagioclase phenocrysts from the 1980 eruptions of Mount St. Helens, USA: Contributions to Mineralogy and Petrology v. 154, no. 3, p. 291–308, doi:10.1007/s00410-007-0194-8.

Blundy, J., and Cashman, K.V., 2001, Ascent-driven crystallisation of dacite magmas at Mount St. Helens, 1980–1986: Contributions to Mineralogy and Petrology, v. 140, no. 6, p. 631–650, doi:10.1007/s004100000219.

Blundy, J., and Cashman, K., 2005, Rapid decompression-driven crystallization recorded by melt inclusions from Mount St. Helens volcano: Geology, v. 33, no. 10, p. 793–796, doi:10.1130/G21668.1.

Blundy, J.D., and Wood, B.J., 1991, Crystal-chemical controls on the partitioning of Ba and Sr between plagioclase feldspar, silicate melts and hydrothermal solutions: Geochimica et Cosmochimica Acta, v. 55, p. 193–209.

Blundy, J., Cashman, K., and Humphreys, M., 2006, Magma heating by decompression-driven crystallization beneath andesite volcanoes: Nature, v. 443, p. 76–80, doi:10.1038/nature05100.

Burgisser, A. and Scaillet, B., 2007, Redox evolution of a degassing magma rising to the surface: Nature, v. 445, no. 7124, p. 194–197, doi:10.1038/nature05509.

Candela, P.A., 1986, The evolution of aqueous vapor from silicate melts; effect on oxygen fugacity: Geochimica et Cosmochimica Acta, v. 50, p. 1205–1211.

Carroll, M.R., and Rutherford, M.J., 1985, Sulfide and sulfate saturation in hydrous silicate melts, *in* Proceedings of 15th Lunar and Planetary Science Conference, part 2: Journal of Geophysical Research, v. 90, supplement, p. C601–C612.

Cashman, K.V., 1992, Groundmass crystallization of Mount St. Helens dacite, 1980–1986; a tool for interpreting shallow magmatic processes: Contributions to Mineralogy and Petrology, v. 109, no. 4, p. 431–449, doi:10.1007/BF00306547.

Cashman, K.V., and Hoblitt, R.P., 2004, Magmatic precursors to the 18 May 1980 eruption of Mount St. Helens, USA: Geology, v. 32, no. 2, p. 141–144.

Cashman, K.V., and McConnell, S.M., 2005, Multiple levels of magma storage during the 1980 summer eruptions of Mount St. Helens, WA: Bulletin of Volcanology, v. 68, no. 1, p. 57–75, doi:10.1007/s00445-005-0422-x.

Cashman, K.V., and Taggart, J.E., 1983, Petrologic monitoring of 1981 and 1982 eruptive products from Mount St. Helens: Science, v. 221, p. 1385–1387.

Cashman, K.V., Thornber, C.R., and Pallister, J.S., 2008, From dome to dust; shallow crystallization and fragmentation of conduit magma during the 2004–2006 dome extrusion of Mount St. Helens, Washington, chap. 19 *of* Sherrod, D.R., Scott, W.E., and Stauffer, P.H., eds., A volcano rekindled; the renewed eruption of Mount St. Helens, 2004–2006: U.S. Geological Survey Professional Paper 1750 (this volume).

Clemente, B., Scaillet, B., and Pichavant, M., 2004, The solubility of sulphur in hydrous rhyolitic melts: Journal of Petrology, v. 45, p. 2171–2196.

Clynne, M.A., Calvert, A.T., Wolfe, E.W., Evarts, R.C., Fleck, R.J., and Lanphere, M.A., 2008, The Pleistocene eruptive history of Mount St. Helens, Washington, from 300,000 to 12,800 years before present, chap. 28 *of* Sherrod, D.R.,

Scott, W.E., and Stauffer, P.H., eds., A volcano rekindled; the renewed eruption of Mount St. Helens, 2004–2006: U.S. Geological Survey Professional Paper 1750 (this volume).

Criswell, C.W., 1987, Chronology and pyroclastic stratigraphy of the May 18, 1980, eruption of Mount St. Helens, Washington: Journal of Geophysical Research, v. 92, p. no. B10, 10237–10266.

Dolejš, D., and Baker, D.R., 2006, Fluorite solubility in hydrous haplogranitic melts at 100 MPa: Chemical Geology, v. 225, nos. 1–2, p. 40–60, doi:10.1016/j.chemgeo.2005.08.00.

Endo, E.T., Dzurisin, D., and Swanson, D.A., 1990, Geophysical and observational constraints for ascent rates of dacitic magma at Mount St. Helens, *in* Ryan, M.P., ed., Magma transport and storage: New York, John Wiley, p. 317–334.

Fruchter, J.S., Robertson, D.E., Evans, J.C., Olsen, K.B., Lepel, E.A., Laul, J.C., Abel, K.H., Sanders, R.W., Jackson, P.O., Wogman, N.S., Perkins, R.W., Vantuyl, H.H., Beauchamp, R.H., Shade, J.W., Daniel, J.L., Erikson, R.L., Sehmel, G.A., Lee, R.N., Robinson, A.V., Moss, O.R., Briant, J.K., and Cannon, W.C., 1980, Mount St. Helens ash from the 18 May 1980 eruption—chemical, physical, mineralogical and biological properties: Science, v. 209, p. 1116–1125.

Gardner, J.E., Carey, S., Rutherford, M.J., and Sigurdsson, H., 1995, Petrologic diversity in Mount St. Helens dacites during the last 4,000 years; implications for magma mixing: Contributions to Mineralogy and Petrology, v. 119, nos. 2–3, p. 224–238.

Gerlach, T.M., and Casadevall, T.J., 1986, Evaluation of gas data from high-temperature fumaroles at Mount St. Helens, 1980–1982: Journal of Volcanology and Geothermal Research, v. 28, nos. 1–2, p. 107–140, doi:10.1016/0377-0273(86)90008-9.

Geschwind, C.-H., and Rutherford, M.J., 1995, Crystallization of microlites during magma ascent; the fluid mechanics of 1980–1986 eruptions at Mount St. Helens: Bulletin of Volcanology, v. 57, no. 5, p. 356–370.

Giletti, B.J., and Shanahan, T.M., 1997, Alkali diffusion in plagioclase feldspar: Chemical Geology, v. 139, p. 3–20.

Halliday, A.N., Fallick, A.E., Dickin, A.P., Mackenzie, A.B., Stephens, W.E., and Hildreth, W., 1983, The isotopic and chemical evolution of Mount St. Helens: Earth and Planetary Science Letters, v. 63, no. 2, p. 241–256, doi:10.1016/0012-821X(83)90040-7.

Heinrich, C.A., Günther, D., Audétat, A., Ulrich, T., and Frischknecht, D., 1999, Metal fractionation between magmatic brine and vapor, determined by microanalysis of fluid inclusions: Geology, v. 27, p. 755–758.

Hinton, R.W., 1990, Ion microprobe trace-element analysis of silicates; measurement of multi-element glasses: Chemical Geology, v. 83, p. 11–25.

Hooper, P.R., Herrick, I.W., Laskowski, E.R., and Knowles, C.R., 1980, Composition of the Mount St. Helens ashfall in the Moscow-Pullman area on 18 May 1980: Science, v. 209, p. 1125–1126.

Humphreys, M.C.S., Kearns, S.L., and Blundy, J.D., 2006, SIMS investigation of electron-beam damage to hydrous, rhyolitic glasses; implications for melt inclusion analysis: American Mineralogist, v. 91, p. 667–679.

Humphreys, M.C.S., Blundy, J.D., and Sparks, R.S.J., 2008, Shallow-level decompression crystallisation and deep magma supply at Shiveluch Volcano: Contributions to Mineralogy and Petrology, v. 155, no. 1, p. 45–61, doi:10.1007/s00410-007-0223-7.

Icenhower, J., and London, D., 1995, An experimental study of element partitioning among biotite, muscovite, and coexisting peraluminous silicic melt at 200 MPa (H_2O): American Mineralogist, v. 80, p. 1229–1251.

Irving, A.J., Rhodes, J.M., and Sparks, J.W., 1980, Mount St. Helens lava dome, pyroclastic flow and ash samples; major and trace element chemistry [abs.]: Eos (American Geophysical Union Transactions), v. 61, no. 46, p. 1138.

Iverson, R.M., 2008, Dynamics of seismogenic volcanic extrusion resisted by a solid surface plug, Mount St. Helens, 2004–2005, chap. 21 *of* Sherrod, D.R., Scott, W.E., and Stauffer, P.H., eds., A volcano rekindled; the renewed eruption of Mount St. Helens, 2004–2006: U.S. Geological Survey Professional Paper 1750 (this volume).

Iverson, R.M., Dzurisin, D., Gardner, C.A., Gerlach, T.M., LaHusen, R.G., Lisowski, M., Major, J.J., Malone, S.D., Messerich, J.A., Moran, S.C., Pallister, J.S., Qamar, A.I., Schilling, S.P., and Vallance, J.W., 2006, Dynamics of seismogenic volcanic extrusion at Mount St. Helens in 2004–05: Nature, v. 444, no. 7118, p. 439–443, doi:10.1038/nature05322.

Johannes, W., and Holtz, F., 1996, Petrogenesis and experimental petrology of granitic rocks: Berlin, Springer-Verlag, 335 p.

Kent, A.J.R., Blundy, J., Cashman, K.V., Cooper, K.M., Donnelly, C., Pallister, J.S., Reagan, M., Rowe, M.C., and Thornber, C.R., 2007, Vapor transfer prior to the October 2004 eruption of Mount St. Helens, Washington: Geology, v. 35, no. 3, p. 231–234, doi:10.1130/G22809A.1.

Kent, A.J.R., Rowe, M.C., Thornber, C.R., and Pallister, J.S., 2008, Trace element and Pb isotope composition of plagioclase from dome samples from the 2004–2005 eruption of Mount St Helens, Washington, chap. 35 *of* Sherrod, D.R.,

Scott, W.E., and Stauffer, P.H., eds., A volcano rekindled; the renewed eruption of Mount St. Helens, 2004–2006: U.S. Geological Survey Professional Paper 1750 (this volume).

Kuntz, M.A., Rowley, P.D., MacLeod, N.S., Reynolds, R.L., MacBroome, L.A., Kaplan, A.M., and Lidke, D.J., 1981, Petrography and particle-size distribution of pyroclastic-flow, ash-cloud, and surge deposits, *in* Lipman, P.W., and Mullineaux, D.R., eds., The 1980 eruptions of Mount St. Helens, Washington: U.S. Geological Survey Professional Paper 1250, p. 525–539.

Leeman, W.P., Smith, D.R., Hildreth, W., Palacz, Z., and Rogers, N., 1990, Compositional diversity of late Cenozoic basalts in a transect across the southern Washington Cascades—implications for subduction zone magmatism: Journal of Geophysical Research, v. 95, p. 19561–19582.

Lees, J.M., 1992, The magma system of Mount St. Helens; non-linear high-resolution P-wave tomography: Journal of Volcanology and Geothermal Research, v. 53, nos. 1–4, p. 103–116.

Luhr, J.F., 1990, Experimental phase relations of water- and sulphur-saturated arc magmas and the 1982 eruptions of El Chichón Volcano: Journal of Petrology, v. 31, p. 1071–1114.

Malone, S.D., Boyko, C., and Weaver, C.S., 1983, Seismic precursors to the Mount St. Helens eruptions in 1981 and 1982: Science, v. 221, p. 1376–1378.

Massol, H., and Jaupart, C., 1999, The generation of gas overpressure in volcanic eruptions: Earth and Planetary Science Letters, v. 166, p. 57–70.

Mastin, L.G., Roeloffs, E., Beeler, N.M., and Quick, J.E., 2008, Constraints on the size, overpressure, and volatile content of the Mount St. Helens magma system from geodetic and dome-growth measurements during the 2004–2006+ eruption, chap. 22 *of* Sherrod, D.R., Scott, W.E., and Stauffer, P.H., eds., A volcano rekindled; the renewed eruption of Mount St. Helens, 2004–2006: U.S. Geological Survey Professional Paper 1750 (this volume).

McGee, K.A., and Casadevall, T.J., 1994, A compilation of sulfur dioxide and carbon dioxide emission-rate data from Mount St. Helens during 1980–88: U.S. Geological Survey Open-File Report 94–212, 24 p.

Melson, W.G., 1983, Monitoring the 1980–1982 eruptions of Mount St. Helens; compositions and abundances of glass: Science, v. 221, p. 1387–1391.

Melson, W.G., and Hopson, C.A., 1981, Preeruption temperatures and oxygen fugacities in the 1980 eruptive sequence, *in* Lipman, P.W., and Mullineaux, D.R., eds., The 1980 eruptions of Mount St. Helens, Washington: U.S. Geological Survey Professional Paper 1250, p. 641–648.

Metrich, N., and Rutherford, M.J., 1992, Experimental study of chlorine behavior in hydrous silicic melts: Geochimica et Cosmochimica Acta, v. 56, p. 607–616.

Moore, J.G., and Albee, W.C., 1981, Topographic and structural changes, March–July 1980 photogrammetric data, *in* Lipman, P.W., and Mullineaux, D.R., eds., The 1980 eruptions of Mount St. Helens, Washington: U.S. Geological Survey Professional Paper 1250, p. 123–134.

Moran, S.C., 1994, Seismicity at Mount St. Helens, 1987–1992; evidence for repressurization of an active magmatic system: Journal of Geophysical Research, v. 99, no. B3, p. 4341–4354, doi:10.1029/93JB02993.

Moran, S.C., Malone, S.D., Qamar, A.I., Thelen, W.A., Wright, A.K., and Caplan-Auerbach, J., 2008, Seismicity associated with renewed dome building at Mount St. Helens, 2004–2005, chap. 2 *of* Sherrod, D.R., Scott, W.E., and Stauffer, P.H., eds., A volcano rekindled; the renewed eruption of Mount St. Helens, 2004–2006: U.S. Geological Survey Professional Paper 1750 (this volume).

Müntener, O., Kelemen, P. B., and Grove, T. L., 2001, The role of H_2O during crystallisation of primitive arc magmas under uppermost mantle conditions and genesis of igneous pyroxenites; an experimental study: Contributions to Mineralogy and Petrology, v. 141, p. 643–658.

Musumeci, C., Gresta, S., and Malone, S.D., 2002, Magma system recharge of Mount St. Helens from precise relative hypocenter location of microearthquakes: Journal of Geophysical Research, v. 107, no. B10, 2264, p. ESE 16-1–ESE 16-9, doi:10.1029/2001JB000629.

Newman, S., and Lowenstern, J.B., 2002, VolatileCalc; a silicate melt-H_2O-CO_2 solution model written in Visual Basic for Excel®: Computers and Geosciences, v. 28, no. 5, p. 597–604, doi:10.1016/S0098-3004(01)00081-4.

Pallister, J.S., Hoblitt, R.P., Crandell, D.R., and Mullineaux, D.R., 1992, Mount St. Helens a decade after the 1980 eruptions; magmatic models, chemical cycles, and a revised hazards assessment: Bulletin of Volcanology, v. 54, no. 2, p. 126–146, doi:10.1007/BF00278003.

Pallister, J.S., Thornber, C.R., Cashman, K.V., Clynne, M.A., Lowers, H.A., Mandeville, C.W., Brownfield, I.K., and Meeker, G.P., 2008, Petrology of the 2004–2006 Mount St. Helens lava dome—implications for magmatic plumbing and eruption triggering, chap. 30 *of* Sherrod, D.R., Scott, W.E., and Stauffer, P.H., eds., A volcano rekindled; the renewed eruption of Mount St. Helens, 2004–2006: U.S. Geological Survey Professional Paper 1750 (this volume).

Pinel, V., and Jaupart, C., 2000, The effect of edifice load on magma ascent beneath a volcano: Philosophical Transactions of the Royal Society, v. 358, p. 1515–1532.

Pinel, V., and Jaupart, C., 2005. Some consequences of volcanic edifice destruction for eruption conditions: Journal of Volcanology and Geothermal Research, v. 145, p. 68–80.

Price, J.D., Hogan, J.P., Gilbert, M.C., London, D., and Morgan, G.B., VI, 1999, Experimental study of titanite-fluorite equilibria in the A-type Mount Scott Granite; implications for assessing F contents of felsic magma: Geology, v. 27, no. 10, p. 951–954.

Rust, A.C., Cashman, K.V., and Wallace, P.J., 2004, Magma degassing buffered by vapor flow through brecciated conduit margins: Geology, v. 32, p. 349–352.

Rutherford, M.D., and Devine, J.D., 1988, The May 18, 1980 eruption of Mount St. Helens 3. Stability and chemistry of amphibole in the magma chamber: Journal of Geophysical Research, v. 93, p. 11949–11959.

Rutherford, M.D., and Hill, P.M., 1993, Magma ascent rates from amphibole breakdown; an experimental study applied to the 1980–1986 Mount St. Helens eruption: Journal of Geophysical Research, v. 98, no. B11, p. 19667–19685.

Rutherford, M.D., Sigurdsson, H., Carey, S., and Davis, A., 1985, The May 18, 1980 eruption of Mount St. Helens 1. Melt composition and experimental phase equilibria: Journal of Geophysical Research, v. 90, p. 2929–2947.

Sarna-Wojcicki, A.M., Meyer, C.E., Woodward, M.J., and Lamothe, P.J., 1981, Composition of air-fall ash erupted on May 18, May 25, June 12, July 22, and August 7, *in* Lipman, P.W., and Mullineaux, D.R., eds., The 1980 eruptions of Mount St. Helens, Washington: U.S. Geological Survey Professional Paper 1250, p. 667–681.

Scaillet, B., and Pichavant, M., 2005, A model of sulphur solubility for hydrous mafic melts; application to the determination of magmatic fluid compositions of Italian volcanoes: Annals of Geophysics, v. 48, p. 671–698.

Scandone, R., and Malone, S.D., 1985, Magma supply, magma discharge and readjustment of the feeding system of Mount St. Helens during 1980: Journal of Volcanology and Geothermal Research, v. 23, nos. 3–4, p. 239–262, doi:10.1016/0377-0273(85)90036-8.

Scandone, R., Cashman, K.V., and Malone, S.D., 2006, Magma supply, magma ascent and the style of volcanic eruptions: Earth and Planetary Science Letters, v. 253, p. 513–529.

Scheidegger, K.F., Federman, A.N., and Tallman, A.M., 1982, Compositional heterogeneity of tephras from the 1980 eruptions of Mount St. Helens: Journal of Geophysical Research, v. 87, p. 10861–10881.

Shinohara, H., 1994, Exsolution of immiscible vapor and liquid phases from a crystallizing silicate melt; implications for chlorine and metal transport: Geochimica et Cosmochimica Acta, v. 58, p. 5215–5221.

Shinohara, H., Iiyama, J.T., and Matsuo, S., 1989, Partition of chlorine compounds between silicate melt and hydrothermal solutions—1. Partition of NaCl-KCl: Geochimica et Cosmochimica Acta, v. 53, p. 2617–2630.

Sisson, T.W., 1994, Hornblende-melt trace-element partitioning measured by ion microprobe: Chemical Geology, v. 117, v. 331–344.

Smith, D.R., and Leeman, W.P., 1987, Petrogenesis of Mount St. Helens dacitic magmas: Journal of Geophysical Research, v. 92, no. B10, p. 10313–10334.

Smith, D.R., and Leeman, W.P., 1993, The origin of Mount St. Helens andesites: Journal of Volcanology and Geothermal Research, v. 55, nos. 3–4, p. 271–303, doi:10.1016/0377-0273(93)90042-P.

Smithsonian Institution, 1980, Mount St. Helens: Washington, D.C., National Museum of Natural History, Smithsonian Institution, Scientific Event Alert Network (SEAN) Bulletin 5, no. 11, p. 2–4.

Spencer, K.J., and Lindsley, D.H., 1981, A solution model for coexisting iron-titanium oxides: American Mineralogist, v. 66, p. 1189–1201.

Stewart, M.L., and Pearce, T.H., 2004, Sieve-textured plagioclase in dacitic magma; interference imaging results: American Mineralogist v. 89, p. 348–351.

Sun, S.-s., and McDonough, W.F., 1989, Chemical and isotopic systematics of oceanic basalts; implications for mantle composition and processes, *in* Saunders, A.D., and Norry, M.J., eds., Magmatism in the ocean basins: Geological Society of London Special Publication 42, p. 313–345.

Swanson, D.A., and Holcomb, R.T., 1990, Regularities in growth of the Mount St. Helens dacite dome, 1980–1986, *in* Fink, J.H., ed., Lava flows and domes, emplacement mechanisms and hazard implications: Berlin, Springer-Verlag, International Association of Volcanology and Chemistry of the Earth's Interior, Proceedings in Volcanology 2, p. 3–24.

Swanson, D.A., Dzurisin, D., Holcomb, R.T., Iwatsubo, E.Y., Chadwick, W.W., Jr., Casadevall, T.J., Ewert, J.W., and Heliker, C.C., 1987, Growth of the lava dome at Mount St. Helens, Washington, (USA), 1981–1983, *in* Fink, J.H., ed., The emplacement of silicic domes and lava flows: Geological Society of America Special Paper 212, p. 1–16.

Symonds, R.B., and Reed, M.H., 1993, Calculation of multicomponent chemical equilibria in gas-solid-liquid systems; calculation methods, thermochemical data, and applications to studies of high-temperature volcanic gases with examples from Mount St. Helens: American Journal of Science, v. 293, no. 8, p. 758–864.

Venezky, D.Y., and Rutherford, M.J., 1999, Petrology and Fe-Ti oxide reequilibration of the 1991 Mount Unzen mixed magma: Journal of Volcanology and Geothermal Research, v. 89, p. 213–230, doi:10.1016/S0377-0273(98)00133-4.

Wallace, P.J., 2001, Volcanic SO_2 emissions and the abundance and distribution of exsolved gas in magma bodies: Journal of Volcanology and Geothermal Research, v. 108, nos. 1–4, p. 85–106, doi:10.1016/S0377-0273(00)00279-1.

Watson, E.B., and Harrison, T.M., 1983, Zircon saturation revisited; temperature and composition effects in a variety of crustal magma types: Earth and Planetary Science Letters, v. 64, p. 295–304.

Weaver, C.S., Zollweg, J.E., and Malone, S.D., 1983, Deep earthquakes beneath Mount St. Helens; evidence for magmatic gas transport?: Science, v. 221, p. 1391–1394.

Weaver, C.S., Grant, W.C., and Shemeta, J.E., 1987, Local crustal extension at Mount St. Helens, Washington: Journal of Geophysical Research, v. 92, no. B10, p. 10170–10178.

Webster, J.D., 2004, The exsolution of magmatic hydrosaline chloride liquids: Chemical Geology, v. 210, p. 33–48.

Whitney, J.A., 1984, Fugacities of sulfurous gases in pyrrhotite-bearing silicic magmas: American Mineralogist, v. 69, p. 69–78.

Williams, D.L., Abrams, G., Finn, C., Dzurisin, D., Johnson, D.J., and Denlinger, R., 1987, Evidence from gravity data for an intrusive complex beneath Mount St. Helens: Journal of Geophysical Research, v. 92, no. B10, p. 10207–10222.

Appendix 1. Chemical Analyses of Glassy Melt Inclusions, Groundmass Glass, and Fe-Ti Oxide Pairs from the 1980–86 and 2004–2006 Eruptions of Mount St. Helens, Washington

[This appendix appears only in the digital versions of this work—in the DVD-ROM that accompanies the printed volume and as a separate file accompanying this chapter on the Web at: http://pubs.usgs.gov/pp/1750.]

Appendix 1 is a spreadsheet file that contains the entire dataset of major, trace-element, and volatiles analyses, a selection of which is in tables 2 and 3 in the text. See tables for analytical details.

Appendix 2. Chemical Analyses of Fe-Ti Oxide Pairs from the 1980–86 and 2004–2006 Eruptions of Mount St. Helens, Washington

[This appendix appears only in the digital versions of this work—in the DVD-ROM that accompanies the printed volume and as a separate file accompanying this chapter on the Web at: http://pubs.usgs.gov/pp/1750.]

Appendix 2 is a spreadsheet file that contains the entire dataset of Fe-Ti analyses and calculated temperature and oxygen fugacity, a selection of which is in table 4 in the text. See table for analytical details.

A Volcano Rekindled: The Renewed Eruption of Mount St. Helens, 2004–2006
Edited by David R. Sherrod, William E. Scott, and Peter H. Stauffer
U.S. Geological Survey Professional Paper 1750, 2008

Chapter 34

Plagioclase Populations and Zoning in Dacite of the 2004–2005 Mount St. Helens Eruption: Constraints for Magma Origin and Dynamics

By Martin J. Streck[1], Cindy A. Broderick[1], Carl R. Thornber[2], Michael A. Clynne[3], and John S. Pallister[2]

Abstract

We investigated plagioclase phenocrysts in dacite of the 2004–5 eruption of Mount St. Helens to gain insights into the magmatic processes of the current eruption, which is characterized by prolonged, nearly solid-state extrusion, low gas emission, and shallow seismicity. In addition, we investigated plagioclase of 1980–86 dacite.

Light and Nomarski microscopy were used to texturally characterize plagioclase crystals. Electron microprobe analyses measured their compositions. We systematically mapped and categorized all plagioclase phenocrysts in a preselected area according to the following criteria: (1) occurrence of zones of acicular orthopyroxene inclusions, (2) presence of dissolution surface(s), and (3) spatial association of 1 and 2. Phenocrysts fall into three main categories; one category contains four subcategories.

The range of anorthite (An) content in 2004–5 plagioclase is about An_{57-35} during the last 30–40 percent crystallization of plagioclase phenocrysts. Select microphenocrysts (10–50 μm) range from An_{30} to An_{42}. Anorthite content is lowest near outermost rims of phenocrysts, but zonation patterns between interior and rim indicate variable trends that correlate with textural features. Crystals without dissolution surfaces (about 14 percent of total) show steadily decreasing An content outward to the crystal rim (outer ~80 μm). All other crystals are banded as a consequence of dissolution; dissolution surfaces are band boundaries. Such crystals display normal outward An zoning within a single band that, following dissolution, is then overgrown abruptly by high-An material of the next band. Swarms of acicular orthopyroxene inclusions in plagioclase are characteristic of 2004–5 dacite. They occur mostly inward of dissolution surfaces, where band composition reaches lowest An content. The relative proportions of the three crystal types are distinctly different between 2004–5 dacite and 1980s dome dacite.

We propose that crystals with no dissolution surfaces are those that were supplied last to the shallow reservoir, whereas plagioclase with increasingly more complex zoning patterns (that is, the number of zoned bands bounded by dissolution surfaces) result from prolonged residency and evolution in the reservoir. We propose that banding and An zoning across multiple bands are primarily a response to thermally induced fluctuations in crystallinity of the magma in combination with recharge; a lesser role is ascribed to cycling crystals through pressure gradients. Crystals without dissolution surfaces, in contrast, could have grown only in response to steady(?) decompression. Some heating-cooling cycles probably postdate the final eruption in 1986. They resulted from small recharge events that supplied new crystals that then experienced resorption-growth cycles. We suggest that magmatic events shortly prior to the current eruption, recorded in the outermost zones of plagioclase phenocrysts, began with the incorporation of acicular orthopyroxene, followed by last resorption, and concluded with crystallization of euhedral rims. Finally, we propose that 2004–5 dacite is composed mostly of dacite magma that remained after 1986 and underwent subsequent magmatic evolution but, more importantly, contains a component of new dacite from deeper in the magmatic system, which may have triggered the new eruption.

Introduction

The 2004 eruption of Mount St. Helens is remarkable for several reasons. Nearly solid, gas-poor dacite lava has been

[1] Department of Geology, Portland State University, Portland, OR 97207

[2] U.S. Geological Survey, 1300 SE Cardinal Court, Vancouver, WA 98683

[3] U.S. Geological Survey, 345 Middlefield Road, Menlo Park, CA 94025

extruded continuously for 28 months (at time of this writing, early 2007). Earthquakes are limited to the upper 3 km, with most located less than 1 km below the surface; no deeper seismicity has been observed (Moran and others, this volume, chap. 2). Emissions of SO_2, H_2S, and CO_2 are extremely low, indicating eruption of degassed magma (Gerlach and others, this volume, chap. 26). Low gas emission argues against the possibility of proximal mafic magma at depth, which might be called upon to have initiated the current eruption, and is consistent with an apparent lack of direct evidence for mingling with more mafic magma. This combination raises two important questions: (1) what is the driving force for the current eruption, and (2) is there petrologic evidence for magma recharge as an eruption trigger?

We studied plagioclase phenocrysts in 2004–5 dacite (fig. 1) and 1980–86 dacite dome rocks with the goal of using these data to investigate magma origin and reservoir dynamics, including evidence for recharge. We used polarized light and Nomarski microscopy in combination with detailed microprobe traverses to texturally and compositionally characterize single plagioclase crystals, focusing on areas near phenocryst rims. In addition, we systematically mapped and classified all plagioclase phenocrysts along thin-section traverses to evaluate variability in plagioclase crystal populations. On the basis of these datasets, we infer that the new dacite is composed of three components. The first is magma that remained in the reservoir after 1986 and whose plagioclase crystals typically underwent crystallization and resorption as crystals cycled through cooler and hotter (and possibly deeper) parts of the reservoir, respectively. Whether or not some of this magma was isolated and escaped any modification remains open to debate. The second component is magma that was probably supplied recently by recharge of the shallow Mount St. Helens magma chamber. This magma carried plagioclase phenocrysts that grew continuously and are compatible with crystallization controlled largely by decompression (Blundy and Cashman, 2001). In addition to these magmatic components, there is evidence that some plagioclase in erupting dacite magmas was derived by disintegration of wall-rock xenoliths constituting the third component. These include crystals with distinct sieve-textured cores probably derived from gabbroic source rocks (Heliker, 1995) and older Mount St. Helens dacite containing plagioclase with unusually low An content and sporadically hosting quartz inclusions (M.J. Streck, unpub. data; Clynne and others, this volume, chap. 28). Our data are compatible with recharge-driven initiation of the current eruption. We suggest that new magma is dacite and is hotter than and has fewer crystals than the resident dacite with which it has blended.

Samples and Analytical Procedures

Samples for this study are splits of samples collected by the staff of the Cascades Volcano Observatory (CVO) as the eruption proceeded (table 1). We report collection dates for 2004–5 samples and eruption dates for 1980–86 samples. The full sample names are given in table 1 but are abbreviated. The reader is referred to Pallister and others (this volume, chap. 30) for information about likely eruption dates for 2004–5 samples. For most of our samples, the estimated eruption date precedes collection date by 1–3 weeks. Sample localities are

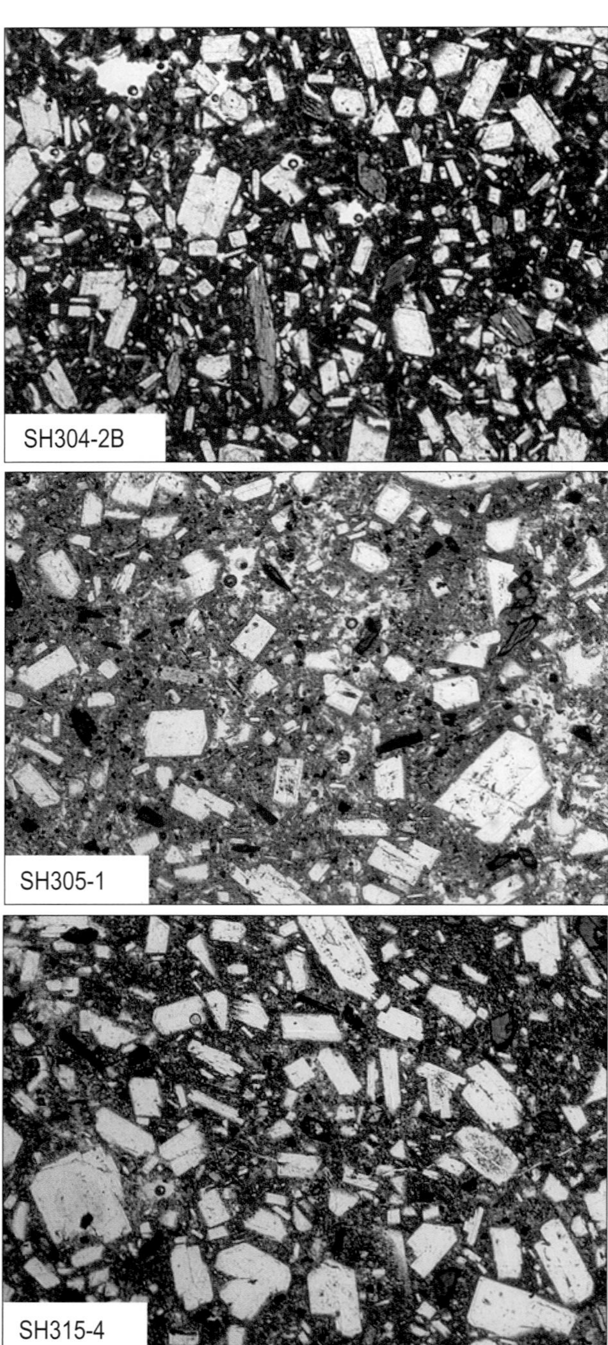

Figure 1. Thin sections of dacite from 2004–5 Mount St. Helens eruption showing crystal-rich nature and plagioclase occurrence mostly as single, equant phenocrysts. Note sporadic plagioclase with sieved interior and clear overgrowth.

Table 1. Samples analyzed in this study and results of crystal mapping.

[All plagioclase assigned to crystal type: Type 1, dissolution surfaces; Type 2, dissolution surfaces and acicular orthopyroxene (opx); Type 3, no dissolution surface and with or without acicular opx. Type 2 crystals further grouped by position of acicular opx relative to dissolution surface(s): A, opx abundant at outermost dissolution surface; B, opx at some surface inboard of the outermost; C, opx is near rim but dissolution surface is near core of crystal; D, opx is near core but dissolution surface is near rim of crystal. EMP, electron microprobe analyses; dashes indicate no analysis. Column for sheets shows total number of images from two transects across each thin section (see fig. 2). Column for indeterminate crystals shows proportion (percent) of unresolved assignments relative to total plagioclase content.]

2004–5 Dacite samples							Normalized abundance, in %, with parenthetical 1σ deviation				Dissolution association in Type 2 crystals, in % (see table notes)			
Sample No.	Collection date	EMP analyses	Sheets per thin section	Total crystals examined	Crystals per sheet	1σ dev.	Type 1 crystals	Type 2 crystals	Type 3 crystals	Indeterminate crystals	A	B	C	D
SH304-2B	Nov. 4, 2004	16	17	1,939	114	17	66 (7)	24 (7)	10 (5)	12	70	18	11	2
SH305-1	Jan. 3, 2005	6	16	1,118	70	8	40 (6)	29 (6)	31 (6)	20	75	9	12	4
SH308-3	Feb. 22, 2005	--	18	1,653	92	12	52 (6)	28 (8)	20 (6)	11	70	11	18	2
SH311-1B	Jan. 19, 2005	9	--	--	--	--	--	--	--	--	--	--	--	--
SH315-4	Apr. 19, 2005	8	13	1,354	104	21	57 (11)	34 (10)	9 (4)	8	69	21	11	0
SH321	Aug. 19, 2005	--	17	1,275	75	18	52 (5)	37 (7)	11 (5)	5	69	23	6	2
SH323-2	Oct. 18, 2005	--	16	1,213	76	15	65 (6)	27 (6)	8 (2)	7	82	14	4	0
SH324-3	Dec. 15, 2005	--	16	1,290	81	6	66 (5)	28 (4)	6 (3)	5	77	20	3	0
						average	57 (10)	30 (4)	14 (9)					

1980–86 Dacite samples							Normalized abundance, in %, with parenthetical 1σ deviation				Dissolution association in Type 2 crystals, in % (see table notes)			
Sample No.	Eruption date	EMP analyses	Sheets per thin section	Total crystals examined	Crystals per sheet	1σ dev.	Type 1 crystals	Type 2 crystals	Type 3 crystals	Indeterminate crystals	A	B	C	D
SH226	October 1986	--	17	747	44	12	80 (10)	4 (3)	16 (9)	16	36	36	28	0
SH157	June 1984	--	15	490	33	7	91 (4)	5 (3)	4 (3)	7	14	81	0	5
SH131	August 1982	--	10	326	33	6	88 (7)	5 (5)	7 (4)	12	19	75	6	0
SC334-99B	~April 1981	9	14	835	60	8	89 (4)	1 (1)	10 (4)	16	50	50	0	0
SH52	December 1980	--	10	181	18	6	84 (9)	9 (6)	7 (5)	11	8	67	0	25
						average	86 (6)	5 (3)	9 (6)					

shown on photogeologic maps in Herriott and others (this volume, chap. 10).

We prepared polished thin sections that were etched in concentrated hydrofluoroboric acid for 25 s in preparation for Nomarski differential interference contrast (NDIC or Nomarski, for brevity) microscopy. This microscopy, in combination with transmitted-light microscopy, was employed to investigate textural aspects of plagioclase crystals. To associate textural characteristics with composition, we performed microprobe analyses along traverses in crystals representative of the range of textural features displayed. Point spacing along analytical traverses was 3–4 μm, concentrating on the outer ~100 μm of the crystal. We analyzed 39 crystals from 2004–5 samples and 9 crystals from 1981 dome lava (table 1). Analyses were done using the five-spectrometer CAMECA SX100 electron microprobe housed at Oregon State University, which was mostly operated remotely from Portland State University. Some additional crystals were analyzed in single-point mode at the University of Stuttgart, Germany, to characterize very small plagioclase crystals. Natural mineral standards were used to calibrate the instruments. Analytical conditions included an accelerating voltage of 15 kV, a beam current of 15 nA, and a focused (~1 μm diameter) beam. Collection times on peak and background positions were 10 and 5 s for Na (counted first), Si, Al, and Ca; times were 30 and 15 s for K, Mg, and Fe.

Encouraged by initial efforts to categorize plagioclase phenocrysts into different textural types (see below), we designed a mapping procedure to determine proportions of plagioclase crystal types. For each thin section, we used transmitted-light images at magnification × 25 and mapped two separate transects, comprising a total of 10–18 adjacent images, or sheets (table 1, fig. 2). In each × 25 sheet, we inspected every plagioclase phenocryst (≥80 μm) with transmitted and Nomarski microscopy and categorized crystals according to selected textural features. In this way, we obtained textural data on all plagioclase phenocrysts within an area covering roughly one-third of each thin section (table 1).

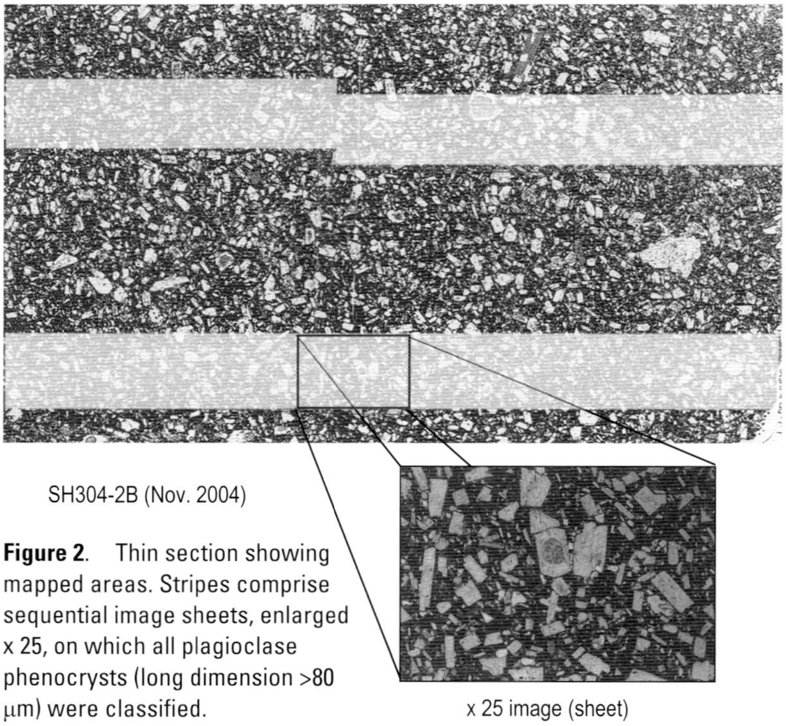

SH304-2B (Nov. 2004)

x 25 image (sheet)

Figure 2. Thin section showing mapped areas. Stripes comprise sequential image sheets, enlarged x 25, on which all plagioclase phenocrysts (long dimension >80 μm) were classified.

Plagioclase in 2004–2005 Mount St. Helens Dacite

The phenocryst assemblage of 2004–5 dacite is dominated by plagioclase with subordinate amounts of orthopyroxene, amphibole, and Fe–Ti oxides. Plagioclase consists dominantly (≥90 percent) of single, euhedral, clear, equant phenocrysts 80–800 μm across (fig. 1). Equant plagioclase also occurs as smaller crystals between 80 and 10 μm. We call these microphenocrysts even though they overlap in size with microlites in the surrounding interstitial groundmass. A few plagioclase crystals are texturally (and likely compositionally) distinct. Typically these are considerably larger (≥1 mm), subhedral to anhedral, and commonly display a sieved-textured interior. Plagioclase glomerocrysts are rare.

Textural Features

Individual plagioclase phenocrysts are characterized by growth features in the form of oscillatory zoning (parallel lines in Nomarski images) or by practically textureless parts (thus appearing as flat areas in Nomarski images) (fig. 3). Resorption textures are commonly found within crystals as dissolution surfaces that cut obliquely across oscillatory growth zones (figs. 3*A–D*) (note: we use the term "resorption" for the general process that creates a "dissolution surface"). The extent of resorption varies and most commonly is expressed as variable degrees of rounding of the corners of interior zones within a crystal. Commonly the phenocrysts have multiple dissolution surfaces; examples with four or more were observed. Sieved or pitted textures are rare in crystals of the dominant population, especially near their rims, but occur frequently in the interiors of the large crystals (>800 μm). Plagioclase phenocrysts may contain inclusions of orthopyroxene, Fe–Ti oxide, amphibole, apatite, and glass (melt). A characteristic feature of plagioclase of the 2004–5 eruption is the occurrence and distribution of tiny orthopyroxene inclusions. They are acicular, with length-to-width ratios of ~10 or greater. Their length is variable but typically about 30 μm. Their maximum widths are on the order of 4–5 μm. Acicular orthopyroxene inclusions occur mostly in swarms and are concentrated in bands close to dissolution surfaces (figs. 3*C*, 3*D*), although they also occur independently of the surfaces (figs. 3*E*, 3*F*). Where associated with a dissolution surface, acicular orthopyroxene bands are, in most cases, inward of the dissolution surface, toward the center of the crystal (figs. 3, 4).

Compositional Features

The overall compositional range for the outer 80–100 μm of plagioclase phenocrysts in the 2004–5 dacite ranges from An_{32-38} to An_{55-60} (figs. 4, 5, 6). At or near the rim (that is, within one traverse step of ~3 μm), compositions are

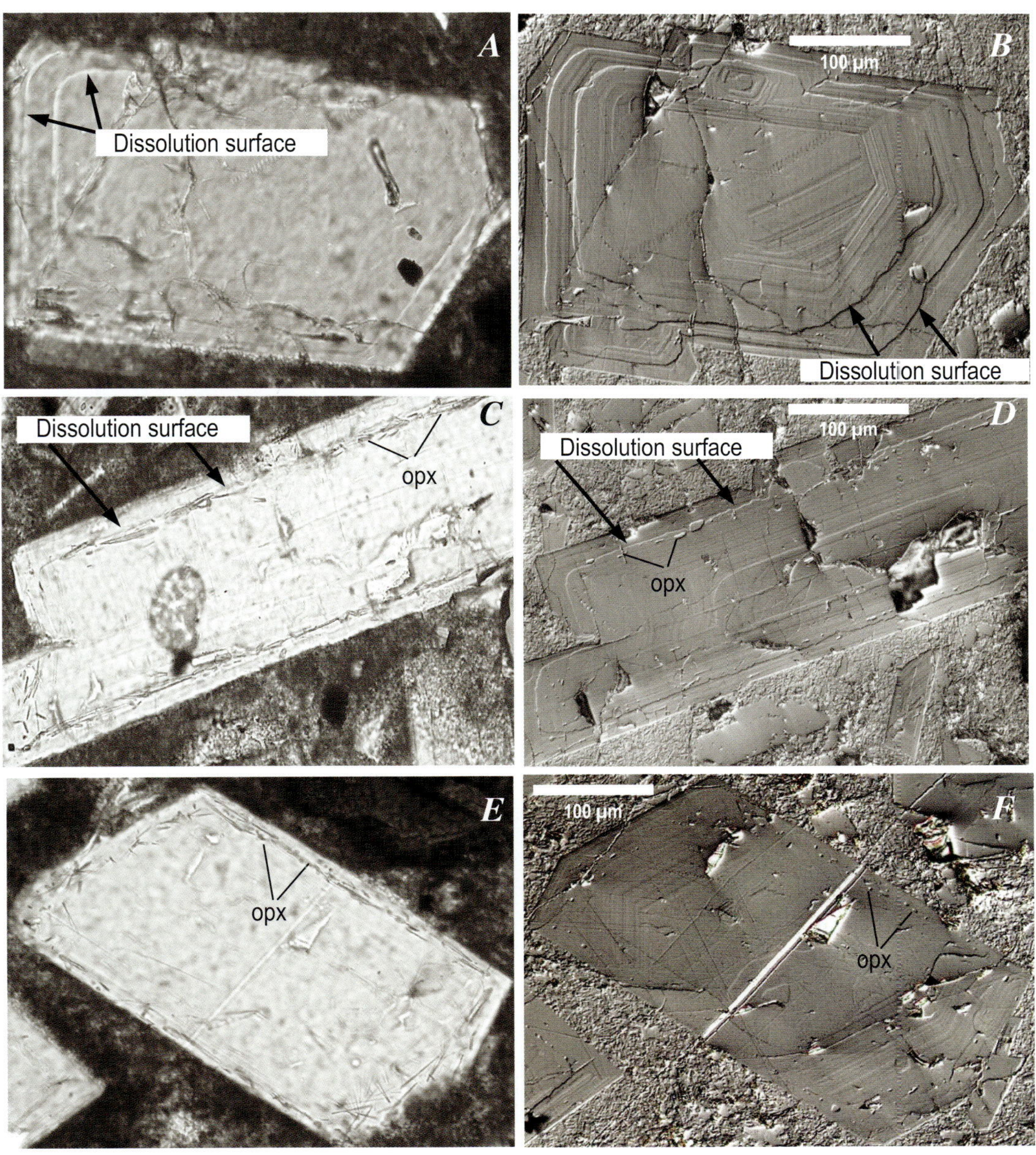

Figure 3. Plagioclase types distinguished by combination of dissolution surfaces (arrows) and presence of acicular orthopyroxene inclusions (opx). Scale bars are 100 μm. Left column, transmitted light images; right column, corresponding Nomarski differential interference contrast images. *A*, *B*, Type 1 plagioclase, with two dissolution surfaces but without acicular orthopyroxene inclusions. *C*, *D*, Type 2 plagioclase, with acicular orthopyroxene inclusions inbound of dissolution surface. *E*, *F*, Type 3 plagioclase with no dissolution surface but containing, in this example, acicular orthopyroxene inclusions near rim.

$An_{35–44}$, although $An_{37–38}$ is most common. Analyzed microphenocrysts are 10 to 50 μm in size and range from ~An_{30} to ~An_{42} (fig. 6). Compositions of microphenocrysts or at the rims of phenocrysts in 2004–5 samples have a wider range in An content than that reported for samples of 1980s dome dacite (Cashman, 1992), but one of our comparison samples of 1980–86 dome dacites (SC-99-334b; table 1, fig. 6) suggests a similar range with minima of $An_{38–40}$ and maxima of $An_{60–65}$ and outermost rim compositions of $An_{35–48}$. We exclude the large and sieve-textured plagioclase crystals from our analysis because they are thought to be derived from disaggregated plutonic or cumulate inclusions (Heliker, 1995). Contrasting with the above range in An content of phenocrysts are fairly sodic compositions of $An_{24–32}$ that we found in the interior parts of some phenocrysts. Such phenocrysts have not been reported previously from Mount St. Helens dacite. They are compositionally distinct but texturally indistinguishable from typical phenocrysts unless they contain abundant mineral inclusions (some of which are acicular). We also exclude these because we believe that the unusually sodic crystal interiors represent recycled older crystals derived from more-silicic magma (see below).

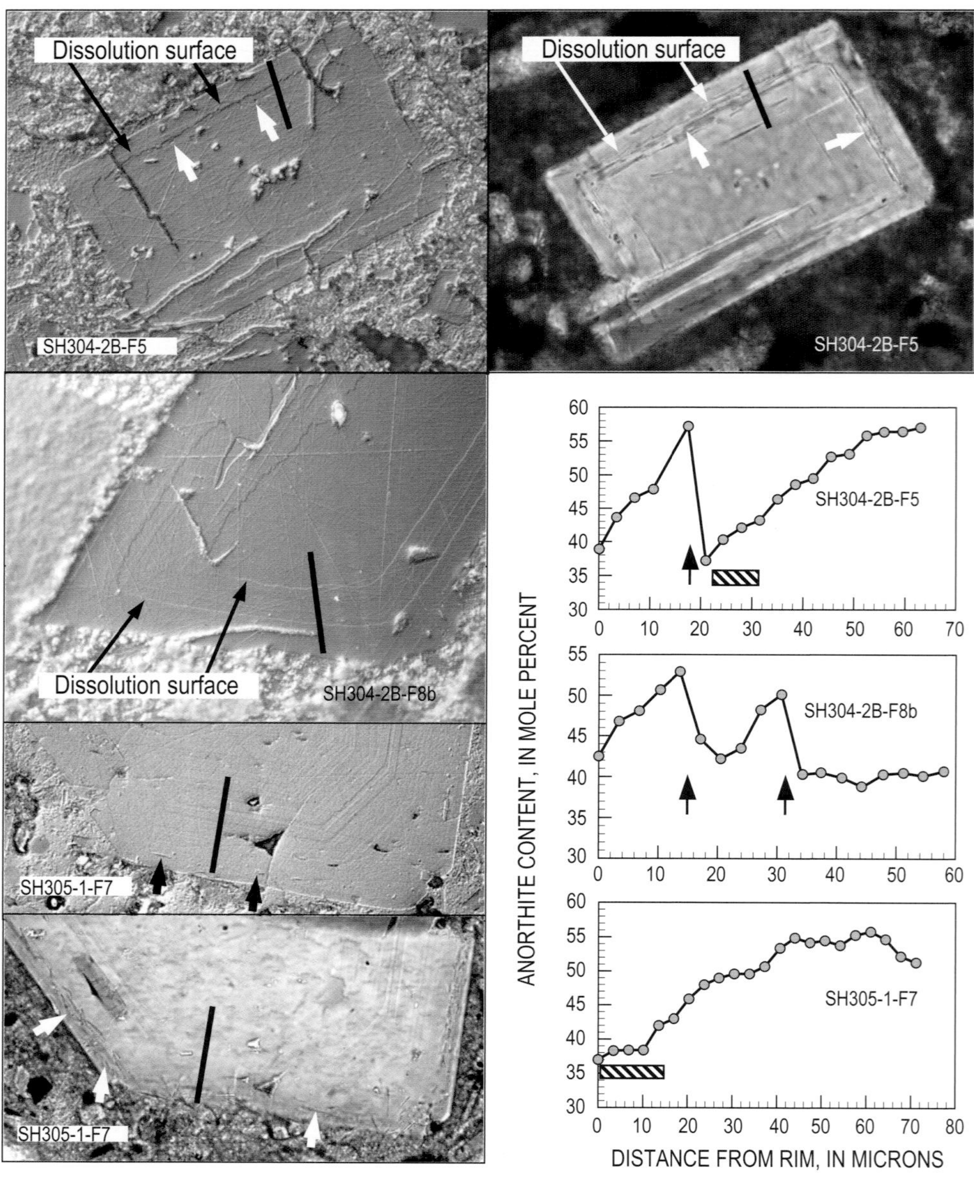

Figure 4. Correlation of textures and composition. Solid lines on Nomarski images indicate location of analytical traverses, and short arrows point to acicular orthopyroxene inclusions. Arrows in graphs indicate location of dissolution (resorption) surfaces, and bars show location of acicular orthopyroxene inclusions.

Near their rims, all plagioclase phenocrysts are compositionally normally zoned within bands that show oscillatory zoning or flat textures. We distinguish compositional from textural zoning because texturally flat areas are frequently compositionally zoned (for example, fig. 4, sample SH304-2B-F5; table 2). Band boundaries are dissolution surfaces. Band widths are variable and can be as narrow as ~10–15 µm. Some smaller crystals do not show any dissolution surface and therefore can be considered to consist of a single, broader band (about 200–300 µm). Compositional changes within a single band, regardless of width, in most cases display An decreases from 7 to 20 mol percent and thus may encompass the entire range of An variability of plagioclase in 2004–5 dacite (table 2). Compositionally uniform bands and bands with slight reverse zoning (Δ ~An_5) are rare. The initial overgrowth on a dissolution surface always has the highest An content; last growth is the lowest An content

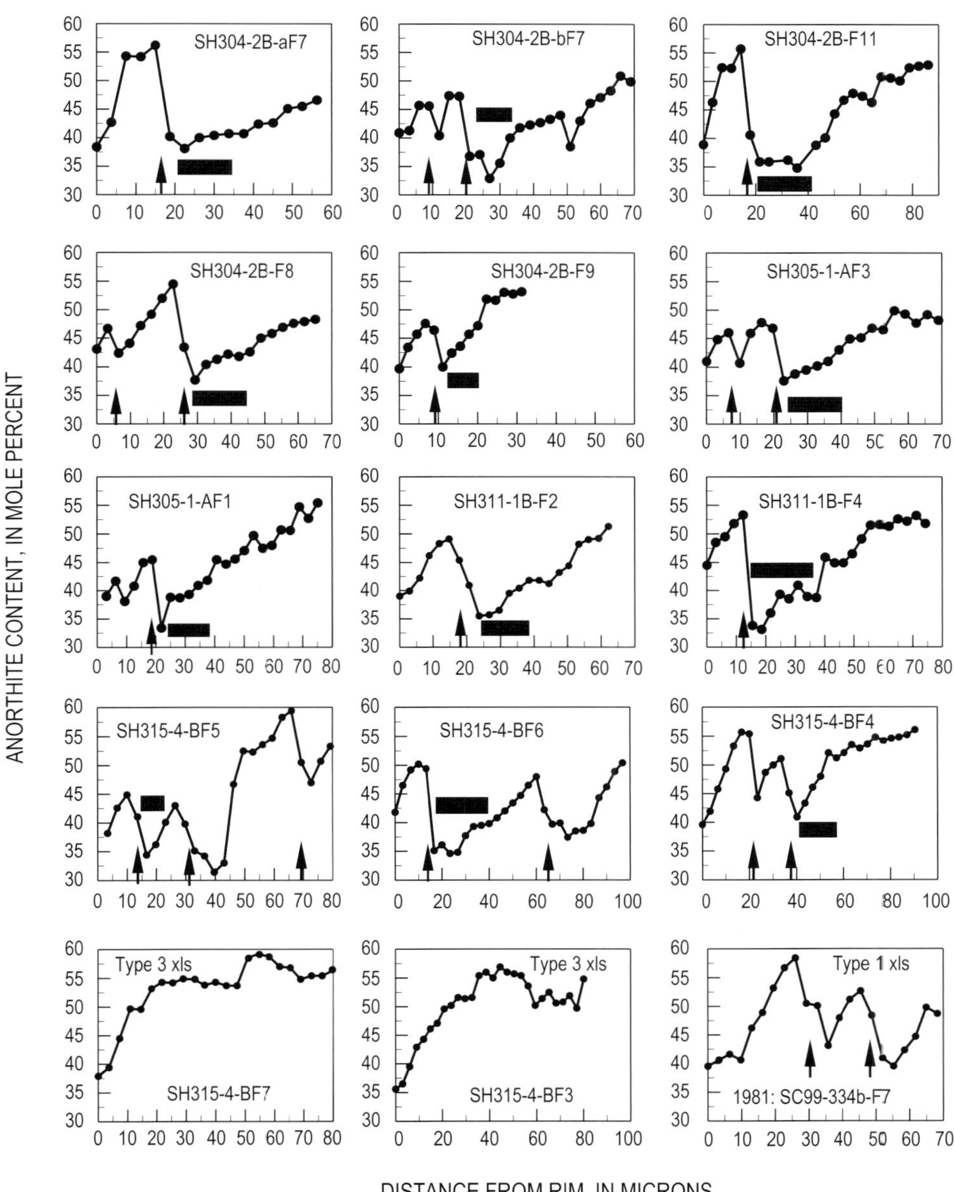

Figure 5. An profiles of Type 2 crystals—those with dissolution surfaces and acicular orthopyroxene inclusions—except bottom row, which depicts two Type 3 crystals (no resorption). Lower right, one 1981 Type 1 crystal (dissolution surface but no inclusions). Arrows indicate location of dissolution surface and bars show location of acicular orthopyroxene inclusions. Resorption is typically followed by abrupt increase in An content. Sequential growth is rimward, toward left on each graph.

within a band—a feature also observed in May 18, 1980, dacite (Pearce and others, 1987). In fact, it is an often-observed feature in volcanic plagioclase with dissolution surfaces (Pearce, 1994). Along a single analytical traverse, abrupt An increases of 5 to 25 mol percent were observed where crossing from the lowest An content of an inner band to the highest An content of the next outer band (figs. 4, 5). Thus the profiles undulate, depending on whether one or multiple dissolution surfaces exist. Rarely, overgrowth on a more interior dissolution surface can be of distinctly lower An content than inward of the dissolution surface.

Acicular orthopyroxene inclusions are consistently associated with the lower-An parts of bands. They occur where the plagioclase composition reaches An_{33-40}. The composition of acicular orthopyroxene inclusions is similar to the composition of orthopyroxene phenocrysts (table 3), although Al and perhaps Ca are slightly higher. It is uncertain whether the Ca and Al variation of acicular inclusions compared to orthopyroxene phenocrysts is significant given the spatial difficulties in analyzing small crystals embedded in plagioclase.

Crystal Mapping

The mapped crystal populations are distinguished by presence or absence of near-rim features produced by alternating growth and resorption events and by the presence or absence of acicular orthopyroxene inclusions. On the basis of these features, we can distinguish three crystal types and determine their proportions (table 1):

- Most abundant are plagioclase crystals containing one or several dissolution surfaces but lacking acicular orthopyroxene; they are designated Type 1 crystals.
- Second in abundance are plagioclase crystals that show dissolution surfaces and contain acicular orthopyroxene inclusions; they are designated Type 2 crystals. We further distinguished subcategories of Type 2 crystals according to location of the orthopyroxene inclusions with respect to dissolution surfaces: (A) inboard of last dissolution surface, (B) only associated with an older dissolution surface, (C) near the rim and not associated with a dissolution surface (that is, the dissolution surface is near the core of the crystals and orthopyroxene inclusions occur near the rim), and (D) near the crystal core and the dissolution surface is near rim.
- Least abundant are crystals lacking clearly discernible dissolution surfaces; they are designated Type 3 crystals. For the Type 3 category, we established subcategories based on whether acicular orthopyroxene inclusions are present or absent.

In some cases, categorization was difficult owing to poor crystal polish, fracturing, disadvantageous cutting of the crys-

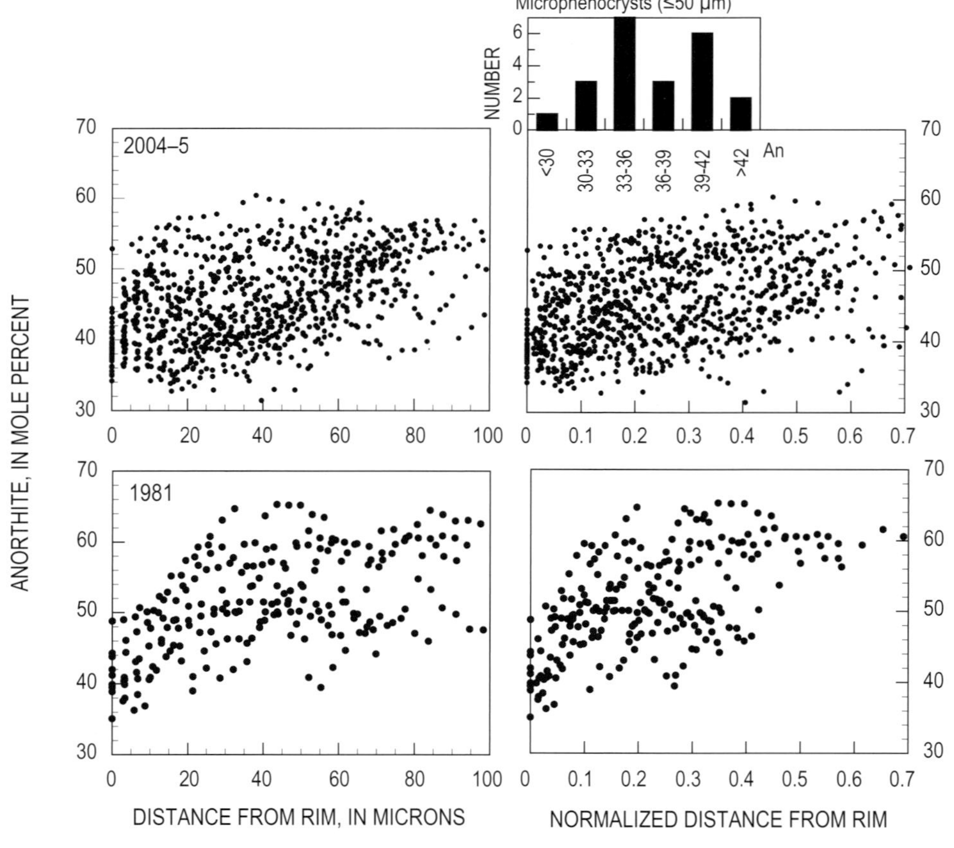

Figure 6. Anorthite content in plagioclase, showing all data of this study. Plots in left column show An content versus distance to rim; in right column, An content versus normalized distance to rim. To normalize distance to rim, we connected traverse end point at rim with center of crystals and took fraction that was covered by traverse. We projected beginning of traverse into "rim – center" line along growth zones in case where analysis traverse was not parallel to "rim – center" line. Histogram shows plagioclase composition of 22 microphenocrysts (~<50 μm) in SH321 (table 1), similar to the two observed in center and along left side of groundmass picture of sample SC99-334A shown in figure 8A. All microphenocrysts were analyzed in center and rim.

Table 2. Representative plagioclase compositions along profiles of two crystals shown in figure 4, starting at ~30 μm from the rim.

[FeO*, total iron as Fe^{2+}. Molecular components for plagioclase shown calculated: An, anorthite; Ab, albite; Or, orthoclase.]

SH304-2B-F5 (Type 2 crystal)										
Distance to rim (μm)-------	**31.5**	**28.0**	**24.5**	**21.0**	**17.5**	**14.0**	**10.5**	**7.0**	**3.5**	**0**
SiO_2	58.3	58.7	59.1	60.1	54.9	55.7	57.1	57.5	58.4	59.8
Al_2O_3	26.7	26.3	26.2	25.4	28.6	27.6	27.0	26.8	26.4	25.4
FeO*	0.29	0.28	0.34	0.30	0.50	0.48	0.47	0.48	0.45	0.49
MgO	0.01	0.01	0.02	0.02	0.04	0.04	0.04	0.03	0.03	0.02
CaO	8.7	8.5	8.2	7.5	11.6	10.6	9.7	9.4	8.8	7.8
Na_2O	6.2	6.4	6.6	6.9	4.8	5.2	5.7	5.9	6.2	6.7
K_2O	0.18	0.20	0.21	0.23	0.12	0.13	0.15	0.17	0.20	0.29
Total	100.3	100.3	100.6	100.4	100.5	99.9	100.2	100.2	100.5	100.5
An	43.2	42.1	40.4	37.2	57.2	52.6	47.9	46.6	43.7	38.8
Ab	55.7	56.8	58.3	61.4	42.1	46.7	51.3	52.4	55.1	59.5
Or	1.1	1.2	1.2	1.4	0.7	0.8	0.9	1.0	1.2	1.7

SH305-1-F7 (Type 3 crystal)										
Distance to rim (μm)------	**30.4**	**27.0**	**23.7**	**20.3**	**16.9**	**13.5**	**10.1**	**6.8**	**3.4**	**0**
SiO_2	55.5	55.6	55.8	56.5	56.8	57.5	58.0	58.1	58.7	58.9
Al_2O_3	27.8	28.1	27.8	27.2	26.9	26.7	26.2	25.5	25.7	25.8
FeO*	0.27	0.34	0.33	0.22	0.35	0.30	0.28	0.79	0.27	0.34
MgO	0.01	0.01	0.01	0.01	0.01	0.02	0.02	0.51	0.04	0.01
CaO	9.9	9.8	9.7	9.1	8.4	8.5	7.7	7.5	7.6	7.5
Na_2O	5.5	5.5	5.7	5.8	6.1	6.4	6.7	6.5	6.7	6.9
K_2O	0.14	0.14	0.16	0.19	0.18	0.19	0.23	0.22	0.23	0.25
Total	99.2	99.5	99.5	99.0	98.6	99.7	99.2	99.2	99.2	99.7
An	49.6	49.0	48.0	45.9	43.0	42.0	38.4	38.4	38.3	37.0
Ab	49.5	50.1	51.1	53.0	55.9	56.8	60.2	60.2	60.4	61.5
Or	0.8	0.8	0.9	1.1	1.1	1.1	1.4	1.3	1.4	1.5

tal leading to obliteration near the rim, and other ambiguities. Crystals that could not be categorized clearly are considered indeterminate crystals; their proportions ranged from 5 to 20 percent (table 1). In subsequent analysis, we assumed that the indeterminate crystals are proportionally distributed among the other populations and therefore normalized the other three categories to their sum to investigate changes in their proportions.

Comparing mapping results among sheets (images at × 25 magnification) that make up surveyed transects yielded standard deviations of mapped crystal types for a single thin section (table 1); 1σ standard deviations are typically on the order of 5–10 percent of the normalized abundance, and this appears to be the natural variation on the level of a single thin section, including the error associated with recognition.

An exception to Type 1 and Type 2 crystals being first and second in abundance is sample SH305-2 (lava collected Jan. 3, 2005), in which Type 3 crystals are slightly more abundant or subequal to Type 2 crystals (fig. 7).

Variations among crystal types in samples of the 2004–5 dacite indicate some trends after apparent natural variation within individual samples (based on 1σ errors) is taken into consideration. Notable are (1) an increase in the abundance of Type 3 crystals in SH305, which taper back to the level observed at the onset of the eruption at the expense of Type 1 crystals, and (2) a possible slight increase in the abundance of Type 2 crystals from SH304 through SH321. Interestingly, the increase of Type 3 crystals from SH304 (November 2004) to SH305 (January 3, 2005) correlates with an increase in magma

Table 3. Compositions of representative orthopyroxene phenocryst and acicular orthopyroxene inclusions in plagioclase phenocrysts.

[Features described as acicular inclusions are typical; those described simply as inclusions are also acicular but slightly larger. FeO*, total iron as Fe^{2+}. Molecular components for pyroxene shown calculated: En, enstatite; Fs, ferrosilite; Wo, wollastonite. Magnesium number, Mg# = (MgO×100)/(MgO+FeO*).]

	Phenocryst		Inclusion		Acicular Inclusion
	Core	Rim	Point 1	Point 2	Point 1
SiO_2	54.31	53.5	53.31	54.15	53.6
TiO_2	0.21	0.14	0.28	0.21	0.1
Al_2O_3	0.41	0.57	2.14	1.2	1.25
FeO*	21.38	23.74	20.02	20.66	23.17
MnO	0.66	0.79	0.47	0.44	0.76
MgO	23.72	21.68	23.45	23.57	22.08
CaO	0.86	0.73	1.59	1.24	0.73
En	65.3	61.0	65.5	65.4	62.0
Fs	33.0	37.5	31.4	32.2	36.5
Wo	1.7	1.5	3.2	2.5	1.5
Mg #	66.4	61.9	67.6	67.0	62.9

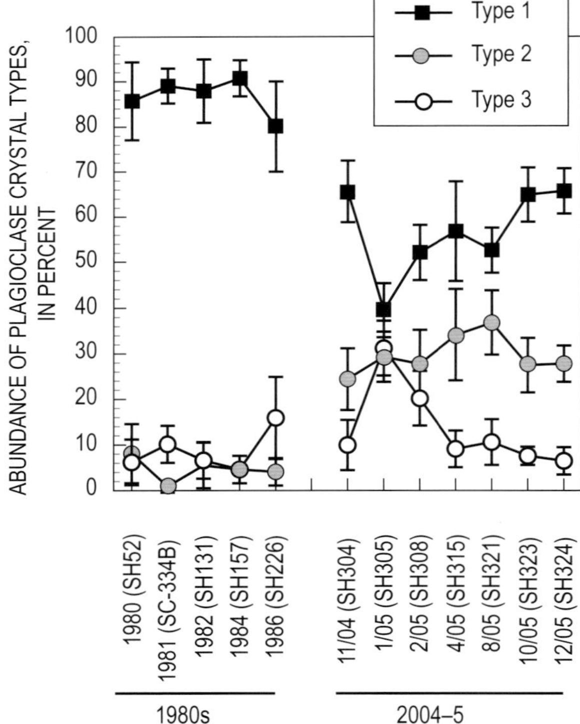

Figure 7. Proportions of different plagioclase types from crystal mapping. Bars showing 1σ error are based on variations measured among mapped sheets (25x images).

temperature as obtained from two-oxide geothermometry, whereas the tapering off to the initial abundance correlates with a drop in magma temperature in the spring of 2005 (Pallister and others, this volume, chap. 30). In other words, the sample in which crystals devoid of dissolution surfaces are most abundant is also the sample from which the highest temperature values were obtained. We will revisit this relation below.

Comparison of crystal populations of 2004–5 dacites with samples of 1980s dome dacite reveals a striking difference, even if all 2004–5 samples are averaged (fig. 7, table 1). The Type 2 crystals are sparse in 1980s dacite, which is dominated by Type 1 crystals. Type 3 crystals display comparable abundances except a temporary increase in samples collected in January and February 2005. In essence, the main difference between 2004–5 and 1980 dacites is an absence of orthopyroxene inclusions in 1980s lava.

Discussion

Acicular Orthopyroxene Inclusions as Probable Markers of Cooling Events

The presence of acicular orthopyroxene inclusions in plagioclase phenocrysts of the 2004–5 dacite is a striking feature (figs. 3, 4, 8). They are also present in plagioclase of 1980s dome dacite, although much rarer than in 2004–5 samples (table 1), and have since been observed by the first author elsewhere in andesite from Mount Hood, Oregon, and Volcán Arenal, Costa Rica. Thus, acicular orthopyroxene inclusions in plagioclase are not unique to this eruption, but their abundance and systematics of occurrence are presently unrivaled. Texturally identical orthopyroxene crystals occur in interstitial glass or groundmass in dacite of the current eruption, as well as in 1980s dome dacite (fig. 8). In particular, samples composed of interstitial glass laced by acicular orthopyroxene microlites and of scattered plagioclase microphenocrysts (<70 μm, either dimension) such as sample SH304-2G of the current eruption (Pallister and others, this volume, chap. 30) and SC99-334A (fig. 8), a 1981 sample, are important because they demonstrate that conditions exist in which interstitial melts of Mount St. Helens dacite primarily nucleate orthopyroxene that grew rapidly (as suggested by being acicular; for example, see Lofgren, 1980).

The supersaturation required to nucleate and rapidly grow orthopyroxene may be caused by a drop in temperature, by decompression associated with degassing, or by a combination of both. Samples with a more crystalline groundmass (for example, SH305-1, fig. 8) contain larger acicular orthopyroxene, which indicate that growth of acicular orthopyroxene continued as groundmass crystallinity increased. Plagioclase did not undergo a concurrent nucleation and rapid-growth event; instead of acicular crystals, equant plagioclase crystals continued to grow. Plagioclase growth in interstitial melt is strongly governed by the rate of decompression and devolatilization as magma ascends to the surface (Hammer and Rutherford,

2002). In general, rapid nucleation rate and acicular growth of plagioclase are induced by faster decompression and devolatilization rates. The occurrence of acicular groundmass orthopyroxene in the absence of acicular plagioclase in SH304-2G and SC99-334A (both representing magma seemingly saturated in orthopyroxene and plagioclase) suggests that temperature may have played an equal or more important role than decompression and devolatilization to induce supersaturation in orthopyroxene but not in plagioclase. Only slow and steady or small decompression steps are compatible with equant shapes of plagioclase microphenocrysts (Hammer and Rutherford, 2002).

An alternative interpretation, that a boundary layer enriched in orthopyroxene components rejected by growing plagioclase and subsequent local saturation and crystallization, is unlikely. A few orthopyroxene crystals may be generated this way but not the swarms of inclusions observed (fig. 8). Constant or decreasing Fe content in profiles approaching bands of orthopyroxene inclusions (fig. 8*D*) suggests no major enrichment of total Fe in the boundary layer.

In conclusion, we believe that the presence of acicular orthopyroxene in some plagioclase phenocryst bands reflects an abundance of acicular orthopyroxene microlites in the interstitial melt at the time of embedding. Therefore, acicular orthopyroxene-rich zones in plagioclase record rapid orthopyroxene-nucleation events that were probably induced in large part by rapid cooling.

Production of Near-Rim Plagioclase—an Evaluation of Processes and Natural Constraints

Cooling, decompression, compositional and volatile fluxes, and kinetic effects all may control compositional and textural features of plagioclase—although we consider kinetic effects (for example, see Pearce, 1994) at best a secondary cause for the abrupt increase of An content by more than 2–4 mol percent (for example, see Ginibre and others, 2002). It is

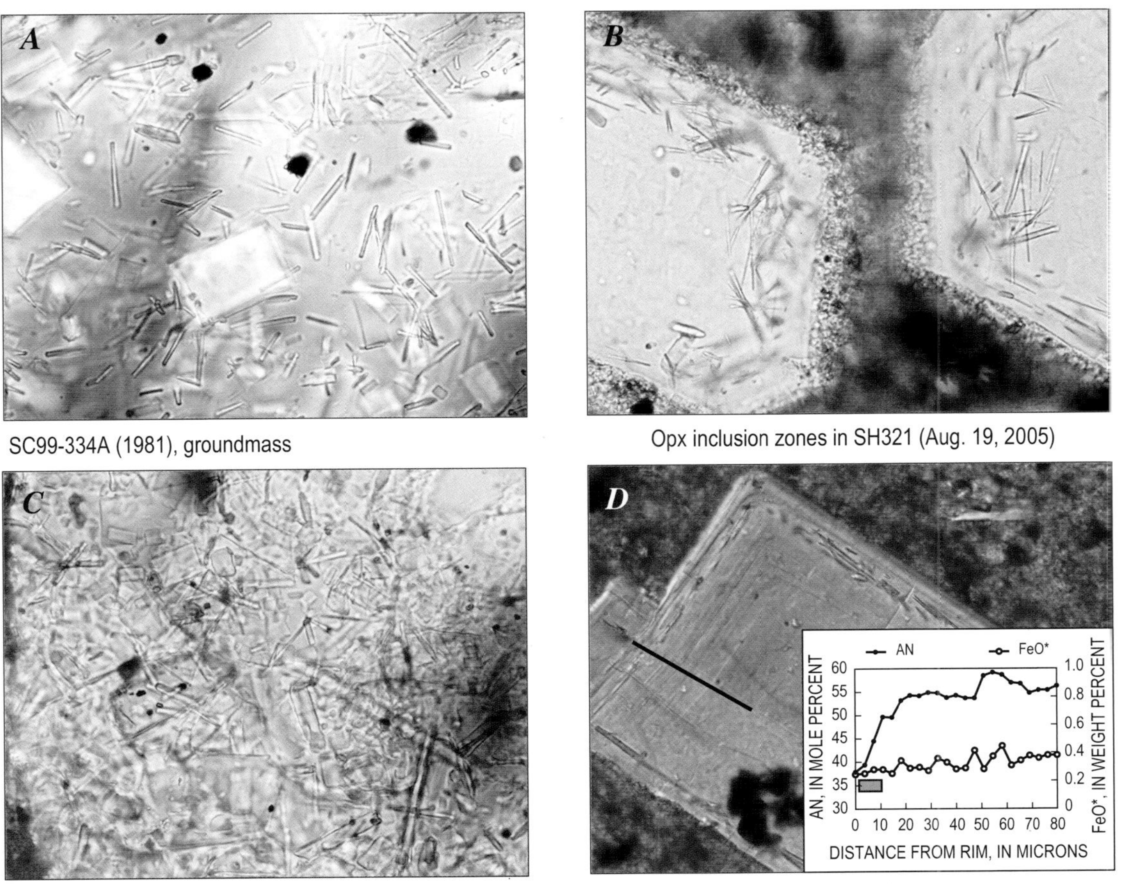

Figure 8. Occurrence of acicular orthopyroxene crystals in groundmass (*A*, *C*) and as inclusions in plagioclase (*B*, *D*). All pictures in transmitted light. *A* and *C* at x 1000 magnification, *B* at x 500 magnification, and *D* at x 200 magnification. Inset in *D* shows analysis traverse along solid line.

typically a certain combination of features that narrows down which parameter exerted greater control.

Below we make the case that the characteristic features of Types 1 and 2 crystals—multiple, normally zoned bands separated by dissolution surfaces within the outer ~80 µm of crystals, combined with marked declines in An content within variably thick bands (as thin as 10–20 µm)—are most consistent with fluctuations in crystallinity as primarily induced by temperature, with other parameters contributing in secondary roles. On the other hand, normal zoning (that is, progressive outward decrease of An content toward rim) over wider (>~50 µm) distances without dissolution surfaces—as observed in Type 3 crystals—is less constrained and may record times when other parameters such as pressure outweigh temperature changes.

If the magmatic system were closed, then higher and lower An content would imply lower or higher crystallinity, respectively, at the time of crystallization. To correlate the degree of crystallinity with a particular An content in plagioclase, we calculated melt composition at a variety of crystallinities and varied the partition coefficient, Kd (Kd = Ca/Na_{plag}/ Ca/Na_{melt}) (Sisson and Grove, 1993), to calculate equilibrium compositions of plagioclase (fig. 9). For our model calculations, we used an average bulk composition from initial analyses of November 4, 2004, dacite (SH304) as starting composition (final analyses in Thornber and others, 2008b). A fixed mineral assemblage was removed from the bulk composition to calculate interstitial melt composition. The assemblage consisted of 6 percent amphibole, 9 percent orthopyroxene, 18 percent An_{53} plagioclase, 65 percent An_{42} plagioclase, and 2 percent titanomagnetite and is based on mineral modes established for 2004–5 dacite (Pallister and others, this volume, chap. 30). Although the extraction oversimplifies any natural process, certain important features are illustrated. If SH304 ever existed as pure liquid, it would initially crystallize An_{53} (at Kd=2) to An_{75} (at Kd=5) under lower to higher water-saturated conditions, respectively (Sisson and Grove, 1993) (fig. 9). We estimate that our investigation applies to approximately the last 30–40 percent of plagioclase phenocryst crystallization (synonymous with whole-rock crystallinities above ~30 percent), as suggested by lengths of microprobe traverses combined with range of phenocryst sizes studied. Thus, the highest commonly observed An content of 55 to 60 mol percent was achieved when crystallinity of SH304 dacite was already at or near 30 percent. This crystallinity requires a minimum Kd of 3, or higher at higher crystallinities, in order to generate An_{55-60} at water-saturated conditions (fig. 9), an interpretation supported by water-saturated experimental results obtained on dacite SH305, in which conditions of 870°C and 200 MPa produced An_{50} plagioclase at a crystallinity of ~30 percent (Rutherford and Devine, this volume, chap. 31). On the other hand, an An content of 37 mol percent requires crystallinity near 50 percent, in keeping with the observation that 2004–5 dacite consists of ~45 percent groundmass (interstitial glass and/or groundmass crystals), and An_{37} is the typical rim and microphenocryst composition. As a consequence, crystals that have equally low or even lower An content further inward than at the rim (figs. 4, 5, 6) mark earlier times when crystal growth occurred at crystallinities between 50 and 60 percent.

A decrease of An content from 55 to 37 mol percent, as is observed commonly within single compositionally zoned bands, requires the following conditions or some combination thereof: (1) ~25 percent crystallization at constant Kd or (2) decreasing Kd at constant crystallinity (for example, at 40 percent crystallinity, Kd would need to decrease from ~4.5 to 2). A decrease in Kd at water-saturated conditions and a given melt composition is synonymous with a decrease in water concentration and thus decrease in P_{total} (Sisson and Grove, 1993). To explain crystals with several dissolution surfaces by changes in Kd would be problematic, as changes in Kd would need to be dramatic and cyclic. If Kd exerted a dominant control on observed An content, then a return to An_{50-55} after resorption would require a substantially higher Kd and would require the crystal to return to a greater depth (Hattori and Sato, 1996). Water-saturated experiments indicate that an increase in pressure of 60 MPa would increase An content by 5 mol percent in Mount St. Helens dacite magmas (Rutherford and Devine, this volume, chap. 31). Thus crystals with bands with An contents ≥5 mol percent higher after resorption would require a depth increase of ~2 km or more, and crystals that display several such bands would have been cycled numerous times. In fact, to

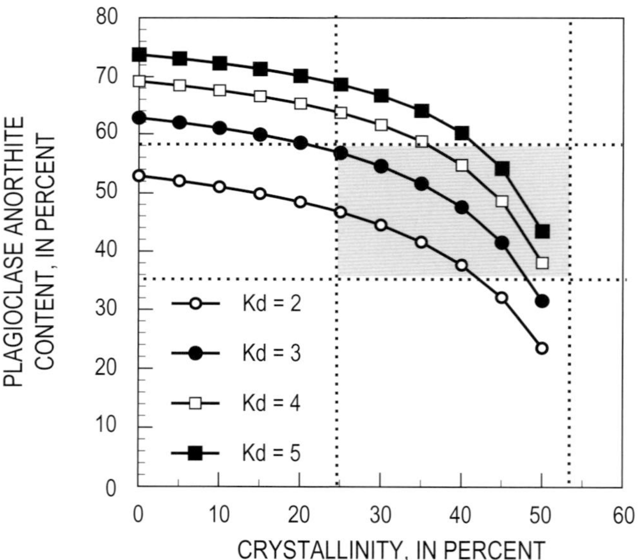

Figure 9. Variation of An content in plagioclase versus degree of crystallinity based on model calculations using variable Kd (=(Ca/Na_{plag})/(Ca/Na_{melt})), bulk composition of SH304 as starting composition (table 1), and removal of a fixed mineral assemblage (see text for details). Model simulates correlation of degree of crystallinity with plagioclase An composition in equilibrium with corresponding interstitial melt. Shaded zone marks conditions covered by this study, as suggested by lengths of microprobe traverses combined with range of phenocryst sizes investigated.

explain the entire An range of An_{55} to An_{37} would require pressure to fluctuate by 150 MPa, equivalent to a depth change of ~5.5 km (Rutherford and Devine, this volume, chap. 31).

An additional complicating factor is that once magma has reached water saturation and begins to degas at shallow depth, it will become undersaturated as it reaches greater depths unless volatiles are added to keep it saturated. If it did not gain volatiles, descent towards higher degree of undersaturation would promote crystallization as the liquidus is raised and likely would crystallize plagioclase of lower An content (for example, Blundy and Cashman, 2001). To return multiple times from An_{37} to An_{55} at a constant Kd poses comparably little difficulty. The only requirement is that crystallinity needs to fluctuate by ~25 percent or less to return to an An content of An_{55}; this could be achieved by local cooling and subsequent entrainment into more interior and hotter parts of the magmatic reservoir (Singer and others, 1995; Couch and others, 2001). In fact, Rb concentrations in melt inclusions of 1980s dacite suggest crystallinity variation by 20 percent at a constant pressure over the pressure interval from 200 to 100 MPa (Blundy and others, 2006)—the inferred pressure of the upper part of the 2004–5 magmatic reservoir (Pallister and others, this volume, chap. 30). A temperature change of about 45ºC would be needed to achieve this, consistent with experimental results showing that An_{55} plagioclase crystallizes at 890ºC and An_{37} crystallizes at 845ºC (Rutherford and Devine, this volume, chap. 31). Such temperatures are also within the range deduced from oxide geothermometry of 2004–5 dacite (Pallister and others, this volume, chap. 30) and are similar to isobaric variations deduced from plagioclase-liquid geothermometry on 1980s dacite (Blundy and others, 2006). Latent heat of crystallization (Blundy and others, 2006) may have contributed to the increase in temperature. On the other hand, magma heating by decompression-driven crystallization (Blundy and others, 2006) appears minimal above 50 MPa and is most significant from about 40 MPa to the surface. Therefore the greatest impact of latent heat is taking place at pressure significantly shallower than conditions of the magma reservoir. Consequently, variation of magma temperatures observed at pressures above 50 MPa require additional explanation (see section "New Versus 1980s Residual Magma and Evidence for Magmatic Recharge," below).

Returning to the discussion of our compositional data, alternative possibilities under conditions of an open system (that is, involving magma and (or) volatile flux into or out of the system) include: (1) an influx of higher Ca/Na magma and (2) switching between water-undersaturated and saturated conditions as the system ranges between lithostatic and hydrostatic conditions. The latter is the only instance where a decrease in P_{total} is not synonymous with decreasing depth as the system degasses under hydrostatic conditions and then is repressurized as connection to the surface ceases and the system returns to lithostatic conditions. Periodic influx (recharge) of more mafic (higher Ca/Na) magma may help to reset conditions for crystallization of a more An-rich plagioclase onto dissolution surfaces, and there is circumstantial evidence that this effect is occurring (see section "New Versus 1980s Residual Magma and Evidence for Magmatic Recharge"). Furthermore, this mechanism works in concert with the notion that abrupt near-rim decrease in An content within single bands is driven mostly by increased crystallinity owing to cooling. The other possibility—in essence reflecting shallow and periodic degassing events—has been advocated to occur at El Chichón volcano during eruption and repose cycles (Tepley and others, 2000). Degassing would promote crystallization, and resorption would then need to occur during repressurization of the system. This process may have contributed to features observed in plagioclase of the 2004–5 dacite at Mount St. Helens (see below) but cannot serve as sole explanation as clearly evidenced by juxtaposed plagioclase phenocrysts with no, single, or multiple dissolution surfaces, therefore requiring a range in the number of degassing events.

Crystal Histories and Populations

On the basis of our textural and compositional analysis, it appears that all plagioclase phenocrysts share, at best, only the last An decrease over the last 5–20 μm. Thus, it seems impossible to generate the diverse features in plagioclase described above during a single ascent in which essentially all phenocrysts grow—as is envisioned for plagioclase of the dome dacite of the 1980s (Blundy and Cashman, 2001). It appears that the only plagioclase crystals for which a single-ascent history is conceivable are crystals that display monotonically decreasing An content (our Type 3) and probably crystals that show mostly continuously decreasing An content but with a dissolution surface deeper in the core of the crystal. These could be a product of continuous crystallization driven by decompression (Blundy and Cashman, 2001). In our view, plagioclase crystals that are poorly explained by a continuous ascent-driven crystallization are those with multiple, normally zoned bands separated by dissolution surfaces. Nearly isobaric temperature fluctuations (corresponding to degree of crystallinity) could account for multiple dissolution surfaces as discussed above. On the other hand, such zonation patterns (also known as sawtooth patterns) have recently been attributed to processes of magma heating by decompression-driven crystallization (Blundy and others, 2006). As argued above, such processes are strongest at depths of less than 1 km and therefore would occur in the conduit and would impact all plagioclase during their final ascent.

In the discussion of crystal populations, two important questions concern the significance of any recognized crystal population and the significance of variations from it. The answers to both questions depend on the processes controlling the features that define crystal types, the minimal changes needed to induce these features, and the minimal distances needed to see a response to differing environmental conditions. As presented above, we based our crystal types on existence of dissolution surfaces separating growth bands and the presence of acicular orthopyroxene. This is analogous to plagioclase crystal populations established by Pearce and others (1987) for dacite of May 18, 1980. The abundance of dissolution surfaces in plagioclase from Mount St. Helens dacite and from dacite elsewhere (for example, see Pearce, 1994) suggests that these features do not require major changes in magmatic conditions but are produced rather easily. Therefore, neighboring crystals with a variable number of dissolution surfaces likely experienced different growth histories and were subsequently juxtaposed by mixing. We propose that crystals with no dissolution surface are those that were supplied to the erupting dacite magma last, whereas increasingly more complex textures, especially several zoned bands bound by dissolution surfaces, are evidence of a prolonged residency and evolution in a shallow reservoir (for example, Tepley and others, 2000). Crystals with multiple bands can be explained solely by temperature gradients and, thus, by crystallinity gradients across the reservoir, in combination with recharge by higher Ca/Na melt (fig. 10). Cycling through polybaric conditions, seemingly required to explain amphibole compositions in 2004–5 dacite (Rutherford and Devine, this volume, chap. 31), is permissible as an influence on the development of bands and zonation. However, narrow (~10–15 μm) bands with strong zonation (for example, $\Delta An \geq 10$ mol percent), which suggest rapid, back-and-forth changes in growth conditions, argue against pressure as a principal control because the required cycling through a vertical distance of several kilometers (~4 km) is unrealistic.

New Versus 1980s Residual Magma and Evidence for Magmatic Recharge

One of the main questions asked about the renewed activity at Mount St. Helens is whether dacite lava that has extruded since October 2004 is magma that was stored in the subvolcanic reservoir since Mount St. Helens erupted in 1986 or is freshly supplied magma. Bulk chemical analyses demonstrate that there are chemical differences between 1980s and 2004–5 lava; for example, SiO_2 is about 1.5–2.5 wt. percent higher in 2004–5 dacite than in most 1980s dome dacite (Pallister and others, this volume, chap. 30). Results from our crystal mapping hold clues to answering the question of new versus residual magma. The high ratio of Type 1 to Type 2 crystals in 1986 versus 2004–5 lava in general and the higher proportion of Type 3 crystals in January and February 2005 samples (table 1, fig. 7) suggest that lava extruded during the current activity is not from the same magma that was extruded during the final year of dome growth in 1986. Closed-system evolution from 1986 to today is one conceivable possibility to explain the observed differences in plagioclase phenocryst populations. Yet, any increases in Type 3 crystals in 2004–5 lava cannot be due to modification of crystals with dissolutions surfaces, which makes the higher proportion of Type 3 crystals early in the 2004–5 eruption in comparison to 1980s sample indicative of freshly supplied crystals. Furthermore, to explain increases in the ratio of Type 2 to Type 1 crystals by growth evolution since 1986, the following would be required: crystallization to trap orthopyroxene followed by some resorption, in turn followed by crystallization of more plagioclase. From the above, it seems likely that 2004–5 dacite is composed mostly of variable proportions of magmatic components that have undergone shallow evolution (that is, modified, residual magma) and components that have been added from deeper parts (new magma). In other words, various magmatic sources provided plagioclase phenocrysts to explain multiple crystal histories, and phenocrysts were juxtaposed by mixing events (additionally, crustal sources supplied xenocrystic plagioclase, but we neglect these in the discussion here).

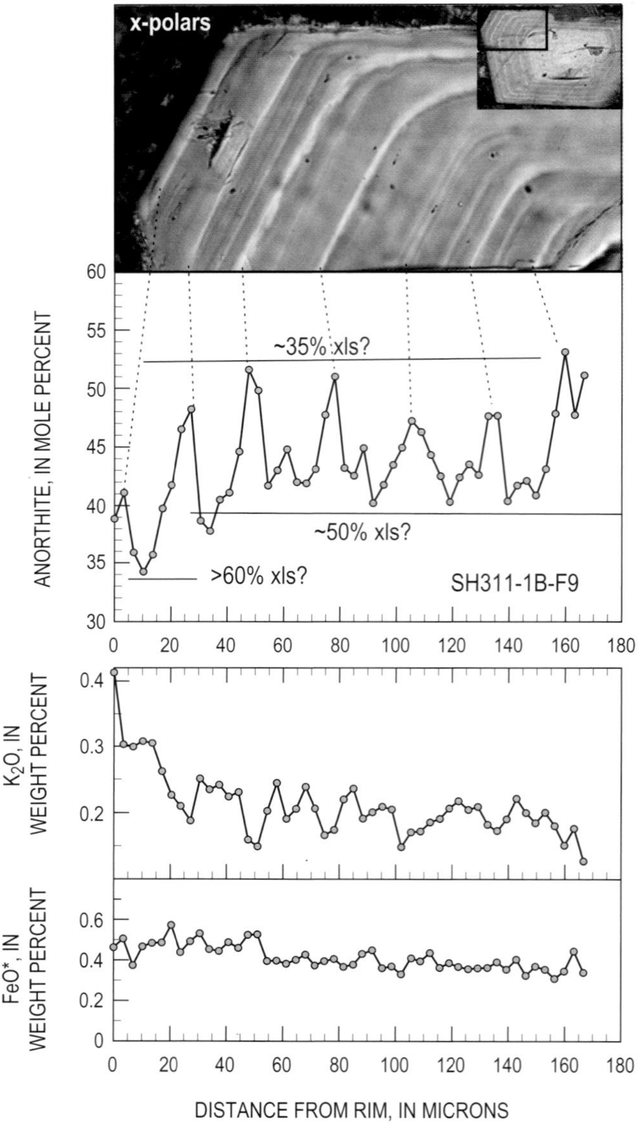

Figure 10. Analytical traverse of plagioclase SH311-1B-F9 showing multiple normally zoned bands bounded by mild dissolution (resorption) surfaces. An peaks correlate inversely with K but not with Fe. We propose that highest An contents record magmatic conditions of low crystallinities (~35 percent crystals) whereas low An contents record high crystallinities (50–60 percent crystals). FeO*, total iron as Fe^{2+}.

There is additional circumstantial evidence that the current eruption has experienced magmatic recharge by hotter magmas with more calcic melts (but not necessarily more calcic bulk composition). Assume that a magma batch undergoes closed-system crystallization to produce the same growth features in equally sized crystals. If growth were continuous, we would expect decreasing An content in the plagioclase crystals as fractional crystallization progresses and the melt fraction decreases (if crystal-melt equilibrium is not maintained). If the same system were to oscillate between higher and lower crystallinity during its course of crystallization, owing to temperature fluctuations, we would expect profiles of overall An decrease toward crystal rims but modulated by resorption and precipitation of higher-An bands (Pearce, 1994; Johannes and others, 1994). Partial plagioclase dissolution would raise the Ca/Na in the melt, and therefore initial overgrowth would be higher in An content than that before resorption. The An content of the initial overgrowth will depend on how much dissolution occurred and may be also influenced by nonequilibrium crystallization effects related to the kinetics of the system (Stewart and Fowler, 2001), but it could never return to the most calcic composition unless all plagioclase dissolved (neglecting the effect of volumetrically less significant calcic phases, for example hornblende or augite, on Ca/Na ratios). Subsequent growth would rapidly decrease An content to lower values as the system increased in crystallinity. This plagioclase response is illustrated schematically in figure 11 as profile A, which is rarely seen in plagioclase of the current

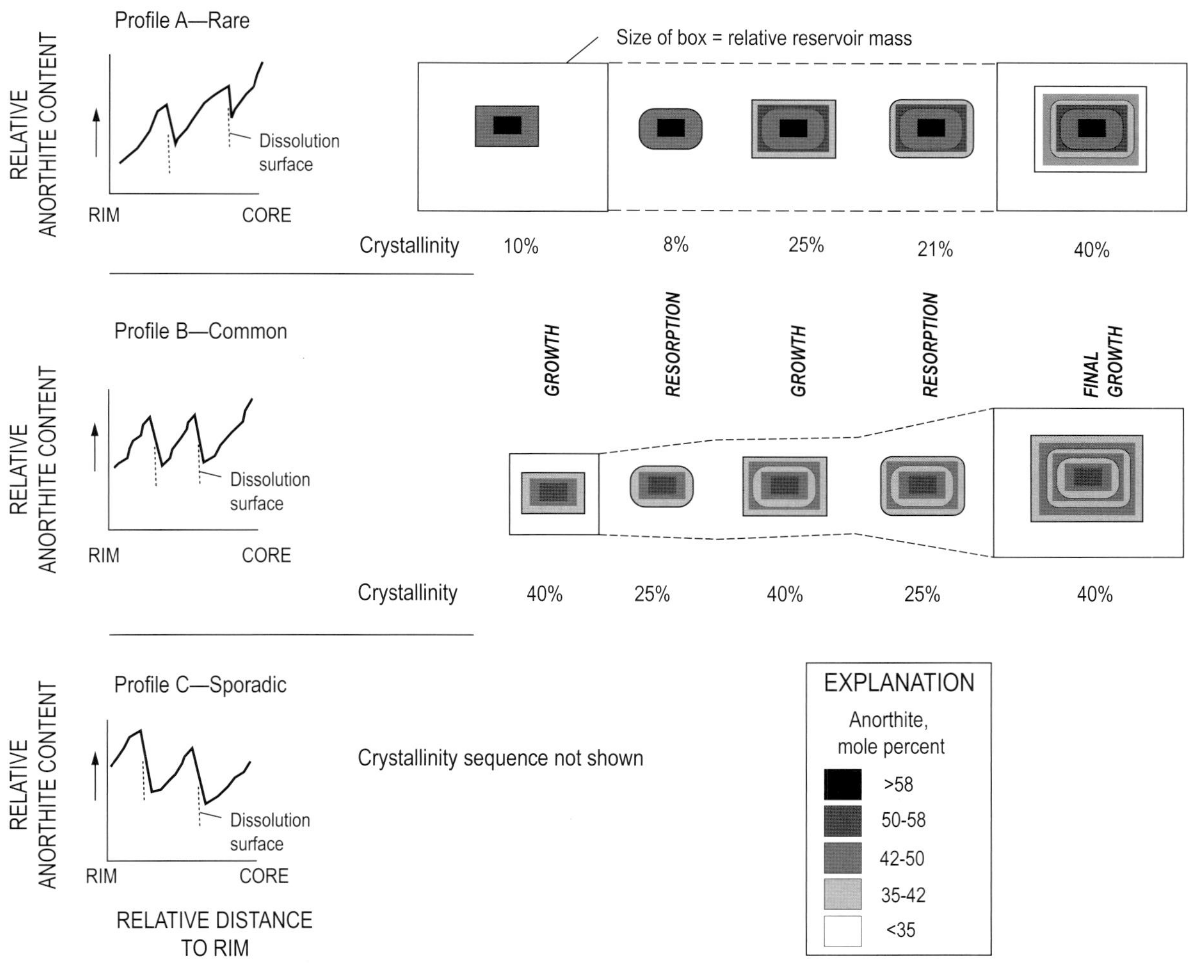

Figure 11. Schematic scenarios to produce common An profiles observed in 2004–5 plagioclase. Given An ranges shown in legend and crystallinity proportions are approximate values. To generate profile B, often observed in plagioclase of 2004–5 dacites, probably requires influx of melt (that is, an increase in reservoir mass) to buffer Ca/Na. If a closed system were to fluctuate in its degree of crystallinity due to temperature variations, profile A would be expected to result, which is only rarely observed. We therefore propose that profile B and, even more so, profile C, are likely the signs of a recharged system rather than one that is closed for magma input.

eruption but is common elsewhere (for example, Tatara dacite, see Singer and others, 1995). A common An profile among 2004–5 phenocrysts, profile B (fig. 11), shows An oscillations with minima and maxima immediately inward and outward of the dissolution surface, respectively, and the range of An content is similar over the course of crystallization (fig. 10). This constant An range is important because, as plagioclase on the whole crystallizes, the system can only produce similar An maxima if there is an influx of melt to buffer melt Ca/Na. The influx needed depends on the Ca/Na ratio in the melt that is recharged and other phases that may be crystallizing. In general, this requires an open system in which the overall crystal mass increases but where melts are buffered to produce the same An range during crystallization of multiple bands (fig. 10). Plagioclase simply convecting through a thermal regime (Singer and others, 1995) would not work because, if balanced, the amount of crystallization on a cooling path and the amount of resorption during the heating stage would not yield an overall growing crystal with return to similar An minima and maxima unless some phenocrysts grow while others are increasingly dissolved, for which evidence is lacking. Shifting crystallization to progressively lower pressures over the course of growth of multiple bands would make it increasingly more difficult to return to comparable An maxima. Plagioclase crystals with compositional profiles similar to schematic profile C (fig. 11)—with a baseline composition that is more calcic towards rim—carry even stronger evidence for an open-system behavior concurrently and (or) preceding the 2004–5 extrusion of dacite magma. The only alternate explanation for crystals to oscillate compositionally around comparable An minima and maxima or around an increasing An baseline with time during ~30 percent of plagioclase crystallization (fig. 10) appears to be decompression-driven crystallization in a heating environment (Blundy and others, 2006). However, the lack of a rim overgrowth of high An on all crystals during the last ascent of 1,000 m (that is, where this affect would be strongest; fig. 2a in Blundy and others, 2006) and the observed low An of tiny microphenocrysts of this study (for example, figs. 6, 8*A*) rather excludes the "latent-heat" explanation. We therefore take the compositional features of profiles B and C (fig. 11) as evidence for magma recharge either of hotter and less crystalline dacitic magma of similar bulk composition as the 2004–5 eruption or of more mafic, Ca-richer magma that has not yet been sampled as extruded lava. Dissolution of plagioclase from gabbroic xenoliths may help buffer Ca/Na as well, but only if the system is sufficiently hot.

Plagioclase View of the Mount St. Helens Eruption

On the basis of the discussion above, we infer the following. Subsequent to the last extrusive event in 1986, remaining dacite magma began cooling. Crystal growth was intermittent as crystals cycled through the interior, hotter parts of the reservoir/conduit system, causing resorption. Temperature gradients across the reservoir were possibly maintained by minor recharge events of deeper dacite magma, which also supplied some plagioclase phenocrysts that were subjected to the same subsequent cycles of resorption and growth as the resident crystals. Seismic evidence also suggests that recharge may have occurred in the middle to late 1990s (Moran and others, this volume, chap. 2). Prior to the renewed eruptive activity in 2004, a relatively widespread crystallization event caused growth and incorporation of acicular orthopyroxene inclusions as some magma experienced rapid cooling, possibly associated with ascent. Subsequent arrival and mixing of new dacite magma remobilized more crystalline parts of the system, causing resorption as new magma mixed with resident magma, ultimately causing the final ascent to the surface immediately or within weeks. During the final ascent, crystals grew euhedral rims. We attribute the last growth cycle—in which plagioclase of lowest An content incorporates acicular orthopyroxene inclusions, is partially resorbed, overgrown with higher An content, and subsequently normally zoned—to magmatic processes that triggered the onset of extrusion in October 2004; but it predated the eruption by months to weeks. Some (as many as three?) of the older, more interior dissolution surfaces, but still within the outer ~80 μm of crystals, may postdate the last eruption in 1986 but predate the last growth cycle. Simply zoned crystals with continuously decreasing An content (that is, Type 3 crystals) were carried by recharging dacite, grew largely in response to decompression, and thus may track the amount of recharged magma. They were stirred into the residing magma and, together with already existing phenocrysts, underwent crystallization to develop a common growth history during final ascent. Earlier recharge events may have carried similar plagioclase but, unless erupted immediately, that plagioclase was texturally modified by resorption-and-growth events, thereby losing its distinct textural character. This model is compatible with results from other petrologic studies of 2004–5 dacite (this volume: Pallister and others, chap. 30; Rutherford and Devine, chap. 31; Thornber and others, chap. 32; Cooper and Donnelly, chap. 36; Reagan and others, chap. 37).

Conclusions

We investigated plagioclase, focusing on near-rim areas of phenocrysts in dacite of the 2004–5 eruption, and compared those to plagioclase in selected dacite samples from the dome that grew in the 1980s. The results of our textural and compositional study are the following:

1. On the basis of distinguishing several plagioclase textural types in combination with a newly developed crystal mapping procedure, we show that 2004–5 dacite contains a different crystal population than 1980s dacite.

2. Observed An range of plagioclase near rim (≤80 μm) in 2004–5 dacite is An_{57-35}, and minima correspond with compositions of smallest microphenocrysts (≤20 μm) at overall crystal contents of ~50 percent. Location of

a given An composition is largely independent of the distance to the rim of crystals, except in texturally simple crystals without dissolution surfaces that are normally zoned (that is, highest An content in innermost reach and lowest An content at the rim). Crystals with dissolution surfaces possess normal zonation within bands bounded by dissolution surfaces, so that highest An content is the immediate overgrowth on a dissolution surface and lowest An content within a band is last to crystallize, leading to one or several An oscillations toward the rim.

3. Acicular orthopyroxene inclusions in plagioclase are characteristic of 2004–5 dacite, and they are consistently embedded in plagioclase with lowest An content. Orthopyroxene inclusions have textural counterparts in glassy groundmass of a rare 2004 sample and also in samples from the 1980s. The orthopyroxene occurrences suggest that inclusions in plagioclase track previous magmatic conditions at which acicular orthopyroxene crystals were temporarily abundant in interstitial melt.

4. We attribute An oscillations with comparable An minima and maxima mostly to changes in crystallinity as induced largely by temperature fluctuations in combination with recharge to maintain Ca/Na as crystallization generally progresses. Plagioclase of lowest An content and with acicular orthopyroxene inclusions may record higher crystallinity and lower temperature conditions (lower Ca/Na in melt), whereas plagioclase of highest An content overgrowing dissolution surfaces crystals may track conditions of lower crystallinity and higher temperature (higher Ca/Na in melt). Convection along a pressure gradient may aid the process through ascent-induced crystallization and descent-induced resorption. Crystals with normal An zonation and essentially no dissolution surface likely crystallized entirely in a decompressing environment.

5. The assemblage of phenocrysts with one or more growth bands composed of similar An range requires localized and repetitive processes, including mixing, to juxtapose crystals with different growth histories. Crystallization of the outermost ~5–15 µm developed during a common growth history among phenocrysts.

6. We envision a scenario in which residual 1980s magma continued to evolve subsequent to the last extrusion in 1986 and was maintained by small recharge events. A cycle of pronounced cooling/heating/cooling (possibly associated with ascent) shortly (months?) before the current eruptive activity can be inferred from the characteristic textural features of 2004–5 plagioclase, namely acicular orthopyroxene inclusions embedded prior to the last dissolution surface, which in turn was overgrown by euhedral rims. Our data are compatible with recharge-driven initiation of the current eruption and that recharged magma may also be dacitic but poorer in crystals and hotter than resident dacite into which it has been blended.

Acknowledgments

We acknowledge support for the remote-access electron microprobe laboratory at Portland State University through a National Science Foundation grant, EAR-0320863. M.J. Streck acknowledges support from the Eidgenössische Technische Hochschule (ETH) Zürich as Gastdozent (guest professor) during preparation of this manuscript and thanks W. Halter and C. Heinrich at the ETH and H.-J. Massone and T. Theye at the University of Stuttgart for their hospitality. Reviews by Maggie Mangan and Frank Tepley were very helpful and improved the paper significantly.

References Cited

Blundy, J., and Cashman, K., 2001, Ascent-driven crystallisation of dacite magmas at Mount St. Helens, 1980–1986: Contributions to Mineralogy and Petrology, v. 140, no. 6, p. 631–650, doi:10.1007/s004100000219.

Blundy, J., Cashman, K., and Humphreys, M., 2006, Magma heating by decompression-driven crystallization beneath andesite volcanoes: Nature, v. 443, no. 7107, p. 76–80, doi:10.1038/nature05100.

Cashman, K.V., 1992, Groundmass crystallization of Mount St. Helens dacite, 1980–1986; a tool for interpreting shallow magmatic processes: Contributions to Mineralogy and Petrology, v. 109, no. 4, p. 431–449, doi:10.1007/BF00306547.

Clynne, M.A., Calvert, A.T., Wolfe, E.W., Evarts, R.C., Fleck, R.J., and Lanphere, M.A., 2008, The Pleistocene eruptive history of Mount St. Helens, Washington, from 300,000 to 12,800 years before present, chap. 28 *of* Sherrod, D.R., Scott, W.E., and Stauffer, P.H., eds., A volcano rekindled; the renewed eruption of Mount St. Helens, 2004–2006: U.S. Geological Survey Professional Paper 1750 (this volume).

Cooper, K.M., and Donnelly, C.T., 2008, ^{238}U-^{230}Th-^{226}Ra disequilibria in dacite and plagioclase from the 2004–2005 eruption of Mount St. Helens, chap. 36 *of* Sherrod, D.R., Scott, W.E., and Stauffer, P.H., eds., A volcano rekindled; the renewed eruption of Mount St. Helens, 2004–2006: U.S. Geological Survey Professional Paper 1750 (this volume).

Couch, S., Sparks, R.S.J., and Carroll, M.R., 2001, Mineral disequilibrium in lavas explained by convective self-mixing in open magma chambers: Nature, v. 411, p. 1037–1039.

Gerlach, T.M., McGee, K.A., and Doukas, M.P., 2008, Emission rates of CO_2, SO_2, and H_2S, scrubbing, and preeruption excess volatiles at Mount St. Helens, 2004–2005, chap. 26 *of* Sherrod, D.R., Scott, W.E., and Stauffer, P.H., eds., A volcano rekindled; the renewed eruption of Mount St. Helens, 2004–2006: U.S. Geological Survey Professional Paper 1750 (this volume).

Ginibre, C., Kronz, A., and Wörner, G., 2002, High resolution quantitative imaging of plagioclase composition using accumulated backscattered electron images; new constraints on oscillatory zoning: Contributions to Mineralogy and Petrology, v. 142, p. 436–448.

Hammer, J.E., and Rutherford, M.J., 2002, An experimental study of the kinetics of decompression-induced crystallization in silicic melt: Journal of Geophysical Research, v. 107, no. B1, p. ECV 8-1–8-24, doi:10.1029/2001JB000281.

Hattori, K., and Sato, H., 1996, Magma evolution recorded in plagioclase zoning in 1991 Pinatubo eruption products: American Mineralogist, v. 81, p. 982–994.

Heliker, C., 1995, Inclusions in the Mount St. Helens dacite erupted from 1980 through 1983: Journal of Volcanology and Geothermal Research, v. 66, nos. 1–3, p. 115–135, doi:10.1016/0377-0273(94)00074-Q.

Herriott, T.M., Sherrod, D.R., Pallister, J.S., and Vallance, J.W., 2008, Photogeologic maps of the 2004–2005 Mount St. Helens eruption, chap. 10 *of* Sherrod, D.R., Scott, W.E., and Stauffer, P.H., eds., A volcano rekindled; the renewed eruption of Mount St. Helens, 2004–2006: U.S. Geological Survey Professional Paper 1750 (this volume).

Johannes, W., Koepke, J., and Behrens, H., 1994, Partial melting reactions of plagioclase and plagioclase-bearing systems, *in* Parsons, I., ed., Feldspars and their reactions: Dordrecht, Netherlands, Kluwer Academic Publishers, NATO Advanced Study Institute series, v. 421, p. 161–194.

Lofgren, G., 1980, Experimental studies on the dynamic crystallization of silicate melts, *in* Hargraves, R.B., ed., Physics of magmatic processes: Princeton, New Jersey, Princeton University Press, p. 478–551.

Moran, S.C., Malone, S.D., Qamar, A.I., Thelen, W.A., Wright, A.K., and Caplan-Auerbach, J., 2008, Seismicity associated with renewed dome building at Mount St. Helens, 2004–2005, chap. 2 *of* Sherrod, D.R., Scott, W.E., and Stauffer, P.H., eds., A volcano rekindled; the renewed eruption of Mount St. Helens, 2004–2006: U.S. Geological Survey Professional Paper 1750 (this volume).

Pallister, J.S., Thornber, C.R., Cashman, K.V., Clynne, M.A., Lowers, H.A., Mandeville, C.W., Brownfield, I.K., and Meeker, G.P., 2008, Petrology of the 2004–2006 Mount St. Helens lava dome—implications for magmatic plumbing and eruption triggering, chap. 30 *of* Sherrod, D.R., Scott, W.E., and Stauffer, P.H., eds., A volcano rekindled; the renewed eruption of Mount St. Helens, 2004–2006: U.S. Geological Survey Professional Paper 1750 (this volume).

Pearce, T.H., 1994, Recent work on oscillatory zoning in plagioclase, *in* Parsons, I., ed., Feldspars and their reactions: Dordrecht, Netherlands, Kluwer Academic Publishers, NATO Advanced Study Institute series, v. 421, p. 313–349.

Pearce, T.H., Russell, J.K., and Wolfson, I., 1987, Laser-interference and Nomarski interference imaging of zoning profiles in plagioclase phenocrysts from the May 18, 1980, eruption of Mount St. Helens, Washington: American Mineralogist, v. 72, p. 1131–1143.

Reagan, M.K., Cooper, K.M., Pallister, J.S., Thornber, C.R., and Wortel, M., 2008, Timing of degassing and plagioclase growth in lavas erupted from Mount St. Helens, 2004–2005, from ^{210}Po-^{210}Pb-^{226}Ra disequilibria, chap. 37 *of* Sherrod, D.R., Scott, W.E., and Stauffer, P.H., eds., A volcano rekindled; the renewed eruption of Mount St. Helens, 2004–2006: U.S. Geological Survey Professional Paper 1750 (this volume).

Rutherford, M.J., and Devine, J.D., III, 2008, Magmatic conditions and processes in the storage zone of the 2004–2006 Mount St. Helens dacite, chap. 31 *of* Sherrod, D.R., Scott, W.E., and Stauffer, P.H., eds., A volcano rekindled; the renewed eruption of Mount St. Helens, 2004–2006: U.S. Geological Survey Professional Paper 1750 (this volume).

Singer, B.S., Dungan, M.A., and Layne, G.D., 1995, Textures and Sr, Ba, Mg, Fe, K, and Ti compositional profiles in volcanic plagioclase; clues to the dynamics of calc-alkaline magma chambers: American Mineralogist, v. 80, p. 776–798.

Sisson, T.W., and Grove, T.L., 1993, Experimental investigations of the role of H_2O in calc-alkaline differentiation and subduction zone magmatism: Contributions to Mineralogy and Petrology, v. 113, p. 143–166.

Stewart, M.L., and Fowler, A.D., 2001, The nature and occurrence of discrete zoning in plagioclase from recently erupted andesitic volcanic rocks, Montserrat: Journal of Volcanology and Geothermal Research, v. 106, p. 243–253.

Tepley, F.J., III, Davidson, J.P., Tilling, R.I., and Arth, J.G., 2000, Magma mixing, recharge and eruption histories recorded in plagioclase phenocrysts from El Chichón volcano, Mexico: Journal of Petrology, v. 41, no. 9, p. 1397–1411, doi:10.1093/petrology/41.9.1397.

Thornber, C.R., Pallister, J.S., Lowers, H.A., Rowe, M.C., Mandeville, C.W., and Meeker, G.P., 2008a, Chemistry, mineralogy, and petrology of amphibole in Mount St. Helens 2004–2006 dacite, chap. 32 *of* Sherrod, D.R., Scott, W.E., and Stauffer, P.H., eds., A volcano rekindled; the renewed eruption of Mount St. Helens, 2004–2006: U.S. Geological Survey Professional Paper 1750 (this volume).

Thornber, C.R., Pallister, J.S., Rowe, M.C., McConnell, S., Herriott, T.M., Eckberg, A., Stokes, W.C., Johnson Cornelius, D., Conrey, R.M., Hannah, T., Taggart, J.E., Jr., Adams, M., Lamothe, P.J., Budahn, J.R., and Knaack, C.M., 2008b, Catalog of Mount St. Helens 2004–2007 dome samples with major- and trace-element chemistry: U.S. Geological Survey Open-File Report 2008–1130, 9 p., with digital database.

A Volcano Rekindled: The Renewed Eruption of Mount St. Helens, 2004–2006
Edited by David R. Sherrod, William E. Scott, and Peter H. Stauffer
U.S. Geological Survey Professional Paper 1750, 2008

Chapter 35

Trace Element and Pb Isotope Composition of Plagioclase from Dome Samples from the 2004–2005 Eruption of Mount St. Helens, Washington

By Adam J.R. Kent[1], Michael C. Rowe[2], Carl. R. Thornber[3], and John S. Pallister[3]

Abstract

We report the results of in-situ laser ablation ICP–MS analyses of anorthite content, trace-element (Li, Ti, Sr, Ba, La, Pr, Ce, Nd, Eu, Pb) concentrations, and Pb-isotope compositions in plagioclase from eight dome-dacite samples collected from the 2004–5 eruption of Mount St. Helens and, for comparison, from three dome samples from 1981–85. For 2004–5 samples, plagioclase phenocrysts range in composition from An_{30} to An_{80}, with the majority An_{42}–An_{65}. With the exception of Li, the range of trace-element abundances in plagioclase phenocrysts is largely constant in material erupted between October 2004 and April 2005 and is broadly consistent with the 1983–85 dome samples. Anomalously high Li contents in the early stage of the eruption are thought to reflect addition of Li to the upper part of the magma chamber immediately before eruption (within ~1 year) by transfer of an alkali-enriched, exsolved vapor from deep within the magma chamber. Other trace elements show significant correlations (at >99 percent confidence limits) with anorthite content in plagioclase phenocrysts—Ba, light rare-earth elements (LREE), and Pb show positive correlations, whereas Ti and Sr correlate negatively. Variations in plagioclase-melt partitioning as a function of anorthite content cannot explain trace-element variations—in particular predicting trends for Ti and Sr opposite to those observed. A simple model involving closed-system fractional crystallization of plagioclase + hypersthene + amphibole + oxides largely reproduces the observed trends. The model requires no gain or loss of plagioclase and is consistent with the lack of europium anomalies in bulk dacite samples. Analytical traverses within individual plagioclase phenocrysts support this model but also point to a diversity of melt compositions present within the magma storage zone in which plagioclase crystallized.

Plagioclase crystals from gabbronorite inclusions in three dacite samples have markedly different trace-element and Pb-isotope compositions from those of plagioclase phenocrysts, despite having a similar range of anorthite contents. Inclusions show some systematic differences from each other but typically have higher Ti, Ba, LREE, and Pb and lower Sr and have lower $^{208}Pb/^{206}Pb$ and $^{207}Pb/^{206}Pb$ ratios than coexisting plagioclase phenocrysts. The compositions of plagioclase from inclusions cannot be related to phenocryst compositions by any reasonable petrologic model. From this we suggest that they are unlikely to represent magmatic cumulates or restite inclusions but instead are samples of mafic Tertiary basement from beneath the volcano.

Introduction

Samples obtained from the 2004 eruption of Mount St. Helens provide an invaluable sample suite for application of petrological and geochemical techniques to examine the eruption of a silicic volcano. A wide range of approaches are detailed in this volume, and they provide valuable insight for monitoring of active and erupting volcanoes and for elucidating past eruptive histories on the basis of examination and analysis of eruptive materials.

This study reports measurements of trace-element abundances and Pb-isotope compositions in plagioclase from dome material erupted at Mount St. Helens from October 2004 to April 2005. The goals of the study are to apply the techniques of trace-element and isotope geochemistry to better

[1] Department of Geosciences, 104 Wilkinson Hall, Oregon State University, Corvallis, OR 97331

[2] Department of Geosciences, 104 Wilkinson Hall, Oregon State University, Corvallis, OR 97331; now at Department of Geoscience, 121 Trowbridge Hall, University of Iowa, Iowa City, IA 52242

[3] U.S. Geological Survey, 1300 SE Cardinal Court, Vancouver, WA 98683

understand origin and evolution of magma produced by the current eruption, as well as to demonstrate the utility of in-situ trace-element analyses by using laser-ablation inductively coupled plasma mass spectrometry (LA–ICP–MS) in petrological volcano-monitoring applications. The rapidity of this technique and relatively simple sample-processing requirements mean that, in the future, LA–ICP–MS could yield trace-element analyses of volcanic products on short time scales, providing an additional tool for monitoring anticipated and ongoing volcanic eruptions. Rowe and others (this volume, chap. 29) report on the application of these same techniques to document the chemistry of ash samples.

Samples and Methods

Samples

We have analyzed plagioclase in eight different dome samples collected between October 2004 and April 2005 and in a smaller number of plagioclase phenocrysts from three samples of earlier dome material erupted in September 1981 (SH100), May–June 1983 (SH141), and May 1985 (SH187) (table 1). Textural and compositional information from plagioclase is commonly used to elucidate the compositions of volcanic rocks (for example, Pearce and Kolisnik, 1990; Zellmer and others, 2003; Triebold and others, 2005; Browne and others, 2006; Streck and others, this volume, chap. 34). Our decision to concentrate on analysis of plagioclase reflects both the ubiquity of this mineral in all erupted products (typically ~80 percent of all crystalline phases and ~40 percent of the rock as a whole), as well as the observed textural diversity of plagioclase in dome samples. Plagioclase analyses, in conjunction with information on plagioclase-melt partition coefficients, also have the potential to act as a monitor of magma chemistry during crystallization (for example, Bindeman and others, 1998; Browne and others, 2006). In most of these samples, widespread groundmass crystallization makes direct analysis of liquid compositions difficult or impossible. Most dome samples contain little glass for analysis and, even where glass is found, it generally occurs only in restricted interstitial locations and has been clearly affected by late crystallization of groundmass phases. Our data supplement the extensive whole-rock geochemical datasets available for these samples (Pallister and others, this volume, chap. 30).

Textural Classification

Studies of the Mount St. Helens dacite have shown some textural complexity in plagioclase and other crystalline phases (for example, Streck and others, this volume, chap. 34). However, in general, many of these features are observed at scales smaller than the 50–70-μm spatial resolution of the laser-ablation analysis used in this study. For this reason we have adopted a simplified textural classification for use with

Table 1. Details of samples analyzed for this study.

[Estimates of eruption date are discussed in Pallister and others (this volume, chap. 30). Inclusions are from sample listed immediately above.]

Sample No.	Collection date	Estimated eruption date	Sample type	Number of analyses
2004–2005				
SH300-1A	10/20/04	<1986	Dacite dome	13
SH304-2A	11/4/04	10/18/04	Dacite dome	35[1]
SH304-2C	11/4/04	10/18/04	Dacite dome	17
Inclusion			Gabbronorite	15
SH305-1	1/3/05	11/20/04	Dacite dome	28
SH305-2	1/3/05	11/20/04	Dacite dome	10
Inclusion			Gabbronorite	10
SH306-1	1/14/05	12/15/04	Dacite dome	22
Inclusion			Gabbronorite	17
SH311-1	1/19/05	01/16/05	Dacite dome	17
SH315-1	4/19/05	04/1/05	Dacite dome	19
1981–85				
SH 100	9/8/81	September 1981	Dacite dome	6
SH 141	6/27/83	May–June 1983	Dacite dome lobe	8
SH 187	6/6/89	May 1985	Dacite dome	14

[1] Does not include 54 analyses from grain traverses.

2004–5 dome samples. This classification is also applicable to grains when polished sample mounts were viewed in reflected light. Most plagioclase occurs as euhedral or subhedral, equant to tabular phenocrysts less than 2 mm long. These display many of the features common in plagioclase phenocrysts from silicic magma, such as oscillatory zoning, spongy-textured zones, entrapment of melt inclusions, and some breakage of grains due to flow processes; but rounding of grains and resorbed zones are relatively uncommon. We refer herein to these crystals as plagioclase phenocrysts and interpret them as the result of crystallization of plagioclase directly from melt.

Plagioclase also is present in numerous crystal-rich inclusions in many recent Mount St. Helens lavas (Heliker, 1995). These generally are referred to as gabbroic inclusions, although many actually have gabbronoritic or noritic compositions and may be hornblende rich. Inclusions from the 2004–5 dacite appear similar to gabbroic and noritic inclusions from the 1980–86 dacite documented by Heliker (1995). In the 2004–5 dome material, inclusions occur in most recovered samples, although they are more abundant in some than others (for example, SH304-2C). We analyzed three hornblende-bearing gabbronorite inclusions from different samples (table 1) for this study. In these, plagioclase is relatively coarse (long axis as much as several millimeters) and subhedral to anhedral in form. Evidence of melt reaction and resorption is common along grain boundaries, suggesting that the inclusions are melting or reacting with the melt that transports them (Heliker, 1995). In thin sections, the inclusions can be seen to be in the process of actively disaggregating. Disaggregation results in a third textural type of plagioclase that we refer to as disaggregated inclusions. Plagioclase crystals of this type occur isolated within the groundmass and are typically much larger than phenocrysts, as large as several millimeters, are subhedral or anhedral, and commonly show indications of significant resorption, disruption of zoning, and/or growth of new plagioclase on rims.

Analytical Methods

Samples were prepared for analysis by selecting small (~5–20 mm) pieces of dome lava from each sample and setting these in 25-mm-diameter epoxy mounts. In most cases, material was chosen because it was macroscopically representative of the larger sample, although in some cases pieces were selected to sample coarse-grained gabbroic inclusions. Once mounted in epoxy, samples were ground down several millimeters to expose the inside of the selected dacite piece by using coarse (240) grit paper before polishing with 300–600 grit paper and, finally, a 1-μm alumina powder and water slurry. Samples were then cleaned for ~5 minutes in distilled water in an ultrasonic bath, and mounts were photographed in reflected light and examined using backscattered electron imagery before analysis.

Trace-element measurements were made by LA–ICP–MS. All measurements were made in the W.M. Keck Collaboratory for Plasma Mass Spectrometry at Oregon State University using a DUV 193 nm ArF Excimer laser and a VG ExCell quadrupole ICP–MS. A general outline of the analytical techniques used for this instrument is given in Kent and others (2004a) and Kent and Ungerer (2006). Ablation was conducted under a He atmosphere, and He also was used to sweep resulting particulate into the ICP–MS at a flow rate of ~0.75 L/min.

During LA–ICP–MS, ~20–25 trace-element and internal-standard isotope masses were monitored (Kent and others, 2004a). Before each ablation, count rates were measured at each mass for 45 s to determine background count rates; these were then directly subtracted from the rates measured during ablation to account for the instrumental background. Following ablation, 45 s was allowed to elapse for signal washout before starting the next analysis. For all trace-element analyses the laser was held stationary relative to the sample so progressive ablation produced a circular crater. Ablation rates in silicate glasses and minerals are on the order of 0.1–0.2 μm per pulse, and a full ablation thus produced a crater 20–30 μm deep and resulted in ablation of ~100–400 ng of material. Two different analytical approaches were taken. First, in order to document trace-element variations between plagioclase phenocrysts and between these and plagioclase in gabbroic inclusions, a large number of analyses of plagioclase from multiple samples were made using 50–80-μm-diameter laser spots. During LA–ICP–MS analysis, detection limits depend largely on the rate at which material is removed, and these spot sizes provided sufficiently low detection limits to enable analysis of a range of trace elements (see below). Samples underwent ablation for 30–40 s with a laser pulse rate of 4 Hz. In addition, for sample SH304-2A a number of selected grains were analyzed along core-rim traverses using a smaller spot size (20 μm) and 7-Hz pulse rate. The smaller spot size allowed consistent detection of only the most abundant trace elements (Li, Ti, Sr, Ba, La, and Ce), but it provided higher spatial resolution to allow study of trace-element variations during progressive plagioclase crystallization. Plagioclase textures and major-element compositions of the same crystals analyzed in the trace-element traverse also were investigated using techniques similar to those detailed in Rowe and others (this volume, chap. 29) with backscattered electron imagery and wavelength-dispersive analysis using a Cameca SX-100 electron microprobe (EMPA).

Before calculation of trace-element abundances, background intensities for each mass were subtracted directly from those measured during ablation, and signals during ablation were only considered to be above background if they were greater than the background count rate plus three standard deviations (calculated from counting statistics). Estimates of minimum detection limits are: <1.5 μg/g for Ti and Li; <0.4 μg/g for Ba, and Rb; <0.1 μg/g for V, Sr, and Nd; and <0.05 μg/g for Y, Zr, Nb, Cs, La, Ce, Pr, Sm, Eu, Pb, Th, and U. In general, only Li, Ti, Sr, Ba, the light rare-earth elements (LREE: La, Ce, Pr, Nd), Eu, and Pb were consistently detectable, and we have restricted our study to these elements. Trace-element abundances were calculated with reference to NIST 612 glass with ^{29}Si as the internal standardizing isotope. Calculation of trace-element abundances required independent knowledge of the average SiO_2 content of each ablation volume, although in zoned plagioclase this may vary on spatial scales smaller than the laser spot size. For this reason, SiO_2 contents were determined directly from LA–ICP–MS analysis by exploiting the stoichiometric relation between anorthite content, CaO/SiO_2, and SiO_2 contents in plagioclase. Measured $^{43}Ca^+/^{29}Si^+$ ratios from plagioclase were converted to CaO/SiO_2 ratios by using the measurement of NIST 612 and application of equation 1:

$$\left(\frac{CaO}{SiO_2}\right)^{Calculated}_{Plagioclase} = \frac{\left(\frac{CaO}{SiO_2}\right)^{Known}_{NIST\_612}}{\left(\frac{^{43}Ca^+}{^{29}Si^+}\right)^{Measured}_{NIST\_612}} \times \left(\frac{^{43}Ca^+}{^{29}Si^+}\right)^{Measured}_{Plagioclase}, \quad (1)$$

where

$\left(\frac{CaO}{SiO_2}\right)^{Calculated}_{Plagioclase}$ is the calculated CaO/SiO_2 of the unknown plagioclase (with oxides in weight percent),

$\left(\frac{CaO}{SiO_2}\right)^{Known}_{NIST\_612}$ is the known CaO/SiO_2 of NIST 612 (we used 0.1594; Pearce and others 1997),

$\left(\frac{^{43}Ca^+}{^{29}Si^+}\right)^{Measured}_{NIST\_612}$ is the measured $^{43}Ca^+/^{29}Si^+$ ratio from NIST 612, and

$\left(\frac{^{43}Ca^+}{^{29}Si^+}\right)^{Measured}_{Plagioclase}$ is the measured $^{43}Ca^+/^{29}Si^+$ ratio in the unknown plagioclase.

We then calculated anorthite and SiO_2 contents of plagioclase from measured CaO/SiO_2 using equations 2 and 3:

$$SiO_2 = 36.02 \times \left(\frac{CaO}{SiO_2}\right)^{Calculated}_{Plagioclase} + 67.82\ , \qquad (2)$$

and

$$An = 2.25 \times \left(\frac{CaO}{SiO_2}\right)^{Calculated}_{Plagioclase} + 0.019. \qquad (3)$$

Equations 2 and 3 are based on empirical relations observed for Mount St. Helens plagioclase from electron microprobe analyses (M.C. Rowe and A.J.R. Kent, unpub. data, 2005) and are close to the those expected from stoichiometric considerations.

Results of measurement of USGS BCR-2G standard glass using the above protocol are shown in appendix 1. We also show CaO/SiO_2 ratios for these glasses calculated from equation 1, and these ratios are within uncertainty of the reported composition of this glass. In general, measured values agree closely with accepted values, and nearly all elements are within ± 5–10 percent of the accepted values.

One test of this analytical procedure is the comparison between anorthite contents measured by EMPA and LA–ICP–MS along the traverses in five plagioclase grains in sample SH304-2A (figs. 1, 2; appendix 2). Overall, there is good agreement between the two techniques, and where differences are apparent, they are most likely because the analyzed volume for LA–ICP–MS is significantly greater than the analyzed volume for EMPA. On the basis of reproducibility of CaO/SiO_2 ratios in BCR-2G, we believe that uncertainties in measured anorthite contents are ±5 percent mole fraction. Overall, we estimate uncertainties in trace-element measurements in plagioclase as $\leq$10 percent (at 2σ) for Sr, Ti, Ba, La, and Ce and $\leq$15–20 percent for Nd, Eu, Pb, and Li. Spot compositions of other Mount St. Helens plagioclase from 1981–85 and 2004–5 are given in appendix 3.

Lead isotope compositions of plagioclase phenocrysts, plagioclase in gabbroic inclusions, and groundmass were analyzed by laser-ablation multicollector ICP–MS (LA–MC–ICP–MS), using a NuPlasma multicollector ICP–MS at Oregon State University. Measurements were made using the same laser systems described above and using 80–100 μm laser spot size, pulse rate of 10–15 Hz, and a lateral translation rate of 5 μm/s. Individual measurements involved from three to five blocks, with each block consisting of two separate 10-s measurements, generally resulting in ablation along a track length of 300–500 μm. For measurement of groundmass composition, a relatively finely crystallized region was chosen and the laser spot simply was translated across the region while using the same ablation conditions. Although this produced some variation in signal intensity, the generally higher Pb content of this material resulted in data of relatively high quality. For most samples, signal intensity was too low (<<100 mV total Pb) to enable sufficiently precise measurement of the minor isotope ^{204}Pb, and thus we report only $^{208}Pb/^{206}Pb$ and $^{207}Pb/^{206}Pb$ ratios (appendix 1).

All ion beams were measured using Faraday collectors. Instrument mass bias was corrected by frequent measurement of NIST 612 and NIST 610 glass and by using the measured $^{208}Pb/^{206}Pb$ ratio to apply an exponential mass-bias correction to Pb-isotope ratios measured in unknown samples. Ratios of 2.1694 and 2.1651 for $^{208}Pb/^{206}Pb$ were measured by Baker and others (2004) in NIST 610 and NIST 612 and were used as the correct composition of this glass. Backgrounds were corrected by on-peak zero measurements for 30 s without the laser firing prior to analysis, with measured signals directly subtracted from signals measurement during ablation. Precision for individual analyses is strongly dependent on signal size and Pb abundance but is generally better than 0.2 percent for $^{208}Pb/^{206}Pb$ and $^{207}Pb/^{206}Pb$ ratios. Analysis of the BCR-2G glass standard gave results that are well within uncertainty of measurements made using solution techniques (Paul and others, 2005).

Results

Measured anorthite content for all plagioclase types ranges between An_{30} and An_{80}, with most between An_{42} and An_{68} (figs. 2, 3). Anorthite contents of plagioclase phenocrysts and those present within gabbroic inclusions show considerable overlap, although inclusions appear to show a somewhat more restricted range of compositions and may range to more anorthite-rich compositions (for example, grain 1 in fig. 2). Significant variations are evident in trace-element abundances in plagioclase, even where these are from the same sample, although the range of trace-element abundances from plagioclase phenocrysts from each sample is broadly similar, with the exception of Li. Lithium contents for dome samples erupted in October and November 2004 are consistently higher than those from subsequently erupted material (fig. 4; Kent and others, 2007; Rowe and others, this volume, chap. 29). Our results for plagioclase phenocrysts are indistinguishable from the composition of a smaller number of samples from the 1981–86 dome complex (fig. 3) and from sample SH300-1A, which is also considered to be a part of the 1980s dome complex pushed ahead of new erupting magma (Pallister and others, this volume, chap 30).

A correlation matrix for anorthite and trace-element abundances in plagioclase phenocrysts from all 2004–5 samples (a total of 138 analyses) shows significant correlations between anorthite content and the abundances of all trace elements other than Li in plagioclase phenocrysts (table 2; fig. 3): Sr and Ti are positively correlated and Ba, LREE, Eu, and Pb are negatively correlated with anorthite. For this relatively large number of analyses, correlation coefficients >0.17 and >0.23 are significant at the 95-percent and 99-percent confidence levels, respectively. Lithium shows no significant correlations with other elements, whereas Ba, LREE, and Pb are strongly positively correlated with each other. Strontium shows relatively poor correlations with Ti and La but significant correlations with Ba, Eu, and Pb. Titanium shows significant negative correlations with Ba, LREE, Eu, and Pb.

There are clear differences in trace-element abundances between plagioclase phenocrysts and plagioclase from gabbroic inclusions. Plagioclase from inclusions typically has higher Ti, Ba, LREE, and Pb and lower Sr contents than phenocrysts with the same anorthite contents, and there also are some systematic differences between different inclusions (figs. 3, 4).

In general, analyses of groundmass and phenocrysts typically show similar Pb isotope composition, whereas plagioclase from gabbronorite inclusions have significantly different Pb-isotope compositions with lower $^{208}Pb/^{206}Pb$ and $^{207}Pb/^{206}Pb$ (fig. 5; appendix 1). In cases where groundmass was analyzed directly adjacent to disaggregating and reacting inclusions (for example, SH304-2C), groundmass compositions appear to lie along mixing lines between inclusions and groundmass from other samples.

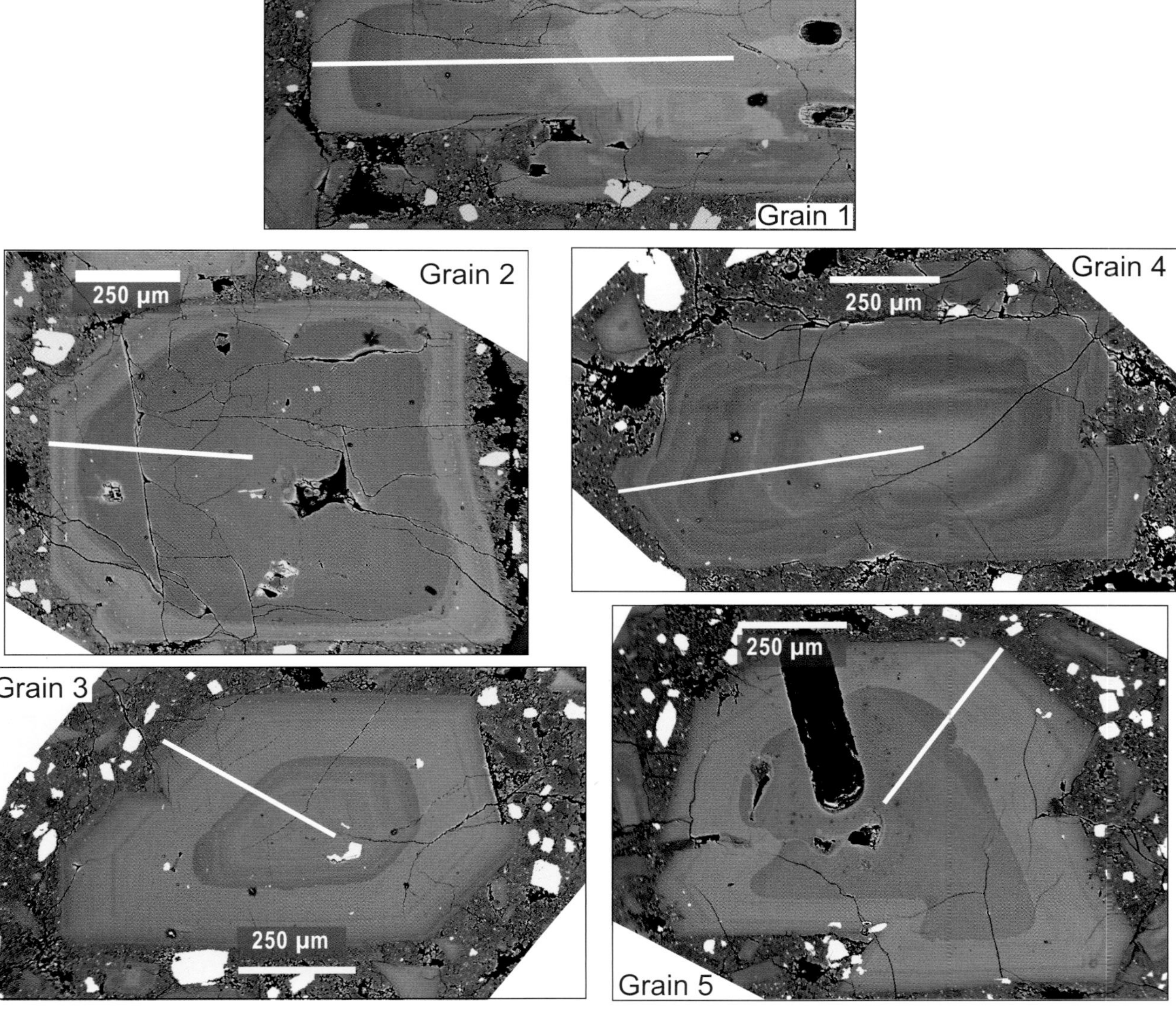

Figure 1. Backscattered electron images of five plagioclase grains from Mount St. Helens sample SH304-2A analyzed for major- and trace-element abundances along traverses. White line in each photograph shows location of analytical traverse.

Discussion

Compositional Variations Among Plagioclase Phenocrysts

Plagioclase phenocrysts from the 2004–5 dome samples show considerable variation in trace-element compositions, with abundances ranging by factors of ~3–5 over the range of anorthite contents recorded. Even at constant anorthite there is a factor of ~2–3 variation in trace-element abundances (fig. 3), which is far outside analytical errors. With the exception of Li, there is no systematic variation in the range of trace-element (fig. 4) or anorthite content in plagioclase phenocrysts over the course of the eruption, consistent with the lack of variation in whole-rock compositions (Pallister and others, this volume, chap. 30). In addition, there is no clear difference in trace-element composition of plagioclase

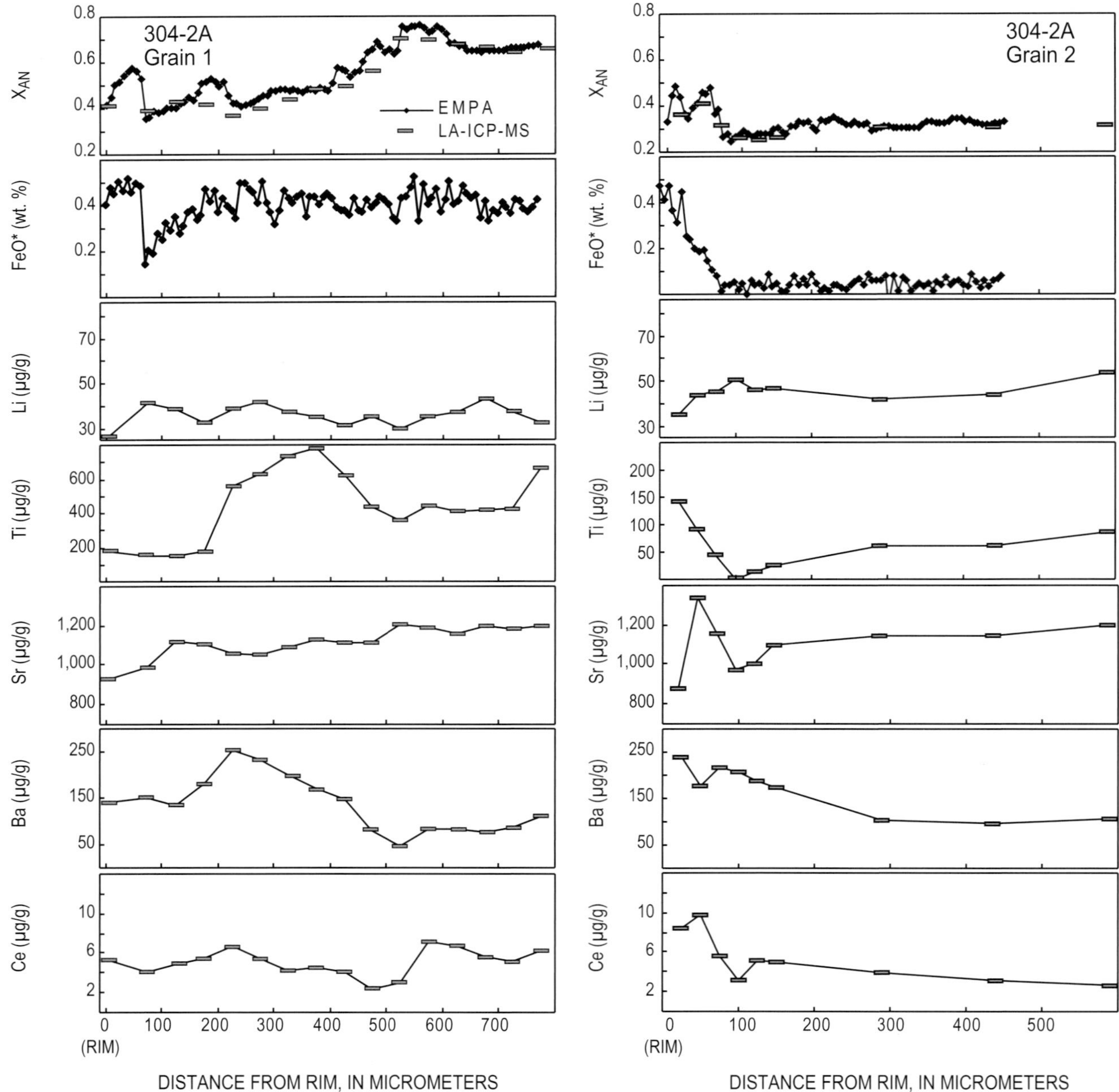

Figure 2. Mole-fraction anorthite (X_{AN}), FeO, Li, Ti, Sr, Ba, and Ce concentrations measured along traverses in five plagioclase grains from Mount St. Helens dacite sample SH304-2A (fig. 1). Symbol width for LA–ICP–MS data is the same size as the laser spot used. 0 is rim. All data except FeO are in appendix 2.

phenocrysts analyzed from 1981–85 dome samples and the 2004–5 samples (fig. 3), although there are suggestions that these samples originate from distinct magma batches (for example, Pallister and others, this volume, chap. 30; Blundy and others, this volume, chap. 33).

Abundances of trace elements other than Li show significant negative (Ba, LREE, Pb) or positive (Sr, Ti) correlations with anorthite content (table 2; fig. 3). One explanation for this is that the correlations simply reflect changes in plagioclase-melt partitioning with changing anorthite content (Blundy and Wood, 1994; Bindeman and others, 1998). However, although calculated plagioclase compositions (determined using the partitioning models in the preceding references and the bulk composition of 2004 dacite as a proxy for melt composition) are a reasonable match for the more incompatible elements (REE, Ba and Pb), the predicted trends for Sr and Ti are reverse to those evident in plagioclase phenocrysts (fig. 3).

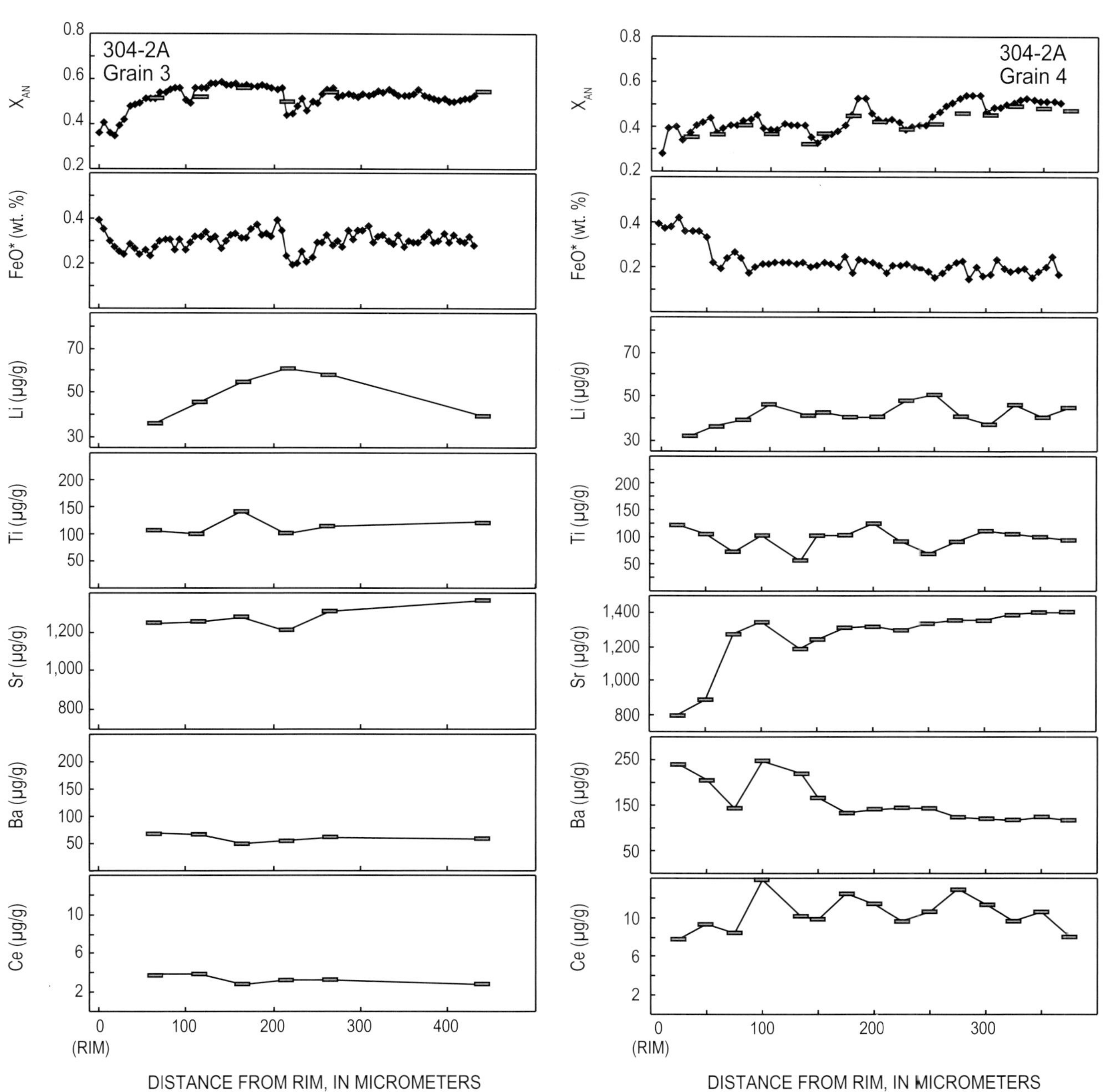

Figure 2.—Continued.

The simplest explanation for this observation is that decreases in Ti and Sr reflect removal of these elements from the melt during progressive closed-system crystallization of phenocryst phases. Because formation of crystals will sequester elements according to their partition coefficients, we do not need subsequent separation of crystals and liquid (as required to change the bulk composition) in order to change the composition of residual melt and subsequent crystals. The lack of europium anomalies in bulk dacite compositions (Pallister and others, this volume, chap. 30), together with simple calculations based on the Nd/Eu ratios of bulk dacite and feldspar, suggest that the 2004–5 dacite has lost <<5–10 percent plagioclase. The modal abundances of plagioclase and other phenocrysts observed in dacite samples thus probably approximate the overall proportions in which they have crystallized, a view broadly consistent with experimental investigations (Rutherford and Devine, this volume, chap. 31).

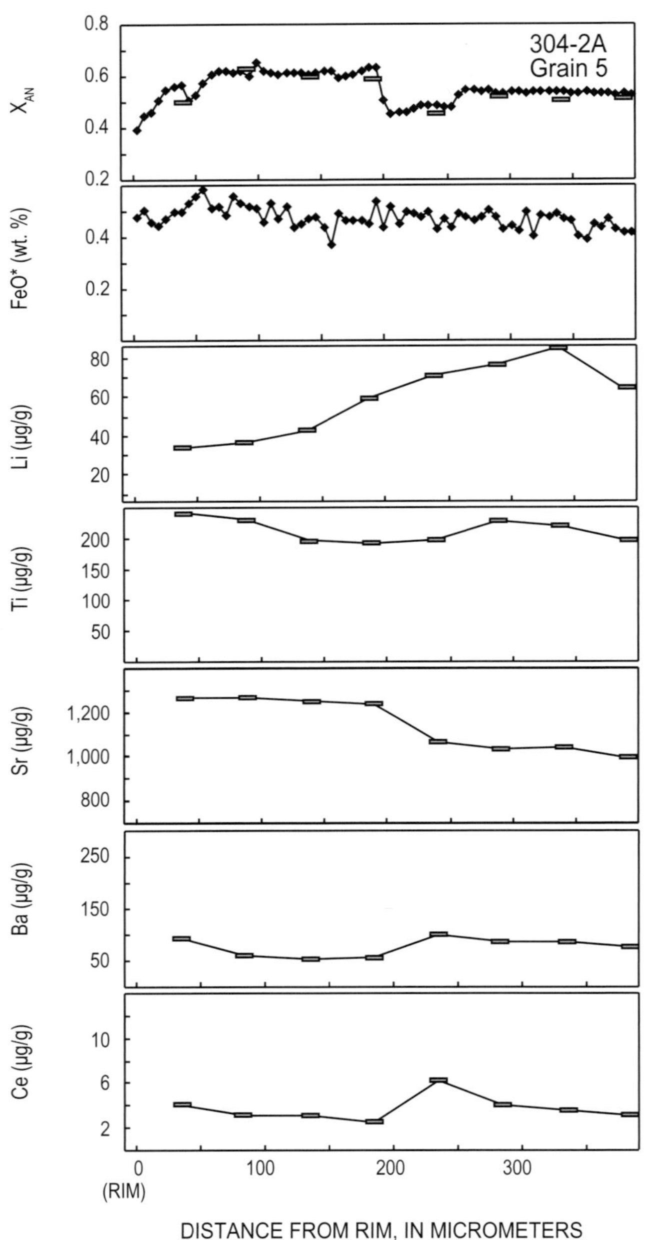

Figure 2.—Continued.

We have calculated changes in plagioclase composition using a simple model involving progressive crystallization of the observed phenocryst phases in the proportions in which they occur within the dacite from a melt with an initial composition that is the same as the bulk composition of dome dacite (fig. 6, table 3). Of the trace elements analyzed, Sr and Ti are the most compatible in the crystallizing assemblage of plagioclase, hypersthene, hornblende, and magnetite-ilmenite, with Sr entering plagioclase and Ti entering hornblende and ilmenite. We also note that our calculations are unlikely to fully explain all variations, given that we assume constant phase proportions and starting melt composition and that no accounting is made for differences in temperature, pressure, or reequilibration between plagioclase and melt (which may be significant for fast-diffusing elements such as Sr, according to Cherniak and Watson, 1994). However, the calculations do suggest that positive trends between anorthite contents and Sr and Ti, at least below ~An_{60}, could result from sequestration of these elements from melt during phenocryst growth and thus are linked to total crystallinity. Strontium/barium ratios in plagioclase also depart significantly from the trends expected from partitioning and are also largely replicated by our model. The negative correlations with anorthite shown by more incompatible elements (Pb, La, Ba) also are reproduced by our model, although these correlations do not differ significantly from those predicted by partitioning alone (fig. 3). Overall, we suggest that crystallization of the observed phenocryst phases, together with the control of anorthite content on crystal-liquid partitioning, exerts strong control over plagioclase trace-element abundances.

Control of mineral compositions by closed-system equilibrium crystallization is recognized in other crystal-rich, silicic magma systems (for example, Zellmer and others, 2003; Treibold and others, 2006), including Mount St Helens. Blundy and others (this volume, chap. 33) also suggest that closed-system crystallization controls glass inclusion compositions in 1980–86 Mount St. Helens lavas. Streck and others (this volume, chap. 34) argue that increases in crystallinity are the primary control on anorthite zoning in the outer ~80 µm of plagioclase phenocrysts in the 2004–5 eruption. Moreover this simple model does not necessarily conflict with more complex crystallization histories, as long as we consider trends shown by plagioclase to represent the range of histories experienced by individual plagioclase grains. Note that we do not visualize a simple "freezing" model in which a single homogenous melt crystallizes progressively until the current crystallinity is reached. Rather, as suggested by zoning and resorption features

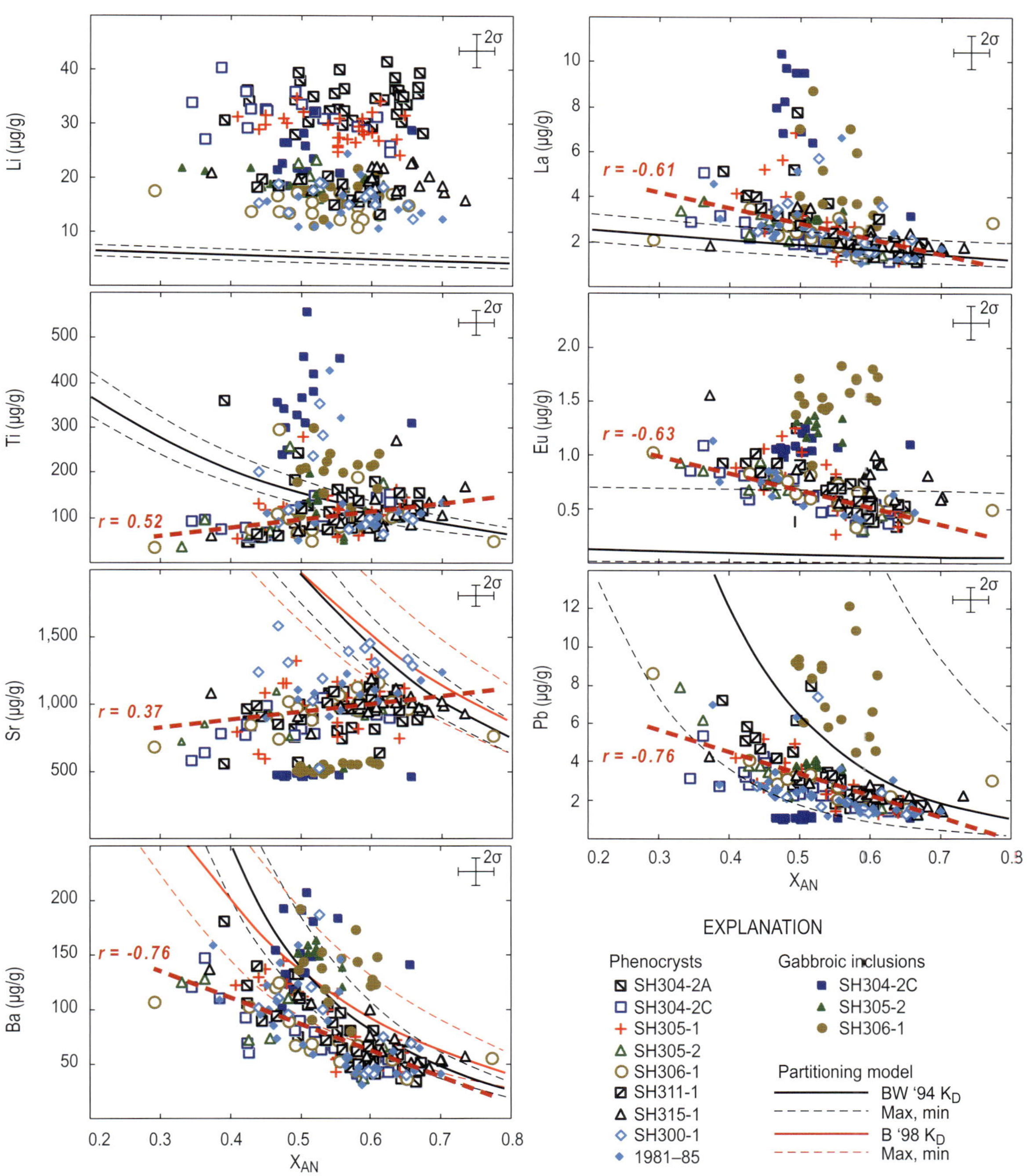

Figure 3. Trace-element abundances and anorthite content measured in plagioclase samples from Mount St. Helens dacite of 2004–5. Data shown for plagioclase present as phenocrysts and within gabbroic inclusions. Thick dashed red lines show linear least-squares fit to phenocryst data, with the value of the correlation coefficient *r* listed. No correlation shown for Li. Solid red and black lines show predicted elemental abundances in plagioclase calculated using plagioclase-melt partitioning models of Bindeman and others (1998; B '98) and, for Sr and Ba, Blundy and Wood (1994; BW '94), and the trace-element abundances measured in dacite sample SH304-2A (Pallister and others, this volume, chap. 30) as the estimated bulk melt composition (see text for explanation). All partition coefficients calculated at 850°C. Results for three dome samples (SH100, SH141, and SH187) from 1981–85 eruptions shown for comparison. Representative error bars (2σ) shown for each plot.

Table 2. Correlation matrix for anorthite and selected trace elements for plagioclase phenocrysts from 2004–2005 Mount St. Helens dome samples.

[Values shown are the calculated linear correlation coefficient r. For the number of analyses (n = 138) $|r| > 0.17$ is significant at 95-percent confidence, $|r| > 0.23$ is significant at 99-percent confidence.]

	Anorthite	Li	Ti	Sr	Ba	La	Eu	Pb
Anorthite	1	-0.04	0.52	0.37	-0.76	-0.61	-0.63	-0.76
Li	-0.04	1	0.14	-0.05	0.06	0.06	-0.04	-0.05
Ti	0.52	0.14	1	0.07	-0.23	-0.38	-0.31	-0.57
Sr	0.37	-0.05	0.07	1	-0.23	-0.11	-0.20	-0.24
Ba	-0.76	0.06	-0.23	-0.23	1	0.83	0.80	0.69
La	-0.61	0.06	-0.38	-0.11	0.83	1	0.74	0.66
Eu	-0.63	-0.04	-0.31	-0.20	0.80	0.74	1	0.68
Pb	-0.76	-0.05	-0.57	-0.24	0.69	0.66	0.68	1

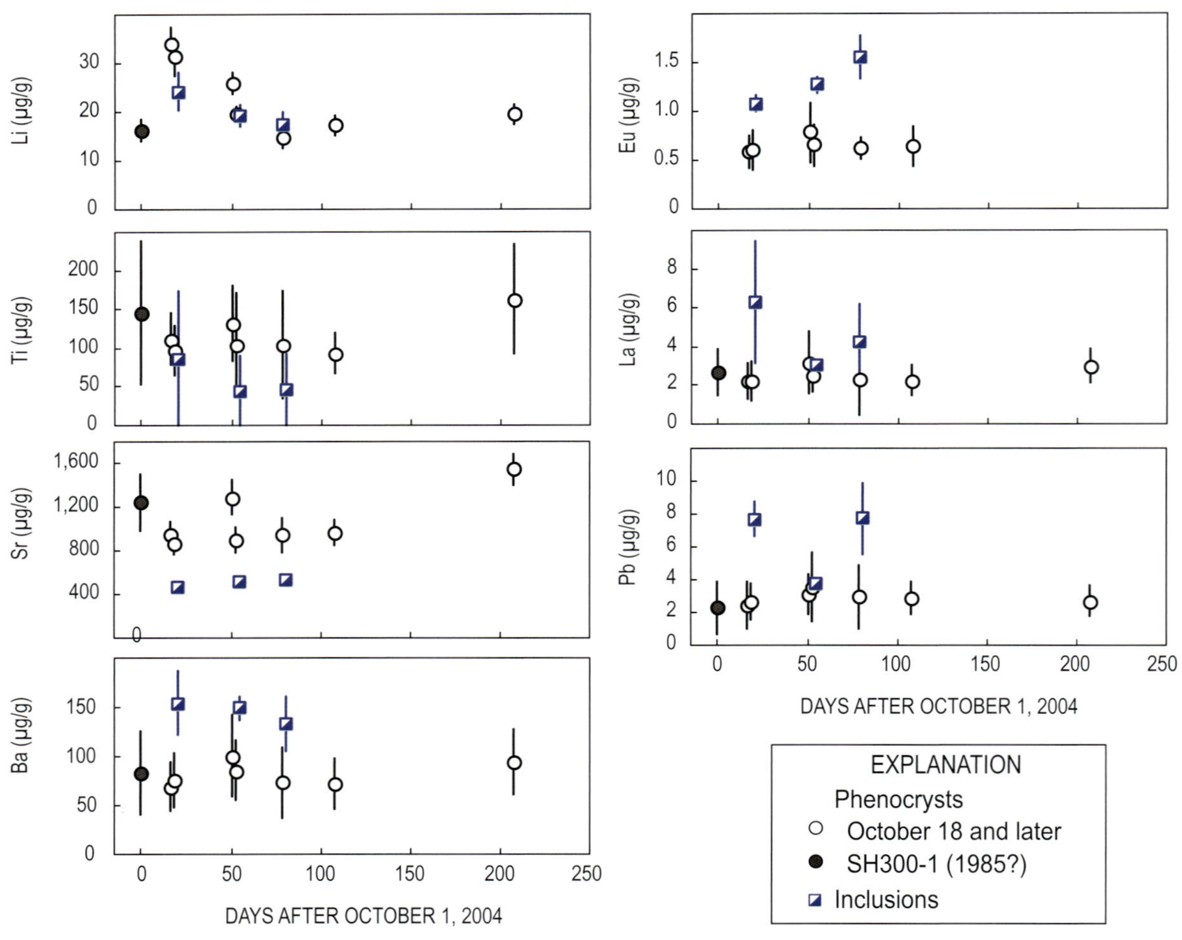

Figure 4. Average trace-element compositions of plagioclase phenocrysts and within gabbronorite inclusions from Mount St. Helens dacite collected between October 2004 and April 2005 as a function of estimated eruption date (Pallister and others, this volume, chap. 30). Symbols represent average composition ±1σ.

in plagioclase and other phenocrysts (see below; Rutherford and Devine, this volume, chap. 31; Streck and others, this volume, chap. 34), plagioclase phenocrysts experienced a range of pressure and temperature conditions and coexisted with a range of melt compositions within a convecting and self-mixing magma chamber (Couch and others, 2001; Rutherford and Devine, this volume, chap. 31). We discuss this further below.

Departures of Li and Eu in plagioclase from the predicted equilibrium partitioning values (fig. 3) are related to other factors. Variations in Li contents are discussed in further detail below and in Kent and others (2007). For Eu, the plagioclase-melt partition coefficients used in figure 3 are from the study of Bindeman and others (1998) and were measured from experiments conducted in the presence of atmospheric oxygen. In this case all Eu was present in the trivalent form, and thus Eu behaves consistently with the other moderately incompatible middle REE (K_D = ~0.1). In most volcanic systems, conditions are more reducing, significant amounts of more compatible divalent Eu are present, and Eu typically is more compatible in plagioclase than other REE (for example, Rollinson, 1993). If we use a general partition coefficient value of 2 for the plagioclase-melt partition coefficient (Rollinson, 1993), then we calculate more reasonable plagioclase Eu contents of 1–2 µg/g.

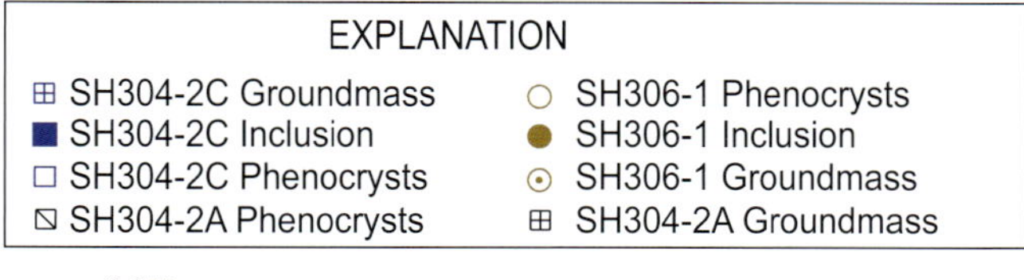

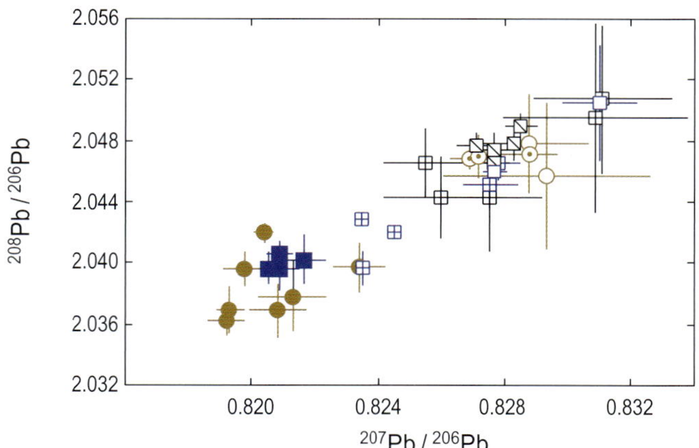

Figure 5. Measured $^{208}Pb/^{207}Pb$ and $^{207}Pb/^{206}Pb$ ratios of groundmass and plagioclase from phenocrysts and inclusions in three samples of 2004–5 Mount St. Helens dacite. Error bars represent 2σ error.

Compositional Variations Within Plagioclase Crystals

Anorthite, FeO, and trace elements were measured along traverses in selected plagioclase phenocrysts from SH304-2A to investigate changes in trace-element composition during progressive crystallization (figs. 1, 2). The grains chosen represent the general classes of phenocryst types recognized by Rutherford and Devine (this volume, chap. 31) and Streck and others (this volume, chap. 34).

The most common compositional feature of plagioclase phenocrysts is cyclic zoning, starting with an abrupt increase in An contents, sometimes also in conjunction with indications of mineral dissolution or resorption (for example, grain 5 in fig. 1), followed by more gradual decrease in An content until the start of the next cycle. Variations in the composition, number, and width of cycles are apparent in individual phenocrysts but, in general, the first plagioclase is $\geq An_{50}$, decreasing outward to ~An_{40-20}. This pattern recurs frequently; grain 4 shows multiple cycles, and grains 2, 3, and 5 show one or two cycles. Such cyclic compositional variation is common in plagioclase phenocrysts from the 2004–5 Mount St Helens dome, although there are subtle differences of opinion regarding their origin. Rutherford and others (this volume, chap. 31) suggest that these cycles represent plagioclase crystallizing during cycles of convection from deeper, hotter parts of the magma chamber to shallower and cooler conditions, whereas Streck and others (this volume, chap. 34) argue that anorthite cycles in the outer 80 µm of phenocrysts largely represent changes in crystallinity rather than changes in external conditions.

Although LA–ICP–MS analyses do not have sufficient spatial resolution to examine individual anorthite cycles in detail, trace-element abundances measured along traverses through individual grains can be examined in light of the variations evident between phenocrysts (figs. 3, 6). We have used the covariation between An contents and trace-element abundance as the basis for comparisons (fig. 7).

With some exceptions, trace-element variations within individual phenocrysts broadly follow the same general trends evident between plagioclase phenocrysts (fig. 2). Thus, within individual grains, Ti and Sr are positively correlated with anorthite, and An contents are broadly anticorrelated with Ba and La (for example, grains 2, 5). This relation also supports a model in which largely closed-system crystallization controls trace-element composition in coexisting liquid and subsequently formed plagioclase. However, in detail, individual crystals define separate subparallel trends (fig. 7). For example, Sr contents in grain 1 form a linear trend with positive slope that is offset to lower Sr contents at a given An than are similar trends in grains 2 and 4. In some cases, as with grain 4, analyses from a short segment of the traverse lie off the trend defined by the other analyses—specifically, the two outermost points measured on the rim have lower Sr and slightly higher Ti than the interior of the grain (figs. 2, 7). It is unlikely that changes in element partitioning related solely to anorthite or temperature

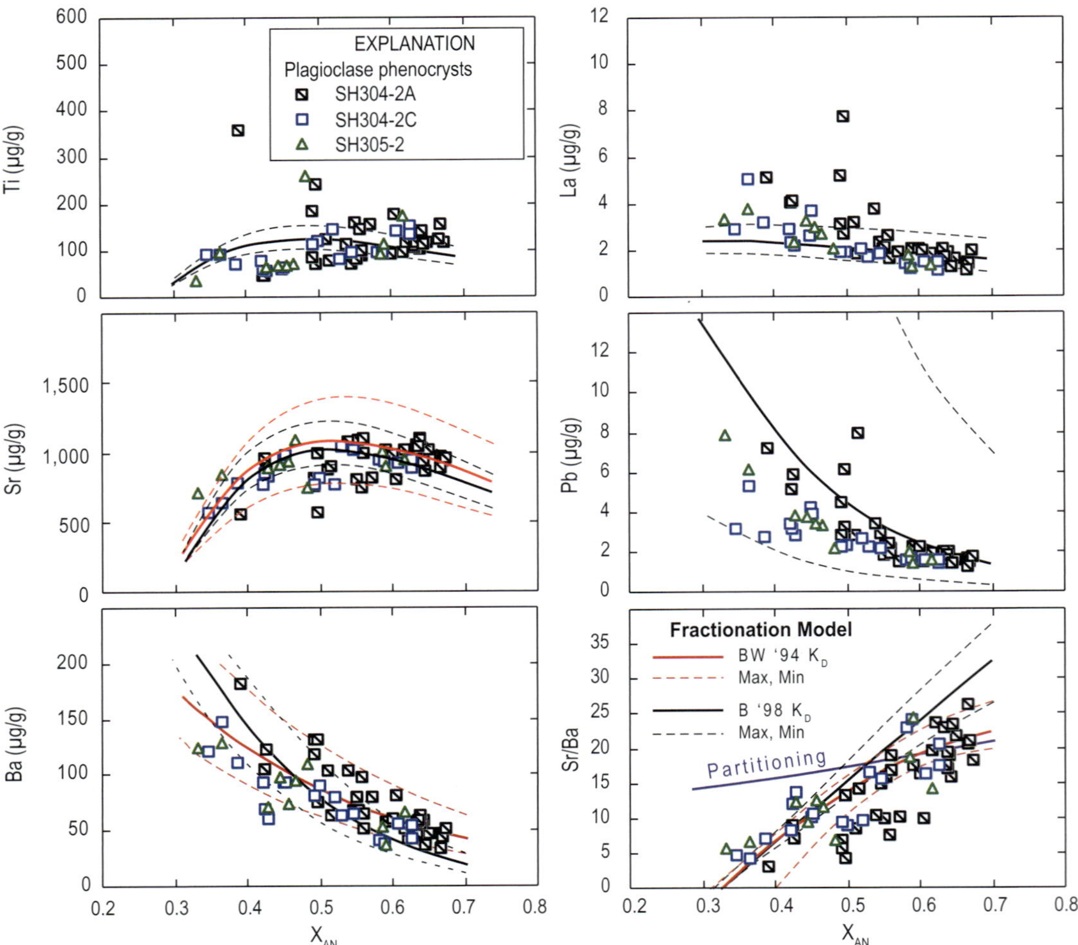

Figure 6. Comparison of selected trace elements and Sr/Ba ratios in plagioclase phenocrysts with trends predicted by a simple closed-system crystallization model. Only Mount St. Helens samples SH304-2A, SH304-2C, and SH305-2 are shown, for clarity, although these are broadly representative of other 2004–5 dome samples. Potential liquid lines of descent were calculated by incrementally removing plagioclase, hornblende, hypersthene, and oxides (magnetite and ilmenite in ratio 1: 5) from an initial melt of bulk composition similar to SH304-2. All phases were removed in the proportions in which they occur as phenocrysts within the dacite (table 3). Trace-element contents of ferromagnesian and oxide phases are given in table 3 and are based on preliminary analyses of these phases by electron microprobe (for Ti) and LA–ICP–MS. Note that the calculation is not particularly sensitive to variations in ferromagnesian and oxide compositions owing to the low modal proportions of these phases and their generally low trace-element contents. The exception is Ti, which is relatively abundant in hornblende (TiO_2 ~2–3 wt. percent) and in ilmenite (TiO_2 ~50 wt. percent). For every 2-percent increment of crystallization, trace-element abundances of equilibrium plagioclase were calculated using the partitioning models of Bindeman and others (1998; black lines) and, for Sr and Ba, Blundy and Wood (1994; red lines). All partition coefficients were calculated at 850°C, consistent with current estimates of magmatic temperatures for 2004–5 (Pallister and others, this volume, chap. 30), although the model is not significantly different at higher temperatures. Uncertainties in partition coefficients shown by dashed lines associated with predicted trends from each partitioning model. Because the anorthite content of crystallizing plagioclase is dictated by several factors (for example, volatile contents, pressure, temperature, and composition), we chose to crystallize the first plagioclase at An_{70} composition and to have the anorthite content decrease linearly and progressively until the final plagioclase has a composition of An_{35} after crystallization of 54 weight percent, the total amount of phenocrysts observed in sample SH304-2A on a void-free basis (Pallister and others, this volume, chap. 30). The change in Sr/Ba ratio predicted by partitioning (using the partition coefficients of Bindeman and others, 1998) is shown by the purple line.

Table 3. Mineral and magma compositions used for crystal-fractionation model shown in figure 6.

[Column labeled Crystal proportion is that observed in dacite sample SH304-2A (Pallister and others this volume, chap. 30), calculated on a groundmass-free basis and not including plagioclase microphenocrysts in groundmass. For oxide minerals, Ti content represents crystallization of magnetite:ilmenite in ratio of ~5:1 (Pallister and others, this volume, chap. 30). Not shown are plagioclase trace-element contents, which were calculated separately for each increment of plagioclase crytallized from the coexisting melt composition, using the partitioning relations of Bindeman and others, (1998). Starting magma composition based on whole-rock analyses of 2004–2005 dome material (Pallister and others, this volume, chap. 30).]

Phase	Crystal proportion	Ti	Sr	Ba	La	Ce	Eu	Pb
Hypersthene	0.10	900	10	1	1	2	0.1	0.1
Hornblende	0.06	30,000	50	70	1	2	0.3	1.7
Oxide	0.02	100,000	0	0	0	0	0	0
Plagioclase	0.82							
Starting magma		4,000	400	336	15	30	1.3	9.8

variations are sufficient to produce the variations found between crystals. We suggest that plagioclase compositions also reflect variations in the composition of coexisting melt from which plagioclase crystallized. Although compositional variations could be inherited partly from the mid or lower crustal source of the dacitic magmas, the near-constant composition of 2004–5 bulk dacite samples argues against large source-derived variation (Pallister and others, this volume, chap. 30). We suggest instead that localized variations in *P* and *T*, crystallinity, and proportions of crystallizing phases within the magma storage zone result in localized variations in melt composition. Crystals reflect the composition of localized melt(s) from which they grow, and thus individual crystals record variable composition trends. Occasional juxtaposition of crystals with new melt compositions, possibly related to convective stirring, also results in crystals with compositions that depart from well-defined trends on variation diagrams, as seen in Sr and Ti in grain 4. We note that melt inclusions from 1980–86 and 2004–5 samples also show large differences in Ba and REE abundances at similar SiO_2, consistent with diverse melt compositions during mineral growth (Blundy and others, this volume, chap. 33).

Grain 1 is slightly different from the other grains analyzed. It is part of a large, complex plagioclase glomerocryst and has a complex anorthite-rich core (as high as An_{75}) with an adjacent low-anorthite central part and then two cycles of An_{55-60} to An_{38-40} (fig. 2). This grain has Ti contents as high as ~600 µg/g in its inner region (from ~200 to 700 µm from the rim), which are considerably higher than the Ti contents of other plagioclase phenocrysts (fig. 3). High Ti suggests that the core of this crystal might have been derived from a disaggregated gabbroic inclusion, although other trace elements do not have inclusion-like compositions. In particular, Sr abundances in the core of this grain are ~1,000–1,200 µg/g, unlike the ~500 µg/g contents seen in plagioclase within gabbroic inclusions (fig. 3). Although the origin of this grain is uncertain, the high Sr might reflect further heterogeneity among inclusions (fig. 3), or it could be due to reequilibration of Sr in plagioclase with melt after disaggregation, with more slowly diffusing Ti not yet reequilibrated (compare with Zellmer and others, 2003). The latter explanation requires a residence time of several thousand years to reequilibrate over distances of hundreds of microns.

Lithium Variations in Plagioclase Phenocrysts

Variations in the Li contents in 2004–5 dome and ash samples are of particular interest and have been discussed in detail by Kent and others (2007) and Rowe and others (this volume, chap. 29). As shown in figure 4, Li contents in plagioclase phenocrysts erupted at the onset of dome extrusion are anomalously high (samples SH304-2A, SH304-2C). These concentrations are higher, by about a factor of two, than those seen in subsequently erupted material and in sample SH300-1 (interpreted to be a remnant of 1980s dome material), and this difference is significant to >99 percent confidence. The increase in Li in October–November 2004 samples mirrors that reported by Berlo and others (2004) in plagioclase from the 1980 eruption of Mount St. Helens, in which high Li contents in plagioclase phenocrysts erupted prior to May 18 and cryptodome material erupted May 18 are thought to reflect vapor-phase transport of alkali metals during degassing from deep within the magma storage zone before eruption (Berlo and others 2004; Blundy and others, this volume, chap. 33). Kent and others (2007) suggest a similar model to explain the 2004–5 material. Although Li contents in the bulk magma from October and November 2004 are not elevated (Pallister and others, this volume, chap. 30), this is probably as a result of vapor loss during late shallow (< ~10 MPa) degassing (Kent and others, 2007). Lithium diffusion in plagioclase is slower than in melt, and thus plagioclase preserves the high Li signature, provided decompression and cooling are sufficiently rapid. This model is supported by the measurement of Li concentrations as high as 207 µg/g in melt inclusions from SH304-2A (Kent and others, 2007) and in Li-loss profiles evident in the outer 100–300 µm of plagioclase transects (fig. 2). High Li signatures also are evident in ~20 percent of pla-

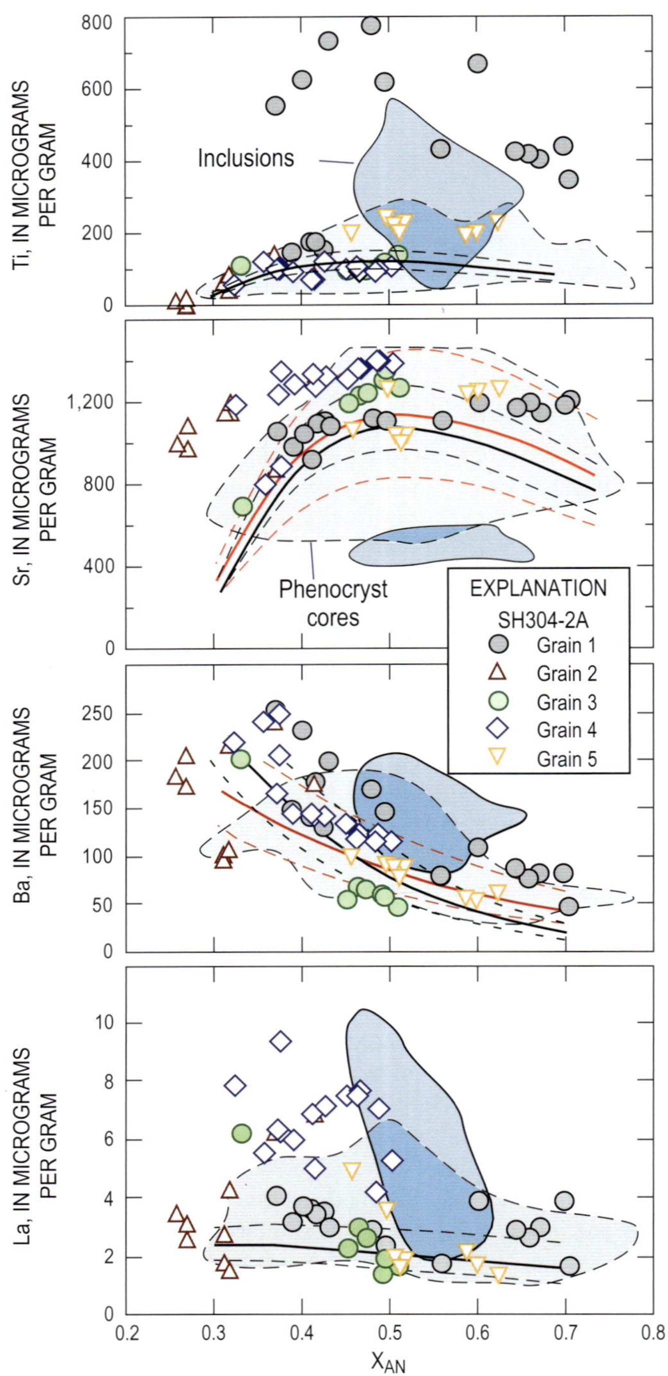

Figure 7. Ti, Sr, Ba, and La versus mole fraction anorthite (X_{AN}) content measured along plagioclase traverses (see figs. 1, 2). Fractionation models from figure 6 are shown as black and red lines (see fig. 6 caption for details). Fields show the range of compositions measured in plagioclase phenocrysts (gray field, dashed line) and gabbroic inclusions (blue field, solid line), from figure 3.

gioclase in ash from explosive eruptions on October 1–5, 2004, as noted by Rowe and others (this volume, chap. 29), who suggest that these explosions were phreatomagmatic in origin. Finally, diffusion modeling based on differences between Li contents in plagioclase phenocrysts and gabbroic inclusions in SH304-2C (fig. 4) suggests that Li enrichment occurred relatively recently—probably within a year of eruption (Kent and others, 2007). One plausible scenario is that the accumulation and phase separation of vapor in the apical part of the shallow Mount St. Helens magma chamber (~5 km) resulted in increased fluid pressure before eruption. Rupturing of wallrocks in late September 2004, perhaps induced by increases in fluid pressure, resulted in loss of the low-density vapor and reequilibration between a high-density, Li-bearing vapor phase and magma. After upward movement of magma commenced in late September or early October, Li-enriched apical magma contributed to initial phreatomagmatic explosions in early October (Rowe and others, this volume; chap. 29) and was the first material erupted once extrusion commenced. Comparison with eruption rates suggests that Li-enriched magma represents ~15–20 percent of the volume of the total material erupted.

Composition and Origin of Gabbronorite Inclusions

Mafic plutonic inclusions are a common feature of Mount St. Helens lavas from the last ~3,000 years and are relatively common in 2004–5 dome samples (Pallister and others, this volume, chap. 30). The potential sources for mafic inclusions include crystalline cumulates and crystal-rich wallrock zones (Heliker, 1995; Cooper and Donnelly, this volume, chap. 36) and fragments of basement rock removed from conduit walls and transported within the magmatic system. One key issue is whether these inclusions represent parts of the same magmatic system responsible for generation and transport of Mount St. Helens magma or represent unrelated rocks from the Tertiary Cascade crust beneath the volcano. Heliker (1995) argued that the former might be the case. However, preliminary U-Pb zircon ages of ~25 Ma from three gabbronorite inclusions from the 1980–86 dome complex (Pallister and others, this volume, chap. 30) suggest that these are derived from Tertiary basement incorporated into the Mount St. Helens magmatic system, and trace-element and Pb-isotope analyses of inclusions and plagioclase phenocrysts support this model. Plagioclase crystals analyzed from three gabbronorite inclusions have significantly different trace-element compositions than coexisting plagioclase phenocrysts, with lower Sr and generally higher Ti, Ba, REE, and Pb (fig. 3). There are also small but consistent differences among inclusions, suggesting that some heterogeneity exists in their source (figs. 3, 4). Differences in trace-element abundances between phenocrysts and inclusions suggest that inclusions have equilibrated with a melt of significantly different composition than that from which coexisting phenocryst phases crystallized. Overall, the compositions of plagioclase in gabbroic inclusions are difficult to relate to those of phenocrysts and to bulk magma composition by any reasonable petrologic model.

The Pb-isotope compositions of plagioclase from inclusions also are consistently different from those of plagioclase phenocrysts and groundmass (fig. 5), with inclusions having lower $^{208}Pb/^{206}Pb$ and $^{207}Pb/^{206}Pb$ than groundmass and phenocrysts. This difference is inconsistent with a simple petrologic relation between inclusions and the host melt, and it specifically argues against inclusions representing a "restite"-like material remaining from melting of metabasalt to produce dacite. Such restite would be expected to have the same Pb-isotope composition as melts unless significant mixing with additional melt or crustal assimilation had occurred.

Lead-isotope composition of groundmass material shows that disaggregation of inclusions also effects the composition of the groundmass on relatively small spatial scales. This phenomenon is particularly evident in SH304-2C, where measurements of the groundmass composition made adjacent to the inclusion lie on an apparent mixing line between the compositions of phenocrysts and plagioclase within gabbroic inclusions (fig. 5). Contributions from disaggregating inclusions also may influence variations in measured $(^{230}Th)/(^{232}Th)$ in plagioclase separates (Cooper and Donnelly, this volume, chap. 36). Such contributions from disaggregation of gabbroic inclusions probably limit the utility of conventional bulk rock or mineral separate-based isotopic measurements for estimating magmatic composition, as these will invariably represent a mixture between the true isotopic composition of the magma and various admixtures of disaggregated and remelted inclusions.

Conclusions

Laser ablation ICP–MS analyses of anorthite content, trace-element (Li, Ti, Sr, Ba, LREE, Pb) concentrations, and Pb-isotope compositions in plagioclase from dacite of the 2004–5 and 1981–86 eruptions of Mount St. Helens provide insight into the petrologic processes leading to formation and eruption of these magmas. Anomalously high Li contents in the early stage of the eruption are thought to reflect addition of Li to the upper part of the magma chamber immediately before eruption (within ~1 year) by transfer of an alkali-enriched exsolved vapor from deep within the mama chamber. Accumulation of Li-rich vapor in the apical part of the magma storage zone may have increased fluid pressures, perhaps helping to initiate eruption. The compositional ranges of other trace elements in plagioclase phenocrysts remain largely constant in material erupted between October 2004 and April 2005 and are broadly similar to those measured in 1981–85 dome samples. These elements show significant correlations with anorthite content that, particularly for Sr and Ti, cannot be described solely by variations in plagioclase–melt partitioning. A simple model involving closed-system fractional crystallization of plagioclase + hypersthene + amphibole + oxides largely reproduces the observed trends, suggesting that plagioclase compositions are predominantly controlled by the degree of crystallinity of the magma and sequestration of compatible elements during crystallization. Analyses from traverses within individual plagioclase phenocrysts generally support this model but also suggest that localized variations exist in the composition of melt from which individual plagioclase crystallize. These analytical differences probably reflect localized variations in phase proportions and crystallinity during magma residence.

Plagioclase from gabbronorite inclusions in three samples has markedly different trace-element and Pb-isotope compositions compared to plagioclase phenocrysts. Inclusions typically have higher Ti, Ba, REE, and Pb and lower Sr and have lower $^{208}Pb/^{206}Pb$ and $^{207}Pb/^{206}Pb$ ratios than coexisting plagioclase phenocrysts. The compositions of plagioclase from gabbroic inclusions appear to be unrelated to phenocryst compositions. We suggest that gabbroic inclusions are samples of the mafic Tertiary basement from beneath the volcano.

Acknowledgments

The facilities of the W.M. Keck Collaboratory for Plasma Mass Spectrometry were used in this work. We would also like to thank the staff of the U.S. Geological Survey David A. Johnston Cascades Volcano Observatory for providing a unique sample set, and the Mount St Helens petrology working group (you know who you are!) for feedback and comments. This work was funded in part by National Science Foundation grant EAR 0440382.

References Cited

Baker, J.A., Peate, D.W., Waight, T., and Meyzen, C., 2004, Pb isotopic analysis of standards and samples using a ^{207}Pb-^{204}Pb double spike and thallium to correct for mass bias with a double-focusing MC–ICP–MS: Chemical Geology, v. 211, p. 275–303.

Berlo, K., Blundy, J., Turner, S., Cashman, K., Hawkesworth, C., and Black, S., 2004, Geochemical precursors to volcanic activity at Mount St. Helens, USA: Science, v. 306, p. 1167–1169.

Bindeman, I.N., Davis, A.M., and Drake, M.J., 1998, Ion microprobe study of plagioclase-basalt partition experiments at natural concentration levels of trace elements: Geochimica et Cosmochimica Acta, v. 62, p. 1175–1193.

Blundy, J.D., and Wood, B.J., 1994, Prediction of crystal–melt partition coefficients from elastic moduli: Nature, v. 372, p. 452–454.

Blundy, J., Cashman, K.V., and Berlo, K., 2008, Evolving magma storage conditions beneath Mount St. Helens inferred from chemical variations in melt inclusions from the 1980–1986 and current (2004–2006) eruptions, chap. 33 *of* Sherrod, D.R., Scott, W.E., and Stauffer, P.H., eds., A volcano rekindled; the renewed eruption of Mount St. Helens, 2004–2006: U.S. Geological Survey Professional Paper 1750 (this volume).

Browne, B.L., Eichelberger, J.C., Patino, L.C., Vogel, T.A., Uto, K., and Hoshizumi, H., 2006, Magma mingling as indicated by texture and Sr /Ba ratios of plagioclase phenocrysts from Unzen volcano, SW Japan: Journal of Volcanology and Geothermal Research, v. 113, p. 103–116.

Cherniak, D.J., and Watson E.B., 1994, A study of strontium diffusion in plagioclase using Rutherford backscattering spectroscopy: Geochimica et Cosmochimica Acta, v. 58, p. 5179–5190.

Cooper, K.M., and Donnelly, C.T., 2008, ^{238}U-^{230}Th-^{226}Ra disequilibria in dacite and plagioclase from the 2004–2005 eruption of Mount St. Helens, chap. 36 *of* Sherrod, D.R., Scott, W.E., and Stauffer, P.H., eds., A volcano rekindled; the renewed eruption of Mount St. Helens, 2004–2006: U.S. Geological Survey Professional Paper 1750 (this volume).

Couch, S., Sparks, R.S.J., and Carroll, M.R., 2001, Mineral disequilibrium in lavas explained by convective self-mixing in open magma chambers: Nature, v. 411, p. 1037–1039.

Heliker, C., 1995, Inclusions in the Mount St. Helens dacite erupted from 1980 through 1983: Journal of Volcanology and Geothermal Research, v. 66, nos. 1–3, p. 115–135, doi:10.1016/0377-0273(94)00074-Q.

Kelley, K.A., Plank, T., Ludden, J., and Staudigel, H., 2003, The composition of altered oceanic crust at OPD sites 801 and 1149: Geochemistry Geophysics Geosystems, v. 4, no. 6, 21 p., doi:10.1029/2002GC000435.

Kent, A.J.R., and Ungerer, C.A., 2006, Analysis of light lithophile elements (Li, Be, B) by laser ablation ICP–MS; comparison between magnetic sector and quadrupole ICP–MS: American Mineralogist, v. 91, p. 1401–1411.

Kent, A.J.R., Stolper, E.M., Francis, D., Woodhead, J., Frei, R., and Eiler, J., 2004a, Mantle heterogeneity during the formation of the North Atlantic Igneous Province; constraints from trace-element and Sr-Nd-Os-O isotope systematics of Baffin Island picrites: Geochemistry Geophysics Geosystems, v. 5, 26 p., doi:10.1029/2004GC000743.

Kent, A.J.R., Jacobsen, B., Peate, D.W., Waight, T.E., and Baker, J.A., 2004b, Isotope dilution MC–ICP–MS rare earth element analysis of geochemical reference materials NIST SRM 610, NIST SRM 612, NIST SRM 614, BHVO-2G, BHVO-2, BCR-2G, JB-2, WS-1, W-2, AGV-1, AGV-2: Geostandards Newsletter, v. 28, p. 417–430.

Kent, A.J.R., Blundy, J., Cashman, K.V., Cooper, K.M., Donnelly, C., Pallister, J.S., Reagan, M., Rowe, M.C., and Thornber, C.R., 2007, Vapor transfer prior to the October 2004 eruption of Mount St. Helens, Washington: Geology, v. 35, no. 3, p. 231–234, doi:10.1130/G22809A.1.

Pallister, J.S., Thornber, C.R., Cashman, K.V., Clynne, M.A., Lowers, H.A., Mandeville, C.W., Brownfield, I.K., and Meeker, G.P., 2008, Petrology of the 2004–2006 Mount St. Helens lava dome—implications for magmatic plumbing and eruption triggering, chap. 30 *of* Sherrod, D.R., Scott, W.E., and Stauffer, P.H., eds., A volcano rekindled; the renewed eruption of Mount St. Helens, 2004–2006: U.S. Geological Survey Professional Paper 1750 (this volume).

Paul, B., Woodhead, J., and Hergt, J.M., 2005, Improved *in situ* isotope analysis of low-Pb materials using LA–MC–ICP–MS with parallel ion counter and Faraday detection: Journal of Analytical Atomic Spectroscopy, v. 20, p. 1350–1357.

Pearce, N.J.G., Perkins, W.T., Westgate, J.A., Gorton, M.P., Jackson, S.E., Neal, C.R., and Chenery, S.P., 1997, A compilation of new and published major and trace-element data for NIST SRM 610 and NIST SRM 612 glass reference materials: Geostandards Newsletter, v. 21, p. 115–144.

Pearce, T.H., and Kolisnik, A.M., 1990, Observations of plagioclase zoning using interference imaging: Earth Science Reviews, v. 29, p. 9–26.

Rocholl, A., 1998, Major and trace-element composition and homogeneity of microbeam reference material; basalt glass USGS BCR-2G: Geostandards Newsletter, v. 22, p. 33–45.

Rollinson, H., 1993, Using geochemical data; evaluation, presentation, interpretation: Harlow, U.K., Longman Scientific and Technical, 352 p.

Rowe, M.C., Thornber, C.R., and Kent, A.J.R., 2008, Identification and evolution of the juvenile component in 2004–2005 Mount St. Helens ash, chap. 29 *of* Sherrod, D.R., Scott, W.E., and Stauffer, P.H., eds., A volcano rekindled; the renewed eruption of Mount St. Helens, 2004–2006: U.S. Geological Survey Professional Paper 1750 (this volume).

Rutherford, M.J., and Devine, J.D., III, 2008, Magmatic conditions and processes in the storage zone of the 2004–2006 Mount St. Helens dacite, chap. 31 *of* Sherrod, D.R., Scott, W.E., and Stauffer, P.H., eds., A volcano rekindled; the renewed eruption of Mount St. Helens, 2004–2006: U.S. Geological Survey Professional Paper 1750 (this volume).

Streck, M.J., Broderick, C.A., Thornber, C.R., Clynne, M.A., and Pallister, J.S., 2008, Plagioclase populations and zoning in dacite of the 2004–2005 Mount St. Helens eruption; constraints for magma origin and dynamics, chap. 34 *of* Sherrod, D.R., Scott, W.E., and Stauffer, P.H., eds., A volcano rekindled; the renewed eruption of Mount St. Helens, 2004–2006: U.S. Geological Survey Professional Paper 1750 (this volume).

Triebold, S., Kronz, A., and Wörner, G., 2005, Anorthite-calibrated backscattered electron profiles, trace elements and growth textures in feldspars from the Teide-Pico Viejo volcanic complex (Tenerife): Journal of Volcanology and Geothermal Research, v. 154, p. 117–130.

Zellmer, G.F., Sparks, R.S.J., Hawkesworth, C.J., and Wiedenbeck, M., 2003, Magma emplacement and remobilization timescales beneath Montserrat; insights from Sr and Ba zonations in plagioclase phenocrysts: Journal of Petrology, v. 44, p. 1413–1431.

Appendix 1. Supplementary Analytical Data for Glass Standard BCR-2G and for Pb-Isotope Compositions of Plagioclase and Groundmass in 2004–2005 Mount St. Helens Dome Samples

Data for seven replicate analyses of glass standard BCR-2G were determined during this study, and a comparison with accepted concentrations is listed in table 4. Table 5 lists $^{208}Pb/^{206}Pb$ and $^{207}Pb/^{206}Pb$ ratios of plagioclase phenocrysts, groundmass, and plagioclase within gabbroic inclusions from three samples of the Mount St. Helens dome erupted in 2004–2005 measured by laser-ablation multicollector ICP–MS. The average of four replicate isotopic analyses from glass standard BCR-2G is included in table 5 for reference.

Table 4. Analytical data from replicate analysis of USGS glass standard BCR-2G.

[Average of seven analyses. CaO/SiO_2 ratios calculated from equation 1 (see text). "Accepted values" compiled from these sources: rare-earth elements from Kent and others (2004b); Li from Kent and Ungerer (2006); Si from Rocholl (1998); all other elements from Kelley and others (2003).]

BCR-2G ----------	Accepted (µg/g)	Measured (µg/g)	± 2σ
Li	10.5	11.2	3.0
Ti	13,500	12,047	490
Sr	346	339	13
Ba	674	624	25
La	25.3	23.1	0.9
Ce	53.7	50.8	2.5
Pr	6.9	6.3	0.5
Nd	28.8	26.2	1.8
Eu	1.9	1.8	0.2
Pb	11.0	11.8	0.7
CaO/SiO_2	0.13	0.12	0.02

Table 5. Pb-isotope compositions of plagioclase and groundmass in 2004–2005 Mount St. Helens dome samples.

[Analysis by laser-ablation multicollector ICP–MS at Oregon State University. Values are isotopic ratios and, parenthetically, their 1σ uncertainties expressed in the final decimal places. "Inclusions" refers to plagioclase in gabbroic inclusions. Average of four replicate isotopic analyses from glass standard BCR-2G included for reference.]

	$^{208}Pb/^{206}Pb$		$^{207}Pb/^{206}Pb$	
SH304-2A				
Phenocryst	2.0495	(62)	0.8309	(29)
Phenocryst	2.0507	(48)	0.8311	(22)
Phenocryst	2.0443	(35)	0.8275	(16)
Phenocryst	2.0443	(27)	0.8260	(18)
Phenocryst	2.0466	(22)	0.8255	(14)
Groundmass	2.0478	(11)	0.8283	(6)
Groundmass	2.0489	(9)	0.8285	(5)
Groundmass	2.0474	(11)	0.8276	(5)
Groundmass	2.0466	(5)	0.8277	(5)
Groundmass	2.0477	(8)	0.8271	(7)
SH304-2C				
Phenocryst	2.0459	(10)	0.8277	(4)
Phenocryst	2.0505	(38)	0.8310	(12)
Groundmass	2.0451	(15)	0.8275	(9)
Groundmass	2.0465	(11)	0.8278	(8)
Groundmass	2.0451	(9)	0.8275	(1)
Groundmass	2.0465	(8)	0.8278	(1)
Groundmass	2.0429	(12)	0.8234	(1)
Groundmass	2.0420	(4)	0.8245	(1)
Groundmass	2.0398	(12)	0.8234	(1)
Inclusion	2.0407	(9)	0.8209	(4)
Inclusion	2.0397	(11)	0.8206	(4)
Inclusion	2.0403	(17)	0.8216	(7)
Inclusion	2.0397	(14)	0.8209	(6)
SH306-1				
Phenocryst	2.0478	(33)	0.8288	(19)
Phenocryst	2.0457	(49)	0.8293	(33)
Groundmass	2.0468	(7)	0.8269	(6)
Groundmass	2.0470	(14)	0.8272	(5)
Groundmass	2.0472	(15)	0.8287	(9)
Inclusion	2.0420	(7)	0.8204	(3)
Inclusion	2.0369	(15)	0.8193	(5)
Inclusion	2.0362	(9)	0.8192	(6)
Inclusion	2.0396	(12)	0.8198	(7)
Inclusion	2.0378	(23)	0.8213	(11)
Inclusion	2.0369	(17)	0.8208	(9)
Inclusion	2.0397	(17)	0.8234	(9)
BCR-2G (n=4)	2.0637	(10)	0.8316	(5)

Appendix 2. Anorthite Content and Trace-Element Abundances in Five Plagioclase Grains from Dome Sample SH304-2A

[This appendix appears only in the digital versions of this work—in the DVD-ROM that accompanies the printed volume and as a separate file accompanying this chapter on the Web: at http://pubs.usgs.gov/pp/1750.]

Appendix 2 is a spreadsheet that lists the mole fraction anorthite and measured concentrations for six elements (Li, Ti, Sr, Ba, La, Ce) from one traverse across each of five plagioclase grains. Traverses range in length from 375 to 775 μm.

Appendix 3. Anorthite and Trace Element Abundances in Plagioclase from 2004–2005 and 1981–1985 Dome Samples from Mount St. Helens

[This appendix appears only in the digital versions of this work—in the DVD-ROM that accompanies the printed volume and as a separate file accompanying this chapter on the Web at http://pubs.usgs.gov/pp/1750.]

Appendix 3 is a spreadsheet that lists the mole fraction anorthite and analytical data for 10 elements (Li, Ti, Sr, Ba, La, Ce, Pr, Nd, Eu, Pb) from 203 analyses of plagioclase phenocryst cores, margins, and inclusions in eight sample erupted in 2004–2005. Also shown are 28 analyses of plagioclase phenocryst cores in three samples erupted during the period 1981–85.

A Volcano Rekindled: The Renewed Eruption of Mount St. Helens 2004–2006
Edited by David R. Sherrod, William E. Scott, and Peter H. Stauffer
U.S. Geological Survey Professional Paper 1750, 2008

Chapter 36

^{238}U-^{230}Th-^{226}Ra Disequilibria in Dacite and Plagioclase from the 2004–2005 Eruption of Mount St. Helens

By Kari M. Cooper[1] and Carrie T. Donnelly[2]

Abstract

Uranium-series disequilibria in whole-rock samples and mineral separates provide unique insights into the time scales and processes of magma mixing, storage, and crystallization. We present ^{238}U-^{230}Th-^{226}Ra data for whole-rock dacite and gouge samples and for plagioclase separated from two dacite samples, all erupted from Mount St. Helens between October 2004 and April 2005. We also present new ^{238}U-^{230}Th disequilibria for a suite of four reference samples from the 1980–86 eruption of Mount St. Helens. We use the U-series data to evaluate the origin of the 2004–5 magma, its relation to the 1980–86 magma, and the relation of 2004–5 phenocrysts to their host magmas. Dacite samples from 2004–5 show variable (^{230}Th)/(^{238}U), ranging from ^{238}U-enriched to ^{230}Th-enriched. (^{230}Th)/(^{232}Th) ratios in 2004–5 dacite and gouge samples do not vary outside of analytical error and are within the range of (^{230}Th)/(^{232}Th) measured for the 1980s reference suite. However, (^{230}Th)/(^{232}Th) for plagioclase separates for dome samples erupted during October and November 2004 are significantly different from corresponding whole-rock values, which suggests that a large fraction (>30 percent) of crystals in each sample are foreign to the host liquid. Furthermore, plagioclase in the two 2004 samples have U-series characteristics distinct from each other and from plagioclase in dacite erupted in 1982, indicating that (1) the current eruption must include a component of crystals (and potentially associated magma) that were not sampled by the 1980–86 eruption, and (2) dacite magmas erupted only a month apart in 2004 contain different populations of crystals, indicating that this foreign component is highly heterogeneous within the 2004–5 magma reservoir.

[1]Department of Earth and Space Sciences, University of Washington, Box 351310, Seattle, WA 98195; now at Geology Department, University of California, One Shields Avenue, Davis, CA 95616

[2] Department of Earth and Space Sciences, University of Washington, Box 351310, Seattle, WA 98195

Introduction

After an 18-year hiatus, Mount St. Helens erupted in October 2004, beginning a period of dacite dome extrusion that produced more than 70 million cubic meters of crystal-rich, gas-poor dacite during the first 18 months of eruption (Pallister and others, this volume, chap. 30). Extrusion continues at the time of this writing (2007). The dome has erupted as essentially a solid plug, extruding a series of spines mantled by meter-thick fault gouge (for example, Pallister and others, this volume, chap. 30; Cashman and others, this volume, chap. 19). Samples have been collected by the staff at the U.S. Geological Survey Cascades Volcano Observatory and distributed to a group of ~25 investigators working on various petrologic and geochemical investigations aimed at understanding the origin and characteristics of the newly erupted material and the relation of the currently erupting magma to that erupted in the 1980–86 eruptive cycle. Major- and trace-element compositions of the 2004–5 dacite whole-rock samples are similar to those of the 1980–86 dacite dome (for example, Pallister and others, 2005; and this volume, chap. 30), suggesting the possibility that the current eruption is tapping magma that remained in the reservoir after the 1980s. In this chapter, we present ^{238}U-^{230}Th-^{226}Ra data for a suite of samples from the first six months (October 2004–April 2005) of the ongoing eruption of Mount St. Helens, and ^{238}U-^{230}Th data for a suite of reference samples from the 1980–86 eruption. We focus here on whole-rock data for dacite dome and gouge samples for the 2004–5 eruption; we also present data for plagioclase separated from two dacite samples. These data complement other analyses by the Mount St. Helens petrology working group presented in this volume. We use these data to address the following questions: (1) Is the current eruption fed by a new batch of magma previously unseen at Mount St. Helens, and/or is this eruption tapping a remnant magma body from the 1980–86 eruption? (2) What is the relation of plagioclase phenocrysts to the host magmas in the 2004 dome samples?

Background: U-Series Disequilibria in Older Mount St. Helens Lavas

U-series Disequilibria in Volcanic Rocks

U-series disequilibria in volcanic rocks have been used for decades as a tool for understanding magmatic processes (see reviews by Bourdon and others, 2003; Ivanovich and Harmon, 1992, and references therein). Disequilibria measured in whole-rock, glass, and mineral separates can be used both as tracers of chemically distinct magmas or crystals (for example, Cooper and Reid, 2003; Turner and others, 2003c) and to provide temporal and chemical information about magmatic processes ranging from melt generation (Bourdon and Sims, 2003; Lundstrom, 2003; Sims and others, 2003; Sims and others, 2002; Turner and others, 2003a) to magma residence and differentiation within the crust (Blake and Rogers, 2005; Condomines and others, 2003; Cooper and others, 2001; Hawkesworth and others, 2004; Reid, 2003; Reid and others, 1997; Rogers and others, 2004; Turner and others, 2003b; Turner and others, 2003c; Vazquez and Reid, 2004) to degassing and related crystal growth (Berlo and others, 2004; Reagan and others, this volume, chap. 37; Turner and others, 2004). A unique aspect of U-series studies is that they allow connection between chemical variations within crystals and absolute ages (for example, Vazquez and Reid, 2004).

U-series studies of magmatic processes are based on the fact that ^{238}U decays to ^{206}Pb through a series of intermediate daughter isotopes with half-lives ranging from less than one second to as much as 0.245 m.y. (^{234}U; Cheng and others, 2000). Any U-bearing system, given sufficient time as a closed system, will attain a state of radioactive or secular equilibrium where the rate of disintegration of each of the nuclides in the chain is the same. Magmatic processes, such as melt generation, crystallization, and degassing, can fractionate the different nuclides in the chain, creating disequilibria between individual parent-daughter pairs. Such disequilibria will return to radioactive equilibrium at a rate dictated by the half-life of the daughter isotope; thus the degree of disequilibrium preserved in erupted lavas contains information about the time since the last fractionation event, and each parent-daughter pair is sensitive to a different time scale. In particular, ^{230}Th-^{238}U disequilibria can record events that occurred within the past ~10,000 years to ~350,000 years, whereas ^{230}Th-^{226}Ra disequilibria are sensitive to time scales of a few hundred years to ~10,000 years. This range of hundreds to hundreds of thousands of years is commensurate with time scales of magma differentiation and storage in many systems (for example, recent reviews by Condomines and others, 2003; Hawkesworth and others, 2004; Reid, 2003; Zellmer and others, 2005), including that of older Mount St. Helens lavas (Cooper and Reid, 2003; Volpe and Hammond, 1991).

U-series Disequilibria in Older Mount St. Helens Lavas

U-series data in older Mount St. Helens lavas have been discussed previously (Bennett and others, 1982; Cooper and Reid, 2003; Volpe and Hammond, 1991), which provides an excellent context for our analyses of the 2004–5 samples. Volpe and Hammond (1991) analyzed ^{238}U-^{230}Th-^{226}Ra disequilibria in whole-rock samples, groundmass, and mineral separates for seven lavas erupted from Mount St. Helens within the past ~2,000 years (figs. 1*A*, 2*A*). Data for whole-rock and groundmass samples span an analytically significant range of $^{230}Th/^{232}Th$ ratios (fig. 1*A*), indicating that the different magmas had different source regions (Volpe and Hammond, 1991). These samples are also significantly enriched in ^{226}Ra compared to radioactive equilibrium with ^{230}Th (that is, $(^{226}Ra)/(^{230}Th) > 1$, where by convention parentheses around the chemical symbols represent activities) with $(^{226}Ra)/(^{230}Th)$ ranging from 1.07 in an andesite of Castle Creek age (MSH 90-4) to 1.55 in a sample of dacite erupted in 1982 (MSH 90-9; fig. 2*A*). The preservation of these ^{226}Ra excesses requires that the time between the last fractionation event (likely to be melt generation) and eruption was less than about 10,000 years.

Volpe and Hammond's (1991) ^{238}U-^{230}Th data for mineral separates and whole-rock samples define linear arrays on a ^{238}U-^{230}Th isochron diagram, with slopes corresponding to apparent ages of 2–6 ka for most samples (fig. 1A). In contrast, two samples of Castle Creek age (erupted ~2 ka) yield apparent ages of 34–27 ka (Volpe and Hammond, 1991). At the same time, all of the mineral separates preserve ^{226}Ra-^{230}Th disequilibria indicating fractionation of Ra from Th within the past 10,000 years (fig. 2*A*), which is in conflict with the ^{230}Th-^{238}U apparent ages for Castle Creek samples. In detail, the ^{226}Ra-^{230}Th data for minerals and whole-rock analyses of the same samples do not define linear arrays on a Ba-normalized ^{226}Ra-^{230}Th isochron diagram (fig. 2*A*), which Volpe and Hammond (1991) interpreted as evidence of addition of a ^{226}Ra-enriched fluid to the liquid after crystallization of the minerals. Cooper and Reid (2003) reexamined Volpe and Hammond's data by using a new method of calculating ^{226}Ra-^{230}Th ages that accounts for impurities in the mineral separates and for differences in partitioning behavior of Ra and Ba. After applying this method, all of the Mount St. Helens data can be explained by crystallization and aging alone, without requiring late-stage addition of Ra to the system. All of the revised ^{226}Ra-^{230}Th ages are consistent with recent (less than a few thousand years) crystal growth, and, with the exception of the two Castle Creek samples, are concordant with ^{230}Th-^{238}U ages. ^{226}Ra-^{230}Th and ^{230}Th-^{238}U disequilibria return to secular equilibrium on different time scales; thus average ages for bulk separates with a protracted growth history will weight the old and young components differently for the two parent-daughter pairs, resulting in different average ages. Cooper and Reid (2003) interpreted the discordant ^{226}Ra-^{230}Th and ^{230}Th-^{238}U ages in the Castle Creek samples to reflect multiple phases of crystallization within the bulk mineral separate, either crystal populations of differing ages or old cores with younger overgrowths. In addition, plagioclase in the 1982 dacite (MSH90-9) has anomalously high Ra/Ba compared to what would be expected for equilibrium partitioning, which may reflect crystallization that was rapid enough to prevent chemical equilibrium between liquid and crystals (Cooper and Reid, 2003). These observations would predict that if the 2004–5 magmas were simply remnant magma from the 1980–86 eruption, then (1) whole-rock isotopic compositions (including (^{230}Th)/(^{232}Th)) would be identical in 2004–5 and 1980–86 samples, and (2) crystals within the 2004–5 dacite would have ^{238}U-^{230}Th-^{226}Ra characteristics like those in crystals erupted in the 1980s. Our new data for 2004–5 samples provide a test of these predictions.

Analytical Methods

Chemical separation of U-series elements and isotopic analysis by multicollector inductively coupled plasma mass spectrometry (MC-ICP-MS) were conducted at the University of Washington. Mass-spectrometry protocols and results for rock and solution standards are detailed in appendix 1. Chemical separation procedures were modified from published procedures (Goldstein and Stirling, 2003; Pietruszka and others, 2002) and are also detailed in the appendix. Briefly, the elements of interest were separated from the rock or mineral matrix using ion-exchange chromatography, conducted in class-100 laboratory facilities (low-particulate facilities, designed to minimize trace-metal contamination). Rock chips or mineral separates (0.5–1.5 g) were dissolved in concentrated hydrofluoric+nitric acids, followed by evaporation and dissolution in hydrochloric acid. Resulting sample solutions were split into three aliquots:

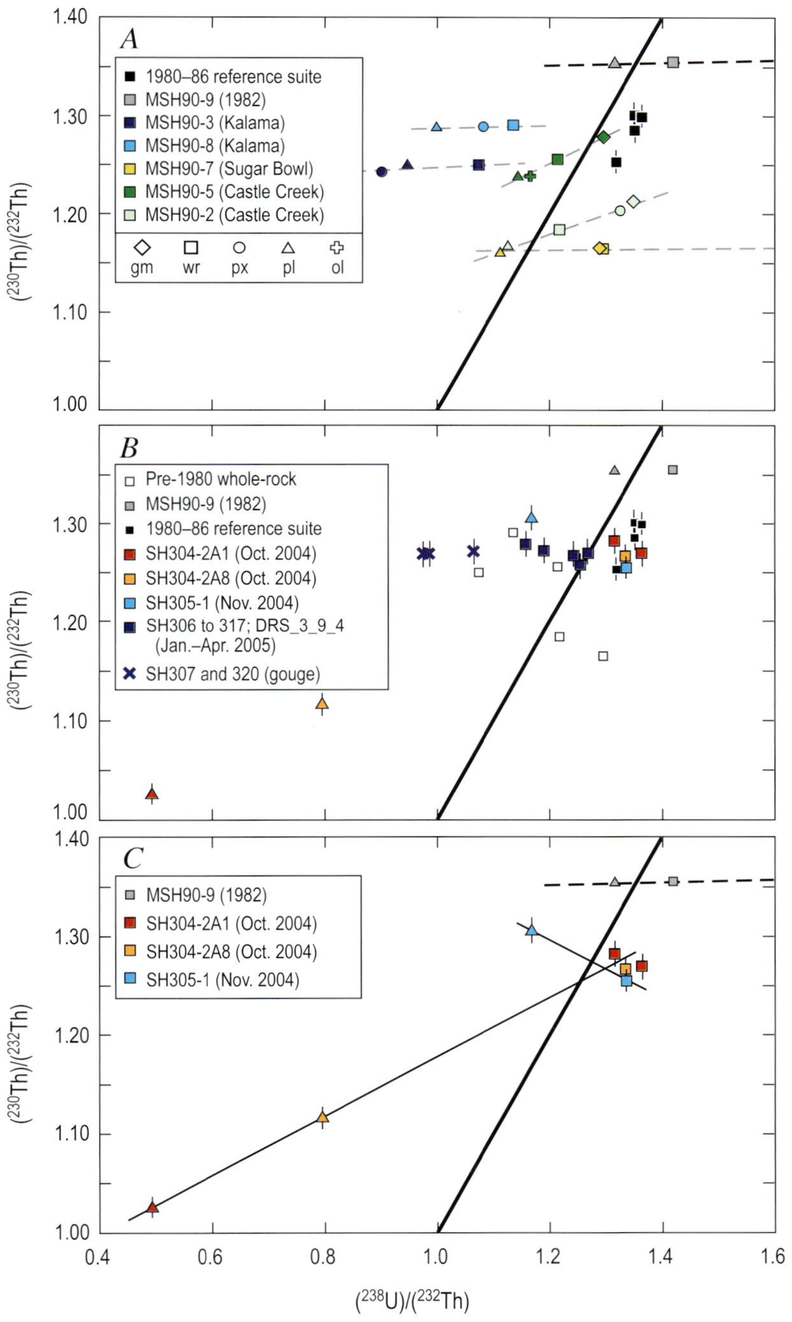

Figure 1. ^{238}U-^{230}Th isochron diagrams for Mount St. Helens samples. Solid bold line with slope 1 on all panels is the equiline (representing radioactive equilibrium). Thin solid and dashed lines are fits to the mineral-separate data for each sample. *A*, Pre-2004 samples. Black squares are analyses of 1980–86 samples from this study; error bars are shown for ±1-percent uncertainties. "MSH90-X" data are from Volpe and Hammond (1991); error bars for those samples are omitted for clarity but are similar in size to those shown for the 1980–86 reference-suite samples. Symbols for different phases are as follows: diamonds, groundmass (gm); squares, whole-rock (wr); circles, pyroxene (px); triangles, plagioclase (pl); cross, olivine (ol). *B*, Data for 1980–2005 samples. Shown for reference are pre-1980 samples (whole-rock data only; open squares) and 1982 dacite (MSH90-9; gray symbols; from Volpe and Hammond, 1991). Error bars for 2004–5 samples are shown only where larger than plotted symbol. Symbols for plagioclase and whole-rock data as in panel *A*; gouge samples indicated by "x" symbols. *C*, Whole-rock data and plagioclase separates for October 2004 dome (SH304-2A) and November 2004 dome (SH305-1). The 1982 dacite sample is shown for reference (Volpe and Hammond, 1991). Symbols as in panels *A* and *B*.

one small aliquot was spiked with ^{233}U and ^{229}Th for U and Th concentration measurement by isotope dilution, a second small aliquot was spiked with ^{135}Ba for Ba concentration measurement by isotope dilution, and the largest aliquot was spiked with ^{228}Ra and used for measurement of Ra concentration by isotope dilution and U and Th isotopic compositions. Uranium and thorium (both for measurement of isotopic composition and for isotope dilution) were separated from the rock matrix and from each other using Eichrom TRU™ resin. Radium was subsequently separated from the rock matrix washed from the TRU column of the Th and U isotopic-composition aliquot using cation-exchange resin and was purified using Eichrom Sr-spec™resin and a final cation-exchange microcolumn. Isotopic ratios were measured using a Nu Plasma MC-ICP-MS equipped with three ion counters and an energy filter on the high-mass ion counter for increased abundance sensitivity.

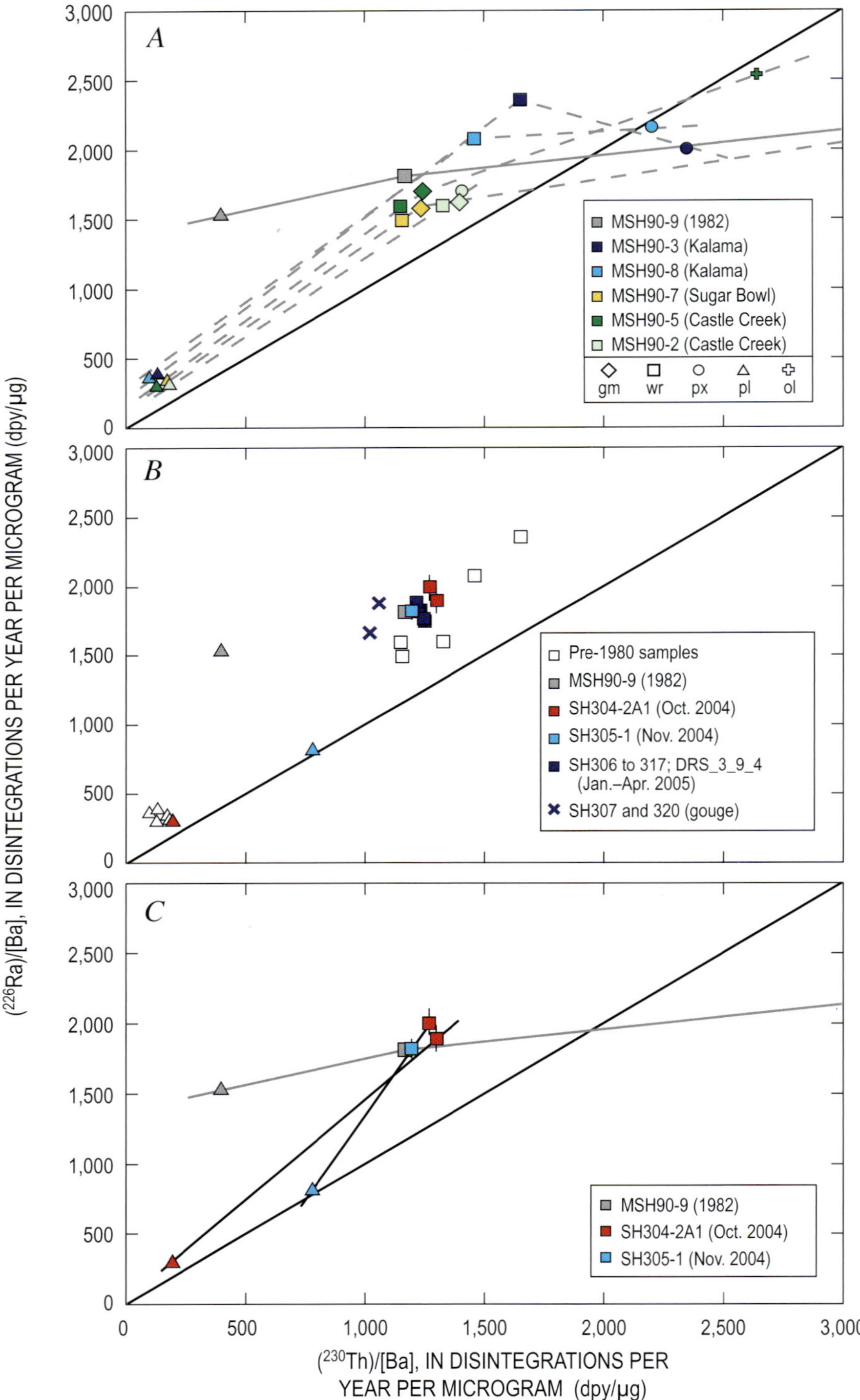

Figure 2. ^{226}Ra-^{230}Th-Ba isochron diagrams for Mount St. Helens samples. Solid line with slope 1 (the equiline, representing radioactive equilibrium) is shown on all panels. *A*, Pre-2004 samples. Symbols as in figure 1 and shown in the legend. *B*, Data for 1980–2005 samples. Pre-1980 samples (whole-rock and plagioclase data only; open symbols) are shown for reference. Error bars are shown where they are larger than the size of the symbols. *C*, Whole-rock data and plagioclase separates for October 2004 dome (SH304-2A) and November 2004 dome (SH305-1). The 1982 dacite sample (Volpe and Hammond, 1991) is shown for reference (gray symbols). Symbols as in panels *A* and *B*.

Results

^{238}U-^{230}Th Disequilibria

2004–2005 Dome Samples

^{230}Th-^{238}U disequilibria for 2004–5 Mount St. Helens dome dacites are within the range of those measured in older Mount St. Helens lavas (Volpe and Hammond, 1991; table 1, fig. 1*B*). $(^{230}Th)/(^{232}Th)$ ratios measured in 2004–5 whole-rock dacite samples span a range of ~2 percent (from 1.257 to 1.282), analytically indistinguishable from each other given our reproducibility of ±1 percent. The dome samples show some variation in U/Th ratio, $((^{238}U)/(^{232}Th) = 1.159–1.366)$, resulting in a variation in ^{230}Th-^{238}U disequilibria from ^{238}U-enriched $((^{230}Th)/(^{238}U) = 0.929)$ to ^{230}Th-enriched $((^{230}Th)/(^{238}U) = 1.103)$. The majority of arc lavas are ^{238}U enriched, which is generally attributed to the influence of subduction-zone fluids, but ^{230}Th-enriched lavas have been observed in some arc settings (Turner and others, 2003a). It is also possible, given the presence of zircon in a sample of 2004–6 dome material (C. Miller, written commun., 2006), that some of the variation in U/Th ratios is due to differences in percentage of zircon and/or incomplete dissolution of zircon in different samples. No systematic decrease in U/Th ratio or ^{230}Th-^{238}U disequilibria over time is observed (not shown), although the two earliest samples (October–November 2004 lava spines) have the highest U/Th ratios and are the only samples that are ^{238}U-enriched.

1980–1986 Reference Suite

The four reference samples from the 1980–86 eruption have thorium isotopic compositions that overlap $^{230}Th/^{232}Th$ measured in the 2004–5 samples (fig. 1*B*). Three samples (SH32, SH131, and SH157, erupted in 1980, 1982, and 1984, respectively) have $^{230}Th/^{232}Th$ ratios at the high end of those measured in 2004–5 dome samples, though they overlap within measurement error. The 1986 sample has $(^{230}Th)/(^{232}Th)$ ~4 percent lower than the other three 1980s samples, but it is within error of the lowest $(^{230}Th)/(^{232}Th)$ ratio measured in 2004–5 dome samples. Our measurement of ^{230}Th-^{238}U disequilibria in SH131 (1982 dome) is not within error of the measurement of the 1982 dome sample (MSH90-9) reported by Volpe and Hammond (1991). This discrepancy could be due to thorium isotopic heterogeneity within the 1982 dome, or it could indicate that one of the measurements is in error. Thorium and U concentrations and Th/U ratios in the two samples of the 1982 dome are similar but not identical, which may support the former interpretation. For the purposes of this paper, we will focus on comparisons of 2004–5 samples with our measurements of the 1980s reference suite because they were performed in the same lab using the same methods.

Plagioclase Separates for 2004 Dome Samples

Plagioclase separates from two subsamples of dome rock erupted in October 2004 (SH304-2A1 and SH304-2A8) have U/Th ratios significantly lower than the whole-rock values for the same samples, qualitatively consistent with relative partitioning of U and Th in plagioclase (Blundy and Wood, 2003). $^{230}Th/^{232}Th$ ratios in the plagioclase separates are also low compared to the corresponding whole-rock values (table 1; fig. 1), and both plagioclase separates have large ^{230}Th-enrichments ($(^{230}Th)/(^{238}U) = 2.087$ and 1.404, respectively). A plagioclase separate from the dome erupted in November 2004 (SH305-1) is also ^{230}Th enriched ($(^{230}Th)/(^{238}U) = 1.117$), with U/Th ratio lower than the corresponding whole-rock measurement but higher than that in plagioclase from SH304-2A. The $^{232}Th/^{230}Th$ ratios in plagioclase and whole-rock samples of SH305-1 differ by about 4 percent, outside of analytical uncertainty. The U/Th ratios measured in plagioclase separates for the October 2004 dome (SH304-2A1 and SH304-2A8) are significantly lower than U/Th ratios measured by Volpe and Hammond (1991) in plagioclase separated from older Mount St. Helens samples, whereas plagioclase in the November 2004 dome sample (SH305-1) has U/Th ratio similar to those measured in plagioclase by Volpe and Hammond (1991). These differences in U/Th most likely reflect differences in the percentage or nature of impurities (groundmass and/or inclusions of glass or other mineral phases) in the plagioclase separates, although some part of the variation may reflect differences in U/Th of the magmas from which they crystallized.

2004–2005 Gouge Samples

The $(^{230}Th)/(^{232}Th)$ ratios measured in gouge samples (SH307-2A and SH320-1) are within error of those measured in the 2004–5 dacites, although $(^{238}U)/(^{232}Th)$ ratios are significantly lower than those measured in dome samples. Concentrations of both uranium and thorium are lower in gouge samples than in dacite samples (table 1). Sample SH320-1 also has lower barium and radium concentrations than do dome samples, although SH307-2A has barium and radium concentrations within the range of dome whole-rock samples.

^{226}Ra-^{230}Th Disequilibria

All whole-rock dome and gouge samples are enriched in ^{226}Ra relative to equilibrium with ^{230}Th, with ^{226}Ra excesses of 40–55 percent for whole-rock samples (similar to those measured by Volpe and Hammond (1991) for older whole-rock samples) and 60–77 percent for gouge samples (table 1; fig. 2*B*). Gouge samples have $(^{230}Th)/[Ba]$ ratios lower than those of dacite dome samples, but broadly similar $(^{226}Ra)/[Ba]$ ratios (fig. 2). (Brackets around the chemical symbol, by convention, indicate concentration.)

A bulk plagioclase separate from the October 2004 dome sample (SH304-2A1) has ^{226}Ra-^{230}Th-Ba characteristics similar to plagioclase separates from older Mount St. Helens samples, but it has lower $(^{226}Ra)/[Ba]$ and $(^{230}Th)/[Ba]$ than Volpe and Hammond's (1991) measurements of plagioclase in the 1982 dome (MSH90-9; fig. 2). The plagioclase separate for the November 2004 dome (SH305-1), in contrast, is within error of radioactive equilibrium ($(^{226}Ra)/(^{230}Th) = 1.039$), with significantly higher $(^{230}Th)/[Ba]$ than any of the other Mount St. Helens plagioclase separates.

Discussion

Origin of the 2004–2005 Dacite: Remnant Magma from 1980–1986?

Whole-Rock Data

Major- and trace-element composition of the 2004–5 dacite whole-rock samples are similar to those of the 1980–86 dacite dome (for example, Pallister and others, 2005; this volume, chap. 30), suggesting the possibility that the cur-

Table 1. Concentrations, isotopic compositions, and activity ratios measured in Mount St. Helens samples.

[See appendix 1 for analytical details. WR, whole-rock; Pl, plagioclase. For duplicate sample names, #1 or #2 indicate chemical separation and analysis of splits of the same solution; "replicate" indicates separate dissolution and analysis of splits of the same rock or mineral separate. Accuracy and reproducibility of measurements was <0.5 percent for Th and U concentrations, <2 percent for Ba concentrations, <1 percent for $^{230}Th/^{232}Th$, and <0.6 percent for $^{234}U/^{238}U$ (see appendix 1 for details). Uncertainties in Ra concentrations were limited by in-run errors during mass spectrometry, which are quoted here as 1 standard error (SE) of the mean (relative). Decay constants used in calculations were $\lambda_{234}=2.82629\times10^{-6}$ (Cheng and others, 2000), $\lambda_{230}=9.158\times10^{-6}$ (Cheng and others, 2000), $\lambda_{232}=4.933\times10^{-11}$, $\lambda_{238}=1.551\times10^{-10}$, and $\lambda_{226}=4.332\times10^{-4}$. Dashes indicate no data.]

Sample No.	Eruption date	Ba, in ppm	Ra, in fg/g	Ra %SE	Th, in ppm	U, in ppm	$^{230}Th/^{232}Th$ (10^{-6})	(^{234}U)/(^{238}U)	(^{238}U)/(^{232}Th)	(^{230}Th)/(^{232}Th)	(^{230}Th)/(^{238}U)	(^{226}Ra)/(^{230}Th)	(^{230}Th)/[Ba], in dpy/μg	(^{226}Ra)/[Ba], in dpy/μg
1980–1986 samples														
SH52	1980	--	--	--	2.049	0.911	7.010	--	1.353	1.301	0.962	--	--	--
SH131	1982	--	--	--	1.974	0.885	7.002	--	1.364	1.300	0.953	--	--	--
SH157	1984	--	--	--	2.390	1.063	6.928	--	1.353	1.286	0.950	--	--	--
SH226	1986	--	--	--	2.496	1.084	6.752	--	1.322	1.253	0.948	--	--	--
2004–2005 samples														
SH304-2A1 WR #1	10/18/04	338.6	555.0[1]	0.61	2.685	1.162	6.906	1.002	1.317	1.282	0.974	1.454	1,301	1,892
SH304-2A1 WR #2	10/18/04	332.2	575.1[2]	2.4	2.598	1.166	6.839	1.002	1.366	1.270	0.930	1.572	1,271	1,998
SH304-2A1 Pl #1	10/18/04	117.9	30.1[1]	1.6	0.175	0.028	5.529	1.004	0.492	1.026	2.087	1.514	195	295
SH304-2A1 Pl #2	10/18/04	116.4	--	--	--	0.029	5.528	1.001	--	1.026	--	--	--	--
SH304-2A8 WR	10/18/04	327.8	--	--	2.581	1.134	6.826	1.001	1.337	1.267	0.948	--	1,277	--
SH304-2A8 Pl	10/18/04	118.1	--	--	0.198	0.052	6.015	1.001	0.795	1.117	1.404	--	240	--
SH305-1 WR	11/20/04	330.9	521.2[1]	1.8	2.585	1.131	--	1.005	--	--	--	--	--	--
SH305-1 WR replicate	11/20/04	--			2.465	1.083	6.770	--	1.338	1.257	0.939	1.517[4]	1,198	1,818[4]
SH305-1 Pl	11/20/04	113.4	79.8[1]	1.3	0.531	0.204	7.034	1.005	1.169	1.306	1.117	1.039	782	813
SH306	12/15/04	329.6	538.0[2]	0.43	2.464	0.965	6.854[3]	1.002	1.191	1.272	1.068	1.547	1,218	1,884
SH307-2A gouge		315.9	514.0[2]	1.4	2.065	0.663	6.836	1.003	0.977	1.269	1.299	1.768	1,062	1,878
SH307-2A gouge replicate		332.6	--	--	2.137	0.693	--	--	0.987	--	--	--	--	--
SH311-1B WR	01/16/05	327.9	496.3[1]	2.4	2.504	0.953	6.888	1.007	1.159	1.279	1.104	1.397	1,250	1,747
MSH05DRS_3_9_4 WR	03/08/05	326.9	515.0[2]	1.1	2.513	1.036	6.776	1.004	1.255	1.258	1.002	1.469	1,238	1,818
SH316-1A WR	04/15/05	331.5	505.7[2]	0.44	2.544	1.061	6.842	1.002	1.269	1.270	1.001	1.411	1,248	1,761
SH317-1A WR	05/01/05	331.5	520.2[2]	0.49	2.504	1.023	6.830	1.000	1.244	1.268	1.019	1.477	1,226	1,811
SH320-1 gouge		283.2	406.0[2]	1.2	1.783	0.625	6.849	1.000	1.066	1.271	1.193	1.615	1,025	1,655
Rock standards														
TML		--	3627[1]	0.19	31.780	11.201	5.763	--	1.073	1.070	0.997	0.962	--	--
TML replicate		--	3707[2]	1.3	31.119	10.944	5.806	1.002[5]	1.070	1.078	1.007	0.996	--	--
BHVO-1		--	163.3[2]	1.1	1.214	0.421	5.784	1.003[5]	1.057	1.074	1.016	1.130	--	--
BHVO-1 replicate		--	--	--	1.213	0.421	--	--	1.056	--	--	--	--	--
BCR-2		672.8	--	--	5.879	1.701	4.745	--	0.880	0.881	1.001	--	--	--

[1] Ra analyses by static, multi-ion-counting routine, as described in appendix 1.

[2] Ra analyses by dynamic routine using only IC0, as described in appendix 1.

[3] Average of two measurements of the same solution during the same day. Individual measurements differed by 0.9 percent.

[4] Calculated using Ra concentration measured for SH305-1 WR.

[5] (^{234}U)/(^{238}U) of rock standards represents the mean of eight measurements of the same solution over four analytical sessions. Relative standard deviation of replicate measurements was 0.17 percent for sample TML and 0.24 percent for BHVO-1.

rent eruption is tapping magma that remained in the reservoir after the 1980s. If the current eruption is tapping magma that is either unmodified from the 1980s or has been modified only by fractional crystallization, one prediction would be that isotopic compositions of the 1980–86 dacite would be identical to those in the 2004–5 dacite. In the case that the two magmas are related by cooling and fractional crystallization, but without significant influence of open-system processes such as wall-rock assimilation or mixing with compositionally distinct batches of magma, some variation in trace-element concentrations of the residual liquid would also be predicted. Kent and others (this volume, chap. 35) propose a model in which the 1980s and 2004–5 magmas are related by fractional crystallization that occurred primarily by chemical isolation of grain interiors from the host magma, without volumetrically significant gain or loss of plagioclase crystals, but with a small volume of an additional crystal component added to the magma through disaggregation of xenoliths. In this scenario, because crystals are not lost from or appreciably added to the bulk magma, whole-rock trace-element ratios would be unmodified during crystallization. In detail, however, a simple model of fractional crystallization would predict higher concentrations of incompatible elements (such as Ra, Th, U, and Ba) in the 2004–5 samples compared to the 1980–86 samples. Although Ra, Th, and U concentrations are indeed higher in the 2004–5 samples (table 1; Volpe and Hammond, 1991), Ba concentrations are lower, which suggests that a more complex explanation is necessary.

Nevertheless, the similarities between magmas erupted during the 1980s and the 2004–5 dacite (for example, major- and trace-element data in Pallister and others, this volume, chap. 30) suggest that the 2004–5 eruption is tapping at least some component of magma that remained in the reservoir after the 1980–86 eruption. The U-series data are consistent with this hypothesis but require some additional component(s) in the plagioclase populations (see below). Thorium isotopic compositions that we measured in whole-rock samples from 1980–86 samples span a small, but analytically significant, range ($^{230}Th/^{232}Th$ ratios vary by ~4 percent), overlapping the thorium isotopic compositions that we measured in the 2004–5 samples, with (^{238}U)/(^{232}Th) similar to the October–November 2004 dome (SH304-2A1 and SH305-1; fig. 1*B*). Later-erupted 2004–5 samples have lower (^{238}U)/(^{232}Th), with no change in (^{230}Th)/(^{232}Th), suggesting that the 2004–5 magma has some trace-element heterogeneity, but that different magmas erupted are all closely related. ^{226}Ra-^{232}Th disequilibria are also similar in all 2004–5 and 1982 dacites, consistent with the similarity in thorium isotopic compositions. Interestingly, there appears to have been a slight decrease in $^{230}Th/^{232}Th$ ratios during the course of the 1980–86 eruption (fig. 1; table 1), suggesting that at least two magmas with different origins were involved in that eruption (and perhaps more, if the much higher $^{230}Th/^{232}Th$ measured in a 1982 dacite sample by Volpe and Hammond (1991) also reflects compositional heterogeneity).

Volpe and Hammond's (1991) measurements of (^{226}Ra)/[Ba] and (^{230}Th)/[Ba] in their sample of 1982 dacite do not overlap with our measurements of 2004–5 samples (fig. 2*B*). Whether there is significant heterogeneity within the 1980–86 and 2004–5 suites, as suggested above for ^{230}Th-^{238}U disequilibria, cannot be assessed at this time because we do not yet have ^{226}Ra data for the 1980–86 reference suite. However, the 2004–5 samples fall in a relatively tight cluster with the exception of the October 2004 dome (SH304-2A1), which has similar (^{226}Ra)/[Ba] but slightly higher (^{230}Th)/[Ba], possibly due to more plagioclase fractionation from this sample than seen in the other dacites.

Plagioclase Separates

When crystal compositions are considered in addition to whole-rock compositions, the 2004–5 magma must contain a component not observed in the 1980–86 magmas. The 2004–5 magmas contain plagioclase with compositions unlike those in older Mount St. Helens samples, which would require addition of crystals to a putative remnant 1980–86 magma. This is most dramatically illustrated by $^{230}Th/^{232}Th$ measured in plagioclase separated from the October 2004 dome (SH304-2A1), which is substantially lower than $^{230}Th/^{232}Th$ measured in any recently erupted samples of Mount St. Helens lavas (figs. 1*B*, *C*). Whether this lower $^{230}Th/^{232}Th$ ratio is attributed to an old component in the plagioclase separate or to the addition of a population of plagioclase unrelated to the host magma, the low-$^{230}Th/^{232}Th$ component is not present to any significant degree in the plagioclase separate from the 1982 dacite measured by Volpe and Hammond (1991). Plagioclase in the November 2004 dome (SH305-1) has $^{230}Th/^{232}Th$ higher than the whole rock, also consistent with a plagioclase component that is foreign to the host liquid, although the foreign crystal component must be of a significantly different composition than that in SH304-2A1. In contrast to differences in their ^{230}Th-^{238}U signatures, the ^{226}Ra-^{230}Th-Ba composition of plagioclase in the October 2004 dome (SH304-2A1) is similar to plagioclase in samples erupted before 1980, but distinct from plagioclase in the 1982 dome sample (MSH90-9; fig. 2). In addition, the ^{226}Ra-^{230}Th-Ba signature of plagioclase of the November 2004 dome (SH305-1) is different from all measurements of plagioclase in older Mount St. Helens samples, including MSH90-9 (Volpe and Hammond, 1991) and SH-04-2A1 (fig. 2).

The presence of a foreign plagioclase component in the 2004–5 lavas is supported by Pb isotopic heterogeneity between plagioclase crystals and groundmass (Kent and others, this volume, chap. 35), by high Al in amphibole crystals that is not in equilibrium with the host liquid at pressures <300 MPa (Rutherford and Devine, this volume, chap. 31), by variable pressure-temperature conditions of crystallization of amphibole (Thornber and others, 2005), and by textures and zoning in plagioclase in the 2004–5 dacite that are distinct from the patterns observed in 1980–86 dacites (Streck and others, this volume, chap. 34). Therefore, the 2004–5 eruption clearly samples multiple crystal populations and, potentially, some associated liquid fractions that were not present in the eruptive products from 1980–86. However, given the similarity in whole-rock U-series compositions of the dacites, any liquid fraction associated with the crystals must be volumetrically minor, suggesting that the crystals were incorporated largely as a crystal mush or cumulate.

One potential scenario to account for these observations is that the 2004–5 magma is dominated volumetrically by remnant magma from 1980–86 but that it incorporated disaggregated crystal mush from within the reservoir system during the 18-year hiatus between eruptions, consistent with the presence of gabbroic inclusions within many of the 2004–5 dacite samples. In this case, the crystal mush must be genetically distinct from the 1980–86 magmas in order to explain the difference between (^{230}Th)/(^{232}Th) measured in the 2004–5 plagioclase separates and that measured in 1980–86 and 2004–5 whole-rock samples. It is also possible that the 2004–5 eruption is at least partially tapping new magma introduced into the reservoir system, perhaps associated with some of the deep earthquake swarms between 1986 and 2004 (Moran and others, 2005). Considering the similarity in major- and trace-element compositions of the 2004–5 dacite to dacites erupted earlier at Mount St. Helens, this new component may have originated through partial melting in the lower crust (see, for example, Pallister and others, 1992; Smith and Leeman, 1987). The range in (^{230}Th)/(^{238}U) and (^{226}Ra)/(^{230}Th) ratios observed in the 2004–5 samples is within the predicted range for incongruent dehydration melting of lower crustal amphibolite (Dufek and Cooper, 2005). However, we cannot rule out an origin through fractional crystallization of a garnet-bearing assemblage from a mantle-derived magma at lower crustal depths, as argued by Blundy and others (this volume, chap. 33). Finally, it is possible that our plagioclase separates contain a component of plagioclase from disaggregated xenoliths, either incorporated from Tertiary basement rocks or from the plutonic roots of the Mount St. Helens reservoir system (Kent and others, this volume, chap. 35; Pallister and others, this volume, chap. 30). In any case, the preservation of significant ^{226}Ra excesses in all of the 2004–5 whole-rock samples indicates that the time between melt generation and eruption for the bulk of the magma was short, less than one or two half-lives of ^{226}Ra (that is, less than a few thousand years).

Plagioclase in 2004–2005 Dacite: Effects of Impurities and Crystal Ages

Plagioclase in October 2004 Dome Samples

Plagioclase separates for the October 2004 dome subsamples (SH304-2A1 and SH304-2A8) have strikingly different thorium isotopic compositions than any of the 2004–5 whole-rock samples (fig. 1). Taken at face value, the slope of the two-point plagioclase-whole-rock isochron would correspond to an apparent crystallization age of ~42 ka. However, this apparent age is inconsistent with the preservation of ^{226}Ra excess measured in the same separates, precluding a simple history of crystal growth over a short time interval (less than a few hundred years) that occurred tens of thousands of years ago. Instead, this anomalously old apparent age likely indicates that the plagioclase separates include some percentage of older and/or foreign crystals in addition to plagioclase crystallized recently from the host liquid.

We estimate, on the basis of examination with binocular microscope, that the bulk plagioclase separate for SH304-2A1 is >95 percent pure. However, there are a number of components that could be present in small quantities in the bulk plagioclase separate, and the data plotted in figure 1 reflect the mixture of all of these; thus, in order to discriminate the effects of plagioclase aging from the effects of impurities, we must consider the U-series signature of each potential contributor. The bulk plagioclase separate could comprise a combination of plagioclase crystallized from the host liquid (at or near the time of eruption, and/or during storage in the crustal reservoir system); plagioclase that is foreign to the host liquid (either as a separate population of plagioclase crystals and/or as cores of crystals with multiple growth stages); groundmass adhering to the outside of plagioclase grains; and microscopic inclusions of melt or other phases within the plagioclase crystals. These in turn could include small amounts of the other major crystallizing phases, for example, amphibole, pyroxene, and Fe-Ti oxides (Pallister and others, this volume, chap. 30; Rutherford and Devine, this volume, chap. 31), and small mass fractions of accessory phases: apatite and zircon (C. Miller, written commun., 2006). Concentrations of Th, U, and Ra in pyroxene or Fe-Ti oxides will be low enough that a few percent of each would not significantly affect the ^{238}U-^{230}Th-^{226}Ra systematics of the bulk plagioclase separate (see also Blundy and Wood, 2003; Cooper and others, 2001); therefore, we will not consider them further. We discuss the U-series signatures and effects of each of the other components below.

Zero-Age Plagioclase

Plagioclase textures and rim compositions that are in equilibrium with the host liquid indicate that some fraction of plagioclase in each of the dome samples grew within a short time of eruption (for example, Pallister and others, this volume, chap. 30; Streck and others, this volume, chap. 34), at least partly as a result of decompression-induced crystallization that occurred during ascent of the 2004–5 magma (Blundy and others, this volume, chap. 33; Pallister and others, this volume, chap. 30). In addition, the lack of europium anomalies in REE patterns for whole-rock samples indicates that gain or loss of plagioclase to the magma must have been volumetrically minor (Blundy and others, this volume, chap. 33; Kent and others, this volume, chap. 35; Pallister and others, this volume, chap. 30), far less than the ~40 percent by volume of plagioclase crystals present in the magmas. In addition, plagioclase separates for 2004–5 samples have ^{210}Pb/^{226}Ra ratios that are not in radioactive equilibrium, indicating that some component of the plagioclase grew within decades of eruption (Reagan, 2005; Reagan and others, this volume, chap. 37). Therefore, the plagioclase separates certainly contain some plagioclase that crystallized from the host liquid at effectively zero age with respect to ^{238}U-^{230}Th-^{226}Ra disequilibria (that is, less than ~10 ka for ^{238}U-^{230}Th and less than a few hundred years for ^{230}Th-^{226}Ra). Such zero-age plagioclase would have $^{230}Th/^{232}Th$ equal to that in the host liquid, and $^{238}U/^{232}Th$ consistent with partitioning of Th and U between plagioclase and liquid at low pressure at ~850°C (based on oxide thermometry; Pallister and others, this volume, chap. 30; Rutherford and Devine, this volume, chap. 31). Blundy and Wood (2003) estimate D_U/D_{Th} in plagioclase to be ~0.18 at 900°C for An_{40}, similar to the temperatures and compositions appropriate for 2004–5 Mount St. Helens lavas. Using these data, we calculate (^{238}U)/(^{232}Th) in plagioclase in equilibrium with the October 2004 dome sample to be ~0.24 (fig. 3, table 2). Absolute values for D_U and D_{Th} are less well constrained, but by using $D_U = 6.0 \pm 3.7 \times 10^{-4}$ (measured in An_{58} plagioclase at 950°C; Blundy and Wood, 2003), we estimate Th and U concentrations of roughly 1–2 ppb in pure plagioclase (table 2). These calculations provide minimum estimates of Th and U concentrations in plagioclase in equilibrium with the liquid fraction of the magma, as the whole rock contains ~30–40 percent crystals and Th and U are incompatible in all of the major crystallizing phases. However, the Th/U ratio will likely be similar in the liquid and whole rock, and calculated (^{238}U)/(^{232}Th) is likely more robust to changes in mineral mode than are concentrations of U or Th. The bulk plagioclase separate, therefore, must contain some phase with (^{238}U)/(^{232}Th) higher than ~0.24 and (^{230}Th)/(^{232}Th) lower than that measured in the bulk separate (1.026).

Using the elastic-strain model and the latest fitting parameters for plagioclase (Blundy and Wood, 2003), we calculate (^{226}Ra)/[Ba] in plagioclase in equilibrium with a liquid of the October 2004 whole-rock composition to be ~330 dpy/µg (An_{40} at 850°C), and (^{230}Th)/[Ba] of ~1–2 dpy/µg (disintegrations per year per microgram). Calculated (^{226}Ra)/[Ba] is slightly higher than that measured in the bulk mineral separate, which could reflect some aging of the plagioclase since crystallization (as much as ~500 years), and/or the effects of other, low-Ra/Ba phases in the bulk separate. Th/Ba ratios could be significantly different in melt and whole-rock, considering that Ba is several orders of magnitude less incompatible than Th in plagioclase and amphibole, which dominate the crystal mode. Th/Ba in the liquid will therefore be higher than that in the whole-rock, leading to higher (^{230}Th)/[Ba] in plagioclase in equilibrium with the liquid. This is consistent with ion microprobe measurements of Th and Ba in plagioclase in older Mount St. Helens samples, where (^{230}Th)/[Ba] ratios were 10–50 for the 1982 dome and ~40–75 for older samples (Cooper and Reid, 2003). We estimate that (^{230}Th)/[Ba] in plagioclase crystallizing from the October 2004 magma is likely ~10–100, lower than the ratio of ~200 in the bulk separate.

Other Populations of Plagioclase

In addition to zero-age plagioclase crystallized from the host liquid, the bulk plagioclase separate may contain some older plagioclase, which would have lower (^{226}Ra)/[Ba] and (if older than ~5–10 ka) lower (^{230}Th)/(^{232}Th) than zero-age plagioclase. There are three possible origins for older crystals in the October 2004 dome plagioclase separate: (1) crystals that precipitated from the host magma and subsequently aged; (2) plagioclase crystallized from a different magma within the Mount St. Helens system ("antecrysts" in the terminology of W. Hildreth, as cited in Charlier and others (2005)); or (3) crystals incorporated from wall rocks unrelated to the Mount St. Helens magmatic system (xenocrysts). Gabbroic to dioritic xenoliths have been observed both in the 1980s eruptive products (Heliker, 1995) and in the current eruption (Kent and others, this volume, chap. 35; Pallister and others, this volume, chap. 30). Note that these are termed "inclusions" by Kent and others (this volume) and Pallister and others (this volume), but we use the term "xenoliths" instead to avoid confusion with microscopic inclusions within plagioclase crystals. Pallister and others (this volume, chap. 30) estimate the abundance of gabbroic to dioritic xenoliths in the 2004–6 dacite at 1–5 percent. They report ion microprobe U-Pb ages of 25 Ma for zircon separated from xenoliths in the 1980–86 lava dome, suggesting that the zircons are samples of Tertiary intrusions unrelated to the Mount St. Helens magmatic system. Kent and others (this volume, chap. 35) interpret the disaggregated xenoliths within the 2004–5 dome to have a similar origin. However, no xenoliths from the 2004–5 dome have been dated and they could, in theory, be of any age as old as the age of the basement rocks. In the case of Mount St. Helens, antecrysts could have ages as old as ~300 ka (Clynne and others, this volume, chap. 28), but older crystals (ranging back to Tertiary in age) would be xenocrysts. Regardless of origin, old plagioclase would likely have low (^{230}Th)/(^{232}Th) and low (^{238}U)/(^{232}Th), which makes it the only one of the likely components in the bulk plagioclase separate that could explain the low (^{230}Th)/(^{232}Th) measured in that separate (fig. 3*A*).

If the older plagioclase crystallized from the host liquid, it would have (^{238}U)/(^{232}Th) like that in zero-age plagioclase but with lower (^{230}Th)/(^{232}Th). Assuming that thorium concentrations are the same in old and young populations, we calculate that (^{230}Th)/(^{232}Th) of the bulk separate could be produced by a mixture of ~70 percent zero-age plagioclase with ~30 percent plagioclase in ^{238}U-^{230}Th radioactive equilibrium. The percentage of old crystals in the mixture would be higher if they were not in radioactive equilibrium; for example, a mix with 200-ka crystals would require ~40 percent old crystals, whereas a mix with ~100-ka crystals would require ~50 percent old crystals. Conversely, the percentage of old crystals may be lower if the thorium concentrations in the old crystals are higher, as suggested by the trace-element data for plagioclase interpreted by Kent and others (this volume, chap. 35) as disaggregated gabbroic xenoliths. For example, if the old crystals had thorium concentrations twice as high as the zero-age crystals, which may be reasonable given the factor of 2–4 enrichment in incompatible elements, such as Pb and La, relative to the zero-age crystals (Kent and others, this volume, chap. 35), the percentage of old crystals required would

Table 2. Calculated compositions of mineral phases in chemical equilibrium with Mount St. Helens sample SH304-2A1.

Phase	Ba, in ppm	Ra, in fg/g	Th, in ppm	U, in ppm	(^{238}U)/(^{232}Th)	(^{230}Th)/(^{232}Th)[1]	(^{230}Th)/(^{238}U)	(^{230}Th)/[Ba], in dpy/μg	(^{226}Ra)/[Ba], in dpy/μg
Zero-age plagioclase	193	56	0.001	0.001	0.24–0.41	1.270	3.10–5.29	1.1 [2]	332
Zero-age amphibole	34	4.4	0.010	0.005	1.37	1.270	0.929	51	154
Zero-age apatite (L)[3]	100	no data	4.57	2.12	1.41	1.270	0.899	7.5×10^3	0 [4]
Zero-age apatite (M&S)[3]	149	no data	4.16	3.03	2.22	1.270	0.572	4.5×10^3	0 [4]
Zero age zircon	1.3	0.0	43.3	117	8.20	1.270	0.155	5.3×10^6	0 [4]
2000 yr apatite (L)	100	373	4.57	2.12	1.41	1.272	0.901	7.5×10^3	4.3×10^3
2000 yr apatite (M&S)	149	226	4.16	3.03	2.22	1.287	0.580	4.6×10^3	2.6×10^3
2000 yr zircon	1.3	3.5×10^3 [5]	43.3	117	8.20	1.395	0.170	5.8×10^6	3.1×10^6

[1] (^{230}Th)/(^{232}Th) for zero-age phases assumed to be equal to that in whole rock.

[2] (^{230}Th)/Ba for zero-age plagioclase calculated from whole-rock composition; actual value may be somewhat higher in plagioclase in equilibrium with liquid (see text for discussion).

[3] Calculated using partition coefficients of Luhr and others, 1984 (L), and Mahood and Stimac, 1990 (M&S), respectively.

[4] (^{226}Ra)/Ba assumed to be zero for apatite and zircon at time of crystallization; this assumption makes little difference in the values calculated for older crystals.

[5] Ra concentration in 2,000-yr-old zircon calculated by assuming constant (^{230}Th), which gives a minimum value; because of the high U/Th ratio in zircon, ^{230}Th activity increases by ~10 percent over 2,000 years.

decrease by a factor of two. Kent and others (this volume, chap. 35) interpreted the lack of Eu anomalies in REE patterns in the whole-rock data for the 2004–5 dacite to indicate that only a small percentage of plagioclase can have been added to or lost from the magma, which would suggest that any older crystals present are near radioactive equilibrium (that is, hundreds of thousands of years old) and/or that they have high concentrations of thorium and presumably other trace elements. However, given the uncertainties in the thorium concentrations of different potential populations of plagioclase, coupled with the possibility that other phases are present in the bulk separates, we cannot uniquely determine whether the old crystals are older than ~300 ka and therefore must be xenocrystic.

Any old-plagioclase component, regardless of origin, with (^{230}Th)/(^{232}Th) lower than the bulk plagioclase separate is likely to be older than ~10 ka and therefore the ^{230}Th-^{226}Ra parent-daughter pair will be in radioactive equilibrium. If we assume that plagioclase in the bulk separate is a mixture of (1) plagioclase rims or crystals that grew immediately before or during eruption in chemical equilibrium with the host liquid and (2) an old plagioclase component (cores or crystals) that is >10 ka and therefore in ^{226}Ra-^{230}Th equilibrium, and if we further assume that both components have the same thorium and barium concentrations and (^{230}Th)/[Ba] ratios, we calculate that the bulk separate contains 25–40 percent old plagioclase (where the range encompasses variations in crystallization temperature from 850°C to 900°C and plagioclase from An_{50} to An_{40}). If the old component is <10 ka, or if the young component has (^{226}Ra)/[Ba] higher than predicted by equilibrium (a potential consequence of rapid crystallization (Cooper and Reid, 2003)), the proportion of old crystals would be higher.

However, such calculations are sensitive to assumptions about (^{230}Th)/[Ba] and barium concentrations in each population of plagioclase, and the mixing proportions are therefore only broadly constrained by this analysis. An additional complication is that radium concentrations in the bulk plagioclase separate will be sensitive to the effects of inclusions of other phases (for example, zircon, allanite, and groundmass) within the separate. Therefore, we do not attempt to interpret the percentage of old plagioclase crystals derived from ^{230}Th-^{226}Ra-Ba relations, except to note that the possible range in the percentage of old crystals is similar to the range that we calculated using thorium isotopic compositions.

Groundmass or Melt Inclusions

In addition to zero-age plagioclase and older plagioclase, some amount of groundmass or melt is likely to be present in the plagioclase separate as adherents to the outside of grains and/or as melt inclusions within plagioclase. The colinearity of the two plagioclase separates for subsamples of the October 2004 dome (SH304-2A1 and SH304-2A8) with the whole-rock data (fig. 1), together with higher concentrations of thorium, uranium, and barium in sample 2A8 compared to 2A1, suggests that SH304-2A8 plagioclase contains a higher percentage of included groundmass or melt inclusions. The difference in concentrations of thorium, barium, and uranium between the two subsamples is consistent with the presence of 1–2 percent more groundmass (with the composition of the whole rock) in SH304-2A8 plagioclase than in the separate from SH304-2A1, and it is possible that SH304-2A8 plagioclase itself contains a few percent by mass of groundmass.

The presence of groundmass will not affect the slope of the two-point plagioclase-whole rock ^{238}U-^{230}Th isochron and therefore will not change the apparent age of the plagioclase separate (~42 ka). As demonstrated by a comparison of the two plagioclase separates for the October dome samples, the presence of groundmass or melt inclusions will shift the bulk separate toward higher $^{230}Th/^{232}Th$ and $^{238}U/^{232}Th$, and therefore the pure plagioclase will have $^{230}Th/^{232}Th$ and $^{238}U/^{232}Th$ even lower than those measured in the bulk separate (fig 3). The presence of groundmass would also lead to higher (^{226}Ra)/[Ba] and (^{230}Th)/[Ba] in the bulk plagioclase separate compared to that in pure, zero-age plagioclase. This presence of groundmass is qualitatively consistent with the observations, but a mixing line on a ^{230}Th-^{226}Ra-Ba isochron diagram between zero-age plagioclase and the whole rock does not pass through the bulk separate (fig. 3) indicating that some other phase(s) must be present in the bulk separate.

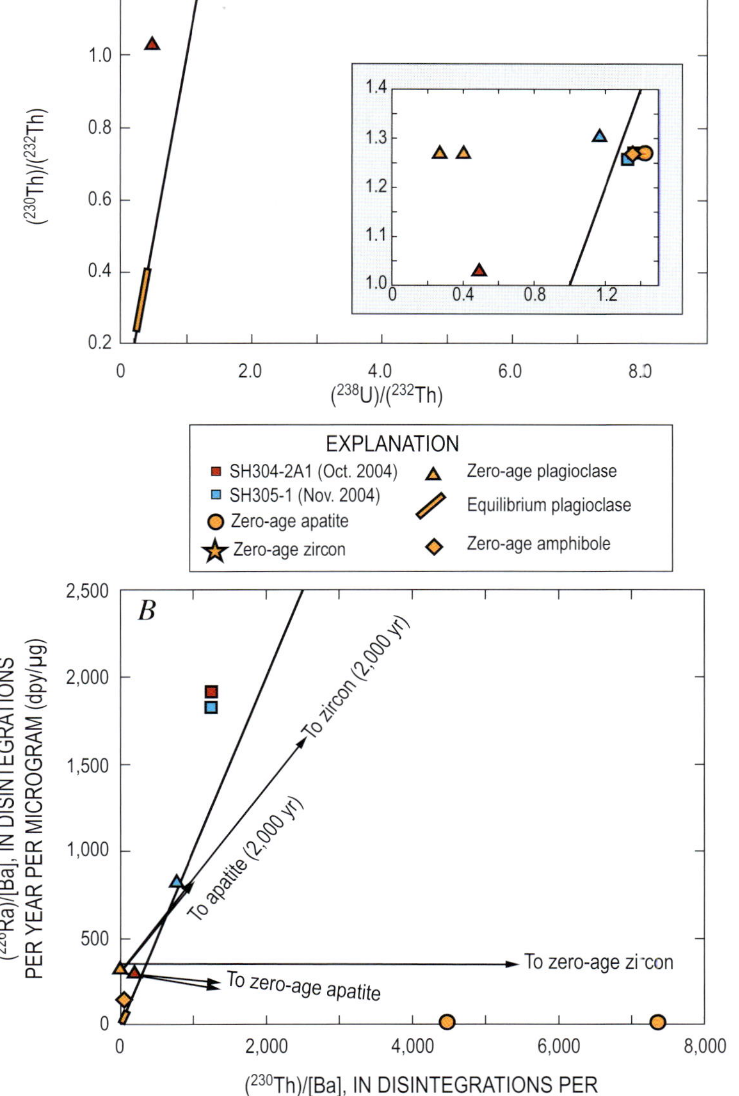

Amphibole

Thorium and uranium are moderately incompatible in amphibole (LaTourrette and others, 1995; Tiepolo and others, 2000), and although the absolute value of the partition coefficients vary with SiO_2, the partitioning behavior of U is similar to that of Th in all compositions. Therefore, amphibole does not appreciably fractionate U from Th (Blundy and Wood, 2003, and references therein), and the effect of amphibole on the ^{238}U-^{230}Th systematics of the plagioclase separate will be similar to, but of a much smaller magnitude than, that of groundmass (fig. 3*A*).

Radium and barium are incompatible in amphibole, and D_{Ra}/D_{Ba} in amphibole is ~0.08 regardless of crystal composition (Blundy and Wood, 2003). Absolute values of D_{Ba} range from 0.10 to 0.72, similar to the range of D_{Ba} in plagioclase. Therefore, at the time of crystallization, amphibole would have (^{226}Ra)/[Ba] slightly lower than that in coexisting plagioclase, with (^{230}Th)/[Ba] similar to, or slightly higher than, that in plagioclase (fig. 3*B*). However, because of the

Figure 3. *A*, ^{238}U-^{230}Th; *B*, ^{230}Th-^{226}Ra isochron diagrams illustrating the effects of different types of impurities in the bulk plagioclase separates. Orange symbols are calculated values for zero-age apatite, zircon, plagioclase, and amphibole, in chemical equilibrium with October 2004 whole-rock (SH304-2A1) and plagioclase in radioactive equilibrium; for calculated values see table 2. The explanation applies to both panels; multiple symbols are shown for zero-age plagioclase and apatite where a range of partition coefficients are considered. The inset in panel *A* shows detail of upper-left corner of the larger diagram. Mixing trajectories on both diagrams will be straight lines; arrows shown in panel *B* illustrate mixing lines between zero-age plagioclase (orange triangle) and either zero-age or 2,000-year-old apatite and zircon. Length of arrows schematically indicates that (because of its higher concentrations of Th and U) zircon will have more leverage on the composition of the bulk plagioclase separate than will apatite.

similarity of the magnitude of radium and barium partition coefficients in amphibole and plagioclase, the effects of a few percent amphibole on the ^{226}Ra-^{230}Th-Ba systematics of the bulk plagioclase separate would be negligible.

Apatite and Zircon

Thorium and uranium are compatible in apatite and zircon, which results in orders of magnitude difference between thorium or uranium concentrations in plagioclase and in these accessory phases. Therefore, even small mass fractions of apatite and zircon could have significant effects on ^{238}U-^{230}Th-^{226}Ra disequilibria in the bulk plagioclase separate.

No experimental data exist for partition coefficients of the U-series nuclides in apatite or zircon. However, studies of coexisting apatite and glass in natural systems yield D_{Th}=1.6–1.7, with uranium somewhat more compatible (D_U=1.8–2.6; Luhr and others, 1984; Mahood and Stimac, 1990). Although some caution is warranted because these data were collected from trachytic to pantelleritic samples, the relative partitioning behavior when comparing two elements should be broadly similar in other compositions. This will lead to (^{238}U)/(^{232}Th) in apatite that is higher than that in the coexisting liquid at the time of crystallization (fig. 3*A*). On the basis of microbeam studies of natural systems, partition coefficients for thorium and uranium in zircon are higher than those for apatite, and D_U/D_{Th} will also be higher than in apatite (D_U ~100 and D_U/D_{Th} ~6; Blundy and Wood, 2003). Ion microprobe measurements of ^{238}U-^{230}Th disequilibria in magmatic zircon crystals confirm that (^{238}U)/(^{232}Th) is high, although the range of (^{238}U)/(^{232}Th) (~2 to >10, compared to ~1 for coexisting glass; for example, Bacon and Lowenstern, 2005; Charlier and others, 2003; Reid and others, 1997) is typically greater than predicted by equilibrium partitioning and may reflect local effects (for example, Bacon and Lowenstern, 2005). On the basis of partitioning data and previous measurements of magmatic zircon, (^{238}U)/(^{232}Th) in zircon coexisting with the October 2004 magma will likely be higher by a factor of 2–6 than that in the whole rock, and therefore zircon or apatite inclusions would elevate (^{238}U)/(^{232}Th) of the bulk plagioclase separate compared to that in pure plagioclase. The effect on (^{230}Th)/(^{232}Th) will depend on the age of the accessory phases; zero-age zircon or apatite will not change (^{230}Th)/(^{232}Th) compared to zero-age plagioclase, but because of their high (^{238}U)/(^{232}Th) ratios, both zircon and apatite will rapidly evolve to higher (^{230}Th)/(^{232}Th) with time. Therefore, addition of older zircon or apatite will increase (^{230}Th)/(^{232}Th) in the bulk separate. The only way that addition of zircon or apatite could explain the low (^{230}Th)/(^{232}Th) in the bulk separate would be if they were xenocrystic and had crystallized from a magma which itself had unusually low (^{230}Th)/(^{232}Th).

In detail, this scenario is difficult to reconcile with the position of the bulk plagioclase on a ^{238}U-^{230}Th isochron diagram (fig. 3*A*). Global compilations of U-series disequilibria in volcanic rocks (for example, Lundstrom, 2003, and references therein) show that all samples measured to date have (^{230}Th)/(^{232}Th) ratios above ~0.5. The high D_U/D_{Th} (and correspondingly high (^{238}U)/(^{232}Th)) for apatite and zircon means that even if they crystallized from a magma with (^{230}Th)/(^{232}Th) of approximately 0.5, a mixing line between pure plagioclase and these accessory phases would not pass through the point for the bulk plagioclase separate. Therefore, an additional phase or phases with low (^{230}Th)/(^{232}Th) and low (^{238}U)/(^{232}Th) (for example, old plagioclase crystals, as argued above) must be present in the bulk plagioclase separate. Even if apatite or zircon are present, they must make up a small percentage of the bulk plagioclase separate. A maximum of 1.4 percent or 0.025 percent (by weight) of apatite or zircon, respectively, could be present if we assume that all of the uranium in the bulk plagioclase separate resides in apatite or zircon; the presence of other impurities (such as groundmass) would decrease the allowable percentage of these phases.

Although apatite or zircon alone cannot be controlling the ^{238}U-^{230}Th disequilibria in the bulk plagioclase separate, small mass fractions of these accessory phases may be present and could influence the ^{230}Th-^{226}Ra disequilibria of the bulk separate. Barium is incompatible in both apatite (D_{Ba} <0.3; Luhr and others, 1984) and zircon (D_{Ba} = 0.003–0.005; Blundy and Wood, 2003), and Blundy and Wood (2003) estimate that D_{Ra} in zircon will be ~10^{-6}. Radium partitioning in apatite has not been measured or estimated, but it is likely to be more incompatible than barium, and both phases will likely have very low (^{226}Ra)/[Ba] at the time of crystallization, effectively zero for zircon. However, considering that thorium is compatible in apatite and zircon, both phases will have extremely high (^{230}Th)/[Ba] compared to coexisting plagioclase (or liquid), and they will evolve rapidly to high (^{226}Ra)/[Ba]. Mixing trajectories for zero-age plagioclase with zircon and apatite are shown on figure 3*B*; contamination with zero-age apatite could reproduce the low (^{226}Ra)/[Ba] of the plagioclase separate. Older apatite or zircon produce mixing trajectories that have slopes too shallow to pass through the data for the bulk plagioclase separate. The interpretation that apatite and zircon are not the dominant control on the ^{226}Ra-^{230}Th-Ba systematics of plagioclase is consistent with the ^{238}U-^{230}Th data, where apatite or zircon in small amounts could contribute to the U-series budget of the bulk plagioclase separate, but an additional component (in addition to zero-age plagioclase and zircon/apatite) is required to explain the data.

^{230}Th-^{226}Ra Age of October 2004 Plagioclase

The bulk plagioclase separate for the October 2004 dome (SH305-1) has (^{226}Ra)/(^{230}Th)>1, indicating that at least some mass fraction of the crystals measured are significantly younger than 10 ka. However, curves for the evolution of melt in equilibrium with plagioclase and curves for the evolution of the whole rock on a (^{226}Ra)/[Ba] evolution diagram for SH304-2A1 do not intersect, even when considering a range of preeruptive temperatures and plagioclase compositions and the potential effects of melt inclusions in the bulk separate (fig. 4). This pattern of data on an evolution diagram could be explained if the melt from which (at least some of) the plagioclase precipitated had significantly lower (^{226}Ra)/[Ba] than the SH304-2A1 whole rock, but such an explanation would require (^{226}Ra)/[Ba] < ~900 dpy/µg in this melt (if we assume some impurities in the bulk separate), lower than that observed in any recent Mount St. Helens lavas (see fig. 2). It is more likely that the plagioclase history and the effects of multiple types of impurities are too complex to allow a meaningful age determination by this method.

Composition of the October 2004 Plagioclase Separate

On the basis of the mixing relations outlined above, the plagioclase separate for the October 2004 dome is composed of at least three components: (1) zero-age plagioclase crystals, (2) older plagioclase crystals (whether xenocrysts or antecrysts), and (3) some groundmass or melt inclusions and/or a minute mass fraction of apatite or zircon. Groundmass, apatite, and zircon will act in a similar way on the ^{238}U-^{230}Th disequilibria, shifting the bulk plagioclase separate toward high (^{238}U)/(^{232}Th) and high (^{230}Th)/(^{232}Th) ratios. The volume of crystals must be dominated by young plagioclase, but there must also be some component of older plagioclase with low (^{230}Th)/(^{232}Th) in order to explain the low (^{230}Th)/(^{232}Th) measured in the bulk separate. The exact age of these foreign crystals cannot be uniquely determined; therefore, they may represent xenocrysts or antecrysts.

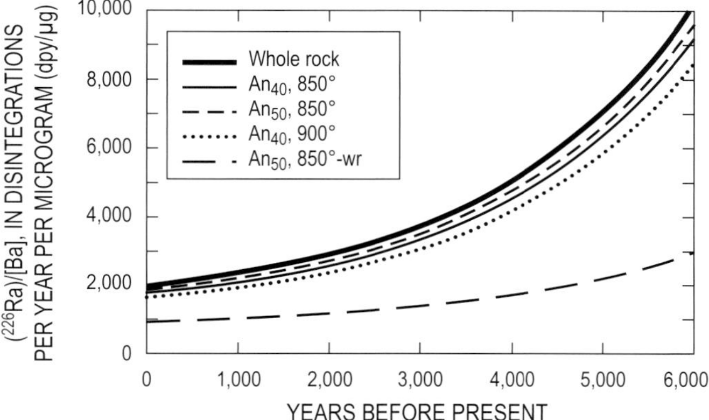

Figure 4. ^{226}Ra evolution diagram for October 2004 dacite (SH304-2A1). Curves shown are for evolution of (^{226}Ra)/[Ba] over time in whole rock (bold line) and for melt in equilibrium with plagioclase with composition of An_{40}–An_{50} at temperatures of 850–900°C. In a case where plagioclase crystallized rapidly within the past ~10,000 years in equilibrium with a liquid having the composition of the whole-rock, the intersection of curves for melt in equilibrium with plagioclase and whole rock would indicate the crystallization age (see Cooper and others, 2001, for details of the technique). The fact that curves for melt in equilibrium with plagioclase in SH304-2A1 do not intersect the whole-rock curve indicates that the bulk plagioclase separate and melt were not in equilibrium, even considering a range of potential crystallization temperatures and compositions of plagioclase. Correcting the plagioclase composition for the effects of having impurities (groundmass, zircon, or apatite) in the bulk separate makes the disequilibrium between melt and plagioclase more extreme. An example is shown by the long-dash curve, calculated assuming 3 percent whole-rock in the bulk separate, which is broadly consistent with concentrations of Th in the plagioclase being below detection limit for laser-ablation ICP-MS analyses (Kent and others, this volume, chap. 35). The lack of equilibrium between plagioclase bulk separate and the likely melt composition suggests that at least some of the crystals are foreign to the host liquid (see text for discussion).

Plagioclase in November 2004 Dacite

In contrast to the low (^{230}Th)/(^{232}Th) measured in the October 2004 plagioclase separate, the (^{230}Th)/(^{232}Th) ratio measured in plagioclase separated from the November 2004 dome sample (SH305-1) is approximately 4 percent higher than that in the host magma. As a result, a two-point plagioclase-whole-rock isochron has a negative slope, yielding a negative apparent age. This observation is inconsistent with crystallization of plagioclase solely from the SH305-1 host liquid, but (as with plagioclase in the October 2004 dome sample) it is consistent with the presence of impurities in the bulk plagioclase separate, which may include an antecrystic or xenocrystic plagioclase component. Interestingly, this foreign component must have higher (^{230}Th)/(^{232}Th) than zero-age plagioclase and, therefore, is compositionally distinct from that present in the October 2004 dome sample, despite the fact that the two dome samples were erupted only a month apart. The plagioclase separate for the November 2005 dome (SH305-1) also has higher (^{226}Ra)/[Ba] and (^{230}Th)/[Ba] than other plagioclase from Mount St. Helens samples (with the exception of Volpe and Hammond's (1991) measurement of MSH90-9; fig. 2), and those ratios are higher than those which would be in equilibrium with the host magma. As argued above for the October 2004 dome, it is likely that the bulk plagioclase separate for the November 2004 dome contains some zero-age plagioclase, and in addition, the separate could contain older plagioclase, zircon, apatite, amphibole, or groundmass in small percentages. The whole-rock October 2004 and November 2004 dome samples have similar U-series characteristics; therefore, the effects of zero-age impurities in the bulk plagioclase separate for the November 2004 dome would be similar to those shown in figure 3 for the October 2004 dome. In the case of the November 2004 plagioclase, the combined ^{238}U-^{230}Th-^{226}Ra-Ba data for the bulk separate are consistent with the presence of a small percentage of apatite, zircon and/or melt inclusions (fig. 3). The presence of less than 1 percent apatite or zircon (±melt) inclusions within the plagioclase separate could explain high (^{238}U)/(^{232}Th), (^{230}Th)/[Ba], and thorium concentrations in the bulk separate; and if the zircon or apatite were a few thousand years old, it could also explain the high (^{230}Th)/(^{232}Th) and (^{226}Ra)/[Ba]. The high (^{230}Th)/(^{232}Th) and (^{226}Ra)/[Ba] could still be consistent with the presence of some old plagioclase in the bulk separate, if offset by the presence of zircon or apatite, but the mixing proportions are difficult to determine because of the complexity of the data. Given the negative apparent ^{230}Th-^{238}U age and the near-equilibrium ^{226}Ra-^{230}Th-Ba data for the SH305-1 plagioclase separate, it is difficult to constrain the age of crystallization of any old component of plagioclase that may be in the bulk separate.

Implications for Magma Reservoir Processes

Age considerations aside, it is striking that plagioclase separates from the October and November 2004 dome samples have quite different U-series characteristics, despite having erupted only one month apart. Evidently, these two magmas entrained different populations of crystals, implying significant heterogeneity within the reservoir system or different transport paths intersecting different resident crystals.

In the case of the October 2004 dome, we can quantify the proportion of old and young crystals, but we cannot uniquely determine the age (and therefore the origin) of the old component. However, we speculate that the percentage of old crystals required (~15–50 percent of the plagioclase separate, depending on Th concentrations and age of the old component) might be higher than is easily explained by disaggregation of xenoliths that are present only in small amounts (1–5 percent of the bulk sample). Considering that 2004–5 dacites have a total of 30–40 percent plagioclase by volume, the assumption that all old crystals represent disaggregated xenoliths would imply that ~5–20 percent of the volume of the whole-rock dacite is composed of these xenocrysts. This, in turn, would imply that at least 1–5 times the volume of xenoliths that are observed has been completely disaggregated and incorporated into the dacite, which would likely produce some trace-element signature of plagioclase addition. Furthermore, we suggest that incorporation of plagioclase from a partially molten crystal mush perhaps may be physically easier than disaggregation of completely solidified xenoliths, and that an antecrystic origin is likely for at least some of the old crystals within the bulk separate. It is likely that there are at least three plagioclase components within the October 2004 dome sample: (1) zero-age plagioclase, (2) antecrystic plagioclase disaggregated from crystal mush, and (3) xenocrystic plagioclase disaggregated from gabbroic xenoliths. The age and origin of the old component(s) may be better constrained by analysis of different size fractions of plagioclase within the dome samples (which could preferentially sample different crystal populations), and work is currently underway to analyze different size fractions of plagioclase in SH304-2A1.

We have found evidence for a xenocrystic or antecrystic component in plagioclase separates in both of the samples from the 2004–5 eruption for which U-series disequilibria in plagioclase have been measured, as well as in at least two of the older Mount St. Helens lavas of Castle Creek age (Cooper and Reid, 2003). Thus, entrainment and disaggregation of crystal mush or xenoliths appears to be a common, if not ubiquitous, process in the Mount St. Helens reservoir system. Furthermore, the heterogeneity of this foreign component within different samples from the 2004–5 eruption suggests that the reservoir system feeding the current eruption is complex and not well mixed.

U-Series Disequilibria in Gouge

The exterior of the Mount St. Helens dome is coated with meter-thick fault gouge, which appears to consist mainly of fragments of dacite dome, as large as several centimeters, within a matrix of finer fragments (Cashman and others, this volume, chap. 19). Gouge samples have ^{230}Th/^{232}Th indistinguishable from that of dacite dome samples (fig. 1*B*), consistent with an origin for the gouge as being dominated by fragmented juvenile dacite. However, lower U/Th and lower U and Th concentrations in gouge compared to dome samples suggests either loss of U and Th (with preferential loss of U) from the gouge material or dilution of dacite fragments within the gouge with some material lower in U and Th concentrations than dome rocks. Similarly, gouge samples have lower (^{230}Th)/[Ba] than dome samples, but they have (^{226}Ra)/[Ba] similar to dome samples (fig. 2*B*), suggesting loss or dilution of Th rather than gain of Ba. Fluxing of gouge with a vapor or fluid could modify trace-element composition of the gouge either by precipitation of phases from the fluid or by leaching of fluid-mobile elements from gouge material. Fluids would be expected to carry U, Ra, and Ba, but not Th; thus, addition of a fluid-derived phase would be expected to add U, Ra, and Ba to the gouge rather than to decrease concentrations relative to the dacite. Leaching of dacite by a fluid could remove U, Ra, and Ba but could not explain the lower concentrations of Th in gouge. Therefore, the observations are most consistent with the presence of a component in the gouge (as yet unidentified) that has low concentrations of U and Th (and, in the case of SH320-1, low concentrations of Ra and Ba) compared to dome dacite.

Conclusions

Juvenile material from the 1980–86 eruption shows heterogeneity in ^{230}Th/^{232}Th ratios. The total range in ^{230}Th/^{232}Th measured in 1980–86 samples overlaps but is larger than the range of ^{230}Th/^{232}Th ratios measured in 2004–5 dacite and dome samples. However, the differences in crystal compositions between 1980s and 2004–5 samples indicates substantial heterogeneity of plagioclase crystals sampled during the two eruptions and even within a short time period during the 2004–5 eruption. This heterogeneity precludes an origin for the 2004–5 magma solely by remobilization of remnant magma from the 1980–86 eruptive cycle. Instead, the U-series data are consistent with a model in which the 2004–5 magma represents a mixture of some remnant 1980s magma with plagioclase crystals (and perhaps associated magma) having an isotopic composition previously unidentified in the erupted products of Mount St. Helens. The U-series data are consistent with an origin for the 2004–5 magma by partial melting of the lower crust, as has been proposed previously for Mount St. Helens dacites. The preservation of significant ^{226}Ra excesses in all measured whole-rock samples of the 2004–5 eruption indicates that the magma was generated recently, likely within the past few thousand years.

In detail, plagioclase separates for October 2004 and November 2004 dome samples (SH304-2A1 and SH305-1) have different U-series characteristics. This suggests that the two dacites, erupted only about a month apart, sample different populations of plagioclase crystals and/or different types of impurities within the bulk plagioclase separates. Plagioclase in both samples is also different in ^{230}Th-^{238}U disequilibria from that measured in older Mount St. Helens samples. Because of the complexities within the crystal populations sampled in the 2004–5 dacites, exact ages for plagioclase cannot be calculated. However, the preservation of ^{226}Ra excess in plagioclase from the October 2004 dome (SH304-2A1) requires that some mass fraction is younger than ~10 ka, and other petrologic constraints suggest that at least some crystallization occurred shortly before or during magma ascent. Simple mass balance calculations suggest that the percentage of a zero-age component is ~60–80 percent, although it could be lower if the older plagioclase component is <10 ka, and/or if the young component has (^{226}Ra)/[Ba] higher than predicted in equilibrium with the whole rock. The bulk plagioclase separate for the November 2004 dome (SH305-1) is within error of ^{226}Ra-^{230}Th equilibrium, and a young component (<10 ka) is not required by the ^{226}Ra-^{230}Th data. However, neither is it precluded by the data, and any older plagioclase is likely less than ~20 ka, if it crystallized from a magma with $^{230}Th/^{232}Th$ similar to that measured in Mount St. Helens whole-rock samples.

The combined whole-rock and plagioclase data for the 1980–86 and 2004–5 eruptions suggest that the crystal populations sampled by Mount St. Helens magmas commonly include a recycled component (whether antecrystic or xenocrystic) and that the magma-storage region beneath Mount St. Helens is complex, preserving chemical distinctions between magmas erupted only a short time apart. Thus, the crystals may contain a longer record of processes within the magma reservoir beneath Mount St. Helens than do the liquid fractions of these magmas. Detailed studies of the crystals may therefore provide insights into the temporal and spatial distribution of magmas and crystal mushes within the reservoir system.

Acknowledgments

We would like to thank the staff at the Cascades Volcano Observatory for providing samples, data, and information about the eruption and for organizing workshops and conference sessions as a venue to discuss recent results. We thank the other members of the Mount St. Helens petrology working group for helpful discussions and open sharing of data and ideas. J. Lowenstern and M. Reagan provided very constructive and helpful reviews. This work was partially supported by NSF EAR-0307691 to K.M. Cooper.

References Cited

Bacon, C.R., and Lowenstern, J.B., 2005, Late Pleistocene granodiorite source for recycled zircon and phenocrysts in rhyodacite lava at Crater Lake, Oregon: Earth and Planetary Science Letters, v. 233, p. 277–293.

Bennett, J.T., Krishnaswami, S., Turekian, K.K., Melson, W.G., and Hopson, C.A., 1982, The uranium and thorium decay series nuclides in Mt. St. Helens effusives Earth and Planetary Science Letters, v. 60, no. 1, p. 61–69.

Berlo, K., Blundy, J., Turner, S., Cashman, K., Hawkesworth, C., and Black, S., 2004, Geochemical precursors to volcanic activity at Mount St. Helens, USA: Science, v. 306, no. 5699, p. 1167–1169.

Blake, S., and Rogers, N., 2005, Magma differentiation rates from (Ra-226/Th-230) and the size and power output of magma chambers: Earth and Planetary Science Letters, v. 236, no. 3–4, p. 654–669.

Blundy, J., and Wood, B., 2003, Mineral-melt partitioning of uranium, thorium and their daughters, *in* Bourdon, B., Henderson, G.M., Lundstrom, C.C., and Turner, S.P., eds., Uranium-series geochemistry: Reviews in Mineralogy and Geochemistry, v. 52, p. 59–123.

Blundy, J., Cashman, K.V., and Berlo, K., 2008, Evolving magma storage conditions beneath Mount St. Helens inferred from chemical variations in melt inclusions from the 1980–1986 and current (2004–2006) eruptions, chap. 33 *of* Sherrod, D.R., Scott, W.E., and Stauffer, P.H., eds., A volcano rekindled; the renewed eruption of Mount St. Helens, 2004–2006: U.S. Geological Survey Professional Paper 1750 (this volume).

Bourdon, B., and Sims, K.W.W., 2003, U-series constraints on intraplate basaltic magmatism, *in* Bourdon, B., Henderson, G.M., Lundstrom, C.C., and Turner, S.P., eds., Uranium-series geochemistry: Reviews in Mineralogy and Geochemistry, v. 52, p. 215–254.

Bourdon, B., Henderson, G.M., Lundstrom, C.C., and Turner, S.P., eds., 2003, Uranium-series geochemistry: Reviews in Mineralogy and Geochemistry, v. 52, 656 p.

Cashman, K.V., Thornber, C.R., and Pallister, J.S., 2008, From dome to dust; shallow crystallization and fragmentation of conduit magma during the 2004–2006 dome extrusion of Mount St. Helens, Washington, chap. 19 *of* Sherrod, D.R., Scott, W.E., and Stauffer, P.H., eds., A volcano rekindled; the renewed eruption of Mount St. Helens, 2004–2006: U.S. Geological Survey Professional Paper 1750 (this volume).

Charlier, B.L.A., Peate, D.W., Wilson, C.J.N., Lowenstern, J.B., Storey, M., and Brown, S.J.A., 2003, Crystallization ages in coeval silicic magma bodies; ^{238}U-^{230}Th disequilibrium evidence from the Rotoiti and Earthquake Flat eruption deposits, Taupo Volcanic Zone, New Zealand: Earth and Planetary Science Letters, v. 206, p. 441–457.

Charlier, B.L.A., Wilson, C.J.N., Lowenstern, J.B., Blake, S., Van Calsteren, P.W., and Davidson, J.P., 2005, Magma generation at a large, hyperactive silicic volcano (Taupo, New Zealand) revealed by U-Th and U-Pb systematics in zircons: Journal of Petrology, v. 46, no. 1, p. 3–32.

Cheng, H., Edwards, R.L., Hoff, J., Gallup, C.D., Richards, D.A., and Asmerom, Y., 2000, The half-lives of uranium-234 and thorium-230: Chemical Geology, v. 169, p. 17–33.

Clynne, M.A., Calvert, A.T., Wolfe, E.W., Evarts, R.C., Fleck, R.J., and Lanphere, M.A., 2008, The Pleistocene eruptive history of Mount St. Helens, Washington, from 300,000 to 12,800 years before present, chap. 28 *of* Sherrod, D.R., Scott, W.E., and Stauffer, P.H., eds., A volcano rekindled; the renewed eruption of Mount St. Helens, 2004–2006: U.S. Geological Survey Professional Paper 1750 (this volume).

Condomines, M., Gauthier, P.J., and Sigmarsson, G., 2003, Timescales of magma chamber processes and dating of young volcanic rocks, *in* Bourdon, B., Henderson, G.M., Lundstrom, C.C., and Turner, S.P., eds., Uranium-Series Geochemistry: Reviews in Mineralogy and Geochemistry, v. 52. p. 125–174.

Cooper, K.M., and Reid, M.R., 2003, Re-examination of crystal ages in recent Mount St. Helens lavas; implications for magma reservoir processes: Earth and Planetary Science Letters, v. 213, nos. 1–2, p. 149–167.

Cooper, K.M., Reid, M.R., Murrell, M.T., and Clague, D.A., 2001, Crystal and magma residence at Kilauea Volcano, Hawaii; ^{230}Th-^{226}Ra dating of the 1955 east rift eruption: Earth and Planetary Science Letters, v. 184, nos. 3–4, p. 703–718.

Dufek, J., and Cooper, K.M., 2005, ^{226}Ra/^{230}Th excess generated in the lower crust; implications for magma transport and storage time scales: Geology, v. 33, no. 10, p. 833–836.

Goldstein, S.J., and Stirling, C.H., 2003, Techniques for measuring uranium-series nuclides; 1992–2002, *in* Bourdon, B., Henderson, G.M., Lundstrom, C.C., and Turner, S.P., eds., Uranium-series geochemistry: Reviews in Mineralogy and Geochemistry, v. 52, p. 23–57.

Hawkesworth, C., George, R., Turner, S., and Zellmer, G., 2004, Time scales of magmatic processes: Earth and Planetary Science Letters, v. 218, p. 1–16.

Heliker, C., 1995, Inclusions in Mount St. Helens dacite erupted from 1980 through 1983: Journal of Volcanology and Geothermal Research, v. 66, nos. 1–4, p. 115–135, doi:10.1016/0377-0273(94)00074-Q.

Ivanovich, M., and Harmon, R.S., eds., 1992, Uranium-series disequilibria; applications to earth, marine, and environmental sciences (2d ed.): Oxford, Oxford University Press, 910 p.

Kent, A.J.R., Rowe, M.C., Thornber, C.R., and Pallister, J.S., 2008, Trace element and Pb isotope composition of plagioclase from dome samples from the 2004–2005 eruption of Mount St Helens, Washington, chap. 35 *of* Sherrod, D.R., Scott, W.E., and Stauffer, P.H., eds., A volcano rekindled; the renewed eruption of Mount St. Helens, 2004–2006: U.S. Geological Survey Professional Paper 1750 (this volume).

LaTourrette, T., Hervig, R.L., and Holloway, J.R., 1995, Trace element partitioning between amphibole, phlogopite, and basanite melt: Earth and Planetary Science Letters, v. 135, p. 13–30.

Luhr, J.F., Carmichael, I.S.E., and Varekamp, J.C., 1984, The 1982 eruptions of El Chichón Volcano, Chiapas, Mexico; mineralogy and petrology of the anhydrite-bearing pumices: Journal of Volcanology and Geothermal Research, v. 23, p. 69–108.

Lundstrom, C.C., 2003, Uranium-series disequilibria in mid-ocean ridge basalts; observations and models of basalt genesis, *in* Bourdon, B., Henderson, G.M., Lundstrom, C.C., and Turner, S.P., eds., Uranium-series geochemistry: Reviews in Mineralogy and Geochemistry, v. 52, p. 175–214.

Mahood, G.A., and Stimac, J.A., 1990, Trace-element partitioning in pantellerites and trachytes: Geochimica et Cosmochimica Acta, v. 54, p. 2257–2276.

Moran, S.C., Qamar, A.I., Thelen, W., Waite, G., Horton, S., LaHusen, R.G., and Major, J.J., 2005, Overview of seismicity associated with the 2004–2005 eruption of Mount St. Helens [abs.]: Eos (American Geophysical Union Transactions), v. 86, no. 52, p. V52B–02.

Pallister, J.S., Hoblitt, R.P., Crandell, D.R., and Mullineaux, D.R., 1992, Mount St. Helens a decade after the 1980 eruptions; magmatic models, chemical cycles, and a revised hazards assessment: Bulletin of Volcanology, v. 54, no. 2, p. 126–146, doi:10.1007/BF00278003.

Pallister, J.S., Reagan, M., and Cashman, K, 2005, A new eruptive cycle at Mount St. Helens?: Eos (American Geophysical Union Transactions), v. 86, no. 48, p. 499–500, doi:10.1029/2005EO480006.

Pallister, J.S., Thornber, C.R., Cashman, K.V., Clynne, M.A., Lowers, H.A., Mandeville, C.W., Brownfield, I.K., and Meeker, G.P., 2008, Petrology of the 2004–2006 Mount St. Helens lava dome—implications for magmatic plumbing and eruption triggering, chap. 30 *of* Sherrod, D.R., Scott, W.E., and Stauffer, P.H., eds., A volcano rekindled; the renewed eruption of Mount St. Helens, 2004–2006: U.S. Geological Survey Professional Paper 1750 (this volume).

Pietruszka, A.J., Carlson, R.W., and Hauri, E.H., 2002, Precise and accurate measurement of ^{226}Ra-^{230}Th-^{238}U disequilibria in volcanic rocks using plasma ionization multicollector mass spectrometry: Chemical Geology, v. 188, p. 171–191.

Reagan, M.K., 2005, Time series ^{210}Pb-^{210}Pb data for lavas erupted from Mount St. Helens volcano; implications for timescales of degassing and crystallization [abs.]: Eos (American Geophysical Union Transactions), v. 86, no. 52, p. V52B–08.

Reagan, M.K., Tepley, F.J., III, Gill, J.B., Wortel, M., and Garrison, J., 2006, Timescales of degassing and crystallization implied by ^{210}Po-^{210}Pb-^{226}Ra disequilibria for andesitic lavas erupted from Arenal volcano: Journal of Volcanology and Geothermal Research, v. 157, p. 135–146.

Reagan, M.K., Cooper, K.M., Pallister, J.S., Thornber, C.R., and Wortel, M., 2008, Timing of degassing and plagioclase growth in lavas erupted from Mount St. Helens, 2004–2005, from ^{210}Po-^{210}Pb-^{226}Ra disequilibria, chap. 37 *of* Sherrod, D.R., Scott, W.E., and Stauffer, P.H., eds., A volcano rekindled; the renewed eruption of Mount St. Helens, 2004–2006: U.S. Geological Survey Professional Paper 1750 (this volume).

Reid, M.R., 2003, Timescales of magma transfer and storage in the crust, *in* Rudnick, R.L., ed., Treatise on geochemistry, volume 3; the crust: Oxford, U.K., p. 167–193.

Reid, M.R., Coath, C.D., Harrison, T.M., and McKeegan, K.D., 1997, Prolonged residence times for the youngest rhyolites associated with Long Valley Caldera; ^{230}Th-^{238}U ion microprobe dating of young zircons: Earth and Planetary Science Letters, v. 150, p. 27–39.

Rogers, N.W., Evans, P.J., Blake, S., Scott, S.C., and Hawkesworth, C.J., 2004, Rates and timescales of fractional crystallization from ^{238}U-^{230}Th-^{226}Ra disequilibria in trachyte lavas from Longonot volcano, Kenya: Journal of Petrology, v. 45, no. 9, p. 1747–1776.

Rutherford, M.J., and Devine, J.D., III, 2008, Magmatic conditions and processes in the storage zone of the 2004–2006 Mount St. Helens dacite, chap. 31 *of* Sherrod, D.R., Scott, W.E., and Stauffer, P.H., eds., A volcano rekindled; the renewed eruption of Mount St. Helens, 2004–2006: U.S. Geological Survey Professional Paper 1750 (this volume).

Sims, K.W.W., Goldstein, S.J., Blichert-Toft, J., Perfit, M.R., Kelemen, P., Fornari, D.J., Michael, P., Murrell, M.T., Hart, S., DePaolo, D.J., Layne, G.D., and Jull, M., 2002, Chemical and isotopic constraints on the generation and transport of melt beneath the East Pacific Rise: Geochimica et Cosmochimica Acta, v. 66, no. 19, p. 3481–3504.

Sims, K.W.W., Blichert-Toft, J., Fornari, D., Perfit, M.R., Goldstein, S., Johnson, P., DePaolo, D.J., Hart, S.R., Murrell, M.T., Michael, P., Layne, G., and Ball, L., 2003, Aberrant youth; chemical and isotopic constraints on the young off-axis lavas from the East Pacific Rise, 9°-10° N: Geochemistry Geophysics Geosystems, v. 4, no. 10, 27 p., doi:8610.1029/2002GC000443.

Smith, D.R., and Leeman, W.P., 1987, Petrogenesis of Mount St. Helens dacitic magmas: Journal of Geophysical Research, v. 92, no. B10, p. 10313–10334.

Streck, M.J., Broderick, C.A., Thornber, C.R., Clynne, M.A., and Pallister, J.S., 2008, Plagioclase populations and zoning in dacite of the 2004–2005 Mount St. Helens eruption; constraints for magma origin and dynamics, chap. 34 *of* Sherrod, D.R., Scott, W.E., and Stauffer, P.H., eds., A volcano rekindled; the renewed eruption of Mount St. Helens, 2004–2006: U.S. Geological Survey Professional Paper 1750 (this volume).

Thornber, C.R., Pallister, J.S., Lowers, H., and Meeker, G.P., 2005, Complex P-T history of amphiboles from the 2004–2005 eruption of Mount St. Helens [abs.]: Eos (American Geophysical Union Transactions), v. 86, no. 52, Fall Meeting Supplement, Abstract V53D–1588.

Tiepolo, M., Vannucci, R., Bottazzi, P., Oberti, R., Zanetti, A., and Foley, S., 2000, Partitioning of rare earth elements, Y, Th, U, and Pb between pargasite, kaersutite, and basanite to trachyte melts; implications for percolated and veined mantle: Geochemistry Geophysics Geosystems, v. 1, 32 p., doi:10.1029/2000GC000064.

Turner, S.P., Bourdon, B., and Gill, J., 2003a, Insights into magma genesis at convergent margins from U-series isotopes, *in* Bourdon, B., Henderson, G.M., Lundstrom, C.C., and Turner, S.P., eds., Uranium-series geochemistry: Reviews in Mineralogy and Geochemistry, v. 52. p. 255–315.

Turner, S., Foden, J., George, R., Evans, P., Varne, R., Elburg, M., and Jenner, G., 2003b, Rates and processes of potassic magma evolution beneath Sangeang Api Volcano, East Sunda Arc, Indonesia: Journal of Petrology, v. 44, no. 3, p. 491–515.

Turner, S., George, R., Jerram, D.A., Carpenter, N., and Hawkesworth, C., 2003c, Case studies of plagioclase growth and residence times in island arc lavas from Tonga and the Lesser Antilles, and a model to reconcile discordant age information: Earth and Planetary Science Letters, v. 214, nos. 1–2, p. 279–294.

Turner, S., Black, S., and Berlo, K., 2004, ^{210}Pb-^{226}Ra and ^{228}Ra-^{232}Th systematics in young arc lavas; implications for magma degassing and ascent rates: Earth and Planetary Science Letters, v. 227, nos. 1–2, p. 1–16, doi:10.1016/j.epsl.2004.08.017.

Vazquez, J.A., and Reid, M.R., 2004, Probing the accumulation history of the voluminous Toba magma: Science, v. 305, p. 991–994.

Volpe, A.M., and Hammond, P.E., 1991, ^{238}U-^{230}Th-^{226}Ra disequilibria in young Mount St. Helens rocks; time constraint for magma formation and crystallization: Earth and Planetary Science Letters, v. 107, p. 475–486.

Zellmer, G.F., Annen, C., Charlier, B.L.A., George, R.M.M., Turner, S.P., and Hawkesworth, C.J., 2005, Magma evolution and ascent at volcanic arcs; constraining petrogenetic processes through rates and chronologies: Journal of Volcanology and Geothermal Research, v. 140, p. 171–191.

Appendix 1. Analytical Methods

Chemical Separations

Procedures for chemical separation were modified from those described by Goldstein and Stirling (2003) and Pietruszka and others (2002). Plagioclase separates were prepared using standard magnetic separation followed by hand-picking using a binocular microscope. Samples (0.5–1.5 g) of mineral separates and whole rocks were cleaned before dissolution using successive baths of distilled acetone, deionized, reverse-osmosis (RO) water, 0.1N HCl + 2 percent H_2O_2, RO water, and distilled acetone. Samples were dissolved in closed Savillex beakers on a hotplate using a 3:1 mixture of concentrated HF:HNO_3. After dissolution, perchloric acid and saturated boric acid were added and samples were evaporated. Samples were treated a second time with perchloric and boric acids, evaporated again, dissolved in 3 N HCl + saturated boric acid, and centrifuged. The solution was decanted, and any residue was dissolved in additional 3N HCl + boric acid (in the proportions 100 mL HCl:5 mL saturated boric acid); this process was repeated until no residue was visible after centrifuging. Sample solutions were split into three aliquots: one small aliquot (corresponding to ~10–100 mg of rock or mineral) was spiked with ^{233}U and ^{229}Th for U and Th concentration measurement by isotope dilution, a second small aliquot (corresponding to ~5–10 mg of rock or mineral) was spiked with ^{135}Ba for Ba concentration measurement by isotope dilution, and the largest aliquot (generally the remainder of the solution, corresponding to ~0.5–1.5 g of rock or mineral) was spiked with ^{228}Ra and used for measurement of Ra concentration by isotope dilution and of U and Th isotopic compositions. All resins used in the chemical separations were precleaned with nitric and hydrochloric acids and RO water, and they were also cleaned and conditioned on the column with the acids used for sample loading and elution.

For the U-Th-Ra aliquot, radium (with major and most trace elements) was separated from Th and U using a column packed with 0.5 mL of Eichrom "pre-filter" (inert beads) and 1–2 mL of Eichrom TRU resin. Samples were loaded in 2–8 column volumes (cv) of 7M HNO_3; the load, together with subsequent washes with 2 cv of 7M HNO_3 and 10 cv of 1.5M HNO_3, was collected and saved for further purification of Ra. This was followed by a wash of 8 cv 3N HCl, which was discarded. Th was eluted from the column in 8 cv 0.2N HCl, followed by U elution from the column in 8 cv 0.1N HCl + 0.05N HF. A second pass through a small TRU column (0.25 mL pre-filter plus 0.5 mL TRU resin) was necessary to remove residual Th from the U fraction.

The thorium and uranium isotope dilution aliquots were spiked with ~1 ng each of ^{229}Th and ^{233}U tracers. Spiked samples were equilibrated by heating for ~48 hours followed by evaporation. Some samples (1980s samples) were treated with 1–2 drops of perchloric acid during equilibration in order to aid sample-spike equilibration. Thorium and uranium were separated using a column loaded with 0.25 mL Eichrom prefilter and 0.5 mL TRU resin. A single pass through the column was generally sufficient to separate U and Th from the matrix.

The radium fraction from the TRU column was dried and redissolved in 1N HCl. Radium was separated from the major elements and most trace elements using a 5–10 mL column loaded with cation-exchange resin (Dowex AG 50-X8). After loading in 1–3 cv 1N HCl, the column was washed with 0–2 cv 1N HCl (adjusted so that the total load + wash was 3 cv), 5 cv 2.0N HCl, 1.5 cv 2.5N HCl, and 1.5 cv 3.0N HCl. The Ra (+Ba) fraction was eluted from the column in 8 cv 6N HCl. For samples larger than 0.5 g, a second, 0.5–1 mL cation-exchange column was run following the same procedure. Radium was separated from barium using a Teflon column packed with 0.45 mL Eichrom Sr-spec resin. The sample was dissolved in 2 cv 2.5N HNO_3 for loading on the column. After loading, Ba was washed from the column with 0.75 cv 2.5N HNO_3 and Ra was eluted from the column in 6 cv 2.5N HNO_3. This column procedure was repeated an additional one to two times, followed by passing the Ra cut through a column loaded with 0.5 mL of Eichrom prefilter before evaporating. A final cation column (0.25 mL) was run 1–4 days prior to mass spectrometry in order to separate ^{228}Th from ^{228}Ra. The sample was loaded on this column in 1 cv 6N HCl; radium was eluted in this fraction plus an additional 6 cv of 6N HCl while Th remained on the column.

The barium isotope dilution aliquot was spiked with a ^{135}Ba-enriched tracer, equilibrated on a hotplate for at least 48 hours, and dried. Barium was separated using a column loaded with 0.65 mL of cation exchange resin (Dowex AG 50-X8). The sample was loaded on the column in 0.65 mL 1.5N HCl (1 cv), followed by washes with 1.5N and 2N HCl. Barium was eluted in 2.5 N HNO_3.

Total-process blanks during the time that the Mount St. Helens samples were run were <20 pg Th and <15 pg U for the large (isotopic composition) aliquots, and <4 pg Th and <6 pg U for the small (isotope dilution) aliquots (compared to typical sample sizes of 0.1–2 μg Th and 0.02–1 μg U in the isotopic composition aliquots and 10–50 ng Th and 2–20 ng U in isotope dilution aliquots). Barium blanks were 5–10 ng, compared to typical sample sizes of 1–2 μg Ba. Radium blanks were always below the limit of detection (~0.1 fg), and sample sizes were a few tens of femtograms Ra for minerals and 200–500 fg Ra for whole-rock samples. Blanks for each measurement were subtracted before calculation of concentrations; in most cases these had a negligible effect on calculated concentrations, but there were small corrections to Ba concentrations.

Mass Spectrometery

All measurements of isotopic ratios for chemically separated samples were performed with a Nu Plasma multicollector-ICP-MS (MC-ICP-MS) at the University of Washington.

This instrument is equipped with three ion counters, one of which (IC0; the high-mass ion counter) is equipped with an energy filter to reduce tailing effects of major peaks. All analyses with the exception of Ba measurements were performed using a desolvating nebulizer (dry plasma), which improves sensitivity by a factor of ~10 compared to use of a peristaltic pump (wet plasma). Ba abundances were high enough that the desolvating nebulizer was unnecessary, and samples were introduced as a wet plasma.

Uranium Isotopic Composition Measurements

$^{234}U/^{238}U$ ratios were measured using a static analysis routine, with ^{238}U measured on a Faraday cup and ^{234}U measured on an ion counter. Instrumental mass bias and ion counter-faraday gain were calibrated using NIST uranium standard CRM-112A with reference to the accepted $^{238}U/^{235}U$ and $^{234}U/^{238}U$ ratios of 137.88 and 5.286×10^{-5}, respectively (Cheng and others, 2000). Rock and solution standards analyzed as unknowns were interspersed with unknowns during a day of analysis, and re-calibrations of mass bias and gain were performed every third or fourth sample. Rock standards known to be in radioactive equilibrium reproducibly yielded (^{234}U)/(^{238}U) ratios within 4–6 per mil of 1.000 (see table 1), which we therefore consider to be our analytical uncertainty for unknowns.

Thorium Isotopic Composition Measurements

$^{230}Th/^{232}Th$ ratios were measured using a static analysis routine with ^{232}Th measured on a Faraday cup and ^{230}Th measured on the high-mass ion counter equipped with an energy filter (IC0). At the beginning of each day of analysis of $^{230}Th/^{232}Th$ ratios, the voltage for the energy filter was tuned in order to optimize the abundance sensitivity, and the instrumental mass bias and ion counter-faraday gain were calibrated using NIST uranium standard CRM-112A. Abundance sensitivity was measured at 400–500 ppb at one AMU during the period of analyses. Correction for tailing of ^{232}Th into the ^{230}Th mass range was done using an exponential fit to the tail, which was measured each day using a Th solution standard (Th 'U' or WUN-1). Solution standards for Th measured as unknowns (Th 'U', WUN-1 (sometimes called ZSR), and IRMM-035) were generally within 1 percent of accepted or certified values (table 1). Rock standards (TML, BHVO-1, BCR-2), which went through the same chemical separation procedure as unknowns and were analyzed as unknowns, yielded (^{230}Th)/(^{238}U) within 1 percent of radioactive equilibrium, or within error of previously measured values (table 1). Therefore, we consider our measurement accuracy and reproducibility on unknowns to be ~1 percent.

Ba Concentration Measurements by Isotope Dilution

Isotopic compositions of sample-spike mixtures were measured using wet plasma and a static routine where all peaks were measured using Faraday cups. Ratios were normalized to the natural ratio of $^{136}Ba/^{138}Ba$ (=0.10954) to correct for instrumental mass bias. Normalized $^{137}Ba/^{138}Ba$ ratios were monitored, and they agreed with the natural ratio to within <0.5 percent for samples. NIST SRM 3104a (barium normal) was run as an unknown throughout the day and always yielded $^{137}Ba/^{138}Ba$ and $^{135}Ba/^{138}Ba$ ratios that were within 0.12 percent and 0.65 percent of the natural ratios, respectively. The barium spike concentration was calibrated with reference to NIST SRM 3104a, which has concentration certified to 0.3 percent at the 95-percent confidence level. Replicate spike calibration measurements agreed to within 0.3 percent. Measurement of USGS standard BCR-2 agreed with the accepted value within 1.6 percent and replicates of the same unknowns agreed within 2 percent. Therefore, measurement precision is better than ~0.5 percent, whereas reproducibility and accuracy is better than 2 percent.

U and Th Concentrations by Isotope Dilution

$^{233}U/^{238}U$ and $^{229}Th/^{232}Th$ ratios were analyzed separately using static routines on Faraday cups. Mass bias was calibrated before analysis and several times over the course of a day of measurements using NIST CRM112A. ^{233}U and ^{229}Th spike concentrations were calibrated using Claritas™ Th and U standard solutions, certified to 0 5 percent, and calculations of concentrations in unknowns included corrections for total-process chemical blanks and evaporation corrections for the spikes. Accuracy was checked by analysis of rock standards BHVO-1, BCR-2 and TML. Our measurements of Th and U concentrations and (^{230}Th)/(^{238}U) of BHVO-1 agree within ~1 percent with published measurements of KIL1919 (collected from the same sample locality as BHVO; Pietruszka and others 2002); both are within error of the recommended value for Th concentration of 1.2±0.3 ppm for USGS standard BHVO-2 and are likely within error of the recommended value for Th concentration in BHVO-1 (of 1.1 ppm), although no error is reported for this value. Certified concentrations of U in BHVO-1 or BHVO-2 are not available. Rock standard TML is known to be slightly heterogeneous in Th and U concentration but to be in radioactive equilibrium; BCR-2 is a sample of a Columbia River Basalt flow erupted before 6 Ma and, therefore, should also be in radioactive equilibrium. Our analyses of TML and of BCR-2 yielded (^{230}Th)/(^{238}U) ratios within ~1 percent of equilibrium; therefore, the combined errors on measured U/Th and $^{230}Th/^{232}Th$ ratios must be better than 1 percent. Thus, accuracy of our measurements of U and Th concentrations must also be better than 1 percent.

Ra Concentrations by Isotope Dilution

$^{226}Ra/^{228}Ra$ measurements were made using two different routines during this study. $^{226}Ra/^{228}Ra$ ratios in the first samples run (including SH304-2A1 whole-rock and plagioclase, SH305-1 whole-rock and plagioclase, and SH311-1B whole-rock) were measured using a static analysis routine in which

^{228}Ra and ^{226}Ra peaks were measured on ion counters IC0 and IC1, respectively. Mass bias and relative ion counter gains were calibrated using NIST CRM112A. After the initial group of samples had high background counts at mass 225.5, we began scanning all samples in the mass range 224.5–229.5 for interferences and found that backgrounds measured at masses 225.5 and 227.5 were significantly lower when using IC0 (which is equipped with an energy filter) than when using IC1. When using IC0, small peaks of ~10 cps are present in some regions of the mass range, but interferences and/or instrumental background at the half-masses used for background measurements were negligible (tenths of counts per second to a few cps, compared to count rates on peaks of hundreds of cps to thousands of cps for most samples). Furthermore, the ion counter gain for IC0 was more stable than that for IC1, so we switched to a dynamic routine where both peaks were measured on IC0. This also has the advantage that ion counter gain calibrations are less critical as long as gains are stable over the time scale of a sample run (~10–15 minutes). The disadvantages of this approach are that the total counting time for each peak is reduced and that the analyses are susceptible to intensity variations due to instability of the plasma; the latter effect was minimized by adding a small amount (a few tens of picograms) of ^{232}Th (as a solution prepared from Ames Th metal) to each unknown and normalizing Ra count rates to the intensity of ^{232}Th measured on a Faraday cup during the same cycle. This analysis routine produces better in-run precision (~0.5–1 percent SE, for peaks of ~200–3000 cps) than the initial routine (~2 percent SE). Concentration of ^{228}Ra in the spike was calibrated with respect to NIST SRM 4965, which has Ra concentration certified to 1.23 percent (3σ). (^{226}Ra)/(^{230}Th) measured in rock standard TML differs from equilibrium by less than 1 percent, and (^{226}Ra)/(^{230}Th) in USGS standard BHVO-1 is within ~2 percent of the previously measured value (Pietruszka and others, 2002). Taking these measurements and the in-run precision into account, we consider our overall uncertainty at the 2σ level to be ~3–5 percent for the early-run samples, and ~1–2 percent for the later samples.

A Volcano Rekindled: The Renewed Eruption of Mount St. Helens, 2004–2006
Edited by David R. Sherrod, William E. Scott, and Peter H. Stauffer
U.S. Geological Survey Professional Paper 1750, 2008

Chapter 37

Timing of Degassing and Plagioclase Growth in Lavas Erupted from Mount St. Helens, 2004–2005, from ^{210}Po-^{210}Pb-^{226}Ra Disequilibria

By Mark K. Reagan[1], Kari M. Cooper[2], John S. Pallister[3], Carl R. Thornber[3], and Matthew Wortel[1]

Abstract

Disequilibrium between ^{210}Po, ^{210}Pb, and ^{226}Ra was measured on rocks and plagioclase mineral separates erupted during the first year of the ongoing eruption of Mount St. Helens. The purpose of this study was to monitor the volatile fluxing and crystal growth that occurred in the weeks, years, and decades leading up to eruption. Whole-rock samples were leached in dilute HCl to remove ^{210}Po precipitated in open spaces. Before leaching, samples had variable initial (^{210}Po) values, whereas after leaching, the groundmasses of nearly all juvenile samples were found to have had (^{210}Po) ≈ 0 when they erupted. Thus, most samples degassed ^{210}Po both before and after the magmas switched from open- to closed-system degassing. All juvenile samples have (^{210}Pb)/(^{226}Ra) ratios within 2σ of equilibrium, suggesting that the magmas involved in the ongoing eruption did not have strong, persistent fluxes of ^{222}Rn in or out of magmas during the decades and years leading to eruption. These equilibrium values also require a period of at least a century after magma generation and the last significant differentiation of the Mount St. Helens dacites. Despite this, the elevated (^{210}Pb)/(^{226}Ra) value measured in a plagioclase mineral separate from lava erupted in 2004 suggests that a significant proportion of this plagioclase grew within a few decades of eruption. The combined dataset suggests that for most 2004–5 lavas, the last stage of open-system degassing of the dacite magmas at Mount St. Helens is confined to the period between 1–2 years and 1–2 weeks before eruption, whereas plagioclase large enough to be included in the mineral separate grew around the time of the 1980s eruption or earlier.

[1] Department of Geoscience, 121 Trowbridge Hall, University of Iowa, Iowa City, IA 52242

[2] Department of Earth and Space Sciences, University of Washington, Box 351310, Seattle, WA 98195; now at Geology Department, University of California, One Shields Ave., Davis, CA 95616

[3] U.S. Geological Survey, 1300 SE Cardinal Court, Vancouver, WA 98683

Introduction

Open- and closed-system degassing occurring during the century before an eruption can be monitored by measuring the relative activities of short-lived radionuclides, such as polonium-210 (^{210}Po; $t_{1/2}$ = 138.4 days), lead-210 (^{210}Pb; $t_{1/2}$ = 22.6 years), and radium-226 (^{226}Ra; $t_{1/2}$ = 1,599 years) in lavas. For example, Po partitions efficiently into exsolving volatile phases and commonly degasses from both mafic and silicic lavas, which results in (^{210}Po)/(^{210}Pb) << 1.0 in erupted lavas. Examples of lavas that have (^{210}Po)/(^{210}Pb) < 0.15 include those erupted from Etna (Lambert and others, 1985; Le Cloarec and Pennisi, 2001), Hawai‘i (Gill and others, 1985), Arenal (Gill and others, 1985; Reagan and others, 2006), Mount St. Helens in 1980 (Bennett and others, 1982), and Anatahan (Reagan and others, 2005). Excesses of ^{210}Po over ^{210}Pb have been observed in some phreatomagmatic tephras because of condensation of ^{210}Po from gases streaming through the shallow conduit system of a volcano before eruption (Reagan and others, 2005).

Radon-222 (^{222}Rn), which lies between ^{226}Ra and ^{210}Pb in the ^{238}U decay series and has a half-life of 3.82 days, strongly partitions into the gas phase (Gill and others, 1985), whereas about 99 percent of Pb stays within the melt (Gauthier and others, 2000). Nevertheless, significant deficits of ^{210}Pb with respect to ^{226}Ra have been observed in magmas with widely varying compositions. Such deficits can result from differential partitioning of these elements between coexisting mineral and melt phases (Williams and others, 1985; Gill and Williams, 1990; Condomines and others, 1995; Sigmarsson, 1996), and/or from persistent (year- to decade-scale) losses of ^{222}Rn by degassing (Gauthier and Condomines, 1999; Gauthier and others, 2000; Le Cloarec and Pennisi, 2001; Le Cloarec and Gauthier, 2003; Turner and others, 2004; Berlo and others, 2004). Deficits in (^{210}Pb) with respect to (^{226}Ra) in midocean-ridge basalts have been attributed to lower partition coefficients for Ra compared to Pb during magma generation (Rubin and others, 2005).

Although large excesses of ^{210}Pb with respect to ^{226}Ra have been reported at some arc volcanoes, including the 1980s lavas and tephras from Mount St. Helens (Berlo and others, 2004), (^{210}Pb/^{226}Ra) values for lavas erupting at many other arc volcanoes are within 2σ error of equilibrium when the error is propagated back to the age of eruption. These near-equilibrium lavas include the silicic andesite tephras erupted from Anatahan in 2004 (Reagan and others, 2005), basalts and andesites erupted from Klyuchevskoy and Bezymianny in Kamchatka (Turner and others, 2007), and most of the basaltic andesites that have erupted from Arenal since 1968 (Reagan and others, 2006). The frequency of near-equilibrium (^{210}Pb)/(^{226}Ra) values in lavas probably reflects the special circumstances needed to supply enough ^{222}Rn to accumulate significant ^{210}Pb excesses (Reagan and others, 2006).

The regular sampling of the ongoing eruption of Mount St. Helens by the U.S. Geological Survey has provided an exceptional suite of samples for applying ^{226}Ra-^{210}Pb-^{210}Po disequilibria to constrain the time scales of degassing and other magmatic processes that have occurred within the century before eruption. Silicic glass inclusions from lavas erupted at Mount St. Helens have as much as 6 weight percent H_2O (Blundy and Cashman, 2005), and degassing of this water has the potential to generate significant disequilibrium between these short-lived nuclides.

Samples and Analytical Procedures

Whole-rock powders analyzed here span the period of the ongoing eruption from October 2004 to December 2005. Most samples are solid juvenile dome samples, but the samples include the phreatomagmatic tephra erupted in October 4, 2004, and March 8, 2005, and two samples of the dome-coating gouge. All dome samples were collected within 2 months of venting at the surface. Other chapters in this volume describe the mineral contents, textures, and chemical compositions of the samples analyzed here in detail (Pallister and others, this volume, chap. 30; Thornber and others, this volume, chap. 32). Briefly, all juvenile samples are dacites with approximately 65 percent SiO_2, 1.4 percent K_2O, and FeO*/MgO ≈2. These samples are highly porphyritic, with approximately 50 percent plagioclase, 3–5 percent hornblende and orthopyroxene, and 1 percent or less each of magnetite and augite phenocrysts, typically in a microlite-choked groundmass. Gabbroic to granodioritic inclusions, some in varying stages of disaggregation, are present in varying amounts in the dacites. These inclusions were avoided in the sampling for this study.

The October 2004 tephra sample (MSH04E2A03_A2) consists of finely pulverized rock fragments, with a variety of mineral textures, reflecting sources for the particles in older Mount St. Helens rocks, as well as juvenile dacite (Rowe and others, this volume, chap. 29). This sample also had organic debris that was removed by hand picking before analysis. The March 2005 tephra sample (MSH05DRS_3_9_4) consisted entirely of fragmented young dome debris and had a high proportion of clasts with lengths from 2 to 6 mm. The coarseness of this sample allowed us to hand-pick fragments for additional fragmentation in a ceramic rotary-ring mill and analysis.

Dome sample preparation began by fragmentation to particle lengths of several millimeters to 2 cm. Unaltered fragments were hand picked for ultrasonic washing in purified water and coarse grinding in a ceramic rotary mill. Gouge sample SH307-2A was indurated, whereas SH314-1G consisted of a collection of particles ranging from silt to about 2 mm in length. The SH307-2A sample was broken up and then coarsely ground. Sample SH314-1G was not additionally comminuted. Except for the initial tephra sample and the first dome sample, all samples were leached with 0.5 N HCl for 10–15 minutes in an ultrasonic agitator, followed by centrifuging and rinsing and centrifuging twice in purified water. This was done to remove ^{210}Po that condensed on surfaces of cracks and vesicles, which proved crucial for determining the initial groundmass (^{210}Po) value.

Plagioclase was separated from sample SH304-2A using standard density and magnetic techniques after grinding and sieving to segregate particles between 170 mesh and 80 mesh. This separate was washed with a 0.5 N HCl–2 percent H_2O_2 mixture for 10 minutes, followed by washing in purified water before analysis.

Analytical techniques for ^{210}Po are discussed in detail elsewhere (Reagan and others, 2005; Reagan and others, 2006). Initial (^{210}Po) and (^{210}Pb) values and errors for samples were calculated using exponential regressions through multiple analyses employing a half-life for ^{210}Po of 138.4 days (Holden, 1990). Rock standard RGM-1 was analyzed six times over the period of analysis. The weighted mean (^{210}Po) value and standard deviation for these analyses are 4.20±0.04 (1σ) decays per minute per gram (dpm/g), which is similar to the measured values for (^{238}U) for this standard (Le Fevre and Pin, 2002). The concentrations of ^{226}Ra in samples discussed here are from Cooper and Donnelly (this volume, chap. 36).

Other Time-Series Data

The variation in major-element, trace-element, and long-lived radiogenic isotopic compositions for juvenile lavas from the ongoing eruption has been minimal (Pallister and others, this volume, chap. 30). However, (^{230}Th)/(^{238}U) values vary from 0.93 to 1.10 at a nearly constant Th isotopic composition in dome samples, which has been attributed to fractionation of U from Th during melting to generate the Mount St. Helens dacites (Cooper and Donnelly, this volume, chap. 36). This Th isotopic composition is similar to the values measured for lavas erupted from Mount St. Helens in the middle 1980s, suggesting that there is a genetic link between the lavas. However, the Th isotopic compositions of plagioclase separates from lavas from the ongoing eruption range from 1.026 to 1.306 (whole-rock values are 1.26–1.28), and some of these values are different than any values measured for 1980s and 2004–5 lavas, indicating that an additional older magma component is involved in the ongoing eruption (Cooper and Donnelly, this volume, chap. 36). A wide range for the average ages of plagioclase mineral separates is supported by their (^{226}Ra)/(^{230}Th) values, which range from 1.51 for plagioclase from sample SH304-2A to 1.04 for a plagioclase from SH305-1 (Cooper and Donnelly, this volume, chap. 36).

^{210}Po-^{210}Pb-^{226}Ra disequilibria

Whole tephras erupted on October 4, 2004, were enriched in ^{210}Po over ^{210}Pb by more than a factor of 2, indicating that significant magmatic ^{210}Po had condensed in the shallow hydrothermal system before the phreatomagmatic explosions began (Reagan and others, 2005). This contrasts with tephras ejected during the phreatomagmatic explosions of March 8, 2005 (MSH05DRS_3_9_4), which were largely degassed of ^{210}Po when they erupted and had very little leachable ^{210}Po (table 1; fig. 1).

The first lavas ejected at the vent (for example, sample SH301-1A7, table 1) had a small excess of ^{210}Po over ^{210}Pb values and (^{210}Pb) that approximately matched (^{210}Pb) values for samples erupted in the 1980s. We interpret these data to indicate that this sample was rock excavated from the dome materials erupted in the 1980s that were in the vent area. The small excess of ^{210}Po for this sample was likely deposited in open spaces from fumarolic gases streaming through the vent area just before eruption. This observation was one of the first indications that this material was not juvenile 2004 material but was excavated from the 1980s dome (see Pallister and others, this volume, chap. 30).

All of the dome samples that were erupted and analyzed after sample SH301-1A7 represented new juvenile magma, and multiple analyses of leached samples produced radioactive equilibration curves that generally demonstrated complete degassing of ^{210}Po before eruption (fig. 1). Plagioclase crystals in sample SH304-2A had initial (^{210}Po) and (^{210}Pb) values of about 0.29 dpm/g (table 1). Assuming that plagioclase in all of the 2004–5 samples have this same (^{210}Po), that plagioclase crystals make up 50 percent of whole rock, and that other coarsely crystalline phases have near zero (^{210}Po), samples with groundmasses that are entirely degassed of ^{210}Po would have (^{210}Po)≈0.14 dpm/g. Therefore, the "no-Po" line on figure 1 is used to represent the approximate value of a whole rock whose groundmass had been entirely degassed of ^{210}Po.

Representative values of (^{210}Po) for whole rocks are compared with the values for leached samples in figure 2. In all cases, the whole-rock values exceed the leached values. For most samples, the values for unleached samples analyzed within two months of eruption are between 5 and 20 percent higher than for the leached samples. For sample SH305-1, the unleached values are more than 50 percent higher; for sample SH316-1A, these values are highly variable and as much as several times higher. These data indicate that a significant amount of ^{210}Po resides in open pore spaces, which indicates that a fraction of the ^{210}Po in all samples degassed into bubbles that never escaped from the magmas. This observation is important from an analytical point of view because it demonstrates the importance of leaching samples in dilute acid to obtain intrinsic ^{210}Po activities in lavas after all gas is lost from the magma. It also is important because it can allow the change from open- to closed-system degassing to be constrained temporally.

Nearly all dome whole-rock samples analyzed had initial (^{210}Po)/(^{210}Pb) ratios near the no-Po value when they vented. That is, the last day of complete degassing of ^{210}Po from the Mount St. Helens dacite, which is represented by the date of intersection of the ^{210}Po ingrowth curves with the no-Po line on figure 1, generally corresponds with their day of eruption within error of analysis and knowledge of eruption day (fig. 3). An exception to this is sample SH305-1, which erupted in mid-November 2004 but apparently had last degassed Po in September 2004.

Like the dome samples, the lithified gouge sample SH307-2A degassed ^{210}Po until the time that it vented to the surface. In contrast, the nonlithified gouge sample SH314-1G either ceased degassing ^{210}Po about a month before it erupted, or gas derived from underlying magma added ^{210}Po to this sample (fig. 3).

All of the calculated initial (^{210}Pb)/(^{226}Ra) values for whole rocks from the ongoing eruption are within 2σ analytical error of equilibrium (table 1). This is in marked contrast with samples erupted from Mount St. Helens in 1980, which had widely varying (^{210}Po)/(^{226}Ra) values (0.8 to 1.4) when they erupted (Berlo and others, 2004).

Discussion

^{210}Po-^{210}Pb Disequilibrium

The tephra sample ejected near the beginning of the ongoing eruption on October 4, 2004, was strongly enriched in ^{210}Po over ^{210}Pb, demonstrating that magmatic Po had condensed on surfaces in the pore space of the shallow fumarolic system shortly before eruption and had erupted along with the pulverized rock fragments. In contrast, the hand-picked tephra fragments erupted on March 8, 2005, during active dome building had low initial (^{210}Po) values, indicating that these fragments were mostly or entirely pieces of shallow dome material that had been emplaced about two weeks before their involvement in the phreatomagmatic explosions (fig. 3).

Table 1. Activities of ^{210}Po and initial (^{210}Pb)/(^{226}Ra) values for samples erupted in 2004–2005 from Mount St. Helens, Washington.

[Eruption day (month/day/year) from Pallister and others (this volume, chap. 30). Day of analysis is number of days after October 1, 2004. Initial (^{210}Pb) values calculated by regressing a best-fit radioactive equilibration curve through leached sample analyses. Values for (^{226}Ra) in dpm/g (disintegrations per minute per gram) from Cooper and Donnelly (this volume, chap. 36).]

Sample No.	Sample type	Eruption day	Analytical treatment	Analysis day	(^{210}Po) dpm/g	$\pm 1\sigma$	(^{210}Pb)	(^{210}Pb)/(^{226}Ra)	$\pm 1\sigma$
MSH04E2A03_A2	Tephra	10/4/04	whole	10	2.361	0.052	~1.17		
			whole	99	1.927	0.044			
			whole	134	1.806	0.041			
SH301-1A7	Dome	1980s	whole	30	1.191	0.026	1.04		
			whole	150	1.131	0.026			
			whole	559	1.043	0.025			
SH304-2A	Dome	10/18/04	whole	42	0.359	0.018	1.19	0.958	0.027
			whole	99	0.574	0.019			
			whole	126	0.642	0.030			
			whole	298	0.966	0.025			
			leached	126	0.593	0.021			
			leached	298	0.949	0.024			
			leached	369	1.015	0.024			
SH304-2A	Plagio-clase	10/18/04	leached	66	0.298	0.010	0.29	4.4	0.1
			leached	188	0.285	0.011			
SH305-1	Dome	11/20/04	whole	99	0.907	0.024	1.17	1.023	0.039
			whole	112	0.845	0.040			
			whole	253	1.036	0.076			
			leached	112	0.621	0.021			
			leached	218	0.863	0.021			
			leached	253	0.913	0.025			
			leached	475	1.061	0.023			
			leached	475	1.084	0.024			
SH306	Dome	12/15/04	whole	126	0.384	0.014	1.15	0.974	0.031
			whole	141	0.486	0.015			
			whole	211	0.708	0.030			
			leached	141	0.445	0.014			
			leached	211	0.681	0.021			
			leached	396	0.938	0.021			
SH307-2A	Gouge	2/12/05	whole	159	0.288	0.030	1.17	1.038	0.033
			whole	218	0.487	0.023			
			leached	159	0.251	0.010			
			leached	218	0.464	0.015			
			leached	475	0.980	0.024			
SH311-1B	Ballistic fragment	1/16/05	whole	159	0.467	0.030	1.15	1.056	0.033
			leached	159	0.438	0.013			
			leached	216	0.611	0.019			
			leached	475	1.001	0.023			
MSH05DRS_3_9_4	Hand-picked clasts	3/8/05	whole	202	0.405	0.028	1.15	1.018	0.032
			leached	202	0.394	0.011			
			leached	483	0.982	0.025			
SH314-1G	Gouge	4/17/05	whole	211	0.360	0.043	1.13		
			leached	211	0.311	0.012			
			leached	396	0.810	0.020			
SH315-1	Dome	4/1/05	whole	211	0.370	0.070	1.13		
			leached	211	0.323	0.013			
			leached	396	0.812	0.020			
			leached	965	1.116	0.022			

Table 1. Activities of ^{210}Po and initial (^{210}Pb)/(^{226}Ra) values for samples erupted in 2004–2005 from Mount St. Helens, Washington.—Continued

[Eruption day (month/day/year) from Pallister and others (this volume, chap. 30). Day of analysis is number of days after October 1, 2004. Initial (^{210}Pb) values calculated by regressing a best-fit radioactive equilibration curve through leached sample analyses. Values for (^{226}Ra) in dpm/g (disintegrations per minute per gram) from Cooper and Donnelly (this volume, chap. 36).]

Sample No.	Sample type	Eruption day	Analytical treatment	Analysis day	(^{210}Po) dpm/g	±1σ	(^{210}Pb)	(^{210}Pb)/(^{226}Ra)	±1σ
SH316-1A	Dome	4/15/05	whole	253	3.642	0.121	1.14	1.028	0.033
			whole	465	1.617	0.076			
			leached	334	0.671	0.018			
			leached	559	0.968	0.024			
			leached	965	1.143	0.023			
SH317-1A	Dome	5/1/05	whole	290	0.543	0.019	1.11	0.973	0.031
			whole	465	1.005	0.068			
			leached	298	0.459	0.014			
			leached	483	0.846	0.022			
			leached	965	1.087	0.020			
MSH319-1	Dome	5/15/05	whole	298	0.534	0.013	1.14		
			whole	465	0.818	0.042			
			leached	298	0.428	0.011			
			leached	516	0.895	0.022			
			leached	978	1.122	0.022			

Although initial whole-rock ^{210}Po activities are variable for dacite lavas from Mount St. Helens, these activities drop to near zero in nearly all samples when ^{210}Po is removed from surfaces by leaching with dilute acid (table 1). Thus, like most other lavas (Gill and others, 1985; Lambert and others, 1985; Le Cloarec and Pennisi, 2001; Bennett and others, 1982; Reagan and others, 2006), the intrinsic initial ^{210}Po activities of Mount St. Helens dacites are near zero. The presence of significant ^{210}Po in pore spaces of the Mount St. Helens dacites implies that the magmas continued to partition ^{210}Po into the gas phase until the magmas arrived at the vent and cooled below the blocking temperature of ^{210}Po.

The activities of ^{210}Po in whole dacite samples were significantly more variable and higher on the day the samples vented to the surface compared with the activities of ^{210}Po in leached samples. These differences probably reflect variations in the depth at which magmas ceased being able to vent gas to their surroundings; that is, when degassing changed from being open-system to closed-system. For most samples, the initial quantity of ^{210}Po in pore spaces was small, which is consistent with closed-system degassing beginning no more than 1–2 weeks before eruption (fig. 2). At an eruption rate of 5–10 meters per day, which is the approximate ascent rate of magmas in the shallow conduit (LaHusen and others, this volume, chap. 16), this switch from open- to closed-system degassing must have typically occurred between about 35 and 150 meters depth, which is similar to the depth where magmas are becoming rheological solids (Moran and others, this volume, chap. 2). However, sample SH305-1, which is unaltered and significantly more vesicular and more glassy than other samples, had much higher leachable ^{210}Po values than less vesicular samples. This sample also has the greatest difference between its eruption day and last degassing day (fig. 3). Therefore, assuming that this sample's velocity was the same as the velocity for other dome dacites, sample SH305-1 might have begun closed-system degassing as much as 200 days before eruption (corresponding to 1–2 km depth) and ceased degassing altogether about 2 months before it erupted (corresponding to about 0.5 km depth). If these assumptions are correct, this dacite chilled deeper within the edifice than other dacites from the ongoing eruption, which also might explain why sample SH305-1 contains fewer groundmass crystals than other samples from the 2004–5 eruption (see Cashman and others, this volume, chap. 19).

One sample with exceptionally high leachable ^{210}Po was sample SH316-1A, which had a whole rock (^{210}Po)/(^{210}Pb) value significantly greater than unity when it erupted. This sample had significant orange staining on fracture surfaces; although these surfaces were avoided during hand picking before analysis, extraneous ^{210}Po from underlying magmas appears to have been deposited heterogeneously in pore spaces throughout this sample. Nevertheless, this extraneous Po did not diffuse into the magma or solidified dacite, because the eruption and Po-degassing dates for sample SH316-1A are within error of each other.

Like the whole-dome samples, the lithified gouge sample SH307-2A degassed ^{210}Po approximately until the day that it vented. Thus, despite its position along the conduit walls, where it quenched to a solid and was ground to gouge, this sample maintained a temperature that was high enough for ^{210}Po to degas completely until it vented. The loose gouge sample SH314-1G appears to have cooled below the ^{210}Po

blocking temperature about a month before eruption, which corresponds to a depth of about 150–300 m below the surface.

^{210}Pb-^{226}Ra Equilibrium

As demonstrated above, the dacites from the ongoing eruption of Mount St. Helens reach the surface nearly degassed of ^{210}Po. Nevertheless, all lavas from the ongoing eruption had near-equilibrium (^{210}Pb)/(^{226}Ra) values when they erupted. Both because ^{222}Rn is a noble gas and because ^{210}Po appears to partition entirely into the gas phase at magmatic temperatures at Mount St. Helens, we assume that ^{222}Rn also strongly partitions from magma into a separate gas phase. If so, then the lack of a measurable ^{210}Pb deficit indicates that open-system degassing of dacites erupting at Mount St. Helens must be confined to the time period between about 1–2 years (the minimum time to produce a measurable ^{210}Pb deficit) before eruption and the start of closed-system degassing near the surface. These equilibrium values also indicate that the lavas from the ongoing eruption did not experience persistent streaming of ^{222}Rn from large volumes of underlying magma, which contrasts with lavas and tephras erupted from Mount St. Helens in 1980 (compare Berlo and others, 2004). Finally, these equilibrium (^{210}Pb)/(^{226}Ra) values indicate that the melting processes that created ^{226}Ra excesses over ^{230}Th (and probably ^{210}Pb) in all of the dacites from the ongoing eruption (Cooper and Donnelly, this volume, chap. 36), as well as the majority of plagioclase fractionation, occurred more than a century before eruption.

The contrast between the lack of (^{210}Pb)/(^{226}Ra) disequilibria during this eruption and the significant disequilibria encountered in samples from the eruption in 1980 (Berlo and others, 2004) is noteworthy. This difference is in stark contrast to Li concentration data, which indicate that plagioclase is enriched in Li at the beginning of both eruptions (compare Berlo and others, 2004; Kent and others, 2007) compared with subsequently erupted samples. The Li data suggest that a Li-enriched fluid pervasively infiltrated the first-erupted magmas and raised Li concentrations in plagioclase through

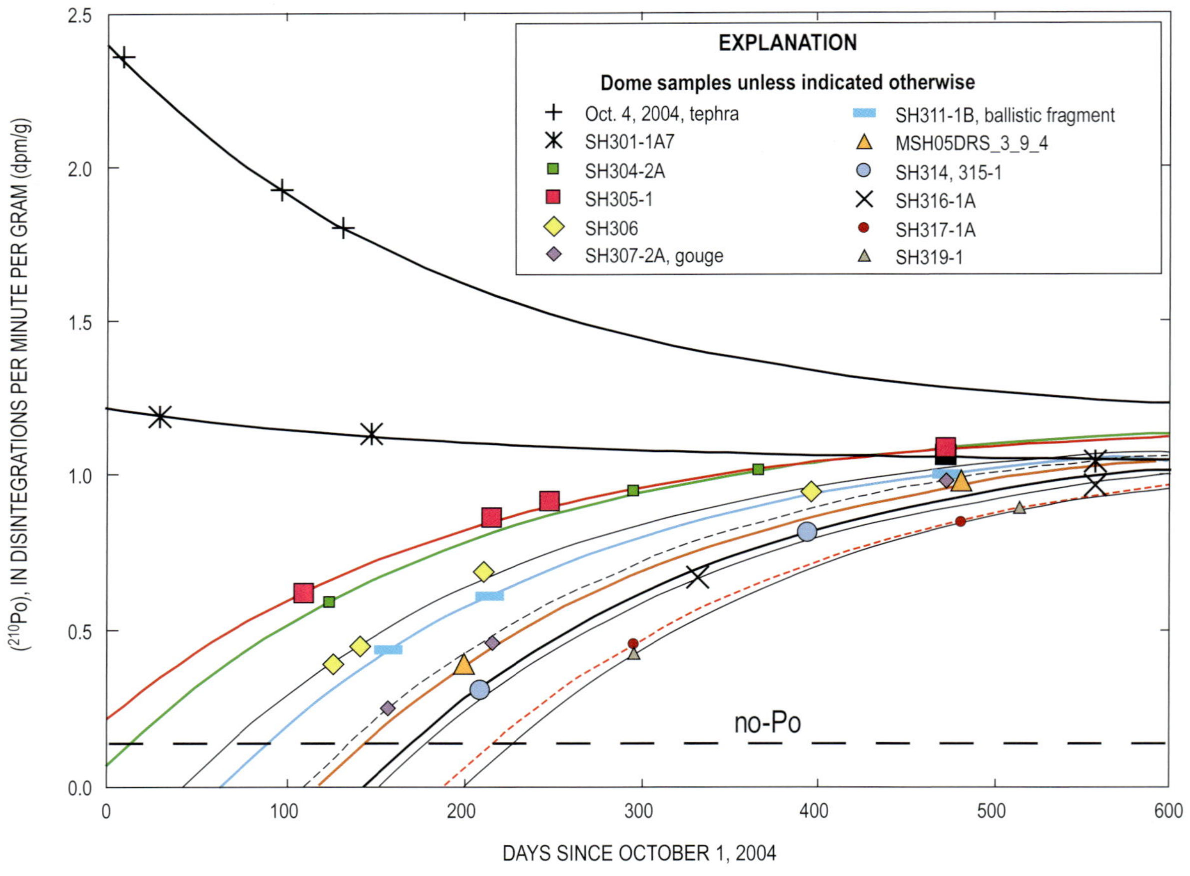

Figure 1. Plot of ^{210}Po activities for leached samples recently erupted from Mount St. Helens, Washington. ^{210}Po ingrowth curves drawn by choosing the day when (^{210}Po) = 0 and the initial (^{210}Pb) value that produced best-fit line through data points for each sample. The "no Po" line represents the approximate whole-rock value when groundmass was entirely degassed of ^{210}Po. Analyses completed more than 600 days after October 1, 2004, are not shown, although they were used to determine the best-fit ingrowth curves. See text for further explanation.

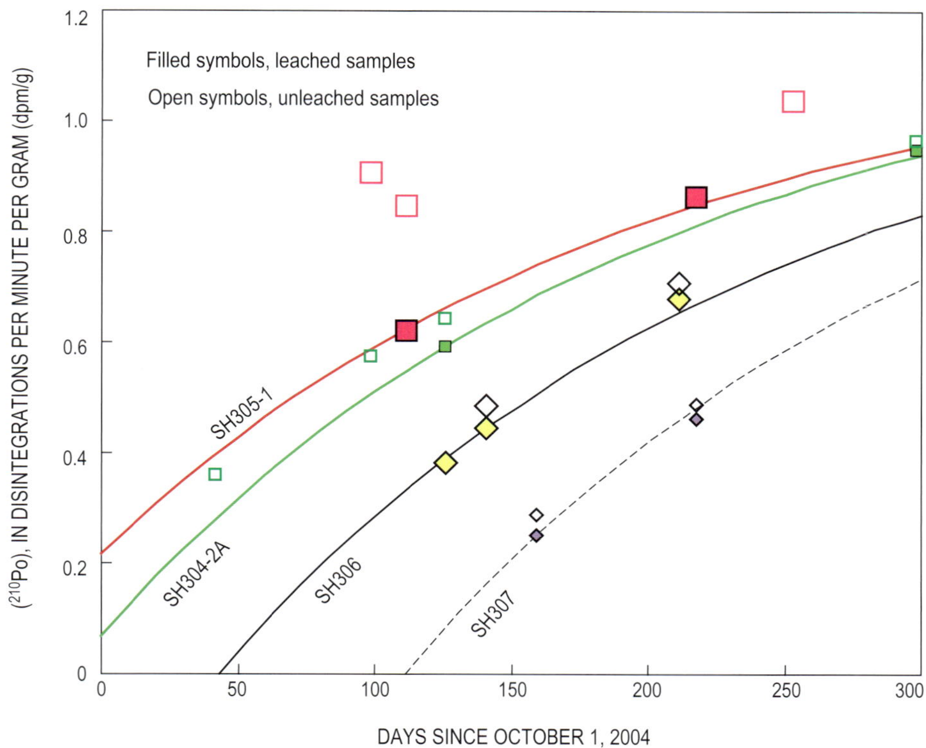

Figure 2. Plot of ^{210}Po activity versus date of analysis in days after Oct. 1, 2004, for representative whole-rock powders from Mount St. Helens, Washington, before (open symbols) and after (filled symbols) leaching (symbols match those in figure 1).

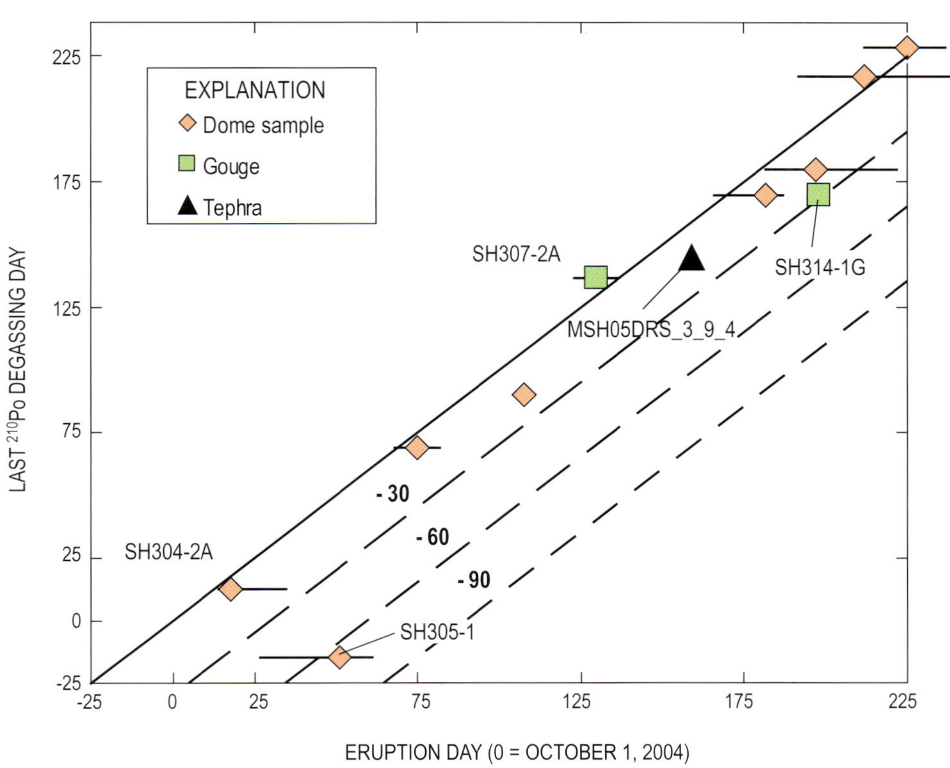

Figure 3. Plot of the last day of ^{210}Po degassing (date of intersection of ^{210}Po ingrowth curves with no-Po line on figure 1) versus the date of eruption for samples from the ongoing eruption of Mount St. Helens, Washington. Numbers for samples mentioned in the text are shown. Symbols show best guess for a sample's eruption date, and lines indicate the range of potential eruption dates. The solid diagonal line marks equivalent last ^{210}Po degassing day and eruption day (^{210}Po ceases degassing on eruption day). Dashed lines show calculated effect if ^{210}Po ceased degassing 30, 60, or 90 days before eruption. Note that most samples of all types degas ^{210}Po by closed- or open-system processes until the magmas are within two weeks of arriving at the surface.

diffusion, whereas this fluid either did not infiltrate subsequent magmas for both eruptions, or it did so for too short a time to affect Li concentrations in plagioclase (Kent and others, 2007). The ^{210}Pb enrichment found in the cryptodome and pumice samples erupted in 1980 was attributed to a Rn flux accompanying the Li flux (Berlo and others, 2004). If so, and if the ^{222}Rn excess required to ingrow ^{210}Pb also was associated with Li-bearing fluid for the current eruption, then this fluxing must have occurred during a much shorter time period before the current eruption than was the case in 1980 (Kent and others, 2007). An alternative possibility is that the ^{222}Rn flux required for the high (^{210}Pb)/(^{226}Ra) values in the 1980 magmas was separate from the Li-bearing fluid. In that case, the ^{222}Rn flux may have been associated with the order-of-magnitude higher rates of gas emission in 1980 compared with emission rates of the ongoing eruption (Gerlach and others, this volume, chap. 26).

The plagioclase mineral separate from sample SH304-2A has (^{210}Po)/(^{210}Pb)≈1, indicating that very little of this plagioclase grew within 1–2 years before eruption. However, comparing the (^{210}Pb) value with the (^{226}Ra) value reported in Cooper and Donnelly (this volume, chap. 36) gives a (^{210}Pb)/(^{226}Ra) value of about 4.4, indicating that a significant proportion of the plagioclase crystals in this lava grew within several decades of eruption. Assuming t=850°C and an average plagioclase An value of 0.5, the D_{Pb}/D_{Ra} value in plagioclase would have been about 9.3 based on the lattice strain method of Blundy and Wood (1994) to calculate D_{Ra} and the partitioning model of Bindeman and others (1998) to calculate D_{Pb}. Reconciling the (^{210}Pb)/(^{226}Ra) values and D_{Pb}/D_{Ra} values produces a model average age of the plagioclase in the mineral separate of about 30 years. Cooper and Donnelly (this volume, chap. 36) show that this plagioclase mineral separate has a (^{226}Ra)/(^{230}Th) value similar to that of the whole rock but a Th isotope ratio that is less than that of the whole rock by about 25 percent. These data were interpreted to suggest that 60–80 percent of the plagioclase is "zero-age" and the rest is older than 10 ka. Assuming that 70 percent of the plagioclase is young and that it grew in a single pulse, the (^{210}Pb)/(^{226}Ra) ratio in the newly grown material would have been about 5.9, which gives a model age of about 17 years, consistent with a large proportion of the plagioclase growing at about the time of the 1980–86 eruption.

Conclusions

1. Leaching of powdered whole-rock samples by dilute acid to remove ^{210}Po deposited in pore spaces is necessary to allow measurement of magmatic ^{210}Po values.

2. ^{210}Po degasses from lavas associated with the ongoing eruption of Mount St. Helens until they vent at the surface. The change from open- to closed-system degassing generally occurs within 150 m of the surface, which is about the depth at which the exterior dome samples become solid. Nevertheless, closed-system degassing began as deep as 1–2 km for some magmas.

3. Our sample of indurated gouge, collected from the surface of the lava dome, continued to degas ^{210}Po until it reached the surface, whereas our sample of loose, more interior gouge appears to have ceased degassing ^{210}Po at a depth of 150–300 m.

4. Magmas erupted in 2004–5 from Mount St. Helens were generated and underwent differentiation more than a century before eruption on the basis of equilibrium (^{210}Pb)/(^{226}Ra) values, but less than a few thousand years before eruption on the basis of disequilibrium (^{226}Ra)/(^{230}Th) values (see Cooper and Donnelly, this volume, chap. 36).

5. The near-equilibrium (^{210}Pb)/(^{226}Ra) ratios for all of the dacites erupted in 2004–5 from Mount St. Helens suggest that the last stage of open-system degassing of these magmas was confined to the time period between about a year before eruption and the start of closed-system degassing near the surface. These values further indicate that persistent streaming of excess ^{222}Rn gas through the magmas did not occur before this eruption, despite Li enrichments observed in plagioclase erupted in October and November 2004 (Kent and others, 2007).

6. The combined dataset of short- and long-lived U-series nuclides suggests that a significant proportion of the coarse plagioclase in a sample erupted in November 2004 grew at about the time of the 1980s eruptions of Mount St. Helens, and not during this last stage of magma rise and degassing.

Acknowledgments

We thank the scientists at the U.S. Geological Survey's Cascades Volcano Observatory and other members of the Mount St. Helens working group for sharing data and information about the ongoing eruption of Mount St. Helens. David Peate, Jennifer Garrison, and Kim Berlo are thanked for insightful discussions. This paper benefited greatly from constructive reviews by Pierre Gauthier and Todd Hinkley. National Science Foundation grants EAR 0504362 and EAR 0609670 funded this research.

References Cited

Bennett, J.T., Krishnaswami, S., Turekian, K.K., Melson, W.G., and Hopson, C.A., 1982, The uranium and thorium decay series nuclides in Mt. St. Helens effusives: Earth and Planetary Science Letters, v. 60, no. 1, p. 61–69.

Berlo, K., Blundy, J., Turner, S., Cashman, K., Hawkesworth, C., and Black, S., 2004, Geochemical precursors to volcanic activity at Mount St. Helens, USA: Science, v. 306, p. 1167–1169.

Blundy, J., and Cashman, K., 2005, Rapid decompression-driven crystallization recorded by melt inclusions from Mount St. Helens volcano: Geology, v. 33, no. 10, p. 793–796, doi:10.1130/G21668.1.

Cashman, K.V., Thornber, C.R., and Pallister, J.S., 2008, From dome to dust; shallow crystallization and fragmentation of conduit magma during the 2004–2006 dome extrusion of Mount St. Helens, Washington, chap. 19 *of* Sherrod, D.R., Scott, W.E., and Stauffer, P.H., eds., A volcano rekindled; the renewed eruption of Mount St. Helens, 2004–2006: U.S. Geological Survey Professional Paper 1750 (this volume).

Condomines, M., Tanguy, J.-C., and Michaud, V., 1995, Magma dynamics at Mt Etna; constraints from U-Th-Ra-Pb radioactive disequilibria and Sr isotopes in historical lavas: Earth and Planetary Science Letters, v. 132, p. 25–41.

Cooper, K.M., and Donnelly, C.T., 2008, ^{238}U-^{230}Th-^{226}Ra disequilibria in dacite and plagioclase from the 2004–2005 eruption of Mount St. Helens, chap. 36 *of* Sherrod, D.R., Scott, W.E., and Stauffer, P.H., eds., A volcano rekindled; the renewed eruption of Mount St. Helens, 2004–2006: U.S. Geological Survey Professional Paper 1750 (this volume).

Gauthier, P.-J., and Condomines, M., 1999, ^{210}Pb-^{226}Ra radioactive disequilibria in recent lavas and radon degassing; inferences on the magma chamber dynamics at Stromboli and Merapi volcanoes: Earth and Planetary Science Letters, v. 172, p. 111–126.

Gauthier, P.-J., Le Cloarec, M.-F., and Condomines, M., 2000, Degassing processes at Stromboli volcano inferred from short-lived disequilibria (^{210}Pb-^{210}Bi-^{210}Po) in volcanic gases: Journal of Volcanology and Geothermal Research, v. 102, p. 1–19.

Gerlach, T.M., McGee, K.A., and Doukas, M.P., 2008, Emission rates of CO_2, SO_2, and H_2S, scrubbing, and preeruption excess volatiles at Mount St. Helens, 2004–2005, chap. 26 *of* Sherrod, D.R., Scott, W.E., and Stauffer, P.H., eds., A volcano rekindled; the renewed eruption of Mount St. Helens, 2004–2006: U.S. Geological Survey Professional Paper 1750 (this volume).

Gill, J., Williams, R., and Bruland, K., 1985, Eruption of basalt and andesite lava degasses ^{222}Rn and ^{210}Po: Geophysical Research Letters, v. 12, p. 17–20.

Holden, N.E., 1990, Total half-lives for selected nuclides: Pure and Applied Chemistry, v. 62, p. 941–958.

Kent, A.J.R., Blundy, J., Cashman, K.V., Cooper, K.M., Donnelly, C., Pallister, J.S., Reagan, M., Rowe, M.C., and Thornber, C.R., 2007, Vapor transfer prior to the October 2004 eruption of Mount St. Helens, Washington: Geology, v. 35, no. 3, p. 231–234, doi:10.1130/G22809A.1.

LaHusen, R.G., Swinford, K.J., Logan, M., and Lisowski, M., 2008, Instrumentation in remote and dangerous settings; examples using data from GPS "spider" deployments during the 2004–2005 eruption of Mount St. Helens, Washington, chap. 16 *of* Sherrod, D.R., Scott, W.E., and Stauffer, P.H., eds., A volcano rekindled; the renewed eruption of Mount St. Helens, 2004–2006: U.S. Geological Survey Professional Paper 1750 (this volume) .

Lambert, G., Le Cloarec, M.F., Ardouin, B., and Le Roulley, J.C., 1985, Volcanic emission of radionuclides and magma dynamics: Earth and Planetary Science Letters, v. 76, p. 185–192.

Le Cloarec, M.-F., and Gauthier, P.-J., 2003, Merapi volcano, central Java, Indonesia; a case study of radionuclide behavior in volcanic gases and its implications for magma dynamics at andesitic volcanoes: Journal of Geophysical Research, v. 108, no. B5, doi:10.1029/2001JB001709, 14 p.

Le Cloarec, M.-F., and Pennisi, M., 2001, Radionuclides and sulfur content in Mount Etna plume in 1983–1995: new constraints on the magma feeding system: Journal of Volcanology and Geothermal Research, v. 108, nos. 1–4, p. 141–155, doi:10.1016/S0377-0273(00)00282-1.

Le Fevre, B., and Pin, C., 2002, Determination of Zr, Hf, Th and U by isotope dilution and inductively coupled plasma-quadrupole mass spectrometry after concomitant separation using extraction chromatography: Geostandards Newsletter, v. 26, p. 161–170.

Moran, S.C., Malone, S.D., Qamar, A.I., Thelen, W.A., Wright, A.K., and Caplan-Auerbach, J., 2008, Seismicity associated with renewed dome building at Mount St. Helens, 2004–2005, chap. 2 *of* Sherrod, D.R., Scott, W.E., and Stauffer, P.H., eds., A volcano rekindled; the renewed eruption of Mount St. Helens, 2004–2006: U.S. Geological Survey Professional Paper 1750 (this volume).

Pallister, J.S., Thornber, C.R., Cashman, K.V., Clynne, M.A., Lowers, H.A., Mandeville, C.W., Brownfield, I.K., and Meeker, G.P., 2008, Petrology of the 2004–2006 Mount St. Helens lava dome—implications for magmatic plumbing and eruption triggering, chap. 30 *of* Sherrod, D.R., Scott, W.E., and Stauffer, P.H., eds., A volcano rekindled; the renewed eruption of Mount St. Helens, 2004–2006: U.S. Geological Survey Professional Paper 1750 (this volume).

Reagan, M., Tepley, F.J., III, Gill, J.B., Wortel., M., and Hartman, B., 2005, Rapid time scales of basalt to andesite differentiation at Anatahan volcano, Mariana Islands: Journal of Volcanology and Geothermal Research, v. 146, nos. 1–3, p. 171–183, doi:10.1016/j.jvolgeores.2004.10.022.

Reagan, M.K., Tepley, F.J., III, Gill, J.B., Wortel., M., and Garrison, J., 2006, Timescales of degassing and crystallization implied by ^{210}Po-^{210}Pb-^{226}Ra disequilibria for andesitic lavas erupted from Arenal volcano: Journal of Volcanology and Geothermal Research, v. 157, p. 135–146, doi:10.1016/j.jvolgeores.2006.03.044.

Rowe, M.C., Thornber, C.R., and Kent, A.J.R., 2008, Identification and evolution of the juvenile component in 2004–2005 Mount St. Helens ash, chap. 29 *of* Sherrod, D.R., Scott, W.E., and Stauffer, P.H., eds., A volcano rekindled; the renewed eruption of Mount St. Helens, 2004–2006: U.S. Geological Survey Professional Paper 1750 (this volume).

Rubin, K.H., van der Zander, I., Smith, M.C., and Bergmanis, E.C., 2005, Minimum speed limit for ocean ridge magmatism from ^{210}Pb-^{226}Ra-^{230}Th disequilibria: Nature, v. 437, p. 534–538.

Sigmarsson, O., 1996, Short magma residence time at an Icelandic volcano inferred from U-series disequilibria: Nature, v. 382, p. 440–442.

Thornber, C.R., Pallister, J.S., Lowers, H.A., Rowe, M.C., Mandeville, C.W., and Meeker, G.P., 2008, Chemistry, mineralogy, and petrology of amphibole in Mount St. Helens 2004–2006 dacite, chap. 32 *of* Sherrod, D.R., Scott, W.E., and Stauffer, P.H., eds., A volcano rekindled; the renewed eruption of Mount St. Helens, 2004–2006: U.S. Geological Survey Professional Paper 1750 (this volume).

Turner, S., Black, S., and Berlo, K., 2004, ^{210}Pb-^{226}Ra and ^{228}Ra-^{232}Th systematics in young arc rocks: Earth and Planetary Science Letters, v. 227, p. 1–16.

Turner, S., Sims, K.W.W., Reagan, M., and Cook, C., 2006, A ^{210}Pb-^{226}Ra-^{230}Th-^{23}8U study of Klyuchevskoy and Bezymianny volcanoes, Kamchatka: Geochimica et Cosmochimica Acta, v. 71, p. 4771-4785, doi:101016/j.gca.2007.08.006.

Williams, R.W., Gill, J.B., and Bruland, K.W., 1986, Ra-Th disequilibria systematics; timescale of carbonatite magma formation at Oldoinyo Lengai volcano, Tanzania: Geochimica et Cosmochimica Acta, v. 50, p. 1249–1259.